CIVIL PROCEDURE

THEORY AND PRACTICE

ASPEN CASEBOOK SERIES

CIVIL PROCEDURE

THEORY AND PRACTICE

SIXTH EDITION

LINDA J. SILBERMAN
NEW YORK UNIVERSITY SCHOOL OF LAW

ALLAN R. STEIN
RUTGERS LAW SCHOOL

TOBIAS BARRINGTON WOLFF
UNIVERSITY OF PENNSYLVANIA LAW SCHOOL

AARON D. SIMOWITZ
WILLAMETTE UNIVERSITY COLLEGE OF LAW

ASPEN PUBLISHING

To contact Customer Service, e-mail customer.service@aspenpublishing.com, call 1-800-950-5259, or mail correspondence to:

Aspen Publishing
Attn: Order Department
PO Box 990
Frederick, MD 21705

Printed in the United States of America.

1 2 3 4 5 6 7 8 9 0

ISBN 978-1-5438-3882-4

Library of Congress Cataloging-in-Publication Data application is in process.

About Aspen Publishing

Aspen Publishing is a leading provider of educational content and digital learning solutions to law schools in the U.S. and around the world. Aspen provides best-in-class solutions for legal education through authoritative textbooks, written by renowned authors, and breakthrough products such as Connected eBooks, Connected Quizzing, and PracticePerfect.

The Aspen Casebook Series (famously known among law faculty and students as the "red and black" casebooks) encompasses hundreds of highly regarded textbooks in more than eighty disciplines, from large enrollment courses, such as Torts and Contracts to emerging electives such as Sustainability and the Law of Policing. Study aids such as the *Examples & Explanations* and *Glannon Guide* series, both highly popular collections, help law students master complex subject matter.

Major products, programs, and initiatives include:

- **Connected eBooks** are enhanced digital textbooks and study aids that come with a suite of online content and learning tools designed to maximize student success. Designed in collaboration with hundreds of faculty and students, the Connected eBook is a significant leap forward in the legal education learning tools available to students.

- **Connected Quizzing** is an easy-to-use formative assessment tool that tests law students' understanding and provides timely feedback to improve learning outcomes. Delivered through CasebookConnect.com, the learning platform already used by students to access their Aspen casebooks, Connected Quizzing is simple to implement and integrates seamlessly with law school course curricula.

- **PracticePerfect** is a visually engaging, interactive study aid to explain commonly encountered legal doctrines through easy-to-understand animated videos, illustrative examples, and numerous practice questions. Developed by a team of experts, PracticePerfect is the ideal study companion for today's law students.

- The **Aspen Learning Library** enables law schools to provide their students with access to the most popular study aids on the market across all of their courses. Available through an annual subscription, the online library consists of study aids in e-book, audio, and video formats with full text search, note-taking, and highlighting capabilities.

- Aspen's **Digital Bookshelf** is an institutional-level online education bookshelf, consolidating everything students and professors need to ensure success. This program ensures that every student has access to affordable course materials from day one.

- **Leading Edge** is a community centered on thinking differently about legal education and putting those thoughts into actionable strategies. At the core of the program is the Leading Edge Conference, an annual gathering of legal education thought leaders looking to pool ideas and identify promising directions of exploration.

To my father, Alfred Silberman (1914–1996), who made all things possible for me. I wish he could have seen this book.

—L. J. S.

To my father, Victor Stein, whose passion for justice and reverence for the rule of law drew all his children to follow his path.

—A. R. S.

To Samuel Emerson Wolff, with the hope that fairness and justice will expand and thrive in the world he has entered.

—T. B. W.

To my mother and father, Amy and Lee Simowitz, and to Emmeline, who daily reminds me to love learning, even (or especially) when it's hard.

—A. D. S.

Summary of Contents

clearly concludes previous cases.

With the Sixth Edition, we are joined by Professor Aaron D. Simowitz of Willamette University College of Law as a co-author and full partner on the casebook. Professor Simowitz is a procedure scholar with particular expertise in personal jurisdiction and the enforcement of judgments in both domestic and transnational settings. We welcome him to the family. His arrival is timely, as our treatment of personal jurisdiction in Chapter 2 required a significant update following the Court's decisions in *Ford Motor Company v. Montana Eighth Judicial District Court* and *Bristol Myers Squibb v. Superior Court of California*. We provide a thorough analytical account of the Court's new "arises out of / relates to" doctrine in Chapter 2 and also endeavor to make sense of its ever-shifting references to federalism and sovereignty in the jurisprudence of *in personam* jurisdiction. We have reworked Chapter 5 in modest ways to make it easier for teachers either to use or not use the case study materials contained therein. Chapter 7 offers a new section on defense preclusion shaped around the Court's recent decision in *Lucky Brand Dungarees v. Marcel Fashions*. Chapter 8 expands its discussion of class action doctrine to include recent developments in the implied requirement of ascertainability under Federal Rule 23 and the statute of limitations tolling doctrine of *American Pipe & Construction Co. v. Utah*. Chapter 10 offers a revised and expanded treatment of the Court's jurisprudence under the Federal Arbitration Act. And, of course, we include recent caselaw from state courts and lower federal courts and other developments in notes and discussion throughout the book.

The first edition of this book was in development for more than a decade. Acknowledgment of everyone who contributed to that effort would run longer than the text. Several, however, stand out: Sam Estreicher at New York University and Pamela Karlan at Stanford University. Other colleagues provided invaluable feedback and advice: Steve Burbank, Perry Dane, Roger Dennis, Michael Dorf, Rochelle Dreyfuss, Jay Feinman, Larry Kramer, Leo Levin, Andy Lowenfeld, Burt Neuborne, Jack Sabatino, Beth Stephens, and Bob Williams. We are also grateful for the heroic efforts of scores of research assistants at NYU and Rutgers, without whom the book would not have been completed—in particular: Helena Almeida, Susan Ciallella, Vangie Cooper, Michael Jordan, Llen Oxman, Eric Posmantier, Tracy Siebold, Chris Svoboda, and Terry Wit. Richard Kelsey, secretary, was instrumental in ensuring that the work was converted into a formal manuscript.

For subsequent editions, we would also like to thank all of the teachers who gave us valuable feedback from prior editions, particularly John Beckerman, Rochelle Dreyfuss, Bill Eskridge, Aviva Orenstein, Rick Swedloff, and Mary Twitchell. For these editions we are also grateful for the dedicated research assistance of Anderson Bailey, Nathaniel Bessey, Jocelyn Burgos, Christopher Campbell, Jacob Karabell, Sean Kiley, Ross Mazer, Kevin Park, Nathaniel Putnam, and Michael Reed. For their research assistance on the Sixth Edition, we are indebted to Louis Bayles at Rutgers, and Mary Rumsey and Amelia Zuidema at Willamette University College of Law. We gratefully acknowledge David Knudsen for granting permission to reprint his photograph of the Rockwell Jet Commander in Chapter 5.

CIVIL PROCEDURE

THEORY AND PRACTICE

CHAPTER 1

INTRODUCTION

A. *OUTLINE OF A LAWSUIT*

1. *What Is Civil Procedure?*

The terms *civil* and *procedure* are broad designations that together describe the process of resolving private disputes in judicial proceedings. Here is what lawyers typically mean when they use each of these terms.

The term *civil* refers to the area of law that defines the rights and obligations that people owe to one another and that they enforce through privately initiated actions. The law that applies in a civil action stands in contrast to *criminal* law, which governs the rules of conduct that the state imposes upon people and enforces through state-initiated prosecutions. (Note, however, that the government is sometimes involved as a party in civil litigation as well.) The main difference between criminal and civil proceedings is the immediate objective of the suit: The object of a criminal proceeding is punishment through fine or imprisonment; the primary object of a civil proceeding is a remedy for an injury in the form of a *judgment*. A person's conduct can have both civil and criminal consequences. If I steal your television set, I can be criminally prosecuted by the state for theft, whereby the state exacts its punishment. I can also be sued by you for the *tort* of *conversion*, and you get your television back or money to buy a new one.

The term *procedure* refers to the system of resolving disputes, usually in a judicial forum. In the broadest sense, this course is about how the judicial machinery works in civil cases. We will focus on what tribunals are available to litigants when they wish to request a remedy and how the litigants present their claims and defenses once they are before the court.

Civil cases and criminal cases are typically governed by different sets of procedural rules. In federal courts, the Federal Rules of Civil Procedure (Fed. R. Civ. P.) apply in civil cases, while the Federal Rules of Criminal Procedure (Fed. R. Crim. P.) apply in criminal cases (though a common set of Federal Rules of Evidence applies in both settings). Moreover, the defendant in a criminal case has the right to have a jury hear the evidence and determine guilt (save for minor misdemeanors), whereas there are significant categories of civil case law where no jury is available. Burdens of proof also differ. The state in a criminal case has the burden of proving the wrongdoer's guilt "beyond a reasonable doubt." The typical burden of proof in a civil case is the considerably less demanding standard of "a fair preponderance of the evidence"—or, in particular cases, a somewhat more demanding standard of "clear and convincing evidence."

2. *Dispute Resolution by Courts Versus Other Agencies*

Our principal focus here will be on formal adjudication in the courts. Courts often make important policy decisions in the course of resolving disputes. However, the principal sources of policy and law are found in the acts of legislatures and executives. Moreover, a great many civil disputes are resolved in our country in nonjudicial tribunals. These are typically administrative agencies staffed by nonjudicial personnel who are responsible for administering particular statutory schemes. For example, claims for government benefits, such as welfare or social security benefits, are resolved in the first instance by state welfare offices and the federal Social Security Administration, respectively. Initial determinations of both the facts and the applicable law are made by these administrative bodies, typically with an opportunity to appeal adverse rulings to the courts. These agency tribunals are the subject of the course in Administrative Law.

In the last chapter of this casebook, we also explore the increasing utilization of alternative methods of dispute resolution, such as mediation and arbitration, which seek to promote resolution of disputes outside the formal process of adjudication.

3. *State Versus Federal Systems*

Another important distinction to keep in mind is the difference between state courts and federal courts. Our country is based on a federal system of government in which power is shared between the 50 states of the union and the federal government. In theory, plenary regulatory authority is vested in the states, with the power of the federal government limited to the areas of responsibility set forth in the Constitution. Over the course of the twentieth century, however, the authority of the federal government expanded considerably—a process facilitated by an expansive interpretation of the legislative authority of Congress under the federal Constitution.

Each of the states and the federal government has its own system of courts. There are, typically, three tiers: a trial court, an intermediate court of appeals, and a supreme court. In the federal system, the trial courts are called *district courts*. The intermediate appeals courts are called *courts of appeals* and generally are responsible for a geographic region called a *circuit*. The high court is the Supreme Court of the United States. The Supreme Court functions as a final appellate authority not only over cases brought in the federal courts, but also over cases brought in the state courts raising questions governed by federal law.

The state courts are considered courts of plenary authority, able to hear cases involving any subject matter not exclusively reserved to the federal courts. The federal courts, by contrast, are courts of limited subject matter authority; they can hear cases only if authorized to do so by federal statute and if the cases otherwise fall within the "judicial power" of the United States as set forth in Article III of the Constitution.

4. The Adversary System

In the Anglo-American legal tradition, the lawyers for each party have the primary responsibility for framing the legal issues and developing the factual foundation for their claim or defense. Lawyers make the necessary investigation, discover the pertinent documents, locate the necessary witnesses, and procure their attendance at trial. At the trial, lawyers formulate questions for the witnesses, including the parties, who give testimony orally before the trier of fact. Lawyers also make decisions about what documents and other evidence to present to the court at trial. Courts have no duty to make an independent investigation and have no facilities for doing so. This contrasts with some civil law systems (sometimes referred to as "inquisitorial" systems), where the court takes the leading role in compiling the dossier, investigating, and questioning witnesses.

Although rules of professional responsibility impose a duty on lawyers to be candid in their representations to the court and their adversaries, the lawyer's primary duty is to frame his or her own client's case in as favorable a light as possible. Neither side, generally, has any obligation to aid its adversary or weaken its own case. The theory of the adversary system is that each party will discover and present everything that will favor its own case and disclose the weakness of its adversary and that truth will be revealed to the impartial decision maker as the result of this bilateral presentation. Note, however, that the accuracy of adjudication depends at least in part on a parity of skill and resources among all counsel.

5. Stages of a Lawsuit

When people suffer injuries caused by the wrongful conduct of another, they can seek a remedy in the courts through the process of *civil litigation*. The aggrieved persons can *sue*, they initiate (through their attorney) a *lawsuit* seeking relief against the wrongdoer. The person or *party* initiating the lawsuit is called the *plaintiff*. The person against whom relief is sought is called the *defendant*.

a. Investigation

Litigation is initiated when the client first consults an attorney. Although the client may want to file a lawsuit immediately, attorneys have a responsibility to ascertain that the client has in fact suffered a wrong for which the courts can offer an effective remedy. The attorney interviews the client to find out his version of the facts, and then conducts legal research to determine whether the client has a viable claim. Professional codes of conduct set standards for lawyers' responsibility as officers of the court. These codes require a lawyer to ascertain that the client has a meritorious claim before initiating litigation. In addition, the rules in federal courts — and some state courts — impose the obligation to certify that the lawyer has conducted an investigation into the facts and the law. *See, e.g.*, Fed. R. Civ. P. 11.

b.   Fee Arrangements

If the lawyer determines that the client has a meritorious claim, the lawyer will make some arrangement for payment of the fee. In this country, the so-called American rule controls: Each side pays its own attorneys' fees, regardless of whether it wins or loses. By contrast, Great Britain and other countries follow the "English rule": Attorneys' fees can be recovered from the losing party. What are the pros and cons of the respective systems?

If clients have sufficient assets, they may agree to pay for the lawyer's time and expenses as they are incurred. In many civil cases, however, a *contingent fee* is typically agreed to, whereby the client agrees to pay the attorney a percentage of the recovery should the client win, but pays nothing if the client loses. (In some cases, a statute may provide for fee-shifting in order to encourage the bringing of certain claims. Federal and state civil rights laws, for example, typically authorize prevailing plaintiffs to recover their attorneys' fees from defendants. *See, e.g.*, 42 U.S.C. §1988.)

Over the last decade, litigants have increasingly turned to third parties for funding of litigation. This alternative litigation funding, or ALF, can take several forms: non-recourse loans, whereby the lender is repaid only in the event that plaintiff obtains a monetary award or settlement; the sale of claims to third parties; or lending by the attorney to the client. Arrangements such as these raise a bevy of ethical issues, including concerns over preservation of the attorney-client privilege, compromising control over the litigation, and historical constraints on financial support for litigation by attorneys and third parties. *See generally*, J. Burton LeBlanc & S. Ann Saucer, *All About Alternative Litigation Financing*, 49 Trial 16 (2013).

c.   Subject Matter Jurisdiction — Federal Court or State Court?

Once the attorney has undertaken the necessary investigation, entered into a satisfactory retainer agreement, and explored without success the prospect of a settlement, she must determine whether to bring this suit in state court or federal court. This raises the question of subject matter jurisdiction. Does the court have authority to hear lawsuits of this type?

When a government creates a court, it may impose limitations on the types of cases the court is authorized to resolve. A familiar example is small claims court. By its statutory charter, a small claims court is authorized to hear claims only involving small amounts in controversy. Similarly, family courts may only have authority to resolve cases involving divorce, child custody, and other domestic relations matters. Bankruptcy courts may only hear claims related to a bankruptcy. These are all limitations on the courts' subject matter jurisdiction.

The state courts, as mentioned above, are courts of plenary (or *general*) subject matter jurisdiction. That is to say, somewhere within a state judicial system, there is generally some court with subject matter jurisdiction to hear every kind of case, except for a small category of claims that must be litigated in the federal courts.

When suit is filed in state court, the attorney will need to review the law of the particular state to determine which court within the state judiciary is appropriate for this type of claim. State systems typically provide for a trial court of general subject matter jurisdiction (in New York, this court is called the Supreme Court of New York) plus courts of more specialized responsibility, such as small claims court, probate court (for the administration of estates), family court (for divorce and other domestic disputes), or court of claims (for claims against state and local governments).

The federal courts, in contrast, are courts of limited subject matter jurisdiction. Most cases cannot be brought in federal court. To bring the case in federal court, the attorney must determine that there is federal subject matter jurisdiction. There are two principal bases of federal subject matter jurisdiction. One is *"arising under" jurisdiction*, provided in 28 U.S.C. §1331. If federal law deems the defendant's conduct wrongful and gives the plaintiff the right to a judicial remedy, the federal courts will normally have arising-under jurisdiction over the plaintiff's claim.

The second basis of federal subject matter jurisdiction is *"diversity" jurisdiction*. The diversity of citizenship jurisdiction provision, 28 U.S.C. §1332, authorizes suit to be brought in federal court when the suit is between "citizens of different states" and the amount in controversy is in excess of $75,000. The statute has been interpreted to require *complete diversity*: All plaintiffs must be from different states than all defendants. Determining the citizenship of a party can be complex, particularly in the case of a business entity.

Most of the subject matter jurisdiction of the federal courts is "concurrent" with that of the state courts. That is to say, both the state and federal courts have authority to resolve such cases. There is a very small category of cases that must be resolved in the federal courts. This includes federal securities, antitrust, patent, and trademark litigation. The federal courts are said to have "exclusive" jurisdiction over these claims. There is a much larger category of cases that can only be brought in the state courts. A Venn diagram of the allocation of subject matter jurisdiction between the state and federal courts would look something like this:

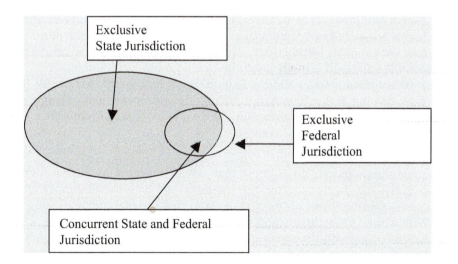

Thus, even if we assume that a case can be brought in federal court, the attorney may also have the option to pursue the case in state court. She might be more familiar with state rules of practice than federal rules, or she might believe that state judges would be more sympathetic to her case. The local state court may be more convenient and might offer a more "localized" jury since a federal district court usually draws its jurors from a broader geographic area. The decision about whether to sue in state or federal court also can be affected by the caseload and backlog in the respective courts. However, some cases filed by a plaintiff in state court can be *removed* to federal court by the defendant under the *removal* procedure authorized by 28 U.S.C. §1441.

d.   Personal Jurisdiction

Whether the case is brought in state or federal courts, plaintiffs often prefer to bring the case in their home state. However, they must determine whether the courts there have *personal jurisdiction* over the defendant; can the defendant be sued within the geographical territory over which the court has authority? This is easily established if the defendant resides in the state, but it can be quite complex in the case of out-of-state defendants.

What should be required in order to exercise judicial authority over a defendant and to force the defendant to defend an action? Should it depend on where the defendant is located at the time the lawsuit begins? Where the defendant acted in causing the alleged injury to the plaintiff? Where the plaintiff was injured or is now residing?

e.   Service of Process

Once the plaintiff has selected the proper court, she must notify the defendant of the commencement of the lawsuit. This is done by what is known as *service of process*. Typically, this process will consist of service of a *summons*, an official document that is issued by the court in which the action has been filed and is then served on the defendants, advising that a lawsuit has been started.

Service of process can be accomplished by several methods. The traditional method is *personal service*. A marshal or sheriff—or, often, a private person authorized by law (in many jurisdictions, any adult who is not otherwise involved in the lawsuit will do)—will actually hand the defendant the summons and complaint. More recently, many states and the federal courts have permitted service through the mail: As long as the defendant returns a signed receipt acknowledging actual receipt of the summons and complaint, personal service is not required.

f.   Pleadings

The summons may do no more than tell an adversary about the commencement of the suit. In some states, the summons will be somewhat more elaborate and give a short synopsis of the type of claim that the plaintiff is alleging against the defendant. Often, the plaintiff is required to serve an initial *pleading*, known as a *complaint*, along with the summons. The complaint informs the defendant of the allegations made against him. A complaint may vary from a simple assertion that the defendant owes the plaintiff a million dollars for injuries suffered to detailing a precise chain of events.

The complaint is the first of the *pleadings*, the documents that set out in writing the claims and defenses of the parties. These pleadings, which include a response by the defendant called an *answer* and perhaps a *reply* by the plaintiff, serve a variety of functions depending on the rules of the particular system. They may: (1) merely apprise the opponent of the general nature of the pleader's claims or defenses; (2) present a detailed account of the factual and legal grounds for the relief sought; or (3) state exactly what the party intends to prove at trial.

The level of detail required in the pleadings is a function of the purpose the particular system intends to further—whether to simply notify the other side or to narrow issues early on so as to facilitate disposition of the case without trial. The federal system generally follows a rule of *notice pleading*, requiring only a "short and plain statement of the claim showing that the pleader is entitled to relief" and of the court's jurisdiction. *See* Fed. R. Civ. P. 8(a). In the federal system, the issue-narrowing function is thought to be better served by a process of pretrial discovery rather than a battle over pleadings. Notwithstanding this liberal pleading standard, the Supreme Court has required that the allegations in a plaintiff's complaint must contain enough factual context to render the claims "plausible" in the eyes of the court. *See Bell Atlantic Corp. v. Twombly*, 550 U.S. 544 (2007).

After the summons and complaint have been served, the defendant in most systems has a choice of responses. The defendant may wish to make a dispositive motion (one that results in the dismissal of the lawsuit) in advance of filing and serving an answer. If the defendant wishes to object to the personal or subject matter jurisdiction of the court, the defendant will then file a *motion to dismiss* for lack of personal or subject matter jurisdiction. If the defendant believes that he cannot be held liable under the applicable law, he will file a *demurrer*, or what is today often called a motion to dismiss for *failure to state a claim. See, e.g.*, Fed. R. Civ. P. 12(b)(6). Such a motion tests the *legal sufficiency* of the complaint: It assumes the facts as alleged by the complaint and asserts "so what," because even on the alleged facts, there is no legal basis for relief. Pursuant to the *Twombly* case, a 12(b)(6) motion may also challenge the factual "plausibility" of the complaint. The court will have to resolve these motions before going ahead—before defendant has even taken a position on the facts of the case.

If such dispositive motions are denied, the defendant will then file and serve an *answer* containing responses that either admit or deny the allegations of the complaint. To preserve certain *affirmative defenses* to the plaintiff's claim, defendant may have to specify the nature of the defense in the answer. *See, e.g.*, Fed. R. Civ. P. 8(c).

The defendant may also assert a *counterclaim* against the plaintiff, alleging that the plaintiff's wrongful conduct injured the defendant. In the federal system, some counterclaims, if closely related to the "transaction" giving rise to the complaint, must be asserted or they are waived. *See* Fed. R. Civ. P. 13(a). Some states do not require assertion of any counterclaims and permit the defendant to press those claims in a separate suit.

g.   Remedies

In the pleadings, the plaintiff may request several different forms of relief. The most common is a request for money *damages*. The plaintiff may also seek an *injunction*, a judicial directive that the defendant act, or refrain from acting, in a particular way. In other circumstances, a party may be able to request a declaration of rights, status, or other legal relationship—for example, that a party is not under an obligation to another party—a remedy known as *declaratory relief.*

In addition to these "final" remedies, a plaintiff may be able to seek certain types of "interim" relief. For example, if it appears that a defendant is likely to remove or dissipate assets, a plaintiff may impose a restraint on those assets prior to commencement of or during the proceedings. Or if the alleged harm is imminent and/or the object of the litigation depends on immediate action, the plaintiff may seek a *temporary restraining order* or a *preliminary injunction.* A temporary restraining order is really "emergency" relief, and as such, may even be granted "*ex parte*" (without consulting the other side). However, it has a limited duration—usually about ten days—during which time a further hearing may be held. A preliminary injunction is the more typical form of interim relief, granted after a hearing. The court directs a party to perform specified acts or refrain from certain action until the court decides the full merits of the action.

h. Pretrial Discovery

In the federal system and in many states the parties may engage in expansive *discovery*—a process of obtaining information from the opposing party and witnesses. The court will assist the parties in obtaining any information that might be useful at trial.

Methods of discovery include *depositions* (recorded examinations of witnesses under oath), *requests for production of documents,* and *interrogatories* (written questions). *See* Fed. R. Civ. P. 26–37. Discovery directed at nonparties may require issuance of a *subpoena* to compel responses. *See, e.g.,* Fed. R. Civ. P. 45.

The theory of expansive discovery is that "trial by surprise" is unfair, and that full exchange of information helps narrow the issues and makes the ultimate trial more manageable. It is also possible that fully informed adversaries are more likely to pursue serious settlement discussions in order to avoid the costs of trial.

There are also disadvantages to discovery. Sometimes little is achieved in discovery other than wasteful expenditure of time and resources for the benefit of attorneys alone. The availability of discovery, standing alone, creates some nuisance value for virtually every lawsuit, irrespective of the merits.

i. Summary Judgment

Sometimes it is possible to avoid trial by showing that there is no genuine material issue for trial—for instance, because one of the parties will not be able to produce any evidence at the trial in support of his position. A party (either a plaintiff or defendant) might then file a pretrial motion for *summary judgment*—judgment without trial. *See* Fed. R. Civ. P. 56. It permits the moving party to go behind the pleadings and test the *factual sufficiency* of the opposing party's position. Often the moving party will employ the fruits of pretrial discovery in support of the motion as well as affidavits of persons having personal knowledge of the facts to show that allegations made in the pleadings have no factual foundation. If the opposing party either by counter-affidavit or other appropriate supporting material can show that there are material factual issues requiring trial, the judge will deny the motion, and the case will proceed to trial.

j. Trial

If the case is not resolved by summary judgment, it will be calendared for trial. The fact finder will be a judge or a jury. In federal courts, the Seventh Amendment of the Constitution assures a right to trial by jury in certain cases to the extent such cases were tried before a jury "at common law." The phrase *at common law* refers to the historical distinction between cases heard in the English law courts and those heard in the Courts of Chancery. As originally constituted, the English law courts were limited to providing relief only in cases falling within the scope of specific "writs" or "forms of action." The Chancery or "Equity" courts developed in order to provide additional remedies in cases not covered by existing writs. The equity courts alone had the power to issue injunctions and other unusual relief. No jury was available in equity proceedings. Thus, most federal cases seeking damages give rise to a right to a jury trial. Many state constitutions contain similar provisions. (By contrast, Great Britain has dispensed with juries in most civil actions.)

Either party may demand a jury trial. In the federal courts, if a seasonable demand is not made, the right to a jury is waived. *See* Fed. R. Civ. P. 38.

The federal civil jury once required 12 members and a unanimous verdict. The Supreme Court has held that the Seventh Amendment permits fewer than 12 jurors in federal civil cases but still requires unanimous verdicts. (The rules governing juries in state courts may be different, and nonunanimous verdicts may be permitted.) If a jury has been demanded, a panel of prospective jurors will be selected. *Voir dire* of the prospective jurors is conducted to determine the juror's bias, prior knowledge of the case, and familiarity with the parties. If the court finds reason to believe that a juror will be unable to hear and decide the case impartially, the juror will be excused for cause. Parties are also permitted a limited number of *peremptory challenges* to strike jurors even without cause. In federal courts, the judge normally conducts the *voir dire*; in many states, this is done by the attorneys for the parties.

At the commencement of the trial, the plaintiff usually makes the *opening statement*, followed by an opening statement by the defendant.

The plaintiff is typically the party with the *burden of persuasion*—the burden of persuading the trier of fact by the requisite degree of certainty. In most civil cases, the burden is one of convincing the trier of fact that "a fair preponderance of the evidence" supports the party's position. The allocation of the burden of persuasion is determined by the applicable substantive law and always remains with the party to whom it is initially assigned.

After the exchange of opening statements, the plaintiff puts on his or her case. The plaintiff's lawyer calls witnesses to testify in open court by *direct examination*. The lawyer for the other side then conducts *cross-examination* of each witness. This is often followed by *redirect* and *re-cross*. The primary responsibility for introducing evidence either through witnesses or documents is with the lawyers. The lawyers are also responsible for *objecting* to evidence that is not permissible under the applicable rules of evidence. For example, an attempt to introduce an out-of-court statement for the purpose of establishing the truth of the statement will often be met with a hearsay objection. A failure to make a timely objection constitutes a waiver. In the federal system, these matters are governed by the Federal Rules of Evidence.

After the plaintiff has called its witnesses, and even before the defendant has put on its case, the defendant may assert that the plaintiff has failed to establish a case for relief and ask for a *judgment as a matter of law* (previously called a *directed verdict*). *See* Fed. R. Civ. P. 50(a). The theory of the judgment as a matter of law is that the function of the jury is to find the facts only when the state of the evidence is such that reasonable persons might differ. If, however, the state of the evidence is such that a reasonable jury could come out only one way, the court should not allow the case to go to the jury. Usually, the court will want to hear the other side's evidence even if it is inclined to grant the motion. The defendant then puts on its case, after which a renewed motion for a judgment as a matter of law might be made.

Usually, the judge errs on the side of allowing the case to go to the jury. This permits the possibility of a verdict in favor of the movant's position and thus may moot the need for the court to rule on the motion. It also helps to preserve a verdict and obviate a retrial should the appeals court reverse the trial court's grant of a post-verdict motion for judgment as a matter of law (previously called a *judgment notwithstanding the verdict (JNOV)*). *See* Fed. R. Civ. P. 50(b).

Before the case goes to the jury, counsel will make closing arguments. The judge and lawyers will also confer with regard to the content of the judge's instructions to the jury. Typically, the lawyers will submit proposed *jury instructions*. The judge instructs the jury on the applicable law. The judge may offer alternative views of the facts and instruct the jury of the legal consequences that attach to those alternative views.

Verdicts can be *general*, merely declaring who won and how much they have been awarded. Alternatively, *special verdicts* require the jury to answer certain questions, e.g., "Was the defendant driving at an excessive speed at the time of the accident?" The judge then must determine how to apply the law to the jury's answers.

After the jury returns with its decision, *post-verdict motions* are entertained. These include (1) a renewed motion for judgment as a matter of law—i.e., the case should not have gone to the jury in the first place; and (2) a *motion for a new trial*—i.e., the judge made some error requiring a new trial or the verdict was against the clear weight of the evidence.

k.   Appeal

Every legal system in the United States provides for review by an appellate court of the decisions of a trial court. In the federal system, the general rule is that appeals are available only from "final decisions" of the district courts. *See* 28 U.S.C. §1291. The upshot of the federal system's finality requirement is that a great many trial court decisions are effectively immune from appellate review. This is true, for example, of a trial court's ruling on discovery motions, which may be quite important to the progress of the litigation but are not likely to dispose of the case. They are thus not considered final decisions.

Once a final judgment is entered, the parties may file their appeal. The appellate court decides the case on the basis of the written *record* of the trial proceeding. It does not hear any witnesses. The record on appeal will contain the pleadings and at least a portion of the transcript of the trial (the court reporter's verbatim record). The parties present their arguments by written briefs supplemented by oral argument. In some appeals courts, oral argument is not available as a matter of right. Appellate courts are typically multi-member tribunals, with appeals heard before panels of the court. In the federal system, appeals are governed by the Federal Rules of Appellate Procedure.

The level of deference that the appeals court gives the trial court's ruling is called the "*standard of review.*" The appellate court reviews most questions of law on a *plenary* basis; the appeals court generally evaluates such questions "*de novo*" (anew) and gives no weight to the trial court's legal conclusions. (However, some legal questions are said to be within the trial court's discretion and hence are treated quite deferentially.) On questions of fact, appeals courts have a more limited role. The trial judge's findings of fact cannot be overturned unless "*clearly erroneous*" (Fed. R. Civ. P. 52(a)(6)), and courts are even more deferential to jury determinations. It is sometimes unclear whether a particular question should be characterized as a question of law or a question of fact for purposes of the standard of review.

An appellate court has power to *affirm, reverse, vacate,* or *modify* the judgment of the trial court. If it reverses, the court may enter judgment accordingly or it may *remand* the case to the trial court for further proceedings.

Decisions are often accompanied by written *opinions* written by one of the judges of the panel hearing the appeal. In some systems, provision is made for summary dispositions of appeals without published opinion.

l.   Enforcement of Judgments

The typical civil judgment for money damages requires an *enforcement proceeding* against the assets of the losing party. State law governs this process, often termed *execution,* and may exempt certain assets of the losing party from execution. As discussed above, state and federal courts owe an obligation to give full faith and credit to the judgment of other American courts.

m.   Finality

A critical characteristic of any dispute-resolution mechanism is finality: Once a court establishes the relative rights of the litigants, the parties will not be permitted to relitigate their claims or defenses. This principle is enforced through the doctrine of *res judicata* (the thing has been decided). *Res judicata,* sometimes referred to as *claim preclusion,* bars claims between the same parties that were, or should have been, asserted in a judicial proceeding that was resolved *on the merits.*

A closely related doctrine of *collateral estoppel* or *issue preclusion* also prevents a party from relitigating particular factual or legal assertions that were decided against that party in a prior proceeding. Unlike *res judicata,* collateral estoppel only precludes assertions that were actually litigated and decided in the earlier proceeding. In many jurisdictions, collateral estoppel may be asserted against a former party by a new litigant who did not participate in the earlier adjudication.

B.   *ILLUSTRATION OF THE STAGES OF A LAWSUIT*—NEW YORK TIMES v. SULLIVAN

In this section, we offer an illustration of the procedural system by tracking the litigation of a single case: a lawsuit in which one of the city commissioners of Montgomery, Alabama claimed that a newspaper advertisement made false and damaging allegations about him. In some ways, *New York Times v. Sullivan,* as the case ultimately came to be known, is one of the most extraordinary cases in modern constitutional law. (Anthony Lewis's book, *Make No Law: The* Sullivan *Case and the First Amendment* (1991), provides a sophisticated but accessible account.) In other ways, the case involved many of the mundane procedural issues that crop up in literally thousands of cases every year. Tracing the case from its beginnings through the judicial system to its final resolution gives us an opportunity to think about a variety of procedural issues that will occupy the remainder of this course. Moreover, by watching the litigation evolve, we try to avoid the sense of inevitability that too often overcomes law students who read nothing but Supreme Court and other appellate opinions. Litigation is a tactical, risky, contingent process, in which the lawyer plays a creative role at almost every turn.

In what follows, we weave together actual documents from the record in *Sullivan*, judicial opinions, narrative information about procedural issues, and questions designed to get you to think about the legal and tactical issues that confronted the lawyers. All of the issues raised in this material will be reconsidered in depth in the course of the book. Don't worry if you do not fully grasp everything now.

1. *The Context of the Lawsuit*

The decade following the Supreme Court's decision in *Brown v. Board of Education*, 347 U.S. 483 (1954), which held racial segregation in public education unconstitutional, was a time of tremendous legal and political ferment. The Montgomery, Alabama, bus boycott galvanized black communities across the country into direct action to break down barriers in transportation, public facilities such as parks and libraries, schools, and restaurants.

These actions included sit-ins, in which black college students demanded to be served by restaurants that were traditionally restricted to whites; "Freedom Rides," in which black and white activists boarded interstate buses and refused to sit in separate seats or to use separate bus waiting rooms; and massive efforts to register black voters, who had been essentially disenfranchised throughout the South.

Courts and state legislatures were as important an arena as streets or lunch counters. On one side, civil rights groups, such as the NAACP Legal Defense and Educational Fund, led by Thurgood Marshall (who later sat as the first African-American member of the Supreme Court), challenged policies that kept blacks from participating fully in civic and political life. On the other side, defenders of segregation engaged in "Massive Resistance." They used the legal system for both defensive and offensive purposes. Defensively, they engaged in protracted litigation designed to delay implementation of *Brown*'s central holding. Offensively, they used criminal prosecutions to impose heavy burdens on civil rights activists.

On February 29, 1960, the State of Alabama charged Dr. Martin Luther King, Jr., the head of the Southern Christian Leadership Conference and a key civil rights leader, with two counts of perjury in connection with the filing of his Alabama state income tax return. King faced ten years in prison if he were convicted of both counts. It was the first felony tax-evasion charge in state history, and it seemed a blatant attempt to incapacitate one of the civil rights movement's most dynamic figures and to intimidate other individuals who might be inclined to challenge segregation's iron hold.

A number of nationally known figures, including Eleanor Roosevelt, Nat King Cole, and Jackie Robinson, formed the Committee to Defend Martin Luther King and the Struggle for Freedom in the South to raise money to aid in King's defense. The Committee's Executive Director, Bayard Rustin, decided to compose and publish an advertisement to solicit contributions. Ultimately, a month after King's indictment, on March 29, 1960, the advertisement, excerpted below, appeared on page 25 of the *New York Times:*

> In Montgomery, Alabama, after students sang "My Country, 'Tis of Thee" on the State Capitol steps, their leaders were expelled from school, and truckloads of police armed with shotguns and tear-gas ringed the Alabama State College Campus. When the entire student body protested to state authorities by refusing to re-register, their dining hall was padlocked in an attempt to starve them into submission. . . .
>
> Again and again the Southern violators have answered Dr. King's peaceful protests with intimidation and violence. They have bombed his home almost killing his wife and child. They have assaulted his person. They have arrested him seven times—for "speeding," "loitering" and similar "offenses." And now they have charged him with "perjury"—a felony under which they could imprison him for ten years.

The Committee paid the Times $4,600 to run the ad. The *Times*'s circulation was 650,000 copies. Fewer than 400 papers went to subscribers in Alabama. One of the subscribers, though, was the company that put out Montgomery, Alabama's two newspapers, the *Montgomery Advertiser* and the *Alabama Journal.*

The *Journal*'s city editor noticed the advertisement and ran a brief story about it on April 5. The story identified some of the Committee members, listed some of the charges in the advertisement, and mentioned some inaccuracies, particularly that students at Alabama State College (an entirely black school) had been expelled for singing "My Country 'Tis of Thee" on the steps of the State Capitol and that college authorities had tried to starve them into submission by padlocking the dining hall.

The *Advertiser's* editor was outraged by what he viewed as the ad's biased treatment of the South, and on April 7, 1960, he ran an editorial denouncing the advertisement as presenting "crude slanders against Montgomery. . . ." One of Montgomery's City Commissioners (the city commission was the three-person board that ran the city) was L. B. Sullivan. Sullivan, who was in charge of the city police force, read that editorial and decided to bring a lawsuit against the Times and four ministers from Alabama whose names appeared on the advertisement.

2.   *The Lawsuit Begins*

Lawsuits normally begin when the plaintiff (the person or entity seeking some form of relief) files a complaint and serves the complaint and a summons, telling the defendant where and when he or she must respond to the complaint.

We reprint below the summons, complaint, and affidavit (a sworn statement) regarding how service was to be accomplished that were used in the *Sullivan* case.

L. B. SULLIVAN

vs.

THE NEW YORK TIMES CO., A CORP., RALPH D. ABERNATHY, FRED L. SHUTTLESWORTH, S.S. SEAY, SR. AND J.E. LOWERY.

SUMMONS AND COMPLAINT

The State of Alabama Montgomery County

To Any Sheriff of the State of Alabama—Greeting:

You are hereby commanded to summon The New York Times Company, a Corporation, Ralph D. Abernathy, Fred L. Shuttlesworth, S. S. Seay, Sr., and J. E. Lowery to appear before the Circuit Court of Montgomery County . . . within thirty days from the service of this summons and complaint, then and there to demur or plead to the complaint of L. B. Sullivan. . . .

Witness my hand this 19 day of April, 1960. John R. Matthews, Clerk.

IN THE CIRCUIT COURT OF MONTGOMERY COUNTY, ALABAMA

[Title omitted]

COMPLAINT—Filed April 19, 1960

Count I

Plaintiff claims of the defendants the sum of Five Hundred Thousand Dollars ($500,000.00) as damages, for that plaintiff avers that defendants falsely and maliciously published in the City of New York, State of New York, and in the City of Montgomery, Alabama, and throughout the State of Alabama of and concerning the plaintiff, in a publication entitled *The New York Times*, in the issue of March 29, 1960, on page 25, in an advertisement entitled, "Heed Their Rising Voices" (a copy of said advertisement being attached hereto and made a part hereof as Exhibit "A"), false and defamatory matter of charges reflecting upon the conduct of the plaintiff as a member of the Board of Commissioners of the City of Montgomery, Alabama, and imputing improper conduct to him, and subjecting him to public contempt, ridicule and shame, and prejudicing the . . . plaintiff in his office, profession, trade, or business, with an intent to defame the plaintiff. . . .

And plaintiff further avers that more than five days before the bringing of this action plaintiff made a written demand for a full and fair public retraction of the aforesaid false and defamatory matter or charges upon defendants and each of them; and defendants, and each of them, have failed or refused to publish a full and fair retraction of such charges or matter in as prominent and public a place or manner as the aforesaid charges or matter occupied as aforesaid;

And plaintiff further avers that he has suffered damage, and embarrassment to his character and reputation, personally and as a public official of the City of Montgomery, Alabama; that he has been subjected to public ridicule and shame; that he has been injured and damaged in the lawful pursuit of his office, profession, trade or business, as a proximate result of the aforesaid false and defamatory publication by the defendants; and plaintiff further claims punitive damages; hence this suit. . . .

Scott, Whitesell & Scott, By: Calvin Whitesell; Steiner, Crum and Baker, By: M. R. Nachman, Jr.; Attorneys for Plaintiff.

Plaintiff demands trial by jury in this cause.

Steiner, Crum & Baker, By: M. R. Nachman, Jr.,

Attorneys for Plaintiff.

AFFIDAVIT

State of Alabama Montgomery County

Before me, Bernice S. Osgoode, a Notary Public in and for said County, in said State, personally appeared M. R. Nachman, Jr., who is known to me, and who, being first duly sworn, deposes and says as follows.

That defendant The New York Times Company, a corporation, is a nonresident of the State of Alabama; that it is not qualified under the Constitution and laws of the State of Alabama as to doing business in the State of Alabama; that it has actually done and is now doing business or performing work or services in the State of Alabama; that this cause of action has arisen out of the doing of such business or as an incident thereof by the said defendant in the State of Alabama, and that by the doing of such business or the performing of such work or services this defendant, in accordance with the Constitution and laws of the State of Alabama, is deemed to have appointed the Secretary of State of Alabama, or her successor or successors in office, to be the true and lawful attorney or agent of this nonresident defendant, upon whom process may be served in this action which has accrued from the performing of such work or services, or as an incident thereof, by this nonresident defendant, acting through its agents, servants, or employees.

And affiant further avers that process should be served upon this defendant, to-wit, The New York Times Company, in the manner prescribed by the laws of Alabama, and particularly in the manner prescribed by Title 7; Sec. 199(1), Code of Alabama 1940 as amended.

Affiant further avers that the residence and the last known address of this defendant is as follows: The New York Times Company, Times Building, 229 West 43d Street, New York, New York.

M. R. Nachman, Jr. . . .

NOTES AND QUESTIONS

1. *The Question of Jurisdiction*

a. *Subject Matter Jurisdiction.* Sullivan chose to file suit in Alabama state court. Could he have filed in federal court? Libel law is state law: Each state decides for itself whether to recognize the tort of defamation, and there is no federal law that gives private individuals a right to seek damages for statements made about them in the press. Thus, Sullivan's suit did not "arise under" federal law for purposes of federal subject matter jurisdiction. (In determining whether a case can be heard in federal court on the theory that it arises under federal law, it is not enough that the defendant has some issue of federal law that it wants to assert, so the fact that the Times might—and ultimately did—argue by way of defense that the First Amendment's guarantee of a free press should limit Sullivan's right to recover does not create "arising under" jurisdiction.)

If Sullivan had sued only the *New York Times*, there would have been diversity jurisdiction. Sullivan was a citizen of Alabama and the Times was a New York corporation and, therefore, for diversity purposes a citizen of New York. But Sullivan chose also to sue four ministers who lived in Alabama and therefore were citizens of the same state as the plaintiff. Why do you think he added these ministers who, after all, were unlikely to have anything near the $500,000 he was seeking in damages?

The answer is a tactical one. Under the federal removal statute, 28 U.S.C. §1441, defendants can *remove* to the federal court system from the state court system cases that the plaintiff could have filed originally in federal court. Think about what the Times could have done if Sullivan had sued it alone. Why might Sullivan have wanted to keep the case in state court? *See* Burt Neuborne, *The Myth of Parity*, 90 Harv. L. Rev. 1105 (1977) (discussing the very different responses of federal and state courts to certain kinds of cases and claims).

The Montgomery County Circuit Court clearly had subject matter jurisdiction over Sullivan's claim. Each state has courts "of general jurisdiction" that can hear cases involving virtually any subject matter.

The New York State Supreme Court, New York's court of general jurisdiction, would also have had subject matter jurisdiction over Sullivan's suit against the Times. So, too, would the California Superior Court, for that matter, since it has the authority to hear tort cases involving significant damages.

b. *Personal Jurisdiction.* But you probably have the intuitive sense that there would be something wrong with Sullivan filing his case in California. Why? Although the subject matter of his case may be the kind of issue California courts deal with all the time, there seems to be something wrong with forcing these defendants to go to California to defend themselves. Thus, we arrive at the second jurisdictional issue in the *Sullivan* case: personal jurisdiction.

A court has *personal jurisdiction* if the parties fall within the geographic reach of the court's authority. The personal jurisdiction of state courts is controlled both by state law and by the United States Constitution. In the first instance, a state decides the reach of its personal jurisdiction. But individuals or entities that think a state's assertion of jurisdiction over them is unfair can argue that, whatever the state's desire, the federal Constitution prevents such an exercise of authority as a matter of "due process of law" under *International Shoe Co. v. Washington*, 326 U.S. 310 (1945).

In a moment, you will be presented with a variety of documents and opinions involving whether the Montgomery County Circuit Court had personal jurisdiction over the *New York Times*. But before you begin reading the documents, put yourself in the positions of the litigants and ask why this matters. Why did Sullivan file his lawsuit in Alabama, rather than New York? Conversely, why might the Times not want to defend itself in Alabama?

2. *Issues of Service and Notice.* Personal service of a summons can provide both notice of the pendency of the litigation, as well as a basis for personal jurisdiction if the process is served within the borders of the state in which the suit was filed. In order for service of process to play this dual role in the *Sullivan* litigation, the

Times or its agent had to have been served in Alabama. In order to facilitate service and provide a basis for personal jurisdiction, many states resort to a legal fiction: Persons or organizations that have engaged in certain activities within the state are deemed to have appointed the Secretary of State (or some other official) as their agent for in-state service of process. The notice function is served as long as the Secretary forwards the summons and complaint to the defendant.

Reread the affidavit filed by M. R. Nachman. How is that affidavit related to the service of process?

In addition to arranging for substituted service of process on the Secretary of State, on April 21, 1960, the Montgomery County Sheriff handed a copy of the summons and complaint to Don McKee "as agent for the *New York Times*." Don McKee was an Alabama newspaperman who served as the Times's "stringer" in Montgomery; he would occasionally submit stories to the Times about local news. Under Ala. Code §7-188 (1960), "[w]hen an action at law is against a corporation the summons may be executed by the delivery of a copy of the summons and complaint to the president, or other head thereof, secretary, cashier, station agent or any other agent thereof." Under what circumstances would service on McKee be adequate service of process? For purposes of notice? Personal jurisdiction?

3. *State Versus Federal Practice.* Note that Sullivan in his complaint demands a trial by jury. In most civil actions seeking money damages, federal or state constitutions guarantee that either party may demand a trial before a jury rather than a trial before the judge (called a *bench trial*), as long as they make a timely demand. *See, e.g.*, Fed. R. Civ. P. 38; Ala. R. Civ. P. 38. It is important to remember that every state has its own rules of procedure that may differ significantly from the federal rules (although some states, such as New Jersey, closely track the federal rules).

3.   *The Defendant's First Response*

Usually, when there is no doubt that the court has personal and subject matter jurisdiction and that the defendant has been properly served with process, the defendant responds to the plaintiff's complaint with an answer. The answer will address the facts alleged in the complaint and may also raise various defenses to the plaintiff's suit.

One of the defendants in the *Sullivan* case was Rev. Ralph D. Abernathy, an Alabama minister. Abernathy was served personally with process and, within the time given under Alabama law, he responded to Sullivan's complaint. (His response was called a *demurrer*, in accordance with Alabama's practice, but you should not worry about such nomenclature at this point in the semester.)

DEMURRER OF RALPH D. ABERNATHY

Now comes Ralph D. Abernathy, one of the defendants in the above entitled cause and demurs to the Complaint filed in the above entitled cause, and separately and severally demurs to each count there, and as grounds of demurrer assigns the following separately and severally:

1. That it does not state a cause of action.
2. That no facts alleged upon which relief sought can be granted. . . .

5. No facts are alleged to show that this defendant published in the City of New York, State of New York, or any place, the advertisement referred to in said Complaint.

6. No facts are alleged to show that this defendant caused to be published in the City of New York, State of New York, or any other place, the advertisement referred to in said Complaint. . . .

. . .

The Times, however, decided not to respond to the merits of Sullivan's complaint. Instead, the Times filed the following document:

MOTION TO QUASH SERVICE OF PROCESS

Comes the New York Times Company, . . . by its attorneys, and appearing solely and specially for the purpose of filing this its motion to quash attempted service of process in this cause and for no other purpose . . . and without making a general appearance . . . alleges the following, separately and severally:

1. On . . . April 26, 1960, The New York Times Company, . . . received by registered mail in New York City, New York, a summons and complaint and affidavit of the Honorable Bettye Frink, Secretary of State of the State of Alabama. . . .

2. . . . a summons and complaint in that cause . . . was (also) served upon one Don McKee by the Sheriff of Montgomery, Alabama, . . . "as agent for the New York Times. . . ."

3. The New York Times Company . . . is a . . . corporation, organized and existing under the laws of the State of New York, with its principal place of business at The Times Building, 229 West 43rd Street, New York, New York, and said corporation . . . has no office or place of business situated in, or employee, agent or servant, in the State of Alabama, and did not have at the time of the service of process as is described in the preceding paragraphs 1 and 2 herein; is not doing business in Alabama or in Montgomery County, Alabama, and was not doing business in Alabama or in Montgomery County at the time of the service of process as described in preceding paragraphs 1 and 2 herein. . . .

6. The New York Times Company, a corporation, is not amenable to service of process in the State of Alabama, and was not at any time pertinent to the alleged cause of action or the purported service in this cause and has not waived service of due process herein by voluntary appearance or otherwise.

7. The cause of action alleged in plaintiff's complaint did not accrue from the doing of any business or the performing of any work or service or as an incident thereto by the defendant, The New York Times Company, a corporation, or its agent, servant or employee in the State of Alabama. . . .

13. Don McKee, upon whom service of process was made, as is described in paragraph 2 herein was not an officer, agent, servant or employee of The New York Times Company . . . at the time of service of process upon him as described in paragraph 2 herein, nor at the time of the accrual of any alleged cause of action set forth in the complaint in this cause nor at the time of the filing of the summons and complaint in this cause. . . .

17. The New York Times Company, a corporation, is not subject to the jurisdiction of this Honorable Court in this cause for this court to assume jurisdiction of

said defendant in this cause would deny to defendant due process of law in contravention of the 14th Amendment to the Constitution of the United States.

Wherefore, The New York Times Company, a corporation, appearing specially for this purpose and no other moves the Court as Follows:

1. That service of process as described in preceding paragraph 1 of this motion be quashed as to the New York Times Company. . . .

2. That service of process as described in preceding paragraph 2 of this motion be quashed as to The New York Times Company. . . .

5. That this court dismiss this action as to The New York Times Company . . . for lack of jurisdiction of the person. . . .

6. That this Court dismiss this action as to The New York Times Company . . . for lack of jurisdiction of the subject matter of said action.

NOTES AND QUESTIONS

1. *Motion to Quash Versus Defense on the Merits.* Notice that the Times does not make any claims in its motion to quash regarding the truth or falsity of the story it published or the story's effect on Sullivan. Would it be inappropriate for the Times both to move to quash the service of process and to argue about the merits of Sullivan's claim?

2. *Special Appearance.* The Times's lawyers were careful to stress that they were appearing "specially for the purpose of filing this its motion . . . and without making a general appearance. . . ." Through this "special appearance" procedure, the newspaper stated it was appearing for the sole purpose of contesting the circuit court's jurisdiction and that such appearance could not be treated as an admission that it was properly served or that the court in fact had jurisdiction. If the Times had entered a general appearance, it would be acknowledging that the circuit court had the authority to dispose of all the issues in the case.

What is the difference between what the Times is asking the court to do in concluding paragraphs 1 and 2 of its prayer for relief and in paragraph 5? What is the difference between what it is asking for in paragraph 5 and what it is asking for in paragraph 6? As we shall see in a moment, paragraph 6 is very significant.

4.   *The Discovery Process*

When a defendant challenges the court's jurisdiction, the merits of the complaint are put to the side while the parties and court deal with the question of jurisdiction.

In response to the Times's motion, Sullivan needed to develop and present to the court sufficient facts to justify the exercise of jurisdiction over the Times. Obviously, many of the relevant facts—whether the Times in fact was doing the kind of business in Alabama that would permit Alabama's exercise of personal jurisdiction and whether Don McKee was in fact the Times's agent—are more within the Times's control than Sullivan's. Accordingly, Sullivan sought discovery of information from the Times that would support the court's exercise of jurisdiction.

Following are some examples of Sullivan's discovery regarding the jurisdictional issues.

MOTION TO PRODUCE

Comes the plaintiff in the above entitled cause and moves this Court for an order requiring the defendant, The New York Times Company . . . to produce the following books, documents, and writings in its possession, custody, control or power, which contain evidence pertinent to the issues in the above styled cause, and which more specifically relate to questions raised and to be presented to this Court by the said defendant's motion to quash . . . :

(1) All issues of the *New York Times* for the following dates: [Here plaintiffs listed several hundred issues during the period Feb. 11, 1956, to April 13, 1960]. . . .

(3) All writings or other documents constituting applications for employment, or contracts of employment, or any business arrangement with the individuals specified in the preceding paragraph as so-called "string-correspondents," or with any other persons who are residents of the State of Alabama and who have been so-called "string correspondents" for the Times since 1956.

(4) All documents or other writings, constituting a statement of rules and regulations from the Times to any "string correspondents" in the State of Alabama during the last four years, regarding the nature of the duties of these "string correspondents". . . .

(6) Copies of all checks, vouchers, and receipts, and any other papers or documents in connection with the payment by the Times to any of the persons named in paragraph 2 of this motion, or any other so-called "string correspondents," resident in Alabama, since January 1, 1956.

(7) All documents and writings constituting expense accounts or statements of expenses submitted for or in behalf of [Times correspondents] . . . relating to expense incurred by them in the State of Alabama since January 1, 1956. . . .

(11) Copies of all writings or other documents evidencing the total receipts by the Times from the sale of its newspaper in Alabama for the year 1959 and the first five months of 1960.

NOTES AND QUESTIONS

What did Sullivan hope to prove with this material? Try to frame how the material sought was relevant to the issue of jurisdiction. At this stage in the lawsuit, how strong a showing of relevancy should be required? Rule 26(b)(1) of the Fed. R. Civ. P. permits discovery of "any nonprivileged matter that is relevant to any party's claim or defense," even if the information sought will be inadmissible at trial.

Sullivan's lawyers also took several *depositions.* Depositions resemble courtroom proceedings in that a court stenographer makes a transcript, and the witnesses are under oath, but they normally take place in private, without a judge being present.

Consider the following excerpts from the deposition of Claude Sitton. (M. Roland Nachman and Sam Rice Baker are Sullivan's attorneys; T. Eric Embry and Thomas Daly are the Times's lawyers.)

THE DEPOSITION OF CLAUDE SITTON

Mr. Nachman: I might state at this point we have stipulated with counsel for The New York Times that we understand that their appearance . . . at this deposition in no manner waives any grounds raised by their Motion to Quash Service and it is stipulated that it shall not be considered as a general appearance in this case. . . .

The witness, CLAUDE F. SITTON, being first duly sworn, testified as follows:

Examination by Mr. Nachman:

Q. . . . How long have you been employed by The New York Times, Mr. Sitton?
A. Since October, 1957. . . . And since May of '58, I have covered the South for The New York Times, southern territory. . . .
Q. In a general way, Mr. Sitton, would you outline what your duties are as Southern Correspondent of The New York Times?
A. Well, to cover news in the South.
Q. Gather news?
A. That's correct.
Q. What area is embraced by the term "South" as you use it?
A. Virginia, Kentucky, North and South Carolina, Tennessee, Georgia, Florida, Alabama, Mississippi, Louisiana, Arkansas. . . .
Q. Mr. Sitton, do you recall that on a Sunday, March 6, 1960, where you covered a so-called demonstration in the City of Montgomery, Alabama?
A. I think I did, yes.
Q. You were present in Montgomery on that date?
A. I think so.
Q. Would you state how that story got to The Times for publication?
A. I called it in.
Q. From Montgomery?
A. That's correct. . . .
Q. In addition to the correspondents . . . does The Times have so-called string correspondents in these states and specifically in Alabama?

Mr. Embry: We object unless it is shown whether he knows whether they have or not.*

Q. Do you know?
A. You refer to my jurisdiction there. This is not really my jurisdiction; I have no — I'm — I'm simply a reporter down here, I cover the South and, as I said before, I told you the basis. I have no — no jurisdiction whatsoever over any other operations that might be conducted in this area.

---

* Unlike at trial, where the judge can immediately rule on an objection, there is no judicial official at a deposition to rule on an objection. The reason Embry has objected here is to preserve the objection for the later hearing in front of the judge. If Nachman asks Sitton this question at a hearing, Embry can raise his objection before the judge then. But if Embry had not objected here, he may have waived his objection at the hearing. There is also a tactical component to objecting. Notice how Embry's objection may subtly signal to Sitton how to answer the question. — EDS.

Q. Well, do you know, or don't you, whether there are located in Alabama certain so-called string correspondents?

A. I know one stringer in Alabama, yes.

Q. What is his name?

A. Don McKee. . . .

Q. Now, am I correct, sir, you covered the Civil Rights Commission hearing in Montgomery which began on December 1, 1958?

A. To the best of my knowledge, I did, sir.

Q. And did that coverage necessitate your physical presence in Montgomery during that time?

A. I was there. . . .

Q. There were also, I believe, some events which took place outside of Montgomery; specifically, there were some events that took place in Barber County?

A. Yes, sir.

Q. And there some took place in the town of Clayton?

A. Yes, sir.

Q. And in the town of Union Springs?

A. Yes, sir.

Q. And you went down to those places?

A. Yes, sir. . . .

Q. Did you interview any persons in Alabama, residents of Alabama, while you were there on this coverage?

A. Yes, sir.

Q. Would you state the names of some of the persons whom you interviewed?

Mr. Embry: We object to this—and direct him not to answer.[**]

A. I decline to answer it.

Mr. Embry: There's a privilege on disclosure of the source of his information. It sheds no light on the issues made under the motion as to the identity of such persons.

Mr. Baker: For the record, we will state that the names of people from whom he has gathered news in Alabama is a material and pertinent inquiry and we think we are entitled to know it.

Mr. Embry: The question doesn't ask what he got from them?

Mr. Nachman: No, I merely asked the persons whom he interviewed and talked to while he was covering these news stories for The Times.

Mr. Embry: We withdraw that objection. . . .

[**] Normally, at a deposition, once an objection has been made and thereby preserved, a lawyer will direct his witness to go ahead and answer the question. But when an objection involves a claim of privilege—the privilege here involves a newsman's right not to be forced to disclose his sources, sometimes called the "reporter's shield"—a lawyer will often simply direct his client not to answer at all, since once the information has been revealed, the privilege is essentially useless. Notice how Embry and Nachman informally negotiate the question into one that Embry will allow Sitton to answer. —Eds.

Q. We're not asking you for the specific things they told you but for the names of the people you talked to.

Mr. Daly: We have no objection.

A. I talked to Sam Lemaistre down in Clayton, isn't it?

Q. Yes.

A. And talked to little George Wallace down at Clayton. . . . And a number of other people. . . .

Q. As best you can estimate it, Mr. Sitton, how frequently have you gone into Alabama during 1960?

A. 1960?

Q. Yes.

A. Four times.

Q. How long have you stayed on those occasions?

A. Time varied. I would have to refresh my memory to give you a—give an estimate. I think the longest period I was there was during that March 6th period. Somewhere in there. I was there, I believe, about three or four days at one time and I left and then I went back and stayed two days, I think, something like that.

Q. Were you there last week in Montgomery? . . .

A. Yes.

Q. What was the purpose of that trip?

A. Cover the King trial.

Q. Gather news for The Times, you're referring to the King trial?

A. Correct.

Q. By the King trial, you're referring to the Martin Luther King trial in Montgomery?

A. That's correct.

Q. What did your news covering activities consist of on that visit?

A. I didn't do anything.

Q. Did you attend the trial?

A. No, sir.

Q. You came to Montgomery and did nothing?

A. That's correct.

Q. Was that the purpose of your coming to Montgomery, to do nothing?

A. No, sir.

Q. What made you decide to do nothing? . . .

A. Well, I was advised that it might be best for me to come back to Atlanta.

Q. Who so advised you?

A. Mr. McLeod.

Q. Who is he?

A. Mr. McLeod.

Mr. Embry: Roderick M. McLeod, Jr., one of my law partners.

Q. Do you customarily confer with lawyers when you go into Alabama to write a news story?

Mr. Embry: We object to that.

Mr. Daly: You didn't get service, you were attempting to serve him down there, you people were or someone was.

Q. Do you adopt the statement of your counsel?
A. I'll say this. I understood that an attempt would be made to serve me and I thought it best that I get in touch with Mr. McLeod.
Q. And he instructed you to leave?
A. That's correct—no, he advised me to leave, he didn't instruct me. . . .

Mr. Nachman: We have no further questions. . . .

NOTES AND QUESTIONS

What relevant information did Nachman obtain from Sitton? How will it help him to show the court that the Times can be sued in Alabama? And what was the final exchange—concerning Sitton's sudden departure from Montgomery the preceding week—all about?

After completion of discovery, the parties appeared before the judge to present evidence and legal arguments regarding the Times's motion. Both the Times and Sullivan put on evidence concerning the Times's amenability to jurisdiction, and each side had the opportunity to cross-examine the witnesses presented by their opponent.

After the court heard the evidence and arguments from the lawyers, it took the matter under advisement, which means it deferred deciding the question until it had time to look at the evidence, read the parties' legal memoranda, and do its own research. Roughly two weeks later, it issued the following decision:

Trial Court's Order and Opinion
WALTER B. JONES, CIRCUIT JUDGE

Plaintiff, a resident of Montgomery, Alabama, has sued the defendant, The New York Times Company . . . and others, in this Court for an allegedly libelous publication specified in the complaint. The matter is now before this Court on the motion and amended motion, of the defendant, The New York Times Company (hereinafter referred to as the "Times"), to quash the service of process upon it. Other defendants are not involved in these motions.

Service was obtained by the Times by serving the Secretary of the State of Alabama pursuant to the provisions of Title 7, Section 199(1), Code of Alabama, 1940, as amended, and by personal service on one Don McKee, as agent for The New York Times. Without dispute, the Secretary of State has performed all acts required of her under the provisions of this section regarding notification to the Times.

GENERAL APPEARANCE

This motion, and its amendment, purport to be a special appearance for the sole purpose of quashing service of process. However, ground 6 of the prayer of this motion asks this Court to "dismiss this action as to The New York Times Company, a corporation, for lack of jurisdiction of the subject matter of said action." Clearly, this ground goes beyond the question of jurisdiction of this Court over the person of the defendant. Plaintiff's attorneys make a threshold argument in opposition to the Times' motion that this defendant has made a general appearance in this case, and has thereby waived any defects in service of process, and has submitted its corporate person to the jurisdiction of the Court.

Plaintiff's contention is sound.

This defendant cannot assert that it is not properly before this Court, and in the same breath argue that if it is, this Court has no jurisdiction of the subject matter of the action.

The Supreme Court of Alabama in *Blankenship v. Blankenship*, 263 Ala. 297, 303, has recently held that a party's appearance in a suit for any purpose other than to contest the Court's jurisdiction over the person of such party, is a general appearance in the cause.

VALIDITY OF SUBSTITUTED SERVICE

In view of the foregoing holding that the Times has made a general appearance in the cause, and has waived its special appearance, it is not essential to a decision on this defendant's motion to consider the matter of whether service of process on the Times is valid. But, in view of the voluminous testimony of this latter question, and in view of the manifold contacts which the Times maintains with the State of Alabama, it seems appropriate to explain why this Court considers that the Times is amenable to process and suit in the Alabama courts regardless of its general appearance.

Our statute, Title 7, Section 199(1) Alabama Code 1940, accords with widespread legislation of recent origin designed to afford state residents the opportunity of maintaining suit against foreign corporations, which . . . maintain significant business contact within the State, . . . if the cause of action sued on arises out of or is incident to the business done in Alabama . . . (and) the suit is not prohibited here by the due process clause (Amendment 14) of the Constitution of the United States. . . .

In order to consider in context the business activities of The New York Times in Alabama, the court adopts the outline of the essential business functions of a newspaper contained in *Consolidated Cosmetics v. D.A. Publishing Co.*, 186 F.2d 906, 908 (7th Cir. 1951):

> The functions of a magazine publishing company obviously include gathering material to be printed, obtaining advertisers and subscribers; printing, selling and delivering the magazines for sale. Each of these, we think, constitutes an essential factor of the magazine publication business. Consequently, if a nonresident corporation sees fit to perform any one of those essential functions in a given jurisdiction, it necessarily follows that it is conducting its activities in such a manner as to be subject to jurisdiction.

The key question is whether The New York Times, by virtue of its business activities in Alabama, maintains sufficient contacts with this State so that suit against it here accords with traditional concepts of fairness and the orderly administration of the laws "which it was the purpose of the due process clause to insure." *International Shoe Co. v. Washington*, 326 U.S. 310, 319.

In the foregoing context, the Court considers the activities of the Times in this State. . . .

To gather news for the Times, eleven admittedly regular staff correspondents have spent 153 days in Alabama. The results of their efforts are revealed in part by the 59 staff news stories in evidence which contain the by-lines of these correspondents. Their news gathering activities have been coordinated and correlated by the Times National News Editor, Harold Faber, who testified in this case; and by the southern regional correspondent, who is regularly assigned to cover news events in this state, among others in the southern region. This present correspondent, Claude Sitton, gave a deposition in this case. He came into Alabama and covered news events in Montgomery in March 1960, relating to certain "demonstrations," which form the basis of a portion of the publication now in suit; and he came into Alabama in May 1960 on assignment to cover the perjury trial of one Martin Luther King, which event is also the subject of a portion of this publication.

In addition to the news gathering activities of its staff correspondents, the Times maintains three so-called "string correspondents," who reside in Montgomery, Birmingham, and Mobile. The state purpose of such "stringers" in this state is to have them available for news stories of note in the area of their residence — subject to call by the Times. The testimony shows that the Times has made an active effort to maintain a "stringer" at these three places in Alabama at all times; has commented upon the value of the services which they have performed; and has actively sought their replacement upon the resignation of any one of them. The testimony is clear that present "stringers" McKee and Chadwick have performed valuable services for the Times' staff correspondents over and above the stories which the stringers themselves sent in for publication. And they performed such services in April 1960. Moreover, "stringer" McKee was entrusted with the delicate task of investigating the facts involved in the instant complaint when the plaintiff demanded that the Times retract the publication.

In search of revenues, the Times actively solicits advertising in the State of Alabama. One representative spent over a week soliciting advertising in Montgomery, Mobile and Birmingham. Another representative spent seven days in Alabama visiting Birmingham, Montgomery and Selma, and a third representative spent three days in Birmingham. All of this business activity occurred in the period from July 1, 1959 through June 3, 1960, after an advertising office was opened in Atlanta, which includes Alabama within its territory. Manager Hurley sold one ad to the State of Alabama which brought between three and five thousand dollars. In 1958, an ad appearing in the Alabama supplement of February 2 brought over $28,000 to the Times. According to its own testimony, the Times received between seventeen and eighteen thousand dollars from ads obtained in Alabama from January 1 through April, 1960. Annualized, these revenues would approximate fifty to fifty-five thousand dollars per year.

A Times witness, Roger Waters, testified that the daily circulation in Alabama was 390 papers per day, and that Sunday circulation was approximately 2,500 papers. This would produce a revenue of $35,884.55 per year, which, when added to the advertising revenue would give the Times a revenue from business activities in Alabama of over $85,000 per year.

The Times contends that the cause of action did not arise out of its conduct of business in Alabama. The Court is of the opinion that the cause of action is "an incident thereto" within the language of Title 7, Section 199(1), Alabama Code, 1940. It is noteworthy that Sitton was assigned to Montgomery by the Times to cover the demonstrations at Alabama State College and the King trial, with which the ad dealt. But, where a corporation is doing business in the State, due process does not require that the cause of action arise out of the business done there.

The Court finds an extensive and continuous course of Alabama business activity — news gathering; solicitation of advertising; circulation of newspapers and other products. These systematic business dealings in Alabama give the Times substantial contact with the State of Alabama, considerably in excess of the minimal contacts required by the Supreme Court decisions. . . . The Times does business in Alabama.

Likewise, the Court finds that to subject the Times to suit in Alabama comports with traditional notions of fair play and the proper administration of justice. Plaintiff resides here, and is a public official of the City of Montgomery. If a reputation has a situs, it is here in Montgomery. The events occurred largely in Montgomery, and witnesses who have knowledge of the truth or falsity of the events as outlined in the advertisement reside in or near Montgomery. Of the four co-defendants, two reside in Montgomery, one in Birmingham and one in Mobile. The Circuit Court of Montgomery County is appropriate and convenient forum to try this action.

This Court has always been a staunch advocate and defender of freedom of the press. But this freedom and other safeguards of the due process clause do not command the plaintiff to carry his witnesses, his evidence, his counsel and himself more than one thousand miles to a distant forum to bring his action for alleged damages to his reputation and to try his case. It is, therefore,

Considered, Ordered, and Adjudged by the Court that the motion of the defendant, The New York Times Company, to quash, and its amended motion to quash, be and the same are hereby denied.

Dated, this the 5th day of August, 1960.

NOTES AND QUESTIONS

1. *Three Theories of Jurisdiction.* Notice that the court justifies its holding that the Times is subject to jurisdiction in three separate ways. First, the Times "waived" its objection to personal jurisdiction and made a "general appearance" by raising an objection to subject matter jurisdiction. Second, even if it hadn't waived its objection, "the cause of action sued on arises out of or is incident to the business done in Alabama." And third, even if the claims were unrelated to the Times's activity in Alabama, "where a corporation is doing business in the State, due process does not require that the cause of action arise out of the business done there."

2. *The Times's "General Appearance."* Judge Jones's first holding is that the Times had made a "general appearance" by challenging the circuit court's subject matter jurisdiction. Why would making arguments beyond those connected with personal jurisdiction operate as a waiver of the Times's objection? Did the Times really mean to consent?* In this connection, consider the analysis offered by the Alabama Supreme Court when it ultimately affirmed the judgment in Sullivan's favor after trial:

> Pleadings based upon lack of jurisdiction of the person are in their nature pleas in abatement, and find no special favor in the law. They are purely

---

* To make sure he was merely entering a special appearance, Embry used the form recommended in a leading text, Alabama Pleading and Practice at Law, which had been written by Judge Jones. Ironically, Judge Jones apparently overruled his own advice in his opinion. *See* Anthony Lewis, *Make No Law: The* Sullivan *Case and the First Amendment* 25–26 (1991).

dilatory and amount to no more than a declaration by a defendant that he
is in court in a proper action, after actual notice, but because of a defect
in service, he is not legally before the court. . . .

We deem the lower court's conclusions correct, that The Times, by
questioning the jurisdiction of the lower court over the subject matter of
this suit, made a general appearance, and thereby submitted itself to the
jurisdiction of the lower court.

New York Times Co. v. Sullivan, 273 Ala. 656, 672, 144 So. 2d 25, 36 (1962).

Do you find the Alabama Supreme Court's reasoning persuasive? What are the
drawbacks of a contrary rule?

The federal system takes a somewhat more permissive approach. Under Fed.
R. Civ. P. 12(b), a defendant can move to dismiss for lack of personal jurisdiction,
insufficient service of process, and lack of subject matter jurisdiction in the same
motion without waiving any defense. However, if defendant omits the defense of
personal jurisdiction or insufficient service of process from a motion to dismiss that
he has filed, or if he fails to raise those defenses in his answer to the complaint, he
will then be deemed to have waived those two objections. *See* Fed. R. Civ. P. 12(g)
and 12(h)(1). At the other end of the spectrum, a motion to dismiss for lack of subject matter jurisdiction can be made at any time. *See* Fed. R. Civ. P. 12(h)(3). Why
are these objections treated so differently?

3. *The Trial Court's Analysis of Its Personal Jurisdiction over the Times.* Notice how
Judge Jones takes the fragmentary bits of evidence in front of him and weaves
them together into a seamless discussion of the Times's connections to Alabama.
Most of your contact with litigation during law school will consist of judicial opinions, primarily appellate ones. It is therefore important to keep in mind, particularly at the beginning of your legal career, how judicial opinions can shape, refine,
and orchestrate the facts to make even very hard cases seem easy. In this case,
however, the facts relevant to the Times's motion were relatively straightforward.

The court's opinion fits the various facts into a legal framework. Where does it
get that framework? Notice how it relies on the Seventh Circuit's opinion in *Consolidated Cosmetics* and the Supreme Court's seminal ruling in *International Shoe.* When
courts use the analysis advanced in prior cases, they are said to be relying on *precedent.* Sometimes, precedent is binding, and a court must follow it. This is especially
true of constitutional rulings by the United states Supreme Court, which *all* lower
courts — state and federal — must follow. Within each state system, state trial courts
are bound by the rulings of state appellate courts. But a court in one system is, for
the most part, not bound by what courts in other systems decide but may treat decisions from sister states and federal courts as persuasive authority.

Judge Jones's alternative holding that the Times's various connections with
Alabama were sufficient to subject it to personal jurisdiction was also affirmed by
the Alabama Supreme Court:

In the present case the evidence shows that the publishing of advertisements was a substantial part of the business of The Times, and its newspapers were regularly sent into Alabama. Advertising was solicited in

Alabama. Its correspondent McKee was called upon by The Times to investigate the truthfulness or falsity of the matters contained in the advertisement after the letter from the plaintiff. The acts therefore disclose not only certain general conditions with reference to newspaper publishing, but also specific acts directly connected with, and directly incident to the business of The Times done in Alabama.

273 Ala. at 673.

How would you evaluate the jurisdictional significance of the Times's connections with Alabama? Do you agree with Judge Jones that plaintiff's claim was sufficiently related to the Times's activity in Alabama to be considered "an incident" of that activity? Why do you think the Alabama statute limits jurisdiction to claims related to a defendant's business in Alabama? Do you agree with Judge Jones that the Times's activity in Alabama was pervasive enough to support jurisdiction even over claims having no connection with that activity?

5. *The Motion to Dismiss*

Having lost its motion to quash, the Times was now obligated to respond to the substance of Sullivan's complaint. (Remember that Abernathy—and the other individual defendants—had already done so, since they were not contesting jurisdiction.)

Accordingly, two weeks after Judge Jones denied the Times's motion to quash, the Times filed its demurrers. A demurrer is a pleading that challenges the legal sufficiency of the complaint. (Its essential equivalent in the federal system, and in most contemporary state systems, is a motion to dismiss for failure to state a claim upon which relief can be granted. *See, e.g.*, Fed. R. Civ. P. 12(b)(6).) In a demurrer or in a motion to dismiss under Federal Rule 12(b)(6), a defendant assumes for purposes of the motion that the factual allegations made by the plaintiff are true. Even on that assumption, defendant argues, the plaintiff's complaint itself shows why the plaintiff is not entitled to recover under the applicable law.

To understand the point of the Times's demurrer, it is necessary to understand the elements of Sullivan's claim. Sullivan alleged that the March 29th advertisement was libelous. Under Alabama law at the time, for Sullivan to be entitled to relief, he had to show that (1) the defendant (2) published in writing (3) a defamatory statement (that is, a statement that would tend to injure the reputation of the person about whom it was falsely made) (4) about the plaintiff. The four numbered items are the elements of Sullivan's claim. If his complaint failed to allege sufficient facts to establish any of these elements, then it would be legally insufficient to make out a claim of libel.

As you read the demurrer filed by the Times and review the demurrer filed by Abernathy, ask yourself which elements of Sullivan's claim each defendant concedes and which elements each defendant attacks.

DEMURRER OF DEFENDANT, THE NEW YORK TIMES COMPANY

Now comes the defendant, The New York Times Company, a corporation, in the above styled cause and demurs to plaintiff's complaint . . . sets down and assigns the following, separately and generally:

1. Said Count fails to state a cause of action. . . .

4. For that it does not appear from the allegations of said Count that the plaintiff was the subject or object of any alleged defamatory or libelous material set forth in said Count.

5. For that it does not appear from the allegations of said Count that any publication of any alleged false and defamatory matter, or libelous matter was of and concerning the plaintiff in this cause.

6. For that the allegations of said Count affirmatively show that the matter complained of as being defamatory, or libelous, set forth in said Count, is not libelous or defamatory per se. . . .

11. For that the allegations of said Count fail to state wherein plaintiff has suffered any damage as a result of any alleged libelous or defamatory matter published by this defendant. . . .

28. For that it affirmatively appears from the allegations of said Count that plaintiff has suffered no injury or damage as a result of the publication of any alleged false and defamatory matter as set out in said Count. . . .

[Later, the Times amended its demurrer to add some additional assertions.]

36. From aught appearing from the allegations of said Count plaintiff is not a "southern violator" referred to in the alleged libelous statement set forth in plaintiff's said Count. . . .

43. For that it affirmatively appears from the allegations of said Count that the alleged libelous matter does not identify plaintiff as being a member of or one of "they" as the same is set forth and contained in the alleged libelous matter set out in said Count. . . .

68. For that the allegations of said Count show that the place of commission of any alleged tort by this defendant was in the City of New York and the State of New York. . . .

69. From aught appearing from the allegations of said Count the subject matter of plaintiff's alleged cause of action is not a tort in the place of its alleged commission, which is alleged to be in the City of New York and the State of New York. . . .

81. For that the allegations of said count, if taken as true, could not authorize the submission to a jury of the questions of whether plaintiff was libeled and suffered any injury or damage therefrom, for as a matter of law the allegation of said count, if proved, could not constitute a cause of action for libel, for so to do would be violative of and contrary to the First Amendment to the Constitution of the United States and constitute an abridgement of the freedom of the press.

NOTES AND QUESTIONS

1. *Choice of Law: Determining the Applicable Law.* Some of the defendant's demurrers attack directly the sufficiency of Sullivan's complaint. Others raise a significantly different kind of attack. Consider, for example, what the Times means by paragraphs 68 and 69. Essentially, the Times is suggesting that because whatever tort was committed occurred in New York, New York's libel law, rather than Alabama's, should apply to this case and that, under New York law, Sullivan had not sufficiently alleged all the elements of a claim of libel. The question of what

substantive tort law applies to a case with multistate connections is known as choice of law. Choice of law questions can play a major role in many kinds of litigation.

In considering paragraphs 68 and 69 of the Times's demurrer, what is the basis for its assertion that New York law, rather than Alabama law, should govern this litigation? Remember that the elements of libel are a matter of state law. Thus, different states can define the tort in very different ways. Because the Supreme Court has been reluctant to police aggressively a state's choice of law decisions, a court that is found to have personal jurisdiction will in a great many cases be able to apply its state's law to the controversy. Later in the course, we shall devote a fair amount of attention to the relationship between jurisdiction and choice of law issues. For the time being, though, you should have at least some sense of why these issues are so important.

2. *The Federal Constitutional Defense.* In addition, consider the argument raised in paragraph 81. What is the Times's contention here? The United States Constitution is the supreme law of the land. That means that states (or Congress, for that matter) cannot enact laws, or create causes of action, that would violate the Constitution. Here, the Times raises, for the first time, the claim that would become central to the ultimate resolution of this case by the United States Supreme Court: To permit plaintiffs to recover libel judgments against defendants in circumstances such as this would violate principles of free speech and the freedom of the press set out in the First Amendment.

6.   *The Answer*

In addition to its demurrers, the Times also responded directly to the factual allegations in Sullivan's complaint. (Although in the Alabama nomenclature of the early 1960s, the document the Times filed was known as its "Pleas," the contemporary term for this pleading is an *answer* to the complaint.)

ANSWER OF THE NEW YORK TIMES CO.

For answer to the complaint . . . defendant, The New York Times Company, a corporation, says:

(1.) It is not guilty of the matters alleged therein. . . .

(2.) [Defendant] did in its issue of its newspaper on March 29, 1960 publish therein the advertisement that made the basis of plaintiff's complaint, but . . . denies that such advertisement or any part thereof was published . . . of and concerning the plaintiff. . . .

(4.) . . . [D]efendant denies that the words in such advertisement or any part thereof complained of by the plaintiff taken in their ordinary or literal sense are libelous or defamatory. . . .

(5.) . . . [D]efendant denies that the words in such advertisement, or any part thereof, taken in their ordinary or literal sense or in the ordinary import of such language damaged the reputation of the plaintiff or injured the plaintiff in his . . . trade, business or profession. . . .

(6.) . . . [D]efendant had no reason to believe, nor did it in fact believe, that any of the matters and things set forth therein or any of the words or language set forth therein was false and, in fact this defendant verily believed them to be true, and as a basis for such belief, this defendant says that said advertisement was proffered to this defendant for publication by it as a paid advertisement by one John Murray, who is an individual whom this defendant believed to be trustworthy; and this defendant further says that said advertisement was published pursuant to an advertising order for the publication of same by Union Advertising Service, which paid this defendant for the publication of said advertisement according to said order, and said Union Advertising Service was by this defendant believed to be a reputable, recognized advertising agency of the City of New York, State of New York, which this defendant believed to be trustworthy; and this defendant further says that said advertisement was, by this defendant believed to be endorsed and signed by individuals, whom this defendant believed to be trustworthy; and this defendant further says that the above and foregoing facts set forth in this, its Plea Six, constitute a defense to this defendant in that the same show that said advertisement complained of by the plaintiff in his complaint was published without malice upon the part of this defendant and in the belief by this defendant that the matters and things contained in said advertisement were true. . . .

NOTES AND QUESTIONS

1. Which, if any, of the elements of Sullivan's case does the Times concede? Why did it concede them? In answering this question, consider how Fed. R. Civ. P. 11 would have affected this question if the case were filed in federal court today.

2. How does paragraph 6 differ from the preceding ones? What is the Times's argument here? If the facts the newspaper alleges here are true, what effect might they have on the outcome of the case?

After considering the Times's demurrers and its answers to the various allegations in the complaint, Judge Jones refused to dismiss the complaint, and decided the case should go forward to trial.

7.   *Pretrial Discovery on the Merits*

You have already observed some discovery in conjunction with the hearing on the personal jurisdiction issue, when Sullivan requested that the Times produce various documents and deposed Claude Sitton to obtain information about the Times's contacts with Alabama. The discovery process was also useful in obtaining information for trial on the merits. Remember that Sullivan had to prove a number of facts to prevail at trial. Moreover, he needed to persuade the jury to award him damages. The following are some examples of the *interrogatories* (written questions) that Sullivan served on the Times.

INTERROGATORIES TO DEFENDANT NEW YORK TIMES

Comes plaintiff L. B. Sullivan, and pursuant to the provisions of Title 7, pp. 477 et seq., Code of Alabama of 1940, propounds the following interrogatories to the defendant, The New York Times Company.

1. Please state your correct corporate name and the name, address, and official position of the person who is answering these interrogatories.

2. Please state all the details, facts, and circumstances under which the advertisement on which this suit is based came to be inserted in the New York Times in the issue of March 29, 1960, on p. 25. In answering this question, please give the names, addresses, and official position of each and every person who had any connection with the handling of the advertisement, and state exactly and in detail what was done by each.

3. Please state exactly and in detail what investigation was made by any person for or on behalf of the New York Times to determine the correctness of the statements contained in said advertisement, prior to its publication. In answering this question, please give the name and address of every person who made any investigation for or on behalf of the New York Times, and state his connection with the New York Times, and state exactly what was done by each such person. Attach to the answers to these interrogatories copies of any written statement which any such person may have made to the New York Times regarding the results of such an investigation.

4. Please state whether or not the New York Times, prior to the publication of the advertisement involved in this suit, carried any news stories in its paper, or received in its files any news coverage or reports from its reporters, news services, or other news gathering media concerning any of the events or occurrences referred to in said advertisement, and if you answer affirmatively please attach to your answers to this interrogatory the original or a true and correct copy of each and every said news story, news account, report, or communication appearing in the New York Times or received by the New York Times or made known to the New York Times prior to the publication of said advertisement on March 29, 1960. . . .

6. Did the New York Times receive from the plaintiff a demand for retraction, by letter dated April 8, 1960? If you answer affirmatively, please attach the original or a true and correct copy of said demand for retraction. . . .

8. After receipt of said demand for retraction from the plaintiff, dated April 8, 1960, did the New York Times make any investigation of the correctness of the statements contained in said advertisement? If you answer affirmatively, please state the name of the person or persons making the investigation, the connection of each with the New York Times, the results of said investigation, and attach to your answers to this interrogatory the originals or true and correct copies of any and all reports, communications, advice, or other writings, informing or apprising you of the results of said investigation.

9. If you have answered that any investigation was made, please advise whether you received any report, verbally or by telephone or otherwise than in writing, and if you answer affirmatively, please state the substance of said verbal or telephonic reports, including the names of the persons who made the report and their connection with the New York Times.

10. Did you in response to plaintiff's demand dated April 8, 1960, publish a retraction in your newspaper? If you answer affirmatively, please attach the original or a true and correct copy of said retraction. . . .

12. Is the following matter contained in the advertisement made the basis of this suit, true:

In Montgomery, Alabama, after students sang, "My Country, 'Tis of Thee" on the Capitol steps, their leaders were expelled from school, and truckloads of police armed with shotguns and tear gas ringed the Alabama State College campus. When the entire student body protested to state authorities by refusing to reregister, their dining hall was padlocked in an attempt to starve them into submission.

Again and again the Southern violators have answered Dr. King's peaceful protests with intimidation and violence. They have bombed his home almost killing his wife and child. They have assaulted his person. They have arrested him seven times—for "speeding," "loitering" and similar "offenses." And now they have charged him with "perjury"—a felony under which they could imprison him for ten years.

Please state each and every fact, statement, or occurrence contained in the foregoing quotation which you say is true; and which are not true. Please state further and fully every source of information upon which you rely for your contention, if you contend that any of the foregoing facts, statements, or occurrences are true. . . .

16. Please state the number of issues of the March 29, 1960 edition of the New York Times which were sold and distributed and give the geographical extent of such sale or distribution. Did the New York Times initiate, by mailing or otherwise arranging for shipment, the distribution of issues of the March 29, 1960, New York Times in the City of Montgomery and State of Alabama? . . .

19. State your gross income during the year 1959 and for the first six months of 1960, and your net earnings for the same period. State your assets, liabilities, and net worth for the year 1959.

NOTES AND QUESTIONS

1. Some of these interrogatories clearly serve an informational purpose. For example, Sullivan had no way of knowing how the Times came to publish the advertisement. Similarly, the Times is in a far better position than Sullivan to know how many issues of the March 29th edition were circulated. Why are these facts relevant to the lawsuit? For one thing, they bear on the issue of damages: If the newspaper knowingly published false and defamatory material, the jury might decide that punitive damages are appropriate to deter it from being so rash in the future. This was also relevant to the newspaper's constitutional defense. And the extent of the damage to Sullivan's reputation would depend, at least in part, on how widely the defamatory story was circulated. Being defamed by a newspaper with nationwide circulation will often be more damaging than being defamed in a letter. Facts regarding the internal operation of the Times are peculiarly within its control, and the discovery process provides an effective mechanism for providing the opposing party with this kind of evidence.

2. Other interrogatories serve very different purposes. For example, why has Sullivan asked the Times for sources it has in its possession regarding the truth or falsity of charges made in the advertisement? Does he not know whether they are true or false? What tactical reasons might he have for wanting to know what the

newspaper knew at the time of publication? Here, the Times's answers may provide Sullivan with material that he in fact could obtain from other sources, but not as easily or cheaply. Moreover, Sullivan may be trying to find out what the Times knows about the underlying facts, as they may be helpful to Sullivan's presentation at trial.

3. Finally, why did Sullivan ask whether the Times had received his demand for retraction (which he had sent by registered mail)? Here, the function of the interrogatories is to bind the defendant. If the Times admits that it received the letter, then Sullivan will have established one element of his claim. In the federal system, interrogatories are often combined with *requests for admission. See* Fed. R. Civ. P. 36. Here, the discovery process serves as a means of winnowing down the issues that will be contested at trial.

The Times responded to the interrogatories by answering some and refusing to answer others:

ANSWERS OF THE NEW YORK TIMES COMPANY TO PLAINTIFF'S INTERROGATORIES

Comes the defendant, The New York Times Company, a corporation, and for answer to the interrogatories heretofore propounded to it by the plaintiff in this cause, says as follows. . . .

2. On or about March 25, 1960, one John Murray brought to The New York Times Plant at 229 West 43rd Street in the City of New York the original copy from which the advertisement referred to in this question was formed. This copy was delivered to one Gerson Aronson, an employee of this defendant, whose title or position with this defendant is a salesman in the National Advertising Department. Mr. Aronson delivered the original of this copy to this defendant's Production Department after making a thermafax copy of such copy, which said thermafax copy was placed on the desk of one D. Vincent Redding, who is an employee of the defendant and whose position is that of Manager of this Defendant's Advertising Acceptability Department.

The Production Department sent the original of such copy to the composing room of this defendant's plant, where some time during the period from about March 25, 1960 to the time of its insertion on March 29, 1960, it was set in type. During this interim of time this defendant's Mr. Redding approved said copy for insertion as a paid advertisement in this defendant's newspaper.

This was all done pursuant to what is called an advertising insertion order for this ad by Union Advertising Service of 302 Fifth Avenue, New York, New York. Said Union Advertising Service was billed by this defendant according to the terms and conditions of said insertion order and was paid by said Union Advertising Service for the publication of said advertisement.

Mr. D. Vincent Redding, who has been previously identified in the foregoing answers, in checking the advertisement inquired about, ascertained that the same was endorsed by a large group of individuals among whom were persons whose general reputation for truth, integrity, and honesty was known to Mr. Redding to be good and on the basis of this he had no reason to believe that anything contained in the ad was false and as the advertisement made no attacks of a personal character upon any individual and otherwise met the advertising acceptability standards promulgated by this defendant he, accordingly, approved it. . . .

4. The New York Times, prior to the publication of the advertisement referred to and insofar as this defendant is able to determine from its records, had received from its reporters, string correspondents and the news service to which it subscribes news stories relating to certain of the events or occurrences referred to in the advertisement. These stories appeared in defendant's newspapers on the dates of February 18, 1960, March 2, 3, 5, 6, 7, 8, 9, 10, 11, 12, 13, 23, 27, 30, 1960, and April 1, 1960. The actual news stories are equally within the knowledge of the plaintiff inasmuch as the same were produced by this defendant in response to this plaintiff's motion to produce same and were introduced into evidence in this cause on a hearing of the defendant's motion to quash service of process herein. . . .

6. Yes. This defendant did receive from plaintiff a demand for retraction by letter dated April 8, 1960, a copy of which is attached hereto as Exhibit "C". . . .

8. Defendant, on advice of counsel, declines to answer this interrogatory inasmuch as the same calls for the results of an investigation initiated and made by the attorneys for this defendant after the publication of the advertisement complained of and in connection with the preparation of the defense of the action which defendant anticipated might be brought by this plaintiff and also calls for a conclusion and for an answer which is the ultimate inquiry before the Court and jury in this cause when the interrogatory makes reference to "correctness of statements contained in said advertisement."

9. Written reports were received by this defendant the substance of which had been telephoned previously. Defendant, on advice of counsel, declines to answer so much of this interrogatory which asks for the substance of the written and telephonic reports for the same reasons outlined in interrogatory 8 above.

10. No. . . .

12. On advice of counsel, this defendant declines to answer this interrogatory as the same is incompetent, irrelevant, and immaterial. It is likewise objectionable as an invasion of the province of the Court and jury and calls for an answer which would be a conclusion as to the ultimate fact to be determined by the Court and jury in this cause on all of the evidence. . . .

19. On advice of counsel defendant declines to answer this interrogatory as the same calls for evidence which is incompetent, irrelevant, and immaterial.

NOTES AND QUESTIONS

1. When a party is served with interrogatories that it feels are inappropriate, it has two options. First, it can simply file "objections" and decline to answer the objectionable interrogatories, explaining briefly the basis for the objection. That is what the Times did in this case. The responsibility then shifts to the party that has propounded the interrogatories to move the court to compel the responding party to answer. *Cf.* Fed. R. Civ. P. 37(a)(3)(B)(iii). Second, the responding party can itself move for a protective order, relieving it of the duty to answer objectionable questions. *Cf.* Fed. R. Civ. P. 26(c).

2. After Sullivan's lawyers received the Times's answers to their interrogatories, they moved to compel the newspaper to answer the questions to which it had objected. Judge Jones heard oral arguments and then ordered the Times to respond to most of the questions to which it had objected. The Times's answers

included two long telegrams from Don McKee and Claude Sitton, which showed that there were several inaccuracies in the advertisement, particularly regarding the incidents at Alabama State University.

8.   *Note on Settlement, Burden of Proof, and Summary Judgment*

a.   Settlement

Very few civil cases actually go to trial. Most lawsuits are either settled voluntarily between the parties or are resolved by the judge prior to trial. Although, as it turns out, the *Sullivan* case in fact was tried to a verdict, it is important to pause at this juncture to identify these two alternative outcomes.

Lawsuits are costly to resolve. Indeed, the time and money expended in pursuing a lawsuit can be enormous: It can take several years from the time a complaint is filed until trial, and appeals and retrials can stretch the process on even further. For example, although Sullivan filed his complaint in April 1960, the Supreme Court's opinion was not handed down until March 1964. Moreover, under the so-called American rule, each party pays its own attorneys' fees, win or lose. In some recent libel cases, defendants have ultimately prevailed, but they have been saddled with over $1 million in defense costs. Although some plaintiffs have sufficient resources to pay their lawyers directly, it is common for plaintiffs to enter into a contingency fee agreement by which the attorney recovers his or her fees only if there is a settlement or judgment in the case.

When both parties' assessments of the likely outcome of trial coincide, the parties will have an incentive to settle the case rather than to fight it out to an inevitable conclusion. (Can you think of circumstances in which this will not be true?) The precise terms of a settlement will depend on a number of factors, such as:

- Each party's assessment of the likely outcomes. A plaintiff who is very optimistic about his potential recovery will demand more in settlement than a plaintiff who has a shakier case. Similarly, a defendant who predicts a likely loss will offer more than a defendant who thinks the plaintiff's case is weak.
- Pressure on the party to resolve the case quickly. For example, an accident victim may need the money quickly to pay medical expenses. If this is so, she may be willing to settle for less money today, even in present value terms, than she would obtain years from now, after a jury verdict and exhaustion of appeals.
- The negotiating skills of each party's representative.
- The effects of settlement on the world beyond this lawsuit. On the one hand, even if a defendant thinks that a particular plaintiff has a strong case, he may decide not to settle, or to offer only a small settlement, because a large settlement might encourage other individuals to file suit as well. On the other hand, a defendant may try to settle a case quietly to avoid bad publicity.
- The incentives of the lawyers themselves. All other things being equal, the contingency fee lawyer prefers to settle rather than litigate because resources devoted to litigation detract from the fee and also entail opportunity costs.

In light of these considerations, and others you can think of, why do you suppose *Sullivan v. New York Times Co.* did not settle? Was there an offer the Times could have made Sullivan that he would have accepted?

As you can see, discovery can serve a critical role in promoting settlement. If both parties base their assumptions about the probable outcome at trial on similar information, at least one source of disagreement can be minimized. In addition, the knowledge that damaging information is discoverable may prompt settlement offers designed to forestall the disclosure of such information. Finally, the fact that discovery itself can be financially costly can prompt parties to settle rather than to incur its costs.

b.   Burden of Proof

Every cause of action consists of a constellation of facts that give rise to a legal claim. As mentioned earlier, Sullivan's claim of libel depended on his showing that the Times and the four ministers published a defamatory statement about him. Put in more formal terms, Sullivan has the burden of proving to a jury, by providing it with sufficient evidence, that the advertisement was about him, that it tended to injure his reputation, and that the newspaper and the four ministers published it. If he cannot meet that burden, then the defendants will win. The term *burden of proof* here means *burden of persuasion*—the party with the burden must persuade the trier of fact by a preponderance of the evidence, the required degree of certainty in civil cases.

The party on whom the burden of proof or persuasion is placed can vary. Normally, the plaintiff bears the burden of proof on the central elements of her cause of action, and the defendant bears the burden of proof on the elements of any affirmative defenses he raises. For example, in libel law, reports of official proceedings are privileged: If a witness at a congressional hearing were to say something false and defamatory about an individual, a newspaper could publish an account of that congressional hearing that contained the false and defamatory statement without being liable to the individual who has been maligned. But the defendant would have to show that the statement had been made during an official proceeding. Thus, he, rather than the plaintiff, would bear the burden of proof on that issue.

c.   Summary Judgment

Discovery and a party's own factual investigation may convince either the plaintiff or the defendant—and sometimes both—that given the facts and the applicable law, there is only one justifiable outcome that a judge or jury presented with all the evidence could reach. In such situations, conducting a full-scale trial would waste both the parties' and the public's resources. Accordingly, a party that believes that the facts would entitle it to a judgment in its favor as a matter of law can move for *summary judgment*. In the federal system, such motions are governed by Fed. R. Civ. P. 56.

Motions for summary judgment tend to be filed in two sets of circumstances. First, a party may move for summary judgment when it bears the burden of proof on particular issues by filing, along with its motion, affidavits (sworn written statements) and other documentary evidence that show that there is no genuine issue as to the facts established and that, on those facts, the moving party is entitled to judgment as a matter of law. Once the motion and supporting papers are filed, the nonmoving party must persuade the court, either through arguments about the moving party's evidence or through providing contradictory evidence, that there are genuine issues of fact that need to be resolved through a trial. When a moving party files a motion for summary judgment in an offensive posture (i.e., one that seeks an order granting the party affirmative relief), its burden is to show that the record establishes such a strong case that *every* element of its claim has been established beyond any genuine dispute of material fact.

Second, a party may move for summary judgment when the *other* party bears the burden of proof by demonstrating that there is insufficient evidence in the record from which a jury could find that the nonmoving party had met its burden of proof. When a moving party files a motion for summary judgment in a defensive posture (i.e., one that seeks to obtain the dismissal of a claim), its burden is to show that the claimant has failed to raise a genuine dispute of material fact as to *any* element of its claim, since a failure of proof with respect to even one element will indicate that the claim must be dismissed.

Again, you should have noticed how critical the discovery process can be to the summary-judgment determination. It enables the parties both to obtain evidence to support their own motions (or to oppose the other party's motions) and to determine whether the other party has evidence to oppose their motions.

Sometimes, both sides will move for summary judgment because each believes that the facts entitle it to victory. Or one or both parties can move for partial summary judgment, seeking merely a declaration that some particular parts of the case—such as liability, but not damages—have been established as a matter of law. Defensive motions for summary judgment are filed more often, and granted with much greater frequency, than offensive motions.

In any event, the task of a court faced with any motion for summary judgment is essentially to ask whether, based on the evidence, a reasonable trier of fact could rule in favor of the nonmovant. If there is only one justifiable outcome to the case, summary judgment is appropriate. But if a jury could reasonably find for either party, depending on how it assessed the evidence, summary judgment is inappropriate, and the judge must deny the motion.

Cases in which the facts are not really in dispute are suitable candidates for summary judgment, whereas cases in which the credibility of conflicting witnesses will determine the outcome are not.

In light of the foregoing necessarily brief discussion, should Sullivan have moved for full or partial summary judgment? Should the Times have? Should the four ministers have? What sorts of affidavits and documents would they have needed to support their motions? How should the court have ruled?

9. *The Trial*

In most civil actions in which the plaintiff is seeking monetary damages, each of the parties has the right to insist on trial before a jury. The Seventh Amendment of the U.S. Constitution guarantees this right for cases tried in federal court, and analogous state constitutional and statutory provisions provide the right in most state courts. (In cases seeking injunctive relief, there is no such right.) Although the parties have the right to insist on trial by jury, they are normally not compelled to do so. Why might a party prefer trial before a judge alone?

If a case is to be tried before a jury—as Sullivan's was—the first order of business is to select a panel of potential jurors. The process of picking a jury begins when a large number of individuals living in the jurisdiction are called for jury duty. Their names are obtained in a variety of ways. In the federal system, since 1968, potential jurors are randomly identified from lists of registered voters. In the states, voting rolls, telephone directories, tax rolls, and lists of motor vehicle license holders are often used, and some states also use the so-called key man system in which the jury commissioners develop lists of appropriate potential jurors.

Once a venire, or group of potential jurors, has been assembled, the prospective jurors are subject to *voir dire* or questioning to determine their fitness to serve. Some jurors may be excused altogether—for example, a juror who cannot understand English or a juror with a medical condition that prevents her from serving. Other jurors will be excused *for cause*—that is, because they should not serve in the particular case—for example, a juror who is related to one of the parties or a witness, or a juror who does not think she could base her decision solely on the evidence. Finally, still other jurors, although they are legally qualified to serve, will be removed by one of the parties exercising a *peremptory* challenge. Each side is given a few peremptory challenges that it can use without providing any reason at all. Although the ostensible reason for peremptory challenges is to help assemble an unbiased jury, one might think of the process as an adversarial attempt by each side to assemble a jury biased in its favor.

Sullivan's lawsuit was tried in a segregated courtroom. Thirty-seven jurors were originally called for service. Among them were two blacks. According to a story in the *Montgomery Advertiser*, "they were immediately struck from the list by attorneys for Sullivan." In 1991, the Supreme Court held that the Equal Protection Clause of the Fourteenth Amendment bars litigants from basing their peremptory challenges on the race of potential jurors. *See Edmondson v. Leesville Concrete Co.*, 500 U.S. 614 (1991). Prior to *Edmondson*, however, the Supreme Court had not limited private litigant's use of peremptory challenges.

After a jury is sworn in, the lawyers for each party have the opportunity to make opening statements to the jury. The opening statements are not evidence in the case; rather, they give each side an opportunity to provide a preview of the evidence it intends to present and its theories as to why the jury should decide in its favor.

Once the opening statements are completed, the plaintiff presents the evidence supporting his case. Often, the parties will agree that particular documents or physical objects are admissible, and they will all be placed into evidence through stipulation—that is, agreement—between the parties. Both sides are then free to refer to the evidence and show it to the jury. In Sullivan's case, for example, the advertisement was clearly an admissible piece of evidence.

The *Sullivan* trial took roughly three days, including the selection of the jury, the presentation of evidence, the arguments, and the jury's deliberations. The story elicited from witnesses at a trial does not unfold as a structured narrative. Individual witnesses may know only small pieces of the entire story, and the order in which they testify and are asked questions may have little to do with the order in which an author would present her readers with the facts. Ultimately, it will be the job of the lawyers in their closing arguments to weave together bits of various witnesses' testimony into a coherent account.

Following the attorneys' summations, the judge instructed the jury on the law it was required to apply to the facts. At the same time, the jury was given control over fact finding. The jury instructions in *Sullivan* ran over five single-spaced typed pages. The following is excerpted from the instructions:

> Now, the plea filed by the defendants in this case or what we call the general issue, raises the question of the truth of the things published. Now, we have a law in Alabama that in an action of this kind the truth of the words written or published, or the circumstances under which they were published, may be given in evidence under the plea of the general issue in mitigation of damages. Those are the words of the statute.
>
> Now, the Court is of the opinion and so charges you, gentlemen of the jury, that the matter complained of in Plaintiff's Exhibit No. 347, that's the controversial ad which you will have before you, and parts of which are set out in the Counts here in the Complaint, belongs to that class of defamation called in law, libel per se. Now, defamatory words to be actionable per se are those which on their face and without the aid of any other evidence or any other extrinsic proof are recognized by the law as being injurious. Writings libelous per se carry the presumption of falsity and of malice. Now, in the case of words actionable per se, that is, actionable by themselves, their injurious character is a fact of common notoriety, established by the general consent of men. The libel in a case of this kind is such that in the natural and proximate consequences it will necessarily cause injury and damage to the person concerned in his official, public or social relations. And the law in such a case implies legal injury from the bare fact of publication itself. We can say, as part of the law in this case, that a publication is libelous per se when they are such as to degrade the plaintiff in the estimation of his friends and the people of the place where he lives, as injure him in his public office, or impute misconduct to him in his office, or want of official integrity, or want of fidelity to a public trust or such as will subject the plaintiff to ridicule or public distrust. All those kind of charges are called, libelous per se.

NOTE AND QUESTIONS

This charge was given to the jury orally. Did you understand all the legal instructions in the charge? Did you have to read it very carefully to comprehend it? How well do you think a group of a dozen laypeople, many without substantial formal education, would understand what they are expected to do?

Following the charge, the jury withdrew to the jury room to deliberate. Juries confer in secret, and no records whatsoever are kept of their discussions. After two hours and 20 minutes, the jury returned with its verdict. It found for the plaintiff and against all of the defendants and awarded Sullivan the entire sum he had claimed as damages: $500,000.

10.   Post-Trial Proceedings

In light of the jury's verdict, the court entered judgment for Sullivan:

FINAL JUDGMENT, JURY AND VERDICT —

November 3, 1960

This day . . . Joseph W. McDade Sr., and eleven others who having been duly empanelled and sworn according to law upon their oaths do say: "We the jury find in favor of the plaintiff and assess his damages at $500,000.00."

It is therefore considered, ordered, and adjudged by the Court that the plaintiff have and recover of the defendant the said sum of Five Hundred Thousand and no/100 ($500,000.00) Dollars together with the cost in this behalf expended, for all of which let execution issue.

NOTES AND QUESTIONS

The defendants, needless to say, were upset by the verdict. The first step they took was to move for a new trial. A judge may decide to set aside a jury's verdict and grant a new trial for a number of reasons. For example, he may conclude that erroneously admitted or excluded evidence might have affected the verdict; he may conclude that something that happened in the jury's presence improperly influenced them; he may be concerned that the jury's verdict was the product of irrationality or prejudice; or he may conclude that the verdict is simply "against the weight of the evidence." In the federal system, motions for a new trial are governed by Fed. R. Civ. P. 59.

In some cases, a judge may be so convinced that no reasonable jury could possibly have found for the prevailing party that he will go beyond ordering a new trial and simply enter judgment notwithstanding the verdict in favor of the other party. In the federal system, the court in such a circumstance would enter a "judgment as a matter of law" under Fed. R. Civ. P. 50(b). Such devices may be viewed as the means by which the court polices the jury system, and they raise significant questions about the allocation of power between judges and juries.

Following oral argument, the court denied the Times's motion.

11.   The Appeals

Parties who are dissatisfied with the outcome of a trial normally have the right to appeal and have a higher court review the result. Appeals courts, unlike trial courts, do not hear additional evidence. Their decisions are based on the record developed in the trial court. The parties have the opportunity to present written arguments in the form of briefs and, sometimes but not always, to give oral arguments as well.

A trial usually takes place before a single judge, sitting with or without a jury. Appeals, on the other hand, are normally decided by multi-judge panels. The entire Alabama Supreme Court considered the Times's and the ministers' appeals and affirmed the judgment.

If the only questions in *Sullivan v. New York Times Co.* had been issues of state law, the Alabama Supreme Court's decision would have been the end of the case. But in our federal system, the Constitution and laws of the United States are the supreme law of the land, *see* U.S. Const., art. VI, cl. 2, and the United States Supreme Court is the final arbiter of the Constitution's meaning. Therefore, a litigant who believes that a state supreme court's decision does not properly apply the Constitution's standards can seek review of that decision in the United States Supreme Court.

Except in a very narrow class of cases, the United States Supreme Court's jurisdiction is discretionary rather than mandatory. A court with mandatory jurisdiction *must* consider a case on the merits. Over time, Congress abolished the Supreme Court's mandatory appellate jurisdiction, and now (with few exceptions) the High Court can choose for itself which cases to hear. Several thousand petitions for a *writ of certiorari* (requests for review) are filed each year, and the United States Supreme Court usually agrees to full consideration of only about 70 to 100. *See generally* Samuel Estreicher & John Sexton, *Rethinking the Supreme Court's Role: A Theory of Managing the Federal Judicial Process* (1986).

The Times filed its petition for certiorari in November 1962. The four ministers also filed a petition. In January 1963, the United States Supreme Court granted the petitions for a *writ of certiorari* and set the case for oral argument. On March 9, 1964, nearly four years after the Times published the advertisement, the Court announced its landmark decision reversing the Alabama judgment on the grounds that the advertisement was protected by the First Amendment of the United States Constitution. *New York Times Co. v. Sullivan*, 376 U.S. 254 (1964).

C. READING A CIVIL PROCEDURE CASE

As in other areas of the law, there are numerous sources of procedural law. A given procedural question may turn on the meaning of a statute, a rule of court, a constitutional provision, or judicially crafted legal doctrine. At various points in this book, we will examine all of those sources. However, as in your other law school courses, we will obtain much of our understanding of the law of civil procedure by reading judicial opinions. The art of reading a judicial opinion and anticipating how that opinion might be used in a subsequent, different case is at the core of a lawyer's craft.

In this section, we provide an example of the kind of case you will read throughout this book. We will try to make explicit the type of insights we can learn from reading procedural opinions and the kinds of questions you should pursue while reading and reviewing cases.

1. Stare Decisis *and the Legal Method*

The primary reason lawyers read legal opinions is because of the principle of *stare decisis* ("abide by a decision"), a commitment to resolving similar cases consistently. In our legal culture, whenever a court is faced with a question of law that is not clearly resolved by the text of a statute (or some other binding text), it will consider how other courts, in similar cases, have resolved the issue. If a higher court in the same jurisdiction has addressed the question, the lower court is obligated to decide the question consistent with that earlier, higher court opinion. Even when the earlier opinion was not written by a higher court in the same jurisdiction, the court may be influenced (although it is not bound) by the earlier decision.

But what makes an earlier case sufficiently "similar" to a subsequent case to bind the lower court to the earlier decision? Cases rarely involve identical facts. One case may involve a red car, another a blue car. One case may involve a bus, another a car. Which of these differences matter? The answer cannot be determined in the abstract; *the factual differences between cases must be evaluated in reference to the legal principle for which the earlier case is cited.*

For example, the difference between a car and a bus might not be considered significant if Case 1 is cited for the proposition that a seller who had been paid in full for a bus must deliver the bus to the buyer. If Case 2 involved a seller's failure to deliver a car, the two cases would probably be considered indistinguishable. However, if Case 1 stands for the proposition that it is reckless to drive a bus at 85 mph, a judge in a subsequent case involving a car traveling at 85 mph might conclude that the earlier case is "distinguishable" because of the different handling characteristics of buses and cars. On the other hand, if the court in the bus case reasoned that 85 mph was far in excess of the human capacity to react safely, the court in the car case might conclude that the difference between buses and cars is not significant in that regard.

A lawyer must be able to construe judicial decisions in a manner helpful to her client. In the last car/bus example, a lawyer for the car driver would argue that the bus-court's reasoning was either implicitly or explicitly dependent on the handling characteristics of buses — i.e., the "holding" of the case is that 85 mph is too fast for a bus. Opposing counsel would offer a construction of the "holding" that is broader and less contextual — i.e., 85 mph is a reckless driving speed.

Note that neither interpretation is in bad faith. In writing the opinion, the bus-judge did not have to think about how the reasoning would apply to different facts. The true "meaning" of the decision in regard to later cases is thus, to a certain extent, indeterminate.

What are the implications of all of this for reading cases? A lawyer's ability to construe judicial decisions requires meticulous attention to both law and fact. She must be able not only to understand which of the facts were important to the court's reasoning, but, ideally, should be able to offer alternative accounts of the court's reasoning that render certain factual characteristics of the decision either extraneous or critical.

She must also be able to evaluate critically the wisdom of the earlier decision. *Stare decisis* notwithstanding, courts are quite reasonably reluctant to follow a badly reasoned precedent. Thus, whenever a lawyer cites a case to a court, she is not only asserting that the precedent is applicable, but that it is sound. Opposing counsel may assert the precedent is both distinguishable and badly reasoned.

As you read the cases in this book, we challenge you to develop these types of analytical skills. How does the case contribute to our understanding of the law? What is the range of credible interpretations of a court's decision? Which facts were important? How would the court's reasoning apply to different facts? How compelling was the court's decision? Is it logically consistent? Is it based on an accurate understanding of the applicable law and facts? Does it reach a desirable result in this case? Does its logic lead to desirable results in other cases?

2. *Reading a Sample Case*

One of the trickier aspects of mastering the case method in Civil Procedure is that the "issue" addressed by the decision is typically not about the underlying rights of the parties to the relief sought in their pleadings. Rather, the opinions are typically about *how* the case will be litigated, such as: Has the case been brought in the appropriate court; have the parties filed appropriate documents with the court; have certain issues or claims been resolved by some earlier litigation; are the parties entitled to seek certain information in discovery? When you learn to "brief" cases in your other courses, the procedural context of the case will typically form the backdrop to understanding the substantive issues in the case. In Civil Procedure, the substantive rights of the parties form the backdrop for understanding their procedural rights.

The following case involves the investigation of Pete Rose by Commissioner of Baseball A. Bartlett Giamatti, which ultimately resulted in Rose's lifetime ban from Major League Baseball for gambling. As you will read in the opinion, Rose attempted to derail the Commissioner's investigation by filing a lawsuit in state court in Ohio. The defendants—Giamatti, the Cincinnati Reds, and Major League Baseball—attempted to "remove" that case to a federal court in Ohio. The following opinion was written in response to Rose's motion to *remand* (return) the case to state court on the ground that the federal court did not have jurisdiction over the case.

Because this decision is in a Civil Procedure book, we know that the point of the decision is not about whether Rose could be banned from baseball for gambling. If this were a Contracts book, a case like this might be included to tell us something about the terms and conditions of an employment contract. The reason we ask you to read this case is because of a procedural issue: Is the case in the proper court? In attempting to answer that question, we don't really care whether Giamatti breached his contractual obligations to Rose. While the substantive rights of the parties may be relevant to the central procedural issue (as indeed is the case here), our primary focus will always be procedural.

As we discussed above, the federal courts are courts of *limited jurisdiction*. Only a small percentage of litigation qualifies for adjudication in federal court. By statute, the federal courts are limited to hearing cases falling within a few narrowly defined categories. The defendants in *Rose* argue that the federal court has jurisdiction because of "diversity of citizenship"; the federal courts are authorized to hear cases between citizens of different states where a sufficient amount of money is at stake.

Although Rose and Giamatti were, in fact, citizens of different states, and a sufficient amount of money was at stake, Rose had included additional defendants in his suit—the Cincinnati Reds and Major League Baseball—whose citizenship may overlap with Rose's, destroying complete diversity. In order for a case to fall within a federal court's diversity jurisdiction, *all* plaintiffs must be diverse from *all* defendants. The court was thus faced with two procedural questions: (1) how does a court evaluate the citizenship of a business entity; and (2) must the court always consider the citizenship of all named parties?

Rose v. Giamatti

721 F. Supp. 906 (S.D. Ohio 1989)

HOLSCHUH, DISTRICT JUDGE. . . .

II. PROCEDURAL HISTORY

Plaintiff, Peter Edward Rose, is the Field Manager of the Cincinnati Reds baseball team. In February of this year, then Commissioner of Baseball Peter V. Ueberroth and then Commissioner of Baseball-elect A. Bartlett Giamatti initiated an investigation regarding allegations that Rose wagered on major league baseball games. On February 23, 1989, Giamatti retained John M. Dowd as Special Counsel for the purpose of conducting the investigation. On May 9, 1989 Dowd submitted a report to Giamatti summarizing the evidence obtained during the investigation. Commissioner Giamatti ultimately scheduled a hearing concerning the allegations for June 26, 1989.

In an effort to prevent Commissioner Giamatti from conducting the June 26 hearing, Rose filed an action in the Court of Common Pleas of Hamilton County, Ohio, on June 19, 1989, seeking a temporary restraining order and preliminary injunction against the pending disciplinary proceedings. Named as defendants in that action were A. Bartlett Giamatti, Major League Baseball, and the Cincinnati Reds. The crux of the complaint[1] is Rose's contention that he is being denied the right to a fair hearing on the gambling allegations by an unbiased decisionmaker. The complaint requests permanent injunctive relief, which, if granted, would prevent Commissioner Giamatti from ever conducting a hearing to determine whether Rose has engaged in gambling activities in violation of the Rules of Major League Baseball. Rose asks that the Court of Common Pleas of Hamilton County, Ohio determine whether he has wagered on major league baseball games, including those of the Cincinnati Reds.

Subsequent to a two-day evidentiary hearing, Common Pleas Court Judge Norbert Nadel issued a temporary restraining order on June 25, 1989. The order enjoined all defendants (1) from any involvement in deciding whether Rose should be disciplined or suspended from participation in baseball and (2) from terminating Rose's employment as Field Manager of the Cincinnati Reds, or interfering

---

1. The complaint alleges seven causes of action based upon state law claims of breach of contract, breach of an implied covenant of good faith and fair dealing, breach of fiduciary duty, promissory estoppel, tortious interference with contract, negligence, and the common law of "due process and natural justice."

with his employment in response to any action taken by Giamatti, or in retaliation for Rose having filed the action. Judge Nadel set July 6, 1989 as the date for a hearing on plaintiff Rose's motion for a preliminary injunction. Commissioner Giamatti and Major League Baseball unsuccessfully sought review of the temporary restraining order in the Ohio Court of Appeals, First Judicial District, in Hamilton County, Ohio; the Court of Appeals held on June 28, 1989 that the temporary restraining order was not an appealable order.

On July 3, 1989, defendant Giamatti filed a notice of removal of the action . . . contending that the federal court has diversity jurisdiction over this action. . . .

On July 5, 1989, Rose filed a motion to remand this action to the Court of Common Pleas of Hamilton County, Ohio, asserting that there is a lack of complete diversity of citizenship between himself and the defendants. . . .

III. DIVERSITY JURISDICTION

The United States district courts are courts of limited jurisdiction, and the federal statute permitting removal of cases filed in state court restricts the types of cases which may be removed from state court to federal court. The removal statute provides in pertinent part that "any civil action brought in a State court of which the district courts of the United States have original jurisdiction, may be removed by the defendant or the defendants to the district court of the United States for the district and division embracing the place where such action is pending." 28 U.S.C. §1441(a). The statute also provides that except for a civil action founded on a claim arising under federal law, "[a]ny other such action shall be removable only if none of the parties in interest properly joined and served as defendants is a citizen of the State in which such action is brought." 28 U.S.C. §1441(b).

Defendant Giamatti contends in his notice of removal that the district court has original jurisdiction of this action by virtue of 28 U.S.C. §1332(a), which grants original jurisdiction to the district courts in civil actions where the amount in controversy exceeds $50,000 and the action is between citizens of different states. This jurisdiction of federal courts is commonly known as "diversity" jurisdiction. The reason for granting diversity jurisdiction to federal courts was stated many years ago by Chief Justice Marshall:

> However true the fact may be, that the tribunals of the states will administer justice as impartially as those of the nation, to parties of every description, it is not less true that the Constitution itself either entertains apprehensions on this subject, or views with such indulgence the possible fears and apprehensions of suitors, that it has established national tribunals for the decision of controversies between aliens and a citizen, or between citizens of different States.

Bank of the United States v. Deveaux, 5 Cranch 61, 87 (1809). The diversity statute has historically been interpreted to require complete diversity of citizenship: . . . diversity jurisdiction does not exist unless *each* defendant is a citizen of a different state from *each* plaintiff. . . . If diversity of citizenship is found to exist among the parties to this action and none of the defendants in interest properly joined and served is a citizen of Ohio, then the action is properly removable from the state court. If the required diversity of citizenship does not exist, then the action is not properly removable and must be remanded to the state court. . . .

The Court will accept as true for purposes of ruling on the motion to remand that plaintiff Rose is a citizen of the State of Ohio, that defendant Giamatti is a citizen of the State of New York, that defendant Cincinnati Reds is a citizen of the State of Ohio,[3] and that defendant Major League Baseball, assuming it exists as a legal entity, is comprised of the two major professional baseball leagues and their constituent twenty-six major league baseball clubs, at least one of which, the Cincinnati Reds, is a citizen of the State of Ohio.

In the present case, it appears from the allegations of the complaint that defendant Cincinnati Reds and defendant Major League Baseball are citizens of the same state as plaintiff Rose. Recognizing that diversity jurisdiction is not demonstrated on the face of the complaint, defendant Giamatti includes in his notice of removal a number of allegations in support of his contention that this Court has diversity jurisdiction over this action such that it is properly removable. First, with respect to the defendant identified as Major League Baseball, the notice asserts that defendant Major League Baseball is not a "juridical entity," but is only a trade name utilized by the professional baseball clubs of the American and National Leagues and thus has no citizenship for diversity purposes. Notice of Removal, ¶7. Second, the notice asserts that any citizenship ascribed to Major League Baseball should be disregarded for purposes of removal, "since Major League Baseball is not a proper party to this action and is at most a nominal party against which no claim or cause of action has been asserted." *Id.* Finally, the notice asserts that Major League Baseball was "fraudulently joined" as a defendant for the purpose of attempting to defeat the removal jurisdiction of this Court. In a similar vein, the notice asserts that the defendant Cincinnati Reds is not a proper party to this action, is only a nominal party, and was fraudulently joined for the same purpose of defeating this Court's removal jurisdiction. *Id.*, at ¶8. . . .

A. The Citizenship of Defendant Major League Baseball

. . . [T]he Court, for purposes of this motion, will accept Rose's contention that the twenty-six major league professional baseball clubs joined together in the Major League Agreement to form an unincorporated association known as Major League Baseball, and that the unincorporated association known as Major League Baseball is before this Court as a properly served defendant in this case.

It is undisputed that, for purposes of determining the citizenship of an unincorporated association, an unincorporated association has no citizenship of its own, but is a citizen of every state in which each of its constituent members is a citizen. . . .

---

3. For purposes of diversity, a limited partnership is considered to be a citizen of each state in which its partners are citizens. *See Bedell v. H.R.C. Ltd.*, 522 F. Supp. 732, 736 n. 8 (E.D. Ky. 1981). Although there is no indication in the record of the state or states of citizenship of the partners in the Cincinnati Reds, the parties agree that the Cincinnati Reds is an Ohio resident. Therefore, the Court will assume for purposes of this motion that at least one of those partners is a citizen of the State of Ohio.

The Cincinnati Reds Baseball Club, a citizen of Ohio, is one of the twenty-six major league baseball clubs which are members of the association doing business as Major League Baseball. Therefore, Major League Baseball is deemed to be a citizen of Ohio for diversity purposes. Because plaintiff Rose and the defendants Major League Baseball and the Cincinnati Reds are all citizens of Ohio, if either Major League Baseball or the Cincinnati Reds is a party properly joined in this action and whose citizenship, for diversity purposes, cannot be ignored, the lack of diversity of citizenship between plaintiff and all defendants would require the Court to conclude that the removal of the case to this Court was improper. Consequently, the Court must determine whether, as the Commissioner contends, the citizenship of these defendants should be ignored for the purpose of determining whether the removal of this case to this Court was proper.

B.   Determination of Proper Parties to This Action from "The Principal Purpose of the Suit"

It is fundamental law that a plaintiff cannot confer jurisdiction upon the federal court, nor prevent a defendant from removing a case to the federal court on diversity grounds, by plaintiff's own determination as to who are proper plaintiffs and defendants to the action. . . .

In considering whether diversity of citizenship exists with respect to the "principal purpose of the suit," certain doctrines are well established. First, a plaintiff cannot defeat a defendant's right of removal on the basis of diversity of citizenship by the "fraudulent joinder" of a non-diverse defendant against whom the plaintiff has no real cause of action. *See Wilson v. Republic Iron & Steel Co.*, 257 U.S. 92, 97 (1921); *Allied Programs Corp. v. Puritan Ins. Co.*, 592 F. Supp. 1274, 1276 (S.D.N.Y. 1984). . . .

In many cases, removability may be determined from the original pleadings, and normally an allegation of a cause of action against the resident defendant will be sufficient to prevent removal. But when a defendant alleges that there has been fraudulent joinder, the court "may pierce the pleadings, consider the entire record, and determine the basis of joinder by any means available." *Dodd v. Fawcett Publications, Inc.*, 329 F.2d at 85 (citations omitted).

Used in this sense, the term "fraudulent joinder" is a term of art and is not intended to impugn the integrity of a plaintiff or plaintiff's counsel. . . .

Second, it is also a long-established doctrine that a federal court, in its determination of whether there is diversity of citizenship between the parties, must disregard nominal or formal parties to the action and determine jurisdiction based only upon the citizenship of the real parties to the controversy. *Navarro Savings Ass'n v. Lee*, 446 U.S. 458 (1980). . . . A real party in interest defendant is one who, by the substantive law, has the duty sought to be enforced or enjoined. . . . In contrast to a "real party in interest," a formal or nominal party is one who, in a genuine legal sense, has no interest in the result of the suit, . . . or no actual interest or control over the subject matter of the litigation. . . .

The Court turns, then, to the realities of the record in this case to determine the real parties to this controversy.

1. Defendant Giamatti

It is apparent from the complaint that the actual controversy in this case is between Rose and Commissioner Giamatti. The complaint is replete with allegations of wrongdoing on the part of Giamatti. . . .

The critical question now before the Court is whether, in this controversy between Rose and Giamatti, there is "the necessary collision of interests" between Rose on the one hand and the Cincinnati Reds and Major League Baseball on the other hand so that the citizenship of these defendants may not be disregarded by the Court. . . .

2. The Cincinnati Reds

Just as it is clear that the crux of the present controversy is between Rose and Giamatti, it is equally clear that, in reality, there is no controversy between Rose and the Cincinnati Reds. The complaint explicitly asserts that Rose "alleges no wrongful conduct on the part of the Reds.". . . Despite this explicit assertion, Rose contends that "all defendants herein owe Pete Rose the contractual duty to ensure that the Commissioner adheres to the Major League Agreement and discharges his duties in accordance with the Rules of Procedure.". . . In essence, Rose asserts that the Commissioner's rules of procedure concerning fair disciplinary hearings are incorporated as a part of his employment contract with the Cincinnati Reds, and that any action by Commissioner Giamatti in violation of his own rules of procedure would constitute a breach of Rose's contract with the Cincinnati Reds. It is Rose's position that the Cincinnati Reds owes him a contractual duty to see that the procedural rules are not violated, and that if Giamatti violates these rules by holding an unfair hearing and, as a result, sanctions Rose, the Reds will have failed in its duty and will have breached his contract. Rose's claim against the Cincinnati Reds, involving no present wrongful conduct on the part of the Reds, is for "anticipatory breach" of his contract.

The Major League Agreement, which unquestionably is incorporated as a part of Rose's contract with the Cincinnati Reds, creates the office of Commissioner of Baseball and vests extraordinary power in the Commissioner. The Commissioner has unlimited authority to investigate any act, transaction or practice that is even suspected to be "not in the best interests" of baseball. In connection with this authority, the Commissioner may (1) summon persons and order the production of documents, and, in case of refusal to appear or produce, impose penalties; (2) determine after investigation what preventative, remedial, or punitive action is appropriate; and (3) take such action against the leagues, the clubs, or individuals. Major League Agreement, Art. 1, Sec. 2. The Commissioner is given virtually unlimited authority to formulate his own rules of procedure for conducting those investigations, the only limitations being that whatever rules he adopts must recognize the right of any party in interest to appear before him and be heard, and the right of the presidents of the two major leagues to appear and be heard on any matter affecting the interests of the leagues. *Id.* at Sec. 2(e). These rules of procedure are not rules adopted by the members of Major League Baseball; they are rules promulgated solely by the Commissioner of Baseball.

In contrast to the Commissioner's own rules of procedure, the members of Major League Baseball have formally adopted extensive rules governing relations between clubs and their employees, misconduct of players and other persons, and many other matters. These rules are known as the "Major League Rules." These detailed rules governing major league professional baseball have been accepted by the twenty-six major league professional baseball clubs and are recognized as binding upon them.

Rose's contract with the Cincinnati Reds provides in relevant part:

> The National League Constitution, Regulations and/or Rules and the *Major League* and Professional Baseball *Agreements and Rules,* and all amendments thereto hereafter adopted, are hereby made a part of this contract. . . .

Considering the Major League Agreement, with its provisions vesting in the Commissioner the authority to promulgate his own procedural rules governing his investigation of matters not in the best interests of baseball, and its provisions for the adoption of Major League Rules binding upon every league, club, and player in major league professional baseball, it is apparent that "the Major League . . . Rules" which are expressly incorporated into Rose's contract with the Cincinnati Reds are the extensive rules of conduct formally adopted by the members of Major League Baseball and not the procedural rules independently promulgated by the Commissioner which govern only his own proceedings. Furthermore, and of greater importance, there is nothing in the Major League Agreement, the Major League Rules, or in Rose's contract with the Cincinnati Reds which gives the Reds any right to prevent the Commissioner from holding a disciplinary hearing or to interfere with proceedings within the jurisdiction of the Commissioner. In fact, the parties are in agreement that the Cincinnati Reds has no such right.

Rose concedes that the Cincinnati Reds has done nothing that would be considered a breach of his contract at this time, nor does he allege that the Cincinnati Reds has taken any action that indicates an intention to refuse to perform its contract with him in the future so as to constitute an anticipatory breach of his contract under Ohio law. . . . Rose's argument that any violation by Giamatti of the Commissioner's own procedural rules would somehow constitute an automatic breach of Rose's contract with the Cincinnati Reds is without legal basis.

It is undeniable that the Cincinnati Reds has, as a practical matter, an interest in the outcome of these proceedings, but not in the legal sense that requires its joinder as a defendant in this action. Rose's complaint specifically alleges that there has been no wrongdoing on the part of the Cincinnati Reds, and the Reds specifically states that it will comply with the terms and conditions of its contract with Rose; there is no real controversy between these parties. The Court concludes that, for the purpose of determining diversity of citizenship, the defendant Cincinnati Reds was, in a legal sense, fraudulently joined as a defendant and that it is, at best, a nominal party in this action. Consequently, the citizenship of the Cincinnati Reds as a defendant may be disregarded for the purpose of determining whether there is complete diversity of citizenship among the parties to this action. In addition to being sued individually as a defendant, the Cincinnati Reds, for the purpose of this analysis of diversity of citizenship, is also a member of Major League Baseball, and the Court turns next to the consideration of that named defendant.

3. Major League Baseball

If Major League Baseball were a typical unincorporated association, its jurisdictional status would be more easily determined. The reality, however, is that Major League Baseball is a unique organization. . . .

The Commissioner's jurisdiction under the Major League Agreement to investigate violations of Major League Rules, or any activity he believes is "not in the best interests" of baseball, is exclusive. The major leagues and the twenty-six major league clubs have absolutely no control over such an investigation or the manner in which the Commissioner conducts it.[10] Rose does not challenge any provision of the Major League Agreement or the Major League Rules, including the rule prohibiting wagering on major league baseball games, nor does he challenge the Commissioner's authority under Article I, Section 2(e) of the Major League Agreement to promulgate his own rules of procedure dealing with investigations of suspected violations of the Major League Rules. What Rose challenges is Commissioner Giamatti's conduct of the investigation and disciplinary proceedings in his particular case. In short, Rose's controversy is not with Major League Baseball, but is with the office of the Commissioner of Baseball for the Commissioner's alleged failure to follow his own procedural rules in conducting the investigation of Rose's alleged gambling activities. Clearly, complete relief can be afforded with regard to the primary relief sought in the complaint — preventing Commissioner Giamatti from conducting a disciplinary hearing — without the need for any order against Major League Baseball or its constituent major league professional baseball clubs.

There is nothing in Rose's contract with the Cincinnati Reds or in the Major League Agreement which gives to the Cincinnati Reds or any other member of Major League Baseball any right, much less a duty, to prevent the Commissioner from conducting hearings concerning conduct "deemed by the Commissioner not to be in the best interests of Baseball." Major League Agreement, Art. I, Sec 3. . . . Accordingly, disregard of those procedural rules by the Commissioner, while it may be the basis for an action against the Commissioner, would not impose contractual liability on the Cincinnati Reds or the other members of Major League Baseball based on either the Major League Agreement or Rose's own contract.

Rose contends that Commissioner Giamatti, in conducting disciplinary proceedings, is acting as the agent for Major League Baseball, and that Major League Baseball is therefore liable for any violation of a duty owed by the Commissioner to Rose to follow his own procedural rules. . . . Under Ohio law, it is clear that a party cannot be held liable for the conduct of such a person over whom the party has no control. . . .

Finally, Rose argues that, "[m]ost important to the present case is the fact that it is the members of [Major League Baseball] who must act if any action is to be taken against Pete Rose." Reply Memorandum at 20. However, it is only if the Commissioner is allowed to proceed with a hearing, finds Rose has violated the Major League Rules concerning wagering on major league baseball games, and places him on the ineligible list does any obligation to take any action arise on the part

---

10. One indicia of the complete independence of the Commissioner is Art. IX of the Major League Agreement, which provides that neither the Commissioner's powers nor his compensation may be diminished during the term of his office.

of the major league baseball clubs. In the meantime, the member clubs of Major League Baseball occupy a necessarily neutral role in the dispute between Rose and the Commissioner. As neutral bystanders to the battle between Rose and the Commissioner which is the subject of this action, the member clubs of Major League Baseball have no legal interest in the controversy, and at most would be considered to be nominal parties for the purpose of determining diversity of citizenship. . . .

The Court has examined the above authorities cited by Rose, as well as others, and concludes that none supports Rose's claims against Major League Baseball in this case. The controversy here, as stated, is between Rose and Commissioner Giamatti and not between Rose and the Cincinnati Reds or between Rose and Major League Baseball. Major League Baseball is, at best, a nominal party in this action. Therefore, the citizenship of Major League Baseball may be disregarded for diversity purposes. . . .

NOTES AND QUESTIONS

1. *Understanding the Procedural Posture of the Case*

a. What part of the decision identifies the court? What kind of court is the United States District Court for the Southern District of Ohio, a state or federal court?

b. How did the case get there? Did Rose file his complaint in that court?

c. What kind of motion is the judge responding to in writing this decision? What did the parties ask him to do?

d. What did the judge decide to do? What happens next?

e. What precise claim or claims did Rose have against Giamatti, the Reds, and Major League Baseball? Did his claims arise under state or federal law?

f. What is the defect in the court's authority that is cured by disregarding the citizenship of the Reds and Major League Baseball?

2. *Understanding the Holding of the Decision*

a. Why do judges write such expansive explanations of their decisions? What function do judicial opinions have other than providing the parties with an account of why they won or lost?

b. Which of the following sentences best captures the significance of this decision for purposes of this course?

i. Rose's primary dispute was with Giamatti, not the Reds or Major League Baseball.

ii. A federal court sitting in diversity only has jurisdiction if all of the plaintiffs are from different states than all the defendants.

iii. In evaluating its diversity jurisdiction, a federal court may disregard the citizenship of any defendant that the plaintiff does not have a real dispute with.

iv. Under Ohio law, a party cannot be held liable for the conduct of someone over whom he has no control.

3. *Thinking Critically About the Decision*

a. If Rose had no real dispute with the Reds or Major League Baseball, why did he join them as defendants? Are you persuaded that he did not need to join those defendants in order to get complete relief?

b. Why do you think the defendants removed the case to federal court?

c. What is the purpose of diversity jurisdiction? Why should the federal courts be dealing at all with cases governed entirely by state law? Is it likely that Ohio state courts would be prejudiced in Rose's favor? Does it make sense today to believe that state courts are predisposed to favor their citizens over citizens from other states? Why would a federal court be more neutral?

d. Could Rose have filed his complaint against Giamatti in federal court in Ohio? Why should the federal courts have authority to hear such a claim?

e. The court states that in order for it to assert jurisdiction, all defendants must be diverse from the plaintiff. Is that rule found in the statutes relied on by the court, 28 U.S.C. §1332, or 28 U.S.C. §1441? Do either of those statutes give the court authority to disregard the claims asserted by the plaintiff against the nondiverse defendants?

f. Note that 28 U.S.C. §1359 requires a federal court to scrutinize the improper or collusive joinder of a party when that joinder was made for the purpose of *creating* jurisdiction. Why do you suppose there is no counterpart in the statute authorizing a court to disregard a joinder designed to *destroy* jurisdiction?

g. If the court had granted the motion to remand the case to state court, could Giamatti have taken any steps in state court to make the case removable? What would have happened if the state court dismissed Rose's claims against the other defendants? Could Giamatti have removed the case at that point?

h. Could the defendants in *Sullivan v. New York Times Co.* have used the "fraudulent joinder" doctrine to get their case into federal court? Are the cases distinguishable?

CHAPTER 2

PERSONAL JURISDICTION AND OTHER COURT-ACCESS RULES

We begin our in-depth study of Civil Procedure with the question of where a lawsuit may be filed. Recall in the *Sullivan v. New York Times* materials that the Times objected to the Alabama court's exercise of authority over it. The Times was raising an objection based on lack of personal jurisdiction, the territorial reach of a court's authority.

That is a particularly important question in the context of a federal system such as the United States, with separate court systems in the individual states. At the international level, the question as to what country can exercise authority over the parties and the transaction is a question of private international law.

These territorial limits on judicial authority are the subject of personal jurisdiction and related court-access rules considered in this chapter. We will study here the evolution of American courts' attempts to define what connections between the parties and the state give that state's courts the legitimate authority to adjudicate.

In one sense, judicial proceedings are exercises of governmental power, and one might want to think about the question of "territorial jurisdiction" as one that concerns the legitimacy of governmental authority to act coercively. To what extent does the assertion of jurisdiction by one state impair the sovereignty of another? To what extent does the assertion of jurisdiction undermine personal freedom? To what extent does our commitment to a national economy and travel necessitate expansive assertions of jurisdiction? At the same time, considerations of convenience might be relevant to the question of where a suit may be brought. As you read these cases, consider the appropriate response to these concerns.

Think also about the possible sources of law that might prevent a state from asserting illegitimate authority over a defendant. Suppose a particular state—say, California—with an imperialistic sense of dispensing justice to all attempted to assert jurisdiction over anyone in the United States, regardless of any connection with California. Would such an assertion of authority be illegitimate? Why? Would any provision of the Constitution prohibit the California courts from asserting jurisdiction?

Two constitutional provisions, in particular, are thought by courts to be relevant to overreaching by state courts. First, the Full Faith and Credit Clause, Article IV, Section 1 provides: "Full Faith and Credit shall be given in each State to the public Acts, Records, and judicial Proceedings of every other State." This provision does not appear on its face to help a defendant: It *compels* the enforcement of one state's judicial proceedings in every other state. However, as we will see, it has been construed not to require the out-of-state enforcement of judgments where the court issuing the judgment lacked jurisdiction over the defendant.

The second pertinent constitutional provision is the Due Process Clause of the Fourteenth Amendment, which ensures that "no State shall . . . deprive any person of life, liberty, or property, without due process of law." While a judicial proceeding in a court lacking jurisdiction may follow the same procedures as any other court, this guarantee of "due process" has been used to prohibit excessive assertions of jurisdiction by state courts.

As you read the first principal case, *Pennoyer v. Neff,* think about potential problems in using these provisions to curtail territorial overreaching by a state court. Neither the Due Process Clause nor the Full Faith and Credit Clause defines when an assertion of jurisdiction is constitutionally excessive. From what source should the court derive standards for evaluating jurisdictional excessiveness?

Keep in mind as you read all of the cases in this chapter that we are looking at an evolution of legal concepts, not a static picture of the law as it stands now. Some of the cases you will read have been overruled, others significantly limited. This can be quite frustrating for beginning law students, particularly since you are typically tested on your ability to apply the current law, not your knowledge of legal history. Why, then, would we ask you to read cases that do not represent the current state of law?

The answer is complex. First is the historian's answer: We cannot understand the present without understanding the past. We cannot fully comprehend the meaning of judicial decisions without understanding the evolution of the legal rules at play in those cases.

Second, and perhaps more significantly, we learn a great deal about the legal process by looking at the evolution of law over time. Given *stare decisis,* how is it that law can change? By examining the evolution of legal doctrine, we get an invaluable window into the ways that precedent does and does not constrain courts. We can learn a great deal about how lawyers and judges apply legal rules to new situations, sometimes extending by analogy, sometimes distinguishing cases, and sometimes departing from existing law.

Finally, it is critical that you develop the ability to assemble a picture of the law from the cumulative data points of multiple cases decided over time. Law is iterative: It builds on itself. There is no authoritative, master list of all current legal rules. Lawyers find the law by reading multiple cases and understanding their relationship. That relationship is itself the subject of effective advocacy: A later case may appear to drain an earlier precedent of its vitality, yet a skilled advocate can demonstrate how they can be reconciled. What are the limits of that advocacy? How do we recognize when a case is no longer good law?

As you read the cases in this chapter, it is important that you understand each case on its own terms, as well as in the context of the other cases.

A. FROM POWER TO FAIRNESS

1. Traditional Bases of Jurisdiction: Power, Presence, Domicile, and Consent

a. Power over the Person or Property of the Defendant

We begin with the Supreme Court's initial effort to develop a conceptual framework for allocating adjudicatory authority among the states, *Pennoyer v. Neff.* Some of the background facts may assist your reading of the decision.

In an earlier action a lawyer, John H. Mitchell, sued Marcus Neff for attorneys' fees allegedly due Mitchell. Neff was an Oregon homesteader who had acquired real property in Oregon under the Donation Law of Oregon. Mitchell had performed certain services for Neff. Mitchell brought suit to recover his legal fees in Oregon state court, but Neff (who by then had moved to California) was never personally served, nor was his Oregon property attached. Instead, Mitchell secured jurisdiction under an Oregon statute that provided that if the defendant, after due diligence, could not be found within the state, he could be served by publication in local newspapers.

In accordance with the Oregon statute, notice of Mitchell's suit against Neff was published in the *Pacific Christian Advocate*, a weekly religious newspaper. Neff did not appear in the suit, and Mitchell obtained a default judgment. Five months later, Mitchell attempted to execute on the judgment by attaching Neff's Oregon real property. Apparently, Neff had only received formal title to the property after Mitchell's judgment against him was issued. Somewhat unusually, Neff's property was actually sold to Mitchell at a sheriff's sale. Mitchell then sold the property to Sylvester Pennoyer. Eight years after the judgment, Neff returned to Oregon and brought suit in federal court to eject Pennoyer from the land. Neff claimed that Mitchell's original judgment was invalid because the court lacked jurisdiction over Neff. This collateral attack eventually reached the Supreme Court as *Pennoyer v. Neff.*

Pennoyer v. Neff

95 U.S. 714 (1877)

Error to the Circuit Court of the United States for the District of Oregon.
MR. JUSTICE FIELD delivered the opinion of the court.

This is an action to recover the possession of a tract of land, of the alleged value of $15,000, situated in the State of Oregon. The plaintiff asserts title to the premises by a patent of the United States issued to him in [March] 1866, under the act of Congress of Sept. 27, 1850, usually known as the Donation Law of Oregon. The defendant claims to have acquired the premises under a sheriff's deed, made upon a sale of the property on execution issued upon a judgment recovered against the plaintiff in one of the circuit courts of the State. The case turns upon the validity of this judgment.

It appears from the record that the judgment was rendered in February, 1866, in favor of J. H. Mitchell, for less than $300, including costs, in an action brought by him upon a demand for services as an attorney; that, at the time the action was commenced and the judgment rendered, the defendant therein, the plaintiff here, was a nonresident of the State; that he was not personally served with process, and did not appear therein; and that the judgment was entered upon his default in not answering the complaint, upon a constructive service of summons by publication.

The Code of Oregon provides for such service when an action is brought against a nonresident and absent defendant, who has property within the State. It also provides, where the action is for the recovery of money or damages, for the attachment of the property of the nonresident. And it also declares that no natural person is subject to the jurisdiction of a court of the State, "unless he appear in the court, or be found within the State, or be a resident thereof, or have property therein; and, in the last case, only to the extent of such property at the time the jurisdiction attached." Construing this latter provision to mean, that, in an action for money or damages where a defendant does not appear in the court, and is not found within the State, and is not a resident thereof, but has property therein, the jurisdiction of the court extends only over such property, the declaration expresses a principle of general, if not universal, law. The authority of every tribunal is necessarily restricted by the territorial limits of the State in which it is established. Any attempt to exercise authority beyond those limits would be deemed in every other forum, as has been said by this court, an illegitimate assumption of power, and be resisted as mere abuse. . . . In the case against the plaintiff, the property here in controversy sold under the judgment rendered was not attached, nor in any way brought under the jurisdiction of the court. Its first connection with the case was caused by a levy of the execution. It was not, therefore, disposed of pursuant to any adjudication, but only in enforcement of a personal judgment, having no relation to the property, rendered against a nonresident without service of process upon him in the action, or his appearance therein. The court below did not consider that an attachment of the property was essential to its jurisdiction or to the validity of the sale, but held that the judgment was invalid from defects in the affidavit upon which the order of publication was obtained, and in the affidavit by which the publication was proved.

There is some difference of opinion among the members of this court as to the rulings upon these alleged defects. The majority are of opinion that inasmuch as the statute requires, for an order of publication, that certain facts shall appear by affidavit *to the satisfaction of the court or judge*, defects in such affidavit can only be taken advantage of on appeal, or by some other direct proceeding, and cannot be urged to impeach the judgment collaterally. The majority of the court are also of opinion that the provision of the statute requiring proof of the publication in a newspaper to be made by the "affidavit of the printer, or his foreman, or his principal clerk," is satisfied when the affidavit is made by the editor of the paper. . . .

If, therefore, we were confined to the rulings of the court below upon the defects in the affidavits mentioned, we should be unable to uphold its decision. But it was also contended in that court, and is insisted upon here, that the judgment in the State court against the plaintiff was void for want of personal service of process on him, or of his appearance in the action in which it was rendered, and that the premises in controversy could not be subjected to the payment of the demand of a resident creditor except by a proceeding *in rem*; that is, by a direct proceeding against the property for that purpose. If these positions are sound, the ruling of the Circuit Court as to the invalidity of that judgment must be sustained, notwithstanding our dissent from the reasons upon which it was made. And that they are sound would seem to follow from two well-established principles of public law respecting the jurisdiction of an independent State over persons and property. The several States of the Union are not, it is true, in every respect independent, many of the rights and powers which originally belonged to them being now vested in the government created by the Constitution. But, except as restrained and limited by that instrument, they possess and exercise the authority of independent States, and the principles of public law to which we have referred are applicable to them. One of these principles is, that every State possesses exclusive jurisdiction and sovereignty over persons and property within its territory. As a consequence, every State has the power to determine for itself the civil *status* and capacities of its inhabitants; to prescribe the subjects upon which they may contract, the forms and solemnities with which their contracts shall be executed, the rights and obligations arising from them, and the mode in which their validity shall be determined and their obligations enforced; and also to regulate the manner and conditions upon which property situated within such territory, both personal and real, may be acquired, enjoyed, and transferred. The other principle of public law referred to follows from the one mentioned; that is, that no State can exercise direct jurisdiction and authority over persons or property without its territory. Story, Confl. Laws, c. 2; Wheat. Int. Law, pt. 2, c. 2. The several States are of equal dignity and authority, and the independence of one implies the exclusion of power from all others. And so it is laid down by jurists, as an elementary principle, that the laws of one State have no operation outside of its territory, except so far as is allowed by comity; and that no tribunal established by it can extend its process beyond that territory so as to subject either persons or property to its decisions. . . .

But as contracts made in one State may be enforceable only in another State, and property may be held by nonresidents, the exercise of the jurisdiction which every State is admitted to possess over persons and property within its own territory will often affect persons and property without it. To any influence exerted in this way by a State affecting persons resident or property situated elsewhere, no objection can be justly taken; whilst any direct exertion of authority upon them, in an attempt to give ex-territorial operation to its laws, or to enforce an ex-territorial jurisdiction by its tribunals, would be deemed an encroachment upon the independence of the State in which the persons are domiciled or the property is situated, and be resisted as usurpation.

Thus the State, through its tribunals, may compel persons domiciled within its limits to execute, in pursuance of their contracts respecting property elsewhere situated, instruments in such form and with such solemnities as to transfer the title, so far as such formalities can be complied with; and the exercise of this jurisdiction in no manner interferes with the supreme control over the property by the State within which it is situated. *Penn v. Lord Baltimore*, 1 Ves. 444; *Massie v. Watts*, 6 Cranch. 148; *Watkins v. Holman*, 16 Pet. 25; *Corbett v. Nutt*, 10 Wall. 864.

So the State, through its tribunals, may subject property situated within its limits owned by nonresidents to the payment of the demand of its own citizens against them; and the exercise of this jurisdiction in no respect infringes upon the sovereignty of the State where the owners are domiciled. Every State owes protection to its own citizens; and, when nonresidents deal with them, it is a legitimate and just exercise of authority to hold and appropriate any property owned by such nonresidents to satisfy the claims of its citizens. It is in virtue of the State's jurisdiction over the property of the nonresident situated within its limits that its tribunals can inquire into that nonresident's obligations to its own citizens, and the inquiry can then be carried only to the extent necessary to control the disposition of the property. If the nonresidents have no property in the State, there is nothing upon which the tribunals can adjudicate. . . .

If, without personal service, judgments *in personam*, obtained *ex parte* against nonresidents and absent parties, upon mere publication of process, which, in the great majority of cases, would never be seen by the parties interested, could be upheld and enforced, they would be the constant instruments of fraud and oppression. Judgments for all sorts of claims upon contracts and for torts, real or pretended, would be thus obtained, under which property would be seized, when the evidence of the transactions upon which they were founded, if they ever had any existence, had perished.

Substituted service by publication, or in any other authorized form, may be sufficient to inform parties of the object of proceedings taken where property is once brought under the control of the court by seizure or some equivalent act. The law assumes that property is always in the possession of its owner, in person or by agent; and it proceeds upon the theory that its seizure will inform him, not only that it is taken into the custody of the court, but that he must look to any proceedings authorized by law upon such seizure for its condemnation and sale. Such service may also be sufficient in cases where the object of the action is to reach and dispose of property in the State, or of some interest therein, by enforcing a contract or a lien respecting the same, or to partition it among different owners, or, when the public is a party, to condemn and appropriate it for a public purpose. In other words, such service may answer in all actions which are substantially proceedings *in rem*. But where the entire object of the action is to determine the personal rights and obligations of the defendants, that is, where the suit is merely *in personam*, constructive service in this form upon a nonresident is ineffectual for any purpose. Process from the tribunals of one State cannot run into another State, and summon parties there domiciled to leave its territory and respond to proceedings against them. Publication of process or notice within the State where the tribunal sits cannot create any greater obligation upon the nonresident to appear. Process sent to him out of the State, and process published within it, are equally unavailing in proceedings to establish his personal liability.

The want of authority of the tribunals of a State to adjudicate upon the obligations of nonresidents, where they have no property within its limits, is not denied by the court below: but the position is assumed, that, where they have property within the State, it is immaterial whether the property is in the first instance brought under the control of the court by attachment or some other equivalent act, and afterwards applied by its judgment to the satisfaction of demands against its owner; or such demands be first established in a personal action, and the property of the nonresident be afterwards seized and sold on execution. But the answer to this position has already been given in the statement, that the jurisdiction of the court to inquire into and determine his obligations at all is only incidental to its jurisdiction over the property. Its jurisdiction in that respect cannot be made to depend upon facts to be ascertained after it has tried the cause and rendered the judgment. If the judgment be previously void, it will not become valid by the subsequent discovery of property of the defendant, or by his subsequent acquisition of it. The judgment, if void when rendered, will always remain void: it cannot occupy the doubtful position of being valid if property be found, and void if there be none. Even if the position assumed were confined to cases where the nonresident defendant possessed property in the State at the commencement of the action, it would still make the validity of the proceedings and judgment depend upon the question whether, before the levy of the execution, the defendant had or had not disposed of the property. If before the levy the property should be sold, then, according to this position, the judgment would not be binding. This doctrine would introduce a new element of uncertainty in judicial proceedings. The contrary is the law: the validity of every judgment depends upon the jurisdiction of the court before it is rendered, not upon what may occur subsequently. . . .

The force and effect of judgments rendered against nonresidents without personal service of process upon them, or their voluntary appearance, have been the subject of frequent consideration in the courts of the United States and of the several States, as attempts have been made to enforce such judgments in States other than those in which they were rendered, under the provision of the Constitution requiring that "full faith and credit shall be given in each State to the public acts, records, and judicial proceedings of every other State;" and the act of Congress providing for the mode of authenticating such acts, records, and proceedings, and declaring that, when thus authenticated, "they shall have such faith and credit given to them in every court within the United States as they have by law or usage in the courts of the State from which they are or shall be taken." In the earlier cases, it was supposed that the act gave to all judgments the same effect in other States which they had by law in the State where rendered. But this view was afterwards qualified so as to make the act applicable only when the court rendering the judgment had jurisdiction of the parties and of the subject-matter, and not to preclude an inquiry into the jurisdiction of the court in which the judgment was rendered, or the right of the State itself to exercise authority over the person or the subject-matter. *M'Elmoyle v. Cohen*, 13 Pet. 312. . . .

Since the adoption of the Fourteenth Amendment to the Federal Constitution, the validity of such judgments may be directly questioned, and their enforcement in the State resisted, on the ground that proceedings in a court of justice to determine the personal rights and obligations of parties over whom that court has no jurisdiction do not constitute due process of law. Whatever difficulty may be experienced in giving to those terms a definition which will embrace every permissible exertion of power affecting private rights, and exclude such as is forbidden, there can be no doubt of their meaning when applied to judicial proceedings. They then mean a course of legal proceedings according to those rules and principles which have been established in our systems of jurisprudence for the protection and enforcement of private rights. To give such proceedings any validity, there must be a tribunal competent by its constitution — that is, by the law of its creation — to pass upon the subject-matter of the suit; and, if that involves merely a determination of the personal liability of the defendant, he must be brought within its jurisdiction by service of process within the State, or his voluntary appearance.

Except in cases affecting the personal *status* of the plaintiff, and cases in which that mode of service may be considered to have been assented to in advance, as hereinafter mentioned, the substituted service of process by publication, allowed by the law of Oregon and by similar laws in other States, where actions are brought against nonresidents, is effectual only where, in connection with process against the person for commencing the action, property in the State is brought under the control of the court, and subjected to its disposition by process adapted to that purpose, or where the judgment is sought as a means of reaching such property or affecting some interest therein; in other words, where the action is in the nature of a proceeding *in rem*. . . .

It is true that, in a strict sense, a proceeding *in rem* is one taken directly against property, and has for its object the disposition of the property, without reference to the title of individual claimants; but, in a larger and more general sense, the terms are applied to actions between parties, where the direct object is to reach and dispose of property owned by them, or of some interest therein. Such are cases commenced by attachment against the property of debtors, or instituted to partition real estate, foreclose a mortgage, or enforce a lien. So far as they affect property in the State, they are substantially proceedings *in rem* in the broader sense which we have mentioned. . . .

It follows from the views expressed that the personal judgment recovered in the State court of Oregon against the plaintiff herein, then a nonresident of the State, was without any validity, and did not authorize a sale of the property in controversy.

To prevent any misapplication of the views expressed in this opinion, it is proper to observe that we do not mean to assert, by any thing we have said, that a State may not authorize proceedings to determine the *status* of one of its citizens towards a nonresident, which would be binding within the State, though made without service of process or personal notice to the nonresident. The jurisdiction which every State possesses to determine the civil *status* and capacities of all its inhabitants involves authority to prescribe the conditions on which proceedings affecting them may be commenced and carried on within its territory. The State, for example, has absolute right to prescribe the conditions upon which the marriage relation between its own citizens shall be created, and the causes for which it may be dissolved. One of the parties guilty of acts for which, by the law of the State, a dissolution may be granted, may have removed to a State where no dissolution is permitted. . . .

Neither do we mean to assert that a State may not require a nonresident entering into a partnership or association within its limits, or making contracts enforceable there, to appoint an agent or representative in the State to receive service of process and notice in legal proceedings instituted with respect to such partnership, association, or contracts, or to designate a place where such service may be made and notice given, and provide, upon their failure, to make such appointment or to designate such place that service may be made upon a public officer designated for that purpose, or in some other prescribed way, and that judgments rendered upon such service may not be binding upon the nonresidents both within and without the State. . . . Nor do we doubt that a State, on creating corporations or other institutions for pecuniary or charitable purposes, may provide a mode in which their conduct may be investigated, their obligations enforced, or their charters revoked, which shall require other than personal service upon their officers or members. . . .

In the present case, there is no feature of this kind, and, consequently, no consideration of what would be the effect of such legislation in enforcing the contract of a nonresident can arise. The question here respects only the validity of a money judgment rendered in one State, in an action upon a simple contract against the resident of another, without service of process upon him, or his appearance therein.

Judgment affirmed.

NOTES AND QUESTIONS

1. The protagonists in *Pennoyer* were a colorful lot. In 1872, Mitchell was elected a United States Senator. Allegations of vote fraud were made against Mitchell, and indictments were sought but later dismissed. Interestingly, federal judge Deady—who rendered the lower court decision in *Pennoyer*—actively supported the attempts to seek indictments for vote fraud. Mitchell was a shady character in other ways. He abandoned his first wife, a 15-year-old girl he was forced to marry, and entered into a bigamous marriage. Sylvester Pennoyer was also a public figure and politician. He was Governor of Oregon and Mayor of Portland. Something of a political maverick, Pennoyer proclaimed Oregon's Thanksgiving Day holiday one week later than the rest of the nation's. For more on the background of *Pennoyer, see* Linda J. Silberman, Shaffer v. Heitner: *The End of an Era*, 53 N.Y.U. L. Rev. 33, 44–48 (1978). *See also* Wendy Collins Perdue, *Sin, Scandal, and Substantive Due Process: Personal Jurisdiction and* Pennoyer *Reconsidered*, 62 Wash. L. Rev. 479 (1987).

2. *Categories of Adjudicatory Jurisdiction.* Justice Field identified three categories of judicial action in *Pennoyer.* The first are actions *in personam,* whereby a court can impose a personal liability or obligation on a defendant or require a defendant to act or refrain from doing an act. The second are proceedings *in rem,* which declare the rights of all persons to a thing. Such actions are based on the court's jurisdiction over the *res,* or thing, at issue. Examples of *in rem* actions include actions under land-registration statutes or *in rem* libels in admiralty. The third type of action, actions *quasi in rem,* result in judgments affecting the interests of particular persons in a thing. (Justice Field described this type of action in *Pennoyer* though he did not use the term *quasi in rem.*) As in pure *in rem* actions, jurisdiction in *quasi in rem* actions is predicated on the court's power over property physically situated or deemed to be situated within the forum state. In theory, *in rem* actions bind the entire world, even those not formally parties to the suit, whereas actions *quasi in rem* bind only the particular parties to the action.

Quasi in rem actions may be further divided into two types. The first type settles claims to the property on which jurisdiction is based, most frequently in actions to quiet title, partition land, or foreclose mortgages. The second type of *quasi in rem* action, the type involved in *Pennoyer,* seeks to obtain a personal judgment on a claim unrelated to the property on which the jurisdiction is based. Recovery in this type of *quasi in rem* action is limited to the value of property that can be found and attached within the state boundary.

3. *The "Power Theory" of Jurisdiction.* Justice Field tells us that the territorial limits of a particular sovereign define its jurisdictional boundaries. In his view, jurisdiction is a function of physical power over persons and things within the territory of the state. Why should "power" be a basis for adjudicatory jurisdiction? Justice Field indicated that this principle was one of general acceptance and recognition. He asserted that it would be an "encroachment upon the independence" of a sister state for a forum to exercise jurisdiction over persons or property outside its borders. Do you agree?

Consider Article 14 of the French Civil Code (Code Napoleon of 1804), which provides: "An alien, though not residing in France, can be cited before the French courts for the performance of obligations contracted by him in France with a Frenchman; he can be brought before French courts on obligations contracted by him in a foreign country toward Frenchmen." What principle supports this exercise of jurisdiction by a French court? Would you expect other countries to recognize French judgments where jurisdiction is predicated on this principle?

If power over persons or property is the basis of jurisdiction in *Pennoyer*, why didn't Neff's ownership of land suffice as a basis of jurisdiction? Why should it matter whether the property was "attached" before or after the judgment so long as Neff owned it at the time the lawsuit was commenced?

4. *Notice of the Pendency of the Action.* Power is only one part of the jurisdictional equation of *Pennoyer*. The Supreme Court also requires that requisite notice be given to the defendant. For Justice Field, the type of notice required depends on the category of jurisdiction that is being exercised. If *in personam* jurisdiction is to be obtained, personal service must be given. (For an example of personal service, *see* Fed. R. Civ. P. 4(e)(2).) If the jurisdiction is *in rem* or *quasi in rem*, publication seems to suffice. Why should notice by publication ever be sufficient? What reasons does Justice Field offer? Does the requirement that property be attached at the outset have relevance to the notice question?

Was the underlying defect in the *Mitchell v. Neff* proceeding one of notice rather than jurisdiction? Would the result in *Pennoyer* have been different if Mitchell had sent Neff a telegram informing him of the filing of the action along with a copy of the summons and complaint? Should it? *See* Robin J. Effron, *The Lost Story of Notice and Personal Jurisdiction*, 74 N.Y.U. Ann. Surv. Am. L. 23 (2018).

5. *"Full Faith and Credit" and Collateral Attack.* Justice Field concluded that the Oregon federal court was not required to recognize the prior Oregon state court judgment notwithstanding the Full Faith and Credit Clause of the United States Constitution, which provides: "Full Faith and Credit shall be given in each State to the public Acts, Records, and judicial Proceedings of every other State. And the Congress may by general Laws prescribe the Manner in which such Acts, Records and Proceedings shall be proved, and the Effect thereof." U.S. Const., art. IV, §1. Congress also passed a Full Faith and Credit statute in 1790, 1 Stat. 122, May 26, 1790. The statute appears today in 28 U.S.C. §1738.

The framers believed the Full Faith and Credit Clause to be essential to the formation of a unified nation because prior to the American Revolution, the colonies were considered foreign to each other. Thus, judgments rendered in one colony were deemed foreign judgments by other colonies and were subject to reexamination in proceedings in a second colony as to both the jurisdiction of the court and the merits of the controversy. *See* 2 J. Story, Commentaries on the Constitution of the United States 183 (3d ed. 1858).

Pennoyer, as a full faith and credit case, recognizes as an exception to full faith and credit any judgment wherein the court did not have personal (or subject matter) jurisdiction and where the jurisdictional objection was not (and could not be) raised in the initial action—in effect, a default judgment. *Pennoyer* was a collateral attack on a prior judgment, and the full faith and credit inquiry was the proper vehicle to question the jurisdiction of the earlier proceeding. *See D'Arcy v. Ketchum*, 52 U.S. (11 How.) 165 (1850) (full faith and credit does not require enforcement of a judgment where the rendering court lacked jurisdiction over the defendant's person or property). Justice Field also comments on an alternative way of bringing these questions to the U.S. Supreme Court in the initial proceeding itself—namely, the newly enacted Due Process Clause of the Fourteenth Amendment. Curiously, however, the Fourteenth Amendment had not even been ratified at the time of the Oregon judgment against Neff. Today, as you will see, challenges to jurisdiction, whether in the initial proceeding or on collateral attack, are often based on the Due Process Clause.

6. How would you apply the rules set forth in *Pennoyer*? Assume that you were Mr. Mitchell's attorney and were trying to bring suit on Mr. Mitchell's claims for attorneys' fees against Mr. Neff, who is off in California. What various options are available to you? How can you bring the suit and enforce the judgment so that Mr. Mitchell gets his money?

7. Justice Field's opinion suggests that different rules might govern cases affecting "the personal status of the plaintiff," such as actions to dissolve a marriage or cases against nonresident corporations or partnerships that may be required by state law to designate an agent for service of process. Are these rules reconcilable with the "power" theory of jurisdiction? Would the outcome in *Pennoyer* have been different if Oregon had enacted a law providing that one who receives legal services in Oregon is deemed to have consented to the jurisdiction of the Oregon courts? Reconsider this question after you read the materials on consent and *Hess v. Pawloski*, at p. 69.

b. Raising Jurisdictional Objections

As we have just seen, one option for a defendant who believes that jurisdiction over him is improper is to decline to appear in the action. A default judgment will then be entered against the defendant. However, the defendant can still raise any jurisdictional objections in a proceeding by the judgment winner to enforce the judgment, or if the property is sold, he may bring a second, collateral suit and try to recover the property, as Neff did in the *Pennoyer* case. Remember, this option is only available if the defendant never comes in and completely defaults in the original action. This default and collateral attack strategy is risky; the only attack on the judgment available to the defaulting party is the jurisdictional ground. If the defendant loses the jurisdictional issue, the judgment is subject to enforcement, and the defendant never has the opportunity to contest the merits of the action.

Read Fed. R. Civ. P. 12(b)(2) in your supplement. What other options does a defendant have if suit is brought against him in a forum that he believes is without power over him? In every state of the United States, there is a provision for the defendant to come in and raise the jurisdictional objection in the initial proceeding. In some states, the defendant must make a *special appearance*—that is, to appear only for the purpose of objecting to the jurisdiction; this was the Alabama practice at the time of *Sullivan v. New York Times*. In other jurisdictions, the defendant merely makes a timely jurisdictional objection by way of motion or in the answer but is permitted also to defend on the merits. What is the effect if the defendant fails to make the jurisdictional objection and then wants to raise the issue at trial or on appeal? *See, e.g.*, Fed. R. Civ. P. 12(b), (g), and (h)(1).

If the defendant is successful on the motion to dismiss for lack of jurisdiction, the case is dismissed. Should the plaintiff be permitted to bring the action in another forum?

If the defendant loses the jurisdictional motion, the defendant may immediately appeal the issue in those jurisdictions that permit appeals from interlocutory—i.e., nonfinal—orders (or otherwise treat the ruling on the jurisdictional motion as an appealable order). However, if a final judgment is required and no immediate appeal is permitted, the defendant will usually want to defend on the merits of the action. At one time this situation posed something of a dilemma for the defendant because some states considered a subsequent defense to the merits of the action a "waiver" of the right to appeal the issue of jurisdiction. Today, almost all states allow the defendant to defend on the merits and preserve the right to appellate review of the jurisdictional objection after the judgment. *See, e.g., Harkness v. Hyde,* 98 U.S. (8 Otto) 476 (1878); *Konicki v. Wirta,* 169 Ill. App. 3d 21, 523 N.E.2d 160 (Ill. App. Ct. 1988).

Keep in mind that the collateral attack option discussed in the first paragraph is only available when the defendant completely stays out of the first proceeding. Once a defendant unsuccessfully moves to dismiss for lack of personal jurisdiction, he is bound by that jurisdictional determination whether he defends on the merits or not and whether or not he appeals the jurisdictional ruling. In any subsequent suit to enforce the judgment in a sister state, the defendant is bound by the determination of the first court that it had jurisdiction over him. In *Baldwin v. Iowa State Traveling Men's Ass'n,* 283 U.S. 522 (1931), the Court stated the general rule:

> Public policy dictates that there be an end of litigation; that those who have contested an issue shall be bound by the result of the contest, and that matters once tried shall be considered forever settled as between the parties. We see no reason why this doctrine should not apply in every case where one voluntarily appears, presents his case and is fully heard, and why he should not, in the absence of fraud, be thereafter concluded by the judgment of the tribunal to which he has submitted his cause.

Id. at 525-526.

c.   Domicile

Does the "power theory" of jurisdiction as expressed in *Pennoyer* justify a state's exercise of authority over one of its domiciliaries, even if he is not personally served within the state? In *Milliken v. Meyer,* 311 U.S. 457 (1940), Milliken brought suit against Meyer in a Wyoming state court. Meyer, who was alleged to be a resident of Wyoming, was personally served with process in Colorado pursuant to a Wyoming statute permitting out-of-state service on its residents in certain circumstances. Meyer did not appear in the Wyoming action, and a judgment was entered against him. Later, Meyer brought suit in Colorado to nullify the Wyoming judgment on the ground that Wyoming had been without jurisdiction over him. The Colorado Supreme Court found the Wyoming judgment invalid, but the U.S. Supreme Court reversed:

> The responsibilities of . . . citizenship arise out of the relationship to the state which domicile creates. That relationship is not dissolved by mere absence from the state. The attendant duties, like the rights and privileges

incident to domicile, are not dependent on continuous presence in the state. One such incident of domicile is amenability to suit within the state even during sojourns without the state, where the state has provided and employed a reasonable method for apprising such an absent party of the proceedings against him.

Id. at 463–464. This same principle was invoked in *Blackmer v. United States,* 284 U.S. 421 (1932), to enforce a contempt conviction of an American citizen who had refused to comply with a subpoena issued by an American court and served on him in France, where he lived.

Milliken and *Blackmer* both deal with out-of-state service on citizens of the forum issuing the process. State citizenship or domicile is usually defined as the place where the person resides and intends to remain for the indefinite future. It is possible for an individual to be a resident of a state without establishing a domicile in that state — e.g., a college student or summer tourist. Would out-of-state service of such a resident be sufficient for personal jurisdiction? Can such a result be squared with the "power theory" of *Pennoyer?*

d. Consent

The Court in *Pennoyer* asserted that a state may determine the personal liability of the defendant by his "voluntary appearance." By what means does a defendant "voluntarily appear" in the action? Suppose the defendant wishes to object to the court's jurisdiction. Might such an objection itself be considered a "voluntary appearance" in the action? After all, if a defendant shows up in court to contest jurisdiction, we can be sure that she is neither unaware of nor unable to participate in the proceeding. *See* Fed. R. Civ. P. 12(b)(2), (g), and (h)(1). The Supreme Court held in York v. Texas, 137 U.S. 15 (1890), that states may constitutionally treat an appearance even for the purpose of contesting jurisdiction as a general appearance. No state currently does.

Suppose a nonresident plaintiff brings suit against a defendant in the defendant's home state. If the defendant now tries to assert a claim (a counterclaim or cross-complaint, as it is often known) against the nonresident plaintiff, can the original plaintiff object to personal jurisdiction over it? In *Adam v. Saenger,* 303 U.S. 59 (1938), the Supreme Court held that the plaintiff, by the voluntary act of bringing suit in California against the defendant, had submitted himself to the jurisdiction of the court on the cross-complaint and that California had acted constitutionally in exacting such submission as the condition of opening its courts to the plaintiff. The counterclaim in *Adam* arose out of the same factual circumstances as the claim asserted by the plaintiff. Would there have been jurisdiction on this theory over wholly unrelated counterclaims? Would the same principle support jurisdiction over a litigating plaintiff by a third person with no connection to the lawsuit?

Can a defendant consent to jurisdiction in advance of litigation? Such consent typically occurs in commercial settings where parties to a transaction agree to a "choice of forum" clause. In *The Bremen v. Zapata Off-Shore Co.,* 407 U.S. 1 (1972), the Supreme Court upheld such a choice of forum clause in an international commercial contract even though neither the parties nor the transaction had any connection with the chosen forum.

Forum selection clauses serve two functions: They confer jurisdiction on the chosen forum and preclude jurisdiction that could otherwise be asserted in a different forum. This type of forum-precluding agreement has become more important in modern cases where, as we will see shortly, the jurisdictional rules have evolved to provide the plaintiff with a greater choice of forums. The Supreme Court sustained use of such a clause in a personal injury action arising out of a passenger cruise in *Carnival Cruise Lines, Inc. v. Shute*, 499 U.S. 585 (1991). In *Shute*, plaintiff sued Carnival Cruise Lines in federal court in her home state of Washington for injuries she sustained off the Mexican coast on a cruise originating in California. Under the jurisdictional standards as they evolved in the modern cases, Carnival may have been amenable to jurisdiction in Washington state. The Supreme Court nonetheless held that plaintiff was obligated to bring suit in Florida, Carnival's principal place of business, by virtue of the forum selection clause printed in fine print on the back of her nonrefundable ticket, which she had not even seen prior to paying for the cruise. The Court held, as a matter of federal admiralty law, that plaintiff failed to carry her "heavy burden" of demonstrating that being forced to litigate in Florida pursuant to the forum selection clause would inflict "unreasonable hardship" on her. The Court noted the desirability of having a clear venue in cases involving a mobile defendant like Carnival, who would then be in a position to pass the litigation cost-savings on to passengers in the form of lower ticket prices.

A different type of question is presented by "confession of judgment" or "*cognovit* note clauses," whereby a loan agreement includes a provision permitting the creditor, in the event of a default on the loan, to have judgment entered against the debtor in a forum without service of process or notice being given to the debtor. In two cases, *D.H. Overmyer Co. v. Frick Co.*, 405 U.S. 174 (1972) and *Swarb v. Lennox*, 405 U.S. 191 (1972), the Supreme Court indicated that *cognovit* clauses did not *per se* violate Due Process, but the Court would look to a variety of factors, including the relative bargaining power of the parties, to determine their validity.

Does the consent basis of jurisdiction also include instances of coerced consent? The Supreme Court in *Pennoyer* expressly stated that a state could require a nonresident entering into a partnership in the state or making contracts enforceable there to appoint an agent to receive process within the state, or upon the creation of domestic corporations could provide a method of enforcing their obligations without personal service on its officers or members. Thus, appointments of local agents to receive service of process as a condition of doing business in the state were viewed as consent to jurisdiction and the fact that consent was extracted by compulsion did not matter.

Suppose, however, that the corporation or nonresident did not in fact appoint an agent for service in the state. You may recall that that was the situation in the *Sullivan v. New York Times* litigation. Can the notion of consent still support jurisdiction over the foreign corporation or nonresident? As regards foreign corporations, the *Pennoyer* Court would have answered "Yes," because it was thought at the time that corporations had no legal existence beyond the state of their charter or incorporation, and hence another state had the power to exclude foreign corporations from doing business within its territory. However, under the compulsion of the Privileges and Immunities Clause, U.S. Const., art. IV, §2, a state could not exclude individuals—or a group of individuals comprising a partnership or other unincorporated association—who conducted business in a state other than their place of domicile. Without such power of exclusion, the Supreme Court held that a state had no right to subject nonresident partners to jurisdiction in its courts—absent personal service in the state—even for claims arising from the partnership's in-state business. *See Flexner v. Farson*, 248 U.S. 289 (1919). The increasing mobility of individuals and businesses, facilitated by the advent of the automobile, began to place pressure on these principles of jurisdiction.

e. Implied Consent

In the 1920s, many states enacted nonresident motorist statutes. The statutes sought to guarantee jurisdiction over motorists from other states who entered the state, caused an injury, and then left. For example, the Massachusetts statute stated that "the operation by a nonresident of a motor vehicle on a public way in the commonwealth . . . shall be deemed equivalent to an appointment by such nonresident of the registrar or his successor in office, to be his true and lawful attorney upon whom may be served all lawful processes in any action or proceeding against him." General Laws of Massachusetts, as amended by Stat. 1923, c. 431, §2. That "appointment" would guarantee jurisdiction in Massachusetts for any action "growing out of any accident or collision in which said nonresident may be involved while operating a motor vehicle on such a way," because "said acceptance or operation shall be a signification of his agreement that any such process against him which is so served shall be of the same legal force and validity as if served on him personally." *Pennoyer*'s "power" framework had no space for jurisdiction over a person in another state who had no property in the state. Therefore, Massachusetts turned to this fiction of implied consent—that driving on Massachusetts roads was the equivalent of submitting to the jurisdiction of Massachusetts courts for actions arising out of that drive.

Leo Pawloski alleged that H.W. Hess "negligently and wantonly drove a motor vehicle on a public highway in Massachusetts" and injured Pawloski. Hess was not personally served and did not own property in Massachusetts. So, Mr. Pawloski used the Massachusetts nonresident motorist statute to ground jurisdiction over Hess in Massachusetts court. In *Hess v. Pawloski* 274 U.S. 352 (1927), the Supreme Court held that this application of the statute was constitutional under the Fourteenth Amendment. The Court noted that this seemed in tension with *Pennoyer*'s vision: "The process of a court of one State cannot run into another and summon a party there domiciled to respond to proceedings against him." The use of implied consent in the nonresident motorist statutes was acceptable because cars "are dangerous machines; and, even when skillfully and carefully operated, their use is attended by serious dangers to persons and property." A state "may make and enforce regulations reasonably calculated to promote care on the part of all, residents and non-residents alike, who use its highways." *Id.* at 355. The Court observed that, "in advance of the operation of a motor vehicle on its highway by a nonresident, the State may require him to appoint one of its officials as his agent on whom process may be served in proceedings growing out of such use. . . . The difference between the formal and implied appointment is not substantial so far as concerns the application of the due process clause of the Fourteenth Amendment." In the Court's view, all Massachusetts was doing was placing its own residents who caused car accidents, who could always be sued in Massachusetts, on equal footing with out-of-staters who caused car accidents.

NOTES AND QUESTIONS

1. The Supreme Court strives to adhere to the "consent" theory, premised on the state's power to exclude nonresident drivers from the state, as its justification for upholding jurisdiction in *Hess*. Would the case be decided differently today if contemporary notions of a right to travel would prevent the state from excluding drivers who drive through the state?

2. How far does this theory of coerced implied consent extend? Would jurisdiction have been found if:

a. No accident occurred, but Pawloski sued Hess for assault and battery after Hess punched Pawloski in an altercation in the parking lot of a roadside diner?

b. Pawloski sued Hess in Massachusetts for an accident that occurred in Vermont, but Hess had driven through Massachusetts on his way to Vermont?

3. Is there a better justification for jurisdiction implicit in *Hess*? How would you articulate it?

f.   Jurisdiction over Out-of-State Corporations

As we have already seen, jurisdiction over corporations presented particular problems in the *Pennoyer* world. A domestic corporation, seen as analogous to an individual domiciliary, was subject to jurisdiction in its state of incorporation, whether service was made inside or outside the state. Jurisdiction over *foreign* corporations (corporations incorporated in another state) was more difficult. Where *Pennoyer* tested an individual's amenability to jurisdiction outside of the home by the location of the body at the moment of service of process, that measure obviously could not be used on corporations; there is no physical manifestation of a corporation's "person" equivalent to an individual's body. Courts were thus forced to look to alternative measures of a corporation's amenability to jurisdiction.

Often, a foreign corporation—sometimes under compulsion and sometimes not—would appoint an agent for service of process in a state in which it did business. In such cases, jurisdiction over such corporations was exercised with regard to any claim against the corporation on a theory of express (even if coerced) consent. When no agent was appointed, states asserted jurisdiction under two basic theories, with somewhat different consequences. If the corporation had extensive activities within the state—and the corporation continued to have activities when the lawsuit was commenced—the corporation was said to have an established "presence" in the state similar to an individual who could be said to be "found" within the state. The corporation, under this theory, could be sued on any claim asserted against it—in today's terms, it was subject to "general jurisdiction." However, if the corporation had less activity in the state but the claim arose from that particular activity, the corporation was said to have "impliedly consented" to suits arising out of that activity and was therefore subject to jurisdiction on related claims only. Today, this jurisdiction over claims relating to the particular activity that took place in the state is referred to as "specific jurisdiction." Finally, if a foreign corporation's activity was so limited that it was neither "present" in the state nor "impliedly consent[ed]" to jurisdiction, it was not subject to jurisdiction in that state.

The rules governing jurisdiction over corporations were (and are), in the first instance, a matter of state law. Individual state law would dictate the level of activity that would be necessary before a corporation would be said to be "present" or to have "impliedly consented." However, since the Due Process Clause provided the outer limits on how far a state could extend its jurisdiction, the constitutional limits of presence and implied consent were questions for the Supreme Court. For an excellent discussion of the history of jurisdiction over corporations, *see* Philip Kurland, *The Supreme Court, The Due Process Clause and the In Personam Jurisdiction of State Courts; From* Pennoyer *to* Denckla: *A Review*, 25 U. Chi. L. Rev. 569, 577–586 (1958).

2. The "Minimum Contacts" Standard: The Expansion of Personal Jurisdiction

International Shoe Co. v. Washington

326 U.S. 310 (1945)

Appeal from the Supreme Court for the State of Washington.

MR. CHIEF JUSTICE STONE delivered the opinion of the Court.

The questions for decision are (1) whether, within the limitations of the due process clause of the Fourteenth Amendment, appellant, a Delaware corporation, has by its activities in the State of Washington rendered itself amenable to proceedings in the courts of that state to recover unpaid contributions to the state unemployment compensation fund exacted by state statutes, Washington Unemployment Compensation Act, Washington Revised Statutes, §9998-103a through §9998-123a, 1941 Supp., and (2) whether the state can exact those contributions consistently with the due process clause of the Fourteenth Amendment.

The statutes in question set up a comprehensive scheme of unemployment compensation, the costs of which are defrayed by contributions required to be made by employers to a state unemployment compensation fund. The contributions are a specified percentage of the wages payable annually by each employer for his employees' services in the state. The assessment and collection of the contributions and the fund are administered by appellees. . . .

In this case notice of assessment for the years in question was personally served upon a sales solicitor employed by appellant in the State of Washington, and a copy of the notice was mailed by registered mail to appellant at its address in St. Louis, Missouri. Appellant appeared specially before the office of unemployment and moved to set aside the order and notice of assessment on the ground that the service upon appellant's salesman was not proper service upon appellant; that appellant was not a corporation of the State of Washington and was not doing business within the state; that it had no agent within the state upon whom service could be made; and that appellant is not an employer and does not furnish employment within the meaning of the statute.

The motion was heard on evidence and a stipulation of facts by the appeal tribunal which denied the motion and ruled that appellee Commissioner was entitled to recover the unpaid contributions. That action was affirmed by the Commissioner; both the Superior Court and the Supreme Court affirmed. 22 Wash. 2d 146,

154 P.2d 801. Appellant in each of these courts assailed the statute as applied, as a violation of the due process clause of the Fourteenth Amendment, and as imposing a constitutionally prohibited burden on interstate commerce. The cause comes here on appeal under §237(a) of the Judicial Code, 28 U.S.C. §344(a), appellant assigning as error that the challenged statutes as applied infringe the due process clause of the Fourteenth Amendment and the commerce clause.

The facts as found by the appeal tribunal and accepted by the state Superior Court and Supreme Court are not in dispute. Appellant is a Delaware corporation, having its principal place of business in St. Louis, Missouri, and is engaged in the manufacture and sale of shoes and other footwear. It maintains places of business in several states, other than Washington, at which its manufacturing is carried on and from which its merchandise is distributed interstate through several sales units or branches located outside the State of Washington.

Appellant has no office in Washington and makes no contracts either for sale or purchase of merchandise there. It maintains no stock of merchandise in that state and makes there no deliveries of goods in intrastate commerce. During the years from 1937 to 1940, now in question, appellant employed eleven to thirteen salesmen under direct supervision and control of sales managers located in St. Louis. These salesmen resided in Washington; their principal activities were confined to that state; and they were compensated by commissions based upon the amount of their sales. The commissions for each year totaled more than $31,000. Appellant supplies its salesmen with a line of samples, each consisting of one shoe of a pair, which they display to prospective purchasers. On occasion they rent permanent sample rooms, for exhibiting samples, in business buildings, or rent rooms in hotels or business buildings temporarily for that purpose. The cost of such rentals is reimbursed by appellant.

The authority of the salesmen is limited to exhibiting their samples and soliciting orders from prospective buyers, at prices and on terms fixed by appellant. The salesmen transmit the orders to appellant's office in St. Louis for acceptance or rejection, and when accepted the merchandise for filling the orders is shipped f.o.b. from points outside Washington to the purchasers within the state. All the merchandise shipped into Washington is invoiced at the place of shipment from which collections are made. No salesman has authority to enter into contracts or to make collections.

The Supreme Court of Washington was of opinion that the regular and systematic solicitation of orders in the state by appellant's salesmen, resulting in a continuous flow of appellant's product into the state, was sufficient to constitute doing business in the state so as to make appellant amenable to suit in its courts. But it was also of opinion that there were sufficient additional activities shown to bring the case within the rule frequently stated, that solicitation within a state by the agents of a foreign corporation plus some additional activities there are sufficient to render the corporation amenable to suit brought in the courts of the state to enforce an obligation arising out of its activities there. . . . The court found such additional activities in the salesmen's display of samples sometimes in permanent display rooms, and the salesmen's residence within the state, continued over a period of years, all resulting in a substantial volume of merchandise regularly shipped by appellant to purchasers within the state. The court also held that the statute as applied did not invade the constitutional power of Congress to regulate interstate commerce and did not impose a prohibited burden on such commerce.

Appellant's argument, renewed here, that the statute imposes an unconstitutional burden on interstate commerce need not detain us. . . .

Appellant also insists that its activities within the state were not sufficient to manifest its "presence" there and that in its absence the state courts were without jurisdiction, that consequently it was a denial of due process for the state to subject appellant to suit. It refers to those cases in which it was said that the mere solicitation of orders for the purchase of goods within a state, to be accepted without the state and filled by shipment of the purchased goods interstate, does not render the corporation seller amenable to suit within the state. . . . And appellant further argues that since it was not present within the state, it is a denial of due process to subject it to taxation or other money exaction. It thus denies the power of the state to lay the tax or to subject appellant to a suit for its collection.

Historically the jurisdiction of courts to render judgment *in personam* is grounded on their de facto power over the defendant's person. Hence his presence within the territorial jurisdiction of a court was prerequisite to its rendition of a judgment personally binding him. *Pennoyer v. Neff*, 95 U.S. 714, 733. But now that the *capias ad respondendum* has given way to personal service of summons or other form of notice, due process requires only that in order to subject a defendant to a judgment *in personam*, if he be not present within the territory of the forum, he have certain minimum contacts with it such that the maintenance of the suit does not offend "traditional notions of fair play and substantial justice." *Milliken v. Meyer*, 311 U.S. 457, 463. See Holmes, J., in *McDonald v. Mabee*, 243 U.S. 90, 91. Compare *Hoopeston Canning Co. v. Cullen*, 318 U.S. 313, 316, 319. See *Blackmer v. United States*, 284 U.S. 421; *Hess v. Pawloski*, 274 U.S. 352; *Young v. Masci*, 289 U.S. 253.

Since the corporate personality is a fiction, although a fiction intended to be acted upon as though it were a fact, . . . it is clear that unlike an individual its "presence" without, as well as within, the state of its origin can be manifested only by activities carried on in its behalf by those who are authorized to act for it. To say that the corporation is so far "present" there as to satisfy due process requirements, for purposes of taxation or the maintenance of suits against it in the courts of the state, is to beg the question to be decided. For the terms "present" or "presence" are used merely to symbolize those activities of the corporation's agent within the state which courts will deem to be sufficient to satisfy the demands of due process. . . . Those demands may be met by such contacts of the corporation with the state of the forum as make it reasonable, in the context of our federal system of government, to require the corporation to defend the particular suit which is brought there. An "estimate of the inconveniences" which would result to the corporation from a trial away from its "home" or principal place of business is relevant in this connection. . . .

While it has been held, in cases on which appellant relies, that continuous activity of some sorts within a state is not enough to support the demand that the corporation be amenable to suits unrelated to that activity, . . . there have been instances in which the continuous corporate operations within a state were thought so substantial and of such a nature as to justify suit against it on causes of action arising from dealings entirely distinct from those activities. . . .

Finally, although the commission of some single or occasional acts of the corporate agent in a state sufficient to impose an obligation or liability on the corporation has not been thought to confer upon the state authority to enforce it, *Rosenberg Bros. & Co. v. Curtis Brown Co.*, 260 U.S. 516, other such acts, because of their nature and quality and the circumstances of their commission, may be deemed sufficient to render the corporation liable to suit. Cf. *Kane v. New Jersey*, 242 U.S. 160; *Hess v. Pawloski, supra; Young v. Masci, supra.* True, some of the decisions holding the corporation amenable to suit have been supported by resort to the legal fiction that it has given its consent to service and suit, consent being implied from its presence in the state through the acts of its authorized agents. . . . But more realistically it may be said that those authorized acts were of such a nature as to justify the fiction. . . .

It is evident that the criteria by which we mark the boundary line between those activities which justify the subjection of a corporation to suit, and those which do not, cannot be simply mechanical or quantitative. The test is not merely, as has sometimes been suggested, whether the activity, which the corporation has seen fit to procure through its agents in another state, is a little more or a little less. . . . Whether due process is satisfied must depend rather upon the quality and nature of the activity in relation to the fair and orderly administration of the laws which it was the purpose of the due process clause to insure. That clause does not contemplate that a state may make binding a judgment *in personam* against an individual or corporate defendant with which the state has no contacts, ties, or relations. . . .

But to the extent that a corporation exercises the privilege of conducting activities within a state, it enjoys the benefits and protection of the laws of that state. The exercise of that privilege may give rise to obligations, and, so far as those obligations arise out of or are connected with the activities within the state, a procedure which requires the corporation to respond to a suit brought to enforce them can, in most instances, hardly be said to be undue. . . .

Applying these standards, the activities carried on in behalf of appellant in the State of Washington were neither irregular nor casual. They were systematic and continuous throughout the years in question. They resulted in a large volume of interstate business, in the course of which appellant received the benefits and protection of the laws of the state, including the right to resort to the courts for the enforcement of its rights. The obligation which is here sued upon arose out of those very activities. It is evident that these operations establish sufficient contacts or ties with the state of the forum to make it reasonable and just, according to our traditional conception of fair play and substantial justice, to permit the state to enforce the obligations which appellant has incurred there. Hence we cannot say that the maintenance of the present suit in the State of Washington involves an unreasonable or undue procedure. . . .

NOTES AND QUESTIONS

1. *"General" Versus "Specific" Jurisdiction.* When a state asserts jurisdiction over a defendant on all claims against the defendant—whether or not related to the defendant's in-state activity—the state is said to assert "general" or all-purpose

jurisdiction over the defendant. An individual defendant is subject to a state's general jurisdiction when the defendant is physically present and served within the state, or when the defendant is domiciled there. *International Shoe* reflects the attempt to find appropriate analogues for a corporation. A corporation is said to be subject to general jurisdiction in the state where it is "domiciled"—i.e., where it is incorporated or has its principal place of business—and "present" where it engages in substantial and extensive activity that manifests that "presence." When a state asserts jurisdiction over the defendant with regard to claims "arising from" the defendant's activity in the forum state, the state is said to be asserting "specific" jurisdiction. An example of specific jurisdiction is a nonresident motorist statute, such as the one in *Hess v. Pawloski*; another is the "implied consent" theory used to assert jurisdiction over a corporation when the claim "arises from" the corporation's activity in the state (as discussed in the earlier Note on Jurisdiction over Out-of-State Corporations). The analytic framework of general and specific jurisdiction was first clearly articulated by Professors Arthur T. von Mehren and Donald T. Trautman in *Jurisdiction to Adjudicate: A Suggested Analysis*, 79 Harv. L. Rev. 1121 (1966). *See also* Mary Twitchell, *The Myth of General Jurisdiction*, 101 Harv. L. Rev. 610 (1988).

International Shoe, which involved jurisdiction over an out-of-state corporation, addressed the constitutional limitations on the exercise of that jurisdiction. How does the analytical approach of the Supreme Court in *International Shoe* differ from that in *Pennoyer v. Neff* and *Hess v. Pawloski*? Is such an approach desirable? For an argument that the Court's approach to personal jurisdiction in *International Shoe* actually restricted states' abilities to exercise jurisdiction over out-of-state defendants in certain cases, and that a return to a territorial model of assessing personal jurisdiction such as that exemplified by *Pennoyer* would allow for a broader assertion of jurisdiction, simplify jurisdictional determinations, and be more predictable for potential defendants, *see* Cody J. Jacobs, *In Defense of Territorial Jurisdiction*, 85 U. Chi. L. Rev. 1589 (2018).

2. *International Shoe* interpreted Due Process to require that an absent defendant have certain "minimum contacts" with the forum state such that the maintenance of the suit does not offend "traditional notions of fair play and substantial justice." How can anyone quarrel with the notion that an assertion of jurisdiction should be "fair"?

Suppose you are counsel to the Local Shoe Company, a local company that wants to expand its business and sell its shoes nationwide. The company is worried that expanding its business activities might make it amenable to lawsuits in far-off places in the United States and particularly in some states that are known for large jury verdicts. Does *International Shoe* offer guidance for the Company (or for you as its counsel) as to how it should structure its manufacturing and sales activity? Did the preexisting jurisdictional law offer clearer, more predictable rules?

3. How would you articulate the Court's test for jurisdiction? What is the relationship between the defendant's forum-state activities and the fairness of asserting jurisdiction? Is evaluation of the "quality and nature" of the defendant's activities in the forum state a means of assessing the litigation burden of defending in that state? Is it also intended as a means of determining the forum state's interest in adjudicating the controversy? How do you understand the Court's suggestion that

the "quality and nature of the activity" of the defendant should be considered in relation to "the fair and orderly administration of the laws which it was the purpose of the due process clause to insure"?

4. Justice Black, in a separate concurrence in *International Shoe*, argued that Washington plainly had jurisdiction because it had the constitutional power to tax the company's activities in the state:

> I believe that the Federal Constitution leaves to each State, without any "ifs" or "buts," a power to tax and to open the doors of its courts for its citizens to sue corporations whose agents do business in those States. Believing that the Constitution gave the States that power, I think it a judicial deprivation to condition its exercise upon this Court's notion of "fair play," however appealing that term may be.

326 U.S. at 324–325. Do you agree?

5. There are generally two distinct inquiries that are part of ascertaining whether jurisdiction exists over a defendant. The first is whether the state authorizes an assertion of jurisdiction, which could be either by a common law rule or a statutory basis. The second inquiry is whether the state's assertion of jurisdiction is consistent with constitutional Due Process. The *International Shoe* decision deals only with the latter inquiry.

6. In each of the following examples, assume that the facts concerning the International Shoe Company are the same as stated in the *International Shoe* decision with the following variations. Also assume that the State of Washington would assert jurisdiction in each of the cases as a matter of state law. Would such an assertion of jurisdiction be constitutional in each instance? Explain your answer.

a. A Washington woman sues the International Shoe Company in the state court of Washington for: (1) breach of contract for failure to deliver shoes that she ordered from one of the salespeople who took her order; (2) negligence and breach of warranty for defective shoes that have caused her serious physical injury.

b. A California woman who ordered the shoes from the salespeople in Washington while she was on a visit to the State of Washington is attempting to sue the company in a Washington court for injuries she suffered in Washington.

c. A California woman bought shoes from the International Shoe Company in California. In this example, both the breach and injury occur in *California*, but she sues, as in example a., for breach of contract and/or tortious injury in the courts of Washington. (The International Shoe Company engages in the same activities in California as it does in Washington, but for some reason, the California plaintiff chooses to sue in Washington.)

7. As the above examples illustrate, the claim being sued on sometimes is related to the defendant's activity in the forum state and sometimes it is not. Does the connection (or lack of connection) between the claim being asserted and the defendant's activity in the forum state have a bearing on the fairness of asserting such jurisdiction? How so?

B.   COURTS' POWER TO HEAR ALL CLAIMS AGAINST A DEFENDANT: ALL-PURPOSE JURISDICTION

1.   General Jurisdiction

a.   Introduction

The traditional bases of jurisdiction discussed earlier in this chapter—presence, domicile, and consent—provided for the assertion of authority over *any claim*, whether or not related to defendant's activities in the forum state. This type of jurisdiction is referred to as *case all-purpose jurisdiction*. In the context of power over out-of-state corporations, this application of the minimum contacts framework is referred to as *general jurisdiction*. You will recall that a corporation, like an individual, was held to be subject to jurisdiction wherever it was domiciled—its place of incorporation—or "present." "Corporate presence" was said to exist wherever the corporation had "systematic and continuous activities"—often referred to as "doing business" jurisdiction. A number of states, such as Florida and New York, provided for general jurisdiction as a statutory matter:

> Fla. Stat. Ann. §48.193(2): "A defendant who is engaged in substantial and not isolated activity within this state, whether such activity is wholly interstate, intrastate, or otherwise, is subject to the jurisdiction of the courts of this state, whether or not the claim arises from that activity."
>
> N.Y. C.P.L.R. §301: "A court may exercise such jurisdiction over persons, property or status as might have been exercised heretofore."

In general jurisdiction cases involving a corporation, a first issue to be determined was whether the corporation met the test of "systematic or continuous activities" under state law, or in the case of the statute, satisfied the statute on the particular facts. The second issue was whether the assertion of jurisdiction was consistent with Due Process. With the *International Shoe* decision, the Due Process "minimum contacts" test became the relevant inquiry for both general as well as specific jurisdiction, although application of the test was necessarily different for the type of unrelated claim that characterizes general jurisdiction.

b.   History

In one of the first general jurisdiction cases to reach the Supreme Court, *Perkins v. Benguet Consolidated Mining Co.*, 342 U.S. 437 (1952), a nonresident of Ohio brought suit in Ohio against a mining company of the Philippines to recover certain dividends and damages as a result of the company's failure to issue her stock certificates. The company's operations in the Philippines had been halted during occupation of the Philippines by the Japanese during World War II, and many of the company's operations were conducted in Ohio during that period. The claims asserted did not relate to the activities of the corporation in Ohio. The Supreme Court addressed competing contentions from the parties that federal Due Process required the Ohio courts to take jurisdiction and that federal Due Process prohibited the Ohio courts from acting. As to the former contention, the Court found that the "suggestion that federal due process *compels* the State to open its courts . . . has no substance." As to the latter, the Court held that, because the company carried on "continuous and systematic" activities in Ohio, Ohio would not violate federal Due Process if it were to decide to take jurisdiction.

The Supreme Court did not take another general jurisdiction case until 30 years later, in *Helicopteros Nacionales de Colombia S.A. v. Hall*, 466 U.S. 408 (1984). The defendant, Helicol, was a Colombian corporation with its principal place of business in Bogota. Helicol provided helicopter transportation for companies in South America. One of its helicopters crashed in Peru and four U.S. citizens were killed. Representatives of the four decedents initiated wrongful death actions against, *inter alia*, Helicol, alleging jurisdiction on the basis of Helicol's "continuous and systematic contacts" with Texas. These included: Helicol sending its CEO to Texas to negotiate the terms of the deal that ultimately resulted in the crash (although the contract was signed in Peru), sourcing 80 percent of its fleet of helicopters from Texas for a seven-year period, and purchasing millions of dollars' worth of spare parts from Texas-based Bell Helicopter over the years. When the case reached the Texas Supreme Court, it upheld jurisdiction, and the Supreme Court granted certiorari.

Because the plaintiffs had conceded that the claims against Helicol did not "arise out of" and were not related to Helicol's activities within Texas, the Court considered only whether Helicol's contacts with the State of Texas could be characterized as "continuous and systematic general business contacts" so as to justify the assertion of general jurisdiction. The Texas Supreme Court had relied on the regular purchases of helicopters and other equipment in Texas, and on the related training trips, to justify the assertion of jurisdiction. However, the Supreme Court of the United States disagreed, holding that "mere purchases, even if occurring at regular intervals, are not enough to warrant a State's assertion of *in personam* jurisdiction over a nonresident corporation in a cause of action not related to those purchase transactions," and characterizing the training trips as "a part of the package of goods and services purchased by Helicol."

In dissent, Justice Brennan criticized the majority for failing to consider that "[t]he vast expansion of our national economy during the past several decades has provided the primary rationale for expanding the permissible reach of a State's jurisdiction under the Due Process Clause." Given that recent business growth and diversification had led to more foreign companies engaging in U.S. transactions, he wrote, "it has become both necessary and . . . desirable to allow the States more leeway in bringing the activities of these nonresident corporations within the scope of their respective jurisdictions." Justice Brennan also criticized the majority for not considering specific jurisdiction. (He did not agree that the plaintiffs had conceded that the cause of action did not "arise of out" Helicol's contacts with Texas.) For Justice Brennan, specific jurisdiction was applicable whenever the cause of action arises out of or "relates to" the contacts between the defendant and the forum. In his view, Helicol's contacts with Texas — the contract negotiations, its purchases of the aircraft that was involved in the crash, and the fact that the pilot whose negligence allegedly caused the crash was trained in Texas — were contacts between Helicol and the forum that directly related to the negligence alleged in the complaint.

Although the Supreme Court in *Helicopteros* found the assertion of general jurisdiction unconstitutional, the fact-specific inquiry as to what level of "continuous and systematic contacts" would suffice created much uncertainty, leading to divergent and inconsistent results, and gave rise to opportunity for broad forum shopping. Moreover, multinational corporations with offices and/or various levels of activity in the United States were often found to be "doing business" and subject to suit on claims that had no relationship to their activities in this country, giving rise to substantial criticism abroad.

In a pair of decisions in 2011 and 2014, the Supreme Court upended decades of general jurisdiction case law. The first decision was *Goodyear Dunlop Tires Operations, S.A. v. Brown*, 564 U.S. 915 (2011). The case arose out of a bus accident in France that injured several members of a North Carolina soccer team. Claiming that a defective tire caused the accident, plaintiffs brought suit in a North Carolina state court against Goodyear and three of its foreign subsidiaries. The state court upheld jurisdiction on the basis that thousands of tires manufactured by the defendants were shipped into North Carolina (albeit through distributors), and that the defendants "on a continuous and systematic basis caused [these] tires to be sent into the United States for sale," and further that defendants "knew or should have known" that such distribution would result in tires being sent to North Carolina. The state appellate court affirmed.

The Supreme Court granted certiorari on the question of whether these sales could be used to support the exercise of *general jurisdiction*. The Court answered no. However, Justice Ginsburg — writing for a unanimous Court — went further, ultimately re-formulating the standards for exercising general jurisdiction across the board. She wrote, "A court may assert general jurisdiction over foreign (sister-state or foreign-country) corporations to hear any and all claims against them when their affiliations with the State are so 'continuous and systematic' as to render them essentially at home in the forum State." Although the Court failed to specify what it meant by "at home," or which fora might qualify, the Court analogized the "paradigm" forum for general jurisdiction over a corporation with the domicile of a natural person: "For an individual, the paradigm forum for the exercise of general jurisdiction is the individual's domicile; for a corporation, it is an equivalent place, one in which the corporation is fairly regarded as at home," identifying domicile, place of incorporation, and principal place of business as "paradigm" bases for general jurisdiction. Referring to *Perkins* in this framework, Justice Ginsburg noted that "Ohio was the corporation's principal, if temporary, place of business," making it a "textbook case of general jurisdiction."

In *Goodyear*, the Court clearly signaled that general jurisdiction was to be curtailed; however, the extent of the limitations and the acceptable bases of jurisdiction post-*Goodyear* were not spelled out. Following *Goodyear*, courts divided on the crucial question of whether any role remained for the traditional concept of "corporate presence" based on the corporation's "continuous and systematic contacts with the forum." However, it did not take long for the Court to deliver further guidance. In 2014, the Court revisited general jurisdiction in a case in which it was not even necessary to address the issue.

c.   The End of an Era

Daimler AG v. Bauman → not applied to individual ; until Burham (P.104)

571 U.S. 117, 134 S.Ct. 746 (2014)

JUSTICE GINSBURG delivered the opinion of the Court.

This case concerns the authority of a court in the United States to entertain a claim brought by foreign plaintiffs against a foreign defendant based on events occurring entirely outside the United States. The litigation commenced in 2004, when twenty-two Argentinian residents filed a complaint in the United States District Court for the Northern District of California against DaimlerChrysler Aktiengesellschaft (Daimler),[2] a German public stock company, headquartered in Stuttgart, that manufactures Mercedes-Benz vehicles in Germany. The complaint alleged that during Argentina's 1976–1983 "Dirty War," Daimler's Argentinian subsidiary, Mercedes-Benz Argentina (MB Argentina) collaborated with state security forces to kidnap, detain, torture, and kill certain MB Argentina workers, among them, plaintiffs or persons closely related to plaintiffs. Damages for the alleged human-rights violations were sought from Daimler under the laws of the United States, California, and Argentina. Jurisdiction over the lawsuit was predicated on the California contacts of Mercedes-Benz USA, LLC (MBUSA), a subsidiary of Daimler incorporated in Delaware with its principal place of business in New Jersey. MBUSA distributes Daimler-manufactured vehicles to independent dealerships throughout the United States, including California.

The question presented is whether the Due Process Clause of the Fourteenth Amendment precludes the District Court from exercising jurisdiction over Daimler in this case, given the absence of any California connection to the atrocities, perpetrators, or victims described in the complaint. Plaintiffs invoked the court's general or all-purpose jurisdiction. California, they urge, is a place where Daimler may be sued on any and all claims against it, wherever in the world the claims may arise. For example, as plaintiffs' counsel affirmed, under the proffered jurisdictional theory, if a Daimler-manufactured vehicle overturned in Poland, injuring a Polish driver and passenger, the injured parties could maintain a design defect suit in California. . . . Exercises of personal jurisdiction so exorbitant, we hold, are barred by due process constraints on the assertion of adjudicatory authority.

In *Goodyear Dunlop Tires Operations, S.A. v. Brown*, 131 S.Ct. 2846 (2011), we addressed the distinction between general or all-purpose jurisdiction, and specific or conduct-linked jurisdiction. As to the former, we held that a court may assert jurisdiction over a foreign corporation "to hear any and all claims against [it]" only when the corporation's affiliations with the State in which suit is brought are so constant and pervasive "as to render [it] essentially at home in the forum State." *Id.* at 2851. Instructed by *Goodyear*, we conclude Daimler is not "at home" in California, and cannot be sued there for injuries plaintiffs attribute to MB Argentina's conduct in Argentina.

---

2. Daimler was restructured in 2007 and is now known as Daimler AG. No party contends that any postsuit corporate reorganization bears on our disposition of this case. This opinion refers to members of the Daimler corporate family by the names current at the time plaintiffs filed suit.

I

In 2004, plaintiffs (respondents here) filed suit in the United States District Court for the Northern District of California, alleging that MB Argentina collaborated with Argentinian state security forces to kidnap, detain, torture, and kill plaintiffs and their relatives during the military dictatorship in place there from 1976 through 1983, a period known as Argentina's "Dirty War.". . . The incidents recounted in the complaint center on MB Argentina's plant in Gonzalez Catan, Argentina; no part of MB Argentina's alleged collaboration with Argentinian authorities took place in California or anywhere else in the United States.

Plaintiffs' operative complaint names only one corporate defendant: Daimler, the petitioner here. Plaintiffs seek to hold Daimler vicariously liable for MB Argentina's alleged malfeasance. Daimler is a German [public stock company] that manufactures Mercedes-Benz vehicles in Germany and has its headquarters in Stuttgart. At times relevant to this case, MB Argentina was a subsidiary wholly owned by Daimler's predecessor in interest.

Daimler moved to dismiss the action for want of personal jurisdiction. Opposing the motion, plaintiffs submitted declarations and exhibits purporting to demonstrate the presence of Daimler itself in California. Alternatively, plaintiffs maintained that jurisdiction over Daimler could be founded on the California contacts of MBUSA, a distinct corporate entity that, according to plaintiffs, should be treated as Daimler's agent for jurisdictional purposes.

MBUSA, an indirect subsidiary of Daimler, is a Delaware limited liability corporation. MBUSA serves as Daimler's exclusive importer and distributor in the United States, purchasing Mercedes-Benz automobiles from Daimler in Germany, then importing those vehicles, and ultimately distributing them to independent dealerships located throughout the Nation. Although MBUSA's principal place of business is in New Jersey, MBUSA has multiple California-based facilities, including a regional office in Costa Mesa, a Vehicle Preparation Center in Carson, and a Classic Center in Irvine. According to the record developed below, MBUSA is the largest supplier of luxury vehicles to the California market. In particular, over 10% of all sales of new vehicles in the United States take place in California, and MBUSA's California sales account for 2.4% of Daimler's worldwide sales.

The relationship between Daimler and MBUSA is delineated in a General Distributor Agreement, which sets forth requirements for MBUSA's distribution of Mercedes-Benz vehicles in the United States. That agreement established MBUSA as an "independent contracto[r]" that "buy[s] and sell[s] [vehicles] . . . as an independent business for [its] own account.". . . The agreement "does not make [MBUSA] . . . a general or special agent, partner, joint venturer or employee of DaimlerChrysler or any DaimlerChrysler Group Company"; MBUSA "ha[s] no authority to make binding obligations for or act on behalf of DaimlerChrysler or any DaimlerChrysler Group Company.". . .

After allowing jurisdictional discovery on plaintiffs' agency allegations, the District Court granted Daimler's motion to dismiss. Daimler's own affiliations with California, the court first determined, were insufficient to support the exercise of all-purpose jurisdiction over the corporation. . . . Next, the court declined to attribute MBUSA's California contacts to Daimler on an agency theory, concluding that plaintiffs failed to demonstrate that MBUSA acted as Daimler's agent. . . .

The Ninth Circuit at first affirmed the District Court's judgment. Addressing solely the question of agency, the Court of Appeals held that plaintiffs had not shown the existence of an agency relationship of the kind that might warrant attribution of MBUSA's contacts to Daimler. *Bauman v. DaimlerChrysler Corp.*, 579 F.3d 1088, 1096–1097 (2009). Judge Reinhardt dissented. In his view, the agency test was satisfied and considerations of "reasonableness" did not bar the exercise of jurisdiction. *Id.* at 1098–1106. Granting plaintiffs' petition for rehearing, the panel withdrew its initial opinion and replaced it with one authored by Judge Reinhardt, which elaborated on reasoning he initially expressed in dissent. *Bauman v. Daimler-Chrysler Corp.*, 644 F.3d 909 (C.A.9 2011).

Daimler petitioned for rehearing and rehearing en banc, urging that the exercise of personal jurisdiction over Daimler could not be reconciled with this Court's decision in *Goodyear Dunlop Tires Operations, S.A. v.* Brown. . . . Over the dissent of eight judges, the Ninth Circuit denied Daimler's petition. See *Bauman v. DaimlerChrysler Corp.*, 676 F.3d 774 (2011) (O'Scannlain, J., dissenting from denial of rehearing en banc).

We granted certiorari to decide whether, consistent with the Due Process Clause of the Fourteenth Amendment, Daimler is amenable to suit in California courts for claims involving only foreign plaintiffs and conduct occurring entirely abroad. . . .

II

[margin annotation: Federal Rule of Civil Procedure]

[margin annotation: 84(k)(1)(A)]

← Federal courts ordinarily follow state law in determining the bounds of their jurisdiction over persons. . . . Under California's long-arm statute, California state courts may exercise personal jurisdiction "on any basis not inconsistent with the Constitution of this state or of the United States." Cal. Civ. Proc. Code Ann. § 410.10 (West 2004). California's long-arm statute allows the exercise of personal jurisdiction to the full extent permissible under the U.S. Constitution. We therefore inquire whether the Ninth Circuit's holding comports with the limits imposed by federal due process. . . .

III

In *Pennoyer v. Neff*, 95 U.S. 714 (1878), decided shortly after the enactment of the Fourteenth Amendment, the Court held that a tribunal's jurisdiction over persons reaches no farther than the geographic bounds of the forum. *See id.* at 720 ("The authority of every tribunal is necessarily restricted by the territorial limits of the State in which it is established."). . . . In time, however, that strict territorial approach yielded to a less rigid understanding, spurred by "changes in the technology of transportation and communication, and the tremendous growth of interstate business activity." *Burnham v. Superior Court of Cal., County of Marin*, 495 U.S. 604, 617 (1990) (opinion of SCALIA, J.).

"The canonical opinion in this area remains *International Shoe* in which we held that a State may authorize its courts to exercise personal jurisdiction over an out-of-state defendant if the defendant has 'certain minimum contacts with [the State] such that the maintenance of the suit does not offend "traditional notions of fair play and substantial justice." ' " *Goodyear*, 131 S.Ct. at 2853 (quoting *International Shoe*, 326 U.S. at 316). Following *International Shoe*, "the relationship among the defendant, the forum, and the litigation, rather than the mutually exclusive sovereignty of the States on which the rules of *Pennoyer* rest, became the central concern of the inquiry into personal jurisdiction." *Shaffer*, 433 U.S. at 204. . . .

International Shoe distinguished between . . . exercises of specific jurisdiction, as just described, and . . . situations where a foreign corporation's "continuous corporate operations within a state [are] so substantial and of such a nature as to justify suit against it on causes of action arising from dealings entirely distinct from those activities." 326 U.S. at 318. As we have since explained, "[a] court may assert general jurisdiction over foreign (sister-state or foreign-country) corporations to hear any and all claims against them when their affiliations with the State are so 'continuous and systematic' as to render them essentially at home in the forum State." *Goodyear*, 131 S.Ct. at 2851; *see id.* at 2853–2854; *Helicopteros*, 466 U.S. at 414, n. 9. . . .

As is evident from *Perkins*, *Helicopteros*, and *Goodyear*, general and specific jurisdiction have followed markedly different trajectories post-*International Shoe*. Specific jurisdiction has been cut loose from *Pennoyer*'s sway, but we have declined to stretch general jurisdiction beyond limits traditionally recognized. As this Court has increasingly trained on the "relationship among the defendant, the forum, and the litigation," *Shaffer*, 433 U.S. at 201, *i.e.*, specific jurisdiction,[10] general jurisdiction has come to occupy a less dominant place in the contemporary scheme.[12]

IV

With this background, we turn directly to the question whether Daimler's affiliations with California are sufficient to subject it to the general (all-purpose) personal jurisdiction of that State's courts. In the proceedings below, the parties agreed on, or failed to contest, certain points we now take as given. Plaintiffs have never attempted to fit this case into the *specific* jurisdiction category. Nor did plaintiffs challenge on appeal the District Court's holding that Daimler's own contacts with California were, by themselves, too sporadic to justify the exercise of general jurisdiction. While plaintiffs ultimately persuaded the Ninth Circuit to impute MBUSA's California contacts to Daimler on an agency theory, at no point have they maintained that MBUSA is an alter ego of Daimler.

Daimler, on the other hand, failed to object below to plaintiffs' assertion that the California courts could exercise all-purpose jurisdiction over MBUSA. . . . We will assume then, for purposes of this decision only, that MBUSA qualifies as at home in California.

A

In sustaining the exercise of general jurisdiction over Daimler, the Ninth Circuit relied on an agency theory, determining that MBUSA acted as Daimler's agent for jurisdictional purposes and then attributing MBUSA's California contacts to

---

10. Remarkably, Justice SOTOMAYOR treats specific jurisdiction as though it were barely there. . . .

12. As the Court made plain in Goodyear and repeats here, general jurisdiction requires affiliations " 'so continuous and systematic' as to render [the foreign corporation] essentially at home in the forum State." 131 S.Ct. at 2851, *i.e.*, comparable to a domestic enterprise in that State.

Daimler. The Ninth Circuit's agency analysis derived from Circuit precedent considering principally whether the subsidiary "performs services that are sufficiently important to the foreign corporation that if it did not have a representative to perform them, the corporation's own officials would undertake to perform substantially similar services." 644 F.3d at 920 [citation omitted].

This Court has not yet addressed whether a foreign corporation may be subjected to a court's general jurisdiction based on the contacts of its in-state subsidiary. Daimler argues, and several Courts of Appeals have held, that a subsidiary's jurisdictional contacts can be imputed to its parent only when the former is so dominated by the latter as to be its alter ego. The Ninth Circuit adopted a less rigorous test based on what it described as an "agency" relationship. . . . But we need not pass judgment on invocation of an agency theory in the context of general jurisdiction, for in no event can the appeals court's analysis be sustained.

The Ninth Circuit's agency finding rested primarily on its observation that MBUSA's services were "important" to Daimler, as gauged by Daimler's hypothetical readiness to perform those services itself if MBUSA did not exist. Formulated this way, the inquiry into importance stacks the deck, for it will always yield a pro-jurisdiction answer: "Anything a corporation does through an independent contractor, subsidiary, or distributor is presumably something that the corporation would do 'by other means' if the independent contractor, subsidiary, or distributor did not exist." 676 F.3d at 777 (O'Scannlain, J., dissenting from denial of rehearing en banc). The Ninth Circuit's agency theory thus appears to subject foreign corporations to general jurisdiction whenever they have an in-state subsidiary or affiliate, an outcome that would sweep beyond even the "sprawling view of general jurisdiction" we rejected in *Goodyear*. 131 S.Ct. at 2856.[15]

B

Even if we were to assume that MBUSA is at home in California, and further to assume MBUSA's contacts are imputable to Daimler, there would still be no basis to subject Daimler to general jurisdiction in California, for Daimler's slim contacts with the State hardly render it at home there.

Goodyear made clear that only a limited set of affiliations with a forum will render a defendant amenable to all-purpose jurisdiction there. . . . Those affiliations have the virtue of being unique—that is, each ordinarily indicates only one place—as well as easily ascertainable. *Cf. Hertz Corp. v. Friend*, 559 U.S. 77, 94 (2010) ("Simple jurisdictional rules . . . promote greater predictability."). These bases afford plaintiffs recourse to at least one clear and certain forum in which a corporate defendant may be sued on any and all claims.

Goodyear did not hold that a corporation may be subject to general jurisdiction *only* in a forum where it is incorporated or has its principal place of business;

---

15. The Ninth Circuit's agency analysis also looked to whether the parent enjoys "the right to substantially control" the subsidiary's activities. *Bauman v. DaimlerChrysler Corp.*, 644 F.3d 909, 924 (2011). The Court of Appeals found the requisite "control" demonstrated by the General Distributor Agreement between Daimler and MBUSA, which gives Daimler the right to oversee certain of MBUSA's operations, even though that agreement expressly disavowed the creation of any agency relationship. Thus grounded, the separate inquiry into control hardly curtails the overbreadth of the Ninth Circuit's agency holding.

it simply typed those places paradigm all-purpose forums. Plaintiffs would have us look beyond the exemplar bases *Goodyear* identified, and approve the exercise of general jurisdiction in every State in which a corporation "engages in a substantial, continuous, and systematic course of business.". . . That formulation, we hold, is unacceptably grasping.

As noted . . . the words "continuous and systematic" were used in *International Shoe* to describe instances in which the exercise of *specific* jurisdiction would be appropriate. . . . Turning to all-purpose jurisdiction, in contrast, *International Shoe* speaks of "instances in which the continuous corporate operations within a state [are] so substantial and of such a nature as to justify suit . . . *on causes of action arising from dealings entirely distinct from those activities.*" *Id.* at 318 (emphasis added). . . . Accordingly, the inquiry under *Goodyear* is not whether a foreign corporation's in-forum contacts can be said to be in some sense "continuous and systematic," it is whether that corporation's "affiliations with the State are so 'continuous and systematic' as to render [it] essentially at home in the forum State." 131 S.Ct. at 2851.[19]

Here, neither Daimler nor MBUSA is incorporated in California, nor does either entity have its principal place of business there. If Daimler's California activities sufficed to allow adjudication of this Argentina-rooted case in California, the same global reach would presumably be available in every other State in which MBUSA's sales are sizable. Such exorbitant exercises of all-purpose jurisdiction would scarcely permit out-of-state defendants "to structure their primary conduct with some minimum assurance as to where that conduct will and will not render them liable to suit." *Burger King Corp.*, 471 U.S. at 472 (internal quotation marks omitted).

It was therefore error for the Ninth Circuit to conclude that Daimler, even with MBUSA's contacts attributed to it, was at home in California, and hence subject to suit there on claims by foreign plaintiffs having nothing to do with anything that occurred or had its principal impact in California.[20]

---

19. We do not foreclose the possibility that in an exceptional case, *see, e.g., Perkins* . . . a corporation's operations in a forum other than its formal place of incorporation or principal place of business may be so substantial and of such a nature as to render the corporation at home in that State. But this case presents no occasion to explore that question, because Daimler's activities in California plainly do not approach that level. It is one thing to hold a corporation answerable for operations in the forum State . . . quite another to expose it to suit on claims having no connection whatever to the forum State.

20. To clarify in light of Justice SOTOMAYOR's opinion concurring in the judgment, the general jurisdiction inquiry does not "focu[s] solely on the magnitude of the defendant's in-state contacts.". . . General jurisdiction instead calls for an appraisal of a corporation's activities in their entirety, nationwide and worldwide. A corporation that operates in many places can scarcely be deemed at home in all of them. Otherwise, "at home" would be synonymous with "doing business" tests framed before specific jurisdiction evolved in the United States. . . .

Justice SOTOMAYOR would reach the same result, but for a different reason. . . . Justice SOTOMAYOR would hold that the exercise of general jurisdiction over Daimler would be unreasonable "in the unique circumstances of this case.". . . When a corporation is genuinely at home in the forum State, however, any second-step inquiry would be superfluous.

. . . Justice SOTOMAYOR's proposal to import Asahi's "reasonableness" check into the general jurisdiction determination [would] compound the jurisdictional inquiry. . . . Imposing such a checklist in cases of general jurisdiction would hardly promote the efficient disposition of an issue that should be resolved expeditiously at the outset of litigation.

C

Finally, the transnational context of this dispute bears attention. . . .

The Ninth Circuit . . . paid little heed to the risks to international comity its expansive view of general jurisdiction posed. Other nations do not share the uninhibited approach to personal jurisdiction advanced by the Court of Appeals in this case. In the European Union, for example, a corporation may generally be sued in the nation in which it is "domiciled," a term defined to refer only to the location of the corporation's "statutory seat," "central administration," or "principal place of business." European Parliament and Council Reg. 1215/2012, Arts. 4(1), and 63(1), 2012 O.J. (L. 351) 7, 18. . . . The Solicitor General informs us, in this regard, that "foreign governments' objections to some domestic courts' expansive views of general jurisdiction have in the past impeded negotiations of international agreements on the reciprocal recognition and enforcement of judgments.". . . Considerations of international rapport thus reinforce our determination that subjecting Daimler to the general jurisdiction of courts in California would not accord with the "fair play and substantial justice" due process demands. *International Shoe*, 326 U.S. at 316 (quoting *Milliken v. Meyer*, 311 U.S. 457, 463 (1940)).

For the reasons stated, the judgment of the United States Court of Appeals for the Ninth Circuit is *Reversed.*

Justice SOTOMAYOR, concurring in the judgment.

I agree with the Court's conclusion that the Due Process Clause prohibits the exercise of personal jurisdiction over Daimler in light of the unique circumstances of this case. I concur only in the judgment, however, because I cannot agree with the path the Court takes to arrive at that result. . . .

The Court can and should decide this case on the far simpler ground that, no matter how extensive Daimler's contacts with California, that State's exercise of jurisdiction would be unreasonable given that the case involves foreign plaintiffs suing a foreign defendant based on foreign conduct, and given that a more appropriate forum is available. . . .

We identified the factors that bear on reasonableness in *Asahi Metal Industry Co. v. Superior Court of Cal., Solano Cty.*, 480 U.S. 102. . . .

The same considerations resolve this case. It involves Argentine plaintiffs suing a German defendant for conduct that took place in Argentina. Like the plaintiffs in *Asahi*, respondents have failed to show that it would be more convenient to litigate in California than in Germany, a sovereign with a far greater interest in resolving the dispute. *Asahi* thus makes clear that it would be unreasonable for a court in California to subject Daimler to its jurisdiction.

III

While the majority's decisional process is problematic enough, I fear that process leads it to an even more troubling result.

A

Until today, our precedents had established a straightforward test for general jurisdiction: Does the defendant have "continuous corporate operations within a state" that are "so substantial and of such a nature as to justify suit against it on causes of action arising from dealings entirely distinct from those activities. . . . In every case where we have applied this test, we have focused solely on the magnitude of the defendant's in-state contacts, not the relative magnitude of those contacts in comparison to the defendant's contacts with other States. . . .

Had the majority applied our settled approach, it would have had little trouble concluding that Daimler's California contacts rise to the requisite level, given the majority's assumption that MBUSA's contacts may be attributed to Daimler and given Daimler's concession that those contacts render MBUSA "at home" in California. Our cases have long stated the rule that a defendant's contacts with a forum State must be continuous, substantial, and systematic in order for the defendant to be subject to that State's general jurisdiction. See *Perkins*, 342 U.S. at 446. We offered additional guidance in *Goodyear*, adding the phrase "essentially at home" to our prior formulation of the rule. . . .

Under this standard, Daimler's concession that MBUSA is subject to general jurisdiction in California . . . should be dispositive. For if MBUSA's California contacts are so substantial and the resulting benefits to MBUSA so significant as to make MBUSA "at home" in California, the same must be true of Daimler when MBUSA's contacts and benefits are viewed as its own. Indeed, until a footnote in its brief before this Court, even Daimler did not dispute this conclusion for eight years of the litigation.

B

The majority today concludes otherwise. Referring to the "continuous and systematic" contacts inquiry that has been taught to generations of first-year law students as "unacceptably grasping," . . . the majority announces the new rule that in order for a foreign defendant to be subject to general jurisdiction, it must not only possess continuous and systematic contacts with a forum State, but those contacts must also surpass some unspecified level when viewed in comparison to the company's "nationwide and worldwide" activities. . . .

Neither of the majority's two rationales for this proportionality requirement is persuasive. First, the majority suggests that its approach is necessary for the sake of predictability. . . . But there is nothing unpredictable about a rule that instructs multinational corporations that if they engage in continuous and substantial contacts with more than one State, they will be subject to general jurisdiction in each one. The majority may not favor that rule as a matter of policy, but such disagreement does not render an otherwise routine test unpredictable.

Nor is the majority's proportionality inquiry any more predictable than the approach it rejects. If anything, the majority's approach injects an additional layer of uncertainty because a corporate defendant must now try to foretell a court's analysis as to both the sufficiency of its contacts with the forum State itself, as well as the relative sufficiency of those contacts in light of the company's operations elsewhere. Moreover, the majority does not even try to explain just how extensive the company's in-state contacts must be in the context of its global operations in order for general jurisdiction to be proper. . . .

Absent the predictability rationale, the majority's sole remaining justification for its proportionality approach is its unadorned concern for the consequences. "If Daimler's California activities sufficed to allow adjudication of this Argentina-rooted case in California," the majority laments, "the same global reach would presumably be available in every other State in which MBUSA's sales are sizable." *Ante* at 761.

The majority characterizes this result as "exorbitant," *ibid.*, but in reality it is an inevitable consequence of the rule of due process we set forth nearly 70 years ago, that there are "instances in which [a company's] continuous corporate operations within a state" are "so substantial and of such a nature as to justify suit against it on causes of action arising from dealings entirely distinct from those activities," *International Shoe*, 326 U.S. In the era of *International Shoe*, it was rare for a corporation to have such substantial nationwide contacts that it would be subject to general jurisdiction in a large number of States. Today, that circumstance is less rare. But that is as it should be. What has changed since *International Shoe* is not the due process principle of fundamental fairness but rather the nature of the global economy. Just as it was fair to say in the 1940's that an out-of-state company could enjoy the benefits of a forum State enough to make it "essentially at home" in the State, it is fair to say today that a multinational conglomerate can enjoy such extensive benefits in multiple forum States that it is "essentially at home" in each one.

In any event, to the extent the majority is concerned with the modern-day consequences of *International Shoe*'s conception of personal jurisdiction, there remain other judicial doctrines available to mitigate any resulting unfairness to large corporate defendants. Here, for instance, the reasonableness prong may afford petitioner relief. . . .

C

The majority's concern for the consequences of its decision should have led it the other way, because the rule that it adopts will produce deep injustice in at least four respects.

First, the majority's approach unduly curtails the States' sovereign authority to adjudicate disputes against corporate defendants who have engaged in continuous and substantial business operations within their boundaries. The majority does not dispute that a State can exercise general jurisdiction where a corporate defendant has its corporate headquarters, and hence its principal place of business within the State. . . . Yet it never explains why the State should lose that power when, as is increasingly common, a corporation "divide[s] [its] command and coordinating functions among officers who work at several different locations." *Id.* at 95–96, 130 S.Ct. 1181. Suppose a company divides its management functions equally among three offices in different States, with one office nominally deemed the company's corporate headquarters. If the State where the headquarters is located can exercise general jurisdiction, why should the other two States be constitutionally forbidden to do the same? Indeed, under the majority's approach, the result would be unchanged even if the company has substantial operations within the latter two States (and even if the company has no sales or other business operations in the first State). Put simply, the majority's rule defines the Due Process Clause so narrowly and arbitrarily as to contravene the States' sovereign prerogative to subject to judgment defendants who have manifested an unqualified "intention to benefit from and thus an intention to submit to the[ir] laws," *J. McIntyre*, 131 S.Ct. at 2787 (plurality opinion).

Second, the proportionality approach will treat small businesses unfairly in comparison to national and multinational conglomerates. Whereas a larger company will often be immunized from general jurisdiction in a State on account of its extensive contacts outside the forum, a small business will not be. For instance, the majority holds today that Daimler is not subject to general jurisdiction in California despite its multiple offices, continuous operations, and billions of dollars' worth of sales there. But imagine a small business that manufactures luxury vehicles principally targeting the California market and that has substantially all of its sales and operations in the State—even though those sales and operations may amount to one-thousandth of Daimler's. Under the majority's rule, that small business will be subject to suit in California on any cause of action involving any of its activities anywhere in the world, while its far more pervasive competitor, Daimler, will not be. That will be so even if the small business incorporates and sets up its headquarters elsewhere (as Daimler does), since the small business' California sales and operations would still predominate when "apprais[ed]" in proportion to its minimal "nationwide and worldwide" operations, *ante* at 762, n. 20.

Third, the majority's approach creates the incongruous result that an individual defendant whose only contact with a forum State is a one-time visit will be subject to general jurisdiction if served with process during that visit, *Burnham v. Superior Court of Cal., County of Marin*, 495 U.S. 604 (1990), but a large corporation that owns property, employs workers, and does billions of dollars' worth of business in the State will not be, simply because the corporation has similar contacts elsewhere (though the visiting individual surely does as well).

Finally, it should be obvious that the ultimate effect of the majority's approach will be to shift the risk of loss from multinational corporations to the individuals harmed by their actions. Under the majority's rule, for example, a parent whose child is maimed due to the negligence of a foreign hotel owned by a multinational conglomerate will be unable to hold the hotel to account in a single U.S. court, even if the hotel company has a massive presence in multiple States. . . . Similarly, a U.S. business that enters into a contract in a foreign country to sell its products to a multinational company there may be unable to seek relief in any U.S. court if the multinational company breaches the contract, even if that company has considerable operations in numerous U.S. forums. See, *e.g.*, *Walpex Trading Co. v. Yacimientos Petroliferos Fiscales Bolivianos*, 712 F.Supp. 383 (S.D.N.Y. 1989). Indeed, the majority's approach would preclude the plaintiffs in these examples from seeking recourse anywhere in the United States even if no other judicial system was available to provide relief. I cannot agree with the majority's conclusion that the Due Process Clause requires these results.

. . . Because I would reverse the Ninth Circuit's decision on the narrower ground that the exercise of jurisdiction over Daimler would be unreasonable in any event, I respectfully concur in the judgment only.

NOTES AND QUESTIONS

1. *A New Era for General Jurisdiction.* The Supreme Court's *Daimler* decision confirmed what the Court had hinted at in its earlier *Goodyear* opinion—that a corporation must be sued "essentially at home" unless the claims being asserted

relate to the corporation's activity in the forum state. Together, the decisions put an end to an era of general jurisdiction jurisprudence that, as Justice Sotomayor put it, "has been taught to generations of first-year law students." Why do you think Justice Ginsburg and the majority reject the traditional "systematic and continuous activities" standard that had been consistently used in the lower courts? What are the advantages of this "new" approach? Can you think of disadvantages?

Not surprisingly, there has been endless commentary on this sea change. For just a few examples *see* Linda J. Silberman, *The End of Another Era: Reflections on* Daimler *and Its Implications for Judicial Jurisdiction in the United States*, 19 Lewis & Clark L. Rev. 675 (2015); Richard D. Freer, *Some Specific Concerns with the New General Jurisdiction*, 15 Nev. L.J. 1161 (2015); Tanya J. Monestier, *Where Is Home Depot "At Home"?:* Daimler v. Bauman *and the End of Doing Business Jurisdiction*, 66 Hastings L.J. 233 (2014); Edward D. Cavanagh, *General Jurisdiction 2.0: The Updating and Uprooting of the Corporate Presence Doctrine*, 68 Me. L. Rev. 287 (2016); Walter W. Heiser, *General Jurisdiction in the Place of Incorporation: An Artificial "Home" for an Artificial Person*, 53 Hous. L. Rev. 631 (2016).

2. *The EU Comparison.* Justice Ginsburg and the Court apparently believe that specific jurisdiction has come to play the dominant role in contemporary jurisdiction and that general jurisdiction is less significant. The opinion notes that the European Union (as well as many other countries) limits general jurisdiction over a corporation to its statutory seat, central administration, or principal place of business. For a discussion of jurisdiction in the European Union, *see* pp. 217–222, *infra*. However, the Court may have overlooked the lack of convergence on specific jurisdiction between the United States and other countries. In the United States, for example, the place of injury may not be sufficient for specific jurisdiction in the absence of purposeful activity on the part of the defendant. We will see later, by comparison, that special (i.e., specific) jurisdiction over a corporate defendant pursuant to the EU Recast is not hampered by Due Process concerns, and thus the court in the country of the place of injury is always available as a possible forum. Additionally, in the multiple defendant cases, the EU Recast permits jurisdiction over all defendants when any one of them is domiciled in the forum state, if the claims are so closely connected that they should be heard together in order to avoid the risk of irreconcilable judgments resulting from separate proceedings. Thus general jurisdiction may be of minimal importance in the European Union. But specific jurisdiction in the United States remains much narrower than in the European Union and may not compensate for the new restrictions on general jurisdiction. *See generally* Linda J. Silberman, *The End of Another Era: Reflections on* Daimler *and Its Implications for Judicial Jurisdiction in the United States*, 19 Lewis & Clark L. Rev. 675, 681–683 (2015).

3. *Paradigm Bases for General Jurisdiction?* Daimler makes clear that only a "limited set of affiliations" with the forum renders a defendant subject to "all-purpose" (i.e., general) jurisdiction. That "limited set" includes the place of incorporation and principal place of business, which the Court called "paradigm all-purpose forums." As the Court explained, "place of incorporation and principal place of business [are] paradigm . . . bases for general jurisdiction. . . . Those affiliations have the virtue of being unique—that is, each ordinarily indicates only one place—as well as easily ascertainable." 134 S.Ct. at 761. At the end of this line, the Court included a "*cf.*" citation to *Hertz Corp. v. Friend*, 559 U.S. 77 (2010). In *Hertz,*

the Court held that in the context of *diversity* jurisdiction (a basis of subject matter, rather than personal, jurisdiction), "principal place of business" refers to the place where a corporation's officers coordinate corporate activities—in other words, the corporation's "nerve center." Pre-*Daimler*, when "doing business" was a viable basis of jurisdiction, principal place of business and the related notion of the corporate "nerve center" did not typically feature in the general jurisdiction analysis. Yet the meaning of the Court's "*cf.*" citation is unclear. Did the Court mean to suggest that corporations are subject to general jurisdiction in the forum where its "nerve center" is located? What if this is different from both the state of incorporation and the state where most of its business activities take place? At least three lower courts have explicitly defined "principal place of business" for purposes of general jurisdiction as the corporate "nerve center," despite the fact that the *Daimler* Court did not once use the phrase "nerve center" in its opinion. *See Google Inc. v. Rockstar Consortium, U.S. LP*, 2014 WL 1571807 (N.D. Ca. Apr. 17, 2014) (rejecting defendants' assertion that Texas is its principal place of business because it does not meet the "nerve center" test from *Hertz*); *Flynn v. Hovensa, LLC*, 2014 WL 3375238 (W.D. Pa. July 3, 2014); *Allstate Ins. Co. v. Electrolux Home Products, Inc.*, 2014 WL 3615382 (N.D. Oh. July 18, 2014).

4. *The "Exceptional" Case for General Jurisdiction.* Regarding the "exceptional case" that permits general jurisdiction beyond the paradigmatic affiliations discussed above, the Court cited *Perkins* as the "textbook case." *Daimler*, 134 S.Ct. at 755. Consider what an exceptional case might be today. Would the "home" of the Boeing Corporation be an "exceptional case" outside the "textbook" example of *Perkins*? Although incorporated in Delaware and headquartered in Illinois, Boeing was founded in Washington State and is purported to have the world's largest building by volume located in that state. Is Boeing subject to general jurisdiction in Washington? *See* John T. Parry, *Introduction: Due Process, Borders, and the Qualities of Sovereignty—Some Thoughts on* J. McIntyre Machinery v. Nicastro, 16 Lewis & Clark L. Rev. 827, 829 n.6 (2012). What else might qualify as an "exceptional case"? *See* Judy M. Cornett & Michael H. Hoffheimer, *Good-bye Significant Contacts: General Personal Jurisdiction after* Daimler AG v. Bauman, 76 Ohio St. L.J. 101 (2015) (suggesting five situations that may qualify as "exceptional cases").

5. *Comparative Analysis Versus Quantum of Local Activity.* As mentioned above, *Daimler* provides little guidance when it comes to identifying the "exceptional case" that permits the exercise of general jurisdiction in fora outside the place of incorporation and principal place of business. One direction comes in a footnote, where the majority writes, "the general jurisdiction inquiry does not focus solely on the magnitude of the defendant's in-state contacts. General jurisdiction instead calls for an appraisal of a corporation's activities in their entirety, nationwide and worldwide." 134 S.Ct. at 762 n. 20. Such an inquiry requires comparing the magnitude of the foreign defendant's in-state activities to the magnitude of its activities elsewhere, rather than simply looking for "a particular quantum of local activity." *Id.* This leads Justice Sotomayor to suggest the majority "deems *Daimler* too big for general jurisdiction." *Id.* at 764 (Sotomayor, J., concurring) (internal quotations omitted). Is it fair that a plaintiff's right to sue locally depends on the proportion of a defendant's activities that take place abroad? Isn't such an approach likely to mean that foreign country defendants are unlikely to be subject to general jurisdiction in the United States? *But see In re Hellas Telecommunications (Lux) IISCA*, 524 B.R.

488 (S.D.N.Y. 2015) (finding general jurisdiction over German company Deutsche Bank AG by evaluating the bank's nationwide contacts under federal Bankruptcy Rule and determining that the bank was "at home" in the United States because it had a regional head office in New York with $5 billion in assets, a 1.6 million square foot office, 1,600 personnel, and 1,000 executives and maintained a substantial long-term presence in the United States not limited to the in-state operations of an affiliate as in *Daimler*). Some courts have taken footnote 20 to call for assessing in-state contacts as a percentage of global activities of the same type. *See, e.g., Wurth Adams Nut & Bolt Co. v. Seastrom Mfg. Co., Inc.*, 2015 WL 1530969 (D.N.J. Apr. 6, 2015) ("Although Defendant has continuing relationships with vendors in New Jersey, only 1.3% of Defendant's total vendors are located in New Jersey. Moreover, from 2010 through 2014, only 3.3% of Defendant's total revenue was derived from New Jersey customers") (internal citations omitted). Other courts have read the comparative inquiry to implicate *Daimler*'s suggestion that the "limited set of affiliations" appropriately giving rise to general jurisdiction "have the virtue of being unique—that is, each ordinarily indicates only one place." 134 S.Ct. at 760. A follow-up question is whether the alleged basis of jurisdiction would create grounds for general jurisdiction in many fora. *See, e.g., In re Roman Catholic Diocese of Albany, N.Y., Inc.*, 745 F.3d 30 (2d Cir. 2014) ("If the Diocese is at home in Vermont, it begs the question: how many homes might it have? . . . It is difficult to see where jurisdiction would end; foreign-state and foreign-country corporations could be found at home essentially anywhere. . . . The Supreme Court explicitly rejected such an expansion of general jurisdiction").

6. Daimler *and Venue Statutes.* In its 2017 decision in *BNSF Ry. Co. v. Tyrell*, 137 S. Ct. 1549 (2017), the Supreme Court affirmed that it meant what it said in *Daimler*. In the opinion below, the Montana Supreme Court had justified exercising general jurisdiction over BNSF Railway Co., incorporated in Delaware and with a principal place of business in Texas, because BNSF had 6 percent of its track, 5 percent of its workers, and generated 10 percent of its revenue in Montana. The Montana court's basis for deviating from *Daimler* was that §56 of the Federal Employer Liability Act (FELA) explicitly authorized state courts to exercise jurisdiction over railroads "doing business" within the state. The Court reversed on statutory grounds. According to a unanimous Court, the §56 formulation of "an action may be brought in a district court . . . in which the defendant shall be doing business" indicated §56 was merely a venue provision (see casebook at p. 252) rather than a conferral of personal jurisdiction. As such, it did not seek to address the jurisdictional standard.

7. Daimler *and Unincorporated Associations. Daimler* has also been taken to govern the jurisdictional analysis for entities other than corporations, with similar results. As stated in *Waldman v. Palestine Liberation Org.*, 835 F.3d 317 (2d Cir. 2016), "[W]hile *Daimler* involved corporations . . . *Daimler*'s reasoning was based on an analogy to general jurisdiction over individuals, and there is no reason to invent a different test for general personal jurisdiction depending on whether the defendant is an individual, a corporation, or another entity."

8. *The Attribution/Imputation Issue.* In attempting to ascertain the "presence" of a defendant for general jurisdiction purposes under state law, questions have arisen when activity is conducted in the state by agents, representatives, or subsidiary companies. Various relationships have yielded different results in the case law—at least

partly a reflection of differences in state law. The general proposition is stated in an early Supreme Court case, *Cannon Mfg. Co. v. Cudahy Packing Co.*, 267 U.S. 333 (1925), which holds that jurisdiction over a parent company does not, standing alone, establish jurisdiction over a subsidiary company, and jurisdiction over the subsidiary is not equivalent to jurisdiction over a parent, unless the parent so controls and dominates the subsidiary to justify disregard of the latter's independent existence. As *Daimler* indicates, there is a Due Process element to the question.

The question presented in Daimler's petition for certiorari was "whether it violates Due Process for a court to exercise general personal jurisdiction over a foreign corporation based solely on the fact than an indirect corporate subsidiary performs services on behalf of the defendant in the forum state." (MBUSA was an "indirect corporate subsidiary" in that it was wholly owned by DaimlerChrysler North America Holding Corporation, a subsidiary directly owned by the Daimler parent corporation.) The Court of Appeals for the Ninth Circuit held that Mercedes, the California corporation, was to be treated as Daimler's agent because (a) Mercedes was performing services sufficiently important to Daimler that would be performed by other means if Mercedes did not exist; and (b) Daimler exercised some degree of control over Mercedes. The Supreme Court described that view as creating an "outcome that would sweep beyond even the sprawling view of general jurisdiction" it had previously rejected in *Goodyear*. The Court referred to other Court of Appeals cases that had adopted "alter ego" or narrower "agency" theories of imputation in the context of general jurisdiction, but indicated it need not address the issue here.

After *Daimler*, most courts have adopted a restrictive approach to imputation in the general jurisdiction context. *See, e.g., Viega Gmbh v. Eighth Judicial District Court*, 328 P.3d 1152 (Nev. 2014) (where neither the German parent company nor its U.S. subsidiary was incorporated or had its principal place of business in Nevada and there was no showing of a relationship with Nevada so continuous and systematic to be considered at home in Nevada, general jurisdiction could not lie); *Sonera Holding B.V. v. Çukurova Holding A.S.*, 750 F.3d 221 (2d Cir. 2014), *cert. denied*, 134 S.Ct. 2888 (2014) ("[E]ven assuming that the activities of Çukurova's affiliates can be ascribed to it for the purposes of a general jurisdictional analysis, Çukurova lacks sufficient contacts with New York to render it 'at home' there."). These cases show that *Daimler* made it more difficult to establish general jurisdiction by imputing jurisdictional contacts.

Imputation of a subsidiary's contacts to the parent for purpose of specific jurisdiction may be easier than for general jurisdiction. In *Daimler*, the Court dropped a footnote stating that "agency relationships . . . may be relevant to the existence of specific jurisdiction. . . . As such a corporation can purposefully avail itself of a forum by directing its agents or distributors to take action there." 134 S.Ct. at 759 n.13. In *In re Chinese-Manufactured Drywall Products Liability Litigation*, 753 F.3d 521 (5th Cir. 2014), the Court of Appeals for the Fifth Circuit held that a Chinese manufacturer of drywall was subject to jurisdiction in Louisiana and Florida based on sales in those states by its Chinese wholly owned subsidiary. The court concluded that the subsidiary's contacts could be imputed to the parent because the subsidiary used the parent's name and trademark, the subsidiary acted only to serve the parent, and the parent and subsidiary held themselves out as the same entity to customers.

For a more thorough discussion of these issues, generally, *see* Lonny Sheinkopf Hoffman, *The Case Against Vicarious Jurisdiction*, 152 U. Pa. L. Rev. 1023 (2004); Lea Brilmayer & Kathleen Paisley, *Personal Jurisdiction and Substantive Legal Relations: Corporations, Conspiracies, and Agency*, 74 Cal. L. Rev. 1 (1986); *see also* Lonny Hoffman, *Further Thinking About Vicarious Jurisdiction: Reflecting on* Goodyear Dunlop Tire Operations, S.A. v. Brown *and Looking Ahead to* DaimlerChrysler AG v. Bauman, 34 U. Pa. J. Int'l L.765 (2013).

     9. *Using Consent to Avoid* Daimler. Most states have statutes requiring that a corporation doing business in the state appoint a registered agent on whom process can be served. Some states, such as California, had interpreted their statute as merely authorization for service, whereas other states, such as New York, had held such registration to be consent to general jurisdiction. Even prior to *Daimler*, the issue arose whether a corporation's act of registering an agent under such a statute was constitutionally sufficient as a ground for a state's exercise of general jurisdiction and gave rise to conflicting decisions. *Compare Knowlton v. Allied Van Lines, Inc.*, 900 F.2d 1196 (8th Cir. 1990) (appointment of an agent for service of process under Minnesota's registration statute represents consent to jurisdiction in Minnesota with respect to any cause of action, and such consent is a valid basis of personal jurisdiction without resort to an analysis of minimum contacts) *with Wenche Siemer v. Learjet Acquisition Corp.*, 966 F.2d 179 (5th Cir. 1992) (foreign corporation that properly complies with Texas registration statute only consents to personal jurisdiction where there are sufficient minimum contacts and jurisdiction is otherwise constitutionally permissible); *Ratliff v. Cooper Laboratories, Inc.*, 444 F.2d 745, 748 (4th Cir. 1971) (the mere presence of agents in the state or even the regular flow of products shipped into a state by the agents is insufficient to confer general jurisdiction and principles of Due Process require a firmer foundation than mere compliance with state domestication statutes).

     Post-*Daimler*, the registration-as-consent statutes as a basis for general jurisdiction raise the question as to whether they overcome the requirement that a corporation be "at home" in the forum state to satisfy the Due Process requirements for general jurisdiction. Decisions on the point are split. *Compare Cooper Tire & Rubber Co. v. McCall*, __ S.E.2d __, 2021 WL 4268074, at *1 (Ga. Sept. 21, 2021) (interpreting the Georgia registration statute to authorize general jurisdiction and holding that it does not violate Due Process after *Daimler*) *with Aybar v. Aybar*, __ N.E.3d __, 2021 WL 4596367, at *6 (N.Y. Oct. 7, 2021) (reinterpreting prior precedent and holding that, "under existing New York law, a foreign corporation does not consent to general jurisdiction in this state merely by complying with the Business Corporation Law's registration provisions"); *Genuine Parts Co. v. Cepec*, 137 A.3d 123 (Del. 2016) (overruling prior precedent, finding that consent-by-registration to general jurisdiction violates Due Process, and interpreting Delaware's registration statute to establish consent to service only); *see also Brown v. Lockheed Martin Corp.*, 814 F.3d 619, 634, 640 (2d Cir. 2016) (interpreting Connecticut's registration statute as "designed to confer what can fairly be characterized as specific jurisdiction" but declining to rule on the constitutionality of consent-by-registration while noting that the issue creates "precisely the result that the Court so roundly rejected in *Daimler*"). For an insightful discussion of the issue and a comprehensive overview of all the state registration statutes, *see* Kevin D. Benish, Pennoyer*'s Ghost: Consent, Registration Statutes, and General Jurisdiction after* Daimler AG v. Bauman, 90 N.Y.U. L. Rev. 1609 (2015). *See also* Tanya Monestier, *Registration Statutes, General Jurisdiction,* *and the Fallacy of Consent*, 36 Cardozo L. Rev. 1343 (2015) (arguing that registering to do business pursuant to a statute does not amount to consent as the term is understood in the context of jurisdiction). For an argument that exercises of general jurisdiction based on consent-by-registration are still valid and a defense of their constitutionality, *see* Oscar G. Chase, *Consent to Judicial Jurisdiction: The Foundation of "Registration" Statutes*, 73 N.Y.U. Ann. Surv. Am. L. 159 (2018) (relying on consent as a viable basis of jurisdiction notwithstanding *Daimler*).

How should courts treat state corporate registration statutes that, prior to *Daimler*, had been construed to subject defendants to general jurisdiction? Even courts within the same district appear to disagree as to how *Daimler* should affect the interpretation of such statutes. *Compare Aetna Inc. v. Kurtzman Carson Consultants, LLC*, No. 18-470, 2019 WL 1440046 (E.D. Pa., Mar. 29, 2019) (finding the Third Circuit's pre-*Daimler* holding that Pennsylvania's registration statute creates general personal jurisdiction over foreign corporations remains good law despite *Daimler*) *with Sullivan v. A. W. Chesterton, Inc.* (*In re Asbestos Prods. Liab. Litig. No.*), 384 F. Supp. 3d 532 (E.D. Pa. 2019) (setting aside Third Circuit precedent to hold that Pennsylvania's registration statute can no longer be interpreted to provide for general personal jurisdiction over foreign corporations given the ruling in *Daimler*).

One factor that may emerge is whether the statute *explicitly* purports to confer general jurisdiction. *Compare Waite v. All Acquisition Corp.*, 901 F.3d 1307 (11th Cir. 2018) (holding that the plain language of Florida's registration statute does not specifically provide for general jurisdiction over a corporation, and thus the court could not exercise jurisdiction over a foreign corporation that was registered to do business in Florida but caused injury to the plaintiff in Massachusetts) *with Gorton v. Air & Liquid Sys. Corp.*, 303 F. Supp. 3d 278 (M.D. Pa. 2018) (asserting jurisdiction based on a Pennsylvania registration statute's explicit language conferring general jurisdiction).

2.   *Property-Based Jurisdiction*

Recall that in the discussion of *Pennoyer*, we distinguished between *in personam* jurisdiction, based on power over the defendant, and *in rem* or *quasi in rem* type I or II jurisdiction, based on power over property. Unlike *in personam* jurisdiction, which requires that the defendant be present in or have significant contacts with the forum, the latter types of jurisdiction traditionally required no more than that some property could be found and (in some instances) attached (seized) within the state.

The classic definition of the pure *in rem* action is found in Justice Holmes' opinion in *Tyler v. Judges of the Court of Registration*, 55 N.E. 812, 812–814 (Mass.), *aff'd*, 179 U.S. 405 (1900). In *Tyler*, plaintiff sought to enjoin proceedings conducted pursuant to a Massachusetts statute providing for the registration and confirmation of title to parcels of real estate, on the grounds that the statute was unconstitutional. In discussing the nature of the challenged proceedings, the court stated:

> There is no dispute that the object of the [challenged statute] . . . is that the "decree of registration shall bind the land and quiet title thereto" and "shall be conclusive upon and against all persons," *whether named in the proceeding or not*. . . . If . . . the object is to bar indifferently all who might be minded to make an objection . . . the proceeding is *in rem*.

In an *in rem* action, the court determines all rights held by anyone in the world in an attached piece of property. In a *quasi in rem* I action, the court seeks to determine only the rights of the named parties to the attached property. In a *quasi in rem* II action, the court seeks to determine the rights of named parties in a matter *unrelated* to the property attached. The attached property served only as the basis for jurisdiction (and as limitation on the amount of any eventual judgment). As in *Mitchell v. Neff*, the subject of a *quasi in rem* II attachment might be a parcel of real estate owned by an out-of-state defendant. In such cases, the concept of *quasi in rem* II jurisdiction was relatively simple. If the defendant owned property within a given state, that state could exercise jurisdiction over that property—that is, the state was empowered to render a valid judgment against the defendant but only to the extent of the in-state property.

The concept of "property," however, encompasses much more than just real property or tangible things:

> Most people . . . conceive of property as *things* that are *owned by persons*. . . . But . . . most property in a modern capitalist society is intangible. Consider . . . shares of stock . . . bonds . . . bank accounts, insurance policies. . . . In our everyday language, we tend to speak of these rights as though they were attached to things. Thus we "deposit our money in a bank," as if we were putting a thing in a place; but really we are creating a complex set of abstract claims against an abstract legal institution. We are told that as insurance policy holders we "own a piece of the rock"; but we really have other abstract claims against another abstract institution.

Thomas C. Grey, *The Disintegration of Property*, in Nomos XXII: Property 69–73 (J. Pennock & J. Chapman, eds., 1980). Can these and other alternate forms of "property" be attached in order to acquire *quasi in rem* jurisdiction? If so, where should such property be considered to be located? *See* Aaron D. Simowitz, *Siting Intangibles*, 48 N.Y.U. J. Int'l L. & Pol. 259 (2015).

In a 1905 ruling, *Harris v. Balk*, 198 U.S. 215, the Supreme Court held that intangible obligations traveled with the obligor, could be attached by personal service of the obligor wherever found, and such attachment provided a basis for *quasi in rem* II jurisdiction. In that case, Harris, a North Carolina resident, owed Balk, also a resident of that state, the sum of $180. Balk, in turn, was indebted to Epstein, a Maryland resident, on an unrelated transaction for a sum over $300. In August 1896, while Harris was in Baltimore on business, Epstein served him with a foreign or nonresident writ of attachment, attaching the debt due Balk from Harris, thus acquiring *quasi in rem* jurisdiction over Balk. Harris did not contest that he owed Balk $180 and allowed a judgment in Maryland for that amount to be entered in favor of Epstein. After Harris had paid that amount, he was sued by Balk in North Carolina for the $180 sum. Harris pleaded in the North Carolina proceeding that the action should be barred because of the Maryland judgment. The North Carolina courts rejected the plea on the ground that Maryland lacked jurisdiction because Harris was only temporarily in Maryland and the situs of the debt was in North Carolina. The Supreme Court, in an opinion by Justice Peckham, reversed. The Court explained that "[t]he obligation of the debtor to pay his debt clings to and accompanies him wherever he goes," and that since Maryland had jurisdiction over the debtor (Harris) through personal service while in that state, Maryland has jurisdiction over property belonging to Balk (the debt owed by Harris) and could adjudicate the *Epstein v. Balk* dispute to the extent of the property before it. The Court further noted that Harris had given Balk notice of the Maryland judgment, and that Balk had, under the Maryland procedure, a year to appear in Maryland for the purpose of contesting the debt to Epstein but had not availed himself of this opportunity.

An important extension of the *Harris v. Balk* rationale occurred in *Seider v. Roth*, 17 N.Y.2d 111, 216 N.E.2d 312 (1966). New York plaintiffs in that case obtained jurisdiction by attaching the contractual obligation of an insurance company, doing business in New York, to defend and indemnify the out-of-state defendant for potential liability arising out of an out-of-state accident. Since most major insurance companies do business throughout the country, *Seider*-type attachment could render policyholders amenable to suit in any forum the plaintiff might choose. However, the doctrine was limited to cases in which plaintiff was a resident of the forum. The *Seider* doctrine represented perhaps the high-water mark of expansive *quasi in rem* jurisdiction, but it was eventually held unconstitutional in *Rush v. Savchuk*, 444 U.S. 320 (1980).

Quasi in rem II jurisdiction provides a mechanism for suing nonresident defendants who might otherwise be beyond the *in personam* jurisdiction of the forum state. A distinguishing feature of this form of jurisdiction is that the defendant's liability is limited to the value of the property before the court. It was also common for many jurisdictions to permit the defendant to make what was called a "limited appearance," to appear solely to defend the merits of the lawsuit without conferring *in personam* jurisdiction on the court. *See, e.g.*, N.Y. C.P.L.R. §320(c). (The fiction was that the defendant was only contesting the rights to the property before the court.)

Quasi in rem II jurisdiction suffers from several procedural deficiencies. First, as applied to certain types of intangibles, a defendant has no control over the movements of its debtors, and hence can be sued in jurisdictions having no connection to the defendant or the underlying dispute. (When *quasi in rem* II jurisdiction is based on more traditional types of property, such as land or bank accounts, there is a greater likelihood that the defendant had some prior connection with the forum in which property was found. *See, e.g.*, *Pennington v. Fourth National Bank*, 243 U.S. 269 (1917).) Second, not all states provide for a limited appearance. *See, e.g.*, Minn. R. Civ. P. 4.04(a)(2) (2005); Miss. Code Ann. §11-31-1 (2004). (There is no statute or federal rule relating to limited appearances in federal courts, but federal courts appear to allow limited appearances under some circumstances while denying them in others.) Finally, it is unclear whether a plaintiff obtaining a judgment in an action in which the defendant had been permitted to make a limited appearance can use issue preclusion to prevent the defendant from relitigating the issues decided in plaintiff's favor. Even though allowing such preclusion would largely vitiate the purpose of the limited appearance procedure, that position enjoys the support of the American Law Institute. *See* Restatement (Second) of Judgments §32, comment d.

In addition to these deficiencies, the analytical underpinnings of *quasi in rem* jurisdiction were being eroded. The Supreme Court in *Mullane v. Central Hanover Bank & Trust Co.*, 339 U.S. 306 (1950), rejected the position of the Court in *Pennoyer* that in a case where jurisdiction was based on the property of the defendant, the law could presume that the caretaker of the property would furnish its owner with notice of the pendency of the action. *See also Schroeder v. City of New York*, 371 U.S. 208 (1962); *Walker v. City of Hutchinson*, 352 U.S. 112 (1956). A number of the lower courts were also raising questions whether *International Shoe* principles could be confined to personal jurisdiction and have no application to property-based jurisdiction. *See, e.g., Jonnet v. Dollar Savings Bank of New York*, 530 F.2d 1123 (3d Cir. 1976) (Gibbons, J., concurring).

In 1977, the Supreme Court decided *Shaffer v. Heitner*, 433 U.S. 186, and essentially eliminated *quasi in rem* II jurisdiction. *Shaffer* was a shareholder derivative suit. This type of action is termed a "derivative action" because the shareholders are asserting the interests of the corporation itself against the officers and directors who have shown themselves unable or unwilling to keep the corporation on the right side of the law. In a derivative action, the shareholders themselves sue the corporations's officers and directors (in addition to the corporation itself) to stop the corporation from doing something bad. Defendant Greyhound Lines, Inc. had engaged in some bad conduct. Specifically, Greyhound had engaged in anticompetitive behavior to crush smaller bus lines, had signed an agreement with the U.S. Department of Justice to stop doing that, and then did that some more.

In *Shaffer v. Heitner*, Heitner purchased one share of Greyhound stock and brought suit in Delaware. Greyhound was (and is) a Delaware corporation. That made jurisdiction over Greyhound simple. But a shareholder derivative suit requires that the court have jurisdiction over all the directors of the corporations — essentially all the people who failed to stop the corporation from misbehaving in the first place. The corporate directors were all over the country. If Heitner could not assert jurisdiction over those directors, the suit could not proceed.

Heitner turned to the Delaware "sequestration" statute, Del. Code Ann., Tit. 8, §169 (1975), which "makes Delaware the situs of ownership of all stock in Delaware corporations." *Shaffer*, 433 U.S. at 192. None of these shares were physically located in Delaware. (It is rare for shares of stock to be represented by physical pieces of paper.) The sequestration statute deemed all of Greyhound stock to be located in Delaware and therefore subject to attachment in Delaware. That enabled Heitner to use *quasi in rem* II jurisdiction to obtain jurisdiction over all the out-of-state Greyhound directors (who were also stockholders) that he needed to sue to bring his shareholder derivative suit. Twenty-one of the 28 defendants entered a special appearance to contest jurisdiction, asserting that "under the rule of *International Shoe Co. v. Washington* . . . they did not have sufficient contacts with Delaware to sustain the jurisdiction of that State's courts." Heitner's principal argument was that *quasi in rem* II jurisdiction was permissible under *Pennoyer* (indeed, recall that Justice Field had pointed to *quasi in rem* II jurisdiction as the appropriate way to bring that action) and that *International Shoe* had only required that, for *in personam* jurisdiction, an absent defendant have minimum contacts in the forum state.

Justice Marshall wrote the majority opinion. He observed that Heitner's "categorical analysis assumes the continued soundness of the conceptual structure founded on the century-old case of *Pennoyer v. Neff*," but that "the law of state-court jurisdiction no longer stands securely on the foundation established in *Pennoyer*." Therefore, "the time is ripe to consider whether the standard of fairness and substantial justice set forth in *International Shoe* should be held to govern actions *in rem* as well as *in personam*."

The Court held that it did. The Court observed that asset jurisdiction is not really just asserting power over a thing. Rather, asset jurisdiction is the power to decide the rights of persons in a thing. Therefore, it is perfectly natural that *International Shoe* should govern assertions of *quasi in rem*, as well as *in personam*, jurisdiction. Nonetheless, "the presence of property in a State may bear on the existence of jurisdiction by providing contacts among the forum State, the defendant, and the litigation." For example, "when claims to the property itself are the source of the underlying controversy between the plaintiff and the defendant, it would be unusual for the State where the property is located not to have jurisdiction." *Shaffer*, 433 U.S. at 207. Therefore, classic *in rem* or *quasi in rem* I jurisdiction would survive—litigation that would determine to rights in the property itself located in the forum state. But *quasi in rem* II "cases where the property which now serves as the basis for state-court jurisdiction is completely unrelated to the plaintiff's cause of action" could not survive *International Shoe*. Power over the property was not sufficient to justify deciding the rights of owners of the property if those rights were unrelated to the property. Fairness—as articulated in *International Shoe*—would be the standard. The Court closed by holding that the Delaware courts could not assert jurisdiction over the out-of-state defendants under the *International Shoe* minimum contacts framework: "Appellants have simply had nothing to do with the State of Delaware. Moreover, appellants had no reason to expect to be haled before a Delaware court. Delaware, unlike some States, has not enacted a statute that treats acceptance of a directorship as consent to jurisdiction in the State. . . . Appellants, who were not required to acquire interests in Greyhound in order to hold their positions, did not by acquiring those interests surrender their right to be brought to judgment only in States with which they had had 'minimum contacts.'" Id. at 216.

Justice Marshall's majority opinion attracted three concurrences. Justice Powell wrote separately to argue that the Court should "explicitly reserve judgment, however, on whether the ownership of some forms of property whose situs is indisputably and permanently located within a State may," such as land, "without more, provide the contacts necessary to subject a defendant to jurisdiction within the State to the extent of the value of the property." Justice Stevens wrote to argue that the Court's opinion should have been limited to "a purchase of securities in the domestic market" because a mere purchase of a share of stock in a Delaware corporation could not reasonably anticipate litigation unrelated to the stock in Delaware.

Justice Brennan—ever the advocate of a broad reading of minimum contacts—wrote to argue that the Court should not have reached the question of whether Delaware's assertion of jurisdiction could satisfy *International Shoe*, but rather should have simply held that sequestration statute unconstitutional. Justice Brennan argued that purchasers of stock in a Delaware corporation, particularly a director, "voluntarily associated themselves with the State of Delaware."

NOTES AND QUESTIONS

1. The *Shaffer* decision truly marked the "The End of an Era." *See* Linda. J. Silberman, Shaffer v. Heitner: *The End of an Era*, 53 N.Y.U. L. Rev. 33 (1978). Recall that *Pennoyer* itself endorsed the attachment of property in the forum as the basis to hear an unrelated claim. This basis of jurisdiction was well-known in

English courts, was adopted throughout the colonies, and then by every U.S. state. *Id.* at 42–43. Two of the concurrences in *Shaffer* attempted to preserve something of *quasi-in-rem* II jurisdiction, either by carving out a special rule for real property (per Justice Powell) or by limiting *Shaffer's* holding to certain forms of intangible property (per Justice Stevens). For several years after *Shaffer,* lower courts tried to preserve some form of *quasi-in-rem* II jurisdiction as a basis to adjudicate claims, *see Intermeat, Inc. v. American Poultry Inc.,* 575 F.2d 1017 (2d Cir. 1978), though these efforts ultimately failed.

2. Recall that *Shaffer* is a shareholder's derivative suit — an action brought by one shareholder on behalf of other shareholders of the corporation against the management of the corporation. Although the corporation is formally made a defendant, the real targets of a derivative suit are the allegedly culpable officers and directors, who are also joined as defendants. None of the Greyhound officers or directors in *Shaffer* was a resident of Delaware. Does this background explain why the plaintiff tried to use the Delaware sequestration statute to obtain *quasi in rem* jurisdiction over the directors *individually*? Did plaintiff have an alternative forum in which to bring this suit? Is the availability of an alternative forum a relevant factor in determining whether jurisdiction by attachment is constitutional?

3. *Shaffer's Impact on* Quasi in Rem *I Jurisdiction. Shaffer* itself involved a purported exercise of *quasi in rem* II jurisdiction, and Justice Marshall does emphasize the fact that events giving rise to the shareholder derivative action had nothing to do with the sequestered property or with Delaware. Does *Shaffer* nevertheless spell the demise of *quasi in rem* I jurisdiction as well, on the theory that "minimum contacts" is now the universal standard for any exercise of jurisdiction over a defendant?

Consider in this regard the pre-*Shaffer* ruling in *Atkinson v. Superior Court,* 49 Cal. 2d 338, 316 P.2d 960 (1957). In that case two groups of Californian musicians brought class actions attacking collective bargaining contracts between their California employers and their union and, in particular, seeking recovery of monies to be remitted to a New York trustee for the benefit of unemployed union musicians nationwide. California had jurisdiction over all of the parties save the New York trustee whose only contact with the state was the receipt of the monies in question — a contact held insufficient for personal jurisdiction in the *Hanson v. Denckla* case. Justice Traynor held that the action could proceed on a *quasi in rem* I theory and found such an assertion of power reasonable under the circumstances:

> The present case is not one in which an obligor has invoked the jurisdiction of a court remote from the obligee solely for the purpose of terminating his obligations or sought to compel conflicting claimants to adjudicate their rights in a forum of his own choice. The obligation plaintiffs seek to enforce grows out of their employment by defendants here. The payments involved are alleged to be consideration for work performed in this state. The [union] defendant is before the court. Under these circumstances, fairness to plaintiffs demands that they be able to reach the fruits of their labors before they are removed from the state. Moreover, fairness to the defendants who are personally before the court also demands that the conflicting claims of the trustee be subject to final adjudication.

49 Cal. 2d at 347.

4. Shaffer*'s Impact on Consent Jurisdiction.* Shortly after the decision in *Shaffer*, the Delaware legislature passed a statute that provided that every nonresident who "accepts appointment as a director, trustee, or member of the governing body of a corporation organized under the laws of this State" is deemed to have "consented to appointment of the registered agent of such corporation as his agent upon whom service of process may be made in all civil actions or proceedings brought in this State, by or on behalf of, or against such corporation, in which any such director, trustee, or member is a necessary or proper party, or in any action against such director, trustee or member for violation of his duty in such capacity." Del. Code. Ann. Tit. 10 §3114(a).

Assuming that the nonresident officers and directors of Greyhound in a *Shaffer*-type derivative suit would be subject to jurisdiction in Delaware under this statute, does the statute violate Due Process? The Delaware Supreme Court thought not. *See Armstrong v. Pomerance*, 423 A.2d 174 (Del. 1980). Would the Supreme Court of the United States that decided *Shaffer* agree?

5. Quasi in Rem *II Post-Judgment.* In a footnote, the Court was careful to clarify that, "[o]nce it has been determined by a court of competent jurisdiction that the defendant is a debtor of the plaintiff, there would seem to be no unfairness in allowing an action to realize on that debt in a State where the defendant has property, whether or not that State would have jurisdiction to determine the existence of the debt as an original matter." *Shaffer*, 433 U.S. at 210 n.36. The Restatement of Conflict of Laws provides a practical rationale for permitting post-judgment attachment wherever the debtor's assets are found: "A debtor should not be able to avoid payment of his obligations by the expedient of removing his assets to a place where he is not subject to an in personam suit." Restatement (Second) of Conflict of Laws §66 cmt. a (1971). And yet this prompts a question: Why is there no unfairness associated with *quasi in rem* II jurisdiction post-judgment, whereas prejudgment the *Shaffer* Court essentially eliminated *quasi in rem* II jurisdiction? Does the rendering of a judgment extinguish the Due Process rights of a defendant turned debtor, at least for jurisdictional purposes? If so, can a judgment debtor be haled into any court, anywhere? *See* Linda J. Silberman & Aaron D. Simowitz, *Recognition and Enforcement of Foreign Judgments and Awards: What Hath Daimler Wrought?*, 91 N.Y.U. L. Rev. 344 (2016) (arguing in favor of *Shaffer*'s distinction, but disputing latter case law that dispensed entirely with jurisdictional requirements post-judgment).

6. *The Anti-Cybersquatting Consumer Protection Act.* In 1999, Congress enacted the Anti-Cybersquatting Consumer Protection Act (ACPA), which provides for an *in rem* action to determine the ownership of intellectual property rights in an Internet domain name. 15 U.S.C. §1125(d)(2) permits a claimant to file such an action in "the judicial district in which the domain name registrar, domain name registry, or other domain name authority that registered or assigned the domain name is located" if the claimant is otherwise unable to obtain personal jurisdiction over the defendant.

Note that in many cases, a defendant's action in registering the domain name in the forum might provide sufficient contact to sustain *in personam* jurisdiction there (in which case the *in rem* provisions of the Act would not be applicable or necessary). However, in some cases the registration may have been achieved through an intermediary, and the registrant may have had no direct contact with the forum. In such cases, could an *in rem* action under the Act constitutionally extinguish the rights of a "cybersquatter"? Should *Shaffer* be construed to require minimum contacts when the property attached is related to the underlying claim? *Compare Porsche Cars North America, Inc. v. Porsche.net*, 302 F.3d 248, 259–260 (4th Cir. 2002) (distinguishing *Shaffer* and upholding Act on the basis that property attached under the Cybersquatting Act is directly related to the underlying claim) *with Fleet Boston Financial Corp. v. Fleetbostonfinancial.com*, 138 F. Supp. 2d 121, 134 (D. Mass. 2001) (*Shaffer* requires that defendant have purposeful contacts with the forum even where property attached is related to claim). *Compare* Catherine Struve & R. Polk Wagner, *Realspace Sovereigns in Cyberspace: Problems with the Anticybersquatting Consumer Protection Act*, 17 Berkeley Tech. L.J. 989 (2002) (arguing that the ACPA could not constitutionally be applied to a foreign registrant who was totally unaware that the domain name was administered by an American registry) *and* Michael P. Allen, *In Rem Jurisdiction from* Pennoyer *to* Shaffer *to the Anti-Cybersquatting Consumer Protection Act*, 11 Geo. Mason L. Rev. 243 (2002) (arguing that the ACPA's *in rem* provisions are unconstitutional) *with* Bhanu K. Sadasivan, *Jurisprudence Under the In Rem Provision of the Anticybersquatting Consumer Protection Act*, 18 Berkeley Tech. L.J. 237 (2003) (arguing that the ACPA's *in rem* provisions should withstand constitutional challenge).

NOTE ON SECURITY ATTACHMENTS

The attachment of property can be used for purposes other than jurisdiction. As we saw at the outset of this chapter, after a judgment is rendered, property may be attached to enforce a judgment. In addition, if there is reason to believe that property may be disposed of prior to a judgment, thereby rendering enforcement impossible, a plaintiff may request an attachment of property for security. Historically, such a security attachment could be obtained in an *ex parte* proceeding, often tying up the defendant's property without prior notice or a hearing. In the late 1960s and early 1970s, the Supreme Court rendered a series of decisions, finding certain state attachment procedures unconstitutional for inadequate notice and hearing provisions. In the first of these cases, *Sniadach v. Family Finance Corp.*, 395 U.S. 337 (1969), a creditor of the defendant garnished the defendant's wages pursuant to a Wisconsin garnishment statute. The only opportunity for the defendant wage earner to contest the garnishment or offer a defense came later, after the action for debt was filed. The Supreme Court held that this prejudgment deprivation of property without opportunity for notice and a prior hearing violated Due Process. Later, the Court expanded this ruling relating to the deprivation of wages to consumer goods purchased under conditional sales contracts. In *Fuentes v. Shevin*, 407 U.S. 67 (1972), a four-person majority of a seven-member Supreme Court held that two state replevin statutes—one from Florida and one from Pennsylvania—were unconstitutional. Both cases involved creditors who had reclaimed goods from consumers under conditional sales contracts in which the plaintiff creditors had retained title to the property. Under both schemes, the creditors were required only to make broad conclusory allegations before a court clerk and post a bond for the property to be seized. In order to reclaim the property, the defendant had to post a bond, and any hearing on the merits would take place in either the plaintiff's suit for repossession or an independent action by the debtor for return of the property. Again, the Supreme Court held that the requirements of Due Process mandated an opportunity for a hearing before the property was taken.

Two years later, a reconstituted nine-person Supreme Court (Justices Powell and Rehnquist having since joined the Court) reviewed another state's sequestration procedure in *Mitchell v. W.T. Grant Co.*, 416 U.S. 600 (1974). Although upholding the basic requirement of procedural Due Process in prejudgment attachment procedures, the Court held that Louisiana's requirements—that a judge issue the summons, that the creditor submit an affidavit setting forth the claim to the goods, and that a post-seizure hearing be held—satisfied the constitutional standard.

The Court subsequently imposed procedural safeguards in nonconsumer cases as well. In *North Georgia Finishing Inc. v. Di-Chem, Inc.*, 419 U.S. 601 (1975), the plaintiff, as part of its commercial dispute with the defendant, attached the defendant's bank account as security for any potential judgment. Under the Georgia statute, a court clerk could issue the writ on conclusory allegations of the plaintiff, and the defendant could regain the property only by posting a bond. Without any view commanding a full majority, the Supreme Court struck down the statute because of the lack of opportunity for an early hearing. Specifics, such as whether the hearing must be prior to or immediately after the attachment and what the hearing should entail, were left open in the various opinions by members of the Court.

The Court further constrained prejudgment attachment in *Connecticut v. Doehr*, 501 U.S. 1 (1991). In that case, the Court struck down a Connecticut statute that authorized prejudgment attachment of real property without prior notice, hearing, or bond. Under the statute, the plaintiff in an assault and battery case was permitted to obtain a lien on defendant's home upon filing an affidavit with a judge attesting to the basis of the complaint. The Court struck down the statute notwithstanding its provision for an expeditious post-attachment hearing and financial penalties if the complaint is deemed to be without probable cause. Distinguishing commercial debt cases like *Mitchell v. W.T. Grant Co.*, the Court held that the risk of an erroneous deprivation was too great in a tort case to justify an attachment upon the unilateral assertions of the plaintiff, at least absent a showing of some exceptional circumstance.

Several excellent articles trace these developments in more depth. *See* Robert S. Catz & Edmund H. Robinson, *Due Process and Creditor's Remedies: From* Sniadach *and* Fuentes *to* Mitchell, North Georgia *and Beyond*, 28 Rutgers L. Rev. 541, 556–562 (1975); Robert E. Scott, *Constitutional Regulation of Provisional Remedies: The Cost of Procedural Due Process*, 61 Va. L. Rev. 807 (1975).

This line of cases from *Sniadach* to *Di-Chem* did not technically address either the procedural requirements or the constitutional standard for *jurisdictional* attachments. In each of the security cases, the defendant was subject to personal jurisdiction in the court issuing the attachment writ; the attachment was designed to assure that there would be property to satisfy an eventual judgment. Indeed, in *Fuentes*, the Supreme Court distinguished its earlier ruling in *Ownbey v. Morgan*, 256 U.S. 94 (1921), a case involving a jurisdictional attachment, stating that such situations warranted postponement of any hearing requirement. Not surprisingly, however, some courts and commentators speculated as to whether the procedural safeguards, such as notice and hearing, might also be required when a jurisdictional attachment was sought. *See, e.g., Jonnet v. Dollar Savings Bank*, 530 F.2d 1123 (3d Cir. 1976) (pre-attachment hearing not necessary but other procedural safeguards would be required to ensure Due Process in a jurisdictional attachment). And indeed it was this issue that occupied most of the Delaware Supreme Court's time in the *Shaffer* case, where the state court ultimately held that the prior notice and hearing requirements were not constitutionally compelled in an attachment for jurisdiction. Because the Supreme Court decided *Shaffer* on "minimum contacts" grounds, it did not reach the issue.

3.   *Transient Service*

You may notice a family resemblance between *Shaffer* and *Daimler*, although they are separated by almost 40 years. Each decision marked the "end of an era," essentially eliminating an entire category of jurisdiction that had supported litigation in American courts for decades. Each decision also expressed a strong preference for limiting litigation in a forum state's courts to those actions *related* to an out-of-state defendant's contacts in the forum state. Both general jurisdiction and *quasi in rem* II jurisdiction are bases of *unrelated*, all-purpose jurisdiction. The contacts in the forum that support jurisdiction are unrelated to the content of the action brought in the forum's courts. Justice Marshall and his successor on the Court, Justice Ginsburg, both seemed skeptical that broad all-purpose jurisdiction had a prominent place in the *International Shoe* framework.

After *Shaffer*, many commentators thought that the next all-purpose basis of jurisdiction to fall would be transient service, often called "tag jurisdiction." In short, tag jurisdiction exists when a natural person (a human being, as opposed to juridical person, like a corporation) enters a state and is personally served in the state in a connection with an action that is currently pending in the state's courts. (Hence the tag-you're-it moniker.) Tag jurisdiction can provide jurisdiction for *any* action. The suit does not have to be related to the purpose of the defendant's visit to the forum state or his other contacts there. The defendant's mere physical presence in the forum (coupled with personal service) is enough.

The Court took up the validity of tag jurisdiction in *Burnham v. Superior Court of California*, 495 U.S. 604 (1990), which presented the question of "whether the Due Process Clause of the Fourteenth Amendment denies California courts jurisdiction over a nonresident who was personally served with process while temporarily in that State, in a suit unrelated to his activities in the State." Dennis and Francie Burnham decided to split after 12 years of marriage, most of it in New Jersey. They agreed that Francie, who intended to move to California, would take custody of their children. They also agreed to file for divorce on the grounds of "irreconcilable differences." Dennis did not do so and instead filed for divorce in New Jersey on the ground of "desertion." Francie filed for divorce in California. A few weeks later, Dennis visited California on business, where he was served with a copy of the California divorce petition after visiting his children. Then he went back to New Jersey. Dennis made a special appearance in California to contest jurisdiction and lost that argument before the California courts.

The Supreme Court unanimously upheld jurisdiction, although with a head-scratching split of opinions. Justice Scalia wrote for plurality of the Court and quickly disassociated himself from *Shaffer*'s reasoning, noting at the outset that "[t]o determine whether the assertion of personal jurisdiction is consistent with due process, we have long relied on the principles traditionally followed by American courts in marking out the territorial limits of each State's authority," invoking

Pennoyer. Justice Scalia's opinion uses some variation of the word "tradition" almost 20 times. Justice Scalia's starting point (and perhaps his ending point) was that tag jurisdiction is "[a]mong the most firmly established principles of personal jurisdiction in American tradition" and that "[t]he view developed early that each State had the power to hale before its courts any individual who could be found within its borders, and that once having acquired jurisdiction over such a person by properly serving him with process, the State could retain jurisdiction to enter judgment against him, no matter how fleeting his visit." Justice Scalia acknowledged that the historical pedigree of tag jurisdiction may have been more myth than fact, but dismissed that, noting support for tag jurisdiction was "shared by American courts at the crucial time for present purposes: 1868, when the Fourteenth Amendment was adopted." Justice Scalia emphasized: "This American jurisdictional practice is, moreover, not merely old; it is continuing. It remains the practice of not only a substantial number of the States, but as far as we are aware all the States and the Federal Government — if one disregards (as one must for this purpose) the few opinions since 1978 that have erroneously said, on grounds similar to those that petitioner presses here, that this Court's due process decisions render the practice unconstitutional." (Justice Scalia did not explain why those post-*Shaffer* decisions "must" be disregarded.) In sum, Justice Scalia viewed *International Shoe* as teaching that physical presence was no longer *necessary* for jurisdiction, not that it was no longer *sufficient.*

Justice Scalia acknowledged that the best critique of tag jurisdiction flowed from *Shaffer,* but that "while our holding today does not contradict Shaffer, our basic approach to the due process question is different." Courts need conduct "no independent inquiry into the desirability or fairness of the prevailing in-state service rule," but should rather leave "that judgment to the legislatures that are free to amend it; for our purposes, its validation is its pedigree," as *International Shoe*'s appeal to "traditional notions of fair play and substantial justice" suggests. Justice White concurred in part and concurred in the judgment to note that the "rule allowing jurisdiction to be obtained over a nonresident by personal service in the forum State, without more, has been and is so widely accepted throughout this country that I could not possibly strike it down, either on its face or as applied in this case, on the ground that it denies due process of law guaranteed by the Fourteenth Amendment."

Justice Brennan, ever the advocate of a broad conception of minimum contacts, concurred in the judgment, joined by three justices. Justice Brennan noted at the outset that "I believe that the approach adopted by Justice Scalia's opinion today — reliance solely on historical pedigree — is foreclosed by our decisions in *International Shoe Co. v. Washington.* . . . The critical insight of *Shaffer* is that all rules of jurisdiction, even ancient ones, must satisfy contemporary notions of due process." Nonetheless, "as a rule the exercise of personal jurisdiction over a defendant based on his voluntary presence in the forum will satisfy the requirements of due process." Justice Brennan argued that, "[b]y visiting the forum State," a person avails himself "of significant benefits provided by the State," including "the State's police, fire, and emergency medical services," travel on "the State's roads and waterways," and "access to its courts." In addition, the fact that the "defendant has already journeyed at least once before to the forum . . . is an indication that suit in the forum likely would not be prohibitively inconvenient."

Justice Scalia dismissed this argument: "Three days' worth of these benefits strike us as powerfully inadequate to establish, as an abstract matter, that it is 'fair' for California to decree the ownership of all Mr. Burnham's worldly goods acquired during the 10 years of his marriage, and the custody over his children. We daresay a contractual exchange swapping those benefits for that power would not survive the "unconscionability" provision of the Uniform Commercial Code. . . ." Justice Stevens concurred to note, as he did in *Shaffer*, that the Court was being a bit overbroad, and need not settle the battle between "tradition" and "fairness."

NOTES AND QUESTIONS

1. *The Scalia Opinion.* Justice Scalia's opinion states that the "minimum contacts" test does not apply at all when a natural person who voluntarily enters the forum is personally served there. Justice Brennan's opinion argues that voluntary presence in the forum state satisfies "minimum contacts." Is Justice Scalia's opinion a reaffirmation of power and territorial theories of jurisdiction?

Is Justice Scalia's reliance on history and tradition a sufficient response to the constitutional challenge? After all, couldn't the same argument about tradition have been made in *Shaffer v. Heitner*? Moreover, the Court has continuously recognized the need to reexamine existing Due Process principles in light of changing political and social needs. Is there a significant reason why tradition should suffice in *Burnham* but not in *Shaffer*? Or is the cynical answer just that Justice Scalia was not on the Court when *Shaffer* was decided? What implications does Justice Scalia's vision have for other issues of constitutional law? *See* Martin H. Redish, *Tradition, Fairness and Personal Jurisdiction: Due Process and Constitutional Theory After* Burnham v. Superior Court, 22 Rutgers L.J. 675 (1991).

2. *The Brennan Opinion.* Is the position of the "Brennan four" any more persuasive? What reasons does Justice Brennan give that make it "fair" to subject Mr. Burnham to jurisdiction in California? Consider, for example, Justice Brennan's argument that Mr. Burnham has a "benefit" because he has a right of access to California courts. That "benefit" is available to all nonresidents regardless of whether they were or have ever been in California. Does Justice Brennan's argument therefore require that all U.S. nationals be subject to jurisdiction in California courts because all U.S. nationals have the right to access California courts?

3. Burnham *as a Matrimonial Case.* Consider also that *Burnham* is a matrimonial case and involved a number of issues: marital status, spousal and child support, determination of marital property rights, and custody. Because traditionally marital status has been thought of as a "*res*," the domicile of either party is sufficient to provide a basis for jurisdiction for divorce. Similarly, a child's presence in the state was historically sufficient for an adjudication of custody. More recently, under the modern Uniform Child Custody Jurisdiction and Enforcement Act, the child's home state is given adjudicatory power in an action by one parent for custody without regard to the contacts of the defendant parent. Notwithstanding the fact that such jurisdictional bases might seem suspect after *Shaffer*, they have continued to survive without further review from the Supreme Court. Thus, although the status

and custody issues in *Burnham* might have been litigated in California without regard to personal jurisdiction over Mr. Burnham, the question of the economic rights between the parties required *in personam* jurisdiction and sufficient contacts between the defendant and California. *Compare Kulko v. Superior Court, supra,* pp. 125–126. Is there any sense to a system that allows status and custody issues to be litigated in California but would require the economic issues between the parties to be litigated in New York? *Compare* the provision in the European Regulation (of 18 December 2008) on jurisdiction, applicable law, recognition and enforcement of decisions, and cooperation in matters relating to maintenance obligations, which provides that in matters relating to maintenance obligations in Member States, jurisdiction lies with either the court for the place where the defendant is habitually resident, or the court for the place where the creditor is habitually resident, or the place where the maintenance proceeding is ancillary to jurisdiction over the question of status or parental responsibility. For a discussion of *Burnham* as a matrimonial case, *see* Linda J. Silberman, *Reflections on* Burnham v. Superior Court: *Toward Presumptive Rules of Jurisdiction and Implications for Choice of Law,* 22 Rutgers L.J. 569, 590–595 (1991).

4. *Service on a Corporate Official.* How far does the concept of service in the forum extend? What if the plaintiff serves an official of a corporation who happens to be within the forum state? In *C.S.B. Commodities v. Urban Trend (HK) Ltd.,* 626 F. Supp. 2d 837 (N.D. Ill. 2009), a knife manufacturer brought an unfair competition claim against a foreign manufacturer of a similar product. The foreign company's president was served while in Illinois and the court found jurisdiction over the individual defendant. However, jurisdiction over the president did not establish jurisdiction over the company, which still required an independent finding of minimum contacts between the company and the forum.

5. *Did* Burnham *survive* Daimler*?* Recall that the rationale for justifying jurisdiction over corporations based on "corporate presence" was drawn from an analogy to justifying the jurisdiction over individuals based on physical presence within the jurisdiction. In minimizing the continued relevance of the foundational cases establishing the corporate presence doctrine, the Supreme Court in *Daimler* wrote, "these cases . . . [were] decided in an era dominated by *Pennoyer*'s territorial thinking . . . [and] should not attract heavy reliance today." Similarly, Scalia's opinion in *Burnham* is predicated on the territorial power theory of jurisdiction. Does *Daimler* presage the death of *Burnham*? Consider *Roch v. Mollica,* in which a New Jersey plaintiff who was injured in Florida brought a negligence action in Massachusetts against New Hampshire defendants who were served while voluntarily visiting the forum. The Supreme Judicial Court of Massachusetts upheld jurisdiction citing *Burnham,* and in a footnote clarified that its "holding applies only to individuals," and that the court did "not address whether presence in the forum State when served with process confers personal jurisdiction over corporations," for which it intimated that *Daimler* would be controlling, 113 N.E.3d 820, 822 n.3 (Mass. 2019); *see also Mohamad v. Rajoub,* No. 17 Civ. 2385, 2018 WL 1737219 (S.D.N.Y., Mar. 12, 2018) (declining to extend *Daimler* to restrict *Burnham* to bar jurisdiction over a Palestinian defendant served process while visiting New York).

C.   COURTS' POWER TO HEAR SPECIFIC CLAIMS AGAINST A DEFENDANT: CASE-LINKED JURISDICTION

1.   Specific-Act Statutes

a.   Constitutionality

International Shoe set up a dichotomy: general jurisdiction and specific jurisdiction. As you have seen, general jurisdiction empowered courts to hear any claim against a corporation where it had "continuous and systematic" contacts. In *Daimler*, the Court redefined "continuous and systematic" contacts to limit it to only those states where the corporation was "essentially at home." Justice Ginsburg justified this contraction, in part, because "general jurisdiction has come to occupy a less dominant place in the contemporary scheme," 571 U.S. at 133, after "the many decades in which specific jurisdiction has flourished." Id. at 133, n.10. As you will see, this constitutional test for specific jurisdiction has evolved over time into a three-part inquiry: (i) Did the defendant purposefully direct its conduct to the forum state? (ii) Did the defendant have minimum contacts in the forum state "arising out of or related" to the claim? and (iii) Would the exercise of jurisdiction by the state's courts be "reasonable"?

But the constitutional inquiry can only limit jurisdiction — it does not authorize courts to exercise power of a defendant. That requires a statute. Statutes that authorize jurisdiction are often called "long-arm statutes," although the term "long-arm" can be used to refer to statutes authorizing service outside the state for both related and unrelated claims. *See, e.g.*, Fla. Stat. Ann. §48.193(2). Statutes that limit jurisdiction to claims arising from specified activity are more accurately known as specific-act or single-act statutes.

Before *International Shoe*, a number of states enacted statutes that authorized jurisdiction over claims against individuals, partnerships, or unincorporated associations that did business in the state where the claim arose from in-state activity. Some statutes also included claims against nonresident motorists arising from accidents in the state, as we saw in *Hess v. Pawloski*. However, in light of the analytical approach in *International Shoe* permitting the assumption of jurisdiction over any matter that bears a reasonable and substantial connection to the forum community, states began to expand the situations in which they asserted jurisdictional authority over nonresidents where the claim arose from minimal and even single acts within the state.

In *McGee v. International Life Insurance Co.*, 355 U.S. 220 (1957), the Supreme Court sustained a state's assertion of jurisdiction over a foreign corporation based on a single act within the state. International Life Insurance, a Texas company, mailed a certificate to Lulu McGee's son in California to offer him life insurance. McGee's son paid premiums under the insurance contract until his death. McGee was the beneficiary under the policy. When she attempted to collect under the policy, International Life refused, claiming that McGee's son had committed suicide. The record disclosed no contacts between International Life and California other than this one life insurance contract. McGee sued in California court and obtained a judgment. Unable to satisfy the judgment in

California, she sought to enforce it in Texas. The Texas courts refused to give Full Faith and Credit to the California judgment on the basis that California had lacked jurisdiction over International Life. That constitutional issue went before the Supreme Court.

Writing only 12 years after *International Shoe*, the Court observed that "[l]ooking back over this long history of litigation a trend is clearly discernible toward expanding the permissible scope of state jurisdiction over foreign corporations and other nonresidents." The Court attributed this trend "to the fundamental transformation of our national economy over the years." The Court observed that commercial transactions crisscrossed the country, were often conducted by mail, and that "modern transportation and communication have made it much less burdensome for a party sued to defend himself in a State where he engages in economic activity." Therefore, there was no unfairness in California courts hearing and deciding the case. The Court emphasized that California "has a manifest interest in providing effective means of redress for its residents when their insurers refuse to pay claims," and that California "residents would be at a severe disadvantage if they were forced to follow the insurance company to a distant State in order to hold it legally accountable." This would be especially true for small claims. If plaintiffs lacked sufficient incentive to cross the country to litigate, the insurance company could be effectively judgment-proof.

NOTES AND QUESTIONS

1. *The Concept of Specific Jurisdiction.* The statute in *McGee* based jurisdiction on claims arising out of insurance contracts made with residents. Unlike *general jurisdiction* over defendants based on extensive activities subjecting them to jurisdiction on any claim, the jurisdiction in *McGee* can be said to be specific—i.e., limited to particular claims (suit on an insurance contract) arising from particular but limited activity in the state (offering an insurance contract). Does specific jurisdiction rest on the "implied consent" doctrine articulated in *Hess v. Pawloski* indicating that the state has the authority to exclude this activity from its borders? Or does the broader analysis of interests discussed in *International Shoe* offer a better rationale?

2. *Limits of* McGee *?* How far does the holding of *McGee* extend? Does it support jurisdiction over a foreign corporation whenever that corporation solicits a contract in a state? What if Lowell Franklin had initiated the communication that led to reinstatement of the insurance policy? Can the case be limited to insurance companies on the theory that the forum state has a strong interest in regulating the conduct of such companies on behalf of resident insureds?

3. As a general matter, the federal courts do not have their own specific-act statutes. Absent a specific statutory authorization, the jurisdictional reach of the federal courts is limited to that of the states, and the federal courts are authorized to serve process outside the state under the authority of the specific-act statute of the state in which it sits. *See* Fed. R. Civ. P. 4(k)(1)(A). Thus, statutes like the one in *McGee* are available to a plaintiff in state and federal court. You will see a more detailed discussion about adjudicatory jurisdiction in the federal courts and the expansion of federal process later in the chapter.

b.　Specific-Act Statutes: Statutory Interpretation

As already noted, post–*International Shoe*, several states passed statutes expanding the jurisdiction of their courts to encompass claims over nonresidents "arising from" particular activities that occurred within the state—e.g., claims arising from the defendant's transaction of any business in the state or the defendant's commission of a tortious act within the state. In addition to issues of interpretation of these statutes, state courts also had to decide whether the statutes, as applied, were consistent with constitutional Due Process standards.[1]

The Illinois statute, one of the first specific-act statutes, contained a number of specific grounds on which the Illinois courts could exercise jurisdiction over a defendant.[2] In *Gray v. American Radiator & Standard Sanitary Corp.*, 22 Ill. 2d 432, 176 N.E.2d 761 (1961), the defendant challenged that portion of the Illinois specific-act statute that provided that a nonresident who, either in person or through an agent, committed a tortious act within the state of Illinois submitted to the jurisdiction of the Illinois courts. The Supreme Court of Illinois considered whether this language provided a basis for jurisdiction over a non-Illinois component manufacturer whose product caused an injury in Illinois; the precise question of statutory interpretation before the court was "whether a tortious act was committed [in Illinois], within the meaning of the statute, despite the fact that the [defendant] had no agent in Illinois." The plaintiff, Mrs. Gray, was injured by a water heater that exploded in Illinois. The safety valve for the heater was manufactured by the Titan Valve Company, an Ohio company; the valve was sold to American Radiator, a Pennsylvania company, that incorporated the valve into the heater, which in the course of commerce was sold to Mrs. Gray in Illinois. The lower court had dismissed the case against Titan on the ground that it had not committed a tortious act in Illinois so as to justify the assertion of jurisdiction pursuant to the Illinois long-arm statute. Because Titan also raised a constitutional objection, the appeal bypassed the intermediate-level court and was heard directly by the Supreme Court of Illinois.

---

1. After reading the cases discussed in this section, you may well appreciate why some states have merely enacted what might be termed "sky's the limit" statutes, which authorize a state to assert jurisdiction on "any basis not inconsistent with the Constitution of this state or of the United States." *See, e.g.*, Cal. Civ. Proc. Code §410.10 (2000). In 1989, Illinois added a catch-all provision to its specific-act statute; in addition to specifically enumerating certain actions that vest Illinois courts with jurisdiction over out-of-state defendants, the Illinois statute was amended to authorize Illinois courts to "exercise jurisdiction on any other basis now or hereafter permitted by the Illinois Constitution and the Constitution of the United States." 735 ILCS 5/2-209(c) (2012).

2. statute provided as follows:

> (1) Any person, whether or not a citizen or resident of this State, who in person or through an agent does any of the acts hereinafter enumerated, thereby submits said person, and, if an individual, his personal representative, to the jurisdiction of the courts of this State as to any course of action arising from doing any of the said acts: (a) The transaction of any business within this State; (b) The commission of a tortious act within this State; (c) The ownership, use, or possession of any real estate situated in this State; (d) Contracting to insure any person, property or risk located within this State at the time of contracting.

Ill. Rev. Stat. 1959, chap. 110, par. 17(1)(a)–(d).

Acknowledging that "the wrong . . . arose . . . from acts performed at the place of manufacture" and that "[o]nly the consequences occurred in Illinois," the Illinois Supreme Court nevertheless took the position that "the alleged negligence in manufacturing cannot be separated from the resulting injury" and, thus, that the tort was committed in Illinois for purposes of the statute—i.e., that the phrase "tortious act" encompassed both the "act" and the "injury." The court relied on both the Restatement of Conflict of Laws, which provides that the place of a wrong is where the last event takes place that is necessary to render the actor liable, and the more general rules governing the computation of time for purposes of determining whether an action has been brought within the applicable statute of limitation to arrive at its holding.

The Titan Company also challenged the assertion of jurisdiction on Due Process grounds. The Illinois Supreme Court rejected this challenge based on the general proposition that "if a corporation elects to sell its products for ultimate use in another State, it is not unjust to hold it answerable there for any damages caused by defects in those products." The court noted that Titan did not claim that the use of its product in Illinois was an isolated instance and found that it was reasonable to infer that defendant's valves resulted in "substantial use and consumption" in Illinois. As you will see, *infra* at pp. 186-210, the requirement that defendant's contacts "arise out of or relate to" the claim will become a key part of the constitutional inquiry for specific jurisdiction. For guidance on this constitutional question, the lower courts initially turned to cases like *Gray* and their consideration of the appropriate test when interpreting the specific-act statutes. The Supreme Court would not consider this "nexus requirement" until several decades later.

NOTES AND QUESTIONS

1. *"Tortious Act:" Statutory Interpretation.* Several years after *Gray*, the New York Court of Appeals took a different position on the meaning of the phrase "tortious act" with respect to New York's specific-act statute, N.Y. C.P.L.R. §302(a), which contained identical language to the statute challenged in *Gray*. In *Feathers v. McLucas*, 15 N.Y.2d 443, 209 N.E.2d 68 (1965), the New York Court of Appeals held that §302(a) did not authorize jurisdiction over a nonresident manufacturer of a tractor-drawn steel propane gas tank that exploded on a New York highway en route to Vermont and injured the New York plaintiffs. The court held that "[t]he mere occurrence of an injury in [New York] certainly cannot serve to transmute an out-of-state tortious act into one committed in [New York] within the sense of the statutory wording." 15 N.Y.2d at 460.

The New York legislature responded to *Feathers* by amending the state's specific-act statute to provide for jurisdiction both over a defendant who "commits a tortious act within the state" (except for defamation of character), N.Y. C.P.L.R. §302(a)(2), and over a defendant who:

> commits a tortious act *without* the state causing injury to person or property *within* the state . . . (except for defamation), if he
>
> > (i) regularly does or solicits business, or engages in any other persistent course of conduct, or derives substantial revenue from goods used or consumed or services rendered, in the state, or

(ii) expects or should reasonably expect the act to have consequences in the state and derives substantial revenue from interstate or international commerce.

N.Y. C.P.L.R. §302(a)(3) (emphasis added). This amendment would presumably have changed the result in *Feathers* so long as the defendant satisfied the requirements of (i) or (ii). Do you think such an assertion of jurisdiction also satisfies the Due Process requirements articulated in *International Shoe*?

    2. *"Transacting Any Business in the State:" Statutory Interpretation.* In addition to the tortious act provisions noted above, state specific-act statutes included numerous other bases for the assertion of jurisdiction over nonresidents. For example, the New York long-arm statute authorized jurisdiction over claims that "arise from" the defendant's "transacting any business in the state." N.Y. C.P.L.R. §302(a)(1). These provisions also raised important questions of statutory interpretation. One such question was whether the "transaction of business" provision in a specific-act statute authorized the assertion of jurisdiction over a nonresident manufacturer who shipped a defective product into the state where it was purchased. It is interesting to compare two decisions issued by the New York Court of Appeals. In one case, a New York child was injured in Connecticut by a geologist's hammer, which had been purchased for him in New York. Finding that the defendant had shipped its products into New York and had engaged in solicitation and advertising in New York and that the sale of the product took place in New York, the court held that there was specific jurisdiction under N.Y. C.P.L.R. §302(a)(1). *Singer v. Walker*, 15 N.Y.2d 443, 209 N.E.2d 68 (1965). But in another case, a New York infant was injured in Canada by a malfunctioning fondue pot, which had been shipped into New York by the defendant Japanese export company and was later purchased at a New York department store. Here, the New York Court of Appeals held there was no specific jurisdiction under N.Y. C.P.L.R. §302(a)(1) because the mere shipment of goods into the state was insufficient to satisfy the statutory standard of "transaction of business" in the state. Although the Japanese exporter had sent representatives into New York to do general market research, this activity, held the court, did not "bear a substantial relationship to the transaction out of which the instant cause of action arose." *McGowan v. Smith*, 52 N.Y.2d 268, 419 N.E.2d 321 (1981). Would the later amendment to N.Y. C.P.L.R. §302(a)(1) — providing for jurisdiction when a defendant "contracts anywhere to supply goods or services within the state" — have changed the result in *McGowan*?

    Does a foreign bank's maintenance of a correspondent bank account at a New York financial institution and use of that account to effect wire transfers on behalf of a foreign client constitute a "transaction of business" under the New York specific-act statute? In *Licci v. Lebanese Canadian Bank*, 20 N.Y.3d 327, 984 N.E.2d 893 (2012), the New York Court of Appeals answered "yes" to that question, which had been certified to it by the Court of Appeals for the Second Circuit. In *Licci*, U.S., Canadian, and Israeli citizens killed or injured by Hizballah rocket attacks during the 2006 Israel-Hizballah conflict brought suit in New York against a Lebanese bank for allegedly aiding and abetting terrorist activities. Plaintiffs alleged that the Lebanese bank had supported the financial branch of Hizballah with its "deliberate use" of a correspondent bank account with American Express Bank (AmEx) through which it maintained bank accounts and secured wire transfers on Hizballah's behalf.

The federal district court dismissed the case for lack of personal jurisdiction, stating that (1) the maintenance of a correspondent bank account with a financial institution in New York did not constitute the "transaction of business" in New York, and (2) the plaintiffs' claims did not "arise from" the bank's maintenance and use of the correspondent account. On appeal, the Court of Appeals for the Second Circuit certified both issues to the New York Court of Appeals. On the first point, the New York Court of Appeals held that while "mere maintenance" of a correspondent account would not subject the foreign bank to jurisdiction, its "repeated use of a correspondent account in New York on behalf of a client" shows "purposeful availment of New York's dependable and transparent banking system, the dollar as a stable and fungible currency, and the predictable jurisdictional and commercial law of New York and the United States." 20 N.Y.3d at 339. Thus, the frequency and deliberate nature of the bank's use of its correspondent account subjected it to jurisdiction. Indeed, in a later 2016 decision, *Al Rushaid v. Pictet & Cie*, 2016 WL 6837930 (N.Y. 2016), the New York Court of Appeals (in a 4-3 ruling) confirmed its position that the bank's use of the correspondent account even if it did not direct the money into the account was sufficient to meet the statutory standard of transacting business in New York.

On the "arising from" issue in *Licci*, the New York Court of Appeals looked to whether there was an "articulable nexus" or "substantial relationship" between the business transaction and the claims asserted. On the facts of *Licci*, the Court held that the plaintiffs alleged that the defendant violated various statutory duties owed to plaintiffs and that those claims had a sufficient connection to the maintenance and use of the correspondent account. The Court noted that although the rockets launched by Hizballah were the alleged immediate cause of the damages claimed, the plaintiffs were suing the bank "for its role in the transfer of funds to Hizballah." Accordingly, the jurisdictional nexus analysis required consideration of the relationship between plaintiffs' claims and the alleged transactions in New York.

Following the state court's response to the certified questions relating to the interpretation of the New York specific-act statute, the Court of Appeals for the Second Circuit proceeded to determine whether subjecting the bank to personal jurisdiction in New York comported with due process. The Second Circuit concluded that the "minimum contacts" requirement was met, and in terms of fairness emphasized the U.S. and state interests in preventing the U.S. banking system from becoming an instrument in support of terrorism. *See Licci ex rel. Licci v. Lebanese Canadian Bank, SAL*, 732 F.3d 161 (2d Cir. 2013).

3. *"Arising Out Of" Forum Activities: Statutory Interpretation.* In both *Singer* and *McGowan*, the New York Court of Appeals addressed only whether there was sufficient activity to satisfy the statutory standard of "transaction of business." Note that under the New York statute — as under most specific-act jurisdictional statutes — it is also necessary that the claim at issue "arise out of" the specified forum state activity. What is the rationale for this "arising out of" or "nexus" requirement? Does satisfaction of such a requirement contribute to litigational convenience? In what way?

Determining whether a cause of action "arises from" specified activity presents its own set of problems. After all, causes of action are not like jacks-in-the-boxes that physically pop up so that they can be located in a particular jurisdiction. Is it clear to you that the claims in *Singer* and *McGowan* "arose from" New York activity when in fact the injuries took place outside New York? Numerous courts have struggled with the interpretation of when a claim can be said to "arise out" of particular activity and, as you will see, have adopted different tests to determine whether a claim "arises out" of particular activity. You will also note that these tests often differ depending on whether the claim is one sounding in tort or in contract.

Some other courts have recognized that tort claims can "arise from" a defendant's transaction of business in the state. In *Shute v. Carnival Cruise Lines*, 897 F.2d 377 (9th Cir. 1990), *rev'd on other grounds*, 499 U.S. 585 (1991), a Washington plaintiff was injured aboard a cruise ship in international waters. The defendant, a Panamanian corporation with its principal place of business in Florida, had engaged in promotional activities and advertising in Washington State. Plaintiff purchased tickets through a local Washington travel agent. The Ninth Circuit Court of Appeals certified the question of whether there was jurisdiction under state law to the Washington Supreme Court, which held that "but for" Carnival's transaction of business within the state, plaintiff would not have been injured on defendant's cruise ship and therefore the claim "arose from" Carnival's Washington contacts. *See Shute v. Carnival Cruise Lines*, 783 P.2d 78 (Wash. 1989).

4. *Choice of Law and Jurisdiction.* We will look at the developments regarding "what law applies" later in this chapter—a subject known as *conflict of laws* or *choice of law*. For the present, however, it is important to understand that the forum does not necessarily apply its own law to a case before it. Instead, it applies its conflict of laws rules to determine what the governing law should be. Can you think of any good reasons why the forum does not just apply its own law when a case is before it?

2.   *The Supreme Court Imposes Limits: The Requirement of a Purposeful Act* 'purposeful availment'

a.   Origins—*Hanson v. Denckla*

The Supreme Court's 1957 ruling in *McGee* suggested that the constitutional Due Process requirement of "minimum contacts" could be satisfied by a single contact with the forum state. The next year, however, the Supreme Court reviewed a very complicated jurisdictional case—*Hanson v. Denckla*, 357 U.S. 235 (1958)—in which two different states, Delaware and Florida, asserted jurisdictional authority to determine the validity of appointments made under a Delaware trust and each claimed its decision was entitled to full faith and credit. The case involved the wealthy Dora Browning Donner, a resident of Pennsylvania, who established a trust in Delaware with a Delaware trust company. Under the terms of the trust, Mrs. Donner reserved certain powers to herself, among them an *inter vivos* power of appointment, which gave her the ability to designate beneficiaries of the trust during her lifetime. Mrs. Donner later moved to Florida, where she executed an *inter vivos* appointment or transfer of approximately one-half million dollars to certain trusts previously established for her daughter, Elizabeth. The appointment appeared to result in an estate plan that left one-third of the estate to each of three daughters; under her will Mrs. Donner had established two trusts for the two other daughters, Katherine and Dorothy, each of whom would also receive about one-half million dollars. Katherine and Dorothy, however, challenged the validity of the *inter vivos* appointment in a suit against Elizabeth and the Delaware trustee in Florida, claiming that the appointment was invalid and the one-half-million-dollar bequest passed to them under the residuary clause of the will. Elizabeth challenged the Florida court's power to proceed on the ground that there was no jurisdiction over the Delaware trustee, whose only connection with Florida was its continuing relationship with the settlor, Mrs. Donner, who had moved there after the trust was established. Meanwhile, Elizabeth, as executrix of the estate, instituted a declaratory judgment action in Delaware to establish the validity of the *inter vivos* appointment. Conflicting decisions on the merits were reached by the supreme courts in the respective states. Delaware decided that Delaware law applied and the appointment was valid, and Florida held that Florida law applied and as such the appointment was invalid.

Challenges to both decisions on full faith and credit and jurisdictional Due Process grounds were asserted in the United States Supreme Court. The Supreme Court held that the Florida decision was not entitled to full faith and credit because Florida could not constitutionally assert jurisdiction over the Delaware trustee. The Supreme Court explained:

> The agreement was executed in Delaware by a trust company incorporated in that State and a settlor domiciled in Pennsylvania. The first relationship Florida had to the agreement was years later when the settlor became domiciled there, and the trustee remitted the trust income to her in that State. . . . But the record discloses no instance in which the trustee performed any acts in Florida that bear the same relationship to the agreement as the solicitation in *McGee*. . . . The unilateral activity of those who claim some relationship with a nonresident defendant cannot satisfy the requirement of contact with the forum State. The application of that rule will vary with the quality and nature of the defendant's activity, but it is essential in each case that there be some act by which the defendant purposefully avails itself of the privilege of conducting activities with the forum State, thus invoking the benefits and protections of its laws.

357 U.S. at 252–253.

Although the greedy sisters lose in *Hanson*, is the Supreme Court's decision jurisdictionally correct? Is it really factually distinguishable from *McGee*? One point of difference emphasized by the Court was that in *McGee*, California had enacted special legislation (the Unauthorized Insurers Process Act) to assert California's interest "in providing effective redress for citizens who had been injured by nonresidents engaged in an activity that the State treats as exceptional and subject to regulation." There was, of course, no specific-act statute in *Hanson*. Why should that make a difference to the question of constitutional Due Process? Consider again the fact that some states, like California and Rhode Island, have enacted "the sky's the limit" jurisdictional statutes. Indeed, unlike the situation in *McGee*, the forum whose substantive law could govern the controversy (Florida) was held to lack personal jurisdiction. The *Hanson* Court insisted on keeping separate the jurisdiction and choice of law issues:

> As we understand [Florida] law, the trustee is an indispensable party over whom the court must acquire jurisdiction before it is empowered to enter judgment in a proceeding affecting the validity of a trust. [Florida] does not

acquire that jurisdiction by being the "center of gravity" of the controversy, or the most convenient location for litigation. The issue is personal jurisdiction, not choice of law. It is resolved in this case by considering the acts of the trustee. As we have indicated, they are insufficient to sustain the jurisdiction.

357 U.S. at 254.

Because *Hanson* was a complicated and difficult case and its rationale somewhat murky, its impact on the run-of-the-mill tort and contract jurisdiction cases seemed minimal. The lower courts continued to exercise jurisdiction over nonresident sellers whose products were shipped into another state and caused injury there; the commercial cases were somewhat less clear, with jurisdiction often more likely to be found in suits by resident buyers against nonresident sellers than in suits by resident sellers against nonresident buyers. Guidance for these types of cases did not come for over two decades.

b.   Portable Tort Cases

World-Wide Volkswagen Corp. v. Woodson

444 U.S. 286 (1980) *before Daimer (2014)*

Certiorari to the Supreme Court of Oklahoma.

Mr. Justice White delivered the opinion of the Court.

The issue before us is whether, consistently with the Due Process Clause of the Fourteenth Amendment, an Oklahoma court may exercise *in personam* jurisdiction over a nonresident automobile retailer and its wholesale distributor in a products-liability action, when the defendants' only connection with Oklahoma is the fact that an automobile sold in New York to New York residents became involved in an accident in Oklahoma.

I

Respondents Harry and Kay Robinson purchased a new Audi automobile from petitioner Seaway Volkswagen, Inc. (Seaway), in Massena, N.Y., in 1976. The following year the Robinson family, who resided in New York, left that State for a new home in Arizona. As they passed through the State of Oklahoma, another car struck their Audi in the rear, causing a fire which severely burned Kay Robinson and her two children.

The Robinsons subsequently brought a products-liability action in the District Court for Creek County, Okla., claiming that their injuries resulted from defective design and placement of the Audi's gas tank and fuel system. They joined as defendants the automobile's manufacturer, Audi NSU Auto Union Aktiengesellschaft (Audi); its importer, Volkswagen of America, Inc. (Volkswagen); its regional distributor, petitioner World-Wide Volkswagen Corp. (World-Wide); and its retail dealer, petitioner Seaway. Seaway and World-Wide entered special appearances,[3] claiming

---

3. Volkswagen also entered a special appearance in the District Court, but unlike World-Wide and Seaway did not seek review in the Supreme Court of Oklahoma and is not a petitioner here. Both Volkswagen and <u>Audi</u> remain as defendants in the litigation pending before the District Court in Oklahoma. *did not argue jurisdiction*

that Oklahoma's exercise of jurisdiction over them would offend the limitations on the State's jurisdiction imposed by the Due Process Clause of the Fourteenth Amendment.

The facts presented to the District Court showed that World-Wide is incorporated and has its business office in New York. It distributes vehicles, parts, and accessories, under contract with Volkswagen, to retail dealers in New York, New Jersey, and Connecticut. Seaway, one of these retail dealers, is incorporated and has its place of business in New York. Insofar as the record reveals, Seaway and World-Wide are fully independent corporations whose relations with each other and with Volkswagen and Audi are contractual only. Respondents adduced no evidence that either World-Wide or Seaway does any business in Oklahoma, ships or sells any products to or in that State, has an agent to receive process there, or purchases advertisements in any media calculated to reach Oklahoma. In fact, . . . there was no showing that any automobile sold by World-Wide or Seaway has ever entered Oklahoma with the single exception of the vehicle involved in the present case.

Despite the apparent paucity of contacts between petitioners and Oklahoma, the District Court rejected their constitutional claim and reaffirmed that ruling in denying petitioners' motion for reconsideration. Petitioners then sought a writ of prohibition in the Supreme Court of Oklahoma to restrain the District Judge, respondent Charles S. Woodson, from exercising *in personam* jurisdiction over them. They renewed their contention that, because they had no "minimal contacts" . . . with the State of Oklahoma, the actions of the District Judge were in violation of their rights under the Due Process Clause.

The Supreme Court of Oklahoma denied the writ, 585 P.2d 351 (1978), holding that personal jurisdiction over petitioners was authorized by Oklahoma's "long-arm" statute, Okla. Stat., Tit. 12, §1701.03 (a)(4) (1971)[7]. Although the court noted that the proper approach was to test jurisdiction against both statutory and constitutional standards, its analysis did not distinguish these questions, probably because §1701.03(a)(4) has been interpreted as conferring jurisdiction to the limits permitted by the United States Constitution.[8] The court's rationale was contained in the following paragraph, 585 P.2d, at 354:

> In the case before us, the product being sold and distributed by the petitioners is by its very design and purpose so mobile that petitioners can foresee its possible use in Oklahoma. This is especially true of the

---

7. This subsection provides:

A court may exercise personal jurisdiction over a person, who acts directly or by an agent, as to a cause of action or claim for relief arising from the person's . . . causing tortious injury in this state by an act or omission outside this state if he regularly does or solicits business or engages in any other persistent course of conduct, or derives substantial revenue from goods used or consumed or services rendered, in this state. . . .

The State Supreme Court rejected jurisdiction based on §1701.03(a)(3), which authorizes jurisdiction over any person "causing tortious injury in this state by an act or omission in this state." Something in addition to the infliction of tortious injury was required.

8. *Fields v. Volkswagen of America, Inc.*, 555 P.2d 48 (Okla. 1976); *Carmack v. Chemical Bank New York Trust Co.*, 536 P.2d 897 (Okla. 1975); *Hines v. Clendenning*, 465 P.2d 460 (Okla. 1970).

distributor, who has the exclusive right to distribute such automobile in New York, New Jersey and Connecticut. The evidence presented below demonstrated that goods sold and distributed by the petitioners were used in the State of Oklahoma, and under the facts we believe it reasonable to infer, given the retail value of the automobile, that the petitioners derive substantial income from automobiles which from time to time are used in the State of Oklahoma. This being the case, we hold that under the facts presented, the trial court was justified in concluding that the petitioners derive substantial revenue from goods used or consumed in this State.

We granted certiorari . . . to consider an important constitutional question with respect to state-court jurisdiction and to resolve a conflict between the Supreme Court of Oklahoma and the highest courts of at least four other States. We reverse.

II

. . . As has long been settled, and as we reaffirm today, a state court may exercise personal jurisdiction over a nonresident defendant only so long as there exist "minimum contacts" between the defendant and the forum State. *International Shoe Co. v. Washington,* . . . The concept of minimum contacts, in turn, can be seen to perform two related, but distinguishable, functions. It protects the defendant against the burdens of litigating in a distant or inconvenient forum. And it acts to ensure that the States, through their courts, do not reach out beyond the limits imposed on them by their status as coequal sovereigns in a federal system.

The protection against inconvenient litigation is typically described in terms of "reasonableness" or "fairness." We have said that the defendant's contacts with the forum State must be such that maintenance of the suit "does not offend 'traditional notions of fair play and substantial justice.' " *International Shoe Co. v. Washington, supra,* at 316, quoting *Milliken v. Meyer,* 311 U.S. 457, 463 (1940). The relationship between the defendant and the forum must be such that it is "reasonable . . . to require the corporation to defend the particular suit which is brought there." 326 U.S., at 317. Implicit in this emphasis on reasonableness is the understanding that the burden on the defendant, while always a primary concern, will in an appropriate case be considered in light of other relevant factors, including the forum State's interest in adjudicating the dispute, *see McGee v. International Life Ins. Co.,* 355 U.S. 220, 223 (1957); the plaintiff's interest in obtaining convenient and effective relief, *see Kulko v. California Superior Court, supra,* at 92, at least when that interest is not adequately protected by the plaintiff's power to choose the forum . . . ; the interstate judicial system's interest in obtaining the most efficient resolution of controversies; and the shared interest of the several States in furthering fundamental substantive social policies, *see Kulko v. California Superior Court, supra,* at 93, 98.

The limits imposed on state jurisdiction by the Due Process Clause, in its role as a guarantor against inconvenient litigation, have been substantially relaxed over the years. . . . The historical developments noted in *McGee,* of course, have only accelerated in the generation since that case was decided.

Nevertheless, we have never accepted the proposition that state lines are irrelevant for jurisdictional purposes, nor could we, and remain faithful to the principles of interstate federalism embodied in the Constitution. The economic interdependence of the States was foreseen and desired by the Framers. In the Commerce Clause, they provided that the Nation was to be a common market, a "free trade unit" in which the States are debarred from acting as separable economic entities. *H. P. Hood & Sons, Inc. v. Du Mond*, 336 U.S. 525, 538 (1949). But the Framers also intended that the States retain many essential attributes of sovereignty, including, in particular, the sovereign power to try causes in their courts. The sovereignty of each State, in turn, implied a limitation on the sovereignty of all of its sister States—a limitation express or implicit in both the original scheme of the Constitution and the Fourteenth Amendment. . . .

Thus, the Due Process Clause "does not contemplate that a state may make binding a judgment *in personam* against an individual or corporate defendant with which the state has no contacts, ties, or relations." *International Shoe Co. v. Washington, supra*, at 319. Even if the defendant would suffer minimal or no inconvenience from being forced to litigate before the tribunals of another State; even if the forum State has a strong interest in applying its law to the controversy; even if the forum State is the most convenient location for litigation, the Due Process Clause, acting as an instrument of interstate federalism, may sometimes act to divest the State of its power to render a valid judgment. *Hanson v. Denckla*, . . .

III

Applying these principles to the case at hand, we find in the record before us a total absence of those affiliating circumstances that are a necessary predicate to any exercise of state-court jurisdiction. Petitioners carry on no activity whatsoever in Oklahoma. They close no sales and perform no services there. They avail themselves of none of the privileges and benefits of Oklahoma law. They solicit no business there either through salespersons or through advertising reasonably calculated to reach the State. Nor does the record show that they regularly sell cars at wholesale or retail to Oklahoma customers or residents or that they indirectly, through others, serve or seek to serve the Oklahoma market. In short, respondents seek to base jurisdiction on one, isolated occurrence and whatever inferences can be drawn therefrom: the fortuitous circumstance that a single Audi automobile, sold in New York to New York residents, happened to suffer an accident while passing through Oklahoma.

It is argued, however, that because an automobile is mobile by its very design and purpose it was "foreseeable" that the Robinsons' Audi would cause injury in Oklahoma. Yet "foreseeability" alone has never been a sufficient benchmark for personal jurisdiction under the Due Process Clause. In *Hanson v. Denckla, supra*, it was no doubt foreseeable that the settlor of a Delaware trust would subsequently move to Florida and seek to exercise a power of appointment there; yet we held that Florida courts could not constitutionally exercise jurisdiction over a Delaware trustee that had no other contacts with the forum State. In *Kulko v. California Superior Court*, 436 U.S. 84 (1978), it was surely "foreseeable" that a divorced wife would move to California from New York, the domicile of the marriage, and that a minor daughter would live with the mother. Yet we held that California could not exercise jurisdiction in a child-support action over the former husband who had remained in New York.

If foreseeability were the criterion, a local California tire retailer could be forced to defend in Pennsylvania when a blowout occurs there, *see Erlanger Mills, Inc. v. Cohoes Fibre Mills, Inc.*, 239 F.2d 502, 507 (CA4 1956); a Wisconsin seller of a defective automobile jack could be hauled before a distant court for damage caused in New Jersey, *Reilly v. Phil Tolkan Pontiac, Inc.*, 372 F. Supp. 1205 (NJ 1974); or a Florida soft-drink concessionaire could be summoned to Alaska to account for injuries happening there, *see Uppgren v. Executive Aviation Services, Inc.*, 304 F. Supp. 165, 170–171 (Minn. 1969). Every seller of chattels would in effect appoint the chattel his agent for service of process. His amenability to suit would travel with the chattel. . . .

This is not to say, of course, that foreseeability is wholly irrelevant. But the foreseeability that is critical to due process analysis is not the mere likelihood that a product will find its way into the forum State. Rather, it is that the defendant's conduct and connection with the forum State are such that he should reasonably anticipate being hauled into court there. *See Kulko v. California Superior Court, supra*, at 97–98. . . . The Due Process Clause, by ensuring the "orderly administration of the laws," *International Shoe Co. v. Washington*, 326 U.S., at 319, gives a degree of predictability to the legal system that allows potential defendants to structure their primary conduct with some minimum assurance as to where that conduct will and will not render them liable to suit.

When a corporation "purposefully avails itself of the privilege of conducting activities within the forum State," *Hanson v. Denckla*, 357 U.S., at 253, it has clear notice that it is subject to suit there, and can act to alleviate the risk of burdensome litigation by procuring insurance, passing the expected costs on to customers, or, if the risks are too great, severing its connection with the State. Hence if the sale of a product of a manufacturer or distributor such as Audi or Volkswagen is not simply an isolated occurrence, but arises from the efforts of the manufacturer or distributor to serve, directly or indirectly, the market for its product in other States, it is not unreasonable to subject it to suit in one of those States if its allegedly defective merchandise has there been the source of injury to its owner or to others. The forum State does not exceed its powers under the Due Process Clause if it asserts personal jurisdiction over a corporation that delivers its products into the stream of commerce with the expectation that they will be purchased by consumers in the forum State. *Cf. Gray v. American Radiator & Standard Sanitary Corp.*, 22 Ill. 2d 432, 176 N.E.2d 761 (1961).

But there is no such or similar basis for Oklahoma jurisdiction over World-Wide or Seaway in this case. Seaway's sales are made in Massena, N.Y. World-Wide's market, although substantially larger, is limited to dealers in New York, New Jersey, and Connecticut. There is no evidence of record that any automobiles distributed by World-Wide are sold to retail customers outside this tristate area. It is foreseeable that the purchasers of automobiles sold by World-Wide and Seaway may take them to Oklahoma. But the mere "unilateral activity of those who claim some relationship with a nonresident defendant cannot satisfy the requirement of contact with the forum State." *Hanson v. Denckla, supra*, at 253.

In a variant on the previous argument, it is contended that jurisdiction can be supported by the fact that petitioners earn substantial revenue from goods used in Oklahoma. The Oklahoma Supreme Court so found, 585 P.2d, at 354–355, drawing the inference that because one automobile sold by petitioners had been used in

Oklahoma, others might have been used there also. While this inference seems less than compelling on the facts of the instant case, we need not question the court's factual findings in order to reject its reasoning.

This argument seems to make the point that the purchase of automobiles in New York, from which the petitioners earn substantial revenue, would not occur *but for* the fact that the automobiles are capable of use in distant States like Oklahoma. Respondents observe that the very purpose of an automobile is to travel, and that travel of automobiles sold by petitioners is facilitated by an extensive chain of Volkswagen service centers throughout the country, including some in Oklahoma. However, financial benefits accruing to the defendant from a collateral relation to the forum State will not support jurisdiction if they do not stem from a constitutionally cognizable contact with that State. *See Kulko v. California Superior Court,* 436 U.S., at 94–95. In our view, whatever marginal revenues petitioners may receive by virtue of the fact that their products are capable of use in Oklahoma is far too attenuated a contact to justify that State's exercise of *in personam* jurisdiction over them.

Because we find that petitioners have no "contacts, ties, or relations" with the State of Oklahoma, *International Shoe Co. v. Washington, supra,* at 319, the judgment of the Supreme Court of Oklahoma is
    Reversed.

MR. JUSTICE BRENNAN, dissenting.
    . . . The petitioners are not unconnected with the forum. Although both sell automobiles within limited sales territories, each sold the automobile which in fact was driven to Oklahoma where it was involved in an accident.[8] It may be true, as the Court suggests, that each sincerely intended to limit its commercial impact to the limited territory, and that each intended to accept the benefits and protection of the laws only of those States within the territory. But obviously these were unrealistic hopes that cannot be treated as an automatic constitutional shield.[9]

An automobile simply is not a stationary item or one designed to be used in one place. An automobile is *intended* to be moved around. Someone in the business of selling large numbers of automobiles can hardly plead ignorance of their mobility or pretend that the automobiles stay put after they are sold. It is not merely that a dealer in automobiles foresees that they will move. . . . The dealer actually intends that the purchasers will use the automobiles to travel to distant States where the dealer does not directly "do business." The sale of an automobile does *purposefully* inject the vehicle into the stream of interstate commerce so that it can travel to distant States. *See Kulko,* 436 U.S., at 94; *Hanson v. Denckla,* 357 U.S. 235, 253 (1958). . . .

---

8. On the basis of this fact, the state court inferred that the petitioners derived substantial revenue from goods used in Oklahoma. The inference is not without support. Certainly, were use of goods accepted as a relevant contact, a plaintiff would not need to have an exact count of the number of petitioners' cars that are used in Oklahoma.

9. Moreover, imposing liability in this case would not so undermine certainty as to destroy an automobile dealer's ability to do business. According jurisdiction does not expand liability except in the marginal case where a plaintiff cannot afford to bring an action except in the plaintiff's own State. In addition, these petitioners are represented by insurance companies. They not only could, but did, purchase insurance to protect them should they stand trial and lose the case. The costs of the insurance no doubt are passed on to customers.

The Court accepts that a State may exercise jurisdiction over a distributor which "serves" that State "indirectly" by "[delivering] its products into the stream of commerce with the expectation that they will be purchased by consumers in the forum State.". . . It is difficult to see why the Constitution should distinguish between a case involving goods which reach a distant State through a chain of distribution and a case involving goods which reach the same State because a consumer, using them as the dealer knew the customer would, took them there.[11] In each case the seller purposefully injects the goods into the stream of commerce and those goods predictably are used in the forum State.[12]

Furthermore, an automobile seller derives substantial benefits from States other than its own. A large part of the value of automobiles is the extensive, nationwide network of highways. Significant portions of that network have been constructed by and are maintained by the individual States, including Oklahoma. The States, through their highway programs, contribute in a very direct and important way to the value of petitioners' businesses. Additionally, a network of other related dealerships with their service departments operates throughout the country under the protection of the laws of the various States, including Oklahoma, and enhances the value of petitioners' businesses by facilitating their customers' traveling.

Thus, the Court errs in its conclusion . . . that "petitioners have *no* 'contacts, ties, or relations' " with Oklahoma. There obviously are contacts, and, given Oklahoma's connection to the litigation, the contacts are sufficiently significant to make it fair and reasonable for the petitioners to submit to Oklahoma's jurisdiction.

III

It may be that affirmance of the judgments . . . would approach the outer limits of *International Shoe*'s jurisdictional principle. But that principle, with its almost exclusive focus on the rights of defendants, may be outdated. . . . The model of society on which the *International Shoe* Court based its opinion is no longer accurate. Business people, no matter how local their businesses, cannot assume that goods remain in the business' locality. Customers and goods can be anywhere else in the country usually in a matter of hours and always in a matter of a very few days.

In answering the question whether or not it is fair and reasonable to allow a particular forum to hold a trial binding on a particular defendant, the interests of the forum State and other parties loom large in today's world and surely are entitled to as much weight as are the interests of the defendant. The "orderly administration of the laws" provides a firm basis for according some protection to the interests of plaintiffs and States as well as of defendants. Certainly, I cannot see how a defendant's right to due process is violated if the defendant suffers no inconvenience. . . .

---

11. For example, I cannot understand the constitutional distinction between selling an item in New Jersey and selling an item in New York expecting it to be used in New Jersey.

12. The manufacturer in the case cited by the Court, *Gray v. American Radiator & Standard Sanitary Corp.*, 22 Ill. 2d 432, 176 N.E.2d 761 (1961), had no more control over which States its goods would reach than did the petitioners in this case.

The Court's opinion in No. 78-1078 suggests that the defendant ought to be subject to a State's jurisdiction only if he has contacts with the State "such that he should reasonably anticipate being haled into court there."[18]. . . There is nothing unreasonable or unfair, however, about recognizing commercial reality. Given the tremendous mobility of goods and people, and the inability of businessmen to control where goods are taken by customers (or retailers), I do not think that the defendant should be in complete control of the geographical stretch of his amenability to suit. Jurisdiction is no longer premised on the notion that nonresident defendants have somehow impliedly consented to suit. People should understand that they are held responsible for the consequences of their actions and that in our society most actions have consequences affecting many States. When an action in fact causes injury in another State, the actor should be prepared to answer for it there unless defending in that State would be unfair for some reason other than that a state boundary must be crossed.[19]

In effect the Court is allowing defendants to assert the sovereign rights of their home States. The expressed fear is that otherwise all limits on personal jurisdiction would disappear. But the argument's premise is wrong. I would not abolish limits on jurisdiction or strip state boundaries of all significance, *see Hanson, supra*, at 260 (Black, J., dissenting); I would still require the plaintiff to demonstrate sufficient contacts among the parties, the forum, and the litigation to make the forum a reasonable State in which to hold the trial.[20]

I would also, however, strip the defendant of an unjustified veto power over certain very appropriate fora—a power the defendant justifiably enjoyed long ago when communication and travel over long distances were slow and unpredictable and when notions of state sovereignty were impractical and exaggerated. But I repeat that that is not today's world. If a plaintiff can show that his chosen forum State has a sufficient interest in the litigation (or sufficient contacts with the defendant), then the defendant who cannot show some real injury to a constitutionally protected interest . . . should have no constitutional excuse not to appear.[21] . . .

[The dissenting opinions of JUSTICE MARSHALL and JUSTICE BLACKMUN are omitted.]

NOTES AND QUESTIONS

1. *Is* Gray *Still Good Law?* Does *World-Wide Volkswagen* suggest that *Gray* (discussed at pp. 110–111) is no longer good law? In *Gray*, the nonresident manufacturer of a component part had its valve incorporated into a product that was

---

18. The Court suggests that this is the critical foreseeability rather than the likelihood that the product will go to the forum State. But the reasoning begs the question. A defendant cannot know if his actions will subject him to jurisdiction in another State until we have declared what the law of jurisdiction is.

19. One consideration that might create some unfairness would be if the choice of forum also imposed on the defendant an unfavorable substantive law which the defendant could justly have assumed would not apply. . . .

20. For instance, . . . I might reach a different result if the accident had not occurred in Oklahoma.

21. Frequently, of course, the defendant will be able to influence the choice of forum through traditional doctrines, such as venue or *forum non conveniens*, permitting the transfer of litigation. . . .

eventually sold and caused injury in the forum state. In *World-Wide Volkswagen*, a nonresident distributor and dealer sold its product to the plaintiff, who subsequently brought the product into the state where she was injured due to the alleged defect. If jurisdiction in *Volkswagen* was inappropriate, does it follow that there should not have been jurisdiction in *Gray*? If not, what principle justifies a distinction between them? Note that the Supreme Court in *Volkswagen* cited *Gray* with apparent approval.

2. *The Role of State Sovereignty Considerations.* Quite apart from the tension in outcomes between *Gray* and *Volkswagen*, the Supreme Court's opinion in *Volkswagen* seems to move away from *Gray* in spirit as well. The Court did not view "minimum contacts" merely as a means of "protecting defendants against the burden of litigating in a distant or inconvenient forum" but also as the vehicle to "ensure that the States, through their courts, do not reach out beyond the limits imposed on them by their status as co-equal sovereigns in a federal system." Indeed, the Court reemphasized the federalism point when it stated that regardless of the inconvenience to the defendant, the litigational convenience of the forum, or the forum's interest in the application of its own law, "the Due Process Clause, acting as an instrument of interstate federalism, may sometimes act to divest the state of its power to render a valid judgment." 444 U.S. at 294.

Does the Court's emphasis on sovereignty and federalism represent a return to the power philosophy of *Pennoyer*? What "federalism" interests are at stake anyhow? The sovereignty emphasis may have been short-lived because two years later, Justice White — the author of the majority opinion in *World-Wide Volkswagen* — appeared to recant. In *Insurance Corp. of Ireland v. Compagnie des Bauxites de Guinee*, 456 U.S. 694 (1982) (the Court holding that a federal court may order discovery in determining a jurisdictional challenge and may impose a finding of jurisdiction as a sanction against the defendant who failed to comply with the discovery order), Justice White included the following footnote:

> It is true that we have stated that the requirement of personal jurisdiction, as applied to state courts, reflects an element of federalism and the character of state sovereignty vis-à-vis other States. . . . The restriction on state sovereign power described in *World-Wide Volkswagen Corp.*, however, must be seen as ultimately a function of the individual liberty interest preserved by the Due Process Clause. That clause is the only source of the personal jurisdiction requirement and the Clause itself makes no mention of federalism concerns. Furthermore, if the federalism concept operated as an independent restriction on the sovereign power of the court, it would not be possible to waive the personal jurisdiction requirement: Individual actions cannot change the powers of sovereignty, although the individual can subject himself to powers from which he may otherwise be protected.

456 U.S. at 702-703 n.10.

3. *Foreseeability.* In *Volkswagen*, plaintiffs argued that the defendant distributor and dealer should be subject to jurisdiction in Oklahoma because it was foreseeable that when they sold the car to plaintiffs in New York the purchasers might take it to another state and suffer injury there. The Court seemingly rejected foreseeability as the appropriate test but suggested that foreseeability is not completely irrelevant:

> [T]he foreseeability that is critical to due process analysis is not the mere
> likelihood that a product will find its way into the forum State. Rather, it
> is that the defendant's conduct and connection with the forum State are
> such that he should reasonably anticipate being haled into court there.

444 U.S. at 297. How are the two "tests" different? Moreover, isn't foreseeability
a completely circular test, however it is put? The defendant will anticipate being
haled into court if the legal rule defines the defendant's activities as sufficient to
subject him to jurisdiction. So long as there is a clear rule, a defendant will be able
to "anticipate" jurisdiction. But how does a standard like "minimum contacts" permit you to "anticipate" anything?

4. *"Portable Torts."* The *Volkswagen* case is often described as necessary to prevent jurisdiction over "portable torts"; otherwise, every seller or manufacturer of a
product will have to defend anywhere the product is eventually taken and causes
injury. Should it matter whether the defendant is a manufacturer or seller who
directly sends the product into the state where the injury occurs, or only a component manufacturer or indirect seller who puts the product generally into the
"stream of commerce" with no designation or control as to where the product eventually winds up? Are the defendant's expectations relevant? Does the level of sales
or amount of product use in the forum state matter?

Suppose Mrs. Robinson had requested that the car be shipped to her in
Oklahoma, where she was going to be on vacation before moving out to Arizona;
the New York dealer delivers the car to her there and then the accident occurs.
Can Oklahoma now assert jurisdiction over the New York dealer? Or suppose
Mrs. Robinson is a resident of Connecticut and comes to New York to buy the
car. The New York distributor also services the Connecticut market, and the
New York dealer is likely to have sold some cars to other Connecticut residents.
If an accident occurs in Connecticut, would it be constitutional for Connecti-
cut to assert jurisdiction over the New York distributor and dealer? Reconsider
these questions after reading two later principal cases in this chapter, *Asahi Metal
Industry v. Superior Court of California*, at p. 127, and *J. McIntyre Machinery, Ltd. v.
Nicastro*, at p. 137.

5. *"Foreseeability" and Family Law Disputes.* In its "foreseeability" discussion in
Volkswagen, the Supreme Court cited its 1978 decision in *Kulko v. Superior Court of
California*, 436 U.S. 84. The plaintiff in that case, a California mother, brought suit
against her New York ex-husband for a modification of child support. The New
York separation agreement, incorporated into a Haitian divorce, provided that the
husband pay the wife $3,000 a year in child support during the time the children
were with her. The parties had lived in New York, but after the divorce the wife
moved to California. The two children remained in New York with their father
during the school year and visited their mother during vacation periods. When the
daughter asked to go live with her mother in California, the father bought her
a one-way plane ticket. Subsequently, the son also went to California to live with
his mother. When the wife brought suit against the ex-husband in California to
increase the amount of child support, the ex-husband moved to dismiss for lack of
jurisdiction. The California Supreme Court found that the defendant had caused
an effect in California by sending his daughter to California and that it was fair to

subject him to personal jurisdiction for the support of both children since he had also in effect consented to his son's change of residence. The Supreme Court of the United States reversed:

> [A]ppellant did no more than acquiesce in the stated preference of one of his children to live with her mother in California. This single act is surely not one that a reasonable parent would expect to result in the substantial financial burden and personal strain of litigating a child-support suit in a forum 3,000 miles away, and we therefore see no basis on which it can be said that appellant could reasonably have anticipated being "haled before a [California] court" (citations omitted). To make jurisdiction in a case such as this turn on whether appellant bought his daughter her ticket or instead unsuccessfully sought to prevent her departure would impose an unreasonable burden on family relations, and one wholly unjustified by the "quality and nature" of appellant's activities in or relating to the State of California.

436 U.S. at 97-98.

What alternative to bringing suit in California does the wife have? In most situations, she would have to bring suit where the husband was present or domiciled—in *Kulko*, that would mean New York.

Under California law at the time of *Kulko*, the Uniform Reciprocal Enforcement of Support Act (URESA) was in effect and permitted a plaintiff in a child support case to use a bi-state mechanism to bring suit. Under that Act, the plaintiff mother could file a petition in her home state—here, California—claiming support from the nonresident father; the merits are then adjudicated in the state of the obligor's residence—here, New York. Thus, neither party had to leave his or her home state. Do you think the existence of this alternative procedure influenced the court in deciding whether assertion of jurisdiction by California in *Kulko* was constitutional?

URESA was replaced by a new Uniform Act, the Uniform Interstate Family Support Act (UIFSA). There are different versions of UIFSA, but all states in the United States have one or another version, as they are required to do under federal law in order to receive federal funding for child support enforcement. The bi-state procedure under UIFSA continues but may be less important because of UIFSA's attempt to expand personal jurisdiction over nonresidents in support cases in a one-state proceeding. To that end, UIFSA adds the following as bases of jurisdiction over nonresidents in support matters: (a) the child resides in this state as a result of the acts or directives of the individual; (b) the individual engaged in sexual intercourse in this state and the child may have been conceived by that act of intercourse; and (c) there is any other basis consistent with the constitutions of this state and the United States for the exercise of personal jurisdiction. Does UIFSA withstand constitutional scrutiny in light of *Kulko*? Why should the Supreme Court view the "sky's the limit" provision of UIFSA any more favorably than it did the California statute involved in *Kulko*? Are either of the more specific provisions listed above any more likely to survive constitutional challenge?

6. *Why Was There a Jurisdictional Battle over the "Little Guys"?* In *Volkswagen*, the German manufacturer did not contest jurisdiction, and the New Jersey importer did not pursue an initial jurisdictional challenge on appeal. Did these defendants make a mistake in not pursuing jurisdictional objections? Or was it absolutely clear that these defendants would be subject to jurisdiction in Oklahoma? How are they distinguishable from the local distributor and dealer?

Can you think of any reason why the New York dealer and distributor were joined in the first place? In some instances, a plaintiff may not be sure which of several defendants is responsible for an alleged defect, or occasionally a plaintiff may try to join additional "deep-pocket" defendants. However, in the *Volkswagen* case, the plaintiffs' claim was that the gas tank was defectively structured or placed — a manufacturing or design defect — and it was unlikely that the local dealer and distributor were more culpable or more solvent than the defendant manufacturer. A different concern was likely at work: It appears that jury verdicts in the local Oklahoma state court were particularly generous to plaintiffs, and thus the plaintiffs' lawyers wanted to assure that the case would stay in state court in Oklahoma. How does jurisdiction over the New York dealer and distributor achieve that end? Reconsider this question after reading the material on the diversity jurisdiction of federal courts in Chapter 3.

Of course, in many cases where joint or alternative liability is at stake, decisions like *Volkswagen* may make it impossible to find a single forum where all defendants can be joined in a single action. What are the drawbacks of bringing separate product liability suits against individual defendants in separate fora? Should the jurisdictional rules be more expansive in multiparty cases? *Compare* Fed. R. Civ. P. 4(k)(1)(B), providing for an additional 100-mile territorial reach where additional parties are joined under Fed. R. Civ. P. 14 or 19.

7. *Consideration of Factors Other Than Defendant's Contacts.* Justice White's citation to *Erlanger Mills, Inc. v. Cohoes Fibre Mills, Inc.*, 239 F.2d 502 (4th Cir. 1956), suggests a concern that finding sellers of chattels suable wherever the chattels end up would impose serious litigation burdens on such sellers and stymie the flow of interstate commerce. On the facts in *Volkswagen*, this concern may have been misplaced because the New York dealers and franchisers were represented by the same New York law firm appearing on behalf of the manufacturer and distributor, and any liability assessed against the New York companies would have been picked up by the manufacturer or importer.

Is there a means of dealing with such concerns as part of the jurisdictional inquiry while acknowledging that the defendant's contacts with the forum state would otherwise be sufficient? What do you think of Justice Brennan's suggested rule of presumptive jurisdiction absent a showing of actual inconvenience or other unfairness — such as unreasonable choice of law rules in the forum state? On the other hand, do we undermine the kind of certainty that would enable individuals and businesses to plan their affairs in an interstate market by adopting such an individualized, fact-specific approach to jurisdiction? Bear these concerns in mind as you read the Supreme Court's adoption of a "reasonableness" test in the next principal case.

c. The "Stream of Commerce" and "Reasonableness"

Asahi Metal Indus. Co. v. Superior Court of California

480 U.S. 102 (1987)

Certiorari to the Supreme Court of California.   ᐟ J. O'Connor's plurality' (4?)

JUSTICE O'CONNOR announced the judgment of the Court and delivered the unanimous opinion of the Court with respect to Part I, the opinion of the Court with respect to Part II-B, in which THE CHIEF JUSTICE, JUSTICE BRENNAN, JUSTICE WHITE, JUSTICE MARSHALL, JUSTICE BLACKMUN, JUSTICE POWELL, and JUSTICE

STEVENS join, and an opinion with respect to Parts II-A and III, in which THE CHIEF JUSTICE, JUSTICE POWELL, and JUSTICE SCALIA join. . . .

I

On September 23, 1978, on Interstate Highway 80 in Solano County, California, Gary Zurcher lost control of his Honda motorcycle and collided with a tractor. Zurcher was severely injured, and his passenger and wife, Ruth Ann Moreno, was killed. In September 1979, Zurcher filed a product liability action in the Superior Court of the State of California in and for the County of Solano. Zurcher alleged that the 1978 accident was caused by a sudden loss of air and an explosion in the rear tire of the motorcycle, and alleged that the motorcycle tire, tube, and sealant were defective. Zurcher's complaint named, *inter alia*, Cheng Shin Rubber Industrial Co., Ltd. (Cheng Shin), the Taiwanese manufacturer of the tube. Cheng Shin in turn filed a cross-complaint seeking indemnification from its codefendants and from petitioner, Asahi Metal Industry Co., Ltd. (Asahi), the manufacturer of the tube's valve assembly. Zurcher's claims against Cheng Shin and the other defendants were eventually settled and dismissed, leaving only Cheng Shin's indemnity action against Asahi.

California's long-arm statute authorizes the exercise of jurisdiction "on any basis not inconsistent with the Constitution of this state or of the United States." Cal. Civ. Proc. Code Ann. §410.10 (West 1973). Asahi moved to quash Cheng Shin's service of summons, arguing the State could not exert jurisdiction over it consistent with the Due Process Clause of the Fourteenth Amendment.

In relation to the motion, the following information was submitted by Asahi and Cheng Shin. Asahi is a Japanese corporation. It manufactures tire valve assemblies in Japan and sells the assemblies to Cheng Shin, and to several other tire manufacturers, for use as components in finished tire tubes. Asahi's sales to Cheng Shin took place in Taiwan. The shipments from Asahi to Cheng Shin were sent from Japan to Taiwan. Cheng Shin bought and incorporated into its tire tubes 150,000 Asahi valve assemblies in 1978; 500,000 in 1979; 500,000 in 1980; 100,000 in 1981; and 100,000 in 1982. Sales to Cheng Shin accounted for 1.24 percent of Asahi's income in 1981 and 0.44 percent in 1982. Cheng Shin alleged that approximately 20 percent of its sales in the United States are in California. Cheng Shin purchases valve assemblies from other suppliers as well, and sells finished tubes throughout the world.

In 1983 an attorney for Cheng Shin conducted an informal examination of the valve stems of the tire tubes sold in one cycle store in Solano County. The attorney declared that of the approximately 115 tire tubes in the store, 97 were purportedly manufactured in Japan or Taiwan, and of those 97, 21 valve stems were marked with the circled letter "A," apparently Asahi's trademark. Of the 21 Asahi valve stems, 12 were incorporated into Cheng Shin tire tubes. The store contained 41 other Cheng Shin tubes that incorporated the valve assemblies of other manufacturers. Declaration of Kenneth B. Shepard in Opposition to Motion to Quash Subpoena, App. to Brief for Respondent 5-6. An affidavit of a manager of Cheng Shin whose duties included the purchasing of component parts stated: " 'In discussions with Asahi regarding the purchase of valve stem assemblies the fact that my Company sells tubes throughout the world and specifically the United States has been discussed. I am informed and believe that Asahi was fully aware that valve stem assemblies sold to my Company and to others would end up throughout the

United States and in California.' " 39 Cal. 3d 35, 48, n. 4, 702 P.2d 543, 549–550, n. 4 (1985). An affidavit of the president of Asahi, on the other hand, declared that Asahi " 'has never contemplated that its limited sales of tire valves to Cheng Shin in Taiwan would subject it to lawsuits in California.' " *Ibid.* The record does not include any contract between Cheng Shin and Asahi. Tr. of Oral Arg. 24.

Primarily on the basis of the above information, the Superior Court denied the motion to quash summons, stating: "Asahi obviously does business on an international scale. It is not unreasonable that they defend claims of defect in their product on an international scale." Order Denying Motion to Quash Summons, *Zurcher v. Dunlop Tire & Rubber Co.*, No. 76180 (Super. Ct., Solano County, Cal., Apr. 20, 1983).

The Court of Appeals of the State of California issued a peremptory writ of mandate commanding the Superior Court to quash service of summons. The court concluded that "it would be unreasonable to require Asahi to respond in California solely on the basis of ultimately realized foreseeability that the product into which its component was embodied would be sold all over the world including California." App. to Pet. for Cert. B5–B6.

The Supreme Court of the State of California reversed and discharged the writ issued by the Court of Appeal. 39 Cal. 3d 35, 702 P.2d 543 (1985). . . . We granted certiorari, 475 U.S. 1044 (1986), and now reverse.

II

A

The Due Process Clause of the Fourteenth Amendment limits the power of a state court to exert personal jurisdiction over a nonresident defendant. "[The] constitutional touchstone" of the determination whether an exercise of personal jurisdiction comports with due process "remains whether the defendant purposefully established 'minimum contacts' in the forum State." *Burger King Corp. v. Rudzewicz*, 471 U.S. 462, 474 (1985), quoting *International Shoe Co. v. Washington*, 326 U.S., at 316. . . .

Applying the principle that minimum contacts must be based on an act of the defendant, the Court in *World-Wide Volkswagen Corp. v. Woodson*, 444 U.S. 286 (1980), rejected the assertion that a *consumer's* unilateral act of bringing the defendant's product into the forum State was a sufficient constitutional basis for personal jurisdiction over the defendant. It had been argued in *World-Wide Volkswagen* that because an automobile retailer and its wholesale distributor sold a product mobile by design and purpose, they could foresee being haled into court in the distant States into which their customers might drive. The Court rejected this concept of foreseeability as an insufficient basis for jurisdiction under the Due Process Clause. *Id.,* at 295–296. The Court disclaimed, however, the idea that "foreseeability is wholly irrelevant" to personal jurisdiction, concluding that "[the] forum State does not exceed its powers under the Due Process Clause if it asserts personal jurisdiction over a corporation that delivers its products into the stream of commerce with the expectation that they will be purchased by consumers in the forum State." *Id.,* at 297–298 (citation omitted). . . .

In *World-Wide Volkswagen* itself, the state court sought to base jurisdiction not on any act of the defendant, but on the foreseeable unilateral actions of the consumer. Since *World-Wide Volkswagen,* lower courts have been confronted with cases in which the defendant acted by placing a product in the stream of commerce, and the stream eventually swept defendant's product into the forum State, but the defendant did nothing else to purposefully avail itself of the market in the forum State. Some courts have understood the Due Process Clause, as interpreted in *World-Wide Volkswagen*, to allow an exercise of personal jurisdiction to be based on no more than the defendant's act of placing the product in the stream of commerce. Other courts have understood the Due Process Clause and the above-quoted language in *World-Wide Volkswagen* to require the action of the defendant to be more purposefully directed at the forum State than the mere act of placing a product in the stream of commerce.

The reasoning of the Supreme Court of California in the present case illustrates the former interpretation of *World-Wide Volkswagen*. The Supreme Court of California held that, because the stream of commerce eventually brought some valves Asahi sold Cheng Shin into California, Asahi's awareness that its valves would be sold in California was sufficient to permit California to exercise jurisdiction over Asahi consistent with the requirements of the Due Process Clause. . . .

Other courts, however, have understood the Due Process Clause to require something more than that the defendant was aware of its product's entry into the forum State through the stream of commerce in order for the State to exert jurisdiction over the defendant. . . . In *Humble v. Toyota Motor Co.*, 727 F.2d 709 (CA8 1984), an injured car passenger brought suit against Arakawa Auto Body Company, a Japanese corporation that manufactured car seats for Toyota. Arakawa did no business in the United States; it had no office, affiliate, subsidiary, or agent in the United States; it manufactured its component parts outside the United States and delivered them to Toyota Motor Company in Japan. The Court of Appeals, adopting the reasoning of the District Court in that case, noted that although it "does not doubt that Arakawa could have foreseen that its product would find its way into the United States," it would be "manifestly unjust" to require Arakawa to defend itself in the United States. *Id.*, at 710–711, quoting 578 F. Supp. 530, 533 (ND Iowa 1982). . . .

We now find this latter position to be consonant with the requirements of due process. The "substantial connection," *Burger King*, 471 U.S., at 475; *McGee*, 355 U.S., at 223, between the defendant and the forum State necessary for a finding of minimum contacts must come about by *an action of the defendant purposefully directed toward the forum State. Burger King, supra*, at 476; *Keeton v. Hustler Magazine, Inc.*, 465 U.S. 770, 774 (1984). The placement of a product into the stream of commerce, without more, is not an act of the defendant purposefully directed toward the forum State. Additional conduct of the defendant may indicate an intent or purpose to serve the market in the forum State, for example, designing the product for the market in the forum State, advertising in the forum State, establishing channels for providing regular advice to customers in the forum State, or marketing the product through a distributor who has agreed to serve as the sales agent in the forum State. But a defendant's awareness that the stream of commerce may or will sweep the product into the forum State does not convert the mere act of placing the product into the stream into an act purposefully directed toward the forum State.

Assuming, *arguendo*, that respondents have established Asahi's awareness that some of the valves sold to Cheng Shin would be incorporated into tire tubes sold in California, respondents have not demonstrated any action by Asahi to purposefully avail itself of the California market. Asahi does not do business in California.

It has no office, agents, employees, or property in California. It does not advertise or otherwise solicit business in California. It did not create, control, or employ
the distribution system that brought its valves to California. *Cf. Hicks v. Kawasaki
Heavy Industries*, 452 F. Supp. 130 (MD Pa. 1978). There is no evidence that Asahi
designed its product in anticipation of sales in California. *Cf. Rockwell International
Corp. v. Costruzioni Aeronautiche Giovanni Agusta*, 553 F. Supp. 328 (ED Pa. 1982). On
the basis of these facts, the exertion of personal jurisdiction over Asahi by the Superior Court of California* exceeds the limits of due process.

B   8/9 agree.

The strictures of the Due Process Clause forbid a state court from exercising
personal jurisdiction over Asahi under circumstances that would offend " 'traditional notions of fair play and substantial justice.' " *International Shoe Co. v. Washington*, 326 U.S., at 316, quoting *Milliken v. Meyer*, 311 U.S., at 463.

We have previously explained that the determination of the reasonableness
of the exercise of jurisdiction in each case will depend on an evaluation of several
factors. A court must consider the burden on the defendant, the interests of the
forum State, and the plaintiff's interest in obtaining relief. It must also weigh in its
determination "the interstate judicial system's interest in obtaining the most efficient resolution of controversies; and the shared interest of the several States in furthering fundamental substantive social policies." *World-Wide Volkswagen*, 444 U.S., at
292 (citations omitted).

A consideration of these factors in the present case clearly reveals the unreasonableness of the assertion of jurisdiction over Asahi, even apart from the question of the placement of goods in the stream of commerce.

Certainly the burden on the defendant in this case is severe. Asahi has been
commanded by the Supreme Court of California not only to traverse the distance
between Asahi's headquarters in Japan and the Superior Court of California in and
for the County of Solano, but also to submit its dispute with Cheng Shin to a foreign
nation's judicial system. The unique burdens placed upon one who must defend one-
self in a foreign legal system should have significant weight in assessing the reasonableness of stretching the long arm of personal jurisdiction over national borders.

When minimum contacts have been established, often the interests of the
plaintiff and the forum in the exercise of jurisdiction will justify even the serious burdens placed on the alien defendant. In the present case, however, the
interests of the plaintiff and the forum in California's assertion of jurisdiction
over Asahi are slight. All that remains is a claim for indemnification asserted by
Cheng Shin, a Taiwanese corporation, against Asahi. The transaction on which

---

* We have no occasion here to determine whether Congress could, consistent with the
Due Process Clause of the Fifth Amendment, authorize federal court personal jurisdiction
over alien defendants based on the aggregate of national contacts, rather than on the con-
tacts between the defendant and the State in which the federal court sits. *See Max Daetwyler
Corp. v. R. Meyer*, 762 F.2d 290, 293–295 (CA3 1985); *DeJames v. Magnificence Carriers, Inc.*, 654
F.2d 280, 283 (CA3 1981); *see also* Born, Reflections on Judicial Jurisdiction in International
Cases, to be published in 17 Ga. J. Int'l & Comp. L. 1 (1987); Lilly, Jurisdiction Over Domestic and Alien Defendants, 69 Va. L. Rev. 85, 127–145 (1983).

the indemnification claim is based took place in Taiwan; Asahi's components were shipped from Japan to Taiwan. Cheng Shin has not demonstrated that it is more convenient for it to litigate its indemnification claim against Asahi in California rather than in Taiwan or Japan.

Because the plaintiff is not a California resident, California's legitimate interests in the dispute have considerably diminished. The Supreme Court of California argued that the State had an interest in "protecting its consumers by ensuring that foreign manufacturers comply with the state's safety standards." 39 Cal. 3d, at 49, 702 P.2d, at 550. The State Supreme Court's definition of California's interest, however, was overly broad. The dispute between Cheng Shin and Asahi is primarily about indemnification rather than safety standards. Moreover, it is not at all clear at this point that California law should govern the question whether a Japanese corporation should indemnify a Taiwanese corporation on the basis of a sale made in Taiwan and a shipment of goods from Japan to Taiwan. *Phillips Petroleum Co. v. Shutts*, 472 U.S. 797, 821–822 (1985); *Allstate Insurance Co. v. Hague*, 449 U.S. 302, 312–313 (1981). The possibility of being haled into a California court as a result of an accident involving Asahi's components undoubtedly creates an additional deterrent to the manufacture of unsafe components; however, similar pressures will be placed on Asahi by the purchasers of its components as long as those who use Asahi components in their final products, and sell those products in California, are subject to the application of California tort law.

World-Wide Volkswagen also admonished courts to take into consideration the interests of the "several States," in addition to the forum State, in the efficient judicial resolution of the dispute and the advancement of substantive policies. In the present case, this advice calls for a court to consider the procedural and substantive policies of other *nations* whose interests are affected by the assertion of jurisdiction by the California court. The procedural and substantive interests of other nations in a state court's assertion of jurisdiction over an alien defendant will differ from case to case. In every case, however, those interests, as well as the Federal Government's interest in its foreign relations policies, will be best served by a careful inquiry into the reasonableness of the assertion of jurisdiction in the particular case, and an unwillingness to find the serious burdens on an alien defendant outweighed by minimal interests on the part of the plaintiff or the forum State. "Great care and reserve should be exercised when extending our notions of personal jurisdiction into the international field." *United States v. First National City Bank*, 379 U.S. 378, 404 (1965) (Harlan, J., dissenting). *See* Born, Reflections on Judicial Jurisdiction in International Cases, to be published in 17 Ga. J. Int'l & Comp. L. 1 (1987).

Considering the international context, the heavy burden on the alien defendant, and the slight interests of the plaintiff and the forum State, the exercise of personal jurisdiction by a California court over Asahi in this instance would be unreasonable and unfair.

III

Because the facts of this case do not establish minimum contacts such that the exercise of personal jurisdiction is consistent with fair play and substantial justice, the judgment of the Supreme Court of California is reversed, and the case is remanded for further proceedings not inconsistent with this opinion.

It is so ordered.

JUSTICE BRENNAN, with whom JUSTICE WHITE, JUSTICE MARSHALL, and JUSTICE BLACKMUN join, concurring in part and concurring in the judgment.

I do not agree with the interpretation in Part II-A of the stream-of-commerce theory, nor with the conclusion that Asahi did not "purposely avail itself of the California market.". . . I do agree, however, with the Court's conclusion in Part II-B that the exercise of personal jurisdiction over Asahi in this case would not comport with "fair play and substantial justice," *International Shoe Co. v. Washington,* 326 U.S. 310, 320 (1945). This is one of those rare cases in which "minimum requirements inherent in the concept of 'fair play and substantial justice' . . . defeat the reasonableness of jurisdiction even [though] the defendant has purposefully engaged in forum activities." *Burger King Corp. v. Rudzewicz,* 471 U.S. 462, 477–478 (1985). I therefore join Parts I and II-B of the Court's opinion, and write separately to explain my disagreement with Part II-A.

Part II-A states that "a defendant's awareness that the stream of commerce may or will sweep the product into the forum State does not convert the mere act of placing the product into the stream into an act purposefully directed toward the forum State.". . . Under this view, a plaintiff would be required to show "[additional] conduct" directed toward the forum before finding the exercise of jurisdiction over the defendant to be consistent with the Due Process Clause. . . . I see no need for such a showing, however. The stream of commerce refers not to unpredictable currents or eddies, but to the regular and anticipated flow of products from manufacture to distribution to retail sale. As long as a participant in this process is aware that the final product is being marketed in the forum State, the possibility of a lawsuit there cannot come as a surprise. Nor will the litigation present a burden for which there is no corresponding benefit. A defendant who has placed goods in the stream of commerce benefits economically from the retail sale of the final product in the forum State, and indirectly benefits from the State's laws that regulate and facilitate commercial activity. These benefits accrue regardless of whether that participant directly conducts business in the forum State, or engages in additional conduct directed toward that State. . . .

The Court in *World-Wide Volkswagen* thus took great care to distinguish "between a case involving goods which reach a distant State through a chain of distribution and a case involving goods which reach the same State because a consumer . . . took them there." *Id.,* at 306–307 (Brennan, J., dissenting). The California Supreme Court took note of this distinction, and correctly concluded that our holding in *World-Wide Volkswagen* preserved the stream-of-commerce theory. . . .

In this case, the facts found by the California Supreme Court support its finding of minimum contacts. The court found that "[although] Asahi did not design or control the system of distribution that carried its valve assemblies into California, Asahi was aware of the distribution system's operation, and it knew that it would benefit economically from the sale in California of products incorporating its components." App. to Pet. for Cert. C-11.[4] Accordingly, I cannot join the determination

---

4. Moreover, the Court found that "at least 18 percent of the tubes sold in a particular California motorcycle supply shop contained Asahi valve assemblies," App. to Pet. for Cert. C-1 1, n. 5, and that Asahi had an ongoing business relationship with Cheng Shin involving average annual sales of hundreds of thousands of valve assemblies, *id.,* at C-2.

in Part II-A that Asahi's regular and extensive sales of component parts to a manufacturer it knew was making regular sales of the final product in California is insufficient to establish minimum contacts with California.

JUSTICE STEVENS, with whom JUSTICE WHITE and JUSTICE BLACKMUN join, concurring in part and concurring in the judgment.

The judgment of the Supreme Court of California should be reversed for the reasons stated in Part II-B of the Court's opinion. While I join Parts I and II-B, I do not join Part II-A for two reasons. First, it is not necessary to the Court's decision. An examination of minimum contacts is not always necessary to determine whether a state court's assertion of personal jurisdiction is constitutional. *See Burger King Corp. v. Rudzewicz*, 471 U.S. 462, 476-478 (1985). Part II-B establishes, after considering the factors set forth in *World-Wide Volkswagen Corp. v. Woodson*, 444 U.S. 286, 292 (1980), that California's exercise of jurisdiction over Asahi in this case would be "unreasonable and unfair.". . . This finding alone requires reversal; this case fits within the rule that "minimum requirements inherent in the concept of 'fair play and substantial justice' may defeat the reasonableness of jurisdiction even if the defendant has purposefully engaged in forum activities." *Burger King*, 471 U.S., at 477-478 (quoting *International Shoe Co. v. Washington*, 326 U.S. 310, 320 (1945)). Accordingly, I see no reason in this case for the plurality to articulate "purposeful direction" or any other test as the nexus between an act of a defendant and the forum State that is necessary to establish minimum contacts.

Second, even assuming that the test ought to be formulated here, Part II-A misapplies it to the facts of this case. The plurality seems to assume that an unwavering line can be drawn between "mere awareness" that a component will find its way into the forum State and "purposeful availment" of the forum's market. . . . Over the course of its dealings with Cheng Shin, Asahi has arguably engaged in a higher quantum of conduct than "[the] placement of a product into the stream of commerce, without more. . . ." Whether or not this conduct rises to the level of purposeful availment requires a constitutional determination that is affected by the volume, the value, and the hazardous character of the components. In most circumstances I would be inclined to conclude that a regular course of dealing that results in deliveries of over 100,000 units annually over a period of several years would constitute "purposeful availment" even though the item delivered to the forum State was a standard product marketed throughout the world.

NOTES AND QUESTIONS

1. *A New Test for Personal Jurisdiction? Asahi* is one of those cases where you need a score card to sort out the various opinions of the individual Justices. Can you define the disagreement between Justice O'Connor's opinion and the opinions filed by Justices Brennan and Stevens? Are there any parts of Justice O'Connor's opinion that command five or more votes?

Ever since the decision in *International Shoe*, the Supreme Court's constitutional test for jurisdiction has required that a defendant have certain minimum contacts with the forum such that the maintenance of the suit does not offend " 'traditional notions of fair play and substantial justice.' " Has the Court in *Asahi* established a new test? How would you articulate it? Justice Scalia is the one Justice who does not join Part II-B of the opinion. Why did he refuse to join? Is he saying that jurisdiction over Asahi in California would in fact be "reasonable"?

2. *Stream of Commerce.* Apart from the "reasonableness inquiry," what is the Court's position on whether a defendant has "minimum contacts" with the forum state for purposes of specific jurisdiction if that defendant put goods into the stream of interstate commerce and the goods ended up in the forum state and caused injury there? Justice Stevens writes separately to say it is unnecessary to decide the question in *Asahi*, but he seems to think there will be the requisite contacts if a sufficient quantity of the product is sold in the forum state.

The argument in favor of jurisdiction in both *Volkswagen* and *Asahi* turns in part on the fact that the injury occurs in the forum state; the state has an interest in regulating conduct within its borders and applying its law to that conduct, and witnesses are likely to be available to testify in that state. Why isn't that enough? Even if the focus of the jurisdictional inquiry is on the defendant and its activities, why isn't the defendant's "purposeful activity" of disseminating its products to the forum state through the stream of commerce sufficient? Does *Asahi* place in question the continued viability of *Gray*? After *Asahi*, many lower courts appeared to be protective of component manufacturers unless they personally directed their conduct to the forum state. *See, e.g., Lesnick v. Hollingsorth & Vose Co.*, 35 F.3d 939 (4th Cir. 1994) (Massachusetts maker of filter medium for manufacturer's cigarettes that were distributed nationwide not subject to jurisdiction in forum state); *Falkirk Mining Co. v. Japan Steel Works, Ltd.*, 906 F.2d 369 (8th Cir. 1990) (Japanese manufacturer of component part incorporated by third party into piece of equipment sold to plaintiff in forum state and causing injury there not subject to jurisdiction).

What about a small manufacturer that contracts to sell its product to Wal-Mart, at which point Wal-Mart takes ownership of the goods, delivers them to several distribution centers throughout the country, and repackages the goods under the Wal-Mart brand name? Is that manufacturer amenable to jurisdiction in every state given Wal-Mart's nationwide profile? In *Luv N' Care, Ltd. v. Insta-Mix, Inc.*, 438 F.3d 465 (5th Cir. 2006), *cert. denied*, 540 U.S. 904 (2006), the Fifth Circuit, using a stream of commerce theory, held that Insta-Mix—a small Colorado corporation that produces plastic bottles—had purposefully availed itself of the Louisiana market because Wal-Mart decided to send 65 shipments of Insta-Mix's product to a distribution center in Louisiana. Responding to the defendant's concerns that the court's ruling would force businesses to choose either to be subject to suit in all 50 states or refuse to do business with Wal-Mart, the court noted that Insta-Mix could have bargained for a contractual condition preventing Wal-Mart from distributing the bottles in circuits that utilize a "stream of commerce" test for jurisdiction. Is this suggestion realistic? How do you think Wal-Mart would respond to this demand in negotiations with a small company like Insta-Mix? In a special concurring opinion, Judge DeMoss acknowledged that *stare decisis* forced the court to find that personal jurisdiction existed over Insta-Mix because of circuit precedent but nonetheless expressed his frustration with the "stream of commerce" approach, calling this case the "proverbial straw that breaks the camel's back" because Insta-Mix had absolutely no ties with Louisiana absent Wal-Mart's actions.

Other courts have disagreed with the Fifth Circuit's analysis and have formally adopted Justice O'Connor's "stream of commerce plus" plurality opinion in *Asahi. See, e.g., Fortis Corp. Ins. v. Viken Ship Mgmt.*, 450 F.3d 214 (6th Cir. 2006) (finding the defendant cargo-vessel owners to be subject to jurisdiction in Ohio because they specifically rigged their vessels to travel to the Great Lakes).

3. *End-Product Manufacturers Compared.* Are component manufacturers substantially different from end-product manufacturers who market through distributors who take control of decision making with respect to distribution of the final product? If a manufacturer sells directly to a distributor in the forum state, that would appear to be direct contact with the forum state without the need to invoke the "stream of commerce" theory. But where the defendant uses a foreign distributor or a distributor in another state to market to the forum state, the defendant's conduct is one step removed in the chain; and the case is usually characterized as a "stream of commerce" case. What factors should determine when a defendant, who has placed its product in the "stream of commerce," intended to serve the forum market? The courts have relied on such factors as the establishment of a network of distributors to market the product, *see, e.g., Barone v. Rich Bros. Interstate Display Fireworks Co.*, 25 F.3d 610 (8th Cir. 1994) (Japanese manufacturer of fireworks subject to jurisdiction in Nebraska where plaintiff was injured and manufacturer had used a network of U.S. distributors to place its products in the stream of commerce in the Midwest, including the forum state); or the custom-designing of the product for the forum market, *see In re Perrier Bottled Water*, 754 F. Supp. 264 (D. Conn. 1990) (product was designed for the U.S. market, including the forum state). *But compare Jennings v. AC Hydraulic*, 383 F.3d 546 (7th Cir. 2004), where Danish manufacturer of a floor jack that collapsed and led to the death of plaintiff's husband was held not subject to jurisdiction in Indiana where the accident occurred. The defendant advertised on a passive website and sold its products to two distributors in Florida, but in the absence of information in the record as to where the distributors resold their products and the source of this floor jack, the court held that the "purposeful availment" showing required by *Volkswagen* had not been satisfied. Subsequently, the Supreme Court of the United States decided a case that presented the issue whether Due Process was satisfied when a foreign manufacturer directly marketed its product through a U.S. distributor who sold the product in the forum state where the injury occurred. *See J. McIntyre Machinery, Ltd. v. Nicastro*, 564 U.S. 873 (2011), *infra* at p. 137.

4. *The Relationship of "Minimum Contacts" and Reasonableness.* What is the relationship between the "minimum contacts" and "reasonableness" strands of the Due Process test as articulated in *Asahi*? Suppose, for example, that the injured plaintiff in *Asahi* had initially joined the defendant Asahi and that no claims had been settled. Would jurisdiction over Asahi in California be constitutional? Is that because of Asahi's "minimum contacts" with the state of California? Or because of the "reasonableness" assessment?

Similarly, is it relevant that the defendant is a Japanese company? Does that fact affect whether the defendant has "minimum contacts" with the state? Whether jurisdiction is reasonable? Both?

Because the defendant is a Japanese company, the Supreme Court suggests that the defendant would have a difficult burden in defending in the United States. By the same token, wouldn't there be a special hardship on the plaintiff if forced to litigate in a foreign country, possibly in a foreign language and without some of the procedural devices common to the American courts, such as broad discovery and jury trials? Perhaps the absence of an alternative forum in the United States should make it more — rather than less — reasonable to exercise jurisdiction over a foreign defendant.

Consider the following observations on the *Asahi* decision by one of the authors of this casebook:

> Although minimum contacts was hardly a litmus paper test for jurisdiction, it did impart a measure of predictability to an area of law where rules of some kind are important. The addition of a separate "reasonableness" criterion, although perhaps only a semantic change, tends to suggest a free-form "fairness" inquiry where additional criteria such as choice-of-law, over-all convenience, and specific individual characteristics might be considered. Although *Asahi* suggests only a declination of jurisdiction on "fairness" grounds, it is possible that assertions of jurisdiction may be invited on subjective notions of fairness even in the absence of minimum contacts. Under this standard, jurisdictional inquiries will encompass every aspect of the relationship and the transaction between the parties. Such inquiries would lead to high transaction costs that should not be imposed on questions which must be determined quickly and efficiently at the outset of the litigation.

Linda J. Silberman, *Reflections on* Burnham v. Superior Court: *Toward Presumptive Rules of Jurisdiction and Implications for Choice-of-Law*, 22 Rutgers L.J. 569, 581–582 (1991).

Is this an accurate characterization of the likely impact of *Asahi?*

d. Specific Jurisdiction and the Single Sale

J. McIntyre Machinery, Ltd. v. Nicastro

564 U.S. 873 (2011)

Justice Kennedy announced the judgment of the Court and delivered an opinion, in which The Chief Justice, Justice Scalia, and Justice Thomas join.

Whether a person or entity is subject to the jurisdiction of a state court despite not having been present in the State either at the time of suit or at the time of the alleged injury, and despite not having consented to the exercise of jurisdiction, is a question that arises with great frequency in the routine course of litigation. The rules and standards for determining when a State does or does not have jurisdiction over an absent party have been unclear because of decades-old questions left open in *Asahi Metal Industry Co. v. Superior Court of Cal., Solano Cty.,* 480 U.S. 102 (1987).

Here, the Supreme Court of New Jersey, relying in part on *Asahi*, held that New Jersey's courts can exercise jurisdiction over a foreign manufacturer of a product so long as the manufacturer "knows or reasonably should know that its products are distributed through a nationwide distribution system that might lead to those products being sold in any of the fifty states." *Nicastro v. McIntyre Machinery America, Ltd.,* 201 N.J. 48, 76, 77, 987 A.2d 575, 591, 592 (2010). Applying that test, the court concluded that a British manufacturer of scrap metal machines was subject to jurisdiction in New Jersey, even though at no time had it advertised in, sent goods to, or in any relevant sense targeted the State.

That decision cannot be sustained. Although the New Jersey Supreme Court issued an extensive opinion with careful attention to this Court's cases and to its own precedent, the "stream of commerce" metaphor carried the decision far afield. Due process protects the defendant's right not to be coerced except by lawful judicial power. As a general rule, the exercise of judicial power is not lawful unless the defendant "purposefully avails itself of the privilege of conducting activities within the forum State, thus invoking the benefits and protections of its laws." *Hanson v. Denckla*, 357 U.S. 235, 253 (1958). There may be exceptions, say, for instance, in cases involving an intentional tort. But the general rule is applicable in this products-liability case, and the so-called "stream-of-commerce" doctrine cannot displace it.

I

This case arises from a products-liability suit filed in New Jersey state court. Robert Nicastro seriously injured his hand while using a metal-shearing machine manufactured by J. McIntyre Machinery, Ltd. (J. McIntyre). The accident occurred in New Jersey, but the machine was manufactured in England, where J. McIntyre is incorporated and operates. The question here is whether the New Jersey courts have jurisdiction over J. McIntyre, notwithstanding the fact that the company at no time either marketed goods in the State or shipped them there. Nicastro was a plaintiff in the New Jersey trial court and is the respondent here; J. McIntyre was a defendant and is now the petitioner.

At oral argument in this Court, Nicastro's counsel stressed three primary facts in defense of New Jersey's assertion of jurisdiction over J. McIntyre. See Tr. of Oral Arg. 29-30.

First, an independent company agreed to sell J. McIntyre's machines in the United States. J. McIntyre itself did not sell its machines to buyers in this country beyond the U.S. distributor, and there is no allegation that the distributor was under J. McIntyre's control.

Second, J. McIntyre officials attended annual conventions for the scrap recycling industry to advertise J. McIntyre's machines alongside the distributor. The conventions took place in various States, but never in New Jersey.

Third, no more than four machines (the record suggests only one, see App. to Pet. for Cert. 130a), including the machine that caused the injuries that are the basis for this suit, ended up in New Jersey.

In addition to these facts emphasized by petitioner, the New Jersey Supreme Court noted that J. McIntyre held both United States and European patents on its recycling technology. 201 N.J., at 55. It also noted that the U.S. distributor "structured [its] advertising and sales efforts in accordance with" J. McIntyre's "direction and guidance whenever possible," and that "at least some of the machines were sold on consignment to" the distributor. *Id.*, at 55, 56.

In light of these facts, the New Jersey Supreme Court concluded that New Jersey courts could exercise jurisdiction over petitioner without contravention of the Due Process Clause. Jurisdiction was proper, in that court's view, because the injury occurred in New Jersey; because petitioner knew or reasonably should have known "that its products are distributed through a nationwide distribution system that might lead to those products being sold in any of the fifty states"; and because petitioner failed to "take some reasonable step to prevent the distribution of its products in this State." *Id.*, at 772.

Both the New Jersey Supreme Court's holding and its account of what it called "[t]he stream-of-commerce doctrine of jurisdiction," *id.*, at 80, 987 A.2d, at 594, were incorrect, however. This Court's *Asahi* decision may be responsible in part for that court's error regarding the stream of commerce, and this case presents an opportunity to provide greater clarity.

II

A court may subject a defendant to judgment only when the defendant has sufficient contacts with the sovereign "such that the maintenance of the suit does not offend 'traditional notions of fair play and substantial justice.'" *International Shoe Co. v. Washington*, 326 U.S. 310, 316 (1945) (quoting *Milliken v. Meyer*, 311 U.S. 457 (1940)). Freeform notions of fundamental fairness divorced from traditional practice cannot transform a judgment rendered in the absence of authority into law. As a general rule, the sovereign's exercise of power requires some act by which the defendant "purposefully avails itself of the privilege of conducting activities within the forum State, thus invoking the benefits and protections of its laws," *Hanson*, 357 U.S., at 253, though in some cases, as with an intentional tort, the defendant might well fall within the State's authority by reason of his attempt to obstruct its laws. In products-liability cases like this one, it is the defendant's purposeful availment that makes jurisdiction consistent with "traditional notions of fair play and substantial justice."

A person may submit to a State's authority in a number of ways. There is, of course, explicit consent. *E.g., Insurance Corp. of Ireland v. Compagnie des Bauxites de Guinee*, 456 U.S. 694 (1982). Presence within a State at the time suit commences through service of process is another example. See *Burnham, supra.* Citizenship or domicile — or, by analogy, incorporation or principal place of business for corporations — also indicates general submission to a State's powers. *Goodyear Dunlop Tires Operations, S. A. v. Brown,* [564 U.S. 915 (2011)]*. Each of these examples reveals circumstances, or a course of conduct, from which it is proper to infer an intention to benefit from and thus an intention to submit to the laws of the forum State. Cf. *Burger King Corp. v. Rudzewicz*, 471 U.S. 462, 476 (1985). These examples support exercise of the general jurisdiction of the State's courts and allow the State to resolve both matters that originate within the State and those based on activities and events elsewhere. *Helicopteros Nacionales de Colombia, S. A. v. Hall,* 466 U.S. 408, 414 (1984). By contrast, those who live or operate primarily outside a State have a due process right not to be subjected to judgment in its courts as a general matter.

There is also a more limited form of submission to a State's authority for disputes that "arise out of or are connected with the activities within the state." *International Shoe Co., supra* at 319. Where a defendant "purposefully avails itself of the

---

* The *Goodyear* case is discussed *infra*, at p. 79. –Eds.

privilege of conducting activities within the forum State, thus invoking the benefits and protections of its laws," *Hanson, supra*, at 253, it submits to the judicial power of an otherwise foreign sovereign to the extent that power is exercised in connection with the defendant's activities touching on the State. <u>In other words, submission through contact with and activity directed at a sovereign may justify specific jurisdiction</u> "in a suit arising out of or related to the defendant's contacts with the forum." *Helicopteros, supra*, at 414, n. 8; . . .

The imprecision arising from *Asahi*, for the most part, results from its statement of the relation between jurisdiction and the "stream of commerce.". . . This Court has stated that a defendant's placing goods into the stream of commerce "with the expectation that they will be purchased by consumers within the forum State" may indicate purposeful availment. *World-Wide Volkswagen Corp. v. Woodson*, 444 U.S. 286, 298 (1980) (finding that expectation lacking). But that statement does not amend the general rule of personal jurisdiction. It merely observes that a defendant may in an appropriate case be subject to jurisdiction without entering the forum — itself an unexceptional proposition — as where manufacturers or distributors "seek to serve" a given State's market. *Id.*, at 295. The principal inquiry in cases of this sort is <u>whether the defendant's activities manifest an intention to submit to the power of a sovereign</u>. In other words, the defendant must "purposefully avai[l] itself of the privilege of conducting activities within the forum State, thus invoking the benefits and protections of its laws." *Hanson, supra*, at 253; *Insurance Corp., supra*, at 704–705 ("[A]ctions of the defendant may amount to a legal submission to the jurisdiction of the court"). Sometimes a defendant does so by sending its goods rather than its agents. The defendant's transmission of goods permits the exercise of jurisdiction only where the defendant can be said to have targeted the forum; as a general rule, it is not enough that the defendant might have predicted that its goods will reach the forum State.

In *Asahi*, an opinion by Justice Brennan for four Justices outlined a different approach. It discarded the central concept of sovereign authority in favor of considerations of fairness and foreseeability. As that concurrence contended, "jurisdiction premised on the placement of a product into the stream of commerce [without more] is consistent with the Due Process Clause," for "[a]s long as a participant in this process is aware that the final product is being marketed in the forum State, the possibility of a lawsuit there cannot come as a surprise." 480 U.S., at 117 (opinion concurring in part and concurring in judgment). It was the premise of the concurring opinion that the defendant's ability to anticipate suit renders the assertion of jurisdiction fair. In this way, the opinion made foreseeability the touchstone of jurisdiction.

The standard set forth in Justice Brennan's concurrence was rejected in an opinion written by Justice O'Connor; but the relevant part of that opinion, too, commanded the assent of only four Justices, not a majority of the Court. That opinion stated: "The 'substantial connection' between the defendant and the forum State necessary for a finding of minimum contacts must come about by an action of the defendant purposefully directed toward the forum State. The placement of a product into the stream of commerce, without more, is not an act of the defendant purposefully directed toward the forum State." *Id.*, at 112.

Since *Asahi* was decided, the courts have sought to reconcile the competing opinions. But Justice Brennan's concurrence, advocating a rule based on general notions of fairness and foreseeability, is inconsistent with the premises of lawful judicial power. This Court's precedents make clear that it is the defendant's actions, not his expectations, that empower a State's courts to subject him to judgment.

The conclusion that jurisdiction is in the first instance a question of authority rather than fairness explains, for example, why the principal opinion in *Burnham* "conducted no independent inquiry into the desirability or fairness" of the rule that service of process within a State suffices to establish jurisdiction over an otherwise foreign defendant. 495 U.S., at 621. . . . Furthermore, were general fairness considerations the touchstone of jurisdiction, a lack of purposeful availment might be excused where carefully crafted judicial procedures could otherwise protect the defendant's interests, or where the plaintiff would suffer substantial hardship if forced to litigate in a foreign forum. That such considerations have not been deemed controlling is instructive. *See, e.g., World-Wide Volkswagen, supra,* at 294.

Two principles are implicit in the foregoing. First, personal jurisdiction requires a forum-by-forum, or sovereign-by-sovereign, analysis. The question is whether a defendant has followed a course of conduct directed at the society or economy existing within the jurisdiction of a given sovereign, so that the sovereign has the power to subject the defendant to judgment concerning that conduct. . . .

The second principle is a corollary of the first. Because the United States is a distinct sovereign, a defendant may in principle be subject to the jurisdiction of the courts of the United States but not of any particular State. This is consistent with the premises and unique genius of our Constitution. Ours is "a legal system unprecedented in form and design, establishing two orders of government, each with its own direct relationship, its own privity, its own set of mutual rights and obligations to the people who sustain it and are governed by it." *U.S. Term Limits, Inc. v. Thornton,* 514 U.S. 779, 838 (1995) (KENNEDY, J., concurring). For jurisdiction, a litigant may have the requisite relationship with the United States Government but not with the government of any individual State. That would be an exceptional case, however. If the defendant is a domestic domiciliary, the courts of its home State are available and can exercise general jurisdiction. And if another State were to assert jurisdiction in an inappropriate case, it would upset the federal balance, which posits that each State has a sovereignty that is not subject to unlawful intrusion by other States. Furthermore, foreign corporations will often target or concentrate on particular States, subjecting them to specific jurisdiction in those forums.

It must be remembered, however, that although this case and *Asahi* both involve foreign manufacturers, the undesirable consequences of Justice Brennan's approach are no less significant for domestic producers. The owner of a small Florida farm might sell crops to a large nearby distributor, for example, who might then distribute them to grocers across the country. If foreseeability were the controlling criterion, the farmer could be sued in Alaska or any number of other States' courts without ever leaving town. And the issue of foreseeability may itself be contested so that significant expenses are incurred just on the preliminary issue of jurisdiction. Jurisdictional rules should avoid these costs whenever possible.

The conclusion that the authority to subject a defendant to judgment depends on purposeful availment, consistent with Justice O'Connor's opinion in *Asahi,* does not by itself resolve many difficult questions of jurisdiction that will arise in particular cases. The defendant's conduct and the economic realities of the market the defendant seeks to serve will differ across cases, and judicial exposition will, in common-law fashion, clarify the contours of that principle.

III

In this case, petitioner directed marketing and sales efforts at the United States. . . . Here the question concerns the authority of a New Jersey state court to exercise jurisdiction, so it is petitioner's purposeful contacts with New Jersey, not with the United States, that alone are relevant.

Respondent has not established that J. McIntyre engaged in conduct purposefully directed at New Jersey. Recall that respondent's claim of jurisdiction centers on three facts: The distributor agreed to sell J. McIntyre's machines in the United States; J. McIntyre officials attended trade shows in several States but not in New Jersey; and up to four machines ended up in New Jersey. The British manufacturer had no office in New Jersey; it neither paid taxes nor owned property there; and it neither advertised in, nor sent any employees to, the State. Indeed, after discovery the trial court found that the "defendant does not have a single contact with New Jersey short of the machine in question ending up in this state." App. to Pet. for Cert. 130a. These facts may reveal an intent to serve the U.S. market, but they do not show that J. McIntyre purposefully availed itself of the New Jersey market.

It is notable that the New Jersey Supreme Court appears to agree, for it could "not find that J. McIntyre had a presence or minimum contacts in this State — in any jurisprudential sense — that would justify a New Jersey court to exercise jurisdiction in this case." 201 N.J., at 61. The court nonetheless held that petitioner could be sued in New Jersey based on a "stream-of-commerce theory of jurisdiction." *Ibid.* As discussed, however, the stream-of-commerce metaphor cannot supersede either the mandate of the Due Process Clause or the limits on judicial authority that Clause ensures. The New Jersey Supreme Court also cited "significant policy reasons" to justify its holding, including the State's "strong interest in protecting its citizens from defective products." *Id.*, at 75. That interest is doubtless strong, but the Constitution commands restraint before discarding liberty in the name of expediency.

. . .

Due process protects petitioner's right to be subject only to lawful authority. At no time did petitioner engage in any activities in New Jersey that reveal an intent to invoke or benefit from the protection of its laws. New Jersey is without power to adjudge the rights and liabilities of J. McIntyre, and its exercise of jurisdiction would violate due process. The contrary judgment of the New Jersey Supreme Court is

Reversed.

JUSTICE BREYER, with whom JUSTICE ALITO joins, concurring in the judgment.

The Supreme Court of New Jersey adopted a broad understanding of the scope of personal jurisdiction based on its view that "[t]he increasingly fast-paced globalization of the world economy has removed national borders as barriers to trade." *Nicastro v. McIntyre Machinery America, Ltd.*, 201 N.J. 48, 52 (2010). I do not doubt that there have been many recent changes in commerce and communication, many of which are not anticipated by our precedents. But this case does not present any of those issues. So I think it unwise to announce a rule of broad applicability without full consideration of the modern-day consequences.

In my view, the outcome of this case is determined by our precedents. Based on the facts found by the New Jersey courts, respondent Robert Nicastro failed to meet his burden to demonstrate that it was constitutionally proper to exercise jurisdiction over petitioner J. McIntyre Machinery, Ltd. (British Manufacturer), a British firm that manufactures scrap-metal machines in Great Britain and sells them through an independent distributor in the United States (American Distributor). On that basis, I agree with the plurality that the contrary judgment of the Supreme Court of New Jersey should be reversed.

I

In asserting jurisdiction over the British Manufacturer, the Supreme Court of New Jersey relied most heavily on three primary facts as providing constitutionally sufficient "contacts" with New Jersey, thereby making it fundamentally fair to hale the British Manufacturer before its courts: (1) The American Distributor on one occasion sold and shipped one machine to a New Jersey customer, namely, Mr. Nicastro's employer, Mr. Curcio; (2) the British Manufacturer permitted, indeed wanted, its independent American Distributor to sell its machines to anyone in America willing to buy them; and (3) representatives of the British Manufacturer attended trade shows in "such cities as Chicago, Las Vegas, New Orleans, Orlando, San Diego, and San Francisco." *Id.*, at 54–55. In my view, these facts do not provide contacts between the British firm and the State of New Jersey constitutionally sufficient to support New Jersey's assertion of jurisdiction in this case.

None of our precedents finds that a single isolated sale, even if accompanied by the kind of sales effort indicated here, is sufficient. Rather, this Court's previous holdings suggest the contrary. The Court has held that a single sale to a customer who takes an accident-causing product to a different State (where the accident takes place) is not a sufficient basis for asserting jurisdiction. See *World-Wide Volkswagen Corp. v. Woodson*, 444 U.S. 286 (1980). And the Court, in separate opinions, has strongly suggested that a single sale of a product in a State does not constitute an adequate basis for asserting jurisdiction over an out-of-state defendant, even if that defendant places his goods in the stream of commerce, fully aware (and hoping) that such a sale will take place. . . .

Here, the relevant facts found by the New Jersey Supreme Court show no "regular . . . flow" or "regular course" of sales in New Jersey; and there is no "something more," such as special state-related design, advertising, advice, marketing, or anything else. Mr. Nicastro, who here bears the burden of proving jurisdiction, has shown no specific effort by the British Manufacturer to sell in New Jersey. He has introduced no list of potential New Jersey customers who might, for example, have regularly attended trade shows. And he has not otherwise shown that the British Manufacturer "purposefully avail[ed] itself of the privilege of conducting activities" within New Jersey, or that it delivered its goods in the stream of commerce "with the expectation that they will be purchased" by New Jersey users. *World-Wide Volkswagen, supra*, at 297–298. . . .

Accordingly, on the record present here, resolving this case requires no more than adhering to our precedents.

II

I would not go further. Because the incident at issue in this case does not implicate modern concerns, and because the factual record leaves many open questions, this is an unsuitable vehicle for making broad pronouncements that refashion basic jurisdictional rules.

A

The plurality seems to state strict rules that limit jurisdiction where a defendant does not "inten[d] to submit to the power of a sovereign" and cannot "be said to have targeted the forum.". . . But what do those standards mean when a company targets the world by selling products from its Web site? And does it matter if, instead of shipping the products directly, a company consigns the products through an intermediary (say, Amazon.com) who then receives and fulfills the orders? And what if the company markets its products through popup advertisements that it knows will be viewed in a forum? Those issues have serious commercial consequences but are totally absent in this case.

B

But though I do not agree with the plurality's seemingly strict no-jurisdiction rule, I am not persuaded by the absolute approach adopted by the New Jersey Supreme Court and urged by respondent and his *amici.* Under that view, a producer is subject to jurisdiction for a products-liability action so long as it "knows or reasonably should know that its products are distributed through a nationwide distribution system that *might* lead to those products being sold in any of the fifty states." 201 N.J., at 76–77. In the context of this case, I cannot agree.

For one thing, to adopt this view would abandon the heretofore accepted inquiry of whether, focusing upon the relationship between "the defendant, the *forum*, and the litigation," it is fair, in light of the defendant's contacts *with that forum*, to subject the defendant to suit there. *Shaffer v. Heitner*, 433 U.S. 186, 204 (1977). . . .

For another, I cannot reconcile so automatic a rule with the constitutional demand for "minimum contacts" and "purposefu[l] avail[ment]," each of which rest upon a particular notion of defendant-focused fairness. *Id.*, at 291, 297. A rule like the New Jersey Supreme Court's would permit every State to assert jurisdiction in a products-liability suit against any domestic manufacturer who sells its products (made anywhere in the United States) to a national distributor, no matter how large or small the manufacturer, no matter how distant the forum, and no matter how few the number of items that end up in the particular forum at issue. What might appear fair in the case of a large manufacturer which specifically seeks, or expects, an equal-sized distributor to sell its product in a distant State might seem unfair in the case of a small manufacturer (say, an Appalachian potter) who sells his product (cups and saucers) exclusively to a large distributor, who resells a single item (a coffee mug) to a buyer from a distant State (Hawaii). I know too little about the range of these or in-between possibilities to abandon in favor of the more absolute rule what has previously been this Court's less absolute approach.

Further, the fact that the defendant is a foreign, rather than a domestic, manufacturer makes the basic fairness of an absolute rule yet more uncertain. I am again less certain than is the New Jersey Supreme Court that the nature of international commerce has changed so significantly as to require a new approach to personal jurisdiction.

It may be that a larger firm can readily "alleviate the risk of burdensome litigation by procuring insurance, passing the expected costs on to customers, or, if the risks are too great, severing its connection with the State." *World-Wide Volkswagen*, *supra*, at 297. But manufacturers come in many shapes and sizes. It may be fundamentally unfair to require a small Egyptian shirt maker, a Brazilian manufacturing cooperative, or a Kenyan coffee farmer, selling its products through international distributors, to respond to products-liability tort suits in virtually every State in the United States, even those in respect to which the foreign firm has no connection at all but the sale of a single (allegedly defective) good. . . .

Accordingly, though I agree with the plurality as to the outcome of this case, I concur only in the judgment of that opinion and not its reasoning.

JUSTICE GINSBURG, with whom JUSTICE SOTOMAYOR and JUSTICE KAGAN join, dissenting. (New Jersey back then is metal capital of the U.S.)

A foreign industrialist seeks to develop a market in the United States for machines it manufactures. It hopes to derive substantial revenue from sales it makes to United States purchasers. Where in the United States buyers reside does not matter to this manufacturer. Its goal is simply to sell as much as it can, wherever it can. It excludes no region or State from the market it wishes to reach. But, all things considered, it prefers to avoid products liability litigation in the United States. To that end, it engages a U.S. distributor to ship its machines stateside. Has it succeeded in escaping personal jurisdiction in a State where one of its products is sold and causes injury or even death to a local user?

Under this Court's pathmarking precedent in *International Shoe Co. v. Washington*, 326 U.S. 310 (1945), and subsequent decisions, one would expect the answer to be unequivocally, "No." But instead, six Justices of this Court, in divergent opinions, tell us that the manufacturer has avoided the jurisdiction of our state courts, except perhaps in States where its products are sold in sizeable quantities. Inconceivable as it may have seemed yesterday, the splintered majority today "turn[s] the clock back to the days before modern long-arm statutes when a manufacturer, to avoid being haled into court where a user is injured, need only Pilate-like wash its hands of a product by having independent distributors market it." Weintraub, *A Map Out of the Personal Jurisdiction Labyrinth*, 28 U.C. Davis L. Rev. 531, 555 (1995).

I

Nicastro operated the 640 Shear in the course of his employment at Curcio Scrap Metal (CSM) in Saddle Brook, New Jersey. *Id.*, at 7a, 43a. "New Jersey has long been a hotbed of scrap-metal businesses. . . ." See Drake, The Scrap-Heap Rollup Hits New Jersey, Business News New Jersey, June 1, 1998, p. 1. In 2008, New Jersey recycling facilities processed 2,013,730 tons of scrap iron, steel, aluminum, and other metals—more than any other State—outpacing Kentucky, its nearest competitor, by nearly 30 percent. Von Haaren, Themelis, & Goldstein, The State of Garbage in America, BioCycle, Oct. 2010, p. 19. . . .

McIntyre UK representatives attended every ISRI convention from 1990 through 2005. *Id.*, at 114a–115a. These annual expositions were held in diverse venues across the United States; in addition to Las Vegas, conventions were held 1990–2005 in New Orleans, Orlando, San Antonio, and San Francisco. *Ibid.* McIntyre UK's president, Michael Pownall, regularly attended ISRI conventions. *Ibid.* He attended ISRI's Las Vegas convention the year CSM's owner first learned of, and saw, the 640 Shear. *Id.*, at 78a–79a, 115a. McIntyre UK exhibited its products at ISRI trade shows, the company acknowledged, hoping to reach "anyone interested in the machine from anywhere in the United States." *Id.*, at 161a.

Although McIntyre UK's U.S. sales figures are not in the record, it appears that for several years in the 1990's, earnings from sales of McIntyre UK products in the United States "ha[d] been good" in comparison to "the rest of the world." *Id.*, at 136a (Letter from Sally Johnson, McIntyre UK's Managing Director, to Gary and Mary Gaither, officers of McIntyre UK's exclusive distributor in the United States (Jan. 13, 1999)). In response to interrogatories, McIntyre UK stated that its commissioning engineer had installed the company's equipment in several States—Illinois, Iowa, Kentucky, Virginia, and Washington. *Id.*, at 119a. . . .

In a November 23, 1999 letter to McIntyre America, McIntyre UK's president spoke plainly about the manufacturer's objective in authorizing the exclusive distributorship: "All we wish to do is sell our products in the [United] States—and get paid!" *Id.*, at 134a. . . . Answering jurisdictional interrogatories, McIntyre UK stated that it had been named as a defendant in lawsuits in Illinois, Kentucky, Massachusetts, and West Virginia. *Id.*, at 98a, 108a. And in correspondence with McIntyre America, McIntyre UK noted that the manufacturer had products liability insurance coverage. *Id.*, at 129a. . . .

In sum, McIntyre UK's regular attendance and exhibitions at ISRI conventions was surely a purposeful step to reach customers for its products "anywhere in the United States." At least as purposeful was McIntyre UK's engagement of McIntyre America as the conduit for sales of McIntyre UK's machines to buyers "throughout the United States." Given McIntyre UK's endeavors to reach and profit from the United States market as a whole, Nicastro's suit, I would hold, has been brought in a forum entirely appropriate for the adjudication of his claim. He alleges that McIntyre UK's shear machine was defectively designed or manufactured and, as a result, caused injury to him at his workplace. The machine arrived in Nicastro's New Jersey workplace not randomly or fortuitously, but as a result of the U.S. connections and distribution system that McIntyre UK deliberately arranged.[3] On what

---

3. McIntyre UK resisted Nicastro's efforts to determine whether other McIntyre machines had been sold to New Jersey customers. See *id.*, at 100a–101a. McIntyre did allow that McIntyre America "may have resold products it purchased from [McIntyre UK] to a buyer in New Jersey," *id.*, at 117a, but said it kept no record of the ultimate destination of machines it shipped to its distributor, *ibid.* A private investigator engaged by Nicastro found at least one McIntyre UK machine, of unspecified type, in use in New Jersey. *Id.*, at 140a–144a. But McIntyre UK objected that the investigator's report was "unsworn and based upon hearsay." Reply Brief 10. Moreover, McIntyre UK maintained, no evidence showed that the machine the investigator found in New Jersey had been "sold into [that State]." *Ibid.*

sensible view of the allocation of adjudicatory authority could the place of Nicastro's injury within the United States be deemed off limits for his products liability claim against a foreign manufacturer who targeted the United States (including all the States that constitute the Nation) as the territory it sought to develop?

II

A few points on which there should be no genuine debate bear statement at the outset. First, all agree, McIntyre UK surely is not subject to general (all-purpose) jurisdiction in New Jersey courts, for that foreign-country corporation is hardly "at home" in New Jersey. See *Goodyear Dunlop Tires Operations, S. A. v. Brown, post,* at 2–3, 9–13. The question, rather, is one of specific jurisdiction, which turns on an "affiliatio[n] between the forum and the underlying controversy." *Goodyear Dunlop, post,* at 2 (quoting von Mehren & Trautman, *Jurisdiction to Adjudicate: A Suggested Analysis,* 79 Harv. L. Rev. 1121, 1136 (1966) (hereinafter von Mehren & Trautman); internal quotation marks omitted); see also *Goodyear Dunlop, post,* at 7–8.

Second, no issue of the fair and reasonable allocation of adjudicatory authority among States of the United States is present in this case. New Jersey's exercise of personal jurisdiction over a foreign manufacturer whose dangerous product caused a workplace injury in New Jersey does not tread on the domain, or diminish the sovereignty, of any sister State. Indeed, among States of the United States, the State in which the injury occurred would seem most suitable for litigation of a products liability tort claim. See *World-Wide Volkswagen Corp. v. Woodson,* 444 U.S. 286, 297 (1980) (if a manufacturer or distributor endeavors to develop a market for a product in several States, it is reasonable "to subject it to suit in one of those States if its allegedly defective [product] has there been the source of injury"); 28 U.S.C. §1391(a)–(b) (in federal-court suits, whether resting on diversity or federal-question jurisdiction, venue is proper in the judicial district "in which a substantial part of the events or omissions giving rise to the claim occurred").

Third, the constitutional limits on a state court's adjudicatory authority derive from considerations of due process, not state sovereignty. As the Court clarified in *Insurance Corp. of Ireland v. Compagnie des Bauxites de Guinee,* 456 U.S. 694 (1982):

> "The restriction on state sovereign power described in *World-Wide Volkswagen Corp.* . . . . must be seen as ultimately a function of the individual liberty interest preserved by the Due Process Clause. That Clause is the only source of the personal jurisdiction requirement and the Clause itself makes no mention of federalism concerns. Furthermore, if the federalism concept operated as an independent restriction on the sovereign power of the court, it would not be possible to waive the personal jurisdiction requirement: Individual actions cannot change the powers of sovereignty, although the individual can subject himself to powers from which he may otherwise be protected." *Id.,* at 703, n. 10.

Finally, in *International Shoe* itself, and decisions thereafter, the Court has made plain that legal fictions, notably "presence" and "implied consent," should be discarded, for they conceal the actual bases on which jurisdiction rests. . . .

[T]he plurality's notion that consent is the animating concept draws no support from controlling decisions of this Court. Quite the contrary, the Court has explained, a forum can exercise jurisdiction when its contacts with the controversy are sufficient; invocation of a fictitious consent, the Court has repeatedly said, is unnecessary and unhelpful. *See, e.g., Burger King Corp. v. Rudzewicz*, 471 U.S. 462, 472 (1985) (Due Process Clause permits "forum . . . to assert specific jurisdiction over an out-of-state defendant who has not consented to suit there"); *McGee v. International Life Ins. Co.*, 355 U.S. 220, 222, 78 S.Ct. 199, 2 L. Ed. 2d 223 (1957) ("[T]his Court [has] abandoned 'consent,' 'doing business,' and 'presence' as the standard for measuring the extent of state judicial power over [out-of-state] corporations.").[5]

III

This case is illustrative of marketing arrangements for sales in the United States common in today's commercial world. A foreign-country manufacturer engages a U.S. company to promote and distribute the manufacturer's products, not in any particular State, but anywhere and everywhere in the United States the distributor can attract purchasers. The product proves defective and injures a user in the State where the user lives or works. Often, as here, the manufacturer will have liability insurance covering personal injuries caused by its products. See Cupp, Redesigning Successor Liability, 1999 U. Ill. L. Rev. 845, 870–871 (noting the ready availability of products liability insurance for manufacturers and citing a study showing, "between 1986 and 1996, [such] insurance cost manufacturers, on average, only sixteen cents for each $100 of product sales"); App. 129–130.

When industrial accidents happen, a long-arm statute in the State where the injury occurs generally permits assertion of jurisdiction, upon giving proper notice, over the foreign manufacturer. . . .

The modern approach to jurisdiction over corporations and other legal entities, ushered in by *International Shoe*, gave prime place to reason and fairness. Is it not fair and reasonable, given the mode of trading of which this case is an example, to require the international seller to defend at the place its products cause injury?[9] Do not litigational convenience and choice-of-law[11] considerations point in that direction? On what measure of reason and fairness can it be considered undue to require McIntyre UK to defend in New Jersey as an incident of its efforts to develop

---

5. But see *ante*, at 4-8 (plurality opinion) (maintaining that a forum may be fair and reasonable, based on its links to the episode in suit, yet off limits because the defendant has not submitted to the State's authority). The plurality's notion that jurisdiction over foreign corporations depends upon the defendant's "submission," *ante*, at 6, seems scarcely different from the long-discredited fiction of implied consent. It bears emphasis that a majority of this Court's members do not share the plurality's view.

9. The plurality objects to a jurisdictional approach "divorced from traditional practice." But "the fundamental transformation of our national economy," this Court has recognized, warrants enlargement of "the permissible scope of state jurisdiction over foreign corporations and other nonresidents." *McGee v. International Life Ins. Co.*, 355 U.S. 220, 222–223 (1957).

11. Historically, "tort cases were governed by the place where the last act giving rise to a claim occurred—that is, the place of injury." Brilmayer 1291–1292. Even as many jurisdictions have modified the traditional rule of *lex loci delicti*, the location of injury continues to hold sway in choice-of-law analysis in tort cases. See generally Whytock, *Myth of Mess? International Choice of Law in Action*, 84 N.Y.U. L. Rev. 719 (2009).

a market for its industrial machines anywhere and everywhere in the United States?[12] Is not the burden on McIntyre UK to defend in New Jersey fair, *i.e.*, a reasonable cost of transacting business internationally, in comparison to the burden on Nicastro to go to Nottingham, England to gain recompense for an injury he sustained using McIntyre's product at his workplace in Saddle Brook, New Jersey?

McIntyre UK dealt with the United States as a single market. Like most foreign manufacturers, it was concerned not with the prospect of suit in State X as opposed to State Y, but rather with its subjection to suit anywhere in the United States. *See* Hay, *Judicial Jurisdiction Over Foreign-Country Corporate Defendants — Comments on Recent Case Law*, 63 Ore. L. Rev. 431, 433 (1984) (hereinafter Hay). As a McIntyre UK officer wrote in an e-mail to McIntyre America: "American law — who needs it?!" App. 129a–130a (e-mail dated April 26, 1999 from Sally Johnson to Mary Gaither). If McIntyre UK is answerable in the United States at all, is it not "perfectly appropriate to permit the exercise of that jurisdiction . . . at the place of injury"? See Hay 435; Degnan & Kane, *The Exercise of Jurisdiction Over and Enforcement of Judgments Against Alien Defendants*, 39 Hastings L.J. 799, 813–815 (noting that "[i]n the international order," the State that counts is the United States, not its component States, and that the fair place of suit within the United States is essentially a question of venue).

In sum, McIntyre UK, by engaging McIntyre America to promote and sell its machines in the United States, "purposefully availed itself" of the United States market nationwide, not a market in a single State or a discrete collection of States. McIntyre UK thereby availed itself of the market of all States in which its products were sold by its exclusive distributor. "Th[e] 'purposeful availment' requirement," this Court has explained, simply "ensures that a defendant will not be haled into a jurisdiction solely as a result of 'random,' 'fortuitous,' or 'attenuated' contacts." *Burger King*, 471 U.S., at 475. Adjudicatory authority is appropriately exercised where "actions by the defendant *himself*" give rise to the affiliation with the forum. *Ibid.* How could McIntyre UK not have intended, by its actions targeting a national market, to sell products in the fourth largest destination for imports among all States of the United States and the largest scrap metal market? See *supra*, at 3, 10, n. 6. But see *ante*, at 11 (plurality opinion) (manufacturer's purposeful efforts to sell its products nationwide are "not . . . relevant" to the personal jurisdiction inquiry). . . .

IV

A

While this Court has not considered in any prior case the now-prevalent pattern presented here — a foreign-country manufacturer enlisting a U.S. distributor to develop a market in the United States for the manufacturer's products — none

---

12. The plurality suggests that the Due Process Clause might permit a federal district court in New Jersey, sitting in diversity and applying New Jersey law, to adjudicate McIntyre UK's liability to Nicastro. . . . In other words, McIntyre UK might be compelled to bear the burden of traveling to New Jersey and defending itself there under New Jersey's products liability law, but would be entitled to federal adjudication of Nicastro's state-law claim. I see no basis in the Due Process Clause for such a curious limitation.

of the Court's decisions tug against the judgment made by the New Jersey Supreme Court. McIntyre contends otherwise, citing *World-Wide Volkswagen,* and *Asahi Metal Industry Co. v. Superior Court of Cal., Solano Cty.,* 480 U.S. 102 (1987).

World-Wide Volkswagen concerned a New York car dealership that sold solely in the New York market, and a New York distributor who supplied retailers in three States only: New York, Connecticut, and New Jersey. . . . [T]his Court observed that the defendants had done nothing to serve the market for cars in Oklahoma. Jurisdiction, the Court held, could not be based on the *customer's* unilateral act of driving the vehicle to Oklahoma . . . see *Asahi,* 480 U.S., at 109 (opinion of O'Connor, J.) (*World-Wide Volkswagen* "rejected the assertion that a *consumer's* unilateral act of bringing the defendant's product into the forum State was a sufficient constitutional basis for personal jurisdiction over the defendant").

Notably, the foreign manufacturer of the Audi in *World-Wide Volkswagen* did not object to the jurisdiction of the Oklahoma courts and the U.S. importer abandoned its initially stated objection. 444 U.S., at 288. And most relevant here, the Court's opinion indicates that an objection to jurisdiction by the manufacturer or national distributor would have been unavailing. To reiterate, the Court said in *World-Wide Volkswagen* that, when a manufacturer or distributor aims to sell its product to customers in several States, it is reasonable "to subject it to suit in [any] one of those States if its allegedly defective [product] has there been the source of injury." *Id.,* at 297.

Asahi arose out of a motorcycle accident in California. Plaintiff, a California resident injured in the accident, sued the Taiwanese manufacturer of the motorcycle's tire tubes, claiming that defects in its product caused the accident. . . .

The decision was not a close call . . . All agreed on the bottom line: The Japanese valve-assembly manufacturer was not reasonably brought into the California courts to litigate a dispute with another foreign party over a transaction that took place outside the United States. . . .

In any event, Asahi, unlike McIntyre UK, did not itself seek out customers in the United States, it engaged no distributor to promote its wares here, it appeared at no tradeshows in the United States, and, of course, it had no Web site advertising its products to the world. Moreover, Asahi was a component-part manufacturer with "little control over the final destination of its products once they were delivered into the stream of commerce." [Citation omitted.] It was important to the Court in *Asahi* that "those who use Asahi components in their final products, and sell those products in California, [would be] subject to the application of California tort law." 480 U.S., at 115 (majority opinion). To hold that *Asahi* controls this case would, to put it bluntly, be dead wrong.[15]

---

15. The plurality notes the low volume of sales in New Jersey, *ante,* at 3, 11. A $24,900 shearing machine, however, is unlikely to sell in bulk worldwide, much less in any given State. By dollar value, the price of a single machine represents a significant sale. Had a manufacturer sold in New Jersey $24,900 worth of flannel shirts, see *Nelson v. Park Industries, Inc.,* 717 F.2d 1120 (CA7 1983), cigarette lighters, see *Oswalt v. Scripto, Inc.,* 616 F.2d 191 (CA5 1980), or wire-rope splices, see *Hedrick v. Daiko Shoji Co.,* 715 F.2d 1355 (CA9 1983), the Court would presumably find the defendant amenable to suit in that State.

B

The Court's judgment also puts United States plaintiffs at a disadvantage in comparison to similarly situated complainants elsewhere in the world. Of particular note, within the European Union, in which the United Kingdom is a participant, the jurisdiction New Jersey would have exercised is not at all exceptional. The European Regulation on Jurisdiction and the Recognition and Enforcement of Judgments provides for the exercise of specific jurisdiction "in matters relating to tort . . . in the courts for the place where the harmful event occurred." Council Reg. 44/2001, Art. 5, 2001 O. J. (L. 12) 4. The European Court of Justice has interpreted this prescription to authorize jurisdiction either where the harmful act occurred or at the place of injury. See *Handelskwekerij G. J., Bier B. V. v. Mines de Potasse d'Alsace S. A.*, 1976 E. C. R. 1735, 1748–1749.

V

The commentators who gave names to what we now call "general jurisdiction" and "specific jurisdiction" anticipated that when the latter achieves its full growth, considerations of litigational convenience and the respective situations of the parties would determine when it is appropriate to subject a defendant to trial in the plaintiff's community. See von Mehren & Trautman 1166–1179. Litigational considerations include "the convenience of witnesses and the ease of ascertaining the governing law." *Id.*, at 1168–1169. As to the parties, courts would differently appraise two situations: (1) cases involving a substantially local plaintiff, like Nicastro, injured by the activity of a defendant engaged in interstate or international trade; and (2) cases in which the defendant is a natural or legal person whose economic activities and legal involvements are largely home-based, *i.e.*, entities without designs to gain substantial revenue from sales in distant markets. See *id.*, at 1167–1169.[18] As the attached appendix of illustrative cases indicates, courts presented with von Mehren and Trautman's first scenario — a local plaintiff injured by the activity of a manufacturer seeking to exploit a multistate or global market — have repeatedly confirmed that jurisdiction is appropriately exercised by courts of the place where the product was sold and caused injury.

. . .

For the reasons stated, I would hold McIntyre UK answerable in New Jersey for the harm Nicastro suffered at his workplace in that State using McIntyre UK's shearing machine. While I dissent from the Court's judgment, I take heart that the plurality opinion does not speak for the Court, for that opinion would take a giant step away from the "notions of fair play and substantial justice" underlying *International Shoe*, 326 U.S., at 316.

---

18. Assigning weight to the local or international stage on which the parties operate would, to a considerable extent, answer the concerns expressed by JUSTICE BREYER.

NOTES AND QUESTIONS

1. *Untangling the Opinions in* McIntyre. Justice Kennedy's opinion is a plurality opinion of four Justices (Kennedy, Chief Justice Roberts, Scalia, and Thomas). The "Kennedy four" view of personal jurisdiction is predicated upon sovereign authority and not fairness. They emphasize the need for a defendant to "submit to the power of a sovereign" and discuss various ways in which the defendant may do so. The proxy for submission in cases of specific jurisdiction is "purposeful availment," which the plurality finds is not met on these facts because the defendant did not "target" the forum state. Has the plurality's emphasis on sovereignty undermined the basic lesson of *International Shoe* that Due Process is a function of certain minimum contacts with the forum state such that maintenance of the suit does not offend "traditional notions of fair play and substantial justice"? Can the philosophies in the two cases be reconciled?

Justice Ginsburg's dissent (joined by Justices Kagan and Sotomayor) is critical of the plurality in just this respect: "The plurality's notion that jurisdiction over foreign corporations depends upon the defendant's 'submission' . . . seems scarcely different from the long-discredited fiction of implied consent. It bears emphasis that a majority of this Court's members do not share the plurality's views." As she emphasizes, "the modern approach to jurisdiction over corporations and other legal entities, ushered in *International Shoe*, gave prime place to reason and fairness." Moreover, Justice Ginsburg finds this case substantially different than *Asahi*, which she characterizes as "not a close call." As Justice Ginsburg points out, *Asahi* was a component-part manufacturer with little control over the final destination of the product, whereas McIntyre UK sought out customers in the United States by engaging a distributor to promote its products in the United States. Moreover, by promoting and selling its machines in the nationwide U.S. market, McIntyre UK availed itself of the market in all states in which its products were sold by its exclusive distributor, especially where, as here, the forum state is the largest market for the manufacturer's product.

Where do the concurring Justices Breyer and Alito stand in this debate? Why are they unwilling to join the majority opinion even though they agree that New Jersey cannot take jurisdiction on the facts as presented? Justice Breyer resists making any broad pronouncements about jurisdiction. He seems to want to distinguish different commercial contexts (e.g., the Internet) from more traditional applications. Justice Breyer also thinks it may matter whether the defendant is a large or small manufacturer and the manner in which the goods are distributed. Can these factors be distilled into jurisdictional rules? What of the need for predictability in advising a client as to its amenability to suit in a state of the United States?

Justice Breyer's opinion clearly criticizes the reasoning put forward by the Kennedy plurality. Is the only real difference between the concurring opinion and the dissent a disagreement regarding the factual record? Compare Justice Breyer's portrayal of McIntyre UK's contacts with New Jersey with that of Justice Ginsburg.

For a more in-depth analysis of the three opinions, *see* Adam N. Steinman, *The Lay of the Land: Examining the Three Opinions in* J. McIntyre Machinery, Ltd. v. Nicastro, 63 S.C. L. Rev. 481 (2012). For further analysis of how the three opinions are being interpreted in the lower courts, *see* Adam N. Steinman, *The Meaning of*

McIntyre, 18 Sw. J. Int'l L. 417 (2012). For a discussion of state court jurisdiction in the post-*McIntyre* era that accounts for sovereignty/federalism concerns, *see* Geoffrey P. Miller, *In Search of the Most Adequate Forum: State Court Personal Jurisdiction*, 2 Stan. J. Complex Litig. 1 (2014).

2. *Comparison with* Asahi. The *Asahi* case was the Supreme Court's last word on specific jurisdiction until *McIntyre* in 2011. *McIntyre* was a variant of the "stream of commerce" line of cases presented by *Asahi*. In *Asahi*, Justice O'Connor's opinion directed to "minimum contacts" stated that the placement of a product into the stream of commerce, without more, was not sufficient to satisfy Due Process; however, she noted that additional conduct of the defendant directed at the forum state might reflect the requisite intent to serve the market. Indeed, she specifically referred to a defendant who markets the product through a distributor who has agreed to serve as the sales agent in the forum state. McIntyre America was an Ohio distributor who sold McIntyre UK's machines throughout the United States, including to New Jersey, where Nicastro was injured. Why doesn't McIntyre UK's use of an Ohio distributor (McIntyre America) suffice as such "additional conduct"? Is it because only one machine was actually shown to end up in New Jersey?

What else might constitute "additional conduct"? The First Circuit discussed the topic in *Knox v. MetalForming, Inc.*, 914 F.3d 685 (1st Cir. 2019), when it upheld jurisdiction in Massachusetts over a foreign defendant whose product, sold throughout the United States via an American distributor, caused injury to the plaintiff in Massachusetts. The defendant, Shechtl, a German manufacturer, had an exclusive contract with MetalForming, a Georgia distributor, for the sale and advertising of its metal-bending machines throughout the United States. Although Schechtl did not target any state in particular and conducted nearly all of its activities in Germany, it retained the right to reject any purchase order MetalForming submitted on behalf of a customer and constructed its machines according to each buyer's technical specifications. Moreover, Schechtl provided its direct contact information on its products packaging and materials, and expressly instructed purchasers to contact it in Germany for spare parts, troubleshooting, or the repair of significant malfunctions.

The Court of Appeals ruled that Schechtl's ability to reject purchase orders created a voluntary connection between it and any forum in which it opted to sell its machines. It further found that the fact Schechtl approved purchases and manufactured its products based on a buyer's specifications added another level of conduct targeting the forum of sale. Finally, the court held that by providing its direct contact information and instructing buyers to reach out to it for parts and repairs, Schechtl had opened direct lines of communication between itself and the forum. In the case of Massachusetts, 45 machines had been sold, creating as many channels of communication between Schechtl and the forum. For these reasons, the First Circuit found Schechtl had purposefully availed itself of the Massachusetts forum.

Do these facts show Shechtl's contacts were significantly distinguishable from those in *McIntyre*? Had McIntyre made itself a point of contact for providing replacement parts, would it have been subject to jurisdiction in New Jersey? What other types of activities might expose foreign defendants like Schechtl and McIntyre to jurisdiction in states in which their products are sold via distributors?

3. *An alternate forum for Nicastro?* If the defendant McIntyre UK is not subject to jurisdiction in New Jersey, can it be sued in Ohio? It is clear that McIntyre UK's sales of its products to the Ohio distributor will not subject it to general jurisdiction on an unrelated claim, but perhaps the injury in New Jersey can be said to "arise" from the shipment of this machine by McIntyre UK to Ohio and thus would be an example of specific jurisdiction. Or is that connection too attenuated? Is this situation more like the *World-Wide Volkswagen* scenario where the fact that the product ends up in the state where the injury occurred cannot be attributed to the activity of the defendant McIntyre UK at all? See below at pages 195–196 for further discussion about when a claim can be said to "arise out of" particular connections with the forum in order to satisfy Due Process.

4. *Uncertainties After* McIntyre. Unfortunately, *McIntyre* did little to clarify many of the issues that arose prior to and after the *Asahi* decision. Nor have five years of post-*McIntyre* cases brought about additional clarity. The splintered opinion in *McIntyre* has led three circuit courts to view the Court's holding as the "position taken by those Members who concurred in the judgment on the narrowest grounds," meaning Justice Breyer's opinion focusing on the fact that the record indicated only a single New Jersey sale in *McIntyre*. *See In re Chinese-Manufactured Drywall Prods. Liab. Litig.*, 753 F.3d 521, 541 (5th Cir. 2014); *Williams v. Romarm, SA,* 756 F.3d 777, 784 (D.C. Cir. 2014); *AFTG-TG, LLC v. Nuvoton Tech. Corp.*, 689 F.3d 1358, 1363 (Fed. Cir. 2012).

Several state courts have followed suit. In *Willemsen v. Invacare*, 282 P.3d 867 (Or. 2012), plaintiff's mother died in a fire allegedly caused by a defective battery charger in her motorized wheelchair. The Oregon Supreme Court (en banc) upheld jurisdiction over the Taiwanese manufacturer who made the battery chargers, which it sold to an Ohio manufacturer of motorized wheelchairs. Over a two-year period, the Ohio wheelchair manufacturer sold more than 1,000 motorized wheelchairs with battery chargers in Oregon. Relying on Justice Breyer's *McIntyre* concurrence, the court held this "regular course of sales" was sufficient to establish the requisite "minimum contacts" such that Oregon could assert jurisdiction over the Taiwanese manufacturer.

In *Book v. Doublestar Dongfeng Tyre Co., Ltd.* 860 N.W.2d 576 (Iowa 2015), the Iowa Supreme Court addressed how the specific business arrangement between a foreign manufacturer and a U.S. distributor affects the jurisdictional analysis. Book filed a products liability action in Iowa after a tire explosion permanently disabled him. The tire was made by Doublestar—a Chinese manufacturer—which sells hundreds of thousands of tires annually to two U.S. distributors. Voma, a Tennessee corporation with its principal place of business in Memphis, is one of the distributors, and the owner of the "Treadstone" brand. When Voma orders tires, Doublestar stamps Voma's logo on the sidewall, and Voma specifies the shipping destination.

In the year before the accident, Doublestar provided Voma 7,008 tires of the model at issue in the case, 999 of which Voma sold into Iowa. To save costs, Voma often "instructed Doublestar to ship the tires directly from China to . . . Des Moines, bypassing Voma's Tennessee facility." However, none of the 12,681 tires shipped in this fashion were the same model as the one that exploded. Moreover, Doublestar testified that it "knew some containers of tires were shipped directly to 'Des Moines, IA' but denied [it] knew 'IA' meant the State of Iowa." The trial court granted its motion to dismiss, relying on Doublestar's lack of awareness or targeting of Iowa, and the fact that the tire causing the accident was shipped to Tennessee first. Plaintiffs' subsequent appeal was granted.

After a sweeping review of federal stream of commerce jurisprudence, the Iowa Supreme Court stated that Justice Breyer's concurrence in *McIntyre* "limited the holding to the facts of the case and declined to adopt any broader rules." *Id.* at 591. As a result, it noted, "other state appellate courts . . . have interpreted [*McIntyre*] to conclude their existing precedent on the stream-of-commerce test remains good law." *Id.* at 592 (collecting cases). In deciding to adopt this approach itself, the Iowa Supreme Court emphasized three factors: First, the court rejected Doublestar's "lack of awareness" argument because of its direct shipments to Iowa, despite the fact that Doublestar "sold the tires to Voma in China and . . . delivered [them] F.O.B at the Chinese port." *Id.* at 597. Second, it pointed out that Breyer's concurrence referenced the "volume, value, and hazardous character" test first articulated by Justice Stevens in *Asahi. Id.* at 596. The Court emphasized this point because the tire allegedly had a "dangerous design" given that a recent change had left it "prone to explode during reasonably foreseeable mounting mistakes." *Id.* at 595. Third, it suggested that "fairness is the crux of the minimum-contacts analysis"—a notion it imported from its pre-*McIntyre* cases—and held that the volume of sales mitigated unfairness concerns. The Court found the fairness factors overwhelmingly supported Iowa as a forum, invoking Justice Ginsburg's dissent in *McIntyre* to suggest a manufacturer cannot "Pilate-like wash its hands of a product by having independent distributors market it." *Id.* at 592 (internal citation omitted). Should it affect the analysis that Doublestar conceded it would be amenable to suit in Tennessee? To the extent personal jurisdiction accounts for burden on the defendant of litigating in the forum, it is not clear that Doublestar would be more inconvenienced by litigating in Tennessee than in Iowa.

Although many lower courts have distinguished *McIntyre* on the facts, one case in which a court followed *McIntyre*'s lead in finding no jurisdiction over a foreign manufacturer is *State v. NV Sumatra Tobacco Trading*, 403 S.W.3d 726 (Tenn. 2013). The State of Tennessee sued NV Sumatra, an Indonesian manufacturer of cigarettes, to collect unpaid contributions to a state-run fund for treating tobacco-related health conditions. Although 11.5 million of NV Sumatra's cigarettes had been sold in Tennessee, the cigarettes in question passed through two layers of foreign distributors before first entering the U.S. market, after which an independent Florida-based tobacco distributor directed domestic sales. Emphasizing NV Sumatra's lack of contractual relationships with an American distributor and the fact that it never directed any of its distributors to target Tennessee specifically, the court held that the defendant did not have sufficient purposeful contacts to justify jurisdiction.

NV Sumatra stakes out a clear position on another important issue on which post-*McIntyre* courts have split: whether the "plus" element from Justice O'Connor's "stream of commerce plus" test can be satisfied simply by *additional sales*, or whether a different type of forum-directed activity is necessary. The court in *NV Sumatra* required specific forum-directed "effort." By contrast, the Washington Supreme Court, sitting en banc, came out the opposite way on this question in *State v. LG Electronics*, 375 P.3d 1035 (Wash. 2016). Upholding jurisdiction over foreign electronics manufacturers, the six-justice majority wrote: "[S]ale of products through an independent nationwide distribution system is not sufficient, absent something more, for a State to assert personal jurisdiction over a manufacturer when only one product enters a state and causes injury." But the majority held that the "something more" could be that "a substantial volume of sales took place in a state as part of the regular flow of commerce." Three justices suggested the majority misinterpreted *McIntyre* on this point:

> [T]he Court ruled that the plaintiff must show that the defendant did "something more" than just sell its products through a nationwide distributor with the hope that they might be sold in the forum state to support forum jurisdiction. . . . The majority then . . . holds that the trial court has jurisdiction over Defendants in this case because the State alleged that Defendants placed large quantities of their products into international streams of commerce with the knowledge that they will likely enter the Washington market at some point, and that many more than one of them did enter our state. This is probably a correct application of Justice Brennan's [chain of distribution] test. But *McIntyre* did not silently adopt Justice Brennan's *Asahi* concurrence.

The partial dissent stated that the "something more" should be equivalent to Justice O'Connor's "plus" factor. Does the *McIntyre* concurrence pick a side in the *Asahi* debate? Justice Breyer explicitly rejects what he calls the "absolute approach" to personal jurisdiction, which would subject a producer to jurisdiction whenever it "knows or reasonably should know that its products are distributed through a nationwide distribution system that *might* lead to those products being sold to any of the fifty states." Some lower courts have read the concurrence as affirmatively adopting the "stream of commerce plus" theory of minimum contacts and finally settling the disagreement in *Asahi*, while others believe that Breyer declined to choose between the *Asahi* opinions. *See* Adam N. Steinman, *The Meaning of* McIntyre, 18 Sw. J. Int'l L. 417 (2012).

How does Justice Ginsburg's dissent square with the "stream of commerce plus" approach? The dissent states that by "purposefully avail[ing] itself" of the United States market nationwide, McIntyre UK "thereby availed itself of the market of *all* States in which its products were sold." In other words, Justice Ginsburg believes that targeted efforts to serve the United States as a whole are effectively targeted efforts to serve the individual states that comprise it. However, Justice Ginsburg's approach is not essentially inconsistent with Justice O'Connor's *Asahi* opinion. Recall that Justice O'Connor's *Asahi* opinion specifically referred to a defendant who markets the product through a distributor who has agreed to serve as the sales agent in the forum state as providing the "something more" her "stream of commerce plus" test required. By relying on the targeted nature of McIntyre UK's conduct, Justice Ginsburg seems to embrace Justice O'Connor's requirement that the defendant must "indicate an intent or purpose to serve the market in the forum State," in addition to merely placing the product into the stream of commerce. *Asahi*, at p. 135.

One federal Court of Appeals has emphasized a different issue: the control exercised by a foreign manufacturer over the distributor in a stream of commerce case. In *Polar Electro Oy v. Suunto Oy*, 2016 WL 3913449 (Fed. Cir. July 20, 2016), plaintiffs filed a patent infringement claim in Delaware on the basis of, *inter alia*, 94 allegedly infringing products that Suunto, the foreign manufacturer, had sold to Delaware retailers. Under the distribution arrangement, the distributor provided destination addresses, took title to the goods in Finland, and directed and paid for shipping. Suunto, by contrast, fulfilled, packaged, and invoiced the orders and took care of other administrative issues related to export processing. The court's reasoning is illustrative: "This is not a case where a small manufacturer sells its products to an independent distributor, who then distributes the products to consumers across the nation. Suunto did not simply place its products in the stream of commerce, with the products fortuitously reaching Delaware as a result of the unilateral effort of [its distributor]. Rather, acting in consort with [its distributor], Suunto deliberately and purposefully shipped the accused products to Delaware retailers." Does this result shed any light on the *Asahi* debate discussed in the context of *State v. LG Electronics*?

For further analysis of *McIntyre* and its implications for the doctrine of specific jurisdiction, *see* Adam N. Steinman et al., in Symposium, *Personal Jurisdiction for the Twenty-First Century: The Implications of* McIntyre *and* Goodyear Dunlop Tires, 63 S.C. L. Rev. 463 *et seq.* (2012). For a discussion of how *McIntyre* has been and could be interpreted in lower courts, *see* Kaitlyn Findley, *Paddling Past* Nicastro *in the Stream of Commerce Doctrine: Interpreting Justice Breyer's Concurrence as Implicitly Inviting Lower Courts to Develop Alternative Jurisdictional Standards*, 63 Emory L.J. 695 (2014).

5. *What Type of Role for Reasonableness?* You will recall that *Asahi* seemed to call for a two-step analysis for specific jurisdiction to meet the test of Due Process. First, "minimum contacts" had to be satisfied and second, a determination must be made that the exercise of jurisdiction would be "reasonable." Reasonableness concerns seem to be most salient in transnational cases where one or more defendants are foreign. *See, e.g., TH Agric. & Nutrition, LLC v. Ace European Grp. Ltd.*, 488 F.3d 1282, 1295-1296 (10th Cir. 2007) ("Even though modern technology and the worldwide nature of the Insurers' business minimize the burden of litigating in a foreign forum, they do not completely remove the burden."); *see also* Linda J. Silberman & Nathan D. Yaffe, *The Transnational Case in Conflict of Laws: Two Suggestions for the New Restatement Third of Conflict of Laws-Judicial Jurisdiction over Foreign Defendants and Party Autonomy in International Contracts*, 27 Duke J. Comp. & Int'l L. 405, 408 (2017) ("[C]ourts in practice only dismiss on reasonableness grounds where the defendant is foreign, whereas they effectively never dismiss domestic defendants on grounds of reasonableness. That is not to say that most foreign defendants in specific jurisdiction cases are dismissed on reasonableness grounds. . . ."). Of course, in *McIntyre* the second step of "reasonableness" is not discussed because both the plurality and the concurrence found that "minimum contacts" were not satisfied. For more on this point, *see* Howard B. Stravitz, *Sayonara to Fair Play and Substantial Justice?*, 63 S.C. L. Rev. 754 (2012).

6. *The Comparative Perspective.* In her dissent, Justice Ginsburg also notes that the "place where the harmful event occurred" is a common basis for jurisdiction in other countries and, in particular, under the European Union Regulation on Jurisdiction and Judgments. (Comparative jurisdiction regimes are discussed more extensively *infra*, at pp. 217-222.) Her point here is that plaintiffs injured in the United States are at a disadvantage because they cannot sue in the place where they are injured, usually their home, whereas foreign plaintiffs will be able to sue where they suffer the harm. But, of course, there may be major procedural differences

in the legal systems of other countries that make suit at the place of injury there less burdensome and/or expensive than if suit were brought in the United States. For further discussion of these issues, *see* "Why Litigants Care About Choice of Forum" *infra*, at pp. 223-229. For a more comprehensive discussion on comparative regimes and why transnational cases raise special considerations, *see* Linda J. Silberman, Goodyear *and* Nicastro: *Observations from a Transnational and Comparative Perspective*, 63 S.C. L. Rev. 591 (2012).

7. *A Role for Congress?* Justice Kennedy's opinion acknowledges that McIntyre UK directed marketing and sales efforts at the *United States*, even if not New Jersey, and suggests, as Justice O'Connor did in an asterisk footnote in *Asahi*, that *Congress* might be able to authorize jurisdiction in an appropriate court based on nationwide contacts. As you will see, *infra*, at pp. 210-217, such nationwide jurisdiction in federal courts has previously been enacted by Congress or the Rulemakers for certain claims arising under federal law.

Some members of Congress have recognized the need for such legislation in these product liability cases, though their call for action has not been taken up in the years since *McIntyre*. First introduced in 2011, the Foreign Manufacturers Legal Accountability Act would require foreign manufacturers that desire to distribute certain products in the United States to establish registered agents in the United States, specifically in a state with "a substantial connection to the importation, distribution, or sale of the products." Noting that many Americans are unable to recover damages from foreign manufacturers for lack of jurisdiction and that the inability to apply U.S. tort law to such manufacturers places domestic manufacturers at a competitive disadvantage, the bill seeks to ensure that foreign manufacturers are subject to the jurisdiction of state and federal courts in at least one state. By registering an agent for service of process, the bill establishes that "the foreign manufacturer or producer . . . thereby consents to the personal jurisdiction of the State and Federal courts of the State in which the registered agent is located." And while the bill has not been enacted, it has been introduced in every legislative session since the Supreme Court announced its decision in *McIntyre*. *See* H.R. 3304 114th Cong. (2015); H.R. 1910 113th Cong. (2013); H.R. 3646, 112th Cong. (2011).

Does this bill go too far in that it appears not to limit jurisdiction to cases where the injury occurs in the United States as the result of the distribution of the product in the United States? Does this type of "coerced" consent meet the constitutional standard of Due Process? Might this bill require the Supreme Court to confront the tension that now exists as a result of *McIntyre* as to whether jurisdiction is to be considered a function of "sovereign authority" and consent or instead predicated upon minimum contacts and fairness?

8. McIntyre *and Internet-Based Commercial Activity*. In *McIntyre*, Justice Breyer, joined by Justice Alito, did not embrace the plurality opinion, in part because the case did "not implicate modern concerns." In particular, Justice Breyer referenced the Internet, questioning how to understand the jurisdictional standards applied "when a company targets the world by selling products from its Web site" or, "instead of shipping the products directly, . . . consigns the products through an intermediary (say, Amazon.com) who then receives and fulfills the orders." Does the plurality opinion in *McIntyre* affect the cases applying *Calder*'s "express aiming and targeting" requirement in the Internet context, discussed earlier at pp. 170-174. Do you think that any of those cases would be decided differently?

Consider the post-*McIntyre* decision, *Mavrix Photo, Inc. v. Brand Technologies, Inc.*, 647 F.3d 1218 (9th Cir. 2011), *cert. denied*, 132 S.Ct. 1101 (2012). In *Mavrix*, the Ninth Circuit held that a California court could exercise specific jurisdiction over an Ohio corporation, Brand Technologies, Inc., in a copyright infringement action in which the plaintiff, Mavrix Photo, Inc., alleged that Brand unlawfully posted numerous pictures of celebrity Stacy Ferguson, better known as "Fergie," on its website, celebrity-gossip.net. Celebrity-gossip.net was an exceptionally popular website with nationwide viewership and scope, on which Brand posted content about celebrity activity occurring primarily around the Southern California area. Notably, however, the pictures at issue in *Mavrix* were all taken outside of California. Nevertheless, the court held that these pictures, and presumably any of the content posted on the website, were "expressly aimed" at California because Brand was clearly exploiting the market there. The court determined that it was clear from "the website's subject matter, as well as the size and commercial value of the California market . . . that Brand anticipated, desired, and achieved a substantial California viewer base." The court found that Brand "sought and attracted nationwide audiences" for commercial gain and therefore could not characterize the consumption of its products as "random, fortuitous, or attenuated." In light of celebrity-gossip.net's popularity, does the court's analysis subject Brand to personal jurisdiction in every forum? For a detailed analysis of how the peculiarities of cyberspace affect jurisdictional analysis post-*McIntyre* and an argument for a narrower use of Internet contacts to support personal jurisdiction, *see* Alan M. Trammell & Derek E. Bambauer, *Personal Jurisdiction and the "Interwebs,"* 100 Cornell L. Rev. 1129 (2015).

Note that the court in *Mavrix* found that *McIntyre* was "consistent" with the line of cases upholding personal jurisdiction on the basis of a "purposefully directed" intentional tort and therefore did not alter the Ninth Circuit's case law. Indeed, the court found that *McIntyre* affirmatively recognized an exception to the purposeful availment requirement in intentional tort cases and, on that basis, applied the effects-based "purposeful direction" test to analyze whether a California court could exercise personal jurisdiction over Brand. Consider that Brand targeted a nationwide audience through celebrity-gossip.net and that McIntyre UK targeted the United States as a whole through its American distributor. How would you explain the different outcomes? Bear these considerations in mind as read the next principal case on purposeful availment and intentional torts.

e.   Defamation and Targeted Wrongdoing

Calder v. Jones   `Calder Effect Test`

465 U.S. 783 (1984)

Justice Rehnquist delivered the opinion of the Court.

Respondent Shirley Jones brought suit in California Superior Court claiming that she had been libeled in an article written and edited by petitioners in Florida. The article was published in a national magazine with a large circulation in California. Petitioners were served with process by mail in Florida and caused special appearances to be entered on their behalf, moving to quash the service of process for lack of personal jurisdiction. The superior court granted the motion on the ground that First Amendment concerns weighed against an assertion of jurisdiction otherwise proper under the Due Process Clause. The California Court of Appeal reversed, rejecting the suggestion that First Amendment considerations enter into the jurisdictional analysis. We now affirm.

Respondent lives and works in California. She . . . brought this suit against the National Enquirer, Inc., its local distributing company, and petitioners for libel, invasion of privacy, and intentional infliction of emotional harm. The Enquirer is a Florida corporation with its principal place of business in Florida. It publishes a national weekly newspaper with a total circulation of over 5 million. About 600,000 of those copies, almost twice the level of the next highest State, are sold in California. Respondent's and her husband's claims were based on an article that appeared in the Enquirer's October 9, 1979 issue. Both the Enquirer and the distributing company answered the complaint and made no objection to the jurisdiction of the California court.

Petitioner South is a reporter employed by the Enquirer. He is a resident of Florida, though he frequently travels to California on business. South wrote the first draft of the challenged article, and his byline appeared on it. He did most of his research in Florida, relying on phone calls to sources in California for the information contained in the article. Shortly before publication, South called respondent's home and read to her husband a draft of the article so as to elicit his comments upon it. Aside from his frequent trips and phone calls, South has no other relevant contacts with California.

Petitioner Calder is also a Florida resident. He has been to California only twice — once, on a pleasure trip, prior to the publication of the article and once after to testify in an unrelated trial. Calder is president and editor of the Enquirer. He "oversee[s] just about every function of the Enquirer.". . . He reviewed and approved the initial evaluation of the subject of the article and edited it in its final form. He also declined to print a retraction requested by respondent. Calder has no other relevant contacts with California.

In considering petitioners' motion to quash service of process, the superior court surmised that the actions of petitioners in Florida, causing injury to respondent in California, would ordinarily be sufficient to support an assertion of jurisdiction over them in California.[5] But the court felt that special solicitude was necessary because of the potential "chilling effect" on reporters and editors which would result from requiring them to appear in remote jurisdictions to answer for the content of articles upon which they worked. The court also noted that respondent's rights could be "fully satisfied" in her suit against the publisher without requiring petitioners to appear as parties. The superior court, therefore, granted the motion.

The California Court of Appeal reversed. 138 Cal. App. 3d 128, 187 Cal. Rptr. 825 (1982). The court agreed that neither petitioner's contacts with California would be sufficient for an assertion of jurisdiction on a cause of action unrelated to those contacts. . . . But the court concluded that a valid basis for jurisdiction existed on the theory that petitioners intended to, and did, cause tortious injury to

---

5. California's "long-arm" statute permits an assertion of jurisdiction over a nonresident defendant whenever permitted by the state and federal Constitutions. Section 410.10 of the California Code of Civil Procedure provides: "A court of this state may exercise jurisdiction on any basis not inconsistent with the Constitution of this state or of the United States."

respondent in California. The fact that the actions causing the effects in California were performed outside the State did not prevent the State from asserting jurisdiction over a cause of action arising out of those effects. The court rejected the superior court's conclusion that First Amendment considerations must be weighed in the scale against jurisdiction. . . .

The Due Process Clause of the Fourteenth Amendment to the United States Constitution permits personal jurisdiction over a defendant in any State with which the defendant has "certain minimum contacts . . . such that the maintenance of the suit does not offend 'traditional notions of fair play and substantial justice.' ". . . In judging minimum contacts, a court properly focuses on "the relationship among the defendant, the forum, and the litigation." *Shaffer v. Heitner*, 433 U.S. 186 (1977). *See also Rush v. Savchuk*, 444 U.S. 320 (1980). The plaintiff's lack of "contacts" will not defeat otherwise proper jurisdiction, *see Keeton v. Hustler Magazine, Inc.*, 465 U.S. 770 (1984), but they may be so manifold as to permit jurisdiction when it would not exist in their absence. Here, the plaintiff is the focus of the activities of the defendants out of which the suit arises. *See McGee v. International Life Ins. Co.*, 355 U.S. 220 (1957).

The allegedly libelous story concerned the California activities of a California resident. It impugned the professionalism of an entertainer whose television career was centered in California. The article was drawn from California sources, and the brunt of the harm, in terms both of respondent's emotional distress and the injury to her professional reputation, was suffered in California. In sum, California is the focal point both of the story and of the harm suffered. Jurisdiction over petitioner is therefore proper in California based on the "effects" of their Florida conduct in California. *World-Wide Volkswagen Corp. v. Woodson*, 444 U.S. 286, 297–298 (1980); Restatement (Second) of Conflicts of Law §37.

Petitioners argue that they are not responsible for the circulation of the article in California. A reporter and an editor, they claim, have no direct economic stake in their employer's sales in a distant State. Nor are ordinary employees able to control their employer's marketing activity. The mere fact that they can "foresee" that the article will be circulated and have an effect in California is not sufficient for an assertion of jurisdiction. . . . Petitioners liken themselves to a welder employed in Florida who works on a boiler which subsequently explodes in California. Cases which hold that jurisdiction will be proper over the manufacturer, *Buckeye Boiler Co. v. Superior Court*, 71 Cal. 2d 893, 80 Cal. Rptr. 113, 458 P.2d 57 (1969); *Gray v. American Radiator & Standard Sanitary Corp.*, 22 Ill. 2d 432, 176 N.E.2d 761 (1961), should not be applied to the welder who has no control over and derives no direct benefit from his employer's sales in that distant State.

Petitioners' analogy does not wash. Whatever the status of their hypothetical welder, petitioners are not charged with mere untargeted negligence. Rather, their intentional, and allegedly tortious, actions were expressly aimed at California. Petitioner South wrote and petitioner Calder edited an article that they knew would have a potentially devastating impact upon respondent. And they knew that the brunt of that injury would be felt by respondent in the State in which she lives and works and in which the National Enquirer has its largest circulation. Under the circumstances, petitioners must "reasonably anticipate being haled into court there" to answer for the truth of the statements made in their article. . . . An individual injured in California need not go to Florida to seek redress from persons who, though remaining in Florida, knowingly cause the injury in California.

Petitioners are correct that their contacts with California are not to be judged according to their employer's activities there. On the other hand, their status as employees does not somehow insulate them from jurisdiction. Each defendant's contacts with the forum State must be assessed individually. . . . In this case, petitioners are primary participants in an alleged wrongdoing intentionally directed at a California resident, and jurisdiction over them is proper on that basis.

We also reject the suggestion that First Amendment concerns enter into the jurisdictional analysis. The infusion of such considerations would needlessly complicate an already imprecise inquiry. . . . Moreover, the potential chill on protected First Amendment activity stemming from libel and defamation actions is already taken into account in the constitutional limitations on the substantive law governing such suits. *See New York Times, Co. v. Sullivan*, 376 U.S. 254 (1964); *Gertz v. Robert Welch, Inc.*, 418 U.S. 323 (1974). To reintroduce those concerns at the jurisdictional stage would be a form of double counting. We have already declined in other contexts to grant special procedural protections to defendants in libel and defamation actions in addition to the constitutional protections embodied in the substantive laws. . . .

We hold that jurisdiction over petitioners in California is proper because of their intentional conduct in Florida calculated to cause injury to respondent in California. The judgment of the California Court of Appeal is

Affirmed.

NOTES AND QUESTIONS

1. *Analyzing (and Limiting?)* Calder. How does the Supreme Court's decision in *Calder* square with the requirement of purposeful availment laid down in *World-Wide Volkswagen*? The Supreme Court in *Calder* emphasizes that the defendants were not charged with "untargeted negligence" but rather their "intentional, and allegedly tortious, actions were expressly aimed at California." Is that the equivalent of "purposeful availment"? If the concern behind the requirement of "purposeful availment" is that a defendant have some control over its amenability to suit, *see World-Wide Volkswagen*, how can it be said that the defendant writer and editor of the National Enquirer exercise such control? Isn't it the National Enquirer that directs activity to California and not the writer and editor? Or does the court in fact fail to draw any distinction between the magazine and its writer/editor? The Court says that the writer and editor "knew" that the brunt of the injury would be felt by Ms. Jones in California where she lived. But isn't that just another way of saying that the defendants had reason to foresee injury to the plaintiff in California—a standard that the Court found to be insufficient in *World-Wide Volkswagen*?

In addition to citing the "effects" of the story in California, the Court notes that the defendants made calls to, and researched and wrote about, the State of California. Is that activity crucial to the finding that jurisdiction is proper? Alternately, some courts have held that *Calder*'s "effects" test is limited to cases of libel/defamation. *See United States v. Swiss Am. Bank*, 274 F.3d 610, 624 (1st Cir. 2001) (the effects test is "specifically designed for use in a defamation case . . . [and] whether

[it] was ever intended to apply to numerous other torts, such as conversion or breach of contract, is unclear.").

The Supreme Court did not revisit the "effects test" until its decision in *Walden v. Fiore*, 134 S.Ct. 1115 (2014). *Walden* arose from incidents that occurred when Gina Fiore and Keith Gipson traveled back from a visit to San Juan, Puerto Rico, to their residences in Nevada. Transportation Security Administration agents in San Juan searched their carry-on luggage, finding $97,000 in cash. Plaintiffs Fiore and Gipson explained they were professional gamblers, and that these were their winnings. Although respondents were cleared for departure, law enforcement in San Juan notified a Drug Enforcement Administration (DEA) task force in Atlanta, Georgia, where plaintiffs landed for a connecting flight to Nevada. Once in Atlanta, the defendant—working as part of the DEA task force—questioned plaintiffs and eventually seized their cash. Plaintiffs were informed they could retrieve the funds upon showing they came from a legitimate source. Afterwards, defendant drafted an affidavit to show probable cause for the seizure of funds, which was filed with the U.S. Attorney's Office. According to plaintiffs, the affidavit contained false and misleading statements, omitting exculpatory information that showed a lack of evidence linking the funds to drugs. Ultimately, no formal complaint was filed, and the DEA returned the funds seven months later.

Plaintiffs filed suit in district court in Nevada, seeking money damages for violations of their Fourth Amendment rights against an illegal "search and seizure." The district court dismissed, concluding that even if the DEA agent caused harm to the plaintiffs in Nevada because he knew they lived in Nevada, that fact was insufficient to confer jurisdiction. A divided panel of the Ninth Circuit Court of Appeals reversed. Although it found the search and seizure in Georgia did not support jurisdiction in Nevada, it held that the district court could properly exercise jurisdiction over the "false probable cause affidavit aspect of the case." Invoking language from *Calder*, the Ninth Circuit found that petitioner "expressly aimed" the submission of his allegedly false affidavit at Nevada by submitting the affidavit knowing that it would affect persons with a "significant connection" to Nevada.

The Supreme Court granted certiorari and reversed. The Court noted that "defendant's suit-related conduct must create a substantial connection with the forum State," referring to this as the "necessary relationship" for jurisdictional purposes. The Court went on to highlight two aspects of the relationship: *First*, that it "must arise out of contacts that the defendant *himself* creates with the forum State" (emphasis in original); and *second*, that that "minimum contacts analysis" generally "looks to the defendant's contacts with the forum State itself, not the defendant's contacts with persons who reside there." Although the defendant may "reach out beyond their State" to create jurisdictionally relevant contacts without physically entering the forum state, the Court clarified that "the plaintiff cannot be the only link between the defendant and the forum."

Rather than limiting *Calder* to the libel context, the Court sought to distinguish the present case from *Calder*:

> Although we recognized that the [*Calder*] defendants' activities focused on the plaintiff, our jurisdictional inquiry "focused on 'the relationship among the defendant, the forum, and the litigation.' " Specifically, we examined the various contacts the defendants had created with California

(and not just with the plaintiff) by writing the allegedly libelous story. We found those forum contacts to be ample: The defendants relied on phone calls to "California sources" for the information in their article; they wrote the story about the plaintiff's activities in California; they caused reputational injury in California by writing an allegedly libelous article that was widely circulated in the State; and the "brunt" of that injury was suffered by the plaintiff in that State.

By contrast, in *Walden*, the Court found that "no part of petitioner's course of conduct occurred in Nevada. . . . Petitioner never traveled to, conducted activities within, contacted anyone in, or sent anything or anyone to Nevada." Emphasizing that the appropriate question is "whether the *defendant's* actions connect him to the *forum*," the Court found "no jurisdictionally relevant contacts with Nevada." In so finding, the Court rejected respondents' reliance on "the injury caused by petitioner's allegedly tortious conduct (*i.e.*, the delayed return of their gambling funds) while they were residing in the forum."

2. *The "Effects" Test Post-*Walden. Courts have regularly invoked *Walden* to reject jurisdiction where the primary link between the defendant and the forum state is defendant's knowledge that plaintiff resides in the forum, coupled with (intentional or unintentional) wrongful conduct. In *Waldman v. Palestine Liberation Org.*, 835 F.3d 317 (2d Cir. 2016), eleven families sued the PLO for terror attacks in Israel that injured or killed plaintiffs or their family members. Although the plaintiffs contended that attackers "intended to hit American citizens," the court cited *Walden* as foreclosing jurisdiction based on "defendant's mere knowledge that a plaintiff resides in a specific jurisdiction." Unlike in *Calder*, the court noted that the United States was not the "focal point" of the harm in *Waldman. See also Fastpath v. Arbela*, 760 F.3d 816 (8th Cir. 2014) (in a contract action, rejecting jurisdiction in Iowa over Arbela based on its "aggressive pursuit" of a business relationship with Fastpath, which included initiating contact at various trade shows, conferences, and presentations, where none of these contacts occurred in Iowa, despite the fact that Arbela knew Fastpath was an Iowa corporation).

The precise relationship between *Walden* and *Calder* is still being worked out by courts. In *Acorda Therapeutics, Inc. v. Mylan Pharmaceuticals, Inc.*, 817 F.3d 755 (Fed. Cir. 2016), the Court of Appeals for the Federal Circuit considered whether Delaware could exercise jurisdiction over Mylan for a patent infringement claim brought by a Delaware corporation. The suit was brought after Mylan filed an "Abbreviated New Drug Application" with the FDA, with plans to market the drug nationwide — including in Delaware, where plaintiff was incorporated — upon obtaining FDA approval. In a separate concurrence, Judge O'Malley discussed the relationship between *Calder* and *Walden*:

> *Walden* serves to clarify *Calder*, but does not overrule it or limit its holding exclusively to libel cases. Rather, it makes clear that due process is not satisfied by a showing of "mere injury to a forum resident"; a court must examine "whether the defendant's conduct connects him to the forum in a meaningful way." In *Calder*, the defendants "expressly aimed their intentional, and allegedly tortious, actions at California because they knew the National Enquirer had its largest circulation in California, and that the article would have a potentially devastating impact there." The nature of ANDA litigation

is such that, as in *Calder*, "the focal point both of the filing of the ANDA and of the harm suffered" is Delaware. Jurisdiction over Mylan is proper in Delaware based on the "effects" of the conduct it aimed at Delaware.

Does *Walden* merely "clarify" *Calder*, or does it do more? For another take, see *ClearOne, Inc. v. RevoLabs, Inc.*, 369 P.3d 1269 (Utah 2016). Plaintiff ClearOne brought suit in Utah against the subsequent employer of its ex-employee for tortious interference with a contractual relationship. The employee lived and worked remotely from Texas, and the subsequent employer — RevoLabs — was a Massachusetts corporation. Prior to joining RevoLabs, the employee discussed the move with several RevoLabs personnel located in a variety of jurisdictions, none of which included Utah. The Utah court acknowledged that its leading pre-*Walden* precedent held the "effects test permitted jurisdiction over a defendant so long as the defendant's tortious act targeted a resident of the forum and the injury was suffered by the plaintiff in the forum state." Although the Utah court suggested this pre-*Walden* test would be met on the facts of the case, the court found that *Walden* "significantly narrowed the broadly formulated effects test" it had previously adopted. Thus it held there was no jurisdiction where none of the relevant conduct occurred in the state, nor had the defendant established any other contact with the state. Is this case consistent with *Acorda v. Mylan*?

A recent Fifth Circuit case, *Trois v. Apple Tree Auction Ctr.*, 882 F.3d 485 (5th Cir. 2018), illustrates some of the difficulties courts still have in assessing what constitutes purposeful activity. A Texas man brought suit in Texas against an Ohio auctioneer for fraudulent misrepresentation. The allegedly fraudulent statements had been made during a three-way conference call to Texas initiated not by the defendant himself but by a third party, located in Kentucky. The Fifth Circuit upheld the District Court's exercise of personal jurisdiction in Texas, stating, "Although [the defendant] did not initiate the conference call to Trois in Texas, [he] was not a passive participant on the call." *Id.* at 491. Is this convincing? Arguably, the defendant did not create the relevant contacts with Texas himself. On the other hand, the court wrote, "we are somewhat wary of drawing a bright line at who may push the buttons on the telephone." *Id.* What might explain this reluctance?

In *Pakootas v. Teck Cominco Metals, Ltd.*, 905 F.3d 565 (9th Cir. 2018), *cert. denied sub nom. Teck Metals Ltd. v. Confederated Tribes of the Colville Reservation*, 139 S. Ct. 2693 (2019), the Ninth Circuit, citing *Calder* but not referencing *Walden*, upheld jurisdiction in the place of injury over a foreign defendant for injuries suffered there on the basis that the defendant was fully aware of the potential consequences of its acts elsewhere. The defendant, Teck Metals, was a Canadian smelter that had dumped millions of tons of industrial waste into the Columbia River over the course of the twentieth century. The dumping occurred in Canada, just north of the border with Washington State, and the river naturally carried the waste into the United States, where it broke down into hazardous substances. The plaintiffs, various Native American tribes and the State of Washington, sought to hold the smelter liable for "response costs" under the Comprehensive Environmental Response, Compensation, and Liability Act (CERCLA).

The Ninth Circuit concluded that Teck expressly aimed its waste at the State of Washington since it was "inconceivable" that Teck did not know its waste, once deposited in the powerful Columbia River just miles upstream from the border, would end up in Washington. It was also clear that, despite this knowledge, Teck continued its activities over the course of almost a century. Therefore, the court found it could exercise jurisdiction over the Canadian corporation. What exactly satisfied the "express aiming" requirement? Was it Teck's knowledge or something more? How does "knowledge" square with the Supreme Court's decision in *Walden?* Teck's petition for certiorari argued strongly that the Ninth Circuit's decision is inconsistent with *Walden* (as well as *Calder*).*See* Petition for Writ of Certiorari at 5, *Teck Metals Ltd. v. Confederated Tribes of the Colville Reservation,* 139 S.Ct. 2693 (2019) (No. 18-1160), but certiorari was denied. Can you distinguish *Teck* from *Walden?*

3. *Special Concerns in Libel Cases.* As illustrated by the *Sullivan v. New York Times* litigation in Chapter 1, libel/defamation cases present a special difficulty because the multistate dissemination of newspapers, magazines, and broadcast media might render publishers and broadcasters suable in virtually every state, and First Amendment considerations are thought to require special protections. Thus, some states expressly exclude defamation cases from the tortious act and injury provisions of their specific-act statutes. *See, e.g.,* N.Y. C.P.L.R. §§302(a)(2) and (3). In addition, a number of lower-court decisions prior to *Calder* had sought to develop a specialized set of rules for jurisdiction in libel and defamation cases. For example, consider *Curtis Publishing Co. v. Birdsong,* 360 F.2d 344 (5th Cir. 1966), where the Fifth Circuit held that Alabama did not have jurisdiction over a libel action brought by Mississippi highway patrol members against the *Saturday Evening Post* for an article concerning the desegregation of the University of Mississippi. The court explained that there was "no rational nexus between Alabama and the parties or the injury":

> The only interest Alabama might have is to protect its citizens against reading libels distributed in Alabama about persons not present in this State. That interest in this litigation is shared by 49 other States, including Mississippi, and a number of foreign countries where the Post is sold. . . . [W]e must be careful to evolve a rule that will be fair both to those injured and those who through normal commercial activity are exposed to the specter of multi-state litigation. . . . Any other ruling would involve the danger of severe burdens on and impediments to interstate commerce. It takes no great stretch of the imagination to see that businesses operating throughout the United States could be exposed to numerous frivolous and harassing lawsuits. . . .

360 F.2d at 347. Do you think such a ruling was constitutionally compelled?

In the same year that it decided *Calder,* the Supreme Court rendered an opinion on jurisdiction in another defamation case, *Keeton v. Hustler Magazine, Inc.,* 465 U.S. 770 (1984). In *Keeton,* a New York resident sued Hustler Magazine, an Ohio corporation with its principal place of business in California, in New Hampshire federal district court. Hustler Magazine had sold between 10 and 15 thousand copies of its magazine in New Hampshire each month. Ms. Keeton had selected New Hampshire because of its unusually long (six-year) statute of limitations; her claim was time-barred elsewhere. The First Circuit held that an exercise of jurisdiction by New Hampshire, which had but an attenuated interest in the controversy, would be unfair, particularly in view of the fact that the "single publication rule" in effect in New Hampshire would permit the plaintiff to recover for damages caused in all 50 states. The Supreme Court reversed. Justice Rehnquist's majority opinion explained that New Hampshire had an interest in redressing injury to reputation that occurs within its borders, and in "cooperating with other States, through the 'single publication rule,' to provide a forum for efficiently litigating all issues and damages arising out of a libel in a unitary proceeding." Moreover, any issues concerning the permissibility of New Hampshire's application of its limitations period involved a question of choice of law that should not "complicate or distort the jurisdictional inquiry." The fact that the plaintiff was not a resident of the forum state "will not defeat jurisdiction established on the basis of defendant's contacts." Here, Hustler Magazine indisputably sought to exploit the New Hampshire market and hence "must reasonably anticipate being haled into court there in a libel action based on the contents of its magazine."

Neither in *Calder* nor in *Keeton* did the Supreme Court give any special consideration to the role of the First Amendment. Indeed, in *Calder*, the Court expressly rejected the argument by the defendants that the exercise of jurisdiction would have a "chilling effect" on First Amendment rights. The Court opined that First Amendment values were already part of the substantive law of libel and that to reintroduce them at the jurisdictional stage would be "a form of double counting."

Although the Supreme Court in *Walden* does not limit *Calder* to libel cases, it does note that the jurisdictional significance of the defendant's contacts with the forum may differ depending on the cause of action: "The strength of [the defendant's] connection [to California in *Calder*] was largely a function of the nature of the libel tort." Yet some courts seemingly read *Walden* to support limiting jurisdiction even in libel/defamation cases. *See, e.g., Scott v. Lackey*, 587 Fed.Appx. 712 (3d Cir. 2014) (holding that the court did not have jurisdiction over defendant who allegedly defamed plaintiff in online discussion forum).

Defamation cases involving broadcasters present special challenges, as illustrated by *TV Azteca v. Ruiz*, 490 S.W.3d 29 (Tex. 2016). In that case, a Mexican recording artist named Gloria Ruiz, sometimes referred to as "Mexico's Madonna," brought suit against two Mexican broadcasting companies. The plaintiff, who had resided in Texas for years at the time of the events giving rise to the dispute, saw TV segments on an episode from her past in which she had been charged and then jailed for a time in Mexico in connection with sexual assault and kidnapping—charges that were eventually dismissed in their entirety. Asserting that she and others viewed the defamatory programs on their televisions in Texas, Ruiz filed suit in Texas state court. Defendants filed special appearances to challenge the court's jurisdiction. The special appearances were denied, leading to an interlocutory appeal, and after the appellate court affirmed, the Supreme Court of Texas granted review.

The broadcasters resisted jurisdiction on the grounds that the broadcasts were "direct[ed] at viewers in the northeast zone of Mexico, not Texas," but they acknowledged that "households in South Texas may receive the broadcasts due to 'signal spillover.'" Arguing that the lower courts had "erred by equating television broadcast to the distribution of magazines and newspapers" as in *Calder* and *Keeton*, the defendants insisted that in contrast to establishing regular circulation, their broadcast signal had merely "stray[ed] into [the] forum." The court agreed that the spill-over alone was not sufficient—even if the petitioner had knowledge it was occurring—because it failed what it described as *Calder*'s "subject-and-sources" test (which requires that either the *subject of* or the *sources used for* producing the defamatory material have a link to the forum). Noting that there is "a subtle yet crucial difference between directing a tort at an individual who happens to live in a particular state and directing a tort at that state," the court stated that the link must be something more than simply a plaintiff who "feels the brunt of the injury" in the forum.

Nonetheless, the court ultimately upheld jurisdiction. In reaching its decision, the court borrowed heavily from the stream-of-commerce jurisprudence. It found that "evidence of defendants' additional conduct demonstrates that they intended to serve the Texas market," such as selling ad time to Texas businesses and entering into Texas to promote their broadcasts there. This supplemental conduct, rather than the location of Ruiz's residence and the location where the harm was felt, provided the basis for exercising jurisdiction in the case.

4. *The Problem of "Libel Tourism."* Libel cases have presented an additional concern when plaintiffs choose to file their libel actions in foreign jurisdictions where the law is more favorable to the party alleging libel — often referred to as "libel tourism." Plaintiffs then attempt to have those judgments enforced in the United States or elsewhere. In some instances, the defendant has sought protection by bringing an action to have the judgment declared non-enforceable. However, there may be difficulty in obtaining jurisdiction over the foreign libel plaintiff.

A prominent case, *Ehrenfeld v. Mahfouz*, 489 F.3d 542 (2d Cir. 2007) and 518 F.3d 102 (2d Cir. 2007), was the catalyst for changes in New York law on both jurisdiction and recognition of judgments to address the concerns of "libel tourism." The *Ehrenfeld* case involved a nonfiction book about funding terrorism, written by Rachel Ehrenfeld, a New York resident, and published in the United States. Khalid bin Mahfouz, a Saudi Arabian businessman who was accused of funding terrorism in the book, brought a libel action against Ehrenfeld in England, where 23 copies of the book were purchased over the Internet. Ehrenfeld did not appear in the English action, and Mahfouz obtained a default judgment against her. Ehrenfeld then filed her own action in federal district court for the Southern District of New York, seeking a declaration that the English judgment was not enforceable in the United States on the ground that English defamation law does not provide the same free speech protections afforded by the United States Constitution. Relying on both §§302(a)(1) and (a)(3) of the N.Y. C.P.L.R as bases of jurisdiction over Mahfouz, Ehrenfeld pointed to communications about the English action made to her by Mahfouz and the fact that he posted the English court order on his website, which was accessible in New York. The district court dismissed the suit for lack of personal jurisdiction, *Ehrenfeld v. Mahfouz*, 2006 WL 1096816 (S.D.N.Y. 2006), and Ehrenfeld appealed. The Court of Appeals for the Second Circuit held that §302(a)(3) did not confer jurisdiction over Mahfouz because Ehrenfeld had not shown that Mahfouz's actions were tortious. The court then certified the question of whether §302(a)(1) conferred jurisdiction on these facts to the New York Court of Appeals because available state court decisions did not provide a clear answer to what contacts were sufficient for "transaction of business," and because it was an important question of public policy. 489 F.3d 542 (2d Cir. 2007). The New York Court of Appeals held that §302(a)(1) did not confer jurisdiction in this case because Mahfouz did not seek to initiate any business transaction nor did Mahfouz purposefully avail himself of any privileges and benefits of New York's laws. *Ehrenfeld v. Mahfouz*, 9 N.Y.3d 501, 881 N.E.2d 830 (N.Y. 2007). The Second Circuit then affirmed the dismissal for lack of personal jurisdiction over the defendant, notwithstanding the plaintiff's contention that her First Amendment rights were being violated. *Ehrenfeld v. Mahfouz*, 518 F.3d 102 (2d Cir. 2007).

Addressing the jurisdictional limitation in *Ehrenfeld*, New York amended its specific-act statute. The provision, interestingly called the Libel Terrorism Protection Act (and not the Libel Tourism Act), added new subsection (d) to N.Y. C.P.L.R. §302:*

Foreign defamation judgment. The courts of this state shall have personal jurisdiction over any person who obtains a judgment in a defamation proceeding outside the United States against any person who is a resident of New York or is a person or entity amenable to jurisdiction in New York who has assets in New York or may have to take actions in New York to comply with the judgment, for the purposes of rendering declaratory relief with respect to that person's liability for the judgment, and/or for the purpose of determining whether said judgment should be deemed non-recognizable pursuant to section fifty-three hundred four of this chapter, to the fullest extent permitted by the United States Constitution, provided:

1. The publication at issue was published in New York, and
2. That resident or person amenable to jurisdiction in New York (i) has assets in New York which might be used to satisfy the foreign defamation judgment, or (ii) may have to take actions in New York to comply with the foreign defamation judgment.

The Libel Terrorism Protection Act also amended Article 53 of N.Y. C.P.L.R. (New York's version of the Uniform Foreign Money-Judgments Recognition Act). *See* Chapter 7 at p. 895. Section 5304, which provides for both mandatory and discretionary non-recognition of foreign country judgments in certain circumstances, gained an additional discretionary ground for non-recognition in §5304(b). Subsection (9) permits non-recognition of a foreign defamation judgment obtained in a jurisdiction that does not provide the same level of protection for freedom of speech and press as would be provided by both the United States and New York constitutions.

For a more detailed discussion of the New York statute, *see* Todd W. Moore, *Untying Our Hands: The Case for Uniform Personal Jurisdiction over "Libel Tourists,"* 77 Fordham L. Rev. 3207 (2009) (discussing approaches to personal jurisdiction over libel tourists); Sarah Staveley O'Carroll, *Libel Tourism Laws: Spoiling the Holiday and Saving the First Amendment?*, 4 N.Y.U. J.L. & Liberty 252 (2009) (arguing that the amendment to the New York statute may not be constitutional).

In August 2010, federal legislation was also enacted to address the problem of "libel tourism." *See* Securing the Protection of our Enduring and Established Constitutional Heritage Act (the SPEECH Act), 28 U.S.C.A. §§4101–4105. In addition to provisions preventing U.S. courts from recognizing or enforcing a foreign country defamation judgment if the judgment would be inconsistent with the First Amendment (§4102), the legislation creates a cause of action to obtain a declaratory

---

* Other states have followed New York's lead and created similar libel tourism laws. *See* Cal. Civ. Proc. Code §1717 (Deering 2009); Fla. Stat. §55.6055 (LexisNexis 2010); 735 Ill. Comp. Stat. Ann. 5/12-621 (LexisNexis 2010).

judgment to determine that a particular foreign judgment is non-enforceable under the provisions of the Act (§4104(a)). Unlike the amendment to the New York specific-act statute discussed earlier, the federal statute does not have an explicit provision providing for jurisdiction over the judgment-creditor for purposes of the declaratory judgment action. Of course, pursuant to Federal Rule 4(k)(1)(A), a federal court can make use of a state specific-act statute to acquire jurisdiction over a defendant. The federal statute does provide for nationwide service in so far as the defendant is found, resides, has an agent, or transacts business within the United States (§4101(b)). Presumably, pursuant to Rule 4(k)(2), discussed *infra* at pp. 187-191, an action for a declaratory judgment may also be brought against a defendant who is not otherwise subject to jurisdiction in a court in the United States if the defendant's contacts with the United States as a whole would be consistent with Due Process and if the action for declaratory relief can be said to "arise under federal law."

Does the Due Process Clause permit a court in the United States to exercise jurisdiction over a foreign party who merely obtained a judgment against a U.S. party in a foreign court? Is it significant that a party who brings a foreign defamation lawsuit would likely effectuate service of process for that suit in the United States? What other type of additional conduct might be necessary to satisfy Due Process?

5. *The* Calder *Standard and Internet-Based Commercial Activity.* Courts have had significant difficulty with applying the *Calder* standard in the Internet context. The question of how *Calder* affects the assertion of specific jurisdiction over defendants engaging in Internet-based commercial activity arises in a variety of contexts: online defamation, trademark infringement, takedown notices, and online marketplaces where commercial activity gives rise to liability.

One of the earliest cases to address the question of when a website targets, or is "expressly aimed" to, a forum arose in the context of trademark infringement. In *Zippo Mfg. Co. v. Zippo Dot Com, Inc.*, 952 F. Supp. 1119, 1123 (W.D. Pa. 1997), the court characterized activity on the Internet as falling into three categories: (1) "active," that is, repeated transmission of computer files over the Internet; (2) "passive," where the site only made information available to those who wanted to access it; and (3) a "middle ground" of an interactive website where the user exchanges information with the host computer. "Active" sites would generally confer personal jurisdiction, "passive" sites would not, and in the middle category, courts would examine the level of interactivity and the commercial nature of the exchange of information. One concern with this approach is that it overlooks the "express aiming" requirement from *Calder,* with the result that establishing a globally accessible website could expose the operator of such a website to jurisdiction anywhere in the world. *See* Catherine Ross Dunham, *Zippo-ing the Wrong Way: How the Internet Has Misdirected the Federal Courts in Their Personal Jurisdiction Analysis,* 43 U.S.F. L. Rev. 559 (2009) (arguing that the *Zippo* test misdirects the focus of the personal jurisdiction analysis solely to the nature of the website, and so fails to properly consider the defendant's actions in assessing whether there is purposeful availment to the forum); Charles Rhodes, Symposium, Internet and the Law: *Rethinking Personal Jurisdiction over the World Wide Web,* 52 The Advoc. (Texas) 53 (2010) (arguing that courts should look to the quantity and quality of contacts rather than simply looking at the type of website).

a. *Commercial Websites and the Question of Express Aiming.* Courts have split on whether the website must be specifically intended to reach (i.e., be expressly aimed at) customers in the forum state. In *be2 LLC v. Ivanov*, 642 F.3d 555 (7th Cir. 2011), the plaintiff, be2, brought a trademark infringement suit in Illinois against the defendant alleging that he had created a dating site with a similar URL to that of the plaintiff in order to confuse customers. Plaintiff provided evidence that 10 men and 34 women in Illinois had registered for accounts on defendant's website. However, personal jurisdiction failed for lack of Due Process because the plaintiff did not prove that the defendant had purposely targeted Illinois. The court held that a website accessible in the forum state, even if interactive, did not prove that the defendant had targeted that forum.

On the other hand, in *Rilley v. MoneyMutual, LLC*, 863 N.W.2d 789 (Minn. 2015), the court addressed the question of whether a Nevada corporation engaged in online money lending could be sued in Minnesota on claims that its website contained false advertising, that its loans were illegal under Minnesota law, and that it violated Minnesota consumer-protection statutes. In the face of the argument that "basing personal jurisdiction on a website would subject website operators to universal jurisdiction because they could be sued anywhere the website is accessed," the Minnesota court responded, "a website that can be accessed from anywhere cannot provide the sole basis for personal jurisdiction if it has never been visited by a forum resident." Is this a satisfactory response? Is it consistent with Due Process, as elaborated in *Calder* and *Walden*? The court also seemed to have policy factors in mind, opining that "it [is] unwise to disregard contacts through an openly accessible website given the increased tendency for commerce to take place via the Internet, particularly when the website is used to circumvent Minnesota law." Should Minnesota's regulatory interest factor into the analysis? Note also that the court found MoneyMutual had done business with over 1,000 customers that it knew to be Minnesotan. Does that fact make a difference—and if so, is it the quantity or the knowledge of their residence?

These cases evince the conceptual difficulties with the "active/passive" line that *Zippo* asks courts to draw. Technological developments, such as algorithm-generated ad targeting, filtering, real-time bidding-based display advertising, will only exacerbate these difficulties in the future. *See generally* M. Margaret McKeown, *The Internet and the Constitution: A Selective Retrospective*, 9 Wash. J.L. Tech. & Arts 135 (2014) (reviewing the past 20 years of the Internet and its challenge to jurisdiction and other constitutional matters); Annie Soo Yeon Ahn, *Clarifying the Standards for Personal Jurisdiction in Light of Growing Transactions on the Internet: The* Zippo *Test and Pleading of Personal Jurisdiction*, 99 Minn. L. Rev. 2325 (2015).

b. *Online Forums.* The issue of jurisdiction over defendants in libel actions where the allegedly defamatory statements have been made on the Internet has also focused attention on the meaning of *Calder*. For example, in *Griffis v. Luban*, 646 N.W.2d 527 (Minn. 2002), the Minnesota Supreme Court refused to enforce an Alabama state court's default judgment against a Minnesota defendant who had posted statements to an online discussion group that allegedly defamed an Alabama resident. The action, which was brought in Alabama by Griffis, a teacher at the University of Alabama, against Luban, a Minnesota resident, arose from an online discussion group ("sci.archaeology") devoted to the subject of ancient Egypt.

Luban had posted disparaging comments about Griffis's scholarly credentials, and Griffis sued for libel. When Luban did not appear in the Alabama action, the court entered a default judgment. When enforcement was sought in Minnesota, Luban argued that the judgment was invalid because Alabama could not constitutionally exercise jurisdiction over her. The Minnesota Supreme Court agreed. The court acknowledged that Luban had posted comments about Griffis's credentials with full knowledge that Griffis was a resident of Alabama, and that she had placed a telephone call to the University of Alabama, where Griffis was employed, to check on her credentials. Nevertheless, the court found that Luban had not "purposefully availed herself of the privilege of conducting activities within the jurisdiction." *Calder*, the court found, did not authorize jurisdiction whenever a defendant committed an intentional tort with *knowledge* that the victim would feel the effects in a particular forum. Rather, the court found, "[w]hile the record supports the conclusion that Luban's statements were intentionally directed at Griffis, whom she knew to be an Alabama resident, we conclude that the evidence does not demonstrate that Luban's statements were 'expressly aimed' at the State of Alabama."

Other cases involving online forums or discussion groups have followed a similar analysis and reached the same result. *See Scott v. Lackey*, 587 Fed.Appx. 712 (3d Cir. 2014) (rejecting jurisdiction where defendant had no jurisdictionally relevant contacts with forum other than discussion group comments about plaintiff who resided there).

c. *Social Networking.* Social networking websites also implicate Internet jurisdiction. In *Capitol Records, LLC v. VideoEgg, Inc.*, 611 F. Supp. 2d 349 (S.D.N.Y. 2009), a federal district court upheld personal jurisdiction over the defendant for facilitating copyright infringement through its social networking website. The website in question allowed users to share copyrighted video content, none of which was provided or sold by the defendants themselves. The defendants operated and maintained the website and sold advertising embedded in the videos. The court determined that the defendant "transact[ed] business" in New York and therefore fell under New York's long-arm statute, but that the traditional "spectrum of interactivity" test was largely irrelevant to the inquiry. The court likened the video files to defamatory articles, and stated that without more, the transmission of files to New York would not support jurisdiction. However, the selling of advertisements to New York companies and the placement of advertisements targeted to the New York market on the website was sufficient for jurisdiction. The court also pointed to the website's designation of New York as one of its "Top Cities" as a " 'tangible manifestation' of [an] attempt to reach [the] New York market."

In *Triple Up, Ltd. v. Youku Tudou, Inc.*, No. 17-7033, 2018 WL 4440459 (D.C. Cir., Jul. 17, 2018), the D.C. Circuit held that a plaintiff, who had an exclusive right to broadcast certain Taiwanese movies in the United States, could not assert jurisdiction over a Chinese video sharing website, Youku, for an infringement action under the Copyright Act and Lanham Act because there was not a sufficient showing that Youku had purposefully availed itself of the United States forum (for cases involving nationwide jurisdiction such as this, see pages 210–217 of the casebook). The videos were uploaded by independent users in other countries and circumvented the geo-blocking technology Youku generally employed to prevent its service from streaming content in places it was not licensed to do so. Although the videos were promptly removed once Youku was notified of the violation, Triple

Up sued, arguing that the court had jurisdiction because Youku "purposefully availed itself of the United States forum by passively permitting the videos to be streamed in the United States" when it failed to implement its geo-blocking technology. Additionally, Triple Up argued jurisdiction existed because Youku had utilized region-specific advertising. The Court of Appeals held that simply being able to access the videos in the United States was not sufficient to show purposeful availment of the forum, particularly given Youku's limited control over user-uploaded content. Moreover, the court held that although Youku derived revenue from advertisements, it utilized a third-party agency to sell and place them, and thus did not play a material role in pairing advertisements with specific videos or regions. Concluding that it was implausible that Youku had designed its website to target the United States, the D.C. Circuit held that Youku had not purposefully availed itself of the United States forum. *But cf. Plixer Int'l v. Scrutinizer GmbH*, 905 F.3d 1 (1st Cir. 2018) (holding a German company had purposefully availed itself of the United States forum through its globally available Internet service through which it executed voluntary sales of that service to Americans, despite the fact it had not directed its activities toward the United States and accepted payment only in euros).

Compare *Triple Up* with the recent decision in *District of Columbia v. Facebook, Inc.*, No. 2018-CA-008715 B (D.C. Super. Ct., May 31, 2019), in which a District of Columbia Superior Court held that Facebook was subject to specific personal jurisdiction in the District of Columbia. The suit was brought in response to revelations that Facebook had sold D.C. residents' personal information to Cambridge Analytica, which the Attorney General for the District alleged violated those residents' privacy rights. The Court distinguished Facebook's activity from Youku services. Because Facebook had enrolled and gathered information from hundreds of thousands of D.C. residents, had garnered millions of dollars in revenue from the sale of those residents' information, and had registered to do business and made repeated business filings in the forum, the court ruled that jurisdiction over Facebook was proper. Is the court in this case essentially ruling that the volume of users and revenue Facebook draws from the forum is sufficient to create personal jurisdiction?

For an interesting discussion of Internet geolocation technology and how courts have attempted to integrate purposeful availment analysis into rulings involving such technologies, *see* Celia Kaechele, *Traditional Notions of Fair Play and Substantial Justice in the Age of Interconnectivity: How Masking an IP Address Could Constitute Purposeful Availment*, 21 Yale J.L & Tech. 59 (2019).

Where putative contacts are unique to a particular form of social media and cannot be analogized to physical activity such as distributing a publication or mailing a letter, courts have tended to downplay their jurisdictional significance. *See, e.g., Binion v. O'Neal*, 95 F.Supp.3d 1055, 1060 (E.D. Mich. 2015) ("[P]osts on Instagram and Twitter were little more than the posting of information on social media websites, which became accessible to users in Michigan and elsewhere."). If social media is defined by its interactivity, is the reasoning used by these courts running counter to currents in technological development? Or could these cases be analyzed in a different way, such as by invoking a "targeting" requirement?

d. *New Technologies.* Personal jurisdiction will have to adapt to new technologies. Recall that *International Shoe* itself was in part a response — however belated — to rapid changes in commerce, communications, and inter-state travel that had occurred in the first half of the 20th century. In the interim, doctrine lagged behind, hung up on fictions related to corporate presence and consent. So too with the Internet. *Zippo* conceptualized interactivity in terms of "transmission of computer files over the Internet"—a framing that is incapable of capturing the diversity, speed, and type of activity that characterizes modern computer use. Technology today is typified by cloud computing; algorithms that update all manner of companies, from Google to commercial retailers, so that they may display targeted advertisements based on user interests; real-time bidding-based display advertising, in which marketers sell and buy ads live, at the scale of a single user-impression at a time; and personal assistants that record and transmit information about users to other companies. Courts and commentators have begun to call for guidance on these new technologies—or in some cases, to innovate in the absence of such guidance. For a discussion of jurisdiction and new technologies, *see* Scott Isaacson, *Finding Something More in Targeted Cyberspace Activities*, 68 Rutgers U.L. Rev. 905 (2016). *See also* Zoe Niesel, *#Personal Jurisdiction: A New Age of Internet Contacts*, 94 Ind. L.J. 103 (2019) (exploring the relationship between minimum contacts and the development of the Internet and arguing that new Internet technologies have rendered the *Zippo* test inadequate and it should thus be replaced by a "holistic analysis" examining a defendant's expectations and notions of fairness).

f.   The Commercial Contract Cases

Volkswagen and *Calder* both dealt with the constitutional reach of jurisdictional statutes in tort cases. Numerous jurisdictional questions also arise in the commercial context. For example, dissatisfied buyers often seek to assert jurisdiction in their home states over nonresident sellers, and alternatively, commercial sellers of goods often want to assert jurisdiction in their state over purchasers who do not pay. Consider a Washington buyer who orders shoes from a company in the state of Missouri; the seller sends the shoes, but they are defective. Can a Washington state court constitutionally assert jurisdiction over the Missouri seller in such a case? Or suppose the seller sends the shoes after the Washington buyer requests them by letter, but the Washington buyer does not pay. May the Missouri seller obtain jurisdiction over the Washington buyer in a Missouri court?

The United States Supreme Court has not considered a modern case involving such buyer-seller scenarios. In *Lakeside Bridge & Steel Co. v. Mountain State Constr. Co.*, 597 F.2d 596 (7th Cir. 1979), a Wisconsin commercial seller contracted with a West Virginia corporation to sell structural assemblies to the latter for incorporation into a dam in Virginia. The seller's agent visited the buyer's offices in West Virginia, a purchase order was sent to seller in Wisconsin, the goods were shipped F.O.B. Seller's Plant, Milwaukee, Wisconsin, and a provision for Wisconsin law was included in the contract. When the buyer refused to pay, claiming that some of the goods were defective, the seller brought suit in Wisconsin. The Seventh Circuit held that such an assertion of jurisdiction would violate Due Process. Justice White dissented from the Supreme Court's denial of certiorari, arguing that the federal and state courts were deeply divided on the question of personal jurisdiction over nonresident corporate defendants based on contractual dealings with resident plaintiffs, and that the disarray "may well have a disruptive effect on commercial relations in which certainty of result is a prime objective." 445 U.S. at 911.

Consider whether the Supreme Court provided the desired guidance in the next principal case.

Burger King Corp. v. Rudzewicz

471 U.S. 462 (1985)

Appeal from the United States Court of Appeals for the Eleventh Circuit. JUSTICE BRENNAN delivered the opinion of the Court. . . .

I

A

Burger King Corporation is a Florida corporation whose principal offices are in Miami. It is one of the world's largest restaurant organizations, with over 3,000 outlets in the 50 States, the Commonwealth of Puerto Rico, and 8 foreign nations. Burger King conducts approximately 80% of its business through a franchise operation that the company styles the "Burger King System" — "a comprehensive restaurant format and operating system for the sale of uniform and quality food products." App. 46. Burger King licenses its franchisees to use its trademarks and service marks for a period of 20 years and leases standardized restaurant facilities to them for the same term. In addition, franchisees acquire a variety of proprietary information concerning the "standards, specifications, procedures and methods for operating a Burger King Restaurant.". . .

In exchange for these benefits, franchisees pay Burger King an initial $40,000 franchise fee and commit themselves to payment of monthly royalties, advertising and sales promotion fees, and rent computed in part from monthly gross sales. Franchisees also agree to submit to the national organization's exacting regulation of virtually every conceivable aspect of their operations. . . .

Burger King oversees its franchise system through a two-tiered administrative structure. The governing contracts provide that the franchise relationship is established in Miami and governed by Florida law, and call for payment of all required fees and forwarding of all relevant notices to the Miami headquarters. The Miami headquarters sets policy and works directly with its franchisees in attempting to resolve major problems. *See* nn. 7, 9, *infra*. . . .

The instant litigation grows out of Burger King's termination of one of its franchisees, and is aptly described by the franchisee as "a divorce proceeding among commercial partners.". . . The appellee John Rudzewicz, a Michigan citizen and resident, is the senior partner in a Detroit accounting firm. In 1978, he was approached by Brian MacShara, the son of a business acquaintance, who suggested that they jointly apply to Burger King for a franchise in the Detroit area. . . .

Rudzewicz and MacShara jointly applied for a franchise to Burger King's Birmingham, Michigan, district office in the autumn of 1978. Their application was forwarded to Burger King's Miami headquarters, which entered into a preliminary agreement with them in February 1979. During the ensuing four months it was agreed that Rudzewicz and MacShara would assume operation of an existing facility in Drayton Plains, Michigan. MacShara attended the prescribed management courses in Miami during this period, . . . and the franchisees purchased $165,000 worth of restaurant equipment from Burger King's Davmor Industries division in Miami. Even before the final agreements were signed, however, the parties began to disagree over site-development fees, building design, computation of monthly rent, and whether the franchisees would be able to assign their liabilities to a corporation they had formed. During these disputes Rudzewicz and MacShara negotiated both with the Birmingham district office and with the Miami headquarters.[7] With some misgivings, Rudzewicz and MacShara finally obtained limited concessions from the Miami headquarters, signed the final agreements, and commenced operations in June 1979. By signing the final agreements, Rudzewicz obligated himself personally to payments exceeding $1 million over the 20-year franchise relationship.

The Drayton Plains facility apparently enjoyed steady business during the summer of 1979, but patronage declined after a recession began later that year. Rudzewicz and MacShara soon fell far behind in their monthly payments to Miami. Headquarters sent notices of default, and an extended period of negotiations began among the franchisees, the Birmingham district office, and the Miami headquarters. After several Burger King officials in Miami had engaged in prolonged but ultimately unsuccessful negotiations with the franchisees by mail and by telephone,[9] headquarters terminated the franchise and ordered Rudzewicz and MacShara to vacate the premises. They refused and continued to occupy and operate the facility as a Burger King restaurant.

B

Burger King commenced the instant action in the United States District Court for the Southern District of Florida in May 1981, invoking that court's diversity jurisdiction pursuant to 28 U.S.C. §1332(a) and its original jurisdiction over federal trademark disputes pursuant to §1338(a).[10] Burger King alleged that Rudzewicz and MacShara had breached their franchise obligations "within [the jurisdiction of] this district court" by failing to make the required payments "at plaintiffs' place of business in Miami, Dade County, Florida," para. 6, App. 121, and also charged that they were tortiously infringing its trademarks and service marks through their

---

7. Although Rudzewicz and MacShara dealt with the Birmingham district office on a regular basis, they communicated directly with the Miami headquarters in forming the contracts; moreover, they learned that the district office had "very little" decision-making authority and accordingly turned directly to headquarters in seeking to resolve their disputes. . . .

9. Miami's policy was to "deal directly" with franchisees when they began to encounter financial difficulties, and to involve district office personnel only when necessary. . . . In the instant case, for example, the Miami office handled all credit problems, ordered cost-cutting measures, negotiated for a partial refinancing of the franchisees' debts, communicated directly with the franchisees in attempting to resolve the dispute, and was responsible for all termination matters.

10. Rudzewicz and MacShara were served in Michigan with summonses and copies of the complaint pursuant to Federal Rule of Civil Procedure 4. . . .

continued, unauthorized operation as a Burger King restaurant, paras. 35–53, App. 130–135. . . . Rudzewicz and MacShara entered special appearances and argued, *inter alia*, that because they were Michigan residents and because Burger King's claim did not "arise" within the Southern District of Florida, the District Court lacked personal jurisdiction over them. The District Court denied their motions after a hearing. . . .

After a 3-day bench trial, the court again concluded that it had "jurisdiction over the subject matter and the parties to this cause." App. 159. Finding that Rudzewicz and MacShara had breached their franchise agreements with Burger King and had infringed Burger King's trademarks and service marks, the court entered judgment against them, jointly and severally, for $228,875 in contract damages. . . .

Rudzewicz appealed to the Court of Appeals for the Eleventh Circuit.[11] A divided panel of that Circuit reversed the judgment, concluding that the District Court could not properly exercise personal jurisdiction over Rudzewicz . . . because "the circumstances of the Drayton Plains franchise and the negotiations which led to it left Rudzewicz bereft of reasonable notice and financially unprepared for the prospect of franchise litigation in Florida." *Burger King Corp. v. MacShara*, 724 F.2d 1505, 1513 (1984). . . .

II

A

The Due Process Clause protects an individual's liberty interest in not being subject to the binding judgments of a forum with which he has established no meaningful "contacts, ties, or relations." *International Shoe Co. v. Washington*, 326 U.S., at 319.[13] By requiring that individuals have "fair warning that a particular activity may subject [them] to the jurisdiction of a foreign sovereign," *Shaffer v. Heitner*, 433 U.S. 186, 218 (1977) (STEVENS, J., concurring in judgment), the Due Process Clause "gives a degree of predictability to the legal system that allows potential defendants to structure their primary conduct with some minimum assurance as to where that conduct will and will not render them liable to suit," *World-Wide Volkswagen Corp. v. Woodson*, 444 U.S. 286, 297 (1980).

---

11. MacShara did not appeal his judgment. *See Burger King Corp. v. MacShara*, 724 F.2d 1505, 1506, n. 1 (CA11 1984). In addition, Rudzewicz entered into a compromise with Burger King and waived his right to appeal the District Court's finding of trademark infringement and its entry of injunctive relief. . . . Accordingly, we need not address the extent to which the tortious act provisions of Florida's long-arm statute, *see* Fla. Stat. §48.193(1)(b) (Supp. 1984), may constitutionally extend to out-of-state trademark infringement. *Cf. Calder v. Jones*, 465 U.S. 783, 788–789 (1984) (tortious out-of-state conduct); *Keeton v. Hustler Magazine, Inc.*, 465 U.S. 770, 776 (1984) (same).

13. Although this protection operates to restrict state power, it "must be seen as ultimately a function of the individual liberty interest preserved by the Due Process Clause" rather than as a function "of federalism concerns." *Insurance Corp. of Ireland v. Compagnie des Bauxites de Guinee*, 456 U.S. 694, 702–703, n. 10 (1982).

Where a forum seeks to assert specific jurisdiction over an out-of-state defendant who has not consented to suit there,[14] this "fair warning" requirement is satisfied if the defendant has "purposefully directed" his activities at residents of the forum, *Keeton v. Hustler Magazine, Inc.*, 465 U.S. 770, 774 (1984), and the litigation results from alleged injuries that "arise out of or relate to" those activities, *Helicopteros Nacionales de Colombia, S.A. v. Hall*, 466 U.S. 408, 414 (1984). . . .

This "purposeful availment" requirement ensures that a defendant will not be haled into a jurisdiction solely as a result of "random," "fortuitous," or "attenuated" contacts, *Keeton v. Hustler Magazine, Inc.*, 465 U.S., at 774; *World-Wide Volkswagen Corp. v. Woodson, supra*, at 299, or of the "unilateral activity of another party or a third person," *Helicopteros Nacionales de Colombia, S.A. v. Hall, supra*, at 417. Jurisdiction is proper, however, where the contacts proximately result from actions by the defendant himself that create a "substantial connection" with the forum State. *McGee v. International Life Insurance Co., supra*, at 223; *see also Kulko v. California Superior Court, supra*, at 94, n. 7.[18] . . .

Jurisdiction in these circumstances may not be avoided merely because the defendant did not *physically* enter the forum State. Although territorial presence frequently will enhance a potential defendant's affiliation with a State and reinforce the reasonable foreseeability of suit there, it is an inescapable fact of modern commercial life that a substantial amount of business is transacted solely by mail and wire communications across state lines, thus obviating the need for physical presence within a State in which business is conducted. So long as a commercial actor's efforts are "purposefully directed" toward residents of another State, we have consistently rejected the notion that an absence of physical contacts can defeat personal jurisdiction there. *Keeton v. Hustler Magazine, Inc., supra*, at 774–775; *see also Calder v. Jones*, 465 U.S., at 788–790; *McGee v. International Life Insurance Co.*, 355 U.S., at 222-223. *Cf. Hoopeston Canning Co. v. Cullen*, 318 U.S. 313, 317 (1943).

Once it has been decided that a defendant purposefully established minimum contacts within the forum State, these contacts may be considered in light of other factors to determine whether the assertion of personal jurisdiction would

---

14. We have noted that, because the personal jurisdiction requirement is a waivable right, there are a "variety of legal arrangements" by which a litigant may give "express or implied consent to the personal jurisdiction of the court." *Insurance Corp. of Ireland v. Compagnie des Bauxites de Guinee, supra*, at 703. For example, particularly in the commercial context, parties frequently stipulate in advance to submit their controversies for resolution within a particular jurisdiction. *See National Equipment Rental, Ltd. v. Szukhent*, 375 U.S. 311 (1964). Where such forum-selection provisions have been obtained through "freely negotiated" agreements and are not "unreasonable and unjust," *The Bremen v. Zapata Off-Shore Co.*, 407 U.S. 1, 15 (1972), their enforcement does not offend due process.

18. So long as it creates a "substantial connection" with the forum, even a single act can support jurisdiction. *McGee v. International Life Insurance Co.*, 355 U.S., at 223. The Court has noted, however, that "some single or occasional acts" related to the forum may not be sufficient to establish jurisdiction if "their nature and quality and the circumstances of their commission" create only an "attenuated" affiliation with the forum. *International Shoe Co. v. Washington*, 326 U.S. 310, 318 (1945); *World-Wide Volkswagen Corp. v. Woodson*, 444 U.S., at 299. This distinction derives from the belief that, with respect to this category of "isolated" acts, *id.*, at 297, the reasonable foreseeability of litigation in the forum is substantially diminished.

comport with "fair play and substantial justice." *International Shoe Co. v. Washington,* 326 U.S., at 320. Thus courts in "appropriate [cases]" may evaluate "the burden on the defendant," "the forum State's interest in adjudicating the dispute," "the plaintiff's interest in obtaining convenient and effective relief," "the interstate judicial system's interest in obtaining the most efficient resolution of controversies," and the "shared interest of the several States in furthering fundamental substantive social policies." *World-Wide Volkswagen Corp. v. Woodson,* 444 U.S., at 292. These considerations sometimes serve to establish the reasonableness of jurisdiction upon a lesser showing of minimum contacts than would otherwise be required. *See, e.g., Keeton v. Hustler Magazine, Inc., supra,* at 780; *Calder v. Jones, supra,* at 788–789; *McGee v. International Life Insurance Co., supra,* at 223–224. On the other hand, where a defendant who purposefully has directed his activities at forum residents seeks to defeat jurisdiction, he must present a compelling case that the presence of some other considerations would render jurisdiction unreasonable. Most such considerations usually may be accommodated through means short of finding jurisdiction unconstitutional. For example, the potential clash of the forum's law with the "fundamental substantive social policies" of another State may be accommodated through application of the forum's choice-of-law rules.[19] Similarly, a defendant claiming substantial inconvenience may seek a change of venue.[20] Nevertheless, minimum requirements inherent in the concept of "fair play and substantial justice" may defeat the reasonableness of jurisdiction even if the defendant has purposefully engaged in forum activities. *World-Wide Volkswagen Corp. v. Woodson, supra,* at 292; *see also* Restatement (Second) of Conflict of Laws §§36–37 (1971). As we previously have noted, jurisdictional rules may not be employed in such a way as to make litigation "so gravely difficult and inconvenient" that a party unfairly is at a "severe disadvantage" in comparison to his opponent. *The Bremen v. Zapata Off-Shore Co.,* 407 U.S. 1, 18 (1972) (*re* forum-selection provisions); *McGee v. International Life Insurance Co., supra,* at 223–224.

B

(1)

Applying these principles to the case at hand, we believe there is substantial record evidence supporting the District Court's conclusion that the assertion of personal jurisdiction over Rudzewicz in Florida for the alleged breach of his franchise agreement did not offend due process. At the outset, we note a continued division among lower courts respecting whether and to what extent a contract

---

19. *See Allstate Insurance Co. v. Hague,* 449 U.S. 302, 307–313 (1981) (opinion of BRENNAN, J.). *See generally* Restatement (Second) of Conflict of Laws §§ 6, 9 (1971).

20. *See, e.g.,* 28 U.S.C. §1404(a) ("For the convenience of parties and witnesses, in the interest of justice, a district court may transfer any civil action to any other district or division where it might have been brought."). This provision embodies in an expanded version the common-law doctrine of *forum non conveniens,* under which a court in appropriate circumstances may decline to exercise its jurisdiction in the interest of the "easy, expeditious and inexpensive" resolution of a controversy in another forum. *See Gulf Oil Corp. v. Gilbert,* 330 U.S. 501, 508–509 (1947).

can constitute a "contact" for purposes of due process analysis.[21] If the question is whether an individual's contract with an out-of-state party *alone* can automatically establish sufficient minimum contacts in the other party's home forum, we believe the answer clearly is that it cannot. The Court long ago rejected the notion that personal jurisdiction might turn on "mechanical" tests, *International Shoe Co. v. Washington, supra,* at 319, or on "conceptualistic . . . theories of the place of contracting or of performance." *Hoopeston Canning Co. v. Cullen,* 318 U.S., at 316. Instead, we have emphasized the need for a "highly realistic" approach that recognizes that a "contract" is "ordinarily but an intermediate step serving to tie up prior business negotiations with future consequences which themselves are the real object of the business transaction." *Id.,* at 316–317. It is these factors — prior negotiations and contemplated future consequences, along with the terms of the contract and the parties' actual course of dealing — that must be evaluated in determining whether the defendant purposefully established minimum contacts within the forum.

In this case, no physical ties to Florida can be attributed to Rudzewicz other than MacShara's brief training course in Miami. Rudzewicz did not maintain offices in Florida and, for all that appears from the record, has never even visited there. Yet this franchise dispute grew directly out of "a contract which had a *substantial* connection with that State." *McGee v. International Life Insurance Co.,* 355 U.S., at 223 (emphasis added). Eschewing the option of operating an independent local enterprise, Rudzewicz deliberately "[reached] out beyond" Michigan and negotiated with a Florida corporation for the purchase of a long-term franchise and the manifold benefits that would derive from affiliation with a nationwide organization. *Travelers Health Ass'n v. Virginia,* 339 U.S., at 647. Upon approval, he entered into a carefully structured 20-year relationship that envisioned continuing and wide-reaching contacts with Burger King in Florida. In light of Rudzewicz' voluntary acceptance of the long-term and exacting regulation of his business from Burger King's Miami headquarters, the "quality and nature" of his relationship to the company in Florida can in no sense be viewed as "random," "fortuitous," or "attenuated." *Hanson v. Denckla,* 357 U.S., at 253; *Keeton v. Hustler Magazine. Inc.,* 465 U.S., at 774; *World-Wide Volkswagen Corp. v. Woodson,* 444 U.S., at 299. Rudzewicz' refusal to make the contractually required payments in Miami, and his continued use of Burger King's trademarks and confidential business information after his termination, caused foreseeable injuries to the corporation in Florida. For these reasons it was, at the very least, presumptively reasonable for Rudzewicz to be called to account there for such injuries.

The Court of Appeals concluded, however, that in light of the supervision emanating from Burger King's district office in Birmingham, Rudzewicz reasonably believed that "the Michigan office was for all intents and purposes the embodiment of Burger King" and that he therefore had no "reason to anticipate a Burger King suit outside of Michigan." 724 F.2d, at 1511. . . . This reasoning overlooks substantial

---

21. *See, e.g., Lakeside Bridge & Steel Co. v. Mountain State Construction Co.,* 445 U.S. 907, 909–910 (1980) (White, J., dissenting from denial of certiorari) (collecting cases); Brewer, Jurisdiction in Single Contract Cases, 6 U. Ark. Little Rock L.J. 1, 7–11, 13 (1983); Note, Long-Arm Jurisdiction in Commercial Litigation: When is a Contract a Contact?, 61 B.U. L. Rev. 375, 384–388 (1981).

record evidence indicating that Rudzewicz most certainly knew that he was affiliating himself with an enterprise based primarily in Florida. The contract documents themselves emphasize that Burger King's operations are conducted and supervised from the Miami headquarters, that all relevant notices and payments must be sent there, and that the agreements were made in and enforced from Miami. . . . Moreover, the parties' actual course of dealing repeatedly confirmed that decisionmaking authority was vested in the Miami headquarters and that the district office served largely as an intermediate link between the headquarters and the franchisees. When problems arose over building design, site-development fees, rent computation, and the defaulted payments, Rudzewicz and MacShara learned that the Michigan office was powerless to resolve their disputes and could only channel their communications to Miami. Throughout these disputes, the Miami headquarters and the Michigan franchisees carried on a continuous course of direct communications by mail and by telephone, and it was the Miami headquarters that made the key negotiating decisions out of which the instant litigation arose. *See* nn. 7, 9, *supra*.

Moreover, we believe the Court of Appeals gave insufficient weight to provisions in the various franchise documents providing that all disputes would be governed by Florida law. The franchise agreement, for example, stated:

> This Agreement shall become valid when executed and accepted by BKC at Miami, Florida; it shall be deemed made and entered into in the State of Florida and shall be governed and construed under and in accordance with the laws of the State of Florida. The choice of law designation does not require that all suits concerning this Agreement be filed in Florida. App. 72.

The Court of Appeals reasoned that choice-of-law provisions are irrelevant to the question of personal jurisdiction, relying on *Hanson v. Denckla* for the proposition that "the center of gravity for choice-of-law purposes does not necessarily confer the sovereign prerogative to assert jurisdiction." 724 F.2d, at 1511–1512, n. 10, *citing* 357 U.S., at 254. This reasoning misperceives the import of the quoted proposition. The Court in *Hanson* and subsequent cases has emphasized that choice-of-law *analysis*—which focuses on all elements of a transaction, and not simply on the defendant's conduct—is distinct from minimum-contacts jurisdictional analysis—which focuses at the threshold solely on the defendant's purposeful connection to the forum. Nothing in our cases, however, suggests that a choice-of-law *provision* should be ignored in considering whether a defendant has "purposefully invoked the benefits and protections of a State's laws" for jurisdictional purposes. Although such a provision standing alone would be insufficient to confer jurisdiction, we believe that, when combined with the 20-year interdependent relationship Rudzewicz established with Burger King's Miami headquarters, it reinforced his deliberate affiliation with the forum State and the reasonable foreseeability of possible litigation there. As Judge Johnson argued in his dissent below, Rudzewicz "purposefully availed himself of the benefits and protections of Florida's laws" by entering into contracts expressly providing that those laws would govern franchise disputes. 724 F.2d, at 1513.[24]

---

24. In addition, the franchise agreement's disclaimer that the "choice of law designation does not *require* that all suits concerning this Agreement be filed in Florida," App. 72 (emphasis added), reasonably should have suggested to Rudzewicz that by negative implication such suits *could* be filed there. . . .

(2)

Nor has Rudzewicz pointed to other factors that can be said persuasively to outweigh the considerations discussed above and to establish the *unconstitutionality* of Florida's assertion of jurisdiction. We cannot conclude that Florida had no "legitimate interest in holding [Rudzewicz] answerable on a claim related to" the contacts he had established in that State. *Keeton v. Hustler Magazine. Inc.*, 465 U.S., at 776; *see also McGee v. International Life Insurance* Co., 355 U.S., at 223 (noting that State frequently will have a "manifest interest in providing effective means of redress for its residents"). Moreover, although Rudzewicz has argued at some length that Michigan's Franchise Investment Law, Mich. Comp. Laws §445.1501 et seq. (1979), governs many aspects of this franchise relationship, he has not demonstrated how Michigan's acknowledged interest might possibly render jurisdiction in Florida *unconstitutional*.[26] Finally, the Court of Appeals' assertion that the Florida litigation "severely impaired [Rudzewicz'] ability to call Michigan witnesses who might be essential to his defense and counterclaim," 724 F.2d, at 1512–1513, is wholly without support in the record.[27] And even to the extent that it is inconvenient for a party who has minimum contacts with a forum to litigate there, such considerations most frequently can be accommodated through a change of venue. *See* n. 20, *supra.* Although the Court has suggested that inconvenience may at some point become so substantial as to achieve *constitutional* magnitude, *McGee v. International Life Insurance Co., supra*, at 223, this is not such a case.

The Court of Appeals also concluded, however, that the parties' dealings involved "a characteristic disparity of bargaining power" and "elements of surprise," and that Rudzewicz "lacked fair notice" of the potential for litigation in Florida because the contractual provisions suggesting to the contrary were merely "boilerplate declarations in a lengthy printed contract." 724 F.2d, at 1511–1512, and n. 10. . . . Rudzewicz presented many of these arguments to the District Court, contending that Burger King was guilty of misrepresentation, fraud, and duress; that it gave insufficient notice in its dealings with him; and that the contract was one of adhesion. *See* 4 Record 687–691. After a 3-day bench trial, the District Court found that Burger King had made no misrepresentations, that Rudzewicz and MacShara "were and are experienced and sophisticated businessmen," and that "at no time" did they "[act] under economic duress or disadvantage imposed by" Burger King. . . .

---

26. Rudzewicz has failed to show how the District Court's exercise of jurisdiction in this case might have been at all inconsistent with Michigan's interests. To the contrary, the court found that Burger King had fully complied with Michigan law, App. 159, and there is nothing in Michigan's Franchise Act suggesting that Michigan would attempt to assert exclusive jurisdiction to resolve franchise disputes affecting its residents. In any event, minimum-contacts analysis presupposes that two or more States may be interested in the outcome of a dispute, and the process of resolving potentially conflicting "fundamental substantive social policies," *World-Wide Volkswagen Corp. v. Woodson*, 444 U.S., at 292, can usually be accommodated through choice-of-law rules rather than through outright preclusion of jurisdiction in one forum. *See* n. 19, *supra.*

27. The only arguable instance of trial inconvenience occurred when Rudzewicz had difficulty in authenticating some corporate records; the court offered him as much time as would be necessary to secure the requisite authentication from the Birmingham district office, and Burger King ultimately stipulated to their authenticity rather than delay the trial. *See* 7 Record 574–575, 578–579, 582, 598–599.

III

Notwithstanding these considerations, the Court of Appeals apparently believed that it was necessary to reject jurisdiction in this case as a prophylactic measure, reasoning that an affirmance of the District Court's judgment would result in the exercise of jurisdiction over "out-of-state consumers to collect payments due on modest personal purchases" and would "sow the seeds of default judgments against franchisees owing smaller debts." 724 F.2d, at 1511. . . . The "quality and nature" of an interstate transaction may sometimes be so "random," "fortuitous," or "attenuated" that it cannot fairly be said that the potential defendant "should reasonably anticipate being haled into court" in another jurisdiction. *World-Wide Volkswagen Corp. v. Woodson*, 444 U.S., at 297; *see also* n. 18, *supra*. We also have emphasized that jurisdiction may not be grounded on a contract whose terms have been obtained through "fraud, undue influence, or overweening bargaining power" and whose application would render litigation "so gravely difficult and inconvenient that [a party] will for all practical purposes be deprived of his day in court." *The Bremen v. Zapata Off-Shore Co.*, 407 U.S., at 12, 18. *Cf. Fuentes v. Shevin*, 407 U.S. 67, 94–96 (1972); *National Equipment Rental, Ltd. v. Szukhent*, 375 U.S. 311, 329 (1964) (Black, J., dissenting) (jurisdictional rules may not be employed against small consumers so as to "[cripple] their defense"). Just as the Due Process Clause allows flexibility in ensuring that commercial actors are not effectively "judgment proof" for the consequences of obligations they voluntarily assume in other States, *McGee v. International Life Insurance Co.*, 355 U.S., at 223, so too does it prevent rules that would unfairly enable them to obtain default judgments against unwitting customers. *Cf. United States v. Rumely*, 345 U.S. 41, 44 (1953) (courts must not be " 'blind' " to what " '[all] others can see and understand' ").

For the reasons set forth above, however, these dangers are not present in the instant case. . . . The judgment of the Court of Appeals is accordingly reversed, and the case is remanded for further proceedings consistent with this opinion.

It is so ordered.

JUSTICE POWELL took no part in the consideration or decision of this case.

JUSTICE STEVENS, with whom JUSTICE WHITE joins, dissenting.

In my opinion there is a significant element of unfairness in requiring a franchisee to defend a case of this kind in the forum chosen by the franchisor. It is undisputed that appellee maintained no place of business in Florida, that he had no employees in that State, and that he was not licensed to do business there. Appellee did not prepare his French fries, shakes, and hamburgers in Michigan, and then deliver them into the stream of commerce "with the expectation that they [would] be purchased by consumers in" Florida. . . . To the contrary, appellee did business only in Michigan, his business, property, and payroll taxes were payable in that State, and he sold all of his products there.

Throughout the business relationship, appellee's principal contacts with appellant were with its Michigan office. Notwithstanding its disclaimer . . . the Court seems ultimately to rely on nothing more than standard boilerplate language contained in various documents . . . to establish that appellee " 'purposefully availed himself of the benefits and protections of Florida's laws.' " . . . Such superficial analysis creates a potential for unfairness not only in negotiations between franchisors and their franchisees but, more significantly, in the resolution of the disputes that inevitably arise from time to time in such relationships. . . .

Accordingly, I respectfully dissent.

NOTES AND QUESTIONS

1. *Impact of* Burger King. What implications does the *Burger King* case have for the buyer-seller cases, such as *Lakeside Bridge*, referred to on p. 174? Can the decision be read to approve jurisdiction in a breach of contract case over a seller who purposefully sends a product into the state? Over a buyer who refuses to pay? Does *Burger King* suggest that it is easier to acquire jurisdiction over nonresident sellers in commercial cases than it is in product liability/tort cases? Should the jurisdictional result be the same in both types of cases?

Note that in *Burger King*, the parties had contemplated a 20-year continuous relationship between the Michigan franchisee and its Florida franchisor and that all negotiations and disputes were carried out through the Florida office. If specific facts such as these are critical to satisfy Due Process, has the Supreme Court abandoned any attempt to establish broad jurisdictional rules for guidance in other cases? *Compare Chung v. NANA Development Corp.*, 783 F.2d 1124 (4th Cir. 1986) (Alaska seller who shipped single purchase of frozen antlers to Virginia buyer at buyer's request not subject to jurisdiction in Virginia because "if a party's slightest gesture of accommodation were to impose personal jurisdiction, commercial dealings would soon turn unobliging and brusque.") *with Mesalic v. Fiberfloat Corp.*, 897 F.2d 696 (3d Cir. 1990) (Florida boat manufacturer who accommodated buyer by delivering boat in New Jersey was subject to jurisdiction in New Jersey). Is fact-specific, case-by-case adjudication more desirable in any event?

2. *Implications for Consumer Transactions.* Should it be more difficult for sellers to obtain jurisdiction over defaulting consumers? The Court of Appeals for the Eleventh Circuit in *Burger King* found jurisdiction unconstitutional because it feared that a finding of jurisdiction would result in the exercise of jurisdiction over "out-of-state consumers to collect payments due on modest personal purchases" and would "sow the seeds of default judgments against franchisees owing smaller debts." The Supreme Court addressed this concern, emphasizing the "flexibility" of the Due Process Clause to "prevent rules that would unfairly enable them to obtain default judgments against unwitting customers." Does that mean that a Missouri shoe company cannot obtain jurisdiction in Missouri over a Washington buyer who orders shoes and fails to pay? Would your answer change if the buyer were a business rather than an individual consumer? Would it matter if the buyer were the party who initiated the transaction rather than the seller? *See, e.g., Bally Export Corp. v. Balicar, Ltd.*, 804 F.2d 398 (7th Cir. 1986) (court refused to vacate default judgment; jurisdiction in Illinois upheld over nonresident buyer who initiated the transaction and ordered various types of gambling devices from Illinois seller and then refused to pay). What if the transaction took place over the Internet?

3. *Balancing "Reasonableness."* Justice Brennan suggests that not only may certain concepts of "fair play and substantial justice" defeat the reasonableness of jurisdiction even if the defendant has purposefully engaged in forum activities, but also that the reasonableness factors may lead to the establishment of jurisdiction "upon

a lesser showing of minimum contacts than would otherwise be required." How do you understand this statement? Is Justice Brennan's view here consistent with *Volkswagen*?

4. Burger King *after* Walden. In *Burger King*, the Court reasoned that Rudzewicz has purposefully directed his conduct to Florida because "Rudzewicz most certainly knew that he was affiliating himself with an enterprise based primarily in Florida." 471 U.S. at 480. You may recall that in *Walden v. Fiore*, decided in 2014, the Court noted that the appropriate question is "whether the defendant's actions connect him to the forum" itself and not whether the defendant's actions connected him with residents of the forum. In *Walden*, the Court found that the defendant had "no jurisdictionally relevant contacts with Nevada," because "no part of petitioner's course of conduct occurred in Nevada. . . . Petitioner never traveled to, conducted activities within, contacted anyone in, or sent anything or anyone to Nevada." 571 U.S. at 290. What distinguishes *Burger King* from *Walden*? Are contractual affiliations different from intentional torts?

5. *Choice of Law Versus Choice of Forum Clauses.* One of the factors relied on in *Burger King* in finding the exercise of jurisdiction reasonable was the existence of a choice of law clause in the contract designating Florida law. As we noted earlier and as we will see again, the question of which court should adjudicate and the question of what law applies are different. However, the fact that parties chose Florida law to apply in this case was thought to support the plaintiff's argument that Florida was also a "fair" forum. Why?

In commercial transactions, parties often include a choice of law or a choice of forum clause or both in their contracts. A choice of forum clause provides for adjudication in a particular forum whereas a choice of law clause provides for the law of a particular state or nation to govern the transaction. There are two aspects to a forum selection clause. First, it is generally perceived to reflect the consent of the defendant to be sued in that forum, thus providing a "consent" basis for jurisdiction (prorogation). Second, forum selection clauses are generally construed to deprive another forum from exercising jurisdiction (derogation). The leading case arose in the admiralty context, *The Bremen v. Zapata Off-Shore Co.*, 407 U.S. 1 (1972), where the Supreme Court held that a Florida court should dismiss an action brought there when the contract between the parties provided that all disputes should be heard in England. The Supreme Court found forum selection clauses to be valid and enforceable unless the resisting party can show they are unfair or unreasonable.

What kind of showing should be required to establish that a forum selection clause is either unfair or unreasonable? Should it depend on why the particular forum is selected or what connection the forum has to the parties and the transaction? In *The Bremen*, the parties had agreed for towage of a tug from Louisiana to Italy and chose England as the forum, even though England had no other connection with the parties, the transaction, or the lawsuit. Does that seem reasonable? Should there be any judicial scrutiny at all where the contract is between economically sophisticated parties? Suppose, however, that a contract for a passenger cruise contains a forum selection clause providing that the action should be brought in the state where the cruise company is located. Is such a clause reasonable? *See Carnival Cruise Lines v. Shute*, 499 U.S. 585 (1991), discussed at p. 68 (upholding choice of forum clause). Both *The Bremen* and *Carnival Cruise* were federal admiralty actions and delineate a federal standard regarding enforcement of choice of forum clauses. Some states, however, have applied a stricter standard and refused to enforce forum selection clauses when, for instance, the court finds that the clause impairs claims unrelated to the contract. *See, e.g., Morgan Trailer MFG Co. v. Hydraroll, Ltd.*, 759 A.2d 926 (Pa. Super. Ct. 2000) (finding jurisdiction over various tort actions in the face of a forum selection clause stipulating exclusive jurisdiction in England for contractual claims).

Choice of law clauses have also enjoyed a presumption of validity, although the courts usually require that the law chosen have some connection with the parties or the transaction. Why would the parties in *Burger King* have included a choice of law clause and not a choice of forum clause in their franchise agreement?

3.   *The Nexus Requirement: Contacts Arising Out of or Related to the Claim*

At this point, you know the three parts of the test for specific jurisdiction that the Supreme Court has hashed out over the decades since *International Shoe*: (1) Did the defendant purposefully direct its conduct to the forum state; (2) Does the suit arise out of or relate to the defendant's contacts in the forum; and (3) would exercise of jurisdiction over the defendant in the forum state's courts be "reasonable," as defined in *Asahi*? You have read extensive case law on the first prong of the analysis, purposeful availment, from its origins in *World-wide Volkswagen* to its more recent incarnations in *Asahi*, *Nicastro*, *Calder*, and *Burger King*. You have not read much on the second prong, minimum contacts "arising from or related to the forum." Surprisingly, the Supreme Court did not have anything to say about this nexus requirement until quite recently. This is the requirement that the defendant's contacts in the forum state have some *nexus* with the claim itself. You might say that this requirement is the essential distinction between case-linked and all-purpose jurisdiction.

You may recall that the Supreme Court in Daimler severely restricted general jurisdiction and promised an expanded role for specific jurisdiction to meet the concerns expressed by Justice Sotomayor in her dissent. You have also seen the Supreme Court narrow specific jurisdiction over several decades by narrowing the conduct that will demonstrate purposeful availment of the forum state. Given those two points of reference, you might expect the Supreme Court to develop a more liberal interpretation of the nexus requirement to make good on the promise of the *Daimler* majority. *See generally* Charles W. "Rocky" Rhodes & Cassandra Burke Robertson, *Toward a New Equilibrium in Personal Jurisdiction*, 48 U.C. Davis L. Rev. 1, 22-35 (2014).

The Court's silence left many questions open, including: (1) whether a plaintiff's claim always needs to have been caused by defendant's conduct in the forum state, and if so, whether any causal link is sufficient; and (2) what if the case is connected to the forum, but the injury was not caused by defendant's forum conduct? In 2017, the Supreme Court finally took a case on the nexus requirement, although it was not a vehicle well-suited to expanding specific jurisdiction.

a.   Parallel Claims—Contacts Not Sufficiently "Related"

Bristol-Myers Squibb v. Sup. Court of Cal.

137 S. Ct. 1773 (2017)

JUSTICE ALITO delivered the opinion of the Court.

More than 600 plaintiffs, most of whom are not California residents, filed this civil action in a California state court against Bristol–Myers Squibb Company (BMS), asserting a variety of state-law claims based on injuries allegedly caused by a BMS drug called Plavix. The California Supreme Court held that the California courts have specific jurisdiction to entertain the nonresidents' claims. We now reverse.

I

A

BMS . . . is incorporated in Delaware and headquartered in New York. . . . BMS also engages in business activities in other jurisdictions, including California. . . .

One of the pharmaceuticals that BMS manufactures and sells is Plavix. . . . BMS did not develop Plavix in California, did not create a marketing strategy for Plavix in California, and did not manufacture, label, package, or work on the regulatory approval of the product in California. BMS instead engaged in all of these activities in either New York or New Jersey. But BMS does sell Plavix in California. Between 2006 and 2012, it sold almost 187 million Plavix pills in the State and took in more than $900 million from those sales. . . .

B

A group of plaintiffs—consisting of 86 California residents and 592 residents from 33 other States—filed eight separate complaints in California Superior Court, alleging that Plavix had damaged their health. All the complaints asserted 13 claims under California law, including products liability, negligent misrepresentation, and misleading advertising claims. The nonresident plaintiffs did not allege that they obtained Plavix through California physicians or from any other California source; nor did they claim that they were injured by Plavix or were treated for their injuries in California.

Asserting lack of personal jurisdiction, BMS moved to quash service of summons on the nonresidents' claims. . . .

The California Supreme Court affirmed [a lower court decision upholding specific jurisdiction]. . . . The majority applied a "sliding scale approach to specific jurisdiction." Under this approach, "the more wide ranging the defendant's forum contacts, the more readily is shown a connection between the forum contacts and the claim." Applying this test, the majority concluded that "BMS's extensive contacts with California" permitted the exercise of specific jurisdiction "based on a less direct connection between BMS's forum activities and plaintiffs' claims than might otherwise be required." This attenuated requirement was met, the majority found, because the claims of the nonresidents were similar in several ways to the claims of the California residents (as to which specific jurisdiction was uncontested) . . . .

The court noted that "[b]oth the resident and nonresident plaintiffs' claims are based on the same allegedly defective product and the assertedly misleading marketing and promotion of that product.". . .

Three justices dissented. "The claims of . . . nonresidents injured by their use of Plavix they purchased and used in other states," they wrote, "in no sense arise from BMS's marketing and sales of Plavix in California,". . . The dissent accused the majority of "expand[ing] specific jurisdiction to the point that, for a large category of defendants, it becomes indistinguishable from general jurisdiction."

We granted certiorari to decide whether the California courts' exercise of jurisdiction in this case violates the Due Process Clause. . . .

II

A

. . .

Since our seminal decision in *International Shoe*, our decisions have recognized two types of personal jurisdiction: "general" (sometimes called "all-purpose") jurisdiction and "specific" (sometimes called "case-linked"). . . . A court with general jurisdiction may hear any claim against that defendant, even if all the incidents underlying the claim occurred in a different State. . . .

Specific jurisdiction is very different. In order for a state court to exercise specific jurisdiction, "the *suit*" must "aris[e] out of or relat[e] to the defendant's contacts with the *forum*." *Daimler AG v. Bauman*, 134 S. Ct. 746, 754 (2014). In other words, there must be "an affiliation between the forum and the underlying controversy, principally, [an] activity or an occurrence that takes place in the forum State and is therefore subject to the State's regulation." *Goodyear Dunlop Tires Op, S.A. v. Brown*, 131 S. Ct. 2846, 2851 (2011). For this reason, specific jurisdiction is confined to adjudication of issues deriving from, or connected with, the very controversy that establishes jurisdiction.

B

In determining whether personal jurisdiction is present, a court must consider a variety of interests. These include the interests of the forum State and of the plaintiff in proceeding with the cause in the plaintiff's forum of choice. But the primary concern is the burden on the defendant. Assessing this burden obviously requires a court to consider the practical problems resulting from litigating in the forum, but it also encompasses the more abstract matter of submitting to the coercive power of a State that may have little legitimate interest in the claims in question. As we have put it, restrictions on personal jurisdiction "are more than a guarantee of immunity from inconvenient or distant litigation. They are a consequence of territorial limitations on the power of the respective States." *Hanson v. Denckla*, 78 S. Ct. 1227, 1238 . "[T]he States retain many essential attributes of sovereignty, including, in particular, the sovereign power to try causes in their courts. The sovereignty of each State . . . implie[s] a limitation on the sovereignty of all its sister States." *World–Wide Volkswagen Corp. v. Woodson*, 444 U.S. 286, 291 (1980). And at times, this federalism interest may be decisive. As we explained in *World–Wide Volkswagen*, "[e]ven if the defendant would suffer minimal or no inconvenience from being forced to litigate before the tribunals of another State; even if the forum State has a strong interest in applying its law to the controversy; even if the forum State is the most convenient location for litigation, the Due Process Clause, acting as an instrument of interstate federalism, may sometimes act to divest the State of its power to render a valid judgment."

III

A

Our settled principles regarding specific jurisdiction control this case. In order for a court to exercise specific jurisdiction over a claim, there must be an "affiliation between the forum and the underlying controversy, principally, [an] activity or an occurrence that takes place in the forum State." *Goodyear*, 131 S. Ct., at 2851. When there is no such connection, specific jurisdiction is lacking regardless of the extent of a defendant's unconnected activities in the State. . . .

For this reason, the California Supreme Court's "sliding scale approach" is difficult to square with our precedents. Under the California approach, the strength of the requisite connection between the forum and the specific claims at issue is relaxed if the defendant has extensive forum contacts that are unrelated to those claims. Our cases provide no support for this approach, which resembles a loose and spurious form of general jurisdiction. For specific jurisdiction, a defendant's general connections with the forum are not enough. . . .

The present case illustrates the danger of the California approach. The State Supreme Court found that specific jurisdiction was present without identifying any adequate link between the State and the nonresidents' claims. As noted, the nonresidents were not prescribed Plavix in California, did not purchase Plavix in California, did not ingest Plavix in California, and were not injured by Plavix in California. The mere fact that *other* plaintiffs were prescribed, obtained, and ingested Plavix in California—and allegedly sustained the same injuries as did the nonresidents—does not allow the State to assert specific jurisdiction over the nonresidents' claims. . . . What is needed—and what is missing here—is a connection between the forum and the specific claims at issue.

Our decision in *Walden* [*v. Fiore*, 134 S. Ct. 1115 (2014)] illustrates this requirement. In that case, Nevada plaintiffs sued an out-of-state defendant for conducting an allegedly unlawful search of the plaintiffs while they were in Georgia preparing to board a plane bound for Nevada. We held that the Nevada courts lacked specific jurisdiction . . . [b]ecause the *relevant* conduct occurred entirely in Georgia. . . . (emphasis in original).

In today's case, the connection between the nonresidents' claims and the forum is even weaker. The relevant plaintiffs are not California residents and do not claim to have suffered harm in that State. . . .

B

The nonresidents maintain that two of our cases support the decision below, but they misinterpret those precedents.

[The Court then described the facts and holding in *Keeton v. Hustler Magazine, Inc.*, 465 U.S. 770 (1984), *see* casebook pp. 166–167.]

The nonresident plaintiffs in this case point to our holding in *Keeton* that there was jurisdiction in New Hampshire to entertain the plaintiff's request for damages suffered outside the State, but that holding concerned jurisdiction to determine *the scope of a claim* involving in-state injury and injury to residents of the State, not, as in this case, jurisdiction to entertain claims involving no in-state injury and no injury to residents of the forum State. . . .

[The Court then also discussed *Phillips Petroleum v. Shutts, see* casebook at p. 228, which it found "has no bearing on the question presented here" because it concerns Due Process protections for *plaintiffs* rather than *defendants.*]

C

In a last ditch contention, respondents contend that BMS's "decision to contract with a California company [McKesson] to distribute [Plavix] nationally" provides a sufficient basis for personal jurisdiction. But as we have explained, the requirements of *International Shoe* must be met as to each defendant over whom a state court exercises jurisdiction. In this case, it is not alleged that BMS engaged in relevant acts together with McKesson in California. Nor is it alleged that BMS is derivatively liable for McKesson's conduct in California. And the nonresidents have adduced no evidence to show how or by whom the Plavix they took was distributed to the pharmacies that dispensed it to them. . . .

IV

Our straightforward application in this case of settled principles of personal jurisdiction will not result in the parade of horribles that respondents conjure up. Our decision does not prevent the California and out-of-state plaintiffs from joining together in a consolidated action in the States that have general jurisdiction over BMS. BMS concedes that such suits could be brought in either New York or Delaware. Alternatively, the plaintiffs who are residents of a particular State—for example, the 92 plaintiffs from Texas and the 71 from Ohio—could probably sue together in their home States. In addition, since our decision concerns the due process limits on the exercise of specific jurisdiction by a State, we leave open the question whether the Fifth Amendment imposes the same restrictions on the exercise of personal jurisdiction by a federal court.

The judgment of the California Supreme Court is reversed, and the case is remanded for further proceedings not inconsistent with this opinion.

JUSTICE SOTOMAYOR, dissenting.

Three years ago, the Court imposed substantial curbs on the exercise of general jurisdiction in its decision in *Daimler.* Today, the Court takes its first step toward a similar contraction of specific jurisdiction by holding that a corporation that engages in a nationwide course of conduct cannot be held accountable in a state court by a group of injured people unless all of those people were injured in the forum State.

I fear the consequences of the Court's decision today will be substantial. The majority's rule will make it difficult to aggregate the claims of plaintiffs across the country whose claims may be worth little alone. It will make it impossible to bring a nationwide mass action in state court against defendants who are "at home" in different States. And it will result in piecemeal litigation and the bifurcation of claims. None of this is necessary. A core concern in this Court's personal jurisdiction cases is fairness. And there is nothing unfair about subjecting a massive corporation to suit in a State for a nationwide course of conduct that injures both forum residents and nonresidents alike.

I

Bristol–Myers' advertising and distribution efforts were national in scope. It conducted a single nationwide advertising campaign for Plavix, using television, magazine, and Internet ads to broadcast its message. A consumer in California heard the same advertisement as a consumer in Maine about the benefits of Plavix. Bristol–Myers' distribution of Plavix also proceeded through nationwide channels: Consistent with its usual practice, it relied on a small number of wholesalers to distribute Plavix throughout the country. . . .

The plaintiffs in these consolidated cases are 86 people who allege they were injured by Plavix in California and several hundred others who say they were injured by the drug in other States. . . . Their claims are "materially identical," as Bristol–Myers concedes. Bristol–Myers acknowledged it was subject to suit in California state court by the residents of that State. But it moved to dismiss the claims brought by the nonresident plaintiffs — respondents here — for lack of jurisdiction. The question here, accordingly, is not whether Bristol–Myers is subject to suit in California on claims that arise out of the design, development, manufacture, marketing, and distribution of Plavix — it is. The question is whether Bristol–Myers is subject to suit in California only on the residents' claims, or whether a state court may also hear the nonresidents' "identical" claims.

II

A

As the majority explains, since our pathmarking opinion in *International Shoe,* the touchstone of the personal-jurisdiction analysis has been the question whether a defendant has "certain minimum contacts with [the State] such that the maintenance of the suit does not offend 'traditional notions of fair play and substantial justice.'. . ."

Our cases have set out three conditions for the exercise of specific jurisdiction over a nonresident defendant. First, the defendant must have " 'purposefully avail[ed] itself of the privilege of conducting activities within the forum State' " or have purposefully directed its conduct into the forum State. Second, the plaintiff's claim must "arise out of or relate to" the defendant's forum conduct. Finally, the exercise of jurisdiction must be reasonable under the circumstances.

B

Viewed through this framework, the California courts appropriately exercised specific jurisdiction over respondents' claims.

First, there is no dispute that Bristol–Myers purposefully availed itself of California and its substantial pharmaceutical market . . . .

Second, respondents' claims "relate to" Bristol–Myers' in-state conduct. A claim "relates to" a defendant's forum conduct if it has a "connect[ion] with" that conduct. *International Shoe*, 326 U.S. at 319. So respondents could not, for instance, hale Bristol–Myers into court in California for negligently maintaining the sidewalk outside its New York headquarters—a claim that has no connection to acts Bristol–Myers took in California. But respondents' claims against Bristol–Myers look nothing like such a claim. Respondents' claims against Bristol–Myers concern conduct materially identical to acts the company took in California: its marketing and distribution of Plavix, which it undertook on a nationwide basis in all 50 States. That respondents were allegedly injured by this nationwide course of conduct in Indiana, Oklahoma, and Texas, and not California, does not mean that their claims do not "relate to" the advertising and distribution efforts that Bristol–Myers undertook in that State. All of the plaintiffs—residents and nonresidents alike—allege that they were injured by the same essential acts. Our cases require no connection more direct than that.

Finally, and importantly, there is no serious doubt that the exercise of jurisdiction over the nonresidents' claims is reasonable. Because Bristol–Myers already faces claims that are identical to the nonresidents' claims in this suit, it will not be harmed by having to defend against respondents' claims: Indeed, the alternative approach—litigating those claims in separate suits in as many as 34 different States—would prove far more burdensome. . . .

III

Bristol–Myers does not dispute that it has purposefully availed itself of California's markets, nor—remarkably—did it argue below that it would be "unreasonable" for a California court to hear respondents' claims. Instead, Bristol–Myers contends that respondents' claims do not "arise out of or relate to" its California conduct. The majority agrees, explaining that no "adequate link" exists "between the State and the nonresidents' claims,"—a result that it says follows from "settled principles [of] specific jurisdiction." But our precedents do not require this result, and common sense says that it cannot be correct.

A

The majority casts its decision today as compelled by precedent. But our cases point in the other direction. . . .

Walden concerned the requirement that a defendant "purposefully avail" himself of a forum State or "purposefully direc[t]" his conduct toward that State, not the separate requirement that a plaintiff's claim "arise out of or relate to" a defendant's forum contacts. . . . But that holding has nothing to do with the dispute between the parties: Bristol–Myers has purposefully availed itself of California—to the tune of millions of dollars in annual revenue. Only if its language is taken out of context, can *Walden* be made to seem relevant to the case at hand.

[O]ur decision in *Keeton* suggests that there should be no such barrier to the exercise of jurisdiction here. . . . The majority today dismisses *Keeton* on the ground that the defendant there faced one plaintiff's claim arising out of its nationwide course of conduct, whereas Bristol– Myers faces many more plaintiffs' claims. But this is a distinction without a difference: In either case, a defendant will face liability in a single State for a single course of conduct that has impact in many States. *Keeton* informs us that there is no unfairness in such a result.

The majority's animating concern, in the end, appears to be federalism: "[T]erritorial limitations on the power of the respective States," we are informed, may—and today do—trump even concerns about fairness to the parties. . . . I see little reason to apply such a principle in a case brought against a large corporate defendant arising out of its nationwide conduct. What interest could any single State have in adjudicating respondents' claims that the other States do not share? I would measure jurisdiction first and foremost by the yardstick set out in *International Shoe*—"fair play and substantial justice." The majority's opinion casts that settled principle aside.

B

I fear the consequences of the majority's decision today will be substantial. Even absent a rigid requirement that a defendant's in-state conduct must actually cause a plaintiff's claim, the upshot of today's opinion is that plaintiffs cannot join their claims together and sue a defendant in a State in which only some of them have been injured. That rule is likely to have consequences far beyond this case.

First, and most prominently, the Court's opinion in this case will make it profoundly difficult for plaintiffs who are injured in different States by a defendant's nationwide course of conduct to sue that defendant in a single, consolidated action. The holding of today's opinion is that such an action cannot be brought in a State in which only some plaintiffs were injured. . . . What interests are served by preventing the consolidation of claims and limiting the forums in which they can be consolidated? The effect of the Court's opinion today is to eliminate nationwide mass actions in any State other than those in which a defendant is "essentially at home."[4] Such a rule hands one more tool to corporate defendants determined to prevent the aggregation of individual claims, and forces injured plaintiffs to bear the burden of bringing suit in what will often be far flung jurisdictions.

Second, the Court's opinion today may make it impossible to bring certain mass actions at all. After this case, it is difficult to imagine where it might be possible to bring a nationwide mass action against two or more defendants headquartered and incorporated in different States. There will be no State where both defendants are "at home," and so no State in which the suit can proceed. What about a nationwide mass action brought against a defendant not headquartered or incorporated in the United States? Such a defendant is not "at home" in any State. . . .

It "does not offend traditional notions of fair play and substantial justice," to permit plaintiffs to aggregate claims arising out of a single nationwide course of conduct in a single suit in a single State where some, but not all, were injured. But that is exactly what the Court holds today is barred by the Due Process Clause.

This is not a rule the Constitution has required before. I respectfully dissent.

---

4. The Court today does not confront the question whether its opinion here would also apply to a class action in which a plaintiff injured in the forum State seeks to represent a nationwide class of plaintiffs, not all of whom were injured there. *Cf. Devlin v. Scardelletti,* 536 U.S. 1, 9–10 (2005) ("Nonnamed class members . . . may be parties for some purposes and not for others"); *see also* Wood, Adjudicatory Jurisdiction and Class Actions, 62 Ind. L.J. 597, 616–617 (1987).

NOTES AND QUESTIONS

1. *Rejecting a "Sliding Scale" for Specific Jurisdiction.* In *BMS,* Justice Alito writes an opinion for the Court, with the exception of Justice Sotomayor, who dissents. The eight-person majority rejects the approach taken by the California Supreme Court that there is a "sliding scale" for specific jurisdiction such that "the strength of the requisite connection between the forum and the specific claims at issue is relaxed if the defendant has extensive forum contacts that are unrelated to those claims." Under that standard, when a defendant's undifferentiated "nationwide course of conduct" injures people in multiple states, a court may exercise jurisdiction over all claims arising from that course of conduct—even if some plaintiffs' claims do not directly arise from forum activities. Why do you think the U.S. Supreme Court is unwilling to accept this more flexible standard for specific jurisdiction in the aftermath of *Daimler*? Are you surprised that Justice Ginsburg, who emphasized the role that specific jurisdiction has in contemporary jurisdiction jurisprudence, joined the majority?

2. *The Practical Effect of the Majority Rule.* Justice Sotomayor dissents and expresses concern about piecemeal litigation and the inability of plaintiffs to bring a joint action against defendants who are "at home" in different states. There are two defendants in *BMS*; both are Delaware corporations but they have their principal places of business in different states. Does the decision mean that Delaware is likely to be the only place where such suits can be brought? Might there be specific jurisdiction against both defendants in the state where the drug was manufactured?

Another practical effect relates to the case of the foreign defendant who is not "at home" in any state. Recall that in *J. McIntyre Machinery, Ltd. v. Nicastro*, 564 U.S. 873 (2011), *see* casebook at pp. 137–151, a plaintiff injured by a foreign manufacturer's product could not sue in the forum where the injury occurred because New Jersey courts lacked jurisdiction for lack of purposeful conduct—and it was far from clear that the plaintiff's claim could be said to "arise out of its activity in Ohio," where the foreign manufacturer's distributor was located. *See* casebook, p. 154 (note 3). Thus, there may have been no place in the United States for the plaintiff to sue the foreign manufacturer. Does a suit against a foreign country defendant present a more compelling case for broadening the arising out of/related to standard for specific jurisdiction?

3. *Connecting a Defendant's In-State Activity to a Claim.* Recall the tests employed by courts to connect conduct to a claim, addressed on pages 113–114, to interpret nexus requirements in state-specific-act statutes. Courts have used many of these tests to define the "arising out of" limitation that is also critical for assessing the constitutionality of specific jurisdiction. *See generally* Linda Sandstrom Simard, *Meeting Expectations: Two Profiles for Specific Jurisdiction*, 38 Ind. L. Rev. 343, 348–367 (2005).

In upholding jurisdiction in *Carnival Cruise Lines v. Shute* against a Due Process challenge, the Ninth Circuit adopted a "but for" causation test similar to the one used by the Washington Supreme Court in interpreting the specific-act statute. The Ninth Circuit emphasized that the "but for" test "preserves the requirement that there be some nexus between the cause of action and the defendant's activities in

the forum."* The court noted that the basic function of the "arising out of" requirement is preservation of the distinction between general and specific jurisdiction
and that a "but for" interpretation is consistent with that function. However, as
the required "arising out of" relationship becomes more remote, the distinction
between the two types of jurisdiction blurs.

Where the contacts between a defendant and the forum state are, to use the
language of *International Shoe*, "single or isolated," jurisdiction over "unrelated"
claims has been found to be inconsistent with Due Process. How attenuated may
the connection between a jurisdictional contact and a cause of action be? Are the
level of forum activity and the "relatedness" of the claim measured on a sliding
scale, such that a significant amount of in-state activity compensates for a weakly
related claim? Or does Due Process require a minimum degree of relatedness
between the claim and the in-state activity?

The Third Circuit surveyed the differing approaches taken by other state
and federal courts in assessing the "arising out of" requirement for constitutional
purposes. The Third Circuit adopted a reformulated "but for" test that directs the
lower courts to consider more carefully the degree of relatedness between the claim
and the in-state activity alleged to provide a basis for the exercise of jurisdiction. In
O'Connor v. Sandy Lane Hotel Co., 496 F.3d 312 (3d Cir. 2007), O'Connor, a customer
receiving a massage at the Sandy Lane Hotel in Barbados, slipped and injured his
shoulder. The massage had been arranged by telephone after the hotel had mailed
a brochure to O'Connor at his home in Pennsylvania. O'Connor brought negligence claims against Sandy Lane in Pennsylvania federal court.

The Pennsylvania long-arm statute provided for jurisdiction to the extent
allowed under the United States Constitution. In its analysis, the court noted that
while O'Connor's claims had to arise out of or relate to some purposeful contact by Sandy Lane, "the Supreme Court has not yet explained the scope of this
requirement." The court then outlined the three predominate approaches taken
by state and federal courts: (1) the "proximate cause" test, which requires that the
defendant's contacts be relevant to the merits of the plaintiff's claim; (2) the more
relaxed "but for" test; and (3) the "substantial connection" test, which looks solely
to "whether the tie between the defendant's contacts and the plaintiff's claim is
close enough to make jurisdiction fair and reasonable" and calls for a sliding-scale
approach based on whether "the degree of relatedness in a given case is inversely
proportional to the overall 'intensity of [the defendant's] forum contacts.'"

The Third Circuit rejected the sliding-scale approach of the "substantial
connection" test because, in its view, this test eliminated the distinction between
specific and general jurisdiction and this distinction remained necessary to allow
potential defendants to "anticipate and control their jurisdictional exposure." It

---

* On review by the Supreme Court, jurisdiction in Washington was found improper
due to a forum selection clause in the contract that had provided for a Florida forum. The
Supreme Court found that the forum selection clause trumped, and therefore it never
addressed the question whether jurisdiction in Washington on these facts would have met
the constitutional standard. Thus, the Supreme Court has never ruled on the constitutional
test for when a claim "arises from" contacts with the forum.

also rejected the traditional "but for" test as "vastly overinclusive." Noting that the relatedness requirement corresponds to the notion that litigation in the forum is reasonably foreseeable, the court adopted a modified "but for" test in which the analysis would "hew closely to the reciprocity principle upon which specific jurisdiction rests. With each purposeful contact by an out-of-state resident, the forum state's laws will extend certain benefits and impose certain obligations."

Under its reformulated test, the court held that the exercise of personal jurisdiction over Sandy Lane was constitutional. But for Sandy Lane's act of mailing the brochure to Pennsylvania, O'Connor would have never been injured. In determining whether the connection was close enough to support a finding of jurisdiction, the court noted that Sandy Lane had formed a contract for spa services through its mailings and calls to Pennsylvania. Under that contract, it had acquired certain rights and obligations. Implicit in the spa agreement was a promise that Sandy Lane would "exercise due care in performing the services required." As such, O'Connor's claims were found to "directly and closely relate to a continuing contractual obligation that arose in Pennsylvania."

Compare O'Connor with *DeLorenzo v. Viceroy Hotel Grp., LLC*, 757 Fed. App. 6 (2d Cir. 2018), in which the Second Circuit affirmed a lower court's dismissal for lack of personal jurisdiction over two foreign hotel chains in part because the plaintiff's injury, which occurred at one of the hotels, did not arise out of her booking her stay online in New York. The plaintiff, DeLorenzo, had reserved a room at one of the hotels in Anguilla after reading a positive review of it in a New York publication. She booked her reservation via the hotel's website from her office in Manhattan. During her stay, she was drugged and sexually assaulted by an employee of a neighboring hotel. DeLorenzo subsequently sued both hotels for negligence and gross negligence. The court held, *inter alia*, that the cause of action was sufficiently remote from the plaintiff's contracting with the defendants online so as to fail to satisfy the arising from prong. Can you distinguish this case from *O'Connor*?

In the *Licci* decisions (*supra* pp. 112–113), the "arising from" prong was a focus for the New York Court of Appeals on the statutory question and for the Second Circuit on the constitutional inquiry. The New York Court of Appeals noted that the alleged breaches of various statutory obligations by the bank took place when the bank used the New York account and therefore established the relevant nexus to plaintiffs' claims. The court also noted that although not all elements of the causes of action pleaded were related to the bank's use of the correspondent account, "where at least one element arises from the New York contacts, the relationship between the business transaction and the claim assert supports specific jurisdiction under the statute." *Licci*, 20 N.Y.3d at 341. As for the constitutional question, the federal Court of Appeals for the Second Circuit stated that the bank's "repeated use of the correspondent account—and hence New York's banking system—as an instrument to achieve the wrong complained of in this suit satisfies the minimum contacts component of the due process inquiry." *Licci ex rel. Licci v. Lebanese Canadian Bank, SAL*, 732 F.3d 161 (2d Cir. 2013).

The Supreme Court in *Bristol-Myers Squibb* did not offer much guidance as to what would establish the necessary connection between the defendant's activity and the claim. Why was it not sufficient for specific jurisdiction that Bristol-Myers Squibb's distributor McKesson Corp. has its principal place of business in California? The majority addresses that issue toward the end of its opinion and explains that there is no allegation that BMS engaged in relevant acts together with McKesson nor any showing by the nonresidents that the drug they took was distributed by McKesson to the pharmacies that dispensed it.

Other cases post-*Bristol-Myers Squibb* have turned on the issue of whether the claim had a sufficient connection to the defendant's activity to satisfy the "arising out of" requirement. The Illinois Supreme Court took up the task of interpreting this requirement in *Rios v. Bayer*, No. 125020, 2020 WL 2963318 (Ill. June 4, 2020). Both resident and nonresident plaintiffs filed suits against Bayer in Illinois, alleging, amongst other claims, that Bayer failed to properly train physicians on a permanent birth control device and distributed false information concerning the device.

Bayer had run clinical trials for the product in Illinois, contracted with Illinois physicians, and established an accreditation program to train physicians in Illinois. On these facts, the state appellate court held that the case was "easily distinguishable" from *Bristol-Myers*, and allowed jurisdiction over the nonresident claims. But the state supreme court disagreed: Although Bayer had trained physicians in Illinois, it had also trained physicians in other states, and none of the nonresident plaintiffs' physicians had been trained in Illinois. Similarly, Bayer distributed false information in Illinois, but neither the nonresident plaintiffs nor their physicians had received that information in Illinois. Thus, the court found, the nonresident plaintiffs' claims did not arise out of or relate to the defendant's in-state activities, and so Illinois courts were precluded by *Bristol-Myers Squibb* from asserting personal jurisdiction over such claims.

In *Lawson v. Simmons Sporting Goods*, 569 S.W.3d 865 (Ark. 2019), an Arkansas plaintiff broke her arm when she tripped over a rug in Simmons Sporting Goods, located in Louisiana. The plaintiff sued Simmons Sporting Goods on a premises liability claim, arguing that the store breached a duty owed to its customers by not maintaining safe premises. The plaintiff sued in her home state of Arkansas, pointing to the store's advertising within the state as providing a basis for personal jurisdiction. Lawson, however, had not been drawn to the store by any particular advertisement. 511 S.W. 3d 883, 888–889 (2017). A state appellate court held that Arkansas courts had jurisdiction over the claim, but the United States Supreme Court vacated the ruling. 138 S. Ct. 237 (2017), *vacating* 511 S.W.3d 883 (Ark. Ct. App. 2017). Had Lawson been drawn to the store by Simmons' advertisements in Arkansas, would that have changed the outcome?

4. *The Role of Sovereignty and Federalism.* The *BMS* majority suggests that, in addition to weighing the burden on the defendant, jurisdictional analysis requires a consideration of sovereignty and interstate federalism: "The primary concern in assessing personal jurisdiction is the burden on the defendant. Assessing this burden obviously requires a court to consider the practical problems resulting from litigating in the forum, but it also encompasses the more abstract matter of submitting to the coercive power of a State that may have little legitimate interest in the claims in question." The language of "submitting" to the sovereign also featured prominently in Justice Kennedy's opinion in *McIntyre*, thereby highlighting that each state has its own sphere of sovereignty that is both absolute and exclusive.

These ideas find their roots in the traditional "power theory" of jurisdiction associated with *Pennoyer*. In *World-Wide Volkswagen*, the Court revived the sovereignty framework for jurisdiction in language quoted by the *BMS* majority: "The States retain many essential attributes of sovereignty, including, in particular, the sovereign power to try causes in their courts. The sovereignty of each State . . . implies a limitation on the sovereignty of all its sister States." However, two years later, the Court seemed to repudiate in dicta in *Insurance Corp. of Ireland v. Compagnie des Bauxites de Guinee*, 456 U.S. 694 (1982), discussed at p. 124 of the casebook. Justice Ginsburg, dissenting in *McIntyre*, relied on *Insurance Corp.* to reject Justice Kennedy's invocation of the sovereignty framework. Moreover, Justice Breyer's separate opinion in *McIntyre*—joined by Justice Alito, who authored *BMS*—made no mention of sovereignty or interstate federalism. Yet eight members of the court signed off on an opinion which heavily emphasized such concepts in *BMS*. What interests are protected by adding federalism and sovereignty to the mix of considerations, which are not adequately protected by simply "weighing the burden on the defendant"?

5. *Does a Claim Based on an In-State Injury Satisfy the "Arising Out Of" Prong?* In Section III(A) of its opinion, the Court underscores the requirement of an "adequate link" between the state asserting jurisdiction and each plaintiff's claim, the requirement traditionally referred to as the "arising out of or relating to" prong. As the Court notes in discussing the nonresident plaintiffs, "the nonresidents were not prescribed Plavix in California, did not purchase Plavix in California, did not ingest Plavix in California, and were not injured by Plavix in California." But Justice Alito, writing for the majority, then seems to go further, citing *Walden* as requiring the defendant's "relevant conduct" to occur in the forum state. *Walden*, however, was a case on purposeful availment, *not* the link required between the litigation and the forum state. Justice Sotomayor suggests that the majority conflates the two requirements. Her dissent recites the modern three-part framework—minimum contacts, arising from/related to, reasonableness—a framework that is never mentioned in the majority opinion.

The majority's language in *BMS* raised a new question about the "arising out of" prong: namely, does there have to be a connection between the litigation and the defendant's forum-directed *conduct*, or is all that is required a link between the litigation and the forum state? The critical consequence of the question is whether an injury that occurs in the forum can satisfy the prong. In 2021, the Supreme Court took up that question and the broader contours of the nexus requirement in two consolidated cases that truly looked like the return of *World-Wide Volkswagen*. . . .

b.   Contacts That Are Sufficiently "Related"

Ford Motor Company v. Montana Eighth Judicial District Court

141 S. Ct. 1017 (2021)

JUSTICE KAGAN delivered the opinion of the Court.

In each of these two cases, a state court held that it had jurisdiction over Ford Motor Company in a products-liability suit stemming from a car accident. The accident happened in the State where suit was brought. The victim was one of the State's residents. And Ford did substantial business in the State—among other things, advertising, selling, and servicing the model of vehicle the suit claims is defective. Still, Ford contends that jurisdiction is improper because the particular car involved in the crash was not first sold in the forum State, nor was it designed or manufactured there. We reject that argument. When a company like Ford serves a market for a product in a State and that product causes injury in the State to one of its residents, the State's courts may entertain the resulting suit.

I

Ford is a global auto company. It is incorporated in Delaware and headquartered in Michigan. But its business is everywhere. Ford markets, sells, and services its products across the United States and overseas. In this country alone, the company annually distributes over 2.5 million new cars, trucks, and SUVs to over 3,200 licensed dealerships. . . . Ford also encourages a resale market for its products: Almost all its dealerships buy and sell used Fords, as well as selling new ones. To enhance its brand and increase its sales, Ford engages in wide-ranging promotional activities, including television, print, online, and direct-mail advertisements. No matter where you live, you've seen them: "Have you driven a Ford lately?" or "Built Ford Tough." Ford also ensures that consumers can keep their vehicles running long past the date of sale. The company provides original parts to auto supply stores and repair shops across the country. (Goes another slogan: "Keep your Ford a Ford.") And Ford's own network of dealers offers an array of maintenance and repair services, thus fostering an ongoing relationship between Ford and its customers.

Accidents involving two of Ford's vehicles—a 1996 Explorer and a 1994 Crown Victoria—are at the heart of the suits before us. One case comes from Montana. Markkaya Gullett was driving her Explorer near her home in the State when the tread separated from a rear tire. The vehicle spun out, rolled into a ditch, and came to rest upside down. Gullett died at the scene of the crash. The representative of her estate sued Ford in Montana state court, bringing claims for a design defect, failure to warn, and negligence. The second case comes from Minnesota. Adam Bandemer was a passenger in his friend's Crown Victoria, traveling on a rural road in the State to a favorite ice-fishing spot. When his friend rear-ended a snowplow, this car too landed in a ditch. Bandemer's air bag failed to deploy, and he suffered serious brain damage. He sued Ford in Minnesota state court, asserting products-liability, negligence, and breach-of-warranty claims.

Ford moved to dismiss the two suits for lack of personal jurisdiction, on basically identical grounds. According to Ford, the state court (whether in Montana or Minnesota) had jurisdiction only if the company's conduct in the State had given rise to the plaintiff's claims. And that causal link existed, Ford continued, only if the company had designed, manufactured, or—most likely—sold in the State the particular vehicle involved in the accident. In neither suit could the plaintiff make that showing. Ford had designed the Explorer and Crown Victoria in Michigan, and it had manufactured the cars in (respectively) Kentucky and Canada. Still more, the company had originally sold the cars at issue outside the forum States—the Explorer in Washington, the Crown Victoria in North Dakota. Only later resales and relocations by consumers had brought the vehicles to Montana and Minnesota. That meant, in Ford's view, that the courts of those States could not decide the suits.

Both the Montana and the Minnesota Supreme Courts (affirming lower court decisions) rejected Ford's argument. . . .

II

A

The Fourteenth Amendment's Due Process Clause limits a state court's power to exercise jurisdiction over a defendant. The canonical decision in this area remains *International Shoe Co. v. Washington*. . . .

A state court may exercise general jurisdiction only when a defendant is "essentially at home" in the State. Ibid. General jurisdiction, as its name implies, extends to "any and all claims" brought against a defendant. Ibid. Those claims need not relate to the forum State or the defendant's activity there; they may concern events and conduct anywhere in the world. But that breadth imposes a correlative limit: Only a select "set of affiliations with a forum" will expose a defendant to such sweeping jurisdiction. *Daimler AG v. Bauman*, 571 U.S. 117 (2014). In what we have called the "paradigm" case, an individual is subject to general jurisdiction in her place of domicile. Ibid. (internal quotation marks omitted). And the "equivalent" forums for a corporation are its place of incorporation and principal place of business. . . . So general jurisdiction over Ford (as all parties agree) attaches in Delaware and Michigan—not in Montana and Minnesota. . . .

Specific jurisdiction is different: It covers defendants less intimately connected with a State, but only as to a narrower class of claims. The contacts needed for this kind of jurisdiction often go by the name "purposeful availment." *Burger King Corp. v. Rudzewicz*, 471 U.S. 462, 475 (1985). The defendant, we have said, must take "some act by which [it] purposefully avails itself of the privilege of conducting activities within the forum State." *Hanson v. Denckla*, 357 U.S. 235, 253 (1958). The contacts must be the defendant's own choice and not "random, isolated, or fortuitous." *Keeton v. Hustler Magazine, Inc.*, 465 U.S. 770, 774 (1984). They must show that the defendant deliberately "reached out beyond" its home—by, for example, "exploi[ting] a market" in the forum State or entering a contractual relationship centered there. *Walden v. Fiore*, 571 U.S. 277, 285 (2014). Yet even then—because the defendant is not "at home"—the forum State may exercise jurisdiction in only certain cases. The plaintiff's claims, we have often stated, "must arise out of or relate to the defendant's contacts" with the forum. *Bristol-Myers*, 582 U. S., at ——, 137 S.Ct., 1780. Or put just a bit differently, "there must be 'an affiliation between the forum and the underlying controversy, principally, [an] activity or an occurrence that takes place in the forum State and is therefore subject to the State's regulation.'" *Bristol-Myers*, 582 U. S., at —— – ——, ——, 137 S.Ct., at 1780 (quoting *Goodyear*, 564 U.S., at 919).

These rules derive from and reflect two sets of values—treating defendants fairly and protecting "interstate federalism." *World-Wide Volkswagen Corp. v. Woodson*, 444 U. S. 286, 293 (1980). Our decision in *International Shoe* founded specific jurisdiction on an idea of reciprocity between a defendant and a State: When (but only when) a company "exercises the privilege of conducting activities within a state"—thus "enjoy[ing] the benefits and protection of [its] laws"—the State may hold the company to account for related misconduct. 326 U.S., at 319, Later decisions have added that our doctrine similarly provides defendants with "fair warning"—knowledge that "a particular activity may subject [it] to the jurisdiction of a foreign sovereign." Id., at 472, 105 S.Ct. 2174 (internal quotation marks omitted); *World-Wide Volkswagen*, 444 U.S., at 297, 100 S.Ct. 580 (likewise referring to "clear notice"). A defendant can thus "structure [its] primary conduct" to lessen or avoid exposure to a given State's courts. Id., at 297, 100 S.Ct. 580. And this Court has considered alongside defendants' interests those of the States in relation to each other. One State's "sovereign power to try" a suit, we have recognized, may prevent "sister States" from exercising their like authority. Id., at 293, 100 S.Ct. 580. The law of specific jurisdiction thus seeks to ensure that States with "little legitimate interest" in a suit do not encroach on States more affected by the controversy. *Bristol-Myers*, 582 U. S., at ——, 137 S.Ct., at 1780.2

B

Ford contends that our jurisdictional rules prevent Montana's and Minnesota's courts from deciding these two suits. In making that argument, Ford does not contest that it does substantial business in Montana and Minnesota — that it actively seeks to serve the market for automobiles and related products in those States. Or to put that concession in more doctrinal terms, Ford agrees that it has "purposefully avail[ed] itself of the privilege of conducting activities" in both places. *Hanson*, 357 U.S., at 253. Ford's claim is instead that those activities do not sufficiently connect to the suits, even though the resident-plaintiffs allege that Ford cars malfunctioned in the forum States. In Ford's view, the needed link must be causal in nature: Jurisdiction attaches "only if the defendant's forum conduct gave rise to the plaintiff's claims." And that rule reduces, Ford thinks, to locating specific jurisdiction in the State where Ford sold the car in question, or else the States where Ford designed and manufactured the vehicle. On that view, the place of accident and injury is immaterial. So (Ford says) Montana's and Minnesota's courts have no power over these cases.

But Ford's causation-only approach finds no support in this Court's requirement of a "connection" between a plaintiff's suit and a defendant's activities. *Bristol-Myers*, 582 U. S., at ——. That rule indeed serves to narrow the class of claims over which a state court may exercise specific jurisdiction. But not quite so far as Ford wants. None of our precedents has suggested that only a strict causal relationship between the defendant's in-state activity and the litigation will do. As just noted, our most common formulation of the rule demands that the suit "arise out of or relate to the defendant's contacts with the forum." Id., at ——, see supra, at 1025. The first half of that standard asks about causation; but the back half, after the "or," contemplates that some relationships will support jurisdiction without a causal showing. That does not mean anything goes. In the sphere of specific jurisdiction, the phrase "relate to" incorporates real limits, as it must to adequately protect defendants foreign to a forum. But again, we have never framed the specific jurisdiction inquiry as always requiring proof of causation — i.e., proof that the plaintiff's claim came about because of the defendant's in-state conduct. So the case is not over even if, as Ford argues, a causal test would put jurisdiction in only the States of first sale, manufacture, and design. A different State's courts may yet have jurisdiction, because of another "activity [or] occurrence" involving the defendant that takes place in the State.

And indeed, this Court has stated that specific jurisdiction attaches in cases identical to the ones here — when a company like Ford serves a market for a product in the forum State and the product malfunctions there. In World-Wide Volkswagen, the Court held that an Oklahoma court could not assert jurisdiction over a New York car dealer just because a car it sold later caught fire in Oklahoma. 444 U.S., at 295, 100 S.Ct. 580. But in so doing, we contrasted the dealer's position to that of two other defendants — Audi, the car's manufacturer, and Volkswagen, the car's nationwide importer (neither of which contested jurisdiction):

"[I]f the sale of a product of a manufacturer or distributor such as Audi or Volkswagen is not simply an isolated occurrence, but arises from the efforts of the manufacturer or distributor to serve, directly or indirectly, the market for its product in [several or all] other States, it is not unreasonable to subject it to suit in one of those States if its allegedly defective merchandise has there been the source of injury to its owner or to others." Id., at 297, 100 S.Ct. 580.

Or said another way, if Audi and Volkswagen's business deliberately extended into Oklahoma (among other States), then Oklahoma's courts could hold the companies accountable for a car's catching fire there — even though the vehicle had been designed and made overseas and sold in New York. For, the Court explained, a company thus "purposefully avail[ing] itself " of the Oklahoma auto market "has clear notice" of its exposure in that State to suits arising from local accidents involving its cars. Ibid. And the company could do something about that exposure: It could "act to alleviate the risk of burdensome litigation by procuring insurance, passing the expected costs on to customers, or, if the risks are [still] too great, severing its connection with the State." Ibid.

Our conclusion in *World-Wide Volkswagen* — though, as Ford notes, technically "dicta," Brief for Petitioner 34 — has appeared and reappeared in many cases since. So, for example, the Court in *Keeton* invoked that part of *World-Wide Volkswagen* to show that when a corporation has "continuously and deliberately exploited [a State's] market, it must reasonably anticipate being haled into [that State's] court[s]" to defend actions "based on" products causing injury there. On two other occasions, we reaffirmed that rule by reciting the above block-quoted language verbatim. And in *Daimler*, we used the Audi/Volkswagen scenario as a paradigm case of specific jurisdiction (though now naming Daimler, the maker of Mercedes Benzes). Said the Court, to "illustrate[ ]" specific jurisdiction's "province[ ]": A California court would exercise specific jurisdiction "if a California plaintiff, injured in a California accident involving a Daimler-manufactured vehicle, sued Daimler [in that court] alleging that the vehicle was defectively designed." As in *World-Wide Volkswagen*, the Court did not limit jurisdiction to where the car was designed, manufactured, or first sold. Substitute Ford for Daimler, Montana and Minnesota for California, and the Court's "illustrat[ive]" case becomes . . . the two cases before us.

To see why Ford is subject to jurisdiction in these cases (as Audi, Volkswagen, and Daimler were in their analogues), consider first the business that the company regularly conducts in Montana and Minnesota. Small wonder that Ford has here conceded "purposeful availment" of the two States' markets. By every means imaginable — among them, billboards, TV and radio spots, print ads, and direct mail — Ford urges Montanans and Minnesotans to buy its vehicles, including (at all relevant times) Explorers and Crown Victorias. Ford cars — again including those two models — are available for sale, whether new or used, throughout the States, at 36 dealerships in Montana and 84 in Minnesota. And apart from sales, Ford works hard to foster ongoing connections to its cars' owners. The company's dealers in Montana and Minnesota (as elsewhere) regularly maintain and repair Ford cars, including those whose warranties have long since expired. And the company distributes replacement parts both to its own dealers and to independent auto shops in the two States. Those activities, too, make Ford money. And by making it easier to own a Ford, they encourage Montanans and Minnesotans to become lifelong Ford drivers.

Now turn to how all this Montana- and Minnesota-based conduct relates to the claims in these cases, brought by state residents in Montana's and Minnesota's courts. Each plaintiff 's suit, of course, arises from a car accident in one of those States. In each complaint, the resident-plaintiff alleges that a defective Ford vehicle — an Explorer in one, a Crown Victoria in the other — caused the crash and resulting harm. And as just described, Ford had advertised, sold, and serviced those two car models in both States for many years. (Contrast a case, which we do not address, in which Ford marketed the models in only a different State or region.) In other words, Ford had systematically served a market in Montana and Minnesota for the very vehicles that the plaintiffs allege malfunctioned and injured them in those States. So there is a strong "relationship among the defendant, the forum, and the litigation" — the "essential foundation" of specific jurisdiction. That is why this Court has used this exact fact pattern (a resident-plaintiff sues a global car company, extensively serving the state market in a vehicle, for an in-state accident) as an illustration — even a paradigm example — of how specific jurisdiction works.[1]

The only complication here, pressed by Ford, is that the company sold the specific cars involved in these crashes outside the forum States, with consumers later selling them to the States' residents. Because that is so, Ford argues, the plaintiffs' claims "would be precisely the same if Ford had never done anything in Montana and Minnesota." Of course, that argument merely restates Ford's demand for an exclusively causal test of connection — which we have already shown is inconsistent with our caselawAnd indeed, a similar assertion could have been made in *World-Wide Volkswagen* — yet the Court made clear that systematic contacts in Oklahoma rendered Audi accountable there for an in-state accident, even though it involved a car sold in New York. So too here, and for the same reasons — even supposing (as Ford does) that without the company's Montana or Minnesota contacts the plaintiffs' claims would be just the same.

But in any event, that assumption is far from clear. For the owners of these cars might never have bought them, and so these suits might never have arisen, except for Ford's contacts with their home States. Those contacts might turn any

---

1. None of this is to say that any person using any means to sell any good in a State is subject to jurisdiction there if the product malfunctions after arrival. We have long treated isolated or sporadic transactions differently from continuous ones. See, e.g., *World-Wide Volkswagen Corp. v. Woodson*, 444 U.S. 286, 297, 100 S.Ct. 580, 62 L.Ed.2d 490 (1980); supra, at 1025. And we do not here consider internet transactions, which may raise doctrinal questions of their own. See *Walden v. Fiore*, 571 U.S. 277, 290, n. 9, 134 S.Ct. 1115, 188 L.Ed.2d 12 (2014) ("[T]his case does not present the very different questions whether and how a defendant's virtual 'presence' and conduct translate into 'contacts' with a particular State"). So consider, for example, a hypothetical offered at oral argument. "[A] retired guy in a small town" in Maine "carves decoys" and uses "a site on the Internet" to sell them. Tr. of Oral Arg. 39. "Can he be sued in any state if some harm arises from the decoy?" Ibid. The differences between that case and the ones before us virtually list themselves. (Just consider all our descriptions of Ford's activities outside its home bases.) So we agree with the plaintiffs' counsel that resolving these cases does not also resolve the hypothetical. See id., at 39–40.

resident of Montana or Minnesota into a Ford owner—even when he buys his car from out of state. He may make that purchase because he saw ads for the car in local media. And he may take into account a raft of Ford's in-state activities designed to make driving a Ford convenient there: that Ford dealers stand ready to service the car; that other auto shops have ample supplies of Ford parts; and that Ford fosters an active resale market for its old models. The plaintiffs here did not in fact establish, or even allege, such causal links. Nor should jurisdiction in cases like these ride on the exact reasons for an individual plaintiff's purchase, or on his ability to present persuasive evidence about them.[2] But the possibilities listed above—created by the reach of Ford's Montana and Minnesota contacts—underscore the aptness of finding jurisdiction here, even though the cars at issue were first sold out of state.

For related reasons, allowing jurisdiction in these cases treats Ford fairly, as this Court's precedents explain. In conducting so much business in Montana and Minnesota, Ford "enjoys the benefits and protection of [their] laws"—the enforcement of contracts, the defense of property, the resulting formation of effective markets. All that assistance to Ford's in-state business creates reciprocal obligations—most relevant here, that the car models Ford so extensively markets in Montana and Minnesota be safe for their citizens to use there. Thus our repeated conclusion: A state court's enforcement of that commitment, enmeshed as it is with Ford's government-protected in-state business, can "hardly be said to be undue." And as *World-Wide Volkswagen* described, it cannot be thought surprising either. An automaker regularly marketing a vehicle in a State, the Court said, has "clear notice" that it will be subject to jurisdiction in the State's courts when the product malfunctions there (regardless where it was first sold). Precisely because that exercise of jurisdiction is so reasonable, it is also predictable—and thus allows Ford to "structure [its] primary conduct" to lessen or even avoid the costs of state-court litigation. *World-Wide Volkswagen*, 444 U.S., at 297, 100 S.Ct. 580.

Finally, principles of "interstate federalism" support jurisdiction over these suits in Montana and Minnesota. Those States have significant interests at stake—"providing [their] residents with a convenient forum for redressing injuries inflicted by out-of-state actors," as well as enforcing their own safety regulations. Consider, next to those, the interests of the States of first sale (Washington and North Dakota)—which Ford's proposed rule would make the most likely forums. For each of those States, the suit involves all out-of-state parties, an out-of-state accident, and out-of-state injuries; the suit's only connection with the State is that a former owner once (many years earlier) bought the car there. In other words, there is a less significant "relationship among the defendant, the forum, and the litigation." So by channeling these suits to Washington and North Dakota, Ford's regime would undermine, rather than promote, what the company calls the Due Process Clause's "jurisdiction-allocating function."

---

2. It should, for example, make no difference if a plaintiff had recently moved to the forum State with his car, and had not made his purchasing decision with that move in mind—so had not considered any of Ford's activities in his new home State.

C

Ford mainly relies for its rule on two of our recent decisions — *Bristol-Myers* and *Walden*. But those precedents stand for nothing like the principle Ford derives from them. If anything, they reinforce all we have said about why Montana's and Minnesota's courts can decide these cases.

Ford says of *Bristol-Myers* that it "squarely foreclose[s]" jurisdiction. In that case, non-resident plaintiffs brought claims in California state court against Bristol-Myers Squibb, the manufacturer of a nationally marketed prescription drug called Plavix. The plaintiffs had not bought Plavix in California; neither had they used or suffered any harm from the drug there. Still, the California Supreme Court thought it could exercise jurisdiction because Bristol-Myers Squibb sold Plavix in California and was defending there against identical claims brought by the State's residents. This Court disagreed, holding that the exercise of jurisdiction violated the Fourteenth Amendment. In Ford's view, the same must be true here. Each of these plaintiffs, like the plaintiffs in *Bristol-Myers*, alleged injury from a particular item (a car, a pill) that the defendant had sold outside the forum State. Ford reads *Bristol-Myers* to preclude jurisdiction when that is true, even if the defendant regularly sold "the same kind of product" in the State.

But that reading misses the point of our decision. We found jurisdiction improper in *Bristol-Myers* because the forum State, and the defendant's activities there, lacked any connection to the plaintiffs' claims. See 582 U. S., at ——, 137 S.Ct., at 1781 ("What is needed — and what is missing here — is a connection between the forum and the specific claims at issue"). The plaintiffs, the Court explained, were not residents of California. They had not been prescribed Plavix in California. They had not ingested Plavix in California. And they had not sustained their injuries in California. See ibid. (emphasizing these points). In short, the plaintiffs were engaged in forum-shopping — suing in California because it was thought plaintiff-friendly, even though their cases had no tie to the State. See id., at ——, 137 S.Ct., at 1782–1783 (distinguishing the Plavix claims from the litigation in Keeton, see supra, at 1027, because they "involv[e] no in-state injury and no injury to residents of the forum State"). That is not at all true of the cases before us. Yes, Ford sold the specific products in other States, as Bristol-Myers Squibb had. But here, the plaintiffs are residents of the forum States. They used the allegedly defective products in the forum States. And they suffered injuries when those products malfunctioned in the forum States. In sum, each of the plaintiffs brought suit in the most natural State — based on an "affiliation between the forum and the underlying controversy, principally, [an] activity or an occurrence that t[ook] place" there. *Bristol-Myers*, 582 U. S., at —— – ——, ——, 137 S.Ct., at 1779–1780, 1780–1781) (internal quotation marks omitted). So Bristol-Myers does not bar jurisdiction.

Ford falls back on *Walden* as its last resort. In that case, a Georgia police officer working at an Atlanta airport searched, and seized money from, two Nevada residents before they embarked on a flight to Las Vegas. The victims of the search sued the officer in Nevada, arguing that their alleged injury (their inability to use the seized money) occurred in the State in which they lived. This Court held the exercise of jurisdiction in Nevada improper even though "the plaintiff[s] experienced [the] effect[s]" of the officer's conduct there. 571 U.S., at 290, 134 S.Ct.

1115. According to Ford, our ruling shows that a plaintiff's residence and place of injury can never support jurisdiction. And without those facts, Ford concludes, the basis for jurisdiction crumbles here as well.

But *Walden* has precious little to do with the cases before us. In *Walden*, only the plaintiffs had any contacts with the State of Nevada; the defendant-officer had never taken any act to "form[ ] a contact" of his own. 571 U.S., at 290, 134 S.Ct. 1115. The officer had "never traveled to, conducted activities within, contacted anyone in, or sent anything or anyone to Nevada." Id., at 289, 134 S.Ct. 1115. So to use the language of our doctrinal test: He had not "purposefully avail[ed himself] of the privilege of conducting activities" in the forum State. *Hanson*, 357 U.S., at 253, 78 S.Ct. 1228. Because that was true, the Court had no occasion to address the necessary connection between a defendant's in-state activity and the plaintiff's claims. But here, Ford has a veritable truckload of contacts with Montana and Minnesota, as it admits. See supra, at 1027–1028. The only issue is whether those contacts are related enough to the plaintiffs' suits. As to that issue, so what if (as *Walden* held) the place of a plaintiff's injury and residence cannot create a defendant's contact with the forum State? Those places still may be relevant in assessing the link between the defendant's forum contacts and the plaintiff's suit—including its assertions of who was injured where. And indeed, that relevance is a key part of Bristol-Myers' reasoning. See 582 U. S., at ——, 137 S.Ct., at 1782 (finding a lack of "connection" in part because the "plaintiffs are not California residents and do not claim to have suffered harm in that State"). One of Ford's own favorite cases thus refutes its appeal to the other.

· · ·

Here, resident-plaintiffs allege that they suffered in-state injury because of defective products that Ford extensively promoted, sold, and serviced in Montana and Minnesota. For all the reasons we have given, the connection between the plaintiffs' claims and Ford's activities in those States—or otherwise said, the "relationship among the defendant, the forum[s], and the litigation"—is close enough to support specific jurisdiction. *Walden*, 571 U.S., at 284, 134 S.Ct. 1115 (internal quotation marks omitted). The judgments of the Montana and Minnesota Supreme Courts are therefore affirmed.

It is so ordered.

JUSTICE BARRETT took no part in the consideration or decision of these cases.

JUSTICE ALITO, concurring in the judgment.

These cases can and should be decided without any alteration or refinement of our case law on specific personal jurisdiction. To be sure, for the reasons outlined in Justice Gorsuch's thoughtful opinion, there are grounds for questioning the standard that the Court adopted in *International Shoe Co. v. Washington*, 326 U.S. 310 (1945). And there are also reasons to wonder whether the case law we have developed since that time is well suited for the way in which business is now conducted. But there is nothing distinctively 21st century about the question in the cases now before us, and the answer to that question is settled by our case law . . . .

· · ·

To say that the Constitution does not require the kind of proof of causation that Ford would demand—what the majority describes as a "strict causal relationship" . . . is not to say that no causal link of any kind is needed. And here, there is a sufficient link. . . .

Recognizing "relate to" as an independent basis for specific jurisdiction risks needless complications. . . . To rein in this phrase, limits must be found, and the Court assures us that "relate to," as it now uses the concept, "incorporates real limits." But without any indication what those limits might be, I doubt that the lower courts will find that observation terribly helpful. Instead, what limits the potentially boundless reach of "relate to" is just the sort of rough causal connection I have described. . . .

JUSTICE GORSUCH, with whom JUSTICE THOMAS joins, concurring in the judgment.

[Justice Gorsuch's concurrence recounts the *International Shoe* framework and his view of its history, arguing that the majority's decision represents a deviation.]

Where this leaves us is far from clear. For a case to "relate to" the defendant's forum contacts, the majority says, it is enough if an "affiliation" or "relationship" or "connection" exists between them. Ante, at 1025, 1028, 1030. But what does this assortment of nouns mean? Loosed from any causation standard, we are left to guess. The majority promises that its new test "does not mean anything goes," but that hardly tells us what does. Ante, at 1026. In some cases, the new test may prove more forgiving than the old causation rule. But it's hard not to wonder whether it may also sometimes turn out to be more demanding. Unclear too is whether, in cases like that, the majority would treat causation and "affiliation" as alternative routes to specific jurisdiction, or whether it would deny jurisdiction outright.

. . .

Not only does the majority's new test risk adding new layers of confusion to our personal jurisdiction jurisprudence. The whole project seems unnecessary. Immediately after disavowing any need for a causal link between the defendant's forum activities and the plaintiffs' injuries, the majority proceeds to admit that such a link may be present here. Ante, at 1029. The majority stresses that the Montana and Minnesota plaintiffs before us "might" have purchased their cars because of Ford's activities in their home States. They "may" have relied on Ford's local advertising. And they "may" have depended on Ford's promise to furnish in-state servicers and dealers. If the majority is right about these things, that would be more than enough to establish a but-for causal link between Ford's in-state activities and the plaintiffs' decisions to purchase their allegedly defective vehicles. Nor should that result come as a surprise: One might expect such causal links to be easy to prove in suits against corporate behemoths like Ford. All the new euphemisms — "affiliation," "relationship," "connection" — thus seem pretty pointless.

. . .

With the old *International Shoe* dichotomy looking increasingly uncertain, it's hard not to ask how we got here and where we might be headed.

NOTES AND QUESTIONS

1. *Defining "Related."* In *Ford*, the Supreme Court attempted to answer one of the last major questions about specific jurisdiction under the *International Shoe* framework: What kind of connection must there be between the defendant's contacts in the forum and the plaintiff's claim? How tight must this connection be for the contacts to be considered "related to the claim" and therefore grounds for specific jurisdiction? Do not make Justice Alito's mistake in *Bristol-Myers Squibb* and confuse the nexus requirement with the requirement of purposeful conduct directed to the forum. In *Ford*, the defendant conceded that it has purposefully directed its conduct to the forum state. Ford challenged only whether its sales of vehicles that did not cause the accident, and associated activity like advertising, were sufficiently "related" to the plaintiff's claim to satisfy the "arising out of or related to" (nexus) requirement of the minimum contacts test for specific jurisdiction.

2. *Variations on* Ford. Consider three types of cases:

a. Defendant sells a defective car to plaintiff in the state where the car then injures plaintiff. Plaintiff sues for damages for the injuries. These are easy cases for specific jurisdiction as both the sale of the car that caused the injury and the plaintiff's injury are in the forum. What if only the injury were in the forum? That would likely satisfy the nexus requirement (though the separate requirement of purposeful availment might not be satisfied). What if only the sale that led to the injury were in the forum and the injury itself was elsewhere? Neither *Ford* nor *Bristol-Myers Squibb* answers that question. What if defendant had sold similar products in the forum, but the particular sale that caused the injury was not in the forum state? *Bristol-Myers Squibb* seems to say that the nexus requirement would not be satisfied.

b. Defendant mails a brochure to Pennsylvania advertising its Barbados resort, plaintiff books the vacation while in Pennsylvania, then is injured while receiving a negligent massage at the Barbados resort—plaintiff sues in Pennsylvania for the injuries suffered. Are defendant's contacts in the forum sufficiently "related" even though plaintiff's claim does not "arise" from them? In other words, plaintiff would not have been injured but for defendant's conduct in the forum state, but that conduct alone would not be enough the generate a claim. *Compare O'Connor v. Sandy Lane Hotel Co.*, 496 F.3d 312 (3d Cir. 2007) (upholding Pennsylvania jurisdiction over Barbados hotel for negligent massage in Barbados because defendant promoted massage service in brochure mailed to plaintiff's Pennsylvania home) *with Licci v. Lebanese Canadian Bank, SAL*, 732 F.3d 161 (2d Cir. 2013) (suggesting that at least one element of claim against defendant must arise out of defendant's forum conduct). Recall that the lower courts have used different approaches to connecting defendant's conduct to the claim, before and after the Supreme Court's intervention in *Bristol-Myers Squibb*, pp. 187–193.

c. Defendant sells defective cars throughout the country, but did not sell the particular car that caused plaintiff's injury in Montana. Plaintiff sues in Montana for the injuries suffered there. (Note that *World-Wide Volkswagen* does not bar this claim due to the lack of purposeful conduct directed to the forum state—the defendant purposefully sells cars in Montana.) The defendant's argument is that its contacts in the forum—sales of other people's cars—are not sufficiently "related" to satisfy the first prong of the specific jurisdiction inquiry.

This third variation is *Ford*. Ford's lawyers attempted to extend *Bristol-Myers Squibb* into an argument that defendant's contacts in the forum *must* cause plaintiff's injuries. Recall that in *Bristol-Myers Squibb*, plaintiffs had purchased, taken, and allegedly been injured by Plavix in many states other than California. Those plaintiffs sought to bring suit in California, along with California plaintiffs whom Plavix had injured in the forum state. But for the non-California plaintiffs, defendant's conduct in California did not in any way *cause* plaintiffs' injuries. Bristol-Myers just sold a lot of the same drug in California to other people. The Court in *Bristol-Myers Squibb* held that there was no specific jurisdiction in California because "[w]hat is needed — and what is missing here — is a connection between the forum and the specific claims at issue." 137 S. Ct. 1773, 1781. In other words, the defendant's contacts in California were "parallel" to the out-of-state plaintiffs' claims, but not "related."

The Supreme Court in *Ford* unanimously rejected this "causation-only" argument and distinguished *Ford* on the basis that the plaintiffs were actually injured in the forum state. (Arguably, the injury in the forum is the most important fact in *Ford*.) Although Ford did not sell the particular car that injured plaintiffs in the forum state, Ford did sell and advertise the same model of car in the forum. In her majority opinion, Justice Kagan noted: "Ford had systematically served a market in Montana and Minnesota for the very vehicles that the plaintiffs allege malfunctioned and injured them in those States. So there is a strong 'relationship among the defendant, the forum, and the litigation' — the 'essential foundation' of specific jurisdiction." 141 S. Ct. at 1028 (quoting *Helicopteros*, 466 U.S., at 414). Justice Kagan then muddled this point somewhat by suggesting that there was *some* causal connection: "For the owners of these cars might never have bought them, and so these suits might never have arisen, except for Ford's contacts with their home States." 141 S. Ct. at 1029.

3. *Open Questions After* Ford. Consider: What if Ford had only sold F-150 trucks in Montana and Minnesota? Related enough? What if Ford only sold F-150 baseball caps in Montana and Minnesota?

4. *Whither "Reasonableness"?* You will recall that Justice O'Connor in *Asahi* introduced the "reasonableness" factors as a third part of the specific jurisdiction analysis. The Court's decision in *Ford* is the first since then in which the Court found that jurisdiction existed over an out-of-state defendant. The Court noted that Ford conceded the first prong of the "minimum contacts" analysis: that it had purposefully directed its conduct to the forum state. The Court then held that Ford's conduct in the forum, the sale of vehicles identical to those that caused the injuries, was sufficiently related to the plaintiffs' claims. And then the Court simply did not consider whether the *Asahi* "reasonableness" factors were satisfied. The "reasonableness" factors were not mentioned. The majority in *Bristol-Myers Squibb* also failed to mention reasonableness, though perhaps because they did not need to reach it after deciding the case on the nexus requirement.

Lower courts continue to use the "reasonableness" factors, although "the reasonableness inquiry essentially leads to dismissal only when there is a foreign defendant." Linda J. Silberman & Nathan D. Yaffe, *The Transnational Case in Conflict of Laws: Two Suggestions for the New Restatement Third of Conflict of Laws-Judicial Jurisdiction over Foreign Defendants and Party Autonomy in International Contracts*, 27 Duke

J. Comp. & Int'l L. 405, 415 (2017). Even then "courts do not dismiss on reasonableness grounds where the case involves a personal injury claim against a foreign manufacturer whose products injure U.S. consumers or employees and minimum contacts are found." *Id.*

As for general jurisdiction, you may recall that in *Daimler*, Justice Sotomayor concurred in the judgment that California could not constitutionally exercise jurisdiction over Daimler AG, but her reasoning was quite different. Analogizing to *Asahi*, she would have decided the case on the ground that the exercise of jurisdiction in this case would be "unreasonable," given that the case involves foreign plaintiffs suing a foreign defendant based on foreign conduct, and a more appropriate forum is available. One might have thought that Justice Ginsburg's concerns about the transnational context of the case and sensitivity to international comity would have led her to be sympathetic to a "reasonableness" inquiry—the approach developed in *Asahi*, precisely to take account of the procedural and substantive policies of other nations whose interests might be affected by the assertion of jurisdiction.

Taken together, do these developments indicate that "reasonableness" is fading away as a separate inquiry? And is the Court needlessly obsessing over extreme cases like *Nicastro*'s Appalachian potter or *Ford*'s Maine decoy maker that could be better handled by application of the "reasonableness" factors? Is it possible to set out jurisdictional rules, rather than standards, that will deal with every extreme case?

D.   THE SPECIALIZED PROBLEM OF NATIONWIDE JURISDICTION

Would you expect the jurisdictional reach of a federal court to extend nationwide rather than be circumscribed by the boundaries of a particular state? The Due Process Clause of the Fifth Amendment (which relates to actions of the federal government) would appear to be the relevant constitutional limitation on the territorial jurisdiction of the federal courts. The sovereign that established the federal courts is the United States, and if sovereignty is the relevant focus, Due Process should be assessed by examining the defendant's contacts with the United States as a whole rather than with one particular state. This theory, under which jurisdiction is "based on an aggregation of the defendant's contacts with the Nation as a whole," is referred to as the "aggregate contacts" or "national contacts" theory.

Apart from constitutional considerations, the jurisdictional reach of the federal courts is a matter for Congress and/or the Rulemakers in the first instance. *See Omni Capital Int'l v. Rudolf Wolff & Co.*, 484 U.S. 97 (1987) (federal courts must have explicit authorization in a statute or a federal rule in order to effect service beyond state lines). As we have seen from the federal cases on personal jurisdiction, the Federal Rules provide that the federal courts are to use the jurisdictional statutes of the state in which they sit. *See* Fed. R. Civ. P. 4(k)(1)(A). That provision encompasses both diversity of citizenship cases and federal question cases, and in those situations, the constitutionality of the assertion of jurisdiction by a federal court is subject to the same Fourteenth Amendment Due Process standard that measures the jurisdiction of the state courts.

The Federal Rules also provide for the exercise of nationwide jurisdiction by the federal courts when so authorized by Congress. Federal Rule 4(k)(1)(C) provides that "[s]erving a summons or filing a waiver of service establishes personal jurisdiction over a defendant" when authorized by a federal statute. But Congress has authorized such nationwide service in only a limited number of contexts, usually as part of a federal statutory scheme creating a federal cause of action. For example, the Clayton Act provides that in a suit under the antitrust laws against a corporation, process may be served "in the district of which it is an inhabitant, or wherever it may be found." 15 U.S.C. §22. Both the Securities Act (15 U.S.C. §77v) and the Securities Exchange Act (15 U.S.C. §78aa) provide for service on a defendant "in any district of which the defendant is an inhabitant or wherever the defendant may be found." Most of the statutes that authorize nationwide and even worldwide service of process contain specialized venue provisions that provide for the action to be brought in a district with which the defendant does have certain contacts. For example, suits against corporate defendants under the Clayton Act are to be brought in a district where the defendant resides or is found or transacts business (15 U.S.C. §22); the Securities Act provides for venue in the district where the defendant is found, is an inhabitant, transacts business, or where the offer or sale took place (15 U.S.C. §77v); and the Securities Exchange Act provides for venue in the district where defendant is found or is an inhabitant or transacts business (15 U.S.C. §78aa). As a result, it is only in the rare case that the defendant will not have contacts with the particular forum state, but there are such instances.*

There are only a few examples of federal statutes providing for nationwide jurisdiction when the claims are based on *state* law. One is 28 U.S.C. §2361, authorizing nationwide service for claims brought under the federal interpleader statute. *See* 28 U.S.C. §1335. Service on (and accordingly jurisdiction over) potential claimants to the interpleader fund can be made wherever the "claimants reside or may be found." Venue is proper in the judicial district "in which one or more of the claimants reside." *See* 28 U.S.C. §1397. Interpleader is discussed more extensively in Chapter 8 at pp. 981–984. A second example is the Multiparty, Multiforum Trial Jurisdiction Act, 28 U.S.C. §1369, discussed more extensively in Chapter 8 at pp. 1048–1049. This Act provides for a federal forum based on minimal diversity of citizenship whenever a civil action arises from a mass accident involving at least 75 deaths. The Act also authorizes worldwide service and nationwide jurisdiction in such cases. *See* 28 U.S.C. §1697. Venue in such an action

---

* It should be noted that most nationwide service of process statutes contain specialized venue provisions that provide for the action to be brought in a district with which the defendant has certain kinds of contacts. However, since many courts hold that venue in cases brought under these statutes may also be laid pursuant to the general venue statute, 28 U.S.C. §1391, this could include the option of suing a corporation or other entity wherever it is subject to personal jurisdiction, under §1391(c)(2), or suing a "defendant not resident in the United States" in any district under §1391(c)(3). Thus, the nationwide service of process statutes, combined with expansive venue provisions, continue to raise Due Process fairness problems. *See* Jon Heller, Note, *Pendent Personal Jurisdiction and Nationwide Service of Process*, 64 N.Y.U. L. Rev. 113, 120–122 (1989).

is proper "in any district in which any defendant resides or in which a substantial part of the accident giving rise to the action took place." 28 U.S.C. §1391(g). Does a provision for worldwide jurisdiction such as this present constitutional problems? If the defendant is from the United States, there is necessarily a constitutional connection between the defendant and the United States as a whole. But what about with respect to a foreign country defendant? If a foreign defendant is sued in the United States and venue is proper only because another defendant resides there, suit in such a forum may run afoul of generally accepted Due Process principles. And even if the foreign defendant is sued in a place where a substantial part of the accident took place, under *Asahi* such a connection does not necessarily establish the requisite contacts.

Since 1993, there is also a provision for nationwide service and jurisdiction that confers on all federal district courts worldwide jurisdiction over defendants in cases arising under federal law when the defendant is not otherwise subject to jurisdiction in any state. *See* Fed. R. Civ. P. 4(k)(2). An example of how Federal Rule 4(k)(2) works is provided below. For an in-depth discussion of the constitutional limits of nationwide personal jurisdiction, as well as an argument that there is no constitutional barrier to Congress's ability to provide for nationwide jurisdiction over all types of claims, and suggestions as to how Congress might do so, *see* Jonathan Remy Nash, *National Personal Jurisdiction*, 68 Emory L.J. 511 (2019).

NOTE ON APPLICATION OF FEDERAL RULE 4(K)(2)

In *Touchcom, Inc. v. Bereskin & Parr*, 574 F.3d 1403 (Fed. Cir. 2009), a Canadian plaintiff, Peter Hollidge, brought a malpractice action against a Canadian law firm, Bereskin & Parr (B&P), and one of the firm's partners, H. Samuel Frost. Hollidge had retained B&P, and specifically Frost, to file and prosecute patent applications in Canada, the United States, and Europe in connection with one of his inventions. The defendants properly prepared and filed the Canadian patent application, but they failed to include the complete computer source code for the patent applications in Europe and the United States. As a result of the defendant's failure, when the plaintiff filed patent infringement actions in the United States in connection with his invention, the federal court in which he brought suit held that his patent was invalid for indefiniteness. The plaintiff subsequently brought his malpractice suit against the defendants in Virginia, where the United States Patent and Trademark Office (USPTO) is located, but the district court ruled that the requirements of Virginia's specific-act statute were not satisfied and dismissed the case for lack of personal jurisdiction. The Court of Appeals for the Federal Circuit agreed with the district court on this point. The court noted that the defendants' only contacts with Virginia were limited to communications in connection with the filing of a patent application with the USPTO and held that these did not constitute sufficient "minimum contacts" with the State of Virginia to subject the defendants to jurisdiction. But the court did not end its analysis there. After holding that the defendants were not subject to jurisdiction based on Virginia's specific-act statute, the court proceeded to analyze whether jurisdiction would be proper under Federal Rule 4(k)(2) and ultimately held that the very same contacts that were insufficient to establish jurisdiction in Virginia were, in fact, sufficient to establish specific jurisdiction based on nationwide contacts under Rule 4(k)(2). The court reasoned that the defendants had purposefully directed their activities at the United States "by availing themselves of the only agency authorized to issue [U.S.] patents" and that their submission of documents to the USPTO to perfect the U.S. patent application was sufficient to satisfy the "minimum contacts" test.

NOTES AND QUESTIONS

1. *The Aggregate Contacts Theory.* *Touchcom* offers an interesting illustration of a case where the court finds that although the defendant does not have sufficient contacts with a *single state* to satisfy Due Process, its contacts with the United States as a whole do meet the Due Process standard. In most cases, the defendant will have contacts in other states in addition to those in the forum state, and it is the aggregation of those contacts that satisfies Due Process. In *Touchcom*, however, the contacts with Virginia, which the court held were not sufficient minimum contacts with Virginia, are the same contacts that the court finds sufficient to satisfy the "aggregate contacts" test of Rule 4(k)(2). Is the court's explanation that these same Virginia contacts show that the defendants have purposefully directed their activities at the United States convincing? Note that jurisdiction would also be proper in any district court in the United States; venue would not limit the district because a defendant not resident in the United States can be sued in any district under 28 U.S.C. §1391(c)(3). Does this suggest a problem with the "aggregate contacts" theory of jurisdiction in its application to foreign defendants pursuant to Rule 4(k)(2)? For an argument that jurisdiction over an alien defendant should be evaluated with respect to the alien's contacts with the United States as a whole in both federal and state courts, *see* William S. Dodge & Scott Dodson, *Personal Jurisdiction and Aliens*, 116 Mich. L. Rev. 1205 (2018).

2. *A Role for Convenience?* Suppose plaintiff had brought suit against the defendants in Alaska. Under the aggregate contacts theory as explained by the court in *Touchcom*, there would be sufficient contacts between the defendant and the United States to support jurisdiction because the Due Process analysis under Rule 4(k)(2) "contemplates a defendant's contacts with the entire United States, as opposed to the state in which the district court sits." Should concerns about convenience to the defendant limit the reach of nationwide or worldwide process statutes? Justice Stewart, dissenting in *Stafford v. Briggs*, 444 U.S. 527 (1980), thought not. *Stafford* involved interpretation of 28 U.S.C. §1391(e), which permits nationwide process and jurisdiction in certain actions involving federal officers or employees. Venue was permitted at plaintiff's residence, a state with which defendants had no contacts. The majority opinion held the statute was inapplicable in a case in which monetary damages rather than equitable relief was sought. In dissent, after arguing that §1391(e) should apply to such suits, Justice Stewart went on to address the defendants' contention that Due Process was violated:

> The short answer to this argument is that due process requires only certain minimum contacts between the defendant and the sovereign that has created the court [citations omitted]. The issue is not whether it is unfair to require a defendant to assume the burden of litigating in an inconvenient forum, but rather whether the court as a particular sovereign has

power to exercise personal jurisdiction over a named defendant. The cases before us involve suits against residents of the United States in the courts of the United States. No due process problem exists.

444 U.S. at 554.

Do you agree? Wouldn't it be seriously inconvenient and burdensome for the defendants in *Touchcom* to have to litigate in Alaska? Shouldn't the constitutional Due Process inquiry include some consideration of fairness to the defendant even when nationwide or worldwide process is authorized? Some courts and commentators believe that it does. *See, e.g., DeJames v. Magnificent Carriers, Inc.,* 654 F.2d 280, 286 n.3 (3d Cir. 1981) (extreme inconvenience to defendant may violate Due Process even when significant contacts with the United States exist). *See also* Robert A. Lusardi, *Nationwide Service of Process: Due Process Limitations on the Power of the Sovereign,* 33 Vill. L. Rev. 1 (1988); Maryellen Fullerton, *Constitutional Limits on Nationwide Personal Jurisdiction in the Federal Courts,* 79 Nw. U. L. Rev. 1 (1984). Other commentators disagree. *See, e.g.,* A. Benjamin Spencer, *Jurisdiction to Adjudicate: A Revised Analysis,* 73 U. Chi. L. Rev. 617 (2006) (arguing that inconveniencing a defendant fails to implicate a constitutionally protected property interest, particularly given the ease of airplane travel and the widespread accessibility of communication mediums).

Of course, as pointed out earlier, venue provisions in many of the nationwide jurisdiction statutes operate to limit the district in which suit can be brought to one in which the defendant does have contacts. In situations where that might not be true, the federal provision for transfer, 28 U.S.C. §1404(a), may operate to prevent unfairness resulting from the reach of nationwide process. Section 1404 authorizes a federal court that has jurisdiction and venue to transfer an action to any other federal district court in which jurisdiction and venue would also be proper. Does the availability of transfer mean that concerns about serious inconvenience need not be part of a Due Process analysis?

3. *Elements of Rule 4(k)(2).* Note the various requirements of Rule 4(k)(2). A defendant may be served anywhere in the world and jurisdiction will be proper when (1) the case arises under federal law, (2) the defendant is not otherwise subject to jurisdiction in any state of the United States, and (3) the exercise of jurisdiction is consistent with constitutional Due Process standards.

The first requirement means that Rule 4(k)(2) does not apply in diversity cases. Thus, it would not affect the result of such cases as *Asahi* or *McIntyre,* even if such a suit were to be brought in federal court. In *Touchcom,* the court held that the plaintiff's malpractice action (which was based on Virginia law) arose under federal law because Virginia law required a plaintiff in a malpractice action to prove "but for" causation and, in this case, "such a showing would necessarily require an analysis of patent validity." Note that under the Supreme Court's later decision in *Gunn v. Minton,* 133 S.Ct. 1059 (2013), it would have been unlikely that Hollidge's claim would arise under federal law. See Chapter 3, pp. 334–335. For an in-depth discussion of these limitations and a proposal that Rule 4(k)(2) be extended to cover diversity and alienage cases in addition to federal question claims, *see* Patrick J. Borchers, *Extending Federal Rule of Civil Procedure 4(k)(2): A Way to (Partially) Clean Up the Personal Jurisdiction Mess,* 67 Am. U. L. Rev. 413 (2017).

Can a plaintiff assert a speculative federal claim to take advantage of Rule 4(k)(2)? Courts have split on whether Rule 4(k)(2) requires a merits inquiry to determine whether a complaint actually states a viable (or sufficiently important) federal claim before deciding whether 4(k)(2) aggregation is available under the "arises under federal law" standard. *See, e.g., Jahner v. Kumho Tire U.S.A., Inc.*, No. CIV. 18-5036-JLV, 2020 WL 4932832, at *15 (D.S.D. Aug. 24, 2020) ("Because a state forum is always available for [a federal] claim, the court does not agree with those courts which have declined to engage in a merits analysis to determine if a claim arises under federal law for Rule 4(k)(2) purposes.").

The effect of the second requirement is that the rule applies only to foreign country defendants. Note, however, the awkward position in which the respective parties find themselves in arguing about the application of Rule 4(k)(2). To take advantage of the rule, either the plaintiff must show that the defendant is *not* subject to personal jurisdiction in any state, or the defendant, in order to defeat jurisdiction in the forum, must show that it *is* subject to jurisdiction in some other state of the United States. Who has the burden to make the required showing, and how is the unavailability of another forum to be proved? Must a plaintiff introduce evidence that defendant lacks sufficient contacts to sustain jurisdiction in each of the 50 states? Or must a defendant concede that it is subject to jurisdiction in a particular state? The court in *Touchcom* surveyed the different approaches taken by the various Courts of Appeals in determining whether the second requirement of Rule 4(k)(2) is met. The First Circuit placed the burden on the plaintiff, whereas the Fifth, Seventh, Ninth, Eleventh, and D.C. Circuits placed the burden on the defendant. The Federal Circuit in *Touchcom* also placed the burden on the defendant, noting that the purpose behind the Rule was to prevent a foreign defendant from escaping U.S. jurisdiction simply because of a lack of sufficient contacts with any one particular state. The court found that that purpose is best achieved by placing the burden on the defendant because "[i]t is difficult to prove a negative."

4. *Rule 4(k)(2) and Terrorism.* Rule 4(k)(2) has proved increasingly significant in cases based on federal statutes providing for jurisdiction over defendants alleged to commit international terrorist acts. Because few international terrorist groups, or terrorists themselves, have enough discernible contacts with a particular state to confer either specific or general jurisdiction, victims and their families looked to federal law and jurisdiction pursuant to Rule 4(k)(2), where it is contacts with the United States as a whole that can be used to satisfy Due Process. Although several Courts of Appeals have held that foreign states are not entitled to Due Process protection because they are not "persons" within the meaning of the Due Process Clause,* both the Palestine Liberation Organization (PLO) and the Palestinian Authority (PA) have been found to have Due Process protection since they are not formal states.

There is an initial question, of course, as to whether entities such as the PLO or the PA are subject to the *Daimler* rule since they are not corporations. If they are, even under Rule 4(k)(2) which permits the aggregation of national contacts, *general* jurisdiction will be difficult to establish. An illustration is *Waldman v. Palestine*

---

* *See Frontera Res. Azer. Corp. v. State Oil Co. of Azer*, 582 F.3d 393 (2d Cir. 2009); *Price v. Socialist People's Libyan Arab Jamahiriya*, 294 F.3d 82 (D.C. Cir. 2002).

Liberation Org., 835 F.3d 317 (2d Cir. 2016), where 11 American families sued the Palestinian Authority and the Palestine Liberation Organization under the federal Anti-Terrorism Act ("ATA"), 18 U.S.C. §2333(a) for their involvement in a series of terrorist attacks in the West Bank that killed or injured U.S. citizens among others. (Under the ATA, a U.S. national or the estate, survivors, or heirs may sue for injuries and recover three-fold damages by reason of an act of international terrorism.) The district court had found that general jurisdiction could be asserted over both the PA and the PLO because their contacts elsewhere were "insufficient to conclude that either defendant is 'at home' in a particular jurisdiction other than the United States." The Court of Appeals for the Second Circuit reversed, holding that the *Daimler* rule was applicable to the PA and the PLO, and that even applying the aggregate contacts standard of the Fifth Amendment under the ATA, neither could be considered "at home" in the United States. The court found that the evidence demonstrated that the defendants were "at home" in Palestine where the entities were headquartered and from where they were directed. For an argument that *Daimler* should not apply to cases against the PA and PLO because the Supreme Court referred only to corporations, *see* Ariel Winawer, Comment, *Too Far From Home: Why Daimler's "At Home" Standard Does Not Apply to Personal Jurisdiction Challenges in Anti-Terrorism Act Cases*, 66 Emory L.J. 161 (2016).

The assertion of *specific* jurisdiction in terrorist cases like *Waldman* will also be difficult in the face of *Walden v. Fiore*, 134 S.Ct. 1115 (2014), as discussed earlier at pp. 163–164. Prior to *Walden*, several district courts had upheld jurisdiction over terrorist groups under the ATA for attacks in foreign countries that injured Americans on the ground that it was foreseeable that terrorist acts (such as an attack in Israel or a detonation of a bomb on a French airline) would injure U.S. citizens. *See, e.g., Sisso v. Islamic Republic of Iran*, 448 F. Supp. 2d 76, 86–90 (D.D.C. 2006); *Pugh v. Socialist People's Libyan Arab Jamahiriya*, 290 F. Supp. 2d 54 (D.D.C. 2003). However, post-*Walden*, in *Waldman*, the Court of Appeals for the Second Circuit rejected arguments by plaintiff that specific jurisdiction was appropriate because a U.S. citizen was killed in Israel, which constituted a foreseeable effect in the United States. The Court found that the bombings and shootings occurred entirely outside the United States and there was no purposeful connection to the forum. Moreover, the defendant's mere knowledge that a plaintiff resides in the United States would be insufficient to satisfy specific jurisdiction.

4. *Federal Consent Jurisdiction.* The Supreme Court denied certiorari in *Waldman* (by then recaptioned as *Sokolow v. Palestine Liberation Org.*). *See Waldman v. Palestine Liberation Org.*, 835 F.3d 317 (2d Cir. 2016), *cert. denied sub nom. Sokolow v. Palestine Liberation Org.*, 138 S. Ct. 1438 (2018). Congress passed the Anti-terrorism Clarification Act in direct response, followed by several amendments in the Promoting Security and Justice for Victims of Terrorism Act. These statutes provide that a defendant "shall be deemed to have consented to personal jurisdiction" in an action under the Anti-terrorism Act if that defendant has made a payment, anywhere in the world, to a person convicted of an act of terrorism against a U.S. national or that person's family on account of their death. 18 U.S.C. §2334. Does this strain the definition of consent beyond its breaking point? Is this compatible with the Court's vision of limited all-purpose jurisdiction in *Daimler*? Recall that, as discussed at pp. 163–164, many states have attempted to fill the void left by *Daimler*

with consent statutes for corporations. Is this sort of aggressive jurisdictional legislation more acceptable when it comes from the federal government?

In addition, these terrorism statutes seem only apply to a limited class of defendants, covering only the Palestinian Authority, the Palestine Liberation Organization, or any entity that claims to carry out their functions. Does it trouble you that a jurisdictional statute targets only two (or a handful) of entities?

5. *Two Different Due Processes.* In *Omni Capital Int'l v. Rudolf Wolff & Co.*, 484 U.S. 97 (1987), the Supreme Court indicated that federal courts applying federal law could assert broader jurisdiction than their state court counterparts because they were constrained by a different amendment to the Constitution: the Fifth Amendment constrains the federal government, whereas the Fourteenth Amendment applies to the states. Thus, federal courts, if authorized by Congress, could aggregate national contacts, whereas state courts could not (regardless of state statutory authorization). If that were not true, Rule 4(k)(2) could not operate.

Is aggregation of national contacts the only difference between the dictates of the Fifth and the Fourteenth Amendments? Many courts have assumed that they are the same, but only two federal appellate courts have directly considered the issue. *Compare Livnat v. Palestinian Auth.*, 851 F.3d 45, 55 (D.C. Cir. 2017) ("The only difference in the personal-jurisdiction analysis under the two Amendments is the scope of relevant contacts: Under the Fourteenth Amendment, which defines the reach of state courts, the relevant contacts are state-specific. Under the Fifth Amendment, which defines the reach of federal courts, contacts with the United States as a whole are relevant.") *with Douglass v. Nippon Yusen Kabushiki Kaisha*, 996 F.3d 289, 296 (5th Cir.) ("[T]he bounds of Fifth Amendment due process are likely not wholly defined by modern Fourteenth Amendment caselaw."), *reh'g en banc granted, opinion vacated sub nom. Douglass v. Kaisha*, 2 F.4th 525 (5th Cir. 2021).

Every Supreme Court case you have read so far in this chapter applied the Fourteenth Amendment. You may recall that the concurrences from *Ford* expressed deep dissatisfaction with the current state of personal jurisdiction jurisprudence. Could the difference between the Fifth and Fourteenth Amendments be a way to change course, for federal courts at least, without overturning prior case law?

E.   COMPARATIVE JURISDICTION REGIMES

1.   The European Regulation on Jurisdiction and the Recognition and Enforcement of Judgments

Justice Scalia goes to great lengths in *Burnham* to demonstrate the wide acceptance and deep historical roots of "tag" jurisdiction in the United States, but he does not consider how such jurisdiction is regarded elsewhere in the world. Often, one can learn much about one's own judicial system by comparison with other systems; thus, jurisdictional regimes in other countries are likely to offer insights into our own. To this end, we examine one particular model — the European Regulation on Jurisdiction and the Recognition and Enforcement of Judgments in Civil and Commercial Matters, commonly referred to as the "Brussels I" or "European"

Regulation. The latest version of the Regulation, known as the Recast—Regulation (EU) No. 1215/2012—took effect in January, 2015.

The earlier Regulation, which came into effect on March 1, 2002, replaced the former "European" or "Brussels" Convention on Jurisdiction and the Recognition and Enforcement of Judgments, which was a treaty on jurisdiction and enforcement of judgments entered into in 1968 by the original Common Market Countries. That treaty provided for "Convention" rules on jurisdiction among the Member States in any case in which a defendant was domiciled in a Member State, and the Convention replaced national rules of jurisdiction in such cases. With respect to judgments, the Convention (and now the Regulation)—in the manner of the United States' Full Faith and Credit Clause—also required enforcement of Member State judgments. In 1971, a separate Protocol conferred authority upon the European Court of Justice to provide rulings on questions that arose under the Convention, thereby creating a supranational tribunal to resolve issues of interpretation arising under the Convention. As the European Community expanded and countries acceded to the Convention, various modifications were made. In 1988, a parallel convention—the Lugano Convention—adopted the jurisdiction and enforcement provisions of the Brussels Convention for the Member States of the larger European Free Trade Association but without review by the European Court of Justice. Effective March 2002, the Convention was replaced by EU Regulation 44/2001, which altered a number of provisions in the original Convention. The use of a "regulation" rather than a revision of the Convention made the provisions directly effective in Member States without the need for ratification by Member States' parliaments.

The structure of the Recast is the same as its predecessor Brussels I Convention and the prior Regulation. It provides rules for jurisdiction that must be adhered to by the Member States in cases to which the Convention is applicable and also for the recognition and enforcement of judgments by Member States. The jurisdictional provisions—which are the focus of our attention—fall into two basic categories: jurisdiction that is required and jurisdiction that is prohibited. Although only jurisdiction expressly conferred by the Recast is permitted (and all other exercises of jurisdiction are prohibited), the Recast also calls particular attention to rules of exorbitant jurisdiction in certain Member States. *See* Art. 5(2).

One important goal of the Recast (and of the predecessor Convention and prior Regulation) was to limit the number of possible fora in any given case. Consider first these "required" bases of jurisdiction. Do they achieve this objective?

Excerpts from the EU Recast:

a. General Provisions

Article 4

1. Subject to this Regulation, persons domiciled in a Member State shall, whatever their nationality, be sued in the courts of that Member State.

2. Persons who are not nationals of the Member State in which they are domiciled shall be governed by the rules of jurisdiction applicable to nationals of that State.

b.   Special Jurisdiction

Article 7

A person domiciled in a Member State may be sued in another Member State:

> **1. (a)** in matters relating to a contract, in the courts for the place of performance of the obligation in question;
> **(b)** for the purpose of this provision and unless otherwise agreed, the place of performance of the obligation in question shall be:
> — in the case of the sale of goods, the place in a Member State where, under the contract, the goods were delivered or should have been delivered,
> — in the case of the provision of services, the place in a Member State where, under the contract, the services were provided or should have been provided;
> **(c)** if point (b) does not apply then point (a) applies;
> **2.** in matters relating to tort, delict or quasi-delict, in the courts for the place where the harmful event occurred or may occur;
> **3.** as regards a civil claim for damages or restitution which is based on an act giving rise to criminal proceedings, in the court seised of those proceedings, to the extent that that court has jurisdiction under its own law to entertain civil proceedings; [. . .]
> **5.** as regards a dispute arising out of the operations of a branch, agency or other establishment, in the courts for the place in which the branch, agency or other establishment is situated; [. . .]

Article 8

A person domiciled in a Member State may also be sued:

> **1.** where he is one of a number of defendants, in the courts for the place where any one of them is domiciled, provided the claims are so closely connected that it is expedient to hear and determine them together to avoid the risk of irreconcilable judgments resulting from separate proceedings;
> **2.** as a third party in an action on a warranty or guarantee or in any other third-party proceedings, in the court seised of the original proceedings, unless these were instituted solely with the object of removing him from the jurisdiction of the court which would be competent in his case; [. . .]

· · ·

Let us first consider the provisions of Articles 7 and 8, which are delineated as "special jurisdiction" in the Recast and which resemble U.S. specific-act statutes in certain respects. Contract claims under the Recast can be brought "in the courts for the place of performance of the obligation in question." (Art. 7(1)(a).) Note that the Recast also defines the "place of performance" for contracts involving the sale of goods and contracts for services. (Art. 7(1)(b).) Is such a rule preferable to the generic provision that appears in many U.S. state specific-act statutes authorizing jurisdiction over claims "arising out of the transaction of any business"?

For tort claims, the Recast provides for jurisdiction in the courts "for the place where the harmful event occurred or may occur." (Art. 7(2).) Interpretation of that provision raised a question similar to the one presented in the United States by *Gray v. American Radiator* as to whether the harmful event occurred where the defendant acted or where the injury was suffered. In *Bier v. Mines de Potasse d'Alsace S.A.*, [1976] ECR 1735 (1977), Dutch plaintiffs were injured in the Netherlands by the dumping of chemicals into tributaries of the Rhine in France by French defendants. The European Court of Justice held, as the Illinois Supreme Court did in *Gray*, that jurisdiction was authorized under the "harmful event" provision either where the harmful act occurred (France) or at the place of injury (the Netherlands).

A more nuanced rule was announced in libel cases, where the European Court of Justice ruled that although suit was proper in a Member State where the libelous publication was distributed, jurisdiction was limited to recovery of the harm suffered in that state; full damages could be recovered only if the lawsuit were brought in the place where the publisher was located. *See Shevill v. Press Alliance*, [1995] ECR I-415. How does the approach of the European Court in *Shevill* compare with that of the Supreme Court of the United States in *Calder v. Jones*, 465 U.S. 783 (1984) and *Keeton v. Hustler Magazine, Inc.*, 465 U.S. 770 (1984)? What are the respective advantages and disadvantages of the *Shevill* rule?

EU Developments: Application of Shevill *to the Internet.* The *Shevill* rule means that a plaintiff who sues for harm caused by an alleged defamatory statement can only sue for the specific harm suffered in the Member State even when she sues in the court of the Member State where she is a habitual resident. Under the Convention, and now the Regulation and Recast, special (i.e., specific) jurisdiction is appropriate in the court of any Member State in which the material is distributed, including that of the plaintiff's habitual residence, but only with respect to the harm occurring in the particular State in question. The full amount of damage can be recovered only if the lawsuit is brought in the courts of the Member State where the publisher is said to be established (its place of incorporation, statutory seat, or principal place of business).

However, the EU Court of Justice in a subsequent decision announced a slightly different rule in the context of online defamation. In *eDate Advertising and Others*, [2011]C-509/09 and C-161/10, the Court of Justice held that in the event of an infringement of personality rights that takes place online on a website, the person harmed has the option of bringing a suit for damages for all the harm caused in the courts of the Member State in which the "centre of his interests" is based as well as in the courts of the Member State where the publisher is established. For a natural person, the "centre of interests" will usually be the Member State of the person's habitual residence. Moreover, in an even more recent case, *Bolagsupplysningen OU v. Svensk Handel AB*, [2017] C-194/16, the Court modified the rule yet again for a corporate plaintiff that brought suit to rectify incorrect information on the defendant's website and to collect damages for the harm caused. The Court held that the "centre of interests" of the Estonian corporate plaintiff was not Estonia, its place of registration, but rather Sweden, the place where its commercial reputation was firmly established, where it carried out the main part of its economic activities, and where the site that featured the incorrect information was operated. With respect to the injunctive relief that was requested, the Court of Justice held that the "multiple courts" approach in *Shevill* and *eDate* permitting recovery for "partial harm" could not be extended to a claim for removal or rectification. Because information and content placed online is of a "ubiquitous nature," only a single and indivisible application for such relief can be made and thus must be brought before a court which can rule on the entirety of the action (i.e., a court in the Member State which is the "centre of interest of the plaintiff" or a court in the Member State where the publisher is established.

How would you expect cases such as *World-Wide Volkswagen Corp. v. Woodson*, 444 U.S. 286 (1980), *Asahi Metal Indus. Co. v. Superior Court of California*, 480 U.S. 102 (1987), and *J. McIntyre Machinery, Ltd. v. Nicastro*, 564 U.S. 873 (2011), to be decided if the relevant countries were members of the European Union and the provisions of the Recast were applicable? Would you be surprised to find that the rules of jurisdiction under the Recast are often more expansive than rules of jurisdiction in the United States in these contexts? Recall that Justice Ginsburg, in her dissent in *McIntyre*, called attention to the Recast and observed that United States plaintiffs are at a disadvantage in comparison to EU plaintiffs who seek to acquire jurisdiction over foreign defendants who cause an injury in their forum state.

Can you identify other areas where jurisdiction over foreign defendants under the Recast seems broader than would be the case under the U.S. jurisdictional rules that you have learned? Note that Article 8(1), which provides for jurisdiction over a defendant in a multidefendant case in a state in which any one of the defendants is domiciled, provided the claims are so closely connected that it is expedient to determine them together to avoid the risk of irreconcilable judgments; and Article 8(2), which authorizes jurisdiction over a third-party defendant brought into the litigation, unless the third-party proceedings were initiated solely to remove the third-party defendant from the otherwise competent court. Would you favor a similar rule in the United States? Would such a rule be constitutional?

In other provisions of the Recast (not excerpted here), there are several specialized rules of jurisdiction dealing with consumers and insureds. For example, under Article 18, a consumer may bring proceedings against another party either in the courts of the Member State in which that party is domiciled or, *regardless of the domicile of the other party*, in the courts for the place where the consumer is domiciled. Note that this provision is an exception to the rule that the Recast extends only to defendants domiciled in a Member State. Thus, in this situation, jurisdiction at the domicile of the plaintiff may be the relevant criterion for the exercise of jurisdiction over the defendant, including a non-EU defendant.* Does such a rule seem appropriate? Would it be constitutional under U.S. Due Process standards?

Why do you think that certain jurisdictional rules in the United States have been somewhat more restrictive than the provisions in the European Regulation? Recall that in the United States, the constitutional standard of Due Process requires that there be a nexus between the individual defendant and the forum state. Under the Brussels Convention and the subsequent Regulation and the Recast,

---

* Article 17 identifies such a contract as (a) a contract for the sale of goods on installment credit terms; (b) a contract for a loan repayable by instalments, or for any form of credit, made to finance the sale of goods; or (c) a contract concluded with a person who pursues commercial or professional activities in the Member State of the consumer's domicile or, by any means, directs such activities to that Member State or to several States, including that Member State, and the contract falls within the scope of such activities.

jurisdictional rules were designed to ensure that there is a relationship between the controversy and the forum but not necessarily with the particular defendant. Thus, the European rules are not encumbered with particular concerns for an individual defendant or a constitutional overlay of "minimum contacts" and "reasonableness" as in American jurisprudence. As a result, the Recast is able to satisfy its preference for formal rules rather than less predictable standards.

The above discussion has been directed to categories of jurisdiction similar to U.S. "specific jurisdiction." With respect to "general jurisdiction," Article 4 of the Regulation provides for jurisdiction over a defendant in the state of domicile of the defendant. The domicile of an entity other than an individual is defined (in Article 63) as the place where it has its statutory seat or central administration or principal place of business. In addition, Article 25 authorizes jurisdiction based on the agreement of the parties, and Article 26 confers jurisdiction on the court of any Member State "before which a defendant enters an appearance."

How do the bases of "general" jurisdiction in the Recast compare to those authorized under United States law? Note that under the Recast, general jurisdiction over a defendant corporation is limited to suit at its domicile, defined as its statutory seat, central administration, or principal place of business. Until *Goodyear* and *Daimler*, general jurisdiction is the U.S. was not so limited and could be asserted on the basis of defendant's systematic and continuous activity in the forum state, even when the claim is unrelated to those activities. However, the Supreme Court decisions in *Goodyear* and *Daimler* now limit general jurisdiction over a corporation to suit at the defendant's "home." Recall that in *Daimler* Justice Ginsburg referenced the EU Recast, though she referred only to the defendant's place of incorporation and principal place of business as the paradigm examples of "home."

As noted previously, neither the Recast nor the national rules of Member States of the European Union generally impose the kind of constitutional limitations found in the United States law of jurisdiction. However, Article 5(1) states that only assertions of jurisdiction provided for in the Regulation are permitted by courts of Member States in cases against domiciliaries of Member States; in addition, Article 5(2) refers to rules of national jurisdiction of which Member States must notify the Commission and shall not be applied to domiciliaries of Member States. The reference is to "exorbitant" bases of jurisdiction previously set out in the Convention and prior Regulation and include: service on the defendant during his temporary presence in the country, the presence of property belonging to the defendant, and nationality of the plaintiff. Should the fact that "tag" jurisdiction was considered "exorbitant" in the EU system have been relevant to the Supreme Court of the United States in deciding *Burnham*? If the defendant in *Burnham* had been foreign, might the characterization of such jurisdiction as "exorbitant" have been invoked as representing an evolving international norm?

2.   *Initiatives and Harmonization*

The United States has ratified no international treaty on jurisdiction or recognition of judgments with any other country. From 1993 until 2001, the Hague Conference on Private International Law attempted to negotiate a worldwide Convention on Jurisdiction and the Recognition and Enforcement of Foreign Judgments. The objective was a broad international treaty, modeled in part on the original Brussels Convention and the later Regulations discussed above, which would provide for both the regulation of judicial jurisdiction and the enforcement/recognition of judgments. The attempt fell short, in large part because cultural and legal traditions in the wide range of participating countries made it difficult to arrive at any consensus about appropriate bases of jurisdiction — whether "required," "permitted," or "prohibited." Disputes over which direct assertions of jurisdiction were appropriate and from the U.S. perspective whether certain grounds would even be constitutional, created much of the difficulty. In addition, other countries would not agree to respect judgments based on U.S. "doing business" general jurisdiction, which they characterized as exorbitant — a basis of jurisdiction that the Supreme Court in *Daimler* later held to be unconstitutional as a matter of U.S. law. For a discussion of some of the problems confronting the attempt at this kind of international treaty, s*ee generally* Ralf Michaels, *Two Paradigms of Jurisdiction*, 27 Mich. J. Int'l L. 1003 (2006).

Eventually, the Hague Conference adopted a substantially scaled-back convention — the Convention on Choice of Court Agreements (available at 44 I.L.M. 1294 (2005)) — dealing with jurisdiction and recognition of judgments in cases involving international business-to-business transactions that contain an exclusive choice of court clause. The Convention contains provisions both for enforcing forum selection clauses (prorogation), for dismissing proceedings in contravention of a forum selection clause (derogation), and for recognizing judgments. If the United States ratifies the Convention, the enforcement of all forum selection clauses in international cases would be subject to this international, and thus federal, standard. For more on the Hague Choice of Court Convention, *see* Louise Ellen Teitz, *The Hague Choice of Court Convention: Validating Party Autonomy and Providing an Alternative to Arbitration*, 53 Am. J. Comp. L. 543 (2005).

A new effort was begun at the Hague Conference in 2014, this time to attempt a treaty to address only recognition and enforcement of judgments and not the assertion of direct jurisdiction. The Hague Convention on the Recognition and Enforcement of Foreign Judgments in Civil or Commercial Matters was successfully finalized in 2019, but has not yet entered into force as of 2021. Under this Judgments Convention, there is no attempt to identify grounds in the treaty for the assertion of direct jurisdiction, as is done, for example, in the European Regulation and Recast. However, the basis of a court's jurisdiction is still an important question for the recognition and enforcement of any judgment. The Judgments Convention therefore identifies those bases of jurisdiction that a foreign court will find acceptable in order to recognize and enforcement that foreign judgment. The agreed bases are limited and do not include some jurisdictional bases that are acceptable in the United States. See Chapter 7, pages 895–898.

F.   WHY LITIGANTS CARE ABOUT CHOICE OF FORUM: CHOICE OF LAW AND OTHER MATTERS

The extensive number of cases on personal jurisdiction as well as litigants' perseverance to fight the issue of personal jurisdiction through the appellate process and all the way to the Supreme Court (when they can) reflect the perception of litigants that jurisdictional issues are tremendously important. Have the cases we have examined so far revealed just what the stakes are?

1. Convenience

One common explanation for why a litigant may choose a particular forum and why a defendant may resist that choice is that of convenience. Plaintiff will often choose to sue at home and/or in a state where the events occur because such a forum is likely to be less expensive and burdensome for the plaintiff. If the plaintiff must bear greater litigation costs in seeking out the defendant, the plaintiff may decide not to sue at all. This concern can also operate on defendant's side; even institutional defendants may bear extra costs in retaining local counsel and the like if they have to defend in noncustomary fora. The parties may also be using "convenience" as a smokescreen for increasing their adversary's costs and possibly inducing a settlement on favorable terms.

2. Values and Bias

Even assuming the law to be applied does not change with the choice of a particular forum — a premise we will question later in this section — judges and juries do have certain values and even biases. Sometimes all that is involved may be only a kind of "hometown sympathy" that could favor a local plaintiff at the expense of an out-of-state defendant. Indeed, it was precisely this concern about local prejudice that caused the First Congress of the United States to create original federal trial court jurisdiction for diversity of citizenship cases, 28 U.S.C. §1332. Remember, however, that the federal court selected for such diversity suits is still likely to be the one in plaintiff's home state. Conceivably, the "bias" may be of a different order. In custody cases, where the court is often required to determine what custody arrangement is in the child's "best interests," the choice of forum may well determine outcome. For example, the question of whether a child who is in the care of his church-going Iowa grandparents after the death of his mother should be returned to his "hippie" father in California might be evaluated differently in Iowa than in California. *See, e.g., Painter v. Bannister,* 140 N.W.2d 152 (Iowa 1966). Pete Rose obviously had reasons other than "convenience" for trying to litigate his claims against Major League Baseball and Commissioner Giamatti in the local courts of Cincinnati, Ohio. In *Curtis Publishing Co. v. Birdsong,* 360 F.2d 344 (5th Cir. 1966), Mississippi highway patrolmen attempted to find a southern jury to determine their libel claims against the eastern publisher when the jurisdictional reach of their own state was restricted by state law. And in *World-Wide Volkswagen,* a nonresident plaintiff injured in the forum state decided to sue in the local courts in order to take advantage of a high-verdict local jury.

3. *Procedural Advantages*

The structure and character of the judicial process in a particular forum may well induce a choice of forum. Plaintiffs often forsake local convenience in order to take advantage of the procedural advantages of a particular forum. For example, one often finds foreign plaintiffs injured abroad seeking to sue American defendants in the courts of the United States rather than in their home courts in order to take advantage of certain distinctive American procedural devices, such as juries, broad discovery, and contingent-fee arrangements. Similarly, American plaintiffs bringing suit against foreign defendants strongly prefer an American court to one in a foreign country, not only because it is more convenient but because of these distinctively "American" features. Defendants, of course, try to resist jurisdiction in the United States because they perceive many of these devices as pro-plaintiff.

4. *Choice of Law*

a. **Background**

As we observed earlier in this chapter, the question of which court adjudicates and the question of whose law applies are analytically separate. The forum does not automatically apply its own law to a case because it is the forum. Rather, the forum applies what are known as its "conflict of laws" rules to determine what the applicable law should be.

The field of "conflicts" possesses a long and rich history. During the nineteenth and much of the first part of the twentieth century, a series of relatively fixed rules constituted the rules of conflicts of laws. Eventually, these rules were adopted in the Restatement of Conflicts (1934), often now referred to as Restatement I or the First Restatement. In tort cases, the law of the place of injury would apply. In contract cases, the applicable law was usually the place where the contract was made or performed. A territorial conception of rights and state power informed these rules: When certain events occurred within the state, the legal rights of the parties then "vested," and that state provided the appropriate rules for redress. Because the rules of conflicts of law were by and large uniform under the First Restatement approach, choice of forum was not usually dictated by a search for favorable law. There were, however, always certain "escape" hatches from these somewhat rigid choice of law rules, and occasionally a forum might refuse to hear the case if it found that law to be strongly against its own "public policy." In addition, the forum was always permitted to apply its own "rules of procedure," which included such matters as rules of pleading, discovery, motion practice, trial, evidence, and appeals. Also included in the category of "procedural" matters were certain laws such as statutes of limitations. Can you think of reasons for allowing the forum always to apply its own rules in matters of "procedure"? Do statutes of limitations implicate those reasons? Given the forum's power to apply its own law on the limitations question, it was not uncommon for a plaintiff to choose a forum in order to find a limitations period under which suit might still be brought. *Keeton v. Hustler Magazine* is a good example of a plaintiff's forum selection to take advantage of a favorable statute of limitations.

The "vested rights" system of the First Restatement came under attack even before the project had been officially completed. Leading proponents of the legal realist movement such as Walter Wheeler Cook were quick to point out that the First Restatement's traditional approach was overly formalistic and relied exclusively on one particular event and failed to take into account the underlying policies of potentially competing laws. *See* Cook, *The Logical and Legal Bases of the Conflict of Laws*, 33 Yale L.J. 457 (1924); David F. Cavers, *A Critique of the Choice-of-Law Problem*, 47 Harv. L. Rev. 173 (1933).

The critiques that developed during this period ultimately led to a new approach in the late 1950s and early 1960s. Championed by the late Professors Brainerd Currie and David Cavers, this new approach to conflicts advocated that in the case of a conflict between two potentially applicable legal rules, the choice of law decision should be made by looking to the purposes behind each of the respective rules. In some situations, only one state would have an interest in applying its law, and in such a case—termed a "false conflict" situation—that state's law would apply irrespective of where the suit was brought. In other cases, more than one state might have such a "policy" or "interest"—termed a "true conflict" situation—and various solutions for breaking the "tie" were offered. Currie argued that the forum should merely apply its own law in the "true conflict" situation; Cavers offered certain "principles of preference" to be applied by the forum court. Later, other commentators offered suggestions, such as applying the "better law" or "weighing" the competing interests. For examples from the writings of Professors Cavers and Currie, *see* David Cavers, "Adams v. Knickerbocker: Five Imaginary Cases," in *The Choice of Law Process* (1965); Brainerd Currie, *Selected Essays on the Conflict of Laws* (1963).

A related but somewhat different approach also came into vogue at roughly the same time. Rather than rely on a single event to determine the applicable law as the First Restatement did, several courts indicated that the state with the "most significant contacts" or the state with the "most significant relationship" to the parties and the events should apply its law to the controversy. Sometimes this methodology was the result of a "counting" of contacts, and occasionally it included consideration of the "governmental interest" analysis of Professors Currie and Cavers. The "significant relationship" approach became the organizing principle of the Restatement (Second) of Conflicts, published in 1971, under the guidance of its Chief Reporter, the late Professor Willis Reese. The Second Restatement called for application of the law of the state that, with respect to a given issue, had the "most significant relationship" to the occurrence and the parties. In making that determination, a court was to consider: (a) the needs of the interstate and international systems; (b) the relevant policies of the forum; (c) the relevant policies of other interested states and the relative interests of those states in the determination of the particular issue; (d) the protection of justified expectations; (e) the basic policies underlying the particular field of law; (f) certainty, predictability, and uniformity of result; and (g) ease in the determination and application of the law to be applied.

As might be expected, the development of these new "conflict" doctrines had a dramatic impact on forum choice. No longer was there a set of clear and predictable rules that would govern in any forum in which suit is brought. Because a forum might apply any of a number of conflict of law methodologies, the conflict of laws approach of a particular forum has become an important part of litigation strategy and forum choice. Even when all the possible fora have adopted one of the modern approaches, different outcomes on the choice of law question are likely. Different courts may analyze the policies underlying substantive rules differently; and, when state interests are in competition, the tie-breaking formula in different fora may differ.

Often, the plaintiff may sue in his or her home state, particularly if forum law is favorable and the state's conflicts law is inclined—as it may be—to favor forum law. In other situations, however, the instinct to sue at home for "convenience" sake may give way to a calculated decision to seek—not necessarily a forum's favorable substantive law—but rather a forum's favorable choice of law rule. Consider the situation in *Kozoway v. Massey-Ferguson, Inc.*, 722 F. Supp. 641 (D.Colo. 1989), where a Canadian plaintiff was injured operating a hay baler on a farm in Canada. The hay baler was manufactured for the defendant Massey-Ferguson, a Maryland corporation, by Vermeer Manufacturing, an Iowa corporation, and shipped directly to a Canadian dealership for sale in Canada. Perhaps it is not altogether surprising that the Canadian plaintiff chose to sue in the United States rather than in Canada—we have already noted the attractive aspects of American discovery and jury trials for foreign plaintiffs. What is more surprising is that the plaintiff sued in Colorado, where the defendant had no relationship to any of the events giving rise to the lawsuit but was a nationwide corporation and subject to general jurisdiction in any state of the United States pre-*Daimler*. Can you think of a reason why plaintiff sued in Colorado and not Iowa or Canada? Canadian law did not provide for strict liability while the law in every state of the United States did have strict liability. However, both Iowa and Canada adhered to the "place of injury" rule of conflicts of law, which would have pointed to the law of Canada as the applicable rule. Colorado, on the other hand, had adopted the more modern "contacts" and "interest" approach and would apply the law of Iowa as the state of the place where the wrongful manufacturing act occurred. (Although this case is a federal case, federal courts in diversity actions apply "state law," which includes a state's conflict of laws rules. *See Erie Railroad Co. v. Tompkins*, 304 64 (1938), at p. 411, and *Klaxon v. Stentor Electric Manufacturing Co.*, 313 U.S. 487 (1941), at pp. 410–411.)

b. Constitutional Constraints on Choice of Law

We have seen the significant role that the Due Process Clause of the Constitution has played in establishing limits on judicial jurisdiction. Should Due Process have a similar function on the question of what state's law may be applied? Or should a state be permitted to apply its own law so long as it has jurisdiction?

Whether and how the Constitution should limit the issue of the applicable law was an important question in the pre-*Daimler* era. Prior to *Daimler*, the ability of a plaintiff to sue a corporate defendant wherever it had continuous and systematic activities gave a plaintiff a broad opportunity to engage in forum-shopping for favorable choice of law rules. In some of the cases, the connections with the parties and the claim being sued upon had little relationship to the forum, but there was always the possibility that the forum would apply a choice-of-law rule that favored its own law, which, if the plaintiff had guessed correctly, would favor the plaintiff. Today, it would be the unusual case where a forum would have no connection to the parties or the transaction—the most likely candidate being "tag jurisdiction" of an individual defendant that was upheld in *Burnham*. Therefore, the series of modern Supreme Court cases that established the constitutional test for choice of law—all were cases where defendants were subject to general "doing business jurisdiction"—are likely to have limited application today. Nonetheless, it is interesting to compare the Due Process test that the Supreme Court established for choice of law with the one the Court developed for jurisdiction. In *Allstate Insurance Co. v. Hague*, 449 U.S. 302 (1981), the Court articulated the Due Process test for choice of law as follows: "for a State's substantive law to be selected in a constitutionally permissible manner, that State must have a significant contact or significant aggregation of contacts, creating state interests, such that choice of its law is neither arbitrary nor fundamentally unfair." 449 U.S. at 312.

In a later case, *Phillips Petroleum Co. v. Shutts*, 472 U.S. 797 (1985), the Court was more explicit about the relationship between jurisdiction and choice of law. *Shutts* involved a class action by claimants residing in all 50 states against Phillips Petroleum, a Delaware corporation with its principal place of business in Oklahoma. The class action was brought in state court in Kansas where Phillips Petroleum conducted substantial business and where, pre-*Daimler*, Phillips was clearly subject to general jurisdiction. The class claims involved back interest allegedly owed to the class members on royalties they had in mineral rights as owners of gas leases that were located primarily in Oklahoma and Texas, although a miniscule amount of the gas leases involved in the lawsuit were in Kansas. The Kansas Supreme Court applied Kansas law to all of the claims, noting that in addition to having jurisdiction over the defendant Phillips Petroleum, Kansas had jurisdiction over the absent class members even though the absent class members had no contacts or connections with Kansas, other than being made part of the class action. On the constitutionality of asserting jurisdiction over these absent class members, the Supreme Court of the United States held that because the absent members had the opportunity under Kansas procedure to "opt out" of the class by responding to a written notice sent to them by first-class mail, they had been afforded adequate Due Process protection and were subject to jurisdiction so as to be bound by any judgment in the case. (The issues concerning jurisdiction over absent class members is discussed in greater detail in Chapter 8.) As for choice of law, however, the Supreme Court reversed the Kansas Supreme Court's application of Kansas law to class members who had no connection to Canada and whose leases were not located in Kansas, noting that the transactions of most of the absent class members bore no relationship to Kansas. The Court explained that the issue of personal jurisdiction was entirely distinct from the question of the constitutional limits of choice of law and that the "latter calculus is not altered by the fact that it may be more difficult or more burdensome to comply with the constitutional limitations because of the large number of transaction which the State proposes to adjudicate and which have little connection with the forum." 472 U.S. at 821.

The last of the cases, *Sun Oil Co. v. Wortman*, 486 U.S. 717 (1988), involved the same factual situation as *Shutts*: a national class action brought in Kansas state to recover interest on royalty payments involving oil leases located in numerous statutes but against a different defendant. However, this time the issue before the Supreme Court was whether Kansas could apply its statute of limitations—that was longer than the statutes of limitations of the states whose law otherwise applied—to all of the claims. The Supreme Court determined that the forum state's procedural interests in the application of its rule make it "neither arbitrary nor fundamentally unfair" to apply its own statute of limitations. Why does the Supreme Court treat the statute of limitations issue differently than the issue of the law that can apply to the rate of interest?

NOTES AND QUESTIONS

1. *Choice of Law after* Daimler. As noted above, the issue of constitutional limitations on choice of law surfaced primarily in general jurisdiction cases where the defendant was subject to suit based on systematic and continuous activities in the forum state and the forum attempted to apply its own law. Such cases are unlikely to arise post-*Daimler*. But the basic question of what choice of law approach the forum will take and what the applicable law will be continue to be important elements in choosing a forum. In addition, the forum does not necessarily apply its own law, and thus the constitutional limits on choice of law may still have some bearing on what law a court may constitutionally apply. Consider a suit in the defendant's home state where the choice of law rule is the place of injury. Is it sufficient for Due Process that there is a connection with the state whose law is to be applied so that the state has an "interest" in applying its own law? Or should there also be a requirement that the defendant engage in "purposeful conduct" in the state of injury, as might be required in order for the state where the injury occurs to exercise jurisdiction? *Cf. Volkswagen, Asahi,* and *McIntyre*. Professor Silberman offers the following view of the jurisdiction and choice of law questions: "To believe that a defendant's contacts with the forum state should be stronger under the due process clause for jurisdictional purposes than for choice of law is to believe that an accused is more concerned with where he will be hanged than whether." *See* Linda J. Silberman, Shaffer v. Heitner: *The End of an Era,* 53 N.Y.U. L. Rev. 33, 88 (1978).

2. *Statutes of Limitations.* Given the Supreme Court's decision in *Sun Oil* that the forum *may apply* as a matter of procedure its own statute of limitations—even when it is longer than the law in other relevant states—a forum's choice of law rule on statute of limitations will be an important factor in the choice of a forum. That a state "may apply" its own limitations rule does not mean that it necessarily will do so. For example, many states, as a matter of their own conflict of laws rules, follow the approach of the Uniform Conflict of Laws Limitations Act (which chooses the limitations period of the state whose law otherwise governs) or the approach of the Restatement (Second) of Conflicts, 1988 revision (which applies the statute of limitations law of the forum if it is shorter but looks to the law of the most significant relationship in other situations). Nonetheless, the possibility that a forum is constitutionally permitted to apply its longer statute of limitations increases the likelihood that a plaintiff will "forum shop" to obtain this choice of law advantage. Recall *Keeton v. Hustler Magazine, Inc.,* at pp. 166–167.

G.   NOTICE AND THE MECHANICS OF SERVICE OF PROCESS

1.   The Constitutional Requirement of Notice

At the outset of our discussion of adjudicatory jurisdiction, we noted that in order to acquire such jurisdiction, it is necessary both that: (1) the defendant (and possibly the subject matter of the dispute) have some relationship with the forum in which the court sits; and (2) the defendant be given notice of the commencement of the suit. For simplicity, we may simply say that adjudicatory jurisdiction requires both *power* or *contacts* and *notice.* This section focuses on the latter requirement.

The constitutional basis for requiring both a nexus and notice is found in the Due Process Clause of the Fourteenth Amendment. Note, however, the different concepts of "Due Process" in those two contexts. In *Pennoyer*, the Court held that the Due Process Clause requires that a state acting coercively on a defendant have proper authority. As developed in that and subsequent cases, the constitutional propriety of jurisdiction turns primarily on a defendant's connection with the forum. "Due Process" in this sense is not primarily a constraint on *how* a state goes about adjudicating. Rather, it is concerned with *whether* a state may exercise authority at all.

The Due Process Clause, of course, also constrains the means by which a state exercises its authority. Imagine a judge deciding a case by rolling dice or refusing to hear evidence from one side. Regardless of whether such techniques were authorized under state law, the defendant would have a constitutional objection to such adjudications. What values would be undermined by those practices? How are these different from the values protected by *Pennoyer* and *International Shoe?* How are they similar?

Two values in particular are thought to be advanced by fair process. One is accuracy. Although litigants have no assurance that adjudication will result in accurate findings of fact and law, they are entitled to processes designed to reach the correct outcome. A judge who refuses to hear all the evidence is less likely to reach the correct outcome than a judge who hears evidence from both sides. But even if the judge's factual conclusions were accurate, there would be an additional problem with a judge hearing from only one side; and that implicates the second value. We are committed to the right of affected parties to participate in the adjudication. Such participation not only increases the likelihood of an accurate result but also promotes the litigants' acceptance of adjudication.

The full scope of the procedural Due Process right is complex and encompasses many issues beyond the scope of this course. In the context of civil litigation, we will see that procedural Due Process affects numerous aspects of procedure: It may constrain the types of prejudgment remedies available to litigants; require that a person be given a right to participate in a proceeding before being bound by a judgment; and delimit the range of acceptable means of notifying parties of the pendency of the litigation, the subject of this section.

It should be obvious why notice is an essential element of procedural Due Process. If the defendant were unaware of the commencement of suit, it would be impossible for her to participate in the litigation at all. But what form of notice is constitutionally required? Suppose plaintiff mails a summons to defendant's home, but thinking the summons was junk mail, defendant throws away the summons without reading it. We would probably conclude that defendant has received constitutionally sufficient notice, even though defendant was never actually aware of the lawsuit. On the other hand, plaintiff must clearly do more than give a defendant the opportunity to learn of the litigation: No one would contend that a notice posted on a bulletin board at the clerk's office would be a sufficient means of notifying a defendant that it has been sued.

The problem, therefore, is one of allocating responsibility: How much responsibility must plaintiff take to try to bring the matter to defendant's attention, and how much responsibility must defendant exercise to effectively receive the notice? How should a court go about allocating that responsibility? Are there ever circumstances in which it would be appropriate to shift responsibility from plaintiff to defendant or vice versa? What factors would go into that analysis? Consider this question in connection with the following case.

Mullane v. Central Hanover Bank & Trust Co.

339 U.S. 306 (1950)

MR. JUSTICE JACKSON delivered the opinion of the Court.

This controversy questions the constitutional sufficiency of noti[ce] [to bene]ciaries on judicial settlement of accounts by the trustee of a comm[on trust fund] established under the New York Banking Law, Consol. Laws, c. 2. T[he New York] Court of Appeals considered and overruled objections that the stat[ute] contravenes requirements of the Fourteenth Amendment and that by [it] the account beneficiaries were deprived of property without due proce[ss.]

Common trust fund legislation is addressed to a problem appropr[iate for legislative] action. Mounting overheads have made administration of small trusts [unprofitable] to corporate trustees. In order that donors and testators of moderatel[y sized estates] may not be denied the service of corporate fiduciaries, the District of C[olumbia and] some thirty states other than New York have permitted pooling small [trust estates] into one fund for investment administration. The income, capital gains, losses and expenses of the collective trust are shared by the constituent trusts in proportion to their contribution. By this plan, diversification of risk and economy of management can be extended to those whose capital standing alone would not obtain such advantage.

Statutory authorization for the establishment of such common trust funds is provided in the New York Banking Law, §100-c, c. 687, L.1937, as amended by c. 602, L. 1943 and c. 158, L.1944. Under this Act a trust company may, with approval of the State Banking Board, establish a common fund and, within prescribed limits, invest therein the assets of an unlimited number of estates, trusts or other funds of which it is trustee. Each participating trust shares ratably in the common fund, but exclusive management and control is in the trust company as trustee, and neither a fiduciary nor any beneficiary of a participating trust is deemed to have ownership in any particular asset or investment of this common fund. The trust company must keep fund assets separate from its own, and in its fiduciary capacity may not deal with itself or any affiliate. Provisions are made for accountings twelve to fifteen months after the establishment of a fund and triennially thereafter. The decree in each such judicial settlement of accounts is made binding and conclusive as to any matter set forth in the account upon everyone having any interest in the common fund or in any participating estate, trust or fund.

In January 1946, Central Hanover Bank and Trust Company established a common trust fund in accordance with these provisions, and in March 1947, it petitioned the Surrogate's Court for settlement of its first account as common trustee. During the accounting period a total of 113 trusts, approximately half inter vivos and half testamentary, participated in the common trust fund, the gross capital of which was nearly three million dollars. The record does not show the number or residence of the beneficiaries, but they were many and it is clear that some of them were not residents of the State of New York.

The only notice given beneficiaries of this specific application was by publication in a local newspaper in strict compliance with the minimum requirements of N.Y. Banking Law §100-c(12): "After filing such petition [for judicial settlement of its account] the petitioner shall cause to be issued by the court in which the petition is filed and shall publish not less than once in each week for four successive weeks in a newspaper to be designated by the court a notice or citation addressed generally without naming them to all parties interested in such common trust fund and in such estates, trusts or funds mentioned in the petition, all of which may be described in the notice or citation only in the manner set forth in said petition and without setting forth the residence of any such decedent or donor of any such estate, trust or fund." Thus the only notice required, and the only one given, was by newspaper publication setting forth merely the name and address of the trust company, the name and the date of establishment of the common trust fund, and a list of all participating estates, trusts or funds.

At the time the first investment in the common fund was made on behalf of each participating estate, however, the trust company, pursuant to the requirements of §100-c(9), had notified by mail each person of full age and sound mind whose name and address was then known to it and who was "entitled to share in the income therefrom . . . [or] . . . who would be entitled to share in the principal if the event upon which such estate, trust or fund will become distributable should have occurred at the time of sending such notice." Included in the notice was a copy of those provisions of the Act relating to the sending of the notice itself and to the judicial settlement of common trust fund accounts.

Upon the filing of the petition for the settlement of accounts, appellant was, by order of the court pursuant to §100-c(12), appointed special guardian and attorney for all persons known or unknown not otherwise appearing who had or might thereafter have any interest in the income of the common trust fund; and appellee Vaughan was appointed to represent those similarly interested in the principal. There were no other appearances on behalf of any one interested in either interest or principal.

Appellant appeared specially, objecting that notice and the statutory provisions for notice to beneficiaries were inadequate to afford due process under the Fourteenth Amendment, and therefore that the court was without jurisdiction to render a final and binding decree. Appellant's objections were entertained and overruled. . . .

The effect of this decree, as held below, is to settle "all questions respecting the management of the common fund." We understand that every right which beneficiaries would otherwise have against the trust company, either as trustee of the common fund or as trustee of any individual trust, for improper management of the common trust fund during the period covered by the accounting is sealed and wholly terminated by the decree. . . .

We are met at the outset with a challenge to the power of the State—the right of its courts to adjudicate at all as against those beneficiaries who reside without the State of New York. It is contended that the proceeding is one *in personam* in that the decree affects neither title to nor possession of any *res*, but adjudges only personal rights of the beneficiaries to surcharge their trustee for negligence or breach of trust. Accordingly, it is said, under the strict doctrine of *Pennoyer v. Neff*, 95 U.S. 714, the Surrogate is without jurisdiction as to nonresidents upon whom personal service of process was not made. . . .

Judicial proceedings to settle fiduciary accounts have been sometimes termed *in rem*, or more indefinitely *quasi in rem*, or more vaguely still, "in the nature of a proceeding *in rem*." It is not readily apparent how the courts of New York did or would classify the present proceeding, which has some characteristics and is wanting in some features of proceedings both *in rem* and *in personam*. But in any event we think that the requirements of the Fourteenth Amendment to the Federal Constitution do not depend upon a classification for which the standards are so elusive and confused generally and which, being primarily for state courts to define, may and do vary from state to state. Without disparaging the usefulness of distinctions between actions *in rem* and those *in personam* in many branches of law, or on other issues, or the reasoning which underlies them, we do not rest the power of the State to resort to constructive service in this proceeding upon how its courts or this Court may regard this historic antithesis. It is sufficient to observe that, whatever the technical definition of its chosen procedure, the interest of each state in providing means to close trusts that exist by the grace of its laws and are administered under the supervision of its courts is so insistent and rooted in custom as to establish beyond doubt the right of its courts to determine the interests of all claimants, resident or nonresident, provided its procedure accords full opportunity to appear and be heard.

Quite different from the question of a State's power to discharge trustees is that of the opportunity it must give beneficiaries to contest. Many controversies have raged about the cryptic and abstract words of the Due Process Clause but there can be no doubt that at a minimum they require that deprivation of life, liberty or property by adjudication be preceded by notice and opportunity for hearing appropriate to the nature of the case.

In two ways this proceeding does or may deprive beneficiaries of property. It may cut off their rights to have the trustee answer for negligent or illegal impairments of their interests. Also, their interests are presumably subject to diminution in the proceeding by allowance of fees and expenses to one who, in their names but without their knowledge, may conduct a fruitless or uncompensatory contest. Certainly the proceeding is one in which they may be deprived of property rights and hence notice and hearing must measure up to the standards of due process.

Personal service of written notice within the jurisdiction is the classic form of notice always adequate in any type of proceeding. But the vital interest of the State in bringing any issues as to its fiduciaries to a final settlement can be served only if interests or claims of individuals who are outside of the State can somehow be determined. A construction of the Due Process Clause which would place impossible or impractical obstacles in the way could not be justified.

Against this interest of the State we must balance the individual interest sought to be protected by the Fourteenth Amendment. This is defined by our holding that "The fundamental requisite of due process of law is the opportunity to be heard." *Grannis v. Ordean*, 234 U.S. 385. This right to be heard has little reality or worth unless one is informed that the matter is pending and can choose for himself whether to appear or default, acquiesce or contest.

The Court has not committed itself to any formula achieving a balance between these interests in a particular proceeding or determining when constructive notice may be utilized or what test it must meet. Personal service has not in all circumstances been regarded as indispensable to the process due to residents, and it has more often been held unnecessary as to nonresidents. We disturb none of the established rules on these subjects. No decision constitutes a controlling or even a very illuminating precedent for the case before us. But a few general principles stand out in the books.

An elementary and fundamental requirement of due process in any proceeding which is to be accorded finality is notice reasonably calculated, under all the circumstances, to apprise interested parties of the pendency of the action and afford them an opportunity to present their objections. . . . The notice must be of such nature as reasonably to convey the required information, . . . and it must afford a reasonable time for those interested to make their appearance. . . . But if with due regard for the practicalities and peculiarities of the case these conditions are reasonably met the constitutional requirements are satisfied. "The criterion is not the possibility of conceivable injury, but the just and reasonable character of the requirements, having reference to the subject with which the statute deals." *American Land Co. v. Zeiss*, 219 U.S. 47.

But when notice is a person's due, process which is a mere gesture is not due process. The means employed must be such as one desirous of actually informing the absentee might reasonably adopt to accomplish it. The reasonableness and hence the constitutional validity of any chosen method may be defended on the ground that it is in itself reasonably certain to inform those affected, . . . or, where conditions do not reasonably permit such notice, that the form chosen is not substantially less likely to bring home notice than other of the feasible and customary substitutes.

It would be idle to pretend that publication alone as prescribed here, is a reliable means of acquainting interested parties of the fact that their rights are before the courts. It is not an accident that the greater number of cases reaching this Court on the question of adequacy of notice have been concerned with actions founded on process constructively served through local newspapers. Chance alone brings to the attention of even a local resident an advertisement in small type inserted in the back pages of a newspaper, and if he makes his home outside the area of the newspaper's normal circulation the odds that the information will never reach him are large indeed. The chance of actual notice is further reduced when as here the notice required does not even name those whose attention it is supposed to attract, and does not inform acquaintances who might call it to attention. In weighing its sufficiency on the basis of equivalence with actual notice we are unable to regard this as more than a feint.

Nor is publication here reinforced by steps likely to attract the parties' attention to the proceeding. It is true that publication traditionally has been acceptable as notification supplemental to other action which in itself may reasonably be expected to convey a warning. The ways of an owner with tangible property are such that he usually arranges means to learn of any direct attack upon his possessory or proprietary rights. Hence, libel of a ship, attachment of a chattel or entry upon real estate in the name of law may reasonably be expected to come promptly to the owner's attention. When the state within which the owner has located such property seizes it for some reason, publication or posting affords an additional measure of notification. A State may indulge the assumption that one who has left tangible property in the State either has abandoned it, in which case proceedings against it deprive him of nothing, . . . or that he has left some caretaker under a duty to let him know that it is being jeopardized. . . .

In the case before us there is, of course, no abandonment. On the other hand these beneficiaries do have a resident fiduciary as caretaker of their interest in this property. But it is their caretaker who in the accounting becomes their adversary. Their trustee is released from giving notice of jeopardy, and no one else is expected to do so. Not even the special guardian is required or apparently expected to communicate with his ward and client, and, of course, if such a duty were merely transferred from the trustee to the guardian, economy would not be served and more likely the cost would be increased.

This Court has not hesitated to approve of resort to publication as a customary substitute in another class of cases where it is not reasonably possible or practicable to give more adequate warning. Thus it has been recognized that, in the case of persons missing or unknown, employment of an indirect and even a probably futile means of notification is all that the situation permits and creates no constitutional bar to a final decree foreclosing their rights. . . .

Those beneficiaries represented by appellant whose interests or whereabouts could not with due diligence be ascertained come clearly within this category. As to them the statutory notice is sufficient. However great the odds that publication will never reach the eyes of such unknown parties, it is not in the typical case much more likely to fail than any of the choices open to legislators endeavoring to prescribe the best notice practicable.

Nor do we consider it unreasonable for the State to dispense with more certain notice to those beneficiaries whose interests are either conjectural or future or, although they could be discovered upon investigation, do not in due course of business come to knowledge of the common trustee. Whatever searches might be required in another situation under ordinary standards of diligence, in view of the character of the proceedings and the nature of the interests here involved we think them unnecessary. We recognize the practical difficulties and costs that would be attendant on frequent investigations into the status of great numbers of beneficiaries, many of whose interests in the common fund are so remote as to be ephemeral; and we have no doubt that such impracticable and extended searches are not required in the name of due process. The expense of keeping informed from day to day of substitutions among even current income beneficiaries and presumptive remaindermen, to say nothing of the far greater number of contingent beneficiaries, would impose a severe burden on the plan, and would likely dissipate its advantages. These are practical matters in which we should be reluctant to disturb the judgment of the state authorities.

Accordingly, we overrule appellant's constitutional objections to published notice insofar as they are urged on behalf of any beneficiaries whose interests or addresses are unknown to the trustee.

As to known present beneficiaries of known place of residence, however, notice by publication stands on a different footing. Exceptions in the name of necessity do not sweep away the rule that within the limits of practicability notice must be such as is reasonably calculated to reach interested parties. Where the names and post office addresses of those affected by a proceeding are at hand, the reasons disappear for resort to means less likely than the mails to apprise them of its pendency.

The trustee has on its books the names and addresses of the income beneficiaries represented by appellant, and we find no tenable ground for dispensing with a serious effort to inform them personally of the accounting, at least by ordinary mail to the record addresses. Certainly sending them a copy of the statute months and perhaps years in advance does not answer this purpose. The trustee periodically remits their income to them, and we think that they might reasonably expect that with or apart from their remittances word might come to them personally that steps were being taken affecting their interests.

We need not weigh contentions that a requirement of personal service of citation on even the large number of known resident or nonresident beneficiaries would, by reasons of delay if not of expense, seriously interfere with the proper administration of the fund. Of course personal service even without the jurisdiction of the issuing authority serves the end of actual and personal notice, whatever power of compulsion it might lack. However, no such service is required under the circumstances. This type of trust presupposes a large number of small interests. The individual interest does not stand alone but is identical with that of a class. The rights of each in the integrity of the fund and the fidelity of the trustee are shared by many other beneficiaries. Therefore notice reasonably certain to reach most of those interested in objecting is likely to safeguard the interests of all, since any objections sustained would inure to the benefit of all. We think that under such circumstances reasonable risks that notice might not actually reach every beneficiary are justifiable. "Now and then an extraordinary case may turn up, but constitutional law, like other mortal contrivances, has to take some chances, and in the great majority of instances, no doubt, justice will be done." *Blinn v. Nelson*, supra, 222 U.S. at 7.

The statutory notice to known beneficiaries is inadequate, not because in fact it fails to reach everyone, but because under the circumstances it is not reasonably calculated to reach those who could easily be informed by other means at hand. However it may have been in former times, the mails today are recognized as an efficient and inexpensive means of communication. Moreover, the fact that the trust company has been able to give mailed notice to known beneficiaries at the time the common trust fund was established is persuasive that postal notification at the time of accounting would not seriously burden the plan.

[handwritten: Paul to take in advance]

In some situations the law requires greater precautions in its proceedings than the business world accepts for its own purposes. In few, if any, will it be satisfied with less. Certainly it is instructive, in determining the reasonableness of the impersonal broadcast notification here used, to ask whether it would satisfy a prudent man of business, counting his pennies but finding it in his interest to convey information to many persons whose names and addresses are in his files. We are not satisfied that it would. Publication may theoretically be available for all the world to see, but it is too much in our day to suppose that each or any individual beneficiary does or could examine all that is published to see if something may be tucked away in it that affects his property interests. . . .

We hold the notice of judicial settlement of accounts required by the New York Banking Law §100-c(12) is incompatible with the requirements of the Fourteenth Amendment as a basis for adjudication depriving known persons whose whereabouts are also known of substantial property rights. Accordingly, the judgment is reversed and the cause remanded for further proceedings not inconsistent with this opinion.

Reversed.

NOTES AND QUESTIONS

Mullane involved an accounting of a common trust fund, an action with characteristics of both traditional *in rem* and *in personam* proceedings, but the Court makes it clear that the constitutional standard it establishes—notice "reasonably calculated" to apprise interested parties of the suit—applies regardless of the form of action. At the same time, the Court does not mandate a particular manner of giving notice, and plainly states that the nature of the action *is* relevant to a determination of the specific manner of notice required.

Think about why the Court retains such flexibility and how the nature of an action should affect the type of notice constitutionally required, as you consider the following cases.

1. *What Makes Notice "Reasonable Under the Circumstances"?* There are two important applications of the Court's standard of constitutionally sufficient notice in *Mullane*: the Court's conclusion that known beneficiaries must receive individualized notice; and that publication *is* a sufficient means for notifying beneficiaries who cannot be identified through the exercise of reasonable effort. Think about how the Court reached those conclusions. Did the nature of the action—an accounting of a common trust fund—affect the analysis?

[handwritten right margin: known - individualized notice ok; unknown - publication ok]

Suppose a defendant borrowed money from plaintiff and then moved away without providing plaintiff with a forwarding address. If plaintiff wanted to file an action to collect the debt against defendant, and defendant's whereabouts could not be ascertained through the exercise of reasonable effort, would service of process by publication satisfy the *Mullane* standard? Is this situation distinguishable from that of the unknown beneficiaries in *Mullane*? Why?

2. *Vicarious Representation.* Note that the Due Process objection of the unknown beneficiaries is being asserted by a legal representative appointed by the court. If one of those beneficiaries wanted to subsequently file a collateral attack on the

Mullane judgment on the ground that he was deprived of his constitutional right to notice, would he be barred by *res judicata*? If the appointed representative could adequately represent the beneficiary's interest in arguing for individualized notice, why couldn't he also adequately represent the beneficiary's interest on the merits? In other words, ~~why was it important that the unknown beneficiaries receive any notice given the court's ability to appoint counsel to represent their interests?~~

3. *Wuchter v. Pizzutti*, 276 U.S. 13 (1928), was decided before *Mullane* but presaged that holding. In *Wuchter*, the Court held invalid a New Jersey statute providing for notice by service on the Secretary of State, in suits involving negligent operation of automobiles. Distinguishing *Hess v. Pawloski*, p. 69, the Court held that "enforced acceptance of the service of process on a state officer by the defendant would not be fair or due process unless such officer or the plaintiff is required to mail the notice to the defendant, or to advise him, by some written communication, so as to make it reasonably probable that he will receive actual notice."

An interesting aspect of *Wuchter* is that the defendant had, in fact, received actual notice of the suit. The Court held that the fact that such notice was not *required* by the statute required reversal. *Wuchter*, therefore, illustrates two important principles: (1) the giving of actual notice may not save the plaintiff if the statutory scheme for notice is deemed unconstitutional on its face; and (2) defective notice undermines the entire proceeding.

4. *Walker v. City of Hutchinson*, 352 U.S. 112 (1956), and *Schroeder v. New York*, 371 U.S. 208 (1962), both involved actions by a city to condemn real property. In *Walker*, notice of the condemnation proceeding was published in a newspaper; in *Schroeder*, notice was published in several newspapers and the city record, and was posted in several areas in the vicinity of, but not on, the property in question. The Court held the notice inadequate in both cases because the names of the property owners were readily ascertainable. What would be the result if notice had been posted *on* the property [=easily?]? Remember Justice Jackson's statement in *Mullane* that the state may assume that owners will keep track of real property that they do not intend to abandon.

5. In *Greene v. Lindsey*, 456 U.S. 444 (1982), public authorities sought to ~~repossess~~ defendants' apartments in a housing project. ~~Notice was given by posting on the door of each tenant's apartment.~~ While conceding that posting on the door of a person's residence would "in many or perhaps most instances" be sufficient, the Court held that in this particular case it did not satisfy Due Process, because testimony in the record indicated that the posted notices were often removed by children and other tenants. The Court went on to hold that notice by posting would have to be supplemented with notice by mail to pass constitutional muster. [standard]

In dissent, Justice O'Connor stated "the Court . . . holds today that notice via the mails is so far superior to posted notice that the difference is of constitutional dimension. How the Court reaches this judgment remains a mystery." Do you agree with the dissent that the Court should not be prescribing specific methods of furnishing notice? Is this inappropriate judicial micromanagement of government, or was the Court justified in setting the level and form of the notice to the particularized circumstances confronting its intended recipients?

Is it relevant to the Court's holding in *Greene* that the defendants stood to lose something as fundamental as their place of residence? Put another way, does or should the importance to the defendant of the interest that he stands to lose affect what notice is constitutionally required? Consider *War Eagle Village Apartments v. Plummer*, 775 N.W.2d 714 (Iowa 2009). War Eagle brought a forcible entry and detainer (FED) action against tenant Plummer. The Iowa statute governing FED actions provided that the landlord should notify the tenant via certified mail, and that notice was complete upon mailing; no signed return receipt was necessary. A hearing had to commence not later than seven days from the date of the court order for the hearing. Accordingly, on July 24, War Eagle sent notice of the action to Plummer via certified mail and obtained a court order setting the hearing for July 31. No attempt to deliver the mail was made by the post office until July 27, and Plummer failed to appear in court. Plummer challenged the constitutionality of the Iowa statute, arguing that it violated Due Process because it was "not reasonably calculated to give notice in advance of the hearing." War Eagle maintained that Plummer had received adequate notice since Due Process does not require actual notice. Pointing to *Greene*, the Iowa Supreme Court first recognized the interests at stake in FED actions: While there is a desire to quickly determine who is entitled to retain possession of an apartment, the defendant has a significant property interest, and adequate notice of legal action is necessary. The court then turned to the Iowa statute, hinging its decision on two points. First, the statute inappropriately deemed service complete upon mailing, yet "dropping a letter in a mailbox is not notice." Second, the requirement of certified mail made adequate notice even less likely since "the letter cannot be left like regular mail to be examined at the end of the day, and it can only be retrieved from the post office for a specified period of time." The court held that the requirement of certified mail, in conjunction with the requirement for a hearing seven days after the court order, made the Iowa statute unconstitutional on its face. The court, following *Greene*, determined that Plummer had a significant property interest that required Due Process protection, but what of War Eagle's property interest? Should a seven-day time frame be sufficient if regular mail is used instead of certified mail, or is such a short period of time always too brief to provide adequate notice to the defendant? Would your answer change if War Eagle was a smaller operation with fewer apartments to rent out, and thus much hinged on whether it lost rent for a single apartment even for a short period of time?

6. In *Tulsa Professional Collection Services, Inc. v. Pope*, 485 U.S. 478 (1988), a creditor sought to recover a debt from the decedent's estate, after the two-month limitations period provided by Oklahoma's Probate Code had expired. The creditor sought to have the missed deadline excused, claiming inadequate notice. Notice of the entry of the will into probate had been given by publication in a local newspaper. Again noting that "whether a particular method of notice is reasonable depends on the particular circumstances," the Court held the notice insufficient because "known or reasonably ascertainable" creditors were an identifiable group potentially affected by the proceeding, were unlikely to learn of the proceeding through publication notice, and therefore merited "reasonably diligent efforts" at actual notice.

Does the following proposition represent a good crystallization of the "rule" of the above cases? If the name of an individual with a substantial property interest at stake is reasonably ascertainable, an effort must be made to notify that party by mail or personal service.

7. Ordinary use of the mails may pose special problems for individuals who are within institutions and who have no personal addresses of their own, such as inmates or members of the armed forces. Even so, the Court has held that *Mullane*

does not require the government to employ any additional effort in such cases. In *Dusenbury v. United States*, 534 U.S. 161 (2002), the FBI initiated a forfeiture proceeding against the possessions of a federal inmate. It sent notice of the forfeiture to the inmate by certified letter addressed to the prison facility. Because of problems with the internal prison mail system, however, the letter never reached the inmate. The inmate argued that it would have required only slightly more effort for the government to increase the likelihood that notices and other certified letters would reach prisoners—for example, by requiring inmates to sign a logbook acknowledging receipt of such mail, a step that the Federal Bureau of Prisons has since adopted voluntarily.

In a 5-4 decision, however, the Court held that the Constitution did not require this additional step. The majority rejected the position of the dissenters that a method of notice is flawed if it is "substantially less likely to bring home notice than a feasible substitute." Rather, the majority held, Due Process "does not require . . . heroic efforts by the Government; it requires only that the Government's effort be reasonably calculated to apprise a party of the pendency of the action." Responding specifically to the fact that the Bureau of Prisons had since adopted the procedure urged by the inmate, the majority explained that the Court has "never held that improvements in the reliability of new procedures necessarily demonstrate the infirmity of those that were replaced."

Does *Dusenbury* appear less protective of the rights of defendants than *Mullane* did? Given the apparent ease with which the Bureau of Prisons could have increased the likelihood that certified mail would reach inmates, do the old procedures really constitute the method that "one desirous of actually informing" the prisoner would employ? Or do the inmate's arguments rely too much on the benefit of hindsight?

What about the Court's assertion that new and improved procedures do not necessarily demonstrate the inadequacy of old procedures? If a litigant discovers a new method of providing notice that is cheap, easy, and much more effective, doesn't that procedure *necessarily* become the one that a person "desirous of actually informing" the defendant would employ? Consider this question in light of *Rio Properties, Inc. v. Rio International Interlink*, 284 F.3d 1007 (9th Cir. 2002), in which the Ninth Circuit held that a district court's decision to order notice by email (pursuant to Rule 4(f)(3), which allows the Court to direct service to be made in a foreign country through alternative means), satisfied the requirements of Due Process. If email and the Internet become the most effective way to track down some defendants, might they not become constitutionally required in cases where previously acceptable alternatives—like sending ordinary mail to a defendant's last known address—are much less likely to succeed? For an argument that electronic service should be permitted for domestic defendants as well as foreign defendants, *see* Ronald J. Hedges et al., *Electronic Service of Process at Home and Abroad: Allowing Domestic Electronic Service of Process in the Federal Courts*, 2009 Fed. Cts. L. Rev. 55 (2009).

The Supreme Court's stance in *Dusenbery* against taking additional steps to notify an individual of a forfeiture proceeding might have been short-lived. In *Jones v. Flowers*, 547 U.S. 220 (2006), a property owner had his land confiscated by the government after he failed to pay his property taxes; the state of Arkansas had mailed two notification letters to the owner at the property's address via certified mail, but no one had signed for the letters or gone to the post office to retrieve them during the 15-day holding period. Resolving a circuit split, the Court, in a 5-3 decision, held that once cognizant that the letters did not reach the owner "the State should have taken additional reasonable steps to notify [him], if practicable to do so." The Court then enumerated several possible steps that might have satisfied Due Process in this situation, including resending the notice by regular mail, posting a notice on the front door of the property, or addressing the mail to "occupant" at the property's address. Notably, the Court refused the property owner's further suggestion that the State should have searched for his new address, claiming that this would impose a "significantly greater" burden on the state than Due Process required.

Justice Thomas dissented, asserting that the Court's ruling is inconsistent with *Dusenbery* because it requires additional notice after a constitutionally approved method already had been used. In response to one of the majority's solutions—to send the notice by regular mail—Justice Thomas opined that then "petitioner would presumably argue that [the State] should have sent notice by certified mail because it creates a paper trail." What remains of the assertion in *Dusenbery* that Due Process only requires "that the Government's effort be reasonably calculated to apprise a party of the pendency of the action"? At the very least, the constitutional parameters of notice by mail are as muddled as ever. In a post-*Jones* decision, *Luessenhop v. Clinton County*, 466 F.3d 259, 271 (2d Cir. 2006), one plaintiff couple had its initial delinquency letter sent via first-class mail but a second mailing sent via certified mail. As for the certified letter, the government possessed a "Track and Confirm" print-out from the postal service but lacked a signature on the return receipt. How can a court make legitimate constitutional distinctions in these situations? Do you now have greater sympathy for Justice O'Connor's dissent in *Greene v. Lindsey* condemning the judicial micromanagement of notice?

The decision in *Jones v. Flowers* and the questions it raises has attracted recent academic commentary. Professor Patrick Borchers argues that the importance of the interest involved does affect what notice is constitutionally required. Professor Borchers contends that the Court in *Jones* suggests that the cost-benefit analysis used in *Mathews v. Eldridge*, 424 U.S. 319 (1976) (*see* pp. 759-760 for discussion of *Mathews*) is now part of the constitutional standard for notice, meaning that less protection would have been required if the case involved a $25 parking ticket instead of $60,000 worth of equity in a home. Patrick J. Borchers, Jones v. Flowers: *An Essay on a Unified Theory of Procedural Due Process*, 40 Creighton L. Rev. 343, 349 (2007).

Consider the notice regime furnished by Fed. R. Civ. P. 4 in light of *Mullane* and its progeny.

2. The Mechanics of Service of Process

A party is given notice of the commencement of a lawsuit by a procedure generally referred to as *service of process*. The *service* aspect is the delivery to the party; *process* refers to the thing served—a paper giving the party information about the suit commenced. Process may consist solely of a *summons*—a document informing the party of the name and location of the court in which suit is being brought and of the general nature of the action (specific requirements vary by jurisdiction) — and requiring the party to appear in court on a specified day or to serve a response within a specified time period. In many jurisdictions, including the federal courts, service must also include a *complaint* — a more detailed recitation of the claims being brought, the parties involved, and the basis of jurisdiction.

a.   Structure of Fed. R. Civ. P. 4

i.   The Summons and Provisions for Service

Fed. R. Civ. P. 4 provides for a uniform federal form of summons. (Other forms of process now fall under Rule 4.1.) Rule 4(a) provides that a summons shall be signed by a clerk of the court. It also describes the technical requirements of form for a summons and the information that it must contain — the names of the court and the parties, the name and address of plaintiff's attorney, the time within which the defendant must respond, and a statement that failure to respond will result in default.

Rule 4(b) deals with the issuance of the summons and indicates that the complaint must first be filed with the court (filing "commences" the action — *see* Fed. R. Civ. P. 3). The plaintiff or her attorney bears the responsibility of effecting service, which must include the summons and a copy of the complaint. Service is often made by a third party, sometimes a professional process server. This method is authorized by Rule 4(c), which (with some exceptions) allows the summons and complaint to be served by anyone at least 18 years old, as long as he is not a party to the suit. This use of private process servers is a change from earlier federal procedure when all process was served by the U.S. Marshal's office. Note, however, that there are still some special situations in which the marshal or another specially appointed officer must be used.

Rule 4(e) sets forth the federal manner for service upon individuals (*see* Fed. R. Civ. P. 4(e)(2)) and also broadens the methods for effecting service by allowing service to be effected both in conformance with the law of the state in which the court sits (the practice permitted under the prior rule) and also with the law of the state in which service is effected (*see* Fed. R. Civ. P. 4(e)(1)). Thus, a plaintiff who serves a defendant out of state has a choice of methods by which to effect service.

Particular sections of Rule 4 specify methods of service, the availability of which depends on the party to be served. As noted, Rule 4(e)(2) addresses service upon individuals, excluding minors and incompetents; it authorizes service on an individual personally or by leaving copies with a person "of suitable age and discretion" at the "individual's dwelling or usual place of abode." For discussion of cases under the slightly different language of the pre-2007 rules, *see* cases collected at 32 A.L.R.3d 112 (1970), 92 A.L.R 3d 827 (1979). In a case where an individual has appointed an agent to accept service or where an agent is appointed by law (as in *Hess* and *Wuchter*), service may be made upon that agent.

Rule 4(g) deals with service upon minors and incompetents. Such service must be made according to the law of the state where service is effected. For an example of such state law, *see* N.Y. C.P.L.R. §309.

Rule 4(h) addresses service upon corporations and other associations. Service upon these entities is made by serving an "officer, a managing or general agent," or an agent designated to receive service. The question of who constitutes an officer or managing or general agent for these purposes is often litigated. *See* cases collected at 71 A.L.R.2d 178 (1960) (domestic corporations), 17 A.L.R.3d 625 (1968) (foreign corporations). Although they have not articulated a clear rule on the issue, courts will generally consider either: (1) the degree of control and discretion exercised by the putative agent in the association or, more practically, (2) whether the agent's position in the association is such that the service is likely to come to the attention of those responsible for protecting the association's interests in litigation. *Compare, e.g., Grammenos v. Lemos*, 457 F.2d 1067 (2d Cir. 1972) *with Alloway v. Wain-Roy Corp.*, 52 F.R.D. 203 (E.D. Pa. 1971).

Rule 4(i) addresses service upon the United States as a defendant. Service may be made personally upon the U.S. Attorney (or his designee) for the district in which the action is brought or by registered or certified mail, addressed to the civil process clerk at the office of the U.S. Attorney. In addition, a copy of the summons and complaint must be sent by regular or certified mail to the Attorney General of the United States.

Rule 4(j)(2) provides the manner of service upon state or local governments. Such service may be made by serving the chief executive officer (e.g., the state governor) or in whatever manner is prescribed by state law. *See, e.g.,* N.Y. C.P.L.R. §§307, 311. Service upon foreign governments is provided for under the Foreign Sovereign Immunities Act, 28 U.S.C. §1608. In *Republic of Sudan v. Harrison*, 139 S. Ct. 1048 (2018), the Supreme Court interpreted §1608(a)(3), which, absent the existence of a special arrangement or an applicable international convention, provides for service of process by any form of mail to a foreign government's head of foreign affairs. The Court held that the statute requires service upon the foreign minister's office *in the foreign state*, and that mailing service to the state's embassy in the United States did not satisfy the statute's service requirement.

Proof of service is covered by Rule 4(l); and Rule 4(m) establishes time limits for service. Rule 4(l) establishes a system for return of service, intended to facilitate proving that service was actually effected. Note that failure to execute a return of service does not, in and of itself, invalidate the service. Rule 4(m) contains information related to time limits on service. It also requires that service be made within 90 days after the complaint is filed but it explicitly allows the court to extend the time for service beyond that 90 days, upon a showing of good cause for the delay, and to direct that it be effected within a specified period. Employing such discretion, judges can avoid the severe effects that strict application of a deadline might produce, as where the statute of limitations would bar refiling of the claim. Formerly, the only available means of relief was by resort to Rule 6(b)'s general provisions for enlargement of time periods.

ii.   Waiver of Service

An additional method of effecting service upon individuals, corporations, and associations is covered by Fed. R. Civ. P. 4(d). In effect, Rule 4(d) replaced a provision for service by mail under a previous version of Rule 4. Because mail itself without acknowledgment did not perfect service, the provision is now entitled "Waiving service" to make clear that what is being requested is a waiver of formal service. Rule 4(d) creates a procedure for waiver of service, intended to save time, effort, and money in the making of service and not to effect substantive changes in the law relating to process. Therefore, the procedure addresses itself only to the mechanical aspect of service — the waiver provisions have no effect on a defendant's right to object to improper jurisdiction or venue. *See* Fed. R. Civ. P. 4(d)(2), (5). On the other hand, when service is waived (as described below), the waiver would foreclose objections to the sufficiency of the form and method of service. The waiver procedure is not available for service upon the United States.

The procedure for requesting and effecting waiver is as follows. First, a request for waiver of service must be in writing, transmitted by first-class mail or "other equally reliable means." *See* Fed. R. Civ. P. 4(d)(1)(G). Does this include a request transmitted by fax or email? *See* Advisory Committee Notes, 1993 Amendments (approving of service of request for waiver by "electronic means," including facsimile): Comment, *Internet Service of Process: A Constitutionally Adequate Alternative?*, 66 U. Chi. L. Rev. 943 (1999). The request itself must contain a copy of the complaint and must identify the court in which the complaint has been filed. It must inform the defendant of the consequences of compliance and of failure to comply with the request. Finally, the request must provide the defendant with two copies of the waiver form appended to Rule 4 as well as a prepaid means for returning the form. The plaintiff must give the defendant "a reasonable time" in which to return the waiver, but at least 30 days from the date the request is sent, or 60 days if the request was sent to a defendant outside any judicial district of the United States. If the defendant makes a timely return of waiver, he would have 60 days from the date the *request* was sent to serve an answer in the action, or 90 days if outside any judicial district of the United States. Failure to comply with the request will result in the imposition of the costs of subsequent service, unless good cause is shown, but such cost-shifting is permitted only when both the plaintiff and the defendant are located in the United States.

Paragraph (4) purports to specify the effective date of service when the waiver provision is used. (The importance of effective date of service is discussed later in the note on service of process and statutes of limitations.) Paragraph (4) provides that the effective date of service is the date that the *waiver* is filed with the court — the date of the transmission of the *request* is immaterial. The interrelationship of this rule with the statute of limitations is potentially complex; the Advisory Committee therefore advises that the waiver procedure not be utilized when commencing an action for which the statute of limitations may soon expire.

iii. Service in a Foreign Country

Would you expect service of process to be different if the defendant upon whom service is to be made is located in a foreign country? In some countries, service of process is considered to be an act of sovereignty that is only proper if made by an official of the state. Indeed, not only is the service considered "ineffective" if a U.S. judgment is sought to be enforced but also in some instances a private process server attempting to make service in certain foreign countries has been arrested in that country. One approach to resolving the conflict of views in different countries about the appropriate methods for serving process is to adopt an international treaty on service of process. The United States is party to several such treaties, the most important one being the Hague Convention on the Service Abroad of Judicial and Extrajudicial Documents (the Hague Service Convention).

The Hague Service Convention provides for a means of serving judicial process in other contracting States by having each state designate a Central Authority "to receive requests for service coming from other contracting States" (Art. 2) and to arrange for service to be made in a manner compatible with the law of that State (Art. 5). Alternative methods of service through diplomatic or consular agents (Art. 8) or via mail (Art. 10) may also be used, unless the state of destination objects. For a more detailed account of the Hague Service Convention and the background leading up to it, *see* Andreas F. Lowenfeld, *Litigation and Arbitration* (West, 3d ed. 2005) at 248–251.

The Hague Service Convention is the exclusive method for serving process when "there is occasion to transmit a judicial or extrajudicial document for service abroad" (Art. 1). In *Volkswagenwerk Aktiengesellschaft v. Schlunk*, 486 U.S. 694 (1988), the Supreme Court of the United States held that because Illinois state law permitted service on the German defendant's domestic subsidiary as an "agent" for service of process, there was no occasion for "service abroad" and thus the Convention was not applicable.

When the Hague Service Convention or another internationally agreed means for service does not govern, Federal Rule 4(f)(2) authorizes various other methods of service, which include (A) service prescribed by the foreign law, (B) service directed by the foreign authority in response to a letter rogatory or letter of request, or (C) personal service or mail with a signed receipt dispatched by the clerk of the court, if these methods are not prohibited by the law of the foreign country. Finally, Federal Rule 4(f)(3) allows the court to direct a particular type of service that is not prohibited by international agreement. In *Rio Properties, Inc. v. Rio International Interlink*, 284 F.3d 1007 (9th Cir. 2002), the Ninth Circuit concluded that a district court's order of service by e-mail was proper where the plaintiff had failed in its attempts to serve the defendant, a Costa Rican corporation, by conventional means. The court observed that email was the method most likely to reach the foreign defendant, as it had no office in the United States and preferred electronic communication.

In *Water Splash, Inc. v. Menon*, 137 S. Ct. 1504 (2017), the Supreme Court addressed the permissible means of service under the Hague Service Convention. Unanimously resolving a longstanding circuit split, the Court held that Article 10(a) of the Convention does not prohibit service by mail.

iv.   Territorial Limits of Service

The territorial reach of federal service is set out in Rule 4(k), and a more extensive analysis of extraterritorial service is provided at pp. 185–187. Rule 4(k)(1)(A) allows federal courts to "borrow" state long-arm statutes and thereby extend their jurisdiction to a degree exactly co-extensive with the courts of state in which they sit.

Rule 4(k)(1)(B) provides a rule for reaching parties brought into the action pursuant to Rules 14 (third-party practice) or 19 (compulsory joinder of parties); such parties may be served within a 100-mile radius of the courthouse (whether in-state or out-of-state). This provision is intended to facilitate bringing in additional parties who are technically out-of-state but geographically close enough to be required to appear without great inconvenience.

Rule 4(k)(1)(C) authorizes service outside of the state pursuant to certain federal statutes. For example, when defendants have been joined in an "interpleader" proceeding brought under 28 U.S.C. §1335 to resolve conflicting claims to the same property, Rule 4(k)(1)(C), in conjunction with 28 U.S.C. §2361, authorizes service of process without any territorial limitations. Rule 4(k)(1)(C) also incorporates into the rules special service of process provisions included in numerous federal substantive laws. For instance, the Securities Exchange Act, 15 U.S.C. §78aa,

provides that a defen   ct in numerous districts and
authorizes process to   nt may be found.

Rule 4(k)(2), dis   12–217. establishes a federal
provision for extrater   stances. It provides that for
claims arising under   establish jurisdiction if the
exercise of jurisdiction   on and the defendant is not
subject to jurisdiction   States. The purpose of this
provision is to allow th   sdiction over foreign defendants conducting subs   ven when they may lack sufficient contacts with ar

Keep in mind tha   diction, whatever its source,
must still meet the con   cess to have a valid exercise
of personal jurisdictio   defendant is served pursuant to a wholly federal means of service, such as Rule 4(k)(1)(C) or 4(k)(2), jurisdiction may be sustained if defendant has sufficient aggregate contacts with the
United States. (For further discussion of the Due Process limitations on federal
courts in these circumstances, *see* pp. 212–213.)

The Rule also contains subdivision 4(n), providing for the use of attachment
of a defendant's in-district assets as a basis for obtaining jurisdiction to the extent of
those assets. The Rule limits the use of such *quasi in rem* jurisdiction to situations in
which the plaintiff is unable to obtain jurisdiction over the defendant in the district
by other means. The subdivision provides that state law is to define the circumstances and manner in which the attachment is to be made.

v. Try Your Hand

To test your understanding of the technicalities of the service of process provisions, try using the text of Rule 4 as well as the above commentary, to answer the
following questions:

(1) What is the first step an attorney must take to commence a federal court
action? file a complaint + Summon

Rule 4(B) (2) How and when do you obtain a summons to serve upon the defendant?

4(c) → 4(m) (3) When must process be served? 90 days after the complaint is filed.

(4) Who serves the defendant? The plaintiff

Rule 4(e)(2)(Bc) (5) How is service made upon an individual within the state if he cannot be
served personally?

Rule 4(h) (6) How is service effected upon a corporation located in the state?

Rule 4 (3)(2)(A) (7) When may process be served outside of the state in which the court sits?

(8) Are there provisions for mail service in federal court actions? If so, when
and how? Yes, under limited condition.

4(d)(3) (9) What should a defendant do if he receives a request for waiver of service?

4(f) (10) How is service to be made on a defendant in a foreign country?

b. State Service of Process Statutes

Although many state service of process statutes are modeled after the Federal
Rules, even those that most closely resemble the federal approach may differ in
important aspects. This section briefly highlights some of the common similarities
and differences between Fed. R. Civ. P. 4 and various state statutes.

1. *Who Issues the Summons?* While some states follow the federal model and issue summons through the court clerk or judge, *see, e.g.,* Fla. R. Civ. P. 1.070(a), others allow attorneys to issue summons, *see, e.g.,* Colo. R. Civ. P. 4(b), or even allow the plaintiff (or her attorney) to do so, *see, e.g.,* S.C. R. Civ. P. 4(a).

2. *Who Can Serve?* Some jurisdictions, like the federal system rules, allow service to be effected by anyone 18 or older who is not a party to the suit. *See, e.g.,* Cal. Civ. Proc. Code §414.10. Many also include the sheriff or similar officials, *see, e.g.,* S.C. R. Civ. P. 4(c). It is also common to allow the court to appoint an individual to effect service, *see, e.g.,* Fla. R. Civ. P. 1.070(b).

3. *Who May Be Served?* As we have seen, in the case of corporations and other associations, who may be served is a question potentially subject to dispute. Most state statutes are quite similar to the Federal Rules on this point, but the language may vary from state to state. *See, e.g.,* Cal. Civ. Proc. Code §416.10; S.C. R. Civ. P. 4(d)(3). Some statutes may be quite different, *see, e.g.,* N.Y. C.P.L.R. §310, which allows service upon a partnership by serving any of the partners. Before serving a corporation or association under state law, it is crucial to consult the state's service statute and the case law interpreting it to determine who may accept service.

4. *How May Service Be Effected?* We have seen that the Federal Rules allow service upon an individual to be effected by leaving process with a suitable person at the party's abode. Some state statutes are equally liberal. *See, e.g.,* S.C. R. Civ. P. 4(d)(1), but others require more. Florida, for example, requires service upon a party represented by counsel to be made upon the party's attorney, by mailing to the attorney's last known address or delivery to the attorney's office. Fla. R. Civ. P. 1.080(b). Some states require that service left at the party's home or business be accompanied by mail. *See, e.g.,* N.Y. C.P.L.R. §308(2). In other cases, when personal or substituted service cannot be made with due diligence, service may be effected by delivery to a suitable person at the party's home or business, accompanied by mailing. Only if these methods fail may service be effected by affixing process to the door of the party's business or abode and, again, accompanying this by mailing. N.Y. C.P.L.R. §308(4).

A number of state jurisdictions also permit mail service or authorize a waiver of service. California's statute, on which the Federal Rule was modeled, is the most similar. *See, e.g.,* Cal. Code Civ. Proc. Code §415.30; N.Y. C.P.L.R. §312-a.

5. *Is Proof of Service Required?* All jurisdictions require some form of proof of service — usually, an affidavit signed by the process server.

6. *What Must Be Served?* At one time, some jurisdictions required only that the summons, not necessarily the complaint, be served. Where this was the case, however, the summons had to include a brief statement of the nature of the case and the relief sought. Why would it be crucial that the relief sought be stated in the summons?

7. *What Information Must Appear in the Process?* Most state service statutes require essentially the same information as Fed. R. Civ. P. 4(a). The most significant common difference is to require that the basis of venue be stated. *See, e.g.,* N.Y. C.P.L.R. §305(a). It is important to consult the particular state law on this point, however, because the technical requirements may vary, and failure to comply with these requirements will often invalidate the service.

248   Chapter 2. Personal Jurisdiction and Other Court-Access Rules

c. Immunity from Process

In a number of jurisdictions, statutes or case law will provide that process cannot be effectively served upon parties who come into the jurisdiction for reasons entitling them to "immunity" from process. Most commonly, immunity is granted to persons, such as witnesses, parties, and attorneys, who have entered the jurisdiction to participate in unrelated judicial proceedings. The justification for this is to aid the court by encouraging such persons to attend the proceeding, free of concern that they might be served once in the jurisdiction.

If the person would be amenable to service outside the jurisdiction as well, and the justification for immunity is therefore inapplicable, should the court deny immunity? Some courts have so held. *See, e.g., Severn v. Adidas Sportschuhfabriken*, 33 Cal. App. 3d 754, 109 Cal. Rptr. 328 (1973) (service on French citizen, in Florida to give deposition, upheld since amenable to service in France); *Merigone v. Seaboard Capital Corp.*, 85 Misc. 2d 965 (Sup. Ct. 1969) (service on New Jersey resident, in New York to attend hearing, upheld since amenable to service in New Jersey).

Immunity may be granted to other persons as well, such as public officials in the execution of their duty, *see* 45 A.L.R.2d 421 (1956), foreign sovereigns or their representatives, *see* 25 A.L.R.3d 322 (1969), or private persons on certain types of public business (e.g., testifying before a legislative committee). For an interesting application of this type of immunity, *see Kadic v. Karadzic*, 70 F.3d 232, 246–248 (2d Cir. 1995), in which defendant, a self-proclaimed president of an unrecognized state and an alleged war criminal, was deemed *not* immune from process while on a visit to New York to speak at the United Nations. The court held that defendant was not immune from service while outside of the "United Nations District," the several block area surrounding the United Nations building, notwithstanding his immunity while inside the District.

Finally, immunity may also be granted where the party served has been enticed into the jurisdiction by fraud. *See Wyman v. Newhouse*, 93 F.2d 313 (2d Cir. 1937); *Tickle v. Barton*, 142 W. Va. 188, 95 S.E.2d 427 (1956).

d. Service of Process and Statutes of Limitations

In order to avoid having a claim barred by the expiration of the statute of limitations, plaintiff must commence the action before the applicable time period has run out. What act is required, however, to "commence" an action for statute of limitations purposes? We have seen that Fed. R. Civ. P. 3 declares that an action is "commenced" when the complaint is filed with the court. When an action is brought in federal court under federal law, therefore, it is the act of filing that must occur before the limitations period has expired (unless the federal statute itself specifies otherwise). *See West v. Conrail*, 481 U.S. 35 (1987). Filing is said to "toll" the running of the statute of limitations.

When the action is brought in federal court under state law, however, it is necessary to apply the state statute of limitations, including the state law as to tolling. *See Walker v. Armco Steel Corp.*, 446 U.S. 740 (1980), discussed at pp. 446–447. (Also, some federal statutes provide for the borrowing of state limitations periods. Since many states require service upon the defendant to toll the statute of limitations, in such actions it is that act, and not filing, that must precede the expiration of the limitations period.)

Refer back to the discussion above of Fed. R. Civ. P. 4(m). The Rule requires that service must be effected within 90 days of the filing of the complaint. However, if service is required to toll a state statute of limitations, and the statute is about to expire, plaintiff cannot safely wait 90 days but must rather effect service before the statute runs out. Conversely, where filing is required to toll the statute, plaintiff must be careful to effect service within the 90-day period or risk having the filing nullified. If a filing is nullified and the statute has meanwhile expired, plaintiff's claim may be barred.

H.   *LOCAL ACTIONS, VENUE,* FORUM NON CONVENIENS, *AND TRANSFER*

The term *venue* is used to describe a number of quite distinct and different problems. Practically, *venue* might be defined as one more hurdle that must be jumped in order to proceed in a particular court; functionally, it is differentiated in the Federal Rules of Civil Procedure from both subject matter jurisdiction and personal jurisdiction in the Rule 12(b)(3) motion to dismiss for lack of venue. Treatises often refer to *venue* as the doctrine determining the place of trial, but in that sense it seems similar to jurisdiction to adjudicate. *Venue* is often distinguished as being concerned only with the "convenience of trial" whereas *jurisdiction* has been said to concern the "power to adjudicate," but this distinction seems more semantic than real. Historically, the difference between "power to adjudicate" and "place of trial" might have made more sense than it seems to today. In England, for example, an action was commenced in the central courts at Westminster. Since jurors in a civil action originally functioned as witnesses, however, it was necessary that jurors be drawn from the place where the events took place — *nisi prius* ("unless before") the judges on assize had been to the county where the action could be tried. Thus, while the action was brought at Westminster, the venue of the trial was the place where the events occurred. Gradually, as jurors lost their role as witnesses, it was no longer necessary to limit venue in this way, and most actions (except certain actions involving title to real property) were regarded as transitory actions that could be brought anywhere.

The adoption of venue in the United States has common roots with its historical antecedent. In many states, as well as in the federal courts, it was thought desirable to limit the fora in which suit may be brought to those regions of the state (or to particular districts as regards the federal system) that had some connection to the parties and the litigation. The concept of venue to facilitate judicial convenience had additional value in the inter-jurisdictional context of the federal system where adjudicatory jurisdiction of the individual states was based largely on theories of power over the person and/or property rather than litigational convenience. Whether this additional tier of convenience scrutiny is necessary is unclear in light of modern developments in adjudicatory jurisdiction where connections between the defendant, the litigation, and the forum play a more significant role in determining a proper forum, although venue rules may serve to further identify a desirable forum. Moreover, venue rules continue to be important in the intrastate context with respect to both federal and state regimes.

Within the federal judicial system, some states have multiple districts and the venue rules are the only mechanism to allocate a case among the districts of a single state. Similarly, the state venue rules in the state system are important in that they provide the mechanism for determining where a case may be heard within a particular state.

1.   Formal State and Federal Venue Statutes

a.   Venue Rules in State Courts

Venue in the state courts operates intra-jurisdictionally — that is, the venue rules determine where within the state the action should be heard. State venue statutes use a variety of criteria to determine the appropriate location of a lawsuit within a particular state. Sometimes the statutes will limit the forum to the county or district of residency of one or both of the parties (if a resident is party). Occasionally, the venue will be fixed where the events occurred. Often a combination of these factors is used. *See, e.g.,* N.Y. C.P.L.R. §503 (a) (providing that "the place of trial shall be in the county in which one of the parties resided when it was commenced, or, if none of the parties then resided in the state, in any county designated by the plaintiff"). *See generally* Stevens, *Venue Statutes: Diagnosis and Proposed Cure,* 49 Mich. L. Rev. 307 (1951).

b.   Venue Rules in Federal Courts

Venue in the federal courts is governed by the general default venue statute, 28 U.S.C. §1391, as well as by specialized venue provisions that govern particular federal claims. *See, e.g.,* 28 U.S.C. §1401 (specifying venue for stockholder derivative actions). Federal venue operates both *intra*-jurisdictionally, to allocate a case within a multidistrict state, as well as *inter*-jurisdictionally, to allocate a case within the nationwide federal judicial system.

The venue provisions of §1391 serve to limit the plaintiff's choice of federal courts in which an action may be brought. Thus, even if a defendant is subject to jurisdiction in a particular state, the venue rules may operate to exclude the federal court in that state, or in other situations may allocate the case to a particular district in that state.

The venue criteria set out in §1391 are the result of a series of amendments to the federal venue statute passed in the 1990s and again in 2011. The effect of the first round of amendments was, by and large, to relax the venue requirements and broaden plaintiff's choice of forum. This was particularly true with respect to a suit against a corporation. The most recent amendments in the Federal Courts Jurisdiction and Venue Clarification Act of 2011 (hereinafter the "2011 venue amendments") eliminated some anachronistic venue provisions that no longer served a useful function and revised other provisions that had caused confusion in the administration of the statute.

Proper venue in a case against a single defendant is in the judicial district where the defendant resides (28 U.S.C. §1391(b)(1)), or where a "substantial part of the events or omissions giving rise to the claim occurred." 28 U.S.C. §1391(b)(2). The 2011 venue amendments provide that a natural person is "deemed to reside" in the judicial district in which that person is domiciled. 28 U.S.C. §1391(c)(1). With respect to a defendant corporation or other artificial entity with the capacity to sue or be sued, 28 U.S.C. §1391(c)(2) deems its "residence" to be "in any judicial district in which such defendant is subject to personal jurisdiction with respect to the civil action in question." Thus, proper venue for a corporation or other entity, including an unincorporated association — when it is sued as a *defendant*— is anywhere it is subject to personal jurisdiction. In multidistrict states, a defendant corporation is deemed subject to personal jurisdiction in a district if its contacts with the district would be sufficient to subject it to jurisdiction if the district were a separate state.[*] *See* 28 U.S.C. §1391(d). When a corporation or artificial entity (with the capacity to sue or be sued) is a *plaintiff*, 28 U.S.C. §1391(c)(2) limits its "residence" to "the judicial district in which it maintains its principal place of business." An alien lawfully admitted for permanent residence in the United States is "deemed to reside" in the judicial district in which that person is domiciled, and thus is treated the same as a U.S. citizen. 28 U.S.C. §1391(a). Defendants (whether citizens or aliens) not resident in the United States may be sued in any district, and their joinder in the lawsuit is disregarded for purposes of determining venue as to [joinder] other defendants. 28 U.S.C. §1391(c)(3).

Venue problems arise primarily in multi-defendant cases. Venue is proper in the district where any defendant resides, if all defendants reside in the same State in which the district court is located. 28 U.S.C. §1391(b)(1). That means that in a case against defendants *from different states*, suit brought in a district that is the residence of one of the defendants is not a proper venue under §1391(b)(1). However, as noted above, venue is also proper where "a substantial part of the events or omissions giving rise to the claim occurred." 28 U.S.C. §1391(b)(2). Thus, venue in the district where such events or acts occurred is the relevant provision most likely applicable to cases involving multiple defendants from different states.

On occasion, however, particular districts — although they satisfy the venue requirements — are unavailable because the plaintiff is unable to get personal jurisdiction over all defendants there. In such a situation, there is one last venue option. This additional rule provides that "if there is no district in which an action may otherwise be brought," venue will be proper in any district "in which any defendant

---

[*] Note the discrepancy in language between 28 U.S.C. §1391(c) and (d). Section 1391(c) was amended in 2011 to accord parity of treatment to corporations and unincorporated associations. The language of §1391(c) was changed to expressly reach unincorporated associations and make them subject to venue in the same manner as a corporation ("an entity that has the right to sue and be sued in its common name"). Yet the language of §1391(d) remains unaltered, referring only to corporations, and making no reference to unincorporated associations. Does that mean that §1391(d), which effectively *limits* the venue possibilities in multidistrict states, applies only to corporations, or is the incongruity in these provisions the result of congressional oversight in the recent 2011 venue amendments?

is subject to the court's personal jurisdiction with respect to such action." 28 U.S.C. §1391(b)(3).* As a practical matter, §1391(b)(3) is invoked most often against multiple defendants (where defendants are from different jurisdictions) and where the claims arise from conduct overseas.

In 2017, the Court issued two decisions interpreting federal venue provisions. In *TC Heartland LLC v. Kraft Foods Group Brands,* 137 S. Ct. 1514 (2017), the Court considered the venue statute for patent infringement actions, 28 U.S.C. §1400(b), which permits plaintiffs to bring suit in "the judicial district where the defendant resides, or where the defendant has committed acts of infringement and has a regular and established place of business." In a unanimous opinion, the Court held that a corporation "resides" only in its state of incorporation for purposes of the patent venue statute.

In reaching that conclusion, the Court considered plaintiffs' contention that the 1988 amendments to §1391 had changed the original meaning of §1400. The amended text of §1391 states, "[e]xcept as otherwise provided by law" and "[f]or all venue purposes," a corporation "shall be deemed to reside, if a defendant, in any judicial district in which such defendant is subject to the court's personal jurisdiction with respect to the civil action in question." Prior to the amendments resulting in this language, the Court had held that "resides" within the meaning of §1400 was limited to a corporation's place of incorporation. But after the 1988 amendments, the Federal Circuit interpreted the amended text to apply to all venue statutes within the same chapter—including §1400. *See VE Holding Corp. v. Johnson Gas Appliance Co.,* 917 F.2d 1574 (1990), *vacated, TC Heartland,* 137 S. Ct. 1514. As a result, since *VE Holding,* a patent infringement defendant was deemed to "reside," for purposes of §1400, in any judicial district which had jurisdiction over it with respect to the action.

In *TC Heartland,* the Court abrogated *VE Holding,* finding that Congress had not "supplant[ed]" the Court's previous interpretation. As such, venue in patent infringement actions would be limited to the place of incorporation, or where "the defendant has committed acts of infringement and has a regular and established place of business." The decision curtails plaintiffs' ability to forum shop for plaintiff-friendly districts where defendants have limited activities.

The *BNSF* case, discussed earlier at page 92 also concerns venue provisions in federal statutes. That case, however, focuses on the difference between jurisdiction and venue. FELA §56, in specifying where an action "may be brought," includes "in the district of residence of the defendant" and "in which the defendant shall be doing business." In finding that §56 spoke to venue and not jurisdiction, the Court clarified that §56 did not seek to define the jurisdictional reach of courts entertaining FELA actions.

---

* Prior to the 2011 amendments, §1391 contained different subsections for venue depending upon whether a case was in federal court based upon diversity or federal-question jurisdiction. The provisions in these subsections were largely identical, but contained some slight differences. There was never any good reason for the difference, and the 2011 amendments eliminated it, providing for a unitary approach to venue as described above.

2. A Note on the Local Action Rule

The 2011 venue amendments also eliminated an archaic specialized venue rule for actions involving title to land, including *in personam* damage actions for trespass to land (where title to land is an element of plaintiff's claim for damages). This so-called local action rule limited venue in such cases to the district where the land was located. In an era where personal jurisdiction over the defendant was limited to defendant's presence or domicile, jurisdiction over the defendant often could not be obtained in the place where the property was located. In such a case, plaintiff would have no forum at all in which to proceed.* The 2011 venue amendments provide that proper venue "shall be determined without regard to whether the action is local or transitory in nature." 28 U.S.C. §1391(a)(2).

Notwithstanding the abrogation of the local action rule in the federal venue provisions, actions to directly determine rights in real property (as contrasted with actions for damages for trespass to land) may still have to be brought in the place where the real property is located. In such actions, many courts hold that the authority of a court to hear an action to determine rights to real property is a matter of subject matter jurisdiction — not venue — and cannot be waived by the parties. Moreover, some state courts may continue to apply the local action rule in broader contexts, such as actions for damages to land.

3. Forum Non Conveniens

The allocation of cases as between state judicial systems is performed largely through the rules of jurisdiction. Within the federal system, the allocation function is aided by the formal venue rules as well. Nonetheless, those rules often operate to give a plaintiff a choice among several fora, and, as we have seen, a number of factors may influence a plaintiff's choice of a particular forum. One additional doctrine of discretion may further restrict a plaintiff's ultimate selection of a forum and provides a defendant with some counter-control over where suit may be brought. In the state courts and in the international context in federal courts, the doctrine of *forum non conveniens* attempts to direct the litigation to a convenient, if not the most convenient, forum; where both the initial and alternative forums are federal courts, this concern with convenience is served by the mechanism of transfer. 28 U.S.C. §1404.

---

* The most notable example of the local action principle in this context is the early case of *Livingston v. Jefferson*, 15 Fed. Cas. 660 (C. C.D. Va. 1811), involving a lawsuit by Edward Livingston against Thomas Jefferson. Livingston had acquired property in Louisiana, which was claimed by the United States as national property. A U.S. marshal, acting under orders from then-President Jefferson, ejected Livingston from the property. Livingston waited until the end of Jefferson's presidency and then brought suit against Jefferson in federal court in Virginia where Jefferson resided. Livingston sought money damages for trespass to his land in Louisiana. The court (with Chief Justice Marshall sitting as a circuit justice in this case) dismissed the suit because the action was "local" and could only be brought in Louisiana where the land was situated.

The doctrine of *forum non conveniens* was developed at common law to allow courts the discretion to dismiss an action that would be more appropriately litigated in another forum even though the proper jurisdiction and venue requirements were met in the first forum. The earliest cases arose in admiralty where, by physically attaching the vessel, a nation's court could legitimately hear disputes arising from collisions between foreign vessels on the high seas. Any nation's admiralty courts were presumed competent to adjudicate the parties' rights based on the *communis juris*—the common law of nations—which governs maritime cases arising in international water. *See, e.g., The Belgenland*, 114 U.S. 355 (1885).

In the 1930s, there were indications of the Supreme Court's willingness to expand dismissals on grounds of convenience. *Canada Malting Co., Ltd. v. Patterson Steamships, Ltd.*, 285 U.S. 413 (1932), arose after a collision between two Canadian vessels in Lake Superior on the American side of the international boundary line. Canadian authorities investigated the accident, but the owner of cargo lost on board one of the vessels brought an action for damages in a United States district court sitting in New York, hoping to ensure the application of the more favorable American recovery scheme. The Supreme Court affirmed "an unqualified discretion to decline jurisdiction in suits in admiralty between foreigners," entrusting to the Canadian courts the question of which nation's law to apply. 285 U.S. at 421.

Broader application of the doctrine in federal courts was upheld in *Gulf Oil Corp. v. Gilbert*, 330 U.S. 501 (1947). Gilbert was a resident of Virginia where he owned and operated a warehouse. The warehouse was destroyed by a fire, and Gilbert alleged the cause to be Gulf Oil's careless handling of a delivery of gasoline (in violation of a local ordinance). Gilbert brought a diversity action in New York where he apparently believed he would win a larger jury verdict and where Gulf was qualified to do business and had designated an agent to receive process. Gulf, a Pennsylvania corporation, was similarly susceptible to jurisdiction and process in Virginia. Every person charged with participating in the allegedly negligent acts resided in Virginia. Gulf claimed a need to implead the Virginia contractor who made the delivery and approximately 350 persons whose goods were stored at the warehouse resided in Virginia. While accepting the general principle of deference to a plaintiff's choice of forum, the Supreme Court pointed to a variety of private and public interests that justified the district court's dismissal of the action:

> The principal of *forum non conveniens* is simply that a court may resist imposition upon its jurisdiction even when its jurisdiction is authorized by the letter of a general venue statute. . . .
>
> If the combination and weight of factors requisite to given results are difficult to forecast or state, those to be considered are not difficult to name. An interest to be considered, and the one likely to be most pressed, is the private interest of the litigant. Important considerations are the relative ease of access to sources of proof; availability of compulsory process for attendance of unwilling, and the cost of obtaining attendance of willing, witnesses; possibility of viewing the premises, if view would be appropriate to the action; and all other practical problems that make trial of a case easy, expeditious and inexpensive. There may also be questions of enforceability of a judgment if one is obtained. The court will weigh relative advantages and obstacles of a fair trial. It is often said that the plaintiff

may not, by choice of an inconvenient forum, "vex," "harass," or "oppress" the defendant by inflicting upon him expense or trouble not necessary to his own right to pursue his remedy. But unless the balance is strongly in favor of the defendant, the plaintiff's choice of forum should rarely be disturbed.

Factors of public interest also have place in applying the doctrine. Administrative difficulties follow for courts when litigation is piled up in congested centers instead of being handled at its origin. Jury duty is a burden that ought not to be imposed upon the people of a community which has no relation to the litigation. In many cases which touch the affairs of many persons, there is reason for holding the trial in their view and reach rather than in remote parts of the country where they can learn of it by report only.

There is a local interest in having localized controversies decided at home. There is appropriateness, too, in having the trial of a diversity case in a forum that is at home with the state law that must govern the case, rather than having a court in some other forum untangle problems in conflict of laws, and in law foreign to itself.

330 U.S. at 507–509 (footnotes omitted).

Justice Black dissented, arguing that "[n]either the venue statute nor the statute which has governed jurisdiction since 1789 contains any indication or implication that a federal district court, once satisfied that jurisdiction and venue requirements have been met, may decline to exercise its jurisdiction," 330 U.S. at 513, and that recognition of *forum non conveniens* was beyond the power of federal courts without a specific congressional mandate. He also predicted that "[t]he Court's new rule will clutter the very threshold of the federal courts with a preliminary trial of fact concerning the relative convenience of forums." 330 U.S. at 516.

Modern *forum non conveniens* cases often involve multinational corporations and events spanning the globe. Inevitably plaintiffs and defendants prefer different fora, particularly when laws governing liability differ depending upon the sovereign before which the parties litigate their dispute. The following case represents the Supreme Court's attempt to define the proper approach for deciding motions for dismissal based on the doctrine of *forum non conveniens*.

Piper Aircraft Co. v. Reyno

454 U.S. 235 (1981)

JUSTICE MARSHALL delivered the opinion of the Court.

These cases arise out of an air crash that took place in Scotland. Respondent, acting as representative of the estates of several Scottish citizens killed in the accident, brought wrongful-death actions against petitioners that were ultimately transferred to the United States District Court for the Middle District of Pennsylvania. Petitioners moved to dismiss on the ground of *forum non conveniens*. After noting that an alternative forum existed in Scotland, the District Court granted their motions. 479 F. Supp. 727 (1979). The United States Court of Appeals for the Third Circuit reversed. 630 F.2d 149 (1980). The Court of Appeals based its decision, at least in part, on the ground that dismissal is automatically barred where the law of the alternative forum is less favorable to the plaintiff than the law of the forum chosen by the plaintiff. Because we conclude that the possibility of an unfavorable change in law should not, by itself, bar dismissal, and because we conclude that the District Court did not otherwise abuse its discretion, we reverse.

I

A

In July 1976, a small commercial aircraft crashed in the Scottish highlands during the course of a charter flight from Blackpool to Perth. The pilot and five passengers were killed instantly. The decedents were all Scottish subjects and residents, as are their heirs and next of kin. There were no eyewitnesses to the accident. At the time of the crash the plane was subject to Scottish air traffic control.

The aircraft, a twin-engine Piper Aztec, was manufactured in Pennsylvania by petitioner Piper Aircraft Co. (Piper). The propellers were manufactured in Ohio by petitioner Hartzell Propeller, Inc. (Hartzell). At the time of the crash the aircraft was registered in Great Britain and was owned and maintained by Air Navigation and Trading Co., Ltd. (Air Navigation). It was operated by McDonald Aviation, Ltd. (McDonald), a Scottish air taxi service. Both Air Navigation and McDonald were organized in the United Kingdom. The wreckage of the plane is now in a hangar in Farnsborough, England.

The British Department of Trade investigated the accident shortly after it occurred. A preliminary report found that the plane crashed after developing a spin, and suggested that mechanical failure in the plane or the propeller was responsible. At Hartzell's request, this report was reviewed by a three-member Review Board, which held a nine-day adversary hearing attended by all interested parties. The Review Board found no evidence of defective equipment and indicated that pilot error may have contributed to the accident. The pilot, who had obtained his commercial pilot's license only three months earlier, was flying over high ground at an altitude considerably lower than the minimum height required by his company's operations manual.

In July 1977, a California probate court appointed respondent Gaynell Reyno administratrix of the estates of the five passengers. Reyno is not related to and does not know any of the decedents or their survivors; she was a legal secretary to the attorney who filed this lawsuit. Several days after her appointment, Reyno commenced separate wrongful-death actions against Piper and Hartzell in the Superior Court of California, claiming negligence and strict liability. Air Navigation, McDonald, and the estate of the pilot are not parties to this litigation. The survivors of the five passengers whose estates are represented by Reyno filed a separate action in the United Kingdom against Air Navigation, McDonald, and the pilot's estate. Reyno candidly admits that the action against Piper and Hartzell was filed in the United States because its laws regarding liability, capacity to sue, and damages are more favorable to her position than are those of Scotland. Scottish law does not recognize strict liability in tort. Moreover, it permits wrongful-death actions only when brought by a decedent's relatives. The relatives may sue only for "loss of support and society."

On petitioners' motion, the suit was removed to the United States District Court for the Central District of California. Piper then moved for transfer to the United States District Court for the Middle District of Pennsylvania, pursuant to 28 U.S.C. §1404(a).* Hartzell moved to dismiss for lack of personal jurisdiction, or in the alternative, to transfer.[5] In December 1977, the District Court quashed service on Hartzell and transferred the case to the Middle District of Pennsylvania. Respondent then properly served process on Hartzell.

B

In May 1978, after the suit had been transferred, both Hartzell and Piper moved to dismiss the action on the ground of *forum non conveniens.* The District Court granted these motions in October 1979. It relied on the balancing test set forth by this Court in *Gulf Oil Corp. v. Gilbert*, 330 U.S. 501 (1947), and its companion case, *Koster v. Lumbermens Mut. Cas. Co.*, 330 U.S. 518 (1947). . . .

After describing our decisions in *Gilbert* and *Koster*, the District Court analyzed the facts of these cases. It began by observing that an alternative forum existed in Scotland; Piper and Hartzell had agreed to submit to the jurisdiction of the Scottish courts and to waive any statute of limitations defense that might be available. It then stated that plaintiff's choice of forum was entitled to little weight. The court recognized that a plaintiff's choice ordinarily deserves substantial deference. It noted, however, that Reyno "is a representative of foreign citizens and residents seeking a forum in the United States because of the more liberal rules concerning products liability law," and that "the courts have been less solicitous when the plaintiff is not an American citizen or resident, and particularly when the foreign citizens seek to benefit from the more liberal tort rules provided for the protection of citizens and residents of the United States.". . .

The District Court next examined several factors relating to the private interests of the litigants, and determined that these factors strongly pointed towards Scotland as the appropriate forum. Although evidence concerning the design, manufacture, and testing of the plane and propeller is located in the United States, the connections with Scotland are otherwise "overwhelming.". . . The real parties in interest are citizens of Scotland, as were all the decedents. Witnesses who could testify regarding the maintenance of the aircraft, the training of the pilot, and the investigation of the accident — all essential to the defense — are in Great Britain. Moreover, all witnesses to damages are located in Scotland. Trial would be aided by familiarity with Scottish topography, and by easy access to the wreckage.

The District Court reasoned that because crucial witnesses and evidence were beyond the reach of compulsory process, and because the defendants would not be able to implead potential Scottish third-party defendants, it would be "unfair to make

---

*28 U.S.C. §1404(a), which will be discussed in the next section of this chapter, provides for the transfer of a case between federal district courts "[f]or the convenience of parties and witnesses, in the interest of justice" provided that jurisdiction and venue are proper in both districts. — EDS.

5. The District Court concluded that it could not assert personal jurisdiction over Hartzell consistent with due process. However, it decided not to dismiss Hartzell because the corporation would be amenable to process in Pennsylvania.

Piper and Hartzell proceed to trial in this forum.". . . The survivors had brought separate actions in Scotland against the pilot, McDonald, and Air Navigation. "[I]t would be fairer to all parties and less costly if the entire case was presented to one jury with available testimony from all relevant witnesses.". . . Although the court recognized that if trial were held in the United States, Piper and Hartzell could file indemnity or contribution actions against the Scottish defendants, it believed that there was a significant risk of inconsistent verdicts.[7] The District Court concluded that the relevant public interests also pointed strongly towards dismissal. The court determined that Pennsylvania law would apply to Piper and Scottish law to Hartzell if the case were tried in the Middle District of Pennsylvania. As a result, "trial in this forum would be hopelessly complex and confusing for a jury.". . . In addition, the court noted that it was unfamiliar with Scottish law and thus would have to rely upon experts from that country. The court also found that the trial would be enormously costly and time-consuming; that it would be unfair to burden citizens with jury duty when the Middle District of Pennsylvania has little connection with the controversy; and that Scotland has a substantial interest in the outcome of the litigation.

In opposing the motions to dismiss, respondent contended that dismissal would be unfair because Scottish law was less favorable. The District Court explicitly rejected this claim. It reasoned that the possibility that dismissal might lead to an unfavorable change in the law did not deserve significant weight; any deficiency in the foreign law was a "matter to be dealt with in the foreign forum.". . .

C

On appeal, the United States Court of Appeals for the Third Circuit reversed and remanded for trial. The decision to reverse appears to be based on two alternative grounds. First, the Court held that the District Court abused its discretion in conducting the *Gilbert* analysis. Second, the Court held that dismissal is never appropriate where the law of the alternative forum is less favorable to the plaintiff.

The Court of Appeals began its review of the District Court's *Gilbert* analysis by noting that the plaintiff's choice of forum deserved substantial weight, even though the real parties in interest are nonresidents. It then rejected the District Court's balancing of the private interests. It found that Piper and Hartzell had failed adequately to support their claim that key witnesses would be unavailable if trial were held in the United States: they had never specified the witnesses they would call and the testimony these witnesses would provide. The Court of Appeals gave little weight to the fact that Piper and Hartzell would not be able to implead potential Scottish third-party defendants, reasoning that this difficulty would be "burdensome" but not "unfair."[9] . . . Finally, the court stated that resolution of the suit would not be significantly aided by familiarity with Scottish topography, or by viewing the wreckage.

---

7. The District Court explained that inconsistent verdicts might result if petitioners were held liable on the basis of strict liability here, and then required to prove negligence in an indemnity action in Scotland. Moreover, even if the same standard of liability applied, there was a danger that different juries would find different facts and produce inconsistent results.

9. The court claimed that the risk of inconsistent verdicts was slight because Pennsylvania and Scotland both adhere to principles of *res judicata* [which requires each jurisdiction to recognize and enforce judgments of the other].

The Court of Appeals also rejected the District Court's analysis of the public interest factors. It found that the District Court gave undue emphasis to the application of Scottish law: " 'the mere fact that the court is called upon to determine and apply foreign law does not present a legal problem of the sort which would justify the dismissal of a case otherwise properly before the court.' " . . . In any event, it believed that Scottish law need not be applied. After conducting its own choice-of-law analysis, the Court of Appeals determined that American law would govern the actions against both Piper and Hartzell. The same choice-of-law analysis apparently led it to conclude that Pennsylvania and Ohio, rather than Scotland, are the jurisdictions with the greatest policy interests in the dispute, and that all other public interest factors favored trial in the United States.

In any event, it appears that the Court of Appeals would have reversed even if the District Court had properly balanced the public and private interests. The court stated:

> [I]t is apparent that the dismissal would work a change in the applicable law so that the plaintiff's strict liability claim would be eliminated from the case. But . . . a dismissal for *forum non conveniens*, like a statutory transfer, "should not, despite its convenience, result in a change in the applicable law." Only when American law is not applicable, or when the foreign jurisdiction would, as a matter of its own choice of law, give the plaintiff the benefit of the claim to which she is entitled here, would dismissal be justified. . . .

In other words, the court decided that dismissal is automatically barred if it would lead to a change in the applicable law unfavorable to the plaintiff. . . .

II

The Court of Appeals erred in holding that plaintiffs may defeat a motion to dismiss on the ground of *forum non conveniens* merely by showing that the substantive law that would be applied in the alternative forum is less favorable to the plaintiffs than that of the present forum. The possibility of a change in substantive law should ordinarily not be given conclusive or even substantial weight in the *forum non conveniens* inquiry. . . .

. . . [B]y holding that the central focus of the *forum non conveniens* inquiry is convenience, *Gilbert* implicitly recognized that dismissal may not be barred solely because of the possibility of an unfavorable change in law. Under *Gilbert*, dismissal will ordinarily be appropriate where trial in the plaintiff's chosen forum imposes a heavy burden on the defendant or the court, and where the plaintiff is unable to offer any specific reasons of convenience supporting his choice.[15] If substantial weight were given to the possibility of an unfavorable change in law, however, dismissal might be barred even where trial in the chosen forum was plainly inconvenient. . . .

---

15. In other words, *Gilbert* held that dismissal may be warranted where a plaintiff chooses a particular forum, not because it is convenient, but solely in order to harass the defendant or take advantage of favorable law. This is precisely the situation in which the Court of Appeals' rule would bar dismissal.

In fact, if conclusive or substantial weight were given to the possibility of a change in law, the *forum non conveniens* doctrine would become virtually useless. Jurisdiction and venue requirements are often easily satisfied. As a result, many plaintiffs are able to choose from among several forums. Ordinarily, these plaintiffs will select that forum whose choice-of-law rules are most advantageous. Thus, if the possibility of an unfavorable change in substantive law is given substantial weight in the *forum non conveniens* inquiry, dismissal would rarely be proper. . . .

The Court of Appeals' approach is not only inconsistent with the purpose of the *forum non conveniens* doctrine, but also poses substantial practical problems. If the possibility of a change in law were given substantial weight, deciding motions to dismiss on the ground of *forum non conveniens* would become quite difficult. Choice-of-law analysis would become extremely important, and the courts would frequently be required to interpret the law of foreign jurisdictions. First, the trial court would have to determine what law would apply if the case were tried in the chosen forum, and what law would apply if the case were tried in the alternative forum. It would then have to compare the rights, remedies, and procedures available under the law that would be applied in each forum. Dismissal would be appropriate only if the court concluded that the law applied by the alternative forum is as favorable to the plaintiff as that of the chosen forum. The doctrine of *forum non conveniens*, however, is designed in part to help courts avoid conducting complex exercises in comparative law. As we stated in *Gilbert*, the public interest factors point towards dismissal where the court would be required to "untangle problems in conflict of laws, and in law foreign to itself.". . .

Upholding the decision of the Court of Appeals would result in other practical problems. At least where the foreign plaintiff named an American manufacturer as defendant,[17] a court could not dismiss the case on grounds of *forum non conveniens* where dismissal might lead to an unfavorable change in law. The American courts, which are already extremely attractive to foreign plaintiffs, would become even more attractive. The flow of litigation into the United States would increase and further congest already crowded courts.[19] . . .

---

17. In fact, the defendant might not even have to be American. A foreign plaintiff seeking damages for an accident that occurred abroad might be able to obtain service of process on a foreign defendant who does business in the United States. Under the Court of Appeals' holding, dismissal would be barred if the law in the alternative forum were less favorable to the plaintiff—even though none of the parties are American, and even though there is absolutely no nexus between the subject matter of the litigation and the United States.

19. In holding that the possibility of a change in law unfavorable to the plaintiff should not be given substantial weight, we also necessarily hold that the possibility of a change in law favorable to the defendant should not be considered. Respondent suggests that Piper and Hartzell filed the motion to dismiss, not simply because trial in the United States would be inconvenient, but also because they believe the laws of Scotland are more favorable. She argues that this should be taken into account in the analysis of the private interests. We recognize, of course, that Piper and Hartzell may be engaged in reverse forum-shopping. However, this possibility ordinarily should not enter into a trial court's analysis of the private interests. If the defendant is able to overcome the presumption in favor of plaintiff by showing that trial in the chosen forum would be unnecessarily burdensome, dismissal is appropriate—regardless of the fact that defendant may also be motivated by a desire to obtain a more favorable forum. . . .

We do not hold that the possibility of an unfavorable change in law should *never* be a relevant consideration in a *forum non conveniens* inquiry. Of course, if the remedy provided by the alternative forum is so clearly inadequate or unsatisfactory that it is no remedy at all, the unfavorable change in law may be given substantial weight; the District Court may conclude that dismissal would not be in the interests of justice.[22] In these cases, however, the remedies that would be provided by the Scottish courts do not fall within this category. Although the relatives of the decedents may not be able to rely on a strict liability theory, and although their potential damages award may be smaller, there is no danger that they will be deprived of any remedy or treated unfairly.

III

The Court of Appeals also erred in rejecting the District Court's *Gilbert* analysis. The Court of Appeals stated that more weight should have been given to the plaintiff's choice of forum, and criticized the District Court's analysis of the private and public interests. However, the District Court's decision regarding the deference due plaintiff's choice of forum was appropriate. Furthermore, we do not believe that the District Court abused its discretion in weighing the private and public interests.

A

The District Court acknowledged that there is ordinarily a strong presumption in favor of the plaintiff's choice of forum, which may be overcome only when the private and public interest factors clearly point towards trial in the alternative forum. It held, however, that the presumption applies with less force when the plaintiff or real parties in interest are foreign.

The District Court's distinction between resident or citizen plaintiffs and foreign plaintiffs is fully justified. In *Koster*, the Court indicated that a plaintiff's choice of forum is entitled to greater deference when the plaintiff has chosen the home forum. . . . When the home forum has been chosen, it is reasonable to assume that this choice is convenient. When the plaintiff is foreign, however, this assumption is much less reasonable. Because the central purpose of any *forum non conveniens* inquiry is to ensure that the trial is convenient, a foreign plaintiff's choice deserves less deference.

B

The *forum non conveniens* determination is committed to the sound discretion of the trial court. It may be reversed only when there has been a clear abuse of discretion; where the court has considered all relevant public and private interest factors, and where its balancing of these factors is reasonable, its decision deserves

---

22. At the outset of any *forum non conveniens* inquiry, the court must determine whether there exists an alternative forum. Ordinarily, this requirement will be satisfied when the defendant is "amenable to process" in the other jurisdiction. *Gilbert*, 330 U.S. at 506-507. In rare circumstances, however, where the remedy offered by the other forum is clearly unsatisfactory, the other forum may not be an adequate alternative, and the initial requirement may not be satisfied. Thus, for example, dismissal would not be appropriate where the alternative forum does not permit litigation of the subject matter of the dispute. . . .

substantial deference. . . . In examining the District Court's analysis of the public and private interests, however, the Court of Appeals seems to have lost sight of this rule, and substituted its own judgment for that of the District Court.

(1)

In analyzing the private interest factors, the District Court stated that the connections with Scotland are "overwhelming.". . . This characterization may be somewhat exaggerated. Particularly with respect to the question of relative ease of access to sources of proof, the private interests point in both directions. As respondent emphasizes, records concerning the design, manufacture, and testing of the propeller and plane are located in the United States. She would have greater access to sources of proof relevant to her strict liability and negligence theories if trial were held here.[25] However, the District Court did not act unreasonably in concluding that fewer evidentiary problems would be posed if the trial were held in Scotland. A large proportion of the relevant evidence is located in Great Britain.

The Court of Appeals found that the problems of proof could not be given any weight because Piper and Hartzell failed to describe with specificity the evidence they would not be able to obtain if trial were held in the United States. It suggested that defendants seeking *forum non conveniens* dismissal must submit affidavits identifying the witnesses they would call and the testimony these witnesses would provide if the trial were held in the alternative forum. Such detail is not necessary. Piper and Hartzell have moved for dismissal precisely because many crucial witnesses are located beyond the reach of compulsory process, and thus are difficult to identify or interview. Requiring extensive investigation would defeat the purpose of their motion. Of course, defendants must provide enough information to enable the District Court to balance the parties' interests. Our examination of the record convinces us that sufficient information was provided here. Both Piper and Hartzell submitted affidavits describing the evidentiary problems they would face if the trial were held in the United States.

The District Court correctly concluded that the problems posed by the inability to implead potential third-party defendants clearly supported holding the trial in Scotland. Joinder of the pilot's estate, Air Navigation, and McDonald is crucial to the presentation of petitioners' defense. If Piper and Hartzell can show that the accident was caused not by a design defect, but rather by the negligence of the pilot, the plane's owners, or the charter company, they will be relieved of all liability. It is true, of course, that if Hartzell and Piper were found liable after a trial in the United States, they could institute an action for indemnity or contribution against these parties in Scotland. It would be far more convenient, however, to resolve all claims in one trial. The Court of Appeals rejected this argument. Forcing petitioners to rely on actions for indemnity or contributions would be "burdensome" but not "unfair.". . . Finding that trial in the plaintiff's chosen forum would be burdensome, however, is sufficient to support dismissal on grounds of *forum non conveniens*.

---

25. In the future, where similar problems are presented, District Courts might dismiss subject to the condition that defendant corporations agree to provide the records relevant to the plaintiff's claims.

(2)

The District Court's review of the factors relating to the public interest was also reasonable. On the basis of its choice-of-law analysis, it concluded that if the case were tried in the Middle District of Pennsylvania, Pennsylvania law would apply to Piper and Scottish law to Hartzell. It stated that a trial involving two sets of laws would be confusing to the jury. It also noted its own lack of familiarity with Scottish law. Consideration of these problems was clearly appropriate under *Gilbert*; in that case we explicitly held that the need to apply foreign law pointed towards dismissal.[29] The Court of Appeals found that the District Court's choice-of-law analysis was incorrect, and that American law would apply to both Hartzell and Piper. Thus, lack of familiarity with foreign law would not be a problem. Even if the Court of Appeals' conclusion is correct, however, all other public interest factors favored trial in Scotland.

Scotland has a very strong interest in this litigation. The accident occurred in its airspace. All of the decedents were Scottish. Apart from Piper and Hartzell, all potential plaintiffs and defendants are either Scottish or English. As we stated in *Gilbert*, there is "a local interest in having localized controversies decided at home.". . . Respondent argues that American citizens have an interest in ensuring that American manufacturers are deterred from producing defective products, and that additional deterrence might be obtained if Piper and Hartzell were tried in the United States, where they could be sued on the basis of both negligence and strict liability. However, the incremental deterrence that would be gained if this trial were held in an American court is likely to be insignificant. The American interest in this accident is simply not sufficient to justify the enormous commitment of judicial time and resources that would inevitably be required if the case were to be tried here.

IV

The Court of Appeals erred in holding that the possibility of an unfavorable change in law bars dismissal on the ground of *forum non conveniens*. It also erred in rejecting the District Court's *Gilbert* analysis. The District Court properly decided that the presumption in favor of the respondent's forum choice applied with less than maximum force because the real parties in interest are foreign. It did not act unreasonably in deciding that the private interests pointed towards trial in Scotland. Nor did it act unreasonably in deciding that the public interests favored trial in Scotland. Thus, the judgment of the Court of Appeals is

Reversed.

NOTES AND QUESTIONS

1. *Assessing "Convenience."* It seems anomalous that the American defendants in *Piper Aircraft* are arguing that Scotland is a more "convenient" forum over the objections of the Scottish real parties in interest. Remember, however, that a second

---

29. . . . Of course, this factor alone is not sufficient to warrant dismissal when a balancing of all relevant factors shows that the plaintiff's chosen forum is appropriate. . . .

action was pending in Scotland, which included parties beyond the reach of the American courts (the pilot's estate and Scottish air taxi company) from whom Piper would have sought indemnification and contribution in an additional Scottish proceeding had a judgment been rendered against it in the United States. As the Court noted, separate litigation over the same facts and issues creates the possibility of inconsistent results. Without such a compelling reason, should an American corporation being sued by a foreign plaintiff be able to claim that plaintiff's home jurisdiction is more "convenient"? *See Abad v. Bayer Corp.*, 563 F.3d 663 (7th Cir. 2009) (dismissal for *forum non conveniens* was appropriate where law of Argentina would govern the substantive issues, bulk of discovery would be conducted in Argentina, and many witnesses resided in Argentina); *Stewart v. Dow Chemical Co.*, 865 F.2d 103 (6th Cir. 1989) (dismissal for *forum non conveniens* appropriate where evidence of injury and treating physicians were in Canada). Is it also not odd that the Scottish plaintiffs are seeking to litigate in a forum in the United States? What is their motivation in seeking an American court?

2. *Reverse Forum Shopping?* Is Justice Marshall correct in reading *Gilbert* to equate harassment of the defendant with the plaintiff's desire to take advantage of more favorable law? Is that consistent with his later admonition that the defendant's motivation to take advantage of more favorable law in seeking *forum non conveniens* dismissal is not to be considered, notwithstanding the possibility of "reverse forum shopping"? Professor Stein argues that a defendant's "reverse forum shopping" does not precisely mirror a plaintiff's selection of the initial forum:

> Although a defendant moving to dismiss on *forum non conveniens* grounds may be motivated by a desire to have foreign law apply to the controversy, unless that motivation is combined with some presumption in favor of defendant's choice of forums, it does not have the same effect as forum shopping by plaintiffs. The "evil" of forum shopping is not that it is motivated by a desire to manipulate the applicable law. Rather, it is that there is a disproportionate advantage bestowed on the plaintiff by both giving the plaintiff the choice of forums and assigning a presumption in favor of that choice. . . . [W]hen defendants "reverse forum shop" through the *forum non conveniens* doctrine, the parties are on equal footing, and the court can assess the relative advantages of the forums free from the strictures of any presumption. To condemn the *forum non conveniens* doctrine because it permits "reverse forum shopping" is to say that plaintiffs should have an unfettered right to select the applicable law—a proposition that would be difficult to defend.

Allan R. Stein, *Forum Non Conveniens and the Redundancy of Court-Access Doctrine*, 133 U. Pa. L. Rev. 781, 826–827 n.199 (1985).

3. *Discrimination Against Foreign Plaintiffs?* The Second Circuit has expanded upon the majority's holding in *Piper* concerning the deference due to the forum choice of a foreign plaintiff versus a domestic plaintiff. The distinction, the Second Circuit has explained, turns on the legitimacy of the reasons for the plaintiff's choice of forum: "The more it appears that a domestic or foreign plaintiff's choice of forum has been dictated by reasons that the law recognizes as valid, the greater the deference that will be given to the plaintiff's forum choice." *See Iragorri v. United*

Techs. Corp., 274 F.3d 65, 71–72 (2d Cir. 2001) (en banc). Thus, a desire to obtain a forum that is close to home and convenient is a valid reason for a (domestic) plaintiff to file in the United States, but a bare desire to take advantage of the favorable legal system of another country is not a valid reason for a (foreign) plaintiff to do so. Does this refinement make the disparate treatment of foreign and domestic plaintiffs more palatable?

Note that the deference due to a *domestic* plaintiff is not absolute. For example, in *Loya v. Starwood Hotels & Resorts Worldwide, Inc.,* 583 F.3d 656 (9th Cir. 2009), a Washington resident brought suit in Washington for the death of her husband who died while scuba diving off the coast of Mexico on an expedition arranged at the resort at which he was staying in Mexico. Notwithstanding the fact that the plaintiff sued American defendants (rather than their Mexican subsidiaries), the district court dismissed on *forum non conveniens* grounds, and the Court of Appeals held the dismissal was not an abuse of discretion. The Ninth Circuit noted that most of the allegedly wrongful conduct took place in Mexico among non-Washington defendants, that Mexican law would apply to numerous issues, and that the Mexican courts would afford a remedy, even though a lesser amount than would be available in the United States. Notwithstanding examples such as *Loya,* one empirical study suggests that U.S. district court judges are approximately 25 percent more likely to dismiss on *forum non conveniens* grounds when the plaintiff is foreign than when the plaintiff is a U.S. citizen. *See* Christopher A. Whytock, *The Evolving Forum Shopping System,* 96 Cornell L. Rev. 481, 527 (2011).

With respect to the deference due a *foreign* plaintiff's choice of forum, the Second Circuit has ruled that where a foreign plaintiff's choice of a New York forum is motivated, at least in part, by the need to secure jurisdiction over all potential defendants, the foreign plaintiff's choice warrants "substantial deference," although not necessarily the same "high deference" that would be given to a resident plaintiff. *See Norex Petroleum, Ltd. v. Access Indus., Inc.,* 416 F.3d 146 (2d Cir. 2005). In *Norex,* several of the defendants expressed a willingness to submit to the jurisdiction of a foreign court, but the Second Circuit held that this did not affect the deference that was due the plaintiff's choice of forum; rather, this fact was relevant only at the second and third stages of the *forum non conveniens* analysis (i.e., determining the availability of an adequate alternative forum and balancing the public and private factors). The Second Circuit has also ruled that a foreign plaintiff's choice need not be given more deference on the basis of a treaty that gives citizens of the plaintiff's home country "freedom of access" to U.S. courts because these treaties do not go so far as to grant "access to each country's courts on terms no less favorable than those applicable to nationals of the court's country." *See Pollux Holding v. Chase Manhattan Bank,* 329 F.3d 64 (2d Cir. 2003).

Professor Elizabeth Lear argues that the presumption established by *Piper* that a foreign plaintiff's choice of a U.S. forum is entitled to less deference than the choice of a domestic plaintiff subverts the American interest in a foreign accident. Elizabeth T. Lear, *National Interests, Foreign Injuries, and Federal Forum Non Conveniens,* 41 U.C. Davis L. Rev. 559 (2007). Professor Lear argues that if federal courts were to properly consider essential American interests, like the deterrence of multinational corporations producing global products that may have negative impact on the safety of American consumers, a *forum non conveniens* dismissal would be less common. Is this a valid criticism of the current *forum non conveniens* inquiry, or has Professor Lear confused the *forum non conveniens* inquiry with choice of law analysis?

4. *Foreign "Blocking Statutes."* What if a foreign plaintiff is prevented from bringing suit in the courts of his country — an otherwise adequate alternative forum — because of a "blocking statute"? The phrase "blocking statute" in this context refers to foreign legislation that provides for "limits on jurisdiction that apparently preclude their courts from hearing any action by one of their residents that was previously commenced in another country, but dismissed based on *forum non conveniens*," or "authorize[s] their courts to apply tort liability and damages law similar to that of the country in which an action was previously commenced by one of their residents, but subsequently dismissed on *forum non conveniens*." Walter W. Heiser, Forum Non Conveniens *and Retaliatory Legislation: The Impact on the Available Alternative Forum Inquiry and on the Desirability of* Forum Non Conveniens *as a Defense Tactic*, 56 Kan. L. Rev. 609, 610 (2008). How should such a statute affect a court's *forum non conveniens* analysis? Some courts have refused to take into account the existence of a foreign "blocking statute" in assessing the existence of an adequate alternative forum. *See, e.g.*, *Morales v. Ford Motor Co.*, 313 F. Supp. 2d 672 (S.D. Tex. 2004). Other courts have held, however, that the existence of a foreign "blocking statute" means that the proposed alternative forum is "[o]bviously . . . not an adequate alternative forum in which Plaintiffs could litigate [a] dispute." *Carl Schroeter GmbH & KO., KG. v. Crawford & Co.*, 2009 WL 1408100, at *8 (E.D. Pa. May 19, 2009).

5. *Adequacy of the Remedy in the Alternative Forum.* In *Piper*, the Supreme Court noted that if the remedy provided by the alternative forum was "so clearly inadequate or unsatisfactory that it is no remedy at all," the plaintiff might be able to avoid a *forum non conveniens* dismissal. The Court explained, however, that neither differences with respect to legal theory (strict liability vs. negligence) nor differences with respect to the size of the damage award rendered the remedy in a Scottish court "inadequate." Can you think of circumstances that might make the remedy in the foreign court inadequate? Suppose the applicable law in the foreign court limited the plaintiff's recovery to $2,500? In *Gonzalez v. Chrysler Corp.*, 301 F.3d 377 (5th Cir. 2002), Mexican plaintiffs brought suit against a U.S. car manufacturer and a U.S. designer of an airbag for the death of their child who was killed in a car accident in Mexico from the force of an airbag that crushed the child when it opened. Mexican law, which was applicable in the case, capped the maximum award for the loss of a child's life at $2,500. Plaintiffs argued that the damage cap made any recovery "*de minimis*" and that because the cost of litigation would exceed any potential recovery, a lawsuit in Mexico was not economically viable; thus, plaintiffs contended that they fell within the *Piper* exception because there was effectively no alternative forum. Nonetheless, the district court dismissed the action, and the Court of Appeals affirmed. The Court of Appeals held that the "economic viability" of a lawsuit should not determine the adequacy of the alternative forum for two reasons. First, there were too many variables to consider in determining a plaintiff's willingness to maintain suit in a foreign forum; and second, courts should not be forced to engage in a "rudderless exercise of line drawing with respect to a cap on damages."

Another case in which the court did examine the nature of the remedy in the foreign court before dismissing the case on *forum non conveniens* grounds is *In re Factor VIII*, 484 F.3d 951 (7th Cir. 2007). The litigation involved suits by hemophiliacs that allegedly became infected with either HIV or Hepatitis C as a result of contaminated blood products; the plaintiffs, who hailed from several different foreign countries, claimed that the defendant drug companies intentionally recruited blood donors that were at a high risk of carrying the viruses. In an attempt to have the entire case dismissed in the U.S. courts, the defendants began by attempting to dismiss the United Kingdom plaintiffs on grounds of *forum non conveniens*; the district court granted the motion. On appeal, the plaintiffs protested that U.K. courts might not permit market-share tort liability, a necessary theory of recovery for nearly all of the U.K. plaintiffs. The Seventh Circuit upheld the dismissal. Judge Wood examined the district court's conclusion that the U.K. courts could expand a recent decision by the House of Lords, the British high court, that appeared to loosen the country's traditional requirement of "but for" causation. She explained: "We do not know, of course, whether the U.K. courts will apply *Fairchild* to the present case, but that kind of certainty is not required (especially in a common-law system like theirs)." Does this case suggest the potential for a looser standard for dismissal when the alternative forum is a common law country like the United Kingdom or Canada? Is this sort of distinction desirable?

In *Aguinda v. Texaco, Inc.*, 303 F.3d 470 (2d Cir. 2002), defendants moved to dismiss on *forum non conveniens* grounds a class action brought in federal court in New York against Texaco, in which plaintiffs alleged that Texaco's oil operation activities in Ecuador had polluted rain forests and rivers causing injuries to 30,000 Ecuadorians. In resisting the motion, one of plaintiffs' arguments was that Ecuador was an inadequate forum because the courts in Ecuador did not provide for class actions or other mechanisms to handle large-scale litigation. The Court of Appeals for the Second Circuit held that the procedures in Ecuador, although less efficient than its own, did not render Ecuador an inadequate forum. That decision should be compared to a ruling by the House of Lords in England, *Lubbe v. Cape PLC* (2000) [1 WLR 1545], where the highest court in England ruled that even though a group of asbestos victims were from South Africa and had suffered their injuries in South Africa, the lack of a viable legal aid system or group action in South Africa through which to pursue the claims made dismissal on *forum non conveniens* grounds improper. Thus, the English court retained the action.

In *Norex Petroleum, Ltd. v. Access Industries, Inc.*, 416 F.3d 146 (2d Cir. 2005), discussed above, the Second Circuit made clear that if a plaintiff would be barred from bringing an action in an alternative forum on grounds of *res judicata*, the requirement that there be an alternative forum would not be satisfied and a motion to dismiss on grounds of *forum non conveniens* should be denied. Would it be more appropriate for a U.S. court in these circumstances to render a conditional dismissal in order to see if the foreign court would in fact preclude the action? Indeed, if such an action would be precluded in the foreign court due to a prior judgment from that court system, would not an action in the United States also be barred by *res judicata*? In *Norex*, the Second Circuit acknowledged as much but indicated that the question of recognizing the foreign country judgment was different than the issue of *forum non conveniens*, and that that issue would be for the district court on remand.

6. *Public and Private Interest Factors.* Once the adequacy of an alternative forum has been established, the *forum non conveniens* inquiry focuses on the balancing of the public and private interest factors noted in *Gulf Oil v. Gilbert.* The private interest factors have traditionally looked to the convenience and costs to the parties, the availability of witnesses and documents, and the enforceability of a judgment. With respect to the public interest factors, should the nature of the claim being asserted play a role in the *forum non conveniens* calculus? For example, should a court be more reluctant to dismiss a case asserting a claim under the federal antitrust laws than one asserting a private law claim? *Compare Capital Currency Exchange, N.V. v. National Westminster Bank PLC*, 155 F.3d 603 (2d Cir. 1998) (finding that since anti-competitive action may be brought under European law in English forum, dismissal was proper) *with Industrial Investment Development Corp. v. Mitsui*, 671 F.2d 876 (5th Cir. 1982) (holding that *forum non conveniens* is inappropriate as an absolute matter in an antitrust case).

7. *Discretion of the District Court.* Remember that the *Piper Aircraft* case is to some extent about discretion; the Supreme Court held that the choice of law disadvantage that plaintiff would suffer upon dismissal was not a sufficient basis for the appeal's court to reverse their decision to dismiss the action. *Compare Hodson v. A.H. Robins Co.*, 715 F.2d 142 (4th Cir. 1983), where plaintiff, a British subject, brought suit against an American manufacturer in Virginia for injuries caused from the use of a Dalkon Shield intrauterine device. Defendant, an American corporation with its headquarters and principal place of business in Virginia, indicated that it would have consented to jurisdiction and service of process in England, production of evidence "deemed material by the English court," and paid the difference in airfare to London for plaintiff's witnesses to the extent it exceeded the airfare to Richmond. The district court concluded that the balance did not favor the defendants, noting the location of significant evidence in the forum and Virginia's public interest in regulating the safety of locally manufactured products. The Fourth Circuit upheld the district court's refusal to dismiss. Is the case inconsistent with *Piper Aircraft?*

8. *Conditioning Dismissal.* As noted earlier, courts sometimes grant a *forum non conveniens* dismissal subject to conditions. In some instances, these conditions are designed to ensure the availability of an alternative forum. For example, the defendant may be required to submit to jurisdiction in the alternative forum and waive statute of limitations defenses.

In *In re Gas Plant Disaster at Bhopal*, 809 F.2d 195 (2d Cir. 1987), *cert. denied*, 484 U.S. 871 (1987), a terrible industrial accident at a gas plant in Bhopal, India in 1984 was the basis for a lawsuit in the United States brought by thousands of Indian citizens as well as the Government of India against Union Carbide, a U.S.-based defendant. The district court dismissed on grounds of *forum non conveniens* subject to certain conditions, including that the defendant agree to the broader discovery procedures under the Federal Rules of Civil Procedure and to the enforcement of any judgment by the Indian court. On appeal, the Second Circuit evaluated the public and private interests involved and agreed that all relevant factors demonstrated that the case should be heard in India. The court also upheld conditions that the defendant consent to jurisdiction in India and waive the statute of limitations defense. However, the court found the condition regarding enforcement unnecessary because such judgments are generally enforceable, and it found the "one-way" discovery rule unfair, although it opined that the parties might agree to reciprocal discovery under the Federal Rules. The court also rejected a request by the defendant that the district judge retain authority to monitor the Indian proceedings to ensure that the defendant's Due Process rights were protected. It stated:

> The concept of shared jurisdictions is both illusory and unrealistic. The parties cannot simultaneously submit to both jurisdictions the resolution of the pre-trial and trial issues when there is only one consolidated case pending in one court. Any denial by the Indian courts of due process can be raised . . . as a defense to the plaintiffs' later attempt to enforce a resulting judgment . . . in this country.

Id. at 205.

9. *Is* Forum Non Conveniens *Redundant?* In the past, *forum non conveniens* was often used to limit the expansive general "doing business" jurisdiction. After *Daimler*, *forum non conveniens* is likely to have much less significant role to play, although in cases similar to *Piper Aircraft* where a defendant sues an American company in its "home" state for injuries to foreigners abroad, *forum non conveniens* will continue to be an important tool for defendants to control forum choice.

Does *forum non conveniens* have any place in cases of specific jurisdiction? Given the modern expansion of personal jurisdiction to include factors relating to "convenience," "state interests," and possibly "reasonableness," is the doctrine of *forum non conveniens* now redundant? One formal difference, of course, is that *forum non conveniens* almost always requires that there be an "adequate alternative forum," whereas it is unclear whether the existence of an alternative forum is part of the "reasonableness" Due Process inquiry with respect to jurisdiction. Also, jurisdictional issues are issues of "law" and subject to traditional appellate review, whereas rulings on *forum non conveniens* are in the discretion of the trial court with only limited appellate review. Is there much substance to that distinction when the legal standard for jurisdiction includes "fairness" and/or "reasonableness"?

10. *Jurisdiction First?* In *Gulf Oil v. Gilbert*, 330 U.S. 501, 504 (1947), the Supreme Court stated that "the doctrine of *forum non conveniens* can never apply if there is absence of jurisdiction or mistake of venue." What about in a situation in which the court needs to permit discovery in order to resolve a complicated jurisdictional question? Should a court eschew potentially exorbitant discovery if it ultimately will dismiss the case per *forum non conveniens* even should jurisdiction be found? A unanimous Supreme Court answered affirmatively in *Sinochem Int'l Co. v. Malaysia Int'l Shipping Corp.*, 549 U.S. 422 (2007). Instead of ordering the district court to conduct limited discovery to resolve a personal jurisdiction question pertaining to nationwide contacts under Rule 4(k)(2), the Court permitted the lower court to dismiss the "textbook case for immediate *forum non conveniens* dismissal"; the case involved the arrest of the Malaysian plaintiff's vessel pursuant to a Chinese admiralty court order secured by the Chinese defendant. In doing so, the Court focused heavily on considerations of judicial economy, claiming that in situations with a complex jurisdictional problem a court can dismiss a case via *forum non conveniens* if the traditional *Gulf Oil* factors "weigh heavily in favor of dismissal. . . ."

In reaching this conclusion, the Court explained that "[r]esolving a *forum non conveniens* motion does not entail any assumption by the court of substantive 'law-declaring power.'" *Id.* at 1192–1193. Nonetheless, how is a court empowered to make a *forum non conveniens* ruling if it would not have either subject matter or personal jurisdiction in a particular case? If *Sinochem* is such a "textbook" case for *forum non conveniens* dismissal, would it be more in line with traditional jurisdictional principles to find personal jurisdiction lacking under the "reasonableness" inquiry that the Supreme Court pronounced in *Asahi Metal Indus. Co. v. Superior Court of California?* Notably, in *Sinochem* the Court explicitly refused to answer the question of whether a court that had elected to pass on a jurisdictional question could have the authority to condition a *forum non conveniens* dismissal on a defendant's waiver of personal jurisdiction in the alternative forum. It deemed this potential problem irrelevant in this case because the Chinese admiralty court already had concluded that the Malaysian company was subject to personal jurisdiction in the Chinese tribunal. The effect of *Sinochem* on the lower courts is yet unknown; a broad interpretation could spur a slew of immediate *forum non conveniens* dismissals, while a narrower perspective could invoke the *Sinochem* exception only in obvious cases for dismissal.   (slay → slew)

11. *Unintended Consequences?* Are you surprised that American defendants prefer a foreign forum to a U.S. forum? Often the preference by the defendant for the foreign forum is the desire to avoid discovery, juries, class actions, and contingent fees. Recent cases demonstrate, however, that U.S. defendants may have gotten more than they bargained for by exposing themselves to possible exorbitant foreign judgments. There are several notable examples of such cases. In *Osorio v. Dole Food Co.*, 2009 WL 3998931 (S.D. Fla. 2009), *aff'd*, 635 F.3d 1277 (11th Cir. 2011), Nicaraguan plaintiffs, allegedly exposed to a harmful agricultural pesticide while working on banana plantations in Nicaragua, brought suit in federal court against the U.S.-based manufacturer, Dow Chemical, and the U.S.-based plantation owner, Dole Food. Defendants successfully argued that Nicaragua was a more appropriate forum and the district court dismissed the case on *forum non conveniens* grounds. After a favorable new law on liability was enacted in Nicaragua, plaintiffs sued there and obtained a $97 million judgment, which they then sought to enforce in the United States. Defendants resisted enforcement of the judgment on the ground that the procedures in the Nicaraguan courts were unfair. Plaintiffs argued that the defendants themselves chose to litigate in the Nicaraguan courts and could not now object to enforcement of the resulting judgment. The district court rejected plaintiffs' position, stating that "[d]efendants should not be, and are not, estopped from contesting the fairness of Nicaragua's procedures because the "interposition" of Special Law 364 into the DBCP litigation fundamentally altered the legal landscape in Nicaragua." A similar issue arose in *Chevron Corp. v. Naranjo*, 768 F. Supp. 2d 581 (S.D.N.Y. 2011), *rev'd*, 667 F.3d 232 (2d Cir. 2012), in the context of determining the enforceability of an $18 billion Ecuadorian judgment, where defendants had earlier moved to dismiss the U.S. action on *forum non conveniens* grounds. The U.S. defendants, who originally touted the adequacy of the Ecuadorian courts, now claimed that the judiciary was corrupt; the Ecuadorian plaintiffs who had resisted defendants' *forum non conveniens* motion on the ground that the Ecuadorian judiciary was corrupt now argued that the

Ecuadorian judgment in their favor was fair. Noting how both sides had changed their positions 180 degrees, the district court stated that it was not inclined to give much credence to the earlier positions of either party. In their article, *Forum Non Conveniens and the Enforcement of Foreign Judgments,* 111 Colum. L. Rev. 1444 (2011), Professors Christopher Whytock and Cassandra Burke-Robertson identify the gap between the criteria for *forum non conveniens* dismissals and the criteria for enforcement of foreign judgments and suggest an approach to closing that gap. Is there really any way to close that gap given that a court on the *forum non conveniens* motion is being asked to make a prediction whereas a court asked to enforce a foreign judgment is able to evaluate the actual events?

NOTE ON STATE *FORUM NON CONVENIENS* DOCTRINE

Keep in mind that *Piper Aircraft* was an application of *forum non conveniens* doctrine in the federal courts. The federal courts invoke *forum non conveniens* almost exclusively when the alternative forum is foreign because, in the interstate context, a move to another federal court is accomplished through the use of the transfer mechanism, 28 U.S.C. §1404, discussed below. State courts also employ the doctrine of *forum non conveniens,* but the alternative forum may be the court in another state as well as a court in another country. In many states, the doctrine is implemented through statute. State *forum non conveniens* standards, whether set forth in statutes or common law decisions, often differ from the federal one. Some states have accorded different weight to the various factors to be considered in deciding whether or not to dismiss, such as the deference to be given to the forum choice of a foreign plaintiff. *See, e.g., Myers v. Boeing Co.,* 794 P.2d 1272 (Wash. 1990) (affirming dismissal of suit against Japanese airline brought by foreign plaintiff but expressly declining to adopt the lesser deference rule of *Piper*). A few states have rejected the doctrine altogether. What considerations might lead a state judicial system to reject the doctrine completely?

The Texas courts at one time found the doctrine of *forum non conveniens* inapplicable in personal injury or wrongful death actions because the applicable Texas statute was viewed as conferring "obligatory" jurisdiction over out-of-state causes of action. *See Dow Chemical Co. v. Alfaro,* 786 S.W.2d 674 (Tex. 1990) (refusing to dismiss action by Costa Rican employees of Standard Fruit who were injured in Costa Rica by pesticides manufactured by American companies). The statute was subsequently amended, and again in 2005, *see* Tex. Civ. Prac. & Rem. Code §71.051, and now authorizes *forum non conveniens* dismissals except in particular situations, such as when suit is brought by a Texas resident or when particular acts occur in Texas. The Louisiana Supreme Court has ruled that it has no general doctrine of *forum non conveniens* at all. *See Fox v. Board of Supervisors of La. State University,* 576 So. 2d 978 (La. 1991). New York, which as a general matter applies *forum non conveniens,* removes such discretion in certain actions. Under N.Y. C.P.L.R. §327(b) and Gen. Obligations Law 5-1402, parties to contracts valued at $1 million or more who choose New York law to apply may include a provision for New York as the forum for any disputes arising out of the contract even if the contract has no connection whatsoever with the state. Why would New York want to invite litigation in which it has no interest to its courts? *See* Survey of New York Practice, 59 St. John's L. Rev.

411, 413–419 (1985) (suggesting that the law was intended to enhance New York's standing as a commercial center, and criticizing the provisions as burdensome on New York courts).

In addition, several state legislatures have followed Texas's lead by passing statutes specifying factors stating when a *forum non conveniens* dismissal is justified. *See* W. Va. Code Ann. §56-1-1a (West 2012) (providing that a plaintiff's choice of forum should receive significant deference unless the plaintiff is not a resident of West Virginia and the cause of action arose in a different state); *see also* Ga. Code Ann. §9-10-31.1 (2007) (codifying a more expansive doctrine of *forum non conveniens* and requiring that courts consider seven factors reflecting public and private interests—including "[t]he traditional deference given to a plaintiff's choice of forum").

Parties are likely to forum shop as between state and federal court because of the differences between state and federal application of *forum non conveniens*. How does a *forum non conveniens* dismissal of a suit by a federal court in a particular state affect a party's ability to file a subsequent suit in the state courts of that state? Can a federal court enjoin such a state court action? The Anti-Injunction Act, 28 U.S.C. §2283, generally prohibits a federal court from enjoining state proceedings except when "necessary in aid of its jurisdiction, or to protect and effectuate its judgments." In *Chick Kam Choo v. Exxon Corp.*, 486 U.S. 140 (1988), a Singaporean plaintiff brought suit for the alleged wrongful death of her husband, which occurred in Singapore while he was working aboard a ship owned by an Exxon subsidiary. She alleged a variety of claims under federal, state, and general maritime law in the Southern District of Texas. The district court granted the defendants' summary judgment motion on the federal claims, held that Singapore (and not Texas) law should govern the lawsuit, and dismissed the remainder of the case on grounds of *forum non conveniens*. Plaintiff subsequently reinitiated suit in a Texas state court, reiterating the state claim with an additional claim based on Singapore law. Defendants sought and received an injunction from the federal district court enjoining plaintiff from pursuing any claims arising from her husband's death in any American court, and the order was affirmed by the Fifth Circuit. However, the Supreme Court, recognizing that the Texas courts might be more open to foreign plaintiffs than the federal courts, reversed the dismissal on the grounds that the district court had not necessarily used the same factors that a Texas court might have considered in making its *forum non conveniens* decision: "[W]hether the Texas state courts are an appropriate forum for petitioner's Singapore claims has not yet been litigated" and thus the injunction was prohibited by the Anti-Injunction Act. 486 U.S. at 149. But the Supreme Court held the injunction valid to prevent relitigation of the applicability of Texas law, which had already been determined by the federal court in the negative. Is there any justification for the result in *Chick Kam Choo*, which bars the Texas courts from hearing a claim based on Texas law but allows them to consider a claim under Singapore law?

Apart from the Anti-Injunction Act, should one court be permitted to enjoin the parties from proceeding elsewhere in the interests of confining litigation to a convenient forum? What dangers do you envision? *See James v. Grand Trunk Western Railroad Co.*, 14 Ill. 2d 356, 152 N.E.2d 858 (1958) (Illinois court could issue counter-injunction restraining defendant from enforcing Wisconsin injunction against plaintiff, a Wisconsin resident, from pursuing wrongful death action in

Illinois). *See* Comment, *Forum Non Conveniens, Injunctions Against Suit and Full Faith and Credit,* 29 U. Chi. L. Rev. 740 (1962). *See also* David W. Robertson & Paula K. Speck, *Access to State Courts in Transnational Personal Injury Cases: Forum Non Conveniens and Antisuit Injunctions,* 68 Tex. L. Rev. 937 (1990).

4. Transfer *Within* the Federal System

[handwritten: Federal ←only→ Federal]

*[handwritten: §1404(a):
• venue change
• rule applied not change]*

In 1948, one year after *Gulf Oil v. Gilbert,* Congress enacted 28 U.S.C. §1404(a), which provides for transfer from one federal district court to another as an alternative to outright dismissal. Although §1404(a) was drafted with *forum non conveniens* principles in mind, the standards for transferring a case under the statute and for granting outright dismissal on *forum non conveniens* grounds are not necessarily identical. In *Norwood v. Kirkpatrick,* 349 U.S. 29 (1955), the Supreme Court concluded that the courts had broader discretion to transfer an action under §1404(a) than they had for dismissal under *forum non conveniens* since the transfer was a less drastic measure than outright dismissal. Does this federal provision for transfer now give defendants forum shopping rights equal to those of plaintiffs?

In addition to the general transfer provision, 28 U.S.C. §1404, two other provisions, 28 U.S.C. §1406 and 28 U.S.C. §1407, authorize transfer in more particularized situations.

a. Section 1404 Transfer

Until the 2011 venue amendments to 28 U.S.C. §1404, a party's ability to transfer a case pursuant to §1404 was substantially limited. In *Hoffman v. Blaski,* 363 U.S. 335 (1960), the Supreme Court had held that the language of the statute authorizing the court to transfer the case to a district or division "where it might have been brought" meant a district or division where the plaintiff could have brought the case originally, i.e., only if jurisdiction and venue were proper in the proposed transferee forum at the time plaintiff brought the suit. In *Hoffman,* plaintiffs resisted defendants' transfer motion on the ground that the transferee forum did not have jurisdiction and venue over the defendants at the time the action was brought. Thus §1404 presents an interesting contrast with *forum non conveniens.* On a motion to dismiss on the basis of *forum non conveniens,* a defendant can consent to jurisdiction in an alternative forum; however, on a motion to transfer pursuant to 28 U.S.C. §1404, *Hoffman* does not allow a defendant to consent to jurisdiction there. The Federal Courts Jurisdiction and Venue Clarification Act of 2011 amended 28 U.S.C. §1404(a) and now permits transfer — in addition to the district "where it might have been brought" — to "any district or division to which *[handwritten: consent → transfer]* all parties have consented." Note that the amendment will only have an impact in a case where all the parties agree to the transfer and does not effect any change in a case like *Hoffman* where the plaintiff resists the transfer motion. A continuing feature of a §1404 transfer relates to the question of the applicable law. In *Klaxon Co. v. Stentor Elec. Mfg. Co.,* 313 U.S. 487 (1941), the Supreme Court held that in a diversity action, the district court must apply whatever law the state in which it sits would apply. In a case that is transferred, there is the additional question of whether that refers to the law that would be applied by the original transferor court or the subsequent transferee court. In *Van Dusen v. Barrack*, 376 U.S. 612 (1964), the Supreme Court held that, as a general matter, the law selected by the transferor forum would continue to apply after a §1404 transfer:

> The legislative history of §1404(a) certainly does not justify the rather startling conclusion that one might "get a change of law as a bonus for a change of venue." Indeed, an interpretation accepting such a rule would go far to frustrate the remedial purposes of §1404(a). If a change of law were in the offering, the parties might well regard the section primarily as a forum-shopping instrument. And, more importantly, courts would at least be reluctant to grant transfers, despite considerations of convenience, if to do so might conceivably prejudice the claim of a plaintiff who had initially selected a permissible forum. We believe, therefore, that both the history and purposes of §1404(a) indicate that it should be regarded as a federal judicial housekeeping measure, dealing with the placement of litigation in the federal courts and generally intended, on the basis of convenience and fairness, simply to authorize a change of courtrooms.

Id. at 636–637.

Is the *Van Dusen* rule inconsistent with the logic of *Piper Aircraft*? If action is more conveniently litigated in state *B* rather than state *A*, shouldn't state *B*'s choice of law rules be applied?

The limits of *Van Dusen*'s logic were tested in *Ferens v. John Deere Co.*, 494 U.S. 516 (1990). In that case, a Pennsylvania resident injured in Pennsylvania by a combine manufacturer filed suit three years after his accident. The limitations period in Pennsylvania, as well as in the manufacturer's place of incorporation (Delaware), had run. Ferens thus filed a tort claim in federal court in Mississippi, where the limitations period was six years. Given that Mississippi courts viewed statutes of limitation as procedural, the Mississippi court would apply the forum's limitation period rather than that of Pennsylvania, even though Pennsylvania law governed the substance of the claim. Once the court deemed the claim timely, the plaintiff filed a §1404(a) transfer motion, which the court granted, whereupon the proceedings moved to a district court in Pennsylvania. The district court, describing the filing in Mississippi as a "procedural ploy," effectively imposed a good faith limitation on the *Van Dusen* rule. The Third Circuit affirmed.

The Supreme Court took the case and reversed. Writing for a five-justice majority, Justice Kennedy noted that the text of §1404(a) provides no suggestion that plaintiffs should be treated differently from defendants in terms of the law applicable on a transfer. The Court recalled three policies that supported its outcome in *Van Dusen*: (1) that §1404(a) should not deprive parties of state-law advantages that exist absent diversity jurisdiction; (2) that §1404(a) should not multiply opportunities for forum shopping; and (3) the §1404 transfer decision should turn on considerations of convenience and the interest of justice rather than on the possible prejudice resulting from a change of law. It then found that all three policies were furthered by applying *Van Dusen* to plaintiff-initiated transfers. Moreover, the Court suggested that denying Ferens the right to rely on Mississippi's statute of limitations would simply encourage him to continue litigating in Mississippi—an obviously less convenient forum. Moreover, the burden of this inconvenient litigation did not fall on plaintiff alone, and ultimately the systemic costs may be greater if limitations on applicability of transferors' limitations periods regularly drove plaintiffs to litigate in less convenient fora.

Writing in dissent for four justices, Justice Scalia evinced concern about the effects of the decision, noting plaintiffs here "achieved exactly what *Klaxon* was designed to prevent: the use of a Pennsylvania federal court instead of a Pennsylvania state court in order to obtain application of a different substantive law." More troubling was the fact that the "file-and-transfer ploy" could be used beyond the context of statutes of limitations, such as "to bring home to the desired state of litigation all sorts of favorable choice-of-law rules regarding substantive liability—in an era when the diversity among the States in choice-of-law principles has become kaleidoscopic." Commentators have also noted the oddity of the result in *Ferens. See* Kermit Roosevelt III, *Choice of Law in Federal Courts: From Erie and Klaxon to CAFA and Shady Grove*, 106 Nw. U. L. Rev. 1 (2012) ("We are used to the idea that plaintiffs go to a forum in order to get its law, but we are less used to the idea that they can order it for takeout.").

b.   Section 1406 Transfer or Dismissal

In what situations is a transfer appropriate under §1406 rather than §1404? Note that §1406 applies when venue in the original forum is improper; in that circumstance, §1406 gives the district court the option of either dismissing or transferring the case to a proper forum. As to choice of law on a §1406 transfer, courts do not apply the rule of *Van Dusen* (the choice of law rule of the transferor forum), but rather look to the choice of law rules of the transferee court. Do you understand why?

But if the plaintiff has filed in the wrong forum, why shouldn't the court just dismiss the case and require the plaintiff to refile in the proper venue?

In *Goldlawr v. Heiman*, 369 U.S. 463 (1962), the Supreme Court expanded the use of a §1406(a) transfer, holding transfer proper under §1406 in the absence of personal jurisdiction over the defendant as well as the absence of proper venue in the initial forum. Writing in dissent in *Goldlawr*, Justice Harlan criticized the majority for reading the statute to allow for a transfer where "*both* venue and jurisdiction were lacking in the district where the action is commenced, while neglecting to provide any comparable alleviative measures for the plaintiff who selects a district where venue is proper but where personal jurisdiction cannot be obtained." 369 U.S. at 468 (Harlan, J., dissenting). To avoid just that disparity, some courts of appeals have read §1406 to allow for transfer in a situation where the transferor court lacked personal jurisdiction but had proper venue. *See, e.g., Corke v. Sameiet M.S. Song of Norway*, 572 F.2d 77 (2d Cir. 1978); Comment, *Personal Jurisdiction Requirements Under Federal Change of Venue Statutes*, 1962 Wis. L. Rev. 342 (1967).

c.   Which Transfer Remedy for Violation of a Forum-Selection Clause

The recent Supreme Court decision, *Atlantic Marine Construction Co. v. U.S. District Court*, 134 S.Ct. 568 (2013), addressed the question of the appropriate federal procedural mechanism for enforcing a valid forum selection clause when suit is brought in a non-chosen forum. Rejecting arguments that an action brought in contravention of a forum selection clause should be dismissed for lack of venue under Rule 12(b)(3) or 28 U.S.C. §1406, the Court held that such an action should be transferred pursuant to 28 U.S.C. §1404 when the chosen forum is a federal court and via *forum non conveniens* when the chosen forum is a state or foreign court. The Court pointed out that the propriety of "venue" is governed by the federal venue statute (28 U.S.C. §1391) and that a forum selection clause does not render venue in a federal court "wrong" or "improper." However, the Court ruled that the forum selection clause could be enforced through a §1404 motion, which, "for the convenience of parties and witnesses, in the interest of justice," authorizes transfer to a district where the case could have been brought or to which all parties agreed. In deciding that §1404 was the proper mechanism, the Court adjusted the traditional factors that are taken into account on such a motion, stating that the plaintiff bears the burden of showing why the court should not transfer and that only in "extraordinary circumstances unrelated to the convenience of the parties" should a transfer be denied. The Court also created an exception to the *Van Dusen* rule (discussed at p. 274) that requires the transferee court to apply the choice of law rules of the transferor forum. The Court explained that a plaintiff who files suit in violation of a forum selection clause should not be entitled to the privilege of a choice of law selection and such gamesmanship should not be rewarded. Therefore, the court in the contractually selected venue should not apply the choice of law rules of the transferor venue, to which the parties have waived their right. Thus, on a §1404 transfer to the chosen forum, the choice of law rules of the transferee forum were held to apply.

d.   Section 1407 Transfer

A different type of transfer mechanism is provided by 28 U.S.C. §1407, whereby actions pending in different districts can be transferred to a single district for "coordinated or consolidated pretrial purposes." Section 1407 also creates the Judicial Panel on Multidistrict Litigation, which makes the determination as to when multidistricting is appropriate. Note that with a §1407 transfer, the transferee forum is designated to deal with pretrial issues only and that there is no requirement that the transferee forum be one in which the action "could have been brought." If an action is to be tried, it must be sent back to the transferor district. *See Lexecon Inc. v. Milberg Weiss Bershad Hynes & Lerach*, 523 U.S. 26 (1988). In light of *BMS*, do you think the fact that the transferee forum only deals with pretrial issues is sufficient to withstand a challenge to that court's personal jurisdiction over out-of-state plaintiffs' claims? For an in-depth discussion as to why multidistrict litigation has avoided serious Due Process scrutiny, as well as the basis upon which §1407 transfers might be justified in the wake of *BMS, see* Andrew D. Bradt, *The Long Arm of Multidistrict Litigation*, 59 Wm. & Mary L. Rev. 1165 (2018). Typical candidates for §1407 treatment are mass torts, including asbestos, and wide-ranging antitrust cases. *See, e.g., In re Asbestos Products Liability Litigation* (No. VI), 771 F. Supp. 415 (J.P.M.L. 1991). The subject of complex litigation is taken up more extensively in Chapter 8.

NOTES AND QUESTIONS

1. Note that in *Ferens* three different propositions of law contributed to the result. First, plaintiffs were able to sue in Mississippi — a state with no relationship to the transaction — because John Deere was "doing business" nationwide,

and pre-*Daimler*, the company was subject to jurisdiction in any state in which it had continuous and systematic activities. Second, in the *Sun Oil* case, discussed at pp. 228–229, the Supreme Court held that a forum is constitutionally permitted to apply its own statute of limitations as a matter of choice of law. Third, the *Van Dusen* rule provides that the choice of law rules of the transferor forum apply on a 28 U.S.C. §1404 transfer. One can debate the desirability of each of the three rules independently, but the combination certainly led to an odd result. Note, however, that under the new *Daimler* rule for general jurisdiction, Mississippi would not be able to exercise general jurisdiction today. Thus, even assuming an initial forum would apply its own statute of limitations under *Sun Oil* and that statute of limitations law would apply on a transfer motion per *Van Dusen*, there would be a more significant connection between the defendant and the forum whose statute of limitations was being applied than was true in the *Ferens* case itself.

2. In *Atlantic Marine*, the Court held that choice of forum agreements are enforceable except in extraordinary circumstances, and that actions filed in contravention of forum selection clauses are to be transferred pursuant to a §1404(a), rather than dismissed or transferred on a §1406(a) motion. The Court's reasoning is that §1406(a) is reserved for cases when venue is "wrong" or "improper." But isn't §1404 reserved for cases where both jurisdiction and venue are proper in the initial forum? How can jurisdiction be proper in a forum where the parties agreed to a different forum *ex ante*? Is it because there is always an initial question of whether the forum selection clause is valid?

3. *United States Bank Nat'l Ass'n v. Bank of Am. N.A.*, 916 F.3d 143 (2d Cir. 2019) presents an interesting example of how different types of forum transfer affect which choice of law rules apply. In this case, an Indiana district court held it lacked jurisdiction over the defendant and transferred the suit to the Southern District of New York under 28 U.S.C. §1631, which permits transfer if the transferor court lacks jurisdiction.[3] A case transferred under §1631 necessarily applies the applicable law of the transferee court, given that the initial forum never had jurisdiction to apply its own choice of law rules. The trial court in New York had applied New York's six-year statute of limitations and dismissed the case. The plaintiff appealed, arguing that the Indiana court erred in finding it lacked personal jurisdiction and that the case should be retransferred back to Indiana. The Court of Appeals ruled that the plaintiff was correct that the defendant was subject to specific personal jurisdiction in Indiana, but nonetheless upheld the initial transfer under §1404(a). Under §1404(a), however, the law of the transferor court applies. Thus, the appellate court found application of Indiana's choice of law rules and its ten-year statute of limitations were proper. It then vacated the lower court's judgment on the basis of untimeliness and remanded the case for adjudication.

4. Due Process analysis generally focuses only on whether or not a court has jurisdiction over a defendant because a plaintiff presumptively consents to the jurisdiction of the court in which she chooses to file a claim. However, such is not the

---

3. The language of 28 U.S.C. §1631 refers only to "jurisdiction," and the circuits have since split as to whether it applies to a lack of personal jurisdiction or subject matter jurisdiction.

case when a court transfers a plaintiff's suit against her will, which might force her to litigate in a distant forum at great cost and impose significant burdens. For an in-depth discussion on venue transfer and an argument for the need for personal jurisdiction over a transferred plaintiff, *see* Scott Dodson, Essay, *Plaintiff Personal Jurisdiction and Venue Transfer*, 117 Mich. L. Rev. 1463 (2019).

Chapter 3

SUBJECT MATTER JURISDICTION

A. INTRODUCTION

The first requirement for initiating litigation is bringing the action in a court that has jurisdiction over the subject matter. For actions in state courts, subject matter jurisdiction is rarely a problem because state courts are considered courts of *plenary* subject matter jurisdiction. Unless state law has limited the court's jurisdiction to a particular subject matter or a particular federal claim is committed to the exclusive jurisdiction of the federal courts, the state court can resolve disputes over any subject matter. By contrast, federal courts are tribunals of limited subject matter jurisdiction. As we shall see, federal courts have jurisdiction only over categories of cases or controversies set forth in Article III, §2 of the Constitution. Further, the lower federal courts have jurisdiction only if Congress has passed legislation authorizing jurisdiction for the federal courts to hear the particular category of disputes. Thus, questions over a federal court's subject matter jurisdiction appear with some frequency.

The reason for this difference in treatment flows from fundamental principles of our federal system. The founders of the Constitution envisioned a federal government of limited powers with the states serving as the polity with plenary responsibility over the primary behavior of its citizens. Just as the Congress's legislative authority is confined to the particular grants in Article I of the Constitution—which significantly limited federal legislative action up until the 1930s—so, too, the federal courts' adjudicative authority is confined to the grants of jurisdiction in Article III. Moreover, the Constitution provides only for the creation of the Supreme Court, leaving to Congress the decision whether to create "inferior Courts." Because the lower federal courts must be established by congressional act, the subject matter jurisdiction of those courts—even if otherwise within the grant of "judicial Power" provided in Article III—must be affirmatively conferred by legislation. This explains why the federal subject matter jurisdictional inquiry requires two steps: (i) finding congressional authorization of jurisdiction; and (ii) finding that such jurisdiction is within the Article III grant of judicial power.*

---

* A similar two-step approach is followed for the appellate jurisdiction of the Supreme Court, even though that tribunal is in a sense established by the Constitution itself. The second paragraph of Article III, Section 2, states that Congress has a substantial degree of control over its appellate jurisdiction: "the supreme Court shall have appellate Jurisdiction, both as to Law and Fact, with such Exceptions and under such Regulations as the Congress shall make." The extent of congressional control is a matter of considerable controversy best taken up in a course on Federal Courts. For a particularly instructive discussion, *see* Henry H. Hart, *The Power of Congress to Limit the Jurisdiction of Federal Courts: An Exercise in Dialectic*, 66 Harv. L. Rev. 1362 (1953).

Because subject matter jurisdictional limits define the power of the court—and therefore serve to delimit the boundary line between the adjudicative branch and the legislative and executive branches of government—they are treated somewhat specially. Under our adversarial system, the courts generally act as umpires and rarely raise legal issues on their own. However, with respect to questions over whether the court has subject matter jurisdiction, the court has a responsibility to address such matters *sua sponte*—i.e., on its own motion—even where the parties have missed the point entirely or are quite content to have the dispute resolved in that tribunal irrespective of jurisdictional difficulties. For instance, it is not uncommon for the Supreme Court to address a potential subject matter jurisdictional defect on its own even though the dispute has wended its way through several layers of courts without objection from anyone. A corollary proposition is that such defects cannot be waived by the parties, even though many other legal objections can be waived by untimely assertion or acquiescence. Consider, for example, *Capron v. Van Noorden*, 6 U.S. (2 Cranch) 126 (1804), where the *plaintiff* was able to escape an unfavorable outcome in the trial court by arguing on appeal that the forum he chose lacked authority over the subject matter. Note also that a determination that the court lacks subject matter jurisdiction has the effect of nullifying the entire litigation as a decision entitled to any precedential influence or binding effect. (This proposition is subject to certain caveats to be considered later in this chapter.) Typically, the Supreme Court will vacate a judgment rendered by a federal court without subject matter jurisdiction.

B.   JUSTICIABILITY

Article III places two different sets of limits on the cases that may be heard in federal court. One type of constraint, which will be discussed extensively in this chapter, is that the "judicial power of the United States" may only operate on particular types of cases—most commonly cases between citizens of different states (diversity jurisdiction) and cases arising under federal law (federal question jurisdiction). A second constraint, which we treat only briefly, is the requirement of a justiciable "case" or "controversy." Although "justiciability" is a highly complex subject best undertaken in upper-year classes in constitutional law and federal courts, it deserves some coverage here because it is an aspect of federal subject matter jurisdiction.

As developed in early decisions of the Supreme Court, the doctrine of justiciability serves a twofold purpose. First, it serves to "limit the business of federal courts to questions presented in an adversary context and in a form historically viewed as capable of resolution through the judicial process." *Flast v. Cohen*, 392 U.S. 83, 95 (1968). This might be termed the "judicial competence" rationale. Second, the doctrine serves to "define the role assigned to the judiciary in a tripartite allocation of power [so as] to assure that the federal courts will not intrude into areas committed to the other branches of government." *Id.* This might be termed the "separation of powers" rationale.

1.   *Standing to Sue*

The first component of justiciability is *standing*. For a matter to fall within the "case and controversy" scope of judicial power, a case usually must be brought by a plaintiff seeking a remedy for an injury that he himself has actually suffered. The injury must be real, not merely hypothetical, and it must be particular to the plaintiff, not merely an instance of law-breaking with no specific relationship to the plaintiff. This is typically not a problem in private-law cases, where the challenged conduct normally affects only a narrow category of persons, usually including the plaintiff. Standing can be more problematic in public-law cases, where the conduct of the defendant—typically the government—may affect a widely diffuse public. Determining the appropriate person to invoke judicial authority in these circumstances can be complex.

a.   Personal Stake in the Controversy

As a general matter, in cases presenting constitutional challenges to Article III standing, the Court has insisted that the plaintiff allege both (i) that he has a "personal stake" in the controversy because he has suffered a "direct injury" as a result of the defendant's conduct; and (ii) that the relief the plaintiff seeks is likely to redress that injury. *See, e.g., Warth v. Seldin*, 422 U.S. 490 (1975). The effect of this first requirement is to limit standing to litigants who can allege that they have been injured in a particularized manner that distinguishes their claim from a generalized interest in good government or law compliance.

The Court's insistence on particularized harm as a prerequisite to constitutional standing has been criticized on a number of grounds. First, some constitutional violations cause injury to the general public without visiting special harms on any particular individual or group, and limiting the class of litigants to those alleging specific harm may lead to underenforcement of constitutional norms. Second, as Professor Jaffe has argued, ideologically committed litigants who suffered no particularized harm may nonetheless be effective advocates. *See* Louis L. Jaffe, *The Citizen as Litigant in Public Actions: The Non-Hohfeldian or Ideological Plaintiff*, 116 U. Pa. L. Rev. 1033 (1968).

The Court's jurisprudence on the question of what constitutes a justiciable injury has not been entirely consistent. For instance, the Court in *Lujan v. Defenders of Wildlife*, 504 U.S. 555 (1992), held that scientists had no standing to challenge an Interior Department decision that would have allegedly endangered the animals they studied. Similarly, in *United States v. Richardson*, 418 U.S. 166 (1974), a taxpayer had no standing to challenge the practice of the CIA of not providing detailed accounting of its expenditures. In both cases, the loss of information available to the plaintiffs was not considered a justiciable injury. However, the Court subsequently held in *Federal Election Commission v. Akins*, 524 U.S. 11 (1998), that voters *could* challenge a Federal Election Commission decision to not require the American Israel Public Affairs Committee to make the extensive disclosures required of "lobbying organizations." The Court has also held that the stigma allegedly suffered by Black plaintiffs as a result of an IRS policy alleged to have benefitted racially discriminatory schools did not satisfy the injury requirement. *Allen v. Wright*, 468 U.S. 737 (1984).

For commentary on the personal stake in the controversy requirement of standing, *see* Jonathan R. Nash, *Standing and the Precautionary Principle*, 108 Colum. L. Rev. 494 (2008) (arguing that the "precautionary principle" used in environmental law should provide grounds for standing in cases where science is still uncertain about the injury but the potential harms are large and irreversible) and F. Andrew Hessick, *Standing, Injury in Fact, and Private Rights*, 93 Cornell L. Rev. 275 (2008) (arguing that requiring a showing of factual injury in private rights cases undermines the separation of powers by preventing courts from guarding rights and by limiting Congress's power to create rights).

① injury + ②   ③
b. "Causation" and "Redressability"

In several decisions in the 1970s, the Court added requirements that the injury complained of be "fairly traceable" to the challenged conduct and likely to be redressed by a favorable decision. For example, in *Linda R.S. v. Richard D.*, 410 U.S. 614 (1973), plaintiffs brought a class action on behalf of mothers of illegitimate children to require state officials to prosecute the fathers of those children for nonsupport. The Court held that the relief sought might bring about the jailing of the delinquent fathers but "[t]he prospect that prosecution will, at least in the future, result in payment of support can, at best, be termed only speculative." *Id.* at 618. The opinion also states that private citizens generally lack "a judicially cognizable interest in the prosecution or nonprosecution of another." *Id.* at 619. *Accord, Warth v. Seldin, supra* (low-income individuals lacked standing to challenge zoning ordinance that was alleged to prevent them and others similarly situated from living in the town because there was no evidence in the record that overturning the zoning ordinance would result in low-income housing being constructed). On other occasions, the Court has seemingly ignored this requirement. *See, e.g., Massachusetts v. EPA*, 549 U.S. 497 (2007) (granting Massachusetts standing to force the EPA to promulgate carbon emission standards based on Massachusetts's interest in state-owned coastal property that would arguably be imperiled by rising ocean levels caused by global warming); *Regents of the Univ. of California v. Bakke*, 438 U.S. 265 (1978) (entertaining challenge to affirmative-action admissions policy by white student who would not have been admitted even in the absence of racial preference to minorities).

The Supreme Court has also held that, with very few exceptions, standing cannot be based on a plaintiff's mere status as a taxpayer. *See Arizona Christian Sch. Tuition Org. v. Winn*, 563 U.S. 125 (2011) (denying standing to a group of citizens seeking to challenge the constitutionality of the Arizona Tax Code). These causation and redressability prongs have been much criticized in the literature. *See, e.g.*, Abram Chayes, *The Role of the Judge in Public Law Litigation*, 89 Harv. L. Rev. 1281, 1305 (1976); Richard H. Fallon Jr., *Of Justiciability, Remedies, and Public Law Litigation: Notes on the Jurisprudence of Lyons*, 59 N.Y.U. L. Rev. 1 (1984).

c. Prudential Barriers and the Role of Congressional Legislation

On occasion, the Court has recognized additional limitations on standing that are not required by Article III but are thought appropriate for other policy reasons. One such limitation is a general presumption against allowing litigants to assert the rights of third parties. The Court has, however, permitted exceptions to this rule. *See generally* Henry P. Monaghan, *Third Party Standing*, 84 Colum. L. Rev. 277 (1984); Robert Allen Sedler, *The Assertion of Constitutional Jus Tertii: A Substantive Approach*, 70 Cal. L. Rev. 1308 (1982). For example, in *Pierce v. Society of Sisters*, 268 U.S. 510 (1925), owners of a private school were permitted to challenge a state law requiring parents to send their children to public schools even though the constitutional basis of the challenge was the constitutional right of the parents to direct the upbringing of their children.

The Court has also identified what it has called "prudential" limitations against plaintiff raising "generalized grievances." That is to say, the Court has generally required the injury suffered by the plaintiff to be different from the injury suffered by the general population. *See, e.g., Allen v. Wright*, 468 U.S. 737 (1984). However, the Court has indicated more recently that "prudential standing" was always a "misnomer" and an "inapt" label. *Lexmark Int'l, Inc. v. Static Control Components, Inc.*, 572 U.S. 118 (2014). Rather, the Court has said that its task in determining whether a legislatively conferred cause of action encompassed a particular plaintiff's claim was one requiring the use of "traditional tools of statutory interpretation." Justice Scalia, writing for a unanimous Court in *Lexmark*, explained: "Just as a court cannot apply its independent policy judgment to recognize a cause of action that Congress has denied, it cannot limit a cause of action that Congress has created merely because 'prudence' dictates." *Id.* at 128. *See also Bank of America Corp. v. City of Miami, Fla.*, 137 S. Ct. 1296 (2017) (treating "prudential standing" and "statutory standing" as interchangeable concepts and reiterating: "The question is whether the statute grants the plaintiff the cause of action he asserts.").

One implication of this focus on statutory interpretation is that Congress can define the scope of the rights and hence the types of claimants who can recover. In *Trafficante v. Metropolitan Life Ins. Co.*, 409 U.S. 205 (1972), for example, white tenants were found to have standing to challenge a landlord's refusal to rent to nonwhite rental applicants. The Court held that the plaintiffs were "persons aggrieved" under §810 of the Civil Rights Act of 1968, 42 U.S.C. §3610, because Congress's purpose was not only to protect nonwhites from the injury of discriminatory refusals to rent but also to protect the interests of whites and nonwhites alike in interracial association. Can Congress confer standing to sue on the public at large via its power to create new substantive rights? For instance, the federal Clean Air Act provides that "any person may commence a civil action on his own behalf" against any polluter who violates the Act. 42 U.S.C. §7604(a). Do these so-called citizen suits violate Article III in the absence of individualized harm to the plaintiffs? These questions continue to provoke debate, but it is clear that Article III does impose some limits on Congress. *Compare Lujan v. Defenders of Wildlife*, 504 U.S. 555 (1992) (requiring plaintiffs to have suffered particularized harm notwithstanding broad conferral of standing under the applicable federal environmental statute), *with Federal Election Commission v. Akins, supra*, 524 U.S. 11, 19 (1998) (upholding congressional conferral of standing on any "aggrieved" person to challenge Federal Election Commission's refusal to require extensive disclosures by American Israel Public Affairs Committee). *See generally* David P. Currie, *Judicial Review under Federal Pollution Laws*, 62 Iowa L. Rev. 1221 (1977). Consider also the authorization of *qui tam* lawsuits in the False Claims Act, 31 U.S.C. §§3729–3731; these are actions brought by modern-day bounty hunters on behalf of the government to recover for fraud committed on the government. *See Vermont Agency of Natural Resources v. United States*, 529 U.S. 765 (2000) (upholding standing).

2.   *Disputes Appropriate for Judicial Resolution*

In addition to the standing doctrine, the Supreme Court has recognized other justiciability barriers that define the appropriateness of the suit for judicial resolution.

a.   Advisory Opinions

Early in the history of the Republic, the Court made clear that the exercise of "judicial power" within the meaning of Article III requires that judicial action resolve the underlying dispute. As a consequence, the federal courts are prohibited from issuing *advisory opinions* concerning the legality of proposed legislation or executive action. The federal courts are also barred from rendering any judgment subject to change by another branch of government. For example, a federal court could not simply screen claims against the federal government if the ultimate decision whether to honor the claim was made by the executive branch. *See Hayburn's Case*, 2 U.S. (2 Dall.) 408 (1792).

b.   Political Questions

Some matters are deemed nonjusticiable because the courts are not viewed as the appropriate institution to construe the underlying law; although the courts generally have the responsibility for interpreting law, the Constitution is thought to commit the enforcement of some legal provisions to the exclusive authority of the coordinate, so-called political, branches of government. For example, Article I of the Constitution assigns to the Senate the exclusive authority to try the impeachment of federal judges charged with the commission of certain criminal offenses, and the Court has dismissed on *political question* grounds litigation challenging the trial procedure followed by the Senate in such a case. *See Nixon v. United States*, 506 U.S. 224 (1993). *See also Rucho v. Common Cause*, 139 S. Ct. 2484 (2019) (holding that the issue of gerrymandering is a political question beyond the reach of federal courts); *Goldwater v. Carter*, 444 U.S. 996 (1979) (deeming the President's unilateral abrogation of a treaty a political question). *See generally* Louis Henkin, *Is There a Political Question Doctrine?*, 85 Yale L.J. 597 (1976); Tara Leigh Grove, *The Lost History of the Political Question Doctrine*, 90 N.Y.U. L. Rev. 1908 (2015).

3.   *Mootness*

A dispute may at the outset be justiciable but because of subsequent events may later cease to be a "live controversy" before the court. For example, in *DeFunis v. Odegaard*, 416 U.S. 312 (1974), a plaintiff seeking admission into the University of Washington Law School's entering class alleged that he was denied admission because of the defendant's preferential admissions policy for minority group members. Because of interim injunctive relief, DeFunis was permitted to attend the school *pendente lite*. By the time the Supreme Court heard argument in the case, he was in the final semester of his third year, and the defendant represented that the school would not interfere with his graduation. The Court held that since DeFunis had sought only injunctive relief, it lacked jurisdiction to proceed further with the case and vacated the judgment below on grounds of mootness. The Court's opinion states that "[t]he inability of the federal judiciary 'to review moot cases derives from the requirement of Art. III of the Constitution under which the exercise of judicial power depends on the existence of a case or controversy.'" However, a more recent case appears to deem mootness a prudential limitation and not constitutionally compelled. *Friends of the Earth v. Laidlaw Environmental Services*, 528 U.S. 167, 190 (2000) (permitting plaintiffs to continue their suit to enjoin defendant's violation of the Clean Water Act even though the polluting site had been torn down during the litigation, and the only sanction still available was a fine payable to the government, not the plaintiffs).

C.   DIVERSITY OF CITIZENSHIP JURISDICTION

For a federal court to have subject matter jurisdiction, the controversy must not only be justiciable but must also fall within one of the headings of federal judicial power in Article III, §2, and within a statutory grant of jurisdiction. In this section, we consider *diversity* jurisdiction — the branch of the "judicial Power of the United States" that is defined in terms of citizenship of the parties to the dispute. The statutory diversity grant is found in 28 U.S.C. §1332. $75,000↑

1.   *Rationale; Complete Diversity Requirement*

Strawbridge v. Curtiss

7 U.S. (3 Cranch) 267 (1806)

This was an appeal from a decree of the Circuit Court for the District of Massachusetts, which dismissed the complainants' bill in chancery, for want of jurisdiction. Some of the complainants were alleged to be citizens of the state of Massachusetts. The defendants were also stated to be citizens of the same state, excepting Curtiss, who was averred to be a citizen of the state of Vermont, and upon whom the *subpoena* was served in that state.

The question of jurisdiction was submitted to the court, without argument, by *P.B. Key*, for the appellants, and *Harper*, for the appellees.

MARSHALL, CH. J., delivered the opinion of the Court. . . . The court has considered this case, and is of opinion that the jurisdiction cannot be supported.

The words of the act of congress are, "where an alien is a party, or the suit is between a citizen of a state where the suit is brought, and a citizen of another state."

need complete
diversity of each
party.
    ↓ *why?*

fear of being
treated unfairly.
(prevent bias)

The court understands these expressions to mean that each distinct interest should be represented by persons, all of whom are entitled to sue, or may be sued, in the federal courts. That is, that where the interest is joint, each of the persons concerned in that interest must be competent to sue, or liable to be sued, in those courts.

But the court does not mean to give an opinion in the case where several parties represent several distinct interests, and some of those parties are, and others are not, competent to sue, or liable to be sued, in the courts of the United States.

Decree Affirmed.

NOTES AND QUESTIONS

1. *Is* Strawbridge *Constitutionally Compelled?* It was not until 1967, in *State Farm Fire & Cas. Co. v. Tashire*, 386 U.S. 523, 531 (1967), that the Supreme Court made clear that *Strawbridge*'s complete diversity requirement involved an interpretation of the diversity statute rather than the reach of the Article III diversity grant: "Chief Justice Marshall . . . [in *Strawbridge*] purported to construe only 'The words of the act of Congress,' not the Constitution itself. And in a variety of contexts this Court and the lower courts have made clear that Article III poses no obstacle to the legislative extension of diversity, so long as any two adverse parties are not co-citizens." *Tashire* involved the federal interpleader statute, 28 U.S.C. §1335, which is explained in Chapter 8.

Congress has more recently taken advantage of the *Tashire* ruling to make use of "minimal diversity," passing the Multiparty, Multiforum Trial Jurisdiction Act and the Class Action Fairness Act, both discussed later in this chapter. Is this view of federal jurisdiction really authorized by Article III? *See* C. Douglas Floyd, *The Limits of Minimal Diversity*, 55 Hastings L.J. 613 (2004) (arguing that a proper reading of Article III would not authorize the recent congressional expansions of federal diversity jurisdiction).

2. Was *Strawbridge*'s reading compelled by the wording of the diversity statute? The statute requires that a citizen of one state be aligned against a citizen of another state, but as long as at least two adverse parties are of diverse citizenship, does it necessarily foreclose joining additional nondiverse parties? Why do you think the Court adopted the complete diversity requirement? Contemporary thinking does not regard diversity jurisdiction as essential to the federal courts' responsibilities. Attitudes in 1806, however, may have been quite different about the availability of a federal forum free from local bias in favor of citizens of the forum state. *But see* Henry Friendly, *The Historic Basis of Diversity Jurisdiction*, 41 Harv. L. Rev. 483 (1928) (questioning the local-bias justification for the creation of diversity jurisdiction). Was Chief Justice Marshall instead simply seeking to limit the business of the federal courts at a time when the Justices in 1806 were saddled with burdensome circuit-riding responsibilities in addition to hearing appeals? *See* Felix Frankfurter & James M. Landis, *The Business of the Supreme Court of the United States—A Study in the Federal Judicial System*, 40 Harv. L. Rev. 834, 834–835 (1927). Caseload considerations are often unacknowledged factors of considerable importance to the process of interpreting jurisdictional statutes.

3. *Why Diversity Jurisdiction?* Was the Court's reading of the statute consistent with the purpose of creating diversity jurisdiction in the first place? The explanation

usually given for the diversity grant was a concern on the part of the Constitution's drafters that, as James Madison observed, "It may happen that a strong prejudice may arise in some states, against the citizens of others, who may have claims against them." 2 Elliot Debates 391 (1828). On one level, the presence of co-citizens among adverse parties blunts a concern with local bias, at least when the interests of the co-parties are intertwined. On the facts in *Strawbridge*, any tendency toward bias against the Vermont citizen might be negated by the presence of a Massachusetts party on the same side. On the other hand, the complete diversity requirement creates a potential for plaintiffs who are citizens of the forum state to defeat diversity jurisdiction by joining co-citizens as nominal defendants when the dispute is essentially with out-of-staters. Recall *Rose v. Giamatti*, at p. 46.

4. *Critique of the Local-Bias Rationale.* There are a number of difficulties with the local-bias rationale for diversity jurisdiction. First, some of the statutory arrangements are difficult to justify in such terms. For example, although the Judiciary Act of 1789 required that one of the parties to the suit be a citizen of the state where the suit is brought, this requirement has long since been abandoned. Moreover, while removal on diversity grounds to federal court was conditioned on a showing of actual prejudice as far back as the Act of March 2, 1867, 14 Stat. 558, such showings were rarely made, and that provision was eliminated in the 1948 revision of the Judicial Code. Also, plaintiffs who are citizens of the forum state can invoke diversity jurisdiction even though they presumably have no reason to fear local prejudice. And, as we shall see, because corporations are deemed citizens only of their place of incorporation and principal place of business, firms with substantial facilities in a particular state may be beneficiaries of local solicitude without being citizens of that state. *See* American Law Institute, Study of the Division of Jurisdiction Between State and Federal Courts, §1302 (1969) (proposal to bar invocation of diversity jurisdiction by a person in any district in the state of which he is a citizen, by a corporation or other business in any district in a state where it has maintained a local establishment for more than two years in an action arising out of the activities of that establishment, or by a person in a district where he has had his principal place of business or employment for more than two years).

Second, there are reasons for questioning the extent to which state courts today exhibit a systemic tilt in favor of local citizens as such. Affiliations on the basis of race, religion, ethnic origin, occupation, or social class may be considerably more important determinants of values and perceptions than state citizenship. Admittedly, sectional bias as between northerners and southerners may still be quite virulent, yet such bias is not captured by a scheme based on state citizenship rather than regional affiliation. The empirical data on the potency of state citizenship bias is, at best, inconclusive. *See* Jerry Goldman & Kenneth S. Marks, *Diversity Jurisdiction and Local Bias: A Preliminary Empirical Inquiry*, 9 J. Legal Stud. 93 (1980); Marvin R. Summers, *Analysis of Factors that Influence Choice of Forum in Diversity Cases*, 47 Iowa. L. Rev. 933 (1962). Moreover, even if some residual bias in favor of local citizens remains, it is unclear why federal courts are immune from such bias. Federal judges are themselves drawn from the ranks of prominent local practitioners, and federal juries are drawn from local citizens (though from a broader venire than state jurors). *See* David L. Shapiro, *Federal Diversity Jurisdiction: A Survey and a Proposal*, 91 Harv. L. Rev. 317, 329–330 (1977).

Third, the retention of diversity jurisdiction may be a luxury that an overburdened federal judiciary can no longer afford. The Report of the Judicial Conference of the United States in its Long Range Plan for the Federal Courts (1995) (at p. 30) observed that diversity jurisdiction accounts for more than one of every five civil cases filed in the federal district courts, about one of every two civil trials, about one of every ten appeals, and more than one of every ten dollars in the federal judicial budget. *See also* Richard A. Posner, The Federal Courts: Crisis and Reform 85–87 (1985). If the federal caseload is to be cut, diversity cases would seem a relatively preferable candidate for assignment to the state system than cases involving the interpretation and application of federal law.

Because the wholesale elimination of diversity jurisdiction has met both a passionate and successful resistance from the trial bar, *see, e.g.,* John B. Frank, *The Case for Diversity Jurisdiction,* 16 Harv. J. on Legis. 403 (1979), less dramatic reform is more plausible. The Long Range Plan for the Federal Courts (1995) suggested other alternatives, such as (1) eliminating original diversity jurisdiction for cases in which the plaintiff is a citizen of the state in which the federal district court is located; (2) requiring that parties invoking diversity jurisdiction plead specific facts showing that the jurisdictional amount-in-controversy requirement has been satisfied; (3) raising the amount-in-controversy level and indexing the new floor amount to the rate of inflation; and (4) amending the statutory specification of the jurisdictional amount to exclude punitive damages from the calculation of the amount in controversy.

Which, if any, of these proposals would you advocate? In 1996, Congress did raise the amount-in-controversy requirement from $50,000 to $75,000 but did not adopt any indexing formula.

5. *Rethinking Diversity Jurisdiction.* Is there a justification for retaining diversity jurisdiction in some form that does not depend on fear of state citizenship bias? Conceivably, diversity jurisdiction helps promote a nonparochial bar of lawyers able to navigate both federal and state courts as well as a "migration of ideas" between federal and state systems. Also, as the chapters on personal jurisdiction and joinder indicate, federal courts offer a unique capacity for serving as a forum for adjudicating multistate controversies that no single state court can hear. *See* Report of the Federal Courts Study Committee 44–45 (1990) (urging a broadening of federal courts' authority to consolidate litigation "based on minimal, rather than complete, diversity so that parties to a multi-state, multi-party state law litigation can be included even if they are citizens of the same state"). *See also* Long Range Plan for the Federal Courts, 31–32 (1995). In the last few years, Congress has used the constitutional grant of diversity jurisdiction to provide for federal jurisdiction in various types of complex litigation. In 2002, Congress enacted the Multiparty, Multiforum Trial Jurisdiction Act, 28 U.S.C. §1369, which authorizes federal jurisdiction on the basis of minimal diversity in certain tort-death actions having multistate connections. In 2005 Congress also used minimal diversity as a basis for federal jurisdiction in certain multistate class actions where the aggregate amount in controversy is at least $5 million. *See* 28 U.S.C. §1332(d). Specifics of the Multiparty, Multiforum Trial Jurisdiction Act and the Class Action Fairness Act can be found later in this chapter at pp. 317–319 and both statutes are discussed more extensively in Chapter 8.

a. Exceptions to Diversity Jurisdiction

i. Domestic Relations

The federal courts have traditionally refused to hear cases dealing with "domestic relations," even if the requisite diversity of citizenship and amount in controversy have been satisfied. Although there is no constitutional or express statutory limitation on the federal courts' power to hear these suits, the exception was articulated in several nineteenth-century Supreme Court opinions, notably *Barber v. Barber*, 62 U.S. (21 How.) 582 (1858), and has been generally accepted since. *See Ankenbrandt v. Richards*, 504 U.S. 689, 704 (1992) (domestic relations exception "encompasses only cases involving the issuance of a divorce, alimony, or child custody decree"; federal court has jurisdiction under §1332 to hear tort action against former husband for child abuse).

The origins of the "domestic relations" exception are thought to derive from the fact that English courts did not have jurisdiction over domestic affairs disputes, which were then the exclusive province of the ecclesiastical courts. *But see* Anthony B. Ullman, Note, *The Domestic Relations Exception to Diversity Jurisdiction*, 83 Colum. L. Rev. 1824, 1835 n.75 (1983) (indicating that the jurisdiction of the ecclesiastical courts over these matters was one of privilege rather than of right). A modern justification for continuing this practice is that such disputes comprise an area of particular state expertise, often requiring retention of jurisdiction and intervention of social services agencies, and hence call for a federal court's abstention. *See* Rebecca A. Swenson, Note, *Application of the Federal Abstention Doctrines to the Domestic Relations Exception to Federal Diversity Jurisdiction*, 1983 Duke L.J. 1095 (1983). *But see* Jill E. Hasday, *Federalism and the Family Reconstructed*, 45 UCLA L. Rev. 1297 (1998) (arguing that domestic relations exception has its origins in coverture laws, which are now clearly disfavored, and that other arguments from history and social welfare do not justify continued adherence to the doctrine). Does the exception reflect a kind of gender bias? Judith Resnik, *"Naturally" Without Gender: Women, Jurisdiction, and the Federal Courts*, 66 N.Y.U. L. Rev. 1682 (1991).

Earlier rationales may not suffice to explain a recent decision of the Supreme Court that has extended a variation on the "domestic relations" exception to federal question cases. In *Elk Grove Unified School District v. Newdow*, 542 U.S. 1 (2004), the Supreme Court dismissed an Establishment Clause challenge to the use of the words "under God" when public schools lead children in reciting the pledge of allegiance. The challenge was brought by the father of a young student, and the Court dismissed the case on "prudential" standing grounds, explaining that the father did not have full custody over his daughter and so did not possess the authority to bring suit on her behalf. The merits of the case had nothing to do with the custodial rights of either parent—the case came to federal court on a federal question rather than diversity jurisdiction, and it challenged only the constitutionality of the school policy, not the custodial arrangements within the family. Resolution of the standing issue merely required the federal courts to determine what rights the state courts had granted the parents to act on behalf of their daughter.

Nonetheless, in explaining its dismissal, the Court invoked the "domestic relations" exception and held it applicable to federal-question as well as diversity cases. When a case involves "elements of the domestic relationship," the Court said, it is "general[ly] . . . appropriate for the federal courts to leave [those] delicate issues of domestic relations to the state courts." *Id.* at 19. This general presumption may only be overcome in "rare instances in which it is necessary to answer a substantial federal question that transcends or exists apart from the family law issue." *Id.* (citing *Palmore v. Sidoti*, 466 U.S. 429 (1984), which involved a challenge to the consideration of race in a custody proceeding).

The implications of *Newdow* for federal subject matter jurisdiction remain to be determined. Despite its broad statements about the domestic relations exception, the rest of the opinion could be read as a simple interpretation of state law on parental rights (albeit with less deference to the court of appeals than the Supreme Court ordinarily shows on such issues). Given the politically charged atmosphere that surrounded the *Newdow* case, the Court's invocation of the domestic relations exception may be an anomaly best explained by a desire not to reach the merits. Even so, *Newdow* now provides a basis for parties to argue in future cases that federal question jurisdiction is inappropriate in cases that involve "elements of the domestic relationship," even on constitutional claims.

For more on the domestic relations exception as it applies in federal question cases, *see* Meredith Johnson Harbach, *Is the Family a Federal Question?*, 66 Wash. & Lee L. Rev. 131 (2009) (discussing the recent expansion of the domestic relations exception and the consequences for federal questions that implicate the family).

ii.   Probate

The federal courts similarly will refuse to adjudicate probate matters. Although the Supreme Court in *Markham v. Allen*, 326 U.S. 490, 494 (1946), asserted that "a federal court has no jurisdiction to probate a will or administer an estate," the history of this jurisdictional limitation is as subject to debate as the domestic relations exception. *See Dragan v. Miller*, 679 F.2d 712 (7th Cir. 1982). At any rate, the contours of the exception, while reserving for the states all matters directly and ancillarily related to the probate proceeding itself and the state court's custody of the property of the decedent, do allow federal courts to entertain certain actions by plaintiffs seeking to establish claims against an estate. *See, e.g., Giardina v. Fontana*, 733 F.2d 1047 (2d Cir. 1984) (allegation that plaintiff was fraudulently induced to assign the proceeds of a will did not call for federal abstention).

In *Marshall v. Marshall*, 547 U.S. 293 (2006), the Supreme Court described the probate exception as designed only to prevent federal courts from "endeavoring to dispose of property that is in the custody of a state probate court." Accordingly, the Court upheld federal jurisdiction over a claim of tortious interference regarding a potential gift from an estate, noting that this tort claim was for an *in personam* judgment and did not directly interfere with the probate proceedings in a state court. It also brushed aside the suggestion that the probate courts' special expertise should confer jurisdiction in these situations; it observed that probate tribunals would not be better suited to resolving a tort claim than a federal district court, which often hears these types of claims. As a result of *Marshall*, the Second Circuit subsequently allowed a plaintiff to bring claims of a breach of fiduciary duty against an executor even though the issues unquestionably would affect the state-court probate proceedings. *See Lefkowitz v. Bank of New York*, 528 F.3d 102 (2d Cir. 2007). In another post-*Marshall* decision, the Seventh Circuit deemed the probate exception applicable to both diversity-of-citizenship cases (28 U.S.C. §1332) and cases arising under federal law (28 U.S.C. §1331), observing that historical evidence now suggests that the exception is not constitutional. *See Jones v. Brennan*, 465 F.3d 304 (7th Cir. 2006).

2. Determining Citizenship; Joinder Issues

a. Time Frame for Determination

Citizenship for diversity purposes is determined as of the time of the commencement of the lawsuit—i.e., the filing of the complaint, *see* Fed. R. Civ. P. 3—rather than at the time of the underlying events giving rise to the litigation. This approach reflects the local-bias rationale for diversity jurisdiction, for presumably the relevant bias is that which will occur during the lawsuit. This test also has the virtue of being relatively easy to apply. However, it also permits a party to manufacture diversity jurisdiction by moving to another state after the cause of action has accrued but before the action has commenced. If the move involves a bona fide change of domicile, the district court will have jurisdiction. *See, e.g., Janzen v. Goos*, 302 F.2d 421 (8th Cir. 1962). Although many decisions hold that a motive to invoke diversity jurisdiction is immaterial in the case of a bona fide change of domicile, *see, e.g., Peterson v. Allcity Ins. Co.*, 472 F.2d 71 (2d Cir. 1972) (bona fide move at time of commencement of suit even though plaintiff returned to former domicile by time of trial), close scrutiny of activities designed to create diversity jurisdiction would seem to be authorized by 28 U.S.C. §1359.

If complete diversity is present at the time of the commencement of the suit, subsequent events such as the plaintiff's return to her former domicile do not work an ouster of jurisdiction. Although it might be argued that subsequent events may have a bearing on the continuing likelihood of local prejudice, adoption of the converse position would render the court's jurisdiction perpetually unsettled and, in some cases, invite post-suit domicile changes simply for the purpose of defeating jurisdiction. In contrast, subsequent events can render a lawsuit moot and hence nonjusticiable. However, it is more difficult to manufacture such events to defeat jurisdiction than to change one's domicile. Moreover, the Supreme Court has fashioned several exceptions to its mootness doctrine to preserve justiciability in the face of a party's strategic manipulation of subsequent events.

If a district court erroneously takes jurisdiction over a case where diversity does not exist, and subsequent events then occur that cure the jurisdictional problem while the lawsuit is still ongoing, the situation becomes more complex. If the jurisdictional defect is caused by the presence of a nondiverse party, and that party is *dismissed* from the suit when the defect becomes apparent, the federal court may be able to retain jurisdiction even though there was no diversity at the time the suit was filed. *See Caterpillar Inc. v. Lewis*, 519 U.S. 61 (1996). If a nondiverse party *changes* its citizenship or otherwise cures the defect while still remaining in the lawsuit, however, the federal court must dismiss the case nonetheless, even if the case has already gone to trial and a dismissal would result in much wasted effort. Thus, in *Grupo Dataflux v. Atlas Global Group*, 541 U.S. 567 (2004), the Supreme Court required that an action be dismissed for lack of jurisdiction because two partners in the plaintiff partnership were nondiverse from the defendant at the time the case was filed. Although both partners left the partnership before a verdict was rendered, the Court held that the citizenship of the partnership entity was to be determined at the time of filing. Nonetheless, federal courts still sometimes conclude that developments subsequent to the filing of the lawsuit can be taken into account when analyzing diversity. Consider *Wright v. Musanti*, 887 F.3d 577 (2d Cir. 2018). When the lawsuit in that case was filed, federal jurisdiction was premised on federal question claims, *see infra* at 312–341, and complete diversity was lacking. Later, the federal claims were dismissed and only state law claims remained. By that time, however, the parties had moved domiciles such that the requirements of complete diversity were satisfied. The Second Circuit upheld continued federal jurisdiction.

What is the justification for treating the dismissal of a nondiverse party differently from a change in its citizenship or status when it comes to curing jurisdictional defects? Would permitting the court to retain jurisdiction if a nondiverse party changes its citizenship create incentives for bad behavior that are not present when the only option for curing the defect is dismissal? Or is the distinction a purely formal one?

b.   Natural Individuals

The citizenship of a natural individual for diversity purposes is that person's domicile — his place of fixed or habitual residence and the place where, if he is absent, he has the intention of returning. A person has only one domicile at a particular time even though he may have residences in several states. Typically, students, military personnel, and prisoners may reside for extended periods of time at a place other than their domicile. Acquisition of a new domicile requires physical presence at the new location with an intention to remain there indefinitely. The courts generally adopt the conflict of laws convention that a domicile once established continues until a new domicile is acquired. Thus, for example, in the *World-Wide Volkswagen v. Woodson* litigation (discussed in Chapter 2), the fact that the Robinsons never reached Arizona, their chosen new domicile, meant that they retained their New York domicile.

For diversity purposes, an individual must be a citizen both of the United States and one of the states of the Union. In response to *Dred Scott v. Sandford*, 60 U.S. (19 How.) 393 (1857) (enslaved party) (which arose in the context of a ruling on diversity jurisdiction), §1 of the Fourteenth Amendment provides that "all citizens born or naturalized in the United States are citizens of the United States and the state in which they reside." Americans domiciled abroad cannot invoke (and their presence as parties could defeat) diversity jurisdiction because they are neither citizens of a state of the United States nor citizens of a foreign state.

The general rule is to look to the citizenship of the one who has the legal right to sue and to represent those having a beneficial interest in the recovery. *See, e.g., Navarro Sav. Ass'n v. Lee*, 446 U.S. 458 (1980) (citizenship of active trustee of business trust controls); *Mexican Cent. Ry. v. Eckman*, 187 U.S. 429 (1903) (citizenship of guardian controls in suit by guardian in his name to recover damages to ward). In the context of appointment of administrators of estates, this rule created a potential for manufacturing diversity jurisdiction. *See* Linda S. Mullenix, *Creative Manipulation of Federal Jurisdiction: Is There Diversity After Death?*, 70 Cornell L. Rev. 1011 (1985). Congress carved an exception out of this general rule in 1988 by amending

§1332 to provide that "the legal representative of the estate of a decedent shall be deemed to be a citizen only of the same state as the decedent." *See* 28 U.S.C. §1332(c)(2). The amendment also provided a parallel rule for the legal representative of an infant or incompetent.

c. Corporations

Corporations were originally considered citizens only of their state of incorporation. The underlying theory was that a corporation has no legal existence outside of its state of incorporation. From the standpoint of the local-bias rationale for diversity jurisdiction, this theory ignored the fact that a corporation might have a very substantial economic presence in states other than the place of incorporation. Moreover, unlike a natural individual's change of domicile, an act of incorporation is a paper transaction that need involve no change in the firm's activities. During the era prior to *Erie Railroad Co. v. Tompkins*, 304 U.S. 64 (1938), when access to a federal diversity court often entailed a change in substantive law as well as forum, reincorporation for the purpose of creating or defeating diversity was not uncommon. *See, e.g., Black & White Taxicab & Transfer* Co. *v. Brown & Yellow Taxicab & Transfer Co.*, 276 U.S. 518 (1928). This abuse led in part to the *Erie* decision, which as we shall see, held that the diversity court must apply the substantive law that would be applied by the state in which it sits. It also prompted Congress in 1958 to amend the diversity statute to address the citizenship of corporations, providing that "a corporation shall be deemed to be a citizen of any state by which it has been incorporated and of the state where it has its principal place of business. . . ."

The 1958 amendment left several issues ambiguous. First, it failed to solve the problem of determining the citizenship of firms incorporated in more than one state. Although most courts treated the corporation as a citizen of every state in which it was incorporated, a few states adhered to the "forum doctrine," which treated a corporation as incorporated solely in the forum state if suit were brought against the corporation in any one of the fora in which it was incorporated. *See, e.g., Hudak v. Port Authority Trans-Hudson Corp.*, 238 F. Supp. 790 (S.D.N.Y. 1965) (New Jersey plaintiff sued defendant, a firm incorporated in New York and New Jersey with its principal place of business in New York. By suing in New York, defendant's New Jersey incorporation was disregarded and plaintiff was able to establish diversity jurisdiction under the "forum doctrine.").

Second, uncertainty was also created when determining the "citizenship" of a foreign corporation. Some courts had limited the definition of "State" (with a capital "S") to the 50 States of the United States and its territories. Under this interpretation, the provision would not cover a foreign corporation at all (i.e., the provision only applied to corporations incorporated in one of the 50 States or U.S. territories). Even though a foreign corporation is treated as a citizen of the foreign state in which it was incorporated (per the interpretation of the citizenship of a foreign corporation prior to the 1958 amendment), the foreign corporation was not deemed a citizen of a State (of the United States) where it had its principal place of business. Thus diversity jurisdiction would exist even where a foreign corporation had its principal place of business in the same State where its adversary was a citizen. As to a U.S. corporation with a foreign principal place of business, the corporation would not be treated as a citizen of the place where it had its principal place of business since that foreign state would not be a State within the meaning of the provision. Thus diversity would exist between a citizen of a foreign country and a U.S. corporation that had its principal place of business in that foreign country.

In December 2011, Congress enacted the Federal Courts Jurisdiction and Venue Clarification Act of 2011. Under that Act, 28 U.S.C. §1332(c) was amended to clarify that a corporation is a citizen of *every* State *and foreign state* where it is incorporated and of the State *or foreign state* where it has its principal place of business. By clarifying that a corporation is a citizen of "every" State and foreign state where it is incorporated, the Act eliminated the "forum doctrine." By expressly including domestic and foreign connections in assessing diversity, every corporation is now treated as a citizen of every State or foreign state in which it is incorporated and the State or foreign state in which it has its principal place of business. Thus, diversity is eliminated in at least two situations: suits between a foreign corporation with its principal place of business in domestic State *X* and a citizen of that same State *X*; and suits between a citizen of foreign country *A* and a U.S. corporation with its principal place of business in foreign country *A.*

The concept of "principal place of business" had also given rise to conflicting case law. Some courts adopted a "nerve center" test that looked to the place from which the corporation's officers "direct, control and coordinate all activities without regard to locale, in the furtherance of the corporate objective," *see, e.g., Scot Typewriter Co. v. Underwood Corp.*, 170 F. Supp. 862 (1959); while others endorsed a "place of activity" test that focused on where the actual corporate activity took place, at least where the corporation's business activities were predominant in a particular State, *see, e.g., Kelly v. United States Steel Corp.*, 284 F.2d 850 (3d Cir. 1960); and still others invited an inquiry into the "total activity" of the corporation. Congress did not address the issue in the 2011 Clarification Act, presumably because the United States Supreme Court had taken up the issue the previous year. In 2010, the Supreme Court decided *Hertz Corp. v. Friend*, 559 U.S. 77 (2010), and interpreted the phrase "principal place of business" in 28 U.S.C. §1332(c)(1) to mean the "nerve center" of the corporation. The case was filed as a class action in California state court on behalf of California citizens who suffered harm as a result of Hertz's alleged violations of California's wage and hour laws. Hertz removed the case to federal court, claiming that it was a citizen of New Jersey, where it had its corporate headquarters and executive offices. The district court, applying Ninth Circuit precedent, found that the California business activities of Hertz substantially predominated, and thus its principal place of business was California. The Ninth Circuit affirmed, and the Supreme Court granted certiorari. Justice Breyer, writing for a unanimous Court, characterized the pre-*Hertz* approach as one "at war with administrative simplicity" and one that had "failed to achieve a nationally uniform interpretation of federal law." The Court concluded that "principal place of business" was best read to refer to the place where the corporation's officers "direct, control and coordinate the corporation's activities"—i.e., the corporation's nerve center.

The Supreme Court acknowledged that the "nerve center" approach presented its own difficulties but offered three justifications for adopting that test. First, the Court viewed the "nerve center" test as the one most compatible with the text of the statute: The word "place" appears in the singular and not the plural, and the word "principal" indicates the "main, prominent, or leading" place and one located within a State and not the State itself. As the Court explained, the application of a more general business activities test requires courts to look at the State itself to measure the amount of business conducted there in comparison to that of other States, and that approach is inconsistent with the statutory language. Second, the Court explained that the nerve center test is easier to administer, comparatively speaking, and does not require the more complex inquiry of trying to ascertain in which State the corporation has more plants or employees or locations. The Court emphasized the need for simple jurisdictional rules that will promote predictability for both litigants and the court itself. Third, the Court believed its interpretation to be the best match with the statute's legislative history. In 1958, the Judicial Conference's initial proposal had posited a numerical test in which a corporation would be "deemed a citizen of the State that accounted for more than half of its gross income." That proposal was rejected in light of criticism that it would prove too complex and impractical. Therefore, the Court reasoned that the interpretation of "principal place of business" should be no more complex than the "half of gross income" test. The Court thought the nerve center test offered that possibility whereas a "general business activities" test did not.

Of course, the *Hertz* test is not responsive to a more general criticism directed at the ability of out-of-state corporations to invoke diversity and gain an unfair advantage over local companies occupying essentially the same role in the community. To that end, proposals have been offered to make a corporation a citizen of every State in which it is registered to do business. *See, e.g.*, Charles W. Joiner, *Corporations as Citizens of Every State Where They Do Business: A Needed Change in Diversity Jurisdiction*, 70 Judicature 291 (1987). Another alternative was that of the American Law Institute, in its Study of the Division of Jurisdiction Between Federal and State Courts §1302 (1969), which recommended that a corporation be precluded from invoking diversity jurisdiction in any State where it has maintained an establishment for two years in any litigation arising out of the activities of that establishment. Congress, however, when it enacted the 2011 venue amendments, apparently did not find it necessary or wise to move in that direction. Do you find either of the proposals to be more attractive than the solution reached in the *Hertz* case?

Note the difference between a corporation's residence for venue purposes under §1391 and its citizenship for diversity purposes under §1332(c)(1). You will recall that for purposes of venue, a defendant that is a corporation "shall be deemed to reside in any judicial district in which it is subject to personal jurisdiction at the time the action is commenced." 28 U.S.C. §1391(c). Thus, while a corporation may be considered a "resident" of numerous States, it will normally be a "citizen" of only one or two states. While this may appear perverse, there is a consistent policy animating both definitions that maximizes federal jurisdiction over corporations: An *expansive* definition of residence subjects the corporation to venue in more federal districts, while a *restrictive* definition of citizenship makes the corporation diverse from a greater number of opposing parties, thereby increasing federal jurisdiction.

Does the *Hertz* definition of "principal place of business" for purposes of the diversity of citizenship statute have any implications for general personal jurisdiction in light of the *Daimler* rule that general jurisdiction is confined to a defendant corporation's place of incorporation and principal place of business? *See* discussion at pp. 90-91 in Chapter 2. Do any of the rationales, as discussed by the Supreme Court in *Hertz*, argue for the same test in determining the principal place of business of a corporation under *Daimler*?

d.   Direct Actions Against Insurance Companies

Section 1332(c), as amended in 1964, creates a special rule for direct actions against liability insurers in which the insured is not joined as a defendant. The amendment was a response to a problem that had arisen as a result of Louisiana's "direct action" statute. (A direct action statute allows an injured plaintiff to sue the alleged tortfeasor's insurance company before obtaining a judgment against the insured and without joining the insured.) By suing the out-of-state insurance company, a local plaintiff was able to create diversity of citizenship and bring what was actually a controversy between citizens of the same State in federal court, thereby avoiding the broad judicial review of jury verdicts that was often available in the state courts. Section 1332(c) prevents that move by imputing the insured's citizenship to the insurer in addition to the insurer's own citizenship. However, the Supreme Court has held that this imputed citizenship rule of §1332(c) does not extend to actions brought in federal court *by* insurers. In *Northbrook National Ins. Co. v. Brewer*, 493 U.S. 6 (1989), a Texas employee obtained a workers' compensation award from the Texas Industrial Accident Board against his employer's insurer, an Illinois corporation. The insurer then brought an action in federal district court in Texas to obtain *de novo* review of the award (as authorized by state law). The Supreme Court adopted a literal reading of the provision, holding that it did not apply in an action brought by the insurer, even though the proceeding had begun as a claim by the employee against the insurer, with the court action simply providing a form of appellate review of the award.

The Federal Courts Jurisdiction and Venue Clarification Act of 2011 venue amendments, which made a corporation a citizen of every State or foreign state in which it is incorporated or has its principal place of business, also effected equivalent changes with respect to the citizenship of insurers in direct actions against insurers. Under the Act, the insurer is now deemed a citizen of *every* State and *foreign state* of which the insured is a citizen; of *every* State and *foreign state* in which the insurer is incorporated; and of the State or *foreign state* where the insurer has its principal place of business. By expanding the citizenship of insurance companies defending against direct actions, the 2011 Jurisdiction and Venue Clarification Act further limits the ability of plaintiffs to create diversity of citizenship by bringing a direct action against the alleged tortfeasor's insurance company.

e.   Unincorporated Associations

The Supreme Court's general approach to unincorporated associations has been to withhold entity status from such associations for purposes of diversity jurisdiction. For example, in *United Steelworkers of America v. R.H. Bouligny, Inc.*, 382 U.S. 145 (1965), the Court held that the citizenship of an unincorporated labor union was to be determined on the basis of the citizenship of all of its members, thus effectively precluding such an entity (in most cases) from invoking diversity jurisdiction or being sued in federal court on the basis of diversity. Similarly, in *Carden v. Arkoma Associates*, 494 U.S. 185 (1990), the Court in considering the citizenship of a limited partnership organized under the laws of Arizona looked to the citizenship of both the general and limited partners to ascertain citizenship of the partnership.

In light of the fact that many unincorporated associations have some characteristics in common with corporations, what explains the Court's resistance to adopting a rule that would look to the location of the entity itself (for example, its State of establishment and principal place of business) rather than to the citizenship of its individual members?

In the most recent case to come before the Supreme Court, *Americold Realty Trust v. Conagra Foods, Inc.*, 494 U.S. 185 (2016), the Court reaffirmed the "doctrinal wall" between incorporated and unincorporated entities, observing that it "saw no reason to tear it down," and stating that any change should be left to Congress. In *Americold*, a group of corporations filed in Kansas state court a contract action against a "real estate investment trust" (REIT) organized under Maryland law. After the case was removed to federal court and resolved in favor of the realty trust, the case was appealed and eventually reached the Supreme Court. Americold contended a REIT should be treated as a trust and relied on the Supreme Court's earlier decision in *Navarro Savings Association v. Lee*, 446 U.S. 458 (1980), which had looked to the citizenship of the eight trustees of a Massachusetts business trust (rather than the citizenship of all the trust beneficiaries) to determine whether diversity was satisfied. However, in *Navarro*, the trustees had sued in their own name, and the Supreme Court noted that for purposes of the Massachusetts business trust in *Navarro*, the trustees had real and substantial control over the assets and brought them within the rule that trustees generally can sue in their own right. Emphasizing the "oft-repeated rule" that all "artificial entities other than corporations" are citizens wherever they have "members," the Court noted that Maryland law defines real estate investment trusts as unincorporated entities that operate "for the benefit and profit of any person who may become a shareholder." Consequently, the Court found Americold to be a citizen of all the States in which its owners reside for the purposes of diversity jurisdiction.

Note that Congress has changed the rule for unincorporated entities in limited circumstances. Unincorporated associations are given the same treatment as corporations for diversity purposes under the 2005 Class Action Fairness Act (CAFA). Under 28 U.S.C. §1332(d)(10), an unincorporated association that qualifies under CAFA will be treated as a citizen of the State in which it has its principal place of business.

f. Class Actions

The topic of class actions will be taken up in detail in Chapter 8, but for present purposes it is sufficient to know that often when the individual stakes for bringing a lawsuit are unlikely to justify the cost of litigation, a named representative may try to bring an action on behalf of himself and others similarly situated, thus providing a means of consolidating the joinder of many small claims and ensuring the availability of legal counsel. Such a class action may promote not only the private interests of the individual members of the class but also the general interest in ensuring compliance with the law. In the context of diversity of citizenship jurisdiction, the question is whether the citizenship of all class members—as would be true of an unincorporated association—must be taken into account. In an early Supreme Court decision, *Supreme Tribe of Ben-Hur v. Cauble*, 255 U.S. 356 (1921), the Court held that each *named class representative* must be of diverse citizenship from each defendant, but the citizenship of *unnamed class members* is not relevant in determining diversity. Thus in structuring a class action, class counsel can either access or block federal jurisdiction by choosing who the class representatives shall be.

g.   State Law Created Business Entities

State laws have created a variety of business entities that defy easy classification as either corporations or partnerships. For example, many States recognize Limited Liability Companies (LLCs), entities that combine the limited shareholder liability of a corporation with the management flexibility of a partnership. Courts have held that, for purposes of diversity, an LLC should be treated as the rough equivalent of a limited partnership, and its citizenship should be determined with reference to the citizenship of all "members." *See, e.g., Cosgrove v. Barolotta,* 150 F.3d 729, 731 (7th Cir. 1998). In *Cosgrove,* Judge Posner identified the "principle that members of associations are citizens for diversity purposes unless Congress provides otherwise (as it has with respect to corporations, in 28 U.S.C. §1332(c)(1))." *Id.*

The distinction is complicated by the fact that, while §1332(c)(1) provides a clear rule for determining the citizenship of a corporation for diversity purposes, it does not provide a definition of "corporation," this being generally a matter of state law. For example, a "professional corporation" (PC) is an entity that allows professional practitioners to limit their liability and realize certain corporate tax advantages. Like an LLC, a PC is a kind of hybrid entity, combining characteristics of both a partnership and a corporation. Unlike LLCs, however, PCs are identified as "corporations" under state law and have been treated by federal courts as corporations, rather than partnerships, for diversity purposes. *See, e.g., Saxe, Bacon & Bolan, P.C. v. Martindale-Hubbell, Inc.,* 710 F.2d 87 (2d Cir. 1983); *Coté v. Wadel,* 796 F.2d 981 (7th Cir. 1986). The Seventh Circuit has upheld the *Coté* rule for professional corporations despite their economic similarities to LLCs and limited partnerships, noting that "for purposes of diversity jurisdiction a corporation is a corporation is a corporation." *See Hoagland v. Sandberg, Phoenix & Von Gontard, P.C.,* 385 F.3d 737, 739 (7th Cir. 2004). In a concurring opinion, Judge Easterbrook criticized the *Coté* rule as "wrong in principle" but voted to affirm it, lamenting the alternative—undertaking a judicial determination of the legal characteristics that make a business entity a "corporation" for purposes of federal diversity—as "untenable in practice." *Id.* at 747. Do you agree with Judge Easterbrook's suggestion that either Congress or the Supreme Court should provide a positive, federal definition of "corporation" for purposes of determining citizenship in §1332 cases rather than relying on state law characterizations? For commentary on the LLC, *see* Comment, *Shoring Up the "Doctrinal Wall" of* Chapman v. Barney: *In Support of the Aggregate Approach to Limited Liability Company Citizenship for Purposes of Federal Diversity Jurisdiction,* 40 Willamette L. Rev. 739 (2004).

h.   The Role for Congress

Keep in mind that Congress itself is in a position to clarify the citizenship of entities by way of legislation, and Congress has done so on several occasions. For example, in 28 U.S.C. §1348, Congress provided that, for the purposes of most actions by or against national banks, such entities shall be deemed "citizens of the States in which they are respectively located." Conflicting rulings arose as to whether the term "located" referred to the bank's principal location or to any place where it carried on banking business, including its branches. In 2006, the Supreme Court in *Wachovia Bank v. Schmidt*, 546 U.S. 303 (2006) resolved the circuit split and held that a national bank, for §1348 purposes, is a citizen of a State where its main office, as set forth in its articles of incorporation, is located. In a recent decision, *Rouse v. Wachovia Mortg.*, 747 F.3d 707 (9th. Cir. 2014), the Ninth Circuit Court of Appeals held that the Supreme Court's 2006 decision in *Wachovia v. Schmidt* made clear that a national bank's citizenship is determined only by the State it has designated to be its main office and that the bank's citizenship is not affected by its principal place of business. The result is that only when a national bank is sued at its main office can a diverse plaintiff limit a defendant national bank's ability to remove the case to federal court.

REMEMBERING *ROSE*—FURTHER VARIATIONS ON DIVERSITY

Recall *Rose v. Giamatti*, the federal trial court decision from the Southern District of Ohio involving baseball player Pete Rose and Commissioner of Major League Baseball Bart Giamatti that you read as a sample case in the introductory chapter to this casebook. *See supra*, p. 46. That case explores the doctrine of *fraudulent joinder*, under which a federal court may disregard the citizenship of some parties in determining whether the requirement of complete diversity is satisfied when it appears that the plaintiff has no real controversy with the nondiverse defendants. This real-party-in-interest analysis is used to decide whether a given association or other entity should be disregarded altogether because the entire entity has no real dispute with the plaintiff. It is that type of analysis that the district court performed in *Rose*. The question in *Rose* was not whether to count only the citizenship of some owners of the Cincinnati Reds but not others, or only select members of Major League Baseball, in assessing jurisdiction. The question, rather, was whether the Reds and Major League Baseball, in their entirety, should be disregarded because Pete Rose had no real controversy with either of them. This type of fraudulent joinder analysis retains its vitality. *See* 13F C. Wright et al., Federal Practice and Procedure §3641.1 (3d ed. 2009).

Rose highlights the ways in which lawyers may try to structure a lawsuit in order to gain a perceived advantage in either state or federal court. By joining organizational defendants who had Ohio members, Rose was attempting to take advantage of the *Strawbridge* rule as well as the provision in 28 U.S.C. §1441(b), which prevents removal by a citizen defendant, in order to block federal court removal by the nonresident defendant.

In addition to the "fraudulent joinder"/"nominal party" doctrines, courts have also realigned the parties in accordance with their understanding of the ultimate interest of the parties before determining whether complete diversity exists. For example, in an action by an insured against his insurer seeking a declaratory judgment as to policy coverage, the tort claimant will be realigned as co-plaintiff with the insured. The "ultimate interest" test becomes difficult to apply, however, when there are parties on both sides of the controversy with shared interests. A common example occurs in shareholder derivative actions where shareholders sue on behalf of the corporation against its officers or directors for breach of fiduciary duty. In theory, the action is on behalf of the corporation and any recovery would flow, in the first instance, to the corporation itself. Yet the corporation acts through its officers and directors, who plainly are adverse to the plaintiffs; typically, before the derivative action could be instituted, the officers and directors had to have turned down a demand to bring the suit themselves on behalf of the firm or have acted so as to render such a demand futile. In such circumstances, the Supreme Court has held that the corporation, which typically must be joined as an indispensable party (under state law), may be treated as a defendant for diversity purposes. *See Smith v. Sperling*, 354 U.S. 91 (1957). Coupled with the rule of the *Ben-Hur* decision, it is rather easy for the shareholder group to pick as the named representative party a shareholder whose citizenship is diverse from that of the corporation and the individual defendants. However, where the derivative action complains not of misconduct by the corporate officers, but rather the activities of third parties owing an obligation to the firm, the mere fact that the corporate officers choose not to bring suit may not preclude realignment of the corporation as party-plaintiff. *See Lewis v. Odell*, 503 F.2d 445 (2d Cir. 1974) (corporation retained position of neutrality with respect to shareholder action and reserved right to take control of the action). Finally, note that a plaintiff who finds that it has joined a party who destroys diversity may ordinarily just drop that party in order to preserve the court's jurisdiction. *See* Fed. R. Civ. P. 21. The Supreme Court has held that a plaintiff may invoke this option even after judgment or at the appellate level. *See Newman-Green, Inc. v. Alfonzo-Larrain*, 490 U.S. 826 (1989).

Would a legislative framework be preferable to this case-by-case doctrine? Members of Congress have proposed legislation to address the issue of fraudulent joinder at various points, but no bill has yet been enacted. The "Innocent Party Protection Act," known at earlier stages as the "Fraudulent Joinder Prevention Act," would have outlined criteria for federal judges to use in evaluating whether a party was fraudulently joined. *See* H.R. 5345, 116th Cong. (2019) (providing that defendants are fraudulently joined if (a) there is "actual fraud" in the pleadings; (b) "it is not plausible to conclude that applicable State law would impose liability," (c) claims against that defendant are "clearly bar[red]" by state or federal law; or (d) there is "no good faith intention" to obtain a judgment against that defendant).

3. *Alienage Jurisdiction*

In addition to controversies between citizens of different States, 28 U.S.C. §1332(a) confers on the federal courts jurisdiction over controversies between:

> . . . .
>
> (2) citizens of a State and citizens or subjects of a foreign state, except that the district courts shall not have original jurisdiction under this subsection of an action between citizens of a State and citizens or subjects of a foreign state who are lawfully admitted for permanent residence in the United States and are domiciled in the same State;
> (3) citizens of different States and in which citizens or subjects of a foreign state are additional parties; and

(4) a foreign state . . . as plaintiff and citizens of a State or of different States.

28 U.S.C. §§1332(a)(2)–(4).

Two justifications for federal alienage jurisdiction are commonly asserted. One rationale is that local bias against foreigners will be mitigated by enabling foreigners to remove such cases to the federal courts. A second argument is that to compel aliens to litigate in state courts would be an affront to the sovereign nations from which they come. The latter rationale may help explain why merely being a noncitizen of the United States is insufficient to invoke alienage jurisdiction; only those persons who are "citizens or subjects of a foreign state" may take their cases to federal court. But note that the same rationale is undercut by the fact that suits between two aliens are not part of the diversity of citizenship grant under the statute or under Article III of the Constitution.

In 1988, Congress amended 28 U.S.C. §1332(a) to provide that an alien "admitted to the United States for permanent residence shall be deemed a citizen of the State in which such alien was domiciled." The objective was to prevent diversity of citizenship jurisdiction when the alien was domiciled in the same State as the other party. In such a situation, the permanent resident alien has appreciable connections to the State, and there was no perceived need for a federal forum to protect the alien against possible bias in the State. Courts interpreted "permanent aliens" to mean only those aliens who have been given "green cards." *See, e.g., Foy v. Schantz, Schatzman & Aaronson, P.A.*, 108 F.3d 1347, 1349 (11th Cir. 1997). However, an ambiguity remained in the interpretation of this "deeming" provision for resident aliens: Was a resident alien a citizen only of its State of residence or was the alien also a citizen of the foreign state? If the former, then two resident aliens might be able to invoke diversity of citizenship, possibly in violation of Article III since the Constitution does not permit alien versus alien jurisdiction. Moreover, the purpose of the 1988 amendment was to curtail diversity jurisdiction, not to expand it. The 2011 Federal Courts Jurisdiction and Venue Clarification Act addressed the issue by eliminating the "deeming" aspect of the resident alien proviso. A new provision amending §1332(a)(2) provides for diversity jurisdiction between citizens of a State and citizens of a foreign state, but now expressly precludes jurisdiction between citizens of a State and citizens or subjects of a foreign state who are lawfully admitted for permanent residence in the United States and are domiciled in the same State. Because the 1988 "deeming" provision is eliminated by the 2011 Act and the new 2011 amendments are limited to §1332(a)(2), it is also now clear that under §1332(a)(3) diversity jurisdiction will exist where there are U.S. citizens of different states on both sides of the lawsuit and resident aliens appear merely as additional parties to disputes.

Does the joinder of a U.S. citizen to a suit involving an alien plaintiff and alien defendant create diversity jurisdiction? Courts have generally held that suits in which an alien and a citizen of a State are on one side of the dispute and an alien is on the other side are outside the realm of both §§1332(a)(2) and (3). *See, e.g., Ed & Fred, Inc. v. Puritan Marine Ins. Underwriters Corp.*, 506 F.2d 757 (5th Cir. 1975) (requisite maximum diversity absent in a suit brought by a citizen of Netherlands Antilles against two defendants, one a citizen of Bermuda and the other a citizen of Massachusetts); *Fosen v. United Techs. Corp.*, 484 F. Supp. 490 (S.D.N.Y.

1980) (no diversity jurisdiction in a suit by Norwegian plaintiffs against Japanese and U.S. defendants). *See also Field v. Volkswagenwerk AG*, 626 F.2d 293 (3d Cir. 1980) (holding that no diversity exists in a suit brought by a Rhode Island citizen and a Czechoslovakian citizen against a West German defendant).

It generally does not matter on which side the U.S. citizen is present. In *Field* (where the U.S. citizen was one of the plaintiffs), as well as in *Ed & Fred* and *Fosen* (U.S. citizen was one of the defendants), the court determined that diversity jurisdiction was destroyed by alien presence on each side. Might there be another way to get into federal court if the U.S. citizen is joined as one of the plaintiffs? Consider this question during the discussion of supplemental jurisdiction later in this chapter.

When there are U.S. citizens of different States on *both* sides of the lawsuit along with aliens on each side, courts have found jurisdiction under §1332(a)(3). For example, assume that *P1* (a New York citizen) and *P2* (a Canadian citizen) sue *D1* (a California citizen) and *D2* (a German citizen). *See, e.g., Samincorp, Inc. v. Southwire Co.*, 531 F. Supp. 1 (N.D. Ga. 1980); *Clark v. Yellow Freight System, Inc.*, 715 F. Supp. 1377 (E.D. Mich. 1989) (holding that §1332(a)(3) allows aliens as additional parties on both sides of the dispute when there is at least one American party on each side of the dispute).

a.   Citizens of States Not Recognized by the United States

Persons who are citizens of entities not recognized by the United States as free and independent sovereigns are similarly excluded from diversity. In *Windert Watch Co. v. Remex Electronics Ltd.*, 468 F. Supp. 1242 (S.D.N.Y. 1979), the court denied diversity jurisdiction to citizens of Hong Kong, after finding that Hong Kong, a crown colony, was not a political subdivision of the United Kingdom. *Windert Watch* is criticized in *Tetra Finance (HK) Ltd. v. Shaheen*, 584 F. Supp. 847, 848 (S.D.N.Y. 1984) (dictum), where the court observed that "[t]he commercial and cultural realities of the modern world dictate that diversity jurisdiction should be granted to certain governmental entities that have not been formally recognized." The issue of recognition can be quite complicated. In *Iran Handicraft and Carpet Export Center v. Marjan International Corp.*, 655 F. Supp. 1275 (S.D.N.Y. 1987), the court held that the fact the United States had severed diplomatic relations with and declined to recognize the Khomeini regime in Iran did not defeat alienage jurisdiction. The court cited the Restatement (Second) of the Foreign Relations Law of the United States for the proposition that "[o]nce the United States recognizes an entity as a sovereign state . . . a subsequent withdrawal of recognition of that state's government does not effect a change in the underlying recognition of the state as an international juridical entity." 655 F. Supp. at 1281. *Iran Handicraft* is difficult to reconcile, however, with the rationale for alienage diversity that the United States would insult foreign governments if it did not provide their citizens with access to American courts of national prominence.

b.   American Citizens Living Abroad

American citizens living abroad are not aliens for purposes of diversity of citizenship and, although citizens of the United States, they are not citizens of any particular State of the United States. Therefore, they do not fall within any of the categories of diversity of citizenship jurisdiction in 28 U.S.C. §1332(a) and thus cannot sue or be sued in federal court on the basis of diversity. Accordingly, a foreign national may sue an American who is a citizen of a State in diversity, but not an American living abroad. Indeed, Americans living abroad are treated less favorably than foreign nationals in that they cannot invoke diversity jurisdiction in suits against Americans domiciled in the United States. *See, e.g., Smith v. Carter*, 545 F.2d 909 (5th Cir. 1977); *Twentieth Century-Fox Film Corp. v. Taylor*, 239 F. Supp. 913 (S.D.N.Y. 1965).

Additionally, when an American living abroad is a partner of a firm, that member can render the partnership stateless for the purpose of diversity jurisdiction, preventing a foreign plaintiff from bringing suit against the partnership in federal court. *See Thompson v. Deloitte & Touche LLP*, 503 F. Supp. 2d 1118 (S.D. Iowa 2007) (holding that one of 30 partners in a limited liability partnership who is an American citizen domiciled in Asia with no domicile in the United States renders the partnership stateless).

c. Dual Nationals

Every Court of Appeals to have considered the issue has held that for a dual national citizen, only the U.S. citizenship is relevant for purposes of diversity under 28 U.S.C. §1332. *See, e.g., Frett-Smith v. Vanterpool*, 511 F.3d 396 (3d Cir. 2008) (holding that plaintiff could not invoke alien jurisdiction under §1332(a)(2) because she was a citizen of both the British Virgin Islands and the United States). Part of the rationale behind this interpretation of §1332(a)(2) is that if dual nationals were able to invoke alienage jurisdiction, it would give them superior access to the federal forum compared to native-born U.S. citizens. Keep in mind that there is no real interest in allowing dual nationals to invoke alienage jurisdiction — the purpose of which is to allow foreign subjects to avoid real or perceived bias in the state courts — as they are U.S. citizens presumably not subject to any bias against aliens. *See Coury v. Prot*, 85 F.3d 244, 250 (5th Cir. 1996). Thus, in *Vanterpool*, a dual citizen of the British Virgin Islands and the United States living abroad was treated the same as an only-U.S. citizen living abroad for the purposes of diversity jurisdiction: not considered a citizen of any particular State of the United States and unable to sue or be sued in the federal court on the basis of diversity.

d. Alien Corporations

A corporation is a citizen of every State and foreign state where it is incorporated and of the State or foreign state where it has its principal place of business. (Recall that the rule for determining the citizenship of a foreign corporation is now explicit by the amendments in the 2011 Jurisdiction and Venue Clarification Act.)

But whose law should determine whether a particular foreign entity is a "citizen" or "subject" of any particular foreign state for the purpose of the alienage provision, 28 U.S.C. §1332(a)(2)? In *J.P. Morgan Chase Bank v. Traffic Stream (BVI) Infrastructure Limited*, 536 U.S. 88 (2002), the Supreme Court held that the alienage statute may look to foreign law to determine what functional characteristics a foreign entity possesses, but it relies upon U.S. law to decide whether those characteristics make the entity a "citizen" or "subject" of a foreign state. Traffic Stream, a corporation of the British Virgin Islands, sought to resist alienage jurisdiction on the asserted grounds that it was not a "citizen or subject" of a foreign state, as required by §1332(a)(2). The company argued, *inter alia*, that under U.K. law a British Virgin Islands corporation was not a "citizen" of the United Kingdom. The Court rejected this contention, finding that a corporation incorporated under the law of the British Virgin Islands was a "citizen or subject" of the United Kingdom for purposes of 28 U.S.C. §1332(a)(2). Regardless of how U.K. law would characterize Traffic Stream, the Court explained, the terms "citizen" and "subject" in the alienage statute are governed by U.S. law, not the law of a corporation's home State. Thus, whatever treatment a corporation would receive at home, §1332(a)(2) is only concerned with "whether the status [that the corporation] claims under [foreign law] would so operate on the law of the United States as to disqualify it from being a citizen or subject under" §1332.

Is the Court's disposition of this argument consistent with the way it has analyzed diversity questions in the past? Recall the decisions involving unincorporated associations, where the Court has favored a bright line test, adopting limited citizenship treatment only to those entities that qualified as "corporations" in their home state and rejecting a "functional" argument that an entity possessing the same characteristics as a corporation under its local laws should be treated as a corporation under the diversity statute. Why did the Court not adopt a similar bright line test in *Traffic Stream*, asking only whether a foreign entity is a "citizen" or "subject" under the laws of the country that created it?

e.   Foreign States Under §1332(a)(4)

One additional provision of the diversity statute, 28 U.S.C. §1332, is worth noting in light of a recent decision by the Court of Appeals for the Second Circuit, *see European Community v. RJR Nabisco, Inc.*, 764 F.3d 129 (2d Cir. 2014), *rev'd on other grounds*, 136 S.Ct. 2090 (2016). Section 1332(a)(4) provides for federal jurisdiction when the action is between a foreign state as plaintiff and citizens of a State or of different States. The definition of "foreign state" for purposes of this section refers to the definition found in the Foreign Sovereign Immunities Act (FSIA) (28 U.S.C. §1603). In an action brought by the European Community against RJR Nabisco, alleging a sophisticated money-laundering scheme and asserting federal statutory claims as well as state law claims for fraud, public nuisance, and unjust enrichment, the question was whether the European Community was a "foreign state" within the meaning of the diversity statute. For purposes of the FSIA, "foreign state" includes an agency or instrumentality of a foreign state, (28 U.S.C. §1603(a)), which in turn includes an "organ of a foreign state." (28 U.S.C. §1603(b)(2)). The district court, having dismissed the federal claims, also dismissed the state law claims for lack of diversity jurisdiction on the grounds that the European Community did not qualify as a foreign state. The Court of Appeals for the Second Circuit reversed, applying a five-factor test to find that the European Community was indeed an "organ of a foreign state."

4.   *Amount in Controversy*

Although Article III does not condition diversity jurisdiction on the presence of a particular amount in controversy, Congress included an amount-in-controversy requirement (then set at $500) in the Judiciary Act of 1789 (1 Stat. 73) and all sub-sequent versions of the diversity statute. Today, the requisite amount in controversy must be in excess of $75,000. By contrast, as a result of a 1980 amendment (Pub. L. No. 96-486, 94 Stat. 2369) to 28 U.S.C. §1331, there is no amount-in-controversy requirement for actions arising under federal law. A handful of federal statutes, however, still carry an amount requirement. *See, e.g.,* Consumer Product Safety Act of 1972, 15 U.S.C. §2072(a).

a. Calculating the Amount in Controversy

For the purpose of assessing the validity of the plaintiff's assertion of the req-uisite amount in controversy, the courts employ what is known as the "legal cer-tainty" test. "[U]nless the law gives a different rule, the sum claimed by the plaintiff controls if the claim is apparently made in good faith. It must appear to a legal certainty that the claim is really for less than the jurisdictional amount to jus-tify dismissal." *St. Paul Mercury Indem. Co. v. Red Cab Co.,* 303 U.S. 283, 288–289 (1938). The defendant probably must demonstrate the existence of a statutory or contractual limitation on recovery. The jurisdictional amount is to be measured at the commencement of the lawsuit and subsequent events — such as the actual recovery — will not destroy the court's jurisdiction. *See Rosado v. Wyman,* 397 U.S. 397, 405 n.6 (1970). Note, however, the limited cost-shifting provision in 28 U.S.C. §1332(b) in the event that plaintiff is awarded less than the jurisdictional amount.

The statutory language requires only that the "matter in controversy" exceed the requisite amount. The general rule is to look to the value to the plaintiff of the sought-for relief, rather than the cost to the defendant. However, where the object of the suit is injunctive relief, there is some authority for the proposition that "the amount in controversy is the pecuniary result to either party which the judgment would directly produce." *McCarty v. Amoco Pipeline Co.,* 595 F.2d 389, 393 (7th Cir. 1979). This approach is criticized in 14AA C. Wright et al., Federal Practice and Procedure §3703 (4th ed. 2011). *See also Smith v. Washington,* 593 F.2d 1097 (D.C. Cir. 1978). Is there any reason not to adopt a "defendant's viewpoint" or "either party's viewpoint" in calculating amount in controversy?

Determining whether a complaint exceeds $75,000 becomes even more com-plicated when a state-court complaint does not have an *ad damnum* clause, which states the amount of damages claimed by the plaintiff. In fact, some state rules of procedure now forbid *ad damnum* clauses in certain actions even though pleadings in federal court require it, *see* Fed. R. Civ. P. 8(a)(3). When a defendant seeks to remove a case from state to federal court, defendant typically has the responsibility to show that the case was subject to original federal jurisdiction and thus remov-able; the lack of an *ad damnum* clause creates the potentially awkward situation of a defendant trying to develop facts that show that the plaintiff is seeking greater than $75,000 in relief. Consider *Rising-Moore v. Red Roof Inns, Inc.,* 435 F.3d 813 (7th Cir. 2006). Because the plaintiff was forbidden from inserting an *ad damnum* clause in his complaint pursuant to Indiana law, the defendant removed the case on the basis of the plaintiff's demands of $180,000 to $200,000 in early settlement negotiations. Writing for the court, Judge Easterbrook found these statements "close in spirit to the *ad damnum* in a complaint" and found it sufficient to fulfill the defendant's bur-den of proof. Might *Rising-Moore* turn settlement talks into adversarial posturing?

Rising-Moore illustrates the difference in burden for a defendant who attempts to show diversity jurisdiction on removal compared with a plaintiff who attempts to establish diversity as an original matter. As noted, when a plaintiff files a diversity-based complaint, the court evaluates the alleged amount in controversy under a "good faith" standard and the case is dismissed only if the defendant can prove to a "legal certainty" that the amount in controversy is actually less than $75,000. On the other hand, when a defendant attempts to remove a case from state court on the grounds that there is both diversity and the requisite amount in controversy, the federal courts used a number of different standards for reviewing the defendant's alleged amount in controversy. For more on these different standards, *see* Michael W. Lewis, *Comedy or Tragedy: The Tale of Diversity Jurisdiction Removal and the One-Year Bar*, 62 S.M.U. L. Rev. 201 (2009). The 2011 Jurisdiction and Venue Clarification Act created a uniform standard for the federal courts to apply upon removal in a new provision, 28 U.S.C. §1446(c), which requires that a defendant prove the requisite amount in controversy by a "preponderance of the evidence" in order to remove the case. However, that provision does not affect the plausibility pleading requirement in the notice of removal. *See Dart Cherokee Basin Operating Co. v. Owens*, 574 U.S. 81 (2014), discussed at p. 391. Interestingly, however, 28 U.S.C. §1446(c) applies only to 28 U.S.C. §1332(a), the traditional $75,000 diversity jurisdiction section, and does not, at least expressly, apply to suits brought under the Class Action Fairness Act (CAFA), which is 28 U.S.C. §1332(d). Should this "preponderance of the evidence" standard also be read to apply to the removal of class action suits? Might some federal courts find suits brought under CAFA sufficiently analogous to apply §1446(c) to §1332(d) as well?

Asymmetry between plaintiffs and defendants also results from the fact that most of the information probative of the amount in controversy typically rests with the plaintiff. The one-year limitation on removal historically gave plaintiffs an incentive to withhold any information that might suggest the amount in controversy was required for removal until after one year, when the defendant no longer had the option to remove the case. Now the 2011 Jurisdiction and Venue Clarification Act has added a new "bad faith" exception to this one-year limitation, which applies whenever the court "finds that the plaintiff has acted in bad faith in order to prevent a defendant from removing the action." 28 U.S.C. §1446(c)(1). In theory, then, this exception eliminates plaintiffs' incentive to withhold or conceal information relevant to the amount in controversy. Do you think it does?

b. The Pertinence of Counterclaims

There is little case law on the question of whether the amount sought by way of counterclaim should count toward the requisite amount in controversy under the statute. In contrast with the general approach to determining the existence of subject matter jurisdiction by examining the *complaint only*, a few lower courts have counted the amount sought in compulsory counterclaims where the plaintiff filed in federal court originally. *See, e.g., Spectacor Management Group v. Brown*, 131 F.3d 120 (3d Cir. 1997) (amount sought in compulsory counterclaim counts in calculating amount in controversy); *Geoffrey E. Macpherson, Ltd. v. Brinecell, Inc.*, 98 F.3d 1241 (10th Cir. 1996) (same). However, this position has been criticized by commentators. *See* 14A C. Wright et al., Federal Practice and Procedure §3706

(4th ed. 2011). No court has counted the amount sought by way of permissive counterclaim. *See id.*

The Supreme Court has offered little guidance. Its single foray into the area has produced as much confusion as clarity. In *Horton v. Liberty Mutual Insurance Co.*, 367 U.S. 348 (1961), an injured employee filed a workers' compensation claim before the Texas Industrial Accident Board, seeking an award of $14,035. Under Texas law, either party could obtain *de novo* judicial review of a Board proceeding. Shortly after the Commission awarded Horton $1,050, Liberty Mutual filed a federal diversity action to set aside the award. One week later, Horton filed his own action in state court to set aside the award, seeking to increase the award to $14,035. (Note that workers' compensation actions are not removable, *see* 28 U.S.C. §1445(c).) Horton then counterclaimed in the federal proceeding for $14,035, and at the same time moved to dismiss the federal proceeding for lack of adequate amount in controversy. The Court held that the amount-in-controversy requirement (at that time in excess of $10,000) had been met. Should *Horton* be read as authority for counting compulsory counterclaims in assessing the amount in controversy? Or did it make particular sense to view the amount in controversy as the amount sought by Horton once the district court was asked to make a *de novo* review of Horton's claim? Wasn't the amount awarded by the Commission irrelevant at that point?

c.   Attorneys' Fees

In an action where attorneys' fees may be obtained in the event the plaintiff prevails on the merits, should projected attorney fees be included in computing the requisite amount in controversy? The courts are divided on the issue, but the majority rule appears to be that attorneys' fees may be included in the amount in controversy only where they are provided for by contract or state statute. *See* 14A C. Wright et al., Federal Practice and Procedure §3712 (4th ed. 2011).

d.   Aggregation of Claims

When a single plaintiff asserts more than one claim against a single defendant, the amount of the two claims may be aggregated in order to reach the jurisdictional amount. The plaintiff need not show any relationship between the two claims, and under Federal Rule 18, plaintiff may join any claim with any other. However, claims of separate plaintiffs seeking similar but distinct relief cannot be aggregated, even if the claims are transactionally related. Also, a single plaintiff cannot usually aggregate claims against multiple defendants.

The rules on aggregation are easily stated but more difficult to apply. Aggregation of claims by separate plaintiffs is permitted only "when several plaintiffs unite to enforce a single title or right, in which they have a common and undivided interest." *Troy Bank v. G.A. Whitehead & Co.*, 222 U.S. 39, 40–41 (1911). But that requires an understanding of when the underlying rights are "common and undivided." Similarly, with respect to aggregation of claims by a single plaintiff against multiple defendants, the "test of jurisdiction is the joint or several character of the liability to the plaintiff." *Walter v. Northeastern R.R. Co.*, 147 U.S. 370, 373 (1893). Some illustrations of these various rules may be helpful.

In the context of a tort action, multiple plaintiffs will rarely be allowed to aggregate their claims against a single defendant, even if every plaintiff alleges the identical wrongdoing by the defendant. This is because the relief they seek is not "common and undivided" and each plaintiff has an independent claim for relief. *See, e.g., Feikema v. Texaco*, 16 F.3d 1408 (4th Cir. 1994) (denying aggregation to multiple plaintiffs alleging property damage from an oil spill). A single plaintiff's claim against joint tortfeasors is more difficult to analyze. In many situations, joint tortfeasors' liability is said to be "joint and several"; any one of them is liable for the full amount of the damage. Thus, a single plaintiff who sues several defendants for negligence will seek the full amount (assume $100,000) of damage against all defendants. Because each defendant is liable for the full amount of the damage, the plaintiff does not really need aggregation; plaintiff has a claim for $100,000 against each defendant. In the rare case where the amount of damage is different with respect to the individual defendants, aggregation will depend on whether defendants' liability is in fact "joint and several." *Compare Bajowski v. Sysco Corp.*, 115 F. Supp. 2d 133, 139 (D. Mass. 2000) (where defendants' acts were sequential and not concurrent, defendants' liability under state law was not joint and plaintiff was not permitted to aggregate claims) *with Hayfield v. Home Depot U.S.A.*, 168 F. Supp. 2d 436, 447, 452 (E.D. Pa. 2001) (allowing aggregation after determining that negligence claim against one defendant and intentional tort claim against a second defendant created joint and several liability under applicable state law).

Aggregation with respect to multiple plaintiffs' claims for punitive damages may call for a different analysis. Initially, it was suggested that aggregation was possible because punitive damages are awarded for the collective good and not for the benefit of each individual plaintiff, thereby indicating the claims were "common and undivided." *See Allen v. R & H Oil & Gas Co.*, 63 F.3d 1326 (5th Cir. 1995). However, the Fifth Circuit later declined to follow *Allen* as binding precedent, *see H&D Tire & Automotive-Hardware, Inc. v. Pitney Bowes Inc.*, 227 F.3d 326, 330 (5th Cir. 2000), and all courts of appeals that have addressed the issue refuse to permit the aggregation of punitive damages in determining the amount in controversy. *See, e.g., Everett v. Verizon Wireless, Inc.*, 460 F.3d 818 (6th Cir. 2006) (refusing to aggregate punitive damages because, unlike common and undivided interests, a plaintiff's receipt of punitive damages is not contingent on the resolution of previous awards).

For a more detailed discussion of the rules of aggregation, *see* Steven S. Gensler, *Diversity Class Actions, Common Relief, and the Rule of Individual Valuation*, 82 Or. L. Rev. 295 (2003); Jeffrey L. Rensberger, *The Amount in Controversy: Understanding the Rules of Aggregation*, 26 Ariz. St. L.J. 925 (1994).

e.   Class Actions

As we saw earlier in the discussion of whose citizenship is looked to in determining diversity, each named class plaintiff must be of diverse citizenship from each defendant, and the citizenship of unnamed class members is not taken into account in evaluating the diversity requirement. *See Supreme Tribe of Ben-Hur v. Cauble*, 255 U.S. 356 (1921). However, with respect to the amount-in-controversy requirement, the Supreme Court held in *Snyder v. Harris*, 394 U.S. 332 (1969), that each individual plaintiff—including each unnamed absent class member—must have a claim that satisfies the requisite jurisdictional amount. Thus, in *Snyder*, the jurisdictional amount-in-controversy requirement was not satisfied where the named class representative could only show damages of $8,740, even though the potential 4,000 shareholders in the class sought a recovery of approximately $1,200,000. Of course, all *Snyder* did was to apply the traditional rule that multiple plaintiffs cannot aggregate claims unless there is a "common and undivided interest" with respect to plaintiffs' claims. The Supreme Court in *Snyder* rejected the argument that all class action plaintiffs could be treated as having such "joint" or "common" interests because the claims could be brought as a single class action under then recently amended Rule 23. Instead, the Court held that only when the class action consisted of claims by plaintiffs with "common and undivided interests" could the claims of class action plaintiffs be aggregated.

An interesting question then arose as to whether a class action was properly within the federal court's jurisdiction if the named class representative plaintiff asserted a claim that met the requisite jurisdictional amount but the claims of absent class members did not. In *Zahn v. International Paper Co.*, 414 U.S. 291 (1973), the Supreme Court held that, with respect to a Rule 23(b)(3) class, federal jurisdiction existed only with respect to those particular class members whose claims satisfied the amount-in-controversy requirement and did not extend to class members' claims that lacked the requisite amount in controversy. For a time then, many state law diversity-based class actions were not able to be brought in federal court for lack of the requisite jurisdictional amount. Two recent developments, which are discussed in more depth later in this chapter, have changed that landscape. First, in 2005, Congress enacted the Class Action Fairness Act (CAFA), which authorized federal court jurisdiction over class actions when the aggregate amount in controversy exceeds $5 million. (CAFA is discussed at pp. 311–312 in this chapter and again at pp. 1023–1038 in Chapter 8.) Second, the Supreme Court in 2005 rendered a decision, *Exxon Mobil Corp. v. Allapattah Services, Inc.*, 545 U.S. 546 (2005), interpreting 28 U.S.C. §1367—a federal statute passed subsequent to the *Zahn* decision—to permit "supplemental jurisdiction" over claims by absent class plaintiffs for less than the statutory amount in controversy so long as the named plaintiff's claim meets the jurisdictional amount requirement. (You will find a more extensive discussion of supplemental jurisdiction as well as the *Allapattah* decision later in this chapter.)

5. *Diversity Jurisdiction and Complex Litigation*

As noted earlier in this chapter, the constitutional grant of diversity of citizenship jurisdiction offers a basis for Congress to provide for federal jurisdiction over multistate controversies that may well deserve a national forum and often may not even be possible to be heard in a single state court. Congress has exercised that authority in two statutes, the Multiparty, Multiforum Trial Jurisdiction Act (28 U.S.C. §1369) and the Class Action Fairness Act (28 U.S.C. §1332(d)).

a. The Multiparty, Multiforum Trial Jurisdiction Act

In November 2002, Congress enacted the Multiparty, Multiforum Trial Jurisdiction Act, 28 U.S.C. §1369. The objectives of the Act were to achieve judicial efficiency and to avoid multiple state and federal lawsuits arising from the same disaster. Subsection (a) of §1369 provides for original jurisdiction in the federal courts over any civil action that arises from an accident involving at least 75 deaths when there is minimal diversity and certain other conditions are met. Those are: (1) a defendant resides in a State and a substantial part of the accident occurred in a different State, regardless of whether that defendant is also a resident of the State where a substantial part of the accident took place; or (2) any two defendants reside in different States, regardless of whether such defendants are also residents of the same State; or (3) substantial parts of the accident took place in different States.

Note the elaborate requirements of this jurisdictional statute. In addition, subsection (b) of §1369 introduces the concept of "abstention"—meaning that although the court technically has jurisdiction, the district is "required" not to exercise such jurisdiction under certain circumstances. Pursuant to §1369(b) a district court is instructed to "abstain" from hearing the action if the substantial majority of plaintiffs are citizens of the state in which the primary defendants are citizens and the claims will be governed primarily by the laws of that State.

Why did Congress make these latter provisions a matter of "abstention" rather than "jurisdiction"? Are concepts such as "substantial majority" and "primary defendants" appropriate in jurisdictional statutes at all? The first decision interpreting the Multiparty, Multiforum Act, *Passa v. Derderian*, 308 F. Supp. 2d 43 (D.R.I. 2004), is discussed in greater detail in Chapter 8 at p. 1049. In *Passa*, various state and federal lawsuits were brought after a fire at a Rhode Island nightclub that resulted in the death of 100 persons and injuries to more than 200 others. Interpreting §1369(b), the court first observed that subsection (b) was a mandatory abstention clause and not a subject matter jurisdictional requirement—an important distinction because the characterization could have an impact on such questions as when the issue can be raised in the proceeding. The court also held that the federal court was not required to abstain. The "substantial majority of all plaintiffs" referred to all potential plaintiffs and not just those who had already filed a lawsuit, and "primary defendants" was found to refer to all defendants facing direct liability with no obligation on a court to make a pretrial determination of liability or culpability.

Section 1369 was also invoked in litigation brought by victims of Hurricane Katrina against property insurance companies. One issue is whether Hurricane Katrina falls within the statutory definition of "accident" within the meaning of §1369 and the concomitant removal provision, §1441(e). The statute defines "accident" as a "sudden accident, or a natural event culminating in an accident, that results in death incurred at a discrete location by at least 75 natural persons." 28 U.S.C. §1369(c)(4). In *Flint v. Louisiana Farm Bureau Mut. Ins. Co.*, 2006 WL 2375593 (E.D. La. 2006), the district court refused to allow piggy-back removal jurisdiction pursuant to §1441(e) because it found that the main action was not an "accident" and therefore could not have been brought under §1369. In the main action, plaintiffs alleged property damage suffered at their individual residences as the result of Hurricane Katrina. The court found that Hurricane Katrina was the "natural event" that culminated in "many accidents" but not in a single accident resulting in the death of at least 75 natural persons at a discrete location. Because the main action could not have been brought under §1369, there was no vehicle by which the *Flint* action could be removed to federal court. The court distinguished an earlier case, *Wallace v. Louisiana Citizens Prop. Ins. Corp.*, 444 F.3d 697 (5th Cir. 2006), where the Fifth Circuit, without expressly ruling on the definition of "accident," accepted jurisdiction pursuant to §1369 in an action in which plaintiffs sought damages against insurance companies for wrongful death and property damage resulting from a levee break as the result of Hurricane Katrina. The court in *Flint* explained that the "accident" in *Wallace* was the levee break, satisfying the requirement of an accident causing the death of at least 75 natural persons at a discrete location.

b. The Class Action Fairness Act

A parallel type of jurisdiction/abstention structure was adopted in the Class Action Fairness Act of 2005. Section 1332 was amended by subsections (d)(1) and (2) to authorize federal district courts to exercise jurisdiction over class actions with an aggregate amount in controversy of at least $5 million on the basis of minimal diversity—that is, only one plaintiff and one defendant must be citizens of different States. When the class action is fundamentally connected to a single State as identified by criteria in the statute, *see* §§1332(d)(3) and (d)(4), the district court is either authorized ((d)(3)) or required ((d)(4)) to "decline jurisdiction." With respect to the mandatory declination of jurisdiction, the district court is required to decline jurisdiction when over two-thirds of the proposed plaintiff class members are citizens of the State where the action is originally filed and either (1) the "primary defendants" are also citizens of the original forum state, or (2) at least one defendant from whom "significant relief" is sought and who has allegedly engaged in conduct that forms a "significant basis" for the class claim is a citizen of the original forum state. *See* §1332(d)(4). For discretionary declinations of jurisdiction somewhat different criteria are used (between one-third and two-thirds of all proposed plaintiff class members are citizens of the State where the action is originally filed and the primary defendants are citizens of that forum state); in addition, the court is instructed to consider a series of factors to determine whether the proposed class action is national or local in scope. *See* §1332(d)(3).

In 2013, the Supreme Court issued a decision addressing the amount in controversy requirement for cases removed under the Class Action Fairness Act. In *Standard Fire Ins. v. Knowles*, 133 S.Ct. 1345 (2013), the named plaintiff stipulated in the complaint that at no time during the case would the damages sought be in excess of $5,000,000 in the aggregate, thereby attempting to avoid removal to federal court. The Supreme Court held that because the class had not yet been certified, the plaintiff cannot legally bind members of the proposed class, and the stipulation had to be ignored. For a more extensive discussion of the interpretation of the jurisdictional provision of the Class Action Fairness Act, *see* the material in Chapter 8 at pp. 1023–1038.

Has Congress made determinations of jurisdiction under the Multiparty, Multiforum Trial Jurisdiction Act and the Class Action Fairness Act an unnecessarily complicated inquiry? For a critical look at the Class Action Fairness Act *see generally* Symposium, *Fairness to Whom? Perspectives on the Class Action Fairness Act of 2005*, 156 U. Pa. L. Rev. 1439 *et seq.* (2008), and in particular, Stephen B. Burbank, *The Class Action Fairness Act of 2005 in Historical Context: A Preliminary View*, 156 U. Pa.

L. Rev. 1439 (2008) (placing CAFA's jurisdictional provisions within the contexts of the history of federal diversity-of-citizenship litigation in general, and the history of diversity class actions in federal court); Richard L. Marcus, *Assessing CAFA's Stated Jurisdictional Policy*, 156 U. Pa. L. Rev. 1765 (2008) (analyzing what jurisdictional policies CAFA furthers and what implications might follow from the change in jurisdiction after CAFA). *See also* Tanya Pierce, *Dueling Grants: Reimagining CAFA's Jurisdictional Provisions*, 33 Ga. St. U. L. Rev. 723, 723–724 (2017) (assessing problems in the application of CAFA's jurisdictional provisions).

D.   *FEDERAL QUESTION JURISDICTION*

The second major type of federal judicial power involves cases "arising under this Constitution, the laws of these United States, and Treaties made, or which shall be made, under their Authority." The general federal question jurisdictional grant can be found in 28 U.S.C. §1331, although many federal statutes contain their own jurisdictional provisions, which should be consulted as well.

NOTE ON CONCURRENT JURISDICTION OF STATE COURTS

Although there is a tendency to link the existence of federal courts to the need to resolve disputes governed by federal law, that was not the assumption of the Constitution's framers. Article III authorizes Congress to create lower federal courts, but, with the exception of the Supreme Court, does not mandate the establishment of any federal court. Although the 1789 Judiciary Act did establish a system of "inferior" national tribunals, these federal courts had authority over only a limited set of federal questions. It was not until 1875 (18 Stat. 470) that federal courts were given original jurisdiction over suits "arising under" federal law. Hence, for the first century of this nation's existence, the adjudication of disputes governed by federal law was largely committed to the state system—the judges of which were subject to the command of the Constitution's Supremacy Clause—with provision for appellate review by the Supreme Court to ensure the supremacy and uniformity of federal law.

With the enormous growth in federal law following the Civil War—a result both of the needs of a growing national economy and of expanded conceptions of the power of the federal government vis-à-vis the states—the arrangements set as of 1789 were destined to change. A system of federal law adjudication lodged primarily in the state courts placed too great a supervisory responsibility on the Justices of the Supreme Court. Congress's decision in 1875 to vest the federal courts with original general federal question jurisdiction reduced the Court's task to somewhat more manageable proportions by ensuring that federal law would develop in tribunals accustomed to such questions and whose members would be particularly sensitive to supervisory signals from the Court. *See* Paul J. Mishkin, *The Federal "Question" in the District Courts*, 53 Colum. L. Rev. 157, 158 (1953) ("[T]he exercise of federal question jurisdiction by lower federal tribunals presumably permits the Supreme Court to confine itself (insofar as any such distinction can be drawn) to the solving of new problems rather than the policing of old solutions, without the loss that might otherwise be entailed in the effectuation of national rights.").

Today, of course, federal courts play the dominant role in the adjudication of disputes governed by federal law. It is a mistake, however, to read state courts out of the picture. The continued involvement of state courts stems from two principal sources. First, in a great many instances, federal law appears in a case as a defense to a claim or other proceeding based on state law. State criminal trials are a prominent example, but this is also true of many civil claims. In a clash between state law and valid federal requirements, the Supremacy Clause requires that the latter shall prevail. The rule allowing—indeed, requiring—state courts to adjudicate federal defenses avoids the need for a second litigation to test the judgment obtained in the first against the requirements of federal law. Moreover, it promotes adherence to the supremacy of federal law.

Second, even where a plaintiff is asserting a right to recover directly under a federal statute, the assumption of the system is that absent a clear intention on Congress's part to commit the statute to the exclusive jurisdiction of the federal courts, the state courts have concurrent jurisdiction over claims based on federal law. For example, the Supreme Court in 1990 unanimously held that state courts have concurrent jurisdiction over claims arising under Title VII of the Civil Rights Act of 1964, 42 U.S.C. §2000e, *see Yellow Freight Sys., Inc. v. Donnelly*, 494 U.S. 820 (1990), and under the civil recovery provisions of the Racketeer Influenced and Corrupt Organizations Act, 18 U.S.C. §§1961–1968, *see Tafflin v. Levitt*, 493 U.S. 455 (1990). The Supreme Court also decided that a state cannot refuse to hear an entire category of federal claims in its state courts by limiting the scope of its concurrent jurisdiction. *Haywood v. Drown*, 556 U.S. 729 (2009). Examples of exclusive federal jurisdiction are rare. *See, e.g.,* 28 U.S.C. §§1333 (admiralty and maritime), 1334 (bankruptcy), 1338 (patent and copyright), and 1346(b) (tort claims against the United States).

Note that Congress may stipulate a federal rule of decision for disputes that will be adjudicated entirely in the state system. *See Thompson v. Thompson*, 484 U.S. 174 (1988) (enforcement and recognition of child custody decrees is governed by the Parental Kidnapping Prevention Act of 1980, 28 U.S.C. §1738A). Nevertheless, courts are reluctant to interpret federal statutes as limiting jurisdiction only to state courts in the absence of explicit language foreclosing federal jurisdiction. In *Mims v. Arrow Financial Services, LLC*, 565 U.S. 368 (2012), the Supreme Court made clear that a federal district court will presumptively retain §1331 jurisdiction over any federal cause of action unless the federal statute, "expressly or by fair implication, excludes" such jurisdiction. *Mims* involved the Telephone Consumer Protection Act (TCPA), 47 U.S.C. §227, which banned certain invasive telemarketing practices and permitted both States and private individuals to bring suits against companies in violation of any regulations promulgated by the Federal Communications Commission (FCC) under the Act. Section 227(g)(1), the provision by which States may bring suits under the Act, reserved jurisdiction exclusively for "the district courts of the United States." However, §227(b), the provision authorizing individuals to bring private suits for damages, contained no such limitation and stated that these individual suits may be brought "in an appropriate court of that State." Mims filed a §227(b) damages action in Federal District Court against Arrow Financial Services for the use of invasive telemarketing practices and Arrow moved to dismiss the complaint for lack of subject matter jurisdiction. The Eleventh Circuit held that by using the language "in an appropriate court of that State" in §227(b), Congress effectively "vest[ed] jurisdiction over [private actions under] the TCPA exclusively in state courts." Justice Ginsburg, writing a unanimous opinion for the Court, reversed the Eleventh Circuit's determination, stating that like the strong "presumption of concurrent state-court jurisdiction," a similar presumption exists favoring concurrent federal-court jurisdiction on claims that otherwise meet the requirements of §1331 federal-question jurisdiction. In other words, whenever a federal statute creates the cause of action, satisfying the so-called Holmes test, divestment of federal court jurisdiction should be found "no more readily than divestment of state court jurisdiction," with concurrent jurisdiction presumed to exist in the absence of explicit language to the contrary.

There are several advantages to a system that makes federal law the shared province of state and federal courts. First, such an arrangement permits some sharing of workload and thus helps limit the growth of the federal judiciary (thought desirable from the standpoint of preserving the prestige of the federal bench). Second, local state courts may be a more convenient locus for certain litigants than one or two federal courts in a state. Most importantly, concurrent jurisdiction promotes commitment to national law and fosters a unitary legal culture. The states cannot close their courthouse doors to federal claims. *See Testa v. Katt*, 330 U.S. 386 (1947). Perforce, state judges must view themselves as part of the federal law system, and lawyers must be proficient in both federal and state practice.

Generalizations about the comparative qualities of the state and federal courts are somewhat hazardous. There is little doubt that state courts tend to have larger caseloads and employ a more bureaucratized procedure than federal courts. Moreover, because of the life tenure of federal judges and hence their relative immunity from direct political influences, federal courts are often thought to be the preferred forum for vindication of controversial federal law claims. *See* Burt Neuborne, *The Myth of Parity*, 90 Harv. L. Rev. 1105 (1977). Yet, courts in a number of states have developed a strong tradition of judicial independence, have streamlined their procedures, and have provided a hospitable reception for federal law, however controversial.

Scholars continue to debate whether federal fora are preferable for adjudicating claims of federal law. *See, e.g*, Thomas B. Bennett, *The Paradox of Exclusive State-Court Jurisdiction over Federal Claims*, 105 Minn. L. Rev. 1211 (2021); Michael E. Solimine, *The Future of Parity*, 46 Wm. & Mary L. Rev. 1457 (2005) (examining varying perspectives on parity and concluding that an overarching conclusion on the subject is inconceivable). *See also* John F. Preis, *Reassessing the Purposes of Federal Question Jurisdiction*, 42 Wake Forest L. Rev. 247 (2007) (noting that federal courts have more experience in adjudicating certain constitutional and statutory provisions than state courts, and the federal government has a sovereignty interest in ensuring that federal courts control the meaning of federal law).

1.   *"Arising Under" Federal Law*

a.   The Role of a Federal Defense

Louisville & Nashville Railroad Co. v. Mottley

211 U.S. 149 (1908)

The appellees (husband and wife), being residents and citizens of Kentucky, brought this suit in equity in the Circuit Court of the United States for the Western District of Kentucky against the appellant, a railroad company and a citizen of the same state. The object of the suit was to compel the specific performance of the following contract:

> Louisville, Ky., Oct. 2d, 1871
>
> The Louisville & Nashville Railroad Company in consideration that E. L. Mottley and wife, Annie E. Mottley, have this day released Company from all damages or claims for damages for injuries received by them on the 7th of September, 1871, in consequence of a collision of trains on the railroad of said Company at Randolph's Station, Jefferson County, Ky., hereby agrees to issue free passes on said Railroad and branches now existing or to exist, to said E. L. & Annie E. Mottley for the remainder of the present year, and thereafter, to renew said passes annually during the lives of said Mottley and wife or either of them.

The bill alleged that in September 1871, plaintiffs, while passengers upon the defendant railroad, were injured by the defendant's negligence, and released their respective claims for damages in consideration of the agreement for transportation during their lives, expressed in the contract. It is alleged that the contract was performed by the defendant up to January 1, 1907, when the defendant declined to renew the passes. The bill then alleges that the refusal to comply with the contract was based solely upon that part of the act of Congress of June 29, 1906, 34 Stat. 584, which forbids the giving of free passes or free transportation. The bill further alleges: First, that the act of Congress referred to does not prohibit the giving of passes under the circumstances of this case; and, second, that if the law is to be construed as prohibiting such passes, it is in conflict with the Fifth Amendment of the Constitution, because it deprives the plaintiffs of their property without due process of law. The defendant demurred to the bill. The judge of the Circuit Court overruled the demurrer, entered a decree for the relief prayed for, and the defendant appealed directly to this court.

MR. JUSTICE MOODY, after making the foregoing statement, delivered the opinion of the court:

Two questions of law were raised by the demurrer to the bill, were brought here by appeal, and have been argued before us. They are, first, whether that part of the act of Congress of June 29, 1906 (34 Stat. 584), which forbids the giving of free passes or the collection of any different compensation for transportation of passengers than that specified in the tariff filed, makes it unlawful to perform a contract for transportation of persons, who in good faith, before the passage of the act, had accepted such contract in satisfaction of a valid cause of action against the railroad; and, second, whether the statute, if it should be construed to render such a contract unlawful, is in violation of the Fifth Amendment of the Constitution of the United States. We do not deem it necessary, however, to consider either of these questions, because, in our opinion, the court below was without jurisdiction of the cause. Neither party has questioned that jurisdiction, but it is the duty of this Court to see to it that the jurisdiction of the Circuit Court, which is defined and limited by statute, is not exceeded. This duty we have frequently performed of our own motion. . . .

There was no diversity of citizenship and it is not and cannot be suggested that there was any ground of jurisdiction, except that the case was a "suit . . . arising under the Constitution and laws of the United States." Act of August 13, 1888, c. 866, 25 Stat. 433, 434. It is the settled interpretation of these words, as used in this statute, conferring jurisdiction, that a suit arises under the Constitution and laws of the United States only when the plaintiff's statement of his own cause of action shows that it is based upon those laws or that Constitution. It is not enough that the plaintiff alleges some anticipated defense to his cause of action and asserts that the defense is invalidated by some provision of the Constitution of the United States. Although such allegations show that very likely, in the course of the litigation, a question under the Constitution would arise, they do not show that the suit, that is, the plaintiff's original cause of action, arises under the Constitution. . . .

NOTES AND QUESTIONS

1. *A Comparison of §1331 and Article III.* Insofar as Article III is concerned, Chief Justice Marshall wrote in *Osborn v. Bank of the United States,* 22 U.S. (9 Wheat.) 738, 823 (1824), that a case arises under federal law whenever a federal question "forms an ingredient of the original cause." In light of *Osborn,* is *Mottley* a construction of the reach of the Article III grant or of the scope of the federal question statute? Note that after the Supreme Court decision in *Mottley,* the plaintiffs sued in state court — and the litigation turned exclusively on federal issues. The case was ultimately reviewed by the Supreme Court of the United States, *see* 219 U.S. 467 (1911), in the exercise of its appellate jurisdiction. *See* 28 U.S.C. §1257. Of course, that appellate jurisdiction must also fall within the parameters of Article III. Is there any justification for reading the "arising under" language of the statute conferring original jurisdiction on the district courts differently from the virtually identical "arising under" language of the Constitution? For reading the scope of the district court's original jurisdiction differently from the Supreme Court's appellate jurisdiction?

2. *Why a Restrictive Rule for Federal Question Jurisdiction?* One reason for the *Mottley* ruling may have been a fear that extension of the broad *Osborn* formulation to the 1875 grant of general federal question jurisdiction might have overwhelmed federal trial courts and brought local law into the federal courts. The development of the country outside of the original thirteen colonies occurred largely under the auspices of federal land grants, with the result that a great many possessory interests were traceable to law developed by the federal courts. Under *Mottley,* it was not sufficient that federal law formed a background "ingredient" in a claim for ejectment

or trespass that otherwise would be governed by local law. *See Oneida Indian Nation v. County of Oneida*, 414 U.S. 661, 667 (1974) (distinguishing Indian tribe's claim of federally protected possessory right to tribal lands from "the claim of a right to possession derived from a federal grant of title whose scope will be governed by state law").

3. *"Well-Pleaded Complaint" Test. Mottley* is often cited as adopting the "well-pleaded complaint" test: A case "arises under" federal law only if it appears on the face of a "well-pleaded complaint," even if federal law is likely to be determinative of the controversy. On one level, the test conformed to the pleading conventions of the time: "In a complaint for specific performance of a contract, it was necessary only to allege the contract and its breach. The allegations concerning the statute, its construction, and its claimed unconstitutionality were appropriately matters to be raised in the defendant's answer and the plaintiff's reply." William Cohen, *The Broken Compass: The Requirement that a Case Arise "Directly" Under Federal Law*, 115 U. Pa. L. Rev. 890, 893–894 (1967). By shrinking the complaint to its "well-pleaded" essentials, jurisdiction would not turn on a plaintiff's anticipation of what a defendant might plead or speculation as to the subsequent course of the suit. This explanation may not fit well, however, with the proceeding in *Mottley* itself, which arose as a bill in equity. *See* Alfred Hill, *Constitutional Remedies*, 69 Colum. L. Rev. 1109, 1129 (1969) ("The bill, as the initiatory pleading was called, had to allege the special circumstances, including the inadequacy of a remedy at law, that would justify the extraordinary intervention of equity. . . . To give adequate reasons for the intervention of equity, the petitioner had to tell the entire story.").

4. *The Role of Defenses.* Quite aside from pleading conventions, *Mottley* is consistent with a procedure for testing jurisdiction on the face of the complaint without requiring the defendant to answer. It would be cumbersome to suspend resolution of the jurisdictional inquiry until all responsive pleadings were filed, and perhaps defendants might act strategically in withholding potential federal defenses in order to defeat jurisdiction. But why not allow a defendant to remove a case from state court to federal court upon the assertion of a federal defense in the answer? This was apparently the practice prior to the 1887 amendments to the 1875 Judiciary Act and was one of the proposals of the ALI 1969 Study, American Law Institute, Study of the Division of Jurisdiction Between State and Federal Courts §1312 (1969). *See* Herbert Wechsler, *Federal Jurisdiction and the Revision of the Judicial Code*, 13 Law & Contemp. Probs. 216, 233–234 (1948). However, as we shall see, the removal statute is generally limited to cases that could have been brought initially in federal court and does not permit removal based on a federal defense.

b. The Scope of "Arising Under"

Only part of the problem is solved by deciding that the federal claim must "arise on the face of the complaint." A second issue turns on what aspects of a particular claim can be said to "arise under" federal law. Should it be sufficient if an element of the claim is federal or should it be necessary to show that important federal interests are at stake in order for a claim to "arise under" federal law? Alternatively, should the source of the right be the critical factor in determining "arising under" jurisdiction?

The courts, including the Supreme Court, have been somewhat inconsistent in articulating a test. In an early case, Justice Holmes, in *American Well Works Co. v. Layne & Bowler Co.*, 241 U.S. 257, 260 (1916), wrote that "[a] suit arises under the law that creates the cause of action." What advantages are there in defining federal jurisdiction in this manner? Aren't there likely to be important issues of federal law that will often be decided by state courts if federal jurisdiction is limited in this way? Is it sufficient protection that the Supreme Court has the power to review state judgments that raise issues of federal law? *See* Theodore Eisenberg, *Congressional Authority to Restrict Lower Federal Court Jurisdiction*, 83 Yale L.J. 498 (1974) (discussing implications of Supreme Court's limited decisional capacity).

In a later case, *Gully v. First National Bank*, 299 U.S. 109 (1936), the Court, in an opinion by Justice Cardozo, set forth the "arising under" test as requiring that the issue of federal law be an "element, and an essential one of the plaintiff's cause of action," and emphasizing that a suit does not arise under federal law "unless it really and substantially involves a dispute or controversy respecting the validity, construction, or effect of such a law, upon the determination of which the result depends." How helpful is that description? *Gully* involved a lawsuit by the state Collector of Taxes against a national bank to collect various local taxes. The only federal element of plaintiff's claim was a federal statute that authorized states to tax national banks, which otherwise would have been immune from state tax laws. Did the Court even need to inquire about the importance or substantiality of the federal issue in *Gully* at all? Doesn't the question of whether the state is authorized to tax the national bank — if relevant — come up only by way of defense? In that sense, isn't *Gully* just like *Mottley*?

Other cases will involve issues of federal law that do form part of the plaintiff's complaint. Assume, for example, that the capacity of a federal entity to sue or be sued is granted by a federal statute. If the federal entity is required by the pleading convention to allege capacity as part of its claim and sues under state law for breach of contract, should the claim be said to "arise under" federal law? If not, is your answer influenced by the fact that the capacity issue seems a relatively unimportant aspect of the claim? Would your answer differ if the federal "element" had greater importance?

Allegations of capacity based on federal law will generally not confer "arising under" jurisdiction for purposes of 28 U.S.C. §1331. However, federal statutes can provide for an entity to "sue or be sued"; the question is whether such clauses should be construed as an *express* grant of federal jurisdiction. The Supreme Court distinguishes between clauses providing for an entity to "sue or be sued in courts of law and equity, State or Federal, within the jurisdiction of the United States," *American National Red Cross v. S.G.*, 505 U.S. 247 (1992) (holding that such a clause provides an express grant of federal jurisdiction), and clauses authorizing an entity to "sue and to be sued . . . in any court of competent jurisdiction, State or Federal," *Crystal Monique Lightfoot v. Cendant Mortgage Corp.*, 137 S.Ct. 553 (2017) (holding that the phrase "court of competent jurisdiction" means an existing source of subject-matter jurisdiction requiring an independent basis of jurisdiction apart from the clause). If capacity alone cannot ground jurisdiction under the "arising under" language of 28 U.S.C. §1331, how does the express grant of federal jurisdiction found in *American National Red Cross* satisfy the "arising under" requirement of Article III?

The next three cases offer examples of federal law as an ingredient of the plaintiff's claim and all reached the Supreme Court of the United States. Is the Court consistent in the requirements it sets for "arising under" jurisdiction?

Smith v. Kansas City Title & Trust Co.

255 U.S. 180 (1920)

MR. JUSTICE DAY delivered the opinion of the Court.

A bill was filed in the United States District Court for the Western Division of the Western District of Missouri by a shareholder in the Kansas City Title & Trust Company to enjoin the Company, its officers, agents and employees from investing the funds of the Company in farm loan bonds issued by Federal Land Banks or Joint Stock Land Banks under authority of the Federal Farm Loan Act of July 17, 1916, c. 245, 39 Stat. 360, as amended January 18, 1918, c. 9, 40 Stat. 431.

The relief was sought on the ground that these acts were beyond the constitutional power of Congress. The bill avers that the Board of Directors of the Company is about to invest its funds in the bonds to the amount of $10,000 in each of the classes described, and will do so unless enjoined by the court in this action. . . .

Section 27 of the act provides that Farm Loan Bonds issued under the provisions of the act by Federal Land Banks or Joint Stock Land Banks shall be a lawful investment for all fiduciary and trust funds, and may be accepted as security for all public deposits. The bill avers that the defendant Trust Company is authorized to buy, invest in and sell government, state and municipal and other bonds, but it cannot buy, invest in or sell any such bonds, papers, stocks or securities which are not authorized to be issued by a valid law or which are not investment securities, but that nevertheless it is about to invest in Farm Loan Bonds; that the Trust Company has been induced to direct its officers to make the investment by reason of its reliance upon the provisions of the Farm Loan Acts, especially §§21, 26 and 27, by which the Farm Loan Bonds are declared to be instrumentalities of the Government of the United States, and as such, with the income derived therefrom, are declared to be exempt from federal, state, municipal and local taxation, and are further declared to be lawful investments for all fiduciary and trust funds. The bill further avers that the acts by which it is attempted to authorize the bonds are wholly illegal, void and unconstitutional and of no effect because unauthorized by the Constitution of the United States.

The bill prays that the acts of Congress authorizing the creation of the banks, especially §§21, 26 and 27 thereof, shall be adjudged and decreed to be unconstitutional, void and of no effect, and that the issuance of the Farm Loan Bonds, and the taxation exemption feature thereof, shall be adjudged and decreed to be invalid.

The First Joint Stock Land Bank of Chicago and the Federal Land Bank of Wichita, Kansas, were allowed to intervene and became parties defendant to the suit. The Kansas City Title & Trust Company filed a motion to dismiss in the nature of a general demurrer, and upon hearing the District Court entered a decree dismissing the bill. From this decree appeal was taken to this court.

No objection is made to the federal jurisdiction, either original or appellate, by the parties to this suit, but that question will be first examined. The Company is authorized to invest its funds in legal securities only. The attack upon the proposed investment in the bonds described is because of the alleged unconstitutionality of the acts of Congress undertaking to organize the banks and authorize the issue of the bonds. No other reason is set forth in the bill as a ground of objection to the proposed investment by the Board of Directors acting in the Company's behalf. As diversity of citizenship is lacking, the jurisdiction of the District Court depends upon whether the cause of action set forth arises under the Constitution or laws of the United States. Judicial Code, §24.

The general rule is that, where it appears from the bill or statement of the plaintiff that the right to relief depends upon the construction or application of the Constitution or laws of the United States, and that such federal claim is not merely colorable, and rests upon a reasonable foundation, the District Court has jurisdiction under this provision.

At an early date, considering the grant of constitutional power to confer juris-diction upon the federal courts, Chief Justice Marshall said: "A case in law or equity consists of the right of the one party, as well as of the other, and may truly be said to arise under the Constitution or a law of the United States, whenever its correct decision depends on the construction of either," *Cohens v. Virginia*, 6 Wheat. 264, 379; and again, when "the title or right set up by the party, may be defeated by one construction of the Constitution or law of the United States, and sustained by the opposite construction." *Osborn v. Bank of the United States*, 9 Wheat. 738, 822. . . .

The jurisdiction of this court is to be determined upon the principles laid down in the cases referred to. In the instant case the averments of the bill show that the directors were proceeding to make the investments in view of the act authoriz-ing the bonds about to be purchased, maintaining that the act authorizing them was constitutional and the bonds valid and desirable investments. The objecting shareholder avers in the bill that the securities were issued under an unconstitu-tional law, and hence of no validity. It is, therefore, apparent that the controversy concerns the constitutional validity of an act of Congress which is directly drawn in question. The decision depends upon the determination of this issue. . . .

MR. JUSTICE BRANDEIS took no part in the consideration or decision of this case.

MR. JUSTICE HOLMES, dissenting.

No doubt it is desirable that the question raised in this case should be set at rest, but that can be done by the Courts of the United States only within the limits of the jurisdiction conferred upon them by the Constitution and the laws of the United States. As this suit was brought by a citizen of Missouri against a Missouri corporation the single ground upon which the jurisdiction of the District Court can be maintained is that the suit "arises under the Constitution or laws of the United States" within the meaning of §24 of the Judicial Code. I am of opinion that this case does not arise in that way and therefore that the bill should have been dismissed.

It is evident that the cause of action arises not under any law of the United States but wholly under Missouri law. The defendant is a Missouri corporation and the right claimed is that of a stockholder to prevent the directors from doing an act, that is, making an investment, alleged to be contrary to their duty. But the scope of their duty depends upon the charter of their corporation and other laws of Missouri. If those laws had authorized the investment in terms the plaintiff would have had no case, and this seems to me to make manifest what I am unable to deem even debatable, that, as I have said, the cause of action arises wholly under Missouri law. If the Missouri law authorizes or forbids the investment according to the determination of this Court upon a point under the Constitution or acts of Congress, still that point is material only because the Missouri law saw fit to make it so. The whole foundation of the duty is Missouri law, which at its sole will incorporate the other law as it might incorporate a document. The other law or document depends for its relevance and effect not on its own force but upon the law that took it up, so I repeat once more the cause of action arises wholly from the law of the State.

But it seems to me that a suit cannot be said to arise under any other law than that which creates the cause of action. It may be enough that the law relied upon creates a part of the cause of action although not the whole, as held in *Osborn v. Bank of the United States*, 9 Wheat. 738, 819–823, which perhaps is all that is meant by the less guarded expressions in *Cohens v. Virginia*, 6 Wheat. 264, 379. I am content to assume this to be so, although the *Osborn Case* has been criticized and regretted. But the law must create at least a part of the cause of action by its own force, for it is the suit, not a question in the suit, that must arise under the law of the United States. The mere adoption by a state law of a United States law as a criterion or test, when the law of the United States has no force *proprio vigore*, does not cause a case under the state law to be also a case under the law of the United States. . . .

Merrell Dow Pharmaceuticals Inc. v. Thompson

478 U.S. 804 (1986)

JUSTICE STEVENS delivered the opinion of the Court.

The question presented is whether the incorporation of a federal standard in a state-law private action, when Congress has intended that there not be a federal private action for violations of that federal standard, makes the action one "arising under the Constitution, laws, or treaties of the United States," 28 U.S.C. §1331.

I

The Thompson respondents are residents of Canada and the MacTavishes reside in Scotland. They filed virtually identical complaints against petitioner, a corporation, that manufactures and distributes the drug Bendectin. The complaints were filed in the Court of Common Pleas in Hamilton County, Ohio. Each complaint alleged that a child was born with multiple deformities as a result of the mother's ingestion of Bendectin during pregnancy. In five of the six counts, the recovery of substantial damages was requested on common-law theories of negligence, breach of warranty, strict liability, fraud, and gross negligence. In Count IV, respondents alleged that the drug Bendectin was "misbranded" in violation of the Federal Food, Drug, and Cosmetic Act (FDCA), 52 Stat. 1040, as amended, 21 U.S.C. §301 *et seq.* (1982 ed. and Supp. III), because its labeling did not provide adequate warning that its use was potentially dangerous. Paragraph 26 alleged that the violation of the FDCA "in the promotion" of Bendectin "constitutes a

Chapter 3. Subject Matter Jurisdiction

rebuttable presumption of negligence." Paragraph 27 alleged that the "violation of said federal statutes directly and proximately caused the injuries suffered" by the two infants. . . .

Petitioner filed a timely petition for removal from the state court to the Federal District Court alleging that the action was "founded, in part, on an alleged claim arising under the laws of the United States."[1] After removal, the two cases were consolidated. Respondents filed a motion to remand to the state forum on the ground that the federal court lacked subject matter jurisdiction. Relying on our decision in *Smith v. Kansas City Title & Trust Co.*, 255 U.S. 180 (1921), the District Court held that Count IV of the complaint alleged a cause of action arising under federal law and denied the motion to remand. It then granted petitioner's motion to dismiss on *forum non conveniens* grounds.

The Court of Appeals for the Sixth Circuit reversed. After . . . noting "that the FDCA does not create or imply . . . a private right of action for individuals injured as a result of violations of the Act," it explained:

> Federal question jurisdiction would, thus, exist only if plaintiffs' right to relief depended necessarily on a substantial question of federal law. Plaintiffs' causes of action referred to the FDCA merely as one available criterion for determining whether Merrell Dow was negligent. Because the jury could find negligence on the part of Merrell Dow without finding a violation of the FDCA, the plaintiffs' causes of action did not depend necessarily upon a question of federal law. Consequently, the causes of action did not arise under federal law and, therefore, were improperly removed to federal court.

We granted certiorari, and we now affirm.

II

. . . Although the constitutional meaning of "arising under" may extend to all cases in which a federal question is "an ingredient" of the action, . . . we have long construed the statutory grant of federal-question jurisdiction as conferring a more limited power. . . .

[T]he propriety of the removal in this case thus turns on whether the case falls within the original "federal question" jurisdiction of the federal courts. There is no "single, precise definition" of that concept; rather, "the phrase 'arising under' masks a welter of issues regarding the interrelation of federal and state authority and the proper management of the federal judicial system." . . .

This much, however, is clear. The "vast majority" of cases that come within this grant of jurisdiction are covered by Justice Holmes's statement that a "'suit arises under the law that creates the cause of action.'" *Franchise Tax Board v. Construction Laborers Vacation Trust*, 463 U.S. 1, 8–9 (1983), quoting *American Well Works Co. v. Layne & Bowler Co.*, 241 U.S. 257, 260 (1916). Thus, the vast majority of cases

---

1. The petition also alleged that the action "is between citizens of a State and citizens or subjects of a foreign state." . . . Because petitioner is a corporation with its principal place of business in Ohio, however, the removal was not proper unless the action was founded on a claim arising under federal law. . . .

brought under the general federal-question jurisdiction of the federal courts are those in which federal law creates the cause of action.

We have, however, also noted that a case may arise under federal law "where the vindication of a right under state law necessarily turned on some construction of federal law." *Franchise Tax Board*, 463 U.S. at 9.[5] Our actual holding in *Franchise Tax Board* demonstrates that this statement must be read with caution; the central issue presented in that case turned on the meaning of the Employee Retirement Income Security Act of 1974, 29 U.S.C. §1001 *et seq.* (1982 ed. and Supp. III), but we nevertheless concluded that federal jurisdiction was lacking. . . .

In this case, both parties agree with the Court of Appeals' conclusion that there is no federal cause of action for FDCA violations. For purposes of our decision, we assume that this is a correct interpretation of the FDCA. Thus, as the case comes to us, it is appropriate to assume that, under the settled framework for evaluating whether a federal cause of action lies, some combination of the following factors is present: (1) the plaintiffs are not part of the class for whose special benefit the statute was passed; (2) the indicia of legislative intent reveal no congressional purpose to provide a private cause of action; (3) a federal cause of action would not further the underlying purposes of the legislative scheme; and (4) the respondents' cause of action is a subject traditionally relegated to state law. In short, Congress did not intend a private federal remedy for violations of the statute that it enacted. . . .

The significance of the necessary assumption that there is no federal private cause of action thus cannot be overstated. For the ultimate import of such a conclusion, as we have repeatedly emphasized, is that it would flout congressional intent to provide a private federal remedy for the violation of the federal statute. We think it would similarly flout, or at least undermine, congressional intent to conclude that the federal courts might nevertheless exercise federal-question jurisdiction and provide remedies for violations of that federal statute solely because the violation of the federal statute is said to be a "rebuttable presumption" or a "proximate cause" under state law, rather than a federal action under federal law.

---

5. The case most frequently cited for that proposition is *Smith v. Kansas City Title & Trust Co.*, 255 U.S. 180 (1921). In that case the Court upheld federal jurisdiction of a shareholder's bill to enjoin the corporation from purchasing bonds issued by the federal land banks under the authority of the Federal Farm Loan Act on the ground that the federal statute that authorized the issuance of the bonds was unconstitutional. The Court stated:

> The general rule is that where it appears from the bill or statement of the plaintiff that the right to relief depends upon the construction or application of the Constitution or laws of the United States, and that such federal claim is not merely colorable, and rests upon a reasonable foundation, the District Court has jurisdiction under this provision. *Id.* at 199.

The effect of this view, expressed over Justice Holmes' vigorous dissent, on his *American Well Works* formulation has been often noted. *See, e.g., Franchise Tax Board*, 463 U.S. at 9 ("[I]t is well settled that Justice Holmes' test is more useful for describing the vast majority of cases that come within the district courts' original jurisdiction than it is for describing which cases are beyond district court jurisdiction"); *T.B. Harms Co. v. Eliscu*, 339 F.2d 823, 827 (CA2 1964) (Friendly, J.) ("It has come to be realized that Mr. Justice Holmes' formula is more useful for inclusion than for the exclusion for which it was intended.").

III

Petitioner advances three arguments to support its position that, even in the face of this congressional preclusion of a federal cause of action for a violation of the federal statute, federal question jurisdiction may lie for the violation of the federal statute as an element of a state cause of action.

First, petitioner contends that the case represents a straightforward application of the statement in *Franchise Tax Board* that federal question jurisdiction is appropriate when "it appears that some substantial, disputed question of federal law is a necessary element of one of the well-pleaded state claims." 463 U.S. at 13. *Franchise Tax Board*, however, did not purport to disturb the long-settled understanding that the mere presence of a federal issue in a state cause of action does not automatically confer federal-question jurisdiction. . . .

Far from creating some kind of automatic test, *Franchise Tax Board* thus candidly recognized the need for careful judgments about the exercise of federal judicial power in an area of uncertain jurisdiction. Given the significance of the assumed congressional determination to preclude federal private remedies, the presence of the federal issue as an element of the state tort is not the kind of adjudication for which jurisdiction would serve congressional purposes and the federal system. This conclusion is fully consistent with the very sentence relied on so heavily by petitioner. We simply conclude that the congressional determination that there should be no federal remedy for the violation of this federal statute is tantamount to a congressional conclusion that the presence of a claimed violation of the statute as an element of a state cause of action is insufficiently "substantial" to confer federal-question jurisdiction.

Second, petitioner contends that there is a powerful federal interest in seeing that the federal statute is given uniform interpretations, and that federal review is the best way of insuring such uniformity. In addition to the significance of the congressional decision to preclude a federal remedy, we do not agree with petitioner's characterization of the federal interest and its implications for federal-question jurisdiction. To the extent that petitioner is arguing that state use and interpretation of the FDCA pose a threat to the order and stability of the FDCA regime, petitioner should be arguing, not that federal courts should be able to review and enforce state FDCA-based causes of action as an aspect of federal-question jurisdiction, but that the FDCA pre-empts state-court jurisdiction over the issue in dispute. Petitioner's concern about the uniformity of interpretation, moreover, is considerably mitigated by the fact that, even if there is no original district court jurisdiction for these kinds of action, this Court retains power to review the decision of a federal issue in a state cause of action.

Finally, petitioner argues that, whatever the general rule, there are special circumstances that justify federal-question jurisdiction in this case. Petitioner emphasizes that it is unclear whether the FDCA applies to sales in Canada and Scotland; there is, therefore, a special reason for having a federal court answer the novel federal question relating to the extraterritorial meaning of the Act. We reject this argument. We do not believe the question whether a particular claim arises under federal law depends on the novelty of the federal issue. Although it is true that federal jurisdiction cannot be based on a frivolous or insubstantial federal question, "the interrelation of federal and state authority and the proper management of the federal judicial system," *Franchise Tax Board*, 463 U.S. at 8, would be ill served by a rule that made the existence of federal-question jurisdiction depend on the district court's case-by-case appraisal of the novelty of the federal question asserted as an element of the state tort. The novelty of an FDCA issue is not sufficient to give it status as a federal cause of action; nor should it be sufficient to give a state-based FDCA claim status as a jurisdiction-triggering federal question.

IV

We conclude that a complaint alleging a violation of a federal statute as an element of a state cause of action, when Congress has determined that there should be no private, federal cause of action for the violation, does not state a claim "arising under the Constitution, laws, or treaties of the United States." 28 U.S.C. §1331.

The judgment of the Court of Appeals is affirmed.

JUSTICE BRENNAN, with whom JUSTICE WHITE, JUSTICE MARSHALL, and JUSTICE BLACKMUN join, dissenting. . . .

II

A

By making federal law an essential element of a state-law claim, the State places the federal law into a context where it will operate to shape behavior: the threat of liability will force individuals to conform their conduct to interpretations of the federal law made by courts adjudicating the state-law claim. It will not matter to an individual found liable whether the officer who arrives at his door to execute judgment is wearing a state or a federal uniform; all he cares about is the fact that a sanction is being imposed—and may be imposed again in the future—because he failed to comply with the federal law. Consequently, the possibility that the federal law will be incorrectly interpreted in the context of adjudicating the state-law claim implicates the concerns that led Congress to grant the district courts power to adjudicate cases involving federal questions in precisely the same way as if it was federal law that "created" the cause of action. It therefore follows that there is federal jurisdiction under §1331.

B

The only remaining question is whether the assumption that Congress decided not to create a private cause of action alters this analysis in a way that makes it inappropriate to exercise original federal jurisdiction. According to the Court, "the very reasons for the development of the modern implied remedy doctrine" support the conclusion that, where the legislative history of a particular law shows (whether expressly or by inference) that Congress intended that there be no private federal remedy, it must also mean that Congress would not want federal courts to exercise jurisdiction over a state-law claim making violations of that federal law actionable. . . . These reasons are "'the increased complexity of federal legislation,'" "'the increased volume of federal litigation,'" and "'the desirability of a more careful scrutiny of legislative intent.'" . . . (*quoting Merrill Lynch, Pierce, Fenner & Smith, Inc. v. Curran*, 456 U.S. 353, 377 (1982)).

These reasons simply do not justify the Court's holding. Given the relative expertise of the federal courts in interpreting federal law, . . . the increased complexity of federal legislation argues rather strongly in *favor* of recognizing federal jurisdiction. And, while the increased volume of litigation may appropriately be considered in connection with reasoned arguments that justify limiting the reach of §1331, I do not believe that the day has yet arrived when this Court may trim a statute solely because it thinks that Congress made it too broad. . . .

The enforcement scheme established by the FDCA is typical of other, similarly broad regulatory schemes. Primary responsibility for overseeing implementation of the Act has been conferred upon a specialized administrative agency, here the Food and Drug Administration (FDA). Congress has provided the FDA with a wide-ranging arsenal of weapons to combat violations of the FDCA, including authority to obtain an *ex parte* court order for the seizure of goods subject to the Act, see 21 U.S.C. §334, authority to initiate proceedings in a federal district court to enjoin continuing violations of the FDCA, see §332, and authority to request a United States Attorney to bring criminal proceedings against violators, see §333. See generally 1 J. O'Reilly, Food and Drug Administration, chs. 6–10 (1979 and Supp. 1985). Significantly, the FDA has no independent enforcement authority; final enforcement must come from the federal courts, which have exclusive jurisdiction over actions under the FDCA. See §§332(a), 333, 334(a)(1). Thus, while the initial interpretive function has been delegated to an expert administrative body whose interpretations are entitled to considerable deference, final responsibility for interpreting the statute in order to carry out the legislative mandate belongs to the federal courts. Cf. *Chevron U.S.A. Inc. v. Natural Resources Defense Council, Inc.,* 467 U.S. 837, 843, n. 9 (1984) ("The judiciary is the final authority on issues of statutory construction and must reject administrative constructions which are contrary to clear congressional intent").

Given that Congress structured the FDCA so that all express remedies are provided by the federal courts, it seems rather strange to conclude that it either "flout[s]" or "undermine[s]" congressional intent for the federal courts to adjudicate a private state-law remedy that is based upon violating the FDCA. . . . That is, assuming that a state cause of action based on the FDCA is not preempted, it is entirely consistent with the FDCA to find that it "arises under" federal law within the meaning of §1331. Indeed, it is the Court's conclusion that such a state cause of action must be kept *out* of the federal courts that appears contrary to legislative intent inasmuch as the enforcement provisions of the FDCA quite clearly express a preference for having federal courts interpret the FDCA and provide remedies for its violation.

It may be that a decision by Congress not to create a private remedy is intended to preclude all private enforcement. If that is so, then a state cause of action that makes relief available to private individuals for violations of the FDCA is preempted. But if Congress' decision not to provide a private federal remedy does *not* preempt such a state remedy, then, in light of the FDCA's clear policy of relying on the federal courts for enforcement, it also should not foreclose federal jurisdiction over that state remedy. Both §1331 and the enforcement provisions of the FDCA reflect Congress' strong desire to utilize the federal courts to interpret and enforce the FDCA, and it is therefore at odds with both these statutes to recognize a private state-law remedy for violating the FDCA but to hold that this remedy cannot be adjudicated in the federal courts.

The Court's contrary conclusion requires inferring from Congress' decision not to create a private federal remedy that, while some private enforcement is permissible in state courts, it is "bad" if that enforcement comes from the *federal* courts. But that is simply illogical. Congress' decision to withhold a private right of action and to rely instead on public enforcement reflects congressional concern with obtaining more accurate implementation and more coordinated enforcement of a regulatory scheme. . . . These reasons are closely related to the Congress' reasons for giving federal courts original federal-question jurisdiction. Thus, if anything, Congress' decision not to create a private remedy *strengthens* the argument in favor of finding federal jurisdiction over a state remedy that is not pre-empted.

NOTES AND QUESTIONS

1. *Comparing* Smith *and* Merrell Dow. Does *Merrell Dow* overrule *Smith v. Kansas City Title & Trust Co.*? Both cases seem to involve state laws that incorporate by reference federal norms—in *Smith*, a Missouri law requiring local banks to invest in legal obligations of the United States; in *Merrell Dow*, Ohio tort law presumably treating violations of federal regulatory standards as negligence *per se*. Is there a basis for distinguishing between the two cases in terms of the impact on federal interests of an erroneous state court ruling? In *Smith*, an erroneous ruling would certainly have deterred local banks from making investments in the federal farm loan program. By contrast, in *Merrell Dow*, an erroneous state ruling was not likely to have a significant impact on the Federal Food and Drug Administration's regulatory standards. To put the point somewhat differently, the Supreme Court very likely would have heard the *Smith* case on appeal if the farm loan program were held unconstitutional, whereas there would be no similar imperative to correct an erroneous state tort ruling in *Merrell Dow*. Nevertheless, is it appropriate (or wise) to make the existence of jurisdiction—inquiry into which normally occurs at the outset of the litigation and by motion in advance of responsive pleadings or evidentiary hearings—turn on this type of assessment of likely impact? Does the language of §1331 invite such an impact-based approach to jurisdiction?

2. *Ascertaining the Test. Merrell Dow* lends some credence to Holmes's dissent in *Smith* that federal jurisdiction depends on whether federal law provides the remedy. In *Merrell Dow*, where there is a federal standard but no federal remedy, the Holmes view rejects federal jurisdiction. But what about the flip side of the Holmes test: when federal law "creates" the remedy but state law is used as the standard? Consider *Shoshone Mining Co. v. Rutter*, 177 U.S. 505 (1900), where the Supreme Court held that there was no federal jurisdiction where a federal statute provided that adverse suits between miners could be determined by reference to local customs and mining practices so long as they were not inconsistent with the laws of the United States. Because the claims presented only questions of local rules and the effect of state statutes, the Court held that the suit did not arise under the Constitution and laws of the United States.

Would it be more accurate to characterize the *Merrell Dow* test as requiring that not only the standard but also the remedy be grounded in federal law? Or can *Merrell Dow* still be explained by reference to a test that measures "federal interests"? What are the advantages of the more formal requirement that both the standard and the remedy be derived from federal law? Is it likely that under such a test some cases that should get federal treatment will fall short of the federal jurisdictional line? Is *Smith v. Kansas City Title & Trust* such a case?

3. *The Latest Word.* Assume an action is brought to quiet title under state law. The plaintiff contends that the defendant's record title to the property is based on a tax seizure that was invalid because the seizure failed to comply with the statutory notice in the federal tax law. Does such a case "arise under" federal law? Is it closer to *Smith* or to *Merrell Dow?* The Supreme Court discusses this precise fact scenario in its 2005 decision below addressing federal question jurisdiction.

Grable & Sons Metal Products v. Darue

545 U.S. 308 (2005)

JUSTICE SOUTER delivered the opinion of the Court.

The question is whether want of a federal cause of action to try claims of title to land obtained at a federal tax sale precludes removal to federal court of a state action with non-diverse parties raising a disputed issue of federal title law. We answer no, and hold that the national interest in providing a federal forum for federal tax litigation is sufficiently substantial to support the exercise of federal question jurisdiction over the disputed issue on removal, which would not distort any division of labor between the state and federal courts, provided or assumed by Congress.

I

In 1994, the Internal Revenue Service seized Michigan real property belonging to petitioner Grable & Sons Metal Products, Inc., to satisfy Grable's federal tax delinquency. Title 26 U.S.C. §6335 required the IRS to give notice of the seizure, and there is no dispute that Grable received actual notice by certified mail before the IRS sold the property to respondent Darue Engineering & Manufacturing. Although Grable also received notice of the sale itself, it did not exercise its statutory right to redeem the property within 180 days of the sale, §6337(b)(1), and after that period had passed, the Government gave Darue a quitclaim deed. §6339.

Five years later, Grable brought a quiet title action in state court, claiming that Darue's record title was invalid because the IRS had failed to notify Grable of its seizure of the property in the exact manner required by §6335(a), which provides that written notice must be "given by the Secretary to the owner of the property [or] left at his usual place of abode or business." Grable said that the statute required personal service, not service by certified mail.

Darue removed the case to Federal District Court as presenting a federal question, because the claim of title depended on the interpretation of the notice statute in the federal tax law. The District Court declined to remand the case at Grable's behest after finding that the "claim does pose a significant question of federal law," . . . and ruling that Grable's lack of a federal right of action to enforce its claim against Darue did not bar the exercise of federal jurisdiction. On the merits, the court granted summary judgment to Darue, holding that although §6335 by its terms required personal service, substantial compliance with the statute was enough.

The Court of Appeals for the Sixth Circuit affirmed. . . . On the jurisdictional question, the panel thought it sufficed that the title claim raised an issue of federal law that had to be resolved, and implicated a substantial federal interest (in construing federal tax law). The court went on to affirm the District Court's judgment on the merits. We granted certiorari on the jurisdictional question alone to resolve a split within the Courts of Appeals on whether *Merrell Dow Pharmaceuticals Inc. v. Thompson,* 478 U.S. 804 (1986), always requires a federal cause of action as a condition for exercising federal-question jurisdiction.[2] We now affirm.

II

Darue was entitled to remove the quiet title action if Grable could have brought it in federal district court originally, 28 U.S.C. §1441(a), as a civil action "arising under the Constitution, laws, or treaties of the United States," §1331. This provision for federal-question jurisdiction is invoked by and large by plaintiffs pleading a cause of action created by federal law. . . . There is, however, another longstanding, if less frequently encountered variety of federal "arising under" jurisdiction, this Court having recognized for nearly 100 years that in certain cases federal-question jurisdiction will lie over state-law claims that implicate significant federal issues. *E.g., Hopkins v. Walker,* 244 U.S. 486, 490–491 (1917). The doctrine captures the commonsense notion that a federal court ought to be able to hear claims recognized under state law that nonetheless turn on substantial questions of federal law, and thus justify resort to the experience, solicitude, and hope of uniformity that a federal forum offers on federal issues, see ALI, Study of the Division of Jurisdiction Between State and Federal Courts 164–166 (1968).

The classic example is *Smith v. Kansas City Title and Trust Co.,* 255 U.S. 180 (1921), a suit by a shareholder claiming that the defendant corporation could not lawfully buy certain bonds of the National Government because their issuance was unconstitutional. Although Missouri law provided the cause of action, the Court recognized federal-question jurisdiction because the principal issue in the case was the federal constitutionality of the bond issue. *Smith* thus held, in a somewhat generous statement of the scope of the doctrine, that a state-law claim could give rise to federal-question jurisdiction so long as it "appears from the [complaint] that the right to relief depends upon the construction or application of [federal law]." *Id.,* at 199.

The *Smith* statement has been subject to some trimming to fit earlier and later cases recognizing the vitality of the basic doctrine, but shying away from the expansive view that mere need to apply federal law in a state-law claim will suffice to open the "arising under" door. As early as 1912, this Court had confined federal-question jurisdiction over state-law claims to those that "really and substantially involv[e] a dispute or controversy respecting the validity, construction or effect of [federal] law." *Shulthis v. McDougal,* 225 U.S. 561, 569 (1912). This limitation was the ancestor of Justice Cardozo's later explanation that a request to exercise federal-question jurisdiction over a state action calls for a "Common-sense accommodation of judgment

---

2. Compare *Seinfeld v. Austen,* 39 F.3d 761, 764 (CA7 1994) (finding that federal-question jurisdiction over a state-law claim requires a parallel federal private right of action), with *Ormet Corp. v. Ohio Power Co.,* 98 F.3d 799, 806 (CA4 1996) (finding that a federal private action is not required).

to [the] kaleidoscopic situations" that present a federal issue, in "a selective process which picks the substantial causes out of the web and lays the other ones aside." *Gully v. First Nat. Bank in Meridian*, 299 U.S. 109, 117–118 (1936). It has in fact become a constant refrain in such cases that federal jurisdiction demands not only a contested federal issue, but a substantial one, indicating a serious federal interest in claiming the advantages thought to be inherent in a federal forum. [Citations omitted.]

But even when the state action discloses a contested and substantial federal question, the exercise of federal jurisdiction is subject to a possible veto. For the federal issue will ultimately qualify for a federal forum only if federal jurisdiction is consistent with congressional judgment about the sound division of labor between state and federal courts governing the application of §1331. Thus, *Franchise Tax Bd.* explained that the appropriateness of a federal forum to hear an embedded issue could be evaluated only after considering the "welter of issues regarding the inter-relation of federal and state authority and the proper management of the federal judicial system." . . . Because arising-under jurisdiction to hear a state-law claim always raises the possibility of upsetting the state-federal line drawn (or at least assumed) by Congress, the presence of a disputed federal issue and the ostensible importance of a federal forum are never necessarily dispositive; there must always be an assessment of any disruptive portent in exercising federal jurisdiction. . . .

These considerations have kept us from stating a "single, precise, all-embracing" test for jurisdiction over federal issues embedded in state-law claims between non-diverse parties. . . . We have not kept them out simply because they appeared in state raiment, as Justice Holmes would have done, see *Smith, supra*, at 214 (dissenting opinion), but neither have we treated "federal issue" as a password opening federal courts to any state action embracing a point of federal law. Instead, the question is, does a state-law claim necessarily raise a stated federal issue, actually disputed and substantial, which a federal forum may entertain without disturbing any congressionally approved balance of federal and state judicial responsibilities.

III

A

This case warrants federal jurisdiction. Grable's state complaint must specify "the facts establishing the superiority of [its] claim," Mich. Ct. Rule 3.411(B)(2)(c) (West 2005), and Grable has premised its superior title claim on a failure by the IRS to give it adequate notice, as defined by federal law. Whether Grable was given notice within the meaning of the federal statute is thus an essential element of its quiet title claim, and the meaning of the federal statute is actually in dispute; it appears to be the only legal or factual issue contested in the case. The meaning of the federal tax provision is an important issue of federal law that sensibly belongs in a federal court. The Government has a strong interest in the "prompt and certain collection of delinquent taxes," *United States v. Rodgers*, 461 U.S. 677, 709 (1983), and the ability of the IRS to satisfy its claims from the property of delinquents requires clear terms of notice to allow buyers like Darue to satisfy themselves that the Service has touched the bases necessary for good title. The Government thus has a direct interest in the availability of a federal forum to vindicate its own administrative action, and buyers (as well as tax delinquents) may find it valuable to come before judges used to federal tax matters. Finally, because it will be the rare state title case that raises a contested matter of federal law, federal jurisdiction to resolve genuine disagreement over federal tax title provisions will portend only a microscopic effect on the federal-state division of labor. See n. 3, *infra*. . . .

[I]n this case, "the facts showing the plaintiffs' title and the existence and invalidity of the instrument or record sought to be eliminated as a cloud upon the title are essential parts of the plaintiffs' cause of action."[3] . . .

B

Merrell Dow Pharmaceuticals Inc. v. Thompson, 478 U.S. 804 (1986), on which Grable rests its position, is not to the contrary. *Merrell Dow* considered a state tort claim resting in part on the allegation that the defendant drug company had violated a federal misbranding prohibition, and was thus presumptively negligent under Ohio law. . . . The Court assumed that federal law would have to be applied to resolve the claim, but after closely examining the strength of the federal interest at stake and the implications of opening the federal forum, held federal jurisdiction unavailable. Congress had not provided a private federal cause of action for violation of the federal branding requirement, and the Court found "it would . . . flout, or at least undermine, congressional intent to conclude that federal courts might nevertheless exercise federal-question jurisdiction and provide remedies for violations of that federal statute solely because the violation . . . is said to be a . . . 'proximate cause' under state law." . . .

Because federal law provides for no quiet title action that could be brought against Darue,[4] Grable argues that there can be no federal jurisdiction here, stressing some broad language in *Merrell Dow* (including the passage just quoted) that on its face supports Grable's position, see Note, Mr. *Smith* Goes to Federal Court: Federal Question Jurisdiction over State Law Claims Post-*Merrell Dow*, 115 Harv. L. Rev. 2272, 2280–2282 (2002) (discussing split in Circuit Courts over private right of action requirement after *Merrell Dow*). But an opinion is to be read as a whole, and Merrell Dow cannot be read whole as overturning decades of precedent, as it would have done by effectively adopting the Holmes dissent in *Smith*, . . . and converting a federal cause of action from a sufficient condition for federal-question jurisdiction[5] into a necessary one.

---

3. The quiet title cases also show the limiting effect of the requirement that the federal issue in a state-law claim must actually be in dispute to justify federal-question jurisdiction. In *Shulthis v. McDougal*, 225 U.S. 561 (1912), this Court found that there was no federal-question jurisdiction to hear a plaintiff's quiet title claim in part because the federal statutes on which title depended were not subject to "any controversy respecting their validity, construction, or effect." *Id.*, at 570. As the Court put it, the requirement of an actual dispute about federal law was "especially" important in "suits involving rights to land acquired under a law of the United States," because otherwise "every suit to establish title to land in the central and western states would so arise [under federal law], as all titles in those States are traceable back to those laws." *Id.*, at 569–570.

4. Federal law does provide a quiet title cause of action against the Federal Government. 28 U.S.C. §2410. That right of action is not relevant here, however, because the federal government no longer has any interest in the property, having transferred its interest to Darue through the quitclaim deed.

5. For an extremely rare exception to the sufficiency of a federal right of action, see *Shoshone Mining Co. v. Rutter*, 177 U.S. 505, 507 (1900).

In the first place, *Merrell Dow* disclaimed the adoption of any bright-line rule, as when the Court reiterated that "in exploring the outer reaches of §1331, determinations about federal jurisdiction require sensitive judgments about congressional intent, judicial power, and the federal system." . . . And as a final indication that it did not mean to make a federal right of action mandatory, it expressly approved the exercise of jurisdiction sustained in *Smith*, despite the want of any federal cause of action available to *Smith*'s shareholder plaintiff. . . . *Merrell Dow* then, did not toss out, but specifically retained the contextual enquiry that had been *Smith*'s hallmark for over 60 years. At the end of *Merrell Dow*, Justice Holmes was still dissenting.

Accordingly, *Merrell Dow* should be read in its entirety as treating the absence of a federal private right of action as evidence relevant to, but not dispositive of, the "sensitive judgments about congressional intent" that §1331 requires. The absence of any federal cause of action affected *Merrell Dow*'s result two ways. The Court saw the fact as worth some consideration in the assessment of substantiality. But its primary importance emerged when the Court treated the combination of no federal cause of action and no preemption of state remedies for misbranding as an important clue to Congress's conception of the scope of jurisdiction to be exercised under §1331. The Court saw the missing cause of action not as a missing federal door key, always required, but as a missing welcome mat, required in the circumstances, when exercising federal jurisdiction over a state misbranding action would have attracted a horde of original filings and removal cases raising other state claims with embedded federal issues. For if the federal labeling standard without a federal cause of action could get a state claim into federal court, so could any other federal standard without a federal cause of action. And that would have meant a tremendous number of cases.

One only needed to consider the treatment of federal violations generally in garden variety state tort law. The violation of federal statutes and regulations is commonly given negligence per se effect in state tort proceedings. . . . A general rule of exercising federal jurisdiction over state claims resting on federal mislabeling and other statutory violations would thus have heralded a potentially enormous shift of traditionally state cases into federal courts. Expressing concern over the "increased volume of federal litigation," and noting the importance of adhering to "legislative intent," *Merrell Dow* thought it improbable that the Congress, having made no provision for a federal cause of action, would have meant to welcome any state-law tort case implicating federal law "solely because the violation of the federal statute is said to [create] a rebuttable presumption [of negligence] . . . under state law." . . . In this situation, no welcome mat meant keep out. *Merrell Dow*'s analysis thus fits within the framework of examining the importance of having a federal forum for the issue, and the consistency of such a forum with Congress's intended division of labor between state and federal courts.

As already indicated, however, a comparable analysis yields a different jurisdictional conclusion in this case. Although Congress also indicated ambivalence in this case by providing no private right of action to Grable, it is the rare state quiet title action that involves contested issues of federal law, see n. 3, *supra*. Consequently, jurisdiction over actions like Grable's would not materially affect, or threaten to affect, the normal currents of litigation. Given the absence of threatening structural consequences and the clear interest the Government, its buyers, and its delinquents have in the availability of a federal forum, there is no good reason to shirk from federal jurisdiction over the dispositive and contested federal issue at the heart of the state-law title claim.

IV

The judgment of the Court of Appeals, upholding federal jurisdiction over Grable's quiet title action, is affirmed. . . .

JUSTICE THOMAS, concurring.

The Court faithfully applies our precedents interpreting 28 U.S.C. §1331 to authorize federal-court jurisdiction over some cases in which state law creates the cause of action but requires determination of an issue of federal law, e.g., *Smith v. Kansas City Title & Trust Co.*, 255 U.S. 180 (1921); *Merrell Dow Pharmaceuticals Inc. v. Thompson*, 478 U.S. 804 (1986). In this case, no one has asked us to overrule those precedents and adopt the rule Justice Holmes set forth in *American Well Works Co. v. Layne & Bowler Co.*, 241 U.S. 257 (1916), limiting §1331 jurisdiction to cases in which federal law creates the cause of action pleaded on the face of the plaintiff's complaint. *Id.*, at 260. In an appropriate case, and perhaps with the benefit of better evidence as to the original meaning of §1331's text, I would be willing to consider that course.*

Jurisdictional rules should be clear. Whatever the virtues of the *Smith* standard, it is anything but clear. . . . Whatever the vices of the *American Well Works* rule, it is clear. Moreover, it accounts for the "'vast majority'" of cases that come within §1331 under our current case law . . . —further indication that trying to sort out which cases fall within the smaller *Smith* category may not be worth the effort it entails. See R. Fallon, D. Meltzer, & D. Shapiro, Hart and Wechsler's The Federal Courts and the Federal System 885–886 (5th ed. 2003). Accordingly, I would be willing in appropriate circumstances to reconsider our interpretation of §1331.

NOTES AND QUESTIONS

1. *Evaluating* Grable. *Grable* seems to have put to rest the view advanced by some after *Merrell Dow* that both the remedy and the standard must be grounded in federal law in order to satisfy "arising under" jurisdiction. But what test has it erected in its place? The Court says that federal jurisdiction demands a "serious federal interest in claiming the advantages thought to be inherent in a federal forum," and, in addition, that "any congressionally approved balance of federal and state

---

* This Court has long construed the scope of the statutory grant of federal-question jurisdiction more narrowly than the scope of the constitutional grant of such jurisdiction. See *Merrell Dow Pharmaceuticals Inc. v. Thompson*, 478 U.S. 804, 807 (1986). I assume for present purposes that this distinction is proper—that is, that the language of 28 U.S.C. §1331, "the district courts shall have original jurisdiction of all *civil actions arising under* the Constitution, laws, or treaties of the United States" (emphasis added), is narrower than the language of Art. III, §2, cl. 1, of the Constitution, "[t]he judicial Power shall extend to all *Cases*, in Law and Equity, *arising under* this Constitution, the Laws of the United States, and Treaties made, or which shall be made, under their Authority. . . ." (emphases added).—EDS.

judicial responsibility possibilities" should not be disturbed. What is the federal interest at stake in *Grable*? Why is that a more substantial federal interest than the federal regulatory scheme at issue in *Merrell Dow*? Or is it the second prong of the analysis that distinguishes the two cases? It is true that in *Merrell Dow* the majority saw the absence of a federal cause of action under the Food, Drug and Cosmetic Act as undermining the claim for federal jurisdiction. But there is no federal private right of action in *Grable* either. So why is the federal-state balance undermined in *Merrell Dow* but not in *Grable*?

Professor Richard D. Freer argues that a multifactor "standard" like the *Grable* test, as opposed to a hard-and-fast "rule," is necessary for federal courts to determine whether they should accept §1331 subject matter jurisdiction. *See* Richard D. Freer, *Of Rules and Standards: Reconciling Statutory Limitations on "Arising Under" Jurisdiction*, 82 Ind. L.J. 309 (2007). *But see* Douglas D. McFarland, *The True Compass: No Federal Question in a State Law Claim*, 55 U. Kan. L. Rev. 1, 34 (2006) (denouncing the *Grable* rule as "no more than pure equity, with the federal chancellor standing at the gate to decide based on a personal sense of fairness whether a case shall enter").

2. Are you persuaded that extending federal jurisdiction to a case like *Grable* will not shift traditionally state cases into federal courts? After all, doesn't plaintiff's quiet title action in *Grable* amount to collateral attack of a sale of property on the basis of improper notice? Although in *Grable* the notice defect was statutory, in other cases the failure of notice might be one of federal constitutional due process. Can such cases now be brought in federal court in reliance on *Grable*? Or is *Grable* different because the initial sale of Grable's property was based on a federal tax delinquency and Grable would have had a statutory right to bring an action in federal court against the government to redeem the property?

3. Are you sympathetic with Justice Thomas's desire for a clearer standard? Would adoption of the test articulated by Justice Holmes — that federal law create the cause of action — be desirable?

4. *Limiting* Grable. Subsequent decisions by the Supreme Court appear to have interpreted *Grable* narrowly. *See Empire Healthchoice Assurance, Inc. v. McVeigh*, 547 U.S. 677 (2006) and *Gunn v. Minton*, 133 S.Ct. 1059 (2013). *Gunn v. Minton* was unusual in that the federal "arising under" issue came up on appeal through the state courts. The case involved a dispute between a client and his lawyers over the unsuccessful prosecution of a patent claim in an earlier proceeding. Patent cases are governed by a federal statute that provides for exclusive jurisdiction in the federal courts for "any civil action arising under any Act of Congress relating to patents." 28 U.S.C. §1338(a). Accordingly, the first lawsuit over the patent itself was in federal court. When Minton lost that case, he sued his lawyers in Texas state court for malpractice, claiming that their failure to raise certain arguments in a timely fashion in the patent suit had been responsible for the outcome. The state trial court ruled against Minton on the merits, granting summary judgment to the lawyers. On appeal, Minton made a surprising argument. For the first time, he claimed that the state courts, where he himself had filed suit, did not have jurisdiction to hear his malpractice claim. Because the malpractice suit related to the lawyers' alleged negligence in prosecuting a patent claim, Minton argued, the suit "arose under" the federal patent laws and was subject to the grant of exclusive jurisdiction in §1338(a). Minton was attempting a second bite at the apple on his malpractice claim by arguing that the court in which he filed suit never had jurisdiction in the

first place and thus he should be allowed to file a new lawsuit in federal court. Since defects of subject-matter jurisdiction cannot be waived — and there would be no jurisdiction in state court if the case were within the exclusive federal jurisdiction — Minton was able to raise the claim for the first time on appeal. Because the Supreme Court had previously held that the "arising under" standard of §1338(a) is identical to that under §1331, the issue of subject matter jurisdiction depended on an interpretation of *Grable*. The intermediate state appellate court rejected Minton's argument, but a divided Supreme Court of Texas agreed that the case arose under federal patent law and hence could not be heard by the state courts.

In a unanimous ruling, the Supreme Court reversed the Texas Supreme Court, finding that that Minton's malpractice suit did not satisfy the "arising under" standard of *Grable*. Summarizing that standard, the Court explained that

> federal jurisdiction over a state law claim will lie if a federal issue is:
> (1) necessarily raised, (2) actually disputed, (3) substantial, and (4) capable of resolution in federal court without disrupting the federal-state balance approved by Congress. Where all four of these requirements are met, we held, jurisdiction is proper because there is a "serious federal interest in claiming the advantages thought to be inherent in a federal forum," which can be vindicated without disrupting Congress's intended division of labor between state and federal courts.

133 S.Ct. at 1065 (quoting *Grable*, 545 U.S. at 313–314). Continuing a shift in terminology that first appeared in *Grable*, the Court appeared to characterize the "federal interest" in jurisdiction as the product of the four other requirements, with the type of consideration that carried the day in *Smith* now a part of the inquiry into how "substantial" the disputed federal issue is. *See id.* at 1066.

This more robust requirement for a "substantial" federal issue drove the Court's conclusion that federal jurisdiction did not lie over Minton's malpractice claim and that state legal malpractice claims based on underlying patent matters will rarely, if ever, arise under federal law. Expanding on the substantiality requirement, the Court explained:

> It is not enough that the federal issue be significant to the particular parties in the immediate suit; that will *always* be true when the state claim necessarily raises a disputed federal issue, as *Grable* separately requires. The substantiality inquiry under *Grable* looks instead to the importance of the issue to the federal system as a whole.

Id. at 1066 (quotation omitted). Here, the Court found, there was an absence of any such systemic federal concerns. Federal patent issues would arise in malpractice suits only in the hypothetical "case within a case" where the state court would try to determine what might have happened if the lawyer had litigated a prior case differently. A state court's conclusions on these questions would have no impact on real-world patent disputes. Neither would they threaten the uniform interpretation of patent laws or the administration of patent claims, since Congress had already provided for exclusive federal jurisdiction over all such disputes. In the absence of any federal question with broader significance to systemic federal interests, jurisdiction does not lie over a state claim.

How broadly significant to systemic federal interests must an issue be to support federal question jurisdiction over state law claims? Would climate change be such an issue? In *Mayor & City of Baltimore v. BP P.L.C.*, 388 F.Supp.3d 538 (D. Md. June 20, 2019), *aff'd*, 952 F.3d 452 (4th Cir. 2020), a Maryland district court remanded to state court the City of Baltimore's suit against various oil and energy corporations for damages resulting from climate change, in part because the resolution of those claims did not necessarily implicate significant issues of federal law. The Mayor and City Council of Baltimore had filed state law nuisance claims against 26 corporations in state court for damages resulting from their substantial contributions to global warming and climate change. The defendants removed the case to federal court, arguing, *inter alia*, that the case has significant implications for foreign policy, requires a cost-benefit analyses of regulatory policy based on federal law, collaterally attacks federal regulatory oversight of the energy sector and environment, and implicates issues relating to federal navigable waters. The district court, citing *Gunn*, found that the City's state law nuisance claims did not "necessarily raise" any issues of federal law nor rely on any federal statutes or regulations and held that the defendants had not established a federal issue was a "necessary element" of the City's suit despite the general federal interest in the problem of climate change. The appellate court upheld the district court's conclusion that §1442 did not apply (and thus was not a proper basis for removal). Note that decisions to remand a case to state court are generally not reviewable on appeal, *see* 42 U.S.C. §1447(d), but there is an exception for cases involving federal officers or agencies as defendants removed under §1442 on which defendants in this case relied. Consistent with the interpretation of §1447(d) used by most circuits, the Fourth Circuit refused to consider any other bases for removal that the defendant had invoked, dismissing the appeal with regard to those other grounds for lack of jurisdiction. 952 F.3d 452, 461. *But see Lu Junhong v. Boeing Co.*, 792 F.3d 805, 813 (7th Cir. 2015) (allowing review of *all* grounds for removal if §1442 is *one* of the grounds).

5. *Extending the §1331 Test.* As noted earlier, the Supreme Court has held that the "arising under" standard of the federal patent statute (28 U.S.C. §1338) at issue in *Gunn* is identical to that standard under §1331. Most recently, the Supreme Court held in *Merrill Lynch, Pierce, Fenner & Smith Inc. v. Manning*, 578 U.S. 901 (2016), that the same standard also applies to §27 of the Securities Exchange Act of 1934 (SEA). In *Manning*, shareholders brought suit against broker-dealers, suing in New Jersey state court under state law for illegally manipulating stock prices. Defendant Merrill Lynch removed the case to federal court, asserting two bases of federal jurisdiction: Section 27, which confers exclusive jurisdiction on the federal courts, as well as the general "arising under" grant of jurisdiction contained in §1331. The plaintiffs moved to remand the case to state court, which was denied. The Third Circuit reversed, finding that federal jurisdiction was improper under both §1331 and §27.

The Supreme Court affirmed, holding that the test for federal jurisdiction under §27 is the same as the "arising under" test for §1331, and that state claims asserted with reference to violations of federal securities law are insufficient to meet that test. In an opinion written by Justice Kagan, the Supreme Court found that an identical reading of the two statutes was compelled both by precedent, as well as by the Court's "practice of reading jurisdictional laws, so long as consistent with their language, to respect the traditional role of state courts in our federal system and to establish clear and administrable rules." Furthermore, by highlighting the "ready answers" that §1331's "arising under" standard provides to courts as a result of its long history, the Supreme Court further emphasized the value it places in consistent and predictable results with regard to jurisdictional questions.

c. Implied Rights of Action

Because the existence of a federal remedy is often the key to federal jurisdiction, courts look to determine whether or not there is a private cause of action as a matter of federal law. As the Court indicated in *Merrell Dow* and *Grable*, usually if there is such a private cause of action under federal law, the standard for federal jurisdiction will be met.

If Congress has expressly provided for a private cause of action, the point is clear. However, often Congress will not have made provision for a private remedy for violation of a federal statute, and the Constitution itself does not as a rule confer a private remedy. Thus, it falls to the courts to determine whether some type of federal remedy should be authorized. When such a remedy is "implied" by the court, it serves the same function with respect to jurisdiction as an express remedy. Often, with little or no fanfare, federal courts will impose injunctive relief in favor of private parties against the federal government when there has been a violation of the Constitution. Occasionally, when it is thought that the particular party is not of the protected class to request such relief, the defect is characterized as one of standing.

With respect to "implying" a private remedy for damages against federal officials for a violation of the Constitution, the question is more difficult. (Note that 42 U.S.C. §1983 authorizes a private right of action to redress constitutional and federal statutory violations committed "under color of" state law, but §1983 does not apply to *federal* governmental action.) A 1971 Supreme Court decision, *Bivens v. Six Unknown Named Agents of Federal Bureau of Narcotics*, 403 U.S. 388 (1971), was the first case to recognize a private damage remedy for a violation of constitutional rights. It did so in the context of a violation of the Fourth Amendment prohibition against unreasonable searches and seizures, even though the constitutional provision, by its terms, makes no reference to damages or other remedy and Congress had not provided a statutory remedy. The Court reasoned that the "absence of affirmative action by Congress" did not bar judicial creation of the damage remedy when the Court deemed the remedy an appropriate means of enforcing the constitutional right. However, later cases refuse to imply a damage remedy if the area is one in which Congress has legislated generally. Thus, in *Bush v. Lucas*, 462 U.S. 367 (1983), the Court held that a *Bivens* remedy was not available under the First Amendment for damages by a federal employee who had been demoted for making critical statements. The Court found that federal personnel policy was involved and Congress had been active in the field, providing mechanisms by which employees' rights were protected that it viewed as equally effective. The Court has been skeptical of expanding *Bivens* ever since. As one Court of Appeals has put it, "What started out as a presumption in favor of implied rights of action has become a firm presumption against them. The Supreme Court has not recognized a new *Bivens* action [since 1980]." *Callahan v. Fed. Bureau of Prisons*, 965 F.3d 520, 523 (6th Cir. 2020).

Whether the courts should imply a private right of action for purely statutory violations—a context where Congress itself has already provided a form of administrative enforcement by public suit or by a limited class of private agents—has also given rise to numerous cases. In *Cort v. Ash*, 422 U.S. 66 (1975), the Court offered a four-part test, the elements of which are discussed by the majority in *Merrell Dow*: (1) is plaintiff one of the class for whose benefit the statute was enacted; (2) is there legislative intent to create or deny a remedy; (3) is a private remedy consistent with the underlying purposes of the legislative scheme; and (4) is state or federal law the appropriate regulator of this area? In that case, a private right of action in a shareholder's suit seeking to recover for corporate money illegally spent in a presidential election was rejected. For a time, the Supreme Court appeared to be more receptive to such "implied rights" of action, *see, e.g., Cannon v. University of Chicago*, 441 U.S. 677 (1979) (private damages remedy implied under Title IX of the Education Act). Since its ruling in *Alexander v. Sandoval*, 532 U.S. 275 (2001), however, that door has been largely closed with the Court demanding explicit "rights-creating language" before it will recognize a private right of action, leaving little room for implied private rights of action under statutes.

d. The Distinction Between "Jurisdiction" and "Merits"

A federal court will necessarily have "jurisdiction" to determine whether there is a private right of action. In *Bell v. Hood*, 327 U.S. 678 (1946), the Supreme Court reversed a federal court's jurisdictional dismissal where the plaintiffs had brought a suit for damages against FBI officials for alleged violations of constitutional rights under the Fourth and Fifth Amendments. The Court observed that the legal issue of whether federal courts could grant money recovery for damages suffered as the result of federal officers violating the Fourth and Fifth Amendments was one of first impression. But the Supreme Court stressed that even if it were to be decided that plaintiffs had failed to state a cause of action, the dismissal would be on the merits and not for lack of jurisdiction. As the Supreme Court explained:

> Jurisdiction . . . is not defeated as respondents seem to contend, by the possibility that the averments might fail to state a cause of action on which petitioners could actually recover. For it is well settled that the failure to state a proper cause of action calls for a judgment on the merits and not for a dismissal for want of jurisdiction. . . . Nor can we say that the cause of action alleged is so patently without merit as to justify . . . the court's dismissal for want of jurisdiction.

Id. at 682–683.

Thus, keep in mind the importance of the concession by both parties in *Merrell Dow* that there was no private cause of action under the FDCA for purposes of the jurisdictional question. Had the plaintiff alleged a private cause of action for damages under the federal FDCA, "arising under" jurisdiction would have existed for the federal claim. *See, e.g., In re Bendectin Litigation*, 857 F.2d 290 (6th Cir. 1988). Although the court ultimately may have determined that no such implied remedy was appropriate, the dismissal would have been for failure to state a cause of action and not for lack of jurisdiction. That distinction may be significant in terms of a court's power to hear related state claims. We will take this issue up in greater detail in the discussion of supplemental jurisdiction later in this chapter.

The Supreme Court returned to the jurisdiction/merits point in *Arbaugh v. Y&H Corp.*, 546 U.S. 500 (2006). Arbaugh filed a claim in federal court alleging that her employer, Y&H, discriminated against her on the basis of sex in violation of Title VII of the Civil Rights Act of 1964. Two weeks after a judgment in Arbaugh's favor, Y&H moved to dismiss the case for lack of federal subject matter jurisdiction (remember that Federal Rule 12(h)(3) allows the parties to suggest that subject matter jurisdiction is lacking at any time during the litigation). Y&H's claim was based on the fact that it had less than 15 employees, which would exempt the corporation from Title VII claims. The lower courts reluctantly dismissed the case, but the Supreme Court reversed, holding that the 15-employee provision was an element of the plaintiff's claim for relief; therefore, the court reinstated the jury verdict because Rule 12(h)(2) does not allow a party to make a 12(b)(6) motion to dismiss a claim after the conclusion of a trial. Writing for a unanimous Court, Justice Ginsburg explained that "when Congress does not rank a statutory limitation on coverage as jurisdictional, courts should treat the restriction as nonjurisdictional in character." *Id.* at 516.

In a more recent case, the Supreme Court has held that the registration requirement in the Copyright Act is not jurisdictional. *See Reed Elsevier, Inc. v. Muchnick*, 559 U.S. 154 (2010). Following *Arbaugh*, the Court rested its conclusion on two grounds. First, the statute did not clearly state that the registration requirement was jurisdictional. Second, the registration requirement, like the numerosity requirement of Title VII at issue in *Arbaugh*, was located in a provision separate from those provisions granting subject matter jurisdiction.

e. The Effect of Declaratory Judgments on "Arising Under" Jurisdiction

One of the most confusing aspects of the "arising under" jurisdiction involves the use of the declaratory judgment procedure. A suit for declaratory relief often reverses the usual order of a lawsuit by permitting the party who would have been the defendant in the traditional "coercive" action to initiate the proceeding and obtain a declaration of rights rather than wait to find itself a defendant in a lawsuit. Under the federal declaratory judgment statute, 28 U.S.C. §§2201-2202, the declaratory judgment plaintiff need not seek any relief other than a declaration of rights. For example, insurance companies frequently request a declaration of nonliability with respect to their insured. In such a situation, the assertion of the defense is the basis for the declaratory judgment complaint. On the facts of *Mottley*, the Railroad might have been able to request a declaration that the federal statute permitted the Railroad to revoke the Mottleys' free passes. The federal issue would thereby appear on the face of the Railroad's declaratory judgment complaint. Should such an action be found to "arise under" federal law?

The law appears to be that an action for declaratory relief arises under federal law only when the "coercive" action that it anticipates would itself be deemed to arise under federal law. (Of course, if the declaratory plaintiff is asserting its own federal cause of action, that action would also be deemed to arise under federal law.) In *Skelly Oil Co. v. Phillips Petroleum Co.*, 339 U.S. 667, 673-674 (1950), the Supreme Court wrote that to allow the Declaratory Judgment Act to create federal jurisdiction through artful pleading that anticipates a defense based on federal law would "contravene the whole trend of jurisdictional legislation by Congress, disregard the effective functioning of the federal judicial system, and distort the limited procedural purpose of the Declaratory Judgment Act." For the Supreme Court's most recent attempt at identifying the "coercive action" in order to ascertain whether the action "arises under" federal law, *see Franchise Tax Board v. Construction Laborers Vacation Trust*, 463 U.S. 1 (1983).

f.   Outer Limits of Article III

In light of *Mottley* and related decisions, the §1331 grant of "arising under" jurisdiction falls considerably short of the Article III grant and thus does not implicate the outer bounds of constitutional "arising under" jurisdiction. That question was implicated in *Textile Workers Union v. Lincoln Mills*, 353 U.S. 448 (1957), a decision also discussed in *Franchise Tax Board*. The statutory provision in *Lincoln Mills*, §301 of the Labor Management Relations Act (LMRA), conferred jurisdiction on the federal courts to adjudicate disputes under collective bargaining contracts but was silent on whether federal law or state law would govern such disputes. Prior to the LMRA, collective bargaining agreements were treated as a species of contract governed by state contract law. The Article III issue was whether Congress could create a federal forum to adjudicate issues of state law in the absence of diversity of citizenship. To meet Article III objections, prominent scholars have offered a theory of "protective jurisdiction." Wherever Congress has legislative authority to promulgate rules of decision, that greater power includes the lesser power to provide a protective federal forum for the application of state law. *See* Herbert Wechsler, *Federal Jurisdiction and the Revision of the Judicial Code*, 13 Law & Contemp. Probs. 216, 224–225 (1948); Paul J. Mishkin, *The Federal "Question" in the District Courts*, 53 Colum. L. Rev. 157, 189 (1953) (articulating somewhat narrower theory requiring presence of substantive federal law in the background of the dispute). Justice Douglas's opinion for the majority, however, sidestepped the issue by finding that federal common law would govern such disputes. Justice Frankfurter, dissenting, argued that Congress did not authorize a change in the substantive law of collective bargaining agreements and proceeded to consider and reject the protective-jurisdiction theory as inconsistent with the constitutional division of federal and state judicial power.

A similar issue arose again in connection with the Foreign Sovereign Immunities Act of 1976 (FSIA), 28 U.S.C. §§1330, 1332(a)(4), 1391(f), 1441(d), and 1602–1611, which governs suits against foreign states brought in American courts. The FSIA provides that federal district courts "shall have original jurisdiction . . . of any nonjury civil action against a foreign state . . . as to any claim . . . with respect to which the foreign state is not entitled to [sovereign] immunity" either under the occasions for immunity recognized by the FSIA or applicable international agreement. §1330(a). In *Verlinden B.V. v. Central Bank of Nigeria*, 461 U.S. 480 (1983), the Court unanimously rejected a lower court holding that the FSIA's grant of federal jurisdiction to entertain a dispute between a foreign plaintiff and a foreign state where the substantive law was not itself based on federal law exceeded Article III limits. Chief Justice Burger's opinion relied on *Osborn* for the proposition that constitutional "arising under" jurisdiction is present whenever a case "might call for the application of federal law." Here, the need to apply federal law was not "a mere speculative possibility" because it would have to be determined at the very outset whether the foreign state could invoke sovereign immunity consistent with the FSIA. *See generally* Carole E. Goldberg-Ambrose, *The Protective Jurisdiction of the Federal Courts*, 30 UCLA L. Rev. 542 (1983); Scott A. Rosenberg, Note, *The Theory of Protective Jurisdiction*, 57 N.Y.U. L. Rev. 933 (1982).

As Justice Douglas's decision in *Lincoln Mills* illustrates, Article III subject matter jurisdiction extends to actions arising under federal common law — there, the newly minted federal common law of collective bargaining agreements. Does it also extend to actions arising under customary international law? That issue arose in *Filartiga v. Pena-Irala*, 630 F.2d 876 (2d Cir. 1980), an action brought by citizens of Paraguay against a Paraguayan national for torture allegedly committed by the defendant in Paraguay in violation of universally recognized international human-rights norms. The Second Circuit held that the Alien Tort Statute (ATS), 28 U.S.C. §1350, conferred federal jurisdiction and that such jurisdiction was consistent with Article III: "The constitutional basis for the [statute] is the law of nations, which has always been part of the federal common law." 630 F.2d at 885. *See generally* Anne-Marie Burley, *The Alien Tort Statute and the Judiciary Act of 1789: A Badge of Honor*, 83 Am. J. Int'l L. 461 (1989). That view was confirmed by the Supreme Court of the United States in *Sosa v. Alvarez-Machain*, 542 U.S. 692 (2004). Although the Supreme Court did not address the Article III point directly, it did confirm that the Alien Tort Statute is a grant of jurisdiction for a limited set of actions alleging violations of the law of nations and that the law of nations is part of the federal common law. The Court has continued to narrow the scope for application of the Alien Tort Statute. In *Kiobel v. Royal Dutch Petroleum Co.*, 569 U.S. 108 (2013), the Court held that the ATS did not extend to claims arising outside the territory of the United States unless they sufficiently "touched and concerned" the United States. More recently, in *Nestle USA, Inc. v. Doe*, 141 S.Ct. 1931 (2021), the Court determined that the general corporate activity of a U.S. corporation was not sufficient to constitute a domestic application of the statute where other conduct and/or injury occurred abroad. Earlier, in *Jesner v. Arab Bank, PLC*, 138 S.Ct. 1386 (2018), the Court ruled that the creation of a private right of action against a foreign corporation under the ATS must be left to Congress, and in its absence, no such action could be brought against a foreign corporation.

Although beyond the scope of this book, Article III may also place limits on the power of Congress to assign certain federal law disputes to federal tribunals whose judges do not enjoy life tenure. *See, e.g., Commodity Futures Trading Comm'n v. Schor*, 478 U.S. 833 (1986) (administrative agency); *Northern Pipeline Construction Co. v. Marathon Pipeline Co.*, 458 U.S. 50 (1982) (bankruptcy court).

E.   *SUPPLEMENTAL JURISDICTION*

This section of the materials addresses the question whether the limited subject matter jurisdiction of the federal courts precludes authority over additional claims between plaintiffs and defendants or over third parties that, standing alone, could not be asserted in such tribunals.

NOTE ON JOINDER OF CLAIMS AND PARTIES UNDER THE FEDERAL RULES OF CIVIL PROCEDURE

We will study the Federal Rules governing joinder of claims and parties in Chapter 8. However, in order to understand the doctrine of supplemental jurisdiction, it is necessary to provide a brief introduction to those techniques here.

Litigation in the Anglo-American system was originally quite simple—in most cases a single plaintiff was permitted to sue a single defendant concerning a single matter. Litigation in the twentieth century became considerably more complex, culminating in the liberal joinder policies of the Federal Rules of Civil Procedure. Under the Federal Rules, multiple plaintiffs may assert numerous claims against multiple defendants, who are in turn permitted to assert "counterclaims" against the plaintiffs, "cross-claims" against co-parties, and to bring additional parties into the litigation.

Under the Federal Rules, a plaintiff can assert all claims plaintiff has against a defendant, regardless of whether the claims have any relationship to each other. *See* Fed. R. Civ. P. 18. Joinder of parties is also expansive but somewhat less so. Under Federal Rule 20, parties may be joined as plaintiffs or defendants only if the claims by or against the joined parties must have some connection to each other—the claims must concern the same transaction or "series of transactions" and must share a common question of law or fact.

Rule 13 authorizes a party to assert counterclaims against anyone who has asserted a claim against it. If the counterclaim "arises out of the transaction or occurrence that is the subject matter of the opposing party's claim" and does not fall within certain limitations/exceptions set forth in Rule 13(a)(1)(B) and Rule 13(a)(2), it is a compulsory counterclaim and must be asserted. Rule 13(b) permits, but does not require, the assertion of any counterclaim that is not compulsory. Parties are further permitted under Rule 13(g) to assert "cross-claims" against non-adverse parties (such as co-defendants), but only if those cross-claims are related to the original action.

A plaintiff, subject to the requirements of Rule 20, has the initial choice of whom to include as a plaintiff or defendant, but additional parties may be brought in by other parties. Rule 14 allows any party defending a claim to bring in a third-party defendant who "is or may be liable" for indemnity on that claim. For instance, a defendant-driver in an auto collision case is permitted under Rule 14 to implead as a third-party defendant the insurance company. In many states, a tortfeasor may seek indemnity against other joint tortfeasors, and thus may bring in the third-party joint tortfeasor under Rule 14. Rule 13(h) further allows a party to join additional parties to a counterclaim or cross-claim.

Under some circumstances, the joinder of certain parties is required. Rule 19(a) authorizes the court to order the joinder of a party who is necessary to accord complete relief or who, if not joined, could have its interests impaired. Thus, a defendant might be able to force additional plaintiffs or defendants to be added to the litigation.

Even if none of the parties to the litigation wants to join an additional party, a person may be able to inject himself into the litigation as an "intervenor" under Rule 24. A person may intervene as a plaintiff or defendant.

The Rules also provide some unconventional joinder techniques. Rule 23 allows a plaintiff, in some circumstances, to "represent" similarly situated claimants in a "class action." While the class members do not normally participate in the litigation, they may be bound by the judgment, and may share in the underlying recovery. Finally, Rule 22 (as well as a federal statute, 28 U.S.C. §1335) permits a plaintiff to join multiple defendants to an "interpleader" where those defendants may have competing claims to the same property held by the plaintiff. For instance, a bank may file an interpleader against all claimants to a given bank account.

However, just because a claim is authorized by the Rules does not mean that the court has jurisdiction over it. That is the issue to which we now turn.

1.   The Origins of Supplemental Jurisdiction: Pendent/Ancillary Claims

United Mine Workers of America v. Gibbs

383 U.S. 715 (1966)

Mr. Justice Brennan delivered the opinion of the Court.

Respondent Paul Gibbs was awarded compensatory and punitive damages in this action against petitioner United Mine Workers of America (UMW) for alleged violations of §303 of the Labor Management Relations Act, 1947, 61 Stat. 158, as amended,[1] and of the common law of Tennessee. The case grew out of the rivalry between the United Mine Workers and the Southern Labor Union over representation of workers in the southern Appalachian coal fields. Tennessee Consolidated Coal Company, not a party here, laid off 100 miners of the UMW's Local 5881 when it closed one of its mines in southern Tennessee during the spring of 1960. Late that summer, Grundy Company, a wholly owned subsidiary of Consolidated, hired respondent as mine superintendent to attempt to open a new mine on Consolidated's property at nearby Gray's Creek through use of members of the Southern Labor Union. As part of the arrangement, Grundy also gave respondent a contract to haul the mine's coal to the nearest railroad loading point.

On August 15 and 16, 1960, armed members of Local 5881 forcibly prevented the opening of the mine, threatening respondent and beating an organizer for the rival union. The members of the local believed Consolidated had promised them the jobs at the new mine; they insisted that if anyone would do the work, they would. . . .

Respondent lost his job as superintendent, and never entered into performance of his haulage contract. He testified that he soon began to lose other trucking contracts and mine leases he held in nearby areas. Claiming these effects to be the result of a concerted union plan against him, he sought recovery not against Local 5881 or its members, but only against petitioner, the international union. The suit was brought in the United States District Court for the Eastern District of Tennessee . . . and jurisdiction was premised on allegations of secondary boycotts under §303. The state law claim, for which jurisdiction was based upon the

---

1. Section 303 of the Labor Management Relations Act, 1947 [creates a cause of action for individuals and firms injured by unlawful union secondary boycotts].

doctrine of pendent jurisdiction, asserted "an unlawful conspiracy and an unlawful boycott aimed at him and [Grundy] to maliciously, wantonly and willfully interfere with his contract of employment and with his contract of haulage."

The trial judge refused to submit to the jury the claims of pressure intended to cause mining firms other than Grundy to cease doing business with Gibbs; he found those claims unsupported by the evidence. The jury's verdict was that the UMW had violated both §303 and state law. Gibbs was awarded $60,000 as damages under the employment contract and $14,500 under the haulage contract; he was also awarded $100,000 punitive damages. On motion, the trial court set aside the award of damages with respect to the haulage contract on the ground that damage was unproved. It also held that union pressure on Grundy to discharge respondent as supervisor would constitute only a primary dispute with Grundy, as respondent's employer, and hence was not cognizable as a claim under §303. Interference with the employment relationship was cognizable as a state claim, however, and a remitted award was sustained on the state law claim. 220 F. Supp. 871. The Court of Appeals for the Sixth Circuit affirmed. 343 F.2d 609. . . .

I

. . . The Court held in *Hurn v. Oursler*, 289 U.S. 238, that state law claims are appropriate for federal court determination if they form a separate but parallel ground for relief also sought in a substantial claim based on federal law. The Court distinguished permissible from non-permissible exercises of federal judicial power over state law claims by contrasting a case where two distinct grounds in support of a single cause of action are alleged, one only of which presents a federal question, and a case where two separate and distinct causes of action are alleged, one only of which is federal in character. In the former, where the federal question averred is not plainly wanting in substance, the federal court, even though the federal ground be not established, may nevertheless retain and dispose of the case upon the non-federal *ground*; in the latter it may not do so upon the non-federal *cause of action*. 289 U.S. at 246. The question is into which category the present action fell.

Hurn was decided in 1933, before the unification of law and equity by the Federal Rules of Civil Procedure. At the time, the meaning of "cause of action" was a subject of serious dispute; the phrase might "mean one thing for one purpose and something different for another." *United States v. Memphis Cotton Oil Co.*, 288 U.S. 62. The Court in *Hurn* identified what it meant by the term by citation of *Baltimore S.S. Co. v. Phillips*, 274 U.S. 316, a case in which "cause of action" had been used to identify the operative scope of the doctrine of *res judicata*. In that case the Court had noted that "the whole tendency of our decisions is to require a plaintiff to try his whole cause of action and his whole case at one time," 274 U.S. at 320. . . . Had the Court found a jurisdictional bar to reaching the state claim in *Hurn*, we assume that the doctrine of *res judicata* would not have been applicable in any subsequent state suit. But the citation of *Baltimore S.S. Co.* shows that the Court found that the weighty policies of judicial economy and fairness to parties reflected in *res judicata* doctrine were in themselves strong counsel for the adoption of a rule which would permit federal courts to dispose of the state as well as the federal claims.

With the adoption of the Federal Rules of Civil Procedure and the unified form of action, Fed. Rule Civ. Proc. 2, much of the controversy over "cause of action" abated. The phrase remained as the keystone of the *Hurn* test, however, and, as commentators have noted, has been the source of considerable confusion. Under the Rules, the impulse is toward entertaining the broadest possible scope of action consistent with fairness to the parties; joinder of claims, parties and remedies is strongly encouraged.[10] Yet because the *Hurn* question involves issues of jurisdiction as well as convenience, there has been some tendency to limit its application to cases in which the state and federal claims are, as in *Hurn*, "little more than the equivalent of different epithets to characterize the same group of circumstances." 289 U.S. at 246.

This limited approach is unnecessarily grudging. Pendent jurisdiction, in the sense of judicial *power*, exists whenever there is a claim "arising under [the] Constitution, the Laws of the United States, and Treaties made, or which shall be made, under their Authority . . . ," U.S. Const., Art. III, §2, and the relationship between that claim and the state claim permits the conclusion that the entire action before the court comprises but one constitutional "case." The federal claim must have substance sufficient to confer subject matter jurisdiction on the court. *Levering & Garrigiues Co. v. Morrin*, 289 U.S. 103. The state and federal claims must derive from a common nucleus of operative fact. But if, considered without regard to their federal or state character, a plaintiff's claims are such that he would ordinarily be expected to try them all in one judicial proceeding, then, assuming substantiality of the federal issues, there is *power* in federal courts to hear the whole.[13]

That power need not be exercised in every case in which it is found to exist. It has consistently been recognized that pendent jurisdiction is a doctrine of discretion, not of plaintiff's right. Its justification lies in considerations of judicial economy, convenience and fairness to litigants; if these are not present a federal court should hesitate to exercise jurisdiction over state claims, even though bound to apply state law to them. *Erie R. Co. v. Tompkins*, 304 U.S. 64. Needless decisions of state law should be avoided both as a matter of comity and to promote justice between the parties, by procuring for them a surer-footed reading of applicable law. Certainly, if the federal claims are dismissed before trial, even though not insubstantial in a jurisdictional sense, the state claims should be dismissed as well. Similarly, if it appears that the state issues substantially predominate, whether in terms of proof, of the scope of the issues raised, or of the comprehensiveness of the remedy sought, the state claims may be dismissed without prejudice and left for resolution to state tribunals. There may, on the other hand, be situations in which the state claim is so closely tied to questions of federal policy that the argument for exercise of pendent jurisdiction is particularly strong. In the present case, for example, the allowable scope of the state claim implicates the federal doctrine of preemption; while this interrelationship does not create statutory federal-question jurisdiction, *Louisville & N.R. Co. v. Mottley*, 211 U.S. 149, its existence is relevant

---

10. See, e.g., Fed. Rules Civ. Proc. 2, 18–20, 42.

13. Cf. *Amstrong Co. v. Nu-Enamel Corp.*, 305 U.S. 315, 325. Note, Problems of Parallel State and Federal Remedies, 71 Harv. L. Rev. 513, 514 (1958). While it is commonplace that the Federal Rules of Civil Procedure do not expand the jurisdiction of federal courts, they do embody "the whole tendency of our decisions . . . to require a plaintiff to try his . . . whole case at one time," *Baltimore S.S. Co. v. Phillips, supra*, and to that extent emphasize the basis of pendent jurisdiction.

to the exercise of discretion. Finally, there may be reasons independent of jurisdictional considerations, such as the likelihood of jury confusion in treating divergent legal theories of relief, that would justify separating state and federal claims for trial, Fed. Rule Civ. Proc. 42(b). If so, jurisdiction should ordinarily be refused.

The question of power will ordinarily be resolved on the pleadings. But the issue whether pendent jurisdiction has been properly assumed is one which remains open throughout the litigation. Pretrial procedures or even the trial itself may reveal a substantial hegemony of state law claims, or likelihood of jury confusion, which could not have been anticipated at the pleading stage. Although it will of course be appropriate to take account in this circumstance of the already completed course of the litigation, dismissal of the state claim might even then be merited. For example, it may appear that the plaintiff was well aware of the nature of his proofs and the relative importance of his claims; recognition of a federal court's wide latitude to decide ancillary questions of state law does not imply that it must tolerate a litigant's effort to impose upon it what is in effect only a state law case. Once it appears that a state claim constitutes the real body of a case, to which the federal claim is only an appendage, the state claim may fairly be dismissed. . . .

It is true that the §303 claims ultimately failed and that the only recovery allowed respondent was on the state claim. We cannot confidently say, however, that the federal issues were so remote or played such a minor role at the trial that in effect the state claim only was tried. Although the District Court dismissed as unproved the §303 claims that petitioner's secondary activities included attempts to induce coal operators other than Grundy to cease doing business with respondent, the court submitted the §303 claims relating to Grundy to the jury. The jury returned verdicts against petitioner on those §303 claims, and it was only on petitioner's motion for a directed verdict and a judgment n.o.v. that the verdicts on those claims were set aside. The District Judge considered the claim as to the haulage contract proved as to liability, and held it failed only for lack of proof of damages. Although there was some risk of confusing the jury in joining the state and federal claims — especially since, as will be developed, differing standards of proof of UMW involvement applied — the possibility of confusion could be lessened by employing a special verdict form, as the District Court did. Moreover, the question whether the permissible scope of the state claim was limited by the doctrine of preemption afforded a special reason for the exercise of pendent jurisdiction; the federal courts are particularly appropriate bodies for the application of preemption principles. We thus conclude that although it may be that the District Court might, in its sound discretion, have dismissed the state claim, the circumstances show no error in refusing to do so.

[The Court's discussion of the federal preemption issue and the applicability of the Norris-LaGuardia Act, 29 U.S.C. §106, is omitted.]

Moore v. New York Cotton Exchange

270 U.S. 593 (1926)

MR. JUSTICE SUTHERLAND delivered the opinion of the Court.

The Odd-Lot Cotton Exchange is an organization whose members make contracts for themselves and for customers for the future delivery of cotton in lots of not more than 100 nor less than 10 bales. The members of the New York Cotton Exchange, which is organized under a special act of the New York Legislature, c. 365, Laws 1871, p. 724, also make contracts for the purchase and sale of cotton for further delivery, either for themselves or for customers; such contracts being made only upon open *viva voce* bidding, between certain hours of the day and in the rooms of the exchange in New York City. Quotations of prices thus established are collected by the New York exchange, and, under the terms of a written agreement with that exchange, the Western Union company pays $27,500 annually for the privilege of receiving and distributing them throughout the United States, to such persons as the exchange approves. Applicants for such quotations must sign an application and agree not to use them in connection with a bucket shop[*] or to give them out to other persons. The Gold & Stock Telegraph Company, a New York corporation and a subsidiary of, and controlled by, the Western Union, is engaged in disseminating quotations of cotton prices by means of ticker service, owned and operated by it, tickers being located in exchanges, brokerage houses and elsewhere in the several states. The Odd-Lot exchange made application to the two telegraph companies for this service in the form required by the contract with the New York exchange. It was refused, the New York exchange having declined to give its consent to the installation on the ground, among others, that, after investigation, it had ascertained that the Odd-Lot had succeeded another exchange which had been convicted of conducting a bucket shop and that the Odd-Lot had in its membership many members of the convicted exchange and was organized as a cover to enable its members to engage in the same unlawful business.

Federal jurisdiction is invoked under the anti-trust laws of the United States. The bill avers that . . . the New York exchange has a monopoly upon the receipt and dissemination of cotton price quotations, through which quotations and prices of cotton, both spot and for future delivery, are influenced, guided and fixed in the exchanges and markets throughout the United States; that the contract with the Western Union is in restraint of interstate trade and commerce in cotton, and was entered into for the purpose of monopolizing and restraining that commerce. There is an attempt to allege unfair methods of competition, which may be put aside at once, since relief in such cases under the Trade Commission Act must be afforded in the first instance by the commission.

The prayer is for a decree canceling the Western Union contract, adjudging the New York Cotton Exchange to be a monopoly, restraining appellees from refusing to install a ticker and furnish the Odd-Lot and its members, as they do others, with continuous cotton quotations, and for other relief.

The answer, in addition to denials and affirmative defensive matter, sets up a counterclaim to the effect that the Odd-Lot, though it had been refused permission to use the quotations of the New York exchange, was purloining them, or receiving them from some person who was purloining them, and giving them out to its members, who were distributing them to bucket shops, with the consequent

---

* A *bucket shop* was the name given to a form of securities fraud in which someone posing as a securities broker would take money from a customer for the purchase of securities and then simply pocket the money, throwing the purchase order in a "bucket." — EDS.

impairment of the value of appellees' property therein. An injunction against the continuance of this practice was asked.

Both parties moved for interlocutory injunctions. The district court denied appellant's motion and granted that of appellees. 291 F. 681. Upon appeal, both orders were affirmed by the Circuit Court of Appeals. 296 F. 61. . . .

The decree granting an injunction upon the counterclaim is challenged on the grounds, shortly stated: (1) That the court, having dismissed the bill for lack of jurisdictional facts, should have dismissed the counterclaim also, there being no independent basis of jurisdiction; (2) that the counterclaim does not arise out of any transaction which is the subject-matter of the suit; and (3) that the decree is not justified by the allegations of the counterclaim or the proof.

1. We do not understand that the dismissal was for the reason that there was an absence of jurisdiction to entertain the bill. What the court held was that the facts alleged were insufficient to establish a case under the Anti-Trust Act. Whether the objection that a bill of complaint does not state a case within the terms of a federal statute challenges the jurisdiction or goes only to the merits, is not always easy to determine. . . .

Here facts are set forth in a serious attempt to justify the claim that the federal statute has been violated, and, while we hold them to be insufficient to sustain the claim, we are not prepared to say that they are so obviously insufficient as to cause it to be without color of merit and in effect no claim at all. We think there is enough in the bill to call for the exercise of the jurisdiction of a federal court to decide, upon the merits, the issue of the legal sufficiency of the allegations to make out the claim of federal right. This was evidently the view of the court below, and we construe its mandate as a direction to dismiss the bill on the merits and not for want of jurisdiction.

2. Equity rule 30 in part provides:

> The answer must state in short and simple form any counter-claim arising out of the transaction which is the subject matter of the suit, and may, without cross-bill, set up any set-off or counter-claim against the plaintiff which might be the subject of an independent suit in equity against him, and such set-off or counter-claim, so set up, shall have the same effect as a cross-suit, so as to enable the court to pronounce a final decree in the same suit on both the original and the cross-claims.

Two classes of counterclaims thus are provided for: (a) one "arising out of the transaction which is the subject matter of the suit," which must be pleaded, and (b) another "which might be the subject of an independent suit in equity" and which may be brought forward at the option of the defendant. We are of opinion that this counterclaim comes within the first branch of the rule, and we need not consider the point that, under the second branch, federal jurisdiction independent of the original bill must appear, as was held in *Cleveland Engineering Co. v. Galion D. M. Truck Co.*, 243 Fed. 405, 407.

The bill sets forth the contract with the Western Union and the refusal of the New York exchange to allow appellant to receive the continuous cotton quotations, and asks a mandatory injunction to compel appellees to furnish them. The answer admits the refusal and justifies it. The counterclaim sets up that, nevertheless, appellant is purloining or otherwise illegally obtaining them, and asks that this practice be enjoined. "Transaction" is a word of flexible meaning. It may comprehend a series of many occurrences, depending not so much upon the immediateness of their connection as upon their logical relationship. The refusal to furnish the quotations is one of the links in the chain which constitutes the transaction upon which appellant here bases its cause of action. It is an important part of the transaction constituting the subject-matter of the counterclaim. It is the one circumstance without which neither party would have found it necessary to seek relief. Essential facts alleged by appellant enter into and constitute in part the cause of action set forth in the counterclaim. That they are not precisely identical, or that the counterclaim embraces additional allegations, as, for example, that appellant is unlawfully getting the quotations, does not matter. To hold otherwise would be to rob this branch of the rule of all serviceable meaning, since the facts relied upon by the plaintiff rarely, if ever, are, in all particulars, the same as those constituting the defendant's counterclaim. . . .

So close is the connection between the case sought to be stated in the bill and that set up in the counterclaim, that it only needs the failure of the former to establish a foundation for the latter; but the relief afforded by the dismissal of the bill is not complete without an injunction restraining appellant from continuing to obtain by stealthy appropriation what the court had held it could not have by judicial compulsion.

NOTES AND QUESTIONS

1. *Understanding the Terminology.* Both *Gibbs* and *Moore* present questions about the reach of federal subject matter jurisdiction when the case before the court includes claims based on both federal and state law. *Gibbs* presents the situation of a plaintiff who asserts both federal and state claims against a defendant, and *Moore* involves assertion of a federal claim by plaintiff and a counterclaim by defendant. You will also note a difference in terminology in the two cases — *Gibbs* talks about *pendent* jurisdiction and *Moore* refers to the court's *ancillary* jurisdiction.

There has always been some confusion about the difference between the terms *ancillary* and *pendent.* Traditionally, the term *ancillary jurisdiction* was used to describe a variety of situations whereby the federal court adjudicated an entire case or controversy when it had subject matter jurisdiction over only a part of it. *See, e.g., Freeman v. Howe,* 65 U.S. (24 How.) 450 (1861), which involved the replevy of goods by a state sheriff from a U.S. marshal who had seized the goods pursuant to a federal proceeding. Because the replevin action was related to property under the control of the federal court, the replevin was related to and dependent upon the federal proceeding; the federal court was said to have ancillary jurisdiction over the replevin claim even though neither diversity of citizenship nor a federal claim was present.

In the context of various joinder situations, ancillary jurisdiction offers a basis upon which a federal court that has subject matter jurisdiction over certain claims — whether on diversity or federal-question grounds — can adjudicate non-federal claims when they are incidental or related to the federal "anchor" claim. The term *pendent jurisdiction* seems to have been used to describe one particular exercise of this type of jurisdiction — the *Gibbs*-type situation where the plaintiff asserts a claim based on federal law against a nondiverse defendant and seeks to have a related state claim adjudicated in the same lawsuit. If one views the terms in this way, *pendent* jurisdiction is really a sub-category of *ancillary* jurisdiction.

Gradually, however, the terms came to have discrete meanings such that pendent jurisdiction referred to a plaintiff's joinder of a related state claim with a claim based on a federal question, and ancillary jurisdiction referred to the federal court's willingness to hear a jurisdictionally defective claim (whether asserted as a claim, counterclaim, or third-party claim) because of its close relationship to the plaintiff's anchor federal claim (whether based on federal-question or diversity jurisdiction). Thus, counterclaims, cross-claims, and third-party claims, as well as the joinder of parties, some of whom might not meet the jurisdictional amount in a diversity case, were captured by the concept of ancillary jurisdiction.

With the enactment of 28 U.S.C. §1367 in 1990, the term *supplemental jurisdiction* has been adopted to embrace both pendent and ancillary jurisdiction.

2. Compare the respective characterizations of the scope of pendent and ancillary jurisdiction in the two Supreme Court decisions. In *Gibbs*, in the context of joinder of claims by plaintiff, the Supreme Court states that the federal courts have power to hear the case when the "state and federal claims . . . derive from a common nucleus of operative facts." The Court in *Moore*, in the context of a counterclaim by the defendant, refers to claims that arise out of the transaction that is the subject matter of the suit and the "logical relationship" between the claim and the counterclaim. Are the differences in formulation only a matter of semantics or do they suggest a difference in the scope of the jurisdiction? Is there any reason for the scope of supplemental jurisdiction in the one situation to be different from the scope of supplemental jurisdiction in the other?

Moore equates the existence of ancillary (now supplemental) jurisdiction with the status of the counterclaim as a compulsory one. Should the test for what is a compulsory counterclaim necessarily be the same as the test for the exercise of supplemental/ancillary jurisdiction? After all, in asking whether the defendant is required to assert this particular counterclaim, the issue is whether the defendant should be forced to assert the claim in the forum at the time of the plaintiff's choosing on the pain of being precluded from ever asserting the claim. But in asking about the exercise of supplemental jurisdiction where the defendant has opted to assert the counterclaim, the only question is whether there is a sufficient connection with the main claim to make it consistent with a single "constitutional case." Has *Moore* confused the two questions?

3. *The Source of the Power.* Original federal court jurisdiction depends not only on the constitutional grant of jurisdiction in Article III but also on the particular grant of jurisdiction by Congress. *See, e.g.,* 28 U.S.C. §§1331, 1334, 1337, and 1338. In its discussion of pendent jurisdiction in *Gibbs*, the Court refers to the scope of judicial power as authorized in Art. III, §2 of the Constitution of the United States. The constitutional language embraces "all Cases . . . arising under federal law"; ergo the "common nucleus of operative facts" is said to offer parameters of one "constitutional case." But what about the language of the relevant statute, 28 U.S.C. §1331? Is the reach of 28 U.S.C. §1331 in authorizing pendent jurisdiction the same as that of Article III of the Constitution? *Compare Louisville & Nashville R.R. Co. v. Mottley, supra.* Or is the point only that the term "civil action" in 28 U.S.C. §1331 is coextensive with a constitutional "case"?

4. *The "Cause of Action" Test.* In *Hurn v. Oursler*, cited in *Gibbs*, the plaintiff sued to enjoin production of a play on the federal grounds of (1) copyright infringement, and state law theories of (2) unfair competition with his copyrighted play and (3) unfair

competition with a revised, uncopyrighted version of the play. The Court found jurisdiction over grounds (1) and (2) as "but different grounds asserted in support of the same cause of action," but held that ground (3) asserted a "separate and distinct" cause of action falling outside of federal jurisdiction. As Justice Brennan observes in *Gibbs*, the *Hurn* decision was difficult to apply because jurisdiction was made to turn on the elusive concept of "cause of action" rather than policies of efficient adjudication. *Hurn* created further practical difficulties because copyright actions can only be brought in federal court, thus necessitating a separate state court action for separate state causes of action arising out of the same factual dispute. To what extent does *Gibbs* change *Hurn*'s "unnecessarily grudging" approach? In 1948 Congress conferred jurisdiction on the federal courts to hear state-law unfair competition claims when joined with "a substantial and related claim" under the federal copyright, patent, or trademark laws. 28 U.S.C. §1338(b). Is the statutory test for pendent-claim jurisdiction under §1338(b) any different from the test adopted in *Gibbs*? Does the fact that federal copyright and patent claims may be heard only in federal court affect the interpretation of §1338(b)?

5. *Justifications for Pendent Jurisdiction.* As Justice Brennan recognizes, the federal court's pendent-claim jurisdiction cannot be explained in terms of strict necessity or the inherent power of a tribunal. If federal jurisdiction had not been found over Gibbs's state tortious interference claim, Gibbs's later assertion of that claim would not have been precluded by *res judicata*—a doctrine that bars relitigation of a cause of action that has already been adjudicated on the merits. Moreover, given the presumptive concurrent jurisdiction of the state courts, piecemeal litigation need not have occurred; a state court action would have provided a forum for adjudicating both Gibbs's federal and state claims. Nevertheless, are there reasons why litigants who have a federal cause of action should not be put to this choice? Does the Court's reference to the possibility of federal preemption of the state claim provide an independent justification for ensuring access to federal court? Does the policy of minimizing the supervisory burden of the Supreme Court justify the *Gibbs* approach? For criticism of *Gibbs*, *see* Michael Shakman, *The New Pendent Jurisdiction of the Federal Courts*, 20 Stan. L. Rev. 262 (1968).

6. *The Role of Discretion.* Ordinarily, when a court has jurisdiction to hear a case, it does not have discretion to refuse to hear the case. Yet, in the *Gibbs* context, the decision to exercise pendent-claim jurisdiction appears to be committed to the district court's discretion. Does the Court explain why? Is the exercise of discretion standardless? Curiously, the issue of discretion is conspicuously absent from the Supreme Court's discussion in *Moore*. Does that mean that there is no such discretion with respect to related counterclaims?

Under what circumstances would a court exceed its discretion in entertaining the pendent state claim? What if the latter claim raises a novel question of state law? What if it entails resort to a fact-finding procedure, say, the use of a jury trial, that would not be available if the suit had been premised on the federal claim alone?

Is it always the case, as the Court seems to suggest, that if the federal claim has been dismissed before trial, the district court should decline discretionary jurisdiction over the nonfederal claim? What if the statute of limitations would now bar a new suit on the nonfederal claim?

7. *Stating a Colorable Claim.* Given *Bell v. Hood, supra* p. 338, how difficult would it be for a plaintiff to allege a sufficiently colorable federal claim for the purpose of obtaining a federal forum for an essentially state law dispute? Could the district court

proceed to decide the state law claim after finding the federal claim jurisdictionally adequate without ever reaching the merits of the jurisdiction-conferring claim?

2. *Additional Parties*

Owen Equipment & Erection Co. v. Kroger

437 U.S. 365 (1978)

MR. JUSTICE STEWART delivered the opinion of the Court. . . .

I

On January 18, 1972, James Kroger was electrocuted when the boom of a steel crane next to which he was walking came too close to a high-tension electric power line. The respondent (his widow, who is the administratrix of his estate) filed a wrongful-death action in the United States District Court for the District of Nebraska against the Omaha Public Power District (OPPD). Her complaint alleged that OPPD's negligent construction, maintenance, and operation of the power line had caused Kroger's death. Federal jurisdiction was based on diversity of citizenship, since the respondent was a citizen of Iowa and OPPD was a Nebraska corporation.

OPPD then filed a third-party complaint pursuant to Fed. Rule Civ. Proc. 14(a)[2],[*] against the petitioner, Owen Equipment and Erection Co. (Owen), alleging that the crane was owned and operated by Owen, and that Owen's negligence had been the proximate cause of Kroger's death.[3] OPPD later moved for summary

---

2. Rule 14(a) provides in relevant part:

> At any time after commencement of the action a defending party, as a third-party plaintiff, may cause a summons and complaint to be served upon a person not a party to the action who is or may be liable to him for all or part of the plaintiff's claim against him. . . . The person served with the summons and third-party complaint, hereinafter called the third-party defendant, shall make his defenses to the third-party plaintiff's claim as provided in Rule 12 and his counterclaims against the third-party plaintiff and cross-claims against other third-party defendants as provided in Rule 13. The third-party defendant may assert against the plaintiff any defenses which the third-party plaintiff has to the plaintiff's claim. The third-party defendant may also assert any claim against the plaintiff arising out of the transaction or occurrence that is the subject matter of the plaintiff's claim against the third-party plaintiff. The plaintiff may assert any claim against the third-party defendant arising out of the transaction or occurrence that is the subject matter of the plaintiff's claim against the third-party plaintiff, and the third-party defendant thereupon shall assert his defenses as provided in Rule 12 and his counter-claims and cross-claims as provided in Rule 13.

* Rule 14(a) discussed throughout the case was restyled in the 2007 amendments and has been subdivided into various subdivisions. — EDS.

3. Under Rule 14(a), a third-party defendant may not be impleaded merely because he may be liable to the *plaintiff.* See n. 2, *supra,* see also Advisory Committee's Notes on 1946 Amendment to Fed. Rule Civ. Proc. 14, 28 U.S.C. App., pp. 7752–7753. While the third-party complaint in this case alleged merely that Owen's negligence caused Kroger's death, and the basis of Owen's alleged liability to OPPD is nowhere spelled out, OPPD evidently relied upon the state common-law right of contribution among joint tortfeasors. See *Dairyland Ins. Co. v. Mumert*, 212 N.W.2d 436, 438 (Iowa); *Best v. Yerkes*, 247 Iowa 800, 77 N.W.2d 23. The petitioner has never challenged the propriety of the third-party complaint as such.

judgment on the respondent's complaint against it. While this motion was pending, the respondent was granted leave to file an amended complaint naming Owen as an additional defendant. Thereafter, the District Court granted OPPD's motion for summary judgment in an unreported opinion.[4] The case thus went to trial between the respondent and the petitioner alone.

The respondent's amended complaint alleged that Owen was "a Nebraska corporation with its principal place of business in Nebraska." Owen's answer admitted that it was "a corporation organized and existing under the laws of the State of Nebraska," and denied every other allegation of the complaint. On the third day of trial, however, it was disclosed that the petitioner's principal place of business was in Iowa, not Nebraska,[5] and that the petitioner and the respondent were thus both citizens of Iowa.[6] The petitioner then moved to dismiss the complaint for lack of jurisdiction. The District Court reserved decision on the motion, and the jury thereafter returned a verdict in favor of the respondent. In an unreported opinion issued after the trial, the District Court denied the petitioner's motion to dismiss the complaint.

The judgment was affirmed on appeal. . . .

II

It is undisputed that there was no independent basis of federal jurisdiction over the respondent's state-law tort action against the petitioner, since both are citizens of Iowa. And although Fed. Rule Civ. Proc. 14(a) permits a plaintiff to assert a claim against a third-party defendant, see n. 2, *supra*, it does not purport to say whether or not such a claim requires an independent basis of federal jurisdiction. Indeed, it could not determine that question, since it is axiomatic that the Federal Rules of Civil Procedure do not create or withdraw federal jurisdiction.[7] . . .

It is apparent that *Gibbs* delineated the constitutional limits of federal judicial power. But even if it be assumed that the District Court in the present case had constitutional power to decide the respondent's lawsuit against the petitioner,[10] . . . it does not follow that the decision of the Court of Appeals was correct. Constitutional

---

4. Judgment was entered pursuant to Fed. Rule Civ. Proc. 54(b), and the Court of Appeals affirmed. *Kroger v. Omaha Public Power District*, 523 F.2d 161 (CA8).

5. The problem apparently was one of geography. Although the Missouri River generally marks the boundary between Iowa and Nebraska, Carter Lake, Iowa, where the accident occurred and where Owen had its main office, lies west of the river, adjacent to Omaha, Neb. Apparently the river once avulsed at one of its bends, cutting Carter Lake off from the rest of Iowa.

6. Title 28 U.S.C. §1332(c) provides that "[f]or the purposes of [diversity jurisdiction] . . . a corporation shall be deemed a citizen of any State by which it has been incorporated and of the State where it has its principal place of business."

7. Fed. Rule Civ. Proc. 82; see *Snyder v. Harris*, 394 U.S. 332; *Sibbach v. Wilson & Co.*, 312 U.S. 1, 10.

10. Federal jurisdiction in *Gibbs* was based upon the existence of a question of federal law. The Court of Appeals in the present case believed that the "common nucleus of operative fact" test also determines the outer boundaries of constitutionally permissible federal jurisdiction when that jurisdiction is based upon diversity of citizenship. We may assume without deciding that the Court of Appeals was correct in this regard. . . .

power is merely the first hurdle that must be overcome in determining that a federal court has jurisdiction over a particular controversy. For the jurisdiction of the federal courts is limited not only by the provisions of Art. III of the Constitution, but also by Acts of Congress. . . .

That statutory law as well as the Constitution may limit a federal court's jurisdiction over nonfederal claims[11] is well illustrated by two recent decisions of this Court, *Aldinger v. Howard*, 427 U.S. 1, and *Zahn v. International Paper Co.*, 414 U.S. 291.[12] . . .

Aldinger and *Zahn* cases thus make clear that a finding that federal and non-federal claims arise from a "common nucleus of operative fact," the test of *Gibbs*, does not end the inquiry into whether a federal court has power to hear the non-federal claims along with the federal ones. Beyond this constitutional minimum, there must be an examination of the posture in which the nonfederal claim is asserted and of the specific statute that confers jurisdiction over the federal claim, in order to determine whether "Congress in [that statute] has . . . expressly or by implication negated" the exercise of jurisdiction over the particular nonfederal claim. *Aldinger v. Howard, supra*, at 18.

III

The relevant statute in this case, 28 U.S.C. §1332(a)(1), confers upon federal courts jurisdiction over "civil actions where the matter in controversy exceeds the sum or value of $10,000 . . . and is between . . . citizens of different States." This statute and its predecessors have consistently been held to require complete diversity of citizenship. That is, diversity jurisdiction does not exist unless *each* defendant is a citizen of a different State from *each* plaintiff. . . .

Thus it is clear that the respondent could not originally have brought suit in federal court naming Owen and OPPD as codefendants, since citizens of Iowa would have been on both sides of the litigation. Yet the identical lawsuit resulted when she amended her complaint. Complete diversity was destroyed just as surely as if she had sued Owen initially. In either situation, in the plain language of the statute, the "matter in controversy" could not be "between . . . citizens of different States."

It is a fundamental precept that federal courts are courts of limited jurisdiction. The limits upon federal jurisdiction, whether imposed by the Constitution or by Congress, must be neither disregarded nor evaded. Yet under the reasoning

---

11. As used in this opinion, the term "nonfederal claim" means one as to which there is no independent basis for federal jurisdiction. Conversely, a "federal claim" means one as to which an independent basis for federal jurisdiction exists.

12. In *Monell v. New York City Dept. of Social Services*, 436 U.S. 658, we have overruled *Monroe v. Pape*, 365 U.S. 167, insofar as it held that political subdivisions are never amenable to suit under 42 U.S.C. §1983—the basis of the holding in *Aldinger* that 28 U.S.C. §1343(3) does not allow pendent jurisdiction of a state-law claim against a county. But *Monell* in no way qualifies the holding of *Aldinger* that the jurisdictional questions presented in a case such as this one are statutory as well as constitutional, a point on which the dissenters in *Aldinger* agreed with the Court. See 427 U.S. at 22 n. 3, Brennan, J., joined by Marshall and Blackmun, JJ., dissenting.

of the Court of Appeals in this case, a plaintiff could defeat the statutory requirement of complete diversity by the simple expedient of suing only those defendants
who were of diverse citizenship and waiting for them to implead nondiverse defendants.[17] If, as the Court of Appeals thought, a "common nucleus of operative fact"
were the only requirement for ancillary jurisdiction in a diversity case, there would
be no principled reason why the respondent in this case could not have joined her
cause of action against Owen in her original complaint as ancillary to her claim
against OPPD. Congress' requirement of complete diversity would thus have been
evaded completely.

It is true, as the Court of Appeals noted, that the exercise of ancillary jurisdiction over nonfederal claims has often been upheld in situations involving
impleader, cross-claims or counterclaims. But in determining whether jurisdiction
over a nonfederal claim exists, the context in which the nonfederal claim is asserted
is crucial. See *Aldinger v. Howard*, 427 U.S. at 14. And the claim here arises in a setting quite different from the kinds of nonfederal claims that have been viewed in
other cases as falling within the ancillary jurisdiction of the federal courts.

First, the nonfederal claim in this case was simply not ancillary to the federal
one in the same sense that, for example, the impleader by a defendant of a third-
party defendant always is. A third-party complaint depends at least in part upon the
resolution of the primary lawsuit. See n. 3, *supra*. Its relation to the original complaint
is thus not mere factual similarity but logical dependence. Cf. *Moore v. New York Cotton
Exchange*, 270 U.S. 593, 610. The respondent's claim against the petitioner, however,
was entirely separate from her original claim against OPPD, since the petitioner's liability to her depended not at all upon whether or not OPPD was also liable. Far from
being an ancillary and dependent claim, it was a new and independent one.

Second, the nonfederal claim here was asserted by the plaintiff, who voluntarily chose to bring suit upon a state-law claim in a federal court. By contrast,
ancillary jurisdiction typically involves claims by a defending party haled into court
against his will, or by another person whose rights might be irretrievably lost unless
he could assert them in an ongoing action in a federal court. A plaintiff cannot
complain if ancillary jurisdiction does not encompass all of his possible claims in
a case such as this one, since it is he who has chosen the federal rather than the
state forum and must thus accept its limitations. "[T]he efficiency plaintiff seeks so
avidly is available without question in the state courts." *Kenrose Mfg. Co. v. Fred Whitaker Co.*, 512 F.2d 890, 894 (CA4).[20]

---

17. This is not an unlikely hypothesis, since a defendant in a tort suit such as this one
would surely try to limit his liability by impleading any joint tortfeasors for indemnity or contribution. Some commentators have suggested that the possible abuse of third-party practice
could be dealt with under 28 U.S.C. §1359, which forbids collusive attempts to create federal
jurisdiction. . . . The dissenting opinion today also expresses this view. But there is nothing
necessarily collusive about a plaintiff's selectively suing only those tortfeasors of diverse citizenship, or about the named defendants' desire to implead joint tortfeasors. Nonetheless,
the requirement of complete diversity would be eviscerated by such a course of events.

20. Whether Iowa's statute of limitations would now bar an action by the respondent
in an Iowa court is, of course, entirely a matter of state law. See Iowa Code §614.10 (1977).
Compare 558 F.2d at 420, with *id.* at 432 n. 42 (Bright, J., dissenting); cf. *Burnett v. New York
Central R. R. Co.*, 380 U.S. 424, 431–432, and n. 9.

It is not unreasonable to assume that, in generally requiring complete diversity, Congress did not intend to confine the jurisdiction of federal courts so inflexibly that they are unable to protect legal rights or effectively to resolve an entire, logically entwined lawsuit. Those practical needs are the basis of the doctrine of ancillary jurisdiction. But neither the convenience of litigants nor considerations of judicial economy can suffice to justify extension of the doctrine of ancillary jurisdiction to a plaintiff's cause of action against a citizen of the same State in a diversity case. Congress has established the basic rule that diversity jurisdiction exists under 28 U.S.C. §1332 only when there is complete diversity of citizenship. "The policy of the statute calls for its strict construction." *Healy v. Ratta*, 292 U.S. 263. . . . To allow the requirement of complete diversity to be circumvented as it was in this case would simply flout the congressional command.

MR. JUSTICE WHITE, with whom MR. JUSTICE BRENNAN joins, dissenting. . . .

The majority . . . brushes aside . . . considerations of convenience, judicial economy, and fairness because it concludes that recognizing ancillary jurisdiction over a plaintiff's claim against a third-party defendant would permit the plaintiff to circumvent the complete-diversity requirement and thereby "flout the congressional command."[4] Since the plaintiff in such a case does not bring the third-party defendant into the suit, however, there is no occasion for deliberate circumvention of the diversity requirement, absent collusion with the defendant. In the case of such collusion, of which there is absolutely no indication here,[5] the court can dismiss the action under the authority of 28 U.S.C. §1359. In the absence of such collusion, there is no reason to adopt an absolute rule prohibiting the plaintiff from asserting those claims that he may properly assert against the third-party defendant pursuant to Fed. Rule Civ. Proc. 14(a). The plaintiff in such a situation brings suit against the defendant only with absolutely no assurance that the defendant will decide or be able to implead a particular third-party defendant. Since the plaintiff has no control over the defendant's decision to implead a third party, the fact that he could not have originally sued that party in federal court should be irrelevant. Moreover, the fact that a plaintiff in some cases may be able to foresee the subsequent chain of events leading to the impleader does not seem to me

---

4. It is true that prior to trial OPPD was dismissed as a party to the suit and that, as we indicated in *Gibbs*, the dismissal prior to trial of the federal claim will generally require the dismissal of the nonfederal claim as well. See 383 U.S. at 726. Given the unusual facts of the present case, however—in particular, the fact that the actual location of Owens' principal place of business was not revealed until the third day of trial—fairness to the parties would lead me to conclude that the District Court did not abuse its discretion in retaining jurisdiction over Mrs. Kroger's claim against Owen. Under the Court's disposition, of course, it would not matter whether or not the federal claim is tried, for in either situation the court would have no jurisdiction over the plaintiff's non-federal claim against the third-party defendant.

5. When Mrs. Kroger brought suit, it was believed that Owen was a citizen of Nebraska, not Iowa. Therefore, had she desired at that time to make Owen a party to the suit, she would have done so directly by naming Owen as a defendant.

to be a sufficient reason to declare that a district court does not have the power
to exercise ancillary jurisdiction over the plaintiff's claims against the third-party
defendant.[7]

NOTES AND QUESTIONS

1. *The Impleader Backdrop of* Kroger. *Kroger* arose in the context of a procedure
known as *impleader,* which permits a defendant to bring in a third party who, either
by agreement or operation of law, is claimed to owe an indemnification obligation
to the defendant. The antecedents of impleader can be found in the common law
practice of *vouching in*: *B,* whose title was placed in issue in a lawsuit by *A,* would
give notice to *C,* who had sold the property to *B* and warranted that good title had
been conveyed. The purpose of the notice was to bind *C* to the determination of
the issue of *B*'s title in the *A v. B* lawsuit. Impleader pursuant to Rule 14 involves the
joinder of *B*'s indemnitor or warrantor as a formal third party to the action.

Certainly prior to *Kroger,* the lower courts had held uniformly that the
impleader/third-party complaint did not require an independent basis of federal
jurisdiction. Hence, it was not essential that there be an "arising under" claim or
diversity between the defendant/third-party plaintiff and the indemnitor/third-
party defendant, or a showing of any particular amount in controversy. *Kroger,*
which involved a claim by the original plaintiff against the third-party defendant,
as authorized by Rule 14(a) (now Rule 14(a)(3) in the restyled Rule) purports to
leave undisturbed the applicability of ancillary jurisdiction to impleader practice.
Two bases for treating impleader differently are offered: (1) impleader is invoked
by a defendant rather than a plaintiff; and (2) impleader is "logically dependent"
on the outcome of the main action, in the sense that the third party's liability is
triggered by a finding of liability in the main action. Must both of these conditions
be present for ancillary jurisdiction to be invoked or would either, standing alone,
suffice? Is it clear why either of these grounds is important?

2. Soon after *Gibbs* was decided, a number of lower courts began to hold that
the "common nucleus of operative facts" test also applied to a plaintiff's assertion of nonfederal claims against additional, nondiverse parties—what has been
termed "pendent party jurisdiction." However, the Supreme Court in *Aldinger v.
Howard* (cited in *Kroger*), made clear that even where the *Gibbs* test was met, policies
in the jurisdiction-conferring (or "anchor") statute might preclude pendent jurisdiction over additional parties. *Aldinger* involved a federal civil rights claim under
28 U.S.C. §1343 and §1983 against local government officials, coupled with a state
claim based on a theory of *respondeat superior* against the local government. The

---

7. Under the *Gibbs* analysis, recognition of the district court's power to hear a plaintiff's
nonfederal claim against a third-party defendant in a diversity suit would not mean that the
court would be required to entertain such claims in all cases. The district court would have
the discretion to dismiss the nonfederal claim if it concluded that the interests of judicial
economy, convenience, and fairness would not be served by the retention of the claim in the
federal lawsuit. See *Gibbs,* 383 U.S. at 726. Accordingly, the majority's concerns that lead it to
conclude that ancillary jurisdiction should not be recognized in the present situation could
be met on a case-by-case basis, rather than by the absolute rule it adopts.

Supreme Court reasoned that pendent jurisdiction could not be used to circumvent the exclusion of local governmental defendants from the statute. *See* David P. Currie, *Pendent Parties*, 45 U. Chi. L. Rev. 753 (1978).

3. *Kroger* appears to follow the *Aldinger* rationale. (However, note that the third-party defendant was not initially joined by the original plaintiff in *Kroger*. Only after the original defendant brought in the third-party plaintiff did plaintiff assert an additional claim against the third-party defendant.) The Supreme Court concluded that the policies of §1332 "negated" the exercise of jurisdiction over Kroger's amended complaint. What evidence did the Court adduce to support that conclusion? Admittedly, *Strawbridge* requires complete diversity. But was Kroger's lawsuit against OPPD artificially structured so as to circumvent *Strawbridge*? A plaintiff can choose to sue a single joint tortfeasor without joining all others who may have contributed to the injury. Why, as the dissent suggests, doesn't §1359 offer sufficient protection against the collusive manufacture of diversity jurisdiction?

One way to answer the dissent is to consider the impact that allowing supplemental jurisdiction over Kroger's claim against Owen would have on the continued vitality of *Strawbridge*'s complete diversity requirement. In the absence of the kind of blanket prohibition imposed by *Kroger*, wouldn't plaintiffs be able to circumvent *Strawbridge* easily, even without collusion? Couldn't Mrs. Kroger reasonably anticipate that OPPD was likely to implead all joint tortfeasors?

4. What if it was Owen that asserted a claim against Kroger arising out of the same underlying series of events as Kroger's claim? *See, e.g., Revere Copper & Brass, Inc. v. Aetna Cas. & Sur. Co.*, 426 F.2d 709 (5th Cir. 1970). Note that such claims are additional claims that come within Rule 14 (specifically, Rule 14(a)(2)(D) in the restyled Rule), but the Rule cannot confer subject matter jurisdiction. After the decision in *Kroger*, would the district court have ancillary jurisdiction over such a claim? If so, could Kroger at this point amend her complaint to assert a related claim against Owen?

5. Note that Mrs. Kroger's claim against Owen went to trial after OPPD, the diverse defendant, had been dismissed from the litigation. Recall the Court's admonition in *Gibbs*: "Certainly, if the federal claims are dismissed before trial . . . the state claims should be dismissed as well." Why didn't the *Kroger* Court base its holding on this factor? Would the result in *Kroger* have been any different if OPPD had remained in the litigation?

FINLEY v. UNITED STATES

In the wake of *Kroger* and *Aldinger*, there was considerable speculation about the continued viability of any form of pendent party jurisdiction. *Kroger* clearly foreclosed pendent/ancillary jurisdiction over claims by a plaintiff in diversity against any nondiverse party; *Aldinger* similarly forbid pendent party jurisdiction in federal-question cases where assertion of jurisdiction over the nonfederal claim was thought to frustrate congressional intent.

Much of that speculation was laid to rest by the Court's decision in *Finley v. United States*, 490 U.S. 545 (1989). *Finley* arose out of an airplane crash at a San Diego airport. Plaintiff, the spouse and mother of the victims, asserted claims in federal court under the Federal Tort Claims Act against the Federal Aviation

Administration for negligent design and maintenance of the runway lights and the air traffic control system. Federal courts have exclusive jurisdiction over such claims under the Act. Plaintiff asserted additional, state-based tort claims against the City of San Diego and the San Diego Gas and Electric Company. There was no independent basis for federal jurisdiction over these additional claims.

The case thus provided the strongest possible context for pendent party jurisdiction. Unlike Mrs. Kroger, plaintiff did not "choose" federal over state court; she had no choice. Moreover, unless the federal court entertained the state claims, plaintiff would be forced to split her claims between state and federal court, since the state court lacked jurisdiction over the federal claims. Mrs. Kroger, in contrast, could have asserted all of her claims in state court.

The Court nonetheless held that the court lacked authority to assert jurisdiction over the state claims against the nonfederal defendants. The decision, written by Justice Scalia, severely constrained the reach of pendent party jurisdiction:

> Analytically, petitioner's case is fundamentally different from *Gibbs* in that it brings into question what has become known as pendent-party jurisdiction, that is, jurisdiction over parties not named in any claim that is independently cognizable by the federal court. We may assume, without deciding, that the constitutional criterion for pendent-party jurisdiction is analogous to the constitutional criterion for pendent-claim jurisdiction, and that petitioner's state-law claims pass that test. Our cases show, however, that with respect to the addition of parties, as opposed to the addition of only claims, we will not assume that the full constitutional power has been congressionally authorized, and will not read jurisdictional statutes broadly. . . .
>
> The most significant element of "posture" or of "context" . . . in the present case (as in *Zahn, Aldinger*, and *Kroger*) is precisely that the added claims involve added parties over whom no independent basis of jurisdiction exists. While in a narrow class of cases a federal court may assert authority over such a claim "ancillary" to jurisdiction otherwise properly vested — for example, when an additional party has a claim upon contested assets within the court's exclusive control, . . . or when necessary to give effect to the court's judgment, see, e.g., *Local Loan Co. v. Hunt*, 292 U.S. 234, 239 (1934) . . . — we have never reached such a result solely on the basis that the *Gibbs* test has been met. And little more basis than that can be relied upon by petitioner here. As in *Kroger*, the relationship between petitioner's added claims and the original complaint is one of "mere factual similarity," which is of no consequence since "neither the convenience of the litigants nor considerations of judicial economy can suffice to justify extension of the doctrine of ancillary jurisdiction," 437 U.S. at 376-377. It is true that here, unlike in *Kroger*, see *id.* at 376, the party seeking to bring the added claims had little choice but to be in federal rather than state court, since the FTCA permits the Federal Government to be sued only there. But that alone is not enough. . . .
>
> As we noted at the outset, our cases do not display an entirely consistent approach with respect to the necessity that jurisdiction be explicitly conferred. The *Gibbs* line of cases was a departure from prior practice,

and a departure that we have no intent to limit or impair. But *Aldinger* indicated that the *Gibbs* approach would not be extended to the pendent-party field, and we decide today to retain that line. Whatever we say regarding the scope of jurisdiction conferred by a particular statute can of course be changed by Congress. What is of paramount importance is that Congress be able to legislate against a background of clear interpretive rules, so that it may know the effect of the language it adopts. All our cases — *Zahn, Aldinger,* and *Kroger* — have held that a grant of jurisdiction over claims involving particular parties does not itself confer jurisdiction over additional claims by or against different parties. Our decision today reaffirms that interpretive rule; the opposite would sow confusion.

Id. at 549–556.

In the *Finley* opinion, Justice Scalia insists that the conferral of jurisdiction in §1346(b) over "civil actions on claims against the United States" means "against the United States and no one else." Can such a construction be justified? Justice Scalia also purports to establish an interpretative rule for pendent party jurisdiction that requires an affirmative grant from Congress. Is such an approach consistent with *Aldinger* and *Kroger*? With *Gibbs*? Does that interpretation place an unworkable burden on Congress when enacting legislation to foresee potential joinder issues that would better be left to case-by-case adjudication?

The impact of *Finley* for other exercises of pendent party jurisdiction was unclear. For example, would you expect impleader under Rule 14 still to be available between nondiverse parties in the absence of an independent basis of jurisdiction? How is that situation distinguishable from *Finley*? In the aftermath of *Finley* and *Kroger*, most lower courts continued to exercise ancillary jurisdiction over such third-party claims. *See, e.g., King Fisher Marine Service v. 21st Phoenix Corp.,* 893 F.2d 1155 (10th Cir. 1990); *Huberman v. Duane Fellows, Inc.,* 725 F. Supp. 204 (S.D.N.Y. 1989). *But see Community Coffee Co. v. M/S Kriti Amethyst,* 715 F. Supp. 772 (E.D. La. 1989) (independent jurisdiction required). *Cf. W.R. Grace & Co. v. Continental Cas. Co.,* 896 F.2d 865 (5th Cir. 1990) (dismissing third-party complaint upon settlement of the main action).

The congressional response to *Finley* in 28 U.S.C. §1367 resolved many of the unanswered questions.

3. *Congress Responds to* Finley: *"Supplemental" Jurisdiction*

Justice Scalia's opinion in *Finley* purports to establish a comprehensive "interpretive principle" for assertions of jurisdiction over pendent parties, inviting Congress to change that principle if it disagrees. As part of the Judicial Improvements Act of 1990, Pub. L. No. 101-650, 104 Stat. 5089, Congress took up that invitation by adding §1367 to Title 28. The amendment applies to "civil actions commenced on or after the date of the enactment of this Act," the effective date of which is December 1, 1990.

NOTES AND QUESTIONS

1. *The Statutory Terminology.* 28 U.S.C. §1367 adopts the term *supplemental jurisdiction* to refer to claims that do not have an independent basis of federal jurisdiction, but are nonetheless within the federal court's subject matter jurisdiction because of their relationship to an "anchor" claim that falls within the court's federal subject matter jurisdiction. Note also that §1367(a) expressly states that such supplemental jurisdiction may include the joinder of additional parties. Does the statute clearly overrule *Finley*? Can you make an argument based on the language of the Federal Tort Claims Act that *Finley* still survives?

2. *How Does 28 U.S.C. §1367(a) Affect the Decision in* Moore? Federal Rules 13(a) and (b) provide for both compulsory and permissive counterclaims. In what situations may such counterclaims be asserted if there is no independent basis of federal jurisdiction? Are there ever situations when a permissive counterclaim might be within the federal court's supplemental jurisdiction?

The Second Circuit answered "yes" to that question in *Jones v. Ford Motor Credit Co.*, 358 F.3d 205 (2d Cir. 2004). In holding that a counterclaim that was only "permissive" under Rule 13 was nonetheless within "supplemental" jurisdiction, the court observed that 28 U.S.C. §1367 "displaced" prior doctrines of pendent and ancillary jurisdiction. The court ruled that any counterclaim—whether permissive or compulsory—that is so related to the original claim that it "forms part of the same case or controversy under Article III" comes within the grant of supplemental jurisdiction. The plaintiffs in the case were requesting class certification for claims of racial discrimination under the Equal Credit Opportunity Act (ECOA); defendant Ford Motor Credit denied the charge and asserted state law counterclaims for amounts of unpaid car loans of the plaintiffs. The district court determined that the counterclaims were "permissive" and expressed serious doubt as to whether §1367(a) authorized supplemental jurisdiction over permissive counterclaims. If permissive counterclaims claims did fall within supplemental jurisdiction, the district judge ruled that he would exercise his discretion under §1367(c) to dismiss the counterclaims. The Second Circuit reversed, holding that even though the counterclaims did not have a relationship to the main claim that would make them compulsory under Rule 13(a), they had a sufficient factual relationship to constitute the same "case" within the meaning of Article III and hence §1367. Moreover, the Court of Appeals stated that the district court's discretionary dismissal was premature and that the court's exercise of its discretion should not be made until after the ruling on class certification.

3. *The Diversity Exclusion.* Congress's attempt in §1367 to legislate the scope of supplemental jurisdiction was not completely successful. With respect to diversity cases, Congress indicated in the House Report on §1367 an intent, consistent with prior law, not to provide supplemental jurisdiction for diversity claims by plaintiffs:

> In diversity-only actions the district courts may not hear plaintiffs' supplemental claims when exercising supplemental jurisdiction would encourage plaintiffs to evade the jurisdictional requirements of 28 U.S.C. §1332 by the simple expedient of naming initially only those defendants whose joinder satisfies §1332's requirement and later adding claims not within the original federal jurisdiction against other defendants who have intervened or been joined on a supplemental basis.

> In accord with case law, the subsection also prohibits the joinder or intervention of persons as plaintiffs if adding them is inconsistent with §1332's requirements. The section is not intended to affect the jurisdictional requirements of 28 U.S.C. §1332 in diversity-only class actions, as those requirements were interpreted prior to *Finley*. [Citing, in footnote, *Supreme Tribe of Ben Hur v. Cauble*, 255 U.S. 356 (1921); *Zahn v. International Paper Co.*, 414 U.S. 291 (1973).]

H.R. Rep. 101–173, at 29 & n. 17 (1990); 136 Cong. Rec. S17570-02 (Oct. 27, 1990).

But did Congress draft the statute consistent with its intent? Read the statute carefully. Note that §1367(a) confers supplemental jurisdiction over claims so related to other claims within the federal court's "original jurisdiction" that they form part of the same case or controversy under Article III. Section 1367(a) refers to all cases within the original jurisdiction of the federal court, but §1367(b) excludes such jurisdiction in certain diversity-based cases. Now read §1367(b) closely. It clearly forecloses the assertion of supplemental jurisdiction over claims "by plaintiffs against persons made parties under Rule 14, 19, 20, or 24 of the Federal Rules. . . . " Thus, a New York plaintiff with the requisite amount in controversy in a suit against a Pennsylvania defendant will not be able to use supplemental jurisdiction to join a second defendant under Rule 20, if that second defendant lacks complete diversity with the plaintiff or the claim does not have an independent jurisdictional amount.

Consider, however, the application of the statute in a suit against a Pennsylvania defendant brought by two *plaintiffs* who join together under Rule 20. One plaintiff is from New York and has the requisite jurisdictional amount, but the second plaintiff lacks an independent basis of jurisdiction, either because he is from Pennsylvania (and destroys diversity) or because he lacks the necessary jurisdictional amount. Given the structure and policies underlying the statute, one would expect such a claim also to be excluded under §1367(b).

But does that conclusion necessarily follow from the statutory text of §1367? Notice that §1367(b) excludes "claims by plaintiffs *against* persons made parties under Rule 14, 19, 20, or 24" and "claims by persons proposed to be joined as plaintiffs under Rule 19 or Rule 24"—with no mention of Rule 20 plaintiffs. Is there any reading of §1367(b) that would exclude the application of supplemental jurisdiction in such a case? *See generally* James E. Pfander, *Supplemental Jurisdiction and Section 1367: The Case for Sympathetic Textualism*, 148 U. Pa. L. Rev. 109, 114 (1999) (arguing that term "original jurisdiction" in §1367(b) should be understood to refer to the collection of complete diversity and aggregation rules that traditionally defined "original jurisdiction" when parties were joined at the outset of a litigation).

A similar statutory "glitch" occurs with respect to supplemental jurisdiction and class action plaintiffs. Recall that in *Zahn v. International Paper Co.*, 414 U.S. 291 (1973), the Court required that each class member satisfy the jurisdictional amount in a diversity-based class action under Rule 23(b)(3), even where the named plaintiffs have met the requisite amount in controversy. The House Report, cited above, indicated that §1367 was not intended to overrule *Zahn*. But where in §1367(b) is the exclusion for supplemental jurisdiction over Rule 23 class members who lack the jurisdictional amount?

The lower courts struggled with these issues and arrived at conflicting decisions until the Supreme Court finally settled the matter in 2005.

Exxon Mobil Corp. v. Allapattah Services, Inc.
Rosario Ortega v. Star-Kist Foods, Inc.

545 U.S. 546 (2005)

JUSTICE KENNEDY delivered the opinion of the Court.

These consolidated cases present the question whether a federal court in a diversity action may exercise supplemental jurisdiction over additional plaintiffs whose claims do not satisfy the minimum amount-in-controversy requirement, provided the claims are part of the same case or controversy as the claims of plaintiffs who do allege a sufficient amount in controversy. Our decision turns on the correct interpretation of 28 U.S.C. §1367. The question has divided the Courts of Appeals, and we granted certiorari to resolve the conflict. . . .

We hold that, where the other elements of jurisdiction are present and at least one named plaintiff in the action satisfies the amount-in-controversy requirement, §1367 does authorize supplemental jurisdiction over the claims of other plaintiffs in the same Article III case or controversy, even if those claims are for less than the jurisdictional amount specified in the statute setting forth the requirements for diversity jurisdiction. We affirm the judgment of the Court of Appeals for the Eleventh Circuit in No. 04-70, and we reverse the judgment of the Court of Appeals for the First Circuit in No. 04-79.

I

In 1991, about 10,000 Exxon dealers filed a class-action suit against the Exxon Corporation in the United States District Court for the Northern District of Florida. The dealers alleged an intentional and systematic scheme by Exxon under which they were overcharged for fuel purchased from Exxon. The plaintiffs invoked the District Court's §1332(a) diversity jurisdiction. After a unanimous jury verdict in favor of the plaintiffs, the District Court certified the case for interlocutory review, asking whether it had properly exercised §1367 supplemental jurisdiction over the claims of class members who did not meet the jurisdictional minimum amount in controversy.

The Court of Appeals for the Eleventh Circuit upheld the District Court's extension of supplemental jurisdiction to these class members. *Allapattah Services, Inc. v. Exxon Corp.*, 333 F.3d 1248 (2003). "We find," the court held, "that §1367 clearly and unambiguously provides district courts with the authority in diversity class actions to exercise supplemental jurisdiction over the claims of class members who do not meet the minimum amount in controversy as long as the district court has original jurisdiction over the claims of at least one of the class representatives." *Id.*, at 1256. This decision accords with the views of the Courts of Appeals for the Fourth, Sixth, and Seventh Circuits. See *Rosmer v. Pfizer, Inc.*, 263 F.3d 110 (CA4 2001); *Olden v. LaFarge Corp.*, 383 F.3d 495 (CA6 2004); *Stromberg Metal Works, Inc. v. Press Mechanical, Inc.*, 77 F.3d 928 (CA7 1996); *In re Brand Name Prescription*

Drugs Antitrust Litigation, 123 F.3d 599 (CA7 1997). The Courts of Appeals for the Fifth and Ninth Circuits, adopting a similar analysis of the statute, have held that in a diversity class action the unnamed class members need not meet the amount-in-controversy requirement, provided the named class members do. These decisions, however, are unclear on whether all the named plaintiffs must satisfy this requirement. *In re Abbott Labs.*, 51 F.3d 524 (CA5 1995); *Gibson v. Chrysler Corp.*, 261 F.3d 927 (CA9 2001).

In the other case now before us the Court of Appeals for the First Circuit took a different position on the meaning of §1367(a). 370 F.3d 124 (2004). In that case, a 9-year-old girl sued Star-Kist in a diversity action in the United States District Court for the District of Puerto Rico, seeking damages for unusually severe injuries she received when she sliced her finger on a tuna can. Her family joined in the suit, seeking damages for emotional distress and certain medical expenses. The District Court granted summary judgment to Star-Kist, finding that none of the plaintiffs met the minimum amount-in-controversy requirement. The Court of Appeals for the First Circuit, however, ruled that the injured girl, but not her family members, had made allegations of damages in the requisite amount.

The Court of Appeals then addressed whether, in light of the fact that one plaintiff met the requirements for original jurisdiction, supplemental jurisdiction over the remaining plaintiffs' claims was proper under §1367. The court held that §1367 authorizes supplemental jurisdiction only when the district court has original jurisdiction over the action, and that in a diversity case original jurisdiction is lacking if one plaintiff fails to satisfy the amount-in-controversy requirement. Although the Court of Appeals claimed to "express no view" on whether the result would be the same in a class action, . . . its analysis is inconsistent with that of the Court of Appeals for the Eleventh Circuit. The Court of Appeals for the First Circuit's view of §1367 is, however, shared by the Courts of Appeal for the Third, Eighth, and Tenth Circuits, and the latter two Courts of Appeals have expressly applied this rule to class actions. See *Meritcare, Inc. v. St. Paul Mercury Ins. Co.*, 166 F.3d 214 (CA3 1999); *Trimble v. Asarco, Inc.*, 232 F.3d 946 (CA8 2000); *Leonhardt v. Western Sugar Co.*, 160 F.3d 631 (CA10 1998).

II

A

The district courts of the United States, as we have said many times, are "courts of limited jurisdiction. They possess only that power authorized by Constitution and statute," *Kokkonen v. Guardian Life Ins. Co. of America*, 511 U.S. 375, 377 (1994). . . .

Although the district courts may not exercise jurisdiction absent a statutory basis, it is well established — in certain classes of cases — that, once a court has original jurisdiction over some claims in the action, it may exercise supplemental jurisdiction over additional claims that are part of the same case or controversy. The leading modern case for this principle is *Mine Workers v. Gibbs*, 383 U.S. 715 (1966). . . .

As we later noted, the decision allowing jurisdiction over pendent state claims in *Gibbs* did not mention, let alone come to grips with, the text of the jurisdictional statutes and the bedrock principle that federal courts have no jurisdiction without statutory authorization. *Finley v. United States*, 490 U.S. 545, 548 (1989). In *Finley*, we nonetheless reaffirmed and rationalized *Gibbs* and its progeny by inferring from it the interpretive principle that, in cases involving supplemental jurisdiction over additional claims between parties properly in federal court, the jurisdictional statutes should be read broadly, on the assumption that in this context Congress intended to authorize courts to exercise their full Article III power to dispose of an "'entire action before the court [which] comprises but one constitutional case.'" 490 U.S., at 549, (quoting *Gibbs, supra*, at 725).

We have not, however, applied *Gibbs*' expansive interpretive approach to other aspects of the jurisdictional statutes. For instance, we have consistently interpreted §1332 as requiring complete diversity: In a case with multiple plaintiffs and multiple defendants, the presence in the action of a single plaintiff from the same State as a single defendant deprives the district court of original diversity jurisdiction over the entire action. *Strawbridge v. Curtiss*, 7 U.S. (3 Cranch) 267 (1806); *Owen Equipment & Erection Co. v. Kroger*, 437 U.S. 365, 375 (1978). The complete diversity requirement is not mandated by the Constitution, *State Farm Fire & Casualty Co. v. Tashire*, 386 U.S. 523, 530–531 (1967), or by the plain text of §1332(a). The Court, nonetheless, has adhered to the complete diversity rule in light of the purpose of the diversity requirement, which is to provide a federal forum for important disputes where state courts might favor, or be perceived as favoring, home-state litigants. The presence of parties from the same State on both sides of a case dispels this concern, eliminating a principal reason for conferring §1332 jurisdiction over any of the claims in the action. . . . The specific purpose of the complete diversity rule explains both why we have not adopted *Gibbs*' expansive interpretive approach to this aspect of the jurisdictional statute and why *Gibbs* does not undermine the complete diversity rule. In order for a federal court to invoke supplemental jurisdiction under *Gibbs*, it must first have original jurisdiction over at least one claim in the action. Incomplete diversity destroys original jurisdiction with respect to all claims, so there is nothing to which supplemental jurisdiction can adhere.

In contrast to the diversity requirement, most of the other statutory prerequisites for federal jurisdiction, including the federal-question and amount-in-controversy requirements, can be analyzed claim by claim. True, it does not follow by necessity from this that a district court has authority to exercise supplemental jurisdiction over all claims provided there is original jurisdiction over just one. Before the enactment of §1367, the Court declined in contexts other than the pendent-claim instance to follow *Gibbs*' expansive approach to interpretation of the jurisdictional statutes. The Court took a more restrictive view of the proper interpretation of these statutes in so-called pendent-party cases involving supplemental jurisdiction over claims involving additional parties—plaintiffs or defendants—where the district courts would lack original jurisdiction over claims by each of the parties standing alone.

Thus, with respect to plaintiff-specific jurisdictional requirements, the Court held in *Clark v. Paul Gray, Inc.*, 306 U.S. 583 (1939), that every plaintiff must separately satisfy the amount-in-controversy requirement. Though *Clark* was a federal-question case, at that time federal-question jurisdiction had an amount-in-controversy requirement analogous to the amount-in-controversy requirement for diversity cases. "Proper practice," *Clark* held, "requires that where each of several plaintiffs is bound to establish the jurisdictional amount with respect to his own claim, the suit should be dismissed as to those who fail to show that the requisite amount is involved." *Id.*, at 590. The Court reaffirmed this rule, in the context of a class action brought invoking §1332(a) diversity jurisdiction, in *Zahn v. International Paper Co.*, 414 U.S. 291 (1973). It follows "inescapably" from *Clark*, the Court held in *Zahn*, that "any plaintiff without the jurisdictional amount must be dismissed from the case, even though others allege jurisdictionally sufficient claims." 414 U.S., at 300.

The Court took a similar approach with respect to supplemental jurisdiction over claims against additional defendants that fall outside the district courts' original jurisdiction. . . . [The Court then discusses the *Aldinger* and *Finley* cases.]

As the jurisdictional statutes existed in 1989, then, here is how matters stood: First, the diversity requirement in §1332(a) required complete diversity; absent complete diversity, the district court lacked original jurisdiction over all of the claims in the action. *Strawbridge*, 7 U.S. (3 Cranch), at 267–268, *Kroger*, 437 U.S., at 373–374. Second, if the district court had original jurisdiction over at least one claim, the jurisdictional statutes implicitly authorized supplemental jurisdiction over all other claims between the same parties arising out of the same Article III case or controversy. *Gibbs*, 383 U.S., at 725. Third, even when the district court had original jurisdiction over one or more claims between particular parties, the jurisdictional statutes did not authorize supplemental jurisdiction over additional claims involving other parties. [Citing *Clark, Zahn,* and *Finley.*]

B

In *Finley* we emphasized that "whatever we say regarding the scope of jurisdiction conferred by a particular statute can of course be changed by Congress." 490 U.S., at 556. In 1990, Congress accepted the invitation. It passed the Judicial Improvements Act, 104 Stat. 5089, which enacted §1367, the provision which controls these cases. . . .

All parties to this litigation and all courts to consider the question agree that §1367 overturned the result in *Finley.* There is no warrant, however, for assuming that §1367 did no more than to overrule *Finley* and otherwise to codify the existing state of the law of supplemental jurisdiction. We must not give jurisdictional statutes a more expansive interpretation than their text warrants, 490 U.S., at 549, 556; but it is just as important not to adopt an artificial construction that is narrower than what the text provides. No sound canon of interpretation requires Congress to speak with extraordinary clarity in order to modify the rules of federal jurisdiction within appropriate constitutional bounds. Ordinary principles of statutory construction apply. In order to determine the scope of supplemental jurisdiction authorized by §1367, then, we must examine the statute's text in light of context, structure, and related statutory provisions.

Section 1367(a) is a broad grant of supplemental jurisdiction over other claims within the same case or controversy, as long as the action is one in which the district courts would have original jurisdiction. The last sentence of §1367(a) makes it clear that the grant of supplemental jurisdiction extends to claims involving joinder or intervention of additional parties. The single question before us, therefore, is whether a diversity case in which the claims of some plaintiffs satisfy the amount-in-controversy requirement, but the claims of other plaintiffs do not, presents a "civil action of which the district courts have original jurisdiction." If the answer is yes, §1367(a) confers supplemental jurisdiction over all claims, including those that do not independently satisfy the amount-in-controversy requirement, if the claims are part of the same Article III case or controversy. If the answer is no, §1367(a) is inapplicable and, in light of our holdings in *Clark* and *Zahn*, the district court has no statutory basis for exercising supplemental jurisdiction over the additional claims.

We now conclude the answer must be yes. When the well-pleaded complaint contains at least one claim that satisfies the amount-in-controversy requirement, and there are no other relevant jurisdictional defects, the district court, beyond all question, has original jurisdiction over that claim. The presence of other claims in the complaint, over which the district court may lack original jurisdiction, is of no moment. If the court has original jurisdiction over a single claim in the complaint, it has original jurisdiction over a "civil action" within the meaning of §1367(a), even if the civil action over which it has jurisdiction comprises fewer claims than were included in the complaint. Once the court determines it has original jurisdiction over the civil action, it can turn to the question whether it has a constitutional and statutory basis for exercising supplemental jurisdiction over the other claims in the action.

Section 1367(a) commences with the direction that §§1367(b) and (c), or other relevant statutes, may provide specific exceptions, but otherwise §1367(a) is a broad jurisdictional grant, with no distinction drawn between pendent-claim and pendent-party cases. In fact, the last sentence of §1367(a) makes clear that the provision grants supplemental jurisdiction over claims involving joinder or intervention of additional parties. The terms of §1367 do not acknowledge any distinction between pendent jurisdiction and the doctrine of so-called ancillary jurisdiction. Though the doctrines of pendent and ancillary jurisdiction developed separately as a historical matter, the Court has recognized that the doctrines are "two species of the same generic problem," *Kroger*, 437 U.S., at 370. Nothing in §1367 indicates a congressional intent to recognize, preserve, or create some meaningful, substantive distinction between the jurisdictional categories we have historically labeled pendent and ancillary.

If §1367(a) were the sum total of the relevant statutory language, our holding would rest on that language alone. The statute, of course, instructs us to examine §1367(b) to determine if any of its exceptions apply, so we proceed to that section. While §1367(b) qualifies the broad rule of §1367(a), it does not withdraw supplemental jurisdiction over the claims of the additional parties at issue here. The specific exceptions to §1367(a) contained in §1367(b), moreover, provide additional support for our conclusion that §1367(a) confers supplemental jurisdiction over these claims. Section 1367(b), which applies only to diversity cases, withholds supplemental jurisdiction over the claims of plaintiffs proposed to be joined as indispensable parties under Federal Rule of Civil Procedure 19, or who seek to intervene pursuant to Rule 24. Nothing in the text of §1367(b), however, withholds supplemental jurisdiction over the claims of plaintiffs permissively joined under Rule 20 (like the additional plaintiffs in No. 04-79) or certified as class-action members pursuant to Rule 23 (like the additional plaintiffs in No. 04-70). The natural, indeed the necessary, inference is that §1367 confers supplemental jurisdiction over claims by Rule 20 and Rule 23 plaintiffs. This inference, at least with respect to Rule 20 plaintiffs, is strengthened by the fact that §1367(b) explicitly excludes supplemental jurisdiction over claims against defendants joined under Rule 20.

We cannot accept the view, urged by some of the parties, commentators, and Courts of Appeals, that a district court lacks original jurisdiction over a civil action unless the court has original jurisdiction over every claim in the complaint. As we understand this position, it requires assuming either that all claims in the complaint must stand or fall as a single, indivisible "civil action" as a matter of definitional necessity—what we will refer to as the "indivisibility theory"—or else that the inclusion of a claim or party falling outside the district court's original jurisdiction somehow contaminates every other claim in the complaint, depriving the court of original jurisdiction over any of these claims—what we will refer to as the "contamination theory."

The indivisibility theory is easily dismissed, as it is inconsistent with the whole notion of supplemental jurisdiction. If a district court must have original jurisdiction over every claim in the complaint in order to have "original jurisdiction" over a "civil action," then in *Gibbs* there was no civil action of which the district court could assume original jurisdiction under §1331, and so no basis for exercising supplemental jurisdiction over any of the claims. The indivisibility theory is further belied by our practice—in both federal-question and diversity cases—of allowing federal courts to cure jurisdictional defects by dismissing the offending parties rather than dismissing the entire action. *Clark*, for example, makes clear that claims that are jurisdictionally defective as to amount in controversy do not destroy original jurisdiction over other claims. 306 U.S., at 590 (dismissing parties who failed to meet the amount-in-controversy requirement but retaining jurisdiction over the remaining party). If the presence of jurisdictionally problematic claims in the complaint meant the district court was without original jurisdiction over the single, indivisible civil action before it, then the district court would have to dismiss the whole action rather than particular parties.

We also find it unconvincing to say that the definitional indivisibility theory applies in the context of diversity cases but not in the context of federal-question cases. The broad and general language of the statute does not permit this result. The contention is premised on the notion that the phrase "original jurisdiction of all civil actions" means different things in §1331 and §1332. It is implausible, however, to say that the identical phrase means one thing (original jurisdiction in all actions where at least one claim in the complaint meets the following requirements) in §1331 and something else (original jurisdiction in all actions where every claim in the complaint meets the following requirements) in §1332.

The contamination theory, as we have noted, can make some sense in the special context of the complete diversity requirement because the presence of nondiverse parties on both sides of a lawsuit eliminates the justification for providing a federal forum. The theory, however, makes little sense with respect to the amount-in-controversy requirement, which is meant to ensure that a dispute is sufficiently important to warrant federal-court attention. The presence of a single nondiverse party may eliminate the fear of bias with respect to all claims, but the presence of a claim that falls short of the minimum amount in controversy does nothing to reduce the importance of the claims that do meet this requirement.

It is fallacious to suppose, simply from the proposition that §1332 imposes both the diversity requirement and the amount-in-controversy requirement, that the contamination theory germane to the former is also relevant to the latter. There is no inherent logical connection between the amount-in-controversy requirement and §1332 diversity jurisdiction. After all, federal-question jurisdiction once had an amount-in-controversy requirement as well. If such a requirement were revived under §1331, it is clear beyond peradventure that §1367(a) provides supplemental jurisdiction over federal-question cases where some, but not all, of the federal-law claims involve a sufficient amount in controversy. In other words, §1367(a) unambiguously overrules the holding and the result in *Clark*. If that is so, however, it would be quite extraordinary to say that §1367 did not also overrule *Zahn*, a case that was premised in substantial part on the holding in *Clark*.

In addition to the theoretical difficulties with the argument that a district court has original jurisdiction over a civil action only if it has original jurisdiction over each individual claim in the complaint, we have already considered and rejected a virtually identical argument in the closely analogous context of removal jurisdiction. In *Chicago v. International College of Surgeons*, 522 U.S. 156 (1997), the plaintiff brought federal- and state-law claims in state court. The defendant removed to federal court. The plaintiff objected to removal, citing the text of the removal statute, §1441(a). That statutory provision, which bears a striking similarity to the relevant portion of §1367, authorizes removal of "any civil action . . . of which the district courts of the United States have original jurisdiction. . . ." The *College of Surgeons* plaintiff urged that, because its state-law claims were not within the District Court's original jurisdiction, §1441(a) did not authorize removal. We disagreed. The federal law claims, we held, "suffice to make the actions 'civil actions' within the 'original jurisdiction' of the district courts. . . . Nothing in the jurisdictional statutes suggests that the presence of related state law claims somehow alters the fact that [the plaintiff's] complaints, by virtue of their federal claims, were 'civil actions' within the federal courts' 'original jurisdiction.'" *Id.*, at 166. Once the case was removed, the District Court had original jurisdiction over the federal law claims and supplemental jurisdiction under §1367(a) over the state-law claims. *Id.*, at 165. . . .

Although *College of Surgeons* involved additional claims between the same parties, its interpretation of §1441(a) applies equally to cases involving additional parties whose claims fall short of the jurisdictional amount. If we were to adopt the contrary view that the presence of additional parties means there is no "civil action . . . of which the district courts . . . have original jurisdiction," those cases simply would not be removable. To our knowledge, no court has issued a reasoned opinion adopting this view of the removal statute. It is settled, of course, that absent complete diversity a case is not removable because the district court would lack original jurisdiction. . . . A failure of complete diversity, unlike the failure of some claims to meet the requisite amount in controversy, contaminates every claim in the action.

We also reject the argument, similar to the attempted distinction of *College of Surgeons* discussed above, that while the presence of additional claims over which the district court lacks jurisdiction does not mean the civil action is outside the purview of §1367(a), the presence of additional parties does. . . . The argument that the presence of additional parties removes the civil action from the scope of §1367(a) also would mean that §1367 left the *Finley* result undisturbed. . . . Yet all concede that one purpose of §1367 was to change the result reached in *Finley*.

Finally, it is suggested that our interpretation of §1367(a) creates an anomaly regarding the exceptions listed in §1367(b): It is not immediately obvious why Congress would withhold supplemental jurisdiction over plaintiffs joined as parties "needed for just adjudication" under Rule 19 but would allow supplemental jurisdiction over plaintiffs permissively joined under Rule 20. The omission of Rule 20 plaintiffs from the list of exceptions in §1367(b) may have been an "unintentional drafting gap," *Meritcare*, 166 F.3d at 221 and n. 6. If that is the case, it is up to Congress rather than the courts to fix it. The omission may seem odd, but it is not absurd. An alternative explanation for the different treatment of Rule 19 and Rule 20 is that Congress was concerned that extending supplemental jurisdiction to Rule 19 plaintiffs would allow circumvention of the complete diversity rule: A nondiverse plaintiff might be omitted intentionally from the original action, but joined later under Rule 19 as a necessary party. . . . The contamination theory described above, if applicable, means this ruse would fail, but Congress may have wanted to make assurance double sure. More generally, Congress may have concluded that federal jurisdiction is only appropriate if the district court would have original jurisdiction over the claims of all those plaintiffs who are so essential to the action that they could be joined under Rule 19.

To the extent that the omission of Rule 20 plaintiffs from the list of §1367(b) exceptions is anomalous, moreover, it is no more anomalous than the inclusion of Rule 19 plaintiffs in that list would be if the alternative view of §1367(a) were to prevail. If the district court lacks original jurisdiction over a civil diversity action where any plaintiff's claims fail to comply with all the requirements of §1332, there is no need for a special §1367(b) exception for Rule 19 plaintiffs who do not meet these requirements. Though the omission of Rule 20 plaintiffs from §1367(b) presents something of a puzzle on our view of the statute, the inclusion of Rule 19 plaintiffs in this section is at least as difficult to explain under the alternative view.

And so we circle back to the original question. When the well-pleaded complaint in district court includes multiple claims, all part of the same case or controversy, and some, but not all, of the claims are within the court's original jurisdiction, does the court have before it "any civil action of which the district courts have original jurisdiction"? It does. Under §1367, the court has original jurisdiction over the civil action comprising the claims for which there is no jurisdictional defect. No other reading of §1367 is plausible in light of the text and structure of the jurisdictional statute. Though the special nature and purpose of the diversity requirement mean that a single nondiverse party can contaminate every other claim in the lawsuit, the contamination does not occur with respect to jurisdictional defects that go only to the substantive importance of individual claims.

It follows from this conclusion that the threshold requirement of §1367(a) is satisfied in cases, like those now before us, where some, but not all, of the plaintiffs in a diversity action allege a sufficient amount in controversy. We hold that §1367 by its plain text overruled *Clark* and *Zahn* and authorized supplemental jurisdiction over all claims by diverse parties arising out of the same Article III case or controversy, subject only to enumerated exceptions not applicable in the cases now before us.

C

The proponents of the alternative view of §1367 insist that the statute is at least ambiguous and that we should look to other interpretive tools, including the legislative history of §1367, which supposedly demonstrate Congress did not intend §1367 to overrule *Zahn*. We can reject this argument at the very outset simply because §1367 is not ambiguous. For the reasons elaborated above, interpreting §1367 to foreclose supplemental jurisdiction over plaintiffs in diversity cases who do not meet the minimum amount in controversy is inconsistent with the text, read in light of other statutory provisions and our established jurisprudence. Even if we were to stipulate, however, that the reading these proponents urge upon us is textually plausible, the legislative history cited to support it would not alter our view as to the best interpretation of §1367.

Those who urge that the legislative history refutes our interpretation rely primarily on the House Judiciary Committee Report on the Judicial Improvements Act. H. R. Rep. No. 101-734 (1990) (House Report or Report). This Report explained that §1367 would authorize jurisdiction in a case like *Finley*, as well as essentially restore the pre-*Finley* understandings of the authorization for and limits on other forms of supplemental jurisdiction. House Report, at 28. The Report stated that §1367(a) "generally authorizes the district court to exercise jurisdiction over a supplemental claim whenever it forms part of the same constitutional case or controversy as the claim or claims that provide the basis of the district court's original jurisdiction," and in so doing codifies *Gibbs* and fills the statutory gap recognized in *Finley*. House Report, at 28–29, and n. 15. The Report then remarked that §1367(b) "is not intended to affect the jurisdictional requirements of [§1332] in diversity-only class actions, as those requirements were interpreted prior to *Finley*," citing, without further elaboration, *Zahn* and *Supreme Tribe of Ben-Hur v. Cauble*, 255 U.S. 356 (1921). House Report, at 29, and n. 17. The Report noted that the "net effect" of §1367(b) was to implement the "principal rationale" of *Kroger*, House Report, at 29, and n. 16, effecting only "one small change" in pre-*Finley* practice with respect to diversity actions: §1367(b) would exclude "Rule 23(a) plaintiff-intervenors to the same extent as those sought to be joined as plaintiffs under Rule 19." House Report, at 29. (It is evident that the report here meant to refer to Rule 24, not Rule 23.)

As we have repeatedly held, the authoritative statement is the statutory text, not the legislative history or any other extrinsic material. Extrinsic materials have a role in statutory interpretation only to the extent they shed a reliable light on the enacting Legislature's understanding of otherwise ambiguous terms. Not all extrinsic materials are reliable sources of insight into legislative understandings, however, and legislative history in particular is vulnerable to two serious criticisms. First, legislative history is itself often murky, ambiguous, and contradictory. Judicial investigation of legislative history has a tendency to become, to borrow Judge Leventhal's memorable phrase, an exercise in "'looking over a crowd and picking out your friends.'" See Wald, Some Observations on the Use of Legislative History in the 1981 Supreme Court Term, 68 Iowa L. Rev. 195, 214 (1983). Second, judicial reliance on legislative materials like committee reports, which are not themselves subject to the requirements of Article I, may give unrepresentative committee members — or, worse yet, unelected staffers and lobbyists — both the power and the incentive to attempt strategic manipulations of legislative history to secure results they were unable to achieve through the statutory text. We need not comment here on whether these problems are sufficiently prevalent to render legislative history inherently unreliable in all circumstances, a point on which Members of this Court have disagreed. It is clear, however, that in this instance both criticisms are right on the mark.

First of all, the legislative history of §1367 is far murkier than selective quotation from the House Report would suggest. The text of §1367 is based substantially on a draft proposal contained in a Federal Court Study Committee working paper, which was drafted by a Subcommittee chaired by Judge Posner. Report of the Subcommittee on the Role of the Federal Courts and Their Relationship to the States 567–568 (Mar. 12, 1990), reprinted in Judicial Conference of the United States, 1 Federal Courts Study Committee, Working Papers and Subcommittee Reports (July 1, 1990). While the Subcommittee explained, in language echoed by the House Report, that its proposal "basically restores the law as it existed prior to Finley," Subcommittee Working Paper, at 561, it observed in a footnote that its proposal would overrule *Zahn* and that this would be a good idea, Subcommittee Working Paper, at 561, n. 33. Although the Federal Courts Study Committee did not expressly adopt the Subcommittee's specific reference to *Zahn*, it neither explicitly disagreed with the Subcommittee's conclusion that this was the best reading of the proposed text nor substantially modified the proposal to avoid this result. Study Committee Report, at 47–48. Therefore, even if the House Report could fairly be read to reflect an understanding that the text of §1367 did not overrule *Zahn*, the Subcommittee Working Paper on which §1367 was based reflected the opposite understanding. The House Report is no more authoritative than the Subcommittee Working Paper. The utility of either can extend no further than the light it sheds on how the enacting Legislature understood the statutory text. Trying to figure out how to square the Subcommittee Working Paper's understanding with the House Report's understanding, or which is more reflective of the understanding of the enacting legislators, is a hopeless task.

Second, the worst fears of critics who argue legislative history will be used to circumvent the Article I process was realized in this case. The telltale evidence is the statement, by three law professors who participated in drafting §1367, see House Report, at 27, n. 13, that §1367 "on its face" permits "supplemental jurisdiction over claims of class members that do not satisfy section 1332's jurisdictional amount requirement, which would overrule [*Zahn*]. [There is] a disclaimer of intent to accomplish this result in the legislative history. . . . It would have been better had the statute dealt explicitly with this problem, and the legislative history was an attempt to correct the oversight." Rowe, Burbank, & Mengler, Compounding or Creating Confusion About Supplemental Jurisdiction? A Reply to Professor Freer, 40 Emory L. J. 943, 960, n. 90 (1991). The professors were frank to concede that if one refuses to consider the legislative history, one has no choice but to "conclude that section 1367 has wiped *Zahn* off the books." *Ibid.* So there exists an acknowledgment, by parties who have detailed, specific knowledge of the statute and the drafting process, both that the plain text of §1367 overruled *Zahn* and that language to the contrary in the House Report was a *post hoc* attempt to alter that result. One need not subscribe to the wholesale condemnation of legislative history to refuse to give any effect to such a deliberate effort to amend a statute through a committee report.

In sum, even if we believed resort to legislative history were appropriate in these cases—a point we do not concede—we would not give significant weight to the House Report. The distinguished jurists who drafted the Subcommittee

Working Paper, along with three of the participants in the drafting of §1367, agree that this provision, on its face, overrules *Zahn*. This accords with the best reading of the statute's text, and nothing in the legislative history indicates directly and explicitly that Congress understood the phrase "civil action of which the district courts have original jurisdiction" to exclude cases in which some but not all of the diversity plaintiffs meet the amount in controversy requirement.

No credence, moreover, can be given to the claim that, if Congress understood §1367 to overrule *Zahn*, the proposal would have been more controversial. We have little sense whether any Member of Congress would have been particularly upset by this result. This is not a case where one can plausibly say that concerned legislators might not have realized the possible effect of the text they were adopting. Certainly, any competent legislative aide who studied the matter would have flagged this issue if it were a matter of importance to his or her boss, especially in light of the Subcommittee Working Paper. There are any number of reasons why legislators did not spend more time arguing over §1367, none of which are relevant to our interpretation of what the words of the statute mean.

D

Finally, we note that the Class Action Fairness Act (CAFA), Pub. L. 109-2, 119 Stat. 4, enacted this year, has no bearing on our analysis of these cases. Subject to certain limitations, the CAFA confers federal diversity jurisdiction over class actions where the aggregate amount in controversy exceeds $5 million. It abrogates the rule against aggregating claims, a rule this Court recognized in *Ben-Hur* and reaffirmed in *Zahn*. The CAFA, however, is not retroactive, and the views of the 2005 Congress are not relevant to our interpretation of a text enacted by Congress in 1990. The CAFA, moreover, does not moot the significance of our interpretation of §1367, as many proposed exercises of supplemental jurisdiction, even in the class-action context, might not fall within the CAFA's ambit. The CAFA, then, has no impact, one way or the other, on our interpretation of §1367....

The judgment of the Court of Appeals for the Eleventh Circuit is affirmed. The judgment of the Court of Appeals for the First Circuit is reversed, and the case is remanded for proceedings consistent with this opinion.

It is so ordered.

Justice Stevens, with whom Justice Breyer joins, dissenting.

Justice Ginsburg's carefully reasoned opinion . . . demonstrates the error in the Court's rather ambitious reading of this opaque jurisdictional statute. She also has demonstrated that "ambiguity" is a term that may have different meanings for different judges, for the Court has made the remarkable declaration that its reading of the statute is so obviously correct—and Justice Ginsburg's so obviously wrong—that the text does not even qualify as "ambiguous." . . . Because ambiguity is apparently in the eye of the beholder, I remain convinced that it is unwise to treat the ambiguity *vel non* of a statute as determinative of whether legislative history is consulted. Indeed, I believe that we as judges are more, rather than less, constrained when we make ourselves accountable to all reliable evidence of legislative intent. See *Koons Buick Pontiac GMC, Inc. v. Nigh*, 543 U.S. slip op., at 2 and n. 1 (Stevens, J., concurring).

The legislative history of 28 U.S.C. §1367 provides powerful confirmation of Justice Ginsburg's interpretation of that statute. It is helpful to consider in full the relevant portion of the House Report, which was also adopted by the Senate. . . .

Not only does the House Report specifically say that §1367 was not intended to upset *Zahn v. International Paper Co.*, 414 U.S. 291 (1973), but its entire explanation of the statute demonstrates that Congress had in mind a very specific and relatively modest task — undoing this Court's 5-to-4 decision in *Finley v. United States*, 490 U.S. 545 (1989). In addition to overturning that unfortunate and much-criticized decision, the statute, according to the Report, codifies and preserves "the pre-*Finley* understandings of the authorization for and limits on other forms of supplemental jurisdiction," House Report, at 28, with the exception of making "one small change in pre-*Finley* practice," *id.*, at 29, which is not relevant here.

The sweeping purpose that the Court's decision imputes to Congress bears no resemblance to the House Report's description of the statute. But this does not seem to trouble the Court, for its decision today treats statutory interpretation as a pedantic exercise, divorced from any serious attempt at ascertaining congressional intent. . . .

The Court's reasons for ignoring this virtual billboard of congressional intent are unpersuasive. That a subcommittee of the Federal Courts Study Committee believed that an earlier, substantially similar version of the statute overruled *Zahn*, . . . only highlights the fact that the statute is ambiguous. What is determinative is that the House Report explicitly rejected that broad reading of the statutory text. Such a report has special significance as an indicator of legislative intent. In Congress, committee reports are normally considered the authoritative explication of a statute's text and purposes, and busy legislators and their assistants rely on that explication in casting their votes. . . .

The Court's second reason — its comment on the three law professors who participated in drafting §1367 . . . — is similarly off the mark. In the law review article that the Court refers to, the professors were merely saying that the text of the statute was susceptible to an overly broad (and simplistic) reading, and that clarification in the House Report was therefore appropriate. See Rowe, Burbank, & Mengler, Compounding or Creating Confusion About Supplemental Jurisdiction? A Reply to Professor Freer, 40 Emory L. J. 943, 960, n. 90 (1991). Significantly, the reference to *Zahn* in the House Report does not at all appear to be tacked-on or out of place; indeed, it is wholly consistent with the Report's broader explanation of Congress' goal of overruling *Finley* and preserving pre-*Finley* law. To suggest that these professors participated in a "deliberate effort to amend a statute through a committee report," . . . reveals an unrealistic view of the legislative process, not to mention disrespect for three law professors who acted in the role of public servants. To be sure, legislative history can be manipulated. But, in the situation before us, there is little reason to fear that an unholy conspiracy of "unrepresentative committee members," . . . law professors, and "unelected staffers and lobbyists," . . . endeavored to torpedo Congress' attempt to overrule (without discussion) two longstanding features of this Court's diversity jurisprudence.

After nearly 20 pages of complicated analysis, which explores subtle doctrinal nuances and coins various neologisms, the Court announces that §1367 could not reasonably be read another way. . . . That conclusion is difficult to accept. Given JUSTICE GINSBURG's persuasive account of the statutory text and its jurisprudential backdrop, and given the uncommonly clear legislative history, I am confident that the majority's interpretation of §1367 is mistaken. I respectfully dissent.

JUSTICE GINSBURG, with whom JUSTICE STEVENS, JUSTICE O'CONNOR, and JUSTICE BREYER join, dissenting.

These cases present the question whether Congress, by enacting 28 U.S.C. §1367, overruled this Court's decisions in *Clark v. Paul Gray, Inc.*, 306 U.S. 583, 589 (1939) (reaffirming the holding of *Troy Bank v. G. A. Whitehead & Co.*, 222 U.S. 39, 40 (1911)), and *Zahn v. International Paper Co.*, 414 U.S. 291 (1973). *Clark* held that, when federal-court jurisdiction is predicated on a specified amount in controversy, each plaintiff joined in the litigation must independently meet the jurisdictional amount requirement. *Zahn* confirmed that in class actions governed by Federal Rule of Civil Procedure 23(b)(3), "each [class member] . . . must satisfy the jurisdictional amount, and any [class member] who does not must be dismissed from the case." 414 U.S., at 301.

Section 1367, all agree, was designed to overturn this Court's decision in *Finley v. United States*, 490 U.S. 545 (1989). . . .

What more §1367 wrought is an issue on which courts of appeals have sharply divided. . . . The Court today holds that §1367, although prompted by *Finley*, a case in which original access to federal court was predicated on a federal question, notably enlarges federal diversity jurisdiction. The Court reads §1367 to overrule *Clark* and *Zahn*, thereby allowing access to federal court by co-plaintiffs or class members who do not meet the now in excess of $75,000 amount-in-controversy requirement, so long as at least one co-plaintiff, or the named class representative, has a jurisdictionally sufficient claim. . . .

The Court adopts a plausibly broad reading of §1367, a measure that is hardly a model of the careful drafter's art. There is another plausible reading, however, one less disruptive of our jurisprudence regarding supplemental jurisdiction. If one reads §1367(a) to instruct, as the statute's text suggests, that the district court must first have "original jurisdiction" over a "civil action" before supplemental jurisdiction can attach, then *Clark* and *Zahn* are preserved, and supplemental jurisdiction does not open the way for joinder of plaintiffs, or inclusion of class members, who do not independently meet the amount-in-controversy requirement. For the reasons that follow, I conclude that this narrower construction is the better reading of §1367.

I

A

Section 1367, captioned "Supplemental jurisdiction," codifies court-recognized doctrines formerly labeled "pendent" and "ancillary" jurisdiction. Pendent jurisdiction involved the enlargement of federal-question litigation to include related state-law claims. Ancillary jurisdiction evolved primarily to protect defending parties, or others whose rights might be adversely affected if they could not air their claims in an ongoing federal-court action. Given jurisdiction over the principal action, federal courts entertained certain matters deemed ancillary regardless of the citizenship of the parties or the amount in controversy. . . . [Justice Ginsburg discusses *Gibbs*, *Finley*, and *Kroger*.]

In sum, in federal-question cases before §1367's enactment, the Court recognized pendent-claim jurisdiction, *Gibbs*, 383 U.S., at 725, but not pendent-party jurisdiction, *Finley*, 490 U.S., at 555–556. As to ancillary jurisdiction, the Court adhered to the limitation that in diversity cases, throughout the litigation, all plaintiffs must remain diverse from all defendants. See *Kroger*, 437 U.S., at 374.

Although pendent jurisdiction and ancillary jurisdiction evolved discretely, the Court has recognized that they are "two species of the same generic problem: Under what circumstances may a federal court hear and decide a state-law claim arising between citizens of the same State?" *Id.*, at 370. *Finley* regarded that question as one properly addressed to Congress. See 490 U.S., at 549, 556; 13 Wright & Miller §3523, p. 127 (2d ed. Supp. 2005); Hart & Wechsler 924–926. . . .

II

A

Section 1367, by its terms, operates only in civil actions "of which the district courts have original jurisdiction." The "original jurisdiction" relevant here is diversity-of-citizenship jurisdiction, conferred by §1332. The character of that jurisdiction is the essential backdrop for comprehension of §1367. . . .

The statute today governing federal court exercise of diversity jurisdiction in the generality of cases, §1332, like all its predecessors, incorporates both a diverse-citizenship requirement and an amount-in-controversy specification[5]. . . .

This Court has long held that, in determining whether the amount-in-controversy requirement has been satisfied, a single plaintiff may aggregate two or more claims against a single defendant, even if the claims are unrelated. *See, e.g., Edwards v. Bates County*, 163 U.S. 269, 273 (1896). But in multiparty cases, including class actions, we have unyieldingly adhered to the nonaggregation rule stated in *Troy Bank*. See *Clark*, 306 U.S., at 589 (reaffirming the "familiar rule that when several plaintiffs assert separate and distinct demands in a single suit, the amount involved in each separate controversy must be of the requisite amount to be within the jurisdiction of the district court, and that those amounts cannot be added together to satisfy jurisdictional requirements"); *Snyder v. Harris*, 394 U.S. 332, 339–340 (1969) (abandonment of the nonaggregation rule in class actions would undercut the

---

5. Endeavoring to preserve the "complete diversity" rule first stated in *Strawbridge v. Curtiss*, 7 U.S. 267 (1806), the Court's opinion drives a wedge between the two components of 28 U.S.C. §1332, treating the diversity-of-citizenship requirement as essential, the amount-in-controversy requirement as more readily disposable. . . . Section 1332 itself, however, does not rank order the two requirements. What "ordinary principle of statutory construction" or "sound canon of interpretation" . . . allows the Court to slice up §1332 this way? In partial explanation, the Court asserts that amount in controversy can be analyzed claim-by-claim, but the diversity requirement cannot. . . . It is not altogether clear why that should be so. The cure for improper joinder of a nondiverse party is the same as the cure for improper joinder of a plaintiff who does not satisfy the jurisdictional amount. In both cases, original jurisdiction can be preserved by dismissing the nonqualifying party. See *Caterpillar Inc. v. Lewis*, 519 U.S. 61, 64 (1996) (diversity); *Newman-Green, Inc. v. Alfonzo-Larrain*, 490 U.S. 826, 836–838 (1989) (same); *Zahn*, 414 U.S., at 295 (amount in controversy); *Clark v. Paul Gray, Inc.*, 306 U.S. 583, 590 (1939) (same).

congressional "purpose . . . to check, to some degree, the rising caseload of the federal courts").

This Court most recently addressed "the meaning of [§1332's] 'matter in controversy' language" in *Zahn*, 414 U.S., at 298. *Zahn*, like *Snyder* decided four years earlier, was a class action. In *Snyder*, no class member had a claim large enough to satisfy the jurisdictional amount. But in *Zahn*, the named plaintiffs had such claims. 414 U.S., at 292. Nevertheless, the Court declined to depart from its "longstanding construction of the 'matter in controversy' requirement of §1332." *Id.*, at 301. . . .

The rule that each plaintiff must independently satisfy the amount-in-controversy requirement, unless Congress expressly orders otherwise, was thus the solidly established reading of §1332 when Congress enacted the Judicial Improvements Act of 1990, which added §1367 to Title 28.

B

These cases present the question whether Congress abrogated the nonaggregation rule long tied to §1332 when it enacted §1367. In answering that question, "context [should provide] a crucial guide." *Rosario Ortega v. Star-Kist Foods, Inc.*, 370 F.3d 124, 135 (2004). The Court should assume, as it ordinarily does, that Congress legislated against a background of law already in place and the historical development of that law. See *National Archives and Records Admin. v. Favish*, 541 U.S. 157, 169 (2004). Here, that background is the statutory grant of diversity jurisdiction, the amount-in-controversy condition that Congress, from the start, has tied to the grant, and the nonaggregation rule this Court has long applied to the determination of the "matter in controversy." . . .

The Court is unanimous in reading §1367(a) to permit pendent-party jurisdiction in federal-question cases, and thus, to overrule *Finley*. The basic jurisdictional grant, §1331, provides that "the district courts shall have original jurisdiction of all civil actions arising under the Constitution, laws, or treaties of the United States." Since 1980, §1331 has contained no amount-in-controversy requirement. See 94 Stat. 2369 (eliminating §1331's amount-in-controversy requirement). Once there is a civil action presenting a qualifying claim arising under federal law, §1331's sole requirement is met. District courts, we have held, may then adjudicate, additionally, state-law claims "deriving from a common nucleus of operative fact." *Gibbs*, 383 U.S., at 725. Section 1367(a) enlarges that category to include not only state-law claims against the defendant named in the federal claim, but also "[state law] claims that involve the joinder or intervention of additional parties."

The Court divides, however, on the impact of §1367(a) on diversity cases controlled by §1332. Under the majority's reading, §1367(a) permits the joinder of related claims cut loose from the nonaggregation rule that has long attended actions under §1332. Only the claims specified in §1367(b) would be excluded from §1367(a)'s expansion of §1332's grant of diversity jurisdiction. And because §1367(b) contains no exception for joinder of plaintiffs under Rule 20 or class actions under Rule 23, the Court concludes, *Clark* and *Zahn* have been overruled.

The Court's reading is surely plausible, especially if one detaches §1367(a) from its context and attempts no reconciliation with prior interpretations of §1332's amount-in-controversy requirement. But §1367(a)'s text, as the First Circuit held, can be read another way, one that would involve no rejection of *Clark* and *Zahn*.

As explained by the First Circuit in *Ortega*, and applied to class actions by the Tenth Circuit in *Leonhardt*, . . . §1367(a) addresses "civil actions of which the district courts have original jurisdiction," a formulation that, in diversity cases, is sensibly read to incorporate the rules on joinder and aggregation tightly tied to §1332 at the time of §1367's enactment. On this reading, a complaint must first meet that "original jurisdiction" measurement. If it does not, no supplemental jurisdiction is authorized. If it does, §1367(a) authorizes "supplemental jurisdiction" over related claims. In other words, §1367(a) would preserve undiminished, as part and parcel of §1332 "original jurisdiction" determinations, both the "complete diversity" rule and the decisions restricting aggregation to arrive at the amount in controversy.[9] Section 1367(b)'s office, then, would be "to prevent the erosion of the complete diversity [and amount-in-controversy] requirements that might otherwise result from an expansive application of what was once termed the doctrine of ancillary jurisdiction." See Pfander, Supplemental Jurisdiction and Section 1367: The Case for a Sympathetic Textualism, 148 U. Pa. L. Rev. 109, 114 (1999); *infra*, at 17–18. In contrast to the Court's construction of §1367, which draws a sharp line between the diversity and amount-in-controversy components of §1332, . . . the interpretation presented here does not sever the two jurisdictional requirements.

The more restrained reading of §1367 just outlined would yield affirmance of the First Circuit's judgment in *Ortega*, and reversal of the Eleventh Circuit's judgment in *Exxon*. It would not discard entirely, as the Court does, the judicially developed doctrines of pendent and ancillary jurisdiction as they existed when *Finley* was decided. Instead, it would recognize §1367 essentially as a codification of those doctrines, placing them under a single heading, but largely retaining their substance, with overriding *Finley* the only basic change: Supplemental jurisdiction, once the district court has original jurisdiction, would now include "claims that involve the joinder or intervention of additional parties." §1367(a).

Pendent jurisdiction, as earlier explained, . . . applied only in federal-question cases and allowed plaintiffs to attach nonfederal claims to their jurisdiction-qualifying claims. Ancillary jurisdiction applied primarily, although not exclusively, in diversity cases and "typically involved claims by a defending party haled into court against his will." . . . As the First Circuit observed, neither doctrine permitted a plaintiff to circumvent the dual requirements of §1332 (diversity of citizenship and amount in controversy) "simply by joining her [jurisdictionally inadequate] claim in an action brought by [a] jurisdictionally competent diversity plaintiff." *Ortega*, 370 F.3d at 138.

Not only would the reading I find persuasive "align statutory supplemental jurisdiction with the judicially developed doctrines of pendent and ancillary jurisdiction," . . . it would also synchronize §1367 with the removal statute, 28 U.S.C. §1441. . . .

The less disruptive view I take of §1367 also accounts for the omission of Rule 20 plaintiffs and Rule 23 class actions in §1367(b)'s text. If one reads §1367(a) as a

---

9. On this reading of §1367(a), it is immaterial that §1367(b) "does not withdraw supplemental jurisdiction over the claims of the additional parties at issue here." . . . Because those claims would not come within §1367(a) in the first place, Congress would have had no reason to list them in §1367(b). . . .

plenary grant of supplemental jurisdiction to federal courts sitting in diversity, one would indeed look for exceptions in §1367(b). Finding none for permissive joinder of parties or class actions, one would conclude that Congress effectively, even if unintentionally, overruled *Clark* and *Zahn*. But if one recognizes that the nonaggregation rule delineated in *Clark* and *Zahn* forms part of the determination whether "original jurisdiction" exists in a diversity case . . . , then plaintiffs who do not meet the amount-in-controversy requirement would fail at the §1367(a) threshold. Congress would have no reason to resort to a §1367(b) exception to turn such plaintiffs away from federal court, given that their claims, from the start, would fall outside the court's §1332 jurisdiction. See Pfander, 148 U. Pa. L. Rev., at 148.

Nor does the more moderate reading assign different meanings to "original jurisdiction" in diversity and federal-question cases. . . .

What is the utility of §1367(b) under my reading of §1367(a)? Section 1367(a) allows parties other than the plaintiff to assert *reactive* claims once entertained under the heading ancillary jurisdiction. See *supra* . . . (listing claims, including compulsory counterclaims and impleader claims, over which federal courts routinely exercised ancillary jurisdiction). As earlier observed, . . . §1367(b) stops plaintiffs from circumventing §1332's jurisdictional requirements by using another's claim as a hook to add a claim that the plaintiff could not have brought in the first instance. *Kroger* is the paradigm case. . . . There, the Court held that ancillary jurisdiction did not extend to a plaintiff's claim against a nondiverse party who been impleaded by the defendant under Rule 14. Section 1367(b), then, is corroborative of §1367(a)'s coverage of claims formerly called ancillary, but provides exceptions to assure that accommodation of added claims would not fundamentally alter "the jurisdictional requirements of section 1332." See Pfander, supra, at 135–137.

While §1367's enigmatic text[12] defies flawless interpretation,[13] . . . the precedent-preservative reading, I am persuaded, better accords with the historical and legal context of Congress' enactment of the supplemental jurisdiction

---

12. The Court notes the passage this year of the Class Action Fairness Act (CAFA), Pub. L. 109-2, 119 Stat. 4, . . . only to dismiss that legislation as irrelevant. Subject to several exceptions and qualifications, CAFA provides for federal-court adjudication of state-law-based class actions in which diversity is "minimal" (one plaintiff's diversity from one defendant suffices), and the "matter in controversy" is an aggregate amount in excess of $5,000,000. Significant here, CAFA's enlargement of federal-court diversity jurisdiction was accomplished, "clearly and conspicuously," by amending §1332. Cf. *Rosario Ortega*, 370 F.3d 124, 142 (CA1 2004).

13. If §1367(a) itself renders unnecessary the listing of Rule 20 plaintiffs and Rule 23 class actions in §1367(b) . . . then it is similarly unnecessary to refer, as §1367(b) does, to "persons proposed to be joined as plaintiffs under Rule 19." On one account, Congress bracketed such persons with persons "seeking to intervene as plaintiffs under Rule 24" to modify pre-§1367 practice. Before enactment of §1367, courts entertained, under the heading ancillary jurisdiction, claims of Rule 24(a) intervenors "of right," see *Owen Equipment & Erection Co. v. Kroger*, 437 U.S. 365, 375, n. 18 (1978), but denied ancillary jurisdiction over claims of "necessary" Rule 19 plaintiffs, see 13 Wright & Miller §3523, p. 127 (2d ed. Supp. 2005). Congress may have sought simply to underscore that those seeking to join as plaintiffs, whether under Rule 19 or Rule 24, should be treated alike, i.e., denied joinder when "inconsistent with the jurisdictional requirements of section 1332." See *Ortega*, 370 F.3d at 140, and n. 15 (internal quotation marks omitted); H. R. Rep., at 29 ("Subsection (b) makes one small change in pre-*Finley* practice," i.e., it eliminates the Rule 19/Rule 24 anomaly.).

statute . . . and the established limits on pendent and ancillary jurisdiction. . . . It does not attribute to Congress a jurisdictional enlargement broader than the one to which the legislators adverted, cf. *Finley*, 490 U.S., at 549, and it follows the sound counsel that "close questions of [statutory] construction should be resolved in favor of continuity and against change." Shapiro, Continuity and Change in Statutory Interpretation, 67 N. Y. U. L. Rev. 921, 925 (1992).[14]

For the reasons stated, I would hold that §1367 does not overrule *Clark* and *Zahn*. I would therefore affirm the judgment of the Court of Appeals for the First Circuit and reverse the judgment of the Court of Appeals for the Eleventh Circuit.

NOTES AND QUESTIONS

1. *Analyzing the Opinion.* The majority opinion of Justice Kennedy takes a claim-by-claim analysis of federal jurisdiction. Thus, since one of the plaintiffs in the *Ortega* action had the requisite amount in controversy, the Court found that the district court had "original jurisdiction over any civil action" within the meaning of 28 U.S.C. §1367(a). Since 28 U.S.C. §1367(b) does not exclude persons joined as *plaintiffs* under Rule 20, supplemental jurisdiction follows from 28 U.S.C. §1367(a). Shouldn't such an approach also follow if a second plaintiff joined pursuant to Rule 20 lacks the requisite diversity of citizenship? How does the majority avoid overruling the complete diversity rule of *Strawbridge v. Curtiss*, given its approach here?

2. The majority appears to recognize the anomaly of allowing supplemental jurisdiction over a proper party under Rule 20 but not a person "required to be joined if feasible" under Rule 19. How does the majority account for accepting that result?

3. What interpretive move does Justice Ginsburg in dissent make in concluding that a Rule 20 plaintiff with less than the requisite jurisdictional amount does not come within the supplemental jurisdiction provisions of §1367? Does the historical development of ancillary and pendent jurisdiction support Justice Ginsburg's view?

4. Why do Justice Kennedy and the majority reject what appears to be the clear intent of Congress not to overrule *Zahn*? Judge Pollack, reaching the opposite result in an early district court case, observed that to refuse to give effect to the congressional intent expressed in the House Report would be for the courts to say to Congress: "We know what you meant to say, but you didn't quite say it. So the message from us in the judicial branch to you in the legislative branch is 'Gotcha!' And better luck next time." *Russ v. State Farm Mut. Auto Ins. Co.*, 961 F. Supp. 808, 820 (E.D. Pa. 1997). Does Justice Kennedy in *Allapattah* give an adequate response to such criticism?

---

14. While the interpretation of §1367 described in this opinion does not rely on the measure's legislative history, that history, as Justice Stevens has shown, . . . is corroborative of the statutory reading set out above.

5. Several provisions of §1367 gave rise to interpretive difficulties and were the subject of extensive commentary in the cases and academic literature about the scope and meaning of the supplemental jurisdiction statute. For an interesting and provocative exchange between a critic of §1367 and three law professors who participated in the statute's drafting, *see* Richard D. Freer, *Compounding Confusion and Hampering Diversity, Life after* Finley *and the Supplemental Jurisdiction Statute*, 40 Emory L.J. 445 (1991); Thomas D. Rowe Jr. et al., *Compounding or Creating Confusion About Supplemental Jurisdiction? A Reply to Professor Freer*, 40 Emory L.J. 943 (1991); Thomas C. Arthur & Richard D. Freer, *Grasping at Burnt Straws: The Disaster of the Supplemental Jurisdiction Statute*, 40 Emory L.J. 963 (1991); Thomas D. Rowe Jr. et al., *A Coda on Supplemental Jurisdiction*, 40 Emory L.J. 993 (1991); Thomas C. Arthur & Richard D. Freer, *Close Enough for Government Work: What Happens When Congress Doesn't Do Its Job*, 40 Emory L.J. 1007 (1991). Among the issues in play were whether the statute overruled the Supreme Court's decision in *Zahn*, whether the statute had been drafted too hastily, and whether a comment in the legislative history stating Congress's intention not to overrule *Zahn* constituted an inappropriate attempt to circumvent the legislative process and change the meaning of the statute. By the time the Supreme Court decided *Allapattah*, the debate over §1367 had only intensified. *See, e.g.*, Richard D. Freer, *The Cauldron Boils: Supplemental Jurisdiction, Amount in Controversy, and Diversity of Citizenship Class Actions*, 53 Emory L.J. 55 (2004); James E. Pfander, *Supplemental Jurisdiction and Section 1367: The Case for Sympathetic Textualism*, 148 U. Pa. L. Rev. 109 (1999). Many of the controversial issues, including the meaning and relevance of the legislative history, were taken up in the Court's decision.

6. *The Debate about Statutory Interpretation.* Does the majority believe it is ever appropriate for the Court to look to legislative intent in interpreting a statute? Justice Kennedy's refusal to consider legislative history in *Allapattah* is consistent with the view, expressed in *Griffin v. Oceanic Contractors, Inc.*, 458 U.S. 564 (1982), that the best evidence of legislative intent is the language of the statute, and that courts should strictly interpret statutes according to their terms. Although the Court in *Griffin* conceded that it would look to legislative intent in rare instances where a literal reading of a statute would "thwart the obvious purpose of the statute," *id.* at 571, it indicated that, in most instances, it would read statutes narrowly, and if legislatures are unhappy with the results they are welcome to change the statutes. Indeed, Congress passed §1367 because it was unhappy with the results in *Finley*.

As Justice Stevens's dissent in *Allapattah* demonstrates, the debate over the acceptable methods of statutory interpretation is far from settled. Some commentators have argued that legislative history is unreliable as evidence of legislative intent and should be used sparingly, *see* Frederick Schauer, *Statutory Construction and the Coordinating Function of Plain Meaning*, 1990 Sup. Ct. Rev. 231, while others advocate a broader judicial inquiry in interpreting a statute, *see* Cass R. Sunstein, *Interpreting Statutes in the Regulatory State*, 103 Harv. L. Rev. 405 (1989) (arguing that "background norms" should be given substantial weight in interpreting statutes); William N. Eskridge, *Dynamic Statutory Interpretation*, 135 U. Pa. L. Rev. 1479 (1987) (arguing that statutory interpretation should include consideration of both historical and evolutive perspectives). Still others challenge the notion that courts should attempt to discern the intent of Congress, arguing that they should rely solely on the language of the statute, read in context. If such a reading does not produce a clear result in a given case, courts should assume that the statute does not address the issue. *See* Frank H. Easterbrook, *The Role of Original Intent in Statutory Construction*, 11 Harv. J.L. & Pub. Pol'y 59 (1988). While commentators disagree on the extent to which courts should consider legislative intent and the tools it should employ in its interpretation of statutes, it is generally accepted that the court need not adhere strictly to the plain meaning of the statutory language if such adherence will produce an absurd result. *See, e.g.*, Richard A. Posner, *Legal Formalism, Legal Realism, and the Interpretation of Statutes and the Constitution*, 37 Case W. Res. L. Rev. 180 (1986). For a critique of the "absurdity doctrine," *see* John F. Manning, *The Absurdity Doctrine*, 116 Harv. L. Rev. 2387 (2003) (arguing that the doctrine is inconsistent with a textualist approach to statutory interpretation and should be abandoned). Yet absurdity, like ambiguity, is often in the eye of the beholder. The Court in *Allapattah* held that the language of §1367 was unambiguous, and that its reading of the statute produced results that, while "something of a puzzle," were not absurd. Do you agree?

7. *The Class Action Fairness Act.* In the last paragraph of the majority opinion, Justice Kennedy refers to the 2005 Class Action Fairness Act (CAFA), discussed more extensively in Chapter 8. CAFA confers federal jurisdiction over class actions on the basis of minimal diversity where the aggregate amount in controversy exceeds $5 million. *See* §1332(d)(2). Claims of individual class members are aggregated to determine whether the $5 million amount in controversy is met. *See* §1332(d)(6). The Act thus supersedes *Snyder v. Harris* and *Zahn v. International Paper Co.* for actions within its ambit.

Do you understand the significance of the subject matter jurisdiction issues in class action litigation? Although in *Allapattah* it was plaintiffs who were seeking federal court jurisdiction for their class action, in many situations class action plaintiffs prefer state court rather than federal court because the state courts have been more liberal in certifying classes than the federal courts. In such instances, it is defendants who are arguing in favor of supplemental jurisdiction in the context of removal and plaintiffs who are resisting. A more extensive discussion of these issues in the context of the Class Action Fairness Act is found in Chapter 8.

8. *The Effect of §1367(c).* Recall that in *Gibbs* the Supreme Court emphasized that even if there is power to hear a case under (what was then called) pendent jurisdiction, a court always has discretion as to whether to exercise such jurisdiction. Now read 28 U.S.C. §1367(c). How does that provision intersect with the rulings in *Allapattah* and *Ortega*? Even if claims by absent class members or Rule 20 plaintiffs that lack the requisite jurisdictional amount fall within supplemental jurisdiction under §1367(a) and (b), might a court nonetheless exercise its discretion under §1367(c) and refuse to entertain such claims? For example, can a court decline to exercise supplemental jurisdiction because the addition of the claims of absent class members would place too great a burden on the federal court? Do the criteria in §1367 authorize a declination of jurisdiction in such circumstances? Even if so, would such an exercise of discretion undermine the Supreme Court's decision in *Allapattah*?

REVIEW PROBLEMS ON 28 U.S.C. §1367

To test your understanding of 28 U.S.C. §1367 (supplemental jurisdiction), try your hand at the following examples. Given the existence of the statute, is there federal subject matter jurisdiction in the following circumstances? As you answer each of these hypotheticals, try to determine which policies justify the result.

1. A New York employee asserts a federal labor claim and state breach of contract claim arising out of a single set of events against a labor union. May both claims be brought in federal court? What if the federal claim is brought against the labor union and the state contract claim is brought against a different defendant, such as the New York employer?

2. Plaintiff, a citizen of New York, brings a federal court action against the defendant, a citizen of Pennsylvania, for $100,000, asserting that the defendant assaulted him. Defendant counterclaims in that action, asserting a claim for libel growing out of that altercation and claiming damages of $30,000. Can the counterclaim be heard in federal court?

3. A New York resident attempts to bring suit in federal court against a Pennsylvania doctor and a Pennsylvania hospital for medical malpractice. The claim against the doctor is for $100,000. The claim against the hospital is for $10,000 (the result of a damages limit under the relevant statute). May both actions be heard in the federal court?

4. *A* and *B*, citizens of New York, are injured in an automobile accident. They attempt to bring suit in federal court against a Pennsylvania defendant. *A* asserts damages under state tort law for $100,000. *B*'s claim is for $40,000. May both actions be heard in the federal court?

5. *A*, a citizen of New York, and *B*, a citizen of Pennsylvania, are injured in an automobile accident. Each asserts a claim for $100,000 against the Pennsylvania defendant. May the action brought by *A* and *B* be heard in federal court?

6. Plaintiff, a citizen of New York, brings a class action based on state law on behalf of all New Yorkers against a Pennsylvania defendant. The named representative has a claim for $80,000, but the other class members have substantially smaller claims — none individually exceeds $20,000. May the class action be brought in federal court?

7. An Iowa plaintiff brings a state tort claim against a Nebraska defendant for the requisite jurisdictional amount. The Nebraska defendant impleads (under an indemnity contract) a third-party defendant, also from Nebraska. May the federal court hear the third-party action?

What if the third-party defendant is from Iowa? If the Iowa third-party defendant is appropriately brought in by the original Nebraska defendant, may the Iowa plaintiff now assert a state tort claim directly against the Iowa third-party defendant?

If the original claim by the plaintiff against the original defendant is based on "federal-question" jurisdiction (28 U.S.C. §1331) and a third-party defendant is impleaded, may the original plaintiff assert a claim based on state law directly against the third-party defendant?

F.   REMOVAL JURISDICTION

Read 28 U.S.C. §1441 in the Rules Supplement.

1.   *The Structure of Removal*

a.   The Basic Scheme: The Tie to Original Jurisdiction

Generally speaking, removal is tied to the original jurisdiction of the federal courts. Thus, most cases in which a plaintiff could have filed originally in federal court can be removed to federal court by a defendant. In diversity cases, the removal grant is somewhat more limited than the grant of original jurisdiction. Only a defendant who is a noncitizen of the forum has the option to remove in an ordinary diversity case. *See* 28 U.S.C. §1441(b).

The general removal statute, §1441(a), begins with a qualifier: "Except as otherwise expressly provided by Act of Congress. . . . " Thus, Congress can choose to make certain types of suits nonremovable. Congress had done just that for claims brought under the Federal Employers' Liability Act, *see* 28 U.S.C. §1445(a), and under state workers' compensation laws, *see* 28 U.S.C. §1445(c). The Supreme Court has given a strict interpretation to the "exception" language in §1441(a), finding that only an "*express*" statutory bar will prevent a party from removing. *See, e.g.*, 28 U.S.C. §1445(a) ("A civil action in any State court against a railroad . . . may not be removed to any district court of the United States."). In *Breuer v. Jim's Concrete of Brevard*, 538 U.S. 691 (2003), the Court held that a federal statute providing merely that an action "may be maintained . . . in any Federal or State court" does not constitute an exception, and the action may still be removed.

The right of removal is given only to the defendant. In *Shamrock Oil & Gas Corp. v. Sheets*, 313 U.S. 100 (1941), the question arose whether a "defendant" to a counterclaim—i.e., the original plaintiff—could exercise the removal option. The Supreme Court answered the question in the negative because the removal statute prior to the Act of 1887 had in fact authorized removal by "either party" whereas the current version of the removal statute authorizes removal only by the "defendant or defendants." In *Home Depot. U.S.A., Inc. v. Jackson*, 139 S. Ct. 1743 (2019), the Supreme Court extended *Shamrock Oil* to preclude removal by a party who was joined as an additional party to a class action counterclaim against the original plaintiff. Citibank had filed a state court debt-collection action against Jackson for charges incurred for the purchase of a water-treatment system. Jackson joined Home Depot and another company as third-party defendants to a class action claim in which it also named Citibank as a counterclaim defendant, alleging state law deceptive trade practices claims. Home Depot attempted to remove the case to federal court. The Supreme Court acknowledged that a third-party counterclaim defendant in Home Depot's shoes, unlike an original plaintiff, has no role in picking the forum, but the majority emphasized that the text of §1441(a) refers to "defendant[s] in a civil action," not defendants to any claim. Because there was no textual reason to differentiate counterclaim defendants originally part of the lawsuit from counterclaim defendants brought in later, the Court found that third-party counterclaim defendants in Home Depot's shoes are not defendants who can remove under §1441(a). The Court also held that the phrase "any defendant" in the Class Action Fairness Act's removal statute, §1453(b), is similarly constrained and does not permit removal by an additional party to a counterclaim.

b. The Forum Defendant Rule and Snap Removal

As discussed above, the "forum defendant rule," 28 U.S.C. §1441(b)(2), bars removing based on diversity if "any party in interest properly joined and served as a defendant" is domiciled in the forum state. But what if there are forum defendants that have yet to be served? Most courts adhere to the plain language of the statute: If a notice of removal based on diversity is filed prior to a forum defendant being properly joined and served, then the plaintiff will not be able to remand the case. While there is some dissent among district courts, the Second, Third, and Fifth Circuits—the only federal appellate courts to rule on the matter—have explicitly sanctioned this practice, known as "snap removal." *Texas Brine Co. v. Am. Arbitration Ass'n*, 955 F.3d 482 (5th Cir. 2020); *Gibbons v. Bristol-Myers Squibb Co.*, 919 F.3d 699 (2d Cir. 2019); *Encompass Insurance Co. v. Stone Mansion Restaurant Inc.* 902 F.3d 147 (3rd Cir. 2018). In *Texas Brine Co.*, the plaintiff, a Texas limited liability corporation, filed suit in Louisiana state court against three defendants: a New York corporation—the American Arbitration Association (AAA)—and two Louisiana citizens. Before the forum residents had been served, the AAA removed the case to federal court. The district court denied the plaintiff's motion to remand and the Fifth Circuit affirmed, holding that the "oddity" created by the "properly joined and served" language did not rise to the level of an "absurdity" that warranted contradicting the unambiguous text of the statute. *See generally* Valerie M. Nannery, *Closing the Snap Removal Loophole*, 86 U. Cin. L. Rev. 541 (2018).

Does snap removal aid the purpose of removal jurisdiction, namely, protecting foreign litigants from state court prejudice? Why do you think Congress included "properly served and joined" in §1441(b)(2)? In 2020, a bill limiting snap removal was introduced to Congress that would require federal courts to remand cases in which a plaintiff served a forum defendant within a specified period of time (a maximum of 30 days) after the notice of removal was filed. *See* Removal Jurisdiction Clairification Act of 2020, H.R. 5801, 116th Cong. (2020).

c. Broader Removal for Protected Parties

Congress has provided certain exceptions from the general rule that a removable case must be one that could have been filed originally in federal court. Generally, these exceptions refer to situations where Congress has determined there is a special need for a protective federal forum that would be hospitable to the defendant's federal defenses. *See, e.g.,* 28 U.S.C. §1442 (federal officer sued in state court for acts under color of federal authority); §1443 (civil rights removal). On the latter, *see* Martin H. Redish, *Revitalizing Civil Rights Removal Jurisdiction*, 64 Minn. L. Rev. 523 (1980).

d. Reconsidering the Role of Federal Defenses

Would the difficulties previously encountered in connection with *Mottley* and *Franchise Tax Board* be easily resolved if Congress had adopted the 1969 American Law Institute proposal and allowed removal on the basis of a substantive federal defense? Other than legislative inertia, are there good reasons why this proposal has not been enacted into law? Are important federalism values, similar to those invoked in support of the state courts' concurrent jurisdiction over federal claims, served by existing arrangements? Judge Posner suggests that frivolous defenses might be manufactured in order to get into federal court without the costs that attend the assertion of frivolous federal claims: "[I]f the plaintiff gets thrown out of federal court because his claim is frivolous, and must start over again, he has lost time; and the loss may be fatal if meanwhile the statute of limitations has run. But the defendant may be delighted to see the plaintiff's case thrown out of federal court when the court discovers that the federal defense is frivolous." Richard A. Posner, The Federal Courts: Crisis and Reform 190–191 (1985). For criticism of existing federal-question removal doctrine, *see* Michael G. Collins, *The Unhappy History of Federal Question Removal*, 71 Iowa L. Rev. 717 (1986).

e. When Is a Counterclaim Relevant?

The removability of a federal-question case is determined by the plaintiff's complaint. Where jurisdiction is based on §1331, the *plaintiff's* claim must arise under federal law; the defendant cannot remove by asserting a federal counterclaim, even a compulsory one. *See* 14C C. Wright et al., Federal Practice and Procedure §3722 (Revised 4th ed. 2021). The courts almost uniformly require the defendant to file an independent federal action in which presumably the plaintiff (now the defendant) could assert his original claims by way of counterclaim.

Interestingly, the rule involving calculation of the jurisdictional amount on removal in diversity cases is less clear. Recall the Supreme Court's decision in *Horton v. Liberty Mutual Insurance Co.*, 367 U.S. 348 (1961), discussed at p. 307, where the Supreme Court appeared to take into account the compulsory counterclaim asserted by the defendant in determining the jurisdictional amount in a case of original federal jurisdiction. *Horton* presented the unique situation of federal review of a workers' compensation award where the injured worker's original application to the compensation board would have satisfied the amount in controversy and thus *Horton* may be limited to its specific facts. In the removal context, however, most federal courts will not consider a counterclaim in determining the amount in controversy for removal, even when the counterclaim would be compulsory under state law.

f. Removal Based upon Diversity and the "Voluntary-Involuntary" Rule

Think back again to the case of *Rose v. Giamatti* from the introductory chapter, *supra* at p. 46. You will recall that the plaintiff, Pete Rose, brought suit in state court against three defendants, two of which were not diverse: Major League Baseball and the Cincinnati Reds. The defendants removed the case to federal court nonetheless and then argued that the citizenship of the organizational defendants should be disregarded under the "fraudulent joinder" doctrine because Rose had no real controversy with them. But if Rose had no real controversy with the organizational defendants, why did those defendants not simply have the claims against them dismissed in state court, leaving a lawsuit between Rose and Giamatti that would satisfy the requirements of complete diversity? A statute, 28 U.S.C. §1446(b), allows a defendant to remove a case within 30 days after the case becomes removable, even if it was not removable when originally filed (provided, in a case where jurisdiction is based upon diversity, that removal occurs within one year of filing or it is shown that the plaintiff has acted in "bad faith" to avoid removal). This statutory provision would seem to authorize exactly this type of scenario. However, some courts follow a "voluntary-involuntary rule" that would likely have prevented Giamatti from following this course of action. The voluntary-involuntary rule prevents a defendant from removing the lawsuit when the state court dismisses the claims against the nondiverse defendants on the merits, unless the *plaintiff* has taken a voluntary act that makes the case removable. If the case becomes removable solely through actions taken by the defendant (like the dismissal of nondiverse claims), the rule prevents removal. (This judicial gloss can be complicated in its application. For example, some courts force the plaintiff to appeal the state court's dismissal of the nondiverse claims in order for the dismissal to be considered involuntary.) The possibility that a dismissal of the state claims would have been considered an involuntary dismissal and thus would have prevented removal may explain why Giamatti chose not to try to have the claims against Major League Baseball and the Cincinnati Reds dismissed while still in state court.

Recently, another variation of fraudulent joinder in diversity cases has become increasingly prevalent: defendants' removal of a case on the basis that the lack of diversity exists only because the plaintiff has improperly joined a nondiverse party in violation of state joinder rules. Joinder is discussed in greater detail in Chapter 8, but for present purposes it is sufficient to understand that a plaintiff usually can join parties only when there is a transactional nexus among the claims and a common question of law or fact. Thus, the doctrine of "fraudulent misjoinder" allows a defendant to remove a case to federal court when a plaintiff has joined unrelated claims in order to destroy complete diversity. Although some courts have embraced "fraudulent misjoinder," *see, e.g., Tapscott v. MS Dealer Service Corp.*, 77 F.3d 1353 (11th Cir. 1996), others have responded to the misjoinder problem by allowing a defendant to remove the case only after the state court severs the unrelated claims, *see, e.g., Rutherford v. Merck & Co.*, 428 F. Supp. 2d 842 (S.D. Ill. 2006). For an overview of the development of the "fraudulent misjoinder" doctrine and an argument that the standard for "fraudulent misjoinder" should parallel the approach traditionally used for fraudulent joinder, *see* E. Farish Percy, *Defining the Contours of the Emerging Fraudulent Misjoinder Doctrine*, 29 Harv. J.L. & Pub. Pol'y 569 (2006).

In an interesting variation on this scenario, the Supreme Court has held that a case cannot be dismissed or remanded for lack of diversity on the grounds that, although all the parties named by the plaintiff are diverse, there are other, nondiverse parties who have *not* been named but should have been because they are the real parties in interest. Defendant, in other words, cannot be denied a federal forum simply because the court believes that the plaintiff may not have joined the right collection of parties. *See Lincoln Props. v. Roche*, 546 U.S. 81 (2005).

g. Removal and "Complete" Preemption

If a plaintiff files suit in state court, asserting state law claims, and the defendant argues that the claims are preempted by federal law, can the defendant remove the case to federal court on the basis of that preemption issue? Ordinarily, the answer would be no. Although preemption is an issue of federal law, it comes up by way of defense, and we know from *Mottley* that federal defenses do not confer "arising under" jurisdiction in federal court. *See Rivet v. Regions Bank of Lou-isiana,* 522 U.S. 470 (1998). In a narrow category of cases, however, the Supreme Court has permitted defendants to remove state law claims to federal court on the basis of a preemption defense. Where Congress expresses a particularly "powerful" interest in preempting state law, the Court has found, that interest "completely preempts" any state law causes of action, such that "a claim which comes within the scope of [the federal statute], even if pleaded in terms of state law, is in reality based on federal law." *Beneficial Nat'l Bank v. Anderson,* 539 U.S. 1 (2003). In such instances, the Court has permitted defendants to remove a case to federal court, even though the requirements of *Mottley* appear not to be satisfied. Thus far, the Court has limited this poorly defined category of "complete preemption" to certain causes of action under three federal statutes: the Labor Management Relations Act, the Employment Retirement Income Security Act (or ERISA), and the National Bank Act. For a recent example of the Supreme Court rejecting "complete preemption," *see Kircher v. Putnam Funds Trust,* 547 U.S. 633, 637 n. 1 (2006) (stating that the Securities Litigation Uniform Standards Act does not completely preempt state law).

h. Removal and Supplemental Jurisdiction

How does the concept of supplemental jurisdiction affect removal jurisdiction? In *City of Chicago v. International College of Surgeons,* 522 U.S. 156 (1997), the Supreme Court allowed removal of a lawsuit challenging on both state and federal grounds a city's landmark designation of plaintiffs' properties. The Supreme Court reasoned that the district court had "original jurisdiction" over the claims arising under federal law and "could exercise supplemental jurisdiction over the accompanying state law claims" so long as those claims constituted part of the same controversy within the meaning of §1367. The crux of *College of Surgeons* actually turned on whether a state claim involving deferential review of a local administrative decision was ever appropriately within supplemental jurisdiction, and the majority held that it was. But the Court's characterization of the removal process appears to have had broader ramifications. Recall that, in *Ortega,* Justice Kennedy relied on *College of Surgeons* to support his claim-by-claim analysis of original jurisdiction, holding that the federal court had "original jurisdiction" over the claim with the requisite jurisdictional amount and "supplemental jurisdiction" over the related claims without the requisite amount in controversy. However, Justice Kennedy's attempt to draw a distinction between "original jurisdiction" and "supplemental" jurisdiction presents certain conceptual problems under the removal statute for a case like *College of Surgeons.* Section 1441(a) requires that the district court must have "original jurisdiction" of a "civil action" for a case to be removed, and there is no textual basis to remove the entire case on the basis of a single federal claim. *Compare* §1441(c), discussed *infra,* where a claim that arises under federal law provides a basis for removal of the entire case, with those claims "not within the original or supplemental jurisdiction of the district court" to be severed and remanded upon removal. Given the language of the removal statute, "original jurisdiction" in the context of removal may be better understood as encompassing jurisdiction based on a specific grant of jurisdiction, such as §1331, as well as "supplemental jurisdiction."

i. An Empirical Look at Removal

Professors Kevin M. Clermont and Theodore Eisenberg conducted an empirical study that shows that plaintiffs' win rates in removed cases are very low when compared with those cases brought originally in federal or state court (both in federal-question and diversity cases). What might account for such a disparity? Professors Clermont and Eisenberg hypothesize that both forum and case selection are favorable to defendants in removed cases. Not only does the defendant benefit from the elimination of supposed local bias in state court, but the fact that removal is available often means either that the defendant has settled all but the plaintiffs' weakest claims or that the plaintiffs' attorneys are not savvy enough to avoid exposing their claims to removal. *See* Kevin M. Clermont & Theodore Eisenberg, *Do Case Outcomes Really Reveal Anything About the Legal System? Win Rates and Removal Jurisdiction*, 83 Cornell L. Rev. 581 (1998).

A more recent study, however, examines a different angle of removal: the growing problem of defendants improperly removing cases. *See* Theodore Eisenberg & Trevor W. Morrison, *Overlooked in the Tort Reform Debate: The Growth of Erroneous Removal*, 2 J. Empirical Legal Stud. 551 (2005). The authors first note that the number of removed cases that ultimately were remanded to state court increased from 12 percent in 1979 to nearly 20 percent in 2003. Further, a case study of state and federal courts in Alabama highlighted some astonishing trends. While plaintiffs only contested removals in 48 percent of removed diversity cases, they were successful in 82 percent of their challenges. Professors Eisenberg and Morrison speculate about the potential causes for this surprising statistic. One possibility is that because §1446(b) forces a defendant to file a notice of removal within 30 days after the defendant receives the pleading that makes the case removable, defendants might not have enough time to gather the information necessary to make an accurate determination and therefore might remove as a precaution. The other possibility is "removal abuse," when a defendant removes in an effort to delay resolution of the case or attempt to outlast a weary or cash-strapped plaintiff. The authors note that while §1447(c) does permit the district court to require a party that erroneously removes a case to pay the other party's costs and attorneys' fees, this provision is used inconsistently. Further, the Supreme Court held that courts only can award attorneys' fees in situations when "the removing party lacked an objectively reasonable basis for seeking removal." *See Martin v. Franklin Capital Corp.*, 546 U.S. 132 (2005). Given this interpretation of §1447(c), it is unlikely that erroneous removals will be greatly deterred without legislative intervention. *See* Eisenberg & Morrison at 576.

j. Foreign States and §1441(d)

Section 1441 also provides for the removal of lawsuits brought against foreign states. Under §1441(d), "[a]ny civil action brought in a State court against a foreign state . . . may be removed by the foreign state to" a federal district court. For these purposes, "foreign state" includes political subdivisions (such as provinces or cantons) and applies even to corporations owned by a foreign state, so long as a majority of the shares in the corporation are owned directly by the sovereign. *See* 28 U.S.C. §1603(a) (defining "foreign state"); *Dole Food Co. v. Patrickson*, 538 U.S. 468

(2003) (holding that majority of shares in corporation must be owned directly by foreign state in order to qualify for removal under §1441(d)). *Dole Food* also held that the determination as to whether an entity has the status of a "foreign state" is made as of the time an action is filed, rather than as of the time the cause of action arose. (Recall that this same timing rule also applies to the determination of citizenship for purposes of general diversity jurisdiction.)

2. The Conundrum of §1441(c)

28 U.S.C. §§1441(a) and (b) of the removal statute premise removal on the basis that all of the removed claims could have been brought in federal court as an original matter. 28 U.S.C. §1441(c) represents a marked departure from that general philosophy of removal and some clarifications were made to that provision in the Federal Courts Jurisdiction and Venue Clarification Act of 2011. 28 U.S.C. §1441(c) applies to actions where state law claims outside of "the original or supplemental jurisdiction of the district court" or claims made "non-removable by statute" are joined with claims arising under federal law. Note that the state law claims fall outside of the supplemental jurisdiction of the federal court because they are so *unrelated* to the federal claim. Nonetheless, 28 U.S.C. §1441(c) permits the defendant to remove the entire action to federal court under §1441(c)(1), and then under §1441(c)(2) the district court is required to sever the non-removable claims and remand them back to state court. This remand requirement was imposed under the 2011 Clarification Act to ensure that only claims that fall within Article III of the Constitution are heard by a federal court.

Do you understand the purpose of §1441(c)? By making removable an action that arises under federal law even though it is joined with non-removable state law claims, a plaintiff cannot join unrelated state law claims and thereby block a defendant's right to remove a federal-question case to federal court. (Note that §1441(c) does not apply to diversity of citizenship cases, and thus plaintiffs may still join non-diverse defendants to block removal in actions where the claims are based on state law. In such a case, the only remedy for a defendant is to argue "fraudulent joinder," as the defendant successfully did in *Rose v. Giamatti*.)

3. Removal Procedures

The procedure for removal is set out in 28 U.S.C. §§1446, 1447, and 1448. It calls for notice of removal to be filed in the district court and a copy of the notice to be filed in state court. A motion to remand back to state court must be raised within 30 days after the filing of the notice of removal. However, if at any time before final judgment it appears that the district court lacks subject matter jurisdiction, the case shall be remanded to state court. *See* 28 U.S.C. §1447(c).

The notice of removal must be filed within 30 days after receipt by the defendant of a copy of the initial pleading setting forth the claim or, if the case is not initially removable, within 30 days of any filing from which it appears that the case has become removable. The Federal Courts Jurisdiction and Venue Clarification

Act of 2011 expanded the definition of "any filing" within the removal statute such that a "filing" in the literal sense is no longer required. Now a defendant can file for removal within 30 days after any new information obtained during state-court discovery reveals that a case, not initially removable, has become removable. *See* 28 U.S.C. §1446(b)(3). The 2011 Clarification Act also explains how the 30-day removal period applies in cases with multiple defendants. Each defendant is given its own 30-day removal period and earlier-served defendants can join in the removal of later-served defendants, even if the earlier-served defendant's removal period has already expired and regardless of whether he or she had previously waived his or her right of removal. *See* 28 U.S.C. §1441(b)(2)(C); *see generally* Paul E. Lund, *The Timeliness of Removal and Multiple-Defendant Lawsuits*, 64 Baylor L. Rev. 59 (2012). Although a case may not be removed on the basis of diversity jurisdiction more than one year after the commencement of the action, a new provision added by the 2011 Jurisdiction and Venue Clarification Act establishes a "bad faith" exception to this one-year limitation. Removal is now authorized even after one year if the court finds that the plaintiff acted deliberately in "bad faith" to avoid removal. *See* 28 U.S.C. §1446(c)(1).

In *Dart Cherokee Basin Operating Co. v. Owens*, 135 S.Ct. 547 (2014), the Supreme Court held that 28 U.S.C. §1446(a) applies the same plausibility standard to its requirement of a "short and plain statement of the grounds for removal" that Rule 8(a) applies to a claim for relief. The Court disapproved precedent in the Tenth Circuit that had required removing defendants to support a notice of removal with evidence that affirmatively established the amount in controversy in a removal based on diversity. Pointing to provisions of the Federal Courts Jurisdiction and Venue Clarification Act of 2011 that require a removing defendant to prove the amount in controversy by a preponderance of the evidence when the defendant's assertion of that amount is challenged, the Court concluded that no such evidence need be included in the notice of removal itself, before any challenge has been levied. Rather, "a defendant's notice of removal need include only a plausible allegation that the amount in controversy exceeds the jurisdictional threshold." Evidence in support of that allegation is required "only when the plaintiff contests, or the court questions, the defendant's allegation."

An order remanding a case to the state court is generally not reviewable on appeal, except for a case removed under 28 U.S.C. §1443. *See* 28 U.S.C. §1447(d). However, in *Thermtron Products, Inc. v. Hermansdorfer*, 423 U.S. 336 (1976), the Supreme Court held that remand orders entered on grounds not authorized by the removal statute could be reviewed on a *writ of mandamus*. In that case, the Supreme Court reversed a district court's remand of a case properly removed from state to federal court because its docket was overcrowded and it thought the case could be adjudicated more efficiently in state court.

The Supreme Court has been cautious about applying the *Thermtron* exception too expansively. In *Powerex Corp. v. Reliant Energy Servs.*, 551 U.S. 224 (2007), the Court held that §1447(d)'s bar on appellate review of remand orders applies whenever "the District Court relied upon a ground that is colorably characterized as subject-matter jurisdiction." The *Thermtron* doctrine thus appears to be limited to situations where a district court either expressly remands on a ground other than subject matter jurisdiction that is plainly unauthorized (an unlikely scenario, now that *Thermtron* is on the books), or else offers an explanation for its remand that cannot plausibly be characterized as going to its subject matter jurisdiction. However, the Court has also held that the general prohibition contained in §1447(d) may not displace authorizations for appellate review contained in more specific statutes. *See, e.g., Osborn v. Haley,* 549 U.S. 225 (2007).

The Supreme Court revisited the issue of the 28 U.S.C. §1447(d) bar on review of remand orders in *Carlsbad Tech., Inc. v. HIF BIO, Inc.,* 556 U.S. 635 (2009). Upon the removal of a case under 28 U.S.C. §1441(a), in which both federal and state law claims (sufficiently related to satisfy the requirements of 28 U.S.C. §1367) are present, a district court is free to refuse to exercise supplemental jurisdiction over the state claims if all of the federal claims have been dismissed. The Supreme Court held that "such remand orders are not based on a lack of subject-matter jurisdiction," and therefore they are reviewable on appeal. The Court reasoned that a district court unquestionably has jurisdiction over such claims but is merely deciding not to hear them on a discretionary basis. In concurrence, Justice Stevens expressed dissatisfaction with the ruling, stating "[t]oday, as in *Thermtron,* the Court holds that §1447(d) does not mean what it says." Also in concurrence, Justice Scalia called for reconsideration of the *Thermtron* decision. For an interesting solution to the problem of when to allow appellate review of remand orders, *see* James Pfander, *Collateral Review of Remand Orders: Reassessing the Supervisory Role of the Supreme Court,* 159 U. Pa. L. Rev. 493 (2011). Professor Pfander argues that the Supreme Court should assert its supervisory authority to correct lower court errors without complicating the existing doctrine of when remand orders can be reviewed.

Removal is a waivable right. Waiver has occasionally turned on whether the defendant filed a responsive pleading raising a defense that might be conclusive of the merits or whether the defendant sought affirmative relief or took affirmative action to adjudicate the merits.

The removal of a case to federal court can have important implications because federal procedure and remedies will apply. *See* Fed. R. Civ. P. 81(c). In *Avco Corp. v. Aero Lodge No. 735,* 390 U.S. 557 (1968), for example, the defendant union sought removal because federal legislation sharply restricts the availability of federal injunctive relief in labor disputes. (We will be considering in Chapter 4 the limits on a federal court's authority to apply federal procedure with respect to claims governed by state substantive law, as well as the corresponding limits on a state court's authority to apply state procedure with respect to federal claims.)

4. Specialized Removal Provisions Under the Class Action Fairness Act and the Multiparty, Multiforum Trial Jurisdiction Act

In Chapter 8, we will examine in greater detail two recent statutory developments that have expanded federal court jurisdiction in complex litigation. We have already briefly looked at the provisions on original jurisdiction in the Multiparty, Multiforum Trial Jurisdiction Act and in the Class Action Fairness Act, *see* pp. 309-312. In order to ensure a federal forum for these actions brought initially in state court, changes to removal were also part of the statutory architecture.

a. Multiparty, Multiforum Trial Jurisdiction Act

You will recall the provisions of 28 U.S.C. §1369 that provide for a federal forum on the basis of minimal diversity for any civil action arising from an accident involving at least 75 deaths when certain other conditions are met. The Act also includes broad provisions for removal in subdivision (e) of §1441. Pursuant to §1441(e)(1), an action may be removed by a defendant if (a) the action could have been brought in federal court under §1369, or (b) the defendant is a party to an action "which is or could have been brought in whole or in part, under [§]1369 . . . and arises from the same accident as the action in State court, even if the action to be removed could not have been brought in a district court as an original matter." What is the purpose of such broad removal provisions?

Passa v. Derderian, 308 F. Supp. 2d 43 (D.R.I. 2004), was one of the first cases to interpret the removal provisions. Multiple actions were brought by different plaintiffs for claims arising out of a deadly nightclub fire in which 100 people were killed and 200 others injured. Anheuser-Busch was named as a defendant in both state and federal court actions. Defendant Anheuser-Busch was allowed to remove an otherwise unremovable state court action because the state court suit arose from the same accident as the federal court action in which Anheuser-Busch was also a defendant.

Another question concerning the application of §1441(e)(1) arose in *Wallace v. Louisiana Citizens Prop. Ins. Corp.*, 444 F.3d 697 (5th Cir. 2006). The case involved a class of plaintiffs who allegedly suffered flood damage as a result of Hurricane Katrina; the defendant insurance company removed the case to federal court under §1441(e)(1)(B) because it was a party to another Hurricane Katrina-related class action in federal court. The district court remanded the case, declining to exercise jurisdiction pursuant to §1369(b), which provides that district courts must abstain from exercising jurisdiction over certain local actions even after removal. The Court of Appeals reversed, holding that §1441(e)(1)(B) confers removal jurisdiction regardless of any other provision, including the mandatory abstention requirements of §1369(b). The court found this interpretation consistent with the Multiparty, Multiforum Trial Jurisdiction Act's overarching goal of consolidating cases stemming from a common disaster.

For recent developments in the interpretation of the specialized removal provisions contained in the Multiparty, Multiform Trial Jurisdiction Act, *see* Chapter 8 at pp. 1023–1038. Note also the special remand provisions for actions removed under §1441(e). Subdivision (e)(2) provides that when a district court to which an action is removed or transferred has made a liability determination requiring further proceedings as to damages, the district court shall remand the action to the state court from which it has been removed for the determination of damages, unless the court finds that, for the convenience of parties and witnesses and in the interest of justice, the action should be retained for the determination of damages. Subdivision (e)(3) provides for a 60-day window before remand, during which time an appeal may be taken with respect to the district court's determination of liability. Subdivision (e)(4) makes clear that the remand for a determination of damages is not reviewable by appeal or otherwise.

b.   Class Action Fairness Act

As noted at pp. 311–312, the Class Action Fairness Act of 2005 amended the diversity statute to authorize federal district courts to exercise jurisdiction over class actions with an aggregate amount in controversy of at least $5 million where minimal diversity is satisfied. *See* 28 U.S.C. §1332(d)(2). When the class action is fundamentally connected to a single state as identified by criteria in the statute, *see* §§1332(d)(3) and (d)(4), the district court is either authorized ((d)(3)) or required ((d)(4)) to decline jurisdiction.

A special provision on removal, 28 U.S.C. §1453, contains particular criteria to govern removal of national class actions filed in state courts. As with a traditional lawsuit, a defendant may remove a class action that could have been brought initially in federal court. Section 1453 also eliminates a number of barriers that exist with respect to removal in the ordinary case, making removal easier for defendants and providing for discretionary interlocutory review of remand orders. Note that (1) a citizen defendant is permitted to remove in a diversity class action; (2) the consent of all defendants is not required; (3) the one-year time limit on removal in diversity cases does not apply; and (4) interlocutory appeal of an order granting or denying a motion to remand a class action to the state court is permitted if application is made within seven days after the order.

G.   CHALLENGING SUBJECT MATTER JURISDICTION

Unlike most other claims of legal error, defects in a court's subject matter jurisdiction are generally treated as nonwaivable and hence are not subject to waiver because of untimely assertion or acquiescence. Indeed, as illustrated by the *Mottley* and *Smith* cases, *supra*, and reflected in the language of Federal Rule 12(h)(3), the court has a responsibility on its own to ensure that it has jurisdiction over the subject matter of the action. The rule of nonwaivability extends through all appellate stages of the litigation, even on review by the United States Supreme Court.

1.   *Direct Review Versus Collateral Challenge*

The traditional view at common law was that a judgment rendered by a court lacking jurisdiction over the subject matter was null and void, and that a challenge to the court's subject matter jurisdiction could be made directly at any time or via collateral attack. In at least one early Supreme Court case, *Des Moines Navigation & Railroad Co. v. Iowa Homestead Co.*, 123 U.S. 552 (1887), the "null and void" doctrine was qualified, and full faith and credit was given to a judgment in a prior federal court litigation between the same parties that had been reviewed by the Supreme Court on the merits without any objection having been raised as to jurisdiction. (However, because the defect in the federal court's removal jurisdiction in the first proceeding was unclear at the time of the initial proceeding, the *Des Moines* case cannot necessarily be viewed as articulating a general rule.)

Subsequent Supreme Court cases also restricted the availability of collateral attack. *See Chicot County Drainage District v. Baxter State Bank*, 308 U.S. 371 (1940) (disallowing collateral attack on judgment rendered by federal court exercising jurisdiction under a statute later held unconstitutional); *Durfee v. Duke*, 375 U.S. 106 (1963) (rejecting collateral attack in Missouri action challenging Nebraska court's jurisdiction over land determined after contested litigation in Nebraska state court to be located in Nebraska). *See generally* Dan B. Dobbs, *The Validation of Void Judgments: The Bootstrap Principle, Part I, The Rationale of Bootstrap*, 53 Va. L. Rev. 1003 (1967).

The Restatement (Second) of Judgments §12 (1982) has fashioned a modern rule for collateral challenge to subject matter jurisdiction that attempts to balance the need for finality against institutional interests in the particular case. Section 12 provides:

> When a court has rendered a judgment in a contested action, the judgment precludes the parties from litigating the question of the court's subject matter jurisdiction in subsequent litigation except if:
>
> (1) The subject matter of the action was so plainly beyond the court's jurisdiction that its entertaining the action was a manifest abuse of authority; or
>
> (2) Allowing the judgment to stand would substantially infringe the authority of another tribunal or agency of government; or
>
> (3) The judgment was rendered by a court lacking capability to make an adequately informed determination of a question concerning its own jurisdiction and as a matter of procedural fairness the party seeking to avoid the judgment should have opportunity belatedly to attack the court's subject matter jurisdiction.

Section 12, as its express language indicates, is applicable to contested actions. If the defendant has defaulted without appearing at all, the defendant is always permitted to raise lack of subject matter jurisdiction in subsequent litigation and avoid the impact of the judgment. (The rule here with respect to a default in lieu of appearance is similar to the rule for raising objections to personal jurisdiction.) *See generally* Restatement (Second) of Judgments §65.

2. Must Subject Matter Jurisdiction Be Established Before Any Other Issue?

In *Steel Co. v. Citizens for Better Environment*, 523 U.S. 83 (1998), the Supreme Court held that the district court erred in dismissing an action on the merits without first establishing that the plaintiff had standing, an element of the court's subject matter jurisdiction. Even though the defendant would prevail whether or not the court had jurisdiction, *Steel* held that a court simply has no authority to make any ruling on the merits until its subject matter jurisdiction is established.

However, the following term the Court held that a court may dismiss for lack of *personal jurisdiction* without first resolving a complex question of subject matter jurisdiction. In *Ruhrgas A.G. v. Marathon Oil Co.*, 526 U.S. 574 (1999), defendant had removed a case to federal court notwithstanding the joinder of a nondiverse plaintiff and then moved to dismiss for lack of personal jurisdiction. Plaintiff moved to remand back to state court because of the incomplete diversity. Defendant's theory of jurisdiction was that, as in *Rose, supra*, the nondiverse party had been "fraudulently joined" and should not be counted for diversity purposes. In order to determine whether there had been a fraudulent joinder, the court would have been required to resolve a complex question of whether the nondiverse plaintiff had a cause of action under Norwegian law. The Supreme Court, emphasizing the need for judicial efficiency, upheld the district court's decision to resolve the case on the relatively clear basis of lack of personal jurisdiction over the German defendant.

Do you see a principled difference between the two Supreme Court cases? Why should the concern about a court's "lack of authority" be different when the issue is one of personal jurisdiction rather than merits? Note that the decision on personal jurisdiction by the Texas federal court in *Ruhrgas* would operate to preclude the plaintiff from obtaining jurisdiction over the German defendant in a Texas state court as well.

Does *Ruhrgas* suggest an underlying problem with the fraudulent joinder doctrine itself—i.e., that under that doctrine, a court must consider the merits of the case in order to establish its subject matter jurisdiction? Wouldn't the *Ruhrgas* problem be largely eliminated if the Court had simply declined to endorse the fraudulent joinder doctrine? Are there going to be many other situations where it is much easier to resolve the case on personal rather than subject matter jurisdiction grounds?

The Court has continued to reject the notion that a court must first establish subject matter jurisdiction before dismissing a case on select other grounds. In *Tenet v. Doe*, 544 U.S. 1 (2005), the Supreme Court dismissed a case based on a longstanding rule that prevents suits against the government relating to covert espionage agreements; in doing so, the Court resolved the case before addressing whether it had subject matter jurisdiction. The Court followed analogous reasoning in *Sinochem Int'l Co. v. Malaysia Int'l Shipping Corp.*, 549 U.S. 422 (2007). *Sinochem* involved allegations of wrongdoing and negligence stemming from a contract between a Malaysian plaintiff and a Chinese defendant over a boat stationed in Chinese waters. In what Justice Ginsburg termed a "textbook" case for a *forum non conveniens* dismissal, the overarching question concerned whether the Court had to resolve the thorny issues of subject matter and personal jurisdiction before dismissing the case. Unanimously, the Court permitted immediate dismissal, extending *Ruhrgas* and determining that "[r]esolving a *forum non conveniens* motion does not entail any assumption by the court of substantive 'law-declaring power.'" *Id.* at 433. The Court emphasized judicial economy as a basis for its decision.

Chapter 4

THE LAW APPLIED IN FEDERAL COURT

Up to this point, we have focused on where a civil action may be brought. The law of personal jurisdiction and venue defined the geographic options for the place of trial, and the law of subject matter jurisdiction delineated authority between state and federal courts. Selection of the forum, however, does not necessarily resolve which jurisdiction's law will be applied in a given case. Just because a suit is brought in Iowa does not mean that Iowa law will be applied in the case. For instance, suppose that a citizen of Kansas was injured in Kansas by a car driven by a citizen of Iowa. If the Kansas plaintiff chooses to file suit in Iowa, the Iowa courts may well decide to apply Kansas law to some or all of the issues in the lawsuit.

Similarly, a party's selection of a federal, rather than state, forum does not necessarily mean that federal, rather than state, law will be applied to all the issues in the lawsuit. Just as the Iowa court must decide whether to apply Iowa or Kansas law, a federal court must decide whether to apply federal or state law. That determination is the subject of this chapter. The choice between laws of different states is the subject of the advanced course in Conflict of Laws and will only be addressed here in passing.

Two legal texts provide the starting point for identifying the law that should be applied in federal courts: the Constitution of the United States, and §34 of the Judiciary Act of 1789. The Tenth Amendment to the federal Constitution embodies the principle of limited federal power: "The powers not delegated to the United States by the Constitution, nor prohibited by it to the States, are reserved to the States respectively, or to the people." This principle is further reflected in the structure of the Constitution, which sets out the "enumerated powers" of each branch of the federal government. Any federal action not authorized by the enumerated powers is unconstitutional because it is outside of the ambit of governmental powers allocated to the federal government.

The power assigned specifically to the federal courts by the Constitution is at once very simple yet potentially expansive: "The judicial Power of the United States shall be vested in one supreme Court, and in such inferior Courts as the Congress may from time to time ordain and establish." Art. III, §1. That "judicial power" includes the authority to resolve certain kinds of "cases" and "controversies," including, as we have seen, cases arising under federal law, and cases between citizens of different states.

But what does the grant of judicial power authorize a court to do? In the course of resolving legal disputes, courts interpret and articulate rules of law. Does jurisdiction to resolve a case include the power to craft new legal rules—i.e., make law? If so, then any case tried in a federal court could be governed by federal judge-made law. A contract unenforceable in state court might become enforceable in federal court. A plaintiff barred by a contributory negligence rule in state court might recover in federal court. Such a characterization of the federal judicial power would make the federal courts, in some ways, more powerful than Congress because Congress can make law only where authorized by the enumerated powers; the federal courts, under this view, could make law whenever they had subject matter jurisdiction.

If, on the other hand, we conclude that the power to hear a case does not necessarily include the authority to make independent rules of law, where should a federal court look to for legal rules in resolving cases? In addition to the Tenth Amendment's "default setting"—that state law controls in the absence of enumerated federal power—Congress has provided some statutory guidance. Section 34 of the Judiciary Act of 1789, now codified as 28 U.S.C. §1652, provides:

> The laws of the several states, except where the Constitution or treaties of the United States or Acts of Congress otherwise require or provide, shall be regarded as rules of decision in civil actions in the courts of the United States, in cases where they apply.

This provision, commonly known as the "Rules of Decision Act," contains a number of ambiguities that make its application problematic. The last phrase, "in cases where they apply," makes the statute appear circular: State law applies where it applies. The meaning of "rules of decision" is also unclear: Does every law applicable to a legal proceeding constitute a "rule of decision," or only those rules that affect how the case is ultimately decided? For instance, is a rule regarding how process should be served a "rule of decision"? What does the "laws of the several states" mean? Does it mean the law of the state where the court is sitting, or the collective laws of all the states? Finally, what constitutes the "laws"? Specifically, do judicial opinions constitute the law of a state, or are they simply legal interpretations, not binding on the federal courts under the Rules of Decision Act?

A.   THE ORIGINS OF THE DEBATE: SWIFT AND ERIE

1.   Swift v. Tyson

The last question regarding the meaning of the "laws" was the focus of two Supreme Court decisions that have largely defined the terms of the debate over the applicable law in federal courts: *Swift v. Tyson* and *Erie v. Tompkins*. *Swift v. Tyson*, 41 U.S. 1 (1842), held that the judicial—i.e., "common law"—decisions of the state courts did not generally constitute the "law of the several states" for the purposes of the Rules of Decision Act. The case arose out of a dispute over the enforceability of a debt instrument. Tyson, a citizen of New York, had attempted to buy some land in Maine and had signed a "bill of exchange"—basically a mortgage—in payment for the land. This note was in turn assigned to Swift, a citizen of Maine, by the sellers of the land in satisfaction of a prior debt that the sellers owed to Swift. It turned out, however, that the sellers did not, in fact, own the land. When the note came due, Tyson refused to pay Swift on the ground that the sellers' fraud nullified the note and precluded recovery by Swift. Swift filed a diversity suit in New York, asserting that as a purchaser of the note without notice of the underlying fraud, he could enforce the note even if the note would not have been enforceable by the sellers. Tyson countered that while "bona fide purchasers" of bills of exchange could indeed enforce such notes, Swift was not a "bona fide purchaser," as defined by the law of New York, because he took the note in satisfaction of a preexisting debt, not for new consideration.

The decision, written by Justice Story, held that the New York judicial decisions on the meaning of a "bona fide purchaser" were not binding on the federal courts. Specifically, the federal courts were free to hold, contrary to New York judicial decisions, that if a holder of a note received the note in satisfaction of a preexisting debt, he would be considered a "bona fide holder," and could enforce the note free of any defenses that the debtor had against the original holder. The Rules of Decision Act did not require conformity with the New York decisions because common law decisions by state courts did not constitute "laws" for the purpose of the Act:

> It is observable, that the courts of New York do not found their decisions upon this point, upon any local statute, or positive, fixed or ancient local usage; but they deduce the doctrine from the general principles of commercial law. It is, however, contended, that the 34th section of the Judiciary Act of 1789, ch. 20, furnishes a rule obligatory upon this court to follow the decisions of the state tribunals in all cases to which they apply. That section provides "that the laws of the several states, except where the Constitution, treaties or statutes of the United States shall otherwise require or provide, shall be regarded as rules of decision, in trials at common law, in the courts of the United States, in cases where they apply." In order to maintain the argument, it is essential, therefore, to hold, that the word "laws," in this section, includes within the scope of its meaning, the decisions of the local tribunals. In the ordinary use of language, it will hardly be contended, that the decisions of courts constitute laws. They are, at most, only evidence of what the laws are, and are not, of themselves, laws. They are often re-examined, reversed and qualified by the courts themselves, whenever they are found to be either defective, or ill-founded, or otherwise incorrect. The laws of a state are more usually understood to mean the rules and enactments promulgated by the legislative authority thereof, or long-established local customs having the force of laws. In all the various cases, which have hitherto come before us for decision, this court has uniformly supposed, that the true interpretation of the 34th section limited its application to state laws, strictly local, that is to say, to the positive statutes of the state, and the construction thereof adopted by the local tribunals, and to rights and titles to things having a permanent locality, such as the rights and titles to real estate, and other matters immovable and intraterritorial in their nature and character. It never has been supposed by us, that the section did apply, or was designed

to apply, to questions of a more general nature, not at all dependent upon local statutes or local usages of a fixed and permanent operation, as, for example, to the construction of ordinary contracts or other written instruments, and especially to questions of general commercial law, where the state tribunals are called upon to perform the like functions as ourselves, that is, to ascertain, upon general reasoning and legal analogies, what is the true exposition of the contract or instrument, or what is the just rule furnished by the principles of commercial law to govern the case. And we have not now the slightest difficulty in holding, that this section, upon its true intendment and construction, is strictly limited to local statutes and local usages of the character before stated, and does not extend to contracts and other instruments of a commercial nature, the true interpretation and effect whereof are to be sought, not in the decisions of the local tribunals, but in the general principles and doctrines of commercial jurisprudence. Undoubtedly, the decisions of the local tribunals upon such subjects are entitled to, and will receive, the most deliberate attention and respect of this court; but they cannot furnish positive rules, or conclusive authority, by which our own judgments are to be bound up and governed. The law respecting negotiable instruments may be truly declared in the language of Cicero, adopted by Lord Mansfield in Luke v. Lyde, . . . to be in a great measure, not the law of a single country only, but of the commercial world. . . .

Id. at 18.

To the modern reader, Story's rejection of the proposition "that the decisions of courts constitute laws" may seem perplexing. Why does he claim that judicial decisions are "only evidence of what the laws are, and are not, of themselves, laws"? He does not assert that state statutes are "only evidence" of what the law is, and not the actual law and, indeed, treats judicial opinions construing statutes as binding on the federal courts. It is only judicial decisions dealing with "general principles of commercial jurisprudence" that he characterizes as mere "evidence" of the law, not binding on the federal courts. Why should some state judicial opinions be considered "conclusive authority," and others viewed as mere "interpretations"?

The answer appears to be bound up in Story's vision of law. While legislators are capable of creating new law in the form of statutes, there is also a "general" or "common law" that exists in the absence of any legislative act. Common law, in this view, is not the law of any particular state. Rather, it is a set of "just" rules shared by the Anglo-American legal system. When state courts issue common law decisions, they do not "make" law, rather they issue their interpretation of the "existing" common law. As independent tribunals, federal courts are free to issue their own interpretations of this "general" law.

Notice the connection between this view and the constitutional limitations discussed above: If common law adjudication is characterized as mere legal interpretation, as opposed to "law-making," then the power to articulate principles of common law appears authorized by the courts' constitutional authority to exercise "judicial power." While it might be perverse to allow federal courts to "create" legal rules that would be beyond the power of Congress to legislate, the constitutional authority of courts merely to "interpret" law seems obvious.

Story may have had a larger purpose in mind in asserting the authority of federal courts to make their own determinations of "general" common law. The interstate transactions of merchants, he argued in *Swift*, should be governed by uniform principles applicable from state to state and not dependent on the pro-creditor or pro-debtor perspectives of the particular states. Because nonresident merchants would often have access to the federal diversity court, they could escape the reach of such biased state laws. The diversity court would provide both a "neutral" forum and a "neutral" law. Hence, by dint of diversity jurisdiction, the federal courts could play a leading role in promoting a uniform commercial law governing interstate transactions. *See* Tony Freyer, Harmony & Dissonance: The *Swift* & *Erie* Cases in American Federalism (1981).

However beneficial a uniform law may have been to commercial transactions (and there is reason to believe that *Swift* did not in fact promote uniformity in this area), Story's vision of common law adjudication was dependent, as a formal matter, on the notion that common law exists without any "law-making" by a state. The idea had some resonance in the reception statutes by which the newly formed states "received" the common law of Great Britain as their own, and the fact that for the greater part of the nineteenth century very little law was the product of legislation. However, with the rise of "legal positivism" in the late nineteenth century and early twentieth century, the notion of a shared "general law" was increasingly at tension with the emerging consensus that law comes into being solely as a consequence of law-making by a government exercising sovereign authority over its citizens. The new perception that common law adjudication was simply judge-made state law eventually strained the conceptual underpinning of *Swift*.

2. Erie R. Co. v. Tompkins   "Erie Doctrine"

Erie R. Co. v. Tompkins

304 U.S. 64 (1938)

On Certiorari to the United States Circuit Court of Appeals for the Second Circuit.

Mr. Justice Brandeis delivered the opinion of the Court.

The question for decision is whether the oft-challenged doctrine of *Swift v. Tyson* shall now be disapproved.

Tompkins, a citizen of Pennsylvania, was injured on a dark night by a passing freight train of the Erie Railroad Company while walking along its right of way at Hughestown in that state. He claimed that the accident occurred through negligence in the operation, or maintenance, of the train; that he was rightfully on the premises as licensee because on a commonly used beaten footpath which ran for a short distance alongside the tracks; and that he was struck by something which looked like a door projecting from one of the moving cars. To enforce that claim he brought an action in the federal court for Southern New York, which had jurisdiction because the company is a corporation of that state. It denied liability; and the case was tried by a jury.

The Erie insisted that its duty to Tompkins was no greater than that owed to a trespasser. It contended, among other things, that its duty to Tompkins, and hence its liability, should be determined in accordance with the Pennsylvania law; that under the law of Pennsylvania, as declared by its highest court, persons who use pathways along the railroad right of way—that is, a longitudinal pathway as distinguished from a crossing—are to be deemed trespassers; and that the railroad is not liable for injuries to undiscovered trespassers resulting from its negligence, unless it be wanton or willful. Tompkins denied that any such rule had been established by the decisions of the Pennsylvania courts; and contended that, since there was no statute of the state on the subject, the railroad's duty and liability is to be determined in federal courts as a matter of general law.

The trial judge refused to rule that the applicable law precluded recovery. The jury brought in a verdict of $30,000; and the judgment entered thereon was affirmed by the Circuit Court of Appeals, which held, that it was unnecessary to consider whether the law of Pennsylvania was as contended, because the question was one not of local, but of general, law, and that "upon questions of general law the federal courts are free, in absence of a local statute, to exercise their independent judgment as to what the law is; and it is well settled that the question of the responsibility of a railroad for injuries caused by its servants is one of general law. . . . Where the public has made open and notorious use of a railroad right of way for a long period of time and without objection, the company owes to persons on such permissive pathway a duty of care in the operation of its trains. . . . It is likewise generally recognized law that a jury may find that negligence exists toward a pedestrian using a permissive path on the railroad right of way if he is hit by some object projecting from the side of the train."

The Erie had contended that application of the Pennsylvania rule was required, among other things, by section 34 of the Federal Judiciary Act of September 24, 1789, c. 20, 28 U.S.C. §725, 28 U.S.C.A. §725, which provides: "The laws of the several States, except where the Constitution, treaties, or statutes of the United States otherwise require or provide, shall be regarded as rules of decision in trials at common law, in the courts of the United States, in cases where they apply."

Because of the importance of the question whether the federal court was free to disregard the alleged rule of the Pennsylvania common law, we granted certiorari.

First. Swift v. Tyson held that federal courts exercising jurisdiction on the ground of diversity of citizenship need not, in matters of general jurisprudence, apply the unwritten law of the state as declared by its highest court; that they are free to exercise an independent judgment as to what the common law of the state is—or should be; and that, as there stated by Mr. Justice Story, "the true interpretation of the 34th section limited its application to state laws, strictly local, that is to say, to the positive statutes of the state, and the construction thereof adopted by the local tribunals, and to rights and titles to things having a permanent locality, such as the rights and titles to real estate, and other matters immovable and intraterritorial in their nature and character. It never has been supposed by us, that the section did apply, or was designed to apply, to questions of a more general nature, not at all dependent upon local statutes or local usages of a fixed and permanent operation, as, for example, to the construction of ordinary contracts or other written instruments, and especially to questions of general commercial law, where the state tribunals are called upon to perform the like functions as ourselves, that is, to ascertain, upon general reasoning and legal analogies, what is the true exposition of the contract or instrument, or what is the just rule furnished by the principles of commercial law to govern the case."

The Court in applying the rule of §34 to equity cases, in *Mason v. United States,* 260 U.S. 545, said: "The statute, however, is merely declarative of the rule which would exist in the absence of the statute." The federal courts assumed, in the broad field of "general law," the power to declare rules of decision which Congress was confessedly without power to enact as statutes. Doubt was repeatedly expressed as to the correctness of the construction given §34, and as to the soundness of the rule which it introduced. But it was the more recent research of a competent scholar, who examined the original document, which established that the construction given to it by the Court was erroneous; and that the purpose of the section was merely to make certain that, in all matters except those in which some federal law is controlling, the federal courts exercising jurisdiction in diversity of citizenship cases would apply as their rules of decision the law of the state, unwritten as well as written.[5]

Criticism of the doctrine became widespread after the decision of *Black & White Taxicab & Transfer Co. v. Brown & Yellow Taxicab & Transfer Co.,* 276 U.S. 518. There, Brown & Yellow, a Kentucky corporation owned by Kentuckians, and the Louisville & Nashville Railroad, also a Kentucky corporation, wished that the former should have the exclusive privilege of soliciting passenger and baggage transportation at the Bowling Green, Ky., Railroad station; and that the Black & White, a competing Kentucky corporation, should be prevented from interfering with that privilege. Knowing that such a contract would be void under the common law of Kentucky, it was arranged that the Brown & Yellow reincorporate under the law of Tennessee, and that the contract with the railroad should be executed there. The suit was then brought by the Tennessee corporation in the federal court for Western Kentucky to enjoin competition by the Black & White; an injunction issued by the District Court was sustained by the Court of Appeals; and this Court, citing many decisions in which the doctrine of *Swift & Tyson* had been applied, affirmed the decree.

Second. Experience in applying the doctrine of *Swift v. Tyson,* had revealed its defects, political and social; and the benefits expected to flow from the rule did not accrue. Persistence of state courts in their own opinions on questions of common law prevented uniformity; and the impossibility of discovering a satisfactory line of demarcation between the province of general law and that of local law developed a new well of uncertainties.[8]

---

5. Charles Warren, New Light on the History of the Federal Judiciary Act of 1789 (1923) 37 Harv. L. Rev. 49, 51–52, 81–88, 108.

8. Compare 2 Warren, *The Supreme Court in United States History,* Rev. Ed. 1935, 89: "Probably no decision of the Court has ever given rise to more uncertainty as to legal rights; and though doubtless intended to promote uniformity in the operation of business transactions, its chief effect has been to render it difficult for business men to know in advance to what particular topic the Court would apply the doctrine. . . . " The Federal Digest through the 1937 volume, lists nearly 1,000 decisions involving the distinction between questions of general and of local law.

On the other hand, the mischievous results of the doctrine had become apparent. Diversity of citizenship jurisdiction was conferred in order to prevent apprehended discrimination in state courts against those not citizens of the state. *Swift v. Tyson* introduced grave discrimination by noncitizens against citizens. It made rights enjoyed under the unwritten "general law" vary according to whether enforcement was sought in the state or in the federal court; and the privilege of selecting the court in which the right should be determined was conferred upon the noncitizen.[9] Thus, the doctrine rendered impossible equal protection of the law. In attempting to promote uniformity of law throughout the United States, the doctrine had prevented uniformity in the administration of the law of the state.

The discrimination resulting became in practice far-reaching. This resulted in part from the broad province accorded to the so-called "general law" as to which federal courts exercised an independent judgment. In addition to questions of purely commercial law, "general law" was held to include the obligations under contracts entered into and to be performed within the state, the extent to which a carrier operating within a state may stipulate for exemption from liability for his own negligence or that of his employee; the liability for torts committed within the state upon persons resident or property located there, even where the question of liability depended upon the scope of a property right conferred by the state; and the right to exemplary or punitive damages. Furthermore, state decisions construing local deeds, mineral conveyances, and even devises of real estate, were disregarded.

In part the discrimination resulted from the wide range of persons held entitled to avail themselves of the federal rule by resort to the diversity of citizenship jurisdiction. Through this jurisdiction individual citizens willing to remove from their own state and become citizens of another might avail themselves of the federal rule. And, without even change of residence, a corporate citizen of the state could avail itself of the federal rule by reincorporating under the laws of another state, as was done in the *Taxicab* case.

The injustice and confusion incident to the doctrine of *Swift v. Tyson* have been repeatedly urged as reasons for abolishing or limiting diversity of citizenship jurisdiction. Other legislative relief has been proposed. If only a question of statutory construction were involved, we should not be prepared to abandon a doctrine so widely applied throughout nearly a century. But the unconstitutionality of the course pursued has now been made clear, and compels us to do so.

Third. Except in matters governed by the Federal Constitution or by acts of Congress, the law to be applied in any case is the law of the state. And whether the law of the state shall be declared by its Legislature in a statute or by its highest court in a decision is not a matter of federal concern. There is no federal general common law. Congress has no power to declare substantive rules of common law applicable in a state whether they be local in their nature or "general," be they commercial law or a part of the law of torts. And no clause in the Constitution purports to confer such a power upon the federal courts. As stated by Mr. Justice

---

9. It was even possible for a nonresident plaintiff defeated on a point of law in the highest court of a State nevertheless to win out by taking a nonsuit and renewing the controversy in the federal court.

Field when protesting in *Baltimore & Ohio R. Co. v. Baugh*, 149 U.S. 368, 401, against ignoring the Ohio common law of fellow-servant liability: . . . "Supervision over either the legislative or the judicial action of the states is in no case permissible except as to matters by the constitution specifically authorized or delegated to the United States. Any interference with either, except as thus permitted, is an invasion of the authority of the state, and, to that extent, a denial of its independence."

The fallacy underlying the rule declared in *Swift v. Tyson* is made clear by Mr. Justice Holmes.[23] The doctrine rests upon the assumption that there is "a transcendental body of law outside of any particular State but obligatory within it unless and until changed by statute," that federal courts have the power to use their judgment as to what the rules of common law are; and that in the federal courts "the parties are entitled to an independent judgment on matters of general law":

> but law in the sense in which courts speak of it today does not exist without some definite authority behind it. The common law so far as it is enforced in a State, whether called common law or not, is not the common law generally but the law of that State existing by the authority of that State without regard to what it may have been in England or anywhere else. . . . The authority and only authority is the State, and if that be so, the voice adopted by the State as its own (whether it be of its Legislature or of its Supreme Court) should utter the last word.

Thus the doctrine of *Swift v. Tyson* is, as Mr. Justice Holmes said, "an unconstitutional assumption of powers by the Courts of the United States which no lapse of time or respectable array of opinion should make us hesitate to correct." In disapproving that doctrine we do not hold unconstitutional §34 of the Federal Judiciary Act of 1789 or any other act of Congress. We merely declare that in applying the doctrine this Court and the lower courts have invaded rights which in our opinion are reserved by the Constitution to the several States. *There is no general federal common laws.*

> *Reversed.*

MR. JUSTICE CARDOZO took no part in the consideration or decision of this case.

MR. JUSTICE BUTLER (dissenting). . . .

This Court has often emphasized its reluctance to consider constitutional questions and that legislation will not be held invalid as repugnant to the fundamental law if the case may be decided upon any other ground. . . .

The Court's opinion in its first sentence defines the question to be whether the doctrine of *Swift v. Tyson* shall now be disapproved; it recites that Congress is without power to prescribe rules of decision that have been followed by federal courts as a result of the construction of §34 in *Swift v. Tyson* and since; after discussion, it declares that "the unconstitutionality of the course pursued (meaning the rule of decision resulting from that construction) . . . compels" abandonment of the doctrine so long applied; and then near the end of the last page, the Court states

---

23. *Kuhn v. Fairmont Coal Co.*, 215 U.S. 349, 370–372; *Black & White Taxicab, etc., Co. v. Brown & Yellow Taxicab, etc., Co.*, 276 U.S. 518, 532–536.

that it does not hold §34 unconstitutional, but merely that, in applying the doctrine of *Swift v. Tyson* construing it, this Court and the lower courts have invaded rights which are reserved by the Constitution to the several states. But, plainly through the form of words employed, the substance of the decision appears; it strikes down as unconstitutional §34 as construed by our decisions; it divests the Congress of power to prescribe rules to be followed by federal courts when deciding questions of general law. In that broad field it compels this and the lower federal courts to follow decisions of the courts of a particular state.

I am of opinion that the constitutional validity of the rule need not be considered, because under the law, as found by the courts of Pennsylvania and generally throughout the country, it is plain that the evidence required a finding that plaintiff was guilty of negligence that contributed to cause his injuries, and that the judgment below should be reversed upon that ground.

Mr. Justice Reed (concurring in part).

I concur in the conclusion reached in this case, in the disapproval of the doctrine of *Swift v. Tyson*, and in the reasoning of the majority opinion, except in so far as it relies upon the unconstitutionality of the "course pursued" by the federal courts.

The "doctrine of *Swift v. Tyson*," as I understand it, is that the words "the laws," as used in §34, line 1, of the Federal Judiciary Act of September 24, 1789, do not include in their meaning "the decisions of the local tribunals." . . .

To decide the case now before us and to "disapprove" the doctrine of *Swift v. Tyson* requires only that we say that the words "the laws" include in their meaning the decisions of the local tribunals. . . .

The "unconstitutional" course referred to in the majority opinion is apparently the ruling in *Swift v. Tyson* that the supposed omission of Congress to legislate as to the effect of decisions leaves federal courts free to interpret general law for themselves. I am not at all sure whether, in the absence of federal statutory direction, federal courts would be compelled to follow state decisions. There was sufficient doubt about the matter in 1789 to induce the first Congress to legislate. No former opinions of this Court have passed upon it. Mr. Justice Holmes evidently saw nothing "unconstitutional" which required the overruling of *Swift v. Tyson*, for he said in the very opinion quoted by the majority. I should leave *Swift v. Tyson* undisturbed, as I indicated in *Kuhn v. Fairmont Coal Co.*, but I would not allow it to spread the assumed dominion into new fields. *Black & White Taxicab Co. v. Brown & Yellow Taxicab Co.*, 276 U.S. 518, 535. If the opinion commits this Court to the position that the Congress is without power to declare what rules of substantive law shall govern the federal courts, that conclusion also seems questionable. The line between procedural and substantive law is hazy, but no one doubts federal power over procedure. . . . The Judiciary Article, 3, and the "necessary and proper" clause of article 1, Section 8, may fully authorize legislation, such as this section of the Judiciary Act.

In this Court, *stare decisis*, in statutory construction, is a useful rule, not an inexorable command. . . . It seems preferable to overturn an established construction of an act of Congress, rather than, in the circumstances of this case, to interpret the Constitution. . . .

NOTES AND QUESTIONS

1. *The Meaning of "Laws" in the Rules of Decision Act.* As discussed above, *Swift v. Tyson* was premised on an interpretation of the word "laws" in the Rules of Decision Act that did not include judicial decisions dealing with matters of "general common law." Justice Brandeis's contrary conclusion in *Erie* thus represents not only a difference in statutory construction but a fundamentally different view of the nature of law. Contrast Justice Story's observation that judicial opinions are merely "evidence" of the common law with Justice Brandeis's conclusion in *Erie* that "[t]he common law so far as it is enforced in a State, whether called common law or not, is not the common law generally but the law of that State existing by the authority of that State without regard to what it may have been in England or elsewhere . . . the voice adopted by the State as its own (whether it be of its Legislature or of its Supreme Court) should utter the last word."

a. *What Did Congress Intend in 1789?* How persuasive is Justice Brandeis's conclusion that the language of the Rules of Decision Act was misconstrued by *Swift*? Brandeis places considerable reliance on an article written by Professor Charles Warren, *New Light on the History of the Federal Judiciary Act of 1789*, 37 Harv. L. Rev. 49 (1923). Warren had discovered an unsigned, handwritten first draft of the Rules of Decision Act that provided: "the statute law of the several States . . . and their unwritten or common law now in use, whether by adoption from the common law of England . . . or otherwise, . . . shall be regarded as the rules of decision in the trials at common law. . . ." Warren asserted that the substitution of "laws of the several states" in the final draft for "statute law of the several states and their unwritten or common law" meant that the drafters intended laws to include common law. *Id.* at 85. Isn't the opposite conclusion just as plausible?

Warren's research and Brandeis's assumptions about the Rules of Decision Act are challenged in Wilfred J. Ritz et al., Rewriting the History of the Judiciary Act of 1789: Exposing Myths, Challenging Premises, and Using New Evidence (Wythe Holt & L. H. La Rue, eds. 1990). The authors contend that it is unlikely that the Congress even saw the handwritten draft relied on by Warren. Moreover, they assert, Congress could not have intended to make the law of any particular state binding on federal courts when it passed the Rules of Decision Act; there was very little state law in printed circulation. Thus, the federal courts would have had access to neither state statutes nor judicial decisions. The phrase "laws of the several states," the authors conclude, referred to the collective law of the 13 states, not the law of any particular state—i.e., the "general law" recognized by *Swift*. The purpose of the Act was to ensure that American, as opposed to English, law was applied in federal courts in the absence of pertinent federal law. *Cf.* Patrick J. Borchers, *The Origins of Diversity Jurisdiction and the Rise of Legal Positivism, and a Brave New World for* Erie *and* Klaxon, 72 Tex. L. Rev. 79 (1993) (arguing that it was inconceivable that the framers of the Judiciary Act contemplated application of state law in diversity, and that the "in cases where it applies" language of the Act refers to situations governed by the "general" common law); Tony Freyer, Harmony & Dissonance: The *Swift* & *Erie* Cases in American Federalism (1981) (defending the result in *Swift* on the grounds that federal general common law was necessary to clarify and create uniformity in the relatively undeveloped common law of commercial transactions, and justified by the diversity clause interest in preventing discrimination against out-of-state creditors).

Note that if, as this scholarship suggests, "laws of the several states" in the Rules of Decision Act actually means the "general" common law, and thus *mandates* the holding of *Swift v. Tyson*, federal courts would be under no statutory obligation to enforce the law of any individual state, even state statutes. Would such a construction violate the Constitution as construed by Justice Brandeis in *Erie*?

This scholarship is a marked departure from the traditional understanding of the Rules of Decision Act as a significant limitation on the law-making powers of the federal judiciary. The Act was included as §34 of the Judiciary Act of 1789, one of the first pieces of legislation before the First Congress. The power of the federal courts was one of the central battlegrounds of the struggles between the "federalists," who favored more expansive federal power, and the "anti-federalists," who feared the erosion of state autonomy at the hands of unbridled federal power. Brandeis's construction of the Rules of Decision Act is consistent with that concern: It ensures that diversity jurisdiction will not be used as an excuse to make federal law at the expense of state sovereignty.

b. *Implicit Congressional Ratification of* Swift*?* Why was Brandeis not prepared to reverse "a doctrine so widely applied throughout nearly a century," "if only a question of statutory construction were involved"? Why should a long-standing statutory misconstruction have greater *stare decisis* effect than a long-standing constitutional misconstruction? Is it a fair assumption that Congress would have amended the Rules of Decision Act if it found *Swift* objectionable? Should such implicit legislative ratification trump evidence that *Swift* was decided contrary to the intention of the drafters of the statute?

Note Brandeis's statement in conclusion that "[i]n disapproving [the *Swift*] doctrine, we do not hold unconstitutional §34 of the Federal Judiciary Act of 1789 or any other act of Congress." While the Court concludes that *Swift* was unconstitutional, the decision is technically based on statutory interpretation grounds. By overruling *Swift* and reinterpreting the statute, the Court was able to avoid declaring the Act itself unconstitutional. The Court has frequently employed this technique to avoid unnecessary constitutional adjudication. *See Ashwander v. TVA*, 297 U.S. 288, 347 (1936) (Brandeis, J.):

> The Court will not pass upon a constitutional question although properly presented by the record, if there is also present some other ground upon which the case may be disposed of. . . . Thus, if a case can be decided on either of two grounds, one involving a constitutional question, the other a question of statutory construction or general law, the Court will decide only the latter.

2. *The Meaning of Equality in the* Erie *Decision.* Justice Brandeis's central policy objection to the rule of *Swift v. Tyson* was that "the doctrine rendered impossible equal protection of the law." He asserted that "*Swift v. Tyson* introduced grave discrimination *by noncitizens against citizens.* It made rights enjoyed under the unwritten 'general law' vary according to whether enforcement was sought in the state or in the federal court; and the privilege of selecting the court in which the right should be determined was conferred upon the noncitizen" (emphasis added).

Do you find Brandeis's charge of "grave discrimination" persuasive? Brandeis is certainly correct that *Swift* promoted forum shopping between state and federal courts insofar as different law could be applied in each forum. But how is that discriminatory? He does not seem to be suggesting that there was a substantive bias in the general federal common law for or against defendants, or for or against out-of-state parties. What then does he mean by "grave discrimination"? Why did Brandeis think that "the privilege of selecting the court . . . was conferred upon the noncitizen"?

There are two plausible interpretations of the equality problem alluded to in *Erie*: equality between plaintiffs and defendants in the same lawsuit; and equality between diverse and nondiverse litigants in different lawsuits. Consider whether either is compelling.

a. *Equality Between Plaintiffs and Defendants?* Does *Erie* promote equality between plaintiffs and defendants? Under *Swift*, when there was a difference between federal and state common law on the issues in dispute, it would always have been to one party's advantage to litigate in federal court. Since most cases within federal subject matter jurisdiction can be removed to federal court, both plaintiffs and defendants could normally exercise equally the option to litigate in federal court. While the consequent displacement of state law might still have been considered objectionable from a federalist perspective, for the most part, it did not give disproportionate power to either party. However, there is one situation where a plaintiff completely controls the choice of state or federal forum: a diversity suit by an out-of-state plaintiff against an in-state defendant, since resident defendants do not have the power to remove under the removal statute. Thus, in a case where a defendant was sued at home by out-of-state plaintiffs, such plaintiffs could "vertically" forum shop (between state and federal courts) under *Swift* for the most desirable law. Where federal law was to the plaintiffs' advantage, they would sue in federal court, and where federal law was disadvantageous, they would sue in state court. *Erie* undoubtedly helped the resident defendant in that situation.

However, it is not clear whether, in the long run, *Erie* has actually created greater parity between plaintiffs and defendants. While perhaps unforeseen at the time, the elimination of general federal common law may have actually increased the ability of plaintiffs to "horizontally" forum shop between different state courts for the most favorable law. At the time of the *Erie* decision, there was enormous uniformity in choice of law doctrine among the states. Accordingly, plaintiffs, at that time, had little incentive to select a particular state forum in order to manipulate the applicable law; all of the potential state forums were likely to apply the same state's law to the controversy. Some time after *Erie* was decided, however, this uniformity eroded. Once states began to apply different choice of law rules, they created an incentive for plaintiffs to file in a particular state to avail themselves of that state's choice of law rules.

If *Swift* were still controlling, federal common law would have represented an escape from such a tactic; to the extent that a defendant could remove to federal court, it could have done no worse than the liability imposed by federal common law. Plaintiffs would not have been able to forum shop among the state courts for a state law that imposed unusually high liability. In most cases, defendants could remove to federal court and avail themselves of the federal standard. *Swift*'s elimination thus facilitated horizontal forum shopping. The contemporaneous expansion of state court personal jurisdiction in *International Shoe Co. v. Washington* rendered defendants with multistate connections particularly susceptible to horizontal forum shopping, since they were now amenable to suit in many more states. Accordingly,

Erie arguably widened the disparity between the plaintiff's and defendant's ability to manipulate the applicable law. *See generally* John B. Corr, *Thoughts on the Vitality of Erie*, 41 Am. U. L. Rev. 1087 (1992) (arguing that *Erie* engendered greater forum shopping and procedural wrangling than *Swift*). *Accord*, Patrick J. Borchers, *The Origins of Diversity Jurisdiction and the Rise of Legal Positivism, and a Brave New World for* Erie *and* Klaxon, 72 Tex. L. Rev. 79 (1993); Suzanna Sherry, *Wrong, Out of Step, and Pernicious:* Erie *as the Worst Decision of All Time*, 39 Pepp. L. Rev. 129, 138 (2011). *But see* George D. Brown, *The Ideologies of Forum Shopping — Why Doesn't a Conservative Court Protect Defendants?*, 71 N.C. L. Rev. 649 (1993) (arguing that forum shopping between state and federal court was more destructive of federalism than forum shopping between state courts); Ernest A. Young, *A General Defense of Erie Railroad Co. v. Tompkins*, 10 J.L. Econ. & Pol'y 17, 45 (2013) (arguing that horizontal disuniformity is a deliberate feature of federalism).

Note that even after *Erie*, if all federal courts applied the *same* state law to a given case, the plaintiff would still not benefit from shopping for a forum with law advantageous to her case. The defendant's removal to federal court would no longer trigger the application of federal common law, but it might have triggered the application of a different state law than would be applied by the state court. However, in its subsequent decision in *Klaxon Co. v. Stentor Electric Manufacturing Co.*, 313 U.S. 487 (1941), the Supreme Court held that federal courts must apply the same state law as would be applied in the state forum. In other words, federal courts under *Erie* are bound not only by state substantive law but by the forum state's choice of law as well:

> Any other ruling would do violence to the principle of uniformity within a state upon which the *Tompkins* decision is based. Whatever lack of uniformity this may produce between federal courts in different states is attributable to our federal system, which leaves to a state, within the limits permitted by the Constitution, the right to pursue local policies diverging from those of its neighbors. It is not for the federal courts to thwart such local policies by enforcing an independent general law of conflict of laws.

Id. at 496.

Klaxon has come under attack by commentators for encouraging interstate forum shopping, and abdicating federal responsibility for curbing parochial choice of law rules. *See* William F. Baxter, *Choice of Law and the Federal System*, 16 Stan. L. Rev. 1 (1963); Harold W. Horowitz, *Toward a Federal Common Law of Choice of Law — A Suggested Approach*, 14 UCLA L. Rev. 1191 (1967). Others, particularly Professor David Cavers, have defended it as necessary to enforce state policies embodied in their choice of law rules and to avoid forum shopping between state and federal courts. Moreover, reversing *Klaxon* would require the federal courts to craft complex choice of law doctrine, something they are no more qualified to do than their state counterparts. David Cavers, American Law Institute, *Change in Choice-of-Law Thinking and Its Bearing on the Klaxon Problem*, in Study of the Division of Jurisdiction Between State and Federal Courts 154 (Tent. Draft No. 1. 1963). There have also been proposals to federalize conflict of laws problems by way of federal statute. *See, e.g.*, Michael H. Gottesman, *Draining the Dismal Swamp: The Case for Federal Choice of Law Statutes*, 80 Geo. L.J. 1 (1991). The Court has consistently adhered to its holding in *Klaxon. See, e.g., Day & Zimmermann, Inc. v. Challoner*, 423 U.S. 3 (1975) (applying Texas conflict of laws rule notwithstanding absence of any Texas interest in the underlying dispute). Professor Wolff has argued that the Class Action Fairness Act provides a statutory basis for overruling *Klaxon* in the class action context. Tobias Barrington Wolff, *Choice of Law and Jurisdictional Policy in the Federal Courts*, 165 U. Pa. L. Rev. 1847 (2017).

b. *Equality Between Diverse and Nondiverse Litigants: Making the Applicable Law Turn on the "Accident of Diversity."* There is another sense in which federal common law might have been considered unfairly discriminatory: It resulted in different allocation of rights, depending on whether the parties were diverse. Justice Brandeis was particularly troubled by the possibility of manipulation, as in the *Black & White Taxicab* case cited in the *Erie* decision. In that case, a company reincorporated in another state for the sole purpose of creating diversity jurisdiction to enforce a business practice that was illegal under state law, but legal under federal common law.

Would it have been any less objectionable in *Black & White Taxicab* if the defendant really became an out-of-state corporation and had not simply reincorporated as a sham (a practice presumably redressable under 28 U.S.C. §1359)? *Swift*, in effect, permitted diverse defendants to engage in conduct prohibited to nondiverse defendants, and permitted diverse plaintiffs to assert rights not equally available to their nondiverse counterparts. Is that any more objectionable than permitting conduct in New Jersey that would be prohibited in New York? Is it more objectionable than enforcing a claim in New Jersey courts that would not be enforced by New York courts?

3. *Intrastate Uniformity and the Regulation of "Primary Conduct."* The maintenance of two bodies of law for actors in the same state under *Swift*—a separate regime of federal common law alongside the otherwise applicable state law—created an additional problem: the difficulty of conforming conduct to the applicable legal rules. Imagine that, prior to the *Erie* decision, you were the railroad official responsible for maintenance of railroad rights-of-way in Pennsylvania and were trying to decide whether to install costly fencing to keep trespassers away from railroad tracks. Under Pennsylvania common law, the railroad has limited liability to trespassers, so the fence may not be cost-justified. Moreover, you would expect under the conflict of laws jurisprudence of the time (and today) that the railroad's obligations to local pedestrians would be governed by local law. *Swift* introduced a level of uncertainty—because the applicable law might change simply because a particular pedestrian was diverse from the railroad and would thus have access to the higher standard of liability imposed by federal common law. Legal uncertainty of this type will not normally be debilitating to the extent that the railroad can always conform its conduct to the higher standard of care—i.e., install the fence (or pay the occasional verdict to the diverse plaintiff if that were cheaper). However, it does make planning more difficult. Moreover, there may be times when the federal and state rules will be inconsistent, in which case conformity with the applicable law becomes impossible without knowing the citizenship of the opposing party. This dilemma was ameliorated by the *Erie* decision.

However, as in the case of "forum shopping," *Erie* may have also facilitated a new uncertainty; it made possible the application of different state laws in a diversity suit, depending on the plaintiff's choice of forum, and that forum's choice of law rules. Thus, for instance, as a railroad planner today, you would still have to deal with the possibility that a potential plaintiff might be a resident of a state with a high damage standard, and a railroad doing business in that state would be subjected to such a standard if it were sued in that state.

4. *Constitutional Basis for* Erie. Which part of the Constitution did *Swift* violate? When Brandeis stated that "Congress has no power to declare substantive rules of common law applicable in a state," did he mean that it would have been unconstitutional for Congress to pass a statute specifying the level of care that a railroad owes to persons walking along railroad tracks? Note that Congress by that time had used its power under the Commerce Clause to enact many laws governing railroads. *See, e.g.,* the Federal Employers Liability Act of 1908, 45 U.S.C. §§51 *et seq.*; the Hours of Service Act, 45 U.S.C. §§61 *et seq.*; and the Railway Labor Act of 1926, 45 U.S.C. §§151 *et seq.* If Congress *would* have the power to pass a tort code for interstate railroads, wouldn't Congress also have the power to delegate to the federal courts the power to determine the applicable standard of care? Is Brandeis asserting that Congress did not in fact delegate that law-making power to the courts or that it would have been constitutionally prohibited from making that delegation? *See* Aaron Nielson, Erie *as Nondelegation,* 72 Ohio St. L.J. 239 (2011) (arguing that the constitutional component of *Erie* is based on principles limiting Congress's ability to delegate law-making authority to the courts).

Does the constitutional problem arise because the federal rule of decision is available only to litigants who have access to federal diversity court? Could Congress pass a Rules of Decision Act that provided: "federal law shall provide the rules of decision in all actions filed in the federal courts"?

Note in connection with these questions two distinct, if related, issues: (1) federalism, the appropriate allocation of authority between the federal and state governments; and (2) separation of powers, the allocation of authority between the legislative and judicial branches of the federal government. Brandeis's central concern in *Erie* seemed to be about federalism: The Constitution did not authorize wholesale federal law-making by any branch of the federal government. If Congress did not have the power to legislate in the absence of enumerated Article I authority, then the court could exercise no broader authority simply because of the existence of diversity jurisdiction. But even in areas where Congress could legislate, it is not clear that the federal courts have comparable power to craft common law. The power to make federal law is, by and large, vested in Congress pursuant to Article I of the Constitution. *Erie* makes clear that the power of the courts to resolve cases and controversies pursuant to Article III is not a general charter to make law.

Do you see any connection between the federalism and separation of powers concerns? Does the fact that law-making is reserved to Congress help protect state autonomy? Could you argue that Congress is institutionally more sensitive to state autonomy than are the courts?

5. *Should the Court in* Erie *have considered whether Pennsylvania would have considered its law binding on the federal courts?* For an argument that Justice Brandeis implicitly rejected the premise that federal courts should consider the state's view of the binding effect of its law, *see* Michael Steven Green, Erie's *Suppressed Premise,* 95 Minn. L. Rev. 1111 (2011).

6. *Substantive Federal Common Law Based on the Conferral of Jurisdiction.* In other contexts, the Court has inferred the power to craft substantive common law from the mere conferral of subject matter jurisdiction. In the admiralty context, for

instance, the Court has assumed that the vesting of admiralty jurisdiction in the federal courts not only gives the courts the authority to craft uniform federal common law binding on both the state and federal courts but is the basis for congressional authority to pass admiralty legislation. *Southern Pacific Co. v. Jensen*, 244 U.S. 205 (1917). This assumption has survived *Erie. See Pope & Talbot, Inc. v. Hawn*, 346 U.S. 406 (1953). *See generally* David W. Robertson, Admiralty & Federalism (1970). *See also Textile Workers Union v. Lincoln Mills*, 353 U.S. 448 (1957) (federal jurisdiction to enforce collective bargaining agreement gives court authority to create body of law defining parties' rights and remedies under the agreement).

Unlike the "general" common law recognized in *Swift*, these assertions of judicial law-making authority: (1) are predicated on the existence of federal legislative authority; (2) do not depend on the diversity of citizenship of the litigants; and (3) supply rules of decision applicable in both federal and state courts. A further discussion of substantive federal common law appears later in this chapter.

7. *Recent Scholarly Reassessment.* The 75th anniversary of the *Erie* decision in 2013 gave rise to several symposia dedicated to reassessing the decision. *See* 54 Wm. & Mary L. Rev 655 *et seq.* (2013); 10 J.L. Econ. & Pol'y 1, *et seq.* (2013). Although the decision commanded support from many scholars, several viewed it as a significant wrong turn. *See, e.g.*, Samuel Issacharoff, *Federalized America: Reflections on* Erie v. Tompkins *and State-Based Regulation*, 10 J.L. Econ. & Pol'y 199 (2013); Suzanna Sherry, *A Pox on Both Your Houses: Why the Court Can't Fix the* Erie *Doctrine*, 10 J.L. Econ. & Pol'y 173 (2013). *See also*, Suzanna Sherry, *Wrong, Out of Step, and Pernicious:* Erie *as the Worst Decision of All Time*, 39 Pepp. L. Rev. 129 (2011).

A 2019 symposium on *Erie*'s 80th anniversary features articles by Ernest A. Young et al., *Symposium, Erie at Eighty: Choice of Law Across the Disciplines*, 10 ConLawNow 175 *et seq.* (2019). See also, Allan Erbsen, *A Unified Approach to* Erie *Analysis for Federal Statutes, Rules, and Common Law*, 10 UC Irvine L. Rev. 1101 (2020).

B. DETERMINING THE PROCEDURAL LAW APPLICABLE IN FEDERAL COURTS

In his concurrence in *Erie*, Justice Reed wrote "If the opinion commits this Court to the position that the Congress is without power to declare what rules of substantive law shall govern the federal courts, that conclusion also seems questionable. The line between procedural and substantive law is hazy, but no one doubts federal power over procedure." He made that observation in support of his conclusion that the Constitution does not require federal courts to enforce state common law, and that that obligation is only a consequence of the Rules of Decision Act.

It does seem incontrovertible that Congress has the constitutional authority to determine procedures for the federal courts. Articles I and III give Congress the power to create the lower federal courts, and the "necessary and proper" clause cited by Justice Reed also gives Congress the power "to make all Laws which shall be necessary and proper for carrying into Execution . . . all other Powers vested by this Constitution in the Government of the United States, or in any Department or Officer thereof."

Why did Justice Reed think that Congress's procedural authority would have been a sufficient basis to "declare what rules of substantive law shall govern the federal courts"? The implication seems to be that any law passed by Congress that directs federal judges on how to do their jobs is authorized as an incident of Congress's power over federal procedure.

While such an expansive view of Congress's power over federal procedure seems at odds with Brandeis's vision of a federal government with limited powers, Reed's observation that for constitutional purposes there is a distinction between procedural and substantive law, proved highly prescient. Notwithstanding *Erie*'s broad command to follow state law, be it statutory or judge-made, subsequent decisions carved out a prominent exception for federal procedural law. Neither the Rules of Decision Act nor the Constitution were thought to compel federal courts to follow consistently state judicial procedures.

Does the substance-procedure distinction make sense in terms of Brandeis's policy concerns in *Erie*? Is it "discriminatory" for federal courts to make available to federal litigants procedures unavailable in the state courts? Do independent federal procedures undermine state autonomy less than independent federal substantive rules would?

Is there any language in the Rules of Decision Act itself that supports a substance-procedure distinction? There are at least two plausible sources. First, state procedures might not be considered "rules of decision" since they only determine how a pretrial process or trial will be conducted, not how it will be decided. Second, federal trials may not be "cases in which they [state judicial procedures] apply" for purposes of the last clause of the Rules of Decision Act.

Another possible reason for the perception that the Rules of Decision Act did not apply to state procedural law was that another federal statute known as the Conformity Act separately required federal courts in actions at law to follow state judicial procedures, even though under *Swift* federal courts were free to disregard substantive state common law. The statute required federal trial courts to conform to "the practice, pleadings, and forms and modes of proceeding in [state civil proceedings]."* In equity proceedings, the federal courts developed their own "Federal Equity Rules." *See generally* Stephen B. Burbank, *The Rules Enabling Act of 1934*, 130 U. Pa. L. Rev. 1015, 1035–1040 (1982). Thus, courts were accustomed to treating substantive and procedural rules differently before *Erie*. With the Conformity Act's repeal in 1934 and the subsequent adoption of the Federal Rules of Civil Procedure shortly after the *Erie* decision, the tables were turned: *Erie* now obligated federal courts to respect state substantive law, while the Rules Enabling Act relieved the federal courts from following state procedures. The courts were again forced to define the "hazy" line between substance and procedure alluded to by Justice Reed. The methodology adopted, however, was in sharp contrast to Justice Reed's expansive sense of federal authority.

---

* An earlier version of the Act, the Process Act of 1792, required conformity with state procedures as they existed in 1789. This "static conformity" created the anomaly that federal courts were bound to follow state procedures no longer followed by the state courts. The 1872 Act eliminated the anomaly by requiring federal courts to conform to the practices currently followed by state courts. This "dynamic conformity" remained in effect until passage of the Rules Enabling Act in 1934.

1.   Outcome Determination

The Supreme Court's first major post-*Erie* effort to distinguish substantive laws, which were binding on the federal courts, from procedural laws, which the federal courts could develop independently, came in *Guaranty Trust Corp. v. York*, 326 U.S. 99 (1945). The case involved a diversity suit for breach of fiduciary duty against a bank serving as trustee for holders of some commercial paper. Had the claim been heard in state court, it would have been dismissed under the state statute of limitations. The plaintiffs asserted that the federal court was free to apply its own "procedures," one of which was the equitable doctrine of *laches*. That doctrine provided that a claim in equity would not be dismissed as untimely unless defendant had been unfairly prejudiced by plaintiff's delay in bringing suit. Thus, plaintiffs asserted, they should be able to assert a claim in federal court that would have been dismissed in state court because of the absence of prejudice to the defendant under the doctrine of laches.

While acknowledging a tradition of federal independence in equity proceedings, Justice Frankfurter nonetheless held that the state statute of limitations was binding on the federal proceeding.

Guaranty Trust Co. of New York v. York

326 U.S. 99 (1945)

MR. JUSTICE FRANKFURTER delivered the opinion of the Court. . . .

Our starting point must be the policy of federal jurisdiction which *Erie R. Co. v. Tompkins* embodies. In overruling *Swift v. Tyson, Erie R. Co. v. Tompkins* did not merely overrule a venerable case. It overruled a particular way of looking at law which dominated the judicial process long after its inadequacies had been laid bare. . . . Law was conceived as a "brooding omnipresence" of Reason, of which decisions were merely evidence and not themselves the controlling formulations. Accordingly, federal courts deemed themselves free to ascertain what Reason, and therefore Law, required wholly independent of authoritatively declared State law, even in cases where a legal right as the basis for relief was created by State authority and could not be created by federal authority and the case got into a federal court merely because it was "between Citizens of different States" under Art. III, §2 of the Constitution of the United States. . . .

In relation to the problem now here, the real significance of *Swift v. Tyson* lies in the fact that it did not enunciate novel doctrine. Nor was it restricted to its particular situation. It summed up prior attitudes and expressions in cases that had come before this Court and lower federal courts for at least thirty years, at law as well as in equity. . . . The notion was stimulated by the attractive vision of a uniform body of federal law. To such sentiments for uniformity of decision and freedom from diversity in State law the federal courts gave currency, particularly in cases where equitable remedies were sought, because equitable doctrines are so often cast in terms of universal applicability when close analysis of the source of legal enforceability is not demanded.

In exercising their jurisdiction on the ground of diversity of citizenship, the federal courts, in the long course of their history, have not differentiated in their regard for State law between actions at law and suits in equity. Although Section 34 of the Judiciary Act of 1789, directed that the "laws of the several States . . . shall be regarded as rules of decision in trials of common law . . . ," this was deemed, consistently for over a hundred years, to be merely declaratory of what would in any event have governed the federal courts and therefore was equally applicable to equity suits. Indeed, it may fairly be said that the federal courts gave greater respect to State-created "substantive rights" . . . in equity than they gave them on the law side, because rights at law were usually declared by State courts and as such increasingly flouted by extension of the doctrine of *Swift v. Tyson*, while rights in equity were frequently defined by legislative enactment and as such known and respected by the federal courts. . . .

Partly because the States in the early days varied greatly in the manner in which equitable relief was afforded and in the extent to which it was available. . . . Congress provided that "the forms and modes of proceeding in suits . . . of equity" would conform to the settled uses of courts of equity. But this enactment gave the federal courts no power that they would not have had in any event when courts were given "cognizance," by the first Judiciary Act, of "equity." From the beginning there has been a good deal of talk in the cases that federal equity is a separate legal system. And so it is, properly understood. The suits in equity of which the federal courts have had cognizance ever since 1789 constituted the body of law which had been transplanted to this country from the English Court of Chancery. But this system of equity "derived its doctrines, as well as its powers, from its mode of giving relief." Langdell, Summary of Equity Pleading (1877) xxvii. In giving federal courts "cognizance" of equity suits in cases of diversity jurisdiction. Congress never gave, nor did the federal courts ever claim, the power to deny substantive rights created by State law or to create substantive rights denied by State law.

This does not mean that whatever equitable remedy is available in a State court must be available in a diversity suit in a federal court, or conversely, that a federal court may not afford an equitable remedy not available in a State court. Equitable relief in a federal court is of course subject to restrictions: the suit must be within the traditional scope of equity as historically evolved in the English Court of Chancery . . . ; a plain, adequate and complete remedy at law must be wanting . . . ; explicit Congressional curtailment of equity powers must be respected; the constitutional right to trial by jury cannot be evaded. . . . That a State may authorize its courts to give equitable relief unhampered by any or all such restrictions cannot remove these fetters from the federal courts. . . . State law cannot define the remedies which a federal court must give simply because a federal court in diversity jurisdiction is available as an alternative tribunal to the States courts. Contrariwise, a federal court may afford an equitable remedy for a substantive right recognized by a State even though a State court cannot give it. Whatever contradiction or confusion may be produced by a medley of judicial phrases severed from their environment, the body of adjudications concerning equitable relief in diversity cases leaves no doubt that the federal courts enforced State-created substantive rights if the mode of proceeding and remedy were consonant with the traditional body of equitable remedies, practice and procedure, and in so doing they were enforcing rights created by the States and not arising under any inherent or statutory federal law.

Inevitably, therefore, the principle of *Erie R. Co. v. Tompkins*, an action at law, was promptly applied to a suit in equity. . . .

And so this case reduces itself to the narrow question whether, when no recovery could be had in a State court because the action is barred by the statute of limitations, a federal court in equity can take cognizance of the suit because there is diversity of citizenship between the parties. Is the outlawry, according to State law, of a claim created by the States a matter of "substantive rights" to be respected by a federal court of equity when that court's jurisdiction is dependent on the fact that there is a State-created right, or is such statute of "a mere remedial character," . . . which a federal court may disregard? . . .

Here we are dealing with a right to recover derived not from the United States but from one of the States. When, because the plaintiff happens to be a nonresident, such a right is enforceable in a federal as well as in a State court, the forms and mode of enforcing the right may at times, naturally enough, vary because the two judicial systems are not identic. But since a federal court adjudicating a state-created right solely because of the diversity of citizenship of the parties is for that purpose, in effect, only another court of the State, it cannot afford recovery if the right to recover is made unavailable by the State nor can it substantially affect the enforcement of the right as given by the State.

And so the question is not whether a statute of limitations is deemed a matter of "procedure" in some sense. The question is whether such a statute concerns merely the manner and the means by which a right to recover, as recognized by the State, is enforced, or whether such statutory limitation is a matter of substance in the aspect that alone is relevant to our problem, namely, does it significantly affect the result of a litigation for a federal court to disregard a law of a State that would be controlling in an action upon the same claim by the same parties in a State court?

It is therefore immaterial whether statutes of limitation are characterized either as "substantive" or "procedural" in State court opinions in any use of those terms unrelated to the specific issue before us. *Erie R. Co. v. Tompkins* was not an endeavor to formulate scientific legal terminology. It expressed a policy that touches vitally the proper distribution of judicial power between State and federal courts. In essence, the intent of that decision was to insure that, in all cases where a federal court is exercising jurisdiction solely because of the diversity of citizenship of the parties, the outcome of the litigation in the federal court should be substantially the same, so far as legal rules determine the outcome of a litigation, as it would be if tried in a State court. The nub of the policy that underlies *Erie R. Co. v. Tompkins* is that for the same transaction the accident of a suit by a non-resident litigant in a federal court instead of in a State court a block away, should not lead to a substantially different result. And so, putting to one side abstractions regarding "substance" and "procedure," we have held that in diversity cases the federal courts must follow the law of the State as to burden of proof, . . . as to conflict of laws, . . . as to contributory negligence. . . .

Plainly enough, a statute that would completely bar recovery in a suit if brought in a State court bears on a State created right vitally and not merely formally or negligibly. As to consequences that so intimately affect recovery or non-recovery a federal court in a diversity case should follow State law. . . . The fact that under New York law a statute of limitations might be lengthened or shortened, that a security may be foreclosed though the debt be barred, that a barred debt may be used as a set-off, are all matters of local law properly to be respected by federal courts sitting in New York when their incidence comes into play there. Such particular rules of local law, however, do not in the slightest change the crucial consideration that if a plea of the statute of limitations would bar recovery in a State court, a federal court ought not to afford recovery. . . .

To make an exception to *Erie R. Co. v. Tompkins* on the equity side of a federal court is to reject the considerations of policy which, after long travail, led to that decision. . . .

Diversity jurisdiction is founded on assurance to non-resident litigants of courts free from susceptibility to potential local bias. . . . And so Congress afforded out-of-State litigants another tribunal, not another body of law. The operation of a double system of conflicting laws in the same State is plainly hostile to the reign of law. Certainly, the fortuitous circumstance of residence out of a State of one of the parties to a litigation ought not to give rise to a discrimination against others equally concerned but locally resident. The source of substantive rights enforced by a federal court under diversity jurisdiction, it cannot be said too often, is the law of the States. Whenever that law is authoritatively declared by a State, whether its voice be the legislature or its highest court, such law ought to govern in litigation founded on that law, whether the forum of application is a State or a federal court and whether the remedies be sought at law or may be had in equity. . . .

The judgment is reversed and the case is remanded for proceedings not inconsistent with this opinion.

So ordered.

MR. JUSTICE RUTLEDGE.

I dissent. . . .

[T]he decision of today does not in so many words rule that Congress could not authorize the federal courts to administer equitable relief in accordance with the substantive rights of the parties, notwithstanding state courts had been forbidden by local statutes of limitations to do so. Nevertheless the implication to that effect seems strong, in view of the reliance upon *Erie R. Co. v. Tompkins*. In any event, the question looms more largely in the issues than the Court's opinion appears to make it. . . . More is at stake in the implications of the decision, if not in the words of the opinion, than simply bringing federal and local law into accord upon matters clearly and exclusively within the constitutional power of the state to determine. It is one thing to require that kind of an accord in diversity cases when the question is merely whether the federal court must follow the law of the state as to burden of proof, . . . contributory negligence, . . . or perhaps in application of the so-called parol evidence rule. These ordinarily involve matters of substantive law, though nominated in terms of procedure. But in some instances their application may lie along the border between procedure or remedy and substance, where the one may or may not be in fact but another name for the other. It is exactly in this borderland, where procedural or remedial rights may or may not have the effect of determining the substantive ones completely, that caution is required in extending the rule of the *Erie* case by the very rule itself. . . .

It may be true that if the matter were wholly fresh the barring of rights in equity by statutes of limitation would seem to partake more of the substantive than of the remedial phase of law. But the matter is not fresh and it is not without room for debate. A long tradition, in the states and here, as well as in the common law which antedated both state and federal law, has emphasized the remedial character of statutes of limitations, more especially in application to equity causes, on many kinds of issues requiring differentiation of such matters from more clearly and exclusively substantive ones. . . . Nor can I say, as was said in the *Erie* case, that the matter is beyond the power of Congress to control. If that be conceded, I think Congress should make the change if it is to be made. The *Erie* decision was rendered in 1938. Seven years have passed without action by Congress to extend the rule to these matters. That is long enough to justify the conclusion that Congress also regards them as not governed by *Erie* and as wishing to make no change. This should be reason enough for leaving the matter at rest until it decides to act.

Applicable statutes of limitations in state tribunals are not always the ones which would apply if suit were instituted in the courts of the state which creates the substantive rights for which enforcement is sought. The state of the forum is free to apply its own period of limitations, regardless of whether the state originating the right has barred suit upon it. Whether or not *the action* will be held to be barred depends therefore not upon the law of the state which creates the substantive right, but upon the law of the state where suit may be brought. This in turn will depend upon where it may be possible to secure service of process, and thus jurisdiction of the person of the defendant. It may be therefore that because of the plaintiff's inability to find the defendant in the jurisdiction which creates his substantive right, he will be foreclosed of remedy by the sheer necessity of going to the haven of refuge within which the defendant confines its presence for jurisdictional purposes. The law of the latter may bar the suit even though suit still would be allowed under the law of the state creating the substantive right.

It is not clear whether today's decision puts it into the power of corporate trustees, by confining their jurisdictional "presence" to states which allow their courts to give equitable remedies only within short periods of time, to defeat the purpose and intent of the law of the state creating the substantive right. If so, the "right" remains alive, with full-fledged remedy, by the law of its origin, and because enforcement must be had in another state, which affords refuge against it, the remedy and with it the right are nullified. I doubt that the Constitution of the United States requires this or that the Judiciary Acts permit it. A good case can be made, indeed has been made, that the diversity jurisdiction was created to afford protection against exactly this sort of nullifying state legislation.

In my judgment this furnishes added reason for leaving any change, if one is to be made, to the judgment of Congress. The next step may well be to say that in applying the doctrine of laches a federal court must surrender its own judgment and attempt to find out what a state court sitting a block away would do with that notoriously amorphous doctrine. . . .

NOTES AND QUESTIONS

1. *Source of Law in* Guaranty Trust*?* What legal text obligated the federal courts to apply the state statute of limitations in this case? The decision does not appear to rely on the Rules of Decision Act, which, as Frankfurter notes, did not, as worded at

the time of the decision, apply to equity proceedings.* What does Frankfurter mean in observing that the Rules of Decision Act "is merely declaratory of what would in any event have governed the federal courts" (in the absence of the statute)? Is the decision based on constitutional limitations on the courts' law-making authority? Is Frankfurter suggesting that Congress lacks the power to enact a federal statute of limitations governing all claims adjudicated in federal court? If the Constitution would not have prevented Congress from passing such a statute, why were the federal courts constrained from adopting a more limited practice as a matter of judge-made law?

2. *"Outcome Determination"?* Do you agree that the central concern of *Erie* was that "in all cases where a federal court is exercising jurisdiction solely because of the diversity of citizenship of the parties, the outcome of the litigation in the federal court should be substantially the same, so far as legal rules determine the outcome of a litigation, as it would be if tried in a state court"?

Do all differences between outcomes in state and federal courts equally implicate *Erie?* What if the state clerk's office were only open until 3:00? Could a federal court hear a claim filed on 4:00 of the last day before the statute expired? Can you articulate a theory consistent with *Guaranty Trust* that allows a federal court to adjudicate a claim in those circumstances?

Is it clear on the facts of *Guaranty Trust* that plaintiff was seeking an outcome unavailable in the state courts? Should the Court have considered whether the action would have been barred in the state equity courts? Couldn't litigants with the same cause of action have brought suit in state law courts earlier? Are there any differences between federal and state practice that would not affect outcome at the point that a litigant has complied with one set of rules but not the other?

3. *"Door-Closing" Versus "Door-Opening."* How would *Guaranty Trust* have been decided if the state statute of limitations had not run, but the federal court concluded that the case should be dismissed under the equitable doctrine of laches because the defendant was prejudiced by the plaintiff's delay in bringing suit? Would it matter if the plaintiff could refile without prejudice in state court? Is there a difference for *Erie* purposes whether the federal court is asked to adjudicate a case that could not be heard in the state court, and when a federal court is asked to *not* adjudicate a case that *could* be heard in the state court?

4. *Statutes of Limitations in Interstate Conflicts.* As noted by Justice Frankfurter, the substance-procedure distinction is not unique to federal-state relations, and courts have used different definitions of those categories depending on the context. Well before *Erie*, courts used the substance-procedure categories in interstate conflicts of laws to distinguish between *substantive* rights—which would receive interstate enforcement—and *procedural* remedies—which were particular to the court in which the action was brought. *See* Alfred Hill, *The* Erie *Doctrine and the Constitution* (pt. 2), 53 Nw. L. Rev. 541, 574–579 (1958).

---

* The Rules of Decision Act as originally enacted applied only to "trials at common law." Lawsuits seeking "equitable" remedies—generally, anything other than money damages—could not be entertained in actions at common law, but rather would have to be brought as equity claims in the Chancery Courts. The Act was amended in 1948 to apply to all "civil actions." A more complete discussion of the division of law and equity can be found in Chapter 5: Anatomy of a Litigation: Pleading, Discovery, and Adjudication.

The specific issue addressed in *Guaranty Trust*—whether a statute of limitations bar is substantive—has been resolved by the Supreme Court differently in the interstate context than in the *Erie* context. That is to say, when one state entertains a claim arising in another state, it may choose to apply its own statute of limitations to the claim as a "procedural" issue governed by the law of the forum. In *Sun Oil Co. v. Wortman, supra* p. 228, the Court addressed the constitutionality of a forum-state extending the statute of limitations beyond the time permitted by the state in which the claim arose. Citing *Guaranty Trust,* Justice Scalia, writing for the majority, explicitly rejected the notion that the categorization of statutes of limitations as substantive for *Erie* purposes obligates courts to treat them as substantive for interstate purposes:

> *Guaranty Trust* itself rejects the notion that there is an equivalence between what is substantive under the *Erie* doctrine and what is substantive for purposes of conflict of laws. Except at the extremes, the terms "substance" and "procedure" precisely describe very little except a dichotomy, and what they mean in a particular context is largely determined by the purposes for which the dichotomy is drawn. In the context of our *Erie* jurisprudence, that purpose is to establish (within the limits of applicable federal law, including the prescribed Rules of Federal Procedure) substantial uniformity of predictable outcome between cases tried in a federal court and cases tried in the courts of the State in which the federal court sits. . . . The purpose of the substance-procedure dichotomy in the context of the Full Faith and Credit Clause, by contrast, is not to establish uniformity but to delimit spheres of state legislative competence.

Id. at 726–727 (citation omitted). Do you agree that *Erie*'s sole objective was achieving uniformity/predictability and not delimiting spheres of legislative competence? Would your definition of "substantive" be affected if you thought the purpose of the Rules of Decision Act was to delimit spheres of authority between the state and federal governments?

5. Erie *and Equitable Remedies.* As Justice Frankfurter acknowledges, there was a long tradition of federal courts operating independently of state law in equity proceedings. Under the Conformity Act, federal courts in equity were free to develop their own procedures; the Conformity Act only required adherence to state procedures in actions at law. Even after the Conformity Act's repeal and the consolidation of law and equity in the federal courts, courts continued to exercise more independence in adjudicating equitable claims than they would have exercised in hearing legal claims. *See generally* David Crump, *The Twilight Zone of the* Erie *Doctrine: Is There Really a Different Choice of Equitable Remedies in the "Court a Block Away"?*, 1991 Wis. L. Rev. 1233.

In *Guaranty Trust,* Frankfurter goes to great lengths to preserve the right of federal courts, at least in equity, to provide different "remedies" than would be provided by a state court. At the same time, he insists that in order to respect state-created substantive rights, the "outcome" of the federal litigation should not vary from the outcome in state court. How is a "remedy" different from an "outcome"? Isn't a right largely defined by the remedies for its violation? Courts have had difficulty in determining which differences in federal equitable remedies are permitted after *Guaranty Trust. See* David Crump, *The Twilight Zone of the* Erie *Doctrine, supra.*

Several recent Court of Appeals cases have declined to follow state law on the availability of equitable relief. In *Sonner v. Premier Nutrition Corporation*, 962 F.3d 1072 (9th Cir. 2020) *aff'd en banc*, 971 F.3d 834 (9th Cir. 2020), the court declined to follow California's abrogation of the requirement that a party seeking an injunction lack an adequate remedy at law. Plaintiff had dropped her damage claims in order to obtain a bench trial (cases "at law" entitle either litigant to demand a jury trial under the Seventh Amendment). The district court then dismissed plaintiff's claim for injunctive relief on the basis that she had an adequate remedy at law. The Court of Appeals affirmed. Notwithstanding the "outcome determinative" effect of deviating from California Law, the court held that the federal interest in preventing the circumvention of the right to jury trial justified the result. *Cf., Davilla v. Enable Midstream Partners L.P.*, 913 F.3d 959, 972–973 (10th Cir. 2019) (declining to follow Oklahoma law governing issuance of injunctions for trespass).

6. *The 1949 "Trilogy."* Supreme Court decisions following *Guaranty Trust* initially took an expansive view of what constitutes a "substantive" rule binding on the federal courts. In three opinions issued on the same day, the Court required conformity to a variety of state procedures that had a less than dispositive impact on the ultimate outcome of the dispute.

Woods v. Interstate Realty Co., 337 U.S. 535 (1949), held that a federal court could not entertain a claim brought by an out-of-state corporation barred from bringing suit in the state courts because of its failure to "qualify" to do business in the state. Under Mississippi law, an out-of-state corporation was barred from using the state courts unless it appointed an agent for service of process upon it in Mississippi. Plaintiff's failure to do so barred it from using both state and federal courts in Mississippi. Any other result, the Court reasoned, would violate the vertical-uniformity principle established in *Guaranty Trust*.

In *Cohen v. Beneficial Industrial Loan Corp.*, 337 U.S. 541 (1949), the state rule in question had a tenuous connection to the outcome of the litigation. The Court there required a federal plaintiff to comply with a state statute requiring stockholders suing corporate officials on behalf of the corporation to post a bond with the court. The Court reasoned that since New Jersey had a right to impose the cost of such litigation on unsuccessful litigants, it likewise had a right to prescribe a mechanism to collect the cost:

> If all the [state statute] did was to create this liability, it would clearly be substantive. But this new liability would be without meaning and value in many cases if it resulted in nothing but a judgment for expenses at or after the end of the case. Therefore, a procedure is prescribed by which the liability is insured by entitling the corporate defendant to a bond of indemnity before the outlay is incurred. We do not think a statute which so conditions the stockholder's action can be disregarded by the federal court as a mere procedural device.

Id. at 555–556.

The Court found the state statute binding on plaintiff notwithstanding Federal Rule of Civil Procedure 23 (now Fed. R. Civ. P. 23.1), which appeared to regulate the conditions of such suits and did not require the posting of a bond. However, because the Federal Rule did not explicitly address whether a bond was necessary, the Court found no conflict between the state statute and Federal Rule.

The third case, *Ragan v. Merchants Transfer & Warehouse Co.*, 337 U.S. 530 (1949), barred as untimely an action filed before the statute of limitations expired but served on the defendant after its expiration. While Fed. R. Civ. P. 3 deemed an action "commenced" upon filing the complaint with the court, the state rule in question required personal service on the defendant within the statutory period. Without addressing the pertinence of the Federal Rule, the Court held that the state's power to define the underlying cause of action carried with it a right to stipulate the means by which it could be enforced: "Since that cause of action is created by local law, the measure of it is to be found only in local law. It carries the same burden and is subject to the same defenses in the federal court as in the state court. . . . Where local law qualifies or abridges it, the federal court must follow suit."

2. Analyzing State and Federal Interests

In *Guaranty Trust*, it was more or less clear that deviation from the state rule would have changed the outcome of the litigation. How should a court handle practices that less clearly implicate the outcome but nonetheless seem important? For example, what if state practice allows the attorneys to conduct *voir dire* of the jury or follows different evidentiary practices than the federal courts? The Supreme Court confronted such an outcome-ambiguous practice in the following case and ended up crafting an alternative approach to *Guaranty Trust*.

✓Byrd v. Blue Ridge Rural Electric Cooperative, Inc.

356 U.S. 525 (1958)

[Byrd, a lineman for a private contractor, was injured while installing a power line to Blue Ridge's electrical substation and sued Blue Ridge in Federal District Court in a diversity suit. Blue Ridge asserted that Byrd's tort claim against it was barred by the South Carolina Workmen's Compensation Act. While Byrd was not directly employed by Blue Ridge, he could be considered a "statutory employee" for purposes of the Workmen's Compensation Act if he performed work normally done by Blue Ridge's own employees. Following a jury verdict for Byrd, the Court of Appeals reversed and directed entry of judgment for Blue Ridge, holding that Byrd was Blue Ridge's statutory employee as a matter of law.

The Supreme Court first held that the Court of Appeals should have remanded to give Byrd an opportunity to present evidence rebutting Blue Ridge's defense that he was a statutory employee. In Part II of its opinion, it addressed whether on remand the issue of coverage under the workers' compensation law should be decided by a judge or jury.]

MR. JUSTICE BRENNAN delivered the opinion of the Court. . . .

A question is also presented as to whether on remand the factual issue is to be decided by the judge or by the jury. The respondent argues on the basis of the decision of the Supreme Court of South Carolina in *Adams v. Davison-Paxon Co.*, 230 S.C. 532, that the issue of immunity should be decided by the judge and not by the jury. That was a negligence action brought in the state trial court against a store owner by an employee of an independent contractor who operated the store's millinery department. The trial judge denied the store owner's motion for a directed verdict made upon the ground that [the Workmen's Compensation Act] barred the plaintiff's action. The jury returned a verdict for the plaintiff. The South Carolina Supreme Court reversed, holding that it was for the judge and not the jury to decide on the evidence whether the owner was a statutory employer, and that the store owner had sustained his defense. The court rested its holding on decisions . . . involving judicial review of the Industrial Commission and said:

> Thus the trial court should have in this case resolved the conflicts in the evidence and determined the fact of whether (the independent contractor) was performing a part of the "trade, business or occupation" of the department store-appellant and, therefore, whether (the employee's) remedy is exclusively under the Workmen's Compensation Law. . . .

The respondent argues that this state-court decision governs the present diversity case and "divests the jury of its normal function" to decide the disputed fact question of the respondent's immunity under [the Workmen's Compensation Act]. This is to contend that the federal court is bound under *Erie R. Co. v. Tompkins*, to follow the state court's holding to secure uniform enforcement of the immunity created by the State.

First. It was decided in *Erie R. Co. v. Tompkins* that the federal courts in diversity cases must respect the definition of state-created rights and obligations by the state courts. We must, therefore, first examine the rule in *Adams v. Davison-Paxon Co.* to determine whether it is bound up with these rights and obligations in such a way that its application in the federal court is required. *Cities Service Oil Co. v. Dunlap*, 308 U.S. 208.

The Workmen's Compensation Act is administered in South Carolina by its Industrial Commission. The South Carolina courts hold that, on judicial review of actions of the Commission under [the Workmen's Compensation Act] the question whether the claim of an injured workman is within the Commission's jurisdiction is a matter of law for decision by the court, which makes its own findings of fact relating to that jurisdiction. The South Carolina Supreme Court states no reasons in *Adams v. Davison-Paxon Co.* why, although the jury decides all other factual issues raised by the cause of action and defenses, the jury is displaced as to the factual issue raised by the affirmative defense [of whether the defendant is a statutory "employer"]. The decisions cited to support the holding are . . . concerned solely with defining the scope and method of judicial review of the Industrial Commission. A State may, of course, distribute the functions of its judicial machinery as it sees fit. The decisions relied upon, however, furnish no reason for selecting the judge rather than the jury to decide this single affirmative defense in the negligence action. They simply reflect a policy . . . that administrative determination of "jurisdictional facts" should not be final but subject to judicial review. The conclusion is inescapable that the *Adams* holding is grounded in the practical consideration that the question had theretofore come before the South Carolina courts from the Industrial Commission and the courts had become accustomed to deciding the factual issue of immunity without the aid of juries. We find nothing to suggest that this rule was announced as an integral part of the special relationship created by the statute. Thus the requirement appears to be merely a form and mode of enforcing the immunity, *Guaranty Trust Co. v. York*, and not a rule intended to be bound up with the definition of the rights and obligations of the parties. The situation is therefore not analogous to that in *Dice v. Akron, C. & Y.R. Co.*, 342 U.S. 359, where this Court held that the right to trial by jury is so substantial a part of the cause of action created by the Federal Employers' Liability Act, 45 U.S.C.A. §51 et seq., that the Ohio courts could not apply, in an action under that statute, the Ohio rule that the question of fraudulent release was for determination by a judge rather than by a jury.

Second. But cases following *Erie* have evinced a broader policy to the effect that the federal courts should conform as near as may be—in the absence of other considerations—to state rules even of form and mode where the state rules may bear substantially on the question whether the litigation would come out one way in the federal court and another way in the state court if the federal court failed to apply a particular local rule. *E.g., Guaranty Trust Co. v. York, supra; Bernhardt v. Polygraphic Co.*, 350 U.S. 198. Concededly the nature of the tribunal which tries issues may be important in the enforcement of the parcel of rights making up a cause of action or defense, and bear significantly upon achievement of uniform enforcement of the right. It may well be that in the instant personal-injury case the outcome would be substantially affected by whether the issue of immunity is decided by a judge or a jury. Therefore, were "outcome" the only consideration, a strong case might appear for saying that the federal court should follow the state practice.

But there are affirmative countervailing considerations at work here. The federal system is an independent system for administering justice to litigants who properly invoke its jurisdiction. An essential characteristic of that system is the manner in which, in civil common law actions, it distributes trial functions between judge and jury and, under the influence—if not the command[10]—of the Seventh Amendment, assigns the decisions of disputed questions of fact to the jury. *Jacob v. City of New York*, 315 U.S. 752. The policy of uniform enforcement of state-created rights and obligations, *see, e.g., Guaranty Trust Co. v. York, supra*, cannot in every case exact compliance with a state rule[12] not bound up with rights and obligations—which disrupts the federal system of allocating functions between judge and jury. *Herron v. Southern Pacific Co.*, 283 U.S. 91. Thus the inquiry here is whether the federal policy favoring jury decisions of disputed fact questions should yield to the state rule in the interest of furthering the objective that the litigation should not come out one way in the federal court and another way in the state court.

We think that in the circumstances of this case the federal court should not follow the state rule. It cannot be gainsaid that there is a strong federal policy against allowing state rules to disrupt the judge-jury relationship in the federal courts. In

_____

10. Our conclusion makes unnecessary the consideration of—and we intimate no view upon—the constitutional question whether the right of jury trial protected in federal courts by the Seventh Amendment embraces the factual issue of statutory immunity when asserted, as here, as an affirmative defense in a common law negligence action.

12. This Court held in *Sibbach v. Wilson & Co.*, 312 U.S. 1, that Federal Rules of Civil Procedure 35 should prevail over a contrary state rule.

Herron v. Southern Pacific Co., supra, the trial judge in a personal-injury negligence action brought in the District Court for Arizona on diversity grounds directed a verdict for the defendant when it appeared as a matter of law that the plaintiff was guilty of contributory negligence. The federal judge refused to be bound by a provision of the Arizona Constitution which made the jury the sole arbiter of the question of contributory negligence. This Court sustained the action of the trial judge, holding that "state laws cannot alter the essential character or function of a federal court" because that function "is not in any sense a local matter, and state statutes which would interfere with the appropriate performance of that function are not binding upon the federal court under either the Conformity Act or the 'Rules of Decision' Act." *Id.,* 283 U.S. at page 94. Perhaps even more clearly in light of the influence of the Seventh Amendment, the function assigned to the jury "is an essential factor in the process for which the Federal Constitution provides." *Id.,* 283 U.S. at page 95. Concededly the *Herron* case was decided before *Erie R. Co. v. Tompkins,* but even when *Swift v. Tyson* was governing law and allowed federal courts sitting in diversity cases to disregard state decisional law, it was never thought that state statutes or constitutions were similarly to be disregarded. . . . Yet *Herron* held that state statutes and constitutional provisions could not disrupt or alter the essential character or function of a federal court.

Third. We have discussed the problem upon the assumption that the outcome of the litigation may be substantially affected by whether the issue of immunity is decided by a judge or a jury. But clearly there is not present here the certainty that a different result would follow, *cf. Guaranty Trust Co. v. York, supra,* or even the strong possibility that this would be the case, *cf. Bernhardt v. Polygraphic Co., supra.* There are factors present here which might reduce that possibility. The trial judge in the federal system has powers denied the judges of many states to comment on the weight of evidence and credibility of witnesses, and discretion to grant a new trial if the verdict appears to him to be against the weight of the evidence. We do not think the likelihood of a different result is so strong as to require the federal practice of jury determination of disputed factual issues to yield to the state rule in the interest of uniformity of outcome.[15] . . .

Reversed and remanded.

Mr. JUSTICE WHITTAKER concurring in part and dissenting in part. . . .

Inasmuch as the law of South Carolina, as construed by its highest court, requires its courts—not juries—to determine whether jurisdiction over the subject matter of cases like this is vested in its Industrial Commission, and inasmuch as the Court's opinion concedes "that in the instant personal-injury case the outcome

---

15. *Stoner v. New York Life Ins. Co.,* 311 U.S. 464, is not contrary. It was there held that the federal court should follow the state rule defining the evidence sufficient to raise a jury question whether the state-created right was established. But the state rule did not have the effect of nullifying the function of the federal judge to control a jury submission as did the Arizona constitutional provision which was denied effect in *Herron.* The South Carolina rule here involved affects the jury function as the Arizona provision affected the function of the judge: The rule entirely displaces the jury without regard to the sufficiency of the evidence to support a jury finding of immunity.

would be substantially affected by whether the issue of immunity is decided by a judge or a jury," it follows that in this diversity case the jurisdictional issue must be determined by the judge—not by the jury. Insofar as the Court holds that the question of jurisdiction should be determined by the jury, I think the Court departs from its past decisions. I therefore respectfully dissent. . . .

NOTES AND QUESTIONS

1. *The Impact of a Different Trier of Fact on the Outcome of the Litigation.* Had the Court resolved *Byrd*, as Justice Whittaker suggests was appropriate, by a strict application of the outcome-determination test, how would the case have come out? Did the Court in *Byrd* believe that the outcome of the litigation would be affected by letting the jury rather than the judge decide the question of whether Byrd was a statutory employee? Does *Guaranty Trust* require conformity to state practice any time the outcome "may well be . . . substantially affected"?

In an earlier decision, *Bernhardt v. Polygraphic Co.*, 350 U.S. 198, 203 (1956), the Supreme Court held the enforceability of an arbitration clause was a matter of state law since the nature of the tribunal could affect the outcome. The federal district court in Vermont refused to stay an action pending arbitration because Vermont state law would not enforce promises to arbitrate. The Supreme Court agreed: "The nature of the tribunal where suits are tried is an important part of the parcel of rights behind a cause of action. The change from a court of law to an arbitration panel may make a radical difference in ultimate result. Arbitration carries no right to trial by jury that is guaranteed both by the Seventh Amendment and [state law]." Presumably then, the right to jury determination of plaintiff's employment status in *Byrd* could have been considered outcome-determinative under *Bernhardt*.

2. *The Problem of Ascertaining State Interests.* Did the Court persuade you that the only purpose to the South Carolina rule was "the practical consideration" that the state courts "had become accustomed to deciding the factual issue of immunity without the aid of juries"? How does the Court know that South Carolina did not want to favor defendants, or preserve the integrity of the workers' compensation scheme by taking the question away from the jury (which might be inclined to allow injured workers to avoid the limitation on tort recovery)? Who should have the burden of proving the nature of the state interest? What would constitute persuasive evidence of the "actual" state interest underlying a state practice? Problems with ascertaining state interests have led scholars to criticize the use of a similar methodology known as "interest analysis" as a method of resolving interstate choice of law dilemmas. *See, e.g.*, R. Lea Brilmayer, *Interest Analysis and the Myth of Legislative Intent*, 78 Mich. L. Rev. 392 (1980). Are there any differences between the interstate and *Erie* contexts that make the pertinent governmental interests more ascertainable in the *Erie* context?

3. *The Federal Interest in a Right to a Jury Trial.* In footnote 10, the Court emphasizes that it does not reach the issue of whether Byrd had a Seventh Amendment right to have a jury determine whether he was covered by the state workers' compensation law. What, then, did the Court mean when it asserted that the distribution of decision making between the judge and jury is "an essential characteristic" of the federal system "under the influence—if not the command" of the Seventh

Amendment? If Byrd did *not* have a constitutional right to a jury determination, in what sense was it "essential" to provide him with one? If he *did* have such a constitutional right, this is a very easy case, is it not? *Cf.* Peter Westen & Jeffrey S. Lehman, *Is There Life for* Erie *After the Death of Diversity?*, 78 Mich. L. Rev. 311, 345–347 (1980) (criticizing the Court's "balancing" approach in *Byrd*).

3. The Impact of the Federal Rules of Civil Procedure

Consider the suggestion above that *Byrd* would have been a very easy case had the Court determined that Byrd had a constitutional right to a jury determination of his employment status. What would have made it an easy case? Both of the legal texts upon which *Erie* is based contain explicit direction always to apply valid and pertinent federal law, state law to the contrary notwithstanding. Article VI of the Constitution provides:

> This Constitution, and the Laws of the United States which shall be made in Pursuance thereof; and all Treaties made, or which shall be made, under the Authority of the United States, shall be the supreme Law of the Land; and the Judges in every State shall be bound thereby, any Thing in the Constitution or Laws of any State to the Contrary notwithstanding.

The Rules of Decision Act also contains an important proviso: State law shall be regarded as the applicable rule of decision "except where the Constitution or treaties of the United States or Acts of Congress otherwise require or provide."

Accordingly, in any case where a valid and pertinent federal law is created or authorized by the Constitution, statute, or treaty, there is no question that it displaces any inconsistent state law in federal court, and in state court as well.

In *Erie*, *Guaranty Trust*, and *Byrd* (as decided without reaching the Seventh Amendment issue), there was little doubt that the federal law in question would have been "judge-made"; no federal statute created a standard of care for railroads toward pedestrians, adopted the doctrine of laches, or provided a right to jury trial on the issue of plaintiff's employment status. There is, however, a large body of federal procedural law—the Federal Rules of Civil Procedure—that *is* authorized by statute, through the Rules Enabling Act of 1934, 28 U.S.C. §2072. Because the doctrine developed in the cases from *Erie* through *Byrd* addressed only the propriety of federal judge-made law, its applicability to procedures authorized by the Federal Rules was not obvious.

Notwithstanding the proviso of the Rules of Decision Act, early cases did not seem to distinguish the legal analysis applicable to cases governed by a Federal Rule from cases governed solely by judicially crafted procedures. *See, e.g., Ragan v. Merchants Transfer & Warehouse Co.*, p. 455 (*Guaranty Trust* requires that state law defining when action is "commenced" for purposes of statute of limitations takes precedence over contrary Fed. R. Civ. P. 3); *cf. Bernhardt v. Polygraphic Co. of America*, p. 459 (narrowly construing the Federal Arbitration Act, 9 U.S.C. §§1 *et seq.*, to avoid conflict with anti-arbitration policy of forum state). However, the Court eventually concluded that the presence of a valid and pertinent Rule of Procedure was virtually dispositive.

a. The Rule-Making Process

i. Rules Enabling Act of 1934

Rather than providing rules of procedure that would govern proceedings in federal court, Congress delegated rule-making power to the courts themselves. This power was at first extremely limited, but by 1938, a revolution had occurred, which resulted in the Federal Rules of Civil Procedure.

The Rules Enabling Act of 1934 represented a 20-year effort on the part of the American Bar Association to create uniform rules of federal civil procedure. The Act, currently codified as 28 U.S.C. §2072, provides in relevant part:

> (a) The Supreme Court shall have the power to prescribe general rules of practice and procedure and rules of evidence for cases in the United States district courts . . . and courts of appeals.
>
> (b) Such rules shall not abridge, enlarge or modify any substantive right. All laws in conflict with such rules shall be of no further force or effect after such rules have taken effect.

Note that the delegation to the Court of the rule-making power in the Act is not absolute. The Court's rule-making authority is limited in scope to "rules of practice and procedure and rules of evidence," and is subject to the proviso of subsection (b) that no rule may "abridge, enlarge or modify any substantive right." Moreover, every rule promulgated pursuant to the Act is subject to congressional veto. Under 28 U.S.C. §2074, the Court is required to report all proposed rules to Congress "not later than May 1 of the year in which a [proposed rule] is to become effective," and "such rule shall take effect no earlier than December 1 of [that year]." Accordingly, Congress has the opportunity to prevent the operation of any rule that it finds objectionable by passing appropriate veto legislation during the seven-month "layover period."

The Supreme Court, promptly acting on this mandate, issued a formal order appointing the Advisory Committee on Rules of Civil Procedure to draft the original federal rules. The first rules were approved by the Supreme Court, were submitted to Congress, and became effective in 1938. *See generally* Stephen B. Burbank, *The Rules Enabling Act of 1934*, 130 U. Pa. L. Rev. 1015 (1982); Winifred R. Brown, Federal Rulemaking: Problems and Possibilities 1 (1981); Jack B. Weinstein, Reform of Court Rule-Making Procedures 21-71 (1977).

Today, the rule-making process is an ongoing evaluation process set forth in 28 U.S.C §§331–333, 2071–2074, a brief description of which follows.

ii. Layers of Review

By the 1950s, the need for a continuing study of and recommendations about the operation and effects of the Rules was apparent. Congress delegated this responsibility to the Judicial Conference of the United States, which is comprised of the Chief Justice of the United States, the chief judge of each judicial circuit, the chief judge of the Court of International Trade, and a district judge from each circuit. *See* 28 U.S.C. §331. The Conference, in turn, established a Standing Committee to review and present recommendations from Advisory Committees specializing in various areas of federal practice — e.g., civil, appellate, and criminal. Thus, the rule-making process has a pyramidal form: At the bottom of the pyramid are the Advisory Committees; the next level is the Standing Committee of the Conference; the third level is the Judicial Conference; the fourth level is the Supreme Court; and at the top of the pyramid is Congress.

The Advisory Committees are composed of judges, practicing lawyers, and legal academics appointed by the Chief Justice of the United States. Each committee has its own reporter, appointed by the Chief Justice. With the help of the chair of the committee, the reporter prepares draft materials and formulates a program of study based on suggestions for rule changes and independent research. The committee's draft is circulated to the bench and bar. After a period for notice and comment, the advisory committee reconsiders the draft in light of the recommendations. This process repeats itself until the advisory committee is satisfied with its draft proposal.

The Standing Committee reviews the draft, occasionally making technical or substantive changes. Once the draft is approved, it is sent to the Judicial Conference. Generally, the Conference approves the Rules as submitted and submits them to the Supreme Court through the Administrative Office of the United States Courts.

Supreme Court review of the proposed Rules is, like most other actions of the Court, highly mysterious. Sometimes the Court fails to promulgate the proposed Rules, but most often it approves and submits them to Congress. On rare occasions, individual Justices have dissented from the approval of a Rule. These dissents indicate that the Court's debates often focus on the constitutional limits of their rule-making powers.

> We believe that . . . many [rules of civil procedure] determine matters so substantially affecting the rights of litigants in law suits that in practical effect they are the equivalent of new legislation which, in our judgment, the Constitution requires to be introduced and enacted by Congress and approved by the President.

374 U.S. 865, 865-866 (Black, J., and Douglas, J., dissenting from promulgation of amendments to Federal Rules of Civil Procedure) (1963). The Rules that these Justices objected to included Rule 50 (directed verdicts), Rule 56 (summary judgment), Rule 49 (special verdicts), and Rule 41 (dismissals). Unlike the *Erie* federalism problems considered above, Justices Black and Douglas were raising a separation of powers objection.

The last step in the rule-making process is the consideration by Congress of the Rules promulgated by the Supreme Court. Congress has the power to approve, reject, amend, or defer effectiveness of any rule or part of any Rule submitted. Unlike ordinary legislation where inaction by Congress on a bill means it does not become law, the Rules promulgated by the Court are legally effective unless Congress acts affirmatively by legislation either to reject or amend them or to defer their effectiveness.

Until 1973, Congress allowed the statutory period of time to pass without taking any action, thus essentially giving the Judicial Conference and Supreme Court the final word. However, the controversy surrounding the drafting of the Federal Rules of Evidence led Congress to reject proposed rules and enact a statute in their place. The version of the Rules of Evidence promulgated by the Supreme Court contained federal privileges for communications between attorney and client, doctor and patient, and the like, applicable in diversity and federal question cases.

Substituting its own judgment, Congress enacted by statute Federal Rules of Evidence that included a provision that state law governs issues of privilege in diversity actions. Since then, Congress has taken a more active role in the rule-making process. *See* David Siegel, *Commentary on 1988 Revision*, 28 U.S.C.A. §2074 (West Supp. 1991); Stephen B. Burbank, *Procedure, Politics and Power: The Role of Congress*, 79 Notre Dame L. Rev. 1677, 1695–1703 (2004).

For a thorough discussion of the rule-making process, *see* Winifred R. Brown, Federal Rulemaking: Problems and Possibilities 5-32 (1981): Joseph F. Spaniol, Jr., *Making Federal Rules: The Inside Story*, 69 A.B.A. J. 1645 (1983).

iii. Status of the Federal Rules

Rules promulgated by the Supreme Court under §2072 have the status of a congressional statute. The last sentence of §2072(b), known as the supersession clause, states that "all laws in conflict with [the Federal Rules of Civil Procedure] shall be of no further force or effect after such rules have taken effect." Thus, when a federal Rule is passed that conflicts with any procedural component of a previously enacted statute, the rule governs. This is known as the "later in time rule."

When Congress undertook to revise §2072 in 1985, the status of the supersession clause was heavily debated. Some commentators argued that the absence of the constitutional safeguards for enacting laws — majority support in both Houses and presentment to the President — in the federal rule-making process necessarily placed federal Rules on a lower level than statutes. Thus, it was argued, any statute in conflict with a federal Rule must continue to apply. *See* Stephen B. Burbank, *Hold the Corks: A Comment on Paul Carrington's "Substance" and "Procedure" in the Rules Enabling Act*, 1989 Duke L.J. 1012. Others argued that Congress carefully limited the power given to the rule-makers through the abridgment of rights language of §2072(b). *See* Paul D. Carrington, *"Substance" and "Procedure" in the Rules Enabling Act*, 1989 Duke L.J. 281. While there have been proposals to eliminate the supersession language, after years of debate, it remains without any alteration. *See also* Anthony Vitarelli, Comment, *A Blueprint for Applying the Rules Enabling Act's Supersession Clause*, 117 Yale L.J. 1225 (2008).

iv. Criticisms

Criticisms of the rule-making process focused in the 1980s on the lack of public participation, the need for more congressional and judicial oversight, and the dual role of the Supreme Court as rule-maker and ultimate judge of the constitutionality of the rules, and the disappearance of uniformity. *See* Jack B. Weinstein, Reform of Court Rule-Making Procedures (1977); Brown, Federal Rulemaking, *supra*; Burbank, *The Rules Enabling Act of 1934, supra*.

The 1988 amendments to the Enabling Act attempted to open the rule-making process to public scrutiny and input. Section 2073(c) requires that any meeting of any committee (advisory or standing) "be open to the public, except when the committee so meeting, in open session and with a majority present, determines that it is in the public interest" to close all or part of the remaining session. Minutes of all meetings must be kept and made available to the public. Section 2073(d) requires the issuance of proposed Rules along with explanatory notes and a written committee report, including any minority view.

v.   Local Rules

Uniformity in federal procedure was the motivating force behind the initial promulgation of the Federal Rules. However, there has always been sensitivity to the differing procedural concerns of the distinct district and circuit courts. Since the original Judiciary Act of 1789, the lower federal courts have had the right to create procedural rules for their respective courts, and Rule 83, one of the original Federal Rules of Civil Procedure, includes such a provision. Today local rule-making is pervasive in the federal court system.

Local rules are authorized by 28 U.S.C. §2071. Local rules must be consistent with the Rules of Civil Procedure as well as with other federal laws. Some argue that local rules undermine the uniformity of the Federal Rules. *See* Stephen N. Subrin, *Federal Rules, Local Rules, and State Rules: Uniformity, Divergence, and Emerging Procedural Patterns*, 137 U. Pa. L. Rev. 1999, 2011 (1989); Carl Tobias, *Civil Justice Reform and the Balkanization of Federal Civil Procedure*, 24 Ariz. St. L.J. 1393 (1992).

vi.   Validity of the Federal Rules

There have been a number of challenges in litigation to the validity of several Federal Rules of Civil Procedure on the basis that those rules "abridge[d], enlarge[d] or modif[ied]" a substantive right, thereby violating the Enabling Act mandate. Although the Court suggested in *Semtek International Inc. v. Lockheed Martin Corp.*, 531 U.S. 497 (2001), that its construction of Rule 41(b) was informed by the Enabling Act's substantive rights proviso, the Court has never deemed a Federal Rule of Procedure in violation of the Act. The courts have tended to construe broadly the breadth of the rule-making power under the Enabling Act and the Constitution, and have narrowly construed the restraint imposed by the Enabling Act.

Hanna v. Plumer

380 U.S. 460 (1965)

MR. CHIEF JUSTICE WARREN delivered the opinion of the Court.

The question to be decided is whether, in a civil action where the jurisdiction of the United States District Court is based upon diversity of citizenship between the parties, service of process shall be made in the manner prescribed by state law or that set forth in Rule 4(d)(1)* of the Federal Rules of Civil Procedure.

On February 6, 1963, petitioner, a citizen of Ohio, filed her complaint in the District Court for the District of Massachusetts, claiming damages in excess of $10,000 for personal injuries resulting from an automobile accident in South Carolina, allegedly caused by the negligence of one Louise Plumer Osgood, a Massachusetts citizen deceased at the time of the filing of the complaint. Respondent, Mrs. Osgood's executor and also a Massachusetts citizen, was named as defendant. On February 8, service was made by leaving copies of the summons

---

* Rule 4(d)(1) referred to throughout the opinion is now Rule 4(e)(2) of the current Federal Rules. — EDS.

and the complaint with respondent's wife at his residence, concededly in compliance with Rule 4(d)(l), which provides:

> The summons and complaint shall be served together. The plaintiff shall furnish the person making service with such copies as are necessary. Service shall be made as follows: (1) Upon an individual other than an infant or an incompetent person, by delivering a copy of the summons and of the complaint to him personally or by leaving copies thereof at his dwelling house or usual place of abode with some person of suitable age and discretion then residing therein. . . .

Respondent filed his answer on February 26, alleging, *inter alia*, that the action could not be maintained because it had been brought "contrary to and in violation of the provisions of Massachusetts General Laws (Ter.Ed.) Chapter 197, Section 9." That section provides:

> Except as provided in this chapter, an executor or administrator shall not be held to answer to an action by a creditor of the deceased which is not commenced within one year from the time of his giving bond for the performance of his trust, or to such an action which is commenced within said year unless before the expiration thereof the writ in such action has been served by delivery in hand upon such executor or administrator or service thereof accepted by him or a notice stating the name of the estate, the name and address of the creditor, the amount of the claim and the court in which the action has been brought has been filed in the proper registry of probate. . . .

Mass. Gen. Laws Ann., c. 197, §9 (1958). On October 17, 1963, the District Court granted respondent's motion for summary judgment, citing *Ragan v. Merchants Transfer & Warehouse Co.*, 337 U.S. 530, and *Guaranty Trust Co. v. York*, 326 U.S. 99, in support of its conclusion that the adequacy of the service was to be measured by §9, with which, the court held, petitioner had not complied. On appeal, petitioner admitted noncompliance with §9, but argued that Rule 4(d)(l) defines the method by which service of process is to be effected in diversity actions. The Court of Appeals for the First Circuit, finding that "(r)elatively recent amendments (to §9) evince a clear legislative purpose to require personal notification within the year,"[1] concluded that the conflict of state and federal rules was over "a substantive rather than a procedural matter," and unanimously affirmed. 331 F.2d 157. . . .

---

1. Section 9 is in part a statute of limitations, providing that an executor need not "answer to an action . . . which is not commenced within one year from the time of his giving bond. . . ." This part of the statute, the purpose of which is to speed the settlement of estates . . . is not involved in this case, since the action clearly was timely commenced. (Respondent filed bond on March 1, 1962; the complaint was filed February 6, 1963; and the service—the propriety of which is in dispute—was made on February 8, 1963.) 331 F.2d at 159. *Cf. Guaranty Trust Co. of New York v. York, supra, Ragan v. Merchants Transfer & Warehouse Co., supra.* Section 9 also provides for the manner of service. Generally, service of process must be made by "delivery in hand," although there are two alternatives: acceptance of service by the executor, or filing of a notice of claim, the components of which are set out in the statute, in the appropriate probate court. The purpose of this part of the statute, which

We conclude that the adoption of Rule 4(d)(l), designed to control service of process in diversity actions, neither exceeded the congressional mandate embodied in the Rules Enabling Act nor transgressed constitutional bounds, and that the Rule is therefore the standard against which the District Court should have measured the adequacy of the service. Accordingly, we reverse the decision of the Court of Appeals.

The Rules Enabling Act, 28 U.S.C. §2072 (1958 ed.), provides, in pertinent part:

> The Supreme Court shall have the power to prescribe, by general rules, the forms of process, writs, pleadings, and motions, and the practice and procedure of the district courts of the United States in civil actions. Such rules shall not abridge, enlarge or modify any substantive right and shall preserve the right of trial by jury. . . .

Under the cases construing the scope of the Enabling Act, Rule 4(d)(l) clearly passes muster. Prescribing the manner in which a defendant is to be notified that a suit has been instituted against him, it relates to the "practice and procedure of the district courts." *Cf. Insurance Co. v. Bangs*, 103 U.S. 435, 439.

> The test must be whether a rule really regulates procedure — the judicial process for enforcing rights and duties recognized by substantive law and for justly administering remedy and redress for disregard or infraction of them.

Sibbach v. Wilson & Co., 312 U.S. 1, 14.

In Mississippi Pub. Corp. v. Murphree, 326 U.S. 438, this Court upheld Rule 4(f), which permits service of a summons anywhere within the State (and not merely the district) in which a district court sits:

> We think that Rule 4(f) is in harmony with the Enabling Act. . . . Undoubtedly most alterations of the rules of practice and procedure may and often do affect the rights of litigants. Congress' prohibition of any alteration of substantive rights of litigants was obviously not addressed to such incidental effects as necessarily attend the adoption of the prescribed new rules of procedure upon the rights of litigants who, agreeably to rules of practice and procedure, have been brought before a court authorized to determine their rights. *Sibbach v. Wilson & Co.*, 312 U.S. 1, 11–14. The fact that the application of Rule 4(f) will operate to subject petitioner's rights to adjudication by the district court for northern Mississippi will undoubtedly affect those rights. But it does not operate to abridge, enlarge or modify the rules of decision by which that court will adjudicate its rights. *Id.* at 445–446.

---

is involved here, is, as the court below noted, to insure that executors will receive actual notice of claims. *Parker v. Rich*, 8 N.E.2d 345, 347 (1937). Actual notice is of course also the goal of Rule 4(d)(1); however, the Federal Rule reflects a determination that this goal can be achieved by a method less cumbersome than that prescribed in §9. In this case the goal seems to have been achieved: although the affidavit filed by respondent in the district court asserts that he had not been served in hand nor had he accepted service, it does not allege lack of actual notice.

Thus were there no conflicting state procedure, Rule 4(d)(1) would clearly control. *National Equipment Rental, Limited v. Szukhent*, 375 U.S. 311, 316. However, respondent, focusing on the contrary Massachusetts rule, calls to the Court's attention another line of cases, a line which—like the Federal Rules—had its birth in 1938. *Erie R. Co. v. Tompkins*, 304 U.S. 64, overruling *Swift v. Tyson*, 16 Pet. 1, held that federal courts sitting in diversity cases, when deciding questions of "substantive" law, are bound by state court decisions as well as state statutes. The broad command of *Erie* was therefore identical to that of the Enabling Act: federal courts are to apply state substantive law and federal procedural law. However, as subsequent cases sharpened the distinction between substance and procedure, the line of cases following *Erie* diverged markedly from the line construing the Enabling Act. *Guaranty Trust Co. v. York*, 326 U.S. 99, made it clear that *Erie*-type problems were not to be solved by reference to any traditional or common-sense substance-procedure distinction:

> And so the question is not whether a statute of limitations is deemed a matter of "procedure" in some sense. The question is . . . does it significantly affect the result of a litigation for a federal court to disregard a law of a State that would be controlling in an action upon the same claim by the same parties in a State court? 326 U.S. at 109.

Respondent, by placing primary reliance on *York* and *Ragan*, suggests that the *Erie* doctrine acts as a check on the Federal Rules of Civil Procedure, that despite the clear command of Rule 4(d)(1), *Erie* and its progeny demand the application of the Massachusetts rule. Reduced to essentials, the argument is: (1) *Erie*, as refined in *York*, demands that federal courts apply state law whenever application of federal law in its stead will alter the outcome of the case. (2) In this case, a determination that the Massachusetts service requirements obtain will result in immediate victory for respondent. If, on the other hand, it should be held that Rule 4(d)(1) is applicable, the litigation will continue, with possible victory for petitioner. (3) Therefore, *Erie* demands application of the Massachusetts rule. The syllogism possesses an appealing simplicity, but is for several reasons invalid. *[handwritten margin note: District Court Holding]*

In the first place, it is doubtful that, even if there were no Federal Rule making it clear that in-hand service is not required in diversity actions, the *Erie* rule would have obligated the District Court to follow the Massachusetts procedure. "Outcome-determination" analysis was never intended to serve as a talisman. *Byrd v. Blue Ridge Rural Elec. Cooperative*, 356 U.S. 525. Indeed, the message of *York* itself is that choices between state and federal law are to be made not by application of any automatic, "litmus paper" criterion, but rather by reference to the policies underlying the *Erie* rule. *Guaranty Trust Co. v. York, supra*, 326 U.S. at 108–112.

The *Erie* rule is rooted in part in a realization that it would be unfair for the character or result of a litigation materially to differ because the suit had been brought in a federal court.

> Diversity of citizenship jurisdiction was conferred in order to prevent apprehended discrimination in state courts against those not citizens of the state. *Swift v. Tyson* (16 Pet. 1) introduced grave discrimination by noncitizens against citizens. It made rights enjoyed under the unwritten

general law vary according to whether enforcement was sought in the state or in the federal court; and the privilege of selecting the court in which the right should be determined was conferred upon the noncitizen. Thus, the doctrine rendered impossible equal protection of the law. *Erie R. Co. v. Tompkins, supra*, 304 U.S. at 74–75.

The decision was also in part a reaction to the practice of "forum-shopping" which had grown up in response to the rule of *Swift v. Tyson.* 304 U.S. at 73–74. That the *York* test was an attempt to effectuate these policies is demonstrated by the fact that the opinion framed the inquiry in terms of "substantial" variations between state and federal litigation. 326 U.S. at 109. Not only are nonsubstantial, or trivial, variations not likely to raise the sort of equal protection problems which troubled the Court in *Erie*, they are also unlikely to influence the choice of a forum. The "outcome-determination" test therefore cannot be read without reference to the twin aims of the *Erie* rule: discouragement of forum-shopping and avoidance of inequitable administration of the laws.[9]

The difference between the conclusion that the Massachusetts rule is applicable, and the conclusion that it is not, is of course at this point "outcome-determinative" in the sense that if we hold the state rule to apply, respondent prevails, whereas if we hold that Rule 4(d)(1) governs, the litigation will continue. But in this sense *every* procedural variation is "outcome-determinative." For example, having brought suit in a federal court, a plaintiff cannot then insist on the right to file subsequent pleadings in accord with the time limits applicable in state courts, even though enforcement of the federal timetable will, if he continues to insist that he must meet only the state time limit, result in determination of the controversy against him. So it is here. Though choice of the federal or state rule will at this point have a marked effect upon the outcome of the litigation, the difference between the two rules would be of scant, if any, relevance to the choice of a forum. Petitioner, in choosing her forum, was not presented with a situation where application of the state rule would wholly bar recovery;[10] rather, adherence to the state rule would have resulted only in altering the way in which process was

---

9. The Court of Appeals seemed to frame the inquiry in terms of how "important" §9 is to the State. . . . One cannot meaningfully ask how important something is without first asking "important for what purpose"? *Erie* and its progeny make clear that when a federal court sitting in a diversity case is faced with a question of whether or not to apply state law, the importance of a state rule is indeed relevant, but only in the context of asking whether application of the rule would make so important a difference to the character or result of the litigation that failure to enforce it would unfairly discriminate against citizens of the forum State, or whether application of the rule would have so important an effect upon the fortunes of one or both of the litigants that failure to enforce it would be likely to cause a plaintiff to choose the federal court.

10. *See Guaranty Trust Co. v. York, supra*, 326 U.S. at 108–109; *Ragan v. Merchants Transfer & Warehouse Co., supra*, 337 U.S. at 532; *Woods v. Interstate Realty Co., supra*, note 5, 337 U.S. at 538. Similarly, a federal court's refusal to enforce the New Jersey rule involved in *Cohen v. Beneficial Indus. Loan Corp.*, 337 U.S. 541, requiring the posting of security by plaintiffs in stockholders' derivative actions, might well impel a stockholder to choose to bring suit in the federal, rather than the state, court.

served.[11] Moreover, it is difficult to argue that permitting service of defendant's wife to take the place of in-hand service of defendant himself alters the mode of enforcement of state-created rights in a fashion sufficiently "substantial" to raise the sort of equal protection problems to which the *Erie* opinion alluded.

There is, however, a more fundamental flaw in respondent's syllogism: the incorrect assumption that the rule of *Erie R. Co. v. Tompkins* constitutes the appropriate test of the validity and therefore the applicability of a Federal Rule of Civil Procedure. The *Erie* rule has never been invoked to void a Federal Rule. It is true that there have been cases where this Court has held applicable a state rule in the face of an argument that the situation was governed by one of the Federal Rules. But the holding of each such case was not that *Erie* commanded displacement of a Federal Rule by an inconsistent state rule, but rather that the scope of the Federal Rule was not as broad as the losing partly urged, and therefore, there being no Federal Rule which covered the point in dispute. *Erie* commanded the enforcement of state law. . . .

(Here, of course, the clash is unavoidable; Rule 4(d)(1) says—implicitly, but with unmistakable clarity—that in-hand service is not required in federal courts.) At the same time, in cases adjudicating the validity of Federal Rules, we have not applied the *York* rule or other refinements of *Erie*, but have to this day continued to decide questions concerning the scope of the Enabling Act and the constitutionality of specific Federal Rules in light of the distinction set forth in *Sibbach. E.g., Schlagenhauf v. Holder*, 379 U.S. 104.

Nor has the development of two separate lines of cases been inadvertent. The line between "substance" and "procedure" shifts as the legal context changes. "Each implies different variables depending upon the particular problem for which it is used." *Guaranty Trust Co. v. York, supra*, 326 U.S. at 108; Cook, The Logical and Legal Bases of the Conflict of Laws, pp. 154–183 (1942). It is true that both the Enabling Act and the *Erie* rule say, roughly, that federal courts are to apply state "substantive" law and federal "procedural" law, but from that it need not follow that the tests are identical. For they were designed to control very different sorts of decisions. When a situation is covered by one of the Federal Rules, the question facing the court is a far cry from the typical, relatively unguided *Erie* choice: the court has been instructed to apply the Federal Rule, and can refuse to do so only if the Advisory Committee, this Court, and Congress erred in their prima facie judgment that the Rule in question transgresses neither the terms of the Enabling Act nor constitutional restrictions.

We are reminded by the *Erie* opinion that neither Congress nor the federal courts can, under the guise of formulating rules of decision for federal courts, fashion rules which are not supported by a grant of federal authority contained in Article I or some other section of the Constitution; in such areas state law must govern because there can be no other law. But the opinion in *Erie*, which involved

---

11. *Cf. Monarch Insurance Co. of Ohio v. Spach*, 281 F.2d 401, 412 (C.A. 5th Cir. 1960). We cannot seriously entertain the thought that one suing an estate would be led to choose the federal court because of a belief that adherence to Rule 4(d)(1) is less likely to give the executor actual notice than §9, and therefore more likely to produce a default judgment. Rule 4(d)(1) is well designed to give actual notice, as it did in this case. . . .

no Federal Rule and dealt with a question which was "substantive" in every traditional sense (whether the railroad owed a duty of care to Tompkins as a trespasser or a licensee), surely neither said nor implied that measures like Rule 4(d)(1) are unconstitutional. For the constitutional provision for a federal court system (augmented by the Necessary and Proper Clause) carries with it congressional power to make rules governing the practice and pleading in those courts, which in turn includes a power to regulate matters which, though falling within the uncertain area between substance and procedure, are rationally capable of classification as either. *Cf. M'Culloch v. State of Maryland*, 4 Wheat. 316, 421. Neither *York* nor the cases following it ever suggested that the rule there laid down for coping with situations where no Federal Rule applies is coextensive with the limitation on Congress to which *Erie* had adverted. . . .

Erie and its offspring cast no doubt on the long-recognized power of Congress to prescribe housekeeping rules for federal courts even though some of those rules will inevitably differ from comparable state rules. *Cf. Herron v. Southern Pacific Co.*, 283 U.S. 91. "When, because the plaintiff happens to be a non-resident, such a right is enforceable in a federal as well as in a State court, the forms and mode of enforcing the right may at times, naturally enough, vary because the two judicial systems are not identic." *Guaranty Trust Co. v. York, supra*, 326 U.S. at 108; *Cohen v. Beneficial Indus. Loan Corp.*, 337 U.S. 541. Thus, though a court, in measuring a Federal Rule against the standards contained in the Enabling Act and the Constitution, need not wholly blind itself to the degree to which the Rule makes the character and result of the federal litigation stray from the course it would follow in state courts, *Sibbach v. Wilson & Co., supra*, 312 U.S. at 13–14, it cannot be forgotten that the *Erie* rule, and the guidelines suggested in *York*, were created to serve another purpose altogether. To hold that a Federal Rule of Civil Procedure must cease to function whenever it alters the mode of enforcing state-created rights would be to disembowel either the Constitution's grant of power over federal procedure or Congress' attempt to exercise that power in the Enabling Act. Rule 4(d)(1) is valid and controls the instant case.

Reversed.

MR. JUSTICE HARLAN, concurring.

It is unquestionably true that up to now *Erie* and the cases following it have not succeeded in articulating a workable doctrine governing choice of law in diversity actions. I respect the Court's effort to clarify the situation in today's opinion. However, in doing so I think it has misconceived the constitutional premises of *Erie* and has failed to deal adequately with those past decisions upon which the courts below relied.

Erie was something more than an opinion which worried about "forum-shopping and avoidance of inequitable administration of the laws," although to be sure these were important elements of the decision. I have always regarded that decision as one of the modern cornerstones of our federalism, expressing policies that profoundly touch the allocation of judicial power between the state and federal systems. *Erie* recognized that there should not be two conflicting systems of law controlling the primary activity of citizens, for such alternative governing authority must necessarily give rise to a debilitating uncertainty in the planning of everyday affairs. And it recognized that the scheme of our Constitution envisions an allocation of law-making functions between state and federal legislative processes which is undercut if the federal judiciary can make substantive law affecting state affairs beyond the bounds of congressional legislative powers in this regard. Thus, in diversity cases *Erie* commands that it be the state law governing primary private activity which prevails.

The shorthand formulations which have appeared in some past decisions are prone to carry untoward results that frequently arise from oversimplification. The Court is quite right in stating that the "outcome-determinative" test of *Guaranty Trust Co. v. York*, 326 U.S. 99, if taken literally, proves too much, for any rule, no matter how clearly "procedural," can affect the outcome of litigation if it is not obeyed. In turning from the "outcome" test of *York* back to the unadorned forum-shopping rationale of *Erie*, however, the Court falls prey to like oversimplification, for a simple forum-shopping rule also proves too much; litigants often choose a federal forum merely to obtain what they consider the advantages of the Federal Rules of Civil Procedure or to try their cases before a supposedly more favorable judge. To my mind the proper line of approach in determining whether to apply a state or a federal rule, whether "substantive" or "procedural," is to stay close to basic principles by inquiring if the choice of rule would substantially affect those primary decisions respecting human conduct which our constitutional system leaves to state regulation. If so, *Erie* and the Constitution require that the state rule prevail, even in the face of a conflicting federal rule.

The Court weakens, if indeed it does not submerge, this basic principle by finding, in effect, a grant of substantive legislative power in the constitutional provision for a federal court system (*compare Swift v. Tyson*, 16 Pet. 1), and through it, setting up the Federal Rules as a body of law inviolate. . . . So long as a reasonable man could characterize any duly-adopted federal rule as "procedural," the Court, unless I misapprehend what is said, would have it apply no matter how seriously it frustrated a State's substantive regulation of the primary conduct and affairs of its citizens. Since the members of the Advisory Committee, the Judicial Conference, and this Court who formulated the Federal Rules are presumably reasonable men, it follows that the integrity of the Federal Rules is absolute. Whereas the unadulterated outcome and forum-shopping tests may err too far toward honoring state rules, I submit that the Court's "arguably procedural, *ergo* constitutional" test moves too fast and far in the other direction.

The courts below relied upon this Court's decisions in *Ragan v. Merchants Transfer & Warehouse Co.*, 337 U.S. 530, and *Cohen v. Beneficial Indus. Loan Corp.*, 337 U.S. 541. Those cases deserve more attention than this Court has given them, particularly *Ragan* which, if still good law, would in my opinion call for affirmance of the result reached by the Court of Appeals. Further, a discussion of these two cases will serve to illuminate the "diversity" thesis I am advocating.

In *Ragan*, a Kansas statute of limitations provided that an action was deemed commenced when service was made on the defendant. Despite Federal Rule 3 which provides that an action commences with the filing of the complaint, the Court held that for purposes of the Kansas statute of limitations a diversity tort action commenced only when service was made upon the defendant. The effect of this holding was that although the plaintiff had filed his federal complaint within the state period of limitations, his action was barred because the federal marshal did not serve a summons on the defendant until after the limitations period had run. I think that the decision was wrong. At most, application of the Federal Rule would have meant that potential Kansas tort defendants would have to defer for a few days the satisfaction of knowing that they had not been sued within the limitations period. The choice of the Federal Rule would have had no effect on the primary stages of private activity from which torts arise, and only the most minimal effect on behavior following the commission of the tort. In such circumstances the interest of the federal system in proceeding under its own rules should have prevailed.

Cohen v. Beneficial Indus. Loan Corp. held that a federal diversity court must apply a state statute requiring a small stockholder in a stockholder derivative suit to post a bond securing payment of defense costs as a condition to prosecuting an action. Such a statute is not "outcome determinative"; the plaintiff can win with or without it. The Court now rationalizes the case on the ground that the statute might affect the plaintiff's choice of forum . . . , but as has been pointed out, a simple forum-shopping test proves too much. The proper view of *Cohen* is in my opinion, that the statute was meant to inhibit small stockholders from instituting "strike suits," and thus it was designed and could be expected to have a substantial impact on private primary activity. Anyone who was at the trial bar during the period when *Cohen* arose can appreciate the strong state policy reflected in the statute. I think it wholly legitimate to view Federal Rule 23 as not purporting to deal with the problem. But even had the Federal Rules purported to do so, and in so doing provided a substantially less effective deterrent to strike suits, I think the state rule should still have prevailed. That is where I believe the Court's view differs from mine; for the Court attributes such overriding force to the Federal Rules that it is hard to think of a case where a conflicting state rule would be allowed to operate, even though the state rule reflected policy considerations which, under *Erie*, would lie within the realm of state legislative authority.

It remains to apply what has been said to the present case. The Massachusetts rule provides that an executor need not answer suits unless in-hand service was made upon him or notice of the action was filed in the proper registry of probate within one year of his giving bond. The evident intent of this statute is to permit an executor to distribute the estate which he is administering without fear that further liabilities may be outstanding for which he could be held personally liable. If the Federal District Court in Massachusetts applies Rule 4(d)(1) of the Federal Rules of Civil Procedure instead of the Massachusetts service rule, what effect would that have on the speed and assurance with which estates are distributed? As I see it, the effect would not be substantial. It would mean simply that an executor would have to check at his own house or the federal courthouse as well as the registry of probate before he could distribute the estate with impunity. As this does not seem enough to give rise to any real impingement on the vitality of the state policy which the Massachusetts rule is intended to serve, I concur in the judgment of the Court.

NOTES AND QUESTIONS

1. *What Is the Core Holding of* Hanna*?* *Hanna* has been described as establishing a "two-track" resolution of *Erie* problems: one track to resolve the "relatively unguided" choice when no federal rule or statute covers the question; and a second track where there is a pertinent federal rule or statute. *See* John Hart Ely, *The Irrepressible Myth of Erie*, 87 Harv. L. Rev. 693 (1974). *Hanna* appears to be an easy case

in that the application of Federal Rule 4 would not have altered the outcome nor induced the choice of the federal forum. Thus, the Court suggests that federal law would have controlled even on the "unguided" track. To the extent that the Court believed Rule 4 to be controlling here, does that mean that the Court's discussion of *Guaranty Trust* and the "unguided choice" are pure dictum? Or conversely, is the Court's discussion of the case as one governed by a pertinent Federal Rule superfluous in light of the negligible impact of the federal practice on outcome?

2. Hanna*'s Clarification of the "Outcome-Determination" Test.* The Court in *Hanna* recognized the potential overinclusiveness of *Guaranty Trust*'s outcome-determination test. How does the Court limit *Guaranty Trust* to avoid characterizing all differences between state and federal procedure as outcome determinative?

The time frame of the outcome-determination test seems critical in *Hanna*; the impact of the choice between state and federal law must be apparent prior to filing, at the point the litigants are selecting the forum. If, and only if, the difference between state and federal law would, at that time, lead a litigant to select the federal forum, should the difference be considered "outcome determinative" within the meaning of *Guaranty Trust*. Use of such a point of reference, *Hanna* concludes, directly advances the policies underlying *Erie* of maintaining equality in the administration of justice, and deterring forum shopping.

Does the Court's focus on forum shopping and equitable administration of laws clarify the "outcome-ambiguous" cases like *Byrd* and *Bernhardt* discussed above? Does the test apply to practices that could induce forum shopping but would not clearly affect outcome? *See Walker v. Armco Steel Corp.*, 446 U.S. 740, 753 (1980) (deviation from state rule that defendant must be served within statute of limitations period would not necessarily induce forum shopping but would represent "inequitable administration of the law"). In a case like *Byrd*, how would a court determine whether the difference between a judge and jury determination of employment status induced the choice of the federal forum?

Should court-access decisions, such as *forum non conveniens*, that simply affect the place of trial but do not go to the "merits" of the controversy be considered "outcome determinative"? Is it enough under *Hanna* that the difference between state and federal court-access law would have induced the choice of a federal forum, or must the difference also affect ultimate disposition of the controversy?

What about *Guaranty Trust* itself? To the extent that *Hanna*'s clarification of "outcome determination" consists of asking whether the difference between state and federal practice would induce the choice of a federal forum, there is still a time-frame problem. At the point in time that plaintiff in *Guaranty Trust* actually filed suit—after the statute of limitations expired—the difference between state and federal law was critical. But plaintiff *could* have filed before the statute expired, in which case the difference between state and federal law would not have affected her choice of forum. Does *Hanna* provide any guidance as to when the outcome-determinative impact of statutes of limitations should be evaluated?

Given the comprehensiveness of the Federal Rules of Civil Procedure, there are not many procedural issues governed solely by common law, and thus subject to the outcome-determination test articulated by *Guaranty Trust* and *Hanna*. The most notable examples of procedural common law are aspects of *res judicata* and *forum non conveniens*. *See generally* Amy Coney Barrett, *Procedural Common Law*, 94 Va. L.

Rev. 813 (2008). *See also, Dietz v. Bouldin*, 136 S.Ct 1885 (2016) (upholding "inherent power" of court to recall jury to correct error in jury verdict). We will see in the next section, however, that even in regard to matters governed generally by Federal Rule or statute, there still may be room for state law to operate. Accordingly, the outcome-determination test may have broader application than just in regard to purely common law practices.

3. *The Status of* Byrd *after* Hanna. Does consideration of state and federal interests have any place in the *Hanna* analysis? In sharp contrast to *Byrd*'s focus on the intent of the state lawmakers in assigning resolution of the employment status question to the judge, the *Hanna* Court in footnote 9 dismisses the alleged "importance" of the Massachusetts service rule to the Massachusetts legislature. The Court is plainly rejecting a test of validity that turns on the perceived "importance" of the state rule. Note, however, the Court's conclusion in footnote 1 that the underlying purpose of the state service rule—actual notice—was apparently satisfied by the means of service employed in this case. Would it have affected the Court's analysis if it had found that the state purpose was frustrated by application of the Federal Rule? If, as in a case like *Byrd*, a court concludes that the state practice was not intended to give the parties any "rights," would *Hanna* require adherence to a state practice simply to deter forum shopping?

4. *Constitutional and Statutory Limits on Federal Rule-Making.* In contrast to the fairly restrictive "outcome determination" limits that *Hanna* imposes on federal procedural common law, the Court holds that practices authorized by the Federal Rules of Civil Procedure are limited only by the Constitution and the Enabling Act.

a. *Constitutionality.* What is the test of a Federal Rule's constitutionality, according to the *Hanna* majority? How does it differ from Justice Harlan's? Do you understand why the majority thinks that a federal statute governing practice in federal courts is constitutional if it is "capable of rational classification" as "procedural"? Is the effect of such a statute on the substantive rights of the parties totally irrelevant to the majority? Is it to Justice Harlan? Take, for instance, a federal statute that made the losing party in a diversity suit pay the attorneys' fees of the prevailing party. Would such a statute automatically survive constitutional scrutiny under the majority view simply because it governs an aspect of federal practice?

b. *The Enabling Act.* How does the Court construe the requirement of the Rules Enabling Act that a Federal Rule "shall not abridge, enlarge or modify any substantive right"? For Chief Justice Warren, how does the constitutional test differ from the statutory test? Does any Rule that satisfies the statutory test also at the same time satisfy any constitutional requirement?

Notice that the Enabling Act contains two possible constraints on rule-making. First, the Enabling Act appears to limit the types, or categories, of rule that the Supreme Court can enact. Under the provision in §2072(a) that limits the Court to promulgating rules of "practice," "procedure," and "evidence," one might argue that a rule aimed at regulating behavior or interests outside the boundaries of a given proceeding are not "procedural" or "evidentiary" in nature—in other words, that they are directed at a subject that is not authorized by the Act and, hence, are *ultra vires*. Second, the Act might also require exceptions to the Federal Rules, even when they are properly directed at subjects of procedure or evidence, when a particular application of a Rule would interfere with rights or interests created by other sources of authority. The provision in §2072(b) forbidding the Rules to "abridge, enlarge or modify any substantive right" appears to support such a reading. *See generally* John Hart Ely, *The Irrepressible Myth of Erie*, 87 Harv. L. Rev. 693, 718–737 (1974) (arguing that both types of analysis are required by the respective portions of the Enabling Act). Keep these separate constraints in mind as you read the materials that follow.

i. *"Substantive Rights" as a Limit on Rule-Making Authority?* Which of the Rules of Civil Procedure are vulnerable to a Rules Enabling Act challenge? Consider the validity of the discovery rules, which compel disclosure of a party's private information and, in particular, Rule 35, which subjects litigants to mental and physical examination. Consider also Rule 17, which stipulates that the law of a person's domicile shall determine her capacity to sue or be sued, or Rule 23, which allows a court to adjudicate claims of persons not present in the litigation.

The Supreme Court, for the most part, has taken an expansive view of the authority of the Court to promulgate Rules that might have some substantive impact; the Court has never held that any Federal Rule of Civil Procedure was in violation of the Enabling Act. Consider the pre-*Hanna* decision in *Sibbach v. Wilson & Co.*, 312 U.S. 1 (1941). The Court there dismissed the argument that Rule 35 violated the Enabling Act by impermissibly intruding on a litigant's substantive right of privacy:

> We are thrown back, then, to the arguments drawn from the language of the Act of June 19, 1934. Is the phrase "substantive rights" confined to rights conferred by law to be protected and enforced in accordance with the adjective law of judicial procedure? It certainly embraces such rights. One of them is the right not to be injured in one's person by another's negligence, to redress infraction of which the present action was brought. The petitioner says the phrase connotes more; that by its use Congress intended that in regulating procedure this court should not deal with important and substantial rights theretofore recognized. Recognized where and by whom? The state courts are divided as to the power in the absence of statute to order a physical examination. . . .
>
> The asserted right, moreover, is no more important than many others enjoyed by litigants in District Courts sitting in the several states, before the Federal Rules of Civil Procedure altered and abolished old rights or privileges and created new ones in connection with the conduct of litigation. The suggestion that the rule offends the important right to freedom from invasion of the person ignores the fact that as we hold, no invasion of freedom from personal restraint attaches to refusal so to comply with its provisions. If we were to adopt the suggested criterion of the importance of the alleged right we should invite endless litigation and confusion worse confounded. The test must be whether a rule really regulates procedure — the judicial process for enforcing rights and duties recognized by substantive law and for justly administering remedy and redress for disregard or infraction of them. That the rules in question are such is admitted.

312 U.S. at 14.

444   Chapter 4. The Law Applied in Federal Court

How do you understand *Sibbach*'s distinction between substance and procedure for purposes of the Enabling Act? Why should it have mattered that the state
courts were divided as to the propriety of physical exams? Do you find compelling
the Court's assertion that no right of bodily privacy is implicated by Rule 35 because
"no invasion of freedom from personal restraint attaches to refusal so to comply with
its provisions"? The Court is presumably referring to the Rule 37(b)(2)(B) limitation on sanctions available in the event of a party's refusal to submit to a medical
examination; a court may not hold the disobedient party in contempt. Would the
Sibbach Court have struck down Rule 35 if a party refusing to submit to a medical
examination *were* subject to contempt of court? Note that under Rule 35, a party is
subjected to physical exam only once her condition is "in controversy." In *Sibbach*, the
plaintiff placed her own condition in controversy by seeking damages for personal
injury. Accordingly, one might have read *Sibbach* as limited to cases in which the party
subject to physical examination might be deemed to have effectively waived whatever
substantive right of privacy she otherwise had, thus avoiding the Enabling Act limitation. However, the Court rejected this reading in *Schlagenhauf v. Holder*, 379 U.S. 104
(1964) (rejecting such a construction of *Sibbach* and upholding the application of
Rule 35 to a defendant).

The Court's more recent decisions in *Ortiz v. Fibreboard Corp.*, 527 U.S. 815
(1999), and *Semtek International Inc. v. Lockheed Martin Corp.*, 531 U.S. 497 (2001)
were thought to possibly signal a change in the Court's interpretation of §2072(b).
(*Ortiz* is discussed in Chapter 8, and *Semtek* is included as a principal case in Chapter 7.) In both cases, the Court narrowly construed Federal Rules of Civil Procedure to avoid potential Enabling Act problems. At issue in *Semtek* was the preclusive
effect that a prior federal dismissal had on a subsequently filed state lawsuit. A
prior California federal diversity proceeding was dismissed pursuant to the California statute of limitations. Plaintiff then filed a second proceeding in Maryland
state court. The question presented to the Supreme Court on appeal was whether
state or federal law governed the effect of the federal court's dismissal on statute of
limitations grounds. Rule 41(b) deems any nonjurisdictional dismissal by a federal
court, including a statute of limitations dismissal, as "on the merits," unless otherwise designated by the judge. This provision had been interpreted by lower courts
to provide the preclusive effect of a federal dismissal; dismissals on the merits normally are accorded *res judicata* effect. Although ultimately determining that federal
law governed the effect to be given a federal judgment, Justice Scalia held that Rule
41(b) should not be construed to provide the answer, given the constraint of the
Enabling Act:

> [I]t would be peculiar to find a rule governing the effect that must be accorded
> federal judgments by other courts ensconced in rules governing the internal
> procedures of the rendering court itself. Indeed, such a rule would arguably
> violate the jurisdictional limitation of the Rules Enabling Act: that the Rules
> "shall not abridge, enlarge or modify any substantive right," 28 U.S.C. §2072(b).
> Cf. *Ortiz v. Fibreboard Corp.*, 527 U.S. 815, 842 (1999) (adopting a "limiting con-
> struction" of Federal Rule of Civil Procedure 23(b)(1)(B) in order to "mini-
> miz[e] potential conflict with the Rules Enabling Act, and [to] avoi[d] serious
> constitutional concerns"). In the present case, for example, if California law
> left petitioner free to sue on this claim in Maryland even after the California

> statute of limitations had expired, the federal court's extinguishment of that
> right (through Rule 41(b)'s mandated claim-preclusive effect of its judgment)
> would seem to violate this limitation.

541 U.S. at 503. The Court displayed a similar sensitivity in construing Rule 23(b)(1)(B) in *Ortiz*, 527 U.S. at 842.

ii. *"Substantive Rights" as a Separation of Powers Limit on Rule-Making Authority?* Why do you think Congress forbade the promulgation of Rules that affect substantive rights? Although this limitation has traditionally been understood as protecting the same sort of federalism concerns advanced by the Rules of Decision Act, Professor Stephen Burbank has persuasively argued that the purpose of the limitation was to prevent the federal courts from usurping legislative prerogatives properly belonging to Congress. "Substantive rights" in this context would mean matters that are sufficiently important that Congress should retain authority. Professor Burbank suggests that Justice Harlan's "primary conduct" analysis is appropriate as a test for that congressional prerogative in the Enabling Act context. *See* Stephen B. Burbank, *The Rules Enabling Act of 1934*, 130 U. Pa. L. Rev. 1015, 1128 (1982). For an application of this view to Rule 11 sanctions, *see* Stephen B. Burbank, *Sanctions in the Proposed Amendments to the Federal Rules of Civil Procedure: Some Questions About Power*, 11 Hofstra L. Rev. 997 (1983).

Does it make sense to limit the power of the rule-makers in order to protect the prerogatives of Congress when that institution has ample opportunity during the seven-month "layover" period after Supreme Court promulgation to modify or strike down any Rule it disfavors? *See* Karen Nelson Moore, *The Supreme Court's Role in Interpreting the Federal Rules of Civil Procedure*, 44 Hastings L.J. 1039, 1049 (1993). *But see* Stephen B. Burbank, *Rules Enabling Act, supra* at 1102 (arguing that hold-over period is insufficient safeguard, given the difficulty of getting on the congressional agenda); *Sibbach v. Wilson, supra* at 428 ("Having due regard to the mechanics of legislation and the practical conditions surrounding the business of Congress when the Rules were submitted, to draw any inference of tacit approval from non-action by Congress is to appeal to unreality.") (Frankfurter, J., dissenting).

iii. *"Primary Behavior"?* How should Justice Harlan's "primary behavior" test be understood? Might not any procedural Rule affect prelitigation behavior to the extent that individuals might alter their behavior to avoid litigation and the procedures applied therein? On that view, are many of the Federal Rules that facilitate access to the courts and reduce the costs of bringing lawsuits, such as those dealing with pretrial discovery and class actions, in jeopardy under Harlan's approach?

Do you agree that the federal courts, either in their rule-making or common law capacity, should be more constrained from making law that affects primary behavior than in making law that simply affects the manner in which disputes are resolved in litigation? Why?

iv. *When Do We Have a "Direct Collision" Between State and Federal Rules?* How did the *Hanna* Court determine that Rule 4 displaced the state rule requiring personal service? Would personal service have been in violation of Rule 4? In what sense, then, was there a "direct collision"? Consider this question in connection with the following section.

4.   Track Assignment—Determining the Existence of a Pertinent Federal Law

a.   "Direct Collision" Between State and Federal Rules

After *Hanna*, the most important question in resolving a conflict between state and federal procedure is whether a federal statute or rule is "broad enough to cover" the question. If there is a valid and pertinent Rule or statute, federal law will always control; otherwise, state law almost always controls. Given the virtually dispositive impact of that question, it is surprising that the Court has had relatively little to say on how a court should determine whether a case belongs on the statutory or common law track.

Three decisions between 1980 and 1990, all written by Justice Marshall, established the criteria for whether a federal statute or Rule is "broad enough" to displace contrary state law under *Hanna.*

In *Walker v. Armco Steel Co.*, 446 U.S. 740 (1980), the Court held that although Federal Rule of Civil Procedure 3 provides that "a civil action is commenced by filing a complaint with the court," state law governed whether the statute of limitations expired on a claim served after, but filed before the statute ran.* While reiterating *Hanna*'s holding that a pertinent Federal Rule of Civil Procedure controls notwithstanding conflicting state provisions, the Court held that Rule 3 was not broad enough to displace the state tolling rule that the defendant must be served before the statute runs:

> Application of the *Hanna* analysis is premised on a "direct collision" between the Federal rule and the state law. . . . In *Hanna* itself the "clash" between Rule 4(d)(l) and the state in-hand service requirement was "unavoidable." . . .
>
>   As has already been noted, we recognized in *Hanna* that the present case is an instance where "the scope of the Federal Rule [is] not as broad as the losing party urge[s], and therefore, there being no Federal Rule which cover[s] the point in dispute, *Erie* command[s] the enforcement of state law." . . . Rule 3 simply states that "[a] civil action is commenced by filing a complaint with the court." There is no indication that the Rule was intended to toll a state statute of limitations, much less that it purported to displace state tolling rules for purposes of state statutes of limitations. In our view, in diversity actions Rule 3 governs the date from which various timing requirements of the Federal Rules begin to run, but does not affect state statutes of limitations. . . .
>
>   In contrast to Rule 3, the Oklahoma statute is a statement of a substantive decision by that State that actual service on, and accordingly actual notice by, the defendant is an integral part of the several policies served by the statute of limitations. . . . The statute of limitations

---

* The Court had reached the same conclusion in *Ragan v. Merchants Transfer & Warehouse Co.*, 337 U.S. 530 (1949). The plaintiff asserted that *Ragan* was implicitly overruled by *Hanna.* 446 U.S. at 740.

establishes a deadline after which the defendant may legitimately have peace of mind; it also recognizes that after a certain period of time it is unfair to require the defendant to attempt to piece together his defense to an old claim. A requirement of actual service promotes both of those functions of the statute. . . . It is these policy aspects which make the service requirement an "integral" part of the statute of limitations both in this case and in *Ragan.* As such, the service rule must be considered part and parcel of the statute of limitations. Rule 3 does not replace such policy determinations found in state law. Rule 3 and [the Oklahoma statute] can exist side by side, therefore, each controlling its own intended sphere of coverage without conflict.

446 U.S. at 749–752.

Do you agree that the "clash" between state and federal law in *Hanna* was more "unavoidable" than in *Walker?* In both cases, wouldn't compliance with the state rule also satisfy the Federal Rule?

Does the *Walker* decision suggest a methodology for determining whether a federal rule displaces or accommodates a state provision? Do you see any similarity between *Byrd* and *Walker*'s focus on the respective policies behind the state and federal rules? *See* Allan R. Stein, Erie *and Court Access,* 100 Yale L.J. 1935, 1953–1956 (1991) (suggesting that *Byrd* provides an appropriate framework for determining whether federal law displaces or accommodates state law).

On the other hand, does *Walker* strain unduly to avoid a "direct collision" by giving Rule 3 a very narrow reading? In a later case, involving a federal question, the Court held that the mere filing of a complaint under Rule 3 indeed tolls the running of the clock for limitations purposes. *See West v. Conrail,* 481 U.S. 35 (1987). Is *Walker* best understood as a case where the Court felt bound by the *stare decisis* effect of *Ragan v. Merchants Transfer & Warehouse Co., supra* p. 423? *See* Paul D. Carrington, *"Substance" and "Procedure" in the Rules Enabling Act,* 1989 Duke L.J. 281, 316.

The Court's second foray into the problem of track assignment in *Burlington Northern Railroad v. Woods,* 480 U.S. 1 (1987), appeared implicitly to relax the "direct collision" standard articulated in *Hanna* and *Walker.* Plaintiff in that case attempted to recover ten percent damages for defendant's unsuccessful appeal from a federal court judgment. Such damages were mandated by an Alabama statute in any unsuccessful appeal where the original judgment was stayed upon appeal. Federal Rule of Appellate Procedure 38 allows the court of appeals, in its discretion, to award damages amounting to single or double costs in the case of "frivolous" appeals, and Rule 37 provides for award of "whatever interest is allowed by law" on any money judgment affirmed on appeal. Thus, the Supreme Court had to determine whether Rules 37 and 38 displaced the Alabama provision:

Rule 38 affords a court of appeals plenary discretion to assess "just damages" in order to penalize an appellant who takes a frivolous appeal and to compensate the injured appellee for the delay and added expense of defending the district court's judgment. Thus, the Rule's discretionary mode of operation unmistakably conflicts with the mandatory provision of Alabama's affirmance penalty statute. Moreover, the purposes underlying the Rule are sufficiently coextensive with the asserted purposes of the Alabama statute to indicate that the Rule occupies the statute's field of operation so as to preclude its application in federal diversity actions.

480 U.S. at 7. The Court further noted that the compensatory function of the Alabama Rule was already served by the award of interest available under Rule 37. *Id.* at n. 5.

In what sense was the Alabama statute in *Burlington Northern* less compatible with the Federal Rules than was the Oklahoma statute in *Walker*? Did Rule 38 forbid the award of damages in nonfrivolous appeals? Would application of the Alabama statute have nullified the operation of either Rule 38 or Rule 37? Couldn't the court of appeals have awarded 10 percent damages in all unsuccessful appeals, and additionally add costs as provided in Rule 38 in the case of frivolous appeals? Would an award under the Alabama statute have been incompatible with Rule 37's provision for the award of "interest allowed by law"?

Do you find persuasive the Court's reasoning that the Federal Rule displaces the state statute because "the purposes underlying the Rule are sufficiently coextensive with the asserted purposes of the Alabama statute"? If, as the Court concluded, the purpose of the Federal Rule was to deter frivolous appeals, and the purpose of the Alabama provision was, in part, "to provide 'additional damages' as compensation to the appellees for having to suffer the ordeal of defending the judgments on appeal," *id.* at 4, in what sense were the purposes "sufficiently coextensive" to support the conclusion that the Rule displaced the statute? *Cf.* Ralph U. Whitten, *Erie and the Federal Rules: A Review and Reappraisal After* Burlington Northern Railroad v. Woods, 21 Creighton L. Rev. 1, 22 (1987).

The Court's third major inquiry into how to determine whether a federal law was "broad enough" to displace contrary state law involved the interpretation of a statute — 28 U.S.C. 1404(a) — rather than a Rule of Civil Procedure. *Stewart Organization, Inc. v. Ricoh, Corp.*, 487 U.S. 22 (1988), appeared to pull back further from the "direct collision" test articulated in *Hanna* and applied in *Walker*.

The case involved the enforcement of forum selection clause in a dealership agreement. Plaintiff asserted claims under both state and federal law, including federal antitrust claims (over which federal courts have exclusive jurisdiction). Defendant moved under §1404(a) to transfer the case to New York pursuant to the forum selection clause, notwithstanding the fact that the dispute had no connection with New York. The parties were from Alabama and New Jersey. The district court denied the motion, holding that Alabama common law, which outlawed the enforcement of forum selection clauses, invalidated the clause and foreclosed the transfer.

The Supreme Court held that state law had no role to play in the application of the federal transfer statute, and the district court's decision therefore constituted an abuse of discretion. Justice Marshall, again writing for the majority, found the Alabama law inconsistent with the statutory framework of §1404(a):

> Section 1404(a) is intended to place discretion in the district court to adjudicate motions for transfer according to an "individualized, case-by-case consideration of convenience and fairness." . . . A motion to transfer under §1404(a) thus calls on the district court to weigh in the balance a number of case-specific factors. The presence of a forum-selection

clause such as the parties entered into in this case will be a significant factor that figures centrally in the district court's calculus. In its resolution of the §1404(a) motion in this case, for example, the District Court will be called on to address such issues as the convenience of a Manhattan forum given the parties' expressed preference for that venue, and the fairness of transfer in light of the forum-selection clause and the parties' relative bargaining power. The flexible and individualized analysis Congress prescribed in §1404(a) thus encompasses consideration of the parties' private expression of their venue preferences. . . .

The premise of the dispute between the parties is that Alabama law may refuse to enforce forum-selection clauses providing for out-of-state venues as a matter of state public policy. If that is so, the District Court will have either to integrate the factor of the forum-selection clause into its weighing of considerations as prescribed by Congress, or else to apply, as it did in this case, Alabama's categorical policy disfavoring forum-selection clauses. Our cases make clear that, as between these two choices in a single "field of operation," . . . the instructions of Congress are supreme. . . .

487 U.S. at 29–30.

A dissent written by Justice Scalia found no collision between §1404(a) and the state policy, and found the majority's conclusion that §1404 displaced state law to

be[g] the question: what law governs whether the forum-selection clause is a valid or invalid allocation of any inconvenience between the parties. If it is invalid, *i.e.*, should be voided, between the parties, it cannot be entitled to any weight in the §1404(a) determination. Since under Alabama law the forum-selection clause should be voided, . . . in this case the question of what weight should be given the forum-selection clause can be reached only if as a preliminary matter federal law controls the issue of the validity of the clause between the parties.

Justice Scalia asserted that issues of contract validity are normally governed by state law, and that there was no indication in the text or purpose of §1404(a) that Congress intended to displace that authority.

NOTES AND QUESTIONS

1. *Do you agree with Justice Scalia that the majority assumes away the key question of whether Congress intended to displace state law, or accommodate it in the operation of §1404?* How does the Court know whether Congress wanted courts to enforce forum selection clauses through the operation of §1404(a)? Do you find persuasive Justice Marshall's conclusion that incorporating the state law on forum selection clauses into the §1404(a) analysis would "impoverish the flexible and multifaceted analysis that Congress intended to govern motions to transfer within the federal system"? Isn't that a particularly weak argument in a case in which the *only* reason supporting transfer was the existence of a forum selection clause?

2. *Are state interests relevant to whether a federal statute displaces state law?* None of the Justices in *Stewart Organization* paid any attention to the reasons for the Alabama rule. If, as the Court held, the test for track assignment under *Hanna* involves

consideration of whether state and federal rules "can exist side by side . . . each controlling its own intended sphere of coverage without conflict," isn't consideration of the "contours of state law" critical? Would it have been helpful to know that the apparent purpose of the Alabama rule was to prevent private parties from ousting the Alabama courts of jurisdiction they would otherwise exercise? *See Redwing Carriers, Inc. v. Foster,* 382 So. 2d 554, 556 (Ala. 1980). Is it clear that Alabama would care if the federal court chose to allow parties to adjust the venue of the action within the federal system? *Cf. Redwing Carriers, Inc., supra* at 555 (noting enforceability of venue selection clauses that stipulate particular venue within Alabama).

What if, on the other hand, the Alabama rule reflects a concern that forum selection clauses are typically "boiler-plate" provisions and not freely bargained for? Should the Court be less inclined to find such a state policy displaced by the federal transfer statute than a state policy concerned exclusively with the operation of state courts? Would Justice Harlan's approach in *Hanna* suggest a different result depending on the nature of the state policy?

3. *The Constitutional Holding of* Stewart. Assume that Congress, in enacting a statute, intends to displace a state law. Is such a displacement automatically consistent with the Tenth Amendment norms of *Erie* simply because it has some federal procedural purpose and is therefore within Congress's power to implement Article III? Note that, unlike in *Hanna,* the "substantive" rights of the parties were arguably changed by the federal provision in *Stewart.* Justice Marshall nonetheless finds that the federal statute "falls comfortably within Congress' powers under Article III as augmented by the Necessary and Proper Clause" insofar as it "is doubtless capable of classification as a procedural rule."

4. *Does the same analysis apply in federal-question cases?* The Court does not rely on the presence of the federal antitrust question in *Stewart,* and indeed reserves the question whether its approach to conflicts between state and federal procedural regimes should differ depending on the inclusion of a federal claim. Other decisions seem to suggest greater latitude for courts to craft a federal procedural rule where the underlying claim is based on federal law. *See West v. Conrail,* 481 U.S. 35, 39 (1987) (action not barred by statute of limitations if commenced in compliance with Rule 3 in federal questions case notwithstanding *Walker's* apparently contrary holding in diversity case). For a critique of that distinction, *see* Stephen B. Burbank, *Of Rules and Discretion: The Supreme Court, Federal Rules and Common Law,* 63 Notre Dame L. Rev. 693, 702–704 (1988); Martin H. Redish & Carter G. Phillips, Erie *and the Rules of Decision Act: In Search of the Appropriate Dilemma,* 91 Harv. L. Rev. 356 (1977). Note that neither the Rules of Decision Act nor the Rules Enabling Act distinguishes between diversity and federal-question cases. *See generally* Peter Westen & Jeffrey S. Lehman, *Is There Life for* Erie *After the Death of Diversity?,* 78 Mich. L. Rev. 311 (1980). For an argument that *Erie* should not constrain federal courts in the same fashion where subject matter jurisdiction is based on a federal question rather than diversity, *see* Alexander A. Reinhert, Erie *Step Zero,* 85 Fordham L. Rev. 2341 (2017).

5. *Enforceability of Forum Selection Clauses Outside of the §1404(a) Context.* The enforceability of forum selection clauses outside of the §1404(a) context remains an unresolved *Erie* dilemma even after *Stewart.* The problem typically comes up in two related contexts: a defendant moves to dismiss for *forum non conveniens* when the case is filed in a forum other than the *foreign* one stipulated in the forum selection

clause;* or a defendant moves to dismiss for improper venue or jurisdiction when a plaintiff has filed in the stipulated forum, which otherwise is not a proper statutory venue or lacks personal jurisdiction over the defendant. *See, e.g., Alexander Proudfoot Co. World Headquarters L.P. v. Thayer,* 877 F.2d 912 (11th Cir. 1989). Should the federal courts abide by the state rule on whether to enforce a forum selection clause in these situations? Does 28 U.S.C. §1391 serve the same role as §1404 does in Stewart in authorizing a federal standard? Could §1391 serve that function if defendant raises a personal jurisdiction objection instead of an objection to venue? If §1391 is not "broad enough" to cover the question of contractual forum selection, how should the issue be analyzed as a "relatively unguided" *Erie* choice? Would deviation from state law be outcome determinate? Would it induce forum shopping? The lower courts are divided on whether to follow state law. *Compare General Eng'g Corp. v. Martin Marietta Alumina, Inc.,* 783 F.2d 352 (3d Cir. 1986) (applying Virgin Island law to enforceability of forum selection clause; *Preferred Capital, Inc. v. Sarasota Kennel Club, Inc.,* 489 F.3d 303 (6th Cir. 2007) (declining per state law to enforce forum selection clause that would have subjected defendant to personal jurisdiction) *with Manetti-Farrow, Inc. v. Gucci Am., Inc.,* 858 F.2d 509 (9th Cir. 1988) (finding in §1391 authority to develop federal standard for enforceability of forum selection clause). *See generally* Patrick J. Borchers, *Forum Selection Agreements in the Federal Courts After* Carnival Cruise: *A Proposal for Congressional Reform,* 67 Wash. L. Rev. 55 (1992).

Gasperini v. Center for Humanities, Inc.

518 U.S. 415 (1996)

GINSBURG, J., delivered the opinion of the Court, in which O'CONNOR, KENNEDY, SOUTER, and BREYER, JJ., joined. STEVENS, J., filed a dissenting opinion. SCALIA, J., filed a dissenting opinion, in which REHNQUIST, C.J., and THOMAS, J., joined.

JUSTICE GINSBURG delivered the opinion of the Court.
Under the law of New York, appellate courts are empowered to review the size of jury verdicts and to order new trials when the jury's award "deviates materially from what would be reasonable compensation." N.Y. Civ. Prac. Law and Rules (CPLR) §5501(c) (McKinney 1995). Under the Seventh Amendment, which

---

* The Supreme Court held in *Atlantic Marine Construction Co. v. U.S. District Court,* 571 U.S. 49 (2013), *supra.* p. 275, that a defendant cannot obtain a dismissal for improper venue pursuant to Fed. R. Civ. P. 12(b)(3) where the action has been filed in violation of a forum selection clause, but is otherwise consistent with §1391. The Court held that the appropriate enforcement mechanism where the stipulated forum was within the United States, was a motion to transfer pursuant to 28 U.S.C. §1404(a). Accordingly, in any case in which the stipulated forum is a domestic one, federal law will control the enforceability of the forum selection clause pursuant to *Stewart Organization. But see* Adam Steinman, Atlantic Marine *Through the Lens of* Erie, 66 Hastings L.J. 795 (2015) (arguing that state law should control in some circumstances notwithstanding *Stewart Organization*). Where the stipulated forum is a foreign one, defendant would be able to move to dismiss pursuant to *forum non conveniens* to enforce the forum selection clause. Such a motion would not fall within the ambit of the *Stewart Organization* holding.

governs proceedings in federal court, but not in state court, "the right of trial by jury shall be preserved, and no fact tried by a jury, shall be otherwise re-examined in any Court of the United States, than according to the rules of the common law." U.S. Const., Amdt. 7. The compatibility of these provisions, in an action based on New York law but tried in federal court by reason of the parties' diverse citizenship, is the issue we confront in this case. We hold that New York's law controlling compensation awards for excessiveness or inadequacy can be given effect, without detriment to the Seventh Amendment, if the review standard set out in CPLR §5501(c) is applied by the federal trial court judge, with appellate control of the trial court's ruling limited to review for "abuse of discretion."

I

Petitioner William Gasperini, a journalist for CBS News and the Christian Science Monitor, began reporting on events in Central America in 1984. He earned his living primarily in radio and print media and only occasionally sold his photographic work. During the course of his seven-year stint in Central America, Gasperini took over 5,000 slide transparencies, depicting active war zones, political leaders, and scenes from daily life. In 1990, Gasperini agreed to supply his original color transparencies to The Center for Humanities, Inc. (Center) for use in an educational videotape, Conflict in Central America. Gasperini selected 300 of his slides for the Center; its videotape included 110 of them. The Center agreed to return the original transparencies, but upon the completion of the project, it could not find them.

Gasperini commenced suit in the United States District Court for the Southern District of New York, invoking the court's diversity jurisdiction pursuant to 28 U.S.C. §1332.[1] He alleged several state-law claims for relief, including breach of contract, conversion, and negligence. The Center conceded liability for the lost transparencies and the issue of damages was tried before a jury.

At trial, Gasperini's expert witness testified that the "industry standard" within the photographic publishing community valued a lost transparency at $1,500. This industry standard, the expert explained, represented the average license fee a commercial photograph could earn over the full course of the photographer's copyright, i.e., in Gasperini's case, his lifetime plus 50 years. . . . Gasperini estimated that his earnings from photography totaled just over $10,000 for the period from 1984 through 1993. He also testified that he intended to produce a book containing his best photographs from Central America.

After a three-day trial, the jury awarded Gasperini $450,000 in compensatory damages. This sum, the jury foreperson announced, "is [$]1500 each, for 300 slides." Moving for a new trial under Federal Rule of Civil Procedure 59, the Center attacked the verdict on various grounds, including excessiveness. Without comment, the District Court denied the motion.

The Court of Appeals for the Second Circuit vacated the judgment entered on the jury's verdict. 66 F.3d 427 (1995). Mindful that New York law governed the controversy, the Court of Appeals endeavored to apply CPLR §5501(c), which instructs

---

1. Plaintiff Gasperini, petitioner here, is a citizen of California; defendant Center, respondent here, is incorporated, and has its principal place of business, in New York.

that, when a jury returns an itemized verdict, as the jury did in this case, the New York Appellate Division "shall determine that an award is excessive or inadequate if it deviates materially from what would be reasonable compensation." . . . Surveying Appellate Division decisions that reviewed damage awards for lost transparencies, the Second Circuit concluded that testimony on industry standard alone was insufficient to justify a verdict; prime among other factors warranting consideration were the uniqueness of the slides' subject matter and the photographer's earning level.

Guided by Appellate Division rulings, the Second Circuit held that the $450,000 verdict "materially deviates from what is reasonable compensation." Some of Gasperini's transparencies, the Second Circuit recognized, were unique, notably those capturing combat situations in which Gasperini was the only photographer present. But others "depicted either generic scenes or events at which other professional photojournalists were present." No more than 50 slides merited a $1,500 award, the court concluded, after "[g]iving Gasperini every benefit of the doubt." Absent evidence showing significant earnings from photographic endeavors or concrete plans to publish a book, the court further determined, any damage award above $100 each for the remaining slides would be excessive. Remittiturs "presen[t] difficult problems for appellate courts," the Second Circuit acknowledged, for court of appeals judges review the evidence from "a cold paper record." Nevertheless, the Second Circuit set aside the $450,000 verdict and ordered a new trial, unless Gasperini agreed to an award of $100,000.

This case presents an important question regarding the standard a federal court uses to measure the alleged excessiveness of a jury's verdict in an action for damages based on state law. We therefore granted certiorari.

II

Before 1986, state and federal courts in New York generally invoked the same judge-made formulation in responding to excessiveness attacks on jury verdicts: courts would not disturb an award unless the amount was so exorbitant that it "shocked the conscience of the court." As described by the Second Circuit:

> The standard for determining excessiveness and the appropriateness of remittitur in New York is somewhat ambiguous. Prior to 1986, New York law employed the same standard as the federal courts, *see Matthews v. CTI Container Transport Int'l Inc.*, 871 F.2d 270, 278 (2d Cir. 1989), which authorized remittitur only if the jury's verdict was so excessive that it "shocked the conscience of the court." *Id.* at 1012. . . .

In both state and federal courts, trial judges made the excessiveness assessment in the first instance, and appellate judges ordinarily deferred to the trial court's judgment. . . .

In 1986, as part of a series of tort reform measures,[3] New York codified a standard for judicial review of the size of jury awards. Placed in CPLR §5501(c), the prescription reads:

---

3. The legislature sought, particularly, to curtail medical and dental malpractice, and to contain "already high malpractice premiums." Legislative Findings and Declaration, Ch. 266, 1986 N.Y. Laws 470 (McKinney).

> In reviewing a money judgment . . . in which it is contended that the award is excessive or inadequate and that a new trial should have been granted unless a stipulation is entered to a different award, the appellate division shall determine that an award is excessive or inadequate if it deviates materially from what would be reasonable compensation.

As stated in Legislative Findings and Declarations accompanying New York's adoption of the "deviates materially" formulation, the lawmakers found the "shock the conscience" test an insufficient check on damage awards; the legislature therefore installed a standard "invit[ing] more careful appellate scrutiny." At the same time, the legislature instructed the Appellate Division, in amended §5522, to state the reasons for the court's rulings on the size of verdicts, and the factors the court considered in complying with §5501(c). In his signing statement, then-Governor Mario Cuomo emphasized that the CPLR amendments were meant to rachet up the review standard: "This will assure greater scrutiny of the amount of verdicts and promote greater stability in the tort system and greater fairness for similarly situated defendants throughout the State." Memorandum on Approving L.1986, Ch. 682, 1986 N.Y. Laws, at 3184. . . .

New York state-court opinions confirm that §5501(c)'s "deviates materially" standard calls for closer surveillance than "shock the conscience" oversight. . . .

Although phrased as a direction to New York's intermediate appellate courts, §5501(c)'s "deviates materially" standard, as construed by New York's courts, instructs state trial judges as well. *See, e.g., Inya v. Ide Hyundai, Inc.*, 209 App. Div. 2d 1015, 1015, 619 N.Y.S.2d 440, 440 (4th Dept. 1994) (error for trial court to apply "shock the conscience" test to motion to set aside damages; proper standard is whether award "materially deviates from what would be reasonable compensation"). . . . Application of §5501(c) at the trial level is key to this case.

To determine whether an award "deviates materially from what would be reasonable compensation," New York state courts look to awards approved in similar cases. . . . The "deviates materially" standard, however, in design and operation, influences outcomes by tightening the range of tolerable awards. . . .

III

In cases like Gasperini's, in which New York law governs the claims for relief, does New York law also supply the test for federal court review of the size of the verdict? The Center answers yes. The "deviates materially" standard, it argues, is a substantive standard that must be applied by federal appellate courts in diversity cases. The Second Circuit agreed. *See* 66 F.3d at 430. . . . Gasperini, emphasizing that §5501(c) trains on the New York Appellate Division, characterizes the provision as procedural, an allocation of decisionmaking authority regarding damages, not a hard cap on the amount recoverable. Correctly comprehended, Gasperini urges, §5501(c)'s direction to the Appellate Division cannot be given effect by federal appellate courts without violating the Seventh Amendment's re-examination clause.

As the parties' arguments suggest, CPLR §5501(c), appraised under *Erie R. Co. v. Tompkins*, 304 U.S. 64 (1938), and decisions in *Erie*'s path, is both "substantive" and "procedural": "substantive" in that §5501(c)'s "deviates materially" standard controls how much a plaintiff can be awarded; "procedural" in that §5501(c) assigns decisionmaking authority to New York's Appellate Division. Parallel application of

§5501(c) at the federal appellate level would be out of sync with the federal system's division of trial and appellate court functions, an allocation weighted by the Seventh Amendment. The dispositive question, therefore, is whether federal courts can give effect to the substantive thrust of §5501(c) without untoward alteration of the federal scheme for the trial and decision of civil cases.

A

Federal diversity jurisdiction provides an alternative forum for the adjudication of state-created rights, but it does not carry with it generation of rules of substantive law. As *Erie* read the Rules of Decision Act: "Except in matters governed by the Federal Constitution or by Acts of Congress, the law to be applied in any case is the law of the State." Under the *Erie* doctrine, federal courts sitting in diversity apply state substantive law and federal procedural law.

Classification of a law as "substantive" or "procedural" for *Erie* purposes is sometimes a challenging endeavor.[7] *Guaranty Trust Co. v. York*, 326 U.S. 99 (1945), an early interpretation of *Erie*, propounded an "outcome-determination" test: "[D]oes it significantly affect the result of a litigation for a federal court to disregard a law of a State that would be controlling in an action upon the same claim by the same parties in a State court?" Ordering application of a state statute of limitations to an equity proceeding in federal court, the Court said in *Guaranty Trust:* "[W]here a federal court is exercising jurisdiction solely because of the diversity of citizenship of the parties, the outcome of the litigation in the federal court should be substantially the same, so far as legal rules determine the outcome of a litigation, as it would be if tried in a State court." *Ibid; see also Ragan v. Merchants Transfer & Warehouse Co.*, 337 U.S. 530 (1949) (when local law that creates the cause of action qualifies it, "federal court must follow suit," for "a different measure of the cause of action in one court than in the other [would transgress] the principle of *Erie*"). A later pathmarking case, qualifying *Guaranty Trust*, explained that the "outcome-determination" test must not be applied mechanically to sweep in all manner of variations; instead, its application must be guided by "the twin aims of the *Erie* rule: discouragement of forum-shopping and avoidance of inequitable administration of the laws." *Hanna v. Plumer*, 380 U.S. 460 (1965).

Informed by these decisions, we address the question whether New York's "deviates materially" standard, codified in CPLR §5501 (c), is outcome-affective in

---

7. Concerning matters covered by the Federal Rules of Civil Procedure, the characterization question is usually unproblematic: It is settled that if the Rule in point is consonant with the Rules Enabling Act, 28 U.S.C. §2072, and the Constitution, the Federal Rule applies regardless of contrary state law. *See Hanna v. Plumer*, 380 U.S. 460 (1965). . . . Federal courts have interpreted the Federal Rules, however, with sensitivity to important state interests and regulatory policies. *See, e.g., Walker v. Armco Steel Corp.*, 446 U.S. 740 (1980) (reaffirming decision in *Ragan v. Merchants Transfer & Warehouse Co.*, 337 U.S. 530 (1949), that state law rather than Rule 3 determines when a diversity action commences for the purposes of tolling the state statute of limitations; Rule 3 makes no reference to the tolling of state limitations, the Court observed, and accordingly found no "direct conflict"); *S.A. Healy Co. v. Milwaukee Metropolitan Sewerage Dist.*, 60 F.3d 305, 310-312 (C.A.7 1995) (state provision for offers of settlement by plaintiffs is compatible with Federal Rule 68, which is limited to offers by defendants).

this sense: Would "application of the [standard] . . . have so important an effect upon the fortunes of one or both of the litigants that failure to [apply] it would [unfairly discriminate against citizens of the forum state, or] be likely to cause a plaintiff to choose the federal court"? . . .

We start from a point the parties do not debate. Gasperini acknowledges that a statutory cap on damages would supply substantive law for *Erie* purposes. . . . ("[T]he state as a matter of its substantive law may, among other things, eliminate the availability of damages for a particular claim entirely, limit the factors a jury may consider in determining damages, or place an absolute cap on the amount of damages available, and such substantive law would be applicable in a federal court sitting in diversity.") . . . [9] Although CPLR §5501(c) is less readily classified, it was designed to provide an analogous control.

New York's Legislature codified in §5501(c) a new standard, one that requires closer court review than the common law "shock the conscience" test. More rigorous comparative evaluations attend application of §5501(c)'s "deviates materially" standard. To foster predictability, the legislature required the reviewing court, when overturning a verdict under §5501(c), to state its reasons, including the factors it considered relevant. *See* CPLR §5522(b). We think it a fair conclusion that CPLR §5501(c) differs from a statutory cap principally "in that the maximum amount recoverable is not set by statute, but rather is determined by case law." In sum, §5501(c) contains a procedural instruction, but the State's objective is manifestly substantive. . . .

It thus appears that if federal courts ignore the change in the New York standard and persist in applying the "shock the conscience" test to damage awards on claims governed by New York law,[10] "'substantial' variations between state and federal [money judgments]" may be expected. *See Hanna.*[11] We therefore agree with the Second Circuit that New York's check on excessive damages implicates what we have called *Erie*'s "twin aims." . . . [12] Just as the *Erie* principle precludes a federal

---

9. While we have not specifically addressed the issue, courts of appeals have held that district court application of state statutory caps in diversity cases, post verdict, does not violate the Seventh Amendment, *See Davis v. Omitowoju*, 883 F.2d 1155, 1161–1165 (C.A.3 1989) (re-examination clause of Seventh Amendment does not impede federal court's post-verdict application of statutory cap); *Boyd v. Bulala*, 877 F.2d 1191, 1196 (C.A.4 1989) (post-verdict application of statutory cap does not violate Seventh Amendment right of trial by jury).

10. JUSTICE SCALIA questions whether federal *district* courts in New York "actually appl[y]" or "*ought*" to apply the "shock the conscience" test in assessing a jury's award for excessiveness. If there is a federal district court standard, it must come from the Court of Appeals, not from the over 40 district court judges in the Southern District of New York, each of whom sits alone and renders decisions not binding on the others. . . .

11. JUSTICE SCALIA questions whether application of CPLR §5501(c), in lieu of the standard generally used by federal courts within the Second Circuit, will in fact yield consistent outcome differentials. . . . The numbers, as the Second Circuit believed, are revealing. . . . Is the difference between an award of $450,000 and $100,000, or between $1,500 per transparency and $500, fairly described as insubstantial? We do not see how that can be so.

12. For rights that are state-created, state law governs the amount properly awarded as punitive damages, subject to an ultimate federal constitutional check for exorbitancy. . . . An evenhanded approach would require federal court deference to endeavors like New York's to control compensatory damages for excessiveness. . . .

court from giving a state-created claim "longer life . . . than [the claim] would have had in the state court," *Ragan*, 337 U.S. at 533–534, so *Erie* precludes a recovery in federal court significantly larger than the recovery that would have been tolerated in state court.

B

CPLR §5501(c), as earlier noted, is phrased as a direction to the New York Appellate Division. Acting essentially as a surrogate for a New York appellate forum, the Court of Appeals reviewed Gasperini's award to determine if it "deviate[d] materially" from damage awards the Appellate Division permitted in similar circumstances. The Court of Appeals performed this task without benefit of an opinion from the District Court, which had denied "without comment" the Center's Rule 59 motion. Concentrating on the authority §5501(c) gives to the Appellate Division, Gasperini urges that the provision shifts fact-finding responsibility from the jury and the trial judge to the appellate court. Assigning such responsibility to an appellate court, he maintains, is incompatible with the Seventh Amendment's re-examination clause, and therefore, Gasperini concludes, §5501(c) cannot be given effect in federal court. Although we reach a different conclusion than Gasperini, we agree that the Second Circuit did not attend to "[a]n essential characteristic of [the federal court] system," *Byrd v. Blue Ridge Rural Elec. Cooperative, Inc.*, 356 U.S. 525 (1958), when it used §5501(c) as "the standard for [federal] appellate review." . . .

That "essential characteristic" was described in *Byrd*, a diversity suit for negligence in which a pivotal issue of fact would have been tried by a judge were the case in state court. The *Byrd* Court held that, despite the state practice, . . . the plaintiff was entitled to a jury trial in federal court. In so ruling, the Court said that the *Guaranty Trust* "outcome-determination" test was an insufficient guide in cases presenting countervailing federal interests. *See Byrd*, 356 U.S. at 537. The Court described the countervailing federal interests present in *Byrd* this way:

> The federal system is an independent system for administering justice to litigants who properly invoke its jurisdiction. An essential characteristic of that system is the manner in which, in civil common law actions, it distributes trial functions between judge and jury and, under the influence — if not the command — of the Seventh Amendment, assigns the decisions of disputed questions of fact to the jury. *Ibid.*

The Seventh Amendment, which governs proceedings in federal court, but not in state court, bears not only on the allocation of trial functions between judge and jury, the issue in *Byrd;* it also controls the allocation of authority to review verdicts, the issue of concern here. The Amendment reads:

> In Suits at common law, where the value in controversy shall exceed twenty dollars, the right of trial by jury shall be preserved, and no fact tried by a jury, shall be otherwise re-examined in any Court of the United States, than according to the rules of the common law. U.S. Const., Amdt. 7.

Byrd involved the first clause of the Amendment, the "trial by jury" clause. This case involves the second, the "re-examination" clause. In keeping with the historic understanding, the re-examination clause does not inhibit the authority of trial judges to grant new trials "for any of the reasons for which new trials have heretofore been granted in actions at law in the courts of the United States." Fed. Rule Civ. Proc. 59(a). That authority is large. *See* 6A Moore's Federal Practice ¶59.05(2) . . . (2d ed. 1996) ("The power of the English common law trial courts to grant a new trial for a variety of reasons with a view to the attainment of justice was well established prior to the establishment of our Government."); *see also Aetna Casualty & Surety Co. v. Yeatts*, 122 F.2d 350, 353 (C.A.4 1941) ("The exercise of [the trial court's power to set aside the jury's verdict and grant a new trial] is not in derogation of the right of trial by jury but is one of the historic safeguards of that right."). . . . "The trial judge in the federal system," we have reaffirmed, "has . . . discretion to grant a new trial if the verdict appears to [the judge] to be against the weight of the evidence." *Byrd*, 356 U.S. at 540. This discretion includes overturning verdicts for excessiveness and ordering a new trial without qualification, or conditioned on the verdict winner's refusal to agree to a reduction (remittitur). . . .

In contrast, appellate review of a federal trial court's denial of a motion to set aside a jury's verdict as excessive is a relatively late, and less secure, development. Such review was once deemed inconsonant with the Seventh Amendment's re-examination clause. *See, e.g., Lincoln v. Power*, 151 U.S. 436 (1894). . . . We subsequently recognized that, even in cases in which the *Erie* doctrine was not in play — cases arising wholly under federal law — the question was not settled; we twice granted certiorari to decide the unsettled issue, but ultimately resolved the cases on other grounds. . . .

Before today, we have not "expressly [held] that the Seventh Amendment allows appellate review of a district court's denial of a motion to set aside an award as excessive." *Browning-Ferris Industries of Vt., Inc. v. Kelco Disposal, Inc.*, 492 U.S. 257, 279, n. 25 (1989). But in successive reminders that the question was worthy of this Court's attention, we noted, without disapproval, that courts of appeals engage in review of district court excessiveness determinations, applying "abuse of discretion" as their standard. . . .

As the Second Circuit explained, appellate review for abuse of discretion is reconcilable with the Seventh Amendment as a control necessary and proper to the fair administration of justice: "We must give the benefit of every doubt to the judgment of the trial judge; but surely there must be an upper limit, and whether that has been surpassed is not a question of fact with respect to which reasonable men may differ, but a question of law." . . . We now approve this line of decisions, and thus make explicit what Justice Stewart thought implicit in our *Grunenthal* disposition: "[N]othing in the Seventh Amendment . . . precludes appellate review of the trial judge's denial of a motion to set aside [a jury verdict] as excessive." 393 U.S. at 164 (Stewart, J., dissenting).

C

In *Byrd*, the Court faced a one-or-the-other choice: trial by judge as in state court, or trial by jury according to the federal practice. In the case before us, a choice of that order is not required, for the principal state and federal interests can be accommodated. The Second Circuit correctly recognized that when New York substantive law governs a claim for relief, New York law and decisions guide the allowable damages. . . . But that court did not take into account the characteristic of the federal-court system that caused us to reaffirm: "The proper role of the trial and appellate courts in the federal system in reviewing the size of jury verdicts is . . . a matter of federal law." *Donovan v. Penn Shipping Co.*, 429 U.S. 648, 649 (1977) (*per curiam*). . . .

New York's dominant interest can be respected, without disrupting the federal system, once it is recognized that the federal district court is capable of performing the checking function, *i.e.*, that court can apply the State's "deviates materially" standard in line with New York case law evolving under CPLR §5501(c).[22] We recall, in this regard, that the "deviates materially" standard serves as the guide to be applied in trial as well as appellate courts in New York.

Within the federal system, practical reasons combine with Seventh Amendment constraints to lodge in the district court, not the court of appeals, primary responsibility for application of §5501(c)'s "deviates materially" check. Trial judges have the "unique opportunity to consider the evidence in the living courtroom context," while appellate judges see only the "cold paper record."

District court applications of the "deviates materially" standard would be subject to appellate review under the standard the Circuits now employ when inadequacy or excessiveness is asserted on appeal: abuse of discretion. . . . In light of *Erie*'s doctrine, the federal appeals court must be guided by the damage-control standard state law supplies,[23] but as the Second Circuit itself has said: "If we reverse, it must be because of an abuse of discretion. . . . The very nature of the problem counsels restraint. . . . We must give the benefit of every doubt to the judgment of the trial judge." *Dagnello*, 289 F.2d at 806.

---

22. Justice Scalia finds in Federal Rule of Civil Procedure 59 a "federal standard" for new trial motions in "'direct collision'" with, and "'leaving no room for the operation of,'" a state law like CPLR §5501(c) . . . (quoting *Burlington Northern R. Co.*, 480 U.S. at 4-5). The relevant prescription, Rule 59(a), has remained unchanged since the adoption of the Federal Rules by this Court in 1937. 302 U.S. 783. Rule 59(a) is as encompassing as it is uncontroversial. It is indeed "Hornbook" law that a most usual ground for a Rule 59 motion is that "the damages are excessive." *See* C. Wright, Law of Federal Courts 676-677 (5th ed. 1994). Whether damages are excessive for the claim-in-suit must be governed by *some* law. And there is no candidate for that governance other than the law that gives rise to the claim for relief—here, the law of New York. *See* 28 U.S C. §2072(a) and (b) ("Supreme Court shall have the power to prescribe general rules of . . . procedure"; "[s]uch rules shall not abridge, enlarge or modify any substantive right"); *Browning-Ferris*, 492 U.S. at 279 ("standard of excessiveness" is a "matte[r] of state, and not federal, common law"); *see also* R. Fallon, D. Meltzer, & D. Shapiro, Hart and Wechsler's The Federal Courts and the Federal System 729-730 (4th ed. 1996) (observing that the Court "has continued since [*Hanna v. Plumer*, 380 U.S. 460 (1965)] to interpret the federal rules to avoid conflict with important state regulatory policies," citing *Walker v. Armco Steel Corp.*, 446 U.S. 740 (1980)).

23. If liability and damage-control rules are split apart here, as Justice Scalia says they must be to save the Seventh Amendment, then Gasperini's claim and others like it would be governed by a most curious "law." The sphinx-like, damage-determining law he would apply to this controversy has a state forepart, but a federal hindquarter. The beast may not be brutish, but there is little judgment in its creation.

IV

It does not appear that the District Court checked the jury's verdict against the relevant New York decisions demanding more than "industry standard" testimony to support an award of the size the jury returned in this case. As the Court of Appeals recognized, the uniqueness of the photographs and the plaintiff's earnings as photographer — past and reasonably projected — are factors relevant to appraisal of the award. . . . Accordingly, we vacate the judgment of the Court of Appeals and instruct that court to remand the case to the District Court so that the trial judge, revisiting his ruling on the new trial motion, may test the jury's verdict against CPLR §5501(c)'s "deviates materially" standard.

It is so ordered.

JUSTICE STEVENS, dissenting.

While I agree with most of the reasoning in the Court's opinion, I disagree with its disposition of the case. I would affirm the judgment of the Court of Appeals. I would also reject the suggestion that the Seventh Amendment limits the power of a federal appellate court sitting in diversity to decide whether a jury's award of damages exceeds a limit established by state law.

I

. . . Although the majority agrees with the Court of Appeals that New York law establishes the size of the damages that may be awarded, it chooses to vacate and remand. The majority holds that a federal court of appeals should review for abuse of discretion a district court's decision to deny a motion for new trial based on a jury's excessive award. As a result, it concludes that the District Court should be given the opportunity to apply in the first instance the "deviates materially" standard that New York law imposes.

The District Court had its opportunity to consider the propriety of the jury's award, and it erred. The Court of Appeals has now corrected that error after "drawing all reasonable inferences in favor of" petitioner. 66 F.3d at 431. As there is no reason to suppose that the Court of Appeals has reached a conclusion with which the District Court could permissibly disagree on remand, I would not require the District Court to repeat a task that has already been well-performed by the reviewing court. I therefore would affirm the judgment of the Court of Appeals.

II

Although I have addressed the question presented as if our decision in *Erie* alone controlled its outcome, petitioner argues that the second clause of the Seventh Amendment, which states that "no fact tried by jury, shall be otherwise re-examined in any Court of the United States, than according to the rules of the common law," U.S. Const. Amdt. VII, bars the procedure followed by the Court of Appeals. There is no merit to that position. . . .

III

For the reasons set forth above. I agree with the majority that the Reexamination Clause does not bar federal appellate courts from reviewing jury awards for excessiveness. I confess to some surprise, however, at its conclusion that "'the influence—if not the command—of the Seventh Amendment,'" (quoting *Byrd v. Blue Ridge Rural Elec. Cooperative. Inc.*, 356 U.S. 525, 537 (1958)), requires federal courts of appeals to review district court applications of state law excessiveness standards for an "abuse of discretion."

The majority's persuasive demonstration that New York law sets forth a substantive limitation on the size of jury awards seems to refute the contention that New York has merely asked appellate courts to reexamine facts. The majority's analysis would thus seem to undermine the conclusion that the Reexamination Clause is relevant to this case.

Certainly, our decision in *Byrd* does not make the Clause relevant. There, we considered only whether the Seventh Amendment's first clause should influence our decision to give effect to a state-law rule denying the right to a jury altogether. *Byrd v. Blue Ridge Rural Elec. Cooperative, Inc.*, 356 U.S. at 537. That holding in no way requires us to consult the Amendment's second clause to determine the standard of review for a district court's application of state substantive law.

My disagreement is tempered, however, because the majority carefully avoids defining too strictly the abuse of discretion standard it announces. To the extent that the majority relies only on "practical reasons" for its conclusion that the Court of Appeals should give some weight to the District Court's assessment in determining whether state substantive law has been properly applied. . . . I do not disagree with its analysis.

As a matter of federal court administration, we have recognized in other contexts the need for according some deference to the lower court's resolution of legal, yet fact-intensive, questions. *See Ornelas v. United States*, 517 U.S. at 699; *Pierce v. Underwood*, 487 U.S. 552, 558, n. 1 (1988). Indeed, it is a familiar, if somewhat circular, maxim that deems an error of law an abuse of discretion.

In the end, therefore, my disagreement with the label that the majority attaches to the standard of appellate review should not obscure the far more fundamental point on which we agree. Whatever influence the Seventh Amendment may be said to exert, *Erie* requires federal appellate courts sitting in diversity to apply "the damage control standard state law supplies."

IV

Because I would affirm the judgment of the Court of Appeals, and because I do not agree that the Seventh Amendment in any respect influences the proper analysis of the question presented, I respectfully dissent.

Justice Scalia, with whom The Chief Justice and Justice Thomas join, dissenting.

Today the Court overrules a longstanding and well-reasoned line of precedent that has for years prohibited federal appellate courts from reviewing refusals by district courts to set aside civil jury awards as contrary to the weight of the evidence. One reason is given for overruling these cases: that the courts of appeals have, for some time now, decided to ignore them. Such unreasoned capitulation to the nullification of what was long regarded as a core component of the Bill of Rights—the Seventh Amendment's prohibition on appellate reexamination of civil jury awards—is wrong. It is not for us, much less for the courts of appeals, to decide that the Seventh Amendment's restriction on federal-court review of jury findings has outlived its usefulness.

The Court also holds today that a state practice that relates to the division of duties between state judges and juries must be followed by federal courts in diversity cases. On this issue, too, our prior cases are directly to the contrary.

As I would reverse the judgment of the Court of Appeals, I respectfully dissent. . . .

II

The Court's holding that federal courts of appeals may review district court denials of motions for new trials for error of fact is not the only novel aspect of today's decision. The Court also directs that the case be remanded to the District Court, so that it may "test the jury's verdict against CPLR §5501(c)'s 'deviates materially' standard." . . . This disposition contradicts the principle that "[t]he proper role of the trial and appellate courts in the federal system in reviewing the size of jury verdicts is . . . a matter of federal law." *Donovan v. Perm Shipping Co.*, 429 U.S. 648, 649 (1977) (per curiam).

The Court acknowledges that state procedural rules cannot, as a general matter, be permitted to interfere with the allocation of functions in the federal court system. Indeed, it is at least partly for this reason that the Court rejects direct application of §5501(c) at the appellate level as inconsistent with an "'essential characteristic'" of the federal court system—by which the Court presumably means abuse-of-discretion review of denials of motions for new trials. But the scope of the Court's concern is oddly circumscribed. The "'essential characteristic'" of the federal jury, and, more specifically, the role of the federal trial court in reviewing jury judgments, apparently counts for little. The Court approves the "accommodat[ion]" achieved by having district courts review jury verdicts under the "deviates materially" standard, because it regards that as a means of giving effect to the State's purposes "without disrupting the federal system." But changing the standard by which trial judges review jury verdicts does disrupt the federal system, and is plainly inconsistent with "the strong federal policy against allowing state rules to disrupt the judge-jury relationship in federal court." *Byrd v. Blue Ridge Rural Elec. Cooperative, Inc.*, 356 U.S. 525, 538.[9] The Court's opinion does not even acknowledge, let alone address, this dislocation.

We discussed precisely the point at issue here in *Browning-Ferris Industries of Vt., Inc. v. Kelco Disposal, Inc.*, 492 U.S. 257 (1989), and gave an answer altogether contrary to the one provided today. *Browning-Ferris* rejected a request to fashion a federal common law rule limiting the size of punitive-damages awards in federal courts, reaffirming the principle of *Erie R. Co. v. Tompkins*, 304 U.S. 64 (1938), that "[i]n a diversity action, or in any other lawsuit where state law provides the basis of decision, the propriety of an award of punitive damages . . . and the factors the jury may consider in determining their amount, are questions of state law." 492 U.S. at 278. But the opinion expressly stated that "[f]ederal law . . . will control on those issues involving the proper review of the jury award by a federal district court

---

9. Since I reject application of the New York standard on other grounds, I need not consider whether it constitutes "reexamination" of a jury's verdict in a manner "otherwise . . . than according to the rules of the common law."

and court of appeals." *Id.* at 278–279. "In reviewing an award of punitive damages," it said, "the role of the district court is to determine whether the jury's verdict is within the confines of state law, and to determine, by reference to federal standards developed under Rule 59, whether a new trial or remittitur should be ordered." *Id.* at 279. The same distinction necessarily applies where the judgment under review is for compensatory damages: State substantive law controls what injuries are compensable and in what amount; but federal standards determine whether the award exceeds what is lawful to such degree that it may be set aside by order for new trial or remittitur.[10]

The Court does not disavow those statements in *Browning-Ferris* (indeed, it does not even discuss them), but it presumably overrules them, at least where the state rule that governs "whether a new trial or remittitur should be ordered" is characterized as "substantive" in nature. That, at any rate, is the reason the Court asserts for giving §5501(c) dispositive effect. The objective of that provision, the Court states, "is manifestly substantive," since it operates to "contro[l] how much a plaintiff can be awarded" by "tightening the range of tolerable awards." Although "less readily classified" as substantive than "a statutory cap on damages," it nonetheless "was designed to provide an analogous control," by making a new trial mandatory when the award "deviat[es] materially" from what is reasonable . . .

I do not see how this can be so. It seems to me quite wrong to regard this provision as a "substantive" rule for *Erie* purposes. The "analog[y]" to "a statutory cap on damages," fails utterly. There is an absolutely fundamental distinction between a *rule of law* such as that, which would ordinarily be imposed upon the jury in the trial court's instructions, and a *rule of review*, which simply determines how closely the jury verdict will be scrutinized for compliance with the instructions. A tighter standard for reviewing jury determinations can no more plausibly be called a "substantive" disposition than can a tighter appellate standard for reviewing trial-court determinations. The one, like the other, provides additional assurance *that the law has been complied with*, but the other, like the one, *leaves the law unchanged*.

The Court commits the classic *Erie* mistake of regarding whatever changes the outcome as substantive. That is not the only factor to be considered. *See Byrd*, 356 U.S. at 537 ("[W]ere 'outcome' the only consideration, a strong case might appear for saying that the federal court should follow the state practice. But there are affirmative countervailing considerations at work here."). Outcome-determination "was never intended to serve as a talisman," *Hanna v. Plumer*, 380 U.S. 460, 466–467 (1965), and does not have the power to convert the most classic elements of the *process* of assuring that the law is observed into the substantive law itself. The right to have a jury make the findings of fact, for example, is generally thought to favor plaintiffs, and that advantage is often thought significant enough to be the basis for forum selection. But no one would argue that *Erie* confers a right to a jury

---

10. Justice Stevens thinks that if an award "exceeds what is lawful," the result is "legal error" that "may be corrected" by the appellate court. But the sort of "legal error" involved here is the imposition of legal consequences (in this case, damages) in light of facts that, under the law, may not warrant them. To suggest that every fact may be reviewed, because what may ensue from an erroneous factual determination is a "legal error," is to destroy the notion that there is a fact-finding function reserved to the jury.

Chapter 4. The Law Applied in Federal Court

in federal court wherever state courts would provide it; or that, were it not for the Seventh Amendment, *Erie* would require federal courts to dispense with the jury whenever state courts do so.

In any event, the Court exaggerates the difference that the state standard will make. It concludes that different outcomes are likely to ensue depending on whether the law being applied is the state "deviates materially" standard of §5501(c) or the "shocks the conscience" standard. *See ante*, at 429–431. Of course it is not the federal *appellate* standard but the federal *district-court* standard for granting new trials that must be compared with the New York standard to determine whether substantially different results will obtain—and it is far from clear that the district-court standard *ought* to be "shocks the conscience." Indeed, it is not even clear (as the Court asserts) that "shocks the conscience" is the standard (erroneous or not) actually applied by the district courts of the Second Circuit. . . . Moreover, some decisions that *say* "shocks the conscience" in fact apply a rule much less stringent. One case, for example, says that *any* award that would not be sustained under the New York "deviates materially" rule "shocks the conscience." *See In re Joint Eastern & S. Dist. Asbestos Litigation*, 798 F. Supp. 925, 937 (E. & S.D.N.Y. 1992), *rev'd on other grounds*, 95 F.2d 343, 346 (C.A.2 1993). In sum, it is at least highly questionable whether the consistent outcome differential claimed by the Court even exists. What seems to me far more likely to produce forum-shopping is the consistent difference between the state and federal *appellate* standards, which the Court leaves untouched. Under the Court's disposition, the Second Circuit reviews only for abuse of discretion, whereas New York's appellate courts engage in a *de novo* review for material deviation, giving the defendant a double shot at getting the damages award set aside. The only result that would produce the conformity the Court erroneously believes *Erie* requires is the one adopted by the Second Circuit and rejected by the Court: *de novo* federal appellate review under the §5501(c) standard.

To say that application of §5501(c) in place of the federal standard will not consistently produce disparate results is not to suggest that the decision the Court has made today is not a momentous one. The *principle* that the state standard governs is of great importance, since it bears the potential to destroy the uniformity of federal practice and the integrity of the federal court system. Under the Court's view, a state rule that directed courts to determine that an award is excessive or inadequate if it deviates *in any degree* from the *proper measure of compensation* would have to be applied in federal courts, effectively requiring federal judges to determine the amount of damages *de novo*, and effectively taking the matter away from the jury entirely. *Cf. Byrd.* Or consider a state rule that allowed the defendant a second trial on damages, with judgment ultimately in the amount of the lesser of two jury awards. *Cf. United States v. Wonson*, 28 F. Cas., at 747–748 (describing Massachusetts practice by which a second jury trial could be had on appeal). Under the reasoning of the Court's opinion, even such a rule as that would have to be applied in the federal courts.

The foregoing describes why I think the Court's *Erie* analysis is flawed. But in my view, one does not even reach the *Erie* question in this case. The standard to be applied by a district court in ruling on a motion for a new trial is set forth in Rule 59 of the Federal Rules of Civil Procedure, which provides that "[a] new trial may be granted . . . for any of the reasons for which new trials have heretofore been granted in actions at law *in the courts of the United States*" (emphasis added). That is undeniably a federal standard.[12] Federal district courts in the Second Circuit have interpreted that standard to permit the granting of new trials where "'it is quite clear that the jury has reached a seriously erroneous result'" and letting the verdict stand would result in a "miscarriage of justice." . . . Assuming (as we have no reason to question) that this is a correct interpretation of what Rule 59 requires, it is undeniable that the federal rule is "'sufficiently broad' to cause a 'direct collision' with the state law or, implicitly, to 'control the issue' before the court, thereby leaving no room for the operation of that law." *Burlington Northern R. Co. v. Woods*, 480 U.S. 1 (1987). It is simply not possible to give controlling effect both to the federal standard and the state standard in reviewing the jury's award. That being so, the court has no choice but to apply the Federal Rule, which is an exercise of what we have called Congress's "power to regulate matters which, though falling within the uncertain area between substance and procedure, are rationally capable of classification as either," *Hanna*. . . .

There is no small irony in the Court's declaration today that appellate review of refusals to grant new trials for error of fact is "a control necessary and proper to the fair administration of justice." It is objection to *precisely* that sort of "control" by federal appellate judges that gave birth to the Reexamination Clause of the Seventh Amendment. Alas, those who drew the Amendment, and the citizens who approved it, did not envision an age in which the Constitution means whatever this Court thinks it ought to mean — or indeed, whatever the courts of appeals have recently thought it ought to mean.

When there is added to the revision of the Seventh Amendment the Court's precedent-setting disregard of Congress's instructions in Rule 59, one must conclude that this is a bad day for the Constitution's distinctive Article III courts in general, and for the role of the jury in those courts in particular. I respectfully dissent.

NOTES AND QUESTIONS

1. *Track Assignment?* Recall that *Hanna* distinguished between "relatively unguided *Erie* choices" and those governed by positive federal law. On which track does the *Gasperini* Court place the standard of review? Are the standards governing either the trial court's scrutiny of the jury verdict, or the appellate court's scrutiny of the trial court's ruling on the motion governed by federal statute, Federal Rule of Civil Procedure, or constitutional provision?

a. *The Role of the Seventh Amendment in* Gasperini*?* The majority ultimately determines that the Seventh Amendment does not preclude either trial court scrutiny of the jury verdict or appellate scrutiny of the trial court's denial of the Rule 59 motion. Does the Seventh Amendment play any part in the majority's rejection of

---

12. I agree with the Court's entire progression of reasoning in its footnote 22 *ante*, at 437, leading to the conclusion that *state* law must determine "[w]hether damages are excessive." But the question of whether damages are excessive is quite separate from the question of when a jury award may be set aside for excessiveness. *See supra*, at 2237. It is the latter that is governed by Rule 59; as *Browning-Ferris* said, district courts are "to determine, by reference to *federal standards developed under Rule 59*, whether a new trial or remittitur should be ordered," 492 U.S. at 279.

the New York standard of scrutiny for federal courts of appeals? Is the abuse of discretion standard to be applied by the court of appeals constitutionally compelled?

b. *Are the Federal Rules of Civil Procedure "Broad Enough" to Cover the Question?* Are you persuaded by the majority's conclusion that Rule 59 does not provide the standard for granting a motion for new trial? Doesn't Rule 59 provide more of an answer than the transfer statute provided in *Stewart?* Has the Court implicitly tightened the "direct collision" standard after apparently relaxing it in *Stewart?* Does the "track-assignment" methodology employed by the majority in *Gasperini* open the door for state law to inform the meaning of any Federal Rule of Civil Procedure? For an argument that state law should affect the operation of pleading, summary judgment, and class certification practice in the federal courts, *see* Adam N. Steinman, *What Is the* Erie *Doctrine? (And What Does It Mean for the Contemporary Politics of Judicial Federalism?)*, 84 Notre Dame L. Rev. 245, 274–287 (2008).

c. Even if Rule 59 does trump the New York statute, as Justice Scalia concludes, is the Rule in violation of the Enabling Act?

2. Byrd *Revived? Gasperini* is the first post-*Hanna* case in which the Court relies on *Byrd* and focuses extensively on the respective state and federal interests in lieu of outcome determination. Can you articulate when analysis of governmental interests is appropriate after *Gasperini?* Does the *Gasperini* opinion effectively reconcile the disparate approaches taken by *Hanna* and *Byrd,* or does its reliance on *Byrd* create confusion over the weight to be given federal and state interests? For an interesting debate, *compare* Thomas Rowe Jr., *Not Bad for Government Work: Does Anyone Else Think the Supreme Court Is Doing a Halfway Decent Job in Its* Erie-Hanna *Jurisprudence,* 73 Notre Dame L. Rev. 963 (1998) (arguing that the basic framework for analysis that has prevailed since *Hanna* remains intact after *Gasperini*) *with* C. Douglas Floyd, Erie *Awry: A Comment on* Gasperini v. Center for Humanities Inc., 1997 BYU L. Rev. 267 (criticizing the majority opinion in *Gasperini* for the way it "confuses and confounds" the extent to which *Byrd* survives). *See also* Richard Freer, *Federal Practice and Procedure Symposium Honoring Charles Alan Wright: Some Thoughts on the State of* Erie *After* Gasperini, 76 Tex. L. Rev. 1637 (1998) (arguing that *Gasperini* will lead courts to decide more cases under the Rules of Decision Act, with little guidance from the Supreme Court on how to undertake such analysis).

How would the case have come out had the Court relied solely on an outcome determination test? Isn't Justice Scalia right in asserting that plaintiffs after *Gasperini* will be drawn to federal court to avoid appellate review of jury verdicts? Does the majority disagree?

a. *Does the Court Properly Evaluate the Relevant State and Federal Interests?* Are you persuaded that there is no relevant distinction for *Erie* purposes between a New York cap on damages, and a provision for judicial review of jury verdicts for excessiveness? Is there any way the Court could have vindicated the state "substantive" interest in limiting excessive jury verdicts without requiring the trial judge to scrutinize the verdict pursuant to the New York CPLR? Do you agree with Justice Scalia that "[t]here is an absolutely fundamental distinction between a rule of law such as that, which would ordinarily be imposed upon the jury in the trial court's instructions, and a rule of review, which simply determines how closely the jury verdict will be scrutinized for compliance with the instructions"? What is that "fundamental distinction"?

b. *Inherent Federal Procedural Authority?* Central to Justice Ginsburg's analysis is the fact that the New York statute had been interpreted to authorize the trial court to review the jury verdict for excessiveness. What if it had not? Suppose the statute directed "all appellate courts" to scrutinize verdicts for excessiveness *de novo* (without reference to the lower court findings), and trial courts were, under New York law, denied that authority. Would the Court have required federal courts of appeals to engage in that scrutiny?

3. For more scholarship on the evolution of the *Erie* doctrine, *see* Caleb Nelson, *A Critical Guide to Erie Railroad v. Tompkins*, 54 Wm. & Mary L. Rev. 922 (2013); Donald L. Doernberg, *The Unseen Track of* Erie Railroad*: Why History and Jurisprudence Suggest a More Straightforward Form of* Erie *Analysis*, 109 W. Va. L. Rev. 611 (2007); Earl C. Dudley, *Deforming the Federal Rules: An Essay on What's Wrong with the Recent* Erie *Decisions*, 92 Va. L. Rev. 707 (2006); Adam N. Steinman, *What Is the* Erie *Doctrine? (And What Does It Mean for the Contemporary Politics of Judicial Federalism?)*, 84 Notre Dame L. Rev. 245 (2008); Patrick L. Woolley, Erie *and Choice of Law After the Class Action Fairness Act*, 80 Tul. L. Rev. 1723 (2006).

Shady Grove Orthopedic Assocs. v. Allstate Ins.

559 U.S. 393 (2010)

[The case grew out of a reform that the State of New York had enacted in the area of class action litigation, an important and complex area of litigation that is explored in depth in Chapter 8. For purposes of this case, you should understand the following about class action litigation.

In a class action, a small number of individual plaintiffs (called "class representatives" or "named plaintiffs") bring suit on behalf of an entire class of similarly situated claimants. For example, owners of stock in a publicly traded corporation might bring suit on behalf of all shareholders, claiming that the corporation had released false or misleading information about its financial health. Or several female employees in a company might bring suit on behalf of all the company's female employees, claiming that the company follows a pattern or practice of discriminating against women in hiring and promotion. In a class action, the idea is that there is enough commonality among the factual and legal theories of the entire group of people who have allegedly been harmed that it makes sense—both for efficiency and fairness reasons—to permit a small number of individuals to litigate the claims on behalf of the entire class. When a case is "certified" to proceed as a class action, that small number of class representatives will litigate their individual claims, and the result will then bind the entire class (subject to certain potential exceptions). The class action is thus a very powerful litigation device, sometimes authorizing the named plaintiffs to litigate the claims of thousands or even millions of class members and magnifying the potential exposure of the defendants enormously—and hence their motivation to settle the case.

The question of when it is appropriate to certify a class action is a complicated one, which we deal with at length in Chapter 8. For present purposes, you should understand that New York has decided that class actions should not generally be available to enforce statutes that impose damages in the form of a penalty. The reason for this policy is a concern that using a class action to litigate many thousands of penalty claims in a single proceeding might magnify the enforcement of penalty statutes to a point that would be damaging and counterproductive. New York has thus concluded that a penalty provision should only be enforceable through a class action if the legislature uses express statutory language to authorize such a proceeding. In contrast, the federal provision that deals with the certification of class actions, Federal Rule of Civil Procedure 23, contains no such limitation.

As you read *Shady Grove*, ask yourself whether the decision is consistent with *Gasperini* or whether their approaches to the Federal Rules differ in any way. Also pay attention to which parts of the opinion speak for a majority of the Court, which parts commanded only a plurality, and in what respects the separate concurring opinion appears to agree with the four-Justice dissent.]

JUSTICE SCALIA announced the judgment of the Court and delivered the opinion of the Court with respect to Parts I and II-A, an opinion with respect to Parts II-B and II-D, in which THE CHIEF JUSTICE, JUSTICE THOMAS, and JUSTICE SOTOMAYOR join, and an opinion with respect to Part II-C, in which THE CHIEF JUSTICE and JUSTICE THOMAS join.

New York law prohibits class actions in suits seeking penalties or statutory minimum damages.[1] We consider whether this precludes a federal district court sitting in diversity from entertaining a class action under Federal Rule of Civil Procedure 23.[2]

---

1. N.Y. Civ. Prac. Law Ann. §901 (West 2006) provides:

"(a) One or more members of a class may sue or be sued as representative parties on behalf of all if:"

"1. the class is so numerous that joinder of all members, whether otherwise required or permitted, is impracticable;"

"2. there are questions of law or fact common to the class which predominate over any questions affecting only individual members;"

"3. the claims or defenses of the representative parties are typical of the claims or defenses of the class;"

"4. the representative parties will fairly and adequately protect the interests of the class; and"

"5. a class action is superior to other available methods for the fair and efficient adjudication of the controversy."

"(b) Unless a statute creating or imposing a penalty, or a minimum measure of recovery specifically authorizes the recovery thereof in a class action, an action to recover a penalty, or minimum measure of recovery created or imposed by statute may not be maintained as a class action."

2. Rule 23(a) provides:

"(a) Prerequisites. One or more members of a class may sue or be sued as representative parties on behalf of all members only if:"

"(1) the class is so numerous that joinder of all members is impracticable;"

"(2) there are questions of law or fact common to the class;"

"(3) the claims or defenses of the representative parties are typical of the claims or defenses of the class; and"

"(4) the representative parties will fairly and adequately protect the interests of the class."

Subsection (b) says that "[a] class action may be maintained if Rule 23(a) is satisfied and if" the suit falls into one of three described categories (irrelevant for present purposes).

The petitioner's complaint alleged the following: Shady Grove Orthopedic Associates, P. A., provided medical care to Sonia E. Galvez for injuries she suffered in an automobile accident. As partial payment for that care, Galvez assigned to Shady Grove her rights to insurance benefits under a policy issued in New York by Allstate Insurance Co. Shady Grove tendered a claim for the assigned benefits to Allstate, which under New York law had 30 days to pay the claim or deny it. Allstate apparently paid, but not on time, and it refused to pay the statutory interest that accrued on the overdue benefits (at two percent per month).

Shady Grove filed this diversity suit in the Eastern District of New York to recover the unpaid statutory interest. Alleging that Allstate routinely refuses to pay interest on overdue benefits, Shady Grove sought relief on behalf of itself and a class of all others to whom Allstate owes interest. The District Court dismissed the suit for lack of jurisdiction. It reasoned that N.Y. Civ. Prac. Law Ann. §901(b), which precludes a suit to recover a "penalty" from proceeding as a class action, applies in diversity suits in federal court, despite Federal Rule of Civil Procedure 23. Concluding that statutory interest is a "penalty" under New York law, it held that §901(b) prohibited the proposed class action. And, since Shady Grove conceded that its individual claim (worth roughly $500) fell far short of the amount-in-controversy requirement for individual suits under 28 U.S.C. §1332(a), the suit did not belong in federal court.[3]

The Second Circuit affirmed. The court did not dispute that a federal rule adopted in compliance with the Rules Enabling Act, 28 U.S.C. §2072, would control if it conflicted with §901(b). But there was no conflict because (as we will describe in more detail below) the Second Circuit concluded that Rule 23 and §901(b) address different issues. Finding no federal rule on point, the Court of Appeals held that §901(b) is "substantive" within the meaning of *Erie R. Co. v. Tompkins* and thus must be applied by federal courts sitting in diversity.

We granted certiorari.

II

The framework for our decision is familiar. We must first determine whether Rule 23 answers the question in dispute. *Burlington Northern R. Co. v. Woods*, 480 U.S. 1, 4-5 (1987). If it does, it governs — New York's law notwithstanding — unless it exceeds statutory authorization or Congress's rulemaking power. *Id.* at 5; see *Hanna v. Plumer*, 380 U.S. 460, 463-464 (1965). We do not wade into *Erie*'s murky waters unless the federal rule is inapplicable or invalid. See 380 U.S. at 469-471.

A

The question in dispute is whether Shady Grove's suit may proceed as a class action. Rule 23 provides an answer. It states that "[a] class action may be maintained" if two conditions are met: The suit must satisfy the criteria set forth in subdivision (a) (*i.e.*, numerosity, commonality, typicality, and adequacy of representation),

---

3. Shady Grove had asserted jurisdiction under 28 U.S.C. §1332(d)(2), which relaxes, for class actions seeking at least $5 million, the rule against aggregating separate claims for calculation of the amount in controversy. See *Exxon Mobil Corp. v. Allapattah Services, Inc.*, 545 U.S. 546, 571 (2005).

and it also must fit into one of the three categories described in subdivision (b). Fed. Rule Civ. Proc. 23(b). By its terms this creates a categorical rule entitling a plaintiff whose suit meets the specified criteria to pursue his claim as a class action. (The Federal Rules regularly use "may" to confer categorical permission, see, *e.g.*, Fed. Rules Civ. Proc. 8(d)(2)-(3), 14(a)(1), 18(a)-(b), 20(a)(1)-(2), 27(a)(1), 30(a)(1), as do federal statutes that establish procedural entitlements, see, *e.g.*, 29 U.S.C. §626(c)(1); 42 U.S.C. §2000e-5(f)(1).) Thus, Rule 23 provides a one-size-fits-all formula for deciding the class-action question. Because §901(b) attempts to answer the same question — *i.e.*, it states that Shady Grove's suit "may *not* be maintained as a class action" (emphasis added) because of the relief it seeks — it cannot apply in diversity suits unless Rule 23 is ultra vires.

The Second Circuit believed that §901(b) and Rule 23 do not conflict because they address different issues. Rule 23, it said, concerns only the criteria for determining whether a given class can and should be certified; section 901(b), on the other hand, addresses an antecedent question: whether the particular type of claim is eligible for class treatment in the first place — a question on which Rule 23 is silent. Allstate embraces this analysis.

We disagree. To begin with, the line between eligibility and certifiability is entirely artificial. Both are preconditions for maintaining a class action. Allstate suggests that eligibility must depend on the "particular cause of action" asserted, instead of some other attribute of the suit. But that is not so. Congress could, for example, provide that only claims involving more than a certain number of plaintiffs are "eligible" for class treatment in federal court. In other words, relabeling Rule 23(a)'s prerequisites "eligibility criteria" would obviate Allstate's objection — a sure sign that its eligibility-certifiability distinction is made-to-order.

There is no reason, in any event, to read Rule 23 as addressing only whether claims made eligible for class treatment by some *other* law should be certified as class actions. Allstate asserts that Rule 23 neither explicitly nor implicitly empowers a federal court "to certify a class in each and every case" where the Rule's criteria are met. But that is *exactly* what Rule 23 does: It says that if the prescribed preconditions are satisfied "[a] class action *may be maintained*" (emphasis added) — not "*a class action may be permitted*." Courts do not maintain actions; litigants do. The discretion suggested by Rule 23's "may" is discretion residing in the plaintiff: He may bring his claim in a class action if he wishes. And like the rest of the Federal Rules of Civil Procedure, Rule 23 *automatically* applies "in all civil actions and proceedings in the United States district courts," Fed. Rule Civ. Proc. 1. . . .

Allstate points out that Congress has carved out some federal claims from Rule 23's reach, see, *e.g.*, 8 U.S.C. §1252(e)(1)(B) — which shows, Allstate contends, that Rule 23 does not authorize class actions for all claims, but rather leaves room for laws like §901(b). But Congress, unlike New York, has ultimate authority over the Federal Rules of Civil Procedure; it can create exceptions to an individual rule as it sees fit — either by directly amending the rule or by enacting a separate statute overriding it in certain instances. The fact that Congress has created specific exceptions to Rule 23 hardly proves that the Rule does not apply generally. In fact, it proves the opposite. If Rule 23 did *not* authorize class actions across the board, the statutory exceptions would be unnecessary.

Allstate next suggests that the structure of §901 shows that Rule 23 addresses only certifiability. Section 901(*a*), it notes, establishes class-certification criteria roughly analogous to those in Rule 23 (wherefore it agrees *that* subsection is preempted). But §901(b)'s rule barring class actions for certain claims is set off as its own subsection, and where it applies §901(a) does not. This shows, according to Allstate, that §901(b) concerns a separate subject. Perhaps it does concern a subject separate from the subject of §901(a). But the question before us is whether it concerns a subject separate from the subject of *Rule 23*—and for purposes of answering *that* question the way New York has structured its statute is immaterial. Rule 23 permits all class actions that meet its requirements, and a State cannot limit that permission by structuring one part of its statute to track Rule 23 and enacting another part that imposes additional requirements. Both of §901's subsections undeniably answer the same question as Rule 23: whether a class action may proceed for a given suit. Cf. *Burlington*, 480 U.S. at 7-8.

The dissent argues that §901(b) has nothing to do with whether Shady Grove may maintain its suit as a class action, but affects only the *remedy* it may obtain if it wins. Whereas "Rule 23 governs procedural aspects of class litigation" by "prescrib[ing] the considerations relevant to class certification and postcertification proceedings," §901(b) addresses only "the size of a monetary award a class plaintiff may pursue." Accordingly, the dissent says, Rule 23 and New York's law may coexist in peace.

We need not decide whether a state law that limits the remedies available in an existing class action would conflict with Rule 23; that is not what §901(b) does. By its terms, the provision precludes a plaintiff from "maintain[ing]" a class action seeking statutory penalties. Unlike a law that sets a ceiling on damages (or puts other remedies out of reach) in properly filed class actions, §901(b) says nothing about what remedies a court may award; it prevents the class actions it covers from coming into existence at all.[4] Consequently, a court bound by §901(b) could not certify a class action seeking both statutory penalties and other remedies even if it announces in advance that it will refuse to award the penalties in the event the plaintiffs prevail; to do so would violate the statute's clear prohibition on "maintain[ing]" such suits as class actions.

The dissent asserts that a plaintiff can avoid §901(b)'s barrier by omitting from his complaint (or removing) a request for statutory penalties. Even assuming all statutory penalties are waivable, the fact that a complaint omitting them could be brought as a class action would not at all prove that §901(b) is addressed only to remedies. If the state law instead banned class actions for fraud claims, a would-be class-action plaintiff could drop the fraud counts from his complaint and proceed with the remainder in a class action. Yet that would not mean the law provides no remedy for fraud; the ban would affect only the procedural means by which the remedy may be pursued. In short, although the dissent correctly abandons Allstate's eligibility-certifiability distinction, the alternative it offers fares no better.

---

4. Contrary to the dissent's implication, we express no view as to whether state laws that set a ceiling on damages recoverable in a single suit are pre-empted. Whether or not those laws conflict with Rule 23, §901(b) does conflict because it addresses not the remedy, but the procedural right to maintain a class action. . . .

The dissent all but admits that the literal terms of §901(b) address the same subject as Rule 23 — *i.e.*, whether a class action may be maintained — but insists the provision's *purpose* is to restrict only remedies ("[W]hile phrased as responsive to the question whether certain class actions may begin, §901(b) is unmistakably aimed at controlling how those actions must end"). Unlike Rule 23, designed to further procedural fairness and efficiency, §901(b) (we are told) "responds to an entirely different concern": the fear that allowing statutory damages to be awarded on a class-wide basis would "produce overkill." The dissent reaches this conclusion on the basis of (1) constituent concern recorded in the law's bill jacket; (2) a commentary suggesting that the Legislature "apparently fear[ed]" that combining class actions and statutory penalties "could result in annihilating punishment of the defendant," . . . (3) a remark by the Governor in his signing statement that §901(b) "'provides a controlled remedy,'" . . . and (4) a state court's statement that the final text of §901(b) "'was the result of a compromise among competing interests,'" . . .

This evidence of the New York Legislature's purpose is pretty sparse. But even accepting the dissent's account of the Legislature's objective at face value, it cannot override the statute's clear text. Even if its aim is to restrict the remedy a plaintiff can obtain, §901(b) achieves that end by limiting a plaintiff's power to maintain a class action. The manner in which the law "could have been written," has no bearing; what matters is the law the Legislature *did* enact. We cannot rewrite that to reflect our perception of legislative purpose, see *Oncale v. Sundowner Offshore Services, Inc.*, 523 U.S. 75, 79-80, (1998).[6] The dissent's concern for state prerogatives is frustrated rather than furthered by revising state laws when a potential conflict with a Federal Rule arises; the state-friendly approach would be to accept the law as written and test the validity of the Federal Rule.

The dissent's approach of determining whether state and federal rules conflict based on the subjective intentions of the state legislature is an enterprise destined to produce "confusion worse confounded," *Sibbach v. Wilson & Co.*, 312 U.S. 1, 14 (1941). It would mean, to begin with, that one State's statute could survive pre-emption (and accordingly affect the procedures in federal court) while another State's identical law would not, merely because its authors had different aspirations. It would also mean that district courts would have to discern, in every diversity case,

---

6. Our decision in *Walker v. Armco Steel Corp.*, 446 U.S. 740 (1980), discussed by the dissent, *post* at 1462-1463, 1466-1467, n. 8, is not to the contrary. There we held that Rule 3 (which provides that a federal civil action is "'commenced'" by filing a complaint in federal court) did not displace a state law providing that "'[a]n action shall be deemed commenced, *within the meaning of this article [the statute of limitations]*, as to each defendant, at the date of the summons which is served on him. . . .'" 446 U.S. at 743, n. 4 (quoting Okla. Stat., Tit. 12, §97 (1971); alteration in original, emphasis added). Rule 3, we explained, "governs the date from which various timing requirements of the Federal Rules begin to run, but does not affect state statutes of limitations" or tolling rules, which it did not "purpor[t] to displace." 446 U.S. at 751, 750. The texts were therefore not in conflict. While our opinion observed that the State's actual-service rule was (in the State's judgment) an "integral part of the several policies served by the statute of limitations," *id.* at 751, nothing in our decision suggested that a federal court may resolve an obvious conflict between the texts of state and federal rules by resorting to the state law's ostensible objectives.

the purpose behind any putatively pre-empted state procedural rule, even if its text squarely conflicts with federal law. That task will often prove arduous. Many laws further more than one aim, and the aim of others may be impossible to discern. Moreover, to the extent the dissent's purpose-driven approach depends on its characterization of §901(b)'s aims as substantive, it would apply to many state rules ostensibly addressed to procedure. Pleading standards, for example, often embody policy preferences about the types of claims that should succeed—as do rules governing summary judgment, pretrial discovery, and the admissibility of certain evidence. Hard cases will abound. It is not even clear that a state supreme court's pronouncement of the law's purpose would settle the issue, since existence of the factual predicate for avoiding federal pre-emption is ultimately a federal question. Predictably, federal judges would be condemned to poring through state legislative history—which may be less easily obtained, less thorough, and less familiar than its federal counterpart.

But while the dissent does indeed artificially narrow the scope of §901(b) by finding that it pursues only substantive policies, that is not the central difficulty of the dissent's position. The central difficulty is that even artificial narrowing cannot render §901(b) compatible with Rule 23. *Whatever* the policies they pursue, they flatly contradict each other. Allstate asserts (and the dissent implies) that we can (and must) *interpret* Rule 23 in a manner that avoids overstepping its authorizing statute.[7] If the Rule were susceptible of two meanings—one that would violate §2072(b) and another that would not—we would agree. See *Ortiz v. Fibreboard Corp.*, 527 U.S. 815, 842 (1999); cf. *Semtek Int'l Inc. v. Lockheed Martin Corp.*, 531 U.S. 497, 503-504 (2001). But it is not. Rule 23 unambiguously authorizes *any* plaintiff, in *any* federal civil proceeding, to maintain a class action if the Rule's prerequisites are met. We cannot contort its text, even to avert a collision with state law that might render it invalid. See *Walker v. Armco Steel Corp.*, 446 U.S. 740, 750, n. 9.[8] What the dissent's approach achieves is not the avoiding of a "conflict between Rule 23

---

7. The dissent also suggests that we should read the Federal Rules "'with sensitivity to important state interests'" and "'to avoid conflict with important state regulatory policies.'" (quoting *Gasperini v. Center for Humanities, Inc.*, 518 U.S. 415, 427, n. 7 (1996)). The search for state interests and policies that are "important" is just as standardless as the "important or substantial" criterion we rejected in *Sibbach v. Wilson & Co.*, 312 U.S. 1, 13-14 (1941), to define the state-created rights a Federal Rule may not abridge.

If all the dissent means is that we should read an ambiguous Federal Rule to avoid "substantial variations [in outcomes] between state and federal litigation," *Semtek Int'l Inc. v. Lockheed Martin Corp.*, 531 U.S. 497, 504 (2001) (internal quotation marks omitted), we entirely agree. We should do so not to avoid doubt as to the Rule's validity—since a Federal Rule that fails *Erie*'s forum-shopping test is not *ipso facto* invalid, . . . —but because it is reasonable to assume that "Congress is just as concerned as we have been to avoid significant differences between state and federal courts in adjudicating claims," *Stewart Organization, Inc. v. Ricoh Corp.*, 487 U.S. 22, 37-38 (1988) (SCALIA, J., dissenting). The assumption is irrelevant here, however, because there is only one reasonable reading of Rule 23.

8. The cases chronicled by the dissent each involved a Federal Rule that we concluded could fairly be read not to "control the issue" addressed by the pertinent state law, thus avoiding a "direct collision" between federal and state law, *Walker*, 446 U.S. at 749 (internal quotation marks omitted). But here, as in *Hanna, supra* at 470, a collision is "unavoidable."

and §901(b), but rather the invalidation of Rule 23 (pursuant to §2072(b) of the Rules Enabling Act) to the extent that it conflicts with the substantive policies of §901. There is no other way to reach the dissent's destination. We must therefore confront head-on whether Rule 23 falls within the statutory authorization.

B

Erie involved the constitutional power of federal courts to supplant state law with judge-made rules. In that context, it made no difference whether the rule was technically one of substance or procedure; the touchstone was whether it "significantly affect[s] the result of a litigation." *Guaranty Trust Co. v. York*, 326 U.S. 99, 109 (1945). That is not the test for either the constitutionality or the statutory validity of a Federal Rule of Procedure. Congress has undoubted power to supplant state law, and undoubted power to prescribe rules for the courts it has created, so long as those rules regulate matters "rationally capable of classification" as procedure. *Hanna*, 380 U.S. at 472. In the Rules Enabling Act, Congress authorized this Court to promulgate rules of procedure subject to its review, 28 U.S.C. §2072(a), but with the limitation that those rules "shall not abridge, enlarge or modify any substantive right," §2072(b).

We have long held that this limitation means that the Rule must "really regulat[e] procedure — the judicial process for enforcing rights and duties recognized by substantive law and for justly administering remedy and redress for disregard or infraction of them," *Sibbach*, 312 U.S. at 14; see *Hanna*, *supra* at 464; *Burlington*, 480 U.S. at 8. The test is not whether the rule affects a litigant's substantive rights; most procedural rules do. *Mississippi Publishing Corp. v. Murphree*, 326 U.S. 438, 445 (1946). What matters is what the rule itself regulates: If it governs only "the manner and the means" by which the litigants' rights are "enforced," it is valid; if it alters "the rules of decision by which [the] court will adjudicate [those] rights," it is not. *Id.* at 446 (internal quotation marks omitted).

Applying that test, we have rejected every statutory challenge to a Federal Rule that has come before us. We have found to be in compliance with §2072(b) rules prescribing methods for serving process . . . (Fed. Rule Civ. Proc. 4(f)); *Hanna*, *supra* at 463-465 . . . , and requiring litigants whose mental or physical condition is in dispute to submit to examinations, see *Sibbach*, *supra* at 14-16. . . . Likewise, we have upheld rules authorizing imposition of sanctions upon those who file frivolous appeals, see *Burlington*, *supra* at 8, (Fed. Rule App. Proc. 38), or who sign court papers without a reasonable inquiry into the facts asserted, see *Business Guides, Inc. v. Chromatic Communications Enterprises, Inc.*, 498 U.S. 533, 551-554 (1991) (Fed. Rule Civ. Proc. 11). Each of these rules had some practical effect on the parties' rights, but each undeniably regulated only the process for enforcing those rights; none altered the rights themselves, the available remedies, or the rules of decision by which the court adjudicated either.

Applying that criterion, we think it obvious that rules allowing multiple claims (and claims by or against multiple parties) to be litigated together are also valid. See, *e.g.*, Fed. Rules Civ. Proc. 18 (joinder of claims), 20 (joinder of parties), 42(a) (consolidation of actions). Such rules neither change plaintiffs' separate entitlements to relief nor abridge defendants' rights; they alter only how the claims are processed. For the same reason, Rule 23 — at least insofar as it allows willing plaintiffs to join their separate claims against the same defendants in a class action — falls within §2072(b)'s authorization. A class action, no less than traditional joinder (of which it is a species), merely enables a federal court to adjudicate claims of multiple parties at once, instead of in separate suits. And like traditional joinder, it leaves the parties' legal rights and duties intact and the rules of decision unchanged.

Allstate contends that the authorization of class actions is not substantively neutral: Allowing Shady Grove to sue on behalf of a class "transform[s][the] dispute over a five *hundred* dollar penalty into a dispute over a five *million* dollar penalty." Allstate's aggregate liability, however, does not depend on whether the suit proceeds as a class action. Each of the 1,000-plus members of the putative class could (as Allstate acknowledges) bring a freestanding suit asserting his individual claim. It is undoubtedly true that some plaintiffs who would not bring individual suits for the relatively small sums involved will choose to join a class action. That has no bearing, however, on Allstate's or the plaintiffs' legal rights. The likelihood that some (even many) plaintiffs will be induced to sue by the availability of a class action is just the sort of "incidental effec[t]" we have long held does not violate §2072(b), *Mississippi Publishing, supra* at 445.

Allstate argues that Rule 23 violates §2072(b) because the state law it displaces, §901(b), creates a right that the Federal Rule abridges—namely, a "substantive right . . . not to be subjected to aggregated class-action liability" in a single suit. To begin with, we doubt that that is so. Nothing in the text of §901(b) (which is to be found in New York's procedural code) confines it to claims under New York law; and of course New York has no power to alter substantive rights and duties created by other sovereigns. As we have said, the *consequence* of excluding certain class actions may be to cap the damages a defendant can face in a single suit, but the law itself alters only procedure. In that respect, §901(b) is no different from a state law forbidding simple joinder. As a fallback argument, Allstate argues that even if §901(b) is a procedural provision, it was enacted "for *substantive reasons.*" Its end was not to improve "the conduct of the litigation process itself" but to alter "the outcome of that process."

The fundamental difficulty with both these arguments is that the substantive nature of New York's law, or its substantive purpose, *makes no difference.* A Federal Rule of Procedure is not valid in some jurisdictions and invalid in others—or valid in some cases and invalid in others—depending upon whether its effect is to frustrate a state substantive law (or a state procedural law enacted for substantive purposes). That could not be clearer in *Sibbach:*

> The petitioner says the phrase ["substantive rights" in the Rules Enabling Act] connotes more; that by its use Congress intended that in regulating procedure this Court should not deal with important and substantial rights theretofore recognized. Recognized where and by whom? The state courts are divided as to the power in the absence of statute to order a physical examination. In a number such an order is authorized by statute or rule. . . .
>
> The asserted right, moreover, is no more important than many others enjoyed by litigants in District Courts sitting in the several states before the Federal Rules of Civil Procedure altered and abolished old rights or privileges and created new ones in connection with the conduct of litigation. . . . If we were to adopt the suggested criterion of the importance of the alleged right we should invite endless litigation and confusion worse confounded. The test must be whether a rule really regulates procedure. . . . 312 U.S. at 13-14 (footnotes omitted).

Hanna unmistakably expressed the same understanding that compliance of a Federal Rule with the Enabling Act is to be assessed by consulting the Rule itself, and not its effects in individual applications:

> [T]he court has been instructed to apply the Federal Rule, and can refuse to do so only if the Advisory Committee, this Court, and Congress erred in their prima facie judgment that the Rule in question transgresses neither the terms of the Enabling Act nor constitutional restrictions. 380 U.S. at 471.

In sum, it is not the substantive or procedural nature or purpose of the affected state law that matters, but the substantive or procedural nature of the Federal Rule. We have held since *Sibbach*, and reaffirmed repeatedly, that the validity of a Federal Rule depends entirely upon whether it regulates procedure. . . . If it does, it is authorized by §2072 and is valid in all jurisdictions, with respect to all claims, regardless of its incidental effect upon state-created rights.

C

A few words in response to the concurrence. We understand it to accept the framework we apply—which requires first, determining whether the federal and state rules can be reconciled (because they answer different questions), and second, if they cannot, determining whether the Federal Rule runs afoul of §2072(b). (Stevens, J., concurring in part and concurring in judgment). The concurrence agrees with us that Rule 23 and §901(b) conflict, and departs from us only with respect to the second part of the test, *i.e.*, whether application of the Federal Rule violates §2072(b). Like us, it answers no, but for a reason different from ours.

The concurrence would decide this case on the basis, not that Rule 23 is procedural, but that the state law it displaces is procedural, in the sense that it does not "function as a part of the State's definition of substantive rights and remedies." A state procedural rule is not preempted, according to the concurrence, so long as it is "so bound up with," or "sufficiently intertwined with," a substantive state-law right or remedy "that it defines the scope of that substantive right or remedy."

This analysis squarely conflicts with *Sibbach*, which established the rule we apply. The concurrence contends that *Sibbach* did not rule out its approach, but that is not so. Recognizing the impracticability of a test that turns on the idiosyncrasies of state law, *Sibbach* adopted and applied a rule with a single criterion: whether the Federal Rule "really regulates procedure." 312 U.S. at 14. That the concurrence's approach would have yielded the same result in *Sibbach* proves nothing; what matters is the rule we *did* apply, and that rule leaves no room for special exemptions based on the function or purpose of a particular state rule.[10] We have rejected an attempt to read into *Sibbach* an exception with no basis in the opinion, see . . . and we see no reason to find such an implied limitation today.

---

10. The concurrence insists that we have misread *Sibbach*, since surely a Federal Rule that "in most cases" regulates procedure does not do so when it displaces one of those "rare" state substantive laws that are disguised as rules of procedure. This mistakes what the Federal Rule *regulates* for its incidental *effects*. As we have explained, most Rules have some effect on litigants' substantive rights or their ability to obtain a remedy, but that does not mean the Rule itself regulates those rights or remedies.

In reality, the concurrence seeks not to apply *Sibbach*, but to overrule it (or, what is the same, to rewrite it). Its approach, the concurrence insists, gives short shrift to the statutory text forbidding the Federal Rules from "abridg[ing], enlarg[ing], or modify[ing] any substantive right," §2072(b). There is something to that. It is possible to understand how it can be determined whether a Federal Rule "enlarges" substantive rights without consulting State law: If the Rule creates a substantive right, even one that duplicates some state-created rights, it establishes a new *federal* right. But it is hard to understand how it can be determined whether a Federal Rule "abridges" or "modifies" substantive rights without knowing what state-created rights would obtain if the Federal Rule did not exist. *Sibbach*'s exclusive focus on the challenged Federal Rule—driven by the very real concern that Federal Rules which vary from State to State would be chaos . . . is hard to square with §2072(b)'s terms.[11]

Sibbach has been settled law, however, for nearly seven decades. Setting aside any precedent requires a "special justification" beyond a bare belief that it was wrong. . . . And a party seeking to overturn a *statutory* precedent bears an even greater burden, since Congress remains free to correct us, and adhering to our precedent enables it do so, . . . We do Congress no service by presenting it a moving target. In all events, Allstate has not even asked us to overrule *Sibbach*, let alone carried its burden of persuading us to do so. Why we should cast aside our decades-old decision escapes us, especially since (as the concurrence explains) that would not affect the result.[13]

The concurrence also contends that applying *Sibbach* and assessing whether a Federal Rule regulates substance or procedure is not always easy. Undoubtedly some hard cases will arise (though we have managed to muddle through

---

11. The concurrence's approach, however, is itself unfaithful to the statute's terms. Section 2072(b) bans abridgement or modification only of "substantive rights," but the concurrence would prohibit pre-emption of "procedural rules that are intimately bound up in the scope of a substantive right or remedy." This would allow States to force a wide array of parochial procedures on federal courts so long as they are "sufficiently intertwined with a state right or remedy."

13. The concurrence is correct that under our disposition any rule that "really regulates procedure," *Sibbach, supra* at 14, will pre-empt a conflicting state rule, however "bound up" the latter is with substantive law. The concurrence is wrong, however, that that result proves our interpretation of §2072(b) implausible. The result is troubling only if one stretches the term "substantive rights" in §2072(b) to mean not only state-law rights themselves, but also any state-law procedures closely connected to them. Neither the text nor our precedent supports that expansive interpretation. The examples the concurrence offers—statutes of limitations, burdens of proof, and standards for appellate review of damages awards—do not make its broad definition of substantive rights more persuasive. They merely illustrate that in rare cases it may be difficult to determine whether a rule "really regulates" procedure or substance. If one concludes the latter, there is no pre-emption of the state rule; the Federal Rule itself is invalid.

The concurrence's concern would make more sense if many Federal Rules that effectively alter state-law rights "bound up with procedures" would survive under *Sibbach*. But as the concurrence concedes, very few would do so. The possible existence of a few outlier instances does not prove *Sibbach*'s interpretation is absurd. Congress may well have accepted such anomalies as the price of a uniform system of federal procedure.

well enough in the 69 years since *Sibbach* was decided). But as the concurrence acknowledges, the basic difficulty is unavoidable: The statute itself refers to "substantive right[s]," §2072(b), so there is no escaping the substance-procedure distinction. What is more, the concurrence's approach does nothing to diminish the difficulty, but rather magnifies it many times over. Instead of a single hard question of whether a Federal Rule regulates substance or procedure, that approach will present hundreds of hard questions, forcing federal courts to assess the substantive or procedural character of countless state rules that may conflict with a single Federal Rule.[14] And it still does not sidestep the problem it seeks to avoid. At the end of the day, one must come face to face with the decision whether or not the state policy (with which a putatively procedural state rule may be "bound up") pertains to a "substantive right or remedy — that is, whether it is substance or procedure.[15] The more one explores the alternatives to *Sibbach*'s rule, the more its wisdom becomes apparent.

D

We must acknowledge the reality that keeping the federal-court door open to class actions that cannot proceed in state court will produce forum shopping. That is unacceptable when it comes as the consequence of judge-made rules created to fill supposed "gaps" in positive federal law. . . . For where neither the Constitution, a treaty, nor a statute provides the rule of decision or authorizes a federal court to supply one, "state law must govern because there can be no other law." . . . But divergence from state law, with the attendant consequence of forum shopping, is the inevitable (indeed, one might say the intended) result of a uniform system of federal procedure. Congress itself has created the possibility that the same case may follow a different course if filed in federal instead of state court. . . . The short of the matter is that a Federal Rule governing procedure is valid whether or not it alters the outcome of the case in a way that induces forum shopping. To hold otherwise would be to "disembowel either the Constitution's grant of power over federal procedure" or Congress's exercise of it.

. . .

The judgment of the Court of Appeals is reversed, and the case is remanded for further proceedings.

It is so ordered.

---

14. The concurrence argues that its approach is no more "taxing" than ours because few if any Federal Rules that are "facially valid" under the Enabling Act will fail the concurrence's test. But that conclusion will be reached only after federal courts have considered hundreds of state rules applying the concurrence's inscrutable standard.

15. The concurrence insists that the task will be easier if courts can "conside[r] the nature and functions of the state law," regardless of the law's "form," (emphasis deleted), *i.e.*, what the law actually says. We think that amorphous inquiry into the "nature and functions" of a state law will tend to increase, rather than decrease, the difficulty of classifying Federal Rules as substantive or procedural. Walking through the concurrence's application of its test to §901(b) gives little reason to hope that its approach will lighten the burden for lower courts.

JUSTICE STEVENS, concurring in part and concurring in the judgment.

The New York law at issue, N.Y. Civ. Prac. Law Ann. (CPLR) §901(b), is a procedural rule that is not part of New York's substantive law. Accordingly, I agree with JUSTICE SCALIA that Federal Rule of Civil Procedure 23 must apply in this case and join Parts I and II-A of the Court's opinion. But I also agree with JUSTICE GINSBURG that there are some state procedural rules that federal courts must apply in diversity cases because they function as a part of the State's definition of substantive rights and remedies.

I

It is a long-recognized principle that federal courts sitting in diversity "apply state substantive law and federal procedural law." *Hanna v. Plumer*, 380 U.S. 460 (1965). This principle is governed by a statutory framework, and the way that it is administered varies depending upon whether there is a federal rule addressed to the matter. . . . If no federal rule applies, a federal court must follow the Rules of Decision Act, 28 U.S.C. §1652, and make the "relatively unguided *Erie* choice," *Hanna*, 380 U.S. at 471, to determine whether the state law is the "rule of decision." But when a situation is covered by a federal rule, the Rules of Decision Act inquiry by its own terms does not apply. See §1652; *Hanna*, 380 U.S. at 471. Instead, the Rules Enabling Act (Enabling Act) controls. See 28 U.S.C. §2072.

That does not mean, however, that the federal rule always governs. Congress has provided for a system of uniform federal rules under which federal courts sitting in diversity operate as "an independent system for administering justice to litigants who properly invoke its jurisdiction," *Byrd v. Blue Ridge Rural Elec. Cooperative, Inc.*, 356 U.S. 525, 537 (1958), and not as state-court clones that assume all aspects of state tribunals but are managed by Article III judges. See *Hanna*, 380 U.S. at 473-474. But while Congress may have the constitutional power to prescribe procedural rules that interfere with state substantive law in any number of respects, that is not what Congress has done. Instead, it has provided in the Enabling Act that although "[t]he Supreme Court" may "prescribe general rules of practice and procedure," §2072(a), those rules "shall not abridge, enlarge or modify any substantive right," §2072(b). Therefore, "[w]hen a situation is covered by one of the Federal Rules, . . . the court has been instructed to apply the Federal Rule" unless doing so would violate the Act or the Constitution. *Hanna*, 380 U.S. at 471.

Although the Enabling Act and the Rules of Decision Act "say, roughly, that federal courts are to apply state 'substantive' law and federal 'procedural' law," the inquiries are not the same. *Ibid.* . . . The Enabling Act does not invite federal courts to engage in the "relatively unguided *Erie* choice, but instead instructs only that federal rules cannot "abridge, enlarge or modify any substantive right," §2072(b). The Enabling Act's limitation does not mean that federal rules cannot displace state policy judgments; it means only that federal rules cannot displace a State's definition of its own rights or remedies. See *Sibbach v. Wilson & Co.*, 312 U.S. 1, 13-14 (1941) (reasoning that "the phrase 'substantive rights'" embraces only those state rights that are sought to be enforced in the judicial proceedings).

Congress has thus struck a balance: "[H]ousekeeping rules for federal courts" will generally apply in diversity cases, notwithstanding that some federal rules "will inevitably differ" from state rules. . . . But not every federal "rul[e] of practice or procedure,"

§2072(a), will displace state law. To the contrary, federal rules must be interpreted with some degree of "sensitivity to important state interests and regulatory policies," *Gasperini v. Center for Humanities, Inc.*, 518 U.S. 415, 427, n. 7 (1996), and applied to diversity cases against the background of Congress' command that such rules not alter substantive rights and with consideration of "the degree to which the Rule makes the character and result of the federal litigation stray from the course it would follow in state courts," *Hanna*, 380 U.S. at 473. This can be a tricky balance to implement.

It is important to observe that the balance Congress has struck turns, in part, on the nature of the state law that is being displaced by a federal rule. And in my view, the application of that balance does not necessarily turn on whether the state law at issue takes the *form* of what is traditionally described as substantive or procedural. Rather, it turns on whether the state law actually is part of a State's framework of substantive rights or remedies. . . .

Applying this balance, therefore, requires careful interpretation of the state and federal provisions at issue. "The line between procedural and substantive law is hazy," *Erie R. Co. v. Tompkins*, 304 U.S. 64, 92 (1938) (Reed, J., concurring), and matters of procedure and matters of substance are not "mutually exclusive categories with easily ascertainable contents," *Sibbach*, 312 U.S. at 17 (Frankfurter, J., dissenting). Rather, "[r]ules which lawyers call procedural do not always exhaust their effect by regulating procedure," *Cohen v. Beneficial Industrial Loan Corp.*, 337 U.S. 541, 555 (1949), and in some situations, "procedure and substance are so interwoven that rational separation becomes well-nigh impossible," *id.* at 559 (Rutledge, J., dissenting). A "state procedural rule, though undeniably 'procedural' in the ordinary sense of the term," may exist "to influence substantive outcomes," *S.A. Healy Co. v. Milwaukee Metropolitan Sewerage Dist.*, 60 F.3d 305, 310 (C.A.7 1995) (Posner, J.), and may in some instances become so bound up with the state-created right or remedy that it defines the scope of that substantive right or remedy. Such laws, for example, may be seemingly procedural rules that make it significantly more difficult to bring or to prove a claim, thus serving to limit the scope of that claim. See, *e.g.*, *Cohen*, 337 U.S. at 555 (state "procedure" that required plaintiffs to post bond before suing); *Guaranty Trust Co.*, 326 U.S. 99 (state statute of limitations). Such "procedural rules" may also define the amount of recovery. See, *e.g.*, *Gasperini*, 518 U.S. at 427 (state procedure for examining jury verdicts as means of capping the available remedy) . . .

In our federalist system, Congress has not mandated that federal courts dictate to state legislatures the form that their substantive law must take. And were federal courts to ignore those portions of substantive state law that operate as procedural devices, it could in many instances limit the ways that sovereign States may define their rights and remedies. When a State chooses to use a traditionally procedural vehicle as a means of defining the scope of substantive rights or remedies, federal courts must recognize and respect that choice. . . .

II

When both a federal rule and a state law appear to govern a question before a federal court sitting in diversity, our precedents have set out a two-step framework for federal courts to negotiate this thorny area. At both steps of the inquiry, there is a critical question about what the state law and the federal rule mean.

The court must first determine whether the scope of the federal rule is "'sufficiently broad'" to "'control the issue'" before the court, "thereby leaving no room for the operation" of seemingly conflicting state law. . . . If the federal rule does not apply or can operate alongside the state rule, then there is no "Ac[t] of Congress" governing that particular question, 28 U.S.C. §1652, and the court must engage in the traditional Rules of Decision Act inquiry under *Erie* and its progeny. In some instances, the "plain meaning" of a federal rule will not come into "'direct collision'" with the state law, and both can operate. *Walker*, 446 U.S. at 750, n. 9, 749. In other instances, the rule "when fairly construed," *Burlington Northern R. Co.*, 480 U.S. at 4, with "sensitivity to important state interests and regulatory policies," *Gasperini*, 518 U.S. at 427, will not collide with the state law.

If, on the other hand, the federal rule is "sufficiently broad to control the issue before the Court," such that there is a "direct collision," *Walker*, 446 U.S. at 749-750, the court must decide whether application of the federal rule "represents a valid exercise" of the "rulemaking authority . . . bestowed on this Court by the Rules Enabling Act." . . . That Act requires, *inter alia*, that federal rules "not abridge, enlarge or modify *any* substantive right." 28 U.S.C. §2072(b) (emphasis added). Unlike JUSTICE SCALIA, I believe that an application of a federal rule that effectively abridges, enlarges, or modifies a state-created right or remedy violates this command. Congress may have the constitutional power "to supplant state law" with rules that are "rationally capable of classification as procedure," but we should generally presume that it has not done so. . . . Indeed, the mandate that federal rules "shall not abridge, enlarge or modify any substantive right" evinces the opposite intent, as does Congress' decision to delegate the creation of rules to this Court rather than to a political branch. . . .

Thus, the second step of the inquiry may well bleed back into the first. When a federal rule appears to abridge, enlarge, or modify a substantive right, federal courts must consider whether the rule can reasonably be interpreted to avoid that impermissible result. . . . And when such a "saving" construction is not possible and the rule would violate the Enabling Act, federal courts cannot apply the rule. See 28 U.S.C. §2072(b) (mandating that federal rules "shall not" alter "*any* substantive right" (emphasis added)); *Hanna*, 380 U.S. at 473 ("[A] court, in measuring a Federal Rule against the standards contained in the Enabling Act . . . need not wholly blind itself to the degree to which the Rule makes the character and result of the federal litigation stray from the course it would follow in state courts"); see also *Semtek Int'l Inc.*, 531 U.S. at 503-504 (noting that if state law granted a particular right, "the federal court's extinguishment of that right . . . would seem to violate [§2072(b)]"); cf. Statement of Justices Black and Douglas, 374 U.S. 865, 870 (1963) (observing that federal rules "as applied in given situations might have to be declared invalid"). A federal rule, therefore, cannot govern a particular case in which the rule would displace a state law that is procedural in the ordinary use of the term but is so intertwined with a state right or remedy that it functions to define the scope of the state-created right. And absent a governing federal rule, a federal court must engage in the traditional Rules of Decision Act inquiry, under the *Erie* line of cases. This application of the Enabling Act shows "sensitivity to important state interests," and "regulatory policies," but it does so as Congress authorized, by ensuring that federal rules that ordinarily "prescribe general rules of practice and procedure," §2072(a), do "not abridge, enlarge or modify any substantive right," §2072(b).

JUSTICE SCALIA believes that the sole Enabling Act question is whether the federal rule "really regulates procedure," which means, apparently, whether it regulates "the manner and the means by which the litigants' rights are enforced."

I respectfully disagree. This interpretation of the Enabling Act is consonant with the Act's first limitation to "general rules of practice and procedure," §2072(a). But it ignores the second limitation that such rules also "not abridge, enlarge or modify *any* substantive right," §2072(b) (emphasis added),[8] and in so doing ignores the balance that Congress struck between uniform rules of federal procedure and respect for a State's construction of its own rights and remedies. It also ignores the separation-of-powers presumption, . . . and federalism presumption, . . . that counsel against judicially created rules displacing state substantive law.[9]

---

8. JUSTICE SCALIA concedes as much, but argues that insofar as I allow for the possibility that a federal rule might violate the Enabling Act when it displaces a seemingly procedural state rule, my approach is itself "unfaithful to the statute's terms," which cover "substantive rights" but not "procedural rules." This is not an objection to my interpretation of the Enabling Act—that courts must look to whether a federal rule alters substantive rights in a given case—but simply to the way I would apply it, allowing for the possibility that a state rule that regulates something traditionally considered to be procedural might actually define a substantive right. JUSTICE SCALIA's objection, moreover, misses the key point: In some instances, a state rule that appears procedural really is not. A rule about how damages are reviewed on appeal may really be a damages cap. See *Gasperini*, 518 U.S. at 427. A rule that a plaintiff can bring a claim for only three years may really be a limit on the existence of the right to seek redress. A rule that a claim must be proved beyond a reasonable doubt may really be a definition of the scope of the claim. These are the sorts of rules that one might describe as "procedural," but they nonetheless define substantive rights. Thus, if a federal rule displaced such a state rule, the federal rule would have altered the State's "substantive rights."

9. The plurality's interpretation of the Enabling Act appears to mean that no matter how bound up a state provision is with the State's own rights or remedies, any contrary federal rule that happens to regulate "the manner and the means by which the litigants' rights are enforced," must govern. There are many ways in which seemingly procedural rules may displace a State's formulation of its substantive law. For example, statutes of limitations, although in some sense procedural rules, can also be understood as a temporal limitation on legally created rights; if this Court were to promulgate a federal limitations period, federal courts would still, in some instances, be required to apply state limitations periods. Similarly, if the federal rules altered the burden of proof in a case, this could eviscerate a critical aspect—albeit one that deals with *how* a right is enforced—of a State's framework of rights and remedies. Or if a federal rule about appellate review displaced a state rule about how damages are reviewed on appeal, the federal rule might be pre-empting a state damages cap. Cf. *Gasperini*, 518 U.S. at 427.

JUSTICE SCALIA responds that some of these federal rules might be invalid under his view of the Enabling Act because they may not "really regulat[e] procedure." This response, of course, highlights how empty the plurality's test really is. The response is also limited to those rules that can be described as "regulat[ing]" substance; it does not address those federal rules that alter the right at issue in the litigation, see *Sibbach v. Wilson & Co.*, 312 U.S. 1, 13-14 (1941), only when they displace particular state laws. JUSTICE SCALIA speculates that "Congress may well have accepted" the occasional alteration of substantive rights "as the price of a uniform system of federal procedure." Were we forced to speculate about the balance that Congress struck, I might very well agree. But no speculation is necessary because Congress explicitly told us that federal rules "shall not" alter "any" substantive right. §2072(b).

Although the plurality appears to agree with much of my interpretation of §2072, it nonetheless rejects that approach for two reasons, both of which are mistaken. First, JUSTICE SCALIA worries that if federal courts inquire into the effect of federal rules on state law, it will enmesh federal courts in difficult determinations about whether application of a given rule would displace a state determination about substantive rights. I do not see why an Enabling Act inquiry that looks to state law necessarily is more taxing than JUSTICE SCALIA's.[10] But in any event, that inquiry is what the Enabling Act requires: While it may not be easy to decide what is actually a "substantive right," "the designations substantive and procedural become important, for the Enabling Act has made them so." The question, therefore, is not what rule *we* think would be easiest on federal courts. The question is what rule Congress established. Although, JUSTICE SCALIA may generally prefer easily administrable, bright-line rules, his preference does not give us license to adopt a second-best interpretation of the Rules Enabling Act. Courts cannot ignore text and context in the service of simplicity.

Second, the plurality argues that its interpretation of the Enabling Act is dictated by this Court's decision in *Sibbach*, which applied a Federal Rule about when parties must submit to medical examinations. But the plurality misreads that opinion. As Justice Harlan observed in *Hanna*, "shorthand formulations which have appeared in earlier opinions are prone to carry untoward results that frequently arise from oversimplification." 380 U.S. at 475 (concurring opinion). To understand *Sibbach*, it is first necessary to understand the issue that was before the Court. The petitioner raised only the facial question whether "Rules 35 and 37 [of the Federal Rules of Civil Procedure] are . . . within the mandate of Congress to this court" and not the specific question of "the obligation of federal courts to apply the substantive law of a state." 312 U.S. at 9. The Court, therefore, had no occasion to consider whether the particular application of the Federal Rules in question would offend the Enabling Act.

Nor, in *Sibbach*, was any further analysis necessary to the resolution of the case because the matter at issue, requiring medical exams for litigants, did not pertain to "substantive rights" under the Enabling Act. Although most state rules bearing on the litigation process are adopted for some policy reason, few seemingly "procedural" rules define the scope of a substantive right or remedy. The matter at issue in *Sibbach* reflected competing federal and state judgments about privacy interests. Those privacy concerns may have been weighty and in some sense substantive; but they did not pertain to the scope of any state right or remedy at issue in the litigation. Thus, in response to the petitioner's argument in *Sibbach* that "substantive rights" include not only "rights sought to be adjudicated by the litigants" but also

---

10. It will be rare that a federal rule that is facially valid under 28 U.S.C. §2072 will displace a State's definition of its own substantive rights. . . . JUSTICE SCALIA's interpretation, moreover, is not much more determinative than mine. Although it avoids courts' having to evaluate state law, it tasks them with figuring out whether a federal rule is really "procedural." It is hard to know the answer to that question and especially hard to resolve it without considering the nature and functions of the state law that the federal rule will displace. The plurality's "'test' is no test at all-in a sense, it is little more than the statement that a matter is procedural if, by revelation, it is procedural."

"general principle[s]" or "question[s] of public policy that the legislature is able to pass upon," *id*. at 2-3, we held that "the phrase 'substantive rights'" embraces only state rights, such as the tort law in that case, that are sought to be enforced in the judicial proceedings. *Id*. at 13-14. If the Federal Rule had in fact displaced a state rule that was sufficiently intertwined with a state right or remedy, then perhaps the Enabling Act analysis would have been different.[13] Our subsequent cases are not to the contrary.[14]

III

JUSTICE GINSBURG views the basic issue in this case as whether and how to apply a federal rule that dictates an answer to a traditionally procedural question (whether to join plaintiffs together as a class), when a state law that "defines the dimensions" of a state-created claim dictates the opposite answer. As explained above, I readily acknowledge that if a federal rule displaces a state rule that is "'procedural' in the ordinary sense of the term," . . . but sufficiently interwoven with the scope of a substantive right or remedy, there would be an Enabling Act problem, and the federal rule would have to give way. In my view, however, this is not such a case.

Rule 23 Controls Class Certification

When the District Court in the case before us was asked to certify a class action, Federal Rule of Civil Procedure 23 squarely governed the determination whether the court should do so. That is the explicit function of Rule 23. Rule 23, therefore, must apply unless its application would abridge, enlarge, or modify New York rights or remedies.

Notwithstanding the plain language of Rule 23, I understand the dissent to find that Rule 23 does *not* govern the question of class certification in this matter because New York has made a substantive judgment that such a class should not be certified, as a means of proscribing damages. Although, as discussed *infra*, I do not accept the dissent's view of §901(b), I also do not see how the dissent's

---

13. Put another way, even if a federal rule in most cases "really regulates procedure," *Sibbach*, 312 U.S. at 14, it does not "really regulat[e] procedure" when it displaces those rare state rules that, although "procedural" in the ordinary sense of the term, operate to define the rights and remedies available in a case. This is so because what is procedural in one context may be substantive in another. . . .

14. Although this Court's decision in *Hanna* cited *Sibbach*, that is of little significance. *Hanna* did not hold that any seemingly procedural federal rule will always govern, even when it alters a substantive state right; nor, as in *Sibbach*, was the argument that I now make before the Court. Indeed, in *Hanna* we cited *Sibbach*'s statement that the Enabling Act prohibits federal rules that alter the rights to be adjudicated by the litigants, 312 U.S. at 13-14, for the proposition that "a court, in measuring a Federal Rule against the standards contained in the Enabling Act . . . need not wholly blind itself to the degree to which the Rule makes the character and result of the federal litigation stray from the course it would follow in state courts," 380 U.S. at 473. And most of our subsequent decisions that have squarely addressed the framework for applying federal rules in diversity cases have not mentioned *Sibbach* at all but cited only *Hanna*. See, *e.g.*, *Burlington Northern R. Co. v. Woods*, 480 U.S. 1, 5, (1987). . . .

interpretation of Rule 23 follows from that view.[15] I agree with JUSTICE GINSBURG that courts should "avoi[d] immoderate interpretations of the Federal Rules that would trench on state prerogatives," and should in some instances "interpre[t] the federal rules to avoid conflict with important state regulatory policies." But that is not what the dissent has done. Simply because a rule should be read in light of federalism concerns, it does not follow that courts may rewrite the rule.

At bottom, the dissent's interpretation of Rule 23 seems to be that Rule 23 covers only those cases in which its application would create no *Erie* problem. The dissent would apply the Rules of Decision Act inquiry under *Erie* even to cases in which there is a governing federal rule, and thus the Act, by its own terms, does not apply. But "[w]hen a situation is covered by one of the Federal Rules, the question facing the court is a far cry from the typical, relatively unguided *Erie* choice." *Hanna*, 380 U.S. at 471. The question is only whether the Enabling Act is satisfied. Although it reflects a laudable concern to protect "state regulatory policies, JUSTICE GINSBURG's approach would, in my view, work an end run around Congress' system of uniform federal rules, see 28 U.S.C. §2072, and our decision in *Hanna*. Federal courts can and should interpret federal rules with sensitivity to "state prerogatives"; but even when "state interests . . . warrant our respectful consideration," federal courts cannot rewrite the rules. If my dissenting colleagues feel strongly that §901(b) is substantive and that class certification should be denied, then they should argue within the Enabling Act's framework. Otherwise, "the Federal Rule applies regardless of contrary state law." *Gasperini*, 518 U.S. at 427, n. 7; accord, *Hanna*, 380 U.S. at 471.

Applying Rule 23 Does Not Violate the Enabling Act

As I have explained, in considering whether to certify a class action such as this one, a federal court must inquire whether doing so would abridge, enlarge, or modify New York's rights or remedies, and thereby violate the Enabling Act. This inquiry is not always a simple one because "[i]t is difficult to conceive of any rule of procedure that cannot have a significant effect on the outcome of a case," Wright §4508, at 232-233, and almost "any rule can be said to have . . . 'substantive effects,' affecting society's distribution of risks and rewards," Ely 724, n. 170. Faced with a federal rule that dictates an answer to a traditionally procedural question and that displaces a state rule, one can often argue that the state rule was *really* some part of the State's definition of its rights or remedies.

In my view, however, the bar for finding an Enabling Act problem is a high one. The mere fact that a state law is designed as a procedural rule suggests it reflects a judgment about how state courts ought to operate and not a judgment

---

15. Nor do I see how it follows from the dissent's premises that a class cannot be certified. The dissent contends that §901(b) is a damages "limitation," or "proscription," whereas Rule 23 "does not command that a particular remedy be available when a party sues in a representative capacity," and that consequently both provisions can apply. Yet even if the dissent's premises were correct, Rule 23 would still control the question whether petitioner may certify a class, and §901(b) would be relevant only to determine whether petitioner, at the conclusion of a class-action lawsuit, may collect statutory damages.

. . .

about the scope of state-created rights and remedies. And for the purposes of operating a federal court system, there are costs involved in attempting to discover the true nature of a state procedural rule and allowing such a rule to operate alongside a federal rule that appears to govern the same question. The mere possibility that a federal rule would alter a state-created right is not sufficient. There must be little doubt.

The text of CPLR §901(b) expressly and unambiguously applies not only to claims based on New York law but also to claims based on federal law or the law of any other State. And there is no interpretation from New York courts to the contrary. It is therefore hard to see how §901(b) could be understood as a rule that, though procedural in form, serves the function of defining New York's rights or remedies. This is all the more apparent because lawsuits under New York law could be joined in federal class actions well before New York passed §901(b) in 1975, and New York had done nothing to prevent that. It is true, as the dissent points out, that there is a limited amount of legislative history that can be read to suggest that the New York officials who supported §901(b) wished to create a "limitation" on New York's "statutory damages." But, as JUSTICE SCALIA notes, that is not the law that New York adopted.[16]

The legislative history, moreover, does not clearly describe a judgment that §901(b) would operate as a limitation on New York's statutory damages. In evaluating that legislative history, it is necessary to distinguish between procedural rules adopted for *some* policy reason and seemingly procedural rules that are intimately bound up in the scope of a substantive right or remedy. Although almost every rule is adopted for some reason and has some effect on the outcome of litigation, not every state rule "defines the dimensions of [a] claim itself." New York clearly crafted §901(b) with the intent that only certain lawsuits—those for which there were not

---

16. In its *Erie* analysis, the dissent observes that when sovereigns create laws, the enacting legislatures sometimes assume those laws will apply only within their territory. That is a true fact, but it does not do very much work for the dissent's position. For one thing, as the dissent observes, this *Erie* analysis is relevant only if there is no conflict between Rule 23 and §901(b), and the court can thus apply both. But because, in my view, Rule 23 applies, the only question is whether it would violate the Enabling Act. . . . And that inquiry is different from the Rules of Decision Act, or *Erie*, inquiry.

The dissent's citations, moreover, highlight simply that when interpreting statutes, context matters. Thus, we sometimes presume that laws cover only domestic conduct and sometimes do not, depending upon, *inter alia*, whether it makes sense in a given situation to assume that "the character of an act as lawful or unlawful must be determined wholly by the law of the [place] where the act is done," *American Banana Co. v. United Fruit Co.*, 213 U.S. 347, 356 (1909). But in the context of §901(b), a presumption against extraterritoriality makes little sense. That presumption applies almost only to laws governing what people can or cannot do. Section 901(b), however, is not directed to the conduct of persons but is instead directed to New York courts. Thus, §901(b) is, by its own terms, not extraterritorial insofar as it states that it governs *New York* courts. It is possible that the New York Legislature simply did not realize that New York courts hear claims under other sources of law and that other courts hear claims under New York law, and therefore mistakenly believed that they had written a limit on New York remedies. But because New York set up §901(b) as a general rule about how its courts operate, my strong presumption is to the contrary.

statutory penalties—could be joined in class actions in New York courts. That decision reflects a policy judgment about which lawsuits should proceed in New York courts in a class form and which should not. As JUSTICE GINSBURG carefully outlines, §901(b) was "apparently" adopted in response to fears that the class-action procedure, applied to statutory penalties, would lead to "annihilating punishment of the defendant." But statements such as these are not particularly strong evidence that §901(b) serves to define who can obtain a statutory penalty or that certifying such a class would enlarge New York's remedy. Any device that makes litigation easier makes it easier for plaintiffs to recover damages.

In addition to the fear of excessive recoveries, some opponents of a broad class-action device "argued that there was no *need* to permit class actions in order to encourage litigation . . . when statutory penalties . . . provided an aggrieved party with a sufficient economic incentive to pursue a claim . . . But those opponents may have felt merely that, for any number of reasons, New York courts should not conduct trials in the class format when that format is unnecessary to motivate litigation.[17] JUSTICE GINSBURG asserts that this could not be true because "suits seeking statutory damages are arguably *best* suited to the class device because individual proof of actual damages is unnecessary." But some people believe that class actions are inefficient or at least unfair, insofar as they join together slightly disparate claims or force courts to adjudicate unwieldy lawsuits. It is not for us to dismiss the possibility that New York legislators shared in those beliefs and thus wanted to exclude the class vehicle when it appeared to be unnecessary.

The legislative history of §901 thus reveals a classically procedural calibration of making it easier to litigate claims in New York courts (under any source of law) only when it is necessary to do so, and not making it *too* easy when the class tool is not required. This is the same sort of calculation that might go into setting filing fees or deadlines for briefs. There is of course a difference of degree between those examples and class certification, but not a difference of kind; the class vehicle may have a greater practical effect on who brings lawsuits than do low filing fees, but that does not transform it into a damages "proscription," or "limitation."[18]

The difference of degree is relevant to the forum shopping considerations that are part of the Rules of Decision Act or *Erie* inquiry. If the applicable federal rule did not govern the particular question at issue (or could be fairly read not

---

17. To be sure, one could imagine the converse story, that a legislature would create statutory penalties but dictate that such penalties apply only when necessary to overcome the costs and inconvenience of filing a lawsuit, and thus are not necessary in a class action. But it is hard to see how that narrative applies to New York, given that New York's penalty provisions, on their face, apply to all plaintiffs, be they class or individual, and that §901(b) addresses penalties that are created under any source of state or federal law.

18. JUSTICE GINSBURG asserts that class certification in this matter would "transform a $500 case into a $5,000,000 award." But in fact, class certification would transform 10,000 $500 cases into one $5,000,000 case. It may be that without class certification, not all of the potential plaintiffs would bring their cases. But that is true of any procedural vehicle; without a lower filing fee, a conveniently located courthouse, easy-to-use federal procedural rules, or many other features of the federal courts, many plaintiffs would not sue.

to do so), then those considerations would matter, for precisely the reasons given by the dissent. But that is not *this* case. As the Court explained in *Hanna*, it is an "incorrect assumption that the rule of *Erie R. Co. v. Tompkins* constitutes the appropriate test of . . . the applicability of a Federal Rule of Civil Procedure." 380 U.S. at 469–470. "It is true that both the Enabling Act and the *Erie* rule say, roughly, that federal courts are to apply state 'substantive' law and federal 'procedural' law," but the tests are different and reflect the fact that "they were designed to control very different sorts of decisions." *Id.* at 471.

Because Rule 23 governs class certification, the only decision is whether certifying a class in this diversity case would "abridge, enlarge or modify" New York's substantive rights or remedies. §2072(b). Although one can argue that class certification would enlarge New York's "limited" damages remedy, such arguments rest on extensive speculation about what the New York Legislature had in mind when it created §901(b). But given that there are two plausible competing narratives, it seems obvious to me that we should respect the plain textual reading of §901(b), a rule in New York's procedural code about when to certify class actions brought under any source of law, and respect Congress' decision that Rule 23 governs class certification in federal courts. In order to displace a federal rule, there must be more than just a possibility that the state rule is different than it appears.

Accordingly, I concur in part and concur in the judgment.

JUSTICE GINSBURG, with whom JUSTICE KENNEDY, JUSTICE BREYER, and JUSTICE ALITO join, dissenting.

The Court today approves Shady Grove's attempt to transform a $500 case into a $5,000,000 award, although the State creating the right to recover has proscribed this alchemy. If Shady Grove had filed suit in New York state court, the 2% interest payment authorized by New York Ins. Law Ann. §5106(a) as a penalty for overdue benefits would, by Shady Grove's own measure, amount to no more than $500. By instead filing in federal court based on the parties' diverse citizenship and requesting class certification, Shady Grove hopes to recover, for the class, statutory damages of more than $5,000,000. The New York Legislature has barred this remedy, instructing that, unless specifically permitted, "an action to recover a penalty, or minimum measure of recovery created or imposed by statute may not be maintained as a class action." N.Y. Civ. Prac. Law Ann. (CPLR) §901(b). The Court nevertheless holds that Federal Rule of Civil Procedure 23, which prescribes procedures for the conduct of class actions in federal courts, preempts the application of §901(b) in diversity suits.

The Court reads Rule 23 relentlessly to override New York's restriction on the availability of statutory damages. Our decisions, however, caution us to ask, before undermining state legislation: Is this conflict really necessary? Had the Court engaged in that inquiry, it would not have read Rule 23 to collide with New York's legitimate interest in keeping certain monetary awards reasonably bounded. I would continue to interpret Federal Rules with awareness of, and sensitivity to, important state regulatory policies. Because today's judgment radically departs from that course, I dissent.

. . .

In sum, both before and after *Hanna*, . . . federal courts have been cautioned by this Court to "interpre[t] the Federal Rules . . . with sensitivity to important state interests," *Gasperini*, 518 U.S. at 427, n. 7, and a will "to avoid conflict with important state regulatory policies," *id.* at 438, n. 22.[2] The Court veers away from that approach—and conspicuously, its most recent reiteration in *Gasperini*—in favor of a mechanical reading of Federal Rules, insensitive to state interests and productive of discord.

C

Our decisions instruct over and over again that, in the adjudication of diversity cases, state interests—whether advanced in a statute, *e.g., Cohen*, or a procedural rule, *e.g., Gasperini*—warrant our respectful consideration. Yet today, the Court gives no quarter to New York's limitation on statutory damages and requires the lower courts to thwart the regulatory policy at stake: To prevent excessive damages, New York's law controls the penalty to which a defendant may be exposed in a single suit. The story behind §901(b)'s enactment deserves telling.

. . .

"[T]he final bill . . . was the result of a compromise among competing interests." *Sperry*, 8 N.Y.3d at 211. Section 901(a) allows courts leeway in deciding whether to certify a class, but §901(b) rejects the use of the class mechanism to pursue the particular remedy of statutory damages. The limitation was not designed with the fair conduct or efficiency of litigation in mind. Indeed, suits seeking statutory damages are arguably *best* suited to the class device because individual proof of actual damages is unnecessary. New York's decision instead to block class-action proceedings for statutory damages therefore makes scant sense, except as a means to a manifestly substantive end: Limiting a defendant's liability in a single lawsuit

---

2. Justice Stevens stakes out common ground on this point: "[F]ederal rules," he observes, "must be interpreted with some degree of 'sensitivity to important state interests and regulatory policies,' . . . and applied to diversity cases against the background of Congress' command that such rules not alter substantive rights and with consideration of 'the degree to which the Rule makes the character and result of the federal litigation stray from the course it would follow in state courts,' *Hanna* [*v. Plumer*], 380 U.S. 460, 473 (1965)]." (Opinion concurring in part and concurring in judgment.) See also *ante* at 1450 ("A 'state procedural rule, though undeniably procedural in the ordinary sense of the term' may exist 'to influence substantive outcomes,' . . . and may in some instances become so bound up with the state-created right or remedy that it defines the scope of that substantive right or remedy." (some internal quotation marks omitted)); *ante* at 1450 ("When a State chooses to use a traditionally procedural vehicle as a means of defining the scope of substantive rights or remedies, federal courts must recognize and respect that choice."). Nevertheless, JUSTICE STEVENS sees no reason to read Rule 23 with restraint in this particular case; the Federal Rule preempts New York's damages limitation, in his view, because §901(b) is "a procedural rule that is not part of New York's substantive law." This characterization of §901(b) does not mirror reality, as I later explain. . . . But a majority of this Court, it bears emphasis, agrees that Federal Rules should be read with moderation in diversity suits to accommodate important state concerns.

in order to prevent the exorbitant inflation of penalties—remedies the New York Legislature created with individual suits in mind.[3]

D

Shady Grove contends—and the Court today agrees—that Rule 23 unavoidably preempts New York's prohibition on the recovery of statutory damages in class actions. The Federal Rule, the Court emphasizes, states that Shady Grove's suit "may be" maintained as a class action, which conflicts with §901(b)'s instruction that it "may not" so proceed. *Ante* at 1437 (internal quotation marks omitted and emphasis deleted). Accordingly, the Court insists, §901(b) "cannot apply in diversity suits unless Rule 23 is ultra vires." *Ibid.* Concluding that Rule 23 does not violate the Rules Enabling Act, the Court holds that the federal provision controls Shady Grove's ability to seek, on behalf of a class, a statutory penalty of over $5,000,000. *Ante* at 1442-1444 (plurality opinion); *ante* at 1457-1460 (STEVENS, J., concurring in part and concurring in judgment).

The Court, I am convinced, finds conflict where none is necessary. Mindful of the history behind §901(b)'s enactment, the thrust of our precedent, and the substantive-rights limitation in the Rules Enabling Act, I conclude, as did the Second Circuit and every District Court to have considered the question in any detail, that Rule 23 does not collide with §901(b). As the Second Circuit well understood, Rule 23 prescribes the considerations relevant to class certification and postcertification proceedings—but it does not command that a particular remedy be available when a party sues in a representative capacity. . . . Section 901(b), in contrast, trains on that latter issue. Sensibly read, Rule 23 governs procedural aspects of class litigation, but allows state law to control the size of a monetary award a class plaintiff may pursue.

In other words, Rule 23 describes a method of enforcing a claim for relief, while §901(b) defines the dimensions of the claim itself. In this regard, it is immaterial that §901(b) bars statutory penalties in wholesale, rather than retail, fashion. The New York Legislature could have embedded the limitation in every provision creating a cause of action for which a penalty is authorized; §901(b) operates as shorthand to the same effect. It is as much a part of the delineation of the claim for relief as it would be were it included claim by claim in the New York Code.

The Court single-mindedly focuses on whether a suit "may" or "may not" be maintained as a class action. Putting the question that way, the Court does not home in on the reason *why.* Rule 23 authorizes class treatment for suits satisfying its prerequisites because the class mechanism generally affords a fair and efficient

---

3. Even in the mine-run case, a class action can result in "potentially ruinous liability." Advisory Committee's Notes on Fed. Rule Civ. Proc. 23, 28 U.S.C.App., p. 143. A court's decision to certify a class accordingly places pressure on the defendant to settle even unmeritorious claims. See, *e.g., Coopers & Lybrand v. Livesay,* 437 U.S. 463, 476 (1978). When representative plaintiffs seek statutory damages, pressure to settle may be heightened because a class action poses the risk of massive liability unmoored to actual injury. See, *e.g., Ratner v. Chemical Bank New York Trust Co.,* 54 F.R.D. 412, 416 (S.D.N.Y.1972) (exercising "considerable discretion of a pragmatic nature" to refuse to certify a class because the plaintiffs suffered negligible actual damages but sought statutory damages of $13,000,000).

way to aggregate claims for adjudication. Section 901(b) responds to an entirely different concern; it does not allow class members to recover statutory damages because the New York Legislature considered the result of adjudicating such claims en masse to be exorbitant. The fair and efficient *conduct* of class litigation is the legitimate concern of Rule 23; the *remedy* for an infraction of state law, however, is the legitimate concern of the State's lawmakers and not of the federal rulemakers. Cf. Ely, The Irrepressible Myth of *Erie*, 87 Harv. L.Rev. 693, 722 (1974) (It is relevant "whether the state provision embodies a substantive policy or represents only a procedural disagreement with the federal rulemakers respecting the fairest and most efficient way of conducting litigation.").

. . .

The absence of an inevitable collision between Rule 23 and §901(b) becomes evident once it is comprehended that a federal court sitting in diversity can accord due respect to both state and federal prescriptions. Plaintiffs seeking to vindicate claims for which the State has provided a statutory penalty may pursue relief through a class action if they forgo statutory damages and instead seek actual damages or injunctive or declaratory relief; any putative class member who objects can opt out and pursue actual damages, if available, and the statutory penalty in an individual action. In this manner, the Second Circuit explained, "Rule 23's procedural requirements for class actions can be applied along with the substantive requirement of CPLR 901(b)." 549 F.3d, at 144. In sum, while phrased as responsive to the question whether certain class actions may begin, §901(b) is unmistakably aimed at controlling how those actions must end. On that remedial issue, Rule 23 is silent.

Any doubt whether Rule 23 leaves §901(b) in control of the remedial issue at the core of this case should be dispelled by our *Erie* jurisprudence, including *Hanna*, which counsels us to read Federal Rules moderately and cautions against stretching a rule to cover every situation it could conceivably reach.[10] The Court states that "[t]here is no reason . . . to read Rule 23 as addressing only whether claims made eligible for class treatment by some *other* law should be certified as class actions." To the contrary, *Palmer, Ragan, Cohen, Walker, Gasperini*, and *Semtek* provide good reason to look to the law that creates the right to recover. See *supra* at 1437-1439. That is plainly so on a more accurate statement of what is at stake: Is there any reason to read Rule 23 as authorizing a claim for relief when the State that created the remedy disallows its pursuit on behalf of a class? None at all is the answer our federal system should give.

Notably, New York is not alone in its effort to contain penalties and minimum recoveries by disallowing class relief; Congress, too, has precluded class treatment for certain claims seeking a statutorily designated minimum recovery. . . . Cf. *Beard v. Kindler*, 130 S.Ct. 612, 618-19 (2009) ("In light of . . . federalism and comity concerns . . . it would seem particularly strange to disregard state . . . rules that are

---

10. The plurality notes that "we have rejected every statutory challenge to a Federal Rule that has come before us." But it omits that we have interpreted Rules with due restraint, including Rule 23, thus diminishing prospects for the success of such challenges. See *Ortiz v. Fibreboard Corp.*, 527 U.S. 815, 842 (1999); *Amchem Products, Inc. v. Windsor*, 521 U.S. 591, 612-613 (1997). . . .

substantially similar to those to which we give full force in our own courts."). States may hesitate to create determinate statutory penalties in the future if they are impotent to prevent federal-court distortion of the remedy they have shaped.

By finding a conflict without considering whether Rule 23 rationally should be read to avoid any collision, the Court unwisely and unnecessarily retreats from the federalism principles undergirding *Erie.* Had the Court reflected on the respect for state regulatory interests endorsed in our decisions, it would have found no cause to interpret Rule 23 so woodenly—and every reason not to do so. . . .

II

Because I perceive no unavoidable conflict between Rule 23 and §901(b), I would decide this case by inquiring "whether application of the [state] rule would have so important an effect upon the fortunes of one or both of the litigants that failure to [apply] it would be likely to cause a plaintiff to choose the federal court." *Hanna,* 380 U.S. at 468, n. 9. See *Gasperini,* 518 U.S. at 428.

. . .

Shady Grove also ranks §901(b) as "procedural" because "nothing in [the statute] suggests that it is limited to rights of action based on New York state law, as opposed to federal law or the law of other states"; instead it "applies to actions seeking penalties under *any* statute." . . .

It is true that §901(b) is not specifically *limited* to claims arising under New York law. But neither is it expressly *extended* to claims arising under foreign law. The rule prescribes, without elaboration either way, that "an action to recover a penalty . . . may not be maintained as a class action." We have often recognized that "general words" appearing in a statute may, in fact, have limited application; "[t]he words 'any person or persons,'" for example, "are broad enough to comprehend every human being. But general words must not only be limited to cases within the jurisdiction of the state, but also to those objects to which the legislature intended to apply them." *United States v. Palmer,* 3 Wheat. 610, 631 (1818) (opinion for the Court by Marshall, C. J.). . . .

Moreover, Shady Grove overlooks the most likely explanation for the absence of limiting language: New York legislators make law with New York plaintiffs and defendants in mind, *i.e.,* as if New York were the universe. See Baxter, Choice of Law and the Federal System, 16 Stan. L.Rev. 1, 11 (1963) ("[L]awmakers often speak in universal terms but must be understood to speak with reference to their constituents."); cf. *Smith v. United States,* 507 U.S. 197, 204, n. 5 (1993) (presumption against extraterritoriality rooted in part in "the commonsense notion that Congress generally legislates with domestic concerns in mind").

. . .

Shady Grove's suggestion that States must specifically limit their laws to domestic rights of action if they wish their enactments to apply in federal diversity litigation misses the obvious point: State legislators generally do not focus on an interstate setting when drafting statutes.

. . .

In short, Shady Grove's effort to characterize §901(b) as simply "procedural" cannot successfully elide this fundamental norm: When no federal law or rule is dispositive of an issue, and a state statute is outcome affective in the sense our cases on *Erie* (pre- and post-*Hanna*) develop, the Rules of Decision Act commands application of the State's law in diversity suits. . . . As this case starkly demonstrates, if federal courts exercising diversity jurisdiction are compelled by Rule 23 to award statutory penalties in class actions while New York courts are bound by §901(b)'s proscription, "substantial variations between state and federal [money judgments] may be expected." *Gasperini*, 518 U.S. at 430. . . . The "variation" here is indeed "substantial." Shady Grove seeks class relief that is *ten thousand times* greater than the individual remedy available to it in state court. As the plurality acknowledges, forum shopping will undoubtedly result if a plaintiff need only file in federal instead of state court to seek a massive monetary award explicitly barred by state law. . . .

It is beyond debate that "a statutory cap on damages would supply substantive law for *Erie* purposes." *Gasperini*, 518 U.S. at 428. . . . In *Gasperini*, we determined that New York's standard for measuring the alleged excessiveness of a jury verdict was designed to provide a control analogous to a damages cap. 116 S.Ct. 2211. The statute was framed as "a procedural instruction," we noted, "but the State's objective [wa]s manifestly substantive." *Ibid.*

Gasperini's observations apply with full force in this case. By barring the recovery of statutory damages in a class action, §901(b) controls a defendant's maximum liability in a suit seeking such a remedy. The remedial provision could have been written as an explicit cap: "In any class action seeking statutory damages, relief is limited to the amount the named plaintiff would have recovered in an individual suit." That New York's Legislature used other words to express the very same meaning should be inconsequential.

. . .

III

The Court's erosion of *Erie*'s federalism grounding impels me to point out the large irony in today's judgment. Shady Grove is able to pursue its claim in federal court only by virtue of the recent enactment of the Class Action Fairness Act of 2005 (CAFA), 28 U.S.C. §1332(d). In CAFA, Congress opened federal-court doors to state-law-based class actions so long as there is minimal diversity, at least 100 class members, and at least $5,000,000 in controversy. By providing a federal forum, Congress sought to check what it considered to be the overreadiness of some state courts to certify class actions. . . . In other words, Congress envisioned fewer — not more — class actions overall. Congress surely never anticipated that CAFA would make federal courts a mecca for suits of the kind Shady Grove has launched: class actions seeking state-created penalties for claims arising under state law — claims that would be barred from class treatment in the State's own courts. . . .

. . .

I would continue to approach *Erie* questions in a manner mindful of the purposes underlying the Rules of Decision Act and the Rules Enabling Act, faithful to precedent, and respectful of important state interests. I would therefore hold that the New York Legislature's limitation on the recovery of statutory damages applies in this case, and would affirm the Second Circuit's judgment.

NOTES AND QUESTIONS

1. *What is the holding of* Shady Grove*?* Shady Grove grapples with potentially momentous issues regarding the proper interpretation of the Rules Enabling Act and its language forbidding the Federal Rules to "abridge, enlarge or modify any substantive right." It also addresses the proper way to interpret the text of a Federal Rule of Civil Procedure. But the impact of *Shady Grove* is made less clear by the fractured nature of the Court's opinion. Only Part II-A of Justice Scalia's analysis, which dealt with the "direct collision" of Rule 23 and New York CPLR 901(b), commanded a majority. Parts II-B, II-C, and II-D, which addressed the Rules Enabling Act more broadly, spoke only for a plurality. What is more, Justice Stevens indicated in his concurring opinion that he was in agreement with the four Ginsburg dissenters on at least some aspects of the proper interpretation of the Rules Enabling Act. Does that mean that the dissenters' opinion, as qualified by Justice Stevens's concurrence, in fact states the controlling standard for interpreting the limitations of the Enabling Act? As you consider the questions that follow, make sure that you have clearly mapped out what portions of Justice Scalia's opinion spoke for the majority, and what areas of agreement there were between Justice Stevens and the Ginsburg dissenters.

2. *Track Assignment.* Both the plurality and concurring opinions conclude that Rule 23 leaves no room for the operation of state law. How persuasive is that conclusion? Does the Rule require certification whenever the listed criteria are satisfied? *See* Tobias Barrington Wolff, *Discretion in Class Certification*, 162 U. Pa. L. Rev. 1897 (2014) (arguing that courts have discretion to deny certification even when the criteria of Rule 23 are satisfied). Is the Court's decision consistent with its approach in *Gasperini*? Does the text of Rule 59(a)(1) leave more room for the operation of state law than does Rule 23?

In the majority section of his opinion, Justice Scalia places great weight upon the fact that New York appears to have framed CPLR §901(b) as a "procedural" provision, setting policy on class actions in penalty cases by specifying when a class action "may not be maintained." That provision, he concludes, directly conflicts with Rule 23, which provides that a class action "may be maintained" if the requirements of Rule 23(a) and (b) are satisfied. Do you find this analysis convincing?

3. *Should the limitations on rule-making in the Enabling Act be seen as protecting federalism or separation of powers concerns?* One of the major sources of disagreement when it comes to the Rules Enabling Act is the role of state law in the interpretation of the Federal Rules in a diversity case. Broadly speaking, there are two views about the proper interpretation of the Enabling Act's "abridge, enlarge or modify any substantive rights" language: a federalism view and a separation of powers view. The federalism view holds that this language aims to preserve important state policies from being displaced by the Federal Rules. The most notable expositor of that view was Dean John Hart Ely. *See* John Hart Ely, *The Irrepressible Myth of* Erie, 87 Harv. L.Rev. 693 (1974). A major implication of this federalism view is that the validity of a Federal Rule might vary from state to state, depending upon what laws or policies a state has on the books. The separation of powers view, in contrast, interprets the Enabling Act as imposing a categorical limit on the matters that the Federal Rules are permitted to address. The Enabling Act limitation is seen as a constraint on the delegated legislative authority of the Supreme Court and the rule

makers, regardless of the content of the underlying state law. This constraint protects the prerogatives of Congress as the primary source of federal substantive policy. A major implication of this separation of powers view is that the Federal Rules will be uniform, rather than varying from state to state, and that the limitations of the Enabling Act will apply with equal force in federal question and diversity cases. The most notable expositor of the separation of powers view is Professor Stephen Burbank, as set forth in his article, *The Rules Enabling Act of 1934*, 130 U. Penn. L. Rev. 1015 (1982).

Consider whether Justice Scalia's approach to *Shady Grove* constituted a rejection of a federalism reading of the Enabling Act. Speaking for the majority, he makes clear his belief that "determining whether state and federal rules conflict based on the subjective intentions of the state legislature is an enterprise destined to produce 'confusion worse confounded,' [citing *Sibbach*], . . . [because] one State's statute could survive pre-emption (and accordingly affect the procedures in federal court) while another State's identical law would not, merely because its authors had different aspirations." Justice Stevens and the Ginsburg dissenters, however, see at least some role for state law in the interpretation of the Federal Rules. Justice Stevens indicates his agreement with the dissenters on this point, making five votes for the proposition that "a federal rule, like any federal law, must be interpreted in light of many different considerations, including 'sensitivity to important state interests' and 'regulatory policies.'" Is Justice Stevens's construction of Rule 23 consistent with that approach?

4. *Does Rule 23 abridge a substantive right in violation of the Enabling Act?* In enacting CPLR §901(b), New York was concerned about the danger that enforcement of its penalty laws through a class action would produce crippling liability that could destroy businesses, and that is why it passed a law prohibiting such aggregate remedies unless the state legislature expressly authorized them. Doesn't this sound like exactly the kind of "substantive" policy issue that the Federal Rules cannot regulate under the Enabling Act? If the availability of penalty class actions might result in significant harms to New York businesses that New York law does not wish to inflict, how can it possibly comply with the Enabling Act for a federal court to award an aggregate remedy?

But, does this objection prove too much? Ordinary class actions can also have a dramatic impact upon an industry. If you believe that *Shady Grove* was wrongly decided, then how can you justify Federal Rule 23 at all? Note the important difference between the federalism and separation of powers approach to the Enabling Act here. If you embrace the federalism approach, then this concern would only arise in states that do not permit class actions under state law, such that the Federal Rule would be trying to do something that the state would not permit. But if you embrace the separation-of-powers approach, then this concern is something you need to deal with regardless of what state or federal law says—if Rule 23 is setting industry-changing policy, then that might exceed the limitations of the Enabling Act under a separation-of-powers view. For one possible response to this challenge, *see* Stephen B. Burbank & Tobias Barrington Wolff, *Redeeming the Missed Opportunities of* Shady Grove, 159 U. Penn. L. Rev. 17, 21 (2010).

In Justice's Scalia's view, could a Rule of Civil Procedure that, in fact, regulated procedure, ever be in violation of the Enabling Act? Under what circumstances would Justice Stevens conclude that such a Rule violated the Enabling Act?

5. *Should the New York prohibition on punitive-damage class actions be considered "procedural" insofar as it is not limited to claims arising under New York law?* In finding that Rule 23 did not abrogate a substantive right, Justice Stevens puts significant weight on the fact that the provision was not limited to claims arising under New York law. But isn't it clear that the New York legislature was only concerned with New York penalty liability when it drafted CPLR §901(b)? The law requires that any "statute creating or imposing a penalty, or a minimum measure of recovery[,] specifically authorize[] the recovery thereof in a class action" in order for aggregate liability to be available. In so doing, it creates a point of reference—express statutory authorization for aggregate penalty liability—that appears to speak only to the contents of New York law. Why would New Jersey, Montana, or the United States Congress have any reason to include such an express authorization in their penalty statutes, since their law contains no general limitation on the availability of penalties on an aggregate basis? In this regard, notice *Weber v. U.S. Sterling Securities*, 924 A.2d 816, 835–838 (Conn. 2007), a choice of law ruling in which the Connecticut Supreme Court concluded that CPLR §901(b) is a part of the "substantive" law of New York and hence must be applied in the state courts of Connecticut in a multistate case governed by New York law.

6. *Following* Shady Grove, *what options does New York have to limit penalty liability?* If you were a legislator, how would you draft a law that would prevent destructive over-enforcement of penalty liability without eliminating penalty remedies altogether? Justice Ginsburg discusses this issue in her dissenting opinion, suggesting such possibilities as (1) individual provisions in each penalty statute under New York law, prohibiting class actions for that statute; or (2) a damages cap on the total amount that can be recovered under a given statute in a class action. Would these options survive preemption by Rule 23? If so, why didn't CPLR §901(b) survive?

7. *Recent Developments.* A number of lower federal courts have distinguished *Shady Grove* and have continued to deny class certification pursuant to state laws prohibiting or limiting certification. *See, e.g., Bearden v. Honeywell Intern. Inc.*, 2010 WL 3239285, *10 (M.D.Tenn. Aug 16, 2010) (NO. 3:09-1035) (denying certification of class action for claims arising under Tennessee consumer protection act); unlike *Shady Grove*, restriction on class actions was "so intertwined with that statute's rights and remedies that it functions to define the scope of the substantive rights" (*quoting* Stevens, J.); *Tait v. BSH Home Appl. Corp.*, 2011 WL 1832941, *8 (C.D.Cal. May 12, 2011) (NO. SACV 10-711 DOC AN) (same); *In re Digital Music Antitrust Litig.*, 812 F. Supp. 2d 390, 416 (S.D.N.Y., 2011) (Illinois rule prohibiting class actions for private claims brought under Illinois antitrust law was substantive limitation, binding on federal diversity court); *In re Wellbutrin XL Antitrust Litigation*, 756 F.Supp.2d 670, 672 (E.D.Pa. 2010) (same); *McKinney v. Bayer Corp.*, 744 F.Supp.2d 733, 740 (N.D.Ohio 2010) (heightened pleading requirement for class actions brought under Ohio consumer fraud statute is substantive and binding on federal court).

Not surprisingly, outside of the class action context, *Shady Grove* has also led to little consistency, particularly where state Rules attempt to police improper litigation conduct. For example, in *Cooke v. Jackson Nat'l Life Ins. Co.*, 919 F.3d 1024, (7th Cir. 2019), the court held that an Illinois state law penalizing insurance companies for "unreasonable delay in settling a claim" did not apply to defendant's litigation conduct in failing to disclose documents concerning the scope of the insurance coverage. That failure, the court held, was governed exclusively by the Federal

Rules of Civil Procedure. *Cf., Stender v. Archstone-Smith Operating Trust*, 958 F.3d 938, 940 (10th Cir. 2020) (Fed. R. Civ. P. 54(d) precludes the award of costs pursuant to Colorado state law). *Compare* the holding in *Cooke to Showman v. Pressdee*, 922 F.3d 1211, 1223–1225 (2019), in which the court held that plaintiff could recover under a Georgia statute that imposed attorneys' fees on defendants who had asserted frivolous defenses in litigation. The court dismissed the argument that sanctions for such conduct were governed exclusively by Rule 11:

> Rule 11 does not speak to whether a prevailing party is entitled to compensatory damages to remedy any injury inflicted on the prevailing party by the opposing party's frivolous or bad-faith claims and defenses. Instead, Rule 11 answers the question whether punitive sanctions should be imposed on an attorney or unrepresented party for filing a "pleading, written motion, or other paper" that violates the certification standards of Rule 11(b). In contrast, §9-11-68(e) confers on a prevailing party a right to potential compensation for injuries sustained as a result of an opposing party's decision to raise "a frivolous claim or defense." O.C.G.A. §9-11-68(e). It follows that §9-11-68(e) does not "address the same subject" as Rule 11. *Cf. Shady Grove*, 559 U.S. at 402.

In *Pappas v. Philip Morris, Inc.*, 915 F.3d 889 (2019), the court held that a Connecticut law forbidding the *pro se* representation of an estate had no application to practice in federal court, which, the court held, was governed exclusively by the "inherent power" of federal courts "to regulate those who appear before them." *See also, Passmore v. Baylor Health Care System*, 823 F.3d 292 (5th Cir. 2016) (finding inapplicable to federal practice a Texas statute that mandated dismissal of plaintiff's suit for failure to serve expert report within 120 days of the answer).

State "Offer of Judgment" provisions that go beyond Federal Rule 68 and shift attorneys' fees to the prevailing party have also received inconsistent federal enforcement. *Compare Scottsdale Ins. Co. v. Tolliver*, 636 F.3d 1273, 1278 (10th Cir. 2011) (Oklahoma offer of judgment rule provides basis for award of attorneys' fees to prevailing defendant notwithstanding unavailability of award under FRCP 68) *with Goldberg v. Pacific Indem. Co.*, 627 F.3d 752, 755 (9th Cir. 2010) (Arizona offer of judgment rule authorizing award of costs to prevailing defendant is inconsistent with FRCP 68 and cannot, therefore, be enforced by federal court).

The federal courts are similarly split over the enforceability of state "anti-SLAPP" statutes, which provide defendants with the opportunity to have a claim dismissed pursuant to a "special motion" showing that claim arose out of defendant's exercise of constitutional rights. *Compare Godin v. Schencks*, 629 F.3d 79, 86 (1st Cir. 2010) (Rules 12 and 56 do not preempt operation of Maine "Anti-SLAPP" statute,) *with Los Lobos Renewable Power, LLC v. Americulture, Inc.*, 885 F.3d 659, 673 (10th Cir.), *cert. denied*, 139 S. Ct. 591 (2018) (New Mexico anti-SLAPP statute does not apply in federal court); *Klocke v. Watson*, 936 F.3d 240 (5th Cir. 2019) (declining to enforce Texas anti-SLAPP statute); *La Liberte v. Reid*, 866 F.3d 79 (2d Cir. 2020) (California anti-SLAPP law not enforceable in federal court).

State Rules requiring verification and/or evidentiary support for certain types of claims have been a particularly frequent subject of *Erie* analysis, with little apparent consensus. *Compare Garman v. Campbell Cnty. School Dist. No. 1*, 630 F.3d 977, 983 (10th Cir 2010) (complaint against state entity must comply with Wyoming requirement that pleading be signed and certified notwithstanding lack of signing and certification requirements under federal pleading rules); *Liggon-Redding v. Estate of Sugarman*, 659 F.3d 258 (3d Cir. 2011) (malpractice claimant must attach certificate of merit to complaint pursuant to Pennsylvania law), *with Estate of C.A. v. Grier*, 752 F.Supp.2d 763, 767 (S.D. Tex, 2010) (Texas law requiring that malpractice claims be accompanied by "certificate of merit" is preempted by federal pleading rules); *Young v. United States*, 942 F.3d 349 (7th Cir. 2019) (federal prisoner's malpractice claim asserted under the Federal Tort Claims Act should not have been dismissed for failure to attach a certificate of merit, as required under Illinois law); and *Gallivan v. United States*, 943 F.3d 291 (6th Cir. 2019) (Ohio certificate of merit law does not apply in federal court).

In an interesting post–*Shady Grove* decision, the Court of Appeals for the Third Circuit enforced a "notice of motion" requirement under Pennsylvania law. *Schmigel v. Uchai*, 800 F.3d 113 (2015). The Third Circuit had previously enforced a requirement of Pennsylvania Rules of Civil Procedure that plaintiffs in medical malpractice proceedings file within 60 days of their complaint a "Certificate of Merit" signed by a physician opining that there is a reasonable probability that plaintiff suffered injury on account of defendant's negligence. Failure to file a timely Certificate rendered the complaint vulnerable to motion to dismiss pursuant to Fed. R. Civ. P. 12(b)(6). *See Liggon-Redding v. Estate of Sugarman*, 659 F.3d 258, 265 (3d Cir. 2011). However, because many complaints were being dismissed for failure to file the Certificate, Pennsylvania subsequently softened the impact by requiring that defendant notify the plaintiff of the defect 30 days before moving to dismiss on that basis, thus giving plaintiff an opportunity to cure. The *Schmigel* court held the notice of motion condition applicable to federal practice notwithstanding the fact that motions to dismiss pursuant to Fed. R. Civ. P. 12(b) must be filed within 21 days of service of the complaint. The majority held that there was no direct collision with Rule 12 insofar as the motion could be made by way of summary judgment instead, and it would be perverse to enforce the Certificate of Merit requirement, which the court deemed substantive, more rigidly than it would be enforced in state court. Judge Rendell, in dissent, found the Pennsylvania practice inconsistent with Rule 12, and thus preempted. Moreover, even if there were no direct collision, the Pennsylvania rule should not be considered "outcome determinative" *ex ante* under *Hanna*.

8. For scholarly commentary on *Shady Grove*, *see* Symposium on *Shady Grove Orthopedic Associates v. Allstate Insurance*: A Collection of "Opinions," 44 Creighton L. Rev 1 (2010); *Symposium*, Erie *Under Advisement: The Doctrine After* Shady Grove, 44 Akron L. Rev. 999 (2011); Shady Grove *Symposium*, 86 Notre Dame L. Rev. 939 (2011); Patrick Woolley, *The Role of State Law in Determining the Construction and Validity of Federal Rules of Civil Procedure*, 35 Rev. Litig. 207 (2016); Kermit Roosevelt, *Choice of Law in Federal Courts: From* Erie *and* Klaxon *to CAFA and* Shady Grove, 1–6 Nw. U. L. Rev. 1 (2012); Stephen B. Burbank & Tobias Barrington Wolff, *Redeeming the Missed Opportunities of* Shady Grove, 159 U. Pa. L. Rev. 17 (2010); Jeffrey Redfern, *Federal "Procedural" Rules Undermine Important State Interests in* Shady Grove, 34 Harv. J.L. & Pub. Pol'y 393 (2011); Linda S. Mullenix, *Federal Class Actions: A Near-Death Experience in a* Shady Grove, 79 Geo. Wash. L. Rev. 448 (2011); Jay Tidmarsh, *Procedure, Substance and* Erie, 64 Vand. L. Rev. 877 (2011); Helen Herskoff, Shady

Grove: *Duck-Rabbits, Clear Statements, and Federalism,* 74 Alb. L. Rev. 1703 (2011); Frank Blechschmidt, Comment, *All Alone in Arbitration:* AT&T v. Concepcion *and the Substantive Impact of Class Action Waivers,* 160 U. Pa. L. Rev. 541 (2012).

C.   *DETERMINING THE CONTENT OF STATE LAW*

When a federal court determines that state law must be followed, it must then proceed to ascertain the content of that law. In many, perhaps most, cases, this is unproblematic; federal judges can read statutes and reported decisions as well as state judges. There is, however, one key difference between state and federal practice that creates analytical difficulty: A federal case does not wind its way through the state system, and hence federal diversity litigants do not have access to the state appellate courts to clarify unsettled law or reverse outmoded precedents.

Thus, if federal litigants are to be treated the same as similarly situated state litigants, the federal court must do its best to account for the possibility that a state appellate court might change the law. This means the objective of the federal trial court is not to mimic a state trial court (which may well be bound by "outmoded" precedent), but rather to decide the case as would the highest state court. Thus, for instance, a federal court may not be bound by intermediate appellate court precedents as a state trial court would be. *Commissioner v. Estate of Bosch,* 387 U.S. 456 (1967). *But see Zakarian v. Prudential Ins. Co. of Am.,* 652 F. Supp. 1126, 1135 (N.D. Ill. 1987) (a minority view holding that federal court must decide all substantive questions in the same manner as a state trial judge). If a state litigant would not necessarily have access to the highest appellate court, does a federal district court's automatic assumption of appellate-like authority to change the law constitute the "equitable administration of the law" required by *Erie?* In some areas, the federal courts and intermediate state courts may have adopted conflicting views on points of state substantive law that the state's highest court has left unresolved. In such circumstances, is forum shopping between state and federal courts induced? Is this an unavoidable cost of diversity jurisdiction, or should diversity courts be obligated to follow the law prevailing in the state intermediate courts? *See generally* Geri J. Yonover, *Ascertaining State Law: The Continuing* Erie *Dilemma,* 38 DePaul L. Rev. 1 (1988) (arguing that *Erie* requires federal district courts to predict how state supreme court will resolve question).

But even assuming the propriety of a federal court exercising authority normally reserved to the state supreme courts, there is a broader problem: If the law is unsettled, inconsistent, or outmoded, what are the sources of law that the federal court can look to in determining the content of state law? What does it mean to apply "state law" if that law is not ascertainable from existing precedent? How, if at all, is the problem different from resolving an unsettled question of federal law? Should the federal court take account of the political inclinations of the current justices of the state supreme court? Is the federal court's task one of predicting what the current state supreme court will do, or should it simply determine what the "best" answer is, and assume a rational state court would reach the same result?

Consider these questions in connection with the next case.

Salve Regina College v. Russell

499 U.S. 225 (1991)

JUSTICE BLACKMUN delivered the opinion of the Court.

The concept of a federal general common law, lurking (to use Justice Holmes' phrase) as a "brooding omnipresence in the sky," was questioned for some time before being firmly rejected in *Erie R. Co. v. Tompkins*. . . . *Erie* mandates that a federal court sitting in diversity apply the substantive law of the forum State, absent a federal statutory or constitutional directive to the contrary. *See also* 28 U.S.C. §1652 ("The laws of the several states, except where the Constitution or treaties of the United States or Acts of Congress otherwise require or provide, shall be regarded as rules of decision in civil actions in the courts of the United States in cases where they apply."). In decisions after *Erie*, this Court made clear that state law is to be determined in the same manner as a federal court resolves an evolving issue of federal law: "with the aid of such light as [is] afforded by the materials for decision at hand, and in accordance with the applicable principles for determining state law." *Meredith v. Winter Haven*, 320 U.S. 228 (1943). . . .

In this case, we must decide specifically whether a federal court of appeals may review a district court's determination of state law under a standard less probing than that applied to a determination of federal law.

I

The issue presented arises out of a contract dispute between a college and one of its students. Petitioner Salve Regina College is an institution of higher education located in Newport, R.I. Respondent Sharon L. Russell was admitted to the college and began her studies as a freshman in 1982. The following year, respondent sought admission to the college's nursing department in order to pursue a bachelor of science degree in nursing. She was accepted by the department and began her nursing studies in the fall of 1983.

Respondent, who was 5'6" tall, weighed in excess of 300 pounds when she was accepted in the nursing program. Immediately after the 1983 school year began, respondent's weight became a topic of commentary and concern by officials of the nursing program. Respondent's first year in the program was marked by a series of confrontations and negotiations concerning her obesity and its effect upon her ability to complete the clinical requirements safely and satisfactorily. During her junior year, respondent signed a document that was designated as a "contract" and conditioned her further participation in the nursing program upon weekly attendance at a weight-loss seminar and a realized average loss of two pounds per week. When respondent failed to meet these commitments, she was asked to withdraw from the program and did so. She transferred to a nursing program at another college, but had to repeat her junior year in order to satisfy the transferee institution's 2-year residency requirement. As a consequence, respondent's nursing education took five years rather than four. She also underwent surgery for her obesity. In 1987, respondent successfully completed her nursing education and she is now a registered nurse.

Soon after leaving Salve Regina College, respondent filed this civil action in the United States District Court for the District of Rhode Island. She asserted, among others, claims based on (1) intentional infliction of emotional distress, (2) invasion of privacy, and (3) nonperformance by the college of its implied agreement to educate respondent.[1] Subject matter jurisdiction in the District Court was based on diversity of citizenship. *See* 28 U.S.C. §1332. The parties agree that the law of Rhode Island applies to all substantive aspects of the action. *See Erie R. Co. v. Tompkins, supra.*

At the close of plaintiff-respondent's case-in-chief, the District Court directed a verdict for the individual defendants on all three of the remaining claims, and for the college on the claims for intentional infliction of emotional distress and invasion of privacy. App. 82. The court, however, denied the college's motion for a directed verdict on the breach-of-contract claim, reasoning that "a legitimate factual issue" remained concerning whether "there was substantial performance by the plaintiff in her overall contractual relationship at Salve Regina." *Id.* at 88.

At the close of all the evidence, the college renewed its motion for a directed verdict. It argued that under Rhode Island law the strict commercial doctrine of substantial performance did not apply in the general academic context. Therefore, according to petitioner, because respondent admitted she had not fulfilled the terms of the contract, the college was entitled to judgment as a matter of law.

The District Court denied petitioner's motion. *Id.* at 92. Acknowledging that the Supreme Court of Rhode Island, to that point, had limited the application of the substantial-performance doctrine to construction contracts, the District Court nonetheless concluded, as a matter of law, that the Supreme Court of Rhode Island would apply that doctrine to the facts of respondent's case. *Id.* at 90–91. The Federal District Judge based this conclusion, in part, on his observation that "I was a state trial judge for 18 and 1/2 years, and I have a feel for what the Rhode Island Supreme Court will or won't do." *Id.* at 91. Accordingly, the District Court submitted the breach-of-contract claim to the jury. The court instructed the jury:

> The law provides that substantial and not exact performance accompanied by good faith is what is required in a case of a contract of this type. It is not necessary that the plaintiff have fully and completely performed every item specified in the contract between the parties. It is sufficient if there has been substantial performance, not necessarily full performance, so long as the substantial performance was in good faith and in compliance with the contract, except for some minor and relatively unimportant deviation or omission. *Id.* at 97.

The jury returned a verdict for respondent, and determined that the damages were $30,513.40. Judgment was entered. Both respondent and petitioner appealed.

---

1. The amended complaint named the college and five faculty members as defendants, and alleged discrimination in violation of the Rehabilitation Act of 1973, 87 Stat. 355, 29 U.S.C. §701 *et seq.*; denial of due process and unconstitutional interference with her liberty and property interests; negligent and intentional infliction of emotional distress; invasion of privacy; wrongful dismissal; violation of express and implied covenants of good faith and fair dealing; and breach of contract. The District Court entered summary judgment for the defendants except as to the three state-law claims for intentional infliction of emotional distress, invasion of privacy, and breach of contract. 649 F. Supp. 391, 407 (1986). It determined that it need not consider "the plausibility of federal question jurisdiction." *Id.,* at 393, n. 1.

The United States Court of Appeals for the First Circuit affirmed. 890 F.2d 484 (1989). It first upheld the District Court's directed verdict dismissing respondent's claims for intentional infliction of emotional distress and invasion of privacy. *Id.* at 487–488. It then turned to petitioner's argument that the District Court erred in submitting the breach-of-contract claim to the jury. Rejecting petitioner's argument that, under Rhode Island law, the doctrine of substantial performance does not apply in the college-student context, the court stated:

> In this case of first impression, the district court held that the Rhode Island Supreme Court would apply the substantial performance standard to the contract in question. In view of the customary appellate deference accorded to interpretations of state law made by federal judges of that state, *Dennis v. Rhode Island Hospital Trust Nat'l Bank*, 744 F.2d 893, 896 (1st Cir. 1984); *O'Rourke v. Eastern Air Lines, Inc.*, 730 F.2d 842, 847 (2d Cir. 1984), we hold that the district court's determination that the Rhode Island Supreme Court would apply standard contract principles is not reversible error. *Id.* at 489.

Petitioner college sought a writ of certiorari from this Court. It alleged that the Court of Appeals erred in deferring to the District Court's determination of state law.[2] A majority of the Courts of Appeals, although varying in their phraseology, embrace a rule of deference similar to that articulated by the Court of Appeals in this case. *See, e.g., Norton v. St. Paul Fire & Marine Ins. Co.*, 902 F.2d 1355, 1357 (CA8 1990) ("In general, we accord substantial deference to a district court's interpretation of the law of the state in which it sits"), and *Self v. Wal-Mart Stores, Inc.*, 885 F.2d 336, 339 (CA6 1989) ("[W]e should give 'considerable weight' to the trial court's views on such questions of local law."). Two Courts of Appeals, however, have broken ranks recently with their sister Circuits. They have concluded that a district-court determination of state law is subject to plenary review by the appellate court. *See Craig v. Lake Asbestos of Quebec, Ltd.*, 843 F.2d 145, 148 (CA3 1988), and *In re McLinn*, 739 F.2d 1395 (CA9 1984) (en banc, with a divided vote). We granted certiorari to resolve the conflict. . . .

II

We conclude that a court of appeals should review *de novo* a district court's determination of state law. As a general matter, of course, the Courts of Appeals are vested with plenary appellate authority over final decisions of district courts. *See* 28 U.S.C. §1291. The obligation of responsible appellate jurisdiction implies the requisite authority to review independently a lower court's determinations.

---

2. *See* Coenen, *To Defer or Not to Defer: A Study of Federal Circuit Court Deference to District Court Rulings on State Law*, 73 Minn. L. Rev. 899 (1989), and the many cases cited therein. *See also* Note, *What Is the Proper Standard for Reviewing a District Court's Interpretation of State Substantive Law?*, 54 U. Cin. L. Rev. 215 (1985), and Note, *A Nondeferential Standard for Appellate Review of State Law Decisions by Federal District Courts*, 42 Wash. & Lee L. Rev. 1311 (1985). *See,* however, Woods, *The* Erie *Enigma: Appellate Review of Conclusions of Law*, 26 Ariz. L. Rev. 755 (1984), and Note, *The Law/Fact Distinction and Unsettled State Law in the Federal Courts*, 64 Tex. L. Rev 157 (1985).

Independent appellate review of legal issues best serves the dual goals of doctrinal coherence and economy of judicial administration. District judges preside alone over fast-paced trials: of necessity they devote much of their energy and resources to hearing witnesses and reviewing evidence. Similarly, the logistical burdens of trial advocacy limit the extent to which trial counsel is able to supplement the district judge's legal research with memoranda and briefs. Thus, trial judges often must resolve complicated legal questions without benefit of "extended reflection [or] extensive information." Coenen, *To Defer or Not to Defer: A Study of Federal Circuit Court Deference to District Court Rulings on State Law,* 73 Minn. L. Rev. 899, 923 (1989).

Courts of Appeals, on the other hand, are structurally suited to the collaborative juridical process that promotes decisional accuracy. With the record having been constructed below and settled for purposes of the appeal, appellate judges are able to devote their primary attention to legal issues. As questions of law become the focus of appellate review, it can be expected that the parties' briefs will be refined to bring to bear on the legal issues more information and more comprehensive analysis than was provided for the district judge. Perhaps most important, courts of appeals employ multi-judge panels, *see* 28 U.S.C. §§46(b) and (c), that permit reflective dialogue and collective judgment. . . .

Independent appellate review necessarily entails a careful consideration of the district court's legal analysis, and an efficient and sensitive appellate court at least will naturally consider this analysis in undertaking its review. Petitioner readily acknowledges the importance of a district court's reasoning to the appellate court's review. Any expertise possessed by the district court will inform the structure and content of its conclusions of law and thereby become evident to the reviewing court. If the court of appeals finds that the district court's analytical sophistication and research have exhausted the state-law inquiry, little more need be said in the appellate opinion. Independent review, however, does not admit of unreflective reliance on a lower court's inarticulable intuitions. Thus, an appropriately respectful application of *de novo* review should encourage a district court to explicate with care the basis for its legal conclusions. *See* Fed. Rule Civ. Proc. 52(a) (requiring the district court to "state separately its conclusions of law").

Those circumstances in which Congress or this Court has articulated a standard of deference for appellate review of district court determinations reflect an accommodation of the respective institutional advantages of trial and appellate courts. In deference to the unchallenged superiority of the district court's fact-finding ability, Civil Rule 52(a) commands that a trial court's findings of fact "shall not be set aside unless clearly erroneous, and due regard shall be given to the opportunity of the trial court to judge of the credibility of the witnesses." In addition, it is "especially common" for issues involving supervision of litigation to be reviewed for abuse of discretion. See *Pierce v. Underwood,* 487 U.S. 552, 558, n.1 (1988). Finally, we have held that deferential review of mixed questions of law and fact is warranted when it appears that the district court is "better positioned" than the appellate court to decide the issue in question or that probing appellate scrutiny will not contribute to the clarity of legal doctrine. *Miller v. Fenton,* 474 U.S. 104, 114 (1985); *see also Cooler & Gell v. Hartmarx Corp.,* 496 U.S. 384, 402 (1990) ("[T]he district court is better situated than the court of appeals to marshal the pertinent facts and apply the fact-dependent legal standard mandated by Rule 11."). . . .

Nothing about the exercise of diversity jurisdiction alters these functional components of decisionmaking or otherwise warrants departure from a rule of independent appellate review. Actually, appellate deference to the district court's determination of state law is inconsistent with the principles underlying this Court's decision in *Erie.* The twin aims of the *Erie* doctrine — "discouragement of forum-shopping and avoidance of inequitable administration of the laws." *Hanna v. Plumer,* 380 U.S. 460, 468, (1965) — are components of the goal of doctrinal coherence advanced by independent appellate review. As respondent has conceded, deferential appellate review invites divergent development of state law among the federal trial courts even within a single State. Tr. of Oral Arg. 34–36. Moreover, by denying a litigant access to meaningful review of state-law claims, appellate courts that defer to the district courts' state-law determinations create a dual system of enforcement of state-created rights, in which the substantive rule applied to a dispute may depend on the choice of forum. *Cf. Erie,* 304 U.S. at 74–75 ("[The rule of *Swift v. Tyson,* 16 Pet. 1 (1842)] made rights enjoyed under the unwritten 'general law' vary according to whether enforcement was sought in the state or in the federal court"). Neither of these results, unavoidable in the absence of independent appellate review, can be reconciled with the commands of *Erie.* . . .

We do not doubt that in many cases the application of a rule of deference in lieu of independent review will not affect the outcome of an appeal. In many diversity cases the controlling issues of state law will have been squarely resolved by the state courts, and a district court's adherence to the settled rule will be indisputably correct. . . . In a case where the controlling question of state law remains unsettled, it is not unreasonable to assume that the considered judgment of the Court of Appeals frequently will coincide with the reasoned determination of the district court. Where the state-law determinations of the two courts diverge, the choice between these standards of review is of no significance if the appellate court concludes that the district court was clearly wrong.[4]

Thus, the mandate of independent review will alter the appellate outcome only in those few cases where the appellate court would resolve an unsettled issue of state law differently from the district court's resolution, but cannot conclude that the district court's determination constitutes clear error. *See, e.g., In re McLinn,* 739 F.2d at 1397 ("The panel indicated that if the question of law were reviewed under the deferential standard that we have applied in the past, which permits reversal only for clear error, then they would affirm; but if they were to review the determination under an independent de novo standard, they would reverse."). These few instances, however, make firm our conviction that the difference between a rule of deference and the duty to exercise independent review

---

4. Of course, a question of state law usually can be resolved definitively if the litigation is instituted in state court and is not finally removed to federal court, or if a certification procedure is available and is successfully utilized. Rhode Island provides a certification procedure. *See* Rhode Island Supreme Court Rule 6 (1989). *See,* however, *Lehman Brothers v. Schein,* 416 U.S. 386 (1974) ("We do not suggest that where there is doubt as to local law and where the certification procedure is available, resort to it is obligatory. It does, of course, in the long run save time, energy, and resources and helps build a cooperative judicial federalism. Its use in a given case rests in the sound discretion of the federal court.") (footnote omitted).

is "much more than a mere matter of degree." *Bose Corp. v. Consumers Union of United States, Inc.,* 466 U.S. 485, 501 (1984). When *de novo* review is compelled, no form of appellate deference is acceptable.

B

Respondent and her *amicus* also argue that *de novo* review is inappropriate because, as a general matter, a district judge is better positioned to determine an issue of state law than are the judges on the court of appeals. This superior capacity derives, it is said, from the regularity with which a district judge tries a diversity case governed by the law of the forum State, and from the extensive experience that the district judge generally has had as practitioner or judge in the forum State.

We are unpersuaded. As an initial matter, this argument seems to us to be founded fatally on overbroad generalizations. Moreover, and more important, the proposition that a district judge is better able to "intuit" the answer to an unsettled question of state law is foreclosed by our holding in *Erie.* The very essence of the *Erie* doctrine is that the bases of state law are presumed to be communicable by the parties to a federal judge no less than to a state judge. Almost 25 years ago, Professor Kurland stated: "Certainly, if the law is not a brooding omnipresence in the sky over the United States, neither is it a brooding omnipresence in the sky of Vermont, or New York or California." Kurland, *Mr. Justice Frankfurter, the Supreme Court and the* Erie *Doctrine in Diversity Cases,* 67 Yale L.J. 187, 217 (1957). *See Southern Pacific Co.,* 244 U.S. at 222, (Holmes, J., dissenting) ("The common law is not a brooding omnipresence in the sky but the articulate voice of some sovereign or quasi-sovereign that can be identified."). Similarly, the bases of state law are as equally communicable to the appellate judges as they are to the district judge. To the extent that the available state law on a controlling issue is so unsettled as to admit of no reasoned divination, we can see no sense in which a district judge's prior exposure or nonexposure to the state judiciary can be said to facilitate the rule of reason.[5]

---

5. "As a general proposition, a federal court judge who sits in a particular state, especially one who has practiced before its courts, may be better able to resolve complex questions as to the law of that state than is a federal judge who has no such personal acquaintance with the law of the state. For this reason federal appellate courts frequently have voiced reluctance to substitute their own view of the state law for that of the district judge. As a matter of judicial administration, this seems defensible. But there is some tendency to go beyond that proposition and to say that if the trial court has reached a permissible conclusion under state law, the appellate court cannot reverse even if it thinks the state law to be otherwise, thereby treating the question of state law much as if it were a question of fact. The determination of state law, however, is a legal question, and although the considered decision of a district judge experienced in the law of a state naturally commands the respect of an appellate court, a party is entitled to meaningful review of that decision just as he is of any other legal question in the case, and just as he would have been if the case had been tried in a state court." 19 C. Wright, A. Miller, and E. Cooper, Federal Practice and Procedure, §4507, pp. 106–110 (1982).

IV

The obligation of responsible appellate review and the principles of a cooperative judicial federalism underlying *Erie* require that Courts of Appeals review the state-law determinations of district courts *de novo*. The Court of Appeals in this case therefore erred in deferring to the local expertise of the District Court. The judgment of the Court of Appeals is reversed, and the case is remanded for further proceedings consistent with this opinion.

It is so ordered.

CHIEF JUSTICE REHNQUIST, with whom JUSTICE WHITE and JUSTICE STEVENS join, dissenting.

I do not believe we need to delve into such abstractions as "deferential" review, on the one hand, as opposed to what the Court's opinion calls, at various places, "plenary," "independent," and "*de novo*" review, on the other, in order to decide this case. The critical language used by the Court of Appeals, and quoted in this Court's opinion, is this:

In view of the customary appellate deference accorded to interpretations of state law made by federal judges of that state, . . . we hold that the district court's determination that the Rhode Island Supreme Court would apply standard contract principles is not reversible error.

. . . In this case, the court concluded that the opinion of a District Judge with 18 years of experience as a trial judge was entitled to some appellate deference.

This seems to me a rather sensible observation. A district court's insights are particularly valuable to an appellate court in a case such as this where the state law is unsettled. In such cases, the courts' task is to try *to predict* how the highest court of that State would decide the question. A judge attempting to predict how a state court would rule must use not only his legal reasoning skills, but also his experiences and perceptions of judicial behavior in that State. It therefore makes perfect sense for an appellate court judge with no local experience to accord special weight to a local judge's assessment of state court trends.

If we must choose among Justice Holmes' aphorisms to help decide this case, I would opt for his observation that "[t]he life of the law has not been logic: it has been experience." O. Holmes, The Common Law 1 (1881). And it does no harm to recall that the members of this Court have no monopoly on experience; judges of the courts of appeals and of the district courts surely possess it just as we do. That the experience of appellate judges should lead them to rely, in appropriate situations, on the experience of district judges who have practiced law in the State in which they sit before taking the bench seems quite natural.

For this very reason, this Court has traditionally given special consideration or "weight" to the district judge's perspective on local law. . . .

But the Court today decides that this intuitively sensible deference is available only to this Court, and not to the courts of appeals. It then proceeds to instruct the courts of appeals and the district courts on their respective functions in the federal judicial system, and how they should go about exercising them. Questions of law are questions of law, they are told, whether they be of state law or federal law, and must all be processed through an identical decisional mold.

I believe this analysis unduly compartmentalizes things which have up to now been left to common sense and good judgment. Federal courts of appeals perform a different role when they decide questions of state law than they do when they decide questions of federal law. In the former case, these courts are not sources of law but only reflections of the jurisprudence of the courts of a State. While in deciding novel federal questions, courts of appeals are likely to ponder the policy implications as well as the decisional law, only the latter need be considered in deciding questions of state law. To my mind, therefore, it not only violates no positive law but also is a sensible allocation of resources to recognize these differences by deferring to the views of the district court where such deference is felt warranted.

I think we run a serious risk that our reach will exceed our grasp when we attempt to impose a rigid logical framework on the courts of appeals in place of a less precise but tolerably well-functioning approach adopted by those courts. I agree with the Court that a court of appeals should not "abdicate" its obligation to decide questions of state law presented in a diversity case. But according weight to the conclusion of a particular district judge on the basis of his experience and special knowledge of state law, an appellate court does not "suspend [its] own thought processes." *In re McLinn*, 739 F.2d 1395, 1404 (9th Cir. 1984) (Schroeder, J., dissenting). I think the Court of Appeals did no more than that here, and I therefore dissent from the reversal of its judgment.

NOTES AND QUESTIONS

1. *Why Deference?* The issue in *Salve Regina College* is the "standard of review" that a federal appellate court should exercise in reviewing a trial court's determination of state law. The standard of review establishes how much deference an appeals court should give to a lower court's ruling. Generally speaking, when an appeals court reviews findings of fact, it will affirm the lower court's findings of fact, even if it disagrees with them, as long as the findings are not "clearly erroneous." Appeals courts generally subject legal rulings to a "plenary" or "*de novo*" standard of review; the issue on appeal will be considered anew, and the appeals court will substitute its judgment for the lower court's. No deference is typically paid to a lower court's determinations of law.

The different levels of scrutiny are generally considered to reflect the respective institutional competence of the two courts. The trial court had access to live witnesses and real evidence not available to the appellate court. The appellate court in turn benefits from the collective legal analysis of three or more typically distinguished, appellate judges.

Why then had many courts prior to *Salve Regina College* taken the position that the court of appeals should defer to the district court's determination of the content of state law? If the court of appeals is generally given greater authority than trial courts to make legal determinations, why shouldn't it exercise that authority to correct what it perceives to be legal misconstructions of state law by the trial court?

One account is that district court judges, compared to court of appeals judges, are relative experts in the underlying state law. Almost every judicial circuit encompasses more than one state, and virtually no federal district does so.* This not only means that district court judges typically see more state law cases than court of appeals judges see, but that district court judges are far more likely to have been drawn from the state bar and bench; the court of appeals judges are typically drawn from all states falling within the circuit. It is for a similar reason that the Supreme Court itself defers to lower court constructions of state law. *Cf. Butner v. United States*, 440 U.S. 48 (1979). Of course, the fact that the federal trial judge is familiar with legal developments in her home state does not necessarily make her an expert on the future course of state law, but it may give her a somewhat better perspective on the question.

Another explanation may lie in the judicial perceptions of *Erie* itself. One reading of *Erie* is that there is no state common law except as made by state judges. Thus the federal judicial task arguably involves understanding the psychology of the state bench as much or more than understanding the "law" itself. This is particularly so in the case of unsettled questions of state law, where the conventional sources of legal research are *a fortiori* inconclusive. In such a case, the court must not only be familiar with relevant case law and policy arguments, but the predilections of the particular judges of the state supreme court. Even if all case law and policy cut in favor of one result, the federal court, under this view, should resolve the case the other way if it has reason to believe the state court would do so. The appropriate standard of federal appellate review may thus turn on whether the judicial task in "predicting" what the state supreme court might do is more akin to the "factual" determinations typically entrusted to the district court (the "fact" of how the state judges will resolve the question), or the more abstract jurisprudential inquiry typically made by the appellate court (ascertaining the "law" of the state).

For an argument that the federal appellate courts should defer to the state law expertise of district courts in some circumstances, *see* Jonathan Remy Nash, *Resuscitating Deference to Lower Federal Court Judges' Interpretations of State Law*, 77 S. Cal. L. Rev. 975, 1012 (2004).

2. *Predicting Versus Deciding Unsettled Questions of State Law.* Justice Rehnquist's dissent in *Salve Regina College* argues that ascertaining the proper answer to a question of unsettled state law does not involve the same process as resolving an unsettled question of federal law. In his view, where state law is not ascertainable from the conventional sources of legal research, the federal courts must limit their analysis to what they believe the state supreme court will do with the issue. This contrasts with a broader, policy-based analysis that courts employ to resolve unsettled questions of federal law. Thus, the relative expertise of courts of appeals in crafting legal rules, he argues, is not as clear in diversity cases.

Do you agree? In the absence of other evidence of the state court's position, isn't it reasonable to assume that the state court would adopt the "best" law, as determined by the same kind of policy analysis courts employ to resolve unsettled questions of federal law? Should a district court's intuition of the state supreme court's predilections trump a contrary conclusion reached by traditional legal analysis?

---

* The sole exception is the District of Wyoming, which includes portions of Yellowstone National Park located within Montana and Idaho. *See* 28 U.S.C. §131. *See generally* 13 C. Wright & Miller et al., Federal Practice and Procedure, §3505 n.3 (3d ed.).

What does it mean to "predict" how the state supreme court will resolve an issue? How is "prediction" different from the kind of legal determinations that federal courts engage in when they decide an issue of federal law? Is there any reason why a district court judge sitting in diversity should take the personal predilections of the state court judges into account more than she would consider the personal predilections of the United States Supreme Court? Is it significant that the state supreme court does not have an opportunity to reverse the federal court's judgment? For a forceful argument that courts should never try to "predict" how particular appellate judges will dispose of a legal question, *see* Michael C. Dorf, *Prediction and the Rule of Law*, 42 UCLA L. Rev. 651 (1995).

3. *Forum Shopping?* Do you agree with the majority that *de novo* appellate review is necessary to avoid forum shopping? While federal appellate resolution of intra-district conflicts certainly advances federal uniformity, has *Salve Regina College* increased or decreased the incentive to forum shop between state and federal courts? If you were an attorney attempting to overturn an antiquated state precedent, would *Salve Regina College* increase your incentive to litigate in state court? Does the Court's insistence on a textually demonstrable basis for ascertaining state law render the federal courts more rigid and precedent-bound than the state courts? *Cf.* Linda Mullenix, *Supreme Court Review: Forum-Shoppers Should Discover a Wider Market*, Nat'l L.J. at S12 (Aug. 19, 1991). Or is that more than compensated for by the freedom of the federal district courts to deviate from lower state court precedents, a power not possessed by the state trial courts?

4. *Statutory Construction.* When a federal court interprets a state statute, is it bound to adopt the methodology of statutory construction used by the state courts? *See* Abbe R. Gluck, *Intersystemic Statutory Interpretation: Methodology as "Law" and the* Erie *Doctrine*, 120 Yale L.J. 1898 (2011).

5. *Certification.* If federal courts want to know how the state supreme court will resolve an unsettled question, why don't they just ask? In many (though not all) states, there is, in fact, a procedure for either federal district courts or courts of appeals or both to "certify" questions of state law to the state supreme courts. *See* Uniform Certification of Questions of Law [Act] Rule (1995), 12 U.L.A. 67 (1996). *See also* Caroll Seron, Federal Judicial Center, *Certifying Questions of State Law: Experience of Federal Judges* 2 (1983). Where the state court accepts the certification, the federal court suspends its proceedings until the question of law is resolved by the state court. A certification proceeding is a significant deviation from normal appellate procedure: There is no defined appellate record or clear opportunity for oral argument. It is within the federal court's discretion whether to certify a question to the state court. Not all states will accept certified questions. Currently, 48 states entertain certified questions from the federal courts. 17A C. Wright et al., Federal Practice and Procedure §4248 n. 30 (3d ed. 2007) (April 2021 Update). Does certification represent an abdication of the federal courts' obligation to exercise jurisdiction in diversity cases? Delegating even part of the adjudication to the state courts could be seen as undermining the function of diversity jurisdiction; if Congress thought there was a need for an unbiased federal tribunal, doesn't that need extend to an unbiased determination of unsettled legal questions? Even from a "cooperative federalism" perspective, don't the federal courts in diversity have a valuable role to play in contributing to the development of state law? For a scathing

critique of certification written by a judge of the First Circuit, *see* Bruce Selya, *Certified Madness: Ask a Silly Question* . . . , 29 Suffolk U. L. Rev. 677 (1995). *Cf.* Jonathon Remy Nash, *Examining the Power of Federal Courts to Certify Questions of State Law*, 88 Cornell L. Rev. 1672 (2003) (arguing that certification violates the Article III assignment of the federal judicial power to the federal judiciary and is inconsistent with the statutory diversity jurisdiction conferred upon the federal courts); Larry M. Roth, *Certified Questions from the Federal Courts: Review and Re-proposal*, 34 U. Miami L. Rev. 1, 9 (1979). *But see* Judith Kaye & Kenneth Weisman, *Interactive Federalism: Certified Questions in New York*, 69 Fordham L. Rev. 373 (2000) (arguing that certification does not significantly delay litigation and reserves to the state courts authority to resolve important legal questions).

6. *Abstention.* If no certification procedure is available, may the federal court simply decline to assert jurisdiction and direct the litigants to the state court? The answer is normally no. The Supreme Court held in *Meredith v. City of Winter Haven*, 320 U.S. 228 (1943), that a court may not abstain from hearing a case simply because the case involves an unsettled question of state law.

There are, however, a variety of abstention doctrines that do authorize declining or delaying the exercise of jurisdiction in favor of a state forum in particular circumstances, mostly involving federal question cases. In federal question cases, the court may abstain to avoid interfering with a pending criminal or quasi-criminal state proceeding, *see Younger v. Harris*, 401 U.S. 37 (1971); or to avoid an unnecessary constitutional adjudication by giving the state courts an opportunity to construe an unsettled question of state law, *see Railroad Commission of Texas v. Pullman Co.*, 312 U.S. 496 (1941).

In addition, abstention has been approved in matters of crucial importance to the state government, such as questions of state administrative law or eminent domain. *See Burford v. Sun Oil Co.*, 319 U.S. 315 (1943); *Louisiana Power & Light Co. v. City of Thibodaux*, 360 U.S. 25 (1959). In exceptional circumstances, federal courts will abstain to avoid duplicative litigation with a parallel state proceeding, but the norm is that both the state and federal litigation will proceed until one of them comes to a final judgment. *See Colorado River Water Conservation District v. United States*, 424 U.S. 800 (1976). *See generally* Martin H. Redish, Federal Jurisdiction: Tensions in the Allocation of Judicial Power 281–308 (2d ed. 1990). The state courts, of course, are free to suspend their proceedings to avoid such duplication.

D. SUBSTANTIVE FEDERAL COMMON LAW

When Justice Brandeis declared in *Erie* that there was no *general* federal common law, he was not foreclosing federal courts from ever crafting common law rules. The Court's explicit concern in *Erie* was that the mere conferral of diversity jurisdiction not be read as authorizing the federal courts to make rules in areas that would lie beyond the legislative authority of Congress. *Erie* did not purport to address the propriety of federal common law in areas where Congress *could* legislate. Indeed, the same day that *Erie* was decided, the Court held in *Hinderlider v. La Plata River & Cherry Creek Ditch Co.*, 304 U.S. 92, 110 (1938), that federal common law governed interstate water disputes. Since *Erie*, the federal courts have on many occasions created common law based on substantive federal interests. As you read this modern example, consider whether the same policies militating for deference to state law in the procedural context ought to counsel for judicial restraint in creating substantive federal common law.

Boyle v. United Technologies Corp.

487 U.S. 500 (1988)

JUSTICE SCALIA delivered the opinion of the Court.

This case requires us to decide when a contractor providing military equipment to the Federal Government can be held liable under state tort law for injury caused by a design defect.

I

On April 27, 1983, David A. Boyle, a United States Marine helicopter copilot, was killed when the CH-53D helicopter in which he was flying crashed off the coast of Virginia Beach, Virginia, during a training exercise. Although Boyle survived the impact of the crash, he was unable to escape from the helicopter and drowned. Boyle's father, petitioner here, brought this diversity action in Federal District Court against the Sikorsky Division of United Technologies Corporation (Sikorsky), which built the helicopter for the United States.

At trial, petitioner presented two theories of liability under Virginia tort law that were submitted to the jury. First, petitioner alleged that Sikorsky had defectively repaired a device called the servo in the helicopter's automatic flight control system, which allegedly malfunctioned and caused the crash. Second, petitioner alleged that Sikorsky had defectively designed the copilot's emergency escape system: the escape hatch opened out instead of in (and was therefore ineffective in a submerged craft because of water pressure), and access to the escape hatch handle was obstructed by other equipment. The jury returned a general verdict in favor of petitioner and awarded him $725,000. The District Court denied Sikorsky's motion for judgment notwithstanding the verdict.

The Court of Appeals reversed and remanded with directions that judgment be entered for Sikorsky. 792 F.2d 413 (CA4 1986). It found, as a matter of Virginia law, that Boyle had failed to meet his burden of demonstrating that the repair work performed by Sikorsky, as opposed to work that had been done by the Navy, was responsible for the alleged malfunction of the flight control system. *Id.* at 415–416. It also found, as a matter of federal law, that Sikorsky could not be held liable for the allegedly defective design of the escape hatch because, on the evidence presented, it satisfied the requirements of the "military contractor defense," which the court had recognized the same day in *Tozer v. LTV Corp.*, 792 F.2d 403 (CA4 1986). 792 F.2d at 414–415.

Petitioner sought review here, challenging the Court of Appeals' decision on three levels: First, petitioner contends that there is no justification in federal law for shielding Government contractors from liability for design defects in military equipment. Second, he argues in the alternative that even if such a defense should exist, the Court of Appeals' formulation of the conditions for its application is inappropriate. Finally, petitioner contends that the Court of Appeals erred in not remanding for a jury determination of whether the elements of the defense were met in this case. We granted certiorari, 479 U.S. 1029 (1986).

II

Petitioner's broadest contention is that, in the absence of legislation specifically immunizing Government contractors from liability for design defects, there is no basis for judicial recognition of such a defense. We disagree. In most fields of activity, to be sure, this Court has refused to find federal pre-emption of state law in the absence of either a clear statutory prescription, *see, e.g., Jones v. Rath Packing Co.,* 430 U.S. 519, 525 (1977); *Rice v. Santa Fe Elevator Corp.,* 331 U.S. 218, 230 (1947), or a direct conflict between federal and state law, *see, e.g., Florida Lime & Avocado Growers, Inc. v. Paul,* 373 U.S. 132, 142–143 (1963); *Mines v. Davidowitz,* 312 U.S. 52, 67 (1941). But we have held that a few areas, involving "uniquely federal interests," *Texas Industries, Inc. v. Radcliff Materials, Inc.,* 451 U.S. 630, 640 (1981), are so committed by the Constitution and laws of the United States to federal control that state law, is pre-empted and replaced, where necessary, by federal law of a content prescribed (absent explicit statutory directive) by the courts—so-called "federal common law." *See, e.g., United States v. Kimbell Foods, Inc.,* 440 U.S. 715, 726–729 (1979); *Banco Nacional v. Sabbatino,* 376 U.S. 398, 426–427 (1964); *Howard v. Lyons,* 360 U.S. 593, 597 (1959); *Clearfield Trust Co. v. United States,* 318 U.S. 363, 366–367 (1943); *D'Oench, Duhme & Co. v. FDIC,* 315 U.S. 447, 457–458 (1942).

The dispute in the present case borders upon two areas that we have found to involve such "uniquely federal interests." We have held that obligations to and rights of the United States under its contracts are governed exclusively by federal law. . . . The present case does not involve an obligation to the United States under its contract, but rather liability to third persons. That liability may be styled one in tort, but it arises out of performance of the contract—and traditionally has been regarded as sufficiently related to the contract that until 1962 Virginia would generally allow design defect suits only by the purchaser and those in privity with the seller. *See General Bronze Corp. v. Kostopulos,* 203 Va. 66, 69–70 (1961); *see also* Va. Code §8.2-318 (1965) (eliminating privity requirement).

Another area that we have found to be of peculiarly federal concern, warranting the displacement of state law, is the civil liability of federal officials for actions taken in the course of their duty. We have held in many contexts that the scope of that liability is controlled by federal law. . . . The present case involves an independent contractor performing its obligation under a procurement contract, rather than an official performing his duty as a federal employee, but there is obviously implicated the same interest in getting the Government's work done.[1]

---

1. Justice Brennan's dissent misreads our discussion here to "intimat[e] that the immunity [of federal officials] . . . might extend . . . [to] nongovernment employees" such as a Government contractor. . . . But we do not address this issue, as it is not before us. We cite these cases merely to demonstrate that the liability of independent contractors performing work for the Federal Government, like the liability of federal officials, is an area of uniquely federal interest.

We think the reasons for considering these closely related areas to be of "uniquely federal" interest apply as well to the civil liabilities arising out of the performance of federal procurement contracts. We have come close to holding as much. In *Yearsley v. W.A. Ross Construction Co.*, 309 U.S. 18 (1940), we rejected an attempt by a landowner to hold a construction contractor liable under state law for the erosion of 95 acres caused by the contractor's work in constructing dikes for the Government. We said that "if [the] authority to carry out the project was validly conferred, that is, if what was done was within the constitutional power of Congress, there is no liability on the part of the contractor for executing its will." *Id.* at 20–21. The federal interest justifying this holding surely exists as much in procurement contracts as in performance contracts; we see no basis for a distinction.

Moreover, it is plain that the Federal Government's interest in the procurement of equipment is implicated by suits such as the present one—even though the dispute is one between private parties. It is true that where "litigation is purely between private parties and does not touch the rights and duties of the United States," *Bank of America Nat'l Trust & Sav. Ass'n v. Parnell*, 352 U.S. 29, 33 (1956), federal law does not govern. Thus, for example, in *Miree v. DeKalb County*, 433 U.S. 25, 30 (1977), which involved the question whether certain private parties could sue as third-party beneficiaries to an agreement between a municipality and the Federal Aviation Administration, we found that state law was not displaced because "the operations of the United States in connection with FAA grants such as these . . . would [not] be burdened" by allowing state law to determine whether third-party beneficiaries could sue, *id.* at 30, and because "any federal interest in the outcome of the [dispute] before us '[was] far too speculative, far too remote a possibility to justify the application of federal law to transactions essentially of local concern.'" *Id.* at 32–33, quoting *Parnell, supra*, 352 U.S. at 33–34; *see also Wallis v. Pan American Petroleum Corp.*, 384 U.S. 63, 69. But the same is not true here. The imposition of liability on Government contractors will directly affect the terms of Government contracts: either the contractor will decline to manufacture the design specified by the Government, or it will raise its price. Either way, the interests of the United States will be directly affected.

That the procurement of equipment by the United States is an area of uniquely federal interest does not, however, end the inquiry. That merely establishes a necessary, not a sufficient, condition for the displacement of state law. Displacement will occur only where, as we have variously described, a "significant conflict" exists between an identifiable "federal policy or interest and the [operation] of state law," *Wallis, supra*, at 68, or the application of state law would "frustrate specific objectives" of federal legislation, *Kimbell Foods*, 440 U.S. at 728. The conflict with federal policy need not be as sharp as that which must exist for ordinary pre-emption when Congress legislates "in a field which the States have traditionally occupied." *Rice v. Santa Fe Elevator Corp.*, 331 U.S. at 230. Or to put the point differently, the fact that the area in question is one of unique federal concern changes what would otherwise be a conflict that cannot produce pre-emption into one that can. But conflict there must be. In some cases, for example where the federal interest requires a uniform rule, the entire body of state law applicable to the area conflicts and is replaced by federal rules. *See, e.g., Clearfield Trust*, 318 U.S. at 366–367 (rights and obligations of United States with respect to commercial paper must be governed by uniform federal rule). In others, the conflict is more narrow, and only particular elements of state law are superseded. *See, e.g., Little Lake Misere Land Co.*, 412 U.S. at 595 (even assuming state law should generally govern federal land acquisitions, particular state law at issue may not); *Howard v. Lyons*, 360 U.S. at 597 (state defamation law generally applicable to federal official, but federal privilege governs for statements made in the course of federal official's duties).

In *Miree, supra*, the suit was not seeking to impose upon the person contracting with the Government a duty contrary to the duty imposed by the Government contract. Rather, it was the contractual duty *itself* that the private plaintiff (as third-party beneficiary) sought to enforce. Between *Miree* and the present case, it is easy to conceive of an intermediate situation, in which the duty sought to be imposed on the contractor is not identical to one assumed under the contract, but is also not contrary to any assumed. If, for example, the United States contracts for the purchase and installation of an air conditioning-unit, specifying the cooling capacity but not the precise manner of construction, a state law imposing upon the manufacturer of such units a duty of care to include a certain safety feature would not be a duty identical to anything promised the Government, but neither would it be contrary. The contractor could comply with both its contractual obligations and the state-prescribed duty of care. No one suggests that state law would generally be pre-empted in this context.

The present case, however, is at the opposite extreme from *Miree*. Here the state-imposed duty of care that is the asserted basis of the contractor's liability (specifically, the duty to equip helicopters with the sort of escape-hatch mechanism petitioner claims was necessary) is precisely contrary to the duty imposed by the Government contract (the duty to manufacture and deliver helicopters with the sort of escape-hatch mechanism shown by the specifications). Even in this sort of situation, it would be unreasonable to say that there is always a "significant conflict" between the state law and a federal policy or interest. If, for example, a federal procurement officer orders, by model number, a quantity of stock helicopters that happen to be equipped with escape hatches opening outward, it is impossible to say that the Government has a significant interest in that particular feature. That would be scarcely more reasonable than saying that a private individual who orders such a craft by model number cannot sue for the manufacturer's negligence because he got precisely what he ordered. . . .

There is, however, a statutory provision that demonstrates the potential for, and suggests the outlines of, "significant conflict" between federal interests and state law in the context of Government procurement. In the FTCA, Congress authorized damages to be recovered against the United States for harm caused by the negligent or wrongful conduct of Government employees, to the extent that a private person would be liable under the law of the place where the conduct occurred. 28 U.S.C. §1346(b). It excepted from this consent to suit, however,

> [a]ny claim . . . based upon the exercise or performance or the failure to exercise or perform a discretionary function or duty on the part of a federal agency or an employee of the Government, whether or not the discretion involved be abused. 28 U.S.C. §2680(a).

We think that the selection of the appropriate design for military equipment to be used by our Armed Forces is assuredly a discretionary function within the meaning of this provision. It often involves not merely engineering analysis but judgment as to the balancing of many technical, military, and even social considerations, including specifically the trade-off between greater safety and greater combat effectiveness. And we are further of the view that permitting "second-guessing" of these judgments, *see United States v. Varig Airlines*, 467 U.S. 797, 814 (1984), through state tort suits against contractors would produce the same effect sought to be avoided by the FTCA exemption. The financial burden of judgments against the contractors would ultimately be passed through, substantially if not totally, to the United States itself, since defense contractors will predictably raise their prices to cover, or to insure against, contingent liability for the Government-ordered designs. To put the point differently: It makes little sense to insulate the Government against financial liability for the judgment that a particular feature of military equipment is necessary when the Government produces the equipment itself, but not when it contracts for the production. In sum, we are of the view that state law which holds Government contractors liable for design defects in military equipment does in some circumstances present a "significant conflict" with federal policy and must be displaced.

We agree with the scope of displacement adopted by the Fourth Circuit here, which is also that adopted by the Ninth Circuit, *see McKay v. Rockwell Int'l Corp., supra*, at 451. Liability for design defects in military equipment cannot be imposed, pursuant to state law, when (1) the United States approved reasonably precise specifications; (2) the equipment conformed to those specifications; and (3) the supplier warned the United States about the dangers in the use of the equipment that were known to the supplier but not to the United States. The first two of these conditions assure that the suit is within the area where the policy of the "discretionary function" would be frustrated — *i.e.*, they assure that the design feature in question was considered by a Government officer, and not merely by the contractor itself. The third condition is necessary because, in its absence, the displacement of state tort law would create some incentive for the manufacturer to withhold knowledge of risks, since conveying that knowledge might disrupt the contract but withholding it would produce no liability. We adopt this provision lest our effort to protect discretionary functions perversely impede them by cutting off information highly relevant to the discretionary decision.

Accordingly, the judgment is vacated and the case is remanded [to determine whether a reasonable jury could have found for plaintiff in light of the government contractor defense].

So ordered.

JUSTICE BRENNAN, with whom JUSTICE MARSHALL and JUSTICE BLACKMUN join, dissenting.

Lieutenant David A. Boyle died when the CH-53D helicopter he was copiloting spun out of control and plunged into the ocean. We may assume, for purposes of this case, that Lt. Boyle was trapped under water and drowned because respondent United Technologies negligently designed the helicopter's escape hatch. We may further assume that any competent engineer would have discovered and cured the defects, but that they inexplicably escaped respondent's notice. Had respondent designed such a death trap for a commercial firm, Lt. Boyle's family could sue under Virginia tort law and be compensated for his tragic and unnecessary death. But respondent designed the helicopter for the Federal Government, and that, the Court tells us today, makes all the difference: Respondent is immune from liability so long as it obtained approval of "reasonably precise specifications"—perhaps no more than a rubber stamp from a federal procurement officer who might or might not have noticed or cared about the defects, or even had the expertise to discover them.

If respondent's immunity "bore the legitimacy of having been prescribed by the people's elected representatives," we would be duty bound to implement their will, whether or not we approved. *United States v. Johnson*, 481 U.S. 681, 703 (1987) (dissenting opinion of SCALIA, J.). Congress, however, has remained silent—and conspicuously so, having resisted a sustained campaign by Government contractors to legislate for them some defense.[1] The Court—unelected and unaccountable to the people—has unabashedly stepped into the breach to legislate a rule denying Lt. Boyle's family the compensation that state law assures them. This time the injustice is of this Court's own making.

Worse yet, the injustice will extend far beyond the facts of this case, for the Court's newly discovered Government contractor defense is breathtakingly sweeping. It applies not only to military equipment like the CH-53D helicopter, but (so far as I can tell) to any made-to-order gadget that the Federal Government might purchase after previewing plans—from NASA's Challenger space shuttle to the Postal Service's old mail cars. The contractor may invoke the defense in suits brought not only by military personnel like Lt. Boyle, or Government employees, but by anyone injured by a Government contractor's negligent design, including, for example, the children who might have died had respondent's helicopter crashed on the beach. It applies even if the Government has not intentionally sacrificed safety for other interests like speed or efficiency, and, indeed, even if the equipment is not of a type that is typically considered dangerous; thus, the contractor who designs a Government building can invoke the defense when the elevator cable snaps or the walls collapse. And the defense is invocable regardless of how blatant or easily remedied the defect, so long as the contractor missed it and the specifications approved by the Government, however unreasonably dangerous, were "reasonably precise." . . .

In my view, this Court lacks both authority and expertise to fashion such a rule, whether to protect the Treasury of the United States or the coffers of industry. Because I would leave that exercise of legislative power to Congress, where our Constitution places it, I would reverse the Court of Appeals and reinstate petitioner's jury award.

I

Before our decision in *Erie R. Co. v. Tompkins*, 304 U.S. 64 (1938), federal courts sitting in diversity were generally free, in the absence of a controlling state statute, to fashion rules of "general" federal common law. *See, e.g., Swift v. Tyson*, 16

---

1. *See, e.g.,* H.R. 4765, 99th Cong., 2d Sess. (1986) (limitations on civil liability of Government contractors); S. 2441, 99th Cong., 2d Sess. (1986) (same). *See also* H.R. 2378, 100th Cong., 1st Sess. (1987) (indemnification of civil liability for Government contractors); H.R. 5883, 98th Cong., 2d Sess. (1984) (same); H.R. 1504, 97th Cong., 1st Sess. (1981) (same); H.R. 5351, 96th Cong., 1st Sess. (1979) (same).

Pet. 1 (1842). *Erie* renounced the prevailing scheme: "Except in matters governed by the Federal Constitution or by Acts of Congress, the law to be applied in any case is the law of the State." 304 U.S. at 78. The Court explained that the expansive power that federal courts had theretofore exercised was an unconstitutional "'invasion of the authority of the State and, to that extent, a denial of its independence.'" *Id.* at 79. Thus, *Erie* was deeply rooted in notions of federalism, and is most seriously implicated when, as here, federal judges displace the state law that would ordinarily govern with their own rules of federal common law. . . .[2]

In pronouncing that "[t]here is no federal general common law," *Erie* put to rest the notion that the grant of diversity jurisdiction to federal courts is itself authority to fashion rules of substantive law. . . . As the author of today's opinion for the Court pronounced for a unanimous Court just two months ago, "'we start with the assumption that the historic police powers of the States were not to be superseded . . . unless that was the clear and manifest purpose of Congress.'" *Puerto Rico Dept. of Consumer Affairs v. Isla Petroleum Corp.*, 485 U.S. 495 (1988). Just as "[t]here is no federal pre-emption *in vacuo*, without a constitutional text or a federal statute to assert it," *id.* at 503, federal common law cannot supersede state law *in vacuo* out of no more than an idiosyncratic determination by five Justices that a particular area is "uniquely federal."

Accordingly, we have emphasized that federal common law can displace state law in "few and restricted" instances. *Wheeldin v. Wheeler*, 373 U.S. 647 (1963). "[A]bsent some congressional authorization to formulate substantive rules of decision, federal common law exists only in such narrow areas as those concerned with the rights and obligations of the United States, interstate and international disputes implicating conflicting rights of States or our relations with foreign nations, and admiralty cases." *Texas Industries, Inc. v. Radcliff Materials, Inc.*, 451 U.S. 630, 641 (1981). "The enactment of a federal rule in an area of national concern, and the decision whether to displace state law in doing so, is generally made not by the federal judiciary, purposefully insulated from democratic pressures, but by the people through their elected representatives in Congress." *Milwaukee v. Illinois*, 451 U.S. 304, 312–313 (1981). . . . State laws "should be overridden by the federal courts only where clear and substantial interests of the National Government, which cannot be served consistently with respect for such state interests, will suffer major damage if the state law is applied." *United States v. Yazell*, 382 U.S. 341, 352 (1966).

II

Congress has not decided to supersede state law here (if anything, it has decided not to, *see* n. 1, *supra*) and the Court does not pretend that its newly manufactured "Government contractor defense" fits within any of the handful of "narrow

---

2. Not all exercises of our power to fashion federal common law displace state law in the same way. For example, our recognition of federal causes of action based upon either the Constitution, *see, e.g., Bivens v. Six Unknown Fed. Narcotics Agents*, 403 U.S. 388 (1971), or a federal statute, *see Cort v. Ash*, 422 U.S. 66 (1975), supplements whatever rights state law might provide, and therefore does not implicate federalism concerns in the same way as does pre-emption of a state-law rule of decision or cause of action. Throughout this opinion I use the word "displace" in the latter sense.

areas," *Texas Industries, supra,* 451 U.S. at 641, of "uniquely federal interests" in which we have heretofore done so, 451 U.S. at 640. Rather, the Court creates a new category of "uniquely federal interests" out of a synthesis of two whose origins predate *Erie* itself: the interest in administering the "obligations to and rights of the United States under its contracts," and the interest in regulating the "civil liability of federal officials for actions taken in the course of their duty." This case is, however, simply a suit between two private parties. We have steadfastly declined to impose federal contract law on relationships that are collateral to a federal contract, or to extend the federal employee's immunity beyond federal employees. And the Court's ability to list 2, or 10, inapplicable areas of "uniquely federal interest" does not support its conclusion that the liability of Government contractors is so "clear and substantial" an interest that this Court must step in lest state law does "major damage." *Yazell, supra,* 382 U.S. at 352.

A

The proposition that federal common law continues to govern the "obligations to and rights of the United States under its contracts" is nearly as old as *Erie* itself. Federal law typically controls when the Federal Government is a party to a suit involving its rights or obligations under a contract. . . . Any such transaction necessarily "radiate[s] interests in transactions between private parties." *Bank of America Nat'l Trust & Sav. Ass'n v. Parnell,* 352 U.S. 29, 33 (1956). But it is by now established that our power to create federal common law controlling the Federal Government's contractual rights and obligations does not translate into a power to prescribe rules that cover all transactions or contractual relationships collateral to Government contracts. . . .

Here . . . a Government contract governed by federal common law looms in the background. But here, too, the United States is not a party to the suit and the suit neither "touch[es] the rights and duties of the United States," *Parnell, supra,* 352 U.S. at 33, nor has a "direct effect upon the United States or its Treasury," *Miree,* 433 U.S. at 29. The relationship at issue is at best collateral to the Government contract. . . .

That the Government might have to pay higher prices for what it orders if delivery in accordance with the contract exposes the seller to potential liability, does not distinguish this case. [Prior cases] declined to extend the reach of federal common law despite the assertion of comparable interests that would have affected the terms of the Government contract—whether its price or its substance—just as "directly" (or indirectly). . . .

As in each of the cases declining to extend the traditional reach of federal law of contracts beyond the rights and duties of the *Federal Government,* "any federal interest in the outcome of the question before us is far too speculative, far too remote a possibility to justify the application of federal law to transactions essentially of local concern." *Miree, supra,* 433 U.S. at 32-33. . . .

B

[There is no precedent for extending immunity to private parties.]

III

In a valiant attempt to bridge the analytical canyon between what *Yearsley* said and what the Court wishes it had said, the Court invokes the discretionary function exception of the Federal Tort Claims Act (FTCA), 28 U.S.C. §2680(a). The Court does not suggest that the exception has any direct bearing here, for petitioner has sued a private manufacturer (not the Federal Government) under Virginia law (not the FTCA). . . .

IV

At bottom, the Court's analysis is premised on the proposition that any tort liability indirectly absorbed by the Government so burdens governmental functions as to compel us to act when Congress has not. That proposition is by no means uncontroversial. The tort system is premised on the assumption that the imposition of liability encourages actors to prevent any injury whose expected cost exceeds the cost of prevention. If the system is working as it should, Government contractors will design equipment to avoid certain injuries (like the deaths of soldiers or Government employees), which would be certain to burden the Government. The Court therefore has no basis for its assumption that tort liability will result in a net burden on the Government (let alone a clearly excessive net burden) rather than a net gain.

Perhaps tort liability is an inefficient means of ensuring the quality of design efforts, but "[w]hatever the merits of the policy" the Court wishes to implement, "its conversion into law is a proper subject for congressional action, not for any creative power of ours." *Standard Oil*, 332 U.S. at 314–315. It is, after all, "Congress, not this Court or the other federal courts, [that] is the custodian of the national purse. By the same token [Congress] is the primary and most often the exclusive arbiter of federal fiscal affairs. And these comprehend, as we have said, securing the treasury or the Government against financial losses *however inflicted*. . . ." *Ibid.* (emphasis added). *See also Gilman, supra*, 347 U.S. at 510–512. If Congress shared the Court's assumptions and conclusion it could readily enact "A BILL [t]o place limitations on the civil liability of government contractors to ensure that such liability does not impede the ability of the United States to procure necessary goods and services," H.R. 4765, 99th Cong., 2d Sess. (1986); *see also* S. 2441, 99th Cong., 2d Sess. (1986). It has not.

Were I a legislator, I would probably vote against any law absolving multibillion dollar private enterprises from answering for their tragic mistakes, at least if that law were justified by no more than the unsupported speculation that their liability might ultimately burden the United States Treasury. Some of my colleagues here would evidently vote otherwise (as they have here), but that should not matter here. We are judges not legislators, and the vote is not ours to cast.

I respectfully dissent.

[Dissent by Justice Stevens omitted.]

NOTES AND QUESTIONS

1. *Paramount Federal Interest?* The impact of the Court's decision is that plaintiff is foreclosed from asserting a claim for *negligent* design; only claims for failure to warn of *known* defects are actionable. Are you persuaded by Justice Scalia that

insulating the contractor from liability for negligence in this case was necessary to protect an important federal interest? Even assuming that the price of goods to the military would be raised by the imposition of liability for defective design, isn't there a countervailing governmental interest in the safety of goods purchased by the military? Is the government indifferent to whether military personnel can recover damages against a negligent manufacturer? Could judgment for the manufacturer here discourage people from serving in the military, just as a judgment for plaintiff would allegedly deter contractors from doing business with the military? How does Justice Scalia know that imposing a burden on government contractors hurts the military more than imposing the burden of uncompensated injuries on a soldier does? If Congress has not seen fit to strike that balance in favor of the contractor, why should the Supreme Court?

2. *Federal Interest in the Design of the Helicopter?* Is your view of the case on the merits affected by whether the escape hatch was actually designed by the military, or simply "rubber-stamped" by a federal official? Is that distinction relevant to the test for immunity articulated by the Court? Would the government be foreclosed under *Boyle* from suing the contractor for defective design? If not, why should plaintiff be foreclosed?

3. *Relevance of Federal Tort Claims Act?* What is the significance of the Federal Tort Claims Act (FTCA)? Justice Scalia is not asserting that the contractor is covered by the FTCA. Rather, his argument seems to be that the same policies advanced for governmental immunity under the FTCA would also be advanced by immunity for the government contractor. Is Scalia asserting that the omission of private contractors from the FTCA was an oversight? Does the FTCA have some legal force "by analogy" that transcends its literal reach? Would the Court have reached the same result in the absence of the statute? What, if any, attention should the majority in *Boyle* have given to the fact that military contractors apparently lobbied Congress in an unsuccessful attempt to obtain a statutory government-contractor defense?

4. *Ideological Role Reversal?* What do you make of the fact that the leading "liberal" on the Court at the time—Brennan—argues in *Boyle* for deference to Congress, and against judicial activism, while the leading "conservative"—Scalia—asserts more expansive judicial authority to craft a rule of tort law that displaces state law? Not surprisingly, in other cases their positions have been reversed. *See, e.g., Bivens v. Six Unknown Named Agents of Federal Bureau of Narcotics*, 403 U.S. 388 (1971) (Brennan opinion finding implied cause of action for Fourth Amendment violations by federal officials); *Thompson v. Thompson*, 484 U.S. 174, 188–193 (Scalia, J., concurring) (urging that federal courts should not assume the role of creating implied causes of action when Congress has not chosen to create one; "[a]n enactment by implication cannot realistically be regarded as the product of the difficult lawmaking process our Constitution has prescribed. . . . It is . . . dangerous to assume that, even with the utmost self-discipline, judges can prevent . . . mirroring the policies they favor."). Are the Justices simply being unprincipled, invoking federal common law when it furthers their ideological position and renouncing it when it does not? *See* Donald L. Doernberg, *Juridical Chameleons in the "New Erie" Canal*, 1990 Utah L. Rev. 759.

5. *The Proper Role of Courts?* What is the appropriate role for judicial lawmaking outside of the interpretation of the Constitution and statutes? State courts have a rich tradition of making common law in advance of legislation. What is the

justification, if any, for confining federal courts to the role of constitutional and statutory interpretation? Even in the area of statutory interpretation, Justice Scalia has imposed upon Congress the burden of explicit legislative drafting, attempting to dissuade the Court from inferring policies and rules from broad statutory purposes not explicitly stated in the legislation. *See, e.g., Thompson v. Thompson*, 484 U.S. 174, 188–192 (1988) (Scalia, J., concurring) (urging abandonment of doctrine of "implied causes of action"). Is it more justifiable for the Court to deduce implicit congressional preferences in the absence of a pertinent statute, as it arguably did in *Boyle?* Or are congressional preferences irrelevant in the absence of a statute? On the other hand, is there any reason why the federal courts should be more constrained in making federal law in areas of federal competency than state courts are in making state common law? *Compare* Martin H. Redish, *Federal Common Law, Political Legitimacy, and the Interpretive Process: An "Institutionalist" Perspective*, 83 Nw. U. L. Rev. 761 (1989) (federal common law is anti-majoritarian and should be constrained by the Rules of Decision Act) *with* Louise Weinberg, *The Curious Notion That the Rules of Decision Act Blocks Supreme Federal Common Law*, 83 Nw. U. L. Rev. 860 (1989) (advocating expansive federal common law-making on the ground that it is more democratic than the legislative process dominated by private interests); Westen & Lehman, *Is There Life for* Erie *After the Death of Diversity?*, 78 Mich. L. Rev. 311 (1979–1980) (arguing that Rules of Decision Act has no application to federal common law).

NOTE ON OTHER EXAMPLES OF FEDERAL COMMON LAW

An intensive treatment of the subject of federal common law is beyond the scope of this course. As discussed in *Boyle*, federal common law has been developed in a number of contexts. Perhaps most commonly, it is employed when Congress has regulated in an area but has neglected to address some specific problem. Federal common law is used to "fill the gaps" where application of state law to the question would frustrate the legislative purpose. The federal courts in such cases must craft, as a matter of federal common law, rules to fill the void. For instance, in *DelCostello v. International Brotherhood of Teamsters*, 462 U.S. 151 (1983), the Court held, as a matter of federal common law, that the statute of limitations in suits by employees against their employers and unions for breach of labor agreements should be provided by federal law. Because the area of collective bargaining is preempted by federal law, and Congress explicitly provided for a federal cause of action in such cases, the Court in *DelCostello* determined it was appropriate to supply the missing term in the statutory scheme by "borrowing," by analogy, the limitations period used in the federal National Labor Relations Act. *See also Merrill Lynch, Pierce, Fenner & Smith, Inc. v. Curran*, 456 U.S. 353 (1982) (implying private cause of actions for violations of the Commodity Exchange Act).

Federal common law rules have also been crafted to define the legal obligations of the federal government or its officials; *see, e.g., Clearfield Trust Co. v. United States*, 318 U.S. 363 (1943) (federal common law determines the rights and obligations of the United States on commercial paper issued by it); and to protect compelling federal interests, as in *Boyle*, as well as cases touching upon foreign relations, admiralty, and disputes between states. *See* Erwin Chemerinsky, Federal Jurisdiction §6.2 (7th ed. 2016). Some commentators have even referred to some forms

Chapter 4. The Law Applied in Federal Court

of constitutional adjudication as "common law" decisions. *See* Thomas W. Merrill, *The Common Law Powers of Federal Courts*, 52 U. Chi. L. Rev. 1, 5–6 (1985).

Emphasizing that "[t]he cases in which federal courts may engage in common lawmaking are few and far between," the Supreme Court in *Rodriguez Federal Deposit Ins. Corp.*, 140 S.Ct. 713 (2020), declined to follow Circuit Court precedent crafting federal common law to determine the ownership of a tax refund for a consolidated federal corporate tax return.

Although substantive federal common law implicates some of the same concerns that were raised in the *Erie* context, there are notable differences. Federal common law is predicated on the existence of federal legislative authority, with the courts acting in advance, or in the interstices of federal legislation. Moreover, invocation of federal common law is not as problematic in terms of the "equality" and forum shopping concerns voiced in *Erie*. When the Supreme Court issues a common law rule in order to protect a substantive federal interest, that rule is binding on both federal and state courts. Thus, such a ruling provides a rule of decision not dependent on the "accident of diversity" and generates no incentive to forum shop between state and federal courts. *See* Henry J. Friendly, *In Praise of* Erie —*and of the New Federal Common Law*, 39 N.Y.U. L. Rev. 383, 421–422 (1964).

Nevertheless, federal common law does raise federalism and separation of powers concerns. *Boyle* is an example of the former. *See* Martha A. Field, *Sources of Law: The Scope of Federal Common Law*, 99 Harv. L. Rev. 881, 924–925 (1986) (unrestrained federal common law would undermine state law-making). Use of federal common law may also appropriate regulatory authority properly belonging to Congress. *See* George D. Brown, *Of Activism and* Erie — *The Implication Doctrine's Implication for the Nature and Role of the Federal Courts*, 69 Iowa L. Rev. 617 (1984) (federal common law appropriates legislative prerogatives properly belonging to Congress); Doernberg, *Judicial Chameleons, supra*, 1990 Utah L. Rev. 759 (same). Others cite the power of Congress to legislatively overrule any common law adjudication as a check on judicial appropriation of legislative prerogatives. *See, e.g.*, Larry Kramer, *The Lawmaking Power of the Federal Courts*, 12 Pace L. Rev. 263, 271 (1992).

NOTE ON "REVERSE *ERIE*" DOCTRINE

When federal substantive law is applied in state courts, there are occasions when use of state procedure does not adequately vindicate the federal right. In such cases, the state procedure will be preempted pursuant to the "reverse-*Erie*" doctrine. *See generally* Kevin M. Clermont, *Reverse*-Erie, 82 Notre Dame L. Rev. 1 (2006); Omar K. Madhany, Note, *Towards a Unified Theory of "Reverse*-Erie," 162 U. Pa. L. Rev. 1261 (2014).

For instance, in *Felder v. Casey*, 487 U.S. 131 (1988), the Court held that the Wisconsin courts were prohibited from applying the Wisconsin notice-of-claims statute to federal civil rights claims filed in state court. The statute required all plaintiffs with claims against a governmental entity or officer to notify defendant within 120 days of injury. The Court held that while states were generally free to apply their own procedure to federal claims, the notice-of-claim provision "unduly burdened" the federal right. The notice requirement in the statute frustrated congressional intent to provide a timely judicial remedy for civil rights violations; citing

Erie, the Court held that the procedure had an impermissible "outcome determinative" impact on the federal cause of action. *Id.* at 151–153.

Note that in federal question cases, unlike diversity cases, both parties usually have equal access to federal court. Thus, application of state procedure in state court is rarely the consequence of unilateral forum shopping, and could not be said to constitute "grave discrimination" on the basis of citizenship. In light of this difference, was the *Felder* Court's use of the "outcome determination" test appropriate? If plaintiff wanted to avail himself of federal procedures, why didn't he simply file in federal court? Is there any reason to believe that Congress believed it necessary to displace state procedure in state court when a federal forum was available?

CHAPTER 5
ANATOMY OF A LITIGATION: PLEADING, DISCOVERY, AND ADJUDICATION

A. PLEADINGS

1. Introduction

A lawsuit is normally commenced by a plaintiff filing a *complaint* with the court. As you saw in the introductory materials, a complaint is a story; it is plaintiff's initial account of defendant's wrongful behavior toward him. In response, defendant is required to provide her account in an *answer*. Together, these documents (occasionally supplemented by additional documents) form the *pleadings*. The pleadings serve to define the parameters of the lawsuit; the pleadings set forth each party's factual and legal contentions and thus will help to focus discovery and trial and occasionally facilitate the disposition of the lawsuit without trial.

The use of pleadings to frame the litigation has been a constant feature of Anglo-American law for hundreds of years. Why do you suppose that is the case? If you were constructing a dispute resolution system from the ground up, would you include a pleading stage? What problems would the courts and the litigants encounter if pleadings were not submitted? Consider the following:

- It would be difficult, if not impossible, for the parties to prepare their case for trial without knowing the position of their opponents.
- Every case would have to go to trial to determine the legal and/or factual sufficiency of a party's position.
- The parties would waste time proving uncontested facts at trial.
- The court would have no way of determining whether evidence sought in discovery or offered as proof at trial was "relevant."
- It would be difficult to determine the scope of a judgment for preclusion purposes without knowing what the parties attempted to establish.

How do pleadings solve these problems? Are there alternative methods of addressing these concerns? Couldn't the parties simply flesh out their case as the litigation proceeded through discovery and approached trial? What are the advantages and disadvantages of requiring the parties to spell out their positions in the initial pleadings compared with providing that information later in the litigation?

Both the English writ system and early common law pleadings placed the entire pretrial burden on the first stage of the litigation—the pleadings. More modern procedural systems have distributed these functions among different stages of the pretrial phase. In thinking about an "ideal" system of pleadings, remember that the lawsuit is just starting, and it may be difficult for a party to obtain information necessary to its case. At the same time, if the "pleading burden" is too easy, parties may too facilely assert nonmeritorious claims or defenses and use the expense of litigation to force unjustified settlements.

2.   *History of Pleading*

Before grappling with the litigation problem that we will use to illustrate the concepts in this chapter, it is useful to understand the history of litigation as it evolved from common law practice in England. Much of that history is still relevant to various aspects of modern procedure.

a.   The Royal Courts at Common Law

Prior to the Norman Conquest (1066), claims and disputes were decided in local tribunals according to local customary law. After the Conquest (and particularly from about 1160 to 1300), the King's courts developed as a separate, and ultimately supreme, system. The law administered in the royal courts was "common law" because it was common to all of the realm.

The three great "common law" courts and their initial principal business were:

• Court of Common Pleas	disputes over freehold land
• Court of King's Bench	felony prosecutions and breaches of the "King's peace"
• Court of the Exchequer	enforcement of the King's revenue

The Court of Common Pleas was the first to emerge as a court of general jurisdiction. By 1600, all three were courts of general and virtually concurrent jurisdiction.

b.   The Writ System and Common Law "Forms of Action"

The Norman Kings enlarged their authority by resort to the prerogative power of the King as preserver of the peace of the realm. This occurred largely through the issuance of *writs* —written orders that some specific thing be done or not be done —in the name of the King by the Chancellor. The Chancellor, the head of the Chancery, was the Secretary of State for all departments and keeper of the King's great seal.

A claimant could not sue in the Court of Common Pleas without first going to the Chancellor and securing a writ authorizing suit. The writ system was essentially a classification of standardized types of situations in which suit could be brought in the royal courts (ergo "no writ, no right").

Common law litigation was cast into "forms of action," corresponding to the available writs, on the theory that a court could try a claim only if it fell within the bounds of the particular writ plaintiff had secured. The writs contained a capsular and stylized statement of the claim and were viewed as conferring authority or jurisdiction on the King's court to try that case. Unlike the contemporary practice of applying a single procedural model to all types of claims, procedure at common law varied with the type of claim being asserted. Each writ was associated with a particular form of plea, pretrial process, and form of judgment and execution. Moreover, a plaintiff could not recover unless he established all of the elements of the particular writ that he elected to use, regardless of whether the case might have succeeded under a different writ.

The principal writs (and corresponding forms of action) were:

- Trespass — intentional injury to person or property
- Covenant — nonperformance of promise "under seal"
- Debt — nonpayment of loan or other fixed-sum obligation
- Assumpsit — breach of an "informal" contract
- Replevin — personal property taken from plaintiff's possession
- Ejectment — wrongful eviction of occupant of land
- Detinue — unlawful detention of personal property by one to whom it has been entrusted
- Trover — conversion of personal property by a finder or other person not entitled to it
- Action of (or on the) Case — a flexible offshoot of Trespass redressing "indirect injury" to person or property; in time, becomes the form of the general tort action for negligence

By the end of the thirteenth century, the system of writs administered by the King's courts became a formally rigid and closed system, with a limited number of fixed forms of action. With the reinvigoration of royal authority following the civil wars of the fourteenth century, the scope of the common law actions expanded. No new writs were devised, but the old forms of action, especially trespass, were construed to reach situations previously considered outside their terms. By the nineteenth century, many of the writs in common use were ones unknown in the fifteenth century—e.g., ejectment, assumpsit, and trover—and many others had previously fallen by the wayside. Nevertheless, the system failed in many ways to adapt itself rapidly enough to the needs of society, and this failure led to the origin and growth of the competing—and complementary—system of equity.

c. The Rise of Equity

Equity developed in response to the rigidity and formalism of the writ system of the common law courts. Many otherwise meritorious claims could not be satisfactorily adjudicated in the common law courts either because they involved transactions not contemplated in the forms of action or because common law procedure had no device for compelling testimony of the parties or the production of documents. In such situations, a *petition* (or "bill") was made directly to the King and his Council, invoking the traditional royal prerogative to do justice. These petitions were often referred to the Chancellor. In essence, the Chancellor became a supervisory judge, offering to parties relief that was not available at common law.

In processing such petitions, the Chancellor developed a special system of procedures to bring the parties before him, sift out the facts, and implement his decisions. These included the direct personal order to a party, the contempt sanction against disobedience, and the use of sworn pleadings, affidavits, and depositions to develop the facts. The bill was a prolix document in no standard form, setting out every conceivable circumstance that entitled plaintiff to any part of the requested relief. Defendant was summoned by a subpoena to appear and answer under oath to each charge in plaintiff's bill of complaint.

Prior to the hearing before the Chancellor—no jury was available—evidence was collected. Each witness was examined before a judicial officer. These depositions would be considered by the judge at the hearing. There was no oral examination before the court. The ultimate judicial remedy was a personal order to the defendant to do or not do a specific thing, with imprisonment as the ultimate sanction for disobedience.

At common law, by contrast, the pretrial proceedings consisted of a war of pleadings. Every pleading was met with a responsive pleading until issues emerged in proper form for consideration by the jury. It was not until trial that documents were produced and witnesses examined. Oral evidence was meager because neither plaintiff nor defendant nor any other party interested in the result of the action was permitted to give evidence. The ultimate judicial remedy at law was normally a judgment for money damages. A writ of execution could then be brought upon the judgment empowering the sheriff to seize and sell defendant's property to pay the damages, or deliver possession to the plaintiff.

The flexibility of equity compared to law went beyond procedure. The chancellors developed their own system of substantive law to protect interests not recognized in the law courts—e.g., the interests of beneficiaries of trusts created to convey land without incurring feudal restrictions; the recognition of the defense of "fraud in the inducement" to relieve a debtor who had given a bond to secure payment of the purchase price where the creditor had misrepresented the value or quality of what was sold.

However, equity jurisdiction was considered extraordinary and available only when the remedy at law was inadequate; equitable redress was regarded as a privilege to be awarded in the Chancellor's discretion rather than as a right available on the basis of precedent.

d. The Struggle Between Law and Equity

Opposition to the rise of equity came from Parliament and later the law courts. More than territorial authority was at stake. A party employing fraud to induce a contract might win at common law, which did not recognize the defense of "fraud in the inducement," whereas he would suffer a contrary fate in equity. The battleground was typically a controversy first brought in equity, resulting in a decree restraining parties from prosecuting their actions in the law courts. Such a restraint was issued when the Chancellor determined that successful prosecution of the lawsuit would be inequitable because of the existence of an equitable defense that the law court would not recognize. In the 1615 decision *Courtney v. Glanvil*, 79 Eng. Rep. 294 (K.B. 1615), the supremacy of equity received the royal stamp of approval.

Despite equity's ascendancy, the dual system worked hardships. Cases were dismissed in equity because the proper remedy was at law. Parties at law could not in the law action establish equitable claims or defenses pertaining to the same occurrence, requiring the bringing of two actions to resolve a single transaction.

e. The "Reception" of the Common Law in the United States

Common law ideas and methods came to the United States in a variety of ways, the most important being the "reception statutes." These statutes typically provided that "the common law of England (including Acts of Parliament that had become woven into the fabric of common law thought, such as the Statute of Frauds) is received as the law of this State." Such statutes frequently had a cut-off date, usually 1776, after which English decisions were not "received" but treated as persuasive authority. Such statutes often provided that English doctrines and precedents were received only "insofar as equitable to local [state] conditions."

Most American courts, at least initially, recognized the common law writs and required litigants to conform their pleadings to the forms of action. This conformity with English practice started to break down in the mid-nineteenth century, as did the distinction between law and equity.

f. Merger of Law and Equity and the Abandonment of the Forms of Action

The dual system of law and equity prevailed in both England and the United States until the nineteenth century: separate equity courts, different equitable procedures, and different equitable remedies. Even when a state had a single court system, it administered law and equity separately. This began to change with the reform movement in New York, led by David Dudley Field, culminating in the New York Code of 1848 (commonly known as the "Field Code"), authorizing a court in a single action to draw on the applicable rules regardless of whether they were formerly treated as legal or as equitable.

Not only did this merge law and equity, but it also made procedure *transubstantive*. A single form of pleading and pretrial practice would govern all claims, regardless of which "writ" the claim may have been cast as at common law. It also abandoned the attempt of common law pleading to narrow the case to a single issue through continuous rounds of responsive pleading.

The work begun by Field has been widely followed in the United States and England. *See, e.g.*, Fed. R. Civ. P. 2 ("There is one form of action — the civil action.").

g.   Modern Pleading Practice

Pleading under the Field Code was far less stylized than under common law pleading. Where the common law writ specified each required allegation, Code pleading simply required the pleader to include "a plain and concise statement of the facts constituting a cause of action." However, the apparent simplicity of the standard did not prevent the courts from developing highly technical rules. A complaint under Code pleading could be dismissed for being either too conclusory or too detailed.

The adoption of the Federal Rules of Civil Procedure in 1938 significantly liberalized the pleading standard. Under Fed. R. Civ. P. 8(a)(2), a pleading must include: "a short and plain statement of the claim showing that the pleader is entitled to relief." The federal litigant normally has to submit only a single pleading; plaintiff need not file a "reply" to defendant's answer. The intent of the drafters was to get away from the technical pleading requirements of both Code and common law pleading. The Federal Rules also made it easier to amend the pleadings and for proof at trial to be at variance from the assertions of the pleadings. *See* Fed. R. Civ. P. 15(a) and (b).

Pleading under the Federal Rules is often characterized as "notice pleading" — that is, the primary function of the pleadings is to put the other parties on notice of the general nature of the pleader's contentions to enable them to prepare the case against the pleader. Obviously, the more detailed pleading required under prior practice also put the other litigants on notice, indeed much more detailed notice. The significant difference is in what modern pleading does *not* provide. Pleading under the Federal Rules simply gets the action underway. If a litigant wants to find out more detailed information about another party's contentions, she gets that information through discovery, not through the pleadings. If a court wants to scrutinize the legal or factual sufficiency of a litigant's position, it may well have to wait for the case to be fleshed out in discovery; the pleadings on their own may not provide sufficient information.

The modern pleader is at much lesser risk of losing her rights through a technical pleading mistake. Fed. R. Civ. P. 1 states that the Rules "should be construed, and administered, and employed by the court and the parties to secure the just, speedy, and inexpensive determination of every action and proceeding." Does the liberalization of pleading accomplish all of those objectives? Can you think of any ways in which the more detailed pleading required under prior practice was more effective at securing a "just, speedy, and inexpensive" resolution of litigation?

3.   Litigation Problem

Throughout this chapter we will ask you to assume the role of various attorneys responsible for litigating a product liability claim against Rockwell International Corporation arising out of the crash of an FAA plane returning from a flight check mission at various airports in western Pennsylvania. We will be using this fact pattern to frame a set of issues that arise at the pleading, discovery, summary judgment, and trial phases of civil litigation.

a.   The Intake Interview

Assume the role of plaintiff's attorney. You have been approached by Mary Burdick, the surviving spouse of Theodore Burdick, one of the crew members killed in the crash. Mrs. Burdick doesn't know a great deal about the circumstances surrounding the crash, but she provides you with the following information.

Mr. Burdick was one of three FAA crew members assigned the task of calibrating the Instrument Landing Signals (ILS) emitted by airports in the mid-Atlantic region. In order to ensure the accuracy of these signals, the FAA sends crews semiannually to compare the positions indicated by the ILS with global positioning data obtained from satellites.

The crew set out on the morning of November 2, 1988, to calibrate the ILS at Westmorland Airport in western Pennsylvania. They were flying in cold, damp weather conducive to the buildup of ice on airplanes at the time of the accident. After finishing the calibration of the ILS, the plane radioed the Latrobe, Pennsylvania, ground control that they had lost power in both engines. Shortly thereafter, the plane crashed, killing all three crew members.

Mrs. Burdick has gotten a copy of the National Transportation Safety Board (NTSB) investigation report of the accident. The report is based on the NTSB's inspection of the remains of the plane, autopsies of the crew members, and interviews with various witnesses. It concludes that the accident was caused by a number of factors. First, the report notes that both the pilot and copilot had been drinking the night before the accident. The copilot's driver's license had recently been revoked for driving under the influence of alcohol. The autopsy revealed a blood alcohol level of .059 in the pilot's blood (a level that would be obtained by testing someone who had just consumed approximately two drinks) and trace amounts of alcohol in the copilot's blood. Second, the report noted damage to the rotors inside the plane's engines consistent with the ingestion of ice into the engines. The report also questioned the judgment and training of the crew.

The transcript of the pilot's radio transmission also suggested that the crew were not sure where they were when the engines failed. They initially asked for the headings into Johnstown Airport, and seconds before the crash said, "I mean Latrobe."

The report describes the plane as a Rockwell 1121A Jet Commander. The turbojet engines were manufactured by General Electric.

b.   Follow-Up Investigation

Following Mrs. Burdick's meeting with you, you discuss the NTSB report with an aviation expert that you have retained. Your expert tells you the following about how the engines could have failed.

First, ice coming off the wings could have been ingested by the engines, which were situated above and behind each wing. If the pieces of ice were large enough, they could have damaged the engines sufficiently to cause a loss of power. Second, he opines, ice could have accumulated around the front of the engines, depriving the engines of sufficient intake of air to operate.

You, of course, need to establish that the accident was caused by some defect in the manufacture or design of the aircraft. Your expert suggests two such possible flaws.

First, he tells you there may be a problem with how the plane was designed to "deice" itself mid-flight. Ice tends to accumulate in cold weather on any surface of the aircraft exposed to the oncoming air, particularly in damp weather. Ice accumulation on the wing is particularly dangerous because it can result in the loss of lift, causing the plane to fall out of the sky. Therefore, planes are always equipped with some means of either preventing the buildup of ice on the wing or removing it if it accumulates. Rockwell utilized the removal, or deicing, technique on the Jet Commander of installing a pneumatic "boot" on the front of the wing. The boot is inflated by the pilot pressing a button in the cockpit. Any ice that has accumulated is then pushed off the wing. It is much safer, the expert tells you, to heat the wing, and prevent ice buildup altogether. Moreover, the engines were close to the wings, creating the danger that the engines might ingest ice removed from the front of the wing. Thus, if the engine failure is attributable to ingestion of ice, Rockwell was arguably at fault. However, the expert notes that the pilot might have contributed to the crash by waiting too long before inflating the deicing boot, thus creating much larger chunks of ice than the engines could safely ingest.

Second, Rockwell might also conceivably be at fault if the engine failure was caused by ice buildup on the front of the engines. The plane was equipped with "anti-icing" heaters that diverted engine heat from the rear of the engine to the front of the engine. If those heaters failed, the resulting ice buildup on the front of the engines could have suffocated the engines. Alternatively, if the pilot forgot to turn on the heat diverters, the crash may have been attributable solely to his error.

Rockwell Jet Commander

4. Candor in Pleading

Do you, as attorney for Mrs. Burdick, now have enough proof of Rockwell's culpability to justify filing a complaint against them? The question of how much information an attorney must possess before filing suit is one of the central issues in litigation. Two Federal Rules address the issue: Rule 11, which requires that an attorney certify that a claim is well founded; and Rule 8(a), which sets forth the required elements of a complaint. Our initial focus will be on Rule 11.

Pursuant to Rule 11, every paper filed in the course of litigation, with the exception of discovery requests and responses, must be signed by the attorney of record. That signature certifies, to the best of the attorney's "knowledge, information and belief, formed after an inquiry reasonable under the circumstances," that the document "is not being presented for any improper purpose"; that the claims and defenses asserted "are warranted by existing law or by a nonfrivolous argument" for modifying existing law; and that factual contentions "have evidentiary support or . . . will likely have evidentiary support after a reasonable opportunity for investigation or discovery."

Attorneys may be sanctioned if the certification was not warranted. The court may order sanctions *sua sponte* (on its own initiative) or pursuant to motion by an opposing party. However, pursuant to Rule 11(c)(2), before a party can file a sanctions motion, the sanctioned party must be given the opportunity to withdraw the offending document.

The question of what constitutes "reasonable inquiry under the circumstances" is complex. In the course of litigation, attorneys often rely on others for much of the information they collect, including information provided by clients, associates, and experts. As you read the following case, consider when such reliance is inappropriate and what obligation an attorney has once she discovers that the underlying facts do not support her claim or defense.

Christian v. Mattel, Inc.

286 F.3d 1118 (9th Cir. 2002)

McKEOWN, CIRCUIT JUDGE.

It is difficult to imagine that the Barbie doll, so perfect in her sculpture and presentation, and so comfortable in every setting, from "California girl" to "Chief Executive Officer Barbie," could spawn such acrimonious litigation and such egregious conduct on the part of her challenger. In her wildest dreams, Barbie could not have imagined herself in the middle of Rule 11 proceedings. But the intersection of copyrights on Barbie sculptures and the scope of Rule 11 is precisely what defines this case.

James Hicks appeals from a district court order requiring him, pursuant to Federal Rule of Civil Procedure 11, to pay Mattel, Inc. $501,565 in attorneys' fees that it incurred in defending against what the district court determined to be a frivolous action. Hicks brought suit on behalf of Harry Christian, claiming that Mattel's Barbie dolls infringed Christian's Claudene doll sculpture copyright. In its sanctions orders, the district court found that Hicks should have discovered prior to commencing the civil action that Mattel's dolls could not have infringed Christian's copyright because, among other things, the Mattel dolls had been created well prior to the Claudene doll and the Mattel dolls had clearly visible copyright notices on their heads. After determining that Hicks had behaved "boorishly" during discovery and had a lengthy rap sheet of prior litigation misconduct, the district court imposed sanctions.

We hold that the district court did not abuse its discretion in determining that the complaint filed by Hicks was frivolous under Rule 11. In parsing the language of the district court's sanctions orders, however, we cannot determine with any degree of certainty whether the district court grounded its Rule 11 decision on Hicks' misconduct that occurred outside the pleadings, such as in oral argument, at a meeting of counsel, and at a key deposition. This is an important distinction because Rule 11 sanctions are limited to misconduct regarding signed pleadings, motions, and other filings. Fed.R.Civ.P. 11. Consequently, we vacate the district court's orders and remand for further proceedings consistent with this opinion. In so doing, we do not condone Hicks' conduct or suggest that the district court did not have a firm basis for awarding sanctions. Indeed, the district court undertook a careful and exhaustive examination of the facts and the legal underpinnings of the copyright challenge. Rather, the remand is to assure that any Rule 11 sanctions are grounded in conduct covered by Rule 11 and to ensure adequate findings for the sizeable fee award.

BACKGROUND

As context for examining the district court's determination that the underlying copyright action was frivolous, we begin by discussing the long history of litigation between Mattel and Hicks' past and current clients: Harry Christian; Christian's daughter, Claudene; and the Collegiate Doll Company ("CDC"), Claudene's proprietorship.

I. Prior Litigation Between Mattel and CDC

Mattel is a toy company that is perhaps best recognized as the manufacturer of the world-famous Barbie doll. Since Barbie's creation in 1959, Mattel has outfitted her in fashions and accessories that have evolved over time. In perhaps the most classic embodiment, Barbie is depicted as a slender-figured doll with long blonde hair and blue eyes. Mattel has sought to protect its intellectual property by registering various Barbie-related copyrights, including copyrights protecting the doll's head sculpture. Mattel has vigorously litigated against putative infringers.

In 1990, Claudene Christian, then an undergraduate student at the University of Southern California ("USC"), decided to create and market a collegiate cheerleader doll. The doll, which the parties refer to throughout their papers as "Claudene," had blonde hair and blue eyes and was outfitted to resemble a USC cheerleader.

Mattel soon learned about the Claudene doll. After concluding that it infringed certain Barbie copyrights, Mattel brought an administrative action before the United States Customs Service in 1996 in which it alleged that the Claudene doll, manufactured abroad, had pirated the head sculpture of the "Teen Talk" and

"SuperStar" Barbies. The Customs Service ruled in CDC's favor and subsequently released a shipment of Claudene dolls. Undaunted, Mattel commenced a federal court action in 1997 in which it once again alleged that CDC infringed various of Mattel's copyrights. At the time, Claudene Christian was president of CDC and Harry Christian was listed as co-founder of the company and chief financial officer. CDC retained Hicks as its counsel. After the court dismissed CDC's multiple counterclaims, the case was settled. Mattel released CDC from any copyright infringement liability in exchange for, among other things, a stipulation that Mattel was free to challenge CDC's alleged copyright of the Claudene doll should CDC "or any successor in interest" challenge Mattel's right to market its Barbie dolls.

II. The Present Action

Seizing on a loophole in the parties' settlement agreement, within weeks of the agreement, Harry Christian, who was not a signatory to the agreement, retained Hicks as his counsel and filed a federal court action against Mattel. In the complaint, which Hicks signed, Christian alleged that Mattel obtained a copy of the copyrighted Claudene doll in 1996, the year of its creation, and then infringed its overall appearance, including its face paint, by developing a new Barbie line called "Cool Blue" that was substantially similar to Claudene. Christian sought damages in the amount of $2.4 billion and various forms of injunctive relief. In an apparent effort to demonstrate that the action was not a sham, Claudene Christian and CDC were also named as defendants. Subsequently, Hicks alleged in a letter to Mattel's counsel that an additional doll called "Virginia Tech University Barbie" also infringed the Claudene doll copyright. Hicks, however, never amended the complaint to plead allegations about Virginia Tech Barbie.

Two months after the complaint was filed, Mattel moved for summary judgment. In support of its motion, Mattel proffered evidence that the Cool Blue Barbie doll contained a 1991 copyright notice on the back of its head, indicating that it predated Claudene's head sculpture copyright by approximately six years. Mattel therefore argued that Cool Blue Barbie could not as a matter of law infringe Claudene's head sculpture copyright. Mattel similarly contended that the copyright on the Virginia Tech Barbie's head sculpture also significantly predated the purported copyright on the Claudene head sculpture. Virginia Tech Barbie and other Barbie dolls contained a head sculpture that was copyrighted in 1976 and originally appeared on SuperStar Barbie.

At a follow-up counsel meeting required by a local rule, Mattel's counsel attempted to convince Hicks that his complaint was frivolous. During the videotaped meeting, they presented Hicks with copies of various Barbie dolls that not only had been created prior to 1996 (the date of Claudene's creation), but also had copyright designations on their heads that predated Claudene's creation. Additionally, Mattel's counsel noted that the face paint on some of the earlier-created Barbie dolls was virtually identical to that used on Claudene. Hicks declined Mattel's invitation to inspect the dolls and, later during the meeting, hurled them in disgust from a conference table.

Having been unsuccessful in convincing Hicks to dismiss Christian's action voluntarily, Mattel served Hicks with a motion for Rule 11 sanctions. In its motion papers, Mattel argued, among other things, that Hicks had signed and filed a frivolous complaint based on a legally meritless theory that Mattel's prior-created head sculptures infringed Claudene's 1997 copyright. Hicks declined to withdraw the complaint during the 21-day safe harbor period provided by Rule 11, and Mattel filed its motion.

Seemingly unfazed by Mattel's Rule 11 motion, Hicks proceeded with the litigation and filed a motion pursuant to Federal Rule of Civil Procedure 56(f) to obtain additional discovery. In particular, he sought information regarding the face painting on certain Barbie dolls and the face paint/head sculpture combinations used by Mattel after 1996. The district court summarily denied the motion. It later noted, in the context of its summary judgment order, that "it is unclear what [Christian] is requesting when he seeks access to post–1996 Barbies."

Hicks then began filing additional papers that were characterized by frequency and volume. Following official completion of the summary judgment briefing schedule, Hicks filed what was styled as a "supplemental opposition." In those papers, Christian asserted for the first time that the head sculpture of Mattel's CEO Barbie (which was created in 1998) infringed Christian's copyright in the Claudene doll. He did not, however, move for leave to amend the complaint.

Hicks later filed additional papers alleging that several additional Barbie dolls infringed the Claudene sculpture. As with CEO Barbie, no motion for leave to amend the complaint was filed. Then, following oral argument, Hicks filed a copy of a supplemental registration of Claudene that the United States Copyright Office had issued five days *prior* to the argument. The supplemental registration clarified that the nature of the original Claudene copyright "was intended to be the sculpture and the painted face" and that the nature of authorship covered both two-dimensional artwork and three-dimensional sculpture.

III. The District Court's Orders

The district court granted Mattel's motions for summary judgment and Rule 11 sanctions. The court ruled that Mattel did not infringe the 1997 Claudene copyright because it could not possibly have accessed the Claudene doll at the time it created the head sculptures of the Cool Blue (copyrighted in 1991) and Virginia Tech (copyrighted in 1976) Barbies. The court also rejected Christian's theory that the Mattel dolls had infringed the totality of Claudene's appearance, including its face paint, because the copyright is "limited in scope and extends only to 3–dimensional sculptures and not 2–dimensional artwork. . . ." Alternatively, the court found that Mattel had been using lighter-colored face paint "on dolls produced before the Claudene doll was created in 1996, such as Colonial Barbie (1994) and Pioneer Barbie (1995)," and therefore could not have infringed the later-created Claudene doll even if the Claudene copyright protected two-dimensional artwork. Finally, the court found that Mattel, as owner of various Barbie head sculpture copyrights, had "the exclusive right to prepare derivative works of its own copyrighted works. See 17 U.S.C. § 106(2). Thus, Mattel has the right to paint and re-paint its own copyrighted sculptures."

In adjudicating the summary judgment motion, the district court did not consider any of Christian's supplemental summary judgment filings. It noted that the papers not only "exceeded the permissible page limits," but also "failed to adhere to Local Rule 3.4.1," which established various type font requirements.

As for Mattel's Rule 11 motion, the district court found that Hicks had "filed a meritless claim against defendant Mattel. A reasonable investigation by Mr. Hicks would have revealed that there was no factual foundation for [Christian's] copyright claim." Indeed, the district court noted that Hicks needed to do little more than examine "the back of the heads of the Barbie dolls he claims were infringing," because such a perfunctory inquiry would have revealed "the pre–1996 copyright notices on the Cool Blue and [Virginia Tech] Barbie doll heads."

Additionally, the district court made other findings regarding Hicks' misconduct in litigating against Mattel, all of which demonstrated that his conduct fell "below the standards of attorneys practicing in the Central District of California." The district court singled out the following conduct:

- Sanctions imposed by the district court against Hicks in a related action against Mattel for failing, among other things, to file a memorandum of law in support of papers styled as a motion to dismiss and failing to appear at oral argument;
- Hicks' behavior during the Early Meeting of Counsel, in which he "toss[ed] Barbie dolls off a table";
- Hicks' interruption of Christian's deposition after Christian made a "damaging admission . . . that a pre–1996 Barbie doll allegedly infringed the later created Claudene doll head. . . ." When asked whether the prior-created Pioneer Barbie doll infringed Claudene, Christian stated, "I think so . . . [b]ecause it's got the look. . . ." At that juncture, Hicks requested an immediate recess, during which he lambasted his client in plain view of Mattel's attorneys and the video camera.
- Hicks' misrepresentations during oral argument on Mattel's summary judgment motion about the number of dolls alleged in the complaint to be infringing and whether he had ever reviewed a particular Barbie catalogue (when a videotape presented to the district court by Mattel demonstrated that Hicks had reviewed it during a deposition);
- Hicks' misstatement of law in a summary judgment opposition brief about the circuit's holdings regarding joint authorship of copyrightable works.

After Mattel submitted a general description of the fees that it incurred in defending against Christian's action, the court requested Mattel to submit a more specific itemization and description of work performed by its attorneys. Mattel complied.

The district court awarded Mattel $501,565 in attorneys' fees. At the outset of its order, the court summarized the findings in its earlier order, namely that it had "predicated its [Rule 11] decision" on Hicks' filing a frivolous complaint and "further found" that he had " 'behaved boorishly, misrepresented the facts and misstated the law.' " In discussing Rule 11's purpose of deterring such conduct, the district court made further findings about Hicks' behavior during prior proceedings — some of which were completely unrelated to this case. The prior litigation referenced by the district court included the following:

- The district court's earlier award of attorneys' fees to Mattel in a related action, and certain behavior by Hicks during the earlier-settled copyright infringement action that Mattel had filed against CDC;

- Hicks' failure to comply with a briefing schedule established by the First Circuit in an unrelated action in 1996; and
- Hicks' filing of conclusory opposition papers in an unrelated action in the Southern District of New York in response to a summary judgment motion in 1986.

The district court next considered various arguments that Hicks had advanced in opposition to Mattel's fee application. Hicks first contended, without much elaboration, that a fee award would have a "ruinous" effect on his finances and ability to practice law. The district court held, however, that "repeated reprimands and sanctions" imposed in prior litigations "clearly have not had the desired deterrent effect on his behavior," and it concluded that Hicks would not be punished sufficiently if the court were to impose mere "non-monetary sanctions." Hicks also argued (somewhat ironically) that Mattel's fees request was excessive in light of how simplistic it should have been to defend against Christian's action. The district court disagreed, reasoning that like the court in *Brandt v. Schal Assocs., Inc.*, 960 F.2d 640, 648 (7th Cir. 1992), the judiciary has " 'little sympathy for the litigant who fires a big gun, and when the adversary returns fire, complains because he was firing blanks.' " . . .

DISCUSSION

I. Standards of Review

. . . We review the district court's decision to impose Rule 11 sanctions—and, if they are warranted, the reasonableness of the actual amount imposed—for abuse of discretion. *Cooter & Gell v. Hartmarx Corp.*, 496 U.S. 384, 401, 405 (1990). In conducting our review of the district court's factual findings in support of the sanctions, we "would be justified in concluding that [the court] had abused its discretion in making [the findings] only if [they] were clearly erroneous." *Id.* at 386. The district court's legal findings must be affirmed unless they result from a "materially incorrect view of the relevant law." *Id.* at 402.

II. Imposition of Rule 11

The district court found that Hicks "filed a meritless claim against defendant Mattel. A reasonable investigation by Mr. Hicks would have revealed that there was no factual foundation for plaintiff's copyright claim." Hicks challenges these findings, arguing that the issues were "more complex" than the district court recognized. Before considering this operative issue, we first consider Rule 11 principles that guide our review.

A. General Rule 11 Principles

Filing a complaint in federal court is no trifling undertaking. An attorney's signature on a complaint is tantamount to a warranty that the complaint is well grounded in fact and "existing law" (or proposes a good faith extension of the existing law) and that it is not filed for an improper purpose.

Rule 11 provides in pertinent part:

   (a) **Signature.** Every pleading, written motion, and other paper shall be signed by at least one attorney of record in the attorney's individual name. . . .

(b) **Representations to Court.** By presenting to the court (whether by sign-ing, filing, submitting, or later advocating) a pleading, written motion, or other paper, an attorney or unrepresented party is certifying to the best of the person's knowledge, information, and belief, formed after an inquiry reason-able under the circumstances . . .

> (2) the claims, defenses, and other legal contentions therein are war-ranted by existing law or by a nonfrivolous argument for the extension, modification, or reversal of existing law or the establishment of new law;

> (3) the allegations and other factual contentions have evidentiary sup-port or, if specifically so identified, are likely to have evidentiary support after a reasonable opportunity for further investigation or discovery[.]

Fed.R.Civ.P. 11.

The attorney has a duty prior to filing a complaint not only to conduct a rea-sonable factual investigation, but also to perform adequate legal research that con-firms whether the theoretical underpinnings of the complaint are "warranted by existing law or a good faith argument for an extension, modification or reversal of existing law." *Golden Eagle Distrib. Corp. v. Burroughs Corp.*, 801 F.2d 1531, 1537 (9th Cir. 1986). One of the fundamental purposes of Rule 11 is to "reduce frivolous claims, defenses or motions and to deter costly meritless maneuvers, . . . [thereby] avoid[ing] delay and unnecessary expense in litigation." *Id.* at 1536 (internal quo-tation marks and citations omitted). Nonetheless, a finding of significant delay or expense is not required under Rule 11. Where, as here, the complaint is the primary focus of Rule 11 proceedings, a district court must conduct a two-prong inquiry to determine (1) whether the complaint is legally or factually "baseless" from an objective perspective, and (2) if the attorney has conducted "a reasonable and competent inquiry" before signing and filing it. *Buster v. Greisen*, 104 F.3d 1186, 1190 (9th Cir. 1997).

B. The District Court's Findings Regarding the Meritless Claim

1. Did Hicks Have an Adequate Legal or Factual Basis for Filing the Complaint?

Hicks filed a single claim of copyright infringement against Mattel. The com-plaint charges that the Cool Blue Barbie infringed the copyright in the Claudene doll head. In addition, in a subsequent letter to Mattel's counsel, he claimed that Virginia Tech Barbie also infringed Claudene. Hicks cannot seriously dispute the district court's conclusions that, assuming the applicability of the doctrine of prior creation, Christian's complaint was legally and factually frivolous.[6] Indeed, as a mat-ter of copyright law, it is well established that a prior-created work cannot infringe a later-created one. . . .

Copyright infringement requires proof that a plaintiff owns a valid copyright in the work and that the defendant copied the work. . . . Proof of copying often revolves around whether the defendant had sufficient access to copy the work.

---

6. The district court did not explicitly delineate between the two concepts in its order. In ruling, however, that Christian's complaint was factually meritless because the Barbie dolls at issue had, as a matter of fact, been prior-created, it necessarily held, as a matter of law, that the copyright infringement claim was without legal merit as well.

Access is only a theoretical issue in this case, however. By simple logic, it is impossible to *copy* something that does not exist. Thus, if Mattel created its doll sculptures before CDC created Claudene in 1994, it is factually and legally impossible for Mattel to be an infringer.

The record of creation is telling and conclusive. The Cool Blue Barbie doll uses the Neptune's Daughter doll head which was created in 1991, some six years before the Claudene doll. The Virginia Tech Barbie doll uses the SuperStar sculpture which Mattel created in 1976. The SuperStar doll was the subject of the just-completed federal court litigation, and Hicks should have been well aware of the prior creation, not to mention that the copyright notice (including date of creation) appears prominently on the back of the dolls' heads.

Recognizing the futility of attacking prior creation, Hicks argues that the paint on the Claudene doll's face features a light makeup that is distinctive and that the two Barbie dolls thus infringe Claudene's overall appearance and presentation. This argument fails because, among other things, Mattel used the light face paint on the Pioneer Barbie, which was created two years before the Claudene doll, thus defeating once again any claim of copying. It also bears noting that Mattel has been repainting various doll heads for decades. Under Hicks' theory, CDC's use of an infringing doll head coupled with "new" face paint would result in liability for Mattel's repainting of its prior-created Barbie doll sculptures. Neither common sense nor copyright law countenance such a result, even if the Claudene doll were deemed a derivative work. . . .

In the face of facts and law clearly against his client, Hicks sought to resurrect the copyright claim by deluging the district court with supplemental filings, including entirely new claims regarding a different assortment of Barbie dolls and non-Barbie dolls. The dolls included, for example, the CEO doll, which used the 1991 Neptune's Daughter head with a modified mouth.

The district court did not consider any of Hicks' supplemental filings, noting that Hicks failed to comply with local rules regarding page limitations and typefaces. Given the chameleon nature of the claims and Hicks' flip-flop from the sculpture-plus-painting theory back to the sculpture-only theory, the district court was justified in putting an end to Hicks' serial filings. The district court has considerable latitude in managing the parties' motion practice and enforcing local rules that place parameters on briefing. We cannot say that the court abused its discretion by declining to consider Hicks' multitudinous efforts to circumvent the court's local rules and to expand the scope of an already frivolous suit. At some point, enough is enough. . . . Consequently, in the face of undisputed evidence concerning the prior-creation of the Barbie dolls, the district court did not abuse its discretion by ruling that the complaint was frivolous.

2. Did Hicks Conduct an Adequate Factual Investigation?

The district court concluded that Hicks "filed a case without factual foundation." Hicks, having argued unsuccessfully that his failure to perform even minimal due diligence was irrelevant as a matter of copyright law, does not contest that he would have been able to discover the copyright information simply by examining the doll heads. Instead he argues that the district court did not understand certain "complex" issues. Simply saying so does not make it so. The district court well understood the legal and factual background of the case. It was Hicks' absence of investigation, not the district court's absence of analysis, that brought about his downfall.

The district court did not abuse its discretion in concluding that Hicks' failure to investigate fell below the requisite standard established by Rule 11.

III. The District Court's Additional Findings Regarding Misconduct

Hicks argues that even if the district court were justified in sanctioning him under Rule 11 based on Christian's complaint and the follow-on motions, its conclusion was tainted because it impermissibly considered other misconduct that cannot be sanctioned under Rule 11, such as discovery abuses, misstatements made during oral argument, and conduct in other litigation.

Hicks' argument has merit. While Rule 11 permits the district court to sanction an attorney for conduct regarding "pleading[s], written motion[s], and other paper[s]" that have been signed and filed in a given case, Fed.R.Civ.P. 11(a), it does not authorize sanctions for, among other things, discovery abuses or misstatements made to the court during an oral presentation. *See Bus. Guides, Inc. v. Chromatic Communications Enter.*, 892 F.2d 802, 813 (9th Cir. 1989) (holding that misstatements made during oral argument cannot constitute sanctionable offenses under Rule 11); In re Yagman, 796 F.2d at 1187 (holding that discovery abuses cannot be sanctioned under Rule 11); *see also* Fed.R.Civ.P. 11, advisory committee notes, 1993 Amendments, Subdivisions (b) and (c) ("The rule applies only to assertions contained in papers filed with or submitted to the court. It does not cover matters arising for the first time during oral presentations to the court, when counsel may make statements that would not be made if there had been more time for study and reflection.").

. . .

The orders clearly demonstrate that the district court decided, at least in part, to sanction Hicks because he signed and filed a factually and legally meritless complaint and for misrepresentations in subsequent briefing. But the orders, coupled with the supporting examples, also strongly suggest that the court considered extra-pleadings conduct as a basis for Rule 11 sanctions. Although the court also referenced conduct in related litigation, it is unlikely that the court based its order on such conduct because Hicks had already been sanctioned for violating local rules in the context of the related litigation and the court noted that fact.

The laundry list of Hicks' outlandish conduct is a long one and raises serious questions as to his respect for the judicial process. Nonetheless, Rule 11 sanctions are limited to "paper[s]" signed in violation of the rule. Conduct in depositions, discovery meetings of counsel, oral representations at hearings, and behavior in prior proceedings do not fall within the ambit of Rule 11. Because we do not know for certain whether the district court granted Mattel's Rule 11 motion as a result of an impermissible intertwining of its conclusion about the complaint's frivolity and Hicks' extrinsic misconduct, we must vacate the district court's Rule 11 orders.

We decline Mattel's suggestion that the district court's sanctions orders could be supported in their entirety under the court's inherent authority. To impose sanctions under its inherent authority, the district court must "make an explicit finding [which it did not do here] that counsel's conduct constituted or was tantamount to bad faith." *Primus Auto. Fin. Serv., Inc. v. Batarse*, 115 F.3d 644, 648 (9th Cir.1997) (internal quotation marks omitted). We acknowledge that the district court has a broad array of sanctions options at its disposal: Rule 11, 28 U.S.C. § 1927, and the court's inherent authority. Each of these sanctions alternatives has its own particular requirements, and it is important that the grounds be separately articulated to assure that the conduct at issue falls within the scope of the sanctions remedy. *See, e.g., B.K.B. v. Maui Police Dep't.*, 276 F.3d 1091, 1107 (9th Cir. 2002) (holding that misconduct committed "in an unreasonable and vexatious manner" that "multiplies the proceedings" violates § 1927); Fink v. Gomez, 239 F.3d 989, 991–992 (9th Cir. 2001) (holding that sanctions may be imposed under the court's inherent authority for "bad faith" actions by counsel, "which includes a broad range of willful improper conduct"). On remand, the district court will have an opportunity to delineate the factual and legal basis for its sanctions orders.

. . .

NOTES AND QUESTIONS

1. *Non-Delegable Duty to Investigate.* Clearly, at the point that Mattel pointed out the weakness in plaintiff's case, Hicks had a duty to verify the earlier Barbie copyright (which he apparently could have done by examining the back of the doll's neck instead of hurling it "in disgust from a conference table"). Was it unreasonable for Hicks to rely on his client's assertion that the Barbie dolls infringed its patent at the time it filed its complaint? The duty to conduct a reasonable pre-filing investigation is said to be "nondelegable." Thus, courts have held it unreasonable for the lawyer to rely on the client's representation of the facts if some independent corroboration was readily available to the attorney. *See Anderson v. County of Montgomery*, 111 F.3d 494 (7th Cir. 1997) (attorney sanctioned for, among other things, failing to investigate independently client's assertion that a prosecutor, a court reporter, and client's former attorney conspired to produce fabricated judicial transcript). What are the implications of this for the *Burdick* pleading problem? Must you independently verify everything that the aviation expert tells you?

2. *Certifying Claims That Do Not Currently Have Evidentiary Support.* What does Fed. R. Civ. P. 11(b)(3) mean when it permits an attorney to certify that "the factual contentions . . . , if specifically so identified, will likely have evidentiary support after a reasonable opportunity for further investigation or discovery"? Does this Rule require an attorney to parse every allegation of the complaint and specifically identify any contention for which he does not currently have evidentiary support?

If an attorney does not currently have evidentiary support for a given factual contention, how can the attorney certify that he or she is *likely* to obtain such support through discovery? On the facts of the case, could you certify on the basis of information you have, that you are *likely* to discover that Rockwell was at fault? What would be the basis for that assertion? What factors would determine whether your pre-filing investigation was sufficient for Rule 11 purposes?

3. *Safe Harbor Provision.* Note that a motion for sanctions under current Rule 11 may not be filed before the opposing party has an opportunity to withdraw the offending paper. If the paper is withdrawn, the motion may not be filed. Fed. R. Civ. P. 11(c)(2). However, because sanctions may be awarded by the court *sua sponte* (on its own initiative), this "safe harbor" is not absolute. However, even court-initiated

sanctions may not be ordered unless the court issues an "order to show cause" why sanctions should not be imposed prior to voluntary dismissal or settlement of the lawsuit. Fed. R. Civ. P. 11(c)(5)(B).

The Fourth Circuit has held that the 21-day "safe harbor" provision is a waivable requirement; a party may be sanctioned even if the opposing party failed to give the 21-day notice required in Rule 11(c) if the sanctioned party fails to raise the notice defect. *Rector v. Approved Federal Savings Bank*, 265 F.3d 248 (4th Cir. 2001). The ruling is consistent with the Supreme Court's later decision in *Kontrick v. Ryan*, 540 U.S. 443 (2004), in which Justice Ginsburg held that even strict time prescriptions must generally be raised by the parties or they will be waived, even if the time limits are deemed "jurisdictional" for some purposes.

There is a split in the circuits on whether the "safe harbor" provision of Rule 11(c)(2) requires service of a motion on the offending party, or whether some other form of notice of the aggrieved party's intent to pursue Rule 11 sanctions is sufficient. *Compare McGreal v. Village of Orland Park*, 928 F.3d 556, 559 (7th Cir. 2019) (letter and emails to plaintiff complaining of plaintiff's violation of Rule 11 suffice to preserve defendant's right to move for Rule 11 sanctions) *with Penn, LLC v. Prosper Bus. Dev. Corp.*, 773 F.3d 764, 768 (6th Cir. 2014) (noting that the Second, Third, Fourth, Fifth, Sixth, Eighth, Ninth, and Tenth Circuits all require strict compliance by serving the pre-filed motion on the offending party).

4. *Securities Reform Act of 1995.* A 1995 federal statute imposes particular pleading and certification requirements in securities cases. The Securities Reform Act of 1995, Pub. L. No. 104-67, 109 Stat. 737 (1995) (codified in different sections of 15 U.S.C.), requires, in addition to the standard Rule 11 certification, that plaintiff in the first-filed action must certify, among other things, that he is not acting at the behest of counsel; is familiar with the subject matter of the complaint; and has authorized initiation of the litigation. 15 U.S.C. §77z-1(a)(2), §78u-4a(2). At the conclusion of the litigation, the judge must determine whether Rule 11 has been complied with, and if not, is *required* to impose sanctions presumptively in the form of attorneys' fees *paid to defendant.* 15 U.S.C. §77z-(1)(c), §78u-4(c).

Congress has on several occasions considered legislation that strengthens the operation of Rule 11. In March 2011, the Lawsuit Reduction Act of 2011 was introduced. H.R. 966, 112th Cong. (2011); S. 533, 112th Cong. (2011). The Act would have made the award of penalties, including attorneys' fees, mandatory whenever a Rule 11 violation was established and would eliminate the safe harbor provision of Rule 11(c)(2). *See* Lonnie Hoffman, *The Case Against the Lawsuit Reduction Act of 2011*, 48 Hous. L. Rev. 545 (2011). In 2017, the House passed the Lawsuit Abuse Reduction Act of 2017, HR 720. The Act would have amended Rule 11 to make the award of monetary sanctions to the prevailing moving party mandatory, including attorneys' fees, and would have eliminated the "safe harbor" of Rule 11(c)(2). The Senate did not act on the measure.

5. *What Is an Improper Purpose?* Pursuant to Rule 11(b)(1), the offending document cannot be used "for any improper purpose, such as to harass, cause unnecessary delay, or needlessly increase the cost of litigation." What if an attorney files litigation in order to publicize defendant's wrongful conduct? Is that an "improper purpose"? Consider *Whitehead v. Food Max, Inc.*, 332 F.3d 796 (5th Cir. 2003). Plaintiff there obtained a $3.4 million verdict against Kmart for not providing adequate

security in its parking lot. Plaintiff's attorney was sanctioned for attempting to execute on the judgment by bringing a sheriff to a Kmart store, accompanied by reporters, to take money out of the cash registers and store vault. The case was on appeal at the time of the attempted execution, and the court held that the judgment was automatically stayed as a consequence under Mississippi law. Accordingly, plaintiff had no legal basis to seek an execution of the judgment and thus violated Rule 11(b)(2). Moreover, even if plaintiff could have reasonably believed the judgment was then subject to execution, the event was staged in order to embarrass Kmart and to publicize the attorney's success, both of which the court considered to be improper purposes under Rule 11(b)(1).

Consider also the Rule 11 sanctions issued in *King v. Whitmer*, 2021 WL 3771875 (E.D. MI August 25, 2021), against attorneys representing supporters of President Trump in the aftermath of the 2020 election. The sanctioned attorneys there had sought to decertify the Michigan vote and declare Trump the winner because of pervasive fraud and irregularies in the conduct of the election. After dismissing plaintiffs' complaint due to the absence of supporting evidence and legal authority, the court awarded sanctions under Rule 11 as well as 28 U.S.C. §1927, which authorizes a court to impose costs, including attorney fees on any counsel that "multiplies the proceedings in any case unreasonably and vexatiously," and pursuant to the court's "inherent authority." In addition to finding that the claims were filed without any basis in law, and without any evidentiary support, the court found that the attorney had an improper motive in filing the litigation: "this case was never about fraud—it was about undermining the People's faith in our democracy and debasing the judicial process to do so."

6. *Against Whom Can Rule 11 Sanctions Be Imposed?* Is it ever appropriate to award monetary sanctions against a client who is represented by counsel? In *Business Guides, Inc. v. Chromatic Communications Enterprises, Inc.*, 498 U.S. 533 (1991), the Supreme Court upheld the award of sanctions against a represented party who signed an affidavit accompanying a request for a temporary restraining order, but failed to exercise reasonable care in ascertaining the truth of the allegations contained therein. Plaintiff, the publisher of a telephone directory, sought to restrain defendant from distributing its own directory, which, plaintiff alleged, was copied from plaintiff's. Plaintiff alleged that inaccurate listings or "seeds," purposely "planted" in plaintiff's directory, appeared in defendant's directory, proving the illegal copying. After the judge's clerk verified, within one hour, the accuracy of nine out of ten of the allegedly incorrect listings, the complaint was withdrawn. In defending against the subsequent Rule 11 sanctions sought by defendant, plaintiff asserted that the error was attributable to a good faith clerical error by the employee assigned the task of monitoring competing directories for possible copying. The Court held plaintiff to the same duty of reasonable investigation as applied to attorneys and rejected its defense that the mistake was made in good faith.

Note that under Fed. R. Civ. P. 11(c)(5)(A), monetary sanctions against a represented party may *not* be imposed for asserting a *legally* frivolous position, only for an inaccurate *factual* assertion. Why do you suppose the drafters made that distinction?

7. *Does Rule 11 Violate the Enabling Act?* Rule 11 of the Federal Rules of Civil Procedure is promulgated by the Supreme Court pursuant to the Rules Enabling Act, 28 U.S.C. §§2072-2074. The Supreme Court in *Business Guides, Inc. v. Chromatic*

Communications Enterprises, Inc., 498 U.S. 533, 551–553 (1991), rejected an Enabling Act challenge to monetary sanctions awarded under the Rule, holding that any effect on "substantive rights" was "incidental."

8. For a general and comprehensive review of Rule 11, *see* Georgene M. Vairo, Rule 11 Sanctions: Case Law, Perspectives and Preventive Measures (Richard G. Johnson ed., 3d ed. 2004).

BURDENS OF PLEADING AND BURDENS OF PROOF

As we study the strategic considerations attorneys give to the preparation of the pleadings, it is important to understand two related but distinct concepts: burdens of pleading and burdens of proof.

The *burden of pleading* dictates which party is obligated to introduce a particular matter into the litigation by raising that matter in the pleadings. If plaintiff fails to raise a matter for which it has the burden of pleading, the complaint will be vulnerable to a motion to dismiss for failure to state a claim. If defendant fails to raise a matter for which it has the burden of pleading, it will be foreclosed from asserting that defense at trial.

The *burden of proof*, in contrast, allocates the duty of *proving* contested facts. The burden of proof contains two elements: producing evidence (the "burden of production") and persuading the trier of fact (the "burden of persuasion"). In the event there is no proof of a contested allegation, the party with the burden of producing evidence will lose. In the event the proof is in equal balance, the party with the burden of persuading the court will lose.

How are these burdens allocated? The relatively simple principle that plaintiff must plead and prove every essential element of its cause of action, and defendant must aver and prove all defenses, begs a complicated question: How do we know whether a particular question is an essential element of the claim, and thus must be averred in the complaint, or a defense, and thus negated in the answer? Analytically, the negation of virtually every defense *could* be considered an essential element of plaintiff's claim and vice versa.

For instance, we could say contracts entered into by competent persons are enforceable and that competence is an essential element of plaintiff's breach of contract action. Alternatively, we could think of competence as an exception from liability that must be asserted by defendants: Contracts are enforceable unless entered into by incompetent persons. There is no analytical imperative to treat it one way rather than another. *See generally* Edward W. Cleary, *Presuming and Pleading: An Essay on Juristic Immaturity*, 12 Stan. L. Rev. 5 (1959).

Much of our sense of who has the burden is attributable to the way the underlying claim is conceptualized. For example, merely alleging that plaintiff was injured in an airplane accident without an additional allegation that the injury was attributable to a defect in the design or manufacture of the aircraft would not support liability against the manufacturer. Thus, at minimum, plaintiff must plead defendant's violation of plaintiff's legally protected right.

In many cases, legal practice and custom dictate where the burdens lie. In other cases, policy plays an important role in the allocation of pleading and proof burdens. For example, the probability that a given issue will be relevant to the litigation affects whether an element should be part of plaintiff's initial complaint.

It would be inefficient to require plaintiff to allege "competence" in every breach of contract action since it is only infrequently at issue. The issue of lack of competence or capacity is often allocated to the defendant to plead. In many cases, the defendant will also carry the burden of proof.

Although the burden of proof often follows the burden of pleading, the courts sometimes require one party to plead a matter, but the other to prove it. One example is the issue of nonpayment of a debt or a loan. It is obvious that nonpayment is a critical aspect of the plaintiff's claim for relief. But, when it comes to proving payment, defendant is likely to have better access to the proof of payment because he will have a receipt. Thus, the burden of proof of payment is usually on the defendant. At the same time, highlighting the issue of nonpayment may be particularly desirable, so that even when plaintiff alleges nonpayment, defendant may also be assigned the burden of pleading payment. *See* Fed. R. Civ. P. 8(c).

One of the most confusing areas of pleading and proof burdens is in the area of contributory negligence. Most jurisdictions assign both the burden of pleading and proof of contributory negligence to defendant. In a few jurisdictions, freedom from such negligence is made a part of plaintiff's cause of action; thus plaintiff will be required to prove (and usually to plead) absence of contributory negligence. The Federal Rules have designated contributory negligence as an affirmative defense to be pled by defendant in the answer. *See* Fed. R. Civ. P. 8(c). And although it has been held that Rule 8(c) must be followed with respect to "pleading," the burden of proof—which will control the outcome in a case where there is no evidence or it is evenly balanced—is controlled by the underlying state law on allocation of the burden of proof.

As a practical matter, the question of who has the burden of pleading can be immaterial. In order to present their legal positions in the most favorable light, the parties frequently "overplead"; whether or not plaintiff has the burden of raising the issue, its negligence complaint will often aver due care by plaintiff.

Note that the federal pleading system generally requires only two pleadings: a complaint and an answer. When the answer contains a counterclaim (a claim by defendant for relief against plaintiff), there is also an answer to the counterclaim. *See* Fed. R. Civ. P. 7. The practical importance of this is that any defense pled in an answer usually need not be contested by the claimant in the pleadings in order for the claimant to challenge that defense in the litigation. The only exception to this would be when a "reply" is ordered by the court pursuant to Fed. R. Civ. P. 7(a)(7).

5. *The Elements of a Complaint*

Fed. R. Civ. P. 8(a) states the requirements for the complaint: "(1) a short and plain statement of the grounds for the court's jurisdiction . . . , (2) a short and plain statement of the claim showing that the pleader is entitled to relief, and (3) a demand for the relief sought, which may include relief in the alternative or different types of relief."

As you read the material below, consider whether it would be sufficient under Rule 8(a) for the plaintiff in the *Rockwell* litigation to allege: (a) a statement of federal court jurisdiction; (b) an assertion that "the defendant Rockwell was negligent in its design of the deicing and anti-icing systems and that the failure of these systems to operate properly caused the plane to crash"; and (c) a request for damages of $5 million.

a. How Detailed Should the Complaint Be?

i. Statement of a Claim Under Fed. R. Civ. P. 8(a)(2)

Prior to 2007, a mere "bare-bones" complaint — even one as skeletal as suggested by our question above — would probably have sufficed under Fed. R. Civ. P. 8. The level of detail required to avoid dismissal was thought to be quite minimal. Official forms previously appended to the Rules of Civil Procedure suggested that a "bare-bones" approach to the complaint would suffice as long as certain essential elements were alleged.* Much of the case law of "pleadings" referred to a complaint as sufficient if it gave "sufficient notice" of the claim to the defendant. In *Conley v. Gibson*, 355 U.S. 41 (1957), the Supreme Court of the United States upheld a complaint filed by black plaintiffs, employees of the Texas and New Orleans Railroad, against their labor union and certain officers. Plaintiffs alleged that after their wrongful discharge by the railroad, the union refused to protect the jobs and interests of the black employees as they did with respect to white employees. Rejecting defendants' contentions that the complaint failed to set forth any specific facts to support the general allegation of discrimination, the Supreme Court held that a complaint should not be dismissed for failure to state a claim "unless it appears beyond doubt that the plaintiff can prove no set of facts in support of his claim which would entitle him to relief." *Id.* at 45–46.

> [A]ll the Rules require is "a short and plain statement of the claim" that will give the defendant fair notice of what the plaintiffs' claim is and the grounds upon which it rests. The illustrative forms appended to the Rules plainly demonstrate this. Such simplified "notice pleading" is made possible by the liberal opportunity for discovery and the other pretrial procedures established by the Rules to disclose more precisely the basis of both claim and defense and to define more narrowly the disputed facts and issues. Following the simple guide of Rule 8(f)** that "all pleadings shall be construed as to do substantial justice," we have no doubt that petitioners' complaint adequately set forth a claim and gave the respondents fair notice of its basis. The Federal Rules reject the approach that pleading is a game of skill in which one misstep by counsel may be decisive to the outcome and accept the principle that the purpose of pleadings is to facilitate a proper decision on the merits.

Id. at 47–48.

---

* A 2015 Amendment to Rule 84 eliminated the official forms in the Appendix to the Rules.

** Rule 8(f) mentioned by the Supreme Court was revised by the 2007 stylistic amendments to the Federal Rules. It is currently numbered as Rule 8(e). — Eds.

Consider after reading the following cases whether this continues to represent an accurate statement of the law.

Bell Atlantic Corp. v. Twombly

550 U.S. 544 (2007)

SOUTER, J., delivered the opinion of the Court, in which ROBERTS, C.J., and SCALIA, KENNEDY, THOMAS, BREYER, and ALITO, J.J., joined. STEVENS, J., filed a dissenting opinion, in which GINSBURG, J., joined, except as to Part IV.

Justice SOUTER delivered the opinion of the Court.

[Plaintiff brought an antitrust action on behalf of customers of the regional telephone companies, the "baby Bells" formed after the breakup of ATT. The complaint alleged that the defendants, denominated in the complaint as "Independent Local Exchange Carriers" or "ILECs," conspired with each other to restrain trade in telecommunication services, including telephone, fax, and Internet. It stated two separate claims. First, plaintiff alleged that the defendants agreed to make it difficult for third-party service providers, denominated in the Complaint as "Competitive Local Exchange Carriers" or "CLECs," to connect to defendants' switching networks. Second, plaintiff alleged an agreement among all the defendants to not compete with each other. The district court dismissed both claims pursuant to Fed. R. Civ. P. 12(b)(6) for failure to state a claim. The Court of Appeals reversed.]

We granted certiorari to address the proper standard for pleading an antitrust conspiracy through allegations of parallel conduct, . . . and now reverse.

II

A

Because §1 of the Sherman Act "does not prohibit [all] unreasonable restraints of trade . . . but only restraints effected by a contract, combination, or conspiracy," *Copperweld Corp. v. Independence Tube Corp.*, 467 U.S. 752, 775 (1984), "[t]he crucial question" is whether the challenged anticompetitive conduct "stem[s] from independent decision or from an agreement, tacit or express," *Theatre Enterprises*, 346 U.S., at 540. While a showing of parallel "business behavior is admissible circumstantial evidence from which the fact finder may infer agreement," it falls short of "conclusively establish[ing] agreement or . . . itself constitut[ing] a Sherman Act offense." *Id.*, at 540-541. Even "conscious parallelism," a common reaction of "firms in a concentrated market [that] recogniz[e] their shared economic interests and their interdependence with respect to price and output decisions" is "not in itself unlawful." *Brooke Group Ltd. v. Brown & Williamson Tobacco Corp.*, 509 U.S. 209, 227 (1993). . . .

The inadequacy of showing parallel conduct or interdependence, without more, mirrors the ambiguity of the behavior: consistent with conspiracy, but just as much in line with a wide swath of rational and competitive business strategy unilaterally prompted by common perceptions of the market. . . . Accordingly, we have previously hedged against false inferences from identical behavior at a number of points in the trial sequence. An antitrust conspiracy plaintiff with evidence showing nothing beyond parallel conduct is not entitled to a directed verdict, see *Theatre Enterprises, supra*; proof of a §1 conspiracy must include evidence tending to exclude the possibility of independent action, see *Monsanto Co. v. Spray-Rite Service Corp.*, 465 U.S. 752 (1984); and at the summary judgment stage a §1 plaintiff's offer of conspiracy evidence must tend to rule out the possibility that the defendants were acting independently, see *Matsushita Elec. Industrial Co. v. Zenith Radio Corp.*, 475 U.S. 574 (1986).

B

This case presents the antecedent question of what a plaintiff must plead in order to state a claim under §1 of the Sherman Act. Federal Rule of Civil Procedure 8(a)(2)* requires only "a short and plain statement of the claim showing that the pleader is entitled to relief," in order to "give the defendant fair notice of what the . . . claim is and the grounds upon which it rests," *Conley v. Gibson*, 355 U.S. 41 (1957). While a complaint attacked by a Rule 12(b)(6) motion to dismiss does not need detailed factual allegations, *ibid.; Sanjuan v. American Bd. of Psychiatry and Neurology, Inc.*, 40 F.3d 247, 251 (C.A.7 1994), a plaintiff's obligation to provide the "grounds" of his "entitle[ment] to relief" requires more than labels and conclusions, and a formulaic recitation of the elements of a cause of action will not do, see *Papasan v. Allain*, 478 U.S. 265, 286 (1986) (on a motion to dismiss, courts "are not bound to accept as true a legal conclusion couched as a factual allegation"). Factual allegations must be enough to raise a right to relief above the speculative level, see 5 C. Wright & A. Miller, Federal Practice and Procedure §1216, pp. 235–236 (3d ed. 2004) (hereinafter Wright & Miller) ("[T]he pleading must contain something more . . . than . . . a statement of facts that merely creates a suspicion [of] a legally cognizable right of action"),[3] on the assumption that all the allegations in the complaint are true (even if doubtful in fact), see, *e.g., Swierkiewicz v. Sorema N.A.*, 534 U.S. 506, 508, n. 1 (2002); *Neitzke v. Williams*, 490 U.S. 319, 327 (1989) ("Rule 12(b)(6) does not countenance . . . dismissals based on a judge's disbelief of a

---

* The wording of Rule 8 and Rule 12(b)(6) referenced in this case was revised by the 2007 stylistic amendments to the Federal Rules. — EDS.

3. The dissent greatly oversimplifies matters by suggesting that the Federal Rules somehow dispensed with the pleading of facts altogether. See *post*, at 10 (opinion of STEVENS, J.) (pleading standard of Federal Rules "does not require, or even invite, the pleading of facts"). While, for most types of cases, the Federal Rules eliminated the cumbersome requirement that a claimant "set out *in detail* the facts upon which he bases his claim," *Conley v. Gibson*, 355 U.S. 41, 47 (1957) (emphasis added), Rule 8(a)(2) still requires a "showing," rather than a blanket assertion, of entitlement to relief. Without some factual allegation in the complaint, it is hard to see how a claimant could satisfy the requirement of providing not only "fair notice" of the nature of the claim, but also "grounds" on which the claim rests. See 5 Wright & Miller §1202, at 94, 95 (Rule 8(a) "contemplate[s] the statement of circumstances, occurrences, and events in support of the claim presented" and does not authorize a pleader's "bare averment that he wants relief and is entitled to it").

complaint's factual allegations"); *Scheuer v. Rhodes*, 416 U.S. 232, 236 (1974) (a well-pleaded complaint may proceed even if it appears "that a recovery is very remote and unlikely").

In applying these general standards to a §1 claim, we hold that stating such a claim requires a complaint with enough factual matter (taken as true) to suggest that an agreement was made. Asking for plausible grounds to infer an agreement does not impose a probability requirement at the pleading stage; it simply calls for enough fact to raise a reasonable expectation that discovery will reveal evidence of illegal agreement.[4] And, of course, a well-pleaded complaint may proceed even if it strikes a savvy judge that actual proof of those facts is improbable, and "that a recovery is very remote and unlikely." *Ibid.* In identifying facts that are suggestive enough to render a §1 conspiracy plausible, we have the benefit of the prior rulings and considered views of leading commentators, already quoted, that lawful parallel conduct fails to bespeak unlawful agreement. It makes sense to say, therefore, that an allegation of parallel conduct and a bare assertion of conspiracy will not suffice. Without more, parallel conduct does not suggest conspiracy, and a conclusory allegation of agreement at some unidentified point does not supply facts adequate to show illegality. Hence, when allegations of parallel conduct are set out in order to make a §1 claim, they must be placed in a context that raises a suggestion of a preceding agreement, not merely parallel conduct that could just as well be independent action.

The need at the pleading stage for allegations plausibly suggesting (not merely consistent with) agreement reflects the threshold requirement of Rule 8(a)(2) that the "plain statement" possess enough heft to "sho[w] that the pleader is entitled to relief." A statement of parallel conduct, even conduct consciously undertaken, needs some setting suggesting the agreement necessary to make out a §1 claim; without that further circumstance pointing toward a meeting of the minds, an account of a defendant's commercial efforts stays in neutral territory. An allegation of parallel conduct is thus much like a naked assertion of conspiracy in a §1 complaint: it gets the complaint close to stating a claim, but without some further factual enhancement it stops short of the line between possibility and plausibility of "entitle[ment] to relief." Cf. *DM Research, Inc. v. College of Am. Pathologists*, 170 F.3d 53, 56 (C.A.1 1999) ("[T]erms like 'conspiracy,' or even 'agreement,' are border-line: they might well be sufficient in conjunction

---

4. Commentators have offered several examples of parallel conduct allegations that would state a §1 claim under this standard. See, *e.g.*, 6 Areeda & Hovenkamp ¶1425, at 167–185 (discussing "parallel behavior that would probably not result from chance, coincidence, independent responses to common stimuli, or mere interdependence unaided by an advance understanding among the parties"); Blechman, Conscious Parallelism, Signaling and Facilitating Devices: The Problem of Tacit Collusion Under the Antitrust Laws, 24 N.Y.L.S. L. Rev. 881, 899 (1979) (describing "conduct [that] indicates the sort of restricted freedom of action and sense of obligation that one generally associates with agreement"). The parties in this case agree that "complex and historically unprecedented changes in pricing structure made at the very same time by multiple competitors, and made for no other discernible reason" would support a plausible inference of conspiracy. Brief for Respondents 37; see also Reply Brief for Petitioners 12.

with a more specific allegation—for example, identifying a written agreement or even a basis for inferring a tacit agreement, . . . but a court is not required to accept such terms as a sufficient basis for a complaint").[5]

We alluded to the practical significance of the Rule 8 entitlement requirement in *Dura Pharmaceuticals, Inc. v. Broudo*, 544 U.S. 336 (2005), when we explained that something beyond the mere possibility of loss causation must be alleged, lest a plaintiff with "'a largely groundless claim'" be allowed to "'take up the time of a number of other people, with the right to do so representing an *in terrorem* increment of the settlement value.'" *Id.*, at 347 (quoting *Blue Chip Stamps v. Manor Drug Stores*, 421 U.S. 723, 741 (1975)). So, when the allegations in a complaint, however true, could not raise a claim of entitlement to relief, "'this basic deficiency should . . . be exposed at the point of minimum expenditure of time and money by the parties and the court.'" 5 Wright & Miller §1216, at 233–234 (quoting *Daves v. Hawaiian Dredging Co.*, 114 F. Supp. 643, 645 (D. Hawaii 1953)); see also *Dura, supra*, at 346; *Asahi Glass Co. v. Pentech Pharmaceuticals, Inc.*, 289 F.Supp.2d 986, 995 (N.D. Ill. 2003) (Posner, J., sitting by designation) ("[S]ome threshold of plausibility must be crossed at the outset before a patent antitrust case should be permitted to go into its inevitably costly and protracted discovery phase").

Thus, it is one thing to be cautious before dismissing an antitrust complaint in advance of discovery, cf. *Poller v. Columbia Broadcasting System, Inc.*, 368 U.S. 464, 473 (1962), but quite another to forget that proceeding to antitrust discovery can be expensive. . . . That potential expense is obvious enough in the present case: plaintiffs represent a putative class of at least 90 percent of all subscribers to local telephone or high-speed Internet service in the continental United States, in an action against America's largest telecommunications firms (with many thousands of employees generating reams and gigabytes of business records) for unspecified (if any) instances of antitrust violations that allegedly occurred over a period of seven years.

It is no answer to say that a claim just shy of a plausible entitlement to relief can, if groundless, be weeded out early in the discovery process through "careful case management," given the common lament that the success of judicial supervision in checking discovery abuse has been on the modest side. See, *e.g.*, Easterbrook, Discovery as Abuse, 69 B.U. L. Rev. 635, 638 (1989) ("Judges can do little about impositional discovery when parties control the legal claims to be presented and conduct the discovery themselves"). And it is self-evident that the problem of discovery abuse cannot be solved by "careful scrutiny of evidence at the summary judgment stage," much less "lucid instructions to juries," *post*, at 4; the threat of discovery expense will push cost-conscious defendants to settle even anemic cases before reaching those proceedings. Probably, then, it is only by taking care to require allegations that reach the level suggesting conspiracy that we can hope to avoid the potentially enormous expense of discovery in cases with no "'reasonably

---

5. The border in *DM Research* was the line between the conclusory and the factual. Here it lies between the factually neutral and the factually suggestive. Each must be crossed to enter the realm of plausible liability.

founded hope that the [discovery] process will reveal relevant evidence'" to support a §1 claim. *Dura*, 544 U.S., at 347 (quoting *Blue Chip Stamps, supra*, at 741; alteration in *Dura*).[6]

Plaintiffs do not, of course, dispute the requirement of plausibility and the need for something more than merely parallel behavior explained in *Theatre Enterprises, Monsanto*, and *Matsushita*, and their main argument against the plausibility standard at the pleading stage is its ostensible conflict with an early statement of ours construing Rule 8. Justice Black's opinion for the Court in *Conley v. Gibson* spoke not only of the need for fair notice of the grounds for entitlement to relief but of "the accepted rule that a complaint should not be dismissed for failure to state a claim unless it appears beyond doubt that the plaintiff can prove no set of facts in support of his claim which would entitle him to relief." 355 U.S., at 45–46. This "no set of facts" language can be read in isolation as saying that any statement revealing the theory of the claim will suffice unless its factual impossibility may be shown from the face of the pleadings; and the Court of Appeals appears to have read *Conley* in some such way when formulating its understanding of the proper pleading standard, see 425 F.3d, at 106, 114 (invoking *Conley*'s "no set of facts" language in describing the standard for dismissal).

On such a focused and literal reading of *Conley*'s "no set of facts," a wholly conclusory statement of claim would survive a motion to dismiss whenever the pleadings left open the possibility that a plaintiff might later establish some "set of [undisclosed] facts" to support recovery. So here, the Court of Appeals

---

6. The dissent takes heart in the reassurances of plaintiffs' counsel that discovery would be "'phased'" and "'limited to the existence of the alleged conspiracy and class certification.'" . . . But determining whether some illegal agreement may have taken place between unspecified persons at different ILECs (each a multibillion dollar corporation with legions of management level employees) at some point over seven years is a sprawling, costly, and hugely time-consuming undertaking not easily susceptible to the kind of line drawing and case management that the dissent envisions. Perhaps the best answer to the dissent's optimism that antitrust discovery is open to effective judicial control is a more extensive quotation of the authority just cited, a judge with a background in antitrust law. Given the system that we have, the hope of effective judicial supervision is slim: "The timing is all wrong. The plaintiff files a sketchy complaint (the Rules of Civil Procedure discourage fulsome documents), and discovery is launched. A judicial officer does not know the details of the case the parties will present and in theory *cannot* know the details. Discovery is used to find the details. The judicial officer always knows less than the parties, and the parties themselves may not know very well where they are going or what they expect to find. A magistrate supervising discovery does not — cannot — know the expected productivity of a given request, because the nature of the requester's claim and the contents of the files (or head) of the adverse party are unknown. Judicial officers cannot measure the costs and benefits to the requester and so cannot isolate impositional requests. Requesters have no reason to disclose their own estimates because they gain from imposing costs on rivals (and may lose from an improvement in accuracy). The portions of the Rules of Civil Procedure calling on judges to trim back excessive demands, therefore, have been, and are doomed to be, hollow. We cannot prevent what we cannot detect; we cannot detect what we cannot define; we cannot define 'abusive' discovery except in theory, because in practice we lack essential information." Easterbrook, Discovery as Abuse, 69 B.U. L. Rev. 635, 638–639 (1989).

specifically found the prospect of unearthing direct evidence of conspiracy sufficient to preclude dismissal, even though the complaint does not set forth a single fact in a context that suggests an agreement. 425 F.3d, at 106, 114. It seems fair to say that this approach to pleading would dispense with any showing of a "'reasonably founded hope'" that a plaintiff would be able to make a case, *see Dura*, 544 U.S., at 347 (quoting *Blue Chip Stamps*, 421 U.S., at 741); Mr. Micawber's optimism would be enough.

Seeing this, a good many judges and commentators have balked at taking the literal terms of the *Conley* passage as a pleading standard. *See, e.g., Car Carriers*, 745 F.2d, at 1106 ("*Conley* has never been interpreted literally") and, "[i]n practice, a complaint . . . must contain either direct or inferential allegations respecting all the material elements necessary to sustain recovery under *some* viable legal theory" (internal quotation marks omitted; emphasis and omission in original); *Ascon Properties, Inc. v. Mobil Oil Co.*, 866 F.2d 1149, 1155 (C.A.9 1989) (tension between *Conley's* "no set of facts" language and its acknowledgment that a plaintiff must provide the "grounds" on which his claim rests); *O'Brien v. DiGrazia*, 544 F.2d 543, 546, n. 3 (C.A.1 1976) ("[W]hen a plaintiff . . . supplies facts to support his claim, we do not think that *Conley* imposes a duty on the courts to conjure up unpleaded facts that might turn a frivolous claim of unconstitutional . . . action into a substantial one"); . . . We could go on, but there is no need to pile up further citations to show that *Conley's* "no set of facts" language has been questioned, criticized, and explained away long enough. To be fair to the *Conley* Court, the passage should be understood in light of the opinion's preceding summary of the complaint's concrete allegations, which the Court quite reasonably understood as amply stating a claim for relief. But the passage so often quoted fails to mention this understanding on the part of the Court, and after puzzling the profession for 50 years, this famous observation has earned its retirement. The phrase is best forgotten as an incomplete, negative gloss on an accepted pleading standard: once a claim has been stated adequately, it may be supported by showing any set of facts consistent with the allegations in the complaint. *See Sanjuan*, 40 F.3d, at 251 (once a claim for relief has been stated, a plaintiff "receives the benefit of imagination, so long as the hypotheses are consistent with the complaint"). . . . *Conley*, then, described the breadth of opportunity to prove what an adequate complaint claims, not the minimum standard of adequate pleading to govern a complaint's survival.

III

When we look for plausibility in this complaint, we agree with the District Court that plaintiffs' claim of conspiracy in restraint of trade comes up short. To begin with, the complaint leaves no doubt that plaintiffs rest their §1 claim on descriptions of parallel conduct and not on any independent allegation of actual agreement among the ILECs. Although in form a few stray statements speak directly of agreement,[9] on fair reading these are merely legal conclusions resting on the

---

9. See Complaint ¶¶51, 64, App. 27, 30–31 (alleging that ILECs engaged in a "contract, combination or conspiracy" and agreed not to compete with one another).

prior allegations. Thus, the complaint first takes account of the alleged "absence of any meaningful competition between [the ILECs] in one another's markets," "the parallel course of conduct that each [ILEC] engaged in to prevent competition from CLECs," "and the other facts and market circumstances alleged [earlier]"; "in light of" these, the complaint concludes "that [the ILECs] have entered into a contract, combination or conspiracy to prevent competitive entry into their . . . markets and have agreed not to compete with one another." Complaint ¶51, App. 27.[10] The nub of the complaint, then, is the ILECs' parallel behavior, consisting of steps to keep the CLECs out and manifest disinterest in becoming CLECs themselves, and its sufficiency turns on the suggestions raised by this conduct when viewed in light of common economic experience.[11]

We think that nothing contained in the complaint invests either the action or inaction alleged with a plausible suggestion of conspiracy. As to the ILECs' supposed agreement to disobey the 1996 Act and thwart the CLECs' attempts to compete, we agree with the District Court that nothing in the complaint intimates that the resistance to the upstarts was anything more than the natural, unilateral reaction of each ILEC intent on keeping its regional dominance. The 1996 Act did more than just subject the ILECs to competition; it obliged them to subsidize their competitors with their own equipment at wholesale rates. The economic incentive to resist was powerful, but resisting competition is routine market conduct, and even if the ILECs flouted the 1996 Act in all the ways the plaintiffs allege, . . . there is no reason to infer that the companies had agreed among themselves to do what was only natural anyway; so natural, in fact, that if alleging parallel decisions to resist competition were enough to imply an antitrust conspiracy, pleading a §1 violation against almost any group of competing businesses would be a sure thing.

The complaint makes its closest pass at a predicate for conspiracy with the claim that collusion was necessary because success by even one CLEC in an ILEC's

---

10. If the complaint had not explained that the claim of agreement rested on the parallel conduct described, we doubt that the complaint's references to an agreement among the ILECs would have given the notice required by Rule 8. Apart from identifying a seven-year span in which the §1 violations were supposed to have occurred (i.e., "[b]eginning at least as early as February 6, 1996, and continuing to the present," *id.*, ¶64, App. 30), the pleadings mentioned no specific time, place, or person involved in the alleged conspiracies. This lack of notice contrasts sharply with the model form for pleading negligence, Form 9, which the dissent says exemplifies the kind of "bare allegation" that survives a motion to dismiss. *Post*, at 6. Whereas the model form alleges that the defendant struck the plaintiff with his car while plaintiff was crossing a particular highway at a specified date and time, the complaint here furnishes no clue as to which of the four ILECs (much less which of their employees) supposedly agreed, or when and where the illicit agreement took place. A defendant wishing to prepare an answer in the simple fact pattern laid out in Form 9 would know what to answer; a defendant seeking to respond to plaintiffs' conclusory allegations in the §1 context would have little idea where to begin.

11. The dissent's quotations from the complaint leave the impression that plaintiffs directly allege illegal agreement; in fact, they proceed exclusively via allegations of parallel conduct, as both the District Court and Court of Appeals recognized. See 313 F. Supp. 2d 174, 182 (S.D.N.Y. 2003); 425 F.3d 99, 102–104 (C.A. 2005).

territory "would have revealed the degree to which competitive entry by CLECs would have been successful in the other territories." *Id.*, ¶ 50, . . . But, its logic aside, this general premise still fails to answer the point that there was just no need for joint encouragement to resist the 1996 Act; as the District Court said, "each ILEC has reason to want to avoid dealing with CLECs" and "each ILEC would attempt to keep CLECs out, regardless of the actions of the other ILECs." 313 F. Supp. 2d, at 184; . . . [12]

Plaintiffs' second conspiracy theory rests on the competitive reticence among the ILECs themselves in the wake of the 1996 Act, which was supposedly passed in the "'hop[e] that the large incumbent local monopoly companies . . . might attack their neighbors' service areas, as they are the best situated to do so.'" Complaint ¶38, App. 20 (quoting Consumer Federation of America, Lessons from 1996 Telecommunications Act: Deregulation Before Meaningful Competition Spells Consumer Disaster, p. 12 (Feb. 2000)). Contrary to hope, the ILECs declined "'to enter each other's service territories in any significant way,'" Complaint ¶38, App. 20, and the local telephone and high speed Internet market remains highly compartmentalized geographically, with minimal competition. Based on this state of affairs, and perceiving the ILECs to be blessed with "especially attractive business opportunities" in surrounding markets dominated by other ILECs, the plaintiffs assert that the ILECs' parallel conduct was "strongly suggestive of conspiracy." *Id.*, ¶40. . . .

But it was not suggestive of conspiracy, not if history teaches anything. In a traditionally unregulated industry with low barriers to entry, sparse competition among large firms dominating separate geographical segments of the market could very well signify illegal agreement, but here we have an obvious alternative explanation. In the decade preceding the 1996 Act and well before that, monopoly was the norm in telecommunications, not the exception. *See Verizon Communications Inc. v. FCC*, 535 U.S. 467, 477–478 (2002) (describing telephone service providers as traditional public monopolies). The ILECs were born in that world, doubtless liked the world the way it was, and surely knew the adage about him who lives by the sword. Hence, a natural explanation for the noncompetition alleged is that the former Government-sanctioned monopolists were sitting tight, expecting their neighbors to do the same thing.

In fact, the complaint itself gives reasons to believe that the ILECs would see their best interests in keeping to their old turf. Although the complaint says generally that the ILECs passed up "especially attractive business opportunit[ies]" by declining to compete as CLECs against other ILECs, Complaint ¶40, . . . it does not allege that competition as CLECs was potentially any more lucrative than

---

12. From the allegation that the ILECs belong to various trade associations, see Complaint ¶46, App. 23, the dissent playfully suggests that they conspired to restrain trade, an inference said to be "buttressed by the common sense of Adam Smith." *Post*, at 22, 25–26. If Adam Smith is peering down today, he may be surprised to learn that his tongue-in-cheek remark would be authority to force his famous pinmaker to devote financial and human capital to hire lawyers, prepare for depositions, and otherwise fend off allegations of conspiracy; all this just because he belonged to the same trade guild as one of his competitors when their pins carried the same price tag.

other opportunities being pursued by the ILECs during the same period,[13] and the complaint is replete with indications that any CLEC faced nearly insurmountable barriers to profitability owing to the ILECs' flagrant resistance to the network sharing requirements of the 1996 Act, *id.*, ¶47. . . . Not only that, but even without a monopolistic tradition and the peculiar difficulty of mandating shared networks, "[f]irms do not expand without limit and none of them enters every market that an outside observer might regard as profitable, or even a small portion of such markets." Areeda & Hovenkamp ¶307d, at 155 (Supp. 2006) (commenting on the case at bar). The upshot is that Congress may have expected some ILECs to become CLECs in the legacy territories of other ILECs, but the disappointment does not make conspiracy plausible. We agree with the District Court's assessment that antitrust conspiracy was not suggested by the facts adduced under either theory of the complaint, which thus fails to state a valid §1 claim.[14]

Plaintiffs say that our analysis runs counter to *Swierkiewicz v. Sorema N.A.*, 534 U.S. 506, 508 (2002), which held that "a complaint in an employment discrimination lawsuit [need] not contain specific facts establishing a prima facie case of discrimination under the framework set forth in *McDonnell Douglas Corp. v. Green*, 411 U.S. 792 (1973)." They argue that just as the prima facie case is a "flexible evidentiary standard" that "should not be transposed into a rigid pleading standard for discrimination cases," *Swierkiewicz, supra*, at 512, "transpos[ing] 'plus factor' summary judgment analysis woodenly into a rigid Rule 12(b)(6) pleading standard . . . would be unwise," . . . As the District Court correctly understood, however, "*Swierkiewicz* did not change the law of pleading, but simply re-emphasized . . . that the Second Circuit's use of a heightened pleading standard for Title VII cases was

---

13. The complaint quoted a reported statement of Qwest's CEO, Richard Notebaert, to suggest that the ILECs declined to compete against each other despite recognizing that it " 'might be a good way to turn a quick dollar.' " ¶42, App. 22 (quoting *Chicago Tribune*, Oct. 31, 2002, Business Section, p. 1). This was only part of what he reportedly said, however, and the District Court was entitled to take notice of the full contents of the published articles referenced in the complaint, from which the truncated quotations were drawn. See Fed. Rule Evid. 201. Notebaert was also quoted as saying that entering new markets as a CLEC would not be "a sustainable economic model" because the CLEC pricing model is "just . . . nuts." *Chicago Tribune*, Oct. 31, 2002, Business Section, p. 1 (cited at Complaint ¶42, App. 22). Another source cited in the complaint quotes Notebaert as saying he thought it "unwise" to "base a business plan" on the privileges accorded to CLECs under the 1996 Act because the regulatory environment was too unstable. *Chicago Tribune*, Dec. 19, 2002, Business Section, p. 2 (cited at Complaint ¶45, App. 23).

14. In reaching this conclusion, we do not apply any "heightened" pleading standard, nor do we seek to broaden the scope of Federal Rule of Civil Procedure 9, which can only be accomplished " 'by the process of amending the Federal Rules, and not by judicial interpretation.' " *Swierkiewicz v. Sorema N.A.*, 534 U.S. 506, 515 (2002) (quoting *Leatherman v. Tarrant County Narcotics Intelligence and Coordination Unit*, 507 U.S. 163, 168 (1993)). On certain subjects understood to raise a high risk of abusive litigation, a plaintiff must state factual allegations with greater particularity than Rule 8 requires. Fed. Rules Civ. Proc. 9(b)–(c). Here, our concern is not that the allegations in the complaint were insufficiently "particular[ized]," *ibid.*; rather, the complaint warranted dismissal because it failed *in toto* to render plaintiffs' entitlement to relief plausible.

contrary to the Federal Rules' structure of liberal pleading requirements." 313 F. Supp. 2d, at 181 (citation and footnote omitted). Even though Swierkiewicz's pleadings "detailed the events leading to his termination, provided relevant dates, and included the ages and nationalities of at least some of the relevant persons involved with his termination," the Court of Appeals dismissed his complaint for failing to allege certain additional facts that Swierkiewicz would need at the trial stage to support his claim in the absence of direct evidence of discrimination. *Swierkiewicz*, 534 U.S., at 514. We reversed on the ground that the Court of Appeals had impermissibly applied what amounted to a heightened pleading requirement by insisting that Swierkiewicz allege "specific facts" beyond those necessary to state his claim and the grounds showing entitlement to relief. *Id.*, at 508.

Here, in contrast, we do not require heightened fact pleading of specifics, but only enough facts to state a claim to relief that is plausible on its face. Because the plaintiffs here have not nudged their claims across the line from conceivable to plausible, their complaint must be dismissed.

. . .

The judgment of the Court of Appeals for the Second Circuit is reversed, and the cause is remanded for further proceedings consistent with this opinion.

It is so ordered.

JUSTICE STEVENS, with whom JUSTICE GINSBURG joins except as to Part IV, dissenting.

. . .

Thus, this is a case in which there is no dispute about the substantive law. If the defendants acted independently, their conduct was perfectly lawful. If, however, that conduct is the product of a horizontal agreement among potential competitors, it was unlawful. Plaintiffs have *alleged* such an agreement and, because the complaint was dismissed in advance of answer, the allegation has not even been denied. Why, then, does the case not proceed? Does a judicial opinion that the charge is not "plausible" provide a legally acceptable reason for dismissing the complaint? I think not.

Respondents' amended complaint describes a variety of circumstantial evidence and makes the straightforward allegation that petitioners

> entered into a contract, combination or conspiracy to prevent competitive entry in their respective local telephone and/or high speed internet services markets and have agreed not to compete with one another and otherwise allocated customers and markets to one another.

Amended Complaint . . . ¶51, (hereinafter Complaint). The complaint explains that, contrary to Congress' expectation when it enacted the 1996 Telecommunications Act, and consistent with their own economic self-interests, petitioner Incumbent Local Exchange Carriers (ILECs) have assiduously avoided infringing upon each other's markets and have refused to permit nonincumbent competitors to access their networks. The complaint quotes Richard Notebaert, the former CEO of one such ILEC, as saying that competing in a neighboring ILEC's territory "might be a good way to turn a quick dollar but that doesn't make it right." *Id.*, ¶42. Moreover, respondents allege that petitioners "communicate amongst themselves" through numerous industry associations. *Id.*, ¶46. In sum, respondents allege that petitioners entered into an agreement that has long been recognized as a classic *per se* violation of the Sherman Act. . . .

Under rules of procedure that have been well settled since well before our decision in *Theatre Enterprises*, a judge ruling on a defendant's motion to dismiss a complaint, "must accept as true all of the factual allegations contained in the complaint." *Swierkiewicz v. Sorema N. A.*, 534 U.S. 506, 508, n. 1. . . . But instead of requiring knowledgeable executives such as Notebaert to respond to these allegations by way of sworn depositions or other limited discovery—and indeed without so much as requiring petitioners to file an answer denying that they entered into any agreement—the majority permits immediate dismissal based on the assurances of company lawyers that nothing untoward was afoot. The Court embraces the argument of those lawyers that "there is no reason to infer that the companies had agreed among themselves to do what was only natural anyway," . . . ; that "there was just no need for joint encouragement to resist the 1996 Act," . . . ; and that the "natural explanation for the noncompetition alleged is that the former Government-sanctioned monopolists were sitting tight, expecting their neighbors to do the same thing". . . .

The Court and petitioners' legal team are no doubt correct that the parallel conduct alleged is consistent with the absence of any contract, combination, or conspiracy. But that conduct is also entirely consistent with the *presence* of the illegal agreement alleged in the complaint. And the charge that petitioners "agreed not to compete with one another" is not just one of "a few stray statements" . . . ; it is an allegation describing unlawful conduct. As such, the Federal Rules of Civil Procedure, our longstanding precedent, and sound practice mandate that the District Court at least require some sort of response from petitioners before dismissing the case.

. . .

Everything today's majority says would therefore make perfect sense if it were ruling on a Rule 56 motion for summary judgment and the evidence included nothing more than the Court has described. But it should go without saying in the wake of *Swierkiewicz* that a heightened production burden at the summary judgment stage does not translate into a heightened pleading burden at the complaint stage. The majority rejects the complaint in this case because—in light of the fact that the parallel conduct alleged is consistent with ordinary market behavior—the claimed conspiracy is "conceivable" but not "plausible," *ante*, at 24. I have my doubts about the majority's assessment of the plausibility of this alleged conspiracy. See Part III, *infra*. But even if the majority's speculation is correct, its "plausibility" standard is irreconcilable with Rule 8 and with our governing precedents. As we made clear in *Swierkiewicz* and *Leatherman*, fear of the burdens of litigation does not justify factual conclusions supported only by lawyers' arguments rather than sworn denials or admissible evidence.

This case is a poor vehicle for the Court's new pleading rule, for we have observed that "in antitrust cases, where 'the proof is largely in the hands of the alleged conspirators,' . . . dismissals prior to giving the plaintiff ample opportunity for discovery should be granted very sparingly.". . . Moreover, the fact that the Sherman Act authorizes the recovery of treble damages and attorney's fees for successful plaintiffs indicates that Congress intended to encourage, rather than discourage, private enforcement of the law. . . . In the face of such a policy this Court should not add requirements to burden the private litigant beyond what is specifically set forth by Congress in those laws. It is therefore more, not less, important in antitrust cases to resist the urge to engage in armchair economics at the pleading stage.

The same year we decided *Conley*, Judge Clark wrote, presciently,

> I fear that every age must learn its lesson that special pleading cannot be made to do the service of trial and that live issues between active litigants are not to be disposed of or evaded on the paper pleadings, i.e., the formalistic claims of the parties. Experience has found no quick and easy short cut for trials in cases generally *and antitrust cases in particular.*

Special Pleading in the "Big Case" in Procedure—The Handmaid of Justice 147, 148 (C. Wright & H. Reasoner eds. 1965) (hereinafter Clark, Special Pleading in the Big Case) (emphasis added).

In this "Big Case," the Court succumbs to the temptation that previous Courts have steadfastly resisted. While the majority assures us that it is not applying any "'heightened'" pleading standard, see *ante*, at 23, n. 14, I shall now explain why I have a difficult time understanding its opinion any other way.

III

The Court does not suggest that an agreement to do what the plaintiffs allege would be permissible under the antitrust laws. . . . Nor does the Court hold that these plaintiffs have failed to allege an injury entitling them to sue for damages under those laws. . . . Rather, the theory on which the Court permits dismissal is that, so far as the Federal Rules are concerned, no agreement has been alleged at all. This is a mind-boggling conclusion.

As the Court explains, prior to the enactment of the Telecommunications Act of 1996 the law prohibited the defendants from competing with each other. The new statute was enacted to replace a monopolistic market with a competitive one. The Act did not merely require the regional monopolists to take affirmative steps to facilitate entry to new competitors, *see Verizon Communications Inc. v. Law Offices of Curtis v. Trinko, LLP*, 540 U.S. 398, 402 (2004); it also permitted the existing firms to compete with each other and to expand their operations into previously forbidden territory. *See* 47 U.S.C. §271. Each of the defendants decided not to take the latter step. That was obviously an extremely important business decision, and I am willing to presume that each company acted entirely independently in reaching that decision. I am even willing to entertain the majority's belief that any agreement among the companies was unlikely. But the plaintiffs allege in three places in their complaint, ¶¶4, 51, 64, . . . that the ILECs did in fact agree both to prevent competitors from entering into their local markets and to forgo competition with each other. And as the Court recognizes, at the motion to dismiss stage, a judge assumes "that all the allegations in the complaint are true (even if doubtful in fact)." . . .

The majority circumvents this obvious obstacle to dismissal by pretending that it does not exist. The Court admits that "in form a few stray statements in the complaint speak directly of agreement," but disregards those allegations by saying that "on fair reading these are merely legal conclusions resting on the prior allegations" of parallel conduct. . . . The Court's dichotomy between factual allegations and "legal conclusions" is the stuff of a bygone era, *supra*, at 5–7. That distinction was a defining feature of code pleading, *see generally* Clark, The Complaint in Code Pleading, 35 Yale L.J. 259 (1925–1926), but was conspicuously abolished when the Federal Rules were enacted in 1938. . . .

Even if I were inclined to accept the Court's anachronistic dichotomy and ignore the complaint's actual allegations, I would dispute the Court's suggestion that any inference of agreement from petitioners' parallel conduct is "implausible." Many years ago a truly great economist perceptively observed that "[p]eople of the same trade seldom meet together, even for merriment and diversion, but the conversation ends in a conspiracy against the public, or in some contrivance to raise prices." A. Smith, An Inquiry Into the Nature and Causes of the Wealth of Nations, in 39 Great Books of the Western World 55 (R. Hutchins & M. Adler eds. 1952). I am not so cynical as to accept that sentiment at face value, but I need not do so here. Respondents' complaint points not only to petitioners' numerous opportunities to meet with each other, Complaint ¶46, . . . [10] but also to Notebaert's curious statement that encroaching on a fellow incumbent's territory "might be a good way to turn a quick dollar but that doesn't make it right," *id.*, ¶42. . . . What did he mean by that? One possible (indeed plausible) inference is that he meant that while it would be in his company's economic self-interest to compete with its brethren, he had agreed with his competitors not to do so. According to the complaint, that is how the Illinois Coalition for Competitive Telecom construed Notebaert's statement, *id.*, ¶44, . . . (calling the statement "evidence of potential collusion among regional Bell phone monopolies to not compete against one another and kill off potential competitors in local phone service"), and that is how Members of Congress construed his company's behavior, *id.*, ¶45, . . . (describing a letter to the Justice Department requesting an investigation into the possibility that the ILECs' "very apparent non-competition policy" was coordinated).

Perhaps Notebaert meant instead that competition would be sensible in the short term but not in the long run. That's what his lawyers tell us anyway. See Brief for Petitioners 36. But I would think that no one would know better what Notebaert meant than Notebaert himself. Instead of permitting respondents to ask Notebaert, however, the Court looks to other quotes from that and other articles and decides that what he meant was that entering new markets as a CLEC would not be a "'sustainable economic model.'" . . . Never mind that—as anyone ever interviewed knows—a newspaper article is hardly a verbatim transcript; the writer selects quotes to package his story, not to record a subject's views for posterity. But more importantly the District Court was required at this stage of the proceedings to construe Notebaert's ambiguous statement in the plaintiffs' favor. *See Allen v. Wright*, 468 U.S.

---

10. The Court describes my reference to the allegation that the defendants belong to various trade associations as "playfully" suggesting that the defendants conspired to restrain trade. *Ante*, n. 12. Quite the contrary: an allegation that competitors meet on a regular basis, like the allegations of parallel conduct, is consistent with—though not sufficient to prove—the plaintiffs' entirely serious and unequivocal allegation that the defendants entered into an unlawful agreement. Indeed, if it were true that the plaintiffs "rest their §1 claim on descriptions of parallel conduct and not on any independent allegation of actual agreement among the ILECs," *ante*, at 18, there would have been no purpose in including a reference to the trade association meetings in the amended complaint.

737, 768, n. 1 (1984). The inference the statement supports—that simultaneous decisions by ILECs not even to attempt to poach customers from one another once the law authorized them to do so were the product of an agreement—sits comfortably within the realm of possibility. That is all the Rules require.

To be clear, if I had been the trial judge in this case, I would not have permitted the plaintiffs to engage in massive discovery based solely on the allegations in this complaint. On the other hand, I surely would not have dismissed the complaint without requiring the defendants to answer the charge that they "have agreed not to compete with one another and otherwise allocated customers and markets to one another." ¶51. . . . Even a sworn denial of that charge would not justify a summary dismissal without giving the plaintiffs the opportunity to take depositions from Notebaert and at least one responsible executive representing each of the other defendants.

NOTES AND QUESTIONS

1. How do you understand Justice Souter's statement that in order to survive a 12(b)(6) motion to dismiss for failure to state a claim, a plaintiff must "state enough facts to state a claim to relief that is plausible on its face"? Does *Twombly* revive the kind of detailed fact pleading that was required at common law and under the Field Code? Without a developed factual record, how should a court determine the plausibility of a complaint? By forcing the judge to make a plausibility determination at this stage in the proceeding, doesn't *Twombly* risk biasing the adjudication by the judge's experience and preconceptions? Consider, in particular, the dismissal of plaintiffs' "second conspiracy theory" dealing with the alleged agreement of the regional phone companies not to compete in each other's markets. Justice Souter acknowledges that an explicit agreement not to compete in this manner would constitute a violation of the antitrust laws, and plaintiffs alleged the existence of such an agreement. Yet the Court finds the complaint legally insufficient in its failure to plead a factual context that is sufficient to make such an allegation not merely "conceivable but plausible."

Notice that the defendants' decisions not to compete in adjacent markets appear to have been *contrary* to their individual short-term economic interests. (Indeed, plaintiff quoted a phone company official who seemed to acknowledge that the phone companies had bypassed an opportunity to "turn a quick dollar.") Thus, defendants' parallel behavior could not be explained away as the Court did with plaintiffs' first conspiracy claim, by simple market logic; each defendant's decision not to compete in adjacent markets seems irrational in the absence of some reasonable expectation that their competitors would exercise similar restraint—an expectation that might come from an illegal conspiracy.

Justice Souter goes to some length to demonstrate that defendants could form such an expectation in the absence of an actionable conspiracy. But should that render plaintiffs' *pleading* inadequate? Hasn't the Court here imposed an even higher burden on plaintiff than merely setting forth a "plausible" claim?

2. *Is Twombly Consistent with Rule 11?* Recall, that pursuant to Rule 11, a pleader must certify that "the factual contentions have evidentiary support or, if specifically so identified, will likely have evidentiary support after a reasonable opportunity

for . . . discovery." Did the *Twombly* complaint satisfy this standard? Is the *Twombly* standard that plaintiff plead a "plausible" claim a more demanding requirement than the "will likely have evidentiary support" standard of Rule 11?

3. Shortly after issuing its decision in *Twombly*, the Court issued another ruling in a 12(b)(6) case. This time, the Court held that the lower courts had applied an excessively strict pleading standard. *Erickson v. Pardus*, 551 U.S. 89 (2007), involved a complaint filed by a *pro se* plaintiff under 28 U.S.C. §1983, a statute that enables individuals to sue state officials for violations of their constitutional rights. Plaintiff Erickson alleged in his complaint that he contracted Hepatitis C while incarcerated in the State of Colorado and sought treatment from prison officials. The officials placed Erickson on a year-long treatment program but suspended treatment after concluding that Erickson was using illegal drugs. Erickson sued, alleging that the refusal of prison officials to treat his Hepatitis C "endanger[ed his] life," causing "his liver [to] suffer[] irreversible damage" and threatening to impose "irreparable damage if his disease [went] untreated." This conduct, he asserted, violated the Eighth Amendment prohibition against cruel and unusual punishment.

The district court dismissed Erickson's complaint. The court concluded that Erickson had not sufficiently alleged that he would suffer "substantial harm" as a result of the prison doctor's actions. The Tenth Circuit affirmed, explaining that Erickson had made "only conclusory allegations to the effect that he has suffered a cognizable independent harm as a result of his removal from the treatment program."

The Court reversed. In fact, the Court took the unusual step of issuing a summary reversal—granting certiorari and vacating the lower-court judgment without argument or briefing—because the "holding [of the lower courts] depart[ed] in so stark a manner from the pleading standard mandated by the Federal Rules of Civil Procedure." Citing *Twombly* and *Conley v. Gibson*, the Court reiterated that "Federal Rule of Civil Procedure 8(a)(2) requires only 'a short and plain statement of the claim showing that the pleader is entitled to relief.'" Specific facts are not necessary; the statement need only "'give the defendant fair notice of what the . . . claim is and the grounds upon which it rests.'" Erickson's complaint easily satisfied that standard:

> The complaint stated that Dr. Bloor's decision to remove petitioner from his prescribed Hepatitis C medication was "endangering [his] life." It alleged this medication was withheld "shortly after" petitioner had commenced a treatment program that would take one year, that he was "Still in need of treatment for this disease," and that the prison officials were in the meantime refusing to provide treatment. This alone was enough to satisfy Rule 8(a)(2).

Id. (citations omitted).

Does *Erickson v. Pardus* blunt the impact of *Twombly*? Can the difference in outcomes be explained by the fact that, according to "common . . . experience" (a phrase the Court uses in *Twombly*), Hepatitis C is a condition that will cause substantial harm if left untreated, while parallel actions by competitors—even parallel actions that appear to run contrary to the competitors' economic incentives—do not necessarily indicate the existence of an illegal agreement or conspiracy?

Ashcroft v. Iqbal

556 U.S. 662 (2009)

JUSTICE KENNEDY delivered the opinion of the Court.

Respondent Javaid Iqbal is a citizen of Pakistan and a Muslim. In the wake of the September 11, 2001, terrorist attacks he was arrested in the United States on criminal charges and detained by federal officials. Respondent claims he was deprived of various constitutional protections while in federal custody. To redress the alleged deprivations, respondent filed a complaint against numerous federal officials, including John Ashcroft, the former Attorney General of the United States, and Robert Mueller, the Director of the Federal Bureau of Investigation (FBI). Ashcroft and Mueller are the petitioners in the case now before us. As to these two petitioners, the complaint alleges that they adopted an unconstitutional policy that subjected respondent to harsh conditions of confinement on account of his race, religion, or national origin.

In the District Court petitioners raised the defense of qualified immunity and moved to dismiss the suit, contending the complaint was not sufficient to state a claim against them. The District Court denied the motion to dismiss, concluding the complaint was sufficient to state a claim despite petitioners' official status at the times in question. Petitioners brought an interlocutory appeal in the Court of Appeals for the Second Circuit. The court, without discussion, assumed it had jurisdiction over the order denying the motion to dismiss; and it affirmed the District Court's decision.

Respondent's account of his prison ordeal could, if proved, demonstrate unconstitutional misconduct by some governmental actors. But the allegations and pleadings with respect to these actors are not before us here. This case instead turns on a narrower question: Did respondent, as the plaintiff in the District Court, plead factual matter that, if taken as true, states a claim that petitioners deprived him of his clearly established constitutional rights. We hold respondent's pleadings are insufficient.

I

Following the 2001 attacks, the FBI and other entities within the Department of Justice began an investigation of vast reach to identify the assailants and prevent them from attacking anew. The FBI dedicated more than 4,000 special agents and 3,000 support personnel to the endeavor. By September 18 "the FBI had received more than 96,000 tips or potential leads from the public." Dept. of Justice, Office of Inspector General, The September 11 Detainees: A Review of the Treatment of Aliens Held on Immigration Charges in Connection with the Investigation of the September 11 Attacks 1, 11–12 (Apr. 2003). . . .

In the ensuing months the FBI questioned more than 1,000 people with suspected links to the attacks in particular or to terrorism in general. *Id.*, at 1. Of those individuals, some 762 were held on immigration charges; and a 184-member subset of that group was deemed to be "of 'high interest' " to the investigation. *Id.*, at 111. The high-interest detainees were held under restrictive conditions designed to prevent them from communicating with the general prison population or the outside world. *Id.*, at 112–113.

Respondent was one of the detainees. According to his complaint, in November 2001 agents of the FBI and Immigration and Naturalization Service arrested him on charges of fraud in relation to identification documents and conspiracy to defraud the United States. *Iqbal v. Hasty*, 490 F. 3d 143, 147–148 (CA2 2007). Pending trial for those crimes, respondent was housed at the Metropolitan Detention Center (MDC) in Brooklyn, New York. Respondent was designated a person "of high interest" to the September 11 investigation and in January 2002 was placed in a section of the MDC known as the Administrative Maximum Special Housing Unit (ADMAX SHU). *Id.*, at 148. As the facility's name indicates, the ADMAX SHU incorporates the maximum security conditions allowable under Federal Bureau of Prison regulations. *Ibid.* ADMAX SHU detainees were kept in lockdown 23 hours a day, spending the remaining hour outside their cells in handcuffs and leg irons accompanied by a four-officer escort. Ibid.

Respondent pleaded guilty to the criminal charges, served a term of imprisonment, and was removed to his native Pakistan. Id., at 149. He then filed a *Bivens* action in the United States District Court for the Eastern District of New York against 34 current and former federal officials and 19 "John Doe" federal corrections officers. See *Bivens v. Six Unknown Fed. Narcotics Agents*, 403 U.S. 388 (1971). The defendants range from the correctional officers who had day-to-day contact with respondent during the term of his confinement, to the wardens of the MDC facility, all the way to petitioners — officials who were at the highest level of the federal law enforcement hierarchy. First Amended Complaint in No. 04–CV–1809 (JG)(JA), ¶¶1011, App. to Pet. for Cert. 157a (hereinafter Complaint).

The 21-cause-of-action complaint does not challenge respondent's arrest or his confinement in the MDC's general prison population. Rather, it concentrates on his treatment while confined to the ADMAX SHU. The complaint sets forth various claims against defendants who are not before us. For instance, the complaint alleges that respondent's jailors "kicked him in the stomach, punched him in the face, and dragged him across" his cell without justification, *id.*, ¶113, App. to Pet. for Cert. 176a; subjected him to serial strip and body-cavity searches when he posed no safety risk to himself or others, *id.*, ¶¶143–145, App. to Pet. for Cert. 182a; and refused to let him and other Muslims pray because there would be "[n]o prayers for terrorists," *id.*, ¶154, App. to Pet. for Cert. 184a.

The allegations against petitioners are the only ones relevant here. The complaint contends that petitioners designated respondent a person of high interest on account of his race, religion, or national origin, in contravention of the First and Fifth Amendments to the Constitution. The complaint alleges that "the [FBI], under the direction of Defendant Mueller, arrested and detained thousands of Arab Muslim men . . . as part of its investigation of the events of September 11." *Id.*, ¶47, at 164a. It further alleges that "[t]he policy of holding post-September-11th detainees in highly restrictive conditions of confinement until they were 'cleared' by the FBI was approved by Defendants Ashcroft and Mueller in discussions in the weeks after September 11, 2001." *Id.*, ¶69, at 168a. Lastly, the complaint posits that petitioners "each knew of, condoned, and willfully and maliciously agreed to subject" respondent to harsh conditions of confinement "as a matter of policy, solely on account of [his] religion, race, and/or national origin and for no legitimate penological interest." *Id.*, ¶96, at 172a–173a. The pleading names Ashcroft as the "principal architect" of the policy, *id.*, ¶10, at 157a, and identifies Mueller as "instrumental in [its] adoption, promulgation, and implementation." *Id.*, ¶11, at 157a.

Petitioners moved to dismiss the complaint for failure to state sufficient allegations to show their own involvement in clearly established unconstitutional conduct. The District Court denied their motion. Accepting all of the allegations in respondent's complaint as true, the court held that "it cannot be said that there [is] no set of facts on which [respondent] would be entitled to relief as against" petitioners. *Id.*, at 136a–137a (relying on *Conley v. Gibson*, 355 U.S. 41 (1957)). Invoking the collateral-order doctrine petitioners filed an interlocutory appeal in the United States Court of Appeals for the Second Circuit. While that appeal was pending, this Court decided *Bell Atlantic Corp. v. Twombly*, 550 U.S. 544 (2007), which discussed the standard for evaluating whether a complaint is sufficient to survive a motion to dismiss.

The Court of Appeals considered *Twombly*'s applicability to this case. Acknowledging that *Twombly* retired the *Conley* no-set-of-facts test relied upon by the District Court, the Court of Appeals' opinion discussed at length how to apply this Court's "standard for assessing the adequacy of pleadings." 490 F.3d, at 155. It concluded that *Twombly* called for a "flexible 'plausibility standard,' which obliges a pleader to amplify a claim with some factual allegations in those contexts where such amplification is needed to render the claim *plausible*." *Id.*, at 157–158. The court found that petitioners' appeal did not present one of "those contexts" requiring amplification. As a consequence, it held respondent's pleading adequate to allege petitioners' personal involvement in discriminatory decisions which, if true, violated clearly established constitutional law. *Id.*, at 174.

Judge Cabranes concurred. He agreed that the majority's "discussion of the relevant pleading standards reflect[ed] the uneasy compromise . . . between a qualified immunity privilege rooted in the need to preserve the effectiveness of government as contemplated by our constitutional structure and the pleading requirements of Rule 8(a) of the Federal Rules of Civil Procedure." *Id.*, at 178 (internal quotation marks and citations omitted). Judge Cabranes nonetheless expressed concern at the prospect of subjecting high-ranking Government officials — entitled to assert the defense of qualified immunity and charged with responding to "a national and international security emergency unprecedented in the history of the American Republic" — to the burdens of discovery on the basis of a complaint as nonspecific as respondent's. *Id.*, at 179. Reluctant to vindicate that concern as a member of the Court of Appeals, *ibid.*, Judge Cabranes urged this Court to address the appropriate pleading standard "at the earliest opportunity." *Id.*, at 178. We granted certiorari, and now reverse.

. . .

III

In *Twombly*, the Court found it necessary first to discuss the antitrust principles implicated by the complaint. Here too we begin by taking note of the elements a plaintiff must plead to state a claim of unconstitutional discrimination against officials entitled to assert the defense of qualified immunity.

. . .

. . . Based on the rules our precedents establish, respondent correctly concedes that Government officials may not be held liable for the unconstitutional conduct of their subordinates under a theory of *respondeat superior*. . . . Because vicarious liability is inapplicable . . . , a plaintiff must plead that each Government-official defendant, through the official's own individual actions, has violated the Constitution.

The factors necessary to establish a *Bivens* violation will vary with the constitutional provision at issue. Where the claim is invidious discrimination in contravention of the First and Fifth Amendments, our decisions make clear that the plaintiff must plead and prove that the defendant acted with discriminatory purpose. . . . Under extant precedent purposeful discrimination requires more than "intent as volition or intent as awareness of consequences." *Personnel Administrator of Mass. v. Feeney*, 442 U.S. 256, 279 (1979). It instead involves a decisionmaker's undertaking a course of action "'because of,' not merely 'in spite of,' [the action's] adverse effects upon an identifiable group." *Ibid.* It follows that, to state a claim based on a violation of a clearly established right, respondent must plead sufficient factual matter to show that petitioners adopted and implemented the detention policies at issue not for a neutral, investigative reason but for the purpose of discriminating on account of race, religion, or national origin.

Respondent disagrees. He argues that, under a theory of "supervisory liability," petitioners can be liable for "knowledge and acquiescence in their subordinates' use of discriminatory criteria to make classification decisions among detainees." Iqbal Brief 45–46. That is to say, respondent believes a supervisor's mere knowledge of his subordinate's discriminatory purpose amounts to the supervisor's violating the Constitution. We reject this argument. Respondent's conception of "supervisory liability" is inconsistent with his accurate stipulation that petitioners may not be held accountable for the misdeeds of their agents. In a §1983 suit or a *Bivens* action — where masters do not answer for the torts of their servants — the term "supervisory liability" is a misnomer. Absent vicarious liability, each Government official, his or her title notwithstanding, is only liable for his or her own misconduct. In the context of determining whether there is a violation of clearly established right to overcome qualified immunity, purpose rather than knowledge is required to impose *Bivens* liability on the subordinate for unconstitutional discrimination; the same holds true for an official charged with violations arising from his or her superintendent responsibilities.

IV

A

We turn to respondent's complaint. Under Federal Rule of Civil Procedure 8(a)(2), a pleading must contain a "short and plain statement of the claim showing that the pleader is entitled to relief." As the Court held in *Twombly*, 550 U.S. 544, the pleading standard Rule 8 announces does not require "detailed factual allegations," but it demands more than an unadorned, the-defendant-unlawfully-harmed-me accusation. *Id.*, at 555. . . . A pleading that offers "labels and conclusions" or "a formulaic recitation of the elements of a cause of action will not do." 550 U.S., at 555. Nor does a complaint suffice if it tenders "naked assertion[s]" devoid of "further factual enhancement." *Id.*, at 557.

To survive a motion to dismiss, a complaint must contain sufficient factual matter, accepted as true, to "state a claim to relief that is plausible on its face." . . . A claim has facial plausibility when the plaintiff pleads factual content that allows the court to draw the reasonable inference that the defendant is liable for the misconduct alleged. . . . The plausibility standard is not akin to a "probability requirement," but it asks for more than a sheer possibility that a defendant has acted unlawfully. . . . Where a complaint pleads facts that are "merely consistent with" a defendant's liability, it "stops short of the line between possibility and plausibility of 'entitlement to relief.'" . . .

Two working principles underlie our decision in *Twombly*. First, the tenet that a court must accept as true all of the allegations contained in a complaint is inapplicable to legal conclusions. Threadbare recitals of the elements of a cause of action, supported by mere conclusory statements, do not suffice. . . . (Although for the purposes of a motion to dismiss we must take all of the factual allegations in the complaint as true, we "are not bound to accept as true a legal conclusion couched as a factual allegation" (internal quotation marks omitted)). Rule 8 marks a notable and generous departure from the hyper-technical, code-pleading regime of a prior era, but it does not unlock the doors of discovery for a plaintiff armed with nothing more than conclusions. Second, only a complaint that states a plausible claim for relief survives a motion to dismiss. . . . Determining whether a complaint states a plausible claim for relief will, as the Court of Appeals observed, be a context-specific task that requires the reviewing court to draw on its judicial experience and common sense. 490 F.3d, at 157-158. But where the well-pleaded facts do not permit the court to infer more than the mere possibility of misconduct, the complaint has alleged—but it has not "show[n]"—"that the pleader is entitled to relief." Fed. Rule Civ. Proc. 8(a)(2).

In keeping with these principles a court considering a motion to dismiss can choose to begin by identifying pleadings that, because they are no more than conclusions, are not entitled to the assumption of truth. While legal conclusions can provide the framework of a complaint, they must be supported by factual allegations. When there are well-pleaded factual allegations, a court should assume their veracity and then determine whether they plausibly give rise to an entitlement to relief.

Our decision in *Twombly* illustrates the two-pronged approach. There, we considered the sufficiency of a complaint alleging that incumbent telecommunications providers had entered an agreement not to compete and to forestall competitive entry, in violation of the Sherman Act, 15 U.S.C. §1. Recognizing that §1 enjoins only anticompetitive conduct "effected by a contract, combination, or conspiracy," . . . the plaintiffs in *Twombly* flatly pleaded that the defendants "ha[d] entered into a contract, combination or conspiracy to prevent competitive entry . . . and ha[d] agreed not to compete with one another." 550 U.S., at 551 (internal quotation marks omitted). The complaint also alleged that the defendants' "parallel course of conduct . . . to prevent competition" and inflate prices was indicative of the unlawful agreement alleged. *Ibid.* (internal quotation marks omitted).

The Court held the plaintiffs' complaint deficient under Rule 8. In doing so it first noted that the plaintiffs' assertion of an unlawful agreement was a "'legal conclusion'" and, as such, was not entitled to the assumption of truth. . . . Had the Court simply credited the allegation of a conspiracy, the plaintiffs would have stated a claim for relief and been entitled to proceed perforce. The Court next addressed the "nub" of the plaintiffs' complaint—the well-pleaded, nonconclusory factual allegation of parallel behavior—to determine whether it gave rise to a "plausible suggestion of conspiracy." . . . Acknowledging that parallel conduct was consistent with an unlawful agreement, the Court nevertheless concluded that it did not plausibly suggest an illicit accord because it was not only compatible with, but indeed was more likely explained by, lawful, unchoreographed free-market behavior. . . . Because the well-pleaded fact of parallel conduct, accepted as true, did not plausibly suggest an unlawful agreement, the Court held the plaintiffs' complaint must be dismissed. . . .

B

Under *Twombly*'s construction of Rule 8, we conclude that respondent's complaint has not "nudged [his] claims" of invidious discrimination "across the line from conceivable to plausible."

We begin our analysis by identifying the allegations in the complaint that are not entitled to the assumption of truth. Respondent pleads that petitioners "knew of, condoned, and willfully and maliciously agreed to subject [him]" to harsh conditions of confinement "as a matter of policy, solely on account of [his] religion, race, and/or national origin and for no legitimate penological interest." Complaint ¶96. . . . The complaint alleges that Ashcroft was the "principal architect" of this invidious policy, *id.*, ¶10, and that Mueller was "instrumental" in adopting and executing it, *id.*, ¶11. These bare assertions, much like the pleading of conspiracy in *Twombly*, amount to nothing more than a "formulaic recitation of the elements" of a constitutional discrimination claim, 550 U.S., at 555, namely, that petitioners adopted a policy "'because of,' not merely 'in spite of,' its adverse effects upon an identifiable group." *Feeney*, 442 U.S., at 279. As such, the allegations are conclusory and not entitled to be assumed true. *Twombly, supra*, 550 U.S., at 554-555. To be clear, we do not reject these bald allegations on the ground that they are unrealistic or nonsensical. We do not so characterize them any more than the Court in *Twombly* rejected the plaintiffs' express allegation of a "'contract, combination or conspiracy to prevent competitive entry,'" *id.*, at 551, because it thought that claim too chimerical to be maintained. It is the conclusory nature of respondent's allegations, rather than their extravagantly fanciful nature, that disentitles them to the presumption of truth.

We next consider the factual allegations in respondent's complaint to determine if they plausibly suggest an entitlement to relief. The complaint alleges that "the [FBI], under the direction of Defendant Mueller, arrested and detained thousands of Arab Muslim men . . . as part of its investigation of the events of September 11." Complaint ¶47. . . . It further claims that "[t]he policy of holding post-September-11th detainees in highly restrictive conditions of confinement until they were 'cleared' by the FBI was approved by Defendants Ashcroft and Mueller in discussions in the weeks after September 11, 2001." *Id.*, ¶69. . . . Taken as true, these allegations are consistent with petitioners' purposefully designating detainees "of high interest" because of their race, religion, or national origin. But given more likely explanations, they do not plausibly establish this purpose.

The September 11 attacks were perpetrated by 19 Arab Muslim hijackers who counted themselves members in good standing of al Qaeda, an Islamic fundamentalist group. Al Qaeda was headed by another Arab Muslim — Osama bin Laden — and composed in large part of his Arab Muslim disciples. It should come as no surprise that a legitimate policy directing law enforcement to arrest and detain individuals because of their suspected link to the attacks would produce a disparate, incidental impact on Arab Muslims, even though the purpose of the policy was to target neither Arabs nor Muslims. On the facts respondent alleges the arrests Mueller oversaw were likely lawful and justified by his nondiscriminatory intent to detain aliens who were illegally present in the United States and who had potential connections to those who committed terrorist acts. As between that "obvious alternative explanation" for the arrests, *Twombly, supra,* at 567, and the purposeful, invidious discrimination respondent asks us to infer, discrimination is not a plausible conclusion.

But even if the complaint's well-pleaded facts give rise to a plausible inference that respondent's arrest was the result of unconstitutional discrimination, that inference alone would not entitle respondent to relief. It is important to recall that respondent's complaint challenges neither the constitutionality of his arrest nor his initial detention in the MDC. Respondent's constitutional claims against petitioners rest solely on their ostensible "policy of holding post-September-11th detainees" in the ADMAX SHU once they were categorized as "of high interest." Complaint ¶69. . . . To prevail on that theory, the complaint must contain facts plausibly showing that petitioners purposefully adopted a policy of classifying post-September-11 detainees as "of high interest" because of their race, religion, or national origin.

This the complaint fails to do. Though respondent alleges that various other defendants, who are not before us, may have labeled him a person of "of high interest" for impermissible reasons, his only factual allegation against petitioners accuses them of adopting a policy approving "restrictive conditions of confinement" for post-September-11 detainees until they were "'cleared' by the FBI." *Ibid.* Accepting the truth of that allegation, the complaint does not show, or even intimate, that petitioners purposefully housed detainees in the ADMAX SHU due to their race, religion, or national origin. All it plausibly suggests is that the Nation's top law enforcement officers, in the aftermath of a devastating terrorist attack, sought to keep suspected terrorists in the most secure conditions available until the suspects could be cleared of terrorist activity. Respondent does not argue, nor can he, that such a motive would violate petitioners' constitutional obligations. He would need to allege more by way of factual content to "nudg[e]" his claim of purposeful discrimination "across the line from conceivable to plausible." *Twombly,* 550 U.S., at 570.

To be sure, respondent can attempt to draw certain contrasts between the pleadings the Court considered in *Twombly* and the pleadings at issue here. In *Twombly,* the complaint alleged general wrongdoing that extended over a period of years, *id.,* at 551, whereas here the complaint alleges discrete wrongs — for instance, beatings — by lower-level Government actors. The allegations here, if true, and if condoned by petitioners, could be the basis for some inference of wrongful intent on petitioners' part. Despite these distinctions, respondent's pleadings do not suffice to state a claim. Unlike in *Twombly,* where the doctrine of *respondeat superior* could bind the corporate defendant, here, as we have noted, petitioners cannot be held liable unless they themselves acted on account of a constitutionally protected characteristic. Yet respondent's complaint does not contain any factual allegation sufficient to plausibly suggest petitioners' discriminatory state of mind. His pleadings thus do not meet the standard necessary to comply with Rule 8.

It is important to note, however, that we express no opinion concerning the sufficiency of respondent's complaint against the defendants who are not before us. Respondent's account of his prison ordeal alleges serious official misconduct that we need not address here. Our decision is limited to the determination that respondent's complaint does not entitle him to relief from petitioners.

C

Respondent offers three arguments that bear on our disposition of his case, but none is persuasive.

1

Respondent first says that our decision in *Twombly* should be limited to pleadings made in the context of an antitrust dispute. . . . This argument is not supported by *Twombly* and is incompatible with the Federal Rules of Civil Procedure. Though *Twombly* determined the sufficiency of a complaint sounding in antitrust, the decision was based on our interpretation and application of Rule 8. 550 U.S., at 554. That Rule in turn governs the pleading standard "in all civil actions and proceedings in the United States district courts." Fed. Rule Civ. Proc. 1. Our decision in *Twombly* expounded the pleading standard for "all civil actions," *ibid.*, and it applies to antitrust and discrimination suits alike. See 550 U.S., at 555–556, and n. 3.

2

Respondent next implies that our construction of Rule 8 should be tempered where, as here, the Court of Appeals has "instructed the district court to cabin discovery in such a way as to preserve" petitioners' defense of qualified immunity "as much as possible in anticipation of a summary judgment motion." . . . We have held, however, that the question presented by a motion to dismiss a complaint for insufficient pleadings does not turn on the controls placed upon the discovery process. *Twombly, supra,* at 559 ("It is no answer to say that a claim just shy of a plausible entitlement to relief can, if groundless, be weeded out early in the discovery process through careful case management given the common lament that the success of judicial supervision in checking discovery abuse has been on the modest side" (internal quotation marks and citation omitted)).

Our rejection of the careful-case-management approach is especially important in suits where Government-official defendants are entitled to assert the defense of qualified immunity. The basic thrust of the qualified-immunity doctrine is to free officials from the concerns of litigation, including "avoidance of disruptive discovery." *Siegert v. Gilley*, 500 U.S. 226, 236 (1991) (KENNEDY, J., concurring in judgment). There are serious and legitimate reasons for this. If a Government official is to devote time to his or her duties, and to the formulation of sound and responsible policies, it is counterproductive to require the substantial diversion that is attendant to participating in litigation and making informed decisions as to how it should proceed. Litigation, though necessary to ensure that officials comply with the law, exacts heavy costs in terms of efficiency and expenditure of valuable time and resources that might otherwise be directed to the proper execution of the work of the Government. The costs of diversion are only magnified when Government officials are charged with responding to, as Judge Cabranes aptly put it, "a national and international security emergency unprecedented in the history of the American Republic." 490 F.3d, at 179.

It is no answer to these concerns to say that discovery for petitioners can be deferred while pretrial proceedings continue for other defendants. It is quite likely that, when discovery as to the other parties proceeds, it would prove necessary for petitioners and their counsel to participate in the process to ensure the case does not develop in a misleading or slanted way that causes prejudice to their position. Even if petitioners are not yet themselves subject to discovery orders, then, they would not be free from the burdens of discovery.

We decline respondent's invitation to relax the pleading requirements on the ground that the Court of Appeals promises petitioners minimally intrusive discovery. That promise provides especially cold comfort in this pleading context, where we are impelled to give real content to the concept of qualified immunity for high-level officials who must be neither deterred nor detracted from the vigorous performance of their duties. Because respondent's complaint is deficient under Rule 8, he is not entitled to discovery, cabined or otherwise.

3

Respondent finally maintains that the Federal Rules expressly allow him to allege petitioners' discriminatory intent "generally," which he equates with a conclusory allegation. . . . It follows, respondent says, that his complaint is sufficiently well pleaded because it claims that petitioners discriminated against him "on account of [his] religion, race, and/or national origin and for no legitimate penological interest." Complaint ¶96. Were we required to accept this allegation as true, respondent's complaint would survive petitioners' motion to dismiss. But the Federal Rules do not require courts to credit a complaint's conclusory statements without reference to its factual context.

It is true that Rule 9(b) requires particularity when pleading "fraud or mistake," while allowing "[m]alice, intent, knowledge, and other conditions of a person's mind [to] be alleged generally." But "generally" is a relative term. In the context of Rule 9, it is to be compared to the particularity requirement applicable to fraud or mistake. Rule 9 merely excuses a party from pleading discriminatory intent under an elevated pleading standard. It does not give him license to evade the less rigid—though still operative—strictures of Rule 8. See 5A C. Wright & A. Miller, Federal Practice and Procedure §1301, p. 291 (3d ed. 2004) ("[A] rigid rule requiring the detailed pleading of a condition of mind would be undesirable because, absent overriding considerations pressing for a specificity requirement, as in the case of averments of fraud or mistake, the general 'short and plain statement of the claim' mandate in Rule 8(a) . . . should control the second sentence of Rule 9(b)"). And Rule 8 does not empower respondent to plead the bare elements of his cause of action, affix the label "general allegation," and expect his complaint to survive a motion to dismiss.

V

We hold that respondent's complaint fails to plead sufficient facts to state a claim for purposeful and unlawful discrimination against petitioners. The Court of Appeals should decide in the first instance whether to remand to the District Court so that respondent can seek leave to amend his deficient complaint.

The judgment of the Court of Appeals is reversed, and the case is remanded for further proceedings consistent with this opinion.

It is so ordered.

JUSTICE SOUTER, with whom JUSTICE STEVENS, JUSTICE GINSBURG, and JUSTICE BREYER join, dissenting.

. . .

II

. . . Ashcroft and Mueller admit they are liable for their subordinates' conduct if they "had actual knowledge of the assertedly discriminatory nature of the classification of suspects as being 'of high interest' and they were deliberately indifferent to that discrimination." . . . Iqbal alleges that after the September 11 attacks the Federal Bureau of Investigation (FBI) "arrested and detained thousands of Arab Muslim men," Complaint ¶47, that many of these men were designated by high-ranking FBI officials as being " 'of high interest,'" *id.*, ¶¶48, 50, and that in many cases, including Iqbal's, this designation was made "because of the race, religion, and national origin of the detainees, and not because of any evidence of the detainees' involvement in supporting terrorist activity," *id.*, ¶49. The complaint further alleges that Ashcroft was the "principal architect of the policies and practices challenged," *id.*, ¶10, and that Mueller "was instrumental in the adoption, promulgation, and implementation of the policies and practices challenged," *id.*, ¶11. According to the complaint, Ashcroft and Mueller "knew of, condoned, and willfully and maliciously agreed to subject [Iqbal] to these conditions of confinement as a matter of policy, solely on account of [his] religion, race, and/or national origin and for no legitimate penological interest." *Id.*, ¶96. The complaint thus alleges, at a bare minimum, that Ashcroft and Mueller knew of and condoned the discriminatory policy their subordinates carried out. Actually, the complaint goes further in alleging that Ashcroft and Mueller affirmatively acted to create the discriminatory detention policy. If these factual allegations are true, Ashcroft and Mueller were, at the very least, aware of the discriminatory policy being implemented and deliberately indifferent to it.

Ashcroft and Mueller argue that these allegations fail to satisfy the "plausibility standard" of *Twombly.* They contend that Iqbal's claims are implausible because such high-ranking officials "tend not to be personally involved in the specific actions of lower-level officers down the bureaucratic chain of command." . . . But this response bespeaks a fundamental misunderstanding of the enquiry that *Twombly* demands. *Twombly* does not require a court at the motion-to-dismiss stage to consider whether the factual allegations are probably true. We made it clear, on the contrary, that a court must take the allegations as true, no matter how skeptical the court may be. See *Twombly*, 550 U.S., at 555 (a court must proceed "on the assumption that all the allegations in the complaint are true (even if doubtful in fact)"); *id.*, at 556 ("[A] well-pleaded complaint may proceed even if it strikes a savvy judge that actual proof of the facts alleged is improbable"); see also *Neitzke v. Williams*, 490 U.S. 319, 327 (1989) ("Rule 12(b)(6) does not countenance . . . dismissals based on a judge's disbelief of a complaint's factual allegations"). The sole exception to this rule lies with allegations that are sufficiently fantastic to defy reality as we know it: claims about little green men, or the plaintiff's recent trip to Pluto, or experiences in time travel. That is not what we have here.

Under *Twombly*, the relevant question is whether, assuming the factual allegations are true, the plaintiff has stated a ground for relief that is plausible. That is, in *Twombly*'s words, a plaintiff must "allege facts" that, taken as true, are "suggestive of illegal conduct." 550 U.S., at 564, n. 8. In *Twombly*, we were faced with allegations of a conspiracy to violate §1 of the Sherman Act through parallel conduct. The difficulty was that the conduct alleged was "consistent with conspiracy, but just as much in line with a wide swath of rational and competitive business strategy unilaterally prompted by common perceptions of the market." *Id.*, at 554. We held that in that sort of circumstance, "[a]n allegation of parallel conduct is . . . much like a naked assertion of conspiracy in a §1 complaint: it gets the complaint close to stating a claim, but without some further factual enhancement it stops short of the line between possibility and plausibility of 'entitlement to relief.' " *Id.*, at 557 (brackets omitted). Here, by contrast, the allegations in the complaint are neither confined to naked legal conclusions nor consistent with legal conduct. The complaint alleges that FBI officials discriminated against Iqbal solely on account of his race, religion, and national origin, and it alleges the knowledge and deliberate indifference that, by Ashcroft and Mueller's own admission, are sufficient to make them liable for the illegal action. Iqbal's complaint therefore contains "enough facts to state a claim to relief that is plausible on its face." *Id.*, at 570.

I do not understand the majority to disagree with this understanding of "plausibility" under *Twombly*. Rather, the majority discards the allegations discussed above with regard to Ashcroft and Mueller as conclusory, and is left considering only two statements in the complaint: that "the [FBI], under the direction of Defendant Mueller, arrested and detained thousands of Arab Muslim men . . . as part of its investigation of the events of September 11," Complaint ¶47, and that "[t]he policy of holding post-September-11th detainees in highly restrictive conditions of confinement until they were 'cleared' by the FBI was approved by Defendants Ashcroft and Mueller in discussions in the weeks after September 11, 2001," *id.*, ¶69. . . . I think the majority is right in saying that these allegations suggest only that Ashcroft and Mueller "sought to keep suspected terrorists in the most secure conditions available until the suspects could be cleared of terrorist activity and that this produced "a disparate, incidental impact on Arab Muslims[.]" And I agree that the two allegations selected by the majority, standing alone, do not state a plausible entitlement to relief for unconstitutional discrimination.

But these allegations do not stand alone as the only significant, nonconclusory statements in the complaint, for the complaint contains many allegations linking Ashcroft and Mueller to the discriminatory practices of their subordinates. See Complaint ¶10 (Ashcroft was the "principal architect" of the discriminatory policy); *id.*, ¶11 (Mueller was "instrumental" in adopting and executing the discriminatory policy); *id.*, ¶96 (Ashcroft and Mueller "knew of, condoned, and willfully and maliciously agreed to subject" Iqbal to harsh conditions "as a matter of policy, solely on account of [his] religion, race, and/or national origin and for no legitimate penological interest").

The majority says that these are "bare assertions" that, "much like the pleading of conspiracy in *Twombly*, amount to nothing more than a 'formulaic recitation of the elements' of a constitutional discrimination claim" and therefore are "not entitled to be assumed true." *Ante*, at 17. . . . The fallacy of the majority's position, however, lies in looking at the relevant assertions in isolation. The complaint contains specific allegations that, in the aftermath of the September 11 attacks, the Chief of the FBI's International Terrorism Operations Section and the Assistant Special Agent in Charge for the FBI's New York Field Office implemented a policy that discriminated against Arab Muslim men, including Iqbal, solely on account of their race, religion, or national origin. See Complaint ¶¶47–53. Viewed in light of these subsidiary allegations, the allegations singled out by the majority as "conclusory" are no such thing. Iqbal's claim is not that Ashcroft and Mueller "knew of, condoned, and willfully and maliciously agreed to subject" him to a discriminatory practice that is left undefined; his allegation is that "they knew of, condoned, and willfully and maliciously agreed to subject" him to a particular, discrete, discriminatory policy detailed in the complaint. Iqbal does not say merely that Ashcroft was the architect of some amorphous discrimination, or that Mueller was instrumental in an ill-defined constitutional violation; he alleges that they helped to create the discriminatory policy he has described. Taking the complaint as a whole, it gives Ashcroft and Mueller "'fair notice of what the . . . claim is and the grounds upon which it rests.'" *Twombly*, 550 U.S., at 555 (quoting *Conley v. Gibson*, 355 U.S. 41, 47 (1957) (omission in original)).

That aside, the majority's holding that the statements it selects are conclusory cannot be squared with its treatment of certain other allegations in the complaint as nonconclusory. For example, the majority takes as true the statement that "[t]he policy of holding post-September-11th detainees in highly restrictive conditions of confinement until they were 'cleared' by the FBI was approved by Defendants Ashcroft and Mueller in discussions in the weeks after September 11, 2001." Complaint ¶69. . . . This statement makes two points: (1) after September 11, the FBI held certain detainees in highly restrictive conditions, and (2) Ashcroft and Mueller discussed and approved these conditions. If, as the majority says, these allegations are not conclusory, then I cannot see why the majority deems it merely conclusory when Iqbal alleges that (1) after September 11, the FBI designated Arab Muslim detainees as being of " 'high interest'" "because of the race, religion, and national origin of the detainees, and not because of any evidence of the detainees' involvement in supporting terrorist activity," Complaint ¶¶48–50, and (2) Ashcroft and Mueller "knew of, condoned, and willfully and maliciously agreed" to that discrimination, *id.*, ¶96. By my lights, there is no principled basis for the majority's disregard of the allegations linking Ashcroft and Mueller to their subordinates' discrimination.

I respectfully dissent.

JUSTICE BREYER, dissenting.

I agree with JUSTICE SOUTER and join his dissent. I write separately to point out that, like the Court, I believe it important to prevent unwarranted litigation from interfering with "the proper execution of the work of the Government." *Ante*, at 21. But I cannot find in that need adequate justification for the Court's interpretation of *Bell Atlantic Corp. v. Twombly*, 550 U.S. 544 (2007), and Federal Rule of Civil Procedure 8. The law, after all, provides trial courts with other legal weapons designed to prevent unwarranted interference. As the Second Circuit explained, where a Government defendant asserts a qualified immunity defense, a trial court, responsible for managing a case and "mindful of the need to vindicate the purpose of the qualified immunity defense," can structure discovery in ways that diminish the risk of imposing unwarranted burdens upon public officials. See *Iqbal v. Hasty*, 490 F.3d

143, 158 (2007). A district court, for example, can begin discovery with lower-level government defendants before determining whether a case can be made to allow discovery related to higher-level government officials. See *ibid.* Neither the briefs nor the Court's opinion provides convincing grounds for finding these alternative case-management tools inadequate, either in general or in the case before us. For this reason, as well as for the independently sufficient reasons set forth in JUSTICE SOUTER's opinion, I would affirm the Second Circuit.

NOTES AND QUESTIONS

1. Notice the two distinct requirements imposed on a pleader pursuant to *Iqbal:* A pleading must contain factual averments and not mere "conclusions"; and those averments must be "plausible." Does the language of Rule 8(a)(2) support either of those requirements? What makes the averment that Ashcroft adopted the policy in question "solely on account of [plaintiff's] religion, race, and/or national origin and for no legitimate penological interest" a "formulaic recitation" not entitled to a presumption of truth? Isn't that an averment of fact? What more would a plaintiff need to allege in order to survive a 12(b)(6) motion? Some lower courts have construed *Iqbal* to mean that allegations unsupported by factual detail are not entitled a presumption of truth. *Compare Santiago v. Warminster Twp.*, 629 F.3d 121 (3d Cir. 2010) (allegation that police chief ordered officers to "have all occupants exit the Plaintiff's home, one at a time, with hands raised under threat of fire, patted down for weapons, and then handcuffed until the home had been cleared and searched" were "naked assertions" and not entitled to presumption of truth); *Glick v. Western Power Sports, Inc.*, 944 F.3d 714 (8th Cir. 2019) (plaintiff's amended complaint was properly dismissed pursuant to Rule 12(b)(6) because the allegations constituted mere legal conclusions with respect to plaintiff's design defect for a neck brace. The amended complaint did not allege how plaintiff was wearing and using the brace, whether plaintiff purchased the brace, how the accident happened, the nature of plaintiff's injuries, and how the brace caused or failed to prevent those injuries), *with Haley v. City of Boston*, 657 F.3d 39 (1st Cir. 2011) (accepting as true for purpose of 12(b)(6) allegation that Boston Police Department adopted policy of concealing exculpatory evidence from criminal defendants). *See generally* Alex Reinert, *Pleading as Information-Forcing*, 75 Law & Contemp. Probs. 1, 10–16 (2012) (reviewing lower court constructions of "conclusory" allegations).

2. Paragraph 52 of the *Iqbal* complaint, not discussed by the Court, alleged that "within the New York area, all Arab Muslim men arrested on criminal or immigration charges . . . — however unrelated the arrestee was to the investigation — were immediately classified as 'of interest to the post-September-11th investigation' [and thus subject to the confinement policy]." Should that allegation also be considered "conclusory"? If this was an averment of fact entitled to a presumption of truth, wasn't it plausible to infer that the defendants at least tacitly approved a race-conscious policy in deciding whom to detain in the facility? Is it plausible that the Justice Department could have adopted this practice without the FBI director and/or the attorney general knowing of it?

3. In several places, the *Iqbal* majority seems to imply that an inference must be the *most* likely, or at least just as plausible as any competing inference, in order

to satisfy the Rule 8 standard. Consider the following passages from the opinion for the Court, the first offering a description of the *Twombly* ruling, the second describing the allegations in *Iqbal*:

> Acknowledging that parallel conduct was consistent with an unlawful agreement, the Court nevertheless concluded that it did not plausibly suggest an illicit accord because it was not only compatible with, but indeed was more likely explained by, lawful, unchoreographed free-market behavior. *Id.*, at 567. Because the well-pleaded fact of parallel conduct, accepted as true, did not plausibly suggest an unlawful agreement, the Court held the plaintiffs' complaint must be dismissed. *Id.*, at 570.
>
> . . .
>
> Taken as true, these allegations [in *Iqbal*] are consistent with petitioners' purposefully designating detainees "of high interest" because of their race, religion, or national origin. But given more likely explanations, they do not plausibly establish this purpose.

If a plaintiff's allegations of wrongdoing may be dismissed because they are "more likely explained by" innocuous behavior or because there are "more likely explanations" than the one urged by plaintiff, does that not indicate that plaintiff must establish that an inference of wrongdoing is at least as likely as any competing interest? Is that a proper interpretation of Rule 8? What happened to the proposition that a claimant is entitled to have every reasonable inference drawn in her favor when confronted with a motion to dismiss?

Consider the view of the Court of Appeals in *Swanson v. Citibank, N.A*, 614 F.3d 400 (7th Cir. 2010):

> "Plausibility" in this context does not imply that the district court should decide whose version to believe, or which version is more likely than not. Indeed, the Court expressly distanced itself from the latter approach in *Iqbal*, "the plausibility standard is not akin to a probability requirement". . . . As we understand it, the Court is saying instead that the plaintiff must give enough details about the subject-matter of the case to present a story that holds together. In other words, the court will ask itself could these things have happened, not did they happen. For cases governed only by Rule 8, it is not necessary to stack up inferences side by side and allow the case to go forward only if the plaintiff's inferences seem more compelling than the opposing inferences.

Id. at 404. The court in *Swanson* overturned a 12(b)(6) dismissal of a lending discrimination claim brought by an African-American plaintiff whose loan was denied after an appraiser hired by the bank came back with a much lower valuation than plaintiff and her own appraiser had put on her home. Plaintiff alleged a conspiracy between the appraiser and the bank to create an excuse for denying the loan. She had no evidence of such a conspiracy; her sole proof of discrimination was that the loan was conditionally approved prior to the appraisal, the bank had denied her a loan in the past, and both the bank and appraiser were aware of defendant's race. The court held those allegations sufficient to avoid dismissal on the pleadings.

4. Are you persuaded that Rule 9(b), which provides that "malice, intent, knowledge, and other conditions of a person's mind may be alleged generally," does not support the sufficiency of the complaint in *Iqbal*? If, as the Court holds, all averments under Rule 8 must contain sufficient factual specificity to render the complaint "plausible," how much *more* detail must a pleader provide in alleging fraud, mistake, or other matters that must be pled "with particularity" under Rule 9? For an argument that *Iqbal* misread Rule 9(b), *see* Benjamin Spencer, *Pleading Conditions of the Mind Under Rule 9(B): Repairing the Damage Wrought by* Iqbal, 41 Cardozo L. Rev. 1015 (2020).

5. Does the presence of a qualified immunity defense in *Iqbal* limit the scope of cases controlled by its holding? As the Court emphasizes, a central function of official immunity—to relieve a governmental official from the burden and distraction of defending frivolous litigation—would be undermined if there were not a mechanism to extricate the official from the case at an early stage. Thus, the defense would lose much of its value if the official were subjected to extensive discovery in order to determine whether the defense were available. Can *Iqbal* be read as limited to such circumstances? Note that the Court appears to reject a similar contention regarding the scope of its holding in *Twombly*. Despite the suggestions in *Twombly* that the distinctive context of antitrust litigation had influenced the Court's ruling, the *Iqbal* majority makes clear that *Twombly*'s plausibility standard applies generally in federal civil litigation. Is there room to argue nonetheless that *Iqbal* should be confined to cases involving immunity defenses?

The Supreme Court relied on *Twombly* and *Iqbal* in *Wood v. Moss*, 134 S. Ct. 2056 (2014), to dismiss a claim brought against Secret Service agents for allegedly discriminating against protestors opposed to President George W. Bush by requiring the protestors to move to an area further from the president than the area assigned to those demonstrating in support of the president. The unanimous opinion written by Justice Ginsburg dismissed as merely "conclusory" the allegations of the pleading that the Secret Service had a pattern and practice of viewpoint discrimination and that supervisors were deliberately indifferent to the obligation to train agents to avoid such discrimination. The complaint failed to allege any competent basis for concluding that the agents moved the protestors without a legitimate security reason. The agents were thus entitled to immunity from suit as a matter of law.

6. At the summary judgment stage, a claimant is required to raise a genuine issue of material fact as to each element of his claim, based upon the record developed during discovery. As with a motion to dismiss, every reasonable inference must be drawn in the claimant's favor when his opponent seeks to have the claim dismissed on summary judgment. But when deciding a summary judgment motion, a court must still undertake some assessment of the plausibility or believability of the inferences that the claimant seeks to draw from the record. Is it preferable for the court to analyze inferences at the summary judgment stage or on a motion to dismiss? Two considerations seem to point in opposite directions here. On the one hand, by the time summary judgment is reached, the defendant has already been forced to undergo discovery. Getting past a motion to dismiss unlocks the "discovery door," as the *Iqbal* Court puts it. Discovery can be expensive and burdensome, and each party must pay its own costs. Only when the court

polices inferences at the motion to dismiss stage can a defendant be spared those expenses. On the other hand, a judge has much more information on which to base such a judgment when looking at a full discovery record than she does at the motion to dismiss stage. On the pleadings, the court can rely only upon its "experience" and "common sense." Is there a better way to protect defendants from burdensome discovery than requiring judges to assess "plausibility" on the basis of mere pleadings?

7. May the court look beyond the pleadings to inform its plausibility determination? Some scholars have suggested that an appropriate compromise would be for the court to allow limited "plausibility discovery" in order to resolve 12(b)(6) motions. *See* Edward A. Hartnett, *Taming* Twombly, 158 U. Pa. L. Rev. 473, 507-508 (2010); Scott Dodson, *Federal Pleading and State Presuit Discovery*, 14 Lewis & Clark L. Rev. 43 (2010); David L. Noll, *The Indeterminacy of* Iqbal, 99 Geo L.J. 117, 141-143 (2010); Suzette M. Malveaux, *Front Loading and Heavy Lifting: How Pre-Dismissal Discovery Can Address the Detrimental Effect of* Iqbal *on Civil Rights Cases*, 14 Lewis & Clark L. Rev. 65, 123-124 (2010).

Consider in this regard the holding in *Palin v. New York Times Co.*, 940 F.3d 804 (2d Cir. 2019), that the district court committed reversable error in holding an evidentiary hearing before granting defendant's 12(b)(6) motion on the basis of plausibility. Ex-governor and Vice-Presidential candidate Sarah Palin had filed a defamation suit against the Times after the paper published an editorial condemning an ad run by Governor Palin's political action committee that included a graphic of a cross-hair over the district of Congresswoman Gabbi Giffords, prior to the shooting of the Congresswoman. The editorial claimed that the "link to political incitement was clear," and that the graphic "put Ms. Giffords and 19 other Democrats under stylized cross hairs." The Times subsequently entered a correction, stating that "an earlier version of this editorial incorrectly stated that a link existed between political incitement and the 2011 shooting of Representative Gabby Giffords. In fact, no such link was established." The Times also clarified that the Sarah PAC map had overlaid cross-hairs on Democratic congressional districts, not the representatives themselves. Palin alleged that the Times knew the initial claim connecting the ad to the shooting was untrue at the time, and thus the Times acted with actual malice.

Prior to ruling on defendant's motion to dismiss on the ground that the complaint did not plausibly state a claim that the defendant acted with actual malice, the district court, on its own initiative, heard testimony from the editorial's author concerning his knowledge and state of mind surrounding the editorial. The court then granted the Times's motion to dismiss with prejudice.

The Court of Appeals held that once the judge considered matters outside of the pleadings, he should have notified the parties that under Rule 12(d), the 12(b)(6) motion had been converted to one for summary judgment and afforded all parties the opportunity to conduct discovery and present pertinent evidence before disposition of the motion.

Does *Palin* foreclose the possibility of conducting limited "plausibility" discovery discussed above, or could the court still have limited the scope of discovery as long as the parties were appropriately notified that the court was taking matters outside of the pleadings into consideration?

8. Consider Justice Souter's contention that at the pleading stage, a judge should dismiss a claim for lack of plausibility only in cases that are "sufficiently fantastic to defy reality as we know it: claims about little green men, or the plaintiff's recent trip to Pluto, or experiences in time travel." Did the claims dismissed in *Twombly* "defy reality as we know it"? Is there a principled distinction between *Iqbal* and *Twombly* that would support Justice Souter's different positions in the two cases? Were Justice Souter and Justice Breyer (who joined the majority in *Twombly* but dissented in *Iqbal*) having second thoughts?

9. In July 2009, Senator Arlen Specter introduced a bill to undo the result in *Twombly*. S.1504—Notice Pleading Restoration Act of 2009, would have prohibited a court from dismissing "a complaint under rule 12(b)(6) or (e) of the Federal Rules of Civil Procedure, except under the standards set forth by the Supreme Court of the United States in *Conley v. Gibson*, 355 U.S. 41 (1957)." No action was taken on the bill. Do you think the bill was an appropriate response to *Twombly*? Isn't there a middle ground between the "no set of facts" standard of *Conley* and the plausibility test of *Twombly* and *Iqbal*? Other legislative proposals eschewed any reference to the *Conley* standard and instead directed that the law of pleading be returned to where it stood under governing Supreme Court precedent on the day before *Twombly* was decided. In what way does that approach differ from the one that S.1504 employed? Would it be preferable for the rule drafters to take up this issue, rather than Congress? Is that a realistic possibility, given that the Supreme Court ultimately gets to decide what amendments to the Rules will be promulgated? How might Rule 8(a)(2) be rewritten to implement that change?

10. *The Impact of* Twombly *and* Iqbal *on Dismissal Rates.* A subsequent empirical study concluded that rates of dismissal under Rule 12(b)(6) for failure to state a claim have increased significantly in the wake of *Twombly* and *Iqbal*. Alexander Reinert, *Measuring the Impact of Plausibility Pleading*, 101 Va. L. Rev. 2117 (2015). *See also*, Bradley A. Areheart, *Organizational Justice and Antidiscrimination*, 104 Minn. L. Rev. 1921, 1947–1948 (2020) (rate of dismissal of employment discrimination cases has increased from 42 to 52 percent since *Twombly* and *Iqbal*). Another study concluded that the overall impact on the merit of cases surviving 12(b)(6) motions cannot be empirically measured. Jonah B. Gelbach, *Material Facts in the Debate Over* Twombly *and* Iqbal, 68 Stan. L. Rev. 369 (2016). *See also*, Jonah B. Gelbach, Note, *Locking the Doors to Discovery? Assessing the Effects of* Twombly *and* Iqbal *on Access to Discovery*, 121 Yale L.J. 2270 (2012) (noting how changes in party behavior in light of changed pleading standards renders empirical studies of dismissal rates problematic).

11. *Plausibility in Removal.* The Supreme Court in *Dart Cherokee Basin Operating Co. v. Owens,* 574 U.S. 81 (2014), held that the plausibility standard developed in the context of Rule 8(a) had equal application to allegations of the amount in controversy in a removal petition pursuant to 28 U.S.C. 1446(a). Plaintiff there had filed a class-action complaint in state court that did specify the amount in controversy sought for alleged underpayment of royalties owed pursuant to oil and gas leases. Defendant's removal petition alleged, without supporting evidence, that the purported underpayments totaled more than $8.2 million. Overruling the Court of Appeals ruling that proof of the amount in controversy must be contained in the notice of removal, the Court held that the notice "need include only a plausible allegation that the amount in controversy exceeds the jurisdictional threshold."

Further proof is required "only when the plaintiff contests, or the court questions, the defendant's allegation." *Id.* at 554.

12. *Twombly* and *Iqbal* continue to be the subject of a great deal of scholarly commentary, much of it critical. *See, e.g.*, Adam Steinman, *The Rise and Fall of Plausibility Pleading?*, 69 Vand. L. Rev. 333 (2016); William H.J. Hubbard, *A Fresh Look at Plausibility Pleading*, 83 U. Chi. L. Rev. 693 (2016); Alexander A. Reinert, *The Burdens of Pleading*, 162 U. Pa. L. Rev. 1767 (2014); Arthur R. Miller, *From* Conley *to* Twombly *to* Iqbal*: A Double Play on the Federal Rules of Civil Procedure*, 60 Duke L.J. 1 (2010); Kevin M. Clermont, *Three Myths About* Twombly-Iqbal, 45 Wake Forest L. Rev. 1337 (2010); A. Benjamin Spencer, *Understanding Pleading Doctrine*, 108 Mich. L. Rev. 1(2009); Robert G. Bone, *Plausibility Pleading Revisited and Revised: A Comment on* Ashcroft v. Iqbal, 85 Notre Dame L. Rev. 849 (2010); Kevin M. Clermont & Stephen C. Yeazell, *Inventing Tests, Destabilizing Systems*, 95 Iowa L. Rev 821 (2010); Allan R. Stein, *Confining* Iqbal, 45 Tulsa L. Rev. 277 (2010); Adam N. Steinman, *The Pleading Problem*, 62 Stan. L. Rev. 1293 (2010). *But see* Robert G. Bone, Twombly, *Pleading Rules, and the Regulation of Court Access*, 94 Iowa L. Rev. 8743 (2009) (arguing that *Twombly* was a modest departure from existing pleading standards, justified by high discovery costs and the low likelihood that plaintiff had asserted a meritorious claim); Charles B. Campbell, *A "Plausible" Showing After* Bell Atlantic v. Twombly, 9 Nev. L.J. 1, 21 (2008) ("By sweeping away *Conley's* 'no set of facts' standard, *Bell Atlantic* opens the way for the more moderate interpretation of Rule 8(a)(2)"); Douglas G. Smith, *The Evolution of a New Pleading Standard:* Ashcroft v. Iqbal, 36 Pepp. L. Rev. 1063 (2009) (asserting that *Twombly* and *Iqbal* increase efficiency and fairness in modern civil practice); Stephen R. Brown, *Reconstructing Pleading:* Twombly, Iqbal, *and the Limited Role of the Plausibility Inquiry*, 43 Akron L. Rev. 1265 (2010) (plausibility inquiry is not always necessary under *Twombly* and *Iqbal*, and courts have discretion to retain deficient claims pending discovery). Volume 114 of the Pennsylvania State Law Review (2010) and Volume 14 of the Lewis & Clark Law Review (2010) are both devoted to scholarly analysis of *Twombly* and *Iqbal*. A 2020 Cardozo Law Review symposium on the tenth anniversary of *Iqbal* includes articles by Howard Erichson, Brooke Coleman, Alexander Reinert, Robin Effron, A. Benjamin Spencer, and Adam Steinman. 41 Cardozo L. Rev. 899, *et seq.*

13. *Subsequent Developments.* Consider whether the Supreme Court's 2011 decision in *Matrixx Initiatives, Inc. v. Siracusano*, 563 U.S. 27 (2011), clarifies the meaning of the plausibility standard imposed by *Iqbal* and *Twombly*. The Court there sustained the sufficiency of a pleading asserting federal securities fraud claims subject to a heightened pleading requirement under the Private Securities Law Reform Act. (*See infra*, p. 543.) The case involved a claim that a manufacturer of a nasal spray failed to disclose to investors several reports from doctors that the spray adversely affected patients' sense of smell. However, plaintiff did not allege that there was any statistically significant proof that the spray, in fact, caused that condition. The Court found it plausible under *Twombly* that investors might still find that the reports were material to their investment decisions given the number of incidents and expertise of the reporting physicians, and that defendants' concerted efforts to contest the significance of the reports without scientific basis raised a "strong inference" that defendants acted with the level of intent to support a claim

under federal securities law. *See generally* Edward A. Hartnett, *Taming* Twombly: *An Update After Matrixx*, 75 Law & Contemp. Probs. 37 (2012).

In a case closely resembling *Iqbal*, the Court of Appeals for the Second Circuit held in *Hasty v. Turkmen*, 789 F.3d 218 (2015) that plaintiffs in a class action had adequately pled a claim against Attorney General Ashcroft and Director Mueller for implementing a plan to place alien arrestees who appeared to be Arab or Muslim in maximum security detention until cleared by the FBI, regardless of their known connection to terrorism. Unlike the *Iqbal* complaint, plaintiffs' complaint cited a report of the inspector general of the Department of Justice that documented how Ashcroft and Mueller personally closely supervised the Justice Department's investigation and response to the 9/11 attacks, including the practice that "aliens detained as part of the . . . investigation would not be released until they were cleared by the FBI." *Id.* at 227. The Court held that it was reasonable to infer from the report that defendants were aware of the detention of arrestees for whom there was no individualized suspicion of terrorist activities. *Id.* at 240. The case was reversed and remanded on other grounds by the Supreme Court *sub nom Ziglar v. Abbasi*, 137 S.Ct. 1843 (2017).

ii. Pleading "Special Matters"

Notwithstanding Rule 8(a)(2), and the general sufficiency of a "short and plain" statement of a claim, there are certain matters that are subject to more exacting scrutiny under the Rules. Fed. R. Civ. P. 9 sets forth the level of specificity required for various "special matters." Why do you suppose that "a party must state with particularity the circumstances constituting fraud or mistake" under Rule 9(b)? Which, if any, of the Rule 9 matters apply to the *Burdick* complaint?

What are "special damages" under Rule 9(g)? The term, as used in the Rule, seems to have an almost opposite meaning from the way it is used by many personal injury lawyers. When lawyers speak of "specials," they typically mean out-of-pocket, objectively verifiable medical expenses incurred as a result of defendants' wrongful action (in contrast to subjectively valued pain and suffering). The term as used in the Rule refers to items of damages that would not usually result from the conduct alleged. *See* 5A C. Wright et al., Federal Practice and Procedure §1310 (4th ed. & 2021 Update). Thus, for instance, medical expenses to repair a bone broken in a car crash would not be considered "special damages"; such injuries would be recoverable based on the allegation of a car crash. However, a pregnancy lost in the accident would have to be specially pled; defendant would not be on notice of such an injury simply by virtue of the allegation of the crash.

In addition to the matters specifically identified in Rule 9 that must be pled with specificity, the courts have, on occasion, subjected various categories of claims to heightened pleading requirements. In *Leatherman v. Tarrant County Narcotics Intelligence and Coordination Unit*, 507 U.S. 163 (1993), the Supreme Court found that practice at odds with the notice pleading regime of the Rule 8(a)(2). Any heightened pleading requirement must come about through amendment to the Rules, not by judicial fiat, the Court concluded. *Cf. Swierkiewicz v. Sorema N.A.*, 534 U.S. 506 (2002) (no heightened pleading standard required for complaint in employment discrimination case, even though plaintiff bears burden of establishing *prima facie* case to defeat summary judgment). *But see Dura Pharmaceuticals, Inc. v. Broudo*, 544 U.S. 336, 1634 (2005) (plaintiff in securities fraud case must allege how his economic loss was caused by defendant's alleged fraud; mere allegation that he paid an "artificially inflated purchase price" does not provide defendant with sufficient "notice of what the relevant economic loss might be or the causal connection between that loss and the misrepresentation"). *See also* Christopher M. Fairman, *Heightened Pleading*, 81 Tex. L. Rev. 551 (2002) (criticizing the persistence of heightened pleading requirements in the contexts of civil rights and securities fraud actions).

Greater specificity may also be imposed by statute in particular substantive areas. For instance, the Private Securities Litigation Reform Act of 1995 requires that a securities plaintiff "state with particularity facts giving rise to a strong inference that the defendant acted with the required state of mind." (*See* p. 543, *supra.*) In *Tellabs, Inc. v. Makor Issues & Rights, Ltd*, 551 U.S. 308 (2007), the Court held that in order to satisfy this standard, a pleading must allege facts that implied a culpable state of mind at least as strongly as they implied an innocent state of mind. It was not enough, the Court found, that a jury might *reasonably* infer a fraudulent intent from the facts alleged (the standard that would apply in a Rule 50 motion following the presentation of the case at trial); rather, the plaintiff had to allege facts that made the existence of a fraudulent intent as likely as any other inference that a jury might draw. (Justice Scalia, in concurrence, asserted that such a standard was too easily satisfied.)

iii.   Can a Complaint Be Too Detailed?

Although the courts have generally read Rule 8(a)(2) as setting forth the *minimum* level of specificity required to avoid dismissal, courts have occasionally rejected complaints for being too long. Thus, in *Presidio Group, LLC v. GMAC Mortgage, LLC*, 2008 WL 2595675 (W.D. Wash. 2008), the court dismissed without prejudice a 341-page complaint against six defendants that included claims for fraud, which were required to be stated with specificity under Rule 9(b): "[W]hile Rule 9(b) requires particularity, the sheer quantity of redundant material presented here forces the Court and the Defendants to engage in an unreasonable amount of filtering. Plaintiff need only state the circumstances constituting fraud; he does not need to quote every email he intends to present into evidence." *Cf. Armstrong v. Tygart*, 886 F.Supp.2d 572 (W.D. Tex. 2012) (dismissing without prejudice 261-paragraph complaint brought by cyclist Lance Armstrong against the United States Anti-Doping Agency for containing excessive amounts of irrelevant information). *But see Hearns v. San Bernardino Police Dep't*, 530 F.3d 1124, 1139 (9th Cir. 2008) (reversing district court's dismissal *with prejudice* of a 68-page complaint alleging racial discrimination on the ground that it failed to contain "a short and plain statement of the claim" under Rule 8(a)(2); excessive length is not sufficient reason to dismiss a complaint).

THINKING STRATEGICALLY

Although the complaint in the *Presidio Group* case seems to have been unusually detailed, attorneys usually provide considerably more information and tell a fuller story in the complaint (and sometimes even in the answer) than what Rule 8 would require. Can you think of reasons why a lawyer might make this choice? Are there potential strategic dangers in embarking on such a course?

Consider the following:

An effective advocate, above all else, is someone who engenders trust by the court. Her objective, from start to finish, is to persuade the judge and jury that her account of the facts and the law is reliable and that her client is in legitimate need of legal redress. Every decision an effective litigator makes in the course of litigation is calculated to reinforce the impression that she is a careful, knowledgeable, and trustworthy professional. This has a number of implications for drafting the complaint:

- The complaint is the first document the court will read in familiarizing itself with the case. It is thus important for plaintiff to make a powerful "first impression." In some jurisdictions (although not federal) the pleadings are shown to the jury.
- The complaint will signal defendant how knowledgeable and serious a claimant plaintiff is; a bare-bones complaint may not encourage serious settlement offers from the defendant.
- The complaint will set the boundaries for discovery and trial. Plaintiff will only be permitted to compel the discovery of information "relevant to any party's claim or defense." Thus, expanding the range of the complaint may widen the range of evidence relevant to the dispute.
- If plaintiff needs to amend the complaint to add additional information or legal theories later, it may appear that the case was not fully researched and investigated initially.
- If plaintiff makes allegations that turn out not to have legal or factual support, the attorney will lose credibility with the court.

6. *Dissecting the* Rockwell *Complaint*

Read the actual complaint filed in the *Rockwell* litigation, and consider the Notes and Question that follow:

Zeitz & Talty
Glenn A. Zeitz, Esquire
1230 Brace Road
P.O. Box 8445
Cherry Hill, NJ 08002-8445
(215) 569-0700
Attorneys for Plaintiff

Coale, Kananack & Murgatroyd
Phillip B. Allen, Esq.
1507 22nd Street, NW
Washington, DC 20037
(202) 783-6600
Attorneys for Plaintiff

MARY F. BURDICK, Executrix of the :	**IN THE UNITED STATES DISTRICT COURT FOR THE DISTRICT OF NEW JERSEY**
Estate of Theodore L. Burdick, :	
Deceased, :	
:	
:	
Plaintiff, :	
:	**DOCKET NO.** _____
vs. :	
:	
ROCKWELL INTERNATIONAL :	**CIVIL COMPLAINT**
CORPORATION, :	
:	
:	
Defendant. :	Jury Trial Demanded

1. Plaintiff Mary F. Burdick is the Executrix of the Estate of Theodore L. Burdick, Deceased, and duly authorized to act on behalf of the aforesaid estate.

2. Defendant Rockwell International Corporation is a corporation organized and existing under the laws of the State of Delaware with its principal place of business in El Segundo, California.

3a. Jurisdiction is predicated upon the diversity of citizenship of the parties, and the amount in controversy is certified to be in excess of $75,000.00 exclusive of interest and costs. Pursuant to 28 U.S.C.A. Section 1332(c)(2), Plaintiff's decedent was domiciled and resided at 120 Alder Avenue, Pleasantville, Atlantic County, New Jersey at all times relevant hereto. Venue is requested to be allocated to Camden County, New Jersey.

3b. This court also has personal jurisdiction over Defendant because Defendant,
    (a) transacted business in the District of New Jersey and/or,
    (b) committed tortious acts outside the State of New Jersey which caused injury to Plaintiff within the District of New Jersey and Defendant,
        (i) is engaged in a persistent course of conduct in the State of New Jersey and/or,
        (ii) expected or should reasonably have expected its tortious acts to have consequences in the State of New Jersey, and derives substantial revenue from interstate or international commerce.

4. On November 2, 1988, Plaintiff's decedent, Theodore L. Burdick, was the technician of a Rockwell-1121A Jet Commander twin-engine aircraft, FAA Registration No. 44.

5. On November 2, 1988, and at all times relevant hereto, the aircraft was piloted by one James E. Burger and had as its copilot, one Richard M. Wadsworth.

6. While the aircraft being piloted by the said James E. Burger was on a facility check flight, it crashed in Oak Grove, Pennsylvania, killing the Plaintiff's decedent, Theodore L. Burdick, the pilot and the co-pilot.

7. The aircraft crashed as a consequence of inability to sustain flight which developed when both engines flamed out due to icing, thereby causing it to crash.

8. As a result of the conduct more particularly described in the counts which follow, Plaintiff's decedent suffered serious bodily injuries resulting in his death, as a result of which the Plaintiff brings this claim under the Wrongful Death Act of New Jersey, NJS 2A:31.2, on behalf of the heirs-at-law of the Plaintiff's decedent.

9. The Plaintiff's decedent was survived by his wife, Mary F. Burdick and two sons, Ian and Lawrence.

10. This action is brought within two (2) years of the death of the Plaintiff's decedent.

11. The damages of the heirs-at-law include loss of comfort, aid and society, funeral expenses, loss of financial support, loss of care, counseling, advice and guidance.

12. This action is also brought pursuant to the Survival Act of the State of New Jersey in that the Plaintiff's decedent suffered death including pain, suffering, terror, the knowledge of certain death and mutilation, and the Plaintiff's decedent's estate has suffered damages for loss of life's pleasures, loss of enjoyment of life, loss of earnings and earning capacity.

COUNT I
NEGLIGENCE OF ROCKWELL INTERNATIONAL CORPORATION

13. Plaintiff hereby incorporates by reference paragraphs 1 through 12 as fully as though the same were here set forth at length.

14. Defendant Rockwell International Corporation manufactured the aircraft in which the Plaintiff's decedent was riding, and in particular, did furnish both the anti-icing and deicing systems for the aircraft.

15. The anti-icing and deicing systems for the aircraft were negligently designed and manufactured, such negligence consisting of the following:
   a. failing to properly design the anti-icing and deicing systems so as to prevent ice accumulation and subsequent ice ingestion by the engines of the aircraft;
   b. failing to comply with the Federal Aviation Regulations relative to certification of the anti-icing and deicing systems;
   c. failing to use suitable materials for the manufacture of the anti-icing and deicing systems so as to avoid the buildup of ice and the subsequent ingestion of ice by the engines;
   d. failing to select suitable materials for the anti-icing and deicing systems;

e. failing to select and design and manufacture an anti-icing and deicing system which would insure that activation of the deicing system would not result in ice ingestion by the engines;

f. failing as the air-frame manufacturer to utilize the state of art in anti-icing and deicing systems design so as to avoid ice accumulation and subsequent ingestion of ice by the engines including, but not necessarily limited to, failing to select the proper engines for the aircraft;

g. failing to properly investigate and evaluate engine failure due to ice ingestion;

h. failing to properly and adequately notify the FAA and aircraft owners of the danger of defective and inadequate anti-icing and deicing systems;

i. failing to take steps to remedy and modify the anti-icing and deicing systems having once known of the existence of the defective and negligent design of the anti-icing and deicing systems;

j. failing to exercise reasonable care as a manufacturer of aircraft to assure safe and defect-free anti-icing and deicing systems so as to avoid the dangers inherent in unsafe anti-icing and deicing systems;

k. otherwise violating the statutes of the United States of America and regulations promulgated pursuant thereto, standards of aircraft manufacture and design, and negligence at law;

l. failing to warn the Plaintiff's decedent, Theodore L. Burdick, of the defect of the anti-icing and deicing systems;

m. failing to warn operators, owners and mechanics of the defect in the anti-icing and deicing systems;

n. failing to provide proper quality control during manufacture of the anti-icing and deicing systems;

o. failing to take proper cognizance of available governmental and commercial publications reporting the defect of the anti-icing and deicing systems;

p. such other acts of negligence as may be determined during discovery.

16. As a consequence of the negligence of the Defendant Rockwell International Corporation, and the damages, injury, and death suffered by the Plaintiff's decedent, the Plaintiff prays for judgment in excess of $75,000.00 Dollars.

COUNT II
STRICT LIABILITY IN TORT AGAINST DEFENDANT ROCKWELL INTERNATIONAL CORPORATION

17. Plaintiff hereby incorporates by reference paragraphs 1–16 as fully as though same were here set forth at length.

18. Defendant Rockwell International Corporation is engaged in the design, manufacture and sale of general aviation aircraft and business aircraft.

19. The Rockwell-1121A Jet Commander twin-engine aircraft in which the Plaintiff's decedent was killed was designed, manufactured and sold by Defendant Rockwell International Corporation.

20. The Rockwell-1121A Jet Commander twin-engine aircraft was in substantially the same condition at the time of the crash as when it left the control of the Defendant Rockwell International Corporation.

21. The Plaintiff's decedent had no knowledge of any defect and no reason to suspect the defective condition in the aircraft.

22. The Rockwell-1121A Jet Commander twin-engine aircraft was defective and unreasonably dangerous.

23. The said defect caused the death of the Plaintiff's decedent and as a result Defendant Rockwell International Corporation is alleged strictly liable under §402A of the Restatement of Torts, 2d.

WHEREFORE, Plaintiff prays for judgment against the Defendant Rockwell International Corporation in an amount in excess of $75,000.00 Dollars.

COUNT III
BREACH OF WARRANTY AGAINST DEFENDANT ROCKWELL INTERNATIONAL CORPORATION

24. Plaintiff hereby incorporates by reference paragraphs 1–23 as fully as though same were here set forth at length.

25. The Defendant Rockwell International Corporation breached its warranties of fitness for a particular purpose in that:

a. the anti-icing and deicing systems were known by Defendant Rockwell International Corporation to require a safe means by which to prevent ice accumulation and/or alternatively a safe means by which to deice the aircraft;

b. the Defendant Rockwell International Corporation failed to manufacture anti-icing and deicing systems which would prevent ice accumulation and/or alternatively deicing without ice ingestion by the engines of the aircraft;

c. this failure of the Defendant Rockwell International Corporation to design and manufacture adequate and safe anti-icing and deicing systems rendered said systems and therefore the aircraft unfit for the purpose for which it was intended, to wit, safe flight.

26. As a consequence of the breach of warranties by Defendant Rockwell International Corporation, Plaintiff's decedent suffered serious personal injuries and death as a result of which Plaintiff claims for judgment against the Defendant Rockwell International Corporation in an amount in excess of $75,000.00 Dollars.

COUNT IV
EXEMPLARY DAMAGES AGAINST DEFENDANT ROCKWELL INTERNATIONAL CORPORATION

27. Plaintiff hereby incorporates by reference paragraphs 1 through 26 as fully as though same were set forth here at length.

28. Long prior to the accident subject to this lawsuit, the Defendant Rockwell International Corporation was aware of the defective, inadequate, dangerous and unreasonably dangerous and defective design of the anti-icing and deicing systems.

29. In spite of repeated knowledge of the unreasonably dangerous and defective design resulting in accidents, near-accidents, injuries and deaths to various other persons, the Defendant Rockwell International Corporation failed and refused to:

a. notify owners, operators and pilots of the Rockwell 1121A Jet Commander twin-engine aircraft of the unreasonable dangerous and defective design of the anti-icing and deicing systems;

b. notify pilots, aircraft owners and mechanics of the Rockwell 1121A Jet Commander twin-engine aircraft's unreasonably dangerous and defective anti-icing and deicing systems design and manufacture;

c. notify the Plaintiff and the public-at-large of the dangers associated with the anti-icing and deicing systems design and manufacture so as to afford the pilot, co-pilot and aircraft owner an opportunity to avoid the serious and tragic consequences of the unsafe anti-icing and deicing systems; and

d. recall, fix, replace, redesign or take any step whatsoever to make the anti-icing and deicing systems safe after it had actual knowledge of the unreasonably dangerous defect therein.

WHEREFORE, Plaintiff prays for judgment against the Defendant Rockwell International Corporation in an amount in excess of $75,000.00 Dollars.
DATED this 19th of October, 1990.

ZEITZ & TALTY   COALE, KANANACK &
                                       MURGATROYD

_____   _____
GLENN A. ZEITZ, ESQ.   PHILLIP B. ALLEN, ESQ.
Attorney for Plaintiff   Attorney for Plaintiff

NOTES AND QUESTIONS

1. *Asserting "Jurisdiction."* Note that paragraphs 1–3a include allegations that show the existence of diversity of citizenship subject matter jurisdiction, as is required by Rule 8(a)(1). Paragraph 3b of the complaint contains allegations with respect to personal jurisdiction, not required by Rule 8. Why do you think Rule 8 does not require personal jurisdiction to be alleged? Is it proper to plead such allegations? Can you think of reasons why plaintiff would choose to include these allegations?

2. *Specifying a Legal Theory.* Are the allegations in the first 12 paragraphs of the complaint sufficient to survive a motion to dismiss? If so, what is the purpose of then separating the complaint into four different counts: Negligence, Strict Liability, Breach of Warranty, and Exemplary Damages?

In a carryover from the early writ system, some pleading systems did require that the complaint not only allege facts that constituted a cause of action but also that it identify the relevant legal theory.

Would you expect a modern pleading system to require plaintiff to identify the legal theory on which she relies? What would such a requirement achieve? Might there be disadvantages in imposing such a requirement?

Although some state systems continue to impose a requirement that the complaint allege the legal theory or theories on which plaintiff relies, Rule 8 contains no such requirement. *See Johnson v. City of Shelby*, 574 U.S. 10 (2014), in which the Supreme Court issued a unanimous *per curiam* opinion that summarily reversed a lower court's dismissal of a complaint. The complaint was filed by a city employee who alleged that his firing was in retaliation for bringing to light the criminal conduct of a city alderman. Although the complaint detailed the facts surrounding the plaintiff's alleged injury, it did not identify the specific legal basis for the claim: 42 U.S.C. §1983, the federal statute that provides a remedy against someone who violates an individual's constitutional rights under color of state authority. The Court held that federal pleading rules "do not countenance dismissal of a complaint for imperfect statement of the legal theory supporting the claim asserted" in the complaint itself. So long as the plaintiff has pled adequate factual matter in the complaint, disputes over the legal basis for the claim can be addressed in the briefing for the motion to dismiss.

Nonetheless, as the *Rockwell* complaint illustrates, plaintiffs often choose to structure their complaint by identifying the particular legal theories on which they rely. Can you think of reasons why a plaintiff would choose to plead legal theories when the pleading rules do not so require?

In the *Rockwell* complaint, plaintiff used separate counts to set forth the facts and legal theories. Fed. R. Civ. P. 10 describes the form of pleadings, including captions and separate statements. Note that although it is common, as in the *Rockwell* complaint, to use separate counts for separate legal theories, Rule 10(b) mandates separate counts only when the claims are "founded on a separate transaction or occurrence" and "if doing so would promote clarity." Fed. R. Civ. P. 8(d)(2) does permit a party to set forth two or more statements of a claim or defense alternatively or hypothetically, either in one count or defense or in separate counts or defenses.

3. *Pleading in the Alternative.* Notice the repeated statements in the complaint that the anti-icing and deicing systems in the plane were defective. The only "anti-icing" system in the plane was installed on the leading edge of the engine intake. Thus, plaintiff may be suggesting that whether the cause of the crash was buildup of ice on the engine or the wing, Rockwell is still liable.

Unlike the practice at common law, such pleading in the alternative is freely permitted under modern practice. *See* Fed. R. Civ. P. 8(d)(2). However, all pleadings are subject to Rule 11. Thus, plaintiff cannot plead in the alternative when she would be expected to know which averment was accurate. For instance, notwithstanding Rule 8, plaintiff would not be permitted to assert that she was a passenger in a car involved in an accident and plead in the alternative that she was the driver, unless she suffered memory loss.

4. *The Ad Damnum Clause.* Notice the "wherefore" clause at the end of each count. These are called ad damnum, or demand, clauses. They have little practical function, other than to comply with Rule 8(a)(3). In the federal system, the demand may be freely amended at any time, and the court is not limited by the clause in awarding damages or other appropriate relief. Nor will the demand clause be dispositive of the right to jury trial:

> "Although the Rule 8(a)(3) demand for relief often is used by the district court as an aid in determining the nature of the action, the simple expedient of making a demand under that subdivision for equitable relief for an essentially legal claim or seeking money damages in a purely equitable proceeding will not defeat the opposing party's right to demand a jury trial under Rule 38(b) or create such a right in favor of the pleader." 5 C. Wright et al., Federal Practice and Procedure §1260 (3d ed. 2004).

Some districts prohibit the pleader from stating a "sum certain," requiring simply an allegation that the sum requested is in excess of the jurisdictional threshold. *See Doe v. Provident Life & Accident Ins. Co.*, 936 F. Supp. 302, 309 (E.D. Pa. 1996) (enforcing local rule prohibition on asserting specific amount in claim for unliquidated damages).

One practical consequence of the *ad damnum* clause is its effect on a default. In the event that defendant fails to answer the complaint, the clerk will enter a default judgment automatically if a "sum certain" has been demanded in the complaint. Fed. R. Civ. P. 55(b)(1). Otherwise, the court may schedule a hearing to determine the amount of the judgment, the truth of any allegation, or to investigate any other matter. *See* Fed. R. Civ. P. 55(b)(2). In no event may a default judgment exceed or be different in kind from that requested in the complaint. Fed. R. Civ. P. 54(c).

7.   *Filing the Complaint; Assignment of the Judge*

As we saw in Chapter 2, a federal action is commenced by filing the complaint with the court. The procedure for filing is normally specified by local rule. In most districts, filing must be done electronically over the Internet. *See* http://www.uscourts.gov/courtrecords/electronic-filing-cmecf. Typically, the complaint must be accompanied by a Civil Action Cover Sheet, as well as a filing fee. The cover sheet includes information about the nature of the case, as well as any related action filed in the district within the recent past. If the case is connected to pending or recently concluded litigation in the district, the case will typically be assigned to the judge responsible for the related litigation. Otherwise, judicial assignments are typically made by computer; the program tracks each judge's caseload, and spreads the different kinds of cases (as identified on the cover sheet) evenly among the judges in the district. In some districts, the assigned judge conducts both the pretrial and trial. In others, pretrial litigation is overseen by a magistrate-judge, except for adjudication of "dispositive motions."

Federal courts employ an electronic Case Management/Electronic Case Files system (CM/ECF) on a resource called PACER ("Public Access to Court Electronic Records"), which permits the electronic filing, service, and download of case documents. *See* https://www.pacer.gov/cmecf/. When an attorney makes an appearance in an action pending before a federal court, the attorney is added to PACER's email distribution list for that action and receives notifications that include links for downloading electronically filed documents. Any papers filed with the court by a represented party subsequent to the Complaint must be filed electronically, absent of showing of good cause or unless allowed by local rule. Fed. R. Civ. P. 5(d)(3)(A). *Pro se* parties operate under somewhat different requirements. *See* Fed. R. Civ. P. 5(d)(3)(B).

8.   *Motions to Dismiss*

Within 21 days of receiving the complaint (60 days if service was waived under Rule 4(d)), defendant must respond either by filing an answer or a motion under Rule 12. If the complaint is too vague or ambiguous for defendant to frame an answer, defendant can move for a more definite statement under Rule 12(e).

The defenses assertable by pre-answer motion are listed in Rule 12(b). Do the listed defenses have anything in common? What kinds of defenses are not appropriately raised by a Rule 12 motion?

Two of the defenses, *insufficient process* (the form of the summons is defective), and *insufficient service* (the summons was not served in accordance with Rule 4 requirements), would typically only be asserted if the statute of limitations has run, since plaintiff can easily re-serve process. The other available defenses may be harder for plaintiff to cure, particularly 12(b)(6), because the claim may be dismissed "with prejudice," precluding reassertion of the claim in any court.

Rule 12(b)(6) tests the legal sufficiency of the complaint; even assuming the truth of plaintiff's factual allegations, the law does not grant plaintiff a right to relief on those allegations. Defendant, in effect, says "so what?" The complaint may be dismissed for "failure to state a claim" under Rule 12(b)(6) if plaintiff fails to allege the essential elements of the claim, as determined by the governing substantive law. Although courts historically tended to be fairly lenient in construing the complaint in the light most favorable to plaintiff, it remains to be seen whether that lenience will be affected by the *Twombly* decision, which emphasized that "[i]n practice, a complaint . . . must contain either direct or inferential allegations respecting all the material elements necessary to sustain recovery under some viable legal theory." 550 U.S. at 562 (*quoting Car Carriers, Inc. v. Ford Motor Co.*, 745 F.2d 1101, 1106 (7th Cir. 1984)). *See* Lonny Hoffman, Twombly *and* Iqbal's *Measure: An Assessment of the Federal Judicial Center's Study of Motions to Dismiss*, 6 Fed. Cts. L. Rev. 1 (2011); Edward A. Hartnett, *Taming Twombly: An Update After Matrixx*, 75 Law & Contemp. Probs. 37, n.9 (2012) (summarizing inconclusive empirical data on the impact of *Twombly* and *Iqbal* on rates of dismissal pursuant to 12(b)(6)).

One question that arises in the event that defendant moves to dismiss for failure to state a claim is how to know what elements are part of plaintiff's case, and what elements are to be allocated to defendant. (*See* our earlier discussion of burdens of pleading and proof, pp. 545-546.) For example, in *Burdick*, is it up to plaintiff to say that the accident was not caused by the pilot's apparent ingestion of alcohol? Must plaintiff affirmatively state that the action is timely and not barred by any statute of limitations? Must plaintiff allege that the pilot properly operated the deicing gear, or must defendant raise misuse as a matter of defense?

Remember that "pleadings" envision responses by defendants, which include denials and affirmative defenses. One place to find guidance is in Rule 8(c), which reflects some of these policies and allocates certain pleading matters to defendant.

A motion to dismiss under Rule 12(b)(6) must be made before pleading. Thus, once the defendant files an answer, he may not make a Rule 12(b) motion. However, a "motion for judgment on the pleadings" under Rule 12(c) may be made after the pleadings are closed, and a defendant may seek dismissal for failure to state a claim under that provision as well. Rule 12(c) may also be used by plaintiffs to test the legal sufficiency of any defense raised by the answer.

What is the significance of treating the 12(b)(6) and 12(c) motions as Rule 56 summary judgment motions "if matters outside the pleading are presented to and not excluded by the court"? *See* Fed. R. Civ. P. 12(d).

In the event that defendant chooses to make a Rule 12 motion, it must consolidate all of its Rule 12 defenses in that motion. Read Rule 12 very carefully and consider how the following hypotheticals would be affected by the rule:

1. Defendant moves under Rule 12(b)(6). The motion is denied. Defendant files an answer raising lack of personal jurisdiction as a defense. Has he preserved his jurisdiction defense?
2. Defendant files an answer without raising any defenses. He then moves to dismiss the complaint for lack of personal jurisdiction. Has he preserved his jurisdiction defense?
3. Defendant files an answer raising lack of personal jurisdiction as a defense. How can he get the court to address the merits of the defense prior to trial?
4. Defendant moves under Rule 12(b)(2) to dismiss for lack of personal jurisdiction. The motion is denied. He then answers without raising any defenses. May defendant nonetheless raise failure to state a claim as a basis to dismiss the action? Under what provision?
5. Defendant moves to dismiss under Rule 12(b)(6). The motion is denied. He then answers without raising any defenses. If the court notices that parties are not diverse, should the court dismiss for lack of subject matter jurisdiction?
6. Defendant moves to dismiss under Rule 12(b)(2) for lack of personal jurisdiction. The motion is denied. Defendant moves under Rule 12(b)(6) for failure to state a claim. What result? Has defendant lost his defense of failure to state a claim?
7. Defendant files a Rule 12(b)(2) motion to dismiss for lack of personal jurisdiction. The motion is denied. He then files a motion for a more definite statement under Rule 12(e). Will the court consider the Rule 12(e) motion?
8. Defendant files a Rule 12(e) motion for more definite statement. The motion is denied. He then files a Rule 12(b)(2) motion to dismiss for lack of personal jurisdiction. Would it matter if the Rule 12(e) motion were granted?

Does Rule 12 have a consistent pattern? How would you summarize the policy?

THINKING STRATEGICALLY

Under what circumstances would a defendant choose to answer in lieu of a Rule 12(b) motion and pursue Rule 12(b) defenses later? When would defendant favor a motion in lieu of an answer?

The obvious advantage of the Rule 12(b) motion is that a defendant does not need to go through the expense of preparing an answer or responding to discovery if the motion is successful. On the other hand, a moving defendant has not formally responded to plaintiff's allegations. The only "story" the court has seen is that of plaintiff. If defendant has a compelling account of the underlying facts, might it be to his advantage to develop the record more completely prior to pressing his legal defenses?

9. *The Answer*

a. Legal Requirements

The answer is a paragraph-by-paragraph response to the allegations of the complaint. Defendant has three options in responding to a given allegation: admit, deny, or state that defendant is without sufficient information to form a belief as to the truth of the allegation. *See* Fed. R. Civ. P. 8(b). An "insufficient information" response has the same effect as a denial. If an allegation is admitted, plaintiff is relieved of the obligation of proving its truth. If an allegation is denied, the party with the burden of proving the allegation will need to establish evidentiary support.

i. Duty to Investigate

The option of using an "insufficient information" response is tempered by the requirement that defendant make a reasonable investigation into the allegations of the complaint. Thus, if the Rockwell official working with the attorney did not know whether there had been prior reports of icing problems on the Jet Commander, Rockwell could not respond to paragraph 15(o) with a claim of "insufficient information" without making further investigation. On the other hand, the response is appropriate for allegations of the complaint that are not verifiable within the time permitted for the filing of an answer.

ii. Legal Conclusions and Document Characterizations

Although not provided for in Rule 8, it is a common practice for defendants in some parts of the country not to plead in response to allegations of law or to plaintiff's characterization of written attachments to the complaint. For instance, if a plaintiff alleges that "the document attached hereto as Exhibit A is a contract for the sale of goods entered into by defendant," it would be customary for defendant to respond: "Admit that defendant signed Exhibit A. Exhibit A is a writing that speaks for itself. The balance of the paragraph states legal conclusions to which no responsive pleading is required."

The practice seems to be inherited from Code pleading, in which conclusions of law were not permitted in the pleadings. *See* 5 C. Wright et al., Federal Practice and Procedure §1218 n. 1 (3d ed. 2004). At least one court has held that the practice of not pleading to conclusions of law is inappropriate, and it ordered defendants to respond. *See Morrow v. Union Pacific Railroad Co.*, 1997 WL 119996 (N.D. Ill. Mar. 14, 1997) ("nothing entitles counsel for a pleader to decide for himself or herself that 'no responsive pleading is required' because an averment is considered a 'legal conclusion' ").

iii. Partial Denials

Rule 8(b)(2) requires that "[a] denial must fairly respond to the substance of the allegation." Rule 8(b)(4) further requires that "[a] party that intends in good faith to deny only part of an allegation must admit the part that is true and deny the rest." A denial that fails to distinguish between the true and false components of a given allegation will be deemed an "ineffective denial" and will be treated as an admission under Rule 8(b)(6).

The courts thus may deal harshly with attorneys who attempt cleverly to avoid admitting matters that are joined with inaccurate allegations in a complaint. For instance, in *Zielinkski v. Philadelphia Piers, Inc.*, 139 F. Supp. 408 (E.D. Pa. 1956), defendant denied an allegation of the paragraph that "[a] forklift owned, operated and controlled by defendant . . . was so negligently and carelessly managed . . . that [it came] . . . into contact with the plaintiff." In fact, defendant owned the forklift, but had leased it to another company. After the statute of limitations expired on a possible claim against the actual operator, the court held that defendant's denial of operation was ineffective since plaintiff reasonably assumed that the denial went to the allegation of negligence, not to whether defendant operated the forklift.

iv. Affirmative Defenses

All defenses must be included in the answer under Rule 8(b)(1)(A). What then does Rule 8(c) add in requiring a party to "affirmatively state any avoidance or affirmative defense"? Look at the list of defenses considered affirmative defenses in Rule 8(c)(1). Do you see anything in common among them?

An affirmative defense is one that "avoids" rather than "denies" the truth of plaintiff's allegations. The reason why affirmative defenses are set forth affirmatively is directly related to the nature of an affirmative defense. The theory behind the rule is that plaintiff should be placed on notice of the nature of the defense. *Mickowski v. Visi-Trak Worldwide LLC*, 415 F.3d 501 (6th Cir. 2005). If defendant denies particular allegations of the complaint, plaintiff will be effectively notified that defendant plans on contesting those allegations. For example, if the answer simply denies that defendant's negligence caused plaintiff's injuries, plaintiff is on notice that defendant may contest its negligence, causation and/or the fact of plaintiff's injury. However, plaintiff would not thereby be put on notice that defendant plans on asserting the statute of limitations. In order to preserve that defense, defendant would have to assert the statute of limitations as an affirmative defense in the answer.

The consequence of omitting an affirmative defense from the answer is that defendant may be precluded from asserting the defense at trial. However, as we will see, there are many opportunities to cure deficient pleadings as the case advances toward trial.

As you will notice in the *Rockwell* answer, reprinted below, when in doubt, attorneys tend to err on the side of pleading a given defense as an affirmative defense, even such obviously nonaffirmative defenses as "lack of proximate cause." There is little downside risk to this practice, and the court, as well as plaintiff, is thereby "educated" about defendant's position.

Do *Twombly* and *Iqbal* have any implications for how affirmative defenses should be pled? *Compare* Joseph A. Seiner, *Plausibility Beyond the Complaint*, 53 Wm. & Mary L. Rev. 987 (2012) (concluding that defendants must plausibly plead affirmative defenses); Melanie A. Goff & Richard A. Bales, *A "Plausible Defense: Applying* Twombly *and* Iqbal *to Affirmative Defenses*, 34 Am. J. Trial Advoc. 603 (2011) (same) *with* Justin Rand, *Tightening Twiqbal: Why Plausibility Must Be Confined to the Complaint*, 9 Fed. Cts. L. Rev. 79 (2016); Nathan Pysno, Note, *Should* Twombly *and* Iqbal *Apply to Affirmative Defenses?*, 64 Vand. L. Rev. 1663 (2011) (answering in the negative).

The requirement of Rule 8(a) that a "pleading that states a claim for relief" must contain a "statement of the claim showing that the pleader is entitled to relief" would not seem to apply to an answer without a counterclaim. A number of lower courts, nonetheless, have concluded that the same pleading standard applies to both claims and affirmative defenses. *See, e.g., GEOMC Co. v. Calmare Therapeutics, Inc.*, 918 F.3d 92 (2019) (plausibility standard applies to answers, but noting that defendant only has 21 days to respond to complaint, and this may excuse the pleading of a defense with less factual context); *Shinew v. Wszola*, 2009 WL 1076279 (E.D. Mich. 2009); *In re Montagne*, 2010 WL 424224 (Bankr. D. Vt. 2010); *OSF Healthcare System v. Banno*, 2010 WL 431963 (C.D. Ill. 2010). For a survey of the case-law regarding whether *Twombly* applies to pleading affirmative defenses, *see* Brian Soucek & Remington B. Lamons, *Heightened Pleading Standards for Defendants: A Case Study of Court-Counting Precedent*, 70 Ala L. Rev. 875 (2019); Anthony Gambol, *The* Twombly/Iqbal *Plausibility Pleading Standard and Affirmative Defenses: Gooses and Ganders Ten Years Later*, 41 Pace L. Rev. 193 (2020) (lower courts have moved away from applying *Twombly* to affirmative defenses).

v. Counterclaims and Cross-Claims

Pursuant to Rule 13 the answer should also include any *counterclaims* defendant has against the plaintiff and *cross-claims* defendant may have against any co-defendants. The subject of counterclaims and cross-claims will be taken up in detail in Chapter 8.

THINKING STRATEGICALLY

Assume that on receipt of the summons and complaint, you, as the attorney for Rockwell, review the facts surrounding the crash with engineering personnel at Rockwell. They are highly dubious of plaintiff's contention that Rockwell was at fault.

First, they doubt plaintiff's assertion that the engine failure was caused by the ingestion of ice. This plane has been in service for over 15 years without any reports of icing difficulties. The deicing boot was extensively tested by Rockwell. At no time could Rockwell get anything larger than minute ice particles to come off the wing and enter the engine. How could it be, they query, that *both* engines simultaneously ingested huge ice particles at the same time, when Rockwell had *no* prior reported incidence of ice ingestion in this model?

They believe the engines were suffocated due to pilot error in permitting a buildup of ice on the leading edge of the engines. Such ice buildup could have been easily prevented by turning on the engine deicing heater. They note the pilot's alcohol consumption and the general disorientation of the crew at the time of the engine failure. "The pilot simply forgot to turn on the heater," they assert.

Alternatively, they posit, if ice did enter the engines, the accident must have been caused by the pilot's inept operation of the deicing boot. The only way to generate ice particles large enough to conceivably stop the engines is if the pilot delayed activating the deicing boot until a thick layer of ice had formed on the wing. The pilot's manual clearly warns the pilot to activate the deicing boot at the first sign of icing conditions.

The engineers also note that the FAA aircraft in question had been owned by the Israeli Air Force prior to its acquisition by the FAA. It is quite possible that the Israelis made modifications in the type or positioning of the engines that conceivably could have made the plane more vulnerable to deicing problems than it was when it was originally sold by Rockwell.

How, if at all, would your answer differ from the one filed in the *Rockwell* litigation, reproduced below?

ANSWER AND AFFIRMATIVE DEFENSES OF DEFENDANT ROCKWELL INTERNATIONAL CORPORATION TO PLAINTIFF'S COMPLAINT

FIRST DEFENSE

1. Defendant is without knowledge or information sufficient to form a belief as to the truth of the averments of Paragraph 1.

2. Admitted.

3(a). To the extent the averments in Paragraph 3(a) constitute conclusions of law, defendant is not obligated to respond under the Federal Rules of Civil Procedure. To the extent such averments constitute averments of fact, the averments are denied. In particular, defendant is without knowledge or information sufficient to form a belief as to the truth of the averments regarding plaintiff's decedent's domicile and denies that plaintiff suffered any damages as a result of defendant's conduct.

3(b). To the extent the averments of Paragraph 3(b) constitute conclusions of law, defendant is not obligated to respond under the Federal Rules of Civil Procedure. To the extent the averments of Paragraph 3(b) may be construed to constitute averments of fact, Rockwell admits it has transacted business in the State of New Jersey but otherwise denies the allegations of Paragraph 3(b).

4. Defendant is without knowledge or information sufficient to form a belief as to the truth of the averments of Paragraph 4.

5. Defendant is without knowledge or information sufficient to form a belief as to the truth of the averments of Paragraph 5.

6. Defendant admits that a crash of a Jet Commander aircraft occurred in or about Oak Grove, Pennsylvania. Defendant is without knowledge or information sufficient to form a belief as to the truth of the remaining averments of Paragraph 6.

7. Defendant is without knowledge or information sufficient to form a belief as to the truth of the averments of Paragraph 7. Defendant incorporates herein by reference its answer to Paragraph 6.

8. To the extent the averments in Paragraph 8 constitute conclusions of law, defendant is not obligated to respond under the Federal Rules of Civil Procedure. The averments of fact in Paragraph 8 are denied.

9. Defendant is without knowledge or information sufficient to form a belief as to the truth of the averments of Paragraph 9.

10. Admitted.

11. To the extent the averments in Paragraph 11 constitute conclusions of law, defendant is not obligated to respond under the Federal Rules of Civil Procedure. To the extent the averments constitute averments of fact, defendant is without knowledge or information sufficient to form a belief as to the truth of the averments in Paragraph 11. As set forth elsewhere in this Answer, it is specifically denied that plaintiff, plaintiff's decedent or heirs-at-law have sustained actionable damages as alleged against this defendant.

12. To the extent the averments in Paragraph 12 constitute conclusions of law, defendant is not obligated to respond under the Federal Rules of Civil Procedure. To the extent such averments constitute averments of fact, defendant is without knowledge or information sufficient to form a belief as to the truth of such averments. It is specifically denied that plaintiff, plaintiff's decedent or heirs-at-law have sustained actionable damages as alleged against this defendant.

COUNT I
NEGLIGENCE

13. Defendant incorporates by reference its responses to Paragraphs 1 through 12 as if fully set forth herein.

14. Defendant admits that a crash of a Jet Commander aircraft occurred in or about Oak Grove, Pennsylvania. Except for the matter specifically admitted, defendant is without knowledge or information sufficient to form a belief as to the truth of the averments of Paragraph 14.

15. Denied. Defendant incorporates herein its responses to Paragraph 14.

16. Denied.

COUNT II
STRICT LIABILITY IN TORT

17. Defendant incorporates by reference its responses to Paragraphs 1 through 16 as if fully set forth herein.

18. Denied.

19. Defendant admits that Rockwell designed, manufactured and sold 1121-A Jet Commander aircraft. Except as specifically admitted, defendant is without knowledge or information sufficient to form a belief as to the truth of the averments of Paragraph 19.

20. Denied.

21. Defendant denies that any defect or defective condition existed in the aircraft as a result of any conduct by defendant and incorporates herein its denials to Paragraphs 15, 22 and 25 of the Complaint. Defendant is without knowledge or information sufficient to form a belief as to the truth of the remaining averments of Paragraph 21.

22. Denied.

23. Denied. Defendant incorporates herein by reference its answer to Paragraph 21.

COUNT III
BREACH OF WARRANTY

24. Defendant incorporates by reference its responses to Paragraphs 1 through 23 as if fully set forth herein.

25. Denied.

26. Denied.

COUNT IV
EXEMPLARY DAMAGES

27. Defendant incorporates by reference its responses to Paragraphs 1 through 26 as if fully set forth herein.
28. Denied.
29. Denied. By way of further response, defendant incorporates herein its denials to Paragraphs 15, 22 and 25 of the Complaint.

AFFIRMATIVE DEFENSES SECOND DEFENSE

Plaintiff's Complaint fails to state any claim against Rockwell International Corporation upon which relief can be granted, in whole or in part.

THIRD DEFENSE

All alleged damages sustained by plaintiff were directly and proximately caused or directly and proximately contributed to by the negligent acts, omissions or fault of plaintiff's decedent, thereby barring or mitigating plaintiff's claims.

FOURTH DEFENSE

Any losses, damages or injuries allegedly sustained by plaintiff were caused by the acts of others over whom Rockwell International Corporation had no control, no responsibility to control, and for which Rockwell International Corporation is not liable.

FIFTH DEFENSE

If any aircraft, system or component of aircraft designed or manufactured by Rockwell International Corporation was in use or operation at the time of the accident alleged in plaintiff's Complaint, then such aircraft, system or component was misused and abused or used in an unintended, unexpected, and abnormal manner by plaintiff and/or others and, by reason of said misuse, abuse, unintended use, unexpected use, and/or abnormal use, plaintiff is barred from recovery.

SIXTH DEFENSE

If any aircraft, system or component of aircraft designed or manufactured by Rockwell International Corporation was in use or operation at the time of the accident alleged in plaintiff's Complaint, then plaintiff and/or others caused changes and alterations to be made in such aircraft, system or component and said changes and alterations, which were not known or approved by Rockwell International Corporation proximately caused or contributed to the loss, damage or detriment, if any, alleged by the plaintiff, thus barring, diminishing or limiting any recovery by the plaintiff.

SEVENTH DEFENSE

Plaintiff and/or others failed to give timely and/or adequate notice of any alleged defect.

EIGHTH DEFENSE

If any aircraft, system or component of aircraft designed or manufactured by Rockwell International Corporation was in use or operation at the time of the accident alleged in plaintiff's Complaint, then the aircraft, system or component conformed with the state of the industrial and scientific art at the relevant time.

NINTH DEFENSE

If any aircraft, system or component of aircraft manufactured by Rockwell International Corporation was in use or operation at the time of the accident alleged in plaintiff's Complaint, then the aircraft, system or component was in compliance with the regulations and specifications of governmental bodies.

TENTH DEFENSE

To the extent that any of plaintiff's alleged injuries and damages may be attributable to Rockwell International Corporation, which is denied, the involvement of Rockwell International Corporation was *de minimis* and plaintiff is not entitled to recover from Rockwell International Corporation.

ELEVENTH DEFENSE

The negligence of plaintiff's decedent was greater than the negligence of Rockwell International Corporation, it being specifically denied that plaintiff was injured as a result of any act or omission for which Rockwell International Corporation is responsible, and, therefore, plaintiff is not entitled to recover damages against Rockwell International Corporation, or in the alternative, any damages awarded to plaintiff must be reduced in proportion to the percentage of negligence attributable to plaintiff.

TWELFTH DEFENSE

Plaintiff's decedent was the proximate cause of any and all damages alleged in plaintiff's Complaint.

THIRTEENTH DEFENSE

Plaintiff's decedent voluntarily assumed the risk of the harm for which plaintiff seeks to hold Rockwell International Corporation liable in this action.

FOURTEENTH DEFENSE

Some or all of the damages or other relief sought by the plaintiff are not recoverable under applicable law.

FIFTEENTH DEFENSE

If plaintiff sustained injury or damages as alleged, which is denied, the injury and damages were caused by the independent, intervening and/or superseding, actionable conduct of others.

SIXTEENTH DEFENSE

Plaintiff's Complaint fails to state a cause of action upon which exemplary damages may be awarded.

WHEREFORE, defendant Rockwell International Corporation demands judgment in its favor and against plaintiff on the Complaint, together with an award of its costs, reasonable attorneys' fees and such other relief as the Court deems equitable and just.

By:

Thomas J. Duffy, Esquire
Patrick J. Keenan, Esquire
Attorneys for Defendant

Of Counsel:

Alfred A. Gollatz, Esquire
Gollatz, Griffin, Ewing & McCarthy
11-13 S. High Street
P.O. Box 796
West Chester, PA 19381

NOTES AND QUESTIONS

1. Which, if any, of the 15 "Affirmative Defenses" needed to be pled "in the affirmative"? Why do you think Rockwell chose to affirmatively plead the others?

2. Why do you think Rockwell declined to plead to "legal conclusions" in paragraphs 3, 8, 11, and 12? Even if Rockwell is correct in asserting that no responsive pleading was required under the Federal Rules, how would it have disadvantaged them to do so? Wouldn't it be useful to know whether or not they contest plaintiff's account of the law? Do you see any difference between the allegation of the complaint that Rockwell responded to and the allegations that it characterized as "conclusions of law"?

3. Why does Rockwell request the award of attorneys' fees? Recall that the general rule is that each party bears its own legal expenses in the absence of a fee-shifting statute and there is no applicable statute here. Is it a satisfactory answer that such a request appears in a form book?

10.   Amendments to the Pleadings

Consistent with the Federal Rules' de-emphasis on the pleadings as the primary mechanism for defining the parameters of the lawsuit, Rule 15 makes it quite easy for a party to amend its pleading. A party may amend its pleading once "as a matter of course." Fed. R. Civ. P. 15(a)(1). This means the pleader does not require the court's permission; it is an absolute right. A complaint or answer containing a counterclaim may be amended as a matter of course within 21 days of the service of the opponent's responsive pleading or Rule 12(b) motion. An answer without a counterclaim may be amended as a matter of course within 21 days of its service.

Thereafter, a party must seek permission of its opponent or of the court before amending its pleadings. However, "the court should freely grant leave when justice so requires." Fed. R. Civ. P. 15(a)(2). The courts have interpreted this to mean that unless the parties have been significantly prejudiced by their reliance on the existing pleadings, leave to amend should be granted.

Thus, for instance, in *Burdick*, suppose that two weeks before the case was scheduled to go to trial, plaintiff sought leave to amend the complaint, adding allegations that a failure of the plane's hydraulic systems (which are needed to maneuver the plane) caused the crash. The court would typically want to know why plaintiff took so long to add such a theory; how much discovery would have to be redone in light of the new allegations; whether evidence is now unavailable; and whether trial would be delayed as a result of the amendment.

A fairly common use of Rule 15(a) is to cure otherwise deficient pleadings subject to dismissal under Rule 12. *See* 6 C. Wright et al., Federal Practice and Procedure §1474 (3d ed. 2010). Courts frequently conditionally dismiss under Rule 12(b)(6) subject to plaintiff amending the complaint within a given time.

Once an amended complaint is filed, defendant must file a new answer and/or Rule 12 motion.

a. Relation-Back

One of the more complex applications of Rule 15 is when the statute of limitations would bar the amended claim if filed as a new action. You may recall that under most state laws, and in federal-question cases, the statute of limitations is normally satisfied if the complaint is filed prior to the expiration of the statute. In federal court, the defendant in those cases may not receive notice until after the statute expires because Rule 4(m) gives a plaintiff 90 days from the date of filing to effect service of process. What happens if it turns out that the wrong party was sued or additional claims have to be added to the complaint after the statute has run? Rule 15(c), in some circumstances, allows an amended complaint to "relate back" to the time the original complaint was filed for statute of limitation purposes.

In order to relate back under Rule 15(c), the claims asserted in the amended complaint must arise out of the "conduct, transaction, or occurrence set forth or attempted to be set forth in the original pleading." Although courts generally interpret that standard liberally, a claim arising out of completely different circumstances may be denied relation-back. *See Mayle v. Felix*, 545 U.S. 644, 657 (2005) (amended complaint in habeas corpus proceeding based on trial court's admission of evidence seized in an allegedly illegal search by police does not relate back to original complaint based on trial court's admission into evidence of a videotaped testimony of state's witness; relation-back is appropriate "only when the claims added by amendment arise from the same core facts as the timely filed claims, and not when the new claims depend upon events separate in 'both time and type' from the originally raised episodes").

Moreover, if the amended complaint changes the defendant, relation-back is permitted only if:

> within the period provided by Rule 4(m) for service of the summons and complaint, the party to be brought in by amendment (A) has received such notice of the institution of the action that the party will not be prejudiced in maintaining a defense of the merits, and (B) knew or should

have known that, but for a mistake concerning the identity of the proper party, the action would have been brought against the party.

Fed. R. Civ. P. 15(c)(1). It is sufficient under the Rule if the new defendant received notice of the original suit from any source; it does not have to come from plaintiff. *See* 6A C. Wright et al., Federal Practice and Procedure §1498 (3d ed. 2010).

The reference to Rule 4(m) was designed to guarantee that the new defendant receive notice in the same time frame as he would have had he been named as an original defendant in the action, i.e., within 90 days of the filing of the complaint.

Note, however, an anomalous result under a literal reading of this provision for actions filed more than 90 days before the statute of limitations expires: In some circumstances, no relation-back is permitted even if the new defendant receives the requisite notice before the statute runs.

Consider the following hypothetical:

Complaint filed on day 1 against defendant *A*.

Defendant *B* learns that plaintiff has sued the wrong defendant on day 200.

Statute of limitations expires on day 300.

Complaint filed against defendant *B* on day 360.

Because more than 90 days have passed since the filing of the complaint, defendant *B* did not receive the requisite notice "within the period provided by Rule 4(m) for service of the summons and complaint." On the other hand, had the complaint been filed against defendant *A* on day 120, the amended complaint would have related back. Is such a difference justifiable? Isn't it perverse to penalize the plaintiff who filed earlier? *See* David S. Siegel, *The Recent (December 1, 1991) Changes in the Federal Rules of Civil Procedure*, 142 F.R.D. 359, 364 (1992) (suggesting a drafting error in the Rule).

A second issue that arises in connection with Rule 15(c) is the question of what constitutes a "mistake concerning the proper party's identity." Suppose in *Rockwell* that plaintiff learned in the course of discovery that the engines on the Jet Commander were in fact manufactured by General Electric Co. (GE), and that a properly constructed engine would not have failed as a consequence of ice ingestion. Within 90 days of the original complaint, but after the statute of limitations on a claim against GE has run, plaintiff moves to substitute GE as a defendant. Does the claim relate back? *See Soper v. Walmart Stores, Inc.*, 923 F. Supp. 1032 (D. Tenn. 1996) (amended claim against a manufacturer of defective devices does not relate back to filing of claim against vendor, which was not asserted by mistake); *Henry v. Federal Deposit Ins. Co.*, 168 F.R.D. 55 (D. Kan. 1996) (claim against defendant originally named as "John Doe" does not relate back since failure to identify defendant by name was a result of lack of knowledge rather than mistake).

In *Krupski v. Costa Crociere*, 560 U.S. 538 (2010), the Court held relation-back appropriate even though the plaintiff had been repeatedly informed by the original defendant that a different corporate entity was responsible for plaintiff's injuries. Plaintiff ignored that information until the original defendant obtained summary judgment. The district court then granted plaintiff leave to amend, and the new defendant sought dismissal under the statute of limitations. The Supreme Court held that plaintiff's delay in amending the complaint was only relevant to the decision whether to allow the amendment under Rule 15(a); once the district court granted leave to amend, relation-back under Rule 15(c) was mandatory if the conditions of 15(c)(1)(C) were satisfied. The new defendant clearly had timely notice of the mistake under 15(c)(1)(C)(i), and plaintiff had made a "mistake concerning the proper party's identity" under 15(c)(1)(C)(ii) notwithstanding the information provided by defendant; even though plaintiff knew about the existence of the other party, plaintiff continued to misunderstand the role that other party played. Plaintiff's mistake may have been unreasonable, but it was a mistake nonetheless.

The Court of Appeals for the Second Circuit has held that its adoption of the *Henry* rule on relation-back of "John Doe" complaints survived the Supreme Court holding in *Krupsk. Ceara v. DOCCS Officer Joseph Deacon*, 916. F.3d 208 (2d Cir. 2019).

On the other hand, if plaintiff simply "misidentified" the proper name of defendant in the complaint but served the complaint on the correct defendant, an amendment correcting the name in the complaint will automatically relate back and need not satisfy all of the conditions of Rule 15(c). *See, e.g., Brittian v. Belk Gallant Co.*, 301 F. Supp. 478 (D. Ga. 1969) (permitting amendment adding word "Suburban" to defendant's name after statute expired).

b. Supplemental Pleading

Claims that arise from events occurring after the filing of the complaint do not need to be included in the proceedings; they will not be barred by *res judicata*. However, if a party wants to include these "after-acquired" claims, it may, with leave of court, include them through "supplemental pleadings" provided for in Rule 15(d).

Why do you suppose the framers of the Federal Rules made supplemental pleadings optional? If the evidence relevant to the preexisting claims would also be used to litigate the supplemental claim, why shouldn't the parties be required to consolidate *all* claims against an opposing party, including after-acquired ones?

B.   DISCOVERY AND SUMMARY JUDGMENT

After the pleadings have been filed, the parties proceed to prepare the case for trial. They collect evidence in support of their own position and seek to learn as much as possible about the nature of evidence that will be presented by their opponent. Most litigators spend far more time in this process of pretrial discovery than they do trying cases.

At common law (and still in most other countries in the world), litigants were on their own in collecting information about their case. Although they could engage in their own investigations, there were few ways of obtaining information from their opponents or uncooperative witnesses prior to trial. A party with the resources to conduct a thorough investigation thus was in a position to surprise his opponent at trial.

For the modern U.S. litigator, there should be no surprises. It is often said that an effective civil litigator can prepare her closing remarks to the jury before the trial begins; through discovery, she already knows every piece of evidence that will be presented. She has examined all the documents and all other evidence, and has interviewed or deposed every witness.

Compare an expansive discovery system with a limited one. Which one ensures a fairer and more accurate adjudication? One advantage of expansive discovery is that a party can still prevail even if all of the proof of the claim or defense is in the possession of an opponent or an uncooperative nonparty. In a system of limited discovery, a party without possession of supporting evidence would be hard-pressed even to get to trial.

There are also potential disadvantages to expansive discovery. The first is cost. As we will see below, completion of extensive discovery can cost each side a substantial amount of money and inconvenience. Combined with the relatively low threshold for surviving a motion to dismiss for failure to state a claim, modern discovery has the potential for inviting "strike suits": claims filed for the purpose of inducing settlement. It also creates the possibility that the party with greater resources can wear down a poorer opponent through exhaustive discovery.

It is also not obvious that the "no surprises" premise of modern discovery in fact results in a more accurate adjudication. Isn't it harder to discredit (or "impeach") a witness if the opposing party has prior notice of the impeaching evidence? Nonetheless, the nearly universal assumption in modern American litigation is that, within limits, the more the parties know before trial, the better.

Even before the pleadings are filed, parties are able to collect a great deal of information about the case, albeit largely without judicial assistance.[*] Although ethical rules prevent direct discussions with a represented adverse party,[**] there are typically many witnesses willing to discuss what they know without legal compulsion. For the most part, if a witness is willing to co-operate, it is to a party's advantage to obtain information from the witness informally. A phone call is much less expensive than a deposition, and the opposing attorney is not privy to the discussion.

However, where a witness is not willing to cooperate, he can be legally obligated to provide information through the mechanism of discovery. In this section, we will survey the wide array of discovery techniques available to civil litigators. We will again use the case of *Burdick v. Rockwell International* to frame our consideration.

Put yourself in the role of the respective attorneys in the *Rockwell* litigation. The pleadings have been closed. How are you going to prove your case, and how can you find out what kind of proof your opponent is going to offer?

It is important to consider the elements of the claim set forth in the complaint. It is plaintiff's responsibility to prove all of the facts alleged that are not admitted by defendant. Thus, plaintiff must establish that the crash was caused when ice

---

[*] The one mechanism for obtaining judicial assistance with pre-filing discovery is Fed. R. Civ. P. 27, which can only be used to preserve the testimony of witnesses who may not be available by the time an action is commenced. The person taking the deposition must petition the court for permission before taking the deposition and must establish that the deposition is necessary to "prevent a failure or delay of justice."

[**] ABA Model Rule of Professional Conduct 4.2 provides: In representing a client, a lawyer shall not communicate about the subject of the representation with a person the lawyer knows to be represented by another lawyer in the matter, unless the lawyer has the consent of the other lawyer or is authorized by law to do so by law or a court order.

removed from the wing flew into the engine, and that the crash was caused by a defect in the design or performance of the aircraft for which defendant is responsible. Plaintiff must also support any claim for damages by proving the value of the decedent's life. Rockwell, conversely, will want to establish evidentiary support of its assertion that the crash was due to the negligence of the crew; the design and operation of the aircraft were sound; or, if there were defects in the aircraft, they were caused by modification of the plane by the Israeli Air Force. Each side presumably wants to know as much as possible about the precise factual and legal assertions its opponent will make at trial.

Thus, there is important information that must be obtained from both parties and nonparties to the litigation. The attorneys presumably want to talk to the persons that designed, tested, and serviced the plane prior to the accident, witnesses to the crash, control tower personnel, governmental officials who may have investigated the accident, and anyone who interacted with the pilots during or before takeoff. They may also want to see the plane's design, service, and inspection records, any surviving debris from the crash, and any reports of icing problems with this type of aircraft or engine.

Each side will presumably retain aviation experts to examine the data concerning the accident and the aircraft and testify about what caused the crash. Each side will want to know about the other's expert and how the expert will testify at trial.

How do the parties go about getting all of this information?

1. Unilateral Disclosure

a. Required Initial Disclosure

The first opportunity a federal litigant has to learn of information in the opposing party's possession is through initial disclosure under Rule 26(a).

Historically, most discovery in American practice was adversarial; a party would only produce information in response to a request by the opposition. There was little affirmative duty to unilaterally bring facts to the attention of the court or opposing party.

The 2000 amendments to the Federal Rules of Civil Procedure radically altered that model. Under the current Rule 26, each party in federal litigation must, at the outset of the litigation, produce a great deal of information about the case without being asked to do so (except in certain exempt categories of cases). Under Rule 26(a)(1)(A), this includes names of persons "likely to have discoverable information . . . that the disclosing party may use to support its claims or defenses," copies or the location of documents that the disclosing party may use to support its claims or defenses, computation of damages sought by the disclosing party, and any relevant insurance coverage.

Later in the proceeding, the parties must also unilaterally disclose information concerning any experts they have retained, any documents or exhibits they may present at trial, and any fact witnesses they intend to call at trial.

Note that the initial disclosure is limited to information that will be used *in support of* the disclosing party's claims or defenses; information supportive of the opposing parties' case need not be unilaterally disclosed. Under an earlier version implemented in some jurisdictions, initial disclosure was required for *all* relevant witnesses and documents, both in support of, and contrary to, the position of the disclosing party. Why do you suppose that Rule 26(a) was amended in this regard?

Imagine that you are counsel to Rockwell. You have in your possession warehouses full of documents concerning the design and operation of the Jet Commander and the engines used in that plane. How many of those documents must you unilaterally produce or identify under Rule 26(a)? What about documents evidencing the absence of any problems? What about documents concerning the design and performance of other deicing systems in other planes?

What constitutes evidence that the party "may use to support its claims or defenses"? What if a party knows of a witness that it plans on using solely to rebut an assertion by the opposing party? For instance, imagine you are counsel for Mrs. Burdick. Defendant has alleged that the accident was caused by the crew's negligent operation of the aircraft. Defendant has not yet asserted that the pilot was alcohol impaired, but given the autopsy report, you expect such an assertion. What if *you* know, from speaking with the waiter who served him, that the pilot, in fact, had one beer at lunch prior to the crash? You will use the waiter to rebut any assertion that the pilot was drunk, but you would rather not alert defendant to his testimony if you don't have to. Are you required to list the waiter in your initial disclosure?

i.   Timing

The timing of initial disclosure is keyed to the first scheduling conference or order required under Rule 16. At least 21 days prior to the first pretrial conference (the date of which is set by the court), the parties are required under Rule 26(f) to confer and develop a discovery plan. Within 14 days of that discussion, they must provide their initial disclosures, unless otherwise stipulated by agreement or ordered by the court.

b.   Expert Disclosure and Pretrial Disclosures

In addition to the initial disclosure required in conjunction with the discovery plan, Rule 26 also requires additional disclosures by the parties later in proceeding. The parties without being requested to do so must inform each other about any expert witnesses they intend to call at trial. Unlike a fact witness, an expert witness does not report observations of past events. Rather, the expert offers an interpretation of facts that have been otherwise established. For example, an expert on tire skid marks might testify that photographs of skid marks suggest that a car was moving at 50 miles per hour. The expert did not see the car or photograph the skid marks. Rather, the expert interprets the evidence presented to the tribunal and offers opinions, not recollections.

Experts have played an increasingly prominent role in modern litigation. The *Rockwell* case demonstrates why. Plaintiff has alleged that the deicing equipment failed to function properly; defendant asserts the crew failed to use the equipment properly. No one present in the aircraft survived the crash. The information available to the litigants — the remains of the aircraft, the trajectory of the plane before impact, etc. — might provide a clue, but only to someone who knows how to interpret the data. Even a highly educated jury would be at a loss in understanding the implications of the scientific information collected by the litigants. The jury will thus base its decision not on its own interpretations of the evidence, but on its assessment of which expert is most credible.

Under Rule 26(a)(2), a party must disclose the identity of any expert it may call at trial and submit a report outlining the expert's conclusions, basis, and qualifications, at least 90 days before trial or when otherwise directed by the court. The parties may thereafter take further discovery as they deem necessary.

2.   *Adversarial Discovery*

a.   Judicial Management—The Discovery Plan

Historically, the decision of how to proceed with discovery was largely at the discretion of the litigants; they could take as much discovery, in whatever form, as they deemed appropriate. There were many perceived abuses of this power. Litigants were in a position to inflict enormous expense by taking expansive, often unnecessary, discovery. Over the last 20 years, courts have moved away from this model. Today, discovery is subject to extensive judicial control.

In federal practice, the court will typically schedule several pretrial conferences pursuant to Rule 16. The conferences are held in judicial chambers (the judge's office) with the attorneys and are conducted by a district court judge or magistrate-judge. The court will review the discovery plan proposed by the parties and then issue a discovery order. The order will typically identify the scope and timing of discovery: who will be deposed, and when and for how long; what, if any, additional documents will be exchanged; what interrogatories or requests for admissions will be served; and what medical examinations will be ordered. It will also provide for the preservation and disclosure of electronic data and specify when all discovery will be completed. The order must be issued "as soon as practicable," normally within 90 days of the service of any defendant, or within 60 days of the appearance of any defendant, whichever is earlier.

Thereafter, most discovery is conducted outside of the presence of the judge. Although the parties may seek judicial intervention in the event of a dispute, they are expected to conduct discovery on their own.

For the most part, the cost of discovery is absorbed by the producing party. As discussed below, some courts have shifted the expense to the party seeking certain electronic discovery, but the norm remains that each side bear its own discovery expenses. This practice has been criticized as unconstitutional by Professor Martin Redish, in *Discovery Cost Allocation, Due Process, and the Constitution's Role in Civil Litigation*, 71 Vand. L. Rev. 1847 (2018).

b.   Scope

The parties are entitled to seek "any nonprivileged matter that is relevant to any party's claim or defense, and proportional to the needs of the case, considering the importance of the issues at stake in the action, the amount in controversy, the parties' relative access to relevant information, the parties' resources, the importance of the discovery in resolving the issues, and whether the burden or expense of the proposed discovery outweighs its likely benefit." Fed. R. Civ. P. 26(b)(1). How do the parties determine what claims or defenses are present in the litigation for the purpose of Rule 26(b)(1)? Does the Rule affect how a party will draft its pleadings?

What if a party feels that the discovery sought from it is not proportional to the needs of the case? May that party object in lieu of producing the information? An Advisory Committee comment to the Rule states that the Rule does not "permit the opposing party to refuse discovery simply by making a boilerplate objection that it is not proportional. The parties and the court have a collective responsibility to consider the proportionality of all discovery and consider it in resolving discovery disputes." But what if the objection is not "boilerplate"? Does a party have an obligation to seek a protective order under Rule 26(c) when it wants to object based on proportionality, or can the responding party shift the burden of seeking judicial assistance onto the party seeking discovery simply by interposing such an objection? For more on this question, *see infra* pp. 635–638.

Note the emphasis in Rule 26(b)(1) that the discovery does not have to directly produce admissible evidence. On motion or on its own, the court must limit the frequency or extent of discovery otherwise allowed by these rules or by local rule if it determines that: (i) the discovery sought is unreasonably cumulative or duplicative, or can be obtained from some other source that is more convenient, less burdensome, or less expensive; (ii) the party seeking discovery has had ample opportunity to obtain the information by discovery in the action; or (iii) the proposed discovery is outside the scope permitted by 26(b)(1).

How should a court weigh the burden of taking discovery against its benefit to the litigants? Should a court ever authorize discovery when the cost of discovery is more than plaintiff is likely to recover? Should the probability of a party's success on the merits affect the discovery to which they are entitled? What if the plaintiff is not seeking monetary recovery? *See generally*, Stephen B. Burbank, *Proportionality and the Social Benefits of Discovery: Out of Sight and Out of Mind?*, 34 Rev. Litig. 647 (2015) (expressing concern that courts will value cost savings over social benefit of discovery); Bernadette Bollas Genetin, *"Just a Bit Outside!": Proportionality in Federal Discovery and the Institutional Capacity of the Federal Courts*, 34 Rev. Litig. 655 (2015) (expressing concerns about lack of objective standards for assessing proportionality).

c.   Devices

There are five major devices that may be employed by the litigants, in addition to the mandatory disclosures required under the Rules: (i) interrogatories; (ii) depositions; (iii) requests for production of documents; (iv) medical examinations; and (v) requests for admission. The use of all these devices is subject to judicial approval in the discovery plan. How and when to use each device is a matter of important strategic judgment.

i.   Interrogatories

Perhaps the most burdensome device is the written interrogatory. Interrogatories are questions served or "propounded" by one party to another party pursuant to Rule 33. Written responses must be served within 30 days (although the parties usually stipulate to extensions of time). It can take a party many hours to prepare answers to even simple interrogatories.

Under Rule 33, interrogatories may be served only on parties to the litigation, and only 25 total questions may be asked without leave of the court. Interrogatories are normally prefaced with extensive definitions and instructions.

There are two key advantages to interrogatories compared with other discovery devices. First, a party is under an obligation to make a reasonable investigation to determine the answer to an interrogatory; "I don't know" is not an adequate response if the answer can be determined through a reasonable effort. However, in the event that the answer can be derived from business records and the burden of finding the answer would be the same for the party seeking the information as the party answering the interrogatory, the responding party has the option under Rule 33(d) of producing those business records. Thus, for example, if an interrogatory asked for the number of persons employed each month from January to December 1997, the responding party could simply make its payroll records available in lieu of looking through those records for the answer.

The second key advantage to interrogatories is that a party may probe an opponent's legal theory and evidentiary support. Rule 33(a)(2) states that "[a]n interrogatory is not objectionable merely because it asks for an opinion or contention that relates to fact or the application of law to fact. . . . " This allows a party to propound "contention" interrogatories: "If you contend that the design of the aircraft was defective, identify with specificity the nature of the alleged defect, and each and every fact upon which you will rely at trial to establish that defect." In many districts, the court will not require answers to contention interrogatories until the close of discovery. *See* Fed. R. Civ. P. 33(a)(2).

The primary limitation of interrogatories is that a party cannot normally propound follow-up questions on the basis of information received in the answers. It is not unusual for an answer to an interrogatory (usually drafted by the attorney for the responding party) to be evasive or incomplete, or to exploit some technical ambiguity in the question: "The aircraft was defective because it was inadequately tested, designed, and manufactured." Although a party can seek judicial redress for evasive or incomplete answers, most parties are hesitant to involve the court in discovery disputes except in egregious cases.

THINKING STRATEGICALLY

Again, play the role of attorney for defendant in the *Rockwell* case. What types of information do you think would be useful to seek through interrogatories? How would you draft the interrogatories to avoid incomplete or evasive answers by plaintiff?

Assume that the following interrogatories were propounded to Rockwell by plaintiffs. Explain which would be effective and which would be problematic. Would there be better ways of getting at some of the information sought? Assume all the relevant terms have been adequately defined.

1. Identify each and every person who had knowledge of the decision to employ the deicing boot in the Jet Commander.

2. If you contend that the pilot of the plane was alcohol-impaired at times relevant to the accident, identify each and every person and document on which you will rely in establishing that impairment.
3. Justify your decision to employ the deicing boot rather than a mechanism to prevent the buildup of ice on the wing.
4. Identify each and every test you conducted to insure that ice removed from the wing would not be ingested into the engines. Specify the date, methodology, persons who participated, and outcome.
5. If you contend that any of the counts in the Complaint are foreclosed by New Jersey law, identify each and every legal authority upon which you will rely in asserting that position.

ii. Depositions

One of the most useful and commonly employed discovery devices is the deposition pursuant to Rule 30. Depositions are examinations of a witness under oath, recorded for possible later use in the proceedings. *See* Fed. R. Civ. P. 32. Any person with relevant information may be deposed, including parties and nonparties. Any party is entitled to attend the deposition, and each attorney may examine the witness. The deposition may be recorded by a stenographer, audiotape, or videotape. Each party is limited to taking ten depositions without leave of the court (unless otherwise specified in the discovery order). Unless otherwise authorized by the court, no deposition may exceed seven hours.

Depositions have the advantage over interrogatories of allowing a party to follow up a line of questioning. Thus, if a witness provides an incomplete or evasive answer, the attorney may pursue the matter. The attorney can also follow new leads that come out in the testimony. The principal limitation of depositions is that "I don't know" and "I don't recall" are perfectly adequate answers (if true). The deponent is under no obligation to come prepared or to try to find out the answers after the deposition is over.

The first step in taking a deposition is serving a Notice of Deposition on all the parties to the litigation. The notice states who is to be deposed, when and where the deposition will take place, and the means by which the deposition will be recorded. In the case of a party deponent, it is customary for the attorneys to discuss the time and place of the deposition in advance of the notice.

A Rule 45 subpoena is required to compel the attendance of nonparty deponents.* This imposes certain limitations on the mechanics of holding a nonparty deposition. Under Rule 45(c)(1)(A), a nonparty deponent may not be forced to attend a deposition more than 100 miles from his place of residence, employment, or where he regularly transacts business. Subpoenas commanding attendance at a deposition are issued from the court where the action is pending. Fed. R. Civ. P. 45(a)(2). Motions to "quash," which seek to relieve the subpoenaed party from complying with the subpoena, are made in the district where the deposition is to be held. Fed. R. Civ. P. 45(d)(3)(A).

---

* Note that a deponent can voluntarily appear without compulsion of a subpoena. However, this is not the usual course.

U.S. citizens abroad may be subpoenaed when the court determines their appearance is "necessary in the interest of justice," and there is no other means of obtaining their testimony. 28 U.S.C. §1783. For foreign citizens outside of the United States, the cooperation of foreign governments is required. Given the fact that U.S. discovery is far more expansive than is available in most other countries, such assistance is not always forthcoming. The problem of obtaining information located outside of the United States is discussed in greater detail at pp. 640–642.

Both party and nonparty deponents may be asked to bring documents or other tangible evidence in their possession to the deposition. Fed. R. Civ. P. 30(b)(2).

A specific individual deponent is normally identified in the Notice of Deposition. However, a party has the option under Rule 30(b)(6) of naming an organization in the notice or subpoena—a corporation, partnership, or government agency—and describing the nature of information sought. The organization then has the duty, after consultation with the party taking the deposition, to designate a specific individual that it will make available for the deposition to testify on its behalf. This is a particularly useful technique for taking nonparty depositions when there has been no prior discovery against third parties. For instance, in the *Rockwell* case, if plaintiff wanted to depose individuals in the FAA responsible for certifying the plane for its deicing capability, Rule 30(b)(6) would allow plaintiff to describe generically the individuals by the nature of their responsibilities, and the FAA would then be obligated to identify the persons best fitting that description.

Depositions are taken before court reporters, or other "officers authorized to administer oaths." However, the attorneys are in charge of the deposition. If there are disputes about the scope of the questions or the manner in which they are asked, it is up to the attorneys to work out their disagreement or submit their dispute to the court. Attorneys defending depositions are cautioned under Rule 30(c)(2) to state any objections "concisely in a nonargumentative and nonsuggestive manner." They may instruct a deponent not to answer "only when necessary to preserve a privilege, to enforce a limitation ordered by the court," or to terminate a deposition being taken in bad faith.

Courts have grown increasingly intolerant of attorneys who try to coach witnesses during the pendency of depositions. The typical strategy for such attorneys is to ask to go "off the record" to discuss a matter with their client. This can frustrate an otherwise effective cross-examination. The Eastern District of New York adopted a "standing order" prohibiting the attorney for the deponent from initiating a private conference with the deponent during the deposition, except to determine whether a privilege should be asserted. Standing Orders of the Court on Effective Discovery in Civil Cases, 102 F.R.D. 339, 351, no. 13 (E.D.N.Y. 1984). In *Hall v. Clifton Precision*, 150 F.R.D. 525 (E.D. Pa. 1993), the court issued a similar prohibition and held that if attorneys held improper off-the-record discussions with their client during a deposition, those discussions were themselves subject to discovery—i.e., the attorney-client privilege would be waived. A number of courts have followed suit. The lesson for defending attorneys is to prepare in advance of the deposition.

THINKING STRATEGICALLY

Again assume the role of plaintiff's attorney in the *Rockwell* case. What sort of information could best be elicited from the Rockwell design engineer through a deposition compared with interrogatories? How would you prepare to take the deposition? What would your objectives be in the deposition?

Assume you are taking the deposition of the person responsible for designing the wing deicer on the Jet Commander. The deponent is a *fact witness*—his testimony will be relevant because of his knowledge and observations at the time the plane was designed, not for his opinion about the cause of the crash.

Before the deposition, you were advised by your expert that the deicing boot used on the Jet Commander was inferior to an anti-icing design that Rockwell had started to use on some of its more expensive aircraft. The anti-icing design heats the wing to prevent ice buildup, while the deicing boot cracks the ice off the wing, thereby presenting the danger that the cracked ice will enter the engine. In fact, your expert tells you, Rockwell stopped using the deicing boot in favor of anti-icing technology within five years after production of the Jet Commander. The following discussion takes place at the deposition of Rockwell's design engineer:

Q. Did you consider any design for wing deicing on the Jet Commander other than the inflatable boot?

A. No.

Q. Did you consider employing an anti-icing design in lieu of the deicing boot?

A. No. We were satisfied that the deicing boot was a safe and effective technology.

Q. Did Rockwell use an anti-icing technology on other planes that it produced at the time the Jet Commander was designed?

A. Yes. I believe we had just started to use that technology on a few other planes.

Q. Did this anti-icing technology prevent the buildup of ice on the wing by diverting engine heat to the wings?

A. Yes.

Q. So on planes with anti-icing technology, it is not necessary to remove ice from the wing during flight?

A. That's correct.

How much more do you want to ask the witness at this point about the decision to use the deicing boot rather than an anti-icing technology? Have you established negligence in the design of the aircraft, or is there more you need to nail down? Is there any risk in attempting to get the witness to admit that it would have been more effective to use the anti-icing design? If you have enough on the record to establish negligence by Rockwell without even considering an alternative design, is there any benefit to spelling out your argument during the deposition? Is there any benefit in not "destroying the witness" at this time?

Now, put yourself in the role of attorney for Rockwell. You know that although the deponent did not personally evaluate alternative deicing technologies, other engineers at the company did. Should you question the deponent yourself to clarify his answer and explain that other Rockwell engineers did consider alternative designs?

iii. Request for Production

Rule 34 permits a party to inspect and copy documents or other tangible evidence in another party's custody or control. Documents may be obtained from nonparties through a Rule 45 subpoena *duces tecum* ("order to bring with").

A party responding to the request has 30 days from service of the request, although parties frequently agree to a longer period. The request may be served as early as 21 days after service of the summons and complaint. Fed. R. Civ. P. 26(d)(2)(A).

Like interrogatories, requests for production of documents normally include extensive definitions and instructions. For instance:

> "Documents" as used in this Request means all stored information whether written, recorded by analog or digital means, photographed, copied or faxed, including, but not limited to all paper, magnetic or optical media, photocopies, video and audio tape recordings, and photographs, including every nonidentical copy of the same document.

The producing party may not shuffle the documents; they must be produced in the order in which they are normally stored. Fed. R. Civ. P. 34(b)(2)(E)(i). A party may choose to produce documents in electronic rather than paper form. Fed. R. Civ. P. 34(b)(2)(B). Electronic documents must be produced either in the form in which they are normally maintained or in a reasonably usable form. Fed. R. Civ. P. 34(b)(2)(E)(ii). However, the requesting party may specify a particular form for production of electronic documents, Fed. R. Civ. P. 34(b)(1)(C), subject to objection by the responding party. Fed. R. Civ. P. 34(b)(2)(D).

Precision is of crucial importance in drafting a request for production of documents. An underinclusive request could miss critical evidence, and an overinclusive request could deluge a party in irrelevant paper. Think about what documents you would need from Rockwell if you represented plaintiff and how you would effectively describe them in a request for production.

Document productions are often the backbone of discovery, and attorneys can spend hundreds of hours reviewing documents. Given the phenomenal expense of complying with a document production request, why don't litigants simply hand their opponents the keys to their filing cabinets? Sometimes they do. But there may well be information contained in a party's records — either proprietary or privileged — that a party does not want, and is not required, to disclose.

The storing and cataloguing of produced documents is an art. Traditionally, this was done by developing a "taxonomy" or catalog of legal and factual issues in the case, and then coding each document for its probative value in the case. More recently, litigants have begun to digitally scan and store produced documents, facilitating sophisticated database manipulation and retrieval of relevant documents.

iv. Mental and Physical Examinations

Mental and physical examinations pursuant to Rule 35 can be of crucial importance when the mental or physical condition of a party is in issue, as in a personal injury proceeding. Unlike the other discovery devices, mental and physical exams require a prior court order "for good cause shown." This is presumably due to the highly invasive nature of the examination.

Rule 35 is silent on the question of who may be present during the examination. The federal courts will generally not permit the presence of counsel during an examination, even when such a right is expressly provided by state statute. *See, e.g., McDaniel v. Toledo, Peoria & Western Railway Co.*, 97 F.R.D. 525 (C.D. Ill. 1983).

What constitutes "good cause"? Clearly, if plaintiff is suing for her own personal injuries, defendant must have the opportunity to verify her condition. But what if defendant simply alleges that he saw plaintiff run through a red light? May plaintiff obtain an order to have defendant's eyes examined? May she subject defendant to a psychiatric exam to determine whether he is a pathologic liar? Not surprisingly, courts require a much greater showing of good cause when a party does not put her own condition in issue.

In *Schlagenhauf v. Holder*, 379 U.S. 104 (1964), the Supreme Court held that it was an abuse of discretion for the district court to order a battery of nine separate mental and physical exams on a defendant bus driver who was charged with rear-ending a truck, simply on the basis that plaintiff asserted that the bus driver's vision was impaired and that the bus driver had had a prior, similar accident:

> "[G]ood-cause" requirements of Rule 35 [are] . . . not met by mere conclusory allegations of the pleadings — nor by mere relevance to the case — but require an affirmative showing by the movant that each condition as to which the examination is sought is really and genuinely in controversy and that good cause exists for ordering each particular examination. Obviously, what may be good cause for one type of examination may not be so for another. The ability of the movant to obtain the desired information by other means is also relevant. . . .
>
> Rule 35, therefore, requires discriminating application by the trial judge, who must decide, as an initial matter in every case, whether the party requesting a mental or physical examination or examinations has adequately demonstrated the existence of the Rule's requirements of "in controversy" and "good cause," which requirements, as the Court of Appeals in this case itself recognized, are necessarily related. This does not, of course, mean that the movant must prove his case on the merits in order to meet the requirements for a mental or physical examination. Nor does it mean that an evidentiary hearing is required in all cases. This may be necessary in some cases, but in other cases the showing could be made by affidavits or other usual methods short of a hearing. It does mean, though, that the movant must produce sufficient information, by whatever means, so that the district judge can fulfill his function mandated by the Rule.

Id. at 118–119.

Note the elaborate process by which the parties exchange medical reports under Rule 35(b). Why aren't all medical reports exchanged as a matter of course as part of the mandatory disclosures under Rule 26? The reason is concern about the doctor-patient privilege. As Rule 35 is structured, a party is obligated to disclose his own medical records only as a consequence of his request for the report of an examination conducted at the request of another party. Thus, the Rule does not formally abrogate the doctor-patient privilege. Would it have been more problematic for the Rule to abrogate the doctor-patient privilege than to force a party to submit to a medical examination?

One of the earliest challenges to the validity of the Federal Rules of Civil Procedure was a challenge to a Rule 35 medical examination as exceeding the scope of rule-making authority under the Rules Enabling Act. The Supreme Court in *Sibbach v. Wilson*, 312 U.S. 1 (1941), upheld Rule 35 as applied to a plaintiff suing from personal injuries, and then, in the *Schlagenhauf* case, upheld the Rule as applied to a defendant (although the Court reduced the number of examinations ordered). Do you see a difference between applying the Rule to defendants as opposed to plaintiffs? For a discussion of *Sibbach* and other issues related to the validity of the Federal Rules, *see* pp. 443-445.

v. Requests for Admissions

As we saw in the case of "contention interrogatories," discovery can serve two distinct purposes: It can be used not only to collect evidence, but to ascertain precisely what another party's legal and factual contentions are. Before "notice pleading" was permitted under the Federal Rules, this latter function was performed by the pleadings; a party was required to spell out its legal and factual contentions with much greater specificity at the outset of the litigation. Notice pleading greatly reduced the amount of information provided in the pleadings, but much of the slack has been taken up by expansive discovery under the Federal Rules. Specifically, Rule 36 permits requests for admissions to be served on any party, and the party served must admit or deny the truth of any legal or factual issues in the litigation. A Rule 36 request looks a great deal like the pleadings, except in the form of a very specific question.

For example, in the *Rockwell* case, plaintiff might want to pose some of the following questions as part of a Rule 36 request:

- Do you admit that Theodore Burdick was employed by the FAA on the date of the accident?
- Do you admit that the crash was a consequence of a loss of power in the engines?
- Do you admit that the engines lost power as a consequence of ice on or in the engine?
- Do you admit that Rockwell designed the deicing system on the plane?
- Do you admit that there was no significant modification of the design of the deicing system after the plane was sold by Rockwell?
- Do you admit that the deicing boots on the wings were designed to remove ice from the wing by cracking the ice and allowing the cracked ice to fly toward the rear of the aircraft?
- Do you admit that at the time that Rockwell designed the deicing boot for the plane, Rockwell was using an alternative ice prevention technology on other of its planes that prevented the buildup of ice on the wings by diverting engine heat to the wings?
- Do you admit that the ice prevention technology could have been installed on the Jet Commander at the time the plane was manufactured?
- Do you admit that Theodore Burdick had an annual income of $65,000?
- Do you admit that the life expectancy of Theodore Burdick was 20 years?
- Do you admit that Pennsylvania law governs the liability of Rockwell in this case?

- Do you admit that the document attached hereto is a true and correct copy of the accident report prepared in this matter by the National Transportation Safety Board?

As in the case of interrogatories, a party may inquire into the application of law to the facts of the case. The responding party is under a duty of reasonable inquiry to determine the truth of each contention.

As in the case of admissions in the answer, any Rule 36 admission relieves the opposing party of the need to present evidence at trial in support of that matter.

One unique aspect of requests for admission is that they are self-executing: Any matter not denied or objected to in a timely fashion is automatically deemed admitted.

Requests for admissions are enforced with both carrots and sticks. Any matter admitted under Rule 36 is deemed to be established for the purpose of that proceeding only: "An admission under this rule is not an admission for any other purpose and cannot be used against the party in any other proceeding." Fed. R. Civ. P. 36(b). As we will see in Chapter 7, this limitation can represent a significant advantage for the admitting party. If a fact is established at trial, that finding might well be used against the losing party in other litigation.

Moreover, Rule 37(c)(2) provides a financial incentive to admit:

> If a party fails to admit what is requested under Rule 36 and if the requesting party later proves a document to be genuine or the matter true, the requesting party may move that the party who failed to admit pay the reasonable expenses, including attorney's fees, incurred in making that proof. The court must so order unless: (A) the request was held objectionable under Rule 36(a); (B) the admission sought was of no substantial importance; (C) the party failing to admit had a reasonable ground to believe that it might prevail on the matter; or (D) there was other good reason for the failure to admit.

Sanctions for unjustified denials are provided for in Rule 37(c)(2). A party refusing to admit may be assessed attorneys' fees for the cost of proving that matter at trial. What if a party knew that a matter was true, but did not think that the party seeking the admission would be able to establish the matter at trial? Does Rule 36 prohibit a party from denying a request simply in order to preserve the issue for trial? *See* Fed. R. Civ. P. 37(c)(2)(C) (authorizing sanctions unless "the party failing to admit had a reasonable ground to believe that it might prevail on the matter").

vi. Stipulations

A request for admission is not the only circumstance in which a fact might be established for purposes of the litigation without the need for an adversarial presentation of evidence. The parties can choose to enter into a "stipulation"—a written agreement by which the parties jointly consent to treat certain facts as true in their dispute. The parties may enter into a stipulation at the outset of the lawsuit, so as to define the issues more clearly and save unnecessary time and expense. Or they may enter into a stipulation regarding the facts that are uncontested in conjunction with a motion (or cross-motions) for summary judgment. Courts generally hold that such stipulations between parties are binding for purposes of the litigation, meaning that a party who later changes its mind about a stipulation will likely be held to the agreement and prohibited from contesting facts that it has previously agreed to take off the table. *See Christian Legal Society v. Hastings College of the Law*, 561 U.S. 661 (2010).

vii. Electronic Discovery

Ever since Fed. R. Civ. P. 34 was amended in 1970 (to include "data compilations from which information can be obtained"), courts have consistently held that electronic evidence is discoverable. *See Anti-Monopoly, Inc. v. Hasbro, Inc.*, 1995 WL 649934, 2 (S.D.N.Y. Nov. 3, 1995) ("It is blackletter law that computerized data is discoverable."). Consider the Rules' expansive approach to discovery in light of the massive amounts of information that modern commercial entities store in electronic form.

Electronic information has introduced novel problems into the discovery process. *See* Richard L. Marcus, *Confronting the Future: Coping with Discovery of Electronic Material*, 64 Law & Contemp. Probs. 253 (2001); Henry S. Noyes, *Is E-Discovery So Different That It Requires New Discovery Rules? An Analysis of Proposed Amendments to the Federal Rules of Civil Procedure*, 71 Tenn. L. Rev. 585 (2004). Several notable differences include: the sheer volume of information and the cost of sifting through that information (for example, large corporate computer networks store terabytes of backup data, with each terabyte being the equivalent of 500 billion typewritten pages); the durability of electronically stored information; the spoliation of evidence during recycling of memory space and the costs associated with storage once the duty to preserve arises; the need to hire experts to locate, retrieve, and translate requested information; the potential necessity for on-site inspection and resultant potential for the disclosure of privileged information.

Much of the electronic-discovery litigation has focused on the costs that accompany electronic information requests. *See* Laura E. Ellsworth & Robert Pass, *Cost Shifting in Electronic Discovery*, 5 Sedona Conf. J. 125 (2004) (listing relevant cases and journal articles). Does Rule 26(b)(2) provide adequate protection to parties responding to discovery requests? Some courts have held that the costs associated with electronic discovery are no different from costs associated with paper discovery. *See In re Brand Name Prescription Drugs Litigation*, 1995 WL 360526 (N.D. Ill. June 15, 1995) ("[I]f a party chooses an electronic storage method, the necessity for a retrieval program is an ordinary and foreseeable risk."). Other courts have constructed cost-shifting models, in which several factors figure into a determination as to whether the requesting party will have to bear some of the cost. *See Zubulake v. UBS Warburg LLC*, 217 F.R.D. 309 (S.D.N.Y. 2003); *Rowe Entm't, Inc. v. William Morris Agency, Inc.*, 205 F.R.D. 421 (S.D.N.Y. 2002). Some courts have used a "marginal utility" approach. *See McPeek v. Ashcroft*, 202 F.R.D. 31 (D.D.C. 2001) (where the court balanced the likelihood of discovering relevant information against the cost after the defendant produced a sample). Rule 26(c)(1)(B) expressly authorizes the court to allocate discovery costs in a protective order.

Is there a downside to cost-shifting in discovery? Could such a prospect deter plaintiffs from seeking discovery? *See* Martin H. Redish, *Electronic Discovery and the Litigation Matrix*, 51 Duke L.J. 561 (2001); Benjamin Spencer, *Rationalizing Cost*

Allocation in Civil Discovery, 34 Rev. Litig. 769 (2015); Jonathan Remy Nash & Joanna Shepherd, *Aligning Incentives and Cost Allocation in Discovery*, 71 Vand. L. Rev. 2015, 2016 (2018) (arguing for parties to share discovery costs).

Electronic discovery amendments to the Federal Rules of Civil Procedure went into effect in 2006, supplemented by additional provisions in 2015. The Rules now call for early attention to electronic discovery issues. Electronically stored documents must be included in the 26(a)(1) initial disclosures, and the Rule 26(f) initial conference and Rule 16(b) scheduling order should include a plan for electronic discovery, including preservation of data and privilege. *See generally* Lee Rosenthal, *A Few Thoughts on Electronic Discovery After December 1, 2006*, 116 Yale L.J. Forum (2015); *The Sedona Principles, Third Edition: Best Practices, Recommendations & Principles for Addressing Electronic Document Production*, 19 Sedona Conf. J. 1 (2018).

Rule 26(b)(2)(B) relieves a responding party from the duty to produce electronically stored information that is not "reasonably accessible because of undue burden or cost." If such an objection is asserted, the party seeking discovery may then file a motion to compel. Even if the court determines that the information is not reasonably accessible, it may still order discovery for "good cause" and may "specify conditions for the discovery." How, if at all, does that scheme differ from the kind of judicial control over discovery implemented by Rule 26(b)(1) and 26(b)(2)(C)? *See* Henry S. Noyes, *Good Cause Is Bad Medicine for the New E-Discovery Rules*, 248 F.R.D. 1 (2008) (arguing that the "good cause" standard under Rule 26(b)(3)(B) does not adequately protect responding parties from onerous electronic discovery obligations).

Perhaps most significantly, Rule 37 now standardizes sanctions for failure to take "reasonable steps" to preserve electronic and other data "that should have been preserved in the anticipation or conduct of litigation" where that data "cannot be restored or replaced through additional discovery." Fed. R. Civ. P. 37(e). This section makes sanctions available only if the failure to preserve caused "prejudice" or was "with the intent to deprive another party of the information." Sanctions for intentional deprivation include jury instructions to presume the information was unfavorable to the party, or dismissal of the action (in the case of plaintiff's destruction of data), or entry of default judgment (in the case of defendant's destruction of data). For a comprehensive summary of recent developments in electronic discovery, *see* Tanya Pierce, *Righting the Ship: What Courts Are Still Getting Wrong About Electronic Discovery*, 72 SMU L. Rev. 785 (2019); Thomas Y. Allman, *The 2015 Civil Rules Package as Transmitted to Congress*, 16 Sedona Conf. J. 1 (2015); William P. Barnette, *Ghost in the Machine:* Zubulake *Revisited and Other Emerging E-Discovery Issues Under the Amended Federal Rules*, 18 Rich. J.L. & Tech. 11 (2012); Bennett B. Borden, Monica McCarroll, Brian C. Vick & Lauren M. Wheeling, *Four Years Later: How the 2006 Amendments to the Federal Rules Have Reshaped the E-Discovery Landscape and Are Revitalizing the Civil Justice System*, 17 Rich. J.L. & Tech. 10 (2011). *The Sedona Conference Commentary on Legal Holds, Second Edition: The Trigger & The Process: A Project of the Sedona Conference Working Group on Electronic Document Retention and Production*, 20 Sedona Conf. J. 341 (2019), provides practical guidelines for determining (a) when the duty to preserve discoverable information arises, and (b) once that duty is triggered, what should be preserved and how the preservation process should be undertaken.

viii. Document Preservation

It is common, even before a complaint has been filed, for attorneys to send a letter advising defendants of their duty to preserve documents and other information, in anticipation of litigation. Although these "litigation hold" letters do not, by themselves, create an enforceable duty, they do serve to establish that defendants were on notice of the imminence of the litigation for purposes of a sanctions claim in the event that information is not preserved. *See generally*, Jeffrey A. Parness, *Expanding Pre-Suit Discovery and Preservation Orders*, 2019 Mich. St. L. Rev. 651 (2019).

ix. Freedom of Information Act

One additional discovery tool outside of the Federal Rules can occasionally be useful for litigants: the Freedom of Information Act (FOIA), 5 U.S.C. §552. The statute enables any person to request the production of documents, with some exceptions, in the custody of a federal agency (such as the FAA). The primary advantage of FOIA requests is that they can be used prior to filing litigation. However, it can take a long time for the agency to respond, and the person filing the request must pay for the cost of retrieving, reviewing, and copying every document produced. Accordingly, FOIA is rarely preferable over discovery under the Federal Rules. *See generally* 57 A.L.R. Fed. 903 (1982, updated through 2021); Janice Toran, *Information Disclosure in Civil Actions: The Freedom of Information Act and the Federal Discovery Rules*, 49 Geo. Wash. L. Rev. 843 (1981).

3. Crafting a Discovery Plan

Rule 26(d)(2) permits the parties to conduct discovery "in any sequence." Think about the discovery needed in the *Rockwell* case. Is one sequence preferable to another? Do you want the documents produced and interrogatories answered before you take depositions? Are there advantages to taking depositions first? When might requests for admission be most useful?

4. Obstacles to Discovery

A party against whom discovery is sought can resist the disclosure of information protected by a "privilege," as well as information outside the scope of the Rule 26 standard of relevance.

a. Privileges

Privileged communications are protected from disclosure by both statute and common law. The conferral of a privilege represents a sacrifice of the accuracy of the adjudication in order to encourage or facilitate certain relationships—e.g., attorney-client; doctor-patient; priest-parishioner; reporter-source. In diversity litigation, privileges are governed by state law. *See* Fed. R. Evid. 501. Otherwise, federal common law and statutes define which communications are privileged. *Id.*

The most universally recognized privilege is attorney-client communication. All communications between the attorney and client concerning the representation are protected from compelled disclosure. The theory behind the privilege is that a client would not be completely candid with her attorney if she feared that her discussion would later be revealed against her wishes. Does that explain why communications *by* the attorney *to* the client are also protected?

Isn't all the information a client tells a lawyer discoverable directly from the client anyway? For instance, suppose a client admits to her attorney that she committed a tort. If she is served with an interrogatory asking whether she committed the tort, she is under an obligation to admit it. Why should the fact that she admitted it to her attorney be protected if the underlying information is not? Does the privilege have any function other than allowing people to tell one story to their lawyer and another to the court?

The traditional answer is that the privilege prevents a client from self-censoring her discussions with her attorney out of a potentially erroneous understanding of the legal implications of the truth. In order to provide effective advice and representation, an attorney must be armed with all the facts. For example, in the *Rockwell* case, suppose a Rockwell executive was under the misapprehension that Rockwell would be liable for punitive damages if a safer deicing system could have been installed on the plane, regardless of its expense. In the absence of a privilege, the client might be tempted to conceal from the attorney that there was, in fact, a safer deicing system available, although at a prohibitive price. If the attorney knew that fact, she could effectively argue that the design employed was reasonable given the cost of the alternative. Instead, she asserts that no alternative technology existed. Her case is then completely undermined when plaintiff establishes that there was an alternative.

Although the primary function of the attorney-client privilege is to protect the client, the privilege may also help to ensure that the client is candid to the court and parties in the course of the litigation. Armed with the truth, the attorney is in a good position to prevent the client from defrauding the tribunal. If the attorney were in the dark, she could not recognize inaccurate information provided by her client in the litigation.

Do these arguments persuade you that the privilege is necessary? Why shouldn't the law make people who lie to their attorneys do so at their own peril?

i.   Who Is the Client?

Only discussions with the client are protected by the attorney-client privilege. In a corporate context, identifying who the client is can be complex. Suppose in the *Rockwell* case, plaintiff seeks to discover the content of conversations that Rockwell's attorney had with engineers working for the company. Such discussions may be separately protected by the "work product" privilege discussed later, but are the discussions also protected by the attorney-client privilege? Is the engineer the client for the purpose of the privilege?

1. Note on *Upjohn Co. v. United States*

The Supreme Court attempted to answer that question in *Upjohn Co. v. United States*, 449 U.S. 383 (1981). The Internal Revenue Service had attempted to obtain from Upjohn notes and records of communication between its general counsel and various lower-level employees of the company. In an earlier internal investigation by Upjohn, the chairman of the board dispatched the general counsel to determine Upjohn's compliance with the Foreign Corrupt Practices Act by submitting questionnaires and conducting interviews with all foreign managers of the company. Following disclosure of some questionable payments to foreign governments in the company's filings with the Securities and Exchange Commission, the IRS commenced a tax investigation, since such payments would not have been tax deductible. The IRS then sought to obtain all files relative to the investigation, including the questionnaires, as well as the counsel's interview notes.

The lower court determined that Upjohn's assertion of the attorney-client privilege was not warranted because the interviewees were outside of the "control group" responsible for directing company actions in response to legal advice. Thus, these were not communications with "the client." The Supreme Court reversed. Although declining "to lay down a broad rule or series of rules to govern all conceivable future questions in this area," the Court held the communications in question were protected.

The Court held that the "control-group" test applied by the lower court "overlooks the fact that the privilege exists to protect not only the giving of professional advice to those who can act on it, but also the giving of information to the lawyer to enable him to give sound and informed advice." Since information critical to the lawyer's advice is often in the hands of employees outside of the control group, the "test adopted by the court below frustrates the very purpose of the privilege by discouraging the communication of relevant information by employees of the client to attorneys seeking to render legal advice to the client corporation." The Court also noted that the control-group test was too unpredictable; an attorney seeking information from lower-level employees could not reliably determine in advance which communications were protected; "an uncertain privilege, or one which purports to be certain but results in widely varying applications is little better than no privilege at all."

Insofar as the communications at issue "were made by Upjohn employees to counsel for Upjohn acting as such, at the direction of corporate superiors in order to secure legal advice from counsel . . . concern[ing] matters within the scope of the employees' corporate duties, and the employees themselves were sufficiently aware that they were being questioned in order that the corporation could obtain legal advice . . . these communications must be protected against compelled disclosure."

NOTES AND QUESTIONS

1. Are there any lower-level employees that would not be covered by the privilege to the extent that the attorney needed to obtain relevant information from them?

2. In the event that the corporation's lawyer discovers from an employee information concerning wrongdoing by the employee, doesn't the lawyer have to disclose that information to senior management? If so, how does conferral of the privilege facilitate the collection of information? Put another way, if the employee would be inclined to be less than candid in direct discussions with management, merely protecting the employee's discussion with corporate counsel from disclosure to third parties is not apt to increase the employee's candor.

What implications does this have for *Upjohn? See* Elizabeth G. Thornburg, *Sanctifying Secrecy: The Mythology of the Corporate Attorney-Client Privilege*, 69 Notre Dame L. Rev. 157, 190 (1993).

3. If, as the Court notes, predictability is critical to the operation of the attorney-client privilege, why does the Court "decline to lay down a broad rule or series of rules to govern all conceivable future questions in this area"? Do you agree that such an effort would have been inconsistent with the provision of the Federal Rules of Evidence that privileges are to be "governed by the principles of the common law as they may be interpreted by the courts of the United States in light of reason and experience"? Could the Court have provided more guidance for future cases than it did? For a comprehensive analysis of *Upjohn, see* John E. Sexton, *A Post-*Upjohn *Consideration of the Corporate Attorney-Client Privilege*, 57 N.Y.U. L. Rev. 443 (1982).

4. Are all communications with counsel by senior management protected? Suppose during your review of Rockwell documents on behalf of Rockwell you discover a 1964 memorandum from the head of the engineering department to a senior vice president discussing the risks of the wing deicer. A "cc" ("carbon" copy) on the bottom of the page indicates that it was copied to John Jones. Jones was a vice president and general counsel to Rockwell. Should you produce the document or assert an attorney-client privilege? What, if any, additional information would you need to ascertain before deciding whether to assert the privilege?

5. *Privilege Logs.* In the event that a responding party chooses to assert a privilege in lieu of producing the information sought, it must "describe the nature of the documents, communications, or tangible things not produced or disclosed — and do so in a manner that, without revealing information itself privileged or protected, will enable other parties to assess the claim." Fed. R. Civ. P. 26(b)(5)(a)(ii). Note the fine line that an objecting attorney must walk: Too little information about the communication may not enable other parties to assess whether the assertion of the privilege was appropriate; too much information will result in a waiver of the privilege.

6. *Privilege in Complex Litigation.* In large cases, a responding party may claim privilege protection for thousands of pages of documents. How can a court assess the propriety of such claims? A document-by-document review would exhaust available judicial resources. Accordingly, some courts have developed innovative techniques to deal with these situations. For example, in *In re Vioxx Products Liability Litigation*, 501 F. Supp. 2d 789 (E.D. La. 2007), after the magistrate-judge supervising discovery had conducted a review of 500,000 pages of documents over which defendant had asserted a privilege, the Court of Appeals concluded that such a review was impractical for future production, and directed the court to develop an alternative review protocol. Accordingly, the court approved a process by which the magistrate sampled documents withheld from production by defendant. The magistrate then made rulings for different categories of documents within that sample, e.g., emails copied to non-attorneys, or attorney review of advertising copy. Defendant was then instructed to conform its document production to the principles set forth in those rulings, and the court monitored compliance by random checks.

ii.   Waiver

The attorney-client privilege is extremely fragile. The privilege may be wholly or partially destroyed by disclosure of the communication to third parties.

1. Unintentional Production of Documents

Perhaps the most common source of privilege waiver occurs due to inadvertent production of privileged documents in the course of discovery. *See generally* Richard L. Marcus, *The Perils of Privilege: Waiver and the Litigator,* 84 Mich. L. Rev. 1605 (1986). It is not unusual for attorneys to stipulate prior to discovery that the inadvertent production of privileged documents will not result in waiver of the privilege, and the parties agree to return all such documents without making any photocopies. Such agreements are now binding on the parties in all federal proceedings. Fed. R. Evid. 502(e).

Even in the absence of an agreement, the inadvertent production of privileged information may not result in the loss of the privilege. Rule 26(b)(5)(B) provides that the recipient of unintentionally produced privileged information must, upon notification, "promptly return, sequester, or destroy the specified information" and "must not use or disclose the information until the claim is resolved." The rule does not purport to establish whether the privilege has been waived by virtue of the unintentional production. However, Federal Rule of Evidence 502 does establish a federal standard for determining whether the unintentional production of privileged material in a federal proceeding results in a waiver. The Rule provides that a disclosure of information protected by the work-product or attorney-client privileges will *not* result in a waiver of the privilege if (1) the disclosure was inadvertent; (2) the holder of the privilege or protection took reasonable steps to prevent disclosure; and (3) the holder promptly took reasonable steps to rectify the error, including (if applicable) following Fed. R. Civ. P. 26(b)(5)(B). Fed. R. Evid. 502(b). The Rule further provides that in the event of an intentional waiver, the waiver extends only to undisclosed information concerning the same subject matter as the disclosed material. Fed. R. Evid. 502(a). Information inadvertently disclosed in a state proceeding will not result in a waiver in a subsequent federal proceeding unless the disclosure would have resulted in a waiver under the federal standard, or unless the state court has otherwise ordered. Fed. R. Evid. 502(c). And if a federal court orders that disclosures in a federal proceeding have not resulted in a waiver, those disclosures cannot be deemed to constitute a waiver of the privilege in subsequent state proceedings. Fed. R. Evid. 502(d). Note that unlike the Federal Rules of Civil Procedure, the Federal Rules of Evidence are statutes passed by Congress, and thus are not subject to the constraints of the Rules Enabling Act.

2. Disclosure to Third Parties

The attorney-client privilege only applies to communications between attorney and client. If the communication is shared with anyone else, the privilege is destroyed. Thus, if a nonclient is present during an interview between the attorney and client, the interview is discoverable. Even if a client reports a privileged communication to a third party after the communication occurs, the privilege is destroyed.

The privilege does permit disclosure to other attorneys in the same office, as well as paralegals and secretaries working for the attorney. What happens when co-parties meet to discuss the case? Courts have recognized a "joint defense privilege" that permits disclosure of certain confidential communications to co-parties and their counsel without destroying the underlying privilege. *See, e.g., Continental Oil Co. v. United States,* 330 F.2d 347 (9th Cir. 1964); *United States v. Evans,* 113 F.3d 1457 (7th Cir. 1997). *See generally* Howard M. Erichson, *Informal Aggregation: Procedural and Ethical Implications of Coordination Among Counsel in Related Lawsuits,* 50 Duke L.J. 381 (2000); Grace M. Giesel, *End the Experiment: The Attorney-Client Privilege Should Not Protect Communications in the Allied Lawyer Setting,* 95 Marq. L. Rev. 475 (2012).

A 2006 court of appeals case held that the voluntary production of documents subpoenaed by the SEC in a criminal investigation constituted a waiver of work-product and attorney-client privileges. *In Re Qwest Communications Int'l, Inc.,* 450 F.3d 1179 (10th Cir. 2006). The documents in question were produced to the government pursuant to a confidentiality agreement with the SEC, but the court held that the privileges were nonetheless waived for purposes of a subsequent private civil action. *See also, In re Pacific Pictures Corp.,* 679 F.3d 1121 (9th Cir. 2012) (voluntary production of documents in compliance with grand jury subpoena waived privilege notwithstanding confidentiality agreement with prosecutor). Note that in both cases, the companies could have maintained the privilege by asserting it in response to the government subpoenas. What they were unable to do was selectively waive the privilege for the purpose of those investigations only.

3. Implied Waiver

Even without breaching confidentiality, a party can waive the privilege by putting the confidential communication at issue in the litigation. For example, if Rockwell were to try to defend against the award of punitive damages by asserting that it believed it was legally obligated to use that deicing mechanism, such a defense could well open the door to discovery about the basis for its legal belief, including relevant advice of counsel. *See Saint-Gobain/Norton Industrial Ceramics Corp. v. General Electric Co.,* 884 F. Supp. 31 (D. Mass. 1995) ("advice of counsel" defense to charge of willful patent infringement waives attorney-client privilege).

iii.   Self-Incrimination

Perhaps the privilege most familiar to lay persons is the privilege against self-incrimination provided for in the Fifth Amendment of the United States Constitution. The privilege is peculiar to criminal liability: A civil defendant has no right to resist disclosures that would tend to establish civil liability. However, if the disclosure could subject the party to subsequent criminal prosecution, the party may assert the Fifth Amendment privilege in response to civil discovery. The privilege does not apply to incriminating documents; thus, the privilege may not normally be asserted in response to a request for production. *See generally* 8 C. Wright et al., Federal Practice and Procedure §2018 (3d ed. 2010).

b.   Work Product

What if, in order to defend the litigation, Rockwell invested several million dollars digitally scanning and storing all of the documents produced in the litigation? Could plaintiffs obtain through discovery the files in which the documents were stored? The underlying documents are certainly not privileged; they have already been produced. Note that the attorney-client privilege would not apply because the files are not communications to or from the client. Is there some other basis to protect the files from disclosure? Defendants might be able to resist turning over the files on the ground that they constitute "attorney work product."

Rule 26(b)(3)(A) recognizes a presumptive privilege for all materials "prepared in anticipation of litigation . . . [b]ut . . . those materials may be discovered if: (i) they are otherwise discoverable under Rule 26(b)(1); and (ii) the party shows that it has substantial need for the materials to prepare its case and cannot, without undue hardship, obtain their substantial equivalent by other means." Even when such a showing is made, Rule 26(b)(3)(B) provides that the court "shall protect against disclosure of the mental impressions, conclusions, opinions, or legal theories of a party's attorney or other representative concerning the litigation."

If the premise behind expansive discovery is that justice is best served when both parties have complete information, what justifies the work-product privilege? The following case articulates the classic justification for the doctrine.

Hickman v. Taylor

329 U.S. 495 (1947)

MR. JUSTICE MURPHY delivered the opinion of the Court.

This case presents an important problem under the Federal Rules of Civil Procedure,* . . . as to the extent to which a party may inquire into oral and written statements of witnesses, or other information, secured by an adverse party's counsel in the course of preparation for possible litigation after a claim has arisen. Examination into a person's files and records, including those resulting from the professional activities of an attorney, must be judged with care. It is not without reason that various safeguards have been established to preclude unwarranted excursions into the privacy of a man's work. At the same time, public policy supports reasonable and necessary inquiries. Properly to balance these competing interests is a delicate and difficult task.

On February 7, 1943, the tug "J. M. Taylor" sank while engaged in helping to tow a car float of the Baltimore & Ohio Railroad across the Delaware River at Philadelphia. The accident was apparently unusual in nature, the cause of it still being unknown. Five of the nine crew members were drowned. Three days later the tug owners and the underwriters employed a law firm, of which respondent Fortenbaugh is a member, to defend them against potential suits by representatives of the deceased crew members and to sue the railroad for damages to the tug.

A public hearing was held on March 4, 1943, before the United States Steamboat Inspectors, at which the four survivors were examined. This testimony was recorded and made available to all interested parties. Shortly thereafter, Fortenbaugh privately interviewed the survivors and took statements from them with an eye toward the anticipated litigation; the survivors signed these statements on March 29. Fortenbaugh also interviewed other persons believed to have some

---

* Note that both the numbering and substance of the Rules discussed in *Hickman* have been altered by subsequent amendments. — EDS.

information relating to the accident and in some cases he made memoranda of what they told him. At the time when Fortenbaugh secured the statements of the survivors, representatives of two of the deceased crew members had been in communication with him. Ultimately claims were presented by representatives of all five of the deceased; four of the claims, however, were settled without litigation. The fifth claimant, petitioner herein, brought suit in a federal court under the Jones Act on November 26, 1943, naming as defendants the two tug owners, individually and as partners, and the railroad.

One year later, petitioner filed 39 interrogatories directed to the tug owners. The 38th interrogatory read: "State whether any statements of the members of the crews of the Tugs 'J. M. Taylor' and 'Philadelphia' or of any other vessel were taken in connection with the towing of the car float and the sinking of the Tug 'John M. Taylor.' Attach hereto exact copies of all such statements if in writing, and if oral, set forth in detail the exact provisions of any such oral statements or reports."

Supplemental interrogatories asked whether any oral or written statements, records, reports or other memoranda had been made concerning any matter relative to the towing operation, the sinking of the tug, the salvaging and repair of the tug, and the death of the deceased. If the answer was in the affirmative, the tug owners were then requested to set forth the nature of all such records, reports, statements or other memoranda.

The tug owners, through Fortenbaugh, answered all of the interrogatories except No. 38 and the supplemental ones just described. While admitting that statements of the survivors had been taken, they declined to summarize or set forth the contents. They did so on the ground that such requests called "for privileged matter obtained in preparation for litigation" and constituted "an attempt to obtain indirectly counsel's private files." It was claimed that answering these requests "would involve practically turning over not only the complete files, but also the telephone records and, almost, the thoughts of counsel."

In connection with the hearing on these objections, Fortenbaugh made a written statement and gave an informal oral deposition explaining the circumstances under which he had taken the statements. But he was not expressly asked in the deposition to produce the statements. The District Court for the Eastern District of Pennsylvania, sitting *en banc*, held that the requested matters were not privileged. The court then decreed that the tug owners and Fortenbaugh, as counsel and agent for the tug owners forthwith "answer Plaintiff's 38th interrogatory and supplemental interrogatories; produce all written statements of witnesses obtained by Mr. Fortenbaugh, as counsel and agent for Defendants; state in substance any fact concerning this case which Defendants learned through oral statements made by witnesses to Mr. Fortenbaugh whether or not included in his private memoranda and produce Mr. Fortenbaugh's memoranda containing statements of fact by witnesses or to submit these memoranda to the Court for determination of those portions which should be revealed to Plaintiff." Upon their refusal, the court adjudged them in contempt and ordered them imprisoned until they complied.

The Third Circuit Court of Appeals, also sitting *en banc*, reversed the judgment of the District Court. 153 F.2d 212. It held that the information here sought was part of the "work product of the lawyer" and hence privileged from discovery under the Federal Rules of Civil Procedure. The importance of the problem, which has engendered a great divergence of views among district courts, led us to grant certiorari. . . .

The pre-trial deposition-discovery mechanism established by Rules 26 to 37 is one of the most significant innovations of the Federal Rules of Civil Procedure. Under the prior federal practice, the pre-trial functions of notice-giving, issue-formulation and fact-revelation were performed primarily and inadequately by the pleadings.[2] Inquiry into the issues and the facts before trial was narrowly confined and was often cumbersome in method. The new rules, however, restrict the pleadings to the task of general notice-giving and invest the deposition-discovery process with a vital role in the preparation for trial. The various instruments of discovery now serve (1) as a device, along with the pre-trial hearing under Rule 16, to narrow and clarify the basic issues between the parties, and (2) as a device for ascertaining the facts, or information as to the existence or whereabouts of facts, relative to those issues. Thus civil trials in the federal courts no longer need be carried on in the dark. The way is now clear, consistent with recognized privileges, for the parties to obtain the fullest possible knowledge of the issues and facts before trial. . . .

In urging that he has a right to inquire into the materials secured and prepared by Fortenbaugh, petitioner emphasizes that the deposition-discovery portions of the Federal Rules of Civil Procedure are designed to enable the parties to discover the true facts and to compel their disclosure wherever they may be found. It is said that inquiry may be made under these rules, epitomized by Rule 26, as to any relevant matter which is not privileged; and since the discovery provisions are to be applied as broadly and liberally as possible, the privilege limitation must be restricted to its narrowest bounds. On the premise that the attorney-client privilege is the one involved in this case, petitioner argues that it must be strictly confined to confidential communications made by a client to his attorney. And since the materials here in issue were secured by Fortenbaugh from third persons rather than from his clients, the tug owners, the conclusion is reached that these materials are proper subjects for discovery under Rule 26.

As additional support for this result, petitioner claims that to prohibit discovery under these circumstances would give a corporate defendant a tremendous advantage in a suit by an individual plaintiff. Thus in a suit by an injured employee against a railroad or in a suit by an insured person against an insurance company the corporate defendant could pull a dark veil of secrecy over all the pertinent facts it can collect after the claim arises merely on the assertion that such facts were gathered by its large staff of attorneys and claim agents. At the same time, the individual plaintiff, who often has direct knowledge of the matter in issue and has no counsel until some time after his claim arises could be compelled to disclose all the intimate details of his case. By endowing with immunity from disclosure all that a lawyer discovers in the course of his duties, it is said, the rights of individual litigants in such cases are drained of vitality and the lawsuit becomes more of a battle of deception than a search for truth.

But framing the problem in terms of assisting individual plaintiffs in their suits against corporate defendants is unsatisfactory. Discovery concededly may work to the disadvantage as well as to the advantage of individual plaintiffs. Discovery, in

---

2. "The great weakness of pleading as a means for developing and presenting issues of fact for trial lay in its total lack of any means for testing the factual basis for the pleader's allegations and denials." Sunderland, "The Theory and Practice of Pre-Trial Procedure," 36 Mich. L. Rev. 215, 216. See also Ragland, Discovery Before Trial (1932), ch. 1.

other words, is not a one-way proposition. It is available in all types of cases at the behest of any party, individual or corporate, plaintiff or defendant. The problem thus far transcends the situation confronting this petitioner. And we must view that problem in light of the limitless situations where the particular kind of discovery sought by petitioner might be used.

We agree, of course, that the deposition-discovery rules are to be accorded a broad and liberal treatment. No longer can the time-honored cry of "fishing expedition" serve to preclude a party from inquiring into the facts underlying his opponent's case.[8] Mutual knowledge of all the relevant facts gathered by both parties is essential to proper litigation. To that end, either party may compel the other to disgorge whatever facts he has in his possession. The deposition-discovery procedure simply advances the stage at which the disclosure can be compelled from the time of trial to the period preceding it, thus reducing the possibility of surprise. But discovery, like all matters of procedure, has ultimate and necessary boundaries. As indicated by Rules 30(b) and (d) and 31(d), limitations inevitably arise when it can be shown that the examination is being conducted in bad faith or in such a manner as to annoy, embarrass or oppress the person subject to the inquiry. And as Rule 26(b) provides, further limitations come into existence when the inquiry touches upon the irrelevant or encroaches upon the recognized domains of privilege.

We also agree that the memoranda, statements and mental impressions in issue in this case fall outside the scope of the attorney-client privilege and hence are not protected from discovery on that basis. It is unnecessary here to delineate the content and scope of that privilege as recognized in the federal courts. For present purposes, it suffices to note that the protective cloak of this privilege does not extend to information which an attorney secures from a witness while acting for his client in anticipation of litigation. Nor does this privilege concern the memoranda, briefs, communications and other writings prepared by counsel for his own use in prosecuting his client's case; and it is equally unrelated to writings which reflect an attorney's mental impressions, conclusions, opinions or legal theories.

But the impropriety of invoking that privilege does not provide an answer to the problem before us. Petitioner has made more than an ordinary request for relevant, non-privileged facts in the possession of his adversaries or their counsel. He has sought discovery as of right of oral and written statements of witnesses whose identity is well known and whose availability to petitioner appears unimpaired. He has sought production of these matters after making the most searching inquiries of his opponents as to the circumstances surrounding the fatal accident, which inquiries were sworn to have been answered to the best of their information and belief. Interrogatories were directed toward all the events prior to, during and subsequent to the sinking of the tug. Full and honest answers to such broad inquiries would necessarily have included all pertinent information gleaned by Fortenbaugh through his interviews with the witnesses. Petitioner makes no suggestion, and we cannot assume, that the tug owners or Fortenbaugh were incomplete or dishonest

---

8. "One of the chief arguments against the 'fishing expedition' objection is the idea that discovery is mutual—that while a party may have to disclose his case, he can at the same time tie his opponent down to a definite position." Pike and Willis, "Federal Discovery in Operation," 7 Univ. of Chicago L. Rev. 297, 303.

in the framing of their answers. In addition, petitioner was free to examine the public testimony of the witnesses taken before the United States Steamboat Inspectors. We are thus dealing with an attempt to secure the production of written statements and mental impressions contained in the files and the mind of the attorney Fortenbaugh without any showing of necessity or any indication or claim that denial of such production would unduly prejudice the preparation of petitioner's case or cause him any hardship or injustice. For aught that appears, the essence of what petitioner seeks either has been revealed to him already through the interrogatories or is readily available to him direct from the witnesses for the asking.

The District Court, after hearing objections to petitioner's request, commanded Fortenbaugh to produce all written statements of witnesses and to state in substance any facts learned through oral statements of witnesses to him. Fortenbaugh was to submit any memoranda he had made of the oral statements so that the court might determine what portions should be revealed to petitioner. All of this was ordered without any showing by petitioner, or any requirement that he make a proper showing, of the necessity for the production of any of this material or any demonstration that denial of production would cause hardship or injustice. The court simply ordered production on the theory that the facts sought were material and were not privileged as constituting attorney-client communications.

In our opinion, neither Rule 26 nor any other rule dealing with discovery contemplates production under such circumstances. That is not because the subject matter is privileged or irrelevant, as those concepts are used in these rules. Here is simply an attempt, without purported necessity or justification, to secure written statements, private memoranda and personal recollections prepared or formed by an adverse party's counsel in the course of his legal duties. As such, it falls outside the arena of discovery and contravenes the public policy underlying the orderly prosecution and defense of legal claims. Not even the most liberal of discovery theories can justify unwarranted inquiries into the files and the mental impressions of an attorney.

Historically, a lawyer is an officer of the court and is bound to work for the advancement of justice while faithfully protecting the rightful interests of his clients. In performing his various duties, however, it is essential that a lawyer work with a certain degree of privacy, free from unnecessary intrusion by opposing parties and their counsel. Proper preparation of a client's case demands that he assemble information, sift what he considers to be the relevant from the irrelevant facts, prepare his legal theories and plan his strategy without undue and needless interference. That is the historical and the necessary way in which lawyers act within the framework|of our system of jurisprudence to promote justice and to protect their clients' interests. This work is reflected, of course, in interviews, statements, memoranda, correspondence, briefs, mental impressions, personal beliefs, and countless other tangible and intangible ways — aptly though roughly termed by the Circuit Court of Appeals in this case as the "work product of the lawyer." Were such materials open to opposing counsel on mere demand, much of what is now put down in writing would remain unwritten. An attorney's thoughts, heretofore inviolate, would not be his own. Inefficiency, unfairness and sharp practices would inevitably develop in the giving of legal advice and in the preparation of cases for trial. The effect on the legal profession would be demoralizing. And the interests of the clients and the cause of justice would be poorly served.

We do not mean to say that all written materials obtained or prepared by an adversary's counsel with an eye toward litigation are necessarily free from discovery in all cases. Where relevant and non-privileged facts remain hidden in an attorney's file and where production of those facts is essential to the preparation of one's case, discovery may properly be had. Such written statements and documents might, under certain circumstances, be admissible in evidence or give clues as to the existence or location of relevant facts. Or they might be useful for purposes of impeachment or corroboration. And production might be justified where the witnesses are no longer available or can be reached only with difficulty. Were production of written statements and documents to be precluded under such circumstances, the liberal ideals of the deposition-discovery portions of the Federal Rules of Civil Procedure would be stripped of much of their meaning. But the general policy against invading the privacy of an attorney's course of preparation is so well recognized and so essential to an orderly working of our system of legal procedure that a burden rests on the one who would invade that privacy to establish adequate reasons to justify production through a subpoena or court order. That burden, we believe, is necessarily implicit in the rules as now constituted.[10]

Rule 30(b), as presently written, gives the trial judge the requisite discretion to make a judgment as to whether discovery should be allowed as to written statements secured from witnesses. But in the instant case there was no room for that discretion to operate in favor of the petitioner. No attempt was made to establish any reason why Fortenbaugh should be forced to produce the written statements. There was only a naked, general demand for these materials as of right and a finding by the District Court that no recognizable privilege was involved. That was insufficient to justify discovery under these circumstances and the court should have sustained the refusal of the tug owners and Fortenbaugh to produce.

But as to oral statements made by witnesses to Fortenbaugh, whether presently in the form of his mental impressions or memoranda, we do not believe that any showing of necessity can be made under the circumstances of this case so as to justify production. Under ordinary conditions, forcing an attorney to repeat or write out all that witnesses have told him and to deliver the account to his adversary gives rise to grave dangers of inaccuracy and untrustworthiness. No legitimate purpose is served by such production. The practice forces the attorney to testify as to what he remembers or what he saw fit to write down regarding witnesses' remarks. Such testimony could not qualify as evidence; and to use it for impeachment or corroborative purposes would make the attorney much less an officer of the court and much more an ordinary witness. The standards of the profession would thereby suffer.

Denial of production of this nature does not mean that any material, non-privileged facts can be hidden from the petitioner in this case. He need not be unduly hindered in the preparation of his case, in the discovery of facts or in his anticipation of his opponents' position. Searching interrogatories directed to Fortenbaugh and the tug owners, production of written documents and statements upon a proper showing and direct interviews with the witnesses themselves all serve to

---

10. Rule 34 is explicit in its requirements that a party show good cause before obtaining a court order directing another party to produce documents. See Report of Proposed Amendments by Advisory Committee on Rules for Civil Procedure (June, 1946); 5 F.R.D. 433.

reveal the facts in Fortenbaugh's possession to the fullest possible extent consistent with public policy. Petitioner's counsel frankly admits that he wants the oral statements only to help prepare himself to examine witnesses and to make sure that he has overlooked nothing. That is insufficient under the circumstances to permit him an exception to the policy underlying the privacy of Fortenbaugh's professional activities. If there should be a rare situation justifying production of these matters, petitioner's case is not of that type.

We fully appreciate the wide-spread controversy among the members of the legal profession over the problem raised by this case. It is a problem that rests on what has been one of the most hazy frontiers of the discovery process. But until some rule or statute definitely prescribes otherwise, we are not justified in permitting discovery in a situation of this nature as a matter of unqualified right. When Rule 26 and the other discovery rules were adopted, this Court and the members of the bar in general certainly did not believe or contemplate that all the files and mental processes of lawyers were thereby opened to the free scrutiny of their adversaries. And we refuse to interpret the rules at this time so as to reach so harsh and unwarranted a result.

We therefore affirm the judgment of the Circuit Court of Appeals.

Affirmed.

MR. JUSTICE JACKSON, concurring.

The narrow question in this case concerns only one of thirty-nine interrogatories which defendants and their counsel refused to answer. As there was persistence in refusal after the court ordered them to answer it, counsel and clients were committed to jail by the district court until they should purge themselves of contempt.

The interrogatory asked whether statements were taken from the crews of the tugs involved in the accident, or of any other vessel, and demanded, "Attach hereto exact copies of all such statements if in writing, and if oral, set forth in detail the exact provisions of any such oral statements or reports." The question is simply whether such a demand is authorized by the rules relating to various aspects of "discovery."

The primary effect of the practice advocated here would be on the legal profession itself. But it too often is overlooked that the lawyer and the law office are indispensable parts of our administration of justice. Law-abiding people can go nowhere else to learn the ever changing and constantly multiplying rules by which they must behave and to obtain redress for their wrongs. The welfare and tone of the legal profession is therefore of prime consequence to society, which would feel the consequences of such a practice as petitioner urges secondarily but certainly.

"Discovery" is one of the working tools of the legal profession. It traces back to the equity bill of discovery in English Chancery practice and seems to have had a forerunner in Continental practice. See Ragland, Discovery Before Trial (1932) 13–16. Since 1848 when the draftsmen of New York's Code of Procedure recognized the importance of a better system of discovery, the impetus to extend and expand discovery, as well as the opposition to it, has come from within the Bar itself. It happens in this case that it is the plaintiff's attorney who demands such unprecedented latitude of discovery and, strangely enough, *amicus* briefs in his support have been filed by several labor unions representing plaintiffs as a class. It is the history of the movement for broader discovery, however, that in actual experience the chief opposition to its extension has come from lawyers who specialize in representing plaintiffs because defendants have made liberal use of it to force plaintiffs to disclose their cases in advance. See Report of the Commission on the Administration of Justice in New York State (1934) 330, 331; Ragland, Discovery Before Trial (1932) 35, 36. Discovery is a two-edged sword and we cannot decide this problem on any doctrine of extending help to one class of litigants.

It seems clear and long has been recognized that discovery should provide a party access to anything that is evidence in his case. *Cf.* Report of Commission on the Administration of Justice in New York State (1934) 41, 42. It seems equally clear that discovery should not nullify the privilege of confidential communication between attorney and client. But those principles give us no real assistance here because what is being sought is neither evidence nor is it a privileged communication between attorney and client.

To consider first the most extreme aspect of the requirement in litigation here, we find it calls upon counsel, if he has had any conversations with any of the crews of the vessels in question or of any other, to "set forth in detail the exact provision of any such oral statements or reports." Thus the demand is not for the production of a transcript in existence but calls for the creation of a written statement not in being. But the statement by counsel of what a witness told him is not evidence when written. Plaintiff could not introduce it to prove his case. What, then, is the purpose sought to be served by demanding this of adverse counsel?

Counsel for the petitioner candidly said on argument that he wanted this information to help prepare himself to examine witnesses, to make sure he overlooked nothing. He bases his claim to it in his brief on the view that the Rules were to do away with the old situation where a law suit developed into "a battle of wits between counsel." But a common law trial is and always should be an adversary proceeding. Discovery was hardly intended to enable a learned profession to perform its functions either without wits or on wits borrowed from the adversary.

The real purpose and the probable effect of the practice ordered by the district court would be to put trials on a level even lower than a "battle of wits." I can conceive of no practice more demoralizing to the Bar than to require a lawyer to write out and deliver to his adversary an account of what witnesses have told him. Even if his recollection were perfect, the statement would be his language permeated with his inferences. Every one who has tried it knows that it is almost impossible so fairly to record the expressions and emphasis of a witness that when he testifies in the environment of the court and under the influence of the leading question there will not be departures in some respects. Whenever the testimony of the witness would differ from the "exact" statement the lawyer had delivered, the lawyer's statement would be whipped out to impeach the witness. Counsel producing his adversary's "inexact" statement could lose nothing by saying, "Here is a contradiction, gentlemen of the jury. I do not know whether it is my adversary or his witness who is not telling the truth, but one is not." Of course, if this practice were adopted, that scene would be repeated over and over again. The lawyer who delivers such statements often would find himself branded a deceiver afraid to take the stand to support his own version of the witness's conversation with him, or else he will have to go on the stand to defend his own credibility—perhaps against that of his chief witness, or possibly even his client.

Every lawyer dislikes to take the witness stand and will do so only for grave reasons. This is partly because it is not his role; he is almost invariably a poor witness. But he steps out of professional character to do it. He regrets it; the profession discourages it. But the practice advocated here is one which would force him to be a witness, not as to what he has seen or done but as to other witnesses' stories, and not because he wants to do so but in self-defense.

And what is the lawyer to do who has interviewed one whom he believes to be a biased, lying or hostile witness to get his unfavorable statements and know what to meet? He must record and deliver such statements even though he would not vouch for the credibility of the witness by calling him. Perhaps the other side would not want to call him either, but the attorney is open to the charge of suppressing evidence at the trial if he fails to call such a hostile witness even though he never regarded him as reliable or truthful.

Having been supplied the names of the witnesses, petitioner's lawyer gives no reason why he cannot interview them himself. If an employee-witness refuses to tell his story, he, too, may be examined under the Rules. He may be compelled on discovery as fully as on the trial to disclose his version of the facts. But that is his own disclosure — it can be used to impeach him if he contradicts it and such a deposition is not useful to promote an unseemly disagreement between the witness and the counsel in the case. . . .

NOTES AND QUESTIONS

1. Are you persuaded by the Court that conferral of the work-product exception is necessary to facilitate effective representation? Do you think that Fortenbaugh would not have interviewed the witnesses if he knew that a court might later order him to disclose the content of those interviews?

2. Note that under both *Hickman* and present Rule 26(b)(3)(A)(ii), work product, other than an attorney's mental impressions, is only conditionally privileged; the material is subject to discovery if a party can demonstrate "substantial need" and that the party is unable "without undue hardship, [to] obtain their substantial equivalent by other means." This standard will normally be met if an important witness is no longer available or no longer remembers the events in question. *See* 8 C. Wright et al., Federal Practice and Procedure §2025 (3d ed. 2010).

3. Why does the Court (as well as present Rule 26(b)(3)(B)) make an attorney's mental impressions absolutely immune from discovery? Are mental impressions immune from discovery because it is important that they remain confidential or because such discovery would require testimony by the attorney?

4. Don't "contention" interrogatories probe an attorney's mental impressions and legal theories? How are they treated differently from undiscoverable work product?

5. Do you agree that it would be inappropriate to require an opposing attorney to testify? Do attorneys make worse witnesses than other interested parties?

6. Where do you draw the line between discoverable and nondiscoverable work product? What constitutes an attorney's mental impression? Would the Rockwell scanned-document files constitute mental impression? What if the files only included documents that the attorney deemed relevant?

7. Attorney work product is protected to varying degrees in the state courts. In Texas and Pennsylvania, only pure "opinion" work product is protected. *See* Elizabeth G. Thornburg, *Rethinking Work Product*, 77 Va. L. Rev. 1515, 1583 n.31 (1991). It is thus conceivable that an attorney might prepare in anticipation of litigation what she expects to be a confidential document only to find herself litigating in a forum that does not recognize the privilege.

8. A document need not be authored by an attorney in order to qualify for work product protection so long as it was prepared at the request of counsel in contemplation of litigation. *United States v. Nobles*, 422 U.S. 225, 229 (1975).

Suppose Rockwell routinely investigated the accident scene every time one of its planes crashed. Would the investigation report be protected by the work product exception? *Compare Rakus v. Erie-Lackawanna Railroad Co.*, 76 F.R.D. 145 (W.D.N.Y. 1977) (routine railroad accident report prepared in the "ordinary course of business" not protected) *with Suggs v. Whitaker*, 152 F.R.D. 501, 507 (M.D.N.C. 1993) (insurance adjuster's automobile accident report protected since insured's negligence was apparent, "and the prospect of litigation [was] immediate"). The crucial question seems to be whether the "primary purpose" in generating the document was to defend potential litigation:

> ("[T]he anticipation of future litigation must have been the primary motivation which led to the creation of the documents. . . . Documents which do not refer to work product prepared by an attorney or other agent of a party to aid in forthcoming litigation, and which were generated in the ordinary course of business, are discoverable.") . . . The foregoing emphasizes the problematic situation arising when a party's documentation reflects concerns for both safety about the product or workplace in issue and potential litigation. As a practical matter, a company seeking to avoid potential litigation over an unsafe product or workplace will use internal investigations for both purposes simultaneously. Deciphering the "driving force" behind the documentation of such investigations may be difficult indeed.

Cameron v. General Motors Corp., 158 F.R.D. 581, 588–589 (D.S.C. 1994).

9. Why do you think that Fortenbaugh decided to face contempt of court and imprisonment rather than produce the discovery? Recall the final-judgment rule of appellate jurisdiction: An appeal may normally be taken only from a judgment disposing of the entire lawsuit. Discovery orders are not final judgments and are not normally appealable before the conclusion of the litigation (at which point they may be moot). The contempt citation, in contrast, is a free-standing final judgment. Fortenbaugh was thus able to obtain appellate review of the district court's order to produce the discovery. The interlocutory appealability of discovery orders is discussed further in Chapter 9.

5.   *Duty to Update*

What happens if a party learns of new information after responding to discovery? Rule 26(e) requires a party "in a timely manner" to supplement her prior responses and initial disclosures "if the party learns that in some material respect the information disclosed is incomplete or incorrect."

Suppose in your representation of Rockwell, your initial document search yields no evidence that Rockwell knowingly used a dangerous deicing design. Trial has been scheduled in three months, and a settlement conference is scheduled for next week. The day before the settlement conference, you find the "smoking gun": a document that concludes that the cost of fixing the deicing design would not be worth the minimal number of lives saved by a more costly design. Must you deliver the document to plaintiffs before the settlement conference? May you conclude a settlement agreement without disclosing the existence of the document?

6. *Procedures to Block and Compel Discovery*

What happens when a party seeks to obtain discovery arguably beyond the permissible bounds? Who has the burden of seeking judicial intervention: the party seeking discovery or the responding party?

There are two principal blocking devices available to the responding party, depending on the context: objections and protective orders.

a. Objections

Objections are unilateral refusals to produce the requested information; they place the burden of seeking judicial intervention on the party seeking discovery. Objections can be interposed in response to interrogatories, questions at depositions, requests for production of documents, and requests for admissions. Objections may be asserted on the basis that the discovery is beyond the scope permitted under the Federal Rules, is sought in an improper manner, or calls for the disclosure of privileged information. Objections to production of documents must "state whether any responsive materials are being withheld on the basis of that objection." Fed. R. Civ. P. 34(b)(2)(C). With the exception of objections at depositions, the objection is in lieu of a response.

At depositions, the testimony is "taken subject to the objection." That means that the witness must answer the question notwithstanding the objection. An attorney may instruct her client not to answer "only when necessary to preserve a privilege, to enforce a limitation on evidence directed by the court," or to present a motion to the court to terminate a deposition taken "unreasonably to annoy, embarrass, or oppress the deponent." Fed. R. Civ. P. 30(c)(2), 30(d)(3)(A).

b. Orders to Compel

Once a party asserts an objection in lieu of an answer, the validity of that objection can be tested by Motion to Compel under Rule 37(a). If the court finds that the objection was unfounded, it will order a response and award the moving party attorneys' fees incurred in making the motion, unless it finds that the objection was "substantially justified." Fed. R. Civ. P. 37(a)(5)(A). Alternatively, if the court finds that the objection was well founded, it will order attorneys' fees to be paid by the moving party. Fed. R. Civ. P. 37(a)(5)(B).

c.   Protective Orders

Instead of waiting for the party seeking discovery to move to compel, a person against whom discovery is sought can preemptively seek judicial intervention in the form of a protective order under Rule 26(c). Such preemptive intervention is the only way to prevent or limit the scope of a deposition. It is also the only effective relief if the discovery sought is not actually objectionable, but is simply sensitive, embarrassing, or confidential.

The court has a great deal of flexibility under Rule 26(c) to craft effective relief. Not only can the court order that discovery not be conducted into a particular area, but it can limit how the discovery will be taken and who will have access to the discovery. For particularly sensitive matters, the court can order that only the attorneys have access to the information and that they keep the information confidential. As in the case of other discovery disputes, the court has the authority to award attorneys' fees to the prevailing party in a request for a protective order. Fed. R. Civ. P. 26(c)(3).

Rule 26(c) requires that "good cause" be shown for the issuance of a protective order. Parties often seek to establish that the discovery would disclose secret "proprietary information," the disclosure of which would put the party at a commercial disadvantage. Courts will compel such discovery if relevant to the action but frequently limit its dissemination. *See, e.g., Coca-Cola Bottling Co. v. Coca Cola Co.*, 107 F.R.D. 288, 300 (D. Del. 1985) (formula for making Coca Cola must be revealed by defendant, but only to plaintiff's counsel).

What if the "good cause" that defendant asserts is that public dissemination of the discovery will subject defendant to similar suits by other plaintiffs? For example, what if plaintiff discovers a document showing that Rockwell was aware of a significant risk that the deicing boot could result in engine failure in a small number of cases? Could Rockwell ask that the document remain confidential because its dissemination would lead to other "negative publicity"? Would it matter whether the deicing boot was still in use on other aircraft? Does the court have a legitimate interest in the public dissemination of the information, or should it limit its consideration to whether the parties have sufficient information to pursue their own claims?

In *Seattle Times v. Rhinehart*, 467 U.S. 20 (1984), the Supreme Court held that the dissemination of information obtained in discovery was not guaranteed by the First Amendment of the United States Constitution. In that case, the Court upheld a trial court's protective order prohibiting defendant newspaper from publishing information obtained from plaintiff in pretrial discovery: "Liberal discovery is provided for the sole purpose of assisting in the preparation and trial, or the settlement, of litigated disputes." Nonetheless, there remains a heated controversy over whether it is appropriate for the public to have access to discovery material. *Compare* Arthur R. Miller, *Confidentiality, Protective Orders, and Public Access to the Courts*, 105 Harv. L. Rev. 427 (1991); Richard L. Marcus, *Myth and Reality in Protective Order Litigation*, 69 Cornell L. Rev. 1 (1983) (arguing that public dissemination of discovery threatens to undermine volitional compliance with discovery rules) *with* Lloyd Doggett & Michael J. Muchetti, *Public Access to Public Courts: Discouraging Secrecy in the Public Interest*, 69 Tex. L. Rev. 643 (1991) (defending Texas state court rule providing greater public access to discovery documents). *See generally Symposium: Secrecy in Litigation*, 81 Chi.-Kent L. Rev. No. 2 (2006).

Note, however, that even when a protective order issues, it is not all powerful. For example, a subpoena issued by an investigating grand jury may override a protective order in a civil case, requiring production of the requested materials. *See In re: Grand Jury*, 286 F.3d 153 (3d Cir. 2002) (requiring production absent exceptional circumstances); *In re Grand Jury Subpoena (Roach)*, 138 F.3d 442 (1st Cir. 1998) (same); In re *Grand Jury Subpoena Served on Meserve, Mumper & Hughes*, 62 F.3d 1222 (9th Cir. 1995) (grand jury subpoena always trumps civil protective order). *But see Martindell v. International Telephone & Telegraph Corp.*, 594 F.2d 291 (2d Cir. 1979) (grand jury subpoena never trumps civil protective order unless exceptional circumstances exist).

d. Sanctions

Discovery under the Federal Rules relies heavily on the good faith of the litigants. The parties are expected to provide the necessary information without judicial intervention. There are, however, a broad range of judicial sanctions available to the court to enforce the duty to disclose.

Rule 37 provides a two-track response to nondisclosure. First, as we saw above, a party can seek an order to compel a response to discovery under Rule 37(a)(3). Unlike a mere discovery request, an order to compel is a judicial directive, the violation of which can result in contempt of court, as well as a range of other sanctions under Rule 37(b). The court can dismiss the action, preclude the noncomplying party from introducing proof on the matter sought, or deem the matter conclusively established for the opposing party. *See, e.g., Insurance Co. of Ireland Ltd. v. Compagnie de Bauxites*, 456 U.S. 694 (1982) (as sanction for defendant's refusal to provide information concerning its amenability to personal jurisdiction, court held jurisdiction over defendant was conclusively established). In cases of repeated stonewalling, the court can issue a default against the disobedient party—it loses the entire case. *See National Hockey League v. Metropolitan Hockey Club, Inc.*, 429 U.S. 874 (1976) (upholding district court's dismissal of plaintiff's case for failure to answer interrogatories).

Second, in the event of a complete failure of a party to respond to discovery (as opposed to not answering specific questions), the court can impose sanctions directly under Rule 37(d), without first issuing an order to compel. This principle applies to failures to file answers to interrogatories, responses to a request for Rule 34 inspection, or appearances at a deposition. All of the Rule 37(b) sanctions are available in such cases, except contempt of court (because the party has not disobeyed a judicial command).

All of the Rule 37 sanctions require that the party seeking sanctions first make an effort to resolve the dispute with the disobedient party informally. Indeed, most lawyers will not even seek sanctions until they have given their opponent enough rope to hang themselves. Courts are more inclined to issue serious sanctions after a party has been given repeated opportunities to comply with discovery.

In addition to sanctions under the Federal Rules, a number of jurisdictions recognize a common law tort of "spoliation of evidence." In those jurisdictions, an independent claim may be asserted for the intentional destruction of evidence. *See, e.g., Smith v. Superior Court*, 151 Cal. App. 3d 491, 198 Cal. Rptr. 829 (1984). *See also* A. Benjamin Spencer, *The Preservation Obligation: Regulating and Sanctioning Pre-Litigation Spoliation in Federal Court*, 79 Fordham L. Rev. 2005 (2011) (suggesting amendments to Federal Rules to create uniform standards for spoliation in federal court). In some circumstances, the intentional destruction of evidence may also constitute the crime of obstruction of justice. *See Arthur Andersen LLP v. United States*, 544 U.S. 696 (2005) (holding that government must prove conscious wrongdoing in order to convict). For an argument that the threat of sanctions under Rule 37 is insufficient to deter abusive conduct in large-stakes litigation, *see* John S. Beckerman, *Confronting Civil Discovery's Fatal Flaws*, 85 Minn. L. Rev. 505 (2000).

7. *Note on International Discovery*

Up to this point we have focused exclusively on the use of discovery to obtain information from sources within the United States. What happens when information pertinent to a U.S. proceeding is outside of the United States? Discovery in other legal systems is typically far more limited than under U.S. law, and U.S. litigants can encounter conflicting obligations when they seek discovery abroad. We briefly survey here some of those differences and describe the bind in which transnational litigation can place litigants. For a more complete examination of these issues, *see* Gary B. Born & Peter B. Rutledge, International Civil Litigation in United States Courts (5th ed. 2011) at pp.1000–1024.

a. Comparing Common Law and Civil Law Systems

Understanding that there are variations within each system, we can begin by breaking the world into two general legal systems — common law systems and civil law systems.

Perhaps surprisingly, discovery practice even in other common law systems varies significantly from U.S. practice. In both the United States and England, there is a period of information exchange that follows the initial pleading and precedes the trial. In English practice, after the "statements of case" — formerly known as pleadings — there is an exchange of information similar to the unilateral disclosure required in the United States under Fed. R. Civ. P. 26(a). The main form of disclosure concerns documents. Under Civil Procedure Rule (CPR) 31.6, a party, pursuant to court order, may be required to disclose, among other things: (1) the documents on which that party will rely; (2) the documents that adversely affect a party's case; (3) the documents that adversely affect an opponent's case; (4) the documents that support an opponent's case. This form of document disclosure is called "standard disclosure" and is one of several options the court has in managing disclosure. CPR 31.5. Also, the court can order disclosure of documents against a third party. CPR 31.17. Note, however, that depositions as conducted in the United States are not available in British practice. Prehearing examinations are available only upon court order under CPR 34.8. The primary function of the examination is as a substitute for live testimony; it is not a discovery device. For more on disclosure practice in England, *see generally* Neil Andrews, 1 Andrews on Civil Process at pp. 261–285 (2013); Adrian Zuckerman, Zuckerman on Civil Procedure, Chapter 15 (3d ed. 2013).

However, in England, codified practice directives called "Pre-Action Protocols" provide for far more extensive exchange of information *before* the pleadings are filed. The protocols "outline the steps parties should take to seek information from and provide information to each other about a *prospective* legal claim." Practice Direction, Protocols, 1.3 (emphasis added). There are several pre-action protocols that address specific types of claims. For example, the malpractice protocol requires that a claimant write a "Letter of Claim" to the professional that includes: (a) the names of the parties involved; (b) a chronological summary of the key facts on which the claim is based (supplemented by the enclosure of key documents); (c) any reasonable requests which the claimant needs to make for documents relevant to the dispute which are held by the professional; (d) the allegations of wrongdoing against the professional; (e) an explanation of how the alleged error has caused the loss claimed; and (f) an estimate of the financial loss suffered by the claimant (supplemented by supporting documents). Practice Direction, Professional Negligence Pre-Action Protocol, B2.2. The professional must then provide a letter of settlement or letter of response that includes the professional's version of the events and any additional documents that the professional relies upon. Pre-Action Protocol for Professional Negligence, 9.2. Only after the professional responds and only if there is no settlement can the claimant move on to commence proceedings. Note that even if a case is not covered by a Pre-Action Protocol, the parties are still directed to exchange information and documents relevant to the claim. Practice Direction, Pre-Action Conduct and Protocols, 6. Under certain circumstances, a court may order pre-action disclosure. CPR 31.16. A court may also stay any proceeding and impose financial sanctions for noncompliance with Pre-Action Protocols. Practice Direction—Pre-Action Conduct and Protocols, 15.

Civil law systems include most countries on the European continent, including France, Germany, Italy, and Spain, as well as Latin America and North Asia. Civil law discovery practice differs dramatically from American practice. The pleadings in civil law systems are very specific and usually refer to attached documents that establish the facts asserted. The pleadings are based on the independent investigations of the parties, as well as information exchanged by the parties. There is little disclosure from and little participation by nonparties. There is *no* opportunity for pretrial discovery. Instead, the court takes control of the litigation immediately after the pleadings are filed. For a comprehensive overview of civil and common law approaches to obtaining information, *see* Oscar Chase et. al., Civil Litigation in Comparative Context, Chapter 4 (2017).

In civil law systems, the judge actually gathers evidence. The judge may request additional information as he or she sees fit by calling and questioning witnesses or by calling for the production of relevant documents. If a party would like an opponent to produce a document, that party may apply to the court, in a very specific application, to order production. Note that in civil law countries, there is little or no discovery of information unfavorable to a party's case.

Professor Hazard has argued that the absence of discovery in civil law systems is related to the absence of the jury there; he asserts that pretrial discovery is more important in a system based on a jury trial in order efficiently to use the lay jury's time. *See* Geoffrey C. Hazard, Jr., *Discovery and the Role of the Judge in Civil Law Jurisdictions*, 73 Notre Dame L. Rev. 1017, 1020 (1998). *Cf.* Oscar Chase, *American "Exceptionalism" and Comparative Procedure*, 50 Am. J. Comp. L. 277, 292 (2002).

b.   Transnational Discovery

Considering the differences outlined above, it is not surprising that many foreign observers regard U.S.-style discovery as excessive, and foreign governments are not always cooperative in attempts by U.S. courts to obtain information from foreign sources.

Many countries have enacted "blocking statutes"—laws that render entities subject to civil or criminal liability for producing certain documents in their jurisdiction for use in proceedings in another country. What happens when a U.S. court orders the production of information subject to such constraints? The Supreme Court provided some guidance in *Société Internationale Pour Participations Industrielles et Commerciales, S.A. v. Rogers*, 357 U.S. 197 (1958). In *Rogers*, a Swiss corporation brought suit against the U.S. government for recovery of property (valued at more than $100 million) seized under the Trading with the Enemy Act. The U.S. government requested, under Fed. R. Civ. P. 34, that plaintiff produce certain banking records located in Switzerland. Production of the documents may have led to the imposition of criminal sanctions under Swiss law, including fine and imprisonment. After several extensions, the district court granted the U.S. government's motion to dismiss the complaint for failure to comply with the production order.

The Supreme Court reversed, but it declined to create a broad privilege relieving a party from the duty to comply with discovery simply because the discovery would be in violation of foreign law: "United States courts should be free to require claimants of seized assets who face legal obstacles under the laws of their own countries to make all . . . efforts [to obtain a relaxation of the foreign penal law] to the maximum of their ability. . . . " *Id.* at 205. However, the Court did find the dismissal for failure to produce the documents unwarranted: "Rule 37 should not be construed to authorize dismissal of this complaint because of petitioner's noncompliance with a pretrial production order when it has been established that failure to comply has been due to inability, and not to willfulness, bad faith, or any fault of petitioner." *Id.* at 212. The Court suggested that the lower court could consider a range of alternative responses on remand, including precluding plaintiff from relying at trial on any information contained in the documents; it was merely foreclosed from using dismissal on the merits as a discovery sanction.

These kinds of tensions gave rise to a desire for greater international cooperation in providing access to information located abroad. Efforts undertaken at the Hague Conference on Private International Law produced the Hague Convention on the Taking of Evidence Abroad in Civil or Commercial Matters, effective in 1972. The objective of the Convention was to provide procedures for obtaining information and taking evidence located in another country with the cooperation and aid of that country, for use in the country where the proceedings were pending. As of 2016, over 50 countries, including the United States, are parties to that Convention. *See generally* Gary B. Born & Peter B. Rutledge, International Civil Litigation in United States Courts (5th ed. 2011) at pp. 1026–1044.

It should be noted that the procedures of the Hague Evidence Convention are designed for obtaining "evidence" that is intended for "use in judicial proceedings, commenced or contemplated." The Convention provides procedures for obtaining evidence through the use of "letters of request." Under the

Convention each Contracting State designates a Central Authority that under-takes to receive a letter of request — a request for information in the proper form — coming from a judicial authority of another Contracting State. The Cen-tral Authority then transmits the request to the proper authority for execution of the request. Contracting States are required to use methods of compulsion available under their internal law to fulfill the letter of request. Although Con-tracting States were prepared to execute letters of request to provide information *at a trial or hearing*, many States were resistant to assisting U.S. discovery practice. Accordingly, the Convention permits Contracting States to declare that they will not execute letters of request for the purpose of "obtaining *pre-trial* discovery of documents," and a number of States have made this reservation. However, States have not necessarily refused all document discovery requests under the excep-tion, but rather have used it to refuse requests that lack sufficient specificity or that have not been reviewed for relevancy by the requesting court.

In the United States, it was initially unclear whether a party seeking discovery abroad under the Federal Rules of Civil Procedure must first seek the information pursuant to the Evidence Convention. The Supreme Court addressed the issue in *Société Nationale Industrielle Aerospatiale v. United States District Court*, 482 U.S. 522 (1987). In *Aerospatiale*, a U.S. plaintiff, injured in an airplane crash in Iowa, brought a product liability suit against the French manufacturer of the plane. The plaintiff sought discovery of certain documents, answers to interrogatories, and requests for admissions. The French defendant argued that because it was a foreign party and the evidence was located abroad, the plaintiff was required to seek the information through the Evidence Convention. The plaintiff argued that the Convention did not apply when there was jurisdiction over the defendant and the information was to be produced for proceedings in a U.S. court; in those circumstances, plaintiff con-tended, the Federal Rules of Civil Procedure applied. The Supreme Court, in a 5-4 opinion, upheld the order for discovery issued by the magistrate-judge while rejecting the extreme positions of both parties. Justice Stevens for the majority found that the Convention "unambiguously supports the conclusion that it was intended to establish optional procedures that would facilitate the taking of evidence abroad." 482 U.S. at 538. The majority opinion also refused to require a first resort to the Convention and left to the trial court the decision as to how to proceed as between the Federal Rules and the Evidence Convention "based on its knowledge of the cause and of the claims and interests of the parties and the governments whose statutes and policies they invoke." *Id.* at 546. Justice Blackmun's dissent for four Justices urged that in the interest of comity there should be a presumption of first resort to the procedures of the Convention, unless it was clearly inappropriate.

When information is located in the United States, parties to foreign proceed-ings could, of course, proceed via the Hague Convention. However, there is a more direct route available through 28 U.S.C. §1782, which provides:

> the district court of the district in which a person resides or is found may order him to give his testimony or statement or to produce a document or other thing for use in a proceeding in a foreign or international tribunal, including criminal investigations conducted before formal accusation. The order may be made pursuant to a letter rogatory issued, or request made, by a foreign or international tribunal or upon the application of

any interested person and may direct that the testimony or statement be given, or the document or other thing be produced, before a person appointed by the court.

The effect of 28 U.S.C. §1782 is to allow parties to a foreign tribunal to obtain American-style discovery for use in foreign proceedings in situations even where it is unlikely that the foreign court itself would have allowed a request for such information. In the only case to reach the Supreme Court, *Intel Corp. v. Advanced Micro Devices, Inc.*, 542 U.S. 241 (2004), the Court refused to impose a requirement that the information should not be available if the information would not be discoverable in the foreign jurisdiction if the materials were located there. Has §1782 become a means for the United States to impose its broad discovery practice on the rest of the world?

8. *Role of Masters and Magistrate-Judges in the Discovery Process*

We have seen a variety of techniques for judicial intervention in the discovery process. In many cases, it is the judge who makes the relevant rulings and orders, but often another judicial actor—either a magistrate or special master—undertakes this role.

In 1968, the Federal Magistrates Act, 28 U.S.C. §636, created full-time judicial officers who could handle the pretrial activity of civil litigation, along with other duties. The purpose of the Magistrates Act was to relieve district judges of their substantial pretrial burden in civil cases, leaving them free to devote more time to the central task of adjudication—hearing cases and writing opinions. In subsequent revisions to the Act and concomitant Federal Rules of Civil Procedure (Rules 72–76) dealing with procedures to "refer" cases to magistrate-judges, the powers of magistrate-judges were spelled out in greater detail.

For example, magistrate-judges may enter a scheduling order when authorized by local rule. *See* Fed. R. Civ. P. 16(b). A federal district judge may designate a magistrate-judge to supervise discovery and/or to "hear and determine" disputed matters that arise in the course of discovery. Rulings on these nondispositive matters are subject to review by the district judge on a clearly erroneous/contrary to law standard. *See* 28 U.S.C. §636(b)(1)(A).

In addition, the district court may refer to a magistrate-judge a dispositive-type matter, such as summary judgment, judgment on the pleadings, or motion to dismiss; however, in such a case the magistrate-judge makes only a "recommendation" that is then reviewed *de novo* by the district court. 28 U.S.C. §636(b)(1)(B), (C).

Upon consent of the parties, a magistrate-judge can also exercise the full civil jurisdiction of a district judge, including the conduct of a jury or nonjury trial. 28 U.S.C. §636(c)(1). Although the preferred practice in such a case is for the magistrate-judge to obtain the consent of all parties in writing, the Supreme Court has held that parties may also manifest their consent to a proceeding before a magistrate-judge by their conduct—for example, by participating fully in the proceeding and failing to object when the magistrate-judge indicates her belief that all parties have consented. *See Roell v. Withrow*, 538 U.S. 580 (2003).

An alternative to a reference of matters to a magistrate-judge is the use of a special master in the pretrial and discovery phases of litigation. Unlike magistrate-judges, who are salaried judicial officers appointed for a term of years with qualifications established for their selection, special masters are private lawyers, retired judges, or legal academics who are appointed for a particular case to assist the judge. Authorization for appointment of special masters is provided for in Fed. R. Civ. P. 53, but there are few guidelines other than the requirement in Rule 53(a)(1) that appointment of a master be "warranted by . . . some exceptional condition, or . . . the need to perform an accounting or resolve a difficult computation of damages; or . . . address pretrial and posttrial matters that cannot be effectively and timely addressed by an available district judge or magistrate."

As Professor Amalia Kessler has shown, masters and magistrates have sometimes performed functions associated more with "inquisitorial" systems like that in France, where the judge exercises much more control over the content and shape of the evidentiary record than is typical in our party-driven, "adversarial" system. Kessler has argued that some abusive practices in modern litigation can be traced to a poorly considered incorporation of inquisitorial methods into an adversarial framework. *See* Amalia D. Kessler, *Our Inquisitorial Tradition: Equity Procedure, Due Process, and the Search for an Alternative to the Adversarial*, 90 Cornell L. Rev. 1181 (2005). The modern use of special masters has expanded to include their handling of a broad range of tasks, including the management of discovery, facilitation of settlement, and ruling on pretrial motions and discovery disputes. However, the "exceptional condition" limitation provides a restriction on the use of special masters even in this role. Thus, special masters are most commonly found in large complex multiparty cases or those involving complicated technical and scientific issues.

Unless the parties have otherwise stipulated, the court must provide *de novo* review of any factual or legal determination by the master to which any party objects. Only rulings concerning "procedural" matters are subject to an abuse of discretion standard. Rule 53 also imposes constraints on the judge's *ex parte* communications with the master and provides for disqualification of masters who would have been subject to disqualification as judges.

For a general discussion of the roles of magistrates and special masters in the discovery process, *see* Linda Silberman, *Judicial Adjuncts Revisited: The Proliferation of Ad Hoc Procedure*, 137 U. Pa. L. Rev. 2131 (1989). For a fuller treatment of the activities of special masters, *see* Thomas E. Willging et al., Special Masters' Incidence and Activity (Federal Judicial Center 2000).

9.   *Summary Judgment*

The ultimate objective of litigation is the favorable adjudication of the case by the court. That adjudication can come at a number of different stages in litigation. We have already seen in Rule 12 a mechanism for a very early disposition of a case. A motion for failure to state a claim under 12(b)(6) is normally granted before the answer is filed, and motion for judgment on the pleadings under Rule 12(c) can be disposed of shortly thereafter. However, their use is largely limited to testing the *legal sufficiency* of the complaint. In deciding a Rule 12(b)(6) or 12(c) motion, the court normally assumes the truth of the matters alleged in the complaint.

What if a pleading is legally sufficient, but a party lacks evidentiary support for its position, even after conducting discovery? Obviously, such a deficiency could be established at trial. But trials are expensive, and if the result is foreordained, there is no reason to put the parties to the trouble and expense of further litigation. Moreover, if the case is to be tried by a jury, it may be inappropriate to allow the jury to adjudicate when there is legally insufficient evidence for one party.

Accordingly, another pretrial device to test the factual and/or legal sufficiency of a pleading is available in modern practice. This is called a *motion for summary judgment*, provided for by Rule 56 in federal practice. The function of summary judgment is to ascertain whether there are evidentiary disputes that must be resolved by the trier of fact at trial. The court, on summary judgment determines whether a party has satisfied its burden of producing evidence that, if believed by the trier of fact, would support a judgment in its favor. If a party cannot meet that burden (called the *burden of production*), the judge will not allow the case (or parts thereof) to proceed to trial.

How does the court determine the existence of evidence without having a trial? The parties direct the court's attention to the discovery already conducted (e.g., deposition transcripts, documents, answers to interrogatories, etc.), as well as *affidavits*, sworn statements of witnesses whom a party intends to call to testify at trial. Obviously, with the evidence in this form, the court is not in a position to assess how credible or compelling the proof is. The function of the motion is not to determine who has the stronger case, but whether the evidence presents a "genuine dispute as to any material fact" requiring a trial to resolve.

Defendant or plaintiff (or both) may move for summary judgment. The court can use summary judgment to dismiss the case or issue a judgment for the claimant. However, the burden on the moving party will vary significantly depending on whether the moving party has the burden of production at trial. Typically, the plaintiff carries the burden of producing evidence on every contested element of its complaint. In the absence of any evidence, the court will issue judgment for the defendant. Thus, when defendant (or the party defending the claim) moves to dismiss the claim on summary judgment, defendant must demonstrate *the absence* of evidence in the record supporting the claim. Defendant does not have to affirmatively disprove plaintiff's allegations, but only that plaintiff cannot identify sufficient evidence in the record to support its case.

On the other hand, when *plaintiff* (or any claimant) moves for summary judgment, its burden is significantly higher. Plaintiff (or the claimant) must demonstrate not only the existence of supporting evidence, but that the evidence conclusively demonstrates the truth of its allegations — i.e., that *all* of the pertinent evidence points in only one direction. If there is any conflicting evidence, the court will deny the motion. In effect, a moving plaintiff attempts to shift the burden of production to the defendant by presenting overwhelming proof.

Keep these differences in mind as you read the following case.

Celotex Corp. v. Catrett

477 U.S. 317 (1986)

JUSTICE REHNQUIST delivered the opinion of the Court.

The United States District Court for the District of Columbia granted the motion of petitioner Celotex Corporation for summary judgment against respondent Catrett because the latter was unable to produce evidence in support of her allegation in her wrongful-death complaint that the decedent had been exposed to petitioner's asbestos products. A divided panel of the Court of Appeals for the District of Columbia Circuit reversed, however, holding that petitioner's failure to support its motion with evidence tending to *negate* such exposure precluded the entry of summary judgment in its favor. *Catrett v. Johns-Manville Sales Corp.*, 756 F.2d 181 (1985). This view conflicted with that of the Third Circuit in *In re Japanese Electronic Products*, 723 F.2d 238 (1983), rev'd on other grounds *sub nom. Matsushita Electric Industrial Co. v. Zenith Radio Corp.*, 475 U.S. 574 (1986). We granted certiorari to resolve the conflict and now reverse the decision of the District of Columbia Circuit.

Respondent commenced this lawsuit in September 1980, alleging that the death in 1979 of her husband, Louis H. Catrett, resulted from his exposure to products containing asbestos manufactured or distributed by 15 named corporations. Respondent's complaint sounded in negligence, breach of warranty, and strict liability. Two of the defendants filed motions challenging the District Court's *in personam* jurisdiction, and the remaining 13, including petitioner, filed motions for summary judgment. Petitioner's motion, which was first filed in September 1981, argued that summary judgment was proper because respondent had "failed to produce evidence that any [Celotex] product . . . was the proximate cause of the injuries alleged within the jurisdictional limits of [the District] Court." In particular, petitioner noted that respondent had failed to identify, in answering interrogatories specifically requesting such information, any witnesses who could testify about the decedent's exposure to petitioner's asbestos products. In response to petitioner's summary judgment motion, respondent then produced three documents which she claimed "demonstrate that there is a genuine material factual dispute" as to whether the decedent had ever been exposed to petitioner's asbestos products. The three documents included a transcript of a deposition of the decedent, a letter from an official of one of the decedent's former employers whom petitioner planned to call as a trial witness, and a letter from an insurance company to respondent's attorney, all tending to establish that the decedent had been exposed to petitioner's asbestos products in Chicago during 1970–1971. Petitioner, in turn, argued that the three documents were inadmissible hearsay and thus could not be considered in opposition to the summary judgment motion.

In July 1982, almost two years after the commencement of the lawsuit, the District Court granted all of the motions filed by the various defendants. The court explained that it was granting petitioner's summary judgment motion because "there [was] no showing that the plaintiff was exposed to the defendant Celotex's product in the District of Columbia or elsewhere within the statutory period." Respondent appealed only the grant of summary judgment in favor of petitioner, and a divided panel of the District of Columbia Circuit reversed. The majority of the Court of Appeals held that petitioner's summary judgment motion was rendered "fatally defective" by the fact that petitioner "made no effort to adduce *any* evidence, in the form of affidavits or otherwise, to support its motion." According to the majority, Rule 56(e) of the Federal Rules of Civil Procedure,* and this Court's decision in *Adickes v. S.H. Kress & Co.*, 398 U.S. 144 (1970), establish that "the party opposing the motion for summary judgment bears the burden of responding *only after* the moving party has met its burden of coming forward with proof of the absence of any genuine issues of material fact." 756 F.2d at 184 (emphasis in original; footnote omitted). The majority therefore declined to consider petitioner's argument that none of the evidence produced by respondent in opposition to the motion for summary judgment would have been admissible at trial. *Ibid.* The dissenting judge argued that "[t]he majority errs in supposing that a party seeking summary judgment must always make an affirmative evidentiary showing, even in cases where there is not a triable, factual dispute." *Id.* at 167, 756 F.2d at 188 (Bork, J., dissenting). According to the dissenting judge, the majority's decision "undermines the traditional authority of trial judges to grant summary judgment in meritless cases." *Id.* at 166, 756 F.2d at 187.

We think that the position taken by the majority of the Court of Appeals is inconsistent with the standard for summary judgment set forth in Rule 56(c) of the Federal Rules of Civil Procedure. Under Rule 56(c), summary judgment is proper "if the pleadings, depositions, answers to interrogatories, and admissions on file, together with the affidavits, if any, show that there is no genuine issue as to any material fact and that the moving party is entitled to a judgment as a matter of law." In our view, the plain language of Rule 56(c) mandates the entry of summary judgment, after adequate time for discovery and upon motion, against a party who fails to make a showing sufficient to establish the existence of an element essential to that party's case, and on which that party will bear the burden of proof at trial. In such a situation, there can be "no genuine issue as to any material fact," since a complete failure of proof concerning an essential element of the nonmoving party's case necessarily renders all other facts immaterial. The moving party is "entitled to a judgment as a matter of law" because the nonmoving party has failed to make a sufficient showing on an essential element of her case with respect to which she has the burden of proof. "[T]h[e] standard [for granting summary judgment] mirrors the standard for a directed verdict under Federal Rule of Civil Procedure 50(a). . . ." *Anderson v. Liberty Lobby, Inc.,* 477 U.S. 242, 250 (1986).

Of course, a party seeking summary judgment always bears the initial responsibility of informing the district court of the basis for its motion, and identifying those portions of "the pleadings, depositions, answers to interrogatories, and admissions on file, together with the affidavits, if any," which it believes demonstrate the absence of a genuine issue of material fact. But unlike the Court of Appeals, we find no express or implied requirement in Rule 56 that the moving party support its motion with affidavits or other similar materials *negating* the opponent's claim. On the contrary, Rule 56(c), which refers to "the affidavits, *if any*" (emphasis added), suggests the absence of such a requirement. And if there were any doubt about the meaning of Rule 56(c) in this regard, such doubt is clearly removed by Rules 56(a) and (b), which provide that claimants and defendants, respectively, may move for summary judgment "*with or without supporting affidavits*" (emphasis added). The import of these subsections is that, regardless of whether the moving party accompanies its summary judgment motion with affidavits, the motion may, and should, be granted so long as whatever is before the district court demonstrates that the standard for the entry of summary judgment, as set forth in Rule 56(c), is satisfied. One of the principal purposes of the summary judgment rule is to isolate and dispose of factually unsupported claims or defenses, and we think it should be interpreted in a way that allows it to accomplish this purpose.

Respondent argues, however, that Rule 56(e), by its terms, places on the nonmoving party the burden of coming forward with rebuttal affidavits, or other specified kinds of materials, only in response to a motion for summary judgment "made and supported as provided in this rule." According to respondent's argument, since petitioner did not "support" its motion with affidavits, summary judgment was improper in this case. But as we have already explained, a motion for summary judgment may be made pursuant to Rule 56 "with or without supporting affidavits." In cases like the instant one, where the nonmoving party will bear the burden of proof at trial on a dispositive issue, a summary judgment motion may properly be made in reliance solely on the "pleadings, depositions, answers to interrogatories, and admissions on file." Such a motion, whether or not accompanied by affidavits, will be "made and supported as provided in this rule," and Rule 56(e) therefore requires the nonmoving party to go beyond the pleadings and by her own affidavits, or by the "depositions, answers to interrogatories, and admissions on file," designate "specific facts showing that there is a genuine issue for trial."

We do not mean that the nonmoving party must produce evidence in a form that would be admissible at trial in order to avoid summary judgment. Obviously, Rule 56 does not require the nonmoving party to depose her own witnesses. Rule 56(e) permits a proper summary judgment motion to be opposed by any of the kinds of evidentiary materials listed in Rule 56(c), except the mere pleadings themselves, and it is from this list that one would normally expect the nonmoving party to make the showing to which we have referred.

The Court of Appeals in this case felt itself constrained, however, by language in our decision in *Adickes v. S.H. Kress & Co.*, 398 U.S. 144 (1970). There we held that summary judgment had been improperly entered in favor of the defendant restaurant in an action brought under 42 U.S.C. §1983. In the course of its opinion, the *Adickes* Court said that "both the commentary on and the background of the 1963 amendment conclusively show that it was not intended to modify the burden of the moving party . . . to show initially the absence of a genuine issue concerning any material fact." *Id.* at 159. We think that this statement is accurate in a literal sense, since we fully agree with the *Adickes* Court that the 1963 amendment to Rule 56(e) was not designed to modify the burden of making the showing generally required by Rule 56(c). It also appears to us that, on the basis of the showing before the Court in *Adickes*, the motion for summary judgment in that case should have been denied. But we do not think the *Adickes* language quoted above should be construed to mean that the burden is on the party moving for summary judgment to produce evidence showing the absence of a genuine issue of material fact, even with respect to an issue on which the nonmoving party bears the burden of proof. Instead, as we have explained, the burden on the moving party may be discharged by "showing"—that is, pointing out to the district court—that there is an absence of evidence to support the nonmoving party's case.

The last two sentences of Rule 56(e) were added, as this Court indicated in *Adickes*, to disapprove a line of cases allowing a party opposing summary judgment to resist a properly made motion by reference only to its pleadings. While the *Adickes* Court was undoubtedly correct in concluding that these two sentences were not intended to *reduce* the burden of the moving party, it is also obvious that they were not adopted to *add to* that burden. Yet that is exactly the result which the reasoning of the Court of Appeals would produce; in effect, an amendment to Rule 56(e) designed to *facilitate* the granting of motions for summary judgment would be interpreted to make it *more difficult* to grant such motions. Nothing in the two sentences themselves requires this result, for the reasons we have previously indicated, and we now put to rest any inference that they do so.

Our conclusion is bolstered by the fact that district courts are widely acknowledged to possess the power to enter summary judgments *sua sponte*, so long as the losing party was on notice that she had to come forward with all of her evidence. . . . It would surely defy common sense to hold that the District Court could have entered summary judgment *sua sponte* in favor of petitioner in the instant case, but that petitioner's filing of a motion requesting such a disposition precluded the District Court from ordering it.

Respondent commenced this action in September 1980, and petitioner's motion was filed in September 1981. The parties had conducted discovery, and no serious claim can be made that respondent was in any sense "railroaded" by a premature motion for summary judgment. Any potential problem with such premature motions can be adequately dealt with under Rule 56(f), which allows a summary judgment motion to be denied, or the hearing on the motion to be continued, if the nonmoving party has not had an opportunity to make full discovery. . . .

The Federal Rules of Civil Procedure have for almost 50 years authorized motions for summary judgment upon proper showings of the lack of a genuine, triable issue of material fact. Summary judgment procedure is properly regarded not as a disfavored procedural shortcut, but rather as an integral part of the Federal Rules as a whole, which are designed "to secure the just, speedy and inexpensive determination of every action." Fed. Rule Civ. Proc. 1. . . . Before the shift to "notice pleading" accomplished by the Federal Rules, motions to dismiss a complaint or to strike a defense were the principal tools by which factually insufficient claims or defenses could be isolated and prevented from going to trial with the attendant unwarranted consumption of public and private resources. But with the advent of "notice pleading," the motion to dismiss seldom fulfills this function any more, and its place has been taken by the motion for summary judgment. Rule 56 must be construed with due regard not only for the rights of persons asserting claims and defenses that are adequately based in fact to have those claims and defenses tried to a jury, but also for the rights of persons opposing such claims and defenses to demonstrate in the manner provided by the Rule, prior to trial, that the claims and defenses have no factual basis.

The judgment of the Court of Appeals is accordingly reversed, and the case is remanded for further proceedings consistent with this opinion.

It is so ordered.

JUSTICE WHITE, concurring.

I agree that the Court of Appeals was wrong in holding that the moving defendant must always support his motion with evidence or affidavits showing the absence of a genuine dispute about a material fact. I also agree that the movant may rely on depositions, answers to interrogatories, and the like, to demonstrate that the plaintiff has no evidence to prove his case and hence that there can be no factual dispute. But the movant must discharge the burden the Rules place upon him: It is not enough to move for summary judgment without supporting the motion in any way or with a conclusory assertion that the plaintiff has no evidence to prove his case.

A plaintiff need not initiate any discovery or reveal his witnesses or evidence unless required to do so under the discovery Rules or by court order. Of course, he must respond if required to do so; but he need not also depose his witnesses or obtain their affidavits to defeat a summary judgment motion asserting only that he has failed to produce any support for his case. It is the defendant's task to negate, if he can, the claimed basis for the suit.

Petitioner Celotex does not dispute that if respondent has named a witness to support her claim, summary judgment should not be granted without Celotex somehow showing that the named witness' possible testimony raises no genuine issue of material fact. . . . It asserts, however, that respondent has failed on request to produce any basis for her case. Respondent, on the other hand, does not contend that she was not obligated to reveal her witnesses and evidence but insists that she has revealed enough to defeat the motion for summary judgment. Because the Court of Appeals found it unnecessary to address this aspect of the case, I agree that the case should be remanded for further proceedings.

JUSTICE BRENNAN, with whom THE CHIEF JUSTICE and JUSTICE BLACKMUN join, dissenting.

This case requires the Court to determine whether Celotex satisfied its initial burden of production in moving for summary judgment on the ground that the plaintiff lacked evidence to establish an essential element of her case at trial. I do not disagree with the Court's legal analysis. The Court clearly rejects the ruling of the Court of Appeals that the defendant must provide affirmative evidence disproving the plaintiff's case. Beyond this, however, the Court has not clearly explained what is required of a moving party seeking summary judgment on the ground that the non-moving party cannot prove its case.[1] This lack of clarity is unfortunate: district courts must routinely decide summary judgment motions, and the Court's opinion will very likely create confusion. For this reason, even *if* I agreed with the Court's result, I would have written separately to explain more clearly the law in this area. However, because I believe that Celotex did not meet its burden of production under Federal Rule of Civil Procedure 56, I respectfully dissent from the Court's judgment.

I

Summary judgment is appropriate where the Court is satisfied "that there is no genuine issue as to any material fact and that the moving party is entitled to a judgment as a matter of law." Fed. Rule Civ. Proc. 56(c). The burden of establishing the nonexistence of a " 'genuine issue' " is on the party moving for summary

---

1. It is also unclear what the Court of Appeals is supposed to do in this case on remand. Justice White — who has provided the Court's fifth vote — plainly believes that the Court of Appeals should reevaluate whether the defendant met its initial burden of production. However, the decision to reverse rather than to vacate the judgment below implies that the Court of Appeals should assume that Celotex has met its initial burden of production and ask only whether the plaintiff responded adequately, and, if so, whether the defendant has met its ultimate burden of persuasion that no genuine issue exists for trial. Absent some clearer expression from the Court to the contrary, Justice White's understanding would seem to be controlling. Cf. *Marks v. United States*, 430 U.S. 188, 193 (1977).

judgment. . . . This burden has two distinct components: an initial burden of production, which shifts to the nonmoving party if satisfied by the moving party; and an ultimate burden of persuasion, which always remains on the moving party. . . . The court need not decide whether the moving party has satisfied its ultimate burden of persuasion[2] unless and until the Court finds that the moving party has discharged its initial burden of production. *Adickes v. S.H. Kress & Co.*, 398 U.S. 144, 157–161 (1970). . . .

The burden of production imposed by Rule 56 requires the moving party to make a prima facie showing that it is entitled to summary judgment. 10A Wright, Miller & Kane §2727. The manner in which this showing can be made depends upon which party will bear the burden of persuasion on the challenged claim at trial. If the *moving* party will bear the burden of persuasion at trial, that party must support its motion with credible evidence — using any of the materials specified in Rule 56(c) — that would entitle it to a directed verdict if not controverted at trial. *Ibid.* Such an affirmative showing shifts the burden of production to the party opposing the motion and requires that party either to produce evidentiary materials that demonstrate the existence of a "genuine issue" for trial or to submit an affidavit requesting additional time for discovery. *Ibid;* Fed. Rules Civ. Proc. 56(e), (f).

If the burden of persuasion at trial would be on the *nonmoving party,* the party moving for summary judgment may satisfy Rule 56's burden of production in either of two ways. First, the moving party may submit affirmative evidence that negates an essential element of the nonmoving party's claim. Second, the moving party may demonstrate to the Court that the nonmoving party's evidence is insufficient to establish an essential element of the nonmoving party's claim. See 10A Wright, Miller & Kane §2727, pp. 130–131; Louis, Federal Summary Judgment Doctrine: A Critical Analysis, 83 Yale L.J. 745, 750 (1974) (hereinafter Louis). If the nonmoving party cannot muster sufficient evidence to make out its claim, a trial would be useless and the moving party is entitled to summary judgment as a matter of law. *Anderson v. Liberty Lobby, Inc.*, 477 U.S. 242 (1986).

Where the moving party adopts this second option and seeks summary judgment on the ground that the nonmoving party—who will bear the burden of persuasion at trial—has no evidence, the mechanics of discharging Rule 56's burden of production are somewhat trickier. Plainly, a conclusory assertion that the nonmoving party has no evidence is insufficient. . . . Such a "burden" of production is no burden at all and would simply permit summary judgment procedure to be converted

---

2. The burden of persuasion imposed on a moving party by Rule 56 is a stringent one. . . . Summary judgment should not be granted unless it is clear that a trial is unnecessary, *Anderson v. Liberty Lobby, Inc.*, 477 U.S. 242, 255 (1986), and any doubt as to the existence of a genuine issue for trial should be resolved against the moving party. *Adickes v. S.H. Kress & Co.*, 398 U.S. 144, 158–159 (1970). In determining whether a moving party has met its burden of persuasion, the court is obliged to take account of the entire setting of the case and must consider all papers of record as well as any materials prepared for the motion. . . . As explained by the Court of Appeals for the Third Circuit in *In re Japanese Electronic Products Antitrust Litigation,* 723 F.2d 238 (1983), rev'd on other grounds *sub nom. Matsushita Electric Industrial Co. v. Zenith Radio Corp.*, 475 U.S. 574, (1986), "[i]f . . . there is any evidence in the record from any source from which a reasonable inference in the [nonmoving party's] favor may be drawn, the moving party simply cannot obtain a summary judgment. . . ." 723 F.2d at 258.

into a tool for harassment. See Louis 750–751. Rather, as the Court confirms, a party who moves for summary judgment on the ground that the nonmoving party has no evidence must affirmatively show the absence of evidence in the record. . . . This may require the moving party to depose the nonmoving party's witnesses or to establish the inadequacy of documentary evidence. If there is literally no evidence in the record, the moving party may demonstrate this by reviewing for the court the admissions, interrogatories, and other exchanges between the parties that are in the record. Either way, however, the moving party must affirmatively demonstrate that there is no evidence in the record to support a judgment for the nonmoving party.

If the moving party has not fully discharged this initial burden of production, its motion for summary judgment must be denied, and the Court need not consider whether the moving party has met its ultimate burden of persuasion. Accordingly, the nonmoving party may defeat a motion for summary judgment that asserts that the nonmoving party has no evidence by calling the Court's attention to supporting evidence already in the record that was overlooked or ignored by the moving party. In that event, the moving party must respond by making an attempt to demonstrate the inadequacy of this evidence, for it is only by attacking all the record evidence allegedly supporting the nonmoving party that a party seeking summary judgment satisfies Rule 56's burden of production.[3] Thus, if the record disclosed that the moving party had overlooked a witness who would provide relevant testimony for the nonmoving party at trial, the Court could not find that the moving party had discharged its initial burden of production unless the moving party sought to demonstrate the inadequacy of this witness' testimony. Absent such a demonstration, summary judgment would have to be denied on the ground that the moving party had failed to meet its burden of production under Rule 56.

The result in *Adickes v. S.H. Kress & Co.*, supra, is fully consistent with these principles. In that case, petitioner was refused service in respondent's lunchroom and then was arrested for vagrancy by a local policeman as she left. Petitioner brought an action under 42 U.S.C. §1983 claiming that the refusal of service and subsequent arrest were the product of a conspiracy between respondent and the police; as proof of this conspiracy, petitioner's complaint alleged that the arresting officer was in respondent's store at the time service was refused. Respondent subsequently moved for summary judgment on the ground that there was no actual evidence in the record from which a jury could draw an inference of conspiracy. In response, petitioner pointed to a statement from her own deposition and an unsworn statement by a Kress employee, both already in the record and both ignored by respondent, that the policeman who arrested petitioner was in the store at the time she was

---

3. Once the moving party has attacked whatever record evidence — if any — the non-moving party purports to rely upon, the burden of production shifts to the nonmoving party, who must either (1) rehabilitate the evidence attacked in the moving party's papers, (2) produce additional evidence showing the existence of a genuine issue for trial as provided in Rule 56(e), or (3) submit an affidavit explaining why further discovery is necessary as provided in Rule 56(f). . . . Summary judgment should be granted if the nonmoving party fails to respond in one or more of these ways, or if, after the nonmoving party responds, the court determines that the moving party has met its ultimate burden of persuading the court that there is no genuine issue of material fact for trial. . . .

refused service. We agreed that "[i]f a policeman were present . . . it would be open to a jury, in light of the sequence that followed, to infer from the circumstances that the policeman and Kress employee had a 'meeting of the minds' and thus reached an understanding that petitioner should be refused service." 398 U.S. at 158. Consequently, we held that it was error to grant summary judgment "on the basis of this record" because respondent had "failed to fulfill its initial burden" of demonstrating that there was no evidence that there was a policeman in the store. . . .

The opinion in *Adickes* has sometimes been read to hold that summary judgment was inappropriate because the respondent had not submitted affirmative evidence to negate the possibility that there was a policeman in the store. . . . The Court of Appeals apparently read *Adickes* this way and therefore required Celotex to submit evidence establishing that plaintiff's decedent had not been exposed to Celotex asbestos. I agree with the Court that this reading of *Adickes* was erroneous and that Celotex could seek summary judgment on the ground that plaintiff could not prove exposure to Celotex asbestos at trial. However, Celotex was still required to satisfy its initial burden of production.

II

I do not read the Court's opinion to say anything inconsistent with or different than the preceding discussion. My disagreement with the Court concerns the application of these principles to the facts of this case.

Defendant Celotex sought summary judgment on the ground that plaintiff had "failed to produce" any evidence that her decedent had ever been exposed to Celotex asbestos. . . . Celotex supported this motion with a two-page "Statement of Material Facts as to Which There Is No Genuine Issue" and a three-page "Memorandum of Points and Authorities" which asserted that the plaintiff had failed to identify any evidence in responding to two sets of interrogatories propounded by Celotex and that therefore the record was "totally devoid" of evidence to support plaintiff's claim. . . .

Approximately three months earlier, Celotex had filed an essentially identical motion. Plaintiff responded to this earlier motion by producing three pieces of evidence which she claimed "[a]t the very least . . . demonstrate that there is a genuine factual dispute for trial," . . . (1) a letter from an insurance representative of another defendant describing asbestos products to which plaintiff's decedent had been exposed . . . ; (2) a letter from T.R. Hoff, a former supervisor of decedent, describing asbestos products to which decedent had been exposed . . . ; and (3) a copy of decedent's deposition from earlier workmen's compensation proceedings. . . . Plaintiff also apparently indicated at that time that she intended to call Mr. Hoff as a witness at trial. . . .

Celotex subsequently withdrew its first motion for summary judgment. . . .[5] However, as a result of this motion, when Celotex filed its second summary judgment motion, the record *did* contain evidence — including at least one

---

5. Celotex apparently withdrew this motion because, contrary to the assertion made in the first summary judgment motion, its second set of interrogatories had not been served on the plaintiff.

witness— supporting plaintiff's claim. Indeed, counsel for Celotex admitted to this Court at oral argument that Celotex was aware of this evidence and of plaintiff's intention to call Mr. Hoff as a witness at trial when the second summary judgment motion was filed. Tr. of Oral Arg. 5–7. Moreover, plaintiff's response to Celotex' second motion pointed to this evidence—noting that it had already been provided to counsel for Celotex in connection with the first motion—and argued that Celotex had failed to "meet its burden of proving that there is no genuine factual dispute for trial." . . .

On these facts, there is simply no question that Celotex failed to discharge its initial burden of production. Having chosen to base its motion on the argument that there was no evidence in the record to support plaintiff's claim, Celotex was not free to ignore supporting evidence that the record clearly contained. Rather, Celotex was required, as an initial matter, to attack the adequacy of this evidence. Celotex' failure to fulfill this simple requirement constituted a failure to discharge its initial burden of production under Rule 56, and thereby rendered summary judgment improper.[6]

This case is indistinguishable from *Adickes*. Here, as there, the defendant moved for summary judgment on the ground that the record contained no evidence to support an essential element of the plaintiff's claim. Here, as there, the plaintiff responded by drawing the court's attention to evidence that was already in the record and that had been ignored by the moving party. Consequently, here, as there, summary judgment should be denied on the ground that the moving party failed to satisfy its initial burden of production.[7]

[The dissenting opinion of JUSTICE STEVENS is omitted.]

NOTES AND QUESTIONS

1. *What Must the Moving Party Show When It Moves Without Affidavits to Dismiss a Claim?* All of the Justices in *Celotex* appear to agree that a defendant does not assume the burden of disproving the case against it by moving for summary judgment. In other words, Celotex did not have to prove that the decedent was *not* exposed to its product. The Justices also seem to agree that defendant must do

---

6. If the plaintiff had answered Celotex' second set of interrogatories with the evidence in her response to the first summary judgment motion, and Celotex had ignored those interrogatories and based its second summary judgment motion on the first set of interrogatories only, Celotex obviously could not claim to have discharged its Rule 56 burden of production. This result should not be different simply because the evidence plaintiff relied upon to support her claim was acquired by Celotex other than in plaintiff's answers to interrogatories.

7. Although JUSTICE WHITE agrees that "if [plaintiff] has named a witness to support her claim, summary judgment should not be granted without Celotex somehow showing that the named witness' possible testimony raises no genuine issue of material fact," he would remand "[b]ecause the Court of Appeals found it unnecessary to address this aspect of the case." *Ante*, at 2555–2556 (concurring). However, Celotex has admitted that plaintiff had disclosed her intent to call Mr. Hoff as a witness at trial before Celotex filed its second motion for summary judgment. Tr. of Oral Arg. 6–7. Under the circumstances, then, remanding is a waste of time.

more than simply put plaintiff to its proof. Rather, the moving defendant "always bears the initial responsibility of informing the district court of the basis for its motion, and identifying those portions of 'the pleadings, depositions, answers to interrogatories, and admissions on file, together with the affidavits, if any,' which it believes demonstrate the absence of a genuine issue of material fact." This requirement is reinforced by Rule 56(c), which requires both the moving and nonmoving parties to cite "to particular parts of materials in the record." Is that a desirable requirement? Isn't it significantly easier for plaintiff to point to the existence of supporting evidence than it is for defendant to establish its absence?

Would relieving the moving defendant from the burden of making a significant showing of the absence of proof on summary judgment promote abuse of the motion? Would Rule 11 alone deter frivolous summary judgment motions? *Compare* Martin B. Louis, *Federal Summary Judgment Doctrine: A Critical Analysis*, 83 Yale L.J. 745, 749–750 (1974) (arguing that summary judgment motion will be used to harass nonmoving party without requiring substantial showing that there is absence of evidentiary support in the record); Adam M. Steinman, *The Irrepressible Myth of* Celotex: *Reconsidering Summary Judgment Burdens Twenty Years After the Trilogy*, 63 Wash. & Lee L. Rev. 81, 124 (2006) (arguing that moving party "must use Rule 56(c) documents" to support its contention that nonmoving party lacks evidence in support of its claim) *with* Martin H. Redish, *Summary Judgment and the Vanishing Trial: Implications of the Litigation Matrix*, 57 Stan. L. Rev. 1329 (2005) (arguing for a minimal burden on moving party to show absence of evidentiary support; Rule 11 is sufficient to deter frivolous motions); David P. Currie, *Thoughts on Directed Verdicts and Summary Judgments*, 45 U. Chi. L. Rev. 72, 79 (1977) (mere filing of summary judgment motion should be sufficient to require nonmoving party to come forward with evidence).

Do you think that Celotex made a sufficient showing of the absence of evidence that the decedent was injured by its product? Did the majority think so? Given that plaintiff had earlier identified a witness (T.R. Hoff) who would testify about the "asbestos products to which decedent had been exposed," should the Court have required Celotex to depose Mr. Hoff before asserting that there was no evidence supporting plaintiff's claim? Or did plaintiff have a duty to come forward with an affidavit by Mr. Hoff? What if Celotex's lawyers in fact interviewed Mr. Hoff, and he confirmed plaintiff's allegations? Would Celotex be justified in moving for summary judgment as long as Hoff's testimony was not of record in the proceeding?

The Supreme Court remanded *Celotex* for reconsideration of the summary judgment motion in light of its holding. On remand, the Court of Appeals determined that the showing made by plaintiff in opposition to Celotex's summary judgment motion was, in fact, sufficient to raise a genuine issue of material fact and defeat summary judgment. 826 F.2d 33 (D.C. Cir. 1987), *cert. denied*, 484 U.S. 1066 (1988).

2. *How Does the Nonmoving Party Defeat a Summary Judgment Motion?* The challenge for the nonmoving party, whether plaintiff or defendant, is to demonstrate the existence of a "genuine dispute as to any material fact." This is accomplished by producing evidence in support of its claim or defense. The evidence may already be in the record from the discovery conducted, or may be presented in the form of an affidavit based on personal knowledge from a witness whose testimony would

be admissible at trial. (Thus, summary judgment does not create any incentive for a party to take the deposition of its own witness.) On rare occasions, the court will entertain live testimony on summary judgment, although the relative advantage of summary judgment over trial is diminished once live witnesses are examined before the court. The court will give the nonmoving party the benefit of all reasonable doubt and will not assess the credibility of the evidence at the summary judgment stage. If there is any genuine conflict in the evidence, the court will deny summary judgment. However, the nonmoving party may not rest on its pleadings; it must come forth with evidence.

Although the materials presented do not have to be in a form that would be admissible at trial (and indeed most affidavits would not be admissible), pursuant to Rule 56(c)(2), a party may object "that the material cited to support or dispute a fact cannot be presented in a form that would be admissible in evidence."

3. *Obtaining Summary Judgment by Affidavit and Documentary Evidence.* As we saw in *Celotex*, a party without the burden of production (usually defendant) can obtain summary judgment without presenting any affirmative proof simply by demonstrating the absence in the record of evidence supportive of the party with the burden of production (usually plaintiff). In such a case, the burden is on the nonmoving party to present affidavits or other evidence supportive of its contentions. Affidavits and other documentary evidence offered by the nonmoving party serve to *defeat* summary judgment by demonstrating the existence of a genuine dispute of material fact. The case will then proceed to trial, where the witnesses who provided affidavits will be examined before the tribunal.

However, proof offered *in support* of a motion for summary judgment can have a much more dispositive impact on the proceeding; such evidence can establish the truth of the moving party's contentions if no contrary proof is offered by the nonmoving party, and thus demonstrate the absence of a genuine dispute as to any material fact. In that case, summary judgment will be granted, and the evidence on which the summary judgment was based *will never be tested at trial.*

Consider under what circumstances this "trial by affidavit" might present the potential for abuse. Courts are particularly wary of affidavits when the material information is in the exclusive control of the moving party. Thus, in *Cross v. United States*, 336 F.2d 431 (2d Cir. 1964), the court denied summary judgment to defendant taxpayer who asserted in his affidavit that travel expenses he incurred on a trip to Europe with his wife and dog were for business purposes and therefore properly deductible from his income taxes. The IRS, which had the burden of proving that the expenses were for nondeductible purposes, successfully argued that it ought to have the opportunity to cross-examine the taxpayer in court. *Accord, Arnstein v. Porter,* 154 F.2d 464 (2d Cir. 1946) (summary judgment improperly entered on behalf of defendant Cole Porter in action accusing Porter of stealing plaintiff's songs; plaintiff should have the right to cross-examine Porter at trial concerning his assertion that he never heard plaintiff's music).

Normally, however, the nonmoving party cannot defeat summary judgment simply by asserting a right to cross-examine the moving party's proof; obviously, such an argument would completely swallow the rule. At a minimum, the nonmoving party must suggest to the court some basis for discrediting or "impeaching" the moving party's evidence.

Where the nonmoving party carries the burden of production, it cannot normally defeat summary judgment merely by asserting a right to challenge the moving party's proof at trial, even if it can identify a basis for impeaching the proof. Thus, in *Dyer v. MacDougal*, 201 F.2d 265 (2d Cir. 1952), an opinion written by Judge Learned Hand, the court held plaintiff could not defeat summary judgment against him simply by attacking the testimony of witnesses who denied in their affidavits hearing slanderous statements made by defendant. Plaintiff was not present when any of the alleged statements were made and had not deposed defendant's witnesses. In granting summary judgment for defendant, the court reasoned that although a party having the burden of production "might succeed in convincing a jury of the truth of his allegations in spite of the fact that all the witnesses denied them, we think it plain that a verdict would nevertheless have to be directed against him." Is *Dyer* consistent with *Cross*?

4. *What Constitutes a "Genuine Dispute" of Material Fact?* The standard for the issuance of summary judgment — that "there is no genuine dispute as to any material fact" — depends on the judge's conclusion that no reasonable jury could find for the nonmoving party based upon the evidence of record. Is this an empirical question or a normative one? How does a judge know whether her own perception is in accord with others' perceptions?

Consider, in this regard, the Supreme Court's decision in *Scott v. Harris*, 550 U.S. 372 (2007). The Court held there that summary judgment should have been entered for the defendant police officers in an excessive force case brought by a plaintiff who was rendered a quadriplegic when the police intentionally ran him off the road during a high-speed chase. The entire chase was videotaped by a camera mounted in the police car. Under the applicable constitutional law, the police are not deemed to have violated the Fourth Amendment through their use of force if their action is "reasonable" in light of the risk posed by the plaintiff. The Court held that the videotape conclusively established that plaintiff posed a serious safety risk to others, and that the police officers' use of force was thus reasonable as a matter of law. In Justice Scalia's words (writing for the majority), the videotape "speak[s] for itself." A dissent by Justice Stevens asserted that the question of reasonableness was one for the jury, notwithstanding the videotape.

Should the existence of the videotape have affected the allocation of adjudicatory responsibility between the judge and jury? What if there had been no videotape, but the facts were established by uncontradicted affidavits of witnesses? Justice Scalia, writing for the majority, described the contents of the videotape in the following terms:

> . . . There we see Respondent's vehicle racing down narrow, two-lane roads in the dead of night at speeds that are shockingly fast. We see it swerve around more than a dozen other cars, cross the double-yellow line, and force cars traveling in both directions to their respective shoulders to avoid being hit. We see it run multiple red lights and travel for considerable periods of time in the occasional center left-turn-only lane, chased by numerous police cars forced to engage in the same hazardous maneuvers just to keep up.

If these facts had been established by affidavit rather than by videotape, should the court have entered summary judgment, or left the question of the reasonableness of the police action to the jury? Notwithstanding the uncontroverted "fact" of plaintiff's conduct, isn't there still a genuine issue, with or without videotape, as to how serious a risk that conduct posed to others, and how necessary the police response was? As between the judge and jury, who is better situated to evaluate the level of risk posed by this kind of driving? Should it have mattered to the Supreme Court in *Scott v. Harris* that both the district court and the court of appeals thought that a jury could have concluded from the videotape that the police action was unreasonable?

Footage from the videotape is available at https://www.youtube.com/watch?v=qrVKSgRZ2GY. In a provocative empirical study, the videotape was shown to 1,350 participants of diverse backgrounds. Although most agreed with the Court's conclusion that plaintiff's driving posed a serious danger warranting the police action, a significant number disagreed. The authors found that the viewers' interpretations of the tape correlated with race, geography, and political attitudes. Does this undermine the Supreme Court's conclusion that "no reasonable jury" could find for the plaintiff? Dan M. Kahan, David A. Hoffman & Donald Braman, *Whose Eyes Are You Going to Believe?* Scott v. Harris *and the Perils of Cognitive Illiberalism*, 122 Harv. L. Rev. 837 (2009). Given that all judges come to the adjudication with their own cultural and political biases that can affect their cognitive judgment, how can a judge ever reliably conclude that "no reasonable jury" could disagree with his or her understanding of the evidence? *See* Elizabeth Thornburg, *(Un)conscious Judging*, 76 Wash. & Lee L. Rev. 1567 (2019) (analyzing various cognitive biases that may distort a judge's sense what constitutes a reasonable inference).

The propriety of resolving excessive force cases on summary judgment has received considerable attention from the Supreme Court since *Scott v. Harris*. In *Tolan v. Cotton*, 572 U.S. 650 (2014) (*per curiam*), the Supreme Court once again emphasized the requirement that a court considering a summary judgment motion view the facts in the light most favorable to the nonmoving party. Cotton, a police officer, had fired three bullets at Tolan while the latter was sitting on the front porch of his parents' home, causing him serious injury. Tolan sued, claiming that the officer had used excessive force in violation of the Fourth Amendment. The officer responded with a defense of qualified immunity, arguing that the law was not clearly established that the shooting was improper on the facts of the case. The district court granted summary judgment in favor of the officer and the Fifth Circuit affirmed, but the Supreme Court summarily reversed. The lower courts had "fail[ed] to credit evidence that contradicted some of [the] key factual conclusions" in the motion for summary judgment by improperly making its own determinations about the credibility of conflicting witness testimony. "The witnesses on both sides come to this case with their own perceptions, recollections, and even potential biases," the Court explained. "By weighing the evidence and reaching factual inferences contrary to Tolan's competent evidence, the court below neglected to adhere to the fundamental principle that at the summary judgment stage, reasonable inferences should be drawn in favor of the nonmoving party." Justices Alito and Scalia concurred in the judgment but filed a separate opinion objecting to the Court's decision to take the case, saying that there was "no confusion in the courts of appeals about the standard to be applied in ruling on a summary judgment motion" and hence no need for the Court to hear an appeal solely for the purpose of correcting an error.

Compare Plumhoff v. Rickard, 572 U.S. 765 (2014), in which the Court unanimously reversed a denial of summary judgment and granted a dismissal to police officers who had been charged with using excessive force in firing 15 shots at a suspect and his passenger. After leading the police on a high-speed chase, the suspect swerved into a parking lot where he was nearly cornered by the police. The suspect's car rammed one of the police cars in the parking lot, and the suspect was in the process of fleeing when the officers fired. The Court held that the officers' conduct was reasonable as a matter of law, and the record showed no genuine dispute of material fact, notwithstanding the plaintiff's claim that the officers overreacted and continued firing bullets into the car after any reasonable danger to the officers or bystanders had abated.

Later, in *Mullenix v. Luna*, 577 U.S. 7 (2015) (*per curiam*), the majority appeared to strengthen yet further its ruling in *Scott* and *Plumhoff* that the determination whether a given set of facts constitutes the unreasonable use of force under the Fourth Amendment involves the interpretation of a legal standard and not a question of fact. *See id.* at 308 (noting with approval the lower court's ruling "that objective unreasonableness is a question of law that can be resolved on summary judgment" and reviewed de novo by an appellate court).

For an argument that Justices Alito and Scalia were too hasty in asserting in *Tolan* that there is "no confusion in the courts of appeals about the standard to be applied in ruling on a summary judgment motion," *see* Tobias Barrington Wolff, Scott v. Harris *and the Future of Summary Judgment*, 15 Nev. L.J. 1351 (2015). Professor Wolff identifies elements of the Court's ruling in *Scott v. Harris* that threaten to undermine the presumption in favor of the nonmoving party in summary judgment practice, and he traces the impact of those rulings in lower federal courts, suggesting that *Scott* has already introduced confusion that *Plumhoff* threatens to exacerbate. Will *Tolan* serve to eliminate that uncertainty? Professor Wolff is skeptical: "The ruling of the Fifth Circuit in *Tolan* was so obviously incorrect that the rebuke of a summary reversal does little to clarify the proper boundaries of the standard." Wolff, *supra*, at 1367.

5. *Timing.* Either party may move for summary judgment any time up to 30 days after the close of discovery. Fed. R. Civ. P. 56(b). Either party may move as early as they want, even before discovery has commenced. However, this permission is tempered by Rule 56(d), which allows the court to give the nonmoving party additional time to conduct discovery or obtain affidavits before responding to the motion.

Pursuant to Rule 56(f), the court, upon notice to the parties, may issue summary judgment without a motion from the parties. It may also grant summary judgment for the nonmoving party, or grant summary judgment on a ground not raised by the parties.

6. *Partial Summary Judgment.* When there is no genuine factual dispute regarding one element of a claim, but a trial is necessary to resolve other parts of the case, the court may issue an order removing the uncontroverted issue from trial as provided for by Rule 56(g). This is often referred to as *partial summary judgment*, although no formal judgment is entered. For instance, when the amount of damages is uncontroverted, but the parties contest liability, the court may issue an order establishing plaintiff's damages, and the case will proceed to trial to determine liability only, a situation expressly provided for under Rule 56(g).

7. *Appeals.* Think about the implication of the final judgment rule for summary judgment orders. Under some circumstances, a grant of summary judgment might be an appealable order, but only if it disposes of the entire case. (When only one of several claims is resolved on summary judgment, the nonmoving party may have appellate redress pursuant to Rule 54(b).)

A denial of summary judgment, by contrast, is clearly not an appealable order. The only thing that the court decides in denying summary judgment is that the case must proceed to trial, the very antithesis of a final judgment. Although a party denied summary judgment may appeal an adverse judgment following trial on the merits, except in rare circumstances, it cannot avoid the trial by an interlocutory appeal of the summary judgment ruling.

In *Ortiz v. Jordan*, 562 U.S. 180 (2011), the Supreme Court held that defendants could not appeal an order denying summary judgment on qualified immunity grounds even after full trial on the merits. Any appellate review must be based on mistakes at the trial, and the appellants failed to assert their objections to the trial court's findings in an appropriate post-trial motion for judgment as a matter of law under Rule 50(b). Accordingly, they were barred from obtaining appellate review of the court's failure to recognize their qualified immunity defense.

For a recent review of the law governing appealability of summary judgment denials, *see* Joan Steinman, *The Puzzling Appeal of Summary Judgment Denials: When Are Such Denials Reviewable?*, 2014 Mich. St. L. Rev. 895 (2014).

8. *What Constitutes Evidence in Support of Plaintiff's Claim?* One of the important functions of summary judgment is to ensure that the jury's adjudication will be based on the evidence and not simply the result of sympathy or intuition. Yet, much of what a jury does is guess. It guesses which witnesses are telling the truth, it guesses about chains of causation, the appropriate amount of damages, or about the significance of evidence. At what point does that speculation become so inappropriate as to justify the court depriving the jury of the opportunity to adjudicate?

Assume in the *Rockwell* case that even after discovery, evidence of what caused the crash is still fairly inconclusive. There is evidence that ice was ingested by the engine, but there is little proof of where it came from or under what circumstances. Rockwell continues to assert that the plane crashed because the engines were deprived of oxygen, a result they attribute to the pilot's failure to turn on the engine heater, thus allowing ice to form on the intake to the engine. Some of this ice it concedes may have been ingested by the engines, but that did not cause the engine failure. Alternatively, Rockwell argues that even if the crash were caused by the engine's ingestion of ice, that could only happen if the pilot failed to inflate the deicing boot prior to a buildup of excessive ice on the wing. There is no evidence of whether the deicing boots malfunctioned.

Defendant's principal evidence is based on tests run on the plane while it was in development. During these tests, the wings were sprayed with water from a tanker plane flying in front during freezing weather. The deicing boot was then inflated. No ice particles visible to the naked eye were ingested by the engine during this test. Rockwell also points to the near-simultaneous loss of power by both the left and right engines. It asserts that it would be highly unlikely for ice large enough to damage both engines to be ingested at virtually the same time when no other plane ever experienced an ingestion of large ice particles.

Obviously, even if the crash was caused in the ways asserted by Rockwell—namely, as a consequence of the pilot's negligent operation of the plane—plaintiff can still assert that Rockwell was negligent in designing a deicing mechanism so vulnerable to pilot error. However, Rockwell's liability would be significantly reduced. On the other hand, if the crash occurred without any pilot error, Rockwell's liability would be enormous. Under what circumstances will a court determine that the evidence presented on summary judgment is sufficiently probative of the fact in dispute to allow the case to go to trial? To what extent should the jury be allowed to rely on inference or speculation in assessing liability?

Consider in this regard the impact of *Matsushita Electric Industrial Co. v. Zenith Radio Corp.*, 475 U.S. 574 (1986). The Supreme Court there upheld the grant of summary judgment against plaintiff, Zenith, in its antitrust claim against several Japanese television manufacturers. Zenith alleged in its complaint that defendants conspired to lower their prices in the American market below cost in order to drive the U.S. competition out of business and to monopolize the market. In order to prevail, Zenith had to establish that the pricing was the result of an agreement among defendants. Zenith's only evidence of such a conspiracy was proof that defendants met regularly to set *minimum* prices as required under Japanese law, and the parallel behavior of all defendants in lowering the price of their American televisions. Although the parallel pricing could have been the result of each company independently pricing its product in accordance with the market, the court of appeals held the evidence would have also permitted a jury to infer the existence of a conspiracy. The Supreme Court disagreed:

> Respondents correctly note that "[o]n summary judgment the inferences to be drawn from the underlying facts . . . must be viewed in the light most favorable to the party opposing the motion." . . . But antitrust law limits the range of permissible inferences from ambiguous evidence in [an antitrust] case. Thus, in *Monsanto Co. v. Spray-Rite Service Corp.*, 465 U.S. 752 (1984), we held that conduct as consistent with permissible competition as with illegal conspiracy does not, standing alone, support an inference of antitrust conspiracy. . . . To survive a motion for summary judgment or for a directed verdict, a plaintiff seeking damages for a violation of [the antitrust statute] must present evidence "that tends to exclude the possibility" that the alleged conspirators acted independently. 465 U.S. at 764. Respondents in this case, in other words, must show that the inference of conspiracy is reasonable in light of the competing inferences of independent action or collusive action that could not have harmed respondents.

The Court noted that in order for the alleged conspiracy to be economically rational, the conspirators had to be able to reap monopoly profits once the U.S. businesses were put out of business. This would be very difficult to implement because once prices were raised, other competitors would enter the market and undercut the higher prices. Further, the conspirators would have to agree not to compete among each other once American competition was eliminated. Given the implausibility of rational economic actors choosing such a course of conduct, and given the alternative, innocent explanation for their conduct, the Court held that a jury should not be permitted to infer the existence of a conspiracy on the basis of the facts in evidence.

Should Mrs. Burdick, like Zenith, have to negate the "competing inference" raised by the facts established in evidence—namely, the possibility that the crash occurred because the engines were deprived of oxygen, not because of the ingestion of ice? Note the *Matsushita* Court's explicit departure in antitrust cases from the normal benefit of doubt accorded the nonmoving party on summary judgment. Should antitrust cases be treated differently? Is a case like *Matsushita* different insofar as there could have been direct evidence of defendant's behavior? Do courts not want to discourage businesses from lowering prices out of fear that it could be viewed as evidence of an illegal conspiracy? Is there reason to distrust a jury's ability to discount an implausible explanation in an antitrust case more than in other cases? We will revisit these issues in connection with Judgments as a Matter of Law under Rule 50 later in this chapter.

For an argument that *Matsushita* and *Celotex* have led to an overzealous use of summary judgment on behalf of defendants in a wide range of cases, *see* Arthur R. Miller, *The Pretrial Rush to Judgment: Are the "Litigation Explosion," "Liability Crisis," and Efficiency Clichés Eroding Our Day in Court and Jury Trial Commitments?*, 78 N.Y.U. L. Rev. 982 (2003). *Cf.* Stephen B. Burbank, *Vanishing Trials and Summary Judgment in Federal Civil Cases: Drifting Toward Bethlehem or Gomorrah?*, 1 J. Emp. L. Stud. 591, 616–620 (2004) (suggesting that percentage of cases disposed of by summary judgment in the Eastern District of Pennsylvania in the period from 1960 to 2000 may have increased by nearly 400 percent, although questioning whether the increase was attributable to *Matsushita* and *Celotex*); Jonathan Remy Nash, *Unearthing Summary Judgment's Concealed Standard of Review*, 50 U.C. Davis L. Rev. 87, 91 (2016) (empirical study finding that federal courts of appeals reversed denials of summary judgment on the basis of qualified immunity at a rate of almost 50 percent).

9. *The Pertinence of Expert Testimony.* Does the analysis change if the parties present expert testimony on causation? Assume that plaintiff comes forth with the opinion of an aviation expert who opines that the crash was caused by the ingestion of ice by the engines, a process that was possible even if the pilot operated the deicing system properly. Is there now, *per se*, a "genuine dispute of material fact" such that the court must deny defendant's summary judgment motion, or should the judge scrutinize the basis for the expert's testimony?

You will return to this question in the upper-level evidence course. For our purposes, it is sufficient to note that, at least in federal practice, the Court has directed the trial judge to be something of a "gatekeeper" in regard to expert opinion. Before admitting expert testimony into evidence, the court must be satisfied "that an expert, whether basing testimony upon professional studies or personal experience, employs in the courtroom the same level of intellectual rigor that characterizes the practice of an expert in the relevant field." *Kumho Tire Co. v. Carmichael*, 526 U.S. 137 (1999). *Accord, Daubert v. Merrell Dow Pharmaceuticals, Inc.*, 509 U.S. 579 (1993).

In *Kumho Tire*, the Court upheld the trial court's exclusion of expert testimony and subsequent grant of summary judgment. The trial court had concluded that the opinion of plaintiff's expert, that the crash of plaintiff's minivan was caused by a defect in his tire, was insufficiently reliable to allow the jury to consider. The Supreme Court ruled that the trial court had wide discretion in determining the reliability of the expert testimony. It did not abuse its discretion in barring the testimony where the expert, based largely on his own experience, insisted that the crash was due to a defect notwithstanding evidence that the tire was near-bald and had been under-inflated. The Court noted that no other expert in the field employed the methodology used by plaintiff's expert, nor was his approach referred to or validated by any technical journals.

10. *Thinking Strategically.* Put yourself in the shoes of defendant's attorney in *Rockwell.* Given the modern approach of resolving all doubts in plaintiff's favor on summary judgment, and given the opinion of plaintiff's expert that the crash was caused by a design defect, is there anything to be gained by moving for summary judgment?

First, *Kumho Tire* and *Daubert* clearly provide the parties with an opportunity to press the issue of an expert's qualification on summary judgment. If the court finds unreliable the expert's conclusion that the crash was caused by the ingestion of ice, that is tantamount to finding no genuine dispute of material fact. Moreover, even if the court admits into evidence the expert testimony and denies summary judgment, defendant might still persuade the court that plaintiff's case is very weak, even if strong enough to survive summary judgment. Many attorneys value this opportunity to "educate the court," totally apart from whether summary judgment is granted.

Are there disadvantages to making a summary judgment motion? Consider whether a summary judgment motion made primarily to educate the court would violate Rule 11. Consider also whether defendant's credibility with the court would be impaired by asserting that there is no genuine dispute as to any material fact on the record that has been developed. Is the attorney's credibility with the judge important in a jury trial?

10.   *Final Pretrial Order*

Although discovery provides the parties with a great deal of information about evidence the other side has in its possession, a much more precise map of the case each party will present at trial is provided by the Final Pretrial Order under Rule 16(e). The Final Pretrial Order will list every witness to be called by each party and the substance of their testimony. The Final Pretrial Order is the final and definitive statement of a party's legal and factual contentions. Any evidence offered not included in the Final Pretrial Order may be excluded from the trial if the opposing party objects to its introduction. Amendments to pleadings and discovery responses are freely permitted, but the Final Pretrial Order may be modified "only to prevent manifest injustice." Here are excerpts from the Final Pretrial Order in the *Rockwell* case. The complete order was 37 pages, not including witness and exhibit lists.

IN THE UNITED STATES DISTRICT COURT
FOR THE DISTRICT OF NEW JERSEY
CAMDEN VICINAGE
HONORABLE JOSEPH E. IRENAS

GEORGE C. BRADY, III, Esquire
Executor of the Estate of
Theodore L. Burdick, Deceased.

Plaintiff,

v.

ROCKWELL INTERNATIONAL CORPORATION,
Civil No. 90-2321

Defendant.

JOINT FINAL PRE-TRIAL ORDER

The following shall constitute the updated Final Pre-Trial Order pursuant to Rule 16 of the Federal Rules of Civil Procedure, and this Final Pre-Trial Order shall govern the conduct of the . . . trial of this case. Amendments to this Order will be allowed only in exceptional circumstances to prevent manifest injustice. Counsel are urged to move to amend in a timely fashion any portion of the order that must be changed or modified between the filing of the order and the trial date.

APPEARANCES:

For plaintiff George C. Brady, Esquire, Executor of the Estate of Theodore L. Burdick:
[List of plaintiff's and defendant's counsel]

PART I. *NATURE OF THE ACTION AND JURISDICTION OF THE COURT*

Jurisdiction is asserted under 28 U.S.C. §1332. There is diversity of citizenship between plaintiff and defendant and the amount at issue is in excess of the required jurisdictional amounts. Jurisdiction is not contested.

This action seeks wrongful death and survival damages, arising out of Rockwell International Corporation's ("Rockwell") alleged violation of the New Jersey product liability laws. The incident giving rise to this action is the crash of a Jet Commander airplane, serial No. 130. The three occupants of the aircraft died in the crash. Suit was filed by the estate of [Mr. Burdick] in June of 1990.

PART II. *STIPULATED FACTS*

A. Facts as to Liability

The flight crew of N44 crashed in Western Pennsylvania on November 2, 1988. N44 was owned by the Federal Aviation Administration ("FAA"), and the three occupants of the aircraft were FAA employees. The flight crew of N44 had intended to inspect an instrument landing system at Westmoreland Airport in Western Pennsylvania and were flying in icing conditions at the time of the incident. One of the pilots of the aircraft reported that he could not get any power from the engines before the crash occurred. The aircraft is equipped with a deice system which is designed to shed ice from the leading edges of the wings. All three crew members died in the crash and there was a post-crash fire.

The Captain of the aircraft, James Burger, was the pilot in command at the time of the accident. Mr. Burger had approximately 17,000 hours total flight time and over 4,000 hours of flight time in the aircraft which crashed. The Estate of Mr. Burger is not a party in this action.

Serial No. 130 was manufactured by Aero Commander, a division of Rockwell Standard Corporation. Rockwell Standard merged with North American Aviation, Inc. in 1967, and the surviving corporation was known as North American Rockwell Corporation. In 1973, Rockwell Manufacturing Company merged with North American Rockwell Corporation, and the surviving corporation is known as Rockwell International Corporation. Rockwell International Corporation is the only defendant in this case.

PART III. *PLAINTIFF'S CONTESTED FACTS*

A. Plaintiff Intends to Prove the Following Contested Facts with Regard to Liability

Plaintiff's decedent, . . . died on November 2, 1988, in a plane crash near Oak Grove, Pennsylvania. The subject aircraft was a Jet Commander Model 1121-A (converted to 1121-B, serial number 130 and registration N-44) designed and manufactured in the 1960's by defendant Rockwell International Corporation, through its predecessor corporation, Aero Commander, Inc. Prior to the crash, both engines on the subject aircraft ingested large quantities of ice, which were shed from the deice boots, causing the engines to stall and flame out which ultimately caused the aircraft to lose power and crash.

Plaintiff's decedent was employed . . . by the Federal Aviation Administration (FAA). In his employment with the FAA, plaintiff's decedent performed, among other duties, safety checks of airport Instrument Landing Systems (ILS). At the time of the crash which gave rise to this action, decedent was in the third day of a series of missions inspecting airport ILS systems throughout the Commonwealth of Pennsylvania, which missions began on October 31, 1988.

The Rockwell aircraft was equipped with a thermal anti-ice system for the plane's engines and a pneumatic boot deicing system, which was designed to break off any ice which accumulated on the leading edges of the N-44's wings. The deicing boot consisted of thick rubber which is inflated by using engine bleed air to expand the rubber and break off ice which accumulates on the leading edges of the wings. This system was also installed on the subject aircraft by the defendant Rockwell International through its predecessor corporations and was never modified by another subsequent entity.

The plane crash which is the subject of this lawsuit occurred as a result of ice ingestion into the N-44's jet engines, two General Electric Model CJ-610-5 engines, which were selected for use on the Jet Commander by defendant Rockwell as airframe manufacturer. The ingestion of ice occurred after the crew of the N-44 activated the aircraft's pneumatic boot deice system in icing conditions. The ice ingestion caused stall and flameout from which restart and recovery was nearly impossible. Captain James Burger and plaintiff's decedent were fully qualified and experienced crew members.

The design of the Jet Commander 1121 was defective in that the normal operation of the pneumatic boot deice system caused ice to be ingested into the engines, which caused stall and flameout. In this case, this defective condition was the proximate cause of the crash of November 2, 1988, which resulted in the deaths of all three crew members. The design of the pneumatic boot deice system is defective because the engines are located aft of the leading edge of the wings, approximately 10 feet directly behind the area where the ice chunks break away from the wing. The leading edges of the wings should have been thermally anti-iced from engine bleed air, which is the design that Lear Jet utilized at the same time the 1121 was designed and manufactured. Interestingly enough, Aero Commander requested B.F. Goodrich to design a thermal section on the wing in front of the engine to protect it from ice ingestion, but never implemented the design even though it was technically feasible.

The Jet Commander 1121 series aircraft was also equipped with General Electric Model CJ 610-5 powerplants or engines. The selection and application of CJ 610-5 engine also renders the aircraft defective because the engine was susceptible to compressor damage from ice ingestion. As the air frame manufacturer of the Jet Commander line of aircraft, Rockwell International and/or its predecessor corporations failed to select the proper engines for this plane, and/or failed to take into account the susceptibility of stall or flameout. Further, the defendant failed to select and design an ice removal system that would prevent ingestion of ice into the engines.

There were a significant number of tests involved in the FAA certification process for the Jet Commander aircraft. Defendant knew that the testing procedures used for the icing certification process of the aircraft were grossly inadequate. Further the defendants did not provide all material facts relating to the certification process to the FAA at the time the aircraft was certified. Because defendant Rockwell International was aware of the defective and dangerous design of the Jet Commander line of aircraft, and because defendant failed to remedy these defects by simply using a thermal "hot section" in front of the engine, exemplary and/or punitive damages should properly be assessed against Rockwell International. Evidence will also show that top engineering officials at Aero-Commander made misrepresentations to the FAA regarding certain aspects of the certification process.

During the 1960's and early 1970's, Rockwell Spring and Axle Company, Rockwell Standard Corporation, Rockwell Manufacturing Corporation and Aero Commander, Inc., N.A. Aviation, Inc. and N.A. Rockwell were all business entities licensed to do business in the Commonwealth of Pennsylvania. During this period, all of these companies merged and/or consolidated with other corporations to become the company we know today as defendant Rockwell International Corporation. In 1969, the above-referenced predecessor corporations of defendant Rockwell International designed and built the subject Jet Commander aircraft, as well as the airplane's deice/anti-ice systems.

While it is true that there were some unrelated minor modifications performed on the subject aircraft by the FAA in the mid 1970's, there is no question that the deice system was never modified by any other entity which subsequently purchased the aircraft. The Honorable Joseph Irenas has recently ruled that the defendant may not call Wayne Sand, Ph.D. as an expert in connection with his supplemental report dated January 26, 1996. Dr. Sand was the only defense expert who attempted to show some causal relationship between the alleged modifications made by the FAA to the Jet Commander and the ensuing crash which occurred on November 2, 1988. Due to a complete lack of evidence as to any causal relationship, Judge Irenas precluded not only Dr. Sand from testifying on this issue but will also effectively prevent the defendant from contending that any of the alleged modifications made to the Jet Commander had any causal relationship to the crash in question. Therefore, because the component of the plane in question, i.e., the pneumatic deice system, was never modified by the FAA, the defendant's efforts to introduce evidence of alleged modifications made by the FAA is completely irrelevant to this action in light of the Court's prior ruling and existing case law interpreting the New Jersey Product Liability Act. . . .

B. Defendant's Statement of Legal Issues in This Case

In addition to the customary legal issues presented by the assertion of the claims and defenses in the pleadings in this case Rockwell submits the following are significant legal issues in this case:

1. Can Rockwell be liable to plaintiff under New Jersey law where no airworthiness certificate was issued by the FAA to the defendant (or its predecessor) on or before defendant transferred the airplane, serial number 130, in July 1969?

2. Does the transfer of type certificate A2SW in 1969 from Rockwell's predecessor to an unrelated third party limit plaintiff's claims against Rockwell in whole or in part?

3. Where the plane as originally manufactured by Rockwell was sold as part of a bulk sale of a product line, can Rockwell be liable under a strict products liability claim under New Jersey law?

4. How do the many modifications (by STC or TIEO) made on serial number 130 subsequent to the time that serial number 130 left the dominion and control of Rockwell's predecessor affect Rockwell's liability on plaintiff'[s] claims?

5. Does the FAA's negligence in the performance of its duties (statutorily delegated or assumed) bar any recovery against Rockwell in whole or in part?

6. Even if the design of the ice protection system contains a design defect, can the plaintiff recover where the ice protection system conformed with state-of-the-art designs for ice protection systems when the design of the plane was certified, as well as the regulations of government regulatory agencies?

7. Have plaintiff'[s] claims under New Jersey law been preempted in this case by federal statutory scheme and the FAA ownership and control over this particular aircraft?

8. Under the facts of this case, can plaintiff assert any claim against Rockwell based on alleged failure to warn?

9. In the facts presented here, does New Jersey law support a survival action for loss of life's enjoyment or pain and suffering?

10. If the crew of the N44 was negligent, does this negligence defeat plaintiff's cause of action?

11. Can plaintiff's damages under the New Jersey Wrongful Death Act support an award for emotional suffering or loss?

12. Plaintiff is barred from raising a claim for punitive damages in the trial of this case. Further, even if plaintiff was not barred, plaintiff failed to state a claim for punitive damages, and it would be inappropriate to impose punitive damages on Rockwell as a successor corporation under the facts of this case.

13. Should the trial be bifurcated as to liability and damages?

14. Is prejudgment interest available to the plaintiff in the event that plaintiff recovers; and if so, how is it determined?

15. [Are] plaintiff's express warranty claims defeated by the terms of the contract(s) of sale between Rockwell Standard Corp. and Israel/IAI?

16. Can plaintiff rely on an advertising brochure in support of their express warranty claims given the executory nature of the contract of sale terms and the sophistication of the purchaser?

17. Rockwell is entitled to judgment in its favor under the absolute defenses under the New Jersey Product Liability Act.

18. The FAA's alterations to the aircraft were substantial and they directly and adversely affected the safety of the aircraft, entitling Rockwell to judgment in its favor. . . .

19. Plaintiff is unable to meet his burden of proof on product misuse.

20. Plaintiff is precluded from again arguing that Pennsylvania law applies to this case.

21. Plaintiff is precluded from raising or introducing any evidence at the trial of incidents of other aircraft accidents. . . .

JOINT SUBMISSION OF WITNESS LISTS

Witness Name	Summary of Testimony	Objective
Robert Albrecht (J) [Address]	All of the individuals listed on this and the next page are former Aero Commander employees involved in the design, production, testing, certification and sales of the Jet Commander aircraft and Rockwell may call some or all of them to testify about their role in that process. Rockwell expects that Messrs. Merryman and Miller may also testify about their connection with the Jet Commander or any airplanes subsumed under Type Certificate A2SW since leaving the employ of Aero Commander. Rockwell expects Mr. Patras to testify about FAA certification procedures at the time the Jet Commander was certified and his involvement with the Jet Commander project. Plaintiffs and/or defendants may read portions of these witnesses' Deposition testimony into evidence in support of plaintiff's theories of liability.	
Charles Boetteher (J) [Address]	Mr. Ramage or a Flight Safety designee may testify as to Flight Safety's courses to train and update Jet Commander pilots, including FAA flight check pilots.	Plaintiff objects
Witness Name	**Summary of Testimony**	**Objective**
Vic Ramage (D) [Address]	Mr. Ramage or a Flight Safety designee may testfy as to Flight Safety's courses to train and update Jet Commander pilots, including FAA flight check pilots.	Plaintiff objects
Jack Tobin (D) [Address]	Mr. Tobin or a Flight Safety designee may testify as to Flight Safety's courses to train and update Jet Commander pilots, including FAA flight check pilots.	Plaintiff objects
Samuel Mazzei (D) [Address]	Mr. Mazzei may testify that he served Captain Burger on a previous occasion when Captain Burger was intoxicated.	Plaintiff objects
Don Compton (D) Electronics Technician—FAA [Address]	Mr. Compton was the ground technician at the Westmoreland Airport who may testify as to communications with the aircraft.	

NOTES AND QUESTIONS

1. Does the Final Pretrial Order differ in significant respects from the complaint? Which provides a clearer picture of plaintiff's case? Would it have been useful to require parties to draft their pleadings with the kind of detail provided in the Final Pretrial Order? Would it have been unfair?

2. Will the jury see the Final Pretrial Order? What function does it serve? Why will the court allow amendment only in "exceptional circumstances"?

C. TRIAL

Once discovery has been completed, the case is ready for trial. The trial may take place before a jury or might be tried solely by a judge in the case of a "bench trial." Even when there is a jury, the trial judge has a range of mechanisms to exercise control over the jury.

1. The Right to a Jury Trial

Before examining some of the mechanisms for obtaining an adjudication from the court, it is important to understand the role of the jury in American procedure. A distinguishing feature of the Anglo-American judicial system is the division of the lawsuit into two distinct stages of pretrial and trial. (As discussed above, civil law systems typically consist of piecemeal hearings that do not include a main event of a single trial.) As we have seen, the pretrial phase is overseen by the judge or a magistrate-judge. Although trials may also be conducted before a judge alone (a "bench trial"), some trials are conducted before juries. In a jury trial, the judge presides, but some of the decision making is left to the jury.

Many of the adjudication procedures that we will consider serve, at least in part, to demarcate an appropriate role for the jury. For instance, summary judgment has a dual function. It saves the court and litigants time by disposing of clear-cut cases without trial. But it also can function as a device to control the jury, which will never have the opportunity to decide cases in which summary judgment has been granted. The judge's power can, in turn, be constrained by the right of the parties to a trial by jury.

Although the jury is formally a part of the trial process, it influences earlier stages of the litigation. For example, a party may choose to structure the lawsuit and request certain forms of relief to obtain or avoid a jury trial. Numerous devices during and after the trial serve to control the jury and preserve its assigned role.

a. When Do the Parties Have a Right to a Jury Trial?

The use of juries has its origins in English common law. Interestingly, England has abandoned jury trials in most civil cases, while the jury has been used more expansively in the United States than in any other country.

The right to jury trial in civil cases is guaranteed by the Seventh Amendment to the United States Constitution. A separate jury trial right in criminal cases is found in the Sixth Amendment. The Seventh Amendment provides:

> In Suits at common law, where the value in controversy shall exceed twenty dollars, the right of trial by jury shall be preserved, and no fact tried by jury shall be otherwise re-examined in any Court of the United States, than according to the rules of the common law.

Two phrases in the Seventh Amendment are very important. First, the phrase "in any Court of the United States" has been interpreted to refer to *federal courts alone*. Although many state constitutions have parallel provisions, there is no federal right to a civil jury trial in state court. There may be important differences between the federal and state rights. For example, the federal court jury must issue a unanimous verdict or the court will declare a mistrial. Many state courts permit nonunanimous verdicts (e.g., 5/6 verdict in New York, and 3/4 verdict in California). Such differences can often influence a plaintiff to bring suit in state rather than federal court.

It is interesting to note that the Sixth Amendment right to trial by jury in criminal cases *has* been made applicable to the states through the "incorporation" doctrine of the Fourteenth Amendment, which provides that no state shall deny any person "due process of law." *See Duncan v. Louisiana*, 391 U.S. 145 (1968). Although many of the Bill of Rights Amendments have been so "incorporated," the Seventh Amendment has not. For more on the doctrine of "selective incorporation," *see* Jerold H. Israel, *Selective Incorporation Revisited*, 71 Geo. L.J. 253 (1982).

The other critical wording in the Seventh Amendment is that in "*suits at common law*" the right to jury trial shall be "*preserved*." Courts interpret this language to mean that federal litigants have a right to jury trial if, at the time of the adoption of the Seventh Amendment in 1791, a litigant asserting the claim in England would have been entitled to a jury trial.

As discussed earlier in this chapter, the use of juries was confined in English practice to the law courts. Juries were not used in the chancery courts (the equity courts). If a claim fell within one of the "forms of action" recognized at common law, the claim had to be pursued in the law courts. The equity courts had jurisdiction only if there was no adequate remedy at law, and they eventually developed their own system of substantive law to protect interests not recognized by the law courts. One of the central limitations of the law courts was that they could not issue injunctive relief, which was solely the province of the chancery courts.

Use of this historical benchmark to evaluate the right to jury trial in contemporary practice has been difficult. American courts largely abandoned the common law forms of action in the first half of the twentieth century. Moreover, there has been a merger of law and equity in federal and most state court systems, so that the same court can hear both legal and equitable claims. *See* Fed. R. Civ. P. 2. In addition, new causes of action, unknown in 1791, have been created through legislation as well as through the growth of the common law.

Accordingly, the courts have been forced to abandon a strictly historical inquiry in favor of a more flexible approach that takes account of this evolution. Rather than determining whether plaintiff's claim literally could have been brought in the law courts in 1791, the courts focus on whether the cause of action is "analogous" to an action recognized at common law and whether the relief sought could have been "offered in the courts at law." As you read the following case, consider what criteria a court should use in determining whether a statutory claim is sufficiently analogous to a common law right to trigger the Seventh Amendment right to jury trial.

Curtis v. Loether

415 U.S. 189 (1974)

Mr. Justice Marshall delivered the opinion of the Court.

Section 812 of the Civil Rights Act of 1968, 82 Stat. 88, 42 U.S.C. §3612, authorizes private plaintiffs to bring civil actions to redress violations of Title VIII, the fair housing provisions of the Act, and provides that "[t]he court may grant as relief, as it deems appropriate, any permanent or temporary injunction, temporary restraining order, or other order, and may award to the plaintiff actual damages and not more than $1,000 punitive damages, together with court costs and reasonable attorney fees. . . ." The question presented in this case is whether the Civil Rights Act or the Seventh Amendment requires a jury trial upon demand by one of the parties in an action for damages and injunctive relief under this section.

Petitioner, a Negro woman, brought this action under §812, claiming that respondents, who are white, had refused to rent an apartment to her because of her race, in violation of §804 (a) of the Act, 42 U.S.C. §3604 (a). In her complaint she sought only injunctive relief and punitive damages; a claim for compensatory damages was later added.[1] After an evidentiary hearing, the District Court granted preliminary injunctive relief, enjoining the respondents from renting the apartment in question to anyone else pending the trial on the merits. This injunction was dissolved some five months later with the petitioner's consent, after she had finally obtained other housing, and the case went to trial on the issues of actual and punitive damages.

Respondents made a timely demand for jury trial in their answer. The District Court, however, held that jury trial was neither authorized by Title VIII nor required by the Seventh Amendment, and denied the jury request. . . . After trial on the merits, the District Judge found that respondents had in fact discriminated against petitioner on account of her race. Although he found no actual damages,

---

1. Although the lower courts treated the action as one for compensatory and punitive damages, petitioner has emphasized in this Court that her complaint sought only punitive damages. It is apparent, however, that petitioner later sought to recover actual damages as well. The District Court's pretrial order indicates the judge's understanding, following a pretrial conference with counsel, that the question of actual damages would be one of the issues to be tried. App. 18a. Petitioner in fact attempted to prove actual damages, App. 45a, but her testimony was excluded for failure to comply with a pretrial discovery order. The District Judge later dismissed the claim of actual damages for failure of proof. In these circumstances, it is irrelevant that the pleadings were never formally amended. Fed. Rules Civ. Proc. 15(b), 16.

see n. 1, *supra*, he awarded $250 in punitive damages, denying petitioner's request for attorney's fees and court costs.

The Court of Appeals reversed on the jury trial issue. . . . After an extended analysis, the court concluded essentially that the Seventh Amendment gave respondents the right to a jury trial in this action, and therefore interpreted the statute to authorize jury trials so as to eliminate any question of its constitutionality. In view of the importance of the jury trial issue in the administration and enforcement of Title VIII and the diversity of views in the lower courts on the question, we granted certiorari. . . . We affirm.

The legislative history on the jury trial question is sparse, and what little is available is ambiguous. There seems to be some indication that supporters of Title VIII were concerned that the possibility of racial prejudice on juries might reduce the effectiveness of civil rights damages actions. On the other hand, one bit of testimony during committee hearings indicates an awareness that jury trials would have to be afforded in damages actions under Title VIII. Both petitioner and respondents have presented plausible arguments from the wording and construction of §812. We see no point to giving extended consideration to these arguments, however, for we think it is clear that the Seventh Amendment entitles either party to demand a jury trial in an action for damages in the federal courts under §812.[6]

The Seventh Amendment provides that "[i]n suits at common law, where the value in controversy shall exceed twenty dollars, the right of trial by jury shall be preserved." Although the thrust of the Amendment was to preserve the right to jury trial as it existed in 1791, it has long been settled that the right extends beyond the common law forms of action recognized at that time. Mr. Justice Story established the basic principle in 1830:

> The phrase "common law," found in this clause, is used in contradistinction to equity, and admiralty, and maritime jurisprudence. . . . By *common law*, [the Framers of the Amendment] meant . . . not merely suits, which the *common* law recognized among its old and settled proceedings, but suits in which *legal* rights were to be ascertained and determined, in contradistinction to those where equitable rights alone were recognized, and

---

6. We recognize, of course, the "cardinal principle that this Court will first ascertain whether a construction of the statute is fairly possible by which the (constitutional) question may be avoided." *United States v. Thirty-seven Photographs*, 402 U.S. 363, 369 (1971), and cases there cited. In this case, however, the necessity for jury trial is so clearly settled by our prior Seventh Amendment decisions that it would be futile to spend time on the statutory issue, particularly since our result is not to invalidate the Civil Rights Act but only to direct that a certain form of procedure be employed in federal court actions under §812. Moreover, the Seventh Amendment issue in this case is in a very real sense the narrower ground of decision. Section 812(a) expressly authorizes actions to be brought "in appropriate State or local courts of general jurisdiction," as well as in the federal courts. The Court has not held that the right to jury trial in civil cases is an element of due process applicable to state courts through the Fourteenth Amendment. Since we rest our decision on Seventh Amendment rather than statutory grounds, we express no view as to whether jury trials must be afforded in §812 actions in the state courts.

equitable remedies were administered. . . . In a just sense, the amendment then may well be construed to embrace all suits which are not of equity and admiralty jurisdiction, whatever might be the peculiar form which they may assume to settle legal rights. *Parsons v. Bedford*, 3 Pet. 433, 446–447 (1830) (emphasis in original).

Petitioner nevertheless argues that the Amendment is inapplicable to new causes of action created by congressional enactment. As the Court of Appeals observed, however, we have considered the applicability of the constitutional right to jury trial in actions enforcing statutory rights "as a matter too obvious to be doubted." . . . Although the Court has apparently never discussed the issue at any length, we have often found the Seventh Amendment applicable to causes of action based on statutes. See, *e.g., Dairy Queen, Inc. v. Wood*, 369 U.S. 469, 477 (1962) (trademark laws); *Hepner v. United States*, 213 U.S. 103, 115 (1909) (immigration laws); cf. *Fleitmann v. Welsbach Street Lighting Co.*, 240 U.S. 27 (1916) (antitrust laws), and discussion of *Fleitmann* in *Ross v. Bernhard*, 396 U.S. 531, 535–536 (1970). Whatever doubt may have existed should now be dispelled. The Seventh Amendment does apply to actions enforcing statutory rights, and requires a jury trial upon demand, if the statute creates legal rights and remedies, enforceable in an action for damages in the ordinary courts of law.

NLRB v. Jones & Laughlin Steel Corp., 301 U.S. 1 (1937), relied on by petitioner, lends no support to her statutory-rights argument. The Court there upheld the award of backpay without jury trial in an NLRB unfair labor practice proceeding, rejecting a Seventh Amendment claim on the ground that the case involved a "statutory proceeding" and "not a suit at common law or in the nature of such a suit." *Id.*, at 48. *Jones & Laughlin* merely stands for the proposition that the Seventh Amendment is generally inapplicable in administrative proceedings, where jury trials would be incompatible with the whole concept of administrative adjudication[8] and would substantially interfere with the NLRB's role in the statutory scheme. *Katchen v. Landy*, 382 U.S. 323 (1966), also relied upon by petitioner, is to like effect. . . . These cases uphold congressional power to entrust enforcement of statutory rights to an administrative process or specialized court of equity free from the strictures of the Seventh Amendment. But when Congress provides for enforcement of statutory rights in an ordinary civil action in the district courts, where there is obviously no functional justification for denying the jury trial right, a jury trial must be available if the action involves rights and remedies of the sort typically enforced in an action at law.

We think it is clear that a damages action under §812 is an action to enforce "legal rights" within the meaning of our Seventh Amendment decisions. . . . A damages action under the statute sounds basically in tort—the statute merely defines a new legal duty, and authorizes the courts to compensate a plaintiff for the injury caused by the defendant's wrongful breach. As the Court of Appeals noted, this cause of action is analogous to a number of tort actions recognized at common

---

8. "[T]he concept of expertise on which the administrative agency rests is not consistent with the use by it of a jury as fact finder." L. Jaffe, Judicial Control of Administrative Action 90 (1965).

law.[10] More important, the relief sought here—actual and punitive damages—is the traditional form of relief offered in the courts of law.[11]

We need not, and do not, go so far as to say that any award of monetary relief must necessarily be "legal" relief. See, *e.g., Mitchell v. Robert DeMario Jewelry, Inc.,* 361 U.S. 288 (1960); *Porter v. Warner Holding Co.,* 328 U.S. 395 (1946). A comparison of Title VIII with Title VII of the Civil Rights Act of 1964, where the courts of appeals have held that jury trial is not required in an action for reinstatement and backpay, is instructive, although we of course express no view on the jury trial issue in that context. In Title VII cases the courts of appeals have characterized backpay as an integral part of an equitable remedy, a form of restitution. But the statutory language on which this characterization is based—

> "[T]he court may enjoin the respondent from engaging in such unlawful employment practice, and order such affirmative action as may be appropriate, which may include, but is not limited to, reinstatement or hiring of employees, with or without back pay . . . , or any other equitable relief as the court deems appropriate," 42 U.S.C.§2000e-5(g) (1970 ed., Supp. II) —

contrasts sharply with §812's simple authorization of an action for actual and punitive damages. In Title VII cases, also, the courts have relied on the fact that the decision whether to award backpay is committed to the discretion of the trial judge. There is no comparable discretion here: if a plaintiff proves unlawful discrimination and actual damages, he is entitled to judgment for that amount. Nor is there any sense in which the award here can be viewed as requiring the defendant to disgorge funds wrongfully withheld from the plaintiff. Whatever may be the merit of the "equitable" characterization in Title VII cases, there is surely no basis for characterizing the award of compensatory and punitive damages here as equitable relief.

---

10. For example, the Court of Appeals recognized that Title VIII could be viewed as an extension of the common law duty of innkeepers not to refuse temporary lodging to a traveler without justification, a duty enforceable in a damages action triable to a jury, to those who rent apartments on a long-term basis. See 467 F.2d, at 1117. An action to redress racial discrimination may also be likened to an action for defamation or intentional infliction of mental distress. Indeed, the contours of the latter tort are still developing, and it has been suggested that "under the logic of the common law development of a law of insult and indignity, racial discrimination might be treated as a dignitary tort." C. Gregory & H. Kalven, Cases and Materials on Torts 961 (2d ed. 1969).

11. The procedural history of this case generated some question in the courts below as to whether the action should be viewed as one for damages and injunctive relief, or as one for damages alone, for purposes of analyzing the jury trial issue. The Court of Appeals concluded that the right to jury trial was properly tested by the relief sought in the complaint and not by the claims remaining at the time of trial. 467 F.2d, at 1118–1119. We need express no view on this question. If the action is properly viewed as one for damages only, our conclusion that this is a legal claim obviously requires a jury trial on demand. And if this legal claim is joined with an equitable claim, the right to jury trial on the legal claim, including all issues common to both claims, remains intact. The right cannot be abridged by characterizing the legal claim as "incidental" to the equitable relief sought. *Beacon Theatres, Inc. v. Westover,* 359 U.S. 500 (1959); *Dairy Queen, Inc. v. Wood,* 369 U.S. 469, 470–473 (1962).

We are not oblivious to the force of petitioner's policy arguments. Jury trials may delay to some extent the disposition of Title VIII damages actions. But Title VIII actions seeking only equitable relief will be unaffected, and preliminary injunctive relief remains available without a jury trial even in damages actions. *Dairy Queen, Inc. v. Wood*, 369 U.S., at 479 n. 20. Moreover, the statutory requirement of expedition of §812 actions, 42 U.S.C. §3614, applies equally to jury and nonjury trials. We recognize, too, the possibility that jury prejudice may deprive a victim of discrimination of the verdict to which he or she is entitled. Of course, the trial judge's power to direct a verdict, to grant judgment notwithstanding the verdict, or to grant a new trial provides substantial protection against this risk, and respondents' suggestion that jury trials will expose a broader segment of the populace to the example of the federal civil rights laws in operation has some force. More fundamentally, however, these considerations are insufficient to overcome the clear command of the Seventh Amendment. The decision of the Court of Appeals must be

Affirmed.

NOTES AND QUESTIONS

1. *When Is a Statutory Right "Analogous" to a Common Law Cause of Action?* What made plaintiff's discrimination claim sufficiently analogous to a common law right to trigger the jury trial right in *Curtis?* Was it important that there was a nondiscrimination norm in the common law for shopkeepers, as discussed in footnote 10? Or is it enough that the Court could conceptualize the right asserted as in the nature of a tort?

The Court's later decision in *City of Monterey v. Del Monte Dunes at Monterey, Ltd.,* 526 U.S. 687 (1999), suggests that the analogy to a common law right may be made at a fairly high level of abstraction. The Court there held that there was a right to jury trial in a "regulatory taking" proceeding brought under the Federal Civil Right Act, 42 U.S.C. §1983. A landowner brought the action against the city of Monterey, California, complaining that the city had imposed excessive and unreasonable constraints on the use of its property. Those constraints, plaintiff alleged, constituted a "taking" without just compensation in violation of the Fourteenth Amendment. The Court held that the question of the city's liability for damages was appropriately submitted to the jury under the Seventh Amendment. While acknowledging that there was no equivalence to a §1983 claim at the time of the adoption of the Seventh Amendment, the Court found the §1983 claim to be "analogous" to a claim heard by juries because it "sounds basically in tort." *Id.* at 709. "Just as common law tort actions provide redress for interference with protected personal or property interests, §1983 provides relief for invasions of rights protected under federal law." *Id.* Don't all lawsuits seek "redress for interference with protected personal or property interests"?

Although the Court did not retreat from the *Curtis* dictum declining to find that the award of damages necessarily constitutes "legal relief" entitled to a jury trial, it emphasized that the plaintiff "sought legal relief" — monetary compensation for the city's actions. But the Court also acknowledged that had compensation been awarded in the context of a condemnation proceeding initiated by the city, it would have been considered a form of "equitable restitution" not "damages," and the landowner would not have been entitled to a jury trial. The Court emphasized that unlike the condemnation context, the court here had to decide a threshold liability issue: Did the city's restrictions on the use of the property constitute a taking? In the condemnation context the only issue before a court is the amount of compensation due the landowner. Is that a significant difference? As argued by Justice Souter in dissent, isn't the condemnation proceeding nevertheless the closest analogue to plaintiff's §1983 claim? As illustrated by *City of Monterey*, given the indeterminacy of finding any historical analogue, the most significant criterion of the right to jury trial tends to be the form of relief requested. *See Chauffeurs, Teamsters and Helpers, Local No. 391 v. Terry*, 494 U.S. 558, 574 (1990) (Brennan, J. dissenting, advocating complete abandonment of the historical analogue test in favor of one looking to the form of relief requested). If only injunctive relief is sought, the case is characterized as an equitable suit, and there is no right to a jury trial. In most cases where only damages are sought, the parties may demand a jury. There are, however, some notable exceptions, particularly for certain statutory claims. *See Atlas Roofing Co. v. Occupational Safety & Health Review Comm'n*, 430 U.S. 442 (1977) (upholding federal statute that makes judge finder of fact in OSHA penalty proceeding against employer).

2. *Why Originalism?* Are you persuaded that there is a more compelling textual basis in the Seventh Amendment for looking to the original meaning of a "right to jury trial" than there is in the case of other constitutional rights? *Compare* Mathew P. Harrington, *The Economic Origins of the Seventh Amendment*, 87 Iowa L. Rev. 145 (2001) (arguing the framers never intended the right to be tied to historical practice); Akhil Reed Amar, The Bill of Rights: Creation and Reconstruction 89 (1998) (arguing for a "dynamic conformity" of the right to jury trial tied to contemporary state practice) *with* Jay Tidmarsh, *The English Fire Courts and the American Right to Civil Jury Trial*, 83 U. Chi. L. Rev. 1893 (2016) (arguing that historic practice implies a greater right of Congress to constrain the right to a jury in federal civil trials). Is it possible for courts to conform to historical practice in regard to the role of juries when little else in modern litigation does? Not only have substantive rights evolved, and (as we shall see shortly) the role of the jury at trial changed, but plaintiffs in the eighteenth century had little access to discovery, it was much more difficult for them to satisfy their pleading obligations, and the rules of evidence and forms of proof at trial have evolved significantly. Could one argue, therefore, that in no event can the parties be accorded the "same" right to jury trial as they had at common law?

3. *What Attributes of a Common Law Jury Does the Seventh Amendment Preserve?* According to *Capital Traction Co. v. Hof*, 174 U.S. 1, 13 (1899), trial by jury at common law was a "trial by a jury of twelve men." Common law jurors were also required to own property, and "were, in some cases, 'kept without meat, drink, fire, or candle' until they rendered a unanimous verdict." Joan L. Larson, *Ancient Juries and Modern Judges: Originalism's Uneasy Relationship with the Jury*, 71 Ohio St. L.J. 959, 961–962 (2010). The Seventh Amendment has not been thought to require conformity with those practices. Today, juries are obviously not composed exclusively of men, and juries may sit in groups as small as six. *See Colgrove v. Battin*, 413 U.S. 149 (1973) (upholding the constitutionality of a six-person civil jury in federal court); Fed. R. Civ. P. 48 ("The court shall seat a jury of not fewer than six and not more than twelve members. . . ."). Rule 48 does require unanimous verdicts "unless the

parties otherwise stipulate." The Court in *Colgrove* concluded that "the Framers of the Seventh Amendment were concerned with preserving the right of trial by jury in civil cases where it existed at common law, rather than the various incidents of trial by jury." 413 U.S. at 155-156.

4. *Statutory Right to Jury Trial.* Note that in *Curtis*, there were two possible sources of a right to jury trial: the Seventh Amendment and the Civil Rights Act. Even in cases not covered by the Seventh Amendment, Congress may provide a right to jury trial when it creates new causes of action, and Congress has done so on numerous occasions. *See, e.g.*, 46 U.S.C. §30104 ("seaman injured in the course of employment . . . may elect to bring a civil action at law, with the right of trial by jury, against the employer"). Because there is no constitutional right guaranteeing a nonjury trial, this conferral of a right broader than the Seventh Amendment is unproblematic. Congressional power to confer a right to jury trial for statutory claims even extends to trial of those claims in state court, where the Seventh Amendment has no application. This explains the Court's somewhat unusual approach in *Curtis* of deciding the constitutional question before reaching the statutory one; the constitutional holding had more limited reach than a statutory construction would have had.

More complicated are congressional attempts to narrow the right to jury trial. Given the Court's Seventh Amendment approach of looking to whether there was a right to jury trial in the analogous common law action, new statutory claims are not automatically insulated from the Seventh Amendment. However, Congress has the constitutional authority to create nonjury, specialized administrative tribunals for adjudicating some statutory claims. *See NLRB v. Jones & Laughlin Steel Corp.*, 301 U.S. 1 (1937). *But see Granfinanciera, S.A. v. Nordberg*, 492 U.S. 33 (1989) (holding unconstitutional Bankruptcy Act's deprivation of jury trial on claim by bankruptcy trustee against defendant in possession of alleged fraudulently transferred assets). The Supreme Court in *Oil States Energy Services, LLC v. Greene's Energy Group, LLC*, 138 S. Ct. 1365 (2018) upheld the constitutionality of the Leahy-Smith America Invents Act, 35 US.C. §100 *et seq.*, which authorized the Patent and Trademark Office to cancel certain issued patents without a jury. Clarifying the Court's earlier holding in *Granfinanciera*, the Court held that in situations in which Article III does not require a matter to be resolved by an Article III court, the Seventh Amendment imposes no additional constraints on the assignment of an adjudication to a non-Article III tribunal.

You will return to this issue in the upper-level course in federal courts.

5. *Mixed Equitable/Legal Claims.* Note that plaintiff in *Curtis* sought an injunction as well as damages. One of the most perplexing problems facing the courts since the merger of law and equity is the availability of the jury trial when both legal and equitable claims are asserted in a single action. At one time, the courts focused on whether the legal or equitable issues "predominated." If the action was basically legal, the jury decided the legal issues, after which the judge ruled on the remaining equitable issues. If the equitable issues predominated, the judge could decide the entire case without a jury, under the "equitable clean-up doctrine," which authorized judicial adjudication of any "incidental" legal issues. The Supreme Court adopted a different approach in several important decisions, starting in 1959.

In *Beacon Theatres, Inc. v. Westover,* 359 U.S. 500 (1959), the Supreme Court established the principle that in cases involving both legal and equitable claims that turn on overlapping facts, the courts must submit the legal issues to a jury before resolving the equitable issues. The case arose out of dispute between two movie theaters, Fox West Coast Theaters and Beacon Theatres. Fox had entered into agreements with several movie distributors granting Fox the exclusive right to show their first-run movies within Fox's geographic region. Beacon owned a theater 11 miles from the Fox theater and notified Fox that Beacon considered Fox's exclusive distribution agreements in violation of the federal antitrust laws. Anticipating suit by Beacon, Fox filed its own action against Beacon seeking a declaration that Fox's distribution agreements were not in violation of the antitrust laws and an injunction against Beacon barring it from filing suit against Fox. Beacon then asserted a damages counterclaim against Fox. Had Beacon asserted its claim in an independent proceeding, it would have clearly been entitled to the jury trial. Here, however, Beacon's legal claim was asserted in an equitable proceeding brought by Fox, normally heard without a jury.

The trial court held that it would first decide Fox's claim without a jury and then impanel a jury to hear Beacon's counterclaim. The problem was that the court's disposition of Fox's case would effectively dispose of Beacon's counterclaim through application of issue preclusion, particularly on the question of whether Beacon was within the geographic area covered by Fox's exclusive distribution rights. The Supreme Court held that the trial court's plan violated Beacon's right to a jury trial on its damage claim. The trial court was required to submit the legal claims to the jury prior to deciding Fox's equitable claims.

Three years later, the Court reiterated that principle in a case in which the equitable claims were considerably more substantial. In *Dairy Queen, Inc. v. Wood,* 369 U.S. 469 (1962), plaintiff, Dairy Queen, brought suit against one of its franchisees for breach of the franchise agreement (very similar to the kind of claim asserted in *Burger King v. Rudzewicz*). Plaintiff sought an injunction restraining Wood from using or profiting from the Dairy Queen trademark, and for an "accounting" (an equitable remedy) and damages for money owed to Dairy Queen. Thus, unlike *Beacon Theaters*, the equitable claims in *Dairy Queen* were dominant. Nonetheless, the Court held that trial still must be conducted in a manner that preserved the right to jury trial on the legal issues. *Accord Ross v. Bernhard,* 396 U.S. 531 (1970) (requiring jury trial of damage claim asserted in derivative shareholder proceeding, a type of proceeding traditionally conducted in equity).

6. *A Complexity Exception to the Seventh Amendment?* In *Beacon Theatres,* the Court noted that "only under the most imperative circumstances, circumstances which in view of the flexible procedures of the Federal Rules we cannot now anticipate, can the right to a jury trial of legal issues be lost through prior determination of equitable claims." 359 U.S. 500, 510–511 (1959). What constitutes an "imperative circumstance"? In *Dairy Queen,* the Court explained that in order to maintain a suit for an equitable accounting on a cause of action cognizable at law, "the plaintiff must be able to show that the 'accounts between the parties' are of such a 'complicated nature' that only a court of equity can satisfactorily unravel them." 369 U.S. 469, 478 (1962). Is complexity an "imperative circumstance"? Would this exception only apply to actions involving equitable and legal claims? Or might complexity stand as a reason to take issues away from juries in purely legal actions?

Consider *In re Japanese Elec. Prods. Antitrust Litigation*, 631 F.2d 1069 (3d Cir. 1980). The claims involved antitrust and antidumping statutes, and the remedies included treble damages. Accordingly, the parties would normally have the right to a trial by jury. When the plaintiff demanded a jury trial, 14 defendants responded by arguing that the case was too large and complex for a jury. Both the district court and the court of appeals agreed that the Seventh Amendment itself contains no complexity exception. However, the court of appeals left open the possibility that adjudication of a very complex case might violate due process and might thus trump the Seventh Amendment:

> The due process objections to jury trial of a complex case implicate values of fundamental importance. If judicial decisions are not based on factual determinations bearing some reliable degree of accuracy, legal remedies will not be applied consistently with the purposes of the laws. There is a danger that jury verdicts will be erratic and completely unpredictable, which would be inconsistent with even-handed justice. Finally, unless the jury can understand the evidence and the legal rules sufficiently to rest its decision on them, the objective of most rules of evidence and procedure in promoting a fair trial will be lost entirely. We believe that when a jury is unable to perform its decision-making task with a reasonable understanding of the evidence and legal rules, it undermines the ability of a district court to render basic justice.
>
> The loss of the right to jury trial in a suit found too complex for a jury does not implicate the same fundamental concerns.

Id. at 1084.

Other courts have disagreed. *See In re U.S. Financial Securities Litigation*, 609 F.2d 411 (9th Cir. 1979) (holding that a complexity exception is not required by due process and would be at odds with the Court's Seventh Amendment jurisprudence). Commentators appear divided as well. *Compare* Morris S. Arnold, *A Historical Inquiry into the Right to Trial by Jury in Complex Civil Litigation*, 128 U. Pa. L. Rev. 829 (1980) (arguing that there was no complexity exception to the right to trial by jury in England in the eighteenth century); Steven I. Friedland, *The Competency and Responsibility of Jurors in Deciding Cases*, 85 Nw. U. L. Rev. 190 (1990) (arguing against a complexity exception to the Seventh Amendment and in favor of expanded jury activity); James R. Steiner-Dillon, *Epistemic Exceptionalism*, 52 Ind. L. Rev. 207 (2019) (concluding that complexity exceptions to the Seventh Amendment should be rejected when the alternative is fact finding by a generalist judge) *with* Lord Devlin, *Jury Trial of Complex Cases: English Practice at the Time of the Seventh Amendment*, 80 Colum. L. Rev. 43 (1980) (arguing that the practice in England in 1791 was for chancellors to make sure complex cases were tried in equity).

7. *The Jury Demand.* Under Fed. R. Civ. P. 38(d), a party must demand a jury trial or he will waive his right. Pursuant to Fed. R. Civ. P. 38(b), the demand may be made by any party in the pleadings or by separate demand. The jury demand must be made within 14 days after the last pleading has been served. Rule 39(b) provides a safety net: The court in its discretion, may, upon motion, "order a trial by jury on any issue for which a jury might have been demanded."

8. *Thinking Strategically.* Note that in *Curtis*, it was the defendant that wanted the jury trial. Under what circumstances do you think a plaintiff would prefer a

bench trial to a jury trial? Do you think plaintiff made a wise choice in *Curtis*? Is there any way that plaintiff could have structured the lawsuit to ensure that the case was not heard by a jury?

b. Allocating the Responsibilities of Judge and Jury

Once it is determined that a case must be tried by a jury, the role of the jury within this legal framework must still be defined. Even when a jury is impaneled, the trial is presided over by the judge. Think about what the respective roles of judge and jury in the trial process might be.

If a judge impaneled a jury simply to observe the trial, but reserved all decision making to herself, it is unlikely that the parties' right to a jury trial would be satisfied. On the other hand, it should be clear that a judge can make many important rulings in the course of a jury trial consistent with the jury trial right, including ruling on the admissibility of evidence or instructing the jurors on the law.

Historically, the jury has performed a variety of functions. Originally, the jury was assigned a role combining elements of witness, inquisitor, and adjudicator. The jury was selected on the basis of its familiarity with the parties and controversy, and it was expected to use that knowledge to investigate and ultimately determine the merits of the case. At times in both the United States and England, the jury had responsibility for both legal and factual determinations. *See* Thayer, *The Jury and Its Development*, 5 Harv. L. Rev. 249 (1892); William E. Nelson, Americanization of the Common Law, The Impact of Legal Change on Massachusetts Society, 1760–1839, 20–30 (1975).

By the middle of the nineteenth century, the role of the jury in the United States was largely confined to fact finding, and that fact finding was to be performed exclusively on the basis of the evidence presented during trial. The judge in contemporary practice decides all questions of law and accordingly instructs the jury on the law. *See* Fed. R. Civ. P. 51.

This law-fact allocation reflects some sense of the respective competencies of the judge and jury. The jury brings to bear the collective life-experience and judgment of 12 people. Their sense of what happened or of who is telling the truth is determined collectively, with lay intuitions and a sense of community input. The judge, on the other hand, is considered an expert on the "law." Particularly after the rise of legal positivism and the decline of natural law, "correct" legal answers are thought to be obtained through the professional craft of reading cases and statutes, not by a lay sense of fairness.

However, to some degree, the law-fact distinction is a false dichotomy. Some questions arising in the course of a trial are easy to classify: "Was the light red?" is clearly a question of fact; "Does a contract require consideration?" is a matter of pure law. Other issues are less clear-cut and might be classified either way: Is a contract "ambiguous"? Was the product "defective"? Was the defendant's conduct "reasonable"? Inevitably the lines blur. Judges take part in factual determinations, and juries play a role in setting legal standards.

The relationship between judge and jury is thus complex. Their relative responsibilities are as much a function of tradition and expediency as the law-fact distinction. The modern requirement that the jury's decision be based exclusively on the basis of the evidence presented, as well as on its obligation to apply the law as given to it by the judge, has resulted in a variety of judicial "controls" over the jury. Through the rules of evidence, juries hear only what the judge deems appropriate. Juries may be required to answer specific questions rather than merely returning a general verdict for plaintiff or defendant. *See, e.g.*, Fed. R. Civ. P. 49(a) and (b). Under various state procedures, juries may be required to itemize damages in certain kinds of cases. *See, e.g.*, N.Y. C.P.L.R. §4111(d) and (e).

Perhaps the greatest control of the judge over the jury is the power given to the judge to prevent the case from ever reaching the jury, and/or permitting the judge to overturn a jury verdict and render a judgment for the verdict loser. *See, e.g.*, Fed. R. Civ. P. 50(a) and 50(b) (Judgment as a Matter of Law in Jury Trials). Such power is limited and can be invoked by a judge only when the judge is confident that no reasonable jury could find in favor of a particular party on the basis of the evidence presented at the trial.

In contrast to the Court's approach in cases like *Curtis* and *City of Monterey* of erring on the side of finding a right to trial by jury, the Court has been more tolerant of modern practices allocating powers to the judge that would have not been exercised in the same way in jury trials at common law. *See, e.g., Markman v. Westview Instruments, Inc.*, 517 U.S. 370 (1996), in which the Court held that there was no Seventh Amendment right to a jury determination of the scope of a patent in an action for patent infringement. Although infringement cases were tried by a jury at common law, there was no clear precedent for whether the scope of the patent claim was within the province of the jury. Accordingly, the Court turned to "functional" rather than historical considerations of the relative competence of the judge or jury to make the determination, which weighed in favor of giving the decision to the judge. *Cf., Parklane Hosiery Co. v. Shore*, 439 U.S. 322 (1979), *supra* p. 848 (holding that expanding the scope of collateral estoppel did not violate the Seventh Amendment). For an argument that the Seventh Amendment requires greater fidelity to historic practice, *see* Suja A. Thomas, *The Seventh Amendment, Modern Procedure, and the English Common Law*, 82 Wash. U. L.Q. 687 (2005); Suja A. Thomas, *Why Summary Judgment is Unconstitutional*, 93 Va. L. Rev. 119 (2007); Suja A. Thomas, *Why the Motion to Dismiss Is Now Unconstitutional*, 92 Minn. L. Rev. 1851 (2008). *But see*, Edward Brunet, *Summary Judgment Is Constitutional*, 93 Iowa L. Rev. 1625 (2008).

c. The Pros and Cons of the Jury Trial

Discussion of the jury system often evokes passionate debate. The framers of the Constitution clearly believed that the jury plays a critical role in checking governmental tyranny. They preferred that responsibility for enforcing both criminal and civil laws ultimately reside with ordinary citizens of the jury, not in any governmental official. In this sense, the jury represents an important democratic institution.

Other democratic "features" of the jury include its application of societal values and elimination of rigidity in the law, its diverse aspects of community sensibility, and its representative and discontinuous character. *See generally* Harry Kalven, Jr., *The Dignity of the Civil Jury*, 50 Va. L. Rev. 1055 (1964). In addition, the jury is often invoked as a positive force for civic participation and for educating citizens about the operation and importance of the rule of law.

On the other hand, serious questions have been raised about the capacity and effectiveness of juries in the adjudication process. Both the subject matter and the complexities of many cases seem ill-suited to determinations by lay persons. *See* Jerome Frank, Courts on Trial (1949). Juries would also seem to introduce inconsistency and unpredictability into the legal process as well as to draw out the proceedings. *See* Franklin Strier, Reconstructing Justice: An Agenda for Trial Reform (1994). However, others have pointed out that judges are not immune from cognitive mistakes. *See* Chris Guthrie, Jeffrey J. Rachlinski & Andrew Wistrich, *Inside the Judicial Mind*, 86 Cornell L. Rev. 777, 829 (2001) ("Our study demonstrates that judges rely on the same cognitive decision-making process as laypersons and other experts, which leaves them vulnerable to cognitive illusions that can produce poor judgments.").

Empirical studies of the jury have not led to any greater degree of consensus about its value. *Compare* Neil Vidmar, *The Performance of the American Civil Jury: An Empirical Perspective*, 40 Ariz. L. Rev. 849 (1998) (empirical research suggests reasonable level of jury performance); James R. Steiner-Dillon, *Epistemic Exceptionalism*, 52 Ind. L. Rev. 207 (2019) (examining the empirical basis of the assumption that judges are better at cognitive tasks, and finding the premise of judicial cognitive superiority, at best, exaggerated) *with* Matthew A. Reiber & Jill D. Weinberg, *The Complexity of Complexity: An Empirical Study of Juror Competence in Civil Cases*, 78 U. Cin. L. Rev. 929 (2010) (concluding that "comprehension declines as complexity increases, particularly when the complexity arises from the presence of multiple parties or claims. The results also show that comprehension does not improve with education or prior jury experience.") *and* George L. Priest, Justifying the Civil Jury in Verdict Assessing the Civil Jury System (Robert E. Litan, ed. 1993) (questioning the extent to which juries actually impart community values to the deliberation); Joni Hersch & W. Kip Viscusi, *Punitive Damages: How Judges and Juries Perform*, 33 J. Legal Stud. 1 (2004) (finding that juries are significantly more likely to award higher punitive and compensatory damages than judges).

What is your view of the civil jury? Consider the central factual question that the jury in the *Rockwell* case had to decide: What caused the engines to lose power? Expert investigators determined the cause of the crash for the National Transportation Safety Board. The NTSB does not ask 12 people chosen at random off the street to evaluate the evidence.

Why are these methodologies different? Does a civil trial perform a different function than a NTSB investigation? Is the scientific truth that the NTSB presumably strives for different than the legal truth to which judicial adjudication aspires? As between a lay jury and an equally nonexpert judge, is there any reason to believe that the judge would have a better sense of why the engines lost power?

2. *Trial Procedure*

Most of the elements of procedure that we have examined in this chapter are designed to prepare the case for trial. The function of a trial is to resolve conflicting evidence. Since summary judgment and motions on the pleadings (as well as settlement) should filter out any case that is legally or factually one-sided, trials are by their very nature up for grabs. The advocacy skills of an attorney (explaining the case to the judge or jury, preparing the witnesses and trial exhibits, and cross-examining the opponent's proof) can have an enormous impact on the ultimate outcome of the case. The upper-level course in trial advocacy will help you develop some of those skills. Our purpose here is to give you a rough description of the trial process.

As we saw in the Final Pretrial Order, most of the trial is carefully scripted in advance. All parties and the court should have clear notice of every witness and the substance of their testimony. Even evidentiary questions can be settled in advance through the use of *motions in limine* (usually pronounced "in liminay," meaning "at the beginning") provided for in federal practice by Federal Rule of Evidence 104. In the *Rockwell* case, for instance, the court ruled on a motion *in limine* that defendant could not introduce proof of the pilots' ingestion of alcohol. It determined that under a New Jersey statute, evidence of alcohol consumption was admissible only when it resulted in legal intoxication.

Trials, for the most part, are open to the public. *See* Fed. R. Civ. P. 43(a). They can take anywhere from a few hours to several weeks.

a. Jury Selection

If a proper jury demand has been made, the first stage of trial is selection of a jury. The jury is drawn from a pool of adult citizens summoned from throughout the district or division (a subdivision of a district). Federal juries are thus typically drawn from a wider geographic area than state juries. Jurors receive a small *per diem* (daily pay) to compensate them for their service. Pursuant to Fed. R. Civ. P. 48, the court must seat a jury of at least six and no more than twelve jurors.

Modern trial practice goes to great lengths to make sure that all of the information a jury gets about the case comes through the trial, as controlled by the rules of evidence. A juror is normally disqualified from service if she is familiar with any of the parties or has learned too much about the controversy prior to the trial.

A juror's qualification is determined by a process known as *voir dire* (usually pronounced "vwar dear," normally translated as "tell the truth"). *Voir dire* is a brief questioning of the jurors concerning their background, knowledge of the parties or controversy, and ability to render impartial justice. Fed. R. Civ. P. 47 provides that the examination may, in the court's discretion, be done by the judge or the attorneys. Where permitted, many attorneys value the opportunity to conduct *voir dire* as a preliminary opportunity to argue subtly the merits of their position. ("Do you think you could be impartial in a case where the plaintiff's decedent died when their jet slammed into a mountain after the engines lost all power?")

Following *voir dire*, the attorneys may challenge a juror's selection. A juror may be challenged for cause or, on peremptory challenge, without cause. In civil cases, the parties, by statute, are entitled to three peremptory challenges, but the court in its discretion may allow more. 28 U.S.C. §1870. The method of exercising the challenges varies with local practice.

Any juror may be challenged for cause on the basis that he would not be impartial. Thus, any juror having a financial stake in the outcome of the case, a relationship with the parties or attorneys, or preconception about the appropriate disposition of the case, will normally be excused for cause.

b. Opening Statements

Trials normally commence with the presentations of opening statements by counsel for each party. The function of the opening statement is to provide an outline of the case that the attorney intends to present. It normally includes a brief statement of her legal theory, as well as a summary of the testimony that will be presented and its legal relevance.

For instance, defendant's opening in the *Rockwell* case might include the following statements:

> Defendant will show that the most likely cause of this tragic accident was gross incompetence by the pilot and crew in the operation of the airplane. You will hear evidence that this aircraft was certified by the FAA after extensive testing for operation in icing conditions. You will hear from experts in the design of deicing systems that, when used properly, the deicing system on this plane was incapable of releasing ice particles large enough to stop the engines.
>
> You will also see undisputed evidence that both of the engines on this plane lost power at virtually the same time. Keep this fact in mind as you listen to plaintiff's account of this accident. Ask yourselves how likely it was for this to be caused by ice particles released from the wings, an effect that has never been demonstrated on even one wing. You will hear from engineering experts that plaintiff's theory is simply inconsistent with these established facts.
>
> Why then did this plane crash? You will hear testimony that the most likely explanation for the simultaneous loss of power in both engines was that ice had built up on the outside of those engines, depriving the engines of needed oxygen. You will hear unchallenged testimony that there is a very simple and effective way to prevent this suffocation. Had the crew simply turned a switch to divert some of the engine power to heat the outer edge of the engines, ice could not have formed there. You will further hear that if they failed to do so in the conditions in which this plane was flying at the time of the accident, ice buildup on both engines, at the same time, was a virtual certainty.

As we saw in the case of pleading, a party on opening must temper vigorous advocacy with honest objectivity; the opening is a promise to the tribunal. If a party fails to deliver on that promise, it severely undermines its credibility.

c. Presentation of the Evidence

i. Order of Proof; Bifurcation

The normal order of proof at trial is that plaintiff puts on its entire case, then defendant puts on its entire case, following which plaintiff may introduce evidence to rebut defendant's case. The parties then offer a closing summation. Plaintiff is normally accorded the privilege of opening first and closing last.

However, this order may be varied at the court's discretion. In particular, the court may choose to split or "*bifurcate*" the case between various issues, as authorized by Fed. R. Civ. P. 42(b). In a bifurcated trial, the parties present proof on the first issue or issues, and then the court adjudicates that issue. If necessary, the parties then proceed to try subsequent issues. For instance, in *Rockwell*, defendant requested, and the court granted, a bifurcation between liability and damages, a common bifurcation request.

Bifurcation serves two important functions. First, it can save the court and litigants considerable time and money if the first adjudication disposes of the case. For instance, a finding of no liability would render unnecessary litigation of damages. Note, however, that where the same witnesses are called for both issues, a bifurcated trial could take longer than a unified one. Second, bifurcation isolates evidence that is germane to only one of the issues, but might distort adjudication of the other issues. For instance, in *Rockwell*, defendant was undoubtedly concerned that the jury's consideration of liability would be inappropriately affected by evidence of how much the decedents suffered in the crash.

On occasion, courts have "reverse-bifurcated" the trial, allowing the jury to determine the amount of plaintiff's damages before hearing testimony on defendant's liability. Can you think of circumstances in which reverse bifurcation would be appropriate?

ii.   Testimony

One of the most common modes of proof at trial is testimony by witnesses. Each witness is first "sworn in" and then questioned by the attorney who called that witness in a process called *direct examination*. During direct examination ("direct"), the attorney may not ask any question that suggests the answer. This is called a "leading question" and is the most common objection asserted during direct. Witnesses may only testify as to matters within their own knowledge and unless they have been qualified as "experts," may not generally offer their opinions.

Following direct, the witness may be questioned by opposing counsel in a process called *cross-examination*. Leading questions are appropriate on cross-examination. An attorney on cross-examination is normally limited to questioning the witness about matters the witness testified to on direct.

If necessary, the lawyer who called the witness to testify may then question the witness again on *redirect* (after which the witness may again be subjected to cross-examination).

Witnesses may occasionally also be questioned by the judge if there is additional information that the judge would like to obtain from a witness. However, particularly in jury trials, judges are reluctant to inject themselves into the examination of witnesses for fear that they may appear to be signaling their view of the case. Jurors are not permitted to question the witnesses directly, although judges may, at their discretion, ask the witness questions submitted to the judge by the jurors.

There are elaborate rules of evidence governing the admissibility of testimony at trial. In federal court, evidentiary questions are controlled by the Federal Rules of Evidence. When a question or testimony appears to be in violation of any rule of evidence, opposing counsel may raise an *objection*. An attorney's failure to make a timely objection may result in waiver of the objection.

When making an objection, the attorney must state the specific grounds for the objection, but does not normally make an argument. If the court does hear argument on the objection it will do so outside of the hearing of the jury. The judge may call the attorneys to a "sidebar," hear argument "in chambers," or temporarily excuse the jury from the courtroom. The court will either *sustain* (agree with) or *overrule* (disagree with) the objection.

When inadmissible testimony has been presented before the opposing party had an opportunity to object—for instance, when the witness testifies without being asked as to a matter outside of his competence—the court will "strike" the evidence and instruct the jury to disregard the testimony. It is generally thought that such instructions are not very effective.

The attendance of witnesses at a federal trial may be compelled by a subpoena pursuant to Fed. R. Civ. P. 45. Trial subpoenas are subject to most of the same conditions as discovery subpoenas, except that a witness within the state may be required to travel more than 100 miles to testify at trial. Where a witness is outside of the jurisdiction, the court may permit the party to offer his testimony through the transcript or videotape of his deposition.

The court, in its discretion, may exclude a witness from the courtroom prior to testifying. This technique can help prevent a witness from conforming his testimony to that of other witnesses.

iii. Presentation of Real Evidence

The other principal mode of proof at trial is the presentation of tangible objects that help prove a factual contention such as a writing, a scar, a photograph, a bloody glove, a tire track, and so on. This is called *real evidence*. (An attorney may also prepare charts or models to help explain the testimony of witnesses. This is called *demonstrative evidence*.)

Before real evidence can be admitted, the attorney must establish its connection to the controversy and that its condition has not been altered. This is normally done through the testimony of a witness—for example, the photographer or the custodian of records. Once admitted into evidence, real evidence, or the "exhibit," becomes part of the trial record.

d. Summations

After each party finishes presenting its evidence, the attorneys make closing arguments or *summations*. The defendant goes first. Closing arguments are the mirror image of the opening statements. The closing arguments review the evidence presented and highlight its significance. If an attorney elicited a significant concession or contradiction from a witness on cross-examination, the attorney will use the closing argument to explain its importance. The attorney may also emphasize the absence of proof. ("You did not hear a single witness testify that he ever saw, or even heard of, ice particles visible to the naked eye come off the wing of any Jet Commander and go into the engine.")

While the judge is responsible for instructing the jury on the applicable law, attorneys also use summation to argue how the applicable legal standards apply to the evidence presented. Plaintiff's attorney in a jury trial often uses summation to emphasize how low the "preponderance of evidence" standard is, the burden of persuasion applicable to most civil actions. ("Imagine weighing the evidence on a sensitive jeweler's scale. Place plaintiff's evidence on one side, defendant's on the other. Imagine the scale in absolute balance. Now put a feather on one side. That's all it takes to create a preponderance of evidence.")

e. Judgments as a Matter of Law

We have already seen in connection with summary judgment the judge's responsibility for taking the case away from the jury before trial if there is insufficient evidence to support a claim or defense. The judge has a final opportunity to do so during or after trial by issuing a judgment as a matter of law pursuant to Fed. R. Civ. P. 50(a) (judgment before submitting case to jury) and 50(b) (judgment after jury verdict).

Dixon v. Wal-Mart Stores, Inc.

330 F.3d 311 (5th Cir. 2003)

Appeal from the United States District Court for the Eastern District of Texas. Before HIGGINBOTHAM, WIENER, and DENNIS, Circuit Judges.

WIENER, Circuit Judge:

In this simple negligence case, Defendant-Appellant Wal-Mart Stores, Inc. ("Wal-Mart") appeals the district court's denial of its motion for judgment as a matter of law following a jury verdict in favor of Plaintiff-Appellee Billie F. Dixon. She had brought suit against Wal-Mart after she tripped on a strip of plastic that was lying on the floor near a check-out register at a Wal-Mart store in Texas. Concluding that Dixon has not established a sufficient evidentiary basis on which a reasonable jury could find in her favor, we reverse the district court's order and remand for entry of judgment as a matter of law in favor of Wal-Mart.

I. FACTS AND PROCEEDINGS

In July 1996, Dixon tripped and fell at approximately 5:00 p.m. on a Sunday while leaving a Wal-Mart store in Longview, Texas. After checking out at one of the registers, she fell when her feet became entangled in a piece of plastic similar to the rope-like plastic strips that are typically used to bind newspapers or magazines into stacks. The injuries resulting from her fall were relatively severe, requiring Dixon to obtain immediate medical treatment at a nearby hospital. Thereafter, she continued to receive regular medical treatment for maladies related to this incident.

In July 1998, Dixon filed suit against Wal-Mart in Texas state court, alleging injuries resulting from Wal-Mart's negligence in failing to maintain reasonably safe premises at its Longview store. Wal-Mart removed the case to federal court under our diversity jurisdiction. At a two-day trial in October 1999, Dixon claimed that Wal-Mart failed to remove an unreasonable risk of harm to its customers at its Longview store, *viz.*, the plastic binder on the floor near the check-out registers. She did not claim *actual* knowledge by Wal-Mart, instead proffering two evidentiary bases for Wal-Mart's *constructive* knowledge of this unreasonable risk of harm: (1) the close physical proximity of the plastic binder to Wal-Mart employees, i.e., the location of the plastic binder only several feet away from the employees staffing the check-out registers, and (2) the sufficiently long time that the plastic binder had remained on the floor, i.e., the implication that the plastic binder had been dropped at the location of her fall by the magazine and newspaper suppliers who restocked the store between 4:30 and 8:30 a.m. that day, more than eight hours prior to her 5:00 p.m. accident. Wal-Mart countered with uncontroverted testimony that (1) all employees are trained to pick up any debris or trash in the store, (2) managers and employees frequently perform safety inspections of the store, and (3) the particular area in which Dixon fell had been inspected most recently approximately five minutes before her accident. The jury returned a verdict for Dixon, but also found her 50% at fault for the accident. Thus, the jury awarded Dixon one-half of the total damages of $125,000.

Pursuant to Federal Rule of Civil Procedure 50, Wal-Mart moved for judgment as a matter of law both at the close of Dixon's case-in-chief and prior to submission of the case to the jury. The district court denied both of these motions. Following the return of the jury verdict, Wal-Mart renewed its motion for judgment as a matter of law, which was again denied. Wal-Mart timely filed a notice of appeal.

II. ANALYSIS

A. Standard of Review

We review *de novo* rulings on motions for judgment as a matter of law, applying the same standards as the district court. Under Rule 50, judgment as a matter of law should be granted if "a party has been fully heard on an issue and there is no legally sufficient evidentiary basis for a reasonable jury to find for that party on that issue."[2] Accordingly, Rule 50 mandates that we adopt a "sufficiency of the evidence" standard in our *de novo* review.

This standard requires that we consider all evidence in the light most favorable to the opposing party and draw all reasonable inferences in favor of the opposing party. We may not make credibility determinations or weigh any evidence, which are fact-finding judgments to be made by the jury, not by the court.[5] Nonetheless, "[i]f the facts and inferences point so strongly and overwhelmingly in favor of the moving party that the reviewing court believes that reasonable jurors could not have arrived at a contrary verdict, then we will conclude that the motion should have been granted."

B. Sufficiency of the Evidence of Wal-Mart's Negligence

1. Texas Law on Premises-Owner Liability

As this case was removed to federal court under our diversity jurisdiction, we look to Texas law for the substantive standards defining Wal-Mart's duty of care to its customers. In Texas, a customer, such as Dixon, is an invitee. As such, business owners like Wal-Mart owe "a duty to exercise reasonable care to protect her from

---

2. Fed. R. Civ. P. 50(a)(1).
5. *Reeves v. Sanderson Plumbing Prods., Inc.* (2000).

dangerous conditions in the store known or discoverable to it."[7] Notably, this is a duty requiring only *reasonable care* by the business owner: Texas courts have repeatedly stated that businesses are not insurers of an invitee's safety. Therefore, to prove premises liability on the part of a business owner, a plaintiff must show:

(1) Actual or constructive knowledge of some condition on the premises by the owner/operator;
(2) the condition posed an unreasonable risk of harm;
(3) the owner/operator did not exercise reasonable care to reduce or eliminate the risk; and
(4) the owner/operator's failure to use such care proximately caused the plaintiff's injuries.

In this case, Wal-Mart did not contest that the plastic binder on the floor constituted an unreasonable risk of harm or that Dixon was in fact injured in a trip and fall caused by this binder. Wal-Mart disputes only Dixon's allegation that it had constructive knowledge of the presence of the plastic binder on the floor. Therefore, the sole issue on appeal is whether Dixon established a sufficient evidentiary basis on which a reasonable jury could find that Wal-Mart had constructive knowledge of the plastic binder's presence on the floor.

2. Constructive Knowledge

On appeal, Dixon reiterates her trial contention that Wal-Mart had constructive knowledge of the plastic binder's presence, given its proximity to Wal-Mart employees and the length of time — at least eight hours — that inferentially it had been at that spot on the floor. She maintains that either of these propositions establishes a sufficient evidentiary basis for presenting this issue to a jury. We shall deal with each of these claims in order.

a. *Evidence of Proximity of Object to Employees*

The argument that constructive knowledge can be inferred from the close physical proximity of an unreasonable risk to the employees of a premises owner was recently rejected by the Texas Supreme Court in *Wal-Mart Stores, Inc. v. Reece.*[10] In that case, a Wal-Mart employee walked directly past a puddle of liquid on the floor, but did not notice the liquid until after the plaintiff had slipped on it and fallen. The plaintiff maintained that Wal-Mart had constructive knowledge by virtue of the employee's proximity to the puddle, despite the employee's undisputed lack of actual knowledge of the liquid's presence. Wal-Mart argued that, as none of its employees knew of the spill, the plaintiff failed to bear her burden of proving knowledge, constructive or actual, on the part of a premises owner. The plaintiff in *Reece* did not adduce any evidence of what caused the spill or — more importantly — how long prior to her slip and fall the spill had occurred. The jury found in the plaintiff's favor, and the Texas appellate court affirmed the verdict based solely on the proposition that the Wal-Mart employee's proximity to the puddle satisfied the element of Wal-Mart's

---

7. *Wal-Mart Stores, Inc. v. Gonzalez*, 968 S.W.2d 934, 936 (Tex.1998).
10. 81 S.W.3d 812 (Tex. 2002).

constructive knowledge of the puddle's existence. In the Texas Supreme Court, Wal-Mart insisted that alone an employee's proximity to a hazard cannot establish constructive knowledge. Wal-Mart argued that such a rule would (1) require "omniscience" of a premises owner, (2) not a [sic] provide premises owner with a fair opportunity to inspect, correct, or warn invitees of the risk, and (3) impose constructive knowledge *instantly*, at the moment a hazard is created, and thus make a premises owner a *de facto* insurer of invitees' safety. The Texas Supreme Court agreed with all of Wal-Mart's arguments, reversed the trial court and the intermediate appellate court, and rendered a take-nothing judgment against the plaintiff. In so doing, the *Reece* court announced the rule that "proximity evidence alone is insufficient to establish constructive notice absent some indication that the hazard existed long enough to give the premises owner a reasonable opportunity to discover it."[13]

Reece further establishes that physical proximity evidence is relevant only in case-by-case determinations of constructive knowledge based on the length of time that the risk has been present. A plaintiff might be able to show, for instance, that a shorter presence is required to establish constructive knowledge for a conspicuous hazard that is near a premises owner's employees than for an inconspicuous hazard that is remote from such employees. Still, the rule in Texas is that temporal evidence, not proximity evidence, is the *sine qua non* of a premises owner's constructive knowledge.

Dixon argued before the district court that Wal-Mart's motion for judgment as a matter of law should be rejected because the accident "happened two feet from a cashier." She did not argue that this is only an additional factor for determining the reasonableness of Wal-Mart's constructive knowledge based on her temporal evidence. Neither did she adduce any evidence at trial of the conspicuousness of the plastic binder on the floor. She argued only that the plastic binder's proximity to Wal-Mart employees serves as an independent basis for finding that Wal-Mart had constructive knowledge of the plastic binder's presence on the floor. Yet, *Reece* mandates the conclusion that the accident's occurrence just "two feet from a cashier" is, by itself, nondeterminative of Wal-Mart's constructive knowledge. Thus, Dixon's proximity argument and her reliance on proximity evidence fails the legal standard under Texas law for determining a premises owner's constructive knowledge.

b. Temporal Evidence of the Plastic Binder's Presence

Dixon asked the jury to infer that the plastic binder was on the floor constantly for *more than eight hours* until her late afternoon accident, presumably having been dropped there in the early morning by the magazine or newspaper suppliers. This is simply unreasonable, given the totality of the evidence proffered at trial. Our standard of review mandates that we draw all *reasonable* inferences in favor of Dixon, and the applicable substantive law in this case requires a premises owner to "exercise *reasonable* care" vis-à-vis an invitee.[16] Under Texas law, a premises owner's constructive knowledge is predicated on *temporal* evidence because a premises

---

13. *Id.* at 815.
16. *Gonzalez*, 968 S.W.2d at 936.

owner is not an insurer of an invitee's safety, and therefore a premises owner must have the opportunity—sufficient time—to "exercise *reasonable* care to reduce or eliminate the risk."

Most often, the reasonableness of constructive knowledge of a premises owner is defined in terms of the *minimum* time required for a risk to exist before it can constitute constructive knowledge.[18] To establish a premises owner's constructive knowledge of the presence of an unreasonable risk of harm, a plaintiff generally must prove that the risk existed for a time sufficiently long to permit the premises owner (or his employees) to (1) discover it and (2) correct it. For this reason, defendant premises owners often respond, as Wal-Mart did in the instant case, that the risk existed for such a brief period of time that, as premises owner, it had insufficient time for the peril to be recognized and corrected.[19] Fealty to her pleading burden and to the *only* evidence she was able to adduce motivated Dixon to imply at trial that (1) the source of the plastic binder was the magazine and newspaper suppliers who visited the store more than eight hours prior to her accident, and (2) the plastic binder lay there the entire eight hours, just steps from the cash register, without being seen.

For the jury to make this inference, however, was logically unreasonable, particularly in light of the evidence submitted by Wal-Mart, which was undisputed by Dixon. Wal-Mart's front-end manager, Jean Chatham, testified that it is "part of our job" constantly to survey the area in which Dixon fell and to pick up any trash. Chatham's job description required her to patrol this particular area approximately once every five minutes, specifically looking for any trash, debris, puddles, or merchandise that should be removed from the area. She further testified that the cashiers go through the same training regimen as do the managers, and that every employee is responsible for making sure that foreign objects are picked up and that any potential risk is promptly eliminated. This testimony was confirmed by the assistant store manager, Luther Fairley, who noted that "picking stuff up off the floor isn't just one person's responsibility but . . . belongs to all the employees at Wal-Mart."

In addition, the Store Director, Greg Smith, explained that all Wal-Mart employees are trained according to company policy "[t]o be on the look-out at all times" for "merchandise on the floor," including such items as a plastic binder and other "type trash." He confirmed Chatham's testimony that the front-end managers are responsible for patrolling the area around the check-out registers, making rounds approximately every five minutes or so. "[T]hey do make the rounds," he

---

18. *See, e.g., Wright*, 73 S.W.3d at 555 (rejecting plaintiff's argument that the cause of her slip and fall, a french fry, was on the floor a sufficiently long time to establish constructive knowledge given only that the french fry was dirty and that Wal-Mart failed to keep sweeping records of the area).

19. *See, e.g., Brookshire Food Stores, LLC v. Allen*, 93 S.W.3d 897, 2002 WL 31769486, 4 (Tex. App.—Texarkana 2002) (nothing that "the available evidence suggests the grapes [on which the plaintiff slipped and fell] were not on the floor longer than fifteen minutes"); *Garcia*, 30 S.W.3d at 23 ("Wal-Mart argues the jalapeno [on which the plaintiff Garcia slipped and fell] went unnoticed by snack bar personnel because it fell immediately prior to Garcia's accident.").

said, "just like myself even, my assistant managers, all of us make the rounds. We obviously try to keep everything as much as possible a hundred percent free of trash, debris and any type of safety hazard."

Smith noted further that, in addition to giving responsibility for cleaning activities to cashiers, front-end managers, assistant managers and himself, Wal-Mart employs a "safety team," which patrols the entire store and constantly trains the employees. Smith explained:

> What they look for is specific hazards and basically what their job duty is—we cover it every day. It's constant training. We have morning and evening meetings with our associates and the safety team does demonstrations. We do spill demonstrations. We do demonstrations on picking up trash, and we have a specific safety team, but it's everybody's duty to maintain the sales floor, including myself. . . . [I]t's just part of my job and my duties to keep the floor clean.

Also, a maintenance crew, comprising a minimum of two employees, is on duty during the "busy times of the day, between say 10 [in the morning] and eight o'clock at night." Their singular job function is to "walk around with a broom, dust pan and a mop and clean the floors."

The result of Wal-Mart's policies, its training programs, and the cleaning responsibilities of all Wal-Mart employees is palpable. Smith testified that approximately five million customers use the Longview Wal-Mart store each year, averaging about 13,700 customers each day, but that only some 50 accidents occur per year. None of this evidence—none of the testimony of Chatham, Fairley or Smith—was challenged or contradicted by Dixon.

Given this extensive evidence of constant searches for hazards by myriad Wal-Mart employees, and the dearth of temporal evidence by Dixon of the presence of the hazard any closer to her fall in time than eight hours, the conclusion is inescapable that any plastic binder dropped by the vendors that morning could not possibly have remained at the location of her fall for those many hours without being discovered. And, absent evidence of some other, believable period of the plastic binder's presence prior to the fall, no reasonable jury could find negligence by Wal-Mart based on constructive knowledge of the risk. When the sole source of the hazard advanced by Dixon is eliminated as being a virtual impossibility, her burden of proof of constructive knowledge fails.

During argument before the district court on Wal-Mart's renewed motion for judgment as a matter of law, Dixon's attorney explained that Wal-Mart must have had constructive knowledge of the presence of the plastic binder because

> it *might* be something from the magazines. They stock the magazines at eight o'clock. If it was left from eight o'clock that morning to five o'clock that afternoon, that's certainly not prudent (emphasis added).[20]

---

20. Smith earlier testified that the newspaper and magazine vendors restock the area near the check-out registers "early in the morning." He further explained that "[t]he morning run on the newspapers is typically 4:30, five o'clock in the morning. The magazine people usually get there eight, nine o'clock, somewhere around in there."

It strains credulity, let alone the bounds of logic and reason, that a plastic binder large enough to entangle Dixon's feet and cause her to fall could have lain on the floor in such a high-traffic area of the store for at least *eight hours*. This area was traversed by thousands of customers that day, and was under the constant surveillance of numerous Wal-Mart employees as well. Yet, Dixon would have the fact-finder believe that the plastic binder lay there for more than eight hours without a single person noticing it, let alone picking it up and removing it. She adduced no evidence that anyone—neither a customer nor an employee—noticed the plastic binder lying on the floor for over eight hours during the busiest portion of the business day in one of the most heavily trafficked areas of the store.

That is simply not credible. When the only source of the binder on which Dixon presented evidence is eliminated as constituting an impossibility, she is left without proof of a source, and thus without proof that the binder had been in place (1) long enough for knowledge of its presence to be imputed to Wal-Mart, but (2) not so long as to defy reason.

In fact, Dixon's proximity argument works in favor of Wal-Mart on this point, not against it. We have shown that it is a logical impossibility that this plastic binder remained on the floor for at least eight hours when it was only feet away from the cashiers, other Wal-Mart employees, and a legion of customers. Had the binder been dropped no later than 8:00 a.m., then in light of the evidence submitted by Wal-Mart, the plastic binder simply could not have lain there all that time without having been seen and removed. The obvious flaw in Dixon's theory is the premise that the *only* way the binder could have gotten to the place of the accident was to have been dropped there that morning by a vendor. Yet Dixon offered *no evidence of any other source or of any time closer to the accident* to place the plastic binder on the floor at the site of her trip and fall. The result is that Dixon has not met her burden to plead and prove credible facts to support even an inference of constructive knowledge of this risk on the part of Wal-Mart.

In a similar case, *Wal-Mart Stores Inc. v. Gonzalez*, the Texas Supreme Court rejected a plaintiff's "logic" that the presence of "dirt" on spilled macaroni salad justified the inference that the macaroni had been on the floor long enough to impute constructive knowledge to Wal-Mart of this risk to its customers. The court explained that

> [d]irt in macaroni salad lying on a *heavily-traveled aisle* is no evidence of the length of time the macaroni had been on the floor. That evidence can no more support the inference that it accumulated dirt over a long period than it can support the opposite inference that the macaroni had just been dropped on the floor and was quickly contaminated by customers and carts traversing the aisle.[21]

The result of the *Gonzalez* court's rejection of this evidentiary basis for the plaintiff's implying that the risk existed for a long time was that there was "no evidence that the macaroni had been on the floor long enough to charge Wal-Mart with constructive notice of this condition."[22] Concluding that the plaintiff

---

21. *Gonzalez*, 968 S.W.2d at 937 (emphasis added).
22. *Id.* at 938.

thus failed to meet her evidentiary burden in pleading notice, the Supreme Court reversed the trial verdict in her favor.[23]

The instant case presents the logical converse of *Gonzalez*. Simply because most cases focus on the *minimum* time requirement for constructive knowledge does not mean that there is not a *maximum* temporal proximity as well. Put another way, a plaintiff asserting premises-owner liability is not free to assert that a risk continued to exist unabated for some illogically long period, regardless of the factual context. If it were otherwise, plaintiffs could assert constructive knowledge of risks that were proved to have existed days or even weeks earlier. Without any reasonable limit on such temporal arguments, premises owners would indeed become *de facto* insurers of invitees' safety.[24]

In this case, Dixon would infer constructive knowledge from evidence of a span of time that is simply too long to be credible. Moreover, her inference is not supported by the totality of the evidence presented at trial; on the contrary, the inference that she was able to sell to the jury is totally refuted by that very evidence. She simply asks too much of a jury to believe that the only source of the plastic binder on which Dixon tripped—the magazine suppliers—were last present more than *eight hours* before her fall, and that the plastic binder lay there undetected all that time. Dixon's inability to show a credible source of the hazard within a reasonable period—a time *between* (1) the instant before her fall and (2) an hour so remote from her fall that the plastic binder could not help but have been discovered—dooms her case. Once the early morning vendors are eliminated as even a remotely possible source, Dixon can point to no believable proximate explanation for the plastic binder's having come to rest at the point of the accident. We are thus left with a plaintiff who has failed to meet her burden of establishing Wal-Mart's constructive knowledge on the basis of plausible temporal evidence.

---

23. The Texas Supreme Court similarly reversed another trial verdict in favor of a slip-and-fall plaintiff when it ruled that "smushed" grapes were not a sufficient evidentiary basis for inferring a long enough period of time for constructive knowledge. The plaintiff offered no other temporal evidence of constructive knowledge on the part of the premises owner. Thus, her verdict was reversed. *See generally Allen*, 93 S.W.3d 897.

24. It is this essential requirement of Texas's premises-owner liability law that the dissent overlooks in its accusation that we are "crafting a new rule of law" that creates a "presumption in favor of premises owners." To the contrary, we are acting within the province of our mandate under *Erie* to predict how the Texas courts would resolve the novel evidentiary issue presented in this case. In so doing, we are applying (1) the absolute rule stated in every Texas premises-owner-liability case that premises owners are *not* insurers of their invitees' safety and (2) the *reasonableness* standard repeatedly applied by the Texas Supreme Court in such premises-owner liability cases as *Reece, Gonzalez* and *Allen*. The dissent would have us ignore this vital jurisprudence and simply create a *de facto* insurer standard for premises-owner liability in Texas: A plaintiff may claim that a hazard has existed "forever" irrespective of factual context, and a jury is always free to agree with such claims no matter how unreasonable or arbitrary, in imposing liability on a premises owner. This rule, as advocated by the dissent and which is the only basis for finding in favor of Dixon in this case, is clearly proscribed by the Texas jurisprudence on premises-owner liability. Accordingly, we reject it outright for what, in essence, it would be: a judicially-created insurance program for all invitees in Texas.

III. CONCLUSION

The basic standard of tort liability is reasonableness, determined in the discrete factual context of each case. Accordingly, a plaintiff is not free to make just any temporal argument in an attempt to meet her burden of demonstrating constructive knowledge. There has to be a reasonable *minimum* time limit for constructive knowledge to be implied, but, conversely, there has to be a reasonable *maximum* time limit as well—an outside time beyond which there can be no nexus. As with virtually every aspect of tort law, there is no absolute, bright-line rule that establishes these temporal boundaries; unique facts and circumstances control in each case. Just as proximity evidence serves as a "plus factor" for temporal arguments, the minimum and maximum limits on the spectrum of the reasonable time within which constructive knowledge can be imputed is determined by the particular facts of each case.

Although all cases to date have turned on the *minimum* time required to establish a premises owner's constructive knowledge, this case presents the novel question of the reasonable *maximum* time limit, given the totality of evidence presented at trial.[25] It defies common sense, and is against all logic, to infer that the plastic binder on which Dixon tripped could possibly have lain on the floor, just two feet away from the Wal-Mart check-out registers, for over eight hours, without being noticed by at least one of the thousands of individuals traversing that spot, including the many employees who were actively patrolling and surveying it for the very purpose of detecting and eliminating any risk to customer safety. The conclusion is inescapable: The source of the plastic binder could not have been the magazine or newspaper vendors who last visited the store early on the morning of Dixon's afternoon accident; and Dixon has proffered no other, believable source. Whatever or whoever the true source might have been, Dixon failed to adduce any evidence of *how* the plastic binder could have come to rest in that area, much less *when*. It follows inescapably that she has not established a sufficient evidentiary basis for proving Wal-Mart's constructive knowledge of the presence of an unreasonable risk of harm to its invitees. Accordingly, the district court's denial of Wal-Mart's motion for judgment as a matter of law is reversed, and the case is remanded to that court for entry of a take-nothing judgment against Dixon and in favor of Wal-Mart.

REVERSED and REMANDED with instructions.

DENNIS, Circuit Judge, dissenting:

Because I believe the majority does not apply Federal Rule of Civil Procedure 50 as interpreted in *Reeves v. Sanderson Plumbing Prods., Inc.*, 530 U.S. 133 (2000), and therefore encroaches on the province of the jury, I respectfully dissent.

The facts in this slip and fall diversity tort suit are straightforward. On Sunday, July 28, 1996, at about 5:00 p.m., Billie Jo Dixon, a 56-year-old homemaker, tripped and fell while shopping at a Wal-Mart store in Longview, Texas. The accident

---

25. We are, therefore, "required to make an *Erie* guess as to what the Texas Supreme Court would most likely decide." *Herrmann Holdings Ltd. v. Lucent Tech., Inc.*, 302 F.3d 552, 558 (5th Cir. 2002).

occurred when Dixon, after paying for pizza and milk at one of the 29 checkout stands, walked away from the cash register and turned left, intending to exit the store. Approximately two feet from the register, Dixon's feet became entangled in a rope-like piece of plastic lying loose on the floor. As a result of the entanglement, Dixon fell face forward to the floor. The fall rendered her unconscious and caused bleeding from her left eye and knee. Paramedics took Dixon to a local hospital emergency room where she received treatment. After the fall Dixon remained "dazed," and continued to experience dizzy spells, weakness, and tingling in her right arm and hand. The piece of plastic that caused Dixon's fall appeared to be a plastic binder commonly used to hold together stacks of magazines or newspapers, or merchandise.

Dixon filed suit against Wal-Mart in Texas state court seeking recovery for damages she suffered because of the accident. Wal-Mart removed the case to federal court under our diversity jurisdiction. A full jury trial followed, with the jury finding Dixon and Wal-Mart each 50% responsible for the accident. Finding total damages of $125,000, the jury awarded Dixon $62,500. The district judge denied Wal-Mart's Federal Rule of Civil Procedure 50 motion for judgment as a matter of law (JMOL), and Wal-Mart appealed.

The applicable legal standards here are accurately summarized by the majority. When considering a Rule 50 motion for judgment as a matter of law following a jury verdict, we must be "especially deferential" to the jury's findings. *Brown v. Bryan County, Okla.*, 219 F.3d 450, 456 (5th Cir. 2000). We may grant a JMOL only where upon reviewing the entire record, we find that there is no legally sufficient evidentiary basis for a reasonable jury to find for the nonmoving party on an issue. Fed R. Civ. P. 50(a). In evaluating the record, we must make all reasonable inferences for the nonmoving party, and disregard all evidence from the moving party that a jury is not required to credit. *Reeves*, 530 U.S. at 150–151 (2000). And of course, we must remember that "[c]redibility determinations, the weighing of the evidence, and the drawing of legitimate inferences from the facts are jury functions, not those of a judge." *Anderson v. Liberty Lobby, Inc.*, 477 U.S. 242, 255 (1986).

Under Texas state law to recover in this slip and fall suit, Dixon must prove by a preponderance of the evidence:

1. Actual or constructive knowledge of some condition on the premises by the owner/operator;
2. That the condition posed an unreasonable risk of harm;
3. That the owner/operator did not exercise reasonable care to reduce or eliminate the risk; and
4. That the owner/operator's failure to use such care proximately caused the plaintiff's injuries.

Keetch v. Kroger Co., 845 S.W.2d 262, 264 (Tex. 1992). As the majority correctly notes, the only issue on appeal is whether Dixon presented the jury a "legally sufficient evidentiary basis" for it to find that Wal-Mart had constructive notice of the plastic binder's hazardous presence on the store's floor.

Dixon established constructive notice through circumstantial evidence, using the standard provided in *Wal-Mart Stores, Inc. v. Gonzalez*, 968 S.W.2d 934 (Tex. 1998). In that case the Texas Supreme Court explained that to establish constructive notice through circumstantial evidence, that evidence must prove that it is "more likely than not that the dangerous condition existed long enough to give the proprietor a reasonable opportunity to discover the condition." *Id.* at 936. Thus, as the majority notes, Dixon's evidentiary burden is to establish that the plastic binder was on the floor for a sufficiently long period of time that Wal-Mart had a reasonable opportunity to correct that condition. And where, as here, the hazard was in constant close proximity to Wal-Mart employees, the reasonable time period needed to correct the defect is shorter than in cases where there are no agents of the premises owner near the danger. *Wal-Mart Stores, Inc. v. Reece*, 81 S.W.3d 812, 816 (Tex. 2002).

To meet this burden Dixon introduced evidence establishing that the plastic binder on which she tripped was similar to the plastic rope used to tie bundles of magazines and newspapers that are delivered to the registers at least once daily. Greg Smith, Wal-Mart store director, explained that magazine vendors used the plastic binders to bundle their merchandise until they placed the reading materials in racks at the checkout stands. He testified that the magazine handlers would typically "go back to our receiving area with a shopping cart and get the banded magazines together. They take them up front. They bust the bands on them and they stock the registers." He stated that the newspaper racks usually were stocked between 4:30 a.m. and 5:00 a.m., and that the magazines usually were restocked between 8:00 a.m. and 9:00 a.m., but that on occasions of heightened demands either or both might be restocked later in the day.[2] Based on this evidence a jury reasonably could have concluded that the binder was on the floor near the registers from the morning magazine restocking until the 5:00 p.m. accident, and therefore, Wal-Mart had a reasonable amount of time to remedy the danger, making it liable for Dixon's injuries.

In response to Dixon's evidence which supports a jury finding of constructive notice, the majority notes in expansive detail the testimony of various Wal-Mart employees regarding the store cleaning policy. It then uses this uncontradicted testimony to "find" that Dixon's theory that the binder was dropped in the morning magazine delivery cannot be the basis of a reasonable jury finding of constructive notice. The majority is cryptic as to whether this is a "finding" of fact or law. But in either case the majority oversteps its role.

If the majority was making a factual finding on the basis of testimony a jury was required to credit, it misstates the record when it suggests that more than the existence of a store cleaning policy was uncontradicted in the Wal-Mart employee testimony. Wal-Mart cites no employee testimony stating that this policy was carried out on the day in question in the area in which Dixon fell.[3] Rather, the majority

---

2. There was no evidence that there had been an afternoon or late-morning restocking on the day of Dixon's fall because Wal-Mart does not maintain records of magazine and newspaper restocking.

3. Jean Chatham, Wal-Mart front-end manager, indicated in her deposition testimony that she checked the front area of the store five minutes prior to an accident in the store. But her description of the accident and the person who reported falling do not match the incident here, and Wal-Mart itself admits that her testimony is of a different incident. Thus the majority's assertion that "the particular area in which Dixon fell had been inspected most recently approximately five minutes before her accident" is simply not supported by the record.

infers textbook execution of store policies from mere evidence that the policies had been formulated. But the jury was free to believe that the cleaning policy had not been carried out. And therefore this court on review cannot make an inference favorable to Wal-Mart, given the Supreme Court's clear directive that when considering a motion for a JMOL a court cannot make inferences for the moving party that the jury was not required to make. *Reeves*, 530 U.S. at 150-51.

If the majority is crafting a new rule of law, it is on even shakier ground. The majority asserts that it is applying the "converse" principle to *Gonzalez*, which is that there is a maximum time period that a plaintiff may establish a hazard was present and still establish premises liability. The majority gives no support in Texas case law for this proposition.[4] And given that logic belies a converse principle to *Gonzalez*, this is not surprising. *Gonzalez* speaks to the policy determination made in Texas that premises owners are not insurers of their invitees' safety. As a result, a hazard must have been in place sufficiently long that a proprietor has a reasonable opportunity to detect and correct it. There can be no "converse" of this proposition because the greater the amount of time a hazard is present, the more unreasonable is the premises owner for failing to correct it.

I believe the effect of the majority opinion is to apply a new presumption in favor of premises owners: where a premises owner has a policy regarding hazards, it is presumed that policy is carried out in each case. Thus, the existence of a store cleaning policy here means that we presume a plastic binder could not have been on the store floor for eight hours in contravention of the policy (albeit subject to rebuttal by the invitee). By creating such a presumption not only does the majority exceed the bounds of our diversity jurisdiction by creating new, unsupported mandatory inferences in state tort law, *Matador Petroleum Corp. v. St. Paul Surplus Lines Ins. Co.*, 174 F.3d 653, 656 (5th Cir. 1999) (role of federal courts sitting in diversity is to decide cases as the highest state court would decide them), but it also tramples upon the jury's role as arbiter of credibility and fact. *Liberty Lobby*, 477 U.S. at 255. I would, therefore, uphold the jury verdict and affirm the judgment of the district court.

NOTES AND QUESTIONS

1. *Rule 50 Practice.* A Rule 50(a) motion is normally made after the opposing party has put on all of its evidence but before the case has been submitted to the jury. Thus, a defendant can move for a judgment as matter of law without putting on any evidence. Either party can move following the close of defendant's case. If the motion is denied, the party can renew its motion within 28 days of entry of judgment. Fed. R. Civ. P. 50(b). (Prior to the 1991 amendments to Rule 50, a

---

4. In response to this criticism, the majority claims it derives support for this rule from a "reasonableness" principle applied by the Texas Supreme Court. But as I explained above, Dixon's theory of constructive notice is unreasonable only if you infer from the existence of a store cleaning policy, execution of that policy. By so doing, the majority makes an inference the jury was not required to make for the moving party, and therefore oversteps the bounds of its Rule 50 review. *Reeves*, 530 U.S. at 150-151 (2000).

motion made before the case was submitted to the jury was called a motion for a "directed verdict";* the renewed motion made after the verdict was for a "judgment notwithstanding the verdict," or "JNOV." That terminology is still used in some state practice.)

A party cannot move for judgment as a matter of law under Rule 50(b) after the jury verdict unless it made a motion under Rule 50(a) before the case went to the jury. The standards governing both the original and renewed motions are identical. The requirement that a party make a Rule 50(a) motion in order to preserve its right to make a Rule 50(b) motion is to satisfy a constitutional concern. The Supreme Court had ruled at one point that the JNOV was in violation of the Seventh Amendment jury trial right because it was considered a reexamination of a "fact tried by a jury" other "than according to the rules of the common law." *Slocum v. New York Life Ins. Co.*, 228 U.S. 364 (1913). Later, however, the Court analogized the motion to a procedure at common law whereby the judge could render a judgment inconsistent with the jury verdict if a party made a motion for a directed verdict prior to submission of the case to the jury, and the judge reserved his ruling on the motion. *Baltimore & Carolina Line, Inc. v. Redman*, 295 U.S. 654 (1935). Accordingly, Rule 50 was drafted to track this common law procedure. *See also Galloway v. United States*, 319 U.S. 372, 391 (1943) (rejecting Seventh Amendment challenge to Rule 50; "The Amendment was designed to preserve the basic institution of jury trial in only its most fundamental elements, not the great mass of procedural forms and details, varying even then so widely among common law jurisdictions"). For an argument that Rule 50 and Rule 56 are inconsistent with common law practice, *see* Suja A. Thomas, *The Seventh Amendment, Modern Procedure, and the English Common Law*, 82 Wash. U. L.Q. 687 (2005).

Why would a court ever deny the motion before the jury adjudicates, but grant the renewed motion after the verdict is returned? There are two excellent reasons. First, if the jury rules "correctly" (as it in all likelihood will), it moots the need for the motion and eliminates the risk of reversal on appeal. Thus, the judge might only grant the motion when it is necessary to correct an improper jury adjudication. Second, if the judgment as a matter of law *is* reversed on appeal, the jury verdict can be restored if the court granted the motion after the jury rendered a verdict. If the court grants the motion before the jury deliberates and the judgment is then reversed on appeal, there will be no verdict to restore; the jury is discharged when the motion is granted, and there will have to be a completely new trial with a new jury.

Rule 50 motions are only available in jury trials. The judge decides the case in any event in a bench trial. However, if, at the close of plaintiff's case in a bench trial, defendant wants to move for a judgment without putting on its case, it may make a motion for judgment under Rule 52(c).

2. *Rule 50 Standard.* The standards for issuance of a judgment as a matter of law are generally thought to be roughly the same as for issuance of summary judgment. *Anderson v. Liberty Lobby, Inc.*, 477 U.S. 242, 250–253 (1986) (summary

---

* In prior practice, the court actually "directed" the jury to return a verdict for the moving party. *See* William Wirt Blume, *Origin and Development of the Directed Verdict*, 48 Mich. L. Rev. 555, 589 (1950). This formal requirement was eliminated in 1961, after which the court simply entered judgment and excused the jury.

judgment standard "mirrors the standard for a [judgment as a matter of law]"). *See* 9B C. Wright et al., Federal Practice and Procedure §2532 (3d ed. 2008). Even though the judge has now had the opportunity to see the witnesses in person, it is still the province of the jury to weigh the evidence and assess credibility. As with summary judgment, the court must view the evidence most favorably to the non-moving party and must deny the motion if any reasonable jury could find for the nonmoving party on the basis of that evidence. *Reeves v. Sanderson Plumbing Products, Inc.*, 530 U.S. 133 (2000). Note that unlike summary judgment, issuance of a judgment as a matter of law will not save the litigants much time or expense. Although it may obviate the need for a protracted jury deliberation, its primary function is to prevent or cure erroneous adjudications by the jury.

Older cases held that "where proven facts give equal support to each of two inconsistent inferences" the courts should not allow the case to be decided by the jury. *Pennsylvania R.R. v. Chamberlin*, 288 U.S. 333, 393 (1932). Later decisions see a greater role for the jury in resolving such ambiguous proof: "Whenever facts are in dispute or the evidence is such that fair-minded men may draw different inferences, a measure of speculation and conjecture is required on the part of those whose duty it is to settle the dispute by choosing what seems to them to be the most reasonable inference. Only when there is a complete absence of probative facts [should the case be taken from the jury]." *Lavender v. Kurn*, 327 U.S. 645 (1946).

Note, however, even under the more relaxed standard articulated in *Lavender,* the court must determine whether the evidence is "probative"—i.e., that it tends to prove plaintiff's contentions. *Cf.* Fed. R. Evid. 401, 402 (deeming inadmissible evidence that does not have "any tendency to make a fact more or less probable than it would be without the evidence"). *See generally* Edward Cooper, *Directions for Directed Verdicts: A Compass for Federal Courts*, 55 Minn. L. Rev. 903 (1971) (arguing that courts apply flexible standards to determine whether inference is sufficiently reasonable to permit jury adjudication, depending on type of case, issue involved, and totality of circumstances).

3. *When May a Jury Draw an Inference?* Can *Dixon* be fairly characterized as a case in which there was a "complete absence of probative facts"? Doesn't the undisputed fact that the plastic is of the type used to bind magazines, delivered that morning, in the vicinity of the accident, tend to show that the plastic had been on the floor since the morning?

Contrary to the majority opinion, weren't there, in fact, three reasonable explanations for how the plastic binding material came to be on the floor? First, as the majority apparently concludes, a customer could have dropped the plastic on the floor (or perhaps moved it from a less visible location) shortly before plaintiff was injured, thereby depriving Wal-Mart of the opportunity to pick it up. Second, the plastic could have been dropped shortly before the accident by a Wal-Mart employee, in which case Wal-Mart presumably would have been vicariously liable for its employee's negligence regardless of how long the plastic was there. Third, the plastic could have been on the floor for over eight hours, and the Wal-Mart employees did not effectively carry out the store policy of conducting regular inspections. Aren't the second and third explanations just as reasonable as the first? Of the three, isn't the first, in fact, the most improbable insofar as people don't normally carry around plastic strapping material in their pockets? Why wasn't the jury entitled to disbelieve Wal-Mart's claim that the area had been effectively inspected for debris shortly before the accident? Given the relatively small verdict and the jury's conclusion that plaintiff was 50 percent responsible for the accident, isn't it unlikely that the verdict was based on excessive sympathy for the plaintiff? If the jury in fact inferred that the plastic had been on the floor all day, on what basis could the court conclude that such an inference was unreasonable? Isn't the jury just as competent as the court (or even more competent given their collective life experience) to determine the reasonableness of that inference?

4. What kind of proof would have allowed the jury to infer that the plastic had been there all day? What if plaintiff had proven that the plastic material was not simply "consistent with" the kind of material used to bind packages of newspapers, but was identical to the strapping material that Wal-Mart's supplier used to bind its newspapers? Would the court still have imposed the burden on Dixon of explaining how the material could have remained on the floor for over eight hours without being detected?

5. Compare the majority's approach with the Supreme Court's decision in *Reeves v. Sanderson Plumbing Products, Inc.*, 530 U.S. 133 (2000). The Court there held improper the court of appeal's entry of judgment as a matter of law against a plaintiff in an age discrimination case. Plaintiff had put on a "prima facie case" by showing that he was in a group protected by the statute, that he was qualified for the position in question, and that the employee hired to replace plaintiff was younger than plaintiff. Defendant then introduced testimony that it had a nondiscriminatory reason for plaintiff's termination, testimony that the plaintiff contested. The Court of Appeals for the Fifth Circuit held that once defendant demonstrated a nondiscriminatory reason for terminating plaintiff, plaintiff had the burden of proving defendant's discriminatory intent, and that it failed to produce any affirmative evidence of such an intent. The Supreme Court reversed and held that the jury was entitled to infer defendant's discriminatory intent from its disbelief of defendant's testimony. Is *Dixon* consistent with *Reeves*?

6. Consider the potential impact of the Court's decision in *Tellabs, Inc. v. Makor Issues & Rights, Ltd.*, 551 U.S. 308 (2007) (discussed at p. 582, *supra*). Under the Private Securities Litigation Reform Act of 1995 (*see* p. 543, *supra*), a complaint must "state with particularity facts giving rise to a strong inference that the defendant acted with the required state of mind." The Court held that in order to satisfy this standard, a pleading must allege facts from which a reasonable jury was at least as likely to infer a culpable state of mind as an innocent state of mind. Finding that standard too low, Justice Scalia, in concurrence, asserted that in order to create a "strong inference," the facts alleged must make it *more* likely that a reasonable jury would infer a culpable state of mind. He then posed the following hypothetical:

> If a jade falcon were stolen from a room to which only A and B had access, could it *possibly* be said there was a "strong inference" that B was the thief? I think not, and I therefore think that the Court's test must fail. In my view, the test should be whether the inference of scienter (if any) is *more plausible* than the inference of innocence.

The majority rejected Justice Scalia's test partially on the ground that he inappropriately equated the statutory pleading standard with the Rule 50 question of whether a jury verdict was supported by the evidence:

Justice Scalia . . . would transpose to the pleading stage "the test that is used at the summary-judgment and judgment-as-a-matter-of-law stages" [quoting from Justice Alito's concurrence]. . . . But the test at each stage is measured against a different backdrop. It is improbable that Congress, without so stating, intended courts to test pleadings, unaided by discovery, to determine whether there is "no genuine issue as to any material fact." See Fed. Rule Civ. Proc. 56(c). And judgment as a matter of law is a post-trial device, turning on the question whether a party has produced evidence "legally sufficient" to warrant a jury determination in that party's favor. See Rule 50(a)(1). 508 U.S. at 324 n.5.

Does the majority mean to suggest that a jury verdict based on the kind of ambiguous proof offered in Justice Scalia's stolen falcon hypothetical would not survive a Rule 50 motion? Was the proof in *Dixon* any less ambiguous? Does plaintiff's proof that icing caused the crash in the *Rockwell* hypothetical satisfy Justice Scalia's standard?

7. *Relevance of State Law?* Note the majority's reliance on the *Gonzalez* case, a Texas state court decision holding that "[d]irt in macaroni salad lying on a *heavily traveled aisle* is no evidence of the length of time the macaroni had been on the floor." Should that state precedent be binding on the federal court under *Erie*? *See* Edward H. Cooper, *Directions for Directed Verdicts: A Compass for Federal Courts*, 55 Minn. L. Rev. 903, 986–988 (1971) (arguing that federal courts should be bound by state standards for permissible jury inferences on the ground that state law reflects substantive preferences).

8. What implication does *Dixon* have for the *Rockwell* hypothetical? Would the *Dixon* court let a jury infer that the engines failed because they ingested ice coming off the wing deicers?

f. Jury Instructions

Assuming the case is submitted to the jury, the final event prior to the jury's deliberation is the issuance of jury instructions by the court. The jury instructions (sometimes called the "charge") inform the jury of the law applicable to the case. This normally includes a description of the elements of plaintiff's cause of action, as well as legally recognized defenses. Courts try to avoid legal abstractions and frame the instructions in the factual context of the litigation. For instance, in *Rockwell*, the 44-page instructions read to the jury included the following:

The parties have each presented evidence supporting a different theory of why the engines of the Jet Commander known as N44 lost power prior to its crash on November 2, 1998. Plaintiffs contend that ice built up on the leading edge of the wings, which was dislodged by operation of the deicing boots and ingested by the engines, causing a loss of power. Defendant agrees that the engines lost power, but contends that this loss resulted from a buildup of ice on the engine nacelle and inlet guide vanes caused by the pilots' failure to activate the anti-icing switch in the aircraft. Thus, your first task will be to determine whether the plaintiffs have proven by a preponderance of the evidence that it was ice dislodged by the wing deicing boots which contributed to the loss of engine power. If you do not find that plaintiffs have established these facts by a preponderance of the evidence, you must enter a verdict in favor of the defendant. However, if you find that plaintiffs have met their burden of proof on this factual issue, you must then proceed to determine whether the aircraft was defectively designed and manufactured by defendant.

In federal practice (although not necessarily in state courts), the judge may also comment on and summarize the evidence. The judge can offer an opinion of how compelling the proof was, but must make clear that the jury is not bound by that view. Kevin F. O'Malley et al., Federal Jury Practice Instructions, §7.05 (5th ed. 2000).

Under Fed. R. Civ. P. 51, the parties are entitled to submit proposed jury instructions, and they have the opportunity to review and object to the adopted instructions prior to their delivery to the jury. In many cases, the court will decide on jury instructions even before trial is commenced. In order to preserve the right to appeal a jury instruction, a party must make an objection to the instruction "before the instructions and arguments are delivered" to the jury. An exception is provided for a party who has not been informed of an instruction before that time. Even if a party has not made a timely objection, the party may still appeal "plain error in the instructions affecting substantial rights." The rule allows the court to issue instructions at any time after the trial begins and before the jury is discharged.

Many courts employ "pattern jury instructions" for certain categories of cases that tend to be frequently litigated. The court will typically work from these "form" instructions and modify and supplement them as required.

Jury instructions are normally delivered to the jury orally. The judge, by discretion, may also give a written copy to the jury. Courts make some effort to draft the instructions in a manner accessible to lay persons, but instructions in a given case can be quite lengthy and complex. As a result, some commentators have questioned whether juries really understand their legal obligations. *See, e.g.*, Leon Green, *The Submission of Issues in Negligence Cases*, 18 U. Miami L. Rev. 30 (1963); Franklin Strier, Reconstructing Justice: An Agenda for Trial Reform (1994). *But see* Shari Seidman Diamond, Beth Murphy & Mary R. Rose, *The "Kettleful of Law" in Real Jury Deliberations: Successes, Failures, and Next Steps*, 106 Nw. U. L. Rev. 1537, 1542 (2012) (describing results of empirical study suggesting that "juries in typical civil cases pay substantial attention to the instructions and that although they struggle, the juries develop a reasonable grasp of most of the law they are asked to apply"); Neil Vidmar, *The Performance of the American Civil Jury: An Empirical Perspective*, 40 Ariz. L. Rev. 849, 866–868 (1998) (reviewing empirical research suggesting that much of the jury confusion is caused by poorly drafted instructions).

Consider in this regard the jury instructions in the *Rockwell* case. The trial court there read the jury a 20-page description of the elements of plaintiff's cause of action. This included a detailed discussion of the meaning of a product defect, use for intended purpose, and proximate cause.

The court explained that a design defect could be established either by showing that the product did not perform in accordance with the user's reasonable expectation or that the risks of the design outweighed its benefits, taking into account the cost and feasibility of alternative designs:

In applying the risk-utility factors, remember that a product may not be considered reasonably safe unless the risks have been reduced to the greatest extent possible consistent with the product's continued utility, that is, without impairing its usefulness and without making it too expensive for the product to be reasonably marketable.

The court then discussed the legal significance of defendant's evidence that the aircraft's design was in accordance with the industry standards and the state of the art:

There has been evidence presented of the common practice and standards in the industry. That evidence bears on the risk/utility analysis. Compliance with common practice or industry standards does not automatically mean that the product is safe. It may still be found to be defective in design. However, compliance with common practice or industry standards, along with all the other evidence in this case, may satisfy you that the product was properly made. . . .

If the product does contain a defect, and the art of the industry at the time of the manufacture was such that by alternate design, construction, or preparation, the product could reasonably have been made less hazardous, then a manufacturer has a duty to adopt such an alternative.

Plaintiff has alleged that the product involved in this action was defective in design because a feasible alternate design existed at the time the product was designed, and was available to the defendant manufacturer.

The word "feasibility," for this purpose, includes not only elements of economy, effectiveness, and practicality, but also technological possibilities under the state of manufacturing art at the time of its design.

On use for intended purpose, the court stated:

Plaintiffs must show that the product was being used in a way that was either intended or was reasonably foreseeable. . . .

Reasonably foreseeable does not mean that the particular misuse was actually foreseen or could have been actually foreseen by the defendant at the time the product left its control. It is rather a test of objective foreseeability. That is, considering the general experience within the industry when the product was manufactured, sold, or distributed, could the future occurrence of misuse have been anticipated by a reasonably careful manufacturer, seller, or distributor?

As to causation, the court explained that:

the defect, whatever you find it to be, must have been a proximate cause of the accident. By proximate cause, we mean that the defect in the product was a substantial factor which, singly or in combination with another cause, brought about the accident. Plaintiffs need not prove that the very accident which occurred could have been anticipated, so long as it was within the realm of foreseeability that some harm could result from the defect in question. If the product in question does not add to the risk of the occurrence of the particular accident and hence was not a contributing factor in the happening of the accident, then plaintiffs have failed to establish a proximate cause of the accident.

The judge later drew the following distinction:

> You have heard testimony in this case about the actions of the pilots in the cockpit on the day of the accident. I instruct you that if you find that the airplane was defectively designed, and if you also find that that defect in whole or in part proximately caused the accident, it would not be a defense that some of the actions of the pilots on that day might be considered negligent—for example, their decision to land the aircraft at Johnstown Airport rather than Latrobe Airport.
>
> As I instructed you earlier, I have admitted testimony concerning the actions of the pilots for one, limited purpose—to assist you in determining whether the accident was in fact proximately caused by a defect in the airplane. If you find by a preponderance of the evidence that the accident was caused by a defect in the airplane, the negligent actions, if any, of the pilots during the final flight would not be a defense.

Do you understand this relatively small excerpt from the instructions? Do you think you would have had you never attended law school? Is the problem the way the instructions were drafted, or is the law unavoidably complicated? Why should the jury be responsible for applying the law to the facts at all? Wouldn't a judge do a better job at conforming the verdict to these complex legal principles? Consider that question in connection with the next section on Form of the Verdict.

g.   Form of the Verdict

One of the most powerful devices for judicial control over the jury is the form of verdict requested from the jury. Under Fed. R. Civ. P. 49, the court may choose among three forms of verdict to submit to the jury: general verdict, special verdict, and general verdict with answers to written questions.

In a *general verdict*, the jury simply determines who wins, and the amount of damages, if any. This form of verdict is the most commonly employed. As you probably discerned from the *Rockwell* jury instructions, it is also the form most prone to erroneous application of law by the jury.

A *special verdict*, by contrast, only requires the jury to answer, in writing, specific factual questions. *See* Fed. R. Civ. P. 49(a). The court then applies the law to those findings to determine the parties' liability. Obviously, this form is the least prone to legal error by the jury since the jury does not apply the law. Indeed, the jury may not even be aware of the legal implications of certain findings of fact.

The *general verdict with answers to written questions* combines aspects of the general and special verdict. *See* Fed. R. Civ. P. 49(b). The jury is asked for a determination of liability, but that determination is crosschecked against its answers to specific factual questions. Judgment is issued in accordance with the general verdict only when it is logically consistent with the jury's answers to interrogatories. Otherwise, the court will enter a judgment consistent with the answers to interrogatories, or return the case to the jury for further consideration. *Id.*

The parties may request a particular form of verdict, but the form employed is entirely within the discretion of the judge. No case has ever appeared to have been reversed on the basis that the judge abused his discretion in his choice of form of verdict, and there is little case law on when the court should employ a particular form. 9B C. Wright et al., Federal Practice and Procedure §2505 (3d ed. 2008). As a litigator, when would you prefer a general verdict?

If the role of the jury is solely to make factual determinations, why do judges seem to prefer the general verdict? The answer implicates some profound issues regarding the nature of law and justice.

If we conceive of the "best" adjudication as accurate fact finding coupled with a faithful application of legal precedent, the general verdict appears almost irrational. The verdict can mask legal misunderstanding or even deliberate defiance of controlling law. For example, in *Rockwell,* a general verdict for the plaintiff could be the result of: (a) a determination of Rockwell's fault in causing the crash; (b) a misunderstanding of Rockwell's legal responsibility; (c) a sense that plaintiff could use the money more than Rockwell; or (d) some combination of all three. Use of a special verdict would certainly increase the likelihood that the jury in fact believed Rockwell caused the crash (although even there, the jury could anticipate that its factual determination of fault would lead to a verdict for plaintiff; thus their purely factual determination could again be outcome-oriented).

But would we necessarily view a verdict for plaintiff based on any reason other than Rockwell's fault to be undesirable? On a purely formal level, any other reason would seem to represent a legal mistake. From a different perspective, however, the jury might be seen to be performing some needed "fine-tuning" of the formal legal rule. This view is premised on the sense that formal legal rules (such as fault-based liability) are only abstract generalizations. These rules work well in the aggregate, but may not achieve just results in all cases. As long as a jury adjudication is not in transparent defiance of the legal rule, thereby undermining the authority of the rule, might we prefer in some cases to allow the jury to view the equities of the case in their entirety? Does the inscrutability of the general verdict thus provide some useful "play in the joints"? Or does this undermine our commitment to the rule of law?

These perspectives are explored in a wealth of thoughtful literature. *See, e.g.,* Mark S. Brodin, *Accuracy, Efficiency and Accountability in the Litigation Process— The Case for the Fact Verdict,* 59 U. Cin. L. Rev. 15 (1990); Leon Green, *The Submission of Issues in Negligence Cases,* 19 U. Miami L. Rev. 30 (1963); Charles T. McCormick, *Jury Verdicts Upon Special Questions in Civil Cases,* 2 F.R.D. 176 (1973); John H. Wigmore, *A Program for the Trial of a Jury Trial,* 12 Am. Jud. Soc. 166 (1929); Roscoe Pound, *Law in Books and Law in Action,* 44 Am. L. Rev. 12, 18 (1910). *See also* Minority Statement of Justices Black and Douglas opposing the 1963 amendments to the Federal Rules of Procedure, 374 U.S. 865 (1963) (urging abolition of the special verdict).

h.   Jury Deliberation

After the jury is charged, it retires to the jury room to deliberate. At the judge's discretion, it may have access to trial exhibits and portions of the trial transcript. The jury usually has the ability to submit written questions to the judge. When that happens, the judge normally consults the parties before responding in open court. No nonjuror is present during deliberations.

Unless the parties have otherwise stipulated, a federal jury must reach a unanimous verdict. If the jury fails to reach a consensus, the judge will declare a mistrial, and the case will have to be retried before a new jury. If the jury reports a deadlock, the judge will often send the jurors back to the jury room and urge them to reach agreement.

The jury can conduct the deliberation however it sees fit. Normally, an elected foreperson presides over the discussion. There is no minimum time that the jurors must deliberate before reaching a verdict. Every juror must, however, agree on the merits: They cannot toss a coin or trade off votes on one count for votes on another.

Once the jury reaches a unanimous decision, it returns to open court and informs the judge of the verdict. Rule 48 requires the judge, at the request of a party, to poll the jury to ascertain any lack of unanimity in the verdict. Fed. R. Civ. P. 48(c).

i. Findings of Fact and Conclusions of Law in a Bench Trial

If the case has been tried without a jury, the judge decides both the law and facts. Unlike a general verdict, the basis for a judge's decision is made very explicit. Pursuant to Fed. R. Civ. P. 52(a), "In an action tried on the facts without a jury . . . the court must find the facts specially and state its conclusions of law separately."

Prior to issuing such findings, the court normally solicits proposed findings of fact and conclusions of law from the parties. Rule 52(a) findings can be quite extensive. The court may (although is not required to) review in its written findings all of the evidence, and state which evidence it found persuasive. At a minimum, the judge must "indicate the factual basis for the ultimate conclusion." *Kelley v. Everglades Drainage District*, 319 U.S. 415, 422 (1943).

The explicit findings in a bench adjudication have interesting implications for both appeal and preclusion purposes. Although Rule 52(a)(6) clearly protects the judge's factual findings from reversal on appeal "unless clearly erroneous," such error is easier to determine than jury error because the trial court makes explicit the basis for its findings. For instance, if the judge misunderstood the testimony of a particular witness, that error will be discernable on the record, unlike a jury's comparable mistake.

As you will see in Chapter 6, in order for an adjudication to foreclose relitigation of specific facts in a subsequent lawsuit, the second court must determine that issue preclusion and the given finding was "actually decided" and "necessary to the judgment" in the first proceeding. Explicit Rule 52(a) findings and conclusions makes possible a very precise determination of the actual basis for the decision.

j. Entry of Judgment

Once the judge or jury has reached a decision, the clerk enters the judgment in accordance with the order or verdict pursuant to Fed. R. Civ. P. 58. The time for appeal and for post-trial relief normally runs from the entry of judgment.

The prevailing party may then petition the court for award of costs — filing fees, cost of transcripts, witness fees, and so on — which are normally awarded as a matter of course. *See* Fed. R. Civ. P. 54(d). Attorneys' fees may also be awarded when authorized by statute.

3. Post-Trial Relief

We will consider in Chapter 9 the nature of appeals. Even prior to appeal, the losing party may seek a range of post-trial remedies in the trial court.

a. Judgment as a Matter of Law

Recall that if a party made an unsuccessful Rule 50(a) motion for judgment as a matter of law before the case was submitted to the jury, the party can renew its request within 28 days of entry of judgment against it by making a Rule 50(b) motion. A party must make a Rule 50(b) motion to preserve its right to appeal the sufficiency of the evidence. *Unitherm Food Systems, Inc. v. Swift-Eckrich, Inc.*, 546 U.S. 394 (2006). The Court in *Unitherm* held that the court of appeals was without authority to order a new trial where the defendant made an unsuccessful motion for judgment as a matter of law pursuant to Rule 50(a) before the case was submitted to the jury, but failed to make a post-verdict motion under either Rule 50(b) or Rule 59 (motion for new trial).

b. Motion for New Trial

The Rule 50(b) motion may be combined with another important remedy: the motion for new trial under Fed. R. Civ. P. 59 (which can also be asserted without renewing the Rule 50 motion). The new trial remedy gives the court the power to grant relief from a flawed jury verdict on a lesser showing than is required for a judgment as a matter of law. As discussed below, the threat of a new trial can also be used to coerce the parties into accepting a different outcome.

The trial court has the power to grant a new trial, effectively nullifying the jury verdict, whenever it deems that justice so requires. The grant or denial of the motion is in the discretion of the court; there is very little appellate scrutiny of the decision. Rule 59 authorizes a new trial "for any reason for which a new trial has heretofore been granted in an action at law in federal court." The court may grant a new trial if it concludes that the verdict was "against the weight of the evidence," that the size of damages was inappropriate, or where otherwise necessary to prevent injustice, *see* 11 C. Wright et al., Federal Practice and Procedure §2805 (3d ed. 2012), as, for example, where the jury has been exposed to inappropriate evidence through attorney misconduct.

Unlike summary judgment or judgment as a matter of law, the judge may grant a motion for new trial even if there is evidence supporting the nonmoving party. The judge is free to weigh the evidence independently of the jury. Although courts rarely grant the motion in close cases, they have the authority to grant a new trial any time they believe the jury reached a "seriously erroneous" result. *Gasperini v. Center for Humanities*, 518 U.S. 415, 468 (1996) (Scalia, J., dissenting). In deciding the motion, the court may independently evaluate the credibility of witnesses and the weight of the evidence. Thus, the court may well grant a new trial when it would be inappropriate to issue a judgment as a matter of law. 9B C. Wright et al., Federal Practice and Procedure §2531 (3d ed. 2008).

c. Conditional Dispositions of the New Trial Motion

As we saw in the *Gasperini* case, the threat of a new trial can be used to coerce the plaintiff into accepting a lower award than issued by the jury. This practice is referred to as a *remittitur*. The *remittitur* is implemented by the "conditional" denial of a new trial; the court denies the motion on the condition that plaintiff accept a specified smaller award.

If a plaintiff accepts the reduced amount, plaintiff cannot appeal the trial court's conditional ruling. *Donovan v. Penn Shipping Co.*, 429 U.S. 648 (1977). A plaintiff who rejects the lower award and is faced with a new trial may, in contrast, appeal the grant of the new trial following the conclusion of the second trial. However, appellate courts rarely reinstate the original verdict. Thus, the *remittitur* gives the trial court enormous leverage.

The court of appeals too can issue a *remittitur* by conditioning its affirmance of a trial court's denial of a motion for new trial upon plaintiff's agreement to accept a lower damage award. 11 C. Wright et al., Federal Practice and Procedure §2820 (3d ed. 2012). However, as we saw in *Gasperini*, appellate review of new trial denial is subject to the "abuse of discretion" standard. Thus, the appeals court has less ability than does the trial court to reduce a verdict it considers unreasonably high.

In some states, the court can use the threat of granting a new trial to coerce defendant into accepting a *higher* liability than the jury awarded. This is referred to as an *additur*. The Supreme Court has prohibited the use of *additurs* in federal practice as in violation of the Seventh Amendment. *Dimick v. Schiedt*, 293 U.S. 474 (1935).

d.   Motions for Relief from a Judgment

If all else fails, the Federal Rules give the unsuccessful litigant an opportunity to reopen an adverse judgment in the issuing court under Fed. R. Civ. P. 60 (b). Rule 60(b) is expansively worded to authorize the court to "relieve a party" from an adverse judgment or ruling on "just terms." Valid reasons for the grant of a Rule 60(b) order include: "mistake, inadvertence, surprise, or excusable neglect"; "newly discovered evidence"; fraud or misrepresentation; or "any other reason justifying relief." A party normally has one year to seek relief under Rule 60(b), with a longer time in certain situations.

Rule 60(b) applies to all final judicial orders. However, courts apply the rule differently depending on the nature of the order from which the party seeks relief. Courts tend to be quite lenient in allowing relief from default judgments. For instance, some courts have reopened default judgments resulting from an attorney's preoccupation with other matters. *See, e.g., MacEwen Petroleum, Inc. v. Tarbell*, 173 F.R.D. 36 (N.D.N.Y. 1997) (attorney returning from vacation neglected to write down due date of answer). *See also* Fed. R. Civ. P. 55(c) (authorizing court to set aside entry of default for "good cause").

Courts tend to be considerably more demanding before they will set aside judgment on the merits, particularly after trial. Courts are particularly skeptical of new evidence or legal theories not presented during the trial. *See, e.g., Torockio v. Chamberlain Mfg. Co.*, 56 F.R.D. 82 (W.D. Pa. 1977) (failure of plaintiff to inform attorney of critical evidence does not justify Rule 60(b) relief). The moving party must demonstrate that it could not have discovered the material earlier through the "exercise of reasonable diligence."

It is unclear whether a mistake *by the court* justifies relief under Rule 60(b). *Compare Tarkington v. U.S. Lines*, 222 F.2d 358 (2d Cir. 1955) (relief should have been granted when contrary, controlling precedent was decided by Supreme Court 11 days after judgment) *with Silk v. Sandoval*, 435 F.2d 1266 (1st Cir. 1971) (erroneous legal ruling by court does not constitute grounds for relief under Rule 60(b); however, a party may move within ten days to amend a judgment pursuant to Rule 59(e) on account of a court's legal error. *Id.*).

CHAPTER 6

REMEDIES AND
FORMS OF RELIEF

After a lawyer has met with the client, assessed the merits of the client's potential claims, chosen a forum and a court system, and determined what law will likely apply to the dispute, one of the most important tasks still remains: determining what relief the lawyer will request on behalf of the client. Indeed, this is likely to be the most important question from the client's perspective: What will you ask the court to do for me, and when is it likely to happen? Every complaint must contain a prayer for relief as one of the basic requirements of pleading. *See, e.g.*, Fed. R. Civ. P. 8(a) ("A pleading that states a claim for relief must contain: . . . (3) a demand for the relief sought, which may include relief in the alternative or different types of relief."). How does a lawyer know what to ask for? What types of remedy are available for different types of injury? What implications flow from asking for one kind of relief rather than another and how might they affect the course of the lawsuit? What forms of immediate relief are available to protect a party's interests in an emergency? The set of doctrines and procedures that provide answers to these questions constitute the law of *remedies*.

Like the fields of federal jurisdiction and conflict of laws, which we have also alluded to in these materials, remedies warrants treatment as an advanced course of its own in most law school curricula. We will only touch on the basics here. Broadly speaking, the law of remedies deals with two types of issue: (1) the *forms* of relief that are available to litigants, along with the *procedures* one must follow to obtain them; and (2) the *content* of that relief, particularly the appropriate measure of damages or the appropriate boundaries of an injunction. We will focus primarily on the first type of question in this chapter, providing an overview of the forms of relief that a litigant can request in civil litigation and the methods and procedures that govern the availability of such relief.

Discussions of the relief available to a claimant often draw a distinction between "rights" (or "entitlements") and "remedies," so it is useful to start with some basic definitions. When we refer to a "right" or an "entitlement" in legal discourse, what we usually mean is an enforceable prerogative that an individual enjoys to engage in a certain activity, remain free from some form of intrusion, or expect certain behavior from another. Common examples of such entitlements include the right to occupy and exclude others from property to which one holds title, the right to remain free from negligent infliction of bodily injury, and the right to receive the benefit of an agreed upon contractual performance. Many of the courses that you study in law school (property, torts, contracts) are primarily concerned with how rights or entitlements such as these are defined in different situations. When we refer to a "remedy," on the other hand, we usually mean the forms of judicial assistance that a person can obtain when her rights have been traduced, whether that assistance aims to compensate her for the harm she has experienced or to undo that harm and place her back in the position she occupied before her rights were violated.

As you read these materials, think about the relationship between "rights" and "remedies." While courts and commentators often treat these concepts as separate or distinct, they are in fact deeply interrelated. As will quickly become apparent, the nature and scope of the remedy that is appropriate for a particular claim will often depend on the nature and scope of the right that an individual is asserting.

A.   *EQUITABLE RELIEF*

The most basic divide in the law of remedies lies in the distinction between the forms of relief available "at law" and suits that seek relief "in equity." This distinction, which we have alluded to several times throughout this course, arises out of the historic division of authority between the overlapping court systems of England—a division that was replicated in some respects in American courts for a significant portion of our early history. In 1938, the Federal Rules of Civil Procedure formally merged actions at law and suits in equity in the federal courts, following the lead of various States that had already instituted similar reforms. *See* Fed. R. Civ. P. 2 ("There is one form of action—the civil action."); Fed. R. Civ. P. 8(a) & (a)(3) ("A pleading . . . may include relief in the alternative or different types of relief."); Advisory Committee Note 2 to Rule 2 ("Reference to actions at law or suits in equity in all statutes should be treated as referring to the civil action prescribed in these rules."). As a result, litigants need not bring different kinds of lawsuit in order to request multiple types of relief. Initiating a single "civil action" suffices to place all the remedial powers of the court at the plaintiff's disposal.

Nonetheless, the distinction between relief at law, which consists primarily of monetary damages, and equitable relief, which consists primarily of nonmonetary remedies such as the injunction, retains vitality in our legal system. A litigant seeking to obtain equitable relief must satisfy special requirements that go beyond merely proving the elements of his claim, and special defenses apply to such proceedings that could lead a court to refuse the use of its equitable powers. What is more, the judge exercises enormous discretion in issuing and crafting equitable remedies. One of the most frequently quoted statements of this need for flexibility in the exercise of equity comes from the case of *Hecht Co. v. Bowles*, 321 U.S. 321, 329 (1944), in which the Supreme Court construed a federal statute narrowly so as to avoid an interpretation that would have placed strict constraints on the equity discretion of district courts. In justifying that result, the Court explained:

> The essence of equity jurisdiction has been the power of the Chancellor to do equity and to mould each decree to the necessities of the particular

case. Flexibility rather than rigidity has distinguished it. The qualities of mercy and practicality have made equity the instrument for nice adjustment and reconciliation between the public interest and private needs as well as between competing private claims.

This emphasis on the trial court's independent judgment in determining what remedy will serve the needs of the public while also doing justice between the competing litigants is a signature feature of equitable relief. Where monetary relief is concerned, the task of calculating the appropriate measure of damages generally involves the application of a determinate legal standard to a set of facts. When the relevant facts are in dispute, the judge or jury is called on to ascertain those facts with as much certainty and accuracy as possible and to award whatever damages the facts require. That is why a court's factual findings are reviewed for "clear error" rather than "abuse of discretion." *See* Fed. R. Civ. P. 52(a)(6). To be sure, some damage claims require a great deal of interpretation and cannot realistically be characterized as a simple matter of rote calculation, as with an award for pain and suffering in a personal injury case. *See* Catherine M. Sharkey, *Punitive Damages: Should Juries Decide?*, 82 Tex. L. Rev. 381, 398-399 (2003) (reviewing Cass Sunstein et al., Punitive Damages: How Juries Decide (2002)) (arguing that awards for pain and suffering frequently require juries to make moral judgments). Still, among the range of considerations that fact finders must take into account in calculating damages awards, an assessment of private justice and the public good is not generally thought to be of primary importance. In equity practice, in contrast, considerations of private justice and the public good expressly guide the court's discretion in determining the form of relief that is most appropriate.

A request for equitable relief can also play a distinctive role in the procedural dynamics of a civil lawsuit. Most notably, a claim for equitable relief is tried before a judge, who serves as the finder of fact in the place of a jury. Some complicated issues arise when a request for damages is mixed with a request for equitable relief in the same suit, *see* pp. 713–714, but the judge always retains exclusive control over the determination as to whether equitable relief is appropriate and what form any such relief should take.

Moreover, when a litigant wishes to obtain provisional or emergency assistance from a court, that assistance will almost always take the form of an injunction or some other equitable intervention. A litigant must therefore demonstrate an entitlement to equitable relief in order to obtain emergency assistance, and the court's decision to impose (for example) a restraining order at the outset of litigation may significantly shape the course of any subsequent proceedings. Federal Rule of Procedure 65, which we will examine in the next section, sets forth the procedures for granting such provisional injunctions in the federal courts.

In short, the distinction between relief at law and relief in equity retains much practical significance in modern lawsuits. We therefore begin our discussion of the law of remedies with an introduction to the special set of doctrines that continue to govern the availability of equitable relief.

1. *Requirements for Obtaining Equitable Relief*

Walgreen Co. v. Sara Creek Property Co.

966 F.2d 273 (7th Cir. 1992)

RICHARD POSNER, Circuit Judge.

This appeal from the grant of a permanent injunction raises fundamental issues concerning the propriety of injunctive relief. The essential facts are simple. Walgreen has operated a pharmacy in the Southgate Mall in Milwaukee since its opening in 1951. Its current lease, signed in 1971 and carrying a 30-year, 6-month term, contains, as had the only previous lease, a clause in which the landlord, Sara Creek, promises not to lease space in the mall to anyone else who wants to operate a pharmacy or a store containing a pharmacy. Such an exclusivity clause, common in shopping-center leases, is occasionally challenged on antitrust grounds . . . ; but that is an issue for another day, since in this appeal Sara Creek does not press the objection it made below to the clause on antitrust grounds.

In 1990, fearful that its largest tenant—what in real estate parlance is called the "anchor tenant"—having gone broke was about to close its store, Sara Creek informed Walgreen that it intended to buy out the anchor tenant and install in its place a discount store operated by Phar-Mor Corporation, a "deep discount" chain, rather than, like Walgreen, just a "discount" chain. Phar-Mor's store would occupy 100,000 square feet, of which 12,000 would be occupied by a pharmacy the same size as Walgreen's. The entrances to the two stores would be within a couple of hundred feet of each other.

Walgreen filed this diversity suit for breach of contract against Sara Creek and Phar-Mor and asked for an injunction against Sara Creek's letting the anchor premises to Phar-Mor. After an evidentiary hearing, the judge found a breach of Walgreen's lease and entered a permanent injunction against Sara Creek's letting the anchor tenant premises to Phar-Mor until the expiration of Walgreen's lease. He did this over the defendants' objection that Walgreen had failed to show that its remedy at law—damages—for the breach of the exclusivity clause was inadequate. Sara Creek had put on an expert witness who testified that Walgreen's damages could be readily estimated, and Walgreen had countered with evidence from its employees that its damages would be very difficult to compute, among other reasons because they included intangibles such as loss of goodwill.

Sara Creek reminds us that damages are the norm in breach of contract as in other cases. Many breaches, it points out, are "efficient" in the sense that they allow resources to be moved into a more valuable use. *Patton v. Mid-Continent Systems, Inc.*, 841 F.2d 742, 750–51 (7th Cir. 1988). Perhaps this is one—the value of Phar-Mor's occupancy of the anchor premises may exceed the cost to Walgreen of facing increased competition. If so, society will be better off if Walgreen is paid its damages, equal to that cost, and Phar-Mor is allowed to move in rather than being kept out by an injunction. That is why injunctions are not granted as a matter of course, but only when the plaintiff's damages remedy is inadequate. *Northern Indiana Public Service Co. v. Carbon County Coal Co.*, 799 F.2d 265, 279 (7th Cir. 1986). Walgreen's is not, Sara Creek argues; the projection of business losses due to increased competition is a routine exercise in calculation. Damages representing either the present value of lost future profits or (what should be the equivalent, *Carusos v. Briarcliff, Inc.*, 45 S.E.2d 802, 806–07 (1947)) the diminution in the value of the leasehold have either been awarded or deemed the proper remedy in a number of reported cases for breach of an exclusivity clause in a shopping-center lease. . . . Why, Sara Creek asks, should they not be adequate here?

Sara Creek makes a beguiling argument that contains much truth, but we do not think it should carry the day. For if, as just noted, damages have been awarded in some cases of breach of an exclusivity clause in a shopping-center lease, injunctions have been issued in others. . . . The choice between remedies requires a balancing of the costs and benefits of the alternatives. *Hecht Co. v. Bowles*, 321 U.S. 321, 329 (1944); *Yakus v. United States*, 321 U.S. 414, 440 (1944). The task of striking the balance is for the trial judge, subject to deferential appellate review in recognition of its particularistic, judgmental, fact-bound character. *K-Mart Corp. v. Oriental Plaza, Inc.*, 875 F.2d 907, 915 (1st Cir. 1989). As we said in an appeal from a grant of a preliminary injunction — but the point is applicable to review of a permanent injunction as well — "The question for us [appellate judges] is whether the [district] judge exceeded the bounds of permissible choice in the circumstances, not what we would have done if we had been in his shoes." *Roland Machinery Co. v. Dresser Industries, Inc.*, 749 F.2d 380, 390 (7th Cir. 1984).

The plaintiff who seeks an injunction has the burden of persuasion — damages are the norm, so the plaintiff must show why his case is abnormal. But when, as in this case, the issue is whether to grant a permanent injunction, not whether to grant a temporary one, the burden is to show that damages are inadequate, not that the denial of the injunction will work irreparable harm. "Irreparable" in the injunction context means not rectifiable by the entry of a final judgment. *Diginet, Inc. v. Western Union ATS, Inc.*, 958 F.2d 1388, 1393 (7th Cir. 1992); *Vogel v. American Society of Appraisers*, 744 F.2d 598, 599 (7th Cir. 1984). It has nothing to do with whether to grant a permanent injunction, which, in the usual case anyway, *is* the final judgment. The use of "irreparable harm" or "irreparable injury" as synonyms for inadequate remedy at law is a confusing usage. It should be avoided. Owen M. Fiss & Doug Rendleman, *Injunctions* 59 (2d ed. 1984).

The benefits of substituting an injunction for damages are twofold. First, it shifts the burden of determining the cost of the defendant's conduct from the court to the parties. If it is true that Walgreen's damages are smaller than the gain to Sara Creek from allowing a second pharmacy into the shopping mall, then there must be a price for dissolving the injunction that will make both parties better off. Thus, the effect of upholding the injunction would be to substitute for the costly processes of forensic fact determination the less costly processes of private negotiation. Second, a premise of our free-market system, and the lesson of experience here and abroad as well, is that prices and costs are more accurately determined by the market than by government. A battle of experts is a less reliable method of determining the actual cost to Walgreen of facing new competition than negotiations between Walgreen and Sara Creek over the price at which Walgreen would feel adequately compensated for having to face that competition.

That is the benefit side of injunctive relief but there is a cost side as well. Many injunctions require continuing supervision by the court, and that is costly. *Roland Machinery Co. v. Dresser Industries, Inc.*, supra, 749 F.2d at 391–92; *Rodriguez v. VIA Metropolitan Transit System*, 802 F.2d 126, 132 (5th Cir. 1986); *Bethlehem Engineering*

Export Co. v. Christie, 105 F.2d 933, 935 (2d Cir. 1939) (L. Hand, J.). A request for specific performance (a form of mandatory injunction) of a franchise agreement was refused on this ground in *North American Financial Group, Ltd. v. S.M.R. Enterprises, Inc.*, 583 F. Supp. 691, 699 (N.D. Ill.1984); see Edward Yorio, *Contract Enforcement: Specific Performance and Injunctions* §3.3.2 (1989). This ground was also stressed in *Rental Development Corp. v. Lavery*, 304 F.2d 839, 841–42 (9th Cir. 1962), a case involving a lease. Some injunctions are problematic because they impose costs on third parties. *Shondel v. McDermott*, 775 F.2d 859, 868 (7th Cir. 1985). A more subtle cost of injunctive relief arises from the situation that economists call "bilateral monopoly," in which two parties can deal only with each other: the situation that an injunction creates. *Goldstick v. I.C.M. Realty*, 788 F.2d 456, 463 (7th Cir. 1986); *Milbrew, Inc. v. Commissioner*, 710 F.2d 1302, 1306–07 (7th Cir. 1983); *Chicago & North Western Transportation Co. v. United States*, 678 F.2d 665, 667 (7th Cir. 1982). The sole seller of widgets selling to the sole buyer of that product would be an example. But so will be the situation confronting Walgreen and Sara Creek if the injunction is upheld. Walgreen can "sell" its injunctive right only to Sara Creek, and Sara Creek can "buy" Walgreen's surrender of its right to enjoin the leasing of the anchor tenant's space to Phar-Mor only from Walgreen. The lack of alternatives in bilateral monopoly creates a bargaining range, and the costs of negotiating to a point within that range may be high. Suppose the cost to Walgreen of facing the competition of Phar-Mor at the Southgate Mall would be $1 million, and the benefit to Sara Creek of leasing to Phar-Mor would be $2 million. Then at any price between those figures for a waiver of Walgreen's injunctive right both parties would be better off, and we expect parties to bargain around a judicial assignment of legal rights if the assignment is inefficient. R.H. Coase, "The Problem of Social Cost," 3 *J. Law & Econ.* 1 (1960). But each of the parties would like to engross as much of the bargaining range as possible—Walgreen to press the price toward $2 million, Sara Creek to depress it toward $1 million. With so much at stake, both parties will have an incentive to devote substantial resources of time and money to the negotiation process. The process may even break down, if one or both parties want to create for future use a reputation as a hard bargainer; and if it does break down, the injunction will have brought about an inefficient result. All these are in one form or another costs of the injunctive process that can be avoided by substituting damages.

The costs and benefits of the damages remedy are the mirror of those of the injunctive remedy. The damages remedy avoids the cost of continuing supervision and third-party effects, and the cost of bilateral monopoly as well. It imposes costs of its own, however, in the form of diminished accuracy in the determination of value, on the one hand, and of the parties' expenditures on preparing and presenting evidence of damages, and the time of the court in evaluating the evidence, on the other.

The weighing up of all these costs and benefits is the analytical procedure that is or at least should be employed by a judge asked to enter a permanent injunction, with the understanding that if the balance is even the injunction should be withheld. The judge is not required to explicate every detail of the analysis and he did not do so here, but as long we are satisfied that his approach is broadly consistent with a proper analysis we shall affirm; and we are satisfied here. The determination of Walgreen's damages would have been costly in forensic resources and inescapably inaccurate. . . . The lease had ten years to run. So Walgreen would have had to project its sales revenues and costs over the next ten years, and then project the impact on those figures of Phar-Mor's competition, and then discount that impact to present value. All but the last step would have been fraught with uncertainty.

. . . It is difficult to forecast the profitability of a retail store over a decade, let alone to assess the impact of a particular competitor on that profitability over that period. Of course one can hire an expert to make such predictions, Glen A. Stankee, "Econometric Forecasting of Lost Profits: Using High Technology to Compute Commercial Damages," 61 *Fla. B.J.* 83 (1987), and if injunctive relief is infeasible the expert's testimony may provide a tolerable basis for an award of damages. We cited cases [above] in which damages have been awarded for the breach of an exclusivity clause in a shopping-center lease. But they are awarded in such circumstances not because anyone thinks them a clairvoyant forecast but because it is better to give a wronged person a crude remedy than none at all. It is the same theory on which damages are awarded for a disfiguring injury. No one thinks such injuries readily monetizable, . . . but a crude estimate is better than letting the wrongdoer get off scot-free (which, not incidentally, would encourage more such injuries). Randall R. Bovbjerg *et al.*, "Valuing Life and Limb in Tort: Scheduling 'Pain and Suffering,'" 83 *Nw. U. L. Rev.* 908 (1989). Sara Creek presented evidence of what happened (very little) to Walgreen when Phar-Mor moved into other shopping malls in which Walgreen has a pharmacy, and it was on the right track in putting in comparative evidence. But there was a serious question whether the other malls were actually comparable to the Southgate Mall, so we cannot conclude, in the face of the district judge's contrary conclusion, that the existence of comparative evidence dissolved the difficulties of computing damages in this case. Sara Creek complains that the judge refused to compel Walgreen to produce all the data that Sara Creek needed to demonstrate the feasibility of forecasting Walgreen's damages. Walgreen resisted, on grounds of the confidentiality of the data and the cost of producing the massive data that Sara Creek sought. Those are legitimate grounds; and the cost (broadly conceived) they expose of pretrial discovery, in turn presaging complexity at trial, is itself a cost of the damages remedy that injunctive relief saves.

Damages are not always costly to compute, or difficult to compute accurately. In the standard case of a seller's breach of a contract for the sale of goods where the buyer covers by purchasing the same product in the market, damages are readily calculable by subtracting the contract price from the market price and multiplying by the quantity specified in the contract. But this is not such a case and here damages would be a costly and inaccurate remedy; and on the other side of the balance some of the costs of an injunction are absent and the cost that is present seems low. The injunction here, like one enforcing a covenant not to compete (standardly enforced by injunction, Yorio, *supra*, 401–08), is a simple negative injunction—Sara Creek is not to lease space in the Southgate Mall to Phar-Mor during the term of Walgreen's lease—and the costs of judicial supervision and enforcement should be negligible. There is no contention that the injunction will harm an *unrepresented* third party. It may harm Phar-Mor but that harm will be reflected in Sara Creek's offer to Walgreen to dissolve the injunction. (Anyway Phar-Mor *is* a party.) The injunction may also, it is true, harm potential customers of Phar-Mor—people who would prefer to shop at a deep-discount store than an ordinary discount store—but their preferences, too, are registered indirectly. The more business Phar-Mor would have, the more rent it will be willing to pay Sara

Creek, and therefore the more Sara Creek will be willing to pay Walgreen to dissolve the injunction.

The only substantial cost of the injunction in this case is that it may set off a round of negotiations between the parties. In some cases, illustrated by *Boomer v. Atlantic Cement Co.*, 26 N.Y.2d 219, 257 N.E.2d 870 (1970), this consideration alone would be enough to warrant the denial of injunctive relief. The defendant's factory was emitting cement dust that caused the plaintiffs harm monetized at less than $200,000, and the only way to abate the harm would have been to close down the factory, which had cost $45 million to build. An injunction against the nuisance could therefore have created a huge bargaining range (could, not would, because it is unclear what the current value of the factory was), and the costs of negotiating to a point within it might have been immense. If the market value of the factory was actually $45 million, the plaintiffs would be tempted to hold out for a price to dissolve the injunction in the tens of millions and the factory would be tempted to refuse to pay anything more than a few hundred thousand dollars. Negotiations would be unlikely to break down completely, given such a bargaining range, but they might well be protracted and costly. There is nothing so dramatic here. Sara Creek does not argue that it will have to close the mall if enjoined from leasing to Phar-Mor. Phar-Mor is not the only potential anchor tenant. *Liza Danielle, Inc. v. Jamko, Inc.*, 408 So. 2d 735, 740 (Fla. App. 1982), on which Sara Creek relies, presented the converse case where the grant of the injunction would have forced an existing tenant to close its store. The size of the bargaining range was also a factor in the denial of injunctive relief in *Gitlitz v. Plankinton Building Properties, Inc.*, 228 Wis. 334, 339–40, 280 N.W. 415, 418 (1938).

To summarize, the judge did not exceed the bounds of reasonable judgment in concluding that the costs (including forgone benefits) of the damages remedy would exceed the costs (including forgone benefits) of an injunction. We need not consider whether, as intimated by Walgreen, exclusivity clauses in shopping-center leases should be considered presumptively enforceable by injunctions. Although we have described the choice between legal and equitable remedies as one for case-by-case determination, the courts have sometimes picked out categories of case in which injunctive relief is made the norm. The best-known example is specific performance of contracts for the sale of real property. *Anderson v. Onsager*, 155 Wis. 2d 504, 455 N.W.2d 885 (1990); *Okaw Drainage District v. National Distillers & Chemical Corp.*, 882 F.2d 1241, 1248 (7th Cir. 1989); Anthony T. Kronman, "Specific Performance," 45 *U. Chi. L. Rev.* 351, 355 and n. 20 (1978). The rule that specific performance will be ordered in such cases as a matter of course is a generalization of the considerations discussed above. Because of the absence of a fully liquid market in real property and the frequent presence of subjective values (many a homeowner, for example, would not sell his house for its market value), the calculation of damages is difficult; and since an order of specific performance to convey a piece of property does not create a continuing relation between the parties, the costs of supervision and enforcement if specific performance is ordered are slight. The exclusivity clause in Walgreen's lease relates to real estate, but we hesitate to suggest that every contract involving real estate should be enforceable as a matter of course by injunctions. Suppose Sara Creek had covenanted to keep the entrance to Walgreen's store free of ice and snow, and breached the covenant. An injunction would require continuing supervision, and it would be easy enough if the injunction were denied for Walgreen to hire its own ice and snow remover and charge the cost to Sara Creek. Cf. *City of Michigan City v. Lake Air Corp.*, 459 N.E.2d 760 (Ind. App. 1984). On the other hand, injunctions to enforce exclusivity clauses are quite likely to be justifiable by just the considerations present here—damages are difficult to estimate with any accuracy and the injunction is a one-shot remedy requiring no continuing judicial involvement. So there is an argument for making injunctive relief presumptively appropriate in such cases, but we need not decide in this case how strong an argument.

Affirmed.

NOTES AND QUESTIONS

1. *Threat of Future Harm.* The first thing a plaintiff must do in order to obtain injunctive relief is to specify the prospective harm for which the plaintiff seeks a remedy. A court cannot change the past, so a plaintiff requesting an injunction or other mandatory order must identify the harmful circumstance that it wants the court to remedy or prevent going forward. Several types of allegation might satisfy this requirement. If a plaintiff alleges that an interloper is wrongfully occupying a plot of land or that a prison system is pursuing policies that violate the rights of inmates, a plaintiff can ask a court to enjoin that ongoing wrongful behavior. A plaintiff may also allege that the defendant is threatening to do harm in the future and request prospective protection against that threat of future harm. The injunction awarded to Walgreen by the Seventh Circuit served that function: Sara Creek had not yet rented the space to Phar-Mor at the time Walgreen filed suit, and Walgreen sought to prevent the threatened violation of its contractual rights. Finally, a plaintiff can ask a court to use its equitable powers to undo the ongoing harmful effects of past legal violations. The desegregation of public schools in the United States is one of the most important and contentious modern examples of this third category of injunction.

When a litigant offers a pure threat of future harm as the basis for requesting an injunction rather than an ongoing present injury, there may be some question as to whether the litigant can satisfy the doctrine of standing. In particular, a litigant may have to demonstrate that the threat of harm he complains of is specific to him and not merely a generalized complaint about the defendant's behavior. Thus, for example, the Supreme Court has held that an individual could neither satisfy the requirement of standing nor demonstrate a threat of future harm in seeking an injunction against the alleged use of illegal choke holds by the Los Angeles Police Department, despite his claim that he was subjected to such a choke hold in the past, because he had alleged no facts suggesting that he personally was in danger of being mistreated in the future. *City of Los Angeles v. Lyons*, 461 U.S. 95, 105–106 (1983). In contrast, the defendant in *Walgreen* acknowledged that it was planning to rent its store to another pharmacy, eliminating any need for speculation about the likelihood of the threatened harm.

2. *No Adequate Remedy at Law.* Once a plaintiff has defined the harm that she seeks to prevent, she must demonstrate that an injunction is necessary because she would have no adequate remedy at law—i.e., that monetary damages would not make her whole for the harm she complains of. There are a number of different grounds on which one can assert that money would constitute an inadequate remedy.

First, as Judge Posner indicates, there are certain types of claims in which it has traditionally been assumed that money damages would be categorically inadequate and hence equitable relief appropriate. Disputes over title to real property constitute one important example. Threats of harm to one's body or person constitute another. In the case of real property, courts have assumed that every plot of land has unique features that cannot be replicated and that are likely to be important to an owner, such that money damages (with which one could, at best, purchase a different plot of land) will always be inadequate. *See* Robert S. Thompson, John A. Sebert, Leonard Gross & R.J. Robertson, Jr., Remedies: Damages, Equity and Restitution 785–786 (4th ed. 2009) ("A land contract vendee is routinely granted specific performance without any substantial debate about the adequacy of legal remedies, for it is normally assumed that the legal remedies are inadequate."); *Flack v. Laster*, 417 A.2d 393, 400 (D.C. App. 1980) ("When land is the subject matter of the agreement, the legal remedy is assumed to be inadequate, since each parcel of land is unique."). Where injury to the person is concerned, courts assume that the integrity of one's body is a unique and vital condition as to which money damages are always a second-best remedy. Note, however, that courts have generally refused to issue injunctions to prevent alleged criminal activity (as opposed to civil harms), though this doctrine is riddled with exceptions.

More broadly, courts generally hold that equitable relief is appropriate whenever a claimant may be deprived of an item with unique aesthetic, sentimental, or other qualities that make it non-fungible and irreplaceable. *See, e.g.*, Alan Schwartz, *The Case for Specific Performance*, 89 Yale L.J. 271 (1979) (describing such "unique goods" as "the paradigm case" for granting the equitable remedy of specific performance in a contract dispute). As with personal injury, harms to one's reputation also elude quantification, and courts have presumed that damage to the public's perception of a person or a product cannot be adequately remedied with the payment of money. *See, e.g.*, *Abbott Labs v. Mead Johnson & Co.*, 971 F.2d 6 (7th Cir. 1992) (acknowledging a "well-established presumption" that commercial harm flowing from false advertising has no adequate remedy at law) (discussed *infra*). In the case of libel or defamation claims, however, the First Amendment imposes strict limitations on the ability of courts to enjoin noncommercial speech.

Courts may also find that a claimant has no adequate remedy at law when the actions threatened by defendant would cause financial or economic damage that would be impossible to compute with any confidence. Judge Posner relies on this argument in concluding that an injunction is an appropriate means of enforcing the *Walgreen* contract. "It is difficult to forecast the profitability of a retail store over a decade, let alone to assess the impact of a particular competitor on that profitability over that period," he explains. Though finders of fact do their best to make such calculations when a violation has already occurred, that does not indicate that such "crude estimate[s]" are adequate remedies, only that they are "better than letting the wrongdoer get off scot-free." Where a business is threatened with prospective harm and the proper measure of damages would be prohibitively difficult to compute, a court may find that equitable relief is appropriate.

In an important and comprehensive survey of reported decisions, Professor Douglas Laycock has found that "[t]here are very few cases" in which courts have failed to apply "at least one of [the] doctrines for finding legal remedies inadequate or inapplicable" in requests for equitable relief. Douglas Laycock, *The Death of the Irreparable Injury Rule*, 103 Harv. L. Rev. 687, 722 (1990). Laycock, a noted scholar in the field of remedies, concludes that "[t]hese remnants of the irreparable injury rule do not make a persuasive case for retaining the rule." *Id.* at 723. *See also* Abram Chayes, *The Role of the Judge in Public Law Litigation*, 89 Harv. L. Rev. 1281, 1292 (1976) ("It is perhaps too soon to reverse the traditional maxim to read that money damages will be awarded only when no suitable form of specific relief can be devised. But surely, the old sense of equitable remedies as 'extraordinary' has faded.").

Nonetheless, there remains a strong doctrinal presumption that a damages award will provide an adequate remedy for any plaintiff who alleges only that she has been wrongfully deprived of money. This is true even in cases where the loss of funds in the short term might have catastrophic consequences. *See, e.g.*, Rhonda Wasserman, *Equity Transformed: Preliminary Injunctions to Require the Payment of Money*, 70 B.U. L. Rev. 623 (1990) (discussing situations in which a claimant may suffer irreparable injury from a delay in obtaining money damages and criticizing the unwillingness of courts to consider granting preliminary injunctive relief to make a portion of an anticipated damages award available more quickly).

3. *Enforceability.* If a claimant succeeds in establishing that she has no adequate remedy at law, she must next convince the court that the equitable relief she is requesting would be practical and enforceable. The primary concern here is with the level of involvement that will be required of the court and the respect with which the court can expect its orders to be treated. By way of example, imagine a corporation that enters into a contract to merge with another company. At the last minute, the company announces its intention to renege on the contract and merge with one of the corporation's competitors instead. In the ensuing lawsuit, consider two variations on the equitable relief that the corporation might request: (1) an injunction prohibiting the company from entering into a formal merger with the competitor, or with any other entity, for a specified period of time; or (2) an injunction requiring the company to go ahead with the original merger and combine its business operations with those of the plaintiff corporation. The first injunction would be relatively simple to administer. A merger is a readily identifiable event characterized by a high degree of formality. After the injunction forbidding the merger issued, the court's intervention would likely be required only if the company attempted to violate its terms outright, and it seems unlikely that there would be much dispute about whether such a violation had occurred. A straightforward *prohibitory* injunction of this type is attractive where enforceability is concerned. The second injunction, however, is *mandatory* in nature, requiring the company to undertake a complicated series of actions — forced merger with the plaintiff — over an extended period of time. The likelihood is thus much greater that the parties will disagree about what the injunction demands of them, requiring the frequent intervention of the court to resolve disputes and compel obedience. The possibility of outright resistance to the injunction's terms is also much greater in the second variation: The defendant company, compelled to join its business operations with those of the plaintiff corporation, may be inclined to withhold its cooperation or even undermine the merger. A court cannot intervene every time its order is obeyed unenthusiastically or by half measures. As a result, the mandatory order is more likely to result in resistance that can undermine public regard for the court's authority.

This is not to say that courts will refuse to issue mandatory injunctions when it appears that enforcement will be difficult or imperfect. In fact, courts issue such orders in a variety of circumstances. Rather, difficulty of enforcement is a factor that will weigh in the court's decision about how to exercise its discretion. Where enforcement promises to be difficult, a court will want to assure itself that the injunction will nonetheless do more good than harm. *See generally* Tracy A. Thomas, David I. Levine & David J. Jung, Remedies: Public and Private, 89-90 (6th ed. 2007) (discussing how enforceability problems are likely to influence a judge's decision whether to grant an injunction).

How does the injunction in the *Walgreen* case measure up under this standard? Walgreen was seeking specific enforcement of a term in its lease agreement under which Sara Creek was forbidden to rent space in its mall to any other pharmacy. Is the injunction that it was requesting prohibitory or mandatory in nature? Can you anticipate any serious problems of enforcement?

4. *The Balance of Private Equities and the Public Interest.* Perhaps the most characteristic factor that a court will weigh in deciding whether to grant equitable relief is the balance of the private equities between the parties, or the impact of the proposed relief on the public good. It is here that the court asks most directly how justice can be done and what impact an injunction or other equitable order will have on the position of each litigant or on important public values. In *Walgreen*, for example, Judge Posner's decision was influenced by the fact that Sara Creek had no pressing need to violate its contract—it did not claim that it would be driven out of business if it could not rent space to Phar-Mor or that the pharmacy company was the only potential tenant. Had Walgreen been requesting monetary relief, these considerations would presumably have been irrelevant. Walgreen's measure of damages from lost revenue would be the same regardless of whether Sara Creek had a good business reason for wanting to breach its lease agreement or not, and Walgreen would be entitled to those damages even if the effect on Sara Creek would be devastating. In requesting injunctive relief, however, Walgreen asks the court for a remedy that has traditionally been viewed as extraordinary. Equity courts expressly take into account whether justice will be served by granting the plaintiff's request in such a case.

As the term suggests, a court seeking to determine the "balance of the equities" will likely ask what benefit the plaintiff will enjoy from receiving a certain type of equitable relief and how that benefit compares to the detriment, if any, that defendant will experience. *See, e.g., Roodveldt v. Merrill Lynch, Pierce, Fenner & Smith,* 585 F. Supp. 770, 784-785 (E.D. Pa. 1984) (refusing to enjoin state court proceedings in arbitration dispute where plaintiff's rights have been adequately protected through other means and injunction might harm defendant's business). Where appropriate, a court might also take into consideration whether the parties have behaved in a culpable or dishonorable fashion.

Courts also take explicit account of the impact that their equity powers might have on broader public values and will deny an injunction where it clearly disserves the public interest. For example, in a dispute between environmental advocates and the United States Navy over the Navy's use of SONAR technology in training exercises, the Supreme Court found that the public interest in national security and effective Navy training (which the Court found to be at risk in the dispute) trumped the interest in protecting marine mammals under federal environmental laws (which the Court found to be implicated in only an attenuated fashion). It therefore ordered the reversal of a district court injunction, finding that such an injunction would be inappropriate as a matter of law. *Winter v. Nat'l Resources Def. Council*, 555 U.S. 7 (2008). *See also, e.g., John Doe I v. Miller*, 418 F.3d 950 (8th Cir. 2005) (refusing to enjoin statute imposing residency restrictions on sex offenders pending appeal to Supreme Court, despite potential harm to plaintiffs, because of significant public interest in enforcement of statute). As a plurality of the Court has put it, an injunction is "to be ordered only after taking into account all of the circumstances that bear on the need for prospective relief" and "a court should be particularly cautious when contemplating relief that implicates public interests." *Salazar v. Buono*, 559 U.S. 700, 714–715 (2010) (plurality opinion of Justice Kennedy) (finding that a district court had failed to take into account all the circumstances and improperly ascribed illicit motives to Congress when it enjoined a federal statute as a violation of the Establishment Clause).

What justifies this injection of the court's own view of justice into the administration of equitable relief? One explanation may arise from the distributional effects that the award of an injunction can have on the parties. A party who is awarded an injunction may enjoy greater bargaining strength and use that power to secure greater compensation through a subsequent settlement than would be available with a damages remedy. In other words, awarding an injunction may make the plaintiff richer than would a damages award. That being so, it seems intuitively satisfying to say that justice should guide the court's hand in deciding when to confer such a benefit. This dynamic is discussed at greater length in the note below. In addition, many forms of equitable relief involve the active and ongoing participation of the court, as discussed in the previous note. It would be unseemly, and might undermine public regard for the judiciary, for the court to be actively involved in administering an injunction that produced palpably unfair results or disserved the public.

NOTE ON LIABILITY RULES AND PROPERTY RULES

Judge Posner emphasizes several times in *Walgreen v. Sara Creek Property* that courts consider injunctions to be extraordinary remedies that they will only grant if the plaintiff can show that monetary damages will not provide an adequate remedy. What is so special about an injunction as to warrant this treatment? If a party like Sara Creek threatens to violate the terms of a contract, why shouldn't an order forcing the company to satisfy its obligations be the first remedy that the court considers? Part of the answer has to do with the history that we touched on in the first pages of this chapter. In the English tradition, the intervention of the equity courts was an extraordinary event for reasons that were as much institutional and political as legal, and much of the rhetoric and doctrine from that tradition has survived even as the original reasons underlying them have faded. But that answer is far from complete. There are many features of the English legal tradition that modern courts have jettisoned freely when they no longer serve a useful purpose. Why have modern courts continued to treat equitable remedies as extraordinary in nature? Once again, when a party is deprived of the contractual performance that it bargained for, why isn't an order compelling that performance the first type of remedy that we consider?

In a highly influential article, Professor Guido Calabresi and A. Douglas Melamed have offered one answer to that question. *See* Guido Calabresi & A. Douglas Melamed, *Property Rules, Liability Rules, and Inalienability: One View of the Cathedral*, 85 Harv. L. Rev. 1089 (1972). (Professor Calabresi went on to become Dean of Yale Law School and then a judge on the U.S. Court of Appeals for the Second Circuit.) Calabresi and Melamed explained that a party who is able to use an injunction to enforce an entitlement has the power to demand her own price before relinquishing that entitlement. Because a court will use its contempt powers to enforce an injunction (as we discuss below), the party that is subject to the injunction cannot simply violate its terms and choose to pay some expected measure of damages. Rather, the holder of the entitlement can demand that his opponent abide by the injunction unless it meets a price that the holder of the entitlement sets. Calabresi and Melamed describe this consequence of equitable enforcement as the distinction between a "property rule" and a "liability rule."

> An entitlement is protected by a property rule to the extent that someone who wishes to remove the entitlement from its holder must buy it from him in a voluntary transaction in which the value of the entitlement is agreed upon by the seller. It is the form of entitlement which gives rise to the least amount of state intervention: once the original entitlement is decided upon, the state does not try to decide its value. It lets each of the parties say how much the entitlement is worth to him, and gives the seller a veto if the buyer does not offer enough. Property rules involve a collective decision as to who is to be given an initial entitlement but not as to the value of the entitlement.
>
> Whenever someone may destroy the initial entitlement if he is willing to pay an objectively determined value for it, an entitlement is protected by a liability rule. This value may be what it is thought the original holder of the entitlement would have sold it for. But the holder's complaint that he would have demanded more will not avail him once the objectively determined value is set. Obviously, liability rules involve an additional stage of state intervention: not only are entitlements protected, but their transfer or destruction is allowed on the basis of a value determined by some organ of the state rather than by the parties themselves.

Id. at 1092. Judge Posner discusses a further variation on this dynamic in *Walgreen v. Sara Creek Property* when he describes the "bilateral monopoly" that can arise when a court places the power of an injunction in the hands of one party. Even if one party to an agreement could earn a large profit (or avoid a large loss) by violating its obligations under the contract, an injunction means that it can only realize that profit with the other party's permission. The same holds true in a tort dispute, where one party may be able to realize a significant profit by engaging in an activity that inflicts economic harms on another that are much smaller in comparison. A nuisance dispute involving a single homeowner and a polluting factory is the classic example here. When the holder of an entitlement is able to obtain an injunction against tortious activity or a breach of contract, it may demand the lion's share of the extra profits as the price for releasing the adverse party from the injunction, even if that amount far exceeds any losses that the entitlement holder would suffer as a result of the wrongful behavior. As Judge Posner suggests, parties in such a case may engage in inefficient bargaining behavior, expending time and effort fighting over the "rents" that the plaintiff seeks to extract from the defendant after obtaining an injunction.

These insights suggest that we might need to flip our original question on its head: When a party like Walgreen is deprived of the contractual performance that it bargained for, what justifies placing an injunction in its hands that may permit it to extract significantly *more* than the reasonable value of that performance from the other party? What costs will it impose on the parties, and on society more broadly, to make one or another remedy available? How does each type of remedy comport with our sense of justice? Consider these questions as you read the next section, where we analyze the defenses that apply to requests for equitable relief.

2. *Equitable Defenses*

Requests for equitable relief are subject to certain special defenses that do not apply to remedies at law. Such equitable defenses might be thought of as special applications of the "balance of the equities" calculation that a court is called on to conduct in deciding whether to grant the requested relief, for they all essentially speak to the fairness, or justice, of providing the plaintiff with an equitable remedy in light of the plaintiff's own behavior. The doctrines that are commonly recognized as defenses to an equity action—unclean hands, estoppel, and *laches*—receive separate treatment here because they are sometimes given dispositive weight in the fairness calculation.

Remember that these defenses apply only to equitable remedies, not to the plaintiff's underlying cause of action. As discussed above, a court does not have the power to find against a claimant on the merits of his cause of action merely because the court believes that a victory for the claimant will produce an unjust outcome. A plaintiff who is denied an equitable remedy under one of the doctrines discussed below can still pursue damages or any other remedies at law that might be available.

a. Unclean Hands

The "unclean hands" doctrine holds that a plaintiff should not be able to invoke the extraordinary assistance of the court if she herself has engaged in wrongful or dishonest behavior in the events giving rise to her grievance. As the maxim is often stated, "He who comes into equity must come with clean hands." *Keystone Driller Co. v. General Excavator Co.*, 290 U.S. 240, 241 (1933). The doctrine empowers courts to deny an equitable remedy to a misbehaving plaintiff, even when the plaintiff's bad acts do not provide a defense to the underlying claim. Imagine, for example, that a plaintiff induced another to enter into a contract through misrepresentation and deceit and then sought the assistance of the court in obtaining specific performance on the contract. Even if the plaintiff's misrepresentations did not give rise to a defense of fraud in the inducement—perhaps because they were not material or because defendant discovered the misrepresentations before signing the contract and reluctantly decided to go ahead with the deal nonetheless—the plaintiff's morally objectionable behavior might lead a court to withhold an equitable remedy. Justice would not be promoted by giving a deceitful plaintiff the extraordinary assistance of equity—including the greater bargaining power that an injunction often carries with it—and, to the extent that specific performance of the agreement would require the active participation of the court, public regard for the judiciary might suffer if the court appeared to be placing its imprimatur upon deceitful behavior.

Several questions arise when a defendant claims that the plaintiff has come to equity with unclean hands. First, how closely must the plaintiff's bad behavior relate to the subject matter of the dispute? Where plaintiff's behavior involves the very transactions that give rise to his claim, as in the example above, the nexus is obvious. As the connection becomes more attenuated, however, the propriety of the defense becomes less clear. Courts have invoked the doctrine of unclean hands to refuse specific enforcement of a covenant not to compete where the business seeking to enforce the provision had exploited its workers and defrauded its customers, see *North Pac. Lumber Co. v. Oliver*, 596 P.2d 931 (Or. 1979) (affirming order of district court refusing specific enforcement); to refuse to enjoin trademark infringement by a competitor where the court believed the plaintiff's product to be "quack medicine" that plaintiff itself had misrepresented to the public, see *Clinton E. Worden & Co. v. California Fig Syrup Co.*, 187 U.S. 516, 528 (1903) ("We find . . . that if the plaintiff makes any material false statement in connection with the property which he seeks to protect, he loses his right to claim the assistance of a court of equity. . . ."); and to refuse equitable division of marital property in a divorce proceeding where the evidence showed that most of the property was acquired through criminal means or was not reported to the taxing authorities, see *Sheridan v. Sheridan*, 589 A.2d 1067 (N.J. Super. 1990). At the same time, many courts have held that the doctrine of unclean hands applies only where the plaintiff's bad behavior relates to "the very transaction of which [the plaintiff] complains." *Seagirt Realty Corp. v. Chazanof*, 196 N.E.2d 254, 256 (N.Y. 1963) (refusing to apply unclean hands in action to clear title on land where bad behavior relates to earlier conveyances not presently before the court). *See also Republic Molding Corp. v. B.W. Photo Utils.*, 319 F.2d 347, 349 (1963) ("What is material is not that the plaintiff's hands are dirty, but that he dirtied them in acquiring the right he now asserts, or that the manner of dirtying renders inequitable the assertions of such rights against the defendant.").

Second, what constitutes "bad behavior" for purposes of the doctrine? When an unclean hands case involves behavior that is criminal (as in *Sheridan, supra*) or that would itself be actionable in a civil lawsuit (as in *California Fig Syrup, supra*), a court's designation of the behavior as "bad" seems uncontroversial. What about situations where neither condition obtains? Suppose that a 40-year-old woman marries a 15-year-old boy in a state where such marriages are legal, then asks for equitable division of marital assets when the marriage ends in divorce shortly thereafter. The boy claims that the woman used her superior age and experience to induce him into a poorly chosen marriage, but he claims no other misconduct on her part. Could a court invoke the doctrine of unclean hands based simply on its own judgment that the woman had acted improperly in exercising undue influence over a minor? Or does the law authorizing 15-year-olds to marry preclude such a judgment? *See generally* Zachariah Chafee, *Coming into Equity with Clean Hands*, 47 Mich. L. Rev. 1065 (1949) (expressing concern that the unclean hands doctrine invites judges to allow personal notions of morality to guide their equity practice).

b. Laches

The doctrine of *laches* holds that a plaintiff may not invoke equity if she delays seeking relief and, as a consequence of her delay, would cause the defendant to suffer prejudice if the court were to grant the equitable remedy that she requests. The maxim associated with *laches* (the equity tradition is full of maxims) states that "Equity aids the vigilant" and does not pity those who sit on their rights. *Laches* thus acts much like a specialized limitations period on equitable relief. As the Second Restatement of Torts explains, "Even during a period less than that prescribed by an applicable or analogous statute of limitations, delay by the plaintiff in bringing suit, after he knew or should have known of the tort may result in [equitable] relief being denied, wholly or in part, if the delay has operated to the prejudice of the defendant or has weakened the court's facility of administration." Restatement (Second) of Torts §939, comment a. Note that the mere fact of delay will not support a *laches* defense. It is the prejudice resulting from delay that triggers the doctrine. *See, e.g.*, Restatement (Second) of Torts §939, comment a ("If . . . no prejudicial consequences have ensued from the plaintiff's passivity . . . , the plaintiff's tolerance of previous harm does not weigh against a permanent injunction against threatened, repeated or future torts. . . .").

c. Equitable Estoppel

The defense of equitable estoppel implicates another aspect of fairness: the desire to avoid rewarding disingenuous or misleading behavior. When Person *A* induces Person *B* to believe a certain fact, Person *B* relies on that fact in good faith, and it then turns out that Person *A* was either wrong or lying, equitable estoppel may prevent Person *A* from benefiting from the true state of affairs, even if Person *B* is technically in the wrong. As it is usually formulated, the doctrine has four elements: (1) one person knows, or has reason to know, of the existence of a certain fact; (2) he misrepresents that fact to a second person for the purpose of inducing reliance (or under circumstances where he should expect to do so); (3) the second person is ignorant of the true state of affairs or reasonably relies on the first person's account; and (4) the second person suffers a detriment as a result of that reliance. Where these conditions are satisfied, the first person may be prevented from offering the true state of affairs as a basis for obtaining equitable relief, even if he is technically in the right.

The doctrine of equitable estoppel does not only operate as a shield against requests by others for equitable relief, as is the case with unclean hands and *laches*. In appropriate cases, courts may also rely on the doctrine as an independent basis for extending equitable assistance. In one case, for example, the Ninth Circuit Court of Appeals extended affirmative relief to a soldier on an equitable estoppel theory after the military discharged him for being gay. *See Watkins v. United States Army*, 875 F.2d 699 (9th Cir. 1989) (en banc). The court found that the military had acted in such bad faith—repeatedly overlooking the soldier's sexual identity and inducing him to structure his career around the belief that he could serve as an openly gay man, then seeking to discharge him for that very reason—that it was prohibited from applying its ban on gay soldiers against him and had to accept the soldier back into service. The government did not need the equitable assistance of the courts to discharge Perry Watkins, so its behavior did not give Watkins a defense to any kind of equitable proceeding. Rather, the court permitted Watkins to assert that behavior as an affirmative basis for preventing the military from discharging him. Note, however, that the Supreme Court has never formally recognized the existence of such an equitable estoppel action against the government. *See, e.g., Heckler v. Community Health Servs. of Crawford Cty.*, 467 U.S. 51, 60–61 (1984) (noting that the availability of estoppel against the government remains an open question but recognizing the possibility that "the public interest in ensuring that the Government can enforce the law free from estoppel might be outweighed by the countervailing interest of citizens in some minimum standard of decency, honor, and reliability").

3.   *Enforcement of Equitable Orders—The Contempt Power and the Collateral Bar Rule*

a.   The Contempt Power

One of the signature features of an injunction or other court order is the availability of enforcement through the *contempt power*. When a court issues an injunction, it imposes an *in personam* obligation on the enjoined parties to obey the injunction's terms. If the parties violate the injunction, they become personally subject to punishment through fines or even imprisonment. The threat of contempt thus places the starkest form of the state's coercive power behind the authority of the court's order.

Contempt sanctions can be either "civil" or "criminal" in nature, though this terminology can be somewhat counterintuitive. The distinction between civil and criminal contempt does not arise from the nature of the underlying proceeding—a civil lawsuit can give rise to either civil or criminal contempt. Nor does it depend primarily on the nature of the actions undertaken by the individual who violates the injunction, nor even on the use of imprisonment as a sanction, which courts can employ in a limited fashion in a civil as well as a criminal contempt proceeding. Rather, the distinction between "civil" and "criminal" contempt refers to the goal that the court seeks to accomplish by imposing the sanction.

Civil contempt sanctions are remedial in nature and aim to secure compliance with the court's order. When a court imposes fines in a civil contempt proceeding, it does so in order to compensate the injured party for the harm it has suffered as a result of the violator's actions, which may include attorneys' fees and other costs associated with enforcing the order. Courts may also impose a prospective schedule of fines to secure compliance and deter future violations, providing, for example, that a party will be fined some substantial sum of money for every day that it violates the injunction going forward. Courts can even imprison a party who refuses to abide by a court's order. One controversial example of this form of civil contempt can occur when a reporter refuses to comply with a discovery order or subpoena requiring her to reveal her journalistic sources or otherwise disclose information she has promised to keep confidential. Jail time is a proper part of a civil contempt sanction only when it aims to secure compliance with the court's order. Thus, a reporter who is jailed in a civil contempt proceeding retains the ability to release herself at any time by complying with the order of the court, and her imprisonment cannot last longer than the underlying proceeding in any event, since the remedial purpose of her imprisonment ceases once the order or injunction is no longer active.

Criminal contempt sanctions, in contrast, aim to punish parties for flouting the authority of the court. The basic tools of enforcement available to the court in a criminal contempt proceeding—fine and imprisonment—are the same as they would be in a civil proceeding, but the sanctions that the court imposes in a criminal proceeding are not limited to strictly remedial purposes. Thus, a court can impose a period of incarceration in criminal contempt proceedings that will last well beyond the termination of the underlying action, and the target of the criminal sanction cannot win her release by agreeing to comply with the court's order in the future. Similarly, when a court imposes a fine as a criminal contempt sanction, the defendant pays the fine to the court as punishment for his actions, rather than to his adversary as compensation. *See generally Hicks on Behalf of Feiock v. Feiock*, 485 U.S. 624, 631–635 (1988) (discussing distinctions between civil and criminal contempt).

This difference in the purpose underlying each type of sanction, along with the potentially greater deprivations associated with criminal contempt, translate to different procedural requirements that must be satisfied for each type of sanction. Criminal contempt proceedings trigger many of the constitutional protections that would apply to any criminal prosecution, including the right to trial by jury (when the penalty is sufficiently serious) and the requirement that any conviction be supported by proof beyond a reasonable doubt. *See Bloom v. Illinois*, 391 U.S. 194 (1968). A court can impose civil contempt sanctions, in contrast, without complying with these robust procedural protections. *See, e.g., Feiock*, 485 U.S. at 637–641 (finding that civil contempt proceeding, unlike criminal sanction, can impose the burden of persuasion for an element of the offense on the defendant, whereas the State must always bear the burden of persuasion for the elements of an offense in a criminal prosecution). Nonetheless, the federal courts and many states require proof by the elevated standard of clear and convincing evidence in civil contempt proceedings, and various federal and state statutes place limits on the use of extreme sanctions in civil proceedings. *See, e.g.*, 28 U.S.C. §1826 (authorizing federal court to "summarily order [the] confinement" of a recalcitrant witness "until such time as the witness is willing to give such testimony or provide such information" but providing that "in no event shall such confinement exceed eighteen months").

b. The Collateral Bar Rule

Another signature feature of the contempt power as a means of enforcing a court order is the collateral bar rule, which holds that an individual who is subject to the order of a court may only contest that order directly—before the court and on appeal—rather than violating the order and then seeking to challenge its validity as a defense to a contempt proceeding. Such a challenge would be collateral—"from the side"—in that it would contest the validity of the order in a proceeding that concerns enforcement, rather than in the proceeding that produced the order in the first place. Even when an injunction or order is later adjudged to have been invalid, willful violation of the order is still punishable by criminal contempt. *See, e.g., Walker v. City of Birmingham*, 388 U.S. 307, 317 (1967) (upholding contempt sanction against Martin Luther King, Jr., for disobeying state court injunction prohibiting a civil rights demonstration, despite later declaring the ordinance on which the injunction was based to be unconstitutional, because "the way to raise [a constitutional] question was to apply to the Alabama courts to have the injunction modified or dissolved"); *United States v. United Mine Workers of America*, 330 U.S. 258 (1947) (a party is subject to criminal contempt for violating a court order even if the statute under which the order was issued is later found to be unconstitutional). Note, however, that the collateral bar rule does not apply to *civil* contempt sanctions. The rule aims to protect the integrity of the court's processes and public regard for its authority. That justification does not apply to an ongoing effort to enforce a judicial order when the order is later adjudged to have been invalid.

The collateral bar rule has exceptions. If a court attempts to issue an order when it clearly lacks power over the parties or jurisdiction over the subject matter, a collateral challenge may be appropriate. Some courts have also held that the collateral bar rule has no application where an order is "transparently invalid," a phrase used in dictum in the *Walker* opinion. *See, e.g., In re Providence Journal Company*, 820 F.2d 1342, 1346–1348 (1st Cir. 1986) (Wisdom, J.) (recognizing an exception to the collateral bar rule for "transparently invalid orders"). For a good collection of authorities discussing arguments for and against the collateral bar rule and exploring its exceptions, *see* Weaver et al., *Remedies, supra*, at 101–123.

B.   INJUNCTIONS IN CIVIL LITIGATION

1.   *Provisional Injunctive Relief*

When a litigant requests an injunctive remedy from a court, it often will not want to wait until the end of a lawsuit before obtaining the requested relief. If the plaintiff claims to be suffering an ongoing injury—improper competition by a former employee that is harming its business, for example, or abusive conditions in a prison—then a significant delay in obtaining equitable relief will translate into significant additional injury. And if the plaintiff seeks to avert an impending action that would inflict irrevocable harm—the destruction of a natural habitat by real estate developers, or the merger of two corporations that could not readily be undone after the fact—then some form of immediate remedy might be necessary if plaintiff is to preserve any hope of meaningful relief. In such cases, the plaintiff alleges that justice delayed would, quite literally, be justice denied. From the defendant's perspective, however, such an early request for judicial intervention would appear to circumvent its right to a full and fair adjudication. If it turns out that the plaintiff's complaint has no merit, then granting an injunction at the outset of the proceedings would actually harm the defendant, interfering with its ability to engage in lawful activity.

The doctrines that govern such requests for *provisional relief* aim to preserve the ability of plaintiffs to secure effective remedies while also protecting the legitimate interest of defendants against wrongful disruption or interference. In the federal courts and most state courts, two forms of provisional injunctive relief are available to plaintiffs who claim the need for emergency assistance: the *temporary restraining order* (TRO) and the *preliminary injunction*. Both carry with them additional requirements on top of the ordinary standard for granting injunctive relief, and both entail a distinctive set of procedures.

The purpose of a temporary restraining order is to afford emergency relief to a plaintiff who claims to be in immediate danger of suffering some form of irreparable injury (destruction of a natural land feature; execution of an improper corporate merger). A TRO is very short lived. It aims to preserve the status quo until a court has the opportunity to consider whether to issue a preliminary injunction in conjunction with a lawsuit. The purpose of a preliminary injunction, in turn, is to spare the plaintiff potential injury during the pendency of the lawsuit itself. While a TRO can only be prohibitory in nature, preventing the defendant from taking any action to change the present circumstances, a preliminary injunction may also impose affirmative obligations if necessary to spare the plaintiff from the injury of which he complains.

When is it appropriate for a court to grant these provisional forms of injunctive relief? What evidentiary standard should a plaintiff have to satisfy, and what procedural safeguards are necessary to protect the interests of defendants from the misuse or abuse of provisional injunctions by plaintiffs? Consider these questions as you read the following case.

a.   Standards for Granting a Preliminary Injunction

Abbott Laboratories v. Mead Johnson & Co.

971 F.2d 6 (7th Cir. 1992)

JOEL FLAUM, Circuit Judge.

Abbott Laboratories (Abbott) filed this interlocutory appeal, 28 U.S.C. §1292(a)(1), after the district court denied its motion for a preliminary injunction against Mead Johnson & Company (Mead). Abbott seeks relief under §43(a) of the Lanham Act (the Act), 15 U.S.C. §1125(a), to halt Mead's alleged false advertising and trade dress infringement practices in the oral electrolyte maintenance solution (OES) market. . . .

I

Oral electrolyte maintenance solutions are over-the-counter medical products used to prevent dehydration in infants suffering from acute diarrhea or vomiting. They are clear liquids, comprised almost exclusively of water, electrolytes and dissolved carbohydrates, and are ingested orally. While OES products do not actually cure diarrhea or nausea, they maintain the fluid balance of infants inflicted [sic] with these maladies by facilitating the body's absorption of fluids and electrolytes. The OES market is a small (approximately $45 million in annual sales) but important one; dehydration is an especially dangerous medical problem for infants, and as many as ten percent of preventable postnatal infant deaths result from the collateral effects, such as dehydration, of diarrhea. . . .

Abbott and Mead are, for all practical purposes, the only two competitors in the United States OES market. Abbott's product is called "Pedialyte," while Mead's is called "Ricelyte." Competition in this market is of surprisingly recent vintage, as Pedialyte enjoyed a virtual monopoly until Mead introduced Ricelyte in 1990.

The two products are virtually identical; only their carbohydrate components differ. This difference is crucial to understanding the dispute in this case. . . . Pedialyte is known as a "glucose-based solution" because its carbohydrate component is glucose. . . . Ricelyte, unlike Pedialyte, is not a glucose-based solution, for it is manufactured with carbohydrates known as "rice syrup solids." . . .

The OES market, unlike typical consumer product markets, is "professionally driven," meaning that Abbott and Mead do not promote their product directly to consumers, but rather to physicians and nurses, who in turn recommend them to consumers. As is standard practice in the medical products field, both companies send sales representatives to visit physicians, primarily pediatricians, to tout the superiority of their respective products. Both companies also distribute brochures to physicians and place most of their print advertising in medical journals rather than in more broadly based media venues. The plan, apparently, is to convince physicians and nurses to suggest one product rather than the other when approached by parents whose infants are suffering from diarrhea or nausea. This initial recommendation is crucial because parents usually accept their physician's initial recommendation, and furthermore tend to stick with the same product should the problem recur. . . .

[Mead launched a promotional campaign in which it intimated that its product was superior to Pedialyte because it was derived from rice. Abbott sued, contending that Mead's intimations were false, and also that Mead had infringed upon Pedialyte's "trade dress" with its bottle design and packaging.] Abbott asked for a preliminary injunction, seeking a wide variety of relief, ranging in severity from a product recall to modifications in Mead's advertising and promotional materials. The district court approved an expedited discovery schedule submitted by the parties, held a ten-day evidentiary hearing, and heard one day of oral argument. Shortly thereafter it issued an order, accompanied by a lengthy and thorough memorandum opinion, denying Abbott's preliminary injunction motion in full. *Abbott Laboratories v. Mead Johnson & Co.*, No. IP 91-202C (S.D. Ind. Oct. 10, 1991) (hereinafter "Dist. Op.").

. . .

II

Despite our recent efforts to clarify the law of preliminary injunctions, *see, e.g., Lawson Prods., Inc. v. Avnet, Inc., supra; American Hosp. Supply Corp. v. Hospital Prods. Ltd.*, 780 F.2d 589 (7th Cir. 1986); *Roland Mach. Co. v. Dresser Indus., Inc.*, 749 F.2d 380 (7th Cir. 1984), confusion persists, as demonstrated by the contrasting spins both parties place upon the four-part preliminary injunction standard. To guide our analysis, as well as assist litigants in future cases, we briefly outline the following precepts. . . .

As a threshold matter, a party seeking a preliminary injunction must demonstrate (1) some likelihood of succeeding on the merits, and (2) that it has "no adequate remedy at law" and will suffer "irreparable harm" if preliminary relief is denied. *Lawson Prods.*, 782 F.2d at 1433; *Roland Mach.*, 749 F.2d at 386–387. If the moving party cannot establish either of these prerequisites, a court's inquiry is over and the injunction must be denied. If, however, the moving party clears both thresholds, the court must then consider: (3) the irreparable harm the non-moving party will suffer if preliminary relief is granted, balancing that harm against the irreparable harm to the moving party if relief is denied; and (4) the public interest, meaning the consequences of granting or denying the injunction to non-parties. *Lawson Prods.*, 782 F.2d at 1433; *Roland Mach.*, 749 F.2d at 387–388.

The court, sitting as would a chancellor in equity, then "weighs" all four factors in deciding whether to grant the injunction, seeking at all times to "minimize the costs of being mistaken." *American Hosp. Supply*, 780 F.2d at 593. We call this process the "sliding scale" approach: the more likely it is the plaintiff will succeed on the merits, the less the balance of irreparable harms need weigh towards its side; the less likely it is the plaintiff will succeed, the more the balance need weigh towards its side. *Diginet, Inc. v. Western Union ATS, Inc.*, 958 F.2d 1388, 1393 (7th Cir. 1992); *Roland Mach.*, 749 F.2d at 387. This weighing process, as noted, also takes into consideration the consequences to the public interest of granting or denying preliminary relief. *Ping v. National Educ. Ass'n*, 870 F.2d 1369, 1371–1372 (7th Cir. 1989); *American Hosp. Supply*, 780 F.2d at 594, 601. While we have at times framed the sliding scale approach in mathematical terms, *see American Hosp. Supply*, 780 F.2d at 593–594, it is more properly characterized as subjective and intuitive, one which permits district courts to "weigh the competing considerations and mold appropriate relief." *Lawson Prods.*, 782 F.2d at 1436.

We review a district court's decision to grant or deny a preliminary injunction under the abuse of discretion standard. *Id.* at 1436–1437. With regard to analysis of each of the four factors, a court abuses its discretion when it commits a clear error of fact or an error of law. *Lawson Prods.*, 782 F.2d at 1437; *Roland Mach.*, 749 F.2d at 392. Absent any such error, the district court's ultimate weighing of all four factors is entitled to great deference; while our review is more searching than an examination of whether the district court weighed those factors "irrationally or fancifully," we may not "substitute our judgment" for that of the district court. *Roland Mach.*, 749 F.2d at 390; *see also Lawson Prods.*, 782 F.2d at 1437. With this standard in mind, we proceed to the case at hand.

III

The district court, as noted, denied Abbott's request to enter a preliminary injunction under §43(a)(2) of the Act to halt Ricelyte's allegedly false and misleading promotional campaign. The court found that Abbott had demonstrated a likelihood of succeeding on the merits, but determined that the remaining three preliminary injunction factors favored Mead. We find that the court misconstrued the legal principles underlying each of those three factors, and hence that it abused its discretion in completely denying preliminary relief.

A.

[The Seventh Circuit agreed with the district court that Abbott had established a likelihood of succeeding on the merits of its claims.]

B.

The second preliminary injunction threshold requires Abbott to establish that it will be irreparably harmed if it does not receive preliminary relief, and that money damages and/or an injunction ordered at final judgment would not rectify that harm. The district court determined that Abbott did not clear this threshold. In so holding, the court acknowledged the well-established presumption that injuries arising from Lanham Act violations are irreparable, even absent a showing of business loss. . . . This presumption, it appears, is based upon the judgment that it is virtually impossible to ascertain the precise economic consequences of intangible harms, such as damage to reputation and loss of goodwill, caused by such violations. *See Roland Mach.*, 749 F.2d at 386.

There can be no doubt that Mead's Ricelyte campaign, which attempts to convince consumers that Pedialyte is an inferior OES product, has dented Abbott's reputation. *See McNeilab*, 848 F.2d at 38 (comparative advertising "necessarily diminishes [the competing product's] value in the minds of the consumer").[4] The district court nonetheless found the presumption of irreparable harm rebutted owing to the unusual structure of the OES market. It reasoned as follows: Pedialyte enjoyed a virtual monopoly prior to Ricelyte's entry into the market. Any injunction, entered after a full trial, would remove Ricelyte from the market, thereby restoring Pedialyte's monopoly and lost market share. Under these circumstances, one could easily measure the sales Abbott lost while waiting for final judgment. As far as the future is concerned, Abbott's reputational damage will have no tangible economic impact because Pedialyte will have regained its monopoly, leaving those who need OES products with no other choice. It appears, then, that we are faced with a rare situation — any harm to Abbott's reputation and goodwill wreaked by Mead's promotional campaign between now and final judgment will be fully compensable in money damages, and therefore cannot be considered irreparable. Put another way, the fact that injunctive relief in Abbott's favor at final judgment would boot Ricelyte from the market renders compensable any injuries Abbott will have suffered in the interim.

The district court's conclusion rests upon two assumptions. First, the court assumed that if final judgment forced Mead to withdraw Ricelyte, Abbott's losses would be limited to past lost sales in the OES market. In our view, this assumption overlooks the fact that Mead's promotional campaign will probably have lingering, incalculable economic consequences even if final relief on the merits drives Ricelyte from the market. Any monopoly Abbott regains is unlikely to last very long. (We of course do not mean to imply that Abbott deserves a monopoly, or that a monopoly would benefit the OES market, but only that Abbott's damages would be difficult to calculate in the event it could not sustain a monopoly.) It is almost certain that Mead will re-enter, or some other company will enter, the OES market shortly after Ricelyte departs; the market has a proven potential for growth, see Dist. Op. at 80, and the dominant player has proven potentially vulnerable. Pedialyte's loss of goodwill will have tangible economic consequences once competition reemerges, because doubts planted by the Ricelyte campaign will linger in the minds of consumers and physicians, who may avail themselves of an alternative to Pedialyte if given the choice. Moreover, any shifts in the OES market between now

---

4. In holding that Abbott did not demonstrate any injury to its reputation, the district court focused exclusively upon, and dismissed as "hyperbole," Abbott's assertion that Mead's campaign had shaken Abbott's "reputation for innovation." Dist. Op. at 76–77. The court did not address the reputational harm that attends a charge of product inferiority.

and final judgment will affect the closely related competition between Abbott and Mead in the immense infant formula market, which accounts for more than $1.5 billion in annual sales. Mead acknowledged as much in its 1991 Marketing Plan, which opined that "[t]he more market share Ricelyte takes from Pedialyte, the more opportunities Ricelyte creates to" shift infant formula sales from Abbott to Mead. Any suggestion that forcing Ricelyte from the market after a full trial would completely reverse this shift is simply implausible.

The loss of market share Abbott will likely suffer in both the OES market (once competition reemerges) and the infant formula market was not considered by the district court. As an original matter, one could have concluded that Abbott would suffer these harms were preliminary relief denied, and that the difficulty, indeed practical impossibility, of quantifying them would render monetary relief inadequate, and hence Abbott's injuries irreparable. *American Hosp. Supply*, 780 F.2d at 597. It is more difficult, however, to determine whether the court's decision not to consider these harms constitutes an abuse of discretion.

We need not resolve that issue here, for the district court erred by assuming in the first instance that granting final injunctive relief to Abbott would necessarily mean the end of Ricelyte. Granted, some of the relief sought by Abbott — *e.g.*, an order requiring Mead to recall Ricelyte, change its label, and immediately cease use of the "Ricelyte" name — would eliminate Ricelyte from the market at least temporarily, and perhaps permanently. But other relief — *e.g.*, an order prohibiting Mead from purveying the false "rice claims" and directing it to issue corrective advertisements and brochures — would not have such drastic consequences. These less severe remedies would leave Ricelyte a viable, albeit somewhat discredited, competitor with at least part of its current market share.

The district court did not address the possibility of ordering these intermediate forms of relief after a full trial on the merits. *See* Dist. Op. at 78, 101–102; *see also id.* at 79 (enjoining use of current Ricelyte bottle and label), 102–103 (enjoining further use of the name "Ricelyte"). This, we believe, constitutes an error of law. It is axiomatic that injunctions, preliminary as well as permanent, have their basis in equity. *Hecht Co. v. Bowles*, 321 U.S. 321, 329 (1944). When faced with a motion for a preliminary injunction, a district court must remain flexible, and weigh the equities as to each element of preliminary relief sought by the plaintiff. *Lawson Prods.*, 782 F.2d at 1435–1436. The same applies to final relief if, as here, the potential parameters of a permanent injunction will influence the equities that govern the propriety of issuing a preliminary injunction. The importance of flexibility is enhanced where those equities depend in great measure upon which preliminary and permanent remedies are ordered. *See id.* at 1435 ("[a]s the type of relief varies the parameters of the injunction equation will also change"). We therefore find that the district court abused its discretion by restricting its focus to those final remedies, to the exclusion of all others, that would eliminate Ricelyte from the market.

If on remand the district court should revisit the topic of preliminary relief, . . . it should explicitly consider whether Abbott's injuries between now and final judgment would be irreparable if some intermediate form of relief were eventually ordered after a full trial. We take no formal stand on this issue, but offer the following observations. Any inquiry must start with the well-established, and in this case unchallenged, presumption that Lanham Act injuries are irreparable.

See International Kennel Club, 846 F.2d at 1091; *McNeilab*, 848 F.2d at 38. While the district court found this presumption rebutted, we have concluded that an assumption underlying the court's rebuttal was erroneous as a matter of law. Absent any considerations we have not had occasion to address, we can see no reason why the presumption should not stand here. Less severe relief, as we just observed, would leave Ricelyte a viable competitor in the OES market, making it extremely difficult to measure Abbott's damages. Some consumers, particularly new parents, would choose Ricelyte for reasons unrelated to Mead's promotional campaign. Other consumers would inevitably choose Ricelyte on the basis of impressions formed during that campaign; this group includes, for example, consumers who accepted their physicians' initial recommendation to purchase Ricelyte but who were not subsequently informed that the recommendation rested upon false premises. In theory, one could differentiate between the two groups of consumers, and thus calculate the damages arising from Mead's campaign. In practice, however, it would "be very difficult to distinguish the effect of the [campaign] from the effect of other [factors causing consumers to purchase Ricelyte], and to project that effect into the distant future." *Roland Mach.*, 749 F.2d at 386. This difficulty would appear to render monetary relief inadequate, and hence Abbott's injury irreparable. *American Hosp. Supply*, 780 F.2d at 597.

Again, by offering these thoughts we do not intend to foreclose the possibility that Mead could rebut, in some other way, the presumption of irreparable harm. We certainly do not intend to suggest that the court must enter the forms of final relief, if any, that would render Abbott's interim injuries irreparable. Finding that, given certain assumptions regarding the potential scope of final relief, Abbott's injuries are irreparable only would mean that it has cleared the second preliminary injunction threshold; the wisdom of granting preliminary relief would then depend upon the discretionary weighing of all four preliminary injunction factors. *Id.* at 593. We conclude only that the district court's analysis of the second preliminary injunction threshold was erroneous as a matter of law.

C.

We next consider the public interest. The district court concluded that granting Abbott's request for a preliminary injunction would disserve the public interest. Ricelyte, the court reasoned, is a safe and effective product whose presence in the market has promoted the public welfare by focusing attention upon OES products and increasing their use. The court also believed that forcing Ricelyte from the market would restore Abbott's former virtual monopoly, dousing competitive incentives to invest in additional research and develop more effective OES products.

We agree with the district court that forcing Ricelyte from the market would harm the public interest. It is a rare case where purging a safe and effective product serves broad societal interests. This is particularly so when the purged product is one of only two in a given market; monopolies, as a general rule, carry substantial social costs, including higher prices, lower output, and a reduced incentive to engage in product innovation beneficial to consumers. Phillip Areeda & Donald F. Turner, II *Antitrust Law* §403, at 271–272 (1978). The costs are even higher when, as here, important health concerns are involved. . . .

But we decline to accept the court's implicit assumption that granting Abbott preliminary relief would necessarily mean the demise of Ricelyte, for the same reasons we just rejected that assumption with regard to final injunctive relief. As noted, some forms of intermediate relief, such as ordering Mead to purge the false aspects of its promotional campaign and issue corrective advertising, would leave Ricelyte a viable competitor. In fact, such relief would serve, rather than disserve, the public interest in truthful advertising, an interest that lies at the heart of the Lanham Act. *Wojnarowicz v. American Family Ass'n*, 745 F. Supp. 130, 141 (S.D.N.Y. 1990). The court therefore committed an error of law by not addressing less severe remedies that would have addressed the allegedly false and misleading aspects of Ricelyte's campaign without eliminating it from the market.

D.

The district court also determined that the balance of hardships tilted in Mead's favor—in other words, that the irreparable harm to Mead of granting preliminary relief would outweigh the irreparable harm to Abbott of denying such relief. It based this ruling upon a finding that the relief requested by Abbott, most notably an injunction prohibiting Mead's further use of the name Ricelyte, would drive Ricelyte from the market for some period of time, and hence might be "fatal" to the product's survival. This, the court stated, would work a "significant" irreparable harm to Mead, a harm which would far outweigh the "possible damage" to Abbott of denying preliminary relief. Dist. Op. at 78. We believe that the court's analysis contains two legal errors, which led it to understate the harm to Abbott of denying an injunction and to overstate the harm to Mead of granting an injunction.

The first error we have already discussed: the court abused its discretion in concluding that Abbott would not suffer any irreparable harm if preliminary relief were denied. The second we have discussed as well. The district court's assessment that Mead would be significantly harmed by a preliminary injunction purging Ricelyte from the market rests on the supposition that any injunction entered would do just that. This supposition is unfounded, for imposing a less severe remedy would most likely wound, but not kill, Ricelyte. Consequently, the sting of a preliminary injunction would depend upon its scope, and could have been less injurious to Mead than the court surmised. *See* §III.C *supra*. These two errors of law, we believe, distorted the district court's assessment of the balance of irreparable harms.

Having found that the district court (1) overstated the irreparable harm to Mead and the public interest of granting a preliminary injunction, and (2) possibly overlooked the irreparable harm to Abbott of denying an injunction, we cannot accept its conclusion that the equities weigh in Mead's favor as to Abbott's false advertising claim under §43(a)(2).

IV

[The court of appeals went on to find that the district court abused its discretion in a similar fashion in its analysis of Abbott's "trade dress" claim.]

. . .

One final note. As we have emphasized throughout, the district court's analysis suffered from its near exclusive focus upon the most drastic remedies requested by Abbott (*e.g.*, product recall) to the exclusion of less severe remedies (*e.g.*, corrective advertising). This focus, we learned at argument, resulted from the district court's decision to adopt, nearly verbatim, the proposed findings of fact and conclusions of law submitted by the parties; obviously, the court selected some of Abbott's proposals and some of Mead's. Each party, it appears, tried to hit a home run, Abbott by submitting conclusions of law granting it all the relief it sought, and Mead by submitting conclusions of law granting Abbott nothing. Neither offered alternative conclusions that steered a reasonable middle ground. So, when it came time for the court to assess the impact upon the parties and the public of granting or denying preliminary relief, the court considered only the impact of either granting the most severe relief or shutting Abbott out altogether.

Of course there is nothing wrong and everything right with zealous advocacy. But counsel, when drafting proposed conclusions of law for the district court, should bear in mind a crucial observation to which we alluded above: courts retain a great deal of flexibility when fashioning preliminary relief, and the equities weighed under the four-part preliminary injunction standard can shift as the nature of that relief varies. *Lawson Prods.*, 782 F.2d at 1435–1436; *see also Ideal Indus.*, 612 F.2d at 1026–1027. Nor do we cast aspersions upon the widespread practice in the busy district courts of adopting many or most of the parties' proposed findings of fact and conclusions of law, particularly if skillfully and wisely drafted. Nonetheless, district judges also should bear in mind our observations regarding the nature of preliminary relief, and, when presented with proposed findings and conclusions that hug the extremes, consider developing alternatives of their own.

NOTES AND QUESTIONS

1. *Likelihood of Success on the Merits.* The first requirement that a plaintiff must satisfy in order to obtain a preliminary injunction is to demonstrate that she is likely to succeed on the merits of her claim. The reason for having such a requirement is straightforward. In requesting provisional relief, the plaintiff is asking the court to enjoin the defendant before her claim has been fully adjudicated. If it turns out that plaintiff is not entitled to relief (either because the facts are not as she alleges or because the law is not on her side), a preliminary injunction will wrongfully restrict the activities of the defendant and may inflict serious harm. The requirement that plaintiff show a likelihood of success on the merits aims to restrict the issuance of preliminary injunctions to those cases where the risk that the injunction will inflict improper harm on the defendant is justified by the likelihood that it will avert such harm for the plaintiff.

How much "likelihood" does a plaintiff have to demonstrate in order to obtain provisional relief? Clearly the plaintiff cannot be expected to establish her claims by a preponderance of the evidence before there has even been an opportunity for adversarial discovery. As we discuss in more detail in the next section, a court frequently decides whether to issue a preliminary injunction on the basis of a hearing in which the parties must rely primarily on information that is already in their possession. The procedures for ascertaining facts for a TRO are typically even more abbreviated.

Where the basic facts of a controversy are in dispute, most courts have settled on a formulation that requires plaintiff to show "some likelihood" or a "substantial probability" of establishing facts that will entitle her to permanent injunctive relief. In a portion of the *Abbott Labs* opinion not reproduced here, for example, the Seventh Circuit wrote of the need to "keep[] in mind throughout that to pass this threshold Abbott need only demonstrate some likelihood of prevailing on the merits, not that it will definitely prevail." Where the basic facts are largely uncontested and the parties' disagreement centers on the proper application of a legal standard to those facts, the court must come to an initial determination as to what the law requires—subject, of course, to reconsideration as the dispute unfolds and the parties have a fuller opportunity to brief the issues. (While the doctrine of "law of the case" sometimes prevents a court from changing its mind within a given proceeding on an issue of law that it has already decided, that principle has no application in the case of a preliminary injunction, in which any legal judgments are, by definition, preliminary in nature.)

2. *Threat of Irreparable Injury.* Plaintiff's second additional requirement in requesting preliminary injunctive relief is to demonstrate that she will suffer "irreparable injury" if her request is not granted. This requirement represents a special application of the general principle that a court will afford equitable relief only when plaintiff has no adequate remedy at law. When a plaintiff requests an injunction at the outset of the litigation, she must demonstrate that she is in danger of suffering imminent harm that could not be remedied by monetary compensation or even the eventual issuance of a permanent injunction—that is, that she will suffer injury during the pendency of the court's proceedings that will not be remedied by a successful final judgment. As Judge Posner indicated in *Walgreen, supra,* courts and commentators sometimes use the terms "irreparable injury" and "no adequate remedy at law" as though they were synonymous, which is incorrect. The proper usage of "irreparable injury" applies only to requests for provisional relief and describes the particular harm that plaintiff alleges she will suffer while the suit is pending.

A temporary restraining order is a particularly extraordinary form of relief in this regard, especially when it is issued without notice to the opposing party, and hence requires an even more urgent showing of irreparable injury. *See* Fed. R. Civ. P. 65(b) (detailing stringent requirements for issuance of TRO without notice). As Wright and Miller put it, an *ex parte* TRO "is an emergency procedure and is appropriate only when the applicant is in need of immediate relief." 11A Wright and Miller §2951, Westlaw (database updated Apr. 2021).

The relevant time frame for conducting the irreparable injury analysis varies depending on the type of preliminary relief that a party requests. In the case of a TRO, the plaintiff must show that she will suffer the requisite irreparable injury before there is even time for a preliminary injunction hearing. In the case of a preliminary injunction, the plaintiff must show that she will suffer irreparable injury before the suit reaches its conclusion.

The court of appeals in *Abbott Labs* reversed the district court's finding that Abbott had failed to satisfy the irreparable injury requirement. What was the source of their disagreement? As the court of appeals explained, certain causes of action carry a strong presumption of irreparable injury because of the nature of the rights asserted. In false advertising cases, for example, courts have concluded that misleading statements are likely to harm the viability of a product by undermining the confidence of consumers or diminishing the product's appeal in the marketplace—injuries that may be impossible to undo and exceedingly difficult to quantify. The district court did not disagree with this basic observation. Rather, it concluded that the particular shape of the market for oral electrolyte maintenance solution created an exception to this general rule. The court of appeals disagreed, rejecting the district court's conclusions about the market for Abbott's products. Did the court of appeals show the proper deference to the district court? Was one court better situated than the other to assess the parties' arguments about the relevant market?

3. *Risk Assessment and Injury Versus Merits.* One question that frequently arises in applications for preliminary injunctions is how the irreparable injury and likelihood of success requirements interact with each other. Are they completely independent prongs in a multi-factor test, or will a strong showing of irreparable injury relax the requirement for demonstrating a likelihood of success (or vice versa)? And what of the potential injury to the defendant? If a trial court issues a preliminary injunction on the basis of an incorrect assessment of the merits, defendant may be enjoined from undertaking perfectly legal activities, perhaps to its great detriment. How does that potential harm to the defendant factor into the trial court's decision?

The majority view holds that the trial court must analyze the threat of all irreparable injuries—to the plaintiff, if the court does not issue the requested injunction, or to the defendant, if it does—in light of the plaintiff's likelihood of succeeding on the merits. *See* 11A Wright and Miller §2948, Westlaw (database updated Apr. 2021) (describing multi-factor test that measures likelihood of success against likely harm to both parties). As Professor Leubsdorf has explained, this way of framing the inquiry may lead to the conclusion that a court should issue a preliminary injunction even when plaintiff cannot show much likelihood of success, provided that the threat of injury to the plaintiff is great and the harm that defendant would suffer under an injunction is minimal. *See* John Leubsdorf, *The Standard for Preliminary Injunctions*, 91 Harv. L. Rev. 525, 541-542 (1978). In *Abbott, supra*, the court suggests this possibility in describing the relationship between likelihood and injury as a "sliding scale" under which a greater threat of harm to plaintiff if the injunction is denied will lower the threshold showing of likelihood whereas a greater threat of harm to defendant if the injunction is granted will raise that threshold.

In a related circumstance, however, the Supreme Court has disapproved this type of flexibility in defining the standards for preliminary injunctive relief in the federal courts. In *Winter v. Nat'l Resources Def. Council*, 555 U.S. 7 (2008), the Court rejected a lower court's holding that a plaintiff need only show a "possibility of irreparable injury" to obtain a preliminary injunction (rather than a "likelihood" of injury) where the plaintiff could also show a high likelihood of success on the merits. As the Court explained, "[i]ssuing a preliminary injunction based only on a possibility of irreparable harm is inconsistent with our characterization of injunctive relief as an extraordinary remedy that may only be awarded upon a clear showing that the plaintiff is entitled to such relief." *Id.* at 375-376. As it turns out, the result in *Winter* did not hinge on this holding. There was evidence in the record that the lower courts had in fact found a high likelihood of irreparable injury, despite the lower standard that they had articulated, and the Supreme Court ultimately based its reversal on a different ground (the strong public interest it found in rejecting the injunction). Thus, the Court did not have occasion to speak in detail about how and when a district court's assessment of the facts in analyzing one part of the standard for issuing a preliminary injunction might properly impact upon its analysis in any other part. Nonetheless, *Winter* appears to indicate some hostility to this kind of hydraulic approach to the standards for injunctive relief.

4. *Remedies for the Defendant.* What happens if a district court enters a preliminary injunction that turns out not to have been warranted? Say, for example, that the plaintiff secures a preliminary injunction on the strength of affidavits tending to show that the defendant's real estate development project will destroy the habitat for an endangered species, but a full trial on the merits leads the court to conclude that the developer has made adequate provision for preserving the habitat? If the developer has suffered serious financial injury as a consequence of the delay in construction, can it pursue a damages remedy against the plaintiff for its losses?

The answer is yes. When a defendant is "wrongfully enjoined" at the outset of a lawsuit, he may recover from plaintiff the damages that he suffers as a consequence of that error. In most jurisdictions, an ultimate victory on the merits before the trial court will suffice to give defendant a basis for seeking such damages. The defendant need not show that the plaintiff acted in bad faith or without evidentiary support in order to recover; he need only show that he was in the right. Thus, a plaintiff faces some risk of liability when it requests provisional relief.

There are several important limitations on this remedy, however. The first relates to the requirement that the plaintiff provide a security bond in provisional relief proceedings. The Federal Rules explicitly require any party seeking provisional injunctive relief (except the United States) to post a bond as security for the payment of any damages in the event of a wrongful injunction. *See* Fed. R. Civ. P. 65(c). The security requirement is mandatory, but the amount of security rests with the discretion of the district court, *see* Fed. R. Civ. P. 65(c) (security is required "in an amount that the court considers proper"), and district courts sometimes require only minimal or even nominal security, particularly in the case of indigent parties or lawsuits with a clear public purpose. Finally, the majority view is that a defendant cannot obtain any damages in excess of the amount of the bond unless the plaintiff acted in bad faith. Thus, the district court can effectively cap the plaintiff's exposure for damages in the event of a wrongful injunction, if it so desires.

Second, a defendant is not entitled to damages for wrongful injunction if a victory for the plaintiff before the lower court is later reversed on appeal; damages are available only if the defendant prevails before the trial court. Thus, as a practical matter, plaintiff is likely to face exposure for wrongful injunction only if she does not have the facts on her side. While a district court can change its view of the law between the time that it issues a preliminary injunction and the entry of final judgment, it is much more likely that a defendant will be wrongfully enjoined because of a dispute over facts.

b.   Procedures for Obtaining TROs and Preliminary Injunctions

Temporary restraining orders and preliminary injunctions, by their nature, must generally be granted at the outset of a civil suit in order to be useful. Indeed, when an applicant requests a TRO, it is almost always the first event in a proceeding, with the application often filed simultaneously with the complaint. (In a case where the offending behavior only begins after the initiation of a lawsuit, a party might request a TRO or preliminary injunction further into the proceedings.) The procedures for considering applications for a TRO or preliminary injunction in the federal courts are governed by Federal Rule of Civil Procedure 65.

In the case of a preliminary injunction, a federal court is never permitted to issue orders *ex parte*. Rather, a preliminary injunction may issue only after the respondent has received notice and an opportunity to participate in whatever hearing the court conducts before rendering its decision. *See* Fed. R. Civ. P. 65(a)(1). The district court has broad discretion to determine what type of proceeding it will conduct in order to ascertain the relevant facts. The hearing will typically include the submission of documents, affidavits, and even live witness or expert testimony where appropriate. A district court has the option to accelerate the full trial on the merits of the plaintiff's claims if it becomes apparent that the necessary discovery can be accomplished in conjunction with the hearing, and in any event the evidentiary record that is developed in a preliminary injunction hearing becomes a part of the record available at trial. *See id.* §(a)(2).

A TRO, in contrast, may sometimes be issued on an *ex parte* basis — that is, without providing the defendant with notice and an opportunity to be heard — but only when the sworn evidence submitted by the applicant makes it clear that "immediate and irreparable injury, loss, or damage will result to the movant before the adverse party can be heard in opposition." *Id.* §(b)(1)(A). Even then, the applicant's attorney must certify to the court the efforts he has undertaken to provide notice. *Id.* §(b)(1)(B). *Ex parte* restraining orders are highly disfavored, and Rule 65 goes on to require that any court granting such an order must proceed as quickly as possible to hold an adversarial hearing to determine whether a preliminary injunction should issue, and also that the court permit the restrained party to file an application on two days' notice to alter or dissolve the restraining order pending the preliminary injunction hearing. A TRO may also be issued following an adversarial hearing with notice to all parties, though by definition the hearing will happen on a highly expedited basis, since the purpose of a TRO is to preserve the status quo in anticipation of a hearing on a preliminary injunction. Indeed, there are few things that can throw a litigator's office into a more frenzied state than receiving an application for a TRO or, worse, a copy of a restraining order that has already issued. Rule 65(c)'s security requirement applies regardless of whether a TRO is issued *ex parte* or on notice, but a TRO, unlike a preliminary injunction, is generally not subject to appellate review, the theory being that the order will last only long enough to convene a preliminary injunction hearing (and in no event longer than 14 days, *see id.* §(b)(2)), with the results of the preliminary injunction hearing then being appealable on an interlocutory basis. *See* 28 U.S.C. §1292(a)(1) (providing jurisdiction for immediate appeal over any order "granting, continuing, modifying, refusing or dissolving [an] injunction[]"); 15A Wright and Miller §3914.3, Westlaw (database updated Apr. 2021) (provision for immediate appeal in §1292 applies to preliminary injunction but is not generally available for temporary restraining order). As you may recall, the Ohio state courts similarly found that TROs are not appealable when they denied review of the order that Pete Rose obtained against the Commissioner of Baseball in *Rose v. Giamatti, supra.*

A restraining order becomes binding through the criminal contempt power only when the affected individuals receive notice, since it would violate due process to impose criminal penalties upon individuals with no notice of the newly imposed restrictions. *See, e.g.*, Fed. R. Civ. P. 65(d)(2) ("The order binds only the following who receive actual notice of it by personal service or otherwise: (A) the parties; (B) the parties' officers, agents, servants, employees, and attorneys; and (C) other persons who are in active concert or participation with anyone described in Rule 65(d)(2)(A) or (B)."). It is thus not uncommon for an applicant who secures a TRO on an *ex parte* basis to deliver a copy of the order to the offending individuals (or to request law enforcement officials to do so) in order to ensure that they receive actual notice and can be bound by the order as quickly as possible.

2. *Permanent Injunctions*

The injunction that results from a final judgment at the close of a fully litigated dispute is referred to as a *permanent injunction.* The term is something of a misnomer. When a party secures an injunction that prohibits another party from taking certain actions, for example, he can terminate the injunction by selling the rights to his opponent through negotiation, as the excerpt from Calabresi and Melamed indicated earlier in this chapter. Similarly, an injunction that requires a party to take affirmative steps in compliance with the judgment, like specific performance on a contract of determinate length, may expire by its terms once those steps are completed. And it is to be hoped that an injunction aiming to undo the present effects of past illegal actions will eventually accomplish its purpose, at which point the role of the court will cease. Rather than actually being "permanent," the distinctive feature of a permanent injunction is that it extends past the time frame of the civil lawsuit and continues to bind the parties on an ongoing basis.

When a permanent injunction results from a settlement between the parties rather than a judgment at the close of a fully litigated action, it is often referred to as a *consent decree.* As the term implies, a consent decree is generally the product of negotiation between the parties and, in theory, represents a compromise that both are willing to live with. Even so, a consent decree is still an injunction: The court retains continuing jurisdiction over the parties, and the decree is subject to modification and is enforceable through the contempt power.

a. Modification of Injunctions

It is not uncommon for parties to request that a court modify an ongoing injunction. The issuance of an injunction often requires a certain amount of prediction—as to what form of relief will be most effective, what conditions will obtain going forward, or how cooperative the parties will be in complying voluntarily with the letter and spirit of the order. Even if a permanent injunction has not yet accomplished its purpose, expired, or become obsolete, there may be many reasons to consider modifying its terms as the parties and the court gain experience in its enforcement and administration.

In the case of an ongoing proceeding in which the court has issued preliminary injunctive relief, there is no final judgment and the court possesses largely unfettered discretion to modify its decree in response to changing circumstances. After a proceeding has come to a fully litigated conclusion, however, the injunction or consent decree will typically have the force of a final judgment. Where that is so, it may be necessary for a party desiring a modification to file a motion under Federal Rule of Civil Procedure 60(b). Rule 60(b) permits a party to obtain relief from a judgment on a number of grounds, including an assertion that "(5) . . . applying it prospectively is no longer equitable."

The standard for obtaining a modification of a final equitable decree is a matter of some dispute. In one early statement, the Supreme Court set a high bar for such requests, proclaiming that "[n]othing less than a clear showing of grievous wrong evoked by new and unforeseen conditions should lead us to change what was decreed after years of litigation with the consent of all concerned." *See United States v. Swift & Co.*, 286 U.S. 106, 119 (1932) (Cardozo, J.). In a later case involving a mandatory injunction aimed at effectuating institutional reform in a prison, however, the Court relaxed that standard considerably, permitting modification of a final decree whenever "a significant change in facts or law" occurs that "warrants revision of the decree" and "the proposed modification [is] suitably tailored to the changed circumstance." *Rufo v. Inmates of Suffolk County Jail*, 502 U.S. 367, 376 (1992). *See also Agostini v. Felton*, 521 U.S. 203, 215 (1997) (citing *Rufo* in discussing standards for modifying final equitable decree). There has been some disagreement among lower federal courts as to whether *Rufo* overrules and replaces *Swift & Co.* in its entirety or, instead, applies only to final decrees in institutional reform cases, where flexibility in the court's ability to modify orders may be of particular importance. *See* 11A Wright and Miller, *supra*, §2961 (reporting that many courts have continued to apply the *Swift & Co.* standard outside the context of institutional reform cases like *Rufo*). *See generally* Candace S. Kovacic-Fleischer, Jean C. Love & Grant S. Nelson, Equitable Remedies, Restitution and Damages 158–166 (8th ed. 2010).

As a corollary to the collateral bar rule, a party who believes that an injunction has become oppressive or obsolete has an obligation to continue abiding by the injunction's terms until he has sought and obtained a modification from the court, rather than violating the injunction and then presenting arguments about oppression or obsolescence collaterally in an enforcement proceeding. Indeed, most courts refuse to permit a private litigant who stands in contempt of an order to seek modification at all, even by way of separate motion, requiring that the party come back into compliance and cure the contempt before it may seek to invoke the assistance of the court. (Different rules may apply to government litigants in this respect.)

b. Ongoing Mandatory Relief — Structural Injunctions and Institutional Reform

The class of injunction often referred to as "structural" or "institutional" raises some of the most difficult and controversial problems in the law of remedies. A structural injunction is an equitable intervention in which the court imposes far-reaching affirmative obligations on the defendant in order to reform an institution that is characterized either by intractable ongoing legal violations or by the entrenched present effects of past wrongs (or both). Going far beyond the issuance of a simple prohibition on illegal behavior, a structural injunction can sometimes involve the court intimately in the ongoing management of a school district, prison system, or other complex institution as the institution attempts to come into compliance with the requirements of the law.

The advent of the structural injunction is a recent development in the American legal tradition, tracing to the Supreme Court's landmark decision in *Brown v. Board of Education*, 347 U.S. 483 (1954), which declared the state system of mandatory segregated schools to be a violation of the constitutional guarantee of equal protection. In the wake of *Brown*, the federal courts embarked upon a long and painful process of implementing that constitutional vision, using mandatory injunctions to restructure school districts and remedy the continuing harm that many nonwhite students experienced as a result of past policies of discrimination — a remedial process that frequently lasted decades and that still continues in many school districts. As the Court put it in *Swann v. Charlotte-Mecklenburg Board of Education*, 402 U.S. 1, 6 (1971), the scope of the relief demanded in the segregation cases created an "area of evolving remedies" in which "courts had to improvise and experiment." In support of these efforts, the Supreme Court issued a series of opinions, beginning in earnest in *Swann*, in which it authorized highly invasive remedies such as the redrawing of school district lines and compulsory busing of students between districts, remedies that required an unprecedented level of intimate involvement by the district court in the ongoing administration of governmental institutions. As Professor Fiss has put it, a structural injunction frequently involves "the initiation of a relationship between the judge and an institution — a declaration that the judge will henceforth manage the reconstruction of an ongoing social institution." Owen M. Fiss, The Civil Rights Injunction 92 (1978).

Professor William Fletcher, now a judge on the U.S. Court of Appeals for the Ninth Circuit, has offered the following description of the decree that can result from a lawsuit seeking to bring about structural reform. As Professor Fletcher explains, the suits raise significant questions about the proper limits of the judicial role in overseeing the management of public institutions in the course of administering an equitable remedy.

What the remedial decree may seek to accomplish, and the means chosen, vary. A decree may be extremely detailed. In a prison or mental hospital case, for instance, it may specify precise staffing ratios, the temperatures in rooms or cells, the types and quantities of food to be served, the manner of determining types of and times for isolation or solitary confinement, and a variety of other things. Once the decree is issued, the judge sometimes appoints a special master to supervise its implementation, or in certain cases, a "receiver" to take over and run the state institution for a time. Ordinarily, the decree stays in effect for a number of years, and the parties are required periodically to submit to the court reports or other evidence of their compliance. Sometimes the decree is amended as conditions change, or as it becomes apparent that the original decree is inadequate to accomplish its purpose. . . .

[T]he fundamental difficulty with constitutional institutional decrees lies not in the depth of their intrusion into the political affairs of the states, but rather in the manner of their intrusion. In reorganizing and redirecting the governmental functions of a political branch of a state, a federal court must rely largely on its own ingenuity in discovering the likely consequences of its remedial decree, and on its own intuitions in evaluating the desirability of those consequences. . . . In such a role, a judge moves far beyond the normal competence and authority of a judicial officer, into an arena where legal aspirations, bureaucratic possibilities, and political constraints converge, and where ordinary legal rules frequently are inapplicable.

William A. Fletcher, *The Discretionary Constitution: Institutional Remedies and Judicial Legitimacy*, 91 Yale L.J. 635, 638–642 (1982).

For several decades, the structural injunction appeared to be falling out of favor, with the imposition by the Supreme Court of increasing limits on remedies for civil rights violations and the enactment by Congress of a federal statute, the Prison Litigation Reform Act of 1995 or PLRA, 18 U.S.C. §§3626 *et seq.*, that curtailed the ability of federal courts to entertain actions on behalf of incarcerated prisoners. In *Brown v. Plata*, 131 S. Ct. 1910 (2011), however, the Supreme Court upheld an injunction in litigation over the State of California's prison system, reaffirming the role of the federal courts in structural reform of state institutions with intractable constitutional problems in an opinion with far-reaching implications.

The *Plata* decision came in the wake of two decades of litigation over inhumane conditions caused by massive overcrowding and inadequate medical care in the California state prison system. Inmates in the general population in California prisons were packed into gymnasia and other spaces never designed for permanent housing and forced to share inadequate and unsanitary bathroom facilities. Inmates with serious mental illness were not provided with minimally adequate medical care and were sometimes held in cages or relegated to administrative separation for prolonged periods of time, producing an epidemic of suicides and widespread mental and physical injury. An independent review panel appointed by the state concluded that conditions were massively inadequate, a conclusion with which the federal district court agreed, and the State of California ultimately conceded that the circumstances in the state prison system violated the Eighth Amendment rights of inmates. The litigation thus focused on the issue of remedy.

After an extensive trial, a three-judge panel of district judges concluded that these Eighth Amendment violations could only be addressed through a substantial reduction in the prison population, down from the current overcrowding of about 200 percent of the capacity for which facilities were designed to no greater than 137.5 percent of design capacity. The court ordered the state to present a plan to accomplish this reduction in overcrowding within two years, and it declared that between 38,000 and 46,000 inmates would be ordered released if the reductions could not be accomplished through other means. California appealed, challenging the propriety of the court's order under the terms of the PLRA and under general principles of constitutional remedies doctrine.

By a 5-4 vote, the Court affirmed the order of the three-judge panel, finding that the trial record of injurious confinement conditions and abusive deprivation of medical treatment amply supported the conclusion that an order requiring a reduction in the prison population was a necessary and narrowly tailored remedy to the continuing violation of inmates' Eighth Amendment rights. Much of the Court's analysis centered on the PLRA, which imposes special requirements on a court that sought to order a release of prisoners, requirements that the Court found to be satisfied. But the Court also spoke more broadly to the standards for measuring a federal court's remedial authority in any lawsuit seeking a structural injunction. On that issue, the Court returned to statements in some of its earliest cases addressing the power of a federal court to order major changes in state institutions where doing so is necessary to remedy serious constitutional violations—cases from which the Court seemed to have retreated in recent years and the vitality of which had been in some doubt:

> Establishing the population at which the State could begin to provide constitutionally adequate medical and mental health care, and the appropriate time frame within which to achieve the necessary reduction, requires a degree of judgment. The inquiry involves uncertain predictions regarding the effects of population reductions, as well as difficult determinations regarding the capacity of prison officials to provide adequate care at various population levels. Courts have substantial flexibility when making these judgments. "'Once invoked, "the scope of a district court's equitable powers . . . is broad, for breadth and flexibility are inherent in equitable remedies."'" Hutto [v. Finney], 437 U.S. 678, 687, n. 9 [(1979)] (quoting Milliken v. Bradley, 433 U.S. 267, 281, 97 S. Ct. 2749, 53 L. Ed. 2d 745 (1977), in turn quoting Swann v. Charlotte-Mecklenburg Bd. of Ed., 402 U.S. 1, 15, 91 S. Ct. 1267, 28 L. Ed. 2d 554 (1971)).

Plata, 131 S. Ct. at 1944.

The *Plata* opinion, as particularly exemplified by this passage, is a significant event in the law of constitutional remedies. *Plata* has reaffirmed the power of federal judges to employ invasive structural injunctions in cases where no lesser remedy will suffice to redress extreme and intractable constitutional violations like those in the California prisons—violations that were exceptional, to be sure, but neither unprecedented in recent history nor singular in the current state of American mass incarceration. In issuing its ruling, the *Plata* majority rejected the sharply expressed views of the four dissenters, who argued that "[t]he Constitution does not give federal judges authority to run state penal systems," *Plata*, 131 S. Ct. at 1959 (Alito, J., dissenting), and that the order in the case "def[ied] all sound conception of the proper role of judges," *id.* at 1958–1959 (Scalia, J., dissenting). Following *Plata*, the structural injunction still lives as a remedial tool in the federal judicial arsenal. *See* Alexander A. Reinert, *Release as Remedy for Excessive Punishment*, 53 Wm. & Mary L. Rev. 1575 (2012) (exploring appropriate remedies for Eighth Amendment violations and discussing significance of *Plata* for those remedial doctrines).

For further discussion of the virtues and vices of the structural injunction, *see* Owen M. Fiss, *Forward: The Forms of Justice*, 91 Harv. L. Rev. 1 (1978); Abram Chayes, *The Role of the Judge in Public Law Litigation*, 89 Harv. L. Rev. 1281 (1976). *See also* Theodore Eisenberg & Stephen Yeazell, *The Ordinary and the Extraordinary in Institutional Litigation*, 93 Harv. L. Rev. 465 (1980) (arguing that disputes in areas such as bankruptcy, trusts and probate contained strong antecedents of the modern structural injunction).

C.   OTHER FORMS OF EQUITABLE RELIEF

Injunctions are the most common form of equitable relief, but they are not the only alternative to a common law damages remedy. A thorough discussion of alternative equitable remedies would require an analysis of substantive liability regimes like contract, trusts and estates, and tort, exceeding the scope of this course. What follows is a brief description of some of the more common non-injunctive equitable remedies that can involve the active involvement of the court. As with an injunction, a litigant who seeks other forms of equitable relief must satisfy the additional requirements of equity (no adequate remedy at law; promotion of the public interest), is subject to equitable defenses (unclean hands; *laches*), and is not entitled to a jury trial on the equitable portion of the suit.

The law of *restitution* forms one important body of equitable doctrine. Restitution aims to prevent people from benefiting from improper or wrongful behavior. The *Restatement (Third) of Restitution* defines the basic principle in its first section: "A person who is unjustly enriched at the expense of another is subject to liability in restitution." Restatement (Third) of Restitution and Unjust Enrichment §1 (Am. L. Inst. 2011). The doctrine finds particular application in cases where the defendant may reap the benefit of behavior that was unlawful or undertaken in bad faith. A restitution action provides courts with a great deal of power and flexibility in preventing wrongdoers from retaining the proceeds of such bad behavior, particularly when "tainted" funds become intermingled with "untainted" funds over the course of time. Through the device of the *constructive trust*, the court can allocate and divide assets among interested parties in such a dispute. When a court imposes a constructive trust, it takes control of the disputed assets, seeks to disaggregate the legitimate from the illegitimate claims of right, and apportions the assets accordingly. Under the doctrine of *tracing*, a court can also follow the path of tainted proceeds over time and seek to deny a wrongdoer any profit or gainful benefit from their use. Thus, if a person wrongfully acquires another's assets and invests those assets at a profit, a court may require him to return both the assets and the profits to the original owner. If he intermingles the wrongfully acquired assets with his own money, the court may impose a constructive trust on the entire investment in order to determine what portion the original owner should receive.

Even claims that do not depend on a theory of restitution can still benefit from the active participation of the court in apportioning a damages award or helping oversee the dissolution of a complex entity. In such cases, *accounting* and *receivership* may be attractive options. An accounting is a proceeding involving a claim for damages or division of assets in which the matters to be decided are so complex that it would be inappropriate to submit them to a jury for decision. As the name suggests, it is complexity of bookkeeping that has traditionally fallen within the ambit of this remedy. Thus, when a lawsuit involves the separation of business holdings between two entities, a court might undertake an accounting rather than submitting the allocation issue to the jury, often appointing a special master to make a recommendation about the appropriate distribution. The equitable device of receivership is sometimes used in conjunction with an accounting. When a court places an entity or fund into receivership, it takes control away from the current managers and appoints an interim administrator (the *receiver*) to protect interested parties from waste, misappropriation, or other harm. Receivers can also oversee an entity during the administration of a larger equitable remedy, such as a consent decree following a civil rights lawsuit, and receivers are sometimes appointed to take temporary custody of land or other property during trial proceedings or some other period of transition. In all such cases, the receiver is answerable directly to the court. *See, e.g.*, Fed. R. Civ. P. 66 ("An action in which a receiver has been appointed may be dismissed only by court order.").

Receivership is expensive, requiring the court to find and appoint a highly qualified professional who will be free from any appearance of partisanship and willing to devote what might be substantial amounts of time to the administrative duties that the court contemplates. It may also be disruptive, interrupting the operations of the entity, fund, or property and interfering with its ability to pursue its business vigorously and profitably. As a consequence, receivership is generally viewed as a drastic remedy, available only when clearly necessary to protect interested parties or the public good.

D. OTHER FORMS OF PROVISIONAL RELIEF

1. Prejudgment Attachment and Encumbrance of Property

Temporary restraining orders and preliminary injunctions are not the only forms of provisional relief that a litigant can request. For a plaintiff bringing an action at law, a broad array of less dramatic provisional remedies have long been available. Some of these remedies, like garnishment of assets or attachment of property, aim to guarantee the ability and the willingness of the defendant to satisfy a money judgment at the close of litigation. Others, like a writ of replevin or a sequestration order, enable the plaintiff to obtain initial possession of a disputed item of personal property and effectively shift the burden to the defendant to insist on her rights if she wishes to put the plaintiff to the test of his claims. Recall that we described such procedures briefly in Chapter 2, following our discussion of *Shaffer v. Heitner*, 433 U.S. 186 (1977), where we outlined the non-jurisdictional purposes for which a litigant might seek to attach property.

Provisional remedies of this type involve the encumbrance or outright seizure of the defendant's property before the plaintiff has obtained a favorable judgment or, in some cases, before there has even been a hearing. They therefore raise significant concerns under the Due Process Clauses of the Fifth and Fourteenth Amendments to the Constitution, which generally require federal and state governments, respectively, to provide notice and an opportunity to be heard before they may deprive a person of the ownership or beneficial possession of his property. If a merchant claims that a consumer has failed to make a payment on an installment contract for the sale of goods, for example, can the state assist the merchant by seizing the goods and forcing the consumer to initiate an action if she wishes to contest the merchant's claim? Is a consumer always entitled to notice and a hearing before property may be seized? If a class of disputes is likely to involve two sophisticated business entities, rather than a merchant and a consumer, does that change the due process calculus?

In a series of cases decided in the late 1960s and early 1970s, the Supreme Court imposed limits on the ability of state and federal courts to seize property or otherwise deprive persons of substantial property interests without first providing some form of notice and pre-deprivation hearing. (Under Federal Rule of Civil Procedure 64, federal district courts generally employ the provisional remedies that would apply under state law.) In some cases, the Court invalidated provisional remedies that had been in use for hundreds of years. In the following case, the most recent in the series, the Court applies the principles it has developed to a Connecticut law authorizing the prejudgment attachment of real estate.

Connecticut v. Doehr

501 U.S. 1 (1991)

WHITE, J., delivered the opinion for a unanimous Court with respect to Parts I and III, the opinion of the Court with respect to Part II, in which REHNQUIST, C.J., and MARSHALL, BLACKMUN, STEVENS, O'CONNOR, KENNEDY, and SOUTER, J.J., joined, and an opinion with respect to Parts IV and V, in which MARSHALL, STEVENS, and O'CONNOR, J.J., joined. REHNQUIST, C.J., filed an opinion concurring in part and concurring in the judgment, in which BLACKMUN, J., joined. SCALIA, J., filed an opinion concurring in part and concurring in the judgment.

Justice WHITE delivered an opinion, Parts I, II, and III of which are the opinion of the Court.

This case requires us to determine whether a state statute that authorizes prejudgment attachment of real estate without prior notice or hearing, without a showing of extraordinary circumstances, and without a requirement that the person seeking the attachment post a bond, satisfies the Due Process Clause of the Fourteenth Amendment. We hold that, as applied to this case, it does not.

I

On March 15, 1988, petitioner John F. DiGiovanni submitted an application to the Connecticut Superior Court for an attachment in the amount of $75,000 on respondent Brian K. Doehr's home in Meriden, Connecticut. DiGiovanni took this step in conjunction with a civil action for assault and battery that he was seeking to institute against Doehr in the same court. The suit did not involve Doehr's real estate, nor did DiGiovanni have any pre-existing interest either in Doehr's home or any of his other property.

Connecticut law authorizes prejudgment attachment of real estate without affording prior notice or the opportunity for a prior hearing to the individual whose property is subject to the attachment. The State's prejudgment remedy statute provides, in relevant part:

"The court or a judge of the court may allow the prejudgment remedy to be issued by an attorney without hearing as provided in sections 52-278c and 52-278d upon verification by oath of the plaintiff or of some competent affiant, that there is probable cause to sustain the validity of the plaintiff's claims and (1) that the prejudgment remedy requested is for an attachment of real property. . . ." Conn. Gen. Stat. §52-278e (1991).

The statute does not require the plaintiff to post a bond to insure the payment of damages that the defendant may suffer should the attachment prove wrongfully issued or the claim prove unsuccessful.

As required, DiGiovanni submitted an affidavit in support of his application. In five one-sentence paragraphs, DiGiovanni stated that the facts set forth in his previously submitted complaint were true; that "I was willfully, wantonly and maliciously assaulted by the defendant, Brian K. Doehr"; that "[s]aid assault and battery broke my left wrist and further caused an ecchymosis to my right eye, as well as other injuries"; and that "I have further expended sums of money for medical care and treatment." App. 24A. The affidavit concluded with the statement, "In my opinion, the foregoing facts are sufficient to show that there is probable cause that judgment will be rendered for the plaintiff." *Ibid.*

On the strength of these submissions the Superior Court Judge, by an order dated March 17, found "probable cause to sustain the validity of the plaintiff's claim" and ordered the attachment on Doehr's home "to the value of $75,000." The sheriff attached the property four days later, on March 21. Only after this did Doehr receive notice of the attachment. He also had yet to be served with the complaint, which is ordinarily necessary for an action to commence in Connecticut. *Young v. Margiotta*, 136 Conn. 429, 433, 71 A.2d 924, 926 (1950). As the statute further required, the attachment notice informed Doehr that he had the right to a hearing: (1) to claim that no probable cause existed to sustain the claim; (2) to request that the attachment be vacated, modified, or dismissed or that a bond be

substituted; or (3) to claim that some portion of the property was exempt from execution. Conn. Gen. Stat. §52-278e(b) (1991).

Rather than pursue these options, Doehr filed suit against DiGiovanni in Federal District Court, claiming that §52-278e(a)(1) was unconstitutional under the Due Process Clause of the Fourteenth Amendment. The District Court upheld the statute and granted summary judgment in favor of DiGiovanni. *Pinsky v. Duncan*, 716 F. Supp. 58 (Conn. 1989). On appeal, a divided panel of the United States Court of Appeals for the Second Circuit reversed. *Pinsky v. Duncan*, 898 F.2d 852 (1990). . . . We granted certiorari to resolve the conflict of authority [among lower courts].

II

With this case we return to the question of what process must be afforded by a state statute enabling an individual to enlist the aid of the State to deprive another of his or her property by means of the prejudgment attachment or similar procedure. Our cases reflect the numerous variations this type of remedy can entail. In *Sniadach v. Family Finance Corp. of Bay View*, 395 U.S. 337 (1969), the Court struck down a Wisconsin statute that permitted a creditor to effect prejudgment garnishment of wages without notice and prior hearing to the wage earner. In *Fuentes v. Shevin*, 407 U.S. 67 (1972), the Court likewise found a due process violation in state replevin provisions that permitted vendors to have goods seized through an *ex parte* application to a court clerk and the posting of a bond. Conversely, the Court upheld a Louisiana *ex parte* procedure allowing a lienholder to have disputed goods sequestered in *Mitchell v. W.T. Grant Co., supra. Mitchell*, however, carefully noted that *Fuentes* was decided against "a factual and legal background sufficiently different . . . that it does not require the invalidation of the Louisiana sequestration statute." *Id.*, 416 U.S., at 615. Those differences included Louisiana's provision of an immediate postdeprivation hearing along with the option of damages; the requirement that a judge rather than a clerk determine that there is a clear showing of entitlement to the writ; the necessity for a detailed affidavit; and an emphasis on the lienholder's interest in preventing waste or alienation of the encumbered property. *Id.*, at 615–618. In *North Georgia Finishing, Inc. v. Di-Chem, Inc.*, 419 U.S. 601 (1975), the Court again invalidated an *ex parte* garnishment statute that not only failed to provide for notice and prior hearing but also failed to require a bond, a detailed affidavit setting out the claim, the determination of a neutral magistrate, or a prompt postdeprivation hearing. *Id.*, at 606–608.

These cases "underscore the truism that '[d]ue process,' unlike some legal rules, is not a technical conception with a fixed content unrelated to time, place and circumstances." *Mathews v. Eldridge, supra*, 424 U.S., at 334 (quoting *Cafeteria & Restaurant Workers v. McElroy*, 367 U.S. 886, 895 (1961)). In *Mathews*, we drew upon our prejudgment remedy decisions to determine what process is due when the government itself seeks to effect a deprivation on its own initiative. 424 U.S., at 334. That analysis resulted in the now familiar threefold inquiry requiring consideration of "the private interest that will be affected by the official action"; "the risk of an erroneous deprivation of such interest through the procedures used, and the probable value, if any, of additional or substitute safeguards"; and lastly "the Government's interest, including the function involved and the fiscal and administrative burdens that the additional or substitute procedural requirement would entail." *Id.*, at 335.

Here the inquiry is similar, but the focus is different. Prejudgment remedy statutes ordinarily apply to disputes between private parties rather than between an individual and the government. Such enactments are designed to enable one of the parties to "make use of state procedures with the overt, significant assistance of state officials," and they undoubtedly involve state action "substantial enough to implicate the Due Process Clause." *Tulsa Professional Collection Services, Inc. v. Pope,* 485 U.S. 478, 486 (1988). Nonetheless, any burden that increasing procedural safeguards entails primarily affects not the government, but the party seeking control of the other's property. See *Fuentes v. Shevin, supra,* 407 U.S., at 99–101 (White, J., dissenting). For this type of case, therefore, the relevant inquiry requires, as in *Mathews,* first, consideration of the private interest that will be affected by the prejudgment measure; second, an examination of the risk of erroneous deprivation through the procedures under attack and the probable value of additional or alternative safeguards; and third, in contrast to *Mathews,* principal attention to the interest of the party seeking the prejudgment remedy, with, nonetheless, due regard for any ancillary interest the government may have in providing the procedure or forgoing the added burden of providing greater protections.

We now consider the *Mathews* factors in determining the adequacy of the procedures before us, first with regard to the safeguards of notice and a prior hearing, and then in relation to the protection of a bond.

III

We agree with the Court of Appeals that the property interests that attachment affects are significant. For a property owner like Doehr, attachment ordinarily clouds title; impairs the ability to sell or otherwise alienate the property; taints any credit rating; reduces the chance of obtaining a home equity loan or additional mortgage; and can even place an existing mortgage in technical default where there is an insecurity clause. Nor does Connecticut deny that any of these consequences occurs.

Instead, the State correctly points out that these effects do not amount to a complete, physical, or permanent deprivation of real property; their impact is less than the perhaps temporary total deprivation of household goods or wages. See *Sniadach, supra,* 395 U.S., at 340; *Mitchell,* 416 U.S., at 613. But the Court has never held that only such extreme deprivations trigger due process concern. See *Buchanan v. Warley,* 245 U.S. 60, 74 (1917). To the contrary, our cases show that even the temporary or partial impairments to property rights that attachments, liens, and similar encumbrances entail are sufficient to merit due process protection. Without doubt, state procedures for creating and enforcing attachments, as with liens, "are subject to the strictures of due process." . . .

We also agree with the Court of Appeals that the risk of erroneous deprivation that the State permits here is substantial. By definition, attachment statutes premise a deprivation of property on one ultimate factual contingency—the award of damages to the plaintiff which the defendant may not be able to satisfy. See *Ownbey v. Morgan,* 256 U.S. 94, 104–105 (1921); R. Thompson & J. Sebert, Remedies: Damages, Equity and Restitution §5.01 (1983). For attachments before judgment, Connecticut mandates that this determination be made by means of a procedural inquiry that asks whether "there is probable cause to sustain the validity of the plaintiff's claim." Conn. Gen. Stat. §52-278e(a) (1991). The statute elsewhere defines the validity of the claim in terms of the likelihood "that judgment will be rendered in the matter in favor of the plaintiff." Conn. Gen. Stat. §52-278c(a)(2) (1991); *Ledgebrook Condominium Assn. v. Lusk Corp.*, 172 Conn. 577, 584, 376 A.2d 60, 63–64 (1977). What probable cause means in this context, however, remains obscure. The State initially took the position, as did the dissent below, that the statute requires a plaintiff to show the objective likelihood of the suit's success. Brief for Petitioners 12; *Pinsky*, 898 F.2d, at 861–862 (Newman, J., dissenting). Doehr, citing ambiguous state cases, reads the provision as requiring no more than that a plaintiff demonstrate a subjective good-faith belief that the suit will succeed. Brief for Respondent 25–26. *Ledgebrook Condominium Assn., supra*, 172 Conn., at 584, 376 A.2d, at 63–64; *Anderson v. Nedovich*, 19 Conn. App. 85, 88, 561 A.2d 948, 949 (1989). At oral argument, the State shifted its position to argue that the statute requires something akin to the plaintiff stating a claim with sufficient facts to survive a motion to dismiss.

We need not resolve this confusion since the statute presents too great a risk of erroneous deprivation under any of these interpretations. If the statute demands inquiry into the sufficiency of the complaint, or, still less, the plaintiff's good-faith belief that the complaint is sufficient, requirement of a complaint and a factual affidavit would permit a court to make these minimal determinations. But neither inquiry adequately reduces the risk of erroneous deprivation. Permitting a court to authorize attachment merely because the plaintiff believes the defendant is liable, or because the plaintiff can make out a facially valid complaint, would permit the deprivation of the defendant's property when the claim would fail to convince a jury, when it rested on factual allegations that were sufficient to state a cause of action but which the defendant would dispute, or in the case of a mere good-faith standard, even when the complaint failed to state a claim upon which relief could be granted. The potential for unwarranted attachment in these situations is self-evident and too great to satisfy the requirements of due process absent any countervailing consideration.

Even if the provision requires the plaintiff to demonstrate, and the judge to find, probable cause to believe that judgment will be rendered in favor of the plaintiff, the risk of error was substantial in this case. As the record shows, and as the State concedes, only a skeletal affidavit need be, and was, filed. The State urges that the reviewing judge normally reviews the complaint as well, but concedes that the complaint may also be conclusory. It is self-evident that the judge could make no realistic assessment concerning the likelihood of an action's success based upon these one-sided, self-serving, and conclusory submissions. And as the Court of Appeals said, in a case like this involving an alleged assault, even a detailed affidavit would give only the plaintiff's version of the confrontation. Unlike determining the existence of a debt or delinquent payments, the issue does not concern "ordinarily uncomplicated matters that lend themselves to documentary proof." *Mitchell*, 416 U.S., at 609. The likelihood of error that results illustrates that "fairness can rarely be obtained by secret, one-sided determination of facts decisive of rights. . . . [And n]o better instrument has been devised for arriving at truth than to give a person in jeopardy of serious loss notice of the case against him and opportunity to meet it." *Joint Anti-Fascist Refugee Comm. v. McGrath*, 341 U.S. 123, 170–172 (1951) (Frankfurter, J., concurring).

What safeguards the State does afford do not adequately reduce this risk. Connecticut points out that the statute also provides an "expeditiou[s]" postattachment adversary hearing, §52-278e(c); notice for such a hearing, §52-278e(b); judicial review of an adverse decision, §52-278l (a); and a double damages action if the original suit is commenced without probable cause, §52-568(a)(1). Similar considerations were present in *Mitchell*, where we upheld Louisiana's sequestration statute despite the lack of predeprivation notice and hearing. But in *Mitchell*, the plaintiff had a vendor's lien to protect, the risk of error was minimal because the likelihood of recovery involved uncomplicated matters that lent themselves to documentary proof, 416 U.S., at 609–610, and the plaintiff was required to put up a bond. None of these factors diminishing the need for a predeprivation hearing is present in this case. It is true that a later hearing might negate the presence of probable cause, but this would not cure the temporary deprivation that an earlier hearing might have prevented. "The Fourteenth Amendment draws no bright lines around three-day, 10-day or 50-day deprivations of property. Any significant taking of property by the State is within the purview of the Due Process Clause." *Fuentes*, 407 U.S., at 86.

Finally, we conclude that the interests in favor of an *ex parte* attachment, particularly the interests of the plaintiff, are too minimal to supply such a consideration here. The plaintiff had no existing interest in Doehr's real estate when he sought the attachment. His only interest in attaching the property was to ensure the availability of assets to satisfy his judgment if he prevailed on the merits of his action. Yet there was no allegation that Doehr was about to transfer or encumber his real estate or take any other action during the pendency of the action that would render his real estate unavailable to satisfy a judgment. Our cases have recognized such a properly supported claim would be an exigent circumstance permitting postponing any notice or hearing until after the attachment is effected. See *Mitchell, supra*, 416 U.S., at 609; *Fuentes, supra*, 407 U.S., at 90–92; *Sniadach*, 395 U.S., at 339. Absent such allegations, however, the plaintiff's interest in attaching the property does not justify the burdening of Doehr's ownership rights without a hearing to determine the likelihood of recovery.

No interest the government may have affects the analysis. The State's substantive interest in protecting any rights of the plaintiff cannot be any more weighty than those rights themselves. Here the plaintiff's interest is *de minimis*. Moreover, the State cannot seriously plead additional financial or administrative burdens involving predeprivation hearings when it already claims to provide an immediate post-deprivation hearing. Conn. Gen. Stat. §§52-278e(b) and (c) (1991); *Fermont*, 178 Conn., at 397–398, 423 A.2d, at 83.

Historical and contemporary practices support our analysis. Prejudgment attachment is a remedy unknown at common law. Instead, "it traces its origin to the Custom of London, under which a creditor might attach money or goods of the defendant either in the plaintiff's own hands or in the custody of a third person, by proceedings in the mayor's court or in the sheriff's court." *Ownbey*, 256 U.S., at 104. Generally speaking, attachment measures in both England and this country had several limitations that reduced the risk of erroneous deprivation which Connecticut permits. Although attachments ordinarily did not require prior notice or

754 Chapter 6. Remedies and Forms of Relief

a hearing, they were usually authorized only where the defendant had taken or threatened to take some action that would place the satisfaction of the plaintiff's potential award in jeopardy. See C. Drake, Law of Suits by Attachment, §§40–82 (1866) (hereinafter Drake); 1 R. Shinn, Attachment and Garnishment §86 (1896) (hereinafter Shinn). Attachments, moreover, were generally confined to claims by creditors. Drake §§9–10; Shinn §12. As we and the Court of Appeals have noted, disputes between debtors and creditors more readily lend themselves to accurate *ex parte* assessments of the merits. Tort actions, like the assault and battery claim at issue here, do not. See *Mitchell, supra*, 416 U.S., at 609–610. Finally, as we will discuss below, attachment statutes historically required that the plaintiff post a bond. Drake §§114–183; Shinn §153.

Connecticut's statute appears even more suspect in light of current practice. A survey of state attachment provisions reveals that nearly every State requires either a preattachment hearing, a showing of some exigent circumstance, or both, before permitting an attachment to take place. [The Court briefly canvassed the practices followed by the States.] . . . We do not mean to imply that any given exigency requirement protects an attachment from constitutional attack. Nor do we suggest that the statutory measures we have surveyed are necessarily free of due process problems or other constitutional infirmities in general. We do believe, however, that the procedures of almost all the States confirm our view that the Connecticut provision before us, by failing to provide a preattachment hearing without at least requiring a showing of some exigent circumstance, clearly falls short of the demands of due process.

IV

[In an opinion that did not command a majority of the Court, Justices White, Marshall, Stevens, and O'Connor went on to conclude that due process always requires a plaintiff to file a bond to cover any damages that a defendant might suffer from an improper use of prejudgment attachment.]

V

Because Connecticut's prejudgment remedy provision, Conn. Gen. Stat. §52-278e(a)(1), violates the requirements of due process by authorizing prejudgment attachment without prior notice or a hearing, the judgment of the Court of Appeals is affirmed, and the case is remanded to that court for further proceedings consistent with this opinion.

It is so ordered.

. . .

Justice Scalia, concurring in part and concurring in the judgment.

Since the manner of attachment here was not a recognized procedure at common law, cf. *Pacific Mut. Life Ins. Co. v. Haslip*, 499 U.S. 1, 24 (1991) (Scalia, J., concurring in judgment), I agree that its validity under the Due Process Clause should be determined by applying the test we set forth in *Mathews v. Eldridge*, 424 U.S. 319 (1976); and I agree that it fails that test. I join Parts I and III of the Court's opinion, and concur in the judgment of the Court.

NOTES AND QUESTIONS

1. *An Overview of Prejudgment Provisional Remedies.* The provisional remedies that the Court discusses in its analysis of the *Sniadach-Fuentes-Mitchell* line of cases encompass a diverse array of procedures. Some of those procedures are available only in certain types of dispute, while others could in theory be invoked in any law-suit—a fact that played a significant role in the Court's analysis in *Doehr*.

The *Fuentes* and *Mitchell* cases both involved procedures designed for disputes over the ownership of personal property. The *writ of replevin* enables a party to invoke the assistance of a sheriff or other executive official in obtaining physical possession of an item when the party claims that her opponent is in possession of it wrongfully. The language of the Florida statute at issue in *Fuentes* is typical: "Any person whose goods or chattels are wrongfully detained by any other person . . . may have a writ of replevin to recover them." The basic claim in such a case is that the defendant either came into possession of the item wrongfully or, as in *Fuentes*, possessed it subject to certain conditions that he has violated (like a payment plan), such that the plaintiff is now entitled to have physical possession returned to her. A *writ of sequestration* like that in *Mitchell* serves a similar function, enabling a plaintiff to have local officials seize disputed items of property when there is some danger that the defendant in possession will harm the items or abscond with them if given the chance. Today, this remedy is used most frequently in cases involving the sale of goods, whether through installment contracts from retailers (as in *Fuentes* and *Mitchell*) or in transactions between merchants or other business entities. The Uniform Commercial Code, for example, provides:

> Unless otherwise agreed a secured party has on default the right to take possession of the collateral. In taking possession a secured party may proceed without judicial process if this can be done without breach of the peace or may proceed by action. If the security agreement so provides the secured party may require the debtor to assemble the collateral and make it available to the secured party at a place to be designated by the secured party which is reasonably convenient to both parties.

U.C.C. §9-609 (Am. L. Inst. & Unif. L. Comm'n 2020). The "secured party" here refers to the plaintiff, who is owed a debt by defendant (i.e., the payments on the item or good) that is "secured" by the value of the good itself. When a party proceeds "without judicial process" in such a case, it undertakes to repossess the item on its own initiative. *See* Jean Braucher, *The Repo Code: A Study of Adjustment to Uncertainty in Commercial Law*, 75 Wash. U. L.Q. 549 (1997) (discussing competing policies underlying self-help replevin procedures and collecting statutes and other authorities). Note that special rules may apply when the government initiates a *forfeiture* proceeding—a seizure of property that is alleged to have been used in conjunction with criminal activity or other wrongdoing. *Compare Calero-Toledo v. Pearson Yacht Leasing Co.*, 416 U.S. 663, 679 (1974) (authorizing seizure of personal property in forfeiture proceeding "that could be removed to another jurisdiction, destroyed, or concealed, if advance warning of confiscation were given") *with U.S. v. James Daniel Good Real Property*, 510 U.S. 43, 59 (1993) (distinguishing *Calero-Toledo* in cases involving real property because "[i]n the usual case . . . [t]here is no reason to . . . assert[] control over [real] property without first affording notice and an adversary hearing").

Other provisional relief mechanisms seek to ensure that a defendant will be able to satisfy a money judgment in the event that the plaintiff prevails on his claims at trial. The procedures of *garnishment* and *attachment* are prominent examples. The term "garnishment" is frequently associated with a person's wages, but it can also apply to a bank account or other assets. In a garnishment proceeding, plaintiff alleges claims against defendant and asserts that there is a danger that he will be unable to recover on those claims unless the court encumbers the defendant's assets or sources of revenue. A garnishment order is served on a third party who owes a payment obligation to the defendant—most frequently a bank or other financial institution, or the defendant's employer—and the third party must then pay some portion of the obligation to the plaintiff rather than the defendant. The "attachment" device that the Court analyzed in *Connecticut v. Doehr* is a similar process, except that a plaintiff utilizing the procedure seeks to secure the defendant's land or other property directly in order to ensure payment of a judgment, rather than encumbering obligations owed by third parties. Parties may also invoke garnishment and attachment in post-judgment proceedings in order to collect from recalcitrant opponents, but it is the prejudgment use of the procedures that raises the most serious due process concerns. *See, e.g., North Georgia Finishing v. Di-Chem, Inc.*, 419 U.S. 601 (1975) (striking down application of garnishment statute that attached defendant's bank account); *Sniadach v. Family Finance Corp.*, 395 U.S. 337 (1969) (striking down statute that permitted prejudgment garnishment of defendant's wages).

States also employ various procedures that have the effect of encumbering or disabling property as a means of forcing disputants to resolve their disagreements over that property. A person who believes that she has an unsatisfied claim on a parcel of land, for example, can file a notice of *lis pendens* upon it. *Lis pendens* alerts any prospective purchasers of the property that there is an outstanding claim concerning who holds proper title, making it impossible for purchasers to claim that they acquired the property with no knowledge of any cloud on the title and, hence, making it impossible for them to claim the status of "bona fide purchasers for value." For all practical purposes, a *lis pendens* notice usually renders a property impossible to sell, giving the possessor a strong incentive to resolve the outstanding dispute.

2. *The Procedural Elements of Provisional Remedies.* The provisional remedies described above share a set of common procedural elements that have become the Court's primary focus in due process challenges. These elements include:

a. *Security Bond.* States sometimes require an applicant seeking a provisional remedy to file a bond with the court so that funds will be available to compensate the defendant if it turns out that the provisional remedy was wrongfully issued. *Cf.* Fed. R. Civ. P. 65(c) (imposing a similar requirement for preliminary injunctions). As with a preliminary injunction, a defendant who is harmed by a wrongfully issued provisional remedy can collect consequential damages in most jurisdictions.

b. *Notice.* Not surprisingly, whether the plaintiff must attempt to provide notice to the defendant before taking or encumbering her property is an important question in the due process analysis of provisional remedies. Where the purpose of a remedy is to prevent defendant from destroying or hiding the property, however, pre-deprivation notice may defeat the purpose of the procedure. *See, e.g., Mitchell,* 416 U.S. at 607–610 (upholding writ of sequestration despite lack of pre-deprivation notice).

   c.   *Involvement of a Judge.* Provisional remedies sometimes require the approval of a judge or magistrate. Others may require only the signature of a clerk of court or a local sheriff. The greater the involvement of a judicial officer in the decision, the more likely a procedure is to survive a due process challenge, though the involvement of a judge is no guarantee in that respect, as *Connecticut v. Doehr* demonstrates.

   d.   *Factual Showing.* The type of factual showing that a petitioner must make differs across these procedures. Some procedures require sworn affidavits and an objectively satisfactory level of evidentiary support, while others demand only conclusory allegations or a statement of good faith. As the majority implies in *Doehr,* the strong trend in the Court's due process opinions has been toward requiring some form of reliable evidence, or, at least, detailed allegations made under penalty of perjury. Note also that a plaintiff may need to make a showing both as to the merits of his claims and as to his need for provisional relief—issues that likely will not overlap when the underlying dispute does not concern the seized property, as in *Doehr.*

   e.   *Type of Claim.* The Court has suggested more than once that certain types of claims lend themselves more readily to the use of provisional remedies. Where the proof in a claim is likely to be documentary and straightforward, as in a dispute over an installment contract for the purchase of goods, the Court is more likely to approve highly streamlined procedures. Where the underlying claim will involve highly contested proof, as in the personal injury claim in *Doehr,* the likelihood of error associated with streamlined procedures, and hence the threat to due process, is greater. Here, too, the question of whether the plaintiff claims a direct interest in the disputed property may bear on the analysis, as the risk of an erroneous deprivation may be lower in such a case. *See Mitchell,* 416 U.S. 607-610 (describing features of vendor-buyer relationship that support finding that provisional relief is appropriate).

   f.   *Post-Deprivation Hearing.* The availability of a prompt adversarial hearing shortly after a seizure or attachment is another factor in the due process analysis, since a hearing may enable the court to correct any erroneous deprivations promptly. Of particular importance is the question of who must initiate such a hearing. When an individual whose property is seized must initiate an entirely new proceeding to contest the seizure, the value of the adversarial hearing is diminished. When the hearing follows directly on the plaintiff's seizure of the owner's goods, it minimizes the duration of any erroneous deprivation. *See Mitchell,* 416 U.S. at 606 (entitling debtor to seek immediate dissolution of writ of sequestration in original proceeding). The relevance of such a hearing to the constitutional analysis may also depend on how likely it is to avert or correct mistakes. If the defendants in a class of cases are unlikely to have the resources or wherewithal to take affirmative steps to protect their interests, then the availability of a post-deprivation hearing may do little to cure a constitutional problem. *See Fuentes,* 407 U.S. at 84 n. 14 (citing evidence that post-deprivation opportunities for recovery of goods are impractical for most consumers).

   With these procedural elements in mind, the major cases that the Court has decided on the due process requirements for provisional relief map onto the table on the next page.

Major Provisional Remedy Cases

CASE	Provisional Remedy Used	Plaintiff Required to Post Bond	Pre-Deprivation Notice	Decision Maker	Factual Showing Required	Remedy Limited to Certain Claims	Post-Deprivation Hearing	RESULT
Sniadach v. Family Finance	Garnish wages for payment of a claim	No	No	Clerk of court	Conclusory allegations	No	No	**Struck down**
Fuentes v. Shevin	Seize property for replevin	Yes	No	Clerk of court	Conclusory allegations	Yes (recover goods)	Yes in FL, No in PA	**Struck down**
Mitchell v. W.T. Grant Co.	Sequester property for replevin	Yes	No	Judge	Specific facts under penalty of perjury	Yes (recover goods)	Yes	**Upheld**
North Georgia Finishing v. Di-Chem	Garnish assets for payment of a claim	No	No	Clerk of court	Allegations, no need for personal knowledge	No	No	**Struck down**
Connecticut v. Doehr	Attach land for payment of a claim	No	No	Judge	Evidence to support "probable cause"	No	Yes	**Struck down**

What appear to be the critical elements that are necessary for a provisional remedy to comport with due process? Consider that question in light of the next note.

3. Mathews v. Eldridge *and Due Process Analysis.* The majority in *Doehr* conducted its due process analysis under a framework first set forth in the landmark case of *Mathews v. Eldridge*, 424 U.S. 319 (1976). In *Mathews*, a recipient of disability benefits claimed that the government had to provide notice and a hearing before terminating those benefits. The Court disagreed, holding that a pre-deprivation hearing was not required when the hearing would impose added cost and inconvenience and would not significantly increase the likelihood of an accurate determination of the recipient's eligibility for benefits in light of the post-deprivation mechanisms of review that were already available. In reaching that result, the Court held that whenever a litigant argues that a given procedure is required by the Due Process Clause, the court should measure that argument against three considerations: (1) the nature and importance of the individual interest that the state is threatening to compromise; (2) the likelihood that the requested procedure will increase the accuracy of the state's determination and decrease the chances of error or abuse; and (3) the nature and importance of the government's interest, including its interest in refusing to offer the procedure for reasons of efficiency and manageability. In *Mathews*, the Court was analyzing a decision by the government itself to terminate a benefit and deprive the recipient of property, but the analytical framework that it developed also applies to disputes between private parties in which the state is providing the mechanism for resolving disputes.

The statute at issue in *Connecticut v. Doehr* did offer one of the most important procedural safeguards: the requirement that a judge rule on the request for provisional relief, rather than a clerk or other lower-level official. In *Mitchell v. W.T. Grant Co.*, the only one of the major cases in this series in which a provisional remedy was found to comport with due process, the Court placed significant weight on the requirement that a judge serve as gatekeeper, writing: "Mitchell was not at the unsupervised mercy of the creditor and court functionaries. The Louisiana law provides for judicial control of the process from beginning to end. This control is one of the measures adopted by the State to minimize the risk that the *ex parte* procedure will lead to a wrongful taking." 416 U.S. at 616–617. Why did Connecticut's requirement that a judge retain control over the decision not count for more? According to the Court, the Connecticut statute only required a plaintiff to make "skeletal" allegations in satisfying the statute's probable cause standard, rendering any finding that the trial court might make on the plaintiff's likelihood of prevailing inherently unreliable, especially on a claim, like assault, that is likely to involve competing versions of complex events. Under the second part of the *Mathews* inquiry, this lax evidentiary standard was likely to result in significant errors, even with a judge serving as the finder of fact.

The Court also focused on the relationship between the provisional remedy and the underlying claim. Even where there is some increased risk of error, the Court suggested, a procedure might pass constitutional muster if it protects the plaintiff against a significant danger that she will be unable to obtain relief, perhaps because the defendant might sell or "waste" a disputed piece of property in which the plaintiff claims an interest or else hides her assets so as to be effectively judgment-proof. Under the third part of the *Mathews* inquiry, the state has a substantial interest in preventing such harms to creditors or other plaintiffs, perhaps even at the cost of some increased risk that defendant will suffer an unjustified deprivation. In *Connecticut v. Doehr*, neither justification was present: the real estate that plaintiff attached was not the subject of the dispute, and there was no reason to assume that defendant would hide or transfer his assets in an attempt to escape paying a judgment.

4. *History and Tradition.* In his brief concurrence, Justice Scalia explains that he joins the majority's analysis under *Mathews v. Eldridge* only because "the manner of attachment here was not a recognized procedure at common law." This refrain should be familiar by now. Justice Scalia has consistently maintained the view that judicial and quasi-judicial procedures should only be subjected to searching analysis under the Due Process Clause when they represent an innovation or a break from traditional common law practices. In analyzing "tag" personal jurisdiction over an individual who travels on a transitory basis through a state, for example, Justice Scalia wrote that the Court should "conduct[] no independent inquiry into the desirability or fairness of the prevailing in-state service rule," for "its validation is its pedigree." *Burnham v. Superior Court of California*, 495 U.S. 604, 621 (1990) (plurality opinion of Scalia, J.). *See also Sun Oil v. Wortman*, 486 U.S. 717, 728-729 (1988) ("[L]ong established and still subsisting choice-of-law practices that come to be thought, by modern scholars, unwise, do not thereby become unconstitutional. . . . If a thing has been practiced for two hundred years by common consent, it will need a strong case for the Fourteenth Amendment to affect it.") (internal quotation omitted).

Is Justice Scalia's approach to due process analysis well suited to the review of provisional remedies? Justice Blackmun, dissenting in *North Georgia Finishing v. Di-Chem*, criticized the Court for striking down "old and long-unattacked commercial statutes designed to afford a way for relief to a creditor against a delinquent debtor." 419 U.S. 601, 614 (1975) (Blackmun, J., dissenting). If a procedural mechanism has been in place for a very long time without substantial controversy, is that pedigree a good indication that the procedure has struck an appropriate balance between the interests of creditors and debtors? Or is it possible that changed commercial conditions could transform a benign or underutilized procedure into a tool of oppression?

5. *Remedies and Cost Shifting.* What is the likely impact of the Court's decisions striking down streamlined procedures such as the replevin remedies at issue in *Fuentes* and *Mitchell*? Commercial creditors will often still pursue consumers when they default on their payment obligations. The cost of pursuing such remedies will simply be higher, as creditors will have to initiate court proceedings more frequently, rather than relying on a summary seizure provision. The hope, of course, is that the extra procedures will prevent erroneous or abusive seizures of property. In all likelihood, the extra costs of those procedures will be passed along to the consumer in the form of less favorable rates on installment purchase plans. In one sense, then, *Fuentes* and *Mitchell* force consumers to purchase insurance against inaccurate provisional remedies by paying increased rates to retailers in return for better dispute resolution procedures.

6. *Due Process and Individual Dignity.* Do decisions like *Fuentes* and *Connecticut v. Doehr* also help to protect dignitary interests? Professor Jerry Mashaw has argued

that one of the purposes of the Due Process Clause is to guarantee that people will be afforded individual consideration before the state deprives them of their property, not only in order to produce accurate results but also to reaffirm the value of the individual as an end unto himself, rather than merely a means of effectuating state policy. *See generally* Jerry L. Mashaw, Due Process in the Administrative State (1985). Does that concern ring true in the present context? The case for a dignitary argument seems stronger in the case of replevin, where there was evidence that the streamlined seizure provisions at issue in *Fuentes* almost always resulted in the repossession of goods with no meaningful individual adjudication at any stage of the proceeding. *See Fuentes*, 407 U.S. at 84 n.14. Are such concerns less applicable in a case like *Connecticut v. Doehr*, where there was every reason to think that defendant would contest the attachment of his property in a subsequent judicial hearing?

2. *Post-Judgment Execution*

Once a judgment is secured, the attorney's role is not necessarily over. Although some defendants pay their judgments voluntarily, others are not so cooperative. By itself, a money judgment is not spendable currency—you cannot deposit it in a bank or use it to pay your taxes. Rather, securing a judgment is just the first step for the successful claimant (who has now become a creditor) to obtain monetary damages from an unwilling opponent (who is now a debtor). The process of converting a judgment into cash is referred to as *execution* or *enforcement*. Executing upon a judgment against an unwilling opponent can be an arduous and costly process. Indeed, for those willing to live with a certain measure of instability and irregularity in their personal finances, it may be possible to avoid payment on a judgment by making the process of enforcement so difficult and expensive as to be no longer worth the plaintiff's effort.

The basic tools that a successful claimant can use in seeking to enforce a judgment are similar to the provisional remedies discussed in the previous section. A judgment holder can proceed against the debtor directly by attaching his property or other assets and forcing a sale, the proceeds from which will then be available to the creditor as payment of the judgment debt. Or the judgment holder can proceed against third parties who owe a duty of payment to the debtor (banks, employers), seeking an order of garnishment that directs those parties to make their payments to the creditor instead. In both cases, there are three basic steps that the judgment holder must undertake in order to secure payment.

First, the creditor must figure out where the debtor's assets are located. This may turn out to be the most difficult part of the process. Some unwilling judgment debtors actively conceal their assets by spreading money across many different financial institutions, transferring ownership of property to family members or sham business entities, and otherwise making their financial arrangements as obscure and irregular as possible. A judgment creditor has powerful discovery tools at his disposal in the face of such efforts. Under Federal Rule of Civil Procedure 69(a)(2), "[i]n aid of the judgment or execution, the judgment creditor or a successor in interest whose interest appears of record may obtain discovery from any person — including the judgment debtor — as provided in these rules or by the procedure of the state where the court is located." In other words, the judgment creditor can use both state and federal discovery procedures to track down assets. Thus, the creditor can subpoena bank records, business records, tax returns, credit card receipts, and any other material that might disclose the existence of assets that the debtor could use to satisfy the judgment.

Once the creditor has identified the debtor's assets, it is necessary to obtain a judgment against the debtor in every state where the creditor wishes to go after those assets in enforcement proceedings. This second step, which is perhaps the most counterintuitive part of the entire process, stems from the division of authority in our dual system of state and federal governments. When a litigant obtains a judgment in one state, that judgment is directly enforceable only in the state where it was rendered. As we discuss in the next chapter, states have an obligation to recognize valid sister-state judgments under the constitutional and statutory provisions requiring them to give "full faith and credit" to judicial acts from other states. *See* U.S. Const., Art. IV §1; 28 U.S.C. §1738. But a judgment from California cannot command direct enforcement in the courts of New York. Rather, the "recognition" that New York is obliged to extend to that judgment is the willingness of its courts to issue another, local judgment on the California decree that will then be enforceable in New York. The Supreme Court established this principle in the case of *McElmoyle v. Cohen*, 38 U.S. (13 Pet.) 312, 325 (1839), in which it held: "To give it the force of a judgment in another State, [a decree] must be made a judgment there, and can only be executed in the latter [state] as its laws may permit. It must be conceded that the judgment of a State court cannot be enforced out of the State by an execution issued within it." Thus, when a judgment debtor owns property in many different states, it may be necessary to obtain many different local judgments in order to secure payment.

Traditionally, the holder of an out-of-state or "foreign" judgment was required to initiate an entirely new lawsuit on that decree in the courts of the local state to obtain an order that he could enforce. This onerous requirement has been streamlined considerably in recent years. Within the federal system, 28 U.S.C. §1963 authorizes litigants to take any judgment "for the recovery of money or property" issued in one federal court and register it in any federal district court by filing a certified copy of the judgment. Such a judgment has "the same effect as a judgment of the district court in the district where registered and may be enforced in like manner." *Id.* In 1964, the National Conference of Commissioners on Uniform State Laws promulgated the revised Uniform Enforcement of Foreign Judgments Act (UEFJA), which sets forth a similar registration mechanism for the states. Under the Act, a creditor can present a judgment from one state to the clerk of court in another, who will issue a new judgment having the same effect as one produced by a purely local proceeding. *See id.* §2. The creditor must also provide the clerk with contact information for the judgment debtor, which the clerk will use to notify the debtor of the newly registered judgment. *See id.* §3. Once served, the debtor has the burden of challenging the validity of the out-of-state decree or raising any other defenses to the enforcement proceeding, such as an appeal or stay of execution in the original forum indicating that immediate enforcement would be inappropriate. *See id.* §4. Almost every jurisdiction in the United States has now enacted some version of the revised Act. *See, e.g.,* Tex. Civ. Prac. & Rem. §§35.001–35.008 (Vernon

2011). As with other civil claims, there are statutes of limitations on actions for the enforcement of judgments, most imposing a limit of between 10 and 20 years after issuance of the original judgment. *See, e.g.*, N.Y. C.P.L.R. §211(b) (2012) ("A money judgment is presumed to be paid and satisfied after the expiration of twenty years from the time when the party recovering it was first entitled to enforce it."); Ky. Rev. Stat. §413.090(1) (2012) (15 years).

Once a judgment creditor has located the debtor's assets and reduced his original judgment to a local decree, he can undertake the last step in the process and execute upon the assets. As a general matter, the process for executing upon a judgment is governed by state law. Federal Rule of Civil Procedure 69(a)(1) makes the law of the state in which a district court is located applicable to all proceedings "on execution—and in proceedings supplementary to and in aid of judgment or execution," except where federal statutes expressly provide otherwise. Generally, a creditor seeking to enforce against real or personal property first obtains a writ of execution from the local court. *See, e.g., id.* §(a)(2) ("A money judgment is enforced by a writ of execution, unless the court directs otherwise."). Garnishment, encumbrance of property, and forced sale are the most common mechanisms by which the execution will be carried out.

In the case of garnishment, a creditor can apply to the court for a writ of execution directly against a bank, employer, or other third party, who will then pay the requisite assets or wages directly to the creditor. In the case of property or other physical assets, the process involves additional steps. To execute upon the debtor's property, the creditor must obtain a writ of execution that describes the property in question in as much detail as possible. The judgment creditor then takes the writ to a marshal, sheriff, or other executive official who serves the writ on the custodians of the property and seizes it for public sale at the courthouse or another appropriate venue. You may have seen notices in your local newspapers for such "sheriff's sales," where real property, automobiles, or other items that have come into the possession of public officials are sold auction style. In the case of items seized on behalf of a judgment creditor, the proceeds from the sale go directly to satisfy the judgment debt. In fact, if you think back to the Supreme Court's decision in *Pennoyer v. Neff*, you may recall that it was just such a sheriff's sale in which Marcus Neff's land was sold to satisfy the default judgment obtained against him by John Mitchell—and, in fact, that it was Mitchell himself who showed up at the sale to purchase Neff's land. As with the other procedures for enforcement, the sale of seized property to satisfy a judgment is generally governed by state law in the federal courts. *See* 28 U.S.C. §§2001–2007. Differences in state law may be quite significant in this respect, as states have policies that exempt certain property from forced sale (most commonly a home or primary residence) or that place limitations on the amount of certain assets that can be seized or garnished (as with wages). In rare instances, federal law may also impose limits on the types of property that are subject to execution. *See, e.g., Helmsley-Spear, Inc. v. Winter*, 426 N.Y.S.2d 778 (App. Div. 1st Dept. 1980) (holding that federal Employment Retirement Income Security Act of 1974 prevents attachment of retirement assets to satisfy judgment).

Finally, there is always the possibility that a judgment debtor will declare bankruptcy before the creditor can collect. When that happens, matters become more complicated. The law of bankruptcy has its own set of principles and procedures for dividing a limited pool of assets among competing creditors, and a judgment creditor may enjoy a different priority under bankruptcy law (where the judgment makes her a "secured" creditor) than she would under the local jurisdiction's enforcement laws (where some "unsecured" creditors might be ahead of judgment creditors in the payment line). In any enforcement proceeding where there is some possibility that the debtor will become insolvent, a litigator is well advised to consult a bankruptcy expert.

CHAPTER 7

PRIOR ADJUDICATION

Finality is an important value in any system of civil procedure. The litigation process consumes public and private resources. At some point in the process, both winners and losers must accept the outcomes of decisions and be precluded from relitigating. This principle of finality is implemented through the doctrine of *res judicata*—Latin for "the thing has been decided."

Although *res judicata* is a logical and necessary element to dispute resolution, it comes at a cost: The judgment receiving *res judicata* effect may be flawed in some way. For example, the court may have made a mistaken judgment about the facts or the law. Although it might be tempting to except erroneous judgments from *res judicata* treatment, such an exception would swallow the rule. If only "correct" judgments were final, no judgment would preclude relitigation of the controversy. Courts would have to retry every case on the merits in order to determine whether to enforce the prior judgment, thereby negating the very purpose of the doctrine. Parties can ask appellate courts to correct errors by trial courts on direct appellate review. But once a litigant has exhausted or failed to pursue appellate remedies, *res judicata* precludes most *collateral attacks*—attempts to disregard a judgment in a subsequent proceeding.

Res judicata has a somewhat complex terminology. The term *res judicata* is sometimes used to refer generically to all types of prior adjudication or "preclusion" doctrines. This broad category of *res judicata* encompasses two related but distinct kinds of preclusion: claim preclusion and issue preclusion. *Claim preclusion*—itself often referred to as *res judicata*, which can cause some confusion—forbids the relitigation of the "claims" in a subsequent proceeding (for example, a claim for damages based on defendant's alleged negligence). *Issue preclusion*—often referred to as *collateral estoppel*—forbids relitigation of specific factual or legal determinations made in a prior proceeding (e.g., "the defendant was negligent," "there was a contract," or "the document is discoverable").

Claim and issue preclusion, though similar, have distinct characteristics. Claim preclusion prohibits any claim that was *or should have been* asserted in a prior proceeding—it applies both to attempts to relitigate a claim that has already been adjudicated and to attempts to split up closely related claims and litigate them one by one in different proceedings. Issue preclusion, in contrast, only estops parties from relitigating issues that were *actually litigated* in a prior proceeding and were *necessary to the prior judgment*. In addition, claim preclusion generally requires that both parties in a subsequent proceeding have been parties to the initial proceeding (i.e., that there was *mutuality of parties*). Issue preclusion, in contrast, may sometimes be asserted *on behalf of* a litigant who did not participate in the initial proceeding, though it can never be asserted *against* someone who was not a party in the prior proceeding (or deemed to be in a "privity" relationship with such a party).

A. CLAIM PRECLUSION

Modern claim preclusion doctrine advances a variety of policies. At its core, claim preclusion gives effect to judicial authority, whatever the outcome of the lawsuit. Where a plaintiff loses, the judgment is said to act as a "bar" to a second try. Where a plaintiff is successful but wants a second or greater remedy than the court awarded, all subsequent attempts to recover for what is basically the same claim are said to "merge" with the initial judgment. Relitigation in either case could undermine the authority of the first tribunal.

Relitigation also frustrates any sense of repose in the parties. Litigants are entitled to feel that they have put a litigated claim behind them, enabling them to plan their affairs accordingly. Such repose is provided by claim preclusion.

And claim preclusion promotes efficiency: It effectively requires a party to consolidate multiple theories of recovery in a single lawsuit. As a result, the litigants and courts are burdened with fewer lawsuits, and evidence presented as a basis for recovery can be considered in a single trial in connection with all bases of recovery that should be heard together.

1. Same Claim

The definition of what constitutes a "single claim" or "single cause of action" to require joinder in a single litigation is one of the central questions in the law of prior adjudication. The law has shifted over time in response to changing rules on joinder of claims, as well as to the respective weight that courts have given to the different policies served by claim preclusion.

Under the system of writs in the English common law, a party was required to select a single writ or form of action, and only certain legal theories could be asserted in connection with a particular writ. Thus, a plaintiff who brought an action for an intentional tort—the writ of trespass—could not recover if the injury was shown to be only the result of negligence—the writ of case. The writ system did not permit joinder of claims brought under different writs, regardless of whether the claims were based on a single incident. In such a system, it made sense to permit a plaintiff to follow up an unsuccessful action under the writ of trespass with an action under the writ of case. The rigidity of the writ system was thus mitigated by permissive rules of claim preclusion; for the most part, a plaintiff could not lose claims based on alternate legal theories that he failed to assert, because those alternate claims could not have been joined in the initial proceeding.

Beginning in the nineteenth century and continuing into the twentieth, rules of joining claims were greatly liberalized. As courts abandoned the traditional forms of common law pleading, litigants were able for the first time to combine multiple legal theories in connection with a single injury or to seek redress in the alternative or for different kinds of injury, all in a single lawsuit. Once litigants became able to include many different legal theories and requests for relief in one proceeding, court systems began to ask what obligations they should impose on litigants in the interest of efficiency and justice. As a result, the relaxation of joinder rules brought a corresponding tightening of preclusion law: Now that parties were *permitted* to consolidate their claims, preclusion law increasingly *required* them to do so.

We begin the unit on claim preclusion with a decision by a court grappling with this transitional issue—how the newly expanded options available to a party to join claims and arguments in a single proceeding should shape the preclusion doctrine that will apply to the judgment produced by that proceeding.

Rush v. City of Maple Heights

147 N.E.2d 599 (1958)

HERBERT, JUDGE.

[Plaintiff sued the City of Maple Heights for personal injuries sustained when her motorcycle crashed on an allegedly bumpy street. Plaintiff had previously prevailed in an action that she filed against the City in Municipal Court for damage sustained to her motorcycle in the same accident. In the subsequent proceeding, which produced the following opinion on appeal, the City interposed the defense of *res judicata* based on plaintiff's earlier action.]

The eighth error assigned by the defendant is that "the trial and appellate courts committed error in permitting plaintiff to split her cause of action and to file a separate action in the Cleveland Municipal Court for her property damage and reduce same to judgment, and, thereafter, to proceed, in the Cuyahoga County Common Pleas Court, with a separate action for personal injuries, both claims arising out of a single accident."

The reasoning behind the majority rule seems to be well stated in the case of *Mobile & Ohio Rd. Co. v. Matthews* . . . [115 Tenn. 172, 91 S.W. 194 (1906)], as follows:

> The negligent action of the plaintiff in error constituted but one tort. The injuries to the person and property of the defendant in error were the several results and effects of one wrongful act. A single tort can be the basis of but one action. It is not improper to declare in different counts for damages to the person and property when both result from the same tort, and it is the better practice to do so where there is any difference in the measure of damages, and all the damages sustained must be sued for in one suit. This is necessary to prevent multiplicity of suits, burdensome expense, and delays to plaintiffs, and vexatious litigation against defendants. . . .
>
> Indeed, if the plaintiff fail [sic] to sue for the entire damage done him by the tort, a second action for the damages omitted will be precluded by the judgment in the first suit brought and tried.

The minority rule would seem to stem from the English case of *Brunsden v. Humphrey* (1884), 14 Q.B. 141. The facts in that case are set forth in the opinion in [*Vasu v. Kohlers, Inc.*, 145 Ohio St. 321, 329, 61 N.E.2d 707, 713 (1945)], concluding with the statement:

> The Master of the Rolls, in his opinion, stated that the test is "whether the same sort of evidence would prove the plaintiff's case in the two actions," and that, in the action relating to the cab, "it would be necessary to give evidence of the damage done to the plaintiff's vehicle." In the present

action it would be necessary to give evidence of the bodily injury occasioned to the plaintiff, and of the sufferings which he has undergone, and for this purpose to call medical witnesses. This one test shows that the causes of action as to the damage done to the plaintiff's cab, and as to the injury occasioned to the plaintiff's person, are distinct.

The fallacy of the reasoning in the English court is best portrayed in the dissenting opinion of Lord Coleridge, as follows:

> It appears to me that whether the negligence of the servant, or the impact of the vehicle which the servant drove, be the technical cause of action, equally the cause is one and the same: that the injury done to the plaintiff is injury done to him at one and the same moment by one and the same act in respect of different *rights*, i.e., his person and his goods, I do not in the least deny; but it seems to me a subtlety not warranted by law to hold that a man cannot bring two actions, if he is injured in his arm and in his leg, but can bring two, if besides his arm and leg being injured, his trousers which contain his leg, and his coatsleeve which contains his arm, have been torn.

There appears to be no valid reason in these days of code pleading to adhere to the old English rule as to distinctions between injuries to the person and damages to the person's property resulting from a single tort. It would seem that the minority rule is bottomed on the proposition that the right of bodily security is fundamentally different from the right of security of property and, also, that, in actions predicated upon a negligent act, damages are a necessary element of each independent cause of action and no recovery may be had unless and until actual consequential damages are shown. . . .

In the light of the foregoing, it is the view of this court that the so-called majority rule conforms much more properly to modern practice. . . .

We, therefore, conclude and hold that, where a person suffers both personal injuries and property damage as a result of the same wrongful act, only a single cause of action arises, the different injuries occasioned thereby being separate items of damage from such act. . . .

Accordingly, the judgment of the Court of Appeals is reversed, and final judgment is entered for defendant.

NOTES AND QUESTIONS

1. *Why Have Claim Preclusion? Rush* offers a somewhat formalistic explanation of claim preclusion and says little about the policies that the doctrine is designed to implement. What might they be? It is generally said that claim preclusion is designed to ensure that decisions are stable, protect the parties from additional litigation, prevent any double recovery, and alleviate burdens on courts. Which of those policies are furthered by the *Rush* decision? Since plaintiff won the first action, a recovery in the second action would not impair the judgment in the first — that is, it would not undermine the authority of that initial proceeding. In addition, plaintiff sought different items of damage in the second action, and hence could not be

said to be seeking to recover twice for the same injury. Of course, if two actions are permitted, the parties have additional litigation expenses and the court also has the burden of two lawsuits. Do these efficiency concerns justify the result in *Rush*?

Can you conceive of situations in which it might be more efficient to conduct two separate actions in a case like *Rush*? Assume that plaintiff's claim for property damage raises only the question of defendant's negligence but that the personal injury claim presents formidable causation issues—e.g., whether plaintiff's injuries were in fact the result of this accident. Under these circumstances, might it not be easier to adjudicate the relatively simple property damage claim independently of the complex personal injury claim?

Consider the fact that Mrs. Rush's claim for property damage was $100, and the verdict obtained on her personal injury claim was for $12,000. In that situation, does it make sense for Mrs. Rush to try to have her "minor" claim resolved quickly? Might your answer depend on whether a small claims court or specialized procedure for such claims is available for the property damage claim? In fact, wouldn't it undermine the very purpose of a small claims court—quick and efficient adjudication of relatively minor claims—if a plaintiff risked losing more valuable claims by pursuing that avenue? Some jurisdictions have adopted a "jurisdictional competency" exception that might prevent claim preclusion from operating in situations such as these, an issue that we discuss at greater length later in the chapter.

2. *Insurance and Subrogation.* Note also that property damage claims, unlike personal injury claims, are often assignable to an insurance company, which can compensate the insured person for her property damages and then become "subrogated" to any claim for property damage the insured may have. Does the rule of *Rush* apply if the first action for property damage is brought by an insurance company that has already paid the insured for property damage and the second action for personal injury is brought by the insured herself? *Vasu v. Kohlers, Inc.*, 61 N.E.2d 707 (1945), the earlier Ohio Supreme Court case cited in *Rush*, involved the insurance subrogation situation, but the *Vasu* court did not rely on those facts for its decision; rather the *Vasu* court stated broadly that injuries to person and property suffered by the same person as a result of the same wrongful act gave rise to distinct causes of action that did not trigger claim preclusion.

Because the parties in *Vasu* were completely different from the parties in *Rush*, the *Vasu* decision has no *res judicata* effect in *Rush*. However, the *Vasu* decision can still have impact as *stare decisis*. *Stare decisis* serves as the precedential legal rule to be followed in a different case with different parties, although the parties in the later case are free to argue that the law applied in an earlier case should now be changed. In *Rush*, the Ohio Supreme Court rejected the earlier statement of law that it had made in *Vasu*. Given the narrower factual situation of *Vasu*, should the *Vasu* decision have had *stare decisis* effect at all, or should the court's language noted above be regarded only as dictum?

3. *Thinking Tactically.* Can you think of other reasons why Mrs. Rush might wish to bring two separate actions? Would differences in the limitations periods applicable to each of the claims affect the choice about whether a plaintiff would want to proceed with a single lawsuit or separate proceedings?

In the second proceeding in *Rush*, plaintiff might have sought to preclude litigation of the *issue* of negligence on the ground that this issue had already been decided in the first proceeding to recover for property damage. (This second aspect of preclusion law—collateral estoppel or issue preclusion—is taken up later in this chapter.) Is it unfair to the defendant to have an important issue like liability adjudicated against it in the context of a modest claim and then have the determination of that issue used against it later to establish its liability for the more substantial claim? Is it possible that a jury might come out differently on an issue of negligence in the context of a small claim if it knows that substantial liability lurks in the background? Might the *Rush* court have been influenced by such considerations in holding that plaintiff should have brought a single lawsuit?

An alternative way of alleviating unfairness to defendant might be to permit plaintiff to bring a second action for personal injuries but to allow the city to relitigate its liability for negligence in the context of the personal injury suit. Is such a solution preferable to requiring plaintiff to join both claims in the initial proceeding?

4. *The Relationship of Claim Preclusion to the Joinder Rules.* The opinion in *Rush* is devoted to defining the parameters of a "single claim" or the "same cause of action," which has been the traditional way of thinking about preclusion law. But with the development of modern procedure and more expansive joinder rules, why should doctrines of preclusion be so limited? Why shouldn't a plaintiff be forced to bring *any* claim that she is able to assert against a defendant in the same action? Put another way, why shouldn't the mandatory effect of preclusion doctrine be coextensive with the permissive scope of joinder rules? At least part of the answer lies in assessing the potential impact of joinder upon a lawsuit. While it might be possible for a plaintiff to join completely unrelated claims against a defendant, doing so could well impose burdens upon the resulting lawsuit. Defining claim preclusion too broadly could result in less-efficient litigation.

Note that the Federal Rules themselves do not provide for compulsory joinder of claims, although there are rules for compulsory counterclaims and compulsory joinder of parties. *See* Chapter 8 on joinder of claims and parties. The permissive joinder policy of the Federal Rules, however, is quite liberal: Rule 18 permits a plaintiff to join any claim against a defendant, whether or not the claims are related, so long as the federal court has jurisdiction. Does the doctrine of preclusion make compulsory joinder rules unnecessary?

Herendeen v. Champion International Corp.

525 F.2d 130 (2d Cir. 1975)

WATERMAN, CIRCUIT JUDGE.

This appeal is from an order of Judge MacMahon of the Southern District of New York dismissing James Herendeen's complaint against the appellees, Champion International Corporation ("Champion"), Nationwide Papers Incorporated ("Nationwide") and the trustees and administrator of the Retirement Income Plan for Salaried Employees of Certain Subsidiaries of U.S. Plywood-Champion Papers, Inc. ("Plan"), on the ground that the matters complained of were *res judicata*. The court concluded that the issues set forth in plaintiff's complaint had been previously decided in a state court proceeding which had there resulted in a dismissal of Herendeen's state court complaint for failure to state a claim upon which relief could be granted. The single question presented for review is whether the prior state court judgment is *res judicata* as to the action now under consideration. We find that it is not. Accordingly, we reverse the order below and remand the case for further proceedings in the district court.

Herendeen is a former employee of defendant Nationwide. He voluntarily resigned his position as a paper salesman of Nationwide on May 15, 1969, and took new employment with a competitor of Nationwide. He subsequently instituted suit in the Supreme Court, New York County, against U.S. Plywood-Champion Papers, Inc. (now Champion) and its subsidiary Nationwide and several of its officers and employees. He charged that the corporation acted fraudulently by inducing him to leave the paper business in order to deprive him of his employee and pension benefits by promising him that he would receive a new written employment contract and would continue to receive all of his employment benefits; but that after he relied on the promise he did not obtain a new contract. In that complaint Herendeen sought damages of $200,000 for the loss of his commissions in the paper industry, and $75,000 in lost pension benefits. The suit in the state court was determined on the merits against Herendeen, *Herendeen v. U.S. Plywood-Champion Papers, Inc.* (Sup. Ct. N.Y. Co., Nov. 20, 1972), *reported in New York Law Journal,* Jan. 11, 1973, *aff'd,* 41 A.D.2d 1030, 343 N.Y.S.2d 785 (1973). As the complaint alleged only an oral "agreement to agree," rather than an enforceable contract, Justice Markowitz held it failed to state a claim upon which relief could be granted, and, of course, the court did not resolve any issue relative to the kind or amount of damages.

Herendeen subsequently commenced the present diversity action in the United States District Court. In this action he seeks to obtain payments he alleges the defendants owe him under the Plan and have withheld from him. Here he claims that having regularly paid the required contributions into the Plan fund while employed by Nationwide, he is entitled pursuant to the Plan's eligibility rules to receive benefits under it now that he is no longer an employee of the corporation. He seeks $100,000 for the wrongful loss of benefits due him under the Plan, injunctive relief, and $785,000 in exemplary and punitive damages. This complaint was dismissed below on the ground of *res judicata.*

For a judgment in a prior action to be a bar to reaching the merits in a subsequent action it is firmly established that the prior judgment must have been rendered by a court of competent jurisdiction, been a final judgment on the merits, and that the same cause of action and the same parties or their privies were involved in both suits. Only the third element is at issue here; and while we agree with the trial court that the same parties or their privies are defendants in both suits, we do not find the requisite measure of identity of the two causes of action essential to support the trial court's finding of *res judicata.*

The test for determining whether causes of action are the same for purposes of *res judicata* has been variously expressed. Most frequently cited as the relevant criteria by both this court and the New York courts are whether a different judgment in the second action would impair or destroy rights or interests established by the judgment entered in the first action, whether the same evidence is necessary to maintain the second cause of action as was required in the first, and whether the essential facts and issues in the second were present in the first.

In applying these standards we must first determine what the plaintiff claimed and what the court decided in the first action. Herendeen's state court complaint alleged the breach of an oral agreement by which Nationwide promised to appellant that he would be provided with a written contract of employment and would continue to receive all of the employment benefits due him as an employee of the parent corporation Champion. He further alleged that the representations made by the corporation in an effort to persuade him to accept this oral agreement were false and fraudulent, and were made in furtherance of a conspiracy among the defendants designed to induce him to forego certain commissions and to drive him from his employment. Thus, his state action was grounded upon and sought damages for an alleged fraudulent breach of contract, and the pension Plan's benefits allegedly fraudulently lost to plaintiff were mentioned only as an element of all the damages plaintiff allegedly suffered as a consequence of the fraud. The state court judge dismissed the suit on the sole ground that no new written or otherwise enforceable employment contract had been made, and that even if an oral promise had been made to make one, or an oral agreement to agree to make one had been reached, enforcement was barred by the Statute of Frauds.

Appellees contend that Herendeen's present claim for pension benefits, based upon his fifteen years of employment and of participation in the Plan, is but a new claim for relief based upon the same cause of action that was adjudicated previously in the state case, and that the present complaint only presents a new theory for recovering damages for the alleged wrongful acts of defendants that have been already adjudicated. Moreover, they argue that under the applicable rules of procedure Herendeen could have presented all of his grounds for relief in the state court action, and, therefore, the final judgment in defendants' favor in the state court is here conclusive upon Herendeen not only as to the claims there adjudicated, but also as to claims which could have been there adjudicated.

We can agree with appellee that they have correctly stated the law that is applicable when a plaintiff in his second suit, grounded upon the same allegations of defendant liability as alleged in a former suit, advances in the second suit a new theory of damage recovery only.[8] Here, however, plaintiff in his second suit has set forth an independent claim of defendant wrongdoing.

In his state suit Herendeen did not raise, and the trial court did not consider in its adjudicating memorandum, the issue of Herendeen's pension rights pursuant to the contract of employment which he had voluntarily terminated on May 18, 1969—rights which he now claims had vested prior to his resignation. While the same alleged right, the right to receive pension benefits, is involved in both suits, the wrongful acts of defendants alleged in the two complaints are quite different. In the state court proceeding the plaintiff complained that the corporation failed to contract with him as promised, and, as a consequence, he lost pension benefits. In the district court suit here, the plaintiff alleges that the corporation has, as to

---

8. Restatement of Judgments §63 (1942) states:

Where a judgment on the merits is rendered in favor of the defendant, the plaintiff is precluded from subsequently maintaining an action on the same cause of action although he presents a ground for the relief asked other than those presented in the original action. . . .

him, misapplied the Plan regulations, and as a consequence pension benefits his pre-existing employment entitles him to, have been wrongfully denied to him upon his employment by a competitor.

Moreover, there is no "measure of identity" in the two complaints such that a judgment in the district court action could impair the parties' rights established by the judgment entered in the state court in the prior adjudicated state action. A finding in the federal case that defendants had misapplied the Plan regulations and thereby deprived plaintiff of a full participation in the Plan fund would not affect the state court determination that defendants were under no obligation to contract with plaintiff in connection with his resignation, or affect the adjudicated rights of the parties with reference to any alleged fraudulently promised future employment.

Finally, it seems obvious that evidence which would have tended to support or to deny the allegations in the state complaint would not be required to meet the issues presented in the federal complaint, and the evidence plaintiff needs to sustain the allegations of wrongdoing in the present complaint would not have sustained the plaintiff's claims of defendant wrongdoing in the state court complaint.[9] Appellant's inability to establish the existence of a new contract with Champion is in no way dispositive of his alleged vested rights in the Plan, which were built up during his fifteen years of employment. Appellant has not yet had his day in court on the issue of whether he can sustain his claim to pension rights.

Although in the state suit appellant could have joined the present cause of action along with his claim that defendants misled him fraudulently when he resigned, he was not compelled to do so; and the institution of the separate suit seeking unpaid alleged entitlements under the pension Plan is in accord with the holding in an early and leading case, *Secor v. Sturgis*, 16 N.Y. 548 (1858).

> The true distinction between demands or rights of action which are single and entire, and those which are several and distinct is, that the former immediately arise out of one and the same act or contract, and the latter out of different acts or contracts. Perhaps as simple and safe a test as the subject admits of . . . is by inquiring whether it rests upon one or several acts or agreements . . . in respect to contracts, express or implied, each contract affords one and only one cause of action. *Secor v. Sturgis, supra* at 558.

We intimate no view as to the merits of appellant's assertions regarding his pension rights under his terminated employment contract. We hold here only that the present federal complaint alleges and sets forth a separate and distinct cause of action from that adjudicated in the state court, and hence the federal action is not barred by the state court judgment. Accordingly, we reverse the judgment below that appellant's action is barred by *res judicata* and remand for further proceedings.

---

9. Restatement of Judgments §61 (1942) states:

Where a judgment is rendered in favor of the plaintiff or where a judgment on the merits is rendered in favor of the defendant, the plaintiff is precluded from subsequently maintaining a second action based upon the same transaction, if the evidence needed to sustain the second action would have sustained the first action.

NOTES AND QUESTIONS

1. In *Herendeen*, plaintiff was allowed to maintain the second action, while plaintiff in *Rush* was not. Are *Herendeen* and *Rush* inconsistent? Does it matter that plaintiff in *Rush* won in the first action, and plaintiff in *Herendeen* lost? Which subsequent claim would more seriously undermine the earlier judgment if it were allowed to proceed, Herendeen's or Rush's?

2. *Defining the Scope of a "Single Claim" for Preclusion Purposes.* The court concluded that the federal proceeding would not "impair the parties' rights established by the judgment entered in the state court." Do you agree? The initial state proceeding determined that Herendeen was not entitled to recover damages, including loss of pension benefits, as the result of defendants' action in inducing him to leave his job and their refusal to provide him with a new employment contract. In the second action, Herendeen sought benefits under the original employment contract. Although the legal theories are different, don't both actions seek to determine—at least in part—plaintiff's "right to pension benefits"? Had not both claims—the one under the new employment contract and the one under the original contract—fully matured at the time Herendeen brought the first suit? Was there, for instance, any allegation that plaintiff did not find out that defendants were reneging on his pension benefits until after he lost the state proceeding?

And what about the rule announced in footnote 8 of the decision that "the plaintiff is precluded from subsequently maintaining an action on the same cause of action although he presents a ground for the relief asked other than those presented in the original action"? Can *Herendeen* be reconciled with that rule? Notwithstanding the court's disclaimer, doesn't *Herendeen* permit a second action on the basis of an alternative legal theory?

The *Herendeen* court addresses this argument by asserting that the second suit arises from a separate "wrongful act" by defendants. Is that rationale convincing? What does the "separateness" of the acts have to do with the policies of claim preclusion?

Compare Seaboard Coast Line Railroad Co. v. Gulf Oil Corp., 409 F.2d 879 (5th Cir. 1969) to the result in *Herendeen*. The court in *Seaboard Coast Line* held that an earlier declaratory judgment that Gulf was not obligated under one contract to indemnify Coast Line for damages caused by a fire barred a later suit for indemnity based on a different contract:

> [O]ur concern is whether Coast Line had two separate causes of action for indemnity, not whether it can now produce different evidence in support of the claim already litigated in the Florida courts. [As the Third Circuit has said:]
>
> > Reference to the basic theory of tort liability substantiates the position taken here. To put it in rather elementary tort language, the basis of the plaintiff's recovery is liability-creating conduct on the part of the defendant, the invasion of a legally protected interest of the plaintiff and the necessary causal connection between defendant's acts and plaintiff's injury. The plaintiff having alleged operative facts which state a cause of action because he tells of defendant's misconduct and his own harm has had his day in court. He does not get another day after the first lawsuit is concluded by giving a different reason than he gave in the first for recovery of damages for the same invasion

of his rights. The problem of his rights against the defendant based upon the alleged wrongful acts is fully before the court whether all the reasons for recovery were stated to the court or not [*quoting Williamson v. Columbia Gas and Electric Corp.*, 186 F.2d 464, 470 (3d Cir. 1950), *cert. denied*, 341 U.S. 921 (1951)].

The principal test for comparing causes of action is whether or not the primary right and duty, and the delict or wrong are the same in each action. . . . In *Baltimore S.S. Co. v. Phillips*, 1926, 274 U.S. 316 . . . the Supreme Court instructs us:

> A cause of action does not consist of facts, but of the unlawful violation of a right which the facts show. The number and variety of the facts alleged do not establish more than one cause of action so long as their result, whether they be considered severally or in combination, is the violation of but one right by a single legal wrong.

> . . . [W]e find that in both the courts below and [in the earlier proceeding] that the duty alleged was the obligation to indemnify for losses caused by fire and the alleged breach of duty was Gulf's failure to indemnify Coast Line in the amount of $100,000. We therefore conclude that the causes of action were the same.

Id. at 880–881.

In what way is *Herendeen* distinguishable?

3. *The Approach Under the Restatement (Second) of Judgments. Herendeen* was decided five years before approval of the Restatement (Second) of Judgments (1982), section 24 of which provides:

Dimensions of "Claim" for Purposes of Merger or Bar — General Rule Concerning "Splitting"

(1) When a valid and final judgment rendered in an action extinguishes the plaintiff's claim pursuant to the rules of merger or bar (*see* §§18, 19), the claim extinguished includes all rights of the plaintiff to remedies against the defendant with respect to all or any part of the transaction, or series of connected transactions, out of which the action arose.

(2) What factual grouping constitutes a "transaction," and what groupings constitute a "series," are to be determined pragmatically, giving weight to such considerations as whether the facts are related in time, space, origin, or motivation, whether they form a convenient trial unit, and whether their treatment as a unit conforms to the parties' expectations or business understanding or usage.

How does the Restatement's formulation of a "claim" for purposes of *res judicata* differ from the court's discussion in *Herendeen*? What are the respective advantages and disadvantages of each approach? Would the result in *Herendeen* change under the Restatement (Second) test? *Compare, e.g., Soto v. Phillips*, 836 S.W.2d 266 (Tex. App. 1992) (plaintiff's initial lawsuit for (1) workers' compensation benefits against the insurance carrier and (2) wrongful discharge against employer precluded a second action against the same defendants for bad faith denial of medical benefits and conspiracy to deny him civil rights).

Does the Restatement's definition of "transaction" permit preclusion even in the absence of a substantial evidentiary overlap between the litigated and omitted claim? For example, assume that plaintiff is involved in an automobile accident with defendant, and after the parties leave from their cars to exchange insurance information, defendant physically attacks plaintiff. Plaintiff's claim for property damage involves completely different proof than the claim for battery. On the one hand, the failure to bring the claims in a single lawsuit is not particularly inefficient given the particular evidence that will be presented on the various claims. On the other hand, witnesses to the event are likely to be able to offer testimony with respect to both claims, and in that sense, it may be "efficient" to have them testify at a single trial. Might it also be said that relitigation of the battery claim following litigation of the property claim would disrupt defendant's justifiable sense of repose since the parties' dispute arises out of a single incident or event?

What do you make of the reference in Restatement (Second) §24(2) to "parties' expectations" or "business understanding or usage"? Can an argument be made that an employee who believes that he has a renewed employment relationship pursuant to a new contract does not expect to have to sue, at the same time, for retirement benefits under the prior contract? How are such expectations to be determined? Aren't expectations formed as a result of the legal regime? Put differently, won't any definition of the "same controversy," consistently applied, deliver as much finality as parties "reasonably" can expect?

4. *Successive Acts or Events.* The *res judicata* implications of cases involving repetitive conduct or transactions can be particularly troublesome. *See generally* 18 C. Wright et al., Federal Practice and Procedure §4409 (3d ed. 2018). When there are past due installments of a contract, a single suit must usually be brought to recover the entire amount due at time of suit. *See, e.g., Metropolitan Life Ins. Co. v. Fichter*, 78 P.2d 307 (1937). Similarly, if a tenant fails to pay rent for three consecutive months, the landlord must sue for the entire amount due. *See, e.g., Sutcliffe Storage & Wholesale Co. v. United States*, 162 F.2d 849 (1st Cir. 1947). If there is an acceleration clause in the contract, the obligee can, and may have to, sue for all future payments due under the contract. The rule for actions on negotiable instruments is different. If a holder of a bond fails to receive payments on interest coupons due, separate proceedings on each coupon, and on the bond itself when due, are permitted. *See Nesbit v. Riverside Independent Dist.*, 144 U.S. 610 (1892); Restatement (Second) of Judgments §24, comment d. Why are the installment examples viewed as "multiple breaches of the same contract," and the bond example as one where each coupon is seen as a separate contractual obligation? Do considerations of business practice and ordinary commercial understanding explain the difference in treatment? *See, e.g., Petromanagement Corp. v. Acme-Thomas Joint Venture*, 835 F.2d 1329 (10th Cir. 1988) (even if separate contracts governed the drilling and operation of oil wells, the transactions alleged in the two complaints were a sufficiently related series of connected transactions to prohibit piecemeal litigation).

5. *Preclusion and Public Law Litigation.* How should a court address successive constitutional challenges to a statute? Does the distinction between a "facial" challenge and an "as-applied" challenge help to overcome a preclusion defense in successive cases? *Whole Women's Health v. Hellerstedt*, 136 S. Ct. 2292 (2016), spoke to these questions. The case involved a challenge to a Texas law that imposed targeted

restrictions on abortion providers and threatened to close large numbers of clinics that offer abortion services. A group of Texas abortion providers brought suit shortly after the law was enacted to challenge its constitutionality before it took effect. Their suit asserted a "facial challenge" claiming that the Texas law was categorically unconstitutional and could not be enforced against any provider. Plaintiffs lost that first suit when the Fifth Circuit concluded that they had not provided sufficient evidence to demonstrate that the targeted regulations were likely to put affected clinics out of business. Plaintiffs did not ask the Supreme Court to review that holding. One week after the ruling, some of the abortion providers from the first suit joined others in bringing a new case. This second suit asserted an "as applied challenge" to the law, claiming that two specific clinics would be unconstitutionally put out of business by the new restrictions. Here, the plaintiffs relied on evidence from the actual implementation of the Texas law after it went into effect. The suit made it all the way to the Supreme Court, which had to decide whether claim preclusion should prevent the abortion providers who had also been plaintiffs in the first lawsuit from having their claims heard on the merits in this second proceeding.

The Court rejected the preclusion defense, finding no bar to the plaintiffs' claims. It addressed two issues in reaching that result. First, plaintiffs pointed out that their claims in the second suit were based on a new set of facts that were not in existence when the first suit was brought: the actual impact of the Texas law on the operation of the specific clinics that were the focus of the new case. Because the first lawsuit was a "facial challenge" initiated before the law took effect, it had focused on the provisions of the Texas law on a categorical basis. The second suit, in contrast, looked at the facts that developed on the ground after the law became operational. Relying extensively on the Restatement (Second) of Judgments, the Court explained that "development of new material facts can mean that a new case and an otherwise similar previous case do not present the same claim" and found that the plaintiffs' "postenforcement as-applied challenge [was] not 'the very same claim' as their preenforcement facial challenge" and so was not subject to a preclusion bar. *Id.* at 2305 (citing Restatement (Second) of Judgments §24, comment f (1982)).

In addition, plaintiffs in the second lawsuit included a challenge to a provision of the Texas law that had not been placed in issue in the first suit. The first suit challenged only a requirement that abortion providers have admitting privileges in area hospitals. The second suit challenged that requirement but also targeted another regulation in the statute that required facilities that provide abortion to satisfy the building codes that apply to an ambulatory surgical center. These were distinct provisions in a larger body of regulations, and the Court found that fact consequential. "The surgical-center provision and the admitting-privileges provision are separate, distinct provisions of" Texas law, the Court wrote, setting forth "two different, independent requirements with different enforcement dates." The Court rejected the idea that "challenges to two different statutory provisions that serve two different functions must be brought in a single suit." Furthermore, the Court reiterated, facts on the ground had changed since the first lawsuit, and some of the implementing regulations for the surgical-center provision may not even have been finalized when the first suit was brought, further demonstrating that claim preclusion should not apply.

This case is a classic example of public law litigation: a pair of constitutional challenges to a statute, one a pre-enforcement suit seeking to prevent the law from going into effect at all, the other a post-enforcement suit seeking to demonstrate that the actual application of the law to particular parties is unconstitutional. The Court refers repeatedly in its opinion to the special considerations that accompany such constitutional litigation, indicating that its preclusion analysis was influenced by the underlying substantive law. *Cf.* Tobias Barrington Wolff, *Managerial Judging and Substantive Law*, 90 Wash. U. L. Rev. 1027 (2013) (discussing the potential for the underlying substantive law to influence procedural doctrines in a variety of settings). The majority appears to have concluded that litigants should normally be able to bring both pre-enforcement facial challenges and post-enforcement as-applied challenges in constitutional litigation, and it adopted a federal common law preclusion rule that would permit that result.

Is the Court's discussion of the separate provisions of the statute surprising? Assume that the plaintiffs could have challenged both of these restrictions on abortion providers in their first lawsuit. Was the decision not to do so a strategic choice of the kind that should carry a price in preclusion doctrine? In the actual dispute before the Court, changed facts between the first and second lawsuits and incomplete implementation of the surgical-center regulations at the time the first suit was brought may have made it difficult or even impossible for the plaintiffs to include the surgical-center provision in their first lawsuit. If preclusion threatened to impose severe consequences on a litigant who wished to assert a facial constitutional challenge in such a case, litigants might forgo pre-enforcement facial challenges altogether to preserve their ability to challenge the full range of applications of the statute later on. Thus, a strong case can be made in favor of the Court's holding. But was it appropriate for the Court to place so much weight on the fact that the regulations were found in "different statutory provisions" when it ruled that these challenges did not arise out of the "same transaction or series of transactions"? Compare the Court's reasoning in those passages with the discussion of claims arising in separate contract provisions in *Herendeen* and *Seaboard Coast Line, supra.* Is the Court returning to the kind of formalism that the Restatement (Second) of Judgments rejected?

6. *Tort Claims for Nuisance.* When defendant engages in conduct that causes continuing or recurring harm to plaintiff in the use of his land, the plaintiff may bring consecutive actions when the nuisance is "temporary" but must resort to a single action for present and future harm when the nuisance is said to be "permanent." Unfortunately, the distinction is far from clear. To avoid the trap of "splitting," in cases of "continuous or recurrent tortious invasions," the plaintiff may elect to treat the nuisance as temporary and sue successively for damages, or allege continuing harm and sue for present and future damages. *See* Restatement (Second) Torts §930(1) and comment b (1979); Restatement (Second) of Judgments §26(1)(e) and comment h (1982).

7. *Relationship Between* Res Judicata *and Supplemental Jurisdiction.* Recall the courts' attempts to define the boundaries of a "case or controversy" for purposes of supplemental jurisdiction. *See* Chapter 3 at pp. 343–352. To what extent should law developed in that context provide the definition of the "same claim" for purposes of *res judicata?* Are all claims that arise out of "the same nucleus of operative facts" and are *permitted* to be brought under supplemental jurisdiction necessarily *required* to be brought as a matter of *res judicata?* Or is the scope of a "claim" and a "case" different for each purpose?

The two doctrines—supplemental jurisdiction and *res judicata*—certainly share some common goals: Both advance efficient and final dispute resolution. Note, however, the different impact that each doctrine has. With respect to supplemental jurisdiction, the question is whether multiple claims *may* be entertained by the court. The impact of broadly defining "same controversy" is to *permit* a party to join a claim as part of a single federal proceeding instead of either requiring the party to litigate on different fronts or forcing a single action into a state forum. On the other hand, determinations about claim preclusion arise after litigation of an initial claim and determine whether a party should lose a claim omitted from the first proceeding. Once the rules are in place, claim preclusion effectively operates as a rule of compulsory joinder in the first action and *compels* parties to join particular claims at the outset of the litigation in order to avoid losing them altogether.

Should the scope of a claim be defined differently where the question is whether the claim may be asserted or whether it must be asserted? In the former situation, a plaintiff presumably wants to bring both claims in the federal forum. In the latter situation, a plaintiff might prefer not to assert a particular claim in a particular forum; thus, the importance of allowing a party to choose the time and place for litigation is a factor to be weighed against the efficiency values of having both claims heard together.

The Supreme Court in *United Mine Workers v. Gibbs, supra,* sought to advance an approach to supplemental jurisdiction that seemed generally broader than the traditional test of *res judicata* and to permit federal courts to hear pendent claims even where *res judicata* would not require those claims to be asserted in the initial proceeding. The supplemental jurisdiction statute, 28 U.S.C. §1367, carries forward this approach. Nevertheless, once supplemental jurisdiction broadens the authority of the federal court to hear nonfederal claims, an argument can be made from efficiency that plaintiff should be required to assert all transactionally related claims that the federal court has authority to hear.

8. *Alternatives to Preclusion.* Should courts distinguish between attempts to relitigate claims actually litigated, and claims omitted from the prior proceeding? In the latter case, the primary cost of relitigation is the waste of party and judicial resources; the first judgment is not otherwise undermined. Where the cost of inefficient joinder is thus reduced, is dismissal of the omitted claim in the subsequent action still the appropriate remedy, or would award of costs and attorneys' fees to defendant be a more suitable sanction? *See* Edward W. Cleary, *Res Judicata Reexamined,* 57 Yale L.J. 339, 348 (1948) (advocating different sanctions for attempts to relitigate claims than for litigation of previously omitted claims).

2. *Changed Circumstances and Other Countervailing Policies*

Federated Department Stores, Inc. v. Moitie

452 U.S. 394 (1981)

JUSTICE REHNQUIST delivered the opinion of the Court.

The only question presented in this case is whether the Court of Appeals for the Ninth Circuit validly created an exception to the doctrine of *res judicata*. The court held that *res judicata* does not bar relitigation of an unappealed adverse judgment where, as here, other plaintiffs in similar actions against common defendants successfully appeal the judgments against them. We disagree with the view taken by the Court of Appeals for the Ninth Circuit and reverse.

I

In 1976 the United States brought an antitrust action against petitioners, owners of various department stores, alleging that they had violated §1 of the Sherman Act, 15 U.S.C. §1, by agreeing to fix the retail price of women's clothing sold in northern California. Seven parallel civil actions were subsequently filed by private plaintiffs seeking treble damages on behalf of proposed classes of retail purchasers, including that of respondent Moitie in state court *(Moitie I)* and respondent Brown *(Brown I)* in the United States District Court for the Northern District of California. Each of these complaints tracked almost verbatim the allegations of the Government's complaint, though the *Moitie I* complaint referred solely to state law. All of the actions originally filed in the District Court were assigned to a single federal judge, and the *Moitie I* case was removed there on the basis of diversity of citizenship and federal-question jurisdiction. The District Court dismissed all of the actions "in their entirety" on the ground that plaintiffs had not alleged an "injury" to their "business or property" within the meaning of §4 of the Clayton Act, 15 U.S.C. §15. *Weinberg v. Federated Department Stores*, 426 F. Supp. 880 (1977).

Plaintiffs in five of the suits appealed that judgment to the Court of Appeals for the Ninth Circuit. The single counsel representing Moitie and Brown, however, chose not to appeal and instead refiled the two actions in state court, *Moitie II* and *Brown II.* Although the complaints purported to raise only state-law claims, they made allegations similar to those made in the prior complaints, including that of the Government. Petitioners removed these new actions to the District Court for the Northern District of California and moved to have them dismissed on the ground of *res judicata.* In a decision rendered July 8, 1977, the District Court first denied respondents' motion to remand. It held that the complaints, though artfully couched in terms of state law, were "in many respects identical" with the prior complaints, and were thus properly removed to federal court because they raised "essentially federal law" claims. The court then concluded that because *Moitie II* and *Brown II* involved the "same parties, the same alleged offenses, and the same time periods" as *Moitie I* and *Brown I,* the doctrine of *res judicata* required that they be dismissed. This time, Moitie and Brown appealed.

Pending that appeal, this Court on June 11, 1979, decided *Reiter v. Sonotone Corp.*, 442 U.S. 330, holding that retail purchasers can suffer an "injury" to their "business or property" as those terms are used in §4 of the Clayton Act. On June 25, 1979, the Court of Appeals for the Ninth Circuit reversed and remanded the five cases which had been decided with *Moitie I* and *Brown I,* the cases that had been appealed, for further proceedings in light of *Reiter.*

When *Moitie II* and *Brown II* finally came before the Court of Appeals for the Ninth Circuit, the court reversed the decision of the District Court dismissing the cases. 611 F.2d 1267. Though the court recognized that a "strict application of the doctrine of *res judicata* would preclude our review of the instant decision," *id.* at 1269, it refused to apply the doctrine to the facts of this case. It observed that the other five litigants in the *Weinberg* cases had successfully appealed the decision against them. It then asserted that "non-appealing parties may benefit from a reversal when their position is closely interwoven with that of appealing parties," and concluded that "[b]ecause the instant dismissal rested on a case that has been effectively overruled," the doctrine of *res judicata* must give way to "public policy" and "simple justice." *Id.* at 1269–1270. . . .

II

There is little to be added to the doctrine of *res judicata* as developed in the case law of this Court. A final judgment on the merits of an action precludes the parties or their privies from relitigating issues that were or could have been raised in that action. *Commissioner v. Sunnen,* 333 U.S. 591, 597 (1948); *Cromwell v. County of Sac,* 94 U.S. 351, 352–353 (1877). Nor are the *res judicata* consequences of a final, unappealed judgment on the merits altered by the fact that the judgment may have been wrong or rested on a legal principle subsequently overruled in another case. *Angel v. Bullington,* 330 U.S. 183 (1947); *Chicot County Drainage District v. Baxter State Bank,* 308 U.S. 371 (1940); *Wilson's Executor v. Deen,* 121 U.S. 525, 534 (1887). As this Court explained in *Baltimore S.S. Co. v. Phillips,* 274 U.S. 316 (1927), an "erroneous conclusion" reached by the court in the first suit does not deprive the defendants in the second action "of their right to rely upon the plea of *res judicata.* . . . A judgment merely voidable because based upon an erroneous view of the law is not open to collateral attack, but can be corrected only by a direct review and not by bringing another action upon the same cause [of action]." We have observed that "[t]he indulgence of a contrary view would result in creating elements of uncertainty and confusion and in undermining the conclusive character of judgments, consequences which it was the very purpose of the doctrine of *res judicata* to avert." *Reed v. Allen,* 286 U.S. 191, 201 (1932).

In this case, the Court of Appeals conceded that the "strict application of the doctrine of *res judicata*" required that *Brown II* be dismissed. By that, the court presumably meant that the "technical elements" of *res judicata* had been satisfied, namely, that the decision in *Brown I* was a final judgment on the merits and involved the same claims and the same parties as *Brown II*.[3] The court, however, declined to dismiss *Brown II* because, in its view, it would be unfair to bar respondents from relitigating a claim so "closely interwoven" with that of the successfully appealing parties. We believe that such an unprecedented departure from accepted principles of *res judicata* is unwarranted. Indeed, the decision below is all but foreclosed by our prior case law.

Reed v. Allen, supra, this Court addressed the issue presented here. The case involved a dispute over the rights to property left in a will. *A* won an interpleader action for rents derived from the property and, while an appeal [by *B*] was pending, brought an ejectment action against the rival claimant *B*. On the basis of the decree in the interpleader suit *A* won the ejectment action. *B* did not appeal this judgment, but prevailed on his earlier appeal from the interpleader decree and was

---

3. The dismissal for failure to state a claim under Federal Rule of Civil Procedure 12(b)(6) is a "judgment on the merits." See *Angel v. Bullington,* 330 U.S. 183, 190 (1947); *Bell v. Hood,* 327 U.S. 678 (1946).

awarded the rents which had been collected. When *B* sought to bring an ejectment action against *A*, the latter pleaded *res judicata*, based on his previous successful ejectment action. This Court held that *res judicata* was available as a defense and that the property belonged to *A*:

> The judgment in the ejectment action was final and not open to assault collaterally, but subject to impeachment only through some form of direct attack. The appellate court was limited to a review of the interpleader decree; and it is hardly necessary to say that jurisdiction to review one judgment gives an appellate court no power to reverse or modify another and independent judgment. If respondent, in addition to appealing from the [interpleader] decree, had appealed from the [ejectment] judgment, the appellate court, having both cases before it, might have afforded a remedy. . . . But this course respondent neglected to follow.

Id. at 198.

This Court's rigorous application of *res judicata* in *Reed*, to the point of leaving one party in possession and the other party entitled to the rents, makes clear that this Court recognizes no general equitable doctrine, such as that suggested by the Court of Appeals, which countenances an exception to the finality of a party's failure to appeal merely because his rights are "closely interwoven" with those of another party. Indeed, this case presents even more compelling reasons to apply the doctrine of *res judicata* than did *Reed*. Respondents here seek to be the windfall beneficiaries of an appellate reversal procured by other independent parties, who have no interest in respondents' case, not a reversal in interrelated cases procured, as in *Reed*, by the same affected party. Moreover, in contrast to *Reed*, where it was unclear why no appeal was taken, it is apparent that respondents here made a calculated choice to forgo their appeals. See also *Ackermann v. United States*, 340 U.S. 193, 198 (1950) (holding that petitioners were not entitled to relief under Federal Rule of Civil Procedure 60(b) when they made a "free, calculated, deliberate choic[e]" not to appeal).

The Court of Appeals also rested its opinion in part on what it viewed as "simple justice." But we do not see the grave injustice which would be done by the application of accepted principles of *res judicata*. "Simple justice" is achieved when a complex body of law developed over a period of years is evenhandedly applied. The doctrine of *res judicata* serves vital public interests beyond any individual judge's ad hoc determination of the equities in a particular case. There is simply "no principle of law or equity which sanctions the rejection by a federal court of the salutary principle of *res judicata*." *Heiser v. Woodruff*, 327 U.S. 726, 733 (1946). The Court of Appeals' reliance on "'public policy'" is similarly misplaced. This Court has long recognized that "[p]ublic policy dictates that there be an end of litigation; that those who have contested an issue shall be bound by the result of the contest, and that matters once tried shall be considered forever settled as between the parties." *Baldwin v. Traveling Men's Ass'n*, 283 U.S. 522, 525 (1931). We have stressed that "[the] doctrine of *res judicata* is not a mere matter of practice or procedure inherited from a more technical time than ours. It is a rule of fundamental and substantial justice, 'of public policy and of private peace,' which should be cordially regarded and enforced by the courts. . . ." *Hart Steel Co. v. Railroad Supply Co.*, 244 U.S. 294, 299 (1917). . . .

[Respondents also] argue that "the district court's dismissal on grounds of *res judicata* should be reversed, and the district court directed to grant respondent's motion to remand to the California state court." *Ibid.* In their view, *Brown I* cannot be considered *res judicata* as to their *state-law* claims, since *Brown I* raised only federal-law claims and *Brown II* raised additional state-law claims not decided in *Brown I*, such as unfair competition, fraud, and restitution.

It is unnecessary for this Court to reach that issue. It is enough for our decision here that *Brown I* is *res judicata* as to respondents' federal-law claims. Accordingly, the judgment of the Court of Appeals is reversed, and the cause is remanded for proceedings consistent with this opinion.

It is so ordered.

[EDS. — The concurring opinion of JUSTICE BLACKMUN, with whom JUSTICE MARSHALL joins, and the full dissenting opinion of JUSTICE BRENNAN, are omitted. Although Justice Brennan dissented on the grounds that the case should not have been removed because the complaint set forth a claim only under state law, he, along with Justices Blackmun and Marshall, thought that the Court should have gone further and concluded that the first action was also *res judicata* as to any remaining state claims:

> Like Justice Blackmun, I would hold that the dismissal . . . is *res judicata* not only as to every matter that was actually litigated, but also as to every ground or theory of recovery that might also have been presented, (citations omitted). An unqualified dismissal on the merits of a substantive federal antitrust claim precludes relitigation of the same claim on a state-law theory, (citations omitted). The Court's failure to acknowledge this basic principle can only create doubts and confusion where none were before and may encourage litigants to split their causes of action, state from federal, in the hope that they might win a second day in court.

Federated Dep't Stores v. Moitie, 452 U.S. 394, 411 (1981) (Brennan, J., dissenting).]

NOTES AND QUESTIONS

1. Was it a fair result in *Moitie* to bind plaintiffs to a legal conclusion that other litigants had reversed on appeal in a parallel case? Is it any harsher than binding a party to an erroneously decided case? What harm would have flowed from allowing plaintiffs to take advantage of the successful appeal of the *Weinberg* parties?

2. *Change of Law During Litigation.* Compare *Moitie* with the decision of the Sixth Circuit in *Harrington v. Vadallia-Butler School Dist.*, 649 F.2d 434 (6th Cir. 1981). Plaintiff Harrington brought suit against defendants for sex discrimination in violation of Title VII of the Civil Rights Act of 1964, 42 U.S.C. §§2000e *et seq.*, the federal employment discrimination act. She did not assert any claim under 42 U.S.C. §1983 of the Civil Rights Act of 1871 because, at the time of her suit, there was a square holding of the Supreme Court of the United States that municipalities were not subject to liability under §1983. Damages under Title VII were awarded to Harrington by the trial court, but the damage award was reversed by the

court of appeals, which held that Title VII did not authorize compensatory damages. While Harrington's appeal was pending in the court of appeals, the Supreme Court reversed its earlier decision with respect to §1983 and held that municipal governments could be sued for damages under that section of the Civil Rights Act. Harrington then filed a second action alleging that defendants' conduct had also violated her civil rights under §1983. Defendant moved for summary judgment on the ground that the claim was barred by the *res judicata* effect of her first suit. The district court dismissed the suit on that ground, and the court of appeals affirmed.

Is *Harrington* an easier or harder case than *Moitie*? Unlike plaintiffs in *Moitie*, didn't Harrington do all that she could have done to pursue her case diligently? Could she have preserved her civil rights claim by including it in her initial lawsuit, or would it have been considered frivolous, in violation of Rule 11? The court of appeals in *Harrington* thought not, noting that the §1983 theory had been available to her in the first action in that "she was free to challenge the validity of [the earlier Supreme Court case]" in the initial lawsuit. Moreover, the court of appeals found that the two causes of action were sufficiently similar that there was no injustice in penalizing Butler for choosing not to plead the second theory. Was it relevant that Harrington's initial lawsuit was still pending in the court of appeals when the change in the law occurred? Should the appeals court have remanded the case to the district court in light of the new Supreme Court ruling? What could the district court have done at that point? Note also that only the Supreme Court has the authority to reconsider "the validity of" one of its own precedents. The court of appeals was thus suggesting that Harrington should have raised a claim that could only have been considered on review before the Supreme Court (or in the unlikely event that the Supreme Court would change its mind in another case while hers was pending, as in fact wound up happening). Does the Sixth Circuit really want every litigant to throw the kitchen sink into its complaint in order to preserve the ability to benefit from changes in the law while their case is pending? Is that good preclusion policy? Or did the Sixth Circuit simply think that Harrington's situation was unlikely to recur with any frequency?

3. *Subsequent Aggravation of Damages.* Does a change in the underlying facts matter any more than a change of law? The issue typically arises in the tort context where plaintiff's injury is aggravated following the initial litigation. The majority rule appears to be that claim preclusion normally bars any further assertion of claims. Restatement (Second) of Judgments §25 and comment c (1982). *See, e.g., Page v. Illinois Cent. Gulf R.R.*, 516 N.E.2d 431 (Ill. App. 5th Dist. 1987) (barring subsequent suit for aggravated lung condition). Is the court's refusal to make an exception for a change in the underlying facts more or less defensible than the refusal to create an exception for the intervening change in law in *Moitie*? Note that defendant will have no recourse once the money has been paid out in the event that plaintiff's condition improves after the litigation. Does that fact make the rule any fairer?

The rule for aggravated injury cases is complicated by statute of limitations considerations. While the rule might appear to call for restraint in filing until the full measure of damages is apparent, plaintiffs may be under pressure to file before the statute of limitations expires. Most states apply a *discovery rule*—the statute of limitations begins to run when the first manifestation of injury is discoverable. This can be problematic in cases of *latent injuries*—injuries with long incubation periods. For instance, a person who has been exposed to asbestos may quickly develop "pleural thickening"—a lung condition apparent only on x-rays and which alone will not inflict significant discomfort. Over time, however, the person may or may not develop asbestosis or lung cancer. Some jurisdictions may require a person with pleural thickening to file immediately, and *res judicata* would preclude any subsequent claim if the condition were thereafter aggravated. *See, e.g., Joyce v. A.C. & S., Inc.*, 785 F.2d 1200 (4th Cir. 1986) (Virginia statute of limitations on claim for asbestos-related lung cancer commences upon manifestation of pleural thickening).* *Cf. Giddeon v. Johns-Manville Sales Corp.*, 761 F.2d 1129, 1136–1138 (5th Cir. 1985) (dictum). *But see Pierce v. Johns-Manville Sales Corp.*, 464 A.2d 1020 (1983) (allowing suit for lung cancer under Maryland three-year statute of limitations even though plaintiff developed asbestosis seven years earlier but had not filed previous tort action); *Wilson v. Johns-Manville Sales Corp.*, 684 F.2d 111 (D.C. Cir. 1982) (diagnosis of "mild asbestosis" in 1973 did not trigger the statute of limitations on claim for cancer diagnosed in 1978).

While claim preclusion is ostensibly an efficiency maximizing doctrine, notice the inefficient effect of cases like *Joyce*. A plaintiff with a relatively minor injury that may become worse over time is forced to initiate legal proceedings at the first manifestation of injury. If she waits until the injury becomes serious, she runs the risk of being barred by the statute of limitations. If she files for redress of the minor injury, she is thereafter barred by *res judicata* from refiling if her injury worsens. Her only prudent alternative is to sue when she is first injured and seek damages for the fear and risk of future injury. Accordingly, people who may never have resorted to litigation because of the minor nature of their injuries are pressured into litigation prematurely, and courts are forced to calculate and award highly speculative damages.

Would it be more efficient to allow plaintiffs with both actual and potential injuries to split their claims, or at least toll (suspend) the statute of limitations until the injury becomes serious? Would that be unfair to defendants? *See In re Moorenovich*, 634 F. Supp. 634 (D. Me. 1986) (foreclosing "risk of cancer" claim on the ground that it was too speculative, but assuring plaintiff that he could refile if he in fact contracted cancer); *Jackson v. Johns-Manville Sales Corp.*, 727 F.2d 506, 516–522 (5th Cir. 1984), certified to state court, en banc, 750 F.2d 1314 (same). *See generally* Michael D. Green, *The Paradox of Statutes of Limitations in Toxic Substances Litigation*, 76 Cal. L. Rev. 965 (1988); Peter H. Schuck, *The Worst Should Go First: Deferral Registries in Asbestos Litigation*, 15 Harv. J.L. & Pub. Pol'y 541, 571 (1992) (proposing that unimpaired asbestos victims should be permitted to "register" their claims and be placed "on hold" until their condition worsens); Note, *Claim Preclusion in Modern Latent Disease Cases: A Proposal for Allowing Second Suits*, 103 Harv. L. Rev. 1989 (1990).

4. *Newly Discovered Evidence.* If a party discovers evidence not asserted in the first proceeding, *res judicata* still precludes relitigation of the claim. Restatement (Second) of Judgments §25 (1982). However, the potential harshness of that rule is

---

* While the *Joyce* case was pending, the Virginia statute of limitations was amended to provide that the statute begins to run upon the diagnosis of a "disabling asbestos-related injury." Va. Code §8.01-249.

mitigated by Fed. R. Civ. P. 60(b), which permits a court to "relieve a party . . . from a final judgment" for a variety of reasons, including newly discovered evidence that could not have been discovered earlier through the exercise of reasonable diligence. Restatement (Second) of Judgments §25, comment c (1982).

5. *Balancing Finality with Other Countervailing Policies.* As *Moitie* indicates, the judicial system's commitment to finality is extremely strong and not easily displaced by competing concerns. However, occasionally courts have recognized that the underlying substantive law may require that multiple actions be permitted. The case of "nuisance" discussed at Note 6 on p. 778 is one such example. The Restatement (Second) of Judgments §26 lists several exceptions to the general rule against splitting, including §26(1)(d), which provides:

> The judgment in the first action was plainly inconsistent with the fair and equitable implementation of a statutory or constitutional scheme, or it is the sense of the scheme that the plaintiff should be permitted to split his claim.

In this connection, consider *United States v. American Heart Research Fund, Inc.,* 996 F.2d 7 (1st Cir. 1993), where the United States government brought a civil suit pursuant to a federal statute for expedited injunctive relief for mail fraud against purported nonprofit scientific organizations engaging in an alleged swindle. Contemporaneously with a guilty plea to separate criminal charges (and payment of a fine), defendants agreed to a consent order in the civil case enjoining them from future fundraising. Several years later the government brought a separate action for unjust enrichment, seeking damages for the underpayment of postage. The district court dismissed the action on the basis of claim preclusion since both remedies—the injunction and the disgorgement—were premised on the same transaction or series of transactions, but the Court of Appeals for the First Circuit reversed. The Court of Appeals relied on the legislative history of the federal statute, which authorized the Attorney General to put a "speedy end to fraud" by seeking an injunction as soon as practicable. The court believed that these expedited injunctive actions should not be handicapped or delayed by requiring the government to include any damage claims arising from the same transaction. Additionally, the court noted, "the government may want to secure additional facts, including the amount of damages, before asserting such claims and may well wish to negotiate with the defendant as to settlement once the ongoing violation has ceased." *Id.* at 11.

Don't the concerns facing the government in *American Heart* confront many litigants who have claims for both injunctive relief and damages? Has the court in *American Heart* just carved out a special rule for the United States government? Or is the result in that case driven by policies attributable to the federal statute that provides the underlying rule of law?

3. *The Special Problem of Defenses and Counterclaims*

Claim preclusion can extend to both plaintiffs and defendants. In some circumstances, a defendant who bypassed the opportunity to assert a defense or a counterclaim in a proceeding may be precluded thereafter from asserting that defense or counterclaim as a claim for affirmative relief in any subsequent proceeding. Application of preclusion against parties who were defendants in the first proceeding, sometimes referred to as "defense preclusion," is often subsumed under compulsory counterclaim rules like Fed. R. Civ. P. 13(a). Rule 13(a) does not prescribe the penalty for failure to assert a compulsory counterclaim—indeed, following the *Semtek* case, *infra*, it is clear that the Federal Rules could not prescribe a rule of preclusion—but most courts enforce the rule by preventing a party from asserting the omitted counterclaim. Debate remains as to whether courts are relying on a common law rule of preclusion or a waiver principle in such a case. *See* 6 C. Wright et al., Federal Practice and Procedure §§1417–1418 (3d ed. 2018 & Supp. 2020) (noting debate over the source of authority for this result); Restatement (Second) of Judgments §22(2)(a) (1982) (barring assertion of claim that should have been interposed as compulsory counterclaim in earlier proceeding, but only after judgment is rendered in the earlier proceeding).

Application of defense preclusion in the absence of a compulsory counterclaim rule is less clear. The Supreme Court issued a ruling that rejected one party's attempt to invoke this species of "defense preclusion" but left open the question whether the doctrine would be available under the federal common law of preclusion if certain conditions were met.

Lucky Brand Dungarees v. Marcel Fashions Group

140 S.Ct. 1589 (2020)

JUSTICE SOTOMAYOR delivered the opinion of the Court.

This case arises from protracted litigation between petitioners Lucky Brand Dungarees, Inc., and others (collectively Lucky Brand) and respondent Marcel Fashions Group, Inc. (Marcel). In the latest lawsuit between the two, Lucky Brand asserted a defense against Marcel that it had not pressed fully in a preceding suit between the parties. This Court is asked to determine whether Lucky Brand's failure to litigate the defense in the earlier suit barred Lucky Brand from invoking it in the later suit. Because the parties agree that, at a minimum, the preclusion of such a defense in this context requires that the two suits share the same claim to relief—and because we find that the two suits here did not—Lucky Brand was not barred from raising its defense in the later action.

I

Marcel and Lucky Brand both sell jeans and other apparel. Both entities also use the word "Lucky" as part of their marks on clothing. In 1986, Marcel received a federal trademark registration for "Get Lucky"; a few years later, in 1990, Lucky Brand began selling apparel using the registered trademark "Lucky Brand" and other marks that include the word "Lucky."

Three categories of marks are at issue in this case: Marcel's "Get Lucky" mark; Lucky Brand's "Lucky Brand" mark; and various other marks owned by Lucky Brand that contain the word "Lucky." These trademarks have led to nearly 20 years of litigation between the two companies, proceeding in three rounds.

A

In 2001 — the first round — Marcel sued Lucky Brand, alleging that Lucky Brand's use of the phrase "Get Lucky" in advertisements infringed Marcel's trademark. In 2003, the parties signed a settlement agreement. As part of the deal, Lucky Brand agreed to stop using the phrase "Get Lucky." In exchange, Marcel agreed to release any claims regarding Lucky Brand's use of its own trademarks.

B

The ink was barely dry on the settlement agreement when, in 2005, the parties began a second round of litigation (2005 Action). Lucky Brand filed suit, alleging that Marcel and its licensee violated its trademarks by copying its designs and logos in a new clothing line. As relevant here, Marcel filed several counterclaims that all turned, in large part, on Lucky Brand's alleged continued use of "Get Lucky": One batch of allegations asserted that Lucky Brand had continued to use Marcel's "Get Lucky" mark in violation of the settlement agreement, while others alleged that Lucky Brand's use of the phrase "Get Lucky" and "Lucky Brand" together was "confusingly similar to" — and thus infringed — Marcel's "Get Lucky" mark. None of Marcel's counterclaims alleged that Lucky Brand's use of its own marks alone — i.e., independent of any alleged use of "Get Lucky" — infringed Marcel's "Get Lucky" mark.

Lucky Brand moved to dismiss the counterclaims, alleging that they were barred by the release provision of the settlement agreement. After the District Court denied the motion without prejudice, Lucky Brand noted the release defense once more in its answer to Marcel's counterclaims. But as the 2005 Action proceeded, Lucky Brand never again invoked the release defense.

The 2005 Action concluded in two phases. First, as a sanction for misconduct during discovery, the District Court concluded that Lucky Brand violated the settlement agreement by continuing to use "Get Lucky" and permanently enjoined Lucky Brand from copying or imitating Marcel's "Get Lucky" mark. The injunction did not enjoin, or even mention, Lucky Brand's use of any other marks or phrases containing the word "Lucky." The case then proceeded to trial. The jury found against Lucky Brand on Marcel's remaining counterclaims — those that alleged infringement from Lucky Brand's continued use of the "Get Lucky" catchphrase alongside its own marks.

C

In April 2011, the third round of litigation began: Marcel filed an action against Lucky Brand (2011 Action), maintaining that Lucky Brand continued to infringe Marcel's "Get Lucky" mark and, in so doing, contravened the judgment issued in the 2005 Action.

This complaint did not reprise Marcel's earlier allegation (in the 2005 Action) that Lucky Brand continued to use the "Get Lucky" phrase. Marcel argued only that Lucky Brand's continued, post-2010 use of Lucky Brand's own marks — some of which used the word "Lucky" — infringed Marcel's "Get Lucky" mark in a manner that (according to Marcel) was previously found infringing.[1] Marcel requested that the District Court enjoin Lucky Brand from using any of Lucky Brand's marks containing the word "Lucky."

The District Court granted Lucky Brand summary judgment, concluding that Marcel's claims in the 2011 Action were essentially the same as its counterclaims in the 2005 Action.

But the Court of Appeals for the Second Circuit disagreed. The court concluded that Marcel's claims in the 2011 Action were distinct from those it had asserted in the 2005 Action, because the claims at issue in the 2005 Action were "for earlier infringements." As the court noted, "[w]inning a judgment . . . does not deprive the plaintiff of the right to sue" for the defendant's "subsequent similar violations."

The Second Circuit further rejected Marcel's request to hold Lucky Brand in contempt for violating the injunction issued in the 2005 Action. The court noted that the conduct at issue in the 2011 Action was Lucky Brand's use of its own marks—not the use of the phrase "Get Lucky." By contrast, the 2005 injunction prohibited Lucky Brand from using the "Get Lucky" mark—not Lucky Brand's own marks that happened to contain the word "Lucky." Moreover, the court reasoned that the jury in the 2005 Action had been "free to find infringement of Marcel's 'Get Lucky' mark based solely on Lucky Brand's use of [the phrase] 'Get Lucky.'" The court vacated and remanded for further proceedings.

On remand to the District Court, Lucky Brand moved to dismiss, arguing—for the first time since its motion to dismiss and answer in the 2005 Action—that Marcel had released its claims by entering the settlement agreement. Marcel countered that Lucky Brand was precluded from invoking the release defense, because it could have pursued the defense fully in the 2005 Action but had neglected to do so. The District Court granted Lucky Brand's motion to dismiss, holding that it could assert its release defense and that the settlement agreement indeed barred Marcel's claims.

The Second Circuit vacated and remanded, concluding that a doctrine it termed "defense preclusion" prohibited Lucky Brand from raising the release defense in the 2011 Action. Noting that a different category of preclusion—issue preclusion—may be wielded against a defendant, see *Parklane Hosiery Co. v. Shore*, 439 U.S. 322, 99 S.Ct. 645, 58 L.Ed.2d 552 (1979), the court reasoned that the same should be true of claim preclusion: A defendant should be precluded from raising an unlitigated defense that it should have raised earlier. The panel then held that "defense preclusion" bars a party from raising a defense where: "(i) a previous action involved an adjudication on the merits"; "(ii) the previous action involved the same parties"; "(iii) the defense was either asserted or could have been asserted, in the prior action"; and "(iv) the district court, in its discretion, concludes that preclusion of the defense is appropriate." Finding each factor satisfied in this case, the panel vacated the District Court's judgment. We granted certiorari to resolve differences among the Circuits regarding when, if ever, claim preclusion applies to defenses raised in a later suit. Compare [the ruling below] with *Hallco Mfg. Co. v. Foster*, 256 F.3d 1290, 1297–1298 (CA Fed. 2001); *McKinnon v. Blue Cross and Blue Shield of Alabama*, 935 F.2d 1187, 1192 (CA11 1991).

II

A

This case asks whether so-called "defense preclusion" is a valid application of res judicata: a term that now comprises two distinct doctrines regarding the preclusive effect of prior litigation. 18 C. Wright, A. Miller, & E. Cooper, Federal Practice and Procedure § 4402 (3d ed. 2016) (Wright & Miller). The first is issue preclusion (sometimes called collateral estoppel), which precludes a party from relitigating an issue actually decided in a prior case and necessary to the judgment. *Allen v. McCurry*, 449 U.S. 90, 94, 101 S.Ct. 411, 66 L.Ed.2d 308 (1980); see *Parklane Hosiery*, 439 U.S. at 326, n. 5, 99 S.Ct. 645.

The second doctrine is claim preclusion (sometimes itself called res judicata). Unlike issue preclusion, claim preclusion prevents parties from raising issues that could have been raised and decided in a prior action — even if they were not actually litigated. If a later suit advances the same claim as an earlier suit between the same parties, the earlier suit's judgment "prevents litigation of all grounds for, or defenses to, recovery that were previously available to the parties, regardless of whether they were asserted or determined in the prior proceeding." *Brown v. Felsen*, 442 U.S. 127, 131, 99 S.Ct. 2205, 60 L.Ed.2d 767 (1979); see also Wright & Miller § 4407. Suits involve the same claim (or "cause of action") when they " 'aris[e] from the same transaction,' " *United States v. Tohono O'odham Nation*, 563 U.S. 307, 316, 131 S.Ct. 1723, 179 L.Ed.2d 723 (2011) (quoting *Kremer v. Chemical Constr. Corp.*, 456 U.S. 461, 482, n. 22, 102 S.Ct. 1883, 72 L.Ed.2d 262 (1982)), or involve a "common nucleus of operative facts," Restatement (Second) of Judgments § 24, Comment *b*, p. 199 (1982) (Restatement (Second)).

Put another way, claim preclusion "describes the rules formerly known as 'merger' and 'bar.'" *Taylor v. Sturgell*, 553 U.S. 880, 892, n. 5, 128 S.Ct. 2161, 171 L.Ed.2d 155 (2008). "If the plaintiff wins, the entire claim is merged in the judgment; the plaintiff cannot bring a second independent action for additional relief, and the defendant cannot avoid the judgment by offering new defenses." Wright & Miller § 4406. But "[i]f the second lawsuit involves a new claim or cause of action, the parties may raise assertions or defenses that were omitted from the first lawsuit even though they were equally relevant to the first cause of action." *Ibid.*

As the Second Circuit itself seemed to recognize, this Court has never explicitly recognized "defense preclusion" as a standalone category of res judicata, unmoored from the two guideposts of issue preclusion and claim preclusion. Instead, our case law indicates that any such preclusion of defenses must, at a minimum, satisfy the strictures of issue preclusion or claim preclusion. See, *e.g., Davis v. Brown*, 94 U.S. 423, 428, 24 L.Ed. 204 (1877) (holding that where two lawsuits involved different claims, preclusion operates "only upon the matter actually at issue and determined in the original action").[2] The parties thus agree

---

2. There may be good reasons to question any application of claim preclusion to defenses. It has been noted that in suits involving successive claims against the same defendant, courts often "assum[e] that the defendant may raise defenses in the second action that were not raised in the first, even though they were equally available and relevant in both actions." Wright & Miller § 4414. This is because "[v]arious considerations, other than actual merits, may govern" whether to bring a defense, "such as the smallness of the amount or the value of the property in controversy, the difficulty of obtaining the necessary evidence, the expense of the litigation, and [a party's] own situation." *Cromwell v. County of Sac*, 94 U.S. 351, 356, 24 L.Ed. 195 (1877). Here, however, this Court need not determine when (if ever) applying claim preclusion to defenses may be appropriate, because a necessary predicate — identity of claims — is lacking.

that where, as here, issue preclusion does not apply, a defense can be barred only if the "causes of action are the same" in the two suits — that is, where they share a " 'common nucleus of operative fact[s].' " Brief for Respondent 2, 27, 31, 50; accord, Reply Brief 3.

B

Put simply, the two suits here were grounded on different conduct, involving different marks, occurring at different times. They thus did not share a "common nucleus of operative facts." Restatement (Second) § 24, Comment *b*, at 199.

To start, claims to relief may be the same for the purposes of claim preclusion if, among other things, "'a different judgment in the second action would impair or destroy rights or interests established by the judgment entered in the first action.'" Wright & Miller § 4407. Here, however, the 2011 Action did not imperil the judgment of the 2005 Action because the lawsuits involved both different conduct and different trademarks.

In the 2005 Action, Marcel alleged that Lucky Brand infringed Marcel's "Get Lucky" mark both by directly imitating its "Get Lucky" mark and by using the "Get Lucky" slogan alongside Lucky Brand's other marks in a way that created consumer confusion. Brief for Respondent 52. Marcel appears to admit, thus, that its claims in the 2005 Action depended on Lucky Brand's alleged use of "Get Lucky." *Id.*, at 9–10 ("Marcel's reverse-confusion theory [in the 2005 Action] depended, in part, on Lucky's continued imitation of the GET LUCKY mark").

By contrast, the 2011 Action did not involve any alleged use of the "Get Lucky" phrase. Indeed, Lucky Brand had been enjoined in the 2005 Action from using "Get Lucky," and in the 2011 Action, Lucky Brand was found not to have violated that injunction. The parties thus do not argue that Lucky Brand continued to use "Get Lucky" after the 2005 Action concluded, and at oral argument, counsel for Marcel appeared to confirm that Marcel's claims in the 2011 Action did not allege that Lucky Brand continued to use "Get Lucky." Instead, Marcel alleged in the 2011 Action that Lucky Brand committed infringement by using Lucky Brand's own marks containing the word "Lucky" — not the "Get Lucky" mark itself. Plainly, then, the 2011 Action challenged different conduct, involving different marks.

Not only that, but the complained-of conduct in the 2011 Action occurred after the conclusion of the 2005 Action. Claim preclusion generally "does not bar claims that are predicated on events that postdate the filing of the initial complaint." *Whole Woman's Health* v. *Hellerstedt*, 579 U.S. ___, ___, 136 S.Ct. 2292, 2305, 195 L.Ed.2d 665 (2016) (internal quotation marks omitted); *Lawlor v. National Screen Service Corp.*, 349 U.S. 322, 327–328, 75 S.Ct. 865, 99 L.Ed. 1122 (1955) (holding that two suits were not "based on the same cause of action," because "[t]he conduct presently complained of was all subsequent to" the prior judgment and it "cannot be given the effect of extinguishing claims which did not even then exist and which could not possibly have been sued upon in the previous case"). This is for good reason: Events that occur after the plaintiff files suit often give rise to new "[m]aterial operative facts" that "in themselves, or taken in conjunction with the antecedent facts," create a new claim to relief. Restatement (Second) § 24, Comment *f*, at 203; 18 J. Moore, D. Coquillette, G. Joseph, G. Vairo, & C. Varner, Federal Practice § 131.22[1], p. 131–55, n. 1 (3d ed. 2019) (citing cases where "[n]ew facts create[d a] new claim").

This principle takes on particular force in the trademark context, where the enforceability of a mark and likelihood of confusion between marks often turns on extrinsic facts that change over time. As Lucky Brand points out, liability for trademark infringement turns on marketplace realities that can change dramatically from year to year. It is no surprise, then, that the Second Circuit held that Marcel's 2011 Action claims were not barred by the 2005 Action. By the same token, the 2005 Action could not bar Lucky Brand's 2011 defenses.

At bottom, the 2011 Action involved different marks, different legal theories, and different conduct—occurring at different times. Because the two suits thus lacked a "common nucleus of operative facts," claim preclusion did not and could not bar Lucky Brand from asserting its settlement agreement defense in the 2011 Action.

III

Resisting this conclusion, Marcel points to treatises and this Court's cases, arguing that they support a version of "defense preclusion" doctrine that extends to the facts of this case. But these authorities do no such thing. As an initial matter, regardless of what those authorities might imply about "defense preclusion," none of them describe scenarios applicable here. Moreover, we doubt that these authorities stand for anything more than that traditional claim- or issue-preclusion principles may bar defenses raised in a subsequent suit—principles that, as explained above, do not bar Lucky Brand's release defense here.

Take, for example, cases that involve either judgment enforcement or a collateral attack on a prior judgment. In the former scenario, a party takes action to enforce a prior judgment already issued against another; in the latter, a party seeks to avoid the effect of a prior judgment by bringing a suit to undo it. If, in either situation, a different outcome in the second action "would nullify the initial judgment or would impair rights established in the initial action," preclusion principles would be at play. Restatement (Second) § 22(b), at 185; Wright & Miller § 4414. In both scenarios, courts simply apply claim preclusion or issue preclusion to prohibit a claim or defense that would attack a previously decided claim.[3] But these principles do not preclude defendants from asserting defenses to new claims, which is precisely what Marcel would have us do here.

In any event, judgment-enforcement and collateral-attack scenarios are far afield from the circumstances of this case. Lucky Brand's defense in the 2011

---

3. One might ask: If any preclusion of defenses (under the claim-preclusion rubric) requires identity of claims in two suits, how could the second similar suit have avoided standard claim preclusion in the first place? Different contexts may yield different answers. In a judgment-enforcement context, the answer may be that claim preclusion applies only "to a final judgment rendered in an action *separate* from that in which the doctrine is asserted." 18 J. Moore, D. Coquillette, G. Joseph, G. Vairo, & C. Varner, Federal Practice § 131.31[1], p. 131–116 (3d ed. 2019) (emphasis added). Thus—although claim preclusion does apply to a later, standalone suit seeking relief that could have been obtained in the first—it "is not applicable to . . . efforts to obtain supplemental relief in the original action, or direct attacks on the judgment." *Ibid* (footnote deleted). The upshot is that—even if a court deems the underlying core of operative facts to be the same—a plaintiff in that circumstance is not precluded from enforcing its rights with respect to continuing wrongful conduct.

Action did not threaten the judgment issued in the 2005 Action or, as Marcel argues, "achieve the same practical result" that the above-mentioned principles seek to avoid. Brief for Respondent 31–32. Indeed, while the judgment in the 2005 Action plainly prohibited Lucky Brand from using "Get Lucky," it did not do the same with respect to Lucky Brand's continued, standalone use of its own marks containing the word "Lucky"—the only conduct at issue in the 2011 Action. Put simply, Lucky Brand's defense to new claims in the 2011 Action did not risk impairing the 2005 judgment.

· · ·

At bottom, Marcel's 2011 Action challenged different conduct—and raised different claims—from the 2005 Action. Under those circumstances, Marcel cannot preclude Lucky Brand from raising new defenses. The judgment of the Second Circuit is therefore reversed, and the case is remanded for proceedings consistent with this opinion.

It is so ordered.

NOTES AND QUESTIONS

1. *Defense Preclusion, Counterclaims, and* Res Judicata. There are at least three situations in which the doctrine of claim preclusion might operate to the disadvantage of a defendant in a subsequent proceeding. One involves *counterclaims.* Imagine that a plaintiff files a lawsuit against a defendant and the defendant has a claim of his own against the plaintiff that is related to the subject matter of that suit. Instead of asserting his claim in that first action as a counterclaim, however, he waits and files a separate lawsuit in which he is now the plaintiff and his opponent now the defendant. The opponent might argue that the original defendant (now plaintiff) is barred from bringing his claim in the second lawsuit because he could have asserted it as a counterclaim in the first action.

A second situation involves *defenses* in the first action that could also constitute independent claims if filed in a separate lawsuit. The classic example is a set-off. Say plaintiff sues defendant for $50,000 for breach of contract, but defendant has a strong argument that plaintiff failed to perform some of her own obligations under the contract so any amount she recovers should be reduced by $25,000. Defendant could assert that argument in the first action as a partial defense to plaintiff's contract claim—a set-off—or he might wait and file his own $25,000 claim for breach of contract in a separate lawsuit. If the defendant chooses the latter course, withholds the set-off defense in the first action and then files a new lawsuit for breach of contract, his opponent could argue that the new claim should be barred because the defendant could have asserted the substance of that claim as a set-off defense in the first suit. Or the defendant in the initial action might have a set-off that is worth *more* than the claim brought by that plaintiff. If he asserts that set-off as a defense in the first action but fails to ask for the extra amount as a counterclaim, claim preclusion might prevent him from bringing a separate suit to recover that surplus amount.

A third situation is the one involved in *Lucky Brand*: A party does not pursue an affirmative defense in an initial lawsuit but then seeks to raise the same defense based on the same facts in a subsequent lawsuit involving the same opponent, and the opponent argues that the defendant is precluded from raising the defense in the second suit because he could have done so in the first. Here the defense is not a set-off that could be asserted as an independent claim; it is simply a defense to liability. One might refer to this as *defense-alone preclusion.*

Each of these situations presents distinct questions of preclusion doctrine and policy.

2. *Defense-Alone Preclusion After* Lucky Brand. The Court unanimously rejected the preclusion argument in *Lucky Brand.* In doing so, did the Court close the door to this form of defense-alone preclusion altogether? As a formal matter the answer is no, but as a practical matter the path for asserting this form of preclusion in the federal courts appears quite narrow going forward. The Court rejected defense-alone preclusion as a "standalone category of res judicata" and held that "any such preclusion of defenses must, at a minimum, satisfy the strictures of issue preclusion or claim preclusion." The Court's holding that defense preclusion was unavailable in *Lucky Brand* was based on its conclusion that the requirements of claim preclusion were not satisfied. In theory, the Court left the door open for defense-alone preclusion in a case that does satisfy the requirements of claim preclusion. But if an affirmative defense in a second lawsuit is so closely related to an earlier suit that the requirements of claim preclusion would be satisfied, would that not also usually be the case for the plaintiff's claim in the second lawsuit as well? The Court acknowledges as much in footnote 3 of its opinion — "One might ask: If any preclusion of defenses (under the claim-preclusion rubric) requires identity of claims in two suits, how could the second similar suit have avoided standard claim preclusion in the first place?" — and offers a judgment enforcement action as one narrow example of a case where those requirements might be satisfied. Note also that claim preclusion is a waivable defense: A defendant can lose the opportunity to make the argument if he does not assert it in a timely fashion. In the imperfect world of actual litigation, a defendant might assert some other affirmative defense in a second action but fail to recognize that he could also argue claim preclusion. In such a case, an attentive plaintiff might be able to argue that the affirmative defense is barred by *res judicata* but that the defendant has lost the opportunity to assert his own *res judicata* argument.

3. *The "Same Claim" Requirement.* The 2005 Action between Marcel and Lucky Brand was distinct from the 2011 Action in two ways that the Court found significant. First, the 2005 Action involved allegations of trademark infringement from Lucky Brand's use of the phrase "Get Lucky," while the 2011 Action involved allegations that Lucky Brand's own product names involved trademark infringement simply by virtue of including the word "Lucky." Second, the 2011 Action was based on marketing activity undertaken by Lucky Brand after the conclusion of the 2005 Action. The Court found that each of these factors rendered the claims distinct and hence outside the permissible boundaries of claim preclusion. Defense preclusion could only apply, the Court held, "if the 'causes of action are the same' in the two suits — that is, where they share a "'common nucleus of operative fact[s].'"

Compare this result to the Court's ruling on preclusion doctrine in *Whole Woman's Health v. Hellerstedt, supra,* on which *Lucky Brand* relies. The Court found in *Hellerstedt* that claim preclusion did not bar a post-enforcement, as-applied challenge to statutory restrictions on access to abortion despite an earlier, pre-enforcement, facial challenge to those restrictions. *Hellerstedt* relied on two arguments: The second lawsuit included facts that were not present in the first (the record of subsequent enforcement of the abortion restrictions and their actual impact on access to the procedure), and the second lawsuit included a challenge to provisions of the statute that were not challenged in the first, in addition to challenges to provisions that were. That combination of factors led the Court to conclude that the post-enforcement challenge did not raise the "same claims" as the earlier suit.

Consider a question similar to one we posed about the *Hellerstedt* case in the notes following *Herendeen. See supra* at 797–799. If the two lawsuits in *Lucky Brand* had not been separated in time, such that the only difference between them related to the nature of the alleged trademark infringement—Lucky Brand's use of the phrase "Get Lucky" vs. the company's use of the word "Lucky" in their own branded materials—would it still be correct to say that these are not the "same claim" and hence that claim preclusion does not apply? As with the two lawsuits in *Hellerstedt,* there are certainly distinctions between the two trademark claims here; they are not identical claims. But recall the language used in the Restatement (Second) of Judgments to define the boundaries of a "claim" for these purposes:

> What factual grouping constitutes a "transaction" and what groupings constitute a "series [of transactions]" are to be determined pragmatically, giving weight to such considerations as whether the facts are related in time, space, origin, or motivation, whether they form a convenient trial unit, and whether their treatment as a unit conforms to the parties' expectations or business understanding or usage.

Restatement (Second) of Judgments §24(2). If Marcel brought one lawsuit alleging that Lucky Brand was infringing their trademark by using the phrase "Get Lucky" and a subsequent lawsuit alleging that Lucky Brand was infringing their trademark by using the word "Lucky" in their branded materials, would you expect a court to find these claims sufficiently "related in time, space, origin or motivation" to warrant a finding of claim preclusion? As with *Hellerstedt,* we do not know whether the Court would have found such distinctions to be enough by themselves to defeat claim preclusion without the added factor that the second lawsuit rested on events that had not yet occurred when the first lawsuit arrived at a judgment. But is it fair to say that the Court's analysis in both cases appears to adopt a more conservative approach to claim preclusion than §24 of the Second Restatement?

Lucky Brand is a ruling on the federal common law of preclusion, not a constitutional due process decision. This means it applies only in situations where the federal law of preclusion governs. States remain free to adopt their own law of defense preclusion, whether narrower or broader, so long as it is consistent with the requirements of due process.

4. *Counterclaims and Claim Preclusion.* When a party is sued as a defendant in a first lawsuit and has a claim against the plaintiff that is closely related to the subject of the suit that he could assert as a counterclaim, failure to do so may result in

claim preclusion if that party tries to file the claim as a plaintiff in a new lawsuit. The Restatement (Second) of Judgments §22 provides as follows:

Effect of Failure to Interpose Counterclaim

(1) Where the defendant may interpose a claim as a counterclaim but he fails to do so, he is not thereby precluded from subsequently maintaining an action on that claim, except as stated in Subsection (2).

(2) A defendant who may interpose a claim as a counterclaim in an action but fails to do so is precluded, after the rendition of judgment in that action, from maintaining an action on the claim if

(a) The counterclaim is required to be interposed by a compulsory counterclaim statute or rule of court, or

(b) The relationship between the counterclaim and the plaintiff's claim is such that successful prosecution of the second action would nullify the initial judgment or would impair rights established in the initial action.

Federal Rule of Civil Procedure 13(a) generally requires defendants to assert as compulsory counterclaims any claim that "arises out of the transaction or occurrence that is the subject matter of the opposing party's claim." State courts vary in their practice, with some following the federal model and others (e.g., New York and Pennsylvania) imposing no general requirement to assert counterclaims.

If a defendant fails to assert a compulsory counterclaim in federal court and the action goes to judgment, what is the mechanism by which the defendant will be prevented from asserting the claim in a subsequent proceeding? The answer is surprisingly unsettled. Wright & Miller explain that "failure to plead a compulsory counterclaim [in a federal proceeding] bars a party from bringing a later independent action on that claim" but continue: "Although this result is well-established by the cases . . . it is not clear precisely on what authority it is based." Wright & Miller, Federal Practice & Procedure §1417 (3d ed. 2020). Some courts have treated the failure to comply with Rule 13(a) as a waiver while others view the penalty for that failure as a matter of claim preclusion.

Ordinarily, the order in which lawsuits are *filed* does not matter for *res judicata* purposes. Rather, it is the first action to reach a *final judgment* that will have *res judicata* effect in other proceedings. The order in which actions are filed might be relevant for other reasons, however. Under some circumstances, a court will issue a *stay* of an action in order to permit another, related action that was filed earlier to come to completion. (Of course, the stay may effectively determine which action arrives at judgment first, which will have *res judicata* implications.) In addition, if one understands a compulsory counterclaim rule to operate through the principle of *waiver*, rather than the principle of *res judicata*, then the failure to assert a compulsory counterclaim in a first-filed action may have immediate implications even before judgment is rendered. For example, in *Grumman Systems Support Co. v. Data General*, 125 F.R.D. 160 (N.D. Cal. 1988), a California district court dismissed a case in which Grumman was asserting a claim that should have been raised as a compulsory counterclaim in an action filed by Data General in Massachusetts. The Massachusetts case was not yet final, but it was filed first and was currently pending. Based on these facts, the court concluded that a failure by Grumman to assert its claim in the Massachusetts action would constitute a waiver. We discuss *Grumman* and related issues in greater depth at pages 902–911 *infra*.

For one interesting treatment of the issue, *see Paramount Pictures Corp. v. Alliant Risk Transfer AG*, 96 N.E.3d 737 (NY 2018). The case involved an initial proceeding in federal court raising both federal and state securities fraud claims in which the defendant failed to raise a compulsory counterclaim—specifically, a claim that the plaintiff's suit breached a covenant not to sue in a contract between the parties. That was followed by a subsequent proceeding in New York state court, where there is no compulsory counterclaim rule, in which the original defendant (now plaintiff) asserted the covenant-not-to-sue claim under state law. The state trial court refused to preclude the claim, finding that New York's decision not to impose a compulsory counterclaim rule governed, but the Court of Appeals disagreed. After a thorough analysis addressing the source of federal preclusion law and the role of Rule 13(a) in a case of this type, the court concluded that the federal policy controlled through the federal common law of preclusion. Because the covenant-not-to-sue claim "should have been asserted in the parties' federal action" and was closely related to the claims in that action, it was "barred by res judicata."

5. *Set-Off Defenses and Claim Preclusion.* Set-offs present an in-between situation: a legal argument that a defendant might be able to assert as a defense to recovery in whole or in part but could also assert as a claim for relief, whether a counterclaim in an existing action or an independent claim in a newly filed action. Suppose a defendant asserts a set-off as a complete defense to a lawsuit and then seeks to recover additional moneys from his opponent in a separate action on the same theory. Should claim preclusion prevent him from doing so on the theory that he is attempting to split his claim?

That was the situation presented in Mitchell v. Federal Intermediate Credit Bank, 164 S.E. 136 (S.C. 1932), a decision of the South Carolina Supreme Court. Federal Intermediate Credit Bank filed an action in federal court against Mitchell, a farmer, to recover on two outstanding notes totaling $9,000 that Mitchell had executed in order to receive loans from the Bank. Mitchell then commenced an action in state court against the bank for an accounting. Mitchell alleged that, in order to obtain the loans at low rates of interest, he was required to sell his potato crop and assign the proceeds to the bank as security. He also claimed that, while his debt to the bank totaled $9,000, his crop had netted an amount of about $18,000, which the bank (or one of its agents) had already received. Thus, Mitchell claimed, the Bank should pay him the surplus amount of about $9,000. After the pleadings were filed in Mitchell's state-court action, the parties agreed to hold that state case in abeyance pending the outcome of the federal suit. In the federal action, Mitchell pleaded as a defense the same facts he alleged in the state action—the assignment of the proceeds—but he did not counterclaim for the additional amounts of money he thought he was owed. The federal action resulted in a verdict in favor of Mitchell, which was affirmed on appeal. In the pending state action, the Bank then contended that Mitchell's claim for the additional amounts of money had been merged in the prior federal judgment and hence that claim preclusion prevented him from recovering the surplus amount. Mitchell appealed to the Supreme Court of South Carolina and that court affirmed, finding that Mitchell had improperly attempted to split his cause of action.

> In the matter before us, the legal wrong which Mitchell suffered was the violation by the bank of his right to receive the proceeds of his potato crop which had come into the bank's hands, amounting to about $18,000.00,

and for this wrong he had a single indivisible cause of action against the bank. When the bank sued him on his two notes amounting to about $9,000.00, he had the option to interpose his claim as a defense to that suit or to demand judgment against the bank, by way of counterclaim, for the amount owing him by it. He elected to set up his claim as a defense only, and the jury applied it to the payment of the notes held by the bank. The transaction out of which the case at bar arises is the same transaction that Mitchell pleaded as a defense in the Federal suit. He might, therefore, "have recovered in that action, upon the same allegations and proofs which he there made, the judgment which he now seeks, if he had prayed for it." He did not do this, but attempted to split his cause of action, and to use one portion of it for defense in that suit and to reserve the remainder for offense in a subsequent suit, which, under applicable principles, could not be done.

Id. at 143-144. What options did the farmer have in the first action? If he chooses not to raise the defense at all, is it clear he will be able to bring an action for his proceeds in a second action? The South Carolina Supreme Court suggests in *Mitchell* that the claim might then be permitted. Another alternative would be to assert both a defense and a counterclaim in the first action. At the time this suit was adjudicated, South Carolina had no compulsory counterclaim rule. (At the time, The Conformity Act would have required the federal court to look to state law to decide whether counterclaims are compulsory.) Should that fact be relevant to the analysis here?

Mitchell was decided in 1932, when claim preclusion doctrine was more limited than is generally true today. Thus, the South Carolina Supreme Court bases its decision in part on the conclusion that "[t]he transaction out of which the case at bar arises is *the same transaction* that Mitchell pleaded as a defense in the Federal suit" (emphasis added). It seems clear from the rest of the court's analysis that this "same transaction" standard is narrower than the test most courts would use today in applying ordinary claim preclusion. (Recall the discussion of this issue in *Herendeen* and the notes following.) On the other hand, South Carolina had no compulsory counterclaim rule at the time, and Mitchell argued that no rights established in the first action would be impaired by permitting the second: He was neither seeking a double recovery nor making any factual claims that would be inconsistent with the earlier judgment. Would it be enough to say that permitting the second action in this *kind* of situation would risk impairing judgments, since double recovery and inconsistent factual determinations might be difficult to guard against? As is not surprising given the time at which it was writing, the South Carolina Supreme Court frames the issue differently, relying instead on a more formal argument about not splitting claims.

6. "*Saving and Splitting Defenses.*" Can you think of legitimate reasons for allowing a defendant to "save" a defense altogether—i.e., not assert a defense to plaintiff's claim and instead bring a separate action against plaintiff? In comment a to Restatement (Second) of Judgments §22, the following rationale is offered for giving a defendant the option of asserting or not asserting a defense: "The defendant should not be required to assert his claim in the forum or the proceeding chosen by the plaintiff but should be allowed to bring suit at a time and place of his own selection."

Consider, for example, a doctor who brings an action against a patient for an unpaid bill for medical services rendered. The forum has no compulsory counterclaim rule. Defendant offers no defense on the merits, and a judgment is given in the doctor's favor. The patient then attempts to sue the doctor for malpractice on the grounds that the medical services originally sued upon by the doctor were negligent and caused harm. (For present purposes, assume that issue preclusion would create no obstacle here.) Under the Restatement (Second) approach, is the patient free to bring the action? If so, could the patient also seek restitution of the amount for the doctor's bill paid pursuant to the earlier judgment? Presumably not, since doing so would "nullify the initial judgment or . . . impair rights established in the initial action." §22(2)(b).

Does the rationale offered by the Restatement (Second) also justify allowing the defendant to "split the defense," using it first as a shield and then as a sword—the result that *Mitchell* prohibited? Imagine that the doctor brings suit to recover payment for services rendered, and the patient offers a defense that the services were done negligently and carelessly. Assume that the defense is successful and the doctor loses. Under the Restatement (Second), would the patient then be able to bring a second action for malpractice and recover additional damages? Is that a sound result? If so, could the patient also use issue preclusion in his favor, asserting the findings from the first judgment to establish the doctor's negligence in the malpractice action? Would that be fair to the doctor? Did the doctor have sufficient incentive to litigate those issues vigorously in the first suit, where only unpaid fees were at stake?

7. *Nullifying a Prior Judgment.* In what circumstances can the failure to interpose a counterclaim in the earlier action bar the assertion of the claim in a second action because it would nullify the judgment in the first proceeding? In *Martino v. McDonald's System, Inc.*, 598 F.2d 1079 (7th Cir. 1979), the court barred plaintiff Martino's antitrust action, which was based on a noncompete clause in the parties' contract, on the basis of a consent judgment that was entered in an earlier suit brought by defendant McDonald's System to enforce the noncompete clause. The compulsory counterclaim rule did not apply because Martino had never filed a responsive pleading in the earlier action. *See* Fed. R. Civ. P. 13(a) ("A *pleading* must state as a counterclaim any claim that—at the time of its service—the *pleader* has against an opposing party if . . .") (emphasis added). Nonetheless, the court held that the action was barred by "long-standing principles of . . . 'common law compulsory counterclaims.'" *Id.* at 1083. Although the general rule is that a defendant who has failed to plead certain facts as a defense or counterclaim will not be precluded from relying on those facts in a subsequent action against the plaintiff, an exception exists where the subsequent action would "nullify [the] rights established by the prior action." *Id.* at 1085.

4. "On the Merits"

Not all judicial dispositions have preclusive effect. Only those cases finally disposed of "on the merits" will foreclose relitigation of the claim. Thus, for example, if a court dismisses a claim for lack of personal jurisdiction, the dismissal will not be "with prejudice" to the party refiling the claim in another jurisdiction (although as a matter of issue preclusion, plaintiff may be estopped from relitigating the question of personal jurisdiction in another court in the same forum). The meaning of "on the merits" can be a matter of considerable dispute.

Costello v. United States

365 U.S. 265 (1961)

MR. JUSTICE BRENNAN delivered the opinion of the Court.

The petitioner became a naturalized citizen on September 10, 1925. The District Court for the Southern District of New York revoked his citizenship on March 9, 1959, in this proceeding brought by the Government under §340(a) of the Immigration and Nationality Act of 1952. That Act authorizes revocation of naturalized citizenship "on the ground that such order and certificate of naturalization were procured by concealment of a material fact or by willful misrepresentation. . . ."[1] The petitioner, in 1925, swore in his Preliminary Form for Naturalization, and when he appeared before a Naturalization Examiner, that his occupation was "real estate." The District Court found that this was "willful misrepresentation and fraud" and that "his true occupation was bootlegging," 171 F. Supp. 10, 16. The Court of Appeals for the Second Circuit affirmed, 275 F.2d 355. We granted certiorari. 362 U.S. 973.

An earlier denaturalization complaint brought under 8 U.S.C. (1946 ed.) §738(a), the predecessor of §340(a), was dismissed on the ground that wiretapping may have infected both the Government's affidavit of good cause and its evidence. *United States v. Costello*, 145 F. Supp. 892. The Court of Appeals for the Second Circuit reversed on the ground that the Government should have been afforded an opportunity to show that its evidence either was untainted or was admissible in any event. 247 F.2d 384. We granted certiorari and reversed, 356 U.S. 256, on a ground not considered below, namely, that the affidavit of good cause, which is a prerequisite to the initiation of denaturalization proceedings under §340(a), *United States v. Zucca*, 351 U.S. 91, was not filed with the complaint. On remand the District Court declined to enter an order of dismissal "without prejudice" and entered an order which did not specify whether the dismissal was with or without prejudice.

---

1. The statute, 66 Stat. 260, as amended, 68 Stat. 1232; 8 U.S.C. §1451, reads in pertinent part as follows:

(a) *Concealment of material evidence; refusal to testify.* "It shall be the duty of the United States attorneys for the respective districts, upon affidavit showing good cause therefor, to institute proceedings in any court specified in subsection (a) of section 1421 of this title in the judicial district in which the naturalized citizen may reside at the time of bringing suit, for the purpose of revoking and setting aside the order admitting such person to citizenship and canceling the certificate of naturalization on the ground that such order and certificate of naturalization were procured by concealment of a material fact or by willful misrepresentation, and such revocation and setting aside of the order admitting such person to citizenship and such canceling of certificate of naturalization shall be effective as of the original date of the order and certificate, respectively: . . ."

The Government did not appeal from that order but brought this new proceeding under §340(a) by affidavit of good cause and complaint filed on May 1, 1958. . . .

It is the petitioner's contention that the order dismissing the earlier complaint must be construed to be with prejudice because it did not specify that it was without prejudice, and the ground of dismissal was not within one of the exceptions under Rule 41(b) of the Federal Rules of Civil Procedure. That Rule provides:

> For failure of the plaintiff to prosecute or to comply with these rules or any order of court, a defendant may move for dismissal of an action or of any claim against him. After the plaintiff has completed the presentation of his evidence, the defendant, without waiving his right to offer evidence in the event the motion is not granted, may move for a dismissal on the ground that upon the facts and the law the plaintiff has shown no right to relief. . . . Unless the court in its order for dismissal otherwise specifies, a dismissal under this subdivision and any dismissal not provided for in this rule, other than a dismissal for lack of jurisdiction or for improper venue, operates as an adjudication upon the merits.[*]

We hold that a dismissal for failure to file the affidavit of good cause is a dismissal "for lack of jurisdiction," within the meaning of the exception under Rule 41(b). In arguing contra, the petitioner relies on cases which hold that a judgment of denaturalization resulting from a proceeding in which the affidavit of good cause was not filed is not open to collateral attack on that ground. *Title v. United States*, 263 F.2d 28; *United States v. Failla*, 164 F. Supp. 307. We think that petitioner misconceives the scope of this exception from the dismissals under Rule 41(b) which operate as adjudications on the merits unless the court specifies otherwise. It is too narrow a reading of the exception to relate the concept of jurisdiction embodied there to the fundamental jurisdictional defects which render a judgment void and subject to collateral attack, such as lack of jurisdiction over the person or subject matter. We regard the exception as encompassing those dismissals which are based on a plaintiff's failure to comply with a precondition requisite to the Court's going forward to determine the merits of his substantive claim. Failure to file the affidavit of good cause in a denaturalization proceeding falls within this category. *United States v. Zucca, supra; Costello v. United States*, 356 U.S. 256.

At common law dismissal on a ground not going to the merits was not ordinarily a bar to a subsequent action on the same claim. In *Haldeman v. United States*, 91 U.S. 584, 585–586, which concerned a voluntary nonsuit, this Court said, "there must be at least one decision on a right between the parties before there can be said to be a termination of the controversy, and before a judgment can avail as a bar to a subsequent suit. . . . There must have been a right adjudicated or released in the first suit to make it a bar, and this fact must appear affirmatively." A similar view applied to many dismissals on the motion of a defendant. In *Hughes v. United States*, 4 Wall. 232, 237, it was said: "In order that a judgment may constitute a bar to another suit, it must be rendered in a proceeding between the same parties or their

---

[*] The wording and internal numbering of Rule 41 have been changed by the 2007 stylistic revisions to the Federal Rules of Civil Procedure. — Eds.

privies, and the point of controversy must be the same in both cases, and must be determined on its merits. If the first suit was dismissed for defect of pleadings, or parties, or a misconception of the form of proceeding, or the want of jurisdiction, or was disposed of on any ground which did not go to the merits of the action, the judgment rendered will prove no bar to another suit." . . .

We do not discern in Rule 41(b) a purpose to change this common-law principle with respect to dismissals in which the merits could not be reached for failure of the plaintiff to satisfy a precondition. All of the dismissals enumerated in Rule 41(b) which operate as adjudications on the merits—failure of the plaintiff to prosecute, or to comply with the Rules of Civil Procedure, or to comply with an order of the Court, or to present evidence showing a right to the relief on the facts and the law—primarily involve situations in which the defendant must incur the inconvenience of preparing to meet the merits because there is no initial bar to the Court's reaching them. It is therefore logical that a dismissal on one of these grounds should, unless the Court otherwise specifies, bar a subsequent action. In defining the situations where dismissals "not provided for in this rule" also operate as adjudications on the merits, and are not to be deemed jurisdictional, it seems reasonable to confine them to those situations where the policy behind the enumerated grounds is equally applicable. Thus a *sua sponte* dismissal by the Court for failure of the plaintiff to comply with an order of the Court should be governed by the same policy. Although a *sua sponte* dismissal is not an enumerated ground, here too the defendant has been put to the trouble of preparing his defense because there was no initial bar to the Court's reaching the merits. . . .

In contrast, the failure of the Government to file the affidavit of good cause in a denaturalization proceeding does not present a situation calling for the application of the policy making dismissals operative as adjudications on the merits. The defendant is not put to the necessity of preparing a defense because the failure of the Government to file the affidavit with the complaint requires the dismissal of the proceeding. Nothing in the term "jurisdiction" requires giving it the limited meaning that the petitioner would ascribe to it. Among the terms of art in the law, "jurisdiction" can hardly be said to have a fixed content. It has been applied to characterize other prerequisites of adjudication which will not be re-examined in subsequent proceedings and must be brought into controversy in the original action if a defendant is to litigate them at all. *See, e.g., Des Moines Navigation & R. Co. v. Iowa Homestead Co.*, 123 U.S. 552 (diversity of citizenship); *In re Sawyer*, 124 U.S. 200, 220–221 (jurisdictional amount). See generally *Noble v. Union River Logging R. Co.*, 147 U.S. 165, 173–174. . . . We therefore hold that the Government was not barred from instituting the present proceeding.

Affirmed.

[Dissents omitted.]

NOTES AND QUESTIONS

1. *Federal Rule 41(b).* Most questions in federal practice concerning whether the same claim may be refiled following a dismissal require attention to Rule 41(b) of the Federal Rules of Civil Procedure, quoted in the opinion of the Court. The majority opinion undercut the *res judicata* impact of the first dismissal in *Costello* by finding that the government's failure to file an affidavit for good cause fell within

the express exception to Rule 41(b) for dismissals "for lack of jurisdiction" and so was not an adjudication "on the merits." Under the Rule, the default designation for a judgment in an involuntary dismissal is that the dismissal will be with prejudice unless an express exception applies or the court provides otherwise in the order of dismissal. In what sense was the defect in the government's affidavit "jurisdictional"? In what way was the defect distinguishable from a deficiency in the pleading that results in a dismissal for failure to state a claim pursuant to Rule 12(b)(6)?

Rule 41(b) treats a dismissal for failure to comply with the Rules or a court order as a dismissal *with prejudice,* but the case law is not always consistent. *Compare Humphreys v. General Business Services, Inc.,* 1991 WL 186673 (D.N.J. 1991) (dismissal by federal court in Maryland for failure to post nonresident bond as required by court order was "on the merits") *and Nagle v. Lee,* 807 F.2d 435, 442–443 (5th Cir. 1987) (dismissal for failure to prosecute is treated as "on the merits" under Rule 41(b)) *with Saylor v. Lindsley,* 391 F.2d 965 (2d Cir. 1968) (dismissal "with prejudice" of prior derivative action for failure to post bond was not "on the merits" because dismissal occurred at the outset of the proceedings and defendant was not required to respond on the merits) *and In re Daily,* 124 B.R. 325 (D. Haw. 1991) (dismissal of bankruptcy complaint for failure to prosecute initial action before same court was not "on the merits" where lawyer was at fault in first action, plaintiff did not willfully delay, and defendant would suffer no prejudice). Note that a district court always has the option of specifying whether or not its dismissal is "on the merits" rather than relying upon Rule 41(b)'s default provision.

It has been suggested that one criterion often used by the court is whether the dismissal is considered a penalty. *See* 18A C. Wright et al., Federal Practice and Procedure §4440 (3d ed. 2018). Is it fair to consider a dismissal on the merits "punitive" and hence "jurisdictional" under Rule 41(b) when it results from a failure to comply with a Federal Rule of Civil Procedure but not when it results from a failure to comply with a statutory requirement, as in *Costello?* Note in this connection the Supreme Court's holding in *Bowles v. Russell,* 531 U.S. 205 (2007), which involved the effect of a party's failure to meet a deadline when seeking appellate review of a district court ruling. In that context, the Court held that such time limitations are "jurisdictional" (and hence not subject to equitable modification by the courts) when contained in a federal statute, even though a similar time limitation might not be "jurisdictional" if contained in a federal rule. In other words, *Bowles* treated a failure to comply with a statutory requirement as a more serious "jurisdictional" problem than a failure to comply with a federal rule. It seems fair to say that the Supreme Court is not always consistent in the way that it deploys the term "jurisdictional" to describe different aspects of federal practice.

2. In *Semtek International Inc. v. Lockheed Martin Corp.,* 531 U.S. 497 (2001), the Supreme Court further clarified the effect of designating a dismissal as "with prejudice" under Rule 41(b). Such a designation does not automatically mean that a dismissal in federal district court attaches claim preclusive effect to the judgment. Rather, a dismissal "with prejudice" under Rule 41(b) merely bars the renewal or refiling of claims in the same federal court from which the case has just been dismissed—as, for example, if a party sought to amend or "fix" the complaint and try again with the same judge who has just ordered the dismissal. While a dismissal "with prejudice" may contribute to a finding that the claims in the first lawsuit are

barred in a subsequent proceeding, the Rule does not require that result of its own force. A dismissal with prejudice, the *Semtek* Court held, "is undoubtedly a necessary condition, but it is not a sufficient one, for claim-preclusive effect in other courts." We examine the *Semtek* decision at length at the end of this chapter.

3. *Curing Defects in Jurisdictional Dismissals. Compare Dozier v. Ford Motor Co.*, 702 F.2d 1189 (D.C. Cir. 1983) *with Costello.* Plaintiff had previously brought a breach of warranty claim against defendant in the federal district court in Virginia, alleging damages of $7,000 compensatory and $1 million punitive. After determining that punitive damages were unavailable in a breach of warranty case, the court dismissed "without prejudice" for lack of jurisdictional amount and absence of diversity. The court of appeals affirmed. After moving to a state diverse from defendant, plaintiff refiled in federal court in the District of Columbia, this time alleging compensatory damages in excess of the jurisdictional amount. Judge (later Justice) Scalia, writing for the court of appeals, held that plaintiff's claim in federal court was barred by *res judicata* for lack of adequate jurisdictional amount. Without mentioning Rule 41(b), the court concluded that the dismissal "without prejudice" simply permitted plaintiff to refile in state court; it did not authorize relitigation of whether there was federal jurisdiction. The court distinguished *Costello* because the defect there was "curable":

> Appellant portrays his inadequate damage claim in the earlier suit as a mere pleading deficiency which falls within the "curable defect" exception to the *res judicata* effect of jurisdictional dismissals. It does not qualify. The "curable defect" exception applies where a "precondition requisite" to the court's proceeding with the original suit was not alleged or proven, and is supplied in the second suit — for example, the Government's filing of an affidavit of good cause in a denaturalization proceeding, *Costello v. United States*, 365 U.S. 265, 284–88 (1961), proper service of process, *Martin v. Dep't of Mental Hygiene*, 588 F.2d 371, 373 n.3 (2d Cir. 1978), or residency adequate to invoke diversity jurisdiction, see *Napper v. Anderson*, 500 F.2d 634, 637 (5th Cir. 1974), *cert. denied*, 423 U.S. 837 (1975). What all these cases have in common is that the jurisdictional deficiency could be remedied by *occurrences subsequent to the original dismissal.* The deficiency pertained to a fact (filing of affidavit, service of process or present residence) separate and apart from the past and completed transactions that constituted the cause of action. It may be desirable (though not unquestionably so) to give a plaintiff multiple chances to comply with these post-transactional requirements; but it is quite another matter to permit him to change his sworn recitation of past facts. Some very old cases suggest that any "defect in pleading" may be remedied. For example in *Smith v. McNeal*, 109 U.S. 426, 431 (1883), the Supreme Court held that dismissal for failure to allege the jurisdictional prerequisite of disputed title was no bar to a subsequent suit which remedied that "defect in pleading." We regard such cases as superseded, expressing a rule that made sense only in a system where liberal amendment of pleading was not permitted.

Id. at 1192–1193.

Judge Wald, in dissent, saw the two cases as indistinguishable:

More troubling is the majority's view that a new suit should be permitted only when the original jurisdictional defect "could be remedied by *occurrences subsequent to the original dismissal.*" . . . The majority views the total failure to file an affidavit of good cause in *Costello* as such a defect, but does not view the amount in controversy defect at issue here as such. I do not see the policy reasons for distinguishing between *Costello* and *Dozier* on this basis. In both *Dozier* and *Costello,* the complainant could have done it right the first time around and did not. In *Costello,* the government did not file an affidavit of good cause at all, while in *Dozier* the plaintiff filed a manifestly defective complaint. The policy rationale for not permitting a second suit (avoiding nuisance to the defendant) applies in both cases with equal force. Either can be defended by simply asserting the defect, with no need to prepare a defense on the merits. The policy rationale for permitting a second suit (giving an incompetent complainant a full chance to have his day in court) also applies to both cases equally. There seems no reason why a total bumbler should be permitted to refile while a partial bumbler should not.

Id. at 1199 (Wald, J., dissenting).

Does Judge Scalia or Judge Wald have the better of the argument? Would the case have come out differently had plaintiff failed to allege the amount of damages altogether in the first action? *See Mann v. Merrill Lynch, Pierce, Fenner & Smith, Inc.,* 488 F.2d 75 (5th Cir. 1973) (permitting refiling of case dismissed for failure to allege citizenship of parties). If, as Judge Scalia suggests, the distinction between *Costello* and *Dozier* is that Dozier "change[d] his sworn recitation of past facts," shouldn't Dozier have been given the opportunity to explain the apparent inconsistency? Why didn't the court simply treat the prior pleading as evidence that the second pleading was not "in good faith"?

Given the court's conclusion that plaintiff would not be barred from refiling in state court, wouldn't it have been conceptually cleaner for the court to treat the case as a matter of issue preclusion rather than claim preclusion? Would the issue have been considered "actually litigated" and "necessarily decided" for issue preclusion purposes? One federal district court has issued a collateral estoppel ruling along these lines. In *Philips Domestic Appliances and Personal Care v. Salton, Inc.,* 2004 WL 417197 (N.D. Ill., Feb. 2, 2004), the defendant claimed that a ruling in a prior proceeding that a certain party was "indispensable" under Rule 19 (which now uses the term "required") had collateral estoppel effect on a subsequent lawsuit in which the same plaintiff was trying to bring the same parties before the court once again. The earlier suit had been dismissed because that "indispensable" party could not be joined—a type of dismissal that Rule 41(b) treats as "without prejudice." Nonetheless, the Court found that issue preclusion bound the parties to the earlier determination of the issue. On appeal, the Seventh Circuit found that the dismissal of the earlier suit was erroneous, which mooted the preclusion issue. *Salton, Inc. v. Philips Domestic Appliances and Personal Care,* 391 F.3d 871, 879-881 (7th Cir. 2004).

4. *"On the Merits"?* Use of the term "on the merits" may itself be somewhat misleading. Default judgments (in favor of plaintiffs) merge plaintiffs' claims and may bar defendants from litigating an independent action after failing to raise

a defense, notwithstanding the fact that the merits of the litigation are never addressed. Dismissals for violations of court orders or for want of prosecution also carry preclusive effect even though the underlying merits of the dispute are not the basis of the dismissal. Thus, it is probably more fruitful to think generally about the kinds of judgments that should carry preclusive weight or be rendered "with prejudice" rather than to inquire whether they are "on the merits."

Obviously, a judgment based on a trial that goes to the substantive merits of the claims carries preclusive weight. So, too, do judgments based on motions for summary judgments and directed verdicts, which decide that the evidence can only be understood to require a judgment for one of the parties, thus rendering a full trial unnecessary.

Judicial decisions based on the fact that a party has chosen the wrong forum (lack of jurisdiction or venue) or has misjoined or failed to join parties do not usually earn preclusive effect. What characteristics about these determinations justify allowing a litigant the opportunity to bring a second action?

5. *Motions to Dismiss for Failure to State a Claim.* What is the preclusive effect of a dismissal based on a defendant's motion to dismiss for failure to state a claim under Fed. R. Civ. P. 12(b)(6)? The federal courts—based on a reading of Fed. R. Civ. P. 41(b)—have consistently held that a Rule 12(b)(6) dismissal precludes a second action arising out of the same transaction, unless the court otherwise specifies. *See, e.g., Isaac v. Schwartz*, 706 F.2d 15 (1st Cir. 1983); *Weston Funding Corp. v. Lafayette Towers, Inc.*, 550 F.2d 710 (2d Cir. 1977); *Rinehart v. Locke*, 454 F.2d 313 (7th Cir. 1971). *See also* Restatement (Second) of Judgments §19, comment d (1982). *But see Briggs v. Bramley*, 177 F. Supp. 599 (D. Or. 1959).

Consider this treatment of Rule 12(b)(6) dismissals in light of the Supreme Court's holdings in *Bell Atlantic Corp. v. Twombly*, 550 U.S. 544 (2007) and *Ashcroft v. Iqbal*, 556 U.S. 662 (2009). *Twombly* and *Iqbal* rejected the liberal approach to pleading that the Court had followed under the *Conley* standard (*see Conley v. Gibson*, 355 U.S. 41, 45–46 (1957)) under which a pleading should be held sufficient unless "it appears beyond doubt that the plaintiff can prove no set of facts in support of his claim which would entitle him to relief," replacing it with a requirement that the plaintiff allege sufficient facts to establish a context that makes the claim for relief plausible. This newly articulated plausibility standard invites the district court to engage much more actively in policing the inferences to be drawn from factual allegations than was true under the *Conley* standard, requiring lower federal courts to rely upon their "judicial experience and common sense" in assessing the plausibility of complaints that rely in part upon conclusory allegations. *Iqbal*, 556 U.S. at 679. If a plaintiff has her complaint dismissed under the plausibility standard and it later becomes clear that the dismissal was unwarranted (because, for example, the plaintiff is able to get her hands on sufficient facts to allege a plausible complaint), is it fair for the dismissal to be preclusive?

6. *Statutes of Limitations.* As we saw in our discussion of *Sun Oil v. Wortman*, *supra*, some states treat a dismissal on statute of limitations grounds as "procedural" in nature, relating only to the willingness of the forum to entertain a stale cause of action, while others treat the dismissal as reflecting a "substantive" limitation on the extent of the rights granted to a party by state law. How might such a designation affect the treatment of a statute of limitations dismissal for preclusion purposes? Is a "procedural" statute of limitations dismissal similar to a dismissal on *forum non conveniens* grounds, such that a litigant should be able to refile in another forum

that is willing to hear the claim? How should such dismissals be treated under Rule 41(b)? These issues implicate the operation of judgments across jurisdictions (or "inter-jurisdictional preclusion"), which we take up later in the chapter.

7. *The Requirement of a "Final" Judgment.* A judgment is considered "final" for purposes of *res judicata* upon rendition of judgment by the trial court. Pendency of an appeal or motion for reconsideration does not delay or suspend the *res judicata* effect of a judgment. Restatement (Second) of Judgments §13, comment f (1982). That rule creates the possibility that a judgment can have preclusive effect, resulting in a dismissal of a second lawsuit, and then that first judgment can be subsequently reversed on appeal. In such a case, the party who was subject to claim or issue preclusion is normally given relief from the second judgment, either by way of appeal or by a separate suit for "restitution." *Id.* §16.

8. *Voluntary Dismissals under Rule 41(a).* When a plaintiff voluntarily seeks to have the case dismissed, Rule 41(a) governs. Pursuant to that provision, the plaintiff can obtain a dismissal without approval of the court by filing a *notice of dismissal,* but only if the opposing party has filed neither an answer nor a motion for summary judgment. If the case has progressed far enough and defendant has taken one of those steps, voluntary dismissal by plaintiff requires either the stipulation of all parties or an order of the court. In the latter circumstance, issuance of an order of dismissal is in the discretion of the district court taking into account any prejudice the defendant will suffer, whether the plaintiff proceeded diligently, and whether dismissal will impose hardship and expense, for example if the lawsuit has advanced to a late stage. *See Kwan v. Schlein,* 634 F.3d 224, 230–231 (2d Cir. 2011). Voluntary dismissals may issue either with or without prejudice. When the parties agree to a stipulated dismissal, they will often specify that the dismissal is with prejudice. When a plaintiff seeks a voluntary dismissal by leave of court, the Rule gives the judge discretion to determine whether the dismissal is with or without prejudice. And even when a plaintiff takes a *nonsuit*—an early-stage voluntary dismissal that does not require leave of court or the consent of other parties, which typically issues without prejudice—the Rule requires the dismissal to be with prejudice when plaintiff has already secured dismissal of an earlier lawsuit that asserted the same claim. *See* Rule 41(a)(1)(B). When a dismissal issues with prejudice, a subsequent suit on the same claim will ordinarily be precluded, whether in the same court or any other court. When a dismissal issues without prejudice, a subsequent suit on the same claim will ordinarily not be precluded. In both situations, it is the applicable preclusion law and not the Rule itself that dictates that result. *See Semtek,* 531 U.S. at 505–506. Note also that the Rule imposes some limits on voluntary dismissal of suits in which the defendant has asserted a counterclaim. *See* Rule 41(a)(1)(B); 41(a)(2).

B.   COLLATERAL ESTOPPEL/ISSUE PRECLUSION

1.   *Traditional Applications*

Even if a subsequent claim is not barred by claim preclusion—either because the claim is considered distinct from the first proceeding, or because the parties are not the same—an issue adjudicated in the first proceeding may bind a party in subsequent litigation if the same issue arises in the later case. For example, suppose Wife obtains a contested annulment of her marriage from Husband. Subsequently, Wife dies and Husband sues her estate for the percentage of the estate to which a spouse is entitled. Husband will be collaterally estopped (issue precluded) by the annulment proceeding from asserting that he had a valid marriage and remained the legal spouse of the deceased. Husband already had an opportunity to establish that his marriage was valid, and he was unsuccessful. He will be bound to that earlier determination and will not be afforded a second chance.

Little v. Blue Goose Motor Coach Co.

178 N.E. 496 (Ill. 1931)

PER CURIAM:

Plaintiff in error procured a judgment in the city court of East St. Louis against defendant in error in the sum of $5,000 for the death of her husband, Robert M. Little. The Appellate Court reversed the judgment without remanding and with a finding of fact. The cause is here on writ of certiorari.

The declaration consists of two counts. The first is a general charge of negligence, and the second charges that the defendant in error willfully operated its bus, causing injury to the deceased. At the close of plaintiff in error's evidence defendant in error moved to instruct the jury to find defendant not guilty. This motion was denied.

It appears from the undisputed evidence that Dr. Robert M. Little, the deceased, while driving his automobile in the city of East St. Louis collided with a passenger bus owned and operated by defendant in error, at the intersection of Ridge avenue and Twenty-seventh street, in that city. Defendant in error sued Dr. Little before a justice of the peace for damage to its bus caused by that collision. Evidence was heard and a judgment entered in favor of defendant in error against Dr. Little for $139.35. . . . During the pendency of the case before the justice of the peace Dr. Little filed a suit in the city court of East St. Louis to recover damages for personal injuries alleged to have been suffered by him in the collision. Some months later a trial was had. . . . [Dr. Little died prior to the jury verdict, and his widow was substituted as the plaintiff.] Defendant in error filed a special plea . . . setting out the judgment in the justice of the peace court against Dr. Little, alleging that the issue there tried was as to his negligence and that of the driver of the bus, and that that issue was by the judgment of the justice of the peace settled and could not be raised in the present suit. . . .

[The court rejected the special plea and awarded judgment to plaintiff for $5,000.] On appeal from this judgment to the Appellate Court that court reversed the same with the following finding of fact: "The court finds that appellant sued Dr. Robert M. Little, appellee's estate, before a justice of the peace for damages to its bus in the collision which occurred on November 1, 1925, and recovered a judgment therefore in the sum of $139.35, that in the rendition of said judgment it was necessarily determined that the collision and damages occasioned to the bus was due to the negligence of Dr. Little, and that immediately prior to his death he could not have maintained an action for personal injuries growing out of the same collision."

The first question arises on the ruling of the Appellate Court invoking against the claim of plaintiff in error the doctrine of estoppel by verdict. It is argued on behalf of plaintiff in error that where a former adjudication is relied on as a bar to a subsequent action it is essential that there be identity both of the subject matter and of the parties, and that in the instant case the subject matter is not the same, as this is the action for death by wrongful act for the benefit of the widow and next of kin, while the former suit was a claim for damages for injury to personal property. The issue on which this case is bottomed was the issue of fact which lay at the base of the judgment recovered before the justice of the peace. The allegation of the special plea is that the issue there raised was one of negligence on the part of Dr. Little on one hand and the defendant in error on the other, and that issue having been determined against Dr. Little, the fact is forever settled between these parties or their privies. Estoppel by verdict arises when a material fact in any litigation has been determined in a former suit between the same parties or between parties with whom the parties to the subsequent suit are in privity, where the fact was also material to the issue. The Appellate Court found as a matter of fact that the issue tried before the justice of the peace was an issue of negligence and was the same issue, arising on the same facts as those relied upon in the action for the wrongful death of Dr. Little and that the issue of negligence was necessarily determined in the suit by the defendant in error against Dr. Little. That question of fact was tried before the city court in this case, and on the evidence there adduced the Appellate Court made its finding of fact. That issue of fact therefore is not open here, and we are to proceed to further consideration of the cause under the established fact that the issue of negligence, at least under the first count of the declaration, is the same issue tried before the justice of the peace. . . .

[T]he judgment of the justice of the peace became a final determination of that issue between the parties, and is conclusive not only upon the immediate parties to that suit but also upon all persons in privity with them, and cannot be litigated again between the parties to that case or their privies in any subsequent action in the same or other court where that question arises, whether upon the same or a different cause of action or whatever may have been the nature or purpose of the action in which the judgment was rendered or of that in which the estoppel is set up. . . . It follows that Dr. Little could not during his lifetime maintain the action filed by him against the defendant in error, and since plaintiff in error's right to recover damages under the Injuries act depends upon Dr. Little's right, during his lifetime, to recover damages for injuries arising out of the same collision, plaintiff in error cannot recover here. In a suit under the Injuries act the cause of action is the wrongful act and not merely the death itself. . . . Plaintiff in error therefore was not entitled to recover under the first count of her declaration, and the Appellate Court did not err in so holding.

It is contended, however, that as the second count of the declaration charges wanton and willful negligence on the part of defendant in error, contributory negligence on the part of Dr. Little is not a defense, and that the judgment of the city court was therefore right. Contributory negligence is not a defense to willful and wanton conduct, but it does not follow that the judgment of the city court was right because of that fact. In all cases charging willful and wanton negligence it is necessary to make proof of such negligence, and where there is no such proof no recovery under such charge can be had. The finding of the Appellate Court that the collision was caused by the negligence of Dr. Little necessarily was a finding of fact on the willful negligence count as well as the general negligence count. Thus the rule that contributory negligence on the part of the plaintiff is not a defense to a charge of willful negligence does not apply. Whether Dr. Little or the bus driver was responsible for the accident was, as we have seen, settled. The judgment for $139.35 necessarily decided that the bus driver was not guilty of willful negligence. . . .

From what we have said it is clear that the Appellate Court was right in reversing the judgment without remanding the case, and its judgment will be affirmed.

Judgment affirmed.

NOTES AND QUESTIONS

1. *Relationship of Issue Preclusion to Claim/Defense Preclusion.* As is evident from the *Blue Goose* case, the question of issue preclusion arises only after it is assumed or determined that other preclusion doctrines do not bar the suit entirely. For example, in *Blue Goose*, the defendant who lost in the original negligence action was apparently not barred by "defense preclusion" or by a compulsory counterclaim rule from bringing his own action for negligence against the bus company—the plaintiff in the first action. However, the doctrine of issue preclusion in this case provided a second layer of protection against having an issue common to both suits litigated twice and possibly inconsistently. Does issue preclusion always reinforce claim preclusion in this manner? Does the availability of issue preclusion encourage a more lenient approach to claim/defense preclusion? Are there advantages in utilizing issue rather than claim/defense preclusion in the *Blue Goose*-type situation? Are there disadvantages? Reconsider these questions after reviewing the problems in Note 5 below.

2. *Requirements of Issue Preclusion.* The Restatement (Second) of Judgments §27 offers this formulation:

> When an issue of fact or law is actually litigated and determined by a valid and final judgment, and the determination is essential to the judgment, the determination is conclusive in a subsequent action between the parties, whether on the same or a different claim.

In other words, the Restatement imposes the following requirements before issue preclusion may apply: (1) an issue must be actually litigated and determined in the first proceeding; (2) the first proceeding must produce a valid final judgment; (3) the issue must have been essential to that judgment; and (4) the "determination," or issue, must be the same in the second proceeding as it was in the first. Why do you think these limitations have been imposed? Do they operate to restrict the application of issue preclusion unduly?

3. *Dimensions of an "Issue."* Consider first the requirement that the issue must be the "same issue." Assume that in a first action for personal injuries, *P* alleges that *D* was negligent in driving at an excessive speed, and a judgment for *D* is given. In a second action, *P* alleges that *D* was negligent in failing to maintain the brakes of the car. Does the first judgment establish *D*'s lack of "negligence" generally, or does it only establish that *D* was not negligent in driving at an excessive speed? What factors are to be taken into account in determining the scope of an issue?

4. *"Actually Litigated."* What does it mean to "actually litigate" an issue? There is no dispute that when an issue is raised by the pleadings and is submitted for determination—whether on a motion or at trial—the issue is actually litigated. In

addition, a determination may be based on a complete failure of proof or a finding of insufficient proof. *See* Restatement (Second) of Judgments §27, comment d (1982). On the other hand, when a party fails to pursue an issue at trial altogether, stipulates to the existence of a fact, or suffers a default judgment, the matter will normally not be deemed to have been "actually litigated." *See In re McMillan*, 579 F.2d 289 (3d Cir. 1978) (default judgment has no collateral estoppel effect); *Jackson Jordan, Inc. v. Plasser American Corp.*, 747 F.2d 1567 (Fed. Cir. 1984) (findings based on stipulations cannot support collateral estoppel). *See generally* 18A C. Wright et al., Federal Practice and Procedure §4442–4443 (3d ed. 2018). Similarly, an issue is not "actually litigated" if a defendant fails to raise it as an affirmative defense, or if it is raised as an allegation by one party and admitted by the other without adducing evidence, or if it is admitted in response to a request for admission under Federal Rule 36. *See* Restatement (Second) of Judgments §27, comment e (1982).

If one side raises an issue in the pleadings and introduces evidence, may the other side choose to ignore the issue to avoid issue preclusion in a subsequent dispute?

5. *"Necessarily Decided" and "Essential to the Judgment."* Because multiple issues are often decided as part of any judgment, it becomes important to analyze which of the decided issues were also necessary to the judgment. Consider the hypotheticals below. In each example, you should consider the question of issue preclusion alone—assume that other doctrines like claim preclusion or compulsory counterclaim rules would not apply. You should also assume that contributory negligence operates as a complete defense to a negligence action. Finally, you should assume that the "same issue" is involved in each successive case. The point of these exercises is to isolate the different postures in which issues can arise in successive cases and work through the requirements of issue preclusion in each circumstance.

The term *general verdict* in these hypotheticals refers to a type of jury verdict that simply awards a verdict for one of the parties and does not spell out the reasons. The term *special verdict* refers to a verdict in which the jury makes specific findings of fact.

> **Hypothetical 1.** In a first action, Paula sues Dave for property damage, alleging negligence. Paula secures a judgment in her favor on a general verdict finding that Dave's negligence caused her property damage.
> **First Variation.** In a second action, Paula sues Dave for personal injuries, alleging negligence.
> **Second Variation.** In a second action, Dave sues Paula for personal injuries, alleging negligence.

Consider the first variation. If Paula sues Dave in a second action to recover for personal injuries caused by Dave's negligence, Dave should be precluded from relitigating the issue of his negligence, because any judgment for Paula would require that she establish the elements of her claim, including the issue of Dave's negligence. Dave's negligence was "necessarily decided" in the first action. What about the possibility that Paula, too, was negligent? If the absence of contributory negligence by Paula is an element of her case under the governing law—that is, if Paula has to allege in her complaint that she was not negligent in order to recover—then Paula's lack of negligence will also be given issue preclusive effect. It was "necessary to the judgment," because Paula had to establish it to prevail. However, if negligence by

Paula was a defense that Dave had to raise in the first action, then there will be issue preclusion only if Dave actually introduced and litigated the issue.

Now consider the second variation. This time, it is Dave who sues in the second action, claiming that Paula is liable in negligence for Dave's personal injuries. (This is like the *Blue Goose* case.) What result? The verdict in the first action necessarily established Dave's negligence. Therefore, in the second action, Dave should be precluded from relitigating the issue of his own negligence. Dave loses. With respect to Paula's negligence, if the issue was litigated in the first action (see the discussion above in the first variation), then Dave will also be estopped from relitigating that issue. Dave would then lose twice over—the issue preclusive effect of the first judgment holds that Paula was not negligent and that Dave was contributorily negligent.

> **Hypothetical 2.** In a first action, Paula sues Dave for property damage, alleging negligence. Dave secures a judgment in his favor on a general verdict finding no liability.
>> **First Variation.** In a second action, Paula sues Dave for personal injury, alleging negligence.
>> **Second Variation.** In a second action, Dave sues Paula for personal injury, alleging negligence.

In the first variation, will issue preclusion prevent Paula from recovering in her second action for personal injuries, after losing in her first suit for property damages? A general verdict in favor of Dave in the first action means that either Dave was not negligent or that Paula was contributorily negligent or both. In the first variation, *either* Paula's contributory negligence *or* Dave's lack of negligence in the first action (or both) will support a verdict for Dave in the second action. Issue preclusion should thus bar the suit. We know that, in reaching its general verdict of no liability in the first action, the jury necessarily decided a combination of issues that would preclude a finding of liability for Paula in the second action (no negligence for Dave, or contributory negligence by Paula, or both), and that suffices.

In the second variation, however, the result is different. In order for Dave to use issue preclusion to establish liability in the second action, he must show that Paula was negligent and that he was not negligent. But it is not clear which issue was established in the first action. Since a finding in Dave's favor on both issues is necessary to support a judgment in the second action, there is no issue preclusion, because it is impossible to tell from the general verdict whether both were actually decided in his favor.

> **Hypothetical 3.** In a first action, Paula sues Dave for personal injury, alleging negligence. Dave secures a judgment in his favor on a special verdict that specifies that (1) Dave was not negligent and (2) Paula was negligent. In a second action, Dave sues Paula for personal injuries, alleging negligence.

In this hypothetical, the first judgment in favor of Dave specifically established that Dave was not negligent and that Paula was negligent. *Either* of those findings, standing alone, was enough to support the judgment in favor of Dave in the first action. Together, they support that judgment twice over. Can you think of any reason why issue preclusion should *not* attach to these findings in a second action? The Restatement (Second) of Judgments §27, comment i, takes the position that where a judgment of a trial court is based on determinations of two issues, either of which standing independently would support the result, the judgment is not conclusive in a later action with respect to either issue. The concern is that a determination in the alternative may not have been rigorously considered and that if preclusive effect is given, a losing party may have additional incentive to appeal in order to avoid the application of preclusion on specific issues. This position was a reversal from the first Restatement of Judgments, which had extended preclusion to all independently sufficient issues. *See* Restatement (First) of Judgments §68, comment n (1942). Notwithstanding the updated position of the Restatement (Second) of Judgments, some courts continue to give issue preclusion to alternative holdings, each of which independently supported the judgment. *See* 18 C. Wright et al., Federal Practice and Procedure §4421 (3d ed. 2018) (describing changing treatment of this situation and continuing practice of some courts in applying preclusion to all independently sufficient issues). Notice also that the Second Restatement position stands in some tension with Hypothetical 2 above, where the black box of a general verdict can sometimes receive issue preclusive effect even when it could possibly encompass findings on two independently sufficient issues, as in the first variation in that hypothetical.

> **Hypothetical 4.** In a first action, Paula sues Dave for property damage, alleging negligence. Dave secures a judgment in his favor on a special verdict that Paula and Dave were both negligent.
>> **First Variation.** In a second action, Paula sues Dave for personal injury, alleging negligence.
>> **Second Variation.** In a second action, Dave sues Paula for personal injury, alleging negligence.

In the first variation, issue preclusion may prevent Paula's subsequent personal injury suit against Dave. Paula was the loser in the first lawsuit and could have appealed the finding that she was negligent, but she chose not to. Since she had the opportunity to pursue appellate review of the adverse finding, Paula had a full and fair opportunity to litigate the issue and can be bound by the result. In the second variation, Dave should not be precluded from asserting his negligence claim. Dave was the prevailing party in the first lawsuit—even though he had an issue decided against him, he secured a judgment of no liability. Dave therefore had no opportunity to appeal the issue of his negligence in the first proceeding (prevailing parties cannot appeal), so he arguably did not receive a full and fair opportunity to contest the issue. *See* Restatement (Second) of Judgments §28(1) (1982) (arguing that there should be no preclusion if "[t]he party against whom preclusion is sought could not, as a matter of law, have obtained review of the judgment in the initial action"). But Dave may be able to employ preclusion to bind Paula to the finding from the first lawsuit that she was negligent, since Paula could have appealed the finding against her. Note, however, that contributory negligence by Paula does not automatically equate with negligence to Dave. If Paula's contributory negligence in the first lawsuit was a failure to fasten her seatbelt, for example, then such a failure would not have caused Dave's injuries.

2. *Modern Applications*

Today, cases like *Blue Goose* and the problem sets above are often disposed of without raising any question of issue preclusion. Expanded applications of claim preclusion and compulsory counterclaim rules regularly prevent relitigation in successive disputes involving the same parties, rendering issue preclusion unnecessary. The case that follows is more typical of modern applications of issue preclusion.

Often, as in the next case, it is someone who was not a party to the first suit who seeks to invoke issue preclusion in a subsequent proceeding. Issue preclusion can only be used *against* someone who was a party to the first proceeding or otherwise bound by that judgment, but issue preclusion can sometimes be invoked *by* someone who had no role in the first lawsuit. The question of whether and when this *nonmutuality* of parties should be permitted is taken up in greater depth later in this chapter. For the moment, consider whether the requirements of issue preclusion discussed in *Blue Goose* offer sufficient protection when findings are transplanted from one context to another in these more modern settings.

Kaufman v. Eli Lilly & Co.

482 N.E.2d 63 (N.Y. 1985)

SIMONS, J.

This is one of 15 similar actions pending in the First Department seeking to recover from pharmaceutical companies for injuries allegedly sustained by the plaintiff daughters as a result of their mothers' ingestion of the drug diethylstilbestrol (DES) while pregnant. In 1977 the Assistant Administrative Justice designated the actions as "complex litigation cases" and assigned them to Justice Arnold Fraiman, directing him to handle all matters relating to them. The first of the 15 actions chosen to be tried was *Bichler v. Lilly & Co.* (55 NY2d 571) and the rest were held pending its disposition. The principal issue in this appeal is the collateral estoppel effect to be given to certain jury findings in that action.

After we sustained a jury verdict against Lilly in *Bichler*, plaintiff moved for partial summary judgment precluding Lilly from relitigating six issues decided by the *Bichler* jury, a severance of the action against Lilly and an immediate trial on the issues of DES ingestion, causation and damages. Lilly cross-moved to depose two of the jurors in the *Bichler* case to establish that their verdict was a compromise. The remaining defendants cross-moved for a severance in the event the court granted plaintiff's motion for collateral estoppel against Lilly. Special Term granted plaintiff's motion for partial summary judgment, denied Lilly's cross motion and granted the codefendants' motions for a severance. A divided Appellate Division affirmed and granted Lilly leave to appeal to this court on a certified question. We now modify the order of the Appellate Division and hold that Lilly may not be collaterally estopped from relitigating the jury's finding that it acted in concert with other drug manufacturers in testing and marketing DES for use in treating accidents of pregnancy. Our modification is required because the concerted action liability found in *Bichler* was based on an unresolved question of law which should not be given preclusive effect in this litigation.

I

In early 1954, plaintiff's mother, then pregnant with her, was prescribed DES to prevent a miscarriage. In July 1973, when plaintiff was 18 years old, it was discovered that plaintiff had cancer of the cervix. A radical hysterectomy was performed and, as a result, plaintiff will be unable to bear children. She instituted this action in 1976 alleging in her amended complaint that her mother's ingestion of DES while pregnant was the proximate cause of the injuries she sustained. Because she was unable to clearly identify the manufacturer of the DES her mother took, plaintiff joined as defendants nine of the approximately 147 pharmaceutical companies manufacturing and marketing DES for the prevention of miscarriages in pregnant women in 1954. She alleged that the defendants were liable to her, *inter alia*, on a concerted action theory of liability because they had "combined and conspired to obtain the approval for DES" without adequate testing.

The *Bichler* action involved a young woman who developed cervical and vaginal cancer at the age of 17. She brought suit against Eli Lilly & Company and others, alleging that her mother's ingestion of DES in 1953 while she was pregnant with her caused her injuries. Plaintiff's theory was that DES had been marketed without adequate testing to determine its safety. After the plaintiff was unsuccessful in attempting to prove that Lilly manufactured the DES prescribed for her mother, she submitted her case to the jury on a concerted action theory of liability. In addition to returning a general verdict for plaintiff, the *Bichler* jury answered seven special interrogatories in her favor as a basis for imposing liability on Lilly.[1] On appeal the Appellate Division and this court affirmed. The courts below gave collateral estoppel effect in this action to six of the *Bichler* jury's findings.[2]

Lilly raises three grounds for reversal of the order granting that relief. First, it contends that the decision in *Bichler* should not be given collateral estoppel effect

---

1. The interrogatories and the jury's answers to them were as follows:

(1) Was DES reasonably safe in the treatment of accidents of pregnancy when it was ingested by plaintiff's mother in 1953? (No)
(2) Was DES a proximate cause of plaintiff's cancer? (Yes)
(3) In 1953 when plaintiff's mother ingested DES, should the defendant, as a reasonably prudent drug manufacturer, have foreseen that DES might cause cancer in the offspring of pregnant women who took it? (Yes)
(4) Foreseeing that DES might cause cancer in the offspring of pregnant women who took it, would a reasonably prudent drug manufacturer test it on pregnant mice before marketing it? (Yes)
(5) If DES had been tested on pregnant mice, would the tests have shown that DES causes cancer in their offspring? (Yes)
(6) Would a reasonably prudent drug manufacturer have marketed DES for use in treating accidents of pregnancy at the time it was ingested by the plaintiff's mother if it had known that DES causes cancer in the offspring of pregnant mice? (No)
(7) Did defendant and the other drug manufacturers act in concert with each other in the testing and marketing of DES for use in treating accidents of pregnancy? (Yes). (See *Bichler v Lilly & Co.*, 55 NY2d 571, 587, n 10, *supra.*)

2. In her motion for summary judgment, plaintiff deleted the second *Bichler* interrogatory dealing with proximate cause. There is one other difference between the *Bichler* interrogatories and the issues on which plaintiff seeks partial summary judgment in this case. In the first, third and sixth *Bichler* interrogatories, the relevant time period was changed from 1953 (when Mrs. Bichler ingested DES) to 1953–1954 (when plaintiff's mother ingested the drug). Contrary to Lilly's claim, these variations in the years do not destroy the identity of issues. That plaintiff's mother taking the drug in 1954 could not mitigate the failure to test found wanting in 1953 or lessen the basis of knowledge upon which a duty to warn cause of action rests.

because (1) the cases do not raise identical issues, (2) there are indications that the *Bichler* verdict was based on jury compromise, (3) there are adjudications inconsistent with *Bichler* on each of the issues involved and (4) the *Bichler* decision is based on an unresolved and novel application of the law of concerted action not expressly adopted in New York. Second, Lilly asserts that if we find its proof of jury compromise in *Bichler* insufficient as it now exists to defeat the application of collateral estoppel, it should be allowed to depose two named jurors from the *Bichler* jury to demonstrate further its contention. Finally, Lilly urges that the lower court erred in severing plaintiff's action against it from actions against the remaining defendants.

II

The doctrine of collateral estoppel precludes a party from relitigating "an issue which has previously been decided against him in a proceeding in which he had a fair opportunity to fully litigate the point" (*Gilberg v. Barbieri*, 53 NY2d 285, 291; *see, Schwartz v Public Administrator*, 24 NY2d 65, 69). It is a doctrine intended to reduce litigation and conserve the resources of the court and litigants and it is based upon the general notion that it is not fair to permit a party to relitigate an issue that has already been decided against it. There are now but two requirements which must be satisfied before the doctrine is invoked. First, the identical issue necessarily must have been decided in the prior action and be decisive of the present action, and second, the party to be precluded from relitigating the issue must have had a full and fair opportunity to contest the prior determination (*Gilberg v. Barbieri, supra*, at p. 291; *Schwartz v. Public Administrator, supra*, at p. 71; *see, Koch v. Consolidated Edison Co.*, 62 NY2d 548, 554–555, *cert denied* 469 U.S. 1210. *Ryan v. New York Tel. Co.*, 62 NY2d 494, 500–501). The party seeking the benefit of collateral estoppel has the burden of demonstrating the identity of the issues in the present litigation and the prior determination, whereas the party attempting to defeat its application has the burden of establishing the absence of a full and fair opportunity to litigate the issue in the prior action (*see, Ryan v. New York Tel Co., supra*, at p. 501; *Schwartz v. Public Administrator, supra*, at p. 73). Applying these rules, we hold that collateral estoppel effect should be denied for the *Bichler* jury's finding on concerted action but that Lilly should be precluded from relitigating the five remaining issues relevant to this action and decided adversely to it in that trial (*see*, n 2, at p. 455, *supra*).

A

When *Bichler* was before this court Lilly challenged the concerted action theory of liability on two grounds. It claimed that it was not an appropriate theory of liability in DES litigation when the identity of the manufacturer is not established and that the court's charge on the theory was erroneous. Although both of these issues could have been raised by appropriate objection in the trial court, they were not, and because they were not, we did not pass on them. We held only that the evidence was legally sufficient to support the jury's findings of concerted action and foreseeability based on the charge given and that the trial court did not err in refusing Lilly's request to charge on its duty to warn (*see, Bichler v. Lilly & Co.*, 55 NY2d 571, 584–587, *supra*). We noted in a footnote that there were several theories upon which similar DES cases were proceeding or it had been suggested they might proceed but we expressed no view in *Bichler*, and, express none now, on which of the proposed theories—concerted action, alternative liability, enterprise liability or market share liability—if any, should be adopted in this or similar DES cases (*see, Bichler v. Lilly & Co., supra*, at p. 580, n 5). The question is still an open one in New York.

The point is significant because collateral estoppel effect will only be given to matters "actually litigated and determined" in a prior action (*see*, Restatement [Second] of Judgments §27, quoted in *Koch v. Consolidated Edison Co.*, 62 NY2d 548, 554, n 2; *see also, Ryan v. New York Tel. Co.*, 62 NY2d 494, *supra*). If the issue has not been litigated, there is no identity of issues between the present action and the prior determination. An issue is not actually litigated if, for example, there has been a default, a confession of liability, a failure to place a matter in issue by proper pleading or even because of a stipulation (*see*, Restatement [Second] of Judgments §27 comments d, e, at 255–257; *see also, Gilberg v. Barbieri*, 53 NY2d 285, *supra*). Because Lilly did not challenge the appropriateness of the concerted action theory in *Bichler*, it was not actually litigated and there is no identity between that issue in *Bichler* and here. Although it may seem a paradox that we should permit defendant to benefit in this litigation because of its failure to challenge concerted action in the prior litigation, the policy reasons for refusing to do so outweigh the reasons for limiting litigation on the issue. It is of paramount importance that the courts establish and develop the law in this emerging area of mass tort liability, rather than permit it to be fixed, even in this limited number of DES actions, on the basis of the law of the case. The need for uniformity and certainty mandates that in such cases collateral estoppel should be rejected (*see, Schwartz v. Public Administrator*, 24 NY2d 65, 72, *supra*; Restatement [Second] of Judgments §28 comment b, at 275–276; *see*, id. §29 [7] and comment I, at 292, 297). This is particularly so when the other defendants will be free to claim, against this same plaintiff, that concerted action is not an appropriate theory of liability and thereby cause inconsistent results.

B

The fact that no exception was taken to the charge on concerted action, however, has no bearing on the factual issues resolved by the jury when it answered the remaining interrogatories and Lilly should be precluded from relitigating them. Identity of issues does exist as to them because the legal theory in both actions is the same and because there are no significant factual differences between them. The plaintiff in *Bichler*, the first of the 15 related cases chosen to be tried, sought to establish Lilly's negligence in testing and marketing DES. The issues Lilly will be precluded from relitigating in this case relate solely to the facts underlying its negligence in testing, questions found against it by the *Bichler* jury and questions which are also involved in this case. Moreover, both plaintiffs' mothers ingested DES in the same time period (1953–1954), both plaintiffs were born in 1954 within seven months of each other and both developed cancer of the cervix and/or vagina at approximately the same age. The issue of proximate cause has been specifically deleted from the *Bichler* interrogatories by plaintiff's motion and Lilly will have the opportunity to demonstrate that plaintiff's injuries were not caused by her mother's ingestion of DES due to minor differences between the plaintiffs or the circumstances surrounding their mothers' ingestion of DES. . . .

Similarly unpersuasive is Lilly's assertion that the *Bichler* verdict is not entitled to collateral estoppel effect because there are indications it was the result of jury compromise. Although indications of jury compromise is one factor properly to be considered in determining whether a party against whom collateral estoppel is sought had a full and fair opportunity to litigate the issues in the prior determination (*see, Koch v. Consolidated Edison Co.*, 62 NY2d 548, 555, n 4, *supra*, quoting *Schwartz v. Public Administrator*, 24 NY2d 65, 72, *supra*), the evidence offered to defeat application of the doctrine in this case is insufficient. Lilly relies only on inadmissible hearsay allegations contained in an affidavit of its former attorney in which he alleges that he interviewed three *Bichler* jurors immediately after the verdict and that one of them told him there had been a compromise and on Lilly's speculation that a compromise resulted because the jury returned its verdict after five days of apparently hopeless deadlock. As we recently emphasized in *Koch*, evidence of this nature is not sufficient to defeat a motion for partial summary judgment on collateral estoppel grounds (*see, Koch v. Consolidated Edison Co., supra*, at p. 557).

Finally, although adjudications on the same issue inconsistent with the one to be given preclusive effect are relevant evidence that the party contesting estoppel did not have a fair opportunity to litigate the prior determination and may be a factor in refusing to apply the doctrine of collateral estoppel (*see*, id., at p. 555, and n 4, quoting Restatement [Second] of Judgments §29 [4]), the cases relied on by Lilly do not support that result here. Those cited include generally cases in which the jury returned a verdict for Lilly on a failure to warn theory and others in which the court granted Lilly judgment either because concerted action was an inappropriate legal theory for DES litigation or because the evidence was insufficient to raise a factual issue on concerted action. Those in the first group are not inconsistent with the *Bichler* jury's responses to the interrogatories finding Lilly negligent on a theory of inadequate testing. The second group, cases involving summary judgment and directed verdicts in Lilly's favor, support Lilly's contention that it should not be estopped from contesting liability on the theory of concerted action but we have found in its favor on that issue on other grounds. Thus, contrary to its contentions, those cases provide no basis for permitting Lilly to relitigate the remaining issues involving Lilly's negligence. In only one case cited by Lilly did a jury return a verdict inconsistent with *Bichler* on the issue of inadequate testing (*see, Barros v. Squibb & Sons*, Civ Act No. 75-1226 [ED Pa 1976]). Lilly relies on that decision and claims the benefit of that jury determination although it was not a party to the litigation. We find no basis to nullify the jury findings in *Bichler*, the first case tried of the several pending before Justice Fraiman and a case in which Lilly participated fully, on the basis of the *Squibb* verdict, a case in which it did not participate at all. Lilly can hardly claim that the *Squibb* determination provides any indication that it lacked a full and fair opportunity to defend against the issues decided adversely to it in *Bichler.*

III

. . . Accordingly, the order of the Appellate Division should be modified by denying plaintiff summary judgment as to the collateral estoppel effect of the *Bichler* jury's finding that defendant Lilly and other drug manufacturers acted in concert in testing and marketing DES for use in treating accidents in pregnancy (interrogatory No. 7) and, as so modified, the order should be affirmed. The certified question is answered in the negative. . . .

NOTES AND QUESTIONS

1. *Same Issue?* In *Kaufman*, the court held that Lilly was precluded from contesting its negligence in testing DES because the "same issue" had been decided adversely to Lilly in the *Bichler* litigation. However, the court in *Kaufman* does permit Lilly to relitigate the issue of whether plaintiff's injuries were caused by the ingestion of DES, even though proximate cause was established in the prior *Bichler* litigation. Why are the two issues treated differently?

a. *Different Time Periods.* With respect to the issue of Lilly's negligence — where the court held that preclusion applies — the court noted that plaintiffs' mothers ingested DES in the same 1953-1954 period and that plaintiffs were born within seven months of each other, indicating that the issue is the same in both proceedings. Would the court have reached that conclusion if Lilly had demonstrated that it possessed different information about the risks of DES at the time Bichler's mother ingested DES than at the time Kaufman's mother ingested DES? Consider *Anderson v. Eli Lilly & Co.*, 557 N.Y.S.2d 981 (3d Dep't 1980), in which the court held that *Bichler* did not conclusively establish Lilly's negligent testing of DES for purposes of an action brought by a plaintiff whose mother ingested DES in 1950, *three years before* Bichler's mother ingested the drug: "[T]he possibility of scientific advances during the intervening three years raises the question of whether that which was foreseeable and discoverable in 1953 could have been foreseen or discovered in 1950." *Id.* at 984. No proof was cited for the *Anderson* court's conclusion that the three-year gap between Anderson's and Bichler's ingestions was more significant than the one-year gap between Bichler's and Kaufman's ingestions.

b. *Differences in Evidence.* Suppose that in *Bichler* a research paper that showed that DES was dangerous and should have put a manufacturer on notice of that possibility was part of the evidence introduced to prove Lilly's negligence. In *Kaufman*, Lilly argues that other research published between Bichler's and Kaufman's ingestions discredits the earlier paper. Does this mean the "same issue" is no longer involved? Or are there other reasons for not applying issue preclusion?

Should a court hold a hearing to assess the evidence now offered by Lilly in order to determine whether issue preclusion is appropriate? If such a hearing is necessary, is there any value to using issue preclusion rather than having the second trier of fact simply decide the existence of negligence on its own? For a discussion of similar problems involved with establishing the existence of the "same issue" in the context of successive asbestos litigation, *see* Michael D. Green, *The Inability of Offensive Collateral Estoppel to Fulfill Its Promise: An Examination of Estoppel in Asbestos Litigation*, 70 Iowa L. Rev. 141, 186-198 (1984).

Who should bear the burden here? The *Kaufman* court stated that the burden was on the party seeking to establish issue preclusion to show that the same issue was previously decided. Does the burden include proving the absence of distinguishing facts? Wouldn't it have been more efficient to require that Lilly bear the burden of proving the existence of distinguishing facts if it wished to avoid issue preclusion?

c. *Different Burdens.* Subtle differences in the legal context between the two proceedings can also complicate whether the "same issue" was decided in the prior proceeding. For instance, if the party defending against the estoppel carried the burden of proof in the first proceeding, but not in the subsequent proceeding, should issue preclusion be imposed where the factual contexts are otherwise identical? The Restatement (Second) of Judgments §28(4) excepts from issue preclusion a situation where: "The party against whom preclusion is sought had a significantly heavier burden of persuasion with respect to the issue in the initial action than in the subsequent action; the burden has shifted to his adversary; or the adversary has a significantly heavier burden than he had in the first action." Accordingly, criminal proceedings, where the state has the burden of proving guilt beyond a reasonable doubt, generally carry preclusive effect in civil proceedings against a losing defendant, but not against the unsuccessful government. *See, e.g., One Lot Emerald Cut Stones v. United States,* 409 U.S. 232 (1972) (permitting civil forfeiture claim against defendant previously acquitted of criminal smuggling charges); *cf. Allen v. McCurry,* 449 U.S. 90 (1980), discussed at pp. 863–872.

2. *Actually Litigated?* In *Kaufman,* the *Bichler* jury expressly found Lilly liable under a "concerted action" theory of liability. However, the *Kaufman* court refused to give that determination preclusive effect because of a failure to "actually litigate" the issue. Why does the court say the issue was not "actually litigated"? Certainly plaintiff relied on the theory of "concerted action" and the jury was so charged. Does it make sense to allow Lilly to challenge the "concerted action" theory now? Does such a holding relieve a party of putting on its best case in the first proceeding?

As *Kaufman* demonstrates, the "actually litigated" and "necessarily decided" requirements can present a thorny evidentiary problem: How should a court determine what was actually litigated and decided? As noted in *Kaufman,* courts have generally rejected the technique of asking the initial fact finder (either the judge or jury members) what the actual basis for the decision was. What would be the problem in allowing testimony of the initial fact finder?

Given the courts' unwillingness to ask the initial fact finder, must a court examine every piece of evidence introduced in the initial litigation and then analyze which issues the evidence was relevant to? *See Sea-Land Servs., Inc. v. Gaudet,* 414 U.S. 573, 592 n.30 (1974) (suggesting that second court may have to calculate the amount of an earlier judgment attributable to lost wages). *Compare Slater v. Skirving,* 70 N.W. 493 (Neb. 1897) (parties may not use extrinsic proof of what was actually litigated to contradict the formal pleadings) *with Allen v. Zurich Ins. Co.,* 667 F.2d 1162, 1166 (4th Cir. 1982) (denying collateral estoppel because party asserting estoppel failed to prove that issue submitted to the jury in prior proceeding was actually litigated). A bright line rule that the pleadings and pretrial orders are dispositive of what was actually litigated would obviate much of the evidentiary problem, and courts do often rely heavily upon those documents in making such determinations. Would it be unfair to hold that a party has actually litigated any matter actually decided by the court that was not formally withdrawn from the pleadings? Such a rule might give parties a perverse incentive to overlitigate every case for fear of future preclusive effects. In the absence of such a rule, however, the F2 court will generally have to make elusive factual findings as to the content of the first action. Is a preclusion doctrine that requires extensive litigation over the scope of the initial judgment self-defeating to the extent that a central objective of preclusion doctrine is to avoid relitigation?

3. *"Necessarily Decided" and "Essential to the Judgment"?* The use of the special verdict in *Kaufman* clarifies what the jury decided. But those findings are given preclusive effect only when they are essential to the judgment.

How do courts decide whether a particular finding is "essential" to the judgment? Some courts have focused on the importance of the issue to the *initial* proceeding; where the issue was not central to the dispute in that case, preclusion was not imposed. *See, e.g., Moore v. United States*, 246 F. Supp. 19 (N.D. Miss. 1965) (earlier determination of how long defendant held cattle before they were considered "breed cattle" entitled to capital gains tax treatment was not binding on defendant in subsequent case because it was not the "ultimate fact" determined in the earlier proceeding, which was simply whether the taxpayer was entitled to capital gains treatment on the sale of 70 animals). The language in several old decisions referred to a distinction between "mediate" or "evidentiary" effects (not entitled to preclusion) and "ultimate" facts (entitled to preclusion). The Restatement (Second) of Judgments §27, comment j, refocused the inquiry on whether the issue was actually recognized by the parties as important and by the adjudicator as necessary to the first judgment.

Other courts have looked to the importance of the issue in the *subsequent* proceeding and whether it was foreseeable that serious collateral consequences would necessarily flow from the adjudication in the earlier proceeding. *The Evergreens v. Nunan*, 141 F.2d 927 (2d Cir. 1944) ("It is not . . . always fair that every fact—'ultimate' or 'mediate'—decided in [the first suit] shall be conclusively established between the parties in all future suits, just because the decision was necessary to the result. What jural relevance facts may acquire in the future is often impossible even remotely to anticipate."). *See generally* Restatement (Second) of Judgments §27, comment j, and §28 comment i (1982). Under both approaches, the idea is that parties should not be subject to preclusion on an issue unless they had reason to focus careful attention on the issue when it first arose.

4. *Other Limitations on Issue Preclusion.* This general concern—that the ramifications of a particular holding may not be foreseeable—runs throughout preclusion doctrine. The Restatement (Second) of Judgments sets forth a number of factors, including those of foreseeability, which justify exceptions to the general rule of issue preclusion. Section 28 provides as follows:

> Although an issue is actually litigated and determined by a valid and final judgment, and the determination is essential to the judgment, relitigation of the issue in a subsequent action between the parties is not precluded in the following circumstances:
>
> (1) The party against whom preclusion is sought could not, as a matter of law, have obtained review of the judgment in the initial action; or
>
> (2) The issue is one of law and (a) the two actions involve claims that are substantially unrelated, or (b) a new determination is warranted in order to take account of an intervening change in the applicable legal context or otherwise to avoid inequitable administration of the laws; or

(3) A new determination of the issue is warranted by differences in the quality or extensiveness of the procedures followed in the two courts or by factors relating to the allocation of jurisdiction between them; or

(4) The party against whom preclusion is sought had a significantly heavier burden of persuasion with respect to the issue in the initial action than in the subsequent action; the burden has shifted to his adversary; or the adversary has a significantly heavier burden than he had in the first action; or

(5) There is a clear and convincing need for a new determination of the issue (a) because of the potential adverse impact of the determination on the public interest or the interests of persons not themselves parties in the initial action, (b) because it was not sufficiently foreseeable at the time of the initial action that the issue would arise in the context of a subsequent action, or (c) because the party sought to be precluded, as a result of the conduct of his adversary or other special circumstances, did not have an adequate opportunity or incentive to obtain a full and fair adjudication in the initial action.

Moreover, the ramifications of a particular holding may be particularly unforeseeable when preclusion is asserted by a nonparty to the original action. Are we certain the *Bichler* jury would have come out the same way if they knew that their determination would have preclusive effect in future cases brought by different parties? When subsequent litigation involves the assertion of preclusion by a nonparty to the original action, the Restatement (Second) of Judgments offers additional criteria to assess whether or not there was full and fair opportunity to litigate the issue. Section 29 provides, in relevant part, that consideration should be given in such cases to whether:

(1) Treating the issue as conclusively determined would be incompatible with an applicable scheme of administering the remedies in the actions involved;

(2) The forum in the second action affords the party against whom preclusion is asserted procedural opportunities in the presentation and determination of the issue that were not available in the first action and could likely result in the issue being differently determined;

(3) The person seeking to invoke favorable preclusion, or to avoid unfavorable preclusion, could have effected joinder in the first action between himself and his present adversary;

(4) The determination relied on as preclusive was itself inconsistent with another determination of the same issue;

(5) The prior determination may have been affected by relationships among the parties to the first action that are not present in the subsequent action, or apparently was based on a compromise verdict or finding;

(6) Treating the issue as conclusively determined may complicate determination of issues in the subsequent action or prejudice the interests of another party thereto;

(7) The issue is one of law and treating it as conclusively determined would inappropriately foreclose opportunity for obtaining reconsideration of the legal rule upon which it was based;

(8) Other compelling circumstances make it appropriate that the party be permitted to relitigate the issue.

What is the purpose of §29? What does the section add to the exceptions set forth in §28? How useful is the Restatement (Second) approach? Shouldn't parties be able to predict at the outset of a lawsuit the ramifications of having an issue determined when they assess how intensively or extensively to pursue litigation of that issue? Do §§28 and 29 provide such guidance? *See generally* Note, *For One Litigant's Sole Relief: Unforeseeable Preclusion and the Second Restatement,* 77 Cornell L. Rev. 905 (1992).

5. *Reevaluating* Kaufman. Which of the factors in Restatement (Second) §§28 and 29 were available to try to resist preclusion in *Kaufman?*

a. *Compromise Verdicts.* Lilly asserted that the verdict in *Bichler* was based on a compromise by the jury (*see* Restatement (Second) of Judgments §29(5) (1982)). The finding of liability, Lilly argued, was only reached because the jury was, at the same time, awarding relatively low damages to the plaintiff. Thus, Lilly argued, the liability determination was unreliable and should not be used to establish liability in other proceedings.

This argument was rejected in *Kaufman* on the ground that Lilly did not prove that there was indeed a compromise. Given the court's refusal to permit Lilly to depose the jurors, how was Lilly supposed to develop the evidence to support such an argument?

Why should it have mattered anyhow if Lilly *had* been able to establish that the *Bichler* verdict was a "compromise"? As noted earlier in this chapter, courts rarely disregard a prior adjudication merely because it was "wrong." Why should it matter that the initial fact finder was ambivalent, or influenced by other factors such as insurance coverage or the relative financial position of the litigants? Should we be more willing to avoid giving preclusive effect to jury determinations that might be influenced by factors other than the merits?

b. *Inconsistent Adjudications. Bichler* appears to be the first of the DES cases in which Lilly's negligence was adjudicated. In arguing that preclusion should not attach to that finding, Lilly tried to take advantage of the fact that an inconsistent decision on the issue of inadequate testing was reached in a case brought against a *different* manufacturer. The *Kaufman* court does not permit Lilly to invoke the "inconsistent verdict" exception to preclusion, since Lilly was not a party in the other case. Thus, following *Kaufman,* it appears that preclusion will be available in all future cases against Lilly that present the "same issues" of negligence, product defect, and so forth. Did the *Kaufman* court go too far in finding preclusion in this suit, which was brought by a different plaintiff after only a single jury verdict against the defendant? Does this make too much ride on the happenstance that Lilly lost the first time around? *Compare Kortenhaus v. Eli Lilly & Co.,* 549 A.2d 437 (N.J. 1988) (rejecting preclusion because of inconsistent verdicts in other cases involving the same defendant).

The "inconsistent verdict" exception serves two different functions. First, it prevents new plaintiffs from selectively taking advantage of prior judgments against the defendant, picking and choosing the results most favorable to them when they were not even involved in the earlier litigation. This aspect of the doctrine implicates the issue of "mutuality"—the question of when, and under what circumstances, a litigant should be able to take advantage of an earlier judgment to which it was not a party. Litigants may engage in strategic behavior where such "nonmutual" preclusion is possible, as we discuss in the section that follows.

The exception's second function is to increase the reliability of those findings that will receive preclusive effect in a subsequent action. When other verdicts exist that are inconsistent with a particular judgment, there may be reason to question whether the judgment is sufficiently accurate to be given preclusive effect in a subsequent action. That concern was presumably at the core of Lilly's argument that no preclusion should be available in *Kaufman*. Note, however, that the court explained its rejection of Lilly's argument by asserting that Lilly enjoyed a "full and fair opportunity to defend against the issues decided adversely to it in *Bichler*." This explanation appears somewhat nonresponsive. Lilly was arguing that the prior inconsistent verdict called into question the reliability of the *Bichler* verdict, not the quality of the opportunity that Lilly enjoyed to contest the issue in that case.

c. *Adequate Opportunity or Incentive to Litigate?* What does it mean to say that a party against whom preclusion is sought did not have an adequate opportunity or incentive to obtain a full and fair adjudication in the initial proceeding? *See* Restatement (Second) of Judgments §§28(5)(c) and 29 (1982). Were there any such factors that should have prevented preclusion in *Kaufman*?

i. *Adequate Opportunity.* Some courts have declined to give issue preclusive effect to certain arbitration or administrative proceedings that lack trial-type adjudicatory safeguards. *Compare, e.g., McDonald v. City of Westbranch*, 466 U.S. 284 (1984) (finding by labor arbitrator, in which "usual rules of evidence do not apply; and rights and procedures common to civil trials, such as discovery, compulsory process, cross-examination, and testimony under oath, are often severely limited or unavailable" cannot collaterally estop plaintiff from challenging her discharge under 42 U.S.C. §1983); *Alexander v. Gardner-Denver Co.*, 415 U.S. 36 (1974) (results of labor arbitration do not preclude former employee from challenging discharge under Title VII of the Civil Rights Act of 1964); *McMullen v. INS*, 788 F.2d 591, 597 (9th Cir. 1986) (denying collateral estoppel effect to magistrate's administrative determination), *overruled on other grounds, Baranind v. Enomoto*, 400 F.3d 744 (9th Cir. 2005) (en banc) *with University of Tennessee v. Elliott*, 478 U.S. 788, 798 n.6 (1986) ("[w]here an administrative forum has the essential procedural characteristics of a court, . . . its determinations should be accorded the same finality that is accorded the judgment of a court") (*quoting* Restatement (Second) of Judgments §83 (1982)).

ii. *Adequate Incentive.* The incentive to litigate is often a function of the amount in controversy in the initial proceeding. Although denial of preclusion because of the "low stakes" usually involves subsequent litigation with a nonparty, cases involving the same parties have refused preclusion where the amount in controversy is trivial and there was an inadequate incentive to pursue the litigation vigorously. *See Eureka Federal Savings & Loan Ass'n v. American Casualty Co.*, 873 F.2d 229, 233–234 (9th Cir. 1989) (findings in an action in which damages totaled $3,300 were an inappropriate basis for collateral estoppel in a subsequent action in which $100 million was at stake). And in some cases where preclusion is asserted by a nonparty, courts have found an adequate incentive to litigate, notwithstanding a small amount in controversy, solely on the grounds that the collateral estoppel consequences of the judgment were obvious. *See, e.g., Cohen v. Bucci*, 905 F.2d 1111, 1112–1113 (7th Cir. 1990). A relatively small amount in controversy may also diminish the incentive to appeal, and preclusion has been denied on that basis in cases brought by third persons not parties to the original litigation. *See, e.g., Eureka Fed. Sav. and Loan Ass'n v. American Cas. Co. of Reading, Pa.*, 873 F.2d 229, 233 (9th Cir. 1989) ("[D]iscrepancies in amounts at issue between two actions may make application of collateral estoppel inappropriate."); *Berner v. British Commonwealth Pacific Airlines*, 346 F.2d 532 (2d Cir. 1965) (prior judgment of $35,000 does not estop defendant from contesting liability in subsequent air crash litigation by other passengers as defendant lacked incentive to appeal first judgment).

C.   PARTIES BOUND AND ADVANTAGED

One overarching principle pervades the law of preclusion: Only one who is a party to a litigation and subject to the court's jurisdiction, or in privity with such a party, can be bound by a judgment. The due process underpinnings of this rule reach as far back as *Pennoyer v. Neff.* Just who is classified as a "party" or "in privity" with a party comprises an important aspect of preclusion law.

The flip side of the problem—who can *take advantage of a prior adjudication*—also presents interesting questions. Traditionally, both claim and issue preclusion held that only a party, or one in privity with a party to the initial litigation, could take advantage of preclusion doctrines. With respect to claim preclusion, the origins of the mutuality requirement related to the scope of a "single claim," which was usually defined in terms of an identity of parties. With respect to issue preclusion, the animating principle for requiring identity of parties was one of fairness—since a nonparty cannot as a matter of due process be bound by an adverse finding that could be used *against* him, it was considered unfair for the nonparty who faced no risk of preclusion himself to be able to use a prior judgment in his *favor* by binding a party to the original action to an unfavorable determination. No issue of due process is presented in such a case, however, since the party being bound to the judgment had its day in court, albeit against a different opponent.

This principle that only a party can take advantage of an earlier adjudication is referred to as the principle of "mutuality." One consequence of mutuality was that it gave the plaintiff an incentive to file successive actions based on the same injury against different defendants rather than consolidate them in a single proceeding. If plaintiff lost the first proceeding, he could try again against another defendant without being estopped by the first proceeding. In contrast, when applied to multiple plaintiffs suing the same defendant, the mutuality requirement seemed to promote efficiency. Nonparty plaintiffs had no incentive to take a wait and see attitude by staying out of the initial litigation, since they would not be able to derive benefit from favorable determinations in that litigation (except insofar as legal rulings might become *stare decisis*). As we shall see later in this chapter, courts over time modified the mutuality of estoppel requirement. We deal initially with the question of who can be bound by a prior judgment.

1.   *Vicarious Representation, Privity, and the Foundations of Preclusion*

Taylor v. Sturgell

553 U.S. 880 (2008)

JUSTICE GINSBURG delivered the opinion of the Court.

"It is a principle of general application in Anglo-American jurisprudence that one is not bound by a judgment *in personam* in a litigation in which he is not designated as a party or to which he has not been made a party by service of process." *Hansberry v. Lee*, 311 U.S. 32, 40, 61 S. Ct. 115, 85 L. Ed. 22 (1940). Several exceptions, recognized in this Court's decisions, temper this basic rule. In a class action, for example, a person not named as a party may be bound by a judgment on the merits of the action, if she was adequately represented by a party who actively participated in the litigation. See *id.*, at 41, 61 S. Ct. 115. In this case, we consider for the first time whether there is a "virtual representation" exception to the general rule against precluding nonparties. Adopted by a number of courts, including the courts below in the case now before us, the exception so styled is broader than any we have so far approved.

The virtual representation question we examine in this opinion arises in the following context. Petitioner Brent Taylor filed a lawsuit under the Freedom of Information Act seeking certain documents from the Federal Aviation Administration. Greg Herrick, Taylor's friend, had previously brought an unsuccessful suit seeking the same records. The two men have no legal relationship, and there is no evidence that Taylor controlled, financed, participated in, or even had notice of Herrick's earlier suit. Nevertheless, the D.C. Circuit held Taylor's suit precluded by the judgment against Herrick because, in that court's assessment, Herrick qualified as Taylor's "virtual representative."

We disapprove the doctrine of preclusion by "virtual representation," and hold, based on the record as it now stands, that the judgment against Herrick does not bar Taylor from maintaining this suit.

I

The Freedom of Information Act (FOIA) accords "any person" a right to request any records held by a federal agency. 5 U.S.C. §552(a)(3)(A) (2006 ed.). No reason need be given for a FOIA request, and unless the requested materials fall within one of the Act's enumerated exemptions, see §552(a)(3)(E), (b), the agency must "make the records promptly available" to the requester, §552(a)(3)(A). If an agency refuses to furnish the requested records, the requester may file suit in federal court and obtain an injunction "order[ing] the production of any agency records improperly withheld." §552(a)(4)(B).

The courts below held the instant FOIA suit barred by the judgment in earlier litigation seeking the same records. Because the lower courts' decisions turned on the connection between the two lawsuits, we begin with a full account of each action.

A

The first suit was filed by Greg Herrick, an antique aircraft enthusiast and the owner of an F-45 airplane, a vintage model manufactured by the Fairchild Engine and Airplane Corporation (FEAC) in the 1930's. In 1997, seeking information that would help him restore his plane to its original condition, Herrick filed a FOIA request asking the Federal Aviation Administration (FAA) for copies of any technical documents about the F-45 contained in the agency's records.

To gain a certificate authorizing the manufacture and sale of the F-45, FEAC had submitted to the FAA's predecessor, the Civil Aeronautics Authority, detailed specifications and other technical data about the plane. Hundreds of pages of documents produced by FEAC in the certification process remain in the FAA's records. The FAA denied Herrick's request, however, upon finding that the documents he sought are subject to FOIA's exemption for "trade secrets and commercial or financial information obtained from a person and privileged or confidential," 5 U.S.C. §552(b)(4) (2006 ed.). In an administrative appeal, Herrick urged that FEAC and its successors had waived any trade-secret protection. The FAA thereupon contacted FEAC's corporate successor, respondent Fairchild Corporation (Fairchild). Because Fairchild objected to release of the documents, the agency adhered to its original decision.

Herrick then filed suit in the U.S. District Court for the District of Wyoming. Challenging the FAA's invocation of the trade-secret exemption, Herrick placed heavy weight on a 1955 letter from FEAC to the Civil Aeronautics Authority. The letter authorized the agency to lend any documents in its files to the public "for use in making repairs or replacement parts for aircraft produced by Fairchild." This broad authorization, Herrick maintained, showed that the F-45 certification records held by the FAA could not be regarded as "secre[t]" or "confidential" within the meaning of §552(b)(4).

Rejecting Herrick's argument, the District Court granted summary judgment to the FAA. The 1955 letter, the court reasoned, did not deprive the F-45 certification documents of trade-secret status, for those documents were never in fact released pursuant to the letter's blanket authorization. The court also stated that even if the 1955 letter had waived trade-secret protection, Fairchild had successfully "reversed" the waiver by objecting to the FAA's release of the records to Herrick.

On appeal, the Tenth Circuit agreed with Herrick that the 1955 letter had stripped the requested documents of trade-secret protection. But the Court of Appeals upheld the District Court's alternative determination — *i.e.*, that Fairchild had restored trade-secret status by objecting to Herrick's FOIA request. On that ground, the appeals court affirmed the entry of summary judgment for the FAA.

In so ruling, the Tenth Circuit noted that Herrick had failed to challenge two suppositions underlying the District Court's decision. First, the District Court assumed trade-secret status could be "restored" to documents that had lost protection. Second, the District Court also assumed that Fairchild had regained trade-secret status for the documents even though the company claimed that status only "*after* Herrick had initiated his request" for the F-45 records. The Court of Appeals expressed no opinion on the validity of these suppositions.

B

The Tenth Circuit's decision issued on July 24, 2002. Less than a month later, on August 22, petitioner Brent Taylor—a friend of Herrick's and an antique aircraft enthusiast in his own right—submitted a FOIA request seeking the same documents Herrick had unsuccessfully sued to obtain. When the FAA failed to respond, Taylor filed a complaint in the U.S. District Court for the District of Columbia. Like Herrick, Taylor argued that FEAC's 1955 letter had stripped the records of their trade-secret status. But Taylor also sought to litigate the two issues concerning recapture of protected status that Herrick had failed to raise in his appeal to the Tenth Circuit.

After Fairchild intervened as a defendant, the District Court in D.C. concluded that Taylor's suit was barred by claim preclusion; accordingly, it granted summary judgment to Fairchild and the FAA. The court acknowledged that Taylor was not a party to Herrick's suit. Relying on the Eighth Circuit's decision in *Tyus v. Schoemehl*, 93 F.3d 449 (1996), however, it held that a nonparty may be bound by a judgment if she was "virtually represented" by a party. . . .

The record before the District Court in Taylor's suit revealed the following facts about the relationship between Taylor and Herrick: Taylor is the president of the Antique Aircraft Association, an organization to which Herrick belongs; the two men are "close associate[s]"; Herrick asked Taylor to help restore Herrick's F-45, though they had no contract or agreement for Taylor's participation in the restoration; Taylor was represented by the lawyer who represented Herrick in the earlier litigation; and Herrick apparently gave Taylor documents that Herrick had obtained from the FAA during discovery in his suit.

Fairchild and the FAA conceded that Taylor had not participated in Herrick's suit. The D.C. District Court determined, however, that Herrick ranked as Taylor's virtual representative because the facts fit each of the other six indicators on the Eighth Circuit's list. Accordingly, the District Court held Taylor's suit, seeking the same documents Herrick had requested, barred by the judgment against Herrick.

The D.C. Circuit affirmed . . . [and] announced [a] five-factor test. The first two factors—"identity of interests" and "adequate representation"—are necessary but not sufficient for virtual representation. In addition, at least one of three other factors must be established: "a close relationship between the present party and his putative representative," "substantial participation by the present party in the first case," or "tactical maneuvering on the part of the present party to avoid preclusion by the prior judgment."

Applying this test to the record in Taylor's case, the D.C. Circuit found [that Taylor had been "virtually represented" by Herrick and was bound by the judgment in the earlier action]. We granted certiorari to resolve the disagreement among the Circuits over the permissibility and scope of preclusion based on "virtual representation."

II

The preclusive effect of a federal-court judgment is determined by federal common law. See *Semtek Int'l Inc. v. Lockheed Martin Corp.*, 531 U.S. 497, 507–508, 121 S. Ct. 1021, 149 L. Ed. 2d 32 (2001). For judgments in federal-question cases—for example, Herrick's FOIA suit—federal courts participate in developing "uniform federal rule[s]" of *res judicata*, which this Court has ultimate authority to determine and declare. *Id.*, at 508, 121 S. Ct. 1021.[4] The federal common law of preclusion is, of course, subject to due process limitations. See *Richards v. Jefferson County*, 517 U.S. 793, 797, 116 S. Ct. 1761, 135 L. Ed. 2d 76 (1996).

Until now, we have never addressed the doctrine of "virtual representation" adopted (in varying forms) by several Circuits and relied upon by the courts below. Our inquiry, however, is guided by well-established precedent regarding the propriety of nonparty preclusion. We review that precedent before taking up directly the issue of virtual representation.

A

The preclusive effect of a judgment is defined by claim preclusion and issue preclusion, which are collectively referred to as "res judicata." Under the doctrine of claim preclusion, a final judgment forecloses "successive litigation of the very same claim, whether or not relitigation of the claim raises the same issues as the earlier suit." *New Hampshire v. Maine*, 532 U.S. 742, 748, 121 S. Ct. 1808, 149 L. Ed. 2d 968 (2001). Issue preclusion, in contrast, bars "successive litigation of an issue of fact or law actually litigated and resolved in a valid court determination essential to the prior judgment," even if the issue recurs in the context of a different claim. *Id.*, at 748–749, 121 S. Ct. 1808. By "preclud[ing] parties from contesting matters that they have had a full and fair opportunity to litigate," these two doctrines protect against "the expense and vexation attending multiple lawsuits, conserv[e] judicial resources, and foste[r] reliance on judicial action by minimizing the possibility of inconsistent decisions." *Montana v. United States*, 440 U.S. 147, 153–154, 99 S. Ct. 970, 59 L. Ed. 2d 210 (1979).

A person who was not a party to a suit generally has not had a "full and fair opportunity to litigate" the claims and issues settled in that suit. The application of claim and issue preclusion to nonparties thus runs up against the "deep-rooted historic tradition that everyone should have his own day in court." *Richards*, 517 U.S., at 798, 116 S. Ct. 1761 (internal quotation marks omitted). Indicating the strength of that tradition, we have often repeated the general rule that "one is not bound by a judgment *in personam* in a litigation in which he is not designated as a party or to which he has not been made a party by service of process." *Hansberry*, 311 U.S., at 40, 61 S. Ct. 115. See also, *e.g.*, *Richards*, 517 U.S., at 798, 116 S. Ct. 1761; *Martin v. Wilks*, 490 U.S. 755, 761, 109 S. Ct. 2180, 104 L. Ed. 2d 835 (1989); *Zenith Radio Corp. v. Hazeltine Research, Inc.*, 395 U.S. 100, 110, 89 S. Ct. 1562, 23 L. Ed. 2d 129 (1969).

B

Though hardly in doubt, the rule against nonparty preclusion is subject to exceptions. For present purposes, the recognized exceptions can be grouped into six categories.

---

4. For judgments in diversity cases, federal law incorporates the rules of preclusion applied by the State in which the rendering court sits. See *Semtek Int'l Inc. v. Lockheed Martin Corp.*, 531 U.S. 497, 508, 121 S. Ct. 1021, 149 L. Ed. 2d 32 (2001).

First, "[a] person who agrees to be bound by the determination of issues in an action between others is bound in accordance with the terms of his agreement." 1 Restatement (Second) of Judgments §40, p. 390 (1980) (hereinafter Restatement). For example, "if separate actions involving the same transaction are brought by different plaintiffs against the same defendant, all the parties to all the actions may agree that the question of the defendant's liability will be definitely determined, one way or the other, in a 'test case.'" D. Shapiro, Civil Procedure: Preclusion in Civil Actions 77–78 (2001) (hereinafter Shapiro). See also *California v. Texas*, 459 U.S. 1096, 1097, 103 S. Ct. 714, 74 L. Ed. 2d 944 (1983) (dismissing certain defendants from a suit based on a stipulation "that each of said defendants . . . will be bound by a final judgment of this Court" on a specified issue).

Second, nonparty preclusion may be justified based on a variety of pre-existing "substantive legal relationship[s]" between the person to be bound and a party to the judgment. Shapiro 78. See also *Richards*, 517 U.S., at 798, 116 S. Ct. 1761. Qualifying relationships include, but are not limited to, preceding and succeeding owners of property, bailee and bailor, and assignee and assignor. See 2 Restatement §§43–44, 52, 55. These exceptions originated "as much from the needs of property law as from the values of preclusion by judgment." 18A C. Wright, A. Miller, & E. Cooper, Federal Practice and Procedure §4448, p. 329 (2d ed. 2002) (hereinafter Wright & Miller).[8]

Third, we have confirmed that, "in certain limited circumstances," a nonparty may be bound by a judgment because she was "adequately represented by someone with the same interests who [wa]s a party" to the suit. *Richards*, 517 U.S., at 798, 116 S. Ct. 1761 (internal quotation marks omitted). Representative suits with preclusive effect on nonparties include properly conducted class actions, see *Martin*, 490 U.S., at 762, n. 2, 109 S. Ct. 2180 (citing Fed. Rule Civ. Proc. 23), and suits brought by trustees, guardians, and other fiduciaries, see *Sea-Land Services, Inc. v. Gaudet*, 414 U.S. 573, 593, 94 S. Ct. 806, 39 L. Ed. 2d 9 (1974). See also 1 Restatement §41.

Fourth, a nonparty is bound by a judgment if she "assume[d] control" over the litigation in which that judgment was rendered. *Montana*, 440 U.S., at 154, 99 S. Ct. 970. See also *Schnell v. Peter Eckrich & Sons, Inc.*, 365 U.S. 260, 262, n. 4, 81 S. Ct. 557, 5 L. Ed. 2d 546 (1961); 1 Restatement §39. Because such a person has had "the opportunity to present proofs and argument," he has already "had his day in court" even though he was not a formal party to the litigation. *Id.*, Comment *a*, p. 382.

Fifth, a party bound by a judgment may not avoid its preclusive force by relitigating through a proxy. Preclusion is thus in order when a person who did not participate in a litigation later brings suit as the designated representative of a person who was a party to the prior adjudication. See *Chicago, R.I. & P.R. Co. v. Schendel*, 270 U.S. 611, 620, 623, 46 S. Ct. 420, 70 L. Ed. 757 (1926); 18A Wright & Miller §4454,

---

8. The substantive legal relationships justifying preclusion are sometimes collectively referred to as "privity." See, *e.g.*, *Richards v. Jefferson County*, 517 U.S. 793, 798, 116 S. Ct. 1761, 135 L. Ed. 2d 76 (1996); 2 Restatement §62, Comment *a*. The term "privity," however, has also come to be used more broadly, as a way to express the conclusion that nonparty preclusion is appropriate on any ground. See 18A Wright & Miller §4449, pp. 351–353, and n. 33 (collecting cases). To ward off confusion, we avoid using the term "privity" in this opinion.

pp. 433–434. And although our decisions have not addressed the issue directly, it also seems clear that preclusion is appropriate when a nonparty later brings suit as an agent for a party who is bound by a judgment. See *id.*, §4449, p. 335.

Sixth, in certain circumstances a special statutory scheme may "expressly foreclos[e] successive litigation by nonlitigants . . . if the scheme is otherwise consistent with due process." *Martin*, 490 U.S., at 762, n. 2, 109 S. Ct. 2180. Examples of such schemes include bankruptcy and probate proceedings, see *ibid.*, and *quo warranto* actions or other suits that, "under [the governing] law, [may] be brought only on behalf of the public at large," *Richards*, 517 U.S., at 804, 116 S. Ct. 1761.

III

Reaching beyond these six established categories, some lower courts have recognized a "virtual representation" exception to the rule against nonparty preclusion. Decisions of these courts, however, have been far from consistent. See 18A Wright & Miller §4457, p. 513 (virtual representation lacks a "clear or coherent theory"; decisions applying it have "an episodic quality"). Some Circuits use the label, but define "virtual representation" so that it is no broader than the recognized exception for adequate representation. See, *e.g., Becherer v. Merrill Lynch, Pierce, Fenner & Smith, Inc.*, 193 F.3d 415, 423, 427 (C.A.6 1999). But other courts, including the Eighth, Ninth, and D.C. Circuits, apply multifactor tests for virtual representation that permit nonparty preclusion in cases that do not fit within any of the established exceptions.

The D.C. Circuit, the FAA, and Fairchild have presented three arguments in support of an expansive doctrine of virtual representation. We find none of them persuasive.

A

The D.C. Circuit purported to ground its virtual representation doctrine in this Court's decisions stating that, in some circumstances, a person may be bound by a judgment if she was adequately represented by a party to the proceeding yielding that judgment. But the D.C. Circuit's definition of "adequate representation" strayed from the meaning our decisions have attributed to that term.

In *Richards*, we reviewed a decision by the Alabama Supreme Court holding that a challenge to a tax was barred by a judgment upholding the same tax in a suit filed by different taxpayers. 517 U.S., at 795–797, 116 S. Ct. 1761. The plaintiffs in the first suit "did not sue on behalf of a class," their complaint "did not purport to assert any claim against or on behalf of any nonparties," and the judgment "did not purport to bind" nonparties. *Id.*, at 801, 116 S. Ct. 1761. There was no indication, we emphasized, that the court in the first suit "took care to protect the interests" of absent parties, or that the parties to that litigation "understood their suit to be on behalf of absent [parties]." *Id.*, at 802, 116 S. Ct. 1761. In these circumstances, we held, the application of claim preclusion was inconsistent with "the due process of law guaranteed by the Fourteenth Amendment." *Id.*, at 797, 116 S. Ct. 1761.

The D.C. Circuit stated, without elaboration, that it did not "read *Richards* to hold a nonparty . . . adequately represented only if special procedures were followed [to protect the nonparty] or the party to the prior suit understood it was representing the nonparty." As the D.C. Circuit saw this case, Herrick adequately represented Taylor for two principal reasons: Herrick had a strong incentive to litigate; and Taylor later hired Herrick's lawyer, suggesting Taylor's "satisfaction with the attorney's performance in the prior case."

The D.C. Circuit misapprehended *Richards.* As just recounted, our holding that the Alabama Supreme Court's application of *res judicata* to nonparties violated due process turned on the lack of either special procedures to protect the nonparties' interests or an understanding by the concerned parties that the first suit was brought in a representative capacity. See *Richards*, 517 U.S., at 801–802, 116 S. Ct. 1761. *Richards* thus established that representation is "adequate" for purposes of nonparty preclusion only if (at a minimum) one of these two circumstances is present.

We restated *Richards'* core holding in *South Central Bell Telephone Co. v. Alabama*, 526 U.S. 160, 119 S. Ct. 1180, 143 L.Ed.2d 258 (1999). In that case, as in *Richards*, the Alabama courts had held that a judgment rejecting a challenge to a tax by one group of taxpayers barred a subsequent suit by a different taxpayer. See 526 U.S., at 164–165, 119 S. Ct. 1180. In *South Central Bell*, however, the nonparty had notice of the original suit and engaged one of the lawyers earlier employed by the original plaintiffs. See *id.*, at 167–168, 119 S. Ct. 1180. Under the D.C. Circuit's decision in Taylor's case, these factors apparently would have sufficed to establish adequate representation. See 490 F.3d, at 973–975. Yet *South Central Bell* held that the application of *res judicata* in that case violated due process. Our inquiry came to an end when we determined that the original plaintiffs had not understood themselves to be acting in a representative capacity and that there had been no special procedures to safeguard the interests of absentees. See 526 U.S., at 168, 119 S. Ct. 1180.

Our decisions recognizing that a nonparty may be bound by a judgment if she was adequately represented by a party to the earlier suit thus provide no support for the D.C. Circuit's broad theory of virtual representation.

B

Fairchild and the FAA do not argue that the D.C. Circuit's virtual representation doctrine fits within any of the recognized grounds for nonparty preclusion. Rather, they ask us to abandon the attempt to delineate discrete grounds and clear rules altogether. Preclusion is in order, they contend, whenever "the relationship between a party and a non-party is 'close enough' to bring the second litigant within the judgment." Courts should make the "close enough" determination, they urge, through a "heavily fact-driven" and "equitable" inquiry. Only this sort of diffuse balancing, Fairchild and the FAA argue, can account for all of the situations in which nonparty preclusion is appropriate.

We reject this argument for three reasons. First, our decisions emphasize the fundamental nature of the general rule that a litigant is not bound by a judgment to which she was not a party. See, *e.g., Richards*, 517 U.S., at 798–799, 116 S. Ct. 1761; *Martin*, 490 U.S., at 761–762, 109 S. Ct. 2180. Accordingly, we have endeavored to delineate discrete exceptions that apply in "limited circumstances." *Id.*, at 762, n. 2, 109 S. Ct. 2180. Respondents' amorphous balancing test is at odds with the constrained approach to nonparty preclusion our decisions advance.

Resisting this reading of our precedents, . . . Fairchild quotes our statement in *Coryell v. Phipps*, 317 U.S. 406, 411, 63 S. Ct. 291, 87 L. Ed. 363 (1943), that privity "turns on the facts of particular cases." That observation, however, scarcely implies that privity is governed by a diffuse balancing test. Fairchild also cites *Blonder-Tongue Laboratories, Inc. v. University of Ill. Foundation*, 402 U.S. 313, 334, 91 S. Ct. 1434, 28 L. Ed. 2d 788 (1971), which stated that estoppel questions turn on "the trial courts' sense of justice and equity." This passing statement, however, was not made with nonparty preclusion in mind; it appeared in a discussion recognizing district courts' discretion to *limit* the use of issue preclusion against persons who *were* parties to a judgment. See *Blonder-Tongue*, 402 U.S., at 334, 91 S. Ct. 1434. . . .

Our second reason for rejecting a broad doctrine of virtual representation rests on the limitations attending nonparty preclusion based on adequate representation. A party's representation of a nonparty is "adequate" for preclusion purposes only if, at a minimum: (1) the interests of the nonparty and her representative are aligned, see *Hansberry*, 311 U.S., at 43, 61 S. Ct. 115; and (2) either the party understood herself to be acting in a representative capacity or the original court took care to protect the interests of the nonparty, see *Richards*, 517 U.S., at 801–802, 116 S. Ct. 1761. In addition, adequate representation sometimes requires (3) notice of the original suit to the persons alleged to have been represented, see *Richards*, 517 U.S., at 801, 116 S. Ct. 1761. In the class-action context, these limitations are implemented by the procedural safeguards contained in Federal Rule of Civil Procedure 23.

An expansive doctrine of virtual representation, however, would "recogniz[e], in effect, a common-law kind of class action." *Tice*, 162 F.3d, at 972 (internal quotation marks omitted). That is, virtual representation would authorize preclusion based on identity of interests and some kind of relationship between parties and nonparties, shorn of the procedural protections prescribed in *Hansberry, Richards,* and Rule 23. These protections, grounded in due process, could be circumvented were we to approve a virtual representation doctrine that allowed courts to "create *de facto* class actions at will." *Tice*, 162 F.3d, at 973.

Third, a diffuse balancing approach to nonparty preclusion would likely create more headaches than it relieves. Most obviously, it could significantly complicate the task of district courts faced in the first instance with preclusion questions. An all-things-considered balancing approach might spark wide-ranging, time-consuming, and expensive discovery tracking factors potentially relevant under seven- or five-prong tests. And after the relevant facts are established, district judges would be called upon to evaluate them under a standard that provides no firm guidance. See *Tyus*, 93 F.3d, at 455 (conceding that "there is no clear test for determining the applicability of" the virtual representation doctrine announced in that case). Preclusion doctrine, it should be recalled, is intended to reduce the burden of litigation on courts and parties. Cf. *Montana*, 440 U.S., at 153–154, 99 S. Ct. 970. "In this area of the law," we agree, "'crisp rules with sharp corners' are preferable to a round-about doctrine of opaque standards." *Bittinger v. Tecumseh Products Co.*, 123 F.3d 877, 881 (C.A.6 1997).

C

Finally, relying on the Eighth Circuit's decision in *Tyus*, 93 F.3d, at 456, the FAA maintains that nonparty preclusion should apply more broadly in "public-law" litigation than in "private-law" controversies. To support this position, the FAA offers two arguments. First, the FAA urges, our decision in *Richards* acknowledges that, in certain cases, the plaintiff has a reduced interest in controlling the litigation "because of the public nature of the right at issue." When a taxpayer challenges "an alleged misuse of public funds" or "other public action," we observed in *Richards*, the suit "has only an indirect impact on [the plaintiff's] interests." 517 U.S., at 803, 116 S. Ct. 1761. In actions of this character, the Court said, "we may assume that the States have wide latitude to establish procedures . . . to limit the number of judicial proceedings that may be entertained." *Ibid.*

Taylor's FOIA action falls within the category described in *Richards*, the FAA contends, because "the duty to disclose under FOIA is owed to the public generally." The opening sentence of FOIA, it is true, states that agencies "shall make [information] available to the public." 5 U.S.C. §552(a) (2006 ed.). Equally true, we have several times said that FOIA vindicates a "public" interest. *E.g., National Archives and Records Admin. v. Favish*, 541 U.S. 157, 172, 124 S. Ct. 1570, 158 L. Ed. 2d 319 (2004). The Act, however, instructs agencies receiving FOIA requests to make the information available not to the public at large, but rather to the "person" making the request. §552(a)(3)(A). See also §552(a)(3)(B) ("In making any record available *to a person* under this paragraph, an agency shall provide the record in any [readily reproducible] form or format requested *by the person. . . .*" (emphasis added)); Brief for National Security Archive et al. as *Amici Curiae* 10 ("Government agencies do not systematically make released records available to the general public."). Thus, in contrast to the public-law litigation contemplated in *Richards*, a successful FOIA action results in a grant of relief to the individual plaintiff, not a decree benefiting the public at large.

Furthermore, we said in *Richards* only that, for the type of public-law claims there envisioned, States are free to adopt procedures limiting repetitive litigation. See 517 U.S., at 803, 116 S. Ct. 1761. In this regard, we referred to instances in which the first judgment foreclosed successive litigation by other plaintiffs because, "under state law, [the suit] could be brought only on behalf of the public at large." *Id.*, at 804, 116 S. Ct. 1761.[12] *Richards* spoke of state legislation, but it appears equally evident that *Congress*, in providing for actions vindicating a public interest, may "limit the number of judicial proceedings that may be entertained." *Id.*, at 803, 116 S. Ct. 1761. It hardly follows, however, that *this Court* should proscribe or confine successive FOIA suits by different requesters. Indeed, Congress' provision for FOIA suits with no statutory constraint on successive actions counsels against judicial imposition of constraints through extraordinary application of the common law of preclusion.

The FAA next argues that "the threat of vexatious litigation is heightened" in public-law cases because "the number of plaintiffs with standing is potentially limitless." FOIA does allow "any person" whose request is denied to resort to federal court for review of the agency's determination. 5 U.S.C. §552(a)(3)(A), (4)(B) (2006 ed.). Thus it is theoretically possible that several persons could coordinate to mount a series of repetitive lawsuits.

---

12. Nonparty preclusion in such cases ranks under the sixth exception described above: special statutory schemes that expressly limit subsequent suits.

But we are not convinced that this risk justifies departure from the usual rules governing nonparty preclusion. First, *stare decisis* will allow courts swiftly to dispose of repetitive suits brought in the same circuit. Second, even when *stare decisis* is not dispositive, "the human tendency not to waste money will deter the bringing of suits based on claims or issues that have already been adversely determined against others." Shapiro 97. This intuition seems to be borne out by experience: The FAA has not called our attention to any instances of abusive FOIA suits in the Circuits that reject the virtual-representation theory respondents advocate here.

IV

For the foregoing reasons, we disapprove the theory of virtual representation on which the decision below rested. The preclusive effects of a judgment in a federal-question case decided by a federal court should instead be determined according to the established grounds for nonparty preclusion described in this opinion. See Part II-B, *supra.*

Although references to "virtual representation" have proliferated in the lower courts, our decision is unlikely to occasion any great shift in actual practice. Many opinions use the term "virtual representation" in reaching results at least arguably defensible on established grounds. See 18A Wright & Miller §4457, pp. 535–539, and n. 38 (collecting cases). In these cases, dropping the "virtual representation" label would lead to clearer analysis with little, if any, change in outcomes. See *Tice,* 162 F.3d, at 971. ("[T]he term 'virtual representation' has cast more shadows than light on the problem [of nonparty preclusion].").

In some cases, however, lower courts have relied on virtual representation to extend nonparty preclusion beyond the latter doctrine's proper bounds. We now turn back to Taylor's action to determine whether his suit is such a case, or whether the result reached by the courts below can be justified on one of the recognized grounds for nonparty preclusion.

A

It is uncontested that four of the six grounds for nonparty preclusion have no application here: There is no indication that Taylor agreed to be bound by Herrick's litigation, that Taylor and Herrick have any legal relationship, that Taylor exercised any control over Herrick's suit, or that this suit implicates any special statutory scheme limiting relitigation. Neither the FAA nor Fairchild contends otherwise.

It is equally clear that preclusion cannot be justified on the theory that Taylor was adequately represented in Herrick's suit. Nothing in the record indicates that Herrick understood himself to be suing on Taylor's behalf, that Taylor even knew of Herrick's suit, or that the Wyoming District Court took special care to protect Taylor's interests. Under our pathmarking precedent, therefore, Herrick's representation was not "adequate." See *Richards,* 517 U.S., at 801–802, 116 S. Ct. 1761.

That leaves only the fifth category: preclusion because a nonparty to an earlier litigation has brought suit as a representative or agent of a party who is bound by the prior adjudication. Taylor is not Herrick's legal representative and he has not purported to sue in a representative capacity. He concedes, however, that preclusion would be appropriate if respondents could demonstrate that he is acting as Herrick's "undisclosed agen[t]."

Respondents argue here, as they did below, that Taylor's suit is a collusive attempt to relitigate Herrick's action. The D.C. Circuit considered a similar question in addressing the "tactical maneuvering" prong of its virtual representation test. See 490 F.3d, at 976. The Court of Appeals did not, however, treat the issue as one of agency, and it expressly declined to reach any definitive conclusions due to "the ambiguity of the facts." *Ibid.* We therefore remand to give the courts below an opportunity to determine whether Taylor, in pursuing the instant FOIA suit, is acting as Herrick's agent. . . .

We have never defined the showing required to establish that a nonparty to a prior adjudication has become a litigating agent for a party to the earlier case. Because the issue has not been briefed in any detail, we do not discuss the matter elaboratively here. We note, however, that courts should be cautious about finding preclusion on this basis. A mere whiff of "tactical maneuvering" will not suffice; instead, principles of agency law are suggestive. They indicate that preclusion is appropriate only if the putative agent's conduct of the suit is subject to the control of the party who is bound by the prior adjudication. See 1 Restatement (Second) of Agency §14, p. 60 (1957) ("A principal has the right to control the conduct of the agent with respect to matters entrusted to him.").[13]

B

On remand, Fairchild suggests, Taylor should bear the burden of proving he is not acting as Herrick's agent. When a defendant points to evidence establishing a close relationship between successive litigants, Fairchild maintains, "the burden [should] shif[t] to the second litigant to submit evidence refuting the charge" of agency. Fairchild justifies this proposed burden-shift on the ground that "it is unlikely an opposing party will have access to direct evidence of collusion."

We reject Fairchild's suggestion. Claim preclusion, like issue preclusion, is an affirmative defense. See Fed. Rule Civ. Proc. 8(c); *Blonder-Tongue,* 402 U.S., at 350, 91 S. Ct. 1434. Ordinarily, it is incumbent on the defendant to plead and prove such a defense, see *Jones v. Bock,* 549 U.S. 199, 204, 127 S. Ct. 910, 166 L. Ed. 2d 798 (2007), and we have never recognized claim preclusion as an exception to that general rule, see 18 Wright & Miller §4405, p. 83 ("[A] party asserting preclusion must carry the burden of establishing all necessary elements."). We acknowledge

---

13. Our decision in *Montana v. United States,* 440 U.S. 147, 99 S. Ct. 970, 59 L. Ed. 2d 210 (1979), also suggests a "control" test for agency. In that case, we held that the United States was barred from bringing a suit because it had controlled a prior unsuccessful action filed by a federal contractor. See *id.,* at 155, 99 S. Ct. 970. We see no reason why preclusion based on a lesser showing would have been appropriate if the order of the two actions had been switched—that is, if the United States had brought the first suit itself, and then sought to relitigate the same claim through the contractor. See *Schendel,* 270 U.S., at 618, 46 S. Ct. 420 ("[I]f, in legal contemplation, there is identity of parties" when two suits are brought in one order, "there must be like identity" when the order is reversed.).

that direct evidence justifying nonparty preclusion is often in the hands of plaintiffs rather than defendants. See, *e.g.*, *Montana*, 440 U.S., at 155, 99 S. Ct. 970 (listing evidence of control over a prior suit). But "[v]ery often one must plead and prove matters as to which his adversary has superior access to the proof." 2 K. Broun, McCormick on Evidence §337, p. 475 (6th ed. 2006). In these situations, targeted interrogatories or deposition questions can reduce the information disparity. We see no greater cause here than in other matters of affirmative defense to disturb the traditional allocation of the proof burden. . . .

For the reasons stated, the judgment of the United States Court of Appeals for the District of Columbia Circuit is vacated, and the case is remanded for further proceedings consistent with this opinion.

It is so ordered.

NOTES AND QUESTIONS

1. In *Taylor*, the Court describes various categories of exceptions to the general rule that a person can only be bound to an action if he was a party to that action. Those exceptions, in turn, take shape around six concepts: (1) consent; (2) actual control of the litigation; (3) substantive legal relationships; (4) relitigation of a prior judgment through a proxy; (5) adequate representation in a properly structured litigation; and (6) statutory schemes that expressly provide for the binding of nonparties. Examples of each of these concepts should already be familiar to you.

a. *Consent and Control.* Two of these concepts—those involving consent and actual control over the litigation—proceed from the basic proposition that preclusion doctrine is defined in terms of the individual rights of litigants surrounding the effects of a judgment. For example, the principle of consent lies at the foundation of the familiar proposition that preclusion arguments are subject to waiver if not raised in a timely manner. *See* Rule 8(c)(1) ("In responding to a pleading, a party must affirmatively state any avoidance or affirmative defense, including . . . *res judicata*."). Under the same basic principle, multiple parties with claims arising from the same set of transactions or events can sometimes consent to have their common issues or claims against the defendant determined by a "test case" in which one plaintiff litigates and others agree to be bound by the result—a procedure that we saw used in the *Kaufman* litigation at p. 850, *supra*. In the category of control, the *Taylor* Court discusses the privity doctrine, under which a nonparty can be bound to a judgment when it assumes actual control of a litigation to such an extent that it may properly be said to have had its day in court with full opportunity to vindicate its rights. In both types of case, the reason for the exception to preclusion doctrine is that the nonparty has taken steps—through a manifestation of consent, or through *de facto* participation and control of the litigation—that justify compromising the individual right that it would otherwise enjoy not to be bound to a judgment in which it was not properly named and served.

b. *Substantive Legal Relationships and Relitigation Through a Proxy.* Two of the other categories of exception focus attention on the nature of the individual rights that are at stake in preclusion analysis. Under the category of agency or proxy, the Court explains in *Taylor*: "[A] party bound by a judgment may not avoid its preclusive force by relitigating through a proxy. Preclusion is thus in order when a person who did not participate in a litigation later brings suit as the designated representative of a person who was a party to the prior adjudication." *Taylor*, 553 U.S. at 895. The preclusive effect of a judgment, in other words, applies to the person who "owned" the rights that were litigated in the first action. Finding a proxy or agent to litigate those same rights in subsequent action will not alter the outcome: The proxy or agent will be bound, just as the original party would have been. Similarly, under the category of "substantive legal relationships," courts have recognized that the rights owned by one person are sometimes wholly derivative of the rights owned by another. When *A* transfers Blackacre to *B* in a sale of property, she can only transfer those rights in Blackacre that she actually owns. If those property rights have been adjudicated in a lawsuit that binds *A*, then *B* acquires Blackacre subject to that adjudication—his rights are subject to the earlier judgment, meaning that he is effectively bound by it. Again, the individual rights in question "run with" the earlier judgment. Other such relationships include "bailee and bailor, and assignee and assignor." *Id.* at 894.

c. *Adequate Representation and Statutory Schemes.* Finally, the last two categories of exception—adequate representation in a class action, and other specialized statutory schemes—focus attention on the statutory or rule-based policies by which the government can create more sweeping exceptions to the traditional rule. In a class action—a complicated proceeding that we study at length in Chapter 8—absent class plaintiffs can be bound to a judgment even though they never participated as individuals, provided that it was clear that the initial proceeding would be representative in nature and that sufficient safeguards were in place to protect the interests of absentees, including the requirement that they receive adequate representation at all points in the proceeding. And under specialized statutory schemes, federal and state legislatures may create other types of proceedings that can bind nonparties—subject always to the requirements of due process. *See id.* at 894–895 (listing examples of bankruptcy, probate, and *quo warranto* actions). In both types of case, legislatures or rule makers have determined that a carefully administered exception to the general rule is necessary to carry out important public policies.

2. The *Taylor* Court remanded the case to the lower court for further proceedings on the question whether Taylor was acting as Herrick's "undisclosed agent" in the second action—the only basis on which preclusion might be available. Though it did not specify the standard that would govern that inquiry, leaving it to the lower courts to consider the matter in the first instance, it did offer two important qualifiers. First, the Court admonished that mere "tactical maneuvering" between the individuals involved would not suffice to support preclusion. Rather, principles of agency law suggest that preclusion would be appropriate only if Herrick actually directed Taylor's actions in the second lawsuit.

Second, the Court rejected the argument that suspicious circumstances like those arguably present in this case called for the burden of persuasion to be shifted to the party seeking to avoid preclusion. Preclusion, the Court pointed out, is an affirmative defense, *see* Fed. R. Civ. P. 8(c), and defendants bear the burden of persuasion for such defenses. Notice the importance of this holding. As the Court acknowledged, the evidence necessary to make out a showing of agency or control in a preclusion case is "often in the hands of plaintiffs rather than defendants," making it difficult for the party asserting preclusion to prevail. What types of evidence might suffice to make such a showing? Would defendant need to establish that there was an actual agency agreement between Taylor and Herrick in the second action? Would it be enough to show that Taylor accepted some heavy-handed direction from Herrick, or would the defendant need to establish that Herrick was making all the major decisions?

3. *Some Special Cases of Privity.* Courts have found privity relationships to exist in some unusual circumstances. In one case, the Idaho Supreme Court has barred a woman from seeking past child-support expenses from a father on the grounds that the *state* had previously brought a suit to establish the father's paternity and determine his future support obligations. *See Lohman v. Flynn,* 78 P.3d 379 (Idaho 2003). Because the mother "requested the state to initiate the paternity and child support case on her behalf" and "[t]he state's interest derived [entirely] from [the mother's] request," the court concluded that the mother was "in privity with the state" and was bound by the first judgment, causing her claim for past support to merge with that judgment. Can this result be justified on a relitigation-through-proxy theory, because the state was litigating rights "owned" by the mother in the first action? Is an agency theory more convincing? Do you think that the mother exercised the kind of actual control in the first proceeding necessary to justify a finding of agency?

In another case, a Maryland court found a law firm to be in privity with its clients. In *Green v. Ford Motor Credit Company,* 828 A.2d 821 (Md. Ct. App. 2003), the plaintiff sued the Ford Motor Credit Company and its law firm, claiming that the two were jointly pursuing a plan to defraud consumers when repossessing leased automobiles. The plaintiff had previously settled with Ford over the terms of her lease, and that settlement barred her claim. The court found that the law firm (which represented Ford in the first action) possessed such an "identity of interest" with Ford that the two were in privity for purposes of the settlement. Does that sound to you like the type of "vicarious representation" that the Court disapproved in *Taylor?* Does *Taylor* overrule *Green?* Note that *Green* is a state-law decision, while *Taylor* was speaking about the federal common law of preclusion. But is there a constitutional due process element to the ruling in *Taylor* that might bear upon the outcome in *Green?*

4. *Appearing in Different Capacities.* While different parties may sometimes be considered the same party for preclusion purposes, there are also situations where the *same* party appearing in different capacities may be treated as a *different* party for preclusion purposes. For example, a person appearing initially as an agent or trustee of another may be permitted in a subsequent proceeding to assert claims or defenses on her own behalf that would otherwise be precluded if there were an identity of parties.

For an interesting application of this rule, *see Hurt v. Pullman, Inc.,* 764 F.2d 1443 (11th Cir. 1985). Pullman first sued Hurt in an Alabama state proceeding for a declaration of limited liability under workers' compensation law. The state court found Hurt 40 percent impaired and awarded damages. Subsequently, Hurt sued Pullman as a trustee of his pension plan for ERISA benefits due in the event of "total disability." Under Alabama law, binding on the federal court, no party could assert collateral estoppel unless she was a party to the earlier proceeding (i.e., unless there was mutuality of parties). Overruling the district court, the Court of Appeals held that Hurt was not precluded by the first proceeding from contending that he was totally disabled because there was no identity of parties. Although Hurt was a party to both proceedings, he appeared in different capacities. In the first proceeding, Hurt was representing his own interests; in the second, he acted as a fiduciary for all contributors to the pension fund.

The Eighth Circuit Court of Appeals, in contrast, has come to a different conclusion in a similar set of circumstances. In *Friez v. First American Bank & Trust of Minot*, 324 F.3d 580 (8th Cir. 2003), Friez, a bank employee, sued the bank for employment benefits under the federal ERISA law in an initial action. The district court dismissed the suit on the merits. Friez then brought another action for the same damages, this time on a tort theory, arguing that the bank and its officers had acted wrongfully in excluding him from the ERISA plan. This time, he sued the bank President and a personnel officer along with the bank itself. The Eighth Circuit found that the first judgment barred the entire action as a matter of claim preclusion, even though the officers were not parties to the first suit, since "[b]oth lawsuits revolve around [the officers'] statements to Friez as officers and managers of [the bank]." *Id.* at 582. Judge Morris Sheppard Arnold dissented, writing that the record in the second case did not indicate that the officers were sued "solely in their capacity as officers and directors," *id.* at 582–583; rather, Friez alleged that the officers engaged in tortious behavior on their own initiative, not as agents of the bank. On that assumption, Judge Arnold argued that *res judicata* should have presented no bar to Friez's claims.

5. *Preclusion and Class Certification.* The Supreme Court expanded further upon *Taylor*'s holding regarding representative litigation in a complicated class action case, *Smith v. Bayer*, 564 U.S. 299 (2011). *Bayer* involved two putative class action proceedings over a defective drug called Baycol. Both suits were filed in West Virginia state court. The first suit, *McCollins v. Bayer Corp.*, was removed to federal court and transferred to a district court in Minnesota as part of a Multidistrict Litigation proceeding. The federal court ultimately denied certification in *McCollins*, finding that individual issues would predominate over common issues in a class proceeding. The second suit, *Smith*, lay dormant in state court for some time but became active after certification was denied in *McCollins*. When the plaintiffs in *Smith* sought certification of their case, defendant Bayer returned to the federal district court that had issued the denial of certification in *McCollins* and asked that court to issue an injunction prohibiting the West Virginia courts from hearing the request to certify the *Smith* class. According to Bayer, the two class actions were identical in all relevant respects, and the West Virginia courts should be bound by the preclusive effect of the federal district court's order denying certification in *McCollins*. The district court agreed and issued an antisuit injunction, which the Eighth Circuit Court of Appeals affirmed. On certiorari review, the Supreme Court unanimously reversed and vacated the antisuit injunction.

The dispute in *Bayer* raised an array of issues that go beyond the subject of this chapter, sounding in class action policy, due process, and the provisions of a federal statute called the Anti-Injunction Act, which places strict limitations on the circumstances in which a federal court may enjoin state proceedings. (For a description and analysis of many of these issues, *see* Tobias Barrington Wolff, *Federal Jurisdiction and Due Process in the Era of the Nationwide Class Action*, 156 U. Pa. L. Rev. 2035, 2073–2117 (2008).) But the case also raised a question of preclusion doctrine. In order for the order denying certification in *McCollins* to serve as the basis for an antisuit injunction in *Bayer*, the defendants would first have to show that the *McCollins* order was preclusive of the certification issue in *Smith*.

The Court held that Bayer could not do so. "For the federal court's determination of the class issue to have this preclusive effect," the Court explained, "at least two conditions must be met. First, the issue the federal court decided must be the same as the one presented in the state tribunal. And second, Smith must have been a party to the federal suit, or else must fall within one of a few discrete exceptions to the general rule against binding nonparties." *Bayer*, 131 S. Ct. at 2376. The Court found neither requirement satisfied. As to the first, the Court explained that the federal class action provision (Rule 23) and the corresponding West Virginia rule, though similar, need not and in fact did not always apply the same certification standard, defeating the basic requirement of identity for an application of issue preclusion. As to the second, the Court found that absentees in an uncertified class were not "parties" to that proceeding for preclusion purposes, even on the threshold question of certification, and that *Taylor v. Sturgell*'s exceptions for representative actions did not apply.

The *Bayer* case raises many interesting questions about strategy and tactics in class litigation. A complete discussion of those issues must wait for Chapter 8. For now, consider the Court's strong reliance upon Rule 23 in defining the circumstances in which a class proceeding can have preclusive effect. Is that a ruling of federal preclusion law and hence confined to proceedings in federal court? Or does it have a due process dimension as well? If a state court attempted to bind putative class members to an order denying certification, relying entirely upon state preclusion law, could *Taylor* and *Bayer* be cited for the proposition that the court's action violated the constitutional limits of due process?

6. In response to *Taylor v. Sturgell*, some state courts have asserted their prerogative to develop different doctrines of privity and vicarious representation. Recall that *Taylor* was a ruling about the federal common law of preclusion. Its holding is not strictly applicable to cases governed by state preclusion law, and states are free to develop their own rules. *See, e.g., State ex rel. Schachter v. Ohio Pub. Emps. Retirement Bd.*, 905 N.E.2d 1210, 1218 (Ohio 2009) (noting that *Taylor* does not bind state courts and finding that employee was in privity with a co-worker in an earlier employment action and hence could not bring a new lawsuit challenging her own employment status); *Calpine Constr. Fin. Co. v. Arizona Dep't of Revenue*, 221 P.3d 1228 (Ariz. App. Div. 1, 2009) (reiterating that Arizona recognizes a limited doctrine of virtual representation and indicating *Taylor*'s rejection of that doctrine with a "but see" citation). Such state doctrines must always be consistent with the federal constitutional requirements of due process. *See Richards v. Jefferson Cnty.*, 517 U.S. 793, 797 (1996).

Consider *City of Chicago v. St. John's United Church of Christ*, 935 N.E.2d 1158 (Ill. App. 3d 2010). That case involved a pair of successive suits challenging the constitutionality of Chicago's use of eminent domain to condemn a cemetery and take the land for an expansion of O'Hare Airport. In the first action, the church that owned the cemetery and the living relatives of some of those buried there sued in federal court alleging federal constitutional claims. That suit was unsuccessful. In the second action, a different group of living relatives sued in state court alleging state constitutional claims. The city asserted a defense of claim preclusion, arguing that the claims could have been raised in the first proceeding and that the second group of living relatives was "virtually represented" by the first group. The court agreed, holding that "[a] nonparty may be bound pursuant to privity if his interests are so closely aligned with those of a party that the party is the 'virtual representative' of the nonparty." Distinguishing *Taylor*, the court emphasized that the Supreme Court's holding applied only to "the preclusive effects of a judgment in a federal-question case decided by a federal court," *id.* at 1168 (quoting *Taylor*, 553 U.S. at 904), leaving states free to develop their own preclusion doctrines subject only to the limits of due process. But take another look: The appellate court appears to have misapplied these principles. The first judgment *was* the result of a federal-question case decided by a federal court. It is that judgment that controls the preclusion analysis, not the law of the forum where the second suit is brought, as the Illinois court appears to believe. As you will read later in this chapter, in cases where lawsuit number two is in a different court system from lawsuit number one, the full faith and credit principle requires the court to measure the preclusive effects of a prior judgment by the preclusion law that governed in the court that rendered the first judgment. The *St. John's* court was correct to say that states can develop their own law of privity following *Taylor*, but it was incorrect to believe that state privity law controlled the outcome of the case before it.

In another case, the Sixth Circuit has rejected an argument that an expansive application of state preclusion doctrine violated due process. In *Ludwig v. Township of Van Buren*, 682 F.3d 457 (6th Cir. 2012), plaintiff, a dancer at an erotic entertainment establishment called Garter Belt, Inc., sought to challenge the constitutionality of a town ordinance that placed limitations on nude performance. In a previous action, Garter Belt had brought a challenge making the same constitutional arguments, but those arguments failed and the business was placed under an injunction requiring it to comply with the ordinance. When plaintiff brought the second challenge, the town interposed the judgment against Garter Belt and argued that the matter was *res judicata*. The district court and the Sixth Circuit both agreed. The Court of Appeals found, first, that Michigan preclusion law bound the plaintiff to the first judgment because of the combination of two factors: (1) the employer/employee relationship between plaintiff and Garter Belt, and (2) the prospective nature of the relief involved: "an employer can only act through its employees, so prospective relief must bind employees to have any effect." *Id.* at 460-461. The court then held that this state preclusion doctrine did not violate due process, relaying principally upon the policy argument that "[a]n enjoined corporation must effectively bind its future employees; otherwise those seeking an injunction cannot get full relief" and suggesting that this result might fall under *Taylor*'s exception for cases involving "legal relationships" among litigants. *Id.* at 462.

Consider whether the Sixth Circuit should have analyzed this case under *Taylor*'s "litigation by proxy" exception. Would there have been obstacles to applying that doctrine on the facts of this case? Also, note the ease with which the Sixth Circuit uses the enumerated exceptions in *Taylor* as a guide for analyzing constitutional due process limitations on state preclusion cases, even though *Taylor* itself speaks only to the federal common law of preclusion. Other courts have also proceeded on the assumption that *Taylor* speaks directly to due process limitations on preclusion. *See, e.g., Mahnke v. Garrigan*, 428 Fed. Appx. 630 (7th Cir. 2011) (*Taylor* "rejected [virtual representation] as inconsistent with due process").

Taylor ranks as a major opinion in the federal law of preclusion, and the federal courts of appeals now rely heavily upon its analysis in analyzing privity arguments. *See, e.g., Esquire Trading & Finance v. CBQ, Inc.*, 562 F.3d 516 (2d Cir. 2009) (vacating district court ruling that had relied upon virtual representation theory and analyzing privity arguments under the *Taylor* standard); *Pelt v. Utah*, 539 F.3d 1271 (10th Cir. 2008) (analyzing privity arguments under the *Taylor* standard). State courts are also free to incorporate *Taylor*'s holding into the state law of preclusion, of course, as some have done. *See, e.g., Arias v. Superior Court of San Joaquin Cnty.*, 46 Cal. 4th 969, 968–987 (2009) (relying in part upon *Taylor* to define the boundaries of privity and representative actions under a California statute); *id.* at 989–991 (Werdegar, J., concurring in the judgment) (relying even more extensively upon *Taylor* to arrive at a different conclusion about the proper analytical framework under state law).

2.   *Mutuality*

Perhaps the most controversial development in preclusion law in the last hundred years has been the trend of allowing third persons—not prior parties and not considered in privity with earlier parties—to take advantage of prior adjudications against their opponents. Because due process prevented unfavorable findings from being used against people who were not parties to an earlier action, the traditional view was that mutuality prohibited such people from using favorable findings as a basis for issue preclusion *against* a prior party. Nonetheless, there had generally been an exception to strict mutuality in the situation of derivative liability. For example, suppose an action for personal injuries is first brought against a person who bears primary liability, such as an employee who has inflicted some harm, and the judgment is in favor of the employee. If the injured person then tries to bring a second suit against the employer on a *respondeat superior* theory, the action will be precluded. The traditional justification held that, if there were no preclusion and the employer were found liable, it would seek indemnity from the employee, negating the employee's victory in the earlier suit and undermining the judgment. *See* Restatement (Second) of Judgments §51, comment b (1982). A broader departure from the mutuality requirement came in 1942 in the *Bernhard v. Bank of America* case, set forth below.

a.   **Defensive**

Bernhard v. Bank of America Nat'l Trust & Savings Assoc.

122 P.2d 892 (Cal. 1942)

TRAYNOR, J.

In June, 1933, Mrs. Clara Sather, an elderly woman, made her home with Mr. and Mrs. Charles O. Cook in San Dimas, California. Because of her failing health, she authorized Mr. Cook and Dr. Joseph Zeiler to make drafts jointly against her commercial account in the Security First National Bank of Los Angeles. On August 24, 1933, Mr. Cook opened a commercial account at the First National Bank of San Dimas in the name of "Clara Sather by Charles O. Cook." No authorization for this account was ever given to the bank by Mrs. Sather. Thereafter, a number of checks drawn by Cook and Zeiler on Mrs. Sather's commercial account in Los Angeles were deposited in the San Dimas account and checks were drawn upon that account signed "Clara Sather by Charles O. Cook" to meet various expenses of Mrs. Sather.

On October 26, 1933, a teller from the Los Angeles Bank called on Mrs. Sather at her request to assist in transferring her money from the Los Angeles Bank to the San Dimas Bank. In the presence of this teller, the cashier of the San Dimas Bank, Mr. Cook, and her physician, Mrs. Sather signed by mark an authorization directing the Security First National Bank of Los Angeles to transfer the balance of her savings account in the amount of $4,155.68 to the First National Bank of San Dimas. She also signed an order for this amount on the Security First National Bank of San Dimas "for credit to the account of Mrs. Clara Sather." The order was credited by the San Dimas Bank to the account of "Clara Sather by Charles O. Cook." Cook withdrew the entire balance from that account and opened a new account in the same bank in the name of himself and his wife. He subsequently withdrew the funds from this last mentioned account and deposited them in a Los Angeles Bank in the names of himself and his wife.

Mrs. Sather died in November, 1933. Cook qualified as executor of the estate and proceeded with its administration. After a lapse of several years he filed an account at the instance of the probate court accompanied by his resignation. The account made no mention of the money transferred by Mrs. Sather to the San Dimas Bank; and Helen Bernhard, Beaulah Bernhard, Hester Burton, and Iva LeDoux, beneficiaries under Mrs. Sather's will, filed objections to the account for this reason. After a hearing on the objections the court settled the account, and as part of its order declared that the decedent during her lifetime had made a gift to Charles O. Cook of the amount of the deposit in question.

After Cook's discharge, Helen Bernhard was appointed administratrix with the will annexed. She instituted this action against defendant, the Bank of America, successor to the San Dimas Bank, seeking to recover the deposit on the ground that the bank was indebted to the estate for this amount because Mrs. Sather never authorized its withdrawal. In addition to a general denial, defendant pleaded two affirmative defenses: (1) that the money on deposit was paid out to Charles O. Cook with the consent of Mrs. Sather and (2) that this fact is *res judicata* by virtue of the finding of the probate court in the proceeding to settle Cook's account that Mrs. Sather made a gift of the money in question to Charles O. Cook and "owned no sums of money whatsoever" at the time of her death. Plaintiff demurred to both these defenses, and objected to the introduction in evidence of the record of the earlier proceeding to support the plea of *res judicata*. . . . The trial court overruled the demurrers and objection to the evidence, and gave judgment for defendant on the ground that Cook's ownership of the money was conclusively established by the finding of the probate court. Plaintiff has appealed, denying that the doctrine of *res judicata* is applicable to the instant case or that there was a valid gift of the money to Cook by Mrs. Sather.

Plaintiff contends that the doctrine of *res judicata* does not apply because the defendant who is asserting the plea was not a party to the previous action nor in privity with a party to that action and because there is no mutuality of estoppel. . . .

Many courts have stated the facile formula that the plea of *res judicata* is available only when there is privity and mutuality of estoppel. (See cases cited in 2 Black, Judgments (Second ed.), secs. 534, 548, 549; 1 Freeman, Judgments (5th ed.), secs. 407, 428; 35 Yale L.J. 607, 608; 34 C.J. 973, 988.) Under the requirement of privity, only parties to the former judgment or their privies may take advantage of or be bound by it. (Ibid.) A party in this connection is one who is "directly interested in the subject matter, and had a right to make defense, or to control the proceeding, and to appeal from the judgment." (1 Greenleaf, Evidence (15th ed.), sec. 523. . . .) A privy is one who, after rendition of the judgment, has acquired an interest in the subject matter affected by the judgment through or under one of the parties, as by inheritance, succession, or purchase. . . . The estoppel is mutual if the one taking advantage of the earlier adjudication would have been bound by it, had it gone against him. . . .

The criteria for determining who may assert a plea of *res judicata* differ fundamentally from the criteria for determining against whom a plea of *res judicata* may be asserted. The requirements of due process of law forbid the assertion of a plea of *res judicata* against a party unless he was bound by the earlier litigation in which the matter was decided. . . . He is bound by that litigation only if he has been a party thereto or in privity with a party thereto. There is no compelling reason, however, for requiring that the party asserting the plea of *res judicata* must have been a party, or in privity with a party, to the earlier litigation.

No satisfactory rationalization has been advanced for the requirement of mutuality. Just why a party who was not bound by a previous action should be precluded from asserting it as *res judicata* against a party who was bound by it is difficult to comprehend. (See 7 Bentham's Works (Bowring's ed.) 171.) Many courts have abandoned the requirement of mutuality and confined the requirement of privity to the party against whom the plea of *res judicata* is asserted . . . The commentators are almost unanimously in accord. . . . The courts of most jurisdictions have in effect accomplished the same result by recognizing a broad exception to the requirements of mutuality and privity, namely, that they are not necessary where the liability of the defendant asserting the plea of *res judicata* is dependent upon or derived from the liability of one who was exonerated in an earlier suit brought by the same plaintiff upon the same facts. . . . Typical examples of such derivative liability are master and servant, principal and agent, and indemnitor and indemnitee. Thus, if a plaintiff sues a servant for injuries caused by the servant's alleged negligence within the scope of his employment, a judgment against the plaintiff on the grounds that the servant was not negligent can be pleaded by the master as *res judicata* if he is subsequently sued by the same plaintiff for the same injuries. Conversely, if the plaintiff first sues the master, a judgment against the plaintiff on the grounds that the servant was not negligent can be pleaded by the servant as *res judicata* if he is subsequently sued by the plaintiff. In each of these situations the party asserting the plea of *res judicata* was not a party to the previous action nor in privity with such a party under the accepted definition of a privy set forth above. Likewise, the estoppel is not mutual since the party asserting the plea, not having been a party or in privity with a party to the former action, would not have been bound by it had it been decided the other way. The cases justify this exception on the ground that it would be unjust to permit one who has had his day in court to reopen identical issues by merely switching adversaries.

In determining the validity of a plea of *res judicata* three questions are pertinent: Was the issue decided in the prior adjudication identical with the one presented in the action in question? Was there a final judgment on the merits? Was the party against whom the plea is asserted a party or in privity with a party to the prior adjudication? Estate of Smead, 219 Cal. 572 [28 Pac. (2d) 348]; Silva v. Hawkins, 152 Cal. 138 [92 Pac. 72], and People v. Rodgers, 118 Cal. 393 [46 Pac. 740, 50 Pac. 668], to the extent that they are inconsistent with this opinion, are overruled.

In the present case, therefore, the defendant is not precluded by lack of privity or of mutuality of estoppel from asserting the plea of *res judicata* against the plaintiff. Since the issue as to the ownership of the money is identical with the issue raised in the probate proceeding, and since the order of the probate court settling the executor's account was a final adjudication of this issue on the merits . . . , it remains only to determine whether the plaintiff in the present action was a party or in privity with a party to the earlier proceeding. The plaintiff has brought the present action in the capacity of administratrix of the estate. In this capacity she represents the very same persons and interests that were represented in the earlier hearing on the executor's account. In that proceeding plaintiff and the other legatees who objected to the executor's account represented the estate of the decedent. They were seeking not a personal recovery but, like the plaintiff in the present action, as administratrix, a recovery for the benefit of the legatees and creditors of the estate, all of whom were bound by the order settling the account. . . . The plea of *res judicata* is therefore available against plaintiff as a party to the former proceeding, despite her formal change of capacity. "Where a party though appearing in two suits in different capacities is in fact litigating the same right, the judgment in one estops him in the other." (15 Cal. Jur. 189; Williams v. Southern Pacific Co., 54 Cal. App. 571 [202 Pac. 356]). . . .

The judgment is affirmed.

NOTES AND QUESTIONS

1. *Defensive Versus Offensive Nonmutual Estoppel.* The type of preclusion recognized in *Bernhard* is known as "defensive" nonmutual issue preclusion: Defendant is asserting another party's victory against plaintiff as a defense. In this context, Justice Traynor did not think that a change in defendant was a good reason to give plaintiff a second bite at the apple. Do you agree?

Is it troublesome nonetheless that if the beneficiaries had prevailed in the initial proceeding against the estate and then had sued the bank, the bank would have been free to contest their entitlement to the account, but when the beneficiaries lost the initial proceeding, the bank was permitted to take advantage of their defeat in the subsequent suit? Does the decision in *Bernhard* provide an incentive for plaintiff to consolidate claims against multiple defendants in a single proceeding? Would that have been possible in this case?

Consider a different situation where a new plaintiff seeks to take advantage of another party's victory against a defendant to *preclude defendant* from contesting the issue of liability—in other words, a case where plaintiff argues, "Since you've already been found liable by someone else, you cannot now dispute your liability to me." This doctrine is known as "offensive" nonmutual issue preclusion. As discussed below, courts have been more cautious in permitting nonmutual issue preclusion in the offensive context than in the defensive context. If a second plaintiff is permitted to rely on the fruits of an earlier plaintiff's favorable findings against the same defendant, does such a rule discourage joinder in the first action? Has the first plaintiff absorbed a disproportionate share of the litigation costs in establishing the particular facts that enure to the second plaintiff's benefit? Do such concerns warrant the denial of preclusion in the context of offensive nonmutual issue preclusion?

2. Bernhard *and the "Indemnification" Exception.* Didn't Justice Traynor have available to him a narrower rationale, given his discussion of the "derivative liability" exception to the mutuality requirement? What would have happened if Bernhard had prevailed in her claim against the bank? If the bank had already paid the money to Cook, wouldn't it be entitled to seek indemnity from Cook? And yet, such a course would deprive Cook of the fruits of his prior victory. Indeed, doesn't this situation fall into the traditional "indemnity circle" exception to preclusion: Plaintiff loses in a suit against the indemnitor (here, Cook) and then proceeds to sue an indemnitee whose liability is entirely derivative — the bank, which is liable only if Cook improperly appropriated the funds?

3. *Binding the "Same Party" in* Bernhard. Although a nonparty may take advantage of a judgment if the mutuality requirement is abandoned, only a party or one "in privity" with a party can be bound by a judgment to his disadvantage. As discussed earlier in this section, this requirement is one of due process. Note that in the first proceeding, the beneficiaries under the will, including Mrs. Bernhard, filed objections to the account of the executor and lost on the issue of whether or not Mrs. Sather had made a gift to Cook. In the second action, Mrs. Bernhard, as the administrator of the estate, represented the beneficiaries and was therefore "in privity" with them.

Since "representation" of a party implicates due process concerns, assertions of representation must be carefully scrutinized. In *Martin v. Wilks*, 490 U.S. 755 (1989), the Supreme Court permitted white firefighters to challenge a consent decree entered in an employment discrimination suit brought by black employees against the municipal fire department. Although the decision was based on the absence of any duty imposed by the Federal Rules of Civil Procedure for the white firefighters to intervene in the prior proceeding, there was arguably an underlying concern that binding them to the results of a proceeding in which they were not represented would violate due process. The particular result in *Martin* was reversed by the Civil Rights Act of 1991, 42 U.S.C. §2000e-2(n)(1)(A)–(B), which provides that no person may challenge a Civil Rights order or consent decree if that person had a reasonable opportunity to intervene or was adequately represented by another. Does this provision of the Civil Rights Act violate the principle of due process that no one can be bound to a proceeding in which she did not have an opportunity to participate or in which she was not adequately represented? *Martin* is discussed further in Chapter 8.

4. *The "Entire Controversy" Doctrine.* Although defensive nonmutual issue preclusion eliminates the incentive for a plaintiff to proceed one by one against multiple potential adversaries, since it precludes a losing plaintiff from relitigating those issues that meet the requirements of issue preclusion in suits against different defendants, such a plaintiff can still get a fresh hearing on issues that are not the "same" or were not necessarily decided in the first proceeding. (In successive suits against the same defendant, claim preclusion may impose additional constraints.) A *victorious* plaintiff, of course, will generally not suffer any adverse issue preclusion effects in successive suits against different defendants, though she also will not be able to benefit from those earlier victories since nonparties will not be bound by the judgments.

Would it be desirable to force a plaintiff to join all defendants who are part of the same controversy in a single litigation? At least one jurisdiction experimented with doing just that, precluding a party from proceeding against *different defendants* if substantially similar claims against those parties could have been joined in the first action. This "entire controversy" doctrine precluded a second suit even if the plaintiff was successful in the initial suit. *See Cogdell v. Hospital Center*, 560 A.2d 1169 (1989) (prospectively announcing rule that plaintiff is required to join all known parties allegedly responsible for plaintiff's injury and later adopting by Court Rule such mandatory joinder, *see* R. 4:30A). Unlike the required party rule of Federal Rule 19(b), the entire controversy doctrine did not require dismissal of the initial action for failure to join specified parties, nor a shaping of relief to mitigate effects on nonparties. Rather, *Cogdell* enforced its consolidation objective by barring subsequent claims against omitted defendants. New Jersey has applied its "entire controversy" doctrine and refused to entertain an action even where the first action against other parties was brought in a federal court in Pennsylvania. *See Mortgagelinq Corp. v. Commonwealth Land Title Ins. Co.*, 678 A.2d 243 (1995).

The doctrine was roundly criticized by practitioners, judges, and scholars. *See Symposium: Entire Controversy Doctrine*, 28 Rutgers L.J. 1 (1996). New Jersey responded in 1998 by substantially abrogating the doctrine. Changes in the New Jersey Court Rules now require parties to disclose any nonparty who could have been joined in the controversy and the trial court may then compel a party to be joined. *See* N.J. Civil Practice R. 4:5-1(b)(2) (requiring disclosure to court at the time of initial pleading); R. 4:29-1(b) (authorizing joinder by court *sua sponte*). The court may impose sanctions for failure to comply with the notice requirements, including dismissal of the subsequent action or imposing the litigation costs on the noncomplying party. R. 4:5-1(b)(2).

5. *Bernhard* began a dramatic shift in the law of issue preclusion nationwide. Most recent considerations of the mutuality requirement by state courts have resulted in at least a partial abandonment of strict mutuality, especially when collateral estoppel is asserted defensively. *See* 18A C. Wright et al., Federal Practice and Procedure §4464 (3d ed. 2018); 31 A.L.R.3d 1044 (1970). The Supreme Court first endorsed nonmutual defensive issue preclusion in federal-question cases in *Blonder-Tongue Laboratories, Inc. v. University of Illinois Found.*, 402 U.S. 313 (1971) (patent litigation). It then recognized offensive nonmutual issue preclusion as a matter of federal common law in the following case.

b.   Offensive

Parklane Hosiery Co. v. Shore

439 U.S. 322 (1979)

MR. JUSTICE STEWART delivered the opinion of the Court.

This case presents the question whether a party who has had issues of fact adjudicated adversely to it in an equitable action may be collaterally estopped from relitigating the same issues before a jury in a subsequent legal action brought against it by a new party.

The respondent brought this stockholder's class action against the petitioners in a Federal District Court. The complaint alleged that the petitioners, Parklane Hosiery Co., Inc. (Parklane), and 13 of its officers, directors, and stockholders, had issued a materially false and misleading proxy statement in connection with a merger.[1] The proxy statement, according to the complaint, had violated §§14(a), 10(b), and 20(a) of the Securities Exchange Act of 1934, 48 Stat. 895, 891, 899, as amended, 15 U.S.C. §§78n(a), 78j(b), and 78t(a), as well as various rules and regulations promulgated by the Securities and Exchange Commission (SEC). The complaint sought damages, rescission of the merger, and recovery of costs.

Before this action came to trial, the SEC filed suit against the same defendants in the Federal District Court, alleging that the proxy statement that had been issued by Parklane was materially false and misleading in essentially the same respects as those that had been alleged in the respondent's complaint. Injunctive relief was requested. After a 4-day trial, the District Court found that the proxy statement was materially false and misleading in the respects alleged, and entered a declaratory judgment to that effect. *SEC v. Parklane Hosiery Co.*, 422 F. Supp. 477. The Court of Appeals for the Second Circuit affirmed this judgment. 558 F.2d 1083.

The respondent in the present case then moved for partial summary judgment against the petitioners, asserting that the petitioners were collaterally estopped from relitigating the issues that had been resolved against them in the action brought by the SEC.[2] The District Court denied the motion on the ground that such an application of collateral estoppel would deny the petitioners their Seventh Amendment right to a jury trial. The Court of Appeals for the Second Circuit reversed, holding that a party who has had issues of fact determined against him after a full and fair opportunity to litigate in a nonjury trial is collaterally estopped from obtaining a subsequent jury trial of these same issues of fact. 565 F.2d 815. The appellate court concluded that "the Seventh Amendment preserves the right to jury trial only with respect to issues of fact, [and] once those issues have been fully and fairly adjudicated in a prior proceeding, nothing remains for trial, either with or without a jury." Id. at 819. . . .

I

The threshold question to be considered is whether, quite apart from the right to a jury trial under the Seventh Amendment, the petitioners can be precluded

---

1. The amended complaint alleged that the proxy statement that had been issued to the stockholders was false and misleading because it failed to disclose: (1) that the president of Parklane would financially benefit as a result of the company's going private; (2) certain ongoing negotiations that could have resulted in financial benefit to Parklane; and (3) that the appraisal of the fair value of Parklane stock was based on insufficient information to be accurate.

2. A private plaintiff in an action under the proxy rules is not entitled to relief simply by demonstrating that the proxy solicitation was materially false and misleading. The plaintiff must also show that he was injured and prove damages. *Mills v. Electric Auto-Lite Co.*, 396 U.S. 375, 386–390. Since the SEC action was limited to a determination of whether the proxy statement contained materially false and misleading information, the respondent conceded that he would still have to prove these other elements of his prima facie case in the private action. The petitioners' right to a jury trial on those remaining issues is not contested.

from relitigating facts resolved adversely to them in a prior equitable proceeding with another party under the general law of collateral estoppel. Specifically, we must determine whether a litigant who was not a party to a prior judgment may nevertheless use that judgment "offensively" to prevent a defendant from relitigating issues resolved in the earlier proceeding.

A

Collateral estoppel, like the related doctrine of *res judicata*, has the dual purpose of protecting litigants from the burden of relitigating an identical issue with the same party or his privy and of promoting judicial economy by preventing needless litigation. *Blonder-Tongue Laboratories, Inc. v. University of Illinois Foundation*, 402 U.S. 313, 328-329. Until relatively recently, however, the scope of collateral estoppel was limited by the doctrine of mutuality of parties. Under this mutuality doctrine, neither party could use a prior judgment as an estoppel against the other unless both parties were bound by the judgment. Based on the premise that it is somehow unfair to allow a party to use a prior judgment when he himself would not be so bound,[7] the mutuality requirement provided a party who had litigated and lost in a previous action an opportunity to relitigate identical issues with new parties.

By failing to recognize the obvious difference in position between a party who has never litigated an issue and one who has fully litigated and lost, the mutuality requirement was criticized almost from its inception. Recognizing the validity of this criticism, the Court in *Blonder-Tongue Laboratories, Inc. v. University of Illinois Foundation, supra*, abandoned the mutuality requirement, at least in cases where a patentee seeks to relitigate the validity of a patent after a federal court in a previous lawsuit has already declared it invalid. . . .

B

The *Blonder-Tongue* case involved defensive use of collateral estoppel—a plaintiff was estopped from asserting a claim that the plaintiff had previously litigated and lost against another defendant. The present case, by contrast, involves offensive use of collateral estoppel—a plaintiff is seeking to estop a defendant from relitigating the issues which the defendant previously litigated and lost against another plaintiff. In both the offensive and defensive use situations, the party against whom estoppel is asserted has litigated and lost in an earlier action. Nevertheless, several reasons have been advanced why the two situations should be treated differently.

First, offensive use of collateral estoppel does not promote judicial economy in the same manner as defensive use does. Defensive use of collateral estoppel precludes a plaintiff from relitigating identical issues by merely "switching adversaries." *Bernhard v. Bank of America Nat'l Trust & Savings Ass'n*, 19 Cal. 2d, at 813, 122 P.2d,

---

7. It is a violation of due process for a judgment to be binding on a litigant who was not a party or a privy and therefore has never had an opportunity to be heard. *Blonder-Tongue Laboratories, Inc. v. University of Illinois Foundation*, 402 U.S. 313, 329; *Hansberry v. Lee*, 311 U.S. 32, 40.

C. Parties Bound and Advantaged   851

at 895.[12] Thus defensive collateral estoppel gives a plaintiff a strong incentive to join all potential defendants in the first action if possible. Offensive use of collateral estoppel, on the other hand, creates precisely the opposite incentive. Since a plaintiff will be able to rely on a previous judgment against a defendant but will not be bound by that judgment if the defendant wins, the plaintiff has every incentive to adopt a "wait and see" attitude, in the hope that the first action by another plaintiff will result in a favorable judgment. E.g., *Nevarov v. Caldwell*, 161 Cal. App. 2d 762, 767–768, 327 P.2d 111, 115; *Reardon v. Allen*, 88 N.J. Super. 560, 571–572, 213 A.2d 26, 32. Thus offensive use of collateral estoppel will likely increase rather than decrease the total amount of litigation, since potential plaintiffs will have everything to gain and nothing to lose by not intervening in the first action.[13]

A second argument against offensive use of collateral estoppel is that it may be unfair to a defendant. If a defendant in the first action is sued for small or nominal damages, he may have little incentive to defend vigorously, particularly if future suits are not foreseeable. *The Evergreens v. Nunan*, 141 F.2d 927, 929 (CA2); *cf. Berner v. British Commonwealth Pac. Airlines*, 346 F.2d 532 (CA2) (application of offensive collateral estoppel denied where defendant did not appeal an adverse judgment awarding damages of $35,000 and defendant was later sued for over $7 million). Allowing offensive collateral estoppel may also be unfair to a defendant if the judgment relied upon as a basis for the estoppel is itself inconsistent with one or more previous judgments in favor of the defendant.[14] Still another situation where it might be unfair to apply offensive estoppel is where the second action affords the defendant procedural opportunities unavailable in the first action that could readily cause a different result.[15]

---

12. Under the mutuality requirement, a plaintiff could accomplish this result since he would not have been bound by the judgment had the original defendant won.

13. The Restatement (Second) of Judgments §88(3) (Tent. Draft No. 2, Apr. 15, 1975) provides that application of collateral estoppel may be denied if the party asserting it "could have effected joinder in the first action between himself and his present adversary."

14. In Professor Currie's familiar example, a railroad collision injures 50 passengers all of whom bring separate actions against the railroad. After the railroad wins the first 25 suits, a plaintiff wins in suit 26. Professor Currie argues that offensive use of collateral estoppel should not be applied so as to allow plaintiffs 27 through 50 automatically to recover. [Currie, *Mutuality of Estoppel: Limits of the* Bernhard *Doctrine*, 9 Stan. L Rev. 281, 304 (1957).] See Restatement (Second) of Judgments §88(4), *supra*.

15. If, for example, the defendant in the first action was forced to defend in an inconvenient forum and therefore was unable to engage in full scale discovery or call witnesses, application of offensive collateral estoppel may be unwarranted. Indeed, differences in available procedures may sometimes justify not allowing a prior judgment to have estoppel effect in a subsequent action even between the same parties, or where defensive estoppel is asserted against a plaintiff who has litigated and lost. The problem of unfairness is particularly acute in cases of offensive estoppel, however, because the defendant against whom estoppel is asserted typically will not have chosen the forum in the first action. *See id.* §88(2) and comment d.

C

We have concluded that the preferable approach for dealing with these problems in the federal courts is not to preclude the use of offensive collateral estoppel, but to grant trial courts broad discretion to determine when it should be applied. The general rule should be that in cases where a plaintiff could easily have joined in the earlier action or where, either for the reasons discussed above or for other reasons, the application of offensive estoppel would be unfair to a defendant, a trial judge should not allow the use of offensive collateral estoppel.

In the present case, however, none of the circumstances that might justify reluctance to allow the offensive use of collateral estoppel is present. The application of offensive collateral estoppel will not here reward a private plaintiff who could have joined in the previous action, since the respondent probably could not have joined in the injunctive action brought by the SEC even had he so desired.[17] Similarly, there is no unfairness to the petitioners in applying offensive collateral estoppel in this case. First, in light of the serious allegations made in the SEC's complaint against the petitioners, as well as the foreseeability of subsequent private suits that typically follow a successful Government judgment, the petitioners had every incentive to litigate the SEC lawsuit fully and vigorously.[18] Second, the judgment in the SEC action was not inconsistent with any previous decision. Finally, there will in the respondent's action be no procedural opportunities available to the petitioners that were unavailable in the first action of a kind that might be likely to cause a different result.[19]

We conclude, therefore, that none of the considerations that would justify a refusal to allow the use of offensive collateral estoppel is present in this case. Since the petitioners received a "full and fair" opportunity to litigate their claims in the SEC action, the contemporary law of collateral estoppel leads inescapably to the conclusion that the petitioners are collaterally estopped from relitigating the question of whether the proxy statement was materially false and misleading.

II

The question that remains is whether, notwithstanding the law of collateral estoppel, the use of offensive collateral estoppel in this case would violate the petitioners' Seventh Amendment right to a jury trial.[20]

---

17. *SEC v. Everest Management Corp.*, 475 F.2d 1236, 1240 (CA2) ("[T]he complicating effect of the additional issues and the additional parties outweighs any advantage of a single disposition of the common issues"). Moreover, consolidation of a private action with one brought by the SEC without its consent is prohibited by statute 15 U.S.C. §78u(g).

18. After a 4-day trial in which the petitioners had every opportunity to present evidence and call witnesses, the District Court held for the SEC. The petitioners then appealed to the Court of Appeals for the Second Circuit, which affirmed the judgment against them. Moreover, the petitioners were already aware of the action brought by the respondent, since it had commenced before the filing of the SEC action.

19. It is true, of course, that the petitioners in the present action would be entitled to a jury trial of the issues bearing on whether the proxy statement was materially false and misleading had the SEC action never been brought—a matter to be discussed in Part II of this opinion. But the presence or absence of a jury as factfinder is basically neutral, quite unlike, for example, the necessity of defending the first lawsuit in an inconvenient forum.

20. The Seventh Amendment provides: "In suits at common law, where the value in controversy shall exceed twenty dollars, the right to jury trial shall be preserved. . . ."

A

"[T]he thrust of the [Seventh] Amendment was to preserve the right to jury trial as it existed in 1791." *Curtis v. Loether*, 415 U.S. 189, 193. At common law, a litigant was not entitled to have a jury determine issues that had been previously adjudicated by a chancellor in equity. . . .

Recognition that an equitable determination could have collateral-estoppel effect in a subsequent legal action was the major premise of this Court's decision in *Beacon Theatres, Inc. v. Westover*, 359 U.S. 500.

It is thus clear that the Court in the *Beacon Theatres* case thought that if an issue common to both legal and equitable claims was first determined by a judge, relitigation of the issue before a jury might be foreclosed by *res judicata* or collateral estoppel. To avoid this result, the Court held that when legal and equitable claims are joined in the same action, the trial judge has only limited discretion in determining the sequence of trial and "that discretion . . . must, wherever possible, be exercised to preserve jury trial." . . .

B

Despite the strong support to be found both in history and in the recent decisional law of this Court for the proposition that an equitable determination can have collateral-estoppel effect in a subsequent legal action, the petitioners argue that application of collateral estoppel in this case would nevertheless violate their Seventh Amendment right to a jury trial. The petitioners contend that since the scope of the Amendment must be determined by reference to the common law as it existed in 1791, and since the common law permitted collateral estoppel only where there was mutuality of parties, collateral estoppel cannot constitutionally be applied when such mutuality is absent.

The petitioners have advanced no persuasive reason, however, why the meaning of the Seventh Amendment should depend on whether or not mutuality of parties is present. A litigant who has lost because of adverse factual findings in an equity action is equally deprived of a jury trial whether he is estopped from relitigating the factual issues against the same party or a new party. In either case, the party against whom estoppel is asserted has litigated questions of fact, and has had the facts determined against him in an earlier proceeding. . . .

The Seventh Amendment has never been interpreted in the rigid manner advocated by the petitioners. On the contrary, many procedural devices developed since 1791 that have diminished the civil jury's historic domain have been found not to be inconsistent with the Seventh Amendment. . . .

The law of collateral estoppel, like the law in other procedural areas defining the scope of the jury's function, has evolved since 1791. . . . Thus if, as we have held, the law of collateral estoppel forecloses the petitioners from relitigating the factual issues determined against them in the SEC action, nothing in the Seventh Amendment dictates a different result, even though because of lack of mutuality there would have been no collateral estoppel in 1791.

The judgment of the Court of Appeals is *Affirmed*.

MR. JUSTICE REHNQUIST, dissenting. [Justice Rehnquist argued that application of collateral estoppel in the absence of mutuality violated petitioners' right to a jury trial under the Seventh Amendment, and that in any event it would be generally "unfair" to apply offensive collateral estoppel where the party sought to be estopped has not had an opportunity to have the facts of his case determined by a jury. He pointed out that issue preclusion had limited efficiencies in this case since a jury would have to be impaneled on other issues, such as whether the alleged misstatements had caused injury and the amount of damages. Finally, he warned that the result of the decision would be to coerce defendants to agree to consent orders or settlements in agency enforcement actions in order to preserve their right to jury trial in the private actions.]

NOTES AND QUESTIONS

1. *The Problem of Inconsistent Determinations.* Consider the following hypothetical in light of *Parklane.* An Acme Airlines plane crashes, killing 250 people. Acme is liable only if the crash was caused by pilot error. In the first 100 lawsuits filed, the jury determines that the crash was caused by uncontrollable windshear. In the next lawsuit, the jury concludes that the crash was caused by pilot error. Should offensive preclusion be available against Acme in the next 149 cases? *See* Brainerd Currie, *Mutuality of Estoppel: Limits of the* Bernhard *Doctrine,* 9 Stan. L. Rev. 281, 304 (1957) (arguing against the use of offensive collateral estoppel in this context).

As suggested in *Parklane,* one possible response to the perceived unfairness of Professor Currie's mass-tort hypothetical would be to deny offensive issue preclusion in cases where defendant has prevailed on the issue in question in prior lawsuits against different plaintiffs. *See* Restatement (Second) of Judgments §29(4) (1982) ("Consideration should be given [to] whether . . . [t]he determination relied on as preclusive was itself inconsistent with another determination of the same issue."). *Accord Hoppe v. G.D. Searle & Co.,* 779 F. Supp. 1925 (S.D.N.Y. 1991) (manufacturer not collaterally estopped from denying intentional misrepresentation and false advertising on basis of prior plaintiff's verdict where there have been conflicting verdicts and defendant prevailed in 16 of 20 suits); *Sandoval v. Superior Court,* 190 Cal. Rptr. 29 (5th Dist. 1983) (declining to collaterally estop defendant by prior determination that product was defectively designed in light of other contrary judgment in action brought by a different plaintiff); *State Farm Fire & Casualty Co. v. Century Home Components, Inc.,* 550 P.2d 1185 (Ore. 1976) (manufacturer not collaterally estopped by judgment finding warehouse fire was caused by its negligence where manufacturer was exonerated in earlier proceeding). Recall that in *Kaufman,* the court declined to invoke this "contrary authority" exception where the earlier contrary decisions did not clearly exonerate Lilly from negligent testing, and the court refused to extend the contrary authority exception to cases where a different defendant had established the contrary authority.

2. Even if there is no existing contrary authority, is it fair to bind a party to an adverse finding when a second jury could well come to a contrary conclusion in the absence of collateral estoppel? As Professor Green has written in the asbestos context:

Relitigation is unlikely to establish a more correct outcome than did the first suit. From the perspective of an asbestos defendant, however, there is substantial unfairness in universalizing a single adverse jury decision, which experience has demonstrated is not reliable. To be sure, the first day in court is more significant than subsequent ones. But when the disputed matter is one that cannot be convincingly or conclusively resolved, those later opportunities surely contribute to a sense of fairness, particularly when the impact of those subsequent days is to actuarialize the ultimate liability of the defendant for its asbestos activities.

Michael D. Green, *The Inability of Offensive Collateral Estoppel to Fulfill Its Promise: An Examination of Estoppel in Asbestos Litigation*, 70 Iowa L. Rev. 141, 223 (1984).

3. *Offensive Nonmutual Estoppel and Joinder Policy.* The Supreme Court suggested in *Parklane* that it may be appropriate to deny offensive collateral estoppel to plaintiffs who had intentionally adopted a "wait and see" attitude in the earlier proceeding. Insofar as plaintiff in *Parklane* was not *permitted* to be joined as a party in the earlier proceeding, plaintiff could not be accused of adopting such an attitude. Should a plaintiff normally be denied the benefits of offensive collateral estoppel simply because she failed to intervene in the earlier case? *Compare Charles J. Arndt, Inc. v. City of Birmingham*, 748 F.2d 1486 (11th Cir. 1984) (plaintiff denied use of collateral estoppel where it "was aware of the ongoing litigation between the City and the [previous plaintiff]" and where the President of plaintiff corporation testified in the prior litigation); *In re Aircrash Disaster at Stapleton Int'l Airport*, 720 F. Supp. 1505 (D. Colo. 1989) (whether collateral estoppel is available to the "wait and see" plaintiff is a matter for the equitable discretion of the trial court and doctrine was not available to plaintiffs in case at bar as they were aware of consolidated trial and could have joined) *with General Dynamics Corp. v. American Telephone and Telegraph*, 650 F. Supp. 1274 (N.D. Ill. 1986) (although plaintiff could technically have effected joinder in earlier litigation, application of offensive collateral estoppel was not unfair as such joinder could not have been made with ease).

D. JUDICIAL ESTOPPEL

While claim and issue preclusion constitute the principal means by which a prior adjudication can have a preclusive impact on a subsequent case, they are not the only possibilities. In rare cases, another doctrine, *judicial estoppel*, might place additional limits on the positions that a litigant can urge on a court. In order to understand what judicial estoppel is and how it works, it will be helpful to reflect briefly on the preclusion doctrines that we have studied thus far.

Claim preclusion and issue preclusion both concern the effects of earlier *judgments* on subsequent litigation. As you have learned, a litigant generally cannot rely on an earlier proceeding for purposes of preclusion unless that proceeding resulted in a final judgment that resolved the merits of the dispute. And the doctrines of preclusion depend upon judgments in other ways, as well. For example, issue preclusion generally is not available unless the issue in question was "necessary to the judgment" in an earlier proceeding. This is because claim and issue preclusion are primarily concerned with the fairest and most efficient way to adjudicate claims. Claim preclusion, as you have seen, essentially works as a mandatory joinder provision, requiring a litigant to join all her transactionally related claims in one proceeding or else lose the chance to litigate them. Similarly, issue preclusion reduces the need to relitigate an issue over and over, provided that a party has had at least one full and fair opportunity to be heard on the issue before being bound. While there is some question as to whether these doctrines always accomplish their purpose of conserving the resources of parties and the judicial system, there is no doubt that it is one of their principal goals.

There are some circumstances, however, in which another kind of preclusion doctrine is called for, one that is concerned primarily with the integrity of the judicial system rather than the fair and efficient resolution of claims. The name most commonly given to this additional preclusion doctrine is *judicial estoppel.* Judicial estoppel is an equitable doctrine that looks primarily to the behavior of a party, rather than the effect of a judgment, in placing limitations on the positions that the party can take in subsequent litigation. More precisely, judicial estoppel provides that, when a party is involved in successive lawsuits that address the same issue or set of events, that party may not urge one position on the court in the first lawsuit, benefit from that position, and then change its tune and urge a contrary position on the court in the second lawsuit simply because its interests have changed. To reward such inconsistent behavior would threaten the integrity of the judiciary by making judges complicit in the strategic manipulation of the court system. Under judicial estoppel, a party may be *estopped,* or prevented, from taking a position contrary to one that it has successfully urged on a court in an earlier litigation. As one court has put it, the doctrine of judicial estoppel is intended to prevent parties from "playing fast and loose with the courts." *Scarano v. Central R. Co.*, 203 F.2d 510, 513 (3d Cir. 1953) (citation omitted).

The Supreme Court formally recognized the doctrine of judicial estoppel for the first time in *New Hampshire v. Maine*, 532 U.S. 742 (2001). *New Hampshire v. Maine* is a rare example of a dispute between states, a type of case that gets filed directly in the Supreme Court at the trial stage. *See* 28 U.S.C. §1251(a) (Supreme Court has "original and exclusive jurisdiction of all controversies between two or more States"), *codifying* The Judiciary Act of 1789, §13, 1 Stat. 80-81). *See also New York v. New Jersey*, 523 U.S. 767 (1998) (lawsuit concerning ownership of Ellis Island, filed directly in Supreme Court). The case involved a disagreement about the proper boundary between New Hampshire and Maine along the Piscataqua River, which lies at the southeastern end of New Hampshire's boundary with Maine and runs into Portsmouth Harbor. In an earlier lawsuit between the two states concerning lobster fishing rights, New Hampshire had joined with Maine in urging the position that the boundary between the two should be determined with reference to the middle of the Piscataqua's main channel of navigation. *See New Hampshire v. Maine*, 426 U.S. 363, 369 (1976). But in the later case, in which the location of the border was now the primary issue to be resolved, New Hampshire changed its position and argued instead that the border ran along the Maine shore and hence that all of the Piscataqua River and Portsmouth Harbor belonged to New Hampshire. *New Hampshire*, 532 U.S. at 745.

It was unclear in this dispute whether either claim preclusion or issue preclusion would bar New Hampshire's argument. The claim in the second lawsuit over the border between the states was clearly different from the earlier claim over lobster fishing rights, and the two did not appear to be transactionally related. And the dispute over lobster fishing rights ended in a consent decree in which the location of the border was one among several factual issues that the parties stipulated to. Hence, the issue probably was not "actually litigated" for purposes of issue preclusion, and might not even be part of a "final judgment" depending on the terms of the consent decree. What was clear, however, was that New Hampshire had changed its position on the location of the boundary between the two lawsuits, seeking to disavow the version of events that it had successfully urged on the Court 25 years earlier.

The Supreme Court rejected this effort and formally adopted the equitable doctrine of judicial estoppel for use in the federal courts. That doctrine, the Court explained, provides that "where a party assumes a certain position in a legal proceeding, and succeeds in maintaining that position, he may not thereafter, simply because his interests have changed, assume a contrary position, especially if it be to the prejudice of the party who has acquiesced in the position formerly taken by him." This rule was intended "to protect the integrity of the judicial process," and, in the case at hand, "the balance of equities" surrounding New Hampshire's opportunistic change of position "firmly tip[ped] . . . in favor of barring [its] complaint" for that purpose. *Id.* at 749–751 (citations omitted).

In explaining its decision, the Court set forth several factors that federal courts should consider in deciding whether to apply judicial estoppel:

> First, a party's later position must be clearly inconsistent with [the position that it took in the earlier lawsuit]. Second, courts regularly inquire whether the party has succeeded in persuading a court to accept that party's earlier position, so that judicial acceptance of an inconsistent position in a later proceeding would create the perception that either the first or the second court was misled. . . . A third consideration is whether the party seeking to assert an inconsistent position would derive an unfair advantage or impose an unfair detriment on the opposing party if not estopped.

Id. at 750–751 (citations omitted). These factors, the Court explained, are not "inflexible prerequisites or an exhaustive formula" for determining when judicial estoppel applies. Rather, they are a guide for determining when the "balance of equities" should prevent a party from adopting inconsistent positions. *Id.* at 751.

Applying these considerations to the case before it, the Court found that the interpretation of the border that New Hampshire was urging was "clearly inconsistent" with the position it had adopted in the earlier litigation. Although that earlier position had been a compromise that New Hampshire accepted somewhat grudgingly in order to obtain the consent decree, that compromise was "sufficiently favorable to New Hampshire to garner its approval," enabling it to "settle the case on terms beneficial to both States." New Hampshire, the Court concluded, had every incentive to contest the location of the boundary in the first lawsuit and adopted the compromise position that it urged on the Court in order to secure concessions from Maine as part of the final consent decree. That being so, New Hampshire could not come back in the present dispute and change its tune, urging the Court to adopt a contrary position and award New Hampshire the territory as to which it had previously disclaimed ownership.

Like the other types of preclusion that we have studied, judicial estoppel is a judge-made doctrine that can vary between court systems. Although the Supreme

Court's decision in *New Hampshire v. Maine* applies to all proceedings in federal court, state courts may reject the doctrine or apply it in a different form. *See, e.g., Jones Lang Wootton, USA v. LeBoeuf, Lamb, Greene & MacRae*, 674 N.Y.S.2d 280, 286 (1st Dep't) (doctrine of judicial estoppel "precludes a party who assumed a certain position in a prior legal proceeding and who secured a judgment in his or her favor from assuming a contrary position in another action simply because his or her interests have changed"); *International Engine Parts, Inc. v. Feddersen & Co.*, 75 Cal. Rptr. 2d 178 (2d Dist. 1998) (same); *McKay v. Owens*, 937 P.2d 1222, 1229 (Idaho 1997) ("[T]he concept of judicial estoppel takes into account not only what a party states under oath in open court, but also what the party knew, or should have known, at the time the original position was adopted."). In addition, judicial estoppel is an equitable doctrine. Its availability is thus subject to the discretion of the trial court, is reviewed for abuse of discretion, and may be subject to equitable defenses.

E.   THE SPECIAL PROBLEM OF LITIGATING AGAINST THE GOVERNMENT

For the most part, the general principles of claim and issue preclusion that you have studied operate no differently when the government is a litigant. But because the government is the greatest repeat litigant of all, there are certain concerns that play out differently in the application of these various preclusion doctrines. For example, because the government often litigates an issue against different parties in different circuits, an unrestrained use of issue preclusion against the government would allow a decision in one case to bind the government in all subsequent litigation. The result would be to require the government to vigorously contest and appeal every lawsuit in which it is involved, placing an enormous strain on its resources. It would also prevent percolation of important issues of law among the circuits and might create an unnecessary restraint on the ability of the government to change the law. *See generally* Samuel Estreicher & Richard L. Revesz, *Nonacquiescence by Federal Administrative Agencies*, 98 Yale L.J. 679 (1989). Thus, the courts have tried to balance these specific concerns that face the government as litigant with broader preclusion principles.

Certainly, when the government litigates with the same party, claim preclusion should operate to preclude the government from coming back on what is essentially the "same claim." Similarly, issue preclusion functions relatively straightforwardly to estop the government when the "same parties" are involved. In *Montana v. United States*, 440 U.S. 147 (1979), the United States was precluded from relitigating the constitutionality of a state gross receipts tax levied by the State of Montana. In the first action, a federal contractor unsuccessfully challenged the constitutionality of the tax on equal protection and supremacy clause grounds. A second action brought by the same contractor for a tax refund for different years was held to be precluded by "*res judicata*" and "collateral estoppel." (Since different years were involved, collateral estoppel would seem to have been the more relevant doctrine.) A third action, brought by the United States, was precluded on "collateral estoppel" grounds because it was found that the United States, although not a formal party to the first lawsuit, had directed the litigation, including paying the attorneys' fees and costs.

The *Montana* litigation raised other interesting issues in the context of government litigation. One question is whether issues of "law" are appropriate for issue preclusion treatment. Many older cases had held that collateral estoppel applied only to issues of fact, not to issues of law. With respect to legal issues, courts were, of course, restrained by principles of *stare decisis*, but parties were thought free to relitigate an issue of law. However, because in many situations the fact/law distinction is somewhat artificial, more modern cases and the Restatement (Second) of Judgments §28(2) now recognize preclusion for issues of law except when "the two actions involve claims that are substantially unrelated or . . . a new determination is warranted in order to take account of an intervening change in the applicable legal context or otherwise to avoid inequitable administration of the laws."

In *Montana*, the government argued that changes in the tax law subsequent to the first lawsuit changed the context sufficiently so that issue preclusion should not apply. However, the Supreme Court, with Justice White dissenting on the issue, held that the factual and legal context had not materially changed since the first litigation, and relitigation of the issue was thus prohibited. *Compare, e.g., Commissioner v. Sunnen*, 266 U.S. 236 (1948) (permitting government to relitigate tax status of a contract separate from but identical to contract that was the subject of adjudication in a previous tax year because it would be unfair if one litigant had access to a legal tax standard inapplicable to all other litigants).

Suppose that the federal government litigates a novel legal issue against a party in the courts of one circuit and loses. If that same legal issue is presented in subsequent litigation between the government and the same party in a different circuit, should issue preclusion apply? Does it matter if the circuit had previously ruled on that issue in litigation involving the government and other parties? *See United States v. Stauffer Chemical Co.*, 464 U.S. 165 (1984) (binding government to prior adjudication that EPA had no right to use private contractor for inspection of another plant operated by defendant, even though plant in the second suit was located in a different state and the federal appeals court for that state had not yet ruled on the issue; the Court left open the question of whether the EPA would be estopped in subsequent litigation with the same party in a circuit that had previously determined in litigation involving other parties that private contractors could be used for inspections).

Suppose that the government loses on an issue in litigation with *A*. Should the government be estopped to relitigate the same issue with respect to *B*? Should the answer depend on whether relitigation is in the same or a different circuit? In *United States v. Mendoza*, 464 U.S. 154 (1984), the Supreme Court barred the use of nonmutual issue preclusion against the United States in an immigration suit. In *Mendoza*, plaintiff filed a petition for naturalization, claiming that the government's administration of the Nationality Act had denied him due process of law. The lower courts held that the government was estopped from relitigating the issue of due process because a prior decision by the district court in California had found that the government's provisions for the naturalization of alien servicemen violated the Due Process Clause of the Fifth Amendment. In reversing the lower courts, the Supreme Court noted that the government was more likely than any private party to be involved in lawsuits against different parties that involve the same legal issue and that nonmutual preclusion would be inappropriate given the nature of government litigation:

A rule allowing nonmutual collateral estoppel against the Government in such cases would substantially thwart the development of important questions of law by freezing the first final decision rendered on a particular legal issue. Allowing only one final adjudication would deprive this Court of the benefit it receives from permitting several courts of appeals to explore a difficult question before this Court grants certiorari. (citations omitted) Indeed if nonmutual estoppel were routinely applied against the Government, this Court would have to revise its practice of waiting for a conflict to develop before granting the Government's petitions for certiorari. See this Court's Rule 17.1.

The Solicitor General's policy for determining when to appeal an adverse decision would also require substantial revision. The Court of Appeals faulted the Government in this case for failing to appeal a decision that it now contends is erroneous, (citation omitted). But the Government's litigation conduct in a case is apt to differ from that of a private litigant. Unlike a private litigant who generally does not forgo an appeal if he believes that he can prevail, the Solicitor General considers a variety of factors, such as the limited resources of the Government and the crowded dockets of the courts, before authorizing an appeal. . . . The application of nonmutual estoppel against the Government would force the Solicitor General to abandon those prudential concerns and to appeal every adverse decision in order to avoid foreclosing further review.

In addition to those institutional concerns traditionally considered by the Solicitor General, the panoply of important public issues raised in governmental litigation may quite properly lead successive administrations of the Executive Branch to take differing positions with respect to the resolution of a particular issue. While the Executive Branch must of course defer to the Judicial Branch for final resolution of questions of constitutional law, the former nonetheless controls the progress of Government litigation through the federal courts. It would be idle to pretend that the conduct of Government litigation in all its myriad features, from the decision to file a complaint in the United States district court to the decision to petition for certiorari to review a judgment of the court of appeals, is a wholly mechanical procedure which involves no policy choices whatever.

Id. at 160–161.

Mendoza thus holds that offensive nonmutual collateral estoppel cannot be asserted against the federal government. The implications of *Mendoza* for administrative agencies seeking to relitigate rulings of law by courts of appeals reached in litigations involving other parties are discussed in Estreicher & Revesz, *Nonacquiescence by Federal Administrative Agencies, supra.*

F.   INTER-JURISDICTIONAL PRECLUSION

Within a given state, preclusion law binds a court to an earlier adjudication of another court in the same jurisdiction. Intra-jurisdictional preclusion thus contributes to the uniform enforcement of the state's laws (unless there has been an intervening change in the law between the two actions), much like *stare decisis*. Any judicial economies realized through the enforcement of preclusion law inure to the benefit of the same judicial system. The enforcement of a judgment across jurisdictional lines—from one state to another, or from a state to federal court—may have a different impact. The issuing court does not necessarily benefit from economies realized in the enforcing state, and the enforcing state may be willing to expend judicial resources on a matter that it has not previously adjudicated. More significantly, the enforcing court may be bound by a judgment and legal standard with which it disagrees, and which may frustrate its public policies. Thus, in some circumstances inter-jurisdictional preclusion may represent an intrusion into the sovereign prerogatives of the enforcing state.

However, there are great benefits realized by the surrender of judicial independence that is implicit in inter-jurisdictional preclusion: inter-jurisdictional uniformity, as well as protection of reliance interests and stability of outcomes within a federal system. Once adjudicated, a litigant's rights will not vary by jurisdiction. The first court to adjudicate a case is given the authority to act for all jurisdictions that respect and enforce its judgment. This inter-jurisdictional cooperation is one of the defining characteristics of American federalism.

As a doctrinal problem, inter-jurisdictional preclusion significantly complicates the subjects of claim and issue preclusion. When a party asserts that a judgment from one judicial system should have preclusive effect in another judicial system, a series of questions arises concerning the appropriate scope of the preclusion. May the enforcing court give less preclusive effect to the judgment than would the issuing court? May it give the judgment more preclusive effect than would the issuing court? For example, what if the issuing state would consider its disposition "on the merits" but the enforcing state would not? What if the enforcing state uses a different definition of "same claim" for *res judicata* purposes or has a more expansive compulsory counterclaim rule?

When the issuing court is a state court and the enforcing court is federal, additional federalism concerns are implicated: To what extent must federal courts, entrusted with the enforcement of federal rights, recognize a prior adjudication in a state proceeding that would preclude litigation of a federal question in the federal forum?

Interjurisdictional preclusion problems arise in three contexts: interstate enforcement, state/federal enforcement, and international enforcement. Our principal focus here will be on the problem of state/federal preclusion, with short notes on the other two aspects.

1. Full Faith and Credit

The starting point for all domestic problems of inter-jurisdictional preclusion is the Full Faith and Credit Clause of the U.S. Constitution, and an implementing statute passed by Congress shortly after constitutional ratification. Article IV, §1 of the Constitution provides:

> Full Faith and Credit shall be given in each State to the public Acts, Records, and judicial Proceedings of every other State. And the Congress may by general Laws prescribe the Manner in which such Acts, Records and Proceedings shall be proved, and the Effect thereof.

The implementing statute, now codified as 28 U.S.C. §1738, provides:

> . . . The records and judicial proceedings of any court of any such State, Territory or Possession . . . shall have the same full faith and credit in every court within the United States and its Territories and Possessions as they have by law or usage in the courts of such State, Territory or Possession from which they are taken.

There are two important differences between Article IV and §1738. First, the statute makes clear that a judgment must receive the "same" respect that it has received in the issuing state. Second, the statute imposes the duty on "every court within the United States and its Territories"; the Constitution speaks only to "each State." Why are those differences significant?

Why do you suppose it was so important to the framers to ensure that state court judgments would be enforceable nationwide? In what ways do those policies correspond to the values promoted by preclusion law? For a comprehensive review of the history of full faith and credit, *see* Ralph U. Whitten, *The Constitutional Limitations on State-Court Jurisdiction: A Historical-Interpretative Reexamination of the Full Faith and Credit and Due Process Clauses (Part One)*, 14 Creighton L. Rev. 499 (1981).

What is the source of the obligation of state courts to respect federal judgments? Notice that neither Article IV nor §1738 explicitly addresses that issue. Although the existence of the obligation has long been clear, the precise source of that obligation was only identified by the Supreme Court in 2001 in *Semtek Int'l v. Lockheed Martin Corp., infra. See generally* Ronan E. Degnan, *Federalized Res Judicata*, 85 Yale L.J. 741 (1976); Stephen B. Burbank, *Interjurisdictional Preclusion, Full Faith and Credit and Federal Common Law: A General Approach*, 71 Cornell L. Rev. 733 (1986).

Does it ever matter whether the duty to enforce a state judgment is imposed by statute rather than the Constitution? Could Congress make exceptions to the duty to enforce state judgments? Could it decide that *no* judgment need be enforced outside of the state of issue in a particular class of cases? *See* 28 U.S.C. §1738C (part of the so-called Defense of Marriage Act, providing that "No State, territory, or possession of the United States, or Indian tribe, shall be required to give effect to any public act, record, or judicial proceeding of any other State, territory, possession, or tribe respecting a relationship between persons of the same sex that is treated as a marriage under the laws of such other State, territory, possession, or tribe, or a right or claim arising from such relationship"); *but see United States v. Windsor*, 570 U.S. 744 (2013) (holding that another part of that statute that denied all federal recognition to the marriages of same-sex couples violated the Due Process Clause of the Fifth Amendment to the U.S. Constitution). Could Congress exempt federal courts from the obligation of enforcing state judgments altogether?

2.   State/Federal Preclusion

The sacrifice of judicial independence implicit in all cases of inter-jurisdictional preclusion has particular significance where a state adjudication deprives a litigant of the opportunity to litigate a federal question in a federal court. As we saw in the context of supplemental jurisdiction, a high value is placed on enabling litigants to assert their federal claims in a federal forum. Indeed, for that reason, the supplemental jurisdiction statute authorizes federal courts to adjudicate matters outside their ordinary jurisdiction in order to eliminate pressure to litigate federal claims in state courts.

Where a state court adjudicates a matter related to subsequent federal litigation, the federal court is faced with a dilemma: the policy of full faith and credit may defeat the substantive goals of federal law. Indeed, preclusion may occur even where the party to be precluded was an involuntary litigant in the state system. The following case highlights these tensions.

Allen v. McCurry

449 U.S. 90 (1980)

Justice Stewart delivered the opinion of the Court.

At a hearing before his criminal trial in a Missouri court, the respondent, Willie McCurry, invoked the Fourth and Fourteenth Amendments to suppress evidence that had been seized by the police. The trial court denied the suppression motion in part, and McCurry was subsequently convicted after a jury trial. The conviction was later affirmed on appeal. *State v. McCurry*, 587 S.W.2d 337 (Mo. App. 1979). . . . McCurry was barred by this Court's decision in *Stone v. Powell*, 428 U.S. 465, from seeking a writ of habeas corpus in a federal district court. Nevertheless, he sought federal-court redress for the alleged constitutional violation by bringing a damages suit under 42 U.S.C. §1983 against the officers who had entered his home and seized the evidence in question. . . .

I

In April 1977, several undercover police officers, following an informant's tip that McCurry was dealing in heroin, went to his house in St. Louis, Mo., to attempt a purchase. Two officers, petitioners Allen and Jacobsmeyer, knocked on the front door, while the other officers hid nearby. When McCurry opened the door, the two officers asked to buy some heroin "caps." McCurry went back into the house and returned soon thereafter, firing a pistol at and seriously wounding Allen and Jacobsmeyer. After a gun battle with the other officers and their reinforcements, McCurry retreated into the house; he emerged again when the police demanded that he surrender. Several officers then entered the house without a warrant, purportedly to search for other persons inside. One of the officers seized drugs and other contraband that lay in plain view, as well as additional contraband he found in dresser drawers and in auto tires on the porch.

McCurry was charged with possession of heroin and assault with intent to kill. At the pretrial suppression hearing, the trial judge excluded the evidence seized from the dresser drawers and tires, but denied suppression of the evidence found in plain view. McCurry was convicted of both the heroin and assault offenses.

McCurry subsequently filed the present §1983 action for $1 million in damages against petitioners Allen and Jacobsmeyer, other unnamed individual police officers, and the city of St. Louis and its police department. The complaint alleged a conspiracy to violate McCurry's Fourth Amendment rights, an unconstitutional search and seizure of his house, and an assault on him by unknown police officers after he had been arrested and handcuffed. The petitioners moved for summary judgment. The District Court apparently understood the gist of the complaint to be the allegedly unconstitutional search and seizure and granted summary judgment, holding that collateral estoppel prevented McCurry from relitigating the search-and-seizure question already decided against him in the state courts. 466 F. Supp. 514 (ED Mo. 1978).[2] . . .

II

The federal courts have traditionally adhered to the related doctrines of *res judicata* and collateral estoppel. Under *res judicata*, a final judgment on the merits of an action precludes the parties or their privies from relitigating issues that were or could have been raised in that action. *Cromwell v. County of Sac.*, 94 U.S. 351, 352. Under collateral estoppel, once a court has decided an issue of fact or law necessary to its judgment, that decision may preclude relitigation of the issue in a suit on a different cause of action involving a party to the first case. *Montana v. United States*, 440 U.S. 147, 153. As this Court and other courts have often recognized, *res judicata* and collateral estoppel relieve parties of the cost and vexation of multiple lawsuits, conserve judicial resources, and, by preventing inconsistent decisions, encourage reliance on adjudication. *Id.* at 153-154.

In recent years, this Court has reaffirmed the benefits of collateral estoppel in particular, finding the policies underlying it to apply in contexts not formerly recognized at common law. Thus, the Court has eliminated the requirement of mutuality in applying collateral estoppel to bar relitigation of issues decided earlier in federal-court suits, *Blonder-Tongue Laboratories, Inc. v. University of Illinois Foundation*, 402 U.S. 313, and has allowed a litigant who was not a party to a federal case to use collateral estoppel "offensively" in a new federal suit against the party who lost on the decided issue in the first case, *Parklane Hosiery Co. v. Shore*, 439 U.S. 322. But one general limitation the Court has repeatedly recognized is that the concept of collateral estoppel cannot apply when the party against whom the earlier decision

---

2. The merits of the Fourth Amendment claim are discussed in the opinion of the Missouri Court of Appeals. *State v. McCurry*, 587 S.W.2d 337 (1979). The state courts upheld the entry of the house as a reasonable response to emergency circumstances, but held illegal the seizure of any evidence discovered as a result of that entry except what was in plain view. *Id.* at 340. McCurry therefore argues here that even if the doctrine of collateral estoppel generally applies to this case, he should be able to proceed to trial to obtain damages for the part of the seizure declared illegal by the state courts. The petitioners contend, on the other hand, that the complaint alleged essentially an illegal entry, adding that only the entry could possibly justify the $1 million prayer. Since the state courts upheld the entry, the petitioners argue that if collateral estoppel applies here at all, it removes from trial all issues except the alleged assault. The United States Court of Appeals, however, addressed only the broad question of the applicability of collateral estoppel to §1983 suits brought by plaintiffs in McCurry's circumstances, and questions as to the scope of collateral estoppel with respect to the particular issues in this case are not now before us.

is asserted did not have a "full and fair opportunity" to litigate that issue in the earlier case. *Montana v. United States, supra,* at 153; *Blonder-Tongue Laboratories, Inc. v. University of Illinois Foundation, supra,* at 328–329.[7]

The federal courts generally have also consistently accorded preclusive effect to issues decided by state courts. E.g., *Montana v. United States, supra; Angel v. Bullington,* 330 U.S. 183. Thus, *res judicata* and collateral estoppel not only reduce unnecessary litigation and foster reliance on adjudication, but also promote the comity between state and federal courts that has been recognized as a bulwark of the federal system. . . .

Indeed, though the federal courts may look to the common law or to the policies supporting *res judicata* and collateral estoppel in assessing the preclusive effect of decisions of other federal courts, Congress has specifically required all federal courts to give preclusive effect to state-court judgments whenever the courts of the State from which the judgments emerged would do so:

> [j]udicial proceedings [of any court of any state] shall have the same full faith and credit in every court within the United States and its Territories and Possessions as they have by law or usage in the courts of such State . . . 28 U.S.C. §1738.[8]

It is against this background that we examine the relationship of §1983 and collateral estoppel, and the decision of the Court of Appeals in this case.

III

This Court has never directly decided whether the rules of *res judicata* and collateral estoppel are generally applicable to §1983 actions. . . .

Because the requirement of mutuality of estoppel was still alive in the federal courts until well into this century, *see Blonder-Tongue Laboratories, Inc. v. University of Illinois Foundation, supra,* at 322–323, the drafters of the 1871 Civil Rights Act, of which §1983 is a part, may have had less reason to concern themselves with rules

---

7. Other factors, of course, may require an exception to the normal rules of collateral estoppel in particular cases. E.g., *Montana v. United States,* 440 U.S., at 162 (unmixed questions of law in successive actions between the same parties on unrelated claims). Contrary to the suggestion of the dissent, *post,* at 112–113, our decision today does not "fashion" any new, more stringent doctrine of collateral estoppel, nor does it hold that the collateral-estoppel effect of a state-court decision turns on the single factor of whether the State gave the federal claimant a full and fair opportunity to litigate a federal question. Our decision does not "fashion" any doctrine of collateral estoppel at all. Rather, it construes §1983 to determine whether the conventional doctrine of collateral estoppel applies to the case at hand. It must be emphasized that the question whether any exceptions or qualifications within the bounds of that doctrine might ultimately defeat a collateral-estoppel defense in this case is not before us. See n. 2, *supra.*

8. This statute has existed in essentially unchanged form since its enactment just after the ratification of the Constitution, Act of May 26, 1790, ch. 11, 1 Stat. 122, and its reenactment soon thereafter, Act of Mar. 27, 1804, ch. 56, 2 Stat. 298–299. Congress has also provided means for authenticating the records of the state proceedings to which the federal courts are to give full faith and credit. 28 U.S.C. §1738.

of preclusion than a modern Congress would. Nevertheless, in 1871 *res judicata* and collateral estoppel could certainly have applied in federal suits following state-court litigation between the same parties or their privies, and nothing in the language of §1983 remotely expresses any congressional intent to contravene the common-law rules of preclusion or to repeal the express statutory requirements of the predecessor of 28 U.S.C. §1738, see n. 8, *supra*. Section 1983 creates a new federal cause of action.[11] It says nothing about the preclusive effect of state-court judgments.

Moreover, the legislative history of §1983 does not in any clear way suggest that Congress intended to repeal or restrict the traditional doctrines of preclusion. The main goal of the Act was to override the corrupting influence of the Ku Klux Klan and its sympathizers on the governments and law enforcement agencies of the Southern States, . . . and of course the debates show that one strong motive behind its enactment was grave congressional concern that the state courts had been deficient in protecting federal rights. But in the context of the legislative history as a whole, this congressional concern lends only the most equivocal support to any argument that, in cases where the state courts have recognized the constitutional claims asserted and provided fair procedures for determining them, Congress intended to override §1738 or the common-law rules of collateral estoppel and *res judicata*. Since repeals by implication are disfavored, . . . much clearer support than this would be required to hold that §1738 and the traditional rules of preclusion are not applicable to §1983 suits.

As the Court has understood the history of the legislation, Congress realized that in enacting §1983 it was altering the balance of judicial power between the state and federal courts. . . . But in doing so, Congress was adding to the jurisdiction of the federal courts, not subtracting from that of the state courts. See *Monroe v. Pape*, [365 U.S. 167,] at 183 [(1961)] ("The federal remedy is supplementary to the state remedy . . . ").[14] The debates contain several references to the concurrent jurisdiction of the state courts over federal questions, and numerous suggestions that the state courts would retain their established jurisdiction so that they could, when the then current political passions abated, demonstrate a new sensitivity to federal rights.

---

11. "Every person who, under color of any statute, ordinance, regulation, custom, or usage, of any State or Territory, subjects, or causes to be subjected, any citizen of the United States or other person within the jurisdiction thereof to the deprivation of any rights, privileges, or immunities secured by the Constitution and laws, shall be liable to the party injured in an action at law, suit in equity, or other proper proceeding for redress." 42 U.S.C. §1983. It has been argued that, since there remains little federal common law after *Erie R. Co. v. Tompkins*, 304 U.S. 64, to hold that the creation of a federal cause of action by itself does away with the rules of preclusion would take away almost all meaning from §1738. Currie, *Res Judicata: The Neglected Defense*, 45 U. Chi. L. Rev. 317, 328 (1978).

14. To the extent that Congress in the post–Civil War period did intend to deny full faith and credit to state-court decisions on constitutional issues, it expressly chose the very different means of postjudgment removal for state-court defendants whose civil rights were threatened by biased state courts and who therefore "are denied or cannot enforce [their civil rights] in the courts or judicial tribunals of the State." Act of Apr. 9, 1866, ch. 31, §3, 14 Stat. 27.

To the extent that it did intend to change the balance of power over federal questions between the state and federal courts, the 42d Congress was acting in a way thoroughly consistent with the doctrines of preclusion. In reviewing the legislative history of §1983 in *Monroe v. Pape, supra,* the Court inferred that Congress had intended a federal remedy in three circumstances: where state substantive law was facially unconstitutional, where state procedural law was inadequate to allow full litigation of a constitutional claim, and where state procedural law, though adequate in theory, was inadequate in practice. 365 U.S. at 173–174. In short, the federal courts could step in where the state courts were unable or unwilling to protect federal rights. *Id.* at 176. This understanding of §1983 might well support an exception to *res judicata* and collateral estoppel where state law did not provide fair procedures for the litigation of constitutional claims, or where a state court failed to even acknowledge the existence of the constitutional principle on which a litigant based his claim. Such an exception, however, would be essentially the same as the important general limit on rules of preclusion that already exists: Collateral estoppel does not apply where the party against whom an earlier court decision is asserted did not have a full and fair opportunity to litigate the claim or issue decided by the first court. . . . But the Court's view of §1983 in *Monroe* lends no strength to any argument that Congress intended to allow relitigation of federal issues decided after a full and fair hearing in a state court simply because the state court's decision may have been erroneous. . . .

The actual basis of the Court of Appeals' holding appears to be a generally framed principle that every person asserting a federal right is entitled to one unencumbered opportunity to litigate that right in a federal district court, regardless of the legal posture in which the federal claim arises. But the authority for this principle is difficult to discern. It cannot lie in the Constitution, which makes no such guarantee, but leaves the scope of the jurisdiction of the federal district courts to the wisdom of Congress.[21] And no such authority is to be found in §1983 itself. For reasons already discussed at length, nothing in the language or legislative history of §1983 proves any congressional intent to deny binding effect to a state-court judgment or decision when the state court, acting within its proper jurisdiction, has given the parties a full and fair opportunity to litigate federal claims, and thereby has shown itself willing and able to protect federal rights. And nothing in the legislative history of §1983 reveals any purpose to afford less deference to judgments in state criminal proceedings than to those in state civil proceedings. There is, in short, no reason to believe that Congress intended to provide a person claiming a federal right an unrestricted opportunity to relitigate an issue already decided in state court simply because the issue arose in a state proceeding in which he would rather not have been engaged at all. . . .

The Court of Appeals erred in holding that McCurry's inability to obtain federal habeas corpus relief upon his Fourth Amendment claim renders the doctrine of collateral estoppel inapplicable to his §1983 suit.[25] Accordingly, the judgment is reversed, and the case is remanded to the Court of Appeals for proceedings consistent with this opinion.

---

21. U.S. Const., Art. III.

25. We do not decide *how* the body of collateral-estoppel doctrine or 28 U.S.C. §1738 should apply in this case. See n. 2, *supra.*

JUSTICE BLACKMUN, with whom JUSTICE BRENNAN and JUSTICE MARSHALL join, dissenting. . . .

. . . Although the legislators of the 42d Congress did not expressly state whether the then existing common-law doctrine of preclusion would survive enactment of §1983, they plainly anticipated more than the creation of a federal statutory remedy to be administered indifferently by either a state or a federal court. The legislative intent, as expressed by supporters and understood by opponents, was to restructure relations between the state and federal courts. Congress deliberately opened the federal courts to individual citizens in response to the States' failure to provide justice in their own courts. Contrary to the view presently expressed by the Court, the 42d Congress was not concerned solely with procedural regularity. Even where there was procedural regularity, which the Court today so stresses, Congress believed that substantive justice was unobtainable. The availability of the federal forum was not meant to turn on whether, in an individual case, the state procedures were adequate. Assessing the state of affairs as a whole, Congress specifically made a determination that federal oversight of constitutional determinations through the federal courts was necessary to ensure the effective enforcement of constitutional rights.

That the new federal jurisdiction was conceived of as concurrent with state jurisdiction does not alter the significance of Congress' opening the federal courts to these claims. Congress consciously acted in the broadest possible manner. The legislators perceived that justice was not being done in the States then dominated by the Klan, and it seems senseless to suppose that they would have intended the federal courts to give full preclusive effect to prior state adjudications. That supposition would contradict their obvious aim to right the wrongs perpetuated in those same courts. . . .

One should note also that in *England v. Medical Examiners*, 375 U.S. 411 (1964), the Court had affirmed the federal courts' special role in protecting constitutional rights under §1983. In that case it held that a plaintiff required by the abstention doctrine to submit his constitutional claim first to a state court could not be precluded entirely from having the federal court, in which he initially had sought relief, pass on his constitutional claim. The Court relied on "the unqualified terms in which Congress, pursuant to constitutional authorization, has conferred specific categories of jurisdiction upon the federal courts," and on its "fundamental objections to any conclusion that a litigant who has properly invoked the jurisdiction of a Federal District Court to consider federal constitutional claims can be compelled, without his consent and through no fault of his own, to accept instead a state court's determination of those claims." *Id.* at 415. The Court set out its understanding as to when a litigant in a §1983 case might be precluded by prior litigation, holding that "if a party freely and without reservation submits his federal claims for decision by the state courts, litigates them there, and has them decided there, then—whether or not he seeks direct review of the state decision in this Court—he has elected to forgo his right to return to the District Court." *Id.* at 419. I do not understand why the Court today should abandon this approach.

The Court now fashions a new doctrine of preclusion, applicable only to actions brought under §1983, that is more strict and more confining than the federal rules of preclusion applied in other cases. In *Montana v. United States*, 440 U.S.

147 (1979), the Court pronounced three major factors to be considered in determining whether collateral estoppel serves as a barrier in the federal court:

> [Whether] the issues presented . . . are in substance the same . . . ; whether controlling facts or legal principles have changed significantly since the state-court judgment; and finally, whether other special circumstances warrant an exception to the normal rules of preclusion. *Id.* at 155.

But now the Court states that the collateral-estoppel effect of prior state adjudication should turn on only one factor, namely, what it considers the "one general limitation" inherent in the doctrine of preclusion: "that the concept of collateral estoppel cannot apply when the party against whom the earlier decision is asserted did not have a 'full and fair opportunity' to litigate that issue in the earlier case." If that one factor is present, the Court asserts, the litigant properly should be barred from relitigating the issue in federal court.[12] One cannot deny that this factor is an important one. I do not believe, however, that the doctrine of preclusion requires the inquiry to be so narrow, and my understanding of the policies underlying §1983 would lead me to consider all relevant factors in each case before concluding that preclusion was warranted.

In this case, the police officers seek to prevent a criminal defendant from relitigating the constitutionality of their conduct in searching his house, after the state trial court had found that conduct in part violative of the defendant's Fourth Amendment rights and in part justified by the circumstances. I doubt that the police officers, now defendants in this §1983 action, can be considered to have been in privity with the State in its role as prosecutor. Therefore, only "issue preclusion" is at stake.

The following factors persuade me to conclude that this respondent should not be precluded from asserting his claim in federal court. First, at the time §1983 was passed, a nonparty's ability, as a practical matter, to invoke collateral estoppel was nonexistent. One could not preclude an opponent from relitigating an issue in a new cause of action, though that issue had been determined conclusively in a prior proceeding, unless there was "mutuality." Additionally, the definitions of "cause of action" and "issue" were narrow.[16] As a result, and obviously, no preclusive effect could arise out of a criminal proceeding that would affect subsequent *civil* litigation. Thus, the 42d Congress could not have anticipated or approved that a criminal defendant, tried and convicted in state court, would be precluded from raising against police officers a constitutional claim arising out of his arrest.

---

12. This articulation of the preclusion doctrine of course would bar a §1983 litigant from relitigating any issue he *might* have raised, as well as any issue he actually litigated in his criminal trial.

16. Compare McCaskill, Actions and Causes of Action, 34 Yale L.J. 614, 638 (1925) (defining "cause of action" as "that group of operative facts which, standing alone, would show a single right in the plaintiff and a single delict to that right giving cause for the state, through its courts, to afford relief to the party or parties whose right was invaded"), with C. Clark, Handbook on the Law of Code Pleading 84 (1928) (adopting "modern" rule expanding "cause of action" to include more than one "right").

Also, the process of deciding in a state criminal trial whether to exclude or admit evidence is not at all the equivalent of a §1983 proceeding. The remedy sought in the latter is utterly different. In bringing the civil suit the criminal defendant does not seek to challenge his conviction collaterally. At most, he wins damages. In contrast, the exclusion of evidence may prevent a criminal conviction. A trial court, faced with the decision whether to exclude relevant evidence, confronts institutional pressures that may cause it to give a different shape to the Fourth Amendment right from what would result in civil litigation of a damages claim. Also, the issue whether to exclude evidence is subsidiary to the purpose of a criminal trial, which is to determine the guilt or innocence of the defendant, and a trial court, at least subconsciously, must weigh the potential damage to the truth-seeking process caused by excluding relevant evidence. . . .

A state criminal defendant cannot be held to have chosen "voluntarily" to litigate his Fourth Amendment claim in the state court. The risk of conviction puts pressure upon him to raise all possible defenses. He also faces uncertainty about the wisdom of forgoing litigation on *any* issue, for there is the possibility that he will be held to have waived his right to appeal on that issue. The "deliberate bypass" of state procedures, which the imposition of collateral estoppel under these circumstances encourages, surely is not a preferred goal. To hold that a criminal defendant who raises a Fourth Amendment claim at his criminal trial "freely and without reservation submits his federal claims for decision by the state courts," . . . is to deny reality. The criminal defendant is an involuntary litigant in the state tribunal, and against him all the forces of the State are arrayed. To force him to a choice between forgoing either a potential defense or a federal forum for hearing his constitutional civil claim is fundamentally unfair.

I would affirm the judgment of the Court of Appeals.

NOTES AND QUESTIONS

1. *Claim or Issue Preclusion?* In *Allen*, the Supreme Court's opinion focuses on collateral estoppel. Do you understand why *Allen* is a case of "issue preclusion" rather than "claim preclusion"? Note that Allen could not have asserted his claim for civil relief in the same proceeding as his criminal prosecution.

2. *Unavailability of an Initial Federal Forum.* Is there any way that McCurry could have ensured that he would obtain a federal forum for his Fourth Amendment claim, short of abandoning his constitutional objections to the evidence used in the criminal proceeding against him? Should this make a difference in deciding whether or not to grant preclusion?

It is unlikely that the federal courts would have entertained a suit challenging the legality of the police conduct while a prior criminal prosecution against McCurry was pending. *See Samuels v. Mackell*, 401 U.S. 66 (1971) (barring federal declaratory judgment proceeding while state criminal prosecution against federal plaintiff was pending). If McCurry's only judicial relief would indeed depend on the state proceeding, doesn't that substantially undermine §1983's purpose of providing a federal forum?

Is there any reason to think that federal courts would be more sympathetic to McCurry's contention of illegal search than was the state criminal court? Is there any reason to believe that Congress thought so?

3. *State-Law Issues to Be Determined. Allen* decides that §1983 does not contemplate an exception to the full faith and credit command of §1738, and therefore the federal court must give the same preclusive effect to findings as the state court would. As noted in footnote 2, the Supreme Court did not pass judgment on whether issue preclusion was in fact appropriate in the circumstances of this case. What arguments are available to plaintiff's lawyers under state law to defeat the application of issue preclusion? Consider here footnote 2 of the majority opinion and the dissent, as well as *Haring v. Prosise*, 462 U.S. 306 (1983) (criminal defendant's plea of guilty on drug charge does not preclude relitigating issue in later §1983 civil rights action against police officer because under state law "actual litigation" is necessary for issue preclusion).

4. *Claim Preclusion and §1983. Allen* did not squarely address the question of whether a §1983 litigant who could have, but did not, raise that claim in a prior state proceeding can be barred through claim preclusion from bringing the §1983 claim in a federal court. In *Migra v. Warren City School District Bd. of Educ.*, 465 U.S. 75 (1984), plaintiff successfully sued the school board and local officials in Ohio state court for breach of contract for reneging on a promise to renew her contract. She subsequently sought additional damages in federal court for a violation of her civil rights under §1983 involving the same underlying conduct. The Supreme Court held that plaintiff's claims were merged in the first state court judgment; 28 U.S.C. §1738 requires the federal court to give the same preclusive effect to the state judgment as would the state court, and claims brought under §1983 did not constitute an exception to the full faith and credit command.

5. *Litigation Options.* How does the *Migra* decision affect the litigation strategy of a plaintiff asserting both state and federal claims? What should plaintiff in *Migra* have done?

If plaintiff in *Migra* wants to litigate her federal claims in federal court, is she forced to litigate her state claims there as well? Is it clear that the federal court has jurisdiction to hear the state claims as a matter of supplemental jurisdiction? If the federal court refuses to hear the state claims, can plaintiff then bring the state claims in state court?

6. *Must an Override of §1738 Be Express?* Do you read the Court's decision in *Allen* to establish an interpretive rule that the full faith and credit principle of 28 U.S.C. §1738 applies unless express language to the contrary appears in the federal law that is the basis of the second suit? Or has the Court authorized resort beyond express text to permit a full consideration of its text, legislative history, and policies, basing its conclusion that §1983 does not work an override on such broad considerations?

Several post-*Allen* decisions appear to give serious attention to the structure and legislative history of statutes in order to determine whether particular federal statutes contemplate claim and/or issue preclusions exceptions to §1738. In *Kremer v. Chemical Constr. Corp.*, 456 U.S. 461, 470–471 (1982), the Supreme Court in a 5-4 decision held that litigants who *appeal* findings by state administrative agencies through the courts are precluded from relitigating Title VII employment discrimination claims arising from the same facts. The Court found that although initial resort to state administrative remedies was required by Title VII and did not deprive a party of a *de novo* federal trial on a Title VII claim, the federal statute contemplated finality once the state's *judicial* machinery was invoked. *Compare Brown v. Felsen*, 442

U.S. 127, 138–139 (1979) (failure to raise issue of fraud in state court action did not preclude use of fraud to prevent debtor's discharge in bankruptcy; Congress's intention in Bankruptcy Act was that bankruptcy court independently resolve all such issues). *See also Matsushita Elec. Indus. v. Epstein*, 516 U.S. 367, 380–381 (1996) (holding that grant of exclusive federal jurisdiction to a statutory cause of action does not require exception to §1738 *proprio vigore*, noting that "we have seldom, if ever, held that a federal statute impliedly repealed §1738," and reiterating that "there [must] be an irreconcilable conflict" in order to justify an implied repeal).

7. *Adjudication by Administrative Agencies.* In *University of Tennessee v. Elliott*, 478 U.S. 788 (1986), the Court made explicit what it had already suggested in *Kremer*—that *unreviewed* state administrative determinations of "no discrimination" did not collaterally estop a plaintiff in a subsequent Title VII claim. In *Elliott*, the Court first held that §1738 by its express terms did not apply because administrative proceedings were not "judicial proceedings of any court" and therefore state preclusion law was not mandated by §1738. However, the Court observed that a federal common law rule with respect to preclusion was appropriate in the case of unreviewed trial-type administrative agency adjudications. As to the content of that rule with respect to plaintiff's Title VII claims, the Court noted that Title VII's statutory scheme requiring that administrative findings be given "substantial weight" undercut a contention that the findings were entitled to "preclusive effect." Thus, relitigation of unreviewed findings by the agency was permitted in the context of a Title VII claim and no preclusion was required. *See also Astoria Fed. Sav. & Loan Ass'n v. Solimino*, 501 U.S. 104 (1991) (unreviewed state administrative denial of age discrimination claim does not preclude federal Age Discrimination in Employment Act claim). However, as to the plaintiff's §1983 claim asserted in *Elliott*, the Court invoked *Allen*'s determination that nothing in the language, structure, or legislative history of §1983 required a departure from the preclusion law generally applicable in the federal system. Thus, on this point the Court in *Elliott* held as a matter of federal common law that when a state agency acts in a judicial capacity to resolve disputed issues of fact, the federal courts should give fact finding by the agency the same preclusive effect to which it would be entitled in the state's courts. *See generally* Stephen B. Burbank, *Federal Judgments Law: Sources of Authority and Sources of Rules*, 70 Tex. L. Rev. 1551 (1992). In the family law context, the Court has held that adoption decrees are also entitled to full faith and credit, despite the lack of adversarial fact-finding that sometimes characterizes those proceedings, if the rendering forum would treat the decree as binding and preclusive. *See V.L. v. E.L.*, 577 U.S. 404 (2016) (*per curiam*).

8. The Supreme Court's decision in *Elliott* indicates that unless the federal statutory scheme indicates an intent to override federal preclusion law, federal courts will give unreviewed findings of state administrative agencies the *same preclusive effect* that the state courts would give. But how much preclusion should the state courts themselves give? Does your answer depend upon what type of procedures the particular agency makes available for deciding legal claims and issues? *See generally* Restatement (Second) of Judgments §83 (1982) (Adjudicative Determination by Administrative Tribunal).

9. In cases where the federal courts have exclusive jurisdiction over a subsequent federal claim, does that fact militate in favor of an exception from generally applicable preclusion principles? Consider that question in connection with the following case.

Marrese v. American Academy of Orthopaedic Surgeons

470 U.S. 373 (1985)

JUSTICE O'CONNOR delivered the opinion of the Court.

This case concerns the preclusive effect of a state court judgment in a subsequent lawsuit involving federal antitrust claims within the exclusive jurisdiction of the federal courts. The Court of Appeals for the Seventh Circuit, sitting en banc, held as a matter of federal law that the earlier state court judgments barred the federal antitrust suit. 726 F.2d 1150 (1984). Under 28 U.S.C. §1738, a federal court generally is required to consider first the law of the State in which the judgment was rendered to determine its preclusive effect. Because the lower courts did not consider state preclusion law in this case, we reverse and remand.

I

Petitioners are board-certified orthopaedic surgeons who applied for membership in respondent American Academy of Orthopaedic Surgeons (Academy). Respondent denied the membership applications without providing a hearing or a statement of reasons. In November 1976, petitioner Dr. Treister filed suit in the Circuit Court of Cook County, State of Illinois, alleging that the denial of membership in the Academy violated associational rights protected by Illinois common law. Petitioner Dr. Marrese separately filed a similar action in state court. Neither petitioner alleged a violation of state antitrust law in his state court action; nor did either petitioner contemporaneously file a federal antitrust suit. The Illinois Appellate Court ultimately held that Dr. Treister's complaint failed to state a cause of action, *Treister v. American Academy of Orthopaedic Surgeons*, 78 Ill. App. 3d 746, 396 N.E.2d 1225 (1979), and the Illinois Supreme Court denied leave to appeal. 79 Ill. 2d 630 (1980). After the Appellate Court ruled against Dr. Treister, the Circuit Court dismissed Dr. Marrese's complaint.

In March 1980, petitioners filed a federal antitrust suit in the United States District Court for the Northern District of Illinois based on the same events underlying their unsuccessful state court actions. As amended, the complaint alleged that respondent Academy possesses monopoly power, that petitioners were denied membership in order to discourage competition, and that their exclusion constituted a boycott in violation of §1 of the Sherman Act, 15 U.S.C. §1. App. 8, 26–30, 33. Respondent filed a motion to dismiss arguing that claim preclusion barred the federal antitrust claim because the earlier state court actions concerned the same facts and were dismissed with prejudice. In denying this motion, the District Court reasoned that state courts lack jurisdiction over federal antitrust claims, and therefore a state court judgment cannot have claim preclusive effect in a subsequent federal antitrust suit. . . .

In a divided vote, the Court of Appeals held that claim preclusion barred the federal antitrust suit and reversed the contempt order because the discovery order was invalid. 726 F.2d 1150 (1984).

On the claim preclusion issue, no opinion commanded the votes of a majority of the Court of Appeals. A plurality opinion concluded that a state court judgment bars the subsequent filing of a federal antitrust claim if the plaintiff could have brought a state antitrust claim under a state statute "materially identical" to the Sherman Act. *Id.* at 1153. The plurality examined the Illinois Antitrust Act, Ill. Rev. Stat., ch. 38, para. 60-3(2) (1981), and found that it is sufficiently similar to the Sherman Act to bar petitioners' federal antitrust claims in the instant case. *Id.* at 1155–1156. An opinion concurring in part concluded that *res judicata* required petitioners to bring their "entire cause of action within a reasonable period of time." *Id.* at 1166 (Flaum, J.). To avoid preclusion of their federal antitrust claim, petitioners should have either filed concurrent state and federal actions or brought their state claims in federal court pendent to their Sherman Act claim. *Ibid.* . . .

We granted certiorari limited to the question whether the Court of Appeals correctly held that claim preclusion requires dismissal of the federal antitrust action, 467 U.S. 1258 (1984), and we now reverse. . . .

III

The issue presented by this case is whether a state court judgment may have preclusive effect on a federal antitrust claim that could not have been raised in the state proceeding. Although federal antitrust claims are within the exclusive jurisdiction of the federal courts, . . . the Court of Appeals ruled that the dismissal of petitioners' complaints in state court barred them from bringing a claim based on the same facts under the Sherman Act. The Court of Appeals erred by suggesting that in these circumstances a federal court should determine the preclusive effect of a state court judgment without regard to the law of the State in which judgment was rendered.

The preclusive effect of a state court judgment in a subsequent federal lawsuit generally is determined by the full faith and credit statute, which provides that state judicial proceedings "shall have the same full faith and credit in every court within the United States . . . as they have by law or usage in the courts of such State . . . from which they are taken" 28 U.S.C. §1738. This statute directs a federal court to refer to the preclusion law of the State in which judgment was rendered. "It has long been established that §1738 does not allow federal courts to employ their own rules of *res judicata* in determining the effect of state judgments. Rather, it goes beyond the common law and commands a federal court to accept the rules chosen by the State from which the judgment is taken." *Kremer v. Chemical Construction Corp.*, 456 U.S. 461, 481–482 (1982); see also *Allen v. McCurry*, 449 U.S. 90, 96 (1980). Section 1738 embodies concerns of comity and federalism that allow the States to determine, subject to the requirements of the statute and the Due Process Clause, the preclusive effect of judgments in their own courts. *See Kremer, supra,* at 478, 481–483. Cf. *Riley v. New York Trust Co.*, 315 U.S. 343, 349 (1942) (discussing preclusive effect of state judgment in proceedings in another State).

The fact that petitioners' antitrust claim is within the exclusive jurisdiction of the federal courts does not necessarily make §1738 inapplicable to this case. Our decisions indicate that a state court judgment may in some circumstances have preclusive effect in a subsequent action within the exclusive jurisdiction of the federal courts. Without discussing §1738, this Court has held that the issue preclusive effect of a state court judgment barred a subsequent patent suit that could not have been brought in state court. *Becher v. Contoure Laboratories, Inc.*, 279 U.S. 388 (1929). Moreover, *Kremer* held that §1738 applies to a claim of employment discrimination under Title VII of the Civil Rights Act of 1964, 78 Stat. 253, as amended, 42 U.S.C.

§2000e et seq., although the Court expressly declined to decide whether Title VII claims can be brought only in federal courts. 456 U.S. at 479, n. 20. *Kremer* implies that absent an exception to §1738, state law determines at least the issue preclusive effect of a prior state judgment in a subsequent action involving a claim within the exclusive jurisdiction of the federal courts.

More generally, *Kremer* indicates that §1738 requires a federal court to look first to state preclusion law in determining the preclusive effects of a state court judgment. Cf. *Haring v. Prosise*, 462 U.S. 306, 314, and n. 8 (1983); Smith, Full Faith and Credit and Section 1983: A Reappraisal, 63 N.C. L. Rev. 59, 110-111 (1984). The Court's analysis in *Kremer* began with the finding that state law would in fact bar relitigation of the discrimination issue decided in the earlier state proceedings. 456 U.S. at 466-467. That finding implied that the plaintiff could not relitigate the same issue in federal court unless some exception to §1738 applied. *Ibid. Kremer* observed that "an exception to §1738 will not be recognized unless a later statute contains an express or implied repeal." *Id.* at 468; see also *Allen v. McCurry, supra,* at 99. Title VII does not expressly repeal §1738, and the Court concluded that the statutory provisions and legislative history do not support a finding of implied repeal. 456 U.S. at 476. We conclude that the basic approach adopted in *Kremer* applies in a lawsuit involving a claim within the exclusive jurisdiction of the federal courts.

To be sure, a state court will not have occasion to address the specific question whether a state judgment has issue or claim preclusive effect in a later action that can be brought only in federal court. Nevertheless, a federal court may rely in the first instance on state preclusion principles to determine the extent to which an earlier state judgment bars subsequent litigation. Cf. *FDIC v. Eckhardt*, 691 F.2d 245, 247-248 (CA6 1982) (applying state law to determine preclusive effect on claim within concurrent jurisdiction of state and federal courts). *Kremer* illustrates that a federal court can apply state rules of issue preclusion to determine if a matter actually litigated in state court may be relitigated in a subsequent federal proceeding. See 456 U.S. at 467.

With respect to matters that were not decided in the state proceedings, we note that claim preclusion generally does not apply where "[the] plaintiff was unable to rely on a certain theory of the case or to seek a certain remedy because of the limitations on the subject matter jurisdiction of the courts. . . ." Restatement (Second) of Judgments §26(1)(c) (1982). If state preclusion law includes this requirement of prior jurisdictional competency, which is generally true, a state judgment will *not* have claim preclusive effect on a cause of action within the exclusive jurisdiction of the federal courts. Even in the event that a party asserting the affirmative defense of claim preclusion can show that state preclusion rules in some circumstances bar a claim outside the jurisdiction of the court that rendered the initial judgment, the federal court should first consider whether application of the state rules would bar the particular federal claim.

Reference to state preclusion law may make it unnecessary to determine if the federal court, as an exception to §1738, should refuse to give preclusive effect to a state court judgment. The issue whether there is an exception to §1738 arises only if state law indicates that litigation of a particular claim or issue should be barred in the subsequent federal proceeding. To the extent that state preclusion law indicates that a judgment normally does not have claim preclusive effect as to matters that the court lacked jurisdiction to entertain, lower courts and commentators have correctly concluded that a state court judgment does not bar a subsequent federal antitrust claim. . . . Unless application of Illinois preclusion law suggests, contrary to the usual view, that petitioners' federal antitrust claim is somehow barred, there will be no need to decide in this case if there is an exception to §1738.[3]

The Court of Appeals did not apply the approach to §1738 that we have outlined. Both the plurality opinion, see 726 F.2d at 1154, and an opinion concurring in part, *see id.* at 1163–1164 (Flaum, J.), express the view that §1738 allows a federal court to give a state court judgment greater preclusive effect than the state courts themselves would give to it. This proposition, however, was rejected by *Migra v. Warren City School Dist. Bd. of Educ.*, 465 U.S. 75 (1984), a case decided shortly after the Court of Appeals announced its decision in the instant case. In *Migra*, a discharged schoolteacher filed suit under 42 U.S.C. §1983 in federal court after she prevailed in state court on a contract claim involving the same underlying events. The Federal District Court dismissed the §1983 action as barred by claim preclusion. The opinion of this Court emphasized that under §1738, state law determined the preclusive effect of the state judgment. *Id.* at 81. Because it was unclear from the record whether the District Court's ruling was based on state preclusion law, we remanded for clarification on this point. *Id.* at 87. Such a remand obviously would have been unnecessary were a federal court free to give greater preclusive effect to a state court judgment than would the judgment-rendering State. *See id.* at 88 (WHITE, J., concurring).

We are unwilling to create a special exception to §1738 for federal antitrust claims that would give state court judgments greater preclusive effect than would the courts of the State rendering the judgment. Cf. *Haring v. Prosise*, 462 U.S. at 317–318 (refusing to create special preclusion rule for §1983 claim subsequent to plaintiff's guilty plea). The plurality opinion for the Court of Appeals relied on *Federated Department Stores, Inc. v. Moitie*, 452 U.S. 394 (1981), to observe that the doctrine of claim preclusion protects defendants from repetitive lawsuits based on the same conduct, 726 F.2d at 1152, and that there is a practical need to require

---

3. THE CHIEF JUSTICE notes that preclusion rules bar the splitting of a cause of action between a court of limited jurisdiction and one of general jurisdiction, and suggests that state requirements of jurisdictional competency may leave unclear whether a state court action precludes a subsequent federal antitrust claim. *Post*, at 388–390. The rule that the judgment of a court of limited jurisdiction concludes the entire claim assumes that the plaintiff might have commenced his action in a court *in the same system of courts* that was competent to give full relief. See Restatement (Second) of Judgments §24, comment g (1982). Moreover, the jurisdictional competency requirement generally is understood to imply that state court litigation based on a state statute analogous to a federal statute, *e.g.*, a state antitrust law, does not bar subsequent attempts to secure relief in federal court if the state court lacked jurisdiction over the federal statutory claim. *Id.*, §26(1)(c), Illustration 2. Although a particular State's preclusion principles conceivably could support a rule similar to that proposed by The Chief Justice, *post*, at 390–391, where state preclusion rules do not indicate that a claim is barred, we do not believe that federal courts should fashion a federal rule to preclude a claim that could not have been raised in the state proceedings.

plaintiffs "to litigate their claims in an economical and parsimonious fashion." *Id.* at 1153. We agree that these are valid and important concerns, and we note that under §1738 state issue preclusion law may promote the goals of repose and conservation of judicial resources by preventing the relitigation of certain issues in a subsequent federal proceeding. *See Kremer*, 456 U.S. at 485 (state judgment barred subsequent Title VII action in federal court).

If we had a single system of courts and our only concerns were efficiency and finality, it might be desirable to fashion claim preclusion rules that would require a plaintiff to bring suit initially in the forum of most general jurisdiction, thereby resolving as many issues as possible in one proceeding. *See* Restatement (Second) of Judgments §24, comment *g* (1982); C. Wright, A. Miller, & E. Cooper, *supra*, §4407, p. 51; id. §4412, p. 93. The decision of the Court of Appeals approximates such a rule inasmuch as it encourages plaintiffs to file suit initially in federal district court and to attempt to bring any state law claims pendent to their federal antitrust claims. Whether this result would reduce the overall burden of litigation is debatable, see 726 F.2d at 1181–1182 (CUDAHY, J., dissenting); C. Wright, A. Miller, & E. Cooper, *supra*, §4407, pp. 51–52, and we decline to base our interpretation of §1738 on our opinion on this question.

More importantly, we have parallel systems of state and federal courts, and the concerns of comity reflected in §1738 generally allow States to determine the preclusive scope of their own courts' judgments. See *Kremer, supra*, at 481–482; *Allen v. McCurry*, 449 U.S. at 96; cf. Currie, Res Judicata: The Neglected Defense, 45 U. Chi. L. Rev. 317, 327 (1978) (state policies may seek to limit preclusive effect of state court judgment). These concerns certainly are not made less compelling because state courts lack jurisdiction over federal antitrust claims. We therefore reject a judicially created exception to §1738 that effectively holds as a matter of federal law that a plaintiff can bring state law claims initially in state court only at the cost of forgoing subsequent federal antitrust claims. *Federated Department Stores, Inc. v. Moitie* does not suggest a contrary conclusion. That case did not involve §1738; rather it held that "accepted principles of *res judicata*" determine the preclusive effect of a federal court judgment. See 452 U.S. at 401.

In this case the Court of Appeals should have first referred to Illinois law to determine the preclusive effect of the state judgment. Only if state law indicates that a particular claim or issue would be barred, is it necessary to determine if an exception to §1738 should apply. Although for purposes of this case, we need not decide if such an exception exists for federal antitrust claims, we observe that the more general question is whether the concerns underlying a particular grant of exclusive jurisdiction justify a finding of an implied partial repeal of §1738. Resolution of this question will depend on the particular federal statute as well as the nature of the claim or issue involved in the subsequent federal action. Our previous decisions indicate that the primary consideration must be the intent of Congress. *See Kremer, supra*, at 470–476 (finding no congressional intent to depart from §1738 for purposes of Title VII); cf. *Brown v. Felsen*, 442 U.S. 127, 138 (1979) (finding congressional intent that state judgments would not have claim preclusive effect on dischargeability issue in bankruptcy).

IV

The decisions below did not consider Illinois preclusion law in their discussion of the claim preclusion issue. . . . Before this Court, the parties have continued to disagree about the content of Illinois preclusion law. We believe that this dispute is best resolved in the first instance by the District Court. Cf. *Migra v. Warren City School Dist. Bd. of Educ.*, 465 U.S. at 87. . . .

The judgment of the Court of Appeals is reversed, and the case is remanded for further proceedings consistent with this opinion.

JUSTICE BLACKMUN and JUSTICE STEVENS took no part in the consideration or decision of this case.

CHIEF JUSTICE BURGER, concurring in the judgment.

. . . I cannot agree with the Court's interpretation of the jurisdictional competency requirement. If state law provides a cause of action that is virtually identical with a federal statutory cause of action, a plaintiff suing in state court is able to rely on the same theory of the case and obtain the same remedy as would be available in federal court, even when the plaintiff cannot expressly invoke the federal statute because it is within the exclusive jurisdiction of the federal courts. In this situation, the jurisdictional competency requirement is effectively satisfied. Therefore, the fact that state law recognizes the jurisdictional competency requirement does not necessarily imply that a state court judgment has no claim preclusive effect on a cause of action within exclusive federal jurisdiction.

The states that recognize the jurisdictional competency requirement do not all define it in the same terms. Illinois courts have expressed the doctrine in the following manner: The principle [of *res judicata*] extends not only to questions which were actually litigated but also to all *questions* which *could have been raised* or determined. *Spiller v. Continental Tube Co.*, 95 Ill. 2d 423, 432, 447 N.E.2d 834, 838 (1983) (emphasis added); see also, e.g., *LaSalle National Bank v. County Board of School Trustees*, 61 Ill. 2d 524, 529, 337 N.E.2d 19, 22 (1975); *People v. Kidd*, 398 Ill. 405, 408, 75 N.E.2d 851, 853–854 (1947). In the present case, each petitioner could have alleged a cause of action under the Illinois Antitrust Act, Ill. Rev. Stat, ch. 38, para. 60-1 *et seq.* (1981), in his prior state court lawsuit against respondent. The principles of Illinois *res judicata* doctrine appear to be indeterminate as to whether petitioners' ability to raise state antitrust claims in their prior state court suits should preclude their assertion of essentially the same claims in the present federal action. This indeterminacy arises from the fact that the Illinois courts have not addressed whether the notion of "questions which could have been raised" should be applied narrowly[1] or broadly.[2]

---

1. *E.g.*, by inquiring whether the plaintiff could have raised the question whether the defendant violated a particular statute.

2. *E.g.*, by inquiring whether the plaintiff could have raised the question whether the defendant engaged in a group boycott.

No Illinois court has considered how the jurisdictional competency requirement should apply in the type of situation presented by this case, where the same
theory of recovery may be asserted under different statutes. Nor has any Illinois
court considered whether *res judicata* precludes splitting a cause of action between
a court of limited jurisdiction and one of general jurisdiction.[3]

Hence it is likely that the principles of Illinois claim preclusion law do not speak
to the preclusive effect that petitioners' state court judgments should have on the
present action. In this situation, it may be consistent with §1738 for a federal court to
formulate a federal rule to resolve the matter. If state law is simply indeterminate, the
concerns of comity and federalism underlying §1738 do not come into play. At the
same time, the federal courts have direct interests in ensuring that their resources are
used efficiently and not as a means of harassing defendants with repetitive lawsuits, as
well as in ensuring that parties asserting federal rights have an adequate opportunity
to litigate those rights. Given the insubstantiality of the state interests and the weight
of the federal interests, a strong argument could be made that a federal rule would
be more appropriate than a creative interpretation of ambiguous state law.[4] When
state law is indeterminate or ambiguous, a clear federal rule would promote substantive interests as well: "Uncertainty intrinsically works to defeat the opportunities for
repose and reliance sought by the rules of preclusion, and confounds the desire for
efficiency by inviting repetitious litigation to test the preclusive effects of the first
effort." 18 C. Wright, A. Miller, & E. Cooper, *supra* n. 3, §4407, at 49.

A federal rule might be fashioned from the test, which this Court has applied
in other contexts, that a party is precluded from asserting a claim that he had a "full
and fair opportunity" to litigate in a prior action. *See, e.g., Kremer v. Chemical Construction Corp.*, 456 U.S. 461, 485 (1982); *Allen v. McCurry*, 449 U.S. 90, 95 (1980);
Montana v. United States, 440 U.S. 147, 153 (1979); *Blonder-Tongue Laboratories, Inc.
v. University of Illinois Foundation*, 402 U.S. 313, 328 (1971). Thus, if a state statute

---

3. Compare Restatement (Second) of Judgments §24, comment g, Illustration 14, pp.
204–205 (1982):

> In an automobile collision, A is injured and his car damaged as a result of the negligence of
> B. Instead of suing in a court of general jurisdiction of the state, A brings his action for the
> damage to his car in a justice's court, which has jurisdiction in actions for damage to property
> but has no jurisdiction in actions for injury to the person. Judgment is rendered for A for the
> damage to the car. A cannot thereafter maintain an action against B to recover for the injury
> to his person arising out of the same collision.

See also 18 C. Wright, A. Miller, & E. Cooper, Federal Practice and Procedure §4412, p. 95
(1981), stating that the "general rule" in state courts is that "[a] second action will not be
permitted on parts of a single claim that could have been asserted in a court of broader jurisdiction simply because the plaintiff went first to a court of limited jurisdiction in the same
state that could not hear them." . . .

4. By contrast, when a federal court construes substantive rights and obligations under
state law in the context of a diversity action, the federal interest is insignificant and the state's
interest is much more direct than it is in the present situation, even if the relevant state law
is ambiguous.

is identical in all material respects with a federal statute within exclusive federal jurisdiction, a party's ability to assert a claim under the state statute in a prior state court action might be said to have provided, in effect, a "full and fair opportunity" to litigate his rights under the federal statute. . . .

The Court will eventually have to face these questions; I would resolve them now.

NOTES AND QUESTIONS

1. *Is There State Law on the Question?* Justice O'Connor emphasized that "[e]ven in the event that a party asserting the affirmative defense of claim preclusion can show that state preclusion rules in some circumstances bar a claim outside the jurisdiction of the court that rendered the initial judgment, the federal court should first consider whether application of the state rules would bar the particular federal claim." What kind of state precedent would indicate whether this particular federal claim would be barred by the prior state judgment? Given the fact that state courts have no jurisdiction to entertain federal antitrust claims, when would the state ever have occasion to rule on this precise question? Does the requirement of §1738 that federal courts give the state proceeding the "same full faith and credit" as would be given by the "law or usage" in state courts have any meaning in this context? *Cf.* Stephen Burbank, *Interjurisdictional Preclusion, Full Faith and Credit and Federal Common Law: A General Approach*, 71 Cornell L. Rev. 733, 825 (1986) (asserting that §1738 should have no bearing on exclusive federal jurisdiction cases like *Marrese*).

2. As in *Allen*, the Supreme Court's holding in *Marrese* is limited: The federal courts, even when hearing claims within the federal court's exclusive jurisdiction, must follow state preclusion law pursuant to the command of §1738. The question left open is what the scope of state preclusion law (claim preclusion in this case) should be.

Consider the various possibilities:

    a. Although plaintiffs could not have brought their federal antitrust claims in state court, they could have brought a state antitrust claim there. Having failed to bring any antitrust claim in the first suit, they should be precluded. (Can you think of reasons why plaintiffs might choose not to join a state antitrust claim in the first proceeding?)

    b. Plaintiffs could have brought their federal antitrust claims in federal court *at the same time* they brought their state common law proceeding in state court. Having chosen not to do so, they should be precluded.

    c. Plaintiffs could have brought both their federal antitrust claims and state law claims in a *single* federal proceeding under supplemental jurisdiction. Thus, having chosen to split their claims, plaintiffs are barred from bringing a second action.

    d. Because these federal antitrust claims are within the federal court's exclusive jurisdiction, the claims could not have been joined with the state law claims in the state court, and thus plaintiffs remain free to bring the antitrust claims in federal court.

What would be the advantages and disadvantages of each of these preclusion options? Which one would you favor? If the state courts were to bar plaintiffs' claims as a matter of state preclusion law, would you expect the federal courts to find an "exception" to §1738?

3. Does *Marrese* help resolve the question posed earlier whether state judicial findings should receive issue preclusion effect in a subsequent action brought under exclusive federal subject matter jurisdiction? In *Lyons v. Westinghouse Elec. Corp.*, 222 F.2d 184 (2d Cir. 1955), the Court of Appeals indicated, in a federal antitrust proceeding, that it would not give collateral estoppel effect to an earlier state court determination that defendants were not engaged in an illegal conspiracy. The federal defendants had previously sued Lyons and his company in a state court action for breach of contract. Lyons had asserted as a defense that the contract was void because it was in furtherance of a conspiracy to restrain trade in violation of federal antitrust law. The state court rejected the defense, finding no proof of a conspiracy. In the context of requesting a stay of a subsequent federal antitrust action brought by Lyons in federal court, defendants urged that the state determination of no conspiracy should estop Lyons in the later action. The Court of Appeals opined that no estoppel should attach because it would undermine the purpose of vesting federal courts with exclusive jurisdiction over antitrust claims:

> In the case at bar it appears to us that the grant to the district courts of exclusive jurisdiction over the action for treble damages should be taken to imply an immunity of their decisions from any prejudgment elsewhere; at least on occasions, like those at bar, where the putative estoppel includes the whole nexus of facts that makes up the wrong. . . . There are sound reasons for assuming that such recovery should not be subject to the determinations of state courts. It was part of the effort to prevent monopoly and restraints of commerce; and it was natural to wish it to be uniformly administered, being national in scope. Relief by certiorari would still exist, it is true; but that is a remedy burdensome to litigants and to the Supreme Court, already charged with enough. Obviously, an administration of the Acts, at once effective and uniform, would best be accomplished by an untrammeled jurisdiction of the federal courts.

Id. at 189.

If a party is free to relitigate a claim as a matter of claim preclusion because the matter is within the federal court's exclusive jurisdiction, does it make sense to prevent the relitigation of particular facts previously decided by the state court on grounds of issue preclusion? Does your answer depend on the nature of the issue that is being litigated? *See* Restatement (Second) of Judgments §86(2) (1982).

4. Inter-jurisdictional preclusion has had an important impact in other contexts. In *Matsushita Elec. Indus. v. Epstein*, 516 U.S. 367 (1996), the Supreme Court held that 28 U.S.C. §1738 (the Full Faith and Credit statute) applied to class actions (just as to individual actions) and to court approved settlements (just as to litigated actions). In *Matsushita*, a Delaware state court approved a "global" settlement of state law claims brought as a class action in Delaware, and the ruling was affirmed by the Delaware Supreme Court. The settlement released not only state claims that

were the subject of the action but also federal claims, including federal securities claims within the exclusive jurisdiction of the federal court. Parallel litigation in federal district court in California had been brought by other members of the Delaware class for violations of the federal securities laws and had been dismissed for failure to state a claim. On the appeal of that dismissal to the Ninth Circuit, defendant argued that the Delaware settlement barred litigation of claims by all shareholders who failed to opt out of the Delaware class settlement. The Ninth Circuit rejected that argument and held that federal class members — even those who failed to opt out of the state court settlement — were not bound by the release with respect to claims within the exclusive jurisdiction of the federal courts that did not rest on an identical factual predicate. The Supreme Court reversed on the question of the preclusive effect to be given to a state court settlement. Observing that a class action settlement was the product of a "judicial proceeding" within the meaning of 28 U.S.C. §1738, the Supreme Court held that, under *Marrese*, a state class action settlement was entitled to the same effect that it would have in courts of the rendering state. In addition, the Court concluded that, under Delaware law, state courts have power to approve a global settlement that encompasses exclusive federal claims. Justice Ginsburg, joined by Justices Stevens and Souter, concurred but stressed that the Ninth Circuit remained free to consider the due process issue of whether the Delaware courts fully and fairly litigated the adequacy of class representation in deciding the binding effect of the judgment on absent class members.

Has the Supreme Court gone too far in extending preclusion to situations like *Matsushita*? For a more extensive discussion of the ramifications of preclusion in class action settlements, *see* Marcel Kahan & Linda Silberman, Matsushita *and Beyond: The Role of State Courts in Class Actions Involving Exclusive Federal Claims*, 1996 S. Ct. Rev. 219 (1997).

On remand, the Ninth Circuit initially found that due process prevented the release of the exclusively federal claims, but then a reconstituted panel reversed that decision on rehearing and found that no collateral attack was available on due process grounds. *Epstein II*, 126 F.3d 1235 (9th Cir. 1997), *withdrawn on rehearing and superseded by Epstein III*, 179 F.3d 641 (9th Cir. 1999). What kind of "process" defect in the state proceeding, if any, would have rendered that judgment vulnerable to collateral attack on due process grounds? What if the state judge had been defrauded? What if he had been bribed? Is that fundamentally different from the plaintiffs' contention that the state class representative failed to look out for the interests of the class, and that the state judge failed to scrutinize the fairness of the settlement adequately? Should the state judge's approval of the settlement be treated as preclusive of the question of whether the class was adequately represented in that proceeding? Would it preclude a malpractice claim against the attorney for the class? These issues are further discussed in Chapter 8, at pp. 1020–1021.

3. Interstate Preclusion

The Full Faith and Credit Clause and 28 U.S.C. §1738 require that a second state give the "same full faith and credit" that the judgment has in the state "from which they are taken." Does this mean that a second state must apply the preclusion law that would apply in the rendering state?

Certainly, both the wording and purpose of the Full Faith and Credit Clause and the implementing statute indicate that the preclusion law chosen by the rendering state controls at least some questions. For example, if the rendering state would not permit the splitting of personal and property damages claims, it would seem that the recognizing state would be required to apply that same rule.

Does the same hold true if a second state wants to give a judgment *more* respect than it would receive in the issuing state? For example, if the rendering state *permits* a party to split claims of property damage and personal injury, must a second state entertain the later personal injury claim merely because the first state would do so? What interests might lead a second state to refuse to entertain the action? Does such a refusal sufficiently undermine the original party's expectations so as to constitute a violation of due process?

States' differing approaches to nonmutual issue preclusion have squarely presented the issue of such over-enforcement of a judgment. In *Hart v. American Airlines, Inc.*, 304 N.Y.S.2d 810, 61 Misc. 2d 41 (Spec. Term 1969), a New York court permitted the use of nonmutual issue preclusion against a defendant who lost a parallel proceeding in Texas even though Texas would not have granted preclusion in a subsequent litigation on behalf of a plaintiff who was not a party to the first proceeding. *Accord Finley v. Kesling*, 433 N.E.2d 1112 (Ill. App. 1982) (imposing nonmutual defensive estoppel without regard to issuing state's mutuality rule). *But see Clyde v. Hodge*, 413 F.2d 48 (3d Cir. 1969) (Pennsylvania could not use nonmutual issue preclusion since Ohio, the rendering state, would not permit such use). In *Columbia Cas. Co. v. Playtex FP, Inc.*, 584 A.2d 1214 (Del. 1991), the Delaware Supreme Court refused to apply nonmutual issue preclusion in a state court action in Delaware since the law of Kansas, the rendering state, retained a mutuality requirement. The initial action in the *Playtex* case was a federal diversity action, and federal law did not require mutuality; nonetheless, the Delaware Supreme Court held that, under *Erie* principles, a federal diversity judgment could only have the preclusive effect that a state court judgment in that state would have and that Kansas law must be used to determine the preclusive effect of the Kansas federal court judgment. For more discussion of these issues, *see* 18B C. Wright et al., Federal Practice and Procedure §§4467–4469 (3d ed. 2018). *See also* Elvin E. Overton, *The Restatement of Judgments, Collateral Estoppel, and Conflict of Laws*, 44 Tenn. L. Rev. 927, 943–949 (1977); Comment, *Mutuality of Collateral Estoppel in Multi-State Litigation: An Evaluation of the Restatement (Second) of Conflict of Laws*, 35 Wash. & Lee L. Rev. 993 (1978); Howard M. Erichson, *Interjurisdictional Preclusion*, 96 Mich. L. Rev. 945 (1998). For more on the preclusive effect of federal diversity judgments, *see* the *Semtek* case, *infra*.

Aside from claim and issue preclusion, must a state court enforce an out-of-state judgment in precisely the same manner as the issuing state? What if the enforcing state exempts more of defendant's property from execution on a judgment than would the issuing state? Notwithstanding the requirement of the statute to give a judgment the "same" effect as it would have in the issuing state, the enforcing state is not necessarily obligated to enforce the judgment in the same *manner* as would the issuing state. This principle was articulated most strongly by the Supreme Court in *Baker v. General Motors Corp.*, 522 U.S. 222 (1998), where the Court held that a Missouri court was permitted to hear testimony from a witness despite a permanent injunction issued by a Michigan court in an earlier case that forbade him from ever testifying against General Motors (GM). The witness, Ronald Elwell, was a former General Motors employee who had access to a great deal of privileged and confidential information. A conflict arose between Elwell and GM, and Elwell entered into a settlement agreement with GM in which he promised not to testify against GM in any future product liability case. Elwell also agreed to the issuance of a permanent injunction by a Michigan court to enforce that agreement. Later, Elwell appeared as a witness in a Missouri product liability case brought against GM by an unrelated plaintiff named Baker. GM asserted that the Missouri federal court was obligated under the full faith and credit statute to bar Elwell's testimony pursuant to the Michigan injunction. Since Elwell's testimony would be barred from any Michigan proceeding, GM argued, the same result must obtain in Missouri.

The Court disagreed. While the Michigan injunction was entitled to full faith and credit, the Court held, the Missouri court was not obligated to "adopt the practices of other States regarding the time, manner, and mechanisms for enforcing judgments." Although Michigan had the authority to resolve the controversy between Elwell and GM, that court neither purported, nor had the authority, to determine what effect that judgment would have on other litigation involving third parties not privy to the earlier suit. Even if other Michigan courts would have ruled Elwell's testimony inadmissible, such a collateral effect does not travel with the judgment.

What if GM had sought a Missouri injunction directly against Elwell, pursuant to the original judgment? If Missouri would have been obligated to give effect to the Michigan judgment and issue a Missouri injunction, why did the Supreme Court allow the Missouri court in the *Baker* case to hear Elwell's testimony? Did GM simply pursue the wrong avenue in attempting to stop Elwell's testimony? (Justice Scalia appears to suggest as much in a separate concurrence in *Baker*.) Note that even if the Michigan injunction had been converted to a Missouri injunction, that would not automatically have precluded the court in *Baker* from hearing Elwell's testimony. Elwell might be subject to contempt sanctions for violating the injunction, but neither Baker nor the court would be prohibited from using his testimony. Whether his testimony is admissible would be a separate question from what consequences he might suffer for giving it.

4. *Federal/State Preclusion, Diversity Jurisdiction, and the* Erie *Doctrine*

How should a court determine the preclusive effect of an earlier judgment that was issued by a federal court sitting in diversity? Are such judgments governed by federal preclusion law or by state law? On the one hand, preclusion is ordinarily judge-made law. This suggests the possibility that the *Erie* doctrine might be the appropriate place to look in determining whether state or federal law should control the effect of the judgment from a federal diversity court. On the other hand, Federal Rule 41(b), discussed in the *Costello* case, appears to provide a rule for determining when a judgment in a federal case is "an adjudication on the merits"—one of the basic requirements for a judgment to have preclusive effect. Does Rule 41 create a federal law of preclusion? Suppose that a state court in F1 would treat a particular type of dismissal as "without prejudice" or "not on the merits," but

Rule 41 would treat it as a dismissal "on the merits." If a federal diversity court in F1 issues such a dismissal, what preclusive effect should the resulting judgment have in a subsequent action?

The Supreme Court has provided some answers to these questions, but raised new questions in the process.

Semtek International Inc. v. Lockheed Martin Corp.

531 U.S. 497 (2001)

JUSTICE SCALIA delivered the opinion of the Court.

This case presents the question whether the claim-preclusive effect of a federal judgment dismissing a diversity action on statute-of-limitations grounds is determined by the law of the State in which the federal court sits.

I

Petitioner filed a complaint against respondent in California state court, alleging breach of contract and various business torts. Respondent removed the case to the United States District Court for the Central District of California on the basis of diversity of citizenship and successfully moved to dismiss petitioner's claims as barred by California's 2-year statute of limitations. In its order of dismissal, the District Court, adopting language suggested by respondent, dismissed petitioner's claims "in [their] entirety on the merits and with prejudice." Without contesting the District Court's designation of its dismissal as "on the merits," petitioner appealed to the Court of Appeals for the Ninth Circuit, which affirmed the District Court's order. 168 F.3d 501 (1999) (table). Petitioner also brought suit against respondent in the State Circuit Court for Baltimore City, Maryland, alleging the same causes of action, which were not time barred under Maryland's 3-year statute of limitations. [Respondent asked the California federal court to enjoin the Maryland state courts from hearing the action, but the federal court refused.] Following a hearing, the Maryland state court granted respondent's motion to dismiss on the ground of *res judicata*. Petitioner then returned to the California federal court and the Ninth Circuit, unsuccessfully moving both courts to amend the former's earlier order so as to indicate that the dismissal was not "on the merits." Petitioner also appealed the Maryland trial court's order of dismissal to the Maryland Court of Special Appeals. The Court of Special Appeals affirmed, holding that, regardless of whether California would have accorded claim-preclusive effect to a statute-of-limitations dismissal by one of its own courts, the dismissal by the California federal court barred the complaint filed in Maryland, since the *res judicata* effect of federal diversity judgments is prescribed by federal law, under which the earlier dismissal was on the merits and claim preclusive. 736 A.2d 1104 (1999). After the Maryland Court of Appeals declined to review the case, we granted certiorari. 530 U.S. 1260 (2000).

II

Petitioner contends that the outcome of this case is controlled by *Dupasseur v. Rochereau*, 21 Wall. 130, 135 (1875), which held that the *res judicata* effect of a federal diversity judgment "is such as would belong to judgments of the State courts rendered under similar circumstances," and may not be accorded any "higher sanctity or effect." Since, petitioner argues, the dismissal of an action on statute-of-limitations grounds by a California state court would not be claim preclusive, it follows that the similar dismissal of this diversity action by the California federal court cannot be claim preclusive. While we agree that this would be the result demanded by *Dupasseur*, the case is not dispositive because it was decided under the Conformity Act of 1872, 17 Stat. 196, which required federal courts to apply the procedural law of the forum State in nonequity cases. That arguably affected the outcome of the case.

Respondent . . . contends that the outcome of this case is controlled by Federal Rule of Civil Procedure 41(b), which provides as follows:

> Involuntary Dismissal: Effect Thereof. For failure of the plaintiff to prosecute or to comply with these rules or any order of court, a defendant may move for dismissal of an action or of any claim against the defendant. Unless the court in its order for dismissal otherwise specifies, a dismissal under this subdivision and any dismissal not provided for in this rule, other than a dismissal for lack of jurisdiction, for improper venue, or for failure to join a party under Rule 19, operates as an adjudication upon the merits.*

Since the dismissal here did not "otherwise specif[y]" (indeed, it specifically stated that it *was* "on the merits"), and did not pertain to the excepted subjects of jurisdiction, venue, or joinder, it follows, respondent contends, that the dismissal "is entitled to claim preclusive effect."

Implicit in this reasoning is the unstated minor premise that all judgments denominated "on the merits" are entitled to claim-preclusive effect. That premise is not necessarily valid. The original connotation of an "on the merits" adjudication is one that actually "pass[es] directly on the substance of [a particular] claim" before the court. Restatement §19, Comment *a*, at 161. That connotation remains common to every jurisdiction of which we are aware. See *ibid.* ("The prototyp[ical] [judgment on the merits is] one in which the merits of [a party's] claim are in fact adjudicated [for or] against the [party] after trial of the substantive issues"). And it is, we think, the meaning intended in those many statements to the effect that a judgment "on the merits" triggers the doctrine of *res judicata* or claim preclusion. See, *e.g., Parklane Hosiery Co. v. Shore*, 439 U.S. 322, 326, n. 5 (1979) ("Under the doctrine of *res judicata*, a judgment on the merits in a prior suit bars a second suit involving the same parties or their privies based on the same cause of action"); *Goddard v. Security Title Ins. & Guarantee Co.*, 92 P.2d 804, 806 (1939) ("[A] final judgment, rendered upon the merits by a court having jurisdiction of the cause . . . is a complete bar to a new suit between [the parties or their privies] on the same cause of action" (internal quotation marks and citations omitted)).

---

* The wording and internal numbering of Rule 41 have been changed by the 2007 stylistic revisions to the Federal Rules of Civil Procedure. —Eds.

But over the years the meaning of the term "judgment on the merits" "has gradually undergone change," R. Marcus, M. Redish, & E. Sherman, Civil Procedure: A Modern Approach 1140–1141 (3d ed. 2000), and it has come to be applied to some judgments (such as the one involved here) that do *not* pass upon the substantive merits of a claim and hence do *not* (in many jurisdictions) entail claim-preclusive effect. Compare, *e.g., Western Coal & Mining Co. v. Jones*, 167 P.2d 719, 724 (1946), and *Koch v. Rodlin Enterprises, Inc.*, 273 Cal. Rptr. 438, 441 (1990), with *Plaut v. Spendthrift Farm, Inc.*, 514 U.S. 211, 228 (1995) (statute of limitations); *Goddard, supra*, at 50–51, 92 P.2d, at 806–807, and *Allston v. Incorporated Village of Rockville Centre*, 267 N.Y.S.2d 564, 565–566 (1966), with *Federated Department Stores, Inc. v. Moitie*, 452 U.S. 394, 399, n. 3 (1981) (demurrer or failure to state a claim). See also Restatement §19, Comment *a* and Reporter's Note; 18 C. Wright, A. Miller, & E. Cooper, Federal Practice and Procedure §4439, pp. 355–358 (1981) (hereinafter Wright & Miller). That is why the Restatement of Judgments has abandoned the use of the term—"because of its possibly misleading connotations," Restatement §19, Comment *a*, at 161.

In short, it is no longer true that a judgment "on the merits" is necessarily a judgment entitled to claim-preclusive effect; and there are a number of reasons for believing that the phrase "adjudication upon the merits" does not bear that meaning in Rule 41(b). To begin with, Rule 41(b) sets forth nothing more than a default rule for determining the import of a dismissal (a dismissal is "upon the merits," with the three stated exceptions, unless the court "otherwise specifies"). This would be a highly peculiar context in which to announce a federally prescribed rule on the complex question of claim preclusion, saying in effect, "All federal dismissals (with three specified exceptions) preclude suit elsewhere, unless the court otherwise specifies."

And even apart from the purely default character of Rule 41(b), it would be peculiar to find a rule governing the effect that must be accorded federal judgments by other courts ensconced in rules governing the internal procedures of the rendering court itself. Indeed, such a rule would arguably violate the jurisdictional limitation of the Rules Enabling Act: that the Rules "shall not abridge, enlarge or modify any substantive right," 28 U.S.C. §2072(b). Cf. *Ortiz v. Fibreboard Corp.*, 527 U.S. 815, 842 (1999) (adopting a "limiting construction" of Federal Rule of Civil Procedure 23(b)(1)(B) in order to "minimiz[e] potential conflict with the Rules Enabling Act, and [to] avoi[d] serious constitutional concerns"). In the present case, for example, if California law left petitioner free to sue on this claim in Maryland even after the California statute of limitations had expired, the federal court's extinguishment of that right (through Rule 41(b)'s mandated claim-preclusive effect of its judgment) would seem to violate this limitation.

Moreover, as so interpreted, the Rule would in many cases violate the federalism principle of *Erie R. Co. v. Tompkins*, 304 U.S. 64, 78–80 (1938), by engendering "'substantial' variations [in outcomes] between state and federal litigation" which would "[l]ikely . . . influence the choice of a forum," *Hanna v. Plumer*, 380 U.S. 460 (1965). See also *Guaranty Trust Co. v. York*, 326 U.S. 99, 108–110 (1945). Cf. *Walker v. Armco Steel Corp.*, 446 U.S. 740, 748–753 (1980). With regard to the claim-preclusion issue involved in the present case, for example, the traditional rule is that expiration of the applicable statute of limitations merely bars the remedy and does not extinguish the substantive right, so that dismissal on that ground does not have claim-preclusive effect in other jurisdictions with longer, unexpired limitation periods. See Restatement (Second) of Conflict of Laws §§142(2), 143 (1969); Restatement of Judgments §49, Comment *a* (1942). Out-of-state defendants sued on stale claims in California and in other States adhering to this traditional rule would systematically remove state-law suits brought against them to federal court—where, unless otherwise specified, a statute-of-limitations dismissal would bar suit everywhere.

Finally, if Rule 41(b) did mean what respondent suggests, we would surely have relied upon it in our cases recognizing the claim-preclusive effect of federal judgments in federal-question cases. Yet for over half a century since the promulgation of Rule 41(b), we have not once done so. See, *e.g., Heck v. Humphrey*, 512 U.S. 477, 488-489, n. 9 (1994); *Federated Department Stores, Inc. v. Moitie, supra*, at 398; *Blonder-Tongue Laboratories, Inc. v. University of Ill. Foundation*, 402 U.S. 313, 324 (1971).

We think the key to a more reasonable interpretation of the meaning of "operates as an adjudication upon the merits" in Rule 41(b) is to be found in Rule 41(a), which, in discussing the effect of voluntary dismissal by the plaintiff, makes clear that an "adjudication upon the merits" is the opposite of a "dismissal without prejudice":

> Unless otherwise stated in the notice of dismissal or stipulation, the dismissal is without prejudice, except that a notice of dismissal operates as an adjudication upon the merits when filed by a plaintiff who has once dismissed in any court of the United States or of any state an action based on or including the same claim.

See also 18 Wright & Miller, §4435, at 329, n. 4 ("Both parts of Rule 41 . . . use the phrase 'without prejudice' as a contrast to adjudication on the merits"); 9 *id.*, §2373, at 396, n. 4 ("'[W]ith prejudice' is an acceptable form of shorthand for 'an adjudication upon the merits'"). See also *Goddard*, 14 Cal. 2d, at 54, 92 P.2d, at 808 (stating that a dismissal "with prejudice" evinces "[t]he intention of the court to make [the dismissal] on the merits"). The primary meaning of "dismissal without prejudice," we think, is dismissal without barring the defendant from returning later, to the same court, with the same underlying claim. That will also ordinarily (though not always) have the consequence of not barring the claim from *other* courts, but its primary meaning relates to the dismissing court itself. Thus, Black's Law Dictionary (7th ed. 1999) defines "dismissed without prejudice" as "removed from the court's docket in such a way that the plaintiff may refile the same suit on the same claim," *id.*, at 482, 92 P.2d 804, and defines "dismissal without prejudice" as "[a] dismissal that does not bar the plaintiff from refiling the lawsuit within the applicable limitations period," *ibid.*

We think, then, that the effect of the "adjudication upon the merits" default provision of Rule 41(b) — and, presumably, of the explicit order in the present case that used the language of that default provision—is simply that, unlike a dismissal "without prejudice," the dismissal in the present case barred refiling of the same claim in the United States District Court for the Central District of California. That is undoubtedly a necessary condition, but it is not a sufficient one, for claim-preclusive effect in other courts.

III

Having concluded that the claim-preclusive effect, in Maryland, of this California federal diversity judgment is dictated neither by *Dupasseur v. Rochereau*, as petitioner contends, nor by Rule 41(b), as respondent contends, we turn to consideration of what determines the issue. Neither the Full Faith and Credit Clause, U.S. Const., Art. IV, §1, nor the full faith and credit statute, 28 U.S.C. §1738, addresses the question. By their terms they govern the effects to be given only to state-court judgments (and, in the case of the statute, to judgments by courts of territories and possessions). And no other federal textual provision, neither of the Constitution nor of any statute, addresses the claim-preclusive effect of a judgment in a federal diversity action.

It is also true, however, that no federal textual provision addresses the claim-preclusive effect of a federal-court judgment in a federal-question case, yet we have long held that States cannot give those judgments merely whatever effect they would give their own judgments, but must accord them the effect that this Court prescribes. See *Stoll v. Gottlieb*, 305 U.S. 165, 171–172 (1938); *Gunter v. Atlantic Coast Line R. Co.*, 200 U.S. 273, 290–291 (1906); *Deposit Bank v. Frankfort*, 191 U.S. 499, 514–515 (1903). The reasoning of that line of cases suggests, moreover, that even when States are allowed to give federal judgments (notably, judgments in diversity cases) no more than the effect accorded to state judgments, that disposition is by direction of *this* Court, which has the last word on the claim-preclusive effect of *all* federal judgments:

> "It is true that for some purposes and within certain limits it is only required that the judgments of the courts of the United States shall be given the same force and effect as are given the judgments of the courts of the States wherein they are rendered; but it is equally true that whether a Federal judgment has been given due force and effect in the state court is a Federal question reviewable by this court, which will determine for itself whether such judgment has been given due weight or otherwise. . . .
>
> "When is the state court obliged to give to Federal judgments only the force and effect it gives to state court judgments within its own jurisdiction? Such cases are distinctly pointed out in the opinion of Mr. Justice Bradley in *Dupasseur v. Rochereau* [which stated that the case was a diversity case, applying state law under state procedure]." *Deposit Bank*, 191 U.S., at 514–515, 24 S. Ct. 154.

In other words, in *Dupasseur* the State was allowed (indeed, required) to give a federal diversity judgment no more effect than it would accord one of its own judgments only because reference to state law was *the federal rule that this Court deemed appropriate*. In short, federal common law governs the claim-preclusive effect of a dismissal by a federal court sitting in diversity. See generally R. Fallon, D. Meltzer, & D. Shapiro, Hart and Wechsler's The Federal Courts and the Federal System 1473 (4th ed. 1996); Degnan, Federalized Res Judicata, 85 Yale L.J. 741 (1976).

It is left to us, then, to determine the appropriate federal rule. And despite the sea change that has occurred in the background law since *Dupasseur* was decided—not only repeal of the Conformity Act but also the watershed decision of this Court in *Erie*—we think the result decreed by *Dupasseur* continues to be correct for diversity cases. Since state, rather than federal, substantive law is at issue there is no need for a uniform federal rule. And indeed, nationwide uniformity in the substance of the matter is better served by having the same claim-preclusive rule (the state rule) apply whether the dismissal has been ordered by a state or a federal court. This is, it seems to us, a classic case for adopting, as the federally prescribed rule of decision, the law that would be applied by state courts in the State in which the federal diversity court sits. See *Gasperini v. Center for Humanities, Inc.*, 518 U.S. 415, 429–431 (1996); *Walker v. Armco Steel Corp.*, 446 U.S., at 752–753; *Bernhardt v. Polygraphic Co. of America*, 350 U.S. 198, 202–205 (1956); *Palmer v. Hoffman*, 318 U.S. 109, 117 (1943); *Klaxon Co. v. Stentor Elec. Mfg. Co.*, 313 U.S. 487, 496 (1941); *Cities Service Oil Co. v. Dunlap*, 308 U.S. 208, 212 (1939). As we have alluded to above, any other rule would produce the sort of "forum-shopping . . . and . . . inequitable administration of the laws" that *Erie* seeks to avoid, *Hanna*, 380 U.S., at 468, since filing in, or removing to, federal court would be encouraged by the divergent effects that the litigants would anticipate from likely grounds of dismissal. See *Guaranty Trust Co. v. York*, 326 U.S., at 109–110.

This federal reference to state law will not obtain, of course, in situations in which the state law is incompatible with federal interests. If, for example, state law did not accord claim-preclusive effect to dismissals for willful violation of discovery orders, federal courts' interest in the integrity of their own processes might justify a contrary federal rule. No such conflict with potential federal interests exists in the present case. Dismissal of this state cause of action was decreed by the California federal court only because the California statute of limitations so required; and there is no conceivable federal interest in giving that time bar more effect in other courts than the California courts themselves would impose. . . .

Because the claim-preclusive effect of the California federal court's dismissal "upon the merits" of petitioner's action on statute-of-limitations grounds is governed by a federal rule that in turn incorporates California's law of claim preclusion (the content of which we do not pass upon today), the Maryland Court of Special Appeals erred in holding that the dismissal necessarily precluded the bringing of this action in the Maryland courts. The judgment is reversed, and the case remanded for further proceedings not inconsistent with this opinion.

NOTES AND QUESTIONS

1. *Semtek* has it all—a preclusion issue, an *Erie* issue, and an inter-jurisdictional issue. It is important to understand clearly the distinctions between the three in studying the impact of the case.

a. *The Preclusion Issue.* The basic preclusion question in *Semtek* is one of claim preclusion: Was the judgment from California federal court, dismissing the plaintiffs' claims on statute of limitations grounds, a judgment "on the merits" that barred those plaintiffs from refiling their lawsuit and trying again? This question, of course, is implicit in most claim preclusion analysis. A judgment usually cannot bar future claims unless it was a judgment "on the merits." *See* Restatement (Second) of Judgments §19 and comment a (1982). In the *Costello* case, for example, the Court determined that a dismissal for failure to file an affidavit of merit was a judgment "without prejudice" that did not bar refiling. How should a subsequent court treat a dismissal on statute of limitations grounds? In *Semtek*, the Court draws a clear distinction between the effect of Rule 41 itself and the role of preclusion doctrine in determining the impact of a judgment when a party seeks to assert the same claims in a subsequent proceeding. As the notes below explain, *Semtek* holds that the preclusive effect of a judgment comes from preclusion doctrine, not Rule 41. *See also supra* at p. 807, the related discussion of Rule 41(a).

b. *The* Erie *Issue.* The *Erie* question in *Semtek* asks which law of preclusion, state or federal, should govern the effect of a federal diversity judgment. That issue arises in an unusual posture. The question presented was not what law a federal diversity court should apply in the case before it, but rather what law should govern in a state court when a party asserts the preclusive effect of a judgment from an earlier federal diversity proceeding. More precisely, the *Erie* issue arises when the F2 court asks what preclusion law applied at the time that the F1 federal diversity court rendered its judgment. The Court holds that Rule 41(b) does not provide the answer — that a Federal Rule cannot create an independent standard of preclusion. Rather, the answer to that question must come from the applicable common law of preclusion. What, then, does the *Erie* line of cases have to say about whether state or federal judge-made preclusion law should apply to a federal diversity judgment?

c. *The Inter-jurisdictional Issue.* As noted above, the plaintiffs in *Semtek* filed their second lawsuit in Maryland state court, not in California federal court (where the first case was filed). Neither the Full Faith and Credit Clause of the Constitution nor §1738 mentions federal judgments. What obligation does a state court have to give effect to a federal diversity judgment? What is the source of that obligation? The Court holds that federal judgments are binding on state courts through the operation of federal common law. We discuss the what and why of that holding in greater detail below.

Make sure that you understand the differences between these issues — and how they relate to each other — as you read the notes that follow.

2. *Dismissals "On the Merits" and Statutes of Limitations.* The *Semtek* case presented another occasion for courts to decide whether a statute of limitations was "procedural" or "substantive." We have seen this question before — in *Guaranty Trust v. York*, where the Court held that a federal diversity court must apply the limitations period that the local state court would use, and in *Sun Oil v. Wortman*, where the Court held that there were no constitutional restrictions on a state court's ability to apply its own limitations period. In each case, the Court recognized that some states treat their limitations periods as "substantive" restrictions on state-created rights, while others treat them as "procedural" restrictions on the remedies that their court systems will permit litigants to pursue.

Because of the procedural posture of *Semtek*, the Supreme Court sent the case back to the Maryland state court for that court to determine what preclusive effect the dismissal would receive under California law. Part of that inquiry could involve whether California would treat statutes of limitations as "procedural" (i.e., remedial) or "substantive." How should an answer to that question affect the preclusion question? If a State's only interest in dismissing a case on statute of limitations grounds would be to keep stale claims from clogging its courts, is there any reason a plaintiff should not be able to refile its claim in another, willing forum? Or do concerns about burdening defendants with duplicative litigation and conserving judicial resources suggest that a plaintiff should be required to find a hospitable forum on the first try?

3. *A Federal Common Law of Preclusion?* The *Semtek* Court unanimously finds that the preclusive effect of a federal judgment is a matter of federal common law, whether the lawsuit that gave rise to the judgment involved a federal question or was purely a diversity case. That is true whether a subsequent proceeding is brought in federal court or state court. Even though the full faith and credit statute does not apply to federal judgments, the Court finds that federal judgments do have mandatory binding effect in state courts through federal common law. But with regard to diversity judgments like the one at issue in *Semtek* the Court adds a twist. Although the preclusive effect of a diversity judgment is a product of federal common law, the Court holds that federal law should ordinarily look to how the *state* where the rendering court is located would treat one of its own judgments. In other words, while federal law is the source of the binding preclusive effect for a diversity judgment, federal law should normally "borrow" a state standard by looking to what the state in the rendering forum would do. To do otherwise, the *Semtek* Court explains, would "engender[] 'substantial' variations [in outcomes] between state and federal litigation" that would "[l]ikely . . . influence the choice of a forum" *ex ante*, in violation of the federalism principles expressed in *Erie*.

There are a number of issues to take particular note of here.

a. Consider the Court's holding that federal preclusion law should ordinarily incorporate a state standard for federal diversity judgments. This may seem confusing at first—we usually think of *Erie* as a choice between two different rules, one state and one federal. But there are other examples of federal common law doctrines that incorporate a state standard. *See, e.g., Commissioner v. Estate of Bosch*, 387 U.S. 456, 457, 464–465 (1967) (looking to the character of a property interest under state law to determine federal estate tax liability).

Note also, the Court holds that federal preclusion law should incorporate the standard that would apply in the forum that *rendered* the judgment (F1), not the standard that would apply in the forum that gives effect to the judgment (F2) — here, California law rather than Maryland law. This is a natural consequence of the way preclusion works. A recognizing forum must always ask what effect a court in the rendering forum would give to the judgment.

b. Why did the Court hold that federal common law controls this preclusion question, given the broad incorporation of state standards into federal preclusion law that the Court found advisable? Why not simply hold that *Erie* required direct application of state preclusion law? The short answer is that the Court had to identify the source of federal authority that made a federal diversity judgment binding on state courts. Recall the Court's discussion of federal common law in *Boyle v. United Technologies*. There, the Court explained that "a few areas, involving 'uniquely federal interests,' are so committed by the Constitution and laws of the United States to federal control that state law is pre-empted and replaced, where necessary, by federal law of a content prescribed (absent explicit statutory directive) by the courts—so-called 'federal common law.'" *Boyle*, 487 U.S. at 504. The weight that will be accorded to a federal judgment, even one adjudicating state law, is a matter that implicates such "uniquely federal interests." If a federal judgment could be disregarded by a hostile state court, it would undermine the jurisdiction of the federal courts and endanger their effectiveness. Together, Article III of the Constitution (which defines the judicial power), Article I, section 8, clause 9 (which empowers Congress to create lower federal tribunals), and the statutes defining the jurisdiction of the federal courts all "require or provide" a supreme body of federal preclusion law as an inherent part of the federal court system. In Rules of Decision Act terms, there is a body of federal law that "applies" and displaces state law, even though the details of that law have been articulated by the federal courts rather than being embodied in a statute.

In a seminal article, Professor Stephen Burbank suggested that the law of preclusion for federal judgments should be rethought to accommodate both the federal interest in the integrity of federal judgments and, where possible, a state's interest in its underlying substantive policies. *See* Stephen B. Burbank, *Interjurisdictional Preclusion, Full Faith and Credit and Federal Common Law: A General Approach*, 71 Cornell L. Rev. 733 (1986). Professor Burbank advocates the adoption of an approach that always treats the recognition of federal judgments as a matter of federal common law and incorporates state standards, where appropriate, as a matter of federal policy rather than statutory or constitutional imperative. *See* Burbank, *supra*, at 778–797. While it did not cite Professor Burbank, the *Semtek* Court appears to have adopted the broad outlines of his approach. *See* Stephen B. Burbank, *Semtek, Forum Shopping, and Federal Common Law*, 77 Notre Dame L. Rev. 1027 (2002) (analyzing *Semtek* decision in light of his earlier work).

4. *Rule 41(b) and Dismissals "with Prejudice."* In *Costello*, we saw a counterintuitive interpretation of Rule 41(b). The Court there held that the clause of Rule 41(b) referring to dismissals for "lack of jurisdiction" was not limited to jurisdictional dismissals as traditionally understood (i.e., for lack of jurisdiction over the person or the subject matter) but extended to cases where the district court dismissed for some threshold reason that prevented it from addressing the merits of the dispute. In *Semtek*, we see another counterintuitive interpretation of Rule 41(b): When a district court designates a dismisses "with prejudice" under the Rule, that designation does not set preclusion doctrine for any court, even though courts commonly use that term when discussing a judgment's preclusive effect. Rather, the Court has given Rule 41(b) a narrower construction, finding that the Rule's designation of a dismissal "with prejudice" only means that the parties may not "try again" in the same court where they filed their lawsuit—for example, by fixing their complaint to cure the defect that resulted in dismissal and asking the court to consider it anew. In essence, *Semtek* holds that a dismissal "with prejudice" under Rule 41(b) means nothing more than a dismissal "without leave to fix your complaint and try again before the same court." Because the second action in *Semtek* was brought in a different court (state court in Maryland), the dismissal "with prejudice" under Rule 41(b) did not control the question whether plaintiffs could proceed with their suit.

The Court in *Semtek* did not decide what preclusive effect was to be given to the federal judgment, leaving that question to the Maryland courts to determine on remand. The Court simply held that the designation of a judgment as "with prejudice" under Rule 41(b) has no binding effect outside the court where the judgment was rendered.

Does this interpretation make sense? Does the language of Rule 41(b) require (or even justify) this result? The Court relies on two textual arguments in reaching its conclusion. First, it points out that Rule 41(b) does not purport to set forth a comprehensive set of preclusion rules. Rather, it merely creates a default rule on one issue: judgments are rendered "with prejudice" unless one of three specified exceptions applies. Such a default provision, the Court concludes, would be an unusual way of indicating an intention to set forth rules for the complex topic of preclusion. Second, the Court explains that it is the recognizing court (F2), and not the rendering court (F1), that must decide what preclusive effect a judgment will receive. The respondent in *Semtek* tried to argue that Rule 41(b) bound *other* courts to give a certain preclusive effect to the judgments it rendered. This reading of Rule 41(b) would have authorized district courts to determine the future effect of their own judgments, a power that courts are generally assumed not to have. *See, e.g., Matsushita Elec. Indus. v. Epstein*, 516 U.S. 367, 395 (1996) (Ginsburg, J., concurring and dissenting) ("A court conducting an action cannot predetermine the *res judicata* effect of the judgment; that effect can be tested only in a subsequent action."). *But see* Tobias Barrington Wolff, *Preclusion in Class Action Litigation*, 105 Colum. L. Rev. 717, 719–720, 752–767 (2005) (challenging this maxim of preclusion law). The *Semtek* Court found that interpretation particularly unconvincing in a provision "ensconced in rules governing the internal procedures of the rendering court itself."

Do you find these textual arguments convincing? The Court makes a good case that the reading of Rule 41(b) urged by the respondent in *Semtek* would create problems under the Enabling Act. But did it offer strong support for its conclusion that a Rule 41(b) dismissal means nothing more than a dismissal "without leave to try again in the very same court"? That reading is nowhere to be found in the text of the rule and it is counterintuitive. Is it more likely that the drafters of Rule 41(b) intended it to do exactly what it appears to do — create binding law on the question whether a judgment has claim preclusive effect in a subsequent proceeding in a different court — and they simply overstepped their authority under the Enabling Act in this instance? *See* Burbank, 77 Notre Dame L. Rev. at 1046.

5. *New Life for the Rules Enabling Act?* The *Semtek* Court places emphasis on the Rules Enabling Act in concluding that Rule 41(b) cannot bear the interpretation that the respondent urged. Recall that §2072(b) of the Rules Enabling Act provides that no Federal Rule may "abridge, enlarge or modify any substantive right." Following *Sibbach v. Wilson & Co.*, 312 U.S. 1 (1941) and its formalistic interpretation of the Enabling Act, which validates any Rule that "really regulates procedure," the Supreme Court has never held that a Federal Rule violates the Act. In *Semtek*, however, the Court relies on the Act to justify a restrictive and counterintuitive interpretation of Rule 41(b), explaining: "In the present case, for example, if California law left petitioner free to sue on this claim in Maryland even after the California statute of limitations had expired, the federal court's extinguishment of that right (through Rule 41(b)'s mandated claim-preclusive effect of its judgment) would seem to violate [§2072(b)'s] limitation." While the construction of Rule 41(b) that the Court adopts in *Semtek* prevents it from having to rule on this issue, it is rare for the Court to suggest that §2072(b) will influence its construction of a Federal Rule. *See also Wal-Mart Stores v. Dukes*, 564 U.S. 338, 367 (2011) (citing the Enabling Act in rejecting an interpretation of Rule 23(b)(1) that would have

required a restructuring of affirmative defenses under Title VII of the Civil Rights Act of 1964); *Ortiz v. Fibreboard Corp.*, 527 U.S. 815, 842 (1999) (suggesting that Court's construction of Rule 23(b)(1) was chosen in part to "minimiz[e] potential conflict with the Rules Enabling Act").

5. Enforcement and Recognition of Foreign Judgments

a. Law in the United States on Enforcement and Recognition of Foreign Judgments

When a party obtains a judgment outside of the United States, neither the Full Faith and Credit Clause nor 28 U.S.C. §1738 governs in disputes over the enforceability or the preclusive effect of the judgment in American courts, because those provisions do not apply to foreign country judgments. Recognition and enforcement of foreign country judgments is generally a matter of state law, with one exception. That exception, discussed at pp. 168–170 in Chapter 2, involves federal legislation designed to address the problem of "libel tourism." The SPEECH Act (Securing the Protection of our Enduring and Established Constitutional Heritage Act) (28 U.S.C.A. §§4101–4105) provides that courts in the United States shall not recognize or enforce a foreign country defamation judgment if the judgment would be inconsistent with the First Amendment. A similar provision is part of New York's version of the Uniform Foreign Money-Judgments Recognition Act, codified at N.Y. C.P.L.R. §5304(8) (providing for non-enforcement of foreign defamation judgments where the defamation law applied by the foreign court did not "provide[] at least as much protection for freedom of speech and press . . . as would be provided by both the United States and New York constitutions"). Nonetheless, as a general matter, American courts have a pro-enforcement attitude toward foreign judgments.

Unlike the treatment of domestic judgments, a foreign judgment can and often will be scrutinized to ensure that it was rendered under a fair and impartial system of justice, the jurisdictional grounds on which the judgment rests are reasonable, and no strong public policy of the United States would be violated by its enforcement. These principles are part of the Uniform Foreign Money-Judgments Recognition Act, 13 U.L.A. (Part II) 43-80 (2002 ed.) and (2021 Supp. at 47–68), which has been adopted by a significant number of states. Even in states that have not expressly adopted the Act, its principles are frequently applied. A few states have imposed a reciprocity requirement under which they will only honor judgments to the same extent as judgments of their states would be respected by a foreign court. For one of the few cases denying recognition on the grounds of lack of reciprocity, *see Banque Libanaise Pour Le Commerce v. Khreich*, 915 F.2d 1000 (5th Cir. 1990) (denying recognition to Abu Dhabi judgment where Abu Dhabi would not enforce Texas judgments). In 2005, a revised Uniform Act was promulgated; the revised Act introduced a number of changes but continued to reject any requirement of reciprocity. *See* Uniform Foreign-Country Money Judgments Recognition Act, 13 U.L.A. (Part II) (2002 ed.) (2021 Supp. at 22–41).

Why do you think the United States has a different standard for recognition and enforcement of foreign country judgments than for sister-state judgments under full faith and credit? Are domestic judgments, which must abide by all the protections set forth in the U.S. Constitution, more worthy of enforcement (or, less disruptive to sister states) than are foreign judgments?

Are you surprised that the recognition of foreign country judgments is a matter of state rather than federal law? Are there foreign relations interests at stake that suggest recognition and enforcement of foreign country judgments should be governed according to a uniform national standard? In 2005, the American Law Institute put forward a proposal for a federal statute on the recognition and enforcement of foreign country judgments. *See* American Law Institute, Recognition and Enforcement of Foreign Judgments: Analysis and Proposed Federal Statute (2006). For a discussion of some of the details of the ALI proposed statute by one of the Reporters, *see* Linda Silberman, *Transnational Litigation: Is There a "Field"? A Tribute to Hal Maier*, 39 Vand. J. Transnat'l L. 1427, 1432–1437 (2006).

For more on the recognition and enforcement of foreign country judgments, *see* Restatement (Fourth) of the Foreign Relations Law of the United States §§401, 403–404 (Am. L. Inst. 2018); Ronald A. Brand, *Federal Judicial Center International Litigation Guide: Recognition and Enforcement of Foreign Judgments*, 74 U. Pitt. L. Rev. 492 (2013).

As discussed in the materials on comparative jurisdiction in Chapter 2 (pp. 217–222), the European Regulation on Jurisdiction and the Recognition and Enforcement of Judgments in Civil and Commercial Matter (EU No. 1215/2012), known as the "Recast,"—which replaced the original "Brussels" Convention and earlier 2001 Regulation—contains (as did its predecessors) not only provisions for the assertion of jurisdiction but also provisions requiring the recognition and enforcement of judgments of other Member States. Judgments rendered on jurisdictional grounds authorized by the Regulation are entitled to recognition and enforcement in other Member States. Jurisdictional rulings are made by the court that hears the case and renders the judgment. Subject to very limited exceptions, jurisdictional challenges are not permitted in the state in which enforcement is sought, even with respect to default judgments. Certain limited defenses to recognition and enforcement are permitted, including defenses based on: public policy, a failure of service if the judgment was in default of an appearance, or a judgment irreconcilable with another judgment that was issued or would be recognized in the state in which enforcement is sought. The European Court of Justice hears cases on both jurisdiction and recognition/enforcement when referred by the appropriate national court. One change brought about by the 2012 Regulation is an expedited procedure for direct enforcement of judgments of Member States; under the Recast, the burden is now on the judgment debtor to apply for "refusal of enforcement" of the judgment on one of the grounds for non-recognition.

In the absence of a treaty, recognition and enforcement of one country's judgments in another country may be difficult. A number of countries impose a reciprocity requirement—that is, enforcement and recognition depend upon showing that the courts of the country whose judgment is at issue would enforce the judgment of the requested country if the facts were reversed. In some countries, such as England, default judgments are generally not enforced unless the defendant was said to be "present" or if the defendant appeared or contractually consented to the jurisdiction of the foreign court. And "public policy" remains an important limitation for most countries in determining whether or not to recognize or enforce the judgment of another country. For a comparative overview of judgment recognition, *see* Linda J. Silberman, *Some Judgments on Judgments: A View from America*, 19 King's L. J. 235-263 (2008).

The enforcement and recognition of U.S. judgments abroad is particularly difficult. Large tort damage judgments from courts in the United States can be regarded as "excessive" and may not be enforced. The pre-*Daimler* "doing business" jurisdiction was regarded as "exorbitant" and judgments resting on such jurisdiction were generally not respected. (That issue will no longer present a problem post-*Daimler*.) Other types of U.S. judgments — often seen as a product of contingent fees, broad discovery, and jury verdicts — are sometimes viewed with suspicion and not enforced. For a discussion of the challenges faced by U.S. judgment holders when seeking recognition and enforcement abroad, *see* Samuel P. Baumgartner, *Understanding the Obstacles to the Recognition and Enforcement of U.S. Judgments Abroad*, 45 N.Y.U. J. Int'l L. & Pol. 965 (2014).

As described in Chapter 2, efforts were undertaken at the Hague Conference on Private International Law to broaden international recognition and enforcement of foreign country judgments through negotiation of a world-wide Convention that addressed both rules of jurisdiction and the recognition of judgments. The effort failed, largely because parties could not agree on the rules for the assertion of direct jurisdiction. A more limited Convention dealing with jurisdiction and the recognition of judgments in cases involving international business-to-business transactions containing an exclusive choice-of-court clause was completed in 2005. *See* Convention on Choice of Court Agreements, June 30, 2005, 44 I.L.M. 1294 (2005). In addition to provisions for enforcing forum-selection clauses (prorogation) and for dismissing proceedings in contravention of forum-selection clauses (derogation), the Choice of Court Convention imposes an obligation to recognize and enforce a judgment where jurisdiction is based on a forum-selection clause, subject to a limited number of defenses. In addition to defenses based on a prior inconsistent judgment and failure of notice and service, the Convention permits recognition to be refused if "the agreement was null and void under the law of the State of the chosen court, unless the chosen court has determined that the agreement is valid"; or if "recognition or enforcement would be manifestly incompatible with the public policy of the requested State, including situation where the specific proceedings leading to the judgment were incompatible with fundamental principles of procedural fairness of that State." Mexico, Singapore, and the Member States of the European Union have become parties to the Choice of Court Convention. For a more extensive discussion of the Hague Choice-of-Court Convention, *see* Louise Ellen Teitz, *The Hague Choice of Court Convention: Validating Party Autonomy and Providing an Alternative to Arbitration*, 53 Am. J. Comp. L. 543 (2006).

Having successfully achieved the Hague Choice of Court Convention, the Hague Conference reinitiated efforts to negotiate a broader international treaty that would address recognition and enforcement of judgments but not the assertion of direct jurisdiction. Those efforts culminated in the Hague Convention on the Recognition and Enforcement of Foreign Judgments in Civil or Commercial Matters that was successfully finalized in 2019, although as of 2021 the Convention was not yet in force. The Convention requires that all countries party to the treaty recognize "judgments in civil or commercial matters" that come within the scope of the Convention. However, the scope is relatively narrow and many kinds of cases are excluded. More importantly, the Convention provides that only judgments based on specific jurisdictional grounds are "eligible" for recognition and enforcement, and those grounds do not encompass many of the jurisdictional grounds that are accepted in the United States. The Convention also provides grounds on which a country may refuse recognition and enforcement without violating the Treaty. Most of the defenses are similar to those found in the state Uniform Acts as well as the European Regulation. Reciprocity is, of course, established by the Treaty itself. The Convention does provide an opt-out mechanism for a state to object to a relationship with a particular Contracting State. This provision allows a country to avoid having a treaty relationship with any Contracting State where there is concern about the fairness, politicization, and/or corruption in a country's legal and judicial system. The Convention establishes only a floor but not a ceiling for recognition and enforcement. Thus a country can continue to have a more liberal recognition and enforcement regime than that provided by the Convention.

From the perspective of the United States, the significance of the Convention is about reciprocal treatment, and the fact that countries party to the Convention would be required to enforce the judgments of other countries, including those from the United States if the United States were also to become a party.

Note also that if the United States were to become a party to either the Choice of Court or the Judgments Conventions, the enforcement of any judgment falling within those Conventions would be subject to an international and therefore federal standard. Even if the existing state laws on recognition and enforcement would be in compliance with the requirements of the Hague Judgments Convention, would it nonetheless be desirable to have federal legislation to implement the Judgments Convention? Might it also make sense to have broader federal legislation to make all foreign judgments subject to a uniform federal standard (as in the ALI proposed federal statute) rather than to the patchwork of state laws as is now the case?

CHAPTER 8

THE BOUNDARIES OF THE LAWSUIT: JOINDER OF CLAIMS AND PARTIES

In this unit, we consider increasingly complex variations on the simple model of the lawsuit where a single plaintiff is asserting a single claim for relief against a single defendant. As we have seen in the chapters on subject matter jurisdiction and prior adjudication, modern procedural systems have expanded the common law view of what constitutes a "single case." For example, the rules of claim preclusion effectively force plaintiffs to assert in a single lawsuit all claims against a single defendant arising out of a series of related factual occurrences. Rules concerning *joinder* have similarly tended to expand the number of claims and parties that can be included in a single lawsuit. In this chapter, we explore these developments with the objective of determining optimal joinder policy: What are the fairest and most efficient boundaries for a single lawsuit?

A. *REAL PARTY IN INTEREST*

Before turning to joinder policy, we consider whether the parties have been appropriately designated. Fed. R. Civ. P. 17(a) provides that the lawsuit must be brought in the name of the "real party in interest."

In general, Rule 17(a) requires that the lawsuit be brought in the name of the person in possession of the substantive right to recover. This is often (although not always) the person who stands to benefit from the litigation. Consider, for example, a claim by an insured plaintiff against a tortfeasor who damaged the insured's property. Once the insured has been made whole by his insurance company, the company may want to pursue a claim against the tortfeasor to be reimbursed for the insurance benefits it was required to pay out. (This is called a "subrogation" claim.) The "real party in interest" rule would normally consider the insurance company the proper plaintiff, since the insured individual no longer has any stake in the outcome of the litigation. However, as the rule itself indicates, certain representatives can sue in their own names without joining those on whose behalf the action is brought, and the real party in interest may not always be the person with the beneficial interest in the litigation.

The avowed purpose of the doctrine is to prevent relitigation of claims. *See Puerto Rico v. Cordeco Dev. Corp.*, 534 F. Supp. 612, 614 (D.P.R. 1982) ("The purpose of Rule 17(a) is to ensure that the judgment will have proper *res judicata* effect by preventing a party not joined in the complaint from asserting the 'real party in interest' status in an identical future suit."). In our subrogation case, for example, the lawsuit must be brought in the name of the insurer to prevent a strategy whereby the insured might first sue and, if he is unsuccessful, the insurer might attempt to relitigate the claim. Given the doctrine of privity, however, it is questionable whether the "real party in interest" rule is needed for this purpose. *See* Thomas E. Atkinson, *The Real Party in Interest Rule: A Plea for Its Abolition*, 32 N.Y.U. L. Rev. 925 (1957).

The "real party in interest" rule has important implications for diversity of citizenship jurisdiction. The federal courts generally look to the citizenship of the real party in interest to determine whether diversity exists. In some instances, this led to appointment of a particular representative or administrator for the express purpose of manipulating diversity jurisdiction. Such attempts to manipulate jurisdiction are difficult to police. 28 U.S.C. §1359 prohibits "improper or collusive" devices to *create* federal court jurisdiction, but there is no concomitant limitation for devices designed to defeat jurisdiction. (Recall in this context, however, the doctrine of fraudulent joinder, applied in *Rose v. Giamatti*, discussed at pp. 299–300, where the court discounts the citizenship of parties that are only nominal.) Also, courts have been reluctant to apply 28 U.S.C. §1359 in the absence of outright fraud or collusion.

One aspect of the diversity problem was eliminated with the 1988 amendment to 28 U.S.C. §1332, which creates an exception to the real party in interest citizenship rule in cases involving the appointment of a guardian or representative of an estate. 28 U.S.C. §1332(c)(2) provides that "the legal representative of the estate of a decedent shall be deemed to be a citizen only of the same State as the decedent, and the legal representative of an infant or incompetent shall be deemed to be a citizen only of the same State as the infant or incompetent."

B. JOINDER OF CLAIMS

1. By Plaintiffs

At common law, plaintiffs could join claims in a single action only if the claims belonged to the same form of action. For example, an action for slander (asserted in the writ of "action on the case") could not be joined with an action for false imprisonment without a warrant (asserted in the writ of "trespass"), even where the claims arose out of the same factual transaction. However, the claims could have been joined had defendant falsely secured a warrant (because such a claim would have also been brought as an "action on the case").

The Field Code of the mid-nineteenth century moved away from the common law system by developing more practical conceptual categories within which claims could be joined. For example, plaintiffs could join claims if they all arose out of: (i) a contract, express or implied; (ii) injuries by force to person or property; (iii) injuries without force to person or property; (iv) injuries to character; (v) claims to recover real property; (vi) claims to recover personal property; or (vii) claims against a trustee. In 1851, a broader residual category was added to permit joinder of claims "where they arise out of the same transaction or transactions connected with the same subject matter of the action." *See* William Wirt Blume, *A Rational Theory of Joinder of Causes of Action and Defenses, and for the Use of Counterclaims*, 26 Mich. L. Rev. 1 (1927).

Note that Fed. R. Civ. P. 18 does not require any transactional relationship between claims in order for them to be joined. A plaintiff is free to assert as many claims against an opposing party as the plaintiff has, whether those claims are related or unrelated. What justification can there be for permitting joinder of claims that bear no relationship to one another? Notwithstanding the unrestricted scope of Rule 18, the court has discretion to sever claims under Rule 21 or to order separate trials under Rules 20(b) and 42(b). Is there any real difference between a rule that would demand a "transactional" linkage among claims and an unrestricted joinder subject to the court's power to sever or order separate trials?

The joinder rule itself does not confer federal subject matter jurisdiction. A party must satisfy both requirements—jurisdiction and joinder—independently. In a federal-question case with no diversity, any state claim joined by plaintiff to federal claims will be dismissed for lack of subject matter jurisdiction unless it is sufficiently related to the federal claims for supplemental jurisdiction to attach. In a diversity action, plaintiff can aggregate against a single defendant to satisfy the jurisdictional amount, meaning that a plaintiff's unrelated claims can still be asserted so long as they satisfy the jurisdictional amount for diversity when added together. Note also that joinder rules are relevant to some subject matter jurisdiction doctrines, such as supplemental jurisdiction.

Rule 18(a) is permissive rather than compulsory. However, other procedural doctrines effectively compel the plaintiff to bring certain claims at the same time. Claim preclusion (preventing the splitting of a single cause of action) and issue preclusion (prohibiting a party from relitigating an issue that arose in a prior litigation) may prevent a plaintiff from asserting or prevailing on an omitted claim in a second action. Thus, the rules of preclusion effectively operate as rules of compulsory joinder: They induce plaintiff to join all related claims in the initial lawsuit to prevent claim/issue preclusion in a subsequent action.

One state, Michigan, has a compulsory joinder provision that requires the joinder of related claims, whether by plaintiffs or by defendants. *See* Michigan Court Rule 2.203(A). *See generally* Robert Meisenholder, *Joinder of Claims and Parties— The New Michigan Pre-Trial Procedural Rules— Models for Other States?*, 61 Mich. L. Rev. 1389 (1963). Is there any advantage to achieving joinder through a mandatory joinder rule rather than by application of preclusion doctrine? Does a rule like Michigan's put the litigants on better notice of the kind of claims they must assert together?

2.   *By Defendants and Co-Parties*

a.   Counterclaims

Grumman Systems Support Corp. v. Data General Corp.

125 F.R.D. 160 (N.D. Cal. 1988)

FERN M. SMITH, District Judge.

This matter [arose out of] defendant Data General's (DG) motion to dismiss, to stay or to transfer this action to the District of Massachusetts. . . . For the reasons set forth below, the Court grants the motion to dismiss, without prejudice, so that the action may properly be brought as a counterclaim to DG's first-filed action in the District of Massachusetts.

BACKGROUND

Defendant Data General has a valuable computer program called ADEX. DG has a copyright on the program. Grumman, a competitor, allegedly copied ADEX without authorization. DG sued Grumman in the District of Massachusetts (Mass. action) for copyright infringement and related causes of action.

The day after its motion to dismiss in Mass. was denied, Grumman sued DG in California state court for violation of the Cartwright Act, the California equivalent of the Sherman Antitrust Act. The California suit was based, factually, on the behavior of DG with respect to its ADEX product. DG removed the California antitrust action to this Court.

DG then made this motion to dismiss or stay this action asserting that it is a compulsory counterclaim to the Mass. action or to transfer this action to the District of Massachusetts under 28 U.S.C. §1404 for the convenience of the parties and witnesses. Grumman has since amended its complaint to add two new defendants and a number of new allegations of predatory practices assertedly in violation of antitrust laws. DG's behavior with respect to the ADEX product continues to be the core of the amended complaint's allegations, but Grumman now states additional allegations that are wholly apart from ADEX matters.

DG asserts that this action is a compulsory counterclaim to the Mass. action under Fed. R. Civ. P. 13(a) and, therefore, its claims must be brought in the Mass. action or be forever waived. Therefore, DG moves for (1) dismissal of this action without prejudice so that Grumman may bring it in Massachusetts or (2) for a stay of this action or (3) for transfer of this action to Massachusetts pursuant to 28 U.S.C. §1404.

DG has moved for [a] preliminary injunction in the Massachusetts action. Grumman's brief opposing the injunction defended on the grounds that DG's behavior with respect to its ADEX product was an attempt to monopolize, to stifle competition in the relevant market and, thus, constituted antitrust violations. Certain of the issues raised here are already being litigated in the Mass. action.

The litigation became even more tortuous, however, when Grumman amended its complaint here to add two additional defendants (the "AMI defendants") as alleged antitrust co-conspirators of DG. The Massachusetts court probably has no personal jurisdiction over the AMI defendants. Recently, two other plaintiffs (both using Grumman's counsel) have filed similar antitrust suits against DG here in the Northern District of California. . . .

DISCUSSION

Fed. R. Civ. P. 13(a) is concerned with the danger of inconsistent adjudication and with judicial economy. *Pochiro v. Prudential Ins. Co.*, 827 F.2d 1246 (9th Cir. 1987); *Albright v. Gates*, 362 F.2d 928 (9th Cir. 1966). Rule 13(a) states that "a pleading shall state as a counterclaim any claim . . . the pleader has against any opposing party if it arises out of the same transaction or occurrence that is the subject matter of the opposing party's claim and does not require for its adjudication the presence of third parties of whom the court cannot acquire jurisdiction."

In addition to the "same transaction or occurrence" standard of the Rule itself, courts have applied a "logical relationship" test to determine if two actions at issue are sufficiently identical for the second to be a compulsory counterclaim to the first. See *Pochiro*, 827 F.2d at 1249. 6 Wright & Miller, Federal Practice & Procedure Section 1410, p. 46ff. The test is a "flexible" one taking into account all of the circumstances in light of the purposes of Rule 13(a). *Moore v. New York Cotton Exchange*, 270 U.S. 593, 610 (1926).

As a threshold matter, it should be made clear that similarity between the legal theories of recovery advanced in the respective actions is largely irrelevant to Rule 13(a) analysis. The Rule itself refers to similarities among the transactions or occurrences [that] make up the factual bases of the lawsuits. Fed. R. Civ. P. 13(a). The few older federal cases giving weight to similarity of issues have been criticized and are in the minority. See Wright & Miller, *supra*, at p. 44. The test in this circuit is "whether the essential facts of the various claims are so logically connected that considerations of judicial economy and fairness dictate that all the issues be resolved in one lawsuit." *Pochiro*, 827 F.2d at 1249 (citation omitted).

The *Pochiro* court considered whether "the facts necessary to prove the two claims substantially overlap, [whether] the collateral estoppel effect of . . . the first action would preclude [matters in the second action]." *Id.* at 1251. Although in *Pochiro* the court found that the allegations of the second action went beyond the facts appearing in the first action and seemed "a bit removed" from the allegations of the first action, the court found that certain core facts were common to and "inextricably intertwined with" both actions. *Id.*

It is clear from Grumman's recent submissions in the Mass. action, as well as from the pleadings of the two actions, that there is sufficient overlap between the factual underpinnings of the two actions to save a great deal of judicial resources if the California action could be litigated with the Mass. action. In the Mass. action, Grumman's Answer contains an affirmative defense relating to DG's alleged monopolization by copyright misuse. Grumman's opposition briefs to DG's motion for preliminary injunction in the Mass. action argue forcefully from that affirmative defense and indeed recite the substance of the allegations that appear in this action. Later-filed claims are eligible for compulsory counterclaim treatment as defenses to the first-filed action if all other Rule 13(a) criteria are met. . . .

However, Grumman does assert antitrust monopolization claims against DG and the AMI defendants that are unique to the California action and in which

904 Chapter 8. The Boundaries of the Lawsuit: Joinder of Claims and Parties

some acts alleged have nothing to do with ADEX. Rather, those claims involve the more generic allegations of conspiracy to monopolize, such as applying improper pressure to DG's customers so that they would . . . refuse to deal with Grumman.

The central issue is whether there is a logical relationship between the claims in the two actions sufficient to precipitate Rule 13(a) concerns. The Court holds there is.

In this case, as in *Pochiro* which this Court takes as controlling, the "facts underlying the [second-filed action] revolve around" the same occurrences as do the facts of the first action. *Id.* at 1250. In *Pochiro*, it was the plaintiff's unlawful use of confidential information. *Id.* Here, it is Grumman's alleged use of a copyrighted diagnostic computer program. In *Pochiro*, as here, this sort of alleged unauthorized use of non-public proprietary information gave rise to allegations in the second-filed action of unlawful restraint of trade claims. In *Pochiro*, plaintiff alleged facts that were not involved in the first action, just as Grumman has alleged additional facts going to its monopolization claim. Since *Albright*, the Ninth Circuit has taken the expansive view of Rule 13(a) that whether the facts "are not precisely identical or [whether] the counterclaim embraces additional allegations . . . does not matter." [citing *Moore*]. In light of these circumstances, the conclusion that this action is a compulsory counterclaim in the Mass. action seems inescapable.

Grumman relies heavily on . . . [other cases]. In *Mead Data Central v. West Pub. Co.*, 679 F. Supp. 1455 (S.D. Oh. 1987), the situation was very similar to this one. A copyright action in Minn., and a later-filed antitrust action in Ohio were followed by a 13(a) motion. The court held that the antitrust allegations were not compulsory counterclaims. *Id.* at 1461. Although this Court recognizes the similarity between the *Mead* case and the case at bar, the Court can not agree with the analysis of the *Mead* court. The *Mead* court relied on the Sixth Circuit standard for Rule 13(a) as set forth in *United States v. Southern Construction Co.*, 293 F.2d 493, 500 (6th Cir. 1961), *rev'd in part on other grounds*, 371 U.S. 57 (1962) and *Maddox v. Kentucky Finance Co.*, 736 F.2d 380, 383 (6th Cir. 1984). This standard, at least as applied by the *Mead* court, differs from the Ninth Circuit standard in several ways.

First, it accords primary weight to the similarity or dissimilarity of the legal issues involved in the two actions. *Mead*, 679 F. Supp. at 1458, 1461 (first factor in court's analysis); *Maddox*, 736 F.2d at 383. In contrast, this circuit has recognized that legal dissimilarities are often the case in contested Rule 13(a) motions and that the factual underpinnings of the complaint are more properly the focus of Rule 13(a) analysis.

Second, the *Mead* court correctly notes that "judicial economy and efficiency are important considerations in determining whether a particular claim constitutes a compulsory counterclaim." *Mead*, 679 F. Supp. at 1462. But its application of this principle is confusing:

> In this case, defendant West argues that judicial economy requires that the two Complaints be litigated in one forum. This Court cannot agree. Discovery in the Minnesota copyright action is nearly complete. Even if this Court were to transfer the case at bar, as both sides want the Minnesota copyright case to go forward, the chance of the two actions being consolidated is virtually nil. The Court does not dispute West's claim that after two years of litigation, Judge Rosenbaum, Magistrate Cudd, and Special Master Younger of the District Court for the District of Minnesota are intimately

familiar with the law of copyright and the law of unfair competition and misrepresentation. Nor does the Court doubt that those individuals are intimately familiar with the facts of the Minnesota copyright action.

The *Mead* court then went on to conclude that "judicial economy and efficiency would [not] be served by hearing the two claims together." *Id.* at 1462. The *Mead* court apparently took the view that, if it were procedurally feasible to consolidate the two actions, this would somehow lend support to holding that the later-filed claims are compulsory counterclaims in a first-filed action. This view would lead to the conclusion that, if the first-filed action had reached judgment or were at an advanced stage of litigation, the later-filed action should not be held to be a compulsory counterclaim to the first-filed action.

This view is necessarily at odds with the purposes and the mandatory operation of Rule 13(a). Under the *Mead* court's view, litigants would be encouraged to wait until the first-filed proceedings are over to file a second action alleging what would have been compulsory counterclaims to the first action. Under *Mead*, this tactic would increase a litigant's chances of surviving a Rule 13(a) motion to dismiss. Once the first-filed action is already too far along for judicial economies to be served by forcing the later-filed action to be litigated in the same proceeding, the later-action plaintiff is permitted to open up a second "front" of litigation—simply by waiting patiently. Worse yet, what if the first-filed action were over? No judicial economies whatsoever would be served by holding that the later-filed action was a compulsory counterclaim. Yet, as Grumman concedes, that is the situation in a majority of the Rule 13(a) cases.

The better and prevailing view is that an action is either sufficiently related to another action to meet the compulsory counterclaim test or it is not. The status of the first-filed action is irrelevant. To hold otherwise would be a considerable if not fatal blow to Rule 13(a) and the policies it embodies. A close reading of *Mead* reveals that the court seems to have imported into its Rule 13(a) analysis concepts ordinarily involved in transfer of venue motions under 28 U.S.C. §1404. Unlike transfer under Section 1404, Rule 13(a) does not involve notions of convenience, discretion and prospective judicial economy. Rather, Rule 13(a) involves only the question of whether there is a sufficient logical nexus between the subject actions. There is no judicial discretion involved. Any notions of judicial economy are merely retrospective—i.e., an aid in determining the extent to which the actions are related by testing whether judicial economies would have been served had the actions been adjudicated in one proceeding.

Finally, in *Mead*, there seemed to have been appreciably less factual overlap between the copyright and antitrust claims than there is here. In *Mead*, the court found little or no overlapping evidence between the two cases. The antitrust claims in *Mead* involved issues that extended far beyond the subject matter of the Minnesota copyright issues. They included monopolization through predatory pricing and anticompetitive acquisition policies.[2] Here, the monopolization allegation does

---

2. Indeed, Mead had brought a similar antitrust suit against West in the Southern District of New York approximately ten years prior but chose to dismiss the action voluntarily when the court granted West's motion to transfer the action to the District of Minnesota. *Mead Data Central, Inc. v. West Publishing Co.*, 3-78 Civ. 142 (D. Minn. 1978).

not extend as far beyond the ADEX issues. Each of the "non-ADEX" allegations, on which Grumman so heavily relies in opposing this motion, is identical. They all allege that DG threatened its business associates not to deal with Grumman. Thus, the percentage of this action that overlaps the Mass. action is greater than the percentage of the *Mead* action that overlapped the Minnesota copyright action.

In *Mercoid Corp. v. Mid-Continent Co.*, 320 U.S. 661 (1944), the Supreme Court wrote broad sweeping dicta that seemed to state that antitrust claims can never be compulsory counterclaims under Rule 13(a), that antitrust claims were exempt from the operation of Rule 13(a). The case was immediately criticized by the commentators and its holding eroded by the lower courts with time. *E.g., Martino v. McDonald's System, Inc.*, 432 F. Supp. 499 (N.D. Ill. 1977) (many courts have now limited the *Mercoid* dicta to cases involving patent misuse; Sherman Act claims can be 13(a) compulsory counterclaims); *Burlington Indus. v. Milliken & Co.*, 690 F.2d 380 (4th Cir. 1982) ("the *Mercoid* decision has been read narrowly . . . and its continuing validity is open to serious question"). Profs. Wright and Miller are to the same effect. See Wright & Miller, *supra*, at §1412, pp. 61–64. Whatever the continued application of *Mercoid*'s exception in the patent litigation context, it is clear at this point that there is no such general exception to the operation of Rule 13(a) and no case decided in the last twenty years holds to the contrary.

AMI Defendants

Grumman argues that the existence of the AMI defendants takes this case out of Rule 13(a) because of the Rule's exception for situations where the court in the first filed action can not acquire personal jurisdiction over would-be counterclaim defendants.

If this were the law, it would be easy to "end-run" Rule 13(a). It is not the law. DG itself is subject to jurisdiction in Massachusetts; therefore, Grumman's claims against DG can be brought there. The AMI defendants are alleged to be antitrust co-conspirators of DG. As such, they are not indispensable parties to the antitrust action under Rule 19. 7 Wright, Miller & Kane Section 1623, pp. 346–48; *Lawlor v. Nat. Screen Serv. Corp.*, 349 U.S. 322 (1955). Rather, as with joint tortfeasors, an antitrust action may proceed against any combination of co-conspirators.

Two New Identical Cases Against DG

Grumman argues that because DG will have to defend two identical antitrust lawsuits, there is no reason to make Grumman go to Massachusetts to litigate its antitrust claim. The argument makes little sense in light of the objective of Rule 13(a) —judicial economy. It would save considerable judicial effort if Grumman were to litigate in Massachusetts while the Court here consolidates the two new cases with what rémains of this action (Grumman v. AMI defendants) and stays the California proceedings pending the outcome of the Massachusetts litigation. Massachusetts decisions will not be *res judicata*, but they will be helpful in guiding decisions on essentially identical claims, albeit among different parties.

This Court hereby dismisses this action as to DG without prejudice, but permits the action to go forward against the AMI defendants subject to any motions to stay this action. Grumman shall then be free to assert these claims as counterclaims in the Mass. action.

NOTES AND QUESTIONS

1. Under the Federal Rules, counterclaims are divided into two basic categories: compulsory (governed by Rule 13(a)); and permissive (Rule 13(b)). A counterclaim that arises out of the same transaction or occurrence that is the subject matter of the opposing party's claim is compulsory while all other counterclaims are permissive.

In *Grumman*, why was it important, from the perspective of DG, the plaintiff in the original Massachusetts suit, that the subsequent action brought by Grumman in California be identified as a compulsory counterclaim to the first action? What would have happened if Grumman's California lawsuit had been filed first? Would the copyright claim that DG asserted in the Massachusetts action then have been a compulsory counterclaim in the California lawsuit? As we have seen in the earlier chapters, parties often have strong preferences with respect to the choice of a forum. Does the existence of a compulsory counterclaim rule increase the likelihood of a race to the courthouse?

2. *Consequences of Failure to Assert Counterclaim.* Note in *Grumman* that the issue of the compulsoriness of the counterclaim arose in a context where it was still possible for Grumman to assert its antitrust claim as a counterclaim in the previously filed Massachusetts action. Suppose that Grumman brought its antitrust action against DG only after DG's copyright infringement claim had proceeded to final judgment in Massachusetts. Would Grumman have been precluded from bringing this claim against DG altogether?

Curiously, the text of Rule 13 has nothing to say about the impact of a failure to assert a claim that falls within Rule 13(a). At the time of the drafting of the rule, there was apparently some concern that the federal rules not intrude too far in affecting "substantive rights." (In this regard, keep in mind the limitations of the Enabling Act, 28 U.S.C. §2072(b).) Nonetheless, the Advisory Committee Note to Rule 13 states: "If the action proceeds to judgment without the interposition of a counterclaim as required by subdivision (a) of this rule, the counterclaim is barred." A 1936 preliminary draft of the counterclaim rule also used terminology evocative of *res judicata*: "If the action proceeds to judgment without such a claim being set up, the claim shall be barred." 6 C. Wright et al., Federal Practice and Procedure §1417 (3d ed. 2012). Thus, it seems clear that a subsequent filing by Grumman — whether in the Massachusetts, California, or any other federal court — would be precluded through the force of Rule 13(a). (Consider, however, whether the Court's analysis of Rule 41(b) in *Semtek* has any bearing on this question.)

Should the preclusive effect of omitted Rule 13(a) counterclaims depend on whether the first action resulted in a contested adjudication, as opposed to a consent or default judgment? *See* 6 C. Wright et al., Federal Practice and Procedure, *supra*, §1417; *cf.* Fleming James Jr., *Consent Judgments as Collateral Estoppel*, 108 U. Pa. L. Rev. 173 (1959). What if defendant successfully moves to dismiss the first action under Rule 12(b)? *See Mellon Bank v. Ternisky*, 999 F.2d 791, 795 (4th Cir. 1993) ("Rule 13(a) does not come into play when a defendant files a motion to dismiss, instead of a pleading.").

A party who fails to assert a counterclaim as required by Rule 13(a) may still be able to assert the counterclaim belatedly if the original action has not reached final judgment. Rule 13(f) offers the pleader the opportunity — in the case of oversight, inadvertence, or excusable neglect — to assert the counterclaim as an amendment with leave of court. However, if a judgment has been reached, Rule 13(f) is unavailable. The only possible recourse for defendant at that point would be a Rule 60(b) request for relief from a judgment for mistake, inadvertence, excusable neglect, newly discovered evidence, or fraud.

3. *Inter-jurisdictional Consequences.* What if the state antitrust claim filed on behalf of Grumman had remained in California state court rather than being removed to federal court? Does Rule 13(a) preclude a state court from hearing a claim that should have been asserted as a compulsory counterclaim in a prior federal action? Is the federal interest in precluding a subsequent action based on an omitted counterclaim as compelling when the subsequent action is not within the federal system? Are state courts required to dismiss such claims even in the absence of a federal judgment (as when the federal proceeding is still pending)?

The answer may depend on whether Rule 13(a) takes effect as a feature of a judgment that triggers mandatory preclusion and recognition obligations, or simply states a federal policy of waiver, which would be enforceable at the discretion of the second court. Is the latter view more attractive in that it would permit flexibility where, say, an insurer controlled the original litigation and may not have had an incentive to interpose counterclaims in the insured's favor? *Compare Allan Block Corp. v. County Materials Corp.*, 512 F.3d 912, 916–917 (7th Cir. 2008) ("Rule 13(a) does not specify the consequences of failing [to assert compulsory counterclaims]. Those consequences are given by the doctrine of *res judicata.*") *with Reynolds v. Hartford Accident & Indem. Co.*, 278 F. Supp. 331, 333 (S.D.N.Y. 1967) (embracing a waiver approach and permitting exceptions where insurer controls original litigation).

Once the federal proceeding is reduced to a judgment, the preclusive effect of Rule 13(a) would presumably be strengthened. Most state courts have declined to hear any claim not pleaded in a prior federal action in violation of Rule 13(a). *See* 6 C. Wright et al., Federal Practice and Procedure §1417 (3d ed. 2012).

4. *An Antitrust Exception?* As in *Grumman*, it is common practice for a defendant to assert antitrust counterclaims in patent or copyright infringement litigation. In *Mercoid Corp. v. Mid-Continent Co.*, 320 U.S. 661 (1944), cited in *Grumman*, the Supreme Court left open the question of whether antitrust claims are exempt from the operation of Rule 13(a) when asserted in response to a patent infringement lawsuit. In *Mercoid*, plaintiff (Mid-Continent) sued defendant (Mercoid) for contributory infringement of a patent. Mercoid then asserted an antitrust counterclaim against Mid-Continent. Mid-Continent raised the defense of *res judicata* to both Mercoid's defenses and counterclaim since, five years earlier, Mid-Continent had sued Smith (a Mercoid customer) for infringement of the same patent. The Supreme Court, assuming that Mercoid was in privity with Smith, stated:

> [Even if] Mercoid were barred in the present case from asserting any defense which might have been interposed in the earlier litigation, it would not follow that its counterclaim for damages would likewise be barred. That claim for damages is more than a defense; it is a separate statutory cause of action. The fact that it might have been asserted as a counterclaim in the prior suit by reason of Rule 13(b) of the Rules of Civil Procedure . . . does not mean that failure to do so renders a prior judgment *res judicata* as respects it.

320 U.S. at 671.

Some courts have interpreted *Mercoid* as carving out an exception to Rule 13(a) for counterclaims asserted in response to a patent infringement lawsuit. *See Tank Insulation Int'l Inc. v. Insultherm, Inc.*, 104 F.3d 83 (5th Cir. 1997) (holding that antitrust counterclaims asserted in patent infringement litigation can only be permissive—regardless of the "logical relationship" test—in accordance with the holding of *Mercoid*). Do you think it is fair to read *Mercoid* as standing for the rule that all antitrust counterclaims asserted in patent infringement litigation are inherently permissive? Might the *Mercoid* court just have assumed the counterclaim was permissive because the issue of whether the counterclaim was permissive or compulsory was never raised? *Compare Critical-Vac Filtration Corp. v. Minuteman Int'l, Inc.*, 233 F.3d 697, 702 (2000) ("We have observed that *Mercoid* failed to discuss the principles on which its decision rested, and have held that the *Mercoid* exception to Rule 13(a) should be limited to the facts in that case. We reiterate that view here. . . .") (internal quotations omitted). For a discussion of the *Mercoid* case and its various interpretations, *see* Teague I. Donahey, *Antitrust Counterclaims in Patent Infringement Litigation: Clarifying the Supreme Court's Enigmatic* Mercoid *Decision*, 39 J.L. & Tech. 225 (1999).

5. *The Definition of Transaction.* What is the appropriate test for determining when a claim "arises out of the transaction or occurrence that is the subject matter of the opposing party's claim" for purposes of Rule 13(a)? We have seen the "same transaction" test adopted in a number of different procedural contexts. In viewing the relationship between DG's copyright infringement claim and Grumman's antitrust claim, the *Grumman* court cites the Supreme Court decision in *Moore v. New York Cotton Exchange*, pp. 346–352, where the Supreme Court looked to whether the claim and counterclaim were "logically related" in formulating the scope of ancillary (now supplemental) jurisdiction.

Remember, however, that with a question of ancillary or supplemental jurisdiction, as in *Moore*, a court is concerned with the permissive aspects of allowing a claim to proceed, with an eye toward considerations of federalism. In the context of asking whether a particular claim is a compulsory counterclaim, a court is deciding whether to *require* a party to bring a particular claim at a time and place not of his own choosing on pain of forfeiting the claim altogether.

Does the different context suggest a narrower definition when the question is whether a claim *must* be asserted as a compulsory counterclaim than when the issue is whether a particular claim or counterclaim is within the federal court's supplemental jurisdiction? For a general discussion about the need to apply the transaction standard according to the varying doctrines that it serves, *see* Mary Kay Kane, *Federal Practice and Procedure Symposium Honoring Charles Alan Wright: Original Sin and Transaction in Federal Civil Procedure*, 76 Tex. L. Rev. 1723, 1745 (1998) ("courts have refused to adopt as broad an approach to the scope of *res judicata* as typically is utilized to determine when joinder is proper").

Determining the appropriate scope of a compulsory counterclaim requires a balancing of competing interests: on the one hand, a desire to maximize efficiency and avoid duplication of litigation; and on the other, a more general policy of allowing a party to choose the time and place for litigation of claims. Does the "logical relationship" test adopted in *Grumman* help illuminate that inquiry? Consider these other less widely used "tests" for determining what constitutes a transactional relationship for Rule 13(a) purposes: "(1) Are the issues of fact and law raised by the claim and counterclaim largely the same? (2) Would *res judicata* (claim preclusion) bar a subsequent suit on defendant's claim absent the compulsory counterclaim rule? (3) Will substantially the same evidence support or refute plaintiff's claim as well as defendant's counterclaim? (4) Is there any logical relationship between the claim and the counterclaim?" *See* 6 C. Wright et al., Federal Practice and Procedure §1410 (3d ed. 2005 & 2021 Update). Is any of these tests better suited to determining when the claim and counterclaim are transactionally related for purposes of Rule 13(a)? How would Grumman's antitrust counterclaim fare under these respective tests?

6. *Exceptions to Rule 13(a).* Certain counterclaims, notwithstanding their transactional nexus with the main claim, are excepted from the scope of Rule 13(a) — claims that are the subject of another pending action, *see* Fed. R. Civ. P. 13(a)(2)(A); and where the court acquired power over the defendant through attachment or some other form of process that does not establish full *in personam* jurisdiction, *see id.* §(a)(2)(B). What is the reason for not making such claims "compulsory"? Note that Rule 13(b) defines a permissive counterclaim as "any claim that is not compulsory," a definition that would encompass the exceptions to Rule 13(a) and allow the pleader to assert such claims if he desired.

7. Rule 13(h) authorizes joinder of additional parties as parties to a counterclaim or cross-claim in accordance with Rules 19 and 20. The court must have personal jurisdiction over the parties, but note that Rule 4(k)(1)(B) authorizes limited extraterritorial service over parties joined pursuant to Rule 19. Recall that when Grumman added two additional defendants (the AMI defendants) as antitrust co-conspirators of DG, the court ruled that the counterclaim against DG could still be heard in Massachusetts despite the lack of personal jurisdiction over the AMI defendants. The lack of personal jurisdiction over the additional joined defendants did not affect the court's jurisdiction over the original defendants; the AMI defendants were not found to be indispensable parties under Rule 19 since an antitrust action may proceed against any combination of co-conspirators.

8. *The Policy Revisited.* Not all states have adopted a compulsory counterclaim policy. New York, for example, declined to adopt a compulsory counterclaim rule as part of the revisions of New York's Civil Practice Law and Rules (the CPLR), determining that defendants should be allowed the same tactical freedom as plaintiffs in asserting their claims and should not be forced to litigate their claims in the forum of plaintiff's choosing. There was also concern that the freedom to use arbitration agreements and negotiation among insurers might be impaired by a compulsory counterclaim rule. Moreover, the need for a compulsory counterclaim rule was reduced by other incentives to assert the counterclaim (since a defendant interposing a counterclaim avoids the cost and effort of a second action) as well as the pressure of collateral estoppel (since defendants may be barred from re-litigating certain issues in a second action). *See* 5 Weinstein et al., New York Civil Practice: Civil Practice Law and Rules ¶3019.12 (2000).

What consequences flow from the failure to adopt a compulsory counterclaim rule? Recall that whether or not there is "defense preclusion" in a subsequent action often turns on whether the state rendering the initial judgment had a compulsory counterclaim rule. *See* Restatement (Second) of Judgments §22. In *Batavia Kill Dist. v. Desch*, 83 App. Div. 2d 97, 100 (N.Y. App. 3d Dept. 1981), a contractor

(Desch) sued a watershed district to recover damages, claiming wrongful termination of a construction contract. The watershed district did not interpose a counterclaim but defended on the ground that the contractor had failed to perform the contract on a timely basis. The jury found that the watershed district was justified in terminating the contract because of Desch's untimely performance. In a second action by the watershed district for damages for nonperformance of the same contract, the Appellate Division permitted the action to proceed and, indeed, held that Desch could not relitigate the jury's determination that there had been untimely performance and that the watershed district's termination of the contract was justified. Thus, the lack of a compulsory counterclaim rule allowed defendant (the watershed district) to "split the defense," using it first as a shield and then as a sword in a second action for damages. Plaintiff, on the other hand, because of the doctrine of collateral estoppel, was left largely unable to defend himself in the second action. Do you think the *Batavia* decision is fair? How would *Batavia* have been decided according to the Restatement (Second) of Judgments §22, discussed at pp. 795–797?

b.   Cross-Claims

Cross-claims are claims asserted between previously non-adverse co-parties (that is, parties on the same side of the "v."). In contrast to defendant's permissive counterclaims, Rule 13(g) only allows parties to assert cross-claims when they are transactionally related either to plaintiff's claims in the original action or to a counterclaim interposed by the defendant. Moreover, all cross-claims are permissive only—though here, too, rules of collateral estoppel may provide a powerful incentive to interpose the claims. *See Schwartz v. Public Administrator*, 246 N.E.2d 725 (N.Y. 1969) (recognizing applicability of issue preclusion between co-parties in a prior action).

Should the "transaction" requirement for cross-claims be interpreted in the same way as the "transaction" requirement for Rule 13(a) counterclaims? Do cross-claims present a greater potential for unraveling the original lawsuit as structured by plaintiff? *See Old Homestead Bread Co. v. Continental Baker Co.*, 47 F.R.D. 560 (D. Colo. 1969) (holding that added complexity of interjecting a cross-claim in a given suit is overshadowed when a close connection between the complaint and a cross-claim exists). In *Old Homestead*, a retailer alleged conspiracy on the part of defendant wholesalers to restrain and monopolize the production, transportation, and marketing of bakery products as well as an unlawful price discrimination scheme. Defendant Interstate Bakeries Corp. filed a cross-claim against the other defendant corporations (Continental, Campbell Taggart, and Rainbo), alleging monopolization on the part of Continental as well as agreements on the part of Campbell Taggart and Rainbo to restrain competition in the bread market. As a result of these practices, Interstate claimed that it was compelled to meet the unreasonably low prices. Continental, Campbell Taggart, and Rainbo argued that the cross-claim did not arise from the same transaction or occurrence described in the complaint because the complaint alleged a conspiracy and a price discrimination scheme among *all* defendants, whereas the cross-claim charged a unilateral attempt to monopolize by defendant Continental and an agreement between defendants Campbell Taggart and Rainbo to illegally restrain trade and practice discriminatory pricing. The court, resorting to the "logical relationship" test, concluded that the complaint and the cross-claim arose out of the same transaction or occurrence (the distribution of bread products) and that the cross-claim need not be factually identical to the original complaint in order for there to be a transactional relationship.

> Both [the original complaint and cross-claim] appear to be offshoots of the same basic controversy. The practices among wholesalers and retailers in the distribution of bread products are the central issues in both claims. The evidence needed to prove these claims will not be identical, but it will be substantially the same. It therefore seems to us that Interstate's specific allegations closely coincide with and are logically related to the conduct which underlies plaintiff's general charge. Furthermore, allowing this cross-claim will enable us to grant full relief to all parties and make a complete determination of all issues arising out of this basic controversy. Accordingly, we conclude that there is a logical and close relationship between the amended complaint and the cross-claim. . . .

Id. at 563–564.

Does the court's discussion of the "logical relationship" test help to clarify the transaction or occurrence standard as applied to cross-claims? Isn't it possible for a cross-claim to be an "offshoot of the same basic controversy" and still require a great deal of different evidence in order to be proved?

Note that if there are difficulties in allowing the cross-claim to be heard with the main action, a court may sever the cross-claim for trial. Fed. R. Civ. P. 13(i) gives the court discretion to invoke Rule 42(b) and order separate trials in order to avoid prejudice or to promote convenience and judicial economy. Under Rule 13(i), the disposal of plaintiff's claim does not preclude the court from proceeding to judgment on the counterclaim or cross-claim (as long as the court has appropriate jurisdiction over the claim).

If a party fails to assert a cross-claim originally, and seeks later to do so by way of amendment (*see* Fed. R. Civ. P. 15(a)), the court has discretion as to whether or not to allow the assertion of the cross-claim. Permission to assert a cross-claim in this situation may be denied if the cross-claim prevents an equitable determination of the main suit. *See, e.g., United States v. Eight Tracts of Land*, 270 F. Supp. 160 (E.D.N.Y. 1967) (denying defendant's motion to file a cross-claim by way of amendment, on the ground that allowing the cross-claim could easily mislead a jury on the issue of damages and prolong the trial with issues that could more properly be determined in a separate action).

Should a party be permitted to assert a cross-claim even if the party has not been placed in a defensive posture? Should the "same transaction or occurrence" requirement be read narrowly to include only those claims directly asserted against cross-claimants? Consider the Third Circuit's approach in *Danner v. Anskis*, 256 F.2d 123 (3d Cir. 1958). In *Danner*, the passenger and driver of one automobile sued the driver of another vehicle involved in an accident. After the latter's default, the plaintiff-passengers attempted to cross-claim against the plaintiff-driver for the same injuries that formed the basis of the original action. The appeals court held that the cross-claim did not arise out of claims asserted against the cross-claimants:

> The purpose of Rule 13(g) is to permit a defendant to state as a cross-claim a claim against a co-defendant growing out of the transaction or occurrence that is the subject matter of the original action . . . and to permit a plaintiff against whom a defendant has filed a counterclaim to state as a cross-claim against a co-plaintiff a claim growing out of the transaction or occurrence that is the subject matter of the counterclaim. . . . [A] cross-claim is intended to state a claim which is ancillary to a claim stated in a complaint or counterclaim which has previously been filed against the party stating the cross-claim.

256 F.2d at 124. Is *Danner* consistent with the language of Rule 13(g)? *See* 6 C. Wright et al., Federal Practice and Procedure §1432 (3d ed. 2005).

C. *JOINDER OF PARTIES*

1. *Permissive Joinder and Consolidation*

Guedry v. Marino

164 F.R.D. 181 (E.D. La. 1995)

Jones, District Judge

BACKGROUND

. . . Defendant, Johnny Marino, individually and in his official capacity as sheriff of St. Charles Parish, has been sued by seven plaintiffs, George Guedry, Jr., Robert Lewis, Claudette Wilson, Nicholas Vitrano, David Zeringue, Brent Mashia and Orvett Smith, under 42 U.S.C. §§1981 and 1983 for alleged violations of the First and Fourteenth Amendments. Plaintiffs also allege state-law violations. Plaintiffs have brought suit against Marino because their commissions as deputies were not renewed as of July 1, 1992, the date that the sheriff assumed office after his re-election. . . .

George Guedry, Jr. alleges that his commission was terminated by defendant in violation of his First and Fourteenth Amendment rights because of (1) his decision to speak out at a parish council meeting; (2) his membership in and association with members of the New Sarpy Civic Association; and (3) his refusal to participate in the defendant's re-election efforts.

Robert Lewis alleges First and Fourteenth Amendment violations as a result of defendant's harassment and retaliation, because of (1) defendant's belief that plaintiff supported defendant's opponent in the election; (2) defendant's belief that plaintiff influenced his neighbor to support defendant's opponent; (3)

plaintiff's decision to speak out on a matter of public concern; and (4) plaintiff's race.

Nicholas Vitrano also claims violations of his First and Fourteenth Amendment rights as a result of defendant's harassment and retaliation, because of defendant's belief that plaintiff had supported the defendant's opposing candidate.

Claudette Wilson asserts that her First and Fourteenth Amendment rights were violated due to defendant's harassment and retaliation efforts against her because she filed a worker's compensation complaint alleging that defendant refused to pay her medical bills for a job-related injury. Further, plaintiff maintains that her Constitutional rights were violated because defendant terminated her commission because of her race and/or sex.

David Zeringue declares that he has been deprived of his right to equal employment opportunities as a result of defendant's harassment of him solely because of (1) defendant's belief that he had not actively supported defendant's re-election bid; and (2) defendant's belief that plaintiff sought to enforce the law against individuals who were political allies of the defendant.

Brent Mashia proclaims that his First and Fourteenth Amendment rights were violated by defendant's harassment of plaintiff solely because of (1) defendant's belief that plaintiff did not actively support the defendant's re-election bid; (2) plaintiff's decision to speak out against defendant's policies of racial discrimination; and (3) plaintiff's race.

Orvett Smith charges that defendant harassed and retaliated against plaintiff solely because of (1) defendant's belief that plaintiff supported his opponent's bid for election; (2) defendant's belief that plaintiff was closely associated with defendant's opponent; and (3) plaintiff's race in violation of plaintiff's First and Fourteenth Amendment rights.

The defendant has filed a "Motion to Sever/Separate Trials" claiming that the plaintiff's cases are improperly joined, entitling him to have the claims severed under Fed. R. Civ. P. 20 and 21. In the alternative, the defendant claims that sufficient reasons exist to sever each plaintiff's case pursuant to Fed. R. Civ. P. 42(b). The defendant postulates that severance is proper because separate trials will promote judicial economy and will prevent jury confusion.

In their opposition, plaintiffs contend that the claims have been properly joined because each plaintiff was terminated for refusing to support defendant's election bid or for supporting defendant's re-election bid but being accused of not doing so. Further, four plaintiffs also allege that they were discharged because of their race. Thus, plaintiffs argue that there is a common question of law or fact with respect to these claims. In the alternative, plaintiffs argue that severing these claims would result in unnecessary delay and prejudice to the litigants. In addition, plaintiffs argue that any possible confusion to the jury can be handled by the Court through its jury instructions.

LAW AND APPLICATION

I. Misjoinder

Fed. R. Civ. P. 20(a) provides, in pertinent part:

All persons may join in one action as plaintiffs if they assert any right to relief jointly, severally, or in the alternative in respect of or arising out of the same transaction, occurrence, or series of transactions or occurrences and if any question of law or fact common to all these persons will arise in the action....

28 U.S.C. Rule 20(a) (West 1992).*

The purpose of Rule 20(a) is to promote trial convenience and expedite the final determination of disputes, thereby preventing multiple lawsuits. *See Mosley v. General Motors Corp.*, 497 F.2d 1330, 1332 (8th Cir. 1974).... Moreover, under the Federal Rules of Civil Procedure, "joinder of claims, parties and remedies is strongly encouraged." *Mosley*, 497 F.2d at 1332, (citing United Mine Workers v. Gibbs, 383 U.S. 715, 724 (1966)).

The Court in *Mosley* noted that:

> [p]ermissive joinder is not, however, applicable in all cases. The rule imposes two specific requisites to the joinder of parties: (1) a right to relief must be asserted by, or against, each plaintiff or defendant relating to or arising out of the same transaction or occurrence, or series of trans- actions or occurrences; and (2) some question of law or fact common to all the parties must arise in the action.

Mosley, 497 F.2d at 1333.... There is no strict rule for determining what con- stitutes the same occurrence or series of transactions or occurrences for purposes of Rule 20(a). Furthermore, Rule 20(a) does not require that every question of law or fact in the action be common among the parties; rather, the rule permits party joinder whenever there will be at least one common question of law or fact. See 7 Charles A. Wright, Arthur R. Miller and Mary Kay Kane, *Federal Practice and Procedure* §1653, at 387 (1986).

Applying these principles to the present case, the Court rejects defendant's argument that plaintiffs' complaint does not satisfy the tests for joinder because they involve different transactions or occurrences and they do not raise common factual or legal issues except as to plaintiff Claudette Wilson. All of the plaintiffs' claims arise out of separate factual circumstances but all of plaintiffs' allegations revolve around claims of termination after alleged violations of First Amendment rights except Clau- dette Wilson. This includes enforcement of the law as to defendant's supporters and/ or failure to support defendant (or allegations thereto) in his re-election bid and/or speaking at a public meeting. Such conduct may constitute a single transaction or occurrence for purposes of Rule 20(a). The alleged discriminatory activity directly affecting each of them, includes common legal and factual questions.

As to plaintiff Claudette Wilson, however, review of the Complaint clearly seems to indicate that, although she was terminated on the same day as the other plaintiffs, there is no other relevant similarity between her claim and the other plaintiffs' claims. Wilson alleges that she was forced to file a Worker's Compensation

---

* The text and internal numbering of Rule 20 were altered in the restyling of the Rules that took effect in December 2007. The relevant portion of the Rule now reads:

Persons may be joined in one action as plaintiffs if:

(A) they assert any right to relief jointly, severally, or in the alternative with respect to or arising out of the same transaction, occurrence, or series of transactions or occurrences; and

(B) any question of law or fact common to all parties will arise in the action.

Fed. R. Civ. P. 20(a)(1). — Eds.

complaint for defendant's refusal to reimburse her for medical payments related to an on-the-job injury. As noted, Wilson claims that her commission was not renewed in retaliation for filing such a claim and also because of her race and/or sex. Although Wilson makes a claim for violation of First Amendment rights as the other plaintiffs do, it is clear that her claims do not arise out of the same transaction or occurrence as the other plaintiffs, insofar as they make a claim for First Amendment violations as to speaking at civic forums and/or not supporting (or allegedly refusing to support) defendant in his re-election campaign.

However, plaintiff Wilson also makes a claim for racial discrimination, as do plaintiffs Robert Lewis, Orvett Smith and Brent Mashia. Thus, Wilson's claims arise out of similar transactions or occurrences and involve similar questions of fact and law such that joinder of her claims with the other plaintiffs' claims under Rule 20(a) is proper.

Hence, [defendant's] motion to sever under Rule 20(a) fails.

Defendant argues that the evidence used to prove any one plaintiff's claims would not be admissible in a trial of any of the other plaintiffs based on relevancy. In addition to the fact that defendant cites no law in support of this contention, the foregoing discussion belies the fallacy of this contention.

Defendant also argues that exposure to irrelevant evidence would "taint and confuse the jury." This argument is outright rejected because any potential confusion to the jury can surely be remedied at trial through a limiting instruction by the Court. Moreover, courts have broad discretion in interpreting the requirements of Rule 20 in an effort to reduce inconvenience, delay and added expense to the parties and to the court, and to promote judicial economy. The time, expense and inconvenience to the parties associated with seven separate trials is readily apparent in this case. Severance of the plaintiffs' claims at this juncture would be imprudent, as it may result in a waste of judicial time and resources. Moreover, the Court does not agree that joinder of plaintiffs' claims will result in prejudice to the defendant or that his right to a fair trial will be compromised.

II. Separate Trials

Defendant's alternative argument is that sufficient reasons exist to sever each of the plaintiffs' cases for trial under Rule 42(b). The defendant contends that severance is necessary to avoid prejudice, to promote economy and to avoid jury confusion. In support of his argument, defendant notes that seven different factual situations and seven sets of witnesses would cause confusion and prejudice. Moreover, defendant argues that a common trial would be "intolerable and unmanageable."

Rule 42(b) provides that separation is proper when a trial court determines that severance is "in furtherance of convenience or to avoid prejudice, or when separate trials will be conducive to expedition or economy.". . . The decision to grant separate trials rests within the sole discretion of the trial court.

The Court rebuffs defendant's argument that the sheer number of claims presented coupled with the testimony of each plaintiff's witnesses will cause prejudice and confusion. To be sure, judicial economy and prejudice based on these factors can be addressed by instructions. The Fifth Circuit has recognized that "[t]here is an important limitation on ordering a separate trial of issues under Rule 42(b): the issue to be tried must be so distinct and separate from the others that a trial of it alone may be had without injustice." *McDaniel v. Anheuser-Busch, Inc.*, 987 F.2d 298, 305 and n. 22 (5th Cir. 1993) (citations omitted). Moreover, "even if bifurcation might somehow promote judicial economy, courts should not order separate trials when bifurcation would result in unnecessary delay, additional expense, or some other form of prejudice." *Laitram Corp. v. Hewlett-Packard Co.*, 791 F. Supp. 113, 115 (E.D. La. 1992) (citations omitted).

As explained above, the claims of all plaintiffs are not so separate and distinct as to constitute injustice. Further, separate trials will cause needless delay and prejudice, especially due to the age of this case. In the end, defendant's proposition would amount to no more than a complicated legal benediction. This Court fully embraces the time-honored premise that "[a]n unreasonable delay in a case's resolution amounts to prejudice to the one opposing separation. [Such delay] is clearly not in the public interest."

After balancing the two competing claims of prejudice, the convenience of the parties and judicial economy, the Court finds that these considerations weigh against the defendant's motion to sever under Rule 42(b). Rather, the Court finds that the goals of judicial economy, the convenience of the parties and fairness will be best served if it retains one trial.

CONCLUSION

For the foregoing reasons, the Court fathoms no valid notions that favor defendant's motion to sever, whether pursuant to Rule 20(a) or Rule 42(b), with a compelling legal basis. To allow seven individual trials on essentially the same, if not identical, issue could cause this matter to go on forever, case after case. Such would be reminiscent of Dante's Ninth Circle.

Accordingly,

IT IS ORDERED that defendant's "Motion to Sever/Separate Trials" is DENIED.

NOTES AND QUESTIONS

1. *Historical Note.* At common law, joinder of parties was a function of the substantive rights of the parties rather than a reflection of considerations of judicial economy and trial convenience. Moreover, there was no concept of permissive joinder of multiple plaintiffs: Plaintiffs asserting joint rights were required to join their respective claims in the same action. Joinder of multiple defendants was treated somewhat more flexibly. Unless defendants were subject to a joint obligation, plaintiff had the option of suing jointly or severally when proceeding against defendants such as joint tortfeasors whose obligations were joint and several. *See* Charles Edward Clark, Code Pleading §59 (2d ed. 1947). The equity courts sought to avoid multiplicity of actions by allowing all persons with an interest in the subject matter to be joined. *See* Joseph Story, Commentaries on Equity Pleadings §76(c) (9th ed. 1879).

Joinder rules under state pleading codes adopted the equity approach but were construed narrowly to restrict plaintiff joinder to cases where all plaintiffs were interested in both the subject matter of the suit and all the relief demanded, and to restrict defendant joinder to cases of joint liability. *See* 7 C. Wright et al., Federal Practice and Procedure §1651 (3d ed. 2012 & 2021 Update). Legislation in the latter part of the nineteenth century, patterned after English developments, sought to liberalize party joinder. Late nineteenth century jurists began to value litigant autonomy, in particular the freedom of plaintiffs to choose the type of lawsuit they wished to bring and the parties they wished to join. The concept developed that plaintiffs sharing a similar "interest" arising out of the same events as well as defendants with "interests in the subject of the suit" antagonistic to the plaintiff could be joined in the same action. *See* Robert G. Bone, *Mapping the Boundaries of a Dispute: Conceptions of Ideal Lawsuit Structure from the Field Code to the Federal Rules*, 89 Colum. L. Rev. 1, 45–78 (1989).

2. *Assessing* Guedry. Unlike joinder of claims under Rule 18(a), joinder of parties under Rule 20(a) is not unlimited. As the *Guedry* court notes, permissive joinder of parties must meet two requirements imposed by the federal rules: (1) a "transactional" relationship; and (2) some question of law or fact common to all parties.

How does the *Guedry* court measure the relevant "transaction, occurrence, or series of transactions or occurrences" from which all the claims arise? Don't the plaintiffs rely on separate factual circumstances for their respective claims of wrongful termination? In particular, aren't plaintiff Wilson's claims sufficiently distinct from the claims of the other plaintiffs so as not to fall within the transactional rubric?

Even if plaintiff Wilson's claim for racial discrimination falls within the scope of Rule 20, what about the other allegations on which Wilson's claims are based — e.g., that her commission was not renewed in retaliation for filing a workers' compensation claim? Even the court acknowledges that there is no relevant similarity between Wilson's claim and the other plaintiffs' claims in various respects. Should the court have dismissed those allegations as insufficiently related and entertained only the transactionally related claims? Or are they all part and parcel of her claim for racial discrimination?

What is the relationship between Rule 18, which allows a plaintiff to assert any claim, and Rule 20, which requires that joined parties have transactionally related claims? Can a plaintiff, having properly joined defendants because of transactionally related claims, assert unrelated claims against the same defendants? In *Burns v. Int'l Bhd. of Painters and Allied Trades*, 1975 WL 1133 (D. Conn. 1975), the court held that such joinder was permissible: ". . . once it is clear under Rule 20(a) that parties are properly joined, Rule 18(a) permits additional claims related or unrelated, by or against all or fewer than all of the parties to be joined."

Corresponding state rules of party and claim joinder have been similarly interpreted. *See, e.g., McCoy v. Like*, 511 N.E.2d 501 (Ind. Ct. App. 1987) (holding that in an action to contest a will, once a defendant has been properly joined, plaintiff is not restricted from asserting other unrelated claims against the joined defendant). Does the policy of allowing plaintiff to assert unrelated claims against properly joined defendants undermine the effect of Rule 20(a)? Is this policy justified on judicial economy/efficiency grounds?

3. *Defining the "Transaction" or "Occurrence" for Permissive Joinder.* How should a court define the transaction or occurrence (or series of transactions or occurrences) out of which the claims must all arise in order to satisfy the joinder requirements of Rule 20? In *Guedry*, the district court concluded that all the plaintiffs' claims concerning retaliation in the workplace arose out of the same transaction,

even though the retaliation they alleged happened at different times and under different circumstances. The court seems to have concluded that Sheriff Marino was pursuing a continuing policy or practice of misusing his office for political gain and that each specific instance of misconduct constituted part of the same series of occurrences under that policy or practice. Compare that scenario to the situation presented when a large company is accused of a companywide policy or practice of discrimination and multiple plaintiffs join together from different departments within the company to challenge their alleged mistreatment (unlike in *Guedry*, where all the employees worked in the same office). Courts have differed in their conclusions about whether Rule 20 joinder is appropriate in such cases, and their rulings tend to be highly fact-specific. *Compare Smith v. North American Rockwell Corp.*, 50 F.R.D. 515 (N.D. Okla. 1970) (claims by employees in different departments of a single company did not arise out of the same series of transactions or occurrences, even where a companywide policy of discrimination was alleged) *with King v. Pepsi Cola Metro. Bottling Co.*, 86 F.R.D. 4 (E.D. Pa. 1979) (allowing joinder of plaintiffs in different departments with different supervisors based on allegations of a pervasive policy of racial discrimination).

Defining the boundaries of a *series* of transactions or occurrences can be tricky when parties attempt expansive joinder. A group of cases involving illegal downloading of digital content provides a striking example. The practice of bit-torrent or swarm downloading allows people to download large digital files anonymously and quickly. It is a form of distributed computing in which a user downloads fragments of a large file from multiple widely distributed sources and then reassembles the fragments on his computer. The user, in turn, makes his computer available to others as another download source for that file. Bit torrent downloads are increasingly used to download copyrighted materials, particularly pornography, because of the speed and anonymity they provide. In response, some owners of copyrighted materials have brought enforcement actions against all the participants in the swarm, attempting to identify the violators by their IP addresses. An IP address gives information about the Internet source from which the files were downloaded but not necessarily the identity of the individual user, making it an imperfect vehicle for identifying violators. Nonetheless, some aggrieved copyright holders make the attempt, likely more for its *in terrorem* effect than for any hope of compensation from individual users. Plaintiffs typically bring suit against a large number of unknown "Doe" defendants, hoping to use the tools of discovery to identify specific users if the lawsuit is allowed to proceed. The title of one leading case is illustrative: *Digital Sin, Inc. v. Does 1–176*, 279 F.R.D. 239, 244–245 (S.D.N.Y. 2012).

A difficult Rule 20 question arises in these suits: Do the claims against all these defendants arise out of the same series of transactions or occurrences, making their joinder in a single action appropriate? People using bit torrent technology are unknown to one another and widely dispersed geographically, with each illegal download happening at a different time and under different circumstances. It is clear that there are *common questions* in these cases. They share the common facts of downloading the same copyrighted material (a particular movie) through a common method (bit torrent) by means of a shared though ever-changing network of computers. And a common legal question binds all the claims: the standard under copyright law for determining when bit torrent downloads are illegal. But does it stretch the idea of a *series of transactions or occurrences* too far to join all these potential violators in a single action rather than treating the claims as distinct and requiring separate lawsuits?

Lower federal courts have produced widely varying answers to this question. In *Digital Sin*, Judge Nathan of the Southern District of New York viewed the bit torrent as a single distributed transaction undertaken jointly by all the participants. She thus found it "difficult to see how . . . a series of individuals connecting either directly with each other or as part of a chain or 'swarm' of connectivity designed to illegally copy and share the exact same copyrighted file . . . could *not* constitute a 'series of transactions or occurrences' for purposes of Rule 20" and ruled that joinder was appropriate. *Digital Sin*, 279 F.R.D. at 244. Other district courts have come to the opposite conclusion. *See, e.g., A.F. Holdings LLC v. Does 1–97*, 2011 WL 2912909, at *4 (N.D. Cal. 2011) (finding that the lack of any possibility of contact between swarm participants prevents a finding that their actions constitute a series of transactions under Rule 20); *Third Degree Films v. Does 1–131*, 280 F.R.D. 493, 498 (D. Ariz. 2012) (observing that plaintiff sought only to join the Arizona participants in a swarm download, a choice made solely for "Plaintiff's convenience," and concluding that the resulting group of unrelated individuals do not share any meaningful series of transactions and should not be joined under Rule 20).

Note the implication to the plaintiff if joinder is not permitted. Plaintiff's only option may be to file individual lawsuits in the hundreds or even thousands, paying an individual filing fee for each lawsuit of around $400 along with other redundant expenses that would make enforcement of their rights impractical. *See Call of the Wild Movie, LLC v. Does 1–1062*, 770 F. Supp. 2d 332, 344 (D.D.C. 2012) (pointing to these practical concerns and granting broad joinder of defendants in a swarm download case). If a finding of no joinder under Rule 20 would frustrate the ability of copyright holders to enforce their rights, should that fact influence the district court's interpretation of the rule? For a further discussion of these cases and the possibility that underlying principles of copyright law might play a role in guiding district courts on the joinder issue, *see* Tobias Barrington Wolff, *Managerial Judging and Substantive Law*, 90 Wash. U. L. Rev. 1027, 1060–1067 (2013).

4. *Permissive Joinder of Defendants.* Rule 20 adopts the same standard for joining multiple defendants as it uses for joinder of multiple plaintiffs. But consider *Insull v. New York World Telegram Corp.*, 172 F. Supp. 615 (N.D. Ill. 1959). In that case, three different authors and publishers independently published statements about plaintiff. Plaintiff joined defendants on the theory that he was libeled by all of them. Declaring a misjoinder of parties, the court held that plaintiff's claims against defendants did not arise out of the same transaction or occurrence since they were completely independent of one another.

Is the *Insull* case inconsistent with *Guedry*? *Compare Poster v. Central Gulf S.S. Corp.*, 25 F.R.D. 18 (E.D. Pa. 1960). In that case, plaintiff, a steamship employee, brought suit against two separate employers (Sinclair and Gulf), alleging that he contracted a disease known as amoebiasis that was caused by Sinclair's negligence in allowing infected persons to board the ship, aid in the preparation of food, and use the lavatory. The plaintiff alleged that his disease was aggravated by the similar negligence of his second employer (Gulf). Defendants argued that joinder was improper since plaintiff's claim was based on two separate and distinct occurrences. Rejecting this argument, the court allowed the joinder of these defendants, reasoning that "the two occurrences were the same in nature and that the second might result in concurrent liability of both companies. . . ." *Id.* at 20. Indeed, despite the court's characterization of the incidents as two separate occurrences, the court determined that the claims were sufficiently related to meet the transaction requirement of Rule 20(a). Do you see a distinction between *Poster* and *Insull?*

5. *Joinder Rules and the Impact of Subject Matter Jurisdiction Requirements.* Rule 20 (like all of the joinder of claim and party rules) refers solely to the requirements for joinder; it does not create any subject matter jurisdiction. A party who meets the standards of Rule 20 must still satisfy the requirements of subject matter jurisdiction (as well as personal jurisdiction). Thus, when federal jurisdiction depends upon diversity, the suit must exhibit complete diversity after any joinder of parties, and, as we have seen in *Rose v. Giamatti,* joinder strategies may be affected by a party's preference for a state or federal forum. For example, by choosing to join a nondiverse party, a plaintiff may be able to ensure that the case will be heard in a state forum. Alternatively, a plaintiff who seeks a federal court for litigation for the action may intentionally decide not to join a party who would destroy the court's subject matter jurisdiction.

A plaintiff has even been permitted to drop a nondiverse party on appeal in order to preserve the court's subject matter jurisdiction. In *Newman-Green, Inc. v. Alfonzo-Larrain,* 490 U.S. 826 (1989), an Illinois corporation brought a breach of contract action against a Venezuelan corporation, four Venezuelan guarantors, and Bettison, a U.S. citizen guarantor who was domiciled in Venezuela. The joinder of Bettison, a "stateless" American citizen, defeated alienage jurisdiction under 28 U.S.C. §1332(a)(3), but the defect went undetected at the trial level. Having secured partial summary judgment in its favor at trial, plaintiff responded to defendant's motion to dismiss for lack of subject matter jurisdiction on appeal by requesting that Bettison be dropped as a party. In sustaining the Seventh Circuit's willingness to have Bettison dismissed from the action, the Supreme Court explained: "Bettison's presence did not provide [the plaintiff] with a tactical advantage," and "given that all of the guarantors (including Bettison) were jointly and severally liable, it cannot be argued that Bettison was indispensable to the suit." Any impact on Bettison himself was negated by the fact that his dismissal from the action would be with prejudice. Note that the *Newman-Green* principle would not necessarily apply if it were *defendants* who had won at trial and sought to preserve the victory on appeal by seeking Bettison's dismissal as a party. Is the difference in result attributable to the fact that it is plaintiff who is in control of structuring the lawsuit? *See also Grupo Dataflux v. Atlas Global Group,* 541 U.S. 567 (2004) (reiterating that parties may not cure jurisdictional defects by making changes to their status post filing; jurisdiction may only be preserved, if at all, by dropping a non-conforming party).

Even though the joinder rules do not create federal subject matter jurisdiction, the ability to join parties under the "transactional relationship" standard of Rule 20 makes possible the operation of supplemental jurisdiction in cases where it is applicable. Thus, for example, a plaintiff who has a federal claim against defendant *A* can join a transactionally related state claim against defendant *B* under Rule 20. Rule 20 itself does not cure a defect in federal subject matter jurisdiction in the claim against *B,* but 28 U.S.C. §1367(a) will confer supplemental jurisdiction over the claims if both claims arise out of a common nucleus of operative facts—as they normally will if they are transactionally related for purposes of Rule 20—subject, of course, to the court's exercise of discretion under §1367(c).

The general rules against certain forms of aggregation still apply under the supplemental jurisdiction statute. Thus, multiple plaintiffs in a diversity case cannot aggregate claims against a single defendant to reach the requisite jurisdictional amount, nor can a plaintiff aggregate claims against multiple defendants—except, in both cases, if the claims fall within the narrow category of "joint and undivided" rights. Likewise, the statute preserves the complete diversity requirement, requiring all plaintiffs to be diverse from all defendants. 28 U.S.C. §1367 does enable parties to use Rule 20 to circumvent the prohibition on aggregation in one important way, however. Recall that 28 U.S.C. §1367(b) contains the list of exceptions to the general grant of supplemental jurisdiction for diversity cases. That list of exceptions fails to mention claims *by plaintiffs* who join together under Rule 20. *See* 28 U.S.C. §1367(b). By its terms, the statute thus enables a plaintiff whose claims do satisfy the jurisdictional amount to join with other plaintiffs whose claims do not, provided that there is still complete diversity of citizenship between all the parties. The Supreme Court recently confirmed that the statute does have this effect. *See Exxon-Mobil Corp. v. Allapattah Servs.*, 545 U.S. 546 (2005). Section 1367(b) does exclude claims by a plaintiff *against defendants* joined under Rule 20, however—the glitch in the statute only covers claims by Rule 20 plaintiffs.

6. *Other Factors Affecting Joinder Strategy.* Remember that Rule 20 gives a plaintiff substantial autonomy in structuring the lawsuit. Can you think of possible motivations for plaintiffs to join or to refrain from joining persons who would qualify as proper parties under Rule 20, whether as plaintiffs or defendants?

Obviously, litigation is expensive, and rather than bring multiple lawsuits against different defendants, plaintiffs are likely to prefer pursuing all defendants in a single action. Such a strategy also allows a single jury to pinpoint liability when potential defendants attempt to blame each other. Nonetheless, if a particular defendant is likely to increase the cost or delay of litigation, a plaintiff may choose not to join her.

Although multiple lawsuits against different defendants provide plaintiff with the opportunity to relitigate before a different judge or jury, keep in mind that nonmutual issue preclusion may, as a practical matter, undercut any benefit of serial litigation; plaintiff will be bound as to any unfavorable findings on issues common to both suits.

With respect to the choice of co-plaintiffs, a number of considerations may affect how a plaintiff proceeds. Is it advantageous for a plaintiff to sue alone in order to go after limited resources of a defendant? Might a jury view the co-plaintiff as more deserving of damages than plaintiff? Are there features about the co-plaintiff that will negatively affect and prejudice plaintiff's case? For a fuller discussion of these issues, *see* Richard Freer, *Avoiding Duplicative Litigation: Rethinking Plaintiff Autonomy and the Role of the Court in Defining the Litigative Unit,* 50 U. Pitt. L. Rev. 809, 824–825 (1989).

7. *Severance and Consolidation.* Apart from formal joinder under Rule 20, the federal rules offer other alternatives for disaggregating or consolidating litigation. One of these—severance—is covered in Rules 20(b), 21, and 42(b) of the Federal Rules. Can you think of reasons why the court would sever the case or order separate trials once the two-part test of Rule 20 is satisfied? Wouldn't it make more sense to grant the court broader discretion to disallow joinder in the first place? If separate trials are likely to be necessary, then the court could deny joinder at the outset. Are there any efficiencies to be gained from joinder if separate trials are going to be necessary?

The device of consolidation is a close relative of joinder. Under Fed. R. Civ. P. 42(a), a court may order consolidation of actions pending before it when the actions involve a "common question of law or fact." What is the difference between the standards for joinder and consolidation? Would a case that did not meet the requirements for joinder still be an appropriate candidate for consolidation? *See Stanford v. TVA Monsanto Chem. Co.*, 18 F.R.D. 152 (M.D. Tenn. 1955) (holding that although joinder of defendants under Rule 20 was improper since the claims against them did not arise out of the same transaction or occurrence, common questions of law and fact were sufficiently involved to meet the requirements of a joint trial under Rule 42(a)); *Kenvin v. Newburger, Loeb & Co.*, 37 F.R.D. 473 (S.D.N.Y. 1965) (finding a misjoinder of parties in violation of Fed. R. Civ. P. 20(a) but recommending a joint trial of all claims against four defendants in the interest of judicial economy and efficiency).

Is there any good reason to maintain different standards for joinder and consolidation?

8. *Consolidation Across Districts.* Note that consolidation in Rule 42(a) refers to actions pending before a particular court. In the federal system, 28 U.S.C. §1407 authorizes interdistrict consolidation of "pretrial proceedings." *See supra* pp. 1040–1041. Informal consolidation of cases pending in different systems is possible by agreement of the courts. See, for example, the concurrent federal-state proceedings arising out of the L'Ambiance Plaza building collapse, *Russillo v. L'Ambiance Plaza Ltd.*, No. CV B-88-35 (D. Conn. Dec. 1, 1988); *Daddona v. Bridgeport*, No. CV 87-00-82-647 (Conn. Super. Ct. Dec. 1, 1988).

9. *Looking Ahead to Mandatory Joinder.* Does it make sense to give plaintiff the power to structure the lawsuit or should the court have the power to compel joinder of parties in the interest of judicial economy? *Compare* Richard D. Freer, *Avoiding Duplicative Litigation: Rethinking Plaintiff Autonomy and the Court's Role in Defining the Litigative Unit*, 50 U. Pitt. L. Rev. 809 (1989) (arguing that plaintiffs are treated as "prima donnas" in their extensive control over joinder of parties, and that, when necessary, federal courts should have the power to compel "packaging" of lawsuits in the name of efficiency) *with* Roger H. Transgrud, *Joinder Alternatives in Mass Tort Litigation*, 70 Cornell L. Rev. 779 (1985) (arguing that it is undesirable in mass tort cases to order joint trials of plaintiffs' compensatory damage claims because doing so will have a negative impact on plaintiff's control over the lawsuit and compromise overall fairness to litigants).

2. *Compulsory Joinder: Necessary and Indispensable Parties*

It is a background principle of our legal system that the plaintiff is considered the architect of the lawsuit — the plaintiff chooses where suit is to be brought and what claims are to be heard. We have seen a number of instances, however, where plaintiff's design can be altered: (1) with respect to choice of court, defendants can employ mechanisms for removal and transfer/*forum non conveniens*; (2) with respect to what claims are heard, defendants can expand the lawsuit through the assertion of counterclaims, cross-claims, and claims against third parties. Considerations of judicial economy and fairness thus mitigate the basic principle that plaintiff is in complete control of the lawsuit.

The concept of "compulsory joinder" is another example of a situation where plaintiff may not be in control of who will be joined as a party to the action. Rule 19 of the Federal Rules of Civil Procedure identifies a limited set of situations in which certain persons must be joined in an action. The principal concerns under this provision are the possibility that the court may be unable to grant complete relief in the absence of an absent party and the related concern that the absent party's interests may be compromised by the proceeding. If such "required" parties cannot be joined (for example, because they would destroy diversity or they are not amenable to the personal jurisdiction of the forum), it is possible that the action will not be able to proceed at all. In the case that follows, the Supreme Court explores the doctrine of the Rule 19 "required" party in the context of a foreign sovereign entity that claims immunity from suit in U.S. courts under a specialized subject matter jurisdiction law called the Foreign Sovereign Immunities Act.

Republic of the Philippines v. Pimentel

553 U.S. 851 (2008)

JUSTICE KENNEDY delivered the opinion of the Court.

This case turns on the interpretation and proper application of Rule 19 of the Federal Rules of Civil Procedure and requires us to address the Rule's operation in the context of foreign sovereign immunity.

This interpleader action was commenced to determine the ownership of property allegedly stolen by Ferdinand Marcos when he was the President of the Republic of the Philippines. Two entities named in the suit invoked sovereign immunity. They are the Republic of the Philippines and the Philippine Presidential Commission on Good Governance, referred to in turn as the Republic and the Commission. They were dismissed, but the interpleader action proceeded to judgment over their objection. Together with two parties who remained in the suit, the Republic and the Commission now insist it was an error to allow the litigation to proceed. Under Rule 19, they contend, the action should have been dismissed once it became clear they could not be joined as parties without their consent.

The United States Court of Appeals for the Ninth Circuit, agreeing with the District Court, held the action could proceed without the Republic and the Commission as parties. Among the reasons the Court of Appeals gave was that the absent, sovereign entities would not prevail on their claims. We conclude the Court of Appeals gave insufficient weight to the foreign sovereign status of the Republic and the Commission, and that the court further erred in reaching and discounting the merits of their claims.

I

A

When the opinion of the Court of Appeals is consulted, the reader will find its quotations from Rule 19 do not accord with its text as set out here; for after the case was in the Court of Appeals and before it came here, the text of the Rule changed. The Rules Committee advised the changes were stylistic only, see Advisory

Committee's Notes on 2007 Amendment to Fed. Rule Civ. Proc. 19, 28 U.S.C. A., p. 168 (2008); and we agree. These are the three relevant stylistic changes. First, the word "required" replaced the word "necessary" in subparagraph (a). Second, the 1966 Rule set out factors in longer clauses and the 2007 Rule sets out the factors affecting joinder in separate lettered headings. Third, the word "indispensable," which had remained as a remnant of the pre-1966 Rule, is altogether deleted from the current text. Though the word "indispensable" had a lesser place in the 1966 Rule, it still had the latent potential to mislead.

As the substance and operation of the Rule both pre- and post-2007 are unchanged, we will refer to the present, revised version. . . . The current Rule states, in relevant part, as follows:

Rule 19. Required Joinder of Parties.

(a) Persons Required to Be Joined if Feasible.

(1) Required Party. A person who is subject to service of process and whose joinder will not deprive the court of subject-matter jurisdiction must be joined as a party if:

(A) in that person's absence, the court cannot accord complete relief among existing parties; or

(B) that person claims an interest relating to the subject of the action and is so situated that disposing of the action in the person's absence may:

(i) as a practical matter impair or impede the person's ability to protect the interest; or

(ii) leave an existing party subject to a substantial risk of incurring double, multiple, or otherwise inconsistent obligations because of the interest.

(2) Joinder by Court Order. If a person has not been joined as required, the court must order that the person be made a party. A person who refuses to join as a plaintiff may be made either a defendant or, in a proper case, an involuntary plaintiff.

(3) Venue. If a joined party objects to venue and the joinder would make venue improper, the court must dismiss that party.

(b) When Joinder Is Not Feasible. If a person who is required to be joined if feasible cannot be joined, the court must determine whether, in equity and good conscience, the action should proceed among the existing parties or should be dismissed. The factors for the court to consider include:

(1) the extent to which a judgment rendered in the person's absence might prejudice that person or the existing parties;

(2) the extent to which any prejudice could be lessened or avoided by:

(A) protective provisions in the judgment;

(B) shaping the relief; or

(C) other measures;

(3) whether a judgment rendered in the person's absence would be adequate; and

(4) whether the plaintiff would have an adequate remedy if the action were dismissed for nonjoinder.

Fed. Rules Civ. Proc. 19(a)–(b).

See also Rule 19(c) (imposing pleading requirements); Rule 19(d) (creating exception for class actions).

B

In 1972, Ferdinand Marcos, then President of the Republic, incorporated Arelma, S.A. (Arelma), under Panamanian law. Around the same time, Arelma opened a brokerage account with [Merrill Lynch] in New York, in which it deposited $2 million. As of the year 2000, the account had grown to approximately $35 million.

Alleged crimes and misfeasance by Marcos during his presidency became the subject of worldwide attention and protest. A class action by and on behalf of some 9,539 of his human rights victims was filed against Marcos and his estate, among others. The class action was tried in the United States District Court for the District of Hawaii and resulted in a nearly $2 billion judgment for the class. We refer to that litigation as the Pimentel case and to its class members as the Pimentel class. In a related action, the Estate of Roger Roxas and Golden Budha [sic] Corporation (the Roxas claimants) claim a right to execute against the assets to satisfy their own judgment against Marcos' widow, Imelda Marcos.

The Pimentel class claims a right to enforce its judgment by attaching the Arelma assets held by Merrill Lynch. The Republic and the Commission claim a right to the assets under a 1955 Philippine law providing that property derived from the misuse of public office is forfeited to the Republic from the moment of misappropriation.

After Marcos fled the Philippines in 1986, the Commission was created to recover any property he wrongfully took. Almost immediately the Commission asked the Swiss Government for assistance in recovering assets — including shares in Arelma — that Marcos had moved to Switzerland. In compliance the Swiss Government froze certain assets and, in 1990, that freeze was upheld by the Swiss Federal Supreme Court. In 1991, the Commission asked the Sandiganbayan, a Philippine court of special jurisdiction over corruption cases, to declare forfeited to the Republic any property Marcos had obtained through misuse of his office. That litigation is still pending in the Sandiganbayan.

The Swiss assets were transferred to an escrow account set up by the Commission at the Philippine National Banc (PNB), pending the Sandiganbayan's decision as to their rightful owner. The Republic and the Commission requested that Merrill Lynch follow the same course and transfer the Arelma assets to an escrow account at PNB. Merrill Lynch did not do so. Facing claims from various Marcos creditors, including the Pimentel class, Merrill Lynch instead filed an interpleader action under 28 U.S.C. §1335. The named defendants in the interpleader action were, among others, the Republic and the Commission, Arelma, PNB, and the Pimentel class (the respondents here). . . .

After being named as defendants in the interpleader action, the Republic and the Commission asserted sovereign immunity under the Foreign Sovereign Immunities Act of 1976 (FSIA), 28 U.S.C. §1604. They moved to dismiss pursuant to Rule 19(b), based on the premise that the action could not proceed without them. Arelma and PNB also moved to dismiss pursuant to Rule 19(b). Without addressing whether they were entitled to sovereign immunity, [District] Judge Real initially rejected the request by the Republic and the Commission to dismiss the interpleader action. They appealed, and the Court of Appeals reversed. It held the Republic and the Commission are entitled to sovereign immunity and that under Rule 19(a) they are required parties (or "necessary" parties under the old terminology). The Court of Appeals entered a stay pending the outcome of the litigation in the Sandiganbayan over the Marcos assets.

After concluding that the pending litigation in the Sandiganbayan could not determine entitlement to the Arelma assets, Judge Real vacated the stay, allowed the action to proceed, and awarded the assets to the Pimentel class. A week later, in the case initiated before the Sandiganbayan in 1991, the Republic asked that court to declare the Arelma assets forfeited, arguing the matter was ripe for decision. The Sandiganbayan has not yet ruled.

In the interpleader case the Republic, the Commission, Arelma, and PNB appealed the District Court's judgment in favor of the Pimentel claimants. This time the Court of Appeals affirmed. Dismissal of the interpleader suit, it held, was not warranted under Rule 19(b) because, though the Republic and the Commission were required ("necessary") parties under Rule 19(a), their claim had so little likelihood of success on the merits that the interpleader action could proceed without them. One of the reasons the court gave was that any action commenced by the Republic and the Commission to recover the assets would be barred by New York's 6-year statute of limitations for claims involving the misappropriation of public property. See N.Y. Civ. Prac. Law Ann. §213 (West Supp. 2008). The court thus found it unnecessary to consider whether any prejudice to the Republic and the Commission might be lessened by some form of judgment or interim decree in the interpleader action. The court also considered the failure of the Republic and the Commission to obtain a judgment in the Sandiganbayan — despite the Arelma share certificates having been located and held in escrow at the PNB since 1997–1998 — to be an equitable consideration counseling against dismissal of the interpleader suit. The court further found it relevant that allowing the interpleader case to proceed would serve the interests of the Pimentel class, which, at this point, likely has no other available forum in which to enforce its judgment against property belonging to Marcos.

This Court granted certiorari. . . .

III

We turn to the question whether the interpleader action could proceed in the District Court without the Republic and the Commission as parties.

Subdivision (a) of Rule 19 states the principles that determine when persons or entities must be joined in a suit. The Rule instructs that nonjoinder even of a required person does not always result in dismissal. Subdivision (a) opens by noting that it addresses joinder "if feasible." Where joinder is not feasible, the question whether the action should proceed turns on the factors outlined in subdivision (b). The considerations set forth in subdivision (b) are nonexclusive, as made clear by the introductory statement that "[t]he factors for the court to consider include." Fed. Rule Civ. Proc. 19(b). The general direction is whether "in equity and good conscience, the action should proceed among the existing parties or should be dismissed." *Ibid.* The design of the Rule, then, indicates that the determination whether to proceed will turn upon factors that are case specific, which is consistent with a Rule based on equitable considerations. This is also consistent with the fact that the determination of who may, or must, be parties to a suit has consequences for the persons and entities affected by the judgment; for the judicial system and its interest in the integrity of its processes and the respect accorded to its decrees; and for society and its concern for the fair and prompt resolution of disputes. See, *e.g.*, *Illinois Brick Co. v. Illinois*, 431 U.S. 720, 737–739, 97 S. Ct. 2061, 52 L. Ed. 2d 707 (1977). For these reasons, the issue of joinder can be complex, and determinations are case specific. See, *e.g.*, *Provident Bank, supra*, at 118–119, 88 S. Ct. 733.

Under the earlier Rules the term "indispensable party" might have implied a certain rigidity that would be in tension with this case-specific approach. The word "indispensable" had an unforgiving connotation that did not fit easily with a system that permits actions to proceed even when some persons who otherwise should be parties to the action cannot be joined. As the Court noted in *Provident Bank*, the use of "indispensable" in Rule 19 created the "verbal anomaly" of an "indispensable person who turns out to be dispensable after all." 390 U.S., at 117, n. 12, 88 S. Ct. 733. Though the text has changed, the new Rule 19 has the same design and, to some extent, the same tension. Required persons may turn out not to be required for the action to proceed after all.

In all events it is clear that multiple factors must bear on the decision whether to proceed without a required person. This decision "must be based on factors varying with the different cases, some such factors being substantive, some procedural, some compelling by themselves, and some subject to balancing against opposing interests." *Id.*, at 119, 88 S. Ct. 733.

IV

We turn to Rule 19 as it relates to this case. The application of subdivision (a) of Rule 19 is not contested. The Republic and the Commission are required entities because "[w]ithout [them] as parties in this interpleader action, their interests in the subject matter are not protected." *In re Republic of Philippines*, 309 F.3d, at 1152; see Fed. Rule Civ. Proc. 19(a)(1)(B)(i). All parties appear to concede this. The disagreement instead centers around the application of subdivision (b), which addresses whether the action may proceed without the Republic and the Commission, given that the Rule requires them to be parties.

We have not addressed the standard of review for Rule 19(b) decisions. The case-specific inquiry that must be followed in applying the standards set forth in subdivision (b), including the direction to consider whether "in equity and good conscience" the case should proceed, implies some degree of deference to the district court. In this case, however, we find implicit in the District Court's rulings, and explicit in the opinion of the Court of Appeals, errors of law that require reversal. Whatever the appropriate standard of review, a point we need not decide, the judgment could not stand. Cf. *Koon v. United States*, 518 U.S. 81, 99–100, 116 S. Ct. 2035, 135 L. Ed. 2d 392 (1996) (a court "by definition abuses its discretion when it makes an error of law").

The Court of Appeals erred in not giving the necessary weight to the absent entities' assertion of sovereign immunity. The court in effect decided the merits of the Republic and the Commission's claims to the Arelma assets. Once it was recognized that those claims were not frivolous, it was error for the Court of Appeals to address them on their merits when the required entities had been granted sovereign immunity. The court's consideration of the merits was itself an infringement on foreign sovereign immunity; and, in any event, its analysis was flawed. We discuss these errors first in the context of how they affected the Court of Appeals' analysis under the first factor of Rule 19(b). We then explain that the outcome suggested by the first factor is confirmed by our analysis under the other provisions of Rule 19(b). The action may not proceed.

A

As to the first Rule 19(b) factor—the extent to which a judgment rendered in the person's absence might prejudice that person or the existing parties, Fed. Rule Civ. Proc. 19(b)(1)—the judgment of the Court of Appeals is incorrect.

In considering whether the Republic and the Commission would be prejudiced if the action were to proceed in their absence, the Court of Appeals gave insufficient weight to their sovereign status. The doctrine of foreign sovereign immunity has been recognized since early in the history of our Nation. It is premised upon the "perfect equality and absolute independence of sovereigns, and th[e] common interest impelling them to mutual intercourse." *Schooner Exchange v. McFaddon*, 7 Cranch 116, 137, 3 L. Ed. 287 (1812). The Court has observed that the doctrine is designed to "give foreign states and their instrumentalities some protection from the inconvenience of suit," *Dole Food Co. v. Patrickson*, 538 U.S. 468, 479, 123 S. Ct. 1655, 155 L. Ed. 2d 643 (2003).

[The Court went on to explain that the privilege of immunity from jurisdiction in American courts enjoyed by foreign sovereigns is codified in a federal statute, the Foreign Sovereign Immunities Act, 28 U.S.C. §§1330, 1602-1611, and protects the dignity of foreign sovereigns from affront through involuntary subjection to coercive judicial power. Those dignitary interests, the Court explained, take "concrete form in this case" because of the "historical and political significance" of the underlying events to the people of the Philippines.]

Though this Court has not considered a case posing the precise question presented here, there are some authorities involving the intersection of joinder and the governmental immunity of the United States. See, *e.g., Mine Safety Appliances Co. v. Forrestal*, 326 U.S. 371, 373-375, 66 S. Ct. 219, 90 L. Ed. 140 (1945) (dismissing an action where the Under Secretary of the Navy was sued in his official capacity, because the Government was a required entity that could not be joined when it withheld consent to be sued); *Minnesota v. United States*, 305 U.S. 382, 386-388, 59 S. Ct. 292, 83 L. Ed. 235 (1939) (dismissing the action for nonjoinder of a required entity where the United States was the owner of the land in question but had not consented to suit). The analysis of the joinder issue in those cases was somewhat perfunctory, but the holdings were clear: A case may not proceed when a required-entity sovereign is not amenable to suit. These cases instruct us that where sovereign immunity is asserted, and the claims of the sovereign are not frivolous, dismissal of the action must be ordered where there is a potential for injury to the interests of the absent sovereign.

The Court of Appeals accordingly erred in undertaking to rule on the merits of the Republic and the Commission's claims. There may be cases where the person who is not joined asserts a claim that is frivolous. In that instance a court may have leeway under both Rule 19(a)(1), defining required parties, and Rule 19(b), addressing when a suit may go forward nonetheless, to disregard the frivolous claim. Here, the claims of the absent entities are not frivolous; and the Court of Appeals should not have proceeded on the premise that those claims would be determined against the sovereign entities that asserted immunity. . . .

Rule 19 cannot be applied in a vacuum, and it may require some preliminary assessment of the merits of certain claims. For example, the Rule directs a court, in determining who is a required person, to consider whether complete relief can be afforded in their absence. See Fed. Rule Civ. Proc. 19(a)(1)(A). Likewise, in the Rule 19(b) inquiry, a court must examine, to some extent, the claims presented and the interests likely to be asserted both by the joined parties and the absent entities or persons. Here, however, it was improper to issue a definitive holding regarding a nonfrivolous, substantive claim made by an absent, required entity that was entitled by its sovereign status to immunity from suit. That privilege is much diminished if an important and consequential ruling affecting the sovereign's substantial interest is determined, or at least assumed, by a federal court in the sovereign's absence and over its objection.

As explained above, the decision to proceed in the absence of the Republic and the Commission ignored the substantial prejudice those entities likely would incur. This most directly implicates Rule 19(b)'s first factor, which directs consideration of prejudice both to absent persons and those who are parties. We have discussed the absent entities. As to existing parties, we do not discount the Pimentel class's interest in recovering damages it was awarded pursuant to a judgment. Furthermore, combating public corruption is a significant international policy. The policy is manifested in treaties providing for international cooperation in recovering forfeited assets. This policy does support the interest of the Pimentel class in recovering damages awarded to it. But it also underscores the important comity concerns implicated by the Republic and the Commission in asserting foreign sovereign immunity. The error is not that the District Court and the Court of Appeals gave too much weight to the interest of the Pimentel class, but that it did not accord proper weight to the compelling claim of sovereign immunity.

Based on these considerations we conclude the District Court and the Court of Appeals gave insufficient weight to the likely prejudice to the Republic and the Commission should the interpleader proceed in their absence.

B

As to the second Rule 19(b) factor—the extent to which any prejudice could be lessened or avoided by relief or measures alternative to dismissal, Fed. Rule Civ. Proc. 19(b)(2) —there is no substantial argument to allow the action to proceed. No alternative remedies or forms of relief have been proposed to us or appear to be available. See 7 C. Wright, A. Miller, & M. Kane, Federal Practice and Procedure §1608, pp. 106–110 (3d ed. 2001) (collecting cases using alternative forms of relief, including the granting of money damages rather than specific performance, the use of declaratory judgment, and the direction that payment be withheld pending suits against the absent party). If the Marcos estate did not own the assets, or if the Republic owns them now, the claim of the Pimentel class likely fails; and in all events, if there are equally valid but competing claims, that too would require adjudication in a case where the Republic and the Commission are parties. See *State Farm Fire & Casualty Co. v. Tashire*, 386 U.S. 523, 534, and n. 16, 87 S. Ct. 1199, 18 L. Ed. 2d 270 (1967); *Russell v. Clark's Executors*, 7 Cranch 69, 98–99, 3 L. Ed. 271 (1812) (Marshall, C. J.); *Wichita & Affiliated Tribes of Okla. v. Hodel*, 788 F.2d 765, 774 (C.A.D.C.1986) ("Conflicting claims by beneficiaries to a common trust present a textbook example of a case where one party may be severely prejudiced by a decision in his absence" (citing *Williams v. Bankhead*, 19 Wall. 563, 570–571, 22 L. Ed. 184 (1874))).

C

As to the third Rule 19(b) factor—whether a judgment rendered without the absent party would be adequate, Fed. Rule Civ. Proc. 19(b)(3)—the Court of Appeals understood "adequacy" to refer to satisfaction of the Pimentel class' claims. But adequacy refers to the "public stake in settling disputes by wholes, whenever possible." *Provident Bank*, 390 U.S., at 111, 88 S. Ct. 733. This "social interest in the efficient administration of justice and the avoidance of multiple litigation" is an interest that has "traditionally been thought to support compulsory joinder of absent and potentially adverse claimants." *Illinois Brick Co.*, 431 U.S., at 737–738, 97 S. Ct. 2061. Going forward with the action without the Republic and the Commission would not further the public interest in settling the dispute as a whole because the Republic and the Commission would not be bound by the judgment in an action where they were not parties.

D

As to the fourth Rule 19(b) factor—whether the plaintiff would have an adequate remedy if the action were dismissed for nonjoinder, Fed. Rule Civ. Proc. 19(b)(4)—the Court of Appeals made much of what it considered the tort victims' lack of an alternative forum should this action be dismissed. This seems to assume the plaintiff in this interpleader action was the Pimentel class. It is Merrill Lynch, however, that has the statutory status of plaintiff as the stakeholder in the interpleader action.

It is true that, in an interpleader action, the stakeholder is often neutral as to the outcome, while other parties press claims in the manner of a plaintiff. That is insufficient, though, to overcome the statement in the interpleader statute that the stakeholder is the plaintiff. See 28 U.S.C. §1335(a) (conditioning jurisdiction in part upon whether "the plaintiff has deposited such money or property" at issue with the district court or has "given bond payable to the clerk of the court in such amount and with such surety as the court or judge may deem proper"). We do not ignore that, in context, the Pimentel class (and indeed all interpleader claimants) are to some extent comparable to the plaintiffs in noninterpleader cases. Their interests are not irrelevant to the Rule 19(b) equitable balance; but the other provisions of the Rule are the relevant ones to consult.

Merrill Lynch, as the stakeholder, makes the point that if the action is dismissed it loses the benefit of a judgment allowing it to disburse the assets and be done with the matter. Dismissal of the action, it urges, leaves it without an adequate remedy, for it "could potentially be forced . . . to defend lawsuits by the various claimants in different jurisdictions, possibly leading to inconsistent judgments." A dismissal of the action on the ground of nonjoinder, however, will protect Merrill Lynch in some respects. That disposition will not provide Merrill Lynch with a judgment determining the party entitled to the assets, but it likely would provide Merrill Lynch with an effective defense against piecemeal litigation and inconsistent, conflicting judgments. As matters presently stand, in any later suit against it Merrill Lynch may seek to join the Republic and the Commission and have the action dismissed under Rule 19(b) should they again assert sovereign immunity. Dismissal for nonjoinder to some extent will serve the purpose of interpleader, which is to prevent a stakeholder from having to pay two or more parties for one claim.

Any prejudice to Merrill Lynch in this regard is outweighed by prejudice to the absent entities invoking sovereign immunity. Dismissal under Rule 19(b) will mean, in some instances, that plaintiffs will be left without a forum for definitive resolution of their claims. But that result is contemplated under the doctrine of foreign sovereign immunity. See, *e.g.*, *Verlinden*, 461 U.S., at 497, 103 S. Ct. 1962 ("[I]f a court determines that none of the exceptions to sovereign immunity applies, the plaintiff will be barred from raising his claim in any court in the United States").

V

The Court of Appeals' failure to give sufficient weight to the likely prejudice to the Republic and the Commission should the interpleader proceed in their absence would, in the usual course, warrant reversal and remand for further proceedings. In this case, however, that error and our further analysis under the additional provisions of Rule 19(b) lead us to conclude the action must be dismissed. This leaves the Pimentel class, which has waited for years now to be compensated for grievous wrongs, with no immediate way to recover on its judgment against Marcos. And it leaves Merrill Lynch, the stakeholder, without a judgment.

The balance of equities may change in due course. One relevant change may occur if it appears that the Sandiganbayan cannot or will not issue its ruling within a reasonable period of time. Other changes could result when and if there is a ruling. If the Sandiganbayan rules that the Republic and the Commission have no right to the assets, their claims in some later interpleader suit would be less substantial than they are now. If the ruling is that the Republic and the Commission own the assets, then they may seek to enforce a judgment in our courts; or consent to become parties in an interpleader suit, where their claims could be considered; or file in some other forum if they can obtain jurisdiction over the relevant persons. We do note that if Merrill Lynch, or other parties, elect to commence further litigation in light of changed circumstances, it would not be necessary to file the new action in the District Court where this action arose, provided venue and jurisdictional requirements are satisfied elsewhere. The present action, however, may not proceed.

. . .

The judgment of the Court of Appeals for the Ninth Circuit is reversed, and the case is remanded with instructions to order the District Court to dismiss the interpleader action.

It is so ordered.

[The separate opinions of JUSTICE STEVENS and JUSTICE SOUTER, both concurring in part and dissenting in part, are omitted.]

NOTES AND QUESTIONS

1. *The Structure of the Rule 19 Inquiry.* Determining the joinder of persons needed for just adjudication under Rule 19 requires a two-step analysis. First, the court must determine whether the person in question is a "required" party who should be joined if feasible (Rule 19 (a)); and second, if joinder is not feasible, the court must determine whether the action may proceed in the absence of the required party or instead should be dismissed (Rule 19(b)).

As the Court indicates in *Pimentel*, the version of Rule 19 in effect prior to the 2007 restyling used somewhat different language. Old Rule 19(a) referred to "necessary" parties in identifying those who should be joined if feasible, and it then analyzed whether the action could move forward in the absence of the missing party by asking whether that party was "indispensable." The old Rule appeared to create two distinct designations, while the restyled rule specifies the standard for identifying a "required" party and then describes the steps that the court should take if joinder of that party is not feasible.

2. *The Impact of the 2007 Restyling Amendments. Pimentel* is the first case that the Supreme Court decided in which it spoke in detail about the effect of the 2007 restyling upon its interpretation of a Federal Rule. Embracing the qualifier issued in conjunction with the 2007 revisions, which proclaimed that the restyling of the rules was not meant to alter their substance or operation in any way, the Court notes the differences in language between the two versions and then proceeds to use the new version of the Rule in its analysis, even though the lower court rulings were governed by the old Rule.

It is noteworthy that a Rule 19 case served as the occasion for the Court to affirm that the 2007 restyling revisions had no impact on the substance or operation of the Rules, because the change in nomenclature from "necessary" and "indispensable" parties to "required" parties is an unusually important one. The prior terminology had its roots in old forms of equity practice under which courts sought to draw rigid and formal distinctions between different classes of parties. *See, e.g., Shields v. Barrow*, 58 U.S. (17 How.) 130 (1854) (advancing these formal categories and coining the term "indispensable"). *See generally* John W. Reed, *Compulsory Joinder of Parties in Civil Actions*, 55 Mich. L. Rev. 327 (1957); Geoffrey C. Hazard, *Indispensable Party: The Historical Origin of a Procedural Phantom*, 61 Colum. L. Rev. 1254 (1961). These rigid categories were reflected in the original version of Rule 19 that took effect in 1938. In 1966, the Supreme Court promulgated a revised Rule 19 that adopted a more pragmatic approach to the inquiry but still retained the "necessary" and "indispensable" terminology associated with the old version. *See* Benjamin Kaplan, *Continuing Work of the Civil Committee: 1966 Amendments to the Federal Rules of Civil Procedure (I)*, 81 Harv. L. Rev. 356, 381 (1967). As the Court notes in *Pimentel*, although that terminology "had a lesser place in the 1966 Rule, it still had the latent potential to mislead."

In rejecting the prior terminology altogether and replacing it with the single concept of a "required" party, the new version of Rule 19 apparently seeks to make a clean break from that latent potential for confusion. According to the Court, this is not a change in the "substance or operation" of the Rule, but rather a clarification of the manner in which the rule was supposed to be operating all along. Still, the Court's own commentary illustrates that the restyling of Rule 19 was a matter of some moment, more so than was the case for most other Rules.

3. Do joint tortfeasors constitute required parties under Rule 19? In *Temple v. Synthes Corp. Ltd.*, 498 U.S. 5 (1990), the Supreme Court answered that question in the negative. *Synthes* involved a claim by a plaintiff who underwent surgery in a Louisiana hospital and suffered an injury when a device broke off inside his back. Plaintiff filed a diversity action in federal district court against Synthes, the manufacturer of the device, and filed a separate suit in Louisiana state court against the hospital and the doctor who performed the surgery. The Court of Appeals for the Fifth Circuit affirmed the district court's dismissal of the suit for failure to join the doctor and the hospital under Rule 19(b). The Supreme Court reversed the judgment of the court of appeals, holding that joint tortfeasors do not satisfy the threshold requirements of Rule 19(a) and thus the courts should never have reached the Rule 19(b) question.

4. *Determining Whether an Action Must Be Dismissed Under Rule 19(b)*. When a court concludes that a missing party is "required" but cannot be made a party to the action, it must assess the Rule 19(b) factors to determine whether the action should be dismissed. How are the factors weighed against each other? In *Glenny v. American Climax, Inc.*, 494 F.2d 651 (10th Cir. 1974), the court held that the importance of each factor in Rule 19(b) depends on the specifics of the case and must be analyzed according to equitable considerations. Does Rule 19(b) give the parties and the court sufficient guidance about when an action may proceed in the absence of a required party? Is broad discretion desirable with respect to an issue like mandatory joinder? Some courts have adopted a more bright-line approach in some circumstances. *See, e.g., Imperial Appliance Corp. v. Hamilton Mfg. Co.*, 263 F. Supp. 1015, 1018 (E.D. Wis. 1967) (heavily weighing the fact that plaintiff had no other available forum to litigate certain patent claims and allowing the action to proceed without absentee parties).

The Court in *Pimentel* reaffirmed that Rule 19(b) calls for a "case-specific" approach in which competing factors are weighed and an "equitable balance" is struck. Note, however, that the Court declined to specify what standard of review should apply in a Rule 19(b) appeal, concluding that the lower courts had made errors of law in assessing the sovereign immunity dimension of the case that would require reversal even under a deferential standard. What explains the Court's reticence in specifying the applicable standard? Rulings by lower courts that involve the weighing of competing factors to strike an "equitable balance" are ordinarily reviewed for abuse of discretion. What other standard might apply to a Rule 19(b) appeal? Many lower federal courts have found that Rule 19 appeals are subject to an abuse of discretion standard, and they do not appear to believe that *Pimentel* calls that conclusion into question. *See, e.g., Cachil Dehe Band of Wintun Indians of the Colusa Indian Community v. California*, 547 F.3d 962, 969–970 (9th Cir. 2008) (reaffirming abuse of discretion standard and noting that *Pimentel* does not address the issue). Professor Katherine Florey has been sharply critical of *Pimentel*, writing that the Court appears to have validated a recent trend that puts Rule 19 "to a radically different use" from its traditional role as a tool for "promoting complete adjudication." Instead, she argues, the Court has sometimes employed the Rule to "dismiss[] cases that appear politically controversial or beyond areas of core judicial competence," particularly those involving sovereign immunity. Professor Florey argues that "the widespread use of Rule 19 for abstention-like purposes is a misuse of the rule." Katherine Florey, *Making Sovereigns Indispensable:* Pimentel *and the Evolution of Rule 19*, 58 UCLA L. Rev. 667, 670–672 (2011).

5. *How do you assess the Supreme Court's analysis under Rules 19(a) and (b) in* Pimentel? In the first part of its substantive analysis, the Court indicates that all parties conceded the status of the Republic and the Commission as required parties under Rule 19(a). That concession turned on the particular features of an interpleader action, which is discussed at greater length later in this chapter. In an interpleader proceeding, a contested stake of property is deposited with the court and the competing claimants to that stake of property are then compelled to resolve their claims all at once before the same tribunal. Under Rule 19(a)(1)(B), it is easy to see that a person with a claim to contested property who is not made a party to an interpleader action will have its interests impaired (since the property will be awarded to someone else), or that the stakeholder might be subject to multiple liabilities if all potential claimants are not joined (since a claimant who is not bound to the interpleader judgment can sue the stakeholder in a separate action, even after the property is awarded to someone else in the first proceeding). But a finding that missing parties are "required" is only the first part of the Rule 19 inquiry. The *Pimentel* Court also concluded that the action could not go forward in the absence of the Republic and the Commission. Why?

The sharpest point of disagreement between the Supreme Court and the lower courts on this point related specifically to the doctrine of sovereign immunity. In their analysis of the first suggested factor under Rule 19(b) — "the extent to which a judgment rendered in the person's absence might prejudice that person . . ." — the lower courts took the view that the Republic and the Commission were not likely to prevail on their claims, and hence that their absence would not prejudice them unduly (because they did not have much to lose). In the special context of a sovereign immunity claim, the Supreme Court found that analysis to be improper. When sovereign immunity applies, the sovereign is entitled to immunity from suit, meaning that the court should not be ruling on the merits of the claims. By offering an initial opinion as to the merit of the sovereigns' claims against the contested property, the lower courts were effectively violating this principle and giving "insufficient weight to the likely prejudice to the Republic and the Commission should the interpleader proceed in their absence." *Pimentel, supra.* Because the Court framed its analysis on this point with such specific reference to the principles of sovereign immunity, it is unclear whether lower courts would be similarly forbidden from making an initial assessment of the merits of a missing party's claim in a Rule 19 case in which sovereign immunity was not in play.

Having found that the Republic and the Commission had a powerful interest in the outcome of the action, the Court concluded that the desire of Merrill Lynch to achieve a definitive resolution of its liability, though substantial, could not outweigh that interest. Here, the Court's analysis focused again on the particular features of an interpleader action, suggesting that Merrill could continue using Rule 19 to have any subsequent actions dismissed so long as the sovereign parties kept asserting immunity, effectively allowing them to avoid multiple liability until all parties were able to be joined. (Note, however, that it is far from clear whether the competing claimants would all be deemed required parties outside the special context of an interpleader action.) The prejudice that other claimants would suffer from this sequence of events—like the *Pimentel* class members, whose recovery would be seriously delayed—was regrettable, but again not a basis for permitting the action to proceed.

The proposition that Rule 19 requires a highly case-specific analysis was certainly borne out in *Pimentel*. The Court's analysis was almost entirely driven by its assessment of the impact of sovereign immunity and the interpleader action on the interests of the various parties, and the Court suggested that a change in the configuration of foreign lawsuits might alter the Rule 19 calculus.

Note finally that the Court did not remand the case for further proceedings upon concluding that the lower courts had made errors of law. Rather, it pronounced that the Rule 19 analysis admitted of only one outcome and directed that the case be dismissed. In light of the discussion above, was it really so clear that the argument for dismissing the case could only come out one way? In their concurring/dissenting opinions (omitted here), Justices Stevens and Souter discussed the actions of the district court, which seemed particularly hostile to the interests of the foreign sovereigns, along with some details relating to the district judge himself, whose behavior on the bench had been scrutinized on several earlier occasions by the Ninth Circuit and Congress. Though the majority does not say so, it is possible that these circumstances influenced the Court's disposition of the case on remand. (Compare this result to the decision of the Court in *Pullman-Standard v. Swint*, discussed in Chapter 9.)

6. *Raising the Indispensability Issue*. Ordinarily, it will be a defendant who moves to dismiss an action pursuant to Rule 19(b). However, it appears from one Supreme Court decision that the trial or the appellate court may raise the nonjoinder of a required party *sua sponte*. In *Provident Tradesmens Bank & Trust Co. v. Patterson*, 390 U.S. 102 (1968), the court of appeals itself raised the absentee's necessary-party status, an action that the Supreme Court did not challenge. *Provident Tradesmens* involved a collision between a car and a truck. The accident produced a series of overlapping lawsuits among the people who were injured (or the estates of those who were killed), the owner of the car, and their insurance carriers. One lawsuit—brought on behalf of the estate of one deceased passenger in the car against the estate of the deceased driver of the car—produced a settlement of $50,000, but the estate had no assets, and the judgment was not paid. The estate of the deceased passenger then sued the insurance carrier representing the car's owner (Lumbermens Mutual, which represented the owner Dutcher), asking that the owner's insurance cover the $50,000 settlement. Lumbermens Mutual had taken the position that the deceased driver did not have permission to use the car and hence that it had no payment obligation, and the estate of the passenger requested a declaration that the car had been used with permission. Dutcher was not joined as a defendant in the action, presumably because his joinder would have destroyed diversity jurisdiction. The plaintiff prevailed in district court, Lumbermens appealed the judgment to the Third Circuit, and the court of appeals raised the Rule 19 issue on its own, reversing the lower court and dismissing the case based on its conclusion that Dutcher was an indispensable party who could not be joined without destroying the court's diversity jurisdiction.

Ultimately, the Supreme Court in *Provident Tradesmens* reversed the Third Circuit and determined that Dutcher was not indispensable under Rule 19(b). While the Court viewed the late stage at which the Rule 19 issue was raised as a significant factor in its analysis, it did not hold that the objection was waived:

> It is difficult to decide at this stage whether [the plaintiffs] would have had an "adequate" remedy had the action been dismissed before trial for nonjoinder: we cannot here determine whether the plaintiffs could have brought the same action, against the same parties plus Dutcher, in a state court. After trial, however, the "adequacy" of this hypothetical alternative, from the plaintiffs' point of view, was obviously greatly diminished. Their interest in preserving a fully litigated judgment should be overborne only by rather greater opposing considerations than would be required at an earlier stage when the plaintiffs' only concern was for a federal rather than a state forum.

390 U.S. at 112.

In raising the issue on appeal, did the Third Circuit overlook Fed. R. Civ. P. 12(h)(2), which requires a defense of failure to join a party under Rule 19 to be made, at the latest, at the trial on the merits? In reversing on the merits without reaching the waiver issue, did the Supreme Court make the same error? And why is the court permitted to raise the objection at all? Usually it is only a dismissal for lack of subject matter jurisdiction that can be raised by the court *sua sponte*. Is the failure to join an indispensable party similar to a defect of subject matter jurisdiction?

7. *Enabling Act Limitations.* In *Provident Tradesmens*, the Supreme Court also took the opportunity to sustain Rule 19 against a challenge that the Rule invaded "substantive rights" and was therefore outside the scope of rulemaking authority granted to the Supreme Court in 28 U.S.C. §2072. The Third Circuit in that case had ruled that the right that an absentee who "may be affected" by a judgment may have to be joined in the action constitutes a "substantive right" that cannot be affected by the Federal Rules of Civil Procedure. Justice Harlan's opinion for the Supreme Court rejected any such sweeping claim: "Rule 19(b) . . . is . . . a valid statement of the criteria for determining whether to proceed or dismiss in the forced absence of an interested person. It takes, for aught that now appears, adequate account of the very real, very substantive claim to fairness on the part of outsiders that may arise in some cases. . . ." 390 U.S. at 125.

Did the Supreme Court and Justice Harlan give sufficient attention to the concern that Rule 19 may significantly intrude on underlying substantive rights? Recall that the claim in *Provident Tradesmens* was a state law claim brought in federal court on diversity of citizenship grounds. Should the federal court have considered whether Pennsylvania state law would have required the joinder of Dutcher if the action had been brought in a Pennsylvania state court? Or does it follow that once the Supreme Court decided that Rule 19 did not transgress the Rules Enabling Act, Rule 19 necessarily applied under *Hanna v. Plumer*, 380 U.S. 460 (1965)? Is that the response that you would expect from Justice Harlan, who wrote the separate concurring opinion in *Hanna*? What if the source of a "substantive" right is a state law requiring that particular parties be joined before the sought-for relief can be granted? For example, what if a state law required that before a shareholder derivative action seeking to recover a claim owed to a corporation can be brought, a demand must be presented to the board of directors, and if it is refused, each of the directors must be joined as a defendant in the action? Can a federal court disregard the state's demand-and-joinder requirement and allow the action to proceed without running afoul of either Enabling Act or *Erie* limitations? In *Provident Tradesmens*, the Court appears to offer a response to this type of question:

> The decision whether to dismiss . . . must be based on factors varying with the different cases, some such factors being substantive, some procedural, some compelling by themselves, and some subject to balancing against opposing interests. Rule 19 does not prevent the assertion of compelling substantive interests; it merely commands the court to examine each controversy to make certain that the interests really exist.

Provident Tradesmens, 390 U.S. at 743. Would a demand-and-joinder requirement pose a "compelling substantive interest" to which a diversity court would be required to give effect?

8. *Other Approaches to the Problem of Mandatory Joinder.* Rather than dismissing an action for lack of subject matter jurisdiction when joinder of a required party destroys the court's diversity of citizenship jurisdiction, would it make sense to allow for minimal diversity in this situation? Alternatively, would it be desirable to allow the action to proceed without the absent party but give the absentee an opportunity to intervene in the action without destroying diversity of citizenship jurisdiction? For a general discussion of expanding subject matter jurisdiction to permit broader joinder opportunities, *see* Richard D. Freer, *Rethinking Compulsory Joinder: A Proposal to Restructure Federal Rule 19*, 60 N.Y.U. L. Rev. 1061 (1985); *Rethinking Plaintiff Autonomy and the Court's Role in Defining the Litigative Unit*, 50 U. Pitt. L. Rev. 809 (1989).

9. *A Different Kind of Mandatory Joinder.* The compulsory joinder provision in Rule 19 operates to force the joinder of certain persons as either plaintiffs or defendants in an initial action, and, in some cases, the failure to join such persons will prevent the lawsuit from proceeding at all. An alternative, or supplement, to this type of mandatory joinder provision might give a plaintiff freedom to structure the parties to the lawsuit but prevent that plaintiff from bringing subsequent litigation if the plaintiff failed to join other parties in the initial action. Just such an approach was adopted in New Jersey, as an aspect of an expanded doctrine of preclusion. See discussion of the entire controversy doctrine, Note 4, at p. 884 in Chapter 7.

Note the various differences in approach between Rule 19 and the "entire controversy doctrine." Rule 19 is directed at the protection of the interests of the present parties to the action and of the absentee. The emphasis in Rule 19 on shaping relief as well as restricting the action from proceeding at all reflects several concerns: that absentees may, as a practical matter, have their rights affected; that the court will not be able to structure the appropriate relief; and that there will be duplicative litigation. The "entire controversy doctrine" focuses primarily on concerns of judicial efficiency; by using preclusion as the sanction, it allows a plaintiff autonomy in structuring the lawsuit while at the same time assuring that there will not be duplicative litigation. Do the different objectives of the respective doctrines suggest that mandatory joinder rules—such as the "entire controversy doctrine"—are best viewed as supplemental to, rather than a substitute for, Rule 19 compulsory joinder practice?

New Jersey's "entire controversy doctrine" was severely criticized by practitioners, judges, and scholars. *See Symposium: Entire Controversy Doctrine*, 28 Rutgers L.J. 1 (1996). Consider the following commentary:

> [J]udicial economy is not a compelling justification for the doctrine. . . . [P]laintiff already has enormous financial incentive to join all parties without the doctrine. It is just as expensive for a plaintiff to relitigate as for anyone else. Moreover, there is no incentive to leave a defendant out in order to get "two bites at the apple." A plaintiff knows that if he loses against one defendant he runs a high risk of being collaterally estopped from asserting a similar claim in a subsequent proceeding. In most cases, this incentive will insure optimal joinder in the first proceeding. In the unusual case where the courts or witnesses are unduly burdened by repetitive litigation, there is a far less draconian solution than dismissal; make the plaintiff pay. Non-party deponents are already reimbursed for out-of-pocket expenses and lost wages. In addition, a refiling plaintiff could be ordered to pay higher court costs and/or attorney fees where a court determines that the claim should have been included in an earlier proceeding. That is a far more appropriate deterrent than giving the omitted defendant the windfall of dismissal.

Allan R. Stein, *Power, Duty and the Entire Controversy Doctrine*, 28 Rutgers L.J. 27, 39 (1996).

The New Jersey rule was revised in 1998. Preclusion is now generally limited to the nonjoinder of *claims*. *See* Rule 4:30A. As to parties, the rule requires that litigants disclose the identity of persons who should be joined because of potential liability on the basis of the same transactional facts. *See* Rule 4:29-1(b). In addition, the pleading rules require that such persons be notified of the litigation, giving them the opportunity to intervene. *See* Rule 4:5-1. That provision also gives the court authority, under certain circumstances, to compel joinder of these nonparties. Finally, the court may impose sanctions for failure to comply with the notice requirement, including dismissal of the subsequent action or imposition of litigation costs on the noncomplying party. *See* Rule 4:5-1(b)(2). For a discussion of the amendments, *see* Howard M. Erichson, *Of Horror Stories and Happy Endings: The Rise and Fall of Preclusion-Based Compulsory Party Joinder Under the New Jersey Entire Controversy Doctrine*, 9 Seton Hall Const. L.J. 755 (1999).

3. Impleader

Our examination of the rules of joinder of claims and parties revealed a number of instances where defendants are able to alter the design of the action as initially structured by plaintiff. Thus, defendants can expand the action by asserting counterclaims and cross-claims and by joining additional parties to those claims, consistent with the rules governing joinder of parties. In addition, defendants may be able to force a plaintiff to join certain persons, as either plaintiffs or defendants in the action, if those parties fall within the scope of Rule 19.

Here, we look at the additional device of "third-party practice" or impleader as it is called under Rule 14 of the Federal Rules of Civil Procedure. Impleader is a procedure whereby a defendant may bring into an action a third party who is or may be liable to defendant for all or part of a claim asserted by plaintiff against the defendant. It is used largely in situations of indemnification and contribution when the applicable substantive law confers such a right on a defendant party. A typical example would be a restaurant that sells contaminated food to a consumer: When the restaurant is sued by the consumer, the restaurant can "implead" the wholesaler who sold the meat to the restaurant as a third-party defendant in the same action. *See, e.g., Jeub v. B/G Foods*, 2 F.R.D. 238 (D. Minn. 1942).

Impleader has its roots in the common law practice of "vouching in," whereby a defendant could "vouch in" a third party who had given a warranty of title or who had agreed to indemnify the original defendant. Whether or not the third-party defendant appeared in the action, the giving of notice (or "vouching in") for the purpose of having the third party participate in the action precluded the third-party defendant from relitigating in a subsequent action brought by defendant against the third party any determination made in the first action that defendant was liable to plaintiff. *See generally* Ronan E. Degnan & Alan J. Barton, *Vouching to Quality Warranty: Case Law and Commercial Code*, 51 Cal. L. Rev. 471 (1963).

Modern impleader differs from common law "vouching in" in that it allows a defendant to join the third party in the main lawsuit, and it extends to any type of indemnification or contribution relationship. Note, however, that impleader may not be invoked by a defendant who asserts only that plaintiff has sued the wrong party. The third-party plaintiff must assert its own claim against the third-party defendant; a mere allegation of the third-party defendant's liability to plaintiff is insufficient. While Rule 14 itself does not create any right of one party to be indemnified by another, substantive law normally provides that a defendant who incurs liability for the acts of another (as in the case of joint and several liability) has a right of contribution or indemnity against the other. Thus, in a typical tort case, a defendant may implead other alleged joint tortfeasors.

Impleader acts as a kind of accelerator, permitting joinder of a potential indemnitor even if the obligation to indemnify does not ripen under state law until a judgment is obtained against the defendant. *See, e.g., D'Onofrio Constr. Co. v. Recon Co.*, 255 F.2d 904 (1st Cir. 1958) (joint tortfeasor who owes a right of contribution to defendant may be impleaded even if under state law the claim for contribution is contingent until payment is made by the initial defendant).

In order to bring in a third-party defendant, however, there must be both personal and subject matter jurisdiction over the third-party defendant. Federal Rule 4(k)(1)(B) extends service of process 100 miles from the district court even if the third-party defendant is otherwise beyond the territorial reach of the forum state. As for subject matter jurisdiction, as we saw in *Owen Equip. Co. v. Kroger*, 437 U.S. 365 (1978), and in the supplemental jurisdiction statute, 28 U.S.C. §1367(b), a third-party plaintiff's claim against a nondiverse third-party defendant is within the scope of the court's ancillary/supplemental jurisdiction. Of course, under 28 U.S.C. §1367(c), a court might still be able to exercise its discretion and dismiss the third-party claim in an appropriate case.

Rule 14 permits a range of other claims to be asserted once a third party is brought into the action. It allows the original plaintiff to assert any transactionally related claim against the third-party defendant and permits a third-party defendant to assert any claim against plaintiff that arises out of the transaction or occurrence that is the subject matter of plaintiff's claims against the third-party plaintiff. Suppose there is the requisite diversity between plaintiff and defendant, as well as between the defendant/third-party plaintiff and the third-party defendant, but complete diversity is lacking between the plaintiff and the third-party defendant. Is a transactionally related claim asserted by the original plaintiff against the third-party defendant, as permitted under Rule 14, within the federal court's supplemental jurisdiction? Review *Owen Equip. Co. v. Kroger*, 437 U.S. 365 (1978), and 28 U.S.C. §1367(b), where we previously analyzed the issue at length. What about a claim by the third-party defendant against the original plaintiff?

4. Intervention

All the means of joining a party that we have considered thus far involve decisions by the named parties to bring a given person into the litigation. What happens if the parties to the litigation do not want or are unable to join a potential party, but that person wants to interject himself into the litigation? Rule 24 provides a mechanism whereby that person can "intervene" and become a party (either as plaintiff or defendant) on his own initiative.

Rule 24 provides for two categories of intervention: intervention as of right and permissive intervention. The names are somewhat misleading. Both types of intervenors must seek permission of the court in order to intervene, and the court has some discretion to grant or deny the request in both cases, albeit far more discretion in the case of permissive intervention.

a. Intervention as of Right

There are two types of intervention as of right under Rule 24(a): (1) when a federal statute confers a right to intervene; and (more commonly) (2) when any person "claims an interest relating to the property or transaction that is the subject of the action, and is so situated that disposing of the action may as a practical matter impair or impede the movant's ability to protects its interest, unless existing parties adequately represent that interest."

Note how the language of Rule 24(a)(2) mirrors the standard for joining a required party under Rule 19(a)(1). Certainly, anyone who *would* be considered a required party under Rule 19 will have a sufficient interest to support intervention under Rule 24(a)(2). However, Rule 24(a)(2) does not appear to be that limited; the courts have permitted a broader class of intervenors than would be considered necessary parties under Rule 19. For instance, in *Smuck v. Hobson*, 408 F.2d 175 (D.C. Cir. 1969), the Court of Appeals for the District of Columbia permitted intervention by parents of school children to appeal a desegregation order against the school district.

Rule 24(a)(2) does require that the intervenor have a legally protected interest; the intervenor must assert its own rights and will not be permitted to join the litigation simply because its economic interests might be affected by the outcome. *See, e.g., Wodecki v. Nationwide Ins. Co.*, 107 F.R.D. 118 (W.D. Pa. 1985) (medical center unable to intervene in patient's action against insurer to recover hospitalization costs). Intervention as of right has similarly been denied where the intervenor's only interest is in preventing the creation of adverse precedent in a future, unrelated case. *Taylor Communications Group v. Southwestern Bell Tel. Co.*, 172 F.3d 385 (5th Cir. 1999) (intervention denied where intervenor had similar dispute with defendant and sought to avoid adverse judicial construction of Telecommunications Act). Note, however, that such persons are normally permitted to file amicus briefs with the court.

In addition to having an adequate interest in the litigation, the intervenor must also demonstrate that its interests are not adequately represented by the existing parties. This requirement can be satisfied "by proof of collusion between the representative and an opposing party, by having or representing an interest adverse to the intervenor, or by the failure of the representative in the fulfillment of his duty." *Stadin v. Union Electric Co.*, 309 F.2d 912, 919 (8th Cir. 1962) (Blackmun, J.). Intervention has been denied where existing parties' interests appear to coincide with those of the intervenor. For instance, the court denied intervention by electricity customers in an action challenging the state Public Utilities Commission (PUC) plan to introduce competition into the New Hampshire electric market, finding that the PUC's interests coincided with consumers' interests. *Public Service Co. v. Patch*, 136 F.3d 197 (1st Cir. 1998).

If the intervenor is willing to assume the burden and expense of joining the litigation, why should the court second guess the intervenor's sense that its interests are not adequately represented? Do the parties have any legitimate interest in excluding someone with a stake in the outcome of the litigation? How would you articulate that interest? Part of the answer may depend on the status of the intervenor in the litigation. May it seek discovery? Assert new and different claims? Present evidence at trial? Object to stipulations by the other parties? The more the intervenor is treated as a full-fledged litigant, the greater the potential for it to complicate, delay, or disrupt the litigation. On the other hand, the whole point of the intervention is that the original parties have not adequately addressed the intervenor's interests, and one would expect the intervention to alter the focus of the litigation in some respects. In general, an intervenor as of right is accorded all the rights and responsibilities of the original parties. However, some courts have conditioned intervention by limiting the intervenor's participation. *Compare United Nuclear Corp. v. Cransford Ins. Co.*, 905 F.2d 1424 (10th Cir. 1990) (intervention permitted for the sole purpose of giving intervenor access to discovery) *with Columbus-American Discovery Group v. Atlantic Mut. Ins. Co.*, 974 F.2d 450, 469–470 (4th Cir. 1992) (trial court abused its discretion in conditioning intervention at eve of trial on intervenor's waiver of right to conduct discovery. Intervenors of right generally "assume the status of full participants in a lawsuit and are normally treated as if they were original parties once intervention is granted"). *See also* 7C C. Wright et al., Federal Practice and Procedure §1921 (3d ed. 2012 & 2021 update) (arguing against any limitations on claims assertable by Rule 24(a) intervenors as of right).

Should a prospective intervenor have to demonstrate that he would have standing to sue on his own behalf as a condition of joining the lawsuit under Rule 24? Or can a person intervene even if the "interest" he asserts would not enable him to sue in his own right? The Supreme Court has provided only partial answers to these questions. In *Diamond v. Charles*, 476 U.S. 54 (1986), the Court held that if a person joins a lawsuit through intervention and, subsequently, the original parties on his side of the lawsuit decide not to appeal an adverse ruling, the intervenor cannot pursue the appeal himself unless he satisfies the requirements of standing—in other words, there must be at least one party left in the suit who satisfies the Article III "case or controversy" requirement in order to pursue an appeal. And in *Town of Chester v. Laroe Estates*, 137 S. Ct. 1645 (2017), the Court held that "an intervenor of right must demonstrate Article III standing when it seeks additional relief beyond that which the plaintiff requests." That requirement applies equally to "cases in which both the plaintiff and the intervenor seek separate money judgments in their own names." *Id.* at 1651. The case involved a real estate company that intervened in a dispute with a town to assert a regulatory takings claim arising from the town's refusal to approve a development plan. Because it was not clear on the record before the Court whether the intervenor was seeking relief independent from the claims that formed a part of the original lawsuit, the Court remanded the case for further factual development. *Laroe Estates* does not answer the question of standing for claims by intervenors who do not "seek additional relief beyond that which the plaintiff requests." For useful discussions of the issue, *see* Caleb Nelson, *Intervention*, 106 Va. L. Rev. 271 (2020) (criticizing the broad "interest representation" approach to intervention favored by many courts and commentators and arguing that the Federal Rules of Civil Procedure demand that all intervenors satisfy the requirements of full party status); Carl Tobias, *Standing to Intervene*, 1991 Wis. L. Rev. 415 (laying out framework of issue and making suggestions for "pragmatic" approach to intervention in public law cases); Juliet Johnson Karastelev, Note, *On the Outside Seeing In: Must Intervenors Demonstrate Standing to Join a Lawsuit?*, 52 Duke L.J. 455, 458 (2002) (arguing that intervenors should have to demonstrate Article III standing only "when they seek, or may be subject to, some form of relief").

b. Permissive Intervention

A person who does not qualify as an intervenor as of right under Rule 24(a) may still be granted some participation in the litigation as a permissive intervenor under Rule 24(b). Like Rule 24(a), Rule 24(b)(1) provides for two subcategories of permissive intervention: where a person (A) "is given a conditional right to intervene by a federal statute"; or (again, more commonly) (B) "has a claim or defense that shares with the main action a common question of law or fact." Moreover, state or federal officials may intervene when statutes or other governmental regulations are implicated in the litigation.

The grant or denial of permissive intervention is expressly within the discretion of the trial court, and courts have rarely been reversed in the exercise of that discretion. Unlike intervention as of right, which can have a disruptive effect on the litigation, permissive intervention will normally be denied where it "will unduly delay or prejudice the adjudication of the original parties' rights." Rule 24(b)(3).

The class of permissive intervenors is obviously broader than intervenors as of right. The rule does not appear to require the intervenor to have a direct pecuniary interest in the litigation, *SEC v. U.S. Realty & Improvement Co.*, 310 U.S. 434, 459 (1940), and a mere desire to avoid creation of adverse precedent may suffice. *See Textile Workers Union v. Allendale Co.*, 226 F.2d 765 (D.C. Cir. 1955). Note that in contrast with permissive joinder under Rule 20, there is no requirement that the permissive intervenor's claim or defense arise out of the same transaction or series of transactions as the other claims or defenses in the litigation. Moreover, it is not even necessary that the intervenor have a legal "claim" against the original parties. *See, e.g., Pansy v. Borough of Stroudsburg*, 23 F.3d 772 (3d Cir. 1994) (newspaper permitted to intervene to challenge validity of confidentiality restriction on settlement agreement).

Not surprisingly, the participation of permissive intervenors can be severely constrained by the court. *See, e.g., Stringfellow v. Concerned Neighbors in Action*, 480 U.S. 370, 373-374 (1987) (describing strict limitations imposed by district court upon permissive intervenors and finding that order imposing those restrictions was not immediately appealable).

c.   Mandatory Intervention?

Does a potential party to the litigation ever have an obligation to intervene? In *Martin v. Wilks*, 490 U.S. 755 (1989), white firefighters from Birmingham, Alabama, sought to challenge hiring practices adopted by the city pursuant to a consent decree entered into by the city in an earlier racial discrimination class action brought by the NAACP on behalf of black firefighters and job applicants. The decree allegedly caused the city to engage in hiring and promotion practices favoring black applicants at the expense of more qualified white applicants. The trial court dismissed the white firefighters' action, citing, among other reasons, the fact that they failed to seek timely intervention in the original proceeding. The Court reversed and held, in a 5-4 decision, that there was no such duty:

> Joinder as a party, rather than knowledge of a lawsuit and an opportunity to intervene, is the method by which potential parties are subjected to the jurisdiction of the court and bound by a judgment or decree. The parties to a lawsuit presumably know better than anyone else the nature and scope of relief sought in the action, and at whose expense such relief might be granted. It makes sense, therefore, to place on them a burden of bringing in additional parties where such a step is indicated, rather than placing on potential additional parties a duty to intervene when they acquire knowledge of the lawsuit. . . .
>
> The difficulties petitioners foresee in identifying those who could be adversely affected by a decree granting broad remedial relief are undoubtedly present, but they arise from the nature of the relief sought and not because of any choice between mandatory intervention and joinder. Rule 19's provisions for joining interested parties are designed to accommodate the sort of complexities that may arise from a decree affecting numerous people in various ways. We doubt that a mandatory intervention rule would be any less awkward. As mentioned, plaintiffs who seek the aid of the courts to alter existing employment policies, or the employer who might be subject to conflicting decrees, are best able to bear the burden of designating those who would be adversely affected if plaintiffs prevail; these parties will generally have a better understanding of the scope of likely relief than employees who are not named but might be affected. Petitioners' alternative [of requiring intervention] does not eliminate the need for, or difficulty of, identifying persons who, because of their interest, should be included in a lawsuit. It merely shifts that responsibility to less able shoulders.

490 U.S. at 765-767.

Justice Stevens, in dissent, asserted that the trial court had dismissed the claims on the merits, not on the basis of preclusion: "if the race-conscious promotions were a product of the City's adherence to pending court orders (i.e., the consent decrees), it could not be said that the City acted with the requisite racially discriminatory intent." 490 U.S. at 779 n. 15. While the city might not, as a matter of substantive law, be held liable for complying with a consent decree, Justice Stevens argued that the white firefighters were not being "bound" by the earlier proceeding. The consent decree simply resulted in a changed circumstance, which may have had a "practical impact" on plaintiffs' claim. *Id.* at 772. He did not take issue with the majority's holding that there was no duty to intervene: "In these cases there is no dispute about the fact that respondents are not parties to the consent decrees. It follows as a matter of course that they are not bound by those decrees." *Id.*

What do you think of the Court's conclusion that party-initiated joinder is superior to requiring third-party intervention? Are you persuaded that the parties are in a better position than nonparties to determine who needs to be included in the litigation? How could the parties in *Martin* have identified all potential white applicants who might be affected by an affirmative action hiring and promotions preference? Would joinder of all such persons have been desirable? In a case like *Martin*, wouldn't it be more efficient to give notice to all potentially affected by the litigation, and let those people decide whether they need to intervene? *See* George M. Strickler, Jr., Martin v. Wilks, 64 Tul. L. Rev. 1557 (1990) (arguing that *Martin* could have been more soundly decided on the basis of due process than joinder policy).

Does it seem appropriate that nonparties never have an obligation to intervene, even when they know that their rights will be adversely affected by the litigation? Doesn't the Court's approach encourage the kind of "sideline-sitting" behavior of concern to the Court in *Parklane Hosiery v. Shore*: that nonparties will "wait and see" if defendant prevails in the initial litigation, and then get a second "bite at the apple" in their own proceeding? Why should the parties to the first proceeding bear all the costs of an incomplete adjudication if the nonparty was, in fact, in just as good a position to ensure a complete adjudication in the first round?

Are you persuaded by Justice Stevens's argument that plaintiffs were merely "affected" by the earlier proceeding, not "bound" by it, thereby obviating any due process concerns? It certainly is true, isn't it, that a lawsuit can have an adverse effect on nonparty rights without violating due process? Consider a judgment that impoverishes a defendant. Would subsequent creditors have any due process right to challenge the earlier proceeding and recover the funds paid out to satisfy the earlier judgment? Is *Martin* distinguishable? *See* Strickler, *supra* at 1572-1574 (arguing that impact in *Martin* was more analogous to legal preclusion since white firefighters were effectively barred from asserting illegality of hiring practices); Samuel Issacharoff, *When Substance Mandates Procedure:* Martin v. Wilks *and the Rights of Vested Incumbents in Civil Rights Consent Degrees,* 77 Cornell L. Rev. 189 (1992) (arguing that white firefighters had vested property rights in promotion opportunities protected by Due Process Clause).

Congress responded to *Martin v. Wilks* by enacting §108 of the Civil Rights Act of 1991. This provision bars collateral attacks on consent decrees in federal employment discrimination cases when a third party had adequate notice of the proposed judgment and an opportunity to object, or when the third party was "adequately represented" by another third-party challenger. 42 U.S.C. §2000e-2(n)(1)(B). Do you see any due process problems with the statute?

5. Interpleader

A recurrent theme running through many of the joinder techniques we have considered thus far is the problem of ensuring that anyone potentially affected by an adjudication be able to participate in the litigation. Rules 19 and 24 protect these interests by either bringing potentially affected parties into the litigation, or, in the case of Rule 19(b), by dismissing the litigation in their absence.

We consider here a slightly different but related type of concern about including all interested parties in a litigation — the problem of inconsistent obligations. Consider the problem faced by an insurance company with policy benefits claimed by numerous individuals. The company has an obligation to pay out a limited, fixed amount under the policy. It is largely indifferent as to whom it pays the benefits. The one result it cannot abide is an adjudication in one case awarding the insurance benefits to one claimant, and then an award of the same benefits to a different claimant in a separate adjudication.

In situations like this, where a single obligation can give rise to multiple, inconsistent liabilities, potential defendants need to ensure that the adjudication is binding on all persons having claims against it. A remedy is provided by Rule 22 and a related federal "interpleader" statute, 28 U.S.C. §2361 (not to be confused with the quite different practice of "impleader" under Rule 14). *Interpleader* permits someone in possession of a particular piece of property that is subject to potentially conflicting claims to join in one proceeding all potential claimants to that property. Unlike a conventional lawsuit, the owner of the property (called the "stakeholder") is not seeking any particular relief against the claimants, other than a guarantee of finality. Indeed, interpleader permits the stakeholder to deposit the property with the court and walk away from the proceeding.

Interpleader is one of the oldest forms of joining multiple parties in a single proceeding. It was available in equity even when the joinder rules of the common law were highly constrained. Historically, interpleader was subject to a number of stringent limitations, many of which have been abandoned in modern practice:

> The same thing, debt, or duty must be claimed by both or all the parties against whom the relief is demanded; 2. All their adverse titles or claims must be dependent on or be derived from a common source; 3. The person asking the relief — the plaintiff — must not have or claim any interest in the subject-matter; 4. He must have incurred no independent liability to either of the claimants; that is, he must stand perfectly indifferent between them, in the position merely of a stakeholder.

4 John Norton Pomeroy, Equity Jurisprudence (5th ed. 1941), §1322 at 906.

Under modern federal practice, a stakeholder deposits the property with the court (or a bond guaranteeing payment) and then joins all potential claimants, who are enjoined from filing independent proceedings against the stakeholder. Unlike traditional equity practice, the stakeholder may contest liability, may assert its own claim to the property, and may proceed without regard to whether the adverse titles were derived from a common source. A stakeholder may initiate an interpleader proceeding as plaintiff or may convert a conventional proceeding to an interpleader by way of counterclaim or cross-claim. *See* 28 U.S.C. §2361; Fed. R. Civ. P. 22.

Notwithstanding its efforts to narrow diversity jurisdiction in general, Congress has, since 1917, seen a particularly appropriate role for the federal courts in rendering effective interpleader relief. Under the Federal Interpleader Act, the federal courts have subject matter jurisdiction over interpleader proceedings if the stakeholder's total obligation is at least $500 and if any single claimant is diverse from any other claimant; there is no need for complete diversity. 28 U.S.C. §1335. *See State Farm Fire & Cas. Co. v. Tashire*, 386 U.S. 523 (1967) (complete diversity rule of *Strawbridge* is not constitutionally mandated and may be abrogated by interpleader statute). Moreover, the court may issue process against any claimant in the United States; an interpleader court has nationwide personal jurisdiction. 28 U.S.C. §2361. Venue is proper wherever one or more claimants reside. 28 U.S.C. §1397.

These provisions apply only to proceedings brought under the statute. A stakeholder may also initiate an interpleader directly under Rule 22, in which case complete diversity is required and normal venue and personal jurisdiction rules apply. There is accordingly little reason for a party to bring a Rule 22 interpleader rather than a statutory interpleader. *See* 7 C. Wright et al., Federal Practice and Procedure §1703 (3d ed. 2012 & 2021 update) (suggesting possibility that deposit of property may not, in some districts, be required for Rule 22 interpleader). It is possible, however, that where the stakeholder is diverse from claimants, all of whom are citizens of the same state, there would be subject matter jurisdiction for a Rule 22 interpleader but not for statutory interpleader.

Notwithstanding the significant liberalization of interpleader practice, the courts have limited its application to claims on the same property that are inconsistent in strict and immediate terms. Thus, in *Indianapolis Colts v. Mayor & City Council of Baltimore*, 741 F.2d 954 (7th Cir. 1984), the court found interpleader unavailable where the Baltimore Colts football team attempted to use the procedure to enjoin the city from pursuing an eminent domain proceeding to take ownership of the team. The Colts asserted that they faced an inconsistent liability to the owners of the Indianapolis football stadium, with whom they had already signed new lease agreements. Since the stadium owners were not seeking ownership of the team (the claim asserted by the city of Baltimore), the court held that the claims were not for the same property and hence that interpleader was inappropriate.

D.   CLASS ACTIONS AND OTHER COMPLEX JOINDER DEVICES

We have now seen a variety of permissive and compulsory joinder devices, some by plaintiffs and some by defendants, that can be used to expand the paradigmatic single plaintiff versus single defendant lawsuit. But questions remain about how to structure litigation when there are massive numbers of parties. Consider, for example, thousands of individuals who purchase a product and are overcharged a small amount by a defendant. Is it practical or economical for these individual plaintiffs to join formally in a lawsuit? Or, if large numbers of persons are injured in a hotel fire, is it sensible to proceed with hundreds of individual lawsuits in different courts?

Can you think of other ways in which such litigation could be structured? Would it ever be feasible to permit representatives of a group to litigate "on behalf" of others? Or would such a "representative action" be inconsistent with the principle that a person cannot be bound unless he has had a day in court? If such a group or representative action is a possibility, what conditions should be imposed before allowing such an action to proceed? Would you expect a change in the litigative unit to have an impact on the substantive results in the case?

Two basic models come to mind in thinking about how to structure litigation where large numbers of individuals join together against a common adversary. One model would maintain substantial autonomy for the individual litigant within a framework in which individuals pooled their resources to achieve economic benefits. Under this approach, litigation by the group would continue to offer each litigant control over inclusion in the group, the right to his or her own counsel, and significant participation in the litigation. The second type of group litigation would cede decision making about the conduct of the litigation to the entity litigating on behalf of the group; litigation would be carried out by representatives of the group and membership in the group would not be strictly a matter of consent. Thus, the autonomy of individual litigants would be subordinated to the "entity," which would become the primary litigant and client.

Although neither of these models exists anywhere in "pure" form, together they pose the competing tensions in thinking about how collective action for litigation should be structured. Might the choice of model depend on whether plaintiff's claim is a "negative-value" claim—i.e., a small claim in which the cost of individual litigation outweighs the value of the claim—or whether in the absence of collective litigation, plaintiff could proceed with an independently viable claim? For further discussion of these models, *see* David L. Shapiro, *Class Actions: The Class as Party and Client*, 13 Notre Dame L. Rev. 913 (1998); Edward H. Cooper, *The (Cloudy) Future of Class Actions*, 40 Ariz. L. Rev. 923 (1998). *See also* Francis E. McGovern & William B. Rubenstein, *The Negotiation Class: A Cooperative Approach to Class Actions Involving Large Stakeholders*, 99 Tex. L. Rev. 73 (2020) (exploring the relevance of the traditional class action model in cases involving a mix of large and small claims); Richard A. Epstein, *Class Actions: Aggregation, Amplification, and Distortion*, 2003 U. Chi. L. Forum 475 (describing class action as tradeoff between autonomy value of control over individual claim and coordination value of "forced exchange" between class members).

1. A First Look at Class Actions

The most common method of litigating claims on behalf of large numbers of individuals is the representative suit, or class action. In a class suit, named representatives and their counsel conduct litigation on behalf of and for the benefit of a particular group. As suggested above, the rules for the conduct of class actions attempt to strike a proper balance between the autonomy of individual litigants and the benefits of collective action.

Two important academic commentators on class actions, Professor Jack Coffee and Professor Sam Issacharoff, in separate articles, identified three discrete elements that might serve as means of protecting individual autonomy within the framework of a "representative" action. They are: *exit*—the ability of a potential class member to avoid membership in the class; *voice*—the ability of a class member to participate in the litigation; and *loyalty*—the assurance that interests of the named representative (as well as counsel) are the same as those of the absent class members. *See* John C. Coffee, Jr., *Class Action Accountability: Reconciling Exit, Voice, and Loyalty in Representative Litigation*, 100 Colum. L. Rev. 370 (2000), and Samuel Issacharoff, *Governance and Legitimacy in the Law of Class Actions*, 1999 Sup. Ct. Rev. 337. *Cf.* Albert Hirschman, *Exit, Voice and Loyalty: Responses to Decline in Firms, Organizations and States* (1970).

As you read the materials in this chapter, consider the relative role for each of these elements in structuring representative litigation on behalf of others.

HISTORICAL NOTE ON CLASS ACTIONS

The concept of the class action was unknown at English common law, but the English Court of Chancery developed a procedure to enable a court of equity to hear an action by or against representatives of a group. The representative action could be brought only if the number of persons involved was so large that joinder was impractical, if all members of the group possessed a "joint interest" in the question to be adjudicated, and if the named parties adequately represented the absent members of the class. For a comprehensive discussion of the English legal historical tradition, *see* Stephen C. Yeazell, From Medieval Group Litigation to the Modern Class Action (1987).

In the United States, equity courts also adopted a similarly cabined representative suit to ensure that large groups of individuals who were united in interest would not be disabled from bringing suit when joinder was impractical. Note, however, that even this limited concept of a class suit is in tension with a fundamental procedural premise we encountered at the outset of our study of the American legal system — that a party must be brought before the court with appropriate jurisdiction and receive notice in order to be bound by any judgment. The justification for the historical class device was that the class members' interests were joint or undivided—not unlike the joint interest previously required of necessary parties under Rule 19—and that the interests of the absentees were adequately represented even though not all members of the group were formal parties to the action. With the merger of law and equity, the procedural codes of the American states adopted class action provisions that permitted somewhat broader class suits. Many of the codes authorized class actions when the parties were too numerous to be joined and the question in dispute was one of common or general interest. Whether or not a judgment in this more expansive class suit was binding on absent class members was not free from doubt. For a comprehensive historical analysis of the *res judicata* effect of such class suits, *see* Geoffrey C. Hazard, John L. Gedid & Stephen Sowle, *An Historical Analysis of the Binding Effect of Class Suits*, 146 U. Pa. L. Rev. 1849 (1998). *See also* 7A C. Wright et al., Federal Practice and Procedure §1751 (3d ed. 2012 & 2021 update) (providing general historical overview of the class action). The original Federal Rule 23 class action provision, adopted in 1938, reflected some of the confusion concerning the binding effect of class actions. The Rule required that persons constituting a class be so numerous as to make it impracticable to bring them before the court and that one or more of them "fairly insure the adequate representation of all." The Rule set forth three categories of class actions:

(1) joint, or common, or secondary in the sense that the owner of a primary right refuses to enforce that right and a member of the class thereby becomes entitled to enforce it;

(2) several, and the object of the action is the adjudication of claims which do or may affect specific property involved in the action; or

(3) several, and there is a common question of law or fact affecting the several rights and a common relief is sought.

The meaning of these categories, defined in terms of abstract rights, proved "obscure and uncertain," and the categorization carried important consequences. Although the binding effect of a class suit on absent class members was not settled by the rule itself, case law treated the various categories of class actions in distinctive ways.

The first category, which largely tracked the historical equity class, came to be referred to as the "true" class action and bound all members of the class.

The second category, eventually overtaken by the bankruptcy laws, was known as a "hybrid" action and bound members of the class only with respect to the specific property involved.

The third category, known as a "spurious" class action, was used primarily to obviate joinder problems but formally bound only those persons who were named parties to the litigation. An additional feature of the spurious class action was to allow absent class members to intervene *after* the judgment, thereby taking advantage of a favorable outcome in the litigation. *See generally Union Carbide & Carbon Corp. v. Nisely*, 300 F.2d 561 (10th Cir. 1961). Note the similarity of such "one-way" intervention by class plaintiffs and the more general ability of nonparties to take advantage of a favorable judgment with the development of nonmutual offensive preclusion principles.

In 1966, Rule 23 of the Federal Rules of Civil Procedure was revised to construct a new tri-part classification of class actions, some with different requirements, but all imposing the critical feature of binding members of the class. We will subsequently examine specific features of the new rule, but at the outset we focus on the central question of whether it is ever appropriate for a "class representative" to bind class members if they are not before the court. Should it be necessary to obtain some type of consent of the absent class members? Is it fair to impose on defendants the burden of liability to an entire class on the basis of "representative" litigation by only some members of the class?

2.   Thinking About "Loyalty": The Threshold Requirement of Adequacy of Representation

Hansberry v. Lee

311 U.S. 32 (1940)

Certiorari to the Supreme Court of Illinois.

MR. JUSTICE STONE delivered the opinion of the Court.

The question is whether the Supreme Court of Illinois, by its adjudication that petitioners in this case are bound by a judgment rendered in an earlier litigation to which they were not parties, has deprived them of the due process of law guaranteed by the Fourteenth Amendment.

Respondents brought this suit in the Circuit Court of Cook County, Illinois, to enjoin the breach by petitioners of an agreement restricting the use of land within a described area of the City of Chicago, which was alleged to have been entered into by some five hundred of the landowners. The agreement stipulated that for a specified period no part of the land should be "sold, leased to or permitted to be occupied by any person of the colored race," and provided that it should not be effective unless signed by the "owners of 95 per centum of the frontage" within the described area. The bill of complaint set up that the owners of 95 percent of the frontage had signed; that respondents are owners of land within the restricted area who have either signed the agreement or acquired their land from others who did sign; and that petitioners Hansberry, who are Negroes, have, with the alleged aid of the other petitioners and with knowledge of the agreement, acquired and are occupying land in the restricted area formerly belonging to an owner who had signed the agreement.

To the defense that the agreement had never become effective because owners of 95 percent of the frontage had not signed it, respondents pleaded that that issue was *res judicata* by the decree in an earlier suit. *Burke v. Kleiman*, 277 Ill. App. 519. To this petitioners pleaded, by way of rejoinder, that they were not parties to that suit or bound by its decree, and that denial of their right to litigate, in the present suit, the issue of performance of the condition precedent to the validity of the agreement would be a denial of due process of law guaranteed by the Fourteenth Amendment. It does not appear, nor is it contended that any of petitioners is the successor in interest to or in privity with any of the parties in the earlier suit.

The circuit court, after a trial on the merits, found that owners of only about 54 percent of the frontage had signed the agreement, and that the only support of the judgment in the *Burke* case was a false and fraudulent stipulation of the parties that owners of 95 percent had signed. But it ruled that the issue of performance of the condition precedent to the validity of the agreement was *res judicata* as alleged and entered a decree for respondents. The Supreme Court of Illinois affirmed. 372 Ill. 369; 24 N.E.2d 37. We granted certiorari to resolve the constitutional question. 309 U.S. 652.

The Supreme Court of Illinois, upon an examination of the record in *Burke v. Kleiman, supra*, found that that suit, in the Superior Court of Cook County, was brought by a landowner in the restricted area to enforce the agreement, which had been signed by her predecessor in title, in behalf of herself and other property owners in like situation, against four named individuals, who had acquired or asserted an interest in a plot of land formerly owned by another signer of the agreement; that, upon stipulation of the parties in that suit that the agreement had been signed by owners of 95 percent of all the frontage, the court had adjudged that the agreement was in force, that it was a covenant running with the land and binding all the land within the described area in the hands of the parties to the agreement and those claiming under them, including defendants, and had entered its decree restraining the breach of the agreement by the defendants and those claiming under them, and that the appellate court had affirmed the decree. It found that the stipulation was untrue but held, contrary to the trial court, that it was not fraudulent or collusive. It also appears from the record in *Burke v. Kleiman* that the case was tried on an agreed statement of facts which raised only a single issue, whether by reason of changes in the restricted area, the agreement had ceased to be enforcible [sic] in equity.

From this the Supreme Court of Illinois concluded in the present case that *Burke v. Kleiman* was a "class" or "representative" suit, and that in such a suit, "where the remedy is pursued by a plaintiff who has the right to represent the class to which he belongs, other members of the class are bound by the results in the case unless it is reversed or set aside on direct proceedings"; that petitioners in the present suit were members of the class represented by the plaintiffs in the earlier suit and consequently were bound by its decree, which had rendered the issue of performance of the condition precedent to the restrictive agreement *res judicata*, so far as petitioners are concerned. The court thought that the circumstance that the stipulation in the earlier suit that owners of 95 percent of the frontage had signed the agreement was contrary to the fact, as found in the present suit, did not militate against this conclusion, since the court in the earlier suit had jurisdiction to determine the fact as between the parties before it, and that its determination, because of the representative character of the suit, even though erroneous, was binding on petitioners until set aside by a direct attack on the first judgment.

State courts are free to attach such descriptive labels to litigations before them as they may choose and to attribute to them such consequences as they think appropriate under state constitutions and laws, subject only to the requirements of the Constitution of the United States. . . .

It is a principle of general application in Anglo-American jurisprudence that one is not bound by a judgment *in personam* in a litigation in which he is not designated as a party or to which he has not been made a party by service of process. *Pennoyer v. Neff*, 950 U.S. 714; 1 Freeman on Judgments (5th ed.), §407. A judgment rendered in such circumstances is not entitled to the full faith and credit which the Constitution and statute of the United States . . . prescribe, *Pennoyer v. Neff, supra.* . . .

To these general rules there is a recognized exception that, to an extent not precisely defined by judicial opinion, the judgment in a "class" or "representative" suit, to which some members of the class are parties, may bind members of the class or those represented who were not made parties to it. *Smith v. Swormstedt*, 16 How. 288 [other citations omitted].

The class suit was an invention of equity to enable it to proceed to a decree in suits where the number of those interested in the subject of the litigation is so great that their joinder as parties in conformity to the usual rules of procedure is impracticable. . . . In such cases where the interests of those not joined are of the same class as the interests of those who are, and where it is considered that the latter fairly represent the former in the prosecution of the litigation of the issues in which all have a common interest, the court will proceed to a decree. . . .

It is evident that the considerations which may induce a court thus to proceed, despite a technical defect of parties, may differ from those which must be taken into account in determining whether the absent parties are bound by the decree or, if it is adjudged that they are, in ascertaining whether such an adjudication satisfies the requirements of due process and of full faith and credit. Nevertheless, there is scope within the framework of the Constitution for holding in appropriate cases that a judgment rendered in a class suit is *res judicata* as to members of the class who are not formal parties to the suit. Here, as elsewhere, the Fourteenth Amendment does not compel state courts or legislatures to adopt any particular rule for establishing the conclusiveness of judgments in class suits; . . . nor does it compel the adoption of the particular rules thought by this Court to be appropriate for the federal courts. With a proper regard for divergent local institutions and interests, cf. *Jackson County v. United States*, 308 U.S. 343, 351, this Court is justified in saying that there has been a failure of due process only in those cases where it cannot be said that the procedure adopted, fairly insures the protection of the interests of absent parties who are to be bound by it. . . .

It is familiar doctrine of the federal courts that members of a class not present as parties to the litigation may be bound by the judgment where they are in fact adequately represented by parties who are present, or where they actually participate in the conduct of the litigation in which members of the class are present as parties, *Plumb v. Goodnow's Administrator*, 123 U.S. 560; *Confectioners' Machinery Co. v. Racine Engine & Mach. Co.*, 7 Cir., 163 F. 914; Id., 7 Cir., 170 F. 1021; *Bryant Electric Co. v. Marshall*, 169 F. 426, or where the interest of the members of the class, some of whom are present as parties, is joint, or where for any other reason the relationship between the parties present and those who are absent is such as legally to entitle the former to stand in judgment for the latter. *Smith v. Swormstedt, supra; cf. Christopher v. Brusselback, supra*, 503, 504, and cases cited.

In all such cases, so far as it can be said that the members of the class who are present are, by generally recognized rules of law, entitled to stand in judgment for those who are not, we may assume for present purposes that such procedure affords a protection to the parties who are represented, though absent, which would satisfy the requirements of due process and full faith and credit. See *Bernheimer v. Converse*, 206 U.S. 516; *Mann v. Augedahl*, 247 U.S. 142; *Chandler v. Peketz*, 297 U.S. 609. Nor do we find it necessary for the decision of this case to say that, when the only circumstance defining the class is that the determination of the rights of its members turns upon a single issue of fact or law, a state could not constitutionally adopt a procedure whereby some of the members of the class could stand in judgment for all, provided that the procedure were so devised and applied as to insure that those present are of the same class as those absent and that the litigation is so conducted as to insure the full and fair consideration of the common issue. . . . We decide only that the procedure and the course of litigation sustained here by the plea of *res judicata* do not satisfy these requirements.

The restrictive agreement did not purport to create a joint obligation or liability. If valid and effective its promises were the several obligations of the signers and those claiming under them. The promises ran severally to every other signer. It is plain that in such circumstances all those alleged to be bound by the agreement would not constitute a single class in any litigation brought to enforce it. Those who sought to secure its benefits by enforcing it could not be said to be in the same class with or represent those whose interest was in resisting performance, for the agreement by its terms imposes obligations and confers rights on the owner of each plot of land who signs it. If those who thus seek to secure the benefits of the agreement were rightly regarded by the state Supreme Court as constituting a class, it is evident that those signers or their successors who are interested in challenging the validity of the agreement and resisting its performance are not of the same class in the sense that their interests are identical so that any group who had elected to enforce rights conferred by the agreement could be said to be acting in the interest of any others who were free to deny its obligation.

Because of the dual and potentially conflicting interests of those who are putative parties to the agreement in compelling or resisting its performance, it is impossible to say, solely because they are parties to it, that any two of them are of the same class. Nor without more, and with the due regard for the protection of the rights of absent parties which due process exacts, can some be permitted to stand in judgment for all.

It is one thing to say that some members of a class may represent other members in a litigation where the sole and common interest of the class in the litigation is either to assert a common right or to challenge an asserted obligation. *Smith v. Swormstedt, supra, Supreme Tribe of Ben-Hur v. Cauble, supra; Groves v. Farmers State Bank,* 368 Ill. 35, 12 N.E.2d 618. It is quite another to hold that all those who are free alternatively either to assert rights or to challenge them are of a single class, so that any group, merely because it is of the class so constituted, may be deemed adequately to represent any others of the class in litigating their interests in either alternative. Such a selection of representatives for purposes of litigation, whose substantial interests are not necessarily or even probably the same as those whom they are deemed to represent, does not afford that protection to absent parties which due process requires. The doctrine of representation of absent parties in a class suit has not hitherto been thought to go so far. . . . Apart from the opportunities it would afford for the fraudulent and collusive sacrifice of the rights of absent parties, we think that the representation in this case no more satisfies the requirements of due process than a trial by a judicial officer who is in such situation that he may have an interest in the outcome of the litigation in conflict with that of the litigants. *Tumey v. Ohio,* 273 U.S. 510.

The plaintiffs in the *Burke* case sought to compel performance of the agreement in behalf of themselves and all others similarly situated. They did not designate the defendants in the suit as a class or seek any injunction or other relief against others than the named defendants, and the decree which was entered did not purport to bind others. In seeking to enforce the agreement the plaintiffs in that suit were not representing the petitioners here whose substantial interest is in resisting performance. The defendants in the first suit were not treated by the pleadings or decree as representing others or as foreclosing by their defense the rights of others; and, even though nominal defendants, it does not appear that their interest in defeating the contract outweighed their interest in establishing its validity. For a court in this situation to ascribe to either the plaintiffs or defendants the performance of such functions on behalf of petitioners here, is to attribute to them a power that it cannot be said that they had assumed to exercise, and a responsibility which, in view of their dual interests it does not appear that they could rightly discharge.

Reversed.

NOTES AND QUESTIONS

1. *The Demise of Racially Restrictive Covenants.* Enforcement of the type of racially restrictive covenant at issue in *Hansberry* would be unconstitutional today. At the

time of *Hansberry*, however, such covenants were perceived as private arrangements that did not implicate state governmental action, which is required to constitute a due process or equal protection violation of the Fourteenth Amendment. In *Shelley v. Kraemer*, 334 U.S. 1 (1948), the Supreme Court ruled that judicial enforcement of such private covenants satisfied the "state action" requirement and violated the Equal Protection Clause of the Fourteenth Amendment.

What impact did the offensive nature of the covenant (even if not unconstitutional at the time) have on the Supreme Court's disposition in *Hansberry*? Are the same problems presented by other types of covenants, such as those prohibiting the hanging of clothes to dry on outside lines, or limiting subdivisions to a lot of specified size?

2. *Differing Interests Among Class Members.* *Hansberry* represents the need in class suits for the "loyalty" element we identified at the beginning of Section 1. How absolute is the connection between the interests of the class representative and those of absent class members? Does *Hansberry* stand for the proposition that due process is violated by binding class members to a judgment when there is internal division of opinion within the class? Was there any attempt to ascertain whether there was in fact such internal division at the time the initial action, *Burke v. Kleiman*, was being litigated? *Compare, e.g.*, Fed. R. Civ. P. 23(a), which imposes the requirement that there be a determination of adequate representation before an action may proceed as a class suit.

An interesting aspect of the *Hansberry* case never raised in the opinion is the fact that the original proceeding, *Burke v. Kleiman*, was brought by Olive Ida Burke at the behest of the property owner's association, and that it was James Burke, her husband, who sold the property to the Hansberrys and successfully challenged the decree obtained by his wife. Also, Mr. Burke had been a member of the Woodlawn Property Owner's Association, the group originally responsible for covering the South Park neighborhood with the racially restrictive covenant. Mr. Burke's decision to sell the house to Carl Hansberry was the result of both changing demographics in Chicago and the Depression; the demand for housing was so low among whites that Mr. Hansberry was the only prospective buyer for the house. For a closer look at the facts surrounding this case, *see* Allen R. Kamp, *The History Behind Hansberry v. Lee*, 20 U.C. Davis L. Rev. 481 (1987). The human element of the *Hansberry* case is recounted in "A Raisin in the Sun" by Lorraine Hansberry, Carl Hansberry's daughter.

Does the fact of the spousal relationship between Mr. and Mrs. Burke change your view about whether Mr. Burke was "adequately represented"?

3. *Unanimity of Viewpoint?* As a general proposition, class actions require commonality of interest, but it may be unrealistic to expect complete unanimity of viewpoint among the members of the class. Consider a class action by riparian owners seeking to stop the disposal practices of a large upstream industrial firm. Is due process violated if the class includes owners who are also employees of the polluting firm who, if put to the choice, would prefer keeping their jobs to ending the pollution? Consider also the facts in *Supreme Tribe of Ben-Hur v. Cauble*, 255 U.S. 356 (1921), where a class of policyholders in life insurance benefits provided by the defendant fraternal society objected to changes in the benefits instituted to remedy an actuarially unsound plan. (Such societies functioned at the time in part as "the

poor man's life insurance companies," providing inexpensive insurance because they were free of reserve requirements imposed on traditional insurers.) There may well have been a difference of view within the class between those who were interested in preserving their preexisting rights and those who placed a greater weight on the continued solvency of the organization. In general, some degree of dissonance within a class of this sort does not place in question the validity of using a class action because the opposing perspective — in the above examples, the economic health of the polluting firm or the solvency of the organization — is being vigorously represented by the opponent of the class. *See* Jack Weinstein, *Revision of Procedure: Some Problems in Class Actions*, 9 Buff. L. Rev. 433 (1960).

Does the preceding paragraph suggest that the problem in *Hansberry* was the fact that the opponents of the class in *Burke v. Kleiman* did not represent the interests of property owners opposed to enforcement of the covenant? If Mrs. Burke had structured the lawsuit as an action against a defendant class consisting of all property owners who opposed enforcement of the covenant, would due process have been satisfied? Alternatively, would the Court's concerns about adequacy of representation be mitigated if any dissenting member of the class were able to "exit" from the litigation at the outset?

4. *Rule 23 and Adequate Representation.* Note that in *Hansberry*, the state trial court made no inquiry about the propriety of a class suit in the initial proceeding, *Burke v. Kleiman*, which was brought as a class suit to enforce the covenant. The challenge to class action status arose only in the context of whether the original judgment was binding on Mr. Burke.

In contrast, Federal Rule 23 (along with many state variants) requires that a court make a number of findings before an action will be certified as a class, including, in particular, that "the representative parties will fairly and adequately protect the interests of the class." The trial court also has an ongoing responsibility to monitor the conduct of the class action to ensure that these requirements are satisfied. In addition to the certification requirements and its supervisory role, the court has the power to make other orders for the conduct of the action including mandating the use of subclasses or appointing class counsel separate from counsel for the named representatives. Any dismissal or settlement of a class action must have the approval of the court (*see* Fed. R. Civ. P. 23(e)). Given the protections provided in Rule 23 for maintenance of a class suit, should an absent class member be able to challenge the finding of adequacy of representation in a subsequent proceeding? For further discussion of this aspect of *Hansberry, see* pp. 1020–1021. Note that there is cause for concern about the care with which some courts scrutinize adequacy of representation under Rule 23. Professor Robert Klonoff has conducted an analysis of over 700 cases, from 1994 to 2003, in which federal courts conducted an inquiry into adequacy of representation during certification proceedings. *See* Robert H. Klonoff, *The Judiciary's Flawed Application of Rule 23's "Adequacy of Representation" Requirement*, 2004 Mich. St. L. Rev. 671. Klonoff concludes that "the vast majority of courts conduct virtually no gate-keeping function and approve class representatives and class counsel with little or no analysis," and that those courts that do conduct adequacy analysis often make it unnecessarily difficult for those opposing certification to demonstrate that adequacy is lacking. *Id.* at 673.

3. The Requirements for Certification

Rule 23(a) sets forth four requirements applicable to all forms of class actions. In addition, the rule imposes further prerequisites for certification depending on which type of class action is being asserted.

a. Threshold Requirements

The four universal requirements are: numerosity, commonality, typicality, and adequacy of representation.

i. Numerosity

Rule 23(a)(1) states that a class may be certified only if the class "is so numerous that joinder of all members is impracticable." Impracticable does not mean impossible; courts can certify a class where joinder would be extremely difficult or inconvenient. There is no magic number of class members guaranteed to satisfy the numerosity prerequisite. Ordinarily, a court will find joinder impracticable for a class with more than forty putative class members. *See generally* 7A C. Wright et al., Federal Practice and Procedure §1762 (3d ed. 2012 & 2021 update). There are, however, many exceptions to this general statement; for example, courts have certified a class with as few as 14 members, *see Manning v. Princeton Consumer Discount Co., Inc.*, 390 F. Supp. 320 (E.D. Pa. 1975), yet have also found that a class with 200 members failed to satisfy Rule 23(a)(1), *see Hum v. Dericks*, 162 F.R.D. 628 (D. Haw. 1995). In addition, a plaintiff need not plead a precise number of class members; certification is possible in cases where it is difficult to know with certainty the exact number of class members at any given time. One federal district court in Florida held that while only 30 class members were known in the case before it, the presence of unknown numbers of future class members made joinder impracticable. *See Hill v. Butterworth*, 170 F.R.D. 509 (N.D. Fla. 1997), *vacated on other grounds*, 147 F.3d 1337 (11th Cir. 1998).

Several other factors are relevant to the practicability of joinder, including judicial economy, nature of the action, and location of the prospective class members. *See* 7A Wright et al., *supra*, §1762. Joinder is considered less practicable when members of the class reside in different geographic areas. For example, a District Court in Illinois certified a class with only 18 members, in part because the class members resided in three different states. *See Caspar v. Linvatec Corp.*, 167 F.R.D. 51 (N.D. Ill. 1996). On the other hand, in a case in which the proposed class was composed of 35 students of an orthodontic course, a district court in New York denied certification, holding that joinder was not impracticable as all students could easily be contacted and each had the ability and financial incentive to bring suit individually. *See Ansari v. New York University*, 179 F.R.D. 112 (S.D.N.Y. 1998).

ii. Commonality

The second prerequisite, embodied in Rule 23(a)(2), mandates the presence of "questions of law or fact common to the class." Not all questions of law and fact must be common to all class members; rather, most courts require merely that more than one material issue of law or fact be held in common. Often, cases involving civil rights, antitrust, or securities fraud claims will satisfy Rule 23(a)(2) because, by their nature, each of these types of claim involves a common act, conspiracy, or course of conduct by the defendant. Although factual differences among the claims may exist, commonality is satisfied if a substantial issue is common to all. For example, in a proposed class action challenging the State of Delaware's administration of various aid programs, the district court held that factual dissimilarities among the aid recipients were insignificant because all of the factual patterns gave rise to common questions of law. *See Ortiz v. Eichler*, 616 F. Supp. 1046 (D. Del. 1985). Commonality is lacking if factual circumstances not common to all members would require a trial court to make individual determinations on that issue for each class member.

In *Wal-Mart Stores v. Dukes*, 564 U.S. 338 (2011), however, the Supreme Court issued a ruling that ratcheted up the commonality standard. The case involved claims of sex discrimination against Wal-Mart in stores throughout the country, in violation of Title VII of the Civil Rights Act of 1964. A putative class of all female Wal-Mart employees asserted that a storewide policy reposing broad discretion in individual store managers on matters of hiring and promotion resulted in disparate impacts upon women. The Supreme Court held that the class could not be certified, finding that the policy did not satisfy the requirement of commonality, as a court would need to consider different circumstances at each individual store to ascertain the factors influencing employment decisions. We consider the impact of *Wal-Mart* at pp. 979-988, *infra*.

iii. Typicality

Third, the claims or defenses of the representative parties must be "typical" of the claims or defenses of the other class members. Fed. R. Civ. P. 23(a)(3). A court will require the named representative's claims to have the same essential characteristics as those of all other class members, ensuring that the claims of the absent class members are represented in court. Again, courts have interpreted this requirement leniently, and do not require that *all* claims and defenses raised by the class be identical in all respects. *See* 7A Wright et al., *supra*, §1764.

To some degree, typicality replicates aspects of the other requirements. It also serves a distinct function by ensuring that the representative's case, on which the fate of the entire class depends, is a fair sample: If the representative's case were stronger than the typical class member's, it would be unfair to the defendant to generalize the class relief based on that claim; if it were atypically weak, it would be unfair to the class to have its fate tied to such a sample.

If the claims or defenses of the representatives of the class and the members of the class stem from a single event or course of conduct and are based on the same legal theory, the class will ordinarily satisfy the typicality prerequisite. For example, in a suit claiming systemic deficiencies in the provision of child welfare services, a class of children satisfied the typicality prerequisite even though the services required by law differed depending on each child's individual situation. The court found that because all children were victims of the system's failures, and all children potentially faced all of the system's deficiencies, the individual circumstances of each child did not affect the central claim that the children's constitutional and statutory rights had been violated. *See Baby Neal for and by Kanter v. Casey*, 43 F.3d 48 (3d Cir. 1994).

Typicality is lacking in cases in which the class representative has or is subject to material claims or defenses that are "unique" to the representative. For example, in *Hanon v. Dataproducts, Inc.*, 976 F.2d 497 (9th Cir. 1992), a securities fraud action, typicality was not satisfied because the named plaintiff had prior litigation experience that subjected him to a unique defense regarding the reasonability of his reliance on market integrity. Consistent with the goals of Rule 23 to encourage the use of class action procedures in appropriate cases, Rules 23(c)(1) and 23(c)(4) allow courts to reorganize a class that has atypical features by certifying a class for a limited purpose or by splitting a class into subclasses. *See* 7A Wright et al., *supra*, §1764.

iv. Adequacy of Representation

As discussed above, ensuring adequate representation is critical to the fairness of binding absent parties to the adjudication. There are two aspects to this requirement: the adequacy of the named party, as seen in *Hansberry*, and the adequacy and competence of class counsel.

The requirement that the named parties adequately represent the interests of the class is set forth in Rule 23(a)(4). The courts' primary focus in this regard has been possible conflicts of interest between the representative and other members of the class, as we saw in *Hansberry*. The courts have been largely indifferent toward the experience, knowledge, or resources of the named representative.

However, those questions *are* central to the courts' examination of the adequacy of class counsel, as set forth in Rule 23(g)(1)(A)–(B). In addition to looking at possible conflicts of interest between counsel and the class, the courts will also scrutinize the competence and experience of counsel. The courts will consider, in particular, the lawyer's financial resources and prior class action experience.

b. Requirements Specific to the Type of Class Action

As noted above, the original federal class action rule was severely limited. It bound absent class members only in the "true class action," and therefore was not responsive to the growing needs of society in the second half of the twentieth century. Consider, for example, a group of consumers who have been overcharged a minimal amount on their purchase and for whom the only viable litigation is a class suit where an attorney would be willing to take the suit on a contingent fee basis. Such a case could not be effectively maintained under the old rule. Also, civil rights claims and other public law litigation emerging in the 1960s seemed to be perfect candidates for broad class injunctive relief, but were similarly hindered.

Under the 1966 amendments, a new tri-part classification was established that encompasses these and other kinds of litigation and binds absent class members to any judgment. The specific types of class suits are identified in Rule 23(b).

First, Rule 23(b)(1) authorizes a class suit in two types of situations: (A) when separate actions would create a risk of inconsistent or varying adjudications with respect to individual members of the class and establish incompatible standards of conduct for the party opposing the class; and (B) when individual adjudications would, as a practical matter, be dispositive of the interests of nonparties to the action. (Class actions in this group roughly approximated the earlier "true class action," though two such typical class suits—derivative actions by shareholders and actions relating to unincorporated associations—were carved out in special provisions. *See* Fed. R. Civ. P. 23.1 (Derivative Actions by Shareholders) and Fed. R. Civ. P. 23.2 (Actions Relating to Unincorporated Associations).)

A second type of class action—described in Federal Rule 23(b)(2)—is directed toward class suits seeking injunctive and declaratory relief. The Rule 23(b)(2) class action is particularly important in the arena of institutional reform. Since the Federal Rules were amended in 1966, Rule 23(b)(2) has been one of the primary vehicles for desegregating public schools, ameliorating inhumane conditions of confinement for prisoners, and redressing discrimination and other violations in such areas as housing and employment. The injunction (or consent decree) that is issued in such a case may be extremely detailed, and the district court may retain jurisdiction over the remedial phase of the case for an extended period of time, hearing any further disputes that may arise between the parties and issuing orders to enforce its decision. In one much-noted example, Judge Leonard Sand of the Southern District of New York oversaw the desegregation of the Yonkers, New York schools in a case whose remedial phase began in 1985 and lasted until 2002, almost 20 years later. *See Yonkers Branch—NAACP v. Yonkers Bd. of Educ.*, 1986 WL 4894 (S.D.N.Y. Apr. 22, 1986) (setting forth proposed remedy for desegregation of Yonkers, New York schools); *United States v. Yonkers Bd. of Educ.*, 123 F. Supp. 2d 694 (2000) (finding continuing need for monitoring to eliminate vestiges of segregation).

The third type of action, known as the "(b)(3)" action, was the most revolutionary in that it gives binding effect to an adjudication brought as a class where the relationship between the parties is greatly attenuated. The class members are similarly situated largely because of conduct by the defendant. The ability to use a class action in this situation facilitates the aggregation of relatively small claims that individually are not economically viable to pursue, but it also raises more serious questions about the rights of absentees and defendants. The rule makers understood some of the difficulties inherent in class litigation of this variety and imposed a set of specialized requirements for a (b)(3) damages action.

Under Rule 23(b)(3), the court is required to determine that the common class questions "predominate" over issues affecting individuals and that a class action is "superior" to other methods of adjudication. Specifically, the court will consider:

(A) the class members' interest in individually controlling the prosecution or defense of separate actions;
(B) the extent and nature of any litigation concerning the controversy already begun by or against class members;
(C) the desirability or undesirability of concentrating the litigation of the claims in the particular forum;
(D) the likely difficulties in managing a class action.

In addition, certain procedural protections attach uniquely to (b)(3) proceedings, as the next section describes.

c.   Notice and Opt Out

Rule 23 imposes robust requirements for the notification of absent class members in class actions undertaken pursuant to Rule 23(b)(3). Rule 23(c)(2)(B) requires the district court to "direct to class members the best notice that is practicable under the circumstances, including individual notice to all members who can be identified through reasonable effort." The Supreme Court has made clear that this requirement of individual notice to all reasonably identifiable class members applies strictly, even if the due process standards for notice might be satisfied by a less demanding notification scheme. *Cf. Mullane v. Central Hanover Bank*, 339 U.S. 306 (1950) (describing due process standards for notice in a representative action). As the Court explained in one of its early rulings on modern Rule 23, "individual notice to identifiable class members [in a (b)(3) action] is not a discretionary consideration to be waived in a particular case. It is, rather, an unambiguous requirement of Rule 23." *Eisen v. Carlisle & Jacquelin*, 417 U.S. 156, 176 (1974).

Rule 23(c) then sets forth in detail the materials that must be contained in the notice for any class action certified under Rule 23(b)(3). Perhaps most significantly, the rule states that class notice "must clearly and concisely state" certain details "in plain, easily understood language." This direction, as the Advisory Committee Notes explain, is intended "as a reminder of the need to work unremittingly at the difficult task of communicating with class members." Though a class action is far removed from the everyday experience of most absentees, the proceeding is nonetheless conducted on behalf of those individuals, and they retain the right to enter an appearance through counsel, raise objections to a settlement, and, in a (b)(3) action, exempt themselves from the proceeding by opting out of the class altogether. The rule makes explicit the need to notify absentees of these rights in language they will understand, a proposition reinforced by the Advisory Committee Notes, which emphasize that a district court must be attentive to the fact that some classes "justify notice not only in English but also in another language because significant numbers of members are more likely to understand notice in a different language."

The rule then goes on to spell out in some detail the topics that a notification should address in a (b)(3) action. These include:

> **(i)** the nature of the action;
> **(ii)** the definition of the class certified;
> **(iii)** the class claims, issues, or defenses;
> **(iv)** that a class member may enter an appearance through counsel if the member so desires;
> **(v)** that the court will exclude from the class any member who requests exclusion;
> **(vi)** the time and manner for requesting exclusion; and
> **(vii)** the binding effect of a class judgment on members under Rule 23(c)(3).

In sum, the notice in a (b)(3) action must clearly advise class members of what is at stake in the lawsuit, what issues it will resolve, and what opportunities the absentee has to influence or avoid the proceedings, and it must direct that notice individually to all reasonably identifiable class members in a language they are likely to understand.

In contrast, class actions undertaken pursuant to Rule 23(b)(1) or (b)(2) only require the district court to "direct appropriate notice to the class," Fed. R. Civ. Proc. 23(c)(2)(A), leaving the details to the discretion of the district court, and there is no requirement that class members be given the opportunity to opt out. Why the difference? The answer lies in the nature of the relief pursued in each type of action. In a (b)(2) action, the class seeks injunctive or declaratory relief. Particularly following the decision in *Wal-Mart Stores v. Dukes, infra,* there may be few if any circumstances in which plaintiffs can maintain a (b)(2) action when they seek damages for individual class members. This fact has several implications. First, a request for broad injunctive or declaratory relief will often benefit all members of the class regardless of whether they are parties to the action, so binding all class members to the judgment in such a case may be necessary to preserve fairness for the defendant. Second, the interests of each individual class member are often less concrete and quantifiable in a case seeking a broad injunction than in a case seeking damages.

But do class members have a constitutional right to opt out of an injunctive class action under the Due Process Clause? When a class action seeks individual monetary damages, the Supreme Court appears to believe that due process does require an opportunity to opt out. *See Phillips Petroleum Co. v. Shutts,* 472 U.S. 797, 812 (1985) (requiring notice and the opportunity to opt out in a state damages class action, though tying that result to the doctrine of personal jurisdiction); *Dukes, infra* (suggesting in *dictum* that *Shutts* establishes a broad due process right to opt out of damages class actions without regard to personal jurisdiction). The Court granted a writ of certiorari in a case in 1994 in which it might have answered the due process question for injunctive class actions, but it dismissed the writ as improvidently granted and has not taken up the issue since. *See Ticor Title Ins. Co. v. Brown,* 511 U.S. 117 (1994) (*per curiam*).

The plaintiff must ordinarily pay the costs of notice. In a typical case, those costs are fronted by class counsel, as are the other costs of litigation. In *Eisen, supra,* the Court held that district courts could not impose notice costs on the defendant, even if it concluded that plaintiffs were likely to succeed on the merits of their claims. However, a district court may require defendant to provide limited assistance in the identification of class members if defendant has superior access to that information and can furnish it at far less expense than the plaintiff. This was the issue in *Oppenheimer Fund v. Sanders,* 437 U.S. 340 (1978), a class action brought on behalf of 121,000 purchasers of shares in defendant's mutual fund between 1968 and 1970 who asserted violations of the federal securities laws. The names and addresses of the class members were contained in defendant's records and held for them by a transfer agent. The Supreme Court found judicial authority under Rule 23(d) for requiring defendant to help plaintiffs compile a list of names and addresses of class members, though it refused to shift the cost of compiling such a list to the defendant absent "special circumstances."

d.   The Implied Requirement of Ascertainability

An increasing number of federal circuit courts have found another requirement to be necessarily implied for certification of a class seeking monetary damages under Rule 23: the *ascertainability* of class membership. This requirement has no explicit foundation in the text of the Rule and the Supreme Court has not yet spoken to the issue, so it remains to be seen whether this part of the doctrine will endure. Even so, its salience in the intermediate appellate courts means that lawyers must grapple with it. The basic idea of the ascertainability requirement is that a class seeking monetary damages must be defined in such a way that a court can determine at an early stage whether a given person is a member of the class through the application of objective criteria that do not require complex fact-finding or adjudication. Sometimes an ascertainability problem simply requires the plaintiffs or the court to choose a more refined class definition, but the doctrine also has the potential to prevent certification of some claims altogether.

Suppose that a plaintiff wants to represent a class of people who have purchased an automobile that is allegedly defective because it was negligently designed. The suit would seek the economic harm associated with the diminution of the car's value resulting from the defect. Imagine two different proposed class definitions for such a suit. In the first class, plaintiff seeks to represent "all people who purchased a negligently designed Acme vehicle." In the second class, plaintiff seeks to represent "all people who purchased an Acme vehicle of model X and year Y." The first class would encounter ascertainability problems because membership in the class is defined in terms of the allegedly negligent design of the plaintiffs' cars. In order to determine whether a given person is a member of the class, a court would need to make a finding on negligent design that could involve a whole process of adjudication. The second suit, however, should encounter no such problem because membership in the class is defined solely in terms of readily ascertainable and objective facts: Did the person purchase an Acme vehicle of model X and year Y? To succeed on their claims, of course, the class would need to litigate and prevail on the issue of negligent design, but determining who is a member of the class—the issue that ascertainability is concerned with—should be easy. While one could imagine situations where the facts involving ownership of a specific make and model of automobile would be contested, such disputes would likely be rare and any disagreement could be resolved without complex adjudication. Some ascertainability problems, however, cannot be resolved through mere refinement of the class definition. *See, e.g., Grandalski v. Quest Diagnostics*, LLC, 767 F.3d 175, 184-185 (3d Cir. 2014) (affirming district court's refusal to certify unjust enrichment claim on grounds of ascertainability because "determining membership in the class would require individualized analyses into whether each putative class member was wrongfully harmed").

The U.S. Court of Appeals for the Third Circuit has defined one of the most demanding standards for this implied requirement, articulating a "two-fold" ascertainability test that "requires a plaintiff to show that: (1) the class is defined with reference to objective criteria; and (2) there is a reliable and administratively feasible mechanism for determining whether putative class members fall within the class definition." *Byrd v. Aaron's, Inc.*, 784 F.3d 154, 163 (3d Cir. 2015) (quotations omitted). The requirement of administrative feasibility has been described as a "heightened standard for ascertainability" that some courts have rejected, even as they embrace the implied requirement that a plaintiff show class membership to be objectively ascertainable. *See, e.g., Cherry v. Dometic Corp.*, 986 F.3d 1296, 1301-1302 (11th Cir. 2021) (reaffirming that ascertainability "is an implied prerequisite of Rule 23" and class representatives "bear the burden to establish that their proposed class is adequately defined and clearly ascertainable" but rejecting the "heightened standard" of "administrative feasibility" as an element of the requirement).

Finally, note the important limitation on ascertainability: Courts have found the requirement not to apply in class suits seeking only injunctive or declaratory relief. *See, e.g., Shelton v. Bledsoe*, 775 F.3d 554 (3d Cir. 2015). The point of ascertainability is to ensure that claims for monetary damages can be defined and administered accurately. Class suits that seek only injunctive or declaratory relief do not require individual notice to all class members, *compare* Fed. R. Civ. Proc. 23(c)(2)(A) *with id.* §(c)(2)(B), and they often have spillover benefits to people outside the class. Thus, knowing at the outset of the lawsuit which individuals are included in the class definition is less pressing in such cases.

e. The Role of "Exit" and "Voice" in the Class Action

As we have seen, the ability to request exclusion from an action brought as a class attaches only to Rule 23(b)(3) actions. Is such a right of exit meaningful to class members, as in *Eisen*, who have only a small-stakes claim? Why would an absent plaintiff who is unlikely to pursue an individual lawsuit in any event choose to opt out of a class suit? *See* Theodore Eisenberg & Geoffrey Miller, *The Role of Opt-Outs and Objectors in Class Action Litigation: Theoretical and Empirical Issues,* 57 Vand. L. Rev. 1529, 1532 (2004) (finding that class members with small-stakes claims opt out at a rate of only 0.2% on average); *but see* Tobias Barrington Wolff, *Federal Jurisdiction and Due Process in the Era of the Nationwide Class Action,* 156 U. Pa. L. Rev. 2035, 2086–2088 (2008) (describing the "astonishing fact" in *Shutts, supra,* that "approximately 11% of all [class members] to whom notice was delivered chose to execute the opt-out form" even though the average claim for each was about $100). Would a dissenting class member in a potential (b)(1) or (b)(2) action, such as Mr. Burke in *Hansberry,* have a much greater incentive to opt out of a class suit than would a class member in *Eisen?* Do you think a right of exit should be required in all class suits as a matter of due process? Or would extending opt-out rights to class actions seeking broad injunctive relief undermine the whole purpose of those suits?

A class member in a (b)(3) class who does not choose to request exclusion from the class under Rule 23(c)(2)(B)(v) can enter an appearance in the action with representation through his or her own counsel. *See* Rule 23(c)(2)(B)(iv). This provision can be viewed as offering class members a participatory voice in the conduct of the litigation. But is there any incentive for a small-stakes class member, as in *Eisen,* to intervene in the action? Conversely, is there any other meaningful way to obtain the views of the absent class members with respect to the conduct of the litigation? Would it make sense to require trustees or guardians *ad litem* to oversee the interests of the absent class members? Or is the role of voice artificial in these cases? On this view, the interest of litigant autonomy may be unimportant in class actions involving small-stakes claims.

4. Working Through Rule 23

Wal-Mart Stores, Inc. v. Dukes

564 US 338

JUSTICE SCALIA delivered the opinion of the Court.

We are presented with one of the most expansive class actions ever. The District Court and the Court of Appeals approved the certification of a class comprising about one and a half million plaintiffs, current and former female employees of petitioner Wal-Mart who allege that the discretion exercised by their local supervisors over pay and promotion matters violates Title VII by discriminating against women. In addition to injunctive and declaratory relief, the plaintiffs seek an award of backpay. We consider whether the certification of the plaintiff class was consistent with Federal Rules of Civil Procedure 23(a) and (b)(2).

I

A

Petitioner Wal-Mart is the Nation's largest private employer. It operates four types of retail stores throughout the country: Discount Stores, Supercenters, Neighborhood Markets, and Sam's Clubs. Those stores are divided into seven nationwide divisions, which in turn comprise 41 regions of 80 to 85 stores apiece. Each store has between 40 and 53 separate departments and 80 to 500 staff positions. In all, Wal-Mart operates approximately 3,400 stores and employs more than one million people.

Pay and promotion decisions at Wal-Mart are generally committed to local managers' broad discretion, which is exercised "in a largely subjective manner." Local store managers may increase the wages of hourly employees (within limits) with only limited corporate oversight. As for salaried employees, such as store managers and their deputies, higher corporate authorities have discretion to set their pay within preestablished ranges.

Promotions work in a similar fashion. Wal-Mart permits store managers to apply their own subjective criteria when selecting candidates as "support managers," which is the first step on the path to management. Admission to Wal-Mart's management training program, however, does require that a candidate meet certain objective criteria, including an above-average performance rating, at least one year's tenure in the applicant's current position, and a willingness to relocate. But except for those requirements, regional and district managers have discretion to use their own judgment when selecting candidates for management training. Promotion to higher office—*e.g.*, assistant manager, co-manager, or store manager—is similarly at the discretion of the employee's superiors after prescribed objective factors are satisfied.

B

The named plaintiffs in this lawsuit, representing the 1.5 million members of the certified class, are three current or former Wal-Mart employees who allege that the company discriminated against them on the basis of their sex by denying them equal pay or promotions, in violation of Title VII of the Civil Rights Act of 1964. [The Court described the jobs and specific grievances of the named plaintiffs.]

. . .

These plaintiffs, respondents here, do not allege that Wal-Mart has any express corporate policy against the advancement of women. Rather, they claim that their local managers' discretion over pay and promotions is exercised disproportionately in favor of men, leading to an unlawful disparate impact on female employees, see 42 U.S.C. §2000e-2(k). And, respondents say, because Wal-Mart is aware of this effect, its refusal to cabin its managers' authority amounts to disparate treatment, see §2000e-2(a). Their complaint seeks injunctive and declaratory relief, punitive damages, and backpay. It does not ask for compensatory damages.

Importantly for our purposes, respondents claim that the discrimination to which they have been subjected is common to *all* Wal-Mart's female employees. The basic theory of their case is that a strong and uniform "corporate culture" permits bias against women to infect, perhaps subconsciously, the discretionary decision making of each one of Wal-Mart's thousands of managers—thereby making every woman at the company the victim of one common discriminatory practice. Respondents therefore wish to litigate the Title VII claims of all female employees at Wal-Mart's stores in a nationwide class action.

C

Class certification is governed by Federal Rule of Civil Procedure 23. Under Rule 23(a), the party seeking certification must demonstrate, first, that:

"**(1)** the class is so numerous that joinder of all members is impracticable,

"**(2)** there are questions of law or fact common to the class,

"**(3)** the claims or defenses of the representative parties are typical of the claims or defenses of the class, and

"**(4)** the representative parties will fairly and adequately protect the interests of the class" (paragraph breaks added).

Second, the proposed class must satisfy at least one of the three requirements listed in Rule 23(b). Respondents rely on Rule 23(b)(2), which applies when "the party opposing the class has acted or refused to act on grounds that apply generally to the class, so that final injunctive relief or corresponding declaratory relief is appropriate respecting the class as a whole."[2]

Invoking these provisions, respondents moved the District Court to certify a plaintiff class consisting of "'[a]ll women employed at any Wal-Mart domestic retail store at any time since December 26, 1998, who have been or may be subjected to Wal-Mart's challenged pay and management track promotions policies and practices.'" As evidence that there were indeed "questions of law or fact common to" all the women of Wal-Mart, as Rule 23(a)(2) requires, respondents relied chiefly on three forms of proof: statistical evidence about pay and promotion disparities between men and women at the company, anecdotal reports of discrimination from about 120 of Wal-Mart's female employees, and the testimony of a sociologist, Dr. William Bielby, who conducted a "social framework analysis" of Wal-Mart's "culture" and personnel practices, and concluded that the company was "vulnerable" to gender discrimination.

---

2. Rule 23(b)(1) allows a class to be maintained where "prosecuting separate actions by or against individual class members would create a risk of" either "(A) inconsistent or varying adjudications," or "(B) adjudications . . . that, as a practical matter, would be dispositive of the interests of the other members not parties to the individual adjudications or would substantially impair or impeded their ability to protect their interests." Rule 23(b)(3) states that a class may be maintained where "questions of law or fact common to class members predominate over any questions affecting only individual members," and a class action would be "superior to other available methods for fairly and efficiently adjudicating the controversy." The applicability of these provisions to the plaintiff class is not before us.

Wal-Mart . . . offered its own countervailing statistical and other proof in an effort to defeat Rule 23(a)'s requirements of commonality, typicality, and adequate representation. Wal-Mart further contended that respondents' monetary claims for backpay could not be certified under Rule 23(b)(2), first because that Rule refers only to injunctive and declaratory relief, and second because the backpay claims could not be manageably tried as a class without depriving Wal-Mart of its right to present certain statutory defenses. With one limitation not relevant here, the District Court granted respondents' motion and certified their proposed class. [The Court then described the ruling of the Ninth Circuit Court of Appeals, which affirmed the certification order in a divided en banc opinion.]

. . .

II

The class action is "an exception to the usual rule that litigation is conducted by and on behalf of the individual named parties only." *Califano v. Yamasaki,* 442 U.S. 682, 700–701, 99 S. Ct. 2545, 61 L. Ed. 2d 176 (1979). In order to justify a departure from that rule, "a class representative must be part of the class and 'possess the same interest and suffer the same injury' as the class members." *East Tex. Motor Freight System, Inc. v. Rodriguez,* 431 U.S. 395, 403, 97 S. Ct. 1891, 52 L. Ed. 2d 453 (1977) (quoting *Schlesinger v. Reservists Comm. to Stop the War,* 418 U.S. 208, 216, 94 S. Ct. 2925, 41 L. Ed. 2d 706 (1974)). Rule 23(a) ensures that the named plaintiffs are appropriate representatives of the class whose claims they wish to litigate. The Rule's four requirements—numerosity, commonality, typicality, and adequate representation—"effectively 'limit the class claims to those fairly encompassed by the named plaintiff's claims.'" *General Telephone Co. of Southwest v. Falcon,* 457 U.S. 147, 156, 102 S. Ct. 2364, 72 L. Ed. 2d 740 (1982) (quoting *General Telephone Co. of Northwest v. EEOC,* 446 U.S. 318, 330, 100 S. Ct. 1698, 64 L. Ed. 2d 319 (1980)).

A

The crux of this case is commonality—the rule requiring a plaintiff to show that "there are questions of law or fact common to the class." Rule 23(a)(2). That language is easy to misread, since "[a]ny competently crafted class complaint literally raises common 'questions.'" Nagareda, Class Certification in the Age of Aggregate Proof, 84 N.Y.U. L.Rev. 97, 131–132 (2009). For example: Do all of us plaintiffs indeed work for Wal-Mart? Do our managers have discretion over pay? Is that an unlawful employment practice? What remedies should we get? Reciting these questions is not sufficient to obtain class certification. Commonality requires the plaintiff to demonstrate that the class members "have suffered the same injury," *Falcon, supra,* at 157, 102 S. Ct. 2364. This does not mean merely that they have all suffered a violation of the same provision of law. Title VII, for example, can be violated in many ways—by intentional discrimination, or by hiring and promotion criteria that result in disparate impact, and by the use of these practices on the part of many different superiors in a single company. Quite obviously, the mere claim by employees of the same company that they have suffered a Title VII injury, or even a disparate-impact Title VII injury, gives no cause to believe that all their claims can productively be litigated at once. Their claims must depend upon a common contention—for example, the assertion of discriminatory bias on the part of the same supervisor. That common contention, moreover, must be of such a nature that it is capable of classwide resolution—which means that determination of its truth or falsity will resolve an issue that is central to the validity of each one of the claims in one stroke.

> "What matters to class certification . . . is not the raising of common 'questions'—even in droves—but, rather the capacity of a classwide proceeding to generate common *answers* apt to drive the resolution of the litigation. Dissimilarities within the proposed class are what have the potential to impede the generation of common answers." Nagareda, *supra*, at 132.

Rule 23 does not set forth a mere pleading standard. A party seeking class certification must affirmatively demonstrate his compliance with the Rule—that is, he must be prepared to prove that there are *in fact* sufficiently numerous parties, common questions of law or fact, etc. We recognized in *Falcon* that "sometimes it may be necessary for the court to probe behind the pleadings before coming to rest on the certification question," 457 U.S., at 160, 102 S. Ct. 2364, and that certification is proper only if "the trial court is satisfied, after a rigorous analysis, that the prerequisites of Rule 23(a) have been satisfied," *id.*, at 161, 102 S. Ct. 2364; see *id.*, at 160, 102 S. Ct. 2364 ("[A]ctual, not presumed, conformance with Rule 23(a) remains . . . indispensable"). Frequently that "rigorous analysis" will entail some overlap with the merits of the plaintiff's underlying claim. That cannot be helped. "'[T]he class determination generally involves considerations that are enmeshed in the factual and legal issues comprising the plaintiff's cause of action.'" *Falcon, supra*, at 160, 102 S. Ct. 2364 (quoting *Coopers & Lybrand v. Livesay*, 437 U.S. 463, 469, 98 S. Ct. 2454, 57 L. Ed. 2d 351 (1978); some internal quotation marks omitted).[16]

---

16. A statement in one of our prior cases, *Eisen v. Carlisle & Jacquelin*, 417 U.S. 156, 177, 94 S. Ct. 2140, 40 L. Ed. 2d 732 (1974), is sometimes mistakenly cited to the contrary: "We find nothing in either the language or history of Rule 23 that gives a court any authority to conduct a preliminary inquiry into the merits of a suit in order to determine whether it may be maintained as a class action." But in that case, the judge had conducted a preliminary inquiry into the merits of a suit, not in order to determine the propriety of certification under Rules 23(a) and (b) (he had already done that, see *id.*, at 165, 94 S. Ct. 2140), but in order to shift the cost of notice required by Rule 23(c)(2) from the plaintiff to the defendants. To the extent the quoted statement goes beyond the permissibility of a merits inquiry for any other pretrial purpose, it is the purest dictum and is contradicted by our other cases.

Perhaps the most common example of considering a merits question at the Rule 23 stage arises in class-action suits for securities fraud. Rule 23(b)(3)'s requirement that "questions of law or fact common to class members predominate over any questions affecting only individual members" would often be an insuperable barrier to class certification, since each of the individual investors would have to prove reliance on the alleged misrepresentation. But the problem dissipates if the plaintiffs can establish the applicability of the so-called "fraud on the market" presumption, which says that all traders who purchase stock in an efficient market are presumed to have relied on the accuracy of a company's public statements. To invoke this presumption, the plaintiffs seeking 23(b)(3) certification must prove that their shares were traded on an efficient market, *Erica P. John Fund, Inc. v. Halliburton Co.*, 563 U.S. ——, ——, 131 S. Ct. 2179, 2185, —— L. Ed. 2d ——, 2011 WL 2175208 (2011) (slip op., at 5), an issue they will surely have to prove *again* at trial in order to make out their case on the merits.

Nor is there anything unusual about that consequence: The necessity of touching aspects of the merits in order to resolve preliminary matters, *e.g.*, jurisdiction and venue, is a familiar feature of litigation. See *Szabo v. Bridgeport Machines, Inc.*, 249 F.3d 672, 676–677 (C.A.7 2001) (Easterbrook, J.).

In this case, proof of commonality necessarily overlaps with respondents' merits contention that Wal-Mart engages in a *pattern or practice* of discrimination. That is so because, in resolving an individual's Title VII claim, the crux of the inquiry is "the reason for a particular employment decision," *Cooper v. Federal Reserve Bank of Richmond*, 467 U.S. 867, 876, 104 S. Ct. 2794, 81 L. Ed. 2d 718 (1984). Here respondents wish to sue about literally millions of employment decisions at once. Without some glue holding the alleged *reasons* for all those decisions together, it will be impossible to say that examination of all the class members' claims for relief will produce a common answer to the crucial question, *"Why was I disfavored?"*

B

This Court's opinion in *Falcon* describes how the commonality issue must be approached. There an employee who claimed that he was deliberately denied a promotion on account of race obtained certification of a class comprising all employees wrongfully denied promotions and all applicants wrongfully denied jobs. 457 U.S., at 152, 102 S. Ct. 2364. We rejected that composite class for lack of commonality and typicality, explaining:

> "Conceptually, there is a wide gap between (a) an individual's claim that he has been denied a promotion [or higher pay] on discriminatory grounds, and his otherwise unsupported allegation that the company has a policy of discrimination, and (b) the existence of a class of persons who have suffered the same injury as that individual, such that the individual's claim and the class claim will share common questions of law or fact and that the individual's claim will be typical of the class claims." *Id.*, at 157–158, 102 S. Ct. 2364.

Falcon suggested two ways in which that conceptual gap might be bridged. First, if the employer "used a biased testing procedure to evaluate both applicants for employment and incumbent employees, a class action on behalf of every applicant or employee who might have been prejudiced by the test clearly would satisfy the commonality and typicality requirements of Rule 23(a)." *Id.*, at 159, n. 15, 102 S. Ct. 2364. Second, "[s]ignificant proof that an employer operated under a general policy of discrimination conceivably could justify a class of both applicants and employees if the discrimination manifested itself in hiring and promotion practices in the same general fashion, such as through entirely subjective decision making processes." *Ibid.* We think that statement precisely describes respondents' burden in this case. The first manner of bridging the gap obviously has no application here; Wal-Mart has no testing procedure or other companywide evaluation method that can be charged with bias. The whole point of permitting discretionary decision making is to avoid evaluating employees under a common standard.

The second manner of bridging the gap requires "significant proof" that Wal-Mart "operated under a general policy of discrimination." That is entirely absent here. Wal-Mart's announced policy forbids sex discrimination, and as the District

Court recognized the company imposes penalties for denials of equal employment opportunity. The only evidence of a "general policy of discrimination" respondents produced was the testimony of Dr. William Bielby, their sociological expert. Relying on "social framework" analysis, Bielby testified that Wal-Mart has a "strong corporate culture," that makes it "'vulnerable'" to "gender bias." He could not, however, "determine with any specificity how regularly stereotypes play a meaningful role in employment decisions at Wal-Mart. At his deposition . . . Dr. Bielby conceded that he could not calculate whether 0.5 percent or 95 percent of the employment decisions at Wal-Mart might be determined by stereotyped thinking." The parties dispute whether Bielby's testimony even met the standards for the admission of expert testimony under Federal Rule of Civil Procedure 702 and our *Daubert* case, see *Daubert v. Merrell Dow Pharmaceuticals, Inc.*, 509 U.S. 579, 113 S. Ct. 2786, 125 L. Ed. 2d 469 (1993). . . . [E]ven if properly considered, Bielby's testimony does nothing to advance respondents' case. "[W]hether 0.5 percent or 95 percent of the employment decisions at Wal-Mart might be determined by stereotyped thinking" is the essential question on which respondents' theory of commonality depends. If Bielby admittedly has no answer to that question, we can safely disregard what he has to say. It is worlds away from "significant proof" that Wal-Mart "operated under a general policy of discrimination."

C

The only corporate policy that the plaintiffs' evidence convincingly establishes is Wal-Mart's "policy" of *allowing discretion* by local supervisors over employment matters. On its face, of course, that is just the opposite of a uniform employment practice that would provide the commonality needed for a class action; it is a policy *against having* uniform employment practices. It is also a very common and presumptively reasonable way of doing business—one that we have said "should itself raise no inference of discriminatory conduct," *Watson v. Fort Worth Bank & Trust*, 487 U.S. 977, 990, 108 S. Ct. 2777, 101 L. Ed. 2d 827 (1988).

[The Court discusses the relevance of statistical evidence in a Title VII discrimination claim, focusing particular attention on the difference in this case between statistics that speak to store-level, regional-level, and national patterns, finding the evidence inadequate to establish a common basis for liability.]

. . .

There is another, more fundamental, respect in which respondents' statistical proof fails. Even if it established (as it does not) a pay or promotion pattern that differs from the nationwide figures or the regional figures in *all* of Wal-Mart's 3,400 stores, that would still not demonstrate that commonality of issue exists. Some managers will claim that the availability of women, or qualified women, or interested women, in their stores' area does not mirror the national or regional statistics. And almost all of them will claim to have been applying some sex-neutral, performance-based criteria—whose nature and effects will differ from store to store. In the landmark case of ours which held that giving discretion to lower-level supervisors can be the basis of Title VII liability under a disparate-impact theory, the plurality opinion *conditioned* that holding on the corollary that merely proving that the discretionary system has produced a racial or sexual disparity *is not enough.* "[T]he plaintiff must begin by identifying the specific employment practice that is challenged." *Watson,* 487 U.S., at 994, 108 S. Ct. 2777; accord, *Wards Cove Packing Co. v. Atonio,* 490 U.S. 642, 656, 109 S. Ct. 2115, 104 L. Ed. 2d 733 (1989) (approving that statement), superseded by statute on other grounds, 42 U.S.C. §2000e–2(k). That is all the more necessary when a class of plaintiffs is sought to be certified. Other than the bare existence of delegated discretion, respondents have identified no "specific employment practice"—much less one that ties all their 1.5 million claims together. Merely showing that Wal–Mart's policy of discretion has produced an overall sex-based disparity does not suffice. [The Court also rejected anecdotal evidence submitted through affidavit by 120 individual employees, finding it insufficient to establish a "general policy of discrimination."]

. . .

The dissent misunderstands the nature of the foregoing analysis. It criticizes our focus on the dissimilarities between the putative class members on the ground that we have "blend[ed]" Rule 23(a)(2)'s commonality requirement with Rule 23(b)(3)'s inquiry into whether common questions "predominate" over individual ones. See *post,* at 2550–2552 (Ginsburg, J., concurring in part and dissenting in part). That is not so. We quite agree that for purposes of Rule 23(a)(2) "'[e]ven a single [common] question'" will do, *post,* at 2566, n. 9 (quoting Nagareda, The Preexistence Principle and the Structure of the Class Action, 103 Colum. L. Rev. 149, 176, n. 110 (2003)). We consider dissimilarities not in order to determine (as Rule 23(b)(3) requires) whether common questions *predominate,* but in order to determine (as Rule 23(a)(2) requires) whether there *is* "[e]ven a single [common] question." And there is not here. Because respondents provide no convincing proof of a companywide discriminatory pay and promotion policy, we have concluded that they have not established the existence of any common question.

In sum, we agree with Chief Judge Kozinski that the members of the class:

> "held a multitude of different jobs, at different levels of Wal-Mart's hierarchy, for variable lengths of time, in 3,400 stores, sprinkled across 50 states, with a kaleidoscope of supervisors (male and female), subject to a variety of regional policies that all differed. . . . Some thrived while others did poorly. They have little in common but their sex and this lawsuit." 603 F.3d, at 652 (dissenting opinion).

III

We also conclude that respondents' claims for backpay were improperly certified under Federal Rule of Civil Procedure 23(b)(2). Our opinion in *Ticor Title Ins. Co. v. Brown,* 511 U.S. 117, 121, 114 S. Ct. 1359, 128 L. Ed. 2d 33 (1994) (*per curiam*) expressed serious doubt about whether claims for monetary relief may be certified under that provision. We now hold that they may not, at least where (as here) the monetary relief is not incidental to the injunctive or declaratory relief.

A

Rule 23(b)(2) allows class treatment when "the party opposing the class has acted or refused to act on grounds that apply generally to the class, so that final injunctive relief or corresponding declaratory relief is appropriate respecting the class as a whole." One possible reading of this provision is that it applies *only* to requests for such injunctive or declaratory relief and does not authorize the class certification of monetary claims at all. We need not reach that broader question in this case, because we think that, at a minimum, claims for *individualized* relief (like the backpay at issue here) do not satisfy the Rule. The key to the (b)(2) class is "the indivisible nature of the injunctive or declaratory remedy warranted—the notion that the conduct is such that it can be enjoined or declared unlawful only as to all of the class members or as to none of them." Nagareda, 84 N.Y.U. L. Rev., at 132. In other words, Rule 23(b)(2) applies only when a single injunction or declaratory judgment would provide relief to each member of the class. It does not authorize class certification when each individual class member would be entitled to a *different* injunction or declaratory judgment against the defendant. Similarly, it does not authorize class certification when each class member would be entitled to an individualized award of monetary damages.

That interpretation accords with the history of the Rule. Because Rule 23 "stems from equity practice" that predated its codification, *Amchem Products, Inc. v. Windsor*, 521 U.S. 591, 613, 117 S. Ct. 2231, 138 L. Ed. 2d 689 (1997), in determining its meaning we have previously looked to the historical models on which the Rule was based, *Ortiz v. Fibreboard Corp.*, 527 U.S. 815, 841–845, 119 S. Ct. 2295, 144 L. Ed. 2d 715 (1999). As we observed in *Amchem*, "[c]ivil rights cases against parties charged with unlawful, class-based discrimination are prime examples" of what (b)(2) is meant to capture. 521 U.S., at 614, 117 S. Ct. 2231. In particular, the Rule reflects a series of decisions involving challenges to racial segregation—conduct that was remedied by a single classwide order. In none of the cases cited by the Advisory Committee as examples of (b)(2)'s antecedents did the plaintiffs combine any claim for individualized relief with their classwide injunction. See Advisory Committee's Note, 39 F.R.D. 69, 102 (1966) (citing cases); *e.g., Potts v. Flax*, 313 F.2d 284, 289, n. 5 (C.A.5 1963); *Brunson v. Board of Trustees of Univ. of School Dist. No. 1, Clarendon Cty.*, 311 F.2d 107, 109 (C.A.4 1962) (*per curiam*); *Frasier v. Board of Trustees of N.C.*, 134 F. Supp. 589, 593 (NC 1955) (three-judge court), aff'd, 350 U.S. 979, 76 S. Ct. 467, 100 L. Ed. 848 (1956).

Permitting the combination of individualized and classwide relief in a (b)(2) class is also inconsistent with the structure of Rule 23(b). Classes certified under (b)(1) and (b)(2) share the most traditional justifications for class treatment—that individual adjudications would be impossible or unworkable, as in a (b)(1) class,[11]

---

11. Rule 23(b)(1) applies where separate actions by or against individual class members would create a risk of "establish[ing] incompatible standards of conduct for the party opposing the class," Rule 23(b)(1)(A), such as "where the party is obliged by law to treat the members of the class alike," Amchem Products, Inc. v. Windsor, 521 U.S. 591, 614, 117 S. Ct. 2231, 138 L. Ed. 2d 689 (1997), or where individual adjudications "as a practical matter, would be dispositive of the interests of the other members not parties to the individual adjudications or would substantially impair or impede their ability to protect their interests," Rule 23(b)(1)(B), such as in "'limited fund' cases, . . . in which numerous persons make claims against a fund insufficient to satisfy all claims," *Amchem, supra*, at 614, 117 S. Ct. 2231.

or that the relief sought must perforce affect the entire class at once, as in a (b)(2) class. For that reason these are also mandatory classes: The Rule provides no opportunity for (b)(1) or (b)(2) class members to opt out, and does not even oblige the District Court to afford them notice of the action. Rule 23(b)(3), by contrast, is an "adventuresome innovation" of the 1966 amendments, *Amchem*, 521 U.S., at 614, 117 S. Ct. 2231 (internal quotation marks omitted), framed for situations "in which 'class-action treatment is not as clearly called for,'" *id.*, at 615, 117 S. Ct. 2231 (quoting Advisory Committee's Notes, 28 U.S.C. App., p. 697 (1994 ed.)). It allows class certification in a much wider set of circumstances but with greater procedural protections. Its only prerequisites are that "the questions of law or fact common to class members predominate over any questions affecting only individual members, and that a class action is superior to other available methods for fairly and efficiently adjudicating the controversy." Rule 23(b)(3). And unlike (b)(1) and (b)(2) classes, the (b)(3) class is not mandatory; class members are entitled to receive "the best notice that is practicable under the circumstances" and to withdraw from the class at their option. See Rule 23(c)(2)(B).

Given that structure, we think it clear that individualized monetary claims belong in Rule 23(b)(3). The procedural protections attending the (b)(3) class — predominance, superiority, mandatory notice, and the right to opt out — are missing from (b)(2) not because the Rule considers them unnecessary, but because it considers them unnecessary *to a (b)(2) class.* When a class seeks an indivisible injunction benefiting all its members at once, there is no reason to undertake a case-specific inquiry into whether class issues predominate or whether class action is a superior method of adjudicating the dispute. Predominance and superiority are self-evident. But with respect to each class member's individualized claim for money, that is not so — which is precisely why (b)(3) requires the judge to make findings about predominance and superiority before allowing the class. Similarly, (b)(2) does not require that class members be given notice and opt-out rights, presumably because it is thought (rightly or wrongly) that notice has no purpose when the class is mandatory, and that depriving people of their right to sue in this manner complies with the Due Process Clause. In the context of a class action predominantly for money damages we have held that absence of notice and opt-out violates due process. See *Phillips Petroleum Co. v. Shutts*, 472 U.S. 797, 812, 105 S. Ct. 2965, 86 L. Ed. 2d 628 (1985). While we have never held that to be so where the monetary claims do not predominate, the serious possibility that it may be so provides an additional reason not to read Rule 23(b)(2) to include the monetary claims here.

B

[The Court next examined a reference in the Advisory Committee note suggesting that Rule 23(b)(2) might be a permissible avenue for the resolution of damages claims when the damages requested are "incidental" to a larger claim for nonmonetary equitable relief — a proposition that many lower courts, including the Ninth Circuit, had relied upon in permitting class actions to proceed under §(b)(2) rather than §(b)(3). That note, the Court concluded, lent no support to the invocation of Rule 23(b)(2) in this case.]

. . .

Finally, respondents argue that their backpay claims are appropriate for a (b)(2) class action because a backpay award is equitable in nature. The latter may be true, but it is irrelevant. The Rule does not speak of "equitable" remedies generally but of injunctions and declaratory judgments. As Title VII itself makes pellucidly clear, backpay is neither. See 42 U.S.C. §2000e–5(g)(2)(B)(i) and (ii) (distinguishing between declaratory and injunctive relief and the payment of "backpay," see §2000e–5(g)(2)(A)).

C

. . .

Contrary to the Ninth Circuit's view, Wal-Mart is entitled to individualized determinations of each employee's eligibility for backpay. Title VII includes a detailed remedial scheme. [The Court described the remedial scheme, emphasizing that Title VII requires an individualized determination in each case of a plaintiff seeking damages, including claims for backpay.] . . .

The Court of Appeals believed that it was possible to replace such proceedings with Trial by Formula. A sample set of the class members would be selected, as to whom liability for sex discrimination and the backpay owing as a result would be determined in depositions supervised by a master. The percentage of claims determined to be valid would then be applied to the entire remaining class, and the number of (presumptively) valid claims thus derived would be multiplied by the average backpay award in the sample set to arrive at the entire class recovery—without further individualized proceedings. We disapprove that novel project. Because the Rules Enabling Act forbids interpreting Rule 23 to "abridge, enlarge or modify any substantive right," 28 U.S.C. §2072(b); see *Ortiz*, 527 U.S., at 845, 119 S. Ct. 2295, a class cannot be certified on the premise that Wal-Mart will not be entitled to litigate its statutory defenses to individual claims. And because the necessity of that litigation will prevent backpay from being "incidental" to the classwide injunction, respondents' class could not be certified even assuming, *arguendo*, that "incidental" monetary relief can be awarded to a 23(b)(2) class.

. . .

The judgment of the Court of Appeals is
Reversed.

Justice Ginsburg, with whom Justice Breyer, Justice Sotomayor, and Justice Kagan join, concurring in part and dissenting in part.

The class in this case, I agree with the Court, should not have been certified under Federal Rule of Civil Procedure 23(b)(2). The plaintiffs, alleging discrimination in violation of Title VII, 42 U.S.C. §2000e *et seq.*, seek monetary relief that is not merely incidental to any injunctive or declaratory relief that might be available. See *ante*, at 2557–2561. A putative class of this type may be certifiable under Rule 23(b)(3), if the plaintiffs show that common class questions "predominate" over issues affecting individuals—*e.g.*, qualification for, and the amount of, backpay or compensatory damages—and that a class action is "superior" to other modes of adjudication.

Whether the class the plaintiffs describe meets the specific requirements of Rule 23(b)(3) is not before the Court, and I would reserve that matter for consideration and decision on remand. The Court, however, disqualifies the class at the starting gate, holding that the plaintiffs cannot cross the "commonality" line set by Rule 23(a)(2). In so ruling, the Court imports into the Rule 23(a) determination concerns properly addressed in a Rule 23(b)(3) assessment.

I

A

Rule 23(a)(2) establishes a preliminary requirement for maintaining a class action: "[T]here are questions of law or fact common to the class." The Rule "does not require that all questions of law or fact raised in the litigation be common," H. Newberg & A. Conte, Newberg on Class Actions §3.10, pp. 3–48 to 3–49 (3d ed. 1992); indeed, "[e]ven a single question of law or fact common to the members of the class will satisfy the commonality requirement," Nagareda, The Preexistence Principle and the Structure of the Class Action, 103 Colum. L. Rev. 149, 176, n. 110 (2003). See Advisory Committee's 1937 Notes on Fed. Rule Civ. Proc. 23, 28 U.S.C. App., p. 138 (citing with approval cases in which "there was only a question of law or fact common to" the class members).

A "question" is ordinarily understood to be "[a] subject or point open to controversy." American Heritage Dictionary 1483 (3d ed. 1992). See also Black's Law Dictionary 1366 (9th ed. 2009) (defining "question of fact" as "[a] disputed issue to be resolved . . . [at] trial" and "question of law" as "[a]n issue to be decided by the judge"). Thus, a "question" "common to the class" must be a dispute, either of fact or of law, the resolution of which will advance the determination of the class members' claims.[3]

B

The District Court, recognizing that "one significant issue common to the class may be sufficient to warrant certification," found that the plaintiffs easily met that test. Absent an error of law or an abuse of discretion, an appellate tribunal has no warrant to upset the District Court's finding of commonality. See *Califano v. Yamasaki*, 442 U.S. 682, 703, 99 S. Ct. 2545, 61 L. Ed. 2d 176 (1979) ("[M]ost issues arising under Rule 23 . . . [are] committed in the first instance to the discretion of the district court.").

The District Court certified a class of "[a]ll women employed at any Wal-Mart domestic retail store at any time since December 26, 1998." The named plaintiffs, led by Betty Dukes, propose to litigate, on behalf of the class, allegations that Wal-Mart discriminates on the basis of gender in pay and promotions. They allege that

---

3. The Court suggests Rule 23(a)(2) must mean more than it says. See *ante,* at 2550–2552. If the word "questions" were taken literally, the majority asserts, plaintiffs could pass the Rule 23(a)(2) bar by "[r]eciting . . . questions" like "Do all of us plaintiffs indeed work for Wal-Mart?" *Ante,* at 2551. Sensibly read, however, the word "questions" means disputed issues, not any utterance crafted in the grammatical form of a question.

the company "[r]eli[es] on gender stereotypes in making employment decisions such as . . . promotion[s][and] pay." Wal-Mart permits those prejudices to infect personnel decisions, the plaintiffs contend, by leaving pay and promotions in the hands of "a nearly all male managerial workforce" using "arbitrary and subjective criteria." Further alleged barriers to the advancement of female employees include the company's requirement, "as a condition of promotion to management jobs, that employees be willing to relocate." Absent instruction otherwise, there is a risk that managers will act on the familiar assumption that women, because of their services to husband and children, are less mobile than men. See Dept. of Labor, Federal Glass Ceiling Commission, Good for Business: Making Full Use of the Nation's Human Capital 151 (1995).

Women fill 70 percent of the hourly jobs in the retailer's stores but make up only "33 percent of management employees." "[T]he higher one looks in the organization the lower the percentage of women." The plaintiffs' "largely uncontested descriptive statistics" also show that women working in the company's stores "are paid less than men in every region" and "that the salary gap widens over time even for men and women hired into the same jobs at the same time." cf. *Ledbetter v. Goodyear Tire & Rubber Co.*, 550 U.S. 618, 643, 127 S. Ct. 2162, 167 L. Ed. 2d 982 (2007) (Ginsburg, J., dissenting).

The District Court identified "systems for . . . promoting in-store employees" that were "sufficiently similar across regions and stores" to conclude that "the manner in which these systems affect the class raises issues that are common to all class members." The selection of employees for promotion to in-store management "is fairly characterized as a 'tap on the shoulder' process," in which managers have discretion about whose shoulders to tap. Vacancies are not regularly posted; from among those employees satisfying minimum qualifications, managers choose whom to promote on the basis of their own subjective impressions.

Wal-Mart's compensation policies also operate uniformly across stores, the District Court found. The retailer leaves open a $2 band for every position's hourly pay rate. Wal-Mart provides no standards or criteria for setting wages within that band, and thus does nothing to counter unconscious bias on the part of supervisors.

Wal-Mart's supervisors do not make their discretionary decisions in a vacuum. The District Court reviewed means Wal-Mart used to maintain a "carefully constructed . . . corporate culture," such as frequent meetings to reinforce the common way of thinking, regular transfers of managers between stores to ensure uniformity throughout the company, monitoring of stores "on a close and constant basis," and "Wal-Mart TV," "broadcas[t] . . . into all stores."

The plaintiffs' evidence, including class members' tales of their own experiences, suggests that gender bias suffused Wal-Mart's company culture. Among illustrations, senior management often refer to female associates as "little Janie Qs." One manager told an employee that "[m]en are here to make a career and women aren't." A committee of female Wal-Mart executives concluded that "[s]tereotypes limit the opportunities offered to women."

Finally, the plaintiffs presented an expert's appraisal to show that the pay and promotions disparities at Wal-Mart "can be explained only by gender discrimination and not by . . . neutral variables." Using regression analyses, their expert, Richard Drogin, controlled for factors including, *inter alia*, job performance, length of time with the company, and the store where an employee worked. *Id.*, at 159. The results, the District Court found, were sufficient to raise an "inference of discrimination."

C

The District Court's identification of a common question, whether Wal-Mart's pay and promotions policies gave rise to unlawful discrimination, was hardly infirm. The practice of delegating to supervisors large discretion to make personnel decisions, uncontrolled by formal standards, has long been known to have the potential to produce disparate effects. Managers, like all humankind, may be prey to biases of which they are unaware.[6] The risk of discrimination is heightened when those managers are predominantly of one sex, and are steeped in a corporate culture that perpetuates gender stereotypes.

[Justice Ginsburg here offers an account of the impact of discretionary management decisions and stereotype on gender parity in the workplace.]

. . .

The plaintiffs' allegations state claims of gender discrimination in the form of biased decision making in both pay and promotions. The evidence reviewed by the District Court adequately demonstrated that resolving those claims would necessitate examination of particular policies and practices alleged to affect, adversely and globally, women employed at Wal-Mart's stores. Rule 23(a)(2), setting a necessary but not a sufficient criterion for class-action certification, demands nothing further.

II

A

The Court gives no credence to the key dispute common to the class: whether Wal-Mart's discretionary pay and promotion policies are discriminatory. See *ante*, at 2551 ("Reciting" questions like "Is [giving managers discretion over pay] an unlawful employment practice?" "is not sufficient to obtain class certification."). "What matters," the Court asserts, "is not the raising of common 'questions,'" but whether there are "[d]issimilarities within the proposed class" that "have the potential to impede the generation of common answers." *Ante*, at 2551 (quoting Nagareda, Class Certification in the Age of Aggregate Proof, 84 N.Y.U. L. Rev. 97, 132 (2009); some internal quotation marks omitted).

---

6. An example vividly illustrates how subjective decision making can be a vehicle for discrimination. Performing in symphony orchestras was long a male preserve. Goldin and Rouse, Orchestrating Impartiality: The Impact of "Blind" Auditions on Female Musicians, 90 Am. Econ. Rev. 715, 715–716 (2000). In the 1970's orchestras began hiring musicians through auditions open to all comers. *Id.*, at 716. Reviewers were to judge applicants solely on their musical abilities, yet subconscious bias led some reviewers to disfavor women. Orchestras that permitted reviewers to see the applicants hired far fewer female musicians than orchestras that conducted blind auditions, in which candidates played behind opaque screens. *Id.*, at 738.

The Court blends Rule 23(a)(2)'s threshold criterion with the more demanding criteria of Rule 23(b)(3), and thereby elevates the (a)(2) inquiry so that it is no longer "easily satisfied," 5 J. Moore et al., Moore's Federal Practice §23.23[2], p. 23-72 (3d ed. 2011). Rule 23(b)(3) certification requires, in addition to the four 23(a) findings, determinations that "questions of law or fact common to class members predominate over any questions affecting only individual members" and that "a class action is superior to other available methods for . . . adjudicating the controversy."

The Court's emphasis on differences between class members mimics the Rule 23(b)(3) inquiry into whether common questions "predominate" over individual issues. And by asking whether the individual differences "impede" common adjudication, *ante*, at 2551-2552 (internal quotation marks omitted), the Court duplicates 23(b)(3)'s question whether "a class action is superior" to other modes of adjudication. Indeed, Professor Nagareda, whose "dissimilarities" inquiry the Court endorses, developed his position in the context of Rule 23(b)(3). See 84 N.Y.U. L. Rev., at 131 (Rule 23(b)(3) requires "some decisive degree of similarity across the proposed class" because it "speaks of common 'questions' that 'predominate' over individual ones"). "The Rule 23(b)(3) predominance inquiry" is meant to "tes[t] whether proposed classes are sufficiently cohesive to warrant adjudication by representation." *Amchem Products, Inc. v. Windsor,* 521 U.S. 591, 623, 117 S. Ct. 2231, 138 L. Ed. 2d 689 (1997). If courts must conduct a "dissimilarities" analysis at the Rule 23(a)(2) stage, no mission remains for Rule 23(b)(3).

Because Rule 23(a) is also a prerequisite for Rule 23(b)(1) and Rule 23(b)(2) classes, the Court's "dissimilarities" position is far reaching. Individual differences should not bar a Rule 23(b)(1) or Rule 23(b)(2) class, so long as the Rule 23(a) threshold is met. See *Amchem Products,* 521 U.S., at 623, n. 19, 117 S. Ct. 2231 (Rule 23(b)(1)(B) "does not have a predominance requirement"); *Yamasaki,* 442 U.S., at 701, 99 S. Ct. 2545 (Rule 23(b)(2) action in which the Court noted that "[i]t is unlikely that differences in the factual background of each claim will affect the outcome of the legal issue"). For example, in *Franks v. Bowman Transp. Co.,* 424 U.S. 747, 96 S. Ct. 1251, 47 L. Ed. 2d 444 (1976), a Rule 23(b)(2) class of African-American truckdrivers complained that the defendant had discriminatorily refused to hire black applicants. We recognized that the "qualification[s] and performance" of individual class members might vary. *Id.,* at 772, 96 S. Ct. 1251 (internal quotation marks omitted). "Generalizations concerning such individually applicable evidence," we cautioned, "cannot serve as a justification for the denial of [injunctive] relief to the entire class." *Ibid.*

B

The "dissimilarities" approach leads the Court to train its attention on what distinguishes individual class members, rather than on what unites them. Given the lack of standards for pay and promotions, the majority says, "demonstrating the invalidity of one manager's use of discretion will do nothing to demonstrate the invalidity of another's."

Wal-Mart's delegation of discretion over pay and promotions is a policy uniform throughout all stores. The very nature of discretion is that people will exercise it in various ways. A system of delegated discretion, *Watson* held, is a practice actionable under Title VII when it produces discriminatory outcomes. 487 U.S., at 990–991, 108 S. Ct. 2777; see *supra*, at 2564–2565. A finding that Wal-Mart's pay and promotions practices in fact violate the law would be the first step in the usual order of proof for plaintiffs seeking individual remedies for company-wide discrimination. *Teamsters v. United States*, 431 U.S. 324, 359, 97 S. Ct. 1843, 52 L. Ed. 2d 396 (1977); see *Albemarle Paper Co. v. Moody*, 422 U.S. 405, 415–423, 95 S. Ct. 2362, 45 L. Ed. 2d 280 (1975). That each individual employee's unique circumstances will ultimately determine whether she is entitled to backpay or damages, §2000e-5(g)(2)(A) (barring backpay if a plaintiff "was refused . . . advancement . . . for any reason other than discrimination"), should not factor into the Rule 23(a)(2) determination.

. . .

The Court errs in importing a "dissimilarities" notion suited to Rule 23(b)(3) into the Rule 23(a) commonality inquiry. I therefore cannot join Part II of the Court's opinion.

NOTES AND QUESTIONS

1. The *Dukes* majority addressed two major class action issues in its opinion decertifying the class action against Wal-Mart. The first relates to the issue of commonality, a requirement of Rule 23(a) that must be satisfied in every class proceeding. On this issue, the Court was split: Four Justices disagreed with the majority's analysis and would not have reached the issue at all. The second issue relates to the prong of Rule 23(b) under which the plaintiffs had attempted to proceed. On that issue, the Court was unanimous: All of the Justices agreed that a class action that primarily seeks monetary damages (here, back pay awards) cannot proceed under Rule 23(b)(2). We examine those issues closely below, in reverse order. Before doing so, however, it is important to understand the background against which they appear.

The *Dukes* case arose in a context—a claim of workplace discrimination under the federal Civil Rights Act of 1964—for which the Rule 23 class action has long been recognized as an important enforcement tool. At the start of his analysis, Justice Scalia correctly points out that the case against Wal-Mart was an employment action of unprecedented size and scope, raising questions about whether the *Dukes* plaintiffs had attempted to accomplish too much in a single proceeding. The inclusion of damages claims made this particular Title VII case a tough candidate for a class action. But, as a general matter, Rule 23 is often an appropriate vehicle for asserting employment discrimination claims on a classwide basis. In fact, the 1966 revisions to Rule 23, which continue to form the basis for modern class action practice, were drafted with the enforcement of the Civil Rights Act in mind. So what was it about this employment discrimination class action that made it inappropriate for class treatment?

2. *The Prongs of Rule 23(b).* The more straightforward answer to that question relates to the second issue identified above: the prong of Rule 23(b) under which the plaintiffs sought to proceed. As you now know, in order to proceed as a class

action under Rule 23, a putative class representative must satisfy two sets of requirements: all the prongs of Rule 23(a) (numerosity, commonality, typicality, adequacy
of representation), and one of the prongs of Rule 23(b). Rule 23(b)(1) is available
when a class action will eliminate the risk of inconsistent adjudications among class
members (under subsection A) or where the resolution of one person's claim would
effectively dispose of other people's claims (under subsection B). Rule 23(b)(2) is for
actions seeking an injunction, a declaration, or similar equitable relief. And Rule
23(b)(3) permits a class action for any other type of claim—typically claims for
damages—but only when the plaintiff can show that "questions of law or fact common to the class predominate" over individual issues (the "predominance" requirement) and that "a class action is superior to other available methods for fairly and
adequately adjudicating the controversy" (the "superiority" requirement).

The reasons a plaintiff—or, more accurately, plaintiff's counsel—will often
want to proceed under Rule 23(b)(1) or (b)(2) rather than 23(b)(3) are straightforward. The predominance and superiority requirements can be difficult to satisfy, creating the possibility that a class action will be wholly unavailable if it must
proceed under (b)(3). And, as the Supreme Court held in *Eisen*, Rule 23 imposes
a mandatory requirement of individual notice to every class member following
certification of a (b)(3) class action, which can be expensive. A (b)(3) action also
requires that class members have the chance to opt out and pursue their own individual suits, a feature that may be unattractive to plaintiff's counsel who often want
to include as many class members as possible in the action and avoid the interference that competing actions can cause, and also to some defendants, who may want
to use a class action to purchase "total peace" through settlement, a goal that could
be frustrated by opt-out class members.

Rule 23(b)(2), by its terms, appears to be available only for cases where the
plaintiffs are requesting injunctive or declaratory relief—and, by implication,
where they are requesting an injunction or declaration that will apply to all class
members in the same way. Consistent with that language, the Court holds in *Dukes*
that Rule 23(b)(2) "applies only when a single injunction or declaratory judgment
would provide relief to each member of the class. It does not authorize class certification when each individual class member would be entitled to a *different* injunction or declaratory judgment against the defendant. Similarly, it does not authorize
class certification when each class member would be entitled to an individualized
award of monetary damages." In *Dukes* itself, the class plaintiffs were requesting
injunctive relief that would have altered Wal-Mart's personnel policies on a companywide basis (the type of relief for which a (b)(2) action is designed), but they
were also requesting awards of individual back pay that would have entailed individual calculations and the potential for adjudication of individual defenses for
every member of the class. This more atomized type of claim—which, the Court
held, would require individual determinations of relief for each class member—
precluded certification of the class under Rule 23(b)(2).

The *Dukes* Court flagged but did not resolve the question whether a class seeking monetary damages in addition to an injunction or declaration could ever be
certified under Rule 23(b)(2). This is an issue with which lower federal courts have
wrestled for years. Following language contained in the Advisory Committee note
that accompanied the 1966 revisions to Rule 23, some Courts of Appeals (including

the Ninth Circuit in *Dukes*) have concluded that individual damages claims could be certified as part of a 23(b)(2) class action so long as they were only "incidental" to an overarching claim for injunctive relief. (In a somewhat confusing use of terminology, which we have edited out of the case, lower courts sometimes describe such cases by saying that the request for injunctive relief "predominates" over the claims for damages. This issue is wholly separate from the "predominance" requirement of Rule 23(b)(3).) *Dukes* does not reach this question, holding instead that, even assuming it to be permissible to include damages claims that are merely "incidental" to a (b)(2) class seeking injunctive relief, the damages claims in this case clearly fail that requirement.

Why did the Court conclude that the claims for back pay in this sex discrimination case against Wal-Mart were not "incidental" and hence could not be included in a (b)(2) class action? The plaintiffs were seeking an overarching injunction that would require Wal-Mart to alter a core personnel policy throughout the entire company. If female employees also believed that they were owed back pay because of discrimination they suffered under that very personnel policy, why were those damages claims not "incidental" to the injunctive relief? In answering that question, look carefully at the Court's description of the claims for back pay that the plaintiffs were asserting on behalf of the class. Were those claims individual in nature — would they vary in amount and possible defenses depending upon the circumstances of each class member — or were they all merely derivative of a central, uniform injunction? The Court concluded that the former was the case. Make sure you understand why.

3. *Commonality and Rule 23(a)*. Having concluded that the class could not proceed under Rule 23(b)(2), the Court could simply have reversed and sent the case back for the lower courts to consider whether certification might be appropriate under Rule 23(b)(3), the more frequently employed tool for damages class actions. That was the course that Justice Ginsburg's four-Justice opinion urged upon the majority. Instead, the majority reached out to decide another issue with implications that could be far-reaching: the requirement of commonality under Rule 23(a).

Recall that every class action must satisfy all the requirements of Rule 23(a), and also fit into one of the prongs of Rule 23(b), in order to be certified. The requirement of commonality has not generally been considered a demanding one. Rule 23(a) demands only that there be "questions of law or fact common to the class" — seemingly, any common questions that are material to the case. And indeed, courts and commentators have long agreed, and the *Dukes* Court reaffirmed, that even a single issue of law or fact that is common to the entire class can satisfy the commonality requirement. When a class action that also raises other, highly individualized issues proceeds under Rule 23(b)(3), the requirement of predominance will do the work in limiting which actions can be certified. Thus, building upon the discussion of Rule 23(b)(2) above, there have generally been two gatekeepers preventing plaintiffs from certifying a class of damages claims that contain too many individualized issues for aggregate treatment: the requirements of §§(b)(1) or (b)(2), which prevent many class actions from proceeding under those prongs at all; and the requirement of predominance in a (b)(3) action, which will prevent certification of an action dominated by individual issues.

In *Dukes*, the plaintiffs claimed that the common issue that tied together all members of the class was a core, companywide personnel policy that left hiring and promotion decisions to the discretion of store-level managers, resulting in widespread discrimination against female employees in violation of Title VII of the Civil Rights Act. Other, more individual issues might also have arisen when the plaintiffs tried to secure the back pay they thought they were owed—a dispute over whether a given employee was actually harmed by the discriminatory policy, or defenses that the company might be able to assert against a given employee's claim—and the plaintiffs had various arguments about how those individual issues could be dealt with. But the requirement of commonality, plaintiffs asserted, was satisfied by the company's core, companywide personnel policy.

The majority disagreed, finding that the proposed class action failed to satisfy the basic Rule 23(a) requirement of commonality. This holding was in part based on inadequacies that the majority identified in the evidence that the *Dukes* plaintiffs offered in trying to establish a companywide effect. The plaintiffs relied largely upon statistical evidence regarding the discriminatory impact of Wal-Mart's core policy, and the majority held that evidence to be insufficient in both quality and weight. We have largely edited out that discussion, as it bears upon matters relating to the substance of a Title VII claim and different forms of statistical proof (though we address one component of the evidence question below).

But the majority did not rest its commonality ruling solely on these evidentiary problems. Rather, it explained:

> There is another, more fundamental, respect in which respondents' statistical proof fails. Even if it established (as it does not) a pay or promotion pattern that differs from the nationwide figures or the regional figures in *all* of Wal-Mart's 3,400 stores, that would still not demonstrate that commonality of issue exists. Some managers will claim that the availability of women, or qualified women, or interested women, in their stores' area does not mirror the national or regional statistics. And almost all of them will claim to have been applying some sex-neutral, performance-based criteria—whose nature and effects will differ from store to store. In the landmark case of ours which held that giving discretion to lower-level supervisors can be the basis of Title VII liability under a disparate-impact theory, the plurality opinion *conditioned* that holding on the corollary that merely proving that the discretionary system has produced a racial or sexual disparity *is not enough*. "[T]he plaintiff must begin by identifying the specific employment practice that is challenged." *Watson*, 487 U.S., at 994, 108 S. Ct. 2777; accord, *Wards Cove Packing Co. v. Atonio*, 490 U.S. 642, 656, 109 S. Ct. 2115, 104 L. Ed. 2d 733 (1989) (approving that statement), superseded by statute on other grounds, 42 U.S.C. §2000e–2(k). That is all the more necessary when a class of plaintiffs is sought to be certified. Other than the bare existence of delegated discretion, respondents have identified no "specific employment practice"—much less one that ties all their 1.5 million claims together. Merely showing that Wal-Mart's policy of discretion has produced an overall sex-based disparity does not suffice.

Dukes, 564 U.S. at 357. The majority went on to explain that a court must focus on the "dissimilarities" that exist within the overall claims of class members in deciding whether the commonality requirement has been satisfied—a proposition that Justice Ginsburg and her fellow dissenters sharply criticize.

The point of difference between the majority and the dissent relates to the nature of the "issue" that a plaintiff must establish as "common" in order to satisfy Rule 23(a). There was no question in *Dukes* that Wal-Mart had a companywide policy of reposing significant discretion in store managers. The parties disagreed about whether this policy had a discriminatory impact upon female employees. According to the plaintiffs, it was enough for them to show that there was a common companywide policy that had a recognized tendency to produce sex discrimination. According to the defendant, in contrast, commonality would not be satisfied unless the plaintiffs could show that there were "specific employment practice[s]" common to all plaintiffs, on top of the companywide policy of reposing discretion in low-level supervisors, that had produced a discriminatory impact. Thus, the majority held, even though there was admittedly a companywide policy of low-level supervisor discretion, and even if plaintiffs could show a companywide impact on female employees, "[m]erely showing that Wal-Mart's policy of discretion has produced an overall sex-based disparity does not suffice" to satisfy the commonality requirement that is the prerequisite to any type of class treatment whatsoever.

To put this part of the holding in concrete terms, imagine if the plaintiffs had only asked for an injunction requiring Wal-Mart to cease its policy of low-level discretion because of the tendency of that policy to produce sex discrimination—no claims for back pay, no request for damages, just an injunction requiring a change in the companywide policy. That would have been precisely the type of class action that section (b)(2) was designed for—the problems addressed in the second part of the Court's holding would never have arisen. But the first part of the Court's holding, finding no commonality under Rule 23(a), means that this action to enjoin a discriminatory policy still could not be certified. According to the majority, even when the problems raised by individual damages claims are taken out of the equation, this action still cannot satisfy the bare requirement of commonality because "[m]erely showing that Wal-Mart's policy of discretion has produced an overall sex-based disparity does not suffice" to satisfy the commonality requirement.

Is the Court guilty of conflating the merits of the claim with the requirements for certification? If Wal-Mart had a companywide policy of low-level supervisor discretion that controlled the workplace circumstances of all class members, and that policy produced "an overall sex-based disparity" throughout the company, then it sounds like there are important "questions of law or fact common to the class." Those circumstances, by themselves, may not warrant relief under Title VII. But if that is so, isn't the proper course to certify the class, at least with respect to the request for injunctive relief, and then rule against the plaintiffs on the merits of their claims if they are unable to produce additional support?

It remains to be seen how broadly the Supreme Court and lower federal courts will interpret this part of the *Dukes* ruling in future cases. It is possible that the impact of the Court's analysis will be confined largely to Title VII cases, with *Dukes*'s fine-grained reading of commonality limited to the particular features of a disparate impact claim. But the majority does not indicate that its ruling should be so confined. Rather, as the dissent suggests, the majority appears to be taking a type of analysis previously characteristic of the "predominance" requirement under Rule 23(b)(3)—asking whether dissimilarities in the individual circumstances of class members outweigh or overwhelm the common circumstances that they share—and applying that analysis to Rule 23(a) commonality, which serves as a threshold requirement for all class actions, including those filed under Rules 23(b)(1) and (2), which have no predominance requirement and are often seeking purely injunctive relief. If future courts read this part of the *Dukes* ruling broadly, the decision may lead them to place substantial limitations on the types of class proceedings that can be certified under any of Rule 23's provisions.

4. *Evidentiary Requirements for Class Certification.* Two issues have long been clear in the doctrine of class certification. First, a plaintiff cannot secure class certification merely by asserting in her pleadings that the requirements of Rule 23 (numerosity, commonality, typicality, adequacy, and one prong of Rule 23(b)) are satisfied. The class certification hearing requires some kind of evidentiary showing. Second, a plaintiff cannot be required to prove her whole case at the certification stage. The class certification hearing is designed to determine whether it is appropriate for the case to proceed on a classwide basis, not whether the plaintiffs will prevail. A significant amount of space exists between those two poles, however, and the lower federal courts have disagreed sharply about the nature of the evidentiary burden that a plaintiff must satisfy at the certification hearing in order to proceed as a class.

Wal-Mart v. Dukes took a significant step toward raising the evidentiary bar for certification. Drawing upon language found in earlier opinions but giving that language new emphasis, the Court held that a plaintiff seeking certification must "affirmatively demonstrate" at the hearing that she can satisfy the requirements of Rule 23 under the scrutiny of a "rigorous analysis." The Court articulates this new standard in the following passage:

> Rule 23 does not set forth a mere pleading standard. A party seeking class certification must affirmatively demonstrate his compliance with the Rule—that is, he must be prepared to prove that there are *in fact* sufficiently numerous parties, common questions of law or fact, etc. We recognized in *Falcon* that "sometimes it may be necessary for the court to probe behind the pleadings before coming to rest on the certification question," 457 U.S., at 160, 102 S. Ct. 2364, and that certification is proper only if "the trial court is satisfied, after a rigorous analysis, that the prerequisites of Rule 23(a) have been satisfied," *id.*, at 161, 102 S. Ct. 2364; see *id.*, at 160, 102 S. Ct. 2364 ("[A]ctual, not presumed, conformance with Rule 23(a) remains . . . indispensable"). Frequently that "rigorous analysis" will entail some overlap with the merits of the plaintiff's underlying claim. That cannot be helped. "'[T]he class determination generally involves considerations that are enmeshed in the factual and legal issues comprising the plaintiff's cause of action.'"

Wal-Mart itself is one of those cases in which the certification analysis entailed significant overlap with the merits of the plaintiff's claims. In portions of the opinion that we have largely edited out, the Court conducts an analysis of the evidence and expert testimony that the plaintiffs submitted at certification concerning the nature of the disparities that Wal-Mart's policy of store-level discretion allegedly imposed upon female employees. In finding that evidence insufficient to warrant certification, the Court focuses primarily on issues that also go to the merits of the plaintiffs' claims.

In a series of subsequent rulings, the Supreme Court has further specified the methods and requirements of proof at the certification stage. The first, *Amgen, Inc. v. Connecticut Retirement Plans and Trust Funds*, 568 U.S. 455 (2013), rejected an argument that a securities plaintiff seeking class certification needed to prove certain facts bearing on the merits of its claims. The case involved claims under the federal securities laws in which the plaintiff retirement fund sought to represent a class of investors under Rule 23(b)(3), claiming that defendant Amgen had made public statements that were fraudulent and had misled investors. Plaintiff was relying on the well-established "fraud on the market" theory to argue that an efficient market for securities will internalize all publicly available information, meaning that investors need not prove individual reliance on fraudulent public statements in order to recover. Amgen acknowledged this theory but argued that its allegedly fraudulent statements were not material. Immaterial statements do not impact stock price, so a finding that the statements were not material would defeat liability, typically an argument for the merits stage of a lawsuit. Amgen argued that the plaintiff needed to establish materiality at the certification stage in order to demonstrate that the liability question was common to all class members and hence that common questions predominate in the action.

Affirming a ruling of the Ninth Circuit, the Court rejected this argument and ruled that the resolution of the materiality question could not be made a prerequisite for certification.

> Rule 23(b)(3) requires a showing that *questions* common to the class predominate, not that those questions will be answered, on the merits, in favor of the class. Because materiality is judged according to an objective standard, the materiality of Amgen's alleged misrepresentations and omissions is a question common to all members of the class Connecticut Retirement would represent. The alleged misrepresentations and omissions, whether material or immaterial, would be so equally for all investors composing the class. As vital, the plaintiff class's inability to prove materiality would not result in individual questions predominating. Instead, a failure of proof on the issue of materiality would end the case, given that materiality is an essential element of the class members' securities-fraud claims. As to materiality, therefore, the class is entirely cohesive: It will prevail or fail in unison. In no event will the individual circumstances of particular class members bear on the inquiry.

Id. at 459–460. Amgen had attempted to capitalize on the Court's statement in *Dukes* that "Rule 23 does not set forth a mere pleading standard" and that the plaintiff must satisfy a "rigorous" standard of proof that may "entail some overlap with the merits of the plaintiff's underlying claim." *Dukes*, 564 U.S. at 351. The *Amgen* Court reaffirmed that proposition but also emphasized its limitations: "Merits questions may be considered to the extent—but only to the extent—that they are relevant to determining whether the Rule 23 prerequisites for class certification are satisfied." *Amgen*, 568 U.S. at 466. If a question relating to the merits of plaintiff's claims must also be answered in order to determine whether class certification is appropriate in the first place, then the plaintiff must present evidence at the certification hearing and satisfy a rigorous standard of proof. Here, however, the district court could determine from the pleadings that the materiality question was common to the entire class because the plaintiffs' claims all related to the same allegedly fraudulent statements. If plaintiff proved materiality, it would establish the element of reliance for all investors; if it failed to prove materiality, then all investors would lose on the merits. The question was common on its face, and plaintiff could not be required to prove materiality as a prerequisite for certification.

In *Comcast Corp. v. Behrend*, 569 U.S. 27 (2013), in contrast, the Court found that several questions relating to the merits did need to be resolved prior to certification. *Behrend* was an antitrust dispute involving allegations of anti-competitive behavior in the cable industry. Through various abuses of market power, the plaintiffs alleged, Comcast had kept the prices for its cable services at above-market levels. Plaintiffs sought certification of a class of Comcast customers in the affected region during the relevant time period, asserting as damages the difference between what customers actually paid and the lower prices they allegedly would have paid in the absence of defendant's conduct. In order to establish liability under the federal antitrust laws, a plaintiff must demonstrate "antitrust impact" (harm to the customer resulting from anti-competitive behavior), and a plaintiff seeking certification of a class must show that antitrust impact can be proven on a classwide basis. At issue in *Behrend* was the standard of proof that the plaintiff must satisfy for antitrust impact at the certification stage.

The plaintiffs alleged four types of improper behavior by defendant in their complaint, but at the certification stage, they relied on only one of those theories in seeking to establish classwide antitrust injury: an improper practice called "overbuilding." Nonetheless, the expert report that plaintiffs submitted as proof that antitrust injury was a common issue framed its analysis with the assumption that consumers were injured in all four of the ways that had initially been alleged in the complaint. Defendants thus argued that the report failed to establish that antitrust injury could be proven on a classwide basis solely under the plaintiffs' theory of overbuilding, because the report failed to isolate that theory and show classwide impact on that ground alone. Defendants also sought to introduce rebuttal evidence affirmatively demonstrating that damages from overbuilding could not be proven on a common basis. The lower federal courts rejected these arguments and certified the class under Rule 23(b)(3). In a 5-4 opinion, the Supreme Court reversed.

Much of the debate between the majority and the dissent in *Behrend* centers on questions of substantive antitrust law that go beyond the scope of this course. For our purposes, *Behrend* is significant in two respects. First, the majority strictly applies the requirement from *Dukes* that plaintiffs must affirmatively demonstrate compliance with Rule 23, finding error when the lower federal courts failed to demand that plaintiffs offer proof of classwide antitrust injury specifically tied to the overbuilding theory. "There is no question," the Court held, "that the [expert's] model failed to measure damages resulting from the particular antitrust injury on which petitioners' liability in this action is premised." *Id.* at 36. Second, the Court criticized the district court for "refusing to entertain arguments against respondents' damages model that bore on the propriety of class certification, simply because those arguments would also be pertinent to the merits determination." *Id.* at 28. A district court must entertain such arguments regardless of their overlap with the merits, the Court explained, where doing so is necessary to determine whether the requirements of Rule 23 have been satisfied.

The most recent of the cases addressing standards of proof at the certification stage is *Tyson Foods v. Bouaphakeo*, 577 U.S. 442 (2016), a dispute involving a company's failure to pay overtime to its workers in violation of the Fair Labor Standards Act. Tyson Foods employed hourly workers at a pork processing plant but did not pay them overtime for the time they had to spend every day putting on and taking off safety gear and walking to and from their posts. The case was certified as a class and went to trial, producing a jury verdict in favor of the plaintiffs. On appeal, Tyson argued that the class should never have been certified because, they argued, the plaintiffs were not able to prove their membership in the class or their damages on a common basis (in large part because Tyson itself did not keep detailed time sheets). According to Tyson, this meant that common questions did not predominate over individual issues. *See* Fed. R. Civ. Proc. 23(b)(3). In order to resolve the dispute, the Court had to answer questions about the burden of proof under the FLSA where an employer fails to keep detailed time sheets and the role of expert testimony and statistical evidence in the certification process. In *Dukes*, the Court had rejected the plaintiffs' attempt to use statistical evidence to establish commonality and predominance in the particular Title VII claim before it. Tyson sought to expand the holding in *Dukes* into a general rejection of statistical evidence at the certification stage.

In a 6-2 ruling, the Court rejected Tyson's arguments. On the question of using statistical evidence in the certification process, the Court explained that "[w]hether and when statistical evidence can be used to establish classwide liability will depend on the purpose for which the evidence is being introduced and on 'the elements of the underlying cause of action.'" *Id.* at 455 (quoting *Erica P. John Fund v. Halliburton Co.*, 563 U.S. 804, 809 (2011)). As with any form of evidence, the Court explained, the permissibility of statistical proof "turns not on the form a proceeding takes—be it a class or individual action—but on the degree to which evidence is reliable in proving or disproving the elements of the relevant cause of action." *Id.* Tyson failed to show that statistical proof would be improper in an individual action under the FLSA. Therefore, the Court held, it failed to show that such proof was improper in a class proceeding.

A thread runs through all these cases. In each, the standard for satisfying the requirements of Rule 23 is closely tied to the substantive theory of liability underlying the dispute—Title VII in *Wal-Mart*, federal securities law in *Amgen*, federal antitrust law in *Behrend*, and the Fair Labor Standards Act in *Tyson Foods*. As Professor Wolff has explained, there is a necessary interplay between the requirements of Rule 23 and the substantive standards against which the underlying claims are measured, and it is important to identify when class action precedents speak to the former issue and when they speak to the latter. *See* Tobias Barrington Wolff, *Managerial Judging and Substantive Law*, 90 Wash. U. L. Rev. 1027 (2013). Do these three cases suggest that the Court's ruling on commonality in *Wal-Mart v. Dukes* had more to do with the substantive requirements of the Civil Rights Act of 1964 and less to do with Rule 23? Professor Wolff made that argument shortly after the case was decided: "The Court's discussion of the commonality issue in *Dukes* is grounded in Title VII policy and speaks primarily to the federal common law of disparate impact remedies under the Civil Rights Act of 1964." Wolff, *supra*, at 1034. *See also McReynolds v. Merrill Lynch, Pierce, Fenner & Smith*, 672 F.3d 482, 487-489 (7th Cir. 2012) (characterizing *Wal-Mart* as "an important development in the law governing class certification in employment discrimination cases" and giving a narrow construction to its holding regarding certification and discretionary employment policies).

5. *Class Certification and the "Fraud on the Market" Theory.* In another post-*Dukes* case, *Halliburton Co. v. Erica P. John Fund*, 573 U.S. 258 (2014) [*Halliburton II*], the Court provided further guidance about the evidentiary standards associated with the "fraud on the market" in securities actions. That doctrine is the product of a federal common law ruling, *see Basic Inc. v. Levinson*, 485 U.S. 224 (1988), and one question presented in *Halliburton II* was whether the Court should overrule that doctrine. The Court declined to do so, which left it with a class action issue: whether a defendant can argue at the class certification stage that the prerequisites of the *Basic* presumption are not satisfied, or whether instead the defendant can challenge the *Basic* presumption only at the merits phase of the lawsuit, after the court has granted certification.

The Court found that defendants are entitled to challenge the *Basic* presumption in the certification hearing, insofar as the grounds for their challenge goes to the suitability of the lawsuit for class treatment. More precisely, the Court found that a defendant could introduce evidence at the certification hearing that would rebut the *Basic* presumption of an efficient market and thereby show that class certification would be improper because plaintiffs would have to prove individual reliance at the merits phase of the lawsuit. In so holding, the Court distinguished its earlier ruling in *Amgen*, where it had found it improper to force plaintiffs to prove "an objective issue susceptible to common, classwide proof" during the certification hearing. The plaintiff's obligation at the certification stage is only to show that her claim is amenable to classwide proof, not that she will prevail on the merits. In *Halliburton II*, however, the defendant sought to introduce evidence demonstrating that class certification was not appropriate at all. If the *Basic* presumption did not apply, defendant argued, certification would fail because the element of reliance was not "an objective issue susceptible to common, classwide proof" without that presumption. The burden remained on the defendant to rebut the *Basic* presumption to defeat certification. *Halliburton II* thus appears to represent a modest extension of a proposition that the Court set forth in *Dukes*. Although a plaintiff cannot be forced to prove the merits of her claim in order to certify a class, she does need to establish through "rigorous analysis" that her claims can be proven on a classwide basis and hence that class certification is proper. In *Dukes*, the Court made clear that such analysis frequently "will entail some overlap with the merits of the plaintiff's underlying claim." In *Halliburton II*, the Court found this principle to require that defendant have an opportunity to rebut the presumption of an efficient market if the amenability of the claims to classwide treatment depends on that presumption.

5.   *The Role of Attorneys' Fees in Class Actions — Who Pays?*

Wal-Mart and *Eisen* illustrate the economic motivation for collective action through a class suit. In the case of *Eisen*, it would make no economic sense for a single odd-lot investor (or even several investors) to pay the costs of a lawyer to bring an individual lawsuit, nor would any attorney take such a case on a contingent fee because the recovery would be too small. And in the case of *Wal-Mart*, even if some aggrieved employees had claims that might warrant individual litigation even taking into account the costs—*positive-value claims*, as opposed to the *negative-value claims* at issue in *Eisen*—the ability to aggregate many such claims together places much more power and leverage in the hands of plaintiff's counsel. How does the financial incentive for the attorney change if the action proceeds as a class suit? How is the lawyer in a class action compensated? Is the financial incentive adequate? Or is it too great?

a. The Source of the Fee

The fee arrangement between attorney and client in a class suit is quite different than in an individual litigation. In traditional litigation, the attorney and the client usually negotiate the fee. While there are some limitations on these individual arrangements—both legal and ethical—those limitations come into play only rarely, and it is the exceptional case in which the court must concern itself with the fee that a lawyer charges her client. The situation in a class action is very different. The attorneys in a class action may never have any communication with the vast majority of the class members whom they purport to represent; indeed, the attorneys may not even know in any but the most general terms who those absent class members are. And even in those cases where a plaintiff's attorney knows the identity of all the members of the class, it usually would be prohibitively difficult to negotiate fee arrangements with so many individuals.

At the same time, attorneys' fees are often the driving force behind a class action. The contingency fee, which we discussed in Chapter 1, underlies much class litigation; and because damages for the class may be quite large, the incentive for lawyers to bring class suits is high. However, it is generally the case that the court itself must determine, or approve, the fees that plaintiffs' counsel will receive in a federal class action. In a typical class action for money damages—one that proceeds under Rule 23 and involves no other special statutory considerations—the fee that is paid to plaintiffs' counsel comes from the pot of money that counsel has recovered on behalf of the class. If the class action proceeds to a judgment for money damages, the court determines this payment itself, under the "common-fund" doctrine. The common-fund doctrine is a creature of the court's historic equity powers and rests on the theory that, where class counsel has obtained a benefit on behalf of an entire class, it would unjustly enrich the class members if they were able to enjoy that benefit without paying for class counsel's efforts. *See, e.g., Boeing Co. v. Van Gehmert*, 444 U.S. 472, 478–479 (1980) (explaining origins of common-fund doctrine). A plaintiff's lawyer who succeeds in obtaining a recovery for the class may request that the court use its equitable powers to award her a portion of the common fund of damages in payment for her services to the class.

When a class action settles, Rule 23 even more directly governs the court's involvement. In a class action settlement, class counsel and defendants typically negotiate the terms of class counsel's payment as part of the settlement package. Rule 23(e) then requires that the parties obtain the approval of the court for the entire settlement, including the amount of compensation that class counsel will receive. Of course, in such a case, class counsel's payment basically still comes out of the "common fund" of the class recovery, since defendants presumably would be willing to pay the same total amount to settle the case even if all the money went directly to the class. Thus, whether a class action proceeds to judgment or settles, the court must still determine what it believes to be a fair and reasonable fee for class counsel, knowing that any money that counsel receives will come directly out of the class members' recovery.

It is important to note that there are some federal statutes with special provisions that govern the issue of attorneys' fees. Most notably, many civil rights statutes contain "fee-shifting" provisions that require defendants to pay directly for plaintiff's reasonable attorneys' fees, provided that plaintiff is a "prevailing party" in the case. *See, e.g.*, 42 U.S.C. §1988(b) (granting district court discretion to award attorneys' fees to prevailing plaintiff in federal civil rights case); 42 U.S.C. §12205 (same for Americans with Disabilities Act). In such a case, the compensation that plaintiff's counsel receives does not come out of plaintiff's recovery; rather, defendant is forced to pay those attorneys' fees on top of any monetary recovery (whether judgment or settlement) that plaintiffs win. In appropriate cases, these statutes can apply in the class action context as well as in individual litigation. We do not examine fee-shifting provisions at length here, but you should be aware that they exist, as they may have a dramatic impact on the economics of a lawsuit.

b. The Principal-Agent Problem

The interests and incentives affecting class counsel and the absent class members produce some interesting tensions in class litigation, particularly as regards settlements of class actions. In a settlement, class counsel may be able to negotiate a substantial fee, and from the perspective of counsel, settlement is likely to be an attractive option. Settlement of a class action means a significant reduction of time and expense for the lawyers involved. However, things may look very different from the perspective of the members of the class. A settlement offer that undervalues the claims of the class in proportion to the risk of going to trial is one that many class members might well reject if they were in control of their own, individual litigation. In a class action, however, the absent class members must depend heavily on class counsel to protect their interests. When the incentives for class counsel and the class are not aligned, there is a danger that the class will have its claims sold off through settlement at bargain-basement prices. The court, in its role as gatekeeper of settlements in general and attorneys' fees in particular, may be the only protection that absent class members have. *See generally* John C. Coffee, Jr., *Understanding the Plaintiff's Attorney: The Implications of Economic Theory for Private Enforcement of Law Through Class and Derivative Actions*, 86 Colum. L. Rev. 669 (1986). Indeed, this dynamic has led some commentators to conclude that a much more robust scheme of governance is needed in the litigation and settlement of class actions in order to ensure that the larger purposes of such proceedings are well served. *See, e.g.*, Alexandra Lahav, *Fundamental Principles for Class Action Governance*, 37 Ind. L. Rev. 65 (2003) (arguing for "a comprehensive model of governance based on four fundamental principles: mandatory disclosure, an actively adversarial process, expertise, and independence of decision-making" in small-claim class actions). As one of the authors of this casebook has emphasized, such managerial efforts must be attentive to the policies underlying the substantive law that governs a dispute as well as general class action policies. *See* Tobias Barrington Wolff, *Managerial Judging and Substantive Law*, 90 Wash. U. L. Rev. 1027 (2013).

For further reading on the subject of the role attorneys' fees play in class action litigation, *see* Judith Resnik, *Money Matters: Judicial Market Interventions Creating Subsidies and Awarding Fees and Costs in Individual and Aggregate Litigation*, 148 U. Pa. L. Rev. 2119 (2000) (examining significant role of judges in regulating market for attorney's services and calling for explicit recognition of that role in judicial decisions); Judith Resnik, Dennis E. Curtis & Deborah R. Hensler, *Individuals Within the Aggregate: Relationships, Representation, and Fees*, 71 N.Y.U. L. Rev. 296 (1996) (exploring use of regulation of attorneys' fees as means of structuring incentives in class action to enhance satisfaction of litigants); Peter H. Huang, *A New Options Theory for Risk Multipliers of Attorney's Fees in Federal Civil Rights Litigation*, 73 N.Y.U. L. Rev. 1943 (1998) (offering approach based on options speculation for awarding attorneys' fees in civil rights litigation); Bruce L. Hay, *The Theory of Fee Regulation in Class Action Settlements*, 46 Am. U. L. Rev. 1429 (1997) (arguing that incentive for class counsel to "sell out" absent class members for an inadequate settlement can be eliminated by regulating attorneys' fees).

6. Class Actions and Mass Torts

Is the vehicle of the class action appropriate for use by tort claimants against a defendant who distributes a product nationwide — such as asbestos, tobacco, or automobiles — and allegedly causes injury to thousands of people? What about the propriety of class action treatment for persons who are injured in a single accident, such as an airplane crash or hotel fire? One difference between these kinds of lawsuits and *Eisen* is the ability of an individual litigant to obtain representation; the stakes in the personal injury lawsuit are much more likely to justify individual representation. Individual damage issues will also tend to be more significant.

As the Advisory Committee Notes to the 1966 amendments to Rule 23 indicate, personal injury suits, at least in the "mass accident" context, were not contemplated when the Rule was revised in 1966:

> A "mass accident" resulting in injuries to numerous persons is ordinarily not appropriate for a class action because of the likelihood that significant questions, not only of damages but of liability and defenses to liability, would be present, affecting the individuals in different ways. In these circumstances an action conducted nominally as a class action would degenerate in practice into multiple lawsuits separately tried.

Of course, the "mass accident" case referred to in the Advisory Committee Note above is different from a nationwide class of product liability claimants. The "single event" tort has a finite number of litigants and can be handled by a series of multiple lawsuits as well as possible consolidation of some of them. Mass tort actions for alleged defects in nationally distributed products can sometimes appear almost infinite in scope and threaten to overwhelm the judicial system. Class treatment of such cases offers the possibility of a substantially more efficient method of adjudication. On the other hand, there is some fear that class treatment of mass torts will generate unnecessary assertion of claims, and there are serious questions about the possibility of satisfying Rule 23's requirements in litigating such claims.

What are the interests of the respective parties in having mass tort product liability cases certified as class actions? What benefits do you see for plaintiffs (and their attorneys) in bringing such claims as class suits? Will defendants always resist certification, or are there benefits to them as well? What about the interests of the judicial system? Are the answers to these questions different if the parties have negotiated a global settlement of their claims?

In the Matter of Bridgestone/Firestone Tires Products Liability Litigation (Bridgestone/Firestone I)

288 F.3d 1012 (7th Cir. 2002)

FRANK EASTERBROOK, Circuit Judge:

Firestone tires on Ford Explorer SUVs experienced an abnormally high failure rate during the late 1990s. In August 2000, while the National Highway Transportation Safety Administration was investigating, Firestone recalled and replaced some of those tires. Ford and Firestone replaced additional tires during 2001. Many suits have been filed as a result of injuries and deaths related to the tire failures. Other suits were filed by persons who own (or owned) Ford Explorers or Firestone tires that have so far performed properly; these persons seek compensation for the risk of failure, which may be reflected in diminished resale value of the vehicles and perhaps in mental stress. The Judicial Panel on Multidistrict Litigation transferred suits filed in, or removed to, federal court to the Southern District of Indiana for consolidated pretrial proceedings under 28 U.S.C. §1407(a). Once these have been completed, the cases must be returned to the originating districts for decision on the merits. See *Lexecon Inc. v. Milberg Weiss Bershad Hynes & Lerach*, 523 U.S. 26 (1998). In an effort to prevent retransfer, counsel representing many of the plaintiffs filed a new consolidated suit in Indianapolis and asked the judge to certify it as a nationwide class action, which would make all other suits redundant. The district court obliged and certified two nationwide classes: the first includes everyone who owns, owned, leases, or leased a Ford Explorer of model year 1991 through 2001 anytime before the first recall, and the second includes all owners and lessees from 1990 until today of Firestone ATX, ATX II, Firehawk ATX, ATX 23 Degree, Widetrack Radial Baja, or Wilderness tire models, or any other Firestone tire "substantially similar" to them. *In re Bridgestone/Firestone, Inc., Tires Products Liability Litigation*, 205 F.R.D. 503 (S.D. Ind. 2001); see also 155 F. Supp. 2d 1069 (S.D. Ind. 2001). More than 60 million tires and 3 million vehicles fit these definitions.

No class action is proper unless all litigants are governed by the same legal rules. Otherwise the class cannot satisfy the commonality and superiority requirements of Fed. R. Civ. P. 23(a), (b)(3). Yet state laws about theories such as those presented by our plaintiffs differ, and such differences have led us to hold that other warranty, fraud, or products-liability suits may not proceed as nationwide classes. . . . The district judge, well aware of this principle, recognized that uniform law would be essential to class certification. Because plaintiffs' claims rest on state law, the choice-of-law rules come from the state in which the federal court sits.

See *Klaxon v. Stentor Electric Manufacturing Co.*, 313 U.S. 487 (1941). The district judge concluded that Indiana law points to the headquarters of the defendants, because that is where the products are designed and the important decisions about disclosures and sales are made. Ford and Firestone engaged in conduct that was uniform across the nation, which the district court took to imply the appropriateness of uniform law. This ruling means that all claims by the Explorer class will be resolved under Michigan law and all claims by the tire class will be resolved under Tennessee law. According to the district court, other obstacles (such as the fact that the six named tire models represent 67 designs for different sizes and performance criteria, and that half of all 1996 and 1997 model Explorers came with Goodyear tires) are worth overcoming in light of the efficiency of class treatment. Nor did the district court deem it important that Firestone's tires were designed in Ohio, and many were manufactured outside Tennessee, as many of Ford's vehicles are manufactured outside Michigan.

Both Ford and Firestone petitioned for interlocutory review under Fed. R. Civ. P. 23(f). We granted these requests because . . . the suit is exceedingly unlikely to be tried. Aggregating millions of claims on account of multiple products manufactured and sold across more than ten years makes the case so unwieldy, and the stakes so large, that settlement becomes almost inevitable — and at a price that reflects the risk of a catastrophic judgment as much as, if not more than, the actual merit of the claims. Permitting appellate review before class certification can precipitate such a settlement is a principal function of Rule 23(f). Another function is permitting appellate review of important legal issues that otherwise might prove elusive. The district court's conclusion that one state's law would apply to claims by consumers throughout the country — not just those in Indiana, but also those in California, New Jersey, and Mississippi — is a novelty, and, if followed, would be of considerable import to other suits. Our review of this choice-of-law question is plenary, so we start there.

Indiana is a *lex loci delicti* state: in all but exceptional cases it applies the law of the place where harm occurred. Those class members who suffered injury or death as a result of defects were harmed in the states where the tires failed. As a practical matter, these class members can be ignored; they are sure to opt out and litigate independently. These classes therefore effectively include only those consumers whose loss (if any) is financial rather than physical: it is the class of persons whose tires did *not* fail, whose vehicles did *not* roll over. Many class members face no future threat of failure either, because about 30 million tires were recalled and replaced, while other tires have been used up and discarded. Financial loss (if any, a qualification we will not repeat) was suffered in the places where the vehicles and tires were purchased at excessive prices or resold at depressed prices. Those injuries occurred in all 50 states, the District of Columbia, Puerto Rico, and U.S. territories such as Guam. The *lex loci delicti* principle points to the places of these injuries, not the defendants' corporate headquarters, as the source of law. . . .

Because these claims must be adjudicated under the law of so many jurisdictions, a single nationwide class is not manageable. Lest we soon see a Rule 23(f) petition to review the certification of 50 state classes, we add that this litigation is not manageable as a class action even on a statewide basis. About 20% of the Ford Explorers were shipped without Firestone tires. The Firestone tires supplied with the majority of the vehicles were recalled at different times;[2] they may well have differed in their propensity to fail, and this would require sub-subclassing among those owners of Ford Explorers with Firestone tires. Some of the vehicles were resold and others have not been; the resales may have reflected different discounts that could require vehicle-specific litigation. Plaintiffs contend that many of the failures occurred because Ford and Firestone advised the owners to underinflate their tires, leading them to overheat. Other factors also affect heating; the failure rate (and hence the discount) may have been higher in Arizona than in Alaska. Of those vehicles that have not yet been resold, some will be resold in the future (by which time the tire replacements may have alleviated or eliminated any discount) and some never will be resold. Owners who wring the last possible mile out of their vehicles receive everything they paid for and have claims that differ from owners who sold their Explorers to the second-hand market during the height of the publicity in 2000. Some owners drove their SUVs off the road over rugged terrain, while others never used the "sport" or "utility" features; these differences also affect resale prices.

Firestone's tires likewise exhibit variability; that's why fewer than half of those included in the tire class were recalled. The tire class includes many buyers who used Firestone tires on vehicles other than Ford Explorers, and who therefore were not advised to underinflate their tires. (Note that this description does not reflect any view of the merits; we are repeating rather than endorsing plaintiffs' contention that Ford counseled "underinflation.") The six trade names listed in the class certification order comprise 67 master tire specifications: "Firehawk ATX" tires, for example, come in multiple diameters, widths, and tread designs; their safety features and failure modes differ accordingly. Plaintiffs say that all 67 specifications had three particular shortcomings that led to excess failures. But whether a particular feature is required for safe operation depends on other attributes of the tires, and as these other attributes varied across the 67 master specifications it would not be possible to make a once-and-for-all decision about whether all 60 million tires were defective, even if the law were uniform. There are other differences too, but the ones we have mentioned preclude any finding "that the questions of law or fact common to the members of the class predominate over any questions affecting only individual members, and that a class action is superior to other available

---

2. On August 9, 2000, Firestone recalled its Radial ATX and Radial ATX II tires, but only in size P235/75R15, plus its Wilderness AT tires in size P235/75R15 (but only if they had been made in Decatur, Illinois). On January 2, 2001, Firestone recalled Wilderness LE tires, size P265/70R16, that had been manufactured the week of April 23, 2000, in Cuernavaca, Mexico. In February 2001 it recalled approximately 98,500 P205/55R16 Firehawk GTA-02 tires, most of which had been installed on Nissan Altima SE cars sold in the United States, Canada, Puerto Rico, and Guam. Finally, on May 22, 2001, Ford began a replacement program for all Firestone Wilderness AT tires in 15-inch, 16-inch, and 17-inch sizes. Other Firestone models, sizes, and plants were not involved in any recall program and these tires, though included in the class definition, may exhibit different (and lower) failure rates. The NHTSA was satisfied that these recalls removed all potentially defective tires from the road and did not require further action. Yet the tire class includes more than twice as many Firestone tires as were recalled.

methods for the fair and efficient adjudication of the controversy." Fed. R. Civ. P. 23(b)(3). Regulation by the NHTSA, coupled with tort litigation by persons suffering physical injury, is far superior to a suit by millions of *uninjured* buyers for dealing with consumer products that are said to be failure-prone.

The district judge did not doubt that differences within the class would lead to difficulties in managing the litigation. But the judge thought it better to cope with these differences than to scatter the suits to the winds and require hundreds of judges to resolve thousands of claims under 50 or more bodies of law. Efficiency is a vital goal in any legal system — but the vision of "efficiency" underlying this class certification is the model of the central planner. Plaintiffs share the premise of the ALI's *Complex Litigation Project* (1993), which devotes more than 700 pages to an analysis of means to consolidate litigation as quickly as possible, by which the authors mean, before multiple trials break out. The authors take as given the benefits of that step. Yet the benefits are elusive. The central planning model — one case, one court, one set of rules, one settlement price for all involved — suppresses information that is vital to accurate resolution. What is the law of Michigan, or Arkansas, or Guam, as applied to this problem? Judges and lawyers will have to guess, because the central planning model keeps the litigation far away from state courts. (Ford asked us to certify legal questions to the Supreme Court of Michigan, to ensure that genuine state law was applied if Michigan's law were to govern the whole country; the plaintiffs stoutly resisted that proposal.) And if the law were clear, how would the facts (and thus the damages per plaintiff) be ascertained? One suit is an all-or-none affair, with high risk even if the parties supply all the information at their disposal. Getting things right the first time would be an accident. Similarly Gosplan or another central planner may hit on the price of wheat, but that would be serendipity. Markets instead use diversified decision making to supply and evaluate information. Thousands of traders affect prices by their purchases and sales over the course of a crop year. This method looks "inefficient" from the planner's perspective, but it produces more information, more accurate prices, and a vibrant, growing economy. See Thomas Sowell, *Knowledge and Decisions* (1980). When courts think of efficiency, they should think of market models rather than central-planning models.

Our decision in *Rhone-Poulenc Rorer* made this point, and it is worth reiterating: only "a decentralized process of multiple trials, involving different juries, and different standards of liability, in different jurisdictions" (51 F.3d at 1299) will yield the information needed for accurate evaluation of mass tort claims. Once a series of decisions or settlements has produced an accurate evaluation of a subset of the claims (say, 1995 Explorers in Arizona equipped with a particular tire specification) the others in that subset can be settled or resolved at an established price. See David Friedman, *More Justice for Less Money*, 39 J.L. & Econ. 211 (1996).

No matter what one makes of the decentralized approach as an original matter, it is hard to adopt the central-planner model without violence not only to Rule 23 but also to principles of federalism. Differences across states may be costly for courts and litigants alike, but they are a fundamental aspect of our federal republic and must not be overridden in a quest to clear the queue in court. . . . Tempting as it is to alter doctrine in order to facilitate class treatment, judges must resist so that all parties' legal rights may be respected. *Amchem Products, Inc. v. Windsor,* 521 U.S. 591, 613, 117 S. Ct. 2231, 138 L. Ed. 2d 689 (1997).

The motion to certify questions of law to the Supreme Court of Michigan is denied as unnecessary in light of this opinion. The district court's order certifying two nationwide classes is REVERSED.

NOTES AND QUESTIONS

1. *Who Stands to Benefit?* Early in his opinion, Judge Easterbrook draws a distinction between tire owners who "suffered injury or death as a result of defects" and "those consumers whose loss (if any) is financial rather than physical." The former group of class members, he says, can "[a]s a practical matter . . . be ignored; they are sure to opt out and litigate independently." The class action that the court envisions, in other words, is one in which only those who may have suffered a relatively minor financial loss but were *not* seriously injured stand to benefit from the suit.

While this result may seem counterintuitive on one level, since claims of serious injury are clearly more important than minor financial losses, it is a natural expression of the class action principles that we have been studying. Personal injury claims are often poorly suited for class treatment, since issues of causation, comparative fault, and damages may need to be determined separately for each individual claimant—a fact that the Advisory Committee emphasized in promulgating the modern class action rule. *See* Fed. R. Civ. P. 23, Advisory Committee Note to 1966 amendments, quoted *supra.* When it is impossible to certify claims for personal injury or other serious harm in a mass tort action, class counsel may seek to pare the lawsuit down to a certifiable core of more uniform, smaller-stakes claims so long as the aggregate proceeding will still involve significant damages. As a result, the most seriously injured plaintiffs may stand to benefit the least from the class proceeding.

What do you make of Judge Easterbrook's assumption that class members with valuable personal injury claims "are sure to opt out and litigate independently"? To be sure, a person who suffers serious injury has every incentive to hire a lawyer and sue for damages. But why should we assume that such a person would bother to opt out of a class action that offered a free resolution of his relatively insignificant claim for economic damages? *See* Theodore Eisenberg & Geoffrey Miller, *The Role of Opt-Outs and Objectors in Class Action Litigation: Theoretical and Empirical Issues,* 57 Vand. L. Rev. 1529, 1532 (2004) (finding that class members opt out at a rate of about 1 percent on average and only 0.2 percent in negative-value claims). And even if most injured plaintiffs would indeed opt out, is it really safe to assume that they will *always* do so? To avoid uncertainty in situations like this, class counsel sometimes seek to use a more tailored class definition that carves high-stakes claims (or high-stakes claimants) out of the suit from the beginning.

2. *Review of the Nonfinal Order.* Note the use of Rule 23(f) as the appellate vehicle in *Bridgestone/Firestone* to reverse certification of the class, despite the absence of a final judgment in this ongoing proceeding. This provision, added to Rule 23 in 1998, permits an interlocutory appeal from the grant or denial of class action certification at the appellate court's discretion, without any requirement of certification by the district court. Prior to the 1998 amendments, 28 U.S.C. §1292(b) — certification by the district court and acceptance of the appeal by the Court of

Appeals—was the principal vehicle for interlocutory review of certification orders, and the limited nature of that vehicle made appeal from a certification order an uncertain proposition. For a discussion of Rule 23(f), *see* Michael E. Solimine & Chirstin Oliver Hines, *Deciding to Decide: Class Action Certification and Interlocutory Review by the United States Courts of Appeals Under Rule 23(f),* 41 Wm. & Mary L. Rev. 1531 (2000).

The Supreme Court rejected an attempt to circumvent the "careful calibration" of Rule 23(f) in *Microsoft Corp. v. Baker,* 137 S. Ct. 1702 (2017). *Microsoft v. Baker* arose out of a product-defect claim involving the Microsoft X-Box video game system. Plaintiffs filed their putative class action in a federal district court, which rejected their request for class certification. Plaintiffs asked the court of appeals to permit an interlocutory appeal on the certification question, but the court refused. Plaintiffs then took a voluntary dismissal of their individual claims (rather than litigate them on the merits) in an attempt to produce a final judgment from which they could take an appeal. Plaintiffs also indicated that they were reserving the right to revive their claims if the court of appeals reversed the certification ruling, so that they could continue to represent the class and participate in any favorable ruling. If the Supreme Court had permitted this action, it would have allowed plaintiffs to secure an appeal as-of-right from adverse certification decisions, risking only their individual claims, which might not be worth pursuing on an individual basis anyway, and seemingly thwarting the more limited discretionary policy on interlocutory appeals reflected in Rule 23(f). Pointing to these factors, the Court rejected the tactic and concluded that the requirement of a final judgment in 28 U.S.C. §1291 had to be interpreted in light of the appellate policies of Rule 23(f). Three members of the Court would have arrived at the same result through an interpretation of Article III of the Constitution rather than §1291.

Rule 23(f) requires a party to request an appeal from the order granting or denying class certification "within 14 days after the order is entered." That time limitation is not "jurisdictional" in nature, meaning that if the requesting party waits more than 14 days but its opponent fails to raise that objection then the timing requirement may be deemed waived. But the Supreme Court has held that the requirement is "mandatory" in nature, meaning that if a requesting party waits too long and its opponent does object, the court does not have the power to forgive the lateness of the request through doctrines like equitable tolling. *Nutraceutical Corp. v. Lambert,* 139 S. Ct. 710 (2019). *See also* Fed. R. App. P. 5(a)(2) (a petition requesting a discretionary appeal "must be filed within the time specified by the statute or rule authorizing the appeal").

3. *The Requirements of "Superiority" and "Predominance."* Even with the personal injury claims removed from the equation, the Seventh Circuit still finds that the class action for economic loss in *Bridgestone/Firestone* cannot satisfy Rule 23(b)(3)'s requirements of superiority and predominance. The court offers two reasons for this holding.

The first reason relates to choice of law. Contrary to the conclusion of the district court, the Seventh Circuit finds that Indiana's choice of law rules would effectively call for the application of the laws of the place where each consumer purchased the allegedly defective tires—that is, the law of all 50 states. Even if the laws in some states were similar enough to be placed into groups and litigated together, the remaining variations would require the district court to preside over a huge, hydra-headed proceeding that would not be sufficiently "manageable" to warrant class treatment, a key determination in assessing whether the class action represents a "superior" method of adjudication under Rule 23(b)(3).

The second reason relates to the nature of the products involved. There was not just one "tire" at issue in this dispute, but rather a range of models designed for a range of uses, as to which the existence of a defect and the possibility of tire failure varied considerably. Structuring a nationwide class action that would permit reliable factual determinations to be made for each separate subgroup of the defendant's products, the Seventh Circuit found, would once again render the proceeding unmanageable. Moreover, the court found, the determination as to whether a particular tire was "defective" depended in part on the type of vehicle on which a given consumer used the tire, while the measure of damages in such a case depended on the manner in which the consumer used the tires — individualized issues that might defeat the requirement that common issues "predominate," especially given the court's conclusion that there might be few truly "common" issues across the many different tire models in the class. Complications like these — introduced by variations within a product line — are a recurring problem in omnibus product defect class actions at both the nationwide and statewide levels. *See, e.g., Benner v. Becton Dickinson & Co.*, 214 F.R.D. 157, 164–167 (S.D.N.Y. 2003) (denying certification in statewide class action alleging defects in medical blood collection needle devices because variations among different products defeat commonality under Rule 23(a)). Indeed, the Seventh Circuit suggested (though it did not squarely hold) that these product-related problems would make it impossible to maintain a defective tire class action even on a statewide rather than a nationwide basis.

In order to appreciate the significance of the court's Rule 23(b)(3) holding, it is important to remember the procedural posture of the case. When the district court decided to certify the class, it took into account all the potential problems with manageability that the Seventh Circuit identified in its opinion and certified nonetheless. Certification orders, you will recall, are reviewed for abuse of discretion. Thus, *Bridgestone/Firestone* stands for the proposition that it is an abuse of discretion for a district court to certify a defective products class exhibiting the level of variation among claimants — as to both applicable law and product features — that was present here.

4. Several years before *Bridgestone/Firestone*, the Fifth Circuit issued a much-noted decision that addressed some similar class action issues. In *Castano v. The American Tobacco Co.*, 84 F.3d 734 (5th Cir. 1996), the appeals court reversed the certification of a nationwide class action on a novel claim relating to smoking, in which the plaintiffs sought compensation for the harm resulting from a smoker's physical addiction to nicotine. The class that the district court certified was immense, encompassing "[a]ll nicotine-dependent persons in the United States . . . who have purchased and smoked cigarettes manufactured" by the defendant tobacco companies, along with their estates and families. The case presented daunting choice of law problems, with absent class plaintiffs residing in all 50 states and variations in the applicable law potentially destroying any uniformity in the governing legal standard. More fundamentally, the novel, untested nature of the addiction-as-injury claim made it difficult to determine with any confidence whether the proposed classwide resolution of "core liability" issues — did the defendant companies know that smoking was addictive, and did they fail to warn smokers of this fact or even

seek to encourage their addiction—would predominate over the resolution of individual issues like reliance, comparative fault, and determination of damages.

In reversing, the Fifth Circuit concluded that it was legal error for any district court to certify a class without first determining which states' laws would apply to the claims of different class members and how variations in those laws might affect the Rule 23 calculus—a holding that the Seventh Circuit reiterated in *Bridgestone/Firestone.* Does this approach mean that multistate class actions will virtually never meet the requirements of Rule 23(b)(3)? Professor Larry Kramer provides a thorough treatment of this issue in *Choice of Law in Complex Litigation,* 71 N.Y.U. L. Rev. 547 (1996), and Professor Linda Silberman considers further developments, including the impact of the Class Action Fairness Act of 2005, in *The Role of Choice of Law in National Class Actions,* 156 U. Pa. L. Rev. 2001 (2008). The Fifth Circuit also concluded that a court should be particularly skeptical of the superiority of the class action device in the case of novel or "immature" claims that lack an established litigation track record. Such cases, the court held, can usually benefit from being tested through a series of individual lawsuits—a proposition that the Seventh Circuit has also embraced, as Judge Easterbrook indicated in drawing a distinction between the "decentralized process of multiple trials" and the "central-planner model" of class action litigation. *See also* In re *Rhone-Poulenc Rorer, Inc.*, 51 F.3d 1293, 1300 (7th Cir. 1995) ("With the aggregate stakes in the tens or hundreds of millions of dollars, or even in the billions, it is not a waste of judicial resources to conduct more than one trial, before more than six jurors, to determine whether a major segment of the international pharmaceutical industry is to follow the asbestos manufacturers into Chapter 11.").

Despite these disapproving statements from the Fifth and Seventh Circuits, not all nationwide mass tort class actions have met the same fate as *Bridgestone/Firestone* and *Castano.* In *In re Agent Orange Prod. Liab. Litig.*, 818 F.2d 145 (2d Cir. 1987), for example, the Second Circuit affirmed certification of a nationwide class of veterans exposed to Agent Orange in Vietnam. In *In re School Asbestos Litig.*, 789 F.2d 996 (3d Cir.), *cert. denied*, 479 U.S. 852 (1986), the Third Circuit permitted a class action for property damage claims resulting from asbestos exposure (though it rejected the broader class for personal injury claims certified by the district court). And in *Jenkins v. Raymark Indus.*, 782 F.2d 468 (5th Cir. 1986), the Fifth Circuit affirmed certification of an asbestos "mass tort" class action of personal injury asbestos claims.

5. *Other Statewide Injury and Products Suits.* There has been a growing proliferation of statewide class actions raising personal injury and product liability tort claims. Whereas cases involving such products as tobacco, asbestos, Agent Orange, or DES present exceptional problems of national scope that arguably justify greater innovation in the crafting of remedies, these justifications are absent for more run-of-the-mill injury cases. Nonetheless, the promise of generous fees has led plaintiffs' attorneys to pursue ever more ambitious tort claims in class action proceedings in state court.

In response, state courts have begun to impose limits similar to those articulated by the federal courts on the use of class actions to recover damages in personal injury suits. One important example is *Southwestern Refining Co. v. Bernal*, 22 S.W.3d 425 (Tex. 2000). *Bernal* arose out of an explosion at a Texas oil refinery that released a mass of soot and toxic smoke into a residential community. Some

900 local residents joined a lawsuit seeking to recover damages for personal injury, emotional distress, and property damage, as well as a punitive award. Plaintiffs sought certification as a class action. The suit presented seemingly intractable problems of causation and damages, requiring individual hearings for each class member in order to determine what compensation was due, if any. But the trial court did not view these obstacles as insurmountable. It crafted a trial plan that would first have tried the common issues of gross negligence and the total punitive damages award, and only then would have conducted the 900 individual trials necessary to determine causation and damages for each plaintiff. 22 S.W.3d at 428–429. The intermediate appellate court, in upholding the certification, suggested that "models, formulas, and damage brochures" might be used to simplify the task of determining individual causation and damages. *Id.* at 429.

The Supreme Court of Texas reversed, finding that the requirement of predominance (which Texas incorporated into a class action provision patterned after Rule 23) was hopelessly frustrated in a case involving individual trials on causation and damages for each plaintiff. As the court explained, "[t]he predominance requirement is intended to prevent class action litigation when the sheer complexity and diversity of the individual issues would overwhelm or confuse a jury or severely compromise a party's ability to present viable claims or defenses." *Id.* at 434. Responding to the suggestion that the trial court could work out the details of individual issues as they arose, the court "reject[ed] this approach of certify now and worry later," holding that "it is improper to certify a class without knowing how the claims can and will likely be tried." *Id.* at 435. Indeed, the court suggested that the sorts of innovation urged by plaintiffs and the trial court might violate Texas's Rules Enabling Act, which, like its federal counterpart, may "not be construed to enlarge or diminish any substantive right or obligations of any parties to any civil action." *Id.* at 437. Any innovations that would "alter the parties' burden of proof, right to a jury trial, or the substantive prerequisites to recovery under a given tort," the court held, would violate that principle. *Id.*

Given the concerns raised in *Bernal*, should it ever be possible to have a class action to recover damages for personal injury claims? Wouldn't such issues as causation, contributory fault, and damages always require individual determinations that would overwhelm the proceedings?

6. *Attempts to Circumvent 23(b)(3).* Given the stringent requirements unique to Rule 23(b)(3), it should not be surprising that some litigants have attempted to circumvent that provision by drawing on other parts of the Rule. Two such strategies bear particular mention. The first is Rule 23(c)(4), which permits a class action to be brought "with respect to particular issues." Class counsel have sometimes attempted to invoke this provision as a basis for certifying only those portions of complicated cases that arguably satisfy the requirement of commonality (for example, the issue of general causation in a toxic tort case), leaving the highly individual issues in a case for later, case-by-case resolution. The argument is that, in certifying only those "particular issues" that are common, Rule 23(c)(4) allows counsel to carve out only the certifiable portions of complicated cases where individual issues would otherwise predominate. While the Supreme Court has not yet had occasion to speak to the issue, the Fifth Circuit's rejection of this argument in *Castano, supra*, appears to be the majority position: "The proper interpretation of the interaction between subdivisions (b)(3) and (c)(4) is that a cause of action, as a whole, must

satisfy the predominance requirement of (b)(3) and that (c)(4) is a housekeeping rule that allows courts to sever the common issues for a class trial." 84 F.3d at 745 n. 21. The ALI project on principles of aggregate litigation currently under way finds the *Castano* view inadequate, instead embracing the position set forth in the Manual for Complex Litigation that "Rule 23(b)(3) and Rule 23(c)(4) [should be understood] as an integrated whole" and that "courts should undertake aggregate treatment of common issues 'only if it permits fair presentation of the claims and defenses and materially advances the disposition of the litigation as a whole."' American Law Institute, *Principles of Aggregation (Preliminary Draft No. 5)*, §2.02, Reporter's Notes, cmt. a (2008) (quoting Manual for Complex Litigation, Fourth §21.24, at 273). Even if it were possible to certify only the common issues in a complex case, note that question of specific causation and damages would almost never be included among those common issues. Ask yourself how class counsel would get paid in such a proceeding.

A second response to the requirements of Rule 23(b)(3) has been to file under one of the other class action categories — particularly Rule 23(b)(1)(A), which deals with "limited fund" proceedings, and Rule 23(b)(2), the provision governing claims for injunctive relief. We will see the Supreme Court's response to one such attempt to use Rule 23(b)(1)(A) in *Ortiz v. Fibreboard, infra.* Where Rule 23(b)(2) is concerned, a much noted line of cases in the Fifth Circuit has placed significant limitations on the ability of plaintiffs to obtain most forms of monetary compensation under the rubric of an equitable class proceeding. In *Allison v. Citgo Petroleum*, 151 F.3d 402 (5th Cir. 1998), the appellate court upheld a district court's refusal to certify a (b)(2) class action in a case alleging employment discrimination under Title VII of the Civil Rights Act of 1964. Because the plaintiffs were seeking compensatory and punitive damages as well as equitable relief, the court held, they could only enjoy the benefit of a (b)(2) if their damages claims were properly characterized as purely "incidental" to their claims for equitable relief, a standard that the court found they could not meet. It thus affirmed the district court's denial of certification, even though Rule 23 was designed with Title VII suits specifically in mind. The Fifth Circuit has shown a somewhat greater willingness to certify employment discrimination suits under Rule 23(b)(2) in the years following *Allison, see, e.g., In re Monumental Life Ins. Co.*, 365 F.3d 408 (5th Cir. 2004), and some other circuits have expressly rejected the *Allison* approach, *see, e.g., Robinson v. Metro-N. Commuter R.R. Co.*, 267 F.3d 147 (2d Cir. 2001).

7. *Many Bites at the Apple? State Class Actions and Successive Attempts at Certification.* Suppose you're the attorney for the plaintiffs seeking class certification in *Bridgestone/Firestone.* You've just lost your case before the Seventh Circuit, and your class has been decertified. What do you do next? Well, why not find a different injured class member to serve as lead plaintiff, find a more sympathetic court, and ask that court to certify a new class action? We know from the chapter on preclusion that a person is only bound by a judgment to which he was a party (or in privity with a party). The Seventh Circuit decertified the class in *Bridgestone/Firestone* — that is, it declared that the absent members of the class were *not parties.* That would seem to mean that the absent class members were not bound by the judgment in that case. (Remember, it is the class members who are potential "parties" here, not the lawyers.) So long as other members of the class are available to serve as new lead plaintiffs, what's to stop the lawyers from filing their lawsuit in jurisdiction after jurisdiction until they

succeed in finding a court willing to certify the class? As should be clear, this is a potential nightmare scenario for defendants. If class counsel could just keep switching one lead plaintiff for another until they succeeded in getting a class certified, defendants might never get any final resolution on the certification issue, and the judgments of those courts that denied certification would be seriously undermined.

That is, in fact, precisely what happened in the *Bridgestone/Firestone* litigation. Following the Seventh Circuit's reversal of certification in the opinion above, lawyers representing the plaintiffs found new class representatives and started filing suits identical to the first in courts around the country—one of which agreed to certify a nationwide class action mere hours after the complaint was filed, without waiting for a response from the defendants and without holding a hearing! Seeking to stem this tide, the defendants asked the federal district court in Indiana to issue an injunction that would forbid any further class actions from being filed on these claims, arguing that such a step was necessary to protect the integrity of the Seventh Circuit's denial of certification. The district court refused, but, on appeal, the Seventh Circuit granted some of the relief that the defendants were seeking. *See In re Bridgestone/Firestone Tires Products Liability Litigation (Bridgestone/Firestone II)*, 333 F.3d 763 (7th Cir. 2003). The court held that its prior judgment in the case was binding on all potential class members on the specific question of certification that it resolved—the determination that a *nationwide* class action was unavailable in this case—and it directed that an injunction issue to prohibit further state court proceedings.

Several years later, the Supreme Court cast significant doubt on the power of federal courts to take such a step. In *Smith v. Bayer*, 564 U.S. 299 (2011), the Court considered an appeal from an injunction issued in a similar situation. A Minnesota District Court in a Multidistrict Litigation proceeding had denied certification to a statewide class action that had been consolidated before it from West Virginia. Subsequently, another action in a West Virginia state court, which had lain dormant during the MDL process, sought certification for the same statewide class. The defendants obtained an injunction from the Minnesota federal court prohibiting this serial attempt at certification. Plaintiffs appealed, and the Supreme Court found that no injunction could issue. The Court's unanimous decision rested on two grounds: first, that the West Virginia state courts apparently use certification standards different from Federal Rule 23, such that the "same issue" was not present in both cases; and second, that the denial of certification in the first action had no preclusive effect upon the putative absentees, who were nonparties to that action. Under both the Federal Anti-Injunction Act and federal preclusion law, the Court found the injunction impermissible. *But see* Tobias Barrrington Wolff, *Federal Jurisdiction and Due Process in the Era of the Nationwide Class Action*, 156 U. Pa. L. Rev. 2035, 2073–2117 (2008) (arguing that neither the Anti-Injunction Act nor due process principles should prevent such an injunction, at least in some cases). With the enactment of the Class Action Fairness Act, this situation may be less of a problem, since many successive attempts at certification will be removable to federal court, where a judge applying federal standards will perhaps be more likely to follow the lead of the first court. But this will not always be so. Where removal provides no remedy—either because it is not possible or because the proposed class is a settlement-only action where plaintiffs and defendants both wish to stay in state court, *see* Wolff, *supra*— *Smith v. Bayer* appears to leave federal courts powerless to prevent serial attempts at certification.

8. *Mass Torts and Limited-Fund Classes.* Class treatment for mass torts has also been attempted under Rule 23(b)(1)(B). In *In re Northern District of California, Dalkon Shield IUD Products Liab. Litig.*, 693 F.2d 847 (9th Cir. 1982), the district court, on its own motion, certified a nationwide class of punitive damage claimants who had brought suit against the manufacturer of the Dalkon Shield intrauterine device, A.H. Robins. One purpose of the certification was to ensure the rights of all class members to a proportionate share of any punitive damages recovery from the "limited fund" of Robins's assets, where the total potential exposure might have driven the company to bankruptcy. Interestingly, in the *Dalkon Shield* litigation, it was defendant Robins that requested certification of a plaintiff punitive damages class, while plaintiffs from several states moved to decertify the class.

Why might defendants want a class action and plaintiffs resist certification in a case like *Dalkon Shield?* Remember that plaintiffs in a Rule 23(b)(1)(B) proceeding would not be permitted to opt out of the class and would be bound by any determination on punitive damages. (In this type of proceeding, defendants can also obtain an injunction against duplicative litigation elsewhere.)

Should the fact that no plaintiff had appeared in support of certification of the class in *Dalkon Shield* have affected the question of whether a class action is appropriate? The Ninth Circuit certainly thought that "typicality" and "adequacy of representation" requirements were affected by this fact. The appeals court ultimately decertified the class because it found that there had not been a sufficient showing that individual punitive damage claims would necessarily impair the ability of defendant to pay later claims, as is required for a limited-fund proceeding under Rule 23(b)(1)(B).

What showing must the parties make to support a limited-fund class action based on the claim that there will be insufficient assets available to pay all claimants? *See, e.g., In re Agent Orange Product Liab. Litig.*, 100 F.R.D. 718, 726 (E.D.N.Y. 1983), *mandamus denied sub nom. In re Diamond Shamrock Chem. Co.*, 725 F.2d 858 (2d Cir. 1984), "the proper standard is whether there is substantial probability — that is less than a preponderance but more than a mere possibility — that if damages are awarded, the claims of earlier litigants would exhaust the defendants' assets." (In the *Ortiz* case, discussed below, the Supreme Court lent further support to this robust hearing requirement.) Would such a showing require the kind of extensive mini-trial of the merits that was frowned on by the Supreme Court in *Eisen?* Does the Ninth Circuit's criticism of the record that Robins made in *Dalkon Shield* hold up in hindsight, given that A.H. Robins subsequently filed for bankruptcy? Or is the bankruptcy court less well suited to ascertaining and preserving the rights of future mass tort claimants? For a discussion of the intersection of mass tort litigation and the Bankruptcy Code, *see* Troy A. McKenzie, *The Mass Tort Bankruptcy: A Pre-History*, 5 J. Tort L. 59 (2012); Alan N. Resnick, *Bankruptcy as a Vehicle for Resolving Enterprise-Threatening Mass Tort Liability*, 148 U. Pa. L. Rev. 2045 (2000).

7. *The Special Problem of Settlement Classes*

Defendants clearly have incentives to settle a large class action in order to avoid the substantial litigation costs associated with a full defense of the action. And it is not surprising that many class actions are ultimately settled rather than litigated once a class has been certified.

But another strategy has emerged with the increase in the filing of class actions—what is known as the "settlement class action." In a settlement class action, the parties arrive at a settlement before or shortly after the action is commenced and prior to any real adverse litigation over the issue of certification. The parties define the scope of the class and ask the court to certify the class "for purposes of settlement." This procedure allows defendants to attempt to settle the action while preserving the right to contest the propriety and scope of the class allegations if the settlement is not approved. It also typically enables a defendant to withdraw from the settlement if too many class members opt out. If the court finds the settlement to be fair, it can certify the class for settlement purposes only. Class members will be notified of the lawsuit, the provisional certification order, and the settlement simultaneously. The court will then hold a "fairness" hearing, entertaining objections with respect to both the propriety of the class certification and the fairness of the settlement. If the court ultimately finds that the settlement is fair and assures itself that the certification requirements are met, it will enter a final order for class certification and settlement approval. For many years, these practices were the product of judicial innovation. In 2018, a set of amendments to Rule 23(e) authorized the settlement-only class action and codified procedures for conducting the proceedings.

Is it clear that the attorneys proposing the class settlement, who stand to receive a substantial fee once the settlement is concluded, adequately represent the interests of the absent claimants? Put another way, is there sufficient "loyalty" on the part of class counsel to the absent members of the class? Are unnamed class plaintiffs sufficiently protected if they have the right to opt out—the possibility of "exit"—in any class settlement?

In the earlier section on attorneys' fees, we examined the pressures on class counsel, who often has more at stake than any individual member of the class, and as a result may have substantial incentive to settle the class claims cheaply in exchange for a substantial fee. The problem is exacerbated when there is the possibility of multiple class actions commenced on behalf of the same or an overlapping class of plaintiffs. What response can you expect when there is more than one set of lawyers purporting to represent a particular class of plaintiffs? The lawyer representing the class knows that if she does not reach a settlement with defendant, counsel in a competing class action is likely to reach such a settlement. In this regard, consider the following comment by Professor Jack Coffee: "[D]efendants can effectively conduct a reverse auction among plaintiffs' attorneys, seeking the lowest bidder from the large population of plaintiffs' attorneys." See John C. Coffee, Jr., *The Corruption of the Class Action: The New Technology of Collusion*, 80 Cornell L. Rev. 851 (1995). *See also* Rhonda Wasserman, *Dueling Class Actions*, 80 B.U. L. Rev. 461 (2000).

Does the fact that the court has final control over whether a class action is dismissed or compromised (*see* Fed. R. Civ. P. 23(e)) provide the necessary protection? Do the procedures added to the Rule in 2018 provide adequate protection for the interests of class members?

The standards for settlement class actions finally reached the Supreme Court in the next case, *Amchem Products v. Windsor*. *Amchem* predates the 2018 amendments to Rule 23, but its analysis of the core requirements of Rule 23 in the settlement context remain a major point of reference.

Amchem Products, Inc. v. Windsor

521 U.S. 591 (1996)

JUSTICE GINSBURG delivered the opinion of the Court.

This case concerns the legitimacy under Rule 23 of the Federal Rules of Civil Procedure of a class-action certification sought to achieve global settlement of current and future asbestos-related claims. The class proposed for certification potentially encompasses hundreds of thousands, perhaps millions, of individuals tied together by this commonality: each was, or some day may be, adversely affected by past exposure to asbestos products manufactured by one or more of 20 companies. Those companies, defendants in the lower courts, are petitioners here.

The United States District Court for the Eastern District of Pennsylvania certified the class for settlement only, finding that the proposed settlement was fair and that representation and notice had been adequate. That court enjoined class members from separately pursuing asbestos-related personal-injury suits in any court, federal or state, pending the issuance of a final order. The Court of Appeals for the Third Circuit vacated the District Court's orders, holding that the class certification failed to satisfy Rule 23's requirements in several critical respects. [*Georgine v. Amchem Products, Inc.*, 83 F.3d 610 (3d Cir. 1996).] We affirm the Court of Appeals' judgment.

I

A

The settlement-class certification we confront evolved in response to an asbestos-litigation crisis. . . . A United States Judicial Conference Ad Hoc Committee on Asbestos Litigation, appointed by THE CHIEF JUSTICE in September 1990, described facets of the problem in a 1991 report. . . .

Real reform, the report concluded, required federal legislation creating a national asbestos dispute-resolution scheme. . . . To this date, no congressional response has emerged.

In the face of legislative inaction, the federal courts — lacking authority to replace state tort systems with a national toxic tort compensation regime — endeavored to work with the procedural tools available to improve management of federal asbestos litigation. Eight federal judges, experienced in the superintendence of asbestos cases, urged the Judicial Panel on Multidistrict Litigation (MDL Panel), to consolidate in a single district all asbestos complaints then pending in federal courts. Accepting the recommendation, the MDL Panel transferred all asbestos cases then filed, but not yet on trial in federal courts to a single district, the United States District Court for the Eastern District of Pennsylvania; pursuant to the transfer order, the collected cases were consolidated for pretrial proceedings before Judge Weiner. The order aggregated pending cases only; no authority resides in the MDL Panel to license for consolidated proceedings claims not yet filed.

B

After the consolidation, attorneys for plaintiffs and defendants formed separate steering committees and began settlement negotiations. Ronald L. Motley and

Gene Locks—later appointed, along with Motley's law partner Joseph F. Rice, to represent the plaintiff class in this action—co-chaired the Plaintiffs' Steering Committee. Counsel for the Center for Claims Resolution (CCR), the consortium of 20 former asbestos manufacturers now before us as petitioners, participated in the Defendants' Steering Committee. Although the MDL order collected, transferred, and consolidated only cases already commenced in federal courts, settlement negotiations included efforts to find a "means of resolving . . . future cases."

In November 1991, the Defendants' Steering Committee made an offer designed to settle all pending and future asbestos cases by providing a fund for distribution by plaintiffs' counsel among asbestos-exposed individuals. The Plaintiffs' Steering Committee rejected this offer, and negotiations fell apart. CCR, however, continued to pursue "a workable administrative system for the handling of future claims.". . .

[A new round of negotiations] yielded the mass settlement agreement now in controversy. At the time, the former heads of the Plaintiffs' Steering Committee represented thousands of plaintiffs with then-pending asbestos-related claims—claimants the parties to this suit call "inventory" plaintiffs. CCR indicated in these discussions that it would resist settlement of inventory cases absent "some kind of protection for the future.". . .

Settlement talks thus concentrated on devising an administrative scheme for disposition of asbestos claims not yet in litigation. In these negotiations, counsel for masses of inventory plaintiffs endeavored to represent the interests of the anticipated future claimants, although those lawyers then had no attorney-client relationship with such claimants.

Once negotiations seemed likely to produce an agreement purporting to bind potential plaintiffs, CCR agreed to settle, through separate agreements, the claims of plaintiffs who had already filed asbestos-related lawsuits. In one such agreement, CCR defendants promised to pay more than $200 million to gain release of the claims of numerous inventory plaintiffs. After settling the inventory claims, CCR, together with the plaintiffs' lawyers CCR had approached, launched this case, exclusively involving persons outside the MDL Panel's province—plaintiffs without already pending lawsuits.

C

The class action thus instituted was not intended to be litigated. Rather, within the space of a single day, January 15, 1993, the settling parties—CCR defendants and the representatives of the plaintiff class described below—presented to the District Court a complaint, an answer, a proposed settlement agreement, and a joint motion for conditional class certification.

The complaint identified nine lead plaintiffs, designating them and members of their families as representatives of a class comprising all persons who had not filed an asbestos-related lawsuit against a CCR defendant as of the date the class action commenced, but who (1) had been exposed—occupationally or through the occupational exposure of a spouse or household member—to asbestos or products containing asbestos attributable to a CCR defendant, or (2) whose spouse or family member had been so exposed. Untold numbers of individuals may fall within this description. All named plaintiffs alleged that they or a member of their family had been exposed to asbestos-containing products of CCR defendants. More than half of the named plaintiffs alleged that they or their family members had already suffered various physical injuries as a result of the exposure. The others alleged that they had not yet manifested any asbestos-related condition. The complaint delineated no subclasses; all named plaintiffs were designated as representatives of the class as a whole.

The complaint invoked the District Court's diversity jurisdiction and asserted various state-law claims for relief. . . . Each plaintiff requested unspecified damages in excess of $100,000. CCR defendants' answer denied the principal allegations of the complaint and asserted 11 affirmative defenses.

A stipulation of settlement accompanied the pleadings; it proposed to settle, and to preclude nearly all class members from litigating against CCR companies, all claims not filed before January 15, 1993, involving compensation for present and future asbestos-related personal injury or death. An exhaustive document exceeding 100 pages, the stipulation presents in detail an administrative mechanism and a schedule of payments to compensate class members who meet defined asbestos-exposure and medical requirements. The stipulation describes four categories of compensable disease. . . . Persons with "exceptional" medical claims—claims that do not fall within the four described diagnostic categories—may in some instances qualify for compensation, but the settlement caps the number of "exceptional" claims CCR must cover.

For each qualifying disease category, the stipulation specifies the range of damages CCR will pay to qualifying claimants. Payments under the settlement are not adjustable for inflation. Mesothelioma claimants—the most highly compensated category—are scheduled to receive between $20,000 and $200,000. . . .

Compensation above the fixed ranges may be obtained for "extraordinary" claims. But the settlement places both numerical caps and dollar limits on such claims. The settlement also imposes "case flow maximums," which cap the number of claims payable for each disease in a given year.

Class members are to receive no compensation for certain kinds of claims, even if otherwise applicable state law recognizes such claims. Claims that garner no compensation under the settlement include claims by family members of asbestos-exposed individuals for loss of consortium, and claims by so-called "exposure-only" plaintiffs for increased risk of cancer, fear of future asbestos-related injury, and medical monitoring. "Pleural" claims, which might be asserted by persons with asbestos-related plaques on their lungs but no accompanying physical impairment, are also excluded. Although not entitled to present compensation, exposure-only claimants and pleural claimants may qualify for benefits when and if they develop a compensable disease and meet the relevant exposure and medical criteria. Defendants forgo defenses to liability, including statute of limitations pleas.

Class members, in the main, are bound by the settlement in perpetuity, while CCR defendants may choose to withdraw from the settlement after ten years. A small number of class members—only a few per year—may reject the settlement and pursue their claims in court. Those permitted to exercise this option, however, may not assert any punitive damages claim or any claim for increased risk of cancer. Aspects of the administration of the settlement are to be monitored by the AFL-CIO and class counsel. Class counsel are to receive attorneys' fees in an amount to be approved by the District Court.

D

On January 29, 1993, as requested by the settling parties, the District Court conditionally certified, under Federal Rule of Civil Procedure 23(b)(3), an encompassing opt-out class. The certified class included persons occupationally exposed to defendants' asbestos products, and members of their families, who had not filed suit as of January 15. Judge Weiner appointed Locks, Motley, and Rice as class counsel. . . . At no stage of the proceedings, however, were additional counsel in fact appointed. Nor was the class ever divided into subclasses. In a separate order, Judge Weiner assigned to Judge Reed, also of the Eastern District of Pennsylvania, "the task of conducting fairness proceedings and of determining whether the proposed settlement is fair to the class." Various class members raised objections to the settlement stipulation, and Judge Weiner granted the objectors full rights to participate in the subsequent proceedings. . . .

Objectors raised numerous challenges to the settlement. . . . Judge Reed concluded that the settlement terms were fair and had been negotiated without collusion. He also found that adequate notice had been given to class members, and that final class certification under Rule 23(b)(3) was appropriate. . . .

[The District Court found that the requirements of numerosity, commonality, and predominance were satisfied.]

The District Court held next that the claims of the class representatives were "typical" of the class as a whole, a requirement of Rule 23(a)(3), and that, as Rule 23(b)(3) demands, the class settlement was "superior" to other methods of adjudication.

Strenuous objections had been asserted regarding the adequacy of representation, a Rule 23(a)(4) requirement. Objectors maintained that class counsel and class representatives had disqualifying conflicts of interests. In particular, objectors urged, claimants whose injuries had become manifest and claimants without manifest injuries should not have common counsel and should not be aggregated in a single class. Furthermore, objectors argued, lawyers representing inventory plaintiffs should not represent the newly-formed class.

Satisfied that class counsel had ably negotiated the settlement in the best interests of all concerned, and that the named parties served as adequate representatives, the District Court rejected these objections. Subclasses were unnecessary, the District Court held, bearing in mind the added cost and confusion they would entail and the ability of class members to exclude themselves from the class during the three-month opt-out period. Reasoning that the representative plaintiffs "have a strong interest that recovery for all of the medical categories be maximized because they may have claims in any, or several categories," the District Court found "no antagonism of interest between class members with various medical conditions, or between persons with and without currently manifest asbestos impairment." Declaring class certification appropriate and the settlement fair, the District Court preliminarily enjoined all class members from commencing any asbestos-related suit against the CCR defendants in any state or federal court. . . .

The objectors appealed. The United States Court of Appeals for the Third Circuit vacated the certification, holding that the requirements of Rule 23 had not been satisfied. 83 F.3d 610 (1996).

E

[The Supreme Court described the detailed opinion by Judge Becker for the Third Circuit. The Court also disposed of various justiciability issues and provided background on the history and development of Rule 23.]

III

. . . In the decades since the 1966 revision of Rule 23, class action practice has become ever more "adventuresome" as a means of coping with claims too numerous to secure their "just, speedy, and inexpensive determination" one by one. The development reflects concerns about the efficient use of court resources and the conservation of funds to compensate claimants who do not line up early in a litigation queue. See generally J. Weinstein, Individual Justice in Mass Tort Litigation: The Effect of Class Actions, Consolidations, and Other Multiparty Devices (1995); Schwarzer, *Settlement of Mass Tort Class Actions: Order out of Chaos*, 80 Cornell L. Rev. 837 (1995).

Among current applications of Rule 23(b)(3), the "settlement only" class has become a stock device. See, e.g., T. Willging, L. Hooper, & R. Niemic, Empirical Study of Class Actions in Four Federal District Courts: Final Report to the Advisory Committee on Civil Rules 61–62 (1996) (noting large number of such cases in districts studied). Although all Federal Circuits recognize the utility of Rule 23(b)(3) settlement classes, courts have divided on the extent to which a proffered settlement affects court surveillance under Rule 23's certification criteria.

In [*In re General Motors Corp. Pick-Up Truck Fuel Tank Products Liab. Litig.*, 55 F.3d 768 (3d Cir.), *cert. denied*, 516 U.S. 824 (1995)], and in the instant case, 83 F.3d, at 624–626, the Third Circuit held that a class cannot be certified for settlement when certification for trial would be unwarranted. Other courts have held that settlement obviates or reduces the need to measure a proposed class against the enumerated Rule 23 requirements. See, e.g., *In re Asbestos Litigation*, 90 F.3d, at 975 (C.A.5) ("in settlement class context, common issues arise from the settlement itself") (citing H. Newberg & A. Conte, 2 Newberg on Class Actions §11.28, at 11–58 (3d ed. 1992)). . . .

A proposed amendment to Rule 23 would expressly authorize settlement class certification, in conjunction with a motion by the settling parties for Rule 23(b)(3) certification, "even though the requirements of subdivision (b)(3) might not be met for purposes of trial." Proposed Amendment to Fed. Rule Civ. Proc. 23(b), 117 S. Ct. No. 1 CXIX, CLIV to CLV (Aug. 1996) (Request for Comment). In response to the publication of this proposal, voluminous public comments—many of them opposed to, or skeptical of, the amendment—were received by the Judicial Conference Standing Committee on Rules of Practice and Procedure. The Committee has not yet acted on the matter. We consider the certification at issue under the rule as it is currently framed.

IV

We granted review to decide the role settlement may play, under existing Rule 23, in determining the propriety of class certification. The Third Circuit's opinion stated that each of the requirements of Rule 23(a) and (b)(3) "must be satisfied without taking into account the settlement." 83 F.3d at 626 (quoting *GM Trucks*, 55 F.3d, at 799). That statement, petitioners urge, is incorrect.

We agree with petitioners to this limited extent: settlement is relevant to a class certification. The Third Circuit's opinion bears modification in that respect. But . . . the Court of Appeals in fact did not ignore the settlement; instead, that court homed in on settlement terms in explaining why it found the absentees' interests inadequately represented. The Third Circuit's close inspection of the settlement in that regard was altogether proper.

Confronted with a request for settlement-only class certification, a district court need not inquire whether the case, if tried, would present intractable management problems, see Fed. Rule Civ. Proc. 23(b)(3)(D), for the proposal is that there be no trial. But other specifications of the rule — those designed to protect absentees by blocking unwarranted or overbroad class definitions — demand undiluted, even heightened, attention in the settlement context. Such attention is of vital importance, for a court asked to certify a settlement class will lack the opportunity, present when a case is litigated, to adjust the class, informed by the proceedings as they unfold. . . .

And, of overriding importance, courts must be mindful that the rule as now composed sets the requirements they are bound to enforce. Federal Rules take effect after an extensive deliberative process involving many reviewers: a Rules Advisory Committee, public commenters, the Judicial Conference, this Court, the Congress. . . . Courts are not free to amend a rule outside the process Congress ordered, a process properly tuned to the instruction that rules of procedure "shall not abridge . . . any substantive right.". . .

The safeguards provided by the Rule 23(a) and (b) class-qualifying criteria, we emphasize, are not impractical impediments — checks shorn of utility — in the settlement class context. First, the standards set for the protection of absent class members serve to inhibit appraisals of the chancellor's foot kind — class certifications dependent upon the court's gestalt judgment or overarching impression of the settlement's fairness.

Second, if a fairness inquiry under Rule 23(e) controlled certification, eclipsing Rule 23(a) and (b), and permitting class designation despite the impossibility of litigation, both class counsel and court would be disarmed. Class counsel confined to settlement negotiations could not use the threat of litigation to press for a better offer, see Coffee, *Class Wars: The Dilemma of the Mass Tort Class Action*, 95 Colum. L. Rev. 1343, 1379–1380 (1995), and the court would face a bargain proffered for its approval without benefit of adversarial investigation, see, e.g., *Kamilewicz v. Bank of Boston Corp.*, 100 F.3d 1348, 1352 (C.A.7 1996) (Easterbrook, J., dissenting from denial of rehearing en banc) (parties "may even put one over on the court, in a staged performance"), *cert. denied*, 520 U.S. 1204 (1997).

Federal courts, in any case, lack authority to substitute for Rule 23's certification criteria a standard never adopted — that if a settlement is "fair," then certification is proper. Applying to this case criteria the rulemakers set, we conclude that the Third Circuit's appraisal is essentially correct. Although that court should have acknowledged that settlement is a factor in the calculus, a remand is not warranted on that account. The Court of Appeals' opinion amply demonstrates why — with or without a settlement on the table — the sprawling class the District Court certified does not satisfy Rule 23's requirements.

A

We address first the requirement of Rule 23(b)(3) that "[common] questions of law or fact . . . predominate over any questions affecting only individual members." The District Court concluded that predominance was satisfied based on two factors: class members' shared experience of asbestos exposure and their common "interest in receiving prompt and fair compensation for their claims, while minimizing the risks and transaction costs inherent in the asbestos litigation process as it occurs presently in the tort system." The settling parties also contend that the settlement's fairness is a common question, predominating over disparate legal issues that might be pivotal in litigation but become irrelevant under the settlement.

The predominance requirement stated in Rule 23(b)(3), we hold, is not met by the factors on which the District Court relied. The benefits asbestos-exposed persons might gain from the establishment of a grand-scale compensation scheme is a matter fit for legislative consideration, but it is not pertinent to the predominance inquiry. That inquiry trains on the legal or factual questions that qualify each class member's case as a genuine controversy, questions that preexist any settlement.

The Rule 23(b)(3) predominance inquiry tests whether proposed classes are sufficiently cohesive to warrant adjudication by representation. See 7A Wright, Miller, & Kane 518-519. The inquiry appropriate under Rule 23(e), on the other hand, protects unnamed class members "from unjust or unfair settlements affecting their rights when the representatives become fainthearted before the action is adjudicated or are able to secure satisfaction of their individual claims by a compromise." But it is not the mission of Rule 23(e) to assure the class cohesion that legitimizes representative action in the first place. If a common interest in a fair compromise could satisfy the predominance requirement of Rule 23(b)(3), that vital prescription would be stripped of any meaning in the settlement context.

The District Court also relied upon this commonality: "The members of the class have all been exposed to asbestos products supplied by the defendants. . . ." Even if Rule 23(a)'s commonality requirement may be satisfied by that shared experience, the predominance criterion is far more demanding. Given the greater number of questions peculiar to the several categories of class members, and to individuals within each category, and the significance of those uncommon questions, any overarching dispute about the health consequences of asbestos exposure cannot satisfy the Rule 23(b)(3) predominance standard.

The Third Circuit highlighted the disparate questions undermining class cohesion in this case:

> Class members were exposed to different asbestos-containing products, for different amounts of time, in different ways, and over different periods. Some class members suffer no physical injury or have only asymptomatic pleural changes, while others suffer from lung cancer, disabling asbestosis, or from mesothelioma. . . . Each has a different history of cigarette smoking, a factor that complicates the causation inquiry.
>
> The [exposure-only] plaintiffs especially share little in common, either with each other or with the presently injured class members. It is unclear whether they will contract asbestos-related disease and, if so, what

disease each will suffer. They will also incur different medical expenses because their monitoring and treatment will depend on singular circumstances and individual medical histories. Id. at 626.

Differences in state law, the Court of Appeals observed, compound these disparities. . . .

No settlement class called to our attention is as sprawling as this one. . . . Predominance is a test readily met in certain cases alleging consumer or securities fraud or violations of the antitrust laws. Even mass tort cases arising from a common cause or disaster may, depending upon the circumstances, satisfy the predominance requirement. The Advisory Committee for the 1966 revision of Rule 23, it is true, noted that "mass accident" cases are likely to present "significant questions, not only of damages but of liability and defenses of liability, . . . affecting the individuals in different ways." And the Committee advised that such cases are "ordinarily not appropriate" for class treatment. But the text of the rule does not categorically exclude mass tort cases from class certification, and district courts, since the late 1970s, have been certifying such cases in increasing number. The Committee's warning, however, continues to call for caution when individual stakes are high and disparities among class members great. As the Third Circuit's opinion makes plain, the certification in this case does not follow the counsel of caution. That certification cannot be upheld, for it rests on a conception of Rule 23(b)(3)'s predominance requirement irreconcilable with the rule's design.

B

Nor can the class approved by the District Court satisfy Rule 23(a)(4)'s requirement that the named parties "will fairly and adequately protect the interests of the class." The adequacy inquiry under Rule 23(a)(4) serves to uncover conflicts of interest between named parties and the class they seek to represent. . . .

As the Third Circuit pointed out, named parties with diverse medical conditions sought to act on behalf of a single giant class rather than on behalf of discrete subclasses. In significant respects, the interests of those within the single class are not aligned. Most saliently, for the currently injured, the critical goal is generous immediate payments. That goal tugs against the interest of exposure-only plaintiffs in ensuring an ample, inflation-protected fund for the future.

The disparity between the currently injured and exposure-only categories of plaintiffs, and the diversity within each category are not made insignificant by the District Court's finding that petitioners' assets suffice to pay claims under the settlement. Although this is not a "limited fund" case certified under Rule 23(b)(1)(B), the terms of the settlement reflect essential allocation decisions designed to confine compensation and to limit defendants' liability. For example, as earlier described, the settlement includes no adjustment for inflation; only a few claimants per year can opt out at the back end; and loss-of-consortium claims are extinguished with no compensation.

The settling parties, in sum, achieved a global compromise with no structural assurance of fair and adequate representation for the diverse groups and individuals affected. Although the named parties alleged a range of complaints, each served generally as representative for the whole, not for a separate constituency. . . .

C

Impediments to the provision of adequate notice, the Third Circuit emphasized, rendered highly problematic any endeavor to tie to a settlement class persons with no perceptible asbestos-related disease at the time of the settlement. Many persons in the exposure-only category, the Court of Appeals stressed, may not even know of their exposure, or realize the extent of the harm they may incur. Even if they fully appreciate the significance of class notice, those without current afflictions may not have the information or foresight needed to decide, intelligently, whether to stay in or opt out.

Family members of asbestos-exposed individuals may themselves fall prey to disease or may ultimately have ripe claims for loss of consortium. Yet large numbers of people in this category—future spouses and children of asbestos victims—could not be alerted to their class membership. And current spouses and children of the occupationally exposed may know nothing of that exposure.

Because we have concluded that the class in this case cannot satisfy the requirements of common issue predominance and adequacy of representation, we need not rule, definitively, on the notice given here. In accord with the Third Circuit, however, we recognize the gravity of the question whether class action notice sufficient under the Constitution and Rule 23 could ever be given to legions so unself-conscious and amorphous.

V

The argument is sensibly made that a nationwide administrative claims processing regime would provide the most secure, fair, and efficient means of compensating victims of asbestos exposure. Congress, however, has not adopted such a solution. And Rule 23, which must be interpreted with fidelity to the Rules Enabling Act and applied with the interests of absent class members in close view, cannot carry the large load CCR, class counsel, and the District Court heaped upon it. . . .

For the reasons stated, the judgment of the Court of Appeals for the Third Circuit is *Affirmed.*

JUSTICE BREYER, with whom JUSTICE STEVENS joins, concurring in part and dissenting in part.

Although I agree with the Court's basic holding that "settlement is relevant to a class certification," I find several problems in its approach that lead me to a different conclusion. First, I believe that the need for settlement in this mass tort case, with hundreds of thousands of lawsuits, is greater than the Court's opinion suggests. Second, I would give more weight than would the majority to settlement-related issues for purposes of determining whether common issues predominate. Third, I am uncertain about the Court's determination of adequacy of representation, and do not believe it appropriate for this Court to second-guess the District Court on the matter without first having the Court of Appeals consider it. Fourth, I am uncertain about the tenor of an opinion that seems to suggest the settlement is unfair. And fifth, in the absence of further review by the Court of Appeals, I cannot accept the majority's suggestions that "notice" is inadequate. . . .

First, I believe the majority understates the importance of settlement in this case. Between 13 and 21 million workers have been exposed to asbestos in the workplace — over the past 40 or 50 years — but the most severe instances of such exposure probably occurred three or four decades ago. See Report of The Judicial Conference Ad Hoc Committee on Asbestos Litigation, pp. 6–7 (Mar. 1991) (Judicial Conference Report); App. 781–782, 801; B. Castlegar, Asbestos: Medical and Legal Aspects 787–788 (4th ed. 1996). This exposure has led to several hundred thousand lawsuits, about 15% of which involved claims for cancer and about 30% for asbestosis. . . . These lawsuits have taken up more than 6% of all federal civil filings in one recent year, and are subject to a delay that is twice that of other civil suits. Judicial Conference Report 7, 10–11.

Delays, high costs, and a random pattern of noncompensation led the Judicial Conference Ad Hoc Committee on Asbestos Litigation to transfer all federal asbestos personal-injury cases to the Eastern District of Pennsylvania in an effort to bring about a fair and comprehensive settlement. . . .

Although the transfer of the federal asbestos cases did not produce a general settlement, it was intertwined with and led to a lengthy year-long negotiation between the co-chairs of the Plaintiff's Multidistrict Litigation Steering Committee (elected by the Plaintiff's Committee Members and approved by the District Court) and the 20 asbestos defendants who are before us here. These "protracted and vigorous" negotiations led to the present partial settlement, which will pay an estimated $1.3 billion and compensate perhaps 100,000 class members in the first 10 years. "The negotiations included a substantial exchange of information" between class counsel and the 20 defendant companies, including "confidential data" showing the defendants' historical settlement averages, numbers of claims filed and settled, and insurance resources. "Virtually no provision" of the settlement "was not the subject of significant negotiation," and the settlement terms "changed substantially" during the negotiations. In the end, the negotiations produced a settlement that, the District Court determined based on its detailed review of the process, was "the result of arms-length adversarial negotiations by extraordinarily competent and experienced attorneys."

The District Court, when approving the settlement, concluded that it improved the plaintiffs' chances of compensation and reduced total legal fees and other transaction costs by a significant amount. Under the previous system, according to the court, "[t]he sickest of victims often go uncompensated for years while valuable funds go to others who remain unimpaired by their mild asbestos disease." The court believed the settlement would create a compensation system that would make more money available for plaintiffs who later develop serious illnesses.

I mention this matter because it suggests that the settlement before us is unusual in terms of its importance, both to many potential plaintiffs and to defendants, and with respect to the time, effort, and expenditure that it reflects. All of which leads me to be reluctant to set aside the District Court's findings without more assurance than I have that they are wrong. I cannot obtain that assurance through comprehensive review of the record because that is properly the job of the Court of Appeals and that court, understandably, but as we now hold, mistakenly, believed that settlement was not a relevant (and, as I would say, important) consideration.

Second, the majority, in reviewing the District Court's determination that common "issues of fact and law predominate," says that the predominance "inquiry trains on the legal or factual questions that qualify each class member's case as a genuine controversy, questions that preexist any settlement." I find it difficult to interpret this sentence in a way that could lead me to the majority's conclusion. If the majority means that these pre-settlement questions are what matters, then how does it reconcile its statement with its basic conclusion that "settlement is relevant" to class certification, or with the numerous lower court authority that says that settlement is not only relevant, but important?

Nor do I understand how one could decide whether common questions "predominate" in the abstract—without looking at what is likely to be at issue in the proceedings that will ensue, namely, the settlement. Every group of human beings, after all, has some features in common, and some that differ. How can a court make a contextual judgment of the sort that Rule 23 requires without looking to what proceedings will follow? Such guideposts help it decide whether, in light of common concerns and differences, certification will achieve Rule 23's basic objective—"economies of time, effort, and expense.". . . I am not saying that the "settlement counts only one way." Rather, the settlement may simply "add a great deal of information to the court's inquiry and will often expose diverging interests or common issues that were not evident or clear from the complaint" and courts "can and should" look to it to enhance the "ability . . . to make informed certification decisions.". . .

The settlement is relevant because it means that these common features and interests are likely to be important in the proceeding that would ensue—a proceeding that would focus primarily upon whether or not the proposed settlement fairly and properly satisfied the interests class members had in common. That is to say, the settlement underscored the importance of (a) the common fact of exposure, (b) the common interest in receiving some compensation for certain rather than running a strong risk of no compensation, and (c) the common interest in avoiding large legal fees, other transaction costs, and delays.

Of course, as the majority points out, there are also important differences among class members. . . .

These differences might warrant subclasses, though subclasses can have problems of their own. "There can be a cost in creating more distinct subgroups, each with its own representation. . . . [T]he more subclasses created, the more severe conflicts bubble to the surface and inhibit settlement. . . . The resources of defendants and, ultimately, the community must not be exhausted by protracted litigation." Wemstein, Individual Justice in Mass Tort Litigation, at 66. Or these differences may be too serious to permit an effort at group settlement. This kind of determination, as I have said, is one that the law commits to the discretion of the district court—reviewable for abuse of discretion by a court of appeals. I believe that we are far too distant from the litigation itself to reweigh the fact-specific Rule 23 determinations and to find them erroneous without the benefit of the Court of Appeals first having restudied the matter with today's legal standard in mind.

Third, the majority concludes that the "representative parties" will not "fairly and adequately protect the interests of the class." Rule 23(a)(4). It finds a serious conflict between plaintiffs who are now injured and those who may be injured in the future because "for the currently injured, the critical goal is generous immediate payments," a goal that "tugs against the interest of exposure-only plaintiffs in ensuring an ample, inflation-protected fund for the future."

I agree that there is a serious problem, but it is a problem that often exists in toxic tort cases. . . . And it is a problem that potentially exists whenever a single defendant injures several plaintiffs, for a settling plaintiff leaves fewer assets available for the others. With class actions, at least, plaintiffs have the consolation that a district court, thoroughly familiar with the facts, is charged with the responsibility of ensuring that the interests of no class members are sacrificed.

Further, certain details of the settlement that are not discussed in the majority opinion suggest that the settlement may be of greater benefit to future plaintiffs than the majority suggests. The District Court concluded that future plaintiffs receive a "significant value" from the settlement due to variety of its items that benefit future plaintiffs, such as: (1) tolling the statute of limitations so that class members "will no longer be forced to file premature lawsuits or risk their claims being time-barred"; (2) waiver of defenses to liability; (3) payment of claims, if and when members become sick, pursuant to the settlement's compensation standards, which avoids "the uncertainties, long delays and high transaction costs [including attorneys' fees] of the tort system"; (4) "some assurance that there will be funds available if and when they get sick," based on the finding that each defendant "has shown an ability to fund the payment of all qualifying claims" under the settlement; and (5) the right to additional compensation if cancer develops (many settlements for plaintiffs with noncancerous conditions bar such additional claims). For these reasons, and others, the District Court found that the distinction between present and future plaintiffs was "illusory."

I do not know whether or not the benefits are more or less valuable than an inflation adjustment. But I can certainly recognize an argument that they are. . . .

Fourth, I am more agnostic than is the majority about the basic fairness of the settlement. The District Court's conclusions rested upon complicated factual findings that are not easily cast aside. It is helpful to consider some of them, such as its determination that the settlement provided "fair compensation . . . while reducing the delays and transaction costs endemic to the asbestos litigation process" and that "the proposed class action settlement is superior to other available methods for the fair and efficient resolution of the asbestos-related personal injury claims of class members.". . . I do believe that these matters would have to be explored in far greater depth before I could reach a conclusion about fairness. And that task, as I have said, is one for the Court of Appeals.

Finally, I believe it is up to the District Court, rather than this Court, to review the legal sufficiency of notice to members of the class. . . .

II

The issues in this case are complicated and difficult. The District Court might have been correct. Or not. Subclasses might be appropriate. Or not. I cannot tell. And I do not believe that this Court should be in the business of trying to make these fact-based determinations. That is a job suited to the district courts in the first instance, and the courts of appeal on review. But there is no reason in this case to believe that the Court of Appeals conducted its prior review with an understanding that the settlement could have constituted a reasonably strong factor in favor of class certification. For this reason, I would provide the courts below with an opportunity to analyze the factual questions involved in certification by vacating the judgment, and remanding the case for further proceedings.

NOTE ON *ORTIZ v. FIBREBOARD CORP.*

Barely two years after it rejected the Rule 23(b)(3) settlement class in *Amchem*, the Supreme Court once again found itself in the mass asbestos tort arena, in *Ortiz v. Fibreboard Corp.*, 527 U.S. 815 (1999). The case involved a global mandatory class of asbestos claimants attempting to reach settlement with a single former asbestos manufacturer, Fibreboard, and two of its former insurance companies. At the time of settlement negotiations with the class, Fibreboard was involved in protracted litigation (in California state court) with the two insurance companies as to the existence and extent of the indemnification required by two insurance policies that Fibreboard had taken out with the companies in the late 1950s—the most recent of which had expired in 1959.

Prior to any decision in the California indemnity action, Fibreboard, the insurance companies, and the plaintiffs' attorneys negotiated a "Global Settlement Agreement" where the insurance companies agreed to drop the California litigation and commit $1.525 billion to Fibreboard's settlement of the class action, with Fibreboard committing another $10 million. In return for this settlement, the insurance companies demanded permanent "peace" from future asbestos claims against Fibreboard through a mandatory "limited fund" class, which would preclude opt-outs by members of the class and bind all potential plaintiffs to the settlement terms.

Accordingly, a class action in Texas federal court was filed for purposes of settlement under Rule 23(b)(1)(B). Recall from *In re Northern District of California, Dalkon Shield IUD Products Liability Litigation*, discussed at p. 1003, that Rule 23(b)(1)(B) actions typically involve a "limited fund." The settling parties in *Ortiz* contended that theirs was a limited fund case because there were some 186,000 pending or potential asbestos claims against Fibreboard, the total value of which exceeded the net worth of Fibreboard, at $235 million, plus the indemnity settlement between Fibreboard and the insurance companies, at $1.535 billion. The district court certified the class under Rule 23(b)(1)(B) based on the threat that the first claims to get to court, if brought separately, could entail such enormous liability that Fibreboard would be driven into insolvency within a few years, and later claimants would be deprived of any remedy. The Fifth Circuit affirmed the settlement, and when the case initially reached the Supreme Court, the judgment was vacated and remanded to the Fifth Circuit for further consideration in light of the Court's ruling in *Amchem*. On remand, the Fifth Circuit again affirmed, distinguishing *Amchem* on the ground that *Ortiz* was certified under Rule 23(b)(1)(B) and not (b)(3) and that the settlement awards in *Ortiz* were not allocated based on the nature of the claimant's injury, as was the case in *Amchem*.

Once again, the Supreme Court rejected certification of a settlement class and reversed the Fifth Circuit. Noting the limitations of the Rules Enabling Act, the Court cautioned against "adventurous" application of Rule 23(b)(1)(B). The Court also criticized the lower courts for simply relying on the agreement of the parties as to the amount of available funds and ignoring the right of objecting and unidentified class members "to have the issue settled by specific evidentiary findings independent of the agreement of defendants and conflicted class counsel." In addition, the Supreme Court found that the class (which included those with present claims never filed as well as future claimants) failed to include a variety of other potential claimants (about 45,000 inventory plaintiffs) and plaintiffs in unsettled present cases. On the record, it appeared that class members and the outsiders would end up with strikingly different benefits. And in the end, stated the Court, "even ostensible parity between settling nonclass plaintiffs and class members would be insufficient to overcome the failure to provide the structural protection of independent representation as for subclasses with conflicting interests." *See also* American Law Institute, *Principles of Aggregation (Preliminary Draft No. 3), supra,* §2.08 (approving mandatory aggregate treatment for "indivisible remedies" where plaintiffs' claims are interdependent by nature but disapproving mandatory treatment for remedies that are "divisible" and not interdependent).

Justice Breyer, joined by Justice Stevens, dissented and argued that a limited fund class was appropriate as long as there was a "significant 'risk' that the total assets available to satisfy the claims of the class members would fall well below the likely total value of those claims." In such circumstances, it was likely that the money would go to the claimants who proceeded first, thereby substantially impairing the ability of later claimants to protect their interests. Justice Breyer also observed that tort issues have traditionally been amenable to judicial resolution, and thus are appropriate for judicial innovation in the class action area.

NOTES AND QUESTIONS

1. *Competing Interests of Class Members.* What precisely is it about the *Amchem* and *Ortiz* class settlements that the Supreme Court majority finds objectionable? Note that the settlement classes in both cases included individuals who had been injured from exposure to asbestos as well as persons who had been exposed but who had not yet suffered any injury. Unlike the problem in *Hansberry*, all members of the class had the same goal—imposing liability on defendant. So why did the Supreme Court find that the named plaintiffs who had actually suffered injuries could not "adequately represent" those class members who were only exposed? Is the defect that the pay-out allocations to the two groups were different? Recall, however, that in *Ortiz*, the payments were not allocated on the basis of the type of injury.

2. *A Conflict of Interest by Class Counsel?* Is the real difficulty in both cases the fact that the "future claimant" class—regardless of whether they had present or future injuries—received inferior benefits when compared to the settlements negotiated by plaintiffs' counsel for their "inventory" of previously filed individual clients? Should this conflict have presented an ethical concern for the lawyers? *See, e.g.,* Susan P. Koniak, *Feasting While the Widow Weeps:* Georgine v. Amchem Products, Inc., 80 Cornell L. Rev. 1045 (1995); Carrie J. Menkel-Meadow, *Ethics and the Settlement of Mass Torts: Where the Rules Meet the Road,* 80 Cornell L. Rev. 1159 (1995).

3. *Use of Subclasses.* There is some suggestion in *Amchem* that the use of sub-classes could mitigate the problem of intra-class conflict—a suggestion that the Court reiterates strongly in *Ortiz.* Would the use of subclasses also include the appointment of separate counsel for each subclass? Does separate representation increase the amount of lawyers' fees that will have to come out of any settlement?

Some courts and commentators have read *Amchem* and *Ortiz* to mean that a court must provide for separately represented subclasses whenever class counsel would have to allocate different payouts among class members or otherwise trade off their interests in the administration of a complex proceeding. The theory is that any such allocation of money or benefits creates some conflict of interests between the various recipients. Professor Issacharoff, however, has argued against such an interpretation of Rule 23. "In an extreme form," he has written, "this reading of *Amchem* would create a spiral of subclasses and sets of counsel that would not only swamp the incentive to invest in bringing a class action, but would impose tremendous transactional costs on an already vulnerable procedure that turned heavily on its ability to realize economies of scale." Samuel Issacharoff, *Governance and Legitimacy in the Law of Class Actions,* 1999 Sup. Ct. Rev. 377, 380. Do you agree? Assuming Professor Issacharoff is correct in his prediction about the practical consequences of excessive subclassing, does that mean that we should scale back our use of subclasses or rather that we should be more reticent in certifying class actions in the first place? Is the function of subclasses fulfilled, as a practical matter, by the presence of objectors who can appear to challenge the propriety or fairness of a settlement? Rule 23(e) now requires district courts to hold hearings at which such objectors may appear before approving a class action settlement.

4. *The Problem of Claimants with Future Injuries.* Is there any way for a class suit to sever claimants with "future injuries"—i.e., those who do not presently have claims because their injuries are not yet manifested, but are likely to have claims in the future—from "current" claimants and still have defendants willing to participate in mass settlements? Or, is it clear that the class action device, after *Amchem* and *Ortiz,* is doomed in these kinds of cases? Are there more effective solutions for dealing with the problem of "future claimants"? *Compare* Geoffrey C. Hazard, Jr., *The Futures Problem,* 148 U. Pa. L. Rev. 1901 (2000) (proposing federal administrative scheme with limited liability that distributors of products could opt into) *with* Linda S. Mullenix, *Back to the Futures: Privatizing Future Claims Resolution,* 148 U. Pa. L. Rev. 1919 (2000) (suggesting that "future claims" be subject to a bidding process to private "vendors" that would guarantee payment to future claimants). *See also In re Diet Drugs Products Liab. Litig.,* 2000 U.S. Dist. LEXIS 2275 (E.D. Pa. 2000) (approving settlement that provided medical screening to all settlement class members, with further compensation or a provisional opt-out right in the event further damage is discovered in future).

5. *The Role of Settlement.* Moving away from the specific mass tort issues in *Amchem* and *Ortiz,* is there a more general problem with settlement-only classes? Recall the following observation by the Supreme Court in *Amchem:*

> [I]f a fairness inquiry under Rule 23(e) controlled certification, eclipsing Rule 23(a) and (b), and permitting class designation despite the impossibility of litigation, both class counsel and court would be disarmed. Class

counsel confined to settlement negotiations could not use the threat of litigation to press for a better offer, . . . and the court would face a bargain proffered for its approval without benefit of adversarial investigation.

521 U.S. at 621.

Does this concern expressed by the Court suggest that there should be an absolutely identical standard for the certification of litigation and settlement classes? Why, then, does the Court say "settlement is relevant to class certification"? How is it relevant? Should the fact that there is a "settlement class" impose a heightened obligation on the court to investigate the "adequacy of representation" to assure that there are not potential intra-class conflicts? On the other hand, doesn't the existence of a settlement reduce the need for an inquiry about the "superiority" and "manageability" of a class suit?

In the wake of *Amchem*, lower federal courts have explored further the impact of settlement on the specific requirements of Rule 23. In one influential ruling, the *en banc* Third Circuit has given much greater leeway on questions of predominance when a class is proposed for settlement purposes only. *Sullivan v. DB Investments*, 667 F.3d 273 (3d Cir. 2011) (en banc), affirmed the certification of a settlement class in which significant variations in state law might have made litigation of the class unmanageable. The case involved allegations that De Beers, a diamond wholesaler, had used its dominant position in the market to fix prices and manipulate the quality of their product to the detriment of consumers. Plaintiffs filed a class action asserting claims under federal and state law antitrust laws and various state consumer protection and common-law doctrines. The district court certified a settlement-only class, but differences among the many potentially applicable state laws led a panel of the Third Circuit to conclude that certification was improper. The en banc court reversed and reinstated the certification order. On the questions of predominance and manageability, the majority explained that, in a "settlement class action, we are not as concerned with formulating some prediction as to how variances in state law would play out at trial, for the proposal is that there be no trial." Rather, the court held, the possibility that variations in state law might "present the type of insuperable obstacles or intractable management problems pertinent to certification of a litigation class" are "largely irrelevant to certification of a settlement class." *Id.* at 303-304 (quotations and alterations omitted). *See also id.* at 335 (Scirica, J., concurring) ("A key question in a litigation class is manageability—how the case will or can be tried, and whether there are questions of fact or law that are capable of common proof. But the settlement class presents no management problems because the case will not be tried."). Are these more permissive approaches to settlement-only class actions compatible with *Amchem* and *Ortiz*? Judge Scirica noted in *Sullivan* that, "[d]espite initial uncertainty [those] opinions might pose formidable obstacles for settling massive, complex cases, that has not, for the most part, proved to be the case."

6. *Collateral Attacks on Settlement Class Actions.* A judgment in a class action (whether incorporating a settlement or otherwise) is, like other judgments, entitled to full faith and credit. But given the concerns about intra-class conflicts and sell-out settlements, should absent class plaintiffs have greater leeway to challenge a class action judgment asserted by way of *res judicata* when those plaintiffs attempt to bring their own litigation and claim that they were not adequately represented in the original class proceeding? Recall that such a collateral challenge was permitted

in *Hansberry v. Lee*, a class action that involved a stipulation (and possible collusion) but not a settlement. However, in *Hansberry*, which was an early, state version of a class suit, there were no procedures for "testing" the adequacy of representation in the initial proceeding. Today, under Rule 23 (and most state counterparts) a class can only be certified when the requisite standards and procedures have been satisfied—one of which is a finding of adequacy of representation by the certifying court. In addition, where the class action involves a settlement, that settlement is subject to the approval of the court.

The issue of collateral attacks on class action settlements arose in the *Matsushita* litigation, discussed in Chapter 7 at pp. 881–882. The Supreme Court, in *Matsushita Electric Indus. v. Epstein*, 516 U.S. 367 (1996), held that a "global" settlement of a class action, releasing both federal and state claims and approved by the state courts in Delaware, was preclusive of a subsequent federal securities action. That subsequent federal action had been brought by plaintiffs who were members of the earlier class and had not opted out of the Delaware state court action or settlement. Following the Supreme Court ruling and on remand to the Ninth Circuit, the federal plaintiffs claimed that, notwithstanding the preclusive effect of the settlement as a general matter, they had not been adequately represented in the state court proceeding and therefore were not bound by the judgment. A Ninth Circuit panel rejected that argument, distinguishing *Hansberry v. Lee* and finding that due process "requires that an absent class member's right to adequate representation be protected by the adoption of the appropriate procedures by the certifying court and by the courts that review its determinations; due process does not require collateral second-guessing of those determinations and that review." *Epstein v. MCA, Inc. (Epstein III)*, 179 F.3d 641, 648 (9th Cir. 1999). An interesting dialogue on the proper role for collateral attack and opt out in class actions appears in Marcel Kahan & Linda Silberman, *The Inadequate Search for "Adequacy" in Class Actions: A Critique of* Epstein v. MCA, Inc., 73 N.Y.U. L. Rev. 765 (1998); William T. Allen, *Finality of Judgments in Class Actions: A Comment on* Epstein v. MCA, Inc., 73 N.Y.U. L. Rev. 1149 (1998); Geoffrey P. Miller, *Full Faith and Credit to Settlements in Overlapping Class Actions*, 73 N.Y.U. L. Rev. 1167 (1998); Alan B. Morrison, *A Brief Reply to Professors Kahan and Silberman*, 73 N.Y.U. L. Rev. 1179 (1998); Marcel Kahan & Linda Silberman, *The Proper Role for Collateral Attack*, 73 N.Y.U. L. Rev. 1193 (1998). *See also* American Law Institute, *Principles of Aggregation (Preliminary Draft No. 3)*, §4.01 (2005) ("Any approach to settlement that constrains a claimant's ability to mount a collateral challenge must be accompanied by adequate protections on the front end to ensure that the rights of all claimants are protected."); Henry Paul Monaghan, *Antisuit Injunctions and Preclusion Against Absent Nonresident Class Members*, 98 Colum. L. Rev. 1148 (1998).

7. *Collateral Attacks and Future Claimants.* What if a settlement purports to release the claims of "future claimants"—individuals who have not yet manifested their injuries at the time of settlement, but who might become sick in the future? Are there any "appropriate procedures" (*see Epstein III, supra*) that could legitimately authorize a court to release the claims of people who, by definition, cannot even be identified at the time of trial? Following *Amchem*, it may be next to impossible for any federal court to certify a class action settlement including future claimants, particularly in a (b)(3) action for monetary damages. But there are class action settlements predating *Amchem* that have done just that. Is the "future claimant" problem serious enough to warrant the type of collateral attack that was turned away in *Matsushita*?

The Supreme Court dramatically failed to decide this issue in a closely watched case entitled *Dow Chemical v. Stephenson. Stephenson* was one chapter in the long litigation history of Agent Orange, a chemical defoliant used by the U.S. military during the Vietnam War that allegedly caused serious health problems years after exposure. In the first wave of Agent Orange litigation, Judge Jack Weinstein of the Eastern District of New York orchestrated a comprehensive global settlement of all outstanding claims. The settlement, which Judge Weinstein implemented in 1984, established a fund that would pay compensation to any eligible individual who manifested a signature disease identified with Agent Orange through 1994. In return, the defendants obtained a global release that forever protected them from all claims arising out of the use of Agent Orange in the jungles of Vietnam. *See In re Agent Orange Product Liab. Litig.*, 597 F. Supp. 740 (E.D.N.Y. 1984), *aff'd*, 818 F.2d 145 (2d Cir. 1987).

Daniel Stephenson and Joe Isaacson, both Vietnam veterans, were diagnosed with signature diseases in 1998 and 1996, respectively, well after the eligibility period for the Agent Orange settlement had expired. They filed suit against the defendants, who argued that the global release in the settlement shielded them from liability. The district court (Judge Weinstein again) agreed and dismissed the claims, but the Second Circuit reversed. The appeals court held that Stephenson and Isaacson were entitled to attack the settlement collaterally on the ground that they had not received adequate representation in the first proceeding. The Supreme Court, however, divided equally on the question, four to four (with Justice Stevens taking no part in the decision). The Second Circuit's opinion was thus left undisturbed but the Court's disposition had no precedential effect. *See Dow Chemical v. Stephenson*, 539 U.S. 111 (2003) (*per curiam*). *See also State v. Homeside Lending*, 826 A.2d 997 (Vt. 2003) (Vermont residents may bring suit, despite Alabama judgment purporting to resolve all claims, because of inadequate representation and lack of personal jurisdiction in original action); *Kamilewicz v. Bank of Boston*, 92 F.3d 506 (7th Cir. 1996) (rejecting attempt by class member to sue class counsel in same case).

8. *The Welfare of Claimants and the Promise of* Amchem *and* Ortiz. *Amchem* and *Ortiz* aim in part to protect absent class members from having their claims compromised or "sold off" without proper attention to their individual interests. But how have asbestos claimants fared in individual tort litigation since those decisions were handed down? According to Professor Deborah Hensler, one of the leading empirical researchers in the field of complex litigation, the results are decidedly mixed. *See* Deborah R. Hensler, *As Time Goes By: Asbestos Litigation After* Amchem *and* Ortiz, 80 Tex. L. Rev. 1899 (2002). Hensler reports that more defendant companies have declared bankruptcy, leaving fewer resources for future claimants, and that aggregate settlements of individual "inventory" claims have continued largely unabated, presenting many of the same concerns about lack of individualized attention that *Amchem* purported to address. On the other hand, new plaintiffs' attorneys have entered the field, opening up what previously had been a largely closed field of asbestos lawyers on the plaintiffs' side and employing aggressive litigation techniques to obtain some large jury awards. Thus, while there appear to be some potential short-term benefits for present claimants, Hensler concludes that *Amchem* and *Ortiz* put at risk those future victims who have the most at stake. *Id.* at 1924. Do these data lend support to Justice Breyer's dissenting view that the Court has interpreted the requirements of Rule 23 too strictly in the context of this unique litigation crisis?

8. *The Class Action Fairness Act*

In 2005, Congress enacted a major legislative reform in the class action arena, the Class Action Fairness Act. *See* Pub. L. No. 109-2, 119 Stat. 4 (Feb. 18, 2005) (enacting 28 U.S.C. §§1453 & 1711–1715, and amending 28 U.S.C.A. §§1332, 1335, and 1603). The Act significantly expanded the role of federal courts in adjudicating class actions that are based on state law while at the same time placing stricter controls on the approval of settlements by federal courts. The basic spirit animating the Act—hostility toward the perceived abuses of class action proceedings, particularly in the state courts—is perhaps best captured by the factual findings that are recited in its opening passages:

> **(2)** Over the past decade, there have been abuses of the class action device that have—
>
> **(A)** harmed class members with legitimate claims and defendants that have acted responsibly;
>
> **(B)** adversely affected interstate commerce; and
>
> **(C)** undermined public respect for our judicial system.
>
> **(3)** Class members often receive little or no benefit from class actions, and are sometimes harmed, such as where—
>
> **(A)** counsel are awarded large fees, while leaving class members with coupons or other awards of little or no value;
>
> **(B)** unjustified awards are made to certain plaintiffs at the expense of other class members; and
>
> **(C)** confusing notices are published that prevent class members from being able to fully understand and effectively exercise their rights.
>
> **(4)** Abuses in class actions undermine the national judicial system, the free flow of interstate commerce, and the concept of diversity jurisdiction as intended by the framers of the United States Constitution, in that State and local courts are—
>
> **(A)** keeping cases of national importance out of Federal court;
>
> **(B)** sometimes acting in ways that demonstrate bias against out-of-State defendants; and
>
> **(C)** making judgments that impose their view of the law on other States and bind the rights of the residents of those States.

Pub. L. 109-2, §2, Feb. 18, 2005, 119 Stat. 4.

In order to combat these perceived evils, the Act instituted two basic reforms: It expanded the diversity jurisdiction of the federal courts, authorizing them to hear many class actions where only minimal diversity exists; and it targeted certain problematic settlement practices.

a. The Jurisdictional Provisions of the Act

The basic assumption underlying the jurisdictional provisions of the Class Action Fairness Act is that the federal courts, on the whole, will be more cautious than state courts in certifying claims for classwide resolution. We have seen several examples of friction between state and federal courts in this chapter. In *Smith v. Bayer*, 131 S. Ct. 2368 (2011), class counsel sought to have a statewide class certified in state court after the Minnesota District Court denied certification in an earlier action asserting the same claims. The district court issued an injunction prohibiting the second case from going forward, but the Supreme Court reversed. Such cases reflect a general perception among class action lawyers that it is easier to shop for a permissive forum in state court than in federal court. While state appellate courts in many jurisdictions have begun to police certification practices more closely, *see, e.g., Southwestern Refining Co. v. Bernal*, 22 S.W.3d 425 (Tex. 2000), all it may take is a trial court willing to certify a class in order to pressure defendant into settling. The Class Action Fairness Act operates on the assumption that giving defendants broader access to federal court will cut down on abuses by ensuring more responsible certification practices early in the process.

The Act amends the diversity statute, authorizing federal district courts to exercise jurisdiction over class actions with an aggregate amount in controversy of at least $5 million where only minimal diversity standards are satisfied — that is, where at least one plaintiff and one defendant are citizens of different states (or, for alienage jurisdiction, a plaintiff is a citizen of a state and a defendant is a citizen of a foreign state). 28 U.S.C. §1332(d)(2). *But see Johnson v. Advance America*, 549 F.3d 932 (4th Cir. 2008) (dual citizenship of defendant company is not enough under CAFA to establish minimal diversity with co-citizen plaintiffs). The statute thus supersedes *Snyder v. Harris* on the issue of aggregation, adding together the claims of all class members in determining whether the jurisdictional amount is satisfied. *Id.* §(d)(6). The Act also includes exceptions to its jurisdictional provisions, which aim to exclude class actions that are primarily concentrated in a single state. The details of these exceptions are complicated and fall into two categories.

First, the Act authorizes district courts, in their discretion, to decline to exercise jurisdiction over class actions in which two conditions are met: (1) between one-third and two-thirds of all the proposed plaintiff class members are citizens of the state where the action is originally filed, and (2) the "primary defendants" are also citizens of that forum state. 28 U.S.C. §1332(d)(3). The Act lists a series of factors that the district court should consider in deciding whether to decline jurisdiction, the basic thrust of which is to determine whether the proposed class action is fundamentally national or local in scope. *Id.* §(d)(3)(A)–(F).

Second, the Act *requires* district courts to decline jurisdiction when over two-thirds of the proposed plaintiff class members are citizens of the state where the action is originally filed and either (1) the "primary defendants" are also citizens of the original forum state (this is called the "home state" exception), or (2) at least one defendant from whom "significant relief" is sought and who has allegedly engaged in conduct that forms a "significant basis" for the class claims, is a citizen of the original forum state (this is called the "local controversy" exception). *Id.* §(d)(4). The Act does not define the term "primary defendant." *See Hollinger v. Home State Mut. Ins. Co.*, 654 F.3d 564 (5th Cir. 2011) (in a discrimination suit against a large group of insurance providers, explaining that "The County Mutuals are the primary defendants, because all putative class members, by definition, have claims against the County Mutuals, and as the entities that issued the insurance policies, the County Mutuals have a primary role in the alleged discrimination.").

In addition, the Act completely exempts class actions from its new jurisdictional grant where the primary defendants are states or state officials or where the total number of plaintiffs is smaller than 100. *Id.* §(d)(5). The Act also excludes certain actions from its jurisdictional grant that involve traded securities and the internal affairs of corporations. *Id.* §(d)(9).

Finally, the Act identifies "mass actions"—defined as individual lawsuits "in which monetary relief claims of 100 or more persons are proposed to be tried jointly on the ground that the plaintiffs' claims involve common questions of law or fact"—and it extends the grant of minimal diversity to such proceedings. *Id.* §(d)(11). In the case of a mass action, however, the Act requires each plaintiff to satisfy the ordinary jurisdictional amount of $75,000, and certain other exceptions apply. *Id.*

Of course, in order for defendants to take advantage of the jurisdictional provisions of the Act, they must be able to remove cases that plaintiffs have filed in state court. Accordingly, the Act also liberalizes the standards for removal. As with an ordinary lawsuit, defendants may remove any case that could have been filed in federal court originally. The Act expressly authorizes any single defendant to effect such removal without the consent of its co-defendants. 28 U.S.C. §1453(b). Removal ordinarily requires the consent of all defendants, a proposition made explicit in the 2011 amendments to the removal statute. *See* 28 U.S.C. §1446(b)(2)(A). The Act eliminates the in-state defendant exception, expressly authorizing defendants to remove a case "without regard to whether any defendant is a citizen of the State in which the action is brought," and it does away with the one-year time limit that usually applies to removal of a diversity case, authorizing defendants to remove to federal court if the case becomes removable at any point in the proceedings. 28 U.S.C. §1453(b). The Act also creates an exception to the general prohibition against appealing a district court's remand of a case to state court, authorizing the courts of appeals to "accept an appeal from an order of a district court granting or denying a motion to remand a class action to the State court from which it was removed if application is made to the court of appeals not more than 10 days after entry of the order." *Id.* §(c)(1). This provision creates a discretionary avenue of interlocutory appeal for remand orders (which are non-final in nature), with the proviso that the court of appeals is required to complete review of any case it accepts "not later than 60 days after the date on which such appeal was filed," *id.* §(c)(2). *See, e.g., Probola v. Long & Foster Real Estate*, 2012 WL 1959550 (3d Cir. June 1, 2012) (describing discretionary nature of review and collecting cases).

These provisions have the effect of channeling large numbers of class actions based entirely on state law into the federal courts.

b. Limitations on Class Action Settlements

Once a class action gets into federal court, the Act imposes substantive limitations on the types of settlements that the parties may enter into. Note that these sections of the Act apply to all class actions in federal court, not merely those that make it there by way of the jurisdictional provisions described above. But they do not apply to state court proceedings.

The portions of the Act relating to settlement target practices falling into two categories. The first includes practices that the Act treats as suspect—not categorically forbidden, but requiring written findings by the district court that the disputed practices will produce some benefit for the class before they can be employed. One such practice is the award of "coupons" and other "noncash" settlements to class members. In the case of consumer class actions in particular—those arising out of defective products, for example, or improper marketing practices—the only benefit that the lawyers sometimes negotiate for the class in a proposed settlement is a coupon that gives discounts on future purchase of the goods and services that the defendant sells. Such coupons often have restrictions (such as being nontransferable or unable to be combined with any other sales promotion) that reduce them to little more than a marketing tool for the defendants. Even so, courts have sometimes awarded fees to class counsel based on the face value of these coupons, apparently assuming that a nontransferable $300 coupon off your next purchase of a pickup truck (for example) is just as good as a check for $300 in cash. Such coupon settlements have been widely criticized. *See, e.g.*, Christopher R. Leslie, *A Market-Based Approach to Coupon Settlements in Antitrust and Consumer Class Action Litigation*, 49 UCLA L. Rev. 991 (2002).

The Class Action Fairness Act mandates careful judicial scrutiny of coupon payouts, requiring that a court authorize them "only after a hearing to determine whether, and making a written finding that, the settlement is fair, reasonable, and adequate for class members." 28 U.S.C. §1712(e). It also specifies that the attorneys in a coupon settlement may only be awarded a contingency fee "based on the value to class members of the coupons that are *redeemed*," rather than the face value of the total number of coupons *awarded, id.* §(a) (emphasis added); otherwise, the attorneys must be paid only for "the amount of time class counsel reasonably expended working on the action" in a coupon case. *Id.* §(b). The Act also forbids approval of any settlement that would require class members to pay money in return for some noncash relief, resulting in a net cash loss to the class member, unless the court first makes "a written finding that nonmonetary benefits to the class member substantially outweigh the monetary loss." *Id.* §1713. *See, e.g., In re Methyl Tertiary Butyl Ether (MTBE) Products Liability Litigation*, 209 F.R.D. 323, 335, 348 (S.D.N.Y. 2002) (discussing, and rejecting, a proposed class action for purely injunctive relief in which class members would have to pay $100–$200 for a test kit to identify themselves as claimants).

In addition, the Act forbids outright the practice of slanting settlement agreements in favor of local members of the class, declaring "closer geographic proximity to the court" to be an illegitimate basis, without more, for more favorable treatment. 28 U.S.C. §1714. This provision aims to prevent class counsel from giving more favorable treatment to local class members simply to increase the likelihood that class counsel will occupy a leading role in the proceeding and collect larger fees.

c.   Reporting Requirements

The Class Action Fairness Act also includes procedural requirements for the approval of class action settlements that aim to increase public oversight of negotiated classwide agreements. Within ten days of filing a proposed class action settlement, each defendant is now required to serve notice "upon the appropriate State official of each State in which a class member resides and the appropriate Federal official." 28 U.S.C. §1715(b). ("State official" means the state attorney general or other appropriate executive; "federal official" means the Attorney General or an appropriate regulator.) The notice must include a copy of the complaint and any related materials, copies of any notice sent to the class during the course of the lawsuit, any proposed class settlement, copies of any other agreements between class counsel and defendants, the names of all class members in each state (or, if that is not feasible, an estimate of the numbers and locations of the class members), and any judicial opinions, orders, or judgments in the case. The Act then requires the district court to wait at least 90 days following provision of this notice before giving final approval to any class action settlement, in order to give state and federal officials — or other private attorneys — an opportunity to take action if they wish. *Id.* §1715(d).

This notification requirement contains a robust enforcement provision. If defendants fail to provide the required notice, "[a] class member may refuse to comply with and may choose not to be bound by a settlement agreement or consent decree in a class action." *Id.* §1715(e)(1). *See also id.* §(e)(2) (foreclosing this escape clause if notice reached appropriate federal official and state attorney general). In other words, if the defendants fail to comply with the notification requirements, class members can either enjoy the benefit of the settlement or choose to "opt out" and sue again, at their option. Consequently, one can expect that defendants will now provide such notice as a matter of course. Note again, however, that this provision, like 28 U.S.C. §§1712-1714, applies only to proceedings filed in or removed to federal court. Many commentators and state attorneys general have reacted with skepticism toward the notion that the required notice will provide state officials with actionable evidence of collusion, or that the officials will have either the tools or the resources to investigate further. *See* Catherine M. Sharkey, *CAFA Settlement Notice Provision: Optimal Regulatory Policy?*, 156 U. Pa. L. Rev. 1971 (2008) (canvassing initial reactions and using settlement notice provision as a vehicle for analyzing CAFA as regulatory policy).

d.   Removal Under the Act

Interpreting the Class Action Fairness Act in the removal context has been an arduous task, with courts having to craft rules for the Act's complex and poorly drafted provisions:

1. *Burdens of Proof.* One issue that has arisen pertains to which party — the plaintiff or the defendant — bears the burden of the proof when the defendant removes a case to federal court (to produce evidence and persuade the judge as to whether a motion to remand should be granted). Based on pre-CAFA principles, this would have been an easily resolvable issue. The removing party typically has the obligation to demonstrate that the case qualifies for federal jurisdiction under the appropriate statutes. However, the text of CAFA fails to specify where this burden falls, and the Senate Judiciary Committee stated in its report recommending the bill that *plaintiffs* must demonstrate that removal was *unfounded* when they move for remand. *See* S. Rep. No. 109-14, at 42 (2005). Initially, multiple district courts followed this legislative directive and imposed the burden of proof on the plaintiff. *See, e.g., Berry v. Am. Express Publ'g*, 381 F. Supp. 2d 1118 (C.D. Cal. 2005). However, the courts of appeals rejected that view and determined that the legislative history, unattached to any statutory text, did not shift the traditional burden. *See, e.g., Abrego Abrego v. Dow Chem. Co.*, 443 F.3d 676, 686 (9th Cir. 2006); *Miedema v. Maytag Corp.*,

450 F.3d 1322, 1330 (11th Cir. 2006). But there are exceptions. With respect to "declinations" of jurisdiction under §§1332(d)(3) and (d)(4) — which consider, among other things, the proportion of plaintiffs that are citizens of the state where the action is filed — courts have shifted this burden to plaintiffs desiring remand. Courts have distinguished these "declinations" from the prima facie case of jurisdiction, which the party requesting federal jurisdiction must assert. *See, e.g., Serrano v. 180 Connect, Inc.*, 478 F.3d 1018 (9th Cir. 2007) (following the rule that a party seeking an exception to jurisdiction must prove that such an exception exists). *See also Garcia v. Boyar & Miller, P.C.*, 2007 WL 1556961 (N.D. Tex. May 30, 2007) (finding that requirement that class consist of more than 100 members is a "statutory exception" to jurisdiction, rather than a "jurisdictional requirement," and hence that the burden of proof falls on the party opposing jurisdiction, rather than the party seeking to establish it). Note also that the complex factual determinations called for by CAFA's jurisdictional provisions may require the court to make preliminary inquiries into the merits of the suit, just as we saw in the *Rose v. Giamatti* case. *See, e.g., Louisiana ex rel. Caldwell v. Allstate Ins. Co.*, 536 F.3d 418 (5th Cir. 2008) (conducting real-party-in-interest inquiry to determine proper way to frame jurisdictional analysis).

2. *Determining the Aggregate Amount in Plaintiffs' Complaint.* A related issue in removal situations involves determining whether the amount in controversy meets the threshold of an aggregate of $5 million, a recurring problem given that defendants carry the burden of proof as the removing party. Many plaintiffs do not insert an *ad damnum* clause specifying the amount of relief sought in their state-court complaint, requiring defendants to remove cases with limited information about the plaintiffs' suit. Consider *Miedema v. Maytag Corp.*, 450 F.3d 1322 (11th Cir. 2006), where Florida consumers brought a class action against the manufacturer of allegedly defective ovens. Plaintiffs' complaint did not specify any amount of relief. In an attempt to remove the case to federal court, the defendant filed an affidavit detailing the number of ovens sold in Florida and calculated the value of those ovens as surpassing $5 million. The court found this affidavit unconvincing because it was unclear whether the monetary values actually reflected the compensatory damages sought by the plaintiffs. The court also noted that the defendant had used an *estimate* of sales volume in Florida in its computation, which required an assumption that the registration rate by Florida consumers closely paralleled the national average. How specific would the defendant's calculations have to be in order to meet the court's demanding standard of removal? Is the court's approach consistent with the purpose of CAFA to bring more class actions into the federal courts in order to protect defendants from overly lenient class certification in state courts? *See also Lowery v. Alabama Power Co.*, 483 F.3d 1184, 1220–1221 (11th Cir. 2007) (refusing to consider defendants' evidence that the value of similar tort claims in Alabama was indicative of the amount in controversy, questioning "whether such general evidence is ever of much use in establishing the value of claims in any one particular suit").

The Supreme Court has issued a decision on the amount in controversy requirement that imposes some limits on the ability of plaintiffs to avoid removal under the Class Action Fairness Act. In *Standard Fire Ins. v. Knowles*, 133 S. Ct. 1345 (2013), the plaintiff brought a class action in Arkansas state court on behalf of "hundreds, and possibly thousands" of homeowners, claiming that the defendant had violated state law by failing to include certain required payments when reimbursing policyholders. In an attempt to avoid removal to federal court, Knowles stipulated in his complaint that he would "not at any time during this case . . . seek damages for the class . . . in excess of $5,000,000 in the aggregate" and later swore out an affidavit to the same effect. *Id.* at 1347 (alterations in original). At a jurisdictional hearing following removal, the district court found that the aggregate amount in controversy would exceed $5,000,000 in the absence of the stipulation but nonetheless concluded that the stipulation must control. The Eighth Circuit declined to hear a discretionary interlocutory appeal, *see* Rule 23(f), but the Supreme Court granted a petition for writ of certiorari and reversed, finding that the stipulation did not override the district court's finding that the jurisdictional amount was satisfied.

Litigants are ordinarily bound by their stipulations, and the Court had previously held that an individual plaintiff can defeat removal to federal court by binding itself to a stipulation that it will only seek a recovery of less than the jurisdictional amount in a diversity case. The *Knowles* Court reaffirmed that principle as to individual litigants. But the issue in *Knowles* was whether the entire class would recover $5,000,000 in the aggregate. When the plaintiff filed his lawsuit, the Court explained, the action was a putative class action but it had not been certified for class treatment. Prior to certification, Knowles himself was the only party to the action. Citing its earlier ruling in *Smith v. Bayer*, 564 U.S. 299 (2011), the Court explained that "a plaintiff who files a proposed class action cannot legally bind members of the proposed class before the class is certified." That being so, the Court held, Knowles "lacked the authority to concede the amount-in-controversy issue for the absent class members." *Knowles*, 133 S. Ct. at 1349. While it was possible that the state court would certify the class and allow the plaintiff to bind class members to his stipulation — a prospect that the plaintiff had urged as a basis for finding that the stipulation should control the jurisdictional question — it was also possible that the state court would reject the stipulation, or find that Knowles was an inadequate representative for placing an "artificial cap" on the class members' recovery. *Id.* To allow a nonbinding stipulation to control the jurisdictional analysis through speculation about what the state court might do in the future would be to "exalt form over substance" and undermine CAFA's purpose to ensure "federal court consideration of interstate cases of national importance." *Id.* (citing CAFA § 2(b)(2), 119 Stat. 5).

3. *The "Home State" and "Local Controversy" Exceptions.* While defendants have grappled with amount-in-controversy quandaries, plaintiffs have a similarly difficult task if they want to remand the case based on either the §1332(d)(3) or (d)(4) exceptions: They must demonstrate that either one-third or two-thirds of the plaintiff class are citizens of the forum state. In a plaintiff class of thousands of members, this task can approach the impossible given the complexities of determining citizenship. Consider *Evans v. Walter Industries, Inc.*, 449 F.3d 1159 (11th Cir. 2006). The class plaintiffs alleged that defendants released waste substances that caused property damage and personal injuries near a small city in Alabama. Several of the defendants removed the case under CAFA, and plaintiffs looked to remand under the "local controversy" exception, §1332(d)(4). In an attempt to determine that

at least two-thirds of the plaintiffs were citizens of Alabama, an attorney for the plaintiffs interviewed 5,200 members of the class, of whom more than 90 percent resided in Alabama. The plaintiffs contended that if 90 percent of the interviewed class members were Alabama *residents*, it is a valid presumption that more than two-thirds of the total class were Alabama *citizens*. The court rejected this evidence as unpersuasive, questioning the attorney's selection of interviewees. While the court acknowledged that demonstrating the plaintiff class's citizenship was a tall order, these obstacles were "to a considerable degree a function of the composition of the class designed by plaintiffs." *Id.* at 1166. *See also Schwartz v. Comcast Corp.*, 2006 WL 487915 (E.D. Pa. 2006) (refusing to assume that residence is a proxy for domicile, even in the class action context). Won't similar problems of proof affect many large class actions?

The Fifth Circuit seems to have taken a more flexible approach. In *Preston v. Tenet Healthsystem Mem'l Med. Ctr., Inc.*, 485 F.3d 804 (5th Cir. 2007), a class of patients sued a hospital for negligence, intentional misconduct, and other state law claims relating to the chaos surrounding the landfall of Hurricane Katrina. When the plaintiffs attempted to remand the case to state court under the discretionary jurisdiction exception to CAFA, §1332(d)(3), plaintiffs presented several pieces of evidence: data gathered from the plaintiffs' medical records, plaintiffs' listed emergency contact phone numbers, and, most important, eight affidavits out of hundreds of potential class members stating their desire to return to New Orleans even though they currently resided in a different state. (Remember that domicile includes the place to which a person "has the intention of returning.") The court emphasized that "the evidentiary standard for establishing the domicile of more than one hundred plaintiffs must be based on practicality and reasonableness." *Id.* at 816. Distinguishing *Evans*, it declared that the plaintiffs' evidence allowed the district court to reasonably assume that the requisite one-third of the plaintiffs were domiciled in Louisiana, especially given the "shared catalyst" of Hurricane Katrina. Which approach — that of the *Evans* court or the *Preston* court — is preferable? For the view that proof of residency should provide a rebuttable presumption of domicile in these situations, *see* Stephen J. Shapiro, *Applying the Jurisdictional Provisions of the Class Action Fairness Act of 2005: In Search of a Sensible Judicial Approach*, 59 Baylor L. Rev. 77, 132–135 (2007). As with other questions relating to subject matter jurisdiction, the applicability of the home-state exception is measured at the time of removal, and courts have concluded that subsequent changes during the course of litigation cannot bring the case within an exception. *See, e.g., Colomar v. Mercy Hospital*, 2007 WL 2083562 (S.D. Fla. July 20, 2007).

Lower federal courts have also held that the home-state and local-controversy exceptions need not be analyzed exclusively with reference to the allegations made in plaintiff's complaint. Congress's express policy to prevent suits that qualify for the home-state exception from being adjudicated in federal court may require those courts to look outside the allegations of the complaint in assessing jurisdiction. *See, e.g., In re Hannaford Bros. Co. Customer Data Security Breach Litig.*, 564 F.3d 75, 79 (1st Cir. 2009) (acknowledging that federal courts must sometimes look outside the allegations contained in the complaint in jurisdictional disputes, including those under CAFA, but finding such an inquiry unnecessary in the case at bar and holding that home-state exception precludes federal jurisdiction).

In this connection, recall the Supreme Court's decision in *Knowles, supra.* All the plaintiffs in that case were Arkansas policyholders. Diversity was satisfied because the insurance company was an out-of-state citizen. Together, those facts brought the case outside the operation of CAFA's home-state and local-controversy exceptions. *See* 28 U.S.C. §§1332(d)(3) & (4). Was *Knowles* really an "interstate case of national importance," as the Court described it? *Knowles,* 133 S. Ct. at 1349. Leading commentators argue that CAFA's exceptions are poorly drafted and harm federalism values because they fail to exclude cases that involve class plaintiffs from a single state where all the alleged injuries occurred in that state and where the defendant, though incorporated and headquartered elsewhere, has a substantial business presence in the state. *See, e.g.,* Stephen B. Burbank, *Fairness to Whom: The Class Action Fairness Act of 2005 in Historical Context: A Preliminary View,* 156 U. Pa. L. Rev. 1439, 1535–1539 (2008).

4. *The Riddle of "Mass Actions."* Perhaps the most perplexing provision of CAFA is the "mass actions" portion of the statute, §1332(d)(11). This provision allows defendants to remove state-court actions deemed "mass actions" that are not class actions but have at least 100 plaintiffs and common questions of law or fact. Congress implemented this provision to prevent plaintiffs from structuring their lawsuits in state court to avoid the jurisdictional requirements of CAFA. But, as one court grumbled, "CAFA's mass action provisions present an opaque, baroque maze of interlocking cross-references that defy easy interpretation." *Lowery v. Alabama Power Co.,* 483 F.3d 1184, 1198 (11th Cir. 2007). First, under §1332(11)(B)(i), even if a mass action is deemed to be removable under the other provisions of CAFA, there is an additional stipulation that "jurisdiction shall only exist only over those plaintiffs whose claims in a mass action satisfy the jurisdictional amount requirement under subsection (a)." Does this provision require a removing defendant to show that all plaintiffs must exceed the individual jurisdictional amount ($75,000) *and* that there be an aggregate ($5 million) amount in controversy? The Fifth Circuit has harmonized these apparently competing requirements by holding that at least one plaintiff in a mass action (but not all) must have an individual amount in controversy that exceeds $75,000, and also that the aggregate amount of $5,000,000 must be met by the action as a whole. *See Hood ex rel Mississippi v. J.P. Morgan Chase & Co.,* 737 F.3d 78, 85–86 (5th Cir. 2013).

Even more befuddling is the fact that the mass action provision, 28 U.S.C. §1332(d)(11) only refers to removal jurisdiction; the rest of §1332, in contrast, grants federal courts "original jurisdiction." Does this mean that plaintiffs could not bring a mass action in federal court? The issue has yet to be analyzed at any length by a federal court, though a few have mentioned the anomaly, *see, e.g., Lowery* at 1200, n. 41, while a few others have suggested in *dictum* (incorrectly, it appears) that subsection (d)(11) includes a grant of "original jurisdiction." *See, e.g., Mireles v. Wells Fargo Bank,* 845 F. Supp. 2d 1034, 1047–1048 (C.D. Cal. 2012).

Consider also the language in subsection (d)(11), which specifies "claims of 100 or more persons . . . proposed to be *tried jointly*" (emphasis added). Does this term suggest that an action is removable under §(d)(11) only when a trial is imminent, rather than at the initiation of the action when there is not yet a specific "proposal" for a trial, or only when the removed action will involve a single mass trial rather than multiple hearings or trials in the joint resolution of the removed claims? Such arguments have not met with favor. *See Bullard v. Burlington Northern Santa Fe Rwy. Co.*, 535 F.3d 759 (7th Cir. 2008) (rejecting these arguments). However, courts have been less sympathetic to an expansive reading of the "proposed to be tried jointly" language when a defendant seeks to remove several individually filed actions that are formally independent of each other and that each have fewer than a hundred plaintiffs. Even if the defendant will have to respond to multiple actions in state court that assert nearly identical claims and may be consolidated for pretrial discovery, the requirement that the court or the plaintiffs propose a joint *trial* appears to be strict. *See Tanoh v. Dow Chemical Co.*, 561 F.3d 945 (2009). Likewise, the Supreme Court has rejected an attempt to apply the numerosity requirement of the mass action provision to a state asserting claims on behalf of its citizens. *Mississippi ex rel. Hood v. AU Optronics*, 134 S. Ct. 736 (2014), involved state antitrust and unfair competition claims against a manufacturer of liquid-crystal displays. Mississippi sued in state court, alleging the formation of a cartel that drove up prices and seeking damages for many aggrieved customers in the form of restitution. The defendant removed to federal court, relying on the mass action provision for subject matter jurisdiction by arguing that the consumers on whose behalf the state sought restitution were the "real parties in interest," *see* Fed. R. Civ. Proc. 17, and hence that their claims were effectively "proposed to be tried jointly" even though the State of Mississippi was the only plaintiff in the lawsuit. The Court rejected this argument. Pointing out that the mass action provision echoes the text of Rule 20, the Court concluded that it authorizes jurisdiction only over "individuals who are proposing to join as plaintiffs in a single action," *id.* at 742, not absent persons whose interests might be implicated in the case. The Court distinguished some of its earlier precedents that had permitted a "real party in interest" analysis to determine whether the requirements of diversity were satisfied, concluding that "Congress provided express indications [in CAFA] that it did not want [that] principle to apply to the mass action provision." *Id.* at 746.

5. *Allapattah's Influence.* Given the abolition of many of the traditional removal jurisdiction prerequisites in §1453, it is not surprising that defendants have tried to expand §1453's reach to class actions outside of CAFA. Such a statutory hook may exist. *See* Adam N. Steinman, *Sausage-Making, Pigs' Ears, and Congressional Expansions of Federal Jurisdiction:* Exxon Mobil v. Allapattah *and Its Lessons for the Class Action Fairness Act*, 81 Wash. L. Rev. 279 (2006). Look closely at §1453. This provision defines several terms, including "class action," by referring to §1332(d)(1). Section 1332(d)(1), meanwhile, defines class action as "any civil action filed under rule 23 of the Federal Rules of Civil Procedure or similar State statute. . . ." Importantly, this definition does not limit class actions to those included in CAFA, because Rule 23 does not set a monetary bar or provide a minimum number of plaintiffs for class actions (beyond the numerosity requirement of Rule 23(a)). This expanded definition of "class action" appears to affect both §1453(b), which eliminates the traditional removal limitations, and §1453(c), which permits broader appellate review of remand orders. Given the Supreme Court's professed adherence to the plain text of statutes in *Allapattah*, isn't there a legitimate argument that all class actions (aside from some very specific exceptions in §1453(d)) are removable by a defendant? So far, courts have not found this argument persuasive despite the statutory text. *See, e.g., In re UPS Supply Chain Solutions*, 2008 WL 4767817 (6th Cir. Oct. 27, 2008); *Saab v. Home Depot U.S.A., Inc.*, 469 F.3d 758, 759-760 (8th Cir. 2006).

6. *CAFA and Removal of Securities Class Actions.* There are some federal statutes that prevent removal of certain claims from state to federal court, even when
removal would otherwise be proper. When a claim that is subject to such a limitation
on removal is brought as a class action, are such statutory limitations superseded by
the removal provisions of the Class Action Fairness Act? *See* 28 U.S.C. §1453. The
federal courts of appeal are already dividing on that question in the context of securities litigation. A portion of the Securities Act of 1933, section 22(a), provides that
certain cases arising under the federal securities laws are not removable to federal
court when they are properly brought in state court in the first instance. 15 U.S.C.
§77v(a). That restriction was partially lifted by the Securities Litigation Uniform
Standards Act of 1998, *see* 15 U.S.C. §77p(c), but it still forbids removal for some
securities claims. If a securities claim that is otherwise not removable because of
section 22(a) of the Securities Act is brought as a class action, can it now be removed
under §1453? The Ninth Circuit answered that question in the affirmative, but the
Seventh Circuit disagreed. *Compare Luther v. Countrywide Home Loans Servicing LP*,
533 F.3d 1031 (9th Cir. 2008) (finding that more "specific" bar on removal of securities claims trumps more "general" removal provisions of CAFA) *with Katz v. Gerardi*,
552 F.3d 558 (7th Cir. 2009) (finding that §1453 supersedes section 22(a) in cases of
incompatibility and remanding for further analysis by the district court).

The Class Action Fairness Act was hotly contested in Congress for years before
its passage, and the controversy promises to continue as its provisions are implemented. Critics charge that the Act recites a laudable purpose when it claims to
reduce abusive settlement practices but applies an excessively blunt response that
would sweep numerous lawsuits into federal court and usurp the role of state courts
in adjudicating state-law disputes. Supporters of the Act respond that a broad remedy was necessary to stem a mounting tide of abusive suits in state court systems
where trial courts sometimes provide little oversight and even less discipline. Consider both perspectives as you read the following notes.

NOTES AND QUESTIONS

1. *Diversity Jurisdiction and Federalism Values.* The most dramatic consequence
of the Class Action Fairness Act is to move a substantial number of class actions
from state court into federal court, displacing—some might say usurping—the
traditional role of state courts in adjudicating disputes that are based on state law.
See Stephen B. Burbank, *The Class Action Fairness Act of 2005 in Historical Context:
A Preliminary View*, 156 U. Pa. L. Rev. 1439 (2008) (developing this critique). In
our discussion of diversity jurisdiction in Chapter 3, we identified this feature of
diversity as a potential cost to *federalism values*: the theory of governance under
which it is presumptively better for state laws to be interpreted and adjudicated
by state courts, which have the power to issue authoritative interpretations of state
law, are accountable to the state legislature and citizenry, and may have a superior
knowledge of local legal norms. That cost, we said, was mitigated in the case of the
general grant of diversity by the relatively limited nature of that provision (which
requires complete diversity of citizenship) and was justified by the benefit of providing an unbiased tribunal for out-of-state parties that is more likely to be free
from political pressure.

What are the implications of the Class Action Fairness Act for federalism values? Unlike in the run-of-the-mill diversity case, there would seem to be a strong argument that federal courts are inherently *more* appropriate than state courts for the resolution of multistate disputes, even when those disputes are based on state law. In a suit of nationwide scope, it may be preferable for a national forum—with judges appointed and confirmed by national political officials—to be responsible for decisions that could have national economic or social implications. Might it not be argued that the Act is an appropriate, targeted use of diversity jurisdiction designed to respond to a specific problem of national importance?

Even if this is so, the Act appears to sweep more broadly than it needs to in accomplishing its goal. For example, consider a class action in which all the plaintiffs reside in the forum state (say, Texas) and are suing over activity that occurred within the forum, but the defendant, though doing substantial business in the forum, is formally a citizen of another state (say, California). This is a Texas lawsuit in every respect other than the formal citizenship of the defendant, yet it would fall within the Act's jurisdictional grant and could be removed to federal court if the aggregate amount in controversy topped $5,000,000. (Recall that, in the absence of the Act, plaintiffs with claims worth less than $75,000 could not get into federal court through aggregation.) Note that neither the discretionary nor the mandatory abstention provision of the Act applies when all the defendants are formally citizens of states other than the forum, as in this example. Is that an appropriate result?

There may also be a danger that the Act will prevent state courts from determining the appropriate substantive rules of decision for the resolution of multistate disputes. The Act only authorizes federal courts to exercise jurisdiction, it does not create substantive law for the resolution of the dispute, nor does it authorize the federal courts to create such law themselves. Federal courts will thus apply state law and state choice of law rules when they hear cases under the Act. (*See Klaxon v. Stentor Elec. Mfg., supra* Chapter 4.) If most multistate class actions are removed under the Act, state courts may have little opportunity to set forth authoritative rules for determining the applicable law or to articulate the state's substantive policies in disputes of that kind.

How would you characterize the Class Action Fairness Act? Is it a reasonable response to perceived abuses in the administration of class actions by out-of-control state courts? Or is it an overbroad solution to an overstated problem? How serious are the costs to federalism values under the Act?

2. *Determining Jurisdiction.* The new grant of diversity jurisdiction contained in the Class Action Fairness Act is complicated. The statute leaves many terms undefined and many questions unanswered. Who counts as a "primary defendant" under §1332(d)(3)-(4)? If most of the primary defendants satisfy those provisions but a few do not, what is the result? How is the district court to determine what proportion of the plaintiff class members (one-third, two-thirds) are citizens of the forum state? What standard of proof is required and what type of evidence would be sufficient for that determination?

Even after federal courts have had the opportunity to provide guidance about the meaning of these provisions, they will still require many contentious factual questions to be resolved at the outset of the proceeding. Isn't this a serious drawback? We have said that there is value in clear jurisdictional rules that permit a court to determine quickly and with certainty whether it has power to hear a dispute.

We do not want to force courts to expend significant effort on questions that might overlap the merits of the suit before the pleading and discovery stages have narrowed and developed the issues before it, nor do we want to increase the risk that courts will spend significant time and effort on the adjudication of a dispute only to have it reversed for jurisdictional reasons on appeal. The Class Action Fairness Act appears to increase the probability of such inefficiencies.

The Act mitigates these inefficiencies somewhat by authorizing immediate appeals from any order granting or denying a motion to remand a removed case to state court, 28 U.S.C. §1453(c)(1) — a provision that parallels Rule 23(f)'s discretionary appeal of certification rulings in some respects. (Oddly, the Act does not offer a similar avenue of appeal for the denial of a motion to dismiss for lack of subject matter jurisdiction in a case that was filed in federal court in the first instance.) This provision will help guard against the waste of effort that might result from a subsequent reversal of a trial on the merits because of jurisdiction. At the same time, however, the opportunity for such discretionary appeals increases the likelihood that courts will have to expend significant effort on threshold jurisdictional issues before the parties have developed any record on the merits. Is this a serious problem? In a class action proceeding, where the court must take a preliminary look at the nature of the dispute in determining whether to certify the class in any event, is there reason to think that the impact of the jurisdictional provisions will be less serious than first appears? Or do the certification inquiry and the jurisdictional determination involve different factual issues?

Lower federal courts interpreting CAFA have applied the familiar principle that the jurisdiction of the federal courts cannot be ousted by developments subsequent to filing or removal. For example, in *Vega v. T-Mobile USA*, 564 F.3d 1256 (11th Cir. 2009), a question arose as to whether CAFA's numerosity requirement was satisfied in a case that was filed in state court and removed to federal court. The question of numerosity was raised and litigated at the time of removal and the district court found that requirement to be satisfied. The definition of the class in the proposed action was subsequently narrowed, and a question arose as to whether numerosity was still satisfied, with the plaintiff seeking to have the case remanded back to state court. The Eleventh Circuit held that such post-filing or post-removal developments would not divest the court of jurisdiction. "Even if it were later found that the narrowed . . . class numbers fewer than 100," the court held, "the §1332(d)(5)(B) limitation applies only to 'proposed' plaintiff classes (as opposed to classes actually certified or that go to trial); jurisdictional facts are assessed at the time of removal; and post-removal events (including non-certification, de-certification, or severance) do not deprive federal courts of subject matter jurisdiction." *Id.* at 1268 n.12.

As with other questions bearing upon subject matter jurisdiction, the federal courts may raise questions on their own initiative concerning whether the requirements of the Class Action Fairness Act are satisfied. *See, e.g., County of Nassau v. Hotels.com*, 577 F.3d 89 (2d Cir. 2009) (raising *sua sponte* the question whether the numerosity requirement of the Class Action Fairness Act was satisfied and remanding to the district court for further inquiries on the factual basis for jurisdiction).

3. *One-Sided Relief?* Critics of the class action have identified two types of problem that arise from lax certification standards. First, there are class suits that we might label "abusive." These are lawsuits that exhibit serious problems of certification — for example, because choice of law analysis would seem to require the

application of many different legal standards to different parts of the dispute—and arguably should never be certified at all; or, alternatively, they are lawsuits that offer little promise of "superior" relief and are brought primarily to extort large fees from defendants, sometimes producing only nominal benefits to the class. Second, there are class actions that exhibit problems of apparent "collusion." The problem of collusion may arise in suits where a real threat of liability exists, along with a legitimate basis for proceeding on a classwide basis, such that certification of a class appears socially useful. In such cases, defendants will sometimes "shop" among counsel for a cooperative plaintiff's lawyer willing to agree to cheap settlement terms in order to secure a generous fee. Class counsel, in other words, sometimes sell off the interests of class members in order to ensure that they will be the ones to get paid. Even in the absence of collusion, the skewed incentives of class counsel in such cases can result in the interests of class members not receiving proper protection. Suits of this type often take the form of a settlement-only class action, where the plaintiff attorneys and the defendant will present to the court a complaint, an answer, a motion for class certification, and a proposed class settlement as a *fait accompli*. In extreme cases, defendants purchase a global release at bargain basement prices, plaintiff's attorneys secure a contingency fee by winning the race to serve as class counsel, and the class members receive little or no actual payment for their potentially valuable claims. *See, e.g.*, Richard A. Nagareda, *The Preexistence Principle and the Structure of the Class Action*, 103 Colum. L. Rev. 149, 159–181 (2003) (describing the class action as a "market" in which defendants can purchase claim preclusive repose).

The promise of the Class Action Fairness Act is to remedy both of these class action problems by authorizing the removal of class actions into federal court, where the Act then imposes limitations on the types of settlements class counsel can enter into and, more broadly, where the hope is that the federal courts will police the behavior of counsel more closely. But does the Act fulfill that promise for everyone involved? For corporate defendants, the benefits of the Act are clear: They can escape abusive lawsuits at the hands of overreaching state courts by removing to a federal forum so long as they can satisfy the modest requirement of minimal diversity and the other particulars of the statute. But what about absent class plaintiffs who are threatened by collusive or otherwise inadequate settlements? How will the Act protect their interests? When the interests of defendant and class counsel become aligned in the settlement process, the defendant has no incentive to remove the case to the more careful scrutiny of a federal forum, nor does class counsel have any incentive to file in federal court in the first place.

In order to protect absent class members in such cases, the Act would have to authorize absent class *plaintiffs* to remove cases as well, relying on absent class members (or competing attorneys) to monitor class proceedings and seek removal when a collusive or inadequate settlement appears to be in the offing. As enacted, the Act contains no such provision. Thus, the relief offered by the Act appears to be one sided, operating largely to the benefit of defendants who wish to escape from suits that they don't want to litigate while providing no assistance to absent plaintiffs who are being poorly served by their own representatives. *See* Tobias Barrington Wolff, *Federal Jurisdiction and Due Process in the Era of the Nationwide Class Action*, 156 U. Pa. L. Rev. 2035 (2008) (identifying these features of CAFA and exploring their implications).

Earlier versions of the Act did have a provision for removal by absent class plaintiffs. Starting with the proposed Class Action Jurisdiction Act of 1998, first introduced as a bill into the House of Representatives, the statute authorized removal of a class action "by any plaintiff class member who is not a named or representative class member of the action for which removal is sought, without the consent of all members of such class." 1998 Cong. U.S. H.R. 3789 (105th Cong., 2d sess.), §1453(a)(2). Similar provisions may be found in every version of the bill introduced into Congress through 2003. It was only in late 2003 that an amendment was made to the pending bill that eliminated the removal option for absent class plaintiffs. The amendment prevailed, and absent class plaintiff removal was left out of both the 2004 version of the Senate bill and the 2005 version that was finally enacted.

Does that legislative history cause you to rethink your views about the propriety of the current version of the Act as a response to the misuse of class actions? Is it accurate to say that the statute, as passed, offers relief that operates primarily in favor of defendants? In a statement accompanying the 2003 amendment, one member of Congress offered the view that eliminating absent class plaintiff removal was necessary in order to prevent maverick plaintiff attorneys from finding individual class members as clients and extorting money from the parties by threatening to derail the action through removal to federal court. Is this a legitimate concern? If so, could the drafters of the Act have addressed that concern without eliminating absent plaintiff removal altogether?

4. *New Restrictions on Attorneys' Fees.* The restrictions that the Act imposes on attorneys' fees in coupon settlements make it much more difficult for class counsel to secure generous compensation for such arrangements. Counsel who wish to receive a contingency fee for a coupon settlement can only obtain an award "based on the value to class members of the coupons that are redeemed." 28 U.S.C. §1712(a). This provision embodies two revisions to the practice often followed in past coupon settlements: (1) counsel can only be paid for "the value *to class members* of the coupons," rather than the coupons' face value; and (2) counsel can be paid only for the number of coupons "that are redeemed," not for the number that are awarded. Moreover, to the extent that class counsel in a coupon settlement are paid on some basis other than a contingency fee for redeemed coupons, their award cannot simply be a negotiated amount but must be "based upon the amount of time class counsel reasonably expended working on the action" subject to any appropriate multiplier for the risk associated with the suit, and must also be approved by the court. *Id.* §(b). A Senate report accompanying an earlier version of the provision explains that the change aims to respond to the problem of "coupon settlements [that] represent a boon to plaintiff attorneys (who receive the bulk of the benefit) and defendant companies (because coupons are rarely redeemed)."

Does the new provision accomplish its stated goals? Contingency fee arrangements now appear unattractive in coupon settlements, from class counsel's perspective. The requirement that coupons be redeemed before class counsel may be paid a contingent fee not only reduces the compensation that class counsel will receive, it also delays it. Typically, a settlement specifies a window of time within which class members may redeem a coupon (by purchasing more of defendant's product or whatever the case may be). Under the new provision, class counsel working for a contingency fee may have to wait for much of that period to elapse before receiving the bulk of their compensation, even in a case where the redemption rate on coupons is high. And, of course, the redemption rate often will not be high, restricting counsel's fee even further. It thus appears that class counsel will have to rely on an hourly compensation rate, subject to an appropriate multiplier, to get paid in coupon settlements. In the case of settlement-only class actions — in which the proposed settlement is often filed at the same time as the complaint, answer, and motion for class certification — the total number of hours required of class counsel may not add up to much of an incentive to file suit.

These changes aim to eliminate suits in which lawyers secure generous fees while providing little benefit to class members. Such lawsuits do exist. But has the Act hit on the right solution? Recall, first, that absent class plaintiffs cannot remove suits to federal court when class counsel and defendant both wish to stay in state court. The Act's limitations on attorneys' fees will not have any impact in such cases, which may account for a significant proportion of coupon settlements. More broadly, is there a danger that plaintiffs' attorneys will be dissuaded from bringing socially useful class actions by these new restrictions? It is easy to condemn truly abusive lawsuits in which attorneys are using a trumped-up claim as a vehicle for extorting fees from a defendant. But attorneys can also serve an important function as "private attorneys general," policing corporate behavior by helping to implement laws that might otherwise go unenforced. Thus, a suit that appears to offer class members nothing more than low-value coupons may have the additional benefit of pressuring defendants into conforming their behavior to the law in the future. Is there a danger that §1712 will make it economically unfeasible for plaintiff attorneys to fulfill this function? For a skeptical view about the usefulness, or propriety, of ascribing a "private attorney general" function to class counsel under Rule 23, see John H. Beisner, Matthew Shors & Jessica Davidson Miller, *Class Action "Cops": Public Servants or Private Entrepreneurs?*, 57 Stan. L. Rev. 1441 (2005).

5. *CAFA's Impact on Class Action Litigation.* What impact will the Class Action Fairness Act have on the day-to-day business of litigating these large and complex suits? In many respects, it is too early to tell. One measure of the statute's impact, however, can already be assessed: the change in the rate at which class actions are litigated in the federal courts. Under CAFA's expanded jurisdictional provisions, one would expect to see significant increases in that rate, and the most recent interim report of the Federal Judicial Center bears that expectation out. The report indicates that "[t]here has been a dramatic increase in the number of diversity class actions filed as original proceedings in the federal courts in the post-CAFA period" — perhaps on the order of a threefold increase. Thomas E. Willging & Emery G. Lee III, *The Impact of the Class Action Fairness Act of 2005 on the Federal Courts: Fourth Interim Report to the Judicial Conference Advisory Committee on Civil Rules* (April 2008), https://www.fjc.gov/content/impact-class-action-fairness-act-2005-federal-courts-fourth-interim-report-judicial-0.

9. Other Issues in Class Actions

a. Subject Matter Jurisdiction Requirements

You will recall that several Supreme Court decisions in the mid-1970s limited the availability of class actions in the federal courts for lack of subject matter jurisdiction. Although the early Supreme Court decision in *Supreme Tribe of Ben-Hur v. Cauble*, 255 U.S. 356 (1921), held that courts need only consider the citizenship of the named class representatives in determining the requirements of diversity of citizenship, the jurisdictional amount requirements met with a different interpretation. In *Snyder v. Harris*, 394 U.S. 332 (1969), the Supreme Court held that each individual claimant must meet the requisite amount in controversy to satisfy the requirements of the diversity statute. The Court reaffirmed that requirement in *Zahn v. International Paper*, 414 U.S. 291 (1973), even though in *Zahn* one of the named plaintiffs had met the requisite amount in controversy, rejecting the use of "ancillary" jurisdiction to permit federal courts to hear small-stakes claims.

Both of these rulings have now been significantly curtailed. In the case of *Snyder*, the Class Action Fairness Act expressly permits aggregation in cases that fall within its ambit. In the case of *Zahn*, the Court has ruled that the supplemental jurisdiction statute, 28 U.S.C. §1367, overruled the Court's earlier holding and authorized class actions to proceed under the ordinary diversity statute so long as the named plaintiffs could satisfy the jurisdictional amount. *See Exxon-Mobil v. Allapattah Servs.*, 545 U.S. 546 (2005).

b. Personal Jurisdiction over Absent Class Members

One important class action issue that remains unresolved relates to the scope of a court's authority to bind absent class members to the class judgment. We have already examined the requirement of "adequate representation" in *Hansberry v. Lee*, 311 U.S. 32 (1940). But more generally, due process precludes a court from binding any party who is not subject to the court's personal jurisdiction. Does that principle suggest that absent class plaintiffs must be subject to the court's personal jurisdiction in order to be bound by a judgment? Ordinarily, a plaintiff who brings an action "consents" to adjudicatory jurisdiction in that court. But absent class plaintiffs do not necessarily "consent" to anything. Of course, if absent class plaintiffs are residents or domiciliaries of the forum state, they would be subject to the court's adjudicatory authority on the basis of that connection. But what about nonresident plaintiffs in a nationwide class where absent plaintiffs have no connection at all with the forum state? Is there any principled difference between the imposition of liability on a defendant and the foreclosure of a class member's claim, which is the consequence of a class action judgment?

In *Phillips Petroleum Co. v. Shutts*, 472 U.S. 797 (1985), a nationwide class of royalty owners brought suit against Phillips Petroleum in Kansas state court, seeking interest payments on suspended royalties. A large number of the class members were nonresidents of Kansas who owned leases in states other than Kansas. Defendant Phillips Petroleum argued that the nationwide class was inappropriate because absent class members who were nonresidents of Kansas and had no connection with Kansas would not be bound by the judgment, as the Kansas court had no personal jurisdiction over such class members. The Supreme Court held that defendant Phillips had standing to raise the "due process" objections of the absent class members but ultimately ruled that, as to a claim for money damages, absent class plaintiffs need not have "minimum contacts" with the forum state. The Court viewed the procedures afforded to the absent class members under the Kansas rules—individual notice, an opportunity to be heard and participate in the litigation, an opt-out procedure, and an assurance of adequate representation—as sufficient to satisfy due process:

Because States place fewer burdens upon absent class plaintiffs than they do upon absent defendants in nonclass suits, the Due Process Clause need not and does not afford the former as much protection from state-court jurisdiction as it does the latter. . . . In this case we hold that a forum State may exercise jurisdiction over the claim of an absent class-action plaintiff, even though the plaintiff may not possess the minimum contacts with the forum which would support personal jurisdiction over a defendant. If the forum State wishes to bind an absent plaintiff concerning a claim for money damages or similar relief at law, it must provide minimal procedural due process protection. The plaintiff must receive notice plus an opportunity to be heard and participate in the litigation, whether in person or through counsel. . . . Additionally, we hold that due process requires at a minimum that an absent plaintiff be provided with an opportunity to remove himself from the class by executing and returning an "opt out" or "request for exclusion" form to the court. Finally, the Due Process Clause of course requires that the named plaintiff at all times adequately represent the interests of the absent class members.

472 U.S. at 118-119.

The passage from *Shutts* quoted above relies heavily on the ability of absent class members to exclude themselves from the class. Does this suggest that absent class plaintiffs in a Rule 23(b)(1) or (b)(2) class — where there is no opt-out provision — would need to have "minimum contacts" with the forum in order to be bound by the judgment? Can *Shutts* be viewed as endorsing a concept of "variable due process" so that the extent of the nonresident's contacts and the adjudicatory safeguards are a function of the burdens imposed on the nonresident? *See* Tobias Barrington Wolff, *Federal Jurisdiction and Due Process in the Era of the Nationwide Class Action*, 156 U. Pa. L. Rev. 2035, 2076-2100 (2008) (analyzing due process and the role of consent in *Shutts*). Do the Supreme Court's judicial jurisdiction decisions support such a view? For more general commentary on the implications of the *Shutts* decision, *see* Linda S. Mullenix, *Getting to* Shutts, 46 U. Kan. L. Rev. 727 (1998); Michael A. Perino, *Class Action Chaos: The Theory of the Core and an Analysis of Opt-Out Rights in Mass Tort Class Actions*, 46 Emory L.J. 85 (1997); Steven T.O. Cottreau, Note, *The Due Process Right to Opt Out of Class Actions*, 73 N.Y.U. L. Rev. 480 (1998).

c. Claim and Issue Preclusion in the Class Action Context

Throughout our discussion of the class action, we have focused primarily on the implications of the proceeding for those claims that are actually certified for classwide treatment. We have not paid much attention to the effect that claim and issue preclusion might have on the individual, nonclass claims possessed by members of the class. Isn't it possible that the claim or issue preclusive effect of a class action judgment might adversely affect the valuable individual claims of class members, even if those individual claims are not themselves litigated in the original proceeding, when they arise out of the same transaction or share common issues?

For example, consider the class action that was proposed in the *Bridgestone/Firestone* case. The plaintiffs asked the court to certify a class in which they hoped to establish that defendant's tires were defective and to obtain compensation for the financial losses experienced by every consumer who purchased defendant's product. Suppose that the class action had gone forward, the case proceeded to trial, and the jury explicitly found that the plaintiffs were not entitled to relief because defendant's tires were not defective—a definitive resolution of an issue that was necessary to the judgment in the first proceeding. If one of those consumers then brought an individual suit seeking compensation for serious personal injuries resulting from a tire failure, what result? Even if claim preclusion would not bar the suit (since the personal injury claim "could not have been brought" in the first proceeding), would issue preclusion prevent her from establishing the defective nature of the product, thereby defeating her claim? If so, what does that say about the propriety of certifying a class action in the first place?

Indeed, how should claim preclusion operate in successive proceedings involving class actions? Say that class counsel brings a lawsuit under Rule 23(b)(2), seeking injunctive relief to prevent employment discrimination or prisoner abuse. Some members of the class may also possess individual claims arising out of the same set of occurrences, entitling them to substantial damages. Does the existence of the class suit effectively force those individuals to "split" their claims for relief, such that claim preclusion might jeopardize their ability to seek damages in a separate action? Suppose that the issue is not a damages claim (which, perhaps, "could not have been brought" in the class proceeding), but rather another claim for injunctive relief that was omitted from the first lawsuit for some reason. Does the (b)(2) lawsuit—which provides no opportunity to opt out—bind class members to every strategic choice and mistake made by class counsel?

Surprisingly, most courts have not given any clear answer to these questions, leaving litigants and judges to wonder about the effect that a class action might have on factually related individual claims. As one of the authors of this casebook has observed, "[this] omission is a serious one," for "[t]he preclusive effects of a proposed class proceeding, considered ex ante, can sometimes have a dramatic impact upon the certification calculus." Tobias Barrington Wolff, *Preclusion in Class Action Litigation*, 105 Colum. L. Rev. 717, 718 (2005). In the defective tire scenario described above, for example, a conflict of interest would arise: "[S]ome members of the class are asked to assume a greater risk when they participate in the class proceeding, since an adverse finding on key issues in the resolution of the common claim may fatally undermine their ability to recover on their individual claims." *Id.* at 732. A few courts, recognizing this possibility, have actually refused to certify class actions that might otherwise have been desirable or appropriate because of the "risk . . . that [subsequent courts] could determine that the proposed class members would be barred [through claim or issue preclusion] from bringing individual actions for damages." *Zachery v. Texaco Exploration & Production, Inc.*, 185 F.R.D. 230, 243 (W.D. Tex. 1999). *See also In re Methyl Tertiary Butyl Ether (MTBE) Products Liability Litigation*, 209 F.R.D. 323, 339–340 (S.D.N.Y. 2002) (identifying threat posed by claim preclusion to valuable individual claims as one of several reasons for not certifying proposed (b)(2) class action).

Where claim preclusion is concerned, the dominant view among most jurisdictions that have addressed the issue appears to be that a class action will not preclude an individual claim for damages that could not have been certified as part of the original action. *See, e.g., Cooper v. Federal Reserve Bank of Richmond*, 467 U.S. 867, 880 (1984) (holding that class action alleging pattern or practice of discrimination under Title VII of 1964 Civil Rights Act does not bar individual claim for purposeful discrimination); 18A C. Wright et al., Federal Practice and Procedure §4455.2 (3d ed. 2021) ("[A]n individual who has suffered particular injury as a result of practices enjoined in a class action should remain free to seek a damages remedy even though claim preclusion would defeat a second action had the first action been an individual suit for the same injunctive relief."). It is less clear how these principles operate in subsequent claims for injunctive relief. *See, e.g., Hiser v. Franklin*, 94 F.3d 1287, 1292–1293 (9th Cir. 1996) (permitting prisoner to litigate individual claim for injunctive relief despite earlier class action because claims did not arise from the same transaction but recognizing that merger and bar do generally apply in such cases). And problems stemming from issue preclusion can sometimes appear intractable. *See, e.g.,* Wolff, *supra,* at 742–743 (discussing issue preclusion problems presented by MTBE class action seeking injunctive relief).

d. Watching the Watchers—Controls on Class Counsel and Settlement

As we have seen, the responsibility of class counsel to offer zealous representation to class plaintiffs sometimes comes into conflict with their own incentives to obtain reliable and generous compensation. The historical record contains more than a few examples of plaintiff's attorneys who appear to have sold out the interests of their clients in order to safeguard their own fees. In 2003, several amendments to Rule 23 took effect that aim to combat this problem.

i. Rule 23(e)—Settlement

Rule 23(e) seeks to provide additional safeguards for the rights of absentees. As you know from *Amchem Products v. Windsor,* the settlement process can sometimes drive the entire litigation in a class action. Yet earlier versions of Rule 23 provided little guidance to district courts on the issue of settlement, saying only that "A class action shall not be dismissed or compromised without the approval of the court, and notice of the proposed dismissal or compromise shall be given to all members of the class in such manner as the court directs." Old Rule 23(e) did not even explain what standard a district court should apply in deciding whether to approve a class settlement.

Most district courts have adopted the practice of holding a "fairness hearing" when the parties propose a settlement, both to determine whether the settlement is fair to the class and to give absentees an opportunity to appear before the court and lodge objections. In a 23(b)(3) class action, district courts have sometimes included a second opportunity to opt out (that is, to opt out of the settlement) in the notice that Rule 23(e) requires for class members. Prior to 2003, however, none of these procedures was required by the Rule, and actual practice varied considerably among district courts. A few courts of appeal even found it necessary to reverse a district court's approval of a settlement when the procedures employed by the court were inadequate to permit either the trial judge or the appellate judges to make a responsible determination as to the fairness of the settlement. *See, e.g., Reynolds v. Beneficial National Bank*, 288 F.3d 277, 283 (7th Cir. 2002) (Posner, J.) ("Although there is no proof that the settlement was actually collusive . . . , the circumstances demanded closer scrutiny than the district judge gave it. He painted with too broad a brush, substituting intuition for the evidence and careful analysis that a case of this magnitude . . . required.").

Rule 23(e) now seeks to regularize the procedures employed in settling a class action and to avoid the kind of perfunctory review criticized by the Seventh Circuit in *Reynolds*. Rule 23(e)(2) requires that the district court hold a hearing to review any settlement offered by the parties and provides that the court can approve the settlement only if it is "fair, reasonable, and adequate." Rule 23(e)(3) requires disclosure of any side agreements that the parties or their attorneys have made among themselves in conjunction with the proposed settlement—information that may be necessary for the court to evaluate the true benefit of the settlement to all the parties involved. And Rule 23(e)(4) empowers the district court to provide a second opportunity for members of a (b)(3) class to opt out after reviewing the proposed settlement, though it does not require that step. As the Advisory Committee Notes explain, these new procedures are meant to codify the district court's role as a quasi-fiduciary protector of the absent class members. Thus, the Notes disapprove of the practice of permitting parties to stipulate to the facts that would support a favorable assessment of the settlement. "[E]ven if the proponents seek to waive the hearing and no objectors have appeared," the Notes explain, "[a] hearing should be held to explore the proposed settlement" in order to preserve the independent protective role of the district court.

A further amendment to Rule 23 promulgated in 2018 gave federal district courts more explicit authority and guidance for entertaining class actions that are filed for purposes of settlement only. Rule 23(e)(1) now expressly recognizes the existence of "a class proposed to be certified for purposes of settlement" and gives the district court discretion to determine "whether to give notice of the proposal to the class" based on the court's estimation of the likelihood that it could "certify the class for purposes of judgment on the proposal" and that it would "approve the proposal under Rule 23(e)(2)." In plain language, these provisions authorize a district court to make a preliminary determination about the merits and viability of a proposed settlement before the court decides whether to direct that notice be provided to the class so that a more formal process of scrutiny can begin. Many district courts employed this practice under the prior rule, often saying that they were giving "preliminary approval" to a proposed settlement. The new rule validates that practice. It also makes clear that such preliminary determinations are not subject to immediate appellate review under Rule 23(f). The amended rule also imposes a stricter standard for granting preliminary approval than many courts had been using. As one district court in New York has explained, "Rule 23 did not specify a standard" for granting preliminary approval prior to the 2018 amendments "and courts in the Second Circuit interpreted Rule 23 to only require the settlement to be 'within the range of possible final approval.'" In re NASDAQ Market-Makers Antitrust Litig., 176 F.R.D. 99, 102 (S.D.N.Y. 1997). Under the new, more exacting standards, a district court must consider whether the court "will likely be able to: (i) approve the proposal under Rule 23(e)(2); and (ii) certify the class for purposes of judgment on the proposal." *In re GSE Bonds Antitrust Litig.*, 414 F. Supp. 3d 686, 692 (S.D.N.Y. 2019).

The new provisions also significantly expand Rule 23(e)(2), which previously instructed a district court that it could approve a class settlement only if it found the proposed settlement "fair, reasonable, and adequate" but gave no guidance on how to make that determination beyond requiring the court to hold a hearing (often called a "fairness hearing"). The amended rule now requires the court to consider a range of factors that seek to measure the adequacy of the negotiations that produced the settlement, the value of the relief to class members in comparison to the risk of litigation, and practical questions about how relief will be distributed to the class and how much and when the lawyers will get paid. The amendments also give new guidance on the role of objectors in a fairness hearing and place limits on the compensation objectors can receive. The federal circuit courts had adopted their own multi-factors tests for determining the fairness of a class settlement prior to the 2018 amendments and so far the circuits appear to be concluding that the amendments did not materially alter the standards they had adopted. *See, e.g., Campbell v. Facebook, Inc.*, 951 F.3d 1105, 1121 n.10 (9th Cir. 2020) ("After the district court's approval of the settlement in this case, Rule 23(e)(2) was amended. Whereas the rule previously did not expand upon what was necessary for a settlement to be 'fair, reasonable, and adequate,' it now lists criteria that are relevant to that determination. We need not determine whether this amendment should be applied retroactively here because applying the amended version of the rule would not change our conclusions."). *See also* Fed. R. Civ. P. 23 advisory committee note to 2018 amendment ("The goal of this amendment is not to displace" any of the factors historically considered in assessing settlement fairness, "but rather to focus the court and the lawyers on the core concerns of procedure and substance that should guide the decision whether to approve the proposal").

ii.   Rules 23(g) and (h) — Appointment of Class Counsel and Attorneys' Fees

The last two sections of Rule 23, also products of the 2003 amendments, deal with topics that can have a dramatic effect on the dynamics of a class action: the appointment of class counsel and the process for awarding attorneys' fees.

As the cases we have read in this section suggest, class counsel plays a pivotal role in directing the course of a representative litigation. This is certainly true in cases where the stakes for the individual parties are small, as in *Eisen*. The Seventh Circuit has written: "Often the class representative has a merely nominal stake [in the suit], and the real plaintiff in interest is then the lawyer for the class, who may have interests that diverge from those of the class members." *Culver v. City of Milwaukee*, 277 F.3d 908, 910 (7th Cir. 2002). But the nationwide asbestos litigation that culminated in the settlement that the Supreme Court ultimately rejected in *Amchem* demonstrates that lawyers can be the primary players in large-stakes class actions, as well. Indeed, it would not be an exaggeration to say that it is the rare class action in which the named plaintiffs play any significant role in directing the course of the proceedings.

Rule 23(g) provides procedures and standards for the appointment of class counsel. Rule 23(g)(1) begins by placing the responsibility for selecting class counsel squarely on the shoulders of the district court, rather than permitting the parties (or the lawyers) to decide the matter among themselves. Rule 23(g)(1)(B) then makes clear what Rule 23(a) had left somewhat ambiguous: that class counsel has a duty, independent of that owed by the class representative, to "fairly and adequately represent the interests of the class."

Rule 23(g)(1)(A) specifies the procedures for the selection of class counsel, requiring the district court to conduct a serious inquiry in which it must consider:

> **(i)** the work counsel has done in identifying or investigating potential claims in the action;
> **(ii)** counsel's experience in handling class actions, other complex litigation, and claims of the type asserted in the action;
> **(iii)** counsel's knowledge of the applicable law; and
> **(iv)** the resources that counsel will commit to representing the class.

The court may also consider "any other matter pertinent to counsel's ability to fairly and adequately represent the interests of the class." *Id.* §23(g)(1)(B). As the Advisory Notes explain, these provisions respond "to the reality that the selection and activity of class counsel are often critically important to the successful handling of a class action."

By the same token, Rule 23(h) recognizes the importance of fee awards in motivating attorneys to become involved in and then settle class action litigation, and it seeks to respond to that reality by regularizing the process for the consideration and approval of such fees. The rule does not impose standards for calculating the appropriate compensation for class counsel (for example, by choosing between the "lodestar" and percentage methods), nor does it control the availability of attorneys' fees in the first place. Rather, Rule 23(h) brings greater transparency to the calculation and award of attorneys' fees. Thus, the Rule makes clear that a district court must follow the procedure outlined in Rule 54 when it awards fees to class counsel, including a formal motion and provision of reasonable notice to members of the class. Class members (or parties from whom fees are sought) may object to class counsel's request, and the court is authorized to hold hearings and, if necessary, to refer the matter to a magistrate or special master for resolution. (These procedures are partially augmented and partially superseded in coupon settlements subject to the Class Action Fairness Act, *supra.*)

Together, Rules 23(g) and (h) seek to bring the process of settlement and attorney compensation out of the shadows. They impose a strict obligation on the district court to give careful scrutiny to any proposed settlement or dismissal of a class action, and they require that class members be notified of the terms of a settlement or dismissal, including the award of attorneys' fees, in order that they might have the opportunity to protect their interests by raising objections in a truly adversarial posture.

e. Statutes of Limitations and the American Pipe Rule

When a plaintiff files a putative class action, what happens to the statutes of limitations for the claims of class members if the court ultimately denies the request for class certification? Can the absentees intervene in the action at that point to pursue their individual claims? Can they file their own lawsuits and pursue their claims in the forum of their choice? Suppose the proposed class is certified under Rule 23(b)(3) but a class member wants to exercise the right to opt out and pursue her claim on her own terms in a separate action? In each of these scenarios, if the statute of limitations on the class member's claim would have expired during the pendency of the putative class action, does that mean she is foreclosed from pursuing her individual claim?

In an important ruling issued shortly after the 1966 amendments to Rule 23, the Supreme Court established a *tolling* rule that sometimes suspends the running of the statute of limitations for class members and preserves their ability to pursue an individual claim. *American Pipe & Construction Co. v. Utah*, 414 U.S. 536 (1974) explained that a tolling rule was "necessary to insure effectuation of the purposes of litigative efficiency and economy that the Rule . . . was designed to serve" and held that "the commencement of the class action . . . suspended the running of the limitation period" for all members of the putative class. *Id.* at 555–556, 561. In *American Pipe* itself, the absent class members intervened in the original lawsuit to press their individual claims. In a subsequent case, *Crown, Cork & Seal v. Parker*, 462 U.S. 345 (1983), the Court held that absentees could also benefit from the tolling rule when they filed a new lawsuit to pursue their individual claims in a different forum. Tolling applied either if class certification was denied in the original lawsuit or if the absentee chose to exercise the right to opt out of a class action certified under Rule 23(b)(3). There is no requirement that absentees know about the original class proceeding or rely on that proceeding in any way. It is enough that an action was filed seeking class treatment and either class certification was denied or the class member decided to opt out.

More recent rulings by the Court have imposed some limitations on the *American Pipe* rule. *California Public Employees' Retirement System v. ANZ Securities*, 137 S. Ct. 2042 (2017), observed that some federal statutes contain what the Court labeled a *statute of repose*—an additional time limitation on top of the statute of limitations that places a hard stop on any extension or alteration of the time to file—and held that *American Pipe* tolling cannot extend the time to pursue individual claims beyond the period specified in such a provision. And *China Agritech v. Resh*, 138 S. Ct. 1800 (2018), held that *American Pipe* tolling is not available to an absentee who seeks to file a subsequent class action, only to an absentee who seeks to pursue her own individual claim. Professors Burbank and Wolff examine these and many other questions concerning the application of *American Pipe* tolling and the analytical foundations of the rule in Stephen B. Burbank & Tobias Barrington Wolff, *Class Actions, Statutes of Limitations and Repose, and Federal Common Law*, 167 U. Penn. L. Rev. 1 (2018).

10. *Multidistrict Consolidation Under 28 U.S.C. §1407*

The federal courts have considerable capacity to consolidate cases that are brought in different federal district courts. In earlier chapters, we have encountered the federal provisions that authorize transfer of a case to a district and division where it might have been brought—28 U.S.C. §§1404 and 1406. Aggregation of complex litigation, such as securities, antitrust, and mass tort cases, can be achieved through coordination among various district courts to transfer cases to a designated district.

Another federal statute, 28 U.S.C. §1407, creates the Judicial Panel on Multi-district Litigation, made up of federal trial and appellate judges, and authorizes the Panel to order transfer of multiple cases to a single transferee forum if "civil actions involving one or more common questions of fact are pending in different districts" and transfer will further the convenience of the parties and the witnesses. There are no jurisdictional or venue barriers to transfer under §1407.

Section 1407 authorizes consolidation only for the purpose of "coordinated or consolidated" *pretrial* purposes. Many cases settle during the consolidated pretrial proceedings or are terminated by dispositive motions during pretrial. But if the case reaches trial, it must be sent back to the transferor district. In *Lexecon Inc. v. Milberg Weiss Bershad Hynes & Lerach*, 523 U.S. 26 (1998), the Supreme Court prohibited a common practice whereby the transferee forum under §1407 would retain the transferred cases for trial by using 28 U.S.C. §1404 to transfer the case to itself for all purposes. The Supreme Court in *Lexecon* held that there was no such power under 28 U.S.C. §1407. The result of the *Lexecon* case is to prevent §1407 from functioning as a single-forum aggregation mechanism. However, the courts might still be able to achieve such consolidation through consent of all the parties.

Aggregation of individual cases has been a particular challenge in mass tort litigation. *See In re Bendectin Litig.*, 857 F.2d 290 (6th Cir. 1988). Consolidation in these cases presents many of the same concerns we encountered in the discussion of class actions. The efficiency of a mass trial on common issues must be weighed against the continued need for individual trials on other issues. As in class actions, lead counsel usually take over the conduct of the litigation and may operate with divided loyalties; special circumstances attending individual claims are likely to be overshadowed by the interests of the group. Mass trials can also affect the way issues are tried in an individual case—for example, liability issues and damages may be bifurcated, special verdicts are sometimes used, and "sampling" may be employed at trial. But consolidated individual actions lack many of the formal protections that apply to class actions, leading some courts and commentators to explore whether greater judicial supervision is appropriate in such cases. *See, e.g., In re Zyprexa Prods. Liab. Litig.*, 424 F. Supp. 2d 488 (E.D.N.Y. 2006) (Weinstein, J.) (developing "quasi-class" theory for greater judicial management in mass MDL consolidation of individual actions).

Does 28 U.S.C. §1407, as interpreted by the Court in *Lexecon*, strike the proper balance between using consolidation to increase efficiency through the elimination of repetitive discovery at the pretrial stage and preserving the right of the individual plaintiff to control the place and manner of trial? Considering the familiarity of the transferee judge with the proceedings, is it inefficient to disperse the litigation for trial in different districts? Legislation to change the result in *Lexecon* has been proposed before. *See, e.g.*, Multidistrict Litigation Act of 2000, H.R. 5562, 106th Cong. 2d Sess. (2000). Would you favor such legislation?

The consolidating power of the MDL statute can be extraordinary. While each individual case that is consolidated into an MDL theoretically remains independent, in practice the lawyers appointed as liaison counsel to the district judge often control the proceedings. Lawyers for parties who have no leadership role in the consolidated action may be unable to file motions, conduct discovery, or pursue settlement discussions independently. As one scholar has noted, "transferee judges create hierarchies of influence. To streamline cases and avoid having to communicate with hundreds of attorneys, judges appoint steering committees and other lead lawyers to conduct discovery, disseminate information, draft motions, negotiate settlements, and try bellwether cases." These "lead attorneys control the litigation and wrest decision-making power away from plaintiffs' individually retained counsel." Elizabeth Chamblee Burch, *Judging Multidistrict Litigation*, 90 N.Y.U. L. Rev. 71, 73–74 (2015). As a consequence, defendants often view the MDL procedure as beneficial, allowing them to focus their litigation and negotiation efforts on one group of lawyers. Plaintiffs outside the steering committee, however, can view an MDL as a black hole from which they cannot escape and where they must wait for others to litigate their claims and negotiate the terms on which they might settle. Although the Supreme Court has held that actions consolidated through the MDL process retain their character as individual lawsuits, *see Gelboim v. Bank of America*, 574 U.S. 405 (2015) (actions in an MDL proceeding are considered individually when determining whether the final judgment rule is satisfied for each one), the reality is often quite different.

11.   *The Multiparty, Multiforum Act*

Another legislative joinder reform, noted in Chapters 2 and 3, is the Multiparty, Multiforum Trial Jurisdiction Act, 28 U.S.C. §1369, enacted by Congress in 2002. The statute provides broad grants of original jurisdiction, removal, and joinder authority that permit federal courts to hear lawsuits arising out of accidents or disasters involving the death of at least 75 people. The Act is specifically designed to work in tandem with the Judicial Panel on Multidistrict Litigation, requiring that any district court notify the panel when a case brought under the multiparty, multiforum act is pending before it. *See id.* §1369(e). The provisions for nationwide service of process (discussed in Chapter 2) and minimal diversity jurisdiction also work to facilitate the consolidation of complex, potentially duplicative litigation in a single federal forum.

Subsection (a) of §1369 provides for original jurisdiction by the federal district courts over any civil action that arises from an accident involving at least 75 deaths if there is minimal diversity and (1) a defendant resides in a state and a "substantial part" of the accident occurred in a different state, regardless of whether the defendant is also a resident of the state where a substantial part of the accident took place, or (2) any two defendants reside in different states, or (3) "substantial parts" of the accident occurred in different states. §1369(a). Subsection (b) requires the district court to "abstain" from hearing the action if the "substantial majority" of plaintiffs are citizens of the state in which the primary defendants are citizens and the claims will be governed primarily by the laws of that state. When a suit is brought under subsection (a), subsection (d) permits any other party with a claim arising from the same accident to intervene as a party plaintiff in the action. Finally, subsection (e) requires a district court in which an action under the Act is pending to notify the judicial panel on multidistrict litigation promptly of the pendency of the action.

The Act also produced changes in other portions of the Judicial Code. Section 1441(e) has been added to the provisions on removal. Pursuant to subdivision (e)(1), an action may be removed by a defendant if (A) the action could have been brought in federal court under §1369 or (B) defendant is a party to an action which is or could have been brought, in whole or in part, under [§]1369 . . . and "arises from the same accident as the action [in the state court], even if the action to be removed could not have been brought in a district court as an original matter." The Act also includes a special venue provision, §1361(g), which provides for venue in an action under §1369 "in any district in which any defendant resides or in which a substantial part of the accident giving rise to the action took place."

The first decision interpreting and applying these provisions was *Passa v. Derderian*, 308 F. Supp. 2d 43 (D.R.I. 2004). Various state and federal lawsuits arose out of a fire at a Rhode Island nightclub that resulted in the death of 100 persons and injuries to more than 200 others. The interpretation of the Act was before the district court in five cases, two of which were originally filed in federal court and three of which were filed in state court and removed to federal court. Plaintiffs in the five cases were citizens and residents of Rhode Island, and the various defendants were citizens of at least nine states and one foreign country. Thus, the prerequisites of the Act were satisfied. But the court was faced with the question of whether §1369(b) operated as a jurisdictional limitation on the district court or should be construed as only a mandatory abstention doctrine. Believing that the jurisdictional characterization of the provision could have an impact on such questions as when the abstention issue could be raised in the proceeding or whether it could be waived, the court first determined that §1369(b) should be interpreted only as a mandatory abstention provision—a right attaching to the parties opposing the federal forum, not a subject matter jurisdictional requirement stripping federal courts of all power to hear cases within its provisions. *See also Wallace v. Louisiana Citizens Prop. Ins. Corp.*, 444 F.3d 697, 701 (5th Cir. 2006) (adopting *Passa*'s mandatory abstention reading).

The court then turned to construing the mandatory abstention rule of §1369(b) with respect to the facts in the cases before it. Since it was clear that the tort claims would be governed by Rhode Island law, the court was called on to resolve whether the "substantial majority of all plaintiffs" were citizens of Rhode Island and whether the "primary defendants" were also citizens of Rhode Island. The court interpreted "substantial majority of all plaintiffs" to refer to all potential plaintiffs, not just those who had already filed a lawsuit, and observed that such an interpretation was consistent with Congress's desire to consolidate all cases arising from a single disaster into one federal court. The court calculated that Rhode Island plaintiffs made up approximately 44 percent of the known plaintiffs and that this number did not constitute a "simple majority, let alone a substantial majority" of all plaintiffs. Thus abstention was unwarranted on this ground. The court also offered its interpretation of "primary defendants." Defendant night club owners and their real estate company were citizens of Rhode Island as were several other defendants; but the band members and their manager, who are alleged to have started the fire, were citizens of California, and some defendants were citizens of other states. Rather than require a court to make a pretrial determination of liability or culpability with respect to the various defendants, the court interpreted the term "primary defendants" to include all defendants facing direct liability and to exclude all defendants joined as secondary or third-party defendants for purposes of vicarious liability. In *Passa*, the "primary defendants" could not all be said to be citizens of Rhode Island, again meaning that mandatory abstention was not warranted.

After a decision has been rendered by the trial court, a litigant who has received an adverse determination may be able to get that determination reviewed by a court of appeals. This chapter will examine the nature of that right, and the procedures that govern appeals. Appeal is one of the defining characteristics of the American legal system. In the federal courts and every state judicial system, the losing party is entitled to at least one appeal "as of right." A second level of discretionary review by the highest court in each system is also normally available.

Enormous private and public resources are expended on appellate review of lower court proceedings, and appeals can greatly delay the ultimate resolution of cases. From the perspective of guaranteeing a fair adjudication to the parties, one might ask whether the cost of appellate review is justified by its benefits. Given that modern procedure affords the parties a comprehensive adjudication on the trial level, how do appeals add to the accuracy or fairness of litigation? Is there reason to think that appellate determinations are in some sense "better" than those of the trial court?

Recall Justice Blackmun's discussion of appellate review in *Salve Regina College v. Russell*, 499 U.S. 225 (1991), holding that determinations of state law by the federal district courts were subject to a *de novo* standard of review in the appellate courts:

> Independent appellate review of legal issues best serves the dual goals of doctrinal coherence and economy of judicial administration. District judges preside alone over fast-paced trials: Of necessity they devote much of their energy and resources to hearing witnesses and reviewing evidence. Similarly, the logistical burdens of trial advocacy limit the extent to which trial counsel is able to supplement the district judge's legal research with memoranda and briefs. Thus, trial judges often must resolve complicated legal questions without benefit of "extended reflection [or] extensive information." Coenen, To Defer or Not to Defer: A Study of Federal Circuit Court Deference to District Court Rulings on State Law, 73 Minn. L. Rev. 899, 923 (1989).
>
> Courts of appeals, on the other hand, are structurally suited to the collaborative juridical process that promotes decisional accuracy. With the record having been constructed below and settled for purposes of the appeal, appellate judges are able to devote their primary attention to legal issues. As questions of law become the focus of appellate review, it can be expected that the parties' briefs will be refined to bring to bear on the legal issues more information and more comprehensive analysis than was

provided for the district judge. Perhaps most important, courts of appeals employ multi-judge panels, see 28 U.S.C. §§46(b) and (c), that permit reflective dialogue and collective judgment. . . .

499 U.S. at 231–232.

Notwithstanding these benefits, when sophisticated commercial parties arrange *ex ante* for a scheme of dispute resolution — such as private arbitration — they generally do not provide for appellate review of the arbitrator's decision, except for exceptional mistakes going to the very integrity of the process. If appeals are not worth the cost and delay in this situation, why should public, judicial adjudication be structured so differently?

At least one answer is that private and public dispute resolution serve different purposes. Private dispute settlement mechanisms, like courts, are designed to resolve accurately the dispute between the parties. But adjudication in the courts has a dual function. Not only does it settle a private dispute between the parties, but it also articulates legal norms for everyone else in the form of judicial decisions.* While appellate review may only marginally contribute to the accuracy of an adjudication, it is considered central to the law-declaring function. Given the rule that only higher court decisions are binding on lower courts, the only way to maintain uniform judicial interpretation is for an appellate court to issue definitive rulings binding on all the courts within its jurisdiction.

This distinction between the public/norm-declaring function and the private/dispute-resolution function also helps explain the different stances (or "standards of review") that appellate courts generally adopt toward questions of law versus questions of fact. While appellate courts typically give little or no weight to the trial court's view of the law, they defer enormously to trial court findings of fact. This is, in part, attributable to institutional competency: The trial judge had the opportunity to observe the witnesses and judge their credibility with respect to testimony about the facts. But it also reflects the greater systemic significance of legal interpretations. Findings of fact, even if erroneous, will have little effect on other cases. Legal interpretations, in contrast, provide guidance for similarly situated cases in the future.

Other rules of appellate review take account of the respective advantages and disadvantages of an appellate process. The *"final judgment rule,"* which delays appellate intervention until the trial court has completed the case, minimizes disruption of the lower court proceeding and protects the appellate docket from potentially unnecessary burdens. The process of "perfecting" an appeal requires the parties to narrow the issues for review, and imposes rigid procedural hurdles that jealously guard the appellate court door.

---

* As Professor Fiss has written:

Adjudication uses public resources, and employs not strangers chosen by the parties but public officials chosen by a process in which the public participates. These officials, like members of the legislative and executive branches, possess a power that has been defined and conferred by public law, not by private agreement. Their job is not to maximize the ends of private parties, nor simply to secure the peace, but to explicate and give force to the values embodied in authoritative texts such as the Constitution and statutes: to interpret those values and to bring reality into accord with them.

Owen M. Fiss, *Against Settlement*, 93 Yale L.J. 1073, 1085 (1984).

A. THE STRUCTURE OF APPELLATE COURTS

The federal and most state judicial systems have three levels of courts. The federal court system is comprised of the district courts, the courts of appeals, and the United States Supreme Court. (There are also several specialized courts handling matters requiring special expertise, such as the Court of Customs and Patent Appeals.) The state courts usually follow the same tripartite judicial structure. In both systems, a losing party is normally entitled to at least one appeal as of right, normally to the intermediate appeals court.

1. Federal Courts

Determinations made in the federal district courts are ordinarily appealable to the courts of appeals, the intermediate appellate courts of the federal system. Appeals from the district courts are said to be "as of right," suggesting an opportunity for full appellate hearing. However, a number of appeals are disposed of without written opinion or oral argument.

The structure and powers of the appellate courts are set out in Title 28 of the United States Code, which also authorizes the Supreme Court to promulgate Federal Rules of Appellate Procedure. The courts of appeals are primarily organized regionally in groups of states to form a circuit. There are 13 circuits — 11 numbered consecutively, plus the Court of Appeals for the District of Columbia, and the Court of Appeals for the Federal Circuit. The jurisdiction of the first 12 circuits is based on geography while the Federal Circuit's jurisdiction is defined by subject matter. (The Federal Circuit has jurisdiction over patent appeals and certain claims against the federal government.)

Each court of appeals consists of a number of judges who sit in three-judge panels. Cases are usually assigned by some random method to these panels. Occasionally, courts of appeals hear cases en banc (with the entire membership sitting). En banc proceedings are convened when requested by a majority of the judges due to the importance of a case or because the previously selected panel deviated from the established precedent in the circuit. En banc proceedings are normally conducted to review a prior decision of a panel, although in exceptional cases, an appeal may proceed directly to en banc review.

The Supreme Court is the highest court in the federal system. Its jurisdiction is exclusively appellate except in a rare class of cases. It may hear cases originating in the lower federal courts as well as cases originating in state courts that turn on questions of federal law. Most cases that begin in federal district court must pass through the courts of appeals before being reviewed by the Supreme Court. On rare occasion, the Supreme Court may accept an appeal directly from a district court. Review by the Supreme Court is in the discretion of the Court, usually exercised by the grant of a writ of certiorari. See 28 U.S.C. §1254(1). The votes of four out of nine Justices are sufficient to permit such review. This discretion is generally exercised so that only cases with broad legal issues of great importance are taken.

In most civil cases, the time limit for filing an appeal to the Supreme Court by way of a petition for a writ of certiorari is 90 days. See 28 U.S.C. §2101(c). Certain uncommon types of appeal, including those in which an Act of Congress has been declared unconstitutional, have shorter time limits. *See id.* §2101(a)–(b). Either way, the clock starts running as soon as the lower court enters a "genuinely final judgment," that is, one that leaves no "question whether the court will modify the judgment and alter the parties' rights." *Hibbs v. Winn,* 542 U.S. 88 (2004). In *Hibbs,* the Court found that the court of appeals' order to the parties to brief the question of whether the case should be reheard en banc suspended the finality of the prior disposition until the court denied the rehearing en banc.

While in theory the Supreme Court may review both state and federal issues decided in the course of lower federal court proceedings, in practice, the Court almost always defers to lower court conclusions of state law. *But see Leavitt v. Jane L.,* 518 U.S. 137, 145 (1996) (reversing court of appeals' construction of state abortion statute: "Our general presumption that courts of appeals correctly decide questions of state law reflects a judgment as to the utility of reviewing them in most cases. . . . That general presumption is obviously inapplicable where the court of appeals' state-law ruling is plainly wrong.").

When a case originates in state court, only those cases that turn on issues of federal law may be considered by the Supreme Court. Note also that the state decision must be a final judgment and have reached the highest court of the state available to the litigants. *See* 28 U.S.C. §1257. The concept of a "final judgment" includes the requirement that the judgment on appeal terminate the proceedings — that is, that the petitioner have no further avenues for potential relief other than the appeal to the Supreme Court. *See Johnson v. California,* 541 U.S. 428 (2004) (*per curiam*) (dismissing case for want of jurisdiction after it became clear that lower court ruling left petitioner further avenues for potential relief). This variation on the final judgment rule is also subject to various exceptions. *See Cox Broadcasting v. Cohn,* 420 U.S. 469, 477–483 (1975) (outlining four categories of cases in which appeal to U.S. Supreme Court may be had from state court proceeding even without final judgment).

2. *State Courts*

Each state has its own appellate structure. In general, most states have one set of intermediate appellate courts and one supreme court. The intermediate courts are generally called the "courts of appeals," but there are exceptions. For instance, Maryland has the "Court of Special Appeals," and New Jersey and New York have the "Appellate Division." The highest appellate court is usually called the state supreme court (although in New York it is called the "Court of Appeals"). Texas maintains separate highest courts for criminal and civil matters. Like the United States Supreme Court, the exercise of most state supreme court jurisdiction is discretionary.

3. *Rules of Appellate Procedure*

In the federal, as well as many state systems, a separate "Rules of Appellate Procedure" governs the conduct of appeals. In federal practice, a number of Federal Rules of Civil Procedure also affect appeals. *See, e.g.,* Fed. R. Civ. P. 52(a)(6), providing that factual determinations by the district court "shall not be set aside unless clearly erroneous." As in the case of the Federal Rules of Civil Procedure, each circuit is also authorized to promulgate local rules "not inconsistent with" the Federal Rules. Practice before the United States Supreme Court is governed by the Rules of the Supreme Court of the United States.

B. APPEALABILITY

1. Who May Appeal?

Only parties to the original action may appeal. However, a nonparty may participate in the appeal either by intervening in the lower action after judgment or by obtaining permission to appear as *amicus*.

The party seeking to appeal the lower court judgment must have been "aggrieved" by the lower court judgment; this requires that either a judgment has been entered, at least in some respect, against the appellant, or that a party has received less than the amount of relief requested. Ordinarily, a party who has obtained judgment in its favor will not be able to appeal an erroneous finding or ruling; a party only has appellate standing to seek reversal of the judgment. *New York Telephone Co. v. Maltbie*, 291 U.S. 645 (1934) (plaintiff who obtained permanent injunction against enforcement of a rate order could not appeal factual determinations concerning the value of its property). *But see Aetna Casualty & Surety Co. v. Cunningham*, 224 F.2d 478 (5th Cir. 1955) (appeal permitted to challenge grounds of judgment favorable to appellant since grounds of decision would affect appellant's ability to recover in a future bankruptcy case).

It is quite common for both parties to appeal aspects of the lower court proceeding. This is referred to as a "cross-appeal." For instance, plaintiff may appeal the lower court's dismissal of its punitive damage claim, while defendant appeals the compensatory damage award against it. The Supreme Court has clarified, however, that a prevailing party does not need to file a cross-appeal in order to seek review of an argument on which he did not succeed below. Even when a party receives all the relief he has requested, a court sometimes rejects one of the arguments on which he sought to rely. If his opponent files an appeal, then an "appellee who does not take a cross-appeal may [nonetheless] urge in support of a decree any matter appearing before the record, although his argument may involve an attack upon the reasoning of the lower court." *Jennings v. Stephens*, 574 U.S. 271, 275 (2015) (quotation omitted). Only if the appellee "attack[s] the decree with a view either to enlarging his own rights thereunder or of lessening the rights of his adversary" must he file a cross-appeal. *Id.*

Moreover, even a completely successful prevailing party may file a "contingent" cross-appeal to assert issues that would become relevant were the other party successful in its appeal. For instance, if the lower court granted defendant's motion to dismiss on statute of limitations grounds, but denied a motion to dismiss for failure to state a claim, defendant may assert a contingent cross-appeal on the failure to state a claim defense once plaintiff appeals the statute of limitations ruling.

The question of who may appeal becomes somewhat more complicated in the case of a class action. While all members of a class are "parties" to the action in some respects—they have some limited rights to participate in the action and are bound by the result—absentees are not formally identified in the action and do not generally have any power to control the course of the litigation. It is clear, of course, that the class representatives have the right to file an appeal, but what about these other class members? The Supreme Court in *Devlin v. Scardelletti*, 536 U.S. 1 (2002), held that *any* class member could appeal a district court's approval of a settlement provided that he appeared at the fairness hearing and lodged timely objections. The Court found that the class member's status as an objector authorized him to appeal the settlement, even though he had not been granted formal leave to intervene:

> What is most important to this case is that nonnamed class members are parties to the proceedings in the sense of being bound by the settlement. It is this feature of class action litigation that requires that class members be allowed to appeal the approval of a settlement when they have objected at the fairness hearing. To hold otherwise would deprive nonnamed class members of the power to preserve their own interests in a settlement that will ultimately bind them, despite their expressed objections before the trial court.

536 U.S. at 10.

This holding may have significant implications outside the class action context, as well. If objecting class members may appeal in order to "preserve their own interests in a settlement that will ultimately bind them," what about those who are in privity with parties in *individual* litigation? They also are in danger of having their interests compromised by a judgment "that will ultimately bind them." Can parties in privity appeal a judgment or court-ordered settlement, even if they never intervene as parties? *See In Re National Football League Players' Concussion Injury Litigation*, 923 F.3d 96 (3d Cir. 2019), which recognized the appellate standing of litigation-finance companies who issued cash advances to class members secured by their settlement claims, allowing the companies to challenge the order of the trial court negating those loans.

While this broader issue was not presented in *Scardelletti*, the Court hinted at such a result, writing: "It is not at all clear . . . that [those in privity with the named party in traditional litigation] may not themselves appeal. Although this Court has never addressed the issue, nonnamed parties in privity with a named party are often allowed by other courts to appeal from the order that affects them." *Scardelletti* appears to have replaced a simple, bright line rule—only named parties may appeal—with a more pragmatic, case-by-case inquiry.

Is this a sensible rule? It certainly has a certain common-sense appeal—people whose interests may be compromised by a judgment should have a chance to appeal that judgment. But might not such a standard encourage a wait-and-see attitude? If a person knows that a lawsuit is underway that may affect her interests as a privy, but she does not seek timely permission to intervene (as was the case in *Scardelletti*), is there not an argument that we should deem her to have waived her chance to participate? *But see Martin v. Wilks*, 490 U.S. 755 (1989) (no general duty for individuals to intervene in case that may affect their interests), *overruled on other grounds* by Civil Rights Act of 1991, 42 U.S.C. §2000e-2(n)(1)(A). Should a party in privity with another have to demonstrate that its interests have not been adequately represented before appealing a judgment or settlement? *Cf.* Fed. R. Civ. P. 24(a) (person seeking intervention as of right because his or her interests may be impaired by the litigation must demonstrate that those interests are not adequately represented by current parties). Does it make a difference if such a person is seeking to appeal on grounds, such as the fairness of a settlement, that could not have been raised at an earlier stage of the litigation?

2. *When May an Appeal Be Taken?*

The question of when an issue is appealable is of enormous importance. Even if a trial court ruling ultimately can be reversed, a party's inability to appeal that ruling immediately may entail significant expense and delay. Moreover, in a number of contexts, if the trial court decides a question incorrectly, the inability of the losing party to appeal immediately will, as a practical matter, render unenforceable the underlying legal position asserted by the party. Consider, for instance, a motion to dismiss on the ground of *forum non conveniens*. If the trial court denies the motion, the case will proceed to trial. Even if, following judgment for plaintiff, the appellate court were to determine that the court erred in denying the *forum non conveniens* motion, there will be no effective remedy since defendant has already been required to litigate in an inconvenient forum. The same might be said of denials of summary judgment motions to the extent that the function, at least in part, is to relieve the moving party of the burden of proceeding to trial; no appellate decision rendered after trial can fully restore that benefit. In fact, appeals courts normally decline to review denials of summary judgment motions after the case has proceeded to trial; while the propriety of the ultimate disposition may be reviewed, the trial court's decision not to bypass trial through summary judgment has been mooted. *See, e.g., Benner v. Nationwide Mut. Ins. Co.*, 93 F.3d 1228, 1233 (4th Cir. 1996).

The reason why immediate appeals are normally not permitted in those circumstances is a consequence of the "final judgment rule." In the federal, and many state jurisdictions, the appeals courts may, with very limited exceptions, only entertain appeals from "final judgments" of the trial courts. Interlocutory appeals (from nonfinal judgments) are permitted from orders relating to injunctions, orders appointing receivers to direct sales or other disposals of property, and decrees from the district courts determining the rights and liabilities of the parties to admiralty cases. *See* 28 U.S.C. §1292(a). In other situations, a court may certify important nonfinal orders for review. *See, e.g.,* 28 U.S.C. §1292(b), Fed. R. Civ. P. 54(b) and 23(f) (discussed later in this chapter).

The final judgment principle is found in 28 U.S.C. §1291, which provides that "the courts of appeals . . . shall have jurisdiction of appeals from all final decisions of the district courts of the United States." In 1990, Congress gave the Supreme Court rule-making authority to define what constitutes a final judgment. 28 U.S.C. §2072(c).

Federal case law has defined a "final decision" as a disposition that "leaves nothing for the court to do but execute the judgment." *See Catlin v. United States,* 324 U.S. 229, 233 (1945).* Thus, a denial of any motion to dismiss is not immediately appealable since the consequence of the denial is that the litigation will proceed. Similarly, decisions to transfer to a different forum or to remand to a state court cannot normally be appealed. Moreover, even a final disposition of some, but not all, claims in a lawsuit may not be immediately appealable. Thus, for instance, if the court dismisses a claim against one of several defendants, plaintiff may have to wait for the disposition of the claims against the remaining defendants before appealing the dismissal, unless certification for immediate appeal is granted under Rule 54(b) (discussed on pp. 1058–1062). For a comprehensive review of the concept of finality in appellate jurisdiction, *see* Bryan Lammon, *Finality, Appealability, and the Scope of Interlocutory Review,* 93 Wash. L. Rev. 1809 (2018).

What are the advantages and disadvantages of the final judgment rule? As suggested above, one of the principal functions of the final judgment rule is to avoid disruption of the trial court proceeding. Appeals from every nonfinal decision of a trial court might disrupt the litigation and significantly delay the ultimate disposition of the case. The rule also protects the appellate court from unnecessary work. As mentioned above, many issues may be mooted by the judgment. Whatever questions the appellate court does hear will be consolidated into a single appeal with one record, thereby increasing the efficiency of the appellate process. The rule also guarantees that legal determinations by the court of appeals will be made in the context of a fully developed factual record.

Those benefits, however, can come at a high cost. While preserving appellate resources, the rule can entail considerable wasted effort by the trial court. If the trial proceeds under an erroneous legal standard, the trial court on remand may have to re-impanel a jury and recall witnesses. Conversely, if a motion to dismiss is erroneously denied, the trial court will have expended a great deal of resources trying a case that it could have summarily disposed of. The final judgment rule may also frustrate effective appellate review of the underlying rights at issue, as in the case of some discovery disputes. Accordingly, a number of exceptions have developed to mitigate these problems.

3. Multiple Claims/Parties and the Rule of Finality

a. Rule 54(b)

Consider whether the expansive joinder permitted by the Federal Rules of Civil Procedure creates the potential for the final judgment rule to operate

---

* The courts have been flexible in determining whether remaining proceedings, discrete from an earlier adjudication, necessarily render the adjudication nonfinal. Thus, in *Radio Station WOW, Inc. v. Johnson,* 326 U.S. 120 (1945), the Court characterized a state court adjudication ordering the transfer of property as "final" notwithstanding a pending "accounting" in the trial court. *Cf. Brown Shoe Co. v. United States,* 370 U.S. 294 (1962) (court's determination that defendant should be divested of its ownership of another shoe company under the antitrust laws was reviewable notwithstanding that the court had not yet developed a divestiture plan). *But see Cobbledick v. United States,* 309 U.S. 323 (1940) (denial of motion to quash grand jury subpoena not a final judgment).

oppressively. As a result of the joinder provisions of Rules 18 and 20, the claims asserted in a litigation may have only a tangential connection with other claims.* Thus, a court may completely resolve part of a lawsuit having little or no connection with the remaining claims. Is it unfair to force the losing party to that discrete claim to wait for the conclusion of the rest of the lawsuit before pursuing its appellate remedies?

Alternatively, what if a dismissed claim *is* closely connected with the remaining claims? Under what circumstances does it make sense to fully litigate the pending claims before permitting appeal of the dismissed claim? Note the potential waste and duplication of trial court resources if the dismissed claim is reversed on appeal. The trial court may have to retry many of the same questions already litigated. On the other hand, application of the final judgment rule in this circumstance probably conserves appellate resources: Resolution of the remaining claims may moot the need for appeal altogether (for instance, where plaintiff obtains complete relief against the remaining defendants); and at a minimum, the appeals court will only have to review the case once, in a consolidated appeal.

Rule 54(b) gives the trial court the flexibility to weigh these competing considerations on a case-by-case basis. Once there is a final disposition of one of the claims or parties, Rule 54(b) gives the court the power to weigh a variety of factors in determining whether to direct the entry of a final judgment as to those claims and allow the losing party to proceed with a partial appeal. If the court fails to direct entry of a final judgment as to the resolved claims (often called a "certification"), the parties must wait until the conclusion of the rest of the litigation before enforcing or appealing the judgment.

NOTE ON *CURTISS-WRIGHT CORP. v. GENERAL ELECTRIC CO.*

Although the decision whether to direct the entry of a final judgment under Rule 54(b) is vested in the discretion of the trial court, the Supreme Court attempted to provide some guidance for the exercise of that discretion in *Curtiss-Wright Corp. v. General Electric Co.*, 446 U.S. 1 (1980). General Electric had entered into a series of contracts with Curtiss-Wright for the purchase of components used in the construction of a naval vessel. Curtiss-Wright asserted a claim for the $19 million balance due under the contract, as well as fraud and misrepresentation claims against GE. GE then counterclaimed for additional costs that it incurred in the construction. Curtiss-Wright's claim for the balance due under the contracts turned entirely on the scope of a release clause in the contracts, which made Curtiss-Wright's entitlement to final payment contingent on a release of all claims that Curtiss-Wright had against GE. On motion for summary judgment, the district court held that Curtiss-Wright was entitled to payment of the balance due notwithstanding the release clause. Pursuant to motion by Curtiss-Wright, the court then directed the entry of a final judgment under Rule 54(b) on that claim to enable Curtiss-Wright to seek immediate payment of the judgment. Any delay, the court held, would be costly to Curtiss-Wright since the rate of interest applicable to the judgment was significantly lower than market rates. The court of appeals reversed on the ground

---

* Recall that under Rule 18 claims are not required to have any relationship to one another.

that pendency of GE's counterclaim, which could ultimately constitute a setoff of GE's liability of the balance due, precluded the entry of a Rule 54(b) certification.

Holding that the district court's certification must stand absent an abuse of discretion, the Supreme Court reversed:

> The function of the district court under the Rule is to act as a "dispatcher" . . . . It is left to the sound judicial discretion of the district court to determine the "appropriate time" when each final decision in a multiple claims action is ready for appeal. *Ibid.* This discretion is to be exercised "in the interest of sound judicial administration."
>
> Thus, in deciding whether there are no just reasons to delay the appeal of individual final judgments in settings such as this, a district court must take into account judicial administrative interests as well as the equities involved. Consideration of the former is necessary to assure that application of the Rule effectively "preserves the historic federal policy against piecemeal appeals." It was therefore proper for the District Judge here to consider such factors as whether the claims under review were separable from the others remaining to be adjudicated and whether the nature of the claims already determined was such that no appellate court would have to decide the same issues more than once even if there were subsequent appeals.
>
> . . .
>
> Plainly, sound judicial administration does not require that Rule 54(b) requests be granted routinely. That is implicit in commending them to the sound discretion of a district court. Because this discretion "is, with good reason, vested by the rule primarily" in the district courts, . . . and because the number of possible situations is large, we are reluctant either to fix or sanction narrow guidelines for the district courts to follow. We are satisfied, however, that on the record here the District Court's assessment of the equities was reasonable.

NOTES AND QUESTIONS

1. Consider the implications of the abuse of discretion standard applied by the Court. Doesn't the decision to direct the entry of a final judgment virtually always involve trade-offs in judicial efficiency? As in *Curtiss-Wright*, one of the parties will inevitably benefit from a designation of finality under Rule 54(b) either to collect on a judgment (as was the case in *Curtiss-Wright*), or to appeal a dismissed claim in time to try it with the rest of the case. The trial court will similarly benefit from appellate review, particularly if the appeals court were to reverse a dismissed claim. Thus, certification under Rule 54(b) facilitates consolidated trial court proceedings.

On the other hand, grant of a Rule 54(b) motion will often be an inefficient use of appellate resources since it necessitates the piecemeal review of a single case. (Of course, the case might settle after the first appellate review, thus avoiding further appeal.) In a case like *Curtiss-Wright*, where the issues in the adjudicated claim are unrelated to the remaining claims, fewer economies are realized from a consolidated appeal. The Court thus recognized the desirability of facilitating the appeal of "separate and distinct claims." Note, however, that if the claims *were* related, the trial court would recognize greater benefits from early appellate reversal. The trial court could then consolidate trial of all related claims.

Given these inevitable trade-offs, when would the decision to certify ever constitute an "abuse of discretion"? In a rare reversal of a Rule 54(b) certification, the court in *Novick v. AXA Network, LLC*, 642 F.3d 304 (2d Cir. 2011), held that the district court abused its discretion in certifying as a final judgment its grant of summary judgment on a counterclaim. Plaintiff had sued for breach of an employment contract, and the defendant counterclaimed for the unpaid balance on a promissory note given by plaintiff. The court of appeals held that because the duty to repay the counterclaim was connected to whether plaintiff was wrongfully terminated, the counterclaim could not be independently appealed pursuant to Rule 54(b). *Cf. General Ins. Co. of America v. Clark Mall Corp.*, 644 F.3d 375 (7th Cir. 2011) (district court improperly certified for appeal its declaratory judgment that insurance company had a duty to defend when counterclaims by insured were still pending).

2. *What Constitutes a "Final Judgment" on a "Claim for Relief"?* Rule 54(b) does not authorize interlocutory appeals of *all* trial court rulings; only final disposition of discrete "claim[s] for relief" are entitled to a designation as final under the Rule. In the case of multiple parties, such discrete claims are fairly easy to identify. Multiple claims against a single party present more difficulty. What if a plaintiff in a tort suit asserted counts for negligence and strict liability against a defendant? Would the court's dismissal of the strict liability count constitute a final judgment on a "claim for relief"? Or would the court consider the two legal theories simply alternative grounds for a single "claim"?

There is no clear answer. In *Sears, Roebuck & Co. v. Mackey*, 351 U.S. 427 (1956), plaintiff Mackey had asserted a multicount complaint against Sears for a variety of anticompetitive actions, all allegedly in violation of the federal antitrust and state tortious interference laws. The trial court dismissed the counts based on federal law but retained for trial two common law counts redressing some of the same underlying conduct. The Supreme Court upheld the trial court's Rule 54(b) certification of the two dismissed counts, notwithstanding their connections to the remaining counts and Sears' contention that they did not constitute separate "claims for relief" within the meaning of the Rule. "There is no doubt that each of the claims dismissed is a 'claim for relief' within the meaning of Rule 54(b)." *Id.* at 436. *But see In re Southeast Banking Corp.*, 69 F.3d 1539 (11th Cir. 1995) (claim that defendants, bank directors, improperly forced one of their subsidiaries to recklessly increase its lending, could not be certified for appeal under Rule 54(b) since claim was inseparable from remaining claim that defendants improperly failed to pursue a merger possibility on behalf of the bank); *Minority Police Officers Ass'n v. City of South Bend*, 721 F.2d 197 (7th Cir. 1983) (court's ruling that statute of limitations barred claims for acts of discrimination that occurred more than two years before complaint was filed was not appealable under Rule 54(b) since not separable from remaining claims based on discriminatory acts occurring within the statutory period); *CMAX, Inc. v. Drewry Photocolor Corp.*, 295 F.2d 695 (9th Cir. 1961) (multiple legal theories to redress the same underlying facts do not constitute separate claims for purposes of Rule 54(b)). *See generally* 10 C. Wright et al., Federal Practice and Procedure §2657 (4th ed. 2014 & 2021 Update).

We have seen in other contexts the use of the "same claim" concept: Supplemental jurisdiction and *res judicata* both rely on such a characterization. To what extent should the courts borrow from either of those contexts to define appealability under Rule 54(b)?

3. *Consolidated Actions.* Consider also the question of litigation consolidated under Rule 42(a). Must litigants seek Rule 54(b) certification for every decided claim that they wish to immediately appeal, or should consolidated cases be treated as separate actions outside the scope of Rule 54(b)? *Compare Sandwiches Inc. v. Wendy's Int'l*, 822 F.2d 707 (7th Cir. 1987); *Huene v. United States*, 743 F.2d 703 (9th Cir. 1984) (holding that Rule 54(b) applies in consolidated actions under Rule 42(a)) *with Kraft Inc. v. Local Union 327*, 683 F.2d 131 (6th Cir. 1982); *In re Mass. Helicopter Airlines Inc.*, 469 F.2d 439 (1st Cir. 1972) (holding that one action in a consolidated case can be appealed before a final decision has been rendered in the other action without the need for Rule 54(b) certification since the actions are separate and distinct). *See also, Gelboim v. Bank of America Corp.*, 574 U.S. 405 (2015) (dismissed class action complaint consolidated for pretrial proceedings in Multidistrict Litigation is appealable final judgment notwithstanding pendency of other claims in the MDL); *EEOC v. Harris Chernin Inc.*, 10 F.3d 1286 (7th Cir. 1993) (in cases where the court has consolidated two actions for all purposes, a decision disposing of all claims in one of the constituent actions but not the other is not final and requires Rule 54(b) certification for appeal; however, where it is clear that actions are consolidated for only limited purposes, a decision disposing of all claims and parties in only one of the actions is a final decision subject to immediate appeal). For further discussion of this issue, *see* Joan Steinman, *The Effects of Case Consolidation on the Procedural Rights of Litigants: What They Are, What They Might Be, Part 1: Justiciability and Jurisdiction (Original and Appellate)*, 42 UCLA L. Rev. 717 (1995).

4. *Avoidance of Forfeiture.* Besides facilitating appellate review of a partial adjudication, Rule 54(b) provides an additional important benefit to a potential appellant: It creates a safe harbor that relieves a losing party from the uncertainty of determining when to file its appeal. Unless the trial court designates partial adjudication as a "final judgment," a partial disposition "shall not terminate the action as to any of the claims or parties." In other words, the time for appeal does not start to run on a partial disposition unless the court expressly designates the order as "final." Prior to the enactment of Rule 54(b), an appellant was forced to guess whether a particular disposition was an appealable final order. If appellant waited until the entire case was over, there was a risk that an appeal of an earlier ruling would be considered out of time. One of the principal purposes of the Rule was to eliminate that uncertainty and the premature appeals that it engendered. *See* 10 C. Wright et al., Federal Practice and Procedure §2654, at n.10 (4th ed. 2014 & 2021 Update).

4. Collateral Orders

Appeal under Rule 54(b) is limited to situations in which the trial court has made a final disposition of a discrete claim for relief. However expansively the courts construe a "claim for relief," there are numerous trial court rulings that do not fall within that category but nonetheless may have irrevocable consequences on a party's rights. Consider, for instance, a government official's claim of immunity from suit. If that defense is erroneously denied by the trial court, the underlying right to be free from the burden of litigation will be lost if the official has to wait for the conclusion of the case on the merits before being allowed to appeal. Where such a ruling is unrelated to any of the issues remaining in the litigation, the courts may treat such "collateral orders" as appealable final judgments.

Digital Equipment Corp. v. Desktop Direct, Inc.

511 U.S. 863 (1994)

JUSTICE SOUTER delivered the opinion of the Court.

Section 1291 of the Judicial Code confines appeals as of right to those from "final decisions of the district courts." 28 U.S.C. §1291. This case raises the question whether an order vacating a dismissal predicated on the parties' settlement agreement is final as a collateral order even without a district court's resolution of the underlying cause of action. *See Cohen v. Beneficial Industrial Loan Corp.*, 337 U.S. 541, 546 (1949). We hold that an order denying effect to a settlement agreement does not come within the narrow ambit of collateral orders.

I

Respondent, Desktop Direct, Inc. (Desktop), sells computers and like equipment under the trade name "Desktop Direct." Petitioner, Digital Equipment Corporation, is engaged in a similar business and in late 1991 began using that trade name to market a new service it called "Desktop Direct from Digital." In response, Desktop filed this action in the United States District Court for the District of Utah, charging Digital with unlawful use of the Desktop Direct name. Desktop sent Digital a copy of the complaint, and negotiations between officers of the two corporations ensued. Under a confidential settlement reached on March 25, 1992, Digital agreed to pay Desktop a sum of money for the right to use the "Desktop Direct" trade name and corresponding trademark, and for waiver of all damages and dismissal of the suit. That same day, Desktop filed a notice of dismissal in the District Court.

Several months later, Desktop moved to vacate the dismissal and rescind the settlement agreement, alleging misrepresentation of material facts during settlement negotiations. The District Court granted the motion, concluding "that a fact finder could determine that [Digital] failed to disclose material facts to [Desktop] during settlement negotiations which would have resulted in rejection of the settlement offer." . . . After the District Court declined to reconsider that ruling or stay its order vacating dismissal, Digital appealed.

The Court of Appeals for the Tenth Circuit dismissed the appeal for lack of jurisdiction, holding that the District Court order was not appealable under §1291, because it neither "end[ed] the litigation on the merits" nor "[fell] within the long-recognized 'collateral order' exception to the final judgment requirement." 993 F.2d 755, 757 (1993). Applying the three-pronged test for determining when "collateral order" appeal is allowed, see *Cohen, supra; Coopers & Lybrand v. Livesay,* 437 U.S. 463 (1978), the Court of Appeals concluded that any benefits claimed under the settlement agreement were insufficiently "important" to warrant the immediate appeal as of right. Although Digital claimed what it styled a "right not to go to trial," the court reasoned that any such privately negotiated right as Digital sought to vindicate was different in kind from an immunity rooted in an explicit constitutional or statutory provision or "compelling public policy rationale," the denial of which has been held to be immediately appealable. 993 F.2d at 758–760.

The Tenth Circuit recognized that it was thus deviating from the rule followed in some other Courts of Appeals. . . . We granted certiorari . . . to resolve this conflict and now affirm.

II

A

The collateral order doctrine is best understood not as an exception to the "final decision" rule laid down by Congress in §1291, but as a "practical construction" of it, *Cohen, supra,* 337 U.S. at 546; *see, e.g., Coopers & Lybrand, supra,* at 468. We have repeatedly held that the statute entitles a party to appeal not only from a district court decision that "ends the litigation on the merits and leaves nothing more for the court to do but execute the judgment," *Catlin v. United States,* 324 U.S. 229, 233 (1945), but also from a narrow class of decisions that do not terminate the litigation, but must, in the interest of "achieving a healthy legal system," cf. *Cobbledick v. United States,* 309 U.S. 323, 326 (1940), nonetheless be treated as "final." The latter category comprises only those district court decisions that are conclusive, that resolve important questions completely separate from the merits, and that would render such important questions effectively unreviewable on appeal from final judgment in the underlying action. See generally *Coopers & Lybrand, supra.* Immediate appeals from such orders, we have explained, do not go against the grain of §1291, with its object of efficient administration of justice in the federal courts, see generally *Richardson-Merrell, Inc. v. Koller,* 472 U.S. 424 (1985).

But we have also repeatedly stressed that the "narrow" exception should stay that way and never be allowed to swallow the general rule, *id.* at 436, that a party is entitled to a single appeal, to be deferred until final judgment has been entered, in which claims of district court error at any stage of the litigation may be ventilated. . . . We have accordingly described the conditions for collateral order appeal as stringent, see, e.g., *Midland Asphalt Corp. v. United States,* 489 U.S. 794, 799 (1989), and have warned that the issue of appealability under §1291 is to be determined for the entire category to which a claim belongs, without regard to the chance that the litigation at hand might be speeded, or a "particular injustic[e]" averted . . . by a prompt appellate court decision. . . .

B

Here, the Court of Appeals accepted Digital's claim that the order vacating dismissal (and so rescinding the settlement agreement) was the "final word on the subject addressed," . . . and held the second *Cohen* condition, separability, to be satisfied, as well. Neither conclusion is beyond question,[2] but each is best left untouched here, both because Desktop has made no serious effort to defend the Court of Appeals' judgment on those points and because the failure to meet the third condition of the *Cohen* test, that the decision on an "important" question be "effectively unreviewable" upon final judgment, would in itself suffice to foreclose immediate appeal under §1291.[3] Turning to these dispositive factors, we conclude, despite Digital's position that it holds a "right not to stand trial" requiring protection by way of immediate appeal, that rights under private settlement agreements can be adequately vindicated on appeal from final judgment.

C

The roots of Digital's argument that the settlement with Desktop gave it a "right not to stand trial altogether" (and that such a right *per se* satisfies the third *Cohen* requirement) are readily traced to *Abney v. United States*, 431 U.S. 651 (1977), where we held that §1291 entitles a criminal defendant to appeal an adverse ruling on a double jeopardy claim, without waiting for the conclusion of his trial. After holding the second *Cohen* requirement satisfied by the distinction between the former jeopardy claim and the question of guilt to be resolved at trial we emphasized that the Fifth Amendment not only secures the right to be free from multiple punishments, but by its very terms embodies the broader principle, "'deeply ingrained in . . . the Anglo-American system of jurisprudence,'" that it is intolerable for "'the State, with all its resources . . . to make repeated attempts to convict an individual [defendant], thereby subjecting him to embarrassment, expense and ordeal and compelling him to live in a continuing state of anxiety and insecurity.'" 431 U.S. at 661–662. . . . We found that immediate appeal was the only way to give "full protection" to this constitutional right "not to face trial at all." . . .

Abney's rationale was applied in *Nixon v. Fitzgerald*, 457 U.S. 731, 742 (1982), where we held to be similarly appealable an order denying the petitioner absolute immunity from suit for civil damages arising from actions taken while petitioner was President of the United States. Seeing this immunity as a "functionally mandated incident of the President's unique office, rooted in the . . . separation of powers and supported by our history," . . . we stressed that it served "compelling public ends," . . . and would be irretrievably lost if the former President were not allowed

---

2. It might be argued that given the District Court's "somewhat cryptic" reference, 993 F.2d at 757, to what "a trier of fact could determine," its rescission order here was merely "tentative," . . . and thus inadequate under the first *Cohen* test, or that the basis for vacating, Digital's alleged misrepresentations about when it first learned of Desktop's use of the trade name, was so "enmeshed in the factual and legal issues comprising the plaintiff's cause of action," . . . i.e., whether Digital (willfully) misappropriated the name, as to elude *Cohen*'s second requirement for collateral order appeal. Indeed, it is possible that the District Court phrased its order here in equivocal terms precisely because it assumed that this lack of separability would preclude any immediate appeal under §1291.

3. We have of course held that the *Cohen* requirements go to an appellate court's subject-matter jurisdiction, see *Firestone Tire & Rubber Co. v. Risjord*, 449 U.S. 368, 379 (1981), and thus, were it necessary here, we would be obliged to assess whether each condition was met, without regard to whether the parties believe it to be satisfied.

an immediate appeal to vindicate this right to be free from the rigors of trial. . . .
Next, in *Mitchell v. Forsyth*, 472 U.S. 511 (1985), we held that similar considerations
supported appeal under §1291 from decisions denying government officials qualified immunity from damages suits. An "essential attribute" . . . of this freedom
from suit for past conduct not violative of clearly established law, we explained, is
the "entitlement not to stand trial or face the other burdens of litigation," . . . one
which would be "effectively lost if a case [were] erroneously permitted to go to
trial." . . . Echoing the reasoning of *Nixon v. Fitzgerald, supra* . . . we explained that
requiring an official with a colorable immunity claim to defend a suit for damages
would be "peculiarly disruptive of effective government," and would work the very
"distraction . . . from . . . dut[y], inhibition of discretionary action, and deterrence
of able people from public service" that qualified immunity was meant to avoid. . . .

D

Digital puts this case on all fours with *Mitchell*. It maintains that it obtained
dual rights under the settlement agreement with Desktop, not only a broad defense
to liability but the "right not to stand trial," the latter being just like the qualified
immunity held immediately appealable in *Mitchell*. As in *Mitchell*, that right must be
enforceable on collateral order appeal, Digital asserts, or an adverse trial ruling will
destroy it forever.

While Digital's argument may exert some pull on a narrow analysis, it does
not hold up under the broad scrutiny to which all claims of immediate appealability under §1291 must be subjected. To be sure, *Abney* and *Mitchell* are fairly
cited for the proposition that orders denying certain immunities are strong candidates for prompt appeal under §1291. But Digital's larger contention, that a
party's ability to characterize a district court's decision as denying an irreparable
"right not to stand trial" altogether is sufficient as well as necessary for a collateral
order appeal, is neither an accurate distillation of our case law nor an appealing
prospect for adding to it.

Even as they have recognized the need for immediate appeals under §1291
to vindicate rights that would be "irretrievably lost," . . . if review were confined
to final judgments only, our cases have been at least as emphatic in recognizing
that the jurisdiction of the courts of appeals should not, and cannot, depend on a
party's agility in so characterizing the right asserted. This must be so because the
strong bias of §1291 against piecemeal appeals almost never operates without some
cost. A fully litigated case can no more be untried than the law's proverbial bell
can be unrung, and almost every pretrial or trial order might be called "effectively
unreviewable" in the sense that relief from error can never extend to rewriting history. Thus, erroneous evidentiary rulings, grants or denials of attorney disqualification, see, e.g., *Richardson-Merrell, supra*, and restrictions on the rights of intervening
parties, see *Stringfellow v. Concerned Neighbors in Action*, 480 U.S. 370 (1987), may
burden litigants in ways that are only imperfectly reparable by appellate reversal
of a final district court judgment . . . ; and other errors, real enough, will not seem
serious enough to warrant reversal at all, when reviewed after a long trial on the
merits. . . . In still other cases, see *Coopers & Lybrand v. Livesay*, 437 U.S. 463 (1978),
an erroneous district court decision will, as a practical matter, sound the "death
knell" for many plaintiffs' claims that might have gone forward if prompt error

correction had been an option. But if immediate appellate review were available every such time, Congress's final decision rule would end up a pretty puny one, and so the mere identification of some interest that would be "irretrievably lost" has never sufficed to meet the third *Cohen* requirement. . . .

Nor does limiting the focus to whether the interest asserted may be called a "right not to stand trial" offer much protection against the urge to push the §1291 limits. We have, after all, acknowledged that virtually every right that could be enforced appropriately by pretrial dismissal might loosely be described as conferring a "right not to stand trial." . . . Allowing immediate appeals to vindicate every such right would move §1291 aside for claims that the district court lacks personal jurisdiction . . . that the statute of limitations has run, see 15B C. Wright, A. Miller & E. Cooper, Federal Practice and Procedure §3918.5, and n. 65, p. 521 (1992), that the movant has been denied his Sixth Amendment right to a speedy trial, see *MacDonald, supra,* that an action is barred on claim preclusion principles, that no material fact is in dispute and the moving party is entitled to judgment as a matter of law, or merely that the complaint fails to state a claim. Such motions can be made in virtually every case . . . and it would be no consolation that a party's meritless summary judgment motion or *res judicata* claim was rejected on immediate appeal; the damage to the efficient and congressionally mandated allocation of judicial responsibility would be done, and any improper purpose the appellant might have had in saddling its opponent with cost and delay would be accomplished. . . . Thus, precisely because candor forces us to acknowledge that there is no single, "obviously correct way to characterize" an asserted right, . . . we have held that §1291 requires courts of appeals to view claims of a "right not to be tried" with skepticism, if not a jaundiced eye. . . .

Digital answers that the status under §1291 of these other (seemingly analogous) rights should not give us pause, because the text and structure of this particular settlement with Desktop confer what no *res judicata* claimant could ever have, an express right not to stand trial. But we cannot attach much significance one way or another to the supposed clarity of the agreement's terms in this case. To ground a ruling here on whether this settlement agreement in terms confers the prized "right not to stand trial" (a point Desktop by no means concedes) would flout our own frequent admonitions . . . that availability of collateral order appeal must be determined at a higher level of generality. Indeed, just because it would be the rare settlement agreement that could not be construed to include (at least an implicit) freedom-from-trial "aspect," we decide this case on the assumption that if Digital prevailed here, any district court order denying effect to a settlement agreement could be appealed immediately. (And even if form were held to matter, settlement agreements would all include "immunity from suit" language a good deal plainer than what Digital relies on here. . . .) . . .

The more fundamental response, however, to the claim that an agreement's provision for immunity from trial can distinguish it from other arguable rights to be trial-free is simply that such a right by agreement does not rise to the level of importance needed for recognition under §1291. This, indeed, is the bone of the fiercest contention in the case. In disparaging any distinction between an order denying a claim grounded on an explicit constitutional guarantee of immunity from trial and an order at odds with an equally explicit right by private agreement of the parties, Digital stresses that the relative "importance" of these rights, heavily relied upon by the Court of Appeals, is a rogue factor. No decision of this Court, Digital maintains, has held an order unappealable as "unimportant" when it has otherwise met the three *Cohen* requirements, and whether a decided issue is thought "important," it says, should have no bearing on whether it is "final" under §1291.

If "finality" were as narrow a concept as Digital maintains, however, the Court would have had little reason to go beyond the first factor in *Cohen*. . . . And if "importance" were truly aberrational, we would not find it featured so prominently in the *Cohen* opinion itself, which describes the "small class" of immediately appealable prejudgment decisions in terms of rights that are "too important to be denied review" right away. . . . To be sure, Digital may validly question whether "importance" is a factor "beyond" the three *Cohen* conditions or whether it is best considered, as we have sometimes suggested it should be, in connection with the second, "separability," requirement, . . . but neither enquiry could lead to the conclusion that "importance" is itself unimportant. To the contrary, the third *Cohen* question, whether a right is "adequately vindicable" or "effectively reviewable," simply cannot be answered without a judgment about the value of the interests that would be lost through rigorous application of a final judgment requirement. . . .

While there is no need to decide here that a privately conferred right could never supply the basis of a collateral order appeal, . . . there are surely sound reasons for treating such rights differently from those originating in the Constitution or statutes. When a policy is embodied in a constitutional or statutory provision entitling a party to immunity from suit (a rare form of protection), there is little room for the judiciary to gainsay its "importance." Including a provision in a private contract, by contrast, is barely a prima facie indication that the right secured is "important" to the benefited party (contracts being replete with boilerplate), let alone that its value exceeds that of other rights not embodied in agreements (e.g., the right to be free from a second suit based on a claim that has already been litigated), or that it qualifies as "important" in *Cohen*'s sense, as being weightier than the societal interests advanced by the ordinary operation of final judgment principles. Where statutory and constitutional rights are concerned, "irretrievabl[e] los[s]" can hardly be trivial, and the collateral order doctrine might therefore be understood as reflecting the familiar principle of statutory construction that, when possible, courts should construe statutes (here §1291) to foster harmony with other statutory and constitutional law. . . . But it is one thing to say that the policy of §1291 to avoid piecemeal litigation should be reconciled with policies embodied in other statutes or the Constitution, and quite another to suggest that this public policy may be trumped routinely by the expectations or clever drafting of private parties.[7]

---

7. This is not to say that rights originating in a private agreement may never be important enough to warrant immediate appeal. To the contrary. Congress only recently enacted a statute, 102 Stat. 4671, see 9 U.S.C. §16 (1988 ed., Supp. IV), essentially providing for immediate appeal when a district court rejects a party's assertion that, under the Arbitration Act, a case belongs before a commercial arbitrator and not in court, a measure predicted to have a "sweeping impact," 15B C. Wright, A. Miller & E. Cooper, Federal Practice and Procedure §3914.17, p. 11 (1992); see generally *id.* at 7–38. That courts must give full effect to this express congressional judgment that particular policies require that private rights be vindicable immediately, however, by no means suggests that they should now be more ready to make similar judgments for themselves. Congress has expressed no parallel sentiment, to the effect that settlement-agreement rights are, as a matter of federal policy, similarly "too important" to be denied immediate review.

Nor are we swayed by Digital's last-ditch effort to come within *Cohen*'s sense of "importance" by trying to show that settlement-agreement "immunities" merit first-class treatment for purposes of collateral order appeal, because they advance the public policy favoring voluntary resolution of disputes. It defies common sense to maintain that parties' readiness to settle will be significantly dampened (or the corresponding public interest impaired) by a rule that a district court's decision to let allegedly barred litigation go forward may be challenged as a matter of right only on appeal from a judgment for the plaintiff's favor.

III

A

Even, finally, if the term "importance" were to be exorcised from the *Cohen* analysis altogether, Digital's rights would remain "adequately vindicable" or "effectively reviewable" on final judgment to an extent that other immunities, like the right to be free from a second trial on a criminal charge, are not. As noted already, experience suggests that freedom from trial is rarely the *sine qua non* (or "the essence," . . .) of a negotiated settlement agreement. Avoiding the burden of a trial is no doubt a welcome incident of out-of-court dispute resolution (just as it is for parties who prevail on pretrial motions), but in the run-of-the-mill cases this boon will rarely compare with the "'embarrassment'" and "'anxiety'" averted by a successful double jeopardy claimant, . . . or the "'distraction from . . . dut[y],'" . . . avoided by qualified immunity. Judged within the four corners of the settlement agreement, avoiding trial probably pales in comparison with the benefit of limiting exposure to liability (an interest that is fully vindicable on appeal from final judgment). In the rare case where a party had a special reason, apart from the generic desire to triumph early, for having bargained for an immunity from trial, *e.g.*, an unusual interest in preventing disclosure of particular information, it may seek protection from the district court.

The case for adequate vindication without immediate appeal is strengthened, moreover, by recognizing that a settling party has a source of recompense unknown to trial immunity claimants dependent on public law alone. The essence of Digital's claim here is that Desktop, for valuable consideration, promised not to sue, and we have been given no reason to doubt that Utah law provides for the enforcement of that promise in the same way that other rights arising from private agreements are enforced, through an action for breach of contract. . . . And as for Digital's suggestion . . . that Desktop is using this proceeding not to remedy a fraud but merely to renege on a promise because it now thinks it should have negotiated a better deal, when a party claims fraud or otherwise seeks recision of a settlement for such improper purposes, its opponent need not rely on a court of appeals for protection. See Fed. Rule Civ. Proc. 11 (opponent may move for sanction when litigation is motivated by an "improper purpose, such as . . . unnecessary delay or needless increase in the cost of litigation").

B

In preserving the strict limitations on review as of right under §1291, our holding should cause no dismay, for the law is not without its safety valve to deal with cases where the contest over a settlement's enforceability raises serious legal questions taking the case out of the ordinary run. While Digital's insistence that the District Court applied a fundamentally wrong legal standard in vacating the dismissal order here may not be considered in deciding appealability under §1291, . . . it plainly is relevant to the availability of the discretionary interlocutory appeal from particular district court orders "involv[ing] a controlling question of law as to which there is substantial ground for difference of opinion," provided for in §1292(b) of Title 28. Indeed, because we suppose that a defendant's claimed entitlement to a privately negotiated "immunity from suit" could in some instances raise "a controlling question of law . . . [which] . . . may materially advance the ultimate termination of the litigation," the discretionary appeal provision (allowing courts to consider the merits of individual claims) would seem a better vehicle for vindicating serious contractual interpretation claims than the blunt, categorical instrument of §1291 collateral order appeal. . . .

IV

The words of §1291 have long been construed to recognize that certain categories of prejudgment decisions exist for which it is both justifiable and necessary to depart from the general rule, that "the whole case and every matter in controversy in it [must be] decided in a single appeal." *McLish v. Roff,* 141 U.S. 661, 665–666 (1891). But denying effect to the sort of (asserted) contractual right at issue here is far removed from those immediately appealable decisions involving rights more deeply rooted in public policy, and the rights Digital asserts may, in the main, be vindicated through means less disruptive to the orderly administration of justice than immediate, mandatory appeal. We accordingly hold that a refusal to enforce a settlement agreement claimed to shelter a party from suit altogether does not supply the basis for immediate appeal under §1291. The judgment of the Court of Appeals is therefore
Affirmed.

NOTES AND QUESTIONS

1. *Assessing* Digital Equipment. Do you agree with the result of *Digital Equipment?* If the settlement agreement in fact precluded the lawsuit, wouldn't it be much more efficient to find that out before the case was tried on the merits? Was the Court's contrary result based on its understanding of §1291, the force of precedent, or policy? Doesn't the Court's holding undermine significantly the value of the settlement? *See* Margaret Meriwether Corday, *Settlement Agreements and the Supreme Court,* 48 Hastings L.J. 9 (1996).

Does the holding in *Digital Equipment* help you determine what kinds of orders are immediately appealable under §1291? *See* Lloyd C. Anderson, *The Collateral Order Doctrine: A New "Serbonian Bog" and Four Proposals for Reform,* 46 Drake L. Rev. 539 (1998) (discussing post-*Digital Equipment* confusion in the lower courts as to what types of orders can be immediately appealed under the collateral order doctrine).

2. *Rationale for Collateral Order.* As discussed in *Digital Equipment,* the Court has reconciled the collateral order doctrine with the final judgment rule by holding that collateral orders in fact constitute "final judgments" within the meaning of 28 U.S.C. §1291. The doctrine was first articulated in *Cohen v. Beneficial Industrial*

Loan Corp., 337 U.S. 541 (1949). The Court there permitted an immediate appeal from the district court's ruling that plaintiff did not have to post a bond in order to pursue its shareholders' derivative claim, as it would have had to do in a state court:

> This decision appears to fall in that small class which finally determine claims of right separable from, and collateral to, rights asserted in the action, too important to be denied review and too independent of the cause itself to require that appellate consideration be deferred until the whole case is adjudicated. We hold this order appealable because it is a final disposition of a claimed right which is not an ingredient of the cause of action and does not require consideration with it.

337 U.S. at 546–557. While such a formulation might encompass a wide array of trial court rulings, the Court has consistently tried to narrow the reach of the doctrine, as it did in *Digital Equipment.*

The Court extended the holding of *Digital Equipment* to preclude interlocutory review of a claim against United States Customs Service agents, which, defendants asserted, should have been barred by the Federal Tort Claims Act. *Will v. Hallock*, 546 U.S. 345 (2006). Plaintiffs in *Will* had brought a previous action under the Federal Tort Claims Act against the United States government for damage to their computer equipment incurred when the equipment was seized in a customs raid. That action was dismissed on the ground of sovereign immunity. While that action was still pending, plaintiffs filed a separate action against the individual customs agents for violation of their constitutional rights. Following the dismissal of the claim against the government, the individual defendants asserted that the action against them should be dismissed pursuant to the "judgment bar" provision of the Tort Claims Acts, pursuant to which a judgment under the Act bars any action by the claimant "against the employee of the government whose act or omission gave rise to the claim." The district court refused to dismiss the action on the ground that the claim against the government was dismissed on a procedural ground having no preclusive effect under the Act. The court of appeals heard the appeal as a "collateral order" and affirmed.

The Supreme Court reversed. The Court held that the "collateral order" doctrine could not be invoked simply to vindicate a defendant's right not to stand trial. Rather, some additional public interest must be advanced by the appeal:

> In each case [allowing appeal under the collateral order doctrine] some particular value of a high order was marshaled in support of the interest in avoiding trial: honoring the separation of powers, preserving the efficiency of government and the initiative of its officials, respecting a State's dignitary interests, and mitigating the government's advantage over the individual. That is, it is not mere avoidance of a trial, but avoidance of a trial that would imperil a substantial public interest, that counts when asking whether an order is "effectively" unreviewable if review is to be left until later. . . .
>
>   . . .
>
> Although the statutory judgment bar is arguably broader than traditional res judicata, it functions in much the same way, with both rules depending on a prior judgment as a condition precedent and neither reflecting a policy that a defendant should be scot free of any liability. The concern behind both rules is a different one, of avoiding duplicative litigation,

"multiple suits on identical entitlements or obligations between the same parties." 18 C. Wright, A. Miller, & E. Cooper, Federal Practice and Procedure §4402, p. 9 (2d ed. 2002) (internal quotation marks omitted). But this rule of respecting a prior judgment by giving a defense against relitigation has not been thought to protect values so great that only immediate appeal can effectively vindicate them. As we indicated in *Digital Equipment*, in the usual case, absent particular reasons for discretionary appeal by leave of the trial court, a defense of claim preclusion is fairly subordinated to the general policy of deferring appellate review to the moment of final judgment.

Id. at 959–960.

Even after *Will*, the courts continue to treat denials of motions to dismiss based on qualified immunity as appealable collateral orders. *See, e.g., Ashcroft v. Iqbal*, 556 U.S. 662, 671 (2009). For a critique of this doctrine, *see* Michael E. Solimine, *Are Interlocutory Qualified Immunity Appeals Lawful?*, 94 Notre Dame L. Rev. Online 169 (2019).

a. *Discovery Orders.* Decisions compelling discovery might be seen as perfect candidates for the collateral order doctrine: The issues are often independent of other issues in the litigation; and the rights often cannot be effectively vindicated by appeal from a final disposition of the case, particularly where claims of privilege have been overruled. Nonetheless, the courts have generally held that discovery orders do not fall within the collateral order doctrine since the parties have an alternative means of obtaining effective appellate review: They can disobey the discovery order and then appeal the subsequent contempt of court citation. *See Firestone Tire & Rubber Co. v. Risjord*, 449 U.S. 368, 377 (1981) ("[W]e have generally denied review of pretrial discovery orders. . . . Our rationale has been that in the rare case when appeal after final judgment will not cure an erroneous discovery order, a party may defy the order, permit a contempt citation to be entered against him, and challenge the order on direct appeal of the contempt ruling.").

Do you think it is appropriate to treat the option of defying a court order as an adequate method of vindicating a party's rights? Is it fair to subject a party to that choice? Does it undermine judicial authority to treat compliance with a court order as an "option"?

In order to appeal a discovery order, the appellant (or the attorney) must actually be subjected to contempt sanctions: The award of other discovery sanctions under the Federal Rules will not suffice. *See Cunningham v. Hamilton County*, 527 U.S. 198 (1999).

What about appeals from *denials* of motions to compel production of discovery? In such cases, the *Firestone Tire & Rubber* option of appealing from contempt citation is unavailable. Courts have, on rare occasion, treated denials of access to discovery as appealable collateral orders. *See In Re: National Prescription Opiate Litigation*, 927 F.3d 919 (6th Cir. 2019), in which the court reviewed and reversed as an appealable collateral order the district court's entry of a protective order depriving the media access to information produced in discovery.

Should assertions of privilege raise additional concerns and be treated differently? Resolving a circuit split on that issue, the Supreme Court held in *Mohawk Industries v. Carpenter*, 558 U.S. 100 (2009), that an order to compel discovery allegedly in violation of defendant's attorney-client privilege did not qualify for review under the doctrine. The Court held that post-judgment review would adequately, if imperfectly, vindicate defendant's rights; if the district court's order was deemed erroneous, the appellate court could order a new trial and exclude all evidence obtained through the order to compel. Moreover, if the need for interlocutory review was, in an appropriate case, particularly compelling, the court could always certify the case for appeal under §1292(b) (*see* pp. 1076–1078), the appeals court could issue a writ of mandamus or prohibition (*see* pp. 1078–1080), or the appellant could defy the order and appeal the consequent contempt citation.

b. *Jurisdiction and Forum Selection Rulings.* Courts have generally resisted treating jurisdictional and related questions as appealable orders, primarily on the ground that appeal from final judgment provides adequate appellate review. *See Lauro Lines, S.R.L. v. Chasser*, 490 U.S. 495 (1985) (denial of motion to dismiss based on forum selection clause not appealable collateral order). *See also Van Cauwenberghe v. Biard*, 486 U.S. 517 (1988) (denial of *forum non conveniens* motion not collateral order); *Chapple v. Levinsky*, 961 F.2d 372 (2d Cir. 1992) (§1404(a) transfer not appealable order). Do those rulings seem fair? If a party has a right not to be subjected to the personal jurisdiction of a given forum, isn't that right frustrated if a party must try its case in that forum on the merits before it is able to vindicate its jurisdictional right? Is the right not to be subjected to jurisdiction in a particular forum distinguishable from the immunity cases discussed in *Digital Equipment? See Van Cauwenberghe v. Biard, supra* (holding that primary right protected by jurisdiction rules is freedom from binding judgment, not freedom from litigation *per se*).

However, in a later decision, the Supreme Court allowed a "collateral order" appeal of an order remanding a previously removed case back to state court. In *Quackenbush v. Allstate Ins. Co.*, 517 U.S. 706 (1996), the district court's decision to remand was rooted in the doctrine of federal abstention, whereby a federal court surrenders jurisdiction to allow the state court to proceed with an action involving important issues of state concern. The Supreme Court found that the "separate question" of whether the federal court should decline to exercise its jurisdiction in the interest of comity and federalism was sufficient to warrant an immediate appeal. The Court also held that 28 U.S.C. §1447(d) — prohibiting review of any order remanding a case to state review — did not bar appellate review of this remand order because the remand prohibition in §1447(d) extends only to remands described in §1447(c) (remands based on lack of subject matter jurisdiction or defects in removal procedure). Can *Quackenbush* be distinguished from the earlier Supreme Court precedents in *Lauro Lines* and *Van Cauwenberghe? See generally* James E. Pfander, *Collateral Review of Remand Orders: Reasserting the Supervisory Role of the Supreme Court*, 159 U. Pa. L. Rev. 493 (2011).

c. *Motions to Disqualify Counsel.* In *Firestone Tire & Rubber Co. v. Risjord*, 449 U.S. 368 (1981), the Court refused to extend the collateral order doctrine to a *denial* of a motion to disqualify counsel for plaintiffs for an alleged conflict of interest. The Court held that the question could be effectively reviewed on appeal from final judgment. This holding was extended to an order *granting* a motion to disqualify counsel in *Richardson-Merrell, Inc. v. Koller*, 472 U.S. 424 (1985).

d. *Procedures That May Violate Constitutional Rights.* In *Sell v. United States*, 539 U.S. 166 (2003), the Supreme Court identified another circumstance that might qualify as a "collateral order" for purposes of appeal: a court-ordered procedure that itself may violate an individual's constitutional rights. *Sell* involved the criminal prosecution of Charles Sell, who suffered from serious mental illness and was unable to control his behavior during trial proceedings. The government wished to administer antipsychotic medication to Sell, against his will, so that the trial could proceed. A federal district court granted an order to that effect, and Sell sought immediate appellate review, claiming that the order violated his constitutional right to bodily integrity. The same statute that ordinarily prevents interlocutory appeals in civil cases, however, also applies in criminal cases (*see* 28 U.S.C. §1291), and the government argued that the statute barred Sell's appeal.

The Supreme Court disagreed, holding that Sell's claim fell within the scope of the collateral order doctrine:

> The order [compelling Sell to be forcibly medicated] (1) "conclusively determine[s] the disputed question," namely, whether Sell has a legal right to avoid forced medication. The order also (2) "resolve[s] an important issue," for, as this Court's cases make clear, involuntary medical treatment raises questions of clear constitutional importance. At the same time, the basic issue—whether Sell must undergo medication against his will—is "completely separate from the merits of the action," i.e., whether Sell is guilty or innocent of the crimes charged. . . . Finally, the issue is (3) "effectively unreviewable on appeal from a final judgment." By the time of trial Sell will have undergone forced medication—the very harm that he seeks to avoid. He cannot undo that harm even if he is acquitted.

Id. at 176–177.

Justice Scalia, joined by Justices O'Connor and Thomas, issued a strong dissent, arguing that the majority had fatally undermined the final judgment rule:

> The Court's opinion . . . effects a breathtaking expansion of appellate jurisdiction over interlocutory orders. If it is applied faithfully (and some appellate panels will be eager to apply it faithfully), any criminal defendant who asserts that a trial court order will, if implemented, cause an immediate violation of his constitutional (or perhaps even statutory?) rights may immediately appeal. He is empowered to hold up the trial for months by claiming that review after final judgment "would come too late" to prevent the violation. A trial-court order requiring the defendant to wear an electronic bracelet could be attacked as an immediate infringement of the constitutional right to "bodily integrity"; an order refusing to allow the defendant to wear a T-shirt that says "Black Power" in front of the jury could be attacked as an immediate violation of First Amendment rights; and an order compelling testimony could be attacked as an immediate denial of Fifth Amendment rights. All these orders would be immediately appealable.

Id. at 190 (Scalia, J., dissenting).

3. *Class Action Certification.* The appealability of class certification decisions has varied dramatically over time. Because the decision whether to certify a claim as a class action under Rule 23 is closely related to the claim on the merits, the question has never been treated as a "collateral order" under *Cohen*. However, because of its virtually dispositive impact on the litigation, courts have at times entertained appeals

on the theory that the class certification decision was in effect a final order; failure to certify was viewed as the "death knell" of litigation. *See, e.g., Eisen v. Carlisle & Jacquelin,* 370 F.2d 119 (2d Cir. 1966), *cert. denied,* 386 U.S. 1035 (1967). However, the Supreme Court rejected that approach in *Coopers & Lybrand v. Livesay,* 437 U.S. 463 (1978).

Still, the continuing concern over class action certifications and the recognition of the impact of a certification decision on the entire litigation led the Advisory Committee on Civil Rules to address directly the nonappealable status of class action certification rulings. In 1998, subsection (f) was added to Rule 23 on class actions and authorizes a court of appeals, in its discretion, to permit an appeal from an order of a district court granting or denying class action status.* Note that unlike interlocutory appeals under 28 U.S.C. §1292(b), under Rule 23(f) the trial court has no control over appealability, and the determination of whether to permit an appeal is entrusted solely to the appellate court.

The Supreme Court has not yet had occasion to construe Rule 23(f). It did hold in *Microsoft Corp. v. Baker,* 137 S. Ct. 1702 (2017), that the voluntary dismissal of individual claims remaining after a denial of class certification did not convert the case to a final judgment for purposes of 28 U.S.C. §1291. Plaintiffs there were denied permission from the Court of Appeals to file an interlocutory appeal of the class certification denial pursuant to Fed. R. Civ. P. 23(f). They then stipulated to dismiss the remaining individual claims "with prejudice," but "reserved the right to revive their claims should the Court of Appeals reverse the District Court's certification denial." The Court held that the dismissal did not convert the case to a "final decision." To allow such a tactic would, according to Justice Ginsburg, unduly circumvent the final judgment rule, as well as the "careful calibration" of interlocutory appeals of class certification decisions under Rule 23(f).

The courts of appeals have divided somewhat on when they should exercise their discretion to permit an interlocutory appeal of a certification decision. *See generally* 7B C. Wright et al., Federal Practice and Procedure §1802.2 (3d ed. 2005 & April 2021 Update); Michael E. Solimine & Christine Oliver Hines, *Deciding to Decide: Class Action Certification and Interlocutory Review by the United States Courts of Appeals Under Rule 23(f),* 41 Wm. & Mary L. Rev. 1531 (2000). The first court to address the issue was the Seventh Circuit in *Blair v. Equifax Check Servs. Inc.,* 181 F.3d 832 (7th Cir. 1999). The Seventh Circuit rejected any bright line test and instead identified three categories of cases where immediate appeal might be appropriate: first, where the denial of class status would sound the "death knell" of any further litigation (for example, when only small amounts are at stake for each individual, as in *Eisen*); second, where the grant of class status would place inordinate pressure on the defendant to settle, even if the suit has little merit; and third, where an immediate appeal would facilitate the development of class action law. *Id.* at 834-835. As to the first two categories, the Seventh Circuit also found that a petitioner must

---

* Any question of the scope of the rule-making authority to control appealability was mooted by an express congressional grant of rule-making power. In 1992, subsection (e) of 28 U.S.C. §1292 granted to the Supreme Court authority to "prescribe rules, in accordance with Section 2072 . . . , to provide for an appeal of an interlocutory decision to the court of appeals that is not otherwise provided for. . . ."

demonstrate that the district court's certification decision was "questionable." It did not, however, impose such a requirement in the third category, as it found that an affirmance can contribute to the development of the law as well as a reversal.

Other circuits have differed somewhat in how they weigh these factors when deciding whether to grant an appeal. *See, e.g., In re Lorazepam & Clorazepate Antitrust Litig.*, 289 F.3d 98, 104 (D.C. Cir. 2002). Concluding that it was best to approach Rule 23(f) appeals conservatively, *Lorazepam* ratcheted up somewhat the showings required in the *Blair* test. *See also Chamberlan v. Ford Motor Co.*, 402 F.3d 952, 959 (9th Cir. 2005) (manifestly erroneous certification order warrants appellate review even in the absence of other factors).

The courts of appeals have adopted a flexible approach to Rule 23(f) in other respects, as well. Thus, the Seventh Circuit has held that Rule 23(f) authorizes discretionary appeals to those district court orders that constitute the "functional equivalent" of a denial of class certification, even if the order is issued under some other provision. *See In re Bemis Company, Inc.*, 279 F.3d 419, 421 (7th Cir. 2002) (reviewing district court order striking part of defendant's answer on grounds that EEOC complaint is exempt from operation of Rule 23 altogether). *But see In re Complaint of Ingram Barge Co.*, 517 F.3d 246 (5th Cir. 2008) (no jurisdiction under Rule 23(f) to review dismissal of class allegations and jury demand in plaintiff's complaint).

5.   *Interlocutory Appeals*

Recall the Supreme Court's observation that Digital's rights could be adequately vindicated without treating the ruling as a collateral order; Digital could have petitioned the court to certify its ruling as an interlocutory appeal under 28 U.S.C. §1292(b). An interlocutory ("while speaking") appeal is one brought prior to final judgment. The two principal categories of interlocutory appeals authorized by federal statute are: appeals as of right under §1292(a) from grants or denials of injunction; and discretionary appeals approved by both the district court and court of appeals under §1292(b).

a.   Injunctions

The most expansive interlocutory review in the federal system is of grants or denials of injunctions under §1292(a). Appellate review is immediate and of right (meaning it does not require permission of any court). The policy behind this expansive exception to the final judgment rule is that injunctions, unlike most other interlocutory orders, have real, immediate, and possibly irreparable, consequences on the parties. *See Baltimore Contractor, Inc. v. Bodinger*, 348 U.S. 176, 181 (1955).

The definition of an injunction for the purpose of §1292(a)(1) is complex. Temporary restraining orders issued pursuant to Fed R. Civ. P. 65(b) do not normally qualify, although preliminary injunctions do. The "injunction" must seek some of the relief sought in the complaint; requests for "procedural orders," such as motions to stay the trial court proceedings or to enjoin some other proceeding or to compel discovery, do not constitute injunctions for purposes of the section. *See* 16 Wright & Miller, §3922.2 (3d ed. 2018).

A court of appeals will normally limit its review to the propriety of the trial court's injunction ruling. Insofar as "probability of success on the merits" is one element of entitlement to injunctive relief, a §1292(a)(1) review may enmesh the appellate court in the merits of the underlying action. This may occasionally lead the court to dispose of related questions. Thus, for instance, the appellate court may dismiss the complaint for failure to state a claim if, in conjunction with its injunction review, it has concluded that the complaint is legally insufficient. *See, e.g., Doe v. Sundquist*, 106 F.3d 702 (6th Cir. 1997). *Cf. Burlington Indus. v. Maple Indus.*, 97 F.3d 1100 (8th Cir. 1996) (reversing denial of motion to dismiss for lack of personal jurisdiction on interlocutory appeal from grant of preliminary injunction). However, the court will normally decide only that which is necessary to resolve the propriety of the injunction ruling. *See generally* 16 Wright & Miller, §3921.1 (3d ed. 2018). There is thus little strategic benefit to moving for an injunction solely for purpose of obtaining appellate review of the merits of the action.

b. Discretionary Appeals

28 U.S.C. §1292(b) provides:

> When a district judge, in making in a civil action an order not otherwise appealable under this section, shall be of the opinion that such order involves a controlling question of law as to which there is substantial ground for difference of opinion and that an immediate appeal from the order may materially advance the ultimate termination of the litigation, he shall so state in writing in such order. The Court of Appeals . . . may thereupon, in its discretion, permit an appeal to be taken from such order, if application is made to it within ten days after the entry of the order.

Appeals under §1292(b) are very infrequent. *See Koehler v. Bank of Bermuda, Ltd.*, 101 F.3d 863, 866 (2d Cir. 1996) (reporting a total of eight appeals granted in the Second Circuit for 1994–1995, combined). *See also* Michael E. Solimine, *Revitalizing Interlocutory Appeals in the Federal Courts*, 58 Geo. Wash. L. Rev. 1165 (1990) (reporting 100 average annual appeals heard under §1292(b) out of 300 certified by the district courts).

The appellant must first persuade the court that just ruled against it that there is "substantial ground" to believe that its ruling was incorrect and that the litigation would be expedited by appellate review, and then the court of appeals must agree to hear the appeal, an exercise of discretion that the courts have likened to the grant of a writ of certiorari by the Supreme Court. *Kennedy v. Bowser*, 843 F.3d 529, 535 (D.C. Cir. 2016) ("In other words, we 'may deny the appeal for any reason, including docket congestion,' . . . and we are not limited to the statutory criteria that govern the district court's certification decision").

Where the district court's ruling could be subject to reconsideration based on subsequent developments in the litigation, the courts have generally denied interlocutory review. For example, denials of motions to dismiss for lack of personal jurisdiction are often fact dependent and based on a limited record at the outset of the litigation. Courts have thus denied review on the basis that further information produced in the course of discovery could affect the court's jurisdictional assessment, and interlocutory review would not, therefore, necessarily expedite the resolution of the case. *See, e.g., Koehler v. Bank of Bermuda, Ltd., supra*, 101 F.3d at 866.

The district court's refusal to certify is not itself normally appealable, and when appeals are entertained, the district court's refusal to certify is accorded substantial deference. Several significant decisions about whether the district court ever has a duty to certify under §1292(b) were issued in connection with President Trump's ownership of the Trump Hotel in Washington, D.C. The district court there denied the president's motion to dismiss plaintiffs' claims based on the "emoluments clause" of the Constitution and declined to certify that ruling for appeal under §1292(b). In a highly unusual exercise of its appellate jurisdiction (brought by way of a "writ of mandamus," discussed below), a panel of the Court of Appeals for the Fourth Circuit determined that the district court's denial of the president's motion to dismiss was clearly erroneous, and its refusal to certify an appeal from that denial thus constituted an abuse of discretion. *In re Trump*, 928 F.3d 360 (4th Cir. 2019). That decision was itself reversed following an en banc review. 958 F.3d 274 (2020), vacated as moot *sub nom Trump v. District of Columbia*, 141 S. Ct. 1262 (2021). The court en banc held that Congress in §1292(b) vested substantial discretion in the district court, 958 F.3d at 282–283, and its refusal to certify should not be overturned absent evidence that it was "based on nothing more than caprice," or that the court "made its decision in manifest bad faith." *Id.* at 285. A mere "naked error of law" does not suffice. *Id.* at 284.

The courts are split on what constitutes "a controlling question of law" under the statute. *Compare In Nice v. L-3 Communications Vertex Aerospace, LLC*, 885 F.3d 1308 (11th Cir. 2018), where the court declined to exercise appellate authority under §1292(b) because it deemed the issue on appeal—whether the political-question doctrine required dismissal of the action—to be a mixed question of law and fact and therefore outside the ambit of §1292(b), *with In Re Trump*, 874 F.3d 948 (6th Cir. 2017), in which the court accepted an interlocutory appeal from the lower court's denial of a motion to dismiss a tort claim by protestors who were assaulted at a Trump rally on the ground that the candidate's request to "get 'em out of here" did not constitute an incitement to riot under Kentucky law.

Several commentators have urged either replacing or supplementing discretionary appeals with some narrowly drawn categories of mandatory review. *See, e.g.*, Timothy P. Glynn, *Discontent and Indiscretion: Discretionary Review of Interlocutory Orders*, 77 Notre Dame L. Rev. 175 (2001); Bryan Lammon, *Rules, Standards, and Experimentation in Appellate Jurisdiction*, 74 Ohio St. L. J. 423 (2013); Andrew S. Pollis, *The Need for Non-Discretionary Interlocutory Appellate Review in Multidistrict Litigation*, 79 Fordham L. Rev. 1643 (2011); Bryan Lammon, *Three Ideas for Discretionary Appeals*, 53 Akron L. Rev. 639, 643–644 (2019).

The federal model of exceedingly spare interlocutory review is the dominant one throughout the United States. However, some states have adopted a strikingly different approach. In New York, for instance, appeal to the intermediate appellate court may be taken as of right from virtually any order that "affects a substantial right." N.Y. C.P.L.R. §5701(a)(2)(v).

6. *Extraordinary Writs*

A final class of cases used to circumvent the final judgment rule involves the use of "extraordinary writs." These writs, directed to the trial court judge, require or prohibit certain exercises of judicial authority.

Recall that in *World-Wide Volkswagen Corp. v. Woodson, supra,* Woodson was not the plaintiff; he was the trial court judge. The case was so captioned because defendants had brought an independent action in the state supreme court against the judge seeking a "writ of prohibition." 444 U.S. 286, 289 (1980). The writ would have *forbidden* the judge from subjecting defendants to jurisdiction in Oklahoma in the case of *Robinson v. World-Wide Volkswagen.* In effect, the action was an interlocutory appeal. Oklahoma's final judgment rule otherwise precluded immediate appellate review since the judge's denial of defendants' motion to dismiss did not terminate the litigation.

An alternative writ, the "writ of mandamus," is available to *require* a judge to exercise particular authority. The use of these "extraordinary writs" as an interlocutory appellate mechanism has an ancient lineage. The writs were incorporated into federal practice by the "All Writs Act," part of the Judiciary Act of 1789. The All Writs Act is currently codified as 28 U.S.C. §1651(a):

> The Supreme Court and all courts established by Act of Congress may issue all writs necessary or appropriate in aid of their respective jurisdictions and agreeable to the usages and principles of law.

Notwithstanding the statutory limitation that the writ needs to be "in aid of the issuing court's jurisdiction," the writs are available even if no appeal is pending, the rationale being that the writ may be necessary to preserve the ability of the appellate court to grant a remedy in the future. Thus, if some action by the trial court would affect a party's rights in a manner that could not be repaired by appeal upon final judgment, the appeals court may employ the writs to preserve its appellate authority. *See McClellan v. Garland,* 217 U.S. 268 (1910).

Use of the writ is limited to exceptional, "jurisdictional" errors by the trial court. Thus, the writ is available to prevent a trial court from acting beyond its jurisdiction (in the case of a writ of prohibition), or to compel it to exercise jurisdiction (in the case of mandamus). While there is a very hazy line, not every alleged error by the trial court can be characterized as jurisdictional:

> The peremptory writ of mandamus has traditionally been used in the federal courts only "to confine an inferior court to a lawful exercise of its prescribed jurisdiction or to compel it to exercise its authority when it is its duty to do so." . . . While the courts have never confined themselves to an arbitrary and technical definition of "jurisdiction," it is clear that only exceptional circumstances amounting to a judicial "usurpation of power" will justify the invocation of this extraordinary remedy.

Will v. United States, 389 U.S. 90, 95 (1967). The Court in *Cheney v. U.S. District Court,* 542 U.S. 367 (2004), laid out a somewhat circular three-part test for justifying the use of mandamus to obtain interlocutory review: The appellant "must have no other adequate means to attain the desired relief"; appellant's right to issuance of the writ is "clear and indisputable"; and the appellate court "must be satisfied that the writ is appropriate under the circumstances." *Id.* at 380–381. The *Cheney* decision reversed the court of appeals' denial of the writ to Vice President Cheney, who sought review of the district court's grant of limited discovery against the Vice President concerning the development of White House energy policy. *See also, In Re: University of Michigan,* 936 F.3d 460 (6th Cir. 2019), where the Court of Appeals issued a Writ of Mandamus under the All Writs Act to reverse the District Court's

1080 Chapter 9. Appeals

order that the president of the University of Michigan attend a settlement conference, and that the conference be open to the public.

Notwithstanding the holding of *Mohawk Industries* that discovery orders are not appealable "collateral orders" (*supra* pp. 1062–1076), a number of lower courts have entertained interlocutory reviews of discovery orders compelling the production of privileged communications pursuant to a writ of mandamus. *See, e.g., Perry v. Schwarzenegger*, 591 F.3d 1147 (9th Cir. 2010) (review of order compelling discovery of internal strategic documents of political organization, which appellant asserted violated its First Amendment rights); *Hernandez v. Tanninen*, 604 F.3d 1095 (9th Cir. 2010) (mandamus available to review order compelling disclosure of attorney-client communications); *S.E.C. v. Rajaratnam*, 622 F.3d 159 (2d Cir. 2010) (mandamus issued to prevent the disclosure of wiretaps obtained by appellants in criminal prosecution of them). *But see In re Motor Fuel Temperature Sales Practices Litigation*, 641 F.3d 470 (10th Cir. 2011) (mandamus not appropriate to review discovery order allegedly in violation of First Amendment rights of trade association because lower court ruling was not clearly erroneous); *Holt-Orsted v. City of Dickson*, 641 F.3d 230 (6th Cir. 2011) (mandamus unavailable to review order compelling communications between plaintiffs and their attorney).

For a comprehensive review of interlocutory appellate practice in the federal courts, and a proposal for its expansion, *see* Adam Steinman, *Reinventing Appellate Practice*, 48 B.C. L. Rev. 1237 (2007). Professor Steinman argues, in particular, that courts should use the All Writs Act more expansively and should treat interlocutory appeals concerning official immunity as matters of injunctive relief under §1292(a) rather than as "collateral orders." *See also* Aaron R. Petty, *The Hidden Harmony of Appellate Jurisdiction*, 62 S.C. L. Rev. 353 (2010) (reviewing interlocutory devices and proposing modest expansion in scope of collateral orders and reduction of cases heard on mandamus).

7. Appeals from State Courts to the U.S. Supreme Court

As a general matter, the final judgment rule also applies to appeals from state court judgments to the Supreme Court of the United States. *See* 28 U.S.C. §1257(a) ("*Final judgments or decrees*" rendered by the highest court of a state in which a decision could be had, may be reviewed by the Supreme Court by writ of certiorari) (emphasis added). In any such case, of course, it is only issues of federal law (statutory, constitutional, or otherwise) that the Supreme Court will ordinarily have occasion to rule upon. *See* 28 U.S.C. §1257(a) (granting jurisdiction only as to issues of federal law).

C. APPELLATE PRACTICE

1. Perfecting the Appeal

Assuming the appealability of a given order by the trial court, appellate procedure imposes a series of requirements that an appellant must comply with in order effectively to bring its appeal to the appellate court. The process of complying with those requirements is called "perfecting the appeal."

There are three basic elements to perfecting the appeal: making an adequate objection to the trial court's decision; filing a timely and sufficient form of appeal; and assembling an appellate record.

a. Preserving Issues for Appeal

Courts of appeals, both federal and state, will generally not overrule the lower court on any nonjurisdictional error that was not called to the attention of the lower court in a timely fashion. The courts sometimes make exceptions for an error that "is purely one of law and either does not depend on the factual record developed below, or the pertinent record has been fully developed." *A-1 Ambulance Service, Inc. v. County of Monterey*, 90 F.3d 333, 339 (9th Cir. 1996). Courts occasionally make exceptions for particularly egregious mistakes. *See Harden v. Roadway Packaging Systems, Inc.*, 249 F.3d 1127, 1141 (9th Cir. 2001) (recognizing exception for miscarriages of justice); *Douglass v. United States Automobile Ass'n*, 79 F.3d 1415 (5th Cir. 1996) (allowing correction of plain error).

The precise means of raising the issue in the lower court to satisfy the general rule varies by jurisdiction. Under prior practice, the appellant was required to "take an exception" to any adverse ruling. *See, e.g., State v. Lizotte*, 200 Conn. 734, 742, 517 A.2d 610, 614 (1986). While that formality has largely been abandoned, a motion for judgment as a matter of law must sometimes be asserted. *See Thronson v. Meisels*, 800 F.2d 136 (7th Cir. 1986) (sufficiency of evidence not reviewable on appeal unless appellant moved for judgment as a matter of law in the trial court). *Accord* New Jersey Civil Practice Rule 2:10-1 (motion for new trial prerequisite to appealing jury verdict as against weight of the evidence). A party who has made an unsuccessful motion under Rule 50(a) for Judgment as a Matter of Law before the case was submitted to the jury, must, following an adverse jury verdict, renew its motion under Rule 50(b), or file a motion for new trial pursuant to Rule 59, in order to challenge the sufficiency of evidence on appeal. *Unitherm Food Systems, Inc. v. Swift-Eckrich, Inc.*, 546 U.S. 394 (2006). What are the implications of *Unitherm* in cases in which the court of appeals finds error in the trial court's admission of evidence? Does *Unitherm* preclude the appellate court from considering the sufficiency of evidence in light of that error if appellant failed to renew its Rule 50 motion following the adverse jury verdict? The court of appeals held in *Fuesting v. Zimmer, Inc.*, 448 F.3d 936 (7th Cir. 2006), that while *Unitherm* precludes the issuance of a judgment as a matter of law in these circumstances, it does not foreclose the court of appeals from ordering a new trial in light of the evidentiary error. In federal practice, formal exceptions to rulings are not required; it is sufficient that the appellant raised the issue at the time the ruling was made or sought. *See* Fed. R. Civ. P. 46. Several other Federal Rules of Civil Procedure determine how particular issues are preserved for appeal. Objections to jury instructions must normally be made before the jury receives the instructions. *See* Fed. R. Civ. P. 51(c). Pursuant to Rule 12(h)(3), objections to subject matter jurisdiction may be raised at any time, including on appeal.

There must be a written record of the submission of the question to the lower court, and the court's disposition of it. If there was no transcript of the allegedly erroneous ruling, the appellant may reconstruct the substance of the proceedings from memory, and submit a written statement in lieu of a transcript. *See* Fed. R. App. P. 10(c).

The appeals court will generally entertain any argument *in support of* the lower court judgment, whether or not it was raised below.

b.   The Notice of Appeal

Pursuant to Fed. R. App. P. 3(a), an appeal is commenced by the filing of a "Notice of Appeal" with the district court. The Notice is a simple document, which need only specify the party taking the appeal, the judgment appealed from, and the name of the court to which the appeal is taken. Service of the Notice is mailed by the district court clerk to all counsel, and to the clerk of the court of appeals.

Under some state appellate rules, an appellant must also identify the particular trial errors for which review is sought. *See, e.g.,* Ga. Rule 24-3614 (requiring "enumeration of errors" to be filed within 20 days of docketing the appeal). Such identification is provided in federal practice by the briefs. (Although where the appeal is based on an assertion that the verdict was against the weight of the evidence, all evidence relevant to that assertion must be identified in the appellate record. *See* Fed. R. App. P. 10(b)(2).)

One of the most stringently enforced aspects of appellate procedure is the time for filing an appeal. The Notice of Appeal must be filed within 30 days of entry of judgment (or 60 days in a case involving the federal government). Fed. R. App. P. 4(a). Any other party is then given an additional 14 days to file a cross-appeal. Fed. R. App. P. 4(a)(3).

The time for appeal can be affected by the filing of various post-trial motions in the trial court under Fed R. Civ. P. 50(b), 52(b), 54, 59, and 60. *See* Fed. R. App. P. 4(a)(4)(A). An appellant may seek by motion a brief extension of time to appeal if such motion is made within 30 days after the time for appeal has expired. Fed. R. App. P. 4(a)(5).

These time limits are treated as "jurisdictional": The appeals court will dismiss an untimely appeal *sua sponte*, even if no party has objected to the timeliness; and the courts will not vary the time limits, even where justice so requires. *See* Perry Dane, *Jurisdictionality, Time, and the Legal Imagination*, 23 Hofstra L. Rev. 1 (1994) (criticizing judicial rigidity in dealing with jurisdictional questions).

A striking example of the courts' rigid enforcement of jurisdictional time limits can be seen in the Supreme Court's 2007 decision in *Bowles v. Russell*, 551 U.S. 205 (2007). The appellant there successfully moved under Fed. R. App. P. 4(a)(6) for a 14-day extension in which to appeal the district court's denial of his habeas corpus petition, beyond the normal 30-day limit, as provided for in 28 U.S.C. §2107. In granting the 4(a)(6) motion, the court "inexplicably" gave the appellant 17 days to file his appeal instead of the 14 days that the rule and statute authorize. The appellant then filed his appeal 16 days later—within the time specified by the district court, but outside the time authorized by the statute. The Supreme Court held that the appeal was untimely, and that the court of appeals lacked jurisdiction to accept the appeal regardless of equitable considerations. The Court emphasized that the 14-day extension of the time limit for filing of notice of appeals is imposed by 28 U.S.C. §2107(c), thereby creating an inviolate limit on the court of appeals' subject matter jurisdiction. *Cf. John Sand & Gravel Co. v. United States*, 552 U.S. 130 (2008) (holding that statute of limitations on claims against the United States government under the Federal Court of Claims Act is jurisdictional and not subject to waiver).

Compare Bowles with the court of appeals decision in *Wilburn v. Robinson,* 480 F.3d 1140, 1144–1145 (D.C. Cir. 2007), decided a few months before *Bowles.* The court there held that respondent's failure to object to the timeliness of the appeal constituted a waiver. Under Fed. R. App. P. 4(a)(4)(A)(vi), a *timely* motion for reconsideration under Rule 60(b) has the effect of tolling the time for taking an appeal; however, such a motion must be made within ten days of the adverse judgment, and the district court has no authority to extend the time for filing the motion. *Cf. Jenkins v. Bellsouth Corp.,* 491 F.3d 1288 (11th Cir. 2011) (district court's vacating and reissuance of its denial of motion for class certification does not extend ten-day limit for filing appeal under Rule 23(f)). Petitioner in *Wilburn* made a Rule 60(b) motion 11 days after the judgment, but respondent failed to object on timeliness grounds, nor did she raise it in her initial brief to the court of appeals. The court considered the tolling provision of Fed. R. App. P. 4 to be nonjurisdictional, and thus subject to a waiver. The court emphasized that "the tolling language of Rule 4(a)(4)(A)(vi) has not been made jurisdictional by statute."

The courts' rigid enforcement of appellate time limits can create real hardship, particularly where there is some ambiguity as to when an appealable order was issued. For instance, in *Buninich v. Becton Dickinson & Co.,* 486 U.S. 196 (1988), plaintiff had filed post-trial motions for new trial and for attorneys' fees. The district court disposed of the new trial motion on May 14, but did not resolve the attorneys' fee motion until August 1. Plaintiff's appeal, filed on August 29, was ruled untimely since the Court deemed the May 14 order a final judgment, and the time for appeal started to run from that date. The Court considered it irrelevant that plaintiff may have reasonably concluded, based on the state of the law at that time, that the May 14 order was not a final judgment. *See also, Ray Haluch Gravel Co. v. Central Pension Fund,* 571 U.S. 177 (2014) (holding in *Buninich* applies in cases where the right to attorney's fees arises from a contract, rather than from a statute).

The filing of the Notice of Appeal does not suspend the enforceability of the district court's judgment. An appellant may separately seek a stay pending appeal under Fed. R. App. P. 8.

c. The Appellate Record

One of the most time-consuming aspects of an appeal is the preparation of the appellate record. The appellate record consists of all papers and exhibits filed in the district court, a transcript of the proceedings, and a copy of the docket entries. (Notice the advantage of the final judgment rule in ensuring that this need only be done once.) The parties may, with the approval of the district court, submit in lieu of the record a "statement of case showing how the issues presented by the appeal arose and were decided in the district court." Fed. R. App. P. 10(d). During the course of the appeal, the parties may refer only to facts or events documented in the record.

An abbreviated version of the record, called an "Appendix," may be required to be appended to the briefs under Fed. R. App. P. 30.

2. Briefing and Oral Argument

The required form and elements of an appellate brief are spelled out in detail in Rules 28 and 32. The time for filing the briefs is set out in Fed. R. App. P. 31, subject to variation under local rules. Rule 31 requires that appellant file its brief within 40 days after the record is filed. Appellee then has 30 days to respond. A reply brief by appellant may be filed 14 days after that.

After the briefs have been submitted, the case will normally be scheduled for oral argument. However, the court can dispense with argument if the panel assigned to the case determines that: the appeal is frivolous; the law is clear; or the decisional process would not be significantly aided by oral argument. Fed. R. App. P. 34(a)(2). In fact, three-quarters all federal appeals were decided, as of 2012, without oral argument. David R. Cleveland & Steven Wisotsky, *The Decline of Oral Argument in the Federal Courts of Appeals: A Modest Proposal for Reform*, 13 J. App. Prac. & Process 119, 119 (2012). *See* also, John B. Oakley, *The Screening of Appeals: The Ninth Circuit's Experience in the Eighties and Innovations for the Nineties*, 1991 BYU L. Rev. 859 (reporting that as of 1991, nearly two-thirds of appeals were decided without oral argument); James C. Martin et al., *Wither Oral Argument? The American Academy of Appellate Lawyers Say Let's Resurrect It!*, 19 J. App. Prac. & Process 89 (2018) (grants of oral arguments have been steadily decreasing).

The time allowed for argument is set by local rule, subject to adjustment on motion to the court. Most circuits provide for fifteen minutes or less of oral argument. Cleveland & Wisotsky, *Decline of Oral Argument, supra* at 119.

The makeup of the appellate panel (in most cases assigned by computer program) is not disclosed to the parties prior to oral argument.

3. Disposition

The judicial code provides that cases be "heard and determined" by the court of appeals; it does not require any particular form of resolution. 28 U.S.C. §46(c). The court has the option of providing a written opinion, or a mere order of affirmance or reversal without opinion. Each circuit has internal guidelines for issuing orders without opinion. The court also has the option of writing an opinion "not for publication." *See* Robert J. Martineau, *Restrictions on Publication and Citation of Judicial Opinions: A Reassessment*, 28 U. Mich. J.L. Ref. 119 (1994). However, pursuant to Fed. R. App. P. 32.1, adopted in 2006, courts may not prohibit or restrict the citation of "unpublished" federal judicial opinions issued after January 1, 2007. That rule does not prevent other courts from treating such opinions as nonbinding precedent. *See* David R. Cleveland, *Overturning the Last Stone: The Final Step in Returning Precedential Status to All Opinions*, 10 J. App. Prac. & Process 61 (2009); David R. Cleveland, *Appellate Court Rules Governing Publication, Citation, and Precedential Value of Opinions: An Update*, 16 J. App. Prac. & Process 257 (2015).

The use of "unpublished" opinions has been widely criticized as undermining principled decision making and the coherent development of the law. *See* William L. Reynolds & William M. Richman, *An Evaluation of Limited Publication in the United States Court of Appeals: The Price of Reform*, 48 U. Chi. L. Rev. 573 (1981); Thomas E. Baker, *Intramural Reforms: How the U.S. Courts of Appeals Have Helped Themselves*, 22

Fla. St. U. L. Rev. 913 (1995); Lauren Robel, *The Practice of Precedent:* Anastasoff, *Noncitation Rules, and the Meaning of Precedent in an Interpretive Community*, 35 Ind. L. Rev. 399, 402 (2002); Penelope Pether, *Inequitable Injunctions: The Scandal of Private Judging in the U.S. Courts*, 56 Stan. L. Rev. 1435 (2004). *But see* Elizabeth M. Horton, *Selective Publication and the Authority of Precedent in the United States Courts of Appeals*, 42 UCLA L. Rev. 1691 (1995) (defending selective publication as rational allocation of scarce appellate resources); Martineau, *supra* (same). Judge Arnold of the U.S. Court of Appeals for the Eighth Circuit has been an especially outspoken critic of the practice. *See Anastosoff v. United States*, 223 F.3d 898 (8th Cir. 2000) (Arnold, J.) *vacated as moot*, 235 F.3d 1054 (8th Cir. 2000) (holding that Eighth Circuit rule prohibiting citation of unpublished opinions violated Article III).

The award of costs to the prevailing party on appeal is presumptive. Pursuant to Fed. R. App. P. 39, the losing party must pay the cost of filing fees, copying the record, obtaining the transcript, and any bond expenses. Moreover, in the event of a "frivolous" appeal, the court is authorized under Rule 38 to award "just damages" and double costs to the appellee.

4. Rehearing and Rehearing En Banc

Within 14 days after entry of the appellate judgment, a party may seek a rehearing on the ground that the court "overlooked or misunderstood" a point of fact or law. Fed. R. App. P. 40(a). No oral argument is permitted on motion for rehearing. *Id.*

A losing party may also petition the entire court for a Rehearing En Banc pursuant to Fed. R. App. P. 35. An en banc hearing is usually argued to all of the active judges in the circuit — not simply a panel of three. (In some of the larger circuits, the en banc panel may be somewhat smaller than the entire court. *See, e.g.*, Ninth Circuit Rule of Appellate Procedure 35-3 (11 judges).) En banc hearings are reserved for exceptional cases in which it is necessary to achieve uniformity within the circuit (usually caused by a split among different appeals panels), or for cases of unusual importance. En banc hearings are granted on majority vote of all active judges in the circuit. For commentary on the growing trend of judges to write "concurral" or "dissental" opinions on the denial of an en banc hearing, *see* Alex Kozinski & James Burnham, *I Say Dissental, You Say Concurral*, 121 Yale L.J. Online 601 (2012) (approving of the practice).

In extraordinary cases, the court may assign the case initially to the court en banc.

D. STANDARDS OF REVIEW

Once an appellant has successfully navigated the way into the appeals court, she must persuade the court to exercise a sufficient level of scrutiny over the lower court findings to warrant reversal. Even if the trial court arguably erred in some important respect, the appeals court may decline to reverse if it gives a great deal of weight to the trial court's findings. The level of scrutiny that an appeals court adopts is known as the "standard of review." *See generally* Steven A. Childress & Martha S. Davis, *Federal Standards of Review* (4th ed. 2010); Amanda Peters, *The Meaning, Measure, and Misuse of Standards of Review,* 13 Lewis & Clark L. Rev. 233 (2009).

The two basic standards of review are the "clearly erroneous" standard and the "*de novo*" or "plenary" standard. The clearly erroneous standard, usually reserved for findings of fact, defers to the lower court unless the appeals court has a "definite and firm conviction that a mistake has been committed." *United States v. U.S. Gypsum Co.,* 333 U.S. 364, 395 (1948). This deferential standard favors the respondent, who is defending the judgment. The *de novo* or plenary standard is usually applied to questions of law. The appeals court considers the question without giving any weight to the fact that the trial court already made a ruling. The court thus considers the question *de novo* or anew. This standard obviously favors the appellant, who is seeking to undermine the lower court's conclusions.

A third standard of review—an abuse of discretion standard—is used to review legal rulings of the trial judge that involve a balancing of factors where the assessment is said to be left to the discretion of the judge. We have seen such examples of this standard in previous chapters—e.g., dismissals on grounds of *forum non conveniens* and a trial judge's grant or denial of a new trial motion.

Use of the clearly erroneous standard is explicitly specified by Federal Rule of Civil Procedure 52(a)(6) for review of trial court factual determinations:

> In an action tried on the facts without a jury . . . [f]indings of fact, whether based on oral or other evidence, must not be set aside unless clearly erroneous, and the reviewing court must give due regard to the trial court's opportunity to judge the witnesses' credibility.

Pullman-Standard v. Swint

456 U.S. 273 (1982)

JUSTICE WHITE delivered the opinion of the Court.

Respondents were black employees at the Bessemer, Ala., plant of petitioner Pullman-Standard (the Company), a manufacturer of railway freight cars and parts. They brought suit against the Company and the union petitioners—the United Steelworkers of America, AFL-CIO-CLC, and its Local 1466 (collectively USW)—alleging violations of Title VII of the Civil Rights Act of 1964, 78 Stat. 253, as amended, 42 U.S.C. §2000e et seq. (1976 ed. and Supp. IV), and 42 U.S.C. §1981. As they come here, these cases involve only the validity, under Title VII, of a seniority system maintained by the Company and USW. The District Court found "that the differences in terms, conditions or privileges of employment resulting [from the seniority system] are 'not the result of an intention to discriminate' because of race or color," . . . and held, therefore, that the system satisfied the requirements of §703(h) of the Act. The Court of Appeals for the Fifth Circuit reversed:

> Because we find that the differences in the terms, conditions and standards of employment for black workers and white workers at Pullman-Standard resulted from an intent to discriminate because of race, we hold that the system is not legally valid under section 703(h) of Title VII. . . .

We granted the petitions for certiorari filed by USW and by the Company, limited to the first question presented in each petition: whether a court of appeals is bound by the "clearly erroneous" rule of Federal Rule of Civil Procedure 52(a) in reviewing a district court's findings of fact, arrived at after a lengthy trial, as to the motivation of the parties who negotiated a seniority system; and whether the court below applied wrong legal criteria in determining the bona fides of the seniority system. We conclude that the Court of Appeals erred in the course of its review and accordingly reverse its judgment and remand for further proceedings.

I

Title VII is a broad remedial measure, designed "to assure equality of employment opportunities." *McDonnell Douglas Corp. v. Green*, 411 U.S. 792, 800 (1973). The Act was designed to bar not only overt employment discrimination, "but also practices that are fair in form, but discriminatory in operation." *Griggs v. Duke Power Co.*, 401 U.S. 424, 431 (1971). "Thus, the Court has repeatedly held that a prima facie Title VII violation may be established by policies or practices that are neutral on their face and in intent but that nonetheless discriminate in effect against a particular group." *Teamsters v. United States*, 431 U.S. 324, 349 (1977) (hereinafter *Teamsters*). The Act's treatment of seniority systems, however, establishes an exception to these general principles. Section 703(h).78 Stat. 257, as set forth in 42 U.S.C. §2000e-2(h), provides in pertinent part:

> Notwithstanding any other provision of this subchapter, it shall not be an unlawful employment practice for an employer to apply different standards of compensation, or different terms, conditions, or privileges of employment pursuant to a bona fide seniority . . . system . . . provided that such differences are not the result of an intention to discriminate because of race.

Under this section, a showing of disparate impact is insufficient to invalidate a seniority system, even though the result may be to perpetuate pre-Act discrimination. In *Trans World Airlines, Inc. v. Hardison*, 432 U.S. 63, 82 (1977), we summarized the effect of §703(h) as follows: "[A]bsent a discriminatory purpose, the operation of a seniority system cannot be an unlawful employment practice even if the system has some discriminatory consequences." Thus, any challenge to a seniority system under Title VII will require a trial on the issue of discriminatory intent: Was the system adopted because of its racially discriminatory impact?

This is precisely what happened in these cases. Following our decision in *Teamsters*, the District Court held a new trial on the limited question of whether the seniority system was "instituted or maintained contrary to Section 703(h) of the new Civil Rights Act of 1964."[2] That court concluded, as we noted above and will discuss below, that the system was adopted and maintained for purposes wholly independent of any discriminatory intent. The Court of Appeals for the Fifth Circuit reversed.

---

2. The procedural history of these cases is rather complex. The original complaint was filed in 1971. Since that time the case has been tried three times and has twice been reviewed by the Court of Appeals.

II

Petitioners submit that the Court of Appeals failed to comply with the command of Rule 52(a)* that the findings of fact of a district court may not be set aside unless clearly erroneous. We first describe the findings of the District Court and the Court of Appeals.

Certain facts are common ground for both the District Court and the Court of Appeals. The Company's Bessemer plant was unionized in the early 1940's. Both before and after unionization, the plant was divided into a number of different operational departments. USW sought to represent all production and maintenance employees at the plant and was elected in 1941 as the bargaining representative of a bargaining unit consisting of most of these employees. At that same time, IAM became the bargaining representative of a unit consisting of five departments. Between 1941 and 1944, IAM ceded certain workers in its bargaining unit to USW. As a result of this transfer, the IAM bargaining unit became all white.

Throughout the period of representation by USW, the plant was approximately half black. Prior to 1965, the Company openly pursued a racially discriminatory policy of job assignments. Most departments contained more than one job category and as a result most departments were racially mixed. There were no lines of progression or promotion within departments.

The seniority system at issue here was adopted in 1954. Under that agreement, seniority was measured by length of continuous service in a particular department. Seniority was originally exercised only for purposes of layoffs and hirings within particular departments. In 1956, seniority was formally recognized for promotional purposes as well. Again, however, seniority, with limited exceptions, was only exercised within departments; employees transferring to new departments forfeited their seniority. This seniority system remained virtually unchanged until after this suit was brought in 1971.[7]

The District Court approached the question of discriminatory intent in the manner suggested by the Fifth Circuit in *James v. Stockham Valves & Fittings Co.*, 559 F.2d 310 (1977). There, the Court of Appeals stated that under *Teamsters* "the totality of the circumstances in the development and maintenance of the system is relevant to examining that issue." 559 F.2d, at 352. There were, in its view, however, four particular factors that a court should focus on.

First, a court must determine whether the system "operates to discourage all employees equally from transferring between seniority units." Ibid. The District Court held that the system here "was facially neutral and . . . was applied equally to all races and ethnic groups." . . . Although there were charges of racial discrimination in its application, the court held that these were "not substantiated by the evidence." . . . It concluded that the system "applied equally and uniformly to all

---

* The provision of Rule 52(a) discussed throughout the case has been renumbered as Rule 52(a)(6). — Eds.

7. In 1972, the Company entered into an agreement with the Department of Labor to bring its employment practices into compliance with Executive Order No. 11246, 3 CFR 339 (1964–1965 Comp.). This provided an exception to the departmental limit on seniority, allowing certain black employees to make inter-departmental transfers without any loss of seniority.

employees, black and white, and that, given the approximately equal number of employees of the two groups, it was quantitatively neutral as well."[9] . . .

Second, a court must examine the rationality of the departmental structure, upon which the seniority system relies, in light of the general industry practice. . . . The District Court found that linking seniority to "departmental age" was "the modal form of agreements generally, as well as with manufacturers of railroad equipment in particular." . . . Furthermore, it found the basic arrangement of departments at the plant to be rationally related to the nature of the work and to be "consistent with practices which were . . . generally followed at other unionized plants throughout the country." . . . While questions could be raised about the necessity of certain departmental divisions, it found that all of the challenged lines of division grew out of historical circumstances at the plant that were unrelated to racial discrimination.[10] Although unionization did produce an all-white IAM bargaining unit, it found that USW "cannot be charged with racial bias in its response to the IAM situation. [USW] sought to represent all workers, black and white, in the plant." . . . Nor could the Company be charged with any racial discrimination that may have existed in IAM:

> The company properly took a "hands-off" approach towards the establishment of the election units. . . . It bargained with those unions which were afforded representational status by the NLRB and did so without any discriminatory animus. . . .

Third, a court had to consider "whether the seniority system had its genesis in racial discrimination," . . . by which it meant the relationship between the system and other racially discriminatory practices. Although finding ample discrimination by the Company in its employment practices and some discriminatory practices by the union,[11] the District Court concluded that the seniority system was in no way related to the discriminatory practices:

> The seniority system . . . had its genesis . . . at a period when racial segregation was certainly being practiced; but this system was not itself the product of this bias. The system rather came about as a result of colorblind

---

9. The court specifically declined to make any finding on whether the no-transfer provision of the seniority system had a greater relative effect on blacks than on whites, because of qualitative differences in the departments in which they were concentrated. It believed that such an inquiry would have been inconsistent with the earlier Fifth Circuit opinion in this case.

10. In particular, the court focused on the history of the unionization process at the plant and found certain of the departmental divisions to be based on the evolving relationship between USW and IAM.

11. With respect to USW, the District Court found that "[u]nion meetings were conducted with different sides of the hall for white and black members, and social functions of the union were also segregated." . . . It also found, however, that "[w]hile possessing some of the trappings taken from an otherwise segregated society, the USW local was one of the few institutions in the area which did not function in fact to foster and maintain segregation; rather, it served a joint interest of white and black workers which had a higher priority than racial considerations." . . .

objectives of a union which—unlike most structures and institutions of the era—was not an arm of a segregated society. Nor did it foster the discrimination . . . which was being practiced by custom in the plant. . . .

Finally, a court must consider "whether the system was negotiated and has been maintained free from any illegal purpose." *James, supra,* at 352. Stating that it had "carefully considered the detailed record of negotiation sessions and contracts which span a period of some thirty-five years," the court found that the system was untainted by any discriminatory purpose. Thus, although the District Court focused on particular factors in carrying out the analysis required by §703(h), it also looked to the entire record and to the "totality of the system under attack." . . .

The Court of Appeals addressed each of the four factors of the *James* test and reached the opposite conclusion. First, it held that the District Court erred in putting aside qualitative differences between the departments in which blacks were concentrated and those dominated by whites, in considering whether the system applied "equally" to whites and blacks.[12] This is a purported correction of a legal standard under which the evidence is to be evaluated.

Second, it rejected the District Court's conclusion that the structure of departments was rational, in line with industry practice, and did not reflect any discriminatory intent. Its discussion is brief but focuses on the role of IAM and certain characteristics unique to the Bessemer plant. The court concluded:

> The record evidence, generally, indicates arbitrary creation of the departments by the company since unionization and an attendant adverse affect [sic] on black workers. The individual differences between the departmental structure at Pullman-Standard and that of other plants, and as compared with industry practice, are indicative of attempts to maintain one-race departments. 624 F.2d at 532.

In reaching this conclusion, the Court of Appeals did not purport to be correcting a legal error, nor did it refer to or expressly apply the clearly erroneous standard.

Third, in considering the "genesis" of the system, the Court of Appeals held that the District Court erred in holding that the motives of IAM were not relevant.[13] This was the correction of a legal error on the part of the District Court in excluding relevant evidence. The court did not stop there, however. It went on to hold that IAM was acting out of discriminatory intent—an issue specifically not reached by the District Court—and that "considerations of race permeated the

---

12. It does not appear to us that the District Court actually found a qualitative difference but held it to be irrelevant. The relevant passage of the District Court opinion read as follows: "By ranking the twenty-eight USW and IAM departments according to some perceived order of desirability, one could . . . attempt to measure the relative effect of the no-transfer rule on white and black employees. . . . It may well be that a somewhat greater impact was felt by blacks than whites although . . . this conclusion is by no means certain." . . .

13. The original complaint in this case did not mention IAM. Prior to the first trial, respondents sought and received leave to amend their complaint to add IAM as a Rule 19 defendant, "insofar as the relief requested may involve or infringe upon the provisions of such Union's collective bargaining agreement with the Company." Order of the District Court, June 4, 1974 (App. 29).

negotiation and the adoption of the seniority system in 1941 and subsequent negotiations thereafter." *Ibid.*

Fourth, despite this conclusion under the third *James* factor the Court of
Appeals then recited, but did not expressly set aside or find clearly erroneous, the
District Court's findings with respect to the negotiation and maintenance of the
seniority system.

The court then announced that "[h]aving carefully reviewed the evidence
offered to show whether the departmental seniority system in the present case is 'bona
fide' within the meaning of §703(h) of Title VII, we reject the district court's finding."
624 F.2d at 533. Elaborating on its disagreement, the Court of Appeals stated:

> An analysis of the totality of the facts and circumstances surrounding
> the creation and continuance of the departmental system at Pullman-
> Standard leaves us with the definite and firm conviction that a mistake
> has been made. There is no doubt, based upon the record in this case,
> about the existence of a discriminatory purpose. The obvious principal
> aim of the I.A.M. in 1941 was to exclude black workers from its bargaining
> unit. That goal was ultimately reached when maneuvers by the I.A.M. and
> U.S.W. resulted in an all-white I.A.M. unit. The U.S.W., in the interest of
> increased membership, acquiesced in the discrimination while succeed-
> ing in significantly segregating the departments within its own unit.
>
> The district court might have reached a different conclusion had it
> given the IAM's role in the creation and establishment of the seniority
> system its due consideration. Ibid., (footnote omitted).

Having rejected the District Court's finding, the court made its own findings
as to whether the USW seniority system was protected by §703(h):

> We consider significant in our decision the manner by which the two
> seniority units were set up, the creation of the various all-white and all-
> black departments within the U.S.W. unit at the time of certification and
> in the years thereafter, conditions of racial discrimination which affected
> the negotiation and renegotiation of the system, and the extent to which
> the system and the attendant no-transfer rule locked blacks into the least
> remunerative positions within the company. Because we find that the dif-
> ferences in the terms, conditions and standards of employment for black
> workers and white workers at Pullman-Standard resulted from an intent to
> discriminate because of race, we hold that the system is not legally valid
> under section 703(h) of Title VII, 42 U.S.C. §2000e-2(h).

In connection with its assertion that it was convinced that a mistake had
been made, the Court of Appeals, in a footnote, referred to the clearly erroneous
standard of Rule 52(a).[14] . . . It pointed out, however, that if findings "are made

---

14. In *United States v. United States Gypsum Co.*, 333 U.S. 364, 395 (1948), this Court characterized the clearly-erroneous standard as follows:

> A finding is "clearly erroneous" when although there is evidence to support it, the reviewing
> court on the entire evidence is left with the definite and firm conviction that a mistake has
> been committed.

We note that the Court of Appeals quoted this passage at the conclusion of its analysis of the
District Court opinion. . . .

under an erroneous view of controlling legal principles, the clearly erroneous rule does not apply, and the findings may not stand." *Ibid.* Finally, quoting from *East v. Romine, Inc.,* 518 F.2d 332, 339 (CA5 1975), the Court of Appeals repeated the following view of its appellate function in Title VII cases where purposeful discrimination is at issue:

> Although discrimination *vel non* is essentially a question of fact it is, at the same time, the ultimate issue for resolution in this case, being expressly proscribed by 42 U.S.C.A. §2000e-2(a). As such, a finding of discrimination or non-discrimination is a finding of ultimate fact. [Cites omitted.] In reviewing the district court's findings, therefore, we will proceed to make an independent determination of appellant's allegations of discrimination, though bound by findings of subsidiary fact which are themselves not clearly erroneous. 624 F.2d at 533, n. 6.

III

Pointing to the above statement of the Court of Appeals and to similar statements in other Title VII cases coming from that court, petitioners submit that the Court of Appeals made an independent determination of discriminatory purpose, the "ultimate fact" in this case, and that this was error under Rule 52(a). We agree with petitioners that if the Court of Appeals followed what seems to be the accepted rule in that Circuit, its judgment must be reversed.[16]

Rule 52(a) broadly requires that findings of fact not be set aside unless clearly erroneous. It does not make exceptions or purport to exclude certain categories of factual findings from the obligation of a court of appeals to accept a district court's findings unless clearly erroneous. It does not divide facts into categories; in particular, it does not divide findings of fact into those that deal with "ultimate" and those that deal with "subsidiary" facts.

---

16. There is some indication in the opinions of the Court of Appeals for the Fifth Circuit . . . that the Circuit rule with respect to "ultimate facts" is only another way of stating a standard of review with respect to mixed questions of law and fact—the ultimate "fact" is the statutory, legally determinative consideration (here, intentional discrimination) which is or is not satisfied by subsidiary facts admitted or found by the trier of fact. As indicated in the text, however, the question of intentional discrimination under §703(h) is a pure question of fact. Furthermore, the Court of Appeals' opinion in this case appears to address the issue as a question of fact unmixed with legal considerations.

At the same time, this Court has on occasion itself indicated that findings on "ultimate facts" are independently reviewable. In *Baumgartner v. United States,* 322 U.S. 665 (1944), the issue was whether or not the findings of the two lower courts satisfied the clear-and-convincing standard of proof necessary to sustain a denaturalization decree. The Court held that the conclusion of the two lower courts that the exacting standard of proof had been satisfied was not an unreviewable finding of fact but one that a reviewing court could independently assess. The Court referred to the finding as one of "ultimate" fact, which in that case involved an appraisal of the strength of the entire body of evidence. The Court said that the significance of the clear-and-convincing proof standard "would be lost" if the ascertainment by the lower

The Rule does not apply to conclusions of law. The Court of Appeals, therefore, was quite right in saying that if a district court's findings rest on an erroneous view of the law, they may be set aside on that basis. But here the District Court was not faulted for misunderstanding or applying an erroneous definition of intentional discrimination.[17] It was reversed for arriving at what the Court of Appeals thought was an erroneous finding as to whether the differential impact of the seniority system reflected an intent to discriminate on account of race. That question, as we see it, is a pure question of fact, subject to Rule 52(a)'s clearly erroneous standard. It is not a question of law and not a mixed question of law and fact.

The Court has previously noted the vexing nature of the distinction between questions of fact and questions of law. See *Baumgartner v. United States*, 322 U.S. 665, 671 (1944). Rule 52(a) does not furnish particular guidance with respect to distinguishing law from fact. Nor do we yet know of any other rule or principle that will unerringly distinguish a factual finding from a legal conclusion. For the reasons that follow, however, we have little doubt about the factual nature of §703(h)'s requirement that a seniority system be free of an intent to discriminate.

Treating issues of intent as factual matters for the trier of fact is commonplace. In *Dayton Board of Education v. Brinkman*, 443 U.S. 526, 534 (1979), the principal question was whether the defendants had intentionally maintained a racially segregated school system at a specified time in the past. We recognized that issue as essentially factual, subject to the clearly-erroneous rule. In *Commissioner v. Duberstein*, 363 U.S. 278 (1960), the Court held that the principal criterion for identifying a gift under the applicable provision of the Internal Revenue Code was the intent or motive of the donor—"one that inquires what the basic reason for his conduct was in fact." *Id.* at 286. Resolution of that issue determined the ultimate issue of whether a gift had been made. Both issues were held to be questions of fact

---

courts whether that exacting standard of proof had been satisfied on the whole record were to be deemed a "fact" of the same order as all other "facts not open to review here." *Id.* at 671.

The Fifth Circuit's rule on appellate consideration of "ultimate facts" has its roots in this discussion in *Baumgartner*. In *Galena Oaks Corp. v. Scofield*, 218 F.2d 217 (CA5 1954), in which the question was whether the gain derived from the sale of a number of houses was to be treated as capital gain or ordinary income, the Court of Appeals relied directly on *Baumgartner* in holding that this was an issue of "ultimate fact" that an appellate court may review free of the clearly-erroneous rule. *Causey v. Ford Motor Co., supra*, at 421, relying on *Galena Oaks Corp. v. Scofield, supra*, said that "although discrimination *vel non* is essentially a question of fact, it is, at the same time, the ultimate issue for resolution in this case" and as such, was deemed to be independently reviewable. The passage from *East v. Romine, Inc., supra*, at 339, which was repeated in the cases before us now . . . rested on the opinion in *Causey v. Ford Motor Co.*

Whatever *Baumgartner* may have meant by its discussion of "ultimate facts," it surely did not mean that whenever the result in a case turns on a factual finding, an appellate court need not remain within the constraints of Rule 52(a). *Baumgartner*'s discussion of "ultimate facts" referred not to pure findings of fact—as we find discriminatory intent to be in this context—but to findings that "clearly impl[y] the application of standards of law." 322 U.S. at 671.

17. As we noted above, the Court of Appeals did at certain points purport to correct what it viewed as legal errors on the part of the District Court. The presence of such legal errors may justify a remand by the Court of Appeals to the District Court for additional fact finding under the correct legal standard. . . .

subject to the clearly erroneous rule. In *United States v. Yellow Cab Co.*, 338 U.S. 338 (1949), an antitrust case, the Court referred to "[f]indings as to the design, motive and intent with which men act" as peculiarly factual issues for the trier of fact and therefore subject to appellate review under Rule 52.

Justice Black's dissent in *Yellow Cab* suggested a contrary approach. Relying on *United States v. Griffith*, 334 U.S. 100 (1948), he argued that it is not always necessary to prove "specific intent" to restrain trade: it is enough if a restraint is the result or consequence of a defendant's conduct or business arrangements. Such an approach, however, is specifically precluded by §703(h) in Title VII cases challenging seniority systems. Differentials among employees that result from a seniority system are not unlawful employment practices unless the product of an intent to discriminate. It would make no sense, therefore, to say that the intent to discriminate required by §703(h) may be presumed from such an impact. As §703(h) was construed in *Teamsters*, there must be a finding of actual intent to discriminate on racial grounds on the part of those who negotiated or maintained the system. That finding appears to us to be a pure question of fact.

This is not to say that discriminatory impact is not part of the evidence to be considered by the trial court in reaching a finding on whether there was such a discriminatory intent as a factual matter.[18] We do assert, however, that under §703(h) discriminatory intent is a finding of fact to be made by the trial court; it is not a question of law and not a mixed question of law and fact of the kind that in some cases may allow an appellate court to review the facts to see if they satisfy some legal concept of discriminatory intent.[19] Discriminatory intent here means actual motive; it is not a legal presumption to be drawn from a factual showing of something less than actual motive. Thus, a court of appeals may only reverse a district court's finding on discriminatory intent if it concludes that the finding is clearly erroneous under Rule 52(a). Insofar as the Fifth Circuit assumed otherwise, it erred.

IV

Respondents do not directly defend the Fifth Circuit rule that a trial court's finding on discriminatory intent is not subject to the clearly erroneous standard of Rule 52(a).[20] Rather, among other things, they submit that the Court of Appeals

---

18. See, e.g., *Furnco Construction Corp. v. Waters*, 438 U.S. 567, 580 (1978): "Proof that [an employer's] work force was racially balanced or that it contained a disproportionately high percentage of minority employees is not wholly irrelevant on the issue of intent when that issue is yet to be decided."

19. We need not, therefore, address the much-mooted issue of the applicability of the Rule 52(a) standard to mixed questions of law and fact—i.e., questions in which the historical facts are admitted or established, the rule of law is undisputed, and the issue is whether the facts satisfy the statutory standard, or to put it another way, whether the rule of law as applied to the established facts is or is not violated. There is substantial authority in the Circuits on both sides of this question. . . . There is also support in decisions of this Court for the proposition that conclusions on mixed questions of law and fact are independently reviewable by an appellate court. . . .

20. Neither does the dissent contend that Rule 52(a) is inapplicable to findings of discriminatory intent. Rather, it contends, that the Rule was properly applied by the Court of Appeals.

recognized and, where appropriate, properly applied Rule 52(a) in setting aside the findings of the District Court. This position has force, but for two reasons it is not persuasive.

First, although the Court of Appeals acknowledged and correctly stated the controlling standard of Rule 52(a), the acknowledgment came late in the court's opinion. The court had not expressly referred to or applied Rule 52(a) in the course of disagreeing with the District Court's resolution of the factual issues deemed relevant under *James v. Stockham Valves & Fittings Co.*, 559 F.2d 310 (1977).[21] Furthermore, the paragraph in which the court finally concludes that the USW seniority system is unprotected by §703(h) strongly suggests that the outcome was the product of the court's independent consideration of the totality of the circumstances it found in the record.

Second and more fundamentally, when the court stated that it was convinced that a mistake had been made, it then identified not only the mistake but also the source of that mistake. The mistake of the District Court was that on the record there could be no doubt about the existence of a discriminatory purpose. The source of the mistake was the District Court's failure to recognize the relevance of the racial purposes of IAM. Had the District Court "given the I.A.M.'s role in the creation and establishment of the seniority system its due consideration," it "might have reached a different conclusion." *Supra*, at 1787.

When an appellate court discerns that a district court has failed to make a finding because of an erroneous view of the law, the usual rule is that there should be a remand for further proceedings to permit the trial court to make the missing findings:

> [F]act finding is the basic responsibility of district courts, rather than appellate courts, and . . . the Court of Appeals should not have resolved in the first instance this factual dispute which had not been considered by the District Court. *DeMarco v. United States*, 415 U.S. 449, 450 (1974).

Likewise, where findings are infirm because of an erroneous view of the law, a remand is the proper course unless the record permits only one resolution of the factual issue. *Kelley v. Southern Pacific Co.*, 419 U.S. 318, 331–332 (1974). All of this is elementary. Yet the Court of Appeals, after holding that the District Court had failed to consider relevant evidence and indicating that the District Court might have come to a different conclusion had it considered that evidence, failed to remand for further proceedings as to the intent of IAM and the significance, if any, of such a finding with respect to the intent of USW itself. Instead, the Court of

---

21. In particular, in regard to the second *James* factor—whether the departmental structure was rational or in line with industry practice—the Court of Appeals did not focus on the evidentiary basis for any particular finding of the District Court. It appeared to make an independent examination of the record and arrive at its own conclusion contrary to that of the District Court. Likewise, in dealing with the genesis of the seniority system and whether or not the negotiation or maintenance of the system was tainted with racial discrimination, the Court of Appeals, while identifying what it thought was legal error in failing to consider the racial practices and intentions of IAM, did not otherwise overturn any of the District Court's findings as clearly erroneous.

Appeals made its own determination as to the motives of IAM, found that USW had acquiesced in the IAM conduct, and apparently concluded that the foregoing was sufficient to remove the system from the protection of §703(h).[23]

Proceeding in this manner seems to us incredible unless the Court of Appeals construed its own well-established Circuit rule with respect to its authority to arrive at independent findings on ultimate facts free of the strictures of Rule 52(a) also to permit it to examine the record and make its own independent findings with respect to those issues on which the district court's findings are set aside for an error of law. As we have previously said, however, the premise for this conclusion is infirm: whether an ultimate fact or not, discriminatory intent under §703(h) is a factual matter subject to the clearly erroneous standard of Rule 52(a). It follows that when a district court's finding on such an ultimate fact is set aside for an error of law, the court of appeals is not relieved of the usual requirement of remanding for further proceedings to the tribunal charged with the task of fact finding in the first instance.

Accordingly, the judgment of the Court of Appeals is reversed, and the cases are remanded to that court for further proceedings consistent with this opinion.

So ordered.

[Concurrence of JUSTICE STEVENS is omitted.]

JUSTICE MARSHALL, with whom JUSTICE BLACKMUN joins except as to Part I, dissenting.

In 1971, a group of Negro employees at Pullman-Standard's Bessemer, Ala., plant brought this class action against Pullman-Standard, the United Steelworkers of America and its Local 1466 (USW), and the International Association of Machinists and its Local 372 (IAM). The plaintiffs alleged, *inter alia*, that the departmental seniority system negotiated by both unions discriminated against Negroes in violation of Title VII of the Civil Rights Act of 1964, 42 U.S.C. §2000e *et seq.* (1976 ed. and Supp. IV), and the Civil Rights Act of 1866, 42 U.S.C. §1981. In 1974, the District Court for the Northern District of Alabama concluded that the seniority system did not operate to discriminate against Negroes. A unanimous panel of the Fifth Circuit reversed. The court ruled that the District Court had committed several errors of law, including failure to give proper weight to the role of the IAM, and had relied on patently inaccurate factual conclusions. *Swint v. Pullman-Standard,* 539 F.2d 77, 95–96 (1976). On remand, the District Court again ruled that the seniority system was immune from attack under Title VII, this time finding that respondents had failed to show discriminatory intent as required by this Court's decision in *Teamsters v. United States,* 431 U.S. 324 (1977). . . . The Fifth Circuit again unanimously rejected the conclusion of the District Court. 624 F.2d 525 (1980).

---

23. IAM's discriminatory motivation, if it existed, cannot be imputed to USW. It is relevant only to the extent that it may shed some light on the purpose of USW or the Company in creating and maintaining the separate seniority system at issue in these cases. A discriminatory intent on the part of IAM, therefore, does not control the outcome of these cases. Neither does the fact, if true, that USW acquiesced in racially discriminatory conduct on the part of IAM. Such acquiescence is not the equivalent of a discriminatory purpose on the part of USW.

The majority now reverses the Fifth Circuit's second unanimous decision on the ground that the Court of Appeals did not pay sufficient homage to the "clearly erroneous" rule, Fed. Rule Civ. Proc. 52(a), in concluding that the seniority system at Pullman-Standard was the product of intentional discrimination against Negroes. Because I cannot agree with the premise of the majority's decision to remand these cases for yet another trial, or with its application of that premise to the facts of this case, I respectfully dissent.

I

The majority premises its holding on the assumption that "'absent a discriminatory purpose, the operation of a seniority system cannot be an unlawful employment practice even if the system has some discriminatory consequences.'" . . . As I have previously indicated, I do not find anything in the relevant statutory language or legislative history to support the proposition that §703(h) of Title VII immunizes a seniority system that perpetuates past discrimination, as the system at issue here clearly does, simply because the plaintiffs are unable to demonstrate to this Court's satisfaction that the system was adopted or maintained for an invidious purpose. . . . In my opinion, placing such a burden on plaintiffs who challenge seniority systems with admitted discriminatory impact, a burden never before imposed in civil suits brought under Title VII, frustrates the clearly expressed will of Congress and effectively "freeze[s] an entire generation of Negro employees into discriminatory patterns that existed before the Act." *Quarles v. Philip Morris, Inc.*, 279 F. Supp. 505, 516 (ED Va. 1968) (Butzner, J.).

II

Even if I were to accept this Court's decision to impose this novel burden on Title VII plaintiffs, I would still be unable to concur in its conclusion that the Fifth Circuit's decision should be reversed for failing to abide by Rule 52(a). The majority asserts that the Court of Appeals in this action ignored the clearly erroneous rule and made an independent determination of discriminatory purpose. I disagree. In my view, the court below followed well-established legal principles both in rejecting the District Court's finding of no discriminatory purpose and in concluding that a finding of such a purpose was compelled by all of the relevant evidence.

The majority concedes, as it must, that the "Court of Appeals acknowledged and correctly stated the controlling standard of Rule 52(a)."

. . . In a footnote to its opinion, the Court of Appeals plainly states that findings of fact may be overturned only if they are either "clearly erroneous" or "made under an erroneous view of controlling legal principles." 624 F.2d at 533, n. 6. Furthermore, as the majority notes, . . . the Court of Appeals justified its decision to reject the District Court's finding that the seniority system was not the result of purposeful discrimination by stating: "An analysis of the totality of the facts and circumstances surrounding the creation and continuance of the departmental system at Pullman-Standard leaves us with the *definite and firm conviction that a mistake has been made.*" 624 F.2d at 533 (emphasis added; footnote omitted). I frankly am at a loss to understand how the Court of Appeals could have expressed its conclusion that the District Court's finding on the issue of intent was clearly erroneous with any more precision or clarity.

The majority rejects the Court of Appeals' clear articulation and implementation of the clearly erroneous rule on the apparent ground that in the course of correctly setting forth the requirements of Rule 52(a), the court also included the following quotation from its prior decision in *East v. Romine, Inc.*, 518 F.2d 332, 339 (1975):

> Although discrimination *vel non* is essentially a question of fact it is, at the same time, the ultimate issue for resolution in this case, being expressly proscribed by 42 U.S.C.A. §2000e-2(a). As such, a finding of discrimination or nondiscrimination is a finding of ultimate fact. [Cites omitted.] In reviewing the district court's findings, therefore, we will proceed to make an independent determination of appellant's allegations of discrimination, though bound by findings of subsidiary fact which are themselves not clearly erroneous. 624 F.2d at 533, n. 6.

The only question presented by this case, therefore, is whether this reference to *East v. Romine, Inc.* should be read as negating the Court of Appeals' unambiguous acknowledgment of the "controlling standard of Rule 52." . . . The majority bases its affirmative answer to that question on two factors. First, the majority contends that the Court of Appeals must not have properly respected the clearly erroneous rule because its acknowledgment that Rule 52(a) supplied the controlling standard "came late in the court's opinion." . . . Second, the Court of Appeals "identified not only the mistake" that it felt had been made, "but also the source of that mistake." . . . If the Court of Appeals had really been applying the clearly erroneous rule, it should have abided by the "usual requirement of remanding for further proceedings to the tribunal charged with the task of fact finding in the first instance." . . .

Neither of these arguments justifies the majority's conclusion that these cases must be remanded for a fourth trial on the merits. I am aware of no rule of decision embraced by this or any other court that places dispositive weight on whether an accurate statement of controlling principle appears "early" or late in a court's opinion. Nor does the majority suggest a basis for this unique rule of interpretation. So long as a court acknowledges the proper legal standard, I should think it irrelevant whether it chooses to set forth that standard at the beginning or at the end of its opinion. The heart of the majority's argument, therefore, is that the failure to remand the action to the District Court after rejecting its conclusion that the seniority system was "bona fide" within the meaning of §703(h) indicates that the Court of Appeals did not properly follow the clearly erroneous rule. Before addressing this issue, however, it is necessary to examine the nature of the finding of "intent" required by this Court in *Teamsters*, the procedure that courts of appeals should follow in reviewing a district court's finding on intent, and the extent to which the court below adhered to that procedure in this case.

The District Court examined the four factors approved by the Fifth Circuit in *James v. Stockham Valves & Fittings Co.*, . . . to determine whether the departmental seniority system at Pullman-Standard was adopted or maintained for a discriminatory purpose. Although indicating that these four factors are not the only way to demonstrate the existence of discriminatory intent, the Court today implicitly acknowledges that proof of these factors satisfies the requirements of *Teamsters*. In particular, the majority agrees that a finding of discriminatory intent sufficient to satisfy *Teamsters* can be based on circumstantial evidence, including evidence of discriminatory impact. . . .

Given the nature of this factual inquiry, the court of appeals must first determine whether the district court applied correct legal principles and therefore *considered* all of the legally relevant evidence presented by the parties. This, as the majority acknowledges, is a "legal" function that the court of appeals must perform in the first instance. . . . Second, the court of appeals must determine whether the district court's finding with respect to intent is *supported* by all of the legally relevant evidence. This, the Court holds today, is generally a factual determination limited by the dictates of Rule 52(a). Finally, if the court of appeals sets aside the district court's finding with respect to intent, either because that finding is clearly erroneous or because it is based on an erroneous legal standard, it may determine, in the interest of judicial economy, whether the legally relevant evidence presented to the district court "permits only one resolution of the factual issue." . . . If only one conclusion is possible, the reviewing court is free to find the existence of the fact in question as a matter of law. See *Bigelow v. Virginia*, 421 U.S. 809, 826–827 (1975); *Levin v. Mississippi River Fuel Corp.*, 386 U.S. 162, 170 (1967).

A common-sense reading of the opinion below demonstrates that the Court of Appeals followed precisely this course in examining the issue of discriminatory intent. Even the majority concedes that the Court of Appeals determined that the District Court committed "legal error" by failing to consider all of the relevant evidence in resolving the first and the third *James* factors. With respect to the first *James* factor—whether the system inhibits all employees equally from transferring between seniority units—the District Court found that the departmental system "locked" both Negro and white workers into departments by discouraging transfers. The District Court acknowledged that Negroes might suffer a greater impact because the company's previous discriminatory policy of openly maintaining "Negro" jobs and "white" jobs had caused Negroes to be concentrated in less desirable positions. The District Court concluded, however, that this differential impact was irrelevant in determining whether the seniority system operated neutrally. The Court of Appeals properly held that the District Court erred in failing to consider the fact that the departmental system locked Negroes into less desirable jobs.

Similarly, as for the third *James* factor—whether the seniority system had its genesis in racial discrimination—the District Court rejected respondents' argument that the motives of the IAM were relevant. It concluded that the USW could not be charged with the racial bias of the IAM. The Court of Appeals held that this conclusion was erroneous because the "motives and intent of the I.A.M. in 1941 and 1942 are significant in consideration of whether the seniority system has its genesis in racial discrimination."[4] . . .

As the majority acknowledges, where findings of fact "'are made under an erroneous view of controlling legal principles, the clearly erroneous rule does not apply, and the findings may not stand.'" . . . Having found that the District Court's

---

4. As the majority indicates in a footnote, . . . the discriminatory motive of the IAM is "relevant . . . to the extent that it may shed light on the purpose of USW or the Company in creating and maintaining the separate seniority system at issue in this case." I do not read the Court of Appeals opinion in this action as holding anything more than that if the USW participated in establishing a system that was designed for the purpose of perpetuating past discrimination, the third *James* factor would be satisfied. Given that the IAM is a party to this litigation, its participation in the creation of the seniority system can hardly be deemed irrelevant.

findings as to the first and third *James* factors were made under an erroneous view of controlling legal principles, the Court of Appeals was *compelled* to set aside those findings free of the requirements of the clearly erroneous rule.[5] But once these two findings were set aside, the District Court's conclusion that the departmental system was bona fide within the meaning of §703(h) also had to be rejected, since that conclusion was based at least in part on its erroneous determinations concerning the first and the third *James* factors.

At the very least, therefore, the Court of Appeals was entitled to remand this action to the District Court for the purpose of reexamining the bona fides of the seniority system under proper legal standards. However, as we have often noted, in some cases a remand is inappropriate where the facts on the record are susceptible to only one reasonable interpretation. See *Dayton Board of Education v. Brinkman,* 443 U.S. 526, 534–537 (1979). . . . In such cases, "[e]ffective judicial administration" requires that the court of appeals draw the inescapable factual conclusion itself, rather than remand the case to the district court for further needless proceedings. *Levin v. Mississippi River Fuel Corp.,* 386 U.S. at 170. Such action is particularly appropriate where the court of appeals is in as good a position to evaluate the record evidence as the district court. The major premise behind the deference to trial courts expressed in Rule 52(a) is that findings of fact "depend peculiarly upon the credit given to witnesses by those who see and hear them." *United States v. Yellow Cab Co.,* 338 U.S. 338, 341 (1949). . . . Indeed Rule 52(a) expressly acknowledges the importance of this factor by stating that "due regard shall be given to the opportunity of the trial court to judge of the credibility of the witnesses." Consequently, this Court has been especially reluctant to resolve factual issues which depend on the credibility of witnesses. See generally *United States v. Oregon State Medical Society, supra,* at 332.

In the cases before the Court today this usual deference is not required because the District Court's findings of fact were entirely based on documentary evidence.[6] As we noted in *United States v. General Motors Corp., supra,* at 141, n. 16, "the trial court's customary opportunity to evaluate the demeanor and thus the credibility of the witnesses, which is the rationale behind Rule 52(a) . . . , plays only a restricted role [in] a 'paper case.'" . . . [7]

---

5. It is therefore irrelevant that the Court of Appeals did not specifically hold that the District Court's other factual findings were clearly erroneous.

6. Only two witnesses testified during the brief hearing that the District Court conducted on the question whether the seniority system at Pullman-Standard was immune under §703(h). Both of these witnesses were long-time Negro employees of Pullman-Standard who testified on behalf of *respondents* concerning racial segregation at the plant and by the USW. There is no indication in the District Court's opinion that it relied upon the testimony of these two witnesses in concluding that the system was bona fide within the meaning of §703(h). The remainder of the record before the District Court consisted entirely of 139 exhibits submitted by respondents, the company, and the unions concerning the development and maintenance of the seniority system from 1940 through the 1970's.

7. This is not to say that the clearly erroneous rule does not apply to "document" cases. *See United States v. Singer Manufacturing Co.,* 374 U.S. 174, 194, n. 9 (1963). However, "when the decision of the court below rests upon an incorrect reading of an undisputed document, [the appellate] court is free to substitute its own reading of the document." *Eutectic Corp. v. Metco, Inc.,* 579 F.2d 1, 5 (CA2 1978). . . .

I believe that the Court of Appeals correctly determined that a finding of discriminatory intent was compelled by the documentary record presented to the District Court. With respect to three of the four *James* factors, the Court of Appeals found overwhelming evidence of discriminatory intent. First, in ruling that the District Court erred by not acknowledging the legal significance of the fact that the seniority system locked Negroes into the least remunerative jobs in the company, the Court of Appeals determined that such disproportionate impact demonstrated that the system did not "'operat[e] to discourage all employees equally from transferring between seniority units.'" . . . Second, noting that "[n]o credible explanation ha[d] been advanced to sufficiently justify" the existence of two separate Die and Tool Departments and two separate Maintenance Departments, a condition not found at any other Pullman-Standard plant, or the creation of all-white and all-Negro departments at the time of unionization and in subsequent years, the Court of Appeals concluded that the second *James* factor had not been satisfied.[8] Finally, with respect to the third *James* factor the Court of Appeals found that once the role of the IAM was properly recognized, it was "crystal clear that considerations of race permeated the negotiation and the adoption of the seniority system in 1941 and subsequent negotiations thereafter." 624 F.2d at 532.[9]

After reviewing all of the relevant record evidence presented to the District Court, the Court of Appeals concluded: "There is no doubt, based upon the record in this case, about the existence of a discriminatory purpose." . . . Because I fail to see how the Court of Appeals erred in carrying out its appellate function, I respectfully dissent from the majority's decision to prolong respondents' 11-year quest for the vindication of their rights by requiring yet another trial.

NOTES AND QUESTIONS

1. *The Law/Fact Distinction.* As the Court makes clear in *Pullman-Standard*, the appropriate level of appellate scrutiny will turn on the characterization of the district court's finding. Questions of fact are deferred to under the "clearly erroneous"

---

8. Although the majority is correct in stating that the Court of Appeals did not "refer to or *expressly* apply the clearly erroneous standard" in reaching this conclusion (emphasis added), the appellate court's adherence to the requirements of Rule 52(a) is nevertheless apparent from the following statement: "The record evidence indicates that a significant number of one-race departments were established upon unionization at Pullman-Standard, and during the next twenty-five years, one-race departments were carved out of previously mixed departments. The establishment and maintenance of the segregated departments appear to be based on *no other considerations than the objective to separate the races.*" 624 F.2d at 531 (emphasis added).

In my opinion, this statement is sufficient to satisfy the requirements of Rule 52(a), particularly in light of the Court of Appeals' general acknowledgement that it was bound by the clearly erroneous rule. . . .

9. Whether or not the Court of Appeals expressly ruled on the fourth *James* factor is irrelevant. As the Court of Appeals clearly stated, its conclusion was based on "the totality of the facts and circumstances surrounding the creation and continuance of the departmental system at Pullman-Standard." . . . Even assuming that the District Court was correct in concluding that the system had been *maintained* free of any illegal purpose, the Court of Appeals was entitled to conclude that discriminatory intent had been demonstrated on the basis of other relevant evidence.

standard, while questions of law are subjected to the more searching "*de novo*" standard of review. At the extremes, those categories are easy to apply. Findings of fact describe historical events — e.g., the light was green; defendant said that he would pay the plaintiff; plaintiff worked at the defendant's place of business. Findings of law articulate abstract rules, independent of any particular historical event — e.g., the statute requires proof of intent; punitive damages are available for breach of contract; summary judgment is appropriate where there is no genuine issue of material fact.

The problem is at the intersection of those categories. A court finds facts and articulates legal standards, but at some point it must apply the law to the facts. Thus in *Pullman-Standard*, the court had to decide the state of mind of those persons responsible for developing and maintaining the seniority system (finding of fact); it had to articulate the definition of culpable intent under Title VII (conclusion of law); and then it had to decide whether the state of mind of the defendants constituted culpable "intent" within the meaning of Title VII. That last step of applying law to fact defies easy characterization.

Was the disagreement between the court of appeals and the district court in *Pullman-Standard* about the meaning of intent or about the state of mind of particular individuals? Consider Justice Marshall's perspective that the district court could not see the forest for the trees; the record demonstrated pervasive racism at the Pullman-Standard company in 1953, that racism permeated every aspect of social and economic activity, and the decision to design a seniority system that perpetuated inequality cannot be separated from the culture that produced that decision. Is that a dispute about fact or about law? In one sense, Justice Marshall is saying that "we know the defendants had bad intent" — the court got a fact wrong. Yet in another sense, he is saying that the "bad intent" for purposes of the statute is not necessarily located in the conscious decision of any individual — the court looked at the wrong facts.

2. *Mixed Questions of Fact and Law.* As the Court acknowledges in footnote 19, there is a division in the lower courts on the appropriate standard of review for mixed questions of law and fact. (Having found that the question before it was one of pure fact, the Court in *Pullman-Standard* did not need to resolve the division.) *Compare Ashland Oil & Refining Co. v. Kenny Constr. Co.*, 395 F.2d 683 (6th Cir. 1968) (mixed questions of law and fact not subject to clearly erroneous standard of review) *with In re Teranis*, 128 F.3d 469 (7th Cir. 1997) (court reviews mixed question of law and fact for clear error). Some courts address the problem on a "sliding scale": The more fact-dominated the issue, the more deference will be paid to the lower court determination. *See, e.g., Reich v. Newspapers of New England, Inc.*, 44 F.3d 1060 (1st Cir. 1995). *See also, Ornelas v. United States*, 517 U.S. 690, 698 (1996) (whether police officer had probable cause for search was a mixed question of law and fact that required *de novo* appellate review; "where the 'relevant legal principle can be given meaning only through its application to the particular circumstances of a case, the Court has been reluctant to give the trier of fact's conclusions presumptive force and, in so doing, strip a federal appellate court of its primary function as an expositor of law'"), quoting *Miller v. Fenton*, 474 U.S. 104, 114 (1985).

Recall our discussion at the beginning of this chapter on the justifications for appellate review. To the extent that appellate review is important in developing a uniform and consistent interpretation of law, isn't it just as important for an appeals court to articulate how law applies to fact, as to articulate abstract principles of law? What is the justification for deference to trial court determination of mixed questions?

3. *Subsidiary Facts.* "Subsidiary" findings of fact by a district court are always reviewed under the clearly erroneous standard, even when they are closely tied to an "ultimate" question that mixes law and fact. The Court reaffirmed that principle in a case involving the validity of a patent, *Teva Pharmaceuticals v. Sandoz*, 574 U.S. 318 (2015). When a complex dispute includes some questions that require the application of a set of facts to a legal standard—for which more invasive appellate review may be appropriate—the Court of Appeals does not thereby acquire a license to conduct its own independent inquiry into the disputed facts of the case. Rather, *Teva* explained, "[Rule 52(a)(6)] and the standard it sets forth must apply when a court of appeals reviews a district court's resolution of subsidiary factual matters made in the course of its" resolution of any ultimate legal issues. *Teva Pharmaceuticals*, 574 U.S. at 323.

Teva Pharmaceuticals involved a challenge to a patent that turned on a construction of the term "molecular weight"—specifically, whether that term was too indefinite to support a valid patent. After conducting a hearing and taking evidence from experts on the question, the district court concluded that the context in which the term was used made clear that it did have a definite and knowable scientific meaning that could support a patent. The Federal Circuit reversed. In doing so, it "reviewed *de novo* all aspects of the District Court's claim construction, including the District Court's determination of subsidiary facts." *Id.* Because the ultimate question of claim construction in a patent validity challenge is a question of law, the Federal Circuit had decided that it could conduct *de novo* review of any subsidiary findings of fact that inform the claim construction, but the Court categorically rejected this *gestalt* approach to Rule 52. The presence of a contested legal question requiring the resolution of disputed facts—a mixed question of fact and law—does not authorize an appellate court to make independent findings on the disputed facts on which that question depends. In *Teva*, construction of the patent depended not only on the legal meaning of the patent documents themselves but also "extrinsic evidence in order to understand, for example, the background science or the meaning of a term in the relevant art during the relevant time period." *Id.* at 331. The resolution of that "underlying factual dispute" could only be reversed on appeal if "the Court of Appeals [found] that the judge, in respect to those factual findings, has made a clear error." *Id.* Even if it would be "simpler for that appellate court to review the entirety of the district court's [ruling] *de novo* rather than to apply two separate standards," the Courts of Appeals are not "free to ignore the Federal Rule." *Id.* at 327–328.

4. *What Does "Clearly Erroneous" Mean?* How bound is the court of appeals to the trial court's fact finding under Rule 52 in a bench trial? Most courts have held that the clearly erroneous standard requires less deference than would be paid to jury determinations:

> This respect for the findings by the trial court cannot be pressed too far. It is simply wrong to say, as one court has, that the "findings will be given the force and effect of a jury verdict." History is clear that those who drafted the rule rejected proposals to apply the limited review of a jury verdict to

finding of a judge. Thus it is not accurate to say that the appellate court takes that view of the evidence that is most favorable to the appellee, that it assumes that all conflicts in the evidence were resolved in his favor, and that he must be given the benefit of all favorable inferences. . . . Instead, the appellate court . . . must give great weight to the findings made and the inferences drawn by the trial judge, but it must reject those findings if it considers them to be clearly erroneous.

9C Wright & Miller, §2585, at 567–568 (3d ed. 2018). *But see Parts and Elec. Motors, Inc. v. Sterling Elec., Inc.*, 866 F.2d 228, 233 (7th Cir. 1988) ("[t]o be clearly erroneous, a decision must strike us as more than just maybe or probably wrong; it must . . . strike us as wrong with the force of a five-week-old, unrefrigerated dead fish").

5. *How Did the Court of Appeals in* Pullman-Standard *Misapply the Clearly Erroneous Standard?* One unusual aspect of the *Pullman-Standard* case is that the court of appeals purported to apply the clearly erroneous standard of review. The Supreme Court nowhere in the opinion holds that the trial court's findings were *not* clearly erroneous. The Supreme Court, nonetheless, held that the appeals court did not give sufficient deference to the trial court's findings. How then did the Supreme Court know that the appeals court failed to apply the clearly erroneous standard?

The Court emphasizes two points. "First, although the Court of Appeals acknowledged and correctly stated the controlling standard of Rule 52(a), the acknowledgment came late in the court's opinion." Do you think the case would have come out differently had the appeals court stated the standard of review at the outset?

Second, "and more fundamentally," the court of appeals "failed to remand for further proceedings as to the intent of IAM and the significance, if any, of such a finding with respect to the intent of USW itself. Instead, the Court of Appeals made its own determination as to the motives of IAM, found that USW had acquiesced in the IAM conduct, and apparently concluded that the foregoing was sufficient [to sustain a cause of action under Title VII]." Why was the court of appeals' failure to remand (for what would have been the third time) inconsistent with a genuine belief that the trial court's findings were clearly erroneous? Is the Supreme Court suggesting that in cases subject to the clearly erroneous standard, courts of appeals must always remand rather than substituting their own judgment?

6. *Why Deference to Fact Determinations?* Why should courts of appeals defer to fact finding by trial courts? The most commonly articulated justification is that the trial court had a better view of the evidence. In a case such as *Pullman-Standard*, where the proof was largely documentary, why should there be any deference?

Rule 52(a) was amended in 1985 specifically to curtail the practice of not deferring to trial court fact finding made on a documentary record:

No matter what the nature of the evidence or the basis of the finding, an appellate court may set it aside only when it is convinced that the finding is clearly erroneous. . . .

. . . [T]his construction of [Rule 52] always has been required by the language of the rule itself, by the Advisory Committee Notes to the rule, and by the decisions of the Supreme Court. It has been required even more clearly by the essential nature and function of trial courts as distinguished from appellate courts. Even in instances in which an appellate court is in as good a position to decide as the trial court, it should not disregard the trial court's finding, because to do so impairs confidence in the trial courts and multiplies appeals with attendant expense and delay.

9C C. Wright et al., Federal Practice and Procedure §2587, at 435–439 (3d ed. 2018). Do you agree? Doesn't it undermine confidence in the judicial system just as much when, as was apparently the case in *Pullman-Standard*, a single district court judge refuses to see a pattern of discrimination that was apparent to the court of appeals, and the court of appeals is powerless to remedy that mistake?

7. *Fact Review in First Amendment Cases.* Notwithstanding the enormous deference that appellate courts must give to fact finding by the trial court pursuant to Rule 52, the Supreme Court has held that appellate courts should exercise a heightened level of scrutiny in defamation cases because of First Amendment concerns. In *Bose Corp. v. Consumers Union*, 466 U.S. 485 (1984), the Court held that the court of appeals properly rejected the trial court's conclusion that a reviewer for *Consumer Reports* intentionally misstated his reaction to the Bose speakers he evaluated.

The First Amendment requires that a plaintiff in a libel case must prove by "clear and convincing evidence" that defendant acted with "actual malice," defined as knowledge or reckless disregard, of the falsity of defendant's defamatory statement. The trial court had held that there was such evidence, finding the reviewer's denial of intentional wrongdoing "not credible." The court of appeals, however, conducted a *de novo* review of the record and concluded that it was unable to find clear and convincing evidence of actual malice. The Supreme Court affirmed, holding that the deference owed to trial court determinations was variable:

> [T]he presumption of correctness that attaches to factual findings is stronger in some cases than in others. The same "clearly erroneous" standard applies to findings based on documentary evidence as to those based entirely on oral testimony, . . . but the presumption has lesser force in the former situation than in the latter. Similarly, the standard does not change as the trial becomes longer and more complex, but the likelihood that the appellate court will rely on the presumption tends to increase when trial judges have lived with the controversy for weeks or months instead of just a few hours.

Id. at 500. Given the constitutionally guaranteed free speech rights of defendant in a libel case, more searching appellate review is necessary to ensure that the constitutional standards have been appropriately applied:

> The requirement of independent appellate review reiterated in *New York Times Co. v. Sullivan* is a rule of federal constitutional law. It emerged from the exigency of deciding concrete cases; it is law in its purest form under our common-law heritage. It reflects a deeply held conviction that judges—and particularly Members of this Court—must exercise such review in order to preserve the precious liberties established and ordained by the Constitution. The question whether the evidence in the record in a defamation case is of the convincing clarity required to strip the utterance of First Amendment protection is not merely a question for the trier of fact. Judges, as expositors of the Constitution, must independently decide

whether the evidence in the record is sufficient to cross the constitutional threshold that bars the entry of any judgment that is not supported by clear and convincing proof of "actual malice."

Id. at 510–511.

Is *Bose* distinguishable from *Pullman-Standard* simply because of the presence of First Amendment concerns? If searching appellate review of the trial court's findings of fact was necessary to ensure that First Amendment standards were properly applied, why wasn't such review appropriate to ensure that the antidiscrimination norms of Title VII were properly enforced? Did the *Bose* plaintiff's heightened burden of proving malice with "convincing clarity" affect the appropriate standard of appellate review?

8. *Harmless Error.* Not every factual or legal error renders the trial court decision vulnerable to reversal on appeal. Unless an error is deemed to affect the "substantial rights" of the parties, appeals courts will not reverse, even if the lower court ruling is clearly erroneous. *See* 28 U.S.C. §2111 ("On the hearing of any appeal or writ of certiorari in any case, the court shall give judgment after an examination of the record without regard to errors or defects which do not affect the substantial rights of the parties."); *McDonough Power Equipment, Inc. v. Greenwood,* 464 U.S. 548, 553 (1984) ("The harmless error rules adopted by this Court and Congress embody the principle that courts should exercise judgment in preference to the automatic reversal for 'error' and ignore errors that do not affect the essential fairness of the trial.").

9. *Abuse of Discretion.* Besides the clearly erroneous and *de novo* standards of review, the courts employ an "abuse of discretion" standard to review a wide range of procedural rulings by the trial court, including rulings on admissibility of evidence, appealability under Rule 54(b), *forum non conveniens,* and permissive intervention. It is also the standard used to review the grant or denial of preliminary injunctions. *See* Linda J. Silberman, *Injunctions by the Numbers: Less Than the Sum of Its Parts,* 63 Chi.-Kent L. Rev. 279 (1987).

The late Judge Henry Friendly argued that the precise level of deference required by the abuse of discretion standard should vary according to the need for case-specific flexibility versus the desirability of generating uniform legal standards:

> [W]e should recognize that "abuse of discretion," like "jurisdiction," is "a verbal coat of . . . many colors." There are a half dozen different definitions of "abuse of discretion," ranging from ones that would require the appellate court to come close to finding that the trial court had taken leave of its senses to others which differ from the definition of error by only the slightest nuance, with numerous variations between the extremes. . . . In those situations "where the decision depends on first-hand observation or direct contact with the litigation," the trial court's decision "merits a high degree of insulation from appellate revision." At the other extreme, when Congress has declared a national policy and enlisted the aid of the courts' equity powers in its enforcement, the Supreme Court has said that the fact that "the [trial] court's discretion is equitable in nature . . . hardly means that it is unfettered by meaningful standards or shielded from thorough appellate review." In some instances the need for uniformity and predictability demand thorough appellate review. In short, the "abuse of

discretion" standard does not give nearly so complete an immunity both to the trial court's rulings as counsel for appellees would have reviewing courts believe. An appellate court must carefully scrutinize the nature of the trial court's determination and decide whether that court's superior opportunities of observation or other reasons of policy require greater deference than would be accorded to its formulations of law or its application of law to the facts. In cases within the former categories, "abuse of discretion" should be given a broad reading, in others a reading which scarcely differs from the definition of error. Above all, an appellate court should consider whether the lawmaker intended that discretion should be committed solely to the trial judge or to judges throughout the judicial system.

Henry J. Friendly, *Indiscretion About Discretion*, 31 Emory L.J. 747, 763, 783–784 (1982) (footnotes omitted).

10. *Review of Jury Findings.* The most deferential standard of review is employed when the appeals court reviews jury determinations. Recall that pursuant to Fed. R. Civ. P. 50(a) and (b), the trial judge may issue a judgment as a matter of law only where there is *no* evidence in support of the jury determination. The trial judge also exercises control over the jury verdict through the power to grant a motion for a new trial when the verdict is against the great weight of the evidence.

Similarly, the appellate courts have very limited powers in upsetting jury verdicts. As you will recall, the appellate court is perceived to be in the same position as the trial court in determining whether the verdict loser is entitled to a judgment as a matter of law. As for a grant or denial of a new trial, the appellate court must accept the ruling of the trial judge unless it finds an abuse of discretion. 11 C. Wright et al., Federal Practice and Procedure §2818 (3d ed. 2018).

11. *Review of Punitive Damages Awards.* There are, however, occasional exceptions to the general rule that the factual findings of a trial court or a jury are reviewed deferentially. There are some cases in which the finder of fact makes comparative assessments that resemble legal or policy determinations more than traditional determinations of historical fact. In these cases, the fact finding is subject to less deferential review both on the trial and appellate levels.

One example that has received considerable attention is a jury's award of punitive damages. In *BMW of North America v. Gore*, 517 U.S. 559 (1996), the Supreme Court held that the Due Process Clause of the Fourteenth Amendment places substantive limitations on the amount of punitive damages that a jury can award. Specifically, the Court held that a punitive damages award violates due process if it is "grossly excessive." When a defendant challenges a punitive damages award on these grounds, the trial court must consider three factors: (1) how reprehensible the defendant's misconduct was, (2) the disparity between the harm suffered by the plaintiff and the punitive damages award, and (3) the disparity between the punitive damages award and the penalties authorized or imposed in comparable cases. *See id.* at 574–575. Under *Gore*, if a defendant believes that a jury's award of punitive damages violates this limitation, it may request the trial court to reduce the award through a *remittitur* (discussed at pp. 707-708).

The Court constrained the award of punitive damages even further in *State Farm Mutual Automobile Insurance Co. v. Campbell*, 538 U.S. 408 (2003), suggesting that a ratio of ten to one in punitive versus compensatory damages should ordinarily constitute a high-water mark. The Court there held that a state jury's award of $145 million punitive damage award for an insurance company's bad faith refusal to settle an accident claim violated the Due Process Clause where the compensatory damages were only $1 million, thus justifying the trial court's entry of a *remittitur.*

Gore has opened the door for more exacting appellate scrutiny of jury awards as well. In *Cooper Industries, Inc. v. Leatherman Tool Group,* 532 U.S. 424 (2001), the Court found that an appeals court should review the lower court's refusal to lower the jury's punitive damage award *de novo,* rather than for clear error or abuse of discretion. "Unlike the measure of actual damages suffered, which presents a question of historical or predictive fact," the Court explained, "the level of punitive damages is not really a 'fact' 'tried' by the jury." *Id.* at 1683. Hence, an appellate court can review the trial court's review of the punitive damages award without deference, and without concern for the Reexamination Clause of the Seventh Amendment, which ordinarily places limitations on a court's ability to revisit the factual determinations of a jury. In this respect, the Court found, the *Gore* inquiry followed a line of Eighth Amendment cases that provide for *de novo* appellate review of judgments disallowing punishments and fines as excessive. *See, e.g., Enmund v. Florida,* 458 U.S. 782, 787, 801 (1982) (death penalty); *United States v. Bajakajian,* 524 U.S. 321, 324 (1998) (excessive fines).

The Supreme Court articulated further limits on punitive damage awards in two more cases. In *Philip Morris USA v. Williams,* 549 U.S. 346 (2007), the Court reversed a $32 million punitive damage award to the estate of a heavy smoker for the manufacturer's deceit concerning the danger of cigarettes.[*] The Court held that it was a violation of due process to punish defendant for injuries suffered by third parties not present in the lawsuit. The Court, however, drew a somewhat confusing distinction: Although juries are not permitted to "use a punitive damages award to punish a defendant for injury that it inflicts upon nonparties," they may take defendant's conduct toward third parties into account in order to establish "reprehensibility." Moreover, "[e]vidence of actual harm to nonparties can help to show that the conduct that harmed the plaintiff also posed a substantial risk of harm to the general public, and so was particularly reprehensible." Justice Stevens, in dissent, asserted that "[t]his nuance eludes me." Do you understand the distinction the majority is making? Do you think juries will?

In *Exxon Shipping Co. v. Baker,* 554 U.S. 471 (2008), the Court established a ceiling for the award of punitive damages for reckless conduct under federal maritime law, holding that punitive damages may not exceed the amount of compensatory damages awarded. Unlike the *Philip Morris* and *Gore* decisions, the constraint on punitive damages imposed by *Exxon Shipping* was not based on constitutional due process limits. Rather, the limitation was a federal common law ruling derived from the substantive law applicable in maritime cases. Thus, the holding may have

---

[*] On remand, the Oregon Supreme Court reinstated the original damage award on the ground that defendant had waived its objection to the jury award given by the trial court. 176 P.3d 1255 (Or. 2008). For an analysis of the federalism tensions underlying the Supreme Court's punitive damage jurisprudence in the wake of *Williams, see* Catherine M. Sharkey, *Federal Incursions and State Defiance: Punitive Damages in the Wake of* Philip Morris v. Williams, 46 Willamette L. Rev. 449 (2010).

limited impact outside of admiralty. However, the Court's rationale, that the law needs to be consistent and predictable, may have implications for future due process decisions:

> Whatever may be the constitutional significance of the unpredictability of high punitive awards, this feature of happenstance is in tension with the function of the awards as punitive, just because of the implication of unfairness that an eccentrically high punitive damage verdict carries in a system whose commonly held notion of law rests on a sense of fairness in dealing with one another. Thus, a penalty should be reasonably predictable in its severity, so that even Justice Holmes's "bad man" can look ahead with some ability to know what the stakes are in choosing one course of action or another. See *The Path of the Law*, 10 Harv. L. Rev. 457, 459 (1897). And when the bad man's counterparts turn up from time to time, the penalty scheme they face ought to threaten them with a fair probability of suffering in like degree when they wreak like damage. Cf. Koon v. United States, 518 U.S. 81 (1996) (noting the need "to reduce unjustified disparities" in criminal sentencing "and so reach toward the evenhandedness and neutrality that are the distinguishing marks of any principled system of justice"). The common sense of justice would surely bar penalties that reasonable people would think excessive for the harm caused in the circumstances.

554 U.S. at 502–503.

This predictability, the Court concluded, could not consistently be achieved simply by "verbal formulations, superimposed on general jury instructions. . . . Instructions can go just so far in promoting systemic consistency when awards are not tied to specifically proven items of damages." *Id.* at 504.

CHAPTER 10

ALTERNATIVE DISPUTE RESOLUTION

Up to this point, we have focused principally on issues that arise in the context of a lawsuit. We have examined who may sue or be sued, where a lawsuit may be brought, what rules and doctrines will apply to the lawsuit while it proceeds, and what issues might arise after the lawsuit is over and judgment is rendered. These doctrines govern *adjudication*: the resolution of disputes by an arm of government (the court system) that derives its power from the state, operates according to laws and rules enacted by the state, and must always answer to the Constitution and any other applicable limitations on state authority. Adjudication is what most people think of when they envision a formal method of resolving disputes, and it is a vital body of procedure for attorneys to know about when they represent their clients.

But adjudication is not the only formal method for resolving disputes in the United States, nor indeed the only method in which government plays a role. There exists a large body of *alternative dispute resolution* methods, or ADR, to which people and organizations also look for assistance when they become involved in disagreements. We will explore these ADR methods in this chapter. The most basic alternative to civil litigation, of course, is *settlement*—a private agreement between the parties to release their claims in return for some benefit, usually a negotiated sum of money. We begin this chapter by looking at a sample settlement agreement. We then go on to examine the forms of ADR that legislatures, courts, and private parties have developed to resolve disputes. As you will see, attempts to encourage or shape settlement between the parties lie behind many of these ADR methods.

The most consequential form of ADR is *arbitration*. The practice of arbitration borrows its essentials from adjudication, but it occurs before a private referee instead of a judge and typically involves less formal procedures, reduced access to coercive discovery, and few opportunities for appellate review or other forms of intercession by courts. The practice of arbitration enjoys powerful support from the Federal Arbitration Act, 9 U.S.C. §§1–16, a federal statute that the Supreme Court has interpreted broadly to render agreements to arbitrate mandatory in most circumstances. More recent cases have seen corporate defendants using arbitration clauses to shield themselves from the threat of class or aggregate litigation. Those efforts have found favor with the Court, raising the stakes of arbitration considerably.

Throughout this chapter, ask yourself how the different alternatives to formal adjudication may or may not be attractive to potential litigants. What problems do different ADR methods solve? What costs do they save the parties, and what additional costs might they impose? Is anything lost when the parties to a dispute forgo the traditional method of adjudication in favor of a private alternative? There is deep disagreement among courts, commentators, and law makers about these seemingly straightforward questions.

A.   SETTLEMENT

1.   The Settlement as Contract

A settlement is a contract. More specifically, it is an agreement entered into by parties to a dispute (or a potential dispute) for the purpose of resolving some or all of their claims. In the simplest form of settlement, defendant agrees to pay plaintiff a sum of money and plaintiff agrees to *release* the claims that she has brought. When plaintiff releases a claim, she agrees not only to drop the claim in whatever lawsuit or proceeding is currently underway but also to refrain from trying to raise the claim in any future proceeding. If a plaintiff were to renege on her settlement and try to bring a lawsuit even after releasing her claims, defendant could raise an affirmative defense by interposing the settlement and release. In this respect, a settlement has effects similar to the *res judicata* effect of a judgment—it serves as a bar to the claims of the plaintiff in future proceedings.

Settlements can be more complicated than simple money-for-release arrangements. Since settlements are negotiated contracts, the parties can generally agree to whatever terms and obligations they want. But there are exceptions. In some special situations, settlement terms must be approved by a court, *see, e.g.*, Fed. R. Civ. P. 23(e) (class actions); and on rare occasions, a court can refuse to enforce a settlement agreement that it finds to be contrary to basic principles of public policy. *See, e.g., Town of Newton v. Rumery*, 480 U.S. 386, 392 (1987) (explaining that "a promise is unenforceable if the interest in its enforcement is outweighed in the circumstances by a public policy harmed by enforcement of the agreement"); *Davies v. Grossmont Union High Sch. Dist.*, 930 F.2d 1390, 1392 (9th Cir. 1991) (refusing to enforce a settlement that bars an individual from running for public office). But, in general, the parties can specify any terms they want in a settlement. Those terms might relate directly to the dispute in question, in which case they can encompass most of the forms of relief that a court could grant. They also might extend more broadly. In the commercial context, for example, it is not unusual for companies to engage in repeat litigation with each other over the course of a number of years, and a settlement might include terms that relate to any *future* disputes that arise between them, like a provision that, in any such future disputes, the loser will pay any attorneys' fees incurred by the winner.

It might also be important to one or both parties to keep the terms of a settlement confidential. Think of a case involving claims of racial discrimination in the workplace. The defendant company in such a case might want to make the case go away quietly, either because the details are embarrassing or because there may be other employees who have been mistreated and would be emboldened to bring suit themselves if they discovered that one of their peers had obtained a recovery. Plaintiff, too, might prefer confidentiality, perhaps because he values his privacy and does not want the details of the incident or the amount of his compensation to be widely known. In fact, confidentiality is an important example of a form of relief that may not be available at all if the parties proceed to judgment instead of reaching a settlement. Court proceedings are generally open to spectators, and American courts have recognized a general right on the part of the public to inspect and copy court records. *See Nixon v. Warner Communications*, 435 U.S. 589, 597–598 (1978). When the parties settle, however, they can condition their settlement upon a mutual obligation not to disclose its terms. If one of the settling parties violates this confidentiality provision, then, as with any other contract, the other party may be able to recover damages, or it may be released from the other terms of the settlement agreement, perhaps empowering it to bring another lawsuit. *See, e.g., Daines v. Harrison*, 838 F. Supp. 1406, 1409 (D. Colo. 1993) (explaining that, if one party violates a confidentiality provision in a settlement, "the other party will have a cause of action for breach of contract").

Like so much else in the law, the question of what a settlement agreement means can be a matter of dispute in subsequent proceedings. One party might disagree with the other's interpretation of what the settlement requires it to do, or what the settlement prohibits. For example, a settlement agreement might prohibit plaintiff from suing in the future, both over claims that he brought in the settled dispute and over any "related" claims. This would be an important provision for defendant, who would want to make sure that plaintiff could not sue again over the same incident or transaction under a different legal theory. What exactly constitutes a "related" claim, however, might well be the subject of disagreement. (Just think of the difficulty that courts have had in deciding when two claims are sufficiently "related" for purposes of claim preclusion or supplemental jurisdiction.)

As a result, the parties to a settlement will sometimes include a term that gives them "total peace" by releasing all claims that either party ever had against the other at the time of settlement, whether related to the current dispute or not. Such a *global release* has the benefit of removing ambiguity and uncertainty, for each party knows that it will never again have to worry about being sued by the other over something that happened in the past. But, of course, such a release also carries some risk. If one party has committed a wrong that the other has not yet discovered, a global release may prevent the aggrieved party from suing when it discovers that it has a cause of action. For this reason, global releases may be more common in cases involving parties who have no past relationship or history — paradigmatically, in a tort case between strangers. In such a case, the chances are slim that one of the parties has a cause of action against the other that it has not yet discovered. In contrast, two business rivals who have had extensive dealings might be reluctant to include a global release in a settlement, as there may be many dealings between them, like contracts or competition over customers, that could give rise to a cause of action that one or the other party has not yet discovered. For such entities, it may be necessary to draft a release that is broad enough to cover anything related to the dispute being settled but not so broad as to release other potential claims between the parties — a balance that, in practice, may be difficult to find.

Thus, parties must think strategically about their present dispute and issues external to that dispute, like the importance of keeping details confidential or the impact of a settlement on other business dealings.

2.   *Settlement Negotiations and Strategic Behavior*

In theory, many of the disputes that arise between parties "should" settle. The information necessary to determine the likely outcome of a trial on the issues of liability and damages is often readily ascertainable. If the parties can know with some confidence what the outcome of a trial is likely to be, then the "rational" thing to do is to settle the case for something close to that projected outcome and avoid the expense and inconvenience of litigation. And indeed, as we have discussed, many cases do settle before a trial verdict is reached. But in practice, not all cases that "should" settle do, and some cases settle only late in the litigation, after much time and money have already been spent. Why should this be so?

Settlement is the end result of a process of negotiation between the parties, and negotiation involves strategic behavior. The information that each side has available to it, the information that each side chooses to reveal to its opponent, and the tactics that each employs in the course of a negotiation can have a significant impact on the terms of any settlement that the parties ultimately reach. Such strategic behavior can distort the outcome of a settlement negotiation. Consider the following possibilities.

One type of strategic behavior can result from imbalances in the information that each party possesses. There may be information about key issues that is within the exclusive control of one party—for example, information that only defendant has about the level of care it employed, or information that only plaintiff has about the true measure of its damages. For strategic reasons, the party in control of sensitive information may choose not to reveal it, even though it is likely to come out through discovery, for fear of weakening its position. This, in turn, may prevent or delay the settlement that "should" ultimately happen—the contract that rational people would agree to if they had the benefit of all the information.

Another type of strategic behavior may be more purely behavioral, arising out of the personal litigation styles of the attorneys in the case. For example, many practitioners believe that the first settlement offer that either side makes in a negotiation can have the effect of defining the parameters within which future negotiations will proceed. From this belief, they may conclude that an aggressive first settlement offer can result in a better ultimate settlement. Such a tactic, however, can also have the effect of discouraging negotiation altogether or significantly delaying a final resolution, resulting once again in increased litigation costs. *See, e.g.*, M. Neale & M. Bazerman, Cognition and Rationality in Negotiation 48 (1991) (reporting results of negotiating experiments demonstrating these effects).

Serious impediments to settlement may even arise out of problems in the relationship between attorney and client. An attorney bears a *fiduciary* duty to the client—a responsibility to represent the best interests of the client zealously and not allow the attorney's individual interests to affect professional judgment. In practice, however, it may be difficult to adhere to this ideal. The incentives of lawyers and clients to settle a lawsuit can become skewed, leading to a risk that lawyers will not give their clients the best advice. To use two simple examples, consider the contingency fee arrangement, on the one hand, and the payment of legal services on an hourly basis, on the other. In a standard contingency arrangement, the lawyer will receive a certain percentage of plaintiff's recovery—say, 30 percent—regardless of whether that recovery results from a settlement or a verdict. In such a case, the attorney may have a strong incentive to settle the dispute quickly, even if it means settling for a lower recovery, since the attorney will recoup any reduction in the fee through the resources saved by not having to go to trial. In a fee-for-service arrangement, in contrast, the incentives may be skewed in the other direction. Since the attorney is being paid for services provided, the attorney's ability to assess the fairness and reasonableness of a settlement offer may be affected by the knowledge that the fee will be small if the client accepts such an offer too early in the proceedings. Professor Geoffrey Miller explores these and other "agency" problems in the attorney-client relationship in *Some Agency Problems in Settlement*, 16 J. Legal Stud. 189 (1987). *See also* Jonathan Molot, *Litigation Finance: A Market Solution to a Procedural Problem*, 99 Geo. L.J. 65 (2010) (arguing that "imbalances in risk preferences," including those caused by litigation finance methods, can "skew settlements" away from efficient or sensible amounts and proposing market-based solutions).

Is it possible to counteract such impediments to settlement through court reforms, and, if so, are such reforms appropriate? Or are these "impediments" just the natural result of an adversarial bargaining process, a process that should be allowed to unfold naturally in a dispute? These questions have received a considerable amount of attention from scholars in the fields of procedure and negotiation. Some scholars have proposed procedural reforms that they believe would eliminate some of the unnecessary inefficiency from the negotiating process. Professors Robert Gertner and Geoffrey Miller, for example, have called for experimentation with settlement "escrow" accounts. Under the arrangement they propose, parties could make settlement offers to a neutral agent. Neither party would know the amount of her opponent's offer, or even whether or when her opponent has made an offer. Only if the offers cross—if the amount defendant is willing to pay surpasses the amount that plaintiff is willing to accept—will the escrow agent reveal the bids. At that point, the case will settle for the amount midway between the two offers. Gertner and Miller argue that such an arrangement could eliminate certain types of inefficiency that sometimes plague settlement negotiations. *See* Robert Gertner & Geoffrey Miller, *Settlement Escrows*, 24 J. Legal Stud. 87 (1995). *See also* Lewis Kornhauser & Richard Revesz, *Settlements Under Joint and Several Liability*, 68 N.Y.U. L. Rev. 427 (1993) (examining impact of joint and several liability on settlement dynamics); Carrie Menkel-Meadow, *Ethics and the Settlement of Mass Torts: When the Rules Meet the Road*, 80 Cornell L. Rev. 1159 (1995) (exploring diverse interests of different actors in mass tort cases and proposing methods for avoiding settlement problems and encouraging fair and efficient resolutions).

One other influence on the incentives of the parties in considering settlement bears mention—Fed. R. Civ. P. 68. Rule 68 creates a formal mechanism for making a settlement offer (or "offer of judgment") and, at the same time, imposes penalties on a plaintiff who rejects the proposed settlement and then goes on to recover less than the offer. Specifically, Rule 68 requires a plaintiff to pay "the costs incurred [by defendant] after the offer was made" if the plaintiff ultimately obtains a judgment that is not as favorable as the offer. Fed. R. Civ. P. 68(d). These costs do not include attorneys' fees unless the substantive statute underlying the cause of action specifically so provides. *See Nusom v. Comh Woodburn, Inc.*, 122 F.3d 830, 834 (9th Cir. 1997). However, plaintiff's rejection of a Rule 68 offer may result in the forfeit of attorneys' fees otherwise provided by substantive law where the offer exceeds the amount ultimately awarded to plaintiff. *Marek v. Chesney*, 473 U.S. 1 (1985).

Note the limited application of Rule 68. It applies only to offers made by a party "defending" a claim—it has no application to settlement offers made by plaintiff. *See Delta Airlines v. August*, 450 U.S. 346, 350 (1981). Moreover, it applies only when plaintiff "obtain[s]" a judgment—that is, when plaintiff wins. The Rule does not impose costs on plaintiff if plaintiff refuses a settlement offer and subsequently loses altogether. *See Delta Airlines*, 450 U.S. at 351 ("Rule 68 provides an additional inducement to settle in those cases in which there is a strong probability that the plaintiff will obtain a judgment but the amount of recovery is uncertain."). Even so, in cases where smaller amounts of money are at stake, Rule 68 may encourage a plaintiff to accept a borderline settlement offer to avoid the risk of paying defendant's costs. Because of the limited sanctions imposed under Rule 68, it has been widely criticized as ineffective. *See* 12 C. Wright et al., Federal Practice and Procedure §3001 (3d. ed. 2002 & 2021 Update) ("Rule 68 has not played a prominent role in judicial efforts at settlement promotion."); Roy D. Simon, *The Riddle of Rule 68*, 54 Geo. Wash. L. Rev. 1 (1985); Stephen B. Burbank, *Proposals to Amend Rule 68—Time to Abandon Ship*, 19 U. Mich. J.L. Reform 425 (1986). Professor Robert Bone, a leading scholar on the history of procedure in American courts, has argued that Rule 68's apparent ineffectiveness in fact reflects a misunderstanding of its original purpose: "The original FRCP drafters did not adopt Rule 68 for the purpose of promoting settlement . . . but simply adopted the offer of judgment rule that existed in state codes. Those state rules . . . were designed to prevent plaintiffs from imposing costs unfairly when the defendant" refused a reasonable offer and had nothing to do with settlement. Robert G. Bone, *"To Encourage Settlement": Rules 68, Offers of Judgment, and the History of the Federal Rules of Civil Procedure*, 102 Nw. L. Rev. 1561, 1562 (2008).

For a further discussion of the dynamics of settlement from an economic or game theory perspective, *see* Kathryn E. Spier, *The Dynamics of Pretrial Negotiation*, 59 Rev. Econ. Stud. 93 (1992); Barry Nalebuff, *Credible Pretrial Negotiation*, 18 RAND J. Econ. 198 (1987); Jennifer F. Reinganum & Louis L. Wilde, *Settlement, Litigation and the Allocation of Litigation Costs*, 17 RAND J. Econ. 557 (1986); Robert G. Bone, *Modeling Frivolous Lawsuits*, 145 U. Pa. L. Rev. 519 (1997).

3. Special Forms of Settlement Agreements

There are some special forms of settlement agreements that have the potential to change the dynamics of the adversarial process and have received mixed reactions in the courts. One particularly disfavored form of agreement that falls into this category is the so-called *Mary Carter* agreement, named after a litigant in a 1967 case in Florida. *See Booth v. Mary Carter Paint Co.*, 202 So. 2d 8 (Fla. Ct. App. 1967), *overruled by Dosdourian v. Cartsen*, 624 So. 2d 241 (Fla. 1993). A *Mary Carter* agreement arises in a lawsuit that has multiple parties on at least one side of the dispute. Under the agreement, one party, usually a defendant, secretly agrees to settle its claims with its opponent. Unlike in a normal settlement, however, after the parties have settled, they do not ask the court to dismiss the settled claim. Indeed, they do not even alert the court to the settlement. Rather, the settling party remains an active part of the lawsuit, agreeing to have its claims formally dismissed only at a later time. The catch is that, as part of the bargain, the settling party agrees to *help* its nominal opponent in litigating its claims against the other parties. Thus, for example, a settling defendant might agree to give extensive testimony about damaging issues in the case, rather than giving as little information as possible as many litigants would try to do. Even more dramatically, a settling defendant might point the finger at its co-defendants, implicating them to the fullest extent possible. And a settling defendant might cooperate with plaintiff on those ministerial issues that arise during the course of the lawsuit — scheduling, the parameters of discovery, the structure of the trial — that can give a tactical advantage to the prevailing party.

A secret turncoat agreement like this can have a dramatic impact on the adjudicatory process. As one commentator has argued, for example, such an agreement can significantly prejudice nonsettling defendants, who may suddenly find a bipartisan effort opposing their positions during discovery and trial or who may be apportioned an inequitable amount of damages due to the cooperation of one of their joint tortfeasors with the plaintiff. *See* John E. Benedict, Note, *It's a Mistake to Tolerate* Mary Carter *Agreements*, 87 Colum. L. Rev. 368 (1987). And if the court and the other litigants are not aware of a *Mary Carter* agreement, they may be unable accurately to assess the credibility of witness testimony or attorney arguments.

Most courts have met *Mary Carter* agreements with disapproval. Some have banned the arrangements outright, finding that they encourage unfair trials, promote unethical behavior on the part of attorneys, or undermine the integrity of the judicial system. *See, e.g., Dosdourian v. Cartsen*, 624 So. 2d 241 (Fla. 1993); *Elbaor v. Smith*, 845 S.W.2d 240 (Tex. 1992); *Cox v. Kelsey-Hayes Co.*, 594 P.2d 354 (Okla. 1978); *Lum v. Stinnett*, 488 P.2d 347 (Nev. 1971). Others have ruled that, at the very least, parties that enter into such an agreement must disclose the terms to the court and to the jury. *See, e.g., Newman v. Ford Motor Co.*, 975 S.W.2d 147 (Mo. 1998). Clearly, a *Mary Carter* agreement bears on the credibility of a witness's testimony or the reasons for a party's actions in the lawsuit. Disclosure allows the judge and jury to take this information into account.

However, in limited circumstances, courts have found that certain *Mary Carter*-style agreements can actually promote important public policies and should *not* be disclosed to juries. Consider *Icicle Seafoods v. Baker (In re The Exxon Valdez)*, 229 F.3d 790 (9th Cir. 2000). The case involved an attempt by a small group of plaintiffs in a larger class action to settle their claims against Exxon arising out of a massive oil spill into the Prince William Sound. Icicle Seafoods and six other plaintiffs, collectively referred to as the "Seattle Seven," entered into an agreement with Exxon to settle any claims they might have for either compensatory or punitive damages. But the settlement did not formally release the Seattle Seven's punitive damages claims against Exxon. Rather, in return for some $63.75 million, the Seven agreed to remain as parties in the punitive damages class action and to "cede back" to Exxon their portion of any punitive damages that the jury might ultimately award. They also agreed to keep this part of the arrangement secret.

The reason for this arrangement had to do with the anticipated behavior of the jury. Exxon was concerned that settling the punitive damages of the Seattle Seven in the ordinary fashion would not result in a reduction of its liability, since the jury would simply award the same total amount of punitive damages to the nonsettling plaintiffs. Moreover, Exxon feared that disclosure of the "cede back" agreement would defeat its purpose, since the jury, upon learning of it, might increase the punitive damages award in order to offset any benefit to Exxon. Hence, Exxon argued, it was necessary to keep the agreement secret.

The Ninth Circuit agreed and held that "cede back agreements should generally not be revealed to juries deliberating on punitive damages." *Id.* at 799. The court cited the "general policy of federal courts to promote settlement before trial" that "is even stronger in the context of large-scale class actions." *Id.* at 795. It found that "cede back agreements make it easier to administer mandatory class actions for the assessment of punitive damages and encourage settlement in mass tort cases." *Id.* at 798.

An analogous secrecy arrangement has also been recognized as beneficial in the reverse situation, where a plaintiff who has sued multiple defendants agrees to indemnify a settling party for any contribution actions that other, nonsettling defendants may later bring against it. *See, e.g., Pierringer v. Hoger,* 124 N.W.2d 106 (Wis. 1963); *Frey v. Snelgrove,* 269 N.W.2d 918 (Minn. 1978). Thus, while *Mary Carter* agreements remain disfavored as a general matter, there are at least some situations in which courts will give them their blessing. *See also* Lisa Bernstein & Daniel Klerman, *An Economic Analysis of* Mary Carter *Agreements,* 83 Geo. L.J. 2215 (1995) (arguing that *Mary Carter* agreements may have socially desirable effects in some circumstances); Jessica McGrath, *Case Digests Issue,* 84 U. Det. Mercy L. Rev. 61 (2006) (discussing developments in Michigan courts concerning "*Mary Carter*-style" agreements); Victoria Holstein-Childress, Mary Carter's *True Colors: Champertous Settlement Agreements Under Louisiana's Nullity Doctrine,* 77 Tul. L. Rev. 885 (2003) (discussing approval of *Mary Carter* agreements in Louisiana courts and arguing that such agreements should be unenforceable).

Another form of settlement that has become increasingly popular is the *high-low agreement,* in which the parties basically give themselves an insurance policy against extreme results at trial. The high-low agreement sets a range of possible outcomes that the parties find acceptable. For example, a plaintiff in a personal injury suit might insist on recovering no less than $100,000, and defendant may be unwilling to pay any more than $1 million. The parties will specify in the agreement that if the result at trial is lower than the minimum (most commonly, a finding of no liability) then plaintiff will still receive the minimum, but if the result at trial is higher than the maximum (say a verdict of $10 million in the example above) then defendant will be obligated to pay only the maximum.

From the parties' point of view, a high-low agreement may make a lot of sense. From a court's point of view, however, it could seem like a hijacking of the trial process. The parties are using the courtroom to give themselves a hedged outcome, usually without the knowledge of the court or jury and it would seem reasonable to expect that two parties who can come close enough to establish high and low parameters on the outcome might be able to reach an actual settlement with a little more work and compromise. Nonetheless, courts have generally been willing to enforce high-low agreements, concluding that, while such agreements may change the dynamics of a trial, they do not threaten the adversarial process in the same way that a *Mary Carter* agreement would. *See, e.g., Garrett v. Mohammed,* 686 So. 2d 629 (Fla. Ct. App. 1996) (distinguishing high-low agreements from *Mary Carter* agreements and upholding validity of the former). *But see California Union Ins. Co. v. Liberty Mut. Ins. Co.,* 920 F. Supp. 908, *amended on other grounds,* 930 F. Supp. 320 (N.D. Ill. 1996) (holding that high-low agreement proposed by insurance carrier did not satisfy carrier's obligation to employ good faith efforts to settle dispute). *See generally* Andrea Alonso & Kevin Faley, *High-Low Agreements: You Can Have Your Cake and Eat It, Too,* 29 Fall Brief 69 (1999).

4. A Sample Settlement Agreement

Imagine that a dispute has arisen between two parties: plaintiff John Smith, an employee of the Acme Widget Company, and defendant, the Company. Plaintiff claims that Acme fired him because he is a Muslim. A federal statute — the Civil Rights Act of 1964, 42 U.S.C. §§2000e *et seq.* — prohibits employers from discriminating against their workers on the basis of religion, and plaintiff has brought a lawsuit in federal court claiming that the Company violated that statute. The Company denies any wrongdoing. After the parties conduct discovery, however, it appears that the circumstances surrounding plaintiff's dismissal were somewhat suspicious, and defendant decides that the best way to handle this lawsuit is to make it go away quickly and quietly. Plaintiff, for his part, is concerned primarily with being compensated for the financial turmoil and dignitary harm he feels the Company has caused him. Defendant makes some overtures of settlement to plaintiff and after some negotiation they arrive at the following agreement.

Settlement Agreement

WHEREAS—

John Smith was, at all times relevant to this agreement, an employee of the Acme Widget Company ("the Company"); and

Smith was fired from the Acme Widget Company on December 1, 2021; and

Smith claims that he was fired from the Company because of his adherence to the Muslim faith, in violation of his rights under the Federal Civil Rights Act of 1964, and has sued the Company in Federal District Court for the Southern District of New York in a case bearing docket number 2022 Civ. 0103 ("the Lawsuit");

AND WHEREAS—

The Company vigorously denies the allegations contained in Smith's complaint and denies any wrongdoing of any kind whatsoever;

AND WHEREAS—

After due consideration, both parties wish to settle this dispute in order to avoid the expense and burden of litigation;

NOW THEREFORE—

The parties hereby agree as follows:

Payment and Dismissal of the Lawsuit

1. Upon the execution of this agreement, the Company will establish an escrow account with the Acme bank and place in the account the sum of $100,000 (one hundred thousand dollars).

2. After the escrow account has been established, Smith and the Company will petition the Court to enter a dismissal of the Lawsuit with prejudice.

3. Upon the Court's entry of dismissal with prejudice, the Company will instruct the Acme bank to transfer the funds in the escrow account to Smith.

Release

4. Smith, on behalf of himself and his heirs, assigns, agents, estate, beneficiaries and designees, hereby releases and waives any and all claims and causes of action, of any kind whatsoever, whether known or unknown, and whether at law or equity, that Smith has ever had against the Company, from the beginning of time through the date of execution of this agreement, whether or not related in any way to the claims asserted in the Lawsuit.

5. The Company, on behalf of itself and its assigns, agents, subsidiaries, beneficiaries and designees, hereby releases and waives any and all claims and causes of action, of any kind whatsoever, whether known or unknown, and whether at law or equity, that the Company has ever had against Smith, from the beginning of time through the date of execution of this agreement, whether or not related in any way to the claims asserted in the Lawsuit.

6. These releases are conditioned on entry of dismissal of the Lawsuit and the transfer to Smith of the funds in the account, as provided herein; but, upon the satisfaction of those conditions, these releases become effective and irrevocable.

No Admission of Wrongdoing

7. Both parties hereby acknowledge and agree that no part of this agreement, nor the fact of entering into this agreement, constitutes an admission by either party of any fact, or of wrongdoing of any kind.

Confidentiality

8. The parties agree that they will keep all the terms of this agreement confidential. The parties will not disclose or convey to third parties, or cause to be disclosed or conveyed to third parties, any of the terms of this agreement including the amount of money awarded to Smith, except insofar as such disclosure is expressly required by law or judicial process and then only to the extent required.

9. The parties further agree that they will not disclose or convey to third parties, or cause to be disclosed or conveyed to third parties, any information that they have acquired through the discovery process in the Lawsuit, including, without limitation, documents, testimony, interrogatory responses, or any information contained therein, or information obtained in settlement discussions, except insofar as such disclosure is expressly required by law or judicial process and then only to the extent required.

10. This confidentiality provision includes, without limitation, communications with the press, with employees of the Company, and with other individuals suing the Company.

Agreed to this 1st day of June, 2022:

_____   _____

John Smith   Jessica Executive
                                                                   CEO, Acme Widget Co.

NOTES AND QUESTIONS

1. The recitations at the beginning of the sample settlement agreement above—particularly defendant's denial of any wrongdoing and the averment that the parties are settling to avoid the hardship of litigation—are fairly typical. Such recitations are largely window dressing. Only in rare cases would the parties' reasons for settling a dispute be relevant in subsequent proceedings, and it is generally understood that the mere fact that a defendant signed a settlement agreement does not constitute any admission of wrongdoing. But window dressing can be important, particularly in disputes that receive media attention or involve high-profile litigants. The public perception of a settlement may be as important to the long-term health of a company as the terms of the settlement itself. Even a confidentiality provision cannot guarantee that the public will not learn the terms of a settlement agreement, so it may behoove a lawyer to write for multiple audiences.

2. You may have noticed that the terms of this settlement agreement are rather spare, and that they are structured in a regimented fashion—e.g., transfer of funds is conditioned upon dismissal of the lawsuit; the release is conditioned upon the satisfaction of all other conditions; and so forth. This is another reflection of the distinctive nature of settlement agreements. The typical contract outside the settlement context is entered into by parties who intend to have a continuing relationship of some kind and (ideally) to cooperate over time. A settlement agreement, however, is typically entered into by parties who are embroiled in a dispute and may wish to have nothing more to do with each other once they have agreed to settlement terms. Thus, simplicity is a virtue in a settlement agreement.

3. As a general rule, settlement offers and settlement discussions are not admissible as evidence if the parties go on to litigate their dispute. *See, e.g.,* Fed. R. Civ. P. 68(b) ("An unaccepted offer is considered withdrawn, but it does not preclude a later offer. Evidence of an unaccepted offer is not admissible except in a proceeding to determine costs."). The reason for this rule should be clear: It would inhibit candor and prevent honest discussion of differences if the parties had to worry that their statements in settlement negotiations could later be used as evidence against them. The same rule applies to plea bargain discussions in criminal cases, as you may know from watching television crime dramas. *See* Federal Rule of Evidence 410 ("[E]vidence of the following is not, in any civil or criminal proceeding, admissible against the defendant who made [a] plea or was a participant in . . . plea discussions: . . . any statement made in the course of plea discussions with an attorney for the prosecuting authority which do not result in a plea of guilty or which result in a plea of guilty later withdrawn.").

4. Suppose that the Company in our imaginary settlement agreement also wanted to prevent John Smith from testifying against the Company on anyone *else's* behalf. Perhaps many employees have had problems with religious discrimination in the Company and Smith has first-hand knowledge of certain key events. Could the Company demand a settlement that forbids Smith from testifying in any subsequent proceedings:in effect, a term that buys Smith's silence? Would such a provision interfere with the rights of subsequent plaintiffs to gather evidence, or with the prerogatives of subsequent courts to conduct trials in the manner they think appropriate? Would it make a difference if the court in the first lawsuit agreed to

adopt the terms of the settlement as an injunction so that there was an actual judgment compelling Smith's silence?

The Supreme Court considered some of these questions in *Baker v. General Motors Corp.*, 522 U.S. 222 (1998). The plaintiff in *Baker* brought a lawsuit against General Motors (GM) in a Missouri court and tried to subpoena the testimony of one Ronald Elwell. Elwell had sued GM in an earlier action in Michigan. That earlier action settled and, as part of the settlement, Elwell had agreed that he would not testify in any other proceedings against the company. The Michigan court incorporated that agreement into an injunction that barred Elwell from giving such testimony. When Baker sought to compel Elwell's testimony in Missouri, GM attempted to use the Michigan injunction to stop him.

The Supreme Court disallowed GM's attempt to exclude the testimony. The Court held that, although injunctions are judgments entitled to interstate enforcement under the Full Faith and Credit Clause, the Missouri court was not acting in violation of the injunction in ordering Elwell's testimony. Only Elwell was bound by the injunction and he was not a party to the later Missouri proceeding. GM was attempting to go beyond the literal terms of the injunction and bind a Missouri court to its terms, preventing that court from hearing evidence in a matter involving a third party's claim. While the Michigan courts may have chosen to enforce the injunction by crafting an evidentiary rule to reach this result, the Court held that full faith and credit does not require other states to enforce judgments in precisely the manner in which they are enforced by the rendering state.

The Court did not reach the question whether Baker's due process rights would have been violated had he brought his lawsuit in Michigan and had the evidence then been excluded by a Michigan court. Nor did it comment on whether Elwell could be held in contempt by a Michigan court for giving testimony in Missouri if such testimony were found to violate the terms of the Michigan injunction, particularly if Elwell had sought out the opportunity to testify.

B. *THE FORMS AND FUNCTIONS OF ADR*

When people speak of ADR, they usually mean something more than simple settlement. "ADR" usually refers to the range of proceedings and procedures that can augment or substitute for the trial process, sometimes with an eye toward promoting settlement but sometimes as a completely separate mechanism for resolving disputes.

Broadly speaking, ADR falls into three categories. The first category includes those ADR methods that seek to replace the court system with a method of adjudication that is similar in form but that the litigants believe to be better or more efficient. We can refer to these as "adversarial" forms of ADR. Adversarial ADR methods may retain many of the basic features of the trial-court model of adjudication including, for example, the development of evidence through formal discovery, legal briefing and arguments, and a court-like forum presided over by a neutral decision maker who acts as a detached referee. *Arbitration* is the most common example of adversarial ADR and it can look a lot like traditional adjudication.

The second broad category includes ADR methods that more clearly merit the description "alternative." Such methods may reject the strictly adversarial character of civil litigation in favor of a model that places more emphasis on cooperation and compromise. They also may seek to address concerns different from those on which civil litigation has traditionally focused. While courts concentrate principally on money damages and enforceable legal rights, these ADR methods reflect concern about such matters as the health of the parties' ongoing relationship, the parties' reputation and standing within the community as a result of the dispute, or the parties' sense of indignation and their desire for an apology. We can refer to these as "non-adversarial" forms of ADR because they stray further from the traditional head-to-head model of civil litigation, though it would be a mistake to think that these forms of ADR are without disagreement and conflict. *Mediation* is the most prominent example of non-adversarial ADR, and even that term encompasses a broad array of possibilities.

Finally, there are various ADR methods that serve to supplement the more traditional forms of litigation or that operate in parallel with them, rather than seeking to replace them. Some of these involve attempts by the parties to predict the likely outcome of a trial so that they can decide how much it is sensible to spend on litigating or settling the dispute. Other methods actively seek to encourage settlement between the parties, requiring them to go through procedures specially designed for that purpose as a condition of pursuing civil litigation through the courts. These "supplemental" forms of ADR include a broad array of possibilities and they are significant both in the impact they may have on the settlement of civil lawsuits and as forms of dispute resolution in their own right.

1. Adversarial Forms of ADR—Arbitration

As a general matter, adversarial forms of ADR arise out of contractual arrangements: Two parties who have some pre-existing relationship agree ahead of time that any disputes that arise between them will be resolved not in a court of law, but under the auspices of a privately run dispute-resolution organization. In a sense, such a contractual provision (usually referred to as an *arbitration clause*) is similar to the forum selection clauses and choice of law provisions that we have looked at in previous chapters. In those instruments, the parties agreed to waive certain rights they might have asserted in a court proceeding—a right to object to a forum on the basis of personal jurisdiction or venue, or a right to have the law of a certain state apply to a dispute—in favor of an agreed-upon forum and predictable law. The arbitration clause takes this idea further: The parties waive their right to invoke the entire court system in favor of an alternative, private forum.

Historically, there was some question as to whether parties could be forced to arbitrate against their will, even where they had agreed to a facially valid arbitration clause. Arbitration was widely looked upon as a disfavored alternative to adjudication and some courts refused to enforce arbitration clauses on the grounds that they violated public policy. *See Gilmer v. Interstate/Johnson Lane Corp.*, 500 U.S. 20, 23 (1991) (describing "the longstanding judicial hostility to arbitration agreements that had existed at English common law and had been adopted by American courts"). All of that changed when Congress passed the Federal Arbitration Act in 1925, later reenacted and codified as the Arbitration Act of 1947. *See* 9 U.S.C. §§1-11. The Arbitration Act overruled judicial hostility to arbitration and provided that a written agreement to arbitrate controversies arising out of a contract "shall be valid, irrevocable, and enforceable, save upon such grounds as exist at law or in equity for the revocation of any contract." *Id.* §2. In other words, following passage of the Act, parties cannot avoid an arbitration clause except on a basis that would nullify it as a contractual provision, such as fraud or mutual mistake. As the Supreme Court has explained, "[b]y its terms, the Act leaves no place for the exercise of discretion by a district court, but instead mandates that district courts shall direct the parties to proceed to arbitration on issues as to which an arbitration agreement has been signed. [9 U.S.C.] §§3, 4." *Dean Witter Reynolds, Inc. v. Byrd,* 470 U.S. 213, 218 (1985).

If neither party disputes that an arbitration clause is valid and applies, there is no need to invoke the provisions of the Act in order to begin the arbitration. Suppose, however, that one of the parties tries to do an end-run around the arbitration clause by preemptively bringing suit in a court. That's when the enforcement provisions of the Federal Arbitration Act become important. In such a case, defendant would file a *motion to compel arbitration* with the court, asking the court to force the recalcitrant party to abide by the arbitration clause. *See* 9 U.S.C. §4 ("A party aggrieved by the alleged failure, neglect, or refusal of another to arbitrate under a written agreement for arbitration may petition any United States district court . . . for an order directing that such arbitration proceed in the manner provided for in such agreement."). If the court determines that the parties have made an enforceable agreement to arbitrate, it will grant the motion and *stay* the court case—the case remains alive, but inactive—in order to permit the arbitration to proceed. *See id.* §3 (providing for stay of proceedings when motion to compel arbitration is granted). If, instead, the court determines that there is no enforceable agreement to arbitrate, then it will reject the motion. The party alleged to be in default of the arbitration agreement can request a jury trial on the disputed factual issues surrounding the existence of the agreement (except in admiralty cases). *Id.* §4. When a lawsuit includes both claims that are subject to arbitration and claims that are not, the arbitrable claims must be sent to arbitration, "even if this will lead to piecemeal litigation." *KPMG LLP v. Cocchi,* 132 S. Ct. 23, 24 (2011) (*per curiam*).

Here is an example of what a simple arbitration clause might look like:

XII. Dispute Resolution

The parties hereby agree that any controversy or claim arising out of or relating to this contract or any alleged breach thereof shall be submitted for arbitration and decision to the American Arbitration Association ["AAA"]. Any such proceeding shall be governed by the Commercial Arbitration Rules of the AAA. The parties further agree that a judgment on any award rendered by the arbitrators may be entered in any court of competent jurisdiction.

Arbitration clauses of this kind are surprisingly common. You have almost certainly agreed to any number of them yourself. Look at the contract terms printed on the back of your gym membership, or in the lease on your apartment, or on any of the many website portals where you must click a button agreeing to a contract and a set of rules before entering. Chances are that some of those contracts, perhaps most, provide that any disputes that arise between the parties must be resolved through arbitration.

Why are businesses so enamored of these arbitration clauses? The standard answers usually given by both commentators and potential litigants are predictability, a quicker and more efficient mechanism for reaching a final resolution to a dispute, and cost savings. These provisions may also stipulate a convenient place or a tribunal that the author expects to be sympathetic. As we explore the various issues that arise when parties enter arbitration, you can decide for yourself whether you think it likely that arbitration will promote these ends. More recent developments in the Court's treatment of arbitration under the FAA have introduced another factor that may eclipse all others: the possibility that corporate actors can use arbitration clauses to shield themselves from any form of classwide litigation in major components of their business. We address this important topic separately in the next section. First, however, it is necessary to understand how arbitration works and to have a basic understanding of the structure and operation of the FAA.

a. How Arbitration Works

Arbitration proceedings are generally conducted under the auspices of private organizations. Two of the more prominent firms for domestic commercial disputes are the American Arbitration Association (AAA), http://www.adr.org, a New York–based not-for-profit corporation that has offices, and conducts arbitrations, throughout the country, and JAMS (formerly Judicial Arbitration and Mediation Services), http://www.jamsadr.com, also a nationwide commercial provider, based in California.

All the rules that govern such private arbitrations are the result of contracting between the parties. This does not mean that parties reinvent the wheel every time they put an arbitration clause into an agreement. The AAA and organizations like it provide "default rules" for their proceedings, and the parties usually incorporate these default rules by reference when they draft an arbitration clause. But parties have the power to contract around these rules if they choose. Thus, Rule One of the Commercial Arbitration Rules of the AAA provides:

R-1. Agreement of Parties

(a) The parties shall be deemed to have made these rules a part of their arbitration agreement whenever they have provided for arbitration by the American Arbitration Association (hereinafter AAA) under its Commercial Arbitration Rules or for arbitration by the AAA of a domestic commercial dispute without specifying particular rules. These rules and any amendment of them shall apply in the form in effect at the time the administrative requirements are met for a Demand for Arbitration or Submission Agreement received by the AAA. The parties, by written agreement, may vary the procedures set forth in these rules. After appointment of the arbitrator, such modifications may be made only with the consent of the arbitrator.

Notice the next to last sentence of that rule: "The parties, by written agreement, may vary the procedures set forth in these rules." This is one of the signature features of commercial arbitration: The parties can agree ahead of time (or even after a dispute arises) to forgo the procedures they do not want or need and keep only those they desire.

In smaller arbitrations, the parties may even enjoy cost savings by doing without lawyers. The conventional wisdom is that arbitration proceedings are more "informal" than court proceedings, making it more realistic for individuals with no legal background to represent themselves. It is probably true that smaller arbitration proceedings generally involve jumping through fewer hoops than a court proceeding (written submissions, filing deadlines, and so on), making the process more accessible to the average person. Even in a smaller arbitration, however, if the stakes are high from the perspective of the individual involved, it will probably be just as important to have legal representation as it would be in a courtroom.

An arbitration is presided over by one or more arbitrators, neutral decision makers who perform much the same function as a judge in a lawsuit. But there are important differences between arbitrators and judges, starting with how the arbitrators are chosen. In a traditional lawsuit, the parties have very little to say about which judge will preside over the dispute. With the exception of unusual situations where a judge might have to *recuse* herself (ask to be replaced because she has personal knowledge of the dispute or some conflict of interest), parties must accept whatever judge is randomly assigned to their case, even if the judge has little expertise in the substantive area at issue in the dispute or is otherwise an unattractive choice from the parties' perspective.

In some arbitrations, however, particularly commercial arbitrations or other high-stakes disputes, the parties have much more to say about who will resolve their claims. First, the arbitrators for such a dispute are often drawn from a pool of individuals with knowledge and experience in the substantive area in question. The AAA, for example, maintains national panels of arbitrators with expertise in certain fields—commercial transactions, real estate, employment law, and so forth—from which arbitrators can be drawn for particular cases. And parties sometimes employ procedures that give them more control in selecting the arbitrators who will adjudicate their disagreement. One procedure that businesses sometimes use in large commercial disputes involves each party selecting one arbitrator, sometimes from lists of potential candidates that each has compiled. The parties will then agree on a method for selecting a third, "outside" arbitrator, perhaps by drawing randomly from an expert panel put together by an organization like the AAA, or by permitting the first two arbitrators to choose. Of course, all the arbitrators are still responsible for rendering fair and impartial decisions. But being able to have more control over the process of selection can give the parties greater confidence that their dispute is being resolved by competent and trustworthy decision makers.

Arbitrators are paid professionals and the parties pay the arbitrators' salaries and any other expenses associated with the proceeding. Arbitrators are often drawn from the ranks of experienced private attorneys and retired judges, though it is not necessary for an arbitrator to be a lawyer. In a particular case, the parties might select an arbitrator with expertise in a relevant substantive area, like economics or corporate finance. While some individuals work as full-time arbitrators, many do so on the side while maintaining full-time positions as lawyers, academics, or other professionals. (Active-duty federal judges cannot serve as paid private arbitrators and state judges generally operate under a similar restriction.)

b. Discovery in Arbitration

One of the major differences between arbitration and formal adjudication is the extent of discovery. As we saw in Chapter 5, discovery in the United States is often expensive in a large commercial lawsuit. Broad requests for documents and numerous depositions are a hallmark of discovery practice in the United States in such cases. In contrast, discovery during arbitration is often more limited in scope than would be the case under the Federal Rules. Although arbitrators may have power to order discovery under the rules of various arbitral institutions, such discovery often happens more quickly and under tighter constraints. This is particularly true in international commercial arbitration, where arbitration can offer a compromise between the "open" discovery of common law systems and the more restricted approach to the exchange of information in civil law countries. Parties to an arbitration can also agree to keep their discovery and arbitral proceedings confidential, an option over which they have less control in a civil trial.

Arbitrators, or the parties to an arbitration, commonly customize discovery for the particular case. At the outset, they will define the scope and mechanisms of discovery, perhaps authorizing limited exchanges of documents and witness statements supporting the party's own case to begin the process.

Note that the Federal Arbitration Act (§7) authorizes arbitrators to subpoena witnesses and documents, and if the subpoena is not complied with, a court will enforce the order.

c. The Available Relief and the Powers of the Arbitrators

As is the case in lawsuits, parties in arbitration proceedings most commonly seek relief in the form of monetary damages. Generally speaking, this presents no problem. The parties have empowered the arbitrators to resolve their dispute, and that includes awarding appropriate damages. But what about disputes involving requests for equitable relief? When a court grants equitable relief, you will remember, it does something more than award money damages. It issues an order that requires the parties to do something, such as convey property or refrain from taking certain actions. What problems might such a request for relief present in an arbitration proceeding?

First, practical constraints on arbitrators may limit their ability to grant certain forms of equitable relief. Consider a case in which the relief requested would require continuing oversight by the tribunal — for example, a case in which the shareholders in a corporation want to get rid of the managers who are currently in charge and place the business in receivership, temporarily replacing those managers with someone working under the supervision of the tribunal. An arbitrator, unlike a judge, may not be a full-time decision maker and may not wish to make such an open-ended commitment to a case. Courts can transfer cases from one judge to another if they have to, so they can preside over disputes that involve a long commitment, like the institutional reform of a prison, even if particular judges are unable to remain in charge over the course of the entire suit. Practically speaking, there are no similar mechanisms available in private arbitration.

And the limitations on the forms of relief that an arbitrator can award may not simply be a matter of practical constraint. Consider requests for equitable relief that implicate *third-party interests.* For example, suppose that two parties enter into a contract for the sale of a piece of intellectual property, like a patented device. The buyer, let us suppose, acquires the patent, but then completely fails to fulfill any of the contractual obligations (like paying royalties) that he made to the seller. As a result, the seller decides to request something more than monetary damages. Instead, the seller asks for *rescission*—an order that "undoes" the formation of the contract, essentially ruling that the contract never took effect in the first place and the patent rights belonged to the seller all along. After the buyer acquired the patent, however, he entered into contracts with other people (third parties) to produce and sell the device. If the seller succeeds in rescinding the original contract of sale, then the rights of these third parties under their own contracts may be placed in jeopardy—they may suddenly have unenforceable agreements with someone who never (legally) owned the patented device in the first place. What about their rights?

When a court decides a case such as this, it will be obliged to consider the interests of third parties in determining whether equitable relief is appropriate and what form it should take. A court might even bring the third parties into the lawsuit as parties themselves; or, if it is unable to do so, decline to decide the case. (Remember the "required parties" rule—Fed. R. Civ. P. 19—from Chapter 8.) A court is able to take such extraordinary steps—requiring individuals to be added to a lawsuit—because it is an arm of the government and, when it acts within its jurisdiction and other constraints on its authority, it is exercising the power of the state. But an arbitration is the result of a contractual arrangement between the parties, who have agreed to submit their dispute to an arbitrator who is neither an agent of the state nor constrained by rigid procedural safeguards. Why should it be possible for an arbitrator to make demands upon third parties who never agreed to submit to such a private authority?

The answer is that such actions generally are not possible for an arbitrator. As a general matter, arbitrators can only exercise the powers that they have been granted by the parties who have agreed to the arbitration. While this may include granting some forms of equitable relief—like an order that one party stop an activity that infringes on the rights of the other—it generally will not include the power to compromise the rights of third parties.

Finally, as should be obvious, arbitrators have no power to make or invalidate law. Even though an arbitration looks like a court proceeding, arbitrators do not exercise the power of the state, regardless of what individual litigants might agree to. Their opinions are not published like judicial opinions, do not count as "precedent" in the jurisdiction where they operate, and are not "persuasive authority" that litigants or courts can cite in future disputes. While an arbitrator may engage in the interpretive exercise of construing a statute or even deciding constitutional questions for purposes of ruling on a specific claim, an arbitrator cannot establish precedent or invalidate a statute in the way a judge does.

d.   Judicial Review of Arbitration Decisions

The forms of judicial review that are available for the parties to an arbitration are limited. Another signature feature of arbitration, commercial or otherwise, is that decisions rendered by arbitrators are final and unreviewable except in a narrow range of circumstances. In some cases, this feature of arbitration can reduce the overall cost of resolving a dispute. If an arbitrator chooses not to follow the strict letter of the law in deciding cases, however, the aggrieved party may have little recourse, even if the parties have agreed ahead of time that any dispute between them should be governed by the law of a particular state. The Supreme Court has held that an arbitrator's failure to follow the letter of the law is not a ground for denying enforcement to an award under the Federal Arbitration Act unless the arbitrator strays so far as to exhibit "manifest disregard" for the law—a heavy burden. *Wilko v. Swan*, 346 U.S. 427, 436–437 (1953), *overruled on other grounds, Rodriguez de Quijas v. Shearson/American Express*, 490 U.S. 477 (1989). An arbitrator has a duty to follow the law, but she operates under much looser restrictions than would a judge, whose decisions on legal issues are subject to *de novo* appellate review.

Importantly, these constraints on judicial review are not subject to alteration by the parties. The Supreme Court has held that sections 9, 10, and 11 of the Federal Arbitration Act—those responsible for "judicial review to confirm, vacate, or modify arbitration awards"—constitute the "exclusive" means by which parties may obtain such review and may not be supplemented or altered by agreement. *Hall Street Assocs. v. Mattel, Inc.*, 552 U.S. 576, 1400 (2008). Indeed, following *Hall Street*, there may be some question whether "manifest disregard" for the law can still serve as grounds for reversal. That standard, though widely applied, is not expressly set forth in the FAA. *Compare, e.g., Citigroup Global Markets v. Bacon*, 562 F.3d 349 (5th Cir. 2009) (finding that *Hall Street* requires rejection of "manifest disregard" as grounds for reversal) *with Comedy Club Inc. v. Improv West Assocs.*, 553 F.3d 1277 (9th Cir. 2009) (holding that "manifest disregard" can be understood as an interpretation of FAA §10(a)(4), which authorizes reversal "where the arbitrators exceeded their powers, or so imperfectly executed them that a mutual, final, and definite award upon the subject matter submitted was not made," and hence survives *Hall Street*).

Arbitrators often render brief opinions with little explanation for their decision, sometimes announcing only who won and the amount of any award. This reflects the different functions that arbitrators and judges serve. A judicial opinion performs a distinctively public function. The opinion does not merely explain the basis of the decision to the parties (and to a reviewing court, if the parties appeal), it also contributes to the law. Since an arbitrator's decision does not "make law" in this fashion and is ordinarily not subject to judicial review, the arbitrator has little reason to provide a detailed explanation for the result.

A party may also be able to obtain judicial review by claiming that the arbitrators have "exceeded their authority." As we saw in the previous section, there are some forms of relief that an arbitrator cannot grant, perhaps because they implicate the rights of third parties or require a level of supervision and oversight that an arbitrator is not equipped to provide. If an arbitrator attempts to award such relief nonetheless, the losing party might be able to convince a court to invalidate the arbitrator's decision on the grounds that it exceeds the arbitrator's powers. Other bases for invalidating an arbitration award include demonstrable corruption or bias on the part of the arbitrators or fraud perpetrated by one of the parties. *See* 9 U.S.C. §10 (setting forth grounds for vacating or rehearing an arbitration award when enforcement is sought in court).

However, the Supreme Court has made clear the exceedingly narrow scope of these avenues of review. In *Oxford Health Plans v. Sutter*, 569 U.S. 564 (2013), a doctor brought suit against a health insurance company over its alleged failure to satisfy certain payment obligations. The company moved to compel arbitration pursuant to a clause that stated: "No civil action concerning any dispute arising under this Agreement shall be instituted before any court, and all such disputes shall be submitted to final and binding arbitration in New Jersey, pursuant to the rules of the American Arbitration Association with one arbitrator." The doctor asked the arbitrator to undertake a class arbitration, and the company responded by arguing that class arbitration was not authorized under the clause. The arbitrator sided with the plaintiff and agreed to conduct a class proceeding. Oxford then went to federal court and asked for an order vacating the arbitrator's decision on the grounds that he had "exceeded his powers" under FAA §10(a)(4). The lower federal courts refused, and the Supreme Court unanimously affirmed. In a strongly worded opinion, the Court reiterated that §10(a)(4) "permits courts to vacate an arbitral decision only when the arbitrator strayed from his delegated task of interpreting a contract, not when he performed that task poorly." *Sutter*, 133 S. Ct. at 571–572. Only if the arbitrator "issu[es] an award that simply reflects his own notions of economic justice rather than drawing its essence from the contract may a court overturn his determination." *Id.* at 2068 (citations and internal alterations omitted). The "sole question" for a reviewing court "is whether the arbitrator (even arguably) interpreted the parties' contract, not whether he got its meaning right or wrong." *Id.* In this case, the arbitrator had twice relied on the language of the arbitration clause in concluding that he had the authority to conduct a class proceeding. That being so, "[t]he arbitrator's construction holds, however good, bad, or ugly." *Id.* at 572–573.

e.   Collecting on the Award

When a party prevails in an arbitration, it does not obtain a "judgment" but rather an arbitral "award." Only courts are empowered to issue "judgments." The difference is more than semantic. As you have learned, judgments receive special treatment under the Full Faith and Credit Clause, U.S. Const., Art. IV §1, and its implementing statute, the Full Faith and Credit Act, 28 U.S.C. §1738. A litigant who obtains a judgment can go to any state where the defendant has assets and seek enforcement of the judgment, often merely by registering it with the court to secure that court's enforcement assistance. *See* 28 U.S.C. §1963 (registration of federal judgments); Uniform Enforcement of Foreign Judgments Act (1964 Revised Act), 13 U.L.A. 152 (1986), explored in Chapter 6, *supra*.

Congress has created an effective summary enforcement mechanism for arbitration awards as well. So long as the parties agreed in their arbitration clause that judgment may be entered on the arbitral award, the Federal Arbitration Act provides that any court specified by the parties may enter such a judgment within one year of the issuance of the award upon the application of one of the parties. *See* 9 U.S.C. §9. If you look back at the sample arbitration clause at the beginning of this section you will see that it contains such a provision: "The parties further agree that a judgment on any award rendered by the arbitrators may be entered in any court of competent jurisdiction." Once a judgment on the award is entered, it will be treated as any traditional court judgment and enforced accordingly. *See* 9 U.S.C. §13.

In addition, the existence of an international treaty, the United Nations Convention on the Recognition and Enforcement of Foreign Arbitral Awards of June 10, 1958, makes international arbitration awards covered by the Convention enforceable in other countries more easily than are traditional foreign country judgments. *See* 9 U.S.C. §§201–208 (provisions of the Federal Arbitration Act implementing the treaty).

NOTES AND QUESTIONS

1. *Arbitrability and the Scope of the Arbitration Clause.* One issue that has received considerable attention in the courts in recent years is the question of *arbitrability*—that is, what claims come within the ambit of an arbitration clause and what claims do not. Recall our earlier discussion of the party who goes to court and brings a lawsuit in an attempt to preempt an arbitration clause, leading defendant to respond by filing a motion to compel arbitration. Suppose that plaintiff responds to the motion to compel by arguing that his claims are not among those that were meant to be included in the arbitration clause. For example, consider a contract for the performance of some service. A claim that one party has refused to perform those services will pretty clearly be subject to arbitration. But what about a claim that one party was hurt on the other's premises while performing those services? There might be some dispute as to whether that tort claim falls under the arbitration clause. *See, e.g.*, Elizabeth G. Thornburg, *Contracting with Tortfeasors: Mandatory Arbitration Clauses and Personal Injury Claims*, 67 Law & Contemp. Probs. 253 (2004) (discussing proliferation of clauses encompassing tort claims in otherwise contractual relationships). Such questions of arbitrability, analogous to questions of subject matter jurisdiction in civil litigation, must usually be decided at the threshold of the proceedings.

2. *Who Decides the Threshold Issues?* Another threshold question arises when a party invokes an arbitration clause: who should *decide* whether a claim is subject to arbitration. In an example like the one in the previous note, where the parties disagree about whether plaintiff's claim comes within the ambit of the arbitration clause, who should resolve that question? Should a court decide the issue, or should it send the dispute to an arbitrator and let the arbitrator, in effect, rule on the scope of its own authority? The American system of arbitration law provides an idiosyncratic answer to that question.

Beginning with the case of *Prima Paint Corp. v. Flood & Conklin Mfg.*, 388 U.S. 395 (1967), the Supreme Court has interpreted the Arbitration Act to embody a strong preference in favor of having arbitrators decide any questions that fall within the scope of an arbitration clause, including questions about the validity and scope of the clause itself. Thus, arbitrators will often rule on the scope and validity of their own authority to decide the issues in the first place. What is more, the Court has held that this principle demands that fine distinctions be drawn between challenges to the validity of an entire contract and challenges narrowly focused on the validity of an arbitration clause considered in isolation.

Prima Paint involved a claim that a contract containing an arbitration clause had been fraudulently induced by one of the parties. The party claiming fraud argued that the federal courts should resolve this threshold issue, reasoning that the arbitration clause could have no effect if the entire contract had been induced by fraud. The Court disagreed. The FAA, the Court held, requires all issues that the contract commits to the arbitrators to be decided by the arbitrators, including issues that might invalidate the entire contract. If a party claims that an arbitration clause specifically, as a distinct component of the agreement, has been fraudulently induced or is otherwise invalid, then a federal court may decide that claim in the first instance. Such a claim calls into question whether there is any proper basis for the arbitrators to exercise authority at all. But if the party merely claims that there was fraudulent inducement of the entire contract, of which the arbitration clause happens to be one part, then the Arbitration Act requires the arbitrators to rule on that claim (assuming that the clause, by its terms, commits the issue to their decision).

The Supreme Court has reaffirmed this aspect of the *Prima Paint* doctrine even in cases where plaintiff alleges that the contract is prohibited by statute and hence is illegal. *See Buckeye Check Cashing v. Cardegna*, 546 U.S. 440 (2006) (holding that the arbitrators must decide (1) whether a contract violates state usury laws and is void, and also (2) whether the arbitration clause gives them power to determine that voidness question). Similarly, the FAA supersedes state laws that would otherwise vest authority in a specialized administrative agency to hear and resolve disputes between parties. *See Preston v. Ferrer*, 552 U.S. 346, 348 (2008). So long as the agreement between the parties is one that "evidences a transaction involving commerce," 9 U.S.C. §2, and that submits disagreements for resolution by arbitration, all such questions are reserved to the arbitrators for decision.

Notice that the cases cited above raise two issues. The first involves the validity or invalidity of an entire contract that contains an arbitration clause. The *Prima Paint* doctrine holds that the arbitrators decide that question, *if* the arbitration clause commits it to the arbitrator's authority. An arbitration clause need not be an all-or-nothing proposition. Some arbitration clauses commit only specific issues to the arbitrators for decision. *Prima Paint* held that arbitrators can decide threshold questions about the validity of a whole contract (as distinct from the threshold question that focuses specifically on whether the arbitration clause, considered in isolation, is valid), but they can only do so if the arbitration clause grants them that power. Thus, a second question arises: When the clause does not spell out exactly what issues are and are not committed to the arbitrators, how does one interpret its scope?

In *First Options of Chicago v. Kaplan*, 514 U.S. 938 (1995), the Court offered some guidance. *First Options* drew a distinction between two types of question: who decides whether a particular dispute falls within the agreed-upon scope of an arbitration clause (that is, how to *apply* the clause); and who decides the scope of the clause when the parties disagree about even that basic question (that is, who rules upon the *arbitrability* issue). On the former question, the Court continued in a deferential mode. If the parties agree that an arbitration clause governs a certain type of issue, and the only question is whether a particular dispute qualifies for arbitration, then it is for the arbitrators to decide. On the latter question, however, the Court preserved a more active role for the courts. "When deciding whether the parties agreed to arbitrate a certain matter," the Court explained, "courts generally . . . should apply ordinary state-law principles that govern the formation of contracts." *Id.* at 944. And when the question is whether the parties agreed to submit the arbitrability question itself to the arbitrators, the court should be especially cautious. As to that question, the Court explained, the law treats silence or ambiguity about the question "*who* (primarily) should decide arbitrability" differently from the way it treats silence or ambiguity about the question "*whether* a particular merits-related dispute is arbitrable because it is within the scope of a valid arbitration agreement." *Id.* at 944-945. Courts should "hesitate to interpret silence or ambiguity on the 'who should decide arbitrability' point as giving the arbitrators that power," the Court explained, "for doing so might too often force unwilling parties to arbitrate a matter they reasonably would have thought a judge, not an arbitrator, would decide." *Id.* at 945. While "any doubts concerning the scope of arbitrable issues should be resolved in favor of arbitration," *Moses H. Cone Memorial Hosp. v. Mercury Constr. Corp.*, 460 U.S. 1, 24-25 (1983), any doubts concerning who should decide the threshold question of arbitrability should be resolved in favor of court review. This distinction between the application of an arbitration clause of agreed-upon scope and the resolution of a dispute over the scope of a clause when that scope is contested, though perhaps elusive, is important and unavoidable.

The Supreme Court has gone on to rule that a "statute of limitations" contained in an arbitration code is presumptively a matter for the arbitrators themselves to rule upon. In *Howsam v. Dean Witter Reynolds, Inc.*, 537 U.S. 79 (2002), the Court reviewed the six-year deadline on arbitration disputes contained in the National Association of Securities Dealers Arbitration Code. It found that disputes over such a limitations provision — whether it applies in a particular dispute, for example, or whether it has expired — do not present one of those "gateway" issues that parties would normally expect a court to step in and rule on. Rather, the Court found, parties should expect such a provision to be encompassed within the broad language of any standard arbitration clause and hence to be entrusted to the decision of the arbitrators. *Id.* at 83-86. *See also Pacificare Health Systems v. Book*, 538 U.S. 401, 403-407 (2003) (ruling that arbitrators should presumptively be given first opportunity to decide whether arbitral rules permit them to award triple damages on a RICO claim, even though plaintiffs argue that they will be denied "meaningful relief" without such damages); *Vimar Seguros y Reaseguros, S.A. v. M/V Sky Reefer*, 515 U.S. 528, 540 (1995) (refusing to rule on whether arbitration proceeding would violate liability rules contained in federal statute until arbitrators have opportunity to decide whether to apply those liability rules themselves).

Indeed, in one case, the Court vacated and remanded a judgment of the South Carolina Supreme Court simply because it was unsure whether the arbitrators had exercised independent judgment on a threshold issue. In *Green Tree Financial Corp. v. Bazzle*, 539 U.S. 444 (2003), an arbitrator had to decide whether he was authorized to conduct a "class arbitration" — the arbitration version of a class action. The arbitrator granted the plaintiff's request to certify a class, conducted the proceeding, and went on to issue an award and attorneys' fees. One might have thought this indicated that the arbitrator had decided the class arbitration issue in the affirmative. The South Carolina courts rejected the defendant's subsequent attempts to appeal, affirming the arbitrator's award. The Supreme Court of the United States vacated the decision, however, sending it back for further proceedings. The sequence of events in the proceedings below made it unclear whether the arbitrator had exercised independent judgment in determining that class arbitration was authorized, or whether he instead believed that he was required to certify the class by certain orders that had been issued by the state court. That lack of clarity was enough for a plurality of the Court to send the case back in order to ensure that the arbitrator was the true decision maker on all those issues entrusted to him under the parties' contract.

The cases discussed above make clear that the Federal Arbitration Act applies to actions filed in state court as well as actions filed in federal court. Indeed, as the Supreme Court has explained, "[s]tate courts rather than federal courts are most frequently called upon to apply the Federal Arbitration Act." *Nitro-Lift Technologies v. Howard*, 568 U.S. 17, 17-18 (2012) (*per curiam*). In *Nitro-Lift*, two Oklahoma employees received a demand to arbitrate from their former company when they took jobs allegedly in violation of a non-compete provision in their old employment contract. In response, the former employees brought suit in Oklahoma state court to have the non-compete restriction declared void. The trial court dismissed and instructed the parties to arbitrate pursuant to an arbitration clause contained in the same contract, but the Oklahoma Supreme Court reversed, finding that the courts could disregard the arbitration clause and reach the merits, under which the court found the contractual non-compete provision void as against public policy. On the arbitration issue, the Oklahoma court's decision could fairly be characterized as hostile to the Supreme Court's FAA precedents. The Court reversed, strongly reasserting its authority in a *per curiam* opinion in which it emphasized the "great importance . . . that state supreme courts adhere to a correct interpretation of the legislation." *Id.*

The Supreme Court has applied the *Prima Paint/First Options* doctrine in an unyielding fashion, finding that the text of the Federal Arbitration Act does not permit *ad hoc* exceptions. In *Henry Schein, Inc. v. Archer & White Sales*, 139 S. Ct. 524 (2019), the Court rejected an exception adopted by some lower federal courts that permitted a court to reject a motion to compel arbitration if it concluded that the moving party's argument that the dispute was subject to arbitration was "wholly groundless" under the contract. "We must interpret the Act as written," the Court held, and when "the parties' contract delegates the arbitrability question to an arbitrator, a court may not override the contract . . . even if the court thinks that the argument that the arbitration agreement applies to a particular dispute is wholly groundless." *Id.* at 529. Recall, however, that the Court has also identified an important caveat to the enforcement of such delegation provisions, explaining: "we should not assume that the parties agreed to arbitrate arbitrability unless there is clear and unmistakable evidence that they did so." *Rent-A-Center, W. v. Jackson*, 561 U.S. 63, 69 n.1 (2010). *See also In re: Automotive Parts Antitrust Litig.*, 951 F.3d 377, 381-382 (6th Cir. 2020) (finding that "an arbitration clause's incorporation of [the American Arbitration Association's] Commercial Rules suffices as "clear and unmistakable evidence" to delegate arbitrability to an arbitrator.").

The Federal Arbitration Act does specify some narrow exceptions to the *Prima Paint/First Options* rule. The Court explored one such exception in *New Prime, Inc. v. Oliveira*, 139 S. Ct. 532 (2019). *Oliveira* involved §1 of the Federal Arbitration Act, which says that "nothing herein" may compel the parties to arbitrate in a dispute involving "contracts of employment" for workers in certain transportation industries. *See* 9 U.S.C. §1. Oliveira was a driver for a trucking company who participated in a class action against New Prime alleging that the company denied lawful wages to their drivers in violation of the Federal Fair Labor Standards Act and various state laws. Oliveira and the other drivers had contractual relationships with New Prime, but they worked as independent contractors rather than employees, and New Prime argued that the drivers' status as independent contractors brought them outside the carve-out of §1 of the Act. This raised two questions: Does the exception in §1 apply to contracts of employment only for full-time employees or does it also reach the employment contracts of independent contractors; and can a court decide that arbitrability question itself even if the contract appears to assign such questions to an arbitrator? The Supreme Court answered both questions in the affirmative. On the merits question, the Court looked to common usage in 1925, the year the Act was enacted, and found that "contract of employment" would have been understood to describe the subject of the contract (employment), not the status of the contracting party (employee vs. independent contractor). Hence, the statutory exemption applied. On the question of arbitrability, the Court held that the carve-out contained in §1 was a "necessarily antecedent statutory inquiry" to any question of interpretation or enforcement of the arbitration clause. As with the provision requiring that a contract "evidenc[e] a transaction involving commerce," 9 U.S.C. §2, the §1 carve-outs are statutory limitations on the applicability of the Act's mandatory enforcement provisions that the court must adjudicate before giving effect to an arbitration clause.

3. *Separate Arbitration Agreements and the* Rent-A-Center *Doctrine.* In *Rent-A-Center, West v. Jackson*, 561 U.S. 63 (2010), the Supreme Court made the presumption in favor of having the arbitrators rather than the courts decide threshold issues even more robust. *Rent-A-Center* involved a contract entered into between a worker and an employer entitled "Mutual Agreement to Arbitrate Claims." The contract was solely concerned with the agreement of the parties to arbitrate. One clause of the agreement, called the "delegation provision," specified that the arbitrators would have "exclusive authority to resolve any dispute relating to the . . . enforceability . . . of this Agreement." When Jackson filed suit against Rent-A-Center claiming employment discrimination, the company filed a motion to compel arbitration, and Jackson responded by arguing that the agreement to arbitrate was unconscionable under the applicable Nevada law and hence unenforceable. The question before the Supreme Court was who should decide that threshold question of unconscionability: the court, or the arbitrator.

Under *Prima Paint*, when a larger contract contains an arbitration clause, a threshold question about the validity of the entire contract goes to the arbitrators, but a threshold question about the validity of the arbitration clause itself — for example, whether one party was forced to include the arbitration clause under circumstances that are unconscionable — must be decided by the court. Jackson argued that, here, the entire contract was an agreement to arbitrate, so *Prima Paint* required that the threshold question be decided by the court. But the Supreme Court disagreed. Writing for the majority, Justice Scalia drew yet another distinction, this time between the delegation provision — the part of this particular contract that specifically gave the arbitrators the authority to decide threshold issues of validity — and the rest of the agreement to arbitrate, which dealt with such matters as the scope of claims included within the agreement. The *Prima Paint* doctrine, the majority held, applied only to that delegation provision. Applying *Prima Paint*, the Court said:

> Here, the "written provision . . . to settle by arbitration a controversy,"
> 9 U.S.C. §2, that Rent-A-Center asks us to enforce is the delegation
> provision—the provision that gave the arbitrator "exclusive authority to
> resolve any dispute relating to the . . . enforceability . . . of this Agree-
> ment." The "remainder of the contract," *Buckeye,* supra, at 445, 126 S.
> Ct. 1204, is the rest of the agreement to arbitrate claims arising out of
> Jackson's employment with Rent-A-Center. To be sure this case differs
> from *Prima Paint, Buckeye,* and *Preston,* in that the arbitration provisions
> sought to be enforced in those cases were contained in contracts unre-
> lated to arbitration—contracts for consulting services, *see Prima Paint,*
> *supra,* at 397, 87 S. Ct. 1801, check-cashing services, *see Buckeye, supra,* at
> 442, 126 S. Ct. 1204, and "personal management" or "talent agent" ser-
> vices, *see Preston, supra,* at 352, 128 S. Ct. 978. In this case, the underlying
> contract is itself an arbitration agreement. But that makes no difference.
> Application of the severability rule does not depend on the substance of
> the remainder of the contract.

Rent-A-Center, 561 U.S. at 71–72. The four dissenters, led by Justice Stevens, criticized this "breezy assertion," responding that "[t]his written arbitration agreement
is but one part of a broader employment agreement between the parties, just as the
arbitration clause in *Prima Paint* was but one part of a broader contract for services
between those parties. Thus, that the subject matter of the agreement is exclusively
arbitration makes *all* the difference in the *Prima Paint* analysis." *Id.* at 76–77 (Stevens, J., dissenting).

In *Prima Paint,* the arbitration clause (as reproduced in the opinion of the
Court) read in full: "Any controversy or claim arising out of or relating to this
Agreement, or the breach thereof, shall be settled by arbitration in the City of New
York, in accordance with the rules then obtaining of the American Arbitration
Association." It was that clause (and clauses like it) that the Supreme Court found
to require a court hearing when a challenge was raised to its validity. Why did the
Rent-A-Center Court conclude that writing a more extended agreement to arbitrate
calls for courts to be less involved in the decision of threshold questions like unconscionability? The majority's explanation was that the delegation provision related
specifically to the assignment of the decision to the legislators. But *Prima Paint* was
based on the distinction between the arbitration clause and the rest of the contract,
not different components of the arbitration clause. Is the majority splitting hairs
too finely here?

Rent-A-Center will make it difficult to challenge a stand-alone agreement to
arbitrate. It was already difficult to satisfy the requirement in *Prima Paint* that a
litigant develop evidence relating specifically to threshold problems with an arbitration clause, as opposed to an entire contract. When a litigant is seeking to challenge a stand-alone agreement to arbitrate, how frequently will there be evidence
relating specifically to threshold problems with the clause that assigns responsibility
to the arbitrators for addressing validity problems?

4. *Federal Statutory Exceptions to the FAA.* The FAA is a federal statute and, as
with any other statute, Congress can create exceptions or carve-outs to it. If Congress decides that a certain class of claims should not be subject to mandatory arbitration—that plaintiffs should be able to litigate those claims in court, even if they

sign an agreement containing an arbitration clause—then Congress has the power to carve such claims out of the FAA. The Supreme Court has suggested that such exceptions to the FAA are disfavored. The Act established a "federal policy favoring arbitration," *Gilmer v. Interstate/Johnson Lane Corp.*, 500 U.S. 20, 26 (1991), and it places the "burden . . . on the party opposing arbitration . . . to show that Congress intended to preclude a waiver of judicial remedies," focusing in particular on the statute's "text or legislative history, or . . . an inherent conflict between arbitration and the statute's underlying purposes." *Shearson/American Express v. McMahon*, 482 U.S. 220, 227 (1987) (internal quotations omitted). But the Court has not yet given much guidance about exactly how to determine, in the absence of a clear and express statement, when a federal statute should be interpreted to require an exemption from the FAA.

In one case, *CompuCredit Corp. v. Greenwood*, 132 S. Ct. 665 (2012), the Court rejected plaintiffs' claim that a federal consumer protection statute created an exemption. *CompuCredit* may tighten the standard for finding exemptions yet further. The 1996 statute involved in that case, the Credit Repair Organizations Act (CROA), 15 U.S.C. §§1679 *et seq.*, aims to give consumers information about their rights in conjunction with certain types of credit cards and other credit-related products. One of those rights is the "right to sue" if credit companies do not abide by the terms of the CROA. The Act further provides that any waiver of a "right" or "protection" provided by the CROA contained in a consumer contract "shall be treated as void" and "may not be enforced." *Id.* at §1679c(a) and 1679f(a). Plaintiffs in the case were a class of consumers to whom defendant marketed a credit card in alleged violation of the CROA. The plaintiffs had signed an agreement that mandated arbitration of any claims, but they argued that the provisions of the CROA, taken together, granted them a right to sue in court that could not be waived in an arbitration clause and hence constituted an exception to the FAA.

By an 8-1 vote, the Court rejected that argument, holding that a plaintiff's "right to sue" was adequately protected by the option to pursue arbitration. In explaining its reasons for finding the plaintiffs' statutory argument unconvincing, the Court pointed to several examples of other statutes that contain clear and express language mandating exemptions to the FAA. The majority did not squarely hold that such express language was necessary, but its opinion left enough of an implication in that direction that Justices Sotomayor and Kagan concurred only in the judgment, explaining that they did not believe that such express language was necessary for an exemption and did not understand the Court to be so holding, even though they did agree that the CROA, read in light of the Court's earlier precedents, did not create an exemption.

5. *Protecting Your Client's Interests.* Look back to the arbitration clause set forth near the beginning of this section. How can you discern such exquisite distinctions from an arbitration clause written in such general terms? How would you advise a client who is thinking about putting an arbitration clause into a contract? At the very least, it is probably necessary to make it clear in a broadly worded clause that the parties have considered questions of arbitrability and committed them to the arbitrator to decide, if that is your goal; or, in the alternative, that the parties have expressly decided to exempt certain types of question from the clause in order to reserve them for resolution by the courts. In theory, following cases like *Prima Paint* and *Kaplan*, parties ought to know that an arbitration clause must be explicit about

such matters. In practice, parties often fail to pay careful attention. More broadly, contracting parties and their lawyers must always be attentive to the interplay between the default rules of arbitration providers and the terms and exceptions they specify in their contract. *See* W. Mark C. Weidemaier, *The Arbitration Clause in Context: How Contract Terms Do (and Do Not) Define the Process*, 40 Creighton L. Rev. 655 (2007) (discussing practical concerns surrounding the drafting of arbitration clauses and the designated providers' default rules).

6. *Does Arbitration Fulfill Its Promises?* How much time and money do you think arbitration really saves? As we have seen, arbitration presents the potential for litigation on all kinds of collateral issues, like the meaning and scope of the arbitration clause, or whether the award violates one of the narrow principles — bias, fraud, manifest disregard for the law — that would permit a court to set the award aside. While the potential for cost savings in the discovery process in a large commercial case is significant, those savings are not inevitable. Arbitrations can drag on for years and may involve discovery that is just as burdensome as that found in a traditional lawsuit. At the very least, the true efficiency of arbitration will vary greatly from case to case. What does that say about the desirability of arbitration as a general practice?

What about arbitration's promise of greater flexibility? The scope of discovery appears to be expanding in large commercial arbitration. At the same time, civil litigation is becoming more streamlined, with Rule 26 requiring the parties to meet at an early stage in the lawsuit "to discuss the nature and basis of their claims and defenses . . . and to develop a proposed discovery plan," Fed. R. Civ. P. 26(f), based in part on their mandatory initial disclosures under Rule 26(a). If parties work together at the outset of litigation, they can achieve many of the same efficiency gains that are available in arbitration by drafting an appropriate plan under Rule 26.

The importance of these and other questions surrounding the ability of arbitration to fulfill its promises continues to grow as arbitration continues to proliferate. Professor Carrie Menkel-Meadow, a leading scholar in alternative dispute resolution, has identified areas of concern for practitioners and policy makers in the practice of arbitration that range from the danger of coercion in unequal contracting arrangements to the potential for conflicts of interest in the selection of arbitrators. *See* Carrie Menkel-Meadow, *Ethics Issues in Arbitration and Related Dispute Processes: What's Happening and What's Not*, 56 U. Miami L. Rev. 949 (2002).

2. Arbitration and the Class Action

One area of great concern that has emerged in the law of arbitration concerns the impact of the FAA on class action litigation. At various points in the development of the doctrine, arbitration has seemed to present opportunities and risks for both plaintiffs and defendants in its potential impact on the class-wide resolution of disputes. Two Supreme Court decisions now appear to have put much more powerful tools into the hands of corporate defendants. The case that follows, *AT&T Mobility v. Concepcion*, is the leading precedent on the power of an arbitration clause to limit access to classwide relief for consumers and employees. A subsequent decision discussed in the notes below, *American Express v. Italian Colors Restaurant*, makes clear the limited avenues available for challenging an arbitration clause even when the clause might have the practical impact of foreclosing a federal cause of action.

AT&T Mobility v. Concepcion

563 U.S. 333 (2011)

JUSTICE SCALIA delivered the opinion of the Court.

Section 2 of the Federal Arbitration Act (FAA) makes agreements to arbitrate "valid, irrevocable, and enforceable, save upon such grounds as exist at law or in equity for the revocation of any contract." 9 U.S.C. § 2. We consider whether the FAA prohibits States from conditioning the enforceability of certain arbitration agreements on the availability of classwide arbitration procedures.

I

In February 2002, Vincent and Liza Concepcion entered into an agreement for the sale and servicing of cellular telephones with AT&T Mobility LCC (AT&T). The contract provided for arbitration of all disputes between the parties, but required that claims be brought in the parties' "individual capacity, and not as a plaintiff or class member in any purported class or representative proceeding."[2] The agreement authorized AT&T to make unilateral amendments, which it did to the arbitration provision on several occasions. The version at issue in this case reflects revisions made in December 2006, which the parties agree are controlling.

The revised agreement provides that customers may initiate dispute proceedings by completing a one-page Notice of Dispute form available on AT&T's Web site. AT&T may then offer to settle the claim; if it does not, or if the dispute is not resolved within 30 days, the customer may invoke arbitration by filing a separate Demand for Arbitration, also available on AT&T's Web site. In the event the parties proceed to arbitration, the agreement specifies that AT&T must pay all costs for nonfrivolous claims; that arbitration must take place in the county in which the customer is billed; that, for claims of $10,000 or less, the customer may choose whether the arbitration proceeds in person, by telephone, or based only on submissions; that either party may bring a claim in small claims court in lieu of arbitration; and that the arbitrator may award any form of individual relief, including injunctions and presumably punitive damages. The agreement, moreover, denies AT&T any ability to seek reimbursement of its attorney's fees, and, in the event that a customer receives an arbitration award greater than AT&T's last written settlement offer, requires AT&T to pay a $7,500 minimum recovery and twice the amount of the claimant's attorney's fees.

---

2. That provision further states that "the arbitrator may not consolidate more than one person's claims, and may not otherwise preside over any form of a representative or class proceeding."

The Concepcions purchased AT&T service, which was advertised as including the provision of free phones; they were not charged for the phones, but they were charged $30.22 in sales tax based on the phones' retail value. In March 2006, the Concepcions filed a complaint against AT&T in the United States District Court for the Southern District of California. The complaint was later consolidated with a putative class action alleging, among other things, that AT&T had engaged in false advertising and fraud by charging sales tax on phones it advertised as free.

In March 2008, AT&T moved to compel arbitration under the terms of its contract with the Concepcions. The Concepcions opposed the motion, contending that the arbitration agreement was unconscionable and unlawfully exculpatory under California law because it disallowed classwide procedures. The District Court denied AT&T's motion. It described AT&T's arbitration agreement favorably, noting, for example, that the informal dispute-resolution process was "quick, easy to use" and likely to "promp[t] full or . . . even excess payment to the customer *without* the need to arbitrate or litigate"; that the $7,500 premium functioned as "a substantial inducement for the consumer to pursue the claim in arbitration" if a dispute was not resolved informally; and that consumers who were members of a class would likely be worse off. Nevertheless, relying on the California Supreme Court's decision in *Discover Bank v. Superior Court*, 36 Cal.4th 148, 30 Cal.Rptr.3d 76, 113 P.3d 1100 (2005), the court found that the arbitration provision was unconscionable because AT&T had not shown that bilateral arbitration adequately substituted for the deterrent effects of class actions.

The Ninth Circuit affirmed, also finding the provision unconscionable under California law as announced in *Discover Bank*. It also held that the *Discover Bank* rule was not preempted by the FAA because that rule was simply "a refinement of the unconscionability analysis applicable to contracts generally in California." In response to AT&T's argument that the Concepcions' interpretation of California law discriminated against arbitration, the Ninth Circuit rejected the contention that "class proceedings will reduce the efficiency and expeditiousness of arbitration" and noted that "*Discover Bank* placed arbitration agreements with class action waivers on the *exact same footing* as contracts that bar class action litigation outside the context of arbitration."

We granted certiorari.

II

The FAA was enacted in 1925 in response to widespread judicial hostility to arbitration agreements. See *Hall Street Associates, L.L.C. v. Mattel, Inc.*, 552 U.S. 576, 581, 128 S.Ct. 1396, 170 L.Ed.2d 254 (2008). Section 2, the "primary substantive provision of the Act," *Moses H. Cone Memorial Hospital v. Mercury Constr. Corp.*, 460 U.S. 1, 24, 103 S.Ct. 927, 74 L.Ed.2d 765 (1983), provides, in relevant part, as follows:

> "A written provision in any maritime transaction or a contract evidencing a transaction involving commerce to settle by arbitration a controversy thereafter arising out of such contract or transaction . . . shall be valid, irrevocable, and enforceable, save upon such grounds as exist at law or in equity for the revocation of any contract." 9 U.S.C. § 2.

We have described this provision as reflecting both a "liberal federal policy favoring arbitration," Moses H. Cone, supra, at 24, 103 S.Ct. 927, and the "fundamental *principle* that arbitration is a matter of contract," *Rent-A-Center, West, Inc. v. Jackson*, 561 U.S. ___, ___, 130 S.Ct. 2772, 2776, 177 L.Ed.2d 403 (2010). In line with these principles, courts must place arbitration agreements on an equal footing with other contracts, *Buckeye Check Cashing, Inc. v. Cardegna*, 546 U.S. 440, 443, 126 S.Ct. 1204, 163 L.Ed.2d 1038 (2006), and enforce them according to their terms, *Volt Information Sciences, Inc. v. Board of Trustees of Leland Stanford Junior Univ.*, 489 U.S. 468, 478, 109 S.Ct. 1248, 103 L.Ed.2d 488 (1989).

The final phrase of § 2, however, permits arbitration agreements to be declared unenforceable "upon such grounds as exist at law or in equity for the revocation of any contract." This saving clause permits agreements to arbitrate to be invalidated by "generally applicable contract defenses, such as fraud, duress, or unconscionability," but not by defenses that apply only to arbitration or that derive their meaning from the fact that an agreement to arbitrate is at issue. The question in this case is whether § 2 preempts California's rule classifying most collective-arbitration waivers in consumer contracts as unconscionable. We refer to this rule as the *Discover Bank* rule.

Under California law, courts may refuse to enforce any contract found "to have been unconscionable at the time it was made," or may "limit the application of any unconscionable clause." Cal. Civ.Code Ann. § 1670.5(a) (West 1985). A finding of unconscionability requires "a 'procedural' and a 'substantive' element, the former focusing on 'oppression' or 'surprise' due to unequal bargaining power, the latter on 'overly harsh' or 'one-sided' results." *Armendariz v. Foundation Health Pyschcare Servs., Inc.*, 24 Cal.4th 83, 114, 99 Cal.Rptr.2d 745, 6 P.3d 669, 690 (2000); *accord, Discover Bank*, 36 Cal.4th, at 159–161, 30 Cal.Rptr.3d 76, 113 P.3d, at 1108.

In Discover Bank, the California Supreme Court applied this framework to class-action waivers in arbitration agreements and held as follows:

> "[W]hen the waiver is found in a consumer contract of adhesion in a setting in which disputes between the contracting parties predictably involve small amounts of damages, and when it is alleged that the party with the superior bargaining power has carried out a scheme to deliberately cheat large numbers of consumers out of individually small sums of money, then . . . the waiver becomes in practice the exemption of the party 'from responsibility for [its] own fraud, or willful injury to the person or property of another.' Under these circumstances, such waivers are unconscionable under California law and should not be enforced." *Id.*, at 162, 30 Cal.Rptr.3d 76, 113 P.3d, at 1110 (*quoting* Cal. Civ.Code Ann. § 1668).

California courts have frequently applied this rule to find arbitration agreements unconscionable.

III

A

The Concepcions argue that the *Discover Bank* rule, given its origins in California's unconscionability doctrine and California's policy against exculpation, is a ground that "exist[s] at law or in equity for the revocation of any contract" under

FAA § 2. Moreover, they argue that even if we construe the *Discover Bank* rule as a prohibition on collective-action waivers rather than simply an application of unconscionability, the rule would still be applicable to all dispute-resolution contracts, since California prohibits waivers of class litigation as well. See *America Online, Inc. v. Superior Ct.*, 90 Cal.App.4th 1, 17–18, 108 Cal.Rptr.2d 699, 711–713 (2001).

When state law prohibits outright the arbitration of a particular type of claim, the analysis is straightforward: The conflicting rule is displaced by the FAA. *Preston v. Ferrer*, 552 U.S. 346, 353, 128 S.Ct. 978, 169 L.Ed.2d 917 (2008). But the inquiry becomes more complex when a doctrine normally thought to be generally applicable, such as duress or, as relevant here, unconscionability, is alleged to have been applied in a fashion that disfavors arbitration. In *Perry v. Thomas*, 482 U.S. 483, 107 S.Ct. 2520, 96 L.Ed.2d 426 (1987), for example, we noted that the FAA's preemptive effect might extend even to grounds traditionally thought to exist "'at law or in equity for the revocation of any contract.'" *Id.*, at 492, n. 9, 107 S.Ct. 2520 (emphasis deleted). We said that a court may not "rely on the uniqueness of an agreement to arbitrate as a basis for a state-law holding that enforcement would be unconscionable, for this would enable the court to effect what . . . the state legislature cannot." *Id.*, at 493, n. 9, 107 S.Ct. 2520.

An obvious illustration of this point would be a case finding unconscionable or unenforceable as against public policy consumer arbitration agreements that fail to provide for judicially monitored discovery. The rationalizations for such a holding are neither difficult to imagine nor different in kind from those articulated in *Discover Bank*. A court might reason that no consumer would knowingly waive his right to full discovery, as this would enable companies to hide their wrongdoing. Or the court might simply say that such agreements are exculpatory—restricting discovery would be of greater benefit to the company than the consumer, since the former is more likely to be sued than to sue. See *Discover Bank, supra*, at 161, 30 Cal. Rptr.3d 76, 113 P.3d, at 1109 (arguing that class waivers are similarly one-sided). And, the reasoning would continue, because such a rule applies the general principle of unconscionability or public-policy disapproval of exculpatory agreements, it is applicable to "any" contract and thus preserved by § 2 of the FAA. In practice, of course, the rule would have a disproportionate impact on arbitration agreements; but it would presumably apply to contracts purporting to restrict discovery in litigation as well.

Other examples are easy to imagine. The same argument might apply to a rule classifying as unconscionable arbitration agreements that fail to abide by the Federal Rules of Evidence, or that disallow an ultimate disposition by a jury (perhaps termed "a panel of twelve lay arbitrators" to help avoid preemption). Such examples are not fanciful, since the judicial hostility towards arbitration that prompted the FAA had manifested itself in "a great variety" of "devices and formulas" declaring arbitration against public policy. *Robert Lawrence Co. v. Devonshire Fabrics, Inc.*, 271 F.2d 402, 406 (C.A.2 1959). And although these statistics are not definitive, it is worth noting that California's courts have been more likely to hold contracts to arbitrate unconscionable than other contracts. Broome, An Unconscionable Application of the Unconscionability Doctrine: How the California Courts are Circumventing the Federal Arbitration Act, 3 Hastings Bus. L.J. 39, 54, 66 (2006); Randall, Judicial Attitudes Toward Arbitration and the Resurgence of Unconscionability, 52 Buffalo L.Rev. 185, 186–187 (2004).

The Concepcions suggest that all this is just a parade of horribles, and no genuine worry. "Rules aimed at destroying arbitration" or "demanding procedures incompatible with arbitration," they concede, "would be preempted by the FAA because they cannot sensibly be reconciled with Section 2." The "grounds" available under § 2's saving clause, they admit, "should not be construed to include a State's mere preference for procedures that are incompatible with arbitration and 'would wholly eviscerate arbitration agreements.'"

We largely agree. Although § 2's saving clause preserves generally applicable contract defenses, nothing in it suggests an intent to preserve state-law rules that stand as an obstacle to the accomplishment of the FAA's objectives. Cf. *Geier v. American Honda Motor Co.*, 529 U.S. 861, 872, 120 S.Ct. 1913, 146 L.Ed.2d 914 (2000); *Crosby v. National Foreign Trade Council*, 530 U.S. 363, 372–373, 120 S.Ct. 2288, 147 L.Ed.2d 352 (2000). As we have said, a federal statute's saving clause "'cannot in reason be construed as [allowing] a common law right, the continued existence of which would be absolutely inconsistent with the provisions of the act. In other words, the act cannot be held to destroy itself.'" *American Telephone & Telegraph Co. v. Central Office Telephone, Inc.*, 524 U.S. 214, 227–228, 118 S.Ct. 1956, 141 L.Ed.2d 222 (1998) (*quoting Texas & Pacific R. Co. v. Abilene Cotton Oil Co.*, 204 U.S. 426, 446, 27 S.Ct. 350, 51 L.Ed. 553 (1907)).

We differ with the Concepcions only in the application of this analysis to the matter before us. We do not agree that rules requiring judicially monitored discovery or adherence to the Federal Rules of Evidence are "a far cry from this case." Brief for Respondents 32. The overarching purpose of the FAA, evident in the text of §§ 2, 3, and 4, is to ensure the enforcement of arbitration agreements according to their terms so as to facilitate streamlined proceedings. Requiring the availability of classwide arbitration interferes with fundamental attributes of arbitration and thus creates a scheme inconsistent with the FAA.

B

The "principal purpose" of the FAA is to "ensur[e] that private arbitration agreements are enforced according to their terms." *Volt*, 489 U.S., at 478, 109 S.Ct. 1248; *see also Stolt-Nielsen S.A. v. AnimalFeeds Int'l Corp.*, 559 U.S. ___, ___, 130 S.Ct. 1758, 1763, 176 L.Ed.2d 605 (2010). This purpose is readily apparent from the FAA's text. Section 2 makes arbitration agreements "valid, irrevocable, and enforceable" as written (subject, of course, to the saving clause); § 3 requires courts to stay litigation of arbitral claims pending arbitration of those claims "in accordance with the terms of the agreement"; and § 4 requires courts to compel arbitration "in accordance with the terms of the agreement" upon the motion of either party to the agreement (assuming that the "making of the arbitration agreement or the failure . . . to perform the same" is not at issue). In light of these provisions, we have held that parties may agree to limit the issues subject to arbitration, *Mitsubishi Motors Corp. v. Soler Chrysler–Plymouth, Inc.*, 473 U.S. 614, 628, 105 S.Ct. 3346, 87 L.Ed.2d 444 (1985), to arbitrate according to specific rules, *Volt, supra*, at 479, 109 S.Ct. 1248, and to limit *with whom* a party will arbitrate its disputes, *Stolt-Nielsen, supra*, at ___, 130 S.Ct. at 1773.

The point of affording parties discretion in designing arbitration processes is to allow for efficient, streamlined procedures tailored to the type of dispute. It can be specified, for example, that the decisionmaker be a specialist in the relevant field, or that proceedings be kept confidential to protect trade secrets. And the informality of arbitral proceedings is itself desirable, reducing the cost and increasing the speed of dispute resolution. *14 Penn Plaza LLC v. Pyett*, 556 U.S. 247, ___, 129 S.Ct. 1456, 1460, 173 L.Ed.2d 398 (2009); *Mitsubishi Motors Corp., supra*, at 628, 105 S.Ct. 3346.

. . .

California's *Discover Bank* rule . . . interferes with arbitration. Although the rule does not *require* classwide arbitration, it allows any party to a consumer contract to demand it *ex post*. The rule is limited to adhesion contracts, *Discover Bank*, 36 Cal.4th, at 162–163, 30 Cal.Rptr.3d 76, 113 P.3d, at 1110, but the times in which consumer contracts were anything other than adhesive are long past.[6] *Carbajal v. H & R Block Tax Servs., Inc.*, 372 F.3d 903, 906 (7th Cir.2004); *see also Hill v. Gateway 2000, Inc.*, 105 F.3d 1147, 1149 (C.A.7 1997). The rule also requires that damages be predictably small, and that the consumer allege a scheme to cheat consumers. *Discover Bank, supra*, at 162–163, 30 Cal.Rptr.3d 76, 113 P.3d, at 1110. The former requirement, however, is toothless and malleable (the Ninth Circuit has held that damages of $4,000 are sufficiently small, *see Oestreicher v. Alienware Corp.*, 322 Fed. Appx. 489, 492 (2009) (unpublished)), and the latter has no limiting effect, as all that is required is an allegation. Consumers remain free to bring and resolve their disputes on a bilateral basis under *Discover Bank*, and some may well do so; but there is little incentive for lawyers to arbitrate on behalf of individuals when they may do so for a class and reap far higher fees in the process. And faced with inevitable class arbitration, companies would have less incentive to continue resolving potentially duplicative claims on an individual basis.

Although we have had little occasion to examine classwide arbitration, our decision in *Stolt-Nielsen* is instructive. In that case we held that an arbitration panel exceeded its power under § 10(a)(4) of the FAA by imposing class procedures based on policy judgments rather than the arbitration agreement itself or some background principle of contract law that would affect its interpretation. 559 U.S., at ___, 130 S.Ct. at 1773–1776. We then held that the agreement at issue, which was silent on the question of class procedures, could not be interpreted to allow them because the "changes brought about by the shift from bilateral arbitration to class-action arbitration" are "fundamental." *Id.*, at ___, 130 S.Ct. at 1776. This is obvious as a structural matter: Classwide arbitration includes absent parties, necessitating additional and different procedures and involving higher stakes. Confidentiality becomes more difficult. And while it is theoretically possible to select an arbitrator with some expertise relevant to the class-certification question, arbitrators are not generally knowledgeable in the often-dominant procedural aspects of certification, such as the protection of absent parties. The conclusion follows that class arbitration, to the extent it is manufactured by *Discover Bank* rather than consensual, is inconsistent with the FAA.

---

6. Of course States remain free to take steps addressing the concerns that attend contracts of adhesion—for example, requiring class-action-waiver provisions in adhesive arbitration agreements to be highlighted. Such steps cannot, however, conflict with the FAA or frustrate its purpose to ensure that private arbitration agreements are enforced according to their terms.

First, the switch from bilateral to class arbitration sacrifices the principal advantage of arbitration — its informality — and makes the process slower, more costly, and more likely to generate procedural morass than final judgment. "In bilateral arbitration, parties forgo the procedural rigor and appellate review of the courts in order to realize the benefits of private dispute resolution: lower costs, greater efficiency and speed, and the ability to choose expert adjudicators to resolve specialized disputes." 559 U.S., at ___, 130 S.Ct. at 1775. But before an arbitrator may decide the merits of a claim in classwide procedures, he must first decide, for example, whether the class itself may be certified, whether the named parties are sufficiently representative and typical, and how discovery for the class should be conducted. A cursory comparison of bilateral and class arbitration illustrates the difference. According to the American Arbitration Association (AAA), the average consumer arbitration between January and August 2007 resulted in a disposition on the merits in six months, four months if the arbitration was conducted by documents only. AAA, Analysis of the AAA's Consumer Arbitration Caseload, online at http://www.adr.org/si.asp?id=5027 (all Internet materials as visited Apr. 25, 2011, and available in Clerk of Court's case file). As of September 2009, the AAA had opened 283 class arbitrations. Of those, 121 remained active, and 162 had been settled, withdrawn, or dismissed. Not a single one, however, had resulted in a final award on the merits. Brief for AAA as *Amicus Curiae* in *Stolt-Nielsen*, O.T. 2009, No. 08–1198, pp. 22–24. For those cases that were no longer active, the median time from filing to settlement, withdrawal, or dismissal — not judgment on the merits — was 583 days, and the mean was 630 days. *Id.*, at 24.[7]

Second, class arbitration *requires* procedural formality. The AAA's rules governing class arbitrations mimic the Federal Rules of Civil Procedure for class litigation. Compare AAA, Supplementary Rules for Class Arbitrations (effective Oct. 8, 2003), online at http://www.adr.org/sp.asp?id=21936, with Fed. Rule Civ. Proc. 23. And while parties can alter those procedures by contract, an alternative is not obvious. If procedures are too informal, absent class members would not be bound by the arbitration. For a class-action money judgment to bind absentees in litigation, class representatives must at all times adequately represent absent class members, and absent members must be afforded notice, an opportunity to be heard, and a right to opt out of the class. *Phillips Petroleum Co. v. Shutts*, 472 U.S. 797, 811–812, 105 S.Ct. 2965, 86 L.Ed.2d 628 (1985). At least this amount of process would presumably be required for absent parties to be bound by the results of arbitration.

We find it unlikely that in passing the FAA Congress meant to leave the disposition of these procedural requirements to an arbitrator. Indeed, class arbitration was not even envisioned by Congress when it passed the FAA in 1925; as the California Supreme Court admitted in *Discover Bank*, class arbitration is a "relatively recent development." 36 Cal.4th, at 163, 30 Cal.Rptr.3d 76, 113 P.3d, at 1110. And it is at the very least odd to think that an arbitrator would be entrusted with ensuring that third parties' due process rights are satisfied.

---

7. The dissent claims that class arbitration should be compared to class litigation, not bilateral arbitration. *Post*, at 6–7. Whether arbitrating a class is more desirable than litigating one, however, is not relevant. A State cannot defend a rule requiring arbitration-by-jury by saying that parties will still prefer it to trial-by-jury.

Third, class arbitration greatly increases risks to defendants. Informal procedures do of course have a cost: The absence of multilayered review makes it more likely that errors will go uncorrected. Defendants are willing to accept the costs of these errors in arbitration, since their impact is limited to the size of individual disputes, and presumably outweighed by savings from avoiding the courts. But when damages allegedly owed to tens of thousands of potential claimants are aggregated and decided at once, the risk of an error will often become unacceptable. Faced with even a small chance of a devastating loss, defendants will be pressured into settling questionable claims. Other courts have noted the risk of "in terrorem" settlements that class actions entail, see, *e.g., Kohen v. Pacific Inv. Management Co. LLC,* 571 F.3d 672, 677–678 (C.A.7 2009), and class arbitration would be no different.

Arbitration is poorly suited to the higher stakes of class litigation. In litigation, a defendant may appeal a certification decision on an interlocutory basis and, if unsuccessful, may appeal from a final judgment as well. Questions of law are reviewed *de novo* and questions of fact for clear error. In contrast, 9 U.S.C. § 10 allows a court to vacate an arbitral award *only* where the award "was procured by corruption, fraud, or undue means"; "there was evident partiality or corruption in the arbitrators"; "the arbitrators were guilty of misconduct in refusing to postpone the hearing . . . or in refusing to hear evidence pertinent and material to the controversy[,] or of any other misbehavior by which the rights of any party have been prejudiced"; or if the "arbitrators exceeded their powers, or so imperfectly executed them that a mutual, final, and definite award . . . was not made." The AAA rules do authorize judicial review of certification decisions, but this review is unlikely to have much effect given these limitations; review under § 10 focuses on misconduct rather than mistake. And parties may not contractually expand the grounds or nature of judicial review. *Hall Street Assocs.,* 552 U.S., at 578, 128 S.Ct. 1396. We find it hard to believe that defendants would bet the company with no effective means of review, and even harder to believe that Congress would have intended to allow state courts to force such a decision.

The Concepcions contend that because parties may and sometimes do agree to aggregation, class procedures are not necessarily incompatible with arbitration. But the same could be said about procedures that the Concepcions admit States may not superimpose on arbitration: Parties *could* agree to arbitrate pursuant to the Federal Rules of Civil Procedure, or pursuant to a discovery process rivaling that in litigation. Arbitration is a matter of contract, and the FAA requires courts to honor parties' expectations. *Rent-A-Center, West,* 561 U.S., at ___, 130 S.Ct. 2772, 2774. But what the parties in the aforementioned examples would have agreed to is not arbitration as envisioned by the FAA, lacks its benefits, and therefore may not be required by state law.

The dissent claims that class proceedings are necessary to prosecute small-dollar claims that might otherwise slip through the legal system. See *post,* at 9. But States cannot require a procedure that is inconsistent with the FAA, even if it is desirable for unrelated reasons. Moreover, the claim here was most unlikely to go unresolved. As noted earlier, the arbitration agreement provides that AT&T will pay claimants a minimum of $7,500 and twice their attorney's fees if they obtain an arbitration award greater than AT&T's last settlement offer. The District Court found this scheme sufficient to provide incentive for the individual prosecution of meritorious claims that are not immediately settled, and the Ninth Circuit admitted that aggrieved customers who filed claims would be "essentially guarantee[d]" to be made whole, 584 F.3d, at 856, n. 9. Indeed, the District Court concluded that the Concepcions were *better off* under their arbitration agreement with AT&T than they would have been as participants in a class action, which "could take months, if not years, and which may merely yield an opportunity to submit a claim for recovery of a small percentage of a few dollars." *Laster*, 2008 WL 5216255, at *12.

. . .

Because it "stands as an obstacle to the accomplishment and execution of the full purposes and objectives of Congress," *Hines v. Davidowitz*, 312 U.S. 52, 67, 61 S.Ct. 399, 85 L.Ed. 581 (1941), *California's Discover Bank* rule is preempted by the FAA. The judgment of the Ninth Circuit is reversed, and the case is remanded for further proceedings consistent with this opinion.

It is so ordered.

[The concurring opinion of JUSTICE THOMAS is omitted.]

JUSTICE BREYER, with whom JUSTICE GINSBURG, JUSTICE SOTOMAYOR, and JUSTICE KAGAN join, dissenting.

The Federal Arbitration Act says that an arbitration agreement "shall be valid, irrevocable, and enforceable, *save upon such grounds as exist at law or in equity for the revocation of any contract.*" 9 U.S.C. § 2 (emphasis added). California law sets forth certain circumstances in which "class action waivers" in *any* contract are unenforceable. In my view, this rule of state law is consistent with the federal Act's language and primary objective. It does not "stan[d] as an obstacle" to the Act's "accomplishment and execution." *Hines v. Davidowitz*, 312 U.S. 52, 67, 61 S.Ct. 399, 85 L.Ed. 581 (1941). And the Court is wrong to hold that the federal Act pre-empts the rule of state law.

I

. . .

The *Discover Bank* rule does not create a "blanket policy in California against class action waivers in the consumer context." *Provencher v. Dell, Inc.*, 409 F.Supp.2d 1196, 1201 (C.D.Cal.2006). Instead, it represents the "application of a more general [unconscionability] principle." *Gentry v. Superior Ct.*, 42 Cal.4th 443, 457, 64 Cal. Rptr.3d 773, 165 P.3d 556, 564 (2007). Courts applying California law have enforced class-action waivers where they satisfy general unconscionability standards. And even when they fail, the parties remain free to devise other dispute mechanisms, including informal mechanisms, that, in context, will not prove unconscionable. See *Volt Information Sciences, Inc. v. Board of Trustees of Leland Stanford Junior Univ.*, 489 U.S. 468, 479, 109 S.Ct. 1248, 103 L.Ed.2d 488 (1989).

II

A

The *Discover Bank* rule is consistent with the federal Act's language. It "applies equally to class action litigation waivers in contracts without arbitration agreements as it does to class arbitration waivers in contracts with such agreements." 36

Cal.4th, at 165–166, 30 Cal.Rptr.3d 76, 113 P.3d, at 1112. Linguistically speaking, it falls directly within the scope of the Act's exception permitting courts to refuse to enforce arbitration agreements on grounds that exist "for the revocation of *any* contract." 9 U.S.C. § 2 (emphasis added). The majority agrees. *Ante,* at 9.

B

The *Discover Bank* rule is also consistent with the basic "purpose behind" the Act. *Dean Witter Reynolds Inc. v. Byrd,* 470 U.S. 213, 219, 105 S.Ct. 1238, 84 L.Ed.2d 158 (1985). We have described that purpose as one of "ensur[ing] judicial enforcement" of arbitration agreements. *Ibid.;* see also *Marine Transit Corp. v. Dreyfus,* 284 U.S. 263, 274, n. 2, 52 S.Ct. 166, 76 L.Ed. 282 (1932) ("'The purpose of this bill is to make *valid and enforceable* agreements for arbitration'" (quoting H.R.Rep. No. 96, 68th Cong., 1st Sess., 1 (1924); emphasis added)); 65 Cong. Rec.1931 (1924) ("It creates no new legislation, grants no new rights, except a remedy to enforce an agreement in commercial contracts and in admiralty contracts"). As is well known, prior to the federal Act, many courts expressed hostility to arbitration, for example by refusing to order specific performance of agreements to arbitrate. See S.Rep. No. 536, 68th Cong., 1st Sess., 2 (1924). The Act sought to eliminate that hostility by placing agreements to arbitrate "'*upon the same footing as other contracts.*'" *Scherk v. Alberto–Culver Co.,* 417 U.S. 506, 511, 94 S.Ct. 2449, 41 L.Ed.2d 270 (1974) (quoting H.R.Rep. No. 96, at 2; emphasis added).

Congress was fully aware that arbitration could provide procedural and cost advantages. The House Report emphasized the "appropriate[ness]" of making arbitration agreements enforceable "at this time when there is so much agitation against the costliness and delays of litigation." *Id.,* at 2. And this Court has acknowledged that parties may enter into arbitration agreements in order to expedite the resolution of disputes. See *Preston v. Ferrer,* 552 U.S. 346, 357, 128 S.Ct. 978, 169 L.Ed.2d 917 (2008) (discussing "prime objective of an agreement to arbitrate"). *See also Mitsubishi Motors Corp. v. Soler Chrysler–Plymouth, Inc.,* 473 U.S. 614, 628, 105 S.Ct. 3346, 87 L.Ed.2d 444 (1985).

But we have also cautioned against thinking that Congress' primary objective was to guarantee these particular procedural advantages. Rather, that primary objective was to secure the "enforcement" of agreements to arbitrate. *Dean Witter,* 470 U.S., at 221, 105 S.Ct. 1238. *See also id.,* at 219, 105 S.Ct. 1238 (we "reject the suggestion that the overriding goal of the Arbitration Act was to promote the expeditious resolution of claims"); *id.,* at 219, 217–218, 105 S.Ct. 1238 ("[T]he intent of Congress" requires us to apply the terms of the Act without regard to whether the result would be "possibly inefficient"); *cf. id.,* at 220, 105 S.Ct. 1238 (acknowledging that "expedited resolution of disputes" might lead parties to prefer arbitration). The relevant Senate Report points to the Act's basic purpose when it says that "[t]he purpose of the [Act] is *clearly set forth in section 2,*" S.Rep. No. 536, at 2 (emphasis added), namely, the section that says that an arbitration agreement "shall be valid, irrevocable, and enforceable, save upon such grounds as exist at law or in equity for the revocation of any contract," 9 U.S.C. § 2.

Thus, insofar as we seek to implement Congress' intent, we should think more than twice before invalidating a state law that does just what § 2 requires, namely, puts agreements to arbitrate and agreements to litigate "upon the same footing." . . .

NOTES AND QUESTIONS

1. *What Is at Stake in the Debate Over Class Arbitration?* The conventional wisdom holds that arbitration proceedings are preferred by defendants. Arbitration is generally a less expensive proceeding than adjudication and lawyers frequently assume that the absence of a jury trial will decrease the settlement value of a plaintiff's claims, both features that may be particularly attractive to defendants who are repeat litigants. If a plaintiff's attorney is able to proceed on a classwide basis in an arbitration proceeding, however, the picture changes considerably. A class proceeding magnifies the stakes in arbitration, placing the defendant at risk for substantial damage awards, and the distinctive features of arbitration — less rigorous procedural strictures and limitations on judicial review — may deprive defendants of protections against overreach that they would rely on courts to impose in an adjudicated class action.

As plaintiff's attorneys have increasingly sought to pursue classwide arbitration, defendants have argued that such proceedings are impermissible. These arguments have generally taken one of three forms. First, a defendant may argue that a particular arbitration clause does not affirmatively authorize a classwide proceeding and that affirmative authorization is necessary for such a proceeding to occur at all. Second, even if an arbitration clause does purport to license classwide arbitration (or if the arbitral rules that it references provide such authorization — see, for example, the "Supplementary Rules for Class Arbitration" in the rules section of the AAA website, www.adr.org), a defendant may argue that such a proceeding would be inconsistent with other requirements of the FAA or with the purposes underlying the Act. Third, a defendant may argue that the arbitration clause expressly prohibits class arbitration, as was the case in *Concepcion*. As the following notes explain, the Court has found the Federal Arbitration Act to have powerful preemptive effect in all three of these settings.

2. *The Federal Arbitration Act and Preemption.* In *Concepcion*, the majority holds that the FAA preempts California's *unconscionability* doctrine, meaning the Arbitration Act supersedes state law and leaves no room for its operation. The Court reaches this conclusion despite the savings clause in the FAA that permits a party to challenge the validity of an arbitration clause "upon such grounds as exist at law or in equity for the revocation of any contract." The California Supreme Court had held in *Discover Bank v. Superior Court* that a take-it-or-leave-it "contract of adhesion" that gives consumers no meaningful opportunity to negotiate terms is unconscionable if it has the practical effect of insulating the company that drafted the contract from liability. According to California, this was a general principle of contract law that would have applied to any class-action waiver (or any other contract provision that had a similar effect) whether or not it was contained in an arbitration clause. Why, then, did the *Discover Bank* doctrine not survive under the FAA as a "ground[] [that] exist[s] at law or in equity for the revocation of any contract"?

The Court's answer to that question is key to understanding the broader implications of *Concepcion*. Even though *Discover Bank* did not expressly target arbitration clauses, the Court holds, it had a "disproportionate impact" on arbitration. To illustrate this point, the Court poses a series of hypotheticals. What if California interpreted its unconscionability doctrine to forbid contract terms that "fail to provide for judicially monitored discovery"? Even if the doctrine did not expressly target arbitration and applied equally to "contracts purporting to restrict discovery in litigation as well," the Court explains, the effect of the doctrine would be felt most strongly in arbitration, where the whole point is to replace the judge with a private arbitrator. The majority plays out similar hypotheticals involving the Rules of Evidence and the role of the jury. In each case, they conclude, permitting state law to invalidate an arbitration clause "would be absolutely inconsistent with the provisions of" the FAA.

In its most basic form, this argument could be concerned with *pretext*: identifying situations in which state law purports to embody a neutral principle that would apply to any contract but in fact is designed to target arbitration. In its stronger form, this argument might be framed in terms of *disparate impact*: identifying situations in which the impact of state law would fall more heavily on arbitration clauses, even if that is not its design and the law could have legitimate applications outside the arbitration setting. Does the Court adopt the stronger form of the argument here when it emphasizes the need to protect the "overarching purposes" of the Federal Arbitration Act from state-law doctrines that would "interfere[] with fundamental attributes of arbitration and thus create[] a scheme inconsistent with the FAA"—is that language that aims to prevent states from circumventing the FAA with pretextual contract law defenses? Or does the Court mean to reach more broadly?

If the Court does embrace a broader disparate-impact approach to FAA preemption in *Concepcion*, then what are the implications of such a doctrine? What other precepts of state contracts law might be unavailable when challenging the validity of an arbitration clause? Suppose that a state were to adopt a strong rule against contracts of adhesion, finding that any take-it-or-leave-it contract that waives the "fundamental rights" of a party is void unless the party's waiver is knowing and voluntary. If it were shown that the doctrine wound up applying most frequently to arbitration clauses but also had serious application in other settings, would *Concepcion* require that it be set aside? The Ninth Circuit found exactly that in a case involving just such a doctrine of adhesion contracts under Montana law. Even though that doctrine was not a pretext for targeting arbitration clauses, it "disproportionately applies to arbitration agreements, invalidating them at a higher rate than other contract provisions," and the appeals court found that fact alone to require preemption. *Mortensen v. Bresnan Communications*, 722 F.3d 1151, 1160–1161 (9th Cir. 2013).

3. *Class Arbitration in the Absence of Affirmative Authorization.* The *Concepcion* case involved an arbitration clause that expressly prohibited classwide proceedings. What if an arbitration clause is silent on the matter, neither prohibiting nor authorizing class arbitration? The Supreme Court addressed this scenario the year before *Concepcion*, holding that class arbitration is disfavored and cannot proceed in the absence of express contractual authorization. *See Stolt-Nielsen v. AnimalFeeds Int'l*, 559 U.S. 662 (2010). The case involved a dispute between a producer of animal feed products and a shipping company over an alleged price-fixing conspiracy by the shipper. AnimalFeeds brought suit under federal antitrust law and its claims were consolidated with similar claims brought by many other customers, all of which were subject to arbitration clauses and had to be submitted to arbitration panels. AnimalFeeds then served a demand for class arbitration, asking to represent a class of direct purchasers of the defendant's shipping and transportation services.

The arbitration clause that the parties had included in their agreement read as follows:

> Arbitration. Any dispute arising from the making, performance or termination of this Charter Party shall be settled in New York, Owner and Charterer each appointing an arbitrator, who shall be a merchant, broker or individual experienced in the shipping business; the two thus chosen, if they cannot agree, shall nominate a third arbitrator who shall be an Admiralty lawyer. Such arbitration shall be conducted in conformity with the provisions and procedure of the United States Arbitration Act [*i.e.*, the FAA], and a judgment of the Court shall be entered upon any award made by said arbitrator.

Id. at 667 (bracketed alteration in Supreme Court opinion). The clause did not expressly address whether classwide arbitration was an authorized form of proceeding, and the parties submitted this question to the arbitrators. Crucially, the parties agreed that the arbitration clause was "silent" on the question of classwide arbitration—it neither made express provision for such a proceeding nor referenced the rules of an arbitration firm that would authorize class arbitration. (The clause was drafted in 1950, before the rise of the modern class action.) Prior to *Stolt-Nielsen*, the Supreme Court itself had not offered clear guidance on the permissibility of class arbitration in such a case, rendering a series of fractured opinions in *Green Tree Financial Corp. v. Bazzle, supra,* that left these questions unanswered. The arbitrators concluded that classwide arbitration was authorized, pointing to a significant number of post-*Bazzle* rulings that had permitted such relief and finding that these other rulings, though dealing with different arbitration clauses found in different contracts, indicated the existence of an industry practice favoring class arbitration. In light of that industry practice, the arbitrators concluded that the contract before them should likewise be interpreted to authorize class arbitration.

The defendant-petitioner then filed an application in a federal district court, asking that the court vacate the order of the arbitrators. That case eventually came to the Supreme Court, which held that classwide arbitration was impermissible in this dispute. The Court declined to answer the question left open following *Hall Street Associates v. Mattel, Inc.,* 552 U.S. 576 (2008), whether "manifest disregard" of the law constituted a basis for reviewing an arbitral award. Instead, the Court concluded, "what the arbitration panel did was simply to impose its own view of sound policy regarding class arbitration." The Court continued:

> Rather than inquiring whether the [Federal Arbitration Act], maritime law, or New York law contains a "default rule" under which an arbitration clause is construed as allowing class arbitration in the absence of express consent, the panel proceeded as if it had the authority of a common-law court to develop what it viewed as the best rule to be applied in such a situation.

Stolt-Nielsen, 559 U.S. at 673–674. The Court then proceeded to issue its own holding on the availability of classwide arbitration. "While the interpretation of an arbitration agreement is generally a matter of state law," the Court explained, "the FAA imposes certain rules of fundamental importance, including the basic precept that arbitration is a matter of consent, not coercion." *Id.* at 681 (quotation omitted).

That principle of consent, the Court explained, included the right of the parties to "specify *with whom* they choose to arbitrate their disputes." *Id.* at 683. That being so, the Court concluded, the FAA was not neutral on the question of classwide arbitration. Far from it:

> From these principles, it follows that a party may not be compelled under the FAA to submit to class arbitration unless there is a contractual basis for concluding that the party *agreed* to do so. In this case, however, the arbitration panel imposed class arbitration even though the parties concurred that they had reached "no agreement" on that issue. The critical point, in the view of the arbitration panel, was that petitioners did not "establish that the parties to the charter agreements intended to *preclude* class arbitration." Even though the parties are sophisticated business entities, even though there is no tradition of class arbitration under maritime law, and even though AnimalFeeds does not dispute that it is customary for the shipper to choose the charter party that is used for a particular shipment, the panel regarded the agreement's silence on the question of class arbitration as dispositive. The panel's conclusion is fundamentally at war with the foundational FAA principle that arbitration is a matter of consent.

> . . .

> An implicit agreement to authorize class-action arbitration, however, is not a term that the arbitrator may infer solely from the fact of the parties' agreement to arbitrate. This is so because class action arbitration changes the nature of arbitration to such a degree that it cannot be presumed the parties consented to it by simply agreeing to submit their disputes to an arbitrator. In bilateral arbitration, parties forgo the procedural rigor and appellate review of the courts in order to realize the benefits of private dispute resolution: lower costs, greater efficiency and speed, and the ability to choose expert adjudicators to resolve specialized disputes. But the relative benefits of class-action arbitration are much less assured, giving reason to doubt the parties' mutual consent to resolve disputes through class-wide arbitration.

Id. at 684–686.

Stolt-Nielsen represents a major shift in the law of classwide arbitration, but questions remain about how to interpret arbitration clauses of more recent vintage than the one before the Court in *Stolt-Nielsen*, where express or implied references to rules allowing for class arbitration (like the AAA's Supplementary Rules for Class Arbitration, *supra*) may call for a different result. Such was the case in *Oxford Health Plans v. Sutter*, 569 U.S. 564 (2013). The parties in *Oxford* disagreed over whether class arbitration was authorized under a clause requiring any "civil action concerning any dispute arising under this Agreement" to be submitted to arbitration "pursuant to the rules of the American Arbitration Association." The arbitrator found that class arbitration was available and defendant Oxford asked the federal courts to vacate that ruling, citing *Stolt-Nielsen* for the proposition that "a court may . . . vacate 'as *ultra vires*' an arbitral decision . . . misconstruing a contract to approve class proceedings." *Id.* at 571. The Court rejected the argument, emphasizing that the outcome in *Stolt-Nielsen* had depended on "an unusual stipulation" between the parties "that they had never reached an agreement on class arbitration" in their contract at all. *Id.* When parties disagree about whether a contract authorizes class arbitration and they submit that question to the arbitrator, as in *Sutter*, they are bound by the arbitrator's ruling on the matter. A court cannot set aside an arbitrator's ruling merely because the arbitrator has "misinterpreted the contract" on the question of class arbitration, but only where he has "abandoned [the] interpretive role" altogether, as the Court had found to be the case in *Stolt-Nielsen. Id.* at 571–572. Under *Concepcion*, of course, a party can still shield itself from class arbitration by including an express waiver to that effect in the agreement. But the *Sutter* decision makes clear that an area of contestation remains in arbitration proceedings governed by contracts that lack such a waiver.

In a subsequent decision, the Court strengthened the *Stolt-Nielsen* doctrine further, holding that class arbitration was not permitted when a contract is ambiguous on the question, rather than merely silent (as in *Stolt-Nielsen*). *Lamps Plus, Inc. v. Varela*, 139 S. Ct. 1407 (2019), involved a breach of data security at Lamps Plus that released the confidential tax information of about 1,300 employees to scammers. Plaintiffs filed a class action in federal district court asserting claims for damages arising from that breach, and defendant moved to compel arbitration. On appeal, the Ninth Circuit found that certain language in the arbitration clause—for example, a provision explaining that arbitration would be "in lieu of any and all lawsuits or other civil legal proceedings"—was ambiguous on the question whether class arbitration was authorized and hence that the contract language should be construed against the interest of the drafter and in favor of permitting a class proceeding. The Supreme Court disagreed. Over sharp dissents by four Justices, the majority held that class arbitration "undermines the most important benefits of . . . traditional individualized arbitration" and "ambiguity does not provide a sufficient basis to conclude that parties to an arbitration agreement agreed to sacrifice the principal advantage of arbitration," its simplicity and efficiency.*Id.* at 1415–1416. Hence, the Court concluded, when an arbitration clause leaves room for doubt about whether it is authorizing a class proceeding, the strong policy against class arbitration that the Court has attributed to the Federal Arbitration Act prohibits such a proceeding.

Following *Stolt-Nielsen* and *Varela*, must an arbitration clause explicitly authorize class arbitration in order for such a proceeding to be permitted under the Federal Arbitration Act? Given the hostility toward class proceedings that the Court finds in the Act, might even such explicit authorization be preempted? *Varela* does not go that far, but it does move a significant distance toward foreclosing the pathways for class relief in arbitration.

4. Consider the practical impact of the *Concepcion* decision in conjunction with other rulings. *Rent-A-Center* has strengthened the presumption that arbitrators, rather than courts, must determine the validity of an arbitration agreement, presumably making it less likely that consumers will succeed in challenging such agreements. *Stolt-Nielsen* and *Varela* have held that, when an arbitration agreement is silent or ambiguous on the question of classwide arbitration, the FAA prohibits

arbitrators from employing that procedure. And *Concepcion* now holds that consumers are bound by mandatory waivers of class arbitration, notwithstanding any provisions of state law to the contrary, even in contracts of adhesion where it is alleged that the defendant company is seeking to defraud consumers on the expectation that they will not enforce their rights. It appears that a consumer who signs an arbitration agreement will be unable to participate in any form of class proceeding unless the agreement affirmatively provides for class arbitration or references a body of arbitral rules that provide for class arbitration and contains no waiver of that procedure. For a discussion of *Concepcion*'s effect on class litigation in the fields of consumer protection and employment law, *see* Myriam Gilles & Gary Friedman, *After Class: Aggregate Litigation in the Wake of AT&T Mobility v. Concepcion*, 79 U. Chi. L. Rev. 623 (2012) (describing *Concepcion* as "coup de grace administered to consumer class actions" but arguing for a restrained reading of the decision that would not wholly foreclose enforcement of important statutory rights).

The Court closed off another potential avenue for circumventing *Concepcion* in *DirectTV v. Imburgia*, 577 U.S. 47 (2015). That case involved a California contract that included an arbitration requirement with a class arbitration waiver, but the clause specified that the agreement to arbitrate would be of no effect "if the law of your state" (that is, the consumer's state) made the agreement illegal. Prior to the Court's decision in *Concepcion*, the California Supreme Court had held that arbitration clauses that waive class-based relief were invalid under California law. *Concepcion* found that the FAA preempted that ruling and required enforcement of arbitration clauses nonetheless. The question in *DirectTV* was whether the reference in the contract to "the law of your state" would render the arbitration clause invalid under the *Discover Bank* doctrine despite the Court's subsequent ruling in *Concepcion*. (The clause was drafted before *Concepcion*.) The Court found that its preemption ruling in *Concepcion* had rendered invalid state laws that disapproved class arbitration waivers and it concluded that neither the drafters of the contract nor California itself could have meant for "*invalid* California law" to be included in any contractual reference to the laws of that state. *Id.* at 55. Justice Ginsburg issued a strongly worded dissent decrying the Court's "ever-larger expansion of the FAA's scope." *Id.* at 71 (Ginsburg, J., dissenting).

5. *The* Concepcion *Doctrine and Federal Causes of Action.* In another major ruling, the Supreme Court has reaffirmed and expanded on its holding in *Concepcion* regarding waivers of class arbitration and other forms of joint proceedings, this time applying the doctrine to a competing federal cause of action. The case, *American Express v. Italian Colors*, 570 U.S. 228 (2013), involved arbitration provisions contained in an agreement between American Express and merchants who accept AmEx cards at their stores. The merchants claimed that AmEx was abusing its monopoly power by forcing merchants to accept a form contract containing unfair terms, and they brought a class action under federal antitrust law. The contract required such claims to go to arbitration and imposed many restrictions on the types of arbitration proceedings that were available to claimants, including a waiver of class proceedings and a prohibition on joint actions in which multiple claimants pooled their resources. AmEx moved to compel arbitration and the merchants argued in response that enforcing these provisions would make it impossible for the merchants to enforce their rights under the federal antitrust statute because any antitrust claim would require an economic analysis that could cost a

million dollars while the recovery for any individual merchant would only be in the tens of thousands. Thus, the merchants argued, enforcing the arbitration clause would preclude any "effective vindication" of their federal statutory rights. In several earlier decisions, the Court had suggested that arbitration obstacles that "preclude a litigant from . . . effectively vindicating her federal statutory rights" might be unenforceable. *Green Tree Financial v. Randolph*, 531 U.S. 79, 90 (2000). *See also Mitsubishi Motors v. Soler Chrysler-Plymouth*, 473 U.S. 614, 637 & n.19 (1985).

Justice Scalia wrote for the majority in a 5-3 ruling that rejected the merchants' arguments. (Justice Sotomayor had sat on the panel that decided an earlier stage of this case when she was a judge on the Second Circuit, and she therefore recused herself.) The Court focused on language from those earlier opinions concerning potential obstacles to "a party's *right to pursue* statutory remedies" and found that the "effective vindication" exception to the FAA, whatever its scope, applies only to barriers to enforcing one's federal statutory rights that are categorical in nature, like a provision that prospectively waives the right to sue altogether. The antitrust laws and similar federal statutes, however, "do not guarantee an affordable procedural path to the vindication of every claim." *Italian Colors*, 570 U.S. at 228–229. Even insurmountable financial barriers to maintaining an individual claim provided no grounds for the merchants to escape the arbitration clause and the constraints that it contained. "Truth to tell," the Court said, "our decision in *AT&T Mobility [v. Concepcion]* all but resolves this case," since *Concepcion* "specifically rejected the argument that class arbitration was necessary to prosecute claims 'that might otherwise slip through the legal system.'" *Id.* at 238 (quoting *Concepcion*, 131 S. Ct. at 1753).

Concepcion involved claims by consumers rather than merchants. Concerns about a party's lack of opportunity to negotiate the terms of an arbitration agreement might be even more acute in the case of consumers, yet that argument did not carry the day in *Concepcion*. On the other hand, the *Concepcion* Court did emphasize provisions included in AT&T Mobility's consumer contract that theoretically made it possible for customers to pursue financially viable arbitration against the company on an individual basis. The contract in *Italian Colors* included no such provisions and it is unclear whether the merchants retained any viable path to recovery under the federal antitrust laws at all. The majority did not address this potential distinction between the two settings when it invoked *Concepcion* to reject the merchants' "effective vindication" argument.

Justice Kagan dissented in a sharply worded opinion joined by Justices Ginsburg and Breyer that accused the majority of elevating form over reality. The whole point of the lawsuit, she argued, was that AmEx was using its market power to force an unfair contract on the merchants. The constraints that the contract imposed on the ability of the merchants to advance federal statutory claims constituted a part of the unfairness that they alleged as violations of the antitrust laws. Those constraints were not limited to a waiver of class arbitration but also "disallow[ed] any kind of joinder or consolidation of claims or parties" and prevented merchants "from informally arranging with other merchants to produce a common expert report." *Id.* at 246 (Kagan, J., dissenting). In other words, AmEx had taken pains to identify and prohibit every means by which the merchants might be able to afford to assert an antitrust claim. According to the dissenters, the record before the Court made it clear that the "effective vindication" doctrine must apply not only to "baldly exculpatory provisions" like a prospective waiver of liability but also to contract clauses that were designed and would reliably operate to produce the same result. *Id.* at 241–242 (Kagan, J. dissenting). The Federal Arbitration Act, Justice Kagan wrote, "reflects a federal policy favoring actual arbitration — that is, arbitration as a streamlined method of resolving disputes, not as a foolproof way of killing off valid claims." *Id.* at 243–244 (Kagan, J., dissenting).

The sharply differing approaches of the Justices to these questions is again on display in *Epic Systems v. Lewis*, 138 S. Ct. 1612 (2018). *Epic Systems* involved arbitration clauses that several companies had required their workers to sign. In each case, the clause prohibited workers from bringing class action lawsuits or initiating class arbitration proceedings. The workers claimed that their employers had deprived them of wages to which they were entitled in violation of the federal Fair Labor Standards Act, and they argued that a related statute, the National Labor Relations Act, guaranteed their right "to engage in . . . concerted activities" for the purpose of securing their "mutual aid or protection." 29 U.S.C. §157. The question in *Epic Systems* was whether that statutory guarantee included the right to bring class action lawsuits and, if so, whether the Federal Arbitration Act mandated enforcement of the class action waivers nonetheless. The savings clause of the FAA permits courts to decline to enforce arbitration clauses "upon such grounds as exist at law or in equity for the revocation of any contract," 9 U.S.C. §2, and the workers argued that enforcement of the arbitration clause to foreclose a class action in their federal wage claims would violate the NLRA's guarantee of "concerted activity" to enforce their rights and hence was a "ground" that "exists at law for the revocation" of the clause. The availability of concerted activity was crucial here, since the claim of any one worker would be too small to litigate, meaning that the workers would have no effective way to enforce their rights if a class action was unavailable.

In a 5-4 ruling, the Court found that the FAA required exactly that result. Building on its ruling in *Concepcion*, the Court held that the FAA requires courts to "be alert to new devices and formulas" that would have a disparate effect on arbitration clauses and that "an argument that a contract is unenforceable *just because it requires bilateral arbitration* . . . is one that impermissibly disfavors arbitration whether it sounds in illegality or unconscionability." *Epic Systems*, 138 S. Ct. at 1623 (emphasis in original). The fact that a competing federal statute might deem the arbitration clause illegal was irrelevant, the Court found, because "the Arbitration Act seems to protect" arbitration clauses "pretty absolutely" and that protection supersedes the competing statutory command. *Id.* at 1621. The dissenters, led by Justice Ginsburg, insisted that the purpose of the NLRA and the FLSA would be set at naught if employers could require workers to accede to contract clauses that took away their only effective means of enforcing claims for wage theft. The dissenters would have held that the NLRA's requirement that mechanisms for "concerted activity" be preserved was adequate to satisfy the FAA's savings clause. Alternatively, if there was a conflict between the statutes, the dissenters insisted that the more specific and focused command of the labor statutes should prevail over the more generic FAA. They described the majority's ruling to the contrary as "egregiously wrong."

The final chapter has not been written in this energetic area of litigation, but there can be no question that the pendulum has swung in favor of the drafters of contracts, who now have broad powers at their disposal to shield themselves from aggregate liability in their relationships with customers or employees.

6. *Alternatives to Class Arbitration.* The frequent assumption in these discussions is that access to class arbitration will facilitate recovery by injured consumers and that rulings by the Court that empower corporate actors to shield themselves from class arbitration through express waivers, or that establish a presumption against class arbitration where contract language is ambiguous, operate to the consumer's detriment. Professor Myriam Gilles, a prominent scholar and critic of class arbitration waivers, has warned that "class action bans" in arbitration clause waivers "promis[e] virtual immunity from liability, given the certainty that consumers and employers would almost never be able to arbitrate small dollar claims." Myriam Gilles, *The Day Doctrine Died: Private Arbitration and the End of Law*, 2016 U. Ill. L. Rev. 371, 376 (2016). But is the issue so clear? Critics of class arbitration point to the danger that arbitrators may have less experience with complex matters involving the interest of absent claimants and are not subject to appellate review, all of which may make them less reliable adjudicators in these matters. Are there viable alternatives to class arbitration? The provision in *Concepcion* appeared to create an economically viable pathway for individual recovery, though *Italian Colors* makes it clear that drafters of arbitration clauses can close off those avenues. Professor Gilles examines the possibility that state attorneys general might be able to use the authority of their offices in new ways to seek aggregate or group relief for consumers and employees, *see* Myriam Gilles, *Procedure in Eclipse: Group-Based Adjudication in a Post-*Concepcion *Era*, 56 St. Louis L.J. 1203, 1226–1228 (2012), though she is not optimistic. What other alternatives for aggregate recovery might be available in the arbitration setting? Would a major policy initiative to facilitate and fund individual arbitration by consumers make sense?

7. *Regulatory Reform?* In July 2017, the federal Consumer Financial Protection Bureau (CFPB) presented a rule, 12 CFR part 1040, that would have prohibited certain businesses from using mandatory arbitration clauses that block class action relief while also imposing reporting requirements on those businesses designed to permit the CFPB to monitor the impact of arbitration on consumer welfare. The rule would have applied to providers of certain consumer financial products and services including credit cards, automobile loans, and debt consolidation. The rule was drafted following an extensive study that the CFPB began in 2012 into the impact of mandatory arbitration clauses and class action waivers on consumers in the sale of financial products and services. An extensive discussion of the proposed rule, including background and supporting materials, may be found at https://www.consumerfinance.gov/policy-compliance/rulemaking/final-rules/arbitration-agreements/.

Had it gone into effect, the proposed rule would likely have had a significant impact on the affected industries. *Concepcion* and *Italian Colors* have given the drafters of consumer contracts the ability to eliminate class actions, class arbitration, and other forms of aggregate relief in almost all cases, whether plaintiffs seek to proceed on state or federal claims, even in cases (like *Italian Colors*) where plaintiffs had no affordable avenue for pursuing relief on an individual basis. The new regulation would have prevented many of those devices from being included in financial services contracts, presumably making it possible once again for plaintiffs suing businesses in the affected industries to pursue aggregate relief. Before the new rule went into effect, however, the newly constituted Congress and Executive following the 2016 election acted to block it through a fast-track joint resolution process that permits Congress to reject proposed rules more easily. *See* https://www.consumerfinance.gov/policy-compliance/rulemaking/final-rules/arbitration-agreements/. No new rules have been proposed as of this publication, though the change in the Executive and Congress following the 2020 election and subsequent developments from the Supreme Court that empower a President to replace the CFPB Director at will may lead to renewed attention to the topic.

3.   *Non-Adversarial Forms of ADR—Mediation*

a.   Mediation as Compromise and "Reality Check"

Mediation is founded on consensus and compromise. It involves an attempt to encourage the parties in a dispute to find common ground and agree upon a mutually satisfactory solution. A mediation proceeding does not result in a verdict that is imposed upon the parties by a neutral decision-making body. Rather, the neutral figure in a mediation (the mediator) seeks to facilitate an outcome that the parties will agree upon voluntarily—one they believe to be fair, or at least the best that they can hope for. Mediation is thus a true alternative to a traditional lawsuit or an adversarial arbitration. It is an attempt to bring the parties to agreement without imposing that agreement upon them.

Mediation can also provide the parties with an important "reality check" as to the strength and reasonableness of their positions in a dispute, even when it does not result in a final resolution. An adversarial proceeding, by its nature, may push the parties into defensive positions in which they insist tenaciously upon the strength of their respective positions. Mediation, in contrast, provides the disputants with the opinion of a neutral third party, and it does so in a context where the parties can entertain the possibility that their positions may be flawed without necessarily suffering a litigation disadvantage. In this respect, mediation may narrow the issues in a dispute and bring the parties considerably closer to settlement. This function of mediation may be particularly useful to businesses. Assessing litigation positions when a dispute arises is a part of doing business, and it can sometimes be difficult for an attorney to step outside the role of advocate and give a balanced assessment of both sides of a dispute. A mediator can provide this valuable outside perspective.

Thus, mediation and adversarial proceedings like a lawsuit or arbitration are not mutually exclusive—the one can complement the other. It is not uncommon for parties to submit a dispute to mediation in hopes of eliminating the need for a more adversarial mechanism but still to keep the adversarial option in reserve. For this reason, mediation is often described as "nonbinding" because the parties are not compelled or bound to accept the solutions presented to them in the proceeding. If a party leaves a mediation dissatisfied, it retains the option of rejecting the proposed solutions and pursuing the more traditional route of a lawsuit or arbitration. Mediation is an attempt to avoid such an adversarial proceeding, not a substitute for it.

Despite the substantive differences between these two ADR methods, the mechanics for invoking a mediation proceeding are similar in some ways to those for invoking arbitration. Most commonly, the parties to a contract will include a provision that requires them to attempt mediation before resorting to a lawsuit or arbitration. (Of course, parties can also choose to submit a dispute to mediation even in the absence of a contractual provision.) Mediation clauses often appear in conjunction with arbitration clauses, as in the following example, which is modeled after a contract for the sale of a house:

Dispute Resolution:

A. Mediation: Buyer and Seller agree to mediate any dispute or claim arising between them out of this Agreement, or any resulting transaction, before resorting to arbitration or court action. If any party commences an action to which this paragraph applies without first attempting to resolve the matter through mediation, or refuses to mediate in good faith after a request has been made, then that party shall not be entitled to recover attorney's fees, even if they would otherwise be available to that party in any such action.

B. Arbitration of Disputes: Buyer and Seller agree that any dispute or claim arising between them out of this Agreement, or any resulting transaction, which is not settled through mediation, shall be decided by neutral, binding arbitration. The arbitrator shall be a retired judge or justice, or an attorney with at least 5 years of experience in residential real estate law, unless the parties mutually agree to a different arbitrator. The arbitrator shall render an award, and the arbitration shall be conducted, in accordance with New York law. Judgment upon the award of the arbitrator may be entered in any court having jurisdiction. The parties shall have the right to discovery in accordance with the New York Civil Procedure Laws and Rules.

Mediation, like arbitration, is usually conducted under the auspices of a private dispute resolution organization. The manner in which mediation proceedings are conducted varies enormously from case to case. Mediations are not structured around the formal development of evidence, as are lawsuits and arbitrations. Rather, they involve a presentation of points of view that can be quite informal. Much depends on the personal style of the mediator. A mediator might prefer to have frequent, individual meetings with each of the parties, encouraging them to speak candidly about their complaints and trying to bring them to more moderate positions, or a mediator might prefer to bring both parties together from the beginning, allowing them to air their unedited grievances in the open and calling upon them to try to see the other's perspective.

As a general rule, lawyers are less involved in mediation proceedings than they would be in either a lawsuit or an arbitration. The lesser degree of formality in the proceedings and the role of the mediator in attempting to draw the parties toward consensus render lawyers less important in mediations. Indeed, some would argue that the presence of lawyers in a mediation is counterproductive. Nonetheless, parties to a mediation do sometimes secure representation. One of the principal reasons for doing so is to avoid making any damaging *admissions*—statements in which the party admits to taking certain actions that could harm the party's case if mediation fails and litigation follows. While there are some limits on the ability of parties to use statements made in a mediation as evidence against their opponents in future proceedings — particularly when those statements form part of a compromise proposal that effectively constitutes a settlement offer (*see* Fed. R. Evid. 408) — other damaging statements that parties make can come back to haunt them. Thus, in some cases, there can be a tension in mediation between the immediate goals of the proceeding and the long-term interests of the parties in the event that mediation should prove unsuccessful.

Depending on the outcome of the mediation, the parties will likely sign some form of settlement agreement that releases some or all of their claims in return for the compromise solution that the mediation has produced. Because they are founded on consensus, mediation outcomes have no enforcement mechanisms analogous to the statutory enforcement provisions for arbitration awards discussed in the previous section. In theory, the parties to a successful mediation have embraced the outcome as an acceptable one and do not need to be coerced to comply. Enforcement is available when it might be necessary, however. A mediated settlement is still a contract and can be enforced in the same manner as any other contract would be.

Some commentators question whether the mediation model described above is in danger of being eclipsed by a more adversarial approach. Indeed, one expert argues that "American mediation practice is advancing steadily towards the practice zone of arbitration." Jacqueline Nolan-Haley, *Mediation: The "New Arbitration,"* 17 Harv. Neg. L. Rev. 61, 62–63 (2012). Surveying the literature on ADR practices, Professor Nolan-Haley explains that "lawyers [are] becom[ing] increasingly visible representing parties in mediation." She concludes that the widespread participation of lawyers in ADR and a movement toward a more adjudicative model in the internal practices of mediation together threaten to convert mediation into "a surrogate for arbitration." *Id.* at 63. This development, she argues, represents a threat to the distinctive values that mediation seeks to promote. *See also* Jean R. Sternlight, *Lawyerless Dispute Resolution: Rethinking a Paradigm,* 37 Ford. Urb. L.J. 381 (2010) (discussing when attorney representation may or may not be appropriate in mediation and arbitration).

b.   The Diverse Interests of Parties

Another virtue that proponents of mediation point to is the opportunity that mediation provides for the individuals involved in a dispute to explain their point of view outside the rigidly defined boundaries of an adversarial proceeding. In most cases, this is a virtue that will probably be more attractive to individual litigants than to a business entity, for whom the "softer" values of mediation may be of little concern. But for individual litigants, the experience of the dispute resolution process may be quite important. Mediation provides an opportunity for parties to articulate their interests in their own terms and to focus on the facts that are most important to them, even when those facts may have limited legal significance. As one commentator has written: "Typically, mediation takes into account expressions that might be considered irrelevant to adjudication of legal entitlements. Parties often speak for themselves, and mediators often encourage any dialogue that they feel will lead toward potential settlement." Deborah L. Levi, Note, *The Role of Apology in Mediation,* 72 N.Y.U. L. Rev. 1165, 1170–1171 (1997). *See also* Thomas J.

Stipanowich, *The Quiet Revolution Comes to Kentucky: A Case Study in Community Mediation*, 81 Ky. L.J. 855, 870–872 (1993) (concluding, after extensive case study of one community, that mediation can be cathartic because it "may offer parties the first opportunity to express their point of view in the presence of others and be heard by the other party"). *But see* Lee Taft, *Apology Subverted: The Commodification of Apology*, 109 Yale L.J. 1135 (2000) (suggesting that apology inevitably loses much of its moral significance when offered in the context of formal dispute resolution and so is of limited value).

The ability of mediation to provide such a forum may not be solely attributable to its nonlegalistic nature. Some proponents of mediation argue that a lesser degree of formality, more direct participation by the parties, and less involvement by lawyers can combine to remove certain structural impediments to the parties' voices being heard, resulting in more nuanced attention to their interests. Professor Judith Resnik, a leading scholar on courts and court reform, has described this school of thought in the following terms:

> [One form of praise for ADR addresses] its potential for kindness as contrasted (sometimes explicitly) with nastiness, which is associated with adjudication. ADR is perceived to be friendly, flexible, and nicer than the uncivil exchanges that characterize litigation.
>
> This congenial theme contains a bundle of claims, which is worth sorting through. One means by which ADR is believed to achieve a congenial tone is because some forms of ADR have the potential to reduce the role of attorneys. Less lawyering is not only a way to minimize fees and thus make the process less expensive and speedier . . . , but less lawyering is also seen as more civilized and as more responsive to the problems at issue. A world with fewer lawyers is imagined to be less rigid and more inventive. The assumption is that, without lawyers, the disputants are empowered to act, and with that empowerment, can shape solutions more responsive to their needs than third parties, in their role as adjudicators, would impose.
>
> The ADR-as-congenial set of claims is not wholly dependent upon the elimination of lawyers. Rather, ADR is also seen as beneficial when lawyers are present—to educate and civilize lawyers by focusing them on the needs of their clients. Some forms of ADR aspire to teach lawyers that initiating settlement negotiations and engaging in various forms of compromise are not signs of weakness. Other forms of ADR hope to provide clients with information directly, enabling clients to better monitor their lawyers who may not always be loyal agents. While adjudicatory modes increase parties' dependence on lawyers, ADR may, under this view, both lessen parties' dependence on lawyers and focus lawyers' attention more directly on parties' needs and interests. . . .
>
> ADR is thus seen as a set of processes more comfortable than adjudication. Litigant satisfaction and enthusiasm for ADR mechanisms are cited as evidence of ADR's accessibility and intelligibility. The informality of ADR and its potential for privacy are assumed to put parties at their ease, and with that ease, to bring about better resolutions. Conversation and cooperation replace conflict; informality empowers. . . .

The vision of ADR as communicative and congenial comes with a frank critique of many of the attributes of adjudication. The formality of adjudication is perceived as undermining open communication. The procedural requirements of adjudication are described as roadblocks to communication and to fairness. The rights of public access and information are seen as intrusive on private parties, who might otherwise respond to the state in its role as facilitator of agreements. Adjudication is seen as a process that often brings out the worst in its participants, either because it distorts their abilities to pursue self-interest or because it defines self-interest in such a fashion that requires inflicting losses, rather than maximizing gains.

Judith Resnik, *Many Doors? Closing Doors? Alternative Dispute Resolution and Adjudication*, 10 Ohio St. J. on Disp. Resol. 212, 246–250 (1995). In sum, mediation's strongest proponents believe that it not only promotes cost savings and efficiency, but also has the capacity to produce solutions that an adversarial mode of dispute resolution would not allow at all. Having described these arguments, however, Resnik herself goes on to express some skepticism at the ability of mediation to fulfill its promise. *See id.*

NOTES AND QUESTIONS

1. *Can Mediation Work?* How realistic does mediation seem to you? After all, parties to a serious dispute often harbor a great deal of anger toward each other. In fact, as we discussed in the section on settlement agreements, parties to a dispute may want to have nothing more to do with each other once the dispute is resolved. Is it reasonable to expect two people who have been involved in a serious employment dispute, for example, to sit down and arrive at a "compromise" solution when the employee wants justice and vindication and the employer wants to remain firm in order to dissuade other employees from bringing similar lawsuits? Is mediation's usefulness limited to cases where the parties are predisposed to finding a compromise solution in the first place? *Cf.* Laura Nader, *Controlling Processes in the Practice of Law: Hierarchy and Pacification in the Movement to Re-Form Dispute Ideology*, 9 Ohio St. J. on Disp. Resol. 1 (1993) (arguing that "coercive harmony" inherent in mediation is of limited effectiveness and endangers the rights of litigants).

2. *Admissions and Admissibility in Mediation.* Some courts have recognized the potential for tension between a mediation proceeding, which is supposed to be open and candid, and future litigation, in which admissions of wrongdoing can be damning, and they have made provisions for keeping confidential any mediation proceedings that occur under the auspices of the court. The District Court for the Eastern District of New York, for example, provides by local rule for court-annexed mediation in which "the mediation process is confidential, whether or not a settlement is reached." The rule explains:

> Unless the parties otherwise agree, all written and oral communications made by the parties and the mediator in connection with or during any mediation session are confidential and may not be disclosed or used for any purpose unrelated to the mediation.

. . .

No papers generated by the mediation process will be included in Court files, nor shall the Judge or Magistrate Judge assigned to the case have access to them. Information about what transpires during mediation sessions will not at any time be made known to the Court, except to the extent required to resolve issues of noncompliance with the mediation procedures.

U.S. District Court for the Eastern District of New York, Local Rule 83.8(d)(1)(A) & d(3). Are such confidentiality rules advisable? Are they necessary? In their absence, how could a mediation satisfy its goals of encouraging reconciliation and providing a forum for a candid assessment of each party's position?

3. *Business Actors and Good Relations.* Might the "softer" values of mediation have some value to business entities after all? At the outset, this section suggested that the "reality check" that mediation can offer as to the respective positions of two litigants may be more useful to a corporation than the conciliatory tone for which mediation strives. A Fortune 500 company, after all, does not immediately spring to mind as the type of litigant most likely to value conciliation. Corporations are principally concerned with the bottom line. Even so, it may be valuable to a corporation to maintain friendly relations with other companies with which it does business. If a dispute arises between a manufacturing corporation and a supplier, for example, the corporation might be reluctant to bring a lawsuit for fear of alienating an important business partner, and yet equally reluctant to let the matter slide completely. The less accusatory atmosphere of a mediation may provide an attractive means of resolving disputes between companies that wish to maintain ongoing and friendly business relations.

4. Supplemental Forms of ADR

Arbitration and mediation are both methods of ADR that can stand by themselves as alternatives to adjudication. In an arbitration, the parties submit their dispute for resolution and the resulting award is final (with the few exceptions noted above). In a mediation, while the parties are not forced to accept the outcome, the point of the proceeding is to arrive at a consensus that will completely settle the parties' differences. Like a traditional lawsuit, arbitration and mediation aim to resolve all the claims between the parties. But not all the procedures that fall under the heading of "alternative dispute resolution" fit that description. There are many ADR procedures that are not necessarily intended to stand alone in providing a final resolution to the parties' disputes. Rather, as the title of this section suggests, these procedures serve to supplement adjudication and its alternatives.

Generally speaking, these supplemental ADR procedures have two purposes. The first is to give the parties an impression of how their claims are likely to be received by a jury, or what size award a fact finder is likely to return. The hope is that, armed with such information, parties will know when a settlement offer represents a fair portion of the best they are likely to obtain through litigation, making it easier for them to make judgments about when to accept an offer while at the same time protecting themselves against settlements that would undervalue their claims. Related to this goal is the second purpose of supplemental ADR procedures — to save money in the court system and reduce caseloads for judges by encouraging cases to settle out of court without first going through a trial.

a. Federal Court Reforms and the Civil Justice Reform Act of 1990

Many supplemental forms of ADR grow out of attempts by federal and state legislatures to relieve the caseload of overburdened courts. The ever-expanding docket of cases in federal and state courts has become a serious problem. In the federal courts, for example, caseloads of individual district judges and appellate panels have increased by orders of magnitude in the last few decades. *See, e.g.,* William H. Rehnquist, *Seen in a Glass Darkly: The Future of the Federal Courts,* 1993 Wis. L. Rev. 1 (discussing growth of caseloads in federal courts and some solutions that have been proposed). In response, both Congress and various state legislatures have attempted to initiate legislative reforms aimed at reducing caseloads by encouraging parties to settle cases early.

One of the most far-reaching reforms that has been attempted in the federal system was the Civil Justice Reform Act (CJRA), 28 U.S.C. §§471 *et seq.,* enacted by Congress in 1990. The CJRA required federal district courts to experiment with various strategies aimed at facilitating the resolution of disputes and placing limits upon discovery. The CJRA was in effect for seven years, and the effort associated with it was far reaching, but in the end this experiment produced only mixed results. After the CJRA expired in 1997, Congress elected to renew only some of the ADR reforms that had been instituted under it. In the Alternative Dispute Resolution Act of 1998, 28 U.S.C. §§651 *et seq.,* Congress required district courts to pass local rules under which courts must require litigants to *consider* one form of supplemental alternative dispute resolution. (We will look at some specific examples in the next section.) Litigants are not required to take advantage of these ADR opportunities, but the 1998 Act imposes considerable institutional pressure upon them to do so.

While the grand experiment of the CJRA did not result in uniform, system-wide changes to the manner in which litigation is conducted in the federal courts, it certainly left its mark. Federal district courts are more open than ever before to channeling disputes into alternative avenues of resolution, and many individual courts have retained reforms in local rules adopted under the CJRA, even following its expiration. *See, e.g.,* U.S. District Court for the Southern District of New York, Local Rule 83.12, Alternative Dispute Resolution (setting forth procedures for court-annexed arbitration and mediation).

b. Some Examples of Supplemental ADR Methods

i. Mandatory Arbitration with Trial De Novo

There are some jurisdictions that require litigants in civil cases to submit to arbitration before proceeding to a full trial on their claims. This so-called court-annexed arbitration is a less formal affair than a trial. It proceeds before a neutral arbiter, usually a retired judge. The litigants have the chance to present evidence and make their case before the arbiter, though usually in a much more concise fashion than one would expect at a trial. At the end of the proceeding, the arbiter renders a decision. Each party then has a certain amount of time in which it can decide to reject the decision of the arbiter and proceed to trial. If a party elects this option, the decision of the arbiter and all the proceedings (including testimony and other evidence) are inadmissible in the subsequent adjudicatory proceedings. The trial proceeds *de novo*, from the beginning, and the parties proceed as if the arbitration had never happened. The party choosing this option, however, does so at a potential cost. If, at the end of the trial, the party who requested a trial *de novo* does not obtain a more favorable result than the arbitration award, that party must typically pay some of the costs associated with the proceedings. This penalty might include anything from the cost that the state incurred in conducting the arbitration proceedings — e.g., a prorated portion of the arbiter's salary, the expense associated with the facilities, and so forth — to the attorneys' fees of the party's opponent.

Mandatory arbitration of this kind is nonbinding. A party who loses the arbitration and thinks she can win at trial, or who recovers a small award and thinks she can do better, has the option of setting aside the arbitration, subject to the penalty described above. If the parties choose not to exercise the trial *de novo* option, however, then the arbitration award matures into a judgment. Such a judgment is not appealable (the trial *de novo* is the "appeal" that would be available) and it has all the characteristics that a judgment following trial would have. The courts of New York, for example, employ this type of mandatory arbitration system in cases involving smaller amounts of money. *See* N.Y. C.P.L.R.§3405 (empowering chief judge to promulgate mandatory arbitration rules for disputes not exceeding specified dollar amounts).

ii. Mandatory Mediation

Similarly, some states require parties to submit certain types of claims to mediation before they will be allowed to proceed to trial. For example, in North Carolina, family law disputes involving custody and visitation must be submitted to mediation before the parties may receive a hearing in court. *See* N.C. Gen. Stat. §50-13.1. This provision is modeled after a 1981 California law, Cal. Civ. Code §4607, that formed part of a significant reform of that state's family law system at the time. *See generally* Michelle Deis, *California's Answer: Mandatory Mediation of Child Custody and Visitation Disputes,* 1 Ohio St. J. on Disp. Resol. 149 (1985). (The California provision was later repealed.)

As we have seen, mediation is, by its very nature, nonbinding — if the parties are unable to agree to a resolution of their claims, then the mediator has no power to impose a solution upon them. As we have also seen, however, the creation of formal structures that require the parties to pursue the avenue of mediation can also place significant pressure upon the parties, and particularly the party who is most concerned with maintaining interpersonal relationships, to settle the dispute quickly. Indeed, these pressures might be most keenly felt in the family-law context, where the issues at stake are inevitably personal and intimate. *See* Trina Grille, *The Mediation Alternative: Process Dangers for Women,* 100 Yale L.J. 1545 (1991).

iii. Mini Trials and Summary Jury Trials

The mini trial and summary jury trial are both aimed at giving the parties a quick snapshot of the merits of their claims and the likely outcome of a trial. A mini trial is a privately organized event in which the parties to a dispute set up and conduct their own abbreviated trial of the issues. The mini trial is conducted before a neutral figure selected by both parties, usually someone with some degree of expertise in the subject matter of the dispute. The parties engage in a much condensed discovery process by exchanging key documents and, perhaps, giving short presentations of testimony, and the lawyers for each side make their best arguments before the arbiter. The point of the mini trial is not to be comprehensive but rather to hit all the major points that will shape a full trial and likely govern the outcome. At the close of the mini trial, the arbiter will give his overall impressions of the merits of each side's position, explain which arguments he found convincing and which he did not, and explain what type of decision he would be likely to render. The hope is that this exercise will guide the parties' further negotiations and make a settlement more likely.

The summary jury trial is a similar but even more abbreviated exercise that is conducted as part of a formal court proceeding, when a case has proceeded all the way to the eve of trial and appears unlikely to settle. Unlike a mini trial, however, a summary jury trial is ordered by the court. In this procedure, the parties go through the *voir dire* process and empanel a jury in much the same way that they would in a full trial. The lawyers for each side then make an abbreviated presentation to the jury. No live testimony is presented. Rather, the lawyers summarize the testimony that each of their witnesses would offer and make their best arguments for why their side should win. At the end of the presentation—which may last no more than a few hours and would rarely last more than a couple of days—the jury retires to deliberate and returns a verdict. The verdict is not binding in any way, and the parties are free to return to settlement talks or proceed to trial as they wish, though the hope, of course, is that this "first look" will make settlement more likely. Submitting to the summary jury trial itself can be mandatory, however, where the court decides to employ the procedure.

The summary jury trial was first devised by a federal district judge in the Northern District of Ohio. *See* Thomas Lambros, *The Summary Jury Trial and Other Alternative Methods of Dispute Resolution*, 103 F.R.D. 461, 463 (1984). Many judges and scholars have praised the device, arguing that, when properly applied, it provides an effective means of encouraging settlement. *See, e.g.*, Ann Woodley, *Strengthening the Summary Jury Trial: A Proposal to Increase Its Effectiveness and Encourage Uniformity in Its Use,* 12 Ohio St. J. on Disp. Resol. 541 (1997) (embracing summary jury trial and describing broad acceptance among judges). Others have been more cautious, suggesting that the amount of time and government money that must be devoted to a summary jury trial—including the empaneling of a jury, which, after all, is composed of individuals who are taken away from their jobs by the proceeding—might better be spent on other methods of encouraging settlement, like conferences before the court. *See* Richard Posner, *The Summary Jury Trial and Other Methods of Alternative Dispute Resolution: Some Cautionary Observations,* 53 U. Chi. L. Rev. 366, 382 (1986). The summary jury trial is one of the devices with which federal district courts experimented broadly during the years that the Civil Justice Reform Act was in force. *See* Woodley, *supra,* at 548-549.

iv. Rent-a-Judge

Rent-a-judge is the colloquial name for *referencing,* a procedure followed in some states by which courts may, at the parties' request, refer a dispute for resolution to a neutral decision maker who is chosen by the parties, rather than the judge presiding over the lawsuit. The referee shares many of the characteristics of a typical arbitrator. The referee may possess expertise in the subject matter of the dispute and may conduct the proceedings between the parties in a less formal and more expedited manner than would be typical for a trial. The principal difference is that the parties can appeal the decision of the rent-a-judge referee in much the same way that they would appeal the decision of a judge following trial — i.e., on the grounds that an error of law has been committed or that the verdict is against the weight of the factual evidence. Private arbitration awards, as we have seen, can be appealed only on extremely narrow grounds.

Where it is available, the parties may elect the referencing procedure any time between the filing of the complaint and the eve of trial. Obviously, the stage at which the parties elect the option will determine how much of the pretrial process (like motions and discovery) will be handled by the referee. California was one of the first states to adopt such a procedure, *see* Cal. Civ. Proc. §§638 *et seq.*, and it met with approval among many judges and litigators. *See* Eric Green, *Avoiding the Legal Logjam — Private Justice, California Style, reprinted in* Center for Public Resources, Corporate Dispute Management 65–82 (1981).

5. *How Well Does ADR Work? Dispute Resolution and the Social Sciences*

As an increasing number of court systems implement some form of mandatory or supplemental ADR for certain classes of cases, more and more data are available for analyzing how well ADR methods work. In some states, court systems have commissioned studies in order to determine what impact their court-annexed ADR programs have upon the amount of time it takes for cases to be resolved, the expense associated with the proceeding (both for the litigants and for the court system), and the satisfaction of the parties and the lawyers with the alternative procedures. In Arizona, for example, the Supreme Court commissioned a study of that state's mandatory nonbinding arbitration program. The study found that mandatory arbitration did not result in substantial cost savings to litigants, nor in faster dispositions of disputes. The procedure did appear to result in litigants receiving a full hearing on the merits of their dispute more frequently, however, and the study found that arbitration may reduce pretrial expenses (though not trial expenses) for the court system. On the whole, litigants and attorneys were satisfied with the system, which they viewed as offering modest benefits with no serious detriments. *See* Roselle L. Wissler & Bob Dauber, *Court-Related Arbitration: Access, If Not Efficiency*, 13 No. 4 Disp. Res. 35 (Summer, 2007) (summarizing study results).

Researchers are bringing increasingly sophisticated social-science techniques to bear on the study of dispute resolution processes. Professor Carrie Menkel-Meadow was an early pioneer in the field and remains a central figure, but many other researchers have now joined the discussion. Professor Donna Shestowsky, for example, has focused particular attention on the design of social-science experiments and empirical studies, pointing out flaws in earlier approaches and offering prescriptions for more rigorous and effective studies going forward. *See, e.g.,* Donna Shestowsky, *Disputants' Perceptions of Dispute-Resolution Procedures: An Ex Ante and Ex Post Longitudinal Empirical Study*, 41 Conn. L. Rev. 63 (2008); Donna

Shestowsky, *Disputants' Preferences for Court-Connected Dispute Resolution Procedures: Why We Should Care and Why We Know So Little*, 23 Ohio St. J. on Disp. Resol. 549 (2008). Professor Shari Seidman Diamond has helped to translate insights from the field of psychological research into the design of studies aimed at assessing the decision-making processes of juries. *See, e.g.*, Shari Seidman Diamond, *Juror Questions During Trial: A Window into Juror Thinking*, 59 Vand. L. Rev. 1927 (2006). Professor Deborah Hensler, a leading expert in ADR and the legal profession, provides a historical context for these developments in *Our Courts, Ourselves*, 108 Penn. St. L. Rev. 165 (2003), where she traces the rise of the alternative dispute resolution movement in the United States and frames questions about the long-term consequences of this increasing devotion of time and resources to ADR processes.

The work of these important scholars is helping the profession to ask better questions, and to develop techniques for obtaining more useful answers, in determining how best to structure and make use of alternative dispute resolution processes in negotiation and conflict resolution.

C.   ADR AND THE QUESTION OF PUBLIC VALUES

As we have seen, the proponents of ADR argue that nontraditional forms of dispute resolution can sometimes do a better job than the courts at promoting such values as efficiency, attention to a broad range of litigant interests, and civility in the resolution of conflict. Some of ADR's opponents have responded by disputing the claim that ADR actually achieves better or more efficient results, or by claiming that ADR achieves these goals, to the extent that it does, at the expense of accuracy or reliability. These are essentially "internal" critiques of ADR—arguments about whether ADR does a better job at promoting the goals of adjudication than adjudication does itself.

Some critics, however, have raised a more fundamental challenge to ADR. They have argued that ADR subverts one of the basic purposes of adjudication—the public resolution of disputes and the public articulation of legal norms. For these critics, the resolution of disputes in a *public* forum, resulting in the making of *law*, is not just an incidental feature of adjudication, but one of its principal purposes. On this view, delegating the dispute resolution process to a private organization always comes at a cost, no matter how efficient or accurate the result. Professor Owen Fiss is a noted proponent of this critique. He has argued that while ADR focuses principally on "maximiz[ing] the ends of private parties" and perhaps "secur[ing] the peace," adjudication serves an additional and vital function: "to explicate and give force to the values embodied in authoritative texts such as the Constitution and statutes[,] to interpret these values and to bring reality into accord with them." Owen M. Fiss, *Against Settlement*, 93 Yale L.J. 1073, 1085 (1984). To the extent that ADR and settlement preempt this articulation of legal norms, Professor Fiss argues, they do so at a cost to the public. Professor Fiss also raises concerns about the fairness of private dispute resolution and settlement, especially in cases involving poor or disadvantaged litigants. Imbalances in power and resources, he suggests, may force more vulnerable litigants to accept inadequate resolutions when cases are decided outside the view of a judge or a jury. Professor Carrie Menkel-Meadow has raised a similar concern in asking whether powerful litigants are likely to enjoy a disproportionate benefit from alternative mechanisms for dispute resolution. *See* Carrie Menkel-Meadow, *Do the "Haves" Come Out Ahead in Alternative Judicial Systems? Repeat Players in ADR*, 15 Ohio St. J. on Disp. Resol. 19 (2000). Menkel-Meadow concludes that the limited empirical data available do give some cause for concern in this respect. *See also* Judith Resnik, *Procedure as Contract*, 80 Notre Dame L. Rev. 593 (2005) (arguing for closer attention to processes by which private parties fashion alternative mechanisms for dispute resolution through contract). *But see* Katherine V. W. Stone, *Procedural Justice in the Boundaryless Workplace: The Tension Between Due Process and Public Policy*, 80 Notre Dame L. Rev. 501 (2005) (arguing that private ADR can sometimes offer workers superior relief by considering a broader range of evidence and potential remedies).

The combination of these two factors — the cost to the public and the potential for systematic disadvantage to less powerful litigants — leads Professor Fiss to believe that ADR and private settlement should be viewed with skepticism, rather than being encouraged in efforts at court reform.

> I do not believe that settlement as a generic practice is preferable to judgment or should be institutionalized on a wholesale and indiscriminate basis. It should be treated instead as a highly problematic technique for streamlining dockets. Settlement is for me the civil analogue of plea bargaining: Consent is often coerced; the bargain may be struck by someone without authority; the absence of a trial and judgment renders subsequent judicial involvement troublesome; and although dockets are trimmed, justice may not be done. Like plea bargaining, settlement is a capitulation to the conditions of mass society and should be neither encouraged nor praised.

Fiss, *supra*, at 1075.

What do you think of Professor Fiss's view of settlement? Is he correct in suggesting that "settlement as a generic practice" involves a compromise of important public values? Even if so, what about the litigants? If they want to settle their dispute, or pursue avenues that make settlement more likely, shouldn't we permit them that choice? Of course, *Against Settlement* does not suggest that litigants who want to settle should be prevented from doing so and forced to litigate. But it does suggest that the courts should not encourage settlement. Does this amount to paternalism? It might well be argued, after all, that ADR increases the autonomy of litigants — their ability to make the choices that are best for them — when it gives them a broader array of options for settling their disputes.

What is more, Professor Fiss assumes that imbalances in power and resources will disadvantage poor litigants more in private ADR or settlement proceedings than in traditional litigation. This assumption is certainly subject to dispute. It is true that the formality of litigation can, in some instances, level the playing field — for example, by affording litigants opportunities for conducting discovery that they might not have in a private ADR forum. *See, e.g.*, Fed. R. Civ. P. 26(a)(1)(A) and (B) (requiring litigants to identify individuals likely to have knowledge about dispute and documents pertaining to dispute). And, in theory, a judge can oversee the proceedings and guard against the possibility that overreaching by a powerful litigant will lead to unfair results. Nonetheless, a party with superior resources will possess a significant advantage in traditional litigation, both in the vigor with which it can pursue the litigation and in the quality of the representation that it will receive. It is not immediately apparent why these problems would be worse in private dispute resolution than they are in the courtroom. In other writings, Professor Fiss has indicated a greater tolerance for alternative dispute resolution in cases that do not implicate broad public values but are more "purely private . . . —private because only the interests and behavior of the immediate parties are at issue." Owen M. Fiss, *The Forms of Justice*, 93 Harv. L. Rev. 1, 31 (1979). Is this concession consistent with the concerns expressed in *Against Settlement*?

Another assumption implicit in *Against Settlement* is the active role that it envisions for judges in administering courtroom proceedings, whether in pushing the parties down a particular path in conducting the litigation, steering them toward settlement, or guarding against overreaching or unfairness. Such a "managerial" role for judges is a relatively recent development in American courts, as Professor Resnik has observed in a much-noted article. *See* Judith Resnik, *Managerial Judges*, 96 Harv. L. Rev. 374 (1982). One's beliefs about the proper role of judges in the courtroom can have a major impact on one's views about the desirability of ADR and its attempts to maximize the chances of settlement.

Attempts by parties to circumvent judgment through settlement can even include attempts to undo what a court has already done. Even after a trial court enters judgment, the parties may still have strong incentives to settle the dispute. For example, the winning party may accept a somewhat reduced award in return for the loser agreeing to pay the judgment right away rather than appealing the result. As part of such a bargain, the parties might also ask the court to *vacate* the judgment it has already entered. When a court vacates a judgment, the judgment is completely *expunged*—it has no precedential value and no effect on the parties, as though the proceeding never happened. There are any number of reasons why this might be important to a losing party. The court's opinion may have changed the law in ways that would be unfavorable to the losing party going forward, or the losing party may have concerns about the effects that the court's factual findings might have in future disputes against other litigants through the doctrine of collateral estoppel. But, is this proper? Should a court really agree to "erase" a judgment at the parties' request? After all, as Professor Fiss argues, a judgment has public implications that go beyond the interests of individual litigants.

The Supreme Court placed significant limitations on the vacatur of judgments in *U.S. Bancorp Mortgage Co. v. Banner Mall Partnership*, 513 U.S. 18 (1994), holding that it is improper to grant the parties' request that a judgment and opinion be vacated where the only reason for the request is that the parties have settled. As the Court explained, even though a case becomes moot when the parties settle, "[w]here mootness results from settlement . . . the losing party has voluntarily forfeited his legal remedy by the ordinary processes of appeal or certiorari, thereby surrendering his claim to the equitable remedy of vacatur. The judgment is not unreviewable, but simply unreviewed by his own choice." *Id.* at 24. Vacatur, the Court explained, is an extraordinary remedy, and while there are some circumstances in which it is appropriate to vacate a judgment that becomes moot—as when the mootness arises by "happenstance" rather than the deliberate actions of a party, *see United States v. Munsingwear, Inc.*, 340 U.S. 36 (1950)—it is not appropriate in the case of settlement. Professor Resnik considers the question of vacating judgments at length in *Whose Judgment? Vacating Judgments, Preferences for Settlement, and the Role of Adjudication at the Close of the Twentieth Century*, 41 UCLA L. Rev. 1471 (1994).

For a pair of classic discussions on the question of ADR and public values, *see* Harry T. Edwards, *Alternative Dispute Resolution: Panacea or Anathema?*, 99 Harv. L. Rev. 668 (1986) (expressing concern that extrajudicial alternative dispute mechanisms may compromise legal principles; Lon L. Fuller, *The Forms and Limits of Adjudication*, 92 Harv. L. Rev. 353 (1978) (setting forth theory of adjudication as intimately bound up with articulation of legal principles).

Principal cases are in italics.